the grass withers

and the flowers fade

BUT

THE WORD OF OUR GOD

STANDS

FOREVER

ISAIAH 40:8

Presented to . . Xiomara . . Montenegro

by . . . .

on the occasion of . . . .

date . . 1/ 7/ 16 . . . .

New Believer's BIBLE

NEW LIVING TRANSLATION

Tyndale House Publishers, Inc.

WHEATON, ILLINOIS

CONTRIBUTORS

Greg Laurie, General Editor
Karen Dagher, Harvest Ministries Editor
Danny Bond, Harvest Ministries Assistant Editor
Steve Benson, Tyndale House Editor
Timothy R. Botts and David Riley Associates, Graphic Designers

Greg Laurie is not only an evangelist and pastor but he is the president of Harvest Ministries as well. Harvest Ministries sponsors Harvest Crusades. These crusades are public evangelistic events intended to present the message of Jesus Christ to people in a nonreligious environment. Begun in 1990, Harvest Crusades are known for their informal atmosphere, contemporary music, and simple, straightforward messages by Greg Laurie. To date, some 1.5 million people have attended the nondenominational Harvest Crusades. If you would like more information on Harvest Ministries and/or their crusades, write to Harvest Ministries, P.O. Box 4000, Riverside, CA 92514-4000. Or call (909) 687-6595. On the internet, type http://www.harvest.org.

Library of Congress Cataloging-in-Publication Data
Bible. English. New Living Translation. 1996
  The new believer's Bible : New Living Translation.
    p. cm.
    ISBN 0-8423-4567-1 (hc : alk. paper). —ISBN 0-8423-4571-X (pbk. : alk. paper)
  I. Tyndale House Publishers.   II. Title.
BS195.N394 1996c
220.5′208DC20   96-2933

Printed in the United States of America

00 99 98 97
8   7   6   5   4   3

Each sale of the Holy Bible, New Living Translation, benefits Wycliffe Bible Translators, which completed its four hundredth New Testament in 1995 and is currently working in another one thousand languages. Tyndale House Publishers and Wycliffe Bible Translators share the vision for an understandable, accurate translation of the Bible for every person.

CONTENTS

OFF AND RUNNING

BIG QUESTIONS

OLD TESTAMENT

NEW TESTAMENT

CHARTS AND INDEXES

Welcome!

Congratulations! You are holding in your hands the best-selling book in the history of humanity—the Bible. It was given to us by God thousands of years ago. Although the Bible has been around for some time, the wisdom and knowledge contained within is still relevant today. In fact, everything you need to know about God and life is found in the pages of this book. It is the "user's manual of life" that we all have been searching for.

The Bible does not just teach us about life, though. It also shows us how to come into a *personal* relationship with the very God who inspired this book. This particular Bible contains features that have been specially designed to help you understand, discover, and deepen the personal relationship that God wants to have with you.

Perhaps you are not yet a believer in Jesus Christ, but you want to know more about Christianity. You may even want to be a believer, but you just don't know how to become one. In *The New Believer's Bible*, you will find a section entitled "How You Can Know God" (p. A1). Here, you will learn how to establish a life-changing relationship with Jesus.

Maybe you have just started in the Christian faith. You are a new believer. Here you will find out how to lay a good foundation for your faith and walk with God in the years ahead.

You may even be a believer who is mature in the faith. Here you will be refreshed and reminded of the essentials of the Christian faith and life.

THE MAIN FEATURES

The New Believer's Bible contains four reading tracks: "Cornerstones," "First Steps," "Off and Running," and "Big Questions." Each reading track (except "Big Questions") is composed of two kinds of notes: *up-front* and *in-text*. The up-front notes appear before the Bible text and are made up of one to two paragraphs and two to eight numbered points that refer you to Scripture passages and their accompanying in-text notes. ("Big Questions" is composed of an up-front list of questions and the page numbers you can find them on, and the in-text notes that answer those questions.)

READING TRACK ONE: CORNERSTONES

Cornerstones—blocks of stone—were traditionally used to start a building's foundation. Likewise, the "Cornerstones" reading track helps you to begin to lay a solid foundation for your faith. Here you will learn about God's character, Jesus' life, and the Holy Spirit's role in the lives of believers. "Cornerstones" also contains notes on the essential Christian character traits that are developed and nurtured by a personal relationship with Jesus Christ. Some of those traits are love, forgiveness, purity, honesty, wisdom, peace, and joy.

READING TRACK TWO: **FIRST STEPS**

The phrase *first steps* brings to mind the image of a young child taking his or her first unassisted steps. Like this young child, new believers in Christ need to learn how to walk all over again, so to speak. That is because the Christian life for most people is a completely new way of living. To help you learn to live this new life, the "First Steps" reading track gives you valuable building blocks for growing in your faith. Here you will discover the importance of and the "how to" of studying the Bible, praying, finding the right church, resisting temptation, and seeking God's will for your life.

READING TRACK THREE: **OFF AND RUNNING**

"How does God's Word apply to my everyday life?" This is one of the most widely asked questions about the Bible today. The "Off and Running" reading track answers this question. Here you will discover how to put your faith into action. You will see what the Bible has to say about important topics like marriage, parenting, priorities, conversation, and job performance. By helping you apply biblical principles to these aspects of your life, "Off and Running" takes you to the next level of the Christian life—living it day to day.

READING TRACK FOUR: **BIG QUESTIONS**

Life often presents us with difficult situations that cause us to ask hard questions. For instance, you may wonder how a good God could let something bad—like cancer—happen to you. Or you may wonder why Jesus Christ is the only way to God. Aren't other religions just as good? In the "Big Questions" reading track, you will find out what the Bible has to say about tough issues. Everything from alternative lifestyles to the second coming of Christ is covered here.

ADDITIONAL FEATURES

At the back of The New Believer's Bible you will find several features that will help you understand the Bible and your faith better. These features are

- *Table of Weights and Measures*—a chart that gives you the English and metric equivalents of biblical weights and measurements.
- *How to Study the Bible*—a practical way for you to read through the Bible, and a list of questions to ask yourself as you read.
- *52 Great Bible Stories*—a list of well-known Bible stories, where you can find them, and the main lesson you can get out of them.
- *Overview of the Bible*—a chart that gives you a basic understanding of each book of the Bible.
- *Memory Verses*—a list of key Bible verses to commit to memory.
- *Prophecies about Jesus*—a list of Old Testament passages that contain prophecies about Jesus, and the New Testament references that record his fulfillment of those prophecies.
- *Glossary of Christian Terms*—a quick-reference guide to help you understand the meanings of words like *atonement, justification, redemption,* and *sanctification.*

HOW TO USE THE READING TRACKS

The New Believer's Bible is easy to use. Simply turn to p. A11 and begin reading the "Who Is God?" up-front note in the "Cornerstones" reading track. Look up the Scripture passages and in-text notes referred to at the end of this note. After you have read all the Scripture passages and in-text notes for "Who Is God?" move on to the next up-front note ("Who Is Jesus?") and begin the process over again.

You can read one up-front note and its Scripture passages and in-text notes a day. Or, if you prefer, browse through the table of contents and choose the topic(s) that interests you the most for your daily reading.

Colossians 3:16 says, "Let the words of Christ, in all their richness, live in your hearts and make you wise." God wants his Word to permeate every area of your life—your home, your business, your play time as well as your prayer time. So open your Bible and your heart, and God will speak to you from these pages. Don't let anything keep you from spending time each day in God's Word.

Greg Laurie

A Note to Readers

With 40 million copies in print, *The Living Bible* has been meeting a great need in people's hearts for more than thirty years. But even good things can be improved, so ninety evangelical scholars from various theological backgrounds and denominations were commissioned in 1989 to begin revising *The Living Bible*. The end result of this seven-year process is the *Holy Bible, New Living Translation*—a general- purpose translation that is accurate, easy to read, and excellent for study.

The goal of any Bible translation is to convey the meaning of the ancient Hebrew and Greek texts as accurately as possible to the modern reader. The New Living Translation is based on the most recent scholarship in the theory of translation. The challenge for the translators was to create a text that would make the same impact in the life of modern readers that the original text had for the original readers. In the New Living Translation, this is accomplished by translating entire thoughts (rather than just words) into natural, everyday English. The end result is a translation that is easy to read and understand and that accurately communicates the meaning of the original text.

We believe that this new translation, which combines the latest in scholarship with the best in translation style, will speak to your heart. We present the New Living Translation with the prayer that God will use it to speak his timeless truth to the church and to the world in a fresh, new way.

The Publishers
July 1996

Introduction to the New Living Translation

Translation Philosophy and Methodology

There are two general theories or methods of Bible translation. The first has been called "formal equivalence." According to this theory, the translator attempts to render each word of the original language into the receptor language and seeks to preserve the original word order and sentence structure as much as possible. The second has been called "dynamic equivalence" or "functional equivalence." The goal of this translation theory is to produce in the receptor language the closest natural equivalent of the message expressed by the original-language text—both in meaning and in style. Such a translation attempts to have the same impact on modern readers as the original had on its own audience.

A dynamic-equivalence translation can also be called a thought-for-thought translation, as contrasted with a formal-equivalence or word-for-word translation. Of course, to translate the thought of the original language requires that the text be interpreted accurately and then be rendered in understandable idiom. So the goal of any thought-for-thought translation is to be both reliable and eminently readable. Thus, as a thought-for-thought translation, the New Living Translation seeks to be both exegetically accurate and idiomatically powerful.

In making a thought-for-thought translation, the translators must do their best to enter into the thought patterns of the ancient authors and to present the same ideas, connotations, and effects in the receptor language. In order to guard against personal biases and to ensure the accuracy of the message, a thought-for-thought translation should be created by a group of scholars who employ the best exegetical tools and who also understand the receptor language very well. With these concerns in mind, the Bible Translation Committee assigned each book of the Bible to three different scholars. Each scholar made a thorough review of the assigned book and submitted suggested revisions to the appropriate general reviewer. The general reviewer reviewed and summarized these suggestions and then proposed a first-draft revision of the text. This draft served as the basis for several additional phases of exegetical and stylistic committee review. Then the Bible Translation Committee jointly reviewed and approved every verse in the final translation.

A thought-for-thought translation prepared by a group of capable scholars has the potential to represent the intended meaning of the original text even more accurately than a word-for-word translation. This is illustrated by the various renderings of the Hebrew word *hesed*. This term cannot be adequately translated by any single English word because it can connote love, mercy, grace, kindness, faithfulness, and loyalty. The context—not the lexicon—must determine which English term is selected for translation.

The value of a thought-for-thought translation can be illustrated by comparing 1 Kings 2:10 in the King James Version, the New International Version, and the New Living Translation. "So David slept with his fathers, and was buried in the city of David" (KJV). "Then David rested with his fathers and was buried in the City of David" (NIV). "Then David died and was buried in the City of David" (NLT). Only the New Living Translation clearly translates the real meaning of the Hebrew idiom "slept with his fathers" into contemporary English.

Written to Be Read Aloud
It is evident in Scripture that the biblical documents were written to be read aloud, often in public worship (see Nehemiah 8; Luke 4:16-20; 1 Timothy 4:13; Revelation 1:3). It is still the case today that more people will hear the Bible read aloud in church than are likely to read it for themselves. Therefore, a new translation must communicate with clarity and power when it is read aloud. For this reason, the New Living Translation is recommended as a Bible to be used for public reading. Its living language is not only easy to understand, but it also has an emotive quality that will make an impact on the listener.

The Texts behind the New Living Translation
The translators of the Old Testament used the Masoretic Text of the Hebrew Bible as their standard text. They used the edition known as *Biblia Hebraica Stuttgartensia* (1977) with its up-to-date textual apparatus, a revision of Rudolf Kittel's *Biblia Hebraica* (Stuttgart, 1937). The translators also compared the Dead Sea Scrolls, the Septuagint and other Greek manuscripts, the Samaritan Pentateuch, the Syriac Peshitta, the Latin Vulgate, and any other versions or manuscripts that shed light on textual problems.

The translators of the New Testament used the two standard editions of the Greek New Testament: the *Greek New Testament*, published by the United Bible Societies (fourth revised edition, 1993), and *Novum Testamentum Graece*, edited by Nestle and Aland (twenty-seventh edition, 1993). These two editions, which have the same text but differ in punctuation and textual notes, represent the best in modern textual scholarship.

Translation Issues
The translators have made a conscious effort to provide a text that can be easily understood by the average reader of modern English. To this end, we have used the vocabulary and language structures commonly used by the average person. The result is a translation of the Scriptures written generally at the reading level of a junior high school student. We have avoided using language that is likely to become quickly dated or that reflects a narrow subdialect of English, with the goal of making the New Living Translation as broadly useful as possible.

But our concern for readability goes beyond the concerns of vocabulary and sentence structure. We are also concerned about historical and cultural barriers to understanding the Bible, and we have sought to translate terms shrouded in history or culture in ways that can be immediately understood by the contemporary reader. Thus, our goal of easy readability expresses itself in a number of other ways:

- Rather than translating ancient weights and measures literally, which communicates little to the modern reader, we have expressed them by means of recognizable contemporary equivalents. We have converted ancient weights and measures to modern English (American) equivalents, and we have rendered the literal Hebrew or Greek measures, along with metric equivalents, in textual footnotes.
- Instead of translating ancient currency values literally, we have generally expressed them in terms of weights in precious metals. In some cases we have used other common terms to communicate the message effectively. For example, "three shekels of silver" might become "three silver coins" or "three pieces of silver" to convey the intended message. Again, a rendering of the literal Hebrew or Greek is given in textual footnotes.
- Since the Hebrew lunar calendar fluctuates from year to year in relation to the solar calendar used today, we have translated Hebrew dates in a way that communicates with our modern readership. It was clear that we could not use the names of the Hebrew months, such as *Abib,* which are meaningless to the modern reader. Nor could we use a simple designation such as "first month," because the months of the Hebrew lunar calendar do not correspond with the months of our calendar. Thus, we have often used seasonal references to communicate the time of year when something happened. For example, "the first month" (which occurs in March and April) might be translated "early spring." Where it is possible to define a specific ancient date in terms of our modern calendar, we use modern dates in the text. Textual footnotes then give the literal Hebrew date and state the rationale for our rendering. For example, Ezra 7:9 pinpoints the date when Ezra arrived in Jerusalem: "the first day of the fifth month." This was during the seventh year of King Artaxerxes' reign (Ezra 7:7). We translate that lunar date as August 4, with a footnote giving the Hebrew and identifying the year as 458 B.C.
- Since ancient references to the time of day differ from our modern methods of denoting time, we used renderings that are instantly understandable to the modern reader. Accordingly, we have rendered specific times of day by using approximate equivalents in terms of our common "o'clock" system. On occasion, translations such as "at dawn the next morning" or "as the sun began to set" have been used when the biblical reference is general.
- Many words in the original texts made sense to the original audience but communicate something quite different to the modern reader. In such cases, some liberty must be allowed in translation to communicate what was intended. Places identified by the term normally translated "city," for example, are often better identified as "towns" or "villages." Similarly, the term normally translated "mountain" is often better rendered "hill."
- Many words and phrases carry a great deal of cultural meaning that was obvious to the original readers but needs explanation in our own culture. For example, the phrase "they beat their breasts" (Luke 23:48) in ancient times meant that people were very upset. In our translation we chose to translate this phrase dynamically: "They went home *in deep sorrow.*" In some cases, however, we have simply illuminated the existing expression to make it immediately understandable. For example, we might have expanded the literal phrase to read "they beat their breasts *in sorrow.*"
- Metaphorical language is often difficult for contemporary readers to understand, so at times we have chosen to translate or illuminate the metaphor. For example, the ancient poet writes, "Your eyes are doves" (Song of Songs 1:15). To help the modern reader, who

might be confused or distracted by a literal visualization of this image, we converted the metaphor to a simile to make the meaning immediately clear: "Your eyes are soft *like* doves." Here we also added the modifier "soft" to help the modern reader catch the significance of the metaphoric expression. A few chapters later, the poet writes, "Your neck is like the tower of David" (Song of Songs 4:4). We rendered it "Your neck is *as stately as* the tower of David" to clarify the intended positive meaning of the metaphor.

- We did not feel obligated to display all Hebrew poetry in English poetic form. Only the book of Psalms is set entirely in poetic lines. Other books, though poetic in nature, are set in prose for the sake of easier reading. Nonetheless, these prose renderings reflect the poetic language of the original Hebrew. Where a portion of text is explicitly said to be a poem or song, however, it has usually been set as such.

- One challenge we faced was in determining how to translate accurately the ancient biblical text that was originally written in a context where male-oriented terms were used to refer to humanity generally. We needed to respect the nature of the ancient context while also trying to make the translation clear to a modern audience that tends to read male-oriented language as applying only to males. Often the original text, though using masculine nouns and pronouns, clearly intends that the message be applied to both men and women. One example is found in the New Testament epistles, where the believers are called "brothers" *(adelphoi)*. Yet it is clear that these epistles were addressed to all the believers—male and female. Thus, we have usually translated this Greek word "brothers and sisters" in order to represent the historical situation more accurately.

We have also been sensitive to passages where the text applies generally to human beings or to the human condition. In many instances we have used plural pronouns (they, them) in place of the masculine singular (he, him). For example, a traditional rendering of Proverbs 22:6 is: "Train up a child in the way he should go, and when he is old he will not turn from it." We have rendered it: "Teach your children to choose the right path, and when they are older, they will remain upon it." At times, we have also replaced third person pronouns with the second person to ensure clarity. A traditional rendering of Proverbs 26:27 is: "He who digs a pit will fall into it, and he who rolls a stone, it will come back on him." We have rendered it: "If you set a trap for others, you will get caught in it yourself. If you roll a boulder down on others, it will roll back on you." All such decisions were driven by the concern to reflect accurately the intended meaning of the original texts of Scripture.

We should emphasize, however, that all masculine nouns and pronouns used to represent God (for example, "Father") have been maintained without exception. We believe that essential traits of God's revealed character can only be conveyed through the masculine language expressed in the original texts of Scripture.

Lexical Consistency in Terminology

For the sake of clarity, we have maintained lexical consistency in areas such as divine names, synoptic passages, rhetorical structures, and nontheological technical terms (i.e., liturgical, cultic, zoological, botanical, cultural, and legal terms). For theological terms, we have allowed a greater semantic range of acceptable English words or phrases for a single Hebrew or Greek word. We avoided weighty theological terms that do not readily communicate to many modern readers. For example, we avoided using words such as "justification," "sanctification," and "regeneration." In place of these words (which are carryovers from Latin), we provided renderings such as "we are made right with God," "we are made holy," and "we are born anew."

The Spelling of Proper Names

Many individuals in the Bible, especially the Old Testament, are known by more than one name or by a number of variant names (e.g., Uzziah/Azariah). For the sake of clarity, we have tried to use a single spelling for any one individual, footnoting the literal spelling whenever we differ from it. This is especially helpful in delineating the kings of Israel and Judah. King Joash/Jehoash of Israel has been consistently called Jehoash, while King Joash/Jehoash of Judah is called Joash. A similar distinction has been used to distinguish between Joram/Jehoram of Israel and Joram/Jehoram of Judah. All such decisions were made with the goal of clarifying the text for the reader. When the ancient biblical writers clearly had a theological purpose in their choice of a variant name (e.g., Eshbaal/Ishbosheth), the different names have been maintained with an explanatory footnote.

The Rendering of Divine Names

All appearances of *'el, 'elohim,* or *'eloah* have been translated "God," except where the context demands the translation "god(s)." We have rendered the tetragrammaton *(YHWH)* consistently as "the Lord," utilizing a form with small capitals that is common among English translations. This will distinguish it from the name *'adonai,* which we render "Lord." When *'adonai* and *YHWH* appear in conjunction, we have rendered it "Sovereign Lord." This also distinguishes *'adonai YHWH* from cases where *YHWH* appears with *'elohim,* which is rendered "Lord God." When *YH* (the short form of *YHWH*) and *YHWH* appear together, we have rendered it "Lord God." The Hebrew word *'adon* is rendered "lord," or "master," or sometimes "sir."

In the New Testament, the Greek word *Christos* has been translated as "Messiah" when the context assumes a Jewish audience. When a Gentile audience can be assumed, *Christos* has been translated as "Christ." The Greek word *kurios* is consistently translated "Lord," except in four quotations of Psalm 110:1, where it is translated "Lord."

Textual Footnotes

The New Living Translation provides several kinds of textual footnotes:

- All Old Testament passages that are clearly quoted in the New Testament are identified in a textual footnote in the New Testament.
- Some textual footnotes provide cultural and historical information on places, things, and people in the Bible that are probably obscure to modern readers. Such notes should aid the reader in understanding the message of the text. For example, in Acts 12:1, "King Herod" is named in this translation as "King Herod Agrippa" and is identified in a footnote as being "the nephew of Herod Antipas and a grandson of Herod the Great."
- When various ancient manuscripts contain different readings, these differences are often documented in footnotes. For instance, textual variants are footnoted when the variant reading is very familiar (usually through the King James Version). We have used footnotes when we have selected variant readings that differ from the Hebrew and Greek editions normally followed.
- When the meaning of a proper name (or a wordplay inherent in a proper name) is relevant to the meaning of the text, it is illuminated with a textual footnote. For example, the footnote at Genesis 3:20 reads: "*Eve* sounds like a Hebrew term that means 'to give life.' " This wordplay in the Hebrew illuminates the meaning of the text, which goes on to say that Eve "would be the mother of all people everywhere." If the meaning of the name is

more certain, it is stated more simply. For example, the footnote at Genesis 16:11 reads: "*Ishmael* means 'God hears.' " In this case, Hagar named her son Ishmael after realizing that God had heard her cry for help.

- When we translate the meaning of a place-name that is often simply transliterated from the Hebrew or Greek, we provide a textual footnote showing the transliteration that appears in many English translations. For example, the name usually transliterated "Havvoth-jair" in Judges 10:4 has been translated "the Towns of Jair," with a footnote that gives the traditional transliteration: "Hebrew *Havvoth-jair*."

- Textual footnotes are also used to show alternative renderings. These are prefaced with the word "Or." On occasion, we also provide notes on words or phrases that represent a translation that departs from long-standing tradition. These notes are prefaced with the words "traditionally rendered." For example, a footnote to the translation "contagious skin disease" at Leviticus 13:2 says, "Traditionally rendered *leprosy*."

AS WE SUBMIT this translation of the Bible for publication, we recognize that any translation of the Scriptures is subject to limitations and imperfections. Anyone who has attempted to communicate the richness of God's Word into another language will realize it is impossible to make a perfect translation. Recognizing these limitations, we sought God's guidance and wisdom throughout this project. Now we pray that he will accept our efforts and use this translation for the benefit of the Church and of all people.

We pray that the New Living Translation will overcome some of the barriers of history, culture, and language that have kept people from reading and understanding God's Word. We hope that readers unfamiliar with the Bible will find the words clear and easy to understand, and that readers well versed in the Scriptures will gain a fresh perspective. We pray that readers will gain insight and wisdom for living, but most of all that they will meet the God of the Bible and be forever changed by knowing him.

The Bible Translation Committee
July 1996

HOLY BIBLE
NEW LIVING TRANSLATION
BIBLE TRANSLATION TEAM

PENTATEUCH
Daniel I. Block, General Reviewer
The Southern Baptist Theological Seminary

GENESIS
Allan Ross, Trinity Episcopal Seminary
John Sailhamer, Northwestern College
Gordon Wenham, The Cheltenham and
 Gloucester College of Higher Education

EXODUS
Robert Bergen, Hannibal-LaGrange College
Daniel I. Block, The Southern Baptist Theological
 Seminary
Eugene Carpenter, Bethel College, Mishawaka,
 Indiana

LEVITICUS
David Baker, Ashland Theological Seminary
Victor Hamilton, Asbury College
Kenneth Mathews, Beeson Divinity School,
 Samford University

NUMBERS
Dale A. Brueggemann, Assemblies of God,
 Division of Foreign Missions
Roland K. Harrison (deceased), Wycliffe College
Gerald L. Mattingly, Johnson Bible College

DEUTERONOMY
J. Gordon McConville, The Cheltenham and
 Gloucester College of Higher Education
Eugene H. Merrill, Dallas Theological Seminary
John A. Thompson, University of Melbourne

HISTORICAL BOOKS
Barry J. Beitzel, General Reviewer
Trinity Evangelical Divinity School

JOSHUA/JUDGES
Carl E. Armerding, Schloss Mittersill Study Centre
Barry J. Beitzel, Trinity Evangelical Divinity School
Lawson Stone, Asbury Theological Seminary

1 & 2 SAMUEL
Barry J. Beitzel, Trinity Evangelical Divinity School
V. Philips Long, Covenant Theological Seminary
J. Robert Vannoy, Biblical Theological Seminary

1 & 2 KINGS
Bill T. Arnold, Asbury Theological Seminary
William H. Barnes, Southeastern College of the
 Assemblies of God
Frederic W. Bush, Fuller Theological Seminary

1 & 2 CHRONICLES
Raymond B. Dillard (deceased), Westminster
 Theological Seminary
David A. Dorsey, Evangelical School of Theology
Terry Eves, Calvin College

EZRA/NEHEMIAH/ESTHER/RUTH
William C. Williams, Southern California College
Hugh G. M. Williamson, Oxford University

POETRY
Tremper Longman III, General Reviewer
Westminster Theological Seminary

JOB
August Konkel, Providence Theological Seminary
Tremper Longman III, Westminster Theological
 Seminary
Al Wolters, Redeemer College

PSALMS 1–75
Mark D. Futato, Westminster Theological
 Seminary in California
Douglas Green, Westminster Theological Seminary
Richard Pratt, Reformed Theological Seminary

PSALMS 76–150
David M. Howard Jr., Trinity Evangelical Divinity
 School
Raymond C. Ortlund Jr., Trinity Evangelical
 Divinity School
Willem VanGemeren, Trinity Evangelical Divinity
 School

PROVERBS
Ted Hildebrandt, Grace College
Richard Schultz, Wheaton College
Raymond C. Van Leeuwen, Eastern College

ECCLESIASTES/SONG OF SONGS
Daniel C. Fredericks, Belhaven College
David Hubbard (deceased), Fuller Theological
 Seminary
Tremper Longman III, Westminster Theological
 Seminary

PROPHETS
John N. Oswalt, General Reviewer
Asbury Theological Seminary

ISAIAH
John N. Oswalt, Asbury Theological Seminary
Gary Smith, Bethel Theological Seminary
John Walton, Moody Bible Institute

JEREMIAH/LAMENTATIONS
G. Herbert Livingston, Asbury Theological
Seminary
Elmer A. Martens, Mennonite Brethren Biblical
Seminary

EZEKIEL
Daniel I. Block, The Southern Baptist Theological
Seminary
David H. Engelhard, Calvin Theological Seminary
David Thompson, Asbury Theological Seminary

DANIEL/HAGGAI/ZECHARIAH/MALACHI
Joyce Baldwin Caine (deceased), Trinity College,
Bristol
Douglas Gropp, Catholic University of America
Roy Hayden, Oral Roberts School of Theology

HOSEA–ZEPHANIAH
Joseph Coleson, Nazarene Theological Seminary
Andrew Hill, Wheaton College
Richard Patterson, Professor Emeritus, Liberty
University

GOSPELS AND ACTS
Grant R. Osborne, General Reviewer
Trinity Evangelical Divinity School

MATTHEW
Craig Blomberg, Denver Conservative Baptist
Seminary
Donald A. Hagner, Fuller Theological Seminary
David Turner, Grand Rapids Baptist Seminary

MARK
Robert Guelich (deceased), Fuller Theological
Seminary
Grant R. Osborne, Trinity Evangelical Divinity
School

LUKE
Darrel Bock, Dallas Theological Seminary
Scot McKnight, North Park College
Robert Stein, Bethel Theological Seminary

JOHN
Gary M. Burge, Wheaton College
Philip W. Comfort, Wheaton College
Marianne Meye Thompson, Fuller Theological
Seminary

ACTS
D. A. Carson, Trinity Evangelical Divinity School
William J. Larkin, Columbia Biblical Seminary
Roger Mohrlang, Whitworth College

LETTERS AND REVELATION
Norman R. Ericson, General Reviewer
Wheaton College

ROMANS/GALATIANS
Gerald Borchert, The Southern Baptist
Theological Seminary
Douglas J. Moo, Trinity Evangelical Divinity
School
Thomas R. Schreiner, Bethel Theological Seminary

1 & 2 CORINTHIANS
Joseph Alexanian, Trinity International University
Linda Belleville, North Park Theological Seminary
Douglas A. Oss, Central Bible College
Robert Sloan, Baylor University

EPHESIANS–PHILEMON
Harold W. Hoehner, Dallas Theological Seminary
Moises Silva, Gordon-Conwell Theological
Seminary
Klyne Snodgrass, North Park Theological
Seminary

HEBREWS/JAMES/1 & 2 PETER/JUDE
Peter Davids, Canadian Theological Seminary
Norman R. Ericson, Wheaton College
William Lane, Seattle Pacific University
J. Ramsey Michaels, S. W. Missouri State
University

1–3 JOHN/REVELATION
Greg Beale, Gordon-Conwell Theological
Seminary
Robert Mounce, Whitworth College
M. Robert Mulholland Jr., Asbury Theological
Seminary

SPECIAL REVIEWERS
F. F. Bruce (deceased), University of Manchester
Kenneth N. Taylor, Tyndale House Publishers

COORDINATIING TEAM
Mark R. Norton, Managing Editor and O. T.
Coordinating Editor
Philip W. Comfort, N. T. Coordinating Editor
Ronald A. Beers, Executive Director and Stylist
Mark D. Taylor, Director and Chief Stylist
Daniel W. Taylor, Consultant

HOW YOU CAN KNOW GOD

What Is Missing in Our Lives?

Purpose, meaning, a reason for living—these are all things we desire and search for in life. Despite steps each one of us takes to find purpose and meaning in life, we still feel empty, unfulfilled. That is because there is a spiritual emptiness in each of our lives. We each have a hole in our heart, a spiritual vacuum deep within our soul—a "God-shaped blank." Possessions won't fill this hole, nor will success. Relationships alone cannot satisfy this emptiness, and morality, in and of itself, falls miserably short of occupying this space. In fact, even religion cannot fill the void in our heart.

There is only one way to effectively fill that void. This way will not only help us to have a life that is full and rich on this earth, but—more important—will give us the absolute hope of spending eternity in the presence of God. Before we can truly appreciate this good news though, we need to understand the bad news, which is a serious problem we all have.

THE PROBLEM: SIN

The Bible clearly identifies our serious problem as sin. Sin is not just an act but the actual nature of our being. In other words, we are not sinners because we sin. Rather, we sin because we are sinners! We are born with a nature to do wrong. King David, the Old Testament Israelite ruler, wrote, "For I was born a sinner—yes, from the moment my mother conceived me" (Psalm 51:5). Because we are born sinners, sinning comes to all of us naturally. That is why it is futile to think that the answer to all of life's problems comes from "within." According to the Bible, the *problem* is within! Scripture tells us, "The human heart is most deceitful and desperately wicked. Who really knows how bad it is?" (Jeremiah 17:9).

We are not basically good—we are basically sinful. This sinfulness spills out into everything we do. Every problem we experience in our society today can be traced back to our refusal to live God's way. Clear back to the Garden of Eden, Adam made his choice, and he suffered the consequences of it, setting the pattern that all humanity would follow. The Bible explains, "When Adam sinned, sin entered the entire human race. Adam's sin brought death, so death spread to everyone, for everyone sinned. . . . Yes, Adam's one sin brought condemnation upon everyone" (Romans 5:12, 18).

"That's not fair!" you may protest. Why should we suffer because of what someone else has done? Yet, given the opportunity, each one of us would have done the same thing as Adam. In fact, not a single day passes that we do not face the same test that was set before Adam. God has given us the freedom to choose between two separate paths: the path that leads to life and the path that leads to death. The Bible says, "Today, I have given you the choice between life and death, between blessings and curses. I call on heaven and earth to witness the choice you make, Oh, that you would choose life, that you and your descendants might live!" (Deuteronomy 30:19).

WITHOUT A LEG TO STAND ON

Someone may say, "But I live a good life. I try to be kind and considerate to others. I live by the Ten Commandments." But the truth of the matter is that the Ten Commandments, or the law, as they are called in the Bible, were not given to make us good but to show us how bad we are. The Bible tells us, "No one can ever be made right in God's sight by doing what his law commands. For the more we know God's law, the clearer it becomes that we aren't obeying it" (Romans 3:20). The purpose of the law is to make us realize how sinful we are. You might say that God's law was given to "shut our mouths" and show us that we desperately need his help and forgiveness for our terminal condition as sinners.

Look at the passages below to get a better understanding of the nature and seriousness of sin.

1. **We Have All Missed the Mark** (see Romans 3:23, p. 964). Romans 3:23 says, we have *all* sinned. For those that would claim to be the sole exception to this eternal truth, verse ten of this chapter plainly says, "No one is good—not even one (Romans 3:10). Another word for *good* is *righteous*. The word *righteous* means, "One who is as he or she ought to be." When the Bible says that no one is righteous, or good, it is not so much referring to behavior but to inner character.

   What exactly is "God's glorious standard" that Romans 3:23 says we have failed to meet? God's "glorious standard" is absolute perfection. Jesus said, "But you are to be perfect, even as your Father in heaven is perfect" (Matthew 5:48). In other words, anyone who is not as good as God is not acceptable to him.

   One definition of *sin*, derived from the Greek word *hamartia*, is to "miss the mark." As far as the mark of perfection goes, we miss it by a mile. Although our sinful nature makes it impossible for us to live up to God's standard, we cannot blame sin on our nature alone. Sin is also a deliberate act.

2. **Sin Is a Deliberate Act** (see Ephesians 2:1-3, p. 1024). Another word for *sins* in Ephesians 2:1 is *transgressions* or *trespasses*. This word speaks of a lapse or deviation from truth. In contrast to simply "missing the mark," this is a deliberate action. Because sin is a deliberate action, we cannot blame our sin on our society or our environment or our mental or physical state. Everyone has chosen to do what was wrong. If we protest this point, "we are only fooling ourselves and refusing to accept the truth" (1 John 1:8).

3. The Ultimate Penalty for Sin Is Death (see Romans 6:23, p. 968). According to the Bible, we have offended a Holy God. We have not done this once or twice, but so many times that we are unable to keep count. Romans 6:23 says, "The *wages* of sin is death. . . ." Wages are something that you are paid for work rendered. In other words, you earn your wages. Because we have all repeatedly sinned, we have earned the penalty of death, which is eternal torment and punishment in a place called hell.

Amid all this talk about sin and death, there is some good news. God has given us a way to escape the penalty of our sin. He has made it possible for us to have a relationship with him and enjoy the hope of eternal life without punishment.

The Solution: Jesus Christ

God understood our problem and knew that we could do nothing about it. Because God loves us, he sent his own Son, Jesus Christ, to earth to bridge the chasm of sin that separates us from him.

WHY JESUS CAN BRIDGE THE GAP

There has never been anyone like Jesus. For starters, Jesus was not conceived in the womb of his mother through natural means. Rather, he was supernaturally conceived in the womb of a young virgin named Mary. Because of his supernatural conception, Jesus, who is wholly God, also became wholly human.

Though Jesus is God, he chose to lay aside the privileges of his deity to live on earth as a man. The Bible, describing the sacrifice Christ made in becoming a man, says that Jesus "made himself nothing; he took the humble position of a slave and appeared in human form. And in human form he obediently humbled himself even further by dying a criminal's death on a cross" (Philippians 2:7-8). It is extremely important to note that Jesus did not cease to be God when he came to earth. He simply laid aside his divine privileges and walked the earth as a man. In doing so, he was personally able to experience the gamut of human emotions, ranging from happiness to deep sorrow. He felt what it was like to be tired, cold, and hungry.

Moreover, he came to this earth with a clear objective in mind: to bridge that gap between us and God.

When the Israelites of the Old Testament sinned, they would have the high priest go into the Temple and offer an animal sacrifice to God to atone for their sins. In a symbolic sense, this was a way of putting one's sins on the animal, which stood in the place of the guilty person. The Bible teaches, "Without the shedding of blood, there is no forgiveness of sins" (Hebrews 9:22).

The sacrificial rituals carried out by the Israelites in the Old Testament foreshadowed what Jesus would do when he came to this earth. He took the sin of the world upon himself when he hung on the cross so many years ago.

Numerous Old Testament prophecies pointed not only to his birth and life but also to his death, including the way in which he would die.

Jesus knew from the beginning that he had come expressly to die for the sins of humanity. He also knew that this sacrifice would be made on a Roman cross. He began his final journey to the cross of Calvary at a place called Caesarea Philippi, and he often spoke of his impending death with his disciples. Scripture records, "From then on Jesus began to tell his disciples plainly that he had to go to Jerusalem, and he told them what would happen to him there. He would suffer at the hands of the leaders and the leading priests and the teachers of religious law. He would be killed, and he would be raised on the third day" (Matthew 16:21).

He was eventually arrested on false charges after Judas Iscariot, one of his own disciples, betrayed him. But it was no accident. If humanity was going to be put in touch with God and have the barrier that separated them removed, something drastic had to be done. In essence, with one hand Jesus took hold of a Holy God, and with the other hand he took hold of the sinful human race. As crude nails were pounded into his hands, he bridged the gap for us!

We must not forget, however, that three days after his crucifixion, Jesus rose from the dead! If it is true that "you can't keep a good man down," then it is even truer that you can't keep the "God-man" down.

WE PUT JESUS ON THE CROSS

The necessity of the death of Jesus Christ on the cross shows just how radical our situation was as fallen people. It's been said that you can tell the depth of a well by how much rope is lowered. When we look at "how much rope was lowered" from heaven, we realize how grave our situation really was.

For that reason, don't blame the people of that day for putting Jesus on the cross. We are just as guilty as they. In reality, it was not the Roman soldiers who put him on the cross, nor was it the Jewish leaders: it was our sins that made it necessary for Jesus to volunteer for this torturous and humiliating death.

Read the verses and notes below to see exactly what Jesus did for us.

1. The Greatest Demonstration of Love (see Romans 5:6-8, p. 966). Jesus did not die for us while we were his friends, but while we were his enemies, opposing him by our sinfulness. Yet, in spite of all of this, God demonstrated his love for us by dying on the cross. In this verse, the Apostle Paul explains that Jesus did not simply die for humanity as a whole, but that he died for us as individuals. Elsewhere, Paul writes, "[Christ] loved me and gave himself for me" (Galatians 2:20).

Whenever you are tempted to doubt God's love for you, take a long look at the cross on which Jesus died. Then realize that, for all practical purposes, it was not nails that held him to the cross, but love.

2. Forsaken That We Might Be Forgiven (see Luke 23:32-49, p. 890). Many of us have heard this story at some point in our lives. Yet the significance behind this heart-wrenching scene is often missed or misunderstood. This was not simply some "good teacher" being crucified for his beliefs. It was God in human form who hung on that cross, bridging the gap between sinful people and a holy God.

Matthew's Gospel tells us that when Jesus hung on that cross, he cried out, "My God, my God, why have you forsaken me?" (Matthew 27:46). Many Bible scholars believe that those words marked the precise moment at which God placed the sins of the world upon his Son. The Bible, speaking of God, says, "You are of purer eyes than to behold evil, and cannot look on wickedness" (Habakkuk 1:13, NKJV). For that reason, the holy Father had to "turn his face" and pour out his wrath upon his own Son. On the cross, Jesus received the wages that were due us. He was not heard that we might be heard. The ear of God was closed to Jesus for a time that it might never be closed to us.

3. Christ, the Sole Mediator (see 1 Timothy 2:5-6, p. 1056). Why is there only one mediator who is qualified to bridge the gap between God and people? Haven't there been other religious leaders who have claimed to have *the* way to God? Haven't some of them also died as a result of their message?

While the answers to these questions may be yes, the truth is that not one of these other leaders was fully God and fully human. That is why Jesus is uniquely qualified to deal with sin. Jesus said, "I am the way, the truth, and the life. No one can come to the Father except through me" (John 14:6). Acts 4:12 tells us, "There is salvation in no one else! There is no other name in all of heaven for people to call on to save them." And, most important, Jesus Christ rose from the dead!

Though it is true that you must believe Jesus died on the cross for your sins in order to receive eternal life and be a true Christian, there is still something else you must do.

The Response: Accept God's Offer

To know Jesus Christ personally and have your sins forgiven, you must believe that you are a sinner separated from God and that your only hope is Jesus Christ, the Son of God, who came and died for your sins. To stop here, however, would be to stop short of salvation.

There are two things you must now do to enter into a relationship with the God from whom you have been separated.

1. TURN FROM YOUR SINS

As Jesus began his public ministry, his first message was "Turn from your sins" (Mark 1:15). In essence, Jesus was tellling the people to repent— to acknowledge their sinning, change their minds, and change the direction of their lives.

Look at it this way. In the past, we have been blinded by our sins, causing us to run from God. As we repent, we do a "U-turn" and start running toward him. It is not enough just to be sorry for our sins. We must also change our lifestyle, for the Bible teaches that "God can use sorrow in our lives to help us turn away from sin" (2 Corinthians 7:10). In other words, if you are really sorry for something, it will result in a change in your actions.

The apostle Paul summed up this change succinctly when he quoted Jesus, who had said that people must "turn from darkness to light, and from the power of Satan to God. Then they will receive forgiveness for their sins and be given a place among God's people, who are set apart by faith in me (Acts 26:18).

You see, there are some things only God can do and some things only you can do. Only God can remove your sins and give you the gift of eternal life, but only you can turn from your sins and receive Jesus as your Savior. That brings up the second thing you must do to respond to God's offer.

2. BELIEVE IN JESUS CHRIST AND RECEIVE HIM INTO YOUR LIFE

Having seen the enormity of your sin and having decided to turn from it, you then must believe in and receive Jesus Christ as your Lord and Savior. Becoming a Christian, however, is far more than following a creed or trying to live by certain standards. Jesus said that you must be "born again," or more literally, "born from above" (John 3:3). This spiritual rebirth happens when we personally believe in Jesus Christ, receive him by inviting him into our lives, and turn from our sins. In other words, we ask Jesus to come and take residence in our lives, making the changes he deems necessary. A person must take this all-important step in order to become a child of God.

Notice that this offer is yours for the asking, and it is free. You don't have to work for it, trying to clean up your life before you make this life-changing decision. The Bible says, "The free gift of God is eternal life through Christ Jesus our Lord" (Romans 6:23).

Being a Christian also means having a relationship with the living God. In Revelation 3:20, Jesus said, "Look! Here I stand at the door and knock. If you hear me calling and open the door, I will come in, and we will share a meal as friends." To better understand the meaning of this verse, it is important to understand the culture at the time it was written. Eating together in Bible times was a long, drawn-out affair. People would not sit on chairs behind tables in a formal setting as we do, but they would sit on the floor, reclining on pillows around a low table. The relaxed atmosphere made meals a time when you would not only satisfy your appetite but also receive a gratifying serving of enjoyable table conversation. You would share your heart and life with those who sat beside you.

Consequently, when Jesus says that he will "share a meal" with us, it implies intimacy, closeness, and friendship. He offers this to us, but we must first "hear him calling" us.

To hear God calling us, we must know how he speaks. One way in which God speaks to us is described in the Bible as a "still, small voice." This could be described in another way as that tug you may have felt on your heart from the Holy Spirit showing you your need for Jesus. He may even be speaking to you right now! It is at that point that you must "open the door." Only you can do that. Jesus will not force his way in.

RECEIVING JESUS CHRIST INTO YOUR HEART

If you are ready to turn from your sins and believe in Jesus Christ so that you can receive the forgiveness of sin and the hope of eternal life, then take a moment to bow your head and pray a prayer like this one right now:

God, I'm sorry for my sin. I turn from it right now. I thank you for sending Jesus Christ to die on the cross for my sin.

Jesus, I ask you to come into my heart and life right now. Be my Lord, Savior, and friend. Help me to follow you all the days of my life as your disciple.

Thank you for forgiving and receiving me right now. Thank

you that my sin is forgiven and that I am going to heaven. In Jesus' name I pray, amen.

REDEDICATING YOUR LIFE TO JESUS CHRIST

Perhaps you are already a Christian but you have strayed from Jesus Christ. You have been a prodigal son or daughter. God will forgive you right now if you will return to him. He tells us in Scripture, "My wayward children, come back to me and I will heal your wayward hearts" (Jeremiah 3:22). If you would like to return to God and rededicate your life to him right now, you may want to pray something like this:

God, I am sorry for my sin. I am sorry that I have strayed from you. I ask you to forgive me now as I repent of my sin. I don't want to live like a prodigal any longer.

Renew and revive me as I once again follow you as my God. Thank you for your forgiveness. In Jesus' name I pray, amen.

Whether you prayed to make a first time commitment or a recommitment, you have made the right decision. God has forgiven and received you if you really meant it. Know that your relationship with Jesus Christ will bring radical and dramatic changes in your life. Describing this, the Bible says, "Those who become Christians become new persons. They are not the same anymore, for the old life is gone. A new life has begun!" (2 Corinthians 5:17). Now that is good news! But more importantly, God has changed your eternal destiny. Instead of fearing a eternal punishment in a place called hell, you will spend peaceful eternity in his presence in heaven.

Read the next section to see what else God has done for you now that you have taken this step.

What God Has Done for You

What actually happens when Jesus Christ comes into your life? First, he saves you from your sins and the punishment you deserve as a result of them—eternity in hell. This is called salvation, or regeneration, and has to do with what takes place in your heart: God gives you new life.

Second, he justifies you. Justification has to do with your standing before God and includes the complete removal and forgiveness of your sins. Think about it! When you receive Jesus Christ into your life, you are completely forgiven. God's Word tells us, "Brothers, listen! In this man Jesus there is forgiveness for your sins! Everyone who believes in him is freed from all guilt and declared right with God [justified]—something the Jewish law could never do" (Acts 13:38-39). Speaking of our sins, God says, "I will never again remember [your] sins and lawless deeds" (Hebrews 10:17). What a wonderful promise!

Justification, however, is more than just the forgiveness and removal of the guilt and condemnation that accompany sin. While God has removed your sins and forgiven you of them, he has also placed the perfect righteousness of Jesus Christ "into your account," so to speak. You don't have to earn it or try to achieve it. It is yours as a gracious gift from the God who loves you. To understand justification more fully, read the following Scripture passages and notes below.

1. **God Promises Us His Gracious Forgiveness** (see 1 John 1:9, p. 1103). The word *confess* means "to say the same thing as another" or "to agree with." To confess means that we are agreeing with God about our sin. We are seeing it as he does. We know that God hates sin. Therefore, to truly confess our sin means that we essentially feel the same way God feels about what we have done. After committing that sin, we will be determined to put it out of our lives and never do it again. That is true confession in the biblical sense. The reason many believers are not experiencing the forgiveness and joy they desire is because they have not yet truly confessed! Once we have met God's conditions, however, we will know his gracious forgiveness. We may not "feel" forgiven, but we are. We have his word on it.

2. **God Has Balanced Our Moral and Spiritual Budget** (see Romans 5:1-2, p. 966). When God makes us right in his sight, he does so by placing all of the righteousness of Christ to our credit. This balances the moral and spiritual budget for us. We now have sufficient "capital of character" to get on with the business of living.

   Up to this point, salvation has been God's responsibility. From this point on, it continues to be his responsibility except that we are responsible for the wise investment of our "capital of character"—that is, we are responsible for living as God desires us to. It is as if your checking account were empty, but then someone made a $100,000 deposit. What you do with that money is up to you.

3. **God Calls Us His Children** (see Luke 15:11-32, p. 877). This incredible story illustrates what happens when a person turns from sin and returns to God. First, notice that the father in the story did not give this prodigal son what he deserved—banishment. In the same way, we do not receive from God what we deserve—punishment for sin. Second, the young man was given what he did not deserve—the rights and privileges of full sonship. Likewise, although we are not worthy to be called children of God, he calls us sons and daughters. In summary, he doesn't give us what we deserve (judgment). He gives us what we don't deserve (forgiveness and justification).

Speaking of sons and daughters, read on to see how God has adopted you into his family.

Adopted and Assured

We have looked at what happens when we are regenerated (when Christ comes into our lives) and when we are justified (when God forgives our sin and puts his righteousness in its place). Now let us look at another incredible thing God has done for us. He has adopted us into his family as his children!

Adoption means "to be given the rights of a son." In essence, you have been given the full rights of sonship in the family of God as though you were born that way. The story of the Prodigal Son illustrates this (Luke 15:11-32). The wayward son thought that after leaving home, he would no longer be considered a son but would instead be treated as a hired servant. Much to his surprise, when he made the long journey home, his father welcomed him and smothered him with kisses. He then gave orders to bring out the best robe and to put a ring on his finger, signifying full rights as a son. That is exactly what God has done for you! Take some time now to examine three Scripture passages that assure you of your adoption into God's family.

1. **God Disciplines His Children** (see Hebrews 12:5-9, p. 1083). Recognizing you are now a child of God is not some distant hope but a present reality. One of the ways God will remind you of this is by correcting you and bringing you back into line like a loving father when you stray away from him.

   Before we were believers, we may have felt no sense of guilt for certain things we did or did not do. But now that we are Christians, God's Holy Spirit shows us the way to live, which includes correcting us. He does this not because he hates us, but because he loves us as his own dear children. Understanding this truth should help us in the way we behave.

2. **You Have an Approachable Father** (see Galatians 4:6, p. 1018). The Aramaic word translated "dear Father" is *abba,* which is a word of affection that a young child would use endearingly toward his or her father. A western equivalent of that phrase would be "papa" or "daddy." God does not want to be viewed as some distant, disinterested father, but as a loving, approachable father to whom you can turn at any time because you are his child.

3. **His Promises Are Not Based upon Your Feelings** (see 1 John 5:11-13, p. 1109). There will be times as a Christian when you may not "feel" God's presence. You may even be tempted to doubt that he has come into your life. But 1 John 5:13 does not say, "I write this to you who believe in the Son of God so that you may *feel* you have eternal life." This is because feelings come and go. They fluctuate. Nor does the Bible say, "I write this so that you may *hope*—if God is in a really good mood—that you have eternal life." It says, "so that you may *know. . . .*" Eternal life is yours! Stand on God's promise to you. You are forgiven, justified, adopted into his family, and assured of salvation. Now that is reason to rejoice!

To find out more about God, turn to "Who Is God?" p. A11, in the Cornerstones section.

Who Is God?

Thousands of years ago, Pharaoh, the Egyptian ruler, posed a question people are still asking today: "Who is the LORD that I should listen to him?" That's a good question, but it is not an easy subject to tackle. It is difficult for our limited minds to grasp the limitless, eternal God. It has been said, "If God were small enough for your minds, he wouldn't be big enough for your needs." For that reason, don't be exasperated if you can't fully understand who God is or why he does certain things. One day, Scripture promises, everything about God and his character will be made perfectly clear to us (1 Corinthians 13:12). But until then, we will find everything we need to know about him in his Word. Look up the following notes and passages to find out who God is.

1. **God Is All-Knowing, Ever Present, and All-Powerful.** The Creator of the Universe knows every intimate detail of his creation (see Psalm 139, p. 534).
2. **God Is Holy.** God's incomparable holiness merits our worship (see Isaiah 6:1-8, p. 580).
3. **God Is Loving and Just.** God's justice is tempered by his love (see 2 Peter 3:3-9, p. 1100).
4. **God Is Personal.** This characteristic of God sets him apart from the so-called "gods" of other religions (see Acts 17:22-31, p. 948).
5. **God Is in Control.** It is important to remember that God is still in control, even if things around us seem to be in chaos (see Habakkuk 3:3-17, p. 766).
6. **The God of the Bible Is the One True God.** While some insist on the existence of many gods, only the God of the Bible is the true, living God, worthy of our devotion (see Isaiah 45:9-23, p. 608).

Who Is Jesus?

Throughout history many people have attempted to answer this question. Some have done so accurately, but many have not. Our best source for answering this question is—once again—God's own Word. The Bible presents us with some inescapable truths about Jesus that demand a response. Anyone who seriously studies Scripture to learn more about Jesus must answer two probing questions: (1) What do you think of Jesus Christ? and (2) Who is he? The writer C. S. Lewis made this observation: "You must make your choice. Either this man was, and is, the Son of God: or else a madman or something worse. You can shut Him up for a fool, you can spit at Him and kill Him as a demon; or you can fall at His feet and call Him Lord and God. But let us not come with any patronising nonsense about His being a great human teacher. He has not left that open to us. He did not intend to" (*Mere Christianity,* rev. ed. [New York: Macmillan, 1952], 41).

Jesus was not just a good man. He was—and is—the God-man. Let's examine what the Bible has to say about Jesus.

1. **Jesus Is Human.** Jesus became our supreme example as God in human form (see Philippians 2:5-11, p. 1034).
2. **Jesus Is Divine.** Even though Jesus became human, he still remained God (see Colossians 1:15-20, p. 1040).
3. **Jesus Had a Specific Mission to Accomplish.** Jesus came to save humankind from sin (see Luke 4:16-21, p. 856).
4. **Jesus Made the Ultimate Sacrifice.** Jesus endured tremendous pain so that we could enjoy eternity with him (see Isaiah 53, p. 612).
5. **Jesus Has Great Power to Transform People.** Jesus can change the most unlikely person into one of the most powerful witnesses on his behalf (see Acts 4:13, p. 926).
6. **Jesus Has an Eternal Dominion.** Jesus' Kingdom extends beyond the boundaries of space and time (see Revelation 1:4-8, p. 1118).

Who Is the Holy Spirit?

The Holy Spirit is the most mysterious member of the Trinity, which includes God the Father, God the Son (Jesus Christ), and God the Spirit (or the Holy Spirit). Many struggle with the idea of God being three persons, yet one. Quite honestly, we will never fully grasp the concept this side of heaven.

Some, however, have wrongly thought of the Holy Spirit as more of an "it" than a "him." That is probably due in part to biblical descriptions of him as being like the wind or coming upon Jesus in the form of a dove, among other comparisons.

Yet these descriptions must be balanced with the descriptions of the other members of the Trinity. For instance, Jesus referred to himself as "the bread of life" and "the good shepherd." In the same way, God the Father is referred to as "a refuge" and "a consuming fire." Does this mean that Jesus is a loaf of bread or a sheep farmer, or that the Father is a pile of rocks or a blast furnace? Of course not! These are simply metaphors used in Scripture to help communicate God's character. Likewise, the unique descriptions attributed to the Holy Spirit do not imply that the Holy Spirit is merely some "force" or "power." Jesus said this about the Holy Spirit: "When the Spirit of truth comes, he will guide you into all truth. . . . He will tell you about the future" (John 16:13). Note the use of the pronoun *he*. The Holy Spirit has a distinct personality, and he also has specific work that he wants to do in our lives as followers of Jesus Christ. Explore what the Bible says about him.

1. **Who the Holy Spirit Helps.** The Holy Spirit strengthens and empowers followers of Christ (see Acts 2:1-40, p. 922).
2. **How the Holy Spirit Works with the Father and the Son.** The Holy Spirit works alongside God the Father and Jesus, God's Son, to make our lives pleasing to God (see 1 Peter 1:2, p. 1092).
3. **Why God Gives Us the Holy Spirit.** The Holy Spirit's presence in our lives is God's mark of ownership (see Ephesians 1:13-14, p. 1024).
4. **How the Holy Spirit Works in Our Lives.** The Holy Spirit draws us to Christ, enters our life at conversion, and empowers us as we allow him to work in our life (see John 14:15-17, p. 912).
5. **When the Holy Spirit Can Be Sinned Against.** There are six specific ways we can sin against the Holy Spirit (see Acts 5:1-10, p. 928).
6. **Why Christians Need the Holy Spirit.** Living the Christian life is impossible without the Holy Spirit's help (see Galatians 5:16-26, p. 1016).

Who Is the Devil?

What is the Devil like? Does he really look like the red-suited, pitchfork-holding cartoon caricature seated on a throne in hell? Or does he roam through the earth disguised as an angel of light?

Unfortunately, far too many people do not have an accurate view of who the Devil is. Many underestimate him and his prowess, even going as far as to doubt his very existence. Someone once asked the great evangelist Charles Finney, "Mr. Finney, do you believe in a literal Devil?" Finney replied, "You try opposing him for a while, and you see if he's literal or not." You will find out how literal the Devil is the moment you make a commitment to Jesus Christ.

The Bible clearly shows us just how active and conniving the Devil really is. At the same time, Scripture also lets us know about the Devil's limitations and ultimate demise. The more we understand the tactics of this intelligent spirit being, the better equipped we will be to ward off his attacks. Below are some key passages of Scripture that answer some of the most commonly asked questions about the Devil—who is also referred to as Satan.

1. **Where Did Satan Come From?** Satan's pride led to his fall from heaven (see Ezekiel 28:12-19, p. 698).
2. **What Are Satan's Abilities?** Satan does have the power and access to do certain things in this world (see 2 Corinthians 4:3-4, p. 1006).
3. **What Are Satan's Limitations?** While we should not underestimate Satan's power, we should realize that it is limited (see Job 1:1–2:10, p. 440).
4. **How Does Satan Attack People?** Satan masterfully uses manipulation and distortion to deceive people (see Genesis 3:1-7, p. 6).
5. **Who Can Thwart Satan's Agenda?** Those who lay down their lives for Christ will defeat this evil foe (see Revelation 12:10-12, p. 1126).

What Are Angels?

According to recent surveys, most people believe in the existence of angels. A glut of books on the subject fill bookstore shelves. Still, our only reliable source on angels and their activity is the Bible. Just who are these mysterious creatures? What do they look like? Do they wear long, flowing robes and have large birdlike wings? And what is their purpose?

You might call angels "God's secret agents." They basically work undercover. Most of the time these secret agents remain invisible—except on those special occasions when God allows people to see them. No doubt God realized that if we were allowed to see them all of the time, they would become an object of our worship, which is to be reserved for God alone. Let's take some time to see what the Bible has to say about angels and their role in this world.

1. **Why Did God Create Angels?** God created angels as unique spiritual beings who worship Christ and care for his followers (see Hebrews 1:4-14, p. 1072).
2. **What Do Angels Do in the Life of a Christian?** God has ordered the angels to protect his followers and keep them from harm (see Psalm 91:1-16, p. 510).
3. **How Are Angels Involved in Our Prayers?** Our prayers can trigger spiritual warfare (see Daniel 10:1–11:1, p. 730).
4. **What Role Will Angels Play in the End Times?** Angels will play a strategic role in spreading the everlasting gospel (see Revelation 14:6-7, p. 1128).

What Are Demons?

Just as there are angels who look out for your welfare, there are angels who are bent upon your destruction. The Bible teaches that when Satan fell from heaven, he took one-third of the angels with him (Revelation 12:4). Although we do not know their exact number, Scripture tells us there are multitudes (Luke 2:13) and legions (Matthew 26:53) of angels. So Satan has a sizable, highly organized force under his control. These fallen angels, also known as demons, help Satan accomplish his purpose, which, in the words of Christ, is to steal, kill, and destroy. While the Bible does not give us specific details as to how demons work, we can be confident that everything we need to know about them is found in Scripture. We do not need to look elsewhere for insights into the spiritual world. See what God's Word has to say about these evil agents.

1. **What Do Demons Believe?** Strange as it may seem, demons acknowledge that there is only one God (see James 2:19, p. 1090).
2. **Can Demons Personally Harm You?** Those people who have a true relationship with Christ cannot be overcome by demons; those who do not are "fair game" for these servants of Satan (see Acts 19:13-20, p. 950).
3. **What Makes Demons Powerless?** The name of Jesus used by the followers of Jesus makes the demons tremble (see Luke 10:1-20, p. 868).

What Is Heaven?

The Bible gives us wonderful, vivid descriptions of heaven. From Scripture we know that heaven's streets are made of gold, and that pain, fear, and sorrow are not present there. But even with all of this detail, we still fall short of understanding "the big picture." That is because it is difficult for us to grasp the absolute perfection and glory of heaven.

All splendor aside, though, what truly makes heaven spectacular is that we will be forever in God's presence. As the psalmist so poignantly expressed, "You will show me the way of life, granting me the joy of your presence and the pleasures of living with you forever" (Psalm 16:11).

While we may not be able to have all of our questions about heaven answered here on earth, the Bible does answer some of our most probing questions.

1. **Who Will Enter Heaven?** Heaven is a place for those who have received Jesus Christ as Lord (see John 14:1-6, p. 910).
2. **When Does a Christian Enter Heaven?** When we take our last breath on earth, we will take our first breath in heaven (see 2 Corinthians 5:6-9, p. 1008).
3. **Will We Recognize People in Heaven?** While our heavenly bodies may resemble our earthly bodies, we will in some ways be like the angels (see Matthew 22:23-33, p. 816).
4. **What Will Life in Heaven Be Like?** Our lives in heaven will no longer be consumed by the cares of this life, but we will be filled with joy being in the presence of our heavenly Father (see Revelation 7:13-17, p. 1122).

What Is Hell?

According to the Bible, you have two options to choose from when it comes to deciding where you will spend your life after death. One option is heaven. The other is hell. Interestingly enough, while there seems to be an increased belief in a place called hell, most people don't believe that they are headed there. Instead, they believe that hell is reserved for only the most hardened of criminals and other "evil" elements of our society. But God's Word judges people by a different set of criteria. You are not sent to hell for being a bad person any more than you are sent to heaven for being a good person. We all deserve to spend eternity in hell (Romans 3:22-23).

While God clearly says that those who reject the salvation offered through his Son, Jesus Christ, will spend eternity in this place of torment, he repeatedly gives each person ample opportunity to choose life—abundant life on earth and eternal life in heaven (2 Peter 3:9). If you haven't made that choice yet, or if you have decided and want a better understanding of what your nonbelieving friends will have to face, consider these facts about hell from the pages of Scripture.

1. **What Is Hell Like?** Hell is a place of unending, isolated torment (see Luke 16:19-31, p. 878).
2. **Who Will Go to Hell?** Those whose names do not appear in the Book of Life are destined to everlasting punishment (see Revelation 20:11-15, p. 1132).
3. **What Is the Worst Punishment of Hell?** Hell's worst punishment is everlasting separation from God's presence (see 2 Thessalonians 1:7-10, p. 1052).

Love

On one occasion Jesus was asked what commandment was the most important. He replied, "The most important commandment is this: 'Hear, O Israel! The Lord our God is the one and only Lord. And you must love the Lord your God with all your heart, all your soul, all your mind, and all your strength.' The second is equally important: 'Love your neighbor as yourself'." (Mark 12:29-31).

These are the two most important commandments because if you truly love God with all your heart, soul, mind, and strength, you will want to do what pleases him. In the same way, if you really love others as much as you love yourself, you will be concerned for their welfare and will treat them accordingly. Before you can effectively love God, however, you must first realize how much he loves you.

Scripture explains that God showed his great love for us by sending Christ to die for us while we were still sinners who had no relationship with him (Romans 5:8). The more we realize this wonderful truth, the more our love for God will grow. The Bible correctly recognizes that our love for God comes as a result of his loving us first (1 John 4:19). These Scripture passages explore some different facets of the love we should have for God and for others.

1. **God Should Be the Greatest Love of Our Life.** Before we can fully love one another, however, we must fully love God and understand his love for us (see Deuteronomy 6:4-5, p. 158).
2. **Christ's Love Sets the Standard.** Our love for others should model Christ's love for us (see Ephesians 5:1-2, p. 1030).
3. **Love Surpasses All Spiritual Gifts.** A Christian who understands what love truly means and shows love in his or her life is the greatest testimony to others (see 1 Corinthians 13:1-13, p. 1000).
4. **Our Love for God Prepares Us for Service.** The depth of our love for God directly affects our ability to minister to others (see John 21:15-17, p. 918).
5. **Our Love for Others Mirrors the Condition of Our Heart.** The love we have for those around us is an indication of the strength of our Christian walk (see 1 John 2:9-11, p. 1104).
6. **Our Love Should Grow.** The closer we grow to God, the more our love for others should increase (see 1 Thessalonians 3:12-13, p. 1046).

Forgiveness

One of the great principles of the Christian life is forgiveness. Jesus modeled this principle for us when he hung on the cross and prayed for the very people who had put him there (see Luke 23:34, p. 890). His words were so powerful and unexpected that they brought about the conversion of one of the thieves hanging on a cross next to him.

Because Jesus completely forgave us, he wants us to follow his example by forgiving others. As Scripture says: "Be kind to each other, tenderhearted, forgiving one another, just as God through Christ has forgiven you. Follow God's example in everything you do, because you are his dear children" (Ephesians 4:32–5:1). The Bible gives us several important characteristics of the forgiveness we should have for others.

1. **Forgiveness First Comes from God.** Our forgiveness of others should flow from God's forgiveness of us (see Mark 11:25, p. 842).
2. **Forgiveness Knows No Limits.** For a Christian, no wrong is too great or too small to forgive (see Matthew 18:21-35, p. 812).
3. **Forgiveness Is Not Selective.** You can't choose to forgive some people and not forgive others (see Matthew 5:43-48, p. 796).
4. **Forgiveness Breaks Down Walls.** When you choose to forgive, you experience true freedom (see Genesis 45:1-15, p. 42).

Purity

Purity is a quality we hear too little about today. Usually when we do hear something about purity, it is in reference to sexual purity. But purity goes beyond this to include wholesome thoughts, a sincere desire to do what is right, and a commitment to obey God's Word. Jesus alluded to the importance of purity by promising that those whose hearts were pure would see God (Matthew 5:8). In using the word heart, Jesus was saying that the center of our being—our will, our emotions, and our thought processes—needs to be cleansed of sin. The Bible texts below examine the idea of purity and how it affects us as followers of Jesus Christ.

1. **Don't Place Yourself in the Way of Unnecessary Temptation.** Know your moral weaknesses and avoid situations where the temptation to sin would be irresistible (see 2 Samuel 11:1–12:14, p. 272).
2. **Guard the Content of Your Thoughts.** Don't fill your mind with the world's moral filth (see 2 Timothy 2:22, p. 1062).
3. **Beware of the Sins of the Heart.** The person who commits adultery in his heart is just as guilty as the person who actually carries it out (see Matthew 5:27-30, p. 794).
4. **Avoid Adulterous Relationships.** God specifically warns us against living in immoral relationships (see 1 Thessalonians 4:1-8, p. 1048).
5. **If You Fall, Ask God to Forgive You and Purify Your Heart and Desires.** Only God can forgive you, restore your joy, and fill you with the right desires (see Psalm 51:7-15, p. 488).
6. **Keep an Eternal Perspective.** Don't waste your time chasing after earthly pleasures (see 2 Peter 3:10-11, p. 1102).

7. Live to Please God. Surrendering your life to the leading of the Holy Spirit is the only way to live a life that is pleasing to God (see Romans 8:5-8, p. 970).

Perseverance

There will be times in your Christian walk when you will feel emotionally "down." You may think that God has forgotten about you. Or you might become discouraged as you see others who have professed faith in Jesus Christ lose interest in spiritual things and fall away. You may begin to wonder whether you are next on the Devil's "hit list." But God will not allow you to be hit with more than you can handle spiritually. In fact, it is during times of trouble that you will actually be strengthened, not weakened.

As you read your Bible, you will come across words like *endurance* and *perseverance.* These words are often used when the Bible compares the Christian life to a race. The race referred to is a marathon, not a fifty-yard dash. Because the Christian life is a long-distance run, you need to pace yourself, to persevere, and most of all, to *finish* the race. Look up the following passages that describe how and why you need to persevere through the inevitable struggles of life.

1. Perseverance Produces Results. As you steadily grow in your understanding of God's Word and apply it to your life, you will win others to the Lord (see Luke 8:15, p. 864).
2. Life's Trials Will Make You Stronger. You shouldn't view difficulties as obstacles to your faith, but as opportunities for spiritual growth (see James 1:2-4, p. 1085).
3. Christ Endured Great Pain for Us. Jesus modeled the ultimate in endurance so that we would be encouraged to keep our faith strong in the race of life (see Hebrews 12:1-3, p. 1080).
4. God Honors Those Who Persevere. A wholehearted commitment to God will enable you to "finish well" with your faith intact (see Joshua 14:6-14, p. 196).

Honesty and Integrity

Honesty and integrity seem to be in short supply these days. Yet the Bible tells us that they are a part of the godly man's or woman's life. Unfortunately, the world tends to gloss over that aspect of the Christian life. It wants to characterize Christians as people who are out of touch with reality. But the Christian is simply someone who allows God to influence every aspect of his or her life—down to the practical, everyday dealings of business, finances, and relationships. The following passages examine how honesty and integrity should characterize our lives.

1. **We Should Be above Criticism.** Daniel's faithful and honest lifestyle made him "stand apart" from everyone else (see Daniel 6:3-4, p. 726).
2. **Our Conduct Should Cause Others to Glorify Christ.** Living a good, honest life around our unbelieving neighbors will ultimately bring glory to God (see 1 Peter 2:9-12, p. 1096).
3. **We Need to Set an Example for Others.** We must seriously pursue a life of integrity in order to be a solid example for our fellow Christians (see Titus 2:6-8, p. 1066).

Faith and Works

When a person truly comes to Jesus Christ, this relationship will dramatically transform his or her life. We may see this transformation more immediately in the lives of some than others. For those whose lives are characterized by pronounced bad habits and blatant immoral living, the change in lifestyle will show others that something profound has indeed happened within that person's life. For others who may not be known for blatantly sinful living, the change may not be as outwardly pronounced, but it is just as significant. Remember, all of us were separated from God by sin, which was dealt with and atoned for at the cross of Jesus.

Our conversion will show itself in both fruit and works. This concept of "bearing fruit" is used often in Scripture to describe the results of someone's commitment to Jesus Christ. If we do not bear fruit, then it is apparent we have not really come to know Jesus Christ as Lord and Savior. Bearing fruit is not an option. It is the natural result of a person coming into union with God. Sometimes there is confusion in this area of fruit bearing, or works. See what the Bible has to say about the issue.

1. **Our Lives Should Show That God Is at Work in Our Hearts.** God desires that we demonstrate our spiritual growth through our outward actions (see Romans 7:4, p. 968).
2. **We Must Live Out Our Faith.** Faith without deeds is incomplete (see James 2:14-18, p. 1088).
3. **God Saved Us for a Purpose.** While God himself gave us salvation, he planned that our salvation would lead to good works (see Ephesians 2:10, p. 1026).
4. **Our Walk Should Match Our Talk.** God isn't as concerned with what we *say* we believe as with how we *live* what we believe (see Matthew 7:21-23, p. 798).

Discernment

An inspector who worked for Scotland Yard in the counterfeit department was once asked if he spent a lot of time handling counterfeit money. He said, "No." He then explained that he spent so much time handling the "real thing" that he could immediately detect the counterfeit. In the same way, as we become knowledgeable about God's Word, we, too, will be able to detect teachings and concepts that are contrary to Scripture. Make no mistake—counterfeit "truth" is out there in force. Look at the following Scripture passages to find out how you can keep from falling prey to false teachings.

1. **Beware of Satan's Clever Imitations.** Satan's work and agents may appear godly, but in the end they will be exposed for what they really are (see Matthew 13:24-30, p. 806).
2. **Recognize Satan's Strategies.** Lies and deceit are Satan's two main strategies to lead people away from the truth (see 1 Timothy 4:1-2, p. 1056).
3. **Understand the Difference between the True Gospel and a False Gospel.** Scripture provides us with a "litmus test" to distinguish between truth and error (see 1 John 4:1-3, p. 1106).
4. **Use God's Word to Evaluate Someone's Teachings.** The best way to detect a counterfeit is to become more familiar with the "real thing" (see Acts 17:11, p. 946).

Peace

Peace of mind—it seems almost elusive in a day when murders are commonplace, job security is nonexistent, and the moral fabric of society is tearing apart at the seams. Yet Jesus has promised that each one of us can experience true peace: "I am leaving you with a gift—peace of mind and heart. And the peace I give isn't like the peace the world gives. So don't be troubled or afraid" (John 14:27).

Unfortunately, some people are so caught up in the "pursuit of peace," that they have forgotten that Jesus has already given it to them. They have simply left that gift "unopened." And we cannot find peace outside of the parameters God has given us. As Augustine said many years ago, "Our souls are restless until they find their rest in God." Begin to "unwrap" this precious gift by examining what God's Word has to say about it.

1. **Peace Begins When We Relinquish Control of Our Lives to God.** When we give Jesus our burdens and allow him to guide us, we find rest (see Matthew 11:28-30, p. 802).
2. **Perfect Peace Builds upon Total Trust.** As God becomes a regular part of our daily lives, our worries begin to disappear (see Isaiah 26:3, p. 592).

3. Our Peace Continues As We Follow the Holy Spirit. We must stop allowing our old, sinful nature to control us before we can really experience peace (see Romans 8:5-8, p. 974).

4. A Love for God's Word Brings Peace of Mind. The more the Bible becomes a part of our lives, the greater the peace we will experience (see Psalm 119:165-168, p. 528).

5. God's Peace Needs to Rule in Our Hearts. We must constantly keep other things from crowding out God's peace in our lives (see Colossians 3:15, p. 1042).

Joy

One noticeable change that takes place in a new believer's life is the inner joy he or she receives. In fact, joy is listed as part of the "fruit of the Spirit" that should be evident in a believer's life (see Galatians 5:22). But this joy is different from the fleeting and temporary "happiness" that is usually dependent upon "good things" happening in someone's life. While sorrows will come a believer's way, the Holy Spirit gives him or her an inner joy and peace that cannot be taken away. Below are some of the ways in which you can experience God's joy in your life.

1. Studying God's Word Helps Us to Experience His Joy. As we study God's Word and honor God with our lives, we experience his joy in our lives (see Nehemiah 8:1-18, p. 422).

2. Knowing and Trusting God Is the Source of Inexpressible Joy. The greatest joy we can experience comes only from a personal relationship with Jesus Christ (see 1 Peter 1:8, p. 1094).

3. Sharing Your Faith Results in Joy. While laboring to introduce people to Jesus is difficult work, the end result will give you much to celebrate (see Psalm 126:5-6, p. 530).

4. Overlooking Petty Issues Frees Us to Experience Joy. God wants us to experience his joy in our lives and to avoid those things that could hamper that joy (see 1 Corinthians 1:10-17, p. 984).

5. Knowing Whom You Belong to and What the Future Holds Brings True Joy. Realizing that you are a child of God and that you will spend eternity in heaven with him will bring you joy (see Romans 15:13, p. 982).

Accountability

Once you receive Jesus Christ into your life as your personal Lord and Savior, not only do you obtain the privileged gift of eternal life, but you immediately acquire a great responsibility. You have been entrusted with the message of the gospel and are responsible for what you do with it in your life. In the end, we know that what we have done on this earth for Christ will be examined before almighty God and displayed before the rest of the world. The question we must all ask is this: Will what I am doing for Christ and his Kingdom stand the test of time? Those who have done much with what God has given them will be greatly rewarded. Take some time to see what God's Word has to say on this subject.

1. **The More We Know, the Greater Our Responsibility Will Be.** The Lord holds those who have been given positions of spiritual leadership to a higher accountability for what they do (see Luke 12:48, p. 874).
2. **We Are Responsible for Our Own Sins and Mistakes.** We cannot pass blame onto others for our own failings (see Jeremiah 31:30, p. 648).
3. **We Need to Invest Our Abilities and Resources in God's Kingdom.** God has graciously given us abilities and resources to invest in the expansion of his Kingdom (see Luke 19:11-26, p. 882).
4. **The Value of Our Work on Earth Will Be Tested.** On Judgment Day, the quality of our faith and the work we have done for Jesus Christ will be revealed and rewarded accordingly (see 1 Corinthians 3:10-15, p. 986).

What to do after you have accepted Christ . . .

Study the Bible

You might say that the Bible is the "user's manual of life" we have all been searching for. Everything we need to know about God and living a life that pleases him is found in its pages.

Tragically, some of us go through life without so much as picking up this amazing book, whose words were inspired by God. Yet, success or failure in the Christian life is determined by how much of the Bible we get into our hearts and minds and how obedient we are to the principles and teachings found within it. Just as we need to continually breathe oxygen to survive, we need to regularly study the Bible to grow and flourish spiritually. Here are some important reasons why we need to spend time in this life-changing book.

1. **Studying the Bible Is Necessary for Our Spiritual Growth.** The Bible performs three functions to help us mature spiritually (see 2 Timothy 3:16-17, p. 1063).
2. **Studying the Bible Keeps Us Spiritually Strong.** The more we get into this book and apply its teachings, the more we will be able to stand our ground in the storms and trials of life (see Psalm 119:9-18, p. 525).
3. **Studying the Bible Makes Scripture a Central Part of Our Lives.** God desires that we make the Bible an integral part of our lives (see Deuteronomy 11:18-20, p. 165).
4. **Studying the Bible Helps Us Apply Its Truth to Our Lives.** We will notice positive changes in our lives as we apply what we read in Scripture (see Psalm 1:1-3, p. 465).

Pray

The idea of talking to God can be intimidating. But it doesn't have to be. In fact, prayer can be a wonderful experience if we know how to do it God's way. Fortunately, we have God's Word to teach us how to pray. The Bible instructs us to pray at all times, in any posture, in any place, for any reason. In addition, it does not matter whether you pray in King James English or the most contemporary jargon. God only desires that you pray from a pure and sincere heart.

The disciples observed the profound effect prayer had in Jesus' life and ministry. They witnessed how Jesus would often go off by himself to spend time in prayer with his heavenly Father. They saw the power, peace, and tranquillity that emanated from his life, giving him the ability to stay calm in troubled circumstances. Jesus' prayer life so impressed these men that they asked him to teach them to pray (Luke 11:1-13). Certainly if the perfect Son of God often took time to pray during his life here on earth, how much more do we, mere men and women, need to pray?

Because prayer is an essential ingredient to walking with Jesus Christ, we need to examine its elements found in God's Word.

1. **Prayer Was Modeled for Us by Christ.** Jesus took the time to show his followers how to pray (see Matthew 6:5-15, p. 795).
2. **Prayer Is Not a Solitary Experience.** God has given us his Holy Spirit to aid us in prayer, even when we do not know what to pray (see Romans 8:26-27, p. 969).
3. **Prayer Allows Us to Voice Our Requests to God.** Prayer is God's appointed way for us to relate our concerns and present our needs to him (see James 4:2-3, p. 1087).
4. **Prayer Enables Us to Seek Forgiveness.** When we pray sincerely for forgiveness, God will hear our prayers and restore us (see Hosea 14:1-7, p. 741).
5. **Prayer Helps Us Overcome Worry.** In the midst of troubles, we can receive God's peace through prayer (see Philippians 4:6-7, p. 1037).
6. **Prayer Increases Our Spiritual Knowledge and Maturity.** God will give us greater spiritual understanding through prayer (see Jeremiah 33:3, p. 653).

Look for and Attend the Right Church

One of the essential building blocks of spiritual growth is fellowship with other believers by becoming part of a local church. The church (meaning the entire body of Christians) is not really an organization so much as an organism. It thrives by keeping its members spiritually active and well fed. The church provides you with spiritual instruction from God's Word, allows you to worship God with other believers, enables you to use your God-given gifts and abilities as God intended, and makes you accountable to spiritual leadership. Some people think they can get enough spiritual input from Christian television, radio programs, and books. While those things do have value, nothing can replace the need to become an active member of a church. Think about it—if joining in fellowship with other believers was not important, why did Jesus establish the church? (see Matthew 16:18). The Bible has plenty to say about the characteristics of a healthy, vibrant church and the necessity of Christian fellowship. Here are four helpful insights from God's Word on looking for and attending the right church.

1. **What to Look for in a Church.** You should look for a church that has the qualities and characteristics of the first century church (see Acts 2:42, 44-47, p. 925).
2. **Why We Need Fellowship with Other Believers.** Fellowship with other Christians sharpens your spiritual discernment and prepares you for Christ's return (see Hebrews 10:25, p. 1079).
3. **Why the Church Needs You.** Not only will you benefit from the church, but the church will benefit from you and your God-given abilities (see Ephesians 4:11-16, p. 1025).
4. **You Have a Place in the Church.** God has given each one of us a unique role to play in our place of fellowship (see 1 Corinthians 12:12-31, p. 999).

Obey God

The real evidence of a true Christian is a changed life. The great British preacher Charles Haddon Spurgeon once said, "Of what value is the grace I profess to receive if it does not dramatically change the way that I live? If it doesn't change the way that I live, it will never change my eternal destiny."

A changed life begins with obedience to God. This means that you will have to stop doing certain things and start doing others. While God begins to change your heart and desires once you have surrendered your life to him, he still gives you the freedom to decide just how much of your life you will let him control. But know this: Whatever you give up to follow Jesus Christ will pale in comparison to what he will give you in return. For example, when you give up sinful behaviors for God, he will replace your sin with forgiveness and a clear conscience. With this incentive for obedience, look at six specific ways the Bible instructs us to obey God.

1. **Recognize That You Are a New Creation.** When you understand what God has done in your life, obedience becomes more of a desire than a mere duty (see 2 Corinthians 5:14-17, p. 1009).
2. **Follow God Wholeheartedly.** When you follow God completely, you will finish the race of life well (see Joshua 14:6-14, p. 197).

3. **Offer God More than Lip Service.** God looks at your heart more than your religious actions (see 1 Samuel 15:21-23, p. 247).
4. **Live in God's Love.** Discover the secret of true and lasting joy (see John 15:9-11, p. 913).
5. **Put on God's Armor.** Obedience prepares you for the battles of life (see Romans 13:11-14, p. 977).
6. **Let God Occupy Your Thoughts.** Your thoughts will affect your actions (see Colossians 3:1-4, p. 1041).

Resist Temptation

Now that you are a follower of Jesus Christ, Satan is going to try to draw you away by tempting you to disobey God's Word. It is not a sin to be tempted—even Jesus was tempted (see Luke 4:1-13). We sin when we give in to that temptation. The good news is that God will never let a temptation become so strong that we can't handle it. In addition, he has given us specific ways to handle temptation. Here are four things to remember when dealing with temptation.

1. **Realize Who Is Tempting You.** Satan is the mastermind behind all of your temptations (see Ephesians 6:10-12, p. 1029).
2. **Resist the Devil.** The Bible says that if you resist Satan's enticements, he will flee from you (see James 4:7-8, p. 1089).
3. **Rejoice Because Victory Is Yours in Christ Jesus.** God promises that he will always provide a way of escape (see 1 Corinthians 10:13, p. 995).
4. **Remember That Others Have Successfully Dealt with Temptation.** Joseph's example shows us one of the best ways to resist temptation (see Genesis 39:1-23, p. 37).

Live in God's Power

Some people look at the Christian life and say, "I couldn't begin to live that way and hold to those standards. It is too hard!" This is true. It is not hard to be a Christian—it is impossible (that is without the help of the Holy Spirit). You see, God has given you power to live the Christian life. The moment you asked Jesus Christ into your heart, he gave you the gift of his Holy Spirit (see "Who Is the Holy Spirit?" p. A12).

The Holy Spirit not only takes up residence in your heart, but he empowers you to live a holy life and to be an effective witness for Jesus Christ. The Holy Spirit's power is much like an investment. You need to draw upon his power daily to live out your faith. To find out more about how the Holy Spirit can empower and strengthen your Christian walk, look up the following passages of Scripture.

1. **God's Spirit Will Guide You.** The Holy Spirit will help you understand the truths of Scripture and the character of God (see John 16:13-15, p. 915).
2. **God's Spirit Will Empower Your Witness.** The Holy Spirit will give you greater courage and an increased ability to share your faith (see Acts 1:8, p. 923).
3. **God's Spirit Will Encourage You to Be Obedient.** You will have a Holy Spirit-inspired desire to obey God's commands (see Ezekiel 36:26-27, p. 707).
4. **God's Spirit Will Help You Overcome Sin.** Sin will no longer have the power over you it had before you accepted Christ into your life (see Romans 8:9-14, p. 967).

Share Your Faith

Next to personally knowing Jesus and walking with him, one of the greatest blessings of the Christian life is to actually lead someone to Jesus Christ. The good news is that God wants to use you—not just pastors, missionaries, and evangelists—as his instrument to speak to others.

Jesus gave us this very commission in Mark 16:15, where he says, "Go into all the world and preach the Good News to everyone, everywhere." This wonderful charge is known as the "great commission." But the way some Christians follow it, you would think it was the "great suggestion." Sharing our faith, however, is something that Jesus wants—and commands—us to do! How do we do this? First Peter 3:15-16 tells us to be ready to give an answer to anyone who asks us about the hope we have in Jesus. Here are five passages from God's Word that will help you to share your faith.

1. **You Don't Need Any Training to Share.** A changed heart is all you need to begin sharing your faith with others (see John 9:1-41, p. 903).
2. **Be Open to God's Leading.** Effectively sharing your faith begins with a willing heart (see Acts 8:4-8, 26-38, p. 933).
3. **Understand the Simplicity of the Gospel.** The message of the gospel is simple yet powerful (see 1 Corinthians 2:1-5, p. 985).
4. **Share Your Own Story.** Never underestimate the strength of your personal testimony (see Acts 26:1-23, p. 957).

Seek God's Will

Have you ever wondered about the future? Have you pondered the answers to such important, life-changing decisions as whom you should marry or what career path you should pursue? More than likely, most of us have asked these questions and wondered if God has a definite plan or opinion in the matter. With that in mind, here is some good news: God is vitally interested in your life, and he does want to lead you in your decisions.

Jesus called his followers friends (see John 15:15). As God's friend you already have an "inside track" in discovering God's will for your life. It is called the Bible. There you will find God's general will for your life (such as putting God first in all you do and following God's guidelines for marriage), as well as some principles to follow when seeking his specific direction for your life. In the end, finding God's will comes down to living out what you read in the Bible and then living by faith. Here are six steps you can take as you seek God's will.

1. **Unconditionally Surrender Your Life.** Certain conditions must be met if you want to know God's will for your life (see Romans 12:1-2, p. 971).
2. **Realize That God Has a Plan for Your Life.** Your life has purpose and meaning, and God wants to reveal it to you (see Jeremiah 29:11, p. 647).
3. **Act upon What God Has Already Revealed in Scripture.** God has already given us some specific guidelines to follow in his Word (see 1 Thessalonians 4:1-8, p. 1047).
4. **Trust God Completely.** There is nothing more reassuring than entrusting an unknown future to a known God (see Proverbs 3:4-8, p. 543).
5. **Listen for God's Voice.** Sometimes God speaks to us in a quiet voice (see 1 Kings 19:11-13, p. 311).

Live as a Disciple

When you hear the word *disciple,* do you immediately think of the Twelve who followed Jesus during his ministry on earth? Many people do not realize that Jesus still has disciples in this day and age. While every disciple is a believer, not every believer is necessarily a disciple. A disciple is someone who has made a wholehearted commitment to follow Jesus Christ as Savior and Lord. In one sense, you might call discipleship "radical Christian living." When you truly make a commitment to be Christ's disciple, you will be living the Christian life as it was meant to be lived. Anything short of discipleship is settling for less than what God desires. Here are four passages from the Bible that explain what it means to truly be a disciple of Jesus.

1. **A Disciple Takes Up His or Her Cross and Follows Christ.** Being a disciple takes work and commitment (see Luke 9:23-25, p. 867).
2. **A Disciple Counts the Cost.** Jesus' disciples are willing to give up everything to follow him (see Luke 14:25-33, p. 877).
3. **A Disciple Abides in Christ.** The source of a disciple's strength comes from his or her closeness to Christ (see John 15:1-17, p. 911).
4. **A Disciple Walks as Jesus Walked.** Disciples pattern their lives after Jesus, the ultimate example of how to live (see 1 John 2:3-6, p. 1105).

Give to God

Money is such an important topic in the Bible that it is the main subject of nearly *half* the parables Jesus told. In addition, one out of every seven verses in the New Testament deals with the topic. To give you an idea of how this compares with other topics, Scripture offers about five hundred verses on prayer and fewer than five hundred on faith, while there are more than *two thousand* verses on money!

You may be wondering what money has to do with your faith. Now that Jesus Christ has come into your life, he wants to be Lord (to be in command) of every aspect of it. That includes your finances. Martin Luther astutely observed, "There are three conversions necessary: the conversion of the heart, the mind, and the purse [or wallet]." When we experience this "conversion of the purse" and give freely of our finances to the Lord's work (to our church, a missionary, or a ministry), we will make the best investment possible—an investment with eternal dividends. With that in mind, here are five questions to consider about wealth and giving.

1. **Why Should You Give a Portion of Your Financial Resources to God?** God wants to prove his faithfulness through your regular giving, or tithes (see Malachi 3:8-11, p. 785).
2. **How Much Should You Give?** God encourages us to give sacrificially (see Mark 12:41-44, p. 845).
3. **What Happens When You Give?** When you give with the right motives, you will experience joy and God's generous blessings (see 2 Corinthians 9:6-14, p. 1013).
4. **How Should You View Material Wealth?** Accumulating wealth should never be a high priority because it is eternally worthless (see Matthew 6:19-34, p. 797).
5. **Can You Enjoy Wealth?** God may bless you materially, but you are responsible for using your material blessings wisely (see 1 Timothy 6:17-19, p. 1057).

Have Courage in Trials

Many Christians have the mistaken idea that once they make a commitment to Jesus Christ, life will be smooth sailing from that day forward. This is certainly not the case. While it is true that walking with Christ will help us avoid many of the problems we used to face, we are still going to experience what the Bible calls "trials."

Trials may come in the form of a crisis, a sudden illness, the loss of a loved one, or some drastic change in your life. You may go through a difficult time when you don't feel God's presence, when church may not be as exciting as it once was for you, or your prayers seem to go no higher than the ceiling. This may cause you to wonder if you have angered God or if he has left you. But God does not allow us to experience trials because he wants to see us suffer. Rather, he allows these difficulties into our lives to help us grow spiritually—to learn to live by faith, not by feelings. Look up the following passages to see the role trials play in our lives. Notice also God's promise to be with us during these times of trouble.

1. **Trials Sharpen Our Faith.** Hardships develop our character and purify our faith (see 1 Peter 1:3-7, p. 1093).
2. **Trials Help Us Comfort Others.** Experiencing suffering deepens our compassion for others who suffer (see 2 Corinthians 1:3-7, p. 1005).
3. **Trials Are Survivable.** We must keep our eternal perspective through the tough times (see 2 Corinthians 4:7-18, p. 1007).
4. **Trials Test Our Foundation.** When we ground our lives in Christ, we can weather any storm (see Luke 6:47-49, p. 861).
5. **Jesus Is with Us in Life's Storms.** We are never outside of God's watchful eye and his abiding presence (see Mark 4:35-41, p. 833).
6. **God Gives Hope to Our Troubled Hearts.** We can have peace of mind in the middle of our greatest trials (see John 14:1-7, p. 909).

OFF AND RUNNING

How your faith affects the daily aspects of your life

Marriage

How many times have you heard the cliché "They have a marriage made in heaven"? This statement implies that some marriages are destined to be good, while others are destined to be bad. Such thinking assumes that marriage has a life of its own, and the only way to find out if you are to have a "good" one or a "bad" one is to "give it a shot." What most people don't seem to understand, though, is that marriage is like a mirror. It reflects what it sees. If a marriage is strong, it is because the husband and wife have put a lot of hard work into it. If a marriage is weak, it is because the husband or wife or both have neglected it.

God never intended for anyone to have a weak marriage. His design for marriage is lifelong, fulfilling companionship. For a couple's marriage to thrive within his design, the couple must obey God and his Word and lay aside this world's distorted and perverse concept of marriage. The Bible contains truths that will not only help keep a couple together but will also keep their marriage strong. In fact, the lessons this book gives on marriage should serve as the foundation of every Christian couple's relationship. Whether you are married or single, the following verses will give you a godly perspective on marriage relationships.

1. **God Created Marriage.** We can learn more about God's marriage ideal from the world's first husband and wife (see Genesis 2:15-25, p. 4).
2. **Husbands and Wives Have Distinct Roles in Marriage.** A marriage works when a couple follows God's specific design for the husband and the wife (see Ephesians 5:21-33, p. 1028).
3. **The Boundaries of Marriage Are to Be Honored and Enjoyed.** Sexual intimacy is meant to be enjoyed only within the bounds of the marriage relationship (see Proverbs 5:15-21, p. 544).

4. **Keeping Your Marriage Strong.** God promises punishment to those who commit adultery or lead immoral lives (see Hebrews 13:4, p. 1082).

5. **Divorce Is Not Part of God's Plan.** Jesus teaches that marriage is meant to be a life-long commitment (see Mark 10:2-12, p. 840).

6. **A Christian Should Not Leave a Non-Christian Spouse.** An unbelieving husband or wife should not be abandoned, but loved (see 1 Corinthians 7:12-16, p. 992).

7. **Marriage Is Not for Everyone.** Although God blesses many with marriage, some are given a calling or ability to remain single (see 1 Corinthians 7:1-40, p. 990).

8. **Marriage Is for Companionship.** While God has given some the ability to remain happily single, he has given others the gift of a companion for life (see Proverbs 18:22, p. 552).

9. **There Is an Intimacy in Marriage That Can Be Found Nowhere Else.** God wants you to have a fulfilling, enjoyable sex life within the parameters of marriage (see Song of Songs 4:1–5:1, p. 572).

10. **A Strong Marriage Is an Ideal Environment for Raising Godly Children.** Those children who see their parents united by their love for God and one another have a distinct advantage over those who do not (see Malachi 2:15, p. 784).

Children

God's plan is to build, strengthen, and protect the family. Satan's plan is to undermine, weaken, and destroy it. Make no mistake: Satan has declared war on the family. Tragically, many of us have been willing accomplices. Why? Because the bulk of the problems in our culture today can be directly traced to the breakdown of the family or to homes in which biblical principles are ignored or disobeyed. This not only includes husbands and wives splitting apart, but also "alternative families," such as homosexual marriages and "live-in" lovers. Such relationships will never be blessed or honored by God, for they are clearly outside the parameters of his will. It has been said, "A family can survive without a country, but a country cannot survive without the family."

Fortunately, there is hope. The Bible gives us specific guidelines to follow when it comes to parenting. If they are put into practice, we will see amazing results. See what the Bible has to say about raising children who love and revere the Lord in a world that is often hostile to God and his values.

1. **Children Are Never Too Young to Learn about God.** Teaching your children to love the Lord in their early years will help them stay true to the Lord later in life (see Proverbs 22:6, p. 554).

2. **Make Sure Your Children Hear the Gospel Message.** The gospel must first be preached in the home (see Acts 16:29-34, p. 944).

3. **Encourage Your Children's Spiritual Growth.** As the apostle Paul suggests, a

loving father encourages his children to live a life pleasing to God (see 1 Thessalonians 2:11-12, p. 1046).

4. **Watch the Legacy You Leave.** Your devotion to God—or lack of it—will make a resounding impression on the next generation (see 2 Chronicles 17:3-6, p. 388).

5. **Discipline Your Children.** Parents who love their children and want them to grow up into young men and women of character will discipline them (see Proverbs 29:15, p. 560).

6. **Avoid Aggravating Your Children.** Your discipline must be tempered with love so that your children do not become resentful (see Colossians 3:20-21, p. 1042).

Priorities

As a Christian, one of the most dramatic changes in your life will be the way you spend your time. Your pursuits and ambitions in life will be different. After all, you are no longer living for yourself but for God. It may be a difficult transition at first, but here are a few pointers we can glean from God's Word.

1. **Place Christ before All Else.** To be a true follower of Jesus Christ, you need to be wholly devoted to him and let nothing else get in the way of your devotion (see Philippians 3:4-11, p. 1036).

2. **Balance Christian Service with Worship.** Don't get so caught up in "serving" the Lord that you forget to worship him and get to know him better (see Luke 10:38-42, p. 870).

3. **Don't Waste Time Pursuing Things That Won't Last.** Your time on earth is short. Ask God to help you spend it on things that count (see Psalm 39:1-7, p. 480).

4. **Spend Time Feeding Your Soul.** God offers blessings to you if you choose to spend time with him rather than devote your life to the pursuit of temporary satisfaction (see Isaiah 55:1-13, p. 614).

5. **Keep Your Spiritual Zeal Alive.** Work hard to keep that "fire" in your heart burning brightly as you serve the Lord (see Romans 12:11, p. 972).

Prayer Time

Before you became a Christian, you may have prayed before meals, on holidays, or perhaps during times of crisis. As a believer, however, prayer should become second nature. Prayer is no longer an option but should become part of all you do.

As you integrate prayer into every aspect of your life, you will not always see your prayers answered the way you would like them to be. When this happens, it is easy to grow discouraged and give up praying. But Jesus implored us to pray and never give up (Luke 18:1). Paul also instructed believers to "keep on praying"

(1 Thessalonians 5:17). When we fail to pray, we miss out on one of the greatest blessings of the Christian life—fellowship with God himself, our power source for living. In addition, we are going against what God has instructed us to do.

The Bible gives us some perspective on how to experience the power of prayer in our lives. The following is a partial list of what should characterize your prayers as a believer.

1. **Pray Regularly.** God wants to hear our prayers throughout the day—not just in times of crisis or before meals (see Psalm 55:16-17, p. 490).
2. **Pray without Hinderance.** Sins and other distractions can negatively affect your prayer life (see Isaiah 59:1-2, p. 616).
3. **Pray Expecting to Get Answers.** The Bible gives us guidelines to follow so that our prayers will be answered (see 1 John 5:14-15, p. 1108).
4. **Pray Effectively.** Prayer can work powerfully in the face of a crisis when God's people come together and call out to him (see Acts 12:1-17, p. 938).
5. **Pray Persistently.** God honors persistent prayer (see Luke 18:1-8, p. 880).

Conversation

As a Christian, it is extremely important to remember that you are a representative of Jesus Christ. One of the more visible ways you represent him is through your speech or conversations. It has been said that every person speaks about thirty thousand words in an average day. That is a considerable amount of "representation time"—especially when you consider the power of the spoken word. With our mouths we have the power to build up or destroy. This should give you even greater motivation to weigh your words before you speak them.

The Bible shares some practical advice when it comes to controlling the tongue. Below are a few passages of Scripture to guide you in this area.

1. **Think before You Speak.** You demonstrate great wisdom and care when you weigh your words (see Proverbs 16:23-24, p. 550).
2. **Control Your Tongue.** As you learn to control your tongue, you will be able to control other aspects of your life (see James 3:1-12, p. 1088).
3. **Refrain from Idle Talk.** We will be held accountable for every idle word we speak (see Matthew 12:35-37, p. 804).
4. **Make a Habit of Talking about the Lord.** When we talk about the Lord and his blessings with one another, God is pleased (see Malachi 3:16, p. 786).
5. **Keep Your Conversation Gracious.** We should speak gently and sensibly as we share our faith with others (see Colossians 4:6, p. 1044).

6. Never Use Vulgar Speech. Our conversations need to reflect God's goodness, not the world's coarseness (see 1 Peter 3:10, p. 1094).

7. Think of Ways to Encourage, Praise, and Build Up Others. As a Christian, you should use your speech constructively (see 1 Thessalonians 5:11, p. 1050).

Relationships

The people we associate with on a regular basis can either help or hinder our spiritual growth. For that reason God has given us some invaluable advice and strong warnings when it comes to choosing our friends. Look at the following Scripture passages to see what to pursue and what to avoid in your relationships with others.

1. Find a Close Christian Friend. A true Christian friend will help you get through times of trouble and temptation (see Galatians 6:1-3, p. 1018).

2. Don't Associate with Those Who Mock God. God and his Word should be the focus of praise—not mockery—in your friendships (see Psalm 1:1-5, p. 462).

3. Avoid Relationships That Could Cause You to Sin. Bad company corrupts good character (see 2 Corinthians 6:14–7:1, p. 1010).

4. Make Sure Your Friendships Honor God. Seek the friendship of those who live as Christ intended (see 1 John 1:7, p. 1104).

Responsibility

A common question that many new Christians have is, "Can I be a Christian and still do . . . ?" Some questions of "Christian liberty" can be answered easily, because the Bible directly addresses these questions. For instance, if someone asks, "Is it OK, as a Christian, to get drunk?" The answer is clearly no. The Bible says, "Don't be drunk with wine, because that will ruin your life. Instead, let the Holy Spirit fill and control you" (Ephesians 5:18). However, questions like, "Can I be a Christian and still drink alcoholic beverages?" or "Can I listen to any kind of music?" or "Can I go to any movie?" are not answered so easily. They are among the many "gray" areas of the Christian life that do not necessarily have a "chapter and verse" answer.

When you face a situation that the Bible does not directly address, you must consider whether or not your actions will please God. Here is a "litmus test" you can apply to those uncertain areas of life.

1. **Does This Activity Build Me Up Spiritually?** You need to avoid anything that has the potential to dull your spiritual senses and take away your hunger for God and his Word (see 1 Corinthians 10:23, p. 996).
2. **Does This Activity Bring Me under Its Power?** As a Christian, you only want to be controlled by the power of Jesus Christ (see 1 Corinthians 6:12, p. 988).
3. **Do I Have an Uneasy Conscience about This Activity?** You must be obedient to what God has told you to do, not swayed by what others are doing (see Romans 14:23, p. 980).
4. **Could This Activity Cause Other Christians to Stumble in Their Faith?** Stay away from things that could negatively influence other Christians around you (see Romans 14:3-21, p. 978).

Job Performance

Some of the greatest challenges you may ever face as a Christian will come from the workplace. Perhaps you work in an unethical, morally questionable environment. Maybe you find it difficult to respect those who are over you. You might find your job tedious or meaningless. You may even wonder if you are making an impact on your co-workers for Christ. Whatever your vocation, your work can become more fulfilling and rewarding when you follow what the Bible has to say about your attitude toward your job or responsibilities. Take these biblical pointers to heart and see what a difference they will make!

1. **Work As If You Are Working for the Lord.** Keep in mind that you are ultimately serving the Lord, not just people (see Colossians 3:22-24, p. 1044).
2. **Create a Spiritual Hunger in Those around You.** Your godly example can help increase your coworkers' desire to know more about Jesus (see Titus 2:9-10, p. 1066).
3. **Strive to Be Responsible.** People will respect you and your message when you can prove that you are responsible (see 1 Thessalonians 4:11-12, p. 1048).
4. **Honor Christ with Your Hard Work.** Don't allow nonbelievers to criticize the Lord because of your poor witness (see Daniel 6:1-28, p. 724).
5. **Don't Neglect Your Spiritual Health.** Never place your desire for material wealth above your spiritual welfare (see Luke 12:15-21, p. 872).

Attitude toward Self

Many are on a quest today to find personal happiness. They will do whatever is necessary to "find themselves." They are told that the answer is "within," so they search in all the wrong places trying to find meaning and purpose in life. The Bible, however, does not teach that the answer is within us. Rather, it teaches that the *problem* is within us. Jeremiah 17:9 tells us, "The heart is most deceitful and desperately wicked. Who really knows how bad it is?" For that reason, all attempts to reform or improve ourselves will meet with failure. We do not need self-esteem as much as we need a realistic view of who we are and who God is. Once we honestly assess our own sinful condition and come to grips with our built-in weakness and vulnerability to sin, then we will be able to appreciate God's solution. In a nutshell, the way to true happiness comes not from seeking *it* but from seeking *God.* Here's what God's Word has to say about how we can be happy, fulfilled people.

1. **We Need to Recognize Our True Condition.** As we humble ourselves before a holy God, we will be blessed (see Matthew 5:3-5, p. 792).
2. **Our Needs Must Come Last.** Jesus gave us the ultimate example of what it means to be a servant (see Hebrews 13:11-13, p. 1084).
3. **We Will Find Happiness in Loving God and Serving Others.** Loving God and others gives us real purpose and meaning in life (see Matthew 22:37-40, p. 818).
4. **We Must Surrender Our Dreams and Seek God's Will.** True followers of Christ entrust their future into God's hands, because he knows what is best for us (see Matthew 16:24-26, p. 810).

BIG QUESTIONS

*What the Bible has to say about
some of life's troubling issues*

The OLD Testament

Genesis

The Account of Creation

In the beginning God created* the heavens and the earth. ²The earth was empty, a formless mass cloaked in darkness. And the Spirit of God was hovering over its surface. ³Then God said, "Let there be light," and there was light. ⁴And God saw that it was good. Then he separated the light from the darkness. ⁵God called the light "day" and the darkness "night." Together these made up one day.

⁶And God said, "Let there be space between the waters, to separate water from water." ⁷And so it was. God made this space to separate the waters above from the waters below. ⁸And God called the space "sky." This happened on the second day.

⁹And God said, "Let the waters beneath the sky be gathered into one place so dry ground may appear." And so it was. ¹⁰God named the dry ground "land" and the water "seas." And God saw that it was good. ¹¹Then God said, "Let the land burst forth with every sort of grass and seed-bearing plant. And let there be trees that grow seed-bearing fruit. The seeds will then produce the kinds of plants and trees from which they came." And so it was. ¹²The land was filled with seed-bearing plants and trees, and their seeds produced plants and trees of like kind. And God saw that it was good. ¹³This all happened on the third day.

¹⁴And God said, "Let bright lights appear in the sky to separate the day from the night. They will be signs to mark off the seasons, the days, and the years. ¹⁵Let their light shine down upon the earth." And so it was. ¹⁶For God made two great lights, the sun and the moon, to shine down upon the earth. The greater one, the sun, presides during the day; the lesser one, the moon, presides through the night. He also made the stars. ¹⁷God set these lights in the heavens to light the earth, ¹⁸to govern the day and the night, and to separate the light from the darkness. And God saw that it was good. ¹⁹This all happened on the fourth day.

²⁰And God said, "Let the waters swarm with fish and other life. Let the skies be filled with birds of every kind." ²¹So God created great sea creatures and every sort of fish and every kind of bird. And God saw that it was good. ²²Then God blessed them, saying, "Let the fish multiply and fill the oceans. Let the birds increase and fill the earth." ²³This all happened on the fifth day.

²⁴And God said, "Let the earth bring forth every kind of animal—livestock, small animals, and wildlife." And so it was. ²⁵God made all sorts of wild animals, livestock, and small animals, each able to reproduce more of its own kind. And God saw that it was good.

²⁶Then God said, "Let us make people* in our image, to be like ourselves. They will be masters over all life—the fish in the sea, the birds in the sky, and all the livestock, wild animals,* and small animals."

²⁷ So God created people in his own image;
God patterned them after himself;
male and female he created them.

²⁸God blessed them and told them, "Multiply and fill the earth and subdue it. Be masters over the fish and birds and all the animals." ²⁹And God said, "Look! I have given you the seed-bearing plants throughout the earth and all the fruit trees for your food. ³⁰And I have given all the grasses and other green plants to the animals and birds for their food." And so it was. ³¹Then God looked over all he had made, and he saw that it was excellent in every way. This all happened on the sixth day.

1:1 Or *In the beginning when God created,* or *When God began to create,* Hebrew reads *all the earth.*   1:26a Hebrew *man;* also in 1:27.   1:26b As in Syriac version;

CHAPTER **2**

So the creation of the heavens and the earth and everything in them was completed. 2On the seventh day, having finished his task, God rested from all his work. 3And God blessed the seventh day and declared it holy, because it was the day when he rested from his work of creation.

4This is the account of the creation of the heavens and the earth.

The Man and Woman in Eden

When the LORD God made the heavens and the earth, 5there were no plants or grain growing on the earth, for the LORD God had not sent any rain. And no one was there to cultivate the soil. 6But water came up out of the ground and watered all the land. 7And the LORD God formed a man's body from the dust of the ground and breathed into it the breath of life. And the man became a living person.

8Then the LORD God planted a garden in Eden, in the east, and there he placed the man he had created. 9And the LORD God planted all sorts of trees in the garden—beautiful trees that produced delicious fruit. At the center of the garden he placed the tree of life and the tree of the knowledge of good and evil.

10A river flowed from the land of Eden, watering the garden and then dividing into four branches. 11One of these branches is the Pishon, which flows around the entire land of Havilah, where gold is found. 12The gold of that land is exceptionally pure; aromatic resin and onyx stone are also found there. 13The second branch is the Gihon, which flows around the entire land of Cush. 14The third branch is the Tigris, which flows to the east of Asshur. The fourth branch is the Euphrates.

15The LORD God placed the man in the Gar-

den of Eden to tend and care for it. 16But the LORD God gave him this warning: "You may freely eat any fruit in the garden 17except fruit from the tree of the knowledge of good and evil. If you eat of its fruit, you will surely die."

18And the LORD God said, "It is not good for the man to be alone. I will make a companion who will help him." 19So the LORD God formed from the soil every kind of animal and bird. He brought them to Adam* to see what he would call them, and Adam chose a name for each one. 20He gave names to all the livestock, birds, and wild animals. But still there was no companion suitable for him. 21So the LORD God caused Adam to fall into a deep sleep. He took one of Adam's ribs* and closed up the place from which he had taken it. 22Then the LORD God made a woman from the rib and brought her to Adam.

23"At last!" Adam exclaimed. "She is part of my own flesh and bone! She will be called 'woman,' because she was taken out of a man." 24This explains why a man leaves his father and mother and is joined to his wife, and the two are united into one. 25Now, although Adam and his wife were both naked, neither of them felt any shame.

CHAPTER **3**
The Man and Woman Sin

Now the serpent was the shrewdest of all the creatures the LORD God had made. "Really?" he asked the woman. "Did God really say you must not eat any of the fruit in the garden?"

2"Of course we may eat it," the woman told him. 3"It's only the fruit from the tree at the center of the garden that we are not allowed to eat. God says we must not eat it or even touch it, or we will die."

2:19 Hebrew *the man*, and so throughout this chapter. 2:21 Or *took a part of Adam's side.*

OFF AND RUNNING

God Created Marriage Read GENESIS 2:15-25

When Jesus was asked about the issue of divorce, he replied, "It [divorce] was not what God had originally intended" (Matthew 19:8). In other words, "From the beginning it was not so." So what is God's original design for marriage?

God created Eve because he knew that it wasn't "good for [Adam] to be alone" (verse 18). The way God uniquely created Eve from one of Adam's ribs illustrates God's design for marriage: that the husband and wife become one. To "become one" means to "become related to." Achieving oneness in marriage requires couples to do two things:

1. Leave. As verse 24 states, marriage begins when a "man leaves his father and mother." By specifying the parent-child relationship, it is implied that if it is necessary to leave your father and mother, then all lesser ties

4"You won't die!" the serpent hissed. 5"God knows that your eyes will be opened when you eat it. You will become just like God, knowing everything, both good and evil."

6The woman was convinced. The fruit looked so fresh and delicious, and it would make her so wise! So she ate some of the fruit. She also gave some to her husband, who was with her. Then he ate it, too. 7At that moment, their eyes were opened, and they suddenly felt shame at their nakedness. So they strung fig leaves together around their hips to cover themselves.

8Toward evening they heard the LORD God walking about in the garden, so they hid themselves among the trees. 9The LORD God called to Adam,* "Where are you?"

10He replied, "I heard you, so I hid. I was afraid because I was naked."

11"Who told you that you were naked?" the LORD God asked. "Have you eaten the fruit I commanded you not to eat?"

12"Yes," Adam admitted, "but it was the woman you gave me who brought me the fruit, and I ate it."

13Then the LORD God asked the woman, "How could you do such a thing?"

"The serpent tricked me," she replied. "That's why I ate it."

14So the LORD God said to the serpent, "Because you have done this, you will be punished. You are singled out from all the domestic and wild animals of the whole earth to be cursed. You will grovel in the dust as long as you live, crawling along on your belly. 15From now on, you and the woman will be enemies, and your offspring and her offspring will be enemies. He will crush your head, and you will strike his heel."

16Then he said to the woman, "You will bear children with intense pain and suffering. And though your desire will be for your husband,* he will be your master."

17And to Adam he said, "Because you listened to your wife and ate the fruit I told you not to eat, I have placed a curse on the ground. All your life you will struggle to scratch a living from it. 18It will grow thorns and thistles for you, though you will eat of its grains. 19All your life you will sweat to produce food, until your dying day. Then you will return to the ground from which you came. For you were made from dust, and to the dust you will return."

20Then Adam named his wife Eve,* because she would be the mother of all people everywhere. 21And the LORD God made clothing from animal skins for Adam and his wife.

22Then the LORD God said, "The people have become as we are, knowing everything, both good and evil. What if they eat the fruit of the tree of life? Then they will live forever!" 23So the LORD God banished Adam and his wife from the Garden of Eden, and he sent Adam out to cultivate the ground from which he had been made. 24After banishing them from the garden, the LORD God stationed mighty angelic beings* to the east of Eden. And a flaming sword flashed back and forth, guarding the way to the tree of life.

CHAPTER 4
Cain, Abel, and Seth

Now Adam* slept with his wife, Eve, and she became pregnant. When the time came, she gave birth to Cain,* and she said, "With the LORD's help, I have brought forth* a man!" 2Later she gave birth to a second son and named him Abel.

When they grew up, Abel became a shepherd,

3:9 Hebrew *the man,* and so throughout this chapter.   3:16 Or *And though you may desire to control your husband.*   3:20 *Eve* sounds like a Hebrew term that means "to give life."   3:24 Hebrew *cherubim.*   4:1a Hebrew *the man.*   4:1b *Cain* sounds like a Hebrew term that can mean "bring forth" or "acquire."   4:1c Or *I have acquired.*

---

must be broken, changed, or left behind. You will still love and honor your parents. You will still have other friends. But your best friend should be your spouse. And no one or thing—including hobbies, business, or even church activities—should get in the way of that relationship.

2. Cleave. To cleave means "to adhere to, to stick to, to be attached by some strong tie." As the text says, "the two are united into one" when this happens. In the original Hebrew, the word used for cleaving meant an aggressive action, implying that you are holding tightly to your relationship with your spouse. The Greek translation of this same word means "to cement together, to stick like glue, or to be welded together so the two cannot be separated without serious damage to both." For that reason, you must periodically take stock of your life and ask yourself whether your current relationships or pursuits are drawing you and your spouse together or driving you apart.

For the next note on "Marriage," turn to p. 1028.

How Does Satan Attack People? Read GENESIS 3:1-7

This passage records Satan's first tempting of humans, and it provides us with a wealth of information concerning his tactics. Here are four ploys Satan used to bring Eve to her fall:

1. He Questioned God's Word. Satan did not deny that God had spoken. He simply questioned whether God had really said what Eve thought he had said. He wanted her to think that perhaps she had misunderstood God's command. Today Satan still twists the truth to try to alienate people from God.

2. He Questioned God's Love. Satan wanted to make Eve think that God was holding something back. In reality, God had placed those restrictions in Adam and Eve's life to keep them from sinning. Likewise, the barriers God places in our lives are there because he loves us.

3. He Denied God's Word. First Satan questioned God's word, but then he denied God's word. He went from "Did God really say this?" to "That's a lie!" It is a short step from questioning God's word to denying it. If Eve had not listened to Satan's questioning, she would never have fallen into his trap.

4. He Substituted His Own Lie. Satan led Eve to believe that if she ate of the tree she would become like God. At that point Eve had a choice: She could take God at his word or believe Satan's lie.

The Bible calls Satan "the father of lies" and even acknowledges that in the last days Satan will resort to deceiving people through a grand, counterfeit scheme (see 2 Thessalonians 2:9-10, pp. 1051-1052). The best defense against Satan's attack is to fill your mind with the truth found in God's Word.

Satan knows that our minds are "command central." This is where we reason, fantasize, and imagine. He will attempt to make you second-guess what God has said in his Word or try to get you to dwell on the what-ifs in life. Our counterattack is found in 2 Corinthians 10:4-5: "We use God's mighty weapons, not merely worldly weapons, to knock down the Devil's strongholds. With these weapons we break down every proud argument that keeps people from knowing God. With these weapons we conquer their rebellious ideas, and we teach them to obey Christ."

CORNER STONES

For the next note on "Who Is the Devil?" turn to p. 1126.

---

while Cain was a farmer. ³At harvesttime Cain brought to the LORD a gift of his farm produce, ⁴while Abel brought several choice lambs from the best of his flock. The LORD accepted Abel and his offering, ⁵but he did not accept Cain and his offering. This made Cain very angry and dejected.

⁶"Why are you so angry?" the LORD asked him. "Why do you look so dejected? ⁷You will be accepted if you respond in the right way. But if you refuse to respond correctly, then watch out! Sin is waiting to attack and destroy you, and you must subdue it."

⁸Later Cain suggested to his brother, Abel, "Let's go out into the fields."* And while they were there, Cain attacked and killed his brother.

⁹Afterward the LORD asked Cain, "Where is your brother? Where is Abel?"

"I don't know!" Cain retorted. "Am I supposed to keep track of him wherever he goes?"

¹⁰But the LORD said, "What have you done? Listen—your brother's blood cries out to me from the ground! ¹¹You are hereby banished from the ground you have defiled with your brother's blood. ¹²No longer will it yield abundant crops for you, no matter how hard you work! From now on you will be a homeless fugitive on the earth, constantly wandering from place to place."

¹³Cain replied to the LORD, "My punishment* is too great for me to bear! ¹⁴You have banished me from my land and from your presence; you have made me a wandering fugitive. All who see me will try to kill me!"

¹⁵The LORD replied, "They will not kill you, for I will give seven times your punishment to

4:8 As in Samaritan Pentateuch, Greek and Syriac versions, Latin Vulgate; Masoretic Text lacks "Let's go out into the fields." 4:13 Or *My sin.*

anyone who does." Then the LORD put a mark on Cain to warn anyone who might try to kill him. 16So Cain left the LORD's presence and settled in the land of Nod,* east of Eden.

17Then Cain's wife became pregnant and gave birth to a son, and they named him Enoch. When Cain founded a city, he named it Enoch after his son.

18 Enoch was the father of* Irad.

Irad was the father of Mehujael.

Mehujael was the father of Methushael.

Methushael was the father of Lamech.

19Lamech married two women—Adah and Zillah. 20Adah gave birth to a baby named Jabal. He became the first of the herdsmen who live in tents. 21His brother's name was Jubal, the first musician—the inventor of the harp and flute. 22To Lamech's other wife, Zillah, was born Tubal-cain. He was the first to work with metal, forging instruments of bronze and iron. Tubal-cain had a sister named Naamah.

23One day Lamech said to Adah and Zillah, "Listen to me, my wives. I have killed a youth who attacked and wounded me. 24If anyone who kills Cain is to be punished seven times, anyone who takes revenge against me will be punished seventy-seven times!"

25Adam slept with his wife again, and she gave birth to another son. She named him Seth,* for she said, "God has granted me another son in place of Abel, the one Cain killed." 26When Seth grew up, he had a son and named him Enosh. It was during his lifetime that people first began to worship the LORD.

CHAPTER 5
From Adam to Noah

This is the history of the descendants of Adam. When God created people,* he made them in the likeness of God. 2He created them male and female, and he blessed them and called them "human."*

3When Adam was 130 years old, his son Seth was born,* and Seth was the very image of his father.* 4After the birth of Seth,* Adam lived another 800 years, and he had other sons and daughters. 5He died at the age of 930.

6When Seth was 105 years old, his son Enosh was born. 7After the birth of Enosh, Seth lived another 807 years, and he had other sons and daughters. 8He died at the age of 912.

9When Enosh was 90 years old, his son Kenan was born. 10After the birth of Kenan, Enosh lived another 815 years, and he had other sons and daughters. 11He died at the age of 905.

12When Kenan was 70 years old, his son Mahalalel was born. 13After the birth of Mahalalel, Kenan lived another 840 years, and he had other sons and daughters. 14He died at the age of 910.

15When Mahalalel was 65 years old, his son Jared was born. 16After the birth of Jared, Mahalalel lived another 830 years, and he had other sons and daughters. 17He died at the age of 895.

18When Jared was 162 years old, his son Enoch was born. 19After the birth of Enoch, Jared lived another 800 years, and he had other sons and daughters. 20He died at the age of 962.

21When Enoch was 65 years old, his son Methuselah was born. 22After the birth of Methuselah, Enoch lived another 300 years in close fellowship with God, and he had other sons and daughters. 23Enoch lived 365 years in all. 24He enjoyed a close relationship with God throughout his life. Then suddenly, he disappeared because God took him.

25When Methuselah was 187 years old, his son Lamech was born. 26After the birth of Lamech, Methuselah lived another 782 years, and he had other sons and daughters. 27He died at the age of 969.

28When Lamech was 182 years old, his son Noah was born. 29Lamech named his son Noah,* for he said, "He will bring us relief from the painful labor of farming this ground that the LORD has cursed." 30After the birth of Noah, Lamech lived 595 years, and he had other sons and daughters. 31He died at the age of 777.

32By the time Noah was 500 years old, he had three sons: Shem, Ham, and Japheth.

CHAPTER 6
Noah and the Flood

When the human population began to grow rapidly on the earth, 2the sons of God saw the beautiful women of the human race and took any they wanted as their wives. 3Then the LORD said, "My Spirit will not put up with humans for such a long time, for they are only mortal flesh.

4:16 *Nod* means "wandering." 4:18 Or *the ancestor of,* and so throughout the verse. 4:25 *Seth* probably means "granted"; the name may also mean "appointed." 5:1 Hebrew *man.* 5:2 Hebrew *man.* 5:3a Or *his son, the ancestor of Seth, was born;* similarly in 5:6, 9, 12, 15, 18, 21, 25. 5:3b Hebrew *was in his own likeness, after his image.* 5:4 Or *After the birth of this ancestor of Seth;* similarly in 5:7, 10, 13, 16, 19, 22, 26. 5:29 *Noah* sounds like a Hebrew term that can mean "relief" or "comfort."

In the future, they will live no more than 120 years."

4In those days, and even afterward, giants* lived on the earth, for whenever the sons of God had intercourse with human women, they gave birth to children who became the heroes mentioned in legends of old.

5Now the LORD observed the extent of the people's wickedness, and he saw that all their thoughts were consistently and totally evil. 6So the LORD was sorry he had ever made them. It broke his heart. 7And the LORD said, "I will completely wipe out this human race that I have created. Yes, and I will destroy all the animals and birds, too. I am sorry I ever made them." 8But Noah found favor with the LORD.

9This is the history of Noah and his family. Noah was a righteous man, the only blameless man living on earth at the time. He consistently followed God's will and enjoyed a close relationship with him. 10Noah had three sons: Shem, Ham, and Japheth.

11Now the earth had become corrupt in God's sight, and it was filled with violence. 12God observed all this corruption in the world, and he saw violence and depravity everywhere. 13So God said to Noah, "I have decided to destroy all living creatures, for the earth is filled with violence because of them. Yes, I will wipe them all from the face of the earth!

14"Make a boat* from resinous wood and seal it with tar, inside and out. Then construct decks and stalls throughout its interior. 15Make it 450 feet long, 75 feet wide, and 45 feet high.* 16Construct an opening all the way around the boat, 18 inches* below the roof. Then put three decks inside the boat—bottom, middle, and upper—and put a door in the side.

17"Look! I am about to cover the earth with a flood that will destroy every living thing. Everything on earth will die! 18But I solemnly swear to keep you safe in the boat, with your wife and your sons and their wives. 19Bring a pair of every kind of animal—a male and a female—into the boat with you to keep them alive during the flood. 20Pairs of each kind of bird and each kind of animal, large and small alike, will come to you to be kept alive. 21And remember, take enough food for your family and for all the animals."

22So Noah did everything exactly as God had commanded him.

CHAPTER **7**
The Flood Covers the Earth

Finally, the day came when the LORD said to Noah, "Go into the boat with all your family, for among all the people of the earth, I consider you alone to be righteous. 2Take along seven pairs of each animal that I have approved for eating and for sacrifice, and take one pair of each of the others. 3Then select seven pairs of every kind of bird. There must be a male and a female in each pair to ensure that every kind of living creature will survive the flood. 4One week from today I will begin forty days and forty nights of rain. And I will wipe from the earth all the living things I have created."

5So Noah did exactly as the LORD had commanded him. 6He was 600 years old when the flood came, 7and he went aboard the boat to escape—he and his wife and his sons and their wives. 8With them were all the various kinds of animals—those approved for eating and sacrifice and those that were not—along with all the birds and other small animals. 9They came into the boat in pairs, male and female, just as God had commanded Noah. 10One week later, the flood came and covered the earth.

11When Noah was 600 years old, on the seventeenth day of the second month, the underground waters burst forth on the earth, and the rain fell in mighty torrents from the sky. 12The rain continued to fall for forty days and forty nights. 13But Noah had gone into the boat that very day with his wife and his sons—Shem, Ham, and Japheth—and their wives. 14With them in the boat were pairs of every kind of breathing animal—domestic and wild, large and small—along with birds and flying insects of every kind. 15Two by two they came into the boat, 16male and female, just as God had commanded. Then the LORD shut them in.

17For forty days the floods prevailed, covering the ground and lifting the boat high above the earth. 18As the waters rose higher and higher above the ground, the boat floated safely on the surface. 19Finally, the water covered even the highest mountains on the earth, 20standing more than twenty-two feet* above the highest peaks. 21All the living things on earth died—birds, domestic animals, wild animals, all kinds of small animals, and all the people. 22Everything died that breathed and lived on dry land. 23Every living thing on the earth was wiped out—people, animals both large and small, and birds. They were all destroyed, and only Noah

6:4 Hebrew *Nephilim.*   6:14 Traditionally rendered *an ark.*   6:15 Hebrew *300 cubits* [135 meters] *long, 50 cubits* [22.5 meters] *wide, and 30 cubits* [13.5 meters] *high.*   6:16 Hebrew *1 cubit* [45 centimeters].   7:20 Hebrew *15 cubits* [6.8 meters].

was left alive, along with those who were with him in the boat. 24And the water covered the earth for 150 days.

CHAPTER 8
The Flood Recedes

But God remembered Noah and all the animals in the boat. He sent a wind to blow across the waters, and the floods began to disappear. 2The underground water sources ceased their gushing, and the torrential rains stopped. 3So the flood gradually began to recede. After 150 days, 4exactly five months from the time the flood began,* the boat came to rest on the mountains of Ararat. 5Two and a half months later,* as the waters continued to go down, other mountain peaks began to appear.

6After another forty days, Noah opened the window he had made in the boat 7and released a raven that flew back and forth until the earth was dry. 8Then he sent out a dove to see if it could find dry ground. 9But the dove found no place to land because the water was still too high. So it returned to the boat, and Noah held out his hand and drew the dove back inside. 10Seven days later, Noah released the dove again. 11This time, toward evening, the bird returned to him with a fresh olive leaf in its beak. Noah now knew that the water was almost gone. 12A week later, he released the dove again, and this time it did not come back.

13Finally, when Noah was 601 years old, ten and a half months after the flood began,* Noah lifted back the cover to look. The water was drying up. 14Two more months went by,* and at last the earth was dry! 15Then God said to Noah, 16"Leave the boat, all of you. 17Release all the animals and birds so they can breed and reproduce in great numbers." 18So Noah, his wife, and his sons and their wives left the boat. 19And all the various kinds of animals and birds came out, pair by pair.

20Then Noah built an altar to the LORD and sacrificed on it the animals and birds that had been approved for that purpose. 21And the LORD was pleased with the sacrifice and said to himself, "I will never again curse the earth, destroying all living things, even though people's thoughts and actions are bent toward evil from childhood. 22As long as the earth remains, there will be springtime and harvest, cold and heat, winter and summer, day and night."

CHAPTER 9
God's Covenant with Noah

God blessed Noah and his sons and told them, "Multiply and fill the earth. 2All the wild animals, large and small, and all the birds and fish will be afraid of you. I have placed them in your power. 3I have given them to you for food, just as I have given you grain and vegetables. 4But you must never eat animals that still have their lifeblood in them. 5And murder is forbidden. Animals that kill people must die, and any person who murders must be killed. 6Yes, you must execute anyone who murders another person, for to kill a person is to kill a living being made in God's image. 7Now you must have many children and repopulate the earth. Yes, multiply and fill the earth!"

8Then God told Noah and his sons, 9"I am making a covenant with you and your descendants, 10and with the animals you brought with you—all these birds and livestock and wild animals. 11I solemnly promise never to send another flood to kill all living creatures and destroy the earth." 12And God said, "I am giving you a sign as evidence of my eternal covenant with you and all living creatures. 13I have placed my rainbow in the clouds. It is the sign of my permanent promise to you and to all the earth. 14When I send clouds over the earth, the rainbow will be seen in the clouds, 15and I will remember my covenant with you and with everything that lives. Never again will there be a flood that will destroy all life. 16When I see the rainbow in the clouds, I will remember the eternal covenant between God and every living creature on earth." 17Then God said to Noah, "Yes, this is the sign of my covenant with all the creatures of the earth."

Noah's Sons

18Shem, Ham, and Japheth, the three sons of Noah, survived the Flood with their father. (Ham is the ancestor of the Canaanites.) 19From these three sons of Noah came all the people now scattered across the earth.

20After the Flood, Noah became a farmer and planted a vineyard. 21One day he became drunk on some wine he had made and lay naked in his tent. 22Ham, the father of Canaan, saw that his father was naked and went outside and told his brothers. 23Shem and Japheth took a robe, held it over their shoulders, walked backward into the tent, and covered their father's naked body. As they did this, they looked the other way so they

---

8:4 Hebrew *on the seventeenth day of the seventh month;* see 7:11. 8:5 Hebrew *On the first day of the tenth month;* see 7:11 and note on 8:4. 8:13 Hebrew *on the first day of the first month;* see 7:11. 8:14 Hebrew *The twenty-seventh day of the second month arrived;* see note on 8:13.

wouldn't see him naked. ²⁴When Noah woke up from his drunken stupor, he learned what Ham, his youngest son, had done. ²⁵Then he cursed the descendants of Canaan, the son of Ham:

"A curse on the Canaanites!
May they be the lowest of servants
    to the descendants of Shem and
    Japheth."

²⁶Then Noah said,

"May Shem be blessed by the LORD my God;
    and may Canaan be his servant.
²⁷ May God enlarge the territory of Japheth,
    and may he share the prosperity of Shem;*
    and let Canaan be his servant."

²⁸Noah lived another 350 years after the Flood. ²⁹He was 950 years old when he died.

CHAPTER **10**

This is the history of the families of Shem, Ham, and Japheth, the three sons of Noah. Many children were born to them after the Flood.

Descendants of Japheth
²The descendants of Japheth were Gomer, Magog, Madai, Javan, Tubal, Meshech, and Tiras. ³The descendants of Gomer were Ashkenaz, Riphath, and Togarmah. ⁴The descendants of Javan were Elishah, Tarshish, Kittim, and Rodanim.* ⁵Their descendants became the seafaring peoples in various lands, each tribe with its own language.

Descendants of Ham
⁶The descendants of Ham were Cush, Mizraim,* Put, and Canaan. ⁷The descendants of Cush were Seba, Havilah, Sabtah, Raamah, and Sabteca. The descendants of Raamah were Sheba and Dedan.

⁸One of Cush's descendants was Nimrod, who became a heroic warrior. ⁹He was a mighty hunter in the LORD's sight.* His name became proverbial, and people would speak of someone as being "like Nimrod, a mighty hunter in the LORD's sight." ¹⁰He built the foundation for his empire in the land of Babylonia,* with the cities of Babel, Erech, Akkad, and Calneh. ¹¹From there he extended his reign to Assyria, where he built Nineveh, Rehoboth-ir, Calah, ¹²and Resen—the main city of the empire, located between Nineveh and Calah.

¹³Mizraim was the ancestor of the Ludites, Anamites, Lehabites, Naphtuhites, ¹⁴Pathrusites, Casluhites, and the Caphtorites, from whom the Philistines came.* ¹⁵Canaan's oldest son was Sidon, the ancestor of the Sidonians. Canaan was also the ancestor of the Hittites, ¹⁶Jebusites, Amorites, Girgashites, ¹⁷Hivites, Arkites, Sinites, ¹⁸Arvadites, Zemarites, and Hamathites. ¹⁹Eventually the territory of Canaan spread from Sidon to Gerar, near Gaza, and to Sodom, Gomorrah, Admah, and Zeboiim, near Lasha.

²⁰These were the descendants of Ham, identified according to their tribes, languages, territories, and nations.

Descendants of Shem
²¹Sons were also born to Shem, the older brother of Japheth.* Shem was the ancestor of all the descendants of Eber. ²²The descendants of Shem were Elam, Asshur, Arphaxad, Lud, and Aram. ²³The descendants of Aram were Uz, Hul, Gether, and Mash. ²⁴Arphaxad was the father of Shelah,* and Shelah was the father of Eber. ²⁵Eber had two sons. The first was named Peleg—"division"—for during his lifetime the people of the world were divided into different language groups and dispersed. His brother's name was Joktan. ²⁶Joktan was the ancestor of Almodad, Sheleph, Hazarmaveth, Jerah, ²⁷Hadoram, Uzal, Diklah, ²⁸Obal, Abimael, Sheba, ²⁹Ophir, Havilah, and Jobab. ³⁰The descendants of Joktan lived in the area extending from Mesha toward the eastern hills of Sephar.

³¹These were the descendants of Shem, identified according to their tribes, languages, territories, and nations.

³²These are the families that came from Noah's sons, listed nation by nation according

---

9:27 Hebrew *may he live in the tents of Shem.* 10:4 As in some Hebrew manuscripts and Greek version (see also 1 Chr 1:7); most Hebrew manuscripts read *Dodanim.* 10:6 Or *Egypt;* also in 10:13. 10:9 Hebrew *a mighty hunter before the LORD;* also in 10:9b. 10:10 Hebrew *Shinar.* 10:14 Hebrew *Casluhites, from whom the Philistines came, Caphtorites.* Compare Jer 47:4; Amos 9:7. 10:21 Or *Shem, whose older brother was Japheth.* 10:24 Greek version reads *Arphaxad was the father of Cainan, Cainan was the father of Shelah.*

to their lines of descent. The earth was populated with the people of these nations after the Flood.

CHAPTER **11**
The Tower of Babel
At one time the whole world spoke a single language and used the same words. ²As the people migrated eastward, they found a plain in the land of Babylonia* and settled there. ³They began to talk about construction projects. "Come," they said, "let's make great piles of burnt brick and collect natural asphalt to use as mortar. ⁴Let's build a great city with a tower that reaches to the skies—a monument to our greatness! This will bring us together and keep us from scattering all over the world."

⁵But the LORD came down to see the city and the tower the people were building. ⁶"Look!" he said. "If they can accomplish this when they have just begun to take advantage of their common language and political unity, just think of what they will do later. Nothing will be impossible for them! ⁷Come, let's go down and give them different languages. Then they won't be able to understand each other."

⁸In that way, the LORD scattered them all over the earth; and that ended the building of the city. ⁹That is why the city was called Babel,* because it was there that the LORD confused the people by giving them many languages, thus scattering them across the earth.

From Shem to Abram
¹⁰This is the history of Shem's family.

When Shem was 100 years old, his son Arphaxad was born. This happened two years after the Flood. ¹¹After the birth of Arphaxad, Shem lived another 500 years and had other sons and daughters.
¹²When Arphaxad was 35 years old, his son Shelah was born.* ¹³After the birth of Shelah, Arphaxad lived another 403 years and had other sons and daughters.*
¹⁴When Shelah was 30 years old, his son Eber was born. ¹⁵After the birth of Eber, Shelah lived another 403 years and had other sons and daughters.
¹⁶When Eber was 34 years old, his son Peleg was born. ¹⁷After the birth of Peleg, Eber

lived another 430 years and had other sons and daughters.
¹⁸When Peleg was 30 years old, his son Reu was born. ¹⁹After the birth of Reu, Peleg lived another 209 years and had other sons and daughters.
²⁰When Reu was 32 years old, his son Serug was born. ²¹After the birth of Serug, Reu lived another 207 years and had other sons and daughters.
²²When Serug was 30 years old, his son Nahor was born. ²³After the birth of Nahor, Serug lived another 200 years and had other sons and daughters.
²⁴When Nahor was 29 years old, his son Terah was born. ²⁵After the birth of Terah, Nahor lived another 119 years and had other sons and daughters.
²⁶When Terah was 70 years old, he became the father of Abram, Nahor, and Haran.

The Family of Terah
²⁷This is the history of Terah's family. Terah was the father of Abram, Nahor, and Haran; and Haran had a son named Lot. ²⁸But while Haran was still young, he died in Ur of the Chaldeans, the place of his birth. He was survived by Terah, his father. ²⁹Meanwhile, Abram married Sarai, and his brother Nahor married Milcah, the daughter of their brother Haran. (Milcah had a sister named Iscah.) ³⁰Now Sarai was not able to have any children.

³¹Terah took his son Abram, his daughter-in-law Sarai, and his grandson Lot (his son Haran's child) and left Ur of the Chaldeans to go to the land of Canaan. But they stopped instead at the village of Haran and settled there. ³²Terah lived for 205 years* and died while still at Haran.

CHAPTER **12**
The Call of Abram
Then the LORD told Abram, "Leave your country, your relatives, and your father's house, and go to the land that I will show you. ²I will cause you to become the father of a great nation. I will bless you and make you famous, and I will make you a blessing to others. ³I will bless those who bless you and curse those who curse you. All the families of the earth will be blessed through you."

⁴So Abram departed as the LORD had instructed

11:2 Hebrew *Shinar.*   **11:9** *Babel* sounds like a Hebrew term that means "confusion."   **11:12** Or *his son, the ancestor of Shelah, was born;* similarly in 11:14, 16, 18, 20, 22, 24.   **11:12-13** Greek version reads ¹²*When Arphaxad was 135 years old, his son Cainan was born.* ¹³*After the birth of Cainan, Arphaxad lived another 430 years and had other sons and daughters, and then he died. When Cainan was 130 years old, his son Shelah was born. After the birth of Shelah, Cainan lived another 330 years and had other sons and daughters, and then he died.*   **11:32** Some ancient versions read *145 years;* compare 11:26; 12:4.

him, and Lot went with him. Abram was seventy-five years old when he left Haran. 5He took his wife, Sarai, his nephew Lot, and all his wealth—his livestock and all the people who had joined his household at Haran—and finally arrived in Canaan. 6Traveling through Canaan, they came to a place near Shechem and set up camp beside the oak at Moreh. At that time, the area was inhabited by Canaanites.

7Then the LORD appeared to Abram and said, "I am going to give this land to your offspring.*" And Abram built an altar there to commemorate the LORD's visit. 8After that, Abram traveled southward and set up camp in the hill country between Bethel on the west and Ai on the east. There he built an altar and worshiped the LORD. 9Then Abram traveled south by stages toward the Negev.

Abram and Sarai in Egypt

10At that time there was a severe famine in the land, so Abram went down to Egypt to wait it out. 11As he was approaching the borders of Egypt, Abram said to Sarai, "You are a very beautiful woman. 12When the Egyptians see you, they will say, 'This is his wife. Let's kill him; then we can have her!' 13But if you say you are my sister, then the Egyptians will treat me well because of their interest in you, and they will spare my life."

14And sure enough, when they arrived in Egypt, everyone spoke of her beauty. 15When the palace officials saw her, they sang her praises to their king, the pharaoh, and she was taken into his harem. 16Then Pharaoh gave Abram many gifts because of her—sheep, cattle, donkeys, male and female servants, and camels.

17But the LORD sent a terrible plague upon Pharaoh's household because of Sarai, Abram's wife. 18So Pharaoh called for Abram and accused him sharply. "What is this you have done to me?" he demanded. "Why didn't you tell me she was your wife? 19Why were you willing to let me marry her, saying she was your sister? Here is your wife! Take her and be gone!" 20Pharaoh then sent them out of the country under armed escort—Abram and his wife, with all their household and belongings.

CHAPTER 13
Abram and Lot Separate

So they left Egypt and traveled north into the Negev—Abram with his wife and Lot and all that they owned, 2for Abram was very rich in

livestock, silver, and gold. 3Then they continued traveling by stages toward Bethel, to the place between Bethel and Ai where they had camped before. 4This was the place where Abram had built the altar, and there he again worshiped the LORD.

5Now Lot, who was traveling with Abram, was also very wealthy with sheep, cattle, and many tents. 6But the land could not support both Abram and Lot with all their flocks and herds living so close together. There were too many animals for the available pastureland. 7So an argument broke out between the herdsmen of Abram and Lot. At that time Canaanites and Perizzites were also living in the land.

8Then Abram talked it over with Lot. "This arguing between our herdsmen has got to stop," he said. "After all, we are close relatives! 9I'll tell you what we'll do. Take your choice of any section of the land you want, and we will separate. If you want that area over there, then I'll stay here. If you want to stay in this area, then I'll move on to another place."

10Lot took a long look at the fertile plains of the Jordan Valley in the direction of Zoar. The whole area was well watered everywhere, like the garden of the LORD or the beautiful land of Egypt. (This was before the LORD had destroyed Sodom and Gomorrah.) 11Lot chose that land for himself—the Jordan Valley to the east of them. He went there with his flocks and servants and parted company with his uncle Abram. 12So while Abram stayed in the land of Canaan, Lot moved his tents to a place near Sodom, among the cities of the plain. 13The people of this area were unusually wicked and sinned greatly against the LORD.

14After Lot was gone, the LORD said to Abram, "Look as far as you can see in every direction. 15I am going to give all this land to you and your offspring* as a permanent possession. 16And I am going to give you so many descendants that, like dust, they cannot be counted! 17Take a walk in every direction and explore the new possessions I am giving you." 18Then Abram moved his camp to the oak grove owned by Mamre, which is at Hebron. There he built an altar to the LORD.

CHAPTER 14
Abram Rescues Lot

About this time war broke out in the region. King Amraphel of Babylonia,* King Arioch of Ellasar, King Kedorlaomer of Elam, and King

12:7 Hebrew *seed.*   13:15 Hebrew *seed.*   14:1 Hebrew *Shinar;* also in 14:9.

Tidal of Goiim ²fought against King Bera of Sodom, King Birsha of Gomorrah, King Shinab of Admah, King Shemeber of Zeboiim, and the king of Bela (now called Zoar).

³The kings of Sodom, Gomorrah, Admah, Zeboiim, and Bela formed an alliance and mobilized their armies in Siddim Valley (that is, the valley of the Dead Sea*). ⁴For twelve years they had all been subject to King Kedorlaomer, but now in the thirteenth year they rebelled.

⁵One year later, Kedorlaomer and his allies arrived. They conquered the Rephaites in Ashteroth-karnaim, the Zuzites in Ham, the Emites in the plain of Kiriathaim, ⁶and the Horites in Mount Seir, as far as El-paran at the edge of the wilderness. ⁷Then they swung around to Enmishpat (now called Kadesh) and destroyed the Amalekites, and also the Amorites living in Hazazon-tamar.

⁸But now the army of the kings of Sodom, Gomorrah, Admah, Zeboiim, and Bela (now called Zoar) prepared for battle in the valley of the Dead Sea* ⁹against King Kedorlaomer of Elam and the kings of Goiim, Babylonia, and Ellasar—four kings against five. ¹⁰As it happened, the valley was filled with tar pits. And as the army of the kings of Sodom and Gomorrah fled, some slipped into the tar pits, while the rest escaped into the mountains. ¹¹The victorious invaders then plundered Sodom and Gomorrah and began their long journey home, taking all the wealth and food with them. ¹²They also captured Lot—Abram's nephew who lived in Sodom—and took everything he owned. ¹³One of the men who escaped came and told Abram the Hebrew, who was camped at the oak grove belonging to Mamre the Amorite. Mamre and his relatives, Eshcol and Aner, were Abram's allies.

¹⁴When Abram learned that Lot had been captured, he called together the men born into his household, 318 of them in all. He chased after Kedorlaomer's army until he caught up with them in Dan. ¹⁵There he divided his men and attacked during the night from several directions. Kedorlaomer's army fled, but Abram chased them to Hobah, north of Damascus. ¹⁶Abram and his allies recovered everything—the goods that had been taken, Abram's nephew Lot with his possessions, and all the women and other captives.

Melchizedek Blesses Abram

¹⁷As Abram returned from his victory over Kedorlaomer and his allies, the king of Sodom came out to meet him in the valley of Shaveh (that is, the King's Valley). ¹⁸Then Melchizedek, the king of Salem and a priest of God Most High, brought him bread and wine. ¹⁹Melchizedek blessed Abram with this blessing:

"Blessed be Abram by God Most High,
   Creator of heaven and earth.
²⁰ And blessed be God Most High,
   who has helped you conquer your
      enemies."

Then Abram gave Melchizedek a tenth of all the goods he had recovered.

²¹The king of Sodom told him, "Give back my people who were captured. But you may keep for yourself all the goods you have recovered."

²²Abram replied, "I have solemnly promised the Lord, God Most High, Creator of heaven and earth, ²³that I will not take so much as a single thread or sandal thong from you. Otherwise you might say, 'I am the one who made Abram rich!' ²⁴All I'll accept is what these young men of mine have already eaten. But give a share of the goods to my allies—Aner, Eshcol, and Mamre."

CHAPTER 15

The Lord's Covenant with Abram

Afterward the Lord spoke to Abram in a vision and said to him, "Do not be afraid, Abram, for I will protect you, and your reward will be great."

²But Abram replied, "O Sovereign Lord, what good are all your blessings when I don't even have a son? Since I don't have a son, Eliezer of Damascus, a servant in my household, will inherit all my wealth. ³You have given me no children, so one of my servants will have to be my heir."

⁴Then the Lord said to him, "No, your servant will not be your heir, for you will have a son of your own to inherit everything I am giving you." ⁵Then the Lord brought Abram outside beneath the night sky and told him, "Look up into the heavens and count the stars if you can. Your descendants will be like that—too many to count!" ⁶And Abram believed the Lord, and the Lord declared him righteous because of his faith. ⁷Then the Lord told him, "I am the Lord who brought you out of Ur of the Chaldeans to give you this land."

⁸But Abram replied, "O Sovereign Lord, how can I be sure that you will give it to me?"

⁹Then the Lord told him, "Bring me a three-year-old heifer, a three-year-old female goat, a three-year-old ram, a turtledove, and a young

14:3 Hebrew *Salt Sea.* **14:8** Hebrew *in Siddim Valley;* see 14:3.

pigeon." ¹⁰Abram took all these and killed them. He cut each one down the middle and laid the halves side by side. He did not, however, divide the birds in half. ¹¹Some vultures came down to eat the carcasses, but Abram chased them away. ¹²That evening, as the sun was going down, Abram fell into a deep sleep. He saw a terrifying vision of darkness and horror.

¹³Then the LORD told Abram, "You can be sure that your descendants will be strangers in a foreign land, and they will be oppressed as slaves for four hundred years. ¹⁴But I will punish the nation that enslaves them, and in the end they will come away with great wealth. ¹⁵(But you will die in peace, at a ripe old age.) ¹⁶After four generations your descendants will return here to this land, when the sin of the Amorites has run its course."

¹⁷As the sun went down and it became dark, Abram saw a smoking firepot and a flaming torch pass between the halves of the carcasses. ¹⁸So the LORD made a covenant with Abram that day and said, "I have given this land to your descendants, all the way from the border of Egypt* to the great Euphrates River—¹⁹the land of the Kenites, Kenizzites, Kadmonites, ²⁰Hittites, Perizzites, Rephaites, ²¹Amorites, Canaanites, Girgashites, and Jebusites."

CHAPTER 16
The Birth of Ishmael

But Sarai, Abram's wife, had no children. So Sarai took her servant, an Egyptian woman named Hagar, ²and gave her to Abram so she could bear his children. "The LORD has kept me from having any children," Sarai said to Abram. "Go and sleep with my servant. Perhaps I can have children through her." And Abram agreed. ³So Sarai, Abram's wife, took Hagar the Egyptian servant and gave her to Abram as a wife. (This happened ten years after Abram first arrived in the land of Canaan.)

⁴So Abram slept with Hagar, and she became pregnant. When Hagar knew she was pregnant, she began to treat her mistress Sarai with contempt. ⁵Then Sarai said to Abram, "It's all your fault! Now this servant of mine is pregnant, and she despises me, though I myself gave her the privilege of sleeping with you. The LORD will make you pay for doing this to me!*"

⁶Abram replied, "Since she is your servant,

you may deal with her as you see fit." So Sarai treated her harshly, and Hagar ran away.

⁷The angel of the LORD found Hagar beside a desert spring along the road to Shur. ⁸The angel said to her, "Hagar, Sarai's servant, where have you come from, and where are you going?"

"I am running away from my mistress," she replied.

⁹Then the angel of the LORD said, "Return to your mistress and submit to her authority." ¹⁰The angel added, "I will give you more descendants than you can count." ¹¹And the angel also said, "You are now pregnant and will give birth to a son. You are to name him Ishmael,* for the LORD has heard about your misery. ¹²This son of yours will be a wild one—free and untamed as a wild donkey! He will be against everyone, and everyone will be against him. Yes, he will live at odds with the rest of his brothers."

¹³Thereafter, Hagar referred to the LORD, who had spoken to her, as "the God who sees me,"* for she said, "I have seen the One who sees me!" ¹⁴Later that well was named Beer-lahairoi,* and it can still be found between Kadesh and Bered.

¹⁵So Hagar gave Abram a son, and Abram named him Ishmael. ¹⁶Abram was eighty-six years old at that time.

CHAPTER 17
Abram Is Named Abraham

When Abram was ninety-nine years old, the LORD appeared to him and said, "I am God Almighty; serve me faithfully and live a blameless life. ²I will make a covenant with you, by which I will guarantee to make you into a mighty nation." ³At this, Abram fell face down in the dust. Then God said to him, ⁴"This is my covenant with you: I will make you the father of not just one nation, but a multitude of nations! ⁵What's more, I am changing your name. It will no longer be Abram; now you will be known as Abraham,* for you will be the father of many nations. ⁶I will give you millions of descendants who will represent many nations. Kings will be among them!

⁷"I will continue this everlasting covenant between us, generation after generation. It will continue between me and your offspring* forever. And I will always be your God and the God of your descendants after you. ⁸Yes, I will give all this land of Canaan to you and to your offspring forever. And I will be their God.

15:18 Hebrew *the river of Egypt*, referring either to an eastern branch of the Nile River or to the brook of Egypt in the Sinai (see Num 34:5). 16:5 Hebrew *Let the LORD judge between you and me.* 16:11 *Ishmael* means "God hears." 16:13 Hebrew *El-roi.* 16:14 *Beer-lahairoi* means "well of the Living One who sees me." 17:5 *Abram* means "exalted father"; *Abraham* means "father of many." 17:7 Hebrew *seed*; also in 17:8.

The Sign of Circumcision

9"Your part of the agreement," God told Abraham, "is to obey the terms of the covenant. You and all your descendants have this continual responsibility. 10This is the covenant that you and your descendants must keep: Each male among you must be circumcised; 11the flesh of his foreskin must be cut off. This will be a sign that you and they have accepted this covenant. 12Every male child must be circumcised on the eighth day after his birth. This applies not only to members of your family, but also to the servants born in your household and the foreign-born servants whom you have purchased. 13All must be circumcised. Your bodies will thus bear the mark of my everlasting covenant. 14Anyone who refuses to be circumcised will be cut off from the covenant family for violating the covenant."

Sarai Is Named Sarah

15Then God added, "Regarding Sarai, your wife—her name will no longer be Sarai; from now on you will call her Sarah.* 16And I will bless her and give you a son from her! Yes, I will bless her richly, and she will become the mother of many nations. Kings will be among her descendants!"

17Then Abraham bowed down to the ground, but he laughed to himself in disbelief. "How could I become a father at the age of one hundred?" he wondered. "Besides, Sarah is ninety; how could she have a baby?" 18And Abraham said to God, "Yes, may Ishmael enjoy your special blessing!"

19But God replied, "Sarah, your wife, will bear you a son. You will name him Isaac,* and I will confirm my everlasting covenant with him and his descendants. 20As for Ishmael, I will bless him also, just as you have asked. I will cause him to multiply and become a great nation. Twelve princes will be among his descendants. 21But my covenant is with Isaac, who will be born to you and Sarah about this time next year."

22That ended the conversation, and God left Abraham. 23On that very day Abraham took his son Ishmael and every other male in his household and circumcised them, cutting off their foreskins, exactly as God had told him. 24Abraham was ninety-nine years old at that time, 25and Ishmael his son was thirteen. 26Both were circumcised the same day, 27along with all the other men and boys of the household, whether they were born there or bought as servants.

CHAPTER 18

A Son Promised to Sarah

The LORD appeared again to Abraham while he was camped near the oak grove belonging to Mamre. One day about noon, as Abraham was sitting at the entrance to his tent, 2he suddenly noticed three men standing nearby. He got up and ran to meet them, welcoming them by bowing low to the ground. 3"My lord," he said, "if it pleases you, stop here for a while. 4Rest in the shade of this tree while my servants get some water to wash your feet. 5Let me prepare some food to refresh you. Please stay awhile before continuing on your journey."

"All right," they said. "Do as you have said."

6So Abraham ran back to the tent and said to Sarah, "Quick! Get three measures* of your best flour, and bake some bread." 7Then Abraham ran out to the herd and chose a fat calf and told a servant to hurry and butcher it. 8When the food was ready, he took some cheese curds and milk and the roasted meat, and he served it to the men. As they ate, Abraham waited on them there beneath the trees.

9"Where is Sarah, your wife?" they asked him.

"In the tent," Abraham replied.

10Then one of them said, "About this time next year I will return, and your wife Sarah will have a son."

Now Sarah was listening to this conversation from the tent nearby. 11And since Abraham and Sarah were both very old, and Sarah was long past the age of having children, 12she laughed silently to herself. "How could a worn-out woman like me have a baby?" she thought. "And when my master—my husband—is also so old?"

13Then the LORD said to Abraham, "Why did Sarah laugh? Why did she say, 'Can an old woman like me have a baby?' 14Is anything too hard for the LORD? About a year from now, just as I told you, I will return, and Sarah will have a son." 15Sarah was afraid, so she denied that she had laughed. But he said, "That is not true. You did laugh."

Abraham Intercedes for Sodom

16Then the men got up from their meal and started on toward Sodom. Abraham went with them part of the way.

17"Should I hide my plan from Abraham?" the LORD asked. 18"For Abraham will become a great and mighty nation, and all the nations of

17:15 *Sarah* means "princess."   17:19 *Isaac* means "he laughs."   18:6 Hebrew *3 seahs*, about 15 quarts or 18 liters.

the earth will be blessed through him. ¹⁹I have singled him out so that he will direct his sons and their families to keep the way of the LORD and do what is right and just. Then I will do for him all that I have promised." ²⁰So the LORD told Abraham, "I have heard that the people of Sodom and Gomorrah are extremely evil, and that everything they do is wicked. ²¹I am going down to see whether or not these reports are true. Then I will know."

²²The two other men went on toward Sodom, but the LORD remained with Abraham for a while. ²³Abraham approached him and said, "Will you destroy both innocent and guilty alike? ²⁴Suppose you find fifty innocent people there within the city—will you still destroy it, and not spare it for their sakes? ²⁵Surely you wouldn't do such a thing, destroying the innocent with the guilty. Why, you would be treating the innocent and the guilty exactly the same! Surely you wouldn't do that! Should not the Judge of all the earth do what is right?"

²⁶And the LORD replied, "If I find fifty innocent people in Sodom, I will spare the entire city for their sake."

²⁷Then Abraham spoke again. "Since I have begun, let me go on and speak further to my Lord, even though I am but dust and ashes. ²⁸Suppose there are only forty-five? Will you destroy the city for lack of five?"

And the LORD said, "I will not destroy it if I find forty-five."

²⁹Then Abraham pressed his request further. "Suppose there are only forty?"

And the LORD replied, "I will not destroy it if there are forty."

³⁰"Please don't be angry, my Lord," Abraham pleaded. "Let me speak—suppose only thirty are found?"

And the LORD replied, "I will not destroy it if there are thirty."

³¹Then Abraham said, "Since I have dared to speak to the Lord, let me continue—suppose there are only twenty?"

And the LORD said, "Then I will not destroy it for the sake of the twenty."

³²Finally, Abraham said, "Lord, please do not get angry; I will speak but once more! Suppose only ten are found there?"

And the LORD said, "Then, for the sake of the ten, I will not destroy it."

³³The LORD went on his way when he had finished his conversation with Abraham, and Abraham returned to his tent.

CHAPTER **19**
Sodom and Gomorrah Destroyed

That evening the two angels came to the entrance of the city of Sodom, and Lot was sitting there as they arrived. When he saw them, he stood up to meet them. Then he welcomed them and bowed low to the ground. ²"My lords," he said, "come to my home to wash your feet, and be my guests for the night. You may then get up in the morning as early as you like and be on your way again."

"Oh no," they said, "we'll just spend the night out here in the city square."

³But Lot insisted, so at last they went home with him. He set a great feast before them, complete with fresh bread made without yeast. After the meal, ⁴as they were preparing to retire for the night, all the men of Sodom, young and old, came from all over the city and surrounded the house. ⁵They shouted to Lot, "Where are the men who came to spend the night with you? Bring them out so we can have sex with them."

⁶Lot stepped outside to talk to them, shutting the door behind him. ⁷"Please, my brothers," he begged, "don't do such a wicked thing. ⁸Look— I have two virgin daughters. Do with them as you wish, but leave these men alone, for they are under my protection."

⁹"Stand back!" they shouted. "Who do you think you are? We let you settle among us, and now you are trying to tell us what to do! We'll treat you far worse than those other men!" And they lunged at Lot and began breaking down the door. ¹⁰But the two angels reached out and pulled Lot in and bolted the door. ¹¹Then they blinded the men of Sodom so they couldn't find the doorway.

¹²"Do you have any other relatives here in the city?" the angels asked. "Get them out of this place—sons-in-law, sons, daughters, or anyone else. ¹³For we will destroy the city completely. The stench of the place has reached the LORD, and he has sent us to destroy it."

¹⁴So Lot rushed out to tell his daughters' fiancés, "Quick, get out of the city! The LORD is going to destroy it." But the young men thought he was only joking.

¹⁵At dawn the next morning the angels became insistent. "Hurry," they said to Lot. "Take your wife and your two daughters who are here. Get out of here right now, or you will be caught in the destruction of the city."

¹⁶When Lot still hesitated, the angels seized his hand and the hands of his wife and two daughters and rushed them to safety outside the

city, for the LORD was merciful. 17"Run for your lives!" the angels warned. "Do not stop anywhere in the valley. And don't look back! Escape to the mountains, or you will die."

18"Oh no, my lords, please," Lot begged. 19"You have been so kind to me and saved my life, and you have granted me such mercy. But I cannot go to the mountains. Disaster would catch up to me there, and I would soon die. 20See, there is a small village nearby. Please let me go there instead; don't you see how small it is? Then my life will be saved."

21"All right," the angel said, "I will grant your request. I will not destroy that little village. 22But hurry! For I can do nothing until you are there." From that time on, that village was known as Zoar.*

23The sun was rising as Lot reached the village. 24Then the LORD rained down fire and burning sulfur from the heavens on Sodom and Gomorrah. 25He utterly destroyed them, along with the other cities and villages of the plain, eliminating all life—people, plants, and animals alike. 26But Lot's wife looked back as she was following along behind him, and she became a pillar of salt.

27The next morning Abraham was up early and hurried out to the place where he had stood in the LORD's presence. 28He looked out across the plain to Sodom and Gomorrah and saw columns of smoke and fumes, as from a furnace, rising from the cities there. 29But God had listened to Abraham's request and kept Lot safe, removing him from the disaster that engulfed the cities on the plain.

Lot and His Daughters

30Afterward Lot left Zoar because he was afraid of the people there, and he went to live in a cave in the mountains with his two daughters. 31One day the older daughter said to her sister, "There isn't a man anywhere in this entire area for us to marry. And our father will soon be too old to have children. 32Come, let's get him drunk with wine, and then we will sleep with him. That way we will preserve our family line through our father." 33So that night they got him drunk, and the older daughter went in and slept with her father. He was unaware of her lying down or getting up again.

34The next morning the older daughter said to her younger sister, "I slept with our father last night. Let's get him drunk with wine again tonight, and you go in and sleep with him. That

way our family line will be preserved." 35So that night they got him drunk again, and the younger daughter went in and slept with him. As before, he was unaware of her lying down or getting up again. 36So both of Lot's daughters became pregnant by their father.

37When the older daughter gave birth to a son, she named him Moab.* He became the ancestor of the nation now known as the Moabites. 38When the younger daughter gave birth to a son, she named him Ben-ammi.* He became the ancestor of the nation now known as the Ammonites.

CHAPTER **20**

Abraham Deceives Abimelech

Now Abraham moved south to the Negev and settled for a while between Kadesh and Shur at a place called Gerar. 2Abraham told people there that his wife, Sarah, was his sister. So King Abimelech sent for her and had her brought to him at his palace.

3But one night God came to Abimelech in a dream and told him, "You are a dead man, for that woman you took is married."

4But Abimelech had not slept with her yet, so he said, "Lord, will you kill an innocent man? 5Abraham told me, 'She is my sister,' and she herself said, 'Yes, he is my brother.' I acted in complete innocence!"

6"Yes, I know you are innocent," God replied. "That is why I kept you from sinning against me; I did not let you touch her. 7Now return her to her husband, and he will pray for you, for he is a prophet. Then you will live. But if you don't return her to him, you can be sure that you and your entire household will die."

8Abimelech got up early the next morning and hastily called a meeting of all his servants. When he told them what had happened, great fear swept through the crowd. 9Then Abimelech called for Abraham. "What is this you have done to us?" he demanded. "What have I done to you that deserves treatment like this, making me and my kingdom guilty of this great sin? This kind of thing should not be done! 10Why have you done this to us?"

11"Well," Abraham said, "I figured this to be a godless place. I thought, 'They will want my wife and will kill me to get her.' 12Besides, she is my sister—we both have the same father, though different mothers—and I married her. 13When God sent me to travel far from my

19:22 *Zoar* means "little." 19:37 *Moab* sounds like a Hebrew term that means "from father." 19:38 *Ben-ammi* means "son of my people."

father's home, I told her, 'Wherever we go, have the kindness to say that you are my sister.'"

14Then Abimelech took sheep and oxen and servants—both men and women—and gave them to Abraham, and he returned his wife, Sarah, to him. 15"Look over my kingdom, and choose a place where you would like to live," Abimelech told him. 16Then he turned to Sarah. "Look," he said, "I am giving your 'brother' a thousand pieces of silver* to compensate for any embarrassment I may have caused you. This will settle any claim against me in this matter."

17Then Abraham prayed to God, and God healed Abimelech, his wife, and the other women of the household, so they could have children. 18For the LORD had stricken all the women with infertility as a warning to Abimelech for having taken Abraham's wife.

CHAPTER 21
The Birth of Isaac

Then the LORD did exactly what he had promised. 2Sarah became pregnant, and she gave a son to Abraham in his old age. It all happened at the time God had said it would. 3And Abraham named his son Isaac.* 4Eight days after Isaac was born, Abraham circumcised him as God had commanded. 5Abraham was one hundred years old at the time.

6And Sarah declared, "God has brought me laughter! All who hear about this will laugh with me. 7For who would have dreamed that I would ever have a baby? Yet I have given Abraham a son in his old age!"

Hagar and Ishmael Sent Away

8As time went by and Isaac grew and was weaned, Abraham gave a big party to celebrate the happy occasion. 9But Sarah saw Ishmael—the son of Abraham and her Egyptian servant Hagar—making fun of Isaac. 10So she turned to Abraham and demanded, "Get rid of that servant and her son. He is not going to share the family inheritance with my son, Isaac. I won't have it!"

11This upset Abraham very much because Ishmael was his son. 12But God told Abraham, "Do not be upset over the boy and your servant wife. Do just as Sarah says, for Isaac is the son through whom your descendants will be counted. 13But I will make a nation of the descendants of Hagar's son because he also is your son."

14So Abraham got up early the next morning, prepared food for the journey, and strapped a container of water to Hagar's shoulders. He sent her away with their son, and she walked out into the wilderness of Beersheba, wandering aimlessly. 15When the water was gone, she left the boy in the shade of a bush. 16Then she went and sat down by herself about a hundred yards* away. "I don't want to watch the boy die," she said, as she burst into tears.

17Then God heard the boy's cries, and the angel of God called to Hagar from the sky, "Hagar, what's wrong? Do not be afraid! God has heard the boy's cries from the place where you laid him. 18Go to him and comfort him, for I will make a great nation from his descendants."

19Then God opened Hagar's eyes, and she saw a well. She immediately filled her water container and gave the boy a drink. 20And God was with the boy as he grew up in the wilderness of Paran. He became an expert archer, 21and his mother arranged a marriage for him with a young woman from Egypt.

A Treaty with Abimelech

22About this time, Abimelech came with Phicol, his army commander, to visit Abraham. "It is clear that God helps you in everything you do," Abimelech said. 23"Swear to me in God's name that you won't deceive me, my children, or my grandchildren. I have been loyal to you, so now swear that you will be loyal to me and to this country in which you are living."

24Abraham replied, "All right, I swear to it!" 25Then Abraham complained to Abimelech about a well that Abimelech's servants had taken violently from Abraham's servants.

26"This is the first I've heard of it," Abimelech said. "And I have no idea who is responsible. Why didn't you say something about this before?" 27Then Abraham gave sheep and oxen to Abimelech, and they made a treaty. 28But when Abraham took seven additional ewe lambs and set them off by themselves, 29Abimelech asked, "Why are you doing that?"

30Abraham replied, "They are my gift to you as a public confirmation that I dug this well." 31So ever since, that place has been known as Beersheba—"well of the oath"—because that was where they had sworn an oath. 32After making their covenant, Abimelech left with Phicol, the commander of his army, and they returned home to the land of the Philistines. 33Then Abraham planted a tamarisk tree at Beersheba,

20:16 Hebrew *1,000 shekels of silver*, about 25 pounds or 11.4 kilograms in weight.   21:3 *Isaac* means "he laughs."   21:16 Hebrew *a bowshot*.

and he worshiped the LORD, the Eternal God, at that place. ³⁴And Abraham lived in Philistine country for a long time.

CHAPTER 22

Abraham's Obedience Tested

Later on God tested Abraham's faith and obedience. "Abraham!" God called.

"Yes," he replied. "Here I am."

²"Take your son, your only son—yes, Isaac, whom you love so much—and go to the land of Moriah. Sacrifice him there as a burnt offering on one of the mountains, which I will point out to you."

³The next morning Abraham got up early. He saddled his donkey and took two of his servants with him, along with his son Isaac. Then he chopped wood to build a fire for a burnt offering and set out for the place where God had told him to go. ⁴On the third day of the journey, Abraham saw the place in the distance. ⁵"Stay here with the donkey," Abraham told the young men. "The boy and I will travel a little farther. We will worship there, and then we will come right back."

⁶Abraham placed the wood for the burnt offering on Isaac's shoulders, while he himself carried the knife and the fire. As the two of them went on together, ⁷Isaac said, "Father?"

"Yes, my son," Abraham replied.

"We have the wood and the fire," said the boy, "but where is the lamb for the sacrifice?"

⁸"God will provide a lamb, my son," Abraham answered. And they both went on together.

⁹When they arrived at the place where God had told Abraham to go, he built an altar and placed the wood on it. Then he tied Isaac up and laid him on the altar over the wood. ¹⁰And Abraham took the knife and lifted it up to kill his son as a sacrifice to the LORD. ¹¹At that moment the angel of the LORD shouted to him from heaven, "Abraham! Abraham!"

"Yes," he answered. "I'm listening."

¹²"Lay down the knife," the angel said. "Do not hurt the boy in any way, for now I know that you truly fear God. You have not withheld even your beloved son from me."

¹³Then Abraham looked up and saw a ram caught by its horns in a bush. So he took the ram and sacrificed it as a burnt offering on the altar in place of his son. ¹⁴Abraham named the place "The LORD Will Provide."* This name has now become a proverb: "On the mountain of the LORD it will be provided."

22:14 Hebrew *Yahweh Yir'eh*.   22:18 Hebrew *seed*.

¹⁵Then the angel of the LORD called again to Abraham from heaven, ¹⁶"This is what the LORD says: Because you have obeyed me and have not withheld even your beloved son, I swear by my own self that ¹⁷I will bless you richly. I will multiply your descendants into countless millions, like the stars of the sky and the sand on the seashore. They will conquer their enemies, ¹⁸and through your descendants,* all the nations of the earth will be blessed—all because you have obeyed me." ¹⁹Then they returned to Abraham's young men and traveled home again to Beersheba, where Abraham lived for quite some time.

²⁰Soon after this, Abraham heard that Milcah, his brother Nahor's wife, had borne Nahor eight sons. ²¹The oldest was named Uz, the next oldest was Buz, followed by Kemuel (the father of Aram), ²²Kesed, Hazo, Pildash, Jidlaph, and Bethuel. ²³Bethuel became the father of Rebekah. ²⁴In addition to his eight sons from Milcah, Nahor had four other children from his concubine Reumah. Their names were Tebah, Gaham, Tahash, and Maacah.

CHAPTER 23

The Burial of Sarah

When Sarah was 127 years old, ²she died at Kiriath-arba (now called Hebron) in the land of Canaan. There Abraham mourned and wept for her. ³Then, leaving her body, he went to the Hittite elders and said, ⁴"Here I am, a stranger in a foreign land, with no place to bury my wife. Please let me have a piece of land for a burial plot."

⁵The Hittites replied to Abraham, ⁶"Certainly, for you are an honored prince among us. It will be a privilege to have you choose the finest of our tombs so you can bury her there."

⁷Then Abraham bowed low before them and said, ⁸"Since this is how you feel, be so kind as to ask Ephron son of Zohar ⁹to let me have the cave of Machpelah, down at the end of his field. I want to pay the full price, of course, whatever is publicly agreed upon, so I may have a permanent burial place for my family."

¹⁰Ephron was sitting there among the others, and he answered Abraham as the others listened, speaking publicly before all the elders of the town. ¹¹"No, sir," he said to Abraham, "please listen to me. I will give you the cave and the field. Here in the presence of my people, I give it to you. Go and bury your dead."

¹²Abraham bowed again to the people of the land, ¹³and he replied to Ephron as everyone

listened. "No, listen to me," he insisted. "I will buy it from you. Let me pay the full price for the field so I can bury my dead there."

14 "Well," Ephron answered, 15 "the land is worth four hundred pieces* of silver, but what is that between friends? Go ahead and bury your dead."

16 So Abraham paid Ephron the amount he had suggested, four hundred pieces of silver, as was publicly agreed. 17 He bought the plot of land belonging to Ephron at Machpelah, near Mamre. This included the field, the cave that was in it, and all the trees nearby. 18 They became Abraham's permanent possession by the agreement made in the presence of the Hittite elders at the city gate. 19 So Abraham buried Sarah there in Canaan, in the cave of Machpelah, near Mamre, which is at Hebron. 20 The field and the cave were sold to Abraham by the Hittites as a permanent burial place.

CHAPTER 24
Isaac Marries Rebekah

Abraham was now a very old man, and the LORD had blessed him in every way. 2 One day Abraham said to the man in charge of his household, who was his oldest servant, 3 "Swear* by the LORD, the God of heaven and earth, that you will not let my son marry one of these local Canaanite women. 4 Go instead to my homeland, to my relatives, and find a wife there for my son Isaac."

5 The servant asked, "But suppose I can't find a young woman who will travel so far from home? May I then take Isaac there to live among your relatives?"

6 "No!" Abraham warned. "Be careful never to take my son there. 7 For the LORD, the God of heaven, who took me from my father's house and my native land, solemnly promised to give this land to my offspring.* He will send his angel ahead of you, and he will see to it that you find a young woman there to be my son's wife. 8 If she is unwilling to come back with you, then you are free from this oath. But under no circumstances are you to take my son there."

9 So the servant took a solemn oath* that he would follow Abraham's instructions. 10 He loaded ten of Abraham's camels with gifts and set out, taking with him the best of everything his master owned. He traveled to Aram-naharaim* and went to the village where Abra-

ham's brother Nahor had settled. 11 There the servant made the camels kneel down beside a well just outside the village. It was evening, and the women were coming out to draw water.

12 "O LORD, God of my master," he prayed. "Give me success and show kindness to my master, Abraham. Help me to accomplish the purpose of my journey. 13 See, here I am, standing beside this spring, and the young women of the village are coming out to draw water. 14 This is my request. I will ask one of them for a drink. If she says, 'Yes, certainly, and I will water your camels, too!'—let her be the one you have appointed as Isaac's wife. By this I will know that you have shown kindness to my master."

15 As he was still praying, a young woman named Rebekah arrived with a water jug on her shoulder. Her father was Bethuel, who was the son of Abraham's brother Nahor and his wife, Milcah. 16 Now Rebekah was very beautiful, and she was a virgin; no man had ever slept with her. She went down to the spring, filled her jug, and came up again. 17 Running over to her, the servant asked, "Please give me a drink."

18 "Certainly, sir," she said, and she quickly lowered the jug for him to drink. 19 When he had finished, she said, "I'll draw water for your camels, too, until they have had enough!" 20 So she quickly emptied the jug into the watering trough and ran down to the well again. She kept carrying water to the camels until they had finished drinking. 21 The servant watched her in silence, wondering whether or not she was the one the LORD intended him to meet. 22 Then at last, when the camels had finished drinking, he gave her a gold ring for her nose and two large gold bracelets* for her wrists.

23 "Whose daughter are you?" he asked. "Would your father have any room to put us up for the night?"

24 "My father is Bethuel," she replied. "My grandparents are Nahor and Milcah. 25 Yes, we have plenty of straw and food for the camels, and we have a room for guests."

26 The man fell down to the ground and worshiped the LORD. 27 "Praise be to the LORD, the God of my master, Abraham," he said. "The LORD has been so kind and faithful to Abraham, for he has led me straight to my master's relatives."

28 The young woman ran home to tell her

23:15 Hebrew *400 shekels*, about 10 pounds or 4.6 kilograms in weight; also in 23:16.   24:3 Hebrew *Put your hand under my thigh, and I will make you swear.*   24:7 Hebrew *seed.*   24:9 Hebrew *put his hand under the thigh of Abraham his master and swore an oath.*   24:10 Aramnaharaim means "Aram of the two rivers," thought to have been located between the Euphrates and Balih Rivers in northwestern Mesopotamia.   24:22 Hebrew *a gold nose-ring weighing a half shekel* [0.2 ounces or 6 grams] *and two gold bracelets weighing 10 shekels* [4 ounces or 114 grams].

family about all that had happened. ²⁹Now Rebekah had a brother named Laban. ³⁰When he saw the nose-ring and the bracelets on his sister's wrists, and when he heard her story, he rushed out to the spring, where the man was still standing beside his camels. Laban said to him, ³¹"Come and stay with us, you who are blessed by the LORD. Why do you stand here outside the village when we have a room all ready for you and a place prepared for the camels!"

³²So the man went home with Laban, and Laban unloaded the camels, gave him straw to bed them down, fed them, and provided water for the camel drivers to wash their feet. ³³Then supper was served. But Abraham's servant said, "I don't want to eat until I have told you why I have come."

"All right," Laban said, "tell us your mission."

³⁴"I am Abraham's servant," he explained. ³⁵"And the LORD has blessed my master richly; he has become a great man. The LORD has given him flocks of sheep and herds of cattle, a fortune in silver and gold, and many servants and camels and donkeys. ³⁶When Sarah, my master's wife, was very old, she gave birth to my master's son, and my master has given him everything he owns. ³⁷And my master made me swear that I would not let Isaac marry one of the local Canaanite women. ³⁸Instead, I was to come to his relatives here in this far-off land, to his father's home. I was told to bring back a young woman from here to marry his son.

³⁹" 'But suppose I can't find a young woman willing to come back with me?' I asked him. ⁴⁰'You will,' he told me, 'for the LORD, in whose presence I have walked, will send his angel with you and will make your mission successful. Yes, you must get a wife for my son from among my relatives, from my father's family. ⁴¹But if you go to my relatives and they refuse to let her come, you will be free from your oath.'

⁴²"So this afternoon when I came to the spring I prayed this prayer: 'O LORD, the God of my master, Abraham, if you are planning to make my mission a success, please guide me in a special way. ⁴³Here I am, standing beside this spring. I will say to some young woman who comes to draw water, "Please give me a drink of water!" ⁴⁴And she will reply, "Certainly! And I'll water your camels, too!" LORD, let her be the one you have selected to be the wife of my master's son.'

⁴⁵"Before I had finished praying these words, I saw Rebekah coming along with her water jug on her shoulder. She went down to the spring and drew water and filled the jug. So I said to her, 'Please give me a drink.' ⁴⁶She quickly lowered the jug from her shoulder so I could drink, and she said, 'Certainly, sir, and I will water your camels, too!' And she did. ⁴⁷When I asked her whose daughter she was, she told me, 'My father is Bethuel, the son of Nahor and his wife, Milcah.' So I gave her the ring and the bracelets.

⁴⁸"Then I bowed my head and worshiped the LORD. I praised the LORD, the God of my master, Abraham, because he had led me along the right path to find a wife from the family of my master's relatives. ⁴⁹So tell me—will you or won't you show true kindness to my master? When you tell me, then I'll know what my next step should be, whether to move this way or that."

⁵⁰Then Laban and Bethuel replied, "The LORD has obviously brought you here, so what can we say? ⁵¹Here is Rebekah; take her and go. Yes, let her be the wife of your master's son, as the LORD has directed."

⁵²At this reply, Abraham's servant bowed to the ground and worshiped the LORD. ⁵³Then he brought out silver and gold jewelry and lovely clothing for Rebekah. He also gave valuable presents to her mother and brother. ⁵⁴Then they had supper, and the servant and the men with him stayed there overnight. But early the next morning, he said, "Send me back to my master."

⁵⁵"But we want Rebekah to stay at least ten days," her brother and mother said. "Then she can go."

⁵⁶But he said, "Don't hinder my return. The LORD has made my mission successful, and I want to report back to my master."

⁵⁷"Well," they said, "we'll call Rebekah and ask her what she thinks." ⁵⁸So they called Rebekah. "Are you willing to go with this man?" they asked her.

And she replied, "Yes, I will go."

⁵⁹So they said good-bye to Rebekah and sent her away with Abraham's servant and his men. The woman who had been Rebekah's childhood nurse went along with her. ⁶⁰They blessed her with this blessing as she parted:

"Our sister, may you become
    the mother of many millions!
May your descendants overcome
    all their enemies."

⁶¹Then Rebekah and her servants mounted the camels and left with Abraham's servant.

⁶²Meanwhile, Isaac, whose home was in the Negev, had returned from Beer-lahairoi. ⁶³One

evening as he was taking a walk out in the fields, meditating, he looked up and saw the camels coming. 64When Rebekah looked up and saw Isaac, she quickly dismounted. 65"Who is that man walking through the fields to meet us?" she asked the servant.

And he replied, "It is my master." So Rebekah covered her face with her veil. 66Then the servant told Isaac the whole story.

67And Isaac brought Rebekah into his mother's tent, and she became his wife. He loved her very much, and she was a special comfort to him after the death of his mother.

CHAPTER 25

The Death of Abraham

Now Abraham married again. Keturah was his new wife, 2and she bore him Zimran, Jokshan, Medan, Midian, Ishbak, and Shuah. 3Jokshan's two sons were Sheba and Dedan. Dedan's descendants were the Asshurites, Letushites, and Leummites. 4Midian's sons were Ephah, Epher, Hanoch, Abida, and Eldaah. These were all descendants of Abraham through Keturah.

5Abraham left everything he owned to his son Isaac. 6But before he died, he gave gifts to the sons of his concubines and sent them off to the east, away from Isaac.

7Abraham lived for 175 years, 8and he died at a ripe old age, joining his ancestors in death. 9His sons Isaac and Ishmael buried him in the cave of Machpelah, near Mamre, in the field of Ephron son of Zohar the Hittite. 10This was the field Abraham had purchased from the Hittites, where he had buried his wife Sarah. 11After Abraham's death, God poured out rich blessings on Isaac, who settled near Beer-lahairoi in the Negev.

Ishmael's Descendants

12This is the history of the descendants of Ishmael, the son of Abraham through Hagar, Sarah's Egyptian servant. 13Here is a list, by their names and clans, of Ishmael's descendants: The oldest was Nebaioth, followed by Kedar, Abdeel, Mibsam, 14Mishma, Dumah, Massa, 15Hadad, Tema, Jetur, Naphish, and Kedemah. 16These twelve sons of Ishmael became the founders of twelve tribes that bore their names, listed according to the places they settled and camped. 17Ishmael finally died at the age of 137 and joined his ancestors in death. 18Ishmael's descendants were scattered across the country

from Havilah to Shur, which is east of Egypt in the direction of Asshur. The clans descended from Ishmael camped close to one another.*

The Births of Jacob and Esau

19This is the history of the family of Isaac, the son of Abraham. 20When Isaac was forty years old, he married Rebekah, the daughter of Bethuel the Aramean from Paddan-aram and the sister of Laban. 21Isaac pleaded with the LORD to give Rebekah a child because she was childless. So the LORD answered Isaac's prayer, and his wife became pregnant with twins. 22But the two children struggled with each other in her womb. So she went to ask the LORD about it. "Why is this happening to me?" she asked.

23And the LORD told her, "The sons in your womb will become two rival nations. One nation will be stronger than the other; the descendants of your older son will serve the descendants of your younger son."

24And when the time came, the twins were born. 25The first was very red at birth. He was covered with so much hair that one would think he was wearing a piece of clothing. So they called him Esau.* 26Then the other twin was born with his hand grasping Esau's heel. So they called him Jacob.* Isaac was sixty years old when the twins were born.

Esau Sells His Birthright

27As the boys grew up, Esau became a skillful hunter, a man of the open fields, while Jacob was the kind of person who liked to stay at home. 28Isaac loved Esau in particular because of the wild game he brought home, but Rebekah favored Jacob.

29One day when Jacob was cooking some stew, Esau arrived home exhausted and hungry from a hunt. 30Esau said to Jacob, "I'm starved! Give me some of that red stew you've made." (This was how Esau got his other name, Edom—"Red.")

31Jacob replied, "All right, but trade me your birthright for it."

32"Look, I'm dying of starvation!" said Esau. "What good is my birthright to me now?"

33So Jacob insisted, "Well then, swear to me right now that it is mine." So Esau swore an oath, thereby selling all his rights as the firstborn to his younger brother. 34Then Jacob gave Esau some bread and lentil stew. Esau ate and drank and went on about his business, indifferent to the fact that he had given up his birthright.

25:18 The meaning of the Hebrew is uncertain.   25:25 *Esau* sounds like a Hebrew term that means "hair."   25:26 *Jacob* means "he grasps the heel"; this can also figuratively mean "he deceives."

CHAPTER 26

Isaac Deceives Abimelech

Now a severe famine struck the land, as had happened before in Abraham's time. So Isaac moved to Gerar, where Abimelech, king of the Philistines, lived. ²The LORD appeared to him there and said, "Do not go to Egypt. ³Do as I say, and stay here in this land. If you do, I will be with you and bless you. I will give all this land to you and your descendants, just as I solemnly promised Abraham, your father. ⁴I will cause your descendants to become as numerous as the stars, and I will give them all these lands. And through your descendants* all the nations of the earth will be blessed. ⁵I will do this because Abraham listened to me and obeyed all my requirements, commands, regulations, and laws."

⁶So Isaac stayed in Gerar. ⁷And when the men there asked him about Rebekah, he said, "She is my sister." He was afraid to admit that she was his wife. He thought they would kill him to get her, because she was very beautiful. ⁸But some time later, Abimelech, king of the Philistines, looked out a window and saw Isaac fondling Rebekah. ⁹Abimelech called for Isaac and exclaimed, "She is obviously your wife! Why did you say she was your sister?"

"Because I was afraid someone would kill me to get her from me," Isaac replied.

¹⁰"How could you treat us this way!" Abimelech exclaimed. "Someone might have taken your wife and slept with her, and you would have made us guilty of great sin." ¹¹Then Abimelech made a public proclamation: "Anyone who harms this man or his wife will die!"

Conflict over Water Rights

¹²That year Isaac's crops were tremendous! He harvested a hundred times more grain than he planted, for the LORD blessed him. ¹³He became a rich man, and his wealth only continued to grow. ¹⁴He acquired large flocks of sheep and goats, great herds of cattle, and many servants. Soon the Philistines became jealous of him, ¹⁵and they filled up all of Isaac's wells with earth. These were the wells that had been dug by the servants of his father, Abraham.

¹⁶And Abimelech asked Isaac to leave the country. "Go somewhere else," he said, "for you have become too rich and powerful for us."

¹⁷So Isaac moved to the Gerar Valley and lived there instead. ¹⁸He reopened the wells his father had dug, which the Philistines had filled in after Abraham's death. Isaac renamed them, using the names Abraham had given them. ¹⁹His shepherds also dug in the Gerar Valley and found a gushing spring.

²⁰But then the local shepherds came and claimed the spring. "This is our water," they said, and they argued over it with Isaac's herdsmen. So Isaac named the well "Argument,"* because they had argued about it with him. ²¹Isaac's men then dug another well, but again there was a fight over it. So Isaac named it "Opposition."* ²²Abandoning that one, he dug another well, and the local people finally left him alone. So Isaac called it "Room Enough,"* for he said, "At last the LORD has made room for us, and we will be able to thrive."

²³From there Isaac moved to Beersheba, ²⁴where the LORD appeared to him on the night of his arrival. "I am the God of your father, Abraham," he said. "Do not be afraid, for I am with you and will bless you. I will give you many descendants, and they will become a great nation. I will do this because of my promise to Abraham, my servant." ²⁵Then Isaac built an altar there and worshiped the LORD. He set up his camp at that place, and his servants dug a well.

A Treaty with Abimelech

²⁶One day Isaac had visitors from Gerar. King Abimelech arrived with his adviser, Ahuzzath, and also Phicol, his army commander. ²⁷"Why have you come?" Isaac asked them. "This is obviously no friendly visit, since you sent me from your land in a most unfriendly way."

²⁸They replied, "We can plainly see that the LORD is with you. So we decided we should have a treaty, a covenant between us. ²⁹Swear that you will not harm us, just as we did not harm you. We have always treated you well, and we sent you away from us in peace. And now look how the LORD has blessed you!"

³⁰So Isaac prepared a great feast for them, and they ate and drank in preparation for the treaty ceremony. ³¹Early the next morning, they each took a solemn oath of nonaggression. Then Isaac sent them home again in peace. ³²That very day Isaac's servants came and told him about a well they had dug. "We've found water!" they said. ³³So Isaac named the well "Oath,"* and from that time to this, the town that grew up there has been called Beersheba—"well of the oath."

³⁴At the age of forty, Esau married a young

26:4 Hebrew *seed.*   26:20 Hebrew *Esek.*   26:21 Hebrew *Sitnah.*   26:22 Hebrew *Rehoboth.*   26:33 Hebrew *Shibah,* which can mean "oath" or "seven."

woman named Judith, the daughter of Beeri the Hittite. He also married Basemath, the daughter of Elon the Hittite. 35But Esau's wives made life miserable for Isaac and Rebekah.

CHAPTER **27**

Jacob Steals Esau's Blessing

When Isaac was old and almost blind, he called for Esau, his older son, and said, "My son?"

"Yes, Father?" Esau replied.

2"I am an old man now," Isaac said, "and I expect every day to be my last. 3Take your bow and a quiver full of arrows out into the open country, and hunt some wild game for me. 4Prepare it just the way I like it so it's savory and good, and bring it here for me to eat. Then I will pronounce the blessing that belongs to you, my firstborn son, before I die."

5But Rebekah overheard the conversation. So when Esau left to hunt for the wild game, 6she said to her son Jacob, "I overheard your father asking Esau 7to prepare him a delicious meal of wild game. He wants to bless Esau in the LORD's presence before he dies. 8Now, my son, do exactly as I tell you. 9Go out to the flocks and bring me two fine young goats. I'll prepare your father's favorite dish from them. 10Take the food to your father; then he can eat it and bless you instead of Esau before he dies."

11"But Mother!" Jacob replied. "He won't be fooled that easily. Think how hairy Esau is and how smooth my skin is! 12What if my father touches me? He'll see that I'm trying to trick him, and then he'll curse me instead of blessing me."

13"Let the curse fall on me, dear son," said Rebekah. "Just do what I tell you. Go out and get the goats."

14So Jacob followed his mother's instructions, bringing her the two goats. She took them and cooked a delicious meat dish, just the way Isaac liked it. 15Then she took Esau's best clothes, which were there in the house, and dressed Jacob with them. 16She made him a pair of gloves from the hairy skin of the young goats, and she fastened a strip of the goat's skin around his neck. 17Then she gave him the meat dish, with its rich aroma, and some freshly baked bread. 18Jacob carried the platter of food to his father and said, "My father?"

"Yes, my son," he answered. "Who is it—Esau or Jacob?"

19Jacob replied, "It's Esau, your older son. I've done as you told me. Here is the wild game,

cooked the way you like it. Sit up and eat it so you can give me your blessing."

20Isaac asked, "How were you able to find it so quickly, my son?"

"Because the LORD your God put it in my path!" Jacob replied.

21Then Isaac said to Jacob, "Come over here. I want to touch you to make sure you really are Esau." 22So Jacob went over to his father, and Isaac touched him. "The voice is Jacob's, but the hands are Esau's," Isaac said to himself. 23But he did not recognize Jacob because Jacob's hands felt hairy just like Esau's. So Isaac pronounced his blessing on Jacob. 24"Are you really my son Esau?" he asked.

"Yes, of course," Jacob replied.

25Then Isaac said, "Now, my son, bring me the meat. I will eat it, and then I will give you my blessing." So Jacob took the food over to his father, and Isaac ate it. He also drank the wine that Jacob served him. Then Isaac said, 26"Come here and kiss me, my son."

27So Jacob went over and kissed him. And when Isaac caught the smell of his clothes, he was finally convinced, and he blessed his son. He said, "The smell of my son is the good smell of the open fields that the LORD has blessed. 28May God always give you plenty of dew for healthy crops and good harvests of grain and wine. 29May many nations become your servants. May you be the master of your brothers. May all your mother's sons bow low before you. All who curse you are cursed, and all who bless you are blessed."

30As soon as Isaac had blessed Jacob, and almost before Jacob had left his father, Esau returned from his hunting trip. 31Esau prepared his father's favorite meat dish and brought it to him. Then he said, "I'm back, Father, and I have the wild game. Sit up and eat it so you can give me your blessing."

32But Isaac asked him, "Who are you?"

"Why, it's me, of course!" he replied. "It's Esau, your older son."

33Isaac began to tremble uncontrollably and said, "Then who was it that just served me wild game? I have already eaten it, and I blessed him with an irrevocable blessing before you came."

34When Esau understood, he let out a loud and bitter cry. "O my father, bless me, too!" he begged.

35But Isaac said, "Your brother was here, and he tricked me. He has carried away your blessing."

36Esau said bitterly, "No wonder his name is Jacob,* for he has deceived me twice, first taking my birthright and now stealing my blessing. Oh, haven't you saved even one blessing for me?"

37Isaac said to Esau, "I have made Jacob your master and have declared that all his brothers will be his servants. I have guaranteed him an abundance of grain and wine—what is there left to give?"

38Esau pleaded, "Not one blessing left for me? O my father, bless me, too!" Then Esau broke down and wept.

39His father, Isaac, said to him, "You will live off the land and what it yields, 40and you will live by your sword. You will serve your brother for a time, but then you will shake loose from him and be free."

Jacob Flees to Paddan-Aram

41Esau hated Jacob because he had stolen his blessing, and he said to himself, "My father will soon be dead and gone. Then I will kill Jacob."

42But someone got wind of what Esau was planning and reported it to Rebekah. She sent for Jacob and told him, "Esau is threatening to kill you. 43This is what you should do. Flee to your uncle Laban in Haran. 44Stay there with him until your brother's fury is spent. 45When he forgets what you have done, I will send for you. Why should I lose both of you in one day?"

46Then Rebekah said to Isaac, "I'm sick and tired of these local Hittite women. I'd rather die than see Jacob marry one of them."

CHAPTER 28

So Isaac called for Jacob, blessed him, and said, "Do not marry any of these Canaanite women. 2Instead, go at once to Paddan-aram, to the house of your grandfather Bethuel, and marry one of your uncle Laban's daughters. 3May God Almighty bless you and give you many children. And may your descendants become a great assembly of nations! 4May God pass on to you and your descendants the blessings he promised to Abraham. May you own this land where we now are foreigners, for God gave it to Abraham."

5So Isaac sent Jacob away, and he went to Paddan-aram to stay with his uncle Laban, his mother's brother, the son of Bethuel the Aramean.

6Esau heard that his father had blessed Jacob and sent him to Paddan-aram to find a wife, and that he had warned Jacob not to marry a Canaanite woman. 7He also knew that Jacob had obeyed his parents and gone to Paddan-aram.

8It was now very clear to Esau that his father despised the local Canaanite women. 9So he visited his uncle Ishmael's family and married one of Ishmael's daughters, in addition to the wives he already had. His new wife's name was Mahalath. She was the sister of Nebaioth and the daughter of Ishmael, Abraham's son.

Jacob's Dream at Bethel

10Meanwhile, Jacob left Beersheba and traveled toward Haran. 11At sundown he arrived at a good place to set up camp and stopped there for the night. Jacob found a stone for a pillow and lay down to sleep. 12As he slept, he dreamed of a stairway that reached from earth to heaven. And he saw the angels of God going up and down on it.

13At the top of the stairway stood the LORD, and he said, "I am the LORD, the God of your grandfather Abraham and the God of your father, Isaac. The ground you are lying on belongs to you. I will give it to you and your descendants. 14Your descendants will be as numerous as the dust of the earth! They will cover the land from east to west and from north to south. All the families of the earth will be blessed through you and your descendants.* 15What's more, I will be with you, and I will protect you wherever you go. I will someday bring you safely back to this land. I will be with you constantly until I have finished giving you everything I have promised."

16Then Jacob woke up and said, "Surely the LORD is in this place, and I wasn't even aware of it." 17He was afraid and said, "What an awesome place this is! It is none other than the house of God—the gateway to heaven!" 18The next morning he got up very early. He took the stone he had used as a pillow and set it upright as a memorial pillar. Then he poured olive oil over it. 19He named the place Bethel—"house of God"—though the name of the nearby village was Luz.

20Then Jacob made this vow: "If God will be with me and protect me on this journey and give me food and clothing, 21and if he will bring me back safely to my father, then I will make the LORD my God. 22This memorial pillar will become a place for worshiping God, and I will give God a tenth of everything he gives me."

CHAPTER 29

Jacob Arrives at Paddan-Aram

Jacob hurried on, finally arriving in the land of the east. 2He saw in the distance three flocks of sheep

---

27:36 *Jacob* means "he grasps the heel"; this can also figuratively mean "he deceives." 28:14 Hebrew *seed.*

lying in an open field beside a well, waiting to be watered. But a heavy stone covered the mouth of the well. ³It was the custom there to wait for all the flocks to arrive before removing the stone. After watering them, the stone would be rolled back over the mouth of the well. ⁴Jacob went over to the shepherds and asked them, "Where do you live?"

"At Haran," they said.

⁵"Do you know a man there named Laban, the grandson of Nahor?"

"Yes, we do," they replied.

⁶"How is he?" Jacob asked.

"He's well and prosperous. Look, here comes his daughter Rachel with the sheep."

⁷"Why don't you water the flocks so they can get back to grazing?" Jacob asked. "They'll be hungry if you stop so early in the day."

⁸"We don't roll away the stone and begin the watering until all the flocks and shepherds are here," they replied.

⁹As this conversation was going on, Rachel arrived with her father's sheep, for she was a shepherd. ¹⁰And because she was his cousin, the daughter of his mother's brother, and because the sheep were his uncle's, Jacob went over to the well and rolled away the stone and watered his uncle's flock. ¹¹Then Jacob kissed Rachel, and tears came to his eyes. ¹²He explained that he was her cousin on her father's side, her aunt Rebekah's son. So Rachel quickly ran and told her father, Laban.

¹³As soon as Laban heard about Jacob's arrival, he rushed out to meet him and greeted him warmly. Laban then brought him home, and Jacob told him his story. ¹⁴"Just think, my very own flesh and blood!" Laban exclaimed.

Jacob Marries Leah and Rachel

After Jacob had been there about a month, ¹⁵Laban said to him, "You shouldn't work for me without pay just because we are relatives. How much do you want?"

¹⁶Now Laban had two daughters: Leah, who was the oldest, and her younger sister, Rachel. ¹⁷Leah had pretty eyes,* but Rachel was beautiful in every way, with a lovely face and shapely figure. ¹⁸Since Jacob was in love with Rachel, he told her father, "I'll work for you seven years if you'll give me Rachel, your younger daughter, as my wife."

¹⁹"Agreed!" Laban replied. "I'd rather give her to you than to someone outside the family."

²⁰So Jacob spent the next seven years working to pay for Rachel. But his love for her was so strong that it seemed to him but a few days. ²¹Finally, the time came for him to marry her. "I have fulfilled my contract," Jacob said to Laban. "Now give me my wife so we can be married."

²²So Laban invited everyone in the neighborhood to celebrate with Jacob at a wedding feast. ²³That night, when it was dark, Laban took Leah to Jacob, and he slept with her. ²⁴And Laban gave Leah a servant, Zilpah, to be her maid.

²⁵But when Jacob woke up in the morning—it was Leah! "What sort of trick is this?" Jacob raged at Laban. "I worked seven years for Rachel. What do you mean by this trickery?"

²⁶"It's not our custom to marry off a younger daughter ahead of the firstborn," Laban replied. ²⁷"Wait until the bridal week is over, and you can have Rachel, too—that is, if you promise to work another seven years for me."

²⁸So Jacob agreed to work seven more years. A week after Jacob had married Leah, Laban gave him Rachel, too. ²⁹And Laban gave Rachel a servant, Bilhah, to be her maid. ³⁰So Jacob slept with Rachel, too, and he loved her more than Leah. He then stayed and worked the additional seven years.

Jacob's Many Children

³¹But because Leah was unloved, the LORD let her have a child, while Rachel was childless. ³²So Leah became pregnant and had a son. She named him Reuben,* for she said, "The LORD has noticed my misery, and now my husband will love me." ³³She soon became pregnant again and had another son. She named him Simeon,* for she said, "The LORD heard that I was unloved and has given me another son." ³⁴Again she became pregnant and had a son. She named him Levi,* for she said, "Surely now my husband will feel affection for me, since I have given him three sons!" ³⁵Once again she became pregnant and had a son. She named him Judah,* for she said, "Now I will praise the LORD!" And then she stopped having children.

CHAPTER **30**

When Rachel saw that she wasn't having any children, she became jealous of her sister. "Give me children, or I'll die!" she exclaimed to Jacob.

²Jacob flew into a rage. "Am I God?" he

29:17 Or *dull eyes.* The meaning of the Hebrew is uncertain.   29:32 *Reuben* means "Look, a son!" It also sounds like the Hebrew for "He has seen my misery."   29:33 *Simeon* probably means "one who hears."   29:34 *Levi* sounds like a Hebrew term that means "being attached" or "feeling affection for."   29:35 *Judah* sounds like the Hebrew term for "praise."

asked. "He is the only one able to give you children!"

3Then Rachel told him, "Sleep with my servant, Bilhah, and she will bear children for me." 4So Rachel gave him Bilhah to be his wife, and Jacob slept with her. 5Bilhah became pregnant and presented him with a son. 6Rachel named him Dan,* for she said, "God has vindicated me! He has heard my request and given me a son." 7Then Bilhah became pregnant again and gave Jacob a second son. 8Rachel named him Naphtali,* for she said, "I have had an intense struggle with my sister, and I am winning!"

9Meanwhile, Leah realized that she wasn't getting pregnant anymore, so she gave her servant, Zilpah, to Jacob to be his wife. 10Soon Zilpah presented him with another son. 11Leah named him Gad,* for she said, "How fortunate I am!" 12Then Zilpah produced a second son, 13and Leah named him Asher,* for she said, "What joy is mine! The other women will consider me happy indeed!"

14One day during the wheat harvest, Reuben found some mandrakes growing in a field and brought the roots to his mother, Leah. Rachel begged Leah to give some of them to her. 15But Leah angrily replied, "Wasn't it enough that you stole my husband? Now will you steal my son's mandrake roots, too?"

Rachel said, "I will let him sleep with you tonight in exchange for the mandrake roots."

16So that evening, as Jacob was coming home from the fields, Leah went out to meet him. "You must sleep with me tonight!" she said. "I have paid for you with some mandrake roots my son has found." So Jacob slept with her. 17And God answered her prayers. She became pregnant again and gave birth to her fifth son. 18She named him Issachar,* for she said, "God has rewarded me for giving my servant to my husband as a wife." 19Then she became pregnant again and had a sixth son. 20She named him Zebulun,* for she said, "God has given me good gifts for my husband. Now he will honor me, for I have given him six sons." 21Later she gave birth to a daughter and named her Dinah.

22Then God remembered Rachel's plight and answered her prayers by giving her a child. 23She became pregnant and gave birth to a son. "God has removed my shame," she said. 24And she named him Joseph,* for she said, "May the LORD give me yet another son."

Jacob's Wealth Increases

25Soon after Joseph was born to Rachel, Jacob said to Laban, "I want to go back home. 26Let me take my wives and children, for I have earned them from you, and let me be on my way. You know I have fully paid for them with my service to you."

27"Please don't leave me," Laban replied, "for I have learned by divination that the LORD has blessed me because you are here. 28How much do I owe you? Whatever it is, I'll pay it."

29Jacob replied, "You know how faithfully I've served you through these many years, and how your flocks and herds have grown. 30You had little indeed before I came, and your wealth has increased enormously. The LORD has blessed you from everything I do! But now, what about me? When should I provide for my own family?"

31"What wages do you want?" Laban asked again.

Jacob replied, "Don't give me anything at all. Just do one thing, and I'll go back to work for you. 32Let me go out among your flocks today and remove all the sheep and goats that are speckled or spotted, along with all the dark-colored sheep. Give them to me as my wages. 33This will make it easy for you to see whether or not I have been honest. If you find in my flock any white sheep or goats that are not speckled, you will know that I have stolen them from you."

34"All right," Laban replied. "It will be as you have said." 35But that very day Laban went out and removed all the male goats that were speckled and spotted, the females that were speckled and spotted with any white patches, and all the dark-colored sheep. He placed them in the care of his sons, 36and they took them three days' distance from where Jacob was. Meanwhile, Jacob stayed and cared for Laban's flock.

37Now Jacob took fresh shoots from poplar, almond, and plane trees and peeled off strips of the bark to make white streaks on them. 38Then he set up these peeled branches beside the watering troughs so Laban's flocks would see them as they came to drink, for that was when they mated. 39So when the flocks mated in front of the white-streaked branches, all of their offspring were streaked, speckled, and spotted. 40Jacob added them to his own flock, thus separating the lambs from Laban's flock. Then at mating time, he turned the flocks toward the streaked and dark-colored rams in Laban's flock. This is how

30:6 Dan is a play on the Hebrew term meaning "to vindicate" or "to judge." 30:8 Naphtali means "my struggle." 30:11 Gad means "good fortune." 30:13 Asher means "happy." 30:18 Issachar sounds like a Hebrew term that means "reward." 30:20 Zebulun probably means "honor." 30:24 Joseph means "may he add."

he built his flock from Laban's. ⁴¹Whenever the stronger females were ready to mate, Jacob set up the peeled branches in front of them. ⁴²But he didn't do this with the weaker ones, so the weaker lambs belonged to Laban, and the stronger ones were Jacob's. ⁴³As a result, Jacob's flocks increased rapidly, and he became very wealthy, with many servants, camels, and donkeys.

CHAPTER 31

Jacob Flees from Laban

But Jacob soon learned that Laban's sons were beginning to grumble. "Jacob has robbed our father!" they said. "All his wealth has been gained at our father's expense." ²And Jacob began to notice a considerable cooling in Laban's attitude toward him.

³Then the LORD said to Jacob, "Return to the land of your father and grandfather and to your relatives there, and I will be with you."

⁴Jacob called Rachel and Leah out to the field where he was watching the flocks, ⁵so he could talk things over with them. "Your father has turned against me and is not treating me like he used to," he told them. "But the God of my father has been with me. ⁶You know how hard I have worked for your father, ⁷but he has tricked me, breaking his wage agreement with me again and again. But God has not allowed him to do me any harm. ⁸For if he said the speckled animals were mine, the whole flock began to produce speckled lambs. And when he changed his mind and said I could have the streaked ones, then all the lambs were born streaked. ⁹In this way, God has made me wealthy at your father's expense. ¹⁰During the mating season, I had a dream and saw that the male goats mating with the flock were streaked, speckled, and spotted. ¹¹Then in my dream, the angel of God said to me, 'Jacob!' And I replied, 'Yes, I'm listening!' ¹²The angel said, 'Look, and you will see that only the streaked, speckled, and spotted males are mating with the females of your flock. For I have seen all that Laban has done to you. ¹³I am the God you met at Bethel, the place where you anointed the pillar of stone and made a vow to serve me. Now leave this country and return to the land you came from.'"

¹⁴Rachel and Leah said, "That's fine with us! There's nothing for us here—none of our father's wealth will come to us anyway. ¹⁵He has reduced our rights to those of foreign women. He sold us, and what he received for us has disappeared. ¹⁶The riches God has given you from our father are legally ours and our chil-

dren's to begin with. So go ahead and do whatever God has told you."

¹⁷So Jacob put his wives and children on camels. ¹⁸He drove the flocks in front of him—all the livestock he had acquired at Paddan-aram—and set out on his journey to the land of Canaan, where his father, Isaac, lived. ¹⁹At the time they left, Laban was some distance away, shearing his sheep. Rachel stole her father's household gods and took them with her. ²⁰They set out secretly and never told Laban they were leaving. ²¹Jacob took all his possessions with him and crossed the Euphrates River, heading for the territory of Gilead.

Laban Pursues Jacob

²²Laban didn't learn of their flight for three days. ²³But when he did, he gathered a group of his relatives and set out in hot pursuit. He caught up with them seven days later in the hill country of Gilead. ²⁴But the previous night God had appeared to Laban in a dream. "Be careful about what you say to Jacob!" he was told.

²⁵So when Laban caught up with Jacob as he was camped in the hill country of Gilead, he set up his camp not far from Jacob's. ²⁶"What do you mean by sneaking off like this?" Laban demanded. "Are my daughters prisoners, the plunder of war, that you have stolen them away like this? ²⁷Why did you slip away secretly? I would have given you a farewell party, with joyful singing accompanied by tambourines and harps. ²⁸Why didn't you let me kiss my daughters and grandchildren and tell them good-bye? You have acted very foolishly! ²⁹I could destroy you, but the God of your father appeared to me last night and told me, 'Be careful about what you say to Jacob!' ³⁰I know you feel you must go, and you long intensely for your childhood home, but why have you stolen my household gods?"

³¹"I rushed away because I was afraid," Jacob answered. "I said to myself, 'He'll take his daughters from me by force.' ³²But as for your household gods, let the person who has taken them die! If you find anything that belongs to you, I swear before all these relatives of ours, I will give it back without question." But Jacob didn't know that Rachel had taken them.

³³Laban went first into Jacob's tent to search there, then into Leah's, and then he searched the tents of the two concubines, but he didn't find the gods. Finally, he went into Rachel's tent. ³⁴Rachel had taken the household gods and had stuffed them into her camel saddle, and now she

was sitting on them. So although Laban searched all the tents, he couldn't find them. 35 "Forgive my not getting up, Father," Rachel explained. "I'm having my monthly period." So despite his thorough search, Laban didn't find them.

36 Then Jacob became very angry. "What did you find?" he demanded of Laban. "What is my crime? You have chased me as though I were a criminal. 37 You have searched through everything I own. Now show me what you have found that belongs to you! Set it out here in front of us, before our relatives, for all to see. Let them decide who is the real owner!

38 "Twenty years I have been with you, and all that time I cared for your sheep and goats so they produced healthy offspring. In all those years I never touched a single ram of yours for food. 39 If any were attacked and killed by wild animals, did I show them to you and ask you to reduce the count of your flock? No, I took the loss! You made me pay for every animal stolen from the flocks, whether the loss was my fault or not. 40 I worked for you through the scorching heat of the day and through cold and sleepless nights. 41 Yes, twenty years—fourteen of them earning your two daughters, and six years to get the flock. And you have reduced my wages ten times! 42 In fact, except for the grace of God—the God of my grandfather Abraham, the awe-inspiring God of my father, Isaac—you would have sent me off without a penny to my name. But God has seen your cruelty and my hard work. That is why he appeared to you last night and vindicated me."

Jacob's Treaty with Laban

43 Then Laban replied to Jacob, "These women are my daughters, and these children are my grandchildren, and these flocks and all that you have—all are mine. But what can I do now to my own daughters and grandchildren? 44 Come now, and we will make a peace treaty, you and I, and we will live by its terms."

45 So Jacob took a stone and set it up as a monument. 46 He also told his men to gather stones and pile them up in a heap. Jacob and Laban then sat down beside the pile of stones to share a meal. 47 They named it "Witness Pile," which is Jegar-sahadutha in Laban's language and Galeed* in Jacob's.

48 "This pile of stones will stand as a witness to remind us of our agreement," Laban said. 49 This place was also called Mizpah,* for Laban said, "May

the LORD keep watch between us to make sure that we keep this treaty when we are out of each other's sight. 50 I won't know about it if you are harsh to my daughters or if you take other wives, but God will see it. 51 This heap of stones and this pillar 52 stand between us as a witness of our vows. I will not cross this line to harm you, and you will not cross it to harm me. 53 I call on the God of our ancestors—the God of your grandfather Abraham and the God of my grandfather Nahor—to punish either one of us who harms the other."

So Jacob took an oath before the awesome God of his father, Isaac, to respect the boundary line. 54 Then Jacob presented a sacrifice to God and invited everyone to a feast. Afterward they spent the night there in the hills. 55 Laban got up early the next morning, and he kissed his daughters and grandchildren and blessed them. Then he returned home.

CHAPTER **32**

Jacob Sends Gifts to Esau

As Jacob and his household started on their way again, angels of God came to meet him. 2 When Jacob saw them, he exclaimed, "This is God's camp!" So he named the place Mahanaim.*

3 Jacob now sent messengers to his brother, Esau, in Edom, the land of Seir. 4 He told them, "Give this message to my master Esau: 'Humble greetings from your servant Jacob! I have been living with Uncle Laban until recently, 5 and now I own oxen, donkeys, sheep, goats, and many servants, both men and women. I have sent these messengers to inform you of my coming, hoping that you will be friendly to us.'"

6 The messengers returned with the news that Esau was on his way to meet Jacob—with an army of four hundred men! 7 Jacob was terrified at the news. He divided his household, along with the flocks and herds and camels, into two camps. 8 He thought, "If Esau attacks one group, perhaps the other can escape."

9 Then Jacob prayed, "O God of my grandfather Abraham and my father, Isaac—O LORD, you told me to return to my land and to my relatives, and you promised to treat me kindly. 10 I am not worthy of all the faithfulness and unfailing love you have shown to me, your servant. When I left home, I owned nothing except a walking stick, and now my household fills two camps! 11 O LORD, please rescue me from my brother, Esau. I am afraid that he is coming to kill me, along with my wives and

---

31:47 *Jegar-sahadutha* means "witness pile" in Aramaic; *Galeed* means "witness pile" in Hebrew. 31:49 *Mizpah* means "watchtower." 32:2 *Mahanaim* means "two camps."

children. [12]But you promised to treat me kindly and to multiply my descendants until they become as numerous as the sands along the seashore—too many to count."

[13]Jacob stayed where he was for the night and prepared a present for Esau: [14]two hundred female goats, twenty male goats, two hundred ewes, twenty rams, [15]thirty female camels with their young, forty cows, ten bulls, twenty female donkeys, and ten male donkeys. [16]He told his servants to lead them on ahead, each group of animals by itself, separated by a distance in between.

[17]He gave these instructions to the men leading the first group: "When you meet Esau, he will ask, 'Where are you going? Whose servants are you? Whose animals are these?' [18]You should reply, 'These belong to your servant Jacob. They are a present for his master Esau! He is coming right behind us.'" [19]Jacob gave the same instructions to each of the herdsmen and told them, "You are all to say the same thing to Esau when you see him. [20]And be sure to say, 'Your servant Jacob is right behind us.'" Jacob's plan was to appease Esau with the presents before meeting him face to face. "Perhaps," Jacob hoped, "he will be friendly to us." [21]So the presents were sent on ahead, and Jacob spent that night in the camp.

Jacob Wrestles with God

[22]But during the night Jacob got up and sent his two wives, two concubines, and eleven sons across the Jabbok River. [23]After they were on the other side, he sent over all his possessions. [24]This left Jacob all alone in the camp, and a man came and wrestled with him until dawn. [25]When the man saw that he couldn't win the match, he struck Jacob's hip and knocked it out of joint at the socket. [26]Then the man said, "Let me go, for it is dawn."

But Jacob panted, "I will not let you go unless you bless me."

[27]"What is your name?" the man asked.

He replied, "Jacob."

[28]"Your name will no longer be Jacob," the man told him. "It is now Israel,* because you have struggled with both God and men and have won."

[29]"What is your name?" Jacob asked him.

"Why do you ask?" the man replied. Then he blessed Jacob there.

[30]Jacob named the place Peniel—"face of God"—for he said, "I have seen God face to face, yet my life has been spared." [31]The sun rose as he left Peniel,* and he was limping because of his hip. [32]That is why even today the people of Israel don't eat meat from near the hip, in memory of what happened that night.

CHAPTER **33**

Jacob and Esau Make Peace

Then, in the distance, Jacob saw Esau coming with his four hundred men. [2]Jacob now arranged his family into a column, with his two concubines and their children at the front, Leah and her children next, and Rachel and Joseph last. [3]Then Jacob went on ahead. As he approached his brother, he bowed low seven times before him. [4]Then Esau ran to meet him and embraced him affectionately and kissed him. Both of them were in tears.

[5]Then Esau looked at the women and children and asked, "Who are these people with you?"

"These are the children God has graciously given to me," Jacob replied. [6]Then the concubines came forward with their children and bowed low before him. [7]Next Leah came with her children, and they bowed down. Finally, Rachel and Joseph came and made their bows.

[8]"And what were all the flocks and herds I met as I came?" Esau asked.

Jacob replied, "They are gifts, my lord, to ensure your goodwill."

[9]"Brother, I have plenty," Esau answered. "Keep what you have."

[10]"No, please accept them," Jacob said, "for what a relief it is to see your friendly smile. It is like seeing the smile of God! [11]Please take my gifts, for God has been very generous to me. I have more than enough." Jacob continued to insist, so Esau finally accepted them.

[12]"Well, let's be going," Esau said. "I will stay with you and lead the way."

[13]But Jacob replied, "You can see, my lord, that some of the children are very young, and the flocks and herds have their young, too. If they are driven too hard, they may die. [14]So go on ahead of us. We will follow at our own pace and meet you at Seir."

[15]"Well," Esau said, "at least let me leave some of my men to guide and protect you."

"There is no reason for you to be so kind to me," Jacob insisted.

[16]So Esau started back to Seir that same day.

32:28 *Israel* means "God struggles" or "one who struggles with God."   32:31 Hebrew *Penuel*, a variant name for Peniel.

17Meanwhile, Jacob and his household traveled on to Succoth. There he built himself a house and made shelters for his flocks and herds. That is why the place was named Succoth.* 18Then they arrived safely at Shechem, in Canaan, and they set up camp just outside the town. 19Jacob bought the land he camped on from the family of Hamor, Shechem's father, for a hundred pieces of silver.* 20And there he built an altar and called it El-Elohe-Israel.*

CHAPTER **34**

Revenge against Shechem

One day Dinah, Leah's daughter, went to visit some of the young women who lived in the area. 2But when the local prince, Shechem son of Hamor the Hivite, saw her, he took her and raped her. 3But Shechem's love for Dinah was strong, and he tried to win her affection. 4He even spoke to his father about it. "Get this girl for me," he demanded. "I want to marry her."

5Word soon reached Jacob that his daughter had been defiled, but his sons were out in the fields herding cattle so he did nothing until they returned. 6Meanwhile, Hamor, Shechem's father, came out to discuss the matter with Jacob. 7He arrived just as Jacob's sons were coming in from the fields. They were shocked and furious that their sister had been raped. Shechem had done a disgraceful thing against Jacob's family,* a thing that should never have been done.

8Hamor told Jacob and his sons, "My son Shechem is truly in love with your daughter, and he longs for her to be his wife. Please let him marry her. 9We invite you to let your daughters marry our sons, and we will give our daughters as wives for your young men. 10And you may live among us; the land is open to you! Settle here and trade with us. You are free to acquire property among us."

11Then Shechem addressed Dinah's father and brothers. "Please be kind to me, and let me have her as my wife," he begged. "I will give whatever you require. 12No matter what dowry or gift you demand, I will pay it—only give me the girl as my wife."

13But Dinah's brothers deceived Shechem and Hamor because of what Shechem had done to their sister. 14They said to them, "We couldn't possibly allow this, because you aren't circumcised. It would be a disgrace for her to marry a man like you! 15But here is a solution. If every man among you will be circumcised like we are, 16we will intermarry with you and live here and unite with you to become one people. 17Otherwise we will take her and be on our way."

18Hamor and Shechem gladly agreed, 19and Shechem lost no time in acting on this request, for he wanted Dinah desperately. Shechem was a highly respected member of his family, 20and he appeared with his father before the town leaders to present this proposal. 21"Those men are our friends," they said. "Let's invite them to live here among us and ply their trade. For the land is large enough to hold them, and we can intermarry with them. 22But they will consider staying here only on one condition. Every one of us men must be circumcised, just as they are. 23But if we do this, all their flocks and possessions will become ours. Come, let's agree to this so they will settle here among us."

24So all the men agreed and were circumcised. 25But three days later, when their wounds were still sore, two of Dinah's brothers, Simeon and Levi, took their swords, entered the town without opposition, and slaughtered every man there, 26including Hamor and Shechem. They rescued Dinah from Shechem's house and returned to their camp. 27Then all of Jacob's sons plundered the town because their sister had been defiled there. 28They seized all the flocks and herds and donkeys—everything they could lay their hands on, both inside the town and outside in the fields. 29They also took all the women and children and wealth of every kind.

30Afterward Jacob said to Levi and Simeon, "You have made me stink among all the people of this land—among all the Canaanites and Perizzites. We are so few that they will come and crush us. We will all be killed!"

31"Should he treat our sister like a prostitute?" they retorted angrily.

CHAPTER **35**

Jacob's Return to Bethel

God said to Jacob, "Now move on to Bethel and settle there. Build an altar there to worship me— the God who appeared to you when you fled from your brother, Esau."

2So Jacob told everyone in his household, "Destroy your idols, wash yourselves, and put on clean clothing. 3We are now going to Bethel, where I will build an altar to the God who answered my prayers when I was in distress. He has stayed with me wherever I have gone."

33:17 Succoth means "shelters." **33:19** Hebrew *100 kesitahs;* the value or weight of the kesitah is no longer known. **33:20** *El-Elohe-Israel* means "God, the God of Israel." **34:7** Hebrew *in Israel.*

4So they gave Jacob all their idols and their earrings, and he buried them beneath the tree near Shechem. 5When they set out again, terror from God came over the people in all the towns of that area, and no one attacked them. 6Finally, they arrived at Luz (now called Bethel) in Canaan. 7Jacob built an altar there and named it El-bethel,* because God had appeared to him there at Bethel when he was fleeing from Esau.

8Soon after this, Rebekah's old nurse, Deborah, died. She was buried beneath the oak tree in the valley below Bethel. Ever since, the tree has been called the "Oak of Weeping."*

9God appeared to Jacob once again when he arrived at Bethel after traveling from Paddan-aram. God blessed him 10and said, "Your name is no longer Jacob; you will now be called Israel."* 11Then God said, "I am God Almighty. Multiply and fill the earth! Become a great nation, even many nations. Kings will be among your descendants! 12And I will pass on to you the land I gave to Abraham and Isaac. Yes, I will give it to you and your descendants." 13Then God went up from the place where he had spoken to Jacob.

14Jacob set up a stone pillar to mark the place where God had spoken to him. He then poured wine over it as an offering to God and anointed the pillar with olive oil. 15Jacob called the place Bethel—"house of God"—because God had spoken to him there.

The Deaths of Rachel and Isaac

16Leaving Bethel, they traveled on toward Ephrath (that is, Bethlehem). But Rachel's pains of childbirth began while they were still some distance away. 17After a very hard delivery, the midwife finally exclaimed, "Don't be afraid—you have another son!" 18Rachel was about to die, but with her last breath she named him Ben-oni; the baby's father, however, called him Benjamin.* 19So Rachel died and was buried on the way to Ephrath (that is, Bethlehem). 20Jacob set up a stone monument over her grave, and it can be seen there to this day.

21Jacob* then traveled on and camped beyond the tower of Eder. 22While he was there, Reuben slept with Bilhah, his father's concubine, and someone told Jacob about it.

These are the names of the twelve sons of Jacob:

23The sons of Leah were Reuben (Jacob's oldest son), Simeon, Levi, Judah, Issachar, and Zebulun.

24The sons of Rachel were Joseph and Benjamin.

25The sons of Bilhah, Rachel's servant, were Dan and Naphtali.

26The sons of Zilpah, Leah's servant, were Gad and Asher.

These were the sons born to Jacob at Paddan-aram.

27So Jacob came home to his father Isaac in Mamre, which is near Kiriath-arba (now called Hebron), where Abraham had also lived. 28Isaac lived for 180 years, 29and he died at a ripe old age, joining his ancestors in death. Then his sons, Esau and Jacob, buried him.

CHAPTER **36**
Descendants of Esau

This is the history of the descendants of Esau (also known as Edom). 2Esau married two young women from Canaan: Adah, the daughter of Elon the Hittite; and Oholibamah, the daughter of Anah and granddaughter of Zibeon the Hivite. 3He also married his cousin Basemath, who was the daughter of Ishmael and the sister of Nebaioth. 4Esau and Adah had a son named Eliphaz. Esau and Basemath had a son named Reuel. 5Esau and Oholibamah had sons named Jeush, Jalam, and Korah. All these sons were born to Esau in the land of Canaan.

6Then Esau took his wives, children, household servants, cattle, and flocks—all the wealth he had gained in the land of Canaan—and moved away from his brother, Jacob. 7There was not enough land to support them both because of all their cattle and livestock. 8So Esau (also known as Edom) settled in the hill country of Seir.

9This is a list of Esau's descendants, the Edomites, who lived in the hill country of Seir.

10Among Esau's sons were Eliphaz, the son of Esau's wife Adah; and Reuel, the son of Esau's wife Basemath.

11The sons of Eliphaz were Teman, Omar, Zepho, Gatam, and Kenaz. 12Eliphaz had another son named Amalek, born to Timna, his concubine. These were all grandchildren of Esau's wife Adah.

35:7 *El-bethel* means "the God of Bethel." **35:8** Hebrew *Allon-bacuth.* **35:10** *Jacob* means "he grasps the heel"; this can also figuratively mean "he deceives"; *Israel* means "God struggles" or "one who struggles with God." **35:18** *Ben-oni* means "son of my sorrow"; *Benjamin* means "son of my right hand." **35:21** Hebrew *Israel;* also in 35:22a.

13The sons of Reuel were Nahath, Zerah, Shammah, and Mizzah. These were all grandchildren of Esau's wife Basemath. 14Esau also had sons through Oholibamah, the daughter of Anah and granddaughter of Zibeon. Their names were Jeush, Jalam, and Korah.

15Esau's children and grandchildren became the leaders of different clans.

The sons of Esau's oldest son, Eliphaz, became the leaders of the clans of Teman, Omar, Zepho, Kenaz, 16Korah, Gatam, and Amalek. These clans in the land of Edom were descended from Eliphaz, the son of Esau and Adah. 17The sons of Esau's son Reuel became the leaders of the clans of Nahath, Zerah, Shammah, and Mizzah. These clans in the land of Edom were descended from Reuel, the son of Esau and Basemath. 18The sons of Esau and his wife Oholibamah became the leaders of the clans of Jeush, Jalam, and Korah. These are the clans descended from Esau's wife Oholibamah, the daughter of Anah.

19These are all the clans descended from Esau (also known as Edom).

Original Peoples of Edom
20These are the names of the tribes that descended from Seir the Horite, one of the families native to the land of Seir: Lotan, Shobal, Zibeon, Anah, 21Dishon, Ezer, and Dishan. These were the Horite clans, the descendants of Seir, who lived in the land of Edom.

22The sons of Lotan were Hori and Heman. Lotan's sister was named Timna. 23The sons of Shobal were Alvan, Manahath, Ebal, Shepho, and Onam. 24The sons of Zibeon were Aiah and Anah. This is the Anah who discovered the hot springs in the wilderness while he was grazing his father's donkeys. 25The son of Anah was Dishon, and Oholibamah was his daughter. 26The sons of Dishon* were Hemdan, Eshban, Ithran, and Keran. 27The sons of Ezer were Bilhan, Zaavan, and Akan. 28The sons of Dishan were Uz and Aran.

29So the leaders of the Horite clans were Lotan, Shobal, Zibeon, Anah, 30Dishon, Ezer, and Dishan. The Horite clans are named after their clan leaders, who lived in the land of Seir.

Rulers of Edom
31These are the kings who ruled in Edom before there were kings in Israel*:

32Bela son of Beor, who ruled from his city of Dinhabah. 33When Bela died, Jobab son of Zerah from Bozrah became king. 34When Jobab died, Husham from the land of the Temanites became king. 35When Husham died, Hadad son of Bedad became king and ruled from the city of Avith. He was the one who destroyed the Midianite army in the land of Moab. 36When Hadad died, Samlah from the city of Masrekah became king. 37When Samlah died, Shaul from the city of Rehoboth on the Euphrates River* became king. 38When Shaul died, Baal-hanan son of Acbor became king. 39When Baal-hanan died, Hadad* became king and ruled from the city of Pau. Hadad's wife was Mehetabel, the daughter of Matred and granddaughter of Mezahab.

40These are the leaders of the clans of Esau, who lived in the places named for them: Timna, Alvah, Jetheth, 41Oholibamah, Elah, Pinon, 42Kenaz, Teman, Mibzar, 43Magdiel, and Iram. These are the names of the clans of Esau, the ancestor of the Edomites, each clan giving its name to the area it occupied.

C H A P T E R **37**
Joseph's Dreams
So Jacob settled again in the land of Canaan, where his father had lived.

2This is the history of Jacob's family. When Joseph was seventeen years old, he often tended his father's flocks with his half brothers, the sons of his father's wives Bilhah and Zilpah. But Joseph reported to his father some of the bad things his brothers were doing. 3Now Jacob* loved Joseph more than any of his other children because Joseph had been born to him in his old age. So one day he gave Joseph a special gift—a beautiful robe.* 4But his brothers hated

---

36:26 Hebrew *Dishan,* a variant name for Dishon; compare 36:21, 28.   36:31 Or *before an Israelite king ruled over them.*   36:37 Hebrew *the river.*
36:39 As in some Hebrew manuscripts, Samaritan Pentateuch, and Syriac version (see also 1 Chr 1:50); most Hebrew manuscripts read *Hadar.*
37:3a Hebrew *Israel;* also in 37:13.   37:3b Traditionally rendered *a coat of many colors.* The exact meaning of the Hebrew is uncertain.

Joseph because of their father's partiality. They couldn't say a kind word to him.

5One night Joseph had a dream and promptly reported the details to his brothers, causing them to hate him even more. 6"Listen to this dream," he announced. 7"We were out in the field tying up bundles of grain. My bundle stood up, and then your bundles all gathered around and bowed low before it!"

8"So you are going to be our king, are you?" his brothers taunted. And they hated him all the more for his dream and what he had said.

9Then Joseph had another dream and told his brothers about it. "Listen to this dream," he said. "The sun, moon, and eleven stars bowed low before me!"

10This time he told his father as well as his brothers, and his father rebuked him. "What do you mean?" his father asked. "Will your mother, your brothers, and I actually come and bow before you?" 11But while his brothers were jealous of Joseph, his father gave it some thought and wondered what it all meant.

12Soon after this, Joseph's brothers went to pasture their father's flocks at Shechem. 13When they had been gone for some time, Jacob said to Joseph, "Your brothers are over at Shechem with the flocks. I'm going to send you to them."

"I'm ready to go," Joseph replied.

14"Go and see how your brothers and the flocks are getting along," Jacob said. "Then come back and bring me word." So Jacob sent him on his way, and Joseph traveled to Shechem from his home in the valley of Hebron.

15When he arrived there, a man noticed him wandering around the countryside. "What are you looking for?" he asked.

16"For my brothers and their flocks," Joseph replied. "Have you seen them?"

17"Yes," the man told him, "but they are no longer here. I heard your brothers say they were going to Dothan." So Joseph followed his brothers to Dothan and found them there.

Joseph Sold into Slavery

18When Joseph's brothers saw him coming, they recognized him in the distance and made plans to kill him. 19"Here comes that dreamer!" they exclaimed. 20"Come on, let's kill him and throw him into a deep pit. We can tell our father that a wild animal has eaten him. Then we'll see what becomes of all his dreams!"

21But Reuben came to Joseph's rescue. "Let's not kill him," he said. 22"Why should we shed his blood? Let's just throw him alive into this pit here. That way he will die without our having to touch him." Reuben was secretly planning to help Joseph escape, and then he would bring him back to his father.

23So when Joseph arrived, they pulled off his beautiful robe 24and threw him into the pit. This pit was normally used to store water, but it was empty at the time. 25Then, just as they were sitting down to eat, they noticed a caravan of camels in the distance coming toward them. It was a group of Ishmaelite traders taking spices, balm, and myrrh from Gilead to Egypt.

26Judah said to the others, "What can we gain by killing our brother? That would just give us a guilty conscience. 27Let's sell Joseph to those Ishmaelite traders. Let's not be responsible for his death; after all, he is our brother!" And his brothers agreed. 28So when the traders* came by, his brothers pulled Joseph out of the pit and sold him for twenty pieces* of silver, and the Ishmaelite traders took him along to Egypt.

29Some time later, Reuben returned to get Joseph out of the pit. When he discovered that Joseph was missing, he tore his clothes in anguish and frustration. 30Then he went back to his brothers and lamented, "The boy is gone! What can I do now?"

31Then Joseph's brothers killed a goat and dipped the robe in its blood. 32They took the beautiful robe to their father and asked him to identify it. "We found this in the field," they told him. "It's Joseph's robe, isn't it?"

33Their father recognized it at once. "Yes," he said, "it is my son's robe. A wild animal has attacked and eaten him. Surely Joseph has been torn in pieces!" 34Then Jacob tore his clothes and put on sackcloth. He mourned deeply for his son for many days. 35His family all tried to comfort him, but it was no use. "I will die in mourning for my son," he would say, and then begin to weep.

36Meanwhile, in Egypt, the traders sold Joseph to Potiphar, an officer of Pharaoh, the king of Egypt. Potiphar was captain of the palace guard.

CHAPTER 38

Judah and Tamar

About this time, Judah left home and moved to Adullam, where he visited a man named Hirah. 2There he met a Canaanite woman, the

37:28a Hebrew *Midianites*; also in 37:36.   37:28b Hebrew *20 shekels*, about 8 ounces or 228 grams in weight.

daughter of Shua, and he married her. ³She became pregnant and had a son, and Judah named the boy Er. ⁴Then Judah's wife had another son, and she named him Onan. ⁵And when she had a third son, she named him Shelah. At the time of Shelah's birth, they were living at Kezib.

⁶When his oldest son, Er, grew up, Judah arranged his marriage to a young woman named Tamar. ⁷But Er was a wicked man in the LORD's sight, so the LORD took his life. ⁸Then Judah said to Er's brother Onan, "You must marry Tamar, as our law requires of the brother of a man who has died. Her first son from you will be your brother's heir."

⁹But Onan was not willing to have a child who would not be his own heir. So whenever he had intercourse with Tamar, he spilled the semen on the ground to keep her from having a baby who would belong to his brother. ¹⁰But the LORD considered it a wicked thing for Onan to deny a child to his dead brother. So the LORD took Onan's life, too.

¹¹Then Judah told Tamar, his daughter-in-law, not to marry again at that time but to return to her parents' home. She was to remain a widow until his youngest son, Shelah, was old enough to marry her. (But Judah didn't really intend to do this because he was afraid Shelah would also die, like his two brothers.) So Tamar went home to her parents.

¹²In the course of time Judah's wife died. After the time of mourning was over, Judah and his friend Hirah the Adullamite went to Timnah to supervise the shearing of his sheep. ¹³Someone told Tamar that her father-in-law had left for the sheep-shearing at Timnah. ¹⁴Tamar was aware that Shelah had grown up, but they had not called her to come and marry him. So she changed out of her widow's clothing and covered herself with a veil to disguise herself. Then she sat beside the road at the entrance to the village of Enaim, which is on the way to Timnah. ¹⁵Judah noticed her as he went by and thought she was a prostitute, since her face was veiled. ¹⁶So he stopped and propositioned her to sleep with him, not realizing that she was his own daughter-in-law.

"How much will you pay me?" Tamar asked.

¹⁷"I'll send you a young goat from my flock," Judah promised.

"What pledge will you give me so I can be sure you will send it?" she asked.

¹⁸"Well, what do you want?" he inquired.

She replied, "I want your identification seal, your cord, and the walking stick you are carrying." So Judah gave these items to her. She then let him sleep with her, and she became pregnant. ¹⁹Afterward she went home, took off her veil, and put on her widow's clothing as usual.

²⁰Judah asked his friend Hirah the Adullamite to take the young goat back to her and to pick up the pledges he had given her, but Hirah couldn't find her. ²¹So he asked the men who lived there, "Where can I find the prostitute* who was sitting beside the road at the entrance to the village?"

"We've never had a prostitute here," they replied. ²²So Hirah returned to Judah and told him that he couldn't find her anywhere and that the men of the village had claimed they didn't have a prostitute there.

²³"Then let her keep the pledges!" Judah exclaimed. "We tried our best to send her the goat. We'd be the laughingstock of the village if we went back again."

²⁴About three months later, word reached Judah that Tamar, his daughter-in-law, was pregnant as a result of prostitution. "Bring her out and burn her!" Judah shouted.

²⁵But as they were taking her out to kill her, she sent this message to her father-in-law: "The man who owns this identification seal and walking stick is the father of my child. Do you recognize them?"

²⁶Judah admitted that they were his and said, "She is more in the right than I am, because I didn't keep my promise to let her marry my son Shelah." But Judah never slept with Tamar again.

²⁷In due season the time of Tamar's delivery arrived, and she had twin sons. ²⁸As they were being born, one of them reached out his hand, and the midwife tied a scarlet thread around the wrist of the child who appeared first, saying, "This one came out first." ²⁹But then he drew back his hand, and the other baby was actually the first to be born. "What!" the midwife exclaimed. "How did you break out first?" And ever after, he was called Perez.* ³⁰Then the baby with the scarlet thread on his wrist was born, and he was named Zerah.*

CHAPTER **39**

Joseph in Potiphar's House

Now when Joseph arrived in Egypt with the Ishmaelite traders, he was purchased by Potiphar, a

---

38:21 Hebrew *shrine prostitute;* also in 38:21b, 22. **38:29** *Perez* means "breaking out." **38:30** *Zerah* means "scarlet" or "brightness."

member of the personal staff of Pharaoh, the king of Egypt. Potiphar was the captain of the palace guard. ²The LORD was with Joseph and blessed him greatly as he served in the home of his Egyptian master. ³Potiphar noticed this and realized that the LORD was with Joseph, giving him success in everything he did. ⁴So Joseph naturally became quite a favorite with him. Potiphar soon put Joseph in charge of his entire household and entrusted him with all his business dealings. ⁵From the day Joseph was put in charge, the LORD began to bless Potiphar for Joseph's sake. All his household affairs began to run smoothly, and his crops and livestock flourished. ⁶So Potiphar gave Joseph complete administrative responsibility over everything he owned. With Joseph there, he didn't have a worry in the world, except to decide what he wanted to eat!

Now Joseph was a very handsome and well-built young man. ⁷And about this time, Potiphar's wife began to desire him and invited him to sleep with her. ⁸But Joseph refused. "Look," he told her, "my master trusts me with everything in his entire household. ⁹No one here has more authority than I do! He has held back nothing from me except you, because you are his wife. How could I ever do such a wicked thing? It would be a great sin against God."

¹⁰She kept putting pressure on him day after day, but he refused to sleep with her, and he kept out of her way as much as possible. ¹¹One day, however, no one else was around when he was doing his work inside the house. ¹²She came and grabbed him by his shirt, demanding, "Sleep with me!" Joseph tore himself away, but as he did, his shirt came off. She was left holding it as he ran from the house.

¹³When she saw that she had his shirt and that he had fled, ¹⁴she began screaming. Soon all the men around the place came running. "My husband has brought this Hebrew slave here to insult us!" she sobbed. "He tried to rape me, but I screamed. ¹⁵When he heard my loud cries, he ran and left his shirt behind with me."

¹⁶She kept the shirt with her, and when her husband came home that night, ¹⁷she told him her story. "That Hebrew slave you've had around here tried to make a fool of me," she said. ¹⁸"I was saved only by my screams. He ran out, leaving his shirt behind!"

Joseph Put in Prison

¹⁹After hearing his wife's story, Potiphar was furious! ²⁰He took Joseph and threw him into the prison where the king's prisoners were held. ²¹But the LORD was with Joseph there, too, and he granted Joseph favor with the chief jailer. ²²Before long, the jailer put Joseph in charge of all the other prisoners and over everything that happened in the prison. ²³The chief jailer had no more worries after that, because Joseph took care of everything. The LORD was with him, making everything run smoothly and successfully.

CHAPTER 40

Joseph Interprets Two Dreams

Some time later, Pharaoh's chief cup-bearer and chief baker offended him. ²Pharaoh became very angry with these officials, ³and he put them in the prison where Joseph was, in the palace of Potiphar, the captain of the guard. ⁴They remained in prison for quite some time, and Potiphar assigned Joseph to take care of them.

⁵One night the cup-bearer and the baker each had a dream, and each dream had its own meaning. ⁶The next morning Joseph noticed the dejected look on their faces. ⁷"Why do you look so worried today?" he asked.

⁸And they replied, "We both had dreams last night, but there is no one here to tell us what they mean."

"Interpreting dreams is God's business," Joseph replied. "Tell me what you saw."

⁹The cup-bearer told his dream first. "In my dream," he said, "I saw a vine in front of me. ¹⁰It had three branches that began to bud and blossom, and soon there were clusters of ripe grapes. ¹¹I was holding Pharaoh's wine cup in my hand, so I took the grapes and squeezed the juice into it. Then I placed the cup in Pharaoh's hand."

¹²"I know what the dream means," Joseph said. "The three branches mean three days. ¹³Within three days Pharaoh will take you out of prison and return you to your position as his chief cup-bearer. ¹⁴And please have some pity on me when you are back in his favor. Mention me to Pharaoh, and ask him to let me out of here. ¹⁵For I was kidnapped from my homeland, the land of the Hebrews, and now I'm here in jail, but I did nothing to deserve it."

¹⁶When the chief baker saw that the first dream had such a good meaning, he told his dream to Joseph, too. "In my dream," he said, "there were three baskets of pastries on my head. ¹⁷In the top basket were all kinds of bak-

ery goods for Pharaoh, but the birds came and ate them."

18"I'll tell you what it means," Joseph told him. "The three baskets mean three days. 19Three days from now Pharaoh will cut off your head and impale your body on a pole. Then birds will come and peck away at your flesh."

20Pharaoh's birthday came three days later, and he gave a banquet for all his officials and household staff. He sent for his chief cup-bearer and chief baker, and they were brought to him from the prison. 21He then restored the chief cup-bearer to his former position, 22but he sentenced the chief baker to be impaled on a pole, just as Joseph had predicted. 23Pharaoh's cup-bearer, however, promptly forgot all about Joseph, never giving him another thought.

CHAPTER **41**
Pharaoh's Dreams
Two years later, Pharaoh dreamed that he was standing on the bank of the Nile River. 2In his dream, seven fat, healthy-looking cows suddenly came up out of the river and began grazing along its bank. 3Then seven other cows came up from the river, but these were very ugly and gaunt. These cows went over and stood beside the fat cows. 4Then the thin, ugly cows ate the fat ones! At this point in the dream, Pharaoh woke up.

5Soon he fell asleep again and had a second dream. This time he saw seven heads of grain on one stalk, with every kernel well formed and plump. 6Then suddenly, seven more heads appeared on the stalk, but these were shriveled and withered by the east wind. 7And these thin heads swallowed up the seven plump, well-formed heads! Then Pharaoh woke up again and realized it was a dream.

8The next morning, as he thought about it, Pharaoh became very concerned as to what the dreams might mean. So he called for all the magicians and wise men of Egypt and told them about his dreams, but not one of them could suggest what they meant. 9Then the king's cup-bearer spoke up. "Today I have been reminded of my failure," he said. 10"Some time ago, you were angry with the chief baker and me, and you imprisoned us in the palace of the captain of the guard. 11One night the chief baker and I each had a dream, and each dream had a meaning. 12We told the dreams to a young Hebrew man who was a servant of the captain of the guard. He told us what each of our dreams meant, 13and everything happened just as he said it would. I was restored

to my position as cup-bearer, and the chief baker was executed and impaled on a pole."

Remember That Others Have Successfully Dealt with Temptation Read GENESIS 39:1-23

This story identifies one of the most common temptations known to man: the temptation to fall into sexual sin. Yet Joseph passed this test with flying colors. His example gives us three practical ways to deal with this temptation so that we, like Joseph, can stand tall in the end.

1. Joseph Recognized That Committing This Act Would Be a Sin against God. This should be the basis for our fight against temptation. Notice that Scripture doesn't say he was solely afraid of what her husband, Potiphar, would think, or even worried that he might get caught. He realized that—regardless of its immediate outcome—he would be sinning against God (verse 9). Since Joseph loved the Lord so much, that thought alone served as a deterrent against the temptation.

2. Joseph Attempted to Steer Clear of Temptation. Verse 6 says that Joseph was a handsome young man. For that reason, all this attention from Potiphar's wife could have been quite an ego builder. But he deliberately chose not to expose himself to this unnecessary temptation (verse 10). As Joseph's actions illustrate, sometimes the best defense against temptation is to keep clear of it in the first place.

3. Joseph Fled. Even though he was able to keep away from Potiphar's wife for a while, there came a time when he was forced to face her. But, as 1 Corinthians 10:13 says, God will always provide a way out of a potentially sinful situation. In this case, Joseph's only recourse was physically fleeing the scene (verse 12). Likewise, sometimes we may have to take drastic actions to avoid succumbing to the temptations Satan places in our path.

Refusing to give in to a certain temptation may seem extremely difficult. But in the end, you will find that your walk with the Lord will grow deeper if you remain faithful through difficult situations.

To begin the next topic, turn to p. A28.

¹⁴Pharaoh sent for Joseph at once, and he was brought hastily from the dungeon. After a quick shave and change of clothes, he went in and stood in Pharaoh's presence. ¹⁵"I had a dream last night," Pharaoh told him, "and none of these men can tell me what it means. But I have heard that you can interpret dreams, and that is why I have called for you."

¹⁶"It is beyond my power to do this," Joseph replied. "But God will tell you what it means and will set you at ease."

¹⁷So Pharaoh told him the dream. "I was standing on the bank of the Nile River," he said. ¹⁸"Suddenly, seven fat, healthy-looking cows came up out of the river and began grazing along its bank. ¹⁹But then seven other cows came up from the river. They were very thin and gaunt— in fact, I've never seen such ugly animals in all the land of Egypt. ²⁰These thin, ugly cows ate up the seven fat ones that had come out of the river first, ²¹but afterward they were still as ugly and gaunt as before! Then I woke up.

²²"A little later I had another dream. This time there were seven heads of grain on one stalk, and all seven heads were plump and full. ²³Then out of the same stalk came seven withered heads, shriveled by the east wind. ²⁴And the withered heads swallowed up the plump ones! I told these dreams to my magicians, but not one of them could tell me what they mean."

²⁵"Both dreams mean the same thing," Joseph told Pharaoh. "God was telling you what he is about to do. ²⁶The seven fat cows and the seven plump heads of grain both represent seven years of prosperity. ²⁷The seven thin, ugly cows and the seven withered heads of grain represent seven years of famine. ²⁸This will happen just as I have described it, for God has shown you what he is about to do. ²⁹The next seven years will be a period of great prosperity throughout the land of Egypt. ³⁰But afterward there will be seven years of famine so great that all the prosperity will be forgotten and wiped out. Famine will destroy the land. ³¹This famine will be so terrible that even the memory of the good years will be erased. ³²As for having the dream twice, it means that the matter has been decreed by God and that he will make these events happen soon.

³³"My suggestion is that you find the wisest man in Egypt and put him in charge of a nation-wide program. ³⁴Let Pharaoh appoint officials over the land, and let them collect one-fifth of all the crops during the seven good years. ³⁵Have

them gather all the food and grain of these good years into the royal storehouses, and store it away so there will be food in the cities. ³⁶That way there will be enough to eat when the seven years of famine come. Otherwise disaster will surely strike the land, and all the people will die."

Joseph Made Ruler of Egypt

³⁷Joseph's suggestions were well received by Pharaoh and his advisers. ³⁸As they discussed who should be appointed for the job, Pharaoh said, "Who could do it better than Joseph? For he is a man who is obviously filled with the spirit of God." ³⁹Turning to Joseph, Pharaoh said, "Since God has revealed the meaning of the dreams to you, you are the wisest man in the land! ⁴⁰I hereby appoint you to direct this project. You will manage my household and organize all my people. Only I will have a rank higher than yours."

⁴¹And Pharaoh said to Joseph, "I hereby put you in charge of the entire land of Egypt." ⁴²Then Pharaoh placed his own signet ring on Joseph's finger as a symbol of his authority. He dressed him in beautiful clothing and placed the royal gold chain about his neck. ⁴³Pharaoh also gave Joseph the chariot of his second-in-command, and wherever he went the command was shouted, "Kneel down!" So Joseph was put in charge of all Egypt. ⁴⁴And Pharaoh said to Joseph, "I am the king, but no one will move a hand or a foot in the entire land of Egypt without your approval."

⁴⁵Pharaoh renamed him Zaphenath-paneah* and gave him a wife—a young woman named Asenath, the daughter of Potiphera, priest of Heliopolis.* So Joseph took charge of the entire land of Egypt. ⁴⁶He was thirty years old when he entered the service of Pharaoh, the king of Egypt. And when Joseph left Pharaoh's presence, he made a tour of inspection throughout the land.

⁴⁷And sure enough, for the next seven years there were bumper crops everywhere. ⁴⁸During those years, Joseph took a portion of all the crops grown in Egypt and stored them for the government in nearby cities. ⁴⁹After seven years, the granaries were filled to overflowing. There was so much grain, like sand on the seashore, that the people could not keep track of the amount.

⁵⁰During this time, before the arrival of the first of the famine years, two sons were born to

41:45a *Zaphenath-paneah* probably means "God speaks and lives."   41:45b Hebrew *of On;* also in 41:50.

Joseph and his wife, Asenath, the daughter of Potiphera, priest of Heliopolis. 51Joseph named his older son Manasseh,* for he said, "God has made me forget all my troubles and the family of my father." 52Joseph named his second son Ephraim,* for he said, "God has made me fruitful in this land of my suffering."

53At last the seven years of plenty came to an end. 54Then the seven years of famine began, just as Joseph had predicted. There were crop failures in all the surrounding countries, too, but in Egypt there was plenty of grain in the storehouses. 55Throughout the land of Egypt the people began to starve. They pleaded with Pharaoh for food, and he told them, "Go to Joseph and do whatever he tells you." 56So with severe famine everywhere in the land, Joseph opened up the storehouses and sold grain to the Egyptians. 57And people from surrounding lands also came to Egypt to buy grain from Joseph because the famine was severe throughout the world.

CHAPTER **42**

Joseph's Brothers Go to Egypt

When Jacob heard that there was grain available in Egypt, he said to his sons, "Why are you standing around looking at one another? 2I have heard there is grain in Egypt. Go down and buy some for us before we all starve to death." 3So Joseph's ten older brothers went down to Egypt to buy grain. 4Jacob wouldn't let Joseph's younger brother, Benjamin, go with them, however, for fear some harm might come to him. 5So Jacob's* sons arrived in Egypt along with others to buy food, for the famine had reached Canaan as well.

6Since Joseph was governor of all Egypt and in charge of the sale of the grain, it was to him that his brothers came. They bowed low before him, with their faces to the ground. 7Joseph recognized them instantly, but he pretended to be a stranger. "Where are you from?" he demanded roughly.

"From the land of Canaan," they replied. "We have come to buy grain."

8Joseph's brothers didn't recognize him, but Joseph recognized them. 9And he remembered the dreams he had had many years before. He said to them, "You are spies! You have come to see how vulnerable our land has become."

10"No, my lord!" they exclaimed. "We have come to buy food. 11We are all brothers and honest men, sir! We are not spies!"

12"Yes, you are!" he insisted. "You have come to discover how vulnerable the famine has made us."

13"Sir," they said, "there are twelve of us brothers, and our father is in the land of Canaan. Our youngest brother is there with our father, and one of our brothers is no longer with us."

14But Joseph insisted, "As I said, you are spies! 15This is how I will test your story. I swear by the life of Pharaoh that you will not leave Egypt unless your youngest brother comes here. 16One of you go and get your brother! I'll keep the rest of you here, bound in prison. Then we'll find out whether or not your story is true. If it turns out that you don't have a younger brother, then I'll know you are spies."

17So he put them all in prison for three days. 18On the third day Joseph said to them, "I am a God-fearing man. If you do as I say, you will live. 19We'll see how honorable you really are. Only one of you will remain in the prison. The rest of you may go on home with grain for your families. 20But bring your youngest brother back to me. In this way, I will know whether or not you are telling me the truth. If you are, I will spare you." To this they agreed.

21Speaking among themselves, they said, "This has all happened because of what we did to Joseph long ago. We saw his terror and anguish and heard his pleadings, but we wouldn't listen. That's why this trouble has come upon us."

22"Didn't I tell you not to do it?" Reuben asked. "But you wouldn't listen. And now we are going to die because we murdered him."

23Of course, they didn't know that Joseph understood them as he was standing there, for he had been speaking to them through an interpreter. 24Now he left the room and found a place where he could weep. Returning, he talked some more with them. He then chose Simeon from among them and had him tied up right before their eyes.

25Joseph then ordered his servants to fill the men's sacks with grain, but he also gave secret instructions to return each brother's payment at the top of his sack. He also gave them provisions for their journey. 26So they loaded up their donkeys with the grain and started for home.

27But when they stopped for the night and one of them opened his sack to get some grain to feed the donkeys, he found his money in the sack. 28"Look!" he exclaimed to his brothers. "My money is here in my sack!" They were filled

41:51 *Manasseh* sounds like a Hebrew term that means "causing to forget."   41:52 *Ephraim* sounds like a Hebrew term that means "fruitful."   42:5 Hebrew *Israel's.*

with terror and said to each other, "What has God done to us?" 29So they came to their father, Jacob, in the land of Canaan and told him all that had happened.

30"The man who is ruler over the land spoke very roughly to us," they told him. "He took us for spies. 31But we said, 'We are honest men, not spies. 32We are twelve brothers, sons of one father; one brother has disappeared, and the youngest is with our father in the land of Canaan.' 33Then the man, the ruler of the land, told us, 'This is the way I will find out if you are honest men. Leave one of your brothers here with me, and take grain for your families and go on home. 34But bring your youngest brother back to me. Then I will know that you are honest men and not spies. If you prove to be what you say, then I will give you back your brother, and you may come as often as you like to buy grain.'"

35As they emptied out the sacks, there at the top of each one was the bag of money paid for the grain. Terror gripped them, as it did their father. 36Jacob exclaimed, "You have deprived me of my children! Joseph has disappeared, Simeon is gone, and now you want to take Benjamin, too. Everything is going against me!"

37Then Reuben said to his father, "You may kill my two sons if I don't bring Benjamin back to you. I'll be responsible for him."

38But Jacob replied, "My son will not go down with you, for his brother Joseph is dead, and he alone is left of his mother's children. If anything should happen to him, you would bring my gray head down to the grave in deep sorrow."

CHAPTER 43
The Brothers Return to Egypt
But there was no relief from the terrible famine throughout the land. 2When the grain they had brought from Egypt was almost gone, Jacob said to his sons, "Go again and buy us a little food."

3But Judah said, "The man wasn't joking when he warned that we couldn't see him again unless Benjamin came along. 4If you let him come with us, we will go down and buy some food. 5But if you don't let Benjamin go, we may as well stay at home. Remember that the man said, 'You won't be allowed to come and see me unless your brother is with you.'"

6"Why did you ever tell him you had another brother?" Jacob* moaned. "Why did you have to treat me with such cruelty?"

7"But the man specifically asked us about our

family," they replied. "He wanted to know whether our father was still living, and he asked us if we had another brother so we told him. How could we have known he would say, 'Bring me your brother'?"

8Judah said to his father, "Send the boy with me, and we will be on our way. Otherwise we will all die of starvation—and not only we, but you and our little ones. 9I personally guarantee his safety. If I don't bring him back to you, then let me bear the blame forever. 10For we could have gone and returned twice by this time if you had let him come without delay."

11So their father, Jacob, finally said to them, "If it can't be avoided, then at least do this. Fill your bags with the best products of the land. Take them to the man as gifts—balm, honey, spices, myrrh, pistachio nuts, and almonds. 12Take double the money that you found in your sacks, as it was probably someone's mistake. 13Then take your brother and go back to the man. 14May God Almighty give you mercy as you go before the man, that he might release Simeon and return Benjamin. And if I must bear the anguish of their deaths, then so be it."

15So they took Benjamin and the gifts and double the money and hurried to Egypt, where they presented themselves to Joseph. 16When Joseph saw that Benjamin was with them, he said to the manager of his household, "These men will eat with me this noon. Take them inside and prepare a big feast." 17So the man did as he was told and took them to Joseph's palace.

18They were badly frightened when they saw where they were being taken. "It's because of the money returned to us in our sacks," they said. "He plans to pretend that we stole it. Then he will seize us as slaves and take our donkeys."

A Feast at Joseph's Palace
19As the brothers arrived at the entrance to the palace, they went over to the man in charge of Joseph's household. 20They said to him, "Sir, after our first trip to Egypt to buy food, 21as we were returning home, we stopped for the night and opened our sacks. The money we had used to pay for the grain was there in our sacks. Here it is; we have brought it back again. 22We also have additional money to buy more grain. We have no idea how the money got into our sacks."

23"Relax. Don't worry about it," the household manager told them. "Your God, the God of your ancestors, must have put it there. We col-

43:6 Hebrew *Israel;* also in 43:11.

lected your money all right." Then he released Simeon and brought him out to them.

24The brothers were then led into the palace and given water to wash their feet and food for their donkeys. 25They were told they would be eating there, so they prepared their gifts for Joseph's arrival at noon.

26When Joseph came, they gave him their gifts and bowed low before him. 27He asked them how they had been getting along, and then he said, "How is your father—the old man you spoke about? Is he still alive?"

28"Yes," they replied. "He is alive and well." Then they bowed again before him.

29Looking at his brother Benjamin, Joseph asked, "Is this your youngest brother, the one you told me about? May God be gracious to you, my son." 30Then Joseph made a hasty exit because he was overcome with emotion for his brother and wanted to cry. Going into his private room, he wept there. 31Then he washed his face and came out, keeping himself under control. "Bring on the food!" he ordered.

32Joseph ate by himself, and his brothers were served at a separate table. The Egyptians sat at their own table because Egyptians despise Hebrews and refuse to eat with them. 33Joseph told each of his brothers where to sit, and to their amazement, he seated them in the order of their ages, from oldest to youngest. 34Their food was served to them from Joseph's own table. He gave the largest serving to Benjamin—five times as much as to any of the others. So they all feasted and drank freely with him.

CHAPTER **44**

Joseph's Silver Cup

When his brothers were ready to leave, Joseph gave these instructions to the man in charge of his household: "Fill each of their sacks with as much grain as they can carry, and put each man's money back into his sack. 2Then put my personal silver cup at the top of the youngest brother's sack, along with his grain money." So the household manager did as he was told.

3The brothers were up at dawn and set out on their journey with their loaded donkeys. 4But when they were barely out of the city, Joseph said to his household manager, "Chase after them and stop them. Ask them, 'Why have you repaid an act of kindness with such evil? 5What do you mean by stealing my master's personal silver drinking cup, which he uses to predict the future? What a wicked thing you have done!'"

6So the man caught up with them and spoke to them in the way he had been instructed. 7"What are you talking about?" the brothers responded. "What kind of people do you think we are, that you accuse us of such a terrible thing? 8Didn't we bring back the money we found in our sacks? Why would we steal silver or gold from your master's house? 9If you find his cup with any one of us, let that one die. And all the rest of us will be your master's slaves forever."

10"Fair enough," the man replied, "except that only the one who stole it will be a slave. The rest of you may go free."

11They quickly took their sacks from the backs of their donkeys and opened them. 12Joseph's servant began searching the oldest brother's sack, going on down the line to the youngest. The cup was found in Benjamin's sack! 13At this, they tore their clothing in despair, loaded the donkeys again, and returned to the city. 14Joseph was still at home when Judah and his brothers arrived, and they fell to the ground before him.

15"What were you trying to do?" Joseph demanded. "Didn't you know that a man such as I would know who stole it?"

16And Judah said, "Oh, my lord, what can we say to you? How can we plead? How can we prove our innocence? God is punishing us for our sins. My lord, we have all returned to be your slaves— we and our brother who had your cup in his sack."

17"No," Joseph said. "Only the man who stole the cup will be my slave. The rest of you may go home to your father."

Judah Speaks for His Brothers

18Then Judah stepped forward and said, "My lord, let me say just this one word to you. Be patient with me for a moment, for I know you could have me killed in an instant, as though you were Pharaoh himself.

19"You asked us, my lord, if we had a father or a brother. 20We said, 'Yes, we have a father, an old man, and a child of his old age, his youngest son. His brother is dead, and he alone is left of his mother's children, and his father loves him very much.' 21And you said to us, 'Bring him here so I can see him.' 22But we said to you, 'My lord, the boy cannot leave his father, for his father would die.' 23But you told us, 'You may not see me again unless your youngest brother is with you.' 24So we returned to our father and told him what you had said. 25And when he said, 'Go back again

Forgiveness Breaks Down Walls Read GENESIS 45:1-15

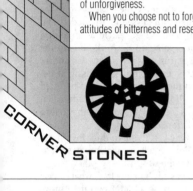

Joseph stands out in Scripture as one of the most amazing examples of a man who extended incredible forgiveness. If anyone could have held a grudge, it certainly would have been this young man. He was sold by his own brothers into slavery because they were jealous of the attention his father, Jacob, heaped upon him. Through an amazing chain of events that were clearly divinely ordered, Joseph was exalted to the second most powerful position in Egypt (and quite possibly in all the world at that time).

In his position, Joseph could have justifiably exacted revenge upon his brothers. Instead, he offered forgiveness to them, saying, "As far as I am concerned, God turned into good what you meant for evil. He brought me to the high position I have today so I could save the lives of many people" (Genesis 50:20). By choosing to forgive his brothers, Joseph refused to become a prisoner of unforgiveness.

When you choose not to forgive those who hurt you, you enslave yourself to the destructive attitudes of bitterness and resentment. These attitudes then begin to eat at you on the inside, day in and day out, to the point that when you see that person or even hear his or her name, it can cause your blood to boil. This is not what God intends for you.

God commanded all of us to forgive. He did this not just so we would show his mercy and grace to others, but to free us from the shackles of unforgiveness. Don't allow yourself to be held captive by an unforgiving heart. Remember, when you forgive someone, you set a prisoner free—yourself.

To begin the next topic, turn to p. A18.

CORNER STONES

---

and buy us a little food,' 26we replied, 'We can't unless you let our youngest brother go with us. We won't be allowed to see the man in charge of the grain unless our youngest brother is with us.' 27Then my father said to us, 'You know that my wife had two sons, 28and that one of them went away and never returned—doubtless torn to pieces by some wild animal. I have never seen him since. 29If you take away his brother from me, too, and any harm comes to him, you would bring my gray head down to the grave in deep sorrow.'

30"And now, my lord, I cannot go back to my father without the boy. Our father's life is bound up in the boy's life. 31When he sees that the boy is not with us, our father will die. We will be responsible for bringing his gray head down to the grave in sorrow. 32My lord, I made a pledge to my father that I would take care of the boy. I told him, 'If I don't bring him back to you, I will bear the blame forever.' 33Please, my lord, let me stay here as a slave instead of the boy, and let the boy return with his brothers. 34For how can I return to my father if the boy is not with me? I cannot bear to see what this would do to him."

CHAPTER **45**
Joseph Reveals His Identity

Joseph could stand it no longer. "Out, all of you!" he cried out to his attendants. He wanted to be alone with his brothers when he told them who he was. 2Then he broke down and wept aloud. His sobs could be heard throughout the palace, and the news was quickly carried to Pharaoh's palace.

3"I am Joseph!" he said to his brothers. "Is my father still alive?" But his brothers were speechless! They were stunned to realize that Joseph was standing there in front of them. 4"Come over here," he said. So they came closer. And he said again, "I am Joseph, your brother whom you sold into Egypt. 5But don't be angry with yourselves that you did this to me, for God did it. He sent me here ahead of you to preserve your lives. 6These two years of famine will grow to seven, during which there will be neither plowing nor harvest. 7God has sent me here to keep you and your families alive so that you will become a great nation. 8Yes, it was God who sent me here, not you! And he has made me a counselor to Pharaoh—manager of his entire household and ruler over all Egypt.

9"Hurry, return to my father and tell him, 'This is what your son Joseph says: God has made me master over all the land of Egypt. Come down to me right away! 10You will live in the land of Goshen so you can be near me with all your children and grandchildren, your flocks and herds, and all that you have. 11I will take care of you there, for there are still five years of famine ahead of us. Otherwise you and your household will come to utter poverty.'"

12Then Joseph said, "You can see for yourselves, and so can my brother Benjamin, that I really am Joseph! 13Tell my father how I am honored here in Egypt. Tell him about everything you have seen, and bring him to me quickly." 14Weeping with joy, he embraced Benjamin, and Benjamin also began to weep. 15Then Joseph kissed each of his brothers and wept over them, and then they began talking freely with him.

Pharaoh Invites Jacob to Egypt

16The news soon reached Pharaoh: "Joseph's brothers have come!" Pharaoh was very happy to hear this and so were his officials.

17Pharaoh said to Joseph, "Tell your brothers to load their pack animals and return quickly to their homes in Canaan. 18Tell them to bring your father and all of their families, and to come here to Egypt to live. Tell them, 'Pharaoh will assign to you the very best territory in the land of Egypt. You will live off the fat of the land!' 19And tell your brothers to take wagons from Egypt to carry their wives and little ones and to bring your father here. 20Don't worry about your belongings, for the best of all the land of Egypt is yours."

21So the sons of Jacob* did as they were told. Joseph gave them wagons, as Pharaoh had commanded, and he supplied them with provisions for the journey. 22And he gave each of them new clothes—but to Benjamin he gave five changes of clothes and three hundred pieces* of silver! 23He sent his father ten donkeys loaded with the good things of Egypt, and ten donkeys loaded with grain and all kinds of other food to be eaten on his journey. 24So he sent his brothers off, and as they left, he called after them, "Don't quarrel along the way!" 25And they left Egypt and returned to their father, Jacob, in the land of Canaan.

26"Joseph is still alive!" they told him. "And he is ruler over all the land of Egypt!" Jacob was stunned at the news—he couldn't believe it. 27But when they had given him Joseph's messages, and when he saw the wagons loaded with the food sent by Joseph, his spirit revived.

28Then Jacob said, "It must be true! My son Joseph is alive! I will go and see him before I die."

CHAPTER 46
Jacob's Journey to Egypt

So Jacob* set out for Egypt with all his possessions. And when he came to Beersheba, he offered sacrifices to the God of his father, Isaac. 2During the night God spoke to him in a vision. "Jacob! Jacob!" he called.

"Here I am," Jacob replied.

3"I am God," the voice said, "the God of your father. Do not be afraid to go down to Egypt, for I will see to it that you become a great nation there. 4I will go with you down to Egypt, and I will bring your descendants back again. But you will die in Egypt with Joseph at your side."

5So Jacob left Beersheba, and his sons brought him to Egypt. They carried their little ones and wives in the wagons Pharaoh had provided for them. 6They brought their livestock, too, and all the belongings they had acquired in the land of Canaan. Jacob and his entire family arrived in Egypt—7sons and daughters, grandsons and granddaughters—all his descendants.

8These are the names of the Israelites, the descendants of Jacob, who went with him to Egypt:

Reuben was Jacob's oldest son. 9The sons of Reuben were Hanoch, Pallu, Hezron, and Carmi.

10The sons of Simeon were Jemuel, Jamin, Ohad, Jakin, Zohar, and Shaul. (Shaul's mother was a Canaanite woman.)

11The sons of Levi were Gershon, Kohath, and Merari.

12The sons of Judah were Er, Onan, Shelah, Perez, and Zerah. (But Er and Onan had died in the land of Canaan.) The sons of Perez were Hezron and Hamul.

13The sons of Issachar were Tola, Puah,* Jashub,* and Shimron.

14The sons of Zebulun were Sered, Elon, and Jahleel.

15These are the sons of Jacob who were born to Leah in Paddan-aram, along with their sister, Dinah. In all, Jacob's descendants through Leah numbered thirty-three.

45:21 Hebrew *Israel*; also in 45:28. 45:22 Hebrew *300 shekels*, about 7.5 pounds or 3.4 kilograms in weight. 46:1 Hebrew *Israel*; also in 46:30. 46:13a As in Syriac version and Samaritan Pentateuch (see also 1 Chr 7:1); Hebrew reads *Puvah*. 46:13b As in some Greek manuscripts and Samaritan Pentateuch (see also Num 26:24; 1 Chr 7:1); Hebrew reads *Iob*.

16The sons of Gad were Zephon,* Haggi, Shuni, Ezbon, Eri, Arodi, and Areli.

17The sons of Asher were Imnah, Ishvah, Ishvi, and Beriah. Their sister was named Serah. Beriah's sons were Heber and Malkiel.

18These sixteen were descendants of Jacob through Zilpah, the servant given to Leah by her father, Laban.

19The sons of Jacob's wife Rachel were Joseph and Benjamin.

20Joseph's sons, born in the land of Egypt, were Manasseh and Ephraim. Their mother was Asenath, daughter of Potiphera, priest of Heliopolis.*

21Benjamin's sons were Bela, Beker, Ashbel, Gera, Naaman, Ehi, Rosh, Muppim, Huppim, and Ard.

22These fourteen were the descendants of Jacob and his wife Rachel.

23The son of Dan was Hushim.

24The sons of Naphtali were Jahzeel, Guni, Jezer, and Shillem.

25These seven were the descendants of Jacob through Bilhah, the servant given to Rachel by her father, Laban.

26So the total number of Jacob's direct descendants who went with him to Egypt, not counting his sons' wives, was sixty-six. 27Joseph also had two sons* who had been born in Egypt. So altogether, there were seventy* members of Jacob's family in the land of Egypt.

Jacob's Family Arrives in Goshen

28Jacob sent Judah on ahead to meet Joseph and get directions to the land of Goshen. And when they all arrived there, 29Joseph prepared his chariot and traveled to Goshen to meet his father. As soon as Joseph arrived, he embraced his father and wept on his shoulder for a long time. 30Then Jacob said to Joseph, "Now let me die, for I have seen you with my own eyes and know you are still alive."

31And Joseph said to his brothers and to all their households, "I'll go and tell Pharaoh that you have all come from the land of Canaan to join me. 32And I will tell him, 'These men are shepherds and livestock breeders. They have brought with them their flocks and herds and everything they own.' 33So when Pharaoh calls

for you and asks you about your occupation, 34tell him, 'We have been livestock breeders from our youth, as our ancestors have been for many generations.' When you tell him this, he will let you live here in the land of Goshen, for shepherds are despised in the land of Egypt."

CHAPTER **47**
Jacob Blesses Pharaoh

So Joseph went to see Pharaoh and said, "My father and my brothers are here from Canaan. They came with all their flocks and herds and possessions, and they are now in the land of Goshen."

2Joseph took five of his brothers with him and presented them to Pharaoh. 3Pharaoh asked them, "What is your occupation?"

And they replied, "We are shepherds like our ancestors. 4We have come to live here in Egypt, for there is no pasture for our flocks in Canaan. The famine is very severe there. We request permission to live in the land of Goshen."

5And Pharaoh said to Joseph, "Now that your family has joined you here, 6choose any place you like for them to live. Give them the best land of Egypt—the land of Goshen will be fine. And if any of them have special skills, put them in charge of my livestock, too."

7Then Joseph brought his father, Jacob, and presented him to Pharaoh, and Jacob blessed Pharaoh. 8"How old are you?" Pharaoh asked him.

9Jacob replied, "I have lived for 130 hard years, but I am still not nearly as old as many of my ancestors." 10Then Jacob blessed Pharaoh again before he left.

11So Joseph assigned the best land of Egypt—the land of Rameses—to his father and brothers, just as Pharaoh had commanded. 12And Joseph furnished food to his father and brothers in amounts appropriate to the number of their dependents.

Joseph's Leadership in the Famine

13Meanwhile, the famine became worse and worse, and the crops continued to fail throughout Egypt and Canaan. 14Joseph collected all the money in Egypt and Canaan in exchange for grain, and he brought the money to Pharaoh's treasure-house. 15When the people of Egypt and Canaan ran out of money, they came to Joseph crying again for food.

46:16 As in Greek version and Samaritan Pentateuch (see also Num 26:15); Hebrew reads *Ziphion*.   46:20 Hebrew *of On*.   46:27a Greek version reads *nine sons*, probably including Joseph's grandsons through Ephraim and Manasseh (see 1 Chr 7:14-20).   46:27b Greek version reads *seventy-five*; see note on Exod 1:5.

"Our money is gone," they said, "but give us bread. Why should we die?"

16 "Well, then," Joseph replied, "since your money is gone, give me your livestock. I will give you food in exchange." 17 So they gave their livestock to Joseph in exchange for food. Soon all the horses, flocks, herds, and donkeys of Egypt were in Pharaoh's possession. But at least they were able to purchase food for that year.

18 The next year they came again and said, "Our money is gone, and our livestock are yours. We have nothing left but our bodies and land. 19 Why should we die before your very eyes? Buy us and our land in exchange for food; we will then become servants to Pharaoh. Just give us grain so that our lives may be saved and so the land will not become empty and desolate."

20 So Joseph bought all the land of Egypt for Pharaoh. All the Egyptians sold him their fields because the famine was so severe, and their land then belonged to Pharaoh. 21 Thus, all the people of Egypt became servants to Pharaoh.* 22 The only land he didn't buy was that belonging to the priests, for they were assigned food from Pharaoh and didn't need to sell their land.

23 Then Joseph said to the people, "See, I have bought you and your land for Pharaoh. I will provide you with seed, so you can plant the fields. 24 Then when you harvest it, a fifth of your crop will belong to Pharaoh. Keep four-fifths for yourselves, and use it to plant the next year's crop and to feed yourselves, your households, and your little ones."

25 "You have saved our lives!" they exclaimed. "May it please you, sir, to let us be Pharaoh's servants." 26 Joseph then made it a law throughout the land of Egypt—and it is still the law—that Pharaoh should receive one-fifth of all the crops grown on his land. But since Pharaoh had not taken over the priests' land, they were exempt from this payment.

27 So the people of Israel settled in the land of Goshen in Egypt. And before long, they began to prosper there, and their population grew rapidly. 28 Jacob lived for seventeen years after his arrival in Egypt, so he was 147 years old when he died. 29 As the time of his death drew near, he called for his son Joseph and said to him, "If you are pleased with me, swear most solemnly that you will honor this, my last request: Do not bury me in Egypt. 30 When I am dead, take me out of Egypt and bury me beside my ancestors." So Joseph promised that he would. 31 "Swear that you will do it," Jacob insisted. So Joseph gave his oath, and Jacob* bowed in worship as he leaned on his staff.*

CHAPTER **48**

Jacob Blesses Manasseh and Ephraim

One day not long after this, word came to Joseph that his father was failing rapidly. So Joseph went to visit him, and he took with him his two sons, Manasseh and Ephraim. 2 When Jacob heard that Joseph had arrived, he gathered his strength and sat up in bed to greet him.

3 Jacob said to Joseph, "God Almighty appeared to me at Luz in the land of Canaan and blessed me. 4 He said to me, 'I will make you a multitude of nations, and I will give this land of Canaan to you and your descendants as an everlasting possession.' 5 Now I am adopting as my own sons these two boys of yours, Ephraim and Manasseh, who were born here in the land of Egypt before I arrived. They will inherit from me just as Reuben and Simeon will. 6 But the children born to you in the future will be your own. The land they inherit will be within the territories of Ephraim and Manasseh. 7 As I was returning from Paddan, Rachel died in the land of Canaan. We were still on the way, just a short distance from Ephrath (that is, Bethlehem). So with great sorrow I buried her there beside the road to Ephrath."

8 Then Jacob* looked over at the two boys. "Are these your sons?" he asked.

9 "Yes," Joseph told him, "these are the sons God has given me here in Egypt."

And Jacob said, "Bring them over to me, and I will bless them."

10 Now Jacob was half blind because of his age and could hardly see. So Joseph brought the boys close to him, and Jacob kissed and embraced them. 11 Then Jacob said to Joseph, "I never thought I would see you again, but now God has let me see your children, too."

12 Joseph took the boys from their grandfather's knees, and he bowed low to him. 13 Then he positioned the boys so Ephraim was at Jacob's left hand and Manasseh was at his right hand. 14 But Jacob crossed his arms as he reached out to lay his hands on the boys' heads. So his right hand was on the head of Ephraim, the younger boy, and his left hand was on the head of Manasseh, the older.

47:21 As in Greek version and Samaritan Pentateuch; Hebrew reads *He moved the people into the towns throughout the land of Egypt.* 47:31a Hebrew *Israel.* 47:31b As in Greek version; Hebrew reads *bowed in worship at the head of his bed.* 48:8 Hebrew *Israel;* also in 48:10, 11, 13, 14, 21.

15Then he blessed Joseph and said, "May God, the God before whom my grandfather Abraham and my father, Isaac, walked, the God who has been my shepherd all my life, 16and the angel who has kept me from all harm—may he bless these boys. May they preserve my name and the names of my grandfather Abraham and my father, Isaac. And may they become a mighty nation."

17But Joseph was upset when he saw that his father had laid his right hand on Ephraim's head. So he lifted it to place it on Manasseh's head instead. 18"No, Father," he said, "this one over here is older. Put your right hand on his head."

19But his father refused. "I know what I'm doing, my son," he said. "Manasseh, too, will become a great people, but his younger brother will become even greater. His descendants will become a multitude of nations!" 20So Jacob blessed the boys that day with this blessing: "The people of Israel will use your names to bless each other. They will say, 'May God make you as prosperous as Ephraim and Manasseh.'" In this way, Jacob put Ephraim ahead of Manasseh.

21Then Jacob said to Joseph, "I am about to die, but God will be with you and will bring you again to Canaan, the land of your ancestors. 22And I give you an extra portion* beyond what I have given your brothers—the portion that I took from the Amorites with my sword and bow."

CHAPTER **49**

Jacob Blesses His Sons

Then Jacob called together all his sons and said, "Gather around me, and I will tell you what is going to happen to you in the days to come.

2 "Come and listen, O sons of Jacob;
  listen to Israel, your father.

3 "Reuben, you are my oldest son,
  the child of my vigorous youth.
  You are first on the list in rank and honor.
4 But you are as unruly as the waves of the sea,
  and you will be first no longer.
  For you slept with one of my wives;
  you dishonored me in my own bed.

5 "Simeon and Levi are two of a kind—
  men of violence.
6 O my soul, stay away from them.

  May I never be a party to their wicked plans.
  For in their anger they murdered men,
  and they crippled oxen just for sport.
7 Cursed be their anger, for it is fierce;
  cursed be their wrath, for it is cruel.
  Therefore, I will scatter their descendants
  throughout the nation of Israel.

8 "Judah, your brothers will praise you.
  You will defeat your enemies.
  All your relatives will bow before you.
9 Judah is a young lion
  that has finished eating its prey.
  Like a lion he crouches and lies down;
  like a lioness—who will dare to rouse him?
10 The scepter will not depart from Judah,
  nor the ruler's staff from his descendants,
  until the coming of the one to whom it belongs,*
  the one whom all nations will obey.
11 He ties his foal to a grapevine,
  the colt of his donkey to a choice vine.
  He washes his clothes in wine
  because his harvest is so plentiful.
12 His eyes are darker than wine,
  and his teeth are whiter than milk.

13 "Zebulun will settle on the shores of the sea
  and will be a harbor for ships;
  his borders will extend to Sidon.

14 "Issachar is a strong beast of burden,
  resting among the sheepfolds.*
15 When he sees how good the countryside is,
  how pleasant the land,
  he will bend his shoulder to the task
  and submit to forced labor.

16 "Dan will govern his people
  like any other tribe in Israel.
17 He will be a snake beside the road,
  a poisonous viper along the path,
  that bites the horse's heels
  so the rider is thrown off.
18 I trust in you for salvation, O LORD!

19 "Gad will be plundered by marauding bands,
  but he will turn and plunder them.

20 "Asher will produce rich foods,
  food fit for kings.

21 "Naphtali is a deer let loose,
  producing magnificent fawns.

48:22 Or *give you the ridge of land.* The meaning of the Hebrew is uncertain. 49:10 Or *until tribute is brought to him and the peoples obey;* traditionally rendered *until Shiloh comes.* 49:14 Or *saddlebags,* or *hearths.*

22 "Joseph is a fruitful tree,
   a fruitful tree beside a fountain.
   His branches reach over the wall.
23 He has been attacked by archers,
   who shot at him and harassed him.
24 But his bow remained strong,
   and his arms were strengthened
   by the Mighty One of Jacob,
   the Shepherd, the Rock of Israel.
25 May the God of your ancestors help you;
   may the Almighty bless you
   with the blessings of the heavens above,
   blessings of the earth beneath,
   and blessings of the breasts and womb.
26 May the blessings of your ancestors
   be greater than the blessings of the
      eternal mountains,
   reaching to the utmost bounds of the
      everlasting hills.
   These blessings will fall on the head of
      Joseph,
   who is a prince among his brothers.

27 "Benjamin is a wolf that prowls.
   He devours his enemies in the morning,
   and in the evening he divides the plunder."

28These are the twelve tribes of Israel, and these are the blessings with which Jacob* blessed his twelve sons. Each received a blessing that was appropriate to him.

Jacob's Death and Burial

29Then Jacob told them, "Soon I will die. Bury me with my father and grandfather in the cave in Ephron's field. 30This is the cave in the field of Machpelah, near Mamre in Canaan, which Abraham bought from Ephron the Hittite for a permanent burial place. 31There Abraham and his wife Sarah are buried. There Isaac and his wife, Rebekah, are buried. And there I buried Leah. 32It is the cave that my grandfather Abraham bought from the Hittites." 33Then when Jacob had finished this charge to his sons, he lay back in the bed, breathed his last, and died.

CHAPTER **50**

Joseph threw himself on his father and wept over him and kissed him. 2Then Joseph told his morticians to embalm the body. 3The embalming process took forty days, and there was a period of national mourning for seventy days. 4When the period of mourning was over, Joseph approached Pharaoh's advisers and asked them

to speak to Pharaoh on his behalf. 5He told them, "Tell Pharaoh that my father made me swear an oath. He said to me, 'I am about to die; take my body back to the land of Canaan, and bury me in our family's burial cave.' Now I need to go and bury my father. After his burial is complete, I will return without delay."

6Pharaoh agreed to Joseph's request. "Go and bury your father, as you promised," he said. 7So Joseph went, with a great number of Pharaoh's counselors and advisers—all the senior officers of Egypt. 8Joseph also took his brothers and the entire household of Jacob. But they left their little children and flocks and herds in the land of Goshen. 9So a great number of chariots, cavalry, and people accompanied Joseph.

10When they arrived at the threshing floor of Atad, near the Jordan River, they held a very great and solemn funeral, with a seven-day period of mourning for Joseph's father. 11The local residents, the Canaanites, renamed the place Abel-mizraim,* for they said, "This is a place of very deep mourning for these Egyptians." 12So Jacob's sons did as he had commanded them. 13They carried his body to the land of Canaan and buried it there in the cave of Machpelah. This is the cave that Abraham had bought for a permanent burial place in the field of Ephron the Hittite, near Mamre.

Joseph Reassures His Brothers

14Then Joseph returned to Egypt with his brothers and all who had accompanied him to his father's funeral. 15But now that their father was dead, Joseph's brothers became afraid. "Now Joseph will pay us back for all the evil we did to him," they said. 16So they sent this message to Joseph: "Before your father died, he instructed us 17to say to you: 'Forgive your brothers for the great evil they did to you.' So we, the servants of the God of your father, beg you to forgive us." When Joseph received the message, he broke down and wept. 18Then his brothers came and bowed low before him. "We are your slaves," they said.

19But Joseph told them, "Don't be afraid of me. Am I God, to judge and punish you? 20As far as I am concerned, God turned into good what you meant for evil. He brought me to the high position I have today so I could save the lives of many people. 21No, don't be afraid. Indeed, I myself will take care of you and your families." And he spoke very kindly to them, reassuring them.

49:28 Hebrew *Israel*.   50:11 *Abel-mizraim* means "mourning of the Egyptians."

The Death of Joseph

22So Joseph and his brothers and their families continued to live in Egypt. Joseph was 110 years old when he died. 23He lived to see three generations of descendants of his son Ephraim and the children of Manasseh's son Makir, who were treated as if they were his own.

24"Soon I will die," Joseph told his brothers, "but God will surely come for you, to lead you out of this land of Egypt. He will bring you back to the land he vowed to give to the descendants of Abraham, Isaac, and Jacob."

25Then Joseph made the sons of Israel swear an oath, and he said, "When God comes to lead us back to Canaan, you must take my body back with you." 26So Joseph died at the age of 110. They embalmed him, and his body was placed in a coffin in Egypt.

Exodus

CHAPTER 1

The Israelites in Egypt

These are the sons of Jacob* who went with their father to Egypt, each with his family: ²Reuben, Simeon, Levi, Judah, ³Issachar, Zebulun, Benjamin, ⁴Dan, Naphtali, Gad, and Asher. ⁵Joseph was already down in Egypt. In all, Jacob had seventy* direct descendants.

⁶In time, Joseph and each of his brothers died, ending that generation. ⁷But their descendants had many children and grandchildren. In fact, they multiplied so quickly that they soon filled the land. ⁸Then a new king came to the throne of Egypt who knew nothing about Joseph or what he had done. ⁹He told his people, "These Israelites are becoming a threat to us because there are so many of them. ¹⁰We must find a way to put an end to this. If we don't and if war breaks out, they will join our enemies and fight against us. Then they will escape from the country."

¹¹So the Egyptians made the Israelites their slaves and put brutal slave drivers over them, hoping to wear them down under heavy burdens. They forced them to build the cities of Pithom and Rameses as supply centers for the king. ¹²But the more the Egyptians oppressed them, the more quickly the Israelites multiplied! The Egyptians soon became alarmed ¹³and decided to make their slavery more bitter still. ¹⁴They were ruthless with the Israelites, forcing them to make bricks and mortar and to work long hours in the fields.

¹⁵Then Pharaoh, the king of Egypt, gave this order to the Hebrew midwives, Shiphrah and Puah: ¹⁶"When you help the Hebrew women give birth, kill all the boys as soon as they are born. Allow only the baby girls to live." ¹⁷But because the midwives feared God, they refused to obey the king and allowed the boys to live, too.

¹⁸Then the king called for the midwives. "Why have you done this?" he demanded. "Why have you allowed the boys to live?"

¹⁹"Sir," they told him, "the Hebrew women are very strong. They have their babies so quickly that we cannot get there in time! They are not slow in giving birth like Egyptian women."

²⁰So God blessed the midwives, and the Israelites continued to multiply, growing more and more powerful. ²¹And because the midwives feared God, he gave them families of their own.

²²Then Pharaoh gave this order to all his people: "Throw all the newborn Israelite boys into the Nile River. But you may spare the baby girls."

CHAPTER 2

The Birth of Moses

During this time, a man and woman from the tribe of Levi got married. ²The woman became pregnant and gave birth to a son. She saw what a beautiful baby he was and kept him hidden for three months. ³But when she could no longer hide him, she got a little basket made of papyrus reeds and waterproofed it with tar and pitch. She put the baby in the basket and laid it among the reeds along the edge of the Nile River. ⁴The baby's sister then stood at a distance, watching to see what would happen to him.

⁵Soon after this, one of Pharaoh's daughters came down to bathe in the river, and her servant girls walked along the riverbank. When the princess saw the little basket among the reeds, she told one of her servant girls to get it for her. ⁶As the princess opened it, she found the baby boy. His helpless cries touched her heart. "He must be one of the Hebrew children," she said.

1:1 Hebrew *Israel*.   1:5 Dead Sea Scrolls and Greek version read *seventy-five*; see notes on Gen 46:27.

7Then the baby's sister approached the princess. "Should I go and find one of the Hebrew women to nurse the baby for you?" she asked.

8"Yes, do!" the princess replied. So the girl rushed home and called the baby's mother.

9"Take this child home and nurse him for me," the princess told her. "I will pay you for your help." So the baby's mother took her baby home and nursed him.

10Later, when he was older, the child's mother brought him back to the princess, who adopted him as her son. The princess named him Moses,* for she said, "I drew him out of the water."

Moses Escapes to Midian

11Many years later, when Moses had grown up, he went out to visit his people, the Israelites, and he saw how hard they were forced to work. During his visit, he saw an Egyptian beating one of the Hebrew slaves. 12After looking around to make sure no one was watching, Moses killed the Egyptian and buried him in the sand.

13The next day, as Moses was out visiting his people again, he saw two Hebrew men fighting. "What are you doing, hitting your neighbor like that?" Moses said to the one in the wrong.

14"Who do you think you are?" the man replied. "Who appointed you to be our prince and judge? Do you plan to kill me as you killed that Egyptian yesterday?"

Moses was badly frightened because he realized that everyone knew what he had done. 15And sure enough, when Pharaoh heard about it, he gave orders to have Moses arrested and killed. But Moses fled from Pharaoh and escaped to the land of Midian.

When Moses arrived in Midian, he sat down beside a well. 16Now it happened that the priest of Midian had seven daughters who came regularly to this well to draw water and fill the water troughs for their father's flocks. 17But other shepherds would often come and chase the girls and their flocks away. This time, however, Moses came to their aid, rescuing the girls from the shepherds. Then he helped them draw water for their flocks.

18When the girls returned to Reuel, their father, he asked, "How did you get the flocks watered so quickly today?"

19"An Egyptian rescued us from the shepherds," they told him. "And then he drew water for us and watered our flocks."

20"Well, where is he then?" their father asked.

"Did you just leave him there? Go and invite him home for a meal!"

21Moses was happy to accept the invitation, and he settled down to live with them. In time, Reuel gave Moses one of his daughters, Zipporah, to be his wife. 22Later they had a baby boy, and Moses named him Gershom,* for he said, "I have been a stranger in a foreign land."

23Years passed, and the king of Egypt died. But the Israelites still groaned beneath their burden of slavery. They cried out for help, and their pleas for deliverance rose up to God. 24God heard their cries and remembered his covenant promise to Abraham, Isaac, and Jacob. 25He looked down on the Israelites and felt deep concern for their welfare.

CHAPTER 3

Moses and the Burning Bush

One day Moses was tending the flock of his father-in-law, Jethro,* the priest of Midian, and he went deep into the wilderness near Sinai,* the mountain of God. 2Suddenly, the angel of the LORD appeared to him as a blazing fire in a bush. Moses was amazed because the bush was engulfed in flames, but it didn't burn up. 3"Amazing!" Moses said to himself. "Why isn't that bush burning up? I must go over to see this."

4When the LORD saw that he had caught Moses' attention, God called to him from the bush, "Moses! Moses!"

"Here I am!" Moses replied.

5"Do not come any closer," God told him. "Take off your sandals, for you are standing on holy ground." 6Then he said, "I am the God of your ancestors—the God of Abraham, the God of Isaac, and the God of Jacob." When Moses heard this, he hid his face in his hands because he was afraid to look at God.

7Then the LORD told him, "You can be sure I have seen the misery of my people in Egypt. I have heard their cries for deliverance from their harsh slave drivers. Yes, I am aware of their suffering. 8So I have come to rescue them from the Egyptians and lead them out of Egypt into their own good and spacious land. It is a land flowing with milk and honey—the land where the Canaanites, Hittites, Amorites, Perizzites, Hivites, and Jebusites live. 9The cries of the people of Israel have reached me, and I have seen how the Egyptians have oppressed them with heavy tasks. 10Now go, for I am sending you to Pha-

---

2:10 *Moses* sounds like a Hebrew term that means "to draw out."   2:22 *Gershom* sounds like a Hebrew term that means "a stranger there."   3:1a Moses' father-in-law went by two names, Jethro and Reuel.   3:1b Hebrew *Horeb*, another name for Sinai.

raoh. You will lead my people, the Israelites, out of Egypt."

¹¹"But who am I to appear before Pharaoh?" Moses asked God. "How can you expect me to lead the Israelites out of Egypt?"

¹²Then God told him, "I will be with you. And this will serve as proof that I have sent you: When you have brought the Israelites out of Egypt, you will return here to worship God at this very mountain."

¹³But Moses protested, "If I go to the people of Israel and tell them, 'The God of your ancestors has sent me to you,' they won't believe me. They will ask, 'Which god are you talking about? What is his name?' Then what should I tell them?"

¹⁴God replied, "I AM THE ONE WHO ALWAYS IS.* Just tell them, 'I AM has sent me to you.'" ¹⁵God also said, "Tell them, 'The LORD,* the God of your ancestors—the God of Abraham, the God of Isaac, and the God of Jacob—has sent me to you.' This will be my name forever; it has always been my name, and it will be used throughout all generations.

¹⁶"Now go and call together all the leaders of Israel. Tell them, 'The LORD, the God of your ancestors—the God of Abraham, Isaac, and Jacob—appeared to me in a burning bush. He said, "You can be sure that I am watching over you and have seen what is happening to you in Egypt. ¹⁷I promise to rescue you from the oppression of the Egyptians. I will lead you to the land now occupied by the Canaanites, Hittites, Amorites, Perizzites, Hivites, and Jebusites—a land flowing with milk and honey."'

¹⁸"The leaders of the people of Israel will accept your message. Then all of you must go straight to the king of Egypt and tell him, 'The LORD, the God of the Hebrews, has met with us. Let us go on a three-day journey into the wilderness to offer sacrifices to the LORD our God.'

¹⁹"But I know that the king of Egypt will not let you go except under heavy pressure. ²⁰So I will reach out and strike at the heart of Egypt with all kinds of miracles. Then at last he will let you go. ²¹And I will see to it that the Egyptians treat you well. They will load you down with gifts so you will not leave empty-handed. ²²The Israelite women will ask for silver and gold jewelry and fine clothing from their Egyptian neighbors and their neighbors' guests. With this clothing, you will dress your sons and daughters. In this way, you will plunder the Egyptians!"

CHAPTER 4
Signs of the LORD's Power

But Moses protested again, "Look, they won't believe me! They won't do what I tell them. They'll just say, 'The LORD never appeared to you.'"

²Then the LORD asked him, "What do you have there in your hand?"

"A shepherd's staff," Moses replied.

³"Throw it down on the ground," the LORD told him. So Moses threw it down, and it became a snake! Moses was terrified, so he turned and ran away.

⁴Then the LORD told him, "Take hold of its tail." So Moses reached out and grabbed it, and it became a shepherd's staff again.

⁵"Perform this sign, and they will believe you," the LORD told him. "Then they will realize that the LORD, the God of their ancestors—the God of Abraham, the God of Isaac, and the God of Jacob—really has appeared to you."

⁶Then the LORD said to Moses, "Put your hand inside your robe." Moses did so, and when he took it out again, his hand was white as snow with leprosy.* ⁷"Now put your hand back into your robe again," the LORD said. Moses did, and when he took it out this time, it was as healthy as the rest of his body.

⁸"If they do not believe the first miraculous sign, they will believe the second," the LORD said. ⁹"And if they do not believe you even after these two signs, then take some water from the Nile River and pour it out on the dry ground. When you do, it will turn into blood."

¹⁰But Moses pleaded with the LORD, "O Lord, I'm just not a good speaker. I never have been, and I'm not now, even after you have spoken to me. I'm clumsy with words."

¹¹"Who makes mouths?" the LORD asked him. "Who makes people so they can speak or not speak, hear or not hear, see or not see? Is it not I, the LORD? ¹²Now go, and do as I have told you. I will help you speak well, and I will tell you what to say."

¹³But Moses again pleaded, "Lord, please! Send someone else."

¹⁴Then the LORD became angry with Moses. "All right," he said. "What about your brother, Aaron the Levite? He is a good speaker. And look! He is on his way to meet you now. And when he sees you, he will be very glad. ¹⁵You will talk to him, giving him the words to say. I will help both of you to speak clearly, and I will tell you what to do. ¹⁶Aaron will be your spokes-

---

3:14 Or *I AM WHO I AM,* or *I WILL BE WHAT I WILL BE.* 3:15 Hebrew *Yahweh*; traditionally rendered *Jehovah.* 4:6 Or *with a contagious skin disease.* The Hebrew word used here can describe various skin diseases.

man to the people, and you will be as God to him, telling him what to say. 17And be sure to take your shepherd's staff along so you can perform the miraculous signs I have shown you."

Moses Returns to Egypt

18Then Moses went back home and talked it over with Jethro, his father-in-law. "With your permission," Moses said, "I would like to go back to Egypt to visit my family. I don't even know whether they are still alive."

"Go with my blessing," Jethro replied.

19Before Moses left Midian, the LORD said to him, "Do not be afraid to return to Egypt, for all those who wanted to kill you are dead."

20So Moses took his wife and sons, put them on a donkey, and headed back to the land of Egypt. In his hand he carried the staff of God.

21Then the LORD reminded him, "When you arrive back in Egypt, go to Pharaoh and perform the miracles I have empowered you to do. But I will make him stubborn so he will not let the people go. 22Then you will tell him, 'This is what the LORD says: Israel is my firstborn son. 23I commanded you to let him go, so he could worship me. But since you have refused, be warned! I will kill your firstborn son!'"

24On the journey, when Moses and his family had stopped for the night, the LORD confronted Moses* and was about to kill him. 25But Zipporah, his wife, took a flint knife and circumcised her son. She threw the foreskin at Moses' feet and said, "What a blood-smeared bridegroom you are to me!" 26(When she called Moses a "blood-smeared bridegroom," she was referring to the circumcision.) After that, the LORD left him alone.

27Now the LORD had said to Aaron, "Go out into the wilderness to meet Moses." So Aaron traveled to the mountain of God, where he found Moses and greeted him warmly. 28Moses then told Aaron everything the LORD had commanded them to do and say. And he told him about the miraculous signs they were to perform.

29So Moses and Aaron returned to Egypt and called the leaders of Israel to a meeting. 30Aaron told them everything the LORD had told Moses, and Moses performed the miraculous signs as they watched. 31The leaders were soon convinced that the LORD had sent Moses and Aaron. And when they realized that the LORD had seen their misery and was deeply concerned for them, they all bowed their heads and worshiped.

4:24 Or *confronted Moses' son;* Hebrew reads *confronted him.*

CHAPTER 5

Moses and Aaron Speak to Pharaoh

After this presentation to Israel's leaders, Moses and Aaron went to see Pharaoh. They told him, "This is what the LORD, the God of Israel, says: 'Let my people go, for they must go out into the wilderness to hold a religious festival in my honor.'"

2"Is that so?" retorted Pharaoh. "And who is the LORD that I should listen to him and let Israel go? I don't know the LORD, and I will not let Israel go."

3But Aaron and Moses persisted. "The God of the Hebrews has met with us," they declared. "Let us take a three-day trip into the wilderness so we can offer sacrifices to the LORD our God. If we don't, we will surely die by disease or the sword."

4"Who do you think you are," Pharaoh shouted, "distracting the people from their tasks? Get back to work! 5Look, there are many people here in Egypt, and you are stopping them from doing their work."

Making Bricks without Straw

6That same day Pharaoh sent this order to the slave drivers and foremen he had set over the people of Israel: 7"Do not supply the people with any more straw for making bricks. Let them get it themselves! 8But don't reduce their production quotas by a single brick. They obviously don't have enough to do. If they did, they wouldn't be talking about going into the wilderness to offer sacrifices to their God. 9Load them down with more work. Make them sweat! That will teach them to listen to these liars!"

10So the slave drivers and foremen informed the people: "Pharaoh has ordered us not to provide straw for you. 11Go and get it yourselves. Find it wherever you can. But you must produce just as many bricks as before!" 12So the people scattered throughout the land in search of straw.

13The slave drivers were brutal. "Meet your daily quota of bricks, just as you did before!" they demanded. 14Then they whipped the Israelite foremen in charge of the work crews. "Why haven't you met your quotas either yesterday or today?" they demanded.

15So the Israelite foremen went to Pharaoh and pleaded with him. "Please don't treat us like this," they begged. 16"We are given no straw, but we are still told to make as many bricks as before. We are beaten for something that isn't our fault! It is the fault of your slave drivers for making such unreasonable demands."

17But Pharaoh replied, "You're just lazy! You obviously don't have enough to do. If you did, you wouldn't be saying, 'Let us go, so we can offer sacrifices to the LORD.' 18Now, get back to work! No straw will be given to you, but you must still deliver the regular quota of bricks."

19Since Pharaoh would not let up on his demands, the Israelite foremen could see that they were in serious trouble. 20As they left Pharaoh's court, they met Moses and Aaron, who were waiting outside for them. 21The foremen said to them, "May the LORD judge you for getting us into this terrible situation with Pharaoh* and his officials. You have given them an excuse to kill us!"

22So Moses went back to the LORD and protested, "Why have you mistreated your own people like this, Lord? Why did you send me? 23Since I gave Pharaoh your message, he has been even more brutal to your people. You have not even begun to rescue them!"

CHAPTER 6
Promises of Deliverance

"Now you will see what I will do to Pharaoh," the LORD told Moses. "When he feels my powerful hand upon him, he will let the people go. In fact, he will be so anxious to get rid of them that he will force them to leave his land!"

2And God continued, "I am the LORD. 3I appeared to Abraham, to Isaac, and to Jacob as God Almighty,* though I did not reveal my name, the LORD,* to them. 4And I entered into a solemn covenant with them. Under its terms, I swore to give them the land of Canaan, where they were living. 5You can be sure that I have heard the groans of the people of Israel, who are now slaves to the Egyptians. I have remembered my covenant with them.

6"Therefore, say to the Israelites: 'I am the LORD, and I will free you from your slavery in Egypt. I will redeem you with mighty power and great acts of judgment. 7I will make you my own special people, and I will be your God. And you will know that I am the LORD your God who has rescued you from your slavery in Egypt. 8I will bring you into the land I swore to give to Abraham, Isaac, and Jacob. It will be your very own property. I am the LORD!'"

9So Moses told the people what the LORD had said, but they wouldn't listen anymore. They

had become too discouraged by the increasing burden of their slavery.

10Then the LORD said to Moses, 11"Go back to Pharaoh, and tell him to let the people of Israel leave Egypt."

12"But LORD!" Moses objected. "My own people won't listen to me anymore. How can I expect Pharaoh to listen? I'm no orator!"

13But the LORD ordered Moses and Aaron to return to Pharaoh, king of Egypt, and to demand that he let the people of Israel leave Egypt.

The Ancestors of Moses and Aaron

14These are the ancestors of clans from some of Israel's tribes:

The descendants of Reuben, Israel's oldest son, included Hanoch, Pallu, Hezron, and Carmi. Their descendants became the clans of Reuben.

15The descendants of Simeon included Jemuel, Jamin, Ohad, Jakin, Zohar, and Shaul (whose mother was a Canaanite). Their descendants became the clans of Simeon.

16These are the descendants of Levi, listed according to their family groups. In the first generation were Gershon, Kohath, and Merari. (Levi, their father, lived to be 137 years old.)

17 The descendants of Gershon included Libni and Shimei, each of whom is the ancestor of a clan.

18 The descendants of Kohath included Amram, Izhar, Hebron, and Uzziel. (Kohath lived to be 133 years old.)

19 The descendants of Merari included Mahli and Mushi.

These are the clans of the Levites, listed according to their genealogies.

20Amram married his father's sister Jochebed, and she bore him Aaron and Moses. (Amram lived to be 137 years old.)

21The descendants of Izhar included Korah, Nepheg, and Zicri.

22The descendants of Uzziel included Mishael, Elzaphan, and Sithri.

23Aaron married Elisheba, the daughter of Amminadab and sister of Nahshon, and she bore him Nadab, Abihu, Eleazar, and Ithamar.

24The descendants of Korah included Assir, Elkanah, and Abiasaph. Their descendants became the clans of Korah.

5:21 Hebrew *for making us a stench in the nostrils of Pharaoh.*   6:3a Hebrew *El Shaddai.*   6:3b Hebrew *Yahweh*; traditionally rendered *Jehovah.*

25Eleazar son of Aaron married one of the daughters of Putiel, and she bore him Phinehas.

These are the ancestors of the Levite clans, listed according to their family groups.

26The Aaron and Moses named in this list are the same Aaron and Moses to whom the LORD said, "Lead all the people of Israel out of the land of Egypt, division by division." 27They are the ones who went to Pharaoh to ask permission to lead the people from the land of Egypt.

28At that time, the LORD had said to them, 29"I am the LORD! Give Pharaoh the message I have given you." 30This is the same Moses who had argued with the LORD, saying, "I can't do it! I'm no orator. Why should Pharaoh listen to me?"

CHAPTER 7
Moses' Staff Becomes a Snake

Then the LORD said to Moses, "Pay close attention to this. I will make you seem like God to Pharaoh. Your brother, Aaron, will be your prophet; he will speak for you. 2Tell Aaron everything I say to you and have him announce it to Pharaoh. He will demand that the people of Israel be allowed to leave Egypt. 3But I will cause Pharaoh to be stubborn so I can multiply my miraculous signs and wonders in the land of Egypt. 4Even then Pharaoh will refuse to listen to you. So I will crush Egypt with a series of disasters, after which I will lead the forces of Israel out with great acts of judgment. 5When I show the Egyptians my power and force them to let the Israelites go, they will realize that I am the LORD."

6So Moses and Aaron did just as the LORD had commanded them. 7Moses was eighty years old, and Aaron was eighty-three at the time they made their demands to Pharaoh.

8Then the LORD said to Moses and Aaron, 9"Pharaoh will demand that you show him a miracle to prove that God has sent you. When he makes this demand, say to Aaron, 'Throw down your shepherd's staff,' and it will become a snake."

10So Moses and Aaron went to see Pharaoh, and they performed the miracle just as the LORD had told them. Aaron threw down his staff before Pharaoh and his court, and it became a snake. 11Then Pharaoh called in his wise men and magicians, and they did the same thing with their secret arts. 12Their staffs became snakes, too! But then Aaron's snake swallowed up their

snakes. 13Pharaoh's heart, however, remained hard and stubborn. He still refused to listen, just as the LORD had predicted.

A Plague of Blood

14Then the LORD said to Moses, "Pharaoh is very stubborn, and he continues to refuse to let the people go. 15So go to Pharaoh in the morning as he goes down to the river. Stand on the riverbank and meet him there. Be sure to take along the shepherd's staff that turned into a snake. 16Say to him, 'The LORD, the God of the Hebrews, has sent me to say, "Let my people go, so they can worship me in the wilderness." Until now, you have refused to listen to him. 17Now the LORD says, "You are going to find out that I am the LORD." Look! I will hit the water of the Nile with this staff, and the river will turn to blood. 18The fish in it will die, and the river will stink. The Egyptians will not be able to drink any water from the Nile.'"

19Then the LORD said to Moses: "Tell Aaron to point his staff toward the waters of Egypt—all its rivers, canals, marshes, and reservoirs. Everywhere in Egypt the water will turn into blood, even the water stored in wooden bowls and stone pots in the people's homes."

20So Moses and Aaron did just as the LORD had commanded them. As Pharaoh and all of his officials watched, Moses raised his staff and hit the water of the Nile. Suddenly, the whole river turned to blood! 21The fish in the river died, and the water became so foul that the Egyptians couldn't drink it. There was blood everywhere throughout the land of Egypt. 22But again the magicians of Egypt used their secret arts, and they, too, turned water into blood. So Pharaoh's heart remained hard and stubborn. He refused to listen to Moses and Aaron, just as the LORD had predicted. 23Pharaoh returned to his palace and put the whole thing out of his mind. 24Then the Egyptians dug wells along the riverbank to get drinking water, for they couldn't drink from the river. 25An entire week passed from the time the LORD turned the water of the Nile to blood.

CHAPTER 8
A Plague of Frogs

Then the LORD said to Moses, "Go to Pharaoh once again and tell him, 'This is what the LORD says: Let my people go, so they can worship me. 2If you refuse, then listen carefully to this: I will send vast hordes of frogs across your entire land from one border to the other. 3The Nile River will swarm with them. They will come up out of the river and into your houses, even into your bedrooms and onto your beds! Every home in Egypt will be filled with them. They will fill even your ovens and your kneading bowls. 4You and your people will be overwhelmed by frogs!'"

5Then the LORD said to Moses, "Tell Aaron to point his shepherd's staff toward all the rivers, canals, and marshes of Egypt so there will be frogs in every corner of the land." 6Aaron did so, and frogs covered the whole land of Egypt! 7But the magicians were able to do the same thing with their secret arts. They, too, caused frogs to come up on the land.

8Then Pharaoh summoned Moses and Aaron and begged, "Plead with the LORD to take the frogs away from me and my people. I will let the people go, so they can offer sacrifices to the LORD."

9"You set the time!" Moses replied. "Tell me when you want me to pray for you, your officials, and your people. I will pray that you and your houses will be rid of the frogs. Then only the frogs in the Nile River will remain alive."

10"Do it tomorrow," Pharaoh said.

"All right," Moses replied, "it will be as you have said. Then you will know that no one is as powerful as the LORD our God. 11All the frogs will be destroyed, except those in the river."

12So Moses and Aaron left Pharaoh, and Moses pleaded with the LORD about the frogs he had sent. 13And the LORD did as Moses had promised. The frogs in the houses, the courtyards, and the fields all died. 14They were piled into great heaps, and a terrible stench filled the land. 15But when Pharaoh saw that the frogs were gone, he hardened his heart. He refused to listen to Moses and Aaron, just as the LORD had predicted.

A Plague of Gnats

16So the LORD said to Moses, "Tell Aaron to strike the dust with his staff. The dust will turn into swarms of gnats throughout the land of Egypt." 17So Moses and Aaron did just as the LORD had commanded them. Suddenly, gnats infested the entire land, covering the Egyptians and their animals. All the dust in the land of Egypt turned into gnats. 18Pharaoh's magicians tried to do the same thing with their secret arts, but this time they failed. And the gnats covered all the people and animals.

19"This is the finger of God!" the magicians exclaimed to Pharaoh. But Pharaoh's heart remained hard and stubborn. He wouldn't listen to them, just as the LORD had predicted.

A Plague of Flies

20Next the LORD told Moses, "Get up early in the morning and meet Pharaoh as he goes down to the river. Say to him, 'This is what the LORD says: Let my people go, so they can worship me. 21If you refuse, I will send swarms of flies throughout Egypt. Your homes will be filled with them, and the ground will be covered with them. 22But it will be very different in the land of Goshen, where the Israelites live. No flies will be found there. Then you will know that I am the LORD and that I have power even in the heart of your land. 23I will make a clear distinction between your people and my people. This miraculous sign will happen tomorrow.'"

24And the LORD did just as he had said. There were terrible swarms of flies in Pharaoh's palace and in every home in Egypt. The whole country was thrown into chaos by the flies.

25Pharaoh hastily called for Moses and Aaron. "All right! Go ahead and offer sacrifices to your God," he said. "But do it here in this land. Don't go out into the wilderness."

26But Moses replied, "That won't do! The Egyptians would detest the sacrifices that we offer to the LORD our God. If we offer them here where they can see us, they will be sure to stone us. 27We must take a three-day trip into the wilderness to offer sacrifices to the LORD our God, just as he has commanded us."

28"All right, go ahead," Pharaoh replied. "I will let you go to offer sacrifices to the LORD your God in the wilderness. But don't go too far away. Now hurry, and pray for me."

29"As soon as I go," Moses said, "I will ask the LORD to cause the swarms of flies to disappear from you and all your people. But I am warning you, don't change your mind again and refuse to let the people go to sacrifice to the LORD."

30So Moses left Pharaoh and asked the LORD to remove all the flies. 31And the LORD did as Moses asked and caused the swarms to disappear. Not a single fly remained in the land! 32But Pharaoh hardened his heart again and refused to let the people go.

CHAPTER 9

A Plague against Livestock

"Go back to Pharaoh," the LORD commanded Moses. "Tell him, 'This is what the LORD, the God of the Hebrews, says: Let my people go, so they can worship me. 2If you continue to oppress them and refuse to let them go, 3the LORD will send a deadly plague to destroy your horses, donkeys, camels, cattle, and sheep. 4But the LORD will again make a distinction between the property of the Israelites and that of the Egyptians. Not a single one of Israel's livestock will die!'"

5The LORD announced that he would send the plague the very next day, 6and he did it, just as he had said. The next morning all the livestock of the Egyptians began to die, but the Israelites didn't lose a single animal from their flocks and herds. 7Pharaoh sent officials to see whether it was true that none of the Israelites' animals were dead. But even after he found it to be true, his heart remained stubborn. He still refused to let the people go.

A Plague of Boils

8Then the LORD said to Moses and Aaron, "Take soot from a furnace, and have Moses toss it into the sky while Pharaoh watches. 9It will spread like fine dust over the whole land of Egypt, causing boils to break out on people and animals alike."

10So they gathered soot from a furnace and went to see Pharaoh. As Pharaoh watched, Moses tossed the soot into the air, and terrible boils broke out on the people and animals throughout Egypt. 11Even the magicians were unable to stand before Moses, because the boils had broken out on them, too. 12But the LORD made Pharaoh even more stubborn, and he refused to listen, just as the LORD had predicted.

A Plague of Hail

13Then the LORD said to Moses, "Get up early in the morning. Go to Pharaoh and tell him, 'The LORD, the God of the Hebrews, says: Let my people go, so they can worship me. 14If you don't, I will send a plague that will really speak to you and your officials and all the Egyptian people. I will prove to you that there is no other God like me in all the earth. 15I could have killed you all by now. I could have attacked you with a plague that would have wiped you from the face of the earth. 16But I have let you live for this reason—that you might see my power and that my fame might spread throughout the earth. 17But you are still lording it over my people, and you refuse to let them go. 18So tomorrow at this time I will send a hailstorm worse than any in all of Egypt's history. 19Quick! Order your livestock and servants to come in from the fields. Every person or animal left outside will die beneath the hail.'"

20Some of Pharaoh's officials believed what the LORD said. They immediately brought their livestock and servants in from the fields. 21But those who had no respect for the word of the LORD left them out in the open.

22Then the LORD said to Moses, "Lift your hand toward the sky, and cause the hail to fall throughout Egypt, on the people, the animals, and the crops."

23So Moses lifted his staff toward the sky, and the LORD sent thunder and hail, and lightning struck the earth. The LORD sent a tremendous hailstorm against all the land of Egypt. 24Never in all the history of Egypt had there been a storm like that, with such severe hail and continuous lightning. 25It left all of Egypt in ruins. Everything left in the fields was destroyed—people, animals, and crops alike. Even all the trees were destroyed. 26The only spot in all Egypt without hail that day was the land of Goshen, where the people of Israel lived.

27Then Pharaoh urgently sent for Moses and Aaron. "I finally admit my fault," he confessed. "The LORD is right, and my people and I are wrong. 28Please beg the LORD to end this terrifying thunder and hail. I will let you go at once."

29"All right," Moses replied. "As soon as I leave the city, I will lift my hands and pray to the LORD. Then the thunder and hail will stop. This will prove to you that the earth belongs to the LORD. 30But as for you and your officials, I know that you still do not fear the LORD God as you should."

31All the flax and barley were destroyed because the barley was ripe and the flax was in bloom. 32But the wheat and the spelt were not destroyed because they had not yet sprouted from the ground.

33So Moses left Pharaoh and went out of the city. As he lifted his hands to the LORD, all at once the thunder and hail stopped, and the downpour ceased. 34When Pharaoh saw this, he and his officials sinned yet again by stubbornly refusing to do as they had promised. 35Pharaoh refused to let the people leave, just as the LORD had predicted.

CHAPTER 10

A Plague of Locusts

Then the LORD said to Moses, "Return to Pharaoh and again make your demands. I have made him and his officials stubborn so I can continue to display my power by performing miraculous signs among them. 2You will be able to tell wonderful stories to your children and grandchildren about the marvelous things I am doing among the Egyptians to prove that I am the LORD."

3So Moses and Aaron went to Pharaoh and said, "This is what the LORD, the God of the Hebrews, says: How long will you refuse to submit to me? Let my people go, so they can worship me. 4If you refuse, watch out! For tomorrow I will cover the whole country with locusts. 5There will be so many that you won't be able to see the ground. They will devour everything that escaped the hailstorm, including all the trees in the fields. 6They will overrun your palaces and the homes of your officials and all the houses of Egypt. Never in the history of Egypt has there been a plague like this one!" And with that, Moses turned and walked out.

7The court officials now came to Pharaoh and appealed to him. "How long will you let these disasters go on? Please let the Israelites go to serve the LORD their God! Don't you realize that Egypt lies in ruins?"

8So Moses and Aaron were brought back to Pharaoh. "All right, go and serve the LORD your God," he said. "But tell me, just whom do you want to take along?"

9"Young and old, all of us will go," Moses replied. "We will take our sons and daughters and our flocks and herds. We must all join together in a festival to the LORD."

10Pharaoh retorted, "The LORD will certainly need to be with you if you try to take your little ones along! I can see through your wicked intentions. 11Never! Only the men may go and serve the LORD, for that is what you requested." And Pharaoh threw them out of the palace.

12Then the LORD said to Moses, "Raise your hand over the land of Egypt to bring on the locusts. Let them cover the land and eat all the crops still left after the hailstorm."

13So Moses raised his staff, and the LORD caused an east wind to blow all that day and through the night. When morning arrived, the east wind had brought the locusts. 14And the locusts swarmed over the land of Egypt from border to border. It was the worst locust plague in Egyptian history, and there has never again been one like it. 15For the locusts covered the surface of the whole country, making the ground look black. They ate all the plants and all the fruit on the trees that had survived the hailstorm. Not one green thing remained, neither tree nor plant, throughout the land of Egypt.

16Pharaoh quickly sent for Moses and Aaron.

10:19 Hebrew *sea of reeds.*

"I confess my sin against the LORD your God and against you," he said to them. 17"Forgive my sin only this once, and plead with the LORD your God to take away this terrible plague."

18So Moses left Pharaoh and pleaded with the LORD. 19The LORD responded by sending a strong west wind that blew the locusts out into the Red Sea.* Not a single locust remained in all the land of Egypt. 20But the LORD made Pharaoh stubborn once again, and he did not let the people go.

A Plague of Darkness

21Then the LORD said to Moses, "Lift your hand toward heaven, and a deep and terrifying darkness will descend on the land of Egypt." 22So Moses lifted his hand toward heaven, and there was deep darkness over the entire land for three days. 23During all that time the people scarcely moved, for they could not see. But there was light as usual where the people of Israel lived.

24Then Pharaoh called for Moses. "Go and worship the LORD," he said. "But let your flocks and herds stay here. You can even take your children with you."

25"No," Moses said, "we must take our flocks and herds for sacrifices and burnt offerings to the LORD our God. 26All our property must go with us; not a hoof can be left behind. We will have to choose our sacrifices for the LORD our God from among these animals. And we won't know which sacrifices he will require until we get there."

27So the LORD hardened Pharaoh's heart once more, and he would not let them go. 28"Get out of here!" Pharaoh shouted at Moses. "Don't ever let me see you again! The day you do, you will die!"

29"Very well," Moses replied. "I will never see you again."

CHAPTER 11
Death for Egypt's Firstborn

Then the LORD said to Moses, "I will send just one more disaster on Pharaoh and the land of Egypt. After that, Pharaoh will let you go. In fact, he will be so anxious to get rid of you that he will practically force you to leave the country. 2Tell all the Israelite men and women to ask their Egyptian neighbors for articles of silver and gold."

3(Now the LORD had caused the Egyptians to look favorably on the people of Israel, and Moses was considered a very great man in the land of Egypt. He was respected by Pharaoh's officials and the Egyptian people alike.)

⁴So Moses announced to Pharaoh, "This is what the LORD says: About midnight I will pass through Egypt. ⁵All the firstborn sons will die in every family in Egypt, from the oldest son of Pharaoh, who sits on the throne, to the oldest son of his lowliest slave. Even the firstborn of the animals will die. ⁶Then a loud wail will be heard throughout the land of Egypt; there has never been such wailing before, and there never will be again. ⁷But among the Israelites it will be so peaceful that not even a dog will bark. Then you will know that the LORD makes a distinction between the Egyptians and the Israelites. ⁸All the officials of Egypt will come running to me, bowing low. 'Please leave!' they will beg. 'Hurry! And take all your followers with you.' Only then will I go!" Then, burning with anger, Moses left Pharaoh's presence.

⁹Now the LORD had told Moses, "Pharaoh will not listen to you. But this will give me the opportunity to do even more mighty miracles in the land of Egypt." ¹⁰Although Moses and Aaron did these miracles in Pharaoh's presence, the LORD hardened his heart so he wouldn't let the Israelites leave the country.

CHAPTER 12
The First Passover

Now the LORD gave the following instructions to Moses and Aaron while they were still in the land of Egypt: ²"From now on, this month will be the first month of the year for you. ³Announce to the whole community that on the tenth day of this month each family must choose a lamb or a young goat for a sacrifice. ⁴If a family is too small to eat an entire lamb, let them share the lamb with another family in the neighborhood. Whether or not they share in this way depends on the size of each family and how much they can eat. ⁵This animal must be a one-year-old male, either a sheep or a goat, with no physical defects.

⁶"Take special care of these lambs until the evening of the fourteenth day of this first month. Then each family in the community must slaughter its lamb. ⁷They are to take some of the lamb's blood and smear it on the top and sides of the doorframe of the house where the lamb will be eaten. ⁸That evening everyone must eat roast lamb with bitter herbs and bread made without yeast. ⁹The meat must never be eaten raw or boiled; roast it all, including the head, legs, and internal organs. ¹⁰Do not leave

any of it until the next day. Whatever is not eaten that night must be burned before morning.

¹¹"Wear your traveling clothes as you eat this meal, as though prepared for a long journey. Wear your sandals, and carry your walking sticks in your hands. Eat the food quickly, for this is the LORD's Passover. ¹²On that night I will pass through the land of Egypt and kill all the firstborn sons and firstborn male animals in the land of Egypt. I will execute judgment against all the gods of Egypt, for I am the LORD! ¹³The blood you have smeared on your doorposts will serve as a sign. When I see the blood, I will pass over you. This plague of death will not touch you when I strike the land of Egypt.

¹⁴"You must remember this day forever. Each year you will celebrate it as a special festival to the LORD. ¹⁵For seven days, you may eat only bread made without yeast. On the very first day you must remove every trace of yeast from your homes. Anyone who eats bread made with yeast at any time during the seven days of the festival will be cut off from the community of Israel. ¹⁶On the first day of the festival, and again on the seventh day, all the people must gather for a time of special worship. No work of any kind may be done on these days except in the preparation of food.

¹⁷"Celebrate this Festival of Unleavened Bread, for it will remind you that I brought your forces out of the land of Egypt on this very day. This festival will be a permanent regulation for you, to be kept from generation to generation. ¹⁸Only bread without yeast may be eaten from the evening of the fourteenth day of the month until the evening of the twenty-first day of the month. ¹⁹During those seven days, there must be no trace of yeast in your homes. Anyone who eats anything made with yeast during this week will be cut off from the community of Israel. These same regulations apply to the foreigners living with you, as if they had been born among you. ²⁰I repeat, during those days you must not eat anything made with yeast. Wherever you live, eat only bread that has no yeast in it."

²¹Then Moses called for the leaders of Israel and said, "Tell each of your families to slaughter the lamb they have set apart for the Passover. ²²Drain each lamb's blood into a basin. Then take a cluster of hyssop branches and dip it into the lamb's blood. Strike the hyssop against the top and sides of the doorframe, staining it with the blood. And remember, no one is allowed to leave the house until morning. ²³For the LORD will pass through the land and strike down the

Egyptians. But when he sees the blood on the top and sides of the doorframe, the LORD will pass over your home. He will not permit the Destroyer to enter and strike down your firstborn.

24"Remember, these instructions are permanent and must be observed by you and your descendants forever. 25When you arrive in the land the LORD has promised to give you, you will continue to celebrate this festival. 26Then your children will ask, 'What does all this mean? What is this ceremony about?' 27And you will reply, 'It is the celebration of the LORD's Passover, for he passed over the homes of the Israelites in Egypt. And though he killed the Egyptians, he spared our families and did not destroy us.'" Then all the people bowed their heads and worshiped.

28So the people of Israel did just as the LORD had commanded through Moses and Aaron. 29And at midnight the LORD killed all the firstborn sons in the land of Egypt, from the firstborn son of Pharaoh, who sat on the throne, to the firstborn son of the captive in the dungeon. Even the firstborn of their livestock were killed. 30Pharaoh and his officials and all the people of Egypt woke up during the night, and loud wailing was heard throughout the land of Egypt. There was not a single house where someone had not died.

Israel's Exodus from Egypt

31Pharaoh sent for Moses and Aaron during the night. "Leave us!" he cried. "Go away, all of you! Go and serve the LORD as you have requested. 32Take your flocks and herds, and be gone. Go, but give me a blessing as you leave." 33All the Egyptians urged the people of Israel to get out of the land as quickly as possible, for they thought, "We will all die!"

34The Israelites took with them their bread dough made without yeast. They wrapped their kneading bowls in their spare clothing and carried them on their shoulders. 35And the people of Israel did as Moses had instructed and asked the Egyptians for clothing and articles of silver and gold. 36The LORD caused the Egyptians to look favorably on the Israelites, and they gave the Israelites whatever they asked for. So, like a victorious army, they plundered the Egyptians!

37That night the people of Israel left Rameses and started for Succoth. There were about 600,000 men, plus all the women and children. And they were all traveling on foot. 38Many people who were not Israelites went with them,

along with the many flocks and herds. 39Whenever they stopped to eat, they baked bread from the yeastless dough they had brought from Egypt. It was made without yeast because the people were rushed out of Egypt and had no time to wait for bread to rise.

40The people of Israel had lived in Egypt for 430 years. 41In fact, it was on the last day of the 430th year that all the LORD's forces left the land. 42This night had been reserved by the LORD to bring his people out from the land of Egypt, so this same night now belongs to him. It must be celebrated every year, from generation to generation, to remember the LORD's deliverance.

Instructions for the Passover

43Then the LORD said to Moses and Aaron, "These are the regulations for the festival of Passover. No foreigners are allowed to eat the Passover lamb. 44But any slave who has been purchased may eat it if he has been circumcised. 45Hired servants and visiting foreigners may not eat it. 46All who eat the lamb must eat it together in one house. You must not carry any of its meat outside, and you may not break any of its bones. 47The whole community of Israel must celebrate this festival at the same time.

48"If there are foreigners living among you who want to celebrate the LORD's Passover, let all the males be circumcised. Then they may come and celebrate the Passover with you. They will be treated just as if they had been born among you. But an uncircumcised male may never eat of the Passover lamb. 49This law applies to everyone, whether a native-born Israelite or a foreigner who has settled among you."

50So the people of Israel followed all the LORD's instructions to Moses and Aaron. 51And that very day the LORD began to lead the people of Israel out of Egypt, division by division.

CHAPTER 13

Dedication of the Firstborn

Then the LORD said to Moses, 2"Dedicate to me all the firstborn sons of Israel and every firstborn male animal. They are mine."

3So Moses said to the people, "This is a day to remember forever—the day you left Egypt, the place of your slavery. For the LORD has brought you out by his mighty power. (Remember, you are not to use any yeast.) 4This day in early spring* will be the anniversary of your exodus. 5You must celebrate this day when the

13:4 Hebrew *in the month of Abib.* This month of the Hebrew lunar calendar usually occurs in March and April.

LORD brings you into the land of the Canaanites, Hittites, Amorites, Hivites, and Jebusites. This is the land he swore to give your ancestors—a land flowing with milk and honey. 6For seven days you will eat only bread without yeast. Then on the seventh day, you will celebrate a great feast to the LORD. 7Eat only bread without yeast during those seven days. In fact, there must be no yeast in your homes or anywhere within the borders of your land during this time.

8"During these festival days each year, you must explain to your children why you are celebrating. Say to them, 'This is a celebration of what the LORD did for us when we left Egypt.' 9This annual festival will be a visible reminder to you, like a mark branded on your hands or your forehead. Let it remind you always to keep the LORD's instructions in your minds and on your lips. After all, it was the LORD who rescued you from Egypt with great power.

10"So celebrate this festival at the appointed time each year. 11And remember these instructions when the LORD brings you into the land he swore to give your ancestors long ago, the land where the Canaanites are now living. 12All firstborn sons and firstborn male animals must be presented to the LORD. 13A firstborn male donkey may be redeemed from the LORD by presenting a lamb in its place. But if you decide not to make the exchange, the donkey must be killed by breaking its neck. However, you must redeem every firstborn son.

14"And in the future, your children will ask you, 'What does all this mean?' Then you will tell them, 'With mighty power the LORD brought us out of Egypt from our slavery. 15Pharaoh refused to let us go, so the LORD killed all the firstborn males throughout the land of Egypt, both people and animals. That is why we now offer all the firstborn males to the LORD—except that the firstborn sons are always redeemed.' 16Again I say, this ceremony will be like a mark branded on your hands or your forehead. It is a visible reminder that it was the LORD who brought you out of Egypt with great power."

Israel's Wilderness Detour

17When Pharaoh finally let the people go, God did not lead them on the road that runs through Philistine territory, even though that was the shortest way from Egypt to the Promised Land. God said, "If the people are faced with a battle, they might change their minds and return to

13:18 Hebrew *sea of reeds.*

Egypt." 18So God led them along a route through the wilderness toward the Red Sea,* and the Israelites left Egypt like a marching army.

19Moses took the bones of Joseph with him, for Joseph had made the sons of Israel swear that they would take his bones with them when God led them out of Egypt—as he was sure God would.

20Leaving Succoth, they camped at Etham on the edge of the wilderness. 21The LORD guided them by a pillar of cloud during the day and a pillar of fire at night. That way they could travel whether it was day or night. 22And the LORD did not remove the pillar of cloud or pillar of fire from their sight.

CHAPTER 14

Then the LORD gave these instructions to Moses: 2"Tell the people to march toward Pi-hahiroth between Migdol and the sea. Camp there along the shore, opposite Baal-zephon. 3Then Pharaoh will think, 'Those Israelites are confused. They are trapped between the wilderness and the sea!' 4And once again I will harden Pharaoh's heart, and he will chase after you. I have planned this so I will receive great glory at the expense of Pharaoh and his armies. After this, the Egyptians will know that I am the LORD!" So the Israelites camped there as they were told.

The Egyptians Pursue Israel

5When word reached the king of Egypt that the Israelites were not planning to return to Egypt after three days, Pharaoh and his officials changed their minds. "What have we done, letting all these slaves get away?" they asked. 6So Pharaoh called out his troops and led the chase in his chariot. 7He took with him six hundred of Egypt's best chariots, along with the rest of the chariots of Egypt, each with a commander. 8The LORD continued to strengthen Pharaoh's resolve, and he chased after the people of Israel who had escaped so defiantly. 9All the forces in Pharaoh's army—all his horses, chariots, and charioteers—were used in the chase. The Egyptians caught up with the people of Israel as they were camped beside the shore near Pi-hahiroth, across from Baal-zephon.

10As Pharaoh and his army approached, the people of Israel could see them in the distance, marching toward them. The people began to panic, and they cried out to the LORD for help. 11Then they turned against Moses and complained, "Why did you bring us out here to die in the wilderness? Weren't there enough graves for us in Egypt? Why did you make us leave? 12Didn't we tell you to leave us alone while we were still in Egypt? Our Egyptian slavery was far better than dying out here in the wilderness!"

13But Moses told the people, "Don't be afraid. Just stand where you are and watch the LORD rescue you. The Egyptians that you see today will never be seen again. 14The LORD himself will fight for you. You won't have to lift a finger in your defense!"

Escape through the Red Sea

15Then the LORD said to Moses, "Why are you crying out to me? Tell the people to get moving! 16Use your shepherd's staff—hold it out over the water, and a path will open up before you through the sea. Then all the people of Israel will walk through on dry ground. 17Yet I will harden the hearts of the Egyptians, and they will follow the Israelites into the sea. Then I will receive great glory at the expense of Pharaoh and his armies, chariots, and charioteers. 18When I am finished with Pharaoh and his army, all Egypt will know that I am the LORD!"

19Then the angel of God, who had been leading the people of Israel, moved to a position behind them, and the pillar of cloud also moved around behind them. 20The cloud settled between the Israelite and Egyptian camps. As night came, the pillar of cloud turned into a pillar of fire, lighting the Israelite camp. But the cloud became darkness to the Egyptians, and they couldn't find the Israelites.

21Then Moses raised his hand over the sea, and the LORD opened up a path through the water with a strong east wind. The wind blew all that night, turning the seabed into dry land. 22So the people of Israel walked through the sea on dry ground, with walls of water on each side! 23Then the Egyptians—all of Pharaoh's horses, chariots, and charioteers—followed them across the bottom of the sea. 24But early in the morning, the LORD looked down on the Egyptian army from the pillar of fire and cloud, and he threw them into confusion. 25Their chariot wheels began to come off, making their chariots impossible to drive. "Let's get out of here!" the Egyptians shouted. "The LORD is fighting for Israel against us!"

26When all the Israelites were on the other side, the LORD said to Moses, "Raise your hand over the sea again. Then the waters will rush back over the Egyptian chariots and chario-

teers." 27So as the sun began to rise, Moses raised his hand over the sea. The water roared back into its usual place, and the LORD swept the terrified Egyptians into the surging currents. 28The waters covered all the chariots and charioteers—the entire army of Pharaoh. Of all the Egyptians who had chased the Israelites into the sea, not a single one survived.

29The people of Israel had walked through the middle of the sea on dry land, as the water stood up like a wall on both sides. 30This was how the LORD rescued Israel from the Egyptians that day. And the Israelites could see the bodies of the Egyptians washed up on the shore. 31When the people of Israel saw the mighty power that the LORD had displayed against the Egyptians, they feared the LORD and put their faith in him and his servant Moses.

CHAPTER **15**
A Song of Deliverance

Then Moses and the people of Israel sang this song to the LORD:

> "I will sing to the LORD, for he has
>   triumphed gloriously;
>   he has thrown both horse and rider into
>   the sea.
> 2 The LORD is my strength and my song;
>   he has become my victory.
>   He is my God, and I will praise him;
>   he is my father's God, and I will exalt him!
> 3 The LORD is a warrior;
>   yes, the LORD is his name!
> 4 Pharaoh's chariots and armies,
>   he has thrown into the sea.
>   The very best of Pharaoh's officers
>   have been drowned in the Red Sea.*
> 5 The deep waters have covered them;
>   they sank to the bottom like a stone.
>
> 6 "Your right hand, O LORD,
>   is glorious in power.
>   Your right hand, O LORD,
>   dashes the enemy to pieces.
> 7 In the greatness of your majesty,
>   you overthrew those who rose against you.
>   Your anger flashed forth;
>   it consumed them as fire burns straw.
> 8 At the blast of your breath, the waters
>   piled up!
>   The surging waters stood straight like a wall;
>   in the middle of the sea the waters
>   became hard.

15:4 Hebrew *sea of reeds;* also in 15:22.

9 "The enemy said, 'I will chase them,
   catch up with them, and destroy them.
I will divide the plunder,
   avenging myself against them.
I will unsheath my sword;
   my power will destroy them.'
10 But with a blast of your breath,
   the sea covered them.
They sank like lead
   in the mighty waters.

11 "Who else among the gods is like you,
   O LORD?
   Who is glorious in holiness like you—
so awesome in splendor,
   performing such wonders?
12 You raised up your hand,
   and the earth swallowed our enemies.

13 "With unfailing love you will lead
   this people whom you have ransomed.
You will guide them in your strength
   to the place where your holiness dwells.
14 The nations will hear and tremble;
   anguish will grip the people of Philistia.
15 The leaders of Edom will be terrified;
   the nobles of Moab will tremble.
All the people of Canaan will melt with
      fear;
16   terror and dread will overcome them.
Because of your great power,
   they will be silent like a stone,
until your people pass by, O LORD,
   until the people whom you purchased
      pass by.
17 You will bring them in and plant them on
      your own mountain—
   the place you have made as your home,
      O LORD,
   the sanctuary, O Lord, that your hands
      have made.
18 The LORD will reign forever and ever!"

19When Pharaoh's horses, chariots, and charioteers rushed into the sea, the LORD brought the
water crashing down on them. But the people of
Israel had walked through on dry land!

20Then Miriam the prophet, Aaron's sister,
took a tambourine and led all the women in
rhythm and dance. 21And Miriam sang this song:

"I will sing to the LORD, for he has
      triumphed gloriously;
   he has thrown both horse and rider into
      the sea."

Bitter Water at Marah

22Then Moses led the people of Israel away
from the Red Sea, and they moved out into the
Shur Desert. They traveled in this desert for
three days without water. 23When they came to
Marah, they finally found water. But the
people couldn't drink it because it was bitter.
(That is why the place was called Marah, which
means "bitter.")

24Then the people turned against Moses.
"What are we going to drink?" they demanded.

25So Moses cried out to the LORD for help, and
the LORD showed him a branch. Moses took the
branch and threw it into the water. This made
the water good to drink.

It was there at Marah that the LORD laid before
them the following conditions to test their faithfulness to him: 26"If you will listen carefully to
the voice of the LORD your God and do what is
right in his sight, obeying his commands and
laws, then I will not make you suffer the diseases
I sent on the Egyptians; for I am the LORD who
heals you."

27After leaving Marah, they came to Elim,
where there were twelve springs and seventy
palm trees. They camped there beside the springs.

CHAPTER 16

Manna and Quail from Heaven

Then they left Elim and journeyed into the Sin*
Desert, between Elim and Mount Sinai. They
arrived there a month after leaving Egypt.*
2There, too, the whole community of Israel
spoke bitterly against Moses and Aaron.

3"Oh, that we were back in Egypt," they
moaned. "It would have been better if the LORD
had killed us there! At least there we had plenty
to eat. But now you have brought us into this
desert to starve us to death."

4Then the LORD said to Moses, "Look, I'm
going to rain down food from heaven for you.
The people can go out each day and pick up as
much food as they need for that day. I will test
them in this to see whether they will follow my
instructions. 5Tell them to pick up twice as
much as usual on the sixth day of each week."

6Then Moses and Aaron called a meeting of
all the people of Israel and told them, "In the
evening you will realize that it was the LORD
who brought you out of the land of Egypt. 7In
the morning you will see the glorious presence
of the LORD. He has heard your complaints,

16:1a Not to be confused with the English word *sin.* 16:1b Hebrew *on the fifteenth day of the second month.* The Exodus had occurred on the
fourteenth day of the first month (see 12:6).

which are against the LORD and not against us. 8The LORD will give you meat to eat in the evening and bread in the morning, for he has heard all your complaints against him. Yes, your complaints are against the LORD, not against us."

9Then Moses said to Aaron, "Say this to the entire community of Israel: 'Come into the LORD's presence, and hear his reply to your complaints.'" 10And as Aaron spoke to the people, they looked out toward the desert. Within the guiding cloud, they could see the awesome glory of the LORD.

11And the LORD said to Moses, 12"I have heard the people's complaints. Now tell them, 'In the evening you will have meat to eat, and in the morning you will be filled with bread. Then you will know that I am the LORD your God.'"

13That evening vast numbers of quail arrived and covered the camp. The next morning the desert all around the camp was wet with dew. 14When the dew disappeared later in the morning, thin flakes, white like frost, covered the ground. 15The Israelites were puzzled when they saw it. "What is it?" they asked.

And Moses told them, "It is the food the LORD has given you. 16The LORD says that each household should gather as much as it needs. Pick up two quarts* for each person."

17So the people of Israel went out and gathered this food—some getting more, and some getting less. 18By gathering two quarts for each person, everyone had just enough. Those who gathered a lot had nothing left over, and those who gathered only a little had enough. Each family had just what it needed.

19Then Moses told them, "Do not keep any of it overnight." 20But, of course, some of them didn't listen and kept some of it until morning. By then it was full of maggots and had a terrible smell. And Moses was very angry with them.

21The people gathered the food morning by morning, each family according to its need. And as the sun became hot, the food they had not picked up melted and disappeared. 22On the sixth day, there was twice as much as usual on the ground—four quarts* for each person instead of two. The leaders of the people came and asked Moses why this had happened. 23He replied, "The LORD has appointed tomorrow as a day of rest, a holy Sabbath to the LORD. On this day we will rest from our normal daily tasks. So

bake or boil as much as you want today, and set aside what is left for tomorrow."

24The next morning the leftover food was wholesome and good, without maggots or odor. 25Moses said, "This is your food for today, for today is a Sabbath to the LORD. There will be no food on the ground today. 26Gather the food for six days, but the seventh day is a Sabbath. There will be no food on the ground for you on that day."

27Some of the people went out anyway to gather food, even though it was the Sabbath day. But there was none to be found. 28"How long will these people refuse to obey my commands and instructions?" the LORD asked Moses. 29"Do they not realize that I have given them the seventh day, the Sabbath, as a day of rest? That is why I give you twice as much food on the sixth day, so there will be enough for two days. On the Sabbath day you must stay in your places. Do not pick up food from the ground on that day."

30So the people rested on the seventh day.

31In time, the food became known as manna.* It was white like coriander seed, and it tasted like honey cakes.

32Then Moses gave them this command from the LORD: "Take two quarts of manna and keep it forever as a treasured memorial of the LORD's provision. By doing this, later generations will be able to see the bread that the LORD provided in the wilderness when he brought you out of Egypt."

33Moses said to Aaron, "Get a container and put two quarts of manna into it. Then store it in a sacred place* as a reminder for all future generations." 34Aaron did this, just as the LORD had commanded Moses. He eventually placed it for safekeeping in the Ark of the Covenant.* 35So the people of Israel ate manna for forty years until they arrived in the land of Canaan, where there were crops to eat. 36(The container used to measure the manna was an omer, which held about two quarts.)*

CHAPTER **17**
Water from the Rock
At the LORD's command, the people of Israel left the Sin* Desert and moved from place to place. Eventually they came to Rephidim, but there was no water to be found there. 2So once more the people grumbled and complained to Moses. "Give us water to drink!" they demanded.

16:16 Hebrew *1 omer* [2 liters]; also in 16:18, 32, 33.   16:22 Hebrew *2 omers* [4 liters].   16:31 *Manna* means "What is it?" See 16:15. 16:33 Hebrew *before the LORD.*   16:34 Hebrew *in front of the Testimony.*   16:36 Hebrew *An omer is one tenth of an ephah.*   17:1 Not to be confused with the English word *sin.*

"Quiet!" Moses replied. "Why are you arguing with me? And why are you testing the LORD?"

3But tormented by thirst, they continued to complain, "Why did you ever take us out of Egypt? Why did you bring us here? We, our children, and our livestock will all die!"

4Then Moses pleaded with the LORD, "What should I do with these people? They are about to stone me!"

5The LORD said to Moses, "Take your shepherd's staff, the one you used when you struck the water of the Nile. Then call some of the leaders of Israel and walk on ahead of the people. 6I will meet you by the rock at Mount Sinai.* Strike the rock, and water will come pouring out. Then the people will be able to drink." Moses did just as he was told; and as the leaders looked on, water gushed out.

7Moses named the place Massah—"the place of testing"—and Meribah—"the place of arguing"—because the people of Israel argued with Moses and tested the LORD by saying, "Is the LORD going to take care of us or not?"

Israel Defeats the Amalekites

8While the people of Israel were still at Rephidim, the warriors of Amalek came to fight against them. 9Moses commanded Joshua, "Call the Israelites to arms, and fight the army of Amalek. Tomorrow, I will stand at the top of the hill with the staff of God in my hand."

10So Joshua did what Moses had commanded. He led his men out to fight the army of Amalek. Meanwhile Moses, Aaron, and Hur went to the top of a nearby hill. 11As long as Moses held up the staff with his hands, the Israelites had the advantage. But whenever he lowered his hands, the Amalekites gained the upper hand. 12Moses' arms finally became too tired to hold up the staff any longer. So Aaron and Hur found a stone for him to sit on. Then they stood on each side, holding up his hands until sunset. 13As a result, Joshua and his troops were able to crush the army of Amalek.

14Then the LORD instructed Moses, "Write this down as a permanent record, and announce it to Joshua: I will blot out every trace of Amalek from under heaven." 15Moses built an altar there and called it "The LORD Is My Banner."* 16He said, "They have dared to raise their fist against the LORD's throne, so now* the LORD will be at war with Amalek generation after generation."

CHAPTER 18
Jethro's Visit to Moses

Word soon reached Jethro, the priest of Midian and Moses' father-in-law, about all the wonderful things God had done for Moses and his people, the Israelites. He had heard about how the LORD had brought them safely out of Egypt.

2Some time before this, Moses had sent his wife, Zipporah, and his two sons to live with Jethro, his father-in-law. 3The name of Moses' first son was Gershom,* for Moses had said when the boy was born, "I have been a stranger in a foreign land." 4The name of his second son was Eliezer,* for Moses had said at his birth, "The God of my fathers was my helper; he delivered me from the sword of Pharaoh." 5Jethro now came to visit Moses, and he brought Moses' wife and two sons with him. They arrived while Moses and the people were camped near the mountain of God. 6Moses was told, "Jethro, your father-in-law, has come to visit you. Your wife and your two sons are with him."

7So Moses went out to meet his father-in-law. He bowed to him respectfully and greeted him warmly. They asked about each other's health and then went to Moses' tent to talk further. 8Moses told his father-in-law about everything the LORD had done to rescue Israel from Pharaoh and the Egyptians. He also told him about the problems they had faced along the way and how the LORD had delivered his people from all their troubles. 9Jethro was delighted when he heard about all that the LORD had done for Israel as he brought them out of Egypt.

10"Praise be to the LORD," Jethro said, "for he has saved you from the Egyptians and from Pharaoh. He has rescued Israel from the power of Egypt! 11I know now that the LORD is greater than all other gods, because his people have escaped from the proud and cruel Egyptians."

12Then Jethro presented a burnt offering and gave sacrifices to God. As Jethro was doing this, Aaron and the leaders of Israel came out to meet him. They all joined him in a sacrificial meal in God's presence.

Jethro's Wise Advice

13The next day, Moses sat as usual to hear the people's complaints against each other. They were lined up in front of him from morning till evening. 14When Moses' father-in-law saw all that Moses was doing for the people, he said, "Why are you trying to do all this alone? The people

---

17:6 Hebrew *Horeb*, another name for Sinai.   17:15 Hebrew *Yahweh Nissi*.   17:16 Or *Hands have been lifted up to the LORD's throne, and now*.   18:3 *Gershom* sounds like a Hebrew term that means "a stranger there."   18:4 *Eliezer* means "God is my helper."

have been standing here all day to get your help."

¹⁵Moses replied, "Well, the people come to me to seek God's guidance. ¹⁶When an argument arises, I am the one who settles the case. I inform the people of God's decisions and teach them his laws and instructions."

¹⁷"This is not good!" his father-in-law exclaimed. ¹⁸"You're going to wear yourself out—and the people, too. This job is too heavy a burden for you to handle all by yourself. ¹⁹Now let me give you a word of advice, and may God be with you. You should continue to be the people's representative before God, bringing him their questions to be decided. ²⁰You should tell them God's decisions, teach them God's laws and instructions, and show them how to conduct their lives. ²¹But find some capable, honest men who fear God and hate bribes. Appoint them as judges over groups of one thousand, one hundred, fifty, and ten. ²²These men can serve the people, resolving all the ordinary cases. Anything that is too important or too complicated can be brought to you. But they can take care of the smaller matters themselves. They will help you carry the load, making the task easier for you. ²³If you follow this advice, and if God directs you to do so, then you will be able to endure the pressures, and all these people will go home in peace."

²⁴Moses listened to his father-in-law's advice and followed his suggestions. ²⁵He chose capable men from all over Israel and made them judges over the people. They were put in charge of groups of one thousand, one hundred, fifty, and ten. ²⁶These men were constantly available to administer justice. They brought the hard cases to Moses, but they judged the smaller matters themselves.

²⁷Soon after this, Moses said good-bye to his father-in-law, who returned to his own land.

CHAPTER **19**

The LORD Reveals Himself at Sinai

The Israelites arrived in the wilderness of Sinai exactly two months after they left Egypt.* ²After breaking camp at Rephidim, they came to the base of Mount Sinai and set up camp there.

³Then Moses climbed the mountain to appear before God. The LORD called out to him from the mountain and said, "Give these instructions to the descendants of Jacob, the people of Israel: ⁴'You have seen what I did to the Egyptians. You know how I brought you to myself and carried you on eagle's wings. ⁵Now if you will obey me and keep my covenant, you will be my own special treasure from among all the nations of the earth; for all the earth belongs to me. ⁶And you will be to me a kingdom of priests, my holy nation.' Give this message to the Israelites."

⁷Moses returned from the mountain and called together the leaders of the people and told them what the LORD had said. ⁸They all responded together, "We will certainly do everything the LORD asks of us." So Moses brought the people's answer back to the LORD.

⁹Then the LORD said to Moses, "I am going to come to you in a thick cloud so the people themselves can hear me as I speak to you. Then they will always have confidence in you."

Moses told the LORD what the people had said. ¹⁰Then the LORD told Moses, "Go down and prepare the people for my visit. Purify them today and tomorrow, and have them wash their clothing. ¹¹Be sure they are ready on the third day, for I will come down upon Mount Sinai as all the people watch. ¹²Set boundary lines that the people may not pass. Warn them, 'Be careful! Do not go up on the mountain or even touch its boundaries. Those who do will certainly die! ¹³Any people or animals that cross the boundary must be stoned to death or shot with arrows. They must not be touched by human hands.' The people must stay away from the mountain until they hear one long blast from the ram's horn. Then they must gather at the foot of the mountain."

¹⁴So Moses went down to the people. He purified them for worship and had them wash their clothing. ¹⁵He told them, "Get ready for an important event two days from now. And until then, abstain from having sexual intercourse."

¹⁶On the morning of the third day, there was a powerful thunder and lightning storm, and a dense cloud came down upon the mountain. There was a long, loud blast from a ram's horn, and all the people trembled. ¹⁷Moses led them out from the camp to meet with God, and they stood at the foot of the mountain. ¹⁸All Mount Sinai was covered with smoke because the LORD had descended on it in the form of fire. The smoke billowed into the sky like smoke from a furnace, and the whole mountain shook with a violent earthquake. ¹⁹As the horn blast grew louder and louder, Moses spoke, and God thundered his reply for all to hear. ²⁰The LORD came

19:1 Hebrew *in the third month . . . on the very day,* i.e., two lunar months to the day after leaving Egypt. This day of the Hebrew lunar calendar occurs in late May or early June; compare note on 13:4.

down on the top of Mount Sinai and called Moses to the top of the mountain. So Moses climbed the mountain.

21Then the LORD told Moses, "Go back down and warn the people not to cross the boundaries. They must not come up here to see the LORD, for those who do will die. 22Even the priests who regularly come near to the LORD must purify themselves, or I will destroy them."

23"But, LORD, the people cannot come up on the mountain!" Moses protested. "You already told them not to. You told me to set boundaries around the mountain and to declare it off limits."

24But the LORD said, "Go down anyway and bring Aaron back with you. In the meantime, do not let the priests or the people cross the boundaries to come up here. If they do, I will punish them."

25So Moses went down to the people and told them what the LORD had said.

CHAPTER 20
The Ten Commandments
Then God instructed the people as follows:

2"I am the LORD your God, who rescued you from slavery in Egypt.

3"Do not worship any other gods besides me.

4"Do not make idols of any kind, whether in the shape of birds or animals or fish. 5You must never worship or bow down to them, for I, the LORD your God, am a jealous God who will not share your affection with any other god! I do not leave unpunished the sins of those who hate me, but I punish the children for the sins of their parents to the third and fourth generations. 6But I lavish my love on those who love me and obey my commands, even for a thousand generations.

7"Do not misuse the name of the LORD your God. The LORD will not let you go unpunished if you misuse his name.

8"Remember to observe the Sabbath day by keeping it holy. 9Six days a week are set apart for your daily duties and regular work, 10but the seventh day is a day of rest dedicated to the LORD your God. On that day no one in your household may do any kind of work. This includes you, your sons and daughters, your male and female servants, your livestock, and any foreigners living among you. 11For in six days the LORD made the heavens, the earth, the sea, and

everything in them; then he rested on the seventh day. That is why the LORD blessed the Sabbath day and set it apart as holy.

12"Honor your father and mother. Then you will live a long, full life in the land the LORD your God will give you.

13"Do not murder.

14"Do not commit adultery.

15"Do not steal.

16"Do not testify falsely against your neighbor.

17"Do not covet your neighbor's house. Do not covet your neighbor's wife, male or female servant, ox or donkey, or anything else your neighbor owns."

18When the people heard the thunder and the loud blast of the horn, and when they saw the lightning and the smoke billowing from the mountain, they stood at a distance, trembling with fear.

19And they said to Moses, "You tell us what God says, and we will listen. But don't let God speak directly to us. If he does, we will die!"

20"Don't be afraid," Moses said, "for God has come in this way to show you his awesome power. From now on, let your fear of him keep you from sinning!"

21As the people stood in the distance, Moses entered into the deep darkness where God was.

Proper Use of Altars
22And the LORD said to Moses, "Say this to the people of Israel: You are witnesses that I have spoken to you from heaven. 23Remember, you must not make or worship idols of silver or gold.

24"The altars you make for me must be simple altars of earth. Offer on such altars your sacrifices to me—your burnt offerings and peace offerings, your sheep and goats and your cattle. Build altars in the places where I remind you who I am, and I will come and bless you there. 25If you build altars from stone, use only uncut stones. Do not chip or shape the stones with a tool, for that would make them unfit for holy use. 26And you may not approach my altar by steps. If you do, someone might look up under the skirts of your clothing and see your nakedness.

CHAPTER 21
Fair Treatment of Slaves
"Here are some other instructions you must present to Israel:

2"If you buy a Hebrew slave, he is to serve for only six years. Set him free in the seventh

What Is Right and Wrong? Read EXODUS 20:1-17

Have you ever tried putting together a do-it-yourself piece of furniture or some of the new "sophisticated" children's toys without a set of instructions? More often than not, if you choose to "go it on your own," you will take twice as long to put the thing together—and you may even make some irreparable mistakes.

Throughout the world today, more and more people seem to lack a set of instructions or absolutes to live by. They have no clear sense of what is right and wrong. But there is good news. God has given us a value system—a "set of instructions"—to live by. It is called the Ten Commandments. This bedrock of spiritual and moral truth clearly distinguishes between good and evil, right and wrong, true and false.

In these commands, God has given us a set of general instructions for just about every aspect of our lives. The first four commands (verses 2-11) show us how we should relate to God. The last six commands (verses 12-17) teach us how to relate to one another. In ten commands, God has clearly shown us what is right and what is wrong.

When Jesus came, he—in a way—simplified these commands by summing them up in two commands: "'You must love the Lord your God with all your heart, all your soul, and all your mind.' This is the first and greatest commandment. A second is equally important: 'Love your neighbor as yourself'" (Matthew 22:37-39). If we live by these commands, we will do what is right and live a life that is pleasing to God.

For the next "Big Question" note, turn to p. 381.

BIG QUESTIONS

---

year, and he will owe you nothing for his freedom. ³If he was single when he became your slave and then married afterward, only he will go free in the seventh year. But if he was married before he became a slave, then his wife will be freed with him.

⁴"If his master gave him a wife while he was a slave, and they had sons or daughters, then the man will be free in the seventh year, but his wife and children will still belong to his master. ⁵But the slave may plainly declare, 'I love my master, my wife, and my children. I would rather not go free.' ⁶If he does this, his master must present him before God.* Then his master must take him to the door and publicly pierce his ear with an awl. After that, the slave will belong to his master forever.

⁷"When a man sells his daughter as a slave, she will not be freed at the end of six years as the men are. ⁸If she does not please the man who bought her, he may allow her to be bought back again. But he is not allowed to sell her to foreigners, since he is the one who broke the contract with her. ⁹And if the slave girl's owner arranges for her to marry his son, he may no longer treat her as a slave girl, but he must treat her as his daughter. ¹⁰If he himself marries her and then takes an-

other wife, he may not reduce her food or clothing or fail to sleep with her as his wife. ¹¹If he fails in any of these three ways, she may leave as a free woman without making any payment.

Cases of Personal Injury

¹²"Anyone who hits a person hard enough to cause death must be put to death. ¹³But if it is an accident and God allows it to happen, I will appoint a place where the slayer can run for safety. ¹⁴However, if someone deliberately attacks and kills another person, then the slayer must be dragged even from my altar and put to death.

¹⁵"Anyone who strikes father or mother must be put to death.

¹⁶"Kidnappers must be killed, whether they are caught in possession of their victims or have already sold them as slaves.

¹⁷"Anyone who curses father or mother must be put to death.

¹⁸"Now suppose two people quarrel, and one hits the other with a stone or fist, causing injury but not death. ¹⁹If the injured person is later able to walk again, even with a crutch, the assailant will be innocent. Nonetheless, the assailant

21:6 Or *before the judges.*

must pay for time lost because of the injury and must pay for the medical expenses.

20"If a male or female slave is beaten and dies, the owner must be punished. 21If the slave recovers after a couple of days, however, then the owner should not be punished, since the slave is the owner's property.

22"Now suppose two people are fighting, and in the process, they hurt a pregnant woman so her child is born prematurely. If no further harm results, then the person responsible must pay damages in the amount the woman's husband demands and the judges approve. 23But if any harm results, then the offender must be punished according to the injury. If the result is death, the offender must be executed. 24If an eye is injured, injure the eye of the person who did it. If a tooth gets knocked out, knock out the tooth of the person who did it. Similarly, the payment must be hand for hand, foot for foot, 25burn for burn, wound for wound, bruise for bruise.

26"If an owner hits a male or female slave in the eye and the eye is blinded, then the slave may go free because of the eye. 27And if an owner knocks out the tooth of a male or female slave, the slave should be released in payment for the tooth.

28"If a bull gores a man or woman to death, the bull must be stoned, and its flesh may not be eaten. In such a case, however, the owner will not be held liable. 29Suppose, on the other hand, that the owner knew the bull had gored people in the past, yet the bull was not kept under control. If this is true and if the bull kills someone, it must be stoned, and the owner must also be killed. 30However, the dead person's relatives may accept payment from the owner of the bull to compensate for the loss of life. The owner will have to pay whatever is demanded.

31"The same principle applies if the bull gores a boy or a girl. 32But if the bull gores a slave, either male or female, the slave's owner is to be given thirty silver coins* in payment, and the bull must be stoned.

33"Suppose someone digs or uncovers a well and fails to cover it, and then an ox or a donkey falls into it. 34The owner of the well must pay in full for the dead animal but then gets to keep it.

35"If someone's bull injures a neighbor's bull and the injured bull dies, then the two owners must sell the live bull and divide the money between them. Each will also own half of the dead bull. 36But if the bull was known from past experience to gore, yet its owner failed to keep it under control, the money will not be divided. The owner of the living bull must pay in full for the dead bull but then gets to keep it.

CHAPTER **22**

Protection of Property

"A fine must be paid by anyone who steals an ox or sheep and then kills or sells it. For oxen the fine is five oxen for each one stolen. For sheep the fine is four sheep for each one stolen.

2"If a thief is caught in the act of breaking into a house and is killed in the process, the person who killed the thief is not guilty. 3But if it happens in daylight, the one who killed the thief is guilty of murder.

"A thief who is caught must pay in full for everything that was stolen. If payment is not made, the thief must be sold as a slave to pay the debt. 4If someone steals an ox or a donkey or a sheep and it is recovered alive, then the thief must pay double the value.

5"If an animal is grazing in a field or vineyard and the owner lets it stray into someone else's field to graze, then the animal's owner must pay damages in the form of high-quality grain or grapes.

6"If a fire gets out of control and goes into another person's field, destroying the sheaves or the standing grain, then the one who started the fire must pay for the lost crops.

7"Suppose someone entrusts money or goods to a neighbor, and they are stolen from the neighbor's house. If the thief is found, the fine is double the value of what was stolen. 8But if the thief is not found, God* will determine whether or not it was the neighbor who stole the property.

9"Suppose there is a dispute between two people as to who owns a particular ox, donkey, sheep, article of clothing, or anything else. Both parties must come before God* for a decision, and the person whom God declares* guilty must pay double to the other.

10"Now suppose someone asks a neighbor to care for a donkey, ox, sheep, or any other animal, but it dies or is injured or gets away, and there is no eyewitness to report just what happened. 11The neighbor must then take an oath of innocence in the presence of the LORD. The owner must accept the neighbor's word, and no payment will be required. 12But if the animal or property was stolen,

---

21:32 Hebrew *30 shekels of silver,* about 12 ounces or 342 grams in weight.   **22:8** Or *the judges.*   **22:9a** Or *before the judges.*   **22:9b** Or *whom the judges declare.*

payment must be made to the owner. ¹³If it was attacked by a wild animal, the carcass must be shown as evidence, and no payment will be required.

¹⁴"If someone borrows an animal from a neighbor and it is injured or killed, and if the owner was not there at the time, the person who borrowed it must pay for it. ¹⁵But if the owner is there, no payment is required. And no payment is required if the animal was rented because this loss was covered by the rental fee.

Social Responsibility

¹⁶"If a man seduces a virgin who is not engaged to anyone and sleeps with her, he must pay the customary dowry and accept her as his wife. ¹⁷But if her father refuses to let her marry him, the man must still pay the money for her dowry.

¹⁸"A sorceress must not be allowed to live.

¹⁹"Anyone who has sexual relations with an animal must be executed.

²⁰"Anyone who sacrifices to any god other than the LORD must be destroyed.

²¹"Do not oppress foreigners in any way. Remember, you yourselves were once foreigners in the land of Egypt.

²²"Do not exploit widows or orphans. ²³If you do and they cry out to me, then I will surely help them. ²⁴My anger will blaze forth against you, and I will kill you with the sword. Your wives will become widows, and your children will become fatherless.

²⁵"If you lend money to a fellow Hebrew in need, do not be like a money lender, charging interest. ²⁶If you take your neighbor's cloak as a pledge of repayment, you must return it by nightfall. ²⁷Your neighbor will need it to stay warm during the night. If you do not return it and your neighbor cries out to me for help, then I will hear, for I am very merciful.

²⁸"Do not blaspheme God* or curse anyone who rules over you.

²⁹"Do not hold anything back when you give me the tithe of your crops and your wine.

"You must make the necessary payment for redemption of your firstborn sons.

³⁰"You must also give me the firstborn of your cattle and sheep. Leave the newborn animal with its mother for seven days; then give it to me on the eighth day.

³¹"You are my own holy people. Therefore, do not eat any animal that has been attacked and killed by a wild animal. Throw its carcass out for the dogs to eat.

A Call for Justice

"Do not pass along false reports. Do not cooperate with evil people by telling lies on the witness stand.

²"Do not join a crowd that intends to do evil. When you are on the witness stand, do not be swayed in your testimony by the opinion of the majority. ³And do not slant your testimony in favor of a person just because that person is poor.

⁴"If you come upon your enemy's ox or donkey that has strayed away, take it back to its owner. ⁵If you see the donkey of someone who hates you struggling beneath a heavy load, do not walk by. Instead, stop and offer to help.

⁶"Do not twist justice against people simply because they are poor.

⁷"Keep far away from falsely charging anyone with evil. Never put an innocent or honest person to death. I will not allow anyone guilty of this to go free.

⁸"Take no bribes, for a bribe makes you ignore something that you clearly see. A bribe always hurts the cause of the person who is in the right.

⁹"Do not oppress the foreigners living among you. You know what it is like to be a foreigner. Remember your own experience in the land of Egypt.

¹⁰"Plant and harvest your crops for six years, ¹¹but let the land rest and lie fallow during the seventh year. Then let the poor among you harvest any volunteer crop that may come up. Leave the rest for the animals to eat. The same applies to your vineyards and olive groves.

¹²"Work for six days, and rest on the seventh. This will give your ox and your donkey a chance to rest. It will also allow the people of your household, including your slaves and visitors, to be refreshed.

¹³"Be sure to obey all my instructions. And remember, never pray to or swear by any other gods. Do not even mention their names.

Three Annual Festivals

¹⁴"Each year you must celebrate three festivals in my honor. ¹⁵The first is the Festival of Unleavened Bread. For seven days you are to eat bread made without yeast, just as I commanded you before. This festival will be an annual event at the appointed time in early spring,* for that is the anniversary of your exodus from Egypt. Everyone must bring me a sacrifice at that time. ¹⁶You must also

---

22:28 Or *Do not revile your judges.*   23:15 Hebrew *in the month of Abib.* This month of the Hebrew lunar calendar usually occurs in March and April.

celebrate the Festival of Harvest,* when you bring me the first crops of your harvest. Finally, you are to celebrate the Festival of the Final Harvest* at the end of the harvest season. ¹⁷At these three times each year, every man in Israel must appear before the Sovereign LORD.

¹⁸"Sacrificial blood must never be offered together with bread that has yeast in it. And no sacrificial fat may be left unoffered until the next morning.

¹⁹"As you harvest each of your crops, bring me a choice sample of the first day's harvest. It must be offered to the LORD your God.

"You must not cook a young goat in its mother's milk.

A Promise of the LORD's Presence

²⁰"See, I am sending my angel before you to lead you safely to the land I have prepared for you. ²¹Pay attention to him, and obey all of his instructions. Do not rebel against him, for he will not forgive your sins. He is my representative— he bears my name. ²²But if you are careful to obey him, following all my instructions, then I will be an enemy to your enemies, and I will oppose those who oppose you. ²³For my angel will go before you and bring you into the land of the Amorites, Hittites, Perizzites, Canaanites, Hivites, and Jebusites, so you may live there. And I will destroy them. ²⁴Do not worship the gods of these other nations or serve them in any way, and never follow their evil example. Instead, you must utterly conquer them and break down their shameful idols.

²⁵"You must serve only the LORD your God. If you do, I will bless you with food and water, and I will keep you healthy. ²⁶There will be no miscarriages or infertility among your people, and I will give you long, full lives.

²⁷"I will send my terror upon all the people whose lands you invade, and they will panic before you. ²⁸I will send hornets ahead of you to drive out the Hivites, Canaanites, and Hittites. ²⁹But I will not do this all in one year because the land would become a wilderness, and the wild animals would become too many to control. ³⁰I will drive them out a little at a time until your population has increased enough to fill the land. ³¹And I will fix your boundaries from the Red Sea to the Mediterranean Sea,* and from the southern deserts to the Euphrates River.* I will help you defeat the people now living in the land, and you will drive them out ahead of you.

³²"Make no treaties with them and have nothing to do with their gods. ³³Do not even let them live among you! If you do, they will infect you with their sin of idol worship, and that would be disastrous for you."

CHAPTER **24**

Israel Accepts the LORD's Covenant

Then the LORD instructed Moses: "Come up here to me, and bring along Aaron, Nadab, Abihu, and seventy of Israel's leaders. All of them must worship at a distance. ²You alone, Moses, are allowed to come near to the LORD. The others must not come too close. And remember, none of the other people are allowed to climb on the mountain at all."

³When Moses had announced to the people all the teachings and regulations the LORD had given him, they answered in unison, "We will do everything the LORD has told us to do."

⁴Then Moses carefully wrote down all the LORD's instructions. Early the next morning he built an altar at the foot of the mountain. He also set up twelve pillars around the altar, one for each of the twelve tribes of Israel. ⁵Then he sent some of the young men to sacrifice young bulls as burnt offerings and peace offerings to the LORD. ⁶Moses took half the blood from these animals and drew it off into basins. The other half he splashed against the altar.

⁷Then he took the Book of the Covenant and read it to the people. They all responded again, "We will do everything the LORD has commanded. We will obey."

⁸Then Moses sprinkled the blood from the basins over the people and said, "This blood confirms the covenant the LORD has made with you in giving you these laws."

⁹Then Moses, Aaron, Nadab, Abihu, and seventy of the leaders of Israel went up the mountain. ¹⁰There they saw the God of Israel. Under his feet there seemed to be a pavement of brilliant sapphire, as clear as the heavens. ¹¹And though Israel's leaders saw God, he did not destroy them. In fact, they shared a meal together in God's presence!

¹²And the LORD said to Moses, "Come up to me on the mountain. Stay there while I give you the tablets of stone that I have inscribed with my instructions and commands. Then you will teach the people from them." ¹³So Moses and his assistant Joshua climbed up the mountain of God.

23:16a Or *Festival of Weeks.* 23:16b This was later called the Festival of Shelters; see Lev 23:33-36. 23:31a Hebrew *from the sea of reeds to the sea of the Philistines.* 23:31b Hebrew *the river.*

14Moses told the other leaders, "Stay here and wait for us until we come back. If there are any problems while I am gone, consult with Aaron and Hur, who are here with you."

15Then Moses went up the mountain, and the cloud covered it. 16And the glorious presence of the LORD rested upon Mount Sinai, and the cloud covered it for six days. On the seventh day the LORD called to Moses from the cloud. 17The Israelites at the foot of the mountain saw an awesome sight. The awesome glory of the LORD on the mountaintop looked like a devouring fire. 18Then Moses disappeared into the cloud as he climbed higher up the mountain. He stayed on the mountain forty days and forty nights.

CHAPTER 25

Offerings for the Tabernacle

The LORD said to Moses, 2"Tell the people of Israel that everyone who wants to may bring me an offering. 3Here is a list of items you may accept on my behalf: gold, silver, and bronze; 4blue, purple, and scarlet yarn; fine linen; goat hair for cloth; 5tanned ram skins and fine goatskin leather; acacia wood; 6olive oil for the lamps; spices for the anointing oil and the fragrant incense; 7onyx stones, and other stones to be set in the ephod and the chestpiece.

8"I want the people of Israel to build me a sacred residence where I can live among them. 9You must make this Tabernacle and its furnishings exactly according to the plans I will show you.

Plans for the Ark

10"Make an Ark of acacia wood—a sacred chest 3¾ feet long, 2¼ feet wide, and 2¼ feet high.* 11Overlay it inside and outside with pure gold, and put a molding of gold all around it. 12Cast four rings of gold for it, and attach them to its four feet, two rings on each side. 13Make poles from acacia wood, and overlay them with gold. 14Fit the poles into the rings at the sides of the Ark to carry it. 15These carrying poles must never be taken from the rings; they are to be left there permanently. 16When the Ark is finished, place inside it the stone tablets inscribed with the terms of the covenant,* which I will give to you.

17"Then make the Ark's cover—the place of atonement—out of pure gold. It must be 3¾ feet long and 2¼ feet wide. 18Then use hammered gold to make two cherubim, and place

them at the two ends of the atonement cover. 19Attach the cherubim to each end of the atonement cover, making it all one piece. 20The cherubim will face each other, looking down on the atonement cover with their wings spread out above it. 21Place inside the Ark the stone tablets inscribed with the terms of the covenant, which I will give to you. Then put the atonement cover on top of the Ark. 22I will meet with you there and talk to you from above the atonement cover between the gold cherubim that hover over the Ark of the Covenant.* From there I will give you my commands for the people of Israel.

Plans for the Table

23"Then make a table of acacia wood, 3 feet long, 1½ feet wide, and 2¼ feet high. 24Overlay it with pure gold and run a molding of gold around it. 25Put around three inches* wide around the top edge, and put a gold molding all around the rim. 26Make four gold rings, and put the rings at the four corners by the four legs, 27close to the rim around the top. These rings will support the poles used to carry the table. 28Make these poles from acacia wood and overlay them with gold. 29And make gold plates and dishes, as well as pitchers and bowls to be used in pouring out drink offerings. 30You must always keep the special Bread of the Presence on the table before me.

Plans for the Lampstand

31"Make a lampstand of pure, hammered gold. The entire lampstand and its decorations will be one piece—the base, center stem, lamp cups, buds, and blossoms. 32It will have six branches, three branches going out from each side of the center stem. 33Each of the six branches will hold a cup shaped like an almond blossom, complete with buds and petals. 34The center stem of the lampstand will be decorated with four almond blossoms, complete with buds and petals. 35One blossom will be set beneath each pair of branches where they extend from the center stem. 36The decorations and branches must all be one piece with the stem, and they must be hammered from pure gold. 37Then make the seven lamps for the lampstand, and set them so they reflect their light forward. 38The lamp snuffers and trays must also be made of pure gold. 39You will need seventy-five pounds* of pure gold for the lampstand and its accessories.

25:10 Hebrew *2½ cubits* [1.1 meters] *long, 1½ cubits* [0.7 meters] *wide, and 1½ cubits high.* In this chapter, the distance measures are calculated from the Hebrew cubit at a ratio of 18 inches or 45 centimeters per cubit.   25:16 Hebrew *place inside it the Testimony;* also in 25:21.   25:22 Or *Ark of the Testimony.*   25:25 Hebrew *a handbreadth* [8 centimeters].   25:39 Hebrew *1 talent* [34 kilograms].

40 "Be sure that you make everything according to the pattern I have shown you here on the mountain.

CHAPTER **26**

Plans for the Tabernacle

"Make the Tabernacle from ten sheets of fine linen. These sheets are to be decorated with blue, purple, and scarlet yarn, with figures of cherubim skillfully embroidered into them. 2Each sheet must be forty-two feet long and six feet wide.* All ten sheets must be exactly the same size. 3Join five of these sheets together into one set; then join the other five sheets into a second set. 4Put loops of blue yarn along the edge of the last sheet in each set. 5The fifty loops along the edge of one set are to match the fifty loops along the edge of the other. 6Then make fifty gold clasps to fasten the loops of the two sets of sheets together, making the Tabernacle a single unit.

7 "Make heavy sheets of cloth from goat hair to cover the Tabernacle. There must be eleven of these sheets, 8each forty-five feet long and six feet wide. All eleven of these sheets must be exactly the same size. 9Join five of these together into one set, and join the other six into a second set. The sixth sheet of the second set is to be doubled over at the entrance of the sacred tent. 10Put fifty loops along the edge of the last sheet in each set, 11and fasten them together with fifty bronze clasps. In this way, the two sets will become a single unit. 12An extra half sheet of this roof covering will be left to hang over the back of the Tabernacle, 13and the covering will hang down an extra eighteen inches on each side. 14On top of these coverings place a layer of tanned ram skins, and over them put a layer of fine goatskin leather. This will complete the roof covering.

15 "The framework of the Tabernacle will consist of frames made of acacia wood. 16Each frame must be 15 feet high and 2¼ feet wide. 17There will be two pegs on each frame so they can be joined to the next frame. All the frames must be made this way. 18Twenty of these frames will support the south side of the Tabernacle. 19They will fit into forty silver bases—two bases under each frame. 20On the north side there will also be twenty of these frames, 21with their forty silver bases, two bases for each frame. 22On the west side there will be six frames, 23along with an extra frame at each corner. 24These corner frames will

be connected at the bottom and firmly attached at the top with a single ring, forming a single unit. Both of these corner frames will be made the same way. 25So there will be eight frames on that end of the Tabernacle, supported by sixteen silver bases—two bases under each frame.

26 "Make crossbars of acacia wood to run across the frames, five crossbars for the north side of the Tabernacle 27and five for the south side. Also make five crossbars for the rear of the Tabernacle, which will face westward. 28The middle crossbar, halfway up the frames, will run all the way from one end of the Tabernacle to the other. 29Overlay the frames with gold and make gold rings to support the crossbars. Overlay the crossbars with gold as well.

30 "Set up this Tabernacle according to the design you were shown on the mountain.

31 "Across the inside of the Tabernacle hang a special curtain made of fine linen, with cherubim skillfully embroidered into the cloth using blue, purple, and scarlet yarn. 32Hang this inner curtain on gold hooks set into four posts made from acacia wood and overlaid with gold. The posts will fit into silver bases. 33When the inner curtain is in place, put the Ark of the Covenant* behind it. This curtain will separate the Holy Place from the Most Holy Place.

34 "Then put the Ark's cover—the place of atonement—on top of the Ark of the Covenant inside the Most Holy Place. 35Place the table and lampstand across the room from each other outside the inner curtain. The lampstand must be placed on the south side, and the table must be set toward the north.

36 "Make another curtain from fine linen for the entrance of the sacred tent, and embroider exquisite designs into it, using blue, purple, and scarlet yarn. 37Hang this curtain on gold hooks set into five posts made from acacia wood and overlaid with gold. The posts will fit into five bronze bases.

CHAPTER **27**

Plans for the Altar of Burnt Offering

"Using acacia wood, make a square altar 7½ feet wide, 7½ feet long, and 4½ feet high.* 2Make a horn at each of the four corners of the altar so the horns and altar are all one piece. Overlay the altar and its horns with bronze. 3The ash buckets, shovels, basins, meat hooks, and firepans will all be

---

26:2 Hebrew *28 cubits* [12.6 meters] *long and 4 cubits* [1.8 meters] *wide.* In this chapter, the distance measures are calculated from the Hebrew cubit at a ratio of 18 inches or 45 centimeters per cubit.   26:33 Or *Ark of the Testimony;* also in 26:34.   27:1 Hebrew *5 cubits* [2.3 meters] *wide, 5 cubits long, and 3 cubits* [1.4 meters] *high.* In this chapter, the distance measures are calculated from the Hebrew cubit at a ratio of 18 inches or 45 centimeters per cubit.

made of bronze. 4Make a bronze grating, with a metal ring at each corner. 5Fit the grating halfway down into the firebox, resting it on the ledge built there. 6For moving the altar, make poles from acacia wood, and overlay them with bronze. 7To carry it, put the poles into the rings at two sides of the altar. 8The altar must be hollow, made from planks. Be careful to build it just as you were shown on the mountain.

Plans for the Courtyard

9 "Then make a courtyard for the Tabernacle, enclosed with curtains made from fine linen. On the south side the curtains will stretch for 150 feet. 10They will be held up by twenty bronze posts that fit into twenty bronze bases. The curtains will be held up with silver hooks attached to the silver rods that are attached to the posts. 11It will be the same on the north side of the courtyard—150 feet of curtains held up by twenty posts fitted into bronze bases, with silver hooks and rods. 12The curtains on the west end of the courtyard will be 75 feet long, supported by ten posts set into ten bases. 13The east end will also be 75 feet long. 14The courtyard entrance will be on the east end, flanked by two curtains. The curtain on the right side will be 22½ feet long, supported by three posts set into three bases. 15The curtain on the left side will also be 22½ feet long, supported by three posts set into three bases.

16 "For the entrance to the courtyard, make a curtain that is 30 feet long. Fashion it from fine linen, and decorate it with beautiful embroidery in blue, purple, and scarlet yarn. It will be attached to four posts that fit into four bases. 17All the posts around the courtyard must be connected by silver rods, using silver hooks. The posts are to be set in solid bronze bases. 18So the entire courtyard will be 150 feet long and 75 feet wide, with curtain walls 7½ feet high, made from fine linen. The bases supporting its walls will be made of bronze.

19 "All the articles used in the work of the Tabernacle, including all the tent pegs used to support the Tabernacle and the courtyard curtains, must be made of bronze.

20 "Tell the people of Israel to bring you pure olive oil for the lampstand, so it can be kept burning continually. 21The lampstand will be placed outside the inner curtain of the Most Holy Place in the Tabernacle.* Aaron and his sons will keep the lamps burning in the LORD's

presence day and night. This is a permanent law for the people of Israel, and it must be kept by all future generations.

CHAPTER **28**

Clothing for the Priests

"Your brother, Aaron, and his sons, Nadab, Abihu, Eleazar, and Ithamar, will be set apart from the common people. They will be my priests and will minister to me. 2Make special clothing for Aaron to show his separation to God—beautiful garments that will lend dignity to his work. 3Instruct all those who have special skills as tailors to make the garments that will set Aaron apart from everyone else, so he may serve me as a priest. 4They are to make a chestpiece, an ephod, a robe, an embroidered tunic, a turban, and a sash. They will also make special garments for Aaron's sons to wear when they serve as priests before me. 5These items must be made of fine linen cloth and embroidered with gold thread and blue, purple, and scarlet yarn.

Design of the Ephod

6 "The ephod must be made of fine linen cloth and skillfully embroidered with gold thread and blue, purple, and scarlet yarn. 7It will consist of two pieces, front and back, joined at the shoulders with two shoulder-pieces. 8And the sash will be made of the same materials: fine linen cloth embroidered with gold thread and blue, purple, and scarlet yarn. 9Take two onyx stones and engrave on them the names of the tribes of Israel. 10Six names will be on each stone, naming all the tribes in the order of their ancestors' births. 11Engrave these names in the same way a gemcutter engraves a seal. Mount the stones in gold settings. 12Fasten the two stones on the shoulder-pieces of the ephod as memorial stones for the people of Israel. Aaron will carry these names before the LORD as a constant reminder. 13The settings are to be made of gold filigree, 14and two cords made of pure gold will be attached to the settings on the shoulders of the ephod.

Design of the Chestpiece

15 "Then, with the most careful workmanship, make a chestpiece that will be used to determine God's will. Use the same materials as you did for the ephod: fine linen cloth embroidered with gold thread and blue, purple, and scarlet yarn. 16This chestpiece will be made of two folds of cloth, forming a pouch nine inches* square.

27:21 Hebrew *in the Tent of Meeting, outside of the inner curtain, in front of the Testimony.*   **28:16** Hebrew *1 span* [23 centimeters].

17Four rows of gemstones* will be attached to it. The first row will contain a red carnelian, a chrysolite, and an emerald. 18The second row will contain a turquoise, a sapphire, and a white moonstone. 19The third row will contain a jacinth, an agate, and an amethyst. 20The fourth row will contain a beryl, an onyx, and a jasper. All these stones will be set in gold. 21Each stone will represent one of the tribes of Israel, and the name of that tribe will be engraved on it as though it were a seal.

22"To attach the chestpiece to the ephod, make braided cords of pure gold. 23Then make two gold rings and attach them to the top corners of the chestpiece. 24The two gold cords will go through the rings on the chestpiece, 25and the ends of the cords will be tied to the gold settings on the shoulder-pieces of the ephod. 26Then make two more gold rings, and attach them to the two lower inside corners of the chestpiece next to the ephod. 27And make two more gold rings and attach them to the ephod near the sash. 28Then attach the bottom rings of the chestpiece to the rings on the ephod with blue cords. This will hold the chestpiece securely to the ephod above the beautiful sash. 29In this way, Aaron will carry the names of the tribes of Israel on the chestpiece over his heart when he goes into the presence of the LORD in the Holy Place. Thus, the LORD will be reminded of his people continually. 30Insert into the pocket of the chestpiece the Urim and Thummim, to be carried over Aaron's heart when he goes into the LORD's presence. Thus, Aaron will always carry the objects used to determine the LORD's will for his people whenever he goes in before the LORD.

Additional Clothing for the Priests

31"Make the robe of the ephod entirely of blue cloth, 32with an opening for Aaron's head in the middle of it. The opening will be reinforced by a woven collar* so it will not tear. 33Make pomegranates out of blue, purple, and scarlet yarn, and attach them to the hem of the robe, with gold bells between them. 34The gold bells and pomegranates are to alternate all the way around the hem. 35Aaron will wear this robe whenever he enters the Holy Place to minister to the LORD, and the bells will tinkle as he goes in and out of the LORD's presence. If he wears it, he will not die.

36"Next make a medallion of pure gold. Using the techniques of an engraver, inscribe it with these words: SET APART AS HOLY TO THE LORD.

37This medallion will be attached to the front of Aaron's turban by means of a blue cord. 38Aaron will wear it on his forehead, thus bearing the guilt connected with any errors regarding the sacred offerings of the people of Israel. He must always wear it so the LORD will accept the people.

39"Weave Aaron's patterned tunic from fine linen cloth. Fashion the turban out of this linen as well. Also make him an embroidered sash.

40"Then for Aaron's sons, make tunics, sashes, and headdresses to give them dignity and respect. 41Clothe Aaron and his sons with these garments, and then anoint and ordain them. Set them apart as holy so they can serve as my priests. 42Also make linen underclothes for them, to be worn next to their bodies, reaching from waist to thigh. 43These must be worn whenever Aaron and his sons enter the Tabernacle* or approach the altar in the Holy Place to perform their duties. Thus they will not incur guilt and die. This law is permanent for Aaron and his descendants.

CHAPTER **29**

Dedication of the Priests

"This is the ceremony for the dedication of Aaron and his sons as priests: Take a young bull and two rams with no physical defects. 2Then using fine wheat flour and no yeast, make loaves of bread, thin cakes mixed with olive oil, and wafers with oil poured over them. 3Place these various kinds of bread in a single basket, and present them at the entrance of the Tabernacle, along with the young bull and the two rams.

4"Present Aaron and his sons at the entrance of the Tabernacle,* and wash them with water. 5Then put Aaron's tunic on him, along with the embroidered robe of the ephod, the ephod itself, the chestpiece, and the sash. 6And place on his head the turban with the gold medallion. 7Then take the anointing oil and pour it over his head. 8Next present his sons, and dress them in their tunics 9with their woven sashes and their headdresses. They will then be priests forever. In this way, you will ordain Aaron and his sons.

10"Then bring the young bull to the entrance of the Tabernacle, and Aaron and his sons will lay their hands on its head. 11You will then slaughter it in the LORD's presence at the entrance of the Tabernacle. 12Smear some of its blood on the horns of the altar with your finger, and pour out the rest at the base of the altar. 13Take all the fat that covers the internal organs, also the long lobe

---

28:17 The identification of some of these gemstones is uncertain. **28:32** The meaning of the Hebrew is uncertain. **28:43** Hebrew *Tent of Meeting.* **29:4** Hebrew *Tent of Meeting;* also in 29:10, 11, 30, 32, 42, 44.

of the liver and the two kidneys with their fat, and burn them on the altar. 14Then take the carcass (including the skin and the dung) outside the camp, and burn it as a sin offering.

15 "Next Aaron and his sons must lay their hands on the head of one of the rams 16as it is slaughtered. Its blood will be collected and sprinkled on the sides of the altar. 17Cut up the ram and wash off the internal organs and the legs. Set them alongside the head and the other pieces of the body, 18and burn them all on the altar. This is a burnt offering to the LORD, which is very pleasing to him.

19 "Now take the other ram and have Aaron and his sons lay their hands on its head 20as it is slaughtered. Collect the blood and place some of it on the tip of the right earlobes of Aaron and his sons. Also put it on their right thumbs and the big toes of their right feet. Sprinkle the rest of the blood on the sides of the altar. 21Then take some of the blood from the altar and mix it with some of the anointing oil. Sprinkle it on Aaron and his sons and on their clothes. In this way, they and their clothing will be set apart as holy to the LORD.

22 "Since this is the ram for the ordination of Aaron and his sons, take the fat of the ram, including the fat tail and the fat that covers the internal organs. Also, take the long lobe of the liver, the two kidneys with their fat, and the right thigh. 23Then take one loaf of bread, one cake mixed with olive oil, and one wafer from the basket of yeastless bread that was placed before the LORD. 24Put all these in the hands of Aaron and his sons to be lifted up as a special gift to the LORD. 25Afterward take the bread from their hands, and burn it on the altar as a burnt offering that will be pleasing to the LORD. 26Then take the breast of Aaron's ordination ram, and lift it up in the LORD's presence as a special gift to him. Afterward keep it for yourself.

27 "Set aside as holy the parts of the ordination ram that belong to Aaron and his sons. This includes the breast and the thigh that were lifted up before the LORD in the ordination ceremony. 28In the future, whenever the people of Israel offer up peace offerings or thanksgiving offerings to the LORD, these parts will be the regular share of Aaron and his descendants.

29 "Aaron's sacred garments must be preserved for his descendants who will succeed him, so they can be anointed and ordained in them. 30Whoever is the next high priest after

Aaron will wear these clothes for seven days before beginning to minister in the Tabernacle and the Holy Place.

31 "Take the ram used in the ordination ceremony, and boil its meat in a sacred place. 32Aaron and his sons are to eat this meat, along with the bread in the basket, at the Tabernacle entrance. 33They alone may eat the meat and bread used for their atonement in the ordination ceremony. The ordinary people may not eat them, for these things are set apart and holy. 34If any of the ordination meat or bread remains until the morning, it must be burned. It may not be eaten, for it is holy.

35 "This is how you will ordain Aaron and his sons to their offices. The ordination ceremony will go on for seven days. 36Each day you must sacrifice a young bull as an offering for the atonement of sin. Afterward make an offering to cleanse the altar. Purify the altar by making atonement for it; make it holy by anointing it with oil. 37Make atonement for the altar every day for seven days. After that, the altar will be exceedingly holy, and whatever touches it will become holy.

38 "This is what you are to offer on the altar. Offer two one-year-old lambs each day, 39one in the morning and the other in the evening. 40With one of them, offer two quarts of fine flour mixed with one quart of olive oil; also, offer one quart of wine* as a drink offering. 41Offer the other lamb in the evening, along with the same offerings of flour and wine as in the morning. It will be a fragrant offering to the LORD, an offering made by fire.

42 "This is to be a daily burnt offering given from generation to generation. Offer it in the LORD's presence at the Tabernacle entrance, where I will meet you and speak with you. 43I will meet the people of Israel there, and the Tabernacle will be sanctified by my glorious presence. 44Yes, I will make the Tabernacle and the altar most holy, and I will set apart Aaron and his sons as holy, that they may be my priests. 45I will live among the people of Israel and be their God, 46and they will know that I am the LORD their God. I am the one who brought them out of Egypt so that I could live among them. I am the LORD their God.

CHAPTER **30**

Plans for the Incense Altar

"Then make a small altar out of acacia wood for burning incense. 2It must be eighteen inches

29:40 Hebrew 1/10 of an ephah [2 liters] of fine flour . . . 1/4 of a hin [1 liter] of olive oil . . . 1/4 of a hin of wine.

square and three feet high,* with horns at the corners carved from the same piece of wood as the altar. ³Overlay the top, sides, and horns of the altar with pure gold, and run a gold molding around the entire altar. ⁴Beneath the molding, on opposite sides of the altar, attach two gold rings to support the carrying poles. ⁵The poles are to be made of acacia wood and overlaid with gold. ⁶Place the incense altar just outside the inner curtain, opposite the Ark's cover—the place of atonement—that rests on the Ark of the Covenant.* I will meet with you there.

⁷"Every morning when Aaron trims the lamps, he must burn fragrant incense on the altar. ⁸And each evening when he tends to the lamps, he must again burn incense in the LORD's presence. This must be done from generation to generation. ⁹Do not offer any unholy incense on this altar, or any burnt offerings, grain offerings, or drink offerings.

¹⁰"Once a year Aaron must purify the altar by placing on its horns the blood from the offering made for the atonement of sin. This will be a regular, annual event from generation to generation, for this is the LORD's supremely holy altar."

Money for the Tabernacle

¹¹And the LORD said to Moses, ¹²"Whenever you take a census of the people of Israel, each man who is counted must pay a ransom for himself to the LORD. Then there will be no plagues among the people as you count them. ¹³His payment to the LORD will be one-fifth of an ounce* of silver. ¹⁴All who have reached their twentieth birthday must give this offering to the LORD. ¹⁵When this offering is given to the LORD to make atonement for yourselves, the rich must not give more, and the poor must not give less. ¹⁶Use this money for the care of the Tabernacle.* It will bring you, the Israelites, to the LORD's attention, and it will make atonement for your lives."

Plans for the Washbasin

¹⁷And the LORD said to Moses, ¹⁸"Make a large bronze washbasin with a bronze pedestal. Put it between the Tabernacle and the altar, and fill it with water. ¹⁹Aaron and his sons will wash their hands and feet there ²⁰before they go into the Tabernacle to appear before the LORD and before they approach the altar to burn offerings to the LORD. They must always wash before ministering

in these ways, or they will die. ²¹This is a permanent law for Aaron and his descendants, to be kept from generation to generation."

The Anointing Oil

²²Then the LORD said to Moses, ²³"Collect choice spices—12½ pounds of pure myrrh, 6¼ pounds* each of cinnamon and of sweet cane, ²⁴12½ pounds of cassia, and one gallon* of olive oil. ²⁵Blend these ingredients into a holy anointing oil. ²⁶Use this scented oil to anoint the Tabernacle, the Ark of the Covenant, ²⁷the table and all its utensils, the lampstand and all its accessories, the incense altar, ²⁸the altar of burnt offering with all its utensils, and the large washbasin with its pedestal. ²⁹Sanctify them to make them entirely holy. After this, whatever touches them will become holy. ³⁰Use this oil also to anoint Aaron and his sons, sanctifying them so they can minister before me as priests. ³¹And say to the people of Israel, 'This will always be my holy anointing oil. ³²It must never be poured on the body of an ordinary person, and you must never make any of it for yourselves. It is holy, and you must treat it as holy. ³³Anyone who blends scented oil like it or puts any of it on someone who is not a priest will be cut off from the community.'"

The Incense

³⁴These were the LORD's instructions to Moses concerning the incense: "Gather sweet spices—resin droplets, mollusk scent, galbanum, and pure frankincense—weighing out the same amounts of each. ³⁵Using the usual techniques of the incense maker, refine it to produce a pure and holy incense. ³⁶Beat some of it very fine and put some of it in front of the Ark of the Covenant, where I will meet with you in the Tabernacle. This incense is most holy. ³⁷Never make this incense for yourselves. It is reserved for the LORD, and you must treat it as holy. ³⁸Those who make it for their own enjoyment will be cut off from the community."

CHAPTER **31**

Craftsmen: Bezalel and Oholiab

The LORD also said to Moses, ²"Look, I have chosen Bezalel son of Uri, grandson of Hur, of the tribe of Judah. ³I have filled him with the Spirit of God, giving him great wisdom, intelligence, and

---

30:2 Hebrew *1 cubit* [45 centimeters] *square and 2 cubits* [90 centimeters] *high.* **30:6** Or *Ark of the Testimony;* also in 30:26, 36. **30:13** Hebrew *half a shekel* [6 grams], *according to the sanctuary shekel, 20 gerahs to each shekel.* **30:16** Hebrew *Tent of Meeting;* also in 30:18, 20, 26, 36. **30:23** Hebrew *500 shekels* [5.7 kilograms] *of pure myrrh, 250 shekels* [2.9 kilograms]. **30:24** Hebrew *500 shekels* [5.7 kilograms] *of cassia, according to the sanctuary shekel, and 1 hin* [3.8 liters].

skill in all kinds of crafts. [4]He is able to create beautiful objects from gold, silver, and bronze. [5]He is skilled in cutting and setting gemstones and in carving wood. Yes, he is a master at every craft!

[6]"And I have appointed Oholiab son of Ahisamach, of the tribe of Dan, to be his assistant. Moreover, I have given special skill to all the naturally talented craftsmen so they can make all the things I have instructed you to make: [7]the Tabernacle itself; the Ark of the Covenant;* the Ark's cover—the place of atonement; all the furnishings of the Tabernacle; [8]the table and all its utensils; the gold lampstand with all its accessories; the incense altar; [9]the altar of burnt offering with all its utensils; the washbasin and its pedestal; [10]the beautifully stitched, holy garments for Aaron the priest, and the garments for his sons to wear as they minister as priests; [11]the anointing oil; and the special incense for the Holy Place. They must follow exactly all the instructions I have given you."

Instructions for the Sabbath

[12]The LORD then gave these further instructions to Moses: [13]"Tell the people of Israel to keep my Sabbath day, for the Sabbath is a sign of the covenant between me and you forever. It helps you to remember that I am the LORD, who makes you holy. [14]Yes, keep the Sabbath day, for it is holy. Anyone who desecrates it must die; anyone who works on that day will be cut off from the community. [15]Work six days only, but the seventh day must be a day of total rest. I repeat: Because the LORD considers it a holy day, anyone who works on the Sabbath must be put to death. [16]The people of Israel must keep the Sabbath day forever. [17]It is a permanent sign of my covenant with them. For in six days the LORD made heaven and earth, but he rested on the seventh day and was refreshed."

[18]Then as the LORD finished speaking with Moses on Mount Sinai, he gave him the two stone tablets inscribed with the terms of the covenant,* written by the finger of God.

CHAPTER **32**
The Calf of Gold

When Moses failed to come back down the mountain right away, the people went to Aaron. "Look," they said, "make us some gods who can lead us. This man Moses, who brought us here from Egypt, has disappeared. We don't know what has happened to him."

[2]So Aaron said, "Tell your wives and sons and daughters to take off their gold earrings, and then bring them to me."

[3]All the people obeyed Aaron and brought him their gold earrings. [4]Then Aaron took the gold, melted it down, and molded and tooled it into the shape of a calf. The people exclaimed, "O Israel, these are the gods who brought you out of Egypt!"

[5]When Aaron saw how excited the people were about it, he built an altar in front of the calf and announced, "Tomorrow there will be a festival to the LORD!"

[6]So the people got up early the next morning to sacrifice burnt offerings and peace offerings. After this, they celebrated with feasting and drinking, and indulged themselves in pagan revelry.

[7]Then the LORD told Moses, "Quick! Go down the mountain! The people you brought from Egypt have defiled themselves. [8]They have already turned from the way I commanded them to live. They have made an idol shaped like a calf, and they have worshiped and sacrificed to it. They are saying, 'These are your gods, O Israel, who brought you out of Egypt.'"

[9]Then the LORD said, "I have seen how stubborn and rebellious these people are. [10]Now leave me alone so my anger can blaze against them and destroy them all. Then I will make you, Moses, into a great nation instead of them."

[11]But Moses pleaded with the LORD his God not to do it. "O LORD!" he exclaimed. "Why are you so angry with your own people whom you brought from the land of Egypt with such great power and mighty acts? [12]The Egyptians will say, 'God tricked them into coming to the mountains so he could kill them and wipe them from the face of the earth.' Turn away from your fierce anger. Change your mind about this terrible disaster you are planning against your people! [13]Remember your covenant with your servants— Abraham, Isaac, and Jacob.* You swore by your own self, 'I will make your descendants as numerous as the stars of heaven. Yes, I will give them all of this land that I have promised to your descendants, and they will possess it forever.'"

[14]So the LORD withdrew his threat and didn't bring against his people the disaster he had threatened.

[15]Then Moses turned and went down the mountain. He held in his hands the two stone tablets inscribed with the terms of the covenant.* They were inscribed on both sides, front and back. [16]These stone tablets were God's

---

31:7 Hebrew *the Tent of Meeting; the Ark of the Testimony.*   31:18 Hebrew *the Testimony.*   32:13 Hebrew *Israel.*   32:15 Hebrew *the Testimony.*

work; the words on them were written by God himself.

17When Joshua heard the noise of the people shouting below them, he exclaimed to Moses, "It sounds as if there is a war in the camp!"

18But Moses replied, "No, it's neither a cry of victory nor a cry of defeat. It is the sound of a celebration."

19When they came near the camp, Moses saw the calf and the dancing. In terrible anger, he threw the stone tablets to the ground, smashing them at the foot of the mountain. 20He took the calf they had made and melted it in the fire. And when the metal had cooled, he ground it into powder and mixed it with water. Then he made the people drink it.

21After that, he turned to Aaron. "What did the people do to you?" he demanded. "How did they ever make you bring such terrible sin upon them?"

22"Don't get upset, sir," Aaron replied. "You yourself know these people and what a wicked bunch they are. 23They said to me, 'Make us some gods to lead us, for something has happened to this man Moses, who led us out of Egypt.' 24So I told them, 'Bring me your gold earrings.' When they brought them to me, I threw them into the fire—and out came this calf!"

25When Moses saw that Aaron had let the people get completely out of control—and much to the amusement of their enemies—26he stood at the entrance to the camp and shouted, "All of you who are on the LORD's side, come over here and join me." And all the Levites came.

27He told them, "This is what the LORD, the God of Israel, says: Strap on your swords! Go back and forth from one end of the camp to the other, killing even your brothers, friends, and neighbors." 28The Levites obeyed Moses, and about three thousand people died that day.

29Then Moses told the Levites, "Today you have been ordained for the service of the LORD, for you obeyed him even though it meant killing your own sons and brothers. Because of this, he will now give you a great blessing."

Moses Intercedes for Israel

30The next day Moses said to the people, "You have committed a terrible sin, but I will return to the LORD on the mountain. Perhaps I will be able to obtain forgiveness for you."

31So Moses returned to the LORD and said, "Alas, these people have committed a terrible

sin. They have made gods of gold for themselves. 32But now, please forgive their sin—and if not, then blot me out of the record you are keeping."

33The LORD replied to Moses, "I will blot out whoever has sinned against me. 34Now go, lead the people to the place I told you about. Look! My angel will lead the way before you! But when I call the people to account, I will certainly punish them for their sins."

35And the LORD sent a great plague upon the people because they had worshiped the calf Aaron had made.

CHAPTER **33**

The LORD said to Moses, "Now that you have brought these people out of Egypt, lead them to the land I solemnly promised Abraham, Isaac, and Jacob. I told them long ago that I would give this land to their descendants. 2And I will send an angel before you to drive out the Canaanites, Amorites, Hittites, Perizzites, Hivites, and Jebusites. 3Theirs is a land flowing with milk and honey. But I will not travel along with you, for you are a stubborn, unruly people. If I did, I would be tempted to destroy you along the way."

4When the people heard these stern words, they went into mourning and refused to wear their jewelry and ornaments. 5For the LORD had told Moses to tell them, "You are an unruly, stubborn people. If I were there among you for even a moment, I would destroy you. Remove your jewelry and ornaments until I decide what to do with you." 6So from the time they left Mount Sinai,* the Israelites wore no more jewelry.

7It was Moses' custom to set up the tent known as the Tent of Meeting far outside the camp. Everyone who wanted to consult with the LORD would go there.

8Whenever Moses went out to the Tent of Meeting, all the people would get up and stand in their tent entrances. They would all watch Moses until he disappeared inside. 9As he went into the tent, the pillar of cloud would come down and hover at the entrance while the LORD spoke with Moses. 10Then all the people would stand and bow low at their tent entrances. 11Inside the Tent of Meeting, the LORD would speak to Moses face to face, as a man speaks to his friend. Afterward Moses would return to the camp, but the young man who assisted him, Joshua son of Nun, stayed behind in the Tent of Meeting.

33:6 Hebrew *Horeb,* another name for Sinai.

Moses Sees the LORD's Glory

12Moses said to the LORD, "You have been telling me, 'Take these people up to the Promised Land.' But you haven't told me whom you will send with me. You call me by name and tell me I have found favor with you. 13Please, if this is really so, show me your intentions so I will understand you more fully and do exactly what you want me to do. Besides, don't forget that this nation is your very own people."

14And the LORD replied, "I will personally go with you, Moses. I will give you rest—everything will be fine for you."

15Then Moses said, "If you don't go with us personally, don't let us move a step from this place. 16If you don't go with us, how will anyone ever know that your people and I have found favor with you? How else will they know we are special and distinct from all other people on the earth?"

17And the LORD replied to Moses, "I will indeed do what you have asked, for you have found favor with me, and you are my friend."

18Then Moses had one more request. "Please let me see your glorious presence," he said.

19The LORD replied, "I will make all my goodness pass before you, and I will call out my name, 'the LORD,' to you. I will show kindness to anyone I choose, and I will show mercy to anyone I choose. 20But you may not look directly at my face, for no one may see me and live." 21The LORD continued, "Stand here on this rock beside me. 22As my glorious presence passes by, I will put you in the cleft of the rock and cover you with my hand until I have passed. 23Then I will remove my hand, and you will see me from behind. But my face will not be seen."

CHAPTER **34**

A New Copy of the Covenant

The LORD told Moses, "Prepare two stone tablets like the first ones. I will write on them the same words that were on the tablets you smashed. 2Be ready in the morning to come up Mount Sinai and present yourself to me there on the top of the mountain. 3No one else may come with you. In fact, no one is allowed anywhere on the mountain. Do not even let the flocks or herds graze near the mountain."

4So Moses cut two tablets of stone like the first ones. Early in the morning he climbed Mount Sinai as the LORD had told him, carrying the two stone tablets in his hands.

5Then the LORD came down in a pillar of cloud and called out his own name, "the LORD," as Moses stood there in his presence. 6He passed in front of Moses and said, "I am the LORD, I am the LORD, the merciful and gracious God. I am slow to anger and rich in unfailing love and faithfulness. 7I show this unfailing love to many thousands by forgiving every kind of sin and rebellion. Even so I do not leave sin unpunished, but I punish the children for the sins of their parents to the third and fourth generations."

8Moses immediately fell to the ground and worshiped. 9And he said, "If it is true that I have found favor in your sight, O Lord, then please go with us. Yes, this is an unruly and stubborn people, but please pardon our iniquity and our sins. Accept us as your own special possession."

10The LORD replied, "All right. This is the covenant I am going to make with you. I will perform wonders that have never been done before anywhere in all the earth or in any nation. And all the people around you will see the power of the LORD—the awesome power I will display through you. 11Your responsibility is to obey all the commands I am giving you today. Then I will surely drive out all those who stand in your way—the Amorites, Canaanites, Hittites, Perizzites, Hivites, and Jebusites.

12"Be very careful never to make treaties with the people in the land where you are going. If you do, you soon will be following their evil ways. 13Instead, you must break down their pagan altars, smash the sacred pillars they worship, and cut down their carved images. 14You must worship no other gods, but only the LORD, for he is a God who is passionate about his relationship with you.

15"Do not make treaties of any kind with the people living in the land. They are spiritual prostitutes, committing adultery against me by sacrificing to their gods. If you make peace with them, they will invite you to go with them to worship their gods, and you are likely to do it. 16And you will accept their daughters, who worship other gods, as wives for your sons. Then they will cause your sons to commit adultery against me by worshiping other gods. 17You must make no gods for yourselves at all.

18"Be sure to celebrate the Festival of Unleavened Bread for seven days, just as I instructed you, at the appointed time each year in early spring,* for that was when you left Egypt.

19"Every firstborn male belongs to me—of both cattle and sheep. 20A firstborn male donkey may be redeemed from the LORD by presenting a

---

34:18 Hebrew *in the month of Abib.* This month of the Hebrew lunar calendar usually occurs in March and April.

lamb in its place. But if you decide not to make the exchange, you must kill the donkey by breaking its neck. However, you must redeem every firstborn son. No one is allowed to appear before me without a gift.

21 "Six days are set aside for work, but on the Sabbath day you must rest, even during the seasons of plowing and harvest. 22And you must remember to celebrate the Festival of Harvest* with the first crop of the wheat harvest, and celebrate the Festival of the Final Harvest* at the end of the harvest season. 23Three times each year all the men of Israel must appear before the Sovereign LORD, the God of Israel. 24No one will attack and conquer your land when you go to appear before the LORD your God those three times each year. I will drive out the nations that stand in your way and will enlarge your boundaries.

25"You must not offer bread made with yeast as a sacrifice to me. And none of the meat of the Passover lamb may be kept over until the following morning. 26You must bring the best of the first of each year's crop to the house of the LORD your God.

"You must not cook a young goat in its mother's milk."

27And the LORD said to Moses, "Write down all these instructions, for they represent the terms of my covenant with you and with Israel."

28Moses was up on the mountain with the LORD forty days and forty nights. In all that time he neither ate nor drank. At that time he wrote the terms of the covenant—the Ten Commandments—on the stone tablets.

29When Moses came down the mountain carrying the stone tablets inscribed with the terms of the covenant,* he wasn't aware that his face glowed because he had spoken to the LORD face to face. 30And when Aaron and the people of Israel saw the radiance of Moses' face, they were afraid to come near him.

31But Moses called to them and asked Aaron and the community leaders to come over and talk with him. 32Then all the people came, and Moses gave them the instructions the LORD had given him on Mount Sinai. 33When Moses had finished speaking with them, he put a veil over his face. 34But whenever he went into the Tent of Meeting to speak with the LORD, he removed the veil until he came out again. Then he would give the people whatever instructions the LORD had given him, 35and the people would see his face

aglow. Afterward he would put the veil on again until he returned to speak with the LORD.

CHAPTER **35**

Instructions for the Sabbath

Now Moses called a meeting of all the people and told them, "You must obey these instructions from the LORD. 2Each week, work for six days only. The seventh day is a day of total rest, a holy day that belongs to the LORD. Anyone who works on that day will die. 3Do not even light fires in your homes on that day."

Gifts for the Tabernacle

4Then Moses said to all the people, "This is what the LORD has commanded. 5Everyone is invited to bring these offerings to the LORD: gold, silver, and bronze; 6blue, purple, and scarlet yarn; fine linen; goat hair for cloth; 7tanned ram skins and fine goatskin leather; acacia wood; 8olive oil for the lamps; spices for the anointing oil and the fragrant incense; 9onyx stones, and other stones to be set in the ephod and the chestpiece.

10"Come, all of you who are gifted craftsmen. Construct everything that the LORD has commanded: 11the entire Tabernacle, including the sacred tent and its coverings, the clasps, frames, crossbars, posts, and bases; 12the Ark and its poles; the Ark's cover—the place of atonement; the inner curtain to enclose the Ark in the Most Holy Place; 13the table, its carrying poles, and all of its utensils; the Bread of the Presence; 14the lampstand and its accessories; the lamp cups and the oil for lighting; 15the incense altar and its carrying poles; the anointing oil and fragrant incense; the curtain for the entrance of the Tabernacle; 16the altar of burnt offering; the bronze grating of the altar and its carrying poles and utensils; the large washbasin with its pedestal; 17the curtains for the walls of the courtyard; the posts and their bases; the curtain for the entrance to the courtyard; 18the tent pegs of the Tabernacle and courtyard and their cords; 19the beautifully stitched clothing for the priests to wear while ministering in the Holy Place; the sacred garments for Aaron and his sons to wear while officiating as priests."

20So all the people left Moses and went to their tents to prepare their gifts. 21If their hearts were stirred and they desired to do so, they brought to the LORD their offerings of materials for the Tabernacle* and its furnishings and for the holy garments. 22Both men and women

34:22a Or *Festival of Weeks.*   34:22b This was later called the Festival of Shelters; see Lev 23:33-36.   34:29 Hebrew *the Testimony.*
35:21 Hebrew *Tent of Meeting.*

came, all whose hearts were willing. Some brought to the LORD their offerings of gold—medallions, earrings, rings from their fingers, and necklaces. They presented gold objects of every kind to the LORD. 23Others brought blue, purple, and scarlet yarn, fine linen, or goat hair for cloth. Some gave tanned ram skins or fine goatskin leather. 24Others brought silver and bronze objects as their offering to the LORD. And those who had acacia wood brought it.

25All the women who were skilled in sewing and spinning prepared blue, purple, and scarlet yarn, and fine linen cloth, and they brought them in. 26All the women who were willing used their skills to spin and weave the goat hair into cloth. 27The leaders brought onyx stones and the other gemstones to be used for the ephod and the chestpiece. 28They also brought spices and olive oil for the light, the anointing oil, and the fragrant incense. 29So the people of Israel—every man and woman who wanted to help in the work the LORD had given them through Moses—brought their offerings to the LORD.

30And Moses told them, "The LORD has chosen Bezalel son of Uri, grandson of Hur, of the tribe of Judah. 31The LORD has filled Bezalel with the Spirit of God, giving him great wisdom, intelligence, and skill in all kinds of crafts. 32He is able to create beautiful objects from gold, silver, and bronze. 33He is skilled in cutting and setting gemstones and in carving wood. In fact, he has every necessary skill. 34And the LORD has given both him and Oholiab son of Ahisamach, of the tribe of Dan, the ability to teach their skills to others. 35The LORD has given them special skills as jewelers, designers, weavers, and embroiderers in blue, purple, and scarlet yarn on fine linen cloth. They excel in all the crafts needed for the work.

CHAPTER **36**

"Bezalel, Oholiab, and the other craftsmen whom the LORD has gifted with wisdom, skill, and intelligence will construct and furnish the Tabernacle, just as the LORD has commanded."

2So Moses told Bezalel and Oholiab to begin the work, along with all those who were specially gifted by the LORD. 3Moses gave them the materials donated by the people for the completion of the sanctuary. Additional gifts were brought each morning. 4But finally the craftsmen left their work to meet with Moses. 5"We have more than enough materials on hand now

to complete the job the LORD has given us to do!" they exclaimed.

6So Moses gave the command, and this message was sent throughout the camp: "Bring no more materials! You have already given more than enough." So the people stopped bringing their offerings. 7Their contributions were more than enough to complete the whole project.

Building the Tabernacle

8The skilled weavers first made ten sheets from fine linen. One of the craftsmen then embroidered blue, purple, and scarlet cherubim into them. 9Each sheet was exactly the same size—forty-two feet long and six feet wide.* 10Five of these sheets were joined together to make one set, and a second set was made of the other five. 11Fifty blue loops were placed along the edge of the last sheet in each set. 12The fifty loops along the edge of the first set of sheets matched the loops along the edge of the second set. 13Then fifty gold clasps were made to connect the loops on the edge of each set. Thus the Tabernacle was joined together in one piece.

14Above the Tabernacle, a roof covering was made from eleven sheets of cloth made from goat hair. 15Each sheet was exactly the same size—forty-five feet long and six feet wide. 16The craftsmen joined five of these sheets together to make one set, and the six remaining sheets were joined to make a second set. 17Then they made fifty loops along the edge of the last sheet in each set. 18They also made fifty small bronze clasps to couple the loops, so the two sets of sheets were firmly attached to each other. In this way, the roof covering was joined together in one piece. 19Then they made two more layers for the roof covering. The first was made of tanned ram skins, and the second was made of fine goatskin leather.

20For the framework of the Tabernacle, they made frames of acacia wood standing on end. 21Each frame was 15 feet high and 2¼ feet wide. 22There were two pegs on each frame so they could be joined to the next frame. All the frames were made this way. 23They made twenty frames to support the south side, 24along with forty silver bases, two for each frame. 25They also made twenty frames for the north side of the Tabernacle, 26along with forty silver bases, two for each frame. 27The west side of the Tabernacle, which was its rear, was made from six frames, 28plus an extra frame at each corner. 29These corner frames were connected at the bottom and

36:9 Hebrew *28 cubits* [12.6 meters] *long and 4 cubits* [1.8 meters] *wide.* In this chapter, the distance measures are calculated from the Hebrew cubit at a ratio of 18 inches or 45 centimeters per cubit.

firmly attached at the top with a single ring, forming a single unit from top to bottom. They made two of these, one for each rear corner. ³⁰So for the west side they made a total of eight frames, along with sixteen silver bases, two for each frame.

³¹Then they made five crossbars from acacia wood to tie the frames on the south side together. ³²They made another five for the north side and five for the west side. ³³The middle crossbar of the five was halfway up the frames, along each side, running from one end to the other. ³⁴The frames and crossbars were all overlaid with gold. The rings used to hold the crossbars were made of pure gold.

³⁵The inner curtain was made of fine linen cloth, and cherubim were skillfully embroidered into it with blue, purple, and scarlet yarn. ³⁶This curtain was then attached to four gold hooks set into four posts of acacia wood. The posts were overlaid with gold and set into four silver bases.

³⁷Then they made another curtain for the entrance to the sacred tent. It was made of fine linen cloth and embroidered with blue, purple, and scarlet yarn. ³⁸This curtain was connected by five hooks to five posts. The posts with their decorated tops and bands were overlaid with gold. The five bases were molded from bronze.

CHAPTER **37**

Building the Ark

Next Bezalel made the Ark out of acacia wood. It was 3¾ feet long, 2¼ feet wide, and 2¼ feet high.* ²It was overlaid with pure gold inside and out, and it had a molding of gold all the way around. ³Four gold rings were fastened to its four feet, two rings at each side. ⁴Then he made poles from acacia wood and overlaid them with gold. ⁵He put the poles into the rings at the sides of the Ark to carry it.

⁶Then, from pure gold, he made the Ark's cover—the place of atonement. It was 3¾ feet long and 2¼ feet wide. ⁷He made two figures of cherubim out of hammered gold and placed them at the two ends of the atonement cover. ⁸They were made so they were actually a part of the atonement cover—it was all one piece. ⁹The cherubim faced each other as they looked down on the atonement cover, and their wings were stretched out above the atonement cover to protect it.

Building the Table

¹⁰Then he made a table out of acacia wood, 3 feet long, 1½ feet wide, and 2¼ feet high. ¹¹It was overlaid with pure gold, with a gold molding all around the edge. ¹²A rim about 3 inches* wide was attached along the edges of the table, and a gold molding ran around the rim. ¹³Then he cast four rings of gold and attached them to the four table legs ¹⁴next to the rim. These were made to hold the carrying poles in place. ¹⁵He made the carrying poles of acacia wood and overlaid them with gold. ¹⁶Next, using pure gold, he made the plates, dishes, bowls, and pitchers to be placed on the table. These utensils were to be used in pouring out drink offerings.

Building the Lampstand

¹⁷Then he made the lampstand, again using pure, hammered gold. Its base, center stem, lamp cups, blossoms, and buds were all of one piece. ¹⁸The lampstand had six branches, three going out from each side of the center stem. ¹⁹Each of the six branches held a cup shaped like an almond blossom, complete with buds and petals. ²⁰The center stem of the lampstand was also decorated with four almond blossoms. ²¹One blossom was set beneath each pair of branches, where they extended from the center stem. ²²The decorations and branches were all one piece with the stem, and they were hammered from pure gold. ²³He also made the seven lamps, the lamp snuffers, and the trays, all of pure gold. ²⁴The entire lampstand, along with its accessories, was made from seventy-five pounds* of pure gold.

Building the Incense Altar

²⁵The incense altar was made of acacia wood. It was eighteen inches square and three feet high, with its corner horns made from the same piece of wood as the altar itself. ²⁶He overlaid the top, sides, and horns of the altar with pure gold and ran a gold molding around the edge. ²⁷Two gold rings were placed on opposite sides, beneath the molding, to hold the carrying poles. ²⁸The carrying poles were made of acacia wood and were overlaid with gold.

²⁹Then he made the sacred oil, for anointing the priests, and the fragrant incense, using the techniques of the most skilled incense maker.

CHAPTER **38**

Building the Altar of Burnt Offering

The altar for burning animal sacrifices also was

37:1 Hebrew *2½ cubits* [1.1 meters] *long, 1½ cubits* [0.7 meters] *wide, and 1½ cubits high.* In this chapter, the distance measures are calculated from the Hebrew cubit at a ratio of 18 inches or 45 centimeters per cubit.   **37:12** Hebrew *a handbreadth* [8 centimeters].   **37:24** Hebrew *1 talent* [34 kilograms].

constructed of acacia wood. It was 7½ feet square at the top and 4½ feet high.* ²There were four horns, one at each of the four corners, all of one piece with the rest. This altar was overlaid with bronze. ³Then he made all the bronze utensils to be used with the altar—the ash buckets, shovels, basins, meat hooks, and firepans. ⁴Next he made a bronze grating that rested on a ledge about halfway down into the firebox. ⁵Four rings were cast for each side of the grating to support the carrying poles. ⁶The carrying poles themselves were made of acacia wood and were overlaid with bronze. ⁷These poles were inserted into the rings at the side of the altar. The altar was hollow and was made from planks.

Building the Washbasin

⁸The bronze washbasin and its bronze pedestal were cast from bronze mirrors donated by the women who served at the entrance of the Tabernacle.*

Building the Courtyard

⁹Then he constructed the courtyard. The south wall was 150 feet long. It consisted of curtains made of fine linen. ¹⁰There were twenty posts, each with its own bronze base, and there were silver hooks and rods to hold up the curtains. ¹¹The north wall was also 150 feet long, with twenty bronze posts and bases and with silver hooks and rods. ¹²The west end was 75 feet wide. The walls were made from curtains supported by ten posts and bases and with silver hooks and rods. ¹³The east end was also 75 feet wide. ¹⁴The courtyard entrance was on the east side, flanked by two curtains. The curtain on the right side was 22½ feet long and was supported by three posts set into three bases. ¹⁵The curtain on the left side was also 22½ feet long and was supported by three posts set into three bases. ¹⁶All the curtains used in the courtyard walls were made of fine linen. ¹⁷Each post had a bronze base, and all the hooks and rods were silver. The tops of the posts were overlaid with silver, and the rods to hold up the curtains were solid silver. ¹⁸The curtain that covered the entrance to the courtyard was made of fine linen cloth and embroidered with blue, purple, and scarlet yarn. It was 30 feet long and 7½ feet high, just like the

curtains of the courtyard walls. ¹⁹It was supported by four posts set into four bronze bases. The tops of the posts were overlaid with silver, and the hooks and rods were also made of silver. ²⁰All the tent pegs used in the Tabernacle and courtyard were made of bronze.

Inventory of Materials

²¹Here is an inventory of the materials used in building the Tabernacle of the Covenant.* Moses directed the Levites to compile the figures, and Ithamar son of Aaron the priest served as recorder. ²²Bezalel son of Uri, grandson of Hur, of the tribe of Judah, was in charge of the whole project, just as the LORD had commanded Moses. ²³He was assisted by Oholiab son of Ahisamach, of the tribe of Dan, a craftsman expert at engraving, designing, and embroidering blue, purple, and scarlet yarn on fine linen cloth.

²⁴The people brought gifts of gold totaling about 2,200 pounds,* all of which was used throughout the Tabernacle.

²⁵The amount of silver that was given was about 7,545 pounds.* ²⁶It came from the tax of one-fifth of an ounce of silver* collected from each of those registered in the census. This included all the men who were twenty years old or older, 603,550 in all. ²⁷The 100 bases for the frames of the sanctuary walls and for the posts supporting the inner curtain required 7,500 pounds of silver, about 75 pounds for each base.* ²⁸The rest of the silver, about 45 pounds,* was used to make the rods and hooks and to overlay the tops of the posts.

²⁹The people also brought 5,310 pounds* of bronze, ³⁰which was used for casting the bases for the posts at the entrance to the Tabernacle, and for the bronze altar with its bronze grating and altar utensils. ³¹Bronze was also used to make the bases for the posts that supported the curtains around the courtyard, the bases for the curtain at the entrance of the courtyard, and all the tent pegs used to hold the curtains of the courtyard in place.

CHAPTER 39
Clothing for the Priests

For the priests, the craftsmen made beautiful garments of blue, purple, and scarlet cloth—

38:1 Hebrew 5 cubits [2.3 meters] square at the top, and 3 cubits [1.4 meters] high. In this chapter, the distance measures are calculated from the Hebrew cubit at a ratio of 18 inches or 45 centimeters per cubit. 38:8 Hebrew Tent of Meeting; also in 38:30. 38:21 Hebrew the Tabernacle, the Tabernacle of the Testimony. 38:24 Hebrew 29 talents [2,175 pounds or 986 kilograms] and 730 shekels [18.3 pounds or 8.3 kilograms], according to the sanctuary shekel. 38:25 Hebrew 100 talents [7,500 pounds or 3,400 kilograms] and 1,775 shekels [44.4 pounds or 20.2 kilograms], according to the sanctuary shekel. 38:26 Hebrew 1 beka [6 grams] per person, that is, half a shekel, according to the sanctuary shekel. 38:27 Hebrew 100 talents [3,400 kilograms] of silver, 1 talent [34 kilograms] for each base. 38:28 Hebrew 1,775 shekels [20.2 kilograms]. 38:29 Hebrew 70 talents [5,250 pounds or 2,380 kilograms] and 2,400 shekels [60 pounds or 27.4 kilograms].

clothing to be worn while ministering in the Holy Place. This same cloth was used for Aaron's sacred garments, just as the LORD had commanded Moses.

Making the Ephod

2The ephod was made from fine linen cloth and embroidered with gold thread and blue, purple, and scarlet yarn. 3A skilled craftsman made gold thread by beating gold into thin sheets and cutting it into fine strips. He then embroidered it into the linen with the blue, purple, and scarlet yarn.

4They made two shoulder-pieces for the ephod, which were attached to its corners so it could be tied down. 5They also made an elaborate woven sash of the same materials: fine linen cloth; blue, purple, and scarlet yarn; and gold thread, just as the LORD had commanded Moses. 6The two onyx stones, attached to the shoulder-pieces of the ephod, were set in gold filigree. The stones were engraved with the names of the tribes of Israel, just as initials are engraved on a seal. 7These stones served as reminders to the LORD concerning the people of Israel. All this was done just as the LORD had commanded Moses.

Making the Chestpiece

8The chestpiece was made in the same style as the ephod, crafted from fine linen cloth and embroidered with gold thread and blue, purple, and scarlet yarn. 9It was doubled over to form a pouch, nine inches* square. 10Four rows of gemstones* were set across it. In the first row were a red carnelian, a chrysolite, and an emerald. 11In the second row were a turquoise, a sapphire, and a white moonstone. 12In the third row were a jacinth, an agate, and an amethyst. 13In the fourth row were a beryl, an onyx, and a jasper. Each of these gemstones was set in gold. 14The stones were engraved like a seal, each with the name of one of the twelve tribes of Israel.

15To attach the chestpiece to the ephod, they made braided cords of pure gold. 16They also made two gold rings and attached them to the top corners of the chestpiece. 17The two gold cords were put through the gold rings on the chestpiece, 18and the ends of the cords were tied to the gold settings on the shoulder-pieces of the ephod. 19Two more gold rings were attached to the lower inside corners of the chestpiece next to the ephod. 20Then two gold rings were attached to the ephod near the sash. 21Blue cords were used to attach the bottom rings of the chestpiece to the rings on the ephod. In this way, the chestpiece was held securely to the ephod above the beautiful sash. All this was done just as the LORD had commanded Moses.

Additional Clothing for the Priests

22The robe of the ephod was woven entirely of blue yarn, 23with an opening for Aaron's head in the middle of it. The edge of this opening was reinforced with a woven collar,* so it would not tear. 24Pomegranates were attached to the bottom edge of the robe. These were finely crafted of blue, purple, and scarlet yarn. 25Bells of pure gold were placed between the pomegranates along the hem of the robe, 26with bells and pomegranates alternating all around the hem. This robe was to be worn when Aaron ministered to the LORD, just as the LORD had commanded Moses.

27Tunics were then made for Aaron and his sons from fine linen cloth. 28The turban, the headdresses, and the underclothes were all made of this fine linen. 29The sashes were made of fine linen cloth and embroidered with blue, purple, and scarlet yarn, just as the LORD had commanded Moses. 30Finally, they made the sacred medallion of pure gold to be worn on the front of the turban. Using the techniques of an engraver, they inscribed it with these words: SET APART AS HOLY TO THE LORD. 31This medallion was tied to the turban with a blue cord, just as the LORD had commanded Moses.

Moses Inspects the Work

32And so at last the Tabernacle* was finished. The Israelites had done everything just as the LORD had commanded Moses. 33And they brought the entire Tabernacle to Moses: the sacred tent with all its furnishings, the clasps, frames, crossbars, posts, and bases; 34the layers of tanned ram skins and fine goatskin leather; the inner curtain that enclosed the Most Holy Place; 35the Ark of the Covenant* and its carrying poles; the Ark's cover—the place of atonement; 36the table and all its utensils; the Bread of the Presence; 37the gold lampstand and its accessories; the lamp cups and the oil for lighting; 38the gold altar; the anointing oil; the fragrant incense; the curtain for the entrance of the sacred tent; 39the bronze altar; the bronze grating; its poles and utensils; the large washbasin and its pedestal; 40the curtains for the walls of

39:9 Hebrew *1 span* [23 centimeters]. 39:10 The identification of some of these gemstones is uncertain. 39:23 The meaning of the Hebrew is uncertain. 39:32 Hebrew *the Tabernacle, the Tent of Meeting;* also in 39:40. 39:35 Or *Ark of the Testimony.*

the courtyard and the posts and bases holding them up; the curtain at the courtyard entrance; the cords and tent pegs; all the articles used in the operation of the Tabernacle; 41the beautifully crafted garments to be worn while ministering in the Holy Place—the holy garments for Aaron the priest and for his sons to wear while on duty.

42So the people of Israel followed all of the LORD's instructions to Moses. 43Moses inspected all their work and blessed them because it had been done as the LORD had commanded him.

CHAPTER **40**

The Tabernacle Completed

The LORD now said to Moses, 2"Set up the Tabernacle* on the first day of the new year.* 3Place the Ark of the Covenant* inside, and install the inner curtain to enclose the Ark within the Most Holy Place. 4Then bring in the table, and arrange the utensils on it. And bring in the lampstand, and set up the lamps.

5"Place the incense altar just outside the inner curtain, opposite the Ark of the Covenant. Set up the curtain made for the entrance of the Tabernacle. 6Place the altar of burnt offering in front of the Tabernacle entrance. 7Set the large washbasin between the Tabernacle* and the altar and fill it with water. 8Then set up the courtyard around the outside of the tent, and hang the curtain for the courtyard entrance.

9"Take the anointing oil and sprinkle it on the Tabernacle and on all its furnishings to make them holy. 10Sprinkle the anointing oil on the altar of burnt offering and its utensils, sanctifying them. Then the altar will become most holy. 11Next anoint the large washbasin and its pedestal to make them holy.

12"Bring Aaron and his sons to the entrance of the Tabernacle, and wash them with water. 13Clothe Aaron with the holy garments and anoint him, setting him apart to serve me as a priest. 14Then bring his sons and dress them in their tunics. 15Anoint them as you did their father, so they may serve me as priests. With this anointing, Aaron's descendants are set apart for the priesthood forever, from generation to generation."

16Moses proceeded to do everything as the LORD had commanded him. 17So the Tabernacle was set up on the first day of the new year.*

18Moses put it together by setting its frames into their bases and attaching the crossbars and raising the posts. 19Then he spread the coverings over the Tabernacle framework and put on the roof layers, just as the LORD had commanded him.

20He placed inside the Ark the stone tablets inscribed with the terms of the covenant,* and then he attached the Ark's carrying poles. He also set the Ark's cover—the place of atonement—on top of it. 21Then he brought the Ark of the Covenant into the Tabernacle and set up the inner curtain to shield it from view, just as the LORD had commanded.

22Next he placed the table in the Tabernacle, along the north side of the Holy Place, just outside the inner curtain. 23And he arranged the Bread of the Presence on the table that stands before the LORD, just as the LORD had commanded.

24He set the lampstand in the Tabernacle across from the table on the south side of the Holy Place. 25Then he set up the lamps in the LORD's presence, just as the LORD had commanded. 26He also placed the incense altar in the Tabernacle, in the Holy Place in front of the inner curtain. 27On it he burned the fragrant incense made from sweet spices, just as the LORD had commanded.

28He attached the curtain at the entrance of the Tabernacle, 29and he placed the altar of burnt offering near the Tabernacle entrance. On it he offered a burnt offering and a grain offering, just as the LORD had commanded.

30Next he placed the large washbasin between the Tabernacle and the altar. He filled it with water so the priests could use it to wash themselves. 31Moses and Aaron and Aaron's sons washed their hands and feet in the basin. 32Whenever they walked past the altar to enter the Tabernacle, they were to stop and wash, just as the LORD had commanded Moses.

33Then he hung the curtains forming the courtyard around the Tabernacle and the altar. And he set up the curtain at the entrance of the courtyard. So at last Moses finished the work.

The LORD's Glory Fills the Tabernacle

34Then the cloud covered the Tabernacle, and the glorious presence of the LORD filled it. 35Moses was no longer able to enter the Tabernacle because the cloud had settled down over

40:2a Hebrew *the Tabernacle, the Tent of Meeting;* also in 40:6, 29. 40:2b Hebrew *the first day of the first month.* This day of the Hebrew lunar calendar occurs in March or early April. 40:3 Or *Ark of the Testimony;* also in 40:5, 21. 40:7 Hebrew *Tent of Meeting;* also in 40:12, 22, 24, 26, 30, 32, 34, 35. 40:17 Hebrew *the first day of the first month, in the second year.* See note on 40:2b. 40:20 Hebrew *the Testimony.*

it, and the Tabernacle was filled with the awesome glory of the LORD.

36Now whenever the cloud lifted from the Tabernacle and moved, the people of Israel would set out on their journey, following it. 37But if the cloud stayed, they would stay until it moved again. 38The cloud of the LORD rested on the Tabernacle during the day, and at night there was fire in the cloud so all the people of Israel could see it. This continued throughout all their journeys.

Leviticus

CHAPTER 1

Procedures for the Burnt Offering

The LORD called to Moses from the Tabernacle* and said to him, 2"Give the following instructions to the Israelites: Whenever you present offerings to the LORD, you must bring animals from your flocks and herds.

3"If your sacrifice for a whole burnt offering is from the herd, bring a bull with no physical defects to the entrance of the Tabernacle so it will be accepted by the LORD. 4Lay your hand on its head so the LORD will accept it as your substitute, thus making atonement for you. 5Then slaughter the animal in the LORD's presence, and Aaron's sons, the priests, will present the blood by sprinkling it against the sides of the altar that stands in front of the Tabernacle. 6When the animal has been skinned and cut into pieces, 7the sons of Aaron the priest will build a wood fire on the altar. 8Aaron's sons will then put the pieces of the animal, including its head and fat, on the wood fire. 9But the internal organs and legs must first be washed with water. Then the priests will burn the entire sacrifice on the altar. It is a whole burnt offering made by fire, very pleasing to the LORD.

10"If your sacrifice for a whole burnt offering is from the flock, bring a male sheep or goat with no physical defects. 11Slaughter the animal on the north side of the altar in the LORD's presence. Aaron's sons, the priests, will sprinkle its blood against the sides of the altar. 12Then you must cut the animal in pieces, and the priests will lay the pieces of the sacrifice, including the head and fat, on top of the wood fire on the altar. 13The internal organs and legs must first be washed with water. Then the priests will burn the entire sacrifice on the altar. It is a whole burnt offering made by fire, very pleasing to the LORD.

14"If you bring a bird as a burnt offering to the LORD, choose either a turtledove or a young pigeon. 15The priest will take the bird to the altar, twist off its head, and burn the head on the altar. He must then let its blood drain out against the sides of the altar. 16The priest must remove the crop and the feathers* and throw them to the east side of the altar among the ashes. 17Then, grasping the bird by its wings, the priest will tear the bird apart, though not completely. Then he will burn it on top of the wood fire on the altar. It is a whole burnt offering made by fire, very pleasing to the LORD.

CHAPTER 2

Procedures for the Grain Offering

"When you bring a grain offering to the LORD, the offering must consist of choice flour. You are to pour olive oil on it and sprinkle it with incense. 2Bring this offering to one of Aaron's sons, and he will take a handful of the flour mixed with olive oil, together with all the incense, and burn this token portion on the altar fire. It is an offering made by fire, very pleasing to the LORD. 3The rest of the flour will be given to Aaron and his sons. It will be considered a most holy part of the offerings given to the LORD by fire.

4"When you present some kind of baked bread as a grain offering, it must be made of choice flour mixed with olive oil but without any yeast. It may be presented in the form of cakes mixed with olive oil or wafers spread with olive oil. 5If your grain offering is cooked on a griddle, it must be made of choice flour and olive oil, and it must contain no yeast. 6Break it into pieces and pour oil on it; it is a kind of grain

1:1 Hebrew *Tent of Meeting;* also in 1:3, 5.   1:16 Or *the crop and its contents.* The meaning of the Hebrew is uncertain.

offering. ⁷If your offering is prepared in a pan, it also must be made of choice flour and olive oil.

⁸"No matter how a grain offering has been prepared before being offered to the LORD, bring it to the priests who will present it at the altar. ⁹The priests will take a token portion of the grain offering and burn it on the altar as an offering made by fire, and it will be very pleasing to the LORD. ¹⁰The rest of the grain offering will be given to Aaron and his sons as their food. It will be considered a most holy part of the offerings given to the LORD by fire.

¹¹"Do not use yeast in any of the grain offerings you present to the LORD, because no yeast or honey may be burned as an offering to the LORD by fire. ¹²You may add yeast and honey to the offerings presented at harvesttime, but these must never be burned on the altar as an offering pleasing to the LORD. ¹³Season all your grain offerings with salt, to remind you of God's covenant. Never forget to add salt to your grain offerings.

¹⁴"If you present a grain offering to the LORD from the first portion of your harvest, bring kernels of new grain that have been roasted on a fire. ¹⁵Since it is a grain offering, put olive oil on it and sprinkle it with incense. ¹⁶The priests will take a token portion of the roasted grain mixed with olive oil, together with all the incense, and burn it as an offering given to the LORD by fire.

CHAPTER **3**

Procedures for the Peace Offering

"If you want to present a peace offering from the herd, use either a bull or a cow. The animal you offer to the LORD must have no physical defects. ²Lay your hand on the animal's head, and slaughter it at the entrance of the Tabernacle.* Aaron's sons, the priests, will then sprinkle the animal's blood against the sides of the altar. ³Part of this peace offering must be presented to the LORD as an offering made by fire. This includes the fat around the internal organs, ⁴the two kidneys with the fat around them near the loins, and the lobe of the liver, which is to be removed with the kidneys. ⁵The sons of Aaron will burn these on the altar on top of the burnt offering on the wood fire. It is an offering made by fire, very pleasing to the LORD.

⁶"If you present a peace offering to the LORD from the flock, you may bring either a goat or a sheep. It may be either male or female, and it must have no physical defects. ⁷If you bring a sheep as your gift, present it to the LORD ⁸by laying your hand on its head and slaughtering it at the entrance of the Tabernacle. The sons of Aaron will then sprinkle the sheep's blood against the sides of the altar. ⁹Part of this peace offering must be presented to the LORD as an offering made by fire. This includes the fat of the entire tail cut off near the backbone, the fat around the internal organs, ¹⁰the two kidneys with the fat around them near the loins, and the lobe of the liver, which is to be removed with the kidneys. ¹¹The priest will burn them on the altar as food, an offering given to the LORD by fire.

¹²"If you bring a goat as your offering to the LORD, ¹³lay your hand on its head, and slaughter it at the entrance of the Tabernacle. Then the sons of Aaron will sprinkle the goat's blood against the sides of the altar. ¹⁴Part of this offering must be presented to the LORD as an offering made by fire. This part includes the fat around the internal organs, ¹⁵the two kidneys with the fat around them near the loins, and the lobe of the liver, which is to be removed with the kidneys. ¹⁶The priest will burn them on the altar as food, an offering made by fire; these will be very pleasing to the LORD. Remember, all the fat belongs to the LORD.

¹⁷"You must never eat any fat or blood. This is a permanent law for you and all your descendants, wherever they may live."

CHAPTER **4**

Procedures for the Sin Offering

Then the LORD said to Moses, ²"Give the Israelites the following instructions for dealing with those who sin unintentionally by doing anything forbidden by the LORD's commands.

³"If the high priest sins, bringing guilt upon the entire community, he must bring to the LORD a young bull with no physical defects. ⁴He must present the bull to the LORD at the entrance of the Tabernacle,* lay his hand on the bull's head, and slaughter it there in the LORD's presence. ⁵The priest on duty will then take some of the animal's blood into the Tabernacle, ⁶dip his finger into the blood, and sprinkle it seven times before the LORD in front of the inner curtain of the Most Holy Place. ⁷The priest will put some of the blood on the horns of the incense altar that stands in the LORD's presence in the Tabernacle. The rest of the bull's blood must be poured out at the base of the altar of burnt offerings at the entrance of the Tabernacle. ⁸The priest must remove all the fat around the bull's internal organs, ⁹the two kidneys with the fat

---

3:2 Hebrew *Tent of Meeting*; also in 3:8, 13.   4:4 Hebrew *Tent of Meeting*; also in 4:5, 7, 14, 16, 18.

around them near the loins, and the lobe of the liver. ¹⁰Then he must burn them on the altar of burnt offerings, just as is done with the bull or cow sacrificed as a peace offering. ¹¹But the rest of the bull—its hide, meat, head, legs, internal organs, and dung—¹²must be carried away to a ceremonially clean place outside the camp, the place where the ashes are thrown. He will burn it all on a wood fire in the ash heap.

¹³"If the entire Israelite community does something forbidden by the LORD and the matter escapes the community's notice, all the people will be guilty. ¹⁴When they discover their sin, the leaders of the community must bring a young bull for a sin offering and present it at the entrance of the Tabernacle. ¹⁵The leaders must then lay their hands on the bull's head and slaughter it there before the LORD. ¹⁶The priest will bring some of its blood into the Tabernacle, ¹⁷dip his finger into the blood, and sprinkle it seven times before the LORD in front of the inner curtain. ¹⁸He will then put some of the blood on the horns of the incense altar that stands in the LORD's presence in the Tabernacle. The rest of the blood must then be poured out at the base of the altar of burnt offerings at the entrance of the Tabernacle. ¹⁹The priest must remove all the animal's fat and burn it on the altar, ²⁰following the same procedure as with the sin offering for the priest. In this way, the priest will make atonement for the people, and they will be forgiven. ²¹The priest must then take what is left of the bull outside the camp and burn it there, just as is done with the sin offering for the high priest. This is a sin offering for the entire community of Israel.

²²"If one of Israel's leaders does something forbidden by the LORD his God, he will be guilty even if he sinned unintentionally. ²³When he becomes aware of his sin, he must bring as his offering a male goat with no physical defects. ²⁴He is to lay his hand on the goat's head and slaughter it before the LORD at the place where burnt offerings are slaughtered. This will be his sin offering. ²⁵Then the priest will dip his finger into the blood of the sin offering, put it on the horns of the altar of burnt offerings, and pour out the rest of the blood at the base of the altar. ²⁶He must burn all the goat's fat on the altar, just as is done with the peace offering. In this way, the priest will make atonement for the leader's sin, and he will be forgiven.

²⁷"If any of the citizens of Israel* do something forbidden by the LORD, they will be guilty even if

they sinned unintentionally. ²⁸When they become aware of their sin, they must bring as their offering a female goat with no physical defects. It will be offered for their sin. ²⁹They are to lay a hand on the head of the sin offering and slaughter it at the place where burnt offerings are slaughtered. ³⁰The priest will then dip his finger into the blood, put the blood on the horns of the altar of burnt offerings, and pour out the rest of the blood at the base of the altar. ³¹Those who are guilty must remove all the goat's fat, just as is done with the peace offering. Then the priest will burn the fat on the altar, and it will be very pleasing to the LORD. In this way, the priest will make atonement for them, and they will be forgiven.

³²"If any of the people bring a sheep as their sin offering, it must be a female with no physical defects. ³³They are to lay a hand on the head of the sin offering and slaughter it at the place where the burnt offerings are slaughtered. ³⁴The priest will then dip his finger into the blood, put it on the horns of the altar of burnt offerings, and pour out the rest of the blood at the base of the altar. ³⁵Those who are guilty must remove all the sheep's fat, just as is done with a sheep presented as a peace offering. Then the priest will burn the fat on the altar on top of the offerings given to the LORD by fire. In this way, the priest will make atonement for them, and they will be forgiven.

CHAPTER **5**

Sins Requiring a Sin Offering

"If any of the people are called to testify about something they have witnessed, but they refuse to testify, they will be held responsible and be subject to punishment.

²"Or if they touch something that is ceremonially unclean, such as the dead body of an animal that is ceremonially unclean—whether a wild animal, a domesticated animal, or an animal that scurries along the ground—they will be considered ceremonially unclean and guilty, even if they are unaware of their defilement.

³"Or if they come into contact with any source of human defilement, even if they don't realize they have been defiled, they will be considered guilty as soon as they become aware of it.

⁴"Or if they make a rash vow of any kind, whether its purpose is for good or bad, they will be considered guilty even if they were not fully aware of what they were doing at the time.

4:27 Hebrew *people of the land.*

5 "When any of the people become aware of their guilt in any of these ways, they must confess their sin 6and bring to the priest as their penalty a female from the flock, either a sheep or a goat. This will be a sin offering to remove their sin, and the priest will make atonement for them.

7 "If any of them cannot afford to bring a sheep, they must bring to the LORD two young turtledoves or two young pigeons as the penalty for their sin. One of the birds will be a sin offering, and the other will be a burnt offering. 8They must bring them to the priest, who will offer one of the birds as the sin offering. The priest will wring its neck but without severing its head from the body. 9Then he will sprinkle some of the blood of the sin offering against the sides of the altar, and the rest will be drained out at the base of the altar. 10The priest will offer the second bird as a whole burnt offering, following all the procedures that have been prescribed. In this way, the priest will make atonement for those who are guilty, and they will be forgiven.

11 "If any of the people cannot afford to bring young turtledoves or pigeons, they must bring two quarts* of choice flour for their sin offering. Since it is a sin offering, they must not mix it with olive oil or put any incense on it. 12They must take the flour to the priest, who will scoop out a handful as a token portion. He will burn this flour on the altar just like any other offering given to the LORD by fire. This will be their sin offering. 13In this way, the priest will make atonement for those who are guilty, and they will be forgiven. The rest of the flour will belong to the priest, just as with the grain offering."

Procedures for the Guilt Offering

14Then the LORD said to Moses, 15 "If any of the people sin by unintentionally defiling the LORD's sacred property, they must bring to the LORD a ram from the flock as their guilt offering. The animal must have no physical defects, and it must be of the proper value in silver as measured by the standard sanctuary shekel.* 16They must then make restitution for whatever holy things they have defiled by paying for the loss, plus an added penalty of 20 percent. When they give their payments to the priest, he will make atonement for them with the ram sacrificed as a guilt offering, and they will be forgiven.

17 "If any of them sin by doing something forbidden by the LORD, even if it is done unintentionally, they will be held responsible. When they become aware of their guilt, 18they must bring to the priest a ram from the flock as a guilt offering. The animal must have no physical defects, and it must be of the proper value. In this way, the priest will make atonement for those who are guilty, and they will be forgiven. 19This is a guilt offering, for they have been guilty of an offense against the LORD."

CHAPTER 6

Sins Requiring a Guilt Offering

And the LORD said to Moses, 2 "Suppose some of the people sin against the LORD by falsely telling their neighbor that an item entrusted to their safekeeping has been lost or stolen. Or suppose they have been dishonest with regard to a security deposit, or they have taken something by theft or extortion. 3Or suppose they find a lost item and lie about it, or they deny something while under oath, or they commit any other similar sin. 4If they have sinned in any of these ways and are guilty, they must give back whatever they have taken by theft or extortion, whether a security deposit, or property entrusted to them, or a lost object that they claimed as their own, 5or anything gained by swearing falsely. When they realize their guilt, they must restore the principal amount plus a penalty of 20 percent to the person they have harmed. 6They must then bring a guilt offering to the priest, who will present it before the LORD. This offering must be a ram with no physical defects or the animal's equivalent value in silver.* 7The priest will then make atonement for them before the LORD, and they will be forgiven."

Further Instructions for the Burnt Offering

8Then the LORD said to Moses, 9 "Give Aaron and his sons the following instructions regarding the whole burnt offering. The burnt offering must be left on the altar until the next morning, and the altar fire must be kept burning all night. 10The next morning, after dressing in his special linen clothing and undergarments, the priest on duty must clean out the ashes of the burnt offering and put them beside the altar. 11Then he must change back into his normal clothing and carry the ashes outside the camp to a place that is ceremonially clean. 12Meanwhile, the fire on the altar must be kept burning; it must never go out. Each morning the priest will add fresh wood to the fire and arrange the daily whole burnt offering on it. He must then burn the fat

---

5:11 Hebrew 1/10 of an ephah [2 liters].   5:15 Each sanctuary shekel was about 0.4 ounces or 11 grams in weight.   6:6 Or and the animal must be of the proper value; Hebrew lacks in silver; compare 5:15.

of the peace offerings on top of this daily whole burnt offering. 13Remember, the fire must be kept burning on the altar at all times. It must never go out.

Further Instructions for the Grain Offering

14"These are the instructions regarding the grain offering. Aaron's sons must present this offering to the LORD in front of the altar. 15The priest on duty will take a handful of the choice flour that has been mixed with olive oil and sprinkled with incense. He will burn this token portion on the altar, and it will be very pleasing to the LORD. 16After burning this handful, the rest of the flour will belong to Aaron and his sons for their food. It must, however, be baked without yeast and eaten in a sacred place within the courtyard of the Tabernacle.* 17Remember, this flour may never be prepared with yeast. I have given it to the priests as their share of the offerings presented to me by fire. Like the sin offering and the guilt offering, it is most holy. 18Any of Aaron's male descendants, from generation to generation, may eat of the grain offering, because it is their regular share of the offerings given to the LORD by fire. Anyone or anything that touches this food will become holy."

Procedures for the Ordination Offering

19And the LORD said to Moses, 20"On the day Aaron and his sons are anointed, they must bring to the LORD a grain offering of two quarts* of choice flour, half to be offered in the morning and half to be offered in the evening. 21It must be cooked on a griddle with olive oil, and it must be well mixed and broken* into pieces. You must present this grain offering, and it will be very pleasing to the LORD. 22As the sons of the priests replace their fathers, they will be inducted into office by offering this same sacrifice on the day they are anointed. It is the LORD's regular share, and it must be completely burned up. 23All such grain offerings of the priests must be entirely burned up. None of the flour may be eaten."

Further Instructions for the Sin Offering

24Then the LORD said to Moses, 25"Give Aaron and his sons these further instructions regarding the sin offering. The animal given as a sin offering is most holy and must be slaughtered in the LORD's presence at the place where the burnt offerings are slaughtered. 26The priest who offers the sacrifice may eat his portion in a sacred place within the courtyard of the Tabernacle.

27Anything or anyone who touches the sacrificial meat will become holy, and if the sacrificial blood splatters anyone's clothing, it must be washed off in a sacred place. 28If a clay pot is used to boil the sacrificial meat, it must be broken. If a bronze kettle is used, it must be scoured and rinsed thoroughly with water. 29Only males from a priest's family may eat of this offering, for it is most holy. 30If, however, the blood of a sin offering has been taken into the Tabernacle to make atonement in the Holy Place for the people's sins, none of that animal's meat may be eaten. It must be completely burned up.

CHAPTER 7

Further Instructions for the Guilt Offering

"These are the instructions for the guilt offering, which is most holy. 2The animal sacrificed as a guilt offering must be slaughtered where the burnt offerings are slaughtered, and its blood sprinkled against the sides of the altar. 3The priest will then offer all its fat on the altar, including the fat from the tail, the fat around the internal organs, 4the two kidneys with the fat around them near the loins, and the lobe of the liver, which is to be removed with the kidneys. 5The priests will burn these parts on the altar as an offering to the LORD made by fire. It is a guilt offering. 6All males from a priest's family may eat the meat, and it must be eaten in a sacred place, for it is most holy.

7"For both the sin offering and the guilt offering, the meat of the sacrificed animal belongs to the priest in charge of the atonement ceremony. 8In the case of the whole burnt offering, the hide of the sacrificed animal also belongs to the priest. 9Any grain offering that has been baked in an oven, prepared in a pan, or cooked on a griddle belongs to the priest who presents it. 10All other grain offerings, whether flour mixed with olive oil or dry flour, are to be shared among all the priests and their sons.

Further Instructions for the Peace Offering

11"These are the instructions regarding the different kinds of peace offerings that may be presented to the LORD. 12If you present your peace offering as a thanksgiving offering, the usual animal sacrifice must be accompanied by various kinds of bread—loaves, wafers, and cakes—all made without yeast and soaked with olive oil. 13This peace offering of thanksgiving must also be accompanied by loaves of yeast bread.

6:16 Hebrew *Tent of Meeting;* also in 6:26, 30.   6:20 Hebrew *1/10 of an ephah* [2 liters].   6:21 The meaning of this Hebrew term is uncertain.

14One of each kind of bread must be presented as a gift to the LORD. This bread will then belong to the priest who sprinkles the altar with blood from the sacrificed animal. 15The animal's meat must be eaten on the same day it is offered. None of it may be saved for the next morning.

16"However, if you bring an offering to fulfill a vow or as a freewill offering, the meat may be eaten on that same day, and whatever is left over may be eaten on the second day. 17But anything left over until the third day must be completely burned up. 18If any of the meat from this peace offering is eaten on the third day, it will not be accepted by the LORD. It will have no value as a sacrifice, and you will receive no credit for bringing it as an offering. By then, the meat will be contaminated; if you eat it, you will have to answer for your sin.

19"Meat that touches anything ceremonially unclean may not be eaten; it must be completely burned up. And as for meat that may be eaten, it may only be eaten by people who are ceremonially clean. 20Anyone who is ceremonially unclean but eats meat from a peace offering that was presented to the LORD must be cut off from the community. 21If anyone touches anything that is unclean, whether it is human defilement or an unclean animal, and then eats meat from the LORD's sacrifices, that person must be cut off from the community."

The Forbidden Blood and Fat

22Then the LORD said to Moses, 23"Give the Israelites these instructions: You must never eat fat, whether from oxen or sheep or goats. 24The fat of an animal found dead or killed by a wild animal may never be eaten, though it may be used for any other purpose. 25Anyone who eats fat from an offering given to the LORD by fire must be cut off from the community. 26Even in your homes, you must never eat the blood of any bird or animal. 27Anyone who eats blood must be cut off from the community."

A Portion for the Priests

28Then the LORD said to Moses, 29"Give these further instructions to the Israelites: When you present a peace offering to the LORD, bring part of it as a special gift to the LORD. 30Present it to him with your own hands as an offering given to the LORD by fire. Bring the fat of the animal, together with the breast, and present it to the LORD by lifting it up before him. 31Then the priest will burn the

fat on the altar, but the breast will belong to Aaron and his sons. 32You are to give the right thigh of your peace offering to the priest as a gift. 33The right thigh must always be given to the priest who sprinkles the blood and offers the fat of the peace offering. 34For I have designated the breast and the right thigh for the priests. It is their regular share of the peace offerings brought by the Israelites. 35This is their share. It has been set apart for Aaron and his descendants from the offerings given to the LORD by fire from the time they were appointed to serve the LORD as priests. 36The LORD commanded that the Israelites were to give these portions to the priests as their regular share from the time of the priests' anointing. This regulation applies throughout the generations to come."

37These are the instructions for the whole burnt offering, the grain offering, the sin offering, the guilt offering, the ordination offering, and the peace offering. 38The LORD gave these instructions to Moses on Mount Sinai when he commanded the Israelites to bring their offerings to the LORD in the wilderness of Sinai.

CHAPTER **8**
Ordination of the Priests

The LORD said to Moses, 2"Now bring Aaron and his sons, along with their special clothing, the anointing oil, the bull for the sin offering, the two rams, and the basket of unleavened bread 3to the entrance of the Tabernacle.* Then call the entire community of Israel to meet you there."

4So Moses followed the LORD's instructions, and all the people assembled at the Tabernacle entrance. 5Moses announced to them, "The LORD has commanded what I am now going to do!" 6Then he presented Aaron and his sons and washed them with water. 7He clothed Aaron with the embroidered tunic and tied the sash around his waist. He dressed him in the robe of the ephod, along with the ephod itself, and attached the ephod with its decorative sash. 8Then Moses placed the chestpiece on Aaron and put the Urim and the Thummim inside it. 9He placed on Aaron's head the turban with the gold medallion at its front, just as the LORD had commanded him.

10Then Moses took the anointing oil and anointed the Tabernacle and everything in it, thus making them holy. 11He sprinkled the altar seven times, anointing it and all its utensils and the washbasin and its pedestal, making them

8:3 Hebrew *Tent of Meeting;* also in 8:4, 31, 33, 35.

holy. ¹²Then he poured some of the anointing oil on Aaron's head, thus anointing him and making him holy for his work. ¹³Next Moses presented Aaron's sons and clothed them in their embroidered tunics, their sashes, and their turbans, just as the LORD had commanded him.

¹⁴Then Moses brought in the bull for the sin offering, and Aaron and his sons laid their hands on its head ¹⁵as Moses slaughtered it. Moses took some of the blood, and with his finger he put it on the four horns of the altar to purify it. He poured out the rest of the blood at the base of the altar. In this way, he set the altar apart as holy and made atonement for it.* ¹⁶He took all the fat around the internal organs, the lobe of the liver, and the two kidneys and their fat, and he burned them all on the altar. ¹⁷The rest of the bull, including its hide, meat, and dung, was burned outside the camp, just as the LORD had commanded Moses.

¹⁸Then Moses presented the ram to the LORD for the whole burnt offering, and Aaron and his sons laid their hands on its head ¹⁹as Moses slaughtered it. Then Moses took the ram's blood and sprinkled it against the sides of the altar. ²⁰Next he cut the ram into pieces and burned the head, some of its pieces, and the fat on the altar. ²¹After washing the internal organs and the legs with water, Moses burned the entire ram on the altar as a whole burnt offering. It was an offering given to the LORD by fire, very pleasing to the LORD. All this was done just as the LORD had commanded Moses.

²²Next Moses presented the second ram, which was the ram of ordination. Aaron and his sons laid their hands on its head ²³as Moses slaughtered it. Then Moses took some of its blood and put it on the lobe of Aaron's right ear, the thumb of his right hand, and the big toe of his right foot. ²⁴Next he presented Aaron's sons and put some of the blood on the lobe of their right ears, the thumb of their right hands, and the big toe of their right feet. He then sprinkled the rest of the blood against the sides of the altar.

²⁵Next he took the fat, including the fat from the tail, the fat around the internal organs, the lobe of the liver, and the two kidneys with their fat, along with the right thigh. ²⁶On top of these he placed a loaf of unleavened bread, a cake of unleavened bread soaked with olive oil, and a thin wafer spread with olive oil. All these were taken from the basket of bread made without yeast that was placed in the LORD's presence.

²⁷He gave all of these to Aaron and his sons, and he presented the portions by lifting them up before the LORD. ²⁸Moses then took all the offerings back and burned them on the altar on top of the burnt offering as an ordination offering. It was an offering given to the LORD by fire, very pleasing to the LORD. ²⁹Then Moses took the breast and lifted it up in the LORD's presence. This was Moses' share of the ram of ordination, just as the LORD had commanded him.

³⁰Next Moses took some of the anointing oil and some of the blood that was on the altar, and he sprinkled them on Aaron and his clothing and on his sons and their clothing. In this way, he made Aaron and his sons and their clothing holy.

³¹Then Moses said to Aaron and his sons, "Boil the rest of the meat at the Tabernacle entrance, and eat it along with the bread that is in the basket of ordination offerings, just as I commanded you. ³²Any meat or bread that is left over must then be burned up. ³³Do not leave the Tabernacle entrance for seven days, for that is the time it will take to complete the ordination ceremony. ³⁴What has been done today was commanded by the LORD in order to make atonement for you. ³⁵Remember, you must stay at the entrance of the Tabernacle day and night for seven days, doing everything the LORD requires. If you fail in this, you will die. This is what the LORD has said." ³⁶So Aaron and his sons did everything the LORD had commanded through Moses.

CHAPTER **9**

The Priests Begin Their Work

After the ordination ceremony, on the eighth day, Moses called together Aaron and his sons and the leaders of Israel. ²He said to Aaron, "Take a young bull for a sin offering and a ram for a whole burnt offering, both with no physical defects, and present them to the LORD. ³Then tell the Israelites to take a male goat for a sin offering for themselves and a year-old calf and a year-old lamb for a whole burnt offering, each with no physical defects. ⁴Also tell them to take a bull* and a ram for a peace offering and flour mixed with olive oil for a grain offering. Tell them to present all these offerings to the LORD because the LORD will appear to them today."

⁵So the people brought all of these things to the entrance of the Tabernacle,* just as Moses had commanded, and the whole community came and stood there in the LORD's presence. ⁶Then Moses told them, "When you have followed these

8:15 Or *that atonement may be made on it.*   9:4 Or *cow;* also in 9:18, 19.   9:5 Hebrew *Tent of Meeting;* also in 9:23.

instructions from the LORD, the glorious presence of the LORD will appear to you."

7Then Moses said to Aaron, "Approach the altar and present your sin offering and your whole burnt offering to make atonement for yourself. Then present the offerings to make atonement for the people, just as the LORD has commanded."

8So Aaron went to the altar and slaughtered the calf as a sin offering for himself. 9His sons brought him the blood, and he dipped his finger into it and put it on the horns of the altar. He poured out the rest of the blood at the base of the altar. 10Then he burned on the altar the fat, the kidneys, and the lobe of the liver from the sin offering, just as the LORD had commanded Moses. 11The meat and the hide, however, he burned outside the camp.

12Next Aaron slaughtered the animal for the whole burnt offering. His sons brought him the blood, and he sprinkled it against the sides of the altar. 13They handed the animal to him piece by piece, including the head, and he burned each part on the altar. 14Then he washed the internal organs and the legs and also burned them on the altar as a whole burnt offering.

15Next Aaron presented the sacrifices for the people. He slaughtered the people's goat and presented it as their sin offering, just as he had done previously for himself. 16Then he brought the whole burnt offering and presented it in the prescribed way. 17He also brought the grain offering, burning a handful of the flour on the altar, in addition to the regular morning burnt offering.

18Then Aaron slaughtered the bull and the ram for the people's peace offering. His sons brought him the blood, and he sprinkled it against the sides of the altar. 19Then he took the fat of the bull and the ram—the fat from the tail and from around the internal organs—along with the kidneys and the lobe of the liver. 20He placed these fat parts on top of the breasts of these animals and then burned them on the altar. 21Aaron then lifted up the breasts and right thighs as an offering to the LORD, just as Moses had commanded.

22After that, Aaron raised his hands toward the people and blessed them. Then, after presenting the sin offering, the whole burnt offering, and the peace offering, he stepped down from the altar. 23Next Moses and Aaron went into the Tabernacle, and when they came back

out, they blessed the people again, and the glorious presence of the LORD appeared to the whole community. 24Fire blazed forth from the LORD's presence and consumed the burnt offering and the fat on the altar. When the people saw all this, they shouted with joy and fell face down on the ground.

CHAPTER 10
The Sin of Nadab and Abihu

Aaron's sons Nadab and Abihu put coals of fire in their incense burners and sprinkled incense over it. In this way, they disobeyed the LORD by burning before him a different kind of fire than he had commanded. 2So fire blazed forth from the LORD's presence and burned them up, and they died there before the LORD.

3Then Moses said to Aaron, "This is what the LORD meant when he said,

'I will show myself holy
　among those who are near me.
I will be glorified
　before all the people.'"

And Aaron was silent.

4Then Moses called for Mishael and Elzaphan, Aaron's cousins, the sons of Aaron's uncle Uzziel. He said to them, "Come and carry the bodies of your relatives away from the sanctuary to a place outside the camp." 5So they came forward and carried them out of the camp by their tunics as Moses had commanded.

6Then Moses said to Aaron and his sons Eleazar and Ithamar, "Do not mourn by letting your hair hang loose* or by tearing your clothes. If you do, you will die, and the LORD will be angry with the whole community of Israel. However, the rest of the Israelites, your relatives, may mourn for Nadab and Abihu, whom the LORD has destroyed by fire. 7But you are not to leave the entrance of the Tabernacle,* under penalty of death, for the anointing oil of the LORD is upon you." So they did as Moses commanded.

Instructions for Priestly Conduct

8Then the LORD said to Aaron, 9"You and your descendants must never drink wine or any other alcoholic drink before going into the Tabernacle. If you do, you will die. This is a permanent law for you, and it must be kept by all future generations. 10You are to distinguish between what is holy and what is ordinary, what is ceremonially unclean and what is clean. 11And you must teach

10:6 Or *by uncovering your heads.*　10:7 Hebrew *Tent of Meeting;* also in 10:9.

the Israelites all the laws that the LORD has given through Moses."

12Then Moses said to Aaron and his remaining sons, Eleazar and Ithamar, "Take what is left of the grain offering after the handful has been presented to the LORD by fire. Make sure there is no yeast in it, and eat it beside the altar, for it is most holy. 13It must be eaten in a sacred place, for it has been given to you and your descendants as your regular share of the offerings given to the LORD by fire. These are the commands I have been given. 14But the breast and thigh that were lifted up may be eaten in any place that is ceremonially clean. These parts have been given to you and to your sons and daughters as your regular share of the peace offerings presented by the people of Israel. 15The thigh and breast that are lifted up must be lifted up to the LORD along with the fat of the offerings given by fire. Then they will belong to you and your descendants forever, just as the LORD has commanded."

16When Moses demanded to know what had happened to the goat of the sin offering, he discovered that it had been burned up. As a result, he became very angry with Eleazar and Ithamar, Aaron's remaining sons. 17"Why didn't you eat the sin offering in the sanctuary area?" he demanded. "It is a holy offering! It was given to you for removing the guilt of the community and for making atonement for the people before the LORD. 18Since the animal's blood was not taken into the Holy Place, you should have eaten the meat in the sanctuary area as I ordered you."

19Then Aaron answered Moses on behalf of his sons. "Today my sons presented both their sin offering and their burnt offering to the LORD," he said. "This kind of thing has also happened to me. Would the LORD have approved if I had eaten the sin offering today?" 20And when Moses heard this, he approved.

CHAPTER **11**

Ceremonially Clean and Unclean Animals

Then the LORD said to Moses and Aaron, 2"Give the following instructions to the Israelites: The animals you may use for food 3include those that have completely divided hooves and chew the cud. 4You may not, however, eat the animals named here* because they either have split hooves or chew the cud, but not both. The camel may not be eaten, for though it chews the cud, it does not have split hooves. 5The same is true of the rock badger* 6and the hare, so they also may never be eaten. 7And the pig may not be eaten, for though it has split hooves, it does not chew the cud. 8You may not eat the meat of these animals or touch their dead bodies. They are ceremonially unclean for you.

9"As for marine animals, you may eat whatever has both fins and scales, whether taken from fresh water or salt water. 10You may not, however, eat marine animals that do not have both fins and scales. You are to detest them, 11and they will always be forbidden to you. You must never eat their meat or even touch their dead bodies. 12I repeat, any marine animal that does not have both fins and scales is strictly forbidden to you.

13"These are the birds you must never eat because they are detestable for you: the eagle, the vulture, the osprey, 14the buzzard, kites of all kinds, 15ravens of all kinds, 16the ostrich, the nighthawk, the seagull, hawks of all kinds, 17the little owl, the cormorant, the great owl, 18the white owl, the pelican, the carrion vulture, 19the stork, herons of all kinds, the hoopoe, and the bat.

20"You are to consider detestable all swarming insects that walk along the ground. 21However, there are some exceptions that you may eat. These include insects that jump with their hind legs: 22locusts of all varieties, crickets, bald locusts, and grasshoppers. All these may be eaten. 23But you are to consider detestable all other swarming insects that walk or crawl.

24"The following creatures make you ceremonially unclean. If you touch any of their dead bodies, you will be defiled until evening. 25If you move the dead body of an unclean animal, you must immediately wash your clothes, and you will remain defiled until evening.

26"Any animal that has divided but unsplit hooves or that does not chew the cud is unclean for you. If you touch the dead body of such an animal, you will be defiled until evening. 27Of the animals that walk on all fours, those that have paws are unclean for you. If you touch the dead body of such an animal, you will be defiled until evening. 28If you pick up and move its carcass, you must immediately wash your clothes, and you will remain defiled until evening.

29"Of the small animals that scurry or creep on the ground, these are unclean for you: the mole, the mouse, the great lizard of all varieties, 30the gecko, the monitor lizard, the common lizard, the sand lizard, and the chameleon. 31All these small animals are unclean for you. If you

11:4 The identification of some of the animals, birds, and insects in this chapter is uncertain.   11:5 Or *coney,* or *hyrax.*

touch the dead body of such an animal, you will be defiled until evening. 32If such an animal dies and falls on something, that object, whatever its use, will be unclean. This is true whether the object is made of wood, cloth, leather, or sackcloth. It must be put into water, and it will remain defiled until evening. After that, it will be ceremonially clean and may be used again.

33 "If such an animal dies and falls into a clay pot, everything in the pot will be defiled, and the pot must be smashed. 34If the water used to cleanse an unclean object touches any food, all of that food will be defiled. And any beverage that is in such an unclean container will be defiled. 35Any object on which the dead body of such an animal falls will be defiled. If it is a clay oven or cooking pot, it must be smashed to pieces. It has become defiled, and it will remain that way.

36 "However, if the dead body of such an animal falls into a spring or a cistern, the water will still be clean. But anyone who removes the dead body will be defiled. 37If the dead body falls on seed grain to be planted in the field, the seed will still be considered clean. 38But if the seed is wet when the dead body falls on it, the seed will be defiled.

39 "If an animal that is permitted for eating dies and you touch its carcass, you will be defiled until evening. 40If you eat any of its meat or carry away its carcass, you must wash your clothes. Then you will remain defiled until evening.

41 "Consider detestable any animal that scurries along the ground; such animals may never be eaten. 42This includes all animals that slither along on their bellies, as well as those with four legs and those with many feet. All such animals are to be considered detestable. 43Never defile yourselves by touching such animals. 44After all, I, the LORD, am your God. You must be holy because I am holy. So do not defile yourselves by touching any of these animals that scurry along the ground. 45I, the LORD, am the one who brought you up from the land of Egypt to be your God. You must therefore be holy because I am holy.

46 "These are the instructions regarding the land animals, the birds, and all the living things that move through the water or swarm over the earth, 47so you can distinguish between what is unclean and may not be eaten and what is clean and may be eaten."

CHAPTER 12
Purification after Childbirth

The LORD said to Moses, "Give these instructions to the Israelites: 2When a woman becomes pregnant and gives birth to a son, she will be ceremonially unclean for seven days, just as she is defiled during her menstrual period. 3On the eighth day, the boy must be circumcised. 4Then the woman must wait for thirty-three days until the time of her purification from the blood of childbirth is completed. During this time of purification, she must not touch anything that is holy. And she must not go to the sanctuary until her time of purification is over. 5If a woman gives birth to a daughter, she will be ceremonially defiled for two weeks, just as she is defiled during her menstrual period. She must then wait another sixty-six days to be purified from the blood of childbirth.

6 "When the time of purification is completed for either a son or a daughter, the woman must bring a year-old lamb for a whole burnt offering and a young pigeon or turtledove for a purification offering. She must take her offerings to the priest at the entrance of the Tabernacle.* 7The priest will then present them to the LORD and make atonement for her. Then she will be ceremonially clean again after her bleeding at childbirth. These are the instructions to be followed after the birth of a son or a daughter.

8 "If a woman cannot afford to bring a sheep, she must bring two turtledoves or two young pigeons. One will be for the whole burnt offering and the other for the purification offering. The priest will sacrifice them, thus making atonement for her, and she will be ceremonially clean."

CHAPTER 13
Contagious Skin Diseases

The LORD said to Moses and Aaron, 2 "If some of the people notice a swelling or a rash or a shiny patch on their skin that develops into a contagious skin disease,* they must be brought to Aaron the priest or to one of his sons. 3The priest will then examine the affected area of a person's skin. If the hair in the affected area has turned white and appears to be more than skin-deep, then it is a contagious skin disease, and the priest must pronounce the person ceremonially unclean.

4 "But if the affected area of the skin is white but does not appear to be more than skin-deep,

12:6 Hebrew *Tent of Meeting.*   13:2 Traditionally rendered *leprosy.* The Hebrew word used throughout this passage is used to describe various skin diseases.

and if the hair in the spot has not turned white, the priest will put the infected person in quarantine for seven days. 5On the seventh day the priest will make another examination. If the affected area has not changed or spread on the skin, then the priest will put the person in quarantine for seven more days. 6The priest will examine the skin again on the seventh day. If the affected area has faded and not spread, the priest will pronounce the person ceremonially clean. It was only a temporary rash. So after washing the clothes, the person will be considered free of disease. 7But if the rash continues to spread after this examination and pronouncement by the priest, the infected person must return to be examined again. 8If the priest notices that the rash has spread, then he must pronounce this person ceremonially unclean, for it is a contagious skin disease.

9 "Anyone who develops a contagious skin disease must go to the priest for an examination. 10If the priest sees that some hair has turned white and an open sore appears in the affected area, 11it is clearly a contagious skin disease, and the priest must pronounce that person ceremonially unclean. In such cases, the person need not be quarantined for further observation because it is clear that the skin is defiled by the disease.

12"Now suppose the priest discovers after his examination that a rash has broken out all over someone's skin, covering the body from head to foot. 13In such cases, the priest must examine the infected person to see if the disease covers the entire body. If it does, he will pronounce the person ceremonially clean because the skin has turned completely white. 14But if any open sores appear, the infected person will be pronounced ceremonially unclean. 15The priest must make this pronouncement as soon as he sees an open sore because open sores indicate the presence of a contagious skin disease. 16However, if the open sores heal and turn white like the rest of the skin, the person must return to the priest. 17If, after another examination, the affected areas have indeed turned completely white, then the priest will pronounce the person ceremonially clean.

18"If anyone has had a boil on the skin that has started to heal, 19but a white swelling or a reddish white spot remains in its place, that person must go to the priest to be examined. 20If the priest finds the disease to be more than skin-deep, and if the hair in the affected area has turned white, then the priest must pronounce that person ceremonially unclean. It is a conta-

gious skin disease that has broken out in the boil. 21But if the priest sees that there is no white hair in the affected area, and if it doesn't appear to be more than skin-deep and has faded, then the priest is to put the person in quarantine for seven days. 22If during that time the affected area spreads on the skin, the priest must pronounce the person ceremonially unclean, because it is a contagious skin disease. 23But if the area grows no larger and does not spread, it is merely the scar from the boil, and the priest will pronounce that person ceremonially clean.

24 "If anyone has suffered a burn on the skin and the burned area changes color, becoming either a shiny reddish white or white, 25then the priest must examine it. If the hair in the affected area turns white and the problem appears to be more than skin-deep, a contagious skin disease has broken out in the burn. The priest must then pronounce that person ceremonially unclean, for it is clearly a contagious skin disease. 26But if the priest discovers that there is no white hair in the affected area and the problem appears to be no more than skin-deep and has faded, then the priest is to put the infected person in quarantine for seven days. 27If at the end of that time the affected area has spread on the skin, the priest must pronounce that person ceremonially unclean, for it is clearly a contagious skin disease. 28But if the affected area has not moved or spread on the skin and has faded, it is simply a scar from the burn. The priest must then pronounce the person ceremonially clean.

29 "If anyone, whether a man or woman, has an open sore on the head or chin, 30the priest must examine the infection. If it appears to be more than skin-deep and fine yellow hair is found in the affected area, the priest must pronounce the infected person ceremonially unclean. The infection is a contagious skin disease of the head or chin. 31However, if the priest's examination reveals that the infection is only skin-deep and there is no black hair in the affected area, then he must put the person in quarantine for seven days. 32If at the end of that time the affected area has not spread and no yellow hair has appeared, and if the infection does not appear to be more than skin-deep, 33the infected person must shave off all hair except the hair on the affected area. Then the priest must put the person in quarantine for another seven days, 34and he will examine the infection again on the seventh day. If it has not spread and appears to be no more than

skin-deep, the priest must pronounce that person ceremonially clean. After washing clothes, that person will be clean. 35But if the infection begins to spread after the person is pronounced clean, 36the priest must do another examination. If the infection has spread, he must pronounce the infected person ceremonially unclean, even without checking for yellow hair. 37But if it appears that the infection has stopped spreading and black hair has grown in the affected area, then the infection has healed. The priest will then pronounce the infected person ceremonially clean.

38"If anyone, whether a man or woman, has shiny white patches on the skin, 39the priest must examine the affected area. If the patch is only a pale white, this is a harmless skin rash, and the person is ceremonially clean.

40"If a man loses his hair and his head becomes bald, he is still ceremonially clean. 41And if he loses hair on his forehead, he simply has a bald forehead; he is still clean. 42However, if a reddish white infection appears on the front or the back of his head, this is a contagious skin disease. 43The priest must examine him, and if he finds swelling around the reddish white sore, 44the man is infected with a contagious skin disease and is unclean. The priest must pronounce him ceremonially unclean because of the infection.

45"Those who suffer from any contagious skin disease must tear their clothing and allow their hair to hang loose.* Then, as they go from place to place, they must cover their mouth and call out, 'Unclean! Unclean!' 46As long as the disease lasts, they will be ceremonially unclean and must live in isolation outside the camp.

Treatment of Contaminated Clothing

47"Now suppose an infectious mildew* contaminates some woolen or linen clothing, 48some woolen or linen fabric, the hide of an animal, or anything made of leather. 49If the affected area in the clothing, the animal hide, the fabric, or the leather has turned bright green or a reddish color, it is contaminated with an infectious mildew and must be taken to the priest to be examined. 50After examining the affected spot, the priest will put it away for seven days. 51On the seventh day the priest must inspect it again. If the affected area has spread, the material is clearly contaminated by an infectious mildew and is unclean. 52The priest must burn the linen or wool clothing or the piece of leather

because it has been contaminated by an infectious mildew. It must be completely destroyed by fire.

53"But if the priest examines it again and the affected spot has not spread in the clothing, the fabric, or the leather, 54the priest will order the contaminated object to be washed and then isolated for seven more days. 55Then the priest must inspect the object again. If he sees that the affected area has not changed appearance after being washed, even if it did not spread, the object is defiled. It must be completely burned up, whether it is contaminated on the inside or outside. 56But if the priest sees that the affected area has faded after being washed, he is to cut the spot from the clothing, the fabric, or the leather. 57If the spot reappears at a later time, however, the mildew is clearly spreading, and the contaminated object must be burned up. 58But if the spot disappears after the object is washed, it must be washed again; then it will be ceremonially clean.

59"These are the instructions for dealing with infectious mildew in woolen or linen clothing or fabric, or in anything made of leather. This is how the priest will determine whether these things are ceremonially clean or unclean."

CHAPTER **14**
Cleansing from Skin Diseases

And the LORD said to Moses, 2"The following instructions must be followed by those seeking purification from a contagious skin disease.* Those who have been healed must be brought to the priest, 3who will examine them at a place outside the camp. If the priest finds that someone has been healed of the skin disease, 4he will perform a purification ceremony, using two wild birds of a kind permitted for food, along with some cedarwood, a scarlet cloth, and a hyssop branch. 5The priest will order one of the birds to be slaughtered over a clay pot that is filled with fresh springwater. 6He will then dip the living bird, along with the cedarwood, the scarlet cloth, and the hyssop branch, into the blood of the slaughtered bird. 7The priest will also sprinkle the dead bird's blood seven times over the person being purified, and the priest will pronounce that person to be ceremonially clean. At the end of the ceremony, the priest will set the living bird free so it can fly away into the open fields.

8"The people being purified must complete

13:45 Or *and uncover their heads.* 13:47 Traditionally rendered *leprosy.* The Hebrew term used throughout this passage is the same term used for the various skin diseases described in 13:1-46. 14:2 Traditionally rendered *leprosy.* See note at 13:2.

the cleansing ceremony by washing their clothes, shaving off all their hair, and bathing themselves in water. Then they will be ceremonially clean and may return to live inside the camp. However, they must still remain outside their tents for seven days. ⁹On the seventh day, they must again shave off all their hair, including the hair of the beard and eyebrows, and wash their clothes and bathe themselves in water. Then they will be pronounced ceremonially clean.

¹⁰"On the next day, the eighth day, each person cured of the skin disease must bring two male lambs and one female year-old lamb with no physical defects, along with five quarts* of choice flour mixed with olive oil and three-fifths of a pint* of olive oil. ¹¹Then the officiating priest will present that person for cleansing, along with the offerings, before the Lord at the entrance of the Tabernacle.* ¹²The priest will take one of the lambs and the olive oil and offer them as a guilt offering by lifting them up before the Lord. ¹³He will then slaughter the lamb there in the sacred area at the place where sin offerings and burnt offerings are slaughtered. As with the sin offering, the guilt offering will be given to the priest. It is a most holy offering. ¹⁴The priest will then take some of the blood from the guilt offering and put it on the tip of the healed person's right ear, on the thumb of the right hand, and on the big toe of the right foot.

¹⁵"Then the priest will pour some of the olive oil into the palm of his own left hand. ¹⁶He will dip his right finger into the oil and sprinkle it seven times before the Lord. ¹⁷The priest will then put some of the oil remaining in his left hand on the tip of the healed person's right ear, on the thumb of the right hand, and on the big toe of the right foot, in addition to the blood of the guilt offering. ¹⁸The oil remaining in the priest's hand will then be poured over the healed person's head. In this way, the priest will make atonement before the Lord for the person being cleansed.

¹⁹"Then the priest must offer the sin offering and again perform the atonement ceremony for the person cured of the skin disease. After that, the priest will slaughter the whole burnt offering ²⁰and offer it on the altar along with the grain offering. In this way, the priest will make atonement for the person being cleansed, and the healed person will be ceremonially clean.

²¹"But anyone who cannot afford two lambs must bring one male lamb for a guilt offering,

along with two quarts* of choice flour mixed with olive oil as a grain offering and three-fifths of a pint of olive oil. The guilt offering will be presented by lifting it up, thus making atonement for the person being cleansed. ²²The person being cleansed must also bring two turtledoves or two young pigeons, whichever the person can afford. One of the pair must be used for a sin offering and the other for a whole burnt offering. ²³On the eighth day, the person being cleansed must bring the offerings to the priest for the cleansing ceremony to be performed in the Lord's presence at the Tabernacle entrance. ²⁴The priest will take the lamb for the guilt offering, along with the olive oil, and lift them up before the Lord as an offering to him. ²⁵Then the priest will slaughter the lamb for the guilt offering and put some of its blood on the tip of the person's right ear, on the thumb of the right hand, and on the big toe of the right foot.

²⁶"The priest will also pour some of the olive oil into the palm of his own left hand. ²⁷He will dip his right finger into the oil and sprinkle some of it seven times before the Lord. ²⁸The priest will then put some of the olive oil from his hand on the lobe of the person's right ear, on the thumb of the right hand, and on the big toe of the right foot, in addition to the blood of the guilt offering. ²⁹The oil that is still in the priest's hand will then be poured over the person's head. In this way, the priest will make atonement for the person being cleansed.

³⁰"Then the priest will offer the two turtledoves or the two young pigeons, whichever the person was able to afford. ³¹One of them is for a sin offering and the other for a whole burnt offering, to be presented along with the grain offering. In this way, the priest will make atonement before the Lord for the person being cleansed. ³²These are the instructions for cleansing those who have recovered from a contagious skin disease but who cannot afford to bring the sacrifices normally required for the ceremony of cleansing."

Treatment of Contaminated Houses

³³Then the Lord said to Moses and Aaron, ³⁴"When you arrive in Canaan, the land I am giving you as an inheritance, I may contaminate some of your houses with an infectious mildew.* ³⁵The owner of such a house must then go to the priest and say, 'It looks like my house has some kind of disease.' ³⁶Before the priest examines the house, he must have the house

---

14:10a Hebrew ³/₁₀ of an ephah [5.4 liters]. **14:10b** Hebrew 1 log [0.3 liters]; also in 14:21. **14:11** Hebrew *Tent of Meeting;* also in 14:23. **14:21** Hebrew ¹/₁₀ of an ephah [2 liters]. **14:34** Traditionally rendered *leprosy.* See note at 13:47.

emptied so everything inside will not be pronounced unclean. Then the priest will go in and inspect the house. 37If he finds bright green or reddish streaks on the walls of the house and the contamination appears to go deeper than the wall's surface, 38he will leave the house and lock it up for seven days. 39On the seventh day the priest must return for another inspection. If the mildew on the walls of the house has spread, 40the priest must order that the stones from those areas be removed. The contaminated material will then be thrown into an area outside the town designated as ceremonially unclean. 41Next the inside walls of the entire house must be scraped thoroughly and the scrapings dumped in the unclean place outside the town. 42Other stones will be brought in to replace the ones that were removed, and the walls will be replastered.

43"But if the mildew reappears after all these things have been done, 44the priest must return and inspect the house again. If he sees that the affected areas have spread, the walls are clearly contaminated with an infectious mildew, and the house is defiled. 45It must be torn down, and all its stones, timbers, and plaster must be carried out of town to the place designated as ceremonially unclean. 46Anyone who enters the house while it is closed will be considered ceremonially unclean until evening. 47All who sleep or eat in the house must wash their clothing.

48"But if the priest returns for his inspection and finds that the affected areas have not reappeared after the fresh plastering, then he will pronounce the house clean because the infectious mildew is clearly gone. 49To purify the house the priest will need two birds, some cedarwood, a scarlet cloth, and a hyssop branch. 50He will slaughter one of the birds over a clay pot that is filled with fresh springwater. 51Then he will dip the cedarwood, the hyssop branch, the scarlet cloth, and the living bird into the blood of the slaughtered bird, and he will sprinkle the house seven times. 52After he has purified the house in this way, 53he will release the living bird in the open fields outside the town. In this way, the priest will make atonement for the house, and it will be ceremonially clean.

54"These are the instructions for dealing with the various kinds of contagious skin disease* and infectious mildew,* 55whether in clothing, in a house, 56in a swollen area of skin, in a skin rash, or in a shiny patch of skin. 57These instruc-tions must be followed when dealing with any contagious skin disease or infectious mildew, to determine when something is ceremonially clean or unclean."

CHAPTER 15
Bodily Discharges

The LORD said to Moses and Aaron, 2"Give these further instructions to the Israelites: Any man who has a genital discharge* is ceremonially unclean because of it. 3This defilement applies whether the discharge continues or is stopped up. In either case the man is unclean. 4Any bedding on which he lies and anything on which he sits will be defiled.

5"So if you touch the man's bedding, you will be required to wash your clothes and bathe in water, and you will remain ceremonially defiled until evening. 6If you sit where the man with the discharge has sat, you will be required to wash your clothes and bathe in water. You will then remain defiled until evening. 7The same instructions apply if you touch the man who has the unclean discharge. 8And if he spits on you, you must undergo the same procedure. 9Any blanket on which the man rides will be defiled. 10If you touch or carry anything that was under him, you will be required to wash your clothes and bathe in water, and you will remain defiled until evening. 11If the man touches you without first rinsing his hands, then you will be required to wash your clothes and bathe in water, and you will remain defiled until evening. 12Any clay pot touched by the man with the discharge must be broken, and every wooden utensil he touches must be rinsed with water.

13"When the man's discharge heals, he must count off a period of seven days. During that time, he must wash his clothes and bathe in fresh springwater. Then he will be ceremonially clean. 14On the eighth day he must bring two turtledoves or two young pigeons and present himself to the LORD at the entrance of the Tabernacle* and give his offerings to the priest. 15The priest will present the offerings there, one for a sin offering and the other for a whole burnt offering. In this way, the priest will make atonement for the man before the LORD for his discharge.

16"Whenever a man has an emission of semen, he must wash his entire body, and he will remain ceremonially defiled until evening. 17Any clothing or leather that comes in contact

14:54 Traditionally rendered *leprosy.* See notes at 13:2 and 13:47.   15:2 Hebrew *a discharge from his flesh;* also in 15:32.   15:14 Hebrew *Tent of Meeting;* also in 15:29.

with the semen must be washed, and it will remain defiled until evening. 18After having sexual intercourse, both the man and the woman must bathe, and they will remain defiled until evening.

19 "Whenever a woman has her menstrual period, she will be ceremonially unclean for seven days. If you touch her during that time, you will be defiled until evening. 20Anything on which she lies or sits during that time will be defiled. 21If you touch her bed, you must wash your clothes and bathe in water, and you will remain defiled until evening. 22The same applies if you touch an object on which she sits, 23whether it is her bedding or any piece of furniture. 24If a man has sexual intercourse with her during this time, her menstrual impurity will be transmitted to him. He will remain defiled for seven days, and any bed on which he lies will be defiled.

25 "If the menstrual flow of blood continues for many days beyond the normal period, or if she discharges blood unrelated to her menstruation, the woman will be ceremonially unclean as long as the discharge continues. 26Anything on which she lies or sits during that time will be defiled, just as it would be during her normal menstrual period. 27If you touch her bed or anything on which she sits, you will be defiled. You will be required to wash your clothes and bathe in water, and you will remain defiled until evening.

28 "When the woman's menstrual discharge stops, she must count off a period of seven days. After that, she will be ceremonially clean. 29On the eighth day, she must bring two turtledoves or two young pigeons and present them to the priest at the entrance of the Tabernacle. 30The priest will offer one for a sin offering and the other for a whole burnt offering. In this way, the priest will make atonement for her before the LORD for her menstrual discharge.

31 "In this way, you will keep the people of Israel separate from things that will defile them, so they will not die as a result of defiling my Tabernacle that is right there among them. 32These are the instructions for dealing with a man who has been defiled by a genital discharge or an emission of semen; 33for dealing with a woman during her monthly menstrual period; for dealing with anyone, man or woman, who has had a bodily discharge of any kind; and for dealing with a man who has had intercourse with a woman during her period."

CHAPTER 16
The Day of Atonement

The LORD spoke to Moses after the death of Aaron's two sons, who died when they burned a different kind of fire than the LORD had commanded.* 2The LORD said to Moses, "Warn your brother Aaron not to enter the Most Holy Place behind the inner curtain whenever he chooses; the penalty for intrusion is death. For the Ark's cover—the place of atonement—is there, and I myself am present in the cloud over the atonement cover.

3 "When Aaron enters the sanctuary area, he must follow these instructions fully. He must first bring a young bull for a sin offering and a ram for a whole burnt offering. 4Then he must wash his entire body and put on his linen tunic and the undergarments worn next to his body. He must tie the linen sash around his waist and put the linen turban on his head. These are his sacred garments. 5The people of Israel must then bring him two male goats for a sin offering and a ram for a whole burnt offering.

6 "Aaron will present the bull as a sin offering, to make atonement for himself and his family. 7Then he must bring the two male goats and present them to the LORD at the entrance of the Tabernacle.* 8He is to cast sacred lots to determine which goat will be sacrificed to the LORD and which one will be the scapegoat.* 9The goat chosen to be sacrificed to the LORD will be presented by Aaron as a sin offering. 10The goat chosen to be the scapegoat will be presented to the LORD alive. When it is sent away into the wilderness, it will make atonement for the people.

11 "Then Aaron will present the young bull as a sin offering for himself and his family. After he has slaughtered this bull for the sin offering, 12he will fill an incense burner with burning coals from the altar that stands before the LORD. Then, after filling both his hands with fragrant incense, he will carry the burner and incense behind the inner curtain. 13There in the LORD's presence, he will put the incense on the burning coals so that a cloud of incense will rise over the Ark's cover—the place of atonement—that rests on the Ark of the Covenant.* If he follows these instructions, he will not die. 14He must dip his finger into the blood of the bull and sprinkle it on the front of the atonement cover and then seven times against the front of the Ark.

15 "Then Aaron must slaughter the goat as a

16:1 Hebrew *when they approached the LORD's presence;* compare 10:1.   16:7 Hebrew *Tent of Meeting;* also in 16:16, 17, 20, 23, 33.
16:8 Hebrew *azazel,* which in this context means "the goat of removal"; also in 16:10, 26.   16:13 Hebrew *on the Testimony,* referring to the terms of God's covenant with Israel, which were kept in the Ark.

sin offering for the people and bring its blood behind the inner curtain. There he will sprinkle the blood on the atonement cover and against the front of the Ark, just as he did with the bull's blood. 16In this way, he will make atonement for the Most Holy Place, and he will do the same for the entire Tabernacle, because of the defiling sin and rebellion of the Israelites. 17No one else is allowed inside the Tabernacle while Aaron goes in to make atonement for the Most Holy Place. No one may enter until he comes out again after making atonement for himself, his family, and all the Israelites.

18"Then Aaron will go out to make atonement for the altar that stands before the LORD by smearing some of the blood from the bull and the goat on each of the altar's horns. 19Then he must dip his finger into the blood and sprinkle it seven times over the altar. In this way, he will cleanse it from Israel's defilement and return it to its former holiness.

20"When Aaron has finished making atonement for the Most Holy Place, the Tabernacle, and the altar, he must bring the living goat forward. 21He is to lay both of his hands on the goat's head and confess over it all the sins and rebellion of the Israelites. In this way, he will lay the people's sins on the head of the goat; then he will send it out into the wilderness, led by a man chosen for this task. 22After the man sets it free in the wilderness, the goat will carry all the people's sins upon itself into a desolate land.

23"As Aaron enters the Tabernacle, he must take off the linen garments he wore when he entered the Most Holy Place, and he must leave the garments there. 24Then he must bathe his entire body with water in a sacred place, put on his garments, and go out to sacrifice his own whole burnt offering and the whole burnt offering for the people. In this way, he will make atonement for himself and for the people. 25He must also burn all the fat of the sin offering on the altar.

26"The man chosen to send the goat out into the wilderness as a scapegoat must wash his clothes and bathe in water. Then he may return to the camp.

27"The bull and goat given as sin offerings, whose blood Aaron brought into the Most Holy Place to make atonement for Israel, will be carried outside the camp to be burned. This includes the animals' hides, the internal organs, and the dung. 28The man who does the burning

must wash his clothes and bathe himself in water before returning to the camp.

29"On the appointed day in early autumn,* you must spend the day fasting and not do any work. This is a permanent law for you, and it applies to those who are Israelites by birth, as well as to the foreigners living among you. 30On this day, atonement will be made for you, and you will be cleansed from all your sins in the LORD's presence. 31It will be a Sabbath day of total rest, and you will spend the day in fasting. This is a permanent law for you. 32In future generations, the atonement ceremony will be performed by the anointed high priest who serves in place of his ancestor Aaron. He will put on the holy linen garments 33and make atonement for the Most Holy Place, the Tabernacle, the altar, the priests, and the entire community. 34This is a permanent law for you, to make atonement for the Israelites once each year."

Moses followed all these instructions that the LORD had given to him.

CHAPTER **17**
Prohibitions against Eating Blood
Then the LORD said to Moses, 2"Give Aaron and his sons and all the Israelites these commands from the LORD. 3If any Israelite sacrifices a bull* or a lamb or a goat anywhere inside or outside the camp 4and does not bring it to the entrance of the Tabernacle* to present it as an offering to the LORD, that person will be guilty of a capital offense.* Such a person has shed blood and must be cut off from the community. 5This rule will stop the Israelites from sacrificing animals in the open fields. It will cause them to bring their sacrifices to the priest at the entrance of the Tabernacle, so he can present them to the LORD as peace offerings. 6That way the priest will be able to sprinkle the blood and burn the fat on the LORD's altar at the entrance of the Tabernacle, and it will be very pleasing to the LORD. 7The people must no longer be unfaithful to the LORD by offering sacrifices to evil spirits* out in the fields. This is a permanent law for them, to be kept generation after generation.

8"Give them this command as well, which applies both to Israelites and to the foreigners living among you. If you offer a whole burnt offering or a sacrifice 9and do not bring it to the entrance of the Tabernacle to offer it to the LORD, you will be cut off from the community.

10"And I will turn against anyone, whether an

16:29 Hebrew *On the tenth day of the seventh month.* This day of the Hebrew lunar calendar occurs in September or early October. 17:3 Or *cow.* 17:4a Hebrew *Tent of Meeting;* also in 17:5, 6, 9. 17:4b Hebrew *blood guilt.* 17:7 Or *goat idols.*

Israelite or a foreigner living among you, who eats or drinks blood in any form. I will cut off such a person from the community, 11for the life of any creature is in its blood. I have given you the blood so you can make atonement for your sins. It is the blood, representing life, that brings you atonement. 12That is why I said to the Israelites: 'You and the foreigners who live among you must never eat or drink blood.'

13"And this command applies both to Israelites and to the foreigners living among you. If you go hunting and kill an animal or bird that is approved for eating, you must drain out the blood and cover it with earth. 14The life of every creature is in the blood. That is why I have told the people of Israel never to eat or drink it, for the life of any bird or animal is in the blood. So whoever eats or drinks blood must be cut off.

15"And this command also applies both to Israelites and the foreigners living among you. If you eat from the carcass of an animal that died a natural death or was killed by a wild animal, you must wash your clothes and bathe yourselves in water. Then you will remain ceremonially unclean until evening; after that, you will be considered clean. 16But if you do not wash your clothes and bathe, you will be held responsible."

CHAPTER **18**

Forbidden Sexual Practices

Then the LORD said to Moses, 2"Say this to your people, the Israelites: I, the LORD, am your God. 3So do not act like the people in Egypt, where you used to live, or like the people of Canaan, where I am taking you. You must not imitate their way of life. 4You must obey all my regulations and be careful to keep my laws, for I, the LORD, am your God. 5If you obey my laws and regulations, you will find life through them. I am the LORD.

6"You must never have sexual intercourse with a close relative, for I am the LORD. 7Do not violate your father by having sexual intercourse with your mother. She is your mother; you must never have intercourse with her. 8Do not have sexual intercourse with any of your father's wives, for this would violate your father.

9"Do not have sexual intercourse with your sister or half sister, whether she is your father's daughter or your mother's daughter, whether she was brought up in the same family or somewhere else.

10"Do not have sexual intercourse with your granddaughter, whether your son's daughter or your daughter's daughter; that would violate you.

11Do not have sexual intercourse with the daughter of any of your father's wives; she is your half sister. 12Do not have intercourse with your aunt, your father's sister, because she is your father's close relative. 13Do not have sexual intercourse with your aunt, your mother's sister, because she is your mother's close relative. 14And do not violate your uncle, your father's brother, by having sexual intercourse with his wife; she also is your aunt. 15Do not have sexual intercourse with your daughter-in-law; she is your son's wife. 16Do not have intercourse with your brother's wife; this would violate your brother.

17"Do not have sexual intercourse with both a woman and her daughter or marry both a woman and her granddaughter, whether her son's daughter or her daughter's daughter. They are close relatives, and to do this would be a horrible wickedness.

18"Do not marry a woman and her sister because they will be rivals. But if your wife dies, then it is all right to marry her sister.

19"Do not violate a woman by having sexual intercourse with her during her period of menstrual impurity.

20"Do not defile yourself by having sexual intercourse with your neighbor's wife.

21"Do not give any of your children as a sacrifice to Molech, for you must not profane the name of your God. I am the LORD.

22"Do not practice homosexuality; it is a detestable sin.

23"A man must never defile himself by having sexual intercourse with an animal, and a woman must never present herself to a male animal in order to have intercourse with it; this is a terrible perversion.

24"Do not defile yourselves in any of these ways, because this is how the people I am expelling from the Promised Land have defiled themselves. 25As a result, the entire land has become defiled. That is why I am punishing the people who live there, and the land will soon vomit them out. 26You must strictly obey all of my laws and regulations, and you must not do any of these detestable things. This applies both to you who are Israelites by birth and to the foreigners living among you.

27"All these detestable activities are practiced by the people of the land where I am taking you, and the land has become defiled. 28Do not give the land a reason to vomit you out for defiling it, as it will vomit out the people who live there now. 29Whoever does any of these detestable things will be cut off from the community of Israel. 30So be careful to obey my laws, and do not practice any of these detestable activities. Do not defile yourselves by doing any of them, for I, the LORD, am your God."

CHAPTER 19

Holiness in Personal Conduct

The LORD also said to Moses, 2 "Say this to the entire community of Israel: You must be holy because I, the LORD your God, am holy. 3Each of you must show respect for your mother and father, and you must always observe my Sabbath days of rest, for I, the LORD, am your God. 4Do not put your trust in idols or make gods of metal for yourselves. I, the LORD, am your God.

5 "When you sacrifice a peace offering to the LORD, offer it properly so it will be accepted on your behalf. 6You must eat it on the same day you offer it or on the next day at the latest. Any leftovers that remain until the third day must be burned. 7If any of the offering is eaten on the third day, it will be contaminated, and I will not accept it. 8If you eat it on the third day, you will answer for the sin of profaning what is holy to the LORD and must be cut off from the community.

9 "When you harvest your crops, do not harvest the grain along the edges of your fields, and do not pick up what the harvesters drop. 10It is the same with your grape crop—do not strip every last bunch of grapes from the vines, and do not pick up the grapes that fall to the ground. Leave them for the poor and the foreigners who live among you, for I, the LORD, am your God.

11 "Do not steal.

"Do not cheat one another.

"Do not lie.

12 "Do not use my name to swear a falsehood and so profane the name of your God. I am the LORD.

13 "Do not cheat or rob anyone.

"Always pay your hired workers promptly.

14 "Show your fear of God by treating the deaf with respect and by not taking advantage of the blind. I am the LORD.

15 "Always judge your neighbors fairly, neither favoring the poor nor showing deference to the rich.

16 "Do not spread slanderous gossip among your people.*

"Do not try to get ahead at the cost of your neighbor's life, for I am the LORD.

17 "Do not nurse hatred in your heart for any of your relatives.

"Confront your neighbors directly so you will not be held guilty for their crimes.

18 "Never seek revenge or bear a grudge against anyone, but love your neighbor as yourself. I am the LORD.

19 "You must obey all my laws.

"Do not breed your cattle with other kinds of animals. Do not plant your field with two kinds of seed. Do not wear clothing woven from two different kinds of fabric.

20 "If a man has sexual intercourse with a slave girl who is committed to become someone else's wife, compensation must be paid. But since she had not been freed at the time, the couple will not be put to death. 21The man, however, must bring a ram as a guilt offering and present it to the LORD at the entrance of the Tabernacle.* 22The priest will then make atonement for him before the LORD with the sacrificial ram of the guilt offering, and the man will be forgiven.

23 "When you enter the land and plant fruit trees, leave the fruit unharvested for the first three years and consider it forbidden.* 24In the fourth year the entire crop will be devoted to the LORD as an outburst of praise. 25Finally, in the fifth year you may eat the fruit. In this way, its yield will be increased. I, the LORD, am your God.

26 "Never eat meat that has not been drained of its blood.

"Do not practice fortune-telling or witchcraft.

27 "Do not trim off the hair on your temples or clip the edges of your beards.

28 "Never cut your bodies in mourning for the dead or mark your skin with tattoos, for I am the LORD.

29 "Do not defile your daughter by making her a prostitute, or the land will be filled with promiscuity and detestable wickedness.

30 "Keep my Sabbath days of rest and show reverence toward my sanctuary, for I am the LORD.

31 "Do not rely on mediums and psychics, for you will be defiled by them. I, the LORD, am your God.

32 "Show your fear of God by standing up in the presence of elderly people and showing respect for the aged. I am the LORD.

33 "Do not exploit the foreigners who live in your land. 34They should be treated like everyone

19:16 Hebrew *Do not act as a merchant toward your own people.*   19:21 Hebrew *Tent of Meeting.*   19:23 Hebrew *consider it uncircumcised.*

else, and you must love them as you love yourself. Remember that you were once foreigners in the land of Egypt. I, the LORD, am your God.

35 "Do not use dishonest standards when measuring length, weight, or volume. 36Your scales and weights must be accurate. Your containers for measuring dry goods or liquids must be accurate.* I, the LORD, am your God, who brought you out of the land of Egypt. 37You must be careful to obey all of my laws and regulations, for I am the LORD."

CHAPTER **20**

Punishments for Disobedience

The LORD said to Moses, 2 "Give the Israelites these instructions, which apply to those who are Israelites by birth as well as to the foreigners living among you. If any among them devote their children as burnt offerings to Molech, they must be stoned to death by people of the community. 3I myself will turn against them and cut them off from the community, because they have defiled my sanctuary and profaned my holy name by giving their children to Molech. 4And if the people of the community ignore this offering of children to Molech and refuse to execute the guilty parents, 5then I myself will turn against them and cut them off from the community, along with all those who commit prostitution by worshiping Molech.

6 "If any among the people are unfaithful by consulting and following mediums or psychics, I will turn against them and cut them off from the community. 7So set yourselves apart to be holy, for I, the LORD, am your God. 8Keep all my laws and obey them, for I am the LORD, who makes you holy.

9 "All who curse their father or mother must be put to death. They are guilty of a capital offense.

10 "If a man commits adultery with another man's wife, both the man and the woman must be put to death. 11If a man has intercourse with his father's wife, both the man and the woman must die, for they are guilty of a capital offense. 12If a man has intercourse with his daughter-in-law, both must be put to death. They have acted contrary to nature and are guilty of a capital offense.

13 "The penalty for homosexual acts is death to both parties. They have committed a detestable act and are guilty of a capital offense. 14If a man has intercourse with both a woman and her mother, such an act is terribly wicked. All three of them must be burned to death to wipe out such wickedness from among you.

15 "If a man has sexual intercourse with an animal, he must be put to death, and the animal must be killed. 16If a woman approaches a male animal to have intercourse with it, she and the animal must both be put to death. Both must die, for they are guilty of a capital offense.

17 "If a man has sexual intercourse with his sister, the daughter of either his father or his mother, it is a terrible disgrace. Both of them must be publicly cut off from the community. Since the man has had intercourse with his sister, he will suffer the consequences of his guilt. 18If a man has intercourse with a woman suffering from a hemorrhage,* both of them must be cut off from the community, because he exposed the source of her flow, and she allowed him to do it.

19 "If a man has sexual intercourse with his aunt, whether his mother's sister or his father's sister, he has violated a close relative. Both parties are guilty of a capital offense. 20If a man has intercourse with his uncle's wife, he has violated his uncle. Both the man and woman involved are guilty of a capital offense and will die childless. 21If a man marries his brother's wife, it is an act of impurity. He has violated his brother, and the guilty couple will remain childless.

22 "You must carefully obey all my laws and regulations; otherwise the land to which I am bringing you will vomit you out. 23Do not live by the customs of the people whom I will expel before you. It is because they do these terrible things that I detest them so much. 24But I have promised that you will inherit their land, a land flowing with milk and honey. I, the LORD, am your God, who has set you apart from all other people.

25 "You must therefore make a distinction between ceremonially clean and unclean animals, and between clean and unclean birds. You must not defile yourselves by eating any animal or bird or creeping creature that I have forbidden. 26You must be holy because I, the LORD, am holy. I have set you apart from all other people to be my very own.

27 "Men and women among you who act as mediums or psychics must be put to death by stoning. They are guilty of a capital offense."

19:36 Hebrew *Use an honest ephah* [a dry measure] *and an honest hin* [a liquid measure]. **20:18** Or *a woman who is menstruating.*

CHAPTER **21**

Instructions for the Priests

The LORD said to Moses, "Tell the priests to avoid making themselves ceremonially unclean by touching a dead relative ²unless it is a close relative—mother or father, son or daughter, brother ³or virgin sister who was dependent because she had no husband. ⁴As a husband among his relatives,* he must not defile himself.

⁵"The priests must never shave their heads, trim the edges of their beards, or cut their bodies. ⁶They must be set apart to God as holy and must never dishonor his name. After all, they are the ones who present the offerings to the LORD by fire, providing God with his food, and they must remain holy.

⁷"The priests must not marry women defiled by prostitution or women who have been divorced, for the priests must be set apart to God as holy. ⁸You must treat them as holy because they offer up food to your God. You must consider them holy because I, the LORD, am holy, and I make you holy. ⁹If a priest's daughter becomes a prostitute, defiling her father's holiness as well as herself, she must be burned to death.

¹⁰"The high priest, who has had the anointing oil poured on his head and has been ordained to wear the special priestly garments, must never let his hair hang loose* or tear his clothing. ¹¹He must never defile himself by going near a dead person, even if it is his father or mother. ¹²He must not desecrate the sanctuary of his God by leaving it to attend his parents' funeral, because he has been made holy by the anointing oil of his God. I am the LORD.

¹³"The high priest must marry a virgin. ¹⁴He must not marry a widow, a divorced woman, or a woman defiled by prostitution. She must be a virgin from his own clan, ¹⁵that he may not dishonor his descendants among the members of his clan, because I, the LORD, have made him holy."

¹⁶Then the LORD said to Moses, ¹⁷"Tell Aaron that in all future generations, his descendants who have physical defects will not qualify to offer food to their God. ¹⁸No one who has a defect may come near to me, whether he is blind or lame, stunted or deformed, ¹⁹or has a broken foot or hand, ²⁰or has a humped back or is a dwarf, or has a defective eye, or has oozing sores or scabs on his skin, or has damaged testicles. ²¹Even though he is a descendant of Aaron, his physical defects disqualify him from presenting offerings to the LORD by fire. Since he has a blemish, he may not offer food to his God. ²²However, he may eat from the food offered to God, including the holy offerings and the most holy offerings. ²³Yet because of his physical defect, he must never go behind the inner curtain or come near the altar, for this would desecrate my holy places. I am the LORD who makes them holy."

²⁴So Moses gave these instructions to Aaron and his sons and to all the Israelites.

CHAPTER **22**

The LORD said to Moses, ²"Tell Aaron and his sons to treat the sacred gifts that the Israelites set apart for me with great care, so they do not profane my holy name. I am the LORD. ³Remind them that if any of their descendants are ceremonially unclean when they approach the sacred food presented by the Israelites, they must be cut off from my presence. I am the LORD!

⁴"If any of the priests have a contagious skin disease* or any kind of discharge that makes them ceremonially unclean, they may not eat the sacred offerings until they have been pronounced clean. If any of the priests become unclean by touching a corpse, or are defiled by an emission of semen, ⁵or by touching a creeping creature that is unclean, or by touching someone who is ceremonially unclean for any reason, ⁶they will remain defiled until evening. They must not eat any of the sacred offerings until they have purified their bodies with water. ⁷When the sun goes down, they will be clean again and may eat the sacred offerings. After all, this food has been set aside for them. ⁸The priests may never eat an animal that has died a natural death or has been torn apart by wild animals, for this would defile them. I am the LORD. ⁹Warn all the priests to follow these instructions carefully; otherwise they will be subject to punishment and die for violating them. I am the LORD who makes them holy.

¹⁰"No one outside a priest's family may ever eat the sacred offerings, even if the person lives in a priest's home or is one of his hired servants. ¹¹However, if the priest buys slaves with his own money, they may eat of his food. And if his slaves have children, they also may share his food. ¹²If a priest's daughter marries someone outside the priestly family, she may no longer eat the sacred offerings. ¹³But if she becomes a widow or is divorced and has no children to support her, and she returns to live in her

21:4 The meaning of the Hebrew is uncertain.   21:10 Or *uncover his head.*   22:4 Traditionally rendered *leprosy.* See note at 13:2.

father's home, she may eat her father's food again. But other than these exceptions, only members of the priests' families are allowed to eat the sacred offerings.

¹⁴"Anyone who eats the sacred offerings without realizing it must pay the priest for the amount eaten, plus an added penalty of 20 percent. ¹⁵No one may defile the sacred offerings brought to the LORD by the Israelites ¹⁶by allowing unauthorized people to eat them. The negligent priest would bring guilt upon the people and require them to pay compensation. I am the LORD, who makes them holy."

Worthy and Unworthy Offerings

¹⁷And the LORD said to Moses, ¹⁸"Give Aaron and his sons and all the Israelites these instructions, which apply to those who are Israelites by birth as well as to the foreigners living among you. If you offer a whole burnt offering to the LORD, whether to fulfill a vow or as a freewill offering, ¹⁹it will be accepted only if it is a male animal with no physical defects. It may be either a bull, a ram, or a male goat. ²⁰Do not bring an animal with physical defects, because it won't be accepted on your behalf.

²¹"If you bring a peace offering to the LORD from the herd or flock, whether to fulfill a vow or as a freewill offering, you must offer an animal that has no physical defects of any kind. ²²An animal that is blind, injured, mutilated, or that has a growth, an open sore, or a scab must never be offered to the LORD by fire on the altar. ²³If the bull* or lamb is deformed or stunted, it may still be offered as a freewill offering, but it may not be offered to fulfill a vow. ²⁴If an animal has damaged testicles or is castrated, it may never be offered to the LORD. ²⁵You must never accept mutilated or defective animals from foreigners to be offered as a sacrifice to your God. Such animals will not be accepted on your behalf because they are defective."

²⁶And the LORD said to Moses, ²⁷"When a bull or a ram or a male goat is born, it must be left with its mother for seven days. From the eighth day on, it will be acceptable as an offering given to the LORD by fire. ²⁸But you must never slaughter a mother animal and her offspring on the same day, whether from the herd or the flock. ²⁹When you bring a thanksgiving offering to the LORD, it must be sacrificed properly so it will be accepted on your behalf. ³⁰Eat the entire sacrificial animal on the day it is presented. Don't

leave any of it until the second day. I am the LORD.

³¹"You must faithfully keep all my commands by obeying them, for I am the LORD. ³²Do not treat my holy name as common and ordinary. I must be treated as holy by the people of Israel. It is I, the LORD, who makes you holy. ³³It was I who rescued you from Egypt, that I might be your very own God. I am the LORD."

CHAPTER 23
The Appointed Festivals

The LORD said to Moses, ²"Give the Israelites instructions regarding the LORD's appointed festivals, the days when all of you will be summoned to worship me. ³You may work for six days each week, but on the seventh day all work must come to a complete stop. It is the LORD's Sabbath day of complete rest, a holy day to assemble for worship. It must be observed wherever you live. ⁴In addition to the Sabbath, the LORD has established festivals, the holy occasions to be observed at the proper time each year.

Passover and the Festival of Unleavened Bread

⁵"First comes the LORD's Passover, which begins at twilight on its appointed day in early spring.* ⁶Then the day after the Passover celebration,* the Festival of Unleavened Bread begins. This festival to the LORD continues for seven days, and during that time all the bread you eat must be made without yeast. ⁷On the first day of the festival, all the people must stop their regular work and gather for a sacred assembly. ⁸On each of the next seven days, the people must present an offering to the LORD by fire. On the seventh day, the people must again stop all their regular work to hold a sacred assembly."

The Festival of Firstfruits

⁹Then the LORD told Moses ¹⁰to give these instructions to the Israelites: "When you arrive in the land I am giving you and you harvest your first crops, bring the priest some grain from the first portion of your grain harvest. ¹¹On the day after the Sabbath, the priest will lift it up before the LORD so it may be accepted on your behalf. ¹²That same day you must sacrifice a year-old male lamb with no physical defects as a whole burnt offering to the LORD. ¹³A grain offering must accompany it consisting of three quarts* of choice flour mixed with olive oil. It will be an

---

22:23 Or *cow*; also in 22:27.   **23:5** Hebrew *on the fourteenth day of the first month.* This day of the Hebrew lunar calendar occurs in late March or early April.   **23:6** Hebrew *On the fifteenth day of the same month.*   **23:13a** Hebrew ²/₁₀ *of an ephah* [3.6 liters]; also in 23:17.

offering given to the LORD by fire, and it will be very pleasing to him. Along with this sacrifice, you must also offer one quart* of wine as a drink offering. 14Do not eat any bread or roasted grain or fresh kernels on that day until after you have brought this offering to your God. This is a permanent law for you, and it must be observed wherever you live.

The Festival of Harvest

15"From the day after the Sabbath, the day the bundle of grain was lifted up as an offering, count off seven weeks. 16Keep counting until the day after the seventh Sabbath, fifty days later, and bring an offering of new grain to the LORD. 17From wherever you live, bring two loaves of bread to be lifted up before the LORD as an offering. These loaves must be baked from three quarts of choice flour that contains yeast. They will be an offering to the LORD from the first of your crops. 18Along with this bread, present seven one-year-old lambs with no physical defects, one bull, and two rams as burnt offerings to the LORD. These whole burnt offerings, together with the accompanying grain offerings and drink offerings, will be given to the LORD by fire and will be pleasing to him. 19Then you must offer one male goat as a sin offering and two one-year-old male lambs as a peace offering.

20"The priest will lift up these offerings before the LORD, together with the loaves representing the first of your later crops. These offerings are holy to the LORD and will belong to the priests. 21That same day, you must stop all your regular work and gather for a sacred assembly. This is a permanent law for you, and it must be observed wherever you live.

22"When you harvest the crops of your land, do not harvest the grain along the edges of your fields, and do not pick up what the harvesters drop. Leave it for the poor and the foreigners living among you. I, the LORD, am your God."

The Festival of Trumpets

23The LORD told Moses 24to give these instructions to the Israelites: "On the appointed day in early autumn,* you are to celebrate a day of complete rest. All your work must stop on that day. You will call the people to a sacred assembly—the Festival of Trumpets—with loud blasts from a trumpet. 25You must do no regular work on that day. Instead, you are to present offerings to the LORD by fire."

The Day of Atonement

26Then the LORD said to Moses, 27"Remember that the Day of Atonement is to be celebrated on the ninth day after the Festival of Trumpets.* On that day you must humble yourselves, gather for a sacred assembly, and present offerings to the LORD by fire. 28Do no work during that entire day because it is the Day of Atonement, when atonement will be made for you before the LORD your God, and payment will be made for your sins. 29Anyone who does not spend that day in humility will be cut off from the community. 30And I will destroy anyone among you who does any kind of work on that day. 31You must do no work at all! This is a permanent law for you, and it must be observed wherever you live. 32This will be a Sabbath day of total rest for you, and on that day you must humble yourselves. This time of rest and fasting will begin the evening before the Day of Atonement* and extend until evening of that day."

The Festival of Shelters

33And the LORD said to Moses, 34"Tell the Israelites to begin the Festival of Shelters on the fifth day after the Day of Atonement.* This festival to the LORD will last for seven days. 35It will begin with a sacred assembly on the first day, and all your regular work must stop. 36On each of the seven festival days, you must present offerings to the LORD by fire. On the eighth day, you must gather again for a sacred assembly and present another offering to the LORD by fire. This will be a solemn closing assembly, and no regular work may be done that day.

37"These are the LORD's appointed annual festivals. Celebrate them by gathering in sacred assemblies to present all the various offerings to the LORD by fire—whole burnt offerings and grain offerings, sacrificial meals and drink offerings—each on its proper day. 38These festivals must be observed in addition to the LORD's regular Sabbath days. And these offerings must be given in addition to your personal gifts, the offerings you make to accompany your vows, and any freewill offerings that you present to the LORD.

39"Now, on the first day of the Festival of Shelters,* after you have harvested all the produce of the land, you will begin to celebrate this seven-day festival to the LORD. Remember that the first day and closing eighth day of the festival will

---

23:13b Hebrew ¼ *of a hin* [1 liter]. 23:24 Hebrew *On the first day of the seventh month.* This day of the Hebrew lunar calendar occurs in September or early October. 23:27 Hebrew *on the tenth day of the seventh month;* see 23:24 and the note there. 23:32 Hebrew *the evening of the ninth day of the month;* see 23:24, 27 and the notes there. 23:34 Hebrew *on the fifteenth day of the seventh month;* see 23:24, 27 and the notes there. 23:39 Hebrew *on the fifteenth day of the seventh month;* see 23:24 and the note there.

be days of total rest. ⁴⁰On the first day, gather fruit from citrus trees,* and collect palm fronds and other leafy branches and willows that grow by the streams. Then rejoice before the LORD your God for seven days. ⁴¹You must observe this seven-day festival to the LORD every year. This is a permanent law for you, and it must be kept by all future generations. ⁴²During the seven festival days, all of you who are Israelites by birth must live in shelters. ⁴³This will remind each new generation of Israelites that their ancestors had to live in shelters when I rescued them from the land of Egypt. I, the LORD, am your God."

⁴⁴So Moses gave these instructions regarding the annual festivals of the LORD to the Israelites.

CHAPTER **24**

Pure Oil and Holy Bread

The LORD said to Moses, ²"Command the people of Israel to provide you with pure olive oil for the lampstand, so it can be kept burning continually. ³Aaron will set it up outside the inner curtain of the Most Holy Place in the Tabernacle* and must arrange to have the lamps tended continually, from evening until morning, before the LORD. This is a permanent law for you, and it must be kept by all future generations. ⁴The lamps on the pure gold lampstand must be tended continually in the LORD's presence.

⁵"You must bake twelve loaves of bread from choice flour, using three quarts* of flour for each loaf. ⁶Place the bread in the LORD's presence on the pure gold table, and arrange the loaves in two rows, with six in each row. ⁷Sprinkle some pure frankincense near each row. It will serve as a token offering, to be burned in place of the bread as an offering given to the LORD by fire. ⁸Every Sabbath day this bread must be laid out before the LORD on behalf of the Israelites as a continual part of the covenant. ⁹The loaves of bread belong to Aaron and his male descendants, who must eat them in a sacred place, for they represent a most holy portion of the offerings given to the LORD by fire."

An Example of Just Punishment

¹⁰One day a man who had an Israelite mother and an Egyptian father got into a fight with one of the Israelite men. ¹¹During the fight, this son of an Israelite woman blasphemed the LORD's name. So the man was brought to Moses for judgment. His mother's name was Shelomith. She was the daughter of Dibri of the tribe of Dan. ¹²They put the man in custody until the LORD's will in the matter should become clear.

¹³Then the LORD said to Moses, ¹⁴"Take the blasphemer outside the camp, and tell all those who heard him to lay their hands on his head. Then let the entire community stone him to death. ¹⁵Say to the people of Israel: Those who blaspheme God will suffer the consequences of their guilt and be punished. ¹⁶Anyone who blasphemes the LORD's name must be stoned to death by the whole community of Israel. Any Israelite or foreigner among you who blasphemes the LORD's name will surely die.

¹⁷"Anyone who takes another person's life must be put to death.

¹⁸"Anyone who kills another person's animal must pay it back in full—a live animal for the animal that was killed.

¹⁹"Anyone who injures another person must be dealt with according to the injury inflicted— ²⁰fracture for fracture, eye for eye, tooth for tooth. Whatever anyone does to hurt another person must be paid back in kind.

²¹"Whoever kills an animal must make full restitution, but whoever kills another person must be put to death.

²²"These same regulations apply to Israelites by birth and foreigners who live among you. I, the LORD, am your God."

²³After Moses gave all these instructions to the Israelites, they led the blasphemer outside the camp and stoned him to death, just as the LORD had commanded Moses.

CHAPTER **25**

The Sabbath Year

While Moses was on Mount Sinai, the LORD said to him, ²"Give these instructions to the Israelites: When you have entered the land I am giving you as an inheritance, the land itself must observe a Sabbath to the LORD every seventh year. ³For six years you may plant your fields and prune your vineyards and harvest your crops, ⁴but during the seventh year the land will enjoy a Sabbath year of rest to the LORD. Do not plant your crops or prune your vineyards during that entire year. ⁵And don't store away the crops that grow naturally or process the grapes that grow on your unpruned vines. The land is to have a year of total rest. ⁶But you, your male and female slaves, your hired servants, and any foreigners who live with you may eat the produce that grows naturally during the Sabbath year. ⁷And your livestock and the wild animals will also be allowed to eat of the land's bounty.

23:40 Or fruit from majestic trees.   24:3 Hebrew the curtain of the Testimony in the Tent of Meeting.   24:5 Hebrew 2/10 of an ephah [3.6 liters].

The Year of Jubilee

8"In addition, you must count off seven Sabbath years, seven years times seven, adding up to forty-nine years in all. 9Then on the Day of Atonement of the fiftieth year,* blow the trumpets loud and long throughout the land. 10This year will be set apart as holy, a time to proclaim release for all who live there. It will be a jubilee year for you, when each of you returns to the lands that belonged to your ancestors and rejoins your clan. 11Yes, the fiftieth year will be a jubilee for you. During that year, do not plant any seeds or store away any of the crops that grow naturally, and do not process the grapes that grow on your unpruned vines. 12It will be a jubilee year for you, and you must observe it as a special and holy time. You may, however, eat the produce that grows naturally in the fields that year. 13In the Year of Jubilee each of you must return to the lands that belonged to your ancestors.

14"When you make an agreement with a neighbor to buy or sell property, you must never take advantage of each other. 15When you buy land from your neighbor, the price of the land should be based on the number of years since the last jubilee. The seller will charge you only for the crop years left until the next Year of Jubilee. 16The more the years, the higher the price; the fewer the years, the lower the price. After all, the person selling the land is actually selling you a certain number of harvests. 17Show your fear of God by not taking advantage of each other. I, the LORD, am your God.

18"If you want to live securely in the land, keep my laws and obey my regulations. 19Then the land will yield bumper crops, and you will eat your fill and live securely in it. 20But you might ask, 'What will we eat during the seventh year, since we are not allowed to plant or harvest crops that year?' 21The answer is, 'I will order my blessing for you in the sixth year, so the land will produce a bumper crop, enough to support you for three years. 22As you plant the seed in the eighth year, you will still be eating the produce of the previous year. In fact, you will eat from the old crop until the new harvest comes in the ninth year.' 23And remember, the land must never be sold on a permanent basis because it really belongs to me. You are only foreigners and tenants living with me.

Redemption of Property

24"With every sale of land there must be a stipulation that the land can be redeemed at any time. 25If any of your Israelite relatives go bank-rupt and are forced to sell some inherited land, then a close relative, a kinsman redeemer, may buy it back for them. 26If there is no one to redeem the land but the person who sold it manages to get enough money to buy it back, 27then that person has the right to redeem it from the one who bought it. The price of the land will be based on the number of years until the next Year of Jubilee. After buying it back, the original owner may then return to the land. 28But if the original owner cannot afford to redeem it, then it will belong to the new owner until the next Year of Jubilee. In the jubilee year, the land will be returned to the original owner.

29"Anyone who sells a house inside a walled city has the right to redeem it for a full year after its sale. During that time, the seller retains the right to buy it back. 30But if it is not redeemed within a year, then the house within the walled city will become the permanent property of the buyer. It will not be returned to the original owner in the Year of Jubilee. 31But a house in a village—a settlement without fortified walls—will be treated like property in the open fields. Such a house may be redeemed at any time and must be returned to the original owner in the Year of Jubilee.

32"The Levites always have the right to redeem any house they have sold within the cities belonging to them. 33And any property that can be redeemed by the Levites—all houses within the Levitical cities—must be returned in the Year of Jubilee. After all, the cities reserved for the Levites are the only property they own in all Israel. 34The strip of pastureland around each of the Levitical cities may never be sold. It is their permanent ancestral property.

Redemption of the Poor and Enslaved

35"If any of your Israelite relatives fall into poverty and cannot support themselves, support them as you would a resident foreigner and allow them to live with you. 36Do not demand an advance or charge interest on the money you lend them. Instead, show your fear of God by letting them live with you as your relatives. 37Remember, do not charge your relatives interest on anything you lend them, whether money or food. 38I, the LORD, am your God, who brought you out of Egypt to give you the land of Canaan and to be your God.

39"If any of your Israelite relatives go bank-rupt and sell themselves to you, do not treat them as slaves. 40Treat them instead as hired servants or as resident foreigners who live with

25:9 Hebrew *on the tenth day of the seventh month, on the Day of Atonement;* see 23:27 and the note there.

you, and they will serve you only until the Year of Jubilee. 41At that time they and their children will no longer be obligated to you, and they will return to their clan and ancestral property. 42The people of Israel are my servants, whom I brought out of the land of Egypt, so they must never be sold as slaves. 43Show your fear of God by treating them well; never exercise your power over them in a ruthless way.

44"However, you may purchase male or female slaves from among the foreigners who live among you. 45You may also purchase the children of such resident foreigners, including those who have been born in your land. You may treat them as your property, 46passing them on to your children as a permanent inheritance. You may treat your slaves like this, but the people of Israel, your relatives, must never be treated this way.

47"If a resident foreigner becomes rich, and if some of your Israelite relatives go bankrupt and sell themselves to such a foreigner, 48they still retain the right of redemption. They may be bought back by a close relative—49an uncle, a nephew, or anyone else who is closely related. They may also redeem themselves if they can get the money. 50The price of their freedom will be based on the number of years left until the next Year of Jubilee—whatever it would cost to hire a servant for that number of years. 51If many years still remain, they will repay most of what they received when they sold themselves. 52If only a few years remain until the Year of Jubilee, then they will repay a relatively small amount for their redemption. 53The foreigner must treat them as servants hired on a yearly basis. You must not allow a resident foreigner to treat any of your Israelite relatives ruthlessly. 54If any Israelites have not been redeemed by the time the Year of Jubilee arrives, then they and their children must be set free at that time. 55For the people of Israel are my servants, whom I brought out of the land of Egypt. I, the LORD, am your God.

CHAPTER **26**

Blessings for Obedience

"Do not make idols or set up carved images, sacred pillars, or shaped stones to be worshiped in your land. I, the LORD, am your God. 2You must keep my Sabbath days of rest and show reverence for my sanctuary. I am the LORD.

3"If you keep my laws and are careful to obey my commands, 4I will send the seasonal rains. The land will then yield its crops, and the trees will produce their fruit. 5Your threshing season will extend until the grape harvest, and your grape harvest will extend until it is time to plant grain again. You will eat your fill and live securely in your land.

6"I will give you peace in the land, and you will be able to sleep without fear. I will remove the wild animals from your land and protect you from your enemies. 7In fact, you will chase down all your enemies and slaughter them with your swords. 8Five of you will chase a hundred, and a hundred of you will chase ten thousand! All your enemies will fall beneath the blows of your weapons.

9"I will look favorably upon you and multiply your people and fulfill my covenant with you. 10You will have such a surplus of crops that you will need to get rid of the leftovers from the previous year to make room for each new harvest. 11I will live among you, and I will not despise you. 12I will walk among you; I will be your God, and you will be my people. 13I, the LORD, am your God, who brought you from the land of Egypt so you would no longer be slaves. I have lifted the yoke of slavery from your neck so you can walk free with your heads held high.

Punishments for Disobedience

14"However, if you do not listen to me or obey my commands, 15and if you break my covenant by rejecting my laws and treating my regulations with contempt, 16I will punish you. You will suffer from sudden terrors, with wasting diseases, and with burning fevers, causing your eyes to fail and your life to ebb away. You will plant your crops in vain because your enemies will eat them. 17I will turn against you, and you will be defeated by all your enemies. They will rule over you, and you will run even when no one is chasing you!

18"And if, in spite of this, you still disobey me, I will punish you for your sins seven times over. 19I will break down your arrogant spirit by making the skies above as unyielding as iron and the earth beneath as hard as bronze. 20All your work will be for nothing, for your land will yield no crops, and your trees will bear no fruit.

21"If even then you remain hostile toward me and refuse to obey, I will inflict you with seven more disasters for your sins. 22I will release wild animals that will kill your children and destroy your cattle, so your numbers will dwindle and your roads will be deserted.

23"And if you fail to learn a lesson from this and continue your hostility toward me, 24then I myself will be hostile toward you, and I will personally strike you seven times over for your sins. 25I will send armies against you to carry out these covenant threats. If you flee to your cities, I will send a plague to destroy you there, and you will be conquered by your enemies. 26I will completely destroy your food supply, so the bread from one oven will have to be stretched to feed ten families. They will ration your food by weight, and even if you have food to eat, you will not be satisfied.

27"If after this you still refuse to listen and still remain hostile toward me, 28then I will give full vent to my hostility. I will punish you seven times over for your sins. 29You will eat the flesh of your own sons and daughters. 30I will destroy your pagan shrines and cut down your incense altars. I will leave your corpses piled up beside your lifeless idols, and I will despise you. 31I will make your cities desolate and destroy your places of worship, and I will take no pleasure in your offerings of incense. 32Yes, I myself will devastate your land. Your enemies who come to occupy it will be utterly shocked at the destruction they see. 33I will scatter you among the nations and attack you with my own weapons. Your land will become desolate, and your cities will lie in ruins. 34Then at last the land will make up for its missed Sabbath years as it lies desolate during your years of exile in the land of your enemies. Then the land will finally rest and enjoy its Sabbaths. 35As the land lies in ruins, it will take the rest you never allowed it to take every seventh year while you lived in it.

36"And for those of you who survive, I will demoralize you in the land of your enemies far away. You will live there in such constant fear that the sound of a leaf driven by the wind will send you fleeing. You will run as though chased by a warrior with a sword, and you will fall even when no one is pursuing you. 37Yes, though no one is chasing you, you will stumble over each other in flight, as though fleeing in battle. You will have no power to stand before your enemies. 38You will die among the foreign nations and be devoured in the land of your enemies. 39Those still left alive will rot away in enemy lands because of their sins and the sins of their ancestors.

40"But at last my people will confess their sins and the sins of their ancestors for betraying me and being hostile toward me. 41Finally, when I have given full expression to my hostility and have brought them to the land of their enemies, then at last their disobedient hearts will be humbled, and they will pay for their sins. 42Then I will remember my covenant with Jacob, with Isaac, and with Abraham, and I will remember the land. 43And the land will enjoy its years of Sabbath rest as it lies deserted. At last the people will receive the due punishment for their sins, for they rejected my regulations and despised my laws.

44"But despite all this, I will not utterly reject or despise them while they are in exile in the land of their enemies. I will not cancel my covenant with them by wiping them out. I, the LORD, am their God. 45I will remember my ancient covenant with their ancestors, whom I brought out of Egypt while all the nations watched. I, the LORD, am their God."

46These are the laws, regulations, and instructions that the LORD gave to the Israelites through Moses on Mount Sinai.

CHAPTER **27**

Redeeming Gifts Offered to the LORD

The LORD said to Moses, 2"Give the following instructions to the Israelites: If you make a special vow to dedicate someone to the LORD by paying the value of that person, 3here is the scale of values to be used. A man between the ages of twenty and sixty is valued at fifty pieces of silver*; 4a woman of that age is valued at thirty pieces of silver. 5A boy between five and twenty is valued at twenty pieces of silver; a girl of that age is valued at ten pieces of silver. 6A boy between the ages of one month and five years is valued at five pieces of silver; a girl of that age is valued at three pieces of silver. 7A man older than sixty is valued at fifteen pieces of silver; a woman older than sixty is valued at ten pieces of silver. 8If you desire to make such a vow but cannot afford to pay the prescribed amount, go to the priest and he will evaluate your ability to pay. You will then pay the amount decided by the priest.

9"If your vow involves giving a clean animal—one that is acceptable as an offering to the LORD—then your gift to the LORD will be considered holy. 10The animal should never be exchanged or substituted for another—neither a good animal for a bad one nor a bad animal for a good one. But if such an exchange is in fact made, then both the original animal and the substitute will be considered holy. 11But if your vow involves an unclean animal—one that is

---

27:3 Hebrew *50 shekels of silver, according to the standard sanctuary shekel,* each about 0.4 ounces or 11 grams in weight. The term *shekels* also appears in 27:4, 5, 6, 7, 16.

not acceptable as an offering to the LORD—then you must bring the animal to the priest. 12He will assess its value, and his assessment will be final. 13If you want to redeem the animal, you must pay the value set by the priest, plus 20 percent.

14"If you dedicate a house to the LORD, the priest must come to assess its value. The priest's assessment will be final. 15If you wish to redeem the house, you must pay the value set by the priest, plus 20 percent. Then the house will again belong to you.

16"If you dedicate to the LORD a piece of your ancestral property, its value will be assessed by the amount of seed required to plant it—fifty pieces of silver for an area that produces* five bushels* of barley seed. 17If the field is dedicated to the LORD in the Year of Jubilee, then the entire assessment will apply. 18But if the field is dedicated after the Year of Jubilee, the priest must assess the land's value in proportion to the years left until the next Year of Jubilee. 19If you decide to redeem the dedicated field, you must pay the land's value as assessed by the priest, plus 20 percent. Then the field will again belong to you. 20But if you decide not to redeem the field, or if the field is sold to someone else by the priests, it can never be redeemed. 21When the field is released in the Year of Jubilee, it will be holy, a field specially set apart* for the LORD. It will become the property of the priests.

22"If you dedicate to the LORD a field that you have purchased but which is not part of your ancestral property, 23the priest must assess its value based on the years until the next Year of Jubilee. You must then give the assessed value of

the land as a sacred donation to the LORD. 24In the Year of Jubilee the field will be released to the original owner from whom you purchased it. 25All the value assessments must be measured in terms of the standard sanctuary shekel.*

26"You may not dedicate to the LORD the firstborn of your cattle or sheep because the firstborn of these animals already belong to him. 27However, if it is the firstborn of a ceremonially unclean animal, you may redeem it by paying the priest's assessment of its worth, plus 20 percent. If you do not redeem it, the priest may sell it to someone else for its assessed value.

28"However, anything specially set apart by the LORD—whether a person, an animal, or an inherited field—must never be sold or redeemed. Anything devoted in this way has been set apart for the LORD as holy. 29A person specially set apart by the LORD for destruction cannot be redeemed. Such a person must be put to death.

30"A tenth of the produce of the land, whether grain or fruit, belongs to the LORD and must be set apart to him as holy. 31If you want to redeem the LORD's tenth of the fruit or grain, you must pay its value, plus 20 percent. 32The LORD also owns every tenth animal counted off from your herds and flocks. They are set apart to him as holy. 33The tenth animal must not be selected on the basis of whether it is good or bad, and no substitutions will be allowed. If any exchange is in fact made, then both the original animal and the substituted one will be considered holy and cannot be redeemed."

34These are the commands that the LORD gave to the Israelites through Moses on Mount Sinai.

27:16a Or *requires.*   27:16b Hebrew *1 homer* [182 liters].   27:21 The Hebrew term used here refers to the complete consecration of things or people to the LORD, either by destroying them or by giving them as an offering; also in 27:28, 29.   27:25 Hebrew *measured according to the sanctuary shekel, 20 gerahs to each shekel.* Each sanctuary shekel was about 0.4 ounces or 11 grams in weight.

Numbers

Israel's First Census

One day in midspring,* during the second year after Israel's departure from Egypt, the LORD spoke to Moses in the Tabernacle* in the wilderness of Sinai. He said, 2"Take a census of the whole community of Israel by their clans and families. List the names of all the men 3twenty years old or older who are able to go to war. You and Aaron are to direct the project, 4assisted by one family leader from each tribe."

5These are the tribes and the names of the leaders chosen for the task:

Tribe	Leader
Reuben	Elizur son of Shedeur
6 Simeon	Shelumiel son of Zurishaddai
7 Judah	Nahshon son of Amminadab
8 Issachar	Nethanel son of Zuar
9 Zebulun	Eliab son of Helon
10 Ephraim son of Joseph . .	Elishama son of Ammihud
Manasseh son of Joseph . .	Gamaliel son of Pedahzur
11 Benjamin	Abidan son of Gideoni
12 Dan	Ahiezer son of Ammishaddai
13 Asher	Pagiel son of Ocran
14 Gad	Eliasaph son of Deuel
15 Naphtali	Ahira son of Enan

16These tribal leaders, heads of their own families, were chosen from among all the people.

17Now Moses and Aaron and the chosen leaders 18called together the whole community of Israel on that very day.* All the people were registered according to their ancestry by their clans and families. The men of Israel twenty years old or older were registered, one by one, 19just as the LORD had commanded Moses. So Moses counted the people there in the wilderness of Sinai.

20-21This is the number of men twenty years old or older who were able to go to war, each listed according to his own clan and family*:

Tribe	Number
Reuben (Jacob's* oldest son)	46,500
22-23 Simeon	59,300
24-25 Gad	45,650
26-27 Judah	74,600
28-29 Issachar	54,400
30-31 Zebulun	57,400
32-33 Ephraim son of Joseph	40,500
34-35 Manasseh son of Joseph	32,200
36-37 Benjamin	35,400
38-39 Dan	62,700
40-41 Asher	41,500
42-43 Naphtali	53,400

44These were the men counted by Moses and Aaron and the twelve leaders of Israel, all listed according to their ancestral descent. 45They were counted by families—all the men of Israel who were twenty years old or older and able to go to war. 46The total number was 603,550.

47But this total did not include the Levites. 48For the LORD had said to Moses, 49"Exempt the tribe of Levi from the census; do not include them when you count the rest of the Israelites. 50You must put the Levites in charge of the Tabernacle of the Covenant,* along with its furnishings and equipment. They must carry the Tabernacle and its equipment as you travel, and they must care for it and camp around it. 51Whenever the Tabernacle is moved, the Levites will take it down and set it up again. Anyone else who goes too near the Tabernacle will be executed. 52Each tribe of Israel will have a designated camping area with its own family banner. 53But the Levites will camp around the Tabernacle of the Covenant to offer the people of Israel protection from the LORD's fierce anger.

1:1a Hebrew *On the first day of the second month.* This day of the Hebrew lunar calendar occurs in April or early May.   1:1b Hebrew *Tent of Meeting.*   1:18 Hebrew *on the first day of the second month;* see 1:1.   1:20-21a In the Hebrew text, *number of men . . . family* is repeated in 1:22, 24, 26, 28, 30, 32, 34, 36, 38, 40, 42.   1:20-21b Hebrew *Israel's.*   1:50 Or *Tabernacle of the Testimony;* also in 1:53.

The Levites are responsible to stand guard around the Tabernacle."

54So the Israelites did everything just as the LORD had commanded Moses.

CHAPTER 2
Organization for Israel's Camp

Then the LORD gave these instructions to Moses and Aaron: 2 "Each tribe will be assigned its own area in the camp, and the various groups will camp beneath their family banners. The Tabernacle* will be located at the center of these tribal compounds.

3-4"The divisions of Judah, Issachar, and Zebulun are to camp toward the sunrise on the east side of the Tabernacle, beneath their family banners. These are the names of the tribes, their leaders, and the number of their available troops:

Tribe	Leader	Number
Judah	Nahshon son of Amminadab	74,600
5-6 Issachar	Nethanel son of Zuar	54,400
7-8 Zebulun	Eliab son of Helon	57,400

9So the total of all the troops on Judah's side of the camp is 186,400. These three tribes are to lead the way whenever the Israelites travel to a new campsite.

10-11"The divisions of Reuben, Simeon, and Gad are to camp on the south side of the Tabernacle, beneath their family banners. These are the names of the tribes, their leaders, and the number of their available troops:

Tribe	Leader	Number
Reuben	Elizur son of Shedeur	46,500
12-13 Simeon	Shelumiel son of Zurishaddai	59,300
14-15 Gad	Eliasaph son of Deuel*	45,650

16So the total of all the troops on Reuben's side of the camp is 151,450. These three tribes will be second in line whenever the Israelites travel.

17"Then the Levites will set out from the middle of the camp with the Tabernacle. All the tribes are to travel in the same order that they camp, each in position under the appropriate family banner.

18-19"The divisions of Ephraim, Manasseh, and Benjamin are to camp on the west side of the Tabernacle, beneath their family banners. These are the names of the tribes, their leaders, and the number of their available troops:

Tribe	Leader	Number
Ephraim	Elishama son of Ammihud	40,500
20-21 Manasseh	Gamaliel son of Pedahzur	32,200
22-23 Benjamin	Abidan son of Gideoni	35,400

24So the total of all the troops on Ephraim's side of the camp is 108,100, and they will follow the Levites in the line of march.

25-26"The divisions of Dan, Asher, and Naphtali are to camp on the north side of the Tabernacle, beneath their family banners. These are the names of the tribes, their leaders, and the number of their available troops:

Tribe	Leader	Number
Dan	Ahiezer son of Ammishaddai	62,700
27-28 Asher	Pagiel son of Ocran	41,500
29-30 Naphtali	Ahira son of Enan	53,400

31So the total of all the troops on Dan's side of the camp is 157,600. They are to bring up the rear whenever the Israelites move to a new campsite."

32In summary, the troops of Israel listed by their families totaled 603,550. 33The Levites were exempted from this census by the LORD's command to Moses. 34So the people of Israel did everything just as the LORD had commanded Moses. Each clan and family set up camp and marched under their banners exactly as the LORD had instructed them.

CHAPTER 3
Levites Appointed for Service

This is the family line of Aaron and Moses as it was recorded when the LORD spoke to Moses on Mount Sinai: 2Aaron's sons were Nadab (the firstborn), Abihu, Eleazar, and Ithamar. 3They were anointed and set apart to minister as priests. 4But Nadab and Abihu died in the LORD's presence in the wilderness of Sinai when they burned before the LORD a different kind of fire than he had commanded. Since they had no sons, this left only Eleazar and Ithamar to serve as priests with their father, Aaron.

5Then the LORD said to Moses, 6 "Call forward the tribe of Levi and present them to Aaron the priest as his assistants. 7They will serve Aaron and the whole community, performing their sacred duties in and around the Tabernacle.* 8They will also maintain all the furnishings of the sacred tent,* serving in the Tabernacle on behalf of all the Israelites. 9Assign the Levites to Aaron and his sons as their assistants. 10Appoint Aaron and his sons to carry out the duties of the priesthood. Anyone else who comes too near the sanctuary must be executed!"

11And the LORD said to Moses, 12 "I have chosen the Levites from among the Israelites as substi-

---

2:2 Hebrew *Tent of Meeting*; also in 2:17.   2:14-15 As in many Hebrew manuscripts, Samaritan Pentateuch, and Latin Vulgate (see also 1:14); most Hebrew manuscripts read *son of Reuel*.   3:7 Hebrew *around the Tent of Meeting, doing service at the Tabernacle*.   3:8 Hebrew *Tent of Meeting*.

tutes for all the firstborn sons of the people of Israel. The Levites are mine [13]because all the firstborn sons are mine. From the day I killed all the firstborn sons of the Egyptians, I set apart for myself all the firstborn in Israel of both men and animals. They are mine; I am the LORD."

The Census of the Levites

[14]The LORD spoke again to Moses, there in the wilderness of Sinai. He said, [15]"Take a census of the tribe of Levi by its families and clans. Count every male who is one month old or older." [16]So Moses counted them, just as the LORD had commanded.

[17]Levi had three sons, who were named Gershon, Kohath, and Merari. [18]The clans descended from Gershon were named for two of his descendants, Libni and Shimei. [19]The clans descended from Kohath were named for four of his descendants, Amram, Izhar, Hebron, and Uzziel. [20]The clans descended from Merari were named for two of his descendants, Mahli and Mushi.

These were the Levite clans, listed according to their family groups.

[21]The descendants of Gershon were composed of the clans descended from Libni and Shimei. [22]There were 7,500 males one month old or older among these Gershonite clans. [23]They were assigned the area to the west of the Tabernacle for their camp. [24]The leader of the Gershonite clans was Eliasaph son of Lael. [25]These two clans were responsible to care for the tent of the Tabernacle with its layers of coverings, its entry curtains, [26]the curtains of the courtyard that surrounded the Tabernacle and altar, the curtain at the courtyard entrance, the cords, and all the equipment related to their use.

[27]The descendants of Kohath were composed of the clans descended from Amram, Izhar, Hebron, and Uzziel. [28]There were 8,600* males one month old or older among these Kohathite clans. They were responsible for the care of the sanctuary. [29]They were assigned the area south of the Tabernacle for their camp. [30]The leader of the Kohathite clans was Elizaphan son of Uzziel. [31]These four clans were responsible for the care of the Ark, the table, the lampstand, the altars, the various utensils used in the sanctuary, the

inner curtain, and all the equipment related to their use. [32]Eleazar the priest, Aaron's son, was the chief administrator over all the Levites, with special responsibility for the oversight of the sanctuary.

[33]The descendants of Merari were composed of the clans descended from Mahli and Mushi. [34]There were 6,200 males one month old or older among these Merarite clans. [35]They were assigned the area north of the Tabernacle for their camp. The leader of the Merarite clans was Zuriel son of Abihail. [36]These two clans were responsible for the care of the frames supporting the Tabernacle, the crossbars, the pillars, the bases, and all the equipment related to their use. [37]They were also responsible for the posts of the courtyard and all their bases, pegs, and cords.

[38]The area in front of the Tabernacle in the east toward the sunrise* was reserved for the tents of Moses and of Aaron and his sons, who had the final responsibility for the sanctuary on behalf of the people of Israel. Anyone other than a priest or Levite who came too near the sanctuary was to be executed.

[39]So among the Levite clans counted by Moses and Aaron at the LORD's command, there were 22,000 males one month old or older.

Redeeming the Firstborn Sons

[40]Then the LORD said to Moses, "Now count all the firstborn sons in Israel who are one month old or older, and register each name. [41]The Levites will be reserved for me as substitutes for the firstborn sons of Israel; I am the LORD. And the Levites' livestock are mine as substitutes for the firstborn livestock of the whole nation of Israel."

[42]So Moses counted the firstborn sons of the people of Israel, just as the LORD had commanded. [43]The total number of firstborn sons who were one month old or older was 22,273.

[44]Now the LORD said to Moses, [45]"Take the Levites in place of the firstborn sons of the people of Israel. And take the livestock of the Levites as substitutes for the firstborn livestock of the people of Israel. The Levites will be mine; I am the LORD. [46]To redeem the 273 firstborn sons of Israel who are in excess of the number of Levites, [47]collect five pieces of silver for each person, each piece weighing the same as the standard sanctuary shekel.* [48]Give the silver to Aaron and his sons as the redemption price for the extra firstborn sons."

[49]So Moses collected redemption money for

3:28 Some Greek manuscripts read 8,300; see total in 3:39. **3:38** Hebrew *toward the sunrise, in front of the Tent of Meeting.* **3:47** Hebrew *5 shekels [2 ounces or 57 grams] apiece, according to the sanctuary shekel, 20 gerahs to each shekel.*

the firstborn sons of Israel who exceeded the number of Levites. ⁵⁰The silver collected on behalf of these firstborn sons of Israel came to about thirty-four pounds in weight.* ⁵¹And Moses gave the redemption money to Aaron and his sons as the LORD had commanded.

Duties of the Kohathite Clan

Then the LORD said to Moses and Aaron, ² "Take a census of the clans and families of the Kohathite division of the Levite tribe. ³Count all the men between the ages of thirty and fifty who qualify to work in the Tabernacle.*

⁴ "The duties of the Kohathites at the Tabernacle will relate to the most sacred objects. ⁵When the camp moves, Aaron and his sons must enter the Tabernacle first to take down the inner curtain and cover the Ark of the Covenant* with it. ⁶Then they must cover the inner curtain with fine goatskin leather, and the goatskin leather with a dark blue cloth. Finally, they must put the carrying poles of the Ark in place.

⁷ "Next they must spread a blue cloth over the table, where the Bread of the Presence is displayed, and place the dishes, spoons, bowls, cups, and the special bread on the cloth. ⁸They must spread a scarlet cloth over that, and finally a covering of fine goatskin leather on top of the scarlet cloth. Then they must insert the carrying poles into the table.

⁹ "Next they must cover the lampstand with a dark blue cloth, along with its lamps, lamp snuffers, trays, and special jars of olive oil. ¹⁰The lampstand with its utensils must then be covered with fine goatskin leather, and the bundle must be placed on a carrying frame.

¹¹ "Aaron and his sons must also spread a dark blue cloth over the gold altar and cover this cloth with a covering of fine goatskin leather. Then they are to attach the carrying poles to the altar. ¹²All the remaining utensils of the sanctuary must be wrapped in a dark blue cloth, covered with fine goatskin leather, and placed on the carrying frame.

¹³ "The ashes must be removed from the altar, and the altar must then be covered with a purple cloth. ¹⁴All the altar utensils—the firepans, hooks, shovels, basins, and all the containers—are to be placed on the cloth, and a covering of fine goatskin leather must be spread over them. Finally, the carrying poles must be put in place. ¹⁵When Aaron

and his sons have finished covering the sanctuary and all the sacred utensils, the Kohathites will come and carry these things to the next destination. But they must not touch the sacred objects, or they will die. So these are the objects of the Tabernacle that the Kohathites must carry.

¹⁶ "Eleazar son of Aaron the priest will be responsible for the oil of the lampstand, the fragrant incense, the daily grain offering, and the anointing oil. In fact, the supervision of the entire Tabernacle and everything in it will be Eleazar's responsibility."

¹⁷Then the LORD said to Moses and Aaron, ¹⁸ "Don't let the Kohathite clans be destroyed from among the Levites! ¹⁹This is what you must do so they will live and not die when they approach the most sacred objects. Aaron and his sons must always go in with them and assign a specific duty or load to each person. ²⁰Otherwise they must not approach the sanctuary and look at the sacred objects for even a moment, or they will die."

Duties of the Gershonite Clan

²¹And the LORD said to Moses, ²² "Take a census of the clans and families of the Gershonite division of the tribe of Levi. ²³Count all the men between the ages of thirty and fifty who are eligible to serve in the Tabernacle.

²⁴ "The duties of the Gershonites will be in the areas of general service and carrying loads. ²⁵They must carry the curtains of the Tabernacle, the Tabernacle itself with its coverings, the outer covering of fine goatskin leather, and the curtain for the Tabernacle entrance. ²⁶They are also to carry the curtains for the courtyard walls that surround the Tabernacle and altar, the curtain across the courtyard entrance, the necessary cords, and all the altar's accessories. The Gershonites are responsible for transporting all these items. ²⁷Aaron and his sons will direct the Gershonites regarding their duties, whether it involves moving or doing other work. They must assign the Gershonites the loads they are to carry. ²⁸So these are the duties assigned to the Gershonites at the Tabernacle. They will be directly responsible to Ithamar son of Aaron the priest.

Duties of the Merarite Clan

²⁹ "Now take a census of the clans and families of the Merarite division of the Levite tribe. ³⁰Count all the men between the ages of thirty and fifty who are eligible to serve in the Tabernacle. ³¹ "Their duties at the Tabernacle will consist

3:50 Hebrew *1,365 shekels* [15.5 kilograms], *according to the sanctuary shekel.*   4:3 Hebrew *Tent of Meeting;* also in 4:4, 15, 23, 25, 28, 30, 31, 33, 35, 37, 39, 41, 43, 47.   4:5 Or *Ark of the Testimony.*

of carrying loads. They will be required to carry the frames of the Tabernacle, the crossbars, the pillars with their bases, 32the posts for the courtyard walls with their bases, pegs, cords, accessories, and everything else related to their use. You must assign the various loads to each man by name. 33So these are the duties of the Merarites at the Tabernacle. They are directly responsible to Ithamar son of Aaron the priest."

The Census of the Levites

34So Moses, Aaron, and the other leaders of the community counted the Kohathite division by its clans and families. 35The count included all the men between thirty and fifty years of age who were eligible for service in the Tabernacle, 36and the total number came to 2,750. 37So this was the total of all those from the Kohathite clans who were eligible to serve at the Tabernacle. Moses and Aaron counted them, just as the LORD had commanded through Moses.

38The Gershonite division was also counted by its clans and families. 39The count included all the men between thirty and fifty years of age who were eligible for service in the Tabernacle, 40and the total number came to 2,630. 41So this was the total of all those from the Gershonite clans who were eligible to serve at the Tabernacle. Moses and Aaron counted them, just as the LORD had commanded.

42The Merarite division was also counted by its clans and families. 43The count included all the men between thirty and fifty years of age who were eligible for service in the Tabernacle, 44and the total number came to 3,200. 45So this was the total of all those from the Merarite clans who were eligible for service. Moses and Aaron counted them, just as the LORD had commanded through Moses.

46So Moses, Aaron, and the leaders of Israel counted all the Levites by their clans and families. 47All the men between thirty and fifty years of age who were eligible for service in the Tabernacle and for its transportation 48numbered 8,580. 49Each man was assigned his task and told what to carry, just as the LORD had commanded through Moses.

And so the census was completed, just as the LORD had commanded Moses.

CHAPTER 5

Purity in Israel's Camp

The LORD gave these instructions to Moses: 2"Command the people of Israel to remove any-

one from the camp who has a contagious skin disease* or a discharge, or who has been defiled by touching a dead person. 3This applies to men and women alike. Remove them so they will not defile the camp, where I live among you." 4So the Israelites did just as the LORD had commanded Moses and removed such people from the camp.

5Then the LORD said to Moses, 6"Give these instructions to the people of Israel: If any of the people—men or women—betray the LORD by doing wrong to another person, they are guilty. 7They must confess their sin and make full restitution for what they have done, adding a penalty of 20 percent and returning it to the person who was wronged. 8But if the person who was wronged is dead, and there are no near relatives to whom restitution can be made, it belongs to the LORD and must be given to the priest, along with a ram for atonement. 9All the sacred gifts that the Israelites bring to a priest will belong to him. 10Each priest may keep the sacred donations that he receives."

Protecting Marital Faithfulness

11And the LORD said to Moses, 12"Say to the people of Israel: 'Suppose a man's wife goes astray and is unfaithful to her husband. 13Suppose she sleeps with another man, but there is no witness since she was not caught in the act. 14If her husband becomes jealous and suspicious of his wife, even if she has not defiled herself, 15the husband must bring his wife to the priest with an offering of two quarts* of barley flour to be presented on her behalf. Do not mix it with olive oil or frankincense, for it is a jealousy offering—an offering of inquiry to find out if she is guilty.

16" 'The priest must then present her before the LORD. 17He must take some holy water in a clay jar and mix it with dust from the Tabernacle floor. 18When he has presented her before the LORD, he must unbind her hair and place the offering of inquiry—the jealousy offering—in her hands to determine whether or not her husband's suspicions are justified. The priest will stand before her, holding the jar of bitter water that brings a curse to those who are guilty. 19The priest will put the woman under oath and say to her, "If no other man has slept with you, and you have not defiled yourself by being unfaithful, may you be immune from the effects of this bitter water that causes the curse. 20But if you have gone astray while under your husband's authority and defiled yourself by sleeping with another man"—21at this point the priest must put the woman under this oath—"then may the people see that the LORD's curse is upon you when he makes you infertile.* 22Now may this water that brings the curse enter your body and make you infertile.*" And the woman will be required to say, "Yes, let it be so." 23Then the priest will write these curses on a piece of leather and wash them off into the bitter water. 24He will then make the woman drink the bitter water, so it may bring on the curse and cause bitter suffering in cases of guilt.

25" Then the priest will take the jealousy offering from the woman's hand, lift it up before the LORD, and carry it to the altar. 26He will take a handful as a token portion and burn it on the altar. Then he will require the woman to drink the water. 27If she has defiled herself by being unfaithful to her husband, the water that brings the curse will cause bitter suffering. She will become infertile,* and her name will become a curse word among her people. 28But if she has not defiled herself and is pure, she will be unharmed and will still be able to have children.

29" This is the ritual law for dealing with jealousy. If a woman defiles herself by being unfaithful to her husband, 30or if a man is overcome with jealousy and suspicion that his wife has been unfaithful, the husband must present his wife before the LORD, and the priest will apply this entire ritual law to her. 31The husband will be innocent of any guilt in this matter, but his wife will be held accountable for her sin.'"

CHAPTER **6**
Nazirite Laws

Then the LORD said to Moses, "Speak to the people of Israel and give them these instructions: 2If some of the people, either men or women, take the special vow of a Nazirite, setting themselves apart to the LORD in a special way, 3they must give up wine and other alcoholic drinks. They must not use vinegar made from wine, they must not drink other fermented drinks or fresh grape juice, and they must not eat grapes or raisins. 4As long as they are bound by their Nazirite vow, they are not allowed to eat or drink anything that comes from a grapevine, not even the grape seeds or skins.

5"They must never cut their hair throughout the time of their vow, for they are holy and set apart to the LORD. That is why they must let their hair grow long. 6And they may not go near a dead body during the entire period of their vow to the LORD, 7even if their own father, mother, brother, or sister has died. They must not defile the hair on their head, because it is the symbol of their separation to God. 8This applies as long as they are set apart to the LORD.

9"If their hair is defiled because someone suddenly falls dead beside them, they must wait for seven days and then shave their heads. Then they will be cleansed from their defilement. 10On the eighth day they must bring two turtledoves or two young pigeons to the priest at the entrance of the Tabernacle.* 11The priest will offer one of the birds for a sin offering and the other for a burnt offering. In this way, he will make atonement for the guilt they incurred from the dead body. Then they must renew their vow that day and let their hair begin to grow again. 12The days of their vow that were completed before their defilement no longer count. They must rededicate themselves to the LORD for the full term of their vow, and each must bring a one-year-old male lamb for a guilt offering.

13"This is the ritual law of the Nazirites. At the conclusion of their time of separation as Nazirites, they must each go to the entrance of the Tabernacle 14and offer these sacrifices to the LORD: a one-year-old male lamb without defect for a burnt offering, a one-year-old female lamb without defect for a sin offering, a ram without defect for a peace offering, 15a basket of bread made without yeast—cakes of choice flour mixed with olive oil and wafers spread with olive oil—along with their prescribed grain offerings and drink offerings. 16The priest will present these offerings before the LORD: first the sin offering and the burnt offering; 17then the ram for a peace offering, along with the basket of bread made without yeast. The priest must also make the prescribed grain offering and drink offering.

18"Then the Nazirites will shave their hair at the entrance of the Tabernacle and put it on the fire beneath the peace-offering sacrifice. 19After each Nazirite's head has been shaved, the priest will take for each of them the boiled shoulder of the ram, one cake made without yeast, and one wafer made without yeast, and put them all into the Nazirite's hands. 20The priest will then lift the gifts up before the LORD in a gesture of offering. These are holy portions for the priest, along with the breast and thigh pieces that were

---

5:21 Hebrew *when he causes your thigh to waste away and your abdomen to swell.* 5:22 Hebrew *enter your body so that your abdomen swells and your thigh wastes away.* 5:27 Hebrew *Her body will swell and her thigh will waste away.* 6:10 Hebrew *Tent of Meeting;* also in 6:13, 18.

lifted up before the LORD. After this ceremony the Nazirites may again drink wine.
21 "This is the ritual law of the Nazirites. If any Nazirites have vowed to give the LORD anything else beyond what is required by their normal Nazirite vow, they must fulfill their special vow exactly as they have promised."

The Priestly Blessing
22Then the LORD said to Moses, 23 "Instruct Aaron and his sons to bless the people of Israel with this special blessing:

24 'May the LORD bless you
and protect you.
25 May the LORD smile on you
and be gracious to you.
26 May the LORD show you his favor
and give you his peace.'

27This is how Aaron and his sons will designate the Israelites as my people,* and I myself will bless them."

CHAPTER **7**
Offerings of Dedication
On the day Moses set up the Tabernacle, he anointed it and set it apart as holy, along with all its furnishings and the altar with its utensils. 2Then the leaders of Israel—the tribal leaders who had organized the census—came and brought their offerings. 3Together they brought six carts and twelve oxen. There was a cart for every two leaders and an ox for each leader. They presented these to the LORD in front of the Tabernacle.
4Then the LORD said to Moses, 5 "Receive their gifts and use these oxen and carts for the work of the Tabernacle.* Distribute them among the Levites according to the work they have to do." 6So Moses presented the carts and oxen to the Levites. 7He gave two carts and four oxen to the Gershonite division for their work, 8and four carts and eight oxen to the Merarite division for their work. All their work was done under the leadership of Ithamar son of Aaron the priest. 9But he gave none of the carts or oxen to the Kohathite division, since they were required to carry the sacred objects of the Tabernacle on their shoulders.
10The leaders also presented dedication gifts for the altar at the time it was anointed. They each placed their gifts before the altar. 11The

LORD said to Moses, "Let each leader bring his gift on a different day for the dedication of the altar."

12On the first day Nahshon son of Amminadab, leader of the tribe of Judah, presented his offering. 13The offering consisted of a silver platter weighing about 3¼ pounds and a silver basin of about 1¾ pounds.* These were both filled with grain offerings of choice flour mixed with olive oil. 14He also brought a gold container weighing about four ounces,* which was filled with incense. 15He brought a young bull, a ram, and a one-year-old male lamb as a burnt offering; 16a male goat for a sin offering; 17and two oxen, five rams, five male goats, and five one-year-old male lambs for a peace offering. This was the offering brought by Nahshon son of Amminadab.

18On the second day Nethanel son of Zuar, leader of the tribe of Issachar, presented his offering. 19The offering consisted of a silver platter weighing about 3¼ pounds and a silver basin of about 1¾ pounds. These were both filled with grain offerings of choice flour mixed with olive oil. 20He also brought a gold container weighing about four ounces, which was filled with incense. 21He brought a young bull, a ram, and a one-year-old male lamb as a burnt offering; 22a male goat for a sin offering; 23and two oxen, five rams, five male goats, and five one-year-old male lambs for a peace offering. This was the offering brought by Nethanel son of Zuar.

24On the third day Eliab son of Helon, leader of the tribe of Zebulun, presented his offering. 25The offering consisted of a silver platter weighing about 3¼ pounds and a silver basin of about 1¾ pounds. These were both filled with grain offerings of choice flour mixed with olive oil. 26He also brought a gold container weighing about four ounces, which was filled with incense. 27He brought a young bull, a ram, and a one-year-old male lamb as a burnt offering; 28a male goat for a sin offering; 29and two oxen, five rams, five male goats, and five one-year-old male lambs for a peace offering. This was the offering brought by Eliab son of Helon.

6:27 Hebrew *will put my name on the people of Israel.*   **7:5** Hebrew *Tent of Meeting;* also in 7:89.   **7:13** Hebrew *silver platter weighing 130 shekels* [1.5 kilograms] *and a silver basin weighing 70 shekels* [0.8 kilograms], *according to the sanctuary shekel;* also in 7:19, 25, 31, 37, 43, 49, 55, 61, 67, 73, 79, 85.   **7:14** Hebrew *10 shekels* [114 grams]; also in 7:20, 26, 32, 38, 44, 50, 56, 62, 68, 74, 80, 86.

³⁰On the fourth day Elizur son of Shedeur, leader of the tribe of Reuben, presented his offering. ³¹The offering consisted of a silver platter weighing about 3¼ pounds and a silver basin of about 1¾ pounds. These were both filled with grain offerings of choice flour mixed with olive oil. ³²He also brought a gold container weighing about four ounces, which was filled with incense. ³³He brought a young bull, a ram, and a one-year-old male lamb as a burnt offering; ³⁴a male goat for a sin offering; ³⁵and two oxen, five rams, five male goats, and five one-year-old male lambs for a peace offering. This was the offering brought by Elizur son of Shedeur.

³⁶On the fifth day Shelumiel son of Zurishaddai, leader of the tribe of Simeon, presented his offering. ³⁷The offering consisted of a silver platter weighing about 3¼ pounds and a silver basin of about 1¾ pounds. These were both filled with grain offerings of choice flour mixed with olive oil. ³⁸He also brought a gold container weighing about four ounces, which was filled with incense. ³⁹He brought a young bull, a ram, and a one-year-old male lamb as a burnt offering; ⁴⁰a male goat for a sin offering; ⁴¹and two oxen, five rams, five male goats, and five one-year-old male lambs for a peace offering. This was the offering brought by Shelumiel son of Zurishaddai.

⁴²On the sixth day Eliasaph son of Deuel, leader of the tribe of Gad, presented his offering. ⁴³The offering consisted of a silver platter weighing about 3¼ pounds and a silver basin of about 1¾ pounds. These were both filled with grain offerings of choice flour mixed with olive oil. ⁴⁴He also brought a gold container weighing about four ounces, which was filled with incense. ⁴⁵He brought a young bull, a ram, and a one-year-old male lamb as a burnt offering; ⁴⁶a male goat for a sin offering; ⁴⁷and two oxen, five rams, five male goats, and five one-year-old male lambs for a peace offering. This was the offering brought by Eliasaph son of Deuel.

⁴⁸On the seventh day Elishama son of Ammihud, leader of the tribe of Ephraim, presented his offering. ⁴⁹The offering consisted of a silver platter

weighing about 3¼ pounds and a silver basin of about 1¾ pounds. These were both filled with grain offerings of choice flour mixed with olive oil. ⁵⁰He also brought a gold container weighing about four ounces, which was filled with incense. ⁵¹He brought a young bull, a ram, and a one-year-old male lamb as a burnt offering; ⁵²a male goat for a sin offering; ⁵³and two oxen, five rams, five male goats, and five one-year-old male lambs for a peace offering. This was the offering brought by Elishama son of Ammihud.

⁵⁴On the eighth day Gamaliel son of Pedahzur, leader of the tribe of Manasseh, presented his offering. ⁵⁵The offering consisted of a silver platter weighing about 3¼ pounds and a silver basin of about 1¾ pounds. These were both filled with grain offerings of choice flour mixed with olive oil. ⁵⁶He also brought a gold container weighing about four ounces, which was filled with incense. ⁵⁷He brought a young bull, a ram, and a one-year-old male lamb as a burnt offering; ⁵⁸a male goat for a sin offering; ⁵⁹and two oxen, five rams, five male goats, and five one-year-old male lambs for a peace offering. This was the offering brought by Gamaliel son of Pedahzur.

⁶⁰On the ninth day Abidan son of Gideoni, leader of the tribe of Benjamin, presented his offering. ⁶¹The offering consisted of a silver platter weighing about 3¼ pounds and a silver basin of about 1¾ pounds. These were both filled with grain offerings of choice flour mixed with olive oil. ⁶²He also brought a gold container weighing about four ounces, which was filled with incense. ⁶³He brought a young bull, a ram, and a one-year-old male lamb as a burnt offering; ⁶⁴a male goat for a sin offering; ⁶⁵and two oxen, five rams, five male goats, and five one-year-old male lambs for a peace offering. This was the offering brought by Abidan son of Gideoni.

⁶⁶On the tenth day Ahiezer son of Ammishaddai, leader of the tribe of Dan, presented his offering. ⁶⁷The offering consisted of a silver platter weighing about 3¼ pounds and a silver basin of about 1¾ pounds. These were both filled with grain offerings of choice flour

mixed with olive oil. 68He also brought a gold container weighing about four ounces, which was filled with incense. 69He brought a young bull, a ram, and a one-year-old male lamb as a burnt offering; 70a male goat for a sin offering; 71and two oxen, five rams, five male goats, and five one-year-old male lambs for a peace offering. This was the offering brought by Ahiezer son of Ammishaddai.

72On the eleventh day Pagiel son of Ocran, leader of the tribe of Asher, presented his offering.
73The offering consisted of a silver platter weighing about 3¼ pounds and a silver basin of about 1¾ pounds. These were both filled with grain offerings of choice flour mixed with olive oil. 74He also brought a gold container weighing about four ounces, which was filled with incense. 75He brought a young bull, a ram, and a one-year-old male lamb as a burnt offering; 76a male goat for a sin offering; 77and two oxen, five rams, five male goats, and five one-year-old male lambs for a peace offering. This was the offering brought by Pagiel son of Ocran.

78On the twelfth day Ahira son of Enan, leader of the tribe of Naphtali, presented his offering.
79The offering consisted of a silver platter weighing about 3¼ pounds and a silver basin of about 1¾ pounds. These were both filled with grain offerings of choice flour mixed with olive oil. 80He also brought a gold container weighing about four ounces, which was filled with incense. 81He brought a young bull, a ram, and a one-year-old male lamb as a burnt offering; 82a male goat for a sin offering; 83and two oxen, five rams, five male goats, and five one-year-old male lambs for a peace offering. This was the offering brought by Ahira son of Enan.

84So this was the dedication offering for the altar, brought by the leaders of Israel at the time it was anointed: twelve silver platters, twelve silver basins, and twelve gold incense containers. 85In all, the silver objects weighed about 60 pounds,* about 3¼ pounds for each platter and 1¾ pounds for each basin. 86The weight of the donated gold came to about three pounds,* about four ounces for each of the gold containers that were filled with incense. 87Twelve bulls, twelve rams, and

twelve one-year-old male lambs were donated for the burnt offerings, along with their prescribed grain offerings. Twelve male goats were brought for the sin offerings. 88Twenty-four young bulls, sixty rams, sixty male goats, and sixty one-year-old male lambs were donated for the peace offerings. This was the dedication offering for the altar after it was anointed.

89Whenever Moses went into the Tabernacle to speak with the LORD, he heard the voice speaking to him from between the two cherubim above the Ark's cover—the place of atonement—that rests on the Ark of the Covenant.* The LORD spoke to him from there.

CHAPTER **8**

Preparing the Lamps

The LORD said to Moses, 2 "Tell Aaron that when he sets up the seven lamps in the lampstand, he is to place them so their light shines forward."
3So Aaron did this. He set up the seven lamps so they reflected their light forward, just as the LORD had commanded Moses. 4The entire lampstand, from its base to its decorative blossoms, was made of beaten gold. It was built according to the exact design the LORD had shown Moses.

The Levites Dedicated

5Then the LORD said to Moses, 6"Now set the Levites apart from the rest of the people of Israel and make them ceremonially clean. 7Do this by sprinkling them with the water of purification. And have them shave their entire body and wash their clothing. Then they will be ceremonially clean. 8Have them bring a young bull and a grain offering of choice flour mixed with olive oil, along with a second young bull for a sin offering. 9Then assemble the whole community of Israel and present the Levites at the entrance of the Tabernacle.* 10When you bring the Levites before the LORD, the people of Israel must lay their hands on them. 11Aaron must present the Levites to the LORD as a special offering from the people of Israel, thus dedicating them to the LORD's service.

12 "Next the Levites will lay their hands on the heads of the young bulls and present them to the LORD. One will be for a sin offering and the other for a burnt offering, to make atonement for the Levites. 13Then have the Levites stand in front of Aaron and his sons, and present them as a special offering to the LORD. 14In this way, you will set the Levites apart from the rest of the people

7:85 Hebrew *2,400 shekels* [27.4 kilograms]. 7:86 Hebrew *120 shekels* [1.4 kilograms]. 7:89 Or *Ark of the Testimony.* 8:9 Hebrew *Tent of Meeting;* also in 8:15, 19, 22, 24, 26.

of Israel, and the Levites will belong to me. 15After this, they may go in and out of the Tabernacle to do their work, because you have purified them and presented them as a special offering.

16"Of all the people of Israel, the Levites are reserved for me. I have claimed them for myself in place of all the firstborn sons of the Israelites; I have taken the Levites as their substitutes. 17For all the firstborn males among the people of Israel are mine, both people and animals. I set them apart for myself on the night I killed all the firstborn sons of the Egyptians. 18Yes, I claim the Levites in place of all the firstborn sons of Israel. 19And of all the Israelites, I have assigned the Levites to Aaron and his sons. They will serve in the Tabernacle on behalf of the Israelites and make atonement for them so no plague will strike them when they approach the sanctuary."

20So Moses, Aaron, and the whole community of Israel dedicated the Levites, carefully following all the LORD's instructions to Moses. 21The Levites purified themselves and washed their clothes, and Aaron presented them to the LORD as a special offering. He then performed the rite of atonement over them to purify them. 22From then on the Levites went into the Tabernacle to perform their duties, helping Aaron and his sons. So they carried out all the commands that the LORD gave Moses concerning the Levites.

23The LORD also instructed Moses, 24"This is the rule the Levites must follow: They must begin serving in the Tabernacle at the age of twenty-five, 25and they must retire at the age of fifty. 26After retirement they may assist their fellow Levites by performing guard duty at the Tabernacle, but they may not officiate in the service. This is how you will assign duties to the Levites."

CHAPTER **9**
The Second Passover

The LORD gave these instructions to Moses in early spring,* during the second year after Israel's departure from Egypt, while he and the rest of the Israelites were in the wilderness of Sinai: 2"Tell the Israelites to celebrate the Passover at the proper time, 3at twilight on the appointed day in early spring.* Be sure to follow all my laws and regulations concerning this celebration."

4So Moses told the people to celebrate the Passover 5in the wilderness of Sinai as twilight fell on the appointed day.* And they celebrated the festival there, just as the LORD had commanded Moses. 6But some of the men had been ceremonially defiled by touching a dead person, so they could not offer their Passover lambs that day. So they came to Moses and Aaron that day 7and said, "We have become ceremonially unclean by touching a dead person. But why should we be excluded from presenting the LORD's offering at the proper time with the rest of the Israelites?"

8Moses answered, "Wait here until I have received instructions for you from the LORD."

9This was the LORD's reply: 10"Say to the Israelites: 'If any of the people now or in future generations are ceremonially unclean at Passover time because of touching a dead body, or if they are on a journey and cannot be present at the ceremony, they may still celebrate the LORD's Passover. 11They must offer the Passover sacrifice one month later,* at twilight on the appointed day. They must eat the lamb at that time with bitter herbs and bread made without yeast. 12They must not leave any of the lamb until the next morning, and they must not break any of its bones. They must follow all the normal regulations concerning the Passover.

13"'But those who are ceremonially clean and not away on a trip, yet still refuse to celebrate the Passover at the regular time, will be cut off from the community of Israel for failing to present the LORD's offering at the proper time. They will suffer the consequences of their guilt. 14And if foreigners living among you want to celebrate the Passover to the LORD, they must follow these same laws and regulations. The same laws apply both to you and to the foreigners living among you.'"

The Fiery Cloud

15The Tabernacle was set up, and on that day the cloud covered it.* Then from evening until morning the cloud over the Tabernacle appeared to be a pillar of fire. 16This was the regular pattern—at night the cloud changed to the appearance of fire. 17When the cloud lifted from over the sacred tent, the people of Israel followed it. And wherever the cloud settled, the people of Israel camped. 18In this way, they traveled at the LORD's command and stopped wherever he told them to. Then they remained

9:1 Hebrew *in the first month*. This month of the Hebrew lunar calendar usually occurs in March and April.   9:3 Hebrew *on the fourteenth day of the first month*. This day of the Hebrew lunar calendar occurs in late March or early April.   9:5 Hebrew *on the fourteenth day of the first month; see note on 9:3*.   9:11 Hebrew *on the fourteenth day of the second month*. This day of the Hebrew lunar calendar occurs in late April or early May.   9:15 Hebrew *covered the Tabernacle, the Tent of the Testimony*.

where they were as long as the cloud stayed over the Tabernacle. 19If the cloud remained over the Tabernacle for a long time, the Israelites stayed for a long time, just as the LORD commanded. 20Sometimes the cloud would stay over the Tabernacle for only a few days, so the people would stay for only a few days. Then at the LORD's command they would break camp. 21Sometimes the cloud stayed only overnight and moved on the next morning. But day or night, when the cloud lifted, the people broke camp and followed. 22Whether the cloud stayed above the Tabernacle for two days, a month, or a year, the people of Israel stayed in camp and did not move on. But as soon as it lifted, they broke camp and moved on. 23So they camped or traveled at the LORD's command, and they did whatever the LORD told them through Moses.

CHAPTER **10**
The Silver Trumpets

Now the LORD said to Moses, 2 "Make two trumpets of beaten silver to be used for summoning the people to assemble and for signaling the breaking of camp. 3When both trumpets are blown, the people will know that they are to gather before you at the entrance of the Tabernacle.* 4But if only one is blown, then only the leaders of the tribes of Israel will come to you.

5 "When you sound the signal to move on, the tribes on the east side of the Tabernacle will break camp and move forward. 6When you sound the signal a second time, the tribes on the south will follow. You must sound short blasts to signal moving on. 7But when you call the people to an assembly, blow the trumpets using a different signal. 8Only the priests, Aaron's descendants, are allowed to blow the trumpets. This is a permanent law to be followed from generation to generation.

9 "When you arrive in your own land and go to war against your enemies, you must sound the alarm with these trumpets so the LORD your God will remember you and rescue you from your enemies. 10Blow the trumpets in times of gladness, too, sounding them at your annual festivals and at the beginning of each month to rejoice over your burnt offerings and peace offerings. The trumpets will remind the LORD your God of his covenant with you. I am the LORD your God."

The Israelites Leave Sinai

11One day in midspring,* during the second year after Israel's departure from Egypt, the cloud lifted from the Tabernacle of the Covenant.* 12So the Israelites set out from the wilderness of Sinai and traveled on in stages until the cloud stopped in the wilderness of Paran.

13When the time to move arrived, the LORD gave the order through Moses. 14The tribes that camped with Judah headed the march with their banner, under the leadership of Nahshon son of Amminadab. 15The tribe of Issachar was led by Nethanel son of Zuar. 16The tribe of Zebulun was led by Eliab son of Helon.

17Then the Tabernacle was taken down, and the Gershonite and Merarite divisions of the Levites were next in the line of march, carrying the Tabernacle with them. 18Then the tribes that camped with Reuben set out with their banner, under the leadership of Elizur son of Shedeur. 19The tribe of Simeon was led by Shelumiel son of Zurishaddai. 20The tribe of Gad was led by Eliasaph son of Deuel.

21Next came the Kohathite division of the Levites, carrying the sacred objects from the Tabernacle. When they arrived at the next camp, the Tabernacle would already be set up at its new location. 22Then the tribes that camped with Ephraim set out with their banner, under the leadership of Elishama son of Ammihud. 23The tribe of Manasseh was led by Gamaliel son of Pedahzur. 24The tribe of Benjamin was led by Abidan son of Gideoni.

25Last of all, the tribes that camped with Dan set out under their banner. They served as the rear guard for all the tribal camps. The tribe of Dan headed this group, under the leadership of Ahiezer son of Ammishaddai. 26The tribe of Asher was led by Pagiel son of Ocran. 27The tribe of Naphtali was led by Ahira son of Enan.

28This was the order in which the tribes marched, division by division.

29One day Moses said to his brother-in-law, Hobab son of Reuel the Midianite, "We are on our way to the Promised Land. Come with us and we will treat you well, for the LORD has given wonderful promises to Israel!"

30But Hobab replied, "No, I will not go. I must return to my own land and family."

31"Please don't leave us," Moses pleaded. "You know the places in the wilderness where we should camp. 32Come, be our guide and we

10:3 Hebrew *Tent of Meeting.* 10:11a Hebrew *On the twentieth day of the second month.* This day of the Hebrew lunar calendar occurs in late April or early May. 10:11b Or *Tabernacle of the Testimony.*

will share with you all the good things that the LORD does for us."

33They marched for three days after leaving the mountain of the LORD, with the Ark of the LORD's covenant moving ahead of them to show them where to stop and rest. 34As they moved on each day, the cloud of the LORD hovered over them. 35And whenever the Ark set out, Moses would cry, "Arise, O LORD, and let your enemies be scattered! Let them flee before you!" 36And when the Ark was set down, he would say, "Return, O LORD, to the countless thousands of Israel!"

CHAPTER 11

The People Complain to Moses

The people soon began to complain to the LORD about their hardships; and when the LORD heard them, his anger blazed against them. Fire from the LORD raged among them and destroyed the outskirts of the camp. 2The people screamed to Moses for help; and when he prayed to the LORD, the fire stopped. 3After that, the area was known as Taberah—"the place of burning"—because fire from the LORD had burned among them there.

4Then the foreign rabble who were traveling with the Israelites began to crave the good things of Egypt, and the people of Israel also began to complain. "Oh, for some meat!" they exclaimed. 5"We remember all the fish we used to eat for free in Egypt. And we had all the cucumbers, melons, leeks, onions, and garlic that we wanted. 6But now our appetites are gone, and day after day we have nothing to eat but this manna!"

7The manna looked like small coriander seeds, pale yellow in color.* 8The people gathered it from the ground and made flour by grinding it with hand mills or pounding it in mortars. Then they boiled it in a pot and made it into flat cakes. These cakes tasted like they had been cooked in olive oil. 9The manna came down on the camp with the dew during the night.

10Moses heard all the families standing in front of their tents weeping, and the LORD became extremely angry. Moses was also very aggravated. 11And Moses said to the LORD, "Why are you treating me, your servant, so miserably? What did I do to deserve the burden of a people like this? 12Are they my children? Am I their father? Is that why you have told me to carry them in my arms—like a nurse carries a baby— to the land you swore to give their ancestors? 13Where am I supposed to get meat for all these

people? They keep complaining and saying, 'Give us meat!' 14I can't carry all these people by myself! The load is far too heavy! 15I'd rather you killed me than treat me like this. Please spare me this misery!"

Moses Chooses Seventy Leaders

16Then the LORD said to Moses, "Summon before me seventy of the leaders of Israel. Bring them to the Tabernacle* to stand there with you. 17I will come down and talk to you there. I will take some of the Spirit that is upon you, and I will put the Spirit upon them also. They will bear the burden of the people along with you, so you will not have to carry it alone.

18"And tell the people to purify themselves, for tomorrow they will have meat to eat. Tell them, 'The LORD has heard your whining and complaints: "If only we had meat to eat! Surely we were better off in Egypt!" Now the LORD will give you meat, and you will have to eat it. 19And it won't be for just a day or two, or for five or ten or even twenty. 20You will eat it for a whole month until you gag and are sick of it. For you have rejected the LORD, who is here among you, and you have complained to him, "Why did we ever leave Egypt?"'"

21But Moses said, "There are 600,000 foot soldiers here with me, and yet you promise them meat for a whole month! 22Even if we butchered all our flocks and herds, would that satisfy them? Even if we caught all the fish in the sea, would that be enough?"

23Then the LORD said to Moses, "Is there any limit to my power? Now you will see whether or not my word comes true!"

24So Moses went out and reported the LORD's words to the people. Then he gathered the seventy leaders and stationed them around the Tabernacle.* 25And the LORD came down in the cloud and spoke to Moses. He took some of the Spirit that was upon Moses and put it upon the seventy leaders. They prophesied as the Spirit rested upon them, but that was the only time this happened.

26Two men, Eldad and Medad, were still in the camp when the Spirit rested upon them. They were listed among the leaders but had not gone out to the Tabernacle, so they prophesied there in the camp. 27A young man ran and reported to Moses, "Eldad and Medad are prophesying in the camp!" 28Joshua son of Nun, who had been Moses' personal assistant since his

---

11:7 Hebrew *the color of gum resin.*   11:16 Hebrew *Tent of Meeting.*   11:24 Hebrew *the tent;* also in 11:26.

youth, protested, "Moses, my master, make them stop!"

29But Moses replied, "Are you jealous for my sake? I wish that all the LORD's people were prophets, and that the LORD would put his Spirit upon them all!" 30Then Moses returned to the camp with the leaders of Israel.

The LORD Sends Quail

31Now the LORD sent a wind that brought quail from the sea and let them fall into the camp and all around it! For many miles in every direction from the camp there were quail flying about three feet above the ground.* 32So the people went out and caught quail all that day and throughout the night and all the next day, too. No one gathered less than fifty bushels*! They spread the quail out all over the camp. 33But while they were still eating the meat, the anger of the LORD blazed against the people, and he caused a severe plague to break out among them. 34So that place was called Kibroth-hattaavah—"the graves of craving"—because they buried the people there who had craved meat from Egypt. 35From there the Israelites traveled to Hazeroth, where they stayed for some time.

CHAPTER 12

The Complaints of Miriam and Aaron

While they were at Hazeroth, Miriam and Aaron criticized Moses because he had married a Cushite woman. 2They said, "Has the LORD spoken only through Moses? Hasn't he spoken through us, too?" But the LORD heard them.

3Now Moses was more humble than any other person on earth. 4So immediately the LORD called to Moses, Aaron, and Miriam and said, "Go out to the Tabernacle,* all three of you!" And the three of them went out. 5Then the LORD descended in the pillar of cloud and stood at the entrance of the Tabernacle.* "Aaron and Miriam!" he called, and they stepped forward. 6And the LORD said to them, "Now listen to me! Even with prophets, I the LORD communicate by visions and dreams. 7But that is not how I communicate with my servant Moses. He is entrusted with my entire house. 8I speak to him face to face, directly and not in riddles! He sees the LORD as he is. Should you not be afraid to criticize him?"

9The LORD was furious with them, and he departed. 10As the cloud moved from above the Tabernacle, Miriam suddenly became white as snow with leprosy.* When Aaron saw what had happened, 11he cried out to Moses, "Oh, my lord! Please don't punish us for this sin we have so foolishly committed. 12Don't let her be like a stillborn baby, already decayed at birth."

13So Moses cried out to the LORD, "Heal her, O God, I beg you!"

14And the LORD said to Moses, "If her father had spit in her face, wouldn't she have been defiled for seven days? Banish her from the camp for seven days, and after that she may return."

15So Miriam was excluded from the camp for seven days, and the people waited until she was brought back before they traveled again. 16Then they left Hazeroth and camped in the wilderness of Paran.

CHAPTER 13

Twelve Scouts Explore Canaan

The LORD now said to Moses, 2"Send men to explore the land of Canaan, the land I am giving to Israel. Send one leader from each of the twelve ancestral tribes." 3So Moses did as the LORD commanded him. He sent out twelve men, all tribal leaders of Israel, from their camp in the wilderness of Paran. 4These were the tribes and the names of the leaders:

Tribe	Leader
Reuben	Shammua son of Zaccur
5 Simeon	Shaphat son of Hori
6 Judah	Caleb son of Jephunneh
7 Issachar	Igal son of Joseph
8 Ephraim	Hoshea son of Nun
9 Benjamin	Palti son of Raphu
10 Zebulun	Gaddiel son of Sodi
11 Manasseh son of Joseph	Gaddi son of Susi
12 Dan	Ammiel son of Gemalli
13 Asher	Sethur son of Michael
14 Naphtali	Nahbi son of Vophsi
15 Gad	Geuel son of Maki

16These are the names of the men Moses sent to explore the land. By this time Moses had changed Hoshea's name to Joshua.*

17Moses gave the men these instructions as he sent them out to explore the land: "Go northward through the Negev into the hill country. 18See what the land is like and find out whether the people living there are strong or weak, few or many. 19What kind of land do they live in? Is it good or bad? Do their towns have walls or are

---

11:31 Or *there were quail 3 feet* [2 cubits or 90 centimeters] *deep on the ground.*   11:32 Hebrew *10 homers* [1.8 kiloliters].   12:4 Hebrew *Tent of Meeting.*   12:5 Hebrew *the tent*; also in 12:10.   12:10 Or *with a contagious skin disease.* The Hebrew word used here can describe various skin diseases.   13:16 *Hoshea* (see 13:8) means "salvation"; *Joshua* means "The LORD is salvation."

they unprotected? 20How is the soil? Is it fertile or poor? Are there many trees? Enter the land boldly, and bring back samples of the crops you see." (It happened to be the season for harvesting the first ripe grapes.)

21So they went up and explored the land from the wilderness of Zin as far as Rehob, near Lebo-hamath. 22Going northward, they passed first through the Negev and arrived at Hebron, where Ahiman, Sheshai, and Talmai—all descendants of Anak—lived. (The ancient town of Hebron was founded seven years before the Egyptian city of Zoan.) 23When they came to what is now known as the valley of Eshcol, they cut down a cluster of grapes so large that it took two of them to carry it on a pole between them! They also took samples of the pomegranates and figs. 24At that time the Israelites renamed the valley Esh-col—"cluster"—because of the cluster of grapes they had cut there.

The Scouting Report

25After exploring the land for forty days, the men returned 26to Moses, Aaron, and the people of Israel at Kadesh in the wilderness of Paran. They reported to the whole community what they had seen and showed them the fruit they had taken from the land. 27This was their report to Moses: "We arrived in the land you sent us to see, and it is indeed a magnificent country—a land flowing with milk and honey. Here is some of its fruit as proof. 28But the people living there are powerful, and their cities and towns are fortified and very large. We also saw the descendants of Anak who are living there! 29The Amalekites live in the Negev, and the Hittites, Jebusites, and Amorites live in the hill country. The Canaanites live along the coast of the Mediterranean Sea* and along the Jordan Valley."

30But Caleb tried to encourage the people as they stood before Moses. "Let's go at once to take the land," he said. "We can certainly conquer it!"

31But the other men who had explored the land with him answered, "We can't go up against them! They are stronger than we are!" 32So they spread discouraging reports about the land among the Israelites: "The land we explored will swallow up any who go to live there. All the people we saw were huge. 33We even saw giants* there, the descendants of Anak. We felt like grasshoppers next to them, and that's what we looked like to them!"

The People Rebel

Then all the people began weeping aloud, and they cried all night. 2Their voices rose in a great chorus of complaint against Moses and Aaron. "We wish we had died in Egypt, or even here in the wilderness!" they wailed. 3"Why is the LORD taking us to this country only to have us die in battle? Our wives and little ones will be carried off as slaves! Let's get out of here and return to Egypt!" 4Then they plotted among themselves, "Let's choose a leader and go back to Egypt!"

5Then Moses and Aaron fell face down on the ground before the people of Israel. 6Two of the men who had explored the land, Joshua son of Nun and Caleb son of Jephunneh, tore their clothing. 7They said to the community of Israel, "The land we explored is a wonderful land! 8And if the LORD is pleased with us, he will bring us safely into that land and give it to us. It is a rich land flowing with milk and honey, and he will give it to us! 9Do not rebel against the LORD, and don't be afraid of the people of the land. They are only helpless prey to us! They have no protection, but the LORD is with us! Don't be afraid of them!"

10But the whole community began to talk about stoning Joshua and Caleb. Then the glorious presence of the LORD appeared to all the Israelites from above the Tabernacle.* 11And the LORD said to Moses, "How long will these people reject me? Will they never believe me, even after all the miraculous signs I have done among them? 12I will disown them and destroy them with a plague. Then I will make you into a nation far greater and mightier than they are!"

Moses Intercedes for the People

13"But what will the Egyptians think when they hear about it?" Moses pleaded with the LORD. "They know full well the power you displayed in rescuing these people from Egypt. 14They will tell this to the inhabitants of this land, who are well aware that you are with this people. They know, LORD, that you have appeared in full view of your people in the pillar of cloud that hovers over them. They know that you go before them in the pillar of cloud by day and the pillar of fire by night. 15Now if you slaughter all these people, the nations that have heard of your fame will say, 16'The LORD was not able to bring them into the land he swore to give them, so he killed them in the wilderness.'

17"Please, Lord, prove that your power is as

13:29 Hebrew *the sea.* 13:33 Hebrew *nephilim.* 14:10 Hebrew *Tent of Meeting.*

great as you have claimed it to be. For you said, ¹⁸'The LORD is slow to anger and rich in unfailing love, forgiving every kind of sin and rebellion. Even so he does not leave sin unpunished, but he punishes the children for the sins of their parents to the third and fourth generations.' ¹⁹Please pardon the sins of this people because of your magnificent, unfailing love, just as you have forgiven them ever since they left Egypt."

²⁰Then the LORD said, "I will pardon them as you have requested. ²¹But as surely as I live, and as surely as the earth is filled with the LORD's glory, ²²not one of these people will ever enter that land. They have seen my glorious presence and the miraculous signs I performed both in Egypt and in the wilderness, but again and again they tested me by refusing to listen. ²³They will never even see the land I swore to give their ancestors. None of those who have treated me with contempt will enter it. ²⁴But my servant Caleb is different from the others. He has remained loyal to me, and I will bring him into the land he explored. His descendants will receive their full share of that land. ²⁵Now turn around and don't go on toward the land where the Amalekites and Canaanites live. Tomorrow you must set out for the wilderness in the direction of the Red Sea.*"

The LORD Punishes the Israelites

²⁶Then the LORD said to Moses and Aaron, ²⁷"How long will this wicked nation complain about me? I have heard everything the Israelites have been saying. ²⁸Now tell them this: 'As surely as I live, I will do to you the very things I heard you say. I, the LORD, have spoken! ²⁹You will all die here in this wilderness! Because you complained against me, none of you who are twenty years old or older and were counted in the census ³⁰will enter the land I swore to give you. The only exceptions will be Caleb son of Jephunneh and Joshua son of Nun.

³¹" 'You said your children would be taken captive. Well, I will bring them safely into the land, and they will enjoy what you have despised. ³²But as for you, your dead bodies will fall in this wilderness. ³³And your children will be like shepherds, wandering in the wilderness forty years. In this way, they will pay for your faithlessness, until the last of you lies dead in the wilderness.

³⁴" 'Because the men who explored the land were there for forty days, you must wander in the wilderness for forty years—a year for each day, suffering the consequences of your sins. You will

discover what it is like to have me for an enemy.' ³⁵I, the LORD, have spoken! I will do these things to every member of the community who has conspired against me. They will all die here in this wilderness!"

³⁶Then the ten scouts who had incited the rebellion against the LORD by spreading discouraging reports about the land ³⁷were struck dead with a plague before the LORD. ³⁸Of the twelve who had explored the land, only Joshua and Caleb remained alive.

³⁹When Moses reported the LORD's words to the Israelites, there was much sorrow among the people. ⁴⁰So they got up early the next morning and set out for the hill country of Canaan. "Let's go," they said. "We realize that we have sinned, but now we are ready to enter the land the LORD has promised us."

⁴¹But Moses said, "Why are you now disobeying the LORD's orders to return to the wilderness? It won't work. ⁴²Do not go into the land now. You will only be crushed by your enemies because the LORD is not with you. ⁴³When you face the Amalekites and Canaanites in battle, you will be slaughtered. The LORD will abandon you because you have abandoned the LORD."

⁴⁴But the people pushed ahead toward the hill country of Canaan, despite the fact that neither Moses nor the Ark of the LORD's covenant left the camp. ⁴⁵Then the Amalekites and the Canaanites who lived in those hills came down and attacked them and chased them as far as Hormah.

CHAPTER 15
Laws concerning Offerings

The LORD told Moses to give these instructions to the people of Israel: ²"When you finally settle in the land I am going to give you, ³and you want to please the LORD with a burnt offering or any other offering given by fire, the sacrifice must be an animal from your flocks of sheep and goats or from your herds of cattle. When it is an ordinary burnt offering, a sacrifice to fulfill a vow, a freewill offering, or a special sacrifice at any of the annual festivals, ⁴whoever brings it must also give to the LORD a grain offering of two quarts* of choice flour mixed with one quart* of olive oil. ⁵For each lamb offered as a whole burnt offering, you must also present one quart of wine for a drink offering.

⁶"If the sacrifice is a ram, give three quarts* of choice flour mixed with two and a half pints* of olive oil, ⁷and give two and a half pints of

---

14:25 Hebrew *sea of reeds.* 15:4a Hebrew ¹/₁₀ *of an ephah* [2 liters]. 15:4b Hebrew ¹/₄ *of a hin* [1 liter]; also in 15:5. 15:6a Hebrew ²/₁₀ *of an ephah* [3.6 liters]. 15:6b Hebrew ¹/₃ *of a hin* [1.3 liters]; also in 15:7.

wine for a drink offering. This sacrifice will be very pleasing to the LORD.

8"When you present a young bull as a burnt offering or a sacrifice in fulfillment of a special vow or as a peace offering to the LORD, 9then the grain offering accompanying it must include five quarts* of choice flour mixed with two quarts* of olive oil, 10plus two quarts of wine for the drink offering. This will be an offering made by fire, very pleasing to the LORD.

11"These are the instructions for what is to accompany each sacrificial bull, ram, lamb, or young goat. 12Each of you must do this with each offering you present. 13If you native Israelites want to present an offering by fire that is pleasing to the LORD, you must follow all these instructions. 14And if any foreigners living among you want to present an offering by fire, pleasing to the LORD, they must follow the same procedures. 15Native Israelites and foreigners are the same before the LORD and are subject to the same laws. This is a permanent law for you. 16The same instructions and regulations will apply both to you and to the foreigners living among you."

17The LORD also said to Moses at this time, 18"Give the people of Israel the following instructions: When you arrive in the land where I am taking you, 19you will eat from the crops that grow there. But you must set some aside as a gift to the LORD. 20Present a cake from the first of the flour you grind and set it aside as a gift, as you do with the first grain from the threshing floor. 21Throughout the generations to come, you are to present this offering to the LORD each year from the first of your ground flour.

22"But suppose some of you unintentionally fail to carry out all these commands that the LORD has given you through Moses. 23And suppose some of your descendants in the future fail to do everything the LORD has commanded through Moses. 24If the mistake was done unintentionally, and the community was unaware of it, the whole community must present a young bull for a burnt offering. It will be pleasing to the LORD, and it must be offered along with the prescribed grain offering and drink offering and with one male goat for a sin offering. 25With it the priest will make atonement for the whole community of Israel, and they will be forgiven. For it was an unintentional sin, and they have corrected it with their offering given to the LORD by fire and by their sin offering. 26The whole community of Israel will be forgiven, including

the foreigners living among you, for the entire population was involved in the sin.

27"If the unintentional sin is committed by an individual, the guilty person must bring a one-year-old female goat for a sin offering. 28The priest will make atonement for the guilty person before the LORD, and that person will be forgiven. 29This same law applies both to native Israelites and the foreigners living among you.

30"But those who brazenly violate the LORD's will, whether native Israelites or foreigners, blaspheme the LORD, and they must be cut off from the community. 31Since they have treated the LORD's word with contempt and deliberately disobeyed his commands, they must be completely cut off and suffer the consequences of their guilt."

Penalty for Breaking the Sabbath

32One day while the people of Israel were in the wilderness, they caught a man gathering wood on the Sabbath day. 33He was apprehended and taken before Moses, Aaron, and the rest of the community. 34They held him in custody because they did not know what to do with him. 35Then the LORD said to Moses, "The man must be put to death! The whole community must stone him outside the camp." 36So the whole community took the man outside the camp and stoned him to death, just as the LORD had commanded Moses.

Tassels on Clothing

37And the LORD said to Moses, 38"Say to the people of Israel: 'Throughout the generations to come you must make tassels for the hems of your clothing and attach the tassels at each corner with a blue cord. 39The tassels will remind you of the commands of the LORD, and that you are to obey his commands instead of following your own desires and going your own ways, as you are prone to do. 40The tassels will help you remember that you must obey all my commands and be holy to your God. 41I am the LORD your God who brought you out of the land of Egypt that I might be your God. I am the LORD your God!'"

CHAPTER **16**
Korah's Rebellion

One day Korah son of Izhar, a descendant of Kohath son of Levi, conspired with Dathan and Abiram, the sons of Eliab, and On son of Peleth, from the tribe of Reuben. 2They incited a rebellion

15:9a Hebrew *3/10 of an ephah* [5.4 liters].   15:9b Hebrew *1/2 of a hin* [2 liters]; also in 15:10.

against Moses, involving 250 other prominent leaders, all members of the assembly. ³They went to Moses and Aaron and said, "You have gone too far! Everyone in Israel has been set apart by the LORD, and he is with all of us. What right do you have to act as though you are greater than anyone else among all these people of the LORD?"

⁴When Moses heard what they were saying, he threw himself down with his face to the ground. ⁵Then he said to Korah and his followers, "Tomorrow morning the LORD will show us who belongs to him and who is holy. The LORD will allow those who are chosen to enter his holy presence. ⁶You, Korah, and all your followers must do this: Take incense burners, ⁷and burn incense in them tomorrow before the LORD. Then we will see whom the LORD chooses as his holy one. You Levites are the ones who have gone too far!"

⁸Then Moses spoke again to Korah: "Now listen, you Levites! ⁹Does it seem a small thing to you that the God of Israel has chosen you from among all the people of Israel to be near him as you serve in the LORD's Tabernacle and to stand before the people to minister to them? ¹⁰He has given this special ministry only to you and your fellow Levites, but now you are demanding the priesthood as well! ¹¹The one you are really revolting against is the LORD! And who is Aaron that you are complaining about him?"

¹²Then Moses summoned Dathan and Abiram, the sons of Eliab, but they replied, "We refuse to come! ¹³Isn't it enough that you brought us out of Egypt, a land flowing with milk and honey, to kill us here in this wilderness, and that you now treat us like your subjects? ¹⁴What's more, you haven't brought us into the land flowing with milk and honey or given us an inheritance of fields and vineyards. Are you trying to fool us? We will not come."

¹⁵Then Moses became very angry and said to the LORD, "Do not accept their offerings! I have not taken so much as a donkey from them, and I have never hurt a single one of them." ¹⁶And Moses said to Korah, "Come here tomorrow and present yourself before the LORD with all your followers. Aaron will also be here. ¹⁷Be sure that each of your 250 followers brings an incense burner with incense on it, so you can present them before the LORD. Aaron will also bring his incense burner."

¹⁸So these men came with their incense burners, placed burning coals and incense on them, and stood at the entrance of the Tabernacle*

with Moses and Aaron. ¹⁹Meanwhile, Korah had stirred up the entire community against Moses and Aaron, and they all assembled at the Tabernacle entrance. Then the glorious presence of the LORD appeared to the whole community, ²⁰and the LORD said to Moses and Aaron, ²¹"Get away from these people so that I may instantly destroy them!"

²²But Moses and Aaron fell face down on the ground. "O God, the God and source of all life," they pleaded. "Must you be angry with all the people when only one man sins?"

²³And the LORD said to Moses, ²⁴"Then tell all the people to get away from the tents of Korah, Dathan, and Abiram."

²⁵So Moses got up and rushed over to the tents of Dathan and Abiram, followed closely by the Israelite leaders. ²⁶"Quick!" he told the people. "Get away from the tents of these wicked men, and don't touch anything that belongs to them. If you do, you will be destroyed for their sins." ²⁷So all the people stood back from the tents of Korah, Dathan, and Abiram. Then Dathan and Abiram came out and stood at the entrances of their tents with their wives and children and little ones.

²⁸And Moses said, "By this you will know that the LORD has sent me to do all these things that I have done—for I have not done them on my own. ²⁹If these men die a natural death, then the LORD has not sent me. ³⁰But if the LORD performs a miracle and the ground opens up and swallows them and all their belongings, and they go down alive into the grave, then you will know that these men have despised the LORD."

³¹He had hardly finished speaking the words when the ground suddenly split open beneath them. ³²The earth opened up and swallowed the men, along with their households and the followers who were standing with them, and everything they owned. ³³So they went down alive into the grave, along with their belongings. The earth closed over them, and they all vanished. ³⁴All of the people of Israel fled as they heard their screams, fearing that the earth would swallow them, too. ³⁵Then fire blazed forth from the LORD and burned up the 250 men who were offering incense.

³⁶And the LORD said to Moses, ³⁷"Tell Eleazar son of Aaron the priest to pull all the incense burners from the fire, for they are holy. Also tell him to scatter the burning incense ³⁸from the burners of these men who have sinned at the

16:18 Hebrew *Tent of Meeting*; also in 16:19, 42, 43, 50.

cost of their lives. He must then hammer the metal of the incense burners into a sheet as a covering for the altar, for these burners have become holy because they were used in the LORD's presence. The altar covering will then serve as a warning to the people of Israel."

39So Eleazar the priest collected the 250 bronze incense burners that had been used by the men who died in the fire, and they were hammered out into a sheet of metal to cover the altar. 40This would warn the Israelites that no unauthorized man—no one who was not a descendant of Aaron—should ever enter the LORD's presence to burn incense. If anyone did, the same thing would happen to him as happened to Korah and his followers. Thus, the LORD's instructions to Moses were carried out.

41But the very next morning the whole community began muttering again against Moses and Aaron, saying, "You two have killed the LORD's people!" 42As the people gathered to protest to Moses and Aaron, they turned toward the Tabernacle and saw that the cloud had covered it, and the glorious presence of the LORD appeared.

43Moses and Aaron came and stood at the entrance of the Tabernacle, 44and the LORD said to Moses, 45"Get away from these people so that I can instantly destroy them!" But Moses and Aaron fell face down on the ground.

46And Moses said to Aaron, "Quick, take an incense burner and place burning coals on it from the altar. Lay incense on it and carry it quickly among the people to make atonement for them. The LORD's anger is blazing among them—the plague has already begun."

47Aaron did as Moses told him and ran out among the people. The plague indeed had already begun, but Aaron burned the incense and made atonement for them. 48He stood between the living and the dead until the plague was stopped. 49But 14,700 people died in that plague, in addition to those who had died in the incident involving Korah. 50Then because the plague had stopped, Aaron returned to Moses at the entrance of the Tabernacle.

CHAPTER **17**
The Budding of Aaron's Staff

Then the LORD said to Moses, 2"Take twelve wooden staffs, one from each of Israel's ancestral tribes, and inscribe each tribal leader's name on his staff. 3Inscribe Aaron's name on the staff

of the tribe of Levi, for there must be one staff for the leader of each ancestral tribe. 4Put these staffs in the Tabernacle in front of the Ark of the Covenant,* where I meet with you. 5Buds will sprout on the staff belonging to the man I choose. Then I will finally put an end to this murmuring and complaining against you."

6So Moses gave the instructions to the people of Israel, and each of the twelve tribal leaders, including Aaron, brought Moses a staff. 7Moses put the staffs in the LORD's presence in the Tabernacle of the Covenant.* 8When he went into the Tabernacle of the Covenant the next day, he found that Aaron's staff, representing the tribe of Levi, had sprouted, blossomed, and produced almonds!

9When Moses brought all the staffs out from the LORD's presence, he showed them to the people. Each man claimed his own staff. 10And the LORD said to Moses: "Place Aaron's staff permanently before the Ark of the Covenant* as a warning to rebels. This should put an end to their complaints against me and prevent any further deaths." 11So Moses did as the LORD commanded him.

12Then the people of Israel said to Moses, "We are as good as dead! We are ruined! 13Everyone who even comes close to the Tabernacle of the LORD dies. We are all doomed!"

CHAPTER **18**
Duties of Priests and Levites

The LORD now said to Aaron: "You, your sons, and your relatives from the tribe of Levi will be held responsible for any offenses related to the sanctuary. But you and your sons alone will be held liable for violations connected with the priesthood.

2"Bring your relatives of the tribe of Levi to assist you and your sons as you perform the sacred duties in front of the Tabernacle of the Covenant.* 3But as the Levites go about their duties under your supervision, they must be careful not to touch any of the sacred objects or the altar. If they do, both you and they will die. 4The Levites must join with you to fulfill their responsibilities for the care and maintenance of the Tabernacle,* but no one who is not a Levite may officiate with you.

5"You yourselves must perform the sacred duties within the sanctuary and at the altar. If you follow these instructions, the LORD's anger will never again blaze against the people of Israel. 6I myself have chosen your fellow Levites from among the Israelites to be your special assistants. They are dedicated to the LORD for service in the Tabernacle. 7But you and your sons, the priests, must personally handle all the sacred service associated with the altar and everything within the inner curtain. I am giving you the priesthood as your special gift of service. Any other person who comes too near the sanctuary will be put to death."

Support for the Priests and Levites

8The LORD gave these further instructions to Aaron: "I have put the priests in charge of all the holy gifts that are brought to me by the people of Israel. I have given these offerings to you and your sons as your regular share. 9You are allotted the portion of the most holy offerings that is kept from the fire. From all the most holy offerings—including the grain offerings, sin offerings, and guilt offerings—that portion belongs to you and your sons. 10You must eat it as a most holy offering. All the males may eat of it, and you must treat it as most holy.

11 "All the other offerings presented to me by the Israelites by lifting them up before the altar also belong to you as your regular share. Any member of your family who is ceremonially clean, male and female alike, may eat of these offerings.

12"I also give you the harvest gifts brought by the people as offerings to the LORD—the best of the olive oil, wine, and grain. 13All the firstfruits of the land that the people present to the LORD belong to you. Any member of your family who is ceremonially clean may eat this food.

14"Whatever is specially set apart for the LORD* also belongs to you.

15 "The firstborn of every mother, whether human or animal, that is offered to the LORD will be yours. But you must always redeem your firstborn sons and the firstborn males of ritually unclean animals. 16Redeem them when they are one month old. The redemption price is five pieces of silver, each piece weighing the same as the standard sanctuary shekel.*

17"However, you may not redeem the firstborn of cattle, sheep, or goats. They are holy and have been set apart for the LORD. Sprinkle their blood on the altar, and burn their fat as an offering given by fire, very pleasing to the LORD. 18The

meat of these animals will be yours, just like the breast and right thigh that are presented by lifting them up before the altar. 19Yes, I am giving you all these holy offerings that the people of Israel bring to the LORD. They are for you and your sons and daughters, to be eaten as your regular share. This is an unbreakable covenant* between the LORD and you and your descendants."

20And the LORD said to Aaron, "You priests will receive no inheritance of land or share of property among the people of Israel. I am your inheritance and your share. 21As for the tribe of Levi, your relatives, I will pay them for their service in the Tabernacle with the tithes from the entire land of Israel.

22"From now on, Israelites other than the priests and Levites are to stay away from the Tabernacle. If they come too near, they will be judged guilty and die. 23The Levites must serve at the Tabernacle, and they will be held responsible for any offenses against it. This is a permanent law among you. But the Levites will receive no inheritance of land among the Israelites, 24because I have given them the Israelites' tithes, which have been set apart as offerings to the LORD. This will be the Levites' share. That is why I said they would receive no inheritance of land among the Israelites."

25The LORD also told Moses, 26"Say this to the Levites: 'When you receive the tithes from the Israelites, give a tenth of the tithes you receive— a tithe of the tithe—to the LORD as a gift. 27The LORD will consider this to be your harvest offering, as though it were the first grain from your own threshing floor or wine from your own winepress. 28You must present one-tenth of the tithe received from the Israelites as a gift to the LORD. From this you must present the LORD's portion to Aaron the priest. 29Be sure to set aside the best portions of the gifts given to you as your gifts to the LORD.'

30"Also say to the Levites: 'When you present the best part, it will be considered as though it came from your own threshing floor or winepress. 31You Levites and your families may eat this food anywhere you wish, for it is your compensation for serving in the Tabernacle. 32You will not be considered guilty for accepting the LORD's tithes if you give the best portion to the priests. But be careful not to treat the holy gifts of the people of Israel as though they were common. If you do, you will die.'"

18:14 The Hebrew term used here refers to the complete consecration of things or people to the LORD, either by destroying them or by giving them as an offering.   18:16 Hebrew *5 shekels* [about 2 ounces or 57 grams] *of silver, according to the sanctuary shekel, 20 gerahs to each shekel.* 18:19 Hebrew *a covenant of salt.*

CHAPTER **19**

The Water of Purification

The LORD said to Moses and Aaron, 2 "Here is another ritual law required by the LORD. Tell the people of Israel to bring you a red heifer that has no physical defects and has never been yoked to a plow. 3 Give it to Eleazar the priest, and it will be taken outside the camp and slaughtered in his presence. 4 Eleazar will take some of its blood on his finger and sprinkle it seven times toward the front of the Tabernacle.* 5 As Eleazar watches, the heifer must be burned—its hide, meat, blood, and dung. 6 Eleazar the priest must then take cedarwood, a hyssop branch, and scarlet thread and throw them into the fire where the heifer is burning.

7 "Then the priest must wash his clothes and bathe himself in water. Afterward he may return to the camp, though he will remain ceremonially unclean until evening. 8 The man who burns the animal must also wash his clothes and bathe in water, and he, too, will remain unclean until evening. 9 Then someone who is ceremonially clean will gather up the ashes of the heifer and place them in a purified place outside the camp. They will be kept there for the people of Israel to use in the water for the purification ceremony. This ceremony is performed for the removal of sin. 10 The man who gathers up the ashes of the heifer must also wash his clothes, and he will remain ceremonially unclean until evening. This is a permanent law for the people of Israel and any foreigners who live among them.

11 "All those who touch a dead human body will be ceremonially unclean for seven days. 12 They must purify themselves on the third and seventh days with the water of purification; then they will be purified. But if they do not do this on the third and seventh days, they will continue to be unclean even after the seventh day. 13 All those who touch a dead body and do not purify themselves in the proper way defile the LORD's Tabernacle and will be cut off from the community of Israel. Since the water of purification was not sprinkled on them, their defilement continues.

14 "This is the ritual law that applies when someone dies in a tent: Those who enter that tent, and those who were inside when the death occurred, will be ceremonially unclean for seven days. 15 Any container in the tent that was not covered with a lid is also defiled. 16 And if someone outdoors touches the corpse of someone who was killed with a sword or who died a natural death, or if someone touches a human bone or a grave, that person will be unclean for seven days.

17 "To remove the defilement, put some of the ashes from the burnt purification offering in a jar and pour fresh water over them. 18 Then someone who is ceremonially clean must take a hyssop branch and dip it into the water. That person must sprinkle the water on the tent, on all the furnishings in the tent, and on anyone who was in the tent, or anyone who has touched a human bone, or has touched a person who was killed or who died naturally, or has touched a grave. 19 On the third and seventh days the ceremonially clean person must sprinkle the water on those who are unclean. Then on the seventh day the people being cleansed must wash their clothes and bathe themselves, and that evening they will be cleansed of their defilement.

20 "But those who become defiled and do not purify themselves will be cut off from the community, for they have defiled the sanctuary of the LORD. Since the water of purification has not been sprinkled on them, they remain defiled. 21 This is a permanent law. Those who sprinkle the water of purification must afterward wash their clothes, and anyone who touches the water of purification will remain defiled until evening. 22 Anything and anyone that a defiled person touches will be ceremonially defiled until evening."

CHAPTER **20**

Moses Strikes the Rock

In early spring* the people of Israel arrived in the wilderness of Zin and camped at Kadesh. While they were there, Miriam died and was buried.

2 There was no water for the people to drink at that place, so they rebelled against Moses and Aaron. 3 The people blamed Moses and said, "We wish we had died in the LORD's presence with our brothers! 4 Did you bring the LORD's people into this wilderness to die, along with all our livestock? 5 Why did you make us leave Egypt and bring us here to this terrible place? This land has no grain, figs, grapes, or pomegranates. And there is no water to drink!"

6 Moses and Aaron turned away from the people and went to the entrance of the Tabernacle,* where they fell face down on the ground. Then the glorious presence of the LORD appeared to them, 7 and the LORD said to Moses, 8 "You and Aaron must take the staff and assemble the en-

---

19:4 Hebrew *Tent of Meeting.*   20:1 Hebrew *In the first month.* This month of the Hebrew lunar calendar usually occurs in March and April. 20:6 Hebrew *Tent of Meeting.*

tire community. As the people watch, command the rock over there to pour out its water. You will get enough water from the rock to satisfy all the people and their livestock."

9So Moses did as he was told. He took the staff from the place where it was kept before the LORD. 10Then he and Aaron summoned the people to come and gather at the rock. "Listen, you rebels!" he shouted. "Must we bring you water from this rock?" 11Then Moses raised his hand and struck the rock twice with the staff, and water gushed out. So all the people and their livestock drank their fill.

12But the LORD said to Moses and Aaron, "Because you did not trust me enough to demonstrate my holiness to the people of Israel, you will not lead them into the land I am giving them!" 13This place was known as the waters of Meribah,* because it was where the people of Israel argued with the LORD, and where he demonstrated his holiness among them.

Edom Refuses Israel Passage

14While Moses was at Kadesh, he sent ambassadors to the king of Edom with this message:

"This message is from your relatives, the people of Israel: You know all the hardships we have been through, 15and that our ancestors went down to Egypt. We lived there a long time and suffered as slaves to the Egyptians. 16But when we cried out to the LORD, he heard us and sent an angel who brought us out of Egypt. Now we are camped at Kadesh, a town on the border of your land. 17Please let us pass through your country. We will be careful not to go through your fields and vineyards. We won't even drink water from your wells. We will stay on the king's road and never leave it until we have crossed the opposite border."

18But the king of Edom said, "Stay out of my land or I will meet you with an army!"

19The Israelites answered, "We will stay on the main road. If any of our livestock drinks your water, we will pay for it. We only want to pass through your country and nothing else."

20But the king of Edom replied, "Stay out! You may not pass through our land." With that he mobilized his army and marched out to meet them with an imposing force. 21Because Edom refused to allow Israel to pass through their country, Israel was forced to turn around.

The Death of Aaron

22The whole community of Israel left Kadesh as a group and arrived at Mount Hor. 23Then the LORD said to Moses and Aaron at Mount Hor on the border of the land of Edom, 24"The time has come for Aaron to join his ancestors in death. He will not enter the land I am giving the people of Israel, because the two of you rebelled against my instructions concerning the waters of Meribah. 25Now take Aaron and his son Eleazar up Mount Hor. 26There you will remove Aaron's priestly garments and put them on Eleazar, his son. Aaron will die there and join his ancestors."

27So Moses did as the LORD commanded. The three of them went up Mount Hor together as the whole community watched. 28At the summit, Moses removed the priestly garments from Aaron and put them on Eleazar, Aaron's son. Then Aaron died there on top of the mountain, and Moses and Eleazar went back down. 29When the people realized that Aaron had died, all Israel mourned for him thirty days.

CHAPTER **21**

Victory over the Canaanites

The Canaanite king of Arad, who lived in the Negev, heard that the Israelites were approaching on the road to Atharim. So he attacked the Israelites and took some of them as prisoners. 2Then the people of Israel made this vow to the LORD: "If you will help us conquer these people, we will completely destroy* all their towns." 3The LORD heard their request and gave them victory over the Canaanites. The Israelites completely destroyed them and their towns, and the place has been called Hormah* ever since.

The Bronze Snake

4Then the people of Israel set out from Mount Hor, taking the road to the Red Sea* to go around the land of Edom. But the people grew impatient along the way, 5and they began to murmur against God and Moses. "Why have you brought us out of Egypt to die here in the wilderness?" they complained. "There is nothing to eat here and nothing to drink. And we hate this wretched manna!"

6So the LORD sent poisonous snakes among them, and many of them were bitten and died. 7Then the people came to Moses and cried out, "We have sinned by speaking against the LORD

20:13 *Meribah* means "arguing."   21:2 The Hebrew term used here refers to the complete consecration of things or people to the LORD, either by destroying them or by giving them as an offering; also in 21:3.   21:3 *Hormah* means "destruction."   21:4 Hebrew *sea of reeds.*

and against you. Pray that the LORD will take away the snakes." So Moses prayed for the people.

8Then the LORD told him, "Make a replica of a poisonous snake and attach it to the top of a pole. Those who are bitten will live if they simply look at it!" 9So Moses made a snake out of bronze and attached it to the top of a pole. Whenever those who were bitten looked at the bronze snake, they recovered!

Israel's Journey to Moab

10The Israelites traveled next to Oboth and camped there. 11Then they went on to Iye-abarim, in the wilderness on the eastern border of Moab. 12From there they traveled to the valley of Zered Brook and set up camp. 13Then they moved to the far side of the Arnon River, in the wilderness adjacent to the territory of the Amorites. The Arnon is the boundary line between the Moabites and the Amorites. 14For this reason *The Book of the Wars of the LORD* speaks of "the town of Waheb in the area of Suphah, and the ravines; and the Arnon River 15and its ravines, which extend as far as the settlement of Ar on the border of Moab."

16From there the Israelites traveled to Beer,* which is the well where the LORD said to Moses, "Assemble the people, and I will give them water." 17There the Israelites sang this song:

"Spring up, O well!
Yes, sing about it!
18 Sing of this well,
which princes dug,
which great leaders hollowed out
with their scepters and staffs."

Then the Israelites left the wilderness and proceeded on through Mattanah, 19Nahaliel, and Bamoth. 20Then they went to the valley in Moab where Pisgah Peak overlooks the wasteland.*

Victory over Sihon and Og

21The Israelites now sent ambassadors to King Sihon of the Amorites with this message:

22"Let us travel through your land. We will stay on the king's road until we have crossed your territory. We will not trample your fields or touch your vineyards or drink your well water."

23But King Sihon refused to let them cross his land. Instead, he mobilized his entire army and attacked Israel in the wilderness, engaging them

in battle at Jahaz. 24But the Israelites slaughtered them and occupied their land from the Arnon River to the Jabbok River. They went only as far as the Ammonite border because the boundary of the Ammonites was fortified.*

25So Israel captured all the towns of the Amorites and settled in them, including the city of Heshbon and its surrounding villages. 26Heshbon had been the capital of King Sihon of the Amorites. He had conquered a former Moabite king and seized all his land as far as the Arnon River. 27For this reason the ancient poets wrote this about him:

"Come to Heshbon, city of Sihon!
May it be restored and rebuilt.
28 A fire flamed forth from Heshbon,
a blaze from the city of Sihon.
It burned the city of Ar in Moab;
it destroyed the rulers of the Arnon
heights.
29 Your destruction is certain, O people of
Moab!
You are finished, O worshipers of
Chemosh!
Chemosh has left his sons as refugees,
and his daughters as captives of Sihon,
the Amorite king.
30 We have utterly destroyed them,
all the way from Heshbon to Dibon.
We have completely wiped them out
as far away as Nophah and Medeba.*"

31So the people of Israel occupied the territory of the Amorites. 32After Moses sent men to explore the Jazer area, they captured all the towns in the region and drove out the Amorites who lived there. 33Then they turned and marched toward Bashan, but King Og of Bashan and all his people attacked them at Edrei. 34The LORD said to Moses, "Do not be afraid of him, for I have given you victory over Og and his entire army, giving you all his land. You will do the same to him as you did to King Sihon of the Amorites, who ruled in Heshbon." 35And Israel was victorious and killed King Og, his sons, and his subjects; not a single survivor remained. Then Israel occupied their land.

CHAPTER 22
Balak Sends for Balaam

Then the people of Israel traveled to the plains of Moab and camped east of the Jordan River,

---

21:16 *Beer* means "well." **21:20** Or *overlooks Jeshimon.* **21:24** Or *because the terrain of the Ammonite frontier was rugged;* Hebrew *because the boundary of the Ammonites was strong.* **21:30** Or *until fire spread to Medeba.* The meaning of the Hebrew is uncertain.

across from Jericho. ²Balak son of Zippor, the Moabite king, knew what the Israelites had done to the Amorites. ³And when they saw how many Israelites there were, he and his people were terrified. ⁴The king of Moab said to the leaders of Midian, "This mob will devour everything in sight, like an ox devours grass!"

So Balak, king of Moab, ⁵sent messengers to Balaam son of Beor, who was living in his native land of Pethor* near the Euphrates River.* He sent this message to request that Balaam come to help him:

"A vast horde of people has arrived from Egypt. They cover the face of the earth and are threatening me. ⁶Please come and curse them for me because they are so numerous. Then perhaps I will be able to conquer them and drive them from the land. I know that blessings fall on the people you bless. I also know that the people you curse are doomed."

⁷Balak's messengers, officials of both Moab and Midian, set out and took money with them to pay Balaam to curse Israel. They went to Balaam and urgently explained to him what Balak wanted. ⁸"Stay here overnight," Balaam said. "In the morning I will tell you whatever the LORD directs me to say." So the officials from Moab stayed there with Balaam.

⁹That night God came to Balaam and asked him, "Who are these men with you?"

¹⁰So Balaam said to God, "Balak son of Zippor, king of Moab, has sent me this message: ¹¹'A vast horde of people has come from Egypt and has spread out over the whole land. Come at once to curse them. Perhaps then I will be able to conquer them and drive them from the land.'"

¹²"Do not go with them," God told Balaam. "You are not to curse these people, for I have blessed them!"

¹³The next morning Balaam got up and told Balak's officials, "Go on home! The LORD will not let me go with you."

¹⁴So the Moabite officials returned to King Balak and reported, "Balaam refused to come with us." ¹⁵Then Balak tried again. This time he sent a larger number of even more distinguished officials than those he had sent the first time. ¹⁶They went to Balaam and gave him this message:

"This is what Balak son of Zippor says: Please don't let anything stop you from coming. ¹⁷I will pay you well and do

anything you ask of me. Just come and curse these people for me!"

¹⁸But Balaam answered them, "Even if Balak were to give me a palace filled with silver and gold, I would be powerless to do anything against the will of the LORD my God. ¹⁹But stay here one more night to see if the LORD has anything else to say to me."

²⁰That night God came to Balaam and told him, "Since these men have come for you, get up and go with them. But be sure to do only what I tell you to do."

Balaam and His Donkey

²¹So the next morning Balaam saddled his donkey and started off with the Moabite officials. ²²But God was furious that Balaam was going, so he sent the angel of the LORD to stand in the road to block his way. As Balaam and two servants were riding along, ²³Balaam's donkey suddenly saw the angel of the LORD standing in the road with a drawn sword in his hand. The donkey bolted off the road into a field, but Balaam beat it and turned it back onto the road. ²⁴Then the angel of the LORD stood at a place where the road narrowed between two vineyard walls. ²⁵When the donkey saw the angel of the LORD standing there, it tried to squeeze by and crushed Balaam's foot against the wall. So Balaam beat the donkey again. ²⁶Then the angel of the LORD moved farther down the road and stood in a place so narrow that the donkey could not get by at all. ²⁷This time when the donkey saw the angel, it lay down under Balaam. In a fit of rage Balaam beat it again with his staff.

²⁸Then the LORD caused the donkey to speak. "What have I done to you that deserves your beating me these three times?" it asked Balaam.

²⁹"Because you have made me look like a fool!" Balaam shouted. "If I had a sword with me, I would kill you!"

³⁰"But I am the same donkey you always ride on," the donkey answered. "Have I ever done anything like this before?"

"No," he admitted.

³¹Then the LORD opened Balaam's eyes, and he saw the angel of the LORD standing in the roadway with a drawn sword in his hand. Balaam fell face down on the ground before him.

³²"Why did you beat your donkey those three times?" the angel of the LORD demanded. "I have come to block your way because you are stubbornly resisting me. ³³Three times the donkey saw

22:5a Or *who was at Pethor in the land of the Amavites.* 22:5b Hebrew *the river.*

me and shied away; otherwise, I would certainly have killed you by now and spared the donkey."

³⁴Then Balaam confessed to the angel of the LORD, "I have sinned. I did not realize you were standing in the road to block my way. I will go back home if you are against my going."

³⁵But the angel of the LORD told him, "Go with these men, but you may say only what I tell you to say." So Balaam went on with Balak's officials. ³⁶When King Balak heard that Balaam was on the way, he went out to meet him at a Moabite town on the Arnon River at the border of his land.

³⁷"Did I not send you an urgent invitation? Why didn't you come right away?" Balak asked Balaam. "Didn't you believe me when I said I would reward you richly?"

³⁸Balaam replied, "I have come, but I have no power to say just anything. I will speak only the messages that God gives me." ³⁹Then Balaam accompanied Balak to Kiriath-huzoth, ⁴⁰where the king sacrificed cattle and sheep. He sent portions of the meat to Balaam and the officials who were with him. ⁴¹The next morning Balak took Balaam up to Bamoth-baal. From there he could see the people of Israel spread out below him.

CHAPTER **23**

Balaam Blesses Israel

Balaam said to King Balak, "Build me seven altars here, and prepare seven young bulls and seven rams for a sacrifice." ²Balak followed his instructions, and the two of them sacrificed a young bull and a ram on each altar.

³Then Balaam said to Balak, "Stand here by your burnt offerings, and I will go to see if the LORD will respond to me. Then I will tell you whatever he reveals to me." So Balaam went alone to the top of a hill, ⁴and God met him there. Balaam said to him, "I have prepared seven altars and have sacrificed a young bull and a ram on each altar."

⁵Then the LORD gave Balaam a message for King Balak and said, "Go back to Balak and tell him what I told you."

⁶When Balaam returned, the king was standing beside his burnt offerings with all the officials of Moab. ⁷This was the prophecy Balaam delivered:

"Balak summoned me to come from Aram;
  the king of Moab brought me from the
    eastern hills.
'Come,' he said, 'curse Jacob for me!
  Come and announce Israel's doom.'

⁸ But how can I curse
  those whom God has not cursed?
How can I condemn
  those whom the LORD has not
    condemned?
⁹ I see them from the cliff tops;
  I watch them from the hills.
I see a people who live by themselves,
  set apart from other nations.
¹⁰ Who can count Jacob's descendants, as
    numerous as dust?
  Who can count even a fourth of Israel's
    people?
Let me die like the righteous;
  let my life end like theirs."

¹¹Then King Balak demanded of Balaam, "What have you done to me? I brought you to curse my enemies. Instead, you have blessed them!"

¹²But Balaam replied, "Can I say anything except what the LORD tells me?"

Balaam's Second Prophecy

¹³Then King Balak told him, "Come with me to another place. There you will see only a portion of the nation of Israel. Curse at least that many!" ¹⁴So Balak took Balaam to the plateau of Zophim on Pisgah Peak. He built seven altars there and offered a young bull and a ram on each altar.

¹⁵Then Balaam said to the king, "Stand here by your burnt offering while I go to meet the LORD."

¹⁶So the LORD met Balaam and gave him a message. Then he said, "Go back to Balak and give him this message."

¹⁷So Balaam returned to the place where the king and the officials of Moab were standing beside Balak's burnt offerings. "What did the LORD say?" Balak asked eagerly.

¹⁸This was the prophecy Balaam delivered:

"Rise up, Balak, and listen!
  Hear me, son of Zippor.
¹⁹ God is not a man, that he should lie.
  He is not a human, that he should
    change his mind.
Has he ever spoken and failed to act?
  Has he ever promised and not carried it
    through?
²⁰ I received a command to bless;
  he has blessed, and I cannot reverse it!
²¹ No misfortune is in sight for Jacob;
  no trouble is in store for Israel.
For the LORD their God is with them;
  he has been proclaimed their king.

22 God has brought them out of Egypt;
he is like a strong ox for them.
23 No curse can touch Jacob;
no sorcery has any power against Israel.
For now it will be said of Jacob,
'What wonders God has done for Israel!'
24 These people rise up like a lioness;
like a majestic lion they stand.
They refuse to rest
until they have feasted on prey,
drinking the blood of the slaughtered!"

25Then Balak said to Balaam, "If you aren't going to curse them, at least don't bless them!" 26But Balaam replied, "Didn't I tell you that I must do whatever the LORD tells me?"

Balaam's Third Prophecy

27Then King Balak said to Balaam, "Come, I will take you to yet another place. Perhaps it will please God to let you curse them from there." 28So Balak took Balaam to the top of Mount Peor, overlooking the wasteland.* 29Balaam again told Balak, "Build me seven altars and prepare me seven young bulls and seven rams for a sacrifice." 30So Balak did as Balaam ordered and offered a young bull and a ram on each altar.

CHAPTER **24**

By now Balaam realized that the LORD intended to bless Israel, so he did not resort to divination as he often did. Instead, he turned and looked out toward the wilderness, 2where he saw the people of Israel camped, tribe by tribe. Then the Spirit of God came upon him, 3and this is the prophecy he delivered:

"This is the prophecy of Balaam son of Beor,
the prophecy of the man whose eyes see clearly,
4 who hears the words of God,
who sees a vision from the Almighty,
who falls down with eyes wide open:
5 How beautiful are your tents, O Jacob;
how lovely are your homes, O Israel!
6 They spread before me like groves of palms,
like fruitful gardens by the riverside.
They are like aloes planted by the LORD,
like cedars beside the waters.
7 Water will gush out in buckets;
their offspring are supplied with all they need.
Their king will be greater than Agag;
their kingdom will be exalted.

23:28 Or *overlooking Jeshimon.*

8 God brought them up from Egypt,
drawing them along like a wild ox.
He devours all the nations that oppose him,
breaking their bones in pieces,
shooting them with arrows.
9 Like a lion, Israel crouches and lies down;
like a lioness, who dares to arouse her?
Blessed is everyone who blesses you,
O Israel,
and cursed is everyone who curses you."

10King Balak flew into a rage against Balaam. He angrily clapped his hands and shouted, "I called you to curse my enemies! Instead, you have blessed them three times. 11Now get out of here! Go back home! I had planned to reward you richly, but the LORD has kept you from your reward."

12Balaam told Balak, "Don't you remember what I told your messengers? I said, 13'Even if Balak were to give me a palace filled with silver and gold, I am powerless to do anything against the will of the LORD.' I told you that I could say only what the LORD says! 14Now I am returning to my own people. But first let me tell you what the Israelites will do to your people in the future."

Balaam's Final Prophecies

15This is the prophecy Balaam delivered:

"This is the message of Balaam son of Beor,
the prophecy of the man whose eyes see clearly,
16 who hears the words of God,
who has knowledge from the Most High,
who sees a vision from the Almighty,
who falls down with eyes wide open:
17 I see him, but not in the present time.
I perceive him, but far in the distant future.
A star will rise from Jacob;
a scepter will emerge from Israel.
It will crush the foreheads of Moab's people,
cracking the skulls of the people of Sheth.
18 Edom will be taken over,
and Seir, its enemy, will be conquered,
while Israel continues on in triumph.
19 A ruler will rise in Jacob
who will destroy the survivors of Ir."

20Then Balaam looked over at the people of Amalek and delivered this prophecy:

"Amalek was the greatest of nations,
but its destiny is destruction!"

²¹Then he looked over at the Kenites and prophesied:

"You are strongly situated;
  your nest is set in the rocks.
²² But the Kenites will be destroyed
  when Assyria* takes you captive."

²³Balaam concluded his prophecies by saying:

"Alas, who can survive when God does this?
²⁴   Ships will come from the coasts of
    Cyprus*;
  they will oppress both Assyria and Eber,
  but they, too, will be utterly destroyed."

²⁵Then Balaam and Balak returned to their homes.

CHAPTER **25**
Moab Seduces Israel

While the Israelites were camped at Acacia,* some of the men defiled themselves by sleeping with the local Moabite women. ²These women invited them to attend sacrifices to their gods, and soon the Israelites were feasting with them and worshiping the gods of Moab. ³Before long Israel was joining in the worship of Baal of Peor, causing the LORD's anger to blaze against his people.

⁴The LORD issued the following command to Moses: "Seize all the ringleaders and execute them before the LORD in broad daylight, so his fierce anger will turn away from the people of Israel." ⁵So Moses ordered Israel's judges to execute everyone who had joined in worshiping Baal of Peor.

⁶Just then one of the Israelite men brought a Midianite woman into the camp, right before the eyes of Moses and all the people, as they were weeping at the entrance of the Tabernacle.* ⁷When Phinehas son of Eleazar and grandson of Aaron the priest saw this, he jumped up and left the assembly. Then he took a spear ⁸and rushed after the man into his tent. Phinehas thrust the spear all the way through the man's body and into the woman's stomach. So the plague against the Israelites was stopped, ⁹but not before 24,000 people had died.

¹⁰Then the LORD said to Moses, ¹¹"Phinehas son of Eleazar and grandson of Aaron the priest has turned my anger away from the Israelites by displaying passionate zeal among them on my behalf. So I have stopped destroying all Israel as I had intended to do in my anger. ¹²So tell him that I am making my special covenant of peace

with him. ¹³In this covenant, he and his descendants will be priests for all time, because he was zealous for his God and made atonement for the people of Israel."

¹⁴The Israelite man killed with the Midianite woman was named Zimri son of Salu, the leader of a family from the tribe of Simeon. ¹⁵The woman's name was Cozbi; she was the daughter of Zur, the leader of a Midianite clan.

¹⁶Then the LORD said to Moses, ¹⁷"Attack the Midianites and destroy them, ¹⁸because they assaulted you with deceit by tricking you into worshiping Baal of Peor, and because of Cozbi, the daughter of a Midianite leader, who was killed on the day of the plague at Peor."

CHAPTER **26**
Israel's Second Census

After the plague had ended, the LORD said to Moses and to Eleazar son of Aaron, the priest, ²"Take a census of all the men of Israel who are twenty years old or older, to find out how many of each family are of military age." ³At that time the entire nation of Israel was camped on the plains of Moab beside the Jordan River, across from Jericho.

So Moses and Eleazar the priest issued these census instructions to the leaders of Israel: ⁴"Count all the men of Israel twenty years old and older, just as the LORD commanded Moses." This is the census record of all the descendants of Israel who came out of Egypt.

The Tribe of Reuben

⁵These were the clans descended from Reuben, Jacob's* oldest son:
  The Hanochite clan, named after its
    ancestor Hanoch.
  The Palluite clan, named after its ancestor
    Pallu.
⁶ The Hezronite clan, named after its ancestor
    Hezron.
  The Carmite clan, named after its ancestor
    Carmi.

⁷The men from all the clans of Reuben numbered 43,730.

⁸Pallu was the ancestor of Eliab, ⁹and Eliab was the father of Nemuel, Dathan, and Abiram. This Dathan and Abiram are the same community leaders who conspired with Korah against Moses and Aaron, defying the LORD. ¹⁰But the earth opened up and swallowed them with Korah, and 250 of their followers were destroyed

24:22 Hebrew *Asshur;* also in 24:24. 24:24 Hebrew *Kittim.* 25:1 Hebrew *Shittim.* 25:6 Hebrew *Tent of Meeting.* 26:5 Hebrew *Israel's.*

that day by fire from the LORD. This served as a warning to the entire nation of Israel. ¹¹However, the sons of Korah did not die that day.

The Tribe of Simeon

¹²These were the clans descended from the sons of Simeon:

The Nemuelite clan, named after its ancestor Nemuel.

The Jaminite clan, named after its ancestor Jamin.

The Jakinite clan, named after its ancestor Jakin.

¹³ The Zerahite clan, named after its ancestor Zerah.

The Shaulite clan, named after its ancestor Shaul.

¹⁴The men from all the clans of Simeon numbered 22,200.

The Tribe of Gad

¹⁵These were the clans descended from the sons of Gad:

The Zephonite clan, named after its ancestor Zephon.

The Haggite clan, named after its ancestor Haggi.

The Shunite clan, named after its ancestor Shuni.

¹⁶ The Oznite clan, named after its ancestor Ozni.

The Erite clan, named after its ancestor Eri.

¹⁷ The Arodite clan, named after its ancestor Arodi.*

The Arelite clan, named after its ancestor Areli.

¹⁸The men from all the clans of Gad numbered 40,500.

The Tribe of Judah

¹⁹Judah had two sons, Er and Onan, who had died in the land of Canaan. ²⁰But the following clans descended from Judah's surviving sons:

The Shelanite clan, named after its ancestor Shelah.

The Perezite clan, named after its ancestor Perez.

The Zerahite clan, named after its ancestor Zerah.

²¹These were the subclans descended from the Perezites:

The Hezronites, named after their ancestor Hezron.

The Hamulites, named after their ancestor Hamul.

²²The men from all the clans of Judah numbered 76,500.

The Tribe of Issachar

²³These were the clans descended from the sons of Issachar:

The Tolaite clan, named after its ancestor Tola.

The Puite clan, named after its ancestor Puah.*

²⁴ The Jashubite clan, named after its ancestor Jashub.

The Shimronite clan, named after its ancestor Shimron.

²⁵The men from all the clans of Issachar numbered 64,300.

The Tribe of Zebulun

²⁶These were the clans descended from the sons of Zebulun:

The Seredite clan, named after its ancestor Sered.

The Elonite clan, named after its ancestor Elon.

The Jahleelite clan, named after its ancestor Jahleel.

²⁷The men from all the clans of Zebulun numbered 60,500.

The Tribe of Manasseh

²⁸Two clans were descended from Joseph through Manasseh and Ephraim.

²⁹These were the clans descended from Manasseh:

The Makirite clan, named after its ancestor Makir.

The Gileadite clan, named after its ancestor Gilead, Makir's son.

³⁰These were the subclans descended from the Gileadites:

The Iezerites, named after their ancestor Iezer.

The Helekites, named after their ancestor Helek.

³¹ The Asrielites, named after their ancestor Asriel.

26:17 As in Samaritan Pentateuch and Syriac version (see also Gen 46:16); Hebrew reads *Arod*.   26:23 As in Samaritan Pentateuch, Greek and Syriac versions, and Latin Vulgate (see also 1 Chr 7:1); Hebrew reads *The Punite clan, named after its ancestor Puvah*.

The Shechemites, named after their ancestor
Shechem.
32 The Shemidaites, named after their ancestor
Shemida.
The Hepherites, named after their ancestor
Hepher.
33 Hepher's son, Zelophehad, had no sons,
but his daughters' names were Mahlah,
Noah, Hoglah, Milcah, and Tirzah.

34The men from all the clans of Manasseh numbered 52,700.

The Tribe of Ephraim

35These were the clans descended from the sons
of Ephraim:
The Shuthelahite clan, named after its
ancestor Shuthelah.
The Bekerite clan, named after its ancestor
Beker.
The Tahanite clan, named after its ancestor
Tahan.

36This was the subclan descended from the
Shuthelahites:
The Eranites, named after their ancestor
Eran.

37The men from all the clans of Ephraim numbered 32,500.

These clans of Manasseh and Ephraim were
all descendants of Joseph.

The Tribe of Benjamin

38These were the clans descended from the sons
of Benjamin:
The Belaite clan, named after its ancestor
Bela.
The Ashbelite clan, named after its ancestor
Ashbel.
The Ahiramite clan, named after its ancestor
Ahiram.
39 The Shuphamite clan, named after its
ancestor Shupham.*
The Huphamite clan, named after its
ancestor Hupham.

40These were the subclans descended from the
Belaites:
The Ardites, named after their ancestor Ard.*
The Naamites, named after their ancestor
Naaman.

41The men from all the clans of Benjamin numbered 45,600.

The Tribe of Dan

42These were the clans descended from the sons
of Dan:
The Shuhamite clan, named after its
ancestor Shuham.

43All the clans of Dan were Shuhamite clans,
and the men from these clans numbered
64,400.

The Tribe of Asher

44These were the clans descended from the sons
of Asher:
The Imnite clan, named after its ancestor
Imnah.
The Ishvite clan, named after its ancestor
Ishvi.
The Beriite clan, named after its ancestor
Beriah.

45These were the subclans descended from the
Beriites:
The Heberites, named after their ancestor
Heber.
The Malkielites, named after their ancestor
Malkiel.

46Asher also had a daughter named Serah.

47The men from all the clans of Asher numbered
53,400.

The Tribe of Naphtali

48These were the clans descended from the sons
of Naphtali:
The Jahzeelite clan, named after its ancestor
Jahzeel.
The Gunite clan, named after its ancestor
Guni.
49 The Jezerite clan, named after its ancestor
Jezer.
The Shillemite clan, named after its
ancestor Shillem.

50The men from all the clans of Naphtali numbered 45,400.

The Census Results

51So the total number of Israelite men counted
in the census numbered 601,730.

52Then the LORD said to Moses, 53"Divide the
land among the tribes in proportion to their
populations, as indicated by the census. 54Give
the larger tribes more land and the smaller tribes
less land, each group's inheritance reflecting the

26:39 As in some Hebrew manuscripts, Samaritan Pentateuch, Greek and Syriac versions, and Latin Vulgate; most Hebrew manuscripts read
Shephupham.   26:40 As in Samaritan Pentateuch, some Greek manuscripts, and Latin Vulgate; Hebrew lacks *named after their ancestor Ard.*

size of its population. ⁵⁵Make sure you assign the land by lot, and define the inheritance of each ancestral tribe by means of the census listings. ⁵⁶Each inheritance must be assigned by lot among the larger and smaller tribal groups."

The Tribe of Levi

⁵⁷This is the census record for the Levites who were counted according to their clans:

The Gershonite clan, named after its ancestor Gershon.

The Kohathite clan, named after its ancestor Kohath.

The Merarite clan, named after its ancestor Merari.

⁵⁸The Libnites, the Hebronites, the Mahlites, the Mushites, and the Korahites were all subclans of the Levites.

Now Kohath was the ancestor of Amram, ⁵⁹and Amram's wife was named Jochebed. She also was a descendant of Levi, born among the Levites in the land of Egypt. Amram and Jochebed became the parents of Aaron, Moses, and their sister, Miriam. ⁶⁰To Aaron were born Nadab, Abihu, Eleazar, and Ithamar. ⁶¹But Nadab and Abihu died when they burned before the LORD a different kind of fire than he had commanded.

⁶²The men from the Levite clans who were one month old or older numbered 23,000. But the Levites were not included in the total census figure of the people of Israel because they were not given an inheritance of land when it was divided among the Israelites.

⁶³So these are the census figures of the people of Israel as prepared by Moses and Eleazar the priest on the plains of Moab beside the Jordan River, across from Jericho. ⁶⁴Not one person that Moses and Aaron counted in this census had been among those counted in the previous census taken in the wilderness of Sinai. ⁶⁵For the LORD had said of them, "They will all die in the wilderness." The only exceptions were Caleb son of Jephunneh and Joshua son of Nun.

CHAPTER **27**
The Daughters of Zelophehad

One day a petition was presented by the daughters of Zelophehad—Mahlah, Noah, Hoglah, Milcah, and Tirzah. Their father, Zelophehad, was the son of Hepher, son of Gilead, son of Makir, son of Manasseh, son of Joseph. ²These women went and stood before Moses, Eleazar

the priest, the tribal leaders, and the entire community at the entrance of the Tabernacle.* ³"Our father died in the wilderness without leaving any sons," they said. "But he was not among Korah's followers, who rebelled against the LORD. He died because of his own sin. ⁴Why should the name of our father disappear just because he had no sons? Give us property along with the rest of our relatives."

⁵So Moses brought their case before the LORD. ⁶And the LORD replied to Moses, ⁷"The daughters of Zelophehad are right. You must give them an inheritance of land along with their father's relatives. Assign them the property that would have been given to their father. ⁸Moreover announce this to the people of Israel: 'If a man dies and has no sons, then give his inheritance to his daughters. ⁹And if he has no daughters, turn his inheritance over to his brothers. ¹⁰If he has no brothers, give his inheritance to his father's brothers. ¹¹But if his father has no brothers, pass on his inheritance to the nearest relative in his clan. The Israelites must observe this as a general legal requirement, just as the LORD commanded Moses.'"

Joshua Chosen to Lead Israel

¹²One day the LORD said to Moses, "Climb to the top of the mountains east of the river,* and look out over the land I have given the people of Israel. ¹³After you have seen it, you will die as Aaron your brother did, ¹⁴for you both rebelled against my instructions in the wilderness of Zin. When the people of Israel rebelled, you failed to demonstrate my holiness to them at the waters." (These are the waters of Meribah at Kadesh* in the wilderness of Zin.)

¹⁵Then Moses said to the LORD, ¹⁶"O LORD, the God of the spirits of all living things, please appoint a new leader for the community. ¹⁷Give them someone who will lead them into battle, so the people of the LORD will not be like sheep without a shepherd."

¹⁸The LORD replied, "Take Joshua son of Nun, who has the Spirit in him, and lay your hands on him. ¹⁹Present him to Eleazar the priest before the whole community, and publicly commission him with the responsibility of leading the people. ²⁰Transfer your authority to him so the whole community of Israel will obey him. ²¹When direction from the LORD is needed, Joshua will stand before Eleazar the priest, who will determine the LORD's will by means of sacred lots.* This is how Joshua and the rest of the

27:2 Hebrew *Tent of Meeting.*   27:12 Hebrew *the mountains of Abarim.*   27:14 Hebrew *waters of Meribath-kadesh.*   27:21 Hebrew *of the Urim.*

community of Israel will discover what they should do."

22So Moses did as the LORD commanded and presented Joshua to Eleazar the priest and the whole community. 23Moses laid his hands on him and commissioned him to his responsibilities, just as the LORD had commanded through Moses.

CHAPTER **28**

The Daily Offerings

The LORD said to Moses, 2"Give these instructions to the people of Israel: The offerings you present to me by fire on the altar are my food, and they are very pleasing to me. See to it that they are brought at the appointed times and offered according to my instructions.

3"Say to them: When you present your daily whole burnt offerings to the LORD, you must offer two one-year-old male lambs with no physical defects. 4One lamb will be sacrificed in the morning and the other in the evening. 5With each lamb you must offer a grain offering of two quarts* of choice flour mixed with one quart* of olive oil. 6This is the regular burnt offering ordained at Mount Sinai, an offering made by fire, very pleasing to the LORD. 7Along with it you must present the proper drink offering, consisting of one quart of fermented drink with each lamb, poured out in the Holy Place as an offering to the LORD. 8Offer the second lamb in the evening with the same grain offering and drink offering. It, too, is an offering made by fire, very pleasing to the LORD.

The Sabbath Offerings

9"On the Sabbath day, sacrifice two one-year-old male lambs with no physical defects. They must be accompanied by a grain offering of three quarts* of choice flour mixed with olive oil, and a drink offering. 10This is the whole burnt offering to be presented each Sabbath day, in addition to the regular daily burnt offering and its accompanying drink offering.

The Monthly Offerings

11"On the first day of each month, present an extra burnt offering to the LORD of two young bulls, one ram, and seven one-year-old male lambs, all with no physical defects. 12These will be accompanied by grain offerings of choice flour mixed with olive oil—five quarts* with

each bull, three quarts with the ram, 13and two quarts with each lamb. This burnt offering must be presented by fire, and it will be very pleasing to the LORD. 14You must also give a drink offering with each sacrifice: two quarts* of wine with each bull, two and a half pints* for the ram, and one quart* for each lamb. Present this monthly burnt offering on the first day of each month throughout the year.

15"Also, on the first day of each month you must offer one male goat for a sin offering to the LORD. This is in addition to the regular daily burnt offering and its accompanying drink offering.

Offerings for the Passover

16"On the appointed day in early spring,* you must celebrate the LORD's Passover. 17On the following day a joyous, seven-day festival will begin, but no bread made with yeast may be eaten. 18On the first day of the festival you must call a sacred assembly of the people. None of your regular work may be done on that day. 19You must present as a burnt offering to the LORD two young bulls, one ram, and seven one-year-old male lambs, all with no physical defects. 20These will be accompanied by grain offerings of choice flour mixed with olive oil— five quarts with each bull, three quarts with the ram, 21and two quarts with each of the seven lambs. 22You must also offer a male goat as a sin offering, to make atonement for yourselves. 23You will present these offerings in addition to your regular morning sacrifices. 24On each of the seven days of the festival, this is how you will prepare the food offerings to be presented by fire, very pleasing to the LORD. These will be offered in addition to the regular whole burnt offerings and drink offerings. 25On the seventh day of the festival you must call another holy assembly of the people. None of your regular work may be done on that day.

Offerings for the Festival of Harvest

26"On the first day of the Festival of Harvest,* when you present the first of your new grain to the LORD, you must call a holy assembly of the people. None of your regular work may be done on that day. 27A special whole burnt offering will be offered that day, very pleasing to the LORD. It will consist of two young bulls, one ram, and seven one-year-old male lambs. 28These will be

28:5a Hebrew *1/10 of an ephah* [2 liters]; also in 28:13, 21, 29.   28:5b Hebrew *1/4 of a hin* [1 liter]; also in 28:7.   28:9 Hebrew *2/10 of an ephah* [3.6 liters]; also in 28:12, 20, 28.   28:12 Hebrew *3/10 of an ephah* [5.4 liters]; also in 28:20, 28.   28:14a Hebrew *1/2 of a hin* [2 liters]. 28:14b Hebrew *1/3 of a hin* [1.3 liters].   28:14c Hebrew *1/4 of a hin* [1 liter].   28:16 Hebrew *On the fourteenth day of the first month.* This day of the Hebrew lunar calendar occurs in late March or early April.   28:26 Or *Festival of Weeks.*

accompanied by grain offerings of choice flour mixed with olive oil—five quarts with each bull, three quarts with the ram, ²⁹and two quarts with each of the seven lambs. ³⁰Also, offer one male goat to make atonement for yourselves. ³¹These special burnt offerings, along with their drink offerings, are in addition to the regular daily burnt offering and its accompanying grain offering. Be sure that all the animals you sacrifice have no physical defects.

CHAPTER **29**

Offerings for the Festival of Trumpets

"The Festival of Trumpets will be celebrated on the appointed day in early autumn* each year. You must call a solemn assembly of all the people on that day, and no regular work may be done. ²On that day you must present a burnt offering, very pleasing to the LORD. It will consist of one young bull, one ram, and seven one-year-old male lambs, all with no physical defects. ³These must be accompanied by grain offerings of choice flour mixed with olive oil—five quarts* with the bull, three quarts* with the ram, ⁴and two quarts* with each of the seven lambs. ⁵In addition, you must sacrifice a male goat as a sin offering, to make atonement for yourselves. ⁶These special sacrifices are in addition to your regular monthly and daily burnt offerings, and they must be given with their prescribed grain offerings and drink offerings. These offerings are given to the LORD by fire and are very pleasing to him.

Offerings for the Day of Atonement

⁷"Ten days later,* you must call another holy assembly of all the people. On that day, the Day of Atonement, the people must go without food, and no regular work may be done. ⁸You must present a burnt offering, very pleasing to the LORD. It will consist of one young bull, one ram, and seven one-year-old male lambs, all with no physical defects. ⁹These offerings must be accompanied by the prescribed grain offerings of choice flour mixed with olive oil—five quarts of choice flour with the bull, three quarts of choice flour with the ram, ¹⁰and two quarts of choice flour with each of the seven lambs. ¹¹You must also sacrifice one male goat for a sin offering. This is in addition to the sin offering of atonement and the regular daily burnt offering with

its grain offering, and their accompanying drink offerings.

Offerings for the Festival of Shelters

¹²"Five days later,* you must call yet another holy assembly of all the people, and on that day no regular work may be done. It is the beginning of the Festival of Shelters, a seven-day festival to the LORD. ¹³That day you must present a special whole burnt offering by fire, very pleasing to the LORD. It will consist of thirteen young bulls, two rams, and fourteen one-year-old male lambs, all with no physical defects. ¹⁴Each of these offerings must be accompanied by a grain offering of choice flour mixed with olive oil—five quarts for each of the thirteen bulls, three quarts for each of the two rams, ¹⁵and two quarts for each of the fourteen lambs. ¹⁶You must also sacrifice a male goat as a sin offering, in addition to the regular daily burnt offering with its accompanying grain offering and drink offering.

¹⁷"On the second day of this seven-day festival, sacrifice twelve young bulls, two rams, and fourteen one-year-old male lambs, all with no physical defects. ¹⁸Each of these offerings of bulls, rams, and lambs must be accompanied by the prescribed grain offering and drink offering. ¹⁹You must also sacrifice a male goat as a sin offering, in addition to the regular daily burnt offering with its accompanying grain offering and drink offering.

²⁰"On the third day of the festival, sacrifice eleven young bulls, two rams, and fourteen one-year-old male lambs, all with no physical defects. ²¹Each of these offerings of bulls, rams, and lambs must be accompanied by the prescribed grain offering and drink offering. ²²You must also sacrifice a male goat as a sin offering, in addition to the regular daily burnt offering with its accompanying grain offering and drink offering.

²³"On the fourth day of the festival, sacrifice ten young bulls, two rams, and fourteen one-year-old male lambs, all with no physical defects. ²⁴Each of these offerings of bulls, rams, and lambs must be accompanied by the prescribed grain offering and drink offering. ²⁵You must also sacrifice a male goat as a sin offering, in addition to the regular daily burnt offering with its accompanying grain offering and drink offering.

²⁶"On the fifth day of the festival, sacrifice nine young bulls, two rams, and fourteen one-

---

29:1 Hebrew *on the first day of the seventh month*. This day of the Hebrew lunar calendar occurs in September or early October. 29:3a Hebrew ³/₁₀ *of an ephah* [5.4 liters]; also in 29:9, 14. 29:3b Hebrew ²/₁₀ *of an ephah* [3.6 liters]; also in 29:9, 14. 29:4 Hebrew ¹/₁₀ *of an ephah* [2 liters]; also in 29:10, 15. 29:7 Hebrew *On the tenth day of the seventh month*; see 29:1 and the note there. 29:12 Hebrew *On the fifteenth day of the seventh month*; see 29:1, 7 and the notes there.

year-old male lambs, all with no physical defects. 27Each of these offerings of bulls, rams, and lambs must be accompanied by the prescribed grain offering and drink offering. 28You must also sacrifice a male goat as a sin offering, in addition to the regular daily burnt offering with its accompanying grain offering and drink offering.

29"On the sixth day of the festival, sacrifice eight young bulls, two rams, and fourteen one-year-old male lambs, all with no physical defects. 30Each of these offerings of bulls, rams, and lambs must be accompanied by the prescribed grain offering and drink offering. 31You must also sacrifice a male goat as a sin offering, in addition to the regular daily burnt offering with its accompanying grain offering and drink offering.

32"On the seventh day of the festival, sacrifice seven young bulls, two rams, and fourteen one-year-old male lambs, all with no physical defects. 33Each of these offerings of bulls, rams, and lambs must be accompanied by the prescribed grain offering and drink offering. 34You must also sacrifice one male goat as a sin offering, in addition to the regular daily burnt offering with its accompanying grain offering and drink offering.

35"On the eighth day of the festival, call all the people to another holy assembly. You must do no regular work on that day. 36You must present a burnt offering, very pleasing to the LORD. It will consist of one young bull, one ram, and seven one-year-old male lambs, all with no physical defects. 37Each of these offerings must be accompanied by the prescribed grain offering and drink offering. 38You must also sacrifice one male goat as a sin offering, in addition to the regular daily burnt offering with its accompanying grain offering and drink offering.

39"You must present these offerings to the LORD at your annual festivals. These are in addition to the sacrifices and offerings you present in connection with vows, or as freewill offerings, burnt offerings, grain offerings, drink offerings, or peace offerings."

40So Moses gave all of these instructions to the people of Israel, just as the LORD had commanded him.

CHAPTER **30**
Laws concerning Vows
Now Moses summoned the leaders of the tribes of Israel and told them, "This is what the LORD has commanded: 2A man who makes a vow to

the LORD or makes a pledge under oath must never break it. He must do exactly what he said he would do.

3"If a young woman makes a vow to the LORD or a pledge under oath while she is still living at her father's home, 4and her father hears of the vow or pledge but says nothing, then all her vows and pledges will stand. 5But if her father refuses to let her fulfill the vow or pledge on the day he hears of it, then all her vows and pledges will become invalid. The LORD will forgive her because her father would not let her fulfill them.

6"Now suppose a young woman takes a vow or makes an impulsive pledge and later marries. 7If her husband learns of her vow or pledge and raises no objections on the day he hears of it, her vows and pledges will stand. 8But if her husband refuses to accept her vow or impulsive pledge on the day he hears of it, he nullifies her commitments, and the LORD will forgive her. 9If, however, a woman is a widow or is divorced, she must fulfill all her vows and pledges no matter what.

10"Suppose a woman is married and living in her husband's home when she makes a vow or pledge. 11If her husband hears of it and does nothing to stop her, her vow or pledge will stand. 12But if her husband refuses to accept it on the day he hears of it, her vow or pledge will be nullified, and the LORD will forgive her. 13So her husband may either confirm or nullify any vows or pledges she makes to deny herself. 14But if he says nothing on the day he hears of it, then he is agreeing to it. 15If he waits more than a day and then tries to nullify a vow or pledge, he will suffer the consequences of her guilt."

16These are the regulations the LORD gave Moses concerning relationships between a man and his wife, and between a father and a young daughter who still lives at home.

CHAPTER **31**
Conquest of the Midianites
Then the LORD said to Moses, 2"Take vengeance on the Midianites for leading the Israelites into idolatry. After that, you will die and join your ancestors."

3So Moses said to the people, "Choose some men to fight the LORD's war of vengeance against Midian. 4From each tribe of Israel, send one thousand men into battle." 5So they chose one thousand men from each tribe of Israel, a total of twelve thousand men armed for battle. 6Then Moses sent them out, a thousand men from each tribe, and Phinehas son of Eleazar the priest led them into battle. They carried along the holy objects of the sanctuary and the trumpets for sounding the charge. 7They attacked Midian just as the LORD had commanded Moses, and they killed all the men. 8All five of the Midianite kings—Evi, Rekem, Zur, Hur, and Reba—died in the battle. They also killed Balaam son of Beor with the sword.

9Then the Israelite army captured the Midianite women and children and seized their cattle and flocks and all their wealth as plunder. 10They burned all the towns and villages where the Midianites had lived. 11After they had gathered the plunder and captives, both people and animals, 12they brought them all to Moses and Eleazar the priest, and to the whole community of Israel, which was camped on the plains of Moab beside the Jordan River, across from Jericho. 13Moses, Eleazar the priest, and all the leaders of the people went to meet them outside the camp. 14But Moses was furious with all the military commanders* who had returned from the battle.

15"Why have you let all the women live?" he demanded. 16"These are the very ones who followed Balaam's advice and caused the people of Israel to rebel against the LORD at Mount Peor. They are the ones who caused the plague to strike the LORD's people. 17Now kill all the boys and all the women who have slept with a man. 18Only the young girls who are virgins may live; you may keep them for yourselves. 19And all of you who have killed anyone or touched a dead body must stay outside the camp for seven days. You must purify yourselves and your captives on the third and seventh days. 20Also, purify all your clothing and everything made of leather, goat hair, or wood."

21Then Eleazar the priest said to the men who were in the battle, "The LORD has given Moses this requirement of the law: 22Anything made of gold, silver, bronze, iron, tin, or lead—23that is, metals that do not burn—must be passed through fire in order to be made ceremonially pure. These metal objects must then be further purified with the water of purification. But everything that burns must be purified by the water alone. 24On the seventh day you must wash your clothes and be purified. Then you may return to the camp."

Division of the Spoils

25And the LORD said to Moses, 26"You and Eleazar the priest and the family leaders of each tribe

are to make a list of all the plunder taken in the battle, including the people and animals. 27Then divide the plunder into two parts, and give half to the men who fought the battle and half to the rest of the people. 28But first give the LORD his share of the captives, cattle, donkeys, sheep, and goats that belong to the army. Set apart one out of every five hundred as the LORD's share. 29Give this share of their half to Eleazar the priest as an offering to the LORD. 30Also take one of every fifty of the captives, cattle, donkeys, sheep, and goats in the half that belongs to the people of Israel. Give this share to the Levites in charge of maintaining the LORD's Tabernacle."

31So Moses and Eleazar the priest did as the LORD commanded Moses.

32The plunder remaining from the spoils that the fighting men had taken totaled 675,000 sheep, 3372,000 cattle, 3461,000 donkeys, 35and 32,000 young girls.

36So the half of the plunder given to the fighting men totaled 337,500 sheep, 37of which 675 were the LORD's share; 3836,000 cattle, of which 72 were the LORD's share; 3930,500 donkeys, of which 61 were the LORD's share; 4016,000 young girls, of whom 32 were the LORD's share. 41Moses gave all the LORD's share to Eleazar the priest, just as the LORD had directed him.

42The half of the plunder belonging to the people of Israel, which Moses had separated from the half belonging to the fighting men, 43amounted to 337,500 sheep, 4436,000 cattle, 4530,500 donkeys, 46and 16,000 young girls. 47From the half-share given to the people, Moses took one of every fifty prisoners and animals and gave them to the Levites who maintained the LORD's Tabernacle. All this was done just as the LORD had commanded Moses.

48Then all the military commanders came to Moses 49and said, "Sir, we have accounted for all the men who went out to battle under our command; not one of us is missing! 50So we are presenting the items of gold we captured as an offering to the LORD from our share of the plunder—armbands, bracelets, rings, earrings, and necklaces. This will make atonement for our lives before the LORD."

51So Moses and Eleazar the priest received the gold from all the military commanders, all kinds of jewelry and crafted objects. 52In all, the gold that the commanders presented as a gift to the LORD weighed about 420 pounds.* 53All the fighting men had taken some of the plunder for

---

31:14 Hebrew *the commanders of thousands, and the commanders of hundreds;* also in 31:48, 52, 54.   31:52 Hebrew *16,750 shekels* [191 kilograms].

themselves. 54So Moses and Eleazar the priest accepted the gifts from the military commanders and brought the gold to the Tabernacle* as a reminder to the LORD that the people of Israel belong to him.

CHAPTER **32**
The Tribes East of the Jordan
Now the tribes of Reuben and Gad owned vast numbers of livestock. So when they saw that the lands of Jazer and Gilead were ideally suited for their flocks and herds, 2they came to Moses, Eleazar the priest, and the other leaders of the people. They said, 3"Ataroth, Dibon, Jazer, Nimrah, Heshbon, Elealeh, Sebam, Nebo, and Beon—4the LORD has conquered this whole area for the people of Israel. It is ideally suited for all our flocks and herds. 5If we have found favor with you, please let us have this land as our property instead of giving us land across the Jordan River."

6"Do you mean you want to stay back here while your brothers go across and do all the fighting?" Moses asked the Reubenites and Gadites. 7"Are you trying to discourage the rest of the people of Israel from going across to the land the LORD has given them? 8This is what your ancestors did when I sent them from Kadesh-barnea to explore the land. 9After they went up to the valley of Eshcol and scouted the land, they discouraged the people of Israel from entering the land the LORD was giving them. 10Then the LORD was furious with them, and he vowed, 11'Of all those I rescued from Egypt, no one who is twenty years old or older will ever see the land I solemnly promised to Abraham, Isaac, and Jacob, for they have not obeyed me completely. 12The only exceptions are Caleb son of Jephunneh the Kenizzite and Joshua son of Nun, for they have wholeheartedly followed the LORD.'

13"The LORD was furious with Israel and made them wander in the wilderness for forty years until the whole generation that sinned against him had died. 14But here you are, a brood of sinners, doing exactly the same thing! You are making the LORD even angrier with Israel. 15If you turn away from him like this and he abandons them again in the wilderness, you will be responsible for destroying this entire nation!"

16But they responded to Moses, "We simply want to build sheepfolds for our flocks and fortified cities for our wives and children. 17Then we will arm ourselves and lead our fellow Israelites into battle until we have brought

them safely to their inheritance. Meanwhile, our families will stay in the fortified cities we build here, so they will be safe from any attacks by the local people. 18We will not return to our homes until all the people of Israel have received their inheritance of land. 19But we do not want any of the land on the other side of the Jordan. We would rather live here on the east side where we have received our inheritance."

20Then Moses said, "If you keep your word and arm yourselves for the LORD's battles, 21and if your troops cross the Jordan until the LORD has driven out his enemies, 22then you may return when the land is finally subdued before the LORD. You will have discharged your duty to the LORD and to the rest of the people of Israel. And the land on the east side of the Jordan will be your inheritance from the LORD. 23But if you fail to keep your word, then you will have sinned against the LORD, and you may be sure that your sin will find you out. 24Go ahead and build towns for your families and sheepfolds for your flocks, but do everything you have said."

25Then the people of Gad and Reuben replied, "We are your servants and will follow your instructions exactly. 26Our children, wives, flocks, and cattle will stay here in the towns of Gilead. 27But, sir, all who are able to bear arms will cross over to fight for the LORD, just as you have said."

28So Moses gave orders to Eleazar, Joshua, and the tribal leaders of Israel. 29He said, "If all the men of Gad and Reuben who are able to fight the LORD's battles cross the Jordan with you, then when the land is conquered, you must give them the land of Gilead as their property. 30But if they refuse to cross over and march ahead of you, then they must accept land with the rest of you in the land of Canaan."

31The tribes of Gad and Reuben said again, "Sir, we will do as the LORD has commanded! 32We will cross the Jordan into Canaan fully armed to fight for the LORD, but our inheritance of land will be here on this side of the Jordan."

33So Moses assigned to the tribes of Gad, Reuben, and half the tribe of Manasseh son of Joseph the territory of King Sihon of the Amorites and the land of King Og of Bashan—the whole land with its towns and surrounding lands.

34The people of Gad built the towns of Dibon, Ataroth, Aroer, 35Atroth-shophan, Jazer, Jogbehah, 36Beth-nimrah, and Beth-haran.

These were all fortified cities with sheepfolds for their flocks.

37The people of Reuben built the towns of Heshbon, Elealeh, Kiriathaim, 38Nebo, Baal-meon, and Sibmah. They changed the names of some of the towns they conquered and rebuilt.

39Then the descendants of Makir of the tribe of Manasseh went to Gilead and conquered it, and they drove out the Amorites, who were living there. 40So Moses gave Gilead to the Makirites, descendants of Manasseh, and they lived there. 41The people of Jair, another clan of the tribe of Manasseh, captured many of the towns in Gilead and changed the name of that region to the Towns of Jair.* 42Meanwhile, a man named Nobah captured the town of Kenath and its surrounding villages, and he renamed that area Nobah after himself.

CHAPTER **33**

Remembering Israel's Journey

This is the itinerary the Israelites followed as they marched out of Egypt under the leadership of Moses and Aaron. 2At the LORD's direction, Moses kept a written record of their progress. These are the stages of their march, identified by the different places they stopped along the way.

3They set out from the city of Rameses on the morning after the first Passover celebration in early spring.* The people of Israel left defiantly, in full view of all the Egyptians. 4Meanwhile, the Egyptians were burying all their firstborn sons, whom the LORD had killed the night before. The LORD had defeated the gods of Egypt that night with great acts of judgment!

5After leaving Rameses, the Israelites set up camp at Succoth.

6Then they left Succoth and camped at Etham on the edge of the wilderness.

7They left Etham and turned back toward Pi-hahiroth, opposite Baal-zephon, and camped near Migdol.

8They left Pi-hahiroth and crossed the Red Sea* into the wilderness beyond. Then they traveled for three days into the Etham wilderness and camped at Marah.

9They left Marah and camped at Elim, where there were twelve springs of water and seventy palm trees.

10They left Elim and camped beside the Red Sea.*

11They left the Red Sea and camped in the Sin* Desert.

12They left the Sin Desert and camped at Dophkah.

13They left Dophkah and camped at Alush.

14They left Alush and camped at Rephidim, where there was no water for the people to drink.

15They left Rephidim and camped in the wilderness of Sinai.

16They left the wilderness of Sinai and camped at Kibroth-hattaavah.

17They left Kibroth-hattaavah and camped at Hazeroth.

18They left Hazeroth and camped at Rithmah.

19They left Rithmah and camped at Rimmon-perez.

20They left Rimmon-perez and camped at Libnah.

21They left Libnah and camped at Rissah.

22They left Rissah and camped at Kehelathah.

23They left Kehelathah and camped at Mount Shepher.

24They left Mount Shepher and camped at Haradah.

25They left Haradah and camped at Makheloth.

26They left Makheloth and camped at Tahath.

27They left Tahath and camped at Terah.

28They left Terah and camped at Mithcah.

29They left Mithcah and camped at Hashmonah.

30They left Hashmonah and camped at Moseroth.

31They left Moseroth and camped at Bene-jaakan.

32They left Bene-jaakan and camped at Hor-haggidgad.

33They left Hor-haggidgad and camped at Jotbathah.

34They left Jotbathah and camped at Abronah.

35They left Abronah and camped at Ezion-geber.

36They left Ezion-geber and camped at Kadesh in the wilderness of Zin.

37They left Kadesh and camped at Mount Hor, at the border of Edom. 38While they were at the foot of Mount Hor, Aaron the priest was directed by the LORD to go up the

32:41 Hebrew *Havvoth-jair*.   33:3 Hebrew *on the fifteenth day of the first month.* This day of the Hebrew lunar calendar occurs in late March or early April.   33:8 Hebrew *the sea.*   33:10 Hebrew *sea of reeds;* also in 33:11.   33:11 Not to be confused with the English word *sin.*

mountain, and there he died. This happened on a day in midsummer,* during the fortieth year after Israel's departure from Egypt. ³⁹Aaron was 123 years old when he died there on Mount Hor.

⁴⁰It was then that the Canaanite king of Arad, who lived in the Negev in the land of Canaan, heard that the people of Israel were approaching his land.

⁴¹Meanwhile, the Israelites left Mount Hor and camped at Zalmonah.

⁴²Then they left Zalmonah and camped at Punon.

⁴³They left Punon and camped at Oboth.

⁴⁴They left Oboth and camped at Iye-abarim on the border of Moab.

⁴⁵They left Iye-abarim* and camped at Dibon-gad.

⁴⁶They left Dibon-gad and camped at Almon-diblathaim.

⁴⁷They left Almon-diblathaim and camped in the mountains east of the river,* near Mount Nebo.

⁴⁸ They left the mountains east of the river and camped on the plains of Moab beside the Jordan River, across from Jericho. ⁴⁹Along the Jordan River they camped from Beth-jeshimoth as far as Abel-shittim on the plains of Moab.

⁵⁰While they were camped near the Jordan River on the plains of Moab opposite Jericho, the LORD said to Moses, ⁵¹ " Speak to the Israelites and tell them: ' When you cross the Jordan River into the land of Canaan, ⁵² you must drive out all the people living there. You must destroy all their carved and molten images and demolish all their pagan shrines. ⁵³ Take possession of the land and settle in it, because I have given it to you to occupy. ⁵⁴ You must distribute the land among the clans by sacred lot and in proportion to their size. A larger inheritance of land will be allotted to each of the larger clans, and a smaller inheritance will be allotted to each of the smaller clans. The decision of the sacred lot is final. In this way, the land will be divided among your ancestral tribes. ⁵⁵ But if you fail to drive out the people who live in the land, those who remain will be like splinters in your eyes and thorns in your sides. They will harass you in the land where you live. ⁵⁶ And I will do to you what I had planned to do to them.' "

CHAPTER 34
Boundaries of the Land

Then the LORD said to Moses, ² "Give these instructions to the Israelites: When you come into the land of Canaan, which I am giving you as your special possession, these will be the boundaries. ³ The southern portion of your country will extend from the wilderness of Zin, along the edge of Edom. The southern boundary will begin on the east at the Dead Sea.* ⁴ It will then run south past Scorpion Pass* in the direction of Zin. Its southernmost point will be Kadesh-barnea, from which it will go to Hazar-addar, and on to Azmon. ⁵ From Azmon the boundary will turn toward the brook of Egypt and end at the Mediterranean Sea.*

⁶ "Your western boundary will be the coastline of the Mediterranean Sea.

⁷ "Your northern boundary will begin at the Mediterranean Sea and run eastward to Mount Hor, ⁸ then to Lebo-hamath, and on through Zedad ⁹ and Ziphron to Hazar-enan. This will be your northern boundary.

¹⁰ "The eastern boundary will start at Hazar-enan and run south to Shepham, ¹¹ then down to Riblah on the east side of Ain. From there the boundary will run down along the eastern edge of the Sea of Galilee,* ¹² and then along the Jordan River to the Dead Sea. These are the boundaries of your land."

¹³ Then Moses told the Israelites, "This is the territory you are to divide among yourselves by sacred lot. The LORD commands that the land be divided up among the nine and a half remaining tribes. ¹⁴ The families of the tribes of Reuben, Gad, and half the tribe of Manasseh have already received their inheritance of land ¹⁵ on the east side of the Jordan River, across from Jericho."

Leaders to Divide the Land

¹⁶ And the LORD said to Moses, ¹⁷ "These are the men who are to divide the land among the people: Eleazar the priest and Joshua son of Nun. ¹⁸ Also enlist one leader from each tribe to help them with the task. ¹⁹ These are the tribes and the names of the leaders:

Tribe	Leader
Judah	Caleb son of Jephunneh
²⁰ Simeon	Shemuel son of Ammihud
²¹ Benjamin	Elidad son of Kislon
²² Dan	Bukki son of Jogli
²³ Manasseh son of Joseph	Hanniel son of Ephod
²⁴ Ephraim son of Joseph . . .	Kemuel son of Shiphtan
²⁵ Zebulun	Elizaphan son of Parnach

33:38 Hebrew *on the first day of the fifth month.* This day of the Hebrew lunar calendar occurs in July or early August. **33:45** As in 33:44; Hebrew reads *Iyim,* another name for Iye-abarim. **33:47** Hebrew *the mountains of Abarim;* also in 33:48. **34:3** Hebrew *Salt Sea;* also in 34:12. **34:4** Hebrew *the ascent of Akrabbim.* **34:5** Hebrew *the sea;* also in 34:6, 7. **34:11** Hebrew *sea of Kinnereth.*

26 Issachar . . . . Paltiel son of Azzan
27 Asher . . . . Ahihud son of Shelomi
28 Naphtali . . . . Pedahel son of Ammihud

29These are the men the LORD has appointed to oversee the dividing of the land of Canaan among the Israelites."

CHAPTER **35**
Towns for the Levites
While Israel was camped beside the Jordan on the plains of Moab, across from Jericho, the LORD said to Moses, 2"Instruct the people of Israel to give to the Levites from their property certain towns to live in, along with the surrounding pasturelands. 3These towns will be their homes, and the surrounding lands will provide pasture for their cattle, flocks, and other livestock. 4The pastureland assigned to the Levites around these towns will extend 1,500 feet* from the town walls in every direction. 5Measure off 3,000 feet* outside the town walls in every direction—east, south, west, north—with the town at the center. This area will serve as the larger pastureland for the towns.

6"You must give the Levites six cities of refuge, where a person who has accidentally killed someone can flee for safety. In addition, give them forty-two other towns. 7In all, forty-eight towns with the surrounding pastureland will be given to the Levites. 8These towns will come from the property of the people of Israel. The larger tribes will give more towns to the Levites, while the smaller tribes will give fewer. Each tribe will give in proportion to its inheritance."

Cities of Refuge
9And the LORD said to Moses, 10"Say this to the people of Israel: 'When you cross the Jordan into the land of Canaan, 11designate cities of refuge for people to flee to if they have killed someone accidentally. 12These cities will be places of protection from a dead person's relatives who want to avenge the death. The slayer must not be killed before being tried by the community. 13Designate six cities of refuge for yourselves, 14three on the east side of the Jordan River and three on the west in the land of Canaan. 15These cities are for the protection of Israelites, resident foreigners, and traveling merchants. Anyone who accidentally kills someone may flee there for safety.

16" 'But if someone strikes and kills another person with a piece of iron, it must be presumed to be murder, and the murderer must be executed. 17Or if someone strikes and kills another person with a large stone, it is murder, and the murderer must be executed. 18The same is true if someone strikes and kills another person with a wooden weapon. It must be presumed to be murder, and the murderer must be executed. 19The victim's nearest relative is responsible for putting the murderer to death. When they meet, the avenger must execute the murderer. 20So if in premeditated hostility someone pushes another person or throws a dangerous object and the person dies, it is murder. 21Or if someone angrily hits another person with a fist and the person dies, it is murder. In such cases, the victim's nearest relative must execute the murderer when they meet.

22" 'But suppose someone pushes another person without premeditated hostility, or throws something that unintentionally hits another person, 23or accidentally drops a stone on someone, though they were not enemies, and the person dies. 24If this should happen, the assembly must follow these regulations in making a judgment between the slayer and the avenger, the victim's nearest relative. 25They must protect the slayer from the avenger, and they must send the slayer back to live in a city of refuge until the death of the high priest.

26" 'But if the slayer leaves the city of refuge, 27and the victim's nearest relative finds him outside the city limits and kills him, it will not be considered murder. 28The slayer should have stayed inside the city of refuge until the death of the high priest. But after the death of the high priest, the slayer may return to his own property. 29These are permanent laws for you to observe from generation to generation, wherever you may live.

30" 'All murderers must be executed, but only if there is more than one witness. No one may be put to death on the testimony of only one witness. 31Also, you must never accept a ransom payment for the life of someone judged guilty of murder and subject to execution; murderers must always be put to death. 32And never accept a ransom payment from someone who has fled to a city of refuge, allowing the slayer to return to his property before the death of the high priest. 33This will ensure that the land where you live will not be polluted, for murder pollutes the land. And no atonement can be made for murder except by the execution of the murderer.

35:4 Hebrew *1,000 cubits* [450 meters].   35:5 Hebrew *2,000 cubits* [900 meters].

34You must not defile the land where you are going to live, for I live there myself. I am the LORD, who lives among the people of Israel.'"

CHAPTER 36
Women Who Inherit Property

Then the heads of the clan of Gilead—descendants of Makir, son of Manasseh, son of Joseph—came to Moses and the family leaders of Israel with a petition. 2They said, "Sir, the LORD instructed you to divide the land by sacred lot among the people of Israel. You were told by the LORD to give the inheritance of our brother Zelophehad to his daughters. 3But if any of them marries a man from another tribe, their inheritance of land will go with them to the tribe into which they marry. In this way, the total area of our tribal land will be reduced. 4Then when the Year of Jubilee comes, their inheritance of land will be added to that of the new tribe, causing it to be lost forever to our ancestral tribe."

5So Moses gave the Israelites this command from the LORD. "The men of the tribe of Joseph are right. 6This is what the LORD commands concerning the daughters of Zelophehad: Let them marry anyone they like, as long as it is within their own ancestral tribe. 7None of the inherited land may pass from tribe to tribe, for the inheritance of every tribe must remain fixed as it was first allotted. 8The daughters throughout the tribes of Israel who are in line to inherit property must marry within their tribe, so that all the Israelites will keep their ancestral property. 9No inheritance may pass from one tribe to another; each tribe of Israel must hold on to its allotted inheritance of land."

10The daughters of Zelophehad did as the LORD commanded Moses. 11Mahlah, Tirzah, Hoglah, Milcah, and Noah all married cousins on their father's side. 12They married into the clans of Manasseh son of Joseph. Thus, their inheritance of land remained within their ancestral tribe.

13These are the commands and regulations that the LORD gave to the people of Israel through Moses while they were camped on the plains of Moab beside the Jordan River, across from Jericho.

Deuteronomy

CHAPTER 1

The Command to Leave Sinai

This book records the words that Moses spoke to all the people of Israel while they were in the wilderness east of the Jordan River. They were camped in the Jordan Valley* near Suph, between Paran on one side and Tophel, Laban, Hazeroth, and Di-zahab on the other. 2Normally it takes only eleven days to travel from Mount Sinai* to Kadesh-barnea, going by way of Mount Seir. 3But forty years after the Israelites left Mount Sinai, on a day in midwinter,* Moses gave these speeches to the Israelites, telling them everything the LORD had commanded him to say. 4This was after he had defeated King Sihon of the Amorites, who had ruled in Heshbon, and King Og of Bashan, who had ruled in Ashtaroth and Edrei.

5So Moses addressed the people of Israel while they were in the land of Moab east of the Jordan River. He began to explain the law as follows: 6"When we were at Mount Sinai, the LORD our God said to us, 'You have stayed at this mountain long enough. 7It is time to break camp and move on. Go to the hill country of the Amorites and to all the neighboring regions—the Jordan Valley, the hill country, the western foothills,* the Negev, and the coastal plain. Go to the land of the Canaanites and to Lebanon, and all the way to the great Euphrates River. 8I am giving all this land to you! Go in and occupy it, for it is the land the LORD swore to give to your ancestors Abraham, Isaac, and Jacob, and to all their descendants.'

Moses Appoints Leaders from Each Tribe

9"At that time I told you, 'You are too great a burden for me to carry all by myself. 10The LORD your God has made you as numerous as the stars! 11And may the LORD, the God of your ancestors, multiply you a thousand times more and bless you as he promised! 12But how can I settle all your quarrels and problems by myself? 13Choose some men from each tribe who have wisdom, understanding, and a good reputation, and I will appoint them as your leaders.'

14"You agreed that my plan was a good one. 15So I took the wise and respected men you had selected from your tribes and appointed them to serve as judges and officials over you. Some were responsible for a thousand people, some for a hundred, some for fifty, and some for ten. 16I instructed the judges, 'You must be perfectly fair at all times, not only to fellow Israelites, but also to the foreigners living among you. 17When you make decisions, never favor those who are rich; be fair to lowly and great alike. Don't be afraid of how they will react, for you are judging in the place of God. Bring me any cases that are too difficult for you, and I will handle them.' 18And at that time I gave you instructions about everything you were to do.

Scouts Explore the Land

19"Then, just as the LORD our God directed us, we left Mount Sinai and traveled through the great and terrifying wilderness, which you yourselves saw, and headed toward the hill country of the Amorites. When we arrived at Kadesh-barnea, 20I said to you, 'You have now reached the land that the LORD our God is giving us. 21Look! He has placed it in front of you. Go and occupy it as the LORD, the God of your ancestors, has promised you. Don't be afraid! Don't be discouraged!'

22"But you responded, 'First, let's send out scouts to explore the land for us. They will advise us on the best route to take and decide which towns we should capture.' 23This seemed like a

---

1:1 Hebrew *the Arabah;* also in 1:7.   1:2 Hebrew *Horeb,* another name for Sinai; also in 1:6, 19.   1:3 Hebrew *on the first day of the eleventh month.* This day of the Hebrew lunar calendar occurs in January or early February.   1:7 Hebrew *the Shephelah.*

good idea to me, so I chose twelve scouts, one from each of your tribes. 24They crossed into the hills and came to the valley of Eshcol and explored it. 25They picked some of its fruit and brought it back to us. And they reported that the land the LORD our God had given us was indeed a good land.

Israel Rebels against the LORD

26"But you rebelled against the command of the LORD your God and refused to go in. 27You murmured and complained in your tents and said, 'The LORD must hate us, bringing us here from Egypt to be slaughtered by these Amorites. 28How can we go on? Our scouts have demoralized us with their report. They say that the people of the land are taller and more powerful than we are, and that the walls of their towns rise high into the sky! They have even seen giants there—the descendants of Anak!'

29"But I said to you, 'Don't be afraid! 30The LORD your God is going before you. He will fight for you, just as you saw him do in Egypt. 31And you saw how the LORD your God cared for you again and again here in the wilderness, just as a father cares for his child. Now he has brought you to this place.' 32But even after all he did, you refused to trust the LORD your God, 33who goes before you looking for the best places to camp, guiding you by a pillar of fire at night and a pillar of cloud by day.

34"When the LORD heard your complaining, he became very angry. So he solemnly swore, 35'Not one of you from this entire wicked generation will live to see the good land I swore to give your ancestors, 36except Caleb son of Jephunneh. He will see this land because he has followed the LORD completely. I will give to him and his descendants some of the land he walked over during his scouting mission.'

37"And the LORD was also angry with me because of you. He said to me, 'You will never enter the Promised Land! 38Instead, your assistant, Joshua son of Nun, will lead the people into the land. Encourage him as he prepares to enter it. 39I will give the land to your innocent children. You were afraid they would be captured, but they will be the ones who occupy it. 40As for you, turn around now and go on back through the wilderness toward the Red Sea.*'

41"Then you confessed, 'We have sinned against the LORD! We will go into the land and fight for it, as the LORD our God has told us.' So

your men strapped on their weapons, thinking it would be easy to conquer the hill country.

42"But the LORD said to me, 'Tell them not to attack, for I will not go with them. If they do, they will be crushed by their enemies.' 43This is what I told you, but you would not listen. Instead, you again rebelled against the LORD's command and arrogantly went into the hill country to fight. 44But the Amorites who lived there came out against you like a swarm of bees. They chased and battered you all the way from Seir to Hormah. 45Then you returned and wept before the LORD, but he refused to listen. 46So you stayed there at Kadesh for a long time.

CHAPTER 2

Remembering Israel's Wanderings

"Then we turned around and set out across the wilderness toward the Red Sea,* just as the LORD had instructed me, and we wandered around Mount Seir for a long time. 2Then at last the LORD said to me, 3'You have been wandering around in this hill country long enough; turn northward. 4Give these orders to the people: "You will be passing through the country belonging to your relatives the Edomites, the descendants of Esau, who live in Seir. The Edomites will feel threatened, so be careful. 5Don't bother them, for I have given them all the hill country around Mount Seir as their property, and I will not give you any of their land. 6Pay them for whatever food or water you use. 7The LORD your God has blessed everything you have done and has watched your every step through this great wilderness. During these forty years, the LORD your God has been with you and provided for your every need so that you lacked nothing." ' 8So we went past our relatives, the descendants of Esau, who live in Seir, and avoided the road through the Arabah Valley that comes up from Elath and Ezion-geber.

"Then as we traveled northward along the desert route through Moab, 9the LORD warned us, 'Do not bother the Moabites, the descendants of Lot, or start a war with them. I have given them Ar as their property, and I will not give you any of their land.'"

10(A numerous and powerful race of giants called the Emites had once lived in the area of Ar. They were as tall as the Anakites, another race of giants. 11Both the Emites and the Anakites are often referred to as the Rephaites, but the Moabites called them Emites. 12In earlier times the Horites had lived at Mount Seir, but they were

1:40 Hebrew *sea of reeds.*   2:1 Hebrew *sea of reeds.*

driven out and displaced by the descendants of Esau. In a similar way the peoples in Canaan were driven from the land that the LORD had assigned to Israel.)

13Moses continued, "Then the LORD told us to cross Zered Brook, and we did. 14So thirty-eight years passed from the time we first arrived at Kadesh-barnea until we finally crossed Zered Brook! For the LORD had vowed that this could not happen until all the men old enough to fight in battle had died in the wilderness. 15The LORD had lifted his hand against them until all of them had finally died.

16"When all the men of fighting age had died, 17the LORD said to me, 18"Today you will cross the border of Moab at Ar 19and enter the land of Ammon. But do not bother the Ammonites, the descendants of Lot, or start a war with them. I have given the land of Ammon to them as their property, and I will not give you any of their land.'"

20(That area, too, was once considered the land of the Rephaites, though the Ammonites referred to them as Zamzummites. 21They were a numerous and powerful race, as tall as the Anakites. But the LORD destroyed them so the Ammonites could occupy their land. 22He had similarly helped the descendants of Esau at Mount Seir, for he destroyed the Horites so they could settle there in their place. The descendants of Esau live there to this day. 23A similar thing happened when the Caphtorites from Crete* invaded and destroyed the Avvites, who had lived in villages in the area of Gaza.)

24Moses continued, "Then the LORD said, 'Now cross the Arnon Gorge! Look, I will help you defeat Sihon the Amorite, king of Heshbon, and I will give you his land. Attack him and begin to occupy the land. 25Beginning today I will make all people throughout the earth terrified of you. When they hear reports about you, they will tremble with dread and fear.'

Victory over Sihon of Heshbon

26"Then from the wilderness of Kedemoth I sent ambassadors to King Sihon of Heshbon with this proposal of peace: 27'Let us pass through your land. We will stay on the main road and won't turn off into the fields on either side. 28We will pay for every bite of food we eat and all the water we drink. All we want is permission to pass through your land. 29The descendants of Esau at Mount Seir allowed us to go through their country, and so did the Moabites, who live in Ar. Let us pass through until we cross the Jordan into the land the LORD our God has given us.' 30But King Sihon refused to allow you to pass through, because the LORD your God made Sihon stubborn and defiant so he could help you defeat them, as he has now done.

31"Then the LORD said to me, 'Look, I have begun to hand King Sihon and his land over to you. Begin now to conquer and occupy his land.' 32Then King Sihon declared war on us and mobilized his forces at Jahaz. 33But the LORD our God handed him over to us, and we crushed him, his sons, and all his people. 34We conquered all his towns and completely destroyed* everyone—men, women, and children. Not a single person was spared. 35We took all the livestock as plunder for ourselves, along with anything of value from the towns we ransacked.

36"The LORD our God helped us conquer Aroer on the edge of the Arnon Gorge, the town in the gorge, and the whole area as far as Gilead. No town had walls too strong for us. 37However, we stayed away from the Ammonites along the Jabbok River and the towns in the hill country— all the places the LORD our God had commanded us to leave alone.

CHAPTER 3
Victory over Og of Bashan

"Next we headed for the land of Bashan, where King Og and his army attacked us at Edrei. 2But the LORD told me, 'Do not be afraid of him, for I have given you victory over Og and his army, giving you his entire land. Treat him just as you treated King Sihon of the Amorites, who ruled in Heshbon.' 3So the LORD our God handed King Og and all his people over to us, and we killed them all. 4We conquered all sixty of his towns, the entire Argob region in his kingdom of Bashan. 5These were all fortified cities with high walls and barred gates. We also took many unwalled villages at the same time. 6We completely destroyed* the kingdom of Bashan, just as we had destroyed King Sihon of Heshbon. We destroyed* all the people in every town we conquered—men, women, and children alike. 7But we kept all the livestock for ourselves and took plunder from all the towns.

8"We now possessed all the land of the two Amorite kings east of the Jordan River—from the Arnon Gorge to Mount Hermon. 9(Mount

2:23 Hebrew from Caphtor. 2:34 The Hebrew term used here refers to the complete consecration of things or people to the LORD, either by destroying them or by giving them as an offering. 3:6 The Hebrew term used here refers to the complete consecration of things or people to the LORD, either by destroying them or by giving them as an offering.

Hermon is called Sirion by the Sidonians; the Amorites call it Senir.) ¹⁰We had now conquered all the cities on the plateau, and all Gilead and Bashan as far as the towns of Salecah and Edrei, which were part of Og's kingdom in Bashan. ¹¹(Incidentally, King Og of Bashan was the last of the giant Rephaites. His iron bed was more than thirteen feet long and six feet wide.* It can still be seen in the Ammonite city of Rabbah.)

Land Division East of the Jordan
¹²"When we took possession of this land, I gave the territory beyond Aroer along the Arnon Gorge, plus half of the hill country of Gilead with its towns, to the tribes of Reuben and Gad. ¹³Then I gave the rest of Gilead and all of Bashan—Og's former kingdom—to the half-tribe of Manasseh. (The Argob region of Bashan used to be known as the land of the Rephaites. ¹⁴Jair, a leader from the tribe of Manasseh, acquired the whole Argob region in Bashan all the way to the borders of the Geshurites and Maacathites. Jair renamed this region after himself, calling it the Towns of Jair,* as it is still known today.) ¹⁵I gave Gilead to the clan of Makir. ¹⁶And to the tribes of Reuben and Gad I gave the area extending from Gilead to the middle of the Arnon Gorge, all the way to the Jabbok River on the Ammonite frontier. ¹⁷They also received the Jordan Valley, including the Jordan River and its eastern banks, all the way from the Sea of Galilee down to the Dead Sea,* with the slopes of Pisgah on the east.

¹⁸"At that time I gave this command to the tribes that will live east of the Jordan: 'Although the LORD your God has given you this land as your property, all your fighting men must cross the Jordan, armed and ready to protect your Israelite relatives. ¹⁹Your wives, children, and numerous livestock, however, may stay behind in the towns I have given you. ²⁰When the LORD has given security to the rest of the Israelites, as he has to you, and when they occupy the land the LORD your God is giving them across the Jordan River, then you may return here to the land I have given you.'

Moses Forbidden to Enter the Land
²¹"At that time I said to Joshua, 'You have seen all that the LORD your God has done to these two kings. He will do the same to all the kingdoms on the west side of the Jordan. ²²Do not be afraid of the nations there, for the LORD your God will fight for you.'

²³"At that time I pleaded with the LORD and said, ²⁴'O Sovereign LORD, I am your servant. You have only begun to show me your greatness and power. Is there any god in heaven or on earth who can perform such great deeds as yours? ²⁵Please let me cross the Jordan to see the wonderful land on the other side, the beautiful hill country and the Lebanon mountains.'

²⁶"But the LORD was angry with me because of you, and he would not listen to me. 'That's enough!' he ordered. 'Speak of it no more. ²⁷You can go to Pisgah Peak and view the land in every direction, but you may not cross the Jordan River. ²⁸But commission Joshua and encourage him, for he will lead the people across the Jordan. He will give them the land you now see before you.' ²⁹So we stayed in the valley near Beth-peor.

CHAPTER **4**
Moses Urges Israel to Obey
"And now, Israel, listen carefully to these laws and regulations that I am about to teach you. Obey them so that you may live, so you may enter and occupy the land the LORD, the God of your ancestors, is giving you. ²Do not add to or subtract from these commands I am giving you from the LORD your God. Just obey them. ³You saw what the LORD did to you at Baal-peor, where the LORD your God destroyed everyone who had worshiped the god Baal of Peor. ⁴But all of you who were faithful to the LORD your God are still alive today.

⁵"You must obey these laws and regulations when you arrive in the land you are about to enter and occupy. The LORD my God gave them to me and commanded me to pass them on to you. ⁶If you obey them carefully, you will display your wisdom and intelligence to the surrounding nations. When they hear about these laws, they will exclaim, 'What other nation is as wise and prudent as this!' ⁷For what great nation has a god as near to them as the LORD our God is near to us whenever we call on him? ⁸And what great nation has laws and regulations as fair as this body of laws that I am giving you today?

⁹"But watch out! Be very careful never to forget what you have seen the LORD do for you. Do not let these things escape from your mind as long as you live! And be sure to pass them on to your children and grandchildren. ¹⁰Tell them especially about the day when you stood before

3:11 Hebrew *9 cubits* [4.1 meters] *long and 4 cubits* [1.8 meters] *wide.*   3:14 Hebrew *Havvoth-jair.*   3:17 Hebrew *from Kinnereth to the sea of the Arabah, the Salt Sea.*

the LORD your God at Mount Sinai,* where he told me, 'Summon the people before me, and I will instruct them. That way, they will learn to fear me as long as they live, and they will be able to teach my laws to their children.' 11You came near and stood at the foot of the mountain, while the mountain was burning with fire. Flames shot into the sky, shrouded in black clouds and deep darkness. 12And the LORD spoke to you from the fire. You heard his words but didn't see his form; there was only a voice. 13He proclaimed his covenant, which he commanded you to keep—the Ten Commandments—and wrote them on two stone tablets. 14It was at that time that the LORD commanded me to issue the laws and regulations you must obey in the land you are about to enter and occupy.

A Warning against Idolatry

15"But be careful! You did not see the LORD's form on the day he spoke to you from the fire at Mount Sinai. 16So do not corrupt yourselves by making a physical image in any form—whether of a man or a woman, 17an animal or a bird, 18a creeping creature or a fish. 19And when you look up into the sky and see the sun, moon, and stars—all the forces of heaven—don't be seduced by them and worship them. The LORD your God designated these heavenly bodies for all the peoples of the earth. 20Remember that the LORD rescued you from the burning furnace of Egypt to become his own people and special possession; that is what you are today.

21"But the LORD was very angry with me because of you. He vowed that I would never cross the Jordan River into the good land the LORD your God is giving you as your special possession. 22Though you will cross the Jordan to occupy the land, I will die here on this side of the river. 23So be careful not to break the covenant the LORD your God has made with you. You will break it if you make idols of any shape or form, for the LORD your God has absolutely forbidden this. 24The LORD your God is a devouring fire, a jealous God.

25"In the future, when you have children and grandchildren and have lived in the land a long time, do not corrupt yourselves by making idols of any kind. This is evil in the sight of the LORD your God and will arouse his anger.

26"Today I call heaven and earth as witnesses against you. If you disobey me, you will quickly disappear from the land you are crossing the Jordan to occupy. You will live there only a short time; then you will be utterly destroyed. 27For the LORD will scatter you among the nations, where only a few of you will survive. 28There, in a foreign land, you will worship idols made from wood and stone, gods that neither see nor hear nor eat nor smell. 29From there you will search again for the LORD your God. And if you search for him with all your heart and soul, you will find him.

30"When those bitter days have come upon you far in the future, you will finally return to the LORD your God and listen to what he tells you. 31For the LORD your God is merciful—he will not abandon you or destroy you or forget the solemn covenant he made with your ancestors.

There Is Only One God

32"Search all of history, from the time God created people on the earth until now. Then search from one end of the heavens to the other. See if anything as great as this has ever happened before. 33Has any nation ever heard the voice of God* speaking from fire—as you did—and survived? 34Has any other god taken one nation for himself by rescuing it from another by means of trials, miraculous signs, wonders, war, awesome power, and terrifying acts? Yet that is what the LORD your God did for you in Egypt, right before your very eyes.

35"He showed you these things so you would realize that the LORD is God and that there is no other god. 36He let you hear his voice from heaven so he could instruct you. He let you see his great fire here on earth so he could speak to you from it. 37Because he loved your ancestors, he chose to bless their descendants and personally brought you out of Egypt with a great display of power. 38He drove out nations far greater than you, so he could bring you in and give you their land as a special possession, as it is today. 39So remember this and keep it firmly in mind: The LORD is God both in heaven and on earth, and there is no other god! 40If you obey all the laws and commands that I will give you today, all will be well with you and your children. Then you will enjoy a long life in the land the LORD your God is giving you for all time."

Eastern Cities of Refuge

41Then Moses set apart three cities of refuge east of the Jordan River, 42where anyone who had accidentally killed someone without having any previous hostility could flee for safety. 43These were the cities: Bezer on the wilderness plateau for the tribe of

---

4:10 Hebrew *Horeb,* another name for Sinai; also in 4:15.   4:33 Or *voice of a god.*

God Should Be the Greatest Love of Our Life Read DEUTERONOMY 6:4-5

The word used for *love* in these verses primarily speaks of an act of mind and will. It is the Hebrew equivalent of the New Testament word for *love, agape,* which speaks of a committed, dedicated love.

Jesus spoke of this love when he quoted verse 5 to a lawyer who asked him, "Teacher, which is the most important commandment in the law of Moses?" Speaking of this commandment from Deuteronomy, Jesus added, "This is the first and greatest commandment" (Matthew 22:37-38). In other words, if you love God with all of your heart, with all of your soul, and with all of your strength, the rest of the commandments will come naturally. But what does it mean to love God with all your heart, soul, and strength?

Love God with All Your *Heart.* To the ancient Hebrews, the heart referred to the core of one's being. Therefore, to love God with all of your heart means that your love for God needs to be at the center of your life.

Love God with All Your *Soul.* The Hebrew word used for *soul* in this text speaks of emotion. To love God with your soul means that you are not afraid of expressing your feelings for God.

Love God with All Your *Strength.* Your strength suggests energy and might, but it also speaks of intellectual commitment and determination. In other words, you will want to fill your mind with the truths of God so that you can love him with your ability to reason.

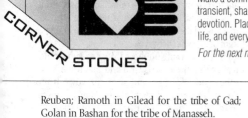

Love for God is the basis for all obedience. If you have an all-consuming love for God, you will want to do what pleases him. Make a commitment today to truly love God—not with some transient, shallow emotion, but with a wholehearted, sincere devotion. Place this holy and noble pursuit at the forefront of your life, and everything else will fall into place.

For the next note on "Love," turn to p. 1030.

CORNER STONES

Reuben; Ramoth in Gilead for the tribe of Gad; Golan in Bashan for the tribe of Manasseh.

Introduction to the Law

⁴⁴This is the law that Moses handed down to the Israelites. ⁴⁵These are the stipulations, laws, and regulations that Moses gave to the people of Israel when they left Egypt, ⁴⁶and as they camped in the valley near Beth-peor east of the Jordan River. (This land was formerly occupied by the Amorites under King Sihon of Heshbon. He and his people had been destroyed by Moses and the Israelites as they came up from Egypt. ⁴⁷Israel conquered his land and that of King Og of Bashan—the two Amorite kings east of the Jordan. ⁴⁸So Israel conquered all the area from Aroer at the edge of the Arnon Gorge to Mount Sirion,* also called Mount Hermon. ⁴⁹And they took the eastern bank of the Jordan Valley as far south as the Dead Sea,* below the slopes of Pisgah.)

CHAPTER **5**
The Ten Commandments

Moses called all the people of Israel together and said, "Listen carefully to all the laws and regulations I am giving you today. Learn them and be sure to obey them!

²"While we were at Mount Sinai,* the LORD our God made a covenant with us. ³The LORD did not make this covenant long ago with our ancestors, but with all of us who are alive today. ⁴The LORD spoke to you face to face from the heart of the fire on the mountain. ⁵I stood as an intermediary between you and the LORD, for you were afraid of the fire and did not climb the mountain. He spoke to me, and I passed his words on to you. This is what he said:

⁶" 'I am the LORD your God, who rescued you from slavery in Egypt.

⁷" 'Do not worship any other gods besides me.

⁸" 'Do not make idols of any kind, whether in the shape of birds or animals or fish. ⁹You

---

4:48 As in Syriac version (see also 3:9); Hebrew reads *Mount Sion.* 4:49 Hebrew *took the Arabah on the east side of the Jordan as far as the sea of the Arabah.* 5:2 Hebrew *Horeb,* another name for Sinai.

must never worship or bow down to them, for I, the LORD your God, am a jealous God who will not share your affection with any other god! I do not leave unpunished the sins of those who hate me, but I punish the children for the sins of their parents to the third and fourth generations. 10But I lavish my love on those who love me and obey my commands, even for a thousand generations.

11" 'Do not misuse the name of the LORD your God. The LORD will not let you go unpunished if you misuse his name.

12" 'Observe the Sabbath day by keeping it holy, as the LORD your God has commanded you. 13Six days a week are set apart for your daily duties and regular work, 14but the seventh day is a day of rest dedicated to the LORD your God. On that day no one in your household may do any kind of work. This includes you, your sons and daughters, your male and female servants, your oxen and donkeys and other livestock, and any foreigners living among you. All your male and female servants must rest as you do. 15Remember that you were once slaves in Egypt and that the LORD your God brought you out with amazing power and mighty deeds. That is why the LORD your God has commanded you to observe the Sabbath day.

16" 'Honor your father and mother, as the LORD your God commanded you. Then you will live a long, full life in the land the LORD your God will give you.

17" 'Do not murder.

18" 'Do not commit adultery.

19" 'Do not steal.

20" 'Do not testify falsely against your neighbor.

21" 'Do not covet your neighbor's wife. Do not covet your neighbor's house or land, male or female servant, ox or donkey, or anything else your neighbor owns.'

22"The LORD spoke these words with a loud voice to all of you from the heart of the fire, surrounded by clouds and deep darkness. This was all he said at that time, and he wrote his words on two stone tablets and gave them to me. 23But when you heard the voice from the darkness, while the mountain was blazing with fire, all your tribal leaders came to me. 24They said, 'The LORD our God has shown us his glory and greatness, and we have heard his voice from the heart of the fire. Today we have seen God speaking to humans, and

yet we live! 25But now, why should we die? If the LORD our God speaks to us again, we will certainly die and be consumed by this awesome fire. 26Can any living thing hear the voice of the living God from the heart of the fire and yet survive? 27You go and listen to what the LORD our God says. Then come and tell us everything he tells you, and we will listen and obey.'

28"The LORD heard your request and said to me, 'I have heard what the people have said to you, and they are right. 29Oh, that they would always have hearts like this, that they might fear me and obey all my commands! If they did, they and their descendants would prosper forever. 30Go and tell them to return to their tents. 31But you stay here with me so I can give you all my commands, laws, and regulations. You will teach them to the people so they can obey them in the land I am giving to them as their inheritance.'"

32So Moses told the people, "You must obey all the commands of the LORD your God, following his instructions in every detail. 33Stay on the path that the LORD your God has commanded you to follow. Then you will live long and prosperous lives in the land you are about to enter and occupy.

CHAPTER 6

A Call for Wholehearted Commitment

"These are all the commands, laws, and regulations that the LORD your God told me to teach you so you may obey them in the land you are about to enter and occupy, 2and so you and your children and grandchildren might fear the LORD your God as long as you live. If you obey all his laws and commands, you will enjoy a long life. 3Listen closely, Israel, to everything I say. Be careful to obey. Then all will go well with you, and you will have many children in the land flowing with milk and honey, just as the LORD, the God of your ancestors, promised you.

4"Hear, O Israel! The LORD is our God, the LORD alone.* 5And you must love the LORD your God with all your heart, all your soul, and all your strength. 6And you must commit yourselves wholeheartedly to these commands I am giving you today. 7Repeat them again and again to your children. Talk about them when you are at home and when you are away on a journey, when you are lying down and when you are getting up again. 8Tie them to your hands as a

6:4 Or *The LORD our God is one LORD*, or *The LORD our God, the LORD is one*, or *The LORD is our God, the LORD is one.*

reminder, and wear them on your forehead. 9Write them on the doorposts of your house and on your gates.

10"The LORD your God will soon bring you into the land he swore to give your ancestors Abraham, Isaac, and Jacob. It is a land filled with large, prosperous cities that you did not build. 11The houses will be richly stocked with goods you did not produce. You will draw water from cisterns you did not dig, and you will eat from vineyards and olive trees you did not plant. When you have eaten your fill in this land, 12be careful not to forget the LORD, who rescued you from slavery in the land of Egypt. 13You must fear the LORD your God and serve him. When you take an oath, you must use only his name.

14"You must not worship any of the gods of neighboring nations, 15for the LORD your God, who lives among you, is a jealous God. His anger will flare up against you and wipe you from the face of the earth. 16Do not test the LORD your God as you did when you complained at Massah. 17You must diligently obey the commands of the LORD your God—all the stipulations and laws he has given you. 18Do what is right and good in the LORD's sight, so all will go well with you. Then you will enter and occupy the good land that the LORD solemnly promised to give your ancestors. 19You will drive out all the enemies living in your land, just as the LORD said you would.

20"In the future your children will ask you, 'What is the meaning of these stipulations, laws, and regulations that the LORD our God has given us?' 21Then you must tell them, 'We were Pharaoh's slaves in Egypt, but the LORD brought us out of Egypt with amazing power. 22Before our eyes the LORD did miraculous signs and wonders, dealing terrifying blows against Egypt and Pharaoh and all his people. 23He brought us out of Egypt so he could give us this land he had solemnly promised to give our ancestors. 24And the LORD our God commanded us to obey all these laws and to fear him for our own prosperity and well-being, as is now the case. 25For we are righteous when we obey all the commands the LORD our God has given us.'

CHAPTER 7
The Privilege of Holiness

"When the LORD your God brings you into the land you are about to enter and occupy, he will clear away many nations ahead of you: the Hittites, Girgashites, Amorites, Canaanites, Perizzites, Hivites, and Jebu-

sites. These seven nations are all more powerful than you. 2When the LORD your God hands these nations over to you and you conquer them, you must completely destroy* them. Make no treaties with them and show them no mercy. 3Do not intermarry with them, and don't let your daughters and sons marry their sons and daughters. 4They will lead your young people away from me to worship other gods. Then the anger of the LORD will burn against you, and he will destroy you. 5Instead, you must break down their pagan altars and shatter their sacred pillars. Cut down their Asherah poles and burn their idols. 6For you are a holy people, who belong to the LORD your God. Of all the people on earth, the LORD your God has chosen you to be his own special treasure.

7"The LORD did not choose you and lavish his love on you because you were larger or greater than other nations, for you were the smallest of all nations! 8It was simply because the LORD loves you, and because he was keeping the oath he had sworn to your ancestors. That is why the LORD rescued you with such amazing power from your slavery under Pharaoh in Egypt. 9Understand, therefore, that the LORD your God is indeed God. He is the faithful God who keeps his covenant for a thousand generations and constantly loves those who love him and obey his commands. 10But he does not hesitate to punish and destroy those who hate him. 11Therefore, obey all these commands, laws, and regulations I am giving you today.

12"If you listen to these regulations and obey them faithfully, the LORD your God will keep his covenant of unfailing love with you, as he solemnly promised your ancestors. 13He will love you and bless you and make you into a great nation. He will give you many children and give fertility to your land and your animals. When you arrive in the land he swore to give your ancestors, you will have large crops of grain, grapes, and olives, and great herds of cattle, sheep, and goats. 14You will be blessed above all the nations of the earth. None of your men or women will be childless, and all your livestock will bear young. 15And the LORD will protect you from all sickness. He will not let you suffer from the terrible diseases you knew in Egypt, but he will bring them all on your enemies!

16"You must destroy all the nations the LORD your God hands over to you. Show them no mercy and do not worship their gods. If you do, they will trap you. 17Perhaps you will think to

---

7:2 The Hebrew term used here refers to the complete consecration of things or people to the LORD, either by destroying them or by giving them as an offering; also in 7:26.

yourselves, 'How can we ever conquer these nations that are so much more powerful than we are?' ¹⁸But don't be afraid of them! Just remember what the LORD your God did to Pharaoh and to all the land of Egypt. ¹⁹Remember the great terrors the LORD your God sent against them. You saw it all with your own eyes! And remember the miraculous signs and wonders, and the amazing power he used when he brought you out of Egypt. The LORD your God will use this same power against the people you fear. ²⁰And then the LORD your God will send hornets* to drive out the few survivors still hiding from you!

²¹"No, do not be afraid of those nations, for the LORD your God is among you, and he is a great and awesome God. ²²The LORD your God will drive those nations out ahead of you little by little. You will not clear them away all at once, for if you did, the wild animals would multiply too quickly for you. ²³But the LORD your God will hand them over to you. He will throw them into complete confusion until they are destroyed. ²⁴He will put their kings in your power, and you will erase their names from the face of the earth. No one will be able to stand against you, and you will destroy them all.

²⁵"You must burn their idols in fire, and do not desire the silver or gold with which they are made. Do not take it or it will become a snare to you, for it is detestable to the LORD your God. ²⁶Do not bring any detestable objects into your home, for then you will be set apart for destruction just like them. You must utterly detest such things, for they are set apart for destruction.

CHAPTER **8**

A Call to Remember and Obey

"Be careful to obey all the commands I am giving you today. Then you will live and multiply, and you will enter and occupy the land the LORD swore to give your ancestors. ²Remember how the LORD your God led you through the wilderness for forty years, humbling you and testing you to prove your character, and to find out whether or not you would really obey his commands. ³Yes, he humbled you by letting you go hungry and then feeding you with manna, a food previously unknown to you and your ancestors. He did it to teach you that people need more than bread for their life; real life comes by feeding on every word of the LORD. ⁴For all these forty years your clothes didn't wear out, and your feet didn't blister or swell. ⁵So you should

realize that just as a parent disciplines a child, the LORD your God disciplines you to help you.

⁶"So obey the commands of the LORD your God by walking in his ways and fearing him. ⁷For the LORD your God is bringing you into a good land of flowing streams and pools of water, with springs that gush forth in the valleys and hills. ⁸It is a land of wheat and barley, of grapevines, fig trees, pomegranates, olives, and honey. ⁹It is a land where food is plentiful and nothing is lacking. It is a land where iron is as common as stone, and copper is abundant in the hills. ¹⁰When you have eaten your fill, praise the LORD your God for the good land he has given you.

¹¹"But that is the time to be careful! Beware that in your plenty you do not forget the LORD your God and disobey his commands, regulations, and laws. ¹²For when you have become full and prosperous and have built fine homes to live in, ¹³and when your flocks and herds have become very large and your silver and gold have multiplied along with everything else, ¹⁴that is the time to be careful. Do not become proud at that time and forget the LORD your God, who rescued you from slavery in the land of Egypt. ¹⁵Do not forget that he led you through the great and terrifying wilderness with poisonous snakes and scorpions, where it was so hot and dry. He gave you water from the rock! ¹⁶He fed you with manna in the wilderness, a food unknown to your ancestors. He did this to humble you and test you for your own good. ¹⁷He did it so you would never think that it was your own strength and energy that made you wealthy. ¹⁸Always remember that it is the LORD your God who gives you power to become rich, and he does it to fulfill the covenant he made with your ancestors.

¹⁹"But I assure you of this: If you ever forget the LORD your God and follow other gods, worshiping and bowing down to them, you will certainly be destroyed. ²⁰Just as the LORD has destroyed other nations in your path, you also will be destroyed for not obeying the LORD your God.

CHAPTER **9**

Victory by God's Grace

"Hear, O Israel! Today you are about to cross the Jordan River to occupy the land belonging to nations much greater and more powerful than you. They live in cities with walls that reach to the sky! ²They are strong and tall—descendants of the famous Anakite giants. You've heard the

7:20 Or *will spread panic,* or *will send a plague.* The meaning of the Hebrew is uncertain.

saying, 'Who can stand up to the Anakites?' 3But the LORD your God will cross over ahead of you like a devouring fire to destroy them. He will subdue them so that you will quickly conquer them and drive them out, just as the LORD has promised.

4"After the LORD your God has done this for you, don't say to yourselves, 'The LORD has given us this land because we are so righteous!' No, it is because of the wickedness of the other nations that he is doing it. 5It is not at all because you are such righteous, upright people that you are about to occupy their land. The LORD your God will drive these nations out ahead of you only because of their wickedness, and to fulfill the oath he had sworn to your ancestors Abraham, Isaac, and Jacob. 6I will say it again: The LORD your God is not giving you this good land because you are righteous, for you are not—you are a stubborn people.

Remembering the Gold Calf

7"Remember how angry you made the LORD your God out in the wilderness. From the day you left Egypt until now, you have constantly rebelled against him. 8Remember how angry you made the LORD at Mount Sinai,* where he was ready to destroy you. 9That was when I was on the mountain receiving the tablets of stone inscribed with the covenant that the LORD had made with you. I was there for forty days and forty nights, and all that time I ate nothing and drank no water. 10The LORD gave me the covenant, the tablets on which God himself had written all the words he had spoken to you from the fire on the mountain.

11"At the end of the forty days and nights, the LORD handed me the two stone tablets with the covenant inscribed on them. 12Then the LORD said to me, 'Go down immediately because the people you led out of Egypt have become corrupt. They have already turned from the way I commanded them to live and have cast an idol for themselves from gold.'

13"The LORD said to me, 'I have been watching this people, and they are extremely stubborn. 14Leave me alone so I may destroy them and erase their name from under heaven. Then I will make a mighty nation of your descendants, a nation larger and more powerful than they are.'

15"So I came down from the fiery mountain, holding in my hands the two stone tablets of the covenant. 16There below me I could see the gold

calf you had made in your terrible sin against the LORD your God. How quickly you had turned from the path the LORD had commanded you to follow! 17So I raised the stone tablets and dashed them to the ground. I smashed them before your very eyes. 18Then for forty days and nights I lay prostrate before the LORD, neither eating bread nor drinking water. I did this because you had sinned by doing what the LORD hated, thus making him very angry. 19How I feared for you, for the LORD was ready to destroy you. But again he listened to me. 20The LORD was so angry with Aaron that he wanted to destroy him. But I prayed for Aaron, and the LORD spared him. 21I took your sin—the calf you had made—and I melted it in the fire and ground it into fine dust. I threw the dust into the stream that cascades down the mountain.

22"You also made the LORD angry at Taberah,* Massah,* and Kibroth-hattaavah.* 23And at Kadesh-barnea the LORD sent you out with this command: 'Go up and take the land I have given you.' But you rebelled against the command of the LORD your God and refused to trust him or obey him. 24Yes, you have been rebelling against the LORD as long as I have known you.

25"That is why I fell down and lay before the LORD for forty days and nights when he was ready to destroy you. 26I prayed to the LORD and said, 'O Sovereign LORD, do not destroy your own people. They are your special possession, redeemed from Egypt by your mighty power and glorious strength. 27Overlook the stubbornness and sin of these people, but remember instead your servants Abraham, Isaac, and Jacob. 28If you destroy these people, the Egyptians will say, "The LORD destroyed them because he wasn't able to bring them to the land he had sworn to give them." Or they might say, "He destroyed them because he hated them; he brought them into the wilderness to slaughter them." 29But they are your people and your special possession, whom you brought from Egypt by your mighty power and glorious strength.'

CHAPTER 10
New Tablets of Stone

"At that time the LORD said to me, 'Prepare two stone tablets like the first ones, and make a sacred chest of wood to keep them in. Return to me on the mountain, 2and I will write on the tablets the same words that were on the ones

9:8 Hebrew *Horeb,* another name for Sinai.   9:22a *Taberah* means "place of burning." See Num 11:1-3.   9:22b *Massah* means "place of testing." See Exod 17:1-7.   9:22c *Kibroth-hattaavah* means "graves of craving." See Num 11:31-34.

you smashed. Then place the tablets in the sacred chest—the Ark of the Covenant.'

3 "So I made a chest of acacia wood and cut two stone tablets like the first two, and I took the tablets up the mountain. 4The LORD again wrote the terms of the covenant—the Ten Commandments—on them and gave them to me. They were the same words the LORD had spoken to you from the heart of the fire on the mountain as you were assembled below. 5Then I came down and placed the tablets in the Ark of the Covenant, which I had made, just as the LORD commanded me. And the tablets are still there in the Ark.

6 "The people of Israel set out from the wells of the people of Jaakan* and traveled to Moserah, where Aaron died and was buried. His son Eleazar became the high priest in his place. 7Then they journeyed to Gudgodah, and from there to Jotbathah, a land with brooks of water. 8At that time the LORD set apart the tribe of Levi to carry the Ark of the LORD's covenant, to minister before the LORD, and to pronounce blessings in his name. These are still their duties. 9That is why the Levites have no share or inheritance reserved for them among the other Israelite tribes. The LORD himself is their inheritance, as the LORD your God told them.

10 "As I said before, I stayed on the mountain in the LORD's presence for forty days and nights, as I had done the first time. And once again the LORD yielded to my pleas and didn't destroy you. 11But the LORD said to me, 'Get up and lead the people into the land I swore to give their ancestors, so they may take possession of it.'

A Call to Love and Obedience

12 "And now, Israel, what does the LORD your God require of you? He requires you to fear him, to live according to his will, to love and worship him with all your heart and soul, 13and to obey the LORD's commands and laws that I am giving you today for your own good. 14The highest heavens and the earth and everything in it all belong to the LORD your God. 15Yet the LORD chose your ancestors as the objects of his love. And he chose you, their descendants, above every other nation, as is evident today. 16Therefore, cleanse your sinful hearts and stop being stubborn.

17 "The LORD your God is the God of gods and Lord of lords. He is the great God, mighty and awesome, who shows no partiality and takes no bribes. 18He gives justice to orphans and widows. He shows love to the foreigners living

among you and gives them food and clothing. 19You, too, must show love to foreigners, for you yourselves were once foreigners in the land of Egypt. 20You must fear the LORD your God and worship him and cling to him. Your oaths must be in his name alone. 21He is your God, the one who is worthy of your praise, the one who has done mighty miracles that you yourselves have seen. 22When your ancestors went down into Egypt, there were only seventy of them. But now the LORD your God has made you as numerous as the stars in the sky!

CHAPTER 11

"You must love the LORD your God and obey all his requirements, laws, regulations, and commands. 2Listen! I am not talking now to your children, who have never experienced the discipline of the LORD your God or seen his greatness and awesome power. 3They weren't there to see the miraculous signs and wonders he performed in Egypt against Pharaoh and all his land. 4They didn't see what the LORD did to the armies of Egypt and to their horses and chariots—how he drowned them in the Red Sea* as they were chasing you, and how he has kept them devastated to this very day! 5They didn't see how the LORD cared for you in the wilderness until you arrived here. 6They weren't there to see what he did to Dathan and Abiram (the sons of Eliab, a descendant of Reuben) when the earth opened up and swallowed them, along with their households and tents and every living thing that belonged to them. 7But you have seen all the LORD's mighty deeds with your own eyes!

The Blessings of Obedience

8 "Therefore, be careful to obey every command I am giving you today, so you may have strength to go in and occupy the land you are about to enter. 9If you obey, you will enjoy a long life in the land the LORD swore to give to your ancestors and to you, their descendants—a land flowing with milk and honey! 10For the land you are about to enter and occupy is not like the land of Egypt from which you came, where you planted your seed and dug out irrigation ditches with your foot as in a vegetable garden. 11It is a land of hills and valleys with plenty of rain—12a land that the LORD your God cares for. He watches over it day after day throughout the year!

13 "If you carefully obey all the commands I am giving you today, and if you love the LORD

10:6 Or *set out from Beeroth of Bene-jaakan.*   11:4 Hebrew *sea of reeds.*

your God with all your heart and soul, and if you worship him, 14then he will send the rains in their proper seasons so you can harvest crops of grain, grapes for wine, and olives for oil. 15He will give you lush pastureland for your cattle to graze in, and you yourselves will have plenty to eat.

16"But do not let your heart turn away from the LORD to worship other gods. 17If you do, the LORD's anger will burn against you. He will shut up the sky and hold back the rain, and your harvests will fail. Then you will quickly die in that good land the LORD is now giving you. 18So commit yourselves completely to these words of mine. Tie them to your hands as a reminder, and wear them on your forehead. 19Teach them to your children. Talk about them when you are at home and when you are away on a journey, when you are lying down and when you are getting up again. 20Write them on the doorposts of your house and on your gates, 21so that as long as the sky remains above the earth, you and your children may flourish in the land the LORD swore to give your ancestors.

22"Be careful to obey all the commands I give you; show love to the LORD your God by walking in his ways and clinging to him. 23Then the LORD will drive out all the nations in your land, though they are much greater and stronger than you. 24Wherever you set your feet, the land will be yours. Your frontiers will stretch from the wilderness in the south to Lebanon in the north, and from the Euphrates River in the east to the Mediterranean Sea in the west.* 25No one will be able to stand against you, for the LORD your God will send fear and dread ahead of you, as he promised you, wherever you go in the whole land.

26"Today I am giving you the choice between a blessing and a curse! 27You will be blessed if you obey the commands of the LORD your God that I am giving you today. 28You will receive a curse if you reject the commands of the LORD your God and turn from his way by worshiping foreign gods.

29"When the LORD your God brings you into the land to possess it, you must pronounce a blessing from Mount Gerizim and a curse from Mount Ebal. 30(These two mountains are west of the Jordan River in the land of the Canaanites who live in the Jordan Valley,* near the town of Gilgal. They are located toward the west, not far from the oaks of Moreh.) 31For you are about to cross the Jordan to occupy the land the LORD

your God is giving you. When you are living in that land, 32you must be careful to obey all the laws and regulations I am giving you today.

CHAPTER **12**

The LORD's Chosen Place for Worship
"These are the laws and regulations you must obey as long as you live in the land the LORD, the God of your ancestors, is giving you.

2"When you drive out the nations that live there, you must destroy all the places where they worship their gods—high on the mountains, high on the hills, and under every green tree. 3Break down their altars and smash their sacred pillars. Burn their Asherah poles and cut down their carved idols. Erase the names of their gods from those places!

4"Do not worship the LORD your God in the way these pagan peoples worship their gods. 5Rather, you must seek the LORD your God at the place he himself will choose from among all the tribes for his name to be honored. 6There you will bring to the LORD your burnt offerings, your sacrifices, your tithes, your special gifts, your offerings to fulfill a vow, your freewill offerings, and your offerings of the firstborn animals of your flocks and herds. 7There you and your families will feast in the presence of the LORD your God, and you will rejoice in all you have accomplished because the LORD your God has blessed you.

8"Today you are doing whatever you please, but that is not how it will be 9when you arrive in the place of rest the LORD your God is giving you. 10You will soon cross the Jordan River and live in the land the LORD your God is giving you as a special possession. When he gives you rest and security from all your enemies, 11you must bring everything I command you—your burnt offerings, your sacrifices, your tithes, your special gifts, and your offerings to fulfill a vow—to the place the LORD your God will choose for his name to be honored. 12You must celebrate there with your sons and daughters and all your servants in the presence of the LORD your God. And remember the Levites who live in your towns, for they will have no inheritance of land as their own. 13Be careful not to sacrifice your burnt offerings just anywhere. 14You may do so only at the place the LORD will choose within one of your tribal territories. There you must offer your burnt offerings and do everything I command you.

15"But you may butcher animals for meat in any town, wherever you want, just as you do

11:24 Hebrew *to the western sea.* 11:30 Hebrew *the Arabah.*

now with gazelle and deer. You may eat as many animals as the LORD your God gives you. All of you, whether ceremonially clean or unclean, may eat that meat. ¹⁶The only restriction is that you are not to eat the blood. You must pour it out on the ground like water.

¹⁷"But your offerings must not be eaten at home—neither the tithe of your grain and new wine and olive oil, nor the firstborn of your flocks and herds, nor an offering to fulfill a vow, nor your freewill offerings, nor your special gifts. ¹⁸You must eat these in the presence of the LORD your God at the place he will choose. Eat them there with your children, your servants, and the Levites who live in your towns, celebrating in the presence of the LORD your God in all you do. ¹⁹Be very careful never to forget the Levites as long as you live in your land.

²⁰"When the LORD your God enlarges your territory as he has promised, you may eat meat whenever you want. ²¹It might happen that the place the LORD your God chooses for his name to be honored is a long way from your home. If so, you may butcher any of the cattle or sheep the LORD has given you, and you may eat the meat at your home as I have commanded you. ²²Anyone, whether ceremonially clean or unclean, may eat that meat, just as you do now with gazelle and deer. ²³The only restriction is never to eat the blood, for the blood is the life, and you must not eat the life with the meat. ²⁴Instead, pour out the blood on the ground like water. ²⁵Do not eat the blood; then all will go well with you and your children, because you will be doing what pleases the LORD. ²⁶Take your sacred gifts and your offerings given to fulfill a vow to the place the LORD chooses to dwell. ²⁷You must offer the meat and blood of your burnt offerings on the altar of the LORD your God. The blood of your other sacrifices must be poured out beside the altar of the LORD your God, but you may eat the meat. ²⁸Be careful to obey all my commands so that all will go well with you and your children, because you will be doing what pleases the LORD your God.

²⁹"When the LORD your God destroys the nations and you drive them out and occupy their land, ³⁰do not be trapped into following their example in worshiping their gods. Do not say, 'How do these nations worship their gods? I want to follow their example.' ³¹You must not do this to the LORD your God. These nations have committed many detestable acts that the LORD hates, all in the name of their gods. They have

Studying the Bible Makes Scripture a Central Part of Our Lives Read DEUTERONOMY 11:18-20

The message God gave the Israelites years ago contains three ways we can keep the truths of the Bible at the center of everything we do:

1. Memorize Scripture. The idea behind verse 18 is to keep Scripture at the forefront of everything we do. Think about it. God told the Israelites to tie these commands to their hands so that the commands would constantly be in their view throughout the day. God also told the Israelites to place his commands on their foreheads so that they would keep his words at the forefront of their thought life. Today the best way to keep God's words at the forefront of our lives is to store them in our hearts and minds. If we memorize his Word, we will find that it will come to mind at just the right time.

2. Talk about the Bible throughout Your Day. Your conversations should be seasoned with the truths you glean from the Bible. Make the most of every opportunity to talk about God's Word during every part of the day (verse 19)! The more you talk about the Bible in your home, at your job, or during your leisure time, the easier it will be for you to make the Bible a central part of your life.

3. Take Notes As You Study God's Word. Even though we may not necessarily write these verses upon the doors of our homes, the idea presented in verse 20 is to etch certain truths from God's Word upon our memory. One of the best ways to remember Scripture is to write it down. Writing something down seems to give that information more "staying power" in our minds. Therefore, you may want to keep a notebook with your Bible to take notes during your study and during church sermons. When you have notes to refer to, you will find it easier to share what you have learned with your family and friends. In addition, you may appreciate your notes later when you need to be reminded of a particular truth from God's Word.

For the next note on "Study the Bible," turn to p. 465.

even burned their sons and daughters as sacrifices to their gods. ³²Carefully obey all the commands I give you. Do not add to them or subtract from them.

CHAPTER **13**

A Warning against Idolatry

"Suppose there are prophets among you, or those who have dreams about the future, and they promise you signs or miracles, ²and the predicted signs or miracles take place. If the prophets then say, 'Come, let us worship the gods of foreign nations,' ³do not listen to them. The LORD your God is testing you to see if you love him with all your heart and soul. ⁴Serve only the LORD your God and fear him alone. Obey his commands, listen to his voice, and cling to him. ⁵The false prophets or dreamers who try to lead you astray must be put to death, for they encourage rebellion against the LORD your God, who brought you out of slavery in the land of Egypt. Since they try to keep you from following the LORD your God, you must execute them to remove the evil from among you.

⁶"Suppose your brother, son, daughter, beloved wife, or closest friend comes to you secretly and says, 'Let us go worship other gods'—gods that neither you nor your ancestors have known. ⁷They might suggest that you worship the gods of peoples who live nearby or who come from the ends of the earth. ⁸If they do this, do not give in or listen, and have no pity. Do not spare or protect them. ⁹You must put them to death! You must be the one to initiate the execution; then all the people must join in. ¹⁰Stone the guilty ones to death because they have tried to draw you away from the LORD your God, who rescued you from the land of Egypt, the place of slavery. ¹¹Then all Israel will hear about it and be afraid, and such wickedness will never again be done among you.

¹²"Suppose you hear in one of the towns the LORD your God is giving you ¹³that some worthless rabble among you have led their fellow citizens astray by encouraging them to worship foreign gods. ¹⁴In such cases, you must examine the facts carefully. If you find it is true and can prove that such a detestable act has occurred among you, ¹⁵you must attack that town and completely destroy* all its inhabitants, as well as all the livestock. ¹⁶Then you must pile all the plunder in the middle of the street and burn it.

Put the entire town to the torch as a burnt offering to the LORD your God. That town must remain a ruin forever; it may never be rebuilt. ¹⁷Keep none of the plunder that has been set apart for destruction. Then the LORD will turn from his fierce anger and be merciful to you. He will have compassion on you and make you a great nation, just as he solemnly promised your ancestors.

¹⁸"The LORD your God will be merciful only if you obey him and keep all the commands I am giving you today, doing what is pleasing to him.

CHAPTER **14**

Ceremonially Clean and Unclean Animals

"Since you are the people of the LORD your God, never cut yourselves or shave the hair above your foreheads for the sake of the dead. ²You have been set apart as holy to the LORD your God, and he has chosen you to be his own special treasure from all the nations of the earth.

³"You must not eat animals that are ceremonially unclean. ⁴These are the animals* you may eat: the ox, the sheep, the goat, ⁵the deer, the gazelle, the roebuck, the wild goat, the ibex, the antelope, and the mountain sheep.

⁶"Any animal that has split hooves and chews the cud may be eaten, ⁷but if the animal doesn't have both, it may not be eaten. So you may not eat the camel, the hare, or the rock badger.* They chew the cud but do not have split hooves. ⁸And the pig may not be eaten, for though it has split hooves, it does not chew the cud. All these animals are ceremonially unclean for you. You may not eat or even touch the dead bodies of such animals.

⁹"As for marine animals, you may eat whatever has both fins and scales. ¹⁰You may not, however, eat marine animals that do not have both fins and scales. They are ceremonially unclean for you.

¹¹"You may eat any bird that is ceremonially clean. ¹²These are the birds you may not eat: the eagle, the vulture, the osprey, ¹³the buzzard, kites of all kinds, ¹⁴ravens of all kinds, ¹⁵the ostrich, the nighthawk, the seagull, hawks of all kinds, ¹⁶the little owl, the great owl, the white owl, ¹⁷the pelican, the carrion vulture, the cormorant, ¹⁸the stork, herons of all kinds, the hoopoe, and the bat.

¹⁹"All flying insects are ceremonially unclean

13:15 The Hebrew term used here refers to the complete consecration of things or people to the LORD, either by destroying them or by giving them as an offering; also in 13:17.   14:4 The identification of some of the animals and birds listed in this chapter is uncertain.   14:7 Or *coney;* or *hyrax.*

for you and may not be eaten. 20But you may eat any winged creature that is ceremonially clean.

21 "Do not eat anything that has died a natural death. You may give it to a foreigner living among you, or you may sell it to a foreigner. But do not eat it yourselves, for you are set apart as holy to the LORD your God.

"Do not boil a young goat in its mother's milk.

The Giving of Tithes

22"You must set aside a tithe of your crops—one-tenth of all the crops you harvest each year. 23Bring this tithe to the place the LORD your God chooses for his name to be honored, and eat it there in his presence. This applies to your tithes of grain, new wine, olive oil, and the firstborn males of your flocks and herds. The purpose of tithing is to teach you always to fear the LORD your God. 24Now the place the LORD your God chooses for his name to be honored might be a long way from your home. 25If so, you may sell the tithe portion of your crops and herds and take the money to the place the LORD your God chooses. 26When you arrive, use the money to buy anything you want—an ox, a sheep, some wine, or beer. Then feast there in the presence of the LORD your God and celebrate with your household. 27And do not forget the Levites in your community, for they have no inheritance as you do.

28"At the end of every third year bring the tithe of all your crops and store it in the nearest town. 29Give it to the Levites, who have no inheritance among you, as well as to the foreigners living among you, the orphans, and the widows in your towns, so they can eat and be satisfied. Then the LORD your God will bless you in all your work.

CHAPTER **15**
Release for Debtors

"At the end of every seventh year you must cancel your debts. 2This is how it must be done. Creditors must cancel the loans they have made to their fellow Israelites. They must not demand payment from their neighbors or relatives, for the LORD's time of release has arrived. 3This release from debt, however, applies only to your fellow Israelites—not to the foreigners living among you. 4There should be no poor among you, for the LORD your God will greatly bless you in the land he is giving you as a special posses-ion. 5You will receive this blessing if you care-ully obey the commands of the LORD your God

that I am giving you today. 6The LORD your God will bless you as he has promised. You will lend money to many nations but will never need to borrow! You will rule many nations, but they will not rule over you!

7"But if there are any poor people in your towns when you arrive in the land the LORD your God is giving you, do not be hard-hearted or tightfisted toward them. 8Instead, be generous and lend them whatever they need. 9Do not be mean-spirited and refuse someone a loan be-cause the year of release is close at hand. If you refuse to make the loan and the needy person cries out to the LORD, you will be considered guilty of sin. 10Give freely without begrudging it, and the LORD your God will bless you in every-thing you do. 11There will always be some among you who are poor. That is why I am commanding you to share your resources freely with the poor and with other Israelites in need.

Release for Hebrew Slaves

12"If an Israelite man or woman voluntarily be-comes your servant and serves you for six years, in the seventh year you must set that servant free.

13"When you release a male servant, do not send him away empty-handed. 14Give him a gen-erous farewell gift from your flock, your threshing floor, and your winepress. Share with him some of the bounty with which the LORD your God has blessed you. 15Remember that you were slaves in the land of Egypt and the LORD your God re-deemed you! That is why I am giving you this command. 16But suppose your servant says, 'I will not leave you,' because he loves you and your family, and he is well off with you. 17In that case, take an awl and push it through his earlobe into the door. After that, he will be your servant for life.

"You must do the same for your female ser-vants.

18"Do not consider it a hardship when you release your servants. Remember that for six years they have given you the services worth double the wages of hired workers, and the LORD your God will bless you in all you do.

Sacrificing Firstborn Male Animals

19"You must set aside for the LORD your God all the firstborn males from your flocks and herds. Do not use the firstborn of your herds to work your fields, and do not shear the firstborn of your flocks. 20Instead, you and your family must eat these animals in the presence of the LORD your God each year at the place he chooses. 21But if this firstborn animal has any defect, such as being lame or blind, or if anything else is wrong with it, you must not sacrifice it to the LORD your God. 22Instead, use it for food for your family at home. Anyone may eat it, whether ceremonially clean or unclean, just as anyone may eat a gazelle or deer. 23But do not eat the blood. You must pour it out on the ground like water.

CHAPTER **16**

Passover and the Festival of Unleavened Bread

"In honor of the LORD your God, always celebrate the Passover at the proper time in early spring,* for that was when the LORD your God brought you out of Egypt by night. 2Your Passover sacrifice may be from either the flock or the herd, and it must be sacrificed to the LORD your God at the place he chooses for his name to be honored. 3Eat it with bread made without yeast. For seven days eat only bread made without yeast, as you did when you escaped from Egypt in such a hurry. Eat this bread—the bread of suffering—so that you will remember the day you departed from Egypt as long as you live. 4Let no yeast be found in any house throughout your land for seven days. And do not let any of the meat of the Passover lamb remain until the next morning.

5"The Passover must not be eaten in the towns that the LORD your God is giving you. 6It must be offered at the place the LORD your God will choose for his name to be honored. Sacrifice it there as the sun goes down on the anniversary of your exodus from Egypt. 7Roast the lamb and eat it in the place the LORD your God chooses. Then go back to your tents the next morning. 8For the next six days you may not eat bread made with yeast. On the seventh day the people must assemble before the LORD your God, and no work may be done on that day.

The Festival of Harvest

9"Count off seven weeks from the beginning of your grain harvest. 10Then you must celebrate the Festival of Harvest* to honor the LORD your God. Bring him a freewill offering in proportion to the blessings you have received from him. 11It is a time to celebrate before the LORD your God at the place he chooses for his name to be honored. Celebrate with your whole family, all your servants, the Levites from your towns, and the foreigners, orphans, and widows who live among you. 12Remember that you were slaves in Egypt, so be careful to obey all these laws.

The Festival of Shelters

13"Another celebration, the Festival of Shelters, must be observed for seven days at the end of the harvest season, after the grain has been threshed and the grapes have been pressed. 14This festival will be a happy time of rejoicing with your family, your servants, and with the Levites, foreigners, orphans, and widows from your towns. 15For seven days celebrate this festival to honor the LORD your God at the place he chooses, for it is the LORD your God who gives you bountiful harvests and blesses all your work. This festival will be a time of great joy for all.

16"Each year every man in Israel must celebrate these three festivals: the Festival of Unleavened Bread, the Festival of Harvest, and the Festival of Shelters. They must appear before the LORD your God at the place he chooses on each of these occasions, and they must bring a gift to the LORD. 17All must give as they are able, according to the blessings given to them by the LORD your God.

Justice for the People

18"Appoint judges and officials for each of your tribes in all the towns the LORD your God is giving you. They will judge the people fairly throughout the land. 19You must never twist justice or show partiality. Never accept a bribe, for bribes blind the eyes of the wise and corrupt the decisions of the godly. 20Let true justice prevail, so you may live and occupy the land that the LORD your God is giving you.

21"You must never set up an Asherah pole beside the altar of the LORD your God. 22And never set up sacred pillars for worship, for the LORD your God hates them.

CHAPTER **17**

"Never sacrifice a sick or defective ox or sheep to the LORD your God, for he detests such gifts.

2"Suppose a man or woman among you, in one of your towns that the LORD your God is giving you, has done evil in the sight of the LORD your God and has violated the covenant 3by serving other gods or by worshiping the sun, the moon, or any of the forces of heaven, which I have strictly forbidden. 4When you hear about it, investigate the matter thoroughly. If it is true that this detestable thing has been done in Israel, 5then that man or woman must be taken to the gates of the town and stoned to death. 6But never put a person to death on the testimony of

16:1 Hebrew *in the month of Abib.* This month of the Hebrew lunar calendar usually occurs in March and April.   16:10 Or *Festival of Weeks;* also in 16:16.

only one witness. There must always be at least two or three witnesses. [7]The witnesses must throw the first stones, and then all the people will join in. In this way, you will purge all evil from among you.

[8]"Suppose a case arises in a local court that is too hard for you to decide—for instance, whether someone is guilty of murder or only of manslaughter, or a difficult lawsuit, or a case involving different kinds of assault. Take such cases to the place the LORD your God will choose, [9]where the Levitical priests and the judge on duty will hear the case and decide what to do. [10]The decision they make at the place the LORD chooses will always stand. You must do exactly what they say. [11]After they have interpreted the law and reached a verdict, the sentence they impose must be fully executed; do not modify it in any way. [12]Anyone arrogant enough to reject the verdict of the judge or of the priest who represents the LORD your God must be put to death. Such evil must be purged from Israel. [13]Then everyone will hear about it and be afraid to act so arrogantly.

Guidelines for a King

[14]"You will soon arrive in the land the LORD your God is giving you, and you will conquer it and settle there. Then you may begin to think, 'We ought to have a king like the other nations around us.' [15]If this happens, be sure that you select as king the man the LORD your God chooses. You must appoint a fellow Israelite, not a foreigner. [16]The king must not build up a large stable of horses for himself, and he must never send his people to Egypt to buy horses there, for the LORD has told you, 'You must never return to Egypt.' [17]The king must not take many wives for himself, because they will lead him away from the LORD. And he must not accumulate vast amounts of wealth in silver and gold for himself.

[18]"When he sits on the throne as king, he must copy these laws on a scroll for himself in the presence of the Levitical priests. [19]He must always keep this copy of the law with him and read it daily as long as he lives. That way he will learn to fear the LORD his God by obeying all the terms of this law. [20]This regular reading will prevent him from becoming proud and acting as if he is above his fellow citizens. It will also prevent him from turning away from these commands in the smallest way. This will ensure that he and his descendants will reign for many generations in Israel.

CHAPTER 18

Gifts for the Priests and Levites

"Remember that the Levitical priests and the rest of the tribe of Levi will not be given an inheritance of land like the other tribes in Israel. Instead, the priests and Levites will eat from the offerings given to the LORD by fire, for that is their inheritance. [2]They will have no inheritance of their own among the Israelites. The LORD himself is their inheritance, just as he promised them.

[3]"These are the parts the priests may claim as their share from the oxen and sheep that the people bring as offerings: the shoulder, the cheeks, and the stomach. [4]You must also give to the priests the first share of the grain, the new wine, the olive oil, and the wool at shearing time. [5]For the LORD your God chose the tribe of Levi out of all your tribes to minister in the LORD's name forever.

[6]"Any Levite who so desires may come from any town in Israel, from wherever he is living, to the place the LORD chooses. [7]He may minister there in the name of the LORD his God, just like his fellow Levites who are serving the LORD there. [8]He may eat his share of the sacrifices and offerings, even if he has a private source of income.

A Call to Holy Living

[9]"When you arrive in the land the LORD your God is giving you, be very careful not to imitate the detestable customs of the nations living there. [10]For example, never sacrifice your son or daughter as a burnt offering.* And do not let your people practice fortune-telling or sorcery, or allow them to interpret omens, or engage in witchcraft, [11]or cast spells, or function as mediums or psychics, or call forth the spirits of the dead. [12]Anyone who does these things is an object of horror and disgust to the LORD. It is because the other nations have done these things that the LORD your God will drive them out ahead of you. [13]You must be blameless before the LORD your God. [14]The people you are about to displace consult with sorcerers and fortune-tellers, but the LORD your God forbids you to do such things.

True and False Prophets

[15]"The LORD your God will raise up for you a prophet like me from among your fellow Israelites, and you must listen to that prophet. [16]For this is what you yourselves requested of the LORD your God when you were assembled at Mount Sinai.* You begged that you might never again

18:10 Or *never make your son or daughter pass through the fire.*   **18:16** Hebrew *Horeb,* another name for Sinai.

have to listen to the voice of the LORD your God or see this blazing fire for fear you would die.

17 "Then the LORD said to me, 'Fine, I will do as they have requested. 18I will raise up a prophet like you from among their fellow Israelites. I will tell that prophet what to say, and he will tell the people everything I command him. 19I will personally deal with anyone who will not listen to the messages the prophet proclaims on my behalf. 20But any prophet who claims to give a message from another god or who falsely claims to speak for me must die.' 21You may wonder, 'How will we know whether the prophecy is from the LORD or not?' 22If the prophet predicts something in the LORD's name and it does not happen, the LORD did not give the message. That prophet has spoken on his own and need not be feared.

CHAPTER 19
Cities of Refuge

"The LORD your God will soon destroy the nations whose land he is giving you, and you will displace them and settle in their towns and homes. 2Then you must set apart three cities of refuge in the land the LORD your God is giving you to occupy. 3Divide the land the LORD your God is giving you into three districts, with one of these cities in each district. Keep the roads to these cities in good repair so that anyone who has killed someone can flee there for safety.

4 "If someone accidentally kills a neighbor without harboring any previous hatred, the slayer may flee to any of these cities and be safe. 5For example, suppose someone goes into the forest with a neighbor to cut wood. And suppose one of them swings an ax and the ax head flies off the handle, killing the other person. In such cases, the slayer could flee to one of the cities of refuge and be safe. 6If the distance to the nearest city of refuge was too far, an enraged avenger might be able to chase down and kill the person who caused the death. The slayer would die, even though there was no death sentence and the first death had been an accident. 7That is why I am commanding you to set aside three cities of refuge.

8 "If the LORD your God enlarges your territory, as he solemnly promised your ancestors, and gives you all the land he promised them, 9you must designate three additional cities of refuge. (He will give you this land if you obey all the commands I have given you—if you always love the LORD your God and walk in his ways.) 10That way you will prevent the death of innocent people in the land the LORD your God is

giving you as a special possession, and you will not be held responsible for murder.

11 "But suppose someone hates a neighbor and deliberately ambushes and murders that neighbor and then escapes to one of the cities of refuge. 12In that case, the leaders of the murderer's hometown must have the murderer brought back from the city of refuge and handed over to the dead person's avenger to be killed. 13Do not feel sorry for that murderer! Purge the guilt of murder from Israel so all may go well with you.

Concern for Justice

14 "When you arrive in the land the LORD your God is giving you as a special possession, never steal someone's land by moving the boundary markers your ancestors set up to mark their property.

15 "Never convict anyone of a crime on the testimony of just one witness. The facts of the case must be established by the testimony of two or three witnesses. 16If a malicious witness comes forward and accuses someone of a crime, 17then both the accuser and accused must appear before the priests and judges who are on duty before the LORD. 18They must be closely questioned, and if the accuser is found to be lying, 19the accuser will receive the punishment intended for the accused. In this way, you will cleanse such evil from among you. 20Those who hear about it will be afraid to do such an evil thing again. 21You must never show pity! Your rule should be life for life, eye for eye, tooth for tooth, hand for hand, foot for foot.

CHAPTER 20
Regulations concerning War

"When you go out to fight your enemies and you face horses and chariots and an army greater than your own, do not be afraid. The LORD your God, who brought you safely out of Egypt, is with you! 2Before you go into battle, the priest will come forward to speak with the troops. 3He will say, 'Listen to me, all you men of Israel! Do not be afraid as you go out to fight today! Do not lose heart or panic. 4For the LORD your God is going with you! He will fight for you against your enemies, and he will give you victory!'

5 "Then the officers of the army will address the troops and say, 'Has anyone just built a new house but not yet dedicated it? If so, go home! You might be killed in the battle, and someone else would dedicate your house! 6Has anyone just planted a vineyard but not yet eaten any of its fruit? If so, go home! You might die in battle,

and someone else would eat from it! ⁷Has anyone just become engaged? Well, go home and get married! You might die in the battle, and someone else would marry your fiancée.' ⁸Then the officers will also say, 'Is anyone terrified? If you are, go home before you frighten anyone else.' ⁹When the officers have finished saying this to their troops, they will announce the names of the unit commanders.

¹⁰"As you approach a town to attack it, first offer its people terms for peace. ¹¹If they accept your terms and open the gates to you, then all the people inside will serve you in forced labor. ¹²But if they refuse to make peace and prepare to fight, you must attack the town. ¹³When the LORD your God hands it over to you, kill every man in the town. ¹⁴But you may keep for yourselves all the women, children, livestock, and other plunder. You may enjoy the spoils of your enemies that the LORD your God has given you. ¹⁵But these instructions apply only to distant towns, not to the towns of nations nearby.

¹⁶"As for the towns of the nations the LORD your God is giving you as a special possession, destroy every living thing in them. ¹⁷You must completely destroy* the Hittites, Amorites, Canaanites, Perizzites, Hivites, and Jebusites, just as the LORD your God has commanded you. ¹⁸This will keep the people of the land from teaching you their detestable customs in the worship of their gods, which would cause you to sin deeply against the LORD your God.

¹⁹"When you are besieging a town and the war drags on, do not destroy the trees. Eat the fruit, but do not cut down the trees. They are not enemies that need to be attacked! ²⁰But you may cut down trees that you know are not valuable for food. Use them to make the equipment you need to besiege the town until it falls.

CHAPTER **21**
Cleansing for Unsolved Murder
"Suppose someone is found murdered in a field in the land the LORD your God is giving you, and you don't know who committed the murder. ²In such cases, your leaders and judges must determine which town is nearest the body. ³Then the leaders of that town must select a young cow that has never been trained or yoked to a plow. ⁴They must lead it to a valley that is neither plowed nor planted with a stream running through it. There they must break the cow's

neck. ⁵The Levitical priests must go there also, for the LORD your God has chosen them to minister before him and to pronounce blessings in the LORD's name. And they are to decide all lawsuits and punishments.

⁶"The leaders of the town nearest the body must wash their hands over the young cow whose neck was broken. ⁷Then they must say, 'Our hands did not shed this blood, nor did we see it happen. ⁸O LORD, forgive your people Israel whom you have redeemed. Do not charge your people Israel with the guilt of murdering an innocent person.' Then they will be absolved of the guilt of this person's blood. ⁹By following these instructions and doing what is right in the LORD's sight, you will cleanse the guilt of murder from your community.

Marriage to a Captive Woman
¹⁰"Suppose you go to war against your enemies and the LORD your God hands them over to you and you take captives. ¹¹And suppose you see among the captives a beautiful woman, and you are attracted to her and want to marry her. ¹²If this happens, you may take her to your home, where she must shave her head, cut her fingernails, ¹³and change all her clothes. Then she must remain in your home for a full month, mourning for her father and mother. After that you may marry her. ¹⁴But if you marry her and then decide you do not like her, you must let her go free. You may not sell her or treat her as a slave, for you have humiliated her.

Rights of the Firstborn
¹⁵"Suppose a man has two wives, but he loves one and not the other, and both have given him sons. And suppose the firstborn son is the son of the wife he does not love. ¹⁶When the man divides the inheritance, he may not give the larger inheritance to his younger son, the son of the wife he loves. ¹⁷He must give the customary double portion to his oldest son, who represents the strength of his father's manhood and who owns the rights of the firstborn son, even though he is the son of the wife his father does not love.

Dealing with a Rebellious Son
¹⁸"Suppose a man has a stubborn, rebellious son who will not obey his father or mother, even though they discipline him. ¹⁹In such cases, the father and mother must take the son before the leaders of the town. ²⁰They must declare: 'This son of ours is stubborn and rebellious and

20:17 The Hebrew term used here refers to the complete consecration of things or people to the LORD, either by destroying them or by giving them as an offering.

refuses to obey. He is a worthless drunkard.' ²¹Then all the men of the town must stone him to death. In this way, you will cleanse this evil from among you, and all Israel will hear about it and be afraid.

Various Regulations

²²"If someone has committed a crime worthy of death and is executed and then hanged on a tree, ²³the body must never remain on the tree overnight. You must bury the body that same day, for anyone hanging on a tree is cursed of God. Do not defile the land the LORD your God is giving you as a special possession.

CHAPTER **22**

"If you see your neighbor's ox or sheep wandering away, don't pretend not to see it. Take it back to its owner. ²If it does not belong to someone nearby or you don't know who the owner is, keep it until the owner comes looking for it; then return it. ³Do the same if you find your neighbor's donkey, clothing, or anything else your neighbor loses. Don't pretend you did not see it.

⁴"If you see your neighbor's ox or donkey lying on the road, do not look the other way. Go and help your neighbor get it to its feet!

⁵"A woman must not wear men's clothing, and a man must not wear women's clothing. The LORD your God detests people who do this.

⁶"If you find a bird's nest on the ground or in a tree and there are young ones or eggs in it with the mother sitting in the nest, do not take the mother with the young. ⁷You may take the young, but let the mother go, so you may prosper and enjoy a long life.

⁸"Every new house you build must have a barrier around the edge of its flat rooftop. That way you will not bring the guilt of bloodshed on your household if someone falls from the roof.

⁹"Do not plant any other crop between the rows of your vineyard. If you do, you are forbidden to use either the grapes from the vineyard or the produce of the other crop.

¹⁰"Do not plow with an ox and a donkey harnessed together.

¹¹"Do not wear clothing made of wool and linen woven together.

¹²"You must put tassels on the four corners of your cloaks.

Regulations for Sexual Purity

¹³"Suppose a man marries a woman and, after sleeping with her, changes his mind about her ¹⁴and falsely accuses her of having slept with another man. He might say, 'I discovered she was not a virgin when I married her.' ¹⁵If the man does this, the woman's father and mother must bring the proof of her virginity to the leaders of the town. ¹⁶Her father must tell them, 'I gave my daughter to this man to be his wife, and now he has turned against her. ¹⁷He has accused her of shameful things, claiming that she was not a virgin when he married her. But here is the proof of my daughter's virginity.' Then they must spread the cloth before the judges. ¹⁸The judges must then punish the man. ¹⁹They will fine him one hundred pieces of silver,* for he falsely accused a virgin of Israel. The payment will be made to the woman's father. The woman will then remain the man's wife, and he may never divorce her.

²⁰"But suppose the man's accusations are true, and her virginity could not be proved. ²¹In such cases, the judges must take the girl to the door of her father's home, and the men of the town will stone her to death. She has committed a disgraceful crime in Israel by being promiscuous while living in her parents' home. Such evil must be cleansed from among you.

²²"If a man is discovered committing adultery, both he and the other man's wife must be killed. In this way, the evil will be cleansed from Israel.

²³"Suppose a man meets a young woman, a virgin who is engaged to be married, and he has sexual intercourse with her. If this happens within a town, ²⁴you must take both of them to the gates of the town and stone them to death. The woman is guilty because she did not scream for help. The man must die because he violated another man's wife. In this way, you will cleanse the land of evil.

²⁵"But if the man meets the engaged woman out in the country, and he rapes her, then only the man should die. ²⁶Do nothing to the young woman; she has committed no crime worthy of death. This case is similar to that of someone who attacks and murders a neighbor. ²⁷Since the man raped her out in the country, it must be assumed that she screamed, but there was no one to rescue her.

²⁸"If a man is caught in the act of raping a young woman who is not engaged, ²⁹he must pay fifty pieces of silver* to her father. Then he must marry the young woman because he vio-

22:19 Hebrew *100 shekels of silver*, about 2.5 pounds or 1.1 kilograms in weight.   22:29 Hebrew *50 shekels of silver*, about 1.25 pounds or 570 grams in weight.

lated her, and he will never be allowed to divorce her.

30 "A man must not have intercourse with his father's wife, for this would violate his father.

CHAPTER **23**

Regulations concerning Worship

"If a man's testicles are crushed or his penis is cut off, he may not be included in the assembly of the LORD.

2 "Those of illegitimate birth and their descendants for ten generations may not be included in the assembly of the LORD.

3 "No Ammonites or Moabites, or any of their descendants for ten generations, may be included in the assembly of the LORD. 4 These nations did not welcome you with food and water when you came out of Egypt. Instead, they tried to hire Balaam son of Beor from Pethor in Aram-naharaim* to curse you. 5 (But the LORD your God would not listen to Balaam. He turned the intended curse into a blessing because the LORD your God loves you.) 6 You must never, as long as you live, try to help the Ammonites or the Moabites in any way.

7 "Do not detest the Edomites or the Egyptians, because the Edomites are your relatives, and you lived as foreigners among the Egyptians. 8 The third generation of Egyptians who came with you from Egypt may enter the assembly of the LORD.

Miscellaneous Regulations

9 "When you go to war against your enemies, stay away from everything impure.

10 "Any man who becomes ceremonially defiled because of a nocturnal emission must leave the camp and stay away all day. 11 Toward evening he must bathe himself, and at sunset he may return to the camp.

12 "Mark off an area outside the camp for a latrine. 13 Each of you must have a spade as part of your equipment. Whenever you relieve yourself, you must dig a hole with the spade and cover the excrement. 14 The camp must be holy, for the LORD your God moves around in your camp to protect you and to defeat your enemies. He must not see any shameful thing among you, or he might turn away from you.

15 "If slaves should escape from their masters and take refuge with you, do not force them to return. 16 Let them live among you in whatever town they choose, and do not oppress them.

17 "No Israelite man or woman may ever become a temple prostitute. 18 Do not bring to the house of the LORD your God any offering from the earnings of a prostitute, whether a man or a woman, for both are detestable to the LORD your God.

19 "Do not charge interest on the loans you make to a fellow Israelite, whether it is money, food, or anything else that may be loaned with interest. 20 You may charge interest to foreigners, but not to Israelites, so the LORD your God may bless you in everything you do in the land you are about to enter and occupy.

21 "When you make a vow to the LORD your God, be prompt in doing whatever you promised him. For the LORD your God demands that you promptly fulfill all your vows. If you don't, you will be guilty of sin. 22 However, it is not a sin to refrain from making a vow. 23 But once you have voluntarily made a vow, be careful to do as you have said, for you have made a vow to the LORD your God.

24 "You may eat your fill of grapes from your neighbor's vineyard, but do not take any away in a basket. 25 And you may pluck a few heads of your neighbor's grain by hand, but you may not harvest it with a sickle.

CHAPTER **24**

"Suppose a man marries a woman but later discovers something about her that is shameful. So he writes her a letter of divorce, gives it to her, and sends her away. 2 If she then leaves and marries another man 3 and the second husband also divorces her or dies, 4 the former husband may not marry her again, for she has been defiled. That would be detestable to the LORD. You must not bring guilt upon the land the LORD your God is giving you as a special possession.

5 "A newly married man must not be drafted into the army or given any other special responsibilities. He must be free to be at home for one year, bringing happiness to the wife he has married.

6 "It is wrong to take a pair of millstones, or even just the upper millstone, as a pledge, for the owner uses it to make a living.

7 "If anyone kidnaps a fellow Israelite and treats him as a slave or sells him, the kidnapper must die. You must cleanse the evil from among you.

8 "Watch all contagious skin diseases* carefully and follow the instructions of the Levitical priests; obey the commands I have given them.

23:4 *Aram-naharaim* means "Aram of the two rivers," thought to have been located between the Euphrates and Balih Rivers in northwestern Mesopotamia. **24:8** Traditionally rendered *leprosy.* The Hebrew word used here can describe various skin diseases.

9Remember what the LORD your God did to Miriam as you were coming from Egypt.

10"If you lend anything to your neighbor, do not enter your neighbor's house to claim the security. 11Stand outside and the owner will bring it out to you. 12If your neighbor is poor and has only a cloak to give as security, do not keep the cloak overnight. 13Return the cloak to its owner by sunset so your neighbor can sleep in it and bless you. And the LORD your God will count it as a righteous act.

14"Never take advantage of poor laborers, whether fellow Israelites or foreigners living in your towns. 15Pay them their wages each day before sunset because they are poor and are counting on it. Otherwise they might cry out to the LORD against you, and it would be counted against you as sin.

16"Parents must not be put to death for the sins of their children, nor the children for the sins of their parents. Those worthy of death must be executed for their own crimes.

17"True justice must be given to foreigners living among you and to orphans, and you must never accept a widow's garment in pledge of her debt. 18Always remember that you were slaves in Egypt and that the LORD your God redeemed you. That is why I have given you this command.

19"When you are harvesting your crops and forget to bring in a bundle of grain from your field, don't go back to get it. Leave it for the foreigners, orphans, and widows. Then the LORD your God will bless you in all you do. 20When you beat the olives from your olive trees, don't go over the boughs twice. Leave some of the olives for the foreigners, orphans, and widows. 21This also applies to the grapes in your vineyard. Do not glean the vines after they are picked, but leave any remaining grapes for the foreigners, orphans, and widows. 22Remember that you were slaves in the land of Egypt. That is why I am giving you this command.

CHAPTER **25**

"Suppose two people take a dispute to court, and the judges declare that one is right and the other is wrong. 2If the person in the wrong is sentenced to be flogged, the judge will command him to lie down and be beaten in his presence with the number of lashes appropriate to the crime. 3No more than forty lashes may ever be given; more than forty lashes would publicly humiliate your neighbor.

4"Do not keep an ox from eating as it treads out the grain.

5"If two brothers are living together on the same property and one of them dies without a son, his widow must not marry outside the family. Instead, her husband's brother must marry her and fulfill the duties of a brother-in-law. 6The first son she bears to him will be counted as the son of the dead brother, so that his name will not be forgotten in Israel. 7But if the dead man's brother refuses to marry the widow, she must go to the town gate and say to the leaders there, 'My husband's brother refuses to preserve his brother's name in Israel—he refuses to marry me.' 8The leaders of the town will then summon him and try to reason with him. If he still insists that he doesn't want to marry her, 9the widow must walk over to him in the presence of the leaders, pull his sandal from his foot, and spit in his face. She will then say, 'This is what happens to a man who refuses to raise up a son for his brother.' 10Ever afterward his family will be referred to as 'the family of the man whose sandal was pulled off'!

11"If two Israelite men are fighting and the wife of one tries to rescue her husband by grabbing the testicles of the other man, 12her hand must be cut off without pity.

13"You must use accurate scales when you weigh out merchandise, 14and you must use full and honest measures. 15Yes, use honest weights and measures, so that you will enjoy a long life in the land the LORD your God is giving you. 16Those who cheat with dishonest weights and measures are detestable to the LORD your God.

17"Never forget what the Amalekites did to you as you came from Egypt. 18They attacked you when you were exhausted and weary, and they struck down those who were lagging behind. They had no fear of God. 19Therefore, when the LORD your God has given you rest from all your enemies in the land he is giving you as a special possession, you are to destroy the Amalekites and erase their memory from under heaven. Never forget this!

CHAPTER **26**

Harvest Offerings and Tithes

"When you arrive in the land the LORD your God is giving you as a special possession and you have conquered it and settled there, 2put some of the first produce from each harvest into a basket and bring it to the place the LORD your God chooses for his name to be honored. 3Go to the priest in charge at that time and say to him, 'With this gift I acknowledge that the LORD your God has brought me into the land he swore to give our ancestors.' ⁴The priest will then take the basket from your hand and set it before the altar of the LORD your God. ⁵You must then say in the presence of the LORD your God, 'My ancestor Jacob was a wandering Aramean who went to live in Egypt. His family was few in number, but in Egypt they became a mighty and numerous nation. ⁶When the Egyptians mistreated and humiliated us by making us their slaves, ⁷we cried out to the LORD, the God of our ancestors. He heard us and saw our hardship, toil, and oppression. ⁸So the LORD brought us out of Egypt with amazing power, overwhelming terror, and miraculous signs and wonders. ⁹He brought us to this place and gave us this land flowing with milk and honey! ¹⁰And now, O LORD, I have brought you a token of the first crops you have given me from the ground.' Then place the produce before the LORD your God and worship him. ¹¹Afterward go and celebrate because of all the good things the LORD your God has given to you and your household. Remember to include the Levites and the foreigners living among you in the celebration.

¹²"Every third year you must offer a special tithe of your crops. You must give these tithes to the Levites, foreigners, orphans, and widows so that they will have enough to eat in your towns. ¹³Then you must declare in the presence of the LORD your God, 'I have taken the sacred gift from my house and have given it to the Levites, foreigners, orphans, and widows, just as you commanded me. I have not violated or forgotten any of your commands. ¹⁴I have not eaten any of it while in mourning; I have not touched it while I was ceremonially unclean; and I have not offered any of it to the dead. I have obeyed the LORD my God and have done everything you commanded me. ¹⁵Look down from your holy dwelling place in heaven and bless your people Israel and the land you have given us—a land flowing with milk and honey—just as you solemnly promised our ancestors.'

A Call to Obey the LORD's Commands

¹⁶"Today the LORD your God has commanded you to obey all these laws and regulations. You must commit yourself to them without reservation. ¹⁷You have declared today that the LORD is your God. You have promised to obey his laws, commands, and regulations by walking in his ways and doing everything he tells you. ¹⁸The LORD has declared today that you are his people, his own special treasure, just as he promised, and that you must obey all his commands. ¹⁹And if you do, he will make you greater than any other nation. Then you will receive praise, honor, and renown. You will be a nation that is holy to the LORD your God, just as he promised."

CHAPTER **27**
The Altar on Mount Ebal

Then Moses and the leaders of Israel charged the people as follows: "Keep all these commands that I am giving you today. ²When you cross the Jordan River and enter the land the LORD your God is giving you, set up some large stones and coat them with plaster. ³Then write all the terms of this law on them. I repeat, you will soon cross the river to enter the land the LORD your God is giving you, a land flowing with milk and honey, just as the LORD, the God of your ancestors, promised you. ⁴When you cross the Jordan, set up these stones at Mount Ebal and coat them with plaster, as I am commanding you today. ⁵Then build an altar there to the LORD your God, using natural stones. ⁶Do not shape the stones with an iron tool. On the altar you must offer burnt offerings to the LORD your God. ⁷Sacrifice peace offerings on it also, and feast there with great joy before the LORD your God. ⁸On the stones coated with plaster, you must clearly write all the terms of this law."

⁹Then Moses and the Levitical priests addressed all Israel as follows: "O Israel, be quiet and listen! Today you have become the people of the LORD your God. ¹⁰So obey the LORD your God by keeping all these commands and laws that I am giving you today."

Curses from Mount Ebal

¹¹That same day Moses gave this charge to the people: ¹²"When you cross the Jordan River, the tribes of Simeon, Levi, Judah, Issachar, Joseph, and Benjamin must stand on Mount Gerizim to proclaim a blessing over the people. ¹³And the tribes of Reuben, Gad, Asher, Zebulun, Dan, and Naphtali must stand on Mount Ebal to proclaim a curse. ¹⁴Then the Levites must shout to all the people of Israel:

¹⁵'Cursed is anyone who carves or casts idols and secretly sets them up. These idols, the work of craftsmen, are detestable to the LORD.'
And all the people will reply, 'Amen.'

¹⁶'Cursed is anyone who despises father or mother.'
And all the people will reply, 'Amen.'

17'Cursed is anyone who steals property from a neighbor by moving a boundary marker.'

And all the people will reply, 'Amen.'

18'Cursed is anyone who leads a blind person astray on the road.'

And all the people will reply, 'Amen.'

19'Cursed is anyone who is unjust to foreigners, orphans, and widows.'

And all the people will reply, 'Amen.'

20'Cursed is anyone who has sexual intercourse with his father's wife, for he has violated his father.'

And all the people will reply, 'Amen.'

21'Cursed is anyone who has sexual intercourse with an animal.'

And all the people will reply, 'Amen.'

22 ' Cursed is anyone who has sexual intercourse with his sister, whether she is the daughter of his father or his mother.'

And all the people will reply, 'Amen.'

23'Cursed is anyone who has sexual intercourse with his mother-in-law.'

And all the people will reply, 'Amen.'

24'Cursed is anyone who kills another person in secret.'

And all the people will reply, 'Amen.'

25'Cursed is anyone who accepts payment to kill an innocent person.'

And all the people will reply, 'Amen.'

26'Cursed is anyone who does not affirm the terms of this law by obeying them.'

And all the people will reply, 'Amen.'

CHAPTER **28**

Blessings for Obedience

"If you fully obey the LORD your God by keeping all the commands I am giving you today, the LORD your God will exalt you above all the nations of the world. 2You will experience all these blessings if you obey the LORD your God:

3 You will be blessed in your towns and in the country.

4 You will be blessed with many children and productive fields.

You will be blessed with fertile herds and flocks.

5 You will be blessed with baskets overflowing with fruit, and with kneading bowls filled with bread.

6 You will be blessed wherever you go, both in coming and in going.

7 "The LORD will conquer your enemies when they attack you. They will attack you from one direction, but they will scatter from you in seven!

8 "The LORD will bless everything you do and will fill your storehouses with grain. The LORD your God will bless you in the land he is giving you.

9 "If you obey the commands of the LORD your God and walk in his ways, the LORD will establish you as his holy people as he solemnly promised to do. 10Then all the nations of the world will see that you are a people claimed by the LORD, and they will stand in awe of you.

11 "The LORD will give you an abundance of good things in the land he swore to give your ancestors—many children, numerous livestock, and abundant crops. 12The LORD will send rain at the proper time from his rich treasury in the heavens to bless all the work you do. You will lend to many nations, but you will never need to borrow from them. 13If you listen to these commands of the LORD your God and carefully obey them, the LORD will make you the head and not the tail, and you will always have the upper hand. 14You must not turn away from any of the commands I am giving you today to follow after other gods and worship them.

Curses for Disobedience

15 "But if you refuse to listen to the LORD your God and do not obey all the commands and laws I am giving you today, all these curses will come and overwhelm you:

16 You will be cursed in your towns and in the country.

17 You will be cursed with baskets empty of fruit, and with kneading bowls empty of bread.

18 You will be cursed with few children and barren fields.

You will be cursed with infertile herds and flocks.

19 You will be cursed wherever you go, both in coming and in going.

20 "The LORD himself will send against you curses, confusion, and disillusionment in everything you do, until at last you are completely destroyed for doing evil and forsaking me. 21The

LORD will send diseases among you until none of you are left in the land you are about to enter and occupy. ²²The LORD will strike you with wasting disease, fever, and inflammation, with scorching heat and drought, and with blight and mildew. These devastations will pursue you until you die. ²³The skies above will be as unyielding as bronze, and the earth beneath will be as hard as iron. ²⁴The LORD will turn your rain into sand and dust, and it will pour down from the sky until you are destroyed.

²⁵"The LORD will cause you to be defeated by your enemies. You will attack your enemies from one direction, but you will scatter from them in seven! You will be an object of horror to all the kingdoms of the earth. ²⁶Your dead bodies will be food for the birds and wild animals, and no one will be there to chase them away.

²⁷"The LORD will afflict you with the boils of Egypt and with tumors, scurvy, and the itch, from which you cannot be cured. ²⁸The LORD will strike you with madness, blindness, and panic. ²⁹You will grope around in broad daylight, just like a blind person groping in the darkness, and you will not succeed at anything you do. You will be oppressed and robbed continually, and no one will come to save you.

³⁰"You will be engaged to a woman, but another man will ravish her. You will build a house, but someone else will live in it. You will plant a vineyard, but you will never enjoy its fruit. ³¹Your ox will be butchered before your eyes, but you won't get a single bite of the meat. Your donkey will be driven away, never to be returned. Your sheep will be given to your enemies, and no one will be there to help you. ³²You will watch as your sons and daughters are taken away as slaves. Your heart will break as you long for them, but nothing you do will help. ³³A foreign nation you have never heard about will eat the crops you worked so hard to grow. You will suffer under constant oppression and harsh treatment. ³⁴You will go mad because of all the tragedy around you. ³⁵The LORD will cover you from head to foot with incurable boils.

³⁶"The LORD will exile you and the king you crowned to a nation unknown to you and your ancestors. Then in exile you will worship gods of wood and stone! ³⁷You will become an object of horror, a proverb and a mockery among all the nations to which the LORD sends you.

³⁸"You will plant much but harvest little, for locusts will eat your crops. ³⁹You will plant vineyards and care for them, but you will not drink the wine or eat the grapes, for worms will destroy the vines. ⁴⁰You will grow olive trees throughout your land, but you will never use the olive oil, for the trees will drop the fruit before it is ripe. ⁴¹You will have sons and daughters, but you will not keep them, for they will be led away into captivity. ⁴²Swarms of insects will destroy your trees and crops. ⁴³The foreigners living among you will become stronger and stronger, while you become weaker and weaker. ⁴⁴They will lend money to you, not you to them. They will be the head, and you will be the tail!

⁴⁵"If you refuse to listen to the LORD your God and to obey the commands and laws he has given you, all these curses will pursue and overtake you until you are destroyed. ⁴⁶These horrors will serve as a sign and warning among you and your descendants forever. ⁴⁷Because you have not served the LORD your God with joy and enthusiasm for the abundant benefits you have received, ⁴⁸you will serve your enemies whom the LORD will send against you. You will be left hungry, thirsty, naked, and lacking in everything. They will oppress you harshly until you are destroyed.

⁴⁹"The LORD will bring a distant nation against you from the end of the earth, and it will swoop down on you like an eagle. It is a nation whose language you do not understand, ⁵⁰a fierce and heartless nation that shows no respect for the old and no pity for the young. ⁵¹Its armies will devour your livestock and crops, and you will starve to death. They will leave you no grain, new wine, olive oil, calves, or lambs, bringing about your destruction. ⁵²They will lay siege to your cities until all the fortified walls in your land—the walls you trusted to protect you—are knocked down. They will attack all the towns in the land the LORD your God has given you. ⁵³The siege will be so severe that you will eat the flesh of your own sons and daughters, whom the LORD your God has given you. ⁵⁴The most tenderhearted man among you will have no compassion for his own brother, his beloved wife, and his surviving children. ⁵⁵He will refuse to give them a share of the flesh he is devouring—the flesh of one of his own children—because he has nothing else to eat during the siege that your enemy will inflict on all your towns. ⁵⁶The most tender and delicate woman among you—so delicate she would not so much as touch her feet to the ground—will be cruel to the husband she loves and to her own son or daughter. ⁵⁷She will hide from them the afterbirth and the new baby she has borne, so that she herself can secretly eat them. She will have noth-

ing else to eat during the siege and terrible distress that your enemy will inflict on all your towns.

58 "If you refuse to obey all the terms of this law that are written in this book, and if you do not fear the glorious and awesome name of the LORD your God, 59then the LORD will overwhelm both you and your children with indescribable plagues. These plagues will be intense and without relief, making you miserable and unbearably sick. 60He will bring against you all the diseases of Egypt that you feared so much, and they will claim you. 61The LORD will bring against you every sickness and plague there is, even those not mentioned in this Book of the Law, until you are destroyed. 62Though you are as numerous as the stars in the sky, few of you will be left because you would not listen to the LORD your God.

63 "Just as the LORD has found great pleasure in helping you to prosper and multiply, the LORD will find pleasure in destroying you, until you disappear from the land you are about to enter and occupy. 64For the LORD will scatter you among all the nations from one end of the earth to the other. There you will worship foreign gods that neither you nor your ancestors have known, gods made of wood and stone! 65There among those nations you will find no place of security and rest. And the LORD will cause your heart to tremble, your eyesight to fail, and your soul to despair. 66Your lives will hang in doubt. You will live night and day in fear, with no reason to believe that you will see the morning light. 67In the morning you will say, 'If only it were night!' And in the evening you will say, 'If only it were morning!' You will say this because of your terror at the awesome horrors you see around you. 68Then the LORD will send you back to Egypt in ships, a journey I promised you would never again make. There you will offer to sell yourselves to your enemies as slaves, but no one will want to buy you."

CHAPTER 29

These are the terms of the covenant the LORD commanded Moses to make with the Israelites while they were in the land of Moab, in addition to the covenant he had made with them at Mount Sinai.*

Moses Reviews the Covenant

2Moses summoned all the Israelites and said to them, "You have seen with your own eyes every-

29:1 Hebrew *Horeb,* another name for Sinai.

thing the LORD did in Egypt to Pharaoh and all his servants and his whole country—3all the great tests of strength, the miraculous signs, and the amazing wonders. 4But to this day the LORD has not given you minds that understand, nor eyes that see, nor ears that hear! 5For forty years I led you through the wilderness, yet your clothes and sandals did not wear out. 6You had no bread or wine or other strong drink, but he gave you food so you would know that he is the LORD your God. 7When we came here, King Sihon of Heshbon and King Og of Bashan came out to fight against us, but we defeated them. 8We took their land and gave it to the tribes of Reuben and Gad and to the half-tribe of Manasseh as their inheritance.

9 "Therefore, obey the terms of this covenant so that you will prosper in everything you do. 10All of you—your tribal leaders, your judges, your officers, all the men of Israel—are standing today before the LORD your God. 11With you are your little ones, your wives, and the foreigners living among you who chop your wood and carry your water. 12You are standing here today to enter into a covenant with the LORD your God. The LORD is making this covenant with you today, and he has sealed it with an oath. 13He wants to confirm you today as his people and to confirm that he is your God, just as he promised you, and as he swore to your ancestors Abraham, Isaac, and Jacob. 14But you are not the only ones with whom the LORD is making this covenant with its obligations. 15The LORD your God is making this covenant with you who stand in his presence today and also with all future generations of Israel.

16 "Surely you remember how we lived in the land of Egypt and how we traveled through the lands of enemy nations as we left. 17You have seen their detestable idols made of wood, stone, silver, and gold. 18The LORD made this covenant with you so that no man, woman, family, or tribe among you would turn away from the LORD our God to worship these gods of other nations, and so that no root among you would bear bitter and poisonous fruit. 19Let none of those who hear the warnings of this curse consider themselves immune, thinking, 'I am safe, even though I am walking in my own stubborn way.' This would lead to utter ruin! 20The LORD will not pardon such people. His anger and jealousy will burn against them. All the curses written in this book will come down on them, and the LORD will erase their names from under heaven.

²¹The LORD will separate them from all the tribes of Israel, to pour out on them all the covenant curses recorded in this Book of the Law.

²²"Then the generations to come, both your own descendants and the foreigners who come from distant lands, will see the devastation of the land and the diseases the LORD will send against it. ²³They will find its soil turned into sulfur and salt, with nothing planted and nothing growing, not even a blade of grass. It will be just like Sodom and Gomorrah, Admah and Zeboiim, which the LORD destroyed in his anger. ²⁴The surrounding nations will ask, 'Why has the LORD done this to his land? Why was he so angry?'

²⁵"And they will be told, 'This happened because the people of the land broke the covenant they made with the LORD, the God of their ancestors, when he brought them out of the land of Egypt. ²⁶They turned to serve and worship other gods that were foreign to them, gods that the LORD had not designated for them. ²⁷That is why the LORD's anger burned against this land, bringing down on it all the curses recorded in this book. ²⁸In great anger and fury the LORD uprooted his people from their land and exiled them to another land, where they still live today!'

²⁹"There are secret things that belong to the LORD our God, but the revealed things belong to us and our descendants forever, so that we may obey these words of the law.

CHAPTER **30**

A Call to Return to the LORD

"Suppose all these things happen to you—the blessings and the curses I have listed—and you meditate on them as you are living among the nations to which the LORD your God has exiled you. ²If at that time you return to the LORD your God, and you and your children begin wholeheartedly to obey all the commands I have given you today, ³then the LORD your God will restore your fortunes. He will have mercy on you and gather you back from all the nations where he has scattered you. ⁴Though you are at the ends of the earth, the LORD your God will go and find you and bring you back again. ⁵He will return you to the land that belonged to your ancestors, and you will possess that land again. He will make you even more prosperous and numerous than your ancestors!

⁶"The LORD your God will cleanse your heart and the hearts of all your descendants so that you will love him with all your heart and soul,

and so you may live! ⁷The LORD your God will inflict all these curses on your enemies and persecutors. ⁸Then you will again obey the LORD and keep all the commands I am giving you today. ⁹The LORD your God will make you successful in everything you do. He will give you many children and numerous livestock, and your fields will produce abundant harvests, for the LORD will delight in being good to you as he was to your ancestors. ¹⁰The LORD your God will delight in you if you obey his voice and keep the commands and laws written in this Book of the Law, and if you turn to the LORD your God with all your heart and soul.

The Choice of Life or Death

¹¹"This command I am giving you today is not too difficult for you to understand or perform. ¹²It is not up in heaven, so distant that you must ask, 'Who will go to heaven and bring it down so we can hear and obey it?' ¹³It is not beyond the sea, so far away that you must ask, 'Who will cross the sea to bring it to us so we can hear and obey it?' ¹⁴The message is very close at hand; it is on your lips and in your heart so that you can obey it.

¹⁵"Now listen! Today I am giving you a choice between prosperity and disaster, between life and death. ¹⁶I have commanded you today to love the LORD your God and to keep his commands, laws, and regulations by walking in his ways. If you do this, you will live and become a great nation, and the LORD your God will bless you and the land you are about to enter and occupy. ¹⁷But if your heart turns away and you refuse to listen, and if you are drawn away to serve and worship other gods, ¹⁸then I warn you now that you will certainly be destroyed. You will not live a long, good life in the land you are crossing the Jordan to occupy.

¹⁹"Today I have given you the choice between life and death, between blessings and curses. I call on heaven and earth to witness the choice you make. Oh, that you would choose life, that you and your descendants might live! ²⁰Choose to love the LORD your God and to obey him and commit yourself to him, for he is your life. Then you will live long in the land the LORD swore to give your ancestors Abraham, Isaac, and Jacob."

CHAPTER **31**

Joshua Becomes Israel's Leader

When Moses had finished saying* these things to all the people of Israel, ²he said, "I am now

31:1 As in Dead Sea Scrolls and Greek version; Masoretic Text reads *Moses went and spoke.*

120 years old and am no longer able to lead you. The LORD has told me that I will not cross the Jordan River. ³But the LORD your God himself will cross over ahead of you. He will destroy the nations living there, and you will take possession of their land. Joshua is your new leader, and he will go with you, just as the LORD promised. ⁴The LORD will destroy the nations living in the land, just as he destroyed Sihon and Og, the kings of the Amorites. ⁵The LORD will hand over to you the people who live there, and you will deal with them as I have commanded you. ⁶Be strong and courageous! Do not be afraid of them! The LORD your God will go ahead of you. He will neither fail you nor forsake you."

⁷Then Moses called for Joshua, and as all Israel watched he said to him, "Be strong and courageous! For you will lead these people into the land that the LORD swore to give their ancestors. You are the one who will deliver it to them as their inheritance. ⁸Do not be afraid or discouraged, for the LORD is the one who goes before you. He will be with you; he will neither fail you nor forsake you."

Public Reading of the Law

⁹So Moses wrote down this law and gave it to the priests, who carried the Ark of the LORD's covenant, and to the leaders of Israel. ¹⁰Then Moses gave them this command: "At the end of every seventh year, the Year of Release, during the Festival of Shelters, ¹¹you must read this law to all the people of Israel when they assemble before the LORD your God at the place he chooses. ¹²Call them all together—men, women, children, and the foreigners living in your towns—so they may listen and learn to fear the LORD your God and carefully obey all the terms of this law. ¹³Do this so that your children who have not known these laws will hear them and will learn to fear the LORD your God. Do this as long as you live in the land you are crossing the Jordan to occupy."

Israel's Disobedience Predicted

¹⁴Then the LORD said to Moses, "The time has come for you to die. Call Joshua and take him with you to the Tabernacle,* and I will commission him there." So Moses and Joshua went and presented themselves at the Tabernacle. ¹⁵And the LORD appeared to them in a pillar of cloud at the entrance to the sacred tent.

¹⁶The LORD said to Moses, "You are about to die and join your ancestors. After you are gone,

31:14 Hebrew *Tent of Meeting;* also in 31:14b.

these people will begin worshiping foreign gods, the gods of the land where they are going. They will abandon me and break the covenant I have made with them. ¹⁷Then my anger will blaze forth against them. I will abandon them, hiding my face from them, and they will be destroyed. Terrible trouble will come down on them, so that they will say, 'These disasters have come because God is no longer among us!' ¹⁸At that time I will hide my face from them on account of all the sins they have committed by worshiping other gods.

¹⁹"Now write down the words of this song, and teach it to the people of Israel. Teach them to sing it, so it may serve as a witness against them. ²⁰For I will bring them into the land I swore to give their ancestors—a land flowing with milk and honey. There they will become prosperous; they will eat all the food they want and become well nourished. Then they will begin to worship other gods; they will despise me and break my covenant. ²¹Then great disasters will come down on them, and this song will stand as evidence against them, for it will never be forgotten by their descendants. I know what these people are like, even before they have entered the land I swore to give them." ²²So that very day Moses wrote down the words of the song and taught it to the Israelites.

²³Then the LORD commissioned Joshua son of Nun with these words: "Be strong and courageous! You must bring the people of Israel into the land I swore to give them. I will be with you."

²⁴When Moses had finished writing down this entire body of law in a book, ²⁵he gave these instructions to the Levites who carried the Ark of the LORD's covenant: ²⁶"Take this Book of the Law and place it beside the Ark of the Covenant of the LORD your God, so it may serve as a witness against the people of Israel. ²⁷For I know how rebellious and stubborn you are. Even now, while I am still with you, you have rebelled against the LORD. How much more rebellious will you be after my death! ²⁸Now summon all the leaders and officials of your tribes so that I can speak to them and call heaven and earth to witness against them. ²⁹I know that after my death you will become utterly corrupt and will turn from the path I have commanded you to follow. In the days to come, disaster will come down on you, for you will make the LORD very angry by doing what is evil in his sight."

The Song of Moses

30So Moses recited this entire song to the assembly of Israel:

CHAPTER **32**

1 "Listen, O heavens, and I will speak!
   Hear, O earth, the words that I say!
2 My teaching will fall on you like rain;
   my speech will settle like dew.
   My words will fall like rain on tender grass,
   like gentle showers on young plants.
3 I will proclaim the name of the LORD;
   how glorious is our God!
4 He is the Rock; his work is perfect.
   Everything he does is just and fair.
   He is a faithful God who does no wrong;
   how just and upright he is!

5 "But they have acted corruptly toward him;
   when they act like that, are they really his
      children?*
   They are a deceitful and twisted
      generation.
6 Is this the way you repay the LORD,
   you foolish and senseless people?
   Isn't he your Father who created you?
   Has he not made you and established you?
7 Remember the days of long ago;
   think about the generations past.
   Ask your father and he will inform you.
   Inquire of your elders, and they will tell
      you.
8 When the Most High assigned lands to the
      nations,
   when he divided up the human race,
   he established the boundaries of the peoples
      according to the number of angelic
      beings.*
9 For the people of Israel belong to the LORD;
   Jacob is his special possession.

10 "He found them in a desert land,
   in an empty, howling wasteland.
   He surrounded them and watched over
      them;
   he guarded them as his most precious
      possession.*
11 Like an eagle that rouses her chicks
   and hovers over her young,
   so he spread his wings to take them in
   and carried them aloft on his pinions.
12 The LORD alone guided them;

they lived without any foreign gods.
13 He made them ride over the highlands;
   he let them feast on the crops of the
      fields.
   He nourished them with honey from the
      cliffs,
   with olive oil from the hard rock.
14 He fed them curds from the herd and milk
      from the flock,
   together with the fat of lambs and goats.
   He gave them choice rams and goats from
      Bashan,
   together with the choicest wheat.
   You drank the finest wine,
   made from the juice of grapes.
15 But Israel* soon became fat and unruly;
   the people grew heavy, plump, and
      stuffed!
   Then they abandoned the God who had
      made them;
   they made light of the Rock of their
      salvation.
16 They stirred up his jealousy by worshiping
      foreign gods;
   they provoked his fury with detestable acts.
17 They offered sacrifices to demons, non-gods,
   to gods they had not known before,
   to gods only recently arrived,
   to gods their ancestors had never feared.
18 You neglected the Rock who had fathered
      you;
   you forgot the God who had given you
      birth.

19 "The LORD saw this and was filled with
      loathing.
   He was provoked to anger by his own
      sons and daughters.
20 He said, 'I will abandon them;
   I will see to their end!
   For they are a twisted generation,
   children without integrity.
21 They have roused my jealousy by
      worshiping non-gods;
   they have provoked my fury with useless
      idols.
   Now I will rouse their jealousy by blessing
      other nations;
   I will provoke their fury by blessing the
      foolish Gentiles.
22 For my anger blazes forth like fire
   and burns to the depths of the grave.*

32:5 The meaning of the Hebrew is uncertain.   32:8 As in Dead Sea Scrolls, which read *of the sons of God,* and Greek version, which reads *of the angels of god;* Masoretic Text reads *of the sons of Israel.*   32:10 Hebrew *as the apple of his eye.*   32:15 Hebrew *Jeshurun,* a term of endearment for Israel.   32:22 Hebrew *of Sheol.*

It devours the earth and all its crops
and ignites the foundations of the
mountains.
23 I will heap disasters upon them
and shoot them down with my arrows.
24 I will send against them wasting famine,
burning fever, and deadly disease.
They will be troubled by the fangs of wild
beasts,
by poisonous snakes that glide in the
dust.
25 Outside, the sword will bring death,
and inside, terror will strike
both young men and young women,
both infants and the aged.
26 I decided to scatter them,*
so even the memory of them would
disappear.
27 But I feared the taunt of the enemy,
that their adversaries might
misunderstand and say,
"Our power has triumphed!
It was not the LORD who did this!" '

28 "Israel is a nation that lacks sense;
the people are foolish, without
understanding.
29 Oh, that they were wise and could
understand this!
Oh, that they might know their fate!
30 How could one person chase a thousand of
them,
and two people put ten thousand to flight,
unless their Rock had sold them,
unless the LORD had given them up?
31 But the rock of our enemies is not like our
Rock,
as even they recognize.*
32 Their vine grows from the vine of Sodom,
from the vineyards of Gomorrah.
Their grapes are poison,
and their clusters are bitter.
33 Their wine is the venom of snakes,
the deadly poison of vipers.

34 " 'I am storing up these things,
sealing them away within my treasury.
35 I will take vengeance; I will repay those who
deserve it.
In due time their feet will slip.
Their day of disaster will arrive,
and their destiny will overtake them.'

36 "Indeed, the LORD will judge his people,
and he will change his mind about* his
servants,
when he sees their strength is gone
and no one is left, slave or free.
37 Then he will ask, 'Where are their gods,
the rocks they fled to for refuge?
38 Where now are those gods,
who ate the fat of their sacrifices
and drank the wine of their offerings?
Let those gods arise and help you!
Let them provide you with shelter!
39 Look now; I myself am he!
There is no god other than me!
I am the one who kills and gives life;
I am the one who wounds and heals;
no one delivers from my power!
40 Now I raise my hand to heaven
and declare, "As surely as I live,
41 when I sharpen my flashing sword
and begin to carry out justice,
I will bring vengeance on my enemies
and repay those who hate me.
42 I will make my arrows drunk with blood,
and my sword will devour flesh—
the blood of the slaughtered and the
captives,
and the heads of the enemy leaders." '

43 "Rejoice with him, O heavens,
and let all the angels of God worship him,*
for he will avenge the blood of his
servants.
He will take vengeance on his enemies
and cleanse his land and his people."

44So Moses came with Joshua* son of Nun
and recited all the words of this song to the
people. 45When Moses had finished reciting
these words to Israel, 46he added: "Take to
heart all the words I have given you today. Pass
them on as a command to your children so
they will obey every word of this law. 47These
instructions are not mere words—they are
your life! By obeying them you will enjoy a
long life in the land you are crossing the Jordan River to occupy."

Moses' Death Foretold

48That same day the LORD said to Moses, 49"Go to
Moab, to the mountains east of the river,* and
climb Mount Nebo, which is across from Jericho.
Look out across the land of Canaan, the land I am

32:26 As in Greek version; the meaning of the Hebrew is uncertain.   32:31 The meaning of the Hebrew is uncertain. Greek version reads
our enemies are fools.   32:36 Or *will take revenge for.*   32:43 As in Dead Sea Scrolls and Greek version; Masoretic Text reads *Rejoice with his
people, O nations.*   32:44 Hebrew *Hoshea,* a variant name for Joshua.   32:49 Hebrew *the mountains of Abarim.*

giving to the people of Israel as their own possession. ⁵⁰Then you must die there on the mountain and join your ancestors, just as Aaron, your
brother, died on Mount Hor and joined his
ancestors. ⁵¹For both of you broke faith with me
among the Israelites at the waters of Meribah at
Kadesh* in the wilderness of Zin. You failed to
demonstrate my holiness to the people of Israel
there. ⁵²So you will see the land from a distance,
but you may not enter the land I am giving to the
people of Israel."

CHAPTER **33**
Moses Blesses the People
This is the blessing that Moses, the man of God,
gave to the people of Israel before his death:

2   "The LORD came from Mount Sinai
        and dawned upon us* from Mount Seir;
     he shone forth from Mount Paran
        and came from Meribah-kadesh
        with flaming fire at his right hand.*
3   Indeed, you love the people;
        all your holy ones are in your hands.
     They follow in your steps
        and accept your instruction.
4   Moses charged us with the law,
        the special possession of the assembly of
        Israel.*
5   The LORD became king in Israel*—
        when the leaders of the people
        assembled,
        when the tribes of Israel gathered."

⁶Moses said this about the tribe of Reuben:*

    "Let the tribe of Reuben live and not die
        out,
     even though their tribe is small."

⁷Moses said this about the tribe of Judah:

    "O LORD, hear the cry of Judah
        and bring them again to their people.
     Give them strength to defend their cause;
        help them against their enemies!"

⁸Moses said this about the tribe of Levi:

    "O LORD, you have given the sacred lots*
        to your faithful servants the Levites.
     You put them to the test at Massah
        and contended with them at the waters
        of Meribah.

9   The Levites obeyed your word
        and guarded your covenant.
     They were more loyal to you
        than to their parents, relatives, and
        children.
10 Now let them teach your regulations to
        Jacob;
     let them give your instructions to Israel.
     They will present incense before you
        and offer whole burnt offerings on the
        altar.
11 Bless the Levites, O LORD,
        and accept all their work.
     Crush the loins of their enemies;
        strike down their foes so they never rise
        again."

¹²Moses said this about the tribe of Benjamin:

    "The people of Benjamin are loved by the
        LORD
     and live in safety beside him.
     He surrounds them continuously
        and preserves them from every harm."

¹³Moses said this about the tribes of Joseph:

    "May their land be blessed by the LORD
        with the choice gift of rain from the
        heavens,
        and water from beneath the earth;
14 with the riches that grow in the sun,
        and the bounty produced each month;
15 with the finest crops of the ancient
        mountains,
        and the abundance from the everlasting
        hills;
16 with the best gifts of the earth and its
        fullness,
        and the favor of the one who appeared
        in the burning bush.
     May these blessings rest on Joseph's head,
        crowning the brow of the prince among
        his brothers.
17 Joseph has the strength and majesty of a
        young bull;
        his power is like the horns of a wild ox.
     He will gore distant nations,
        driving them to the ends of the earth.
     This is my blessing for the multitudes of
        Ephraim
        and the thousands of Manasseh."

32:51 Hebrew *waters of Meribath-kadesh.*   33:2a As in Greek and Syriac versions; Hebrew reads *upon them.*   33:2b Or *came from myriads of holy ones, from the south, from his mountain slopes.* The meaning of the Hebrew is uncertain.   33:4 Hebrew *of Jacob.*   33:5 Hebrew *in Jeshurun,* a term of endearment for Israel.   33:6 Hebrew lacks *Moses said this about the tribe of Reuben.*   33:8 Hebrew *given your Thummim and Urim.* See Exod 28:30.

18Moses said this about the tribes of Zebulun and Issachar*:

"May the people of Zebulun prosper in
their expeditions abroad.
May the people of Issachar prosper at
home in their tents.
19 They summon the people to the mountain
to offer proper sacrifices there.
They benefit from the riches of the sea
and the hidden treasures of the sand."

20Moses said this about the tribe of Gad:

"Blessed is the one who enlarges Gad's
territory!
Gad is poised there like a lion
to tear off an arm or a head.
21 The people of Gad took the best land for
themselves;
a leader's share was assigned to them.
When the leaders of the people were
assembled,
they carried out the LORD's justice
and obeyed his regulations for Israel."

22Moses said this about the tribe of Dan:

"Dan is a lion's cub,
leaping out from Bashan."

23Moses said this about the tribe of Naphtali:

"O Naphtali, you are rich in favor
and full of the LORD's blessings;
may you possess the west and the south."

24Moses said this about the tribe of Asher:

"May Asher be blessed above other sons;
may he be esteemed by his brothers;
may he bathe his feet in olive oil.
25 May the bolts of your gates be of iron and
bronze;
may your strength match the length of
your days!"

26 "There is no one like the God of Israel.*
He rides across the heavens to help you,
across the skies in majestic splendor.
27 The eternal God is your refuge,
and his everlasting arms are under you.
He thrusts out the enemy before you;
it is he who cries, 'Destroy them!'
28 So Israel will live in safety,

prosperous Jacob in security,
in a land of grain and wine,
while the heavens drop down dew.
29 How blessed you are, O Israel!
Who else is like you, a people saved by
the LORD?
He is your protecting shield
and your triumphant sword!
Your enemies will bow low before you,
and you will trample on their backs!"

CHAPTER **34**
The Death of Moses

Then Moses went to Mount Nebo from the plains of Moab and climbed Pisgah Peak, which is across from Jericho. And the LORD showed him the whole land, from Gilead as far as Dan; 2all the land of Naphtali; the land of Ephraim and Manasseh; all the land of Judah, extending to the Mediterranean Sea*; 3the Negev; the Jordan Valley with Jericho—the city of palms—as far as Zoar. 4Then the LORD said to Moses, "This is the land I promised on oath to Abraham, Isaac, and Jacob, and I told them I would give it to their descendants. I have now allowed you to see it, but you will not enter the land."

5So Moses, the servant of the LORD, died there in the land of Moab, just as the LORD had said. 6He was buried* in a valley near Beth-peor in Moab, but to this day no one knows the exact place. 7Moses was 120 years old when he died, yet his eyesight was clear, and he was as strong as ever. 8The people of Israel mourned thirty days for Moses on the plains of Moab, until the customary period of mourning was over.

9Now Joshua son of Nun was full of the spirit of wisdom, for Moses had laid his hands on him. So the people of Israel obeyed him and did everything just as the LORD had commanded Moses.

10There has never been another prophet like Moses, whom the LORD knew face to face. 11The LORD sent Moses to perform all the miraculous signs and wonders in the land of Egypt against Pharaoh, all his servants, and his entire land. 12And it was through Moses that the LORD demonstrated his mighty power and terrifying acts in the sight of all Israel.

33:18 Hebrew lacks *and Issachar.*   **33:26** Hebrew *of Jeshurun,* a term of endearment for Israel.   **34:2** Hebrew *the western sea.*   **34:6** Hebrew *He buried him,* that is, "The LORD buried him." Samaritan Pentateuch and some Greek manuscripts read *They buried him.*

Joshua

CHAPTER 1

The LORD's Charge to Joshua

After the death of Moses the LORD's servant, the LORD spoke to Joshua son of Nun, Moses' assistant. He said, 2"Now that my servant Moses is dead, you must lead my people across the Jordan River into the land I am giving them. 3I promise you what I promised Moses: 'Everywhere you go, you will be on land I have given you—4from the Negev Desert in the south to the Lebanon mountains in the north, from the Euphrates River on the east to the Mediterranean Sea* on the west, and all the land of the Hittites.' 5No one will be able to stand their ground against you as long as you live. For I will be with you as I was with Moses. I will not fail you or abandon you.

6"Be strong and courageous, for you will lead my people to possess all the land I swore to give their ancestors. 7Be strong and very courageous. Obey all the laws Moses gave you. Do not turn away from them, and you will be successful in everything you do. 8Study this Book of the Law continually. Meditate on it day and night so you may be sure to obey all that is written in it. Only then will you succeed. 9I command you—be strong and courageous! Do not be afraid or discouraged. For the LORD your God is with you wherever you go."

Joshua's Charge to the Israelites

10Joshua then commanded the leaders of Israel, 11"Go through the camp and tell the people to get their provisions ready. In three days you will cross the Jordan River and take possession of the land the LORD your God has given you."

12Then Joshua called together the tribes of Reuben, Gad, and the half-tribe of Manasseh. He told them, 13"Remember what Moses, the servant of the LORD, commanded you: 'The LORD your God is giving you rest and has given you this land.' 14Your wives, children, and cattle may remain here on the east side of the Jordan River, but your warriors, fully armed, must lead the other tribes across the Jordan to help them conquer their territory. Stay with them 15until the LORD gives rest to them as he has given rest to you, and until they, too, possess the land the LORD your God is giving them. Only then may you settle here on the east side of the Jordan River in the land that Moses, the servant of the LORD, gave you."

16They answered Joshua, "We will do whatever you command us, and we will go wherever you send us. 17We will obey you just as we obeyed Moses. And may the LORD your God be with you as he was with Moses. 18Anyone who rebels against your word and does not obey your every command will be put to death. So be strong and courageous!"

CHAPTER 2

Rahab Protects the Spies

Then Joshua secretly sent out two spies from the Israelite camp at Acacia.* He instructed them, "Spy out the land on the other side of the Jordan River, especially around Jericho." So the two men set out and came to the house of a prostitute named Rahab and stayed there that night.

2But someone told the king of Jericho, "Some Israelites have come here tonight to spy out the land." 3So the king of Jericho sent orders to Rahab: "Bring out the men who have come into your house. They are spies sent here to discover the best way to attack us."

4Rahab, who had hidden the two men, replied, "The men were here earlier, but I didn't know where they were from. 5They left the city at dusk,

1:4 Hebrew *the Great Sea.* 2:1 Hebrew *Shittim.*

as the city gates were about to close, and I don't know where they went. If you hurry, you can probably catch up with them." 6(But she had taken them up to the roof and hidden them beneath piles of flax.) 7So the king's men went looking for the spies along the road leading to the shallow crossing places of the Jordan River. And as soon as the king's men had left, the city gate was shut.

8Before the spies went to sleep that night, Rahab went up on the roof to talk with them. 9"I know the LORD has given you this land," she told them. "We are all afraid of you. Everyone is living in terror. 10For we have heard how the LORD made a dry path for you through the Red Sea* when you left Egypt. And we know what you did to Sihon and Og, the two Amorite kings east of the Jordan River, whose people you completely destroyed.* 11No wonder our hearts have melted in fear! No one has the courage to fight after hearing such things. For the LORD your God is the supreme God of the heavens above and the earth below. 12Now swear to me by the LORD that you will be kind to me and my family since I have helped you. Give me some guarantee that 13when Jericho is conquered, you will let me live, along with my father and mother, my brothers and sisters, and all their families."

14"We offer our own lives as a guarantee for your safety," the men agreed. "If you don't betray us, we will keep our promise when the LORD gives us the land."

15Then, since Rahab's house was built into the city wall, she let them down by a rope through the window. 16"Escape to the hill country," she told them. "Hide there for three days until the men who are searching for you have returned; then go on your way."

17Before they left, the men told her, "We can guarantee your safety 18only if you leave this scarlet rope hanging from the window. And all your family members—your father, mother, brothers, and all your relatives—must be here inside the house. 19If they go out into the street, they will be killed, and we cannot be held to our oath. But we swear that no one inside this house will be killed—not a hand will be laid on any of them. 20If you betray us, however, we are not bound by this oath in any way."

21"I accept your terms," she replied. And she sent them on their way, leaving the scarlet rope hanging from the window.

22The spies went up into the hill country and stayed there three days. The men who were chasing them had searched everywhere along the road, but they finally returned to the city without success. 23Then the two spies came down from the hill country, crossed the Jordan River, and reported to Joshua all that had happened to them. 24"The LORD will certainly give us the whole land," they said, "for all the people in the land are terrified of us."

CHAPTER 3

The Israelites Cross the Jordan

Early the next morning Joshua and all the Israelites left Acacia* and arrived at the banks of the Jordan River, where they camped before crossing. 2Three days later, the Israelite leaders went through the camp 3giving these instructions to the people: "When you see the Levitical priests carrying the Ark of the Covenant of the LORD your God, follow them. 4Since you have never traveled this way before, they will guide you. Stay about a half mile* behind them, keeping a clear distance between you and the Ark. Make sure you don't come any closer."

5Then Joshua told the people, "Purify yourselves, for tomorrow the LORD will do great wonders among you."

6In the morning Joshua said to the priests, "Lift up the Ark of the Covenant and lead the people across the river." And so they started out.

7The LORD told Joshua, "Today I will begin to make you great in the eyes of all the Israelites. Now they will know that I am with you, just as I was with Moses. 8Give these instructions to the priests who are carrying the Ark of the Covenant: 'When you reach the banks of the Jordan River, take a few steps into the river and stop.'"

9So Joshua told the Israelites, "Come and listen to what the LORD your God says. 10Today you will know that the living God is among you. He will surely drive out the Canaanites, Hittites, Hivites, Perizzites, Girgashites, Amorites, and Jebusites. 11Think of it! The Ark of the Covenant, which belongs to the Lord of the whole earth, will lead you across the Jordan River! 12Now choose twelve men, one from each tribe. 13The priests will be carrying the Ark of the LORD, the Lord of all the earth. When their feet touch the water, the flow of water will be cut off upstream, and the river will pile up there in one heap."

14When the people set out to cross the Jordan, the priests who were carrying the Ark of the Covenant went ahead of them. 15Now it was the harvest season, and the Jordan was overflowing

2:10a Hebrew *sea of reeds.*   2:10b The Hebrew term used here refers to the complete consecration of things or people to the LORD, either by destroying them or by giving them as an offering.   3:1 Hebrew *Shittim.*   3:4 Hebrew *about 2,000 cubits* [900 meters].

its banks. But as soon as the feet of the priests who were carrying the Ark touched the water at the river's edge, 16the water began piling up at a town upstream called Adam, which is near Zarethan. And the water below that point flowed on to the Dead Sea* until the riverbed was dry. Then all the people crossed over near the city of Jericho. 17Meanwhile, the priests who were carrying the Ark of the LORD's covenant stood on dry ground in the middle of the riverbed as the people passed by them. They waited there until everyone had crossed the Jordan on dry ground.

CHAPTER 4
Memorials to the Jordan Crossing

When all the people were safely across the river, the LORD said to Joshua, 2"Now choose twelve men, one from each tribe. 3Tell the men to take twelve stones from where the priests are standing in the middle of the Jordan and pile them up at the place where you camp tonight."

4So Joshua called together the twelve men 5and told them, "Go into the middle of the Jordan, in front of the Ark of the LORD your God. Each of you must pick up one stone and carry it out on your shoulder—twelve stones in all, one for each of the twelve tribes. 6We will use these stones to build a memorial. In the future, your children will ask, 'What do these stones mean to you?' 7Then you can tell them, 'They remind us that the Jordan River stopped flowing when the Ark of the LORD's covenant went across.' These stones will stand as a permanent memorial among the people of Israel."

8So the men did as Joshua told them. They took twelve stones from the middle of the Jordan River, one for each tribe, just as the LORD had commanded Joshua. They carried them to the place where they camped for the night and constructed the memorial there.

9Joshua also built another memorial of twelve stones in the middle of the Jordan, at the place where the priests who carried the Ark of the Covenant were standing. The memorial remains there to this day.

10The priests who were carrying the Ark stood in the middle of the river until all of the LORD's instructions, which Moses had given to Joshua, were carried out. Meanwhile, the people hurried across the riverbed. 11And when everyone was on the other side, the priests crossed over with the Ark of the LORD. 12The armed warriors from the tribes of Reuben, Gad, and the half-tribe of Manasseh led the Israelites across the Jordan, just as Moses had directed. 13These warriors—about forty thousand strong—were ready for battle, and they crossed over to the plains of Jericho in the LORD's presence.

14That day the LORD made Joshua great in the eyes of all the Israelites, and for the rest of his life they revered him as much as they had revered Moses.

15The LORD had said to Joshua, 16"Command the priests carrying the Ark of the Covenant* to come up out of the riverbed." 17So Joshua gave the command. 18And as soon as the priests carrying the Ark of the LORD's covenant came up out of the riverbed, the Jordan River flooded its banks as before.

19The people crossed the Jordan on the tenth day of the first month—the month that marked their exodus from Egypt.* They camped at Gilgal, east of Jericho. 20It was there at Gilgal that Joshua piled up the twelve stones taken from the Jordan River. 21Then Joshua said to the Israelites, "In the future, your children will ask, 'What do these stones mean?' 22Then you can tell them, 'This is where the Israelites crossed the Jordan on dry ground.' 23For the LORD your God dried up the river right before your eyes, and he kept it dry until you were all across, just as he did at the Red Sea* when he dried it up until we had all crossed over. 24He did this so that all the nations of the earth might know the power of the LORD, and that you might fear the LORD your God forever."

CHAPTER 5

When all the Amorite kings west of the Jordan and all the Canaanite kings who lived along the Mediterranean coast* heard how the LORD had dried up the Jordan River so the people of Israel could cross, they lost heart and were paralyzed with fear.

Israel Reestablishes Covenant Ceremonies

2At that time the LORD told Joshua, "Use knives of flint to make the Israelites a circumcised people again." 3So Joshua made flint knives and circumcised the entire male population of Israel at Gibeath-haaraloth.* 4Joshua had to circumcise them because all the men who were old enough to bear arms

---

3:16 Hebrew *the sea of the Arabah, the Salt Sea.* 4:16 Hebrew *Ark of the Testimony.* 4:19 Hebrew *the tenth day of the first month.* This day of the Hebrew lunar calendar occurs in late March or early April. 4:23 Hebrew *sea of reeds.* 5:1 Hebrew *along the sea.* 5:3 *Gibeath-haaraloth* means "hill of foreskins."

when they left Egypt had died in the wilderness. ⁵Those who left Egypt had all been circumcised, but none of those born after the Exodus, during the years in the wilderness, had been circumcised. ⁶The Israelites wandered in the wilderness for forty years until all the men who were old enough to bear arms when they left Egypt had died. For they had disobeyed the LORD, and the LORD vowed he would not let them enter the land he had sworn to give us—a land flowing with milk and honey. ⁷So Joshua circumcised their sons who had not been circumcised on the way to the Promised Land—those who had grown up to take their fathers' places. ⁸After all the males had been circumcised, they rested in the camp until they were healed.

⁹Then the LORD said to Joshua, "Today I have rolled away the shame of your slavery in Egypt." So that place has been called Gilgal* to this day.

¹⁰While the Israelites were camped at Gilgal on the plains of Jericho, they celebrated Passover on the evening of the fourteenth day of the first month—the month that marked their exodus from Egypt.* ¹¹The very next day they began to eat unleavened bread and roasted grain harvested from the land. ¹²No manna appeared that day, and it was never seen again. So from that time on the Israelites ate from the crops of Canaan.

The LORD's Commander Confronts Joshua

¹³As Joshua approached the city of Jericho, he looked up and saw a man facing him with sword in hand. Joshua went up to him and asked, "Are you friend or foe?"

¹⁴"Neither one," he replied. "I am commander of the LORD's army."

At this, Joshua fell with his face to the ground in reverence. "I am at your command," Joshua said. "What do you want your servant to do?"

¹⁵The commander of the LORD's army replied, "Take off your sandals, for this is holy ground." And Joshua did as he was told.

CHAPTER **6**
The Fall of Jericho

Now the gates of Jericho were tightly shut because the people were afraid of the Israelites. No one was allowed to go in or out. ²But the LORD said to Joshua, "I have given you Jericho, its king, and all its mighty warriors. ³Your entire army is to march around the city once a day for six days. ⁴Seven priests will walk ahead of the Ark, each carrying a ram's horn. On the seventh day you are to march around the city seven times, with the priests blowing the horns. ⁵When you hear the priests give one long blast on the horns, have all the people give a mighty shout. Then the walls of the city will collapse, and the people can charge straight into the city."

⁶So Joshua called together the priests and said, "Take up the Ark of the Covenant, and assign seven priests to walk in front of it, each carrying a ram's horn." ⁷Then he gave orders to the people: "March around the city, and the armed men will lead the way in front of the Ark of the LORD."

⁸After Joshua spoke to the people, the seven priests with the rams' horns started marching in the presence of the LORD, blowing the horns as they marched. And the priests carrying the Ark of the LORD's covenant followed behind them. ⁹Armed guards marched both in front of the priests and behind the Ark, with the priests continually blowing the horns. ¹⁰"Do not shout; do not even talk," Joshua commanded. "Not a single word from any of you until I tell you to shout. Then shout!" ¹¹So the Ark of the LORD was carried around the city once that day, and then everyone returned to spend the night in the camp.

¹²Joshua got up early the next morning, and the priests again carried the Ark of the LORD. ¹³The seven priests with the rams' horns marched in front of the Ark of the LORD, blowing their horns. Armed guards marched both in front of the priests with the horns and behind the Ark of the LORD. All this time the priests were sounding their horns. ¹⁴On the second day they marched around the city once and returned to the camp. They followed this pattern for six days.

¹⁵On the seventh day the Israelites got up at dawn and marched around the city as they had done before. But this time they went around the city seven times. ¹⁶The seventh time around, as the priests sounded the long blast on their horns, Joshua commanded the people, "Shout! For the LORD has given you the city! ¹⁷The city and everything in it must be completely destroyed* as an offering to the LORD. Only Rahab the prostitute and the others in her house will be spared, for she protected our spies. ¹⁸Do not take any of the things set apart for destruction, or you yourselves will be completely destroyed, and you will bring trouble on all Israel. ¹⁹Everything made from silver, gold, bronze, or iron is

5:9 *Gilgal* sounds like the Hebrew word *galal*, meaning "to roll."   5:10 Hebrew *the fourteenth day of the first month.* This day of the Hebrew lunar calendar occurs in late March or early April.   6:17 The Hebrew term used here refers to the complete consecration of things or people to the LORD, either by destroying them or by giving them as an offering; also in 6:18, 21.

sacred to the LORD and must be brought into his treasury."

20When the people heard the sound of the horns, they shouted as loud as they could. Suddenly, the walls of Jericho collapsed, and the Israelites charged straight into the city from every side and captured it. 21They completely destroyed everything in it—men and women, young and old, cattle, sheep, donkeys—everything.

22Then Joshua said to the two spies, "Keep your promise. Go to the prostitute's house and bring her out, along with all her family."

23The young men went in and brought out Rahab, her father, mother, brothers, and all the other relatives who were with her. They moved her whole family to a safe place near the camp of Israel.

24Then the Israelites burned the city and everything in it. Only the things made from silver, gold, bronze, or iron were kept for the treasury of the LORD's house. 25So Joshua spared Rahab the prostitute and her relatives who were with her in the house, because she had hidden the spies Joshua sent to Jericho. And she lives among the Israelites to this day.

26At that time Joshua invoked this curse:

"May the curse of the LORD fall on anyone
    who tries to rebuild the city of Jericho.
At the cost of his firstborn son,
    he will lay its foundation.
At the cost of his youngest son,
    he will set up its gates."

27So the LORD was with Joshua, and his name became famous throughout the land.

CHAPTER 7

Ai Defeats the Israelites

But Israel was unfaithful concerning the things set apart for the LORD.* A man named Achan had stolen some of these things, so the LORD was very angry with the Israelites. Achan was the son of Carmi, of the family of Zimri,* of the clan of Zerah, and of the tribe of Judah.

2Joshua sent some of his men from Jericho to spy out the city of Ai, east of Bethel, near Bethaven. 3When they returned, they told Joshua, "It's a small town, and it won't take more than two or three thousand of us to destroy it. There's no need for all of us to go there."

4So approximately three thousand warriors were sent, but they were soundly defeated. The

men of Ai 5chased the Israelites from the city gate as far as the quarries,* and they killed about thirty-six who were retreating down the slope. The Israelites were paralyzed with fear at this turn of events, and their courage melted away.

6Joshua and the leaders of Israel tore their clothing in dismay, threw dust on their heads, and bowed down facing the Ark of the LORD until evening. 7Then Joshua cried out, "Sovereign LORD, why did you bring us across the Jordan River if you are going to let the Amorites kill us? If only we had been content to stay on the other side! 8Lord, what am I to say, now that Israel has fled from its enemies? 9For when the Canaanites and all the other people living in the land hear about it, they will surround us and wipe us off the face of the earth. And then what will happen to the honor of your great name?"

10But the LORD said to Joshua, "Get up! Why are you lying on your face like this? 11Israel has sinned and broken my covenant! They have stolen the things that I commanded to be set apart for me. And they have not only stolen them; they have also lied about it and hidden the things among their belongings. 12That is why the Israelites are running from their enemies in defeat. For now Israel has been set apart for destruction. I will not remain with you any longer unless you destroy the things among you that were set apart for destruction.

13"Get up! Command the people to purify themselves in preparation for tomorrow. For this is what the LORD, the God of Israel, says: Hidden among you, O Israel, are things set apart for the LORD. You will never defeat your enemies until you remove these things. 14In the morning you must present yourselves by tribes, and the LORD will point out the tribe to which the guilty man belongs. That tribe must come forward with its clans, and the LORD will point out the guilty clan. That clan will then come forward, and the LORD will point out the guilty family. Finally, each member of the guilty family must come one by one. 15The one who has stolen what was set apart for destruction will himself be burned with fire, along with everything he has, for he has broken the covenant of the LORD and has done a horrible thing in Israel."

Achan's Sin

16Early the next morning Joshua brought the tribes of Israel before the LORD, and the tribe of Judah was singled out. 17Then the clans of Judah

7:1a The Hebrew term used here refers to the complete consecration of things or people to the LORD, either by destroying them or by giving them as an offering; also in 7:11, 12, 13, 15. 7:1b As in Greek version (see also 1 Chr 2:6); Hebrew reads *Zabdi*. Also in 7:17, 18. 7:5 Or *as far as Shebarim*.

came forward, and the clan of Zerah was singled out. Then the families of Zerah came before the LORD, and the family of Zimri was singled out. 18Every member of Zimri's family was brought forward person by person, and Achan was singled out.

19Then Joshua said to Achan, "My son, give glory to the LORD, the God of Israel, by telling the truth. Make your confession and tell me what you have done. Don't hide it from me."

20Achan replied, "I have sinned against the LORD, the God of Israel. 21For I saw a beautiful robe imported from Babylon,* two hundred silver coins,* and a bar of gold weighing more than a pound.* I wanted them so much that I took them. They are hidden in the ground beneath my tent, with the silver buried deeper than the rest."

22So Joshua sent some men to make a search. They ran to the tent and found the stolen goods hidden there, just as Achan had said, with the silver buried beneath the rest. 23They took the things from the tent and brought them to Joshua and all the Israelites. Then they laid them on the ground in the presence of the LORD.

24Then Joshua and all the Israelites took Achan, the silver, the robe, the bar of gold, his sons, daughters, cattle, donkeys, sheep, tent, and everything he had, and they brought them to the valley of Achor. 25Then Joshua said to Achan, "Why have you brought trouble on us? The LORD will now bring trouble on you." And all the Israelites stoned Achan and his family and burned their bodies. 26They piled a great heap of stones over Achan, which remains to this day. That is why the place has been called the Valley of Trouble* ever since. So the LORD was no longer angry.

CHAPTER **8**

The Israelites Defeat Ai

Then the LORD said to Joshua, "Do not be afraid or discouraged. Take the entire army and attack Ai, for I have given to you the king of Ai, his people, his city, and his land. 2You will destroy them as you destroyed Jericho and its king. But this time you may keep the captured goods and the cattle for yourselves. Set an ambush behind the city."

3So Joshua and the army of Israel set out to attack Ai. Joshua chose thirty thousand fighting men and sent them out at night 4with these orders: "Hide in ambush close behind the city

and be ready for action. 5When our main army attacks, the men of Ai will come out to fight as they did before, and we will run away from them. 6We will let them chase us until they have all left the city. For they will say, 'The Israelites are running away from us as they did before.' 7Then you will jump up from your ambush and take possession of the city, for the LORD your God will give it to you. 8Set the city on fire, as the LORD has commanded. You have your orders."

9So they left that night and lay in ambush between Bethel and the west side of Ai. But Joshua remained among the people in the camp that night. 10Early the next morning Joshua roused his men and started toward Ai, accompanied by the leaders of Israel. 11They camped on the north side of Ai, with a valley between them and the city. 12That night Joshua sent five thousand men to lie in ambush between Bethel and Ai, on the west side of the city. 13So they stationed the main army north of the city and the ambush west of the city. Joshua himself spent that night in the valley.

14When the king of Ai saw the Israelites across the valley, he and all his army hurriedly went out early the next morning and attacked the Israelites at a place overlooking the Jordan Valley.* But he didn't realize there was an ambush behind the city. 15Joshua and the Israelite army fled toward the wilderness as though they were badly beaten, 16and all the men in the city were called out to chase after them. In this way, they were lured away from the city. 17There was not a man left in Ai or Bethel* who did not chase after the Israelites, and the city was left wide open.

18Then the LORD said to Joshua, "Point your spear toward Ai, for I will give you the city." Joshua did as he was commanded. 19As soon as Joshua gave the signal, the men in ambush jumped up and poured into the city. They quickly captured it and set it on fire.

20When the men of Ai looked behind them, smoke from the city was filling the sky, and they had nowhere to go. For the Israelites who had fled in the direction of the wilderness now turned on their pursuers. 21When Joshua and the other Israelites saw that the ambush had succeeded and that smoke was rising from the city, they turned and attacked the men of Ai. 22Then the Israelites who were inside the city came out and started killing the enemy from the rear. So the men of Ai were caught in a trap, and all of them died. Not a single person survived or es-

---

7:21a Hebrew *Shinar.*   7:21b Hebrew *200 shekels of silver,* about 5 pounds or 2.3 kilograms in weight.   7:21c Hebrew *50 shekels,* about 20 ounces or 570 grams in weight.   7:26 Hebrew *valley of Achor.*   8:14 Hebrew *the Arabah.*   8:17 Some manuscripts lack *or Bethel.*

caped. ²³Only the king of Ai was taken alive and brought to Joshua.

²⁴When the Israelite army finished killing all the men outside the city, they went back and finished off everyone inside. ²⁵So the entire population of Ai was wiped out that day—twelve thousand in all. ²⁶For Joshua kept holding out his spear until everyone who had lived in Ai was completely destroyed.* ²⁷Only the cattle and the treasures of the city were not destroyed, for the Israelites kept these for themselves, as the LORD had commanded Joshua. ²⁸So Ai* became a permanent mound of ruins, desolate to this very day.

²⁹Joshua hung the king of Ai on a tree and left him there until evening. At sunset the Israelites took down the body and threw it in front of the city gate. They piled a great heap of stones over him that can still be seen today.

The LORD's Covenant Renewed

³⁰Then Joshua built an altar to the LORD, the God of Israel, on Mount Ebal. ³¹He followed the instructions that Moses the LORD's servant had written in the Book of the Law: "Make me an altar from stones that are uncut and have not been shaped with iron tools." Then on the altar they presented burnt offerings and peace offerings to the LORD. ³²And as the Israelites watched, Joshua copied the law of Moses onto the stones of the altar.*

³³Then all the Israelites—foreigners and citizens alike—along with the leaders, officers, and judges, were divided into two groups. One group stood at the foot of Mount Gerizim, the other at the foot of Mount Ebal. Each group faced the other, and between them stood the Levitical priests carrying the Ark of the LORD's covenant. This was all done according to the instructions Moses, the servant of the LORD, had given for blessing the people of Israel.

³⁴Joshua then read to them all the blessings and curses Moses had written in the Book of the Law. ³⁵Every command Moses had ever given was read to the entire assembly, including the women and children and the foreigners who lived among the Israelites.

CHAPTER **9**

The Gibeonites Deceive Israel

Now all the kings west of the Jordan heard about what had happened. (These were the kings of the Hittites, Amorites, Canaanites, Perizzites,

Hivites, and Jebusites, who lived in the hill country, in the western foothills,* and along the coast of the Mediterranean Sea* as far north as the Lebanon mountains.) ²These kings quickly combined their armies to fight against Joshua and the Israelites.

³But when the people of Gibeon heard what had happened to Jericho and Ai, ⁴they resorted to deception to save themselves. They sent ambassadors to Joshua, loading their donkeys with weathered saddlebags and old patched wineskins. ⁵They put on ragged clothes and worn-out, patched sandals. And they took along dry, moldy bread for provisions. ⁶When they arrived at the camp of Israel at Gilgal, they told Joshua and the men of Israel, "We have come from a distant land to ask you to make a peace treaty with us."

⁷The Israelites replied to these Hivites, "How do we know you don't live nearby? For if you do, we cannot make a treaty with you."

⁸They replied, "We will be your servants."

"But who are you?" Joshua demanded. "Where do you come from?"

⁹They answered, "We are from a very distant country. We have heard of the might of the LORD your God and of all he did in Egypt. ¹⁰We have also heard what he did to the two Amorite kings east of the Jordan River—King Sihon of Heshbon and King Og of Bashan (who lived in Ashtaroth). ¹¹So our leaders and our people instructed us, 'Prepare for a long journey. Go meet with the people of Israel and declare our people to be their servants, and ask for peace.'

¹²"This bread was hot from the ovens when we left. But now, as you can see, it is dry and moldy. ¹³These wineskins were new when we filled them, but now they are old and cracked. And our clothing and sandals are worn out from our long, hard trip."

¹⁴So the Israelite leaders examined their bread, but they did not consult the LORD. ¹⁵Then Joshua went ahead and signed a peace treaty with them, and the leaders of Israel ratified their agreement with a binding oath.

¹⁶Three days later, the facts came out—these people of Gibeon lived nearby! ¹⁷The Israelites set out at once to investigate and reached their towns in three days. The names of these towns were Gibeon, Kephirah, Beeroth, and Kiriath-jearim. ¹⁸But the Israelites did not attack the towns, for their leaders had made a vow to the LORD, the God of Israel.

The people of Israel grumbled against their

8:26 The Hebrew term used here refers to the complete consecration of things or people to the LORD, either by destroying them or by giving them as an offering. **8:28** Ai means "ruin." **8:32** Or *onto stones.* **9:1a** Hebrew *the Shephelah.* **9:1b** Hebrew *the Great Sea.*

leaders because of the treaty. 19But the leaders replied, "We have sworn an oath in the presence of the LORD, the God of Israel. We cannot touch them. 20We must let them live, for God would be angry with us if we broke our oath. 21Let them live. But we will make them chop the wood and carry the water for the entire community."

So the Israelites kept their promise to the Gibeonites. 22But Joshua called together the Gibeonite leaders and said, "Why did you lie to us? Why did you say that you live in a distant land when you live right here among us? 23May you be cursed! From now on you will chop wood and carry water for the house of my God."

24They replied, "We did it because we were told that the LORD your God instructed his servant Moses to conquer this entire land and destroy all the people living in it. So we feared for our lives because of you. That is why we have done it. 25Now we are at your mercy—do whatever you think is right."

26Joshua did not allow the people of Israel to kill them. 27But that day he made the Gibeonites the woodchoppers and water carriers for the people of Israel and for the altar of the LORD—wherever the LORD would choose to build it. That arrangement continues to this day.

CHAPTER **10**
Israel Defeats the Southern Kings
Now Adoni-zedek, king of Jerusalem, heard that Joshua had captured and completely destroyed* Ai and killed its king, just as he had destroyed the city of Jericho and killed its king. He also learned that the Gibeonites had made peace with Israel and were now their allies. 2He and his people became very afraid when they heard all this because Gibeon was a large city—as large as the royal cities and larger than Ai. And the Gibeonite men were mighty warriors. 3So King Adoni-zedek of Jerusalem sent messengers to several other kings: Hoham of Hebron, Piram of Jarmuth, Japhia of Lachish, and Debir of Eglon. 4"Come and help me destroy Gibeon," he urged them, "for they have made peace with Joshua and the people of Israel."

5So these five Amorite kings combined their armies for a united attack. They moved all their troops into place and attacked Gibeon.

6The men of Gibeon quickly sent messengers to Joshua at Gilgal, "Don't abandon your servants now!" they pleaded. "Come quickly and save us! For all the Amorite kings who live in the hill country have come out against us with their armies."

7So Joshua and the entire Israelite army left Gilgal and set out to rescue Gibeon. 8"Do not be afraid of them," the LORD said to Joshua, "for I will give you victory over them. Not a single one of them will be able to stand up to you."

9Joshua traveled all night from Gilgal and took the Amorite armies by surprise. 10The LORD threw them into a panic, and the Israelites slaughtered them in great numbers at Gibeon. Then the Israelites chased the enemy along the road to Beth-horon and attacked them at Azekah and Makkedah, killing them along the way. 11As the Amorites retreated down the road from Beth-horon, the LORD destroyed them with a terrible hailstorm that continued until they reached Azekah. The hail killed more of the enemy than the Israelites killed with the sword.

12On the day the LORD gave the Israelites victory over the Amorites, Joshua prayed to the LORD in front of all the people of Israel. He said,

"Let the sun stand still over Gibeon,
    and the moon over the valley of Aijalon."

13So the sun and moon stood still until the Israelites had defeated their enemies.

Is this event not recorded in *The Book of Jashar*? The sun stopped in the middle of the sky, and it did not set as on a normal day. 14The LORD fought for Israel that day. Never before or since has there been a day like that one, when the LORD answered such a request from a human being.

15Then Joshua and the Israelite army returned to their camp at Gilgal.

Joshua Kills the Five Southern Kings
16During the battle, the five kings escaped and hid in a cave at Makkedah. 17When Joshua heard that they had been found, 18he issued this command: "Cover the opening of the cave with large rocks and place guards at the entrance to keep the kings inside. 19The rest of you continue chasing the enemy and cut them down from the rear. Don't let them get back to their cities, for the LORD your God has given you victory over them."

20So Joshua and the Israelite army continued the slaughter and wiped out the five armies except for a tiny remnant that managed to reach their fortified cities. 21Then the Israelites returned safely to their camp at Makkedah. After that, no one dared to speak a word against Israel.

10:1 The Hebrew term used here refers to the complete consecration of things or people to the LORD, either by destroying them or by giving them as an offering; also in 10:28, 35, 37, 39, 40. **10:13** Or *The Book of the Upright*.

²²Then Joshua said, "Remove the rocks covering the opening of the cave and bring the five kings to me." ²³So they brought the five kings out of the cave—the kings of Jerusalem, Hebron, Jarmuth, Lachish, and Eglon. ²⁴Joshua told the captains of his army, "Come and put your feet on the kings' necks." And they did as they were told. ²⁵"Don't ever be afraid or discouraged," Joshua told his men. "Be strong and courageous, for the LORD is going to do this to all of your enemies." ²⁶Then Joshua killed each of the five kings and hung them on five trees until evening.

²⁷As the sun was going down, Joshua gave instructions for the bodies of the kings to be taken down from the trees and thrown into the cave where they had been hiding. Then they covered the opening of the cave with a large pile of stones, which remains to this very day.

Israel Destroys the Southern Cities
²⁸That same day Joshua completely destroyed the city of Makkedah, killing everyone in it, including the king. Not one person in the city was left alive. He killed the king of Makkedah as he had killed the king of Jericho. ²⁹Then Joshua and the Israelites went to Libnah and attacked it. ³⁰There, too, the LORD gave them the city and its king. They slaughtered everyone in the city and left no survivors. Then Joshua killed the king of Libnah just as he had killed the king of Jericho.

³¹From Libnah, Joshua and the Israelites went to Lachish and attacked it. ³²And the LORD gave it to them on the second day. Here, too, the entire population was slaughtered, just as at Libnah. ³³During the attack on Lachish, King Horam of Gezer had arrived with his army to help defend the city. But Joshua's men killed him and destroyed his entire army.

³⁴Then Joshua and the Israelite army went to Eglon and attacked it. ³⁵They captured it in one day, and as at Lachish, they completely destroyed everyone in the city. ³⁶After leaving Eglon, they attacked Hebron, ³⁷capturing it and all of its surrounding towns. And just as they had done at Eglon, they completely destroyed the entire population. Not one person was left alive. ³⁸Then they turned back and attacked Debir. ³⁹They captured the city, its king, and all of its surrounding villages. And they killed everyone in it, leaving no survivors. They completely destroyed Debir just as they had destroyed Libnah and Hebron.

⁴⁰So Joshua conquered the whole region—

the kings and people of the hill country, the Negev, the western foothills,* and the mountain slopes. He completely destroyed everyone in the land, leaving no survivors, just as the LORD, the God of Israel, had commanded. ⁴¹Joshua slaughtered them from Kadesh-barnea to Gaza and from Goshen to Gibeon. ⁴²In a single campaign Joshua conquered all these kings and their land, for the LORD, the God of Israel, was fighting for his people. ⁴³Then Joshua and the Israelite army returned to their camp at Gilgal.

CHAPTER **11**
Israel Defeats the Northern Kings
When King Jabin of Hazor heard what had happened, he sent urgent messages to the following kings: King Jobab of Madon; the king of Shimron; the king of Acshaph; ²all the kings of the northern hill country; the kings in the Jordan Valley* south of Galilee*; the kings in the western foothills*; the kings of Naphoth-dor on the west; ³the kings of Canaan, both east and west; the kings of the Amorites; the kings of the Hittites; the kings of the Perizzites; the kings in the Jebusite hill country; and the Hivites in the towns on the slopes of Mount Hermon, in the land of Mizpah.

⁴All these kings responded by mobilizing their warriors and uniting to fight against Israel. Their combined armies, along with a vast array of horses and chariots, covered the landscape like the sand on the seashore. ⁵They established their camp around the water near Merom to fight against Israel.

⁶Then the LORD said to Joshua, "Do not be afraid of them. By this time tomorrow they will all be dead. Cripple their horses and burn their chariots."

⁷So Joshua and his warriors traveled to the water near Merom and attacked suddenly. ⁸And the LORD gave them victory over their enemies. The Israelites chased them as far as Great Sidon and Misrephoth-maim, and eastward into the valley of Mizpah, until not one enemy warrior was left alive. ⁹Then Joshua crippled the horses and burned all the chariots, as the LORD had instructed.

¹⁰Joshua then turned back and captured Hazor and killed its king. (Hazor had at one time been the capital of the federation of all these kingdoms.) ¹¹The Israelites completely destroyed* every living thing in the city. Not a

10:40 Hebrew *the Shephelah.* 11:2a Hebrew *the Arabah;* also in 11:16. 11:2b Hebrew *of Kinnereth.* 11:2c Hebrew *the Shephelah;* also in 11:16. 11:11 The Hebrew term used here refers to the complete consecration of things or people to the LORD, either by destroying them or by giving them as an offering; also in 11:12, 20, 21.

single person was spared. And then Joshua burned the city.

¹²Joshua slaughtered all the other kings and their people, completely destroying them, just as Moses, the servant of the LORD, had commanded. ¹³However, Joshua did not burn any of the cities built on mounds except Hazor. ¹⁴And the Israelites took all the captured goods and cattle of the ravaged cities for themselves, but they killed all the people. ¹⁵As the LORD had commanded his servant Moses, so Moses commanded Joshua. And Joshua did as he was told, carefully obeying all of the LORD's instructions to Moses.

¹⁶So Joshua conquered the entire region—the hill country, the Negev, the land of Goshen, the western foothills, the Jordan Valley, and the mountains and lowlands of Israel. ¹⁷The Israelite territory now extended all the way from Mount Halak, which leads up to Seir, to Baal-gad at the foot of Mount Hermon in the valley of Lebanon. Joshua killed all the kings of those territories, ¹⁸waging war for a long time to accomplish this. ¹⁹No one in this region made peace with the Israelites except the Hivites of Gibeon. All the others were defeated. ²⁰For the LORD hardened their hearts and caused them to fight the Israelites instead of asking for peace. So they were completely and mercilessly destroyed, as the LORD had commanded Moses.

²¹During this period, Joshua destroyed all the descendants of Anak, who lived in the hill country of Hebron, Debir, Anab, and the entire hill country of Judah and Israel. He killed them all and completely destroyed their towns. ²²Not one was left in all the land of Israel, though some still remained in Gaza, Gath, and Ashdod. ²³So Joshua took control of the entire land, just as the LORD had instructed Moses. He gave it to the people of Israel as their special possession, dividing the land among the tribes. So the land finally had rest from war.

CHAPTER **12**
Kings Defeated East of the Jordan
These are the kings east of the Jordan River who had been killed and whose land was taken. Their territory extended from the Arnon Gorge to Mount Hermon and included all the land east of the Jordan Valley.*

²King Sihon of the Amorites, who lived in Heshbon, was defeated. His kingdom included Aroer, on the edge of the Arnon Gorge, and extended from the middle of the Arnon Gorge to the Jabbok River, which serves as a boundary for the Ammonites. This territory included half of the present area of Gilead, which lies north of the Jabbok River. ³Sihon also controlled the Jordan Valley as far north as the western shores of the Sea of Galilee* and as far south as the Dead Sea,* from Beth-jeshimoth to the slopes of Pisgah.

⁴King Og of Bashan, the last of the Rephaites, lived at Ashtaroth and Edrei. ⁵He ruled a territory stretching from Mount Hermon to Salecah in the north and to all of Bashan in the east, and westward to the boundaries of the kingdoms of Geshur and Maacah. His kingdom included the northern half of Gilead, the other portion of which was in the territory of King Sihon of Heshbon. ⁶Moses, the servant of the LORD, and the Israelites had destroyed the people of King Sihon and King Og. And Moses gave their land to the tribes of Reuben, Gad, and the half-tribe of Manasseh.

Kings Defeated West of the Jordan
⁷The following is a list of the kings Joshua and the Israelite armies defeated on the west side of the Jordan, from Baal-gad in the valley of Lebanon to Mount Halak, which leads up to Seir. (Joshua allotted this land to the tribes of Israel as their inheritance, ⁸including the hill country, the western foothills,* the Jordan Valley, the mountain slopes, the Judean wilderness, and the Negev. The people who lived in this region were the Hittites, the Amorites, the Canaanites, the Perizzites, the Hivites, and the Jebusites.) These are the kings Israel defeated:

⁹ The king of Jericho
The king of Ai, near Bethel
¹⁰ The king of Jerusalem
The king of Hebron
¹¹ The king of Jarmuth
The king of Lachish
¹² The king of Eglon
The king of Gezer
¹³ The king of Debir
The king of Geder
¹⁴ The king of Hormah
The king of Arad
¹⁵ The king of Libnah
The king of Adullam
¹⁶ The king of Makkedah
The king of Bethel
¹⁷ The king of Tappuah
The king of Hepher
¹⁸ The king of Aphek
The king of Lasharon

12:1 Hebrew *the Arabah;* also in 12:3, 8.   12:3a Hebrew *sea of Kinnereth.*   12:3b Hebrew *the sea of the Arabah, the Salt Sea.*   12:8 Hebrew *the Shephelah.*

19 The king of Madon
  The king of Hazor
20 The king of Shimron-meron
  The king of Acshaph
21 The king of Taanach
  The king of Megiddo
22 The king of Kedesh
  The king of Jokneam in Carmel
23 The king of Dor in the city of Naphoth-dor*
  The king of Goyim in Gilgal*
24 The king of Tirzah.

In all, thirty-one kings and their cities were destroyed.

CHAPTER **13**

The Land Yet to Be Conquered

When Joshua was an old man, the LORD said to him, "You are growing old, and much land remains to be conquered. 2The people still need to occupy the land of the Philistines and the Geshurites—3territory that belongs to the Canaanites. This land extends from the stream of Shihor, which is on the boundary of Egypt, northward to the boundary of Ekron, 4and includes the five Philistine cities of Gaza, Ashdod, Ashkelon, Gath, and Ekron. The land of the Avvites in the south also remains to be conquered. In the north, this area has not yet been conquered: all the land of the Canaanites, including Mearah (which belongs to the Sidonians), stretching northward to Aphek on the border of the Amorites; 5the land of the Gebalites and all of the Lebanon mountain area to the east, from Baal-gad beneath Mount Hermon to Lebo-hamath; 6and all the hill country from Lebanon to Misrephoth-maim, including all the land of the Sidonians.

"I will drive these people out of the land for the Israelites. So be sure to give this land to Israel as a special possession, just as I have commanded you. 7Include all this territory as Israel's inheritance when you divide the land among the nine tribes and the half-tribe of Manasseh."

The Land Divided East of the Jordan

8Half the tribe of Manasseh and the tribes of Reuben and Gad had already received their inheritance on the east side of the Jordan, for Moses, the servant of the LORD, had previously assigned this land to them.

9Their territory extended from Aroer on the edge of the Arnon Gorge (including the town in the middle of the gorge) to the plain beyond Medeba, as far as Dibon. 10It also included all the towns of King Sihon of the Amorites, who reigned in Heshbon, and extended as far as the borders of Ammon. 11It included Gilead, the territory of the kingdoms of Geshur and Maacah, all of Mount Hermon, all of Bashan as far as Salecah, 12and all the territory of King Og of Bashan, who had reigned in Ashtaroth and Edrei. King Og was the last of the Rephaites, for Moses had attacked them and driven them out. 13But the Israelites failed to drive out the people of Geshur and Maacah, so they continue to live among the Israelites to this day.

An Inheritance for the Tribe of Levi

14Moses did not assign any land to the tribe of Levi. Instead, as the LORD had promised them, their inheritance came from the offerings burned on the altar to the LORD, the God of Israel.

The Land Given to the Tribe of Reuben

15Moses had assigned the following area to the families of the tribe of Reuben.

16Their territory extended from Aroer on the edge of the Arnon Gorge (including the town in the middle of the gorge) to the plain beyond Medeba. 17It included Heshbon and the other towns on the plain—Dibon, Bamoth-baal, Beth-baal-meon, 18Jahaz, Kedemoth, Mephaath, 19Kiriathaim, Sibmah, Zereth-shahar on the hill above the valley, 20Beth-peor, the slopes of Pisgah, and Beth-jeshimoth.

21The land of Reuben also included all the towns of the plain and the entire kingdom of Sihon. Sihon was the Amorite king who had reigned in Heshbon and was killed by Moses along with the chiefs of Midian—Evi, Rekem, Zur, Hur, and Reba—princes living in the region who were allied with Sihon. 22The Israelites also killed Balaam the magician, the son of Beor. 23The Jordan River marked the western boundary for the tribe of Reuben. The towns and villages in this area were given as an inheritance to the families of the tribe of Reuben.

The Land Given to the Tribe of Gad

24Moses had assigned the following area to the families of the tribe of Gad.

25Their territory included Jazer, all the towns of Gilead, and half of the land of

12:23a Hebrew *Naphath-dor,* a variant name for Naphoth-dor. 12:23b Greek version reads *Goyim in Galilee.*

God Honors Those Who Persevere Read JOSHUA 14:6-14

This passage briefly recounts one of the "unsung heroes" of the Bible: Caleb. He and Joshua had been part of a group of men Moses had commissioned to explore the Promised Land. When this group had returned, only Caleb and Joshua reported that they could go ahead and take the land with the Lord's help. The others instilled fear in the crowd, insisting that such a mission would be too dangerous. In the end, the Lord punished that entire generation—with the exception of Caleb and Joshua—for refusing to follow his word and enter the land.

What was the secret to Caleb's spiritual success and longevity? He never lost his spiritual edge. Verse 8 gives us further insight: He followed the Lord wholeheartedly. He fully and completely obeyed God in his life. As a result, he "finished well" in the race of life. Below are three lessons from Caleb's life about what it takes to fully follow the Lord:

1. You Will Not Compromise. Caleb refused to go with the majority opinion when it contradicted what he knew to be God's will. He recognized that he had to seek God's approval over man's.

2. You Will Take God at His Word and Stand on It. Caleb had to endure forty years of desert wandering before he could enter the Promised Land. Yet he never doubted God's ability to carry through on his promise.

3. You Will Desire Fellowship and Communion with God. Caleb remained faithful to the very end. He understood the truth behind the verse, "Though our bodies are dying, our spirits are being renewed every day" (2 Corinthians 4:16).

The key to finishing well in this spiritual race is to maintain a committed, close relationship with Jesus Christ. When your love for Jesus is strong, the spiritual distractions of this world will look less and less attractive. May we, like Caleb, be able to say, "I am as strong today as I was in the day that the Lord called me."

To begin the next topic, turn to p. A19.

CORNER STONES

Ammon, as far as the town of Aroer just west of Rabbah. ²⁶It extended from Heshbon to Ramath-mizpeh and Betonim, and from Mahanaim to Lo-debar.* ²⁷In the valley were Beth-haram, Beth-nimrah, Succoth, Zaphon, and the rest of the kingdom of King Sihon of Heshbon. The Jordan River was the western border, extending as far north as the Sea of Galilee.* ²⁸The towns and villages in this area were given as an inheritance to the families of the tribe of Gad.

The Land Given to the Half-Tribe of Manasseh
²⁹Moses had assigned the following area to the families of the half-tribe of Manasseh.

³⁰Their territory extended from Mahanaim, including all of Bashan, all the former kingdom of King Og, and the sixty towns of Jair in Bashan. 31 It also included half of

13:26 Or *to the territory of Debir.* 13:27 Hebrew *sea of Kinnereth.*

Gilead and King Og's royal cities of Ashtaroth and Edrei. All this was given to the descendants of Makir, who was Manasseh's son.

32 These are the allotments Moses had made while he was on the plains of Moab, across the Jordan River, east of Jericho. ³³But Moses gave no land to the tribe of Levi, for the LORD, the God of Israel, had promised to be their inheritance.

CHAPTER **14**
The Land Divided West of the Jordan
The remaining tribes of Israel inherited land in Canaan as allotted by Eleazar the priest, Joshua son of Nun, and the tribal leaders. ²These nine and a half tribes received their inheritance by means of sacred lots, in accordance with the LORD's command through Moses. ³Moses had already given an inheritance of land to the two

and a half tribes on the east side of the Jordan River. ⁴The tribe of Joseph had become two separate tribes—Manasseh and Ephraim. And the Levites were given no land at all, only towns to live in and the surrounding pasturelands for their flocks and herds. ⁵So the distribution of the land was in strict accordance with the LORD's instructions to Moses.

Caleb Requests His Land

⁶A delegation from the tribe of Judah, led by Caleb son of Jephunneh the Kenizzite, came to Joshua at Gilgal. Caleb said to Joshua, "Remember what the LORD said to Moses, the man of God, about you and me when we were at Kadesh-barnea. ⁷I was forty years old when Moses, the servant of the LORD, sent me from Kadesh-barnea to explore the land of Canaan. I returned and gave from my heart a good report, ⁸but my brothers who went with me frightened the people and discouraged them from entering the Promised Land. For my part, I followed the LORD my God completely. ⁹So that day Moses promised me, 'The land of Canaan on which you were just walking will be your special possession and that of your descendants forever, because you wholeheartedly followed the LORD my God.'

¹⁰"Now, as you can see, the LORD has kept me alive and well as he promised for all these forty-five years since Moses made this promise—even while Israel wandered in the wilderness. Today I am eighty-five years old. ¹¹I am as strong now as I was when Moses sent me on that journey, and I can still travel and fight as well as I could then. ¹²So I'm asking you to give me the hill country that the LORD promised me. You will remember that as scouts we found the Anakites living there in great, walled cities. But if the LORD is with me, I will drive them out of the land, just as the LORD said."

¹³So Joshua blessed Caleb son of Jephunneh and gave Hebron to him as an inheritance. ¹⁴Hebron still belongs to the descendants of Caleb son of Jephunneh the Kenizzite because he wholeheartedly followed the LORD, the God of Israel. ¹⁵(Previously Hebron had been called Kiriath-arba. It had been named after Arba, a great hero of the Anakites.)

And the land had rest from war.

CHAPTER **15**

The Land Given to the Tribe of Judah

The land assigned to the families of the tribe of Judah reached southward to the border of

Follow God Wholeheartedly

Read JOSHUA 14:6-14

One of the key phrases in this passage is "I followed the Lord completely." It was that complete obedience and wholehearted commitment that enabled Caleb to finish well in the race of life. If you want to share in Caleb's spiritual stamina, keep the following three lessons in mind:

1. To Fully Follow the Lord Means That You Will Not Compromise. After Caleb returned with his report from the Promised Land, he stood his ground and held fast to the truth at the risk of being ostracized or even killed (see Numbers 13:1–14:10, pp. 127-128). Yet God blessed his obedience: Of the two to three million Israelites who had left Egypt, only Caleb and Joshua made it to the Promised Land. Seek God's approval over man's.

2. To Fully Follow the Lord Means That You Will Take God at His Word. Caleb believed that God would keep his promise to him, even though he had to wait through forty years of wilderness wandering. Yet Caleb was right to put his faith in the Lord. When the Israelites entered the Promised Land, the Lord kept his promise, and Caleb received his portion of the Promised Land.

3. To Fully Follow the Lord Means That You Will Desire Fellowship with Him. When you maintain a personal relationship with Jesus Christ, this world will lose its appeal. Caleb sought fellowship with God, and from this fellowship, God gave Caleb the strength to keep going through even the most discouraging times.

When you are only giving God your bare minimum and your love for Jesus is not burning brightly, this world and its temporary pleasures will look more and more appealing. Remember these lessons from the life of Caleb. Keep your eyes on the Lord, and remember his promises to you when you face difficulties in this life. Fully follow God in all you do, and you will not only survive but thrive in your Christian walk.

For the next note on *"Obey God," turn to p. 247.*

Edom, with the wilderness of Zin being its southernmost point.

2The southern boundary began at the south bay of the Dead Sea,* 3ran south of Scorpion Pass* into the wilderness of Zin and went south of Kadesh-barnea to Hezron. Then it went up to Addar, where it turned toward Karka. 4From there it passed to Azmon, until it finally reached the brook of Egypt, which it followed to the Mediterranean Sea.* This was their* southern boundary.

5The eastern boundary extended along the Dead Sea to the mouth of the Jordan River.

The northern boundary began at the bay where the Jordan River empties into the Dead Sea, 6crossed to Beth-hoglah, then proceeded north of Beth-arabah to the stone of Bohan. (Bohan was Reuben's son.) 7From that point it went through the valley of Achor to Debir, turning north toward Gilgal, which is across from the slopes of Adummim on the south side of the valley. From there the border extended to the springs at En-shemesh and on to En-rogel. 8The boundary then passed through the valley of the son of Hinnom, along the southern slopes of the Jebusites, where the city of Jerusalem is located. Then it went west to the top of the mountain above the valley of Hinnom, and on up to the northern end of the valley of Rephaim. 9From there the border extended from the top of the mountain to the spring at the waters of Nephtoah,* and from there to the towns on Mount Ephron. Then it turned toward Baalah (that is, Kiriath-jearim). 10The border circled west of Baalah to Mount Seir, passed along to the town of Kesalon on the northern slope of Mount Jearim, and went down to Beth-shemesh and on to Timnah. 11The boundary line then proceeded to the slope of the hill north of Ekron, where it turned toward Shikkeron and Mount Baalah. It passed Jabneel and ended at the Mediterranean Sea. 12The western boundary was the shoreline of the Mediterranean Sea.*

These are the boundaries for the families of the tribe of Judah.

The Land Given to Caleb

13The LORD instructed Joshua to assign some of Judah's territory to Caleb son of Jephunneh. So Caleb was given the city of Arba (that is, Hebron), which had been named after Anak's ancestor. 14Caleb drove out the three Anakites—Sheshai, Ahiman, and Talmai—descendants of Anak.

15Then he fought against the people living in the town of Debir (formerly called Kiriath-sepher). 16Caleb said, "I will give my daughter Acsah in marriage to the one who attacks and captures Kiriath-sepher." 17Othniel, the son of Caleb's brother Kenaz, was the one who conquered it, so Acsah became Othniel's wife.

18When Acsah married Othniel, she urged him* to ask her father for an additional field. As she got down off her donkey, Caleb asked her, "What is it? What can I do for you?"

19She said, "Give me a further blessing. You have been kind enough to give me land in the Negev; please give me springs as well." So Caleb gave her the upper and lower springs.

The Towns Judah Inherited

20This was the inheritance given to the families of the tribe of Judah.

21The towns of Judah situated along the borders of Edom in the extreme south are Kabzeel, Eder, Jagur, 22Kinah, Dimonah, Adadah, 23Kedesh, Hazor, Ithnan, 24Ziph, Telem, Bealoth, 25Hazor-hadattah, Kerioth-hezron (that is, Hazor), 26Amam, Shema, Moladah, 27Hazar-gaddah, Heshmon, Beth-pelet, 28Hazar-shual, Beersheba, Biziothiah, 29Baalah, Iim, Ezem, 30Eltolad, Kesil, Hormah, 31Ziklag, Madmannah, Sansannah, 32Lebaoth, Shilhim, Ain, and Rimmon. In all, there were twenty-nine of these towns with their surrounding villages.

33The following towns situated in the western foothills* were also given to Judah: Eshtaol, Zorah, Ashnah, 34Zanoah, En-gannim, Tappuah, Enam, 35Jarmuth, Adullam, Socoh, Azekah, 36Shaaraim, Adithaim, Gederah, and Gederothaim. In all, there were fourteen towns with their surrounding villages.

37Also included were Zenan, Hadashah, Migdal-gad, 38Dilean, Mizpeh, Joktheel, 39Lachish, Bozkath, Eglon, 40Cabbon,

15:2 Hebrew *the Salt Sea*; also in 15:5. 15:3 Hebrew *Akrabbim*. 15:4a Hebrew *the sea*; also in 15:11. 15:4b Hebrew *your*. 15:9 Or *the spring at Me-nephtoah*. 15:12 Hebrew *the Great Sea*; also in 15:47. 15:18 Some Greek manuscripts read *Othniel urged her*. 15:33 Hebrew *the Shephelah*.

Lahmam, Kitlish, 41Gederoth, Beth-dagon, Naamah, and Makkedah—sixteen towns with their surrounding villages. 42Besides these, there were Libnah, Ether, Ashan, 43Iphtah, Ashnah, Nezib, 44Keilah, Aczib, and Mareshah—nine towns with their surrounding villages.

45The territory of the tribe of Judah also included all the towns and villages of Ekron. 46From Ekron the boundary extended west and included the towns near Ashdod with their surrounding villages. 47It also included Ashdod with its towns and villages and Gaza with its towns and villages, as far as the brook of Egypt and along the coast of the Mediterranean Sea.

48Judah also received the following towns in the hill country: Shamir, Jattir, Socoh, 49Dannah, Kiriath-sannah (that is, Debir), 50Anab, Eshtemoh, Anim, 51Goshen, Holon, and Giloh—eleven towns with their surrounding villages.

52Also included were the towns of Arab, Dumah, Eshan, 53Janim, Beth-tappuah, Aphekah, 54Humtah, Kiriath-arba (that is, Hebron), and Zior—nine towns with their surrounding villages.

55Besides these, there were Maon, Carmel, Ziph, Juttah, 56Jezreel, Jokdeam, Zanoah, 57Kain, Gibeah, and Timnah—ten towns with their surrounding villages.

58In addition, there were Halhul, Beth-zur, Gedor, 59Maarath, Beth-anoth, and Eltekon—six towns with their surrounding villages. 60There were also Kiriath-baal (that is, Kiriath-jearim) and Rabbah—two towns with their surrounding villages.

61In the wilderness there were the towns of Beth-arabah, Middin, Secacah, 62Nibshan, the City of Salt, and En-gedi—six towns with their surrounding villages.

63But the tribe of Judah could not drive out the Jebusites, who lived in the city of Jerusalem, so the Jebusites live there among the people of Judah to this day.

CHAPTER 16
The Inheritance of Ephraim and West Manasseh
The allotment to the descendants of Joseph extended from the Jordan River near Jericho, east of the waters of Jericho, through the wilderness and into the hill country of Bethel. 2From Bethel (that is, Luz)* it ran over to Ataroth in the territory of the Arkites. 3Then it descended westward to the territory of the Japhletites as far as Lower Beth-horon, then to Gezer and on over to the Mediterranean Sea.*

The Land Given to Ephraim
4The families of Joseph's sons, Manasseh and Ephraim, received their inheritance.

5The following territory was given to the families of the tribe of Ephraim as their inheritance.

The eastern boundary of their inheritance began at Ataroth-addar. From there it ran to Upper Beth-horon, 6then on to the Mediterranean Sea. The northern boundary began at the Mediterranean, ran east past Micmethath, then curved eastward past Taanath-shiloh to the east of Janoah. 7From Janoah it turned southward to Ataroth and Naarah, touched Jericho, and ended at the Jordan River. 8From Tappuah the border extended westward, following the Kanah Ravine to the Mediterranean Sea. This is the inheritance given to the families of the tribe of Ephraim.

9Ephraim was also given some towns with surrounding villages in the territory of the half-tribe of Manasseh. 10They did not drive the Canaanites out of Gezer, however, so the people of Gezer live as slaves among the people of Ephraim to this day.

CHAPTER 17
The Land Given to West Manasseh
The next allotment of land was given to the half-tribe of Manasseh, the descendants of Joseph's older son. Gilead and Bashan on the east side of the Jordan had already been given to the family of Makir because he was a great warrior. (Makir was Manasseh's oldest son and was the father of Gilead.) 2Land on the west side of the Jordan was allotted to the remaining families within the tribe of Manasseh: Abiezer, Helek, Asriel, Shechem, Hepher, and Shemida.

3However, Zelophehad son of Hepher, who was a descendant of Manasseh, Makir, and Gilead, had no sons. Instead, he had five daughters. Their names were Mahlah, Noah, Hoglah, Milcah, and Tirzah. 4These women came to Eleazar the priest, Joshua son of Nun, and the Israelite leaders and said, "The LORD commanded Moses

16:2 As in Greek version (also see 18:13); Hebrew reads *From Bethel to Luz.* 16:3 Hebrew *the sea;* also in 16:6, 8.

to give us an inheritance along with the men of our tribe."

So Joshua gave them an inheritance along with their uncles, as the LORD had commanded. 5As a result, Manasseh's inheritance came to ten parcels of land, in addition to the land of Gilead and Bashan across the Jordan River, 6because the female descendants of Manasseh received an inheritance along with the male descendants. (The land of Gilead was given to the rest of the male descendants of Manasseh.)

7The boundary of the tribe of Manasseh extended from the border of Asher to Micmethath, which is east of Shechem. Then the boundary went south from Micmethath to the people living near the spring of Tappuah. 8(The land surrounding Tappuah belonged to Manasseh, but the town of Tappuah, on the border of Manasseh's territory, belonged to the tribe of Ephraim.) 9From the spring of Tappuah, the border of Manasseh followed the northern side of the Kanah Ravine to the Mediterranean Sea.* (Several towns in Manasseh's territory belonged to the tribe of Ephraim.) 10The land south of the ravine belonged to Ephraim, and the land north of the ravine belonged to Manasseh, with the Mediterranean Sea forming Manasseh's western border. North of Manasseh was the territory of Asher, and to the east was the territory of Issachar.

11The following towns within the territory of Issachar and Asher were given to Manasseh: Beth-shan,* Ibleam, Dor (that is, Naphoth-dor),* Endor, Taanach, and Megiddo, with their respective villages. 12But the descendants of Manasseh were unable to occupy these towns. They could not drive out the Canaanites who continued to live there. 13Later on, however, when the Israelites became strong enough, they forced the Canaanites to work as slaves. But they did not drive them out of the land.

14The descendants of Joseph came to Joshua and asked, "Why have you given us only one portion of land when the LORD has given us so many people?"

15Joshua replied, "If the hill country of Ephraim is not large enough for you, clear out

land for yourselves in the forest where the Perizzites and Rephaites live."

16They said, "The hill country is not enough for us, and the Canaanites in the lowlands around Beth-shan and the valley of Jezreel have iron chariots—they are too strong for us."

17Then Joshua said to the tribes of Ephraim and Manasseh, the descendants of Joseph, "Since you are so large and strong, you will be given more than one portion. 18The forests of the hill country will be yours as well. Clear as much of the land as you wish and live there. And I am sure you can drive out the Canaanites from the valleys, too, even though they are strong and have iron chariots."

CHAPTER **18**

The Allotments of the Remaining Land

Now that the land was under Israelite control, the entire Israelite assembly gathered at Shiloh and set up the Tabernacle.* 2But there remained seven tribes who had not yet been allotted their inheritance.

3Then Joshua asked them, "How long are you going to wait before taking possession of the remaining land the LORD, the God of your ancestors, has given to you? 4Select three men from each tribe, and I will send them out to survey the unconquered territory. They will return to me with a written report of their proposed divisions of the inheritance. 5The scouts will map the land into seven sections, excluding Judah's territory in the south and Joseph's territory in the north. 6Then I will cast sacred lots in the presence of the LORD our God to decide which section will be assigned to each tribe. 7However, the Levites will not receive any land. Their role as priests of the LORD is their inheritance. And the tribes of Gad, Reuben, and the half-tribe of Manasseh won't receive any more land, for they have already received their inheritance, which Moses, the servant of the LORD, gave them on the east side of the Jordan River."

8As the men who were mapping out the land started on their way, Joshua commanded them, "Go and survey the land. Then return to me with your written report, and I will assign the land to the tribes by casting sacred lots in the presence of the LORD here at Shiloh." 9The men did as they were told and mapped the entire territory into seven sections, listing the towns in each section. Then they returned to Joshua in the camp at Shiloh. 10There at Shi-

---

17:9 Hebrew *the sea;* also in 17:10.   17:11a Hebrew *Beth-shean,* a variant name for Beth-shan; also in 17:16.   17:11b The meaning of the Hebrew here is uncertain.   18:1 Hebrew *Tent of Meeting.*

loh, Joshua cast sacred lots in the presence of the LORD to determine which tribe should have each section.

The Land Given to Benjamin

11The first allotment of land went to the families of the tribe of Benjamin. It lay between the territory previously assigned to the tribes of Judah and Joseph.

12The northern boundary began at the Jordan River, went north of the slope of Jericho, then west through the hill country and the wilderness of Beth-aven. 13From there the boundary went south to Luz (that is, Bethel) and proceeded down to Ataroth-addar to the top of the hill south of Lower Beth-horon.

14The boundary then ran south along the western edge of the hill facing Beth-horon, ending at the village of Kiriath-baal (that is, Kiriath-jearim), one of the towns belonging to the tribe of Judah. This was the western boundary.

15The southern boundary began at the outskirts of Kiriath-jearim. From there it ran westward* to the spring at the waters of Nephtoah,* 16and down to the base of the mountain beside the valley of the son of Hinnom, at the northern end of the valley of Rephaim. From there it went down the valley of Hinnom, crossing south of the slope where the Jebusites lived, and continued down to En-rogel. 17From En-rogel the boundary proceeded northeast to En-shemesh and on to Geliloth (which is across from the slopes of Adummim). Then it went down to the stone of Bohan. (Bohan was Reuben's son.) 18From there it passed along the north side of the slope overlooking the Jordan Valley.* The border then went down into the valley, 19ran past the north slope of Beth-hoglah, and ended at the north bay of the Dead Sea,* which is the southern end of the Jordan River.

20The eastern boundary was the Jordan River.

This was the inheritance for the families of the tribe of Benjamin.

The Towns Given to Benjamin

21These were the towns given to the families of the tribe of Benjamin.

Jericho, Beth-hoglah, Emek-keziz, 22Beth-arabah, Zemaraim, Bethel, 23Avvim, Parah, Ophrah, 24Kephar-ammoni, Ophni, and Geba—twelve towns with their villages. 25Also Gibeon, Ramah, Beeroth, 26Mizpeh, Kephirah, Mozah, 27Rekem, Irpeel, Taralah, 28Zela, Haeleph, Jebus (that is, Jerusalem), Gibeah, and Kiriath-jearim*—fourteen towns with their villages.

This was the inheritance given to the families of the tribe of Benjamin.

CHAPTER 19
The Land Given to Simeon

The second allotment of land went to the families of the tribe of Simeon. Their inheritance was surrounded by Judah's territory.

2Simeon's inheritance included Beersheba, Sheba, Moladah, 3Hazar-shual, Balah, Ezem, 4Eltolad, Bethul, Hormah, 5Ziklag, Beth-marcaboth, Hazar-susah, 6Beth-lebaoth, and Sharuhen—thirteen towns with their villages. 7It also included Ain, Rimmon, Ether, and Ashan—four towns with their villages, 8including all the villages as far south as Baalath-beer (also known as Ramah of the Negev).

This was the inheritance of the families of the tribe of Simeon. 9Their inheritance came from part of what had been given to Judah because Judah's territory was too large for them. So the tribe of Simeon received an inheritance within the territory of Judah.

The Land Given to Zebulun

10The third allotment of land went to the families of the tribe of Zebulun.

The boundary of Zebulun's inheritance started at Sarid. 11From there it went west, going past Maralah, touching Dabbesheth, and proceeding to the brook east of Jokneam. 12In the other direction, the boundary line went east from Sarid to the border of Kisloth-tabor, and from there to Daberath and up to Japhia. 13Then it continued east to Gath-hepher, Eth-kazin, and Rimmon and turned toward Neah. 14The northern boundary of Zebulun passed Hannathon and ended at the valley

---

18:15a Or *it went to Ephron, and.* The meaning of the Hebrew is uncertain.   **18:15b** Or *the spring at Me-nephtoah.*   **18:18** Hebrew *the Arabah.*   **18:19** Hebrew *Salt Sea.*   **18:28** As in Greek version; Hebrew reads *Kiriath.*

of Iphtah-el. 15The towns in these areas included Kattath, Nahalal, Shimron, Idalah, and Bethlehem—twelve towns with their surrounding villages.

16This was the inheritance of the families of the tribe of Zebulun.

The Land Given to Issachar

17The fourth allotment of land went to the families of the tribe of Issachar.

18Its boundaries included the following towns: Jezreel, Kesulloth, Shunem, 19Hapharaim, Shion, Anaharath, 20Rabbith, Kishion, Ebez, 21Remeth, En-gannim, En-haddah, and Beth-pazzez. 22The boundary also touched Tabor, Shahazumah, and Beth-shemesh, ending at the Jordan River—sixteen towns with their surrounding villages.

23This was the inheritance of the families of the tribe of Issachar.

The Land Given to Asher

24The fifth allotment of land went to the families of the tribe of Asher.

25Its boundaries included these towns: Helkath, Hali, Beten, Acshaph, 26Allammelech, Amad, and Mishal. The boundary on the west went from Carmel to Shihor-libnath, 27turned east toward Beth-dagon, and ran as far as Zebulun in the valley of Iphtah-el, running north to Beth-emek and Neiel. It then continued north to Cabul, 28Abdon,* Rehob, Hammon, Kanah, and as far as Greater Sidon. 29Then the boundary turned toward Ramah and the fortified city of Tyre and came to the Mediterranean Sea* at Hosah. The territory also included Mehebel, Aczib, 30Ummah, Aphek, and Rehob—twenty-two towns with their surrounding villages.

31This was the inheritance of the families of the tribe of Asher.

The Land Given to Naphtali

32The sixth allotment of land went to the families of the tribe of Naphtali.

33Its boundary ran from Heleph, from the oak at Zaanannim, and extended across to Adami-nekeb, Jabneel, and as far as Lakkum, ending at the Jordan River. 34The western boundary ran past Aznoth-tabor, then to Hukkok, and touched the boundary of Zebulun in the south, the boundary of Asher on the west, and the Jordan River* on the east. 35The fortified cities included in this territory were Ziddim, Zer, Hammath, Rakkath, Kinnereth, 36Adamah, Ramah, Hazor, 37Kedesh, Edrei, En-hazor, 38Yiron, Migdal-el, Horem, Beth-anath, and Beth-shemesh—nineteen cities with their surrounding villages.

39This was the inheritance of the families of the tribe of Naphtali.

The Land Given to Dan

40The seventh and last allotment of land went to the families of the tribe of Dan.

41The towns within Dan's inheritance included Zorah, Eshtaol, Ir-shemesh, 42Shaalabbin, Aijalon, Ithlah, 43Elon, Timnah, Ekron, 44Eltekeh, Gibbethon, Baalath, 45Jehud, Bene-berak, Gath-rimmon, 46and Me-jarkon, also Rakkon along with the territory across from Joppa.

47But the tribe of Dan had trouble taking possession of their land, so they fought against the town of Laish.* They captured it, slaughtered its people, and settled there. They renamed the city Dan after their ancestor.

48This was the inheritance of the families of the tribe of Dan—these towns with their villages.

The Land Given to Joshua

49After all the land was divided among the tribes, the Israelites gave a special piece of land to Joshua as his inheritance. 50For the LORD had said he could have any town he wanted. He chose Timnath-serah in the hill country of Ephraim. He rebuilt the town and lived there.

51These are the territories that Eleazar the priest, Joshua son of Nun, and the tribal leaders gave as an inheritance to the tribes of Israel by casting sacred lots in the presence of the LORD at the entrance of the Tabernacle* at Shiloh. So the division of the land was completed.

CHAPTER **20**
The Cities of Refuge

The LORD said to Joshua, 2"Now tell the Israelites to designate the cities of refuge, as I instructed

---

19:28 As in some Hebrew manuscripts (see also 21:30); most Hebrew manuscripts read *Ebron.* 19:29 Hebrew *the sea.* 19:34 Hebrew *and Judah at the Jordan River.* 19:47 Hebrew *Leshem,* another name for Laish. 19:51 Hebrew *Tent of Meeting.*

Moses. ³Anyone who kills another person unintentionally can run to one of these cities and be protected from the relatives of the one who was killed, for the relatives may seek to avenge the killing.

⁴"Upon reaching one of these cities, the one who caused the accidental death will appear before the leaders at the city gate and explain what happened. They must allow the accused to enter the city and live there among them. ⁵If the relatives of the victim come to avenge the killing, the leaders must not release the accused to them, for the death was accidental. ⁶But the person who caused the death must stay in that city and be tried by the community and found innocent. Then the one declared innocent because the death was accidental must continue to live in that city until the death of the high priest who was in office at the time of the accident. After that, the one found innocent is free to return home."

⁷The following cities were designated as cities of refuge: Kedesh of Galilee, in the hill country of Naphtali; Shechem, in the hill country of Ephraim; and Kiriath-arba (that is, Hebron), in the hill country of Judah. ⁸On the east side of the Jordan River, across from Jericho, the following cities were designated as cities of refuge: Bezer, in the wilderness plain of the tribe of Reuben; Ramoth in Gilead, in the territory of the tribe of Gad; and Golan in Bashan, in the land of the tribe of Manasseh. ⁹These cities were set apart for Israelites as well as the foreigners living among them. Anyone who accidentally killed another person could take refuge in one of these cities. In this way, they could escape being killed in revenge prior to standing trial before the community.

CHAPTER **21**

The Towns Given to the Levites

Then the leaders of the tribe of Levi came to consult with Eleazar the priest, Joshua son of Nun, and the leaders of the other tribes of Israel. ²They spoke to them at Shiloh in the land of Canaan, saying, "The LORD instructed Moses to give us towns to live in and pasturelands for our cattle." ³So by the command of the LORD the Levites were given as their inheritance the following towns with their pasturelands.

⁴The descendants of Aaron, who were members of the Kohathite clan within the tribe of Levi, were given thirteen towns that were originally assigned to the tribes of Judah, Simeon, and Benjamin. ⁵The other families of the Kohathite clan were allotted ten towns from the

territories of Ephraim, Dan, and the half-tribe of Manasseh.

⁶The clan of Gershon received thirteen towns from the tribes of Issachar, Asher, Naphtali, and the half-tribe of Manasseh in Bashan.

⁷The clan of Merari received twelve cities from the tribes of Reuben, Gad, and Zebulun.

⁸So the Israelites obeyed the LORD's command to Moses and assigned these towns and pasturelands to the Levites by casting sacred lots.

⁹The Israelites gave the following towns from the tribes of Judah and Simeon ¹⁰to the descendants of Aaron, who were members of the Kohathite clan within the tribe of Levi, since the sacred lot fell to them first: ¹¹Kiriath-arba (that is, Hebron), in the hill country of Judah, along with its surrounding pasturelands. (Arba was an ancestor of Anak.) ¹²But the fields beyond the city and the surrounding villages were given to Caleb son of Jephunneh.

¹³The following towns with their pasturelands were given to the descendants of Aaron the priest: Hebron (a city of refuge for those who accidentally killed someone), Libnah, ¹⁴Jattir, Eshtemoa, ¹⁵Holon, Debir, ¹⁶Ain, Juttah, and Beth-shemesh—nine towns from these two tribes.

¹⁷From the tribe of Benjamin the priests were given the following towns with their surrounding pasturelands: Gibeon, Geba, ¹⁸Anathoth, and Almon—four towns. ¹⁹So thirteen towns were given to the priests, the descendants of Aaron.

²⁰The rest of the Kohathite clan from the tribe of Levi was allotted these towns and pasturelands from the tribe of Ephraim: ²¹Shechem (a city of refuge for those who accidentally killed someone), Gezer, ²²Kibzaim, and Beth-horon—four towns.

²³The following towns and pasturelands were allotted to the priests from the tribe of Dan: Eltekeh, Gibbethon, ²⁴Aijalon, and Gath-rimmon—four towns.

²⁵The half-tribe of Manasseh allotted the following towns with their pasturelands to the priests: Taanach and Gath-rimmon—two towns. ²⁶So ten towns with their pasturelands were given to the rest of the Kohathite clan.

²⁷The descendants of Gershon, another clan within the tribe of Levi, received two towns with their pasturelands from the half-tribe of Manasseh: Golan in Bashan (a city of refuge) and Be-eshterah.

²⁸From the tribe of Issachar they received

Kishion, Daberath, [29]Jarmuth, and En-gannim—four towns with their pasturelands.

[30]From the tribe of Asher they received Mishal, Abdon, [31]Helkath, and Rehob—four towns and their pasturelands.

[32]From the tribe of Naphtali they received Kedesh in Galilee (a city of refuge), Hammoth-dor, and Kartan—three towns with their pasturelands.

[33]So thirteen towns and their pasturelands were allotted to the clan of Gershon.

[34]The rest of the Levites—the Merari clan—were given the following towns from the tribe of Zebulun: Jokneam, Kartah, [35]Dimnah, and Nahalal—four towns with their pasturelands.

[36]From the tribe of Reuben they received Bezer, Jahaz,* [37]Kedemoth, and Mephaath—four towns with their pasturelands.

[38]From the tribe of Gad they received Ramoth in Gilead (a city of refuge), Mahanaim, [39]Heshbon, and Jazer—four towns with their pasturelands. [40]So twelve towns were allotted to the clan of Merari.

[41]The total number of towns and pasturelands within Israelite territory given to the Levites came to forty-eight. [42]Every one of these towns had pasturelands surrounding it.

[43]So the LORD gave to Israel all the land he had sworn to give their ancestors, and they conquered it and settled there. [44]And the LORD gave them rest on every side, just as he had solemnly promised their ancestors. None of their enemies could stand against them, for the LORD helped them conquer all their enemies. [45]All of the good promises that the LORD had given Israel came true.

CHAPTER **22**

The Eastern Tribes Return Home

Then Joshua called together the tribes of Reuben, Gad, and the half-tribe of Manasseh. [2]He told them, "You have done as Moses, the servant of the LORD, commanded you, and you have obeyed every order I have given you. [3]You have not deserted the other tribes, even though the campaign has lasted for such a long time. You have been careful to obey the commands of the LORD your God up to the present day. [4]And now the LORD your God has given the other tribes rest, as he promised them. So go home now to the land Moses, the servant of the LORD, gave you on the east side of the Jordan River. [5]But be very careful to obey all the commands and the law that Moses gave to you. Love the LORD your God,

walk in all his ways, obey his commands, be faithful to him, and serve him with all your heart and all your soul."

[6]So Joshua blessed them and sent them home. [7]Now Moses had given the land of Bashan to the half-tribe of Manasseh east of the Jordan. The other half of the tribe was given land west of the Jordan. As Joshua sent them away, he blessed them [8]and said, "Share with your relatives back home the great wealth you have taken from your enemies. Share with them your large herds of cattle, your silver and gold, your bronze and iron, and your clothing."

[9]So the men of Reuben, Gad, and the half-tribe of Manasseh left the rest of Israel at Shiloh in the land of Canaan. They started the journey back to their own land of Gilead, the territory that belonged to them according to the LORD's command through Moses.

The Eastern Tribes Build a Memorial

[10]But while they were still in Canaan, before they crossed the Jordan River, Reuben, Gad, and the half-tribe of Manasseh built a very large altar near the Jordan River at a place called Geliloth.

[11]When the rest of Israel heard they had built the altar at Geliloth west of the Jordan River, in the land of Canaan, [12]the whole assembly gathered at Shiloh and prepared to go to war against their brother tribes. [13]First, however, they sent a delegation led by Phinehas son of Eleazar, the priest. They crossed the river to talk with the tribes of Reuben, Gad, and the half-tribe of Manasseh. [14]In this delegation were ten high officials of Israel, one from each of the ten tribes, and each a leader within the family divisions of Israel.

[15]When they arrived in the land of Gilead, they said to the tribes of Reuben, Gad, and the half-tribe of Manasseh, [16]"The whole community of the LORD demands to know why you are betraying the God of Israel. How could you turn away from the LORD and build an altar in rebellion against him? [17]Was our sin at Peor not enough? We are not yet fully cleansed of it, even after the plague that struck the entire assembly of the LORD. [18]And yet today you are turning away from following the LORD. If you rebel against the LORD today, he will be angry with all of us tomorrow. [19]If you need the altar because your land is defiled, then join us on our side of the river, where the LORD lives among us in his Tabernacle, and we will share our land with you. But do not rebel against the LORD or draw us into

21:36 Hebrew *Jahzah,* a variant name for Jahaz.

your rebellion by building another altar for yourselves. There is only one true altar of the LORD our God. 20Didn't God punish all the people of Israel when Achan, a member of the clan of Zerah, sinned by stealing the things set apart for the LORD*? He was not the only one who died because of that sin."

21Then the people of Reuben, Gad, and the half-tribe of Manasseh answered these high officials: 22"The LORD alone is God! The LORD alone is God! We have not built the altar in rebellion against the LORD. If we have done so, do not spare our lives this day. But the LORD knows, and let all Israel know, too, 23that we have not built an altar for ourselves to turn away from the LORD. Nor will we use it for our burnt offerings or grain offerings or peace offerings. If we have built it for this purpose, may the LORD himself punish us.

24"We have built this altar because we fear that in the future your descendants will say to ours, 'What right do you have to worship the LORD, the God of Israel? 25The LORD has placed the Jordan River as a barrier between our people and your people. You have no claim to the LORD.' And your descendants may make our descendants stop worshiping the LORD. 26So we decided to build the altar, not for burnt sacrifices, 27but as a memorial. It will remind our descendants and your descendants that we, too, have the right to worship the LORD at his sanctuary with our burnt offerings, sacrifices, and peace offerings. Then your descendants will not be able to say to ours, 'You have no claim to the LORD.' 28If they say this, our descendants can reply, 'Look at this copy of the LORD's altar that our ancestors made. It is not for burnt offerings or sacrifices; it is a reminder of the relationship both of us have with the LORD.' 29Far be it from us to rebel against the LORD or turn away from him by building our own altar for burnt offerings, grain offerings, or sacrifices. Only the altar of the LORD our God that stands in front of the Tabernacle may be used for that purpose."

30When Phinehas the priest and the high officials heard this from the tribes of Reuben, Gad, and the half-tribe of Manasseh, they were satisfied. 31Phinehas son of Eleazar, the priest, replied to them, "Today we know the LORD is among us because you have not sinned against the LORD as we thought. Instead, you have rescued Israel from being destroyed by the LORD."

32Then Phinehas son of Eleazar, the priest, and the ten high officials left the tribes of Reuben and Gad in Gilead and returned to the land of Canaan to tell the Israelites what had happened. 33And all the Israelites were satisfied and praised God and spoke no more of war against Reuben and Gad. 34The people of Reuben and Gad named the altar "Witness,"* for they said, "It is a witness between us and them that the LORD is our God, too."

CHAPTER 23

Joshua's Final Words to Israel

The years passed, and the LORD had given the people of Israel rest from all their enemies. Joshua, who was now very old, 2called together all the elders, leaders, judges, and officers of Israel. He said to them, "I am an old man now. 3You have seen everything the LORD your God has done for you during my lifetime. The LORD your God has fought for you against your enemies. 4I have allotted to you as an inheritance all the land of the nations yet unconquered, as well as the land of those we have already conquered—from the Jordan River to the Mediterranean Sea* in the west. 5This land will be yours, for the LORD your God will drive out all the people living there now. You will live there instead of them, just as the LORD your God promised you.

6"So be strong! Be very careful to follow all the instructions written in the Book of the Law of Moses. Do not deviate from them in any way. 7Make sure you do not associate with the other people still remaining in the land. Do not even mention the names of their gods, much less swear by them or worship them. 8But be faithful to the LORD your God as you have done until now.

9"For the LORD has driven out great and powerful nations for you, and no one has yet been able to defeat you. 10Each one of you will put to flight a thousand of the enemy, for the LORD your God fights for you, just as he has promised. 11So be very careful to love the LORD your God.

12"But if you turn away from him and intermarry with the survivors of these nations remaining among you, 13then know for certain that the LORD your God will no longer drive them out from your land. Instead, they will be a snare and a trap to you, a pain in your side and a thorn in your eyes, and you will be wiped out from this good land the LORD your God has given you.

14"Soon I will die, going the way of all the earth. Deep in your hearts you know that every

---

22:20 The Hebrew term used here refers to the complete consecration of things or people to the LORD, either by destroying them or by giving them as an offering. 22:34 Hebrew *edh*. Some manuscripts lack this word. 23:4 Hebrew *the Great Sea*.

promise of the LORD your God has come true. Not a single one has failed! 15But as surely as the LORD your God has given you the good things he promised, he will also bring disaster on you if you disobey him. He will completely wipe you out from this good land he has given you. 16If you break the covenant of the LORD your God by worshiping and serving other gods, his anger will burn against you, and you will quickly be wiped out from the good land he has given you."

CHAPTER **24**

The LORD's Covenant Renewed

Then Joshua summoned all the people of Israel to Shechem, along with their elders, leaders, judges, and officers. So they came and presented themselves to God.

2Joshua said to the people, "This is what the LORD, the God of Israel, says: Your ancestors, including Terah, the father of Abraham and Nahor, lived beyond the Euphrates River,* and they worshiped other gods. 3But I took your ancestor Abraham from the land beyond the Euphrates and led him into the land of Canaan. I gave him many descendants through his son Isaac. 4To Isaac I gave Jacob and Esau. To Esau I gave the hill country of Seir, while Jacob and his children went down into Egypt.

5"Then I sent Moses and Aaron, and I brought terrible plagues on Egypt; and afterward I brought you out as a free people. 6But when your ancestors arrived at the Red Sea,* the Egyptians chased after you with chariots and horses. 7When you cried out to the LORD, I put darkness between you and the Egyptians. I brought the sea crashing down on the Egyptians, drowning them. With your very own eyes you saw what I did. Then you lived in the wilderness for many years.

8"Finally, I brought you into the land of the Amorites on the east side of the Jordan. They fought against you, but I gave you victory over them, and you took possession of their land. 9Then Balak son of Zippor, king of Moab, started a war against Israel. He asked Balaam son of Beor to curse you, 10but I would not listen to him. Instead, I made Balaam bless you, and so I rescued you from Balak.

11"When you crossed the Jordan River and came to Jericho, the men of Jericho fought against you. There were also many others who fought you, including the Amorites, the Perizzites, the Canaanites, the Hittites, the Girgashites, the Hivites, and the Jebusites. But I gave you

victory over them. 12And I sent hornets ahead of you to drive out the two kings of the Amorites. It was not your swords or bows that brought you victory. 13I gave you land you had not worked for, and I gave you cities you did not build—the cities in which you are now living. I gave you vineyards and olive groves for food, though you did not plant them.

14"So honor the LORD and serve him wholeheartedly. Put away forever the idols your ancestors worshiped when they lived beyond the Euphrates River and in Egypt. Serve the LORD alone. 15But if you are unwilling to serve the LORD, then choose today whom you will serve. Would you prefer the gods your ancestors served beyond the Euphrates? Or will it be the gods of the Amorites in whose land you now live? But as for me and my family, we will serve the LORD."

16The people replied, "We would never forsake the LORD and worship other gods. 17For the LORD our God is the one who rescued us and our ancestors from slavery in the land of Egypt. He performed mighty miracles before our very eyes. As we traveled through the wilderness among our enemies, he preserved us. 18It was the LORD who drove out the Amorites and the other nations living here in the land. So we, too, will serve the LORD, for he alone is our God."

19Then Joshua said to the people, "You are not able to serve the LORD, for he is a holy and jealous God. He will not forgive your rebellion and sins. 20If you forsake the LORD and serve other gods, he will turn against you and destroy you, even though he has been so good to you."

21But the people answered Joshua, saying, "No, we are determined to serve the LORD!"

22"You are accountable for this decision," Joshua said. "You have chosen to serve the LORD."

"Yes," they replied, "we are accountable."

23"All right then," Joshua said, "destroy the idols among you, and turn your hearts to the LORD, the God of Israel."

24The people said to Joshua, "We will serve the LORD our God. We will obey him alone."

25So Joshua made a covenant with the people that day at Shechem, committing them to a permanent and binding contract between themselves and the LORD. 26Joshua recorded these things in the Book of the Law of God. As a reminder of their agreement, he took a huge stone and rolled it beneath the oak tree beside the Tabernacle of the LORD.

27Joshua said to all the people, "This stone

24:2 Hebrew *the river*; also in 24:3, 14, 15.   24:6 Hebrew *sea of reeds.*

has heard everything the LORD said to us. It will be a witness to testify against you if you go back on your word to God."

28Then Joshua sent the people away, each to his own inheritance.

Leaders Buried in the Promised Land
29Soon after this, Joshua son of Nun, the servant of the LORD, died at the age of 110. 30They buried him in the land he had inherited, at Timnath-serah in the hill country of Ephraim, north of Mount Gaash.

31Israel served the LORD throughout the lifetime of Joshua and of the leaders who outlived him—those who had personally experienced all that the LORD had done for Israel.

32The bones of Joseph, which the Israelites had brought along with them when they left Egypt, were buried at Shechem, in the parcel of ground Jacob had bought from the sons of Hamor for one hundred pieces of silver.* This land was located in the territory allotted to the tribes of Ephraim and Manasseh, the descendants of Joseph.

33Eleazar son of Aaron also died. He was buried in the hill country of Ephraim, in the town of Gibeah, which had been given to his son Phinehas.

24:32 Hebrew *100 kesitahs;* the value or weight of the kesitah is no longer known.

Judges

CHAPTER 1

Judah and Simeon Conquer the Land

After Joshua died, the Israelites asked the LORD, "Which tribe should attack the Canaanites first?"

²The LORD answered, "Judah, for I have given them victory over the land."

³The leaders of Judah said to their relatives from the tribe of Simeon, "Join with us to fight against the Canaanites living in the territory allotted to us. Then we will help you conquer your territory." So the men of Simeon went with Judah.

⁴When the men of Judah attacked, the LORD gave them victory over the Canaanites and Perizzites, and they killed ten thousand enemy warriors at the town of Bezek. ⁵While at Bezek they encountered King Adoni-bezek and fought against him, and the Canaanites and Perizzites were defeated. ⁶Adoni-bezek escaped, but the Israelites soon captured him and cut off his thumbs and big toes. ⁷Adoni-bezek said, "I once had seventy kings with thumbs and big toes cut off, eating scraps from under my table. Now God has paid me back for what I did to them." They took him to Jerusalem, and he died there.

⁸The men of Judah attacked Jerusalem and captured it, killing all its people and setting the city on fire. ⁹Then they turned south to fight the Canaanites living in the hill country, the Negev, and the western foothills.* ¹⁰Judah marched against the Canaanites in Hebron (formerly called Kiriath-arba), defeating the forces of Sheshai, Ahiman, and Talmai. ¹¹From there they marched against the people living in the town of Debir (formerly called Kiriath-sepher).

¹²Then Caleb said, "I will give my daughter Acsah in marriage to the one who attacks and captures Kiriath-sepher." ¹³Othniel, the son of Caleb's younger brother Kenaz, was the one who conquered it, so Acsah became Othniel's wife.

¹⁴When Acsah married Othniel, she urged him* to ask her father for an additional field. As she got down off her donkey, Caleb asked her, "What is it? What can I do for you?"

¹⁵She said, "Give me a further blessing. You have been kind enough to give me land in the Negev; please give me springs as well." So Caleb gave her the upper and lower springs.

¹⁶When the tribe of Judah left Jericho,* the Kenites, who were descendants of Moses' father-in-law, traveled with them into the wilderness of Judah. They settled among the people there, near the town of Arad in the Negev.

¹⁷Then Judah joined with Simeon to fight against the Canaanites living in Zephath, and they completely destroyed* the town. So the town was named Hormah.* ¹⁸In addition, Judah captured the cities of Gaza, Ashkelon, and Ekron, along with their surrounding territories.

Israel Fails to Conquer the Land

¹⁹The LORD was with the people of Judah, and they took possession of the hill country. But they failed to drive out the people living in the plains because the people there had iron chariots. ²⁰The city of Hebron was given to Caleb as Moses had promised. And Caleb drove out the people living there, who were descendants of the three sons of Anak. ²¹The tribe of Benjamin, however, failed to drive out the Jebusites, who were living in Jerusalem. So to this day the Jebusites live in Jerusalem among the people of Benjamin.

²²The descendants of Joseph attacked the town of Bethel, and the LORD was with them.

1:9 Hebrew the Shephelah.   1:14 Greek version and Latin Vulgate read he urged her.   1:16 Hebrew the city of palms.   1:17a The Hebrew term used here refers to the complete consecration of things or people to the LORD, either by destroying them or by giving them as an offering. 1:17b Hormah means "destruction."

²³They sent spies to Bethel (formerly known as Luz), ²⁴who confronted a man coming out of the city. They said to him, "Show us a way into the city, and we will have mercy on you." ²⁵So he showed them a way in, and they killed everyone in the city except for this man and his family. ²⁶Later the man moved to the land of the Hittites, where he built a city. He named the city Luz, and it is known by that name to this day.

²⁷The tribe of Manasseh failed to drive out the people living in Beth-shan,* Taanach, Dor, Ibleam, Megiddo, and their surrounding villages, because the Canaanites were determined to stay in that region. ²⁸When the Israelites grew stronger, they forced the Canaanites to work as slaves, but they never did drive them out of the land.

²⁹The tribe of Ephraim also failed to drive out the Canaanites living in Gezer, and so the Canaanites continued to live there among them.

³⁰The tribe of Zebulun also failed to drive out the Canaanites living in Kitron and Nahalol, who continued to live there among them. But they forced them to work as slaves.

³¹The tribe of Asher also failed to drive out the residents of Acco, Sidon, Ahlab, Aczib, Helbah, Aphik, and Rehob. ³²In fact, because they did not drive them out, the Canaanites dominated the land where the people of Asher lived.

³³The tribe of Naphtali also failed to drive out the residents of Beth-shemesh and Beth-anath. Instead, the Canaanites dominated the land where they lived. Nevertheless, the people of Beth-shemesh and Beth-anath were sometimes forced to work as slaves for the people of Naphtali.

³⁴As for the tribe of Dan, the Amorites forced them into the hill country and would not let them come down into the plains. ³⁵The Amorites were determined to stay in Mount Heres, Aijalon, and Shaalbim, but when the descendants of Joseph became stronger, they forced the Amorites to work as slaves. ³⁶The boundary of the Amorites ran from Scorpion Pass* to Sela and continued upward from there.

CHAPTER 2

The LORD's Messenger Comes to Bokim

The angel of the LORD went up from Gilgal to Bokim with a message for the Israelites. He told them, "I brought you out of Egypt into this land that I swore to give your ancestors, and I said I would never break my covenant with you. ²For

your part, you were not to make any covenants with the people living in this land; instead, you were to destroy their altars. Why, then, have you disobeyed my command? ³Since you have done this, I will no longer drive out the people living in your land. They will be thorns in your sides, and their gods will be a constant temptation to you." ⁴When the angel of the LORD finished speaking, the Israelites wept loudly. ⁵So they called the place "Weeping,"* and they offered sacrifices to the LORD.

The Death of Joshua

⁶After Joshua sent the people away, each of the tribes left to take possession of the land allotted to them. ⁷And the Israelites served the LORD throughout the lifetime of Joshua and the leaders who outlived him—those who had seen all the great things the LORD had done for Israel.

⁸Then Joshua son of Nun, the servant of the LORD, died at the age of 110. ⁹They buried him in the land he had inherited, at Timnath-serah* in the hill country of Ephraim, north of Mount Gaash.

Israel Disobeys the LORD

¹⁰After that generation died, another generation grew up who did not acknowledge the LORD or remember the mighty things he had done for Israel. ¹¹Then the Israelites did what was evil in the LORD's sight and worshiped the images of Baal. ¹²They abandoned the LORD, the God of their ancestors, who had brought them out of Egypt. They chased after other gods, worshiping the gods of the people around them. And they angered the LORD. ¹³They abandoned the LORD to serve Baal and the images of Ashtoreth. ¹⁴This made the LORD burn with anger against Israel, so he handed them over to marauders who stole their possessions. He sold them to their enemies all around, and they were no longer able to resist them. ¹⁵Every time Israel went out to battle, the LORD fought against them, bringing them defeat, just as he promised. And the people were very distressed.

The LORD Rescues His People

¹⁶Then the LORD raised up judges to rescue the Israelites from their enemies. ¹⁷Yet Israel did not listen to the judges but prostituted themselves to other gods, bowing down to them. How quickly they turned away from the path of their ancestors, who had walked in obedience to the LORD's commands. ¹⁸Whenever the LORD placed a judge

---

1:27 Hebrew *Beth-shean,* a variant name for Beth-shan.   1:36 Hebrew *Akrabbim.*   2:5 Hebrew *Bokim.*   2:9 Hebrew *Timnath-heres,* a variant name for Timnath-serah.

over Israel, he was with that judge and rescued the people from their enemies throughout the judge's lifetime. For the LORD took pity on his people, who were burdened by oppression and suffering. ¹⁹But when the judge died, the people returned to their corrupt ways, behaving worse than those who had lived before them. They followed other gods, worshiping and bowing down to them. And they refused to give up their evil practices and stubborn ways.

²⁰So the LORD burned with anger against Israel. He said, "Because these people have violated the covenant I made with their ancestors and have ignored my commands, ²¹I will no longer drive out the nations that Joshua left unconquered when he died. ²²I did this to test Israel—to see whether or not they would obey the LORD as their ancestors did." ²³That is why the LORD did not quickly drive the nations out or allow Joshua to conquer them all.

CHAPTER 3

The Nations Left in Canaan

The LORD left certain nations in the land to test those Israelites who had not participated in the wars of Canaan. ²He did this to teach warfare to generations of Israelites who had no experience in battle. ³These were the nations: the Philistines (those living under the five Philistine rulers), all the Canaanites, the Sidonians, and the Hivites living in the hill country of Lebanon from Mount Baal-hermon to Lebo-hamath. ⁴These people were left to test the Israelites—to see whether they would obey the commands the LORD had given to their ancestors through Moses.

⁵So Israel lived among the Canaanites, Hittites, Amorites, Perizzites, Hivites, and Jebusites, ⁶and they intermarried with them. Israelite sons married their daughters, and Israelite daughters were given in marriage to their sons. And the Israelites worshiped their gods.

Othniel Becomes Israel's Judge

⁷The Israelites did what was evil in the LORD's sight. They forgot about the LORD their God, and they worshiped the images of Baal and the Asherah poles. ⁸Then the LORD burned with anger against Israel, and he handed them over to King Cushan-rishathaim of Aram-naharaim.* And the Israelites were subject to Cushan-rishathaim for eight years.

⁹But when Israel cried out to the LORD for help, the LORD raised up a man to rescue them. His name was Othniel, the son of Caleb's younger brother, Kenaz. ¹⁰The Spirit of the LORD came upon him, and he became Israel's judge. He went to war against King Cushan-rishathaim of Aram, and the LORD gave Othniel victory over him. ¹¹So there was peace in the land for forty years. Then Othniel son of Kenaz died.

Ehud Becomes Israel's Judge

¹²Once again the Israelites did what was evil in the LORD's sight, so the LORD gave King Eglon of Moab control over Israel. ¹³Together with the Ammonites and Amalekites, Eglon attacked Israel and took possession of Jericho.* ¹⁴And the Israelites were subject to Eglon of Moab for eighteen years.

¹⁵But when Israel cried out to the LORD for help, the LORD raised up a man to rescue them. His name was Ehud son of Gera, of the tribe of Benjamin, who was left-handed. The Israelites sent Ehud to deliver their tax money to King Eglon of Moab. ¹⁶So Ehud made himself a double-edged dagger that was eighteen inches* long, and he strapped it to his right thigh, keeping it hidden under his clothing. ¹⁷He brought the tax money to Eglon, who was very fat. ¹⁸After delivering the payment, Ehud sent home those who had carried the tax money.

¹⁹But when Ehud reached the stone carvings near Gilgal, he turned back. He came to Eglon and said, "I have a secret message for you." So the king commanded his servants to be silent and sent them all out of the room. ²⁰Ehud walked over to Eglon as he was sitting alone in a cool upstairs room and said, "I have a message for you from God!" As King Eglon rose from his seat, ²¹Ehud reached with his left hand, pulled out the dagger strapped to his right thigh, and plunged it into the king's belly. ²²The dagger went so deep that the handle disappeared beneath the king's fat. So Ehud left the dagger in, and the king's bowels emptied. ²³Then Ehud closed and locked the doors and climbed down the latrine and escaped through the sewage access.

²⁴After Ehud was gone, the king's servants returned and found the doors to the upstairs room locked. They thought he might be using the latrine, ²⁵so they waited. But when the king didn't come out after a long delay, they became concerned and got a key. And when they opened the door, they found their master dead on the floor.

3:8 *Aram-naharaim* means "Aram of the two rivers," thought to have been located between the Euphrates and Balih Rivers in northwestern Mesopotamia.   3:13 Hebrew *the city of palms*.   3:16 Hebrew *1 cubit* [45 centimeters].

26While the servants were waiting, Ehud escaped, passing the idols on his way to Seirah. 27When he arrived in the hill country of Ephraim, Ehud sounded a call to arms. Then he led a band of Israelites down from the hills. 28"Follow me," he said, "for the LORD has given you victory over Moab your enemy." So they followed him. And the Israelites took control of the shallows of the Jordan River across from Moab, preventing anyone from crossing. 29They attacked the Moabites and killed about ten thousand of their strongest and bravest warriors. Not one of them escaped. 30So Moab was conquered by Israel that day, and the land was at peace for eighty years.

Shamgar Becomes Israel's Judge
31After Ehud, Shamgar son of Anath rescued Israel. He killed six hundred Philistines with an ox goad.

CHAPTER **4**
Deborah Becomes Israel's Judge
After Ehud's death, the Israelites again did what was evil in the LORD's sight. 2So the LORD handed them over to King Jabin of Hazor, a Canaanite king. The commander of his army was Sisera, who lived in Harosheth-haggoyim. 3Sisera, who had nine hundred iron chariots, ruthlessly oppressed the Israelites for twenty years. Then the Israelites cried out to the LORD for help.

4Deborah, the wife of Lappidoth, was a prophet who had become a judge in Israel. 5She would hold court under the Palm of Deborah, which stood between Ramah and Bethel in the hill country of Ephraim, and the Israelites came to her to settle their disputes. 6One day she sent for Barak son of Abinoam, who lived in Kedesh in the land of Naphtali. She said to him, "This is what the LORD, the God of Israel, commands you: Assemble ten thousand warriors from the tribes of Naphtali and Zebulun at Mount Tabor. 7I will lure Sisera, commander of Jabin's army, along with his chariots and warriors, to the Kishon River. There I will give you victory over him."

8Barak told her, "I will go, but only if you go with me!"

9"Very well," she replied, "I will go with you. But since you have made this choice, you will receive no honor. For the LORD's victory over Sisera will be at the hands of a woman." So Deborah went with Barak to Kedesh. 10At Kedesh, Barak called together the tribes of Zebulun and Naphtali, and ten thousand warriors marched up with him. Deborah also marched with them.

11Now Heber the Kenite, a descendant of Moses' brother-in-law* Hobab, had moved away from the other members of his tribe and pitched his tent by the Oak of Zaanannim, near Kedesh.

12When Sisera was told that Barak son of Abinoam had gone up to Mount Tabor, 13he called for all nine hundred of his iron chariots and all of his warriors, and they marched from Harosheth-haggoyim to the Kishon River.

14Then Deborah said to Barak, "Get ready! Today the LORD will give you victory over Sisera, for the LORD is marching ahead of you." So Barak led his ten thousand warriors down the slopes of Mount Tabor into battle. 15When Barak attacked, the LORD threw Sisera and all his charioteers and warriors into a panic. Then Sisera leaped down from his chariot and escaped on foot. 16Barak chased the enemy and their chariots all the way to Harosheth-haggoyim, killing all of Sisera's warriors. Not a single one was left alive.

17Meanwhile, Sisera ran to the tent of Jael, the wife of Heber the Kenite, because Heber's family was on friendly terms with King Jabin of Hazor. 18Jael went out to meet Sisera and said to him, "Come into my tent, sir. Come in. Don't be afraid." So he went into her tent, and she covered him with a blanket.

19"Please give me some water," he said. "I'm thirsty." So she gave him some milk to drink and covered him again.

20"Stand at the door of the tent," he told her. "If anybody comes and asks you if there is anyone here, say no."

21But when Sisera fell asleep from exhaustion, Jael quietly crept up to him with a hammer and tent peg. Then she drove the tent peg through his temple and into the ground, and so he died.

22When Barak came looking for Sisera, Jael went out to meet him. She said, "Come, and I will show you the man you are looking for." So he followed her into the tent and found Sisera lying there dead, with the tent peg through his temple.

23So on that day Israel saw God subdue Jabin, the Canaanite king. 24And from that time on Israel became stronger and stronger against King Jabin, until they finally destroyed him.

4:11 Or *father-in-law.*

CHAPTER **5**

The Song of Deborah

On that day Deborah and Barak son of Abinoam sang this song:

2 "When Israel's leaders take charge,
    and the people gladly follow—
bless the LORD!

3 "Listen, you kings!
    Pay attention, you mighty rulers!
    For I will sing to the LORD.
    I will lift up my song to the LORD, the
        God of Israel.

4 "LORD, when you set out from Seir
    and marched across the fields of Edom,
the earth trembled
    and the cloudy skies poured down rain.

5 The mountains quaked at the coming of the
        LORD.
    Even Mount Sinai shook in the presence
        of the LORD, the God of Israel.

6 "In the days of Shamgar son of Anath, and
        in the days of Jael,
    people avoided the main roads,
    and travelers stayed on crooked side paths.

7 There were few people left in the villages of
        Israel—
    until Deborah arose as a mother for
        Israel.

8 When Israel chose new gods,
    war erupted at the city gates.
    Yet not a shield or spear could be seen
        among forty thousand warriors in Israel!

9 My heart goes out to Israel's leaders,
    and to those who gladly followed.
    Bless the LORD!

10 "You who ride on fine donkeys
    and sit on fancy saddle blankets, listen!
    And you who must walk along the road,
        listen!

11 Listen to the village musicians* gathered at
        the watering holes.
    They recount the righteous victories of
        the LORD,
    and the victories of his villagers in Israel.
    Then the people of the LORD
        marched down to the city gates.

12 "Wake up, Deborah, wake up!
    Wake up, wake up, and sing a song!
    Arise, Barak!
    Lead your captives away, son of Abinoam!

5:11 The meaning of the Hebrew is uncertain.

13 "Down from Tabor marched the remnant
        against the mighty.
    The people of the LORD marched down
        against mighty warriors.

14 They came down from Ephraim—a land
        that once belonged to the Amalekites,
    and Benjamin also followed you.
    From Makir the commanders marched down;
        from Zebulun came those who carry the
        rod of authority.

15 The princes of Issachar were with Deborah
        and Barak.
    They followed Barak, rushing into the
        valley.
    But in the tribe of Reuben
        there was great indecision.

16 Why did you sit at home among the
        sheepfolds—
    to hear the shepherds whistle for their flocks?
    In the tribe of Reuben
        there was great indecision.

17 Gilead remained east of the Jordan.
    And Dan, why did he stay home?
    Asher sat unmoved at the seashore,
        remaining in his harbors.

18 But Zebulun risked his life,
    as did Naphtali, on the battlefield.

19 "The kings of Canaan fought at Taanach
        near Megiddo's springs,
    but they carried off no treasures of battle.

20 The stars fought from heaven.
    The stars in their orbits fought against
        Sisera.

21 The Kishon River swept them away—
    that ancient river, the Kishon.
    March on, my soul, with courage!

22 Then the horses' hooves hammered the ground,
    the galloping, galloping of Sisera's
        mighty steeds.

23 'Let the people of Meroz be cursed,' said the
        angel of the LORD.
    'Let them be utterly cursed
    because they did not come to help the LORD,
        to help the LORD against the mighty warriors.'

24 "Most blessed is Jael,
    the wife of Heber the Kenite.
    May she be blessed above all women
        who live in tents.

25 Sisera asked for water,
    and Jael gave him milk.
    In a bowl fit for kings,
        she brought him yogurt.

26 Then with her left hand she reached for a
    tent peg,
  and with her right hand she reached for
    the workman's hammer.
  She hit Sisera, crushing his head.
  She pounded the tent peg through his
    head, piercing his temples.
27 He sank, he fell,
  he lay dead at her feet.

28 "From the window Sisera's mother looked
    out.
  Through the window she watched for his
    return, saying,
  'Why is his chariot so long in coming?
  Why don't we hear the sound of chariot
    wheels?'
29 A reply comes from her wise women,
  and she repeats these words to herself:
30 'They are dividing the captured goods they
    found—
  a woman or two for every man.
  There are gorgeous robes for Sisera,
  and colorful, beautifully embroidered
    robes for me.'

31 "LORD, may all your enemies die as Sisera did!
  But may those who love you rise like the
    sun at full strength!"

Then there was peace in the land for forty years.

CHAPTER 6

Gideon Becomes Israel's Judge

Again the Israelites did what was evil in the
LORD's sight. So the LORD handed them over to
the Midianites for seven years. 2The Midianites
were so cruel that the Israelites fled to the mountains, where they made hiding places for themselves in caves and dens. 3Whenever the
Israelites planted their crops, marauders from
Midian, Amalek, and the people of the east
would attack Israel, 4camping in the land and
destroying crops as far away as Gaza. They left
the Israelites with nothing to eat, taking all the
sheep, oxen, and donkeys. 5These enemy
hordes, coming with their cattle and tents as
thick as locusts, arrived on droves of camels too
numerous to count. And they stayed until the
land was stripped bare. 6So Israel was reduced to
starvation by the Midianites. Then the Israelites
cried out to the LORD for help.

7When they cried out to the LORD because of
Midian, 8the LORD sent a prophet to the Israel-

6:19 Hebrew *1 ephah* [18 liters].

ites. He said, "This is what the LORD, the God of
Israel, says: I brought you up out of slavery in
Egypt 9and rescued you from the Egyptians and
from all who oppressed you. I drove out your
enemies and gave you their land. 10I told you, 'I
am the LORD your God. You must not worship
the gods of the Amorites, in whose land you now
live.' But you have not listened to me."

11Then the angel of the LORD came and sat
beneath the oak tree at Ophrah, which belonged
to Joash of the clan of Abiezer. Gideon son of
Joash had been threshing wheat at the bottom
of a winepress to hide the grain from the Midianites. 12The angel of the LORD appeared to him
and said, "Mighty hero, the LORD is with you!"

13"Sir," Gideon replied, "if the LORD is with
us, why has all this happened to us? And where
are all the miracles our ancestors told us about?
Didn't they say, 'The LORD brought us up out of
Egypt'? But now the LORD has abandoned us and
handed us over to the Midianites."

14Then the LORD turned to him and said, "Go
with the strength you have and rescue Israel
from the Midianites. I am sending you!"

15"But Lord," Gideon replied, "how can I
rescue Israel? My clan is the weakest in the whole
tribe of Manasseh, and I am the least in my
entire family!"

16The LORD said to him, "I will be with you.
And you will destroy the Midianites as if you
were fighting against one man."

17Gideon replied, "If you are truly going to
help me, show me a sign to prove that it is really
the LORD speaking to me. 18Don't go away until
I come back and bring my offering to you."

The LORD answered, "I will stay here until you
return."

19Gideon hurried home. He cooked a young
goat, and with half a bushel* of flour he baked
some bread without yeast. Then, carrying the
meat in a basket and the broth in a pot, he
brought them out and presented them to the
angel, who was under the oak tree.

20The angel of God said to him, "Place the
meat and the unleavened bread on this rock, and
pour the broth over it." And Gideon did as he was
told. 21Then the angel of the LORD touched the
meat and bread with the staff in his hand, and fire
flamed up from the rock and consumed all he had
brought. And the angel of the LORD disappeared.

22When Gideon realized that it was the angel
of the LORD, he cried out, "Sovereign LORD, I have
seen the angel of the LORD face to face!"

²³"It is all right," the LORD replied. "Do not be afraid. You will not die." ²⁴And Gideon built an altar to the LORD there and named it "The LORD Is Peace."* The altar remains in Ophrah in the land of the clan of Abiezer to this day.

²⁵That night the LORD said to Gideon, "Take the second best bull from your father's herd, the one that is seven years old. Pull down your father's altar to Baal, and cut down the Asherah pole standing beside it. ²⁶Then build an altar to the LORD your God here on this hill, laying the stones carefully. Sacrifice the bull as a burnt offering on the altar, using as fuel the wood of the Asherah pole you cut down." ²⁷So Gideon took ten of his servants and did as the LORD had commanded. But he did it at night because he was afraid of the other members of his father's household and the people of the town. He knew what would happen if they found out who had done it.

²⁸Early the next morning, as the people of the town began to stir, someone discovered that the altar of Baal had been knocked down and that the Asherah pole beside it was gone. In their place a new altar had been built, and it had the remains of a sacrifice on it. ²⁹The people said to each other, "Who did this?" And after asking around and making a careful search, they learned that it was Gideon, the son of Joash.

³⁰"Bring out your son," they shouted to Joash. "He must die for destroying the altar of Baal and for cutting down the Asherah pole."

³¹But Joash shouted to the mob, "Why are you defending Baal? Will you argue his case? Whoever pleads his case will be put to death by morning! If Baal truly is a god, let him defend himself and destroy the one who knocked down his altar!" ³²From then on Gideon was called Jerubbaal, which means "Let Baal defend himself," because he knocked down Baal's altar.

³³Soon afterward the armies of Midian, Amalek, and the people of the east formed an alliance against Israel and crossed the Jordan, camping in the valley of Jezreel. ³⁴Then the Spirit of the LORD took possession of Gideon. He blew a ram's horn as a call to arms, and the men of the clan of Abiezer came to him. ³⁵He also sent messengers throughout Manasseh, Asher, Zebulun, and Naphtali, summoning their warriors, and all of them responded.

³⁶Then Gideon said to God, "If you are truly going to use me to rescue Israel as you promised, ³⁷prove it to me in this way. I will put some wool on the threshing floor tonight. If the fleece is wet with dew in the morning but the ground is dry, then I will know that you are going to help me rescue Israel as you promised." ³⁸And it happened just that way. When Gideon got up the next morning, he squeezed the fleece and wrung out a whole bowlful of water.

³⁹Then Gideon said to God, "Please don't be angry with me, but let me make one more request. This time let the fleece remain dry while the ground around it is wet with dew." ⁴⁰So that night God did as Gideon asked. The fleece was dry in the morning, but the ground was covered with dew.

CHAPTER **7**

Gideon Defeats the Midianites

So Jerubbaal (that is, Gideon) and his army got up early and went as far as the spring of Harod. The armies of Midian were camped north of them in the valley near the hill of Moreh. ²The LORD said to Gideon, "You have too many warriors with you. If I let all of you fight the Midianites, the Israelites will boast to me that they saved themselves by their own strength. ³Therefore, tell the people, 'Whoever is timid or afraid may leave* and go home.'" Twenty-two thousand of them went home, leaving only ten thousand who were willing to fight.

⁴But the LORD told Gideon, "There are still too many! Bring them down to the spring, and I will sort out who will go with you and who will not." ⁵When Gideon took his warriors down to the water, the LORD told him, "Divide the men into two groups. In one group put all those who cup water in their hands and lap it up with their tongues like dogs. In the other group put all those who kneel down and drink with their mouths in the stream." ⁶Only three hundred of the men drank from their hands. All the others got down on their knees and drank with their mouths in the stream. ⁷The LORD told Gideon, "With these three hundred men I will rescue you and give you victory over the Midianites. Send all the others home." ⁸So Gideon collected the provisions and rams' horns of the other warriors and sent them home. But he kept the three hundred men with him.

Now the Midianite camp was in the valley just below Gideon. ⁹During the night, the LORD said, "Get up! Go down into the Midianite camp, for I have given you victory over them! ¹⁰But if you are afraid to attack, go down to the camp with your servant Purah. ¹¹Listen to what

6:24 Hebrew *Yahweh Shalom.*   7:3 Hebrew *leave Mount Gilead.* The identity of Mount Gilead is uncertain in this context. It is perhaps used here as another name for Mount Gilboa.

the Midianites are saying, and you will be greatly encouraged. Then you will be eager to attack."

So Gideon took Purah and went down to the outposts of the enemy camp. 12The armies of Midian, Amalek, and the people of the east had settled in the valley like a swarm of locusts. Their camels were like grains of sand on the seashore—too many to count! 13Gideon crept up just as a man was telling his friend about a dream. The man said, "I had this dream, and in my dream a loaf of barley bread came tumbling down into the Midianite camp. It hit a tent, turned it over, and knocked it flat!"

14His friend said, "Your dream can mean only one thing—God has given Gideon son of Joash, the Israelite, victory over all the armies united with Midian!"

15When Gideon heard the dream and its interpretation, he thanked God. Then he returned to the Israelite camp and shouted, "Get up! For the LORD has given you victory over the Midianites!" 16He divided the three hundred men into three groups and gave each man a ram's horn and a clay jar with a torch in it. 17Then he said to them, "Keep your eyes on me. When I come to the edge of the camp, do just as I do. 18As soon as my group blows the rams' horns, those of you on the other sides of the camp blow your horns and shout, 'For the LORD and for Gideon!'"

19It was just after midnight, after the changing of the guard, when Gideon and the one hundred men with him reached the outer edge of the Midianite camp. Suddenly, they blew the horns and broke their clay jars. 20Then all three groups blew their horns and broke their jars. They held the blazing torches in their left hands and the horns in their right hands and shouted, "A sword for the LORD and for Gideon!" 21Each man stood at his position around the camp and watched as all the Midianites rushed around in a panic, shouting as they ran. 22When the three hundred Israelites blew their horns, the LORD caused the warriors in the camp to fight against each other with their swords. Those who were not killed fled to places as far away as Beth-shittah near Zererah and to the border of Abel-meholah near Tabbath.

23Then Gideon sent for the warriors of Naphtali, Asher, and Manasseh, who joined in the chase after the fleeing army of Midian. 24Gideon also sent messengers throughout the hill country of Ephraim, saying, "Come down to attack the Midianites. Cut them off at the shallows of the Jordan

River at Beth-barah." And the men of Ephraim did as they were told. 25They captured Oreb and Zeeb, the two Midianite generals, killing Oreb at the rock of Oreb, and Zeeb at the winepress of Zeeb. And they continued to chase the Midianites. Afterward the Israelites brought the heads of Oreb and Zeeb to Gideon, who was by the Jordan.

CHAPTER **8**

Gideon Kills Zebah and Zalmunna

Then the people of Ephraim asked Gideon, "Why have you treated us this way? Why didn't you send for us when you first went out to fight the Midianites?" And they argued heatedly with Gideon.

2But Gideon replied, "What have I done compared to you? Aren't the last grapes of Ephraim's harvest better than the entire crop of my little clan of Abiezer? 3God gave you victory over Oreb and Zeeb, the generals of the Midianite army. What have I done compared to that?" When the men of Ephraim heard Gideon's answer, they were no longer angry.

4Gideon then crossed the Jordan River with his three hundred men, and though they were exhausted, they continued to chase the enemy. 5When they reached Succoth, Gideon asked the leaders of the town, "Will you please give my warriors some food? They are very tired. I am chasing Zebah and Zalmunna, the kings of Midian."

6But the leaders of Succoth replied, "You haven't caught Zebah and Zalmunna yet. Catch them first, and then we will feed your warriors."

7So Gideon said, "After the LORD gives me victory over Zebah and Zalmunna, I will return and tear your flesh with the thorns and briers of the wilderness."

8From there Gideon went up to Peniel* and asked for food, but he got the same answer. 9So he said to the people of Peniel, "After I return in victory, I will tear down this tower."

10By this time Zebah and Zalmunna were in Karkor with a remnant of 15,000 warriors—all that remained of the allied armies of the east—for 120,000 had already been killed. 11Gideon circled around by the caravan route east of Nobah and Jogbehah, taking the Midianite army by surprise. 12Zebah and Zalmunna, the two Midianite kings, fled, but Gideon chased them down and captured all their warriors.

13After this, Gideon returned by way of Heres Pass. 14There he captured a young man from Suc-

8:8 Hebrew *Penuel*, a variant name for Peniel; also in 8:9, 17.

coth and demanded that he write down the names of all the seventy-seven rulers and leaders in the town. ¹⁵Gideon then returned to Succoth and said to the leaders, "Here are Zebah and Zalmunna. When we were here before, you taunted me, saying, 'You haven't caught Zebah and Zalmunna yet. Catch them first, and then we will feed your exhausted warriors.'" ¹⁶Then Gideon took the leaders of the town and taught them a lesson, punishing them with thorns and briers from the wilderness. ¹⁷He also knocked down the tower of Peniel and killed all the men in the town.

¹⁸Then Gideon asked Zebah and Zalmunna, "The men you killed at Tabor—what were they like?"

"Like you," they replied. "They all had the look of a king's son."

¹⁹"They were my brothers!" Gideon exclaimed. "As surely as the LORD lives, I wouldn't kill you if you hadn't killed them."

²⁰Turning to Jether, his oldest son, he said, "Kill them!" But Jether did not draw his sword, for he was only a boy and was afraid.

²¹Then Zebah and Zalmunna said to Gideon, "Don't ask a boy to do a man's job! Do it yourself!" So Gideon killed them both and took the royal ornaments from the necks of their camels.

Gideon's Sacred Ephod

²²Then the Israelites said to Gideon, "Be our ruler! You and your son and your grandson will be our rulers, for you have rescued us from Midian."

²³But Gideon replied, "I will not rule over you, nor will my son. The LORD will rule over you! ²⁴However, I have one request. Each of you can give me an earring out of the treasures you collected from your fallen enemies." (The enemies, being Ishmaelites, all wore gold earrings.)

²⁵"Gladly!" they replied. They spread out a cloak, and each one threw in a gold earring he had gathered. ²⁶The weight of the gold earrings was forty-three pounds,* not including the crescents and pendants, the royal clothing of the kings, or the chains around the necks of their camels. ²⁷Gideon made a sacred ephod from the gold and put it in Ophrah, his hometown. But soon all the Israelites prostituted themselves by worshiping it, and it became a trap for Gideon and his family.

²⁸That is the story of how Israel subdued Midian, which never recovered. Throughout the rest of Gideon's lifetime—about forty years— the land was at peace.

²⁹Then Gideon* son of Joash returned home. ³⁰He had seventy sons, for he had many wives. ³¹He also had a concubine in Shechem, who bore him a son named Abimelech. ³²Gideon died when he was very old, and he was buried in the grave of his father, Joash, at Ophrah in the land of the clan of Abiezer.

³³As soon as Gideon was dead, the Israelites prostituted themselves by worshiping the images of Baal, making Baal-berith their god. ³⁴They forgot the LORD their God, who had rescued them from all their enemies surrounding them. ³⁵Nor did they show any loyalty to the family of Jerubbaal (that is, Gideon), despite all the good he had done for Israel.

CHAPTER 9

Abimelech Rules over Shechem

One day Gideon's* son Abimelech went to Shechem to visit his mother's brothers. He said to them and to the rest of his mother's family, ²"Ask the people of Shechem whether they want to be ruled by all seventy of Gideon's sons or by one man. And remember, I am your own flesh and blood!"

³So Abimelech's uncles spoke to all the people of Shechem on his behalf. And after listening to their proposal, they decided in favor of Abimelech because he was their relative. ⁴They gave him seventy silver coins from the temple of Baal-berith, which he used to hire some soldiers who agreed to follow him. ⁵He took the soldiers to his father's home at Ophrah, and there, on one stone, they killed all seventy of his half brothers. But the youngest brother, Jotham, escaped and hid. ⁶Then the people of Shechem and Beth-millo called a meeting under the oak beside the pillar* at Shechem and made Abimelech their king.

Jotham's Parable

⁷When Jotham heard about this, he climbed to the top of Mount Gerizim and shouted, "Listen to me, people of Shechem! Listen to me if you want God to listen to you! ⁸Once upon a time the trees decided to elect a king. First they said to the olive tree, 'Be our king!' ⁹But it refused, saying, 'Should I quit producing the olive oil that blesses both God and people, just to wave back and forth over the trees?'

¹⁰Then they said to the fig tree, 'You be our

8:26 Hebrew *1,700 shekels* [19.4 kilograms].   8:29 Hebrew *Jerubbaal*; see 6:32.   9:1 Hebrew *Jerubbaal's* (see 6:32); also in 9:2, 24.   9:6 The meaning of the Hebrew is uncertain.

king!' ¹¹But the fig tree also refused, saying, 'Should I quit producing my sweet fruit just to wave back and forth over the trees?'

¹²"Then they said to the grapevine, 'You be our king!' ¹³But the grapevine replied, 'Should I quit producing the wine that cheers both God and people, just to wave back and forth over the trees?'

¹⁴"Then all the trees finally turned to the thornbush and said, 'Come, you be our king!' ¹⁵And the thornbush replied, 'If you truly want to make me your king, come and take shelter in my shade. If not, let fire come out from me and devour the cedars of Lebanon.'

¹⁶"Now make sure you have acted honorably and in good faith by making Abimelech your king, and that you have done right by Gideon* and all of his descendants. Have you treated my father with the honor he deserves? ¹⁷For he fought for you and risked his life when he rescued you from the Midianites. ¹⁸But now you have revolted against my father and his descendants, killing his seventy sons on one stone. And you have chosen his slave woman's son, Abimelech, to be your king just because he is your relative. ¹⁹If you have acted honorably and in good faith toward Gideon and his descendants, then may you find joy in Abimelech, and may he find joy in you. ²⁰But if you have not acted in good faith, then may fire come out from Abimelech and devour the people of Shechem and Beth-millo; and may fire come out from the people of Shechem and Beth-millo and devour Abimelech!" ²¹Then Jotham escaped and lived in Beer because he was afraid of his brother Abimelech.

Shechem's Revolt against Abimelech

²²After Abimelech had ruled over Israel for three years, ²³God stirred up trouble* between Abimelech and the people of Shechem, and they revolted. ²⁴In the events that followed, God punished Abimelech and the men of Shechem for murdering Gideon's seventy sons. ²⁵The people of Shechem set an ambush for Abimelech on the hilltops and robbed everyone who passed that way. But someone warned Abimelech about their plot.

²⁶At that time Gaal son of Ebed moved to Shechem with his brothers and gained the confidence of the people of Shechem. ²⁷During the annual harvest festival at Shechem, held in the temple of the local god, the wine flowed freely, and everyone began cursing Abimelech. ²⁸"Who

is Abimelech?" Gaal shouted. "He's not a true descendant of Shechem!* Why should we be Abimelech's servants? He's merely the son of Gideon, and Zebul is his administrator. Serve the men of Hamor, who are Shechem's true descendants. Why should we serve Abimelech? ²⁹If I were in charge, I would get rid of Abimelech. I would say* to him, 'Get some more soldiers, and come out and fight!'"

³⁰But when Zebul, the leader of the city, heard what Gaal was saying, he was furious. ³¹He sent messengers to Abimelech in Arumah,* telling him, "Gaal son of Ebed and his brothers have come to live in Shechem, and now they are inciting the city to rebel against you. ³²Come by night with an army and hide out in the fields. ³³In the morning, as soon as it is daylight, storm the city. When Gaal and those who are with him come out against you, you can do with them as you wish."

³⁴So Abimelech and his men went by night and split into four groups, stationing themselves around Shechem. ³⁵Gaal was standing at the city gates when Abimelech and his army came out of hiding. ³⁶When Gaal saw them, he said to Zebul, "Look, there are people coming down from the hilltops!"

Zebul replied, "It's just the shadows of the hills that look like men."

³⁷But again Gaal said, "No, people are coming down from the hills.* And another group is coming down the road past the Diviners' Oak.*"

³⁸Then Zebul turned on him triumphantly. "Now where is that big mouth of yours?" he demanded. "Wasn't it you that said, 'Who is Abimelech, and why should we be his servants?' The men you mocked are right outside the city! Go out and fight them!"

³⁹Gaal then led the men of Shechem into battle against Abimelech, ⁴⁰but he was defeated and ran away. Many of Shechem's warriors were killed, and the ground was covered with dead bodies all the way to the city gate. ⁴¹Abimelech stayed in Arumah, and Zebul drove Gaal and his brothers out of Shechem.

⁴²The next day the people of Shechem went out into the fields to battle. When Abimelech heard about it, ⁴³he divided his men into three groups and set an ambush in the fields. When Abimelech saw the people coming out of the city, he and his men jumped up from their hiding places and attacked them. ⁴⁴Abimelech and his group stormed the city gate to keep the men of Shechem from getting back in, while Abime-

9:16 Hebrew *Jerubbaal* (see 6:32); also in 9:19, 28, 57.   9:23 Hebrew *sent a disturbing spirit.*   9:28 Hebrew *Who is Shechem?*   9:29 As in Greek version; Hebrew reads *And he said.*   9:31 Hebrew *Tormah;* see 9:41.   9:37a Or *the center of the land.*   9:37b Hebrew *Elon-meonenim.*

lech's other two groups cut them down in the fields. 45The battle went on all day before Abimelech finally captured the city. He killed the people, leveled the city, and scattered salt all over the ground.

46When the people who lived in the tower of Shechem heard what had happened, they took refuge within the walls of the temple of Baalberith.* 47Someone reported to Abimelech that the people were gathered together in the temple, 48so he led his forces to Mount Zalmon. He took an ax and chopped some branches from a tree, and he put them on his shoulder. "Quick, do as I have done!" he told his men. 49So each of them cut down some branches, following Abimelech's example. They piled the branches against the walls of the temple and set them on fire. So all the people who had lived in the tower of Shechem died, about a thousand men and women.

50Then Abimelech attacked the city of Thebez and captured it. 51But there was a strong tower inside the city, and the entire population fled to it. They barricaded themselves in and climbed up to the roof of the tower. 52Abimelech followed them to attack the tower. But as he prepared to set fire to the entrance, 53a woman on the roof threw down a millstone that landed on Abimelech's head and crushed his skull. 54He said to his young armor bearer, "Draw your sword and kill me! Don't let it be said that a woman killed Abimelech!" So the young man stabbed him with his sword, and he died. 55When Abimelech's men saw that he was dead, they disbanded and returned to their homes.

56Thus, God punished Abimelech for the evil he had done against his father by murdering his seventy brothers. 57God also punished the men of Shechem for all their evil. So the curse of Jotham son of Gideon came true.

CHAPTER **10**

Tola Becomes Israel's Judge

After Abimelech's death, Tola, the son of Puah and descendant of Dodo, came to rescue Israel. He was from the tribe of Issachar but lived in the town of Shamir in the hill country of Ephraim. 2He was Israel's judge for twenty-three years. When he died, he was buried in Shamir.

Jair Becomes Israel's Judge

3After Tola died, a man from Gilead named Jair judged Israel for twenty-two years. 4His thirty sons rode around on thirty donkeys, and they owned thirty towns in the land of Gilead, which are still called the Towns of Jair.* 5When Jair died, he was buried in Kamon.

The Ammonites Oppress Israel

6Again the Israelites did evil in the LORD's sight. They worshiped images of Baal and Ashtoreth, and the gods of Aram, Sidon, Moab, Ammon, and Philistia. Not only this, but they abandoned the LORD and no longer served him at all. 7So the LORD burned with anger against Israel, and he handed them over to the Philistines and the Ammonites, 8who began to oppress them that year. For eighteen years they oppressed all the Israelites east of the Jordan River in the land of the Amorites (that is, in Gilead). 9The Ammonites also crossed to the west side of the Jordan and attacked Judah, Benjamin, and Ephraim. The Israelites were in great distress. 10Finally, they cried out to the LORD, saying, "We have sinned against you because we have abandoned you as our God and have served the images of Baal."

11The LORD replied, "Did I not rescue you from the Egyptians, the Amorites, the Ammonites, the Philistines, 12the Sidonians, the Amalekites, and the Maonites? When they oppressed you, you cried out to me, and I rescued you. 13Yet you have abandoned me and served other gods. So I will not rescue you anymore. 14Go and cry out to the gods you have chosen! Let them rescue you in your hour of distress!"

15But the Israelites pleaded with the LORD and said, "We have sinned. Punish us as you see fit, only rescue us today from our enemies." 16Then the Israelites put aside their foreign gods and served the LORD. And he was grieved by their misery.

17At that time the armies of Ammon had gathered for war and were camped in Gilead, preparing to attack Israel's army at Mizpah. 18The leaders of Gilead said to each other, "Whoever attacks the Ammonites first will become ruler over all the people of Gilead."

CHAPTER **11**

Jephthah Becomes Israel's Judge

Now Jephthah of Gilead was a great warrior. He was the son of Gilead, but his mother was a prostitute. 2Gilead's wife also had several sons, and when these half brothers grew up, they chased Jephthah off the land. "You will not get any of our father's inheritance," they said, "for you are the son of a prostitute." 3So Jephthah

9:46 Hebrew El-berith, another name for Baal-berith; compare 9:4.   10:4 Hebrew Havvoth-jair.

fled from his brothers and lived in the land of Tob. Soon he had a large band of rebels following him.

⁴At about this time, the Ammonites began their war against Israel. ⁵When the Ammonites attacked, the leaders of Gilead sent for Jephthah in the land of Tob. They said, ⁶"Come and be our commander! Help us fight the Ammonites!"

⁷But Jephthah said to them, "Aren't you the ones who hated me and drove me from my father's house? Why do you come to me now when you're in trouble?"

⁸"Because we need you," they replied. "If you will lead us in battle against the Ammonites, we will make you ruler over all the people of Gilead."

⁹Jephthah said, "If I come with you and if the LORD gives me victory over the Ammonites, will you really make me ruler over all the people?"

¹⁰"The LORD is our witness," the leaders replied. "We promise to do whatever you say."

¹¹So Jephthah went with the leaders of Gilead, and he became their ruler and commander of the army. At Mizpah, in the presence of the LORD, Jephthah repeated what he had said to the leaders.

¹²Then Jephthah sent messengers to the king of Ammon, demanding to know why Israel was being attacked. ¹³The king of Ammon answered Jephthah's messengers, "When the Israelites came out of Egypt, they stole my land from the Arnon River to the Jabbok River and all the way to the Jordan. Now then, give back the land peaceably."

¹⁴Jephthah sent this message back to the Ammonite king:

¹⁵"This is what Jephthah says: Israel did not steal any land from Moab or Ammon. ¹⁶When the people of Israel arrived at Kadesh on their journey from Egypt after crossing the Red Sea,* ¹⁷they sent messengers to the king of Edom asking for permission to pass through his land. But their request was denied. Then they asked the king of Moab for similar permission, but he wouldn't let them pass through either. So the people of Israel stayed in Kadesh.

¹⁸"Finally, they went around Edom and Moab through the wilderness. They traveled along Moab's eastern border and camped on the other side of the Arnon River. But

they never once crossed the Arnon River into Moab.

¹⁹"Then Israel sent messengers to King Sihon of the Amorites, who ruled from Heshbon, asking for permission to cross through his land to get to their destination. ²⁰But King Sihon didn't trust Israel to pass through his land. Instead, he mobilized his army at Jahaz and attacked them. ²¹But the LORD, the God of Israel, gave his people victory over King Sihon. So Israel took control of all the land of the Amorites, who lived in that region, ²²from the Arnon River to the Jabbok River, and from the wilderness to the Jordan.

²³"So you see, it was the LORD, the God of Israel, who took away the land from the Amorites and gave it to Israel. Why, then, should we give it to you? ²⁴You keep whatever your god Chemosh gives you, and we will keep whatever the LORD our God gives us. ²⁵Are you any better than Balak son of Zippor, king of Moab? Did he try to make a case against Israel for disputed land? Did he go to war? No, of course not. ²⁶But now after three hundred years you make an issue of this! Israel has been living here all this time, spread across the land from Heshbon to Aroer and in all the towns along the Arnon River. Why have you made no effort to recover it before now? ²⁷I have not sinned against you. Rather, you have wronged me by attacking me. Let the LORD, who is judge, decide today which of us is right—Israel or Ammon."

²⁸But the king of Ammon paid no attention to Jephthah's message.

Jephthah's Vow

²⁹At that time the Spirit of the LORD came upon Jephthah, and he went throughout the land of Gilead and Manasseh, including Mizpah in Gilead, and led an army against the Ammonites. ³⁰And Jephthah made a vow to the LORD. He said, "If you give me victory over the Ammonites, ³¹I will give to the LORD the first thing coming out of my house to greet me when I return in triumph. I will sacrifice it as a burnt offering."

³²So Jephthah led his army against the Ammonites, and the LORD gave him victory. ³³He thoroughly defeated the Ammonites from Aroer to an area near Minnith—twenty towns—

11:16 Hebrew *sea of reeds.*

and as far away as Abel-keramim. Thus Israel subdued the Ammonites.

34When Jephthah returned home to Mizpah, his daughter—his only child—ran out to meet him, playing on a tambourine and dancing for joy. 35When he saw her, he tore his clothes in anguish. "My daughter!" he cried out. "My heart is breaking! What a tragedy that you came out to greet me. For I have made a vow to the LORD and cannot take it back."

36And she said, "Father, you have made a promise to the LORD. You must do to me what you have promised, for the LORD has given you a great victory over your enemies, the Ammonites. 37But first let me go up and roam in the hills and weep with my friends for two months, because I will die a virgin."

38"You may go," Jephthah said. And he let her go away for two months. She and her friends went into the hills and wept because she would never have children. 39When she returned home, her father kept his vow, and she died a virgin. So it has become a custom in Israel 40for young Israelite women to go away for four days each year to lament the fate of Jephthah's daughter.

CHAPTER **12**
Ephraim Fights with Jephthah

Then the tribe of Ephraim mobilized its army and crossed over to Zaphon. They sent this message to Jephthah: "Why didn't you call for us to help you fight against Ammon? We are going to burn down your house with you in it!"

2"I summoned you at the beginning of the dispute, but you refused to come!" Jephthah said. "You failed to help us in our struggle against Ammon. 3So I risked my life and went to battle without you, and the LORD gave me victory over the Ammonites. So why have you come to fight me?"

4The leaders of Ephraim responded, "The men of Gilead are nothing more than rejects from Ephraim and Manasseh." So Jephthah called out his army and attacked the men of Ephraim and defeated them.

5Jephthah captured the shallows of the Jordan, and whenever a fugitive from Ephraim tried to go back across, the men of Gilead would challenge him. "Are you a member of the tribe of Ephraim?" they would ask. If the man said, "No, I'm not," 6they would tell him to say "Shibboleth." If he was from Ephraim, he would say "Sibboleth," because people from Ephraim cannot pronounce the word correctly.

Then they would take him and kill him at the shallows of the Jordan River. So forty-two thousand Ephraimites were killed at that time.

7Jephthah was Israel's judge for six years. When he died, he was buried in one of the towns of Gilead.

Ibzan Becomes Israel's Judge

8After Jephthah, Ibzan became Israel's judge. He lived in Bethlehem, 9and he had thirty sons and thirty daughters. He married his daughters to men outside his clan and brought in thirty young women from outside his clan to marry his sons. Ibzan judged Israel for seven years. 10When he died, he was buried at Bethlehem.

Elon Becomes Israel's Judge

11After him, Elon from Zebulun became Israel's judge. He judged Israel for ten years. 12When he died, he was buried at Aijalon in Zebulun.

Abdon Becomes Israel's Judge

13After Elon died, Abdon son of Hillel, from Pirathon, became Israel's judge. 14He had forty sons and thirty grandsons, who rode on seventy donkeys. He was Israel's judge for eight years. 15Then he died and was buried at Pirathon in Ephraim, in the hill country of the Amalekites.

CHAPTER **13**
The Birth of Samson

Again the Israelites did what was evil in the LORD's sight, so the LORD handed them over to the Philistines, who kept them in subjection for forty years.

2In those days, a man named Manoah from the tribe of Dan lived in the town of Zorah. His wife was unable to become pregnant, and they had no children. 3The angel of the LORD appeared to Manoah's wife and said, "Even though you have been unable to have children, you will soon become pregnant and give birth to a son. 4You must not drink wine or any other alcoholic drink or eat any forbidden food. 5You will become pregnant and give birth to a son, and his hair must never be cut. For he will be dedicated to God as a Nazirite from birth. He will rescue Israel from the Philistines."

6The woman ran and told her husband, "A man of God appeared to me! He was like one of God's angels, terrifying to look at. I didn't ask where he was from, and he didn't tell me his name. 7But he told me, 'You will become pregnant and give birth to a son. You must not drink wine or any other alcoholic drink or eat any forbidden food. For your son will be dedicated to God as a Nazirite from the moment of his birth until the day of his death.'"

8Then Manoah prayed to the LORD. He said, "Lord, please let the man of God come back to us again and give us more instructions about this son who is to be born."

9God answered his prayer, and the angel of God appeared once again to his wife as she was sitting in the field. But her husband, Manoah, was not with her. 10So she quickly ran and told her husband, "The man who appeared to me the other day is here again!"

11Manoah ran back with his wife and asked, "Are you the man who talked to my wife the other day?"

"Yes," he replied, "I am."

12So Manoah asked him, "When your words come true, what kind of rules should govern the boy's life and work?"

13The angel of the LORD replied, "Be sure your wife follows the instructions I gave her. 14She must not eat grapes or raisins, drink wine or any other alcoholic drink, or eat any forbidden food."

15Then Manoah said to the angel of the LORD, "Please stay here until we can prepare a young goat for you to eat."

16"I will stay," the angel of the LORD replied, "but I will not eat anything. However, you may prepare a burnt offering as a sacrifice to the LORD." (Manoah didn't realize it was the angel of the LORD.)

17Then Manoah asked the angel of the LORD, "What is your name? For when all this comes true, we want to honor you."

18"Why do you ask my name?" the angel of the LORD replied. "You wouldn't understand if I told you."

19Then Manoah took a young goat and a grain offering and offered it on a rock as a sacrifice to the LORD. And as Manoah and his wife watched, the LORD did an amazing thing. 20As the flames from the altar shot up toward the sky, the angel of the LORD ascended in the fire. When Manoah and his wife saw this, they fell with their faces to the ground.

21The angel did not appear again to Manoah and his wife. Manoah finally realized it was the angel of the LORD, 22and he said to his wife, "We will die, for we have seen God!"

23But his wife said, "If the LORD were going to kill us, he wouldn't have accepted our burnt offering and grain offering. He wouldn't have appeared to us and told us this wonderful thing and done these miracles."

24When her son was born, they named him Samson. And the LORD blessed him as he grew up. 25And in Mahaneh-dan, which is located between the towns of Zorah and Eshtaol, the Spirit of the LORD began to take hold of him.

CHAPTER **14**
Samson's Riddle

One day when Samson was in Timnah, he noticed a certain Philistine woman. 2When he returned home, he told his father and mother, "I want to marry a young Philistine woman I saw in Timnah."

3His father and mother objected strenuously, "Isn't there one woman in our tribe or among all the Israelites you could marry? Why must you go to the pagan Philistines to find a wife?"

But Samson told his father, "Get her for me. She is the one I want." 4His father and mother didn't realize the LORD was at work in this, creating an opportunity to disrupt the Philistines, who ruled over Israel at that time.

5As Samson and his parents were going down to Timnah, a young lion attacked Samson near the vineyards of Timnah. 6At that moment the Spirit of the LORD powerfully took control of him, and he ripped the lion's jaws apart with his bare hands. He did it as easily as if it were a young goat. But he didn't tell his father or mother about it. 7When Samson arrived in Timnah, he talked with the woman and was very pleased with her.

8Later, when he returned to Timnah for the wedding, he turned off the path to look at the carcass of the lion. And he found that a swarm of bees had made some honey in the carcass. 9He scooped some of the honey into his hands and ate it along the way. He also gave some to his father and mother, and they ate it. But he didn't tell them he had taken the honey from the carcass of the lion.

10As his father was making final arrangements for the marriage, Samson threw a party at Timnah, as was the custom of the day. 11Thirty young men from the town were invited to be his companions. 12Samson said to them, "Let me tell you a riddle. If you solve my riddle during these seven days of the celebration, I will give you thirty plain linen robes and thirty fancy robes. 13But if you can't solve it, then you must give me thirty linen robes and thirty fancy robes."

"All right," they agreed, "let's hear your riddle."

14So he said:

"From the one who eats came something to
eat;
out of the strong came something sweet."

Three days later they were still trying to figure
it out. 15On the fourth* day they said to Samson's wife, "Get the answer to the riddle from
your husband, or we will burn down your
father's house with you in it. Did you invite us
to this party just to make us poor?"

16So Samson's wife came to him in tears and
said, "You don't love me; you hate me! You have
given my people a riddle, but you haven't told
me the answer."

"I haven't even given the answer to my father
or mother," he replied. "Why should I tell you?"
17So she cried whenever she was with him and
kept it up for the rest of the celebration. At last,
on the seventh day, he told her the answer because of her persistent nagging. Then she gave
the answer to the young men.

18So before sunset of the seventh day, the men
of the town came to Samson with their answer:

"What is sweeter than honey?
What is stronger than a lion?"

Samson replied, "If you hadn't plowed with
my heifer, you wouldn't have found the answer
to my riddle!" 19Then the Spirit of the LORD
powerfully took control of him. He went down
to the town of Ashkelon, killed thirty men, took
their belongings, and gave their clothing to the
men who had answered his riddle. But Samson
was furious about what had happened, and he
went back home to live with his father and
mother. 20So his wife was given in marriage to
the man who had been Samson's best man at
the wedding.

CHAPTER **15**

Samson's Vengeance on the Philistines
Later on, during the wheat harvest, Samson took
a young goat as a present to his wife. He intended to sleep with her, but her father wouldn't
let him in. 2"I really thought you hated her," her
father explained, "so I gave her in marriage to
your best man. But look, her sister is more beautiful than she is. Marry her instead."

3Samson said, "This time I cannot be blamed
for everything I am going to do to you Philistines." 4Then he went out and caught three hundred foxes. He tied their tails together in pairs,

14:15 As in Greek version; Hebrew reads *seventh.*

and he fastened a torch to each pair of tails.
5Then he lit the torches and let the foxes run
through the fields of the Philistines. He burned
all their grain to the ground, including the grain
still in piles and all that had been bundled. He
also destroyed their grapevines and olive trees.

6"Who did this?" the Philistines demanded.

"Samson," was the reply, "because his father-
in-law from Timnah gave Samson's wife to be
married to his best man." So the Philistines went
and got the woman and her father and burned
them to death.

7"Because you did this," Samson vowed, "I
will take my revenge on you, and I won't stop
until I'm satisfied!" 8So he attacked the Philistines with great fury and killed many of them.
Then he went to live in a cave in the rock of
Etam.

9The Philistines retaliated by setting up camp
in Judah and raiding the town of Lehi. 10The
men of Judah asked the Philistines, "Why have
you attacked us?"

The Philistines replied, "We've come to capture Samson. We have come to pay him back for
what he did to us."

11So three thousand men of Judah went down
to get Samson at the cave in the rock of Etam. They
said to Samson, "Don't you realize the Philistines
rule over us? What are you doing to us?"

But Samson replied, "I only paid them back
for what they did to me."

12But the men of Judah told him, "We have
come to tie you up and hand you over to the
Philistines."

"All right," Samson said. "But promise that
you won't kill me yourselves."

13"We will tie you up and hand you over to
the Philistines," they replied. "We won't kill
you." So they tied him up with two new ropes
and led him away from the rock.

14As Samson arrived at Lehi, the Philistines
came shouting in triumph. But the Spirit of the
LORD powerfully took control of Samson, and he
snapped the ropes on his arms as if they were
burnt strands of flax, and they fell from his
wrists. 15Then he picked up a donkey's jawbone
that was lying on the ground and killed a thousand Philistines with it. 16And Samson said,

"With the jawbone of a donkey,
I've made heaps on heaps!
With the jawbone of a donkey,
I've killed a thousand men!"

17When he finished speaking, he threw away the jawbone; and the place was named Jawbone Hill.*

18Now Samson was very thirsty, and he cried out to the LORD, "You have accomplished this great victory by the strength of your servant. Must I now die of thirst and fall into the hands of these pagan people?" 19So God caused water to gush out of a hollow in the ground at Lehi, and Samson was revived as he drank. Then he named that place "The Spring of the One Who Cried Out,"* and it is still in Lehi to this day.

20Samson was Israel's judge for twenty years, while the Philistines ruled the land.

CHAPTER 16

Samson Removes Gaza's Gates

One day Samson went to the Philistine city of Gaza and spent the night with a prostitute. 2Word soon spread that Samson was there, so the men of Gaza gathered together and waited all night at the city gates. They kept quiet during the night, saying to themselves, "When the light of morning comes, we will kill him."

3But Samson stayed in bed only until midnight. Then he got up, took hold of the city gates with its two posts, and lifted them, bar and all, right out of the ground. He put them on his shoulders and carried them all the way to the top of the hill across from Hebron.

Samson and Delilah

4Later Samson fell in love with a woman named Delilah, who lived in the valley of Sorek. 5The leaders of the Philistines went to her and said, "Find out from Samson what makes him so strong and how he can be overpowered and tied up securely. Then each of us will give you eleven hundred pieces* of silver."

6So Delilah said to Samson, "Please tell me what makes you so strong and what it would take to tie you up securely."

7Samson replied, "If I am tied up with seven new bowstrings that have not yet been dried, I will be as weak as anyone else."

8So the Philistine leaders brought Delilah seven new bowstrings, and she tied Samson up with them. 9She had hidden some men in one of the rooms of her house, and she cried out, "Samson! The Philistines have come to capture you!" But Samson snapped the bowstrings as if they were string that had been burned in a fire. So the secret of his strength was not discovered.

10Afterward Delilah said to him, "You made fun of me and told me a lie! Now please tell me how you can be tied up securely."

11Samson replied, "If I am tied up with brand-new ropes that have never been used, I will be as weak as anyone else."

12So Delilah took new ropes and tied him up with them. The men were hiding in the room as before, and again Delilah cried out, "Samson! The Philistines have come to capture you!" But Samson snapped the ropes from his arms as if they were thread.

13Then Delilah said, "You have been making fun of me and telling me lies! Won't you please tell me how you can be tied up securely?"

Samson replied, "If you weave the seven braids of my hair into the fabric on your loom and tighten it with the loom shuttle,* I will be as weak as anyone else."

So while he slept, Delilah wove the seven braids of his hair into the fabric 14and tightened it with the loom shuttle. Again she cried out, "Samson! The Philistines have come to capture you!" But Samson woke up, pulled back the loom shuttle, and yanked his hair away from the loom and the fabric.

15Then Delilah pouted, "How can you say you love me when you don't confide in me? You've made fun of me three times now, and you still haven't told me what makes you so strong!" 16So day after day she nagged him until he couldn't stand it any longer.

17Finally, Samson told her his secret. "My hair has never been cut," he confessed, "for I was dedicated to God as a Nazirite from birth. If my head were shaved, my strength would leave me, and I would become as weak as anyone else."

18Delilah realized he had finally told her the truth, so she sent for the Philistine leaders. "Come back one more time," she said, "for he has told me everything." So the Philistine leaders returned and brought the money with them. 19Delilah lulled Samson to sleep with his head in her lap, and she called in a man to shave off his hair, making his capture certain. And his strength left him. 20Then she cried out, "Samson! The Philistines have come to capture you!"

When he woke up, he thought, "I will do as before and shake myself free." But he didn't realize the LORD had left him.

21So the Philistines captured him and gouged out his eyes. They took him to Gaza, where he was bound with bronze chains and made to

15:17 Hebrew *Ramath-lehi.*   15:19 Hebrew *En-hakkore.*   16:5 Hebrew *1,100 shekels,* about 28 pounds or 12.5 kilograms in weight.   16:13 As in Greek version; Hebrew lacks *on your loom and tighten it with the loom shuttle.*

grind grain in the prison. 22But before long his hair began to grow back.

Samson's Final Victory

23The Philistine leaders held a great festival, offering sacrifices and praising their god, Dagon. They said, "Our god has given us victory over our enemy Samson!"

24When the people saw him, they praised their god, saying, "Our god has delivered our enemy to us! The one who killed so many of us is now in our power!"

25Half drunk by now, the people demanded, "Bring out Samson so he can perform for us!" So he was brought from the prison and made to stand at the center of the temple, between the two pillars supporting the roof.

26Samson said to the servant who was leading him by the hand, "Place my hands against the two pillars. I want to rest against them." 27The temple was completely filled with people. All the Philistine leaders were there, and there were about three thousand on the roof who were watching Samson and making fun of him.

28Then Samson prayed to the LORD, "Sovereign LORD, remember me again. O God, please strengthen me one more time so that I may pay back the Philistines for the loss of my eyes." 29Then Samson put his hands on the center pillars of the temple and pushed against them with all his might. 30"Let me die with the Philistines," he prayed. And the temple crashed down on the Philistine leaders and all the people. So he killed more people when he died than he had during his entire lifetime.

31Later his brothers and other relatives went down to get his body. They took him back home and buried him between Zorah and Eshtaol, where his father, Manoah, was buried. Samson had been Israel's judge for twenty years.

CHAPTER 17

Micah's Idols

A man named Micah lived in the hill country of Ephraim. 2One day he said to his mother, "I heard you curse the thief who stole eleven hundred pieces* of silver from you. Well, here they are. I was the one who took them."

"The LORD bless you for admitting it," his mother replied. 3He returned the money to her, and she said, "I now dedicate these silver coins to the LORD. In honor of my son, I will have an image carved and an idol cast." 4So his mother

took two hundred of the silver coins to a silversmith, who made them into an image and an idol. And these were placed in Micah's house.

5Micah set up a shrine, and he made a sacred ephod and some household idols. Then he installed one of his sons as the priest. 6In those days Israel had no king, so the people did whatever seemed right in their own eyes.

7One day a young Levite from Bethlehem in Judah 8arrived in that area of Ephraim, looking for a good place to live. He happened to stop at Micah's house as he was traveling through. 9"Where are you from?" Micah asked him.

And he replied, "I am a Levite from Bethlehem in Judah, and I am looking for a place to live."

10"Stay here with me," Micah said, "and you can be a father and priest to me. I will give you ten pieces* of silver a year, plus a change of clothes and your food." 11The Levite agreed to this and became like one of Micah's sons. 12So Micah ordained the Levite as his personal priest, and he lived in Micah's house. 13"I know the LORD will bless me now," Micah said, "because I have a Levite serving as my priest."

CHAPTER 18

Idolatry in the Tribe of Dan

Now in those days Israel had no king. And the tribe of Dan was trying to find a place to settle, for they had not yet driven out the people who lived in the land assigned to them. 2So the men of Dan chose five warriors from among their clans, who lived in the towns of Zorah and Eshtaol, to scout out a land for them to settle in.

When these warriors arrived in the hill country of Ephraim, they came to Micah's home and spent the night there. 3Noticing the young Levite's accent, they took him aside and asked him, "Who brought you here, and what are you doing? Why are you here?" 4He told them about his agreement with Micah and that he was Micah's personal priest.

5Then they said, "Ask God whether or not our journey will be successful."

6"Go in peace," the priest replied. "For the LORD will go ahead of you on your journey."

7So the five men went on to the town of Laish, where they noticed the people living carefree lives, like the Sidonians; they were peaceful and secure. The people were also wealthy because their land was very fertile. And they lived

17:2 Hebrew *1,100 shekels*, about 28 pounds or 12.5 kilograms in weight.   17:10 Hebrew *10 shekels*, about 4 ounces or 114 grams in weight.

a great distance from Sidon and had no allies nearby.

8When the men returned to Zorah and Eshtaol, their relatives asked them, "What did you find?"

9The men replied, "Let's attack! We have seen the land, and it is very good. You should not hesitate to go and take possession of it. 10When you get there, you will find the people living carefree lives. God has given us a spacious and fertile land, lacking in nothing!"

11So six hundred warriors from the tribe of Dan set out from Zorah and Eshtaol. 12They camped at a place west of Kiriath-jearim in Judah, which is called Mahaneh-dan* to this day. 13Then they went up into the hill country of Ephraim and came to the house of Micah.

14The five men who had scouted out the land around Laish said to the others, "There is a shrine here with a sacred ephod, some household idols, a carved image, and a cast idol. It's obvious what we ought to do." 15So the five men went over to Micah's house, where the young Levite lived, and greeted him kindly. 16As the six hundred warriors from the tribe of Dan stood just outside the gate, 17the five spies entered the shrine and took the carved image, the sacred ephod, the household idols, and the cast idol.

18When the priest saw the men carrying all the sacred objects out of Micah's shrine, he said, "What are you doing?"

19"Be quiet and come with us," they said. "Be a father and priest to all of us. Isn't it better to be a priest for an entire tribe of Israel than just for the household of one man?" 20The young priest was quite happy to go with them, so he took along the sacred ephod, the household idols, and the carved image. 21They started on their way again, placing their children, livestock, and possessions in front of them.

22When the people from the tribe of Dan were quite a distance from Micah's home, Micah and some of his neighbors came chasing after them. 23They were shouting as they caught up with them. The men of Dan turned around and said, "What do you want? Why have you called these men together and chased after us like this?"

24"What do you mean, What do I want?" Micah replied. "You've taken away all my gods and my priest, and I have nothing left!"

25The men of Dan said, "Watch what you say! Some of us are short-tempered, and they might get angry and kill you and your family." 26So the men of Dan went on their way. When Micah saw that there were too many of them for him to attack, he turned around and went home.

27Then, with Micah's idols and his priest, the men of Dan came to the town of Laish, whose people were peaceful and secure. They attacked and killed all the people and burned the town to the ground. 28There was no one to rescue the residents of the town, for they lived a great distance from Sidon and had no allies nearby. This happened in the valley near Beth-rehob.

Then the people of the tribe of Dan rebuilt the town and lived there. 29They renamed the town Dan after their ancestor, Israel's son, but it had originally been called Laish.

30Then they set up the carved image, and they appointed Jonathan son of Gershom, a descendant of Moses,* as their priest. This family continued as priests for the tribe of Dan until the Exile. 31So Micah's carved image was worshiped by the tribe of Dan as long as the Tabernacle of God remained at Shiloh.

CHAPTER **19**
The Levite and His Concubine

Now in those days Israel had no king. There was a man from the tribe of Levi living in a remote area of the hill country of Ephraim. One day he brought home a woman from Bethlehem in Judah to be his concubine. 2But she was unfaithful to him and returned to her father's home in Bethlehem. After about four months, 3her husband took a servant and an extra donkey to Bethlehem to persuade her to come back. When he arrived at her father's house, she took him inside, and her father welcomed him. 4Her father urged him to stay awhile, so he stayed three days, eating, drinking, and sleeping there.

5On the fourth day the man was up early, ready to leave, but the woman's father said, "Have something to eat before you go." 6So the two of them sat down together and had something to eat and drink. Then the woman's father said, "Please stay the night and enjoy yourself." 7The man got up to leave, but his father-in-law kept urging him to stay, so he finally gave in and stayed the night. 8On the morning of the fifth day he was up early again, ready to leave, and again the woman's father said, "Have something to eat; then you can leave some time this afternoon." So they had another day of feasting.

9That afternoon, as he and his concubine and

18:12 *Mahaneh-dan* means "the camp of Dan." 18:30 As in an ancient Hebrew tradition, some Greek manuscripts, and Latin Vulgate; Masoretic Text reads *of Manasseh*.

servant were preparing to leave, his father-in-law said, "Look, it's getting late. Stay the night and enjoy yourself. Tomorrow you can get up early and be on your way."

¹⁰But this time the man was determined to leave. So he took his two saddled donkeys and his concubine and headed in the direction of Jebus (that is, Jerusalem). ¹¹It was late in the day when they reached Jebus, and the man's servant said to him, "It's getting too late to travel; let's stay in this Jebusite city tonight."

¹²"No," his master said, "we can't stay in this foreign city where there are no Israelites. We will go on to Gibeah. ¹³We will find a place to spend the night in either Gibeah or Ramah." ¹⁴So they went on. The sun was setting as they came to Gibeah, a town in the land of Benjamin, ¹⁵so they stopped there to spend the night. They rested in the town square, but no one took them in for the night.

¹⁶That evening an old man came home from his work in the fields. He was from the hill country of Ephraim, but he was living in Gibeah in the territory of Benjamin. ¹⁷When he saw the travelers sitting in the town square, he asked them where they were from and where they were going.

¹⁸"We have been in Bethlehem in Judah," the man replied. "We are on our way home to a remote area in the hill country of Ephraim, and we're going to the Tabernacle of the LORD. But no one has taken us in for the night, ¹⁹even though we have everything we need. We have straw and fodder for our donkeys and plenty of bread and wine for ourselves."

²⁰"You are welcome to stay with me," the old man said. "I will give you anything you might need. But whatever you do, don't spend the night in the square." ²¹So he took them home with him and fed their donkeys. After they washed their feet, they had supper together.

²²While they were enjoying themselves, some of the wicked men in the town surrounded the house. They began beating at the door and shouting to the old man, "Bring out the man who is staying with you so we can have sex with him."

²³The old man stepped outside to talk to them. "No, my brothers, don't do such an evil thing. For this man is my guest, and such a thing would be shameful. ²⁴Here, take my virgin daughter and this man's concubine. I will bring them out to you, and you can do whatever you

like to them. But don't do such a shameful thing to this man."

²⁵But they wouldn't listen to him. Then the Levite took his concubine and pushed her out the door. The men of the town abused her all night, taking turns raping her until morning. Finally, at dawn, they let her go. ²⁶At daybreak the woman returned to the house where her husband was staying. She collapsed at the door of the house and lay there until it was light.

²⁷When her husband opened the door to leave, he found her there. She was lying face down, with her hands on the threshold. ²⁸He said, "Get up! Let's go!" But there was no answer.* So he put her body on his donkey and took her home.

²⁹When he got home, he took a knife and cut his concubine's body into twelve pieces. Then he sent one piece to each tribe of Israel. ³⁰Everyone who saw it said, "Such a horrible crime has not been committed since Israel left Egypt. Shouldn't we speak up and do something about this?"

CHAPTER **20**

Israel's War with Benjamin

Then all the Israelites, from Dan to Beersheba and from the land of Gilead, came together in one large assembly and stood in the presence of the LORD at Mizpah. ²The leaders of all the people and all the tribes of Israel—400,000 warriors armed with swords—took their positions in the assembly of the people of God. ³(Word soon reached the land of Benjamin that the other tribes had gone up to Mizpah.) The Israelites then asked how this terrible crime had happened.

⁴The Levite, the husband of the woman who had been murdered, said, "My concubine and I came to Gibeah, a town in the land of Benjamin, to spend the night. ⁵That night some of the leaders of Gibeah surrounded the house, planning to kill me, and they raped my concubine until she was dead. ⁶So I cut her body into twelve pieces and sent the pieces throughout the land of Israel, for these men have committed this terrible and shameful crime. ⁷Now then, the entire community of Israel must decide what should be done about this!"

⁸And all the people stood up together and replied, "Not one of us will return home. ⁹Instead, we will draw lots to decide who will attack Gibeah. ¹⁰One tenth of the men from each tribe will be chosen to supply the warriors with food,

19:28 Greek version adds *for she was dead.*

and the rest of us will take revenge on Gibeah*
for this shameful thing they have done in Israel."
¹¹So all the Israelites were united, and they gathered together to attack the town.

¹²The Israelites sent messengers to the tribe of
Benjamin, saying, "What a terrible thing has
been done among you! ¹³Give up these evil men
from Gibeah so we can execute them and purge
Israel of this evil."

But the people of Benjamin would not listen.
¹⁴Instead, they came from their towns and gathered at Gibeah to fight the Israelites. ¹⁵Twenty-
six thousand of their warriors armed with
swords arrived in Gibeah to join the seven hundred warriors who lived there. ¹⁶Seven hundred
of Benjamin's warriors were left-handed, each of
whom could sling a rock and hit a target within
a hairsbreadth, without missing. ¹⁷Israel had
400,000 warriors armed with swords, not counting Benjamin's warriors.

¹⁸Before the battle the Israelites went to
Bethel and asked God, "Which tribe should lead
the attack against the people of Benjamin?"

The LORD answered, "Judah is to go first."

¹⁹So the Israelites left early the next morning
and camped near Gibeah. ²⁰Then they advanced
toward Gibeah to attack the men of Benjamin.
²¹But Benjamin's warriors, who were defending
the town, came out and killed twenty-two thousand Israelites in the field that day.

²²But the Israelites took courage and assembled at the same place they had fought the
previous day. ²³(For they had gone up to Bethel
and wept in the presence of the LORD until
evening. Then they asked the LORD, "Should we
fight against our relatives from Benjamin
again?" And the LORD said, "Go out and fight
against them.")

²⁴So they went out to fight against the warriors of Benjamin, ²⁵but the men of Benjamin
killed another eighteen thousand Israelites, all
of whom were experienced with a sword.

²⁶Then all the Israelites went up to Bethel and
wept in the presence of the LORD and fasted until
evening. They also brought burnt offerings and
peace offerings to the LORD. ²⁷And the Israelites
went up seeking direction from the LORD. (In
those days the Ark of the Covenant of God was in
Bethel, ²⁸and Phinehas son of Eleazar and grandson of Aaron was the priest.) The Israelites asked
the LORD, "Should we fight against our relatives
from Benjamin again or should we stop?"

20:10 Hebrew *Geba*, in this case, a variant for Gibeah; also in 20:33.

The LORD said, "Go! Tomorrow I will give you
victory over them."

²⁹So the Israelites set an ambush all around
Gibeah. ³⁰They went out on the third day and
assembled at the same place as before. ³¹When
the warriors of Benjamin came out to attack, they
were drawn away from the town. And as they had
done before, they began to kill the Israelites.
About thirty Israelites died in the open fields and
along the roads leading to Bethel and Gibeah.

³²Then the warriors of Benjamin shouted,
"We're defeating them as we did in the first
battle!" But the Israelites had agreed in advance
to run away so that the men of Benjamin would
chase them along the roads and be drawn away
from the town.

³³When the main group of Israelite warriors
reached Baal-tamar, they turned and prepared to
attack. Then the Israelites hiding in ambush west
of Gibeah jumped up from where they were
³⁴and advanced against Benjamin from behind.
The fighting was so heavy that Benjamin didn't
realize the impending disaster. ³⁵So the LORD
helped Israel defeat Benjamin, and that day the
Israelites killed 25,100 of Benjamin's warriors,
all of whom were experienced with a sword.
³⁶Then the men of Benjamin saw that they were
beaten.

The Israelites had retreated from Benjamin's
warriors in order to give those hiding in ambush
more room to maneuver. ³⁷Then those who
were in hiding rushed in from all sides and
killed everyone in the town. ³⁸They sent up a
large cloud of smoke from the town, ³⁹which
was the signal for the Israelites to turn and attack
Benjamin's warriors.

By that time Benjamin's warriors had killed
about thirty Israelites, and they shouted, "We're
defeating them as we did in the first battle!"
⁴⁰But when the warriors of Benjamin looked
behind them and saw the smoke rising into the
sky from every part of the town, ⁴¹the Israelites
turned and attacked. At this point Benjamin's
warriors realized disaster was near and became
terrified. ⁴²So they ran toward the wilderness,
but the Israelites chased after them and killed
them. ⁴³The Israelites surrounded the men of
Benjamin and were relentless in chasing them
down, finally overtaking them east of Gibeah.
⁴⁴Eighteen thousand of Benjamin's greatest
warriors died in that day's battle. ⁴⁵The survivors fled into the wilderness toward the rock
of Rimmon, but Israel killed five thousand

of them along the road. They continued the chase until they had killed another two thousand near Gidom.

46So the tribe of Benjamin lost twenty-five thousand brave warriors that day, 47leaving only six hundred men who escaped to the rock of Rimmon, where they lived for four months. 48Then the Israelites returned and slaughtered every living thing in all the towns—the people, the cattle—everything. They also burned down every town they came to.

CHAPTER 21

Israel Provides Wives for Benjamin

The Israelites had vowed at Mizpah never to give their daughters in marriage to a man from the tribe of Benjamin. 2And the people went to Bethel and sat in the presence of God until evening, raising their voices and weeping bitterly. 3"O LORD, God of Israel," they cried out, "why has this happened? Now one of our tribes is missing!"

4Early the next morning the people built an altar and presented their burnt offerings and peace offerings on it. 5Then they said, "Was any tribe of Israel not represented when we held our council in the presence of the LORD at Mizpah?" At that time they had taken a solemn oath in the LORD's presence, vowing that anyone who refused to come must die.

6The Israelites felt deep sadness for Benjamin and said, "Today we have lost one of the tribes from our family; it is nearly wiped out. 7How can we find wives for the few who remain, since we have sworn by the LORD not to give them our daughters in marriage?"

8So they asked, "Was anyone absent when we presented ourselves to the LORD at Mizpah?" And they discovered that no one from Jabesh-gilead had attended. 9For after they counted all the people, no one from Jabesh-gilead was present. 10So they sent twelve thousand warriors to Jabesh-gilead with orders to kill everyone there, including women and children. 11"This is what you are to do," they said. "Completely destroy* all the males and every woman who is not a virgin." 12Among the residents of Jabesh-gilead

they found four hundred young virgins who had never slept with a man, and they brought them to the camp at Shiloh in the land of Canaan.

13The Israelite assembly sent a peace delegation to the little remnant of Benjamin who were living at the rock of Rimmon. 14Then the men of Benjamin returned to their homes, and the four hundred women of Jabesh-gilead who were spared were given to them as wives. But there were not enough women for all of them.

15The people felt sorry for Benjamin because the LORD had left this gap in the tribes of Israel. 16So the Israelite leaders asked, "How can we find wives for the few who remain, since all the women of the tribe of Benjamin are dead? 17There must be heirs for the survivors so that an entire tribe of Israel will not be lost forever. 18But we cannot give them our own daughters in marriage because we have sworn with a solemn oath that anyone who does this will fall under God's curse."

19Then they thought of the annual festival of the LORD held in Shiloh, between Lebonah and Bethel, along the east side of the road that goes from Bethel to Shechem. 20They told the men of Benjamin who still needed wives, "Go and hide in the vineyards. 21When the women of Shiloh come out for their dances, rush out from the vineyards, and each of you can take one of them home to be your wife! 22And when their fathers and brothers come to us in protest, we will tell them, 'Please be understanding. Let them have your daughters, for we didn't find enough wives for them when we destroyed Jabesh-gilead. And you are not guilty of breaking the vow since you did not give your daughters in marriage to them.'"

23So the men of Benjamin did as they were told. They kidnapped the women who took part in the celebration and carried them off to the land of their own inheritance. Then they rebuilt their towns and lived in them. 24So the assembly of Israel departed by tribes and families, and they returned to their own homes.

25In those days Israel had no king, so the people did whatever seemed right in their own eyes.

21:11 The Hebrew term used here refers to the complete consecration of things or people to the LORD, either by destroying them or by giving them as an offering.

Ruth

CHAPTER 1

Elimelech Moves His Family to Moab

In the days when the judges ruled in Israel, a man from Bethlehem in Judah left the country because of a severe famine. He took his wife and two sons and went to live in the country of Moab. ²The man's name was Elimelech, and his wife was Naomi. Their two sons were Mahlon and Kilion. They were Ephrathites from Bethlehem in the land of Judah. During their stay in Moab, ³Elimelech died and Naomi was left with her two sons. ⁴The two sons married Moabite women. One married a woman named Orpah, and the other a woman named Ruth. But about ten years later, ⁵both Mahlon and Kilion died. This left Naomi alone, without her husband or sons.

Naomi and Ruth Return

⁶Then Naomi heard in Moab that the LORD had blessed his people in Judah by giving them good crops again. So Naomi and her daughters-in-law got ready to leave Moab to return to her homeland. ⁷With her two daughters-in-law she set out from the place where she had been living, and they took the road that would lead them back to Judah.

⁸But on the way, Naomi said to her two daughters-in-law, "Go back to your mothers' homes instead of coming with me. And may the LORD reward you for your kindness to your husbands and to me. ⁹May the LORD bless you with the security of another marriage." Then she kissed them good-bye, and they all broke down and wept.

¹⁰"No," they said. "We want to go with you to your people."

¹¹But Naomi replied, "Why should you go on with me? Can I still give birth to other sons who could grow up to be your husbands? ¹²No, my daughters, return to your parents' homes, for I am too old to marry again. And even if it were possible, and I were to get married tonight and bear sons, then what? ¹³Would you wait for them to grow up and refuse to marry someone else? No, of course not, my daughters! Things are far more bitter for me than for you, because the LORD himself has caused me to suffer."

¹⁴And again they wept together, and Orpah kissed her mother-in-law good-bye. But Ruth insisted on staying with Naomi. ¹⁵"See," Naomi said to her, "your sister-in-law has gone back to her people and to her gods. You should do the same."

¹⁶But Ruth replied, "Don't ask me to leave you and turn back. I will go wherever you go and live wherever you live. Your people will be my people, and your God will be my God. ¹⁷I will die where you die and will be buried there. May the LORD punish me severely if I allow anything but death to separate us!" ¹⁸So when Naomi saw that Ruth had made up her mind to go with her, she stopped urging her.

¹⁹So the two of them continued on their journey. When they came to Bethlehem, the entire town was stirred by their arrival. "Is it really Naomi?" the women asked.

²⁰"Don't call me Naomi," she told them. "Instead, call me Mara,* for the Almighty has made life very bitter for me. ²¹I went away full, but the LORD has brought me home empty. Why should you call me Naomi when the LORD has caused me to suffer* and the Almighty has sent such tragedy?"

²²So Naomi returned from Moab, accompanied by her daughter-in-law Ruth, the young Moabite woman. They arrived in Bethlehem at the beginning of the barley harvest.

1:20 *Naomi* means "pleasant"; *Mara* means "bitter."   **1:21** Or *has testified against me.*

CHAPTER **2**

Ruth Works in Boaz's Field

Now there was a wealthy and influential man in Bethlehem named Boaz, who was a relative of Naomi's husband, Elimelech.

2One day Ruth said to Naomi, "Let me go out into the fields to gather leftover grain behind anyone who will let me do it."

And Naomi said, "All right, my daughter, go ahead." 3So Ruth went out to gather grain behind the harvesters. And as it happened, she found herself working in a field that belonged to Boaz, the relative of her father-in-law, Elimelech.

4While she was there, Boaz arrived from Bethlehem and greeted the harvesters. "The LORD be with you!" he said.

"The LORD bless you!" the harvesters replied.

5Then Boaz asked his foreman, "Who is that girl over there?"

6And the foreman replied, "She is the young woman from Moab who came back with Naomi. 7She asked me this morning if she could gather grain behind the harvesters. She has been hard at work ever since, except for a few minutes' rest over there in the shelter."

8Boaz went over and said to Ruth, "Listen, my daughter. Stay right here with us when you gather grain; don't go to any other fields. Stay right behind the women working in my field. 9See which part of the field they are harvesting, and then follow them. I have warned the young men not to bother you. And when you are thirsty, help yourself to the water they have drawn from the well."

10Ruth fell at his feet and thanked him warmly. "Why are you being so kind to me?" she asked. "I am only a foreigner."

11"Yes, I know," Boaz replied. "But I also know about the love and kindness you have shown your mother-in-law since the death of your husband. I have heard how you left your father and mother and your own land to live here among complete strangers. 12May the LORD, the God of Israel, under whose wings you have come to take refuge, reward you fully."

13"I hope I continue to please you, sir," she replied. "You have comforted me by speaking so kindly to me, even though I am not as worthy as your workers."

14At lunchtime Boaz called to her, "Come over here and help yourself to some of our food. You can dip your bread in the wine if you like." So she sat with his harvesters, and Boaz gave her food—more than she could eat.

15When Ruth went back to work again, Boaz ordered his young men, "Let her gather grain right among the sheaves without stopping her. 16And pull out some heads of barley from the bundles and drop them on purpose for her. Let her pick them up, and don't give her a hard time!"

17So Ruth gathered barley there all day, and when she beat out the grain that evening, it came to about half a bushel.* 18She carried it back into town and showed it to her mother-in-law. Ruth also gave her the food that was left over from her lunch.

19"So much!" Naomi exclaimed. "Where did you gather all this grain today? Where did you work? May the LORD bless the one who helped you!"

So Ruth told her mother-in-law about the man in whose field she had worked. And she said, "The man I worked with today is named Boaz."

20"May the LORD bless him!" Naomi told her daughter-in-law. "He is showing his kindness to us as well as to your dead husband.* That man is one of our closest relatives, one of our family redeemers."

21Then Ruth said, "What's more, Boaz even told me to come back and stay with his harvesters until the entire harvest is completed."

22"This is wonderful!" Naomi exclaimed. "Do as he said. Stay with his workers right through the whole harvest. You will be safe there, unlike in other fields."

23So Ruth worked alongside the women in Boaz's fields and gathered grain with them until the end of the barley harvest. Then she worked with them through the wheat harvest, too. But all the while she lived with her mother-in-law.

CHAPTER **3**

Ruth at the Threshing Floor

One day Naomi said to Ruth, "My daughter, it's time that I found a permanent home for you, so that you will be provided for. 2Boaz is a close relative of ours, and he's been very kind by letting you gather grain with his workers. Tonight he will be winnowing barley at the threshing floor. 3Now do as I tell you—take a bath and put on perfume and dress in your nicest clothes. Then go to the threshing floor, but don't let Boaz see you until he has finished his meal. 4Be sure to notice where he lies down; then go and uncover his feet and lie down there. He will tell you what to do."

2:17 Hebrew *about an ephah* [18 liters].   2:20 Hebrew *to the living and to the dead.*

5 "I will do everything you say," Ruth replied. 6 So she went down to the threshing floor that night and followed the instructions of her mother-in-law.

7 After Boaz had finished his meal and was in good spirits, he lay down beside the heap of grain and went to sleep. Then Ruth came quietly, uncovered his feet, and lay down. 8 Around midnight, Boaz suddenly woke up and turned over. He was surprised to find a woman lying at his feet! 9 "Who are you?" he demanded.

"I am your servant Ruth," she replied. "Spread the corner of your covering over me, for you are my family redeemer."

10 "The LORD bless you, my daughter!" Boaz exclaimed. "You are showing more family loyalty now than ever by not running after a younger man, whether rich or poor. 11 Now don't worry about a thing, my daughter. I will do what is necessary, for everyone in town knows you are an honorable woman. 12 But there is one problem. While it is true that I am one of your family redeemers, there is another man who is more closely related to you than I am. 13 Stay here tonight, and in the morning I will talk to him. If he is willing to redeem you, then let him marry you. But if he is not willing, then as surely as the LORD lives, I will marry you! Now lie down here until morning."

14 So Ruth lay at Boaz's feet until the morning, but she got up before it was light enough for people to recognize each other. For Boaz said, "No one must know that a woman was here at the threshing floor." 15 Boaz also said to her, "Bring your cloak and spread it out." He measured out six scoops* of barley into the cloak and helped her put it on her back. Then Boaz* returned to the town.

16 When Ruth went back to her mother-in-law, Naomi asked, "What happened, my daughter?"

Ruth told Naomi everything Boaz had done for her, 17 and she added, "He gave me these six scoops of barley and said, 'Don't go back to your mother-in-law empty-handed.'"

18 Then Naomi said to her, "Just be patient, my daughter, until we hear what happens. The man won't rest until he has followed through on this. He will settle it today."

CHAPTER **4**
Boaz Marries Ruth

So Boaz went to the town gate and took a seat there. When the family redeemer he had mentioned came by, Boaz called out to him, "Come over here, friend. I want to talk to you." So they sat down together. 2 Then Boaz called ten leaders from the town and asked them to sit as witnesses. 3 And Boaz said to the family redeemer, "You know Naomi, who came back from Moab. She is selling the land that belonged to our relative Elimelech. 4 I felt that I should speak to you about it so that you can redeem it if you wish. If you want the land, then buy it here in the presence of these witnesses. But if you don't want it, let me know right away, because I am next in line to redeem it after you."

The man replied, "All right, I'll redeem it."

5 Then Boaz told him, "Of course, your purchase of the land from Naomi also requires that you marry Ruth, the Moabite widow. That way, she can have children who will carry on her husband's name and keep the land in the family."

6 "Then I can't redeem it," the family redeemer replied, "because this might endanger my own estate. You redeem the land; I cannot do it."

7 In those days it was the custom in Israel for anyone transferring a right of purchase to remove his sandal and hand it to the other party. This publicly validated the transaction. 8 So the other family redeemer drew off his sandal as he said to Boaz, "You buy the land."

9 Then Boaz said to the leaders and to the crowd standing around, "You are witnesses that today I have bought from Naomi all the property of Elimelech, Kilion, and Mahlon. 10 And with the land I have acquired Ruth, the Moabite widow of Mahlon, to be my wife. This way she can have a son to carry on the family name of her dead husband and to inherit the family property here in his hometown. You are all witnesses today."

11 Then the leaders and all the people standing there replied, "We are witnesses! May the LORD make the woman who is now coming into your home like Rachel and Leah, from whom all the nation of Israel descended! May you be great in Ephrathah and famous in Bethlehem. 12 And may the LORD give you descendants by this young woman who will be like those of our ancestor Perez, the son of Tamar and Judah."

The Descendants of Boaz

13 So Boaz married Ruth and took her home to live with him. When he slept with her, the LORD enabled her to become pregnant, and she gave birth

3:15a Hebrew *six measures*, an unknown quantity.   **3:15b** Most Hebrew manuscripts read *he*; many Hebrew manuscripts, Syriac version, and Latin Vulgate read *she*.

to a son. 14And the women of the town said to Naomi, "Praise the LORD who has given you a family redeemer today! May he be famous in Israel. 15May this child restore your youth and care for you in your old age. For he is the son of your daughter-in-law who loves you so much and who has been better to you than seven sons!"

16Naomi took care of the baby and cared for him as if he were her own. 17The neighbor women said, "Now at last Naomi has a son again!" And they named him Obed. He became the father of Jesse and the grandfather of David.

18This is their family line beginning with their ancestor Perez:

Perez was the father of Hezron.
19 Hezron was the father of Ram.
Ram was the father of Amminadab.
20 Amminadab was the father of Nahshon.
Nahshon was the father of Salmon.
21 Salmon was the father of Boaz.
Boaz was the father of Obed.
22 Obed was the father of Jesse.
Jesse was the father of David.

1 Samuel

CHAPTER 1

Elkanah and His Family

There was a man named Elkanah who lived in Ramah* in the hill country of Ephraim. He was the son of Jeroham and grandson of Elihu, from the family of Tohu and the clan of Zuph. 2Elkanah had two wives, Hannah and Peninnah. Peninnah had children, while Hannah did not.

3Each year Elkanah and his family would travel to Shiloh to worship and sacrifice to the LORD Almighty at the Tabernacle. The priests of the LORD at that time were the two sons of Eli—Hophni and Phinehas. 4On the day Elkanah presented his sacrifice, he would give portions of the sacrifice to Peninnah and each of her children. 5But he gave Hannah a special portion* because he loved her very much, even though the LORD had given her no children. 6But Peninnah made fun of Hannah because the LORD had closed her womb. 7Year after year it was the same—Peninnah would taunt Hannah as they went to the Tabernacle.* Hannah would finally be reduced to tears and would not even eat.

8"What's the matter, Hannah?" Elkanah would ask. "Why aren't you eating? Why be so sad just because you have no children? You have me—isn't that better than having ten sons?"

Hannah's Prayer for a Son

9Once when they were at Shiloh, Hannah went over to the Tabernacle* after supper to pray to the LORD. Eli the priest was sitting at his customary place beside the entrance. 10Hannah was in deep anguish, crying bitterly as she prayed to the LORD. 11And she made this vow: "O LORD Almighty, if you will look down upon my sorrow and answer my prayer and give me a son, then I will give him back to you. He will be yours for his entire lifetime, and as a sign that he has been dedicated to the LORD, his hair will never be cut."*

12As she was praying to the LORD, Eli watched her. 13Seeing her lips moving but hearing no sound, he thought she had been drinking. 14"Must you come here drunk?" he demanded. "Throw away your wine!"

15"Oh no, sir!" she replied, "I'm not drunk! But I am very sad, and I was pouring out my heart to the LORD. 16Please don't think I am a wicked woman! For I have been praying out of great anguish and sorrow."

17"In that case," Eli said, "cheer up! May the God of Israel grant the request you have asked of him."

18"Oh, thank you, sir!" she exclaimed. Then she went back and began to eat again, and she was no longer sad.

Samuel's Birth and Dedication

19The entire family got up early the next morning and went to worship the LORD once more. Then they returned home to Ramah. When Elkanah slept with Hannah, the LORD remembered her request, 20and in due time she gave birth to a son. She named him Samuel,* for she said, "I asked the LORD for him."

21The next year Elkanah, Peninnah, and their children went on their annual trip to offer a sacrifice to the LORD. 22But Hannah did not go. She told her husband, "Wait until the baby is weaned. Then I will take him to the Tabernacle and leave him there with the LORD permanently."*

23"Whatever you think is best," Elkanah agreed. "Stay here for now, and may the LORD

1:1 Hebrew *Ramathaim-zophim;* compare 1:19.   1:5 Or *a double portion.* The meaning of the Hebrew is uncertain.   1:7 Hebrew *the house of the LORD;* also in 1:24.   1:9 Hebrew *the Temple of the LORD.*   1:11 Some manuscripts add *He will drink neither wine nor intoxicants.*
1:20 *Samuel* sounds like the Hebrew term for "asked of God" or "heard by God."   1:22 Some manuscripts add *I will offer him as a Nazirite for all time.*

help you keep your promise." So she stayed home and nursed the baby.

24When the child was weaned, Hannah took him to the Tabernacle in Shiloh. They brought along a three-year-old bull* for the sacrifice and half a bushel* of flour and some wine. 25After sacrificing the bull, they took the child to Eli. 26"Sir, do you remember me?" Hannah asked. "I am the woman who stood here several years ago praying to the LORD. 27I asked the LORD to give me this child, and he has given me my request. 28Now I am giving him to the LORD, and he will belong to the LORD his whole life." And they* worshiped the LORD there.

CHAPTER **2**

Hannah's Prayer of Praise

Then Hannah prayed:

"My heart rejoices in the LORD!
  Oh, how the LORD has blessed me!
Now I have an answer for my enemies,
  as I delight in your deliverance.

2 No one is holy like the LORD!
  There is no one besides you;
  there is no Rock like our God.

3 "Stop acting so proud and haughty!
  Don't speak with such arrogance!
The LORD is a God who knows your deeds;
  and he will judge you for what you have
    done.

4 Those who were mighty are mighty no
    more;
  and those who were weak are now strong.

5 Those who were well fed are now starving;
  and those who were starving are now full.
The barren woman now has seven children;
  but the woman with many children will
    have no more.

6 The LORD brings both death and life;
  he brings some down to the grave but
    raises others up.

7 The LORD makes one poor and another rich;
  he brings one down and lifts another up.

8 He lifts the poor from the dust—
  yes, from a pile of ashes!
He treats them like princes,
  placing them in seats of honor.

"For all the earth is the LORD's,
  and he has set the world in order.

9 He will protect his godly ones,

but the wicked will perish in darkness.
No one will succeed by strength alone.

10 Those who fight against the LORD will be
      broken.
He thunders against them from heaven;
  the LORD judges throughout the earth.
He gives mighty strength to his king;
  he increases the might of his anointed one."

11Then Elkanah and Hannah returned home to Ramah without Samuel. And the boy became the LORD's helper, for he assisted Eli the priest.

Eli's Wicked Sons

12Now the sons of Eli were scoundrels who had no respect for the LORD 13or for their duties as priests. Whenever anyone offered a sacrifice, Eli's sons would send over a servant with a three-pronged fork. While the meat of the sacrificed animal was still boiling, 14the servant would stick the fork into the pot and demand that whatever it brought up be given to Eli's sons. All the Israelites who came to worship at Shiloh were treated this way. 15Sometimes the servant would come even before the animal's fat had been burned on the altar. He would demand raw meat before it had been boiled so that it could be used for roasting.

16The man offering the sacrifice might reply, "Take as much as you want, but the fat must first be burned." Then the servant would demand, "No, give it to me now, or I'll take it by force." 17So the sin of these young men was very serious in the LORD's sight, for they treated the LORD's offerings with contempt.

18Now Samuel, though only a boy, was the LORD's helper. He wore a linen tunic just like that of a priest.* 19Each year his mother made a small coat for him and brought it to him when she came with her husband for the sacrifice. 20Before they returned home, Eli would bless Elkanah and his wife and say, "May the LORD give you other children to take the place of this one she gave to the LORD.*" 21And the LORD gave Hannah three sons and two daughters. Meanwhile, Samuel grew up in the presence of the LORD.

22Now Eli was very old, but he was aware of what his sons were doing to the people of Israel. He knew, for instance, that his sons were seducing the young women who assisted at the entrance of the Tabernacle.* 23Eli said to them, "I have been hearing reports from the people about the wicked things you are doing. Why do

---

1:24a As in Dead Sea Scrolls, Greek and Syriac versions; Masoretic Text reads *3 bulls.*   1:24b Hebrew *and an ephah* [18 liters].   1:28 Or *he.*
2:18 Hebrew *He wore a linen ephod.*   2:20 As in Greek version; Hebrew reads *this one she requested of the LORD in prayer.*   2:22 Hebrew *Tent of Meeting.* Some manuscripts lack this entire sentence.

you keep sinning? 24You must stop, my sons! The reports I hear among the LORD's people are not good. 25If someone sins against another person, God* can mediate for the guilty party. But if someone sins against the LORD, who can intercede?" But Eli's sons wouldn't listen to their father, for the LORD was already planning to put them to death.

26Meanwhile, as young Samuel grew taller, he also continued to gain favor with the LORD and with the people.

A Warning for Eli's Family

27One day a prophet came to Eli and gave him this message from the LORD: "Didn't I reveal myself to your ancestors when the people of Israel were slaves in Egypt? 28I chose your ancestor Aaron* from among all his relatives to be my priest, to offer sacrifices on my altar, to burn incense, and to wear the priestly garments* as he served me. And I assigned the sacrificial offerings to you priests. 29So why do you scorn my sacrifices and offerings? Why do you honor your sons more than me—for you and they have become fat from the best offerings of my people!

30"Therefore, the LORD, the God of Israel, says: The terrible things you are doing cannot continue! I had promised that your branch of the tribe of Levi* would always be my priests. But I will honor only those who honor me, and I will despise those who despise me. 31I will put an end to your family, so it will no longer serve as my priests. All the members of your family will die before their time. None will live to a ripe old age. 32You will watch with envy as I pour out prosperity on the people of Israel. But no members of your family will ever live out their days. 33Those who are left alive will live in sadness and grief, and their children will die a violent death.* 34And to prove that what I have said will come true, I will cause your two sons, Hophni and Phinehas, to die on the same day!

35"Then I will raise up a faithful priest who will serve me and do what I tell him to do. I will bless his descendants, and his family will be priests to my anointed kings forever. 36Then all of your descendants will bow before his descendants, begging for money and food. 'Please,' they will say, 'give us jobs among the priests so we will have enough to eat.'"

CHAPTER **3**

The LORD Speaks to Samuel

Meanwhile, the boy Samuel was serving the LORD by assisting Eli. Now in those days messages from the LORD were very rare, and visions were quite uncommon.

2One night Eli, who was almost blind by now, had just gone to bed. 3The lamp of God had not yet gone out, and Samuel was sleeping in the Tabernacle* near the Ark of God. 4Suddenly, the LORD called out, "Samuel! Samuel!"

"Yes?" Samuel replied. "What is it?" 5He jumped up and ran to Eli. "Here I am. What do you need?"

"I didn't call you," Eli replied. "Go on back to bed." So he did.

6Then the LORD called out again, "Samuel!"

Again Samuel jumped up and ran to Eli. "Here I am," he said. "What do you need?"

"I didn't call you, my son," Eli said. "Go on back to bed."

7Samuel did not yet know the LORD because he had never had a message from the LORD before. 8So now the LORD called a third time, and once more Samuel jumped up and ran to Eli. "Here I am," he said. "What do you need?"

Then Eli realized it was the LORD who was calling the boy. 9So he said to Samuel, "Go and lie down again, and if someone calls again, say, 'Yes, LORD, your servant is listening.'" So Samuel went back to bed.

10And the LORD came and called as before, "Samuel! Samuel!"

And Samuel replied, "Yes, your servant is listening."

11Then the LORD said to Samuel, "I am about to do a shocking thing in Israel. 12I am going to carry out all my threats against Eli and his family. 13I have warned him continually that judgment is coming for his family, because his sons are blaspheming God* and he hasn't disciplined them. 14So I have vowed that the sins of Eli and his sons will never be forgiven by sacrifices or offerings."

Samuel Speaks for the LORD

15Samuel stayed in bed until morning, then got up and opened the doors of the Tabernacle* as usual. He was afraid to tell Eli what the LORD had said to him. 16But Eli called out to him, "Samuel, my son."

"Here I am," Samuel replied.

17"What did the LORD say to you? Tell me

2:25 Or the judges. 2:28a Hebrew your father. 2:28b Hebrew an ephod. 2:30 Hebrew that your house and your father's house. 2:33 As in Dead Sea Scrolls, which read die by the sword; Masoretic Text reads die like mortals. 3:3 Hebrew the Temple of the LORD. 3:13 As in Greek version; Hebrew reads his sons have made themselves contemptible. 3:15 Hebrew the house of the LORD.

everything. And may God punish you if you hide anything from me!" 18So Samuel told Eli everything; he didn't hold anything back. "It is the LORD's will," Eli replied. "Let him do what he thinks best."

19As Samuel grew up, the LORD was with him, and everything Samuel said was wise and helpful. 20All the people of Israel from one end of the land to the other knew that Samuel was confirmed as a prophet of the LORD. 21The LORD continued to appear at Shiloh and gave messages to Samuel there at the Tabernacle. 1And Samuel's words went out to all the people of Israel.

CHAPTER **4**

The Philistines Capture the Ark

At that time Israel was at war with the Philistines. The Israelite army was camped near Ebenezer, and the Philistines were at Aphek. 2The Philistines attacked and defeated the army of Israel, killing four thousand men. 3After the battle was over, the army of Israel retreated to their camp, and their leaders asked, "Why did the LORD allow us to be defeated by the Philistines?" Then they said, "Let's bring the Ark of the Covenant of the LORD from Shiloh. If we carry it into battle with us, it* will save us from our enemies."

4So they sent men to Shiloh to bring back the Ark of the Covenant of the LORD Almighty, who is enthroned between the cherubim. Hophni and Phinehas, the sons of Eli, helped carry the Ark of God to where the battle was being fought. 5When the Israelites saw the Ark of the Covenant of the LORD coming into the camp, their shout of joy was so loud that it made the ground shake!

6"What's going on?" the Philistines asked. "What's all the shouting about in the Hebrew camp?" When they were told it was because the Ark of the LORD had arrived, 7they panicked. "The gods have* come into their camp!" they cried. "This is a disaster! We have never had to face anything like this before! 8Who can save us from these mighty gods of Israel? They are the same gods who destroyed the Egyptians with plagues when Israel was in the wilderness. 9Fight as you never have before, Philistines! If you don't, we will become the Hebrews' slaves just as they have been ours!"

10So the Philistines fought desperately, and Israel was defeated again. The slaughter was great; thirty thousand Israelite men died that

4:3 Or *he.* 4:7 Or *A god has.*

day. The survivors turned and fled to their tents. 11The Ark of God was captured, and Hophni and Phinehas, the two sons of Eli, were killed.

The Death of Eli

12A man from the tribe of Benjamin ran from the battlefront and arrived at Shiloh later that same day. He had torn his clothes and put dust on his head to show his grief. 13Eli was waiting beside the road to hear the news of the battle, for his heart trembled for the safety of the Ark of God. When the messenger arrived and told what had happened, an outcry resounded throughout the town. 14"What is all the noise about?" Eli asked.

The messenger rushed over to Eli, 15who was ninety-eight years old and blind. 16He said to Eli, "I have just come from the battlefront—I was there this very day."

"What happened?" Eli demanded.

17"Israel has been defeated," the messenger replied. "Thousands of Israelite troops are dead on the battlefield. Your two sons, Hophni and Phinehas, were killed, too. And the Ark of God has been captured."

18When the messenger mentioned what had happened to the Ark, Eli fell backward from his seat beside the gate. He broke his neck and died, for he was old and very fat. He had led Israel for forty years.

19Eli's daughter-in-law, the wife of Phinehas, was pregnant and near her time of delivery. When she heard that the Ark of God had been captured and that her husband and father-in-law were dead, her labor pains suddenly began. 20She died in childbirth, but before she passed away the midwives tried to encourage her. "Don't be afraid," they said. "You have a baby boy!" But she did not answer or respond in any way.

21She named the child Ichabod—"Where is the glory?"—murmuring, "Israel's glory is gone." She named him this because the Ark of God had been captured and because her husband and her father-in-law were dead. 22Then she said, "The glory has departed from Israel, for the Ark of God has been captured."

CHAPTER **5**

The Ark in Philistia

After the Philistines captured the Ark of God, they took it from the battleground at Ebenezer to the city of Ashdod. 2They carried the Ark of God into the temple of Dagon and placed it beside the idol of Dagon. ³But when the citizens of Ashdod went to see it the next morning, Dagon had fallen with his face to the ground in front of the Ark of the LORD! So they set the idol up again. ⁴But the next morning the same thing happened—the idol had fallen face down before the Ark of the LORD again. This time his head and hands had broken off and were lying in the doorway. Only the trunk of his body was left intact. ⁵That is why to this day neither the priests of Dagon nor anyone who enters the temple of Dagon will step on its threshold.

⁶Then the LORD began to afflict the people of Ashdod and the nearby villages with a plague of tumors.* ⁷When the people realized what was happening, they cried out, "We can't keep the Ark of the God of Israel here any longer! He is against us! We will all be destroyed along with our god Dagon." ⁸So they called together the rulers of the five Philistine cities and asked, "What should we do with the Ark of the God of Israel?"

The rulers discussed it and replied, "Move it to the city of Gath." So they moved the Ark of the God of Israel to Gath. ⁹But when the Ark arrived at Gath, the LORD began afflicting its people, young and old, with a plague of tumors, and there was a great panic.

¹⁰So they sent the Ark of God to the city of Ekron, but when the people of Ekron saw it coming they cried out, "They are bringing the Ark of the God of Israel here to kill us, too!" ¹¹So the people summoned the rulers again and begged them, "Please send the Ark of the God of Israel back to its own country, or it* will kill us all." For the plague from God had already begun, and great fear was sweeping across the city. ¹²Those who didn't die were afflicted with tumors; and there was weeping everywhere.

CHAPTER **6**

The Philistines Return the Ark

The Ark of the LORD remained in Philistine territory seven months in all. ²Then the Philistines called in their priests and diviners and asked them, "What should we do about the Ark of the LORD? Tell us how to return it to its own land."

³"Send the Ark of the God of Israel back, along with a gift," they were told. "Send a guilt offering so the plague will stop. Then, if the plague doesn't stop, you will know that God didn't send the plague after all."

⁴"What sort of guilt offering should we send?" they asked.

And they were told, "Since the plague has struck both you and your five rulers, make five gold tumors and five gold rats, just like those that have ravaged your land. ⁵Make these things to show honor to the God of Israel. Perhaps then he will stop afflicting you, your gods, and your land. ⁶Don't be stubborn and rebellious as Pharaoh and the Egyptians were. They wouldn't let Israel go until God had ravaged them with dreadful plagues. ⁷Now build a new cart, and find two cows that have just had calves. Make sure the cows have never been yoked to a cart. Hitch the cows to the cart, but shut their calves away from them in a pen. ⁸Put the Ark of the LORD on the cart, and beside it place a chest containing the gold rats and gold tumors. Then let the cows go wherever they want. ⁹If they cross the border of our land and go to Beth-shemesh, we will know it was the LORD who brought this great disaster upon us. If they don't, we will know that the plague was simply a coincidence and was not sent by the LORD at all."

¹⁰So these instructions were carried out. Two cows with newborn calves were hitched to the cart, and their calves were shut up in a pen. ¹¹Then the Ark of the LORD and the chest containing the gold rats and gold tumors were placed on the cart. ¹²And sure enough, the cows went straight along the road toward Beth-shemesh, lowing as they went. The Philistine rulers followed them as far as the border of Beth-shemesh.

¹³The people of Beth-shemesh were harvesting wheat in the valley, and when they saw the Ark, they were overjoyed! ¹⁴The cart came into the field of a man named Joshua and stopped beside a large rock. So the people broke up the wood of the cart for a fire and killed the cows and sacrificed them to the LORD as a burnt offering. ¹⁵Several men of the tribe of Levi lifted the Ark of the LORD and the chest containing the gold rats and gold tumors from the cart and placed them on the large rock. Many burnt offerings and sacrifices were offered to the LORD that day by the people of Beth-shemesh. ¹⁶The five Philistine rulers watched all this and then returned to Ekron that same day.

¹⁷The five gold tumors that were sent by the Philistines as a guilt offering to the LORD were gifts from the rulers of Ashdod, Gaza, Ashkelon, Gath, and Ekron. ¹⁸The five gold rats represented the five Philistine cities and their surrounding villages, which were controlled by the five rulers. The large rock at Beth-shemesh,

---

5:6 Greek version and Latin Vulgate read *tumors. And rats appeared in their land, and death and destruction were throughout the city.* 5:11 Or *he.*

where they set the Ark of the LORD, still stands in the field of Joshua as a reminder of what happened there.

The Ark Moved to Kiriath-Jearim

19But the LORD killed seventy men* from Beth-shemesh because they looked into the Ark of the LORD. And the people mourned greatly because of what the LORD had done. 20"Who is able to stand in the presence of the LORD, this holy God?" they cried out. "Where can we send the Ark from here?" 21So they sent messengers to the people at Kiriath-jearim and told them, "The Philistines have returned the Ark of the LORD. Please come here and get it!"

CHAPTER 7

So the men of Kiriath-jearim came to get the Ark of the LORD. They took it to the hillside home of Abinadab and ordained Eleazar, his son, to be in charge of it. 2The Ark remained in Kiriath-jearim for a long time—twenty years in all. During that time, all Israel mourned because it seemed that the LORD had abandoned them.

Samuel Leads Israel to Victory

3Then Samuel said to all the people of Israel, "If you are really serious about wanting to return to the LORD, get rid of your foreign gods and your images of Ashtoreth. Determine to obey only the LORD, then he will rescue you from the Philistines." 4So the Israelites destroyed their images of Baal and Ashtoreth and worshiped only the LORD.

5Then Samuel told them, "Come to Mizpah, all of you. I will pray to the LORD for you." 6So they gathered there and, in a great ceremony, drew water from a well and poured it out before the LORD. They also went without food all day and confessed that they had sinned against the LORD. So it was at Mizpah that Samuel became Israel's judge.

7When the Philistine rulers heard that all Israel had gathered at Mizpah, they mobilized their army and advanced. The Israelites were badly frightened when they learned that the Philistines were approaching. 8"Plead with the LORD our God to save us from the Philistines!" they begged Samuel. 9So Samuel took a young lamb and offered it to the LORD as a whole burnt offering. He pleaded with the LORD to help Israel, and the LORD answered.

10Just as Samuel was sacrificing the burnt of-

fering, the Philistines arrived for battle. But the LORD spoke with a mighty voice of thunder from heaven, and the Philistines were thrown into such confusion that the Israelites defeated them. 11The men of Israel chased them from Mizpah to Beth-car, slaughtering them all along the way.

12Samuel then took a large stone and placed it between the towns of Mizpah and Jeshanah.* He named it Ebenezer—"the stone of help"—for he said, "Up to this point the LORD has helped us!" 13So the Philistines were subdued and didn't invade Israel again for a long time. And throughout Samuel's lifetime, the LORD's powerful hand was raised against the Philistines. 14The Israelite towns near Ekron and Gath that the Philistines had captured were restored to Israel, along with the rest of the territory that the Philistines had taken. And there was also peace between Israel and the Amorites in those days.

15Samuel continued as Israel's judge for the rest of his life. 16Each year he traveled around, setting up his court first at Bethel, then at Gilgal, and then at Mizpah. He judged the people of Israel at each of these places. 17Then he would return to his home at Ramah, and he would hear cases there, too. And Samuel built an altar to the LORD at Ramah.

CHAPTER 8

Israel Requests a King

As Samuel grew old, he appointed his sons to be judges over Israel. 2Joel and Abijah, his oldest sons, held court in Beersheba. 3But they were not like their father, for they were greedy for money. They accepted bribes and perverted justice.

4Finally, the leaders of Israel met at Ramah to discuss the matter with Samuel. 5"Look," they told him, "you are now old, and your sons are not like you. Give us a king like all the other nations have."

6Samuel was very upset with their request and went to the LORD for advice. 7"Do as they say," the LORD replied, "for it is me they are rejecting, not you. They don't want me to be their king any longer. 8Ever since I brought them from Egypt they have continually forsaken me and followed other gods. And now they are giving you the same treatment. 9Do as they ask, but solemnly warn them about how a king will treat them."

Samuel Warns against a Kingdom

10So Samuel passed on the LORD's warning to the people. 11"This is how a king will treat you,"

6:19 As in a few Hebrew manuscripts; most Hebrew manuscripts and Greek version read *50,070 men*. Perhaps the text should be understood to read *the LORD killed 70 men and 50 oxen.* 7:12 As in Greek version; Hebrew reads *Shen.*

Samuel said. "The king will draft your sons into his army and make them run before his chariots. 12Some will be commanders of his troops, while others will be slave laborers. Some will be forced to plow in his fields and harvest his crops, while others will make his weapons and chariot equipment. 13The king will take your daughters from you and force them to cook and bake and make perfumes for him. 14He will take away the best of your fields and vineyards and olive groves and give them to his own servants. 15He will take a tenth of your harvest and distribute it among his officers and attendants. 16He will want your male and female slaves and demand the finest of your cattle* and donkeys for his own use. 17He will demand a tenth of your flocks, and you will be his slaves. 18When that day comes, you will beg for relief from this king you are demanding, but the LORD will not help you."

19But the people refused to listen to Samuel's warning. "Even so, we still want a king," they said. 20"We want to be like the nations around us. Our king will govern us and lead us into battle."

21So Samuel told the LORD what the people had said, 22and the LORD replied, "Do as they say, and give them a king." Then Samuel agreed and sent the people home.

CHAPTER 9

Saul Meets Samuel

Kish was a rich, influential man from the tribe of Benjamin. He was the son of Abiel and grandson of Zeror, from the family of Becorath and the clan of Aphiah. 2His son Saul was the most handsome man in Israel—head and shoulders taller than anyone else in the land.

3One day Kish's donkeys strayed away, and he told Saul, "Take a servant with you, and go look for them." 4So Saul took one of his servants and traveled all through the hill country of Ephraim, the land of Shalishah, the Shaalim area, and the entire land of Benjamin, but they couldn't find the donkeys anywhere. 5Finally, they entered the region of Zuph, and Saul said to his servant, "Let's go home. By now my father will be more worried about us than about the donkeys!"

6But the servant said, "I've just thought of something! There is a man of God who lives here in this town. He is held in high honor by all the people because everything he says comes true. Let's go find him. Perhaps he can tell us which way to go."

7"But we don't have anything to offer him,"

Saul replied. "Even our food is gone, and we don't have a thing to give him."

8"Well," the servant said, "I have one small silver piece.* We can at least offer it to him and see what happens!" 9(In those days if people wanted a message from God, they would say, "Let's go and ask the seer," for prophets used to be called seers.)

10"All right," Saul agreed, "let's try it!" So they started into the town where the man of God was.

11As they were climbing a hill toward the town, they met some young women coming out to draw water. So Saul and his servant asked, "Is the seer here today?"

12"Yes," they replied. "Stay right on this road. He is at the town gates. He has just arrived to take part in a public sacrifice up on the hill. 13Hurry and catch him before he goes up the hill to eat. The guests won't start until he arrives to bless the food."

14So they entered the town, and as they passed through the gates, Samuel was coming out toward them to climb the hill. 15Now the LORD had told Samuel the previous day, 16"About this time tomorrow I will send you a man from the land of Benjamin. Anoint him to be the leader of my people, Israel. He will rescue them from the Philistines, for I have looked down on my people in mercy and have heard their cry."

17When Samuel noticed Saul, the LORD said, "That's the man I told you about! He will rule my people."

18Just then Saul approached Samuel at the gateway and asked, "Can you please tell me where the seer's house is?"

19"I am the seer!" Samuel replied. "Go on up the hill ahead of me to the place of sacrifice, and we'll eat there together. In the morning I will tell you what you want to know and send you on your way. 20And don't worry about those donkeys that were lost three days ago, for they have been found. And I am here to tell you that you and your family are the focus of all Israel's hopes."

21Saul replied, "But I'm only from Benjamin, the smallest tribe in Israel, and my family is the least important of all the families of that tribe! Why are you talking like this to me?"

22Then Samuel brought Saul and his servant into the great hall and placed them at the head of the table, honoring them above the thirty special guests. 23Samuel then instructed the

8:16 As in Greek version; Hebrew reads *young men.*   9:8 Hebrew ¹⁄₄ *shekel of silver,* about 0.1 ounces or 3 grams in weight.

cook to bring Saul the finest cut of meat, the piece that had been set aside for the guest of honor. 24So the cook brought it in and placed it before Saul. "Go ahead and eat it," Samuel said. "I was saving it for you even before I invited these others!" So Saul ate with Samuel.

25After the feast, when they had returned to the town, Samuel took Saul up to the roof of the house and prepared a bed for him there.* 26At daybreak the next morning, Samuel called up to Saul, "Get up! It's time you were on your way." So Saul got ready, and he and Samuel left the house together. 27When they reached the edge of town, Samuel told Saul to send his servant on ahead. After the servant was gone, Samuel said, "Stay here, for I have received a special message for you from God."

CHAPTER 10

Samuel Anoints Saul as King

Then Samuel took a flask of olive oil and poured it over Saul's head. He kissed Saul on the cheek and said, "I am doing this because the LORD has appointed you to be the leader of his people Israel.* 2When you leave me today, you will see two men beside Rachel's tomb at Zelzah, on the border of Benjamin. They will tell you that the donkeys have been found and that your father is worried about you and is asking, 'Have you seen my son?'

3 "When you get to the oak of Tabor, you will see three men coming toward you who are on their way to worship God at Bethel. One will be bringing three young goats, another will have three loaves of bread, and the third will be carrying a skin of wine. 4They will greet you and offer you two of the loaves, which you are to accept.

5 "When you arrive at Gibeah of God,* where the garrison of the Philistines is located, you will meet a band of prophets coming down from the altar on the hill. They will be playing a harp, a tambourine, a flute, and a lyre, and they will be prophesying. 6At that time the Spirit of the LORD will come upon you with power, and you will prophesy with them. You will be changed into a different person. 7After these signs take place, do whatever you think is best, for God will be with you. 8Then go down to Gilgal ahead of me and wait for me there seven days. I will join you there to sacrifice burnt offerings and peace offerings. When I arrive, I will give you further instructions."

Samuel's Signs Are Fulfilled

9As Saul turned and started to leave, God changed his heart, and all Samuel's signs were fulfilled that day. 10When Saul and his servant arrived at Gibeah, they saw the prophets coming toward them. Then the Spirit of God came upon Saul, and he, too, began to prophesy. 11When his friends heard about it, they exclaimed, "What? Is Saul a prophet? How did the son of Kish become a prophet?" 12But one of the neighbors responded, "It doesn't matter who his father is; anyone can become a prophet."* So that is the origin of the saying "Is Saul a prophet?"

13When Saul had finished prophesying, he climbed the hill to the altar. 14"Where in the world have you been?" Saul's uncle asked him.

"We went to look for the donkeys," Saul replied, "but we couldn't find them. So we went to the prophet Samuel to ask him where they were."

15"Oh? And what did he say?" his uncle asked.

16"He said the donkeys had been found," Saul replied. But Saul didn't tell his uncle that Samuel had anointed him to be king.

Saul Is Acclaimed King

17Later Samuel called all the people of Israel to meet before the LORD at Mizpah. 18And he gave them this message from the LORD, the God of Israel: "I brought you from Egypt and rescued you from the Egyptians and from all of the nations that were oppressing you. 19But though I have done so much for you, you have rejected me and said, 'We want a king instead!' Now, therefore, present yourselves before the LORD by tribes and clans."

20So Samuel called the tribal leaders together before the LORD, and the tribe of Benjamin was chosen.* 21Then he brought each family of the tribe of Benjamin before the LORD, and the family of the Matrites was chosen. And finally Saul son of Kish was chosen from among them. But when they looked for him, he had disappeared! 22So they asked the LORD, "Where is he?"

And the LORD replied, "He is hiding among the baggage." 23So they found him and brought him out, and he stood head and shoulders above anyone else.

24Then Samuel said to all the people, "This is the man the LORD has chosen as your king. No one in all Israel is his equal!"

9:25 As in Greek version; Hebrew reads *and talked with him there.* 10:1 Greek version reads *Israel. And you will rule over the LORD's people and save them from their enemies around them. This will be the sign to you that the LORD has appointed you to be leader over his inheritance.* 10:5 Hebrew *Gibeath-elohim.* 10:12 Hebrew *responded, "Who is their father?"* 10:20 Hebrew *chosen by lot;* also in 10:21.

And all the people shouted, "Long live the king!"

25Then Samuel told the people what the rights and duties of a king were. He wrote them down on a scroll and placed it before the LORD. Then Samuel sent the people home again.

26When Saul returned to his home at Gibeah, a band of men whose hearts God had touched became his constant companions. 27But there were some wicked men who complained, "How can this man save us?" And they despised him and refused to bring him gifts. But Saul ignored them.*

CHAPTER 11

Saul Defeats the Ammonites

About a month later,* King Nahash of Ammon led his army against the Israelite city of Jabesh-gilead. But the citizens of Jabesh asked for peace. "Make a treaty with us, and we will be your servants," they pleaded.

2"All right," Nahash said, "but only on one condition. I will gouge out the right eye of every one of you as a disgrace to all Israel!"

3"Give us seven days to send messengers throughout Israel!" replied the leaders of Jabesh. "If none of our relatives will come to save us, we will agree to your terms."

4When the messengers came to Gibeah, Saul's hometown, and told the people about their plight, everyone broke into tears. 5Saul was plowing in the field, and when he returned to town, he asked, "What's the matter? Why is everyone crying?" So they told him about the message from Jabesh.

6Then the Spirit of God came mightily upon Saul, and he became very angry. 7He took two oxen and cut them into pieces and sent the messengers to carry them throughout Israel with this message: "This is what will happen to the oxen of anyone who refuses to follow Saul and Samuel into battle!" And the LORD made the people afraid of Saul's anger, and all of them came out together as one. 8When Saul mobilized them at Bezek, he found that there were 300,000 men of Israel, in addition to 30,000* from Judah.

9So Saul sent the messengers back to Jabesh-gilead to say, "We will rescue you by noontime tomorrow!" What joy there was throughout the city when that message arrived!

10The men of Jabesh then told their enemies, "Tomorrow we will come out to you, and you can do to us as you wish." 11But before dawn the next morning, Saul arrived, having divided his army into three detachments. He launched a surprise attack against the Ammonites and slaughtered them the whole morning. The remnant of their army was so badly scattered that no two of them were left together.

12Then the people exclaimed to Samuel, "Now where are those men who said Saul shouldn't rule over us? Bring them here, and we will kill them!"

13But Saul replied, "No one will be executed today, for today the LORD has rescued Israel!"

14Then Samuel said to the people, "Come, let us all go to Gilgal to reaffirm Saul's kingship." 15So they went to Gilgal, and in a solemn ceremony before the LORD they crowned him king. Then they offered peace offerings to the LORD, and Saul and all the Israelites were very happy.

CHAPTER 12

Samuel's Farewell Address

Then Samuel addressed the people again: "I have done as you asked and given you a king. 2I have selected him ahead of my own sons, and I stand here, an old, gray-haired man. I have served as your leader since I was a boy. 3Now tell me as I stand before the LORD and before his anointed one—whose ox or donkey have I stolen? Have I ever cheated any of you? Have I ever oppressed you? Have I ever taken a bribe? Tell me and I will make right whatever I have done wrong."

4"No," they replied, "you have never cheated or oppressed us in any way, and you have never taken even a single bribe."

5"The LORD and his anointed one are my witnesses," Samuel declared, "that you can never accuse me of robbing you."

"Yes, it is true," they replied.

6"It was the LORD who appointed Moses and Aaron," Samuel continued. "He brought your ancestors out of the land of Egypt. 7Now stand here quietly before the LORD as I remind you of all the great things the LORD has done for you and your ancestors.

8"When the Israelites were* in Egypt and cried out to the LORD, he sent Moses and Aaron to rescue them from Egypt and to bring them into

10:27 Dead Sea Scroll 4QSam^a continues: *Nahash, king of the Ammonites, had been grievously oppressing the Gadites and Reubenites who lived east of the Jordan River. He gouged out the right eye of each of the Israelites living there, and he didn't allow anyone to come and rescue them. In fact, of all the Israelites east of the Jordan, there wasn't a single one whose right eye Nahash had not gouged out. But there were seven thousand men who had escaped from the Ammonites, and they had settled in Jabesh-gilead.* **11:1** As in Greek version; Hebrew lacks *About a month later.* **11:8** Dead Sea Scrolls and Greek version read *70,000.* **12:8** Hebrew *When Jacob was.*

this land. 9But the people soon forgot about the LORD their God, so he let them be conquered by Sisera, the general of Hazor's army, and by the Philistines and the king of Moab.

10"Then they cried to the LORD again and confessed, 'We have sinned by turning away from the LORD and worshiping the images of Baal and Ashtoreth. But we will worship you and you alone if you will rescue us from our enemies.' 11Then the LORD sent Gideon,* Barak,* Jephthah, and Samuel* to save you, and you lived in safety.

12"But when you were afraid of Nahash, the king of Ammon, you came to me and said that you wanted a king to reign over you, even though the LORD your God was already your king. 13All right, here is the king you have chosen. Look him over. You asked for him, and the LORD has granted your request.

14"Now if you will fear and worship the LORD and listen to his voice, and if you do not rebel against the LORD's commands, and if you and your king follow the LORD your God, then all will be well. 15But if you rebel against the LORD's commands and refuse to listen to him, then his hand will be as heavy upon you as it was upon your ancestors.

16"Now stand here and see the great thing the LORD is about to do. 17You know that it does not rain at this time of the year during the wheat harvest. I will ask the LORD to send thunder and rain today. Then you will realize how wicked you have been in asking the LORD for a king!"

18So Samuel called to the LORD, and the LORD sent thunder and rain. And all the people were terrified of the LORD and of Samuel. 19"Pray to the LORD your God for us, or we will die!" they cried out to Samuel. "For now we have added to our sins by asking for a king."

20"Don't be afraid," Samuel reassured them. "You have certainly done wrong, but make sure now that you worship the LORD with all your heart and that you don't turn your back on him in any way. 21Don't go back to worshiping worthless idols that cannot help or rescue you—they really are useless! 22The LORD will not abandon his chosen people, for that would dishonor his great name. He made you a special nation for himself.

23"As for me, I will certainly not sin against the LORD by ending my prayers for you. And I will continue to teach you what is good and right. 24But be sure to fear the LORD and sincerely worship him. Think of all the wonderful things he has done for you. 25But if you continue to sin, you and your king will be destroyed."

CHAPTER 13

Continued War with Philistia

Saul was thirty* years old when he became king, and he reigned for forty-two years.*

2Saul selected three thousand special troops from the army of Israel and sent the rest of the men home. He took two thousand of the chosen men with him to Micmash and the hill country of Bethel. The other thousand went with Saul's son Jonathan to Gibeah in the land of Benjamin.

3Soon after this, Jonathan attacked and defeated the garrison of Philistines at Geba. The news spread quickly among the Philistines that Israel was in revolt, so Saul sounded the call to arms throughout Israel. 4He announced that the Philistine garrison at Geba had been destroyed, and he warned the people that the Philistines now hated the Israelites more than ever. So the entire Israelite army mobilized again and met Saul at Gilgal.

5The Philistines mustered a mighty army of three thousand* chariots, six thousand horsemen, and as many warriors as the grains of sand along the seashore! They camped at Micmash east of Beth-aven. 6When the men of Israel saw the vast number of enemy troops, they lost their nerve entirely and tried to hide in caves, holes, rocks, tombs, and cisterns. 7Some of them crossed the Jordan River and escaped into the land of Gad and Gilead.

Saul's Disobedience and Samuel's Rebuke

Meanwhile, Saul stayed at Gilgal, and his men were trembling with fear. 8Saul waited there seven days for Samuel, as Samuel had instructed him earlier, but Samuel still didn't come. Saul realized that his troops were rapidly slipping away. 9So he demanded, "Bring me the burnt offering and the peace offerings!" And Saul sacrificed the burnt offering himself. 10Just as Saul was finishing with the burnt offering, Samuel arrived. Saul went out to meet and welcome him, 11but Samuel said, "What is this you have done?"

Saul replied, "I saw my men scattering from me, and you didn't arrive when you said you

---

12:11a Hebrew *Jerubbaal*, another name for Gideon; see Judg 7:1. 12:11b As in Greek and Syriac versions; Hebrew reads *Bedan*.
12:11c Greek and Syriac versions read *Samson*. 13:1a As in a few Greek manuscripts; the number is missing in the Hebrew.
13:1b Hebrew *reigned . . . and two*; the number is incomplete in the Hebrew. Compare Acts 13:21. 13:5 As in Greek and Syriac versions; Hebrew reads *30,000*.

would, and the Philistines are at Micmash ready for battle. 12So I said, 'The Philistines are ready to march against us, and I haven't even asked for the LORD's help!' So I felt obliged to offer the burnt offering myself before you came."

13"How foolish!" Samuel exclaimed. "You have disobeyed the command of the LORD your God. Had you obeyed, the LORD would have established your kingdom over Israel forever. 14But now your dynasty must end, for the LORD has sought out a man after his own heart. The LORD has already chosen him to be king over his people, for you have not obeyed the LORD's command."

Israel's Military Disadvantage

15Samuel then left Gilgal and went on his way, but the rest of the troops went with Saul to meet the army. They went up from Gilgal to Gibeah in the land of Benjamin.* When Saul counted the men who were still with him, he found only six hundred left! 16Saul and Jonathan and the troops with them were staying at Geba, near Gibeah, in the land of Benjamin. The Philistines set up their camp at Micmash. 17Three raiding parties soon left the camp of the Philistines. One went north toward Ophrah in the land of Shual, 18another went west to Beth-horon, and the third moved toward the border above the valley of Zeboim near the wilderness.

19There were no blacksmiths in the land of Israel in those days. The Philistines wouldn't allow them for fear they would make swords and spears for the Hebrews. 20So whenever the Israelites needed to sharpen their plowshares, picks, axes, or sickles,* they had to take them to a Philistine blacksmith. 21(The schedule of charges was as follows: a quarter of an ounce of silver* for sharpening a plowshare or a pick, and an eighth of an ounce* for sharpening an ax, a sickle, or an ox goad.) 22So none of the people of Israel had a sword or spear, except for Saul and Jonathan. 23The pass at Micmash had meanwhile been secured by a contingent of the Philistine army.

CHAPTER 14

Jonathan's Daring Plan

One day Jonathan said to the young man who carried his armor, "Come on, let's go over to where the Philistines have their outpost." But Jonathan did not tell his father what he was doing. 2Meanwhile, Saul and his six hundred

men were camped on the outskirts of Gibeah, around the pomegranate tree at Migron. 3(Among Saul's men was Ahijah the priest, who was wearing the linen ephod. Ahijah was the son of Ahitub, Ichabod's brother. Ahitub was the son of Phinehas and the grandson of Eli, the priest of the LORD who had served at Shiloh.)

No one realized that Jonathan had left the Israelite camp. 4To reach the Philistine outpost, Jonathan had to go down between two rocky cliffs that were called Bozez and Seneh. 5The cliff on the north was in front of Micmash, and the one on the south was in front of Geba. 6"Let's go across to see those pagans," Jonathan said to his armor bearer. "Perhaps the LORD will help us, for nothing can hinder the LORD. He can win a battle whether he has many warriors or only a few!"

7"Do what you think is best," the youth replied. "I'm with you completely, whatever you decide."

8"All right then," Jonathan told him. "We will cross over and let them see us. 9If they say to us, 'Stay where you are or we'll kill you,' then we will stop and not go up to them. 10But if they say, 'Come on up and fight,' then we will go up. That will be the LORD's sign that he will help us defeat them."

11When the Philistines saw them coming, they shouted, "Look! The Hebrews are crawling out of their holes!" 12Then they shouted to Jonathan, "Come on up here, and we'll teach you a lesson!"

"Come on, climb right behind me," Jonathan said to his armor bearer, "for the LORD will help us defeat them!" 13So they climbed up using both hands and feet, and the Philistines fell back as Jonathan and his armor bearer killed them right and left. 14They killed about twenty men in all, and their bodies were scattered over about half an acre.* 15Suddenly, panic broke out in the Philistine army, both in the camp and in the field, including even the outposts and raiding parties. And just then an earthquake struck, and everyone was terrified.

Israel Defeats the Philistines

16Saul's lookouts in Gibeah saw a strange sight—the vast army of Philistines began to melt away in every direction. 17"Find out who isn't here," Saul ordered. And when they checked, they found that Jonathan and his armor bearer were gone. 18Then Saul shouted to Ahijah,

13:15 As in Greek version; Hebrew reads *Samuel left Gilgal and went to Gibeah in the land of Benjamin.* 13:20 As in Greek version; Hebrew reads *or plowshares.* 13:21a Hebrew *1 pim* [8 grams]. 13:21b Hebrew *⅓ of a shekel* [4 grams]. 14:14 Hebrew *half a yoke;* a "yoke" was the amount of land plowed by a pair of yoked oxen in one day.

"Bring the ephod here!" For at that time Ahijah was wearing the ephod in front of the Israelites.* ¹⁹But while Saul was talking to the priest, the shouting and confusion in the Philistine camp grew louder and louder. So Saul said to Ahijah, "Never mind; let's get going!"*

²⁰Then Saul and his six hundred men rushed out to the battle and found the Philistines killing each other. There was terrible confusion everywhere. ²¹Even the Hebrews who had gone over to the Philistine army revolted and joined in with Saul, Jonathan, and the rest of the Israelites. ²²Likewise, the men who were hiding in the hills joined the chase when they saw the Philistines running away. ²³So the LORD saved Israel that day, and the battle continued to rage even out beyond Beth-aven.

Saul's Foolish Oath

²⁴Now the men of Israel were worn out that day, because Saul had made them take an oath, saying, "Let a curse fall on anyone who eats before evening—before I have full revenge on my enemies." So no one ate a thing all day, ²⁵even though they found honeycomb on the ground in the forest. ²⁶They didn't even touch the honey because they all feared the oath they had taken.

²⁷But Jonathan had not heard his father's command, and he dipped a stick into a piece of honeycomb and ate the honey. After he had eaten it, he felt much better. ²⁸But one of the men saw him and said, "Your father made the army take a strict oath that anyone who eats food today will be cursed. That is why everyone is weary and faint."

²⁹"My father has made trouble for us all!" Jonathan exclaimed. "A command like that only hurts us. See how much better I feel now that I have eaten this little bit of honey. ³⁰If the men had been allowed to eat freely from the food they found among our enemies, think how many more we could have killed!"

³¹But hungry as they were, they chased and killed the Philistines all day from Micmash to Aijalon, growing more and more faint. ³²That evening they flew upon the battle plunder and butchered the sheep, cattle, and calves, but they ate them without draining the blood. ³³Someone reported to Saul, "Look, the men are sinning against the LORD by eating meat that still has blood in it."

"That is very wrong," Saul said. "Find a large stone and roll it over here. ³⁴Then go out among the troops and tell them, 'Bring the cattle and

sheep here to kill them and drain the blood. Do not sin against the LORD by eating meat with the blood still in it.'" So that night all the troops brought their animals and slaughtered them there. ³⁵And Saul built an altar to the LORD, the first one he had ever built.

³⁶Then Saul said, "Let's chase the Philistines all night and destroy every last one of them."

His men replied, "We'll do whatever you think is best."

But the priest said, "Let's ask God first."

³⁷So Saul asked God, "Should we go after the Philistines? Will you help us defeat them?" But God made no reply that day.

³⁸Then Saul said to the leaders, "Something's wrong! I want all my army commanders to come here. We must find out what sin was committed today. ³⁹I vow by the name of the LORD who rescued Israel that the sinner will surely die, even if it is my own son Jonathan!" But no one would tell him what the trouble was. ⁴⁰Then Saul said, "Jonathan and I will stand over here, and all of you stand over there." And the people agreed.

⁴¹Then Saul prayed, "O LORD, God of Israel, please show us who is guilty and who is innocent. Are Jonathan and I guilty, or is the sin among the others?"* And Jonathan and Saul were chosen* as the guilty ones, and the people were declared innocent.

⁴²Then Saul said, "Now choose* between me and Jonathan." And Jonathan was shown to be the guilty one.

⁴³"Tell me what you have done," Saul demanded of Jonathan.

"I tasted a little honey," Jonathan admitted. "It was only a little bit on the end of a stick. Does that deserve death?"

⁴⁴"Yes, Jonathan," Saul said, "you must die! May God strike me dead if you are not executed for this."

⁴⁵But the people broke in and said to Saul, "Should Jonathan, who saved Israel today, die? Far from it! As surely as the LORD lives, not one hair on his head will be touched, for he has been used of God to do a mighty miracle today." So the people rescued Jonathan, and he was not put to death. ⁴⁶Then Saul called back the army from chasing the Philistines, and the Philistines returned home.

Saul's Military Successes

⁴⁷Now when Saul had secured his grasp on Israel's throne, he fought against his enemies in every

14:18 As in some Greek manuscripts; Hebrew reads *"Bring the Ark of God."* For at that time the Ark of God was with the Israelites.
14:19 Hebrew *Withdraw your hand.*   14:41a Greek version adds *If the fault is with me or my son Jonathan, respond with Urim; but if the men of Israel are at fault, respond with Thummim.*   14:41b Hebrew *chosen by lot.*   14:42 Hebrew *draw lots.*

direction—against Moab, Ammon, Edom, the kings of Zobah, and the Philistines. And wherever he turned, he was victorious. ⁴⁸He did great deeds and conquered the Amalekites, saving Israel from all those who had plundered them.

⁴⁹Saul's sons included Jonathan, Ishbosheth,* and Malkishua. He also had two daughters: Merab, who was older, and Michal. ⁵⁰Saul's wife was Ahinoam, the daughter of Ahimaaz. The commander of Saul's army was his cousin Abner, his uncle Ner's son. ⁵¹Abner's father, Ner, and Saul's father, Kish, were brothers; both were sons of Abiel.

⁵²The Israelites fought constantly with the Philistines throughout Saul's lifetime. So whenever Saul saw a young man who was brave and strong, he drafted him into his army.

CHAPTER **15**

Saul Destroys the Amalekites

One day Samuel said to Saul, "I anointed you king of Israel because the LORD told me to. Now listen to this message from the LORD! ²This is what the LORD Almighty says: 'I have decided to settle accounts with the nation of Amalek for opposing Israel when they came from Egypt. ³Now go and completely destroy* the entire Amalekite nation—men, women, children, babies, cattle, sheep, camels, and donkeys.'"

⁴So Saul mobilized his army at Telaim. There were 200,000 troops in addition to 10,000 men from Judah. ⁵Then Saul went to the city of Amalek and lay in wait in the valley. ⁶Saul sent this message to the Kenites: "Move away from where the Amalekites live or else you will die with them. For you were kind to the people of Israel when they came up from Egypt." So the Kenites packed up and left.

⁷Then Saul slaughtered the Amalekites from Havilah all the way to Shur, east of Egypt. ⁸He captured Agag, the Amalekite king, but completely destroyed everyone else. ⁹Saul and his men spared Agag's life and kept the best of the sheep and cattle, the fat calves and lambs—everything, in fact, that appealed to them. They destroyed only what was worthless or of poor quality.

The LORD Rejects Saul

¹⁰Then the LORD said to Samuel, ¹¹"I am sorry that I ever made Saul king, for he has not been loyal to me and has again refused to obey me."

14:49 Hebrew *Ishvi*, a variant name for Ishbosheth; also known as Eshbaal. 15:3 The Hebrew term used here refers to the complete consecration of things or people to the LORD, either by destroying them or by giving them as an offering; also in 15:8, 9, 15, 18, 20, 21.

Samuel was so deeply moved when he heard this that he cried out to the LORD all night.

¹²Early the next morning Samuel went to find Saul. Someone told him, "Saul went to Carmel

---

Offer God More than Lip Service Read 1 SAMUEL 15:1-23

This passage contains some strong warnings for those who would attempt to appease God with their outward religious practices rather than living a life of heartfelt obedience. The words were directed to King Saul, who had just come back from a mission in which he had almost—but not completely—followed the Lord's instructions to him. What led to Saul's demise?

Saul Did Not Completely Obey God's Command. God had told Saul to completely kill a sinful nation, which included the livestock as well as the people. But Saul disobeyed God and chose to keep the best of the cattle and sheep for himself. Likewise, when God tells us to get rid of sinful practices in our lives, we are disobeying him if we keep on committing certain sins.

Saul Was Filled with Pride. God had made Saul king of Israel when Saul didn't think much of himself. After this successful raid, in which he had followed his own instincts rather than God's, he erected a monument to himself! When faced with temptation, we can make the same mistake if we rely on our own strength instead of God's.

Saul Tried to Rationalize His Actions. To make up for his poor judgment, Saul told Samuel that he had planned to offer to God as a sacrifice the sheep and oxen he had kept. Unfortunately, such an action would not excuse his moment of disobedience. Sometimes we think we can justify our behavior by keeping up a religious front or going through a few rituals. Although you may be able to fool some people, you cannot fool God.

God will honor only those whose hearts are fully devoted to him. If you have been covering up your sin with "lip service" or a "spiritual facade," ask him for forgiveness today. As the passage says, "Obedience is far better than sacrifice."

For the next note on "Obey God," turn to p. 913.

to set up a monument to himself; then he went on to Gilgal."

13When Samuel finally found him, Saul greeted him cheerfully. "May the LORD bless you," he said. "I have carried out the LORD's command!"

14"Then what is all the bleating of sheep and lowing of cattle I hear?" Samuel demanded.

15"It's true that the army spared the best of the sheep and cattle," Saul admitted. "But they are going to sacrifice them to the LORD your God. We have destroyed everything else."

16Then Samuel said to Saul, "Stop! Listen to what the LORD told me last night!"

"What was it?" Saul asked.

17And Samuel told him, "Although you may think little of yourself, are you not the leader of the tribes of Israel? The LORD has anointed you king of Israel. 18And the LORD sent you on a mission and told you, 'Go and completely destroy the sinners, the Amalekites, until they are all dead.' 19Why haven't you obeyed the LORD? Why did you rush for the plunder and do exactly what the LORD said not to do?"

20"But I did obey the LORD," Saul insisted. "I carried out the mission he gave me. I brought back King Agag, but I destroyed everyone else. 21Then my troops brought in the best of the sheep and cattle and plunder to sacrifice to the LORD your God in Gilgal."

22But Samuel replied, "What is more pleasing to the LORD: your burnt offerings and sacrifices or your obedience to his voice? Obedience is far better than sacrifice. Listening to him is much better than offering the fat of rams. 23Rebellion is as bad as the sin of witchcraft, and stubbornness is as bad as worshiping idols. So because you have rejected the word of the LORD, he has rejected you from being king."

Saul Pleads for Forgiveness

24Then Saul finally admitted, "Yes, I have sinned. I have disobeyed your instructions and the LORD's command, for I was afraid of the people and did what they demanded. 25Oh, please, forgive my sin now and go with me to worship the LORD."

26But Samuel replied, "I will not return with you! Since you have rejected the LORD's command, he has rejected you from being the king of Israel."

27As Samuel turned to go, Saul grabbed at him to try to hold him back and tore his robe. 28And Samuel said to him, "See? The LORD has torn the kingdom of Israel from you today and has given it to someone else—one who is better than you. 29And he who is the Glory of Israel will not lie, nor will he change his mind, for he is not human that he should change his mind!"

30Then Saul pleaded again, "I know I have sinned. But please, at least honor me before the leaders and before my people by going with me to worship the LORD your God." 31So Samuel finally agreed and went with him, and Saul worshiped the LORD.

Samuel Executes King Agag

32Then Samuel said, "Bring King Agag to me." Agag arrived full of smiles, for he thought, "Surely the worst is over, and I have been spared!"* 33But Samuel said, "As your sword has killed the sons of many mothers, now your mother will be childless." And Samuel cut Agag to pieces before the LORD at Gilgal. 34Then Samuel went home to Ramah, and Saul returned to his house at Gibeah. 35Samuel never went to meet with Saul again, but he mourned constantly for him. And the LORD was sorry he had ever made Saul king of Israel.

CHAPTER 16
Samuel Anoints David as King

Finally, the LORD said to Samuel, "You have mourned long enough for Saul. I have rejected him as king of Israel. Now fill your horn with olive oil and go to Bethlehem. Find a man named Jesse who lives there, for I have selected one of his sons to be my new king."

2But Samuel asked, "How can I do that? If Saul hears about it, he will kill me."

"Take a heifer with you," the LORD replied, "and say that you have come to make a sacrifice to the LORD. 3Invite Jesse to the sacrifice, and I will show you which of his sons to anoint for me."

4So Samuel did as the LORD instructed him. When he arrived at Bethlehem, the leaders of the town became afraid. "What's wrong?" they asked. "Do you come in peace?"

5"Yes," Samuel replied. "I have come to sacrifice to the LORD. Purify yourselves and come with me to the sacrifice." Then Samuel performed the purification rite for Jesse and his sons and invited them, too.

6When they arrived, Samuel took one look at Eliab and thought, "Surely this is the LORD's anointed!" 7But the LORD said to Samuel, "Don't judge by his appearance or height, for I

15:32 Dead Sea Scrolls and Greek version read *Agag arrived hesitantly, for he thought, "Surely this is the bitterness of death."*

have rejected him. The LORD doesn't make decisions the way you do! People judge by outward appearance, but the LORD looks at a person's thoughts and intentions."

8Then Jesse told his son Abinadab to step forward and walk in front of Samuel. But Samuel said, "This is not the one the LORD has chosen." 9Next Jesse summoned Shammah, but Samuel said, "Neither is this the one the LORD has chosen." 10In the same way all seven of Jesse's sons were presented to Samuel. But Samuel said to Jesse, "The LORD has not chosen any of these." 11Then Samuel asked, "Are these all the sons you have?"

"There is still the youngest," Jesse replied. "But he's out in the fields watching the sheep."

"Send for him at once," Samuel said. "We will not sit down to eat until he arrives."

12So Jesse sent for him. He was ruddy and handsome, with pleasant eyes. And the LORD said, "This is the one; anoint him."

13So as David stood there among his brothers, Samuel took the olive oil he had brought and poured it on David's head. And the Spirit of the LORD came mightily upon him from that day on. Then Samuel returned to Ramah.

David Serves in Saul's Court

14Now the Spirit of the LORD had left Saul, and the LORD sent a tormenting spirit that filled him with depression and fear. 15Some of Saul's servants suggested a remedy. "It is clear that a spirit from God is tormenting you," they said. 16"Let us find a good musician to play the harp for you whenever the tormenting spirit is bothering you. The harp music will quiet you, and you will soon be well again."

17"All right," Saul said. "Find me someone who plays well and bring him here."

18One of the servants said to Saul, "The son of Jesse is a talented harp player. Not only that; he is brave and strong and has good judgment. He is also a fine-looking young man, and the LORD is with him."

19So Saul sent messengers to Jesse to say, "Send me your son David, the shepherd." 20Jesse responded by sending David to Saul, along with a young goat and a donkey loaded down with food and wine. 21So David went to Saul and served him. Saul liked David very much, and David became one of Saul's armor bearers.

22Then Saul sent word to Jesse asking, "Please let David join my staff, for I am very pleased with him." 23And whenever the tormenting spirit from God troubled Saul, David would play the harp. Then Saul would feel better, and the tormenting spirit would go away.

CHAPTER 17

Goliath Challenges the Israelites

The Philistines now mustered their army for battle and camped between Socoh in Judah and Azekah at Ephes-dammim. 2Saul countered by gathering his troops near the valley of Elah. 3So the Philistines and Israelites faced each other on opposite hills, with the valley between them.

4Then Goliath, a Philistine champion from Gath, came out of the Philistine ranks to face the forces of Israel. He was a giant of a man, measuring over nine feet* tall! 5He wore a bronze helmet and a coat of mail that weighed 125 pounds.* 6He also wore bronze leggings, and he slung a bronze javelin over his back. 7The shaft of his spear was as heavy and thick as a weaver's beam, tipped with an iron spearhead that weighed fifteen pounds.* An armor bearer walked ahead of him carrying a huge shield.

8Goliath stood and shouted across to the Israelites, "Do you need a whole army to settle this? Choose someone to fight for you, and I will represent the Philistines. We will settle this dispute in single combat! 9If your man is able to kill me, then we will be your slaves. But if I kill him, you will be our slaves! 10I defy the armies of Israel! Send me a man who will fight with me!" 11When Saul and the Israelites heard this, they were terrified and deeply shaken.

Jesse Sends David to Saul's Camp

12Now David was the son of a man named Jesse, an Ephrathite from Bethlehem in the land of Judah. Jesse was an old man at that time, and he had eight sons in all. 13Jesse's three oldest sons—Eliab, Abinadab, and Shammah—had already joined Saul's army to fight the Philistines. 14David was the youngest of Jesse's sons. Since David's three oldest brothers were in the army, they stayed with Saul's forces all the time. 15But David went back and forth between working for Saul and helping his father with the sheep in Bethlehem.

16For forty days, twice a day, morning and evening, the Philistine giant strutted in front of the Israelite army.

17One day Jesse said to David, "Take this half-bushel* of roasted grain and these ten

---

17:4 Hebrew *6 cubits and 1 span* [which totals about 9.75 feet or 3 meters]; Greek version and Dead Sea Scrolls read *4 cubits and 1 span* [which totals about 6.75 feet or 2 meters].   **17:5** Hebrew *5,000 shekels* [57 kilograms].   **17:7** Hebrew *600 shekels* [6.8 kilograms]. **17:17** Hebrew *ephah* [18 liters].

loaves of bread to your brothers. [18]And give these ten cuts of cheese to their captain. See how your brothers are getting along, and bring me back a letter from them.*"

[19]David's brothers were with Saul and the Israelite army at the valley of Elah, fighting against the Philistines. [20]So David left the sheep with another shepherd and set out early the next morning with the gifts. He arrived at the outskirts of the camp just as the Israelite army was leaving for the battlefield with shouts and battle cries. [21]Soon the Israelite and Philistine forces stood facing each other, army against army. [22]David left his things with the keeper of supplies and hurried out to the ranks to greet his brothers. [23]As he was talking with them, he saw Goliath, the champion from Gath, come out from the Philistine ranks, shouting his challenge to the army of Israel.

[24]As soon as the Israelite army saw him, they began to run away in fright. [25]"Have you seen the giant?" the men were asking. "He comes out each day to challenge Israel. And have you heard about the huge reward the king has offered to anyone who kills him? The king will give him one of his daughters for a wife, and his whole family will be exempted from paying taxes!"

[26]David talked to some others standing there to verify the report. "What will a man get for killing this Philistine and putting an end to his abuse of Israel?" he asked them. "Who is this pagan Philistine anyway, that he is allowed to defy the armies of the living God?" [27]And David received the same reply as before: "What you have been hearing is true. That is the reward for killing the giant."

[28]But when David's oldest brother, Eliab, heard David talking to the men, he was angry. "What are you doing around here anyway?" he demanded. "What about those few sheep you're supposed to be taking care of? I know about your pride and dishonesty. You just want to see the battle!"

[29]"What have I done now?" David replied. "I was only asking a question!" [30]He walked over to some others and asked them the same thing and received the same answer. [31]Then David's question was reported to King Saul, and the king sent for him.

David Kills Goliath

[32]"Don't worry about a thing," David told Saul. "I'll go fight this Philistine!"

[33]"Don't be ridiculous!" Saul replied. "There

17:18 Hebrew *and take their pledge.*

is no way you can go against this Philistine. You are only a boy, and he has been in the army since he was a boy!"

[34]But David persisted. "I have been taking care of my father's sheep," he said. "When a lion or a bear comes to steal a lamb from the flock, [35]I go after it with a club and take the lamb from its mouth. If the animal turns on me, I catch it by the jaw and club it to death. [36]I have done this to both lions and bears, and I'll do it to this pagan Philistine, too, for he has defied the armies of the living God! [37]The LORD who saved me from the claws of the lion and the bear will save me from this Philistine!"

Saul finally consented. "All right, go ahead," he said. "And may the LORD be with you!"

[38]Then Saul gave David his own armor—a bronze helmet and a coat of mail. [39]David put it on, strapped the sword over it, and took a step or two to see what it was like, for he had never worn such things before. "I can't go in these," he protested. "I'm not used to them." So he took them off again. [40]He picked up five smooth stones from a stream and put them in his shepherd's bag. Then, armed only with his shepherd's staff and sling, he started across to fight Goliath.

[41]Goliath walked out toward David with his shield bearer ahead of him, [42]sneering in contempt at this ruddy-faced boy. [43]"Am I a dog," he roared at David, "that you come at me with a stick?" And he cursed David by the names of his gods. [44]"Come over here, and I'll give your flesh to the birds and wild animals!" Goliath yelled.

[45]David shouted in reply, "You come to me with sword, spear, and javelin, but I come to you in the name of the LORD Almighty—the God of the armies of Israel, whom you have defied. [46]Today the LORD will conquer you, and I will kill you and cut off your head. And then I will give the dead bodies of your men to the birds and wild animals, and the whole world will know that there is a God in Israel! [47]And everyone will know that the LORD does not need weapons to rescue his people. It is his battle, not ours. The LORD will give you to us!"

[48]As Goliath moved closer to attack, David quickly ran out to meet him. [49]Reaching into his shepherd's bag and taking out a stone, he hurled it from his sling and hit the Philistine in the forehead. The stone sank in, and Goliath stumbled and fell face downward to the ground. [50]So David triumphed over the Philistine giant with

only a stone and sling. And since he had no sword, ⁵¹he ran over and pulled Goliath's sword from its sheath. David used it to kill the giant and cut off his head.

Israel Routs the Philistines

When the Philistines saw that their champion was dead, they turned and ran. ⁵²Then the Israelites gave a great shout of triumph and rushed after the Philistines, chasing them as far as Gath* and the gates of Ekron. The bodies of the dead and wounded Philistines were strewn all along the road from Shaaraim, as far as Gath and Ekron. ⁵³Then the Israelite army returned and plundered the deserted Philistine camp. ⁵⁴(David took Goliath's head to Jerusalem, but he stored the Philistine's armor in his own tent.)

⁵⁵As Saul watched David go out to fight Goliath, he asked Abner, the general of his army, "Abner, whose son is he?"

"I really don't know," Abner said.

⁵⁶"Well, find out!" the king told him.

⁵⁷After David had killed Goliath, Abner brought him to Saul with the Philistine's head still in his hand. ⁵⁸"Tell me about your father, my boy," Saul said.

And David replied, "His name is Jesse, and we live in Bethlehem."

CHAPTER **18**

Saul Becomes Jealous of David

After David had finished talking with Saul, he met Jonathan, the king's son. There was an immediate bond of love between them, and they became the best of friends. ²From that day on Saul kept David with him at the palace and wouldn't let him return home. ³And Jonathan made a special vow to be David's friend, ⁴and he sealed the pact by giving him his robe, tunic, sword, bow, and belt.

⁵Whatever Saul asked David to do, David did it successfully. So Saul made him a commander in his army, an appointment that was applauded by the fighting men and officers alike. ⁶But something happened when the victorious Israelite army was returning home after David had killed Goliath. Women came out from all the towns along the way to celebrate and to cheer for King Saul, and they sang and danced for joy with tambourines and cymbals.* ⁷This was their song:

"Saul has killed his thousands,
and David his ten thousands!"

⁸This made Saul very angry. "What's this?" he said. "They credit David with ten thousands and me with only thousands. Next they'll be making him their king!" ⁹So from that time on Saul kept a jealous eye on David.

¹⁰The very next day, in fact, a tormenting spirit from God overwhelmed Saul, and he began to rave like a madman. David began to play the harp, as he did whenever this happened. But Saul, who had a spear in his hand, ¹¹suddenly hurled it at David, intending to pin him to the wall. But David jumped aside and escaped. This happened another time, too, ¹²for Saul was afraid of him, and he was jealous because the LORD had left him and was now with David. ¹³Finally, Saul banned him from his presence and appointed him commander over only a thousand men, but David faithfully led his troops into battle.

¹⁴David continued to succeed in everything he did, for the LORD was with him. ¹⁵When Saul recognized this, he became even more afraid of him. ¹⁶But all Israel and Judah loved David because he was so successful at leading his troops into battle.

David Marries Saul's Daughter

¹⁷One day Saul said to David, "I am ready to give you my older daughter, Merab, as your wife. But first you must prove yourself to be a real warrior by fighting the LORD's battles." For Saul thought to himself, "I'll send him out against the Philistines and let them kill him rather than doing it myself."

¹⁸"Who am I, and what is my family in Israel that I should be the king's son-in-law?" David exclaimed. "My father's family is nothing!"

¹⁹So* when the time came for the wedding, Saul gave Merab in marriage to Adriel, a man from Meholah.

²⁰In the meantime, Saul's daughter Michal had fallen in love with David, and Saul was delighted when he heard about it. ²¹"Here's another chance to see him killed by the Philistines!" Saul said to himself. But to David he said, "I have a way for you to become my son-in-law after all!"

²²Then Saul told his men to say confidentially to David, "The king really likes you, and so do we. Why don't you accept the king's offer and become his son-in-law?"

²³When Saul's men said these things to David, he replied, "How can a poor man from a

---

17:52 As in some Greek manuscripts; Hebrew reads *a valley.* **18:6** The type of instrument represented by the final word is uncertain. **18:19** Or *But.*

humble family afford the bride price for the daughter of a king?"

24When Saul's men reported this back to the king, 25he told them, "Tell David that all I want for the bride price is one hundred Philistine foreskins! Vengeance on my enemies is all I really want." But what Saul had in mind was that David would be killed in the fight.

26David was delighted to accept the offer. So before the time limit expired, 27he and his men went out and killed two hundred Philistines and presented all their foreskins to the king. So Saul gave Michal to David to be his wife.

28When the king realized how much the LORD was with David and how much Michal loved him, 29he became even more afraid of him, and he remained David's enemy for the rest of his life. 30Whenever the Philistine army attacked, David was more successful against them than all the rest of Saul's officers. So David's name became very famous throughout the land.

CHAPTER 19

Saul Tries to Kill David

Saul now urged his servants and his son Jonathan to assassinate David. But Jonathan, because of his close friendship with David, 2told him what his father was planning. "Tomorrow morning," he warned him, "you must find a hiding place out in the fields. 3I'll ask my father to go out there with me, and I'll talk to him about you. Then I'll tell you everything I can find out."

4The next morning Jonathan spoke with his father about David, saying many good things about him. "Please don't sin against David," Jonathan pleaded. "He's never done anything to harm you. He has always helped you in any way he could. 5Have you forgotten about the time he risked his life to kill the Philistine giant and how the LORD brought a great victory to Israel as a result? You were certainly happy about it then. Why should you murder an innocent man like David? There is no reason for it at all!"

6So Saul listened to Jonathan and vowed, "As surely as the LORD lives, David will not be killed." 7Afterward Jonathan called David and told him what had happened. Then he took David to see Saul, and everything was as it had been before.

8War broke out shortly after that, and David led his troops against the Philistines. He attacked them with such fury that they all ran away.

9But one day as Saul was sitting at home, the tormenting spirit from the LORD suddenly came upon him again. As David played his harp for the king, 10Saul hurled his spear at David in an attempt to kill him. But David dodged out of the way and escaped into the night, leaving the spear stuck in the wall.

Michal Saves David's Life

11Then Saul sent troops to watch David's house. They were told to kill David when he came out the next morning. But Michal, David's wife, warned him, "If you don't get away tonight, you will be dead by morning." 12So she helped him climb out through a window, and he escaped. 13Then she took an idol* and put it in his bed, covered it with blankets, and put a cushion of goat's hair at its head. 14When the troops came to arrest David, she told them he was sick and couldn't get out of bed.

15"Then bring him to me in his bed," Saul ordered, "so I can kill him as he lies there!" And he sent them back to David's house. 16But when they came to carry David out, they discovered that it was only an idol in the bed with a cushion of goat's hair at its head.

17"Why have you tricked me and let my enemy escape?" Saul demanded of Michal.

"I had to," Michal replied. "He threatened to kill me if I didn't help him."

18So David got away and went to Ramah to see Samuel, and he told him all that Saul had done to him. Then Samuel took David with him to live at Naioth. 19When the report reached Saul that David was at Naioth in Ramah, 20he sent troops to capture him. But when they arrived and saw Samuel and the other prophets prophesying, the Spirit of God came upon Saul's men, and they also began to prophesy. 21When Saul heard what had happened, he sent other troops, but they, too, prophesied! The same thing happened a third time! 22Finally, Saul himself went to Ramah and arrived at the great well in Secu. "Where are Samuel and David?" he demanded.

"They are at Naioth in Ramah," someone told him. 23But on the way to Naioth the Spirit of God came upon Saul, and he, too, began to prophesy! 24He tore off his clothes and lay on the ground all day and all night, prophesying in the presence of Samuel. The people who were watching exclaimed, "What? Is Saul a prophet, too?"

19:13 Hebrew *teraphim;* also in 19:16.

CHAPTER 20
Jonathan Helps David

David now fled from Naioth in Ramah and found Jonathan. "What have I done?" he exclaimed. "What is my crime? How have I offended your father that he is so determined to kill me?"

2 "That's not true!" Jonathan protested. "I'm sure he's not planning any such thing, for he always tells me everything he's going to do, even the little things. I know he wouldn't hide something like this from me. It just isn't so!"

3 Then David took an oath before Jonathan and said, "Your father knows perfectly well about our friendship, so he has said to himself, 'I won't tell Jonathan—why should I hurt him?' But I swear to you that I am only a step away from death! I swear it by the LORD and by your own soul!"

4 "Tell me what I can do!" Jonathan exclaimed.

5 David replied, "Tomorrow we celebrate the new moon festival. I've always eaten with your father on this occasion, but tomorrow I'll hide in the field and stay there until the evening of the third day. 6 If your father asks where I am, tell him I asked permission to go home to Bethlehem for an annual family sacrifice. 7 If he says, 'Fine!' then you will know all is well. But if he is angry and loses his temper, then you will know he was planning to kill me. 8 Show me this kindness as my sworn friend—for we made a covenant together before the LORD—or kill me yourself if I have sinned against your father. But please don't betray me to him!"

9 "Never!" Jonathan exclaimed. "You know that if I had the slightest notion my father was planning to kill you, I would tell you at once."

10 Then David asked, "How will I know whether or not your father is angry?"

11 "Come out to the field with me," Jonathan replied. And they went out there together. 12 Then Jonathan told David, "I promise by the LORD, the God of Israel, that by this time tomorrow, or the next day at the latest, I will talk to my father and let you know at once how he feels about you. If he speaks favorably about you, I will let you know. 13 But if he is angry and wants you killed, may the LORD kill me if I don't warn you so you can escape and live. May the LORD be with you as he used to be with my father. 14 And may you treat me with the faithful love of the LORD as long as I live. But if I die, 15 treat my

family with this faithful love, even when the LORD destroys all your enemies."

16 So Jonathan made a covenant with David,* saying, "May the LORD destroy all your enemies!" 17 And Jonathan made David reaffirm his vow of friendship again, for Jonathan loved David as much as he loved himself.

18 Then Jonathan said, "Tomorrow we celebrate the new moon festival. You will be missed when your place at the table is empty. 19 The day after tomorrow, toward evening, go to the place where you hid before, and wait there by the stone pile.* 20 I will come out and shoot three arrows to the side of the stone pile as though I were shooting at a target. 21 Then I will send a boy to bring the arrows back. If you hear me tell him, 'They're on this side,' then you will know, as surely as the LORD lives, that all is well, and there is no trouble. 22 But if I tell him, 'Go farther—the arrows are still ahead of you,' then it will mean that you must leave immediately, for the LORD is sending you away. 23 And may the LORD make us keep our promises to each other, for he has witnessed them."

24 So David hid himself in the field, and when the new moon festival began, the king sat down to eat. 25 He sat at his usual place against the wall, with Jonathan sitting opposite him* and Abner beside him. But David's place was empty. 26 Saul didn't say anything about it that day, for he said to himself, "Something must have made David ceremonially unclean. Yes, that must be why he's not here." 27 But when David's place was empty again the next day, Saul asked Jonathan, "Why hasn't the son of Jesse been here for dinner either yesterday or today?"

28 Jonathan replied, "David earnestly asked me if he could go to Bethlehem. 29 He wanted to take part in a family sacrifice. His brother demanded that he be there, so I told him he could go. That's why he isn't here."

30 Saul boiled with rage at Jonathan. "You stupid son of a whore!"* he swore at him. "Do you think I don't know that you want David to be king in your place, shaming yourself and your mother? 31 As long as that son of Jesse is alive, you'll never be king. Now go and get him so I can kill him!"

32 "But what has he done?" Jonathan demanded. "Why should he be put to death?" 33 Then Saul hurled his spear at Jonathan, intending to kill him. So at last Jonathan realized that his father was really determined to kill David. 34 Jonathan left the table in fierce anger

20:16 Hebrew *with the house of David.* **20:19** Hebrew *the stone Ezel.* The meaning of the Hebrew is uncertain. **20:25** As in Greek version; Hebrew reads *with Jonathan standing.* **20:30** Hebrew *You son of a perverse and rebellious woman.*

and refused to eat all that day, for he was crushed by his father's shameful behavior toward David.

35The next morning, as agreed, Jonathan went out into the field and took a young boy with him to gather his arrows. 36"Start running," he told the boy, "so you can find the arrows as I shoot them." So the boy ran, and Jonathan shot an arrow beyond him. 37When the boy had almost reached the arrow, Jonathan shouted, "The arrow is still ahead of you. 38Hurry, hurry, don't wait." So the boy quickly gathered up the arrows and ran back to his master. 39He, of course, didn't understand what Jonathan meant; only Jonathan and David knew. 40Then Jonathan gave his bow and arrows to the boy and told him to take them back to the city.

41As soon as the boy was gone, David came out from where he had been hiding near the stone pile.* Then David bowed to Jonathan with his face to the ground. Both of them were in tears as they embraced each other and said good-bye, especially David. 42At last Jonathan said to David, "Go in peace, for we have made a pact in the LORD's name. We have entrusted each other and each other's children into the LORD's hands forever." Then David left, and Jonathan returned to the city.

CHAPTER 21
David Runs from Saul

David went to the city of Nob to see Ahimelech the priest. Ahimelech trembled when he saw him. "Why are you alone?" he asked. "Why is no one with you?"

2"The king has sent me on a private matter," David said. "He told me not to tell anyone why I am here. I have told my men where to meet me later. 3Now, what is there to eat? Give me five loaves of bread or anything else you have."

4"We don't have any regular bread," the priest replied. "But there is the holy bread, which I guess you can have if your young men have not slept with any women recently."

5"Don't worry," David replied. "I never allow my men to be with women when they are on a campaign. And since they stay clean even on ordinary trips, how much more on this one!"

6So, since there was no other food available, the priest gave him the holy bread—the Bread of the Presence that was placed before the LORD in the Tabernacle. It had just been replaced that day with fresh bread.

7Now Doeg the Edomite, Saul's chief herdsman, was there that day for ceremonial purification.*

8David asked Ahimelech, "Do you have a spear or sword? The king's business was so urgent that I didn't even have time to grab a weapon!"

9"I only have the sword of Goliath the Philistine, whom you killed in the valley of Elah," the priest replied. "It is wrapped in a cloth behind the ephod. Take that if you want it, for there is nothing else here."

"There is nothing like it!" David replied. "Give it to me!"

10So David escaped from Saul and went to King Achish of Gath. 11But Achish's officers weren't happy about his being there. "Isn't this David, the king of the land?" they asked. "Isn't he the one the people honor with dances, singing, 'Saul has killed his thousands, and David his ten thousands'?"

12David heard these comments and was afraid of what King Achish might do to him. 13So he pretended to be insane, scratching on doors and drooling down his beard. 14Finally, King Achish said to his men, "Must you bring me a madman? 15We already have enough of them around here! Why should I let someone like this be my guest?"

CHAPTER 22
David at the Cave of Adullam

So David left Gath and escaped to the cave of Adullam. Soon his brothers and other relatives joined him there. 2Then others began coming— men who were in trouble or in debt or who were just discontented—until David was the leader of about four hundred men.

3Later David went to Mizpeh in Moab, where he asked the king, "Would you let my father and mother live here under royal protection until I know what God is going to do for me?" 4The king agreed, and David's parents stayed in Moab while David was living in his stronghold.

5One day the prophet Gad told David, "Leave the stronghold and return to the land of Judah." So David went to the forest of Hereth. 6The news of his arrival in Judah soon reached Saul. At the time, the king was sitting beneath a tamarisk tree on the hill at Gibeah, holding his spear and surrounded by his officers.

7"Listen here, you men of Benjamin!" Saul shouted when he heard the news. "Has David promised you fields and vineyards? Has he

20:41 As in Greek version; Hebrew reads *near the south edge.* 21:7 Hebrew *was detained before the LORD.*

promised to make you commanders in his army? ⁸Is that why you have conspired against me? For not one of you has ever told me that my own son is on David's side. You're not even sorry for me. Think of it! My own son—encouraging David to try and kill me!"

⁹Then Doeg the Edomite, who was standing there with Saul's men, spoke up. "When I was at Nob," he said, "I saw David talking to Ahimelech the priest. ¹⁰Ahimelech consulted the LORD to find out what David should do. Then he gave David food and the sword of Goliath the Philistine."

The Slaughter of the Priests

¹¹King Saul immediately sent for Ahimelech and all his family, who served as priests at Nob. ¹²When they arrived, Saul shouted at him, "Listen to me, you son of Ahitub!"

"What is it, my king?" Ahimelech asked.

¹³"Why have you and David conspired against me?" Saul demanded. "Why did you give him food and a sword? Why have you inquired of God for him? Why did you encourage him to revolt against me and to come here and attack me?"

¹⁴"But sir," Ahimelech replied, "is there anyone among all your servants who is as faithful as David, your son-in-law? Why, he is the captain of your bodyguard and a highly honored member of your household! ¹⁵This was certainly not the first time I had consulted God for him! Please don't accuse me and my family in this matter, for I knew nothing of any plot against you."

¹⁶"You will surely die, Ahimelech, along with your entire family!" the king shouted. ¹⁷And he ordered his bodyguards, "Kill these priests of the LORD, for they are allies and conspirators with David! They knew he was running away from me, but they didn't tell me!" But Saul's men refused to kill the LORD's priests.

¹⁸Then the king said to Doeg, "You do it." So Doeg turned on them and killed them, eighty-five priests in all, all still wearing their priestly tunics. ¹⁹Then he went to Nob, the city of the priests, and killed the priests' families—men and women, children and babies, and all the cattle, donkeys, and sheep.

²⁰Only Abiathar, one of the sons of Ahimelech, escaped and fled to David. ²¹When he told David that Saul had killed the priests of the LORD, ²²David exclaimed, "I knew it! When I saw Doeg there that day, I knew he would tell Saul. Now I have caused the death of all your father's

family. ²³Stay here with me, and I will protect you with my own life, for the same person wants to kill us both."

CHAPTER **23**

David Protects the Town of Keilah

One day news came to David that the Philistines were at Keilah stealing grain from the threshing floors. ²David asked the LORD, "Should I go and attack them?"

"Yes, go and save Keilah," the LORD told him.

³But David's men said, "We're afraid even here in Judah. We certainly don't want to go to Keilah to fight the whole Philistine army!"

⁴So David asked the LORD again, and again the LORD replied, "Go down to Keilah, for I will help you conquer the Philistines."

⁵So David and his men went to Keilah. They slaughtered the Philistines and took all their livestock and rescued the people of Keilah. ⁶Abiathar the priest went to Keilah with David, taking the ephod with him to get answers for David from the LORD.

⁷Saul soon learned that David was at Keilah. "Good!" he exclaimed. "We've got him now! God has handed him over to me, for he has trapped himself in a walled city!"

⁸So Saul mobilized his entire army to march to Keilah and attack David and his men. ⁹But David learned of Saul's plan and told Abiathar the priest to bring the ephod and ask the LORD what he should do. ¹⁰And David prayed, "O LORD, God of Israel, I have heard that Saul is planning to come and destroy Keilah because I am here. ¹¹Will the men of Keilah surrender me to him?* And will Saul actually come as I have heard? O LORD, God of Israel, please tell me."

And the LORD said, "He will come."

¹²Again David asked, "Will these men of Keilah really betray me and my men to Saul?"

And the LORD replied, "Yes, they will betray you."

David Hides in the Wilderness

¹³So David and his men—about six hundred of them now—left Keilah and began roaming the countryside. Word soon reached Saul that David had escaped, so he didn't go to Keilah after all. ¹⁴David now stayed in the strongholds of the wilderness and in the hill country of Ziph. Saul hunted him day after day, but God didn't let him be found.

¹⁵One day near Horesh, David received the news that Saul was on the way to Ziph to search

23:11 Some manuscripts lack the first sentence of 23:11.

for him and kill him. ¹⁶Jonathan went to find David and encouraged him to stay strong in his faith in God. ¹⁷"Don't be afraid," Jonathan reassured him. "My father will never find you! You are going to be the king of Israel, and I will be next to you, as my father is well aware." ¹⁸So the two of them renewed their covenant of friendship before the LORD. Then Jonathan returned home, while David stayed at Horesh.

¹⁹But now the men of Ziph went to Saul in Gibeah and betrayed David to him. "We know where David is hiding," they said. "He is in the strongholds of Horesh on the hill of Hakilah, which is in the southern part of Jeshimon. ²⁰Come down whenever you're ready, O king, and we will catch him and hand him over to you!"

²¹"The LORD bless you," Saul said. "At last someone is concerned about me! ²²Go and check again to be sure of where he is staying and who has seen him there, for I know that he is very crafty. ²³Discover his hiding places, and come back with a more definite report. Then I'll go with you. And if he is in the area at all, I'll track him down, even if I have to search every hiding place in Judah!"

²⁴So the men of Ziph returned home ahead of Saul. Meanwhile, David and his men had moved into the wilderness of Maon in the Arabah Valley south of Jeshimon. ²⁵When David heard that Saul and his men were searching for him, he went even farther into the wilderness to the great rock, and he remained there in the wilderness of Maon. But Saul kept after him. ²⁶He and David were now on opposite sides of a mountain. Just as Saul and his men began to close in on David and his men, ²⁷an urgent message reached Saul that the Philistines were raiding Israel again. ²⁸So Saul quit the chase and returned to fight the Philistines. Ever since that time, the place where David was camped has been called the Rock of Escape.* ²⁹David then went to live in the strongholds of En-gedi.

CHAPTER 24
David Spares Saul's Life

After Saul returned from fighting the Philistines, he was told that David had gone into the wilderness of En-gedi. ²So Saul chose three thousand special troops from throughout Israel and went to search for David and his men near the rocks of the wild goats. ³At the place where the road passes some sheepfolds, Saul went into a cave to relieve himself. But as it happened, David and his men were hiding in that very cave!

23:28 Hebrew *Sela-hammahlekoth.*

⁴"Now's your opportunity!" David's men whispered to him. "Today is the day the LORD was talking about when he said, 'I will certainly put Saul into your power, to do with as you wish.'" Then David crept forward and cut off a piece of Saul's robe.

⁵But then David's conscience began bothering him because he had cut Saul's robe. ⁶"The LORD knows I shouldn't have done it," he said to his men. "It is a serious thing to attack the LORD's anointed one, for the LORD himself has chosen him." ⁷So David sharply rebuked his men and did not let them kill Saul.

After Saul had left the cave and gone on his way, ⁸David came out and shouted after him, "My lord the king!" And when Saul looked around, David bowed low before him.

⁹Then he shouted to Saul, "Why do you listen to the people who say I am trying to harm you? ¹⁰This very day you can see with your own eyes it isn't true. For the LORD placed you at my mercy back there in the cave, and some of my men told me to kill you, but I spared you. For I said, 'I will never harm him—he is the LORD's anointed one.' ¹¹Look, my father, at what I have in my hand. It is a piece of your robe! I cut it off, but I didn't kill you. This proves that I am not trying to harm you and that I have not sinned against you, even though you have been hunting for me to kill me. ¹²The LORD will decide between us. Perhaps the LORD will punish you for what you are trying to do to me, but I will never harm you. ¹³As that old proverb says, 'From evil people come evil deeds.' So you can be sure I will never harm you. ¹⁴Who is the king of Israel trying to catch anyway? Should he spend his time chasing one who is as worthless as a dead dog or a flea? ¹⁵May the LORD judge which of us is right and punish the guilty one. He is my advocate, and he will rescue me from your power!"

¹⁶Saul called back, "Is that really you, my son David?" Then he began to cry. ¹⁷And he said to David, "You are a better man than I am, for you have repaid me good for evil. ¹⁸Yes, you have been wonderfully kind to me today, for when the LORD put me in a place where you could have killed me, you didn't do it. ¹⁹Who else would let his enemy get away when he had him in his power? May the LORD reward you well for the kindness you have shown me today. ²⁰And now I realize that you are surely going to be king, and Israel will flourish under your rule. ²¹Now, swear

to me by the LORD that when that happens you will not kill my family and destroy my line of descendants!"

22So David promised, and Saul went home. But David and his men went back to their stronghold.

CHAPTER 25
The Death of Samuel
Now Samuel died, and all Israel gathered for his funeral. They buried him near his home at Ramah.

Nabal Angers David
Then David moved down to the wilderness of Maon.* 2There was a wealthy man from Maon who owned property near the village of Carmel. He had three thousand sheep and a thousand goats, and it was sheep-shearing time. 3This man's name was Nabal, and his wife, Abigail, was a sensible and beautiful woman. But Nabal, a descendant of Caleb, was mean and dishonest in all his dealings.

4When David heard that Nabal was shearing his sheep, 5he sent ten of his young men to Carmel. He told them to deliver this message: 6"Peace and prosperity to you, your family, and everything you own! 7I am told that you are shearing your sheep and goats. While your shepherds stayed among us near Carmel, we never harmed them, and nothing was ever stolen from them. 8Ask your own servants, and they will tell you this is true. So would you please be kind to us, since we have come at a time of celebration? Please give us any provisions you might have on hand." 9David's young men gave this message to Nabal and waited for his reply.

10"Who is this fellow David?" Nabal sneered. "Who does this son of Jesse think he is? There are lots of servants these days who run away from their masters. 11Should I take my bread and water and the meat I've slaughtered for my shearers and give it to a band of outlaws who come from who knows where?" 12So David's messengers returned and told him what Nabal had said.

13"Get your swords!" was David's reply as he strapped on his own. Four hundred men started off with David, and two hundred remained behind to guard their equipment.

14Meanwhile, one of Nabal's servants went to Abigail and told her, "David sent men from the wilderness to talk to our master, and he insulted them. 15But David's men were very good to us, and we never suffered any harm

from them. Nothing was stolen from us the whole time they were with us. 16In fact, day and night they were like a wall of protection to us and the sheep. 17You'd better think fast, for there is going to be trouble for our master and his whole family. He's so ill-tempered that no one can even talk to him!"

18Abigail lost no time. She quickly gathered two hundred loaves of bread, two skins of wine, five dressed sheep, nearly a bushel* of roasted grain, one hundred raisin cakes, and two hundred fig cakes. She packed them on donkeys and said to her servants, 19"Go on ahead. I will follow you shortly." But she didn't tell her husband what she was doing.

20As she was riding her donkey into a mountain ravine, she saw David and his men coming toward her. 21David had just been saying, "A lot of good it did to help this fellow. We protected his flocks in the wilderness, and nothing he owned was lost or stolen. But he has repaid me evil for good. 22May God deal with me severely if even one man of his household is still alive tomorrow morning!"

Abigail Intercedes for Nabal
23When Abigail saw David, she quickly got off her donkey and bowed low before him. 24She fell at his feet and said, "I accept all blame in this matter, my lord. Please listen to what I have to say. 25I know Nabal is a wicked and ill-tempered man; please don't pay any attention to him. He is a fool, just as his name suggests.* But I never even saw the messengers you sent.

26"Now, my lord, as surely as the LORD lives and you yourself live, since the LORD has kept you from murdering and taking vengeance into your own hands, let all your enemies be as cursed as Nabal is. 27And here is a present I have brought to you and your young men. 28Please forgive me if I have offended in any way. The LORD will surely reward you with a lasting dynasty, for you are fighting the LORD's battles. And you have not done wrong throughout your entire life.

29"Even when you are chased by those who seek your life, you are safe in the care of the LORD your God, secure in his treasure pouch! But the lives of your enemies will disappear like stones shot from a sling! 30When the LORD has done all he promised and has made you leader of Israel, 31don't let this be a blemish on your record. Then you won't have to carry on your conscience the staggering burden of needless bloodshed and

25:1 As in Greek version; Hebrew reads *Paran.*   25:18 Hebrew *5 seahs* [30 liters].   25:25 The name *Nabal* means "fool."

vengeance. And when the LORD has done these great things for you, please remember me!"

32David replied to Abigail, "Praise the LORD, the God of Israel, who has sent you to meet me today! 33Thank God for your good sense! Bless you for keeping me from murdering the man and carrying out vengeance with my own hands. 34For I swear by the LORD, the God of Israel, who has kept me from hurting you, that if you had not hurried out to meet me, not one of Nabal's men would be alive tomorrow morning." 35Then David accepted her gifts and told her, "Return home in peace. We will not kill your husband."

36When Abigail arrived home, she found that Nabal had thrown a big party and was celebrating like a king. He was very drunk, so she didn't tell him anything about her meeting with David until the next morning. 37The next morning when he was sober, she told him what had happened. As a result he had a stroke,* and he lay on his bed paralyzed. 38About ten days later, the LORD struck him and he died.

David Marries Abigail

39When David heard that Nabal was dead, he said, "Praise the LORD, who has paid back Nabal and kept me from doing it myself. Nabal has received the punishment for his sin." Then David wasted no time in sending messengers to Abigail to ask her to become his wife.

40When the messengers arrived at Carmel, they told Abigail, "David has sent us to ask if you will marry him."

41She bowed low to the ground and responded, "Yes, I am even willing to become a slave to David's servants!" 42Quickly getting ready, she took along five of her servant girls as attendants, mounted her donkey, and went with David's messengers. And so she became his wife. 43David also married Ahinoam from Jezreel, making both of them his wives. 44Saul, meanwhile, had given his daughter Michal, David's wife, to a man from Gallim named Palti son of Laish.

CHAPTER **26**
David Spares Saul Again

Now some messengers from Ziph came back to Saul at Gibeah to tell him, "David is hiding on the hill of Hakilah, which overlooks Jeshimon." 2So Saul took three thousand of his best troops and went to hunt him down in the wilderness of Ziph. 3Saul camped along the road beside the

25:37 Hebrew *his heart failed him.*

hill of Hakilah, near Jeshimon, where David was hiding. But David knew of Saul's arrival, 4so he sent out spies to watch his movements.

5David slipped over to Saul's camp one night to look around. Saul and his general, Abner son of Ner, were sleeping inside a ring formed by the slumbering warriors. 6"Will anyone volunteer to go in there with me?" David asked Ahimelech the Hittite and Abishai son of Zeruiah, Joab's brother.

"I'll go with you," Abishai replied. 7So David and Abishai went right into Saul's camp and found him asleep, with his spear stuck in the ground beside his head. Abner and the warriors were lying asleep around him. 8"God has surely handed your enemy over to you this time!" Abishai whispered to David. "Let me thrust that spear through him. I'll pin him to the ground, and I won't need to strike twice!"

9"No!" David said. "Don't kill him. For who can remain innocent after attacking the LORD's anointed one? 10Surely the LORD will strike Saul down someday, or he will die in battle or of old age. 11But the LORD forbid that I should kill the one he has anointed! But I'll tell you what— we'll take his spear and his jug of water and then get out of here!"

12So David took the spear and jug of water that were near Saul's head. Then he and Abishai got away without anyone seeing them or even waking up, because the LORD had put Saul's men into a deep sleep. 13David climbed the hill opposite the camp until he was at a safe distance. 14Then he shouted down to Abner and Saul, "Wake up, Abner!"

"Who is it?" Abner demanded.

15"Well, Abner, you're a great man, aren't you?" David taunted. "Where in all Israel is there anyone as mighty? So why haven't you guarded your master the king when someone came to kill him? 16This isn't good at all! I swear by the LORD that you and your men deserve to die, because you failed to protect your master, the LORD's anointed! Look around! Where are the king's spear and the jug of water that were beside his head?"

17Saul recognized David's voice and called out, "Is that you, my son David?"

And David replied, "Yes, my lord the king. 18Why are you chasing me? What have I done? What is my crime? 19But now let my lord the king listen to his servant. If the LORD has stirred you up against me, then let him accept my offering. But if this is simply a human scheme, then may those involved be cursed by the LORD. For you have driven me from my home, so I can no longer live among the LORD's people and worship as I should. 20Must I die on foreign soil, far from the presence of the LORD? Why has the king of Israel come out to search for a single flea? Why does he hunt me down like a partridge on the mountains?"

21Then Saul confessed, "I have sinned. Come back home, my son, and I will no longer try to harm you, for you valued my life today. I have been a fool and very, very wrong."

22"Here is your spear, O king," David replied. "Let one of your young men come over and get it. 23The LORD gives his own reward for doing good and for being loyal, and I refused to kill you even when the LORD placed you in my power, for you are the LORD's anointed one. 24Now may the LORD value my life, even as I have valued yours today. May he rescue me from all my troubles."

25And Saul said to David, "Blessings on you, my son David. You will do heroic deeds and be a great conqueror." Then David went away, and Saul returned home.

CHAPTER 27
David among the Philistines

But David kept thinking to himself, "Someday Saul is going to get me. The best thing for me to do is escape to the Philistines. Then Saul will stop hunting for me, and I will finally be safe."

2So David took his six hundred men and their families and went to live at Gath under the protection of King Achish. 3David brought his two wives along with him—Ahinoam of Jezreel and Abigail of Carmel, Nabal's widow. 4Word soon reached Saul that David had fled to Gath, so he stopped hunting for him.

5One day David said to Achish, "If it is all right with you, we would rather live in one of the country towns instead of here in the royal city." 6So Achish gave him the town of Ziklag (which still belongs to the kings of Judah to this day), 7and they lived there among the Philistines for a year and four months.

8David and his men spent their time raiding the Geshurites, the Girzites, and the Amalekites—people who had lived near Shur, along the road to Egypt, since ancient times. 9David didn't leave one person alive in the villages he attacked. He took the sheep, cattle, donkeys, camels, and clothing before returning home to see King Achish.

10"Where did you make your raid today?" Achish would ask.

And David would reply, "Against the south of Judah, the Jerahmeelites, and the Kenites."

11No one was left alive to come to Gath and tell where he had really been. This happened again and again while he was living among the Philistines. 12Achish believed David and thought to himself, "By now the people of Israel must hate him bitterly. Now he will have to stay here and serve me forever!"

CHAPTER 28
Saul Consults a Medium

About that time the Philistines mustered their armies for another war with Israel. King Achish told David, "You and your men will be expected to join me in battle."

2"Very well!" David agreed. "Now you will see for yourself what we can do."

Then Achish told David, "I will make you my personal bodyguard for life."

3Meanwhile, Samuel had died, and all Israel had mourned for him. He was buried in Ramah, his hometown. And Saul had banned all mediums and psychics from the land of Israel.

4The Philistines set up their camp at Shunem, and Saul and the armies of Israel camped at Gilboa. 5When Saul saw the vast Philistine army, he became frantic with fear. 6He asked the LORD what he should do, but the LORD refused to answer him, either by dreams or by sacred lots* or by the prophets. 7Saul then said to his advisers, "Find a woman who is a medium, so I can go and ask her what to do."

His advisers replied, "There is a medium at Endor."

8So Saul disguised himself by wearing ordinary clothing instead of his royal robes. Then he went to the woman's home at night, accompanied by two of his men.

"I have to talk to a man who has died," he said. "Will you call up his spirit for me?"

9"Are you trying to get me killed?" the woman demanded. "You know that Saul has expelled all the mediums and psychics from the land. Why are you setting a trap for me?"

10But Saul took an oath in the name of the LORD and promised, "As surely as the LORD lives, nothing bad will happen to you for doing this."

11Finally, the woman said, "Well, whose spirit do you want me to call up?"

"Call up Samuel," Saul replied.

28:6 Hebrew *by Urim.*

¹²When the woman saw Samuel, she screamed, "You've deceived me! You are Saul!"

¹³"Don't be afraid!" the king told her. "What do you see?"

"I see a god* coming up out of the earth," she said.

¹⁴"What does he look like?" Saul asked.

"He is an old man wrapped in a robe," she replied. Saul realized that it was Samuel, and he fell to the ground before him.

¹⁵"Why have you disturbed me by calling me back?" Samuel asked.

"Because I am in deep trouble," Saul replied. "The Philistines are at war with us, and God has left me and won't reply by prophets or dreams. So I have called for you to tell me what to do."

¹⁶But Samuel replied, "Why ask me if the LORD has left you and has become your enemy? ¹⁷The LORD has done just as he said he would. He has taken the kingdom from you and given it to your rival, David. ¹⁸The LORD has done this because you did not obey his instructions concerning the Amalekites. ¹⁹What's more, the LORD will hand you and the army of Israel over to the Philistines tomorrow, and you and your sons will be here with me. The LORD will bring the entire army of Israel down in defeat."

²⁰Saul fell full length on the ground, paralyzed with fright because of Samuel's words. He was also faint with hunger, for he had eaten nothing all day and all night. ²¹When the woman saw how distraught he was, she said, "Sir, I obeyed your command at the risk of my life. ²²Now do what I say, and let me give you something to eat so you can regain your strength for the trip back."

²³But Saul refused. The men who were with him also urged him to eat, so he finally yielded and got up from the ground and sat on the couch. ²⁴The woman had been fattening a calf, so she hurried out and killed it. She kneaded dough and baked unleavened bread. ²⁵She brought the meal to Saul and his men, and they ate it. Then they went out into the night.

CHAPTER **29**
The Philistines Reject David

The entire Philistine army now mobilized at Aphek, and the Israelites camped at the spring in Jezreel. ²As the Philistine rulers were leading out their troops in groups of one hundred and one thousand, David and his men marched at the rear with King Achish. ³But the Philistine com-

28:13 Or *gods.*

manders demanded, "What are these Hebrews doing here?"

And Achish told them, "This is David, the man who ran away from King Saul of Israel. He's been with me for years, and I've never found a single fault in him since he defected to me."

⁴But the Philistine commanders were angry. "Send him back!" they demanded. "He can't go into the battle with us. What if he turns against us? Is there any better way for him to reconcile himself with his master than by turning on us in battle? ⁵Isn't this the same David about whom the women of Israel sing in their dances, 'Saul has killed his thousands, and David his ten thousands'?"

⁶So Achish finally summoned David and his men. "I swear by the LORD," he told them, "you are some of the finest men I've ever met. I think you should go with us, but the other Philistine rulers won't hear of it. ⁷Please don't upset them, but go back quietly."

⁸"What have I done to deserve this treatment?" David demanded. "Why can't I fight the enemies of my lord, the king?"

⁹But Achish insisted, "As far as I'm concerned, you're as perfect as an angel of God. But my commanders are afraid to have you with them in the battle. ¹⁰Now get up early in the morning, and leave with your men as soon as it gets light." ¹¹So David headed back into the land of the Philistines, while the Philistine army went on to Jezreel.

CHAPTER **30**
David Destroys the Amalekites

Three days later, when David and his men arrived home at their town of Ziklag, they found that the Amalekites had made a raid into the Negev and had burned Ziklag to the ground. ²They had carried off the women and children and everyone else but without killing anyone. ³When David and his men saw the ruins and realized what had happened to their families, ⁴they wept until they could weep no more. ⁵David's two wives, Ahinoam of Jezreel and Abigail, the widow of Nabal of Carmel, were among those captured. ⁶David was now in serious trouble because his men were very bitter about losing their wives and children, and they began to talk of stoning him. But David found strength in the LORD his God.

⁷Then he said to Abiathar the priest, "Bring me the ephod!" So Abiathar brought it. ⁸Then

David asked the LORD, "Should I chase them? Will I catch them?"

And the LORD told him, "Yes, go after them. You will surely recover everything that was taken from you!" 9So David and his six hundred men set out, and they soon came to Besor Brook. 10But two hundred of the men were too exhausted to cross the brook, so David continued the pursuit with his four hundred remaining troops.

11Some of David's troops found an Egyptian man in a field and brought him to David. They gave him some bread to eat and some water to drink. 12They also gave him part of a fig cake and two clusters of raisins because he hadn't had anything to eat or drink for three days and nights. It wasn't long before his strength returned.

13"To whom do you belong, and where do you come from?" David asked him.

"I am an Egyptian—the slave of an Amalekite," he replied. "My master left me behind three days ago because I was sick. 14We were on our way back from raiding the Kerethites in the Negev, the territory of Judah, and the land of Caleb, and we had just burned Ziklag."

15"Will you lead me to them?" David asked.

The young man replied, "If you swear by God's name that you will not kill me or give me back to my master, then I will guide you to them."

16So the Egyptian led them to the Amalekite encampment. When David and his men arrived, the Amalekites were spread out across the fields, eating and drinking and dancing with joy because of the vast amount of plunder they had taken from the Philistines and the land of Judah. 17David and his men rushed in among them and slaughtered them throughout that night and the entire next day until evening. None of the Amalekites escaped except four hundred young men who fled on camels. 18David got back everything the Amalekites had taken, and he rescued his two wives. 19Nothing was missing: small or great, son or daughter, nor anything else that had been taken. David brought everything back. 20His troops rounded up all the flocks and herds and drove them on ahead. "These all belong to David as his reward!" they said.

21When they reached Besor Brook and met the two hundred men who had been too tired to go with them, David greeted them joyfully. 22But some troublemakers among David's men said, "They didn't go with us, so they can't have

30:29 Greek version reads *Carmel.*

any of the plunder. Give them their wives and children, and tell them to be gone."

23But David said, "No, my brothers! Don't be selfish with what the LORD has given us. He has kept us safe and helped us defeat the enemy. 24Do you think anyone will listen to you when you talk like this? We share and share alike—those who go to battle and those who guard the equipment." 25From then on David made this a law for all of Israel, and it is still followed.

26When he arrived at Ziklag, David sent part of the plunder to the leaders of Judah, who were his friends. "Here is a present for you, taken from the LORD's enemies," he said. 27The gifts were sent to the leaders of the following towns where David and his men had been: Bethel, Ramoth-negev, Jattir, 28Aroer, Siphmoth, Eshtemoa, 29Racal,* the towns of the Jerahmeelites, the towns of the Kenites, 30Hormah, Bor-ashan, Athach, 31Hebron, and all the other places they had visited.

CHAPTER 31
The Death of Saul

Now the Philistines attacked Israel, forcing the Israelites to flee. Many were slaughtered on the slopes of Mount Gilboa. 2The Philistines closed in on Saul and his sons, and they killed three of his sons—Jonathan, Abinadab, and Malkishua. 3The fighting grew very fierce around Saul, and the Philistine archers caught up with him and wounded him severely. 4Saul groaned to his armor bearer, "Take your sword and kill me before these pagan Philistines run me through and humiliate me." But his armor bearer was afraid and would not do it. So Saul took his own sword and fell on it. 5When his armor bearer realized that Saul was dead, he fell on his own sword and died beside the king. 6So Saul, three of his sons, his armor bearer, and his troops all died together that same day.

7When the Israelites on the other side of the Jezreel Valley and beyond the Jordan saw that their army had been routed and that Saul and his sons were dead, they abandoned their towns and fled. So the Philistines moved in and occupied their towns.

8The next day, when the Philistines went out to strip the dead, they found the bodies of Saul and his three sons on Mount Gilboa. 9So they cut off Saul's head and stripped off his armor. Then they proclaimed the news of Saul's death in their pagan temple and to the people throughout the land of Philistia. 10They placed his armor in the temple of the Ashtoreths, and they fastened his body to the wall of the city of Beth-shan.

¹¹But when the people of Jabesh-gilead heard what the Philistines had done to Saul, ¹²their warriors traveled all night to Beth-shan and took the bodies of Saul and his sons down from the wall. They brought them to Jabesh, where they burned the bodies. ¹³Then they took their remains and buried them beneath the tamarisk tree at Jabesh, and they fasted for seven days.

2 Samuel

CHAPTER **1**

David Learns of Saul's Death

After the death of Saul, David returned from his victory over the Amalekites and spent two days in Ziklag. 2On the third day after David's return, a man arrived from the Israelite battlefront. He had torn his clothes and put dirt on his head to show that he was in mourning. He fell to the ground before David in deep respect.

3 "Where have you come from?" David asked.

"I escaped from the Israelite camp," the man replied.

4 "What happened?" David demanded. "Tell me how the battle went."

The man replied, "Our entire army fled. Many men are dead and wounded on the battlefield, and Saul and his son Jonathan have been killed."

5 "How do you know that Saul and Jonathan are dead?" David demanded.

6The young man answered, "I happened to be on Mount Gilboa. I saw Saul there leaning on his spear with the enemy chariots closing in on him. 7When he turned and saw me, he cried out for me to come to him. 'How can I help?' I asked him. 8And he said to me, 'Who are you?' I replied, 'I am an Amalekite.' 9Then he begged me, 'Come over here and put me out of my misery, for I am in terrible pain and want to die.'

10 "So I killed him," the Amalekite told David, "for I knew he couldn't live. Then I took his crown and one of his bracelets so I could bring them to you, my lord."

11David and his men tore their clothes in sorrow when they heard the news. 12They mourned and wept and fasted all day for Saul and his son Jonathan, and for the LORD's army and the nation of Israel, because so many had died that day.

1:18 Or *The Book of the Upright.*

13Then David said to the young man who had brought the news, "Where are you from?"

And he replied, "I am a foreigner, an Amalekite, who lives in your land."

14 "Were you not afraid to kill the LORD's anointed one?" David asked. 15Then David said to one of his men, "Kill him!" So the man thrust his sword into the Amalekite and killed him. 16 "You die self-condemned," David said, "for you yourself confessed that you killed the LORD's anointed one."

David's Song for Saul and Jonathan

17Then David composed a funeral song for Saul and Jonathan. 18Later he commanded that it be taught to all the people of Judah. It is known as the Song of the Bow, and it is recorded in *The Book of Jashar.**

19 Your pride and joy, O Israel, lies dead on
the hills!
How the mighty heroes have fallen!
20 Don't announce the news in Gath,
or the Philistines will rejoice.
Don't proclaim it in the streets of
Ashkelon,
or the pagans will laugh in triumph.

21 O mountains of Gilboa,
let there be no dew or rain upon you or
your slopes.
For there the shield of the mighty was
defiled;
the shield of Saul will no longer be
anointed with oil.
22 Both Saul and Jonathan killed their
strongest foes;
they did not return from battle
empty-handed.

23 How beloved and gracious were Saul and
Jonathan!
They were together in life and in death.
They were swifter than eagles;
they were stronger than lions.

24 O women of Israel, weep for Saul,
for he dressed you in fine clothing and
gold ornaments.

25 How the mighty heroes have fallen in battle!
Jonathan lies dead upon the hills.
26 How I weep for you, my brother Jonathan!
Oh, how much I loved you!
And your love for me was deep,
deeper than the love of women!

27 How the mighty heroes have fallen!
Stripped of their weapons, they lie dead.

CHAPTER **2**

David Anointed King of Judah

After this, David asked the LORD, "Should I move
back to Judah?"
And the LORD replied, "Yes."
Then David asked, "Which town should I go to?"
And the LORD replied, "Hebron."
2 David's wives were Ahinoam from Jezreel
and Abigail, the widow of Nabal from Carmel.
So David and his wives 3 and his men and their
families all moved to Judah, and they settled
near the town of Hebron. 4 Then Judah's leaders
came to David and crowned him king over the
tribe of Judah.

When David heard that the men of Jabesh-
gilead had buried Saul, 5 he sent them this message: "May the LORD bless you for being so loyal
to your king and giving him a decent burial.
6 May the LORD be loyal to you in return and
reward you with his unfailing love! And I, too,
will reward you for what you have done. 7 And
now that Saul is dead, I ask you to be my strong
and loyal subjects like the people of Judah, who
have anointed me as their new king."

Ishbosheth Crowned King of Israel

8 But Abner son of Ner, the commander of Saul's
army, had already gone to Mahanaim with
Saul's son Ishbosheth.* 9 There he proclaimed
Ishbosheth king over Gilead, Jezreel, Ephraim,
Benjamin, the land of the Ashurites, and all the
rest of Israel. 10 Ishbosheth was forty years old
when he became king, and he ruled from Mahanaim for two years. Meanwhile, the tribe of

Judah remained loyal to David. 11 David made
Hebron his capital, and he ruled as king of
Judah for seven and a half years.

War between Israel and Judah

12 One day Abner led some of Ishbosheth's troops
from Mahanaim to Gibeon. 13 About the same time,
Joab son of Zeruiah led David's troops from Hebron, and they met Abner at the pool of Gibeon.
The two groups sat down there, facing each other
from opposite sides of the pool. 14 Then Abner suggested to Joab, "Let's have a few of our warriors put
on an exhibition of hand-to-hand combat."

"All right," Joab agreed. 15 So twelve men
were chosen from each side to fight against each
other. 16 Each one grabbed his opponent by the
hair and thrust his sword into the other's side so
that all of them died. The place has been known
ever since as the Field of Swords.* 17 The two
armies then began to fight each other, and by the
end of the day Abner and the men of Israel had
been defeated by the forces of David.

The Death of Asahel

18 Joab, Abishai, and Asahel, the three sons of
Zeruiah, were among David's forces that day.
Asahel could run like a deer, 19 and he began
chasing Abner. He was relentless and single-
minded in his pursuit. 20 When Abner looked
back and saw him coming, he called out, "Is that
you, Asahel?"

"Yes, it is," he replied.
21 "Go fight someone else!" Abner warned.
"Take on one of the younger men and strip him
of his weapons." But Asahel refused and kept
right on chasing Abner.

22 Again Abner shouted to him, "Get away
from here! I will never be able to face your
brother Joab if I have to kill you!" 23 But Asahel
would not give up, so Abner thrust the butt end
of his spear through Asahel's stomach, and the
spear came out through his back. He stumbled
to the ground and died there. And everyone who
came by that spot stopped and stood still when
they saw Asahel lying there.

24 When Joab and Abishai found out what
had happened, they set out after Abner. The sun
was just going down as they arrived at the hill of
Ammah near Giah, along the road to the wilderness of Gibeon. 25 Abner's troops from the tribe
of Benjamin regrouped there at the top of the
hill to take a stand. 26 Abner shouted down to
Joab, "Must we always solve our differences with

2:8 Also known as *Eshbaal.* 2:16 Hebrew *Helkath-hazzurim.*

swords? Don't you realize the only thing we will gain is bitterness toward each other? When will you call off your men from chasing their Israelite brothers?"

27Then Joab said, "God only knows what would have happened if you hadn't spoken, for we would have chased you all night if necessary." 28So Joab blew his trumpet, and his men stopped chasing the troops of Israel.

29All that night Abner and his men retreated through the Jordan Valley.* They crossed the Jordan River, traveling all through the morning,* and they did not stop until they arrived at Mahanaim.

30Meanwhile, Joab and his men also returned home. When Joab counted his casualties, he discovered that only nineteen men were missing, in addition to Asahel. 31But three hundred and sixty of Abner's men, all from the tribe of Benjamin, had been killed. 32Joab and his men took Asahel's body to Bethlehem and buried him there beside his father. Then they traveled all night and reached Hebron at daybreak.

CHAPTER **3**

That was the beginning of a long war between those who had been loyal to Saul and those who were loyal to David. As time passed David became stronger and stronger, while Saul's dynasty became weaker and weaker.

David's Sons Born in Hebron

2These were the sons who were born to David in Hebron:

> The oldest was Amnon, whose mother was Ahinoam of Jezreel.
> 3 The second was Kileab, whose mother was Abigail, the widow of Nabal from Carmel.
> The third was Absalom, whose mother was Maacah, the daughter of Talmai, king of Geshur.
> 4 The fourth was Adonijah, whose mother was Haggith.
> The fifth was Shephatiah, whose mother was Abital.
> 5 The sixth was Ithream, whose mother was David's wife Eglah.

These sons were all born to David in Hebron.

Abner Joins Forces with David

6As the war went on, Abner became a powerful leader among those who were loyal to Saul's dy-

nasty. 7One day Ishbosheth,* Saul's son, accused Abner of sleeping with one of his father's concubines, a woman named Rizpah. 8Abner became furious. "Am I a Judean dog to be kicked around like this?" he shouted. "After all I have done for you and your father by not betraying you to David, is this my reward—that you find fault with me about this woman? 9May God deal harshly with me if I don't help David get all that the LORD has promised him! 10I should just go ahead and give David the rest of Saul's kingdom. I should set him up as king over Israel as well as Judah, from Dan to Beersheba." 11Ishbosheth didn't dare say another word because he was afraid of what Abner might do.

12Then Abner sent messengers to David, saying, "Let's make an agreement, and I will help turn the entire nation of Israel over to you."

13"All right," David replied, "but I will not negotiate with you unless you bring back my wife Michal, Saul's daughter, when you come."

14David then sent this message to Ishbosheth, Saul's son: "Give me back my wife Michal, for I bought her with the lives of one hundred Philistines." 15So Ishbosheth took Michal away from her husband Palti* son of Laish. 16Palti followed along behind her as far as Bahurim, weeping as he went. Then Abner told him, "Go back home!" So Palti returned.

17Meanwhile, Abner had consulted with the leaders of Israel. "For some time now," he told them, "you have wanted to make David your king. 18Now is the time! For the LORD has said, 'I have chosen David to save my people from the Philistines and from all their other enemies.'"

19Abner also spoke with the leaders of the tribe of Benjamin. Then he went to Hebron to tell David that all the people of Israel and Benjamin supported him.

20When Abner came to Hebron with his twenty men, David entertained them with a great feast. 21Then Abner said to David, "Let me go and call all the people of Israel to your side. They will make a covenant with you to make you their king. Then you will be able to rule over everything your heart desires." So David sent Abner safely on his way.

Joab Murders Abner

22But just after Abner left, Joab and some of David's troops returned from a raid, bringing much plunder with them. 23When Joab was told that Abner had just been there visiting the king and had been sent away in safety, 24he rushed to

2:29a Hebrew *the Arabah*. 2:29b Or *continued on through the Bithron*. The meaning of the Hebrew is uncertain. 3:7 Also known as *Eshbaal*. 3:15 As in 1 Sam 25:44; Hebrew reads *Paltiel*, a variant name for Palti.

see the king. "What have you done?" he demanded. "What do you mean by letting Abner get away? 25You know perfectly well that he came to spy on you and to discover everything you are doing!"

26Joab then left David and sent messengers to catch up with Abner. They found him at the pool of Sirah and brought him back with them. But David knew nothing about it. 27When Abner arrived at Hebron, Joab took him aside at the gateway as if to speak with him privately. But then he drew his dagger and killed Abner in revenge for killing his brother Asahel.

28When David heard about it, he declared, "I vow by the LORD that I and my people are innocent of this crime against Abner. 29Joab and his family are the guilty ones. May his family in every generation be cursed with a man who has open sores or leprosy* or who walks on crutches* or who dies by the sword or who begs for food!"

30So Joab and his brother Abishai killed Abner because Abner had killed their brother Asahel at the battle of Gibeon.

David Mourns Abner's Death

31Then David said to Joab and all those who were with him, "Tear your clothes and put on sackcloth. Go into deep mourning for Abner." And King David himself walked behind the procession to the grave. 32They buried Abner in Hebron, and the king and all the people wept at his graveside. 33Then the king sang this funeral song for Abner:

"Should Abner have died as fools die?
34 Your hands were not bound;
   your feet were not chained.
No, you were murdered—
   the victim of a wicked plot."

All the people wept again for Abner. 35David had refused to eat anything the day of the funeral, and now everyone begged him to eat. But David had made a vow, saying, "May God kill me if I eat anything before sundown." 36This pleased the people very much. In fact, everything the king did pleased them! 37So everyone in Judah and Israel knew that David was not responsible for Abner's death.

38Then King David said to the people, "Do you not realize that a great leader and a great man has fallen today in Israel? 39And even though I am the anointed king, these two sons

of Zeruiah—Joab and Abishai—are too strong for me to control. So may the LORD repay these wicked men for their wicked deeds."

CHAPTER 4
The Murder of Ishbosheth

When Ishbosheth* heard about Abner's death at Hebron, he lost all courage, and his people were paralyzed with fear. 2Now there were two brothers, Baanah and Recab, who were captains of Ishbosheth's raiding parties. They were sons of Rimmon, a member of the tribe of Benjamin who lived in Beeroth. The town of Beeroth is now part of Benjamin's territory 3because the original people of Beeroth fled to Gittaim, where they still live as foreigners.

4(Saul's son Jonathan had a son named Mephibosheth,* who was crippled as a child. He was five years old when Saul and Jonathan were killed at the battle of Jezreel. When news of the battle reached the capital, the child's nurse grabbed him and fled. But she fell and dropped him as she was running, and he became crippled as a result.)

5One day Recab and Baanah, the sons of Rimmon from Beeroth, went to Ishbosheth's home around noon as he was taking a nap. 6The doorkeeper, who had been sifting wheat, became drowsy and fell asleep. So Recab and Baanah slipped past the doorkeeper, went into Ishbosheth's bedroom, and stabbed him in the stomach. Then they escaped. 7But before leaving, they cut off his head as he lay there on his bed. Taking his head with them, they fled across the Jordan Valley* through the night. 8They arrived at Hebron and presented Ishbosheth's head to David. "Look!" they exclaimed. "Here is the head of Ishbosheth, the son of your enemy Saul who tried to kill you. Today the LORD has given you revenge on Saul and his entire family!"

9But David said to Recab and Baanah, "As surely as the LORD lives, the one who saves me from my enemies, I will tell you the truth. 10Once before, someone told me, 'Saul is dead,' thinking he was bringing me good news. But I seized him and killed him at Ziklag. That's the reward I gave him for his news! 11Now what reward should I give the wicked men who have killed an innocent man in his own house and on his own bed? Should I not also demand your very lives?" 12So David ordered his young men to kill them, and they did. They cut off their hands and feet and hung their bodies

---

3:29a Or *or a contagious skin disease.* The Hebrew word used here can describe various skin diseases. 3:29b Or *who is effeminate;* Hebrew reads *who handles a spindle.* 4:1 Also known as *Eshbaal.* 4:4 Also known as *Meribbaal.* 4:7 Hebrew *the Arabah.*

beside the pool in Hebron. Then they took Ishbosheth's head and buried it in Abner's tomb in Hebron.

CHAPTER 5

David Becomes King of All Israel

Then all the tribes of Israel went to David at Hebron and told him, "We are all members of your family. ²For a long time, even while Saul was our king, you were the one who really led Israel. And the LORD has told you, 'You will be the shepherd of my people Israel. You will be their leader.'" ³So there at Hebron, David made a covenant with the leaders of Israel before the LORD. And they anointed him king of Israel.

⁴David was thirty years old when he began to reign, and he reigned forty years in all. ⁵He had reigned over Judah from Hebron for seven years and six months, and from Jerusalem he reigned over all Israel and Judah for thirty-three years.

David Captures Jerusalem

⁶David then led his troops to Jerusalem to fight against the Jebusites. "You'll never get in here," the Jebusites taunted. "Even the blind and lame could keep you out!" For the Jebusites thought they were safe. ⁷But David captured the fortress of Zion, now called the City of David.

⁸When the insulting message from the defenders of the city reached David, he told his own troops, "Go up through the water tunnel into the city and destroy those 'lame' and 'blind' Jebusites. How I hate them." That is the origin of the saying, "The blind and the lame may not enter the house."* ⁹So David made the fortress his home, and he called it the City of David. He built additional fortifications around the city, starting at the Millo* and working inward. ¹⁰And David became more and more powerful, because the LORD God Almighty was with him.

¹¹Then King Hiram of Tyre sent messengers to David, along with carpenters and stonemasons to build him a palace. Hiram also sent many cedar logs for lumber. ¹²And David realized that the LORD had made him king over Israel and had made his kingdom great for the sake of his people Israel.

¹³After moving from Hebron to Jerusalem, David married more wives and concubines, and he had many sons and daughters. ¹⁴These are the names of David's sons who were born in Jerusalem: Shimea,* Shobab, Nathan, Solomon, ¹⁵Ibhar, Elishua, Nepheg, Japhia, ¹⁶Elishama, Eliada, and Eliphelet.

David Conquers the Philistines

¹⁷When the Philistines heard that David had been anointed king of Israel, they mobilized all their forces to capture him. But David was told they were coming and went into the stronghold. ¹⁸The Philistines arrived and spread out across the valley of Rephaim. ¹⁹So David asked the LORD, "Should I go out to fight the Philistines? Will you hand them over to me?"

The LORD replied, "Yes, go ahead. I will certainly give you the victory."

²⁰So David went to Baal-perazim and defeated the Philistines there. "The LORD has done it!" David exclaimed. "He burst through my enemies like a raging flood!" So David named that place Baal-perazim (which means "the Lord who bursts through"). ²¹The Philistines had abandoned their idols there, so David and his troops confiscated them.

²²But after a while the Philistines returned and again spread out across the valley of Rephaim. ²³And once again David asked the LORD what to do. "Do not attack them straight on," the LORD replied. "Instead, circle around behind them and attack them near the balsam trees. ²⁴When you hear a sound like marching feet in the tops of the balsam trees, attack! That will be the signal that the LORD is moving ahead of you to strike down the Philistines." ²⁵So David did what the LORD commanded, and he struck down the Philistines all the way from Gibeon* to Gezer.

CHAPTER 6

The Ark Brought to Jerusalem

Then David mobilized thirty thousand special troops. ²He led them to Baalah of Judah* to bring home the Ark of God, which bears the name of the LORD Almighty, who is enthroned between the cherubim. ³They placed the Ark of God on a new cart and brought it from the hillside home of Abinadab. Uzzah and Ahio, Abinadab's sons, were guiding the cart ⁴with the Ark of God on it, with Ahio walking in front. ⁵David and all the people of Israel were celebrating before the LORD with all their might, singing songs* and playing all kinds of musical instruments—lyres, harps, tambourines, castanets, and cymbals.

5:8 The meaning of this saying is uncertain.   5:9 Or *the supporting terraces.* The meaning of the Hebrew is uncertain.   5:14 As in parallel text at 1 Chr 3:5; Hebrew reads *Shammua,* a variant name for Shimea.   5:25 As in Greek version (see also 1 Chr 14:16); Hebrew reads *Geba.*   6:2 *Baalah of Judah* is another name for Kiriath-jearim; compare 1 Chr 13:6.   6:5 As in Greek version (see also 1 Chr 13:8); Hebrew reads *cypress trees.*

⁶But when they arrived at the threshing floor of Nacon, the oxen stumbled, and Uzzah put out his hand to steady the Ark of God. ⁷Then the LORD's anger blazed out against Uzzah for doing this, and God struck him dead beside the Ark of God. ⁸David was angry because the LORD's anger had blazed out against Uzzah. He named that place Perez-uzzah (which means "outbreak against Uzzah"). It is still called that today.

⁹David was now afraid of the LORD and asked, "How can I ever bring the Ark of the LORD back into my care?" ¹⁰So David decided not to move the Ark of the LORD into the City of David. He took it instead to the home of Obed-edom of Gath. ¹¹The Ark of the LORD remained there with the family of Obed-edom for three months, and the LORD blessed him and his entire household.

¹²Then King David was told, "The LORD has blessed Obed-edom's home and everything he has because of the Ark of God." So David went there and brought the Ark to the City of David with a great celebration. ¹³After the men who were carrying it had gone six steps, they stopped and waited so David could sacrifice an ox and a fattened calf. ¹⁴And David danced before the LORD with all his might, wearing a priestly tunic.* ¹⁵So David and all Israel brought up the Ark of the LORD with much shouting and blowing of trumpets.

Michal's Contempt for David

¹⁶But as the Ark of the LORD entered the City of David, Michal, the daughter of Saul, looked down from her window. When she saw King David leaping and dancing before the LORD, she was filled with contempt for him.

¹⁷The Ark of the LORD was placed inside the special tent that David had prepared for it. And David sacrificed burnt offerings and peace offerings to the LORD. ¹⁸When he had finished, David blessed the people in the name of the LORD Almighty. ¹⁹Then he gave a gift of food to every man and woman in Israel: a loaf of bread, a cake of dates,* and a cake of raisins. Then everyone went home.

²⁰When David returned home to bless his family, Michal came out to meet him and said in disgust, "How glorious the king of Israel looked today! He exposed himself to the servant girls like any indecent person might do!"

²¹David retorted to Michal, "I was dancing before the LORD, who chose me above your father and his family! He appointed me as the leader of Israel, the people of the LORD. So I am

willing to act like a fool in order to show my joy in the LORD. ²²Yes, and I am willing to look even more foolish than this, but I will be held in honor by the girls of whom you have spoken!" ²³So Michal, the daughter of Saul, remained childless throughout her life.

CHAPTER **7**
The LORD's Covenant Promise to David

When the LORD had brought peace to the land and King David was settled in his palace, ²David summoned Nathan the prophet. "Look!" David said. "Here I am living in this beautiful cedar palace, but the Ark of God is out in a tent!"

³Nathan replied, "Go ahead and do what you have in mind, for the LORD is with you."

⁴But that same night the LORD said to Nathan,

⁵"Go and tell my servant David, 'This is what the LORD says: Are you the one to build me a temple to live in? ⁶I have never lived in a temple, from the day I brought the Israelites out of Egypt until now. My home has always been a tent, moving from one place to another. ⁷And I have never once complained to Israel's leaders, the shepherds of my people Israel. I have never asked them, "Why haven't you built me a beautiful cedar temple?" '

⁸"Now go and say to my servant David, 'This is what the LORD Almighty says: I chose you to lead my people Israel when you were just a shepherd boy, tending your sheep out in the pasture. ⁹I have been with you wherever you have gone, and I have destroyed all your enemies. Now I will make your name famous throughout the earth! ¹⁰And I have provided a permanent homeland for my people Israel, a secure place where they will never be disturbed. It will be their own land where wicked nations won't oppress them as they did in the past, ¹¹from the time I appointed judges to rule my people. And I will keep you safe from all your enemies.

" 'And now the LORD declares that he will build a house for you—a dynasty of kings! ¹²For when you die, I will raise up one of your descendants, and I will make his kingdom strong. ¹³He is the one who will build a house—a temple—for my name. And I will establish the throne of his

---

6:14 Hebrew *a linen ephod.*   6:19 Or *a portion of meat.* The meaning of the Hebrew is uncertain.

kingdom forever. ¹⁴I will be his father, and he will be my son. If he sins, I will use other nations to punish him. ¹⁵But my unfailing love will not be taken from him as I took it from Saul, whom I removed before you. ¹⁶Your dynasty and your kingdom will continue for all time before me, and your throne will be secure forever.'"

¹⁷So Nathan went back to David and told him everything the LORD had said.

David's Prayer of Thanks

¹⁸Then King David went in and sat before the LORD and prayed, "Who am I, O Sovereign LORD, and what is my family, that you have brought me this far? ¹⁹And now, Sovereign LORD, in addition to everything else, you speak of giving me a lasting dynasty! Do you deal with everyone this way,* O Sovereign LORD? ²⁰What more can I say? You know what I am really like, Sovereign LORD. ²¹For the sake of your promise and according to your will, you have done all these great things and have shown them to me.

²²"How great you are, O Sovereign LORD! There is no one like you—there is no other God. We have never even heard of another god like you! ²³What other nation on earth is like Israel? What other nation, O God, have you redeemed from slavery to be your own people? You made a great name for yourself when you rescued your people from Egypt. You performed awesome miracles and drove out the nations and gods that stood in their way. ²⁴You made Israel your people forever, and you, O LORD, became their God.

²⁵"And now, O LORD God, do as you have promised concerning me and my family. Confirm it as a promise that will last forever. ²⁶And may your name be honored forever so that all the world will say, 'The LORD Almighty is God over Israel!' And may the dynasty of your servant David be established in your presence.

²⁷"O LORD Almighty, God of Israel, I have been bold enough to pray this prayer because you have revealed that you will build a house for me—an eternal dynasty! ²⁸For you are God, O Sovereign LORD. Your words are truth, and you have promised these good things to me, your servant. ²⁹And now, may it please you to bless me and my family so that our dynasty may

continue forever before you. For when you grant a blessing to your servant, O Sovereign LORD, it is an eternal blessing!"

CHAPTER **8**

David's Military Victories

After this, David subdued and humbled the Philistines by conquering Gath, their largest city.* ²David also conquered the land of Moab. He made the people lie down on the ground in a row, and he measured them off in groups with a length of rope. He measured off two groups to be executed for every one group to be spared. The Moabites who were spared became David's servants and brought him tribute money.

³David also destroyed the forces of Hadadezer son of Rehob, king of Zobah, when Hadadezer marched out to strengthen his control along the Euphrates River. ⁴David captured seventeen hundred charioteers* and twenty thousand foot soldiers. Then he crippled all but one hundred of the chariot horses.

⁵When Arameans from Damascus arrived to help Hadadezer, David killed twenty-two thousand of them. ⁶Then he placed several army garrisons in Damascus, the Aramean capital, and the Arameans became David's subjects and brought him tribute money. So the LORD gave David victory wherever he went. ⁷David brought the gold shields of Hadadezer's officers to Jerusalem, ⁸along with a large amount of bronze from Hadadezer's cities of Tebah* and Berothai.

⁹When King Toi of Hamath heard that David had destroyed the army of Hadadezer, ¹⁰he sent his son Joram to congratulate David on his success. Hadadezer and Toi had long been enemies, and there had been many wars between them. Joram presented David with many gifts of silver, gold, and bronze. ¹¹King David dedicated all these gifts to the LORD, along with the silver and gold he had set apart from the other nations he had subdued—¹²Edom,* Moab, Ammon, Philistia, and Amalek—and from Hadadezer son of Rehob, king of Zobah.

¹³So David became very famous. After his return he destroyed eighteen thousand Edomites* in the Valley of Salt. ¹⁴He placed army garrisons throughout Edom, and all the Edomites became David's subjects. This was another example of how the LORD made David victorious wherever he went.

7:19 The meaning of the Hebrew is uncertain. 8:1 Hebrew *by conquering Metheg-ammah,* a name which means "the bridle," possibly referring to the size of the city or the tribute money taken from it. Compare 1 Chr 18:1. 8:4 Greek version reads *1,000 chariots and 7,000 charioteers;* compare 1 Chr 18:4. 8:8 As in some Greek manuscripts (see also 1 Chr 18:8); Hebrew reads *Betah.* 8:12 As in a few Hebrew manuscripts and Greek and Syriac versions (see also 8:14; 1 Chr 18:11); most Hebrew manuscripts read *Aram.* 8:13 As in a few Hebrew manuscripts and Greek and Syriac versions (see also 8:14; 1 Chr 18:12); most Hebrew manuscripts read *Arameans.*

15David reigned over all Israel and was fair to everyone. 16Joab son of Zeruiah was commander of the army. Jehoshaphat son of Ahilud was the royal historian. 17Zadok son of Ahitub and Ahimelech son of Abiathar were the priests. Seraiah was the court secretary. 18Benaiah son of Jehoiada was captain of the king's bodyguard.* David's sons served as priestly leaders.*

CHAPTER 9
David's Kindness to Mephibosheth

One day David began wondering if anyone in Saul's family was still alive, for he had promised Jonathan that he would show kindness to them. 2He summoned a man named Ziba, who had been one of Saul's servants. "Are you Ziba?" the king asked.

"Yes sir, I am," Ziba replied.

3The king then asked him, "Is anyone still alive from Saul's family? If so, I want to show God's kindness to them in any way I can."

Ziba replied, "Yes, one of Jonathan's sons is still alive, but he is crippled."

4"Where is he?" the king asked.

"In Lo-debar," Ziba told him, "at the home of Makir son of Ammiel." 5So David sent for him and brought him from Makir's home. 6His name was Mephibosheth*; he was Jonathan's son and Saul's grandson. When he came to David, he bowed low in great fear and said, "I am your servant."

7But David said, "Don't be afraid! I've asked you to come so that I can be kind to you because of my vow to your father, Jonathan. I will give you all the land that once belonged to your grandfather Saul, and you may live here with me at the palace!"

8Mephibosheth fell to the ground before the king. "Should the king show such kindness to a dead dog like me?" he exclaimed.

9Then the king summoned Saul's servant Ziba and said, "I have given your master's grandson everything that belonged to Saul and his family. 10You and your sons and servants are to farm the land for him to produce food for his family. But Mephibosheth will live here at the palace with me."

Ziba, who had fifteen sons and twenty servants, replied, 11"Yes, my lord; I will do all that you have commanded." And from that time on, Mephibosheth ate regularly with David, as though he were one of his own sons. 12Mephibosheth had a young son named Mica. And from then on, all the members of Ziba's household were Mephibosheth's servants. 13And Mephibosheth, who was crippled in both feet, moved to Jerusalem to live at the palace.

CHAPTER 10
David Defeats the Ammonites

Some time after this, King Nahash of the Ammonites died, and his son Hanun became king. 2David said, "I am going to show complete loyalty to Hanun because his father, Nahash, was always completely loyal to me." So David sent ambassadors to express sympathy to Hanun about his father's death.

But when David's ambassadors arrived in the land of Ammon, 3Hanun's advisers said to their master, "Do you really think these men are coming here to honor your father? No! David has sent them to spy out the city so that they can come in and conquer it!" 4So Hanun seized David's ambassadors and shaved off half of each man's beard, cut off their robes at the buttocks, and sent them back to David in shame. 5When David heard what had happened, he sent messengers to tell the men to stay at Jericho until their beards grew out, for they were very embarrassed by their appearance.

6Now the people of Ammon realized how seriously they had angered David, so they hired twenty thousand Aramean mercenaries from the lands of Beth-rehob and Zobah, one thousand from the king of Maacah, and twelve thousand from the land of Tob. 7When David heard about this, he sent Joab and the entire Israelite army to fight them. 8The Ammonite troops drew up their battle lines at the entrance of the city gates, while the Arameans from Zobah and Rehob and the men from Tob and Maacah positioned themselves to fight in the open fields.

9When Joab saw that he would have to fight on two fronts, he chose the best troops in his army. He placed them under his personal command and led them out to fight the Arameans in the fields. 10He left the rest of the army under the command of his brother Abishai, who was to attack the Ammonites. 11"If the Arameans are too strong for me, then come over and help me," Joab told his brother. "And if the Ammonites are too strong for you, I will come and help you. 12Be courageous! Let us fight bravely to save our people and the cities of our God. May the LORD's will be done."

13When Joab and his troops attacked, the Arameans began to run away. 14And when the Ammonites saw the Arameans running, they ran

8:18a Hebrew *of the Kerethites and Pelethites.* 8:18b Hebrew *David's sons were priests;* compare parallel text at 1 Chr 18:17. 9:6 Also known as *Meribbaal.*

from Abishai and retreated into the city. After the battle was over, Joab returned to Jerusalem. ¹⁵The Arameans now realized that they were no match for Israel. So when they regrouped, ¹⁶they were joined by additional Aramean troops summoned by Hadadezer from the other side of the Euphrates River.* These troops arrived at Helam under the command of Shobach, the commander of all Hadadezer's forces. ¹⁷When David heard what was happening, he mobilized all Israel, crossed the Jordan River, and led the army to Helam. The Arameans positioned themselves there in battle formation and then attacked David. ¹⁸But again the Arameans fled from the Israelites. This time David's forces killed seven hundred charioteers and forty thousand horsemen,* including Shobach, the commander of their army. ¹⁹When Hadadezer and his Aramean allies realized they had been defeated by Israel, they surrendered to them and became their subjects. After that, the Arameans were afraid to help the Ammonites.

CHAPTER **11**

David and Bathsheba

The following spring, the time of year when kings go to war, David sent Joab and the Israelite army to destroy the Ammonites. In the process they laid siege to the city of Rabbah. But David stayed behind in Jerusalem.

²Late one afternoon David got out of bed after taking a nap and went for a stroll on the roof of the palace. As he looked out over the city, he noticed a woman of unusual beauty taking a bath. ³He sent someone to find out who she was, and he was told, "She is Bathsheba, the daughter of Eliam and the wife of Uriah the Hittite." ⁴Then David sent for her; and when she came to the palace, he slept with her. (She had just completed the purification rites after having her menstrual period.) Then she returned home. ⁵Later, when Bathsheba discovered that she was pregnant, she sent a message to inform David.

⁶So David sent word to Joab: "Send me Uriah the Hittite." ⁷When Uriah arrived, David asked him how Joab and the army were getting along and how the war was progressing. ⁸Then he told Uriah, "Go on home and relax." David even sent a gift to Uriah after he had left the palace. ⁹But Uriah wouldn't go home. He stayed that night at the palace entrance with some of the king's other servants.

¹⁰When David heard what Uriah had done, he summoned him and asked, "What's the matter with you? Why didn't you go home last night after being away for so long?"

¹¹Uriah replied, "The Ark and the armies of Israel and Judah are living in tents,* and Joab and his officers are camping in the open fields. How could I go home to wine and dine and sleep with my wife? I swear that I will never be guilty of acting like that."

¹²"Well, stay here tonight," David told him, "and tomorrow you may return to the army." So Uriah stayed in Jerusalem that day and the next. ¹³Then David invited him to dinner and got him drunk. But even then he couldn't get Uriah to go home to his wife. Again he slept at the palace entrance.

David Arranges for Uriah's Death

¹⁴So the next morning David wrote a letter to Joab and gave it to Uriah to deliver. ¹⁵The letter instructed Joab, "Station Uriah on the front lines where the battle is fiercest. Then pull back so that he will be killed." ¹⁶So Joab assigned Uriah to a spot close to the city wall where he knew the enemy's strongest men were fighting. ¹⁷And Uriah was killed along with several other Israelite soldiers.

¹⁸Then Joab sent a battle report to David. ¹⁹He told his messenger, "Report all the news of the battle to the king. ²⁰But he might get angry and ask, 'Why did the troops go so close to the city? Didn't they know there would be shooting from the walls? ²¹Wasn't Gideon's son Abimelech killed* at Thebez by a woman who threw a millstone down on him?' Then tell him, 'Uriah the Hittite was killed, too.'"

²²So the messenger went to Jerusalem and gave a complete report to David. ²³"The enemy came out against us," he said. "And as we chased them back to the city gates, ²⁴the archers on the wall shot arrows at us. Some of our men were killed, including Uriah the Hittite."

²⁵"Well, tell Joab not to be discouraged," David said. "The sword kills one as well as another! Fight harder next time, and conquer the city!"

²⁶When Bathsheba heard that her husband was dead, she mourned for him. ²⁷When the period of mourning was over, David sent for her and brought her to the palace, and she became one of his wives. Then she gave birth to a son. But the Lord was very displeased with what David had done.

10:16 Hebrew *the river.*   **10:18** Some Greek manuscripts read *foot soldiers;* compare parallel text at 1 Chr 19:18.   **11:11** Or *at Succoth.*
11:21 Hebrew *Was not Abimelech son of Jerubbesheth killed.*

Don't Place Yourself in the Way of Unnecessary Temptation
Read 2 SAMUEL 11:1–12:14

David fell headlong into temptation without thinking of the consequences. What makes his spiritual descent even more perplexing is that he was known as being "a man after God's own heart." He was the one who, as a boy, had killed the gigantic Philistine, Goliath. David was also the same man who had been divinely appointed to lead the nation of Israel and had guided his army into a string of military victories. How could a man of such character, who often spoke of his love for God, make such a grave mistake? In this story, we find at least four mistakes David made that led him into committing sexual sin:

1. David Lowered His Guard. David was idle. Instead of leading his troops into battle, he was on his roof, taking some time off. In addition, he didn't seem to engage in any of the activities of his youth, like worshiping God in song, spending time alone with God, and depending upon God for strength. By moving away from that intimacy with God, he had become more vulnerable to the pull of temptation.

2. David Entertained Temptation. When David saw Bathsheba bathing herself, he could have turned away, but he didn't. Jesus warns us, "Anyone who even looks at a woman with lust in his eye has already committed adultery with her in his heart" (Matthew 5:28). It is wrong to put yourself in a place where you know you will be exposed to things that could sinfully arouse you or hurt you. He could have left after that first look, but he didn't.

3. David Acted on the Temptation. David had allowed lust to build in his heart to the point that he wanted to act on it. He could have repented right then and there, but he went ahead and entered into an immoral relationship with her.

4. David Developed a Dullness toward Sin. When David found out that Bathsheba was pregnant, instead of making matters right, he went on to commit other sins, including deception and murder. He had allowed this sin to so control him that he could no longer distinguish between right and wrong.

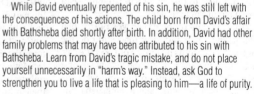

While David eventually repented of his sin, he was still left with the consequences of his actions. The child born from David's affair with Bathsheba died shortly after birth. In addition, David had other family problems that may have been attributed to his sin with Bathsheba. Learn from David's tragic mistake, and do not place yourself unnecessarily in "harm's way." Instead, ask God to strengthen you to live a life that is pleasing to him—a life of purity.

For the next note on "Purity," turn to p. 1062.

CORNER STONES

CHAPTER **12**
Nathan Rebukes David

So the LORD sent Nathan the prophet to tell David this story: "There were two men in a certain town. One was rich, and one was poor. ²The rich man owned many sheep and cattle. ³The poor man owned nothing but a little lamb he had worked hard to buy. He raised that little lamb, and it grew up with his children. It ate from the man's own plate and drank from his cup. He cuddled it in his arms like a baby daughter. ⁴One day a guest arrived at the home of the rich man. But instead of killing a lamb from his own flocks for food, he took the poor man's lamb and killed it and served it to his guest."

⁵David was furious. "As surely as the LORD lives," he vowed, "any man who would do such a thing deserves to die! ⁶He must repay four lambs to the poor man for the one he stole and for having no pity."

⁷Then Nathan said to David, "You are that man! The LORD, the God of Israel, says, 'I anointed you king of Israel and saved you from the power of Saul. ⁸I gave you his house and his wives and the kingdoms of Israel and Judah. And if that had not been enough, I would have given you much, much more. ⁹Why, then, have

you despised the word of the LORD and done this horrible deed? For you have murdered Uriah and stolen his wife. 10From this time on, the sword will be a constant threat to your family, because you have despised me by taking Uriah's wife to be your own.

11 " 'Because of what you have done, I, the LORD, will cause your own household to rebel against you. I will give your wives to another man, and he will go to bed with them in public view. 12You did it secretly, but I will do this to you openly in the sight of all Israel.' "

David Confesses His Guilt

13Then David confessed to Nathan, "I have sinned against the LORD."

Nathan replied, "Yes, but the LORD has forgiven you, and you won't die for this sin. 14But you have given the enemies of the LORD great opportunity to despise and blaspheme him, so your child will die."

15After Nathan returned to his home, the LORD made Bathsheba's baby deathly ill. 16David begged God to spare the child. He went without food and lay all night on the bare ground. 17The leaders of the nation pleaded with him to get up and eat with them, but he refused. 18Then on the seventh day the baby died. David's advisers were afraid to tell him. "He was so broken up about the baby being sick," they said. "What will he do to himself when we tell him the child is dead?"

19But when David saw them whispering, he realized what had happened. "Is the baby dead?" he asked.

"Yes," they replied. 20Then David got up from the ground, washed himself, put on lotions, and changed his clothes. Then he went to the Tabernacle and worshiped the LORD. After that, he returned to the palace and ate. 21His advisers were amazed. "We don't understand you," they told him. "While the baby was still living, you wept and refused to eat. But now that the baby is dead, you have stopped your mourning and are eating again."

22David replied, "I fasted and wept while the child was alive, for I said, 'Perhaps the LORD will be gracious to me and let the child live.' 23But why should I fast when he is dead? Can I bring him back again? I will go to him one day, but he cannot return to me."

24Then David comforted Bathsheba, his wife, and slept with her. She became pregnant and

gave birth to a son, and they named him Solomon. The LORD loved the child 25and sent word through Nathan the prophet that his name should be Jedidiah—"beloved of the LORD"—because the LORD loved him.

David Captures Rabbah

26Meanwhile, Joab and the Israelite army were successfully ending their siege of Rabbah, the capital of Ammon. 27Joab sent messengers to tell David, "I have fought against Rabbah and captured its water supply.* 28Now bring the rest of the army and finish the job, so you will get credit for the victory instead of me."

29So David led the rest of his army to Rabbah and captured it. 30David removed the crown from the king's head,* and it was placed on David's own head. The crown was made of gold and set with gems, and it weighed about seventy-five pounds.* David took a vast amount of plunder from the city. 31He also made slaves of the people of Rabbah and forced them to labor with saws, picks, and axes, and to work in the brick kilns. That is how he dealt with the people of all the Ammonite cities. Then David and his army returned to Jerusalem.

CHAPTER 13

The Rape of Tamar

David's son Absalom had a beautiful sister named Tamar. And Amnon, her half brother, fell desperately in love with her. 2Amnon became so obsessed with Tamar that he became ill. She was a virgin, and it seemed impossible that he could ever fulfill his love for her.

3Now Amnon had a very crafty friend—his cousin Jonadab. He was the son of David's brother Shimea.* 4One day Jonadab said to Amnon, "What's the trouble? Why should the son of a king look so dejected morning after morning?"

So Amnon told him, "I am in love with Tamar, Absalom's sister."

5"Well," Jonadab said, "I'll tell you what to do. Go back to bed and pretend you are sick. When your father comes to see you, ask him to let Tamar come and prepare some food for you. Tell him you'll feel better if she feeds you."

6So Amnon pretended to be sick. And when the king came to see him, Amnon asked him, "Please let Tamar come to take care of me and cook something for me to eat." 7So David

12:27 Or *captured the city of water.* 12:30a Greek version reads *removed the crown of Milcom;* compare 1 Kgs 11:5. Milcom, also called Molech, was the god of the Ammonites. 12:30b Hebrew *1 talent* [34 kilograms]. 13:3 Hebrew *Shimeah* (also in 13:32), a variant name for Shimea; compare 1 Chr 2:13.

agreed and sent Tamar to Amnon's house to prepare some food for him.

8When Tamar arrived at Amnon's house, she went to the room where he was lying down so he could watch her mix some dough. Then she baked some special bread for him. 9But when she set the serving tray before him, he refused to eat. "Everyone get out of here," Amnon told his servants. So they all left. 10Then he said to Tamar, "Now bring the food into my bedroom and feed it to me here." So Tamar took it to him. 11But as she was feeding him, he grabbed her and demanded, "Come to bed with me, my darling sister."

12"No, my brother!" she cried. "Don't be foolish! Don't do this to me! You know what a serious crime it is to do such a thing in Israel. 13Where could I go in my shame? And you would be called one of the greatest fools in Israel. Please, just speak to the king about it, and he will let you marry me."

14But Amnon wouldn't listen to her, and since he was stronger than she was, he raped her. 15Then suddenly Amnon's love turned to hate, and he hated her even more than he had loved her. "Get out of here!" he snarled at her.

16"No, no!" Tamar cried. "To reject me now is a greater wrong than what you have already done to me."

But Amnon wouldn't listen to her. 17He shouted for his servant and demanded, "Throw this woman out, and lock the door behind her!"

18So the servant put her out. She was wearing a long, beautiful robe,* as was the custom in those days for the king's virgin daughters. 19But now Tamar tore her robe and put ashes on her head. And then, with her face in her hands, she went away crying.

20Her brother Absalom saw her and asked, "Is it true that Amnon has been with you? Well, don't be so upset. Since he's your brother anyway, don't worry about it." So Tamar lived as a desolate woman in Absalom's house. 21When King David heard what had happened, he was very angry. 22And though Absalom never spoke to Amnon about it, he hated Amnon deeply because of what he had done to his sister.

Absalom's Revenge on Amnon

23Two years later, when Absalom's sheep were being sheared at Baal-hazor near Ephraim, Absalom invited all the king's sons to come to a feast. 24He went to the king and said, "My sheep-shearers are now at work. Would the king and his servants please come to celebrate the occasion with me?"

25The king replied, "No, my son. If we all came, we would be too much of a burden on you." Absalom pressed him, but the king wouldn't come, though he sent his thanks.

26"Well, then," Absalom said, "if you can't come, how about sending my brother Amnon instead?"

"Why Amnon?" the king asked. 27But Absalom kept on pressing the king until he finally agreed to let all his sons attend, including Amnon.

28Absalom told his men, "Wait until Amnon gets drunk; then at my signal, kill him! Don't be afraid. I'm the one who has given the command. Take courage and do it!" 29So at Absalom's signal they murdered Amnon. Then the other sons of the king jumped on their mules and fled.

30As they were on the way back to Jerusalem, this report reached David: "Absalom has killed all your sons; not one is left alive!" 31The king jumped up, tore his robe, and fell prostrate on the ground. His advisers also tore their clothes in horror and sorrow.

32But just then Jonadab, the son of David's brother Shimea, arrived and said, "No, not all your sons have been killed! It was only Amnon! Absalom has been plotting this ever since Amnon raped his sister Tamar. 33No, your sons aren't all dead! It was only Amnon." 34Meanwhile Absalom escaped.

Then the watchman on the Jerusalem wall saw a great crowd coming toward the city from the west. He ran to tell the king, "I see a crowd of people coming from the Horonaim road* along the side of the hill."

35"Look!" Jonadab told the king. "There they are now! Your sons are coming, just as I said." 36They soon arrived, weeping and sobbing, and the king and his officials wept bitterly with them. 37And David mourned many days for his son Amnon.

Absalom fled to his grandfather, Talmai son of Ammihud, the king of Geshur. 38He stayed there in Geshur for three years. 39And David, now reconciled to Amnon's death, longed to be reunited with his son Absalom.*

CHAPTER 14

Joab Arranges for Absalom's Return

Joab realized how much the king longed to see Absalom. 2So he sent for a woman from Tekoa who had a reputation for great wisdom. He said

---

13:18 Or *a robe with sleeves,* or *an ornamented robe.* The meaning of the Hebrew is uncertain. 13:34 As in Greek version; Hebrew reads *from the road behind him.* 13:39 Or *no longer felt a need to go out after Absalom.*

to her, "Pretend you are in mourning; wear mourning clothes and don't bathe or wear any perfume. Act like a woman who has been in deep sorrow for a long time. ³Then go to the king and tell him the story I am about to tell you." Then Joab told her what to say.

⁴When the woman approached the king, she fell with her face down to the floor in front of him and cried out, "O king! Help me!"

⁵"What's the trouble?" the king asked.

"I am a widow," she replied. ⁶"My two sons had a fight out in the field. And since no one was there to stop it, one of them was killed. ⁷Now the rest of the family is demanding, 'Let us have your son. We will execute him for murdering his brother. He doesn't deserve to inherit his family's property.' But if I do that, I will have no one left, and my husband's name and family will disappear from the face of the earth."

⁸"Leave it to me," the king told her. "Go home, and I'll see to it that no one touches him."

⁹"Oh, thank you, my lord," she replied. "And I'll take the responsibility if you are criticized for helping me like this."

¹⁰"Don't worry about that!" the king said. "If anyone objects, bring them to me. I can assure you they will never complain again!"

¹¹Then she said, "Please swear to me by the LORD your God that you won't let anyone take vengeance against my son. I want no more bloodshed."

"As surely as the LORD lives," he replied, "not a hair on your son's head will be disturbed!"

¹²"Please let me ask one more thing of you!" she said.

"Go ahead," he urged. "Speak!"

¹³She replied, "Why don't you do as much for all the people of God as you have promised to do for me? You have convicted yourself in making this decision, because you have refused to bring home your own banished son. ¹⁴All of us must die eventually. Our lives are like water spilled out on the ground, which cannot be gathered up again. That is why God tries to bring us back when we have been separated from him. He does not sweep away the lives of those he cares about—and neither should you!

¹⁵"But I have come to plead with you for my son because my life and my son's life have been threatened. I said to myself, 'Perhaps the king will listen to me ¹⁶and rescue us from those who would cut us off from God's people. ¹⁷Yes, the king will give us peace of mind again.' I know that

14:26 Hebrew *200 shekels* [2.3 kilograms] *by the royal standard.*

you are like an angel of God and can discern good from evil. May the LORD your God be with you."

¹⁸"I want to know one thing," the king replied.

"Yes, my lord?" she asked.

¹⁹"Did Joab send you here?"

And the woman replied, "My lord the king, how can I deny it? Nobody can hide anything from you. Yes, Joab sent me and told me what to say. ²⁰He did it to place the matter before you in a different light. But you are as wise as an angel of God, and you understand everything that happens among us!"

²¹So the king sent for Joab and told him, "All right, go and bring back the young man Absalom."

²²Joab fell to the ground before the king and blessed him and said, "At last I know that I have gained your approval, for you have granted me this request!"

²³Then Joab went to Geshur and brought Absalom back to Jerusalem. ²⁴But the king gave this order: "Absalom may go to his own house, but he must never come into my presence." So Absalom did not see the king.

Absalom Reconciled to David

²⁵Now no one in Israel was as handsome as Absalom. From head to foot, he was the perfect specimen of a man. ²⁶He cut his hair only once a year, and then only because it was too heavy to carry around. When he weighed it out, it came to five pounds!* ²⁷He had three sons and one daughter. His daughter's name was Tamar, and she was very beautiful.

²⁸Absalom lived in Jerusalem for two years without getting to see the king. ²⁹Then Absalom sent for Joab to ask him to intercede for him, but Joab refused to come. Absalom sent for him a second time, but again Joab refused to come. ³⁰So Absalom said to his servants, "Go and set fire to Joab's barley field, the field next to mine." So they set his field on fire, as Absalom had commanded.

³¹Then Joab came to Absalom and demanded, "Why did your servants set my field on fire?"

³²And Absalom replied, "Because I wanted you to ask the king why he brought me back from Geshur if he didn't intend to see me. I might as well have stayed there. Let me see the king; if he finds me guilty of anything, then let him execute me."

³³So Joab told the king what Absalom had

said. Then at last David summoned his estranged son, and Absalom came and bowed low before the king, and David kissed him.

CHAPTER 15

Absalom's Rebellion

After this, Absalom bought a chariot and horses, and he hired fifty footmen to run ahead of him. ²He got up early every morning and went out to the gate of the city. When people brought a case to the king for judgment, Absalom would ask where they were from, and they would tell him their tribe. ³Then Absalom would say, "You've really got a strong case here! It's too bad the king doesn't have anyone to hear it. ⁴I wish I were the judge. Then people could bring their problems to me, and I would give them justice!" ⁵And when people tried to bow before him, Absalom wouldn't let them. Instead, he took them by the hand and embraced them. ⁶So in this way, Absalom stole the hearts of all the people of Israel.

⁷After four years,* Absalom said to the king, "Let me go to Hebron to offer a sacrifice to the LORD in fulfillment of a vow I made to him. ⁸For while I was at Geshur, I promised to sacrifice to him in Hebron if he would bring me back to Jerusalem."

⁹"All right," the king told him. "Go and fulfill your vow."

So Absalom went to Hebron. ¹⁰But while he was there, he sent secret messengers to every part of Israel to stir up a rebellion against the king. "As soon as you hear the trumpets," his message read, "you will know that Absalom has been crowned king in Hebron." ¹¹He took two hundred men from Jerusalem with him as guests, but they knew nothing of his intentions. ¹²While he was offering the sacrifices, he sent for Ahithophel, one of David's counselors who lived in Giloh. Soon many others also joined Absalom, and the conspiracy gained momentum.

David Escapes from Jerusalem

¹³A messenger soon arrived in Jerusalem to tell King David, "All Israel has joined Absalom in a conspiracy against you!"

¹⁴"Then we must flee at once, or it will be too late!" David urged his men. "Hurry! If we get out of the city before he arrives, both we and the city of Jerusalem will be spared from disaster."

¹⁵"We are with you," his advisers replied. "Do what you think is best." ¹⁶So the king and his household set out at once. He left no one behind except ten of his concubines to keep the palace in order. ¹⁷The king and his people set out on foot, and they paused at the edge of the city ¹⁸to let David's troops move past to lead the way. There were six hundred Gittites who had come with David from Gath, along with the king's bodyguard.*

¹⁹Then the king turned to Ittai, the captain of the Gittites, and asked, "Why are you coming with us? Go on back with your men to King Absalom, for you are a guest in Israel, a foreigner in exile. ²⁰You arrived only yesterday, and now should I force you to wander with us? I don't even know where we will go. Go on back and take your troops with you, and may the LORD show you his unfailing love and faithfulness.*"

²¹But Ittai said to the king, "I vow by the LORD and by your own life that I will go wherever you go, no matter what happens—whether it means life or death."

²²David replied, "All right, come with us." So Ittai and his six hundred men and their families went along.

²³There was deep sadness throughout the land as the king and his followers passed by. They crossed the Kidron Valley and then went out toward the wilderness.

²⁴Abiathar and Zadok and the Levites took the Ark of the Covenant of God and set it down beside the road. Then they offered sacrifices there until everyone had passed by. ²⁵David instructed Zadok to take the Ark of God back into the city. "If the LORD sees fit," David said, "he will bring me back to see the Ark and the Tabernacle again. ²⁶But if he is through with me, then let him do what seems best to him."

²⁷Then the king told Zadok the priest, "Look,* here is my plan. You and Abiathar* should return quietly to the city with your son Ahimaaz and Abiathar's son Jonathan. ²⁸I will stop at the shallows of the Jordan River* and wait there for a message from you. Let me know what happens in Jerusalem before I disappear into the wilderness." ²⁹So Zadok and Abiathar took the Ark of God back to the city and stayed there.

³⁰David walked up the road that led to the Mount of Olives, weeping as he went. His head was covered and his feet were bare as a sign of mourning. And the people who were with him covered their heads and wept as they climbed the mountain. ³¹When someone told David that his adviser Ahithophel was now backing Absa-

---

15:7 As in Greek and Syriac versions; Hebrew reads *40 years.*   **15:18** Hebrew *the Kerethites and Pelethites.*   **15:20** As in Greek version; Hebrew reads *and may unfailing love and faithfulness go with you.*   **15:27a** As in Greek version; Hebrew reads *Are you a seer?* or *Do you see?*   **15:27b** Hebrew lacks *and Abiathar;* compare 15:29.   **15:28** Hebrew *at the crossing points of the wilderness.*

lom, David prayed, "O LORD, let Ahithophel give Absalom foolish advice!"

32As they reached the spot at the top of the Mount of Olives where people worshiped God, David found Hushai the Arkite waiting for him. Hushai had torn his clothing and put dirt on his head as a sign of mourning. 33But David told him, "If you go with me, you will only be a burden. 34Return to Jerusalem and tell Absalom, 'I will now be your adviser, just as I was your father's adviser in the past.' Then you can frustrate and counter Ahithophel's advice. 35Zadok and Abiathar, the priests, are there. Tell them the plans that are being made to capture me, 36and they will send their sons Ahimaaz and Jonathan to find me and tell me what is going on." 37So David's friend Hushai returned to Jerusalem, getting there just as Absalom arrived.

CHAPTER **16**

David and Ziba

David was just past the top of the hill when Ziba, the servant of Mephibosheth,* caught up with him. He was leading two donkeys loaded with two hundred loaves of bread, one hundred clusters of raisins, one hundred bunches of summer fruit, and a skin of wine. 2"What are these for?" the king asked Ziba.

And Ziba replied, "The donkeys are for your people to ride on, and the bread and summer fruit are for the young men to eat. The wine is to be taken with you into the wilderness for those who become faint."

3"And where is Mephibosheth?" the king asked him.

"He stayed in Jerusalem," Ziba replied. "He said, 'Today I will get back the kingdom of my grandfather Saul.'"

4"In that case," the king told Ziba, "I give you everything Mephibosheth owns."

"Thank you, sir," Ziba replied. "I will always do whatever you want me to do."

Shimei Curses David

5As David and his party passed Bahurim, a man came out of the village cursing them. It was Shimei son of Gera, a member of Saul's family. 6He threw stones at the king and the king's officers and all the mighty warriors who surrounded them. 7"Get out of here, you murderer, you scoundrel!" he shouted at David. 8"The LORD is paying you back for murdering Saul and

his family. You stole his throne, and now the LORD has given it to your son Absalom. At last you will taste some of your own medicine, you murderer!"

9"Why should this dead dog curse my lord the king?" Abishai son of Zeruiah demanded. "Let me go over and cut off his head!"

10"No!" the king said. "What am I going to do with you sons of Zeruiah! If the LORD has told him to curse me, who am I to stop him?" 11Then David said to Abishai and the other officers, "My own son is trying to kill me. Shouldn't this relative of Saul* have even more reason to do so? Leave him alone and let him curse, for the LORD has told him to do it. 12And perhaps the LORD will see that I am being wronged and will bless me because of these curses." 13So David and his men continued on, and Shimei kept pace with them on a nearby hillside, cursing as he went and throwing stones at David and tossing dust into the air.

14The king and all who were with him grew weary along the way, so they rested when they reached the Jordan River.*

Ahithophel Advises Absalom

15Meanwhile, Absalom and his men arrived at Jerusalem, accompanied by Ahithophel. 16When David's friend Hushai the Arkite arrived, he went immediately to see Absalom. "Long live the king!" he exclaimed. "Long live the king!"

17"Is this the way you treat your friend David?" Absalom asked him. "Why aren't you with him?"

18"I'm here because I work for the man who is chosen by the LORD and by Israel," Hushai replied. 19"And anyway, why shouldn't I serve you? I helped your father, and now I will help you!"

20Then Absalom turned to Ahithophel and asked him, "What should I do next?"

21Ahithophel told him, "Go and sleep with your father's concubines, for he has left them here to keep the house. Then all Israel will know that you have insulted him beyond hope of reconciliation, and they will give you their support."

22So they set up a tent on the palace roof where everyone could see it, and Absalom went into the tent to sleep with his father's concubines.

23Absalom followed Ahithophel's advice, just as David had done. For every word Ahithophel spoke seemed as wise as though it had come directly from the mouth of God.

16:1 Also known as *Meribbaal.* 16:11 Hebrew *this Benjaminite.* 16:14 As in Greek version (see also 17:16); Hebrew reads *when they reached their destination.*

CHAPTER **17**

Now Ahithophel urged Absalom, "Let me choose twelve thousand men to start out after David tonight. 2I will catch up to him while he is weary and discouraged. He and his troops will panic, and everyone will run away. Then I will kill only the king, 3and I will bring all the people back to you as a bride returns to her husband. After all, it is only this man's life that you seek.* Then all the people will remain unharmed and peaceful." 4This plan seemed good to Absalom and to all the other leaders of Israel.

Hushai Counters Ahithophel's Advice

5But then Absalom said, "Bring in Hushai the Arkite. Let's see what he thinks about this." 6When Hushai arrived, Absalom told him what Ahithophel had said. Then he asked, "What is your opinion? Should we follow Ahithophel's advice? If not, speak up."

7"Well," Hushai replied, "this time I think Ahithophel has made a mistake. 8You know your father and his men; they are mighty warriors. Right now they are probably as enraged as a mother bear who has been robbed of her cubs. And remember that your father is an experienced soldier. He won't be spending the night among the troops. 9He has probably already hidden in some pit or cave. And when he comes out and attacks and a few of your men fall, there will be panic among your troops, and everyone will start shouting that your men are being slaughtered. 10Then even the bravest of them, though they have the heart of a lion, will be paralyzed with fear. For all Israel knows what a mighty man your father is and how courageous his warriors are.

11"I suggest that you mobilize the entire army of Israel, bringing them from as far away as Dan and Beersheba. That way you will have an army as numerous as the sand on the seashore. And I think that you should personally lead the troops. 12When we find David, we can descend on him like the dew that falls to the ground, so that not one of his men is left alive. 13And if David has escaped into some city, you will have the entire army of Israel there at your command. Then we can take ropes and drag the walls of the city into the nearest valley until every stone is torn down."

14Then Absalom and all the leaders of Israel said, "Hushai's advice is better than Ahithophel's." For the LORD had arranged to defeat the counsel of Ahithophel, which really was the better plan, so that he could bring disaster upon Absalom!

Hushai Warns David to Escape

15Then Hushai reported to Zadok and Abiathar, the priests, what Ahithophel had said and what he himself had suggested instead. 16"Quick!" he told them. "Find David and urge him not to stay at the shallows of the Jordan River* tonight. He must go across at once into the wilderness beyond. Otherwise he will die and his entire army with him."

17Jonathan and Ahimaaz had been staying at En-rogel so as not to be seen entering and leaving the city. Arrangements had been made for a servant girl to bring them the message they were to take to King David. 18But a boy saw them leaving En-rogel to go to David, and he told Absalom about it. Meanwhile, they escaped to Bahurim, where a man hid them inside a well in his courtyard. 19The man's wife put a cloth over the top of the well with grain on it to dry in the sun; so no one suspected they were there.

20When Absalom's men arrived, they asked her, "Have you seen Ahimaaz and Jonathan?"

She replied, "They were here, but they crossed the brook." Absalom's men looked for them without success and returned to Jerusalem.

21Then the two men crawled out of the well and hurried on to King David. "Quick!" they told him, "cross the Jordan tonight!" And they told him how Ahithophel had advised that he be captured and killed. 22So David and all the people with him went across the Jordan River during the night, and they were all on the other bank before dawn.

23Meanwhile, Ahithophel was publicly disgraced when Absalom refused his advice. So he saddled his donkey, went to his hometown, set his affairs in order, and hanged himself. He died there and was buried beside his father.

24David soon arrived at Mahanaim. By now, Absalom had mobilized the entire army of Israel and was leading his troops across the Jordan River. 25Absalom had appointed Amasa as commander of his army, replacing Joab, who had been commander under David. (Amasa was Joab's cousin. His father was Jether,* an Ishmaelite.* His mother, Abigail daughter of Nahash, was the sister of Joab's mother, Zeruiah.) 26Absalom and the Israelite army set up camp in the land of Gilead.

27When David arrived at Mahanaim, he was

17:3 As in Greek version; Hebrew reads *like the return of all is the man whom you seek.*   17:16 Hebrew *at the crossing points of the wilderness.*
17:25a Hebrew *Ithra,* a variant name for Jether.   17:25b As in some Greek manuscripts (see also 1 Chr 2:17); Hebrew reads *an Israelite.*

warmly greeted by Shobi son of Nahash of Rabbah, an Ammonite, and by Makir son of Ammiel of Lo-debar, and by Barzillai of Gilead from Rogelim. 28They brought sleeping mats, cooking pots, serving bowls, wheat and barley flour, roasted grain, beans, lentils, 29honey, butter, sheep, and cheese for David and those who were with him. For they said, "You must all be very tired and hungry and thirsty after your long march through the wilderness."

CHAPTER **18**
Absalom's Defeat and Death
David now appointed generals and captains to lead his troops. 2One-third were placed under Joab, one-third under Joab's brother Abishai son of Zeruiah, and one-third under Ittai the Gittite. The king told his troops, "I am going out with you."

3But his men objected strongly. "You must not go," they urged. "If we have to turn and run—and even if half of us die—it will make no difference to Absalom's troops; they will be looking only for you. You are worth ten thousand of us, and it is better that you stay here in the city and send us help if we need it."

4"If you think that's the best plan, I'll do it," the king finally agreed. So he stood at the gate of the city as all the divisions of troops passed by. 5And the king gave this command to Joab, Abishai, and Ittai: "For my sake, deal gently with young Absalom." And all the troops heard the king give this order to his commanders.

6So the battle began in the forest of Ephraim, 7and the Israelite troops were beaten back by David's men. There was a great slaughter, and twenty thousand men laid down their lives that day. 8The battle raged all across the countryside, and more men died because of the forest than were killed by the sword.

9During the battle, Absalom came unexpectedly upon some of David's men. He tried to escape on his mule, but as he rode beneath the thick branches of a great oak, his head got caught. His mule kept going and left him dangling in the air. 10One of David's men saw what had happened and told Joab, "I saw Absalom dangling in a tree."

11"What?" Joab demanded. "You saw him there and didn't kill him? I would have rewarded you with ten pieces of silver* and a hero's belt!"

12"I wouldn't do it for a thousand pieces of silver,*" the man replied. "We all heard the king say to you and Abishai and Ittai, 'For my sake, please don't harm young Absalom.' 13And if I had betrayed the king by killing his son—and the king would certainly find out who did it— you yourself would be the first to abandon me."

14"Enough of this nonsense," Joab said. Then he took three daggers and plunged them into Absalom's heart as he dangled from the oak still alive. 15Ten of Joab's young armor bearers then surrounded Absalom and killed him. 16Then Joab blew the trumpet, and his men returned from chasing the army of Israel. 17They threw Absalom's body into a deep pit in the forest and piled a great heap of stones over it. And the army of Israel fled to their homes.

18During his lifetime, Absalom had built a monument to himself in the King's Valley, for he had said, "I have no son to carry on my name." He named the monument after himself, and it is known as Absalom's Monument to this day.

David Mourns Absalom's Death
19Then Zadok's son Ahimaaz said, "Let me run to the king with the good news that the LORD has saved him from his enemy Absalom."

20"No," Joab told him, "it wouldn't be good news to the king that his son is dead. You can be my messenger some other time, but not today."

21Then Joab said to a man from Cush, "Go tell the king what you have seen." The man bowed and ran off.

22But Ahimaaz continued to plead with Joab, "Whatever happens, please let me go, too."

"Why should you go, my son?" Joab replied. "There will be no reward for you."

23"Yes, but let me go anyway," he begged.

Joab finally said, "All right, go ahead." Then Ahimaaz took a shortcut across the plain of the Jordan and got to Mahanaim ahead of the man from Cush.

24While David was sitting at the city gate, the watchman climbed to the roof of the gateway by the wall. As he looked, he saw a lone man running toward them. 25He shouted the news down to David, and the king replied, "If he is alone, he has news."

As the messenger came closer, 26the watchman saw another man running toward them. He shouted down, "Here comes another one!"

The king replied, "He also will have news."

27"The first man runs like Ahimaaz son of Zadok," the watchman said.

"He is a good man and comes with good news," the king replied.

18:11 Hebrew *10 shekels of silver,* about 4 ounces or 114 grams in weight. **18:12** Hebrew *1,000 shekels,* about 25 pounds or 11.4 kilograms in weight.

²⁸Then Ahimaaz cried out to the king, "All is well!" He bowed low with his face to the ground and said, "Blessed be the LORD your God, who has handed over the rebels who dared to stand against you."

²⁹"What about young Absalom?" the king demanded. "Is he all right?"

Ahimaaz replied, "When Joab told me to come, there was a lot of commotion. But I didn't know what was happening."

³⁰"Wait here," the king told him. So Ahimaaz stepped aside.

³¹Then the man from Cush arrived and said, "I have good news for my lord the king. Today the LORD has rescued you from all those who rebelled against you."

³²"What about young Absalom?" the king demanded. "Is he all right?"

And the Cushite replied, "May all of your enemies, both now and in the future, be as that young man is!"

³³The king was overcome with emotion. He went up to his room over the gateway and burst into tears. And as he went, he cried, "O my son Absalom! My son, my son Absalom! If only I could have died instead of you! O Absalom, my son, my son."

CHAPTER 19

Joab Rebukes the King

Word soon reached Joab that the king was weeping and mourning for Absalom. ²As the troops heard of the king's deep grief for his son, the joy of that day's victory was turned into deep sadness. ³They crept back into the city as though they were ashamed and had been beaten in battle. ⁴The king covered his face with his hands and kept on weeping, "O my son Absalom! O Absalom, my son, my son!"

⁵Then Joab went to the king's room and said to him, "We saved your life today and the lives of your sons, your daughters, and your wives and concubines. Yet you act like this, making us feel ashamed, as though we had done something wrong. ⁶You seem to love those who hate you and hate those who love you. You have made it clear today that we mean nothing to you. If Absalom had lived and all of us had died, you would be pleased. ⁷Now go out there and congratulate the troops, for I swear by the LORD that if you don't, not a single one of them will remain here tonight. Then you will be worse off than you have ever been." ⁸So the king went out

19:20 Hebrew *the house of Joseph.*

and sat at the city gate, and as the news spread throughout the city that he was there, everyone went to him.

Meanwhile, the Israelites who supported Absalom had fled to their homes. ⁹And throughout the tribes of Israel there was much discussion and argument going on. The people were saying, "The king saved us from our enemies, the Philistines, but Absalom chased him out of the country. ¹⁰Now Absalom, whom we anointed to rule over us, is dead. Let's ask David to come back and be our king again."

¹¹Then King David sent Zadok and Abiathar, the priests, to say to the leaders of Judah, "Why are you the last ones to reinstate the king? For I have heard that all Israel is ready, and only you are holding out. ¹²Yet you are my relatives, my own tribe, my own flesh and blood! Why are you the last ones to welcome me back?" ¹³And David told them to tell Amasa, "Since you are my nephew, may God strike me dead if I do not appoint you as commander of my army in place of Joab." ¹⁴Then Amasa convinced all the leaders of Judah, and they responded unanimously. They sent word to the king, "Return to us, and bring back all those who are with you."

David's Return to Jerusalem

¹⁵So the king started back to Jerusalem. And when he arrived at the Jordan River, the people of Judah came to Gilgal to meet him and escort him across the river. ¹⁶Then Shimei son of Gera, the man from Bahurim in Benjamin, hurried across with the men of Judah to welcome King David. ¹⁷A thousand men from the tribe of Benjamin were with him, including Ziba, the servant of Saul, and Ziba's fifteen sons and twenty servants. They rushed down to the Jordan to arrive ahead of the king. ¹⁸They all crossed the ford and worked hard ferrying the king's household across the river, helping them in every way they could.

David's Mercy to Shimei

As the king was about to cross the river, Shimei fell down before him. ¹⁹"My lord the king, please forgive me," he pleaded. "Forget the terrible thing I did when you left Jerusalem. ²⁰I know how much I sinned. That is why I have come here today, the very first person in all Israel* to greet you."

²¹Then Abishai son of Zeruiah said, "Shimei should die, for he cursed the LORD's anointed king!"

²²"What am I going to do with you sons of

Zeruiah!" David exclaimed. "This is not a day for execution but for celebration! I am once again the king of Israel!" 23Then, turning to Shimei, David vowed, "Your life will be spared."

David's Kindness to Mephibosheth

24Now Mephibosheth,* Saul's grandson, arrived from Jerusalem to meet the king. He had not washed his feet or clothes nor trimmed his beard since the day the king left Jerusalem. 25"Why didn't you come with me, Mephibosheth?" the king asked him.

26Mephibosheth replied, "My lord the king, my servant Ziba deceived me. I told him, 'Saddle my donkey so that I can go with the king.' For as you know I am crippled. 27Ziba has slandered me by saying that I refused to come. But I know that you are like an angel of God, so do what you think is best. 28All my relatives and I could expect only death from you, my lord, but instead you have honored me among those who eat at your own table! So how can I complain?"

29"All right," David replied. "My decision is that you and Ziba will divide your land equally between you."

30"Give him all of it," Mephibosheth said. "I am content just to have you back again, my lord!"

David's Kindness to Barzillai

31Barzillai of Gilead now arrived from Rogelim to conduct the king across the Jordan. 32He was very old, about eighty, and very wealthy. He was the one who had provided food for the king during his stay in Mahanaim. 33"Come across with me and live in Jerusalem," the king said to Barzillai. "I will take care of you there."

34"No," he replied, "I am far too old for that. 35I am eighty years old today, and I can no longer enjoy anything. Food and wine are no longer tasty, and I cannot hear the musicians as they play. I would only be a burden to my lord the king. 36Just to go across the river with you is all the honor I need! 37Then let me return again to die in my own town, where my father and mother are buried. But here is my son Kimham. Let him go with you and receive whatever good things you want to give him."

38"Good," the king agreed. "Kimham will go with me, and I will do for him whatever I would have done for you." 39So all the people crossed the Jordan with the king. After David had blessed and embraced him, Barzillai returned to his own home. 40The king then went on to Gilgal, taking Kimham with him. All the army of Judah and half the army of Israel escorted him across the river.

An Argument over the King

41But the men of Israel complained to the king that the men of Judah had gotten to do most of the work in helping him cross the Jordan. 42"Why not?" the men of Judah replied. "The king is one of our own tribe. Why should this make you angry? We have charged him nothing. And he hasn't fed us or even given us gifts!"

43"But there are ten tribes in Israel," the others replied. "So we have ten times as much right to the king as you do. Why did you treat us with such contempt? Remember, we were the first to speak of bringing him back to be our king again." The argument continued back and forth, and the men of Judah were very harsh in their replies.

CHAPTER 20
The Revolt of Sheba

Then a troublemaker named Sheba son of Bicri, a man from the tribe of Benjamin, blew a trumpet and shouted, "We have nothing to do with David. We want no part of this son of Jesse. Come on, you men of Israel, let's all go home!" 2So the men of Israel deserted David and followed Sheba. But the men of Judah stayed with their king and escorted him from the Jordan River to Jerusalem.

3When the king arrived at his palace in Jerusalem, he instructed that the ten concubines he had left to keep house should be placed in seclusion. Their needs were to be cared for, he said, but he would no longer sleep with them. So each of them lived like a widow until she died.

4Then the king instructed Amasa to mobilize the army of Judah within three days and to report back at that time. 5So Amasa went out to notify the troops, but it took him longer than the three days he had been given. 6Then David said to Abishai, "That troublemaker Sheba is going to hurt us more than Absalom did. Quick, take my troops and chase after him before he gets into a fortified city where we can't reach him."

7So Abishai and Joab set out after Sheba with an elite guard from Joab's army and the king's own bodyguard.* 8As they arrived at the great stone in Gibeon, Amasa met them, coming from the opposite direction. Joab was wearing his uniform with a dagger strapped to his belt. As he stepped forward to greet Amasa, he secretly slipped the dagger from its sheath. 9"How are

19:24 Also known as *Meribbaal*.   20:7 Hebrew *the Kerethites and Pelethites*; also in 20:23.

you, my cousin?" Joab said and took him by the beard with his right hand as though to kiss him. ¹⁰Amasa didn't notice the dagger in his left hand, and Joab stabbed him in the stomach with it so that his insides gushed out onto the ground. Joab did not need to strike again, and Amasa soon died. Joab and his brother Abishai left him lying there and continued after Sheba.

¹¹One of Joab's young officers shouted to Amasa's troops, "If you are for Joab and David, come and follow Joab." ¹²But Amasa lay in his blood in the middle of the road, and Joab's officer saw that a crowd was gathering around to stare at him. So he pulled him off the road into a field and threw a cloak over him. ¹³With Amasa's body out of the way, everyone went on with Joab to capture Sheba.

¹⁴Meanwhile, Sheba had traveled across Israel to mobilize his own clan of Bicri at the city of Abel-beth-maacah. ¹⁵When Joab's forces arrived, they attacked Abel-beth-maacah and built a ramp against the city wall and began battering it down. ¹⁶But a wise woman in the city called out to Joab, "Listen to me, Joab. Come over here so I can talk to you." ¹⁷As he approached, the woman asked, "Are you Joab?"

"I am," he replied.

So she said, "Listen carefully to your servant."

"I'm listening," he said.

¹⁸Then she continued, "There used to be a saying, 'If you want to settle an argument, ask advice at the city of Abel.' ¹⁹I am one who is peace loving and faithful in Israel. But you are destroying a loyal city. Why do you want to destroy what belongs to the LORD?"

²⁰And Joab replied, "Believe me, I don't want to destroy your city! ²¹All I want is a man named Sheba son of Bicri from the hill country of Ephraim, who has revolted against King David. If you hand him over to me, we will leave the city in peace."

"All right," the woman replied, "we will throw his head over the wall to you." ²²Then the woman went to the people with her wise advice, and they cut off Sheba's head and threw it out to Joab. So he blew the trumpet and called his troops back from the attack, and they all returned to their homes. Joab returned to the king at Jerusalem.

²³Joab once again became the commander of David's army. Benaiah son of Jehoiada was commander of the king's bodyguard. ²⁴Adoniram* was in charge of the labor force. Jehoshaphat son

of Ahilud was the royal historian. ²⁵Sheva was the court secretary. Zadok and Abiathar were the priests. ²⁶Ira the Jairite was David's personal priest.

CHAPTER 21

David Avenges the Gibeonites

There was a famine during David's reign that lasted for three years, so David asked the LORD about it. And the LORD said, "The famine has come because Saul and his family are guilty of murdering the Gibeonites."

²So King David summoned the Gibeonites. They were not part of Israel but were all that was left of the nation of the Amorites. Israel had sworn not to kill them, but Saul, in his zeal, had tried to wipe them out. ³David asked them, "What can I do for you to make amends? Tell me so that the LORD will bless his people again."

⁴"Well, money won't do it," the Gibeonites replied. "And we don't want to see the Israelites executed in revenge."

"What can I do then?" David asked. "Just tell me and I will do it for you."

⁵Then they replied, "It was Saul who planned to destroy us, to keep us from having any place at all in Israel. ⁶So let seven of Saul's sons or grandsons be handed over to us, and we will execute them before the LORD at Gibeon, on the mountain of the LORD.*"

"All right," the king said, "I will do it." ⁷David spared Jonathan's son Mephibosheth,* who was Saul's grandson, because of the oath David and Jonathan had sworn before the LORD. ⁸But he gave them Saul's two sons Armoni and Mephibosheth, whose mother was Rizpah daughter of Aiah. He also gave them the five sons of Saul's daughter Merab,* the wife of Adriel son of Barzillai from Meholah. ⁹The men of Gibeon executed them on the mountain before the LORD. So all seven of them died together at the beginning of the barley harvest.

¹⁰Then Rizpah, the mother of two of the men, spread sackcloth on a rock and stayed there the entire harvest season. She prevented vultures from tearing at their bodies during the day and stopped wild animals from eating them at night. ¹¹When David learned what Rizpah, Saul's concubine, had done, ¹²he went to the people of Jabesh-gilead and asked for the bones of Saul and his son Jonathan. (When Saul and Jonathan had died in a battle with the Philistines, it was

20:24 As in Greek version (see also 1 Kgs 4:6; 5:14); Hebrew reads *Adoram*. 21:6 As in Greek version (see also 21:9); Hebrew reads *at Gibeah of Saul, the chosen of the LORD*. 21:7 Also known as *Meribbaal*. 21:8 As in a few Hebrew and Greek manuscripts and Syriac version (see also 1 Sam 18:19); most Hebrew manuscripts read *Michal*.

the people of Jabesh-gilead who had retrieved their bodies from the public square of the Philistine city of Beth-shan.) ¹³So David brought the bones of Saul and Jonathan, as well as the bones of the men the Gibeonites had executed. ¹⁴He buried them all in the tomb of Kish, Saul's father, at the town of Zela in the land of Benjamin. After that, God ended the famine in the land of Israel.

Battles against Philistine Giants

¹⁵Once again the Philistines were at war with Israel. And when David and his men were in the thick of battle, David became weak and exhausted. ¹⁶Ishbi-benob was a descendant of the giants*; his bronze spearhead weighed more than seven pounds,* and he was armed with a new sword. He had cornered David and was about to kill him. ¹⁷But Abishai son of Zeruiah came to his rescue and killed the Philistine. After that, David's men declared, "You are not going out to battle again! Why should we risk snuffing out the light of Israel?"

¹⁸After this, there was another battle against the Philistines at Gob. As they fought, Sibbecai from Hushah killed Saph, another descendant of the giants. ¹⁹In still another battle at Gob, Elhanan son of Jair* from Bethlehem killed the brother of Goliath of Gath.* The handle of his spear was as thick as a weaver's beam! ²⁰In another battle with the Philistines at Gath, a huge man with six fingers on each hand and six toes on each foot—a descendant of the giants—²¹defied and taunted Israel. But he was killed by Jonathan, the son of David's brother Shimea.* ²²These four Philistines were descended from the giants of Gath, but they were killed by David and his warriors.

CHAPTER **22**
David's Song of Praise

David sang this song to the LORD after the LORD had rescued him from all his enemies and from Saul. ²These are the words he sang:

"The LORD is my rock, my fortress, and my
savior;
³   my God is my rock, in whom I find
protection.
He is my shield, the strength of my
salvation, and my stronghold,

my high tower, my savior, the one who
saves me from violence.
⁴ I will call on the LORD, who is worthy of
praise,
for he saves me from my enemies.

⁵ "The waves of death surrounded me;
the floods of destruction swept over me.
⁶ The grave* wrapped its ropes around me;
death itself stared me in the face.
⁷ But in my distress I cried out to the LORD;
yes, I called to my God for help.
He heard me from his sanctuary;
my cry reached his ears.

⁸ "Then the earth quaked and trembled;
the foundations of the heavens shook;
they quaked because of his anger.
⁹ Smoke poured from his nostrils;
fierce flames leaped from his mouth;
glowing coals flamed forth from him.
¹⁰ He opened the heavens and came down;
dark storm clouds were beneath his feet.
¹¹ Mounted on a mighty angel,* he flew,
soaring* on the wings of the wind.
¹² He shrouded himself in darkness,
veiling his approach with dense rain
clouds.
¹³ A great brightness shone before him,
and bolts of lightning blazed forth.
¹⁴ The LORD thundered from heaven;
the Most High gave a mighty shout.
¹⁵ He shot his arrows and scattered his
enemies;
his lightning flashed, and they were
confused.
¹⁶ Then at the command of the LORD,
at the blast of his breath,
the bottom of the sea could be seen,
and the foundations of the earth were
laid bare.

¹⁷ "He reached down from heaven and
rescued me;
he drew me out of deep waters.
¹⁸ He delivered me from my powerful enemies,
from those who hated me and were too
strong for me.
¹⁹ They attacked me at a moment when I was
weakest,
but the LORD upheld me.
²⁰ He led me to a place of safety;
he rescued me because he delights in me.

21:16a As in Greek version; Hebrew reads *a descendant of the Rephaites*; also in 21:18, 20, 22.   21:16b Hebrew *300 shekels* [3.4 kilograms].   21:19a As in parallel text at 1 Chr 20:5; Hebrew reads *son of Jaare-oregim.*   21:19b As in parallel text at 1 Chr 20:5; Hebrew reads *killed Goliath of Gath.*   21:21 As in parallel text at 1 Chr 20:7; Hebrew reads *Shimei,* a variant name for Shimea.   22:6 Hebrew *Sheol.*   22:11a Hebrew *cherub.*   22:11b As in some Hebrew manuscripts (see also Ps 18:10); other Hebrew manuscripts read *appearing.*

21 The LORD rewarded me for doing right;
    he compensated me because of my
      innocence.
22 For I have kept the ways of the LORD;
    I have not turned from my God to follow
      evil.
23 For all his laws are constantly before me;
    I have never abandoned his principles.
24 I am blameless before God;
    I have kept myself from sin.
25 The LORD rewarded me for doing right,
    because of my innocence in his sight.

26 "To the faithful you show yourself faithful;
    to those with integrity you show integrity.
27 To the pure you show yourself pure,
    but to the wicked you show yourself hostile.
28 You rescue those who are humble,
    but your eyes are on the proud to
      humiliate them.
29 O LORD, you are my light;
    yes, LORD, you light up my darkness.
30 In your strength I can crush an army;
    with my God I can scale any wall.

31 "As for God, his way is perfect.
    All the LORD's promises prove true.
    He is a shield for all who look to him for
      protection.
32 For who is God except the LORD?
    Who but our God is a solid rock?
33 God is my strong fortress;
    he has made my way safe.
34 He makes me as surefooted as a deer,
    leading me safely along the mountain
      heights.
35 He prepares me for battle;
    he strengthens me to draw a bow of bronze.
36 You have given me the shield of your
      salvation;
    your help* has made me great.
37 You have made a wide path for my feet
    to keep them from slipping.

38 "I chased my enemies and destroyed them;
    I did not stop until they were conquered.
39 I consumed them; I struck them down so
      they could not get up;
    they fell beneath my feet.
40 You have armed me with strength for the
      battle;
    you have subdued my enemies under my
      feet.
41 You made them turn and run;
    I have destroyed all who hated me.

42 They called for help, but no one came to
      rescue them.
    They cried to the LORD, but he refused to
      answer them.
43 I ground them as fine as the dust of the
      earth;
    I swept them into the gutter like dirt.

44 "You gave me victory over my accusers.
    You preserved me as the ruler over
      nations;
    people I don't even know now serve me.
45 Foreigners cringe before me;
    as soon as they hear of me, they submit.
46 They all lose their courage
    and come trembling from their
      strongholds.

47 "The LORD lives! Blessed be my rock!
    May God, the rock of my salvation, be
      exalted!
48 He is the God who pays back those who
      harm me;
    he subdues the nations under me
49   and rescues me from my enemies.
    You hold me safe beyond the reach of my
      enemies;
    you save me from violent opponents.
50 For this, O LORD, I will praise you among
      the nations;
    I will sing joyfully to your name.
51 You give great victories to your king;
    you show unfailing love to your anointed,
    to David and all his descendants forever."

CHAPTER 23

David's Last Words
These are the last words of David:

"David, the son of Jesse, speaks—
    David, the man to whom God gave such
      wonderful success,
David, the man anointed by the God of
      Jacob,
    David, the sweet psalmist of Israel.

2 "The Spirit of the LORD speaks through me;
    his words are upon my tongue.
3 The God of Israel spoke.
    The Rock of Israel said to me:
    'The person who rules righteously,
    who rules in the fear of God,
4 he is like the light of the morning,
    like the sunrise bursting forth in a
      cloudless sky,

22:36 As in Dead Sea Scrolls; most Hebrew manuscripts read *your answering.*

like the refreshing rains that bring tender
grass from the earth.'

5 "It is my family God has chosen!
Yes, he has made an everlasting covenant
with me.
His agreement is eternal, final, sealed.
He will constantly look after my safety
and success.
6 But the godless are like thorns to be thrown
away,
for they tear the hand that touches them.
7 One must be armed to chop them down;
they will be utterly consumed with fire."

David's Mightiest Men

8These are the names of David's mightiest men. The
first was Jashobeam the Hacmonite,* who was commander of the Three—the three greatest warriors
among David's men. He once used his spear to kill
eight hundred enemy warriors in a single battle.*
9Next in rank among the Three was Eleazar
son of Dodai, a descendant of Ahoah. Once Eleazar and David stood together against the Philistines when the entire Israelite army had fled. 10He
killed Philistines until his hand was too tired to
lift his sword, and the LORD gave him a great
victory that day. The rest of the army did not
return until it was time to collect the plunder!
11Next in rank was Shammah son of Agee
from Harar. One time the Philistines gathered at
Lehi and attacked the Israelites in a field full of
lentils. The Israelite army fled, 12but Shammah
held his ground in the middle of the field and
beat back the Philistines. So the LORD brought
about a great victory.
13Once during harvesttime, when David was at
the cave of Adullam, the Philistine army was
camped in the valley of Rephaim. The Three (who
were among the Thirty—an elite group among
David's fighting men) went down to meet him
there. 14David was staying in the stronghold at the
time, and a Philistine detachment had occupied
the town of Bethlehem. 15David remarked longingly to his men, "Oh, how I would love some of
that good water from the well in Bethlehem, the
one by the gate." 16So the Three broke through the
Philistine lines, drew some water from the well,
and brought it back to David. But he refused to

drink it. Instead, he poured it out before the LORD.
17"The LORD forbid that I should drink this!" he
exclaimed. "This water is as precious as the blood
of these men who risked their lives to bring it to
me." So David did not drink it. This is an example
of the exploits of the Three.

David's Thirty Mighty Men

18Abishai son of Zeruiah, the brother of Joab,
was the leader of the Thirty.* He once used his
spear to kill three hundred enemy warriors in a
single battle. It was by such feats that he became
as famous as the Three. 19Abishai was the most
famous of the Thirty* and was their commander, though he was not one of the Three.
20There was also Benaiah son of Jehoiada, a
valiant warrior from Kabzeel. He did many heroic deeds, which included killing two of Moab's
mightiest warriors. Another time he chased a
lion down into a pit. Then, despite the snow and
slippery ground, he caught the lion and killed it.
21Another time, armed only with a club, he
killed a great Egyptian warrior who was armed
with a spear. Benaiah wrenched the spear from
the Egyptian's hand and killed him with it.
22These are some of the deeds that made Benaiah almost as famous as the Three. 23He was
more honored than the other members of the
Thirty, though he was not one of the Three. And
David made him commander of his bodyguard.
24Other members of the Thirty included:

Asahel, Joab's brother;
Elhanan son of Dodo from Bethlehem;
25 Shammah from Harod;
Elika from Harod;
26 Helez from Pelon*;
Ira son of Ikkesh from Tekoa;
27 Abiezer from Anathoth;
Sibbecai* from Hushah;
28 Zalmon from Ahoah;
Maharai from Netophah;
29 Heled* son of Baanah from Netophah;
Ithai* son of Ribai from Gibeah (from the
tribe of Benjamin);
30 Benaiah from Pirathon;
Hurai* from Nahale-gaash*;
31 Abi-albon the Arbathite;
Azmaveth from Bahurim;

23:8a As in parallel text at 1 Chr 11:11; Hebrew reads *Josheb-basshebeth the Tahkemonite.*   23:8b As in some Greek manuscripts (see also
1 Chr 11:11); the Hebrew is uncertain, though it might be rendered *the Three. It was Adino the Eznite who killed eight hundred men at one
time.*   23:18 As in a few Hebrew manuscripts and Syriac version; most Hebrew manuscripts read *the Three.*   23:19 As in Syriac version;
Hebrew reads *the Three.*   23:26 As in parallel text at 1 Chr 11:27 (see also 1 Chr 27:10); Hebrew reads *from Palti.*   23:27 As in some Greek
manuscripts (see also 1 Chr 11:29); Hebrew reads *Mebunnai.*   23:29a As in some Hebrew manuscripts (see also 1 Chr 11:30); most Hebrew
manuscripts read *Heleb.*   23:29b As in parallel text at 1 Chr 11:31; Hebrew reads *Ittai.*   23:30a As in some Greek manuscripts (see also
1 Chr 11:32); Hebrew reads *Hiddai.*   23:30b Or *from the ravines of Gaash.*

³² Eliahba from Shaalbon;
the sons of Jashen;
³³ Jonathan son of Shagee* from Harar;
Ahiam son of Sharar from Harar;
³⁴ Eliphelet son of Ahasbai from Maacah;
Eliam son of Ahithophel from Giloh;
³⁵ Hezro from Carmel;
Paarai from Arba;
³⁶ Igal son of Nathan from Zobah;
Bani from Gad;
³⁷ Zelek from Ammon;
Naharai from Beeroth (Joab's armor bearer);
³⁸ Ira from Jattir;
Gareb from Jattir;
³⁹ Uriah the Hittite.

There were thirty-seven in all.

CHAPTER 24

David Takes a Census

Once again the anger of the LORD burned against Israel, and he caused David to harm them by taking a census. "Go and count the people of Israel and Judah," the LORD told him.

²So the king said to Joab, the commander of his army, "Take a census of all the people in the land—from Dan in the north to Beersheba in the south—so that I may know how many people there are."

³But Joab replied to the king, "May the LORD your God let you live until there are a hundred times as many people in your kingdom as there are now! But why do you want to do this?"

⁴But the king insisted that they take the census, so Joab and his officers went out to count the people of Israel. ⁵First they crossed the Jordan and camped at Aroer, south of the town in the valley, in the direction of Gad. Then they went on to Jazer, ⁶then to Gilead in the land of Tahtim-hodshi* and to Dan-jaan and around to Sidon. ⁷Then they came to the stronghold of Tyre, and all the cities of the Hivites and Canaanites. Finally, they went south to Judah as far as Beersheba. ⁸Having gone through the entire land, they completed their task in nine months and twenty days and then returned to Jerusalem. ⁹Joab reported the number of people to the king. There were 800,000 men of military age in Israel and 500,000 in Judah.

Judgment for David's Sin

¹⁰But after he had taken the census, David's conscience began to bother him. And he said to the LORD, "I have sinned greatly and shouldn't have taken the census. Please forgive me, LORD, for doing this foolish thing."

¹¹The next morning the word of the LORD came to the prophet Gad, who was David's seer. This was the message: ¹²"Go and say to David, 'This is what the LORD says: I will give you three choices. Choose one of these punishments, and I will do it.'"

¹³So Gad came to David and asked him, "Will you choose three* years of famine throughout the land, three months of fleeing from your enemies, or three days of severe plague throughout your land? Think this over and let me know what answer to give the LORD."

¹⁴"This is a desperate situation!" David replied to Gad. "But let us fall into the hands of the LORD, for his mercy is great. Do not let me fall into human hands."

¹⁵So the LORD sent a plague upon Israel that morning, and it lasted for three days. Seventy thousand people died throughout the nation. ¹⁶But as the death angel was preparing to destroy Jerusalem, the LORD relented and said to the angel, "Stop! That is enough!" At that moment the angel of the LORD was by the threshing floor of Araunah the Jebusite.

¹⁷When David saw the angel, he said to the LORD, "I am the one who has sinned and done wrong! But these people are innocent—what have they done? Let your anger fall against me and my family."

David Builds an Altar

¹⁸That day Gad came to David and said to him, "Go and build an altar to the LORD on the threshing floor of Araunah the Jebusite."

¹⁹So David went to do what the LORD had commanded him. ²⁰When Araunah saw the king and his men coming toward him, he came forward and bowed before the king with his face to the ground. ²¹"Why have you come, my lord?" Araunah asked.

And David replied, "I have come to buy your threshing floor and to build an altar to the LORD there, so that the LORD will stop the plague."

²²"Take it, my lord, and use it as you wish," Araunah said to David. "Here are oxen for the burnt offering, and you can use the threshing tools and ox yokes for wood to build a fire on the altar. ²³I will give it all to you, and may the LORD your God accept your sacrifice."

23:33 As in parallel text at 1 Chr 11:34; Hebrew reads *Jonathan, Shammah*; some Greek manuscripts read *Jonathan son of Shammah*.
24:6 Greek version reads *to Gilead and to Kadesh in the land of the Hittites*. 24:13 As in Greek version (see also 1 Chr 21:12); Hebrew reads *seven*.

24But the king replied to Araunah, "No, I insist on buying it, for I cannot present burnt offerings to the LORD my God that have cost me nothing." So David paid him fifty pieces of silver* for the threshing floor and the oxen. 25David built an altar there to the LORD and offered burnt offerings and peace offerings. And the LORD answered his prayer, and the plague was stopped.

24:24 Hebrew *50 shekels of silver,* about 20 ounces or 570 grams in weight.

1 Kings

CHAPTER 1

David in His Old Age

Now King David was very old, and no matter how many blankets covered him, he could not keep warm. 2So his advisers told him, "We will find a young virgin who will wait on you and be your nurse. She will lie in your arms and keep you warm." 3So they searched throughout the country for a beautiful girl, and they found Abishag from Shunem and brought her to the king. 4The girl was very beautiful, and she waited on the king and took care of him. But the king had no sexual relations with her.

Adonijah Claims the Throne

5About that time David's son Adonijah, whose mother was Haggith, decided to make himself king in place of his aged father. So he provided himself with chariots and horses* and recruited fifty men to run in front of him. 6Now his father, King David, had never disciplined him at any time, even by asking, "What are you doing?" Adonijah was a very handsome man and had been born next after Absalom. 7Adonijah took Joab son of Zeruiah and Abiathar the priest into his confidence, and they agreed to help him become king. 8But among those who remained loyal to David and refused to support Adonijah were Zadok the priest, Benaiah son of Jehoiada, Nathan the prophet, Shimei, Rei, and David's personal bodyguard.

9Adonijah went to the stone of Zoheleth* near the spring of En-rogel, where he sacrificed sheep, oxen, and fattened calves. He invited all his brothers—the other sons of King David—and all the royal officials of Judah. 10But he did not invite Nathan the prophet, or Benaiah, or the king's bodyguard, or his brother Solomon.

11Then Nathan the prophet went to Bathsheba, Solomon's mother, and asked her, "Did you realize that Haggith's son, Adonijah, has made himself king and that our lord David doesn't even know about it? 12If you want to save your own life and the life of your son Solomon, follow my counsel. 13Go at once to King David and say to him, 'My lord, didn't you promise me that my son Solomon would be the next king and would sit upon your throne? Then why has Adonijah become king?' 14And while you are still talking with him, I will come and confirm everything you have said."

15So Bathsheba went into the king's bedroom. He was very old now, and Abishag was taking care of him. 16Bathsheba bowed low before him.

"What can I do for you?" he asked her.

17She replied, "My lord, you vowed to me by the LORD your God that my son Solomon would be the next king and would sit on your throne. 18But instead, Adonijah has become the new king, and you do not even know about it. 19He has sacrificed many oxen, fattened calves, and sheep, and he has invited all your sons and Abiathar the priest and Joab, the commander of the army. But he did not invite your servant Solomon. 20And now, my lord the king, all Israel is waiting for your decision as to who will become king after you. 21If you do not act, my son Solomon and I will be treated as criminals as soon as you are dead."

22While she was still speaking with the king, Nathan the prophet arrived. 23The king's advisers told him, "Nathan the prophet is here to see you."

Nathan went in and bowed low before the king. 24He asked, "My lord, have you decided that Adonijah will be the next king and that he will sit on your throne? 25Today he has sacrificed

1:5 Or *and chariateers.*   1:9 Or *to the Serpent's Stone;* Greek version supports reading *Zoheleth* as a proper name.

many oxen, fattened calves, and sheep, and he has invited your sons to attend the celebration. He also invited Joab, the commander of the army,* and Abiathar the priest. They are feasting and drinking with him and shouting, 'Long live King Adonijah!' 26But I myself, your servant, was not invited; neither were Zadok the priest, Benaiah son of Jehoiada, nor Solomon. 27Has my lord really done this without letting any of his servants know who should be the next king?"

David Makes Solomon King

28"Call Bathsheba," David said. So she came back in and stood before the king. 29And the king vowed, "As surely as the LORD lives, who has rescued me from every danger, 30today I decree that your son Solomon will be the next king and will sit on my throne, just as I swore to you before the LORD, the God of Israel."

31Then Bathsheba bowed low before him again and exclaimed, "May my lord King David live forever!"

32Then King David ordered, "Call Zadok the priest, Nathan the prophet, and Benaiah son of Jehoiada." When they came into the king's presence, 33the king said to them, "Take Solomon and my officers down to Gihon Spring. Solomon is to ride on my personal mule. 34There Zadok the priest and Nathan the prophet are to anoint him king over Israel. Then blow the trumpets and shout, 'Long live King Solomon!' 35When you bring him back here, he will sit on my throne. He will succeed me as king, for I have appointed him to be ruler over Israel and Judah."

36"Amen!" Benaiah son of Jehoiada replied. "May the LORD, the God of my lord the king, decree it to be so. 37And may the LORD be with Solomon as he has been with you, and may he make Solomon's reign even greater than yours!"

38So Zadok the priest, Nathan the prophet, Benaiah son of Jehoiada, and the king's bodyguard* took Solomon down to Gihon Spring, and Solomon rode on King David's personal mule. 39There Zadok the priest took a flask of olive oil from the sacred tent and poured it on Solomon's head. Then the trumpets were blown, and all the people shouted, "Long live King Solomon!" 40And all the people returned with Solomon to Jerusalem, playing flutes and shouting for joy. The celebration was so joyous and noisy that the earth shook with the sound.

41Adonijah and his guests heard the celebrating and shouting just as they were finishing their banquet. When Joab heard the sound of trumpets, he asked, "What's going on? Why is the city in such an uproar?"

42And while he was still speaking, Jonathan son of Abiathar the priest arrived. "Come in," Adonijah said to him, "for you are a good man. You must have good news."

43"Not at all!" Jonathan replied. "Our lord King David has just declared Solomon king! 44The king sent him down to Gihon Spring with Zadok the priest, Nathan the prophet, and Benaiah son of Jehoiada, protected by the king's bodyguard. They had him ride on the king's own mule, 45and Zadok and Nathan have anointed him as the new king. They have just returned, and the whole city is celebrating and rejoicing. That's what all the noise is about. 46Moreover, Solomon is now sitting on the royal throne as king. 47All the royal officials went to King David and congratulated him, saying, 'May your God make Solomon's fame even greater than your own, and may Solomon's kingdom be even greater than yours!' Then the king bowed his head in worship as he lay in his bed, 48and he spoke these words: 'Blessed be the LORD, the God of Israel, who today has chosen someone to sit on my throne while I am still alive to see it.'"

49Then all of Adonijah's guests jumped up in panic from the banquet table and quickly went their separate ways. 50Adonijah himself was afraid of Solomon, so he rushed to the sacred tent and caught hold of the horns of the altar. 51Word soon reached Solomon that Adonijah had seized the horns of the altar and that he was pleading, "Let Solomon swear today that he will not kill me!"

52Solomon replied, "If he proves himself to be loyal, he will not be harmed.* But if he does not, he will die." 53So King Solomon summoned Adonijah, and they brought him down from the altar. He came and bowed low before the king, and Solomon dismissed him, saying, "Go on home."

CHAPTER 2

David's Final Instructions to Solomon

As the time of King David's death approached, he gave this charge to his son Solomon: 2"I am going where everyone on earth must someday go. Take courage and be a man. 3Observe the requirements of the LORD your God and follow all his ways. Keep each of the laws, commands, regulations, and stipulations written in the law

---

1:25 As in Greek version; Hebrew reads *invited the commanders of the army.*   1:38 Hebrew *the Kerethites and Pelethites;* also in 1:44.
1:52 Hebrew *not a hair on his head will be touched.*

of Moses so that you will be successful in all you do and wherever you go. 4If you do this, then the LORD will keep the promise he made to me: 'If your descendants live as they should and follow me faithfully with all their heart and soul, one of them will always sit on the throne of Israel.'

5"And there is something else. You know that Joab son of Zeruiah murdered my two army commanders, Abner son of Ner and Amasa son of Jether. He pretended that it was an act of war, but it was done in a time of peace,* staining his belt and sandals with the blood of war. 6Do with him what you think best, but don't let him die in peace.

7"Be kind to the sons of Barzillai of Gilead. Make them permanent guests of the king, for they took care of me when I fled from your brother Absalom.

8"And remember Shimei son of Gera, the man from Bahurim in Benjamin. He cursed me with a terrible curse as I was fleeing to Mahanaim. When he came down to meet me at the Jordan River, I swore by the LORD that I would not kill him. 9But that oath does not make him innocent. You are a wise man, and you will know how to arrange a bloody death for him."

10Then David died and was buried in the City of David. 11He had reigned over Israel for forty years, seven of them in Hebron and thirty-three in Jerusalem. 12Solomon succeeded him as king, replacing his father, David, and he was firmly established on the throne.

Solomon Establishes His Rule

13One day Adonijah, whose mother was Haggith, came to see Bathsheba, Solomon's mother. "Have you come to make trouble?" she asked him.

"No," he said, "I come in peace. 14In fact, I have a favor to ask of you."

"What is it?" she asked.

15He replied, "As you know, the kingdom was mine; everyone expected me to be the next king. But the tables were turned, and everything went to my brother instead; for that is the way the LORD wanted it. 16So now I have just one favor to ask of you. Please don't turn me down."

"What is it?" she asked.

17He replied, "Speak to King Solomon on my behalf, for I know he will do anything you request. Ask him to give me Abishag, the girl from Shunem, as my wife."

18"All right," Bathsheba replied. "I will speak to the king for you."

19So Bathsheba went to King Solomon to speak on Adonijah's behalf. The king rose from his throne to meet her, and he bowed down before her. When he sat down on his throne again, he ordered that a throne be brought for his mother, and she sat at his right hand.

20"I have one small request to make of you," she said. "I hope you won't turn me down."

"What is it, my mother?" he asked. "You know I won't refuse you."

21"Then let your brother Adonijah marry Abishag, the girl from Shunem," she replied.

22"How can you possibly ask me to give Abishag to Adonijah?" Solomon demanded. "You might as well be asking me to give him the kingdom! You know that he is my older brother, and that he has Abiathar the priest and Joab son of Zeruiah on his side." 23Then King Solomon swore solemnly by the LORD: "May God strike me dead if Adonijah has not sealed his fate with this request. 24The LORD has confirmed me and placed me on the throne of my father, David; he has established my dynasty as he promised. So as surely as the LORD lives, Adonijah will die this very day!" 25So King Solomon ordered Benaiah son of Jehoiada to execute him, and Adonijah was put to death.

26Then the king said to Abiathar the priest, "Go back to your home in Anathoth. You deserve to die, but I will not kill you now, because you carried the Ark of the Sovereign LORD for my father, and you suffered right along with him through all his troubles." 27So Solomon deposed Abiathar from his position as priest of the LORD, thereby fulfilling the decree the LORD had made at Shiloh concerning the descendants of Eli.

28Although he had not followed Absalom earlier, Joab had also joined Adonijah's revolt. When Joab heard about Adonijah's death, he ran to the sacred tent of the LORD and caught hold of the horns of the altar. 29When news of this reached King Solomon, he sent Benaiah son of Jehoiada to execute him.

30Benaiah went into the sacred tent of the LORD and said to Joab, "The king orders you to come out!"

But Joab answered, "No, I will die here."

So Benaiah returned to the king and told him what Joab had said.

31"Do as he said," the king replied. "Kill him there beside the altar and bury him. This will remove the guilt of his senseless murders from me and from my father's family. 32Then the LORD

2:5 Or *He murdered them during a time of peace as revenge for deaths they had caused in time of war.*

will repay him for the murders of two men who were more righteous and better than he. For my father was no party to the deaths of Abner son of Ner, commander of the army of Israel, and Amasa son of Jether, commander of the army of Judah. 33May Joab and his descendants be forever guilty of these murders, and may the LORD grant peace to David and his descendants and to his throne forever."

34So Benaiah son of Jehoiada returned to the sacred tent and killed Joab, and Joab was buried at his home in the wilderness. 35Then the king appointed Benaiah to command the army in place of Joab, and he installed Zadok the priest to take the place of Abiathar.

36The king then sent for Shimei and told him, "Build a house here in Jerusalem and live there. But don't step outside the city to go anywhere else. 37On the day you cross the Kidron Valley, you will surely die; your blood will be on your own head."

38Shimei replied, "Your sentence is fair; I will do whatever my lord the king commands." So Shimei lived in Jerusalem for a long time.

39But three years later, two of Shimei's slaves escaped to King Achish of Gath. When Shimei learned where they were, 40he saddled his donkey and went to Gath to search for them. When he had found them, he took them back to Jerusalem.

41Solomon heard that Shimei had left Jerusalem and had gone to Gath and returned. 42So he sent for Shimei and demanded, "Didn't I make you swear by the LORD and warn you not to go anywhere else, or you would surely die? And you replied, 'The sentence is fair; I will do as you say.' 43Then why haven't you kept your oath to the LORD and obeyed my command?"

44The king also said to Shimei, "You surely remember all the wicked things you did to my father, King David. May the LORD punish you for them. 45But may I receive the LORD's rich blessings, and may one of David's descendants always sit on this throne." 46Then, at the king's command, Benaiah son of Jehoiada took Shimei outside and killed him.

So the kingdom was now firmly in Solomon's grip.

CHAPTER 3
Solomon Asks for Wisdom

Solomon made an alliance with Pharaoh, the king of Egypt, and married one of his daughters. He brought her to live in the City of David until he could finish building his palace and the Temple of the LORD and the wall around the city. 2At that time the people of Israel sacrificed their offerings at local altars, for a temple honoring the name of the LORD had not yet been built.

3Solomon loved the LORD and followed all the instructions of his father, David, except that Solomon, too, offered sacrifices and burned incense at the local altars. 4The most important of these altars was at Gibeon, so the king went there and sacrificed one thousand burnt offerings. 5That night the LORD appeared to Solomon in a dream, and God said, "What do you want? Ask, and I will give it to you!"

6Solomon replied, "You were wonderfully kind to my father, David, because he was honest and true and faithful to you. And you have continued this great kindness to him today by giving him a son to succeed him. 7O LORD my God, now you have made me king instead of my father, David, but I am like a little child who doesn't know his way around. 8And here I am among your own chosen people, a nation so great they are too numerous to count! 9Give me an understanding mind so that I can govern your people well and know the difference between right and wrong. For who by himself is able to govern this great nation of yours?"

10The Lord was pleased with Solomon's reply and was glad that he had asked for wisdom. 11So God replied, "Because you have asked for wisdom in governing my people and have not asked for a long life or riches for yourself or the death of your enemies—12I will give you what you asked for! I will give you a wise and understanding mind such as no one else has ever had or ever will have! 13And I will also give you what you did not ask for—riches and honor! No other king in all the world will be compared to you for the rest of your life! 14And if you follow me and obey my commands as your father, David, did, I will give you a long life."

15Then Solomon woke up and realized it had been a dream. He returned to Jerusalem and stood before the Ark of the Lord's covenant, where he sacrificed burnt offerings and peace offerings. Then he invited all his officials to a great banquet.

Solomon Judges Wisely

16Some time later, two prostitutes came to the king to have an argument settled. 17"Please, my lord," one of them began, "this woman and I live in the same house. I gave birth to a baby while she was with me in the house. 18Three days later, she also had a baby. We were alone;

there were only two of us in the house. ¹⁹But her baby died during the night when she rolled over on it. ²⁰Then she got up in the night and took my son from beside me while I was asleep. She laid her dead child in my arms and took mine to sleep beside her. ²¹And in the morning when I tried to nurse my son, he was dead! But when I looked more closely in the morning light, I saw that it wasn't my son at all."

²²Then the other woman interrupted, "It certainly was your son, and the living child is mine."

"No," the first woman said, "the dead one is yours, and the living one is mine." And so they argued back and forth before the king.

²³Then the king said, "Let's get the facts straight. Both of you claim the living child is yours, and each says that the dead child belongs to the other. ²⁴All right, bring me a sword." So a sword was brought to the king. ²⁵Then he said, "Cut the living child in two and give half to each of these women!"

²⁶Then the woman who really was the mother of the living child, and who loved him very much, cried out, "Oh no, my lord! Give her the child—please do not kill him!"

But the other woman said, "All right, he will be neither yours nor mine; divide him between us!"

²⁷Then the king said, "Do not kill him, but give the baby to the woman who wants him to live, for she is his mother!"

²⁸Word of the king's decision spread quickly throughout all Israel, and the people were awed as they realized the great wisdom God had given him to render decisions with justice.

CHAPTER **4**
Solomon's Officials and Governors
So Solomon was king over all Israel, ²and these were his high officials:

Azariah son of Zadok was the priest.
³ Elihoreph and Ahijah, the sons of Shisha, were court secretaries.
Jehoshaphat son of Ahilud was the royal historian.
⁴ Benaiah son of Jehoiada was commander of the army.
Zadok and Abiathar were the priests.
⁵ Azariah son of Nathan presided over the district governors.

Zabud son of Nathan, a priest, was a trusted adviser to the king.
⁶ Ahishar was manager of palace affairs.
Adoniram son of Abda was in charge of the labor force.

⁷Solomon also had twelve district governors who were over all Israel. They were responsible for providing food from the people for the king's household. Each of them arranged provisions for one month of the year.

⁸These are the names of the twelve governors:

Ben-hur, in the hill country of Ephraim.
⁹ Ben-deker, in Makaz, Shaalbim, Beth-shemesh, and Elon-bethhanan.
¹⁰ Ben-hesed, in Arubboth, including Socoh and all the land of Hepher.
¹¹ Ben-abinadab, in Naphoth-dor.* (He was married to Taphath, one of Solomon's daughters.)
¹² Baana son of Ahilud, in Taanach and Megiddo, all of Beth-shan* near Zarethan below Jezreel, and all the territory from Beth-shan to Abel-meholah and over to Jokmeam.
¹³ Ben-geber, in Ramoth-gilead, including the Towns of Jair (named for Jair son of Manasseh) in Gilead, and in the Argob region of Bashan, including sixty great fortified cities with gates barred with bronze.
¹⁴ Ahinadab son of Iddo, in Mahanaim.
¹⁵ Ahimaaz, in Naphtali. (He was married to Basemath, another of Solomon's daughters.)
¹⁶ Baana son of Hushai, in Asher and in Aloth.
¹⁷ Jehoshaphat son of Paruah, in Issachar.
¹⁸ Shimei son of Ela, in Benjamin.
¹⁹ Geber son of Uri, in the land of Gilead,* including the territories of King Sihon of the Amorites and King Og of Bashan.

And there was one governor over the land of Judah.*

Solomon's Prosperity and Wisdom
²⁰The people of Judah and Israel were as numerous as the sand on the seashore. They were very contented, with plenty to eat and drink. ²¹King Solomon ruled all the kingdoms from the Euphrates River* to the land of the Philistines, as far south as the border of Egypt. The conquered peoples of those lands sent tribute money to

4:11 Hebrew *Naphath-dor,* a variant name for Naphoth-dor. 4:12 Hebrew *Beth-shean,* a variant name for Beth-shan; also in 4:12b. 4:19a Greek version reads *of Gad;* compare 4:13. 4:19b As in some Greek manuscripts; Hebrew lacks *of Judah.* The meaning of the Hebrew is uncertain. 4:21 Hebrew *the river;* also in 4:24.

Solomon and continued to serve him throughout his lifetime.

22The daily food requirements for Solomon's palace were 150 bushels of choice flour and 300 bushels of meal,* 23ten oxen from the fattening pens, twenty pasture-fed cattle, one hundred sheep or goats, as well as deer, gazelles, roebucks, and choice fowl.

24Solomon's dominion extended over all the kingdoms west of the Euphrates River, from Tiphsah to Gaza. And there was peace throughout the entire land. 25Throughout the lifetime of Solomon, all of Judah and Israel lived in peace and safety. And from Dan to Beersheba, each family had its own home and garden.

26Solomon had four thousand* stalls for his chariot horses and twelve thousand horses.* 27The district governors faithfully provided food for King Solomon and his court, each during his assigned month. 28They also brought the necessary barley and straw for the royal horses in the stables.

29God gave Solomon great wisdom and understanding, and knowledge too vast to be measured. 30In fact, his wisdom exceeded that of all the wise men of the East and the wise men of Egypt. 31He was wiser than anyone else, including Ethan the Ezrahite and Heman, Calcol, and Darda—the sons of Mahol. His fame spread throughout all the surrounding nations. 32He composed some 3,000 proverbs and wrote 1,005 songs. 33He could speak with authority about all kinds of plants, from the great cedar of Lebanon to the tiny hyssop that grows from cracks in a wall. He could also speak about animals, birds, reptiles, and fish. 34And kings from every nation sent their ambassadors to listen to the wisdom of Solomon.

CHAPTER **5**

Preparations for Building the Temple

King Hiram of Tyre had always been a loyal friend of David, so when he learned that David's son Solomon was the new king of Israel, Hiram sent ambassadors to congratulate him. 2Then Solomon sent this message back to Hiram:

3 "You know that my father, David, was not able to build a Temple to honor the name of the LORD his God because of the many wars he waged with surrounding nations.

He could not build until the LORD gave him victory over all his enemies. 4But now the LORD my God has given me peace on every side, and I have no enemies and all is well. 5So I am planning to build a Temple to honor the name of the LORD my God, just as he instructed my father that I should do. For the LORD told him, 'Your son, whom I will place on your throne, will build the Temple to honor my name.' 6Now please command that cedars from Lebanon be cut for me. Let my men work alongside yours, and I will pay your men whatever wages you ask. As you know, there is no one among us who can cut timber like you Sidonians!"

7When Hiram received Solomon's message, he was very pleased and said, "Praise the LORD for giving David a wise son to be king of the great nation of Israel." 8Then he sent this reply to Solomon:

"I have received your message, and I will do as you have asked concerning the timber. I can supply you with both cedar and cypress. 9My servants will bring the logs from the Lebanon mountains to the Mediterranean Sea and build them into rafts. We will float them along the coast to whatever place you choose. Then we will break the rafts apart and deliver the timber to you. You can pay me with food for my household."

10So Hiram produced for Solomon as much cedar and cypress timber as he desired. 11In return Solomon sent him an annual payment of 100,000 bushels* of wheat for his household and 110,000 gallons* of olive oil. 12So the LORD gave great wisdom to Solomon just as he had promised. And Hiram and Solomon made a formal alliance of peace.

13Then King Solomon enlisted 30,000 laborers from all Israel. 14He sent them to Lebanon in shifts, 10,000 every month, so that each man would be one month in Lebanon and two months at home. Adoniram was in charge of this labor force. 15Solomon also enlisted 70,000 common laborers, 80,000 stonecutters in the hill country, 16and 3,600* foremen to supervise the work. 17At the king's command, the stone-

4:22 Hebrew 30 *cors* [5.5 kiloliters] *of choice flour and 60 cors* [11 kiloliters] *of meal.* 4:26a As in some Greek manuscripts (see also 2 Chr 9:25); Hebrew reads *40,000.* 4:26b Or *12,000 charioteers.* 5:11a Hebrew *20,000 cors* [3,640 kiloliters]. 5:11b As in Greek version, which reads *20,000 baths* [420 kiloliters] (see also 2 Chr 2:10); Hebrew reads *20 cors,* about 800 gallons or 3.6 kiloliters in volume. 5:16 As in some Greek manuscripts (see also 2 Chr 2:2, 18); Hebrew reads *3,300.*

cutters quarried and shaped costly blocks of stone for the foundation of the Temple. ¹⁸Men from the city of Gebal helped Solomon's and Hiram's builders prepare the timber and stone for the Temple.

CHAPTER 6
Solomon Builds the Temple

It was in midspring,* during the fourth year of Solomon's reign, that he began the construction of the Temple of the LORD. This was 480 years after the people of Israel were delivered from their slavery in the land of Egypt.

²The Temple that King Solomon built for the LORD was 90 feet long, 30 feet wide, and 45 feet high.* ³The foyer at the front of the Temple was 30 feet wide, running across the entire width of the Temple. It projected outward 15 feet from the front of the Temple. ⁴Solomon also made narrow, recessed windows throughout Temple.

⁵A complex of rooms was built against the outer walls of the Temple, all the way around the sides and rear of the building. ⁶The complex was three stories high, the bottom floor being 7½ feet wide, the second floor 9 feet wide, and the top floor 10½ feet wide. The rooms were connected to the walls of the Temple by beams resting on ledges built out from the wall. So the beams were not inserted into the walls themselves.

⁷The stones used in the construction of the Temple were prefinished at the quarry, so the entire structure was built without the sound of hammer, ax, or any other iron tool at the building site.

⁸The entrance to the bottom floor* was on the south side of the Temple. There were winding stairs going up to the second floor, and another flight of stairs between the second and third floors. ⁹After completing the Temple structure, Solomon put in a ceiling made of beams and planks of cedar. ¹⁰As already stated, there was a complex of rooms on three sides of the building, attached to the Temple walls by cedar timbers. Each story of the complex was 7½ feet high.

¹¹Then the LORD gave this message to Solomon: ¹²"Concerning this Temple you are building, if you keep all my laws and regulations and obey all my commands, I will fulfill through you the promise I made to your father, David. ¹³I will live among the people of Israel and never forsake my people."

The Temple's Interior

¹⁴So Solomon finished building the Temple. ¹⁵The entire inside, from floor to ceiling, was paneled with wood. He paneled the walls and ceilings with cedar, and he used cypress for the floors. ¹⁶He partitioned off an inner sanctuary—the Most Holy Place—at the far end of the Temple. It was 30 feet deep and was paneled with cedar from floor to ceiling. ¹⁷The main room of the Temple, outside the Most Holy Place, was 60 feet long. ¹⁸Cedar paneling completely covered the stone walls throughout the Temple, and the paneling was decorated with carvings of gourds and open flowers.

¹⁹Solomon prepared the inner sanctuary in the rear of the Temple, where the Ark of the LORD's covenant would be placed. ²⁰This inner sanctuary was 30 feet long, 30 feet wide, and 30 feet high. Solomon overlaid its walls and ceiling with pure gold. He also overlaid the altar made of cedar.* ²¹Then he overlaid the rest of the Temple's interior with pure gold, and he made gold chains to protect the entrance to the Most Holy Place. ²²So he finished overlaying the entire Temple with gold, including the altar that belonged to the Most Holy Place.

²³Within the inner sanctuary Solomon placed two cherubim made of olive wood, each 15 feet tall. ²⁴The wingspan of each of the cherubim was 15 feet, each wing being 7½ feet long. ²⁵The two cherubim were identical in shape and size; ²⁶each was 15 feet tall. ²⁷Solomon placed them side by side in the inner sanctuary of the Temple. Their outspread wings reached from wall to wall, while their inner wings touched at the center of the room. ²⁸He overlaid the two cherubim with gold.

²⁹All the walls of the inner sanctuary and the main room were decorated with carvings of cherubim, palm trees, and open flowers. ³⁰The floor in both rooms was overlaid with gold.

³¹For the entrance to the inner sanctuary, Solomon made double doors of olive wood with five-sided doorposts. ³²These doors were decorated with carvings of cherubim, palm trees, and open flowers, and the doors were overlaid with gold.

³³Then he made four-sided doorposts of olive wood for the entrance to the Temple.

6:1 Hebrew *in the month of Ziv, which is the second month.* This month of the Hebrew lunar calendar usually occurs in April and May.
6:2 Hebrew *60 cubits* [27 meters] *long, 20 cubits* [9 meters] *wide, and 30 cubits* [13.5 meters] *high.* In this chapter, the distance measures are calculated from the Hebrew cubit at a ratio of 18 inches or 45 centimeters per cubit. 6:8 As in Greek version; Hebrew reads *middle floor.*
6:20 Or *overlaid the altar with cedar.* The meaning of the Hebrew is uncertain.

34There were two folding doors of cypress wood, and each door was hinged to fold back upon itself. 35These doors were decorated with carvings of cherubim, palm trees, and open flowers, and the doors were overlaid with gold.

36The walls of the inner courtyard were built so that there was one layer of cedar beams after every three layers of hewn stone.

37The foundation of the LORD's Temple was laid in midspring* of the fourth year of Solomon's reign. 38The entire building was completed in every detail by midautumn* of the eleventh year of his reign. So it took seven years to build the Temple.

CHAPTER 7
Solomon Builds His Palace

Solomon also built a palace for himself, and it took him thirteen years to complete the construction.

2One of Solomon's buildings was called the Palace of the Forest of Lebanon. It was 150 feet long, 75 feet wide, and 45 feet high.* The great cedar ceiling beams rested on four rows of cedar pillars. 3It had a cedar roof supported by forty-five rafters that rested on three rows of pillars, fifteen in each row. 4On each of the side walls there were three rows of windows facing each other. 5All the doorways were rectangular in frame; they were in sets of three, facing each other.

6He also built the Hall of Pillars, which was 75 feet long and 45 feet wide. There was a porch at its front, covered by a canopy that was supported by pillars.

7There was also the Hall of the Throne, also known as the Hall of Judgment, where Solomon sat to hear legal matters. It was paneled with cedar from floor to ceiling.* 8Solomon's living quarters surrounded a courtyard behind this hall; they were built the same way. He also built similar living quarters for Pharaoh's daughter, one of his wives. 9All these buildings were built entirely from huge, costly blocks of stone, cut and trimmed to exact measure on all sides. 10Some of the huge foundation stones were 15 feet long, and some were 12 feet long. 11The costly blocks of stone used in the walls were also cut to measure, and cedar beams were also used.

12The walls of the great courtyard were built so that there was one layer of cedar beams after every three layers of hewn stone, just like the walls of the inner courtyard of the LORD's Temple with its entrance foyer.

Furnishings for the Temple

13King Solomon then asked for a man named Huram* to come from Tyre, 14for he was a craftsman skilled in bronze work. He was half Israelite, since his mother was a widow from the tribe of Naphtali, and his father had been a foundry worker from Tyre. So he came to work for King Solomon.

15Huram cast two bronze pillars, each 27 feet tall and 18 feet in circumference. 16For the tops of the pillars he made capitals of molded bronze, each 7½ feet tall. 17Each capital was decorated with seven sets of latticework and interwoven chains. 18He also made two rows of pomegranates that encircled the latticework to decorate the capitals over the pillars. 19The capitals on the columns inside the foyer were shaped like lilies, and they were 6 feet tall. 20Each capital on the two pillars had two hundred pomegranates in two rows around them, beside the rounded surface next to the latticework. 21Huram set the pillars at the entrance of the Temple, one toward the south and one toward the north. He named the one on the south Jakin, and the one on the north Boaz.* 22The capitals on the pillars were shaped like lilies. And so the work on the pillars was finished.

23Then Huram cast a large round tank, 15 feet across from rim to rim; it was called the Sea. It was 7½ feet deep and about 45 feet in circumference. 24The Sea was encircled just below its rim by two rows of decorative gourds. There were about six gourds per foot* all the way around, and they had been cast as part of the tank.

25The Sea rested on a base of twelve bronze oxen, all facing outward. Three faced north, three faced west, three faced south, and three faced east. 26The walls of the Sea were about three inches* thick, and its rim flared out like a cup and resembled a lily blossom. It could hold about 11,000 gallons* of water.

27Huram also made ten bronze water carts, each 6 feet long, 6 feet wide, and 4½ feet tall.

6:37 Hebrew *in the month of Ziv.* This month of the Hebrew lunar calendar usually occurs in April and May.   6:38 Hebrew *in the month of Bul, which is the eighth month.* This month of the Hebrew lunar calendar usually occurs in October and November.   7:2 Hebrew *100 cubits* [45 meters] *long, 50 cubits* [22.5 meters] *wide, and 30 cubits* [13.5 meters] *high.* In this chapter, the distance measures are calculated from the Hebrew cubit at a ratio of 18 inches or 45 centimeters per cubit.   7:7 As in Syriac version and Latin Vulgate; Hebrew reads *from floor to floor.*   7:13 Hebrew *Hiram* (also in 7:40, 45); compare 2 Chr 2:13. This is not the same person mentioned in 5:1.   7:21 Jakin probably means "he establishes"; Boaz probably means "in him is strength."   7:24 Or *20 gourds per meter;* Hebrew reads *10 per cubit.*   7:26a Hebrew *a handbreadth* [8 centimeters].   7:26b Hebrew *2,000 baths* [42 kiloliters].

28They were constructed with side panels braced with crossbars. 29Both the panels and the crossbars were decorated with carved lions, oxen, and cherubim. Above and below the lions and oxen were wreath decorations. 30Each of these carts had four bronze wheels and bronze axles. At each corner of the carts were supporting posts for the bronze basins; these supports were decorated with carvings of wreaths on each side. 31The top of each cart had a circular frame for the basin. It projected 1½ feet above the cart's top like a round pedestal, and its opening was 2¼ feet across; it was decorated on the outside with carvings of wreaths. The panels of the carts were square, not round. 32Under the panels were four wheels that were connected to axles that had been cast as one unit with the cart. The wheels were 2¼ feet in diameter 33and were similar to chariot wheels. The axles, spokes, rims, and hubs were all cast from molten bronze.

34There were supports at each of the four corners of the carts, and these, too, were cast as one unit with the cart. 35Around the top of each cart there was a rim 9 inches wide.* The supports and side panels were cast as one unit with the cart. 36Carvings of cherubim, lions, and palm trees decorated the panels and supports wherever there was room, and there were wreaths all around. 37All ten water carts were the same size and were made alike, for each was cast from the same mold.

38Huram also made ten bronze basins, one for each cart. Each basin was 6 feet across and could hold 220 gallons* of water. 39He arranged five water carts on the south side of the Temple and five on the north side. The Sea was placed at the southeast corner of the Temple. 40He also made the necessary pots, shovels, and basins.

So at last Huram completed everything King Solomon had assigned him to make for the Temple of the LORD:

41 two pillars,
  two bowl-shaped capitals on top of the
    pillars,
  two networks of chains that decorated the
    capitals,
42 four hundred pomegranates that hung from
    the chains on the capitals (two rows of
    pomegranates for each of the chain
    networks that were hung around the
    capitals on top of the pillars),
43 the ten water carts holding the ten basins,
44 the Sea and the twelve oxen under it,
45 the pots, the shovels, and the basins.

All these utensils for the Temple of the LORD that Huram made for Solomon were made of burnished bronze. 46The king had them cast in clay molds in the Jordan Valley between Succoth and Zarethan. 47Solomon did not weigh all the utensils because there were so many; the weight of the bronze could not be measured.

48So Solomon made all the furnishings of the Temple of the LORD:

  the gold altar,
  the gold table for the Bread of the Presence,
49 the gold lampstands, five on the south and
    five on the north, in front of the Most
    Holy Place,
  the flower decorations, lamps, and tongs, all
    of gold,
50 the cups, lamp snuffers, basins, dishes, and
    firepans, all of pure gold,
  the doors for the entrances to the Most Holy
    Place and the main room of the Temple,
    with their fronts overlaid with gold.

51So King Solomon finished all his work on the Temple of the LORD. Then Solomon brought all the gifts his father, David, had dedicated— the silver, the gold, and the other utensils—and he stored them in the treasuries of the LORD's Temple.

CHAPTER **8**
The Ark Brought to the Temple
Solomon then summoned the leaders of all the tribes and families of Israel to assemble in Jerusalem. They were to bring the Ark of the LORD's covenant from its location in the City of David, also known as Zion, to its new place in the Temple. 2They all assembled before the king at the annual Festival of Shelters in early autumn.* 3When all the leaders of Israel arrived, the priests picked up the Ark. 4Then the priests and Levites took the Ark of the LORD, along with the Tabernacle* and all its sacred utensils, and carried them up to the Temple. 5King Solomon and the entire community of Israel sacrificed sheep and oxen before the Ark in such numbers that no one could keep count!

6Then the priests carried the Ark of the LORD's covenant into the inner sanctuary of the Temple—the Most Holy Place—and placed it

---

7:35 Hebrew *half a cubit wide* [22.5 centimeters]. 7:38 Hebrew *40 baths* [840 liters]. 8:2 Hebrew *at the festival in the month Ethanim, which is the seventh month.* The Festival of Shelters began on the fifteenth day of the seventh month on the Hebrew lunar calendar. This occurs on our calendar in late September or early October. 8:4 Hebrew *Tent of Meeting.*

beneath the wings of the cherubim. 7The cherubim spread their wings over the Ark, forming a canopy over the Ark and its carrying poles. 8These poles were so long that their ends could be seen from the front entrance of the Temple's main room—the Holy Place—but not from outside it. They are still there to this day. 9Nothing was in the Ark except the two stone tablets that Moses had placed there at Mount Sinai,* where the LORD made a covenant with the people of Israel as they were leaving the land of Egypt.

10As the priests came out of the inner sanctuary, a cloud filled the Temple of the LORD. 11The priests could not continue their work because the glorious presence of the LORD filled the Temple.

Solomon Blesses the People

12Then Solomon prayed, "O LORD, you have said that you would live in thick darkness. 13But I have built a glorious Temple for you, where you can live forever!"

14Then the king turned around to the entire community of Israel standing before him and gave this blessing: 15"Blessed be the LORD, the God of Israel, who has kept the promise he made to my father, David. 16For he told my father, 'From the day I brought my people Israel out of Egypt, I have never chosen a city among the tribes of Israel as the place where a temple should be built to honor my name. But now I have chosen David to be king over my people.'"

17Then Solomon said, "My father, David, wanted to build this Temple to honor the name of the LORD, the God of Israel. 18But the LORD told him, 'It is right for you to want to build the Temple to honor my name, 19but you are not the one to do it. One of your sons will build it instead.'

20"And now the LORD has done what he promised, for I have become king in my father's place. I have built this Temple to honor the name of the LORD, the God of Israel. 21And I have prepared a place there for the Ark, which contains the covenant that the LORD made with our ancestors when he brought them out of Egypt."

Solomon's Prayer of Dedication

22Then Solomon stood with his hands lifted toward heaven before the altar of the LORD in front of the entire community of Israel. 23He prayed, "O LORD, God of Israel, there is no God like you in all of heaven or earth. You keep your promises

and show unfailing love to all who obey you and are eager to do your will. 24You have kept your promise to your servant David, my father. You made that promise with your own mouth, and today you have fulfilled it with your own hands. 25And now, O LORD, God of Israel, carry out your further promise to your servant David, my father. For you said to him, 'If your descendants guard their behavior as you have done, they will always reign over Israel.' 26Now, O God of Israel, fulfill this promise to your servant David, my father.

27"But will God really live on earth? Why, even the highest heavens cannot contain you. How much less this Temple I have built! 28Listen to my prayer and my request, O LORD my God. Hear the cry and the prayer that your servant is making to you today. 29May you watch over this Temple both day and night, this place where you have said you would put your name. May you always hear the prayers I make toward this place. 30May you hear the humble and earnest requests from me and your people Israel when we pray toward this place. Yes, hear us from heaven where you live, and when you hear, forgive.

31"If someone wrongs another person and is required to take an oath of innocence in front of the altar at this Temple, 32then hear from heaven and judge between your servants—the accuser and the accused. Punish the guilty party and acquit the one who is innocent.

33"If your people Israel are defeated by their enemies because they have sinned against you, and if they turn to you and call on your name and pray to you here in this Temple, 34then hear from heaven and forgive their sins and return them to this land you gave their ancestors.

35"If the skies are shut up and there is no rain because your people have sinned against you, and then they pray toward this Temple and confess your name and turn from their sins because you have punished them, 36then hear from heaven and forgive the sins of your servants, your people Israel. Teach them to do what is right, and send rain on your land that you have given to your people as their special possession.

37"If there is a famine in the land, or plagues, or crop disease, or attacks of locusts or caterpillars, or if your people's enemies are in the land besieging their towns—whatever the trouble is—38and if your people offer a prayer concerning their troubles or sorrow, raising their hands toward this Temple, 39then hear from heaven where you live, and forgive. Give your people

8:9 Hebrew *at Horeb,* another name for Sinai.

whatever they deserve, for you alone know the human heart. ⁴⁰Then they will fear you and walk in your ways as long as they live in the land you gave to our ancestors.

⁴¹"And when foreigners hear of you and come from distant lands to worship your great name—⁴²for they will hear of you and of your mighty miracles and your power—and when they pray toward this Temple, ⁴³then hear from heaven where you live, and grant what they ask of you. Then all the people of the earth will come to know and fear you, just as your own people Israel do. They, too, will know that this Temple I have built bears your name.

⁴⁴"If your people go out at your command to fight their enemies, and if they pray to the LORD toward this city that you have chosen and toward this Temple that I have built for your name, ⁴⁵then hear their prayers from heaven and uphold their cause.

⁴⁶"If they sin against you—and who has never sinned?—you may become angry with them and let their enemies conquer them and take them captive to a foreign land far or near. ⁴⁷But in that land of exile, they may turn to you again in repentance and pray, 'We have sinned, done evil, and acted wickedly.' ⁴⁸Then if they turn to you with their whole heart and soul and pray toward the land you gave to their ancestors, toward this city you have chosen, and toward this Temple I have built to honor your name, ⁴⁹then hear their prayers from heaven where you live. Uphold their cause ⁵⁰and forgive your people who have sinned against you. Make their captors merciful to them, ⁵¹for they are your people—your special possession—whom you brought out of the iron-smelting furnace of Egypt.

⁵²"May your eyes be open to my requests and to the requests of your people Israel. Hear and answer them whenever they cry out to you. ⁵³For when you brought our ancestors out of Egypt, O Sovereign LORD, you told your servant Moses that you had separated Israel from among all the nations of the earth to be your own special possession."

The Dedication of the Temple

⁵⁴When Solomon finished making these prayers and requests to the LORD, he stood up in front of the altar of the LORD, where he had been kneeling with his hands raised toward heaven. ⁵⁵He stood there and shouted this blessing over the entire community of Israel: ⁵⁶"Praise the LORD who has given rest to his people Israel, just as he promised. Not one word has failed of all the wonderful promises he gave through his servant Moses. ⁵⁷May the LORD our God be with us as he was with our ancestors; may he never forsake us. ⁵⁸May he give us the desire to do his will in everything and to obey all the commands, laws, and regulations that he gave our ancestors. ⁵⁹And may these words that I have prayed in the presence of the LORD be before him constantly, day and night, so that the LORD our God may uphold my cause and the cause of his people Israel, fulfilling our daily needs. ⁶⁰May people all over the earth know that the LORD is God and that there is no other god. ⁶¹And may you, his people, always be faithful to the LORD our God. May you always obey his laws and commands, just as you are doing today."

⁶²Then the king and all Israel with him offered sacrifices to the LORD. ⁶³Solomon sacrificed peace offerings to the LORD numbering 22,000 oxen and 120,000 sheep. And so the king and all Israel dedicated the Temple of the LORD. ⁶⁴That same day the king dedicated the central area of the courtyard in front of the LORD's Temple. He offered burnt offerings, grain offerings, and the fat of peace offerings there, because the bronze altar in the LORD's presence was too small to handle so many offerings.

⁶⁵Then Solomon and all Israel celebrated the Festival of Shelters* in the presence of the LORD their God. A large crowd had gathered from as far away as Lebo-hamath in the north to the brook of Egypt in the south. The celebration went on for fourteen days in all—seven days for the dedication of the altar and seven days for the Festival of Shelters.* ⁶⁶After the festival was over,* Solomon sent the people home. They blessed the king as they went, and they were all joyful and happy because the LORD had been good to his servant David and to his people Israel.

CHAPTER 9

The LORD's Response to Solomon

So Solomon finished building the Temple of the LORD, as well as the royal palace. He completed everything he had planned to do. ²Then the LORD appeared to Solomon a second time, as he had done before at Gibeon. ³The LORD said to him, "I have heard your prayer and your request.

8:65a Hebrew *the festival;* see note on 8:2.   **8:65b** Hebrew *seven days and seven days, fourteen days;* compare parallel text at 2 Chr 7:8-10.
8:66 Hebrew *On the eighth day,* probably referring to the day following the seven-day Festival of Shelters; compare parallel text at 2 Chr 7:9-10.

I have set apart this Temple you have built so that my name will be honored there forever. I will always watch over it and care for it. 4As for you, if you will follow me with integrity and godliness, as David your father did, always obeying my commands and keeping my laws and regulations, 5then I will establish the throne of your dynasty over Israel forever. For I made this promise to your father, David: 'You will never fail to have a successor on the throne of Israel.'

6"But if you or your descendants abandon me and disobey my commands and laws, and if you go and worship other gods, 7then I will uproot the people of Israel from this land I have given them. I will reject this Temple that I have set apart to honor my name. I will make Israel an object of mockery and ridicule among the nations. 8And though this Temple is impressive now, it will become an appalling sight for all who pass by. They will scoff and ask, 'Why did the LORD do such terrible things to his land and to his Temple?' 9And the answer will be, 'Because his people forgot the LORD their God, who brought their ancestors out of Egypt, and they worshiped other gods instead. That is why the LORD has brought all these disasters upon them.'"

Solomon's Agreement with Hiram

10Now at the end of the twenty years during which Solomon built the Temple of the LORD and the royal palace, 11Solomon gave twenty towns in the land of Galilee to King Hiram of Tyre as payment for all the cedar and cypress lumber and gold he had furnished for the construction of the buildings. 12Hiram came from Tyre to see the towns Solomon had given him, but he was not at all pleased with them. 13"What kind of towns are these, my brother?" he asked. "These towns are worthless!" So Hiram called that area Cabul— "worthless"—as it is still known today. 14Hiram had sent Solomon nine thousand pounds* of gold.

Solomon's Many Achievements

15This is the account of the forced labor that Solomon conscripted to build the LORD's Temple, the royal palace, the Millo,* the wall of Jerusalem, and the cities of Hazor, Megiddo, and Gezer. 16(The king of Egypt had attacked and captured Gezer, killing the Canaanite population and burning it down. He gave the city to his daughter as a wedding gift when she married

Solomon. 17So Solomon rebuilt the city of Gezer.) He also built up the towns of Lower Bethhoron, 18Baalath, and Tamar* in the desert, within his land. 19He built towns as supply centers and constructed cities where his chariots and horses* could be kept. He built to his heart's content in Jerusalem and Lebanon and throughout the entire realm.

20There were still some people living in the land who were not Israelites, including Amorites, Hittites, Perizzites, Hivites, and Jebusites. 21These were descendants of the nations that Israel had not completely destroyed.* So Solomon conscripted them for his labor force, and they serve in the labor force to this day. 22But Solomon did not conscript any of the Israelites for forced labor. Instead, he assigned them to serve as fighting men, government officials, officers in his army, commanders of his chariots, and charioteers. 23He also appointed 550 of them to supervise the various projects.

24After Solomon moved his wife, Pharaoh's daughter, from the City of David to the new palace he had built for her, he constructed the Millo.

25Three times each year Solomon offered burnt offerings and peace offerings to the LORD on the altar he had built. He also burned incense to the LORD. And so he finished the work of building the Temple.

26Later King Solomon built a fleet of ships at Ezion-geber, a port near Elath* in the land of Edom, along the shore of the Red Sea.* 27Hiram sent experienced crews of sailors to sail the ships with Solomon's men. 28They sailed to Ophir and brought back to Solomon some sixteen tons* of gold.

CHAPTER **10**
The Queen of Sheba's Visit

When the queen of Sheba heard of Solomon's reputation, which brought honor to the name of the LORD, she came to test him with hard questions. 2She arrived in Jerusalem with a large group of attendants and a great caravan of camels loaded with spices, huge quantities of gold, and precious jewels. When she met with Solomon, they talked about everything she had on her mind. 3Solomon answered all her questions; nothing was too hard for the king to explain to her. 4When the queen of

---

9:14 Hebrew *120 talents* [4 metric tons]. 9:15 Or *the supporting terraces;* also in 9:24. 9:18 The marginal *Qere* reading of the Masoretic Text reads *Tadmor.* 9:19 Or *and charioteers.* 9:21 The Hebrew term used here refers to the complete consecration of things or people to the LORD, either by destroying them or by giving them as an offering. 9:26a As in Greek version (see also 2 Kgs 14:22; 16:6); Hebrew reads *Eloth.* 9:26b Hebrew *sea of reeds.* 9:28 Hebrew *420 talents* [14 metric tons].

Sheba realized how wise Solomon was, and when she saw the palace he had built, [5]she was breathless. She was also amazed at the food on his tables, the organization of his officials and their splendid clothing, the cup-bearers and their robes, and the burnt offerings Solomon made at the Temple of the LORD.

[6]She exclaimed to the king, "Everything I heard in my country about your achievements and wisdom is true! [7]I didn't believe it until I arrived here and saw it with my own eyes. Truly I had not heard the half of it! Your wisdom and prosperity are far greater than what I was told. [8]How happy these people must be! What a privilege for your officials to stand here day after day, listening to your wisdom! [9]The LORD your God is great indeed! He delights in you and has placed you on the throne of Israel. Because the LORD loves Israel with an eternal love, he has made you king so you can rule with justice and righteousness."

[10]Then she gave the king a gift of nine thousand pounds* of gold, and great quantities of spices and precious jewels. Never again were so many spices brought in as those the queen of Sheba gave to Solomon.

[11](When Hiram's ships brought gold from Ophir, they also brought rich cargoes of almug wood and precious jewels. [12]The king used the almug wood to make railings for the Temple of the LORD and the royal palace, and to construct harps and lyres for the musicians. Never before or since has there been such a supply of beautiful almug wood.)

[13]King Solomon gave the queen of Sheba whatever she asked for, besides all the other customary gifts he had so generously given. Then she and all her attendants left and returned to their own land.

Solomon's Wealth and Splendor

[14]Each year Solomon received about twenty-five tons* of gold. [15]This did not include the additional revenue he received from merchants and traders, all the kings of Arabia, and the governors of the land.

[16]King Solomon made two hundred large shields of hammered gold, each containing over fifteen pounds* of gold. [17]He also made three hundred smaller shields of hammered gold, each containing nearly four pounds* of gold.

The king placed these shields in the Palace of the Forest of Lebanon.

[18]Then the king made a huge ivory throne and overlaid it with pure gold. [19]The throne had six steps and a rounded back. On both sides of the seat were armrests, with the figure of a lion standing on each side of the throne. [20]Solomon made twelve other lion figures, one standing on each end of each of the six steps. No other throne in all the world could be compared with it!

[21]All of King Solomon's drinking cups were solid gold, as were all the utensils in the Palace of the Forest of Lebanon. They were not made of silver because silver was considered of little value in Solomon's day!

[22]The king had a fleet of trading ships* that sailed with Hiram's fleet. Once every three years the ships returned, loaded down with gold, silver, ivory, apes, and peacocks.*

[23]So King Solomon became richer and wiser than any other king in all the earth. [24]People from every nation came to visit him and to hear the wisdom God had given him. [25]Year after year, everyone who came to visit brought him gifts of silver and gold, clothing, weapons, spices, horses, and mules.

[26]Solomon built up a huge force of chariots and horses. He had fourteen hundred chariots and twelve thousand horses.* He stationed many of them in the chariot cities, and some near him in Jerusalem. [27]The king made silver as plentiful in Jerusalem as stones. And valuable cedarwood was as common as the sycamore wood that grows in the foothills of Judah.* [28]Solomon's horses were imported from Egypt* and from Cilicia*; the king's traders acquired them from Cilicia at the standard price. [29]At that time, Egyptian chariots delivered to Jerusalem could be purchased for 600 pieces of silver,* and horses could be bought for 150 pieces of silver.* Many of these were then resold to the kings of the Hittites and the kings of Aram.

CHAPTER 11
Solomon's Many Wives

Now King Solomon loved many foreign women. Besides Pharaoh's daughter, he married women from Moab, Ammon, Edom, Sidon, and from among the Hittites. [2]The LORD had clearly instructed his people not to intermarry with those

---

10:10 Hebrew *120 talents* [4 metric tons].   10:14 Hebrew *666 talents* [23 metric tons].   10:16 Hebrew *600 shekels* [6.8 kilograms].   10:17 Hebrew *3 minas* [1.8 kilograms].   10:22a Hebrew *fleet of ships of Tarshish.*   10:22b Or *and baboons.*   10:26 Or *12,000 charioteers.*   10:27 Hebrew *the Shephelah.*   10:28a Possibly *Muzur,* a district near Cilicia; also in 10:29.   10:28b Hebrew *Kue,* probably another name for Cilicia.   10:29a Hebrew *600 shekels of silver,* about 15 pounds or 6.8 kilograms in weight.   10:29b Hebrew *150* [*shekels*], about 3.8 pounds or 1.7 kilograms in weight.

nations, because the women they married would lead them to worship their gods. Yet Solomon insisted on loving them anyway. ³He had seven hundred wives and three hundred concubines. And sure enough, they led his heart away from the LORD. ⁴In Solomon's old age, they turned his heart to worship their gods instead of trusting only in the LORD his God, as his father, David, had done. ⁵Solomon worshiped Ashtoreth, the goddess of the Sidonians, and Molech,* the detestable god of the Ammonites. ⁶Thus, Solomon did what was evil in the LORD's sight; he refused to follow the LORD completely, as his father, David, had done. ⁷On the Mount of Olives, east of Jerusalem, he even built a shrine for Chemosh, the detestable god of Moab, and another for Molech, the detestable god of the Ammonites. ⁸Solomon built such shrines for all his foreign wives to use for burning incense and sacrificing to their gods.

⁹The LORD was very angry with Solomon, for his heart had turned away from the LORD, the God of Israel, who had appeared to him twice. ¹⁰He had warned Solomon specifically about worshiping other gods, but Solomon did not listen to the LORD's command. ¹¹So now the LORD said to him, "Since you have not kept my covenant and have disobeyed my laws, I will surely tear the kingdom away from you and give it to one of your servants. ¹²But for the sake of your father, David, I will not do this while you are still alive. I will take the kingdom away from your son. ¹³And even so, I will let him be king of one tribe, for the sake of my servant David and for the sake of Jerusalem, my chosen city."

Solomon's Enemies

¹⁴Then the LORD raised up Hadad the Edomite, a member of Edom's royal family, to be an enemy against Solomon. ¹⁵Years before, David had gone to Edom with Joab, his army commander, to bury some Israelites who had died in battle. While there, the Israelite army had killed nearly every male in Edom. ¹⁶Joab and the army had stayed there for six months, killing them. ¹⁷But Hadad and a few of his father's royal officials had fled. (Hadad was a very small child at the time.) ¹⁸They escaped from Midian and went to Paran, where others joined them. Then they traveled to Egypt and went to Pharaoh, who gave them a home, food, and some land. ¹⁹Pharaoh grew very fond of Hadad, and he gave him a wife—the sister of Queen Tahpenes. ²⁰She

bore him a son, Genubath, who was brought up in Pharaoh's palace among Pharaoh's own sons.

²¹When the news reached Hadad in Egypt that David and his commander Joab were both dead, he said to Pharaoh, "Let me return to my own country."

²²"Why?" Pharaoh asked him. "What do you lack here? How have we disappointed you that you want to go home?"

"Nothing is wrong," he replied. "But even so, I must return home."

²³God also raised up Rezon son of Eliada to be an enemy against Solomon. Rezon had fled from his master, King Hadadezer of Zobah, ²⁴and had become the leader of a gang of rebels. After David conquered Hadadezer, Rezon and his men fled to Damascus, where he became king. ²⁵Rezon was Israel's bitter enemy for the rest of Solomon's reign, and he made trouble, just as Hadad did. Rezon hated Israel intensely and continued to reign in Aram.

Jeroboam Rebels against Solomon

²⁶Another rebel leader was Jeroboam son of Nebat, one of Solomon's own officials. He came from the city of Zeredah in Ephraim, and his mother was Zeruah, a widow. ²⁷This is the story behind his rebellion. Solomon was rebuilding the Millo* and repairing the walls of the city of his father, David. ²⁸Jeroboam was a very capable young man, and when Solomon saw how industrious he was, he put him in charge of the labor force from the tribes of Ephraim and Manasseh.*

²⁹One day as Jeroboam was leaving Jerusalem, the prophet Ahijah from Shiloh met him on the road, wearing a new cloak. The two of them were alone in a field, ³⁰and Ahijah took the new cloak he was wearing and tore it into twelve pieces. ³¹Then he said to Jeroboam, "Take ten of these pieces, for this is what the LORD, the God of Israel, says: 'I am about to tear the kingdom from the hand of Solomon, and I will give ten of the tribes to you! ³²But I will leave him one tribe for the sake of my servant David and for the sake of Jerusalem, which I have chosen out of all the tribes of Israel. ³³For Solomon has abandoned me and worshiped Ashtoreth, the goddess of the Sidonians; Chemosh, the god of Moab; and Molech, the god of the Ammonites. He has not followed my ways and done what is pleasing in my sight. He has not obeyed my laws and regulations as his father, David, did.

³⁴" 'But I will not take the entire kingdom

11:5 Hebrew *Milcom,* a variant name for Molech; also in 11:33.   11:27 Or *the supporting terraces.*   11:28 Hebrew *from the house of Joseph.*

from Solomon at this time. For the sake of my servant David, the one whom I chose and who obeyed my commands and laws, I will let Solomon reign for the rest of his life. 35But I will take the kingdom away from his son and give ten of the tribes to you. 36His son will have one tribe so that the descendants of David my servant will continue to reign* in Jerusalem, the city I have chosen to be the place for my name. 37And I will place you on the throne of Israel, and you will rule over all that your heart desires. 38If you listen to what I tell you and follow my ways and do whatever I consider to be right, and if you obey my laws and commands, as my servant David did, then I will always be with you. I will establish an enduring dynasty for you as I did for David, and I will give Israel to you. 39But I will punish the descendants of David because of Solomon's sin—though not forever.' "

40Solomon tried to kill Jeroboam, but he fled to King Shishak of Egypt and stayed there until Solomon died.

41The rest of the events in Solomon's reign, including his wisdom, are recorded in *The Book of the Acts of Solomon.* 42Solomon ruled in Jerusalem over all Israel for forty years. 43When Solomon died, he was buried in the city of his father, David. Then his son Rehoboam became the next king.

CHAPTER **12**

The Northern Tribes Revolt

Rehoboam went to Shechem, where all Israel had gathered to make him king. 2When Jeroboam son of Nebat heard of Solomon's death, he returned from Egypt,* for he had fled to Egypt to escape from King Solomon. 3The leaders of Israel sent for Jeroboam, and the whole assembly of Israel went to speak with Rehoboam. 4"Your father was a hard master," they said. "Lighten the harsh labor demands and heavy taxes that your father imposed on us. Then we will be your loyal subjects."

5Rehoboam replied, "Give me three days to think this over. Then come back for my answer." So the people went away.

6Then King Rehoboam went to discuss the matter with the older men who had counseled his father, Solomon. "What is your advice?" he asked. "How should I answer these people?"

7The older counselors replied, "If you are willing to serve the people today and give them a favorable answer, they will always be your loyal subjects."

8But Rehoboam rejected the advice of the elders and instead asked the opinion of the young men who had grown up with him and who were now his advisers. 9"What is your advice?" he asked them. "How should I answer these people who want me to lighten the burdens imposed by my father?"

10The young men replied, "This is what you should tell those complainers: 'My little finger is thicker than my father's waist—if you think he was hard on you, just wait and see what I'll be like! 11Yes, my father was harsh on you, but I'll be even harsher! My father used whips on you, but I'll use scorpions!' "

12Three days later, Jeroboam and all the people returned to hear Rehoboam's decision, just as the king had requested. 13But Rehoboam spoke harshly to them, for he rejected the advice of the older counselors 14and followed the counsel of his younger advisers. He told the people, "My father was harsh on you, but I'll be even harsher! My father used whips on you, but I'll use scorpions!" 15So the king paid no attention to the people's demands. This turn of events was the will of the LORD, for it fulfilled the LORD's message to Jeroboam son of Nebat through the prophet Ahijah from Shiloh.

16When all Israel realized that the king had rejected their request, they shouted, "Down with David and his dynasty! We have no share in Jesse's son! Let's go home, Israel! Look out for your own house, O David!" So the people of Israel returned home. 17But Rehoboam continued to rule over the Israelites who lived in the towns of Judah.

18King Rehoboam sent Adoniram,* who was in charge of the labor force, to restore order, but all Israel stoned him to death. When this news reached King Rehoboam, he quickly jumped into his chariot and fled to Jerusalem. 19The northern tribes of Israel have refused to be ruled by a descendant of David to this day.

20When the people of Israel learned of Jeroboam's return from Egypt, they called an assembly and made him king over all Israel. So only the tribe of Judah remained loyal to the family of David.

Shemaiah's Prophecy

21When Rehoboam arrived at Jerusalem, he mobilized the armies of Judah and Benjamin— 180,000 select troops—to fight against the army

11:36 Hebrew *will continue to have a lamp.*   12:2 As in Greek version and Latin Vulgate (see also 2 Chr 10:2); Hebrew reads *he lived in Egypt.*   12:18 As in some Greek manuscripts and Syriac version (see also 4:6; 5:14); Hebrew reads *Adoram.*

of Israel and to restore the kingdom to himself. 22But God said to Shemaiah, the man of God, 23"Say to Rehoboam son of Solomon, king of Judah, and to all the people of Judah and Benjamin, 24'This is what the LORD says: Do not fight against your relatives, the Israelites. Go back home, for what has happened is my doing!'" So they obeyed the message of the LORD and went home, as the LORD had commanded.

Jeroboam Makes Gold Calves

25Jeroboam then built up the city of Shechem in the hill country of Ephraim, and it became his capital. Later he went and built up the town of Peniel.* 26Jeroboam thought to himself, "Unless I am careful, the kingdom will return to the dynasty of David. 27When they go to Jerusalem to offer sacrifices at the Temple of the LORD, they will again give their allegiance to King Rehoboam of Judah. They will kill me and make him their king instead."

28So on the advice of his counselors, the king made two gold calves. He said to the people, "It is too much trouble for you to worship in Jerusalem. O Israel, these are the gods who brought you out of Egypt!"

29He placed these calf idols at the southern and northern ends of Israel—in Bethel and in Dan. 30This became a great sin, for the people worshiped them, traveling even as far as Dan.

31Jeroboam built shrines at the pagan high places and ordained priests from the rank and file of the people—those who were not from the priestly tribe of Levi. 32Jeroboam also instituted a religious festival in Bethel, held on a day in midautumn,* similar to the annual Festival of Shelters in Judah. There at Bethel he himself offered sacrifices to the calves he had made. And it was at Bethel that he appointed priests for the pagan shrines he had made. 33So on the appointed day in midautumn, a day that he himself had designated, Jeroboam offered sacrifices on the altar at Bethel. He instituted a religious festival for Israel, and he went up to the altar to burn incense.

CHAPTER 13

A Prophet Denounces Jeroboam

At the LORD's command, a man of God from Judah went to Bethel, and he arrived there just as Jeroboam was approaching the altar to offer a sacrifice. 2Then at the LORD's command, he shouted, "O altar, altar! This is what the LORD says: A child named Josiah will be born into the dynasty of David. On you he will sacrifice the priests from the pagan shrines who come here to burn incense, and human bones will be burned on you." 3That same day the man of God gave a sign to prove his message, and he said, "The LORD has promised to give this sign: This altar will split apart, and its ashes will be poured out on the ground."

4King Jeroboam was very angry with the man of God for speaking against the altar. So he pointed at the man and shouted, "Seize that man!" But instantly the king's hand became paralyzed in that position, and he couldn't pull it back. 5At the same time a wide crack appeared in the altar, and the ashes poured out, just as the man of God had predicted in his message from the LORD.

6The king cried out to the man of God, "Please ask the LORD your God to restore my hand again!" So the man of God prayed to the LORD, and the king's hand became normal again.

7Then the king said to the man of God, "Come to the palace with me and have something to eat, and I will give you a gift."

8But the man of God said to the king, "Even if you gave me half of everything you own, I would not go with you. I would not eat any food or drink any water in this place. 9For the LORD gave me this command: 'You must not eat any food or drink any water while you are there, and do not return to Judah by the same way you came.'" 10So he left Bethel and went home another way.

11As it happened, there was an old prophet living in Bethel, and his sons came home and told him what the man of God had done in Bethel that day. They also told him what he had said to the king. 12The old prophet asked them, "Which way did he go?" So they told their father which road the man of God had taken. 13"Quick, saddle the donkey," the old man said. And when they had saddled the donkey for him, 14he rode after the man of God and found him sitting under an oak tree.

The old prophet asked him, "Are you the man of God who came from Judah?"

"Yes," he replied, "I am."

15Then he said to the man of God, "Come home with me and eat some food."

16"No, I cannot," he replied. "I am not allowed to eat any food or drink any water here in

---

12:25 Hebrew *Penuel*, a variant name for Peniel.   12:32 Hebrew *on the fifteenth day of the eighth month* (also in 12:33). This day of the Hebrew lunar calendar occurs in late October or early November, exactly one month after the annual Festival of Shelters in Judah (see Lev 23:34).

this place. ¹⁷For the LORD gave me this command: 'You must not eat any food or drink any water while you are there, and do not return to Judah by the same way you came.'"

¹⁸But the old prophet answered, "I am a prophet, too, just as you are. And an angel gave me this message from the LORD: 'Bring him home with you, and give him food to eat and water to drink.'" But the old man was lying to him. ¹⁹So they went back together, and the man of God ate some food and drank some water at the prophet's home.

²⁰Then while they were sitting at the table, a message from the LORD came to the old prophet. ²¹He cried out to the man of God from Judah, "This is what the LORD says: You have defied the LORD's message and have disobeyed the command the LORD your God gave you. ²²You came back to this place and ate food and drank water where he told you not to eat or drink. Because of this, your body will not be buried in the grave of your ancestors."

²³Now after the man of God had finished eating and drinking, the prophet saddled his own donkey for him, ²⁴and the man of God started off again. But as he was traveling along, a lion came out and killed him. His body lay there on the road, with the donkey and the lion standing beside it. ²⁵People came by and saw the body lying in the road and the lion standing beside it, and they went and reported it in Bethel, where the old prophet lived.

²⁶When the old prophet heard the report, he said, "It is the man of God who disobeyed the LORD's command. The LORD has fulfilled his word by causing the lion to attack and kill him." ²⁷Then the prophet said to his sons, "Saddle a donkey for me." So they saddled a donkey, ²⁸and he went out and found the body lying in the road. The donkey and lion were still standing there beside it, for the lion had not eaten the body nor attacked the donkey. ²⁹So the prophet laid the body of the man of God on the donkey and took it back to the city to mourn over him and bury him. ³⁰He laid the body in his own grave, crying out in grief, "Oh, my brother!"

³¹Afterward the prophet said to his sons, "When I die, bury me in the grave where the man of God is buried. Lay my bones beside his bones. ³²For the message the LORD told him to proclaim against the altar in Bethel and against the pagan shrines in the towns of Samaria will surely come true."

³³But even after this, Jeroboam did not turn from his evil ways. He continued to choose priests from the rank and file of the people. Anyone who wanted to could become a priest for the pagan shrines. ³⁴This became a great sin and resulted in the destruction of Jeroboam's kingdom and the death of all his family.

CHAPTER **14**

Ahijah's Prophecy against Jeroboam

At that time Jeroboam's son Abijah became very sick. ²So Jeroboam told his wife, "Disguise yourself so that no one will recognize you as the queen. Then go to the prophet Ahijah at Shiloh—the man who told me I would become king. ³Take him a gift of ten loaves of bread, some cakes, and a jar of honey, and ask him what will happen to the boy."

⁴So Jeroboam's wife went to Ahijah's home at Shiloh. He was an old man now and could no longer see. ⁵But the LORD had told Ahijah, "Jeroboam's wife will come here, pretending to be someone else. She will ask you about her son, for he is very sick. You must give her the answer that I give you."

⁶So when Ahijah heard her footsteps at the door, he called out, "Come in, wife of Jeroboam! Why are you pretending to be someone else?" Then he told her, "I have bad news for you. ⁷Give your husband, Jeroboam, this message from the LORD, the God of Israel: 'I promoted you from the ranks of the common people and made you ruler over my people Israel. ⁸I ripped the kingdom away from the family of David and gave it to you. But you have not been like my servant David, who obeyed my commands and followed me with all his heart and always did whatever I wanted him to do. ⁹You have done more evil than all who lived before you. You have made other gods and have made me furious with your gold calves. And since you have turned your back on me, ¹⁰I will bring disaster on your dynasty and kill all your sons, slave or free alike. I will burn up your royal dynasty as one burns up trash until it is all gone. ¹¹I, the LORD, vow that the members of your family who die in the city will be eaten by dogs, and those who die in the field will be eaten by vultures.'"

¹²Then Ahijah said to Jeroboam's wife, "Go on home, and when you enter the city, the child will die. ¹³All Israel will mourn for him and bury him. He is the only member of your family who will have a proper burial, for this child is the only good thing that the LORD, the God of Israel, sees in the entire family of Jeroboam. ¹⁴And the LORD will raise up a king over Israel who will

destroy the family of Jeroboam. This will happen today, even now! 15Then the LORD will shake Israel like a reed whipped about in a stream. He will uproot the people of Israel from this good land that he gave their ancestors and will scatter them beyond the Euphrates River,* for they have angered the LORD by worshiping Asherah poles. 16He will abandon Israel because Jeroboam sinned and made all of Israel sin along with him."

17So Jeroboam's wife returned to Tirzah, and the child died just as she walked through the door of her home. 18When the people of Israel buried him, they mourned for him, as the LORD had promised through the prophet Ahijah.

19The rest of the events of Jeroboam's reign, all his wars and how he ruled, are recorded in *The Book of the History of the Kings of Israel.* 20Jeroboam reigned in Israel twenty-two years. When Jeroboam died, his son Nadab became the next king.

Rehoboam Rules in Judah

21Meanwhile, Rehoboam son of Solomon was king in Judah. He was forty-one years old when he became king, and he reigned seventeen years in Jerusalem, the city the LORD had chosen from among all the tribes of Israel as the place to honor his name. Rehoboam's mother was Naamah, an Ammonite woman. 22During Rehoboam's reign, the people of Judah did what was evil in the LORD's sight, arousing his anger with their sin, for it was even worse than that of their ancestors. 23They built pagan shrines and set up sacred pillars and Asherah poles on every high hill and under every green tree. 24There were even shrine prostitutes throughout the land. The people imitated the detestable practices of the pagan nations the LORD had driven from the land ahead of the Israelites.

25In the fifth year of King Rehoboam's reign, King Shishak of Egypt came up and attacked Jerusalem. 26He ransacked the Temple of the LORD and the royal palace and stole everything, including all the gold shields Solomon had made. 27Afterward Rehoboam made bronze shields as substitutes, and he entrusted them to the care of the palace guard officers. 28Whenever the king went to the Temple of the LORD, the guards would carry them along and then return them to the guardroom.

29The rest of the events in Rehoboam's reign and all his deeds are recorded in *The Book of the*

History of the Kings of Judah. 30There was constant war between Rehoboam and Jeroboam. 31When Rehoboam died, he was buried among his ancestors in the City of David. His mother was Naamah, an Ammonite woman. Then his son Abijam* became the next king.

CHAPTER 15

Abijam Rules in Judah

Abijam* began to rule over Judah in the eighteenth year of Jeroboam's reign in Israel. 2He reigned in Jerusalem three years. His mother was Maacah, the daughter of Absalom.* 3He committed the same sins as his father before him, and his heart was not right with the LORD his God, as the heart of his ancestor David had been. 4But for David's sake, the LORD his God allowed his dynasty to continue,* and he gave Abijam a son to rule after him in Jerusalem. 5For David had done what was pleasing in the LORD's sight and had obeyed the LORD's commands throughout his life, except in the affair concerning Uriah the Hittite.

6There was war between Abijam and Jeroboam* throughout Abijam's reign. 7The rest of the events in Abijam's reign and all his deeds are recorded in *The Book of the History of the Kings of Judah.* There was constant war between Abijam and Jeroboam. 8When Abijam died, he was buried in the City of David. Then his son Asa became the next king.

Asa Rules in Judah

9Asa began to rule over Judah in the twentieth year of Jeroboam's reign in Israel. 10He reigned in Jerusalem forty-one years. His grandmother* was Maacah, the daughter of Absalom. 11Asa did what was pleasing in the LORD's sight, as his ancestor David had done. 12He banished the shrine prostitutes from the land and removed all the idols his ancestors had made. 13He even deposed his grandmother Maacah from her position as queen mother because she had made an obscene Asherah pole. He cut down the pole and burned it in the Kidron Valley. 14Although the pagan shrines were not completely removed, Asa remained faithful to the LORD throughout his life. 15He brought into the Temple of the LORD the silver and gold and the utensils that he and his father had dedicated.

16There was constant war between King Asa of Judah and King Baasha of Israel. 17King Baa-

14:15 Hebrew *the river.*   14:31 Also known as *Abijah.*   15:1 Also known as *Abijah.*   15:2 Hebrew *Abishalom* (also in 15:10), a variant name for Absalom; compare 2 Chr 11:20.   15:4 Hebrew *gave him a lamp in Jerusalem.*   15:6 As in a few Hebrew manuscripts; most Hebrew manuscripts read *between Rehoboam and Jeroboam.*   15:10 Hebrew *his mother* (also in 15:13); compare 15:2.

sha of Israel invaded Judah and fortified Ramah in order to prevent anyone from entering or leaving King Asa's territory in Judah. 18Asa responded by taking all the silver and gold that was left in the treasuries of the LORD's Temple and the royal palace. He sent it with some of his officials to Ben-hadad son of Tabrimmon and grandson of Hezion, the king of Aram, who was ruling in Damascus, along with this message:

19 "Let us renew the treaty that existed between your father and my father. See, I am sending you a gift of silver and gold. Break your treaty with King Baasha of Israel so that he will leave me alone."

20Ben-hadad agreed to King Asa's request and sent his armies to attack Israel. They conquered the towns of Ijon, Dan, Abel-beth-maacah, and all Kinnereth, with all the land of Naphtali. 21As soon as Baasha of Israel heard what was happening, he abandoned his project of fortifying Ramah and withdrew to Tirzah. 22Then King Asa sent an order throughout Judah, requiring that everyone, without exception, help to carry away the building stones and timbers that Baasha had been using to fortify Ramah. Asa used these materials to fortify the town of Geba in Benjamin and the town of Mizpah.

23The rest of the events in Asa's reign, the extent of his power, and the names of the cities he built are recorded in *The Book of the History of the Kings of Judah.* In his old age his feet became diseased. 24When Asa died, he was buried with his ancestors in the City of David. Then his son Jehoshaphat became the next king.

Nadab Rules in Israel

25Nadab son of Jeroboam began to rule over Israel in the second year of King Asa's reign in Judah. He reigned in Israel two years. 26But he did what was evil in the LORD's sight and followed the example of his father, continuing the sins of idolatry that Jeroboam had led Israel to commit.

27Then Baasha son of Ahijah, from the tribe of Issachar, plotted against Nadab and assassinated him while he and the Israelite army were laying siege to the Philistine town of Gibbethon. 28Baasha killed Nadab in the third year of King Asa's reign in Judah, and he became the next king of Israel. 29He immediately killed all the descendants of King Jeroboam, so that not one of the royal family was left, just as the LORD had promised concerning Jeroboam by the prophet Ahijah from Shiloh. 30This was done because

Jeroboam had aroused the anger of the LORD, the God of Israel, by the sins he had committed and the sins he had led Israel to commit. 31The rest of the events in Nadab's reign and all his deeds are recorded in *The Book of the History of the Kings of Israel.*

Baasha Rules in Israel

32There was constant war between Asa and King Baasha of Israel. 33Baasha began to rule over Israel in the third year of King Asa's reign in Judah. Baasha reigned in Tirzah twenty-four years. 34But he did what was evil in the LORD's sight and followed the example of Jeroboam, continuing the sins of idolatry that Jeroboam had led Israel to commit.

CHAPTER **16**

This message from the LORD was delivered to King Baasha by the prophet Jehu son of Hanani: 2 "I lifted you out of the dust to make you ruler of my people Israel, but you have followed the evil example of Jeroboam. You have aroused my anger by causing my people to sin. 3So now I will destroy you and your family, just as I destroyed the descendants of Jeroboam son of Nebat. 4Those of your family who die in the city will be eaten by dogs, and those who die in the field will be eaten by the vultures."

5The rest of the events in Baasha's reign and the extent of his power are recorded in *The Book of the History of the Kings of Israel.* 6When Baasha died, he was buried in Tirzah. Then his son Elah became the next king.

7This message from the LORD had been spoken against Baasha and his family through the prophet Jehu son of Hanani. It was delivered because Baasha had done what was evil in the LORD's sight, arousing him to anger by his sins, just like the family of Jeroboam, and also because Baasha had destroyed the family of Jeroboam.

Elah Rules in Israel

8Elah son of Baasha began to rule over Israel from Tirzah in the twenty-sixth year of King Asa's reign in Judah. He reigned in Israel two years. 9Then Zimri, who commanded half of the royal chariots, made plans to kill him. One day in Tirzah, Elah was getting drunk at the home of Arza, the supervisor of the palace. 10Zimri walked in and struck him down and killed him. This happened in the twenty-seventh year of King Asa's reign in Judah. Then Zimri became the next king.

11Zimri immediately killed the entire royal family of Baasha, and he did not leave a single male child. He even destroyed distant relatives and friends. 12So Zimri destroyed the dynasty of Baasha as the LORD had promised through the prophet Jehu. 13This happened because of the sins of Baasha and his son Elah and because of all the sins they led Israel to commit, arousing the anger of the LORD, the God of Israel, with their idols. 14The rest of the events in Elah's reign and all his deeds are recorded in *The Book of the History of the Kings of Israel.*

Zimri Rules in Israel

15Zimri began to rule over Israel from Tirzah in the twenty-seventh year of King Asa's reign in Judah, but he reigned only seven days. When the army of Israel, which was then engaged in attacking the Philistine town of Gibbethon, 16heard that Zimri had assassinated the king, they chose Omri, commander of the army, as their new king. 17So Omri led the army of Israel away from Gibbethon to attack Tirzah, Israel's capital. 18When Zimri saw that the city had been taken, he went into the citadel of the king's house and burned it down over himself and died in the flames. 19For he, too, had done what was evil in the LORD's sight and followed the example of Jeroboam, continuing the sins of idolatry that Jeroboam had led Israel to commit. 20The rest of the events of Zimri's reign and his conspiracy are recorded in *The Book of the History of the Kings of Israel.*

Omri Rules in Israel

21But now the people of Israel were divided into two groups. Half the people tried to make Tibni son of Ginath their king, while the other half supported Omri. 22But Omri's supporters defeated the supporters of Tibni son of Ginath. So Tibni was killed, and Omri became the next king.

23Omri began to rule over Israel in the thirty-first year of King Asa's reign in Judah. He reigned twelve years in all, six of them in Tirzah. 24Then Omri bought the hill now known as Samaria from its owner, Shemer, for 150 pounds of silver.* He built a city on it and called the city Samaria in honor of Shemer. 25But Omri did what was evil in the LORD's sight, even more than any of the kings before him. 26He followed the example of Jeroboam, continuing the sins of idolatry that Jeroboam had led Israel to commit. Thus, he aroused the anger of the LORD, the God

16:24 Hebrew *for 2 talents* [68 kilograms] *of silver.*

of Israel. 27The rest of the events in Omri's reign, the extent of his power, and all his deeds are recorded in *The Book of the History of the Kings of Israel.* 28When Omri died, he was buried in Samaria. Then his son Ahab became the next king.

Ahab Rules in Israel

29Ahab son of Omri began to rule over Israel in the thirty-eighth year of King Asa's reign in Judah. He reigned in Samaria twenty-two years. 30But Ahab did what was evil in the LORD's sight, even more than any of the kings before him. 31And as though it were not enough to live like Jeroboam, he married Jezebel, the daughter of King Ethbaal of the Sidonians, and he began to worship Baal. 32First he built a temple and an altar for Baal in Samaria. 33Then he set up an Asherah pole. He did more to arouse the anger of the LORD, the God of Israel, than any of the other kings of Israel before him.

34It was during his reign that Hiel, a man from Bethel, rebuilt Jericho. When he laid the foundations, his oldest son, Abiram, died. And when he finally completed it by setting up the gates, his youngest son, Segub, died. This all happened according to the message from the LORD concerning Jericho spoken by Joshua son of Nun.

CHAPTER **17**

Elijah Fed by Ravens

Now Elijah, who was from Tishbe in Gilead, told King Ahab, "As surely as the LORD, the God of Israel, lives—the God whom I worship and serve—there will be no dew or rain during the next few years unless I give the word!"

2Then the LORD said to Elijah, 3"Go to the east and hide by Kerith Brook at a place east of where it enters the Jordan River. 4Drink from the brook and eat what the ravens bring you, for I have commanded them to bring you food."

5So Elijah did as the LORD had told him and camped beside Kerith Brook. 6The ravens brought him bread and meat each morning and evening, and he drank from the brook. 7But after a while the brook dried up, for there was no rainfall anywhere in the land.

The Widow at Zarephath

8Then the LORD said to Elijah, 9"Go and live in the village of Zarephath, near the city of Sidon. There is a widow there who will feed you. I have given her my instructions."

10So he went to Zarephath. As he arrived at the

gates of the village, he saw a widow gathering sticks, and he asked her, "Would you please bring me a cup of water?" ¹¹As she was going to get it, he called to her, "Bring me a bite of bread, too."

¹²But she said, "I swear by the LORD your God that I don't have a single piece of bread in the house. And I have only a handful of flour left in the jar and a little cooking oil in the bottom of the jug. I was just gathering a few sticks to cook this last meal, and then my son and I will die."

¹³But Elijah said to her, "Don't be afraid! Go ahead and cook that 'last meal,' but bake me a little loaf of bread first. Afterward there will still be enough food for you and your son. ¹⁴For this is what the LORD, the God of Israel, says: There will always be plenty of flour and oil left in your containers until the time when the LORD sends rain and the crops grow again!"

¹⁵So she did as Elijah said, and she and Elijah and her son continued to eat from her supply of flour and oil for many days. ¹⁶For no matter how much they used, there was always enough left in the containers, just as the LORD had promised through Elijah.

¹⁷Some time later, the woman's son became sick. He grew worse and worse, and finally he died. ¹⁸She then said to Elijah, "O man of God, what have you done to me? Have you come here to punish my sins by killing my son?"

¹⁹But Elijah replied, "Give me your son." And he took the boy's body from her, carried him up to the upper room, where he lived, and laid the body on his bed. ²⁰Then Elijah cried out to the LORD, "O LORD my God, why have you brought tragedy on this widow who has opened her home to me, causing her son to die?"

²¹And he stretched himself out over the child three times and cried out to the LORD, "O LORD my God, please let this child's life return to him." ²²The LORD heard Elijah's prayer, and the life of the child returned, and he came back to life! ²³Then Elijah brought him down from the upper room and gave him to his mother. "Look, your son is alive!" he said.

²⁴Then the woman told Elijah, "Now I know for sure that you are a man of God, and that the LORD truly speaks through you."

CHAPTER **18**

The Contest on Mount Carmel

After many months passed, in the third year of the drought, the LORD said to Elijah, "Go and present yourself to King Ahab. Tell him that I will soon send rain!" ²So Elijah went to appear before Ahab.

Meanwhile, the famine had become very severe in Samaria. ³So Ahab summoned Obadiah, who was in charge of the palace. (Now Obadiah was a devoted follower of the LORD. ⁴Once when Jezebel had tried to kill all the LORD's prophets, Obadiah had hidden one hundred of them in two caves. He had put fifty prophets in each cave and had supplied them with food and water.) ⁵Ahab said to Obadiah, "We must check every spring and valley to see if we can find enough grass to save at least some of my horses and mules." ⁶So they divided the land between them. Ahab went one way by himself, and Obadiah went another way by himself.

⁷As Obadiah was walking along, he saw Elijah coming toward him. Obadiah recognized him at once and fell to the ground before him. "Is it really you, my lord Elijah?" he asked.

⁸"Yes, it is," Elijah replied. "Now go and tell your master I am here."

⁹"Oh, sir," Obadiah protested, "what harm have I done to you that you are sending me to my death at the hands of Ahab? ¹⁰For I swear by the LORD your God that the king has searched every nation and kingdom on earth from end to end to find you. And each time when he was told, 'Elijah isn't here,' King Ahab forced the king of that nation to swear to the truth of his claim. ¹¹And now you say, 'Go and tell your master that Elijah is here'! ¹²But as soon as I leave you, the Spirit of the LORD will carry you away to who knows where. When Ahab comes and cannot find you, he will kill me. Yet I have been a true servant of the LORD all my life. ¹³Has no one told you, my lord, about the time when Jezebel was trying to kill the LORD's prophets? I hid a hundred of them in two caves and supplied them with food and water. ¹⁴And now you say, 'Go and tell your master that Elijah is here'! Sir, if I do that, I'm as good as dead!"

¹⁵But Elijah said, "I swear by the LORD Almighty, in whose presence I stand, that I will present myself to Ahab today."

¹⁶So Obadiah went to tell Ahab that Elijah had come, and Ahab went out to meet him. ¹⁷"So it's you, is it—Israel's troublemaker?" Ahab asked when he saw him.

¹⁸"I have made no trouble for Israel," Elijah replied. "You and your family are the troublemakers, for you have refused to obey the commands of the LORD and have worshiped the images of Baal instead. ¹⁹Now bring all the people of Israel to Mount Carmel, with all 450 prophets of Baal and the 400 prophets of Asherah, who are supported by Jezebel."

²⁰So Ahab summoned all the people and the prophets to Mount Carmel. ²¹Then Elijah stood in front of them and said, "How long are you going to waver between two opinions? If the LORD is God, follow him! But if Baal is God, then follow him!" But the people were completely silent.

²²Then Elijah said to them, "I am the only prophet of the LORD who is left, but Baal has 450 prophets. ²³Now bring two bulls. The prophets of Baal may choose whichever one they wish and cut it into pieces and lay it on the wood of their altar, but without setting fire to it. I will prepare the other bull and lay it on the wood on the altar, but not set fire to it. ²⁴Then call on the name of your god, and I will call on the name of the LORD. The god who answers by setting fire to the wood is the true God!" And all the people agreed.

²⁵Then Elijah said to the prophets of Baal, "You go first, for there are many of you. Choose one of the bulls and prepare it and call on the name of your god. But do not set fire to the wood."

²⁶So they prepared one of the bulls and placed it on the altar. Then they called on the name of Baal all morning, shouting, "O Baal, answer us!" But there was no reply of any kind. Then they danced wildly around the altar they had made.

²⁷About noontime Elijah began mocking them. "You'll have to shout louder," he scoffed, "for surely he is a god! Perhaps he is deep in thought, or he is relieving himself. Or maybe he is away on a trip, or he is asleep and needs to be wakened!"

²⁸So they shouted louder, and following their normal custom, they cut themselves with knives and swords until the blood gushed out. ²⁹They raved all afternoon until the time of the evening sacrifice, but still there was no reply, no voice, no answer.

³⁰Then Elijah called to the people, "Come over here!" They all crowded around him as he repaired the altar of the LORD that had been torn down. ³¹He took twelve stones, one to represent each of the tribes of Israel,* ³²and he used the stones to rebuild the LORD's altar. Then he dug a trench around the altar large enough to hold about three gallons.* ³³He piled wood on the altar, cut the bull into pieces, and laid the pieces on the wood. Then he said, "Fill four large jars with water, and pour the water over the offering and the wood." After they had done this, ³⁴he said, "Do the same thing again!" And when they were finished, he said, "Now do it a third time!"

So they did as he said, ³⁵and the water ran around the altar and even overflowed the trench.

³⁶At the customary time for offering the evening sacrifice, Elijah the prophet walked up to the altar and prayed, "O LORD, God of Abraham, Isaac, and Jacob,* prove today that you are God in Israel and that I am your servant. Prove that I have done all this at your command. ³⁷O LORD, answer me! Answer me so these people will know that you, O LORD, are God and that you have brought them back to yourself."

³⁸Immediately the fire of the LORD flashed down from heaven and burned up the young bull, the wood, the stones, and the dust. It even licked up all the water in the ditch! ³⁹And when the people saw it, they fell on their faces and cried out, "The LORD is God! The LORD is God!"

⁴⁰Then Elijah commanded, "Seize all the prophets of Baal. Don't let a single one escape!" So the people seized them all, and Elijah took them down to the Kishon Valley and killed them there.

Elijah Prays for Rain

⁴¹Then Elijah said to Ahab, "Go and enjoy a good meal! For I hear a mighty rainstorm coming!"

⁴²So Ahab prepared a feast. But Elijah climbed to the top of Mount Carmel and fell to the ground and prayed. ⁴³Then he said to his servant, "Go and look out toward the sea."

The servant went and looked, but he returned to Elijah and said, "I didn't see anything." Seven times Elijah told him to go and look, and seven times he went. ⁴⁴Finally the seventh time, his servant told him, "I saw a little cloud about the size of a hand rising from the sea."

Then Elijah shouted, "Hurry to Ahab and tell him, 'Climb into your chariot and go back home. If you don't hurry, the rain will stop you!'"

⁴⁵And sure enough, the sky was soon black with clouds. A heavy wind brought a terrific rainstorm, and Ahab left quickly for Jezreel. ⁴⁶Now the LORD gave special strength to Elijah. He tucked his cloak into his belt and ran ahead of Ahab's chariot all the way to the entrance of Jezreel.

CHAPTER 19

Elijah Flees to Sinai

When Ahab got home, he told Jezebel what Elijah had done and that he had slaughtered the prophets of Baal. ²So Jezebel sent this message to Elijah: "May the gods also kill me if by this

---

18:31 Hebrew *each of the tribes of the sons of Jacob to whom the LORD had said, "Your name will be Israel."* **18:32** Hebrew *2 seahs* [12 liters] *of seed.* **18:36** Hebrew *and Israel.*

time tomorrow I have failed to take your life like those whom you killed."

3Elijah was afraid and fled for his life. He went to Beersheba, a town in Judah, and he left his servant there. 4Then he went on alone into the desert, traveling all day. He sat down under a solitary broom tree and prayed that he might die. "I have had enough, LORD," he said. "Take my life, for I am no better than my ancestors."

5Then he lay down and slept under the broom tree. But as he was sleeping, an angel touched him and told him, "Get up and eat!" 6He looked around and saw some bread baked on hot stones and a jar of water! So he ate and drank and lay down again.

7Then the angel of the LORD came again and touched him and said, "Get up and eat some more, for there is a long journey ahead of you."

8So he got up and ate and drank, and the food gave him enough strength to travel forty days and forty nights to Mount Sinai,* the mountain of God. 9There he came to a cave, where he spent the night.

The LORD Speaks to Elijah

But the LORD said to him, "What are you doing here, Elijah?"

10Elijah replied, "I have zealously served the LORD God Almighty. But the people of Israel have broken their covenant with you, torn down your altars, and killed every one of your prophets. I alone am left, and now they are trying to kill me, too."

11"Go out and stand before me on the mountain," the LORD told him. And as Elijah stood there, the LORD passed by, and a mighty windstorm hit the mountain. It was such a terrible blast that the rocks were torn loose, but the LORD was not in the wind. After the wind there was an earthquake, but the LORD was not in the earthquake. 12And after the earthquake there was a fire, but the LORD was not in the fire. And after the fire there was the sound of a gentle whisper. 13When Elijah heard it, he wrapped his face in his cloak and went out and stood at the entrance of the cave.

And a voice said, "What are you doing here, Elijah?"

14He replied again, "I have zealously served the LORD God Almighty. But the people of Israel have broken their covenant with you, torn down your altars, and killed every one of your prophets. I alone am left, and now they are trying to kill me, too."

19:8 Hebrew *Horeb,* another name for Sinai.

15Then the LORD told him, "Go back the way you came, and travel to the wilderness of Damascus. When you arrive there, anoint Hazael to be king of Aram. 16Then anoint Jehu son of Nimshi to be king of Israel, and anoint Elisha son of Shaphat from Abel-meholah to replace you as my prophet. 17Anyone who escapes from Hazael will be killed by Jehu, and those who escape Jehu will be killed by Elisha! 18Yet I will preserve seven thousand others in Israel who have never bowed to Baal or kissed him!"

The Call of Elisha

19So Elijah went and found Elisha son of Shaphat plowing a field with a team of oxen. There were eleven teams of oxen ahead of him, and he was plowing with the twelfth team. Elijah went over to him and threw his cloak across his shoulders and walked away again. 20Elisha left the

---

Listen for God's Voice
Read 1 KINGS 19:11-13

The Bible records several instances in which God spoke to people in an audible voice, as in the case of Elijah and Moses. Yet God's voice may not necessarily be audible to the human ear: It may simply be a reinforcement of what he has said in his Word. You might say this is the "gentle whisper" or "still, small voice" of God in the life of the believer today.

Sadly, we often overpower his voice with the constant barrage of "noise" in our lives. We don't have the concentration to meditate on the things of God because we are constantly listening to the TV at home, turning up the radio in the car—or doing all of the talking ourselves.

Yet God wants us to learn to be aggressive listeners. God will not always speak to us in dramatic ways. Many times you will hear his voice in what should be your daily routine as a believer: spending time in prayer; reading God's Word; meditating on his Word; and fellowshiping with other believers.

Work hard at being a listener who has open ears, an open mind, an open heart, and an open Bible. Jesus often said, "Anyone who is willing to hear should listen and understand" (Mark 4:9).

To begin the next topic, turn to p. A30.

oxen standing there, ran after Elijah, and said to him, "First let me go and kiss my father and mother good-bye, and then I will go with you!"

Elijah replied, "Go on back! But consider what I have done to you."

21Elisha then returned to his oxen, killed them, and used the wood from the plow to build a fire to roast their flesh. He passed around the meat to the other plowmen, and they all ate. Then he went with Elijah as his assistant.

CHAPTER 20

Ben-Hadad Attacks Samaria

Now King Ben-hadad of Aram mobilized his army, supported by the chariots and horses of thirty-two allied kings. They went to besiege Samaria, the Israelite capital, and launched attacks against it. 2Ben-hadad sent messengers into the city to relay this message to King Ahab of Israel: "This is what Ben-hadad says: 3'Your silver and gold are mine, and so are the best of your wives and children!'"

4"All right, my lord," Ahab replied. "All that I have is yours!"

5Soon Ben-hadad's messengers returned again and said, "This is what Ben-hadad says: 'I have already demanded that you give me your silver, gold, wives, and children. 6But about this time tomorrow I will send my officials to search your palace and the homes of your people. They will take away everything you consider valuable!'"

7Then Ahab summoned all the leaders of the land and said to them, "Look how this man is stirring up trouble! I already agreed when he sent the message demanding that I give him my wives and children and silver and gold."

8"Don't give in to any more demands," the leaders and people advised.

9So Ahab told the messengers from Ben-hadad, "Say this to my lord the king: 'I will give you everything you asked for the first time, but this last demand of yours I simply cannot meet.'" So the messengers returned to Ben-hadad with the response.

10Then Ben-hadad sent this message to Ahab: "May the gods bring tragedy on me, and even worse than that, if there remains enough dust from Samaria to provide more than a handful for each of my soldiers."

11The king of Israel sent back this answer: "A warrior still dressing for battle should not boast like a warrior who has already won."

12This reply of Ahab's reached Ben-hadad

20:12 Or *in Succoth;* also in 20:16.

and the other kings as they were drinking in their tents.* "Prepare to attack!" Ben-hadad commanded his officers. So they prepared to attack the city.

Ahab's Victory over Ben-Hadad

13Then a prophet came to see King Ahab and told him, "This is what the LORD says: Do you see all these enemy forces? Today I will hand them all over to you. Then you will know that I am the LORD."

14Ahab asked, "How will he do it?"

And the prophet replied, "This is what the LORD says: The troops of the provincial commanders will do it."

"Should we attack first?" Ahab asked.

"Yes," the prophet answered.

15So Ahab mustered the troops of the 232 provincial commanders. Then he called out the rest of his army of seven thousand men. 16About noontime, as Ben-hadad and the thirty-two allied kings were still in their tents getting drunk, 17the troops of the provincial commanders marched out of the city. As they approached, Ben-hadad's scouts reported to him, "Some troops are coming from Samaria."

18"Take them alive," Ben-hadad commanded, "whether they have come for peace or for war."

19But by now Ahab's provincial commanders had led the army out to fight. 20Each Israelite soldier killed his Aramean opponent, and suddenly the entire Aramean army panicked and fled. The Israelites chased them, but King Ben-hadad and a few others escaped on horses. 21However, the other horses and chariots were destroyed, and the Arameans were killed in a great slaughter.

22Afterward the prophet said to King Ahab, "Get ready for another attack by the king of Aram next spring."

Ben-Hadad's Second Attack

23After their defeat, Ben-hadad's officers said to him, "The Israelite gods are gods of the hills; that is why they won. But we can beat them easily on the plains. 24Only this time replace the kings with field commanders! 25Recruit another army like the one you lost. Give us the same number of horses, chariots, and men, and we will fight against them in the plains. There's not a shadow of a doubt that we will beat them." So King Ben-hadad did as they suggested. 26The following spring he called up the Aramean army and marched out against Israel, this time at

Aphek. ²⁷Israel then mustered its army, set up supply lines, and moved into the battle. But the Israelite army looked like two little flocks of goats in comparison to the vast Aramean forces that filled the countryside!

²⁸Then the man of God went to the king of Israel and said, "This is what the LORD says: The Arameans have said that the LORD is a god of the hills and not of the plains. So I will help you defeat this vast army. Then you will know that I am the LORD."

²⁹The two armies camped opposite each other for seven days, and on the seventh day the battle began. The Israelites killed 100,000 Aramean foot soldiers in one day. ³⁰The rest fled behind the walls of Aphek, but the wall fell on them and killed another 27,000. Ben-hadad fled into the city and hid in a secret room. ³¹Ben-hadad's officers said to him, "Sir, we have heard that the kings of Israel are very merciful. So let's humble ourselves by wearing sackcloth and putting ropes on our heads. Then perhaps King Ahab will let you live."

³²So they put on sackcloth and ropes and went to the king of Israel and begged, "Your servant Ben-hadad says, 'Please let me live!'"

The king of Israel responded, "Is he still alive? He is my brother!"

³³The men were quick to grasp at this straw of hope, and they replied, "Yes, your brother Ben-hadad!"

"Go and get him," the king of Israel told them. And when Ben-hadad arrived, Ahab invited him up into his chariot!

³⁴Ben-hadad told him, "I will give back the towns my father took from your father, and you may establish places of trade in Damascus, as my father did in Samaria."

Then Ahab said, "I will let you go under these conditions." So they made a treaty, and Ben-hadad was set free.

A Prophet Condemns Ahab

³⁵Meanwhile, the LORD instructed one of the group of prophets to say to another man, "Strike me!" But the man refused to strike the prophet. ³⁶Then the prophet told him, "Because you have not obeyed the voice of the LORD, a lion will kill you as soon as you leave me." And sure enough, when he had gone, a lion attacked and killed him.

³⁷Then the prophet turned to another man and said, "Strike me!" So he struck the prophet and wounded him.

³⁸The prophet waited for the king beside the road, having placed a bandage over his eyes to disguise himself. ³⁹As the king passed by, the prophet called out to him, "Sir, I was in the battle, and a man brought me a prisoner. He said, 'Guard this man; if for any reason he gets away, you will either die or pay a fine of seventy-five pounds* of silver!' ⁴⁰But while I was busy doing something else, the prisoner disappeared!"

"Well, it's your own fault," the king replied. "You have determined your own judgment."

⁴¹Then the prophet pulled the bandage from his eyes, and the king of Israel recognized him as one of the prophets. ⁴²And the prophet told him, "This is what the LORD says: Because you have spared the man I said must be destroyed,* now you must die in his place, and your people will die instead of his people." ⁴³So the king of Israel went home to Samaria angry and sullen.

CHAPTER **21**
Naboth's Vineyard

King Ahab had a palace in Jezreel, and near the palace was a vineyard owned by a man named Naboth. ²One day Ahab said to Naboth, "Since your vineyard is so convenient to the palace, I would like to buy it to use as a vegetable garden. I will give you a better vineyard in exchange, or if you prefer, I will pay you for it."

³But Naboth replied, "The LORD forbid that I should give you the inheritance that was passed down by my ancestors." ⁴So Ahab went home angry and sullen because of Naboth's answer. The king went to bed with his face to the wall and refused to eat!

⁵"What in the world is the matter?" his wife, Jezebel, asked him. "What has made you so upset that you are not eating?"

⁶"I asked Naboth to sell me his vineyard or to trade it, and he refused!" Ahab told her.

⁷"Are you the king of Israel or not?" Jezebel asked. "Get up and eat and don't worry about it. I'll get you Naboth's vineyard!"

⁸So she wrote letters in Ahab's name, sealed them with his seal, and sent them to the elders and other leaders of the city where Naboth lived. ⁹In her letters she commanded: "Call the citizens together for fasting and prayer and give Naboth a place of honor. ¹⁰Find two scoundrels* who will accuse him of cursing God and the king. Then take him out and stone him to death."

¹¹So the elders and other leaders followed the instructions Jezebel had written in the letters.

20:39 Hebrew *1 talent* [34 kilograms]. 20:42 The Hebrew term used here refers to the complete consecration of things or people to the LORD, either by destroying them or by giving them as an offering. 21:10 Hebrew *two sons of Belial;* also in 21:13.

¹²They called for a fast and put Naboth at a prominent place before the people. ¹³Then two scoundrels accused him before all the people of cursing God and the king. So he was dragged outside the city and stoned to death. ¹⁴The city officials then sent word to Jezebel, "Naboth has been stoned to death."

¹⁵When Jezebel heard the news, she said to Ahab, "You know the vineyard Naboth wouldn't sell you? Well, you can have it now! He's dead!" ¹⁶So Ahab immediately went down to the vineyard to claim it.

¹⁷But the LORD said to Elijah, who was from Tishbe, ¹⁸"Go down to meet King Ahab, who rules in Samaria. He will be at Naboth's vineyard in Jezreel, taking possession of it. ¹⁹Give him this message: 'This is what the LORD says: Isn't killing Naboth bad enough? Must you rob him, too? Because you have done this, dogs will lick your blood outside the city just as they licked the blood of Naboth!'"

²⁰"So my enemy has found me!" Ahab exclaimed to Elijah.

"Yes," Elijah answered, "I have come because you have sold yourself to what is evil in the LORD's sight. ²¹The LORD is going to bring disaster to you and sweep you away. He will not let a single one of your male descendants, slave or free alike, survive in Israel! ²²He is going to destroy your family as he did the family of Jeroboam son of Nebat and the family of Baasha son of Ahijah, for you have made him very angry and have led all of Israel into sin. ²³The LORD has also told me that the dogs of Jezreel will eat the body of your wife, Jezebel, at the city wall. ²⁴The members of your family who die in the city will be eaten by dogs, and those who die in the field will be eaten by vultures."

²⁵No one else so completely sold himself to what was evil in the LORD's sight as did Ahab, for his wife, Jezebel, influenced him. ²⁶He was especially guilty because he worshiped idols just as the Amorites had done—the people whom the LORD had driven from the land ahead of the Israelites.

²⁷When Ahab heard this message, he tore his clothing, dressed in sackcloth, and fasted. He even slept in sackcloth and went about in deep mourning.

²⁸Then another message from the LORD came to Elijah, who was from Tishbe: ²⁹"Do you see how Ahab has humbled himself before me? Because he has done this, I will not do what I promised during his lifetime. It will happen to his sons; I will destroy all his descendants."

CHAPTER 22
Jehoshaphat and Ahab

For three years there was no war between Aram and Israel. ²Then during the third year, King Jehoshaphat of Judah went to visit King Ahab of Israel. ³During the visit, Ahab said to his officials, "Do you realize that the Arameans are still occupying our city of Ramoth-gilead? And we haven't done a thing about it!" ⁴Then he turned to Jehoshaphat and asked, "Will you join me in fighting against Ramoth-gilead?"

And Jehoshaphat replied to King Ahab, "Why, of course! You and I are brothers, and my troops are yours to command. Even my horses are at your service." ⁵Then Jehoshaphat added, "But first let's find out what the LORD says."

⁶So King Ahab summoned his prophets, about four hundred of them, and asked them, "Should I go to war against Ramoth-gilead or not?"

They all replied, "Go right ahead! The Lord will give you a glorious victory!"

⁷But Jehoshaphat asked, "Isn't there a prophet of the LORD around, too? I would like to ask him the same question."

⁸King Ahab replied, "There is still one prophet of the LORD, but I hate him. He never prophesies anything but bad news for me! His name is Micaiah son of Imlah."

"You shouldn't talk like that," Jehoshaphat said. "Let's hear what he has to say."

⁹So the king of Israel called one of his officials and said, "Quick! Go and get Micaiah son of Imlah."

Micaiah Prophesies against Ahab

¹⁰King Ahab of Israel and King Jehoshaphat of Judah, dressed in their royal robes, were sitting on thrones at the threshing floor near the gate of Samaria. All of Ahab's prophets were prophesying there in front of them. ¹¹One of them, Zedekiah son of Kenaanah, made some iron horns and proclaimed, "This is what the LORD says: With these horns you will gore the Arameans to death!"

¹²All the other prophets agreed. "Yes," they said, "go up to Ramoth-gilead and be victorious, for the LORD will give you victory!"

¹³Meanwhile, the messenger who went to get Micaiah said to him, "Look, all the prophets are promising victory for the king. Be sure that you agree with them and promise success."

¹⁴But Micaiah replied, "As surely as the LORD lives, I will say only what the LORD tells me to say."

¹⁵When Micaiah arrived before the king, Ahab asked him, "Micaiah, should we go to war against Ramoth-gilead or not?"

And Micaiah replied, "Go right ahead! The LORD will give the king a glorious victory!"

16But the king replied sharply, "How many times must I demand that you speak only the truth when you speak for the LORD?"

17So Micaiah told him, "In a vision I saw all Israel scattered on the mountains, like sheep without a shepherd. And the LORD said, 'Their master has been killed. Send them home in peace.'"

18"Didn't I tell you?" the king of Israel said to Jehoshaphat. "He does it every time. He never prophesies anything but bad news for me."

19Then Micaiah continued, "Listen to what the LORD says! I saw the LORD sitting on his throne with all the armies of heaven around him, on his right and on his left. 20And the LORD said, 'Who can entice Ahab to go into battle against Ramoth-gilead so that he can be killed there?' There were many suggestions, 21until finally a spirit approached the LORD and said, 'I can do it!'

22" 'How will you do this?' the LORD asked.

"And the spirit replied, 'I will go out and inspire all Ahab's prophets to speak lies.'

" 'You will succeed,' said the LORD. 'Go ahead and do it.'

23"So you see, the LORD has put a lying spirit in the mouths of your prophets. For the LORD has determined disaster for you."

24Then Zedekiah son of Kenaanah walked up to Micaiah and slapped him across the face. "When did the Spirit of the LORD leave me to speak to you?" he demanded.

25And Micaiah replied, "You will find out soon enough when you find yourself hiding in some secret room!"

26King Ahab of Israel then ordered, "Arrest Micaiah and take him back to Amon, the governor of the city, and to my son Joash. 27Give them this order from the king: 'Put this man in prison, and feed him nothing but bread and water until I return safely from the battle!'"

28But Micaiah replied, "If you return safely, the LORD has not spoken through me!" Then he added to those standing around, "Take note of what I have said."

The Death of Ahab

29So the king of Israel and King Jehoshaphat of Judah led their armies against Ramoth-gilead. 30Now King Ahab said to Jehoshaphat, "As we go into battle, I will disguise myself so no one will recognize me, but you wear your royal robes." So Ahab disguised himself, and they went into battle.

31Now the king of Aram had issued these orders to his thirty-two charioteers: "Attack only the king of Israel!" 32So when the Aramean charioteers saw Jehoshaphat in his royal robes, they went after him. "There is the king of Israel!" they shouted. But when Jehoshaphat cried out, 33the charioteers realized he was not the king of Israel, and they stopped chasing him.

34An Aramean soldier, however, randomly shot an arrow at the Israelite troops, and the arrow hit the king of Israel between the joints of his armor. "Get me out of here!" Ahab groaned to the driver of his chariot. "I have been badly wounded!" 35The battle raged all that day, and Ahab was propped up in his chariot facing the Arameans. The blood from his wound ran down to the floor of his chariot, and as evening arrived he died. 36Just as the sun was setting, the cry ran through his troops: "It's all over—return home!" 37So the king died, and his body was taken to Samaria and buried there. 38Then his chariot was washed beside the pool of Samaria, where the prostitutes bathed, and dogs came and licked the king's blood, just as the LORD had promised.

39The rest of the events in Ahab's reign and the story of the ivory palace and the cities he built are recorded in *The Book of the History of the Kings of Israel.* 40When Ahab died, he was buried among his ancestors. Then his son Ahaziah became the next king.

Jehoshaphat Rules in Judah

41Jehoshaphat son of Asa began to rule over Judah in the fourth year of King Ahab's reign in Israel. 42He was thirty-five years old when he became king, and he reigned in Jerusalem twenty-five years. His mother was Azubah, the daughter of Shilhi. 43Jehoshaphat was a good king, following the example of his father, Asa. He did what was pleasing in the LORD's sight. During his reign, however, he failed to remove all the pagan shrines, and the people still offered sacrifices and burned incense there. 44Jehoshaphat also made peace with the king of Israel.

45The rest of the events in Jehoshaphat's reign, the extent of his power, and the wars he waged are recorded in *The Book of the History of the Kings of Judah.* 46He banished from the land the rest of the shrine prostitutes, who still continued their practices from the days of his father, Asa. 47There was no king in Edom at that time, only a deputy.

48Jehoshaphat also built a fleet of trading ships* to sail to Ophir for gold. But the ships never set sail, for they were wrecked at Ezion-geber. 49At that time Ahaziah son of Ahab proposed to Jehoshaphat, "Let my men sail an expedition with your men." But Jehoshaphat refused the offer.

50When Jehoshaphat died, he was buried with his ancestors in the City of David. Then his son Jehoram became the next king.

22:48 Hebrew *fleet of ships of Tarshish.*

Ahaziah Rules in Israel

51Ahaziah son of Ahab began to rule over Israel in the seventeenth year of King Jehoshaphat's reign in Judah. He reigned in Samaria two years. 52But he did what was evil in the LORD's sight, following the example of his father and mother and the example of Jeroboam son of Nebat, who had led Israel into the sin of idolatry. 53He served Baal and worshiped him, arousing the anger of the LORD, the God of Israel, just as his father had done.

2 Kings

CHAPTER 1

Elijah Confronts King Ahaziah

After King Ahab's death, the nation of Moab declared its independence from Israel.

2One day Israel's new king, Ahaziah, fell through the latticework of an upper room at his palace in Samaria, and he was seriously injured. So he sent messengers to the temple of Baal-zebub, the god of Ekron, to ask whether he would recover.

3But the angel of the LORD told Elijah, who was from Tishbe, "Go and meet the messengers of the king of Samaria and ask them, 'Why are you going to Baal-zebub, the god of Ekron, to ask whether the king will get well? Is there no God in Israel? 4Now, therefore, this is what the LORD says: You will never leave the bed on which you are lying, but you will surely die.'" So Elijah went to deliver the message.

5When the messengers returned to the king, he asked them, "Why have you returned so soon?"

6They replied, "A man came up to us and said, 'Go back to the king and give him this message from the LORD: Why are you sending men to Baal-zebub, the god of Ekron, to ask whether you will get well? Is there no God in Israel? Now, since you have done this, you will never leave the bed on which you are lying, but you will surely die.'"

7"Who was this man?" the king demanded. "What did he look like?"

8They replied, "He was a hairy man,* and he wore a leather belt around his waist."

"It was Elijah from Tishbe!" the king exclaimed. 9Then he sent an army captain with fifty soldiers to arrest him. They found him sitting on top of a hill. The captain said to him, "Man of God, the king has commanded you to come along with us."

10But Elijah replied to the captain, "If I am a man of God, let fire come down from heaven and destroy you and your fifty men!" Then fire fell from heaven and killed them all.

11So the king sent another captain with fifty men. The captain said to him, "Man of God, the king says that you must come down right away."

12Elijah replied, "If I am a man of God, let fire come down from heaven and destroy you and your fifty men!" And again the fire of God fell from heaven and killed them all.

13Once more the king sent a captain with fifty men. But this time the captain fell to his knees before Elijah. He pleaded with him, "O man of God, please spare my life and the lives of these, your fifty servants. 14See how the fire from heaven has destroyed the first two groups. But now please spare my life!"

15Then the angel of the LORD said to Elijah, "Don't be afraid. Go with him." So Elijah got up and went to the king.

16And Elijah said to the king, "This is what the LORD says: Why did you send messengers to Baal-zebub, the god of Ekron, to ask whether you will get well? Is there no God in Israel? Now, since you have done this, you will never leave the bed on which you are lying, but you will surely die."

17So Ahaziah died, just as the LORD had promised through Elijah. Since Ahaziah did not have a son to succeed him, his brother Joram* became the next king. This took place in the second year of the reign of Jehoram son of Jehoshaphat, king of Judah. 18The rest of the events in Ahaziah's reign are recorded in *The Book of the History of the Kings of Israel.*

CHAPTER 2

Elijah Taken into Heaven

When the LORD was about to take Elijah up to heaven in a whirlwind, Elijah and Elisha were

---

1:8 Or *He was wearing clothing made of hair.*   **1:17** Hebrew *Jehoram,* a variant name for Joram.

traveling from Gilgal. [2]And Elijah said to Elisha, "Stay here, for the LORD has told me to go to Bethel."

But Elisha replied, "As surely as the LORD lives and you yourself live, I will never leave you!" So they went on together to Bethel.

[3]The group of prophets from Bethel came to Elisha and asked him, "Did you know that the LORD is going to take your master away from you today?"

"Quiet!" Elisha answered. "Of course I know it."

[4]Then Elijah said to Elisha, "Stay here, for the LORD has told me to go to Jericho."

But Elisha replied again, "As surely as the LORD lives and you yourself live, I will never leave you." So they went on together to Jericho.

[5]Then the group of prophets from Jericho came to Elisha and asked him, "Did you know that the LORD is going to take your master away from you today?"

"Quiet!" he answered again. "Of course I know it."

[6]Then Elijah said to Elisha, "Stay here, for the LORD has told me to go to the Jordan River."

But again Elisha replied, "As surely as the LORD lives and you yourself live, I will never leave you." So they went on together.

[7]Fifty men from the group of prophets also went and watched from a distance as Elijah and Elisha stopped beside the Jordan River. [8]Then Elijah folded his cloak together and struck the water with it. The river divided, and the two of them went across on dry ground!

[9]When they came to the other side, Elijah said to Elisha, "What can I do for you before I am taken away?"

And Elisha replied, "Please let me become your rightful successor."*

[10]"You have asked a difficult thing," Elijah replied. "If you see me when I am taken from you, then you will get your request. But if not, then you won't."

[11]As they were walking along and talking, suddenly a chariot of fire appeared, drawn by horses of fire. It drove between them, separating them, and Elijah was carried by a whirlwind into heaven. [12]Elisha saw it and cried out, "My father! My father! The chariots and charioteers of Israel!" And as they disappeared from sight, Elisha tore his robe in two.

[13]Then Elisha picked up Elijah's cloak and returned to the bank of the Jordan River. [14]He

struck the water with the cloak and cried out, "Where is the LORD, the God of Elijah?" Then the river divided, and Elisha went across.

[15]When the group of prophets from Jericho saw what happened, they exclaimed, "Elisha has become Elijah's successor!"* And they went to meet him and bowed down before him. [16]"Sir," they said, "just say the word and fifty of our strongest men will search the wilderness for your master. Perhaps the Spirit of the LORD has left him on some mountain or in some valley."

"No," Elisha said, "don't send them." [17]But they kept urging him until he was embarrassed, and he finally said, "All right, send them." So fifty men searched for three days but did not find Elijah. [18]Elisha was still at Jericho when they returned. "Didn't I tell you not to go?" he asked.

Elisha's First Miracles

[19]Now the leaders of the town of Jericho visited Elisha. "We have a problem, my lord," they told him. "This town is located in beautiful natural surroundings, as you can see. But the water is bad, and the land is unproductive."

[20]Elisha said, "Bring me a new bowl with salt in it." So they brought it to him. [21]Then he went out to the spring that supplied the town with water and threw the salt into it. And he said, "This is what the LORD says: I have made this water wholesome. It will no longer cause death or infertility.*" [22]And sure enough! The water has remained wholesome ever since, just as Elisha said.

[23]Elisha left Jericho and went up to Bethel. As he was walking along the road, a group of boys from the town began mocking and making fun of him. "Go away, you baldhead!" they chanted. "Go away, you baldhead!" [24]Elisha turned around and looked at them, and he cursed them in the name of the LORD. Then two bears came out of the woods and mauled forty-two of them. [25]From there Elisha went to Mount Carmel and finally returned to Samaria.

CHAPTER **3**

War between Israel and Moab

Ahab's son Joram* began to rule over Israel in the eighteenth year of King Jehoshaphat's reign in Judah. He reigned in Samaria twelve years. [2]He did what was evil in the LORD's sight, but he was not as wicked as his father and mother. He at least tore down the sacred pillar of Baal that his father had set up. [3]Nevertheless he contin-

---

2:9 Hebrew *Let me inherit a double share of your spirit.*   2:15 Hebrew *The spirit of Elijah rests upon Elisha.*   2:21 Or *or make the land unproductive.*   3:1 Hebrew *Jehoram,* a variant name for Joram; also in 3:6.

ued in the sins of idolatry that Jeroboam son of Nebat had led the people of Israel to commit.

4King Mesha of Moab and his people were sheep breeders. They used to pay the king of Israel an annual tribute of 100,000 lambs and the wool of 100,000 rams. 5But after Ahab's death, the king of Moab rebelled against the king of Israel. 6So King Joram mustered the army of Israel and marched from Samaria. 7On the way, he sent this message to King Jehoshaphat of Judah: "The king of Moab has rebelled against me. Will you help me fight him?"

And Jehoshaphat replied, "Why, of course! You and I are brothers, and my troops are yours to command. Even my horses are at your service." 8Then Jehoshaphat asked, "What route will we take?"

"We will attack from the wilderness of Edom," Joram replied. 9The king of Edom and his troops joined them, and all three armies traveled along a roundabout route through the wilderness for seven days. But there was no water for the men or their pack animals.

10"What should we do?" the king of Israel cried out. "The LORD has brought the three of us here to let the king of Moab defeat us."

11But King Jehoshaphat of Judah asked, "Is there no prophet of the LORD with us? If there is, we can ask the LORD what to do."

One of King Joram's officers replied, "Elisha son of Shaphat is here. He used to be Elijah's personal assistant.*"

12Jehoshaphat said, "Then the LORD will speak through him." So the kings of Israel, Judah, and Edom went to consult with Elisha.

13"I want no part of you," Elisha said to the king of Israel. "Go to the pagan prophets of your father and mother!"

But King Joram said, "No! For it was the LORD who called us three kings here to be destroyed by the king of Moab!"

14Elisha replied, "As surely as the LORD Almighty lives, whom I serve, I would not bother with you except for my respect for King Jehoshaphat of Judah. 15Now bring me someone who can play the harp."

While the harp was being played, the power of the LORD came upon Elisha, 16and he said, "This is what the LORD says: This dry valley will be filled with pools of water! 17You will see neither wind nor rain, says the LORD, but this valley will be filled with water. You will have plenty for yourselves and for your cattle and your other animals.

18But this is only a simple thing for the LORD, for he will make you victorious over the army of Moab! 19You will conquer the best of their cities, even the fortified ones. You will cut down all their trees, stop up all their springs, and ruin all their good land with stones."

20And sure enough, the next day at about the time when the morning sacrifice was offered, water suddenly appeared! It was flowing from the direction of Edom, and soon there was water everywhere.

21Meanwhile, when the people of Moab heard about the three armies marching against them, they mobilized every man who could fight, young and old, and stationed themselves along their border. 22But when they got up the next morning, the sun was shining across the water, making it look as red as blood. 23"It's blood!" the Moabites exclaimed. "The three armies have attacked and killed each other! Let's go and collect the plunder!"

24When they arrived at the Israelite camp, the army of Israel rushed out and attacked the Moabites, who turned and ran. The army of Israel chased them into the land of Moab, destroying everything as they went. 25They destroyed the cities, covered their good land with stones, stopped up the springs, and cut down the good trees. Finally, only Kir-hareseth was left, but even that came under attack.*

26When the king of Moab saw that he was losing the battle, he led seven hundred of his warriors in a desperate attempt to break through the enemy lines near the king of Edom, but they failed to escape. 27So he took his oldest son, who would have been the next king, and sacrificed him as a burnt offering on the wall. As a result, the anger against Israel was great, so they withdrew and returned to their own land.

CHAPTER **4**

Elisha Helps a Poor Widow

One day the widow of one of Elisha's fellow prophets came to Elisha and cried out to him, "My husband who served you is dead, and you know how he feared the LORD. But now a creditor has come, threatening to take my two sons as slaves."

2"What can I do to help you?" Elisha asked. "Tell me, what do you have in the house?"

"Nothing at all, except a flask of olive oil," she replied.

3And Elisha said, "Borrow as many empty jars

3:11 Hebrew *He used to pour water on the hands of Elijah.*   3:25 Hebrew *until only Kir-hareseth was left, with its stones, but the slingers surrounded and attacked it.*

as you can from your friends and neighbors. 4Then go into your house with your sons and shut the door behind you. Pour olive oil from your flask into the jars, setting the jars aside as they are filled."

5So she did as she was told. Her sons brought many jars to her, and she filled one after another. 6Soon every container was full to the brim!

"Bring me another jar," she said to one of her sons.

"There aren't any more!" he told her. And then the olive oil stopped flowing.

7When she told the man of God what had happened, he said to her, "Now sell the olive oil and pay your debts, and there will be enough money left over to support you and your sons."

Elisha and the Woman from Shunem

8One day Elisha went to the town of Shunem. A wealthy woman lived there, and she invited him to eat some food. From then on, whenever he passed that way, he would stop there to eat.

9She said to her husband, "I am sure this man who stops in from time to time is a holy man of God. 10Let's make a little room for him on the roof and furnish it with a bed, a table, a chair, and a lamp. Then he will have a place to stay whenever he comes by."

11One day Elisha returned to Shunem, and he went up to his room to rest. 12He said to his servant Gehazi, "Tell the woman I want to speak to her." When she arrived, 13Elisha said to Gehazi, "Tell her that we appreciate the kind concern she has shown us. Now ask her what we can do for her. Does she want me to put in a good word for her to the king or to the commander of the army?"

"No," she replied, "my family takes good care of me."

14Later Elisha asked Gehazi, "What do you think we can do for her?"

He suggested, "She doesn't have a son, and her husband is an old man."

15"Call her back again," Elisha told him. When the woman returned, Elisha said to her as she stood in the doorway, 16"Next year at about this time you will be holding a son in your arms!"

"No, my lord!" she protested. "Please don't lie to me like that, O man of God." 17But sure enough, the woman soon became pregnant. And at that time the following year she had a son, just as Elisha had said.

18One day when her child was older, he went out to visit his father, who was working with the harvesters. 19Suddenly he complained, "My head hurts! My head hurts!"

His father said to one of the servants, "Carry him home to his mother."

20So the servant took him home, and his mother held him on her lap. But around noontime he died. 21She carried him up to the bed of the man of God, then shut the door and left him there. 22She sent a message to her husband: "Send one of the servants and a donkey so that I can hurry to the man of God and come right back."

23"Why today?" he asked. "It is neither a new moon festival nor a Sabbath."

But she said, "It's all right." 24So she saddled the donkey and said to the servant, "Hurry! Don't slow down on my account unless I tell you to."

25As she approached the man of God at Mount Carmel, Elisha saw her in the distance. He said to Gehazi, "Look, the woman from Shunem is coming. 26Run out to meet her and ask her, 'Is everything all right with you, with your husband, and with your child?'"

"Yes," the woman told Gehazi, "everything is fine."

27But when she came to the man of God at the mountain, she fell to the ground before him and caught hold of his feet. Gehazi began to push her away, but the man of God said, "Leave her alone. Something is troubling her deeply, and the LORD has not told me what it is."

28Then she said, "It was you, my lord, who said I would have a son. And didn't I tell you not to raise my hopes?"

29Then Elisha said to Gehazi, "Get ready to travel; take my staff and go! Don't talk to anyone along the way. Go quickly and lay the staff on the child's face."

30But the boy's mother said, "As surely as the LORD lives and you yourself live, I won't go home unless you go with me." So Elisha returned with her.

31Gehazi hurried on ahead and laid the staff on the child's face, but nothing happened. There was no sign of life. He returned to meet Elisha and told him, "The child is still dead."

32When Elisha arrived, the child was indeed dead, lying there on the prophet's bed. 33He went in alone and shut the door behind him and prayed to the LORD. 34Then he lay down on the child's body, placing his mouth on the child's mouth, his eyes on the child's eyes, and his hands on the child's hands. And the child's body began to grow warm again! 35Elisha got up and walked back and forth in the room a few times. Then he stretched himself out again on the child. This time the boy sneezed seven times and opened his eyes!

36Then Elisha summoned Gehazi. "Call the child's mother!" he said. And when she came in, Elisha said, "Here, take your son!" 37She fell at his feet, overwhelmed with gratitude. Then she picked up her son and carried him downstairs.

Miracles during a Famine

38Elisha now returned to Gilgal, but there was a famine in the land. One day as the group of prophets was seated before him, he said to his servant, "Put on a large kettle and make some stew for these men."

39One of the young men went out into the field to gather vegetables and came back with a pocketful of wild gourds. He shredded them and put them into the kettle without realizing they were poisonous. 40But after the men had eaten a bite or two they cried out, "Man of God, there's poison in this stew!" So they would not eat it.

41Elisha said, "Bring me some flour." Then he threw it into the kettle and said, "Now it's all right; go ahead and eat." And then it did not harm them!

42One day a man from Baal-shalishah brought the man of God a sack of fresh grain and twenty loaves of barley bread made from the first grain of his harvest. Elisha said, "Give it to the group of prophets* so they can eat."

43"What?" his servant exclaimed. "Feed one hundred people with only this?"

But Elisha repeated, "Give it to the group of prophets so they can eat, for the LORD says there will be plenty for all. There will even be some left over!" 44And sure enough, there was plenty for all and some left over, just as the LORD had promised.

CHAPTER **5**
The Healing of Naaman

The king of Aram had high admiration for Naaman, the commander of his army, because through him the LORD had given Aram great victories. But though Naaman was a mighty warrior, he suffered from leprosy.*

2Now groups of Aramean raiders had invaded the land of Israel, and among their captives was a young girl who had been given to Naaman's wife as a maid. 3One day the girl said to her mistress, "I wish my master would go to see the prophet in Samaria. He would heal him of his leprosy."

4So Naaman told the king what the young girl from Israel had said. 5"Go and visit the prophet," the king told him. "I will send a letter of introduction for you to carry to the king of Israel." So Naaman started out, taking as gifts 750 pounds of silver, 150 pounds of gold,* and ten sets of clothing. 6The letter to the king of Israel said: "With this letter I present my servant Naaman. I want you to heal him of his leprosy."

7When the king of Israel read it, he tore his clothes in dismay and said, "This man sends me a leper to heal! Am I God, that I can kill and give life? He is only trying to find an excuse to invade us again."

8But when Elisha, the man of God, heard about the king's reaction, he sent this message to him: "Why are you so upset? Send Naaman to me, and he will learn that there is a true prophet here in Israel."

9So Naaman went with his horses and chariots and waited at the door of Elisha's house. 10But Elisha sent a messenger out to him with this message: "Go and wash yourself seven times in the Jordan River. Then your skin will be restored, and you will be healed of leprosy."

11But Naaman became angry and stalked away. "I thought he would surely come out to meet me!" he said. "I expected him to wave his hand over the leprosy and call on the name of the LORD his God and heal me! 12Aren't the Abana River and Pharpar River of Damascus better than all the rivers of Israel put together? Why shouldn't I wash in them and be healed?" So Naaman turned and went away in a rage.

13But his officers tried to reason with him and said, "Sir, if the prophet had told you to do some great thing, wouldn't you have done it? So you should certainly obey him when he says simply to go and wash and be cured!" 14So Naaman went down to the Jordan River and dipped himself seven times, as the man of God had instructed him. And his flesh became as healthy as a young child's, and he was healed!

15Then Naaman and his entire party went back to find the man of God. They stood before him, and Naaman said, "I know at last that there is no God in all the world except in Israel. Now please accept my gifts."

16But Elisha replied, "As surely as the LORD lives, whom I serve, I will not accept any gifts." And though Naaman urged him to take the gifts, Elisha refused.

4:42 Hebrew *to the people;* also in 4:43. 5:1 Or *from a contagious skin disease.* The Hebrew word used here and throughout this passage can describe various skin diseases. 5:5 Hebrew *10 talents* [340 kilograms] *of silver, 6,000 shekels* [68 kilograms] *of gold.*

¹⁷Then Naaman said, "All right, but please allow me to load two of my mules with earth from this place, and I will take it back home with me. From now on I will never again offer any burnt offerings or sacrifices to any other god except the LORD. ¹⁸However, may the LORD pardon me in this one thing. When my master the king goes into the temple of the god Rimmon to worship there and leans on my arm, may the LORD pardon me when I bow, too."

¹⁹"Go in peace," Elisha said. So Naaman started home again.

The Greed of Gehazi

²⁰But Gehazi, Elisha's servant, said to himself, "My master should not have let this Aramean get away without accepting his gifts. As surely as the LORD lives, I will chase after him and get something from him." ²¹So Gehazi set off after him.

When Naaman saw him running after him, he climbed down from his chariot and went to meet him. "Is everything all right?" Naaman asked.

²²"Yes," Gehazi said, "but my master has sent me to tell you that two young prophets from the hill country of Ephraim have just arrived. He would like 75 pounds* of silver and two sets of clothing to give to them."

²³"By all means, take 150 pounds* of silver," Naaman insisted. He gave him two sets of clothing, tied up the money in two bags, and sent two of his servants to carry the gifts for Gehazi. ²⁴But when they arrived at the hill, Gehazi took the gifts from the servants and sent the men back. Then he hid the gifts inside the house.

²⁵When he went in to his master, Elisha asked him, "Where have you been, Gehazi?"

"I haven't been anywhere," he replied.

²⁶But Elisha asked him, "Don't you realize that I was there in spirit when Naaman stepped down from his chariot to meet you? Is this the time to receive money and clothing and olive groves and vineyards and sheep and oxen and servants? ²⁷Because you have done this, you and your children and your children's children will suffer from Naaman's leprosy forever." When Gehazi left the room, he was leprous; his skin was as white as snow.

CHAPTER **6**
The Floating Ax Head

One day the group of prophets came to Elisha and told him, "As you can see, this place where we meet with you is too small. ²Let's go down to the Jordan River, where there are plenty of logs. There we can build a new place for us to meet."

"All right," he told them, "go ahead."

³"Please come with us," someone suggested.

"I will," he said.

⁴When they arrived at the Jordan, they began cutting down trees. ⁵But as one of them was chopping, his ax head fell into the river. "Ah, my lord!" he cried. "It was a borrowed ax!"

⁶"Where did it fall?" the man of God asked. When he showed him the place, Elisha cut a stick and threw it into the water. Then the ax head rose to the surface and floated. ⁷"Grab it," Elisha said to him. And the man reached out and grabbed it.

Elisha Traps the Arameans

⁸When the king of Aram was at war with Israel, he would confer with his officers and say, "We will mobilize our forces at such and such a place."

⁹But immediately Elisha, the man of God, would warn the king of Israel, "Do not go near that place, for the Arameans are planning to mobilize their troops there." ¹⁰So the king of Israel would send word to the place indicated by the man of God, warning the people there to be on their guard. This happened several times.

¹¹The king of Aram became very upset over this. He called in his officers and demanded, "Which of you is the traitor? Who has been informing the king of Israel of my plans?"

¹²"It's not us, my lord," one of the officers replied. "Elisha, the prophet in Israel, tells the king of Israel even the words you speak in the privacy of your bedroom!"

¹³The king commanded, "Go and find out where Elisha is, and we will send troops to seize him."

And the report came back: "Elisha is at Dothan." ¹⁴So one night the king of Aram sent a great army with many chariots and horses to surround the city. ¹⁵When the servant of the man of God got up early the next morning and went outside, there were troops, horses, and chariots everywhere.

"Ah, my lord, what will we do now?" he cried out to Elisha.

¹⁶"Don't be afraid!" Elisha told him. "For there are more on our side than on theirs!"

¹⁷Then Elisha prayed, "O LORD, open his eyes and let him see!" The LORD opened his servant's

5:22 Hebrew *1 talent* [34 kilograms].   5:23 Hebrew *2 talents* [68 kilograms].

eyes, and when he looked up, he saw that the hillside around Elisha was filled with horses and chariots of fire.

18As the Aramean army advanced toward them, Elisha prayed, "O LORD, please make them blind." And the LORD did as Elisha asked. 19Then Elisha went out and told them, "You have come the wrong way! This isn't the right city! Follow me, and I will take you to the man you are looking for." And he led them to Samaria. 20As soon as they had entered Samaria, Elisha prayed, "O LORD, now open their eyes and let them see." And the LORD did, and they discovered that they were in Samaria.

21When the king of Israel saw them, he shouted to Elisha, "My father, should I kill them?"

22"Of course not!" Elisha told him. "Do we kill prisoners of war? Give them food and drink and send them home again to their master."

23So the king made a great feast for them and then sent them home to their king. After that, the Aramean raiders stayed away from the land of Israel.

Ben-Hadad Besieges Samaria

24Some time later, however, King Ben-hadad of Aram mobilized his entire army and besieged Samaria. 25As a result there was a great famine in the city. After a while even a donkey's head sold for two pounds of silver, and a cup of dove's dung cost about two ounces* of silver.

26One day as the king of Israel was walking along the wall of the city, a woman called to him, "Please help me, my lord the king!"

27"If the LORD doesn't help you, what can I do?" he retorted. "I have neither food nor wine to give you." 28But then the king asked, "What is the matter?"

She replied, "This woman proposed that we eat my son one day and her son the next. 29So we cooked my son and ate him. Then the next day I said, 'Kill your son so we can eat him,' but she had hidden him."

30When the king heard this, he tore his clothes in despair. And as the king walked along the wall, the people could see that he was wearing sackcloth underneath next to his skin. 31"May God kill me if I don't execute Elisha son of Shaphat this very day," the king vowed.

32Elisha was sitting in his house at a meeting with the leaders of Israel when the king sent a messenger to summon him. But before the messenger arrived, Elisha said to the leaders, "A murderer has sent a man to kill me. When he arrives, shut the door and keep him out. His master will soon follow him."

33While Elisha was still saying this, the messenger arrived. And the king* said, "It is the LORD who has brought this trouble on us! Why should I wait any longer for the LORD?"

CHAPTER **7**

Elisha replied, "Hear this message from the LORD! This is what the LORD says: By this time tomorrow in the markets of Samaria, five quarts of fine flour will cost only half an ounce of silver,* and ten quarts of barley grain will cost only half an ounce of silver.* "

2The officer assisting the king said to the man of God, "That couldn't happen even if the LORD opened the windows of heaven!"

But Elisha replied, "You will see it happen, but you won't be able to eat any of it!"

Lepers Visit the Enemy Camp

3Now there were four men with leprosy* sitting at the entrance of the city gates. "Why should we sit here waiting to die?" they asked each other. 4"We will starve if we stay here, and we will starve if we go back into the city. So we might as well go out and surrender to the Aramean army. If they let us live, so much the better. But if they kill us, we would have died anyway."

5So that evening they went out to the camp of the Arameans, but no one was there! 6For the Lord had caused the whole army of Aram to hear the clatter of speeding chariots and the galloping of horses and the sounds of a great army approaching. "The king of Israel has hired the Hittites and Egyptians* to attack us!" they cried out. 7So they panicked and fled into the night, abandoning their tents, horses, donkeys, and everything else, and they fled for their lives.

8When the lepers arrived at the edge of the camp, they went into one tent after another, eating, drinking wine, and carrying out silver and gold and clothing and hiding it. Finally, they said to each other, "This is not right. This is wonderful news, and we aren't sharing it with anyone! If we wait until morning, some terrible calamity will certainly fall upon us. Come on, let's go back and tell the people at the palace."

10So they went back to the city and told the

6:25 Hebrew *sold for 80 shekels* [0.9 kilograms] *of silver, and* 1/4 *of a cab* [0.3 liters] *of dove's dung cost 5 shekels* [57 grams]. Dove's dung may be a variety of wild vegetable.   6:33 Hebrew *he.*   7:1a Hebrew *1 seah* [6 liters] *of fine flour will cost 1 shekel* [11 grams]; also in 7:16, 18.   7:1b Hebrew *2 seahs* [12 liters] *of barley grain will cost 1 shekel* [11 grams]; also in 7:16, 18.   7:3 Or *with a contagious skin disease.* The Hebrew word used here and throughout this passage can describe various skin diseases.   7:6 Possibly *and the people of Muzur,* a district near Cilicia.

gatekeepers what had happened—that they had gone out to the Aramean camp and no one was there! The horses and donkeys were tethered and the tents were all in order, but there was not a single person around. ¹¹Then the gatekeepers shouted the news to the people in the palace.

Israel Plunders the Camp
¹²The king got out of bed in the middle of the night and told his officers, "I know what has happened. The Arameans know we are starving, so they have left their camp and have hidden in the fields. They are expecting us to leave the city, and then they will take us alive and capture the city."

¹³One of his officers replied, "We had better send out scouts to check into this. Let them take five of the remaining horses. If something happens to them, it won't be a greater loss than if they stay here and die with the rest of us."

¹⁴So two chariots with horses were prepared, and the king sent scouts to see what had happened to the Aramean army. ¹⁵They went all the way to the Jordan River, following a trail of clothing and equipment that the Arameans had thrown away in their mad rush to escape. The scouts returned and told the king about it. ¹⁶Then the people of Samaria rushed out and plundered the Aramean camp. So it was true that five quarts of fine flour were sold that day for half an ounce of silver, and ten quarts of barley grain were sold for half an ounce of silver, just as the LORD had promised. ¹⁷The king appointed his officer to control the traffic at the gate, but he was knocked down and trampled to death as the people rushed out.

So everything happened exactly as the man of God had predicted when the king came to his house. ¹⁸The man of God had said to the king, "By this time tomorrow in the markets of Samaria, five quarts of fine flour will cost half an ounce of silver, and ten quarts of barley grain will cost half an ounce of silver." ¹⁹The king's officer had replied, "That couldn't happen even if the LORD opened the windows of heaven!" And the man of God had said, "You will see it happen, but you won't be able to eat any of it!" ²⁰And so it was, for the people trampled him to death at the gate!

CHAPTER **8**
The Woman from Shunem Returns Home
Elisha had told the woman whose son he had brought back to life, "Take your family and move to some other place, for the LORD has called for a famine on Israel that will last for

seven years." ²So the woman did as the man of God instructed. She took her family and lived in the land of the Philistines for seven years.

³After the famine ended she returned to the land of Israel, and she went to see the king about getting back her house and land. ⁴As she came in, the king was talking with Gehazi, the servant of the man of God. The king had just said, "Tell me some stories about the great things Elisha has done." ⁵And Gehazi was telling the king about the time Elisha had brought a boy back to life. At that very moment, the mother of the boy walked in to make her appeal to the king.

"Look, my lord!" Gehazi exclaimed. "Here is the woman now, and this is her son—the very one Elisha brought back to life!"

⁶"Is this true?" the king asked her. And she told him that it was. So he directed one of his officials to see to it that everything she had lost was restored to her, including the value of any crops that had been harvested during her absence.

Hazael Murders Ben-Hadad
⁷Now Elisha went to Damascus, the capital of Aram, where King Ben-hadad lay sick. Someone told the king that the man of God had come. ⁸When the king heard the news, he said to Hazael, "Take a gift to the man of God. Then tell him to ask the LORD if I will get well again."

⁹So Hazael loaded down forty camels with the finest products of Damascus as a gift for Elisha. He went in to him and said, "Your servant Ben-hadad, the king of Aram, has sent me to ask you if he will recover."

¹⁰And Elisha replied, "Go and tell him, 'You will recover.' But the LORD has shown me that he will actually die!" ¹¹Elisha stared at Hazael* with a fixed gaze until Hazael became uneasy. Then the man of God started weeping.

¹²"What's the matter, my lord?" Hazael asked him.

Elisha replied, "I know the terrible things you will do to the people of Israel. You will burn their fortified cities, kill their young men, dash their children to the ground, and rip open their pregnant women!"

¹³Then Hazael replied, "How could a nobody like me* ever accomplish such a great feat?"

But Elisha answered, "The LORD has shown me that you are going to be the king of Aram."

¹⁴When Hazael went back, the king asked him, "What did Elisha tell you?"

8:11 Hebrew *He stared at him.*   8:13 Hebrew *a dog.*

And Hazael replied, "He told me that you will surely recover."

15But the next day Hazael took a blanket, soaked it in water, and held it over the king's face until he died. Then Hazael became the next king of Aram.

Jehoram Rules in Judah

16Jehoram son of King Jehoshaphat of Judah began to rule over Judah in the fifth year of King Joram's reign in Israel. Joram was the son of Ahab. 17Jehoram was thirty-two years old when he became king, and he reigned in Jerusalem eight years. 18But Jehoram followed the example of the kings of Israel and was as wicked as King Ahab, for he had married one of Ahab's daughters. So Jehoram did what was evil in the LORD's sight. 19But the LORD was not willing to destroy Judah, for he had made a covenant with David and promised that his descendants would continue to rule forever.*

20During Jehoram's reign, the Edomites revolted against Judah and crowned their own king. 21So Jehoram* went with all his chariots to attack the town of Zair.* The Edomites surrounded him and his charioteers, but he escaped at night under cover of darkness. Jehoram's army, however, deserted him and fled. 22Edom has been independent from Judah to this day. The town of Libnah revolted about that same time.

23The rest of the events in Jehoram's reign and all his deeds are recorded in *The Book of the History of the Kings of Judah.* 24When Jehoram died, he was buried with his ancestors in the City of David. Then his son Ahaziah became the next king.

Ahaziah Rules in Judah

25Ahaziah son of Jehoram began to rule over Judah in the twelfth year of King Joram's reign in Israel. King Joram was the son of Ahab. 26Ahaziah was twenty-two years old when he became king, and he reigned in Jerusalem one year. His mother was Athaliah, a granddaughter of King Omri of Israel. 27Ahaziah followed the evil example of King Ahab's family, doing what was evil in the LORD's sight, because he was related by marriage to the family of Ahab.

28Ahaziah joined King Joram of Israel in his war against King Hazael of Aram at Ramothgilead. When King Joram was wounded in the battle, 29he returned to Jezreel to recover from his wounds. While Joram was there, King Ahaziah of Judah went to visit him.

CHAPTER 9

Jehu Anointed King of Israel

Meanwhile, Elisha the prophet had summoned a member of the group of prophets. "Get ready to go to Ramoth-gilead," he told him. "Take this vial of olive oil with you, 2and find Jehu son of Jehoshaphat and grandson of Nimshi. Call him into a back room away from his friends, 3and pour the oil over his head. Say to him, 'This is what the LORD says: I anoint you to be the king over Israel.' Then open the door and run for your life!"

4So the young prophet did as he was told and went to Ramoth-gilead. 5When he arrived there, he found Jehu sitting in a meeting with the other army officers. "I have a message for you, Commander," he said.

"For which one of us?" Jehu asked.

"For you, Commander," he replied.

6So Jehu left the others and went into the house. Then the young prophet poured the oil over Jehu's head and said, "This is what the LORD, the God of Israel, says: I anoint you king over the LORD's people, Israel. 7You are to destroy the family of Ahab, your master. In this way, I will avenge the murder of my prophets and all the LORD's servants who were killed by Jezebel. 8The entire family of Ahab must be wiped out—every male, slave and free alike, in Israel. 9I will destroy the family of Ahab as I destroyed the families of Jeroboam son of Nebat and of Baasha son of Ahijah. 10Dogs will eat Ahab's wife, Jezebel, at the plot of land in Jezreel, and no one will bury her." Then the young prophet opened the door and ran.

11Jehu went back to his fellow officers, and one of them asked him, "What did that crazy fellow want? Is everything all right?"

"You know the way such a man babbles on," Jehu replied.

12"You're lying," they said. "Tell us." So Jehu told them what the man had said and that at the LORD's command he had been anointed king over Israel.

13They quickly spread out their cloaks on the bare steps and blew a trumpet, shouting, "Jehu is king!"

Jehu Kills Joram and Ahaziah

14So Jehu son of Jehoshaphat and grandson of Nimshi formed a conspiracy against King Joram. (Now Joram had been with the army at Ramothgilead, defending Israel against the forces of King Hazael of Aram. 15But Joram* had been wounded in the fighting and had returned to

8:19 Hebrew *promised to give a lamp to David and his descendants forever.*   8:21a Hebrew *Joram,* a variant name for Jehoram; also in 8:23, 24.
8:21b Greek version reads *Seir.*   9:15 Hebrew *Jehoram,* a variant name for Joram; also in 9:17, 21, 22, 23, 24.

Jezreel to recover from his wounds.) So Jehu told the men with him, "Since you want me to be king, don't let anyone escape to Jezreel to report what we have done."

¹⁶Then Jehu got into a chariot and rode to Jezreel to find King Joram, who was lying there wounded. King Ahaziah of Judah was there, too, for he had gone to visit him. ¹⁷The watchman on the tower of Jezreel saw Jehu and his company approaching, so he shouted to Joram, "I see a company of troops coming!"

"Send out a rider to find out if they are coming in peace," King Joram shouted back.

¹⁸So a rider went out to meet Jehu and said, "The king wants to know whether you are coming in peace."

Jehu replied, "What do you know about peace? Get behind me!"

The watchman called out to the king, "The rider has met them, but he is not returning."

¹⁹So the king sent out a second rider. He rode up to them and demanded, "The king wants to know whether you come in peace."

Again Jehu answered, "What do you know about peace? Get behind me!"

²⁰The watchman exclaimed, "The rider has met them, but he isn't returning either! It must be Jehu son of Nimshi, for he is driving so recklessly."

²¹"Quick! Get my chariot ready!" King Joram commanded.

Then King Joram of Israel and King Ahaziah of Judah rode out in their chariots to meet Jehu. They met him at the field that had belonged to Naboth of Jezreel. ²²King Joram demanded, "Do you come in peace, Jehu?"

Jehu replied, "How can there be peace as long as the idolatry and witchcraft of your mother, Jezebel, are all around us?"

²³Then King Joram reined the chariot horses around and fled, shouting to King Ahaziah, "Treason, Ahaziah!" ²⁴Then Jehu drew his bow and shot Joram between the shoulders. The arrow pierced his heart, and he sank down dead in his chariot.

²⁵Jehu said to Bidkar, his officer, "Throw him into the field of Naboth of Jezreel. Do you remember when you and I were riding along behind his father, Ahab? The Lord pronounced this message against him: ²⁶'I solemnly swear that I will repay him here on Naboth's property, says the Lord, for the murder of Naboth and his sons that I saw yesterday.' So throw him out on Naboth's field, just as the Lord said."

²⁷When King Ahaziah of Judah saw what was happening, he fled along the road to Beth-haggan. Jehu rode after him, shouting, "Shoot him, too!" So they shot Ahaziah in his chariot at the Ascent of Gur, near Ibleam. He was able to go on as far as Megiddo, but he died there. ²⁸His officials took him by chariot to Jerusalem, where they buried him with his ancestors in the City of David. ²⁹Ahaziah's reign over Judah had begun in the eleventh year of King Joram's reign in Israel.

The Death of Jezebel

³⁰When Jezebel, the queen mother, heard that Jehu had come to Jezreel, she painted her eyelids and fixed her hair and sat at a window. ³¹When Jehu entered the gate of the palace, she shouted at him, "Have you come in peace, you murderer? You are just like Zimri, who murdered his master!"

³²Jehu looked up and saw her at the window and shouted, "Who is on my side?" And two or three eunuchs looked out at him. ³³"Throw her down!" Jehu yelled. So they threw her out the window, and some of her blood spattered against the wall and on the horses. And Jehu trampled her body under his horses' hooves.

³⁴Then Jehu went into the palace and ate and drank. Afterward he said, "Someone go and bury this cursed woman, for she is the daughter of a king." ³⁵But when they went out to bury her, they found only her skull, her feet, and her hands.

³⁶When they returned and told Jehu, he stated, "This fulfills the message from the Lord, which he spoke through his servant Elijah from Tishbe: 'At the plot of land in Jezreel, dogs will eat Jezebel's flesh. ³⁷Her body will be scattered like dung on the field of Jezreel, so that no one will be able to recognize her.'"

CHAPTER **10**

Jehu Kills Ahab's Family

Now Ahab had seventy sons living in the city of Samaria. So Jehu wrote a letter and sent copies to Samaria, to the officials of the city,* to the leaders of the people, and to the guardians of King Ahab's sons. The letter said, ² "The king's sons are with you, and you have at your disposal chariots, horses, a fortified city, and weapons. As soon as you receive this letter, ³select the best qualified of King Ahab's sons to be your king, and prepare to fight for Ahab's dynasty."

⁴But they were paralyzed with fear and said, "Two kings couldn't stand against this man!

10:1 As in some Greek manuscripts and Latin Vulgate (see also 10:6); Hebrew reads *of Jezreel*.

What can we do?" ⁵So the palace and city administrators, together with the other leaders and the guardians of the king's sons, sent this message to Jehu: "We are your servants and will do anything you tell us. We will not make anyone king; do whatever you think is best."

⁶Jehu responded with a second letter: "If you are on my side and are going to obey me, bring the heads of the king's sons to me at Jezreel at about this time tomorrow."

Now the seventy sons of the king were being cared for by the leaders of Samaria, where they had been raised since childhood. ⁷When the letter arrived, the leaders killed all seventy of the king's sons. They placed their heads in baskets and presented them to Jehu at Jezreel. ⁸A messenger went to Jehu and said, "They have brought the heads of the king's sons."

So Jehu ordered, "Pile them in two heaps at the entrance of the city gate, and leave them there until morning."

⁹In the morning he went out and spoke to the crowd that had gathered around them. "You aren't to blame," he told them. "I am the one who conspired against my master and killed him. But who killed all these? ¹⁰You can be sure that the message of the LORD that was spoken concerning Ahab's family will not fail. The LORD declared through his servant Elijah that this would happen." ¹¹Then Jehu killed all of Ahab's relatives living in Jezreel and all his important officials, personal friends, and priests. So Ahab was left without a single survivor.

¹²Then Jehu set out for Samaria. Along the way, while he was at Beth-eked of the Shepherds, ¹³he met some relatives of King Ahaziah of Judah. "Who are you?" he asked them.

And they replied, "We are relatives of King Ahaziah. We are going to visit the sons of King Ahab and the queen mother."

¹⁴"Take them alive!" Jehu shouted to his men. And they captured all forty-two of them and killed them at the well of Beth-eked. None of them escaped.

¹⁵When Jehu left there, he met Jehonadab son of Recab, who was coming to meet him. After they had greeted each other, Jehu said to him, "Are you as loyal to me as I am to you?"

"Yes, I am," Jehonadab replied.

"If you are," Jehu said, "then give me your hand." So Jehonadab put out his hand, and Jehu helped him into the chariot. ¹⁶Then Jehu said, "Now come with me, and see how devoted I am

10:25 Hebrew *city.*

to the LORD." So Jehonadab rode along with him. ¹⁷When Jehu arrived in Samaria, he killed everyone who was left there from Ahab's family, just as the LORD had promised through Elijah.

Jehu Kills the Priests of Baal

¹⁸Then Jehu called a meeting of all the people of the city and said to them, "Ahab hardly worshiped Baal at all compared to the way I will worship him! ¹⁹Summon all the prophets and worshipers of Baal, and call together all his priests. See to it that every one of them comes, for I am going to offer a great sacrifice to Baal. Any of Baal's worshipers who fail to come will be put to death." But Jehu's plan was to destroy all the worshipers of Baal.

²⁰Then Jehu ordered, "Prepare a solemn assembly to worship Baal!" So they did. ²¹He sent messengers throughout all Israel summoning those who worshiped Baal. They all came and filled the temple of Baal from one end to the other. ²²And Jehu instructed the keeper of the wardrobe, "Be sure that every worshiper of Baal wears one of these robes." So robes were given to them.

²³Then Jehu went into the temple of Baal with Jehonadab son of Recab. Jehu said to the worshipers of Baal, "Make sure that only those who worship Baal are here. Don't let anyone in who worships the LORD!" ²⁴So they were all inside the temple to offer sacrifices and burnt offerings. Now Jehu had surrounded the building with eighty of his men and had warned them, "If you let anyone escape, you will pay for it with your own life."

²⁵As soon as Jehu had finished sacrificing the burnt offering, he commanded his guards and officers, "Go in and kill all of them. Don't let a single one escape!" So they killed them all with their swords, and the guards and officers dragged their bodies outside. Then Jehu's men went into the fortress* of the temple of Baal. ²⁶They dragged out the sacred pillar used in the worship of Baal and destroyed it. ²⁷They broke down the sacred pillar of Baal and wrecked the temple of Baal, converting it into a public toilet. That is what it is used for to this day. ²⁸Thus, Jehu destroyed every trace of Baal worship from Israel. ²⁹He did not, however, destroy the gold calves at Bethel and Dan, the great sin that Jeroboam son of Nebat had led Israel to commit.

³⁰Nonetheless the LORD said to Jehu, "You have done well in following my instructions to destroy the family of Ahab. Because of this I will

cause your descendants to be the kings of Israel down to the fourth generation." ³¹But Jehu did not obey the law of the LORD, the God of Israel, with all his heart. He refused to turn from the sins of idolatry that Jeroboam had led Israel to commit.

The Death of Jehu

³²At about that time the LORD began to reduce the size of Israel's territory. King Hazael conquered several sections of the country ³³east of the Jordan River, including all of Gilead, Gad, Reuben, and Manasseh. He conquered the area from the town of Aroer by the Arnon Gorge to as far north as Gilead and Bashan.

³⁴The rest of the events in Jehu's reign and all his deeds and achievements are recorded in *The Book of the History of the Kings of Israel.* ³⁵When Jehu died, he was buried with his ancestors in Samaria. Then his son Jehoahaz became the next king. ³⁶In all, Jehu reigned over Israel from Samaria for twenty-eight years.

CHAPTER 11
Athaliah Rules in Judah

When Athaliah, the mother of King Ahaziah of Judah, learned that her son was dead, she set out to destroy the rest of the royal family. ²But Ahaziah's sister Jehosheba, the daughter of King Jehoram,* took Ahaziah's infant son, Joash, and stole him away from among the rest of the king's children, who were about to be killed. Jehosheba put Joash and his nurse in a bedroom to hide him from Athaliah, so the child was not murdered. ³Joash and his nurse remained hidden in the Temple of the LORD for six years while Athaliah ruled over the land.

Revolt against Athaliah

⁴In the seventh year of Athaliah's reign, Jehoiada the priest summoned the commanders, the Carite mercenaries, and the guards to come to the Temple of the LORD. He made a pact with them and made them swear an oath of loyalty there in the LORD's Temple; then he showed them the king's son.

⁵Jehoiada told them, "This is what you must do. A third of you who are on duty on the Sabbath are to guard the royal palace itself. ⁶Another third of you are to stand guard at the Sur Gate. And the final third must stand guard behind the palace guard. These three groups will all guard the palace. ⁷The other two units who are off duty on the Sabbath must stand guard for

11:2 Hebrew *Joram,* a variant name for Jehoram.

the king at the LORD's Temple. ⁸Form a bodyguard for the king and keep your weapons in hand. Any unauthorized person who approaches you must be killed. Stay right beside the king at all times."

⁹So the commanders did everything just as Jehoiada the priest ordered. The commanders took charge of the men reporting for duty that Sabbath, as well as those who were going off duty. They brought them all to Jehoiada the priest, ¹⁰and he supplied them with the spears and shields that had once belonged to King David and were stored in the Temple of the LORD. ¹¹The guards stationed themselves around the king, with their weapons ready. They formed a line from the south side of the Temple around to the north side and all around the altar.

¹²Then Jehoiada brought out Joash, the king's son, and placed the crown on his head. He presented Joash with a copy of God's covenant and proclaimed him king. They anointed him, and all the people clapped their hands and shouted, "Long live the king!"

The Death of Athaliah

¹³When Athaliah heard all the noise made by the guards and the people, she hurried to the LORD's Temple to see what was happening. ¹⁴And she saw the newly crowned king standing in his place of authority by the pillar, as was the custom at times of coronation. The officers and trumpeters were surrounding him, and people from all over the land were rejoicing and blowing trumpets. When Athaliah saw all this, she tore her clothes in despair and shouted, "Treason! Treason!"

¹⁵Then Jehoiada the priest ordered the commanders who were in charge of the troops, "Take her out of the Temple, and kill anyone who tries to rescue her. Do not kill her here in the Temple of the LORD." ¹⁶So they seized her and led her out to the gate where horses enter the palace grounds, and she was killed there.

Jehoiada's Religious Reforms

¹⁷Then Jehoiada made a covenant between the LORD and the king and the people that they would be the LORD's people. He also made a covenant between the king and the people. ¹⁸And all the people of the land went over to the temple of Baal and tore it down. They demolished the altars and smashed the idols to pieces, and they killed Mattan the priest of Baal in front of the altars.

Jehoiada the priest stationed guards at the Temple of the LORD. ¹⁹Then the commanders, the Carite mercenaries, the guards, and all the people of the land escorted the king from the Temple of the LORD. They went through the gate of the guards and into the palace, and the king took his seat on the royal throne. ²⁰So all the people of the land rejoiced, and the city was peaceful because Athaliah had been killed at the king's palace.

²¹Joash* was seven years old when he became king.

CHAPTER 12
Joash Repairs the Temple

Joash* began to rule over Judah in the seventh year of King Jehu's reign in Israel. He reigned in Jerusalem forty years. His mother was Zibiah, from Beersheba. ²All his life Joash did what was pleasing in the LORD's sight because Jehoiada the priest instructed him. ³Yet even so, he did not destroy the pagan shrines, and the people still offered sacrifices and burned incense there.

⁴One day King Joash said to the priests, "Collect all the money brought as a sacred offering to the LORD's Temple, whether it is a regular assessment, a payment of vows, or a voluntary gift. ⁵Let the priests take some of that money to pay for whatever repairs are needed at the Temple."

⁶But by the twenty-third year of Joash's reign, the priests still had not repaired the Temple. ⁷So King Joash called for Jehoiada and the other priests and asked them, "Why haven't you repaired the Temple? Don't use any more gifts for your own needs. From now on, it must all be spent on getting the Temple into good condition." ⁸So the priests agreed not to collect any more money from the people, and they also agreed not to undertake the repairs of the Temple themselves.

⁹Then Jehoiada the priest bored a hole in the lid of a large chest and set it on the right-hand side of the altar at the entrance of the Temple of the LORD. The priests guarding the entrance put all of the people's contributions into the chest. ¹⁰Whenever the chest became full, the court secretary and the high priest counted the money that had been brought to the LORD's Temple and put it into bags. ¹¹Then they gave the money to the construction supervisors, who used it to pay the people working on the LORD's Temple—the carpenters, the builders, ¹²the masons, and the stonecutters. They also used the money to buy timber and cut stone for

repairing the LORD's Temple, and they paid any other expenses related to the Temple's restoration.

¹³The money brought to the Temple was not used for making silver cups, lamp snuffers, basins, trumpets, or other articles of gold or silver for the Temple of the LORD. ¹⁴It was paid out to the workmen, who used it for the Temple repairs. ¹⁵No accounting was required from the construction supervisors, because they were honest and faithful workers. ¹⁶However, the money that was contributed for guilt offerings and sin offerings was not brought into the LORD's Temple. It was given to the priests for their own use.

The End of Joash's Reign

¹⁷About this time King Hazael of Aram went to war against Gath and captured it. Then he turned to attack Jerusalem. ¹⁸King Joash collected all the sacred objects that Jehoshaphat, Jehoram, and Ahaziah, the previous kings of Judah, had dedicated, along with what he himself had dedicated. He sent them all to Hazael, along with all the gold in the treasuries of the LORD's Temple and the royal palace. So Hazael called off his attack on Jerusalem.

¹⁹The rest of the events in Joash's reign and all his deeds are recorded in *The Book of the History of the Kings of Judah.* ²⁰But his officers plotted against him and assassinated him at Beth-millo on the road to Silla. ²¹The assassins were Jozabad son of Shimeath and Jehozabad son of Shomer—both trusted advisers. Joash was buried with his ancestors in the City of David. Then his son Amaziah became the next king.

CHAPTER 13
Jehoahaz Rules in Israel

Jehoahaz son of Jehu began to rule over Israel in the twenty-third year of King Joash's reign in Judah. He reigned in Samaria seventeen years. ²But he did what was evil in the LORD's sight. He followed the example of Jeroboam son of Nebat, continuing the sins of idolatry that Jeroboam son of Nebat had led Israel to commit. ³So the LORD was very angry with Israel, and he allowed King Hazael of Aram and his son Ben-hadad to defeat them time after time.

⁴Then Jehoahaz prayed for the LORD's help, and the LORD heard his prayer. The LORD could see how terribly the king of Aram was oppressing Israel. ⁵So the LORD raised up a deliverer to rescue the Israelites from the tyranny of the

---

11:21 Hebrew *Jehoash,* a variant name for Joash.   12:1 Hebrew *Jehoash,* a variant name for Joash; also in 12:2, 4, 6, 7, 18.

2 KINGS 14 ▸▸▸ page 330

Arameans. Then Israel lived in safety again as they had in former days. 6But they continued to sin, following the evil example of Jeroboam. They even set up an Asherah pole in Samaria. 7Finally, Jehoahaz's army was reduced to fifty mounted troops, ten chariots, and ten thousand foot soldiers. The king of Aram had killed the others like they were dust under his feet.

8The rest of the events in Jehoahaz's reign and all his deeds, including the extent of his power, are recorded in *The Book of the History of the Kings of Israel.* 9When Jehoahaz died, he was buried in Samaria with his ancestors. Then his son Jehoash* became the next king.

Jehoash Rules in Israel

10Jehoash son of Jehoahaz began to rule over Israel in the thirty-seventh year of King Joash's reign in Judah. He reigned in Samaria sixteen years. 11But he did what was evil in the LORD's sight. He refused to turn from the sins of idolatry that Jeroboam son of Nebat had led Israel to commit. 12The rest of the events in Jehoash's reign and all his deeds, including the extent of his power and his war with King Amaziah of Judah, are recorded in *The Book of the History of the Kings of Israel.* 13When Jehoash died, he was buried with his ancestors in Samaria. Then his son Jeroboam II became the next king.

Elisha's Final Prophecy

14When Elisha was in his last illness, King Jehoash of Israel visited him and wept over him. "My father! My father! The chariots and charioteers of Israel!" he cried.

15Elisha told him, "Get a bow and some arrows." And the king did as he was told. 16Then Elisha told the king of Israel to put his hand on the bow, and Elisha laid his own hands on the king's hands. 17Then he commanded, "Open that eastern window," and he opened it. Then he said, "Shoot!" So he did.

Then Elisha proclaimed, "This is the LORD's arrow, full of victory over Aram, for you will completely conquer the Arameans at Aphek. 18Now pick up the other arrows and strike them against the ground." So the king picked them up and struck the ground three times. 19But the man of God was angry with him. "You should have struck the ground five or six times!" he exclaimed. "Then you would have beaten Aram until they were entirely destroyed. Now you will be victorious only three times."

20Then Elisha died and was buried.

Groups of Moabite raiders used to invade the land each spring. 21Once when some Israelites were burying a man, they spied a band of these raiders. So they hastily threw the body they were burying into the tomb of Elisha. But as soon as the body touched Elisha's bones, the dead man revived and jumped to his feet!

22King Hazael of Aram had oppressed Israel during the entire reign of King Jehoahaz. 23But the LORD was gracious to the people of Israel, and they were not totally destroyed. He pitied them because of his covenant with Abraham, Isaac, and Jacob. And to this day he still has not completely destroyed them or banished them from his presence.

24King Hazael of Aram died, and his son Ben-hadad became the next king. 25Then Jehoash son of Jehoahaz recaptured from Ben-hadad son of Hazael the towns that Hazael had taken from Jehoash's father, Jehoahaz. Jehoash defeated Ben-hadad on three occasions, and so recovered the Israelite towns.

CHAPTER **14**

Amaziah Rules in Judah

Amaziah son of Joash began to rule over Judah in the second year of the reign of King Jehoash* of Israel. 2Amaziah was twenty-five years old when he became king, and he reigned in Jerusalem twenty-nine years. His mother was Jehoaddin, from Jerusalem. 3Amaziah did what was pleasing in the LORD's sight, but not like his ancestor David. Instead, he followed the example of his father, Joash. 4Amaziah did not destroy the pagan shrines, where the people offered sacrifices and burned incense.

5When Amaziah was well established as king, he executed the men who had assassinated his father. 6However, he did not kill the children of the assassins, for he obeyed the command of the LORD written in the Book of the Law of Moses: "Parents must not be put to death for the sins of their children, nor the children for the sins of their parents. Those worthy of death must be executed for their own crimes."*

7It was Amaziah who killed ten thousand Edomites in the Valley of Salt. He also conquered Sela and changed its name to Joktheel, as it is called to this day.

8One day Amaziah sent this challenge to Israel's king Jehoash, the son of Jehoahaz and grandson of Jehu: "Come and meet me in battle!"

13:9 Hebrew *Joash,* a variant name for Jehoash; also in 13:10, 12, 13, 14, 25. **14:1** Hebrew *Joash,* a variant name for Jehoash; also in 14:13, 23, 27. **14:6** Deut 24:16.

⁹But King Jehoash of Israel replied to King Amaziah of Judah with this story: "Out in the Lebanon mountains a thistle sent a message to a mighty cedar tree: 'Give your daughter in marriage to my son.' But just then a wild animal came by and stepped on the thistle, crushing it! ¹⁰You have indeed destroyed Edom and are very proud about it. Be content with your victory and stay at home! Why stir up trouble that will bring disaster on you and the people of Judah?"

¹¹But Amaziah refused to listen, so King Jehoash of Israel mobilized his army against King Amaziah of Judah. The two armies drew up their battle lines at Beth-shemesh in Judah. ¹²Judah was routed by the army of Israel, and its army scattered and fled for home. ¹³King Jehoash of Israel captured King Amaziah of Judah at Beth-shemesh and marched on to Jerusalem. Then Jehoash ordered his army to demolish six hundred feet* of Jerusalem's wall, from the Ephraim Gate to the Corner Gate. ¹⁴He carried off all the gold and silver and all the utensils from the Temple of the LORD, as well as from the palace treasury. He also took hostages and returned to Samaria.

¹⁵The rest of the events in Jehoash's reign, including the extent of his power and his war with King Amaziah of Judah, are recorded in *The Book of the History of the Kings of Israel.* ¹⁶When Jehoash died, he was buried with his ancestors in Samaria. Then his son Jeroboam II became the next king.

¹⁷King Amaziah of Judah lived on for fifteen years after the death of King Jehoash of Israel. ¹⁸The rest of the events in Amaziah's reign are recorded in *The Book of the History of the Kings of Judah.* ¹⁹There was a conspiracy against Amaziah's life in Jerusalem, and he fled to Lachish. But his enemies sent assassins after him, and they killed him there. ²⁰They brought him back to Jerusalem on a horse, and he was buried with his ancestors in the City of David.

²¹The people of Judah then crowned Amaziah's sixteen-year-old son, Uzziah,* as their next king. ²²After his father's death, Uzziah rebuilt the town of Elath and restored it to Judah.

Jeroboam II Rules in Israel

²³Jeroboam II, the son of Jehoash, began to rule over Israel in the fifteenth year of King Amaziah's reign in Judah. Jeroboam reigned in Samaria forty-one years. ²⁴He did what was evil in the LORD's sight. He refused to turn from the sins of idolatry that Jeroboam son of Nebat had led Israel to commit. ²⁵Jeroboam II recovered the territories of Israel between Lebo-hamath and the Dead Sea,* just as the LORD, the God of Israel, had promised through Jonah son of Amittai, the prophet from Gath-hepher. ²⁶For the LORD saw the bitter suffering of everyone in Israel, and how they had absolutely no one to help them. ²⁷And because the LORD had not said he would blot out the name of Israel completely, he used Jeroboam II, the son of Jehoash, to save them.

²⁸The rest of the events in the reign of Jeroboam II and all his deeds, including the extent of his power, his wars, and how he recovered for Israel both Damascus and Hamath, which had belonged to Judah,* are recorded in *The Book of the History of the Kings of Israel.* ²⁹When Jeroboam II died, he was buried with his ancestors, the kings of Israel. Then his son Zechariah became the next king.

CHAPTER **15**
Uzziah Rules in Judah

Uzziah* son of Amaziah began to rule over Judah in the twenty-seventh year of the reign of King Jeroboam II of Israel. ²He was sixteen years old when he became king, and he reigned in Jerusalem fifty-two years. His mother was Jecoliah, from Jerusalem. ³He did what was pleasing in the LORD's sight, just as his father, Amaziah, had done. ⁴But he did not destroy the pagan shrines, where the people offered sacrifices and burned incense. ⁵The LORD struck the king with leprosy,* which lasted until the day of his death; he lived in a house by himself. The king's son Jotham was put in charge of the royal palace, and he governed the people of the land.

⁶The rest of the events in Uzziah's reign and all his deeds are recorded in *The Book of the History of the Kings of Judah.* ⁷When Uzziah died, he was buried near his ancestors in the City of David. Then his son Jotham became the next king.

Zechariah Rules in Israel

⁸Zechariah son of Jeroboam II began to rule over Israel in the thirty-eighth year of King Uzziah's reign in Judah. He reigned in Samaria six months. ⁹Zechariah did what was evil in the LORD's sight, as his ancestors had done. He refused to turn from the sins of idolatry that Jeroboam son of Nebat had led Israel to commit. ¹⁰Then Shallum son of

14:13 Hebrew *400 cubits* [180 meters].   14:21 Hebrew *Azariah,* a variant name for Uzziah.   14:25 Hebrew *the sea of the Arabah.*   14:28 Or *to Yaudi.*   15:1 Hebrew *Azariah,* a variant name for Uzziah; also in 15:6, 7, 8, 17, 23, 27.   15:5 Or *with a contagious skin disease.* The Hebrew word used here and throughout this passage can describe various skin diseases.

Jabesh conspired against Zechariah, assassinated him in public,* and became the next king. ¹¹The rest of the events in Zechariah's reign are recorded in *The Book of the History of the Kings of Israel.* ¹²So the LORD's message to Jehu came true: "Your descendants will be kings of Israel down to the fourth generation."

Shallum Rules in Israel

¹³Shallum son of Jabesh began to rule over Israel in the thirty-ninth year of King Uzziah's reign in Judah. Shallum reigned in Samaria only one month. ¹⁴Then Menahem son of Gadi went to Samaria from Tirzah and assassinated him, and he became the next king. ¹⁵The rest of the events in Shallum's reign, including his conspiracy, are recorded in *The Book of the History of the Kings of Israel.*

Menahem Rules in Israel

¹⁶At that time Menahem destroyed the town of Tappuah* and all the surrounding countryside as far as Tirzah, because its citizens refused to surrender the town. He killed the entire population and ripped open the pregnant women.

¹⁷Menahem son of Gadi began to rule over Israel in the thirty-ninth year of King Uzziah's reign in Judah. He reigned in Samaria ten years. ¹⁸But Menahem did what was evil in the LORD's sight. During his entire reign, he refused to turn from the sins of idolatry that Jeroboam son of Nebat had led Israel to commit. ¹⁹Then King Tiglath-pileser* of Assyria invaded the land. But Menahem paid him thirty-seven tons* of silver to gain his support in tightening his grip on royal power. ²⁰Menahem extorted the money from the rich of Israel, demanding that each of them pay twenty ounces* of silver in the form of a special tax. So the king of Assyria turned from attacking Israel and did not stay in the land. ²¹The rest of the events in Menahem's reign and all his deeds are recorded in *The Book of the History of the Kings of Israel.* ²²When Menahem died, his son Pekahiah became the next king.

Pekahiah Rules in Israel

²³Pekahiah son of Menahem began to rule over Israel in the fiftieth year of King Uzziah's reign in Judah. He reigned in Samaria two years. ²⁴But Pekahiah did what was evil in the LORD's sight. He refused to turn from the sins of idolatry that Jeroboam son of Nebat had led Israel to commit. ²⁵Then Pekah son of Remaliah, the commander of Pekahiah's army, conspired against him. With fifty men from Gilead, Pekah assassinated the king, along with Argob and Arieh, in the citadel of the palace at Samaria. Pekah then became the next king of Israel. ²⁶The rest of the events in Pekahiah's reign and all his deeds are recorded in *The Book of the History of the Kings of Israel.*

Pekah Rules in Israel

²⁷Pekah son of Remaliah began to rule over Israel in the fifty-second year of King Uzziah's reign in Judah. He reigned in Samaria twenty years. ²⁸But Pekah did what was evil in the LORD's sight. He refused to turn from the sins of idolatry that Jeroboam son of Nebat had led Israel to commit. ²⁹During his reign, King Tiglath-pileser of Assyria attacked Israel again, and he captured the towns of Ijon, Abel-beth-maacah, Janoah, Kedesh, and Hazor. He also conquered the regions of Gilead, Galilee, and Naphtali, and he took the people to Assyria as captives. ³⁰Then Hoshea son of Elah conspired against Pekah and assassinated him. He began to rule over Israel in the twentieth year of Jotham son of Uzziah. ³¹The rest of the events in Pekah's reign and all his deeds are recorded in *The Book of the History of the Kings of Israel.*

Jotham Rules in Judah

³²Jotham son of Uzziah began to rule over Judah in the second year of King Pekah's reign in Israel. ³³He was twenty-five years old when he became king, and he reigned in Jerusalem sixteen years. His mother was Jerusha, the daughter of Zadok.

³⁴Jotham did what was pleasing in the LORD's sight, just as his father Uzziah had done. ³⁵But he did not destroy the pagan shrines, where the people offered sacrifices and burned incense. He was the one who rebuilt the upper gate of the Temple of the LORD.

³⁶The rest of the events in Jotham's reign and all his deeds are recorded in *The Book of the History of the Kings of Judah.* ³⁷In those days the LORD began to send King Rezin of Aram and King Pekah of Israel to attack Judah. ³⁸When Jotham died, he was buried with his ancestors in the City of David. Then his son Ahaz became the next king.

CHAPTER 16

Ahaz Rules in Judah

Ahaz son of Jotham began to rule over Judah in the seventeenth year of King Pekah's reign in Is-

---

15:10 Or *at Ibleam.*   **15:16** As in some Greek manuscripts; Hebrew reads *Tiphsah.*   **15:19a** Hebrew *Pul,* another name for Tiglath-pileser.
15:19b Hebrew *1,000 talents* [34 metric tons].   **15:20** Hebrew *50 shekels* [570 grams].

rael. ²Ahaz was twenty years old when he became king, and he reigned in Jerusalem sixteen years. He did not do what was pleasing in the sight of the LORD his God, as his ancestor David had done. ³Instead, he followed the example of the kings of Israel, even sacrificing his own son in the fire.* He imitated the detestable practices of the pagan nations the LORD had driven from the land ahead of the Israelites. ⁴He offered sacrifices and burned incense at the pagan shrines and on the hills and under every green tree.

⁵Then King Rezin of Aram and King Pekah of Israel declared war on Ahaz. They besieged Jerusalem but did not conquer it. ⁶At that time the king of Edom* recovered the town of Elath for Edom.* He drove out the people of Judah and sent Edomites* to live there, as they do to this day.

⁷King Ahaz sent messengers to King Tiglath-pileser of Assyria with this message: "I am your servant and your vassal.* Come up and rescue me from the attacking armies of Aram and Israel." ⁸Then Ahaz took the silver and gold from the Temple of the LORD and the palace treasury and sent it as a gift to the Assyrian king. ⁹So the Assyrians attacked the Aramean capital of Damascus and led its population away as captives, resettling them in Kir. They also killed King Rezin.

¹⁰King Ahaz then went to Damascus to meet with King Tiglath-pileser of Assyria. While he was there, he noticed an unusual altar. So he sent a model of the altar to Uriah the priest, along with its design in full detail. ¹¹Uriah built an altar just like it by following the king's instructions, and it was ready for the king when he returned from Damascus. ¹²When the king returned, he inspected the altar and made offerings on it. ¹³The king presented a burnt offering and a grain offering, poured a drink offering over it, and sprinkled the blood of peace offerings on it.

¹⁴Then King Ahaz removed the old bronze altar from the front of the LORD's Temple, which had stood between the entrance and the new altar, and placed it on the north side of the new altar. ¹⁵He said to Uriah the priest, "Use the new altar for the morning sacrifices of burnt offering, the evening grain offering, the king's burnt offering and grain offering, and the offerings of the people, including their drink offerings. The blood from the burnt offerings and sacrifices should be sprinkled over the new altar. The old bronze altar will be only for my personal use."

¹⁶Uriah the priest did just as King Ahaz instructed him.

¹⁷Then the king removed the side panels and basins from the portable water carts. He also removed the Sea from the backs of the bronze oxen and placed it on the stone pavement. ¹⁸In deference to the king of Assyria, he also removed the canopy that had been constructed inside the palace for use on the Sabbath day,* as well as the king's outer entrance to the Temple of the LORD.

¹⁹The rest of the events in Ahaz's reign and his deeds are recorded in *The Book of the History of the Kings of Judah.* ²⁰When Ahaz died, he was buried with his ancestors in the City of David. Then his son Hezekiah became the next king.

CHAPTER 17

Hoshea Rules in Israel

Hoshea son of Elah began to rule over Israel in the twelfth year of King Ahaz's reign in Judah. He reigned in Samaria nine years. ²He did what was evil in the LORD's sight, but not as much as the kings of Israel who ruled before him.

³King Shalmaneser of Assyria attacked and defeated King Hoshea, so Israel was forced to pay heavy annual tribute to Assyria. ⁴Then Hoshea conspired against the king of Assyria by asking King So of Egypt* to help him shake free of Assyria's power and by refusing to pay the annual tribute to Assyria. When the king of Assyria discovered this treachery, he arrested him and put him in prison for his rebellion.

⁵Then the king of Assyria invaded the entire land, and for three years he besieged Samaria. ⁶Finally, in the ninth year of King Hoshea's reign, Samaria fell, and the people of Israel were exiled to Assyria. They were settled in colonies in Halah, along the banks of the Habor River in Gozan, and among the cities of the Medes.

Samaria Falls to Assyria

⁷This disaster came upon the nation of Israel because the people worshiped other gods, sinning against the LORD their God, who had brought them safely out of their slavery in Egypt. ⁸They had imitated the practices of the pagan nations the LORD had driven from the land before them, as well as the practices the kings of Israel had introduced. ⁹The people of Israel had also secretly done many things that were not pleasing to the LORD their God. They built pagan shrines for themselves

16:3 Or *even making his son pass through the fire.* 16:6a As in Latin Vulgate; Hebrew reads *Rezin king of Aram.* 16:6b As in Latin Vulgate; Hebrew reads *Aram.* 16:6c As in marginal *Qere* reading of the Masoretic Text, Greek version, and Latin Vulgate; Hebrew reads *Arameans.* 16:7 Hebrew *your son.* 16:18 The meaning of the Hebrew is uncertain. 17:4 Or *by asking the king of Egypt at Sais.*

in all their towns, from the smallest outpost to the largest walled city. [10]They set up sacred pillars and Asherah poles at the top of every hill and under every green tree. [11]They burned incense at the shrines, just like the nations the LORD had driven from the land ahead of them. So the people of Israel had done many evil things, arousing the LORD's anger. [12]Yes, they worshiped idols, despite the LORD's specific and repeated warnings. [13]Again and again the LORD had sent his prophets and seers to warn both Israel and Judah: "Turn from all your evil ways. Obey my commands and laws, which are contained in the whole law that I commanded your ancestors and which I gave you through my servants the prophets."

[14]But the Israelites would not listen. They were as stubborn as their ancestors and refused to believe in the LORD their God. [15]They rejected his laws and the covenant he had made with their ancestors, and they despised all his warnings. They worshiped worthless idols and became worthless themselves. They followed the example of the nations around them, disobeying the LORD's command not to imitate them. [16]They defied all the commands of the LORD their God and made two calves from metal. They set up an Asherah pole and worshiped Baal and all the forces of heaven. [17]They even sacrificed their own sons and daughters in the fire.* They consulted fortune-tellers and used sorcery and sold themselves to evil, arousing the LORD's anger.

[18]And because the LORD was angry, he swept them from his presence. Only the tribe of Judah remained in the land. [19]But even the people of Judah refused to obey the commands of the LORD their God. They walked down the same evil paths that Israel had established. [20]So the LORD rejected all the descendants of Israel. He punished them by handing them over to their attackers until they were destroyed. [21]For when the LORD tore Israel away from the kingdom of David, they chose Jeroboam son of Nebat as their king. Then Jeroboam drew Israel away from following the LORD and made them commit a great sin. [22]And the people of Israel persisted in all the evil ways of Jeroboam. They did not turn from these sins of idolatry [23]until the LORD finally swept them away, just as all his prophets had warned would happen. So Israel was carried off to the land of Assyria, where they remain to this day.

Foreigners Settle in Israel

[24]And the king of Assyria transported groups of people from Babylon, Cuthah, Avva, Hamath,

and Sepharvaim and resettled them in the towns of Samaria, replacing the people of Israel. So the Assyrians took over Samaria and the other towns of Israel. [25]But since these foreign settlers did not worship the LORD when they first arrived, the LORD sent lions among them to kill some of them.

[26]So a message was sent to the king of Assyria: "The people whom you have resettled in the towns of Israel* do not know how to worship the God of the land. He has sent lions among them to destroy them because they have not worshiped him correctly."

[27]The king of Assyria then commanded, "Send one of the exiled priests from Samaria back to Israel. Let him teach the new residents the religious customs of the God of the land." [28]So one of the priests who had been exiled from Samaria returned to Bethel and taught the new residents how to worship the LORD.

[29]But these various groups of foreigners also continued to worship their own gods. In town after town where they lived, they placed their idols at the pagan shrines that the people of Israel had built. [30]Those from Babylon worshiped idols of their god Succoth-benoth. Those from Cuthah worshiped their god Nergal. And those from Hamath worshiped Ashima. [31]The Avvites worshiped their gods Nibhaz and Tartak. And the people from Sepharvaim even burned their own children as sacrifices to Adrammelech and Anammelech.

[32]These new residents worshiped the LORD, but they appointed from among themselves priests to offer sacrifices at the pagan shrines. [33]And though they worshiped the LORD, they continued to follow the religious customs of the nations from which they came. [34]And this is still going on among them today. They follow their former practices instead of truly worshiping the LORD and obeying the laws, regulations, instructions, and commands he gave the descendants of Jacob, whose name he changed to Israel. [35]For the LORD had made a covenant with the descendants of Jacob and commanded them: "Do not worship any other gods or bow before them or serve them or offer sacrifices to them. [36]Worship only the LORD, who brought you out of Egypt with such mighty miracles and power. You must worship him and bow before him; offer sacrifices to him alone. [37]Be careful to obey all the laws, regulations, instructions, and commands that he wrote for you. You must not worship any other gods. [38]Do not forget the covenant I made with you, and do not worship

17:17 Or *They even made their sons and daughters pass through the fire.*   17:26 Hebrew *of Samaria;* also in 17:29.

other gods. ³⁹You must worship only the LORD your God. He is the one who will rescue you from all your enemies."

⁴⁰But the people would not listen and continued to follow their old ways. ⁴¹So while these new residents worshiped the LORD, they also worshiped their idols. And to this day their descendants do the same.

CHAPTER **18**

Hezekiah Rules in Judah

Hezekiah son of Ahaz began to rule over Judah in the third year of King Hoshea's reign in Israel. ²He was twenty-five years old when he became king, and he reigned in Jerusalem twenty-nine years. His mother was Abijah,* the daughter of Zechariah. ³He did what was pleasing in the LORD's sight, just as his ancestor David had done. ⁴He removed the pagan shrines, smashed the sacred pillars, and knocked down the Asherah poles. He broke up the bronze serpent that Moses had made, because the people of Israel had begun to worship it by burning incense to it. The bronze serpent was called Nehushtan.*

⁵Hezekiah trusted in the LORD, the God of Israel. There was never another king like him in the land of Judah, either before or after his time. ⁶He remained faithful to the LORD in everything, and he carefully obeyed all the commands the LORD had given Moses. ⁷So the LORD was with him, and Hezekiah was successful in everything he did. He revolted against the king of Assyria and refused to pay him tribute. ⁸He also conquered the Philistines as far distant as Gaza and its territory, from their smallest outpost to their largest walled city.

⁹During the fourth year of Hezekiah's reign, which was the seventh year of King Hoshea's reign in Israel, King Shalmaneser of Assyria attacked Israel and began a siege on the city of Samaria. ¹⁰Three years later, during the sixth year of King Hezekiah's reign and the ninth year of King Hoshea's reign in Israel, Samaria fell. ¹¹At that time the king of Assyria deported the Israelites to Assyria and put them in colonies in Halah, along the banks of the Habor River in Gozan, and among the cities of the Medes. ¹²For they had refused to listen to the LORD their God. Instead, they had violated his covenant—all the laws the LORD had given through his servant Moses.

Assyria Invades Judah

¹³In the fourteenth year of King Hezekiah's reign, King Sennacherib of Assyria came to attack the fortified cities of Judah and conquered them. ¹⁴King Hezekiah sent this message to the king of Assyria at Lachish: "I have done wrong. I will pay whatever tribute money you demand if you will only go away." The king of Assyria then demanded a settlement of more than eleven tons of silver and about one ton of gold.* ¹⁵To gather this amount, King Hezekiah used all the silver stored in the Temple of the LORD and in the palace treasury. ¹⁶Hezekiah even stripped the gold from the doors of the LORD's Temple and from the doorposts he had overlaid with gold, and he gave it all to the Assyrian king.

¹⁷Nevertheless the king of Assyria sent his commander in chief, his field commander, and his personal representative from Lachish with a huge army to confront King Hezekiah in Jerusalem. The Assyrians stopped beside the aqueduct that feeds water into the upper pool, near the road leading to the field where cloth is bleached. ¹⁸They summoned King Hezekiah, but the king sent these officials to meet with them: Eliakim son of Hilkiah, the palace administrator, Shebna the court secretary, and Joah son of Asaph, the royal historian.

Sennacherib Threatens Jerusalem

¹⁹Then the Assyrian king's personal representative sent this message to King Hezekiah:

"This is what the great king of Assyria says: What are you trusting in that makes you so confident? ²⁰Do you think that mere words can substitute for military skill and strength? Which of your allies will give you any military backing against Assyria? ²¹Will Egypt? If you lean on Egypt, you will find it to be a stick that breaks beneath your weight and pierces your hand. The pharaoh of Egypt is completely unreliable!

²²"But perhaps you will say, 'We are trusting in the LORD our God!' But isn't he the one who was insulted by King Hezekiah? Didn't Hezekiah tear down his shrines and altars and make everyone in Judah worship only at the altar here in Jerusalem?

²³"I'll tell you what! My master, the king of Assyria, will strike a bargain with you. If you can find two thousand horsemen in your entire army, he will give you two thousand horses for them to ride on!

18:2 As in parallel text at 2 Chr 29:1; Hebrew reads *Abi,* a variant name for Abijah.   18:4 *Nehushtan* sounds like the Hebrew terms that mean "snake," "bronze," and "unclean thing."   18:14 Hebrew *300 talents* [10 metric tons] *of silver and 30 talents* [1 metric ton] *of gold.*

24With your tiny army, how can you think of challenging even the weakest contingent of my master's troops, even with the help of Egypt's chariots and horsemen*? 25What's more, do you think we have invaded your land without the LORD's direction? The LORD himself told us, 'Go and destroy it!'"

26Then Eliakim son of Hilkiah, Shebna, and Joah said to the king's representative, "Please speak to us in Aramaic, for we understand it well. Don't speak in Hebrew, for the people on the wall will hear."

27But Sennacherib's representative replied, "My master wants everyone in Jerusalem to hear this, not just you. He wants them to know that if you do not surrender, this city will be put under siege. The people will become so hungry and thirsty that they will eat their own dung and drink their own urine."

28Then he stood and shouted in Hebrew to the people on the wall, "Listen to this message from the great king of Assyria! 29This is what the king says: Don't let King Hezekiah deceive you. He will never be able to rescue you from my power. 30Don't let him fool you into trusting in the LORD by saying, 'The LORD will rescue us! This city will never be handed over to the Assyrian king.'

31"Don't listen to Hezekiah! These are the terms the king of Assyria is offering: Make peace with me—open the gates and come out. Then I will allow each of you to continue eating from your own garden and drinking from your own well. 32Then I will arrange to take you to another land like this one—a country with bountiful harvests of grain and wine, bread and vineyards, olive trees and honey—a land of plenty. Choose life instead of death!

"Don't listen to Hezekiah when he tries to mislead you by saying, 'The LORD will rescue us!' 33Have the gods of any other nations ever saved their people from the king of Assyria? 34What happened to the gods of Hamath and Arpad? And what about the gods of Sepharvaim, Hena, and Ivvah? Did they rescue Samaria from my power? 35What god of any nation has ever been able to save its people from my power? Name just one! So what makes you think that the LORD can rescue Jerusalem?"

36But the people were silent and did not answer because Hezekiah had told them not to speak. 37Then Eliakim son of Hilkiah, the palace administrator, Shebna the court secretary, and Joah son of Asaph, the royal historian, went

back to Hezekiah. They tore their clothes in despair, and they went in to see the king and told him what the Assyrian representative had said.

CHAPTER **19**
Hezekiah Seeks the LORD's Help
When King Hezekiah heard their report, he tore his clothes and put on sackcloth and went into the Temple of the LORD to pray. 2And he sent Eliakim the palace administrator, Shebna the court secretary, and the leading priests, all dressed in sackcloth, to the prophet Isaiah son of Amoz. 3They told him, "This is what King Hezekiah says: This is a day of trouble, insult, and disgrace. It is like when a child is ready to be born, but the mother has no strength to deliver it. 4But perhaps the LORD your God has heard the Assyrian representative defying the living God and will punish him for his words. Oh, pray for those of us who are left!"

5After King Hezekiah's officials delivered the king's message to Isaiah, 6the prophet replied, "Say to your master, 'This is what the LORD says: Do not be disturbed by this blasphemous speech against me from the Assyrian king's messengers. 7Listen! I myself will move against him, and the king will receive a report from Assyria telling him that he is needed at home. Then I will make him want to return to his land, where I will have him killed with a sword.'"

8Meanwhile, the Assyrian representative left Jerusalem and went to consult his king, who had left Lachish and was attacking Libnah. 9Soon afterward King Sennacherib received word that King Tirhakah of Ethiopia* was leading an army to fight against him. Before leaving to meet the attack, he sent this message back to Hezekiah in Jerusalem:

10"This message is for King Hezekiah of Judah. Don't let this God you trust deceive you with promises that Jerusalem will not be captured by the king of Assyria. 11You know perfectly well what the kings of Assyria have done wherever they have gone. They have crushed everyone who stood in their way! Why should you be any different? 12Have the gods of other nations rescued them—such nations as Gozan, Haran, Rezeph, and the people of Eden who were in Tel-assar? The former kings of Assyria destroyed them all! 13What happened to the king of Hamath and the

18:24 Or *and charioteers.* 19:9 Hebrew *of Cush.*

king of Arpad? What happened to the kings of Sepharvaim, Hena, and Ivvah?"

14After Hezekiah received the letter and read it, he went up to the LORD's Temple and spread it out before the LORD. 15And Hezekiah prayed this prayer before the LORD: "O LORD, God of Israel, you are enthroned between the mighty cherubim! You alone are God of all the kingdoms of the earth. You alone created the heavens and the earth. 16Listen to me, O LORD, and hear! Open your eyes, O LORD, and see! Listen to Sennacherib's words of defiance against the living God.

17"It is true, LORD, that the kings of Assyria have destroyed all these nations, just as the message says. 18And they have thrown the gods of these nations into the fire and burned them. But of course the Assyrians could destroy them! They were not gods at all—only idols of wood and stone shaped by human hands. 19Now, O LORD our God, rescue us from his power; then all the kingdoms of the earth will know that you alone, O LORD, are God."

Isaiah Predicts Judah's Deliverance

20Then Isaiah son of Amoz sent this message to Hezekiah: "This is what the LORD, the God of Israel, says: I have heard your prayer about King Sennacherib of Assyria. 21This is the message that the LORD has spoken against him:

The virgin daughter of Zion
   despises you and laughs at you.
The daughter of Jerusalem
   scoffs and shakes her head as you flee.

22 'Whom do you think you have been
      insulting and ridiculing?
   Against whom did you raise your voice?
   At whom did you look in such proud
      condescension?
   It was the Holy One of Israel!

23 By your messengers you have mocked the
      Lord.
   You have said, "With my many chariots
   I have conquered the highest mountains—
      yes, the remotest peaks of Lebanon.
   I have cut down its tallest cedars
      and its choicest cypress trees.
   I have reached its farthest corners
      and explored its deepest forests.

24 I have dug wells in many a foreign land
      and refreshed myself with their water.
   I even stopped up the rivers of Egypt
      so that my armies could go across!"

25 'But have you not heard?
      It was I, the LORD, who decided this long
         ago.
   Long ago I planned what I am now causing
      to happen,
   that you should crush fortified cities into
      heaps of rubble.
26 That is why their people have so little power
      and are such easy prey for you.
   They are as helpless as the grass,
      as easily trampled as tender green shoots.
   They are like grass sprouting on a housetop,
      easily scorched by the sun.

27 'But I know you well—
      your comings and goings and all you do.
   I know the way you have raged against me.
28 And because of your arrogance against me,
      which I have heard for myself,
   I will put my hook in your nose
      and my bridle in your mouth.
   I will make you return
      by the road on which you came.' "

29Then Isaiah said to Hezekiah, "Here is the proof that the LORD will protect this city from Assyria's king. This year you will eat only what grows up by itself, and next year you will eat what springs up from that. But in the third year you will plant crops and harvest them; you will tend vineyards and eat their fruit. 30And you who are left in Judah, who have escaped the ravages of the siege, will take root again in your own soil, and you will flourish and multiply. 31For a remnant of my people will spread out from Jerusalem, a group of survivors from Mount Zion. The passion of the LORD Almighty will make this happen!

32"And this is what the LORD says about the king of Assyria: His armies will not enter Jerusalem to shoot their arrows. They will not march outside its gates with their shields and build banks of earth against its walls. 33The king will return to his own country by the road on which he came. He will not enter this city, says the LORD. 34For my own honor and for the sake of my servant David, I will defend it."

35That night the angel of the LORD went out to the Assyrian camp and killed 185,000 Assyrian troops. When the surviving Assyrians* woke up the next morning, they found corpses everywhere. 36Then King Sennacherib of Assyria broke camp and returned to his own land. He went home to his capital of Nineveh and stayed there. 37One day

19:35 Hebrew *When they.*

while he was worshiping in the temple of his god Nisroch, his sons Adrammelech and Sharezer killed him with their swords. They then escaped to the land of Ararat, and another son, Esarhaddon, became the next king of Assyria.

CHAPTER **20**

Hezekiah's Sickness and Recovery

About that time Hezekiah became deathly ill, and the prophet Isaiah son of Amoz went to visit him. He gave the king this message: "This is what the LORD says: Set your affairs in order, for you are going to die. You will not recover from this illness."

²When Hezekiah heard this, he turned his face to the wall and prayed to the LORD, ³ "Remember, O LORD, how I have always tried to be faithful to you and do what is pleasing in your sight." Then he broke down and wept bitterly.

⁴But before Isaiah had left the middle courtyard, this message came to him from the LORD. ⁵ "Go back to Hezekiah, the leader of my people. Tell him, 'This is what the LORD, the God of your ancestor David, says: I have heard your prayer and seen your tears. I will heal you, and three days from now you will get out of bed and go to the Temple of the LORD. ⁶I will add fifteen years to your life, and I will rescue you and this city from the king of Assyria. I will do this to defend my honor and for the sake of my servant David.'"

⁷Then Isaiah said to Hezekiah's servants, "Make an ointment from figs and spread it over the boil." They did this, and Hezekiah recovered!

⁸Meanwhile, Hezekiah had said to Isaiah, "What sign will the LORD give to prove that he will heal me and that I will go to the Temple of the LORD three days from now?"

⁹Isaiah replied, "This is the sign that the LORD will give you to prove he will do as he promised. Would you like the shadow on the sundial to go forward ten steps or backward ten steps?"

¹⁰ "The shadow always moves forward," Hezekiah replied. "Make it go backward instead."

¹¹So Isaiah asked the LORD to do this, and he caused the shadow to move ten steps backward on the sundial of Ahaz!

Envoys from Babylon

¹²Soon after this, Merodach-baladan son of Baladan, king of Babylon, sent Hezekiah his best wishes and a gift, for he had heard that Hezekiah had been very sick. ¹³Hezekiah welcomed the Babylonian envoys and showed them everything in his treasure-houses—the silver, the gold, the spices, and the aromatic oils. He also took them to see his armory and showed them all his other treasures—everything! There was nothing in his palace or kingdom that Hezekiah did not show them.

¹⁴Then Isaiah the prophet went to King Hezekiah and asked him, "What did those men want? Where were they from?"

Hezekiah replied, "They came from the distant land of Babylon."

¹⁵ "What did they see in your palace?" Isaiah asked.

"They saw everything," Hezekiah replied. "I showed them everything I own—all my treasures."

¹⁶Then Isaiah said to Hezekiah, "Listen to this message from the LORD. ¹⁷The time is coming when everything you have—all the treasures stored up by your ancestors—will be carried off to Babylon. Nothing will be left, says the LORD. ¹⁸Some of your own descendants will be taken away into exile. They will become eunuchs who will serve in the palace of Babylon's king."

¹⁹Then Hezekiah said to Isaiah, "This message you have given me from the LORD is good." But the king was thinking, "At least there will be peace and security during my lifetime."

²⁰The rest of the events in Hezekiah's reign, including the extent of his power and how he built a pool and dug a tunnel to bring water into the city, are recorded in *The Book of the History of the Kings of Judah.* ²¹When Hezekiah died, his son Manasseh became the next king.

CHAPTER **21**

Manasseh Rules in Judah

Manasseh was twelve years old when he became king, and he reigned in Jerusalem fifty-five years. His mother was Hephzibah. ²He did what was evil in the LORD's sight, imitating the detestable practices of the pagan nations whom the LORD had driven from the land ahead of the Israelites. ³He rebuilt the pagan shrines his father, Hezekiah, had destroyed. He constructed altars for Baal and set up an Asherah pole, just as King Ahab of Israel had done. He also bowed before all the forces of heaven and worshiped them. ⁴He even built pagan altars in the Temple of the LORD, the place where the LORD had said his name should be honored. ⁵He built these altars for all the forces of heaven in both courtyards of the LORD's Temple. ⁶Manasseh even sacrificed his own son in the fire.* He practiced sorcery

21:6 Or *even made his son pass through the fire.*

and divination, and he consulted with mediums and psychics. He did much that was evil in the LORD's sight, arousing his anger.

7Manasseh even took an Asherah pole he had made and set it up in the Temple, the very place where the LORD had told David and his son Solomon: "My name will be honored here forever in this Temple and in Jerusalem—the city I have chosen from among all the other tribes of Israel. 8If the Israelites will obey my commands—the whole law that was given through my servant Moses—I will not send them into exile from this land that I gave their ancestors."
9But the people refused to listen, and Manasseh led them to do even more evil than the pagan nations whom the LORD had destroyed when the Israelites entered the land.

10Then the LORD said through his servants the prophets: 11"King Manasseh of Judah has done many detestable things. He is even more wicked than the Amorites, who lived in this land before Israel. He has led the people of Judah into idolatry. 12So this is what the LORD, the God of Israel, says: I will bring such disaster on Jerusalem and Judah that the ears of those who hear about it will tingle with horror. 13I will judge Jerusalem by the same standard I used for Samaria and by the same measure I used for the family of Ahab. I will wipe away the people of Jerusalem as one wipes a dish and turns it upside down. 14Then I will reject even those few of my people who are left, and I will hand them over as plunder for their enemies. 15For they have done great evil in my sight and have angered me ever since their ancestors came out of Egypt."

16Manasseh also murdered many innocent people until Jerusalem was filled from one end to the other with innocent blood. This was in addition to the sin that he caused the people of Judah to commit, leading them to do evil in the LORD's sight.

17The rest of the events in Manasseh's reign and all his deeds, including the sins he committed, are recorded in *The Book of the History of the Kings of Judah.* 18When Manasseh died, he was buried in the palace garden, the garden of Uzza. Then his son Amon became the next king.

Amon Rules in Judah

19Amon was twenty-two years old when he became king, and he reigned in Jerusalem two years. His mother was Meshullemeth, the daughter of Haruz from Jotbah. 20He did what was evil in the LORD's sight, just as his father,

Manasseh, had done. 21He followed the example of his father, worshiping the same idols that his father had worshiped. 22He abandoned the LORD, the God of his ancestors, and he refused to follow the LORD's ways.

23Then Amon's own servants plotted against him and assassinated him in his palace. 24But the people of the land killed all those who had conspired against King Amon, and they made his son Josiah the next king.

25The rest of the events in Amon's reign and all his deeds are recorded in *The Book of the History of the Kings of Judah.* 26He was buried in his tomb in the garden of Uzza. Then his son Josiah became the next king.

CHAPTER **22**
Josiah Rules in Judah

Josiah was eight years old when he became king, and he reigned in Jerusalem thirty-one years. His mother was Jedidah, the daughter of Adaiah from Bozkath. 2He did what was pleasing in the LORD's sight and followed the example of his ancestor David. He did not turn aside from doing what was right.

3In the eighteenth year of his reign, King Josiah sent Shaphan son of Azaliah and grandson of Meshullam, the court secretary, to the Temple of the LORD. He told him, 4"Go up to Hilkiah the high priest and have him count the money the gatekeepers have collected from the people at the LORD's Temple. 5Entrust this money to the men assigned to supervise the Temple's restoration. Then they can use it to pay workers to repair the Temple of the LORD. 6They will need to hire carpenters, builders, and masons. Also have them buy the timber and the cut stone needed to repair the Temple. 7But there will be no need for the construction supervisors to keep account of the money they receive, for they are honest people."

Hilkiah Discovers God's Law

8Hilkiah the high priest said to Shaphan the court secretary, "I have found the Book of the Law in the LORD's Temple!" Then Hilkiah gave the scroll to Shaphan, and he read it.

9Shaphan returned to the king and reported, "Your officials have given the money collected at the Temple of the LORD to the workers and supervisors at the Temple." 10Shaphan also said to the king, "Hilkiah the priest has given me a scroll." So Shaphan read it to the king.

11When the king heard what was written in the Book of the Law, he tore his clothes in despair.

¹²Then he gave these orders to Hilkiah the priest, Ahikam son of Shaphan, Acbor son of Micaiah, Shaphan the court secretary, and Asaiah the king's personal adviser: ¹³"Go to the Temple and speak to the LORD for me and for the people and for all Judah. Ask him about the words written in this scroll that has been found. The LORD's anger is burning against us because our ancestors have not obeyed the words in this scroll. We have not been doing what this scroll says we must do."

¹⁴So Hilkiah the priest, Ahikam, Acbor, Shaphan, and Asaiah went to the newer Mishneh section* of Jerusalem to consult with the prophet Huldah. She was the wife of Shallum son of Tikvah and grandson of Harhas, the keeper of the Temple wardrobe. ¹⁵She said to them, "The LORD, the God of Israel, has spoken! Go and tell the man who sent you, ¹⁶'This is what the LORD says: I will destroy this city and its people, just as I stated in the scroll you read. ¹⁷For my people have abandoned me and worshiped pagan gods, and I am very angry with them for everything they have done. My anger is burning against this place, and it will not be quenched.'

¹⁸"But go to the king of Judah who sent you to seek the LORD and tell him: 'This is what the LORD, the God of Israel, says concerning the message you have just heard: ¹⁹You were sorry and humbled yourself before the LORD when you heard what I said against this city and its people, that this land would be cursed and become desolate. You tore your clothing in despair and wept before me in repentance. So I have indeed heard you, says the LORD. ²⁰I will not send the promised disaster against this city until after you have died and been buried in peace. You will not see the disaster I am going to bring on this place.'" So they took her message back to the king.

CHAPTER **23**

Josiah's Religious Reforms

Then the king summoned all the leaders of Judah and Jerusalem. ²And the king went up to the Temple of the LORD with all the people of Judah and Jerusalem, and the priests, and the prophets—all the people from the least to the greatest. There the king read to them the entire Book of the Covenant that had been found in the LORD's Temple. ³The king took his place of authority beside the pillar and renewed the covenant in the LORD's presence. He pledged to obey the LORD by keeping all his commands, regulations, and laws with all his heart and soul. In this way, he confirmed all the terms of the covenant that were written in the scroll, and all the people pledged themselves to the covenant.

⁴Then the king instructed Hilkiah the high priest and the leading priests and the Temple gatekeepers to remove from the LORD's Temple all the utensils that were used to worship Baal, Asherah, and all the forces of heaven. The king had all these things burned outside Jerusalem on the terraces of the Kidron Valley, and he carried the ashes away to Bethel. ⁵He did away with the pagan priests, who had been appointed by the previous kings of Judah, for they had burned incense at the pagan shrines throughout Judah and even in the vicinity of Jerusalem. They had also offered incense to Baal, and to the sun, the moon, the constellations, and to all the forces of heaven. ⁶The king removed the Asherah pole from the LORD's Temple and took it outside Jerusalem to the Kidron Valley, where he burned it. Then he ground the pole to dust and threw the dust in the public cemetery. ⁷He also tore down the houses of the shrine prostitutes that were inside the Temple of the LORD, where the women wove coverings for the Asherah pole.

⁸Josiah brought back to Jerusalem all the priests of the LORD, who were living in other towns of Judah. He also defiled all the pagan shrines, where they had burned incense, from Geba to Beersheba. He destroyed the shrines at the entrance to the gate of Joshua, the governor of Jerusalem. This gate was located to the left of the city gate as one enters the city. ⁹The priests who had served at the pagan shrines were not allowed to serve at the LORD's altar in Jerusalem, but they were allowed to eat unleavened bread with the other priests.

¹⁰Then the king defiled the altar of Topheth in the valley of Ben-hinnom, so no one could ever again use it to sacrifice a son or daughter in the fire* as an offering to Molech. ¹¹He removed from the entrance of the LORD's Temple the horse statues that the former kings of Judah had dedicated to the sun. They were near the quarters of Nathan-melech the eunuch, an officer of the court. The king also burned the chariots dedicated to the sun.

¹²Josiah tore down the altars that the kings of Judah had built on the palace roof above the upper room of Ahaz. The king destroyed the altars that Manasseh had built in the two courtyards of the LORD's Temple. He smashed them to bits and scattered the pieces in the Kidron Valley.

22:14 Or *the Second Quarter,* a newer section of Jerusalem.   23:10 Or *to make a son or daughter pass through the fire.*

13The king also desecrated the pagan shrines east of Jerusalem and south of the Mount of Corruption, where King Solomon of Israel had built shrines for Ashtoreth, the detestable goddess of the Sidonians; and for Chemosh, the detestable god of the Moabites; and for Molech,* the detestable god of the Ammonites. 14He smashed the sacred pillars and cut down the Asherah poles. Then he desecrated these places by scattering human bones over them.

15The king also tore down the altar at Bethel, the pagan shrine that Jeroboam son of Nebat had made when he led Israel into sin. Josiah crushed the stones to dust and burned the Asherah pole. 16Then as Josiah was looking around, he noticed several tombs in the side of the hill. He ordered that the bones be brought out, and he burned them on the altar at Bethel to desecrate it. This happened just as the LORD had promised through the man of God as Jeroboam stood beside the altar at the festival. Then Josiah turned and looked up at the tomb of the man of God* who had predicted these things. 17"What is that monument over there?" Josiah asked.

And the people of the town told him, "It is the tomb of the man of God who came from Judah and predicted the very things that you have just done to the altar at Bethel!"

18Josiah replied, "Leave it alone. Don't disturb his bones." So they did not burn his bones or those of the old prophet from Samaria.

19Then Josiah demolished all the buildings at the pagan shrines in the towns of Samaria, just as he had done at Bethel. They had been built by the various kings of Israel and had made the LORD very angry. 20He executed the priests of the pagan shrines on their own altars, and he burned human bones on the altars to desecrate them. Finally, he returned to Jerusalem.

Josiah Celebrates Passover

21King Josiah then issued this order to all the people: "You must celebrate the Passover to the LORD your God, as it is written in the Book of the Covenant." 22There had not been a Passover celebration like that since the time when the judges ruled in Israel, throughout all the years of the kings of Israel and Judah. 23This Passover was celebrated to the LORD in Jerusalem during the eighteenth year of King Josiah's reign.

24Josiah also exterminated the mediums and psychics, the household gods, and every other kind of idol worship, both in Jerusalem and throughout the land of Judah. He did this in obedience to all the laws written in the scroll that Hilkiah the priest had found in the LORD's Temple. 25Never before had there been a king like Josiah, who turned to the LORD with all his heart and soul and strength, obeying all the laws of Moses. And there has never been a king like him since.

26Even so, the LORD's anger burned against Judah because of all the great evils of King Manasseh, and he did not hold back his fierce anger from them. 27For the LORD had said, "I will destroy Judah just as I have destroyed Israel. I will banish the people from my presence and reject my chosen city of Jerusalem and the Temple where my name was to be honored."

28The rest of the events in Josiah's reign and all his deeds are recorded in *The Book of the History of the Kings of Judah.*

29While Josiah was king, Pharaoh Neco, king of Egypt, went to the Euphrates River to help the king of Assyria. King Josiah marched out with his army to fight him, but King Neco killed him when they met at Megiddo. 30Josiah's officers took his body back in a chariot from Megiddo to Jerusalem and buried him in his own tomb. Then the people anointed his son Jehoahaz and made him the next king.

Jehoahaz Rules in Judah

31Jehoahaz was twenty-three years old when he became king, and he reigned in Jerusalem three months. His mother was Hamutal, the daughter of Jeremiah from Libnah. 32He did what was evil in the LORD's sight, just as his ancestors had done.

33Pharaoh Neco put Jehoahaz in prison at Riblah in the land of Hamath to prevent him from ruling from Jerusalem. He also demanded that Judah pay 7,500 pounds of silver and 75 pounds of gold* as tribute. 34Pharaoh Neco then installed Eliakim, another of Josiah's sons, to reign in place of his father, and he changed Eliakim's name to Jehoiakim. Jehoahaz was taken to Egypt as a prisoner, where he died.

Jehoiakim Rules in Judah

35In order to get the silver and gold demanded as tribute by Pharaoh Neco, Jehoiakim collected a tax from the people of Judah, requiring them to pay in proportion to their wealth.

36Jehoiakim was twenty-five years old when he became king, and he reigned in Jerusalem

---

23:13 Hebrew *Milcom,* a variant name for Molech.   23:16 As in Greek version; Hebrew lacks *as Jeroboam stood beside the altar at the festival. Then Josiah turned and looked up at the tomb of the man of God.*   23:33 Hebrew *100 talents* [3.4 metric tons] *of silver and 1 talent* [34 kilograms] *of gold.*

eleven years. His mother was Zebidah, the daughter of Pedaiah from Rumah. ³⁷He did what was evil in the LORD's sight, just as his ancestors had done.

CHAPTER 24

During Jehoiakim's reign, King Nebuchadnezzar of Babylon invaded the land of Judah. Jehoiakim surrendered and paid him tribute for three years but then rebelled. ²Then the LORD sent bands of Babylonian,* Aramean, Moabite, and Ammonite raiders against Judah to destroy it, just as the LORD had promised through his prophets. ³These disasters happened to Judah according to the LORD's command. He had decided to remove Judah from his presence because of the many sins of Manasseh. ⁴He had filled Jerusalem with innocent blood, and the LORD would not forgive this.

⁵The rest of the events in Jehoiakim's reign and all his deeds are recorded in *The Book of the History of the Kings of Judah.* ⁶When Jehoiakim died, his son Jehoiachin became the next king. ⁷The king of Egypt never returned after that, for the king of Babylon occupied the entire area formerly claimed by Egypt—from the brook of Egypt to the Euphrates River.

Jehoiachin Rules in Judah

⁸Jehoiachin was eighteen years old when he became king, and he reigned in Jerusalem three months. His mother was Nehushta, the daughter of Elnathan from Jerusalem. ⁹Jehoiachin did what was evil in the LORD's sight, just as his father had done.

¹⁰During Jehoiachin's reign, the officers of King Nebuchadnezzar of Babylon came up against Jerusalem and besieged it. ¹¹Nebuchadnezzar himself arrived at the city during the siege. ¹²Then King Jehoiachin, along with his advisers, nobles, and officials, and the queen mother, surrendered to the Babylonians.

In the eighth year of Nebuchadnezzar's reign, he took Jehoiachin prisoner. ¹³As the LORD had said beforehand, Nebuchadnezzar carried away all the treasures from the LORD's Temple and the royal palace. They cut apart all the gold vessels that King Solomon of Israel had placed in the Temple. ¹⁴King Nebuchadnezzar took ten thousand captives from Jerusalem, including all the princes and the best of the soldiers, craftsmen, and smiths. So only the poorest people were left in the land.

¹⁵Nebuchadnezzar led King Jehoiachin away as a captive to Babylon, along with his wives and officials, the queen mother, and all Jerusalem's elite. ¹⁶He also took seven thousand of the best troops and one thousand craftsmen and smiths, all of whom were strong and fit for war. ¹⁷Then the king of Babylon installed Mattaniah, Jehoiachin's uncle, as the next king, and he changed Mattaniah's name to Zedekiah.

Zedekiah Rules in Judah

¹⁸Zedekiah was twenty-one years old when he became king, and he reigned in Jerusalem eleven years. His mother was Hamutal, the daughter of Jeremiah from Libnah. ¹⁹But Zedekiah did what was evil in the LORD's sight, just as Jehoiakim had done. ²⁰So the LORD, in his anger, finally banished the people of Jerusalem and Judah from his presence and sent them into exile.

The Fall of Jerusalem

Then Zedekiah rebelled against the king of Babylon.

CHAPTER 25

So on January 15,* during the ninth year of Zedekiah's reign, King Nebuchadnezzar of Babylon led his entire army against Jerusalem. They surrounded the city and built siege ramps against its walls. ²Jerusalem was kept under siege until the eleventh year of King Zedekiah's reign.

³By July 18 of Zedekiah's eleventh year,* the famine in the city had become very severe, with the last of the food entirely gone. ⁴Then a section of the city wall was broken down, and all the soldiers made plans to escape from the city. But since the city was surrounded by the Babylonians,* they waited for nightfall and fled through the gate between the two walls behind the king's gardens. They made a dash across the fields, in the direction of the Jordan Valley.*

⁵But the Babylonians chased after them and caught the king on the plains of Jericho, for by then his men had all abandoned him. ⁶They brought him to the king of Babylon at Riblah, where sentence was passed against him. ⁷The king of Babylon made Zedekiah watch as all his

24:2 Or *Chaldean.* 25:1 Hebrew *on the tenth day of the tenth month,* of the Hebrew calendar. A number of events in 2 Kings can be cross-checked with dates in surviving Babylonian records and related accurately to our modern calendar. This event occurred on January 15, 588 B.C. 25:3 Hebrew *By the ninth day,* that is, "of the fourth month of Zedekiah's eleventh year" (compare Jer 52:6 and the note there). This event of the Hebrew lunar calendar occurred on July 18, 586 B.C.; also see note on 25:1. 25:4a Or *the Chaldeans;* also in 25:5, 13, 25, 26. 25:4b Hebrew *the Arabah.*

sons were killed. Then they gouged out Zedekiah's eyes, bound him in bronze chains, and led him away to Babylon.

The Temple Destroyed

8On August 14 of that year,* which was the nineteenth year of Nebuchadnezzar's reign, Nebuzaradan, captain of the guard, an official of the Babylonian king, arrived in Jerusalem. 9He burned down the Temple of the LORD, the royal palace, and all the houses of Jerusalem. He destroyed all the important buildings in the city. 10Then the captain of the guard supervised the entire Babylonian* army as they tore down the walls of Jerusalem. 11Nebuzaradan, captain of the guard, then took as exiles those who remained in the city, along with the rest of the people and the troops who had declared their allegiance to the king of Babylon. 12But the captain of the guard allowed some of the poorest people to stay behind in Judah to care for the vineyards and fields.

13The Babylonians broke up the bronze pillars, the bronze water carts, and the bronze Sea that were at the LORD's Temple, and they carried all the bronze away to Babylon. 14They also took all the pots, shovels, lamp snuffers, dishes, and all the other bronze utensils used for making sacrifices at the Temple. 15Nebuzaradan, captain of the guard, also took the firepans and basins, and all the other utensils made of pure gold or silver.

16The bronze from the two pillars, the water carts, and the Sea was too great to be weighed. These things had been made for the LORD's Temple in the days of King Solomon. 17Each of the pillars was 27 feet* tall. The bronze capital on top of each pillar was 7½ feet* high and was decorated with a network of bronze pomegranates all the way around.

18The captain of the guard took with him as prisoners Seraiah the chief priest, his assistant Zephaniah, and the three chief gatekeepers. 19And of the people still hiding in the city, he took an officer of the Judean army, five of the king's personal advisers, the army commander's chief secretary, who was in charge of recruit-

ment, and sixty other citizens. 20Nebuzaradan the commander took them all to the king of Babylon at Riblah. 21And there at Riblah, in the land of Hamath, the king of Babylon had them all put to death. So the people of Judah were sent into exile from their land.

Gedaliah Governs in Judah

22Then King Nebuchadnezzar appointed Gedaliah son of Ahikam and grandson of Shaphan as governor over the people left in Judah. 23When all the army commanders and their men learned that the king of Babylon had appointed Gedaliah as governor, they joined him at Mizpah. These included Ishmael son of Nethaniah, Johanan son of Kareah, Seraiah son of Tanhumeth the Netophathite, and Jaazaniah son of the Maacathite, and all their men.

24Gedaliah vowed to them that the Babylonian officials meant them no harm. "Live in the land and serve the king of Babylon, and all will go well for you," he promised. 25But in midautumn of that year,* Ishmael son of Nethaniah and grandson of Elishama, who was of the royal family, went to Mizpah with ten men and assassinated Gedaliah and everyone with him, both Judeans and Babylonians.

26Then all the people of Judah, from the least to the greatest, as well as the army commanders, fled in panic to Egypt, for they were afraid of what the Babylonians would do to them.

Hope for Israel's Royal Line

27In the thirty-seventh year of King Jehoiachin's exile in Babylon, Evil-merodach ascended to the Babylonian throne. He was kind to Jehoiachin and released him from prison on April 2 of that year.* 28He spoke pleasantly to Jehoiachin and gave him preferential treatment over all the other exiled kings in Babylon. 29He supplied Jehoiachin with new clothes to replace his prison garb and allowed him to dine at the king's table for the rest of his life. 30The Babylonian king also gave him a regular allowance to cover his living expenses until the day of his death.

25:8 Hebrew *On the seventh day of the fifth month,* of the Hebrew calendar. This day was August 14, 586 B.C.; also see note on 25:1. **25:10** Or *Chaldean;* also in 25:24. **25:17a** Hebrew *18 cubits* [8.1 meters]. **25:17b** As in parallel texts at 1 Kgs 7:16, 2 Chr 3:15, and Jer 52:22, all of which read *5 cubits* [2.3 meters]; Hebrew reads *3 cubits,* which is 4.5 feet or 1.4 meters. **25:25** Hebrew *in the seventh month,* of the Hebrew calendar. This month occurred in October and November 586 B.C. **25:27** Hebrew *on the twenty-seventh day of the twelfth month,* of the Hebrew calendar. This day was April 2, 561 B.C.; also see note on 25:1.

1 Chronicles

CHAPTER 1

From Adam to Noah's Sons

The descendants of Adam were Seth, Enosh, 2Kenan, Mahalalel, Jared, 3Enoch, Methuselah, Lamech, 4and Noah.

The sons of Noah were* Shem, Ham, and Japheth.

Descendants of Japheth

5The descendants of Japheth were Gomer, Magog, Madai, Javan, Tubal, Meshech, and Tiras.

6The descendants of Gomer were Ashkenaz, Riphath,* and Togarmah.

7The descendants of Javan were Elishah, Tarshish, Kittim, and Rodanim.

Descendants of Ham

8The descendants of Ham were Cush, Mizraim,* Put, and Canaan.

9The descendants of Cush were Seba, Havilah, Sabtah, Raamah, and Sabteca. The descendants of Raamah were Sheba and Dedan. 10Cush was also the ancestor of Nimrod, who was known across the earth as a heroic warrior.

11Mizraim was the ancestor of the Ludites, Anamites, Lehabites, Naphtuhites, 12Pathrusites, Casluhites, and the Caphtorites, from whom the Philistines came.*

13Canaan's oldest son was Sidon, the ancestor of the Sidonians. Canaan was also the ancestor of the Hittites, 14Jebusites, Amorites, Girgashites, 15Hivites, Arkites, Sinites, 16Arvadites, Zemarites, and Hamathites.

Descendants of Shem

17The descendants of Shem were Elam, Asshur, Arphaxad, Lud, and Aram.

The descendants of Aram were* Uz, Hul, Gether, and Mash.*

18Arphaxad was the father of Shelah. Shelah was the father of Eber. 19Eber had two sons. The first was named Peleg—"division"— for during his lifetime the people of the world were divided into different language groups and dispersed. His brother's name was Joktan.

20Joktan was the ancestor of Almodad, Sheleph, Hazarmaveth, Jerah, 21Hadoram, Uzal, Diklah, 22Obal,* Abimael, Sheba, 23Ophir, Havilah, and Jobab. All these were descendants of Joktan.

24So this is the family line descended from Shem: Arphaxad, Shelah,* 25Eber, Peleg, Reu, 26Serug, Nahor, Terah, 27and Abram, later known as Abraham.

Descendants of Abraham

28The sons of Abraham were Isaac and Ishmael.

29The sons of Ishmael were Nebaioth (the oldest), Kedar, Adbeel, Mibsam, 30Mishma, Dumah, Massa, Hadad, Tema, 31Jetur, Naphish, and Kedemah. These were the sons of Ishmael.

32The sons of Keturah, Abraham's concubine, were Zimran, Jokshan, Medan, Midian, Ishbak, and Shuah.

The sons of Jokshan were Sheba and Dedan.

1:4 As in Greek version (see also Gen 5:3-32); Hebrew lacks *The sons of Noah were.* 1:6 As in some Hebrew manuscripts and Greek version (see also Gen 10:3); most Hebrew manuscripts read *Diphath.* 1:8 Or *Egypt;* also in 1:11. 1:12 Hebrew *Casluhites, from whom the Philistines came, Caphtorites.* See Jer 47:4; Amos 9:7. 1:17a As in one Hebrew manuscript and some Greek manuscripts (see also Gen 10:23); most Hebrew manuscripts lack *The descendants of Aram were.* 1:17b As in parallel text at Gen 10:23; Hebrew reads *and Meshech.* 1:22 As in some Hebrew manuscripts and Syriac version (see also Gen 10:28); most Hebrew manuscripts read *Ebal.* 1:24 Some Greek manuscripts read *Arphaxad, Cainan, Shelah.* See notes on Gen 10:24; 11:12-13.

33 The sons of Midian were Ephah, Epher, Hanoch, Abida, and Eldaah.

All these were sons of Abraham by his concubine Keturah.

Descendants of Isaac

34 Abraham was the father of Isaac. The sons of Isaac were Esau and Israel.*

Descendants of Esau

35 The sons of Esau were Eliphaz, Reuel, Jeush, Jalam, and Korah.

36 The sons of Eliphaz were Teman, Omar, Zepho,* Gatam, Kenaz, and Amalek, who was born to Timna.*

37 The sons of Reuel were Nahath, Zerah, Shammah, and Mizzah.

Original Peoples of Edom

38 The sons of Seir were Lotan, Shobal, Zibeon, Anah, Dishon, Ezer, and Dishan.

39 The sons of Lotan were Hori and Heman.* Lotan's sister was named Timna.

40 The sons of Shobal were Alvan,* Manahath, Ebal, Shepho,* and Onam.

The sons of Zibeon were Aiah and Anah.

41 The son of Anah was Dishon.

The sons of Dishon were Hemdan,* Eshban, Ithran, and Keran.

42 The sons of Ezer were Bilhan, Zaavan, and Akan.* The sons of Dishan* were Uz and Aran.

Rulers of Edom

43 These are the kings who ruled in Edom before there were kings in Israel*:

Bela son of Beor, who ruled from his city of Dinhabah.

44 When Bela died, Jobab son of Zerah from Bozrah became king.

45 When Jobab died, Husham from the land of the Temanites became king.

46 When Husham died, Hadad son of Bedad became king and ruled from the city of Avith. He was the one who destroyed the Midianite army in the land of Moab.

47 When Hadad died, Samlah from the city of Masrekah became king.

48 When Samlah died, Shaul from the city of Rehoboth on the Euphrates River* became king.

49 When Shaul died, Baal-hanan son of Acbor became king.

50 When Baal-hanan died, Hadad became king and ruled from the city of Pau.* His wife was Mehetabel, the daughter of Matred and granddaughter of Me-zahab. 51 Then Hadad died.

The clan leaders of Edom were Timna, Alvah,* Jetheth, 52 Oholibamah, Elah, Pinon, 53 Kenaz, Teman, Mibzar, 54 Magdiel, and Iram. These were the clan leaders of Edom.

CHAPTER **2**

Descendants of Israel

The sons of Israel* were Reuben, Simeon, Levi, Judah, Issachar, Zebulun, 2 Dan, Joseph, Benjamin, Naphtali, Gad, and Asher.

Descendants of Judah

3 Judah had three sons through Bathshua, a Canaanite woman. Their names were Er, Onan, and Shelah. But the oldest son, Er, was a wicked man, so the LORD killed him. 4 Later Judah had twin sons through Tamar, his widowed daughter-in-law. Their names were Perez and Zerah. So Judah had five sons in all.

5 The sons of Perez were Hezron and Hamul.

6 The sons of Zerah were Zimri, Ethan, Heman, Calcol, and Darda*—five in all.

7 Achan* son of Carmi, one of Zerah's descendants, brought disaster on Israel by taking plunder that had been set apart for the LORD.*

8 The son of Ethan was Azariah.

From Judah's Grandson Hezron to David

9 The sons of Hezron were Jerahmeel, Ram, and Caleb.*

10 Ram was the father of Amminadab. Amminadab was the father of Nahshon, a leader of Judah.

1:34 *Israel* is the name that God gave to Jacob. **1:36a** As in many Hebrew manuscripts and a few Greek manuscripts (see also Gen 36:11); most Hebrew manuscripts read *Zephi*. **1:36b** As in some Greek manuscripts (see also Gen 36:12); Hebrew reads *Kenaz, Timna, and Amalek*. **1:39** As in parallel text at Gen 36:22; Hebrew reads *and Homam*. **1:40a** As in many Hebrew manuscripts and a few Greek manuscripts (see also Gen 36:23); most Hebrew manuscripts read *Alian*. **1:40b** As in some Hebrew manuscripts (see also Gen 36:23); most Hebrew manuscripts read *Shephi*. **1:41** As in many Hebrew manuscripts and some Greek manuscripts (see also Gen 36:26); most Hebrew manuscripts read *Hamran*. **1:42a** As in many Hebrew and Greek manuscripts (see also Gen 36:27); most Hebrew manuscripts read *Jaakan*. **1:42b** Hebrew *Dishon*; compare 1:38 and parallel text at Gen 36:28. **1:43** Or *before an Israelite king ruled over them*. **1:48** Hebrew *the river*. **1:50** As in many Hebrew manuscripts, some Greek manuscripts, Syriac version, and Latin Vulgate (see also Gen 36:39); most Hebrew manuscripts read *Pai*. **1:51** As in parallel text at Gen 36:40; Hebrew reads *Aliah*. **2:1** *Israel* is the name that God gave to Jacob. **2:6** As in many Hebrew manuscripts, some Greek manuscripts, and Syriac version (see also 1 Kgs 4:31); Hebrew reads *Dara*. **2:7a** Hebrew *Achar*; compare Josh 7:1. *Achar* means "disaster." **2:7b** The Hebrew term used here refers to the complete consecration of things or people to the LORD, either by destroying them or by giving them as an offering. **2:9** Hebrew *Kelubai*, a variant name for Caleb; compare 2:18.

11 Nahshon was the father of Salmon.* Salmon was the father of Boaz.
12 Boaz was the father of Obed. Obed was the father of Jesse.

13Jesse's first son was Eliab, his second was Abinadab, his third was Shimea, 14his fourth was Nethanel, his fifth was Raddai, 15his sixth was Ozem, and his seventh was David. 16Their sisters were named Zeruiah and Abigail. Zeruiah had three sons named Abishai, Joab, and Asahel. 17Abigail married a man named Jether, an Ishmaelite, and they had a son named Amasa.

Descendants of Hezron's Son Caleb
18Hezron's son Caleb had two wives named Azubah and Jerioth. Azubah's sons were named Jesher, Shobab, and Ardon. 19After Azubah died, Caleb married Ephrathah,* and they had a son named Hur. 20Hur was the father of Uri. Uri was the father of Bezalel.

21When Hezron was sixty years old, he married Gilead's sister, the daughter of Makir. They had a son named Segub. 22Segub was the father of Jair, who ruled twenty-three towns in the land of Gilead. 23(Later Geshur and Aram captured the Towns of Jair* and also took Kenath and its sixty surrounding villages.) All these were descendants of Makir, the father of Gilead.

24Soon after Hezron died in the town of Caleb-ephrathah, his wife Abijah gave birth to a son named Ashhur (the father of* Tekoa).

Descendants of Hezron's Son Jerahmeel
25The sons of Jerahmeel, the oldest son of Hezron, were Ram (the oldest), Bunah, Oren, Ozem, and Ahijah. 26Jerahmeel had a second wife named Atarah. She was the mother of Onam.

27The sons of Ram, the oldest son of Jerahmeel, were Maaz, Jamin, and Eker.
28The sons of Onam were Shammai and Jada. The sons of Shammai were Nadab and Abishur.
29 The sons of Abishur and his wife Abihail were Ahban and Molid.
30 The sons of Nadab were Seled and Appaim. Seled died without children, 31but Appaim had a son named Ishi. The son

of Ishi was Sheshan. Sheshan had a descendant named Ahlai.

32Shammai's brother, Jada, had two sons named Jether and Jonathan. Jether died without children, 33but Jonathan had two sons named Peleth and Zaza. These were all descendants of Jerahmeel.

34Sheshan had no sons, though he did have daughters. He also had an Egyptian servant named Jarha. 35Sheshan gave one of his daughters to be the wife of Jarha, and they had a son named Attai.

36 Attai was the father of Nathan. Nathan was the father of Zabad.
37 Zabad was the father of Ephlal. Ephlal was the father of Obed.
38 Obed was the father of Jehu. Jehu was the father of Azariah.
39 Azariah was the father of Helez. Helez was the father of Eleasah.
40 Eleasah was the father of Sismai. Sismai was the father of Shallum.
41 Shallum was the father of Jekamiah. Jekamiah was the father of Elishama.

Descendants of Hezron's Son Caleb
42The oldest son of Caleb, the brother of Jerahmeel, was Mesha, the father of Ziph. Caleb's second son was Mareshah, the father of Hebron.* 43The sons of Hebron were Korah, Tappuah, Rekem, and Shema. 44Shema was the father of Raham. Raham was the father of Jorkeam. Rekem was the father of Shammai. 45The son of Shammai was Maon. Maon was the father of Beth-zur.

46Caleb's concubine Ephah gave birth to Haran, Moza, and Gazez. Haran was the father of Gazez.

47The sons of Jahdai were Regem, Jotham, Geshan, Pelet, Ephah, and Shaaph.

48Another of Caleb's concubines, Maacah, gave birth to Sheber and Tirhanah. 49She also gave birth to Shaaph (the father of Madmannah) and Sheva (the father of Macbenah and Gibea). Caleb also had a daughter named Acsah. 50These were all descendants of Caleb.

Descendants of Caleb's Son Hur
The sons of Hur, the oldest son of Caleb's wife Ephrathah, were Shobal (the father of

Kiriath-jearim), ⁵¹Salma (the father of Bethlehem), and Hareph (the father of Beth-gader).

⁵²The descendants of Shobal (the father of Kiriath-jearim) were Haroeh, half the Manahathites, ⁵³and the families of Kiriath-jearim—the Ithrites, Puthites, Shumathites, and Mishraites, from whom came the people of Zorah and Eshtaol.

⁵⁴The descendants of Salma were Bethlehem, the Netophathites, Atroth-beth-joab, the other half of the Manahathites, the Zorites, ⁵⁵and the families of scribes living at Jabez—the Tirathites, Shimeathites, and Sucathites. All these were Kenites who descended from Hammath, the father of the family of Recab.*

CHAPTER **3**

Descendants of David

These were the sons who were born to David in Hebron:

The oldest was Amnon, whose mother was Ahinoam of Jezreel.

The second was Kileab,* whose mother was Abigail from Carmel.

2 The third was Absalom, whose mother was Maacah, the daughter of Talmai, king of Geshur.

The fourth was Adonijah, whose mother was Haggith.

3 The fifth was Shephatiah, whose mother was Abital.

The sixth was Ithream, whose mother was Eglah.

⁴These six sons were born to David in Hebron, where he reigned seven and a half years.

Then David moved the capital to Jerusalem, where he reigned another thirty-three years. ⁵The sons born to David in Jerusalem included Shimea, Shobab, Nathan, and Solomon. Bath-sheba,* the daughter of Ammiel, was the mother of these sons. ⁶David also had nine other sons: Ibhar, Elishua,* Elpelet,* ⁷Nogah, Nepheg, Japhia, ⁸Elishama, Eliada, and Eliphelet.

⁹These were the sons of David, not including the sons of his concubines. David also had a daughter named Tamar.

Descendants of Solomon

¹⁰The descendants of Solomon were Rehoboam, Abijah, Asa, Jehoshaphat, ¹¹Jehoram,* Ahaziah, Joash, ¹²Amaziah, Uzziah,* Jotham, ¹³Ahaz, Hezekiah, Manasseh, ¹⁴Amon, and Josiah.

¹⁵The sons of Josiah were Johanan (the oldest), Jehoiakim (the second), Zedekiah (the third), and Jehoahaz* (the fourth).

¹⁶Jehoiakim was succeeded by his son Jehoiachin; he, in turn, was succeeded by his uncle Zedekiah.*

Descendants of Jehoiachin

¹⁷The sons of Jehoiachin,* who was taken prisoner by the Babylonians, were Shealtiel, ¹⁸Malkiram, Pedaiah, Shenazzar, Jekamiah, Hoshama, and Nedabiah.

¹⁹The sons of Pedaiah were Zerubbabel and Shimei.

The sons of Zerubbabel were Meshullam and Hananiah. He also had a daughter named Shelomith. ²⁰His five other sons were Hashubah, Ohel, Berekiah, Hasadiah, and Jushab-hesed.

²¹The sons of Hananiah were Pelatiah and Jeshaiah. Jeshaiah's son was Rephaiah. Rephaiah's son was Arnan. Arnan's son was Obadiah. Obadiah's son was Shecaniah.

²²Shecaniah's descendants were Shemaiah and his sons, Hattush, Igal, Bariah, Neariah, and Shaphat—six in all.

²³The sons of Neariah were Elioenai, Hizkiah, and Azrikam—three in all.

²⁴The sons of Elioenai were Hodaviah, Eliashib, Pelaiah, Akkub, Johanan, Delaiah, and Anani—seven in all.

CHAPTER **4**

Other Descendants of Judah

Some of the descendants of Judah were Perez, Hezron, Carmi, Hur, and Shobal.

²Shobal's son Reaiah was the father of Jahath. Jahath was the father of Ahumai and Lahad. These were the families of the Zorathites.

³The descendants of* Etam were Jezreel, Ishma, Idbash, Hazzelelponi (his daughter), ⁴Penuel (the father of* Gedor), and Ezer (the father of Hushah). These were

the descendants of Hur (the firstborn of Ephrathah), the ancestor of Bethlehem. [5]Ashhur (the father of Tekoa) had two wives, named Helah and Naarah. [6]Naarah gave birth to Ahuzzam, Hepher, Temeni, and Haahashtari. [7]Helah gave birth to Zereth, Izhar, Ethnan, [8]and Koz, who became the ancestor of Anub, Zobebah, and all the families of Aharhel son of Harum.

[9]There was a man named Jabez who was more distinguished than any of his brothers. His mother named him Jabez* because his birth had been so painful. [10]He was the one who prayed to the God of Israel, "Oh, that you would bless me and extend my lands! Please be with me in all that I do, and keep me from all trouble and pain!" And God granted him his request.

[11]Kelub (the brother of Shuhah) was the father of Mehir. Mehir was the father of Eshton. [12]Eshton was the father of Beth-rapha, Paseah, and Tehinnah. Tehinnah was the father of Ir-nahash. These were the descendants of Recah. [13]The sons of Kenaz were Othniel and Seraiah. Othniel's sons were Hathath and Meonothai.* [14]Meonothai was the father of Ophrah. Seraiah was the father of Joab, the founder of the Valley of Craftsmen,* so called because many craftsmen lived there. [15]The sons of Caleb son of Jephunneh were Iru, Elah, and Naam. The son of Elah was Kenaz. [16]The sons of Jehallelel were Ziph, Ziphah, Tiria, and Asarel. [17]The sons of Ezrah were Jether, Mered, Epher, and Jalon. Mered married an Egyptian woman, who became the mother of Miriam, Shammai, and Ishbah (the father of Eshtemoa). [18]Mered also married a woman of Judah, who became the mother of Jered (the father of Gedor), Heber (the father of Soco), and Jekuthiel (the father of Zanoah). Mered's Egyptian wife was named Bithiah, and she was an Egyptian princess. [19]Hodiah's wife was the sister of Naham. One of her sons was the father of Keilah the Garmite, and another was the father of Eshtemoa the Maacathite. [20]The sons of Shimon were Amnon, Rinnah, Ben-hanan, and Tilon. The descendants of Ishi were Zoheth and Ben-zoheth.

Descendants of Judah's Son Shelah

[21]Shelah was one of Judah's sons. The descendants of Shelah were Er (the father of Lecah), Laadah (the father of Mareshah), the families of linen workers at Beth-ashbea, [22]Jokim, the people of Cozeba, Joash, and Saraph, who ruled over Moab and Jashubi-lehem. These names all come from ancient records. [23]They were the potters who lived in Netaim and Gederah. They all worked for the king.

Descendants of Simeon

[24]The sons of Simeon were Nemuel, Jamin, Jarib, Zerah, and Shaul. [25]The descendants of Shaul were Shallum, Mibsam, and Mishma. [26]The descendants of Mishma were Hammuel, Zaccur, and Shimei. [27]Shimei had sixteen sons and six daughters, but none of his brothers had large families. So Simeon's tribe never became as large as the tribe of Judah.

[28]They lived in Beersheba, Moladah, Hazar-shual, [29]Bilhah, Ezem, Tolad, [30]Bethuel, Hormah, Ziklag, [31]Beth-marcaboth, Hazar-susim, Beth-biri, and Shaaraim. These towns were under their control until the time of King David. [32]Their descendants also lived in Etam, Ain, Rimmon, Token, and Ashan—five towns [33]and their surrounding villages as far away as Baalath.* This was their territory, and these names are recorded in their family genealogy.

[34]Other descendants of Simeon included Meshobab, Jamlech, Joshah son of Amaziah, [35]Joel, Jehu son of Joshibiah, son of Seraiah, son of Asiel, [36]Elioenai, Jaakobah, Jeshohaiah, Asaiah, Adiel, Jesimiel, Benaiah, [37]and Ziza son of Shiphi, son of Allon, son of Jedaiah, son of Shimri, son of Shemaiah.

[38]These were the names of some of the leaders of Simeon's wealthy clans, [39]who traveled to the region of Gedor, in the east part of the valley, seeking pastureland for their flocks. [40]They found lush pastures there, and the land was quiet and peaceful.

Some of Ham's descendants had been living in the region of Gedor. [41]But during the reign of King Hezekiah of Judah, the leaders of Simeon invaded it and completely destroyed* the homes of the descendants of Ham and of the

---

4:9 *Jabez* sounds like a Hebrew term meaning "distress" or "pain." 4:13 As in some Greek manuscripts and Latin Vulgate; Hebrew lacks *and Meonothai.* 4:14 Or *Joab, the father of Ge-harashim.* 4:33 As in some Greek manuscripts (see also Josh 19:8); Hebrew reads *Baal.* 4:41 The Hebrew term used here refers to the complete consecration of things or people to the Lord, either by destroying them or by giving them as an offering.

Meunites. They killed everyone who lived there and took the land for themselves, because they wanted its good pastureland for their flocks. ⁴²Five hundred of these invaders from the tribe of Simeon went to Mount Seir, led by Pelatiah, Neariah, Rephaiah, and Uzziel—all sons of Ishi. ⁴³They destroyed the few Amalekites who had survived, and they have lived there ever since.

CHAPTER **5**
Descendants of Reuben
The oldest son of Israel* was Reuben. But since he dishonored his father by sleeping with one of his father's concubines, his birthright was given to the sons of his brother Joseph. For this reason, Reuben is not listed in the genealogy as the firstborn son. ²It was the descendants of Judah that became the most powerful tribe and provided a ruler for the nation,* but the birthright belonged to Joseph.

³The sons of Reuben, the oldest son of Israel, were Hanoch, Pallu, Hezron, and Carmi.
⁴The descendants of Joel were Shemaiah, Gog, Shimei, ⁵Micah, Reaiah, Baal, ⁶and Beerah.

Beerah was the leader of the Reubenites when they were taken into captivity by King Tiglath-pileser* of Assyria.
⁷Beerah's relatives are listed in their genealogy by their clans: Jeiel (the leader), Zechariah, ⁸and Bela son of Azaz, son of Shema, son of Joel.

These Reubenites lived in the area that stretches from Aroer to Nebo and Baal-meon. ⁹And since they had so many cattle in the land of Gilead, they spread eastward toward the edge of the desert that stretches to the Euphrates River.

¹⁰During the reign of Saul, the Reubenites defeated the Hagrites in battle. Then they moved into the Hagrite settlements all along the eastern edge of Gilead.

Descendants of Gad
¹¹Across from the Reubenites in the land of Bashan lived the descendants of Gad, who were spread as far east as Salecah. ¹²Joel was the leader in the land of Bashan, and Shapham was second-in-command, along with Janai and Shaphat.
¹³Their relatives, the leaders of seven other clans, were Michael, Meshullam, Sheba, Jorai, Jacan, Zia, and Eber. ¹⁴These were all

descendants of Abihail son of Huri, son of Jaroah, son of Gilead, son of Michael, son of Jeshishai, son of Jahdo, son of Buz. ¹⁵Ahi son of Abdiel, son of Guni, was the leader of their clans.

¹⁶The Gadites lived in the land of Gilead, in Bashan and its villages, and throughout the Sharon Plain. ¹⁷All of these were listed in the genealogical records during the days of King Jotham of Judah and King Jeroboam of Israel.

The Tribes East of the Jordan
¹⁸There were 44,760 skilled warriors in the armies of Reuben, Gad, and the half-tribe of Manasseh. They were all skilled in combat and armed with shields, swords, and bows. ¹⁹They waged war against the Hagrites, the Jeturites, the Naphishites, and the Nodabites. ²⁰They cried out to God during the battle, and he answered their prayer because they trusted in him. So the Hagrites and all their allies were defeated. ²¹The plunder taken from the Hagrites included 50,000 camels, 250,000 sheep, 2,000 donkeys, and 100,000 captives. ²²Many of the Hagrites were killed in the battle because God was fighting against them. So they lived in their land until they were taken away into exile.

²³The half-tribe of Manasseh spread through the land from Bashan to Baal-hermon, Senir, and Mount Hermon. They were very numerous. ²⁴These were the leaders of their clans: Epher, Ishi, Eliel, Azriel, Jeremiah, Hodaviah, and Jahdiel. Each of these men had a great reputation as a warrior and leader. ²⁵But they were unfaithful and violated their covenant with the God of their ancestors. They worshiped the gods of the nations that God had destroyed. ²⁶So the God of Israel caused King Pul of Assyria (also known as Tiglath-pileser) to invade the land and lead away the people of Reuben, Gad, and the half-tribe of Manasseh as captives. The Assyrians exiled them to Halah, Habor, Hara, and the Gozan River, where they remain to this day.

CHAPTER **6**
The Priestly Line
The sons of Levi included Gershon, Kohath, and Merari.
²The descendants of Kohath included Amram, Izhar, Hebron, and Uzziel.
³The children of Amram were Aaron, Moses, and Miriam.

5:1 *Israel* is the name that God gave to Jacob. 5:2 Or *and from Judah came a prince.* 5:6 Hebrew *Tilgath-pilneser,* a variant name for Tiglath-pileser; also in 5:26.

The sons of Aaron were Nadab, Abihu, Eleazar, and Ithamar.

4 Eleazar was the father of Phinehas. Phinehas was the father of Abishua.
5 Abishua was the father of Bukki. Bukki was the father of Uzzi.
6 Uzzi was the father of Zerahiah. Zerahiah was the father of Meraioth.
7 Meraioth was the father of Amariah. Amariah was the father of Ahitub.
8 Ahitub was the father of Zadok. Zadok was the father of Ahimaaz.
9 Ahimaaz was the father of Azariah. Azariah was the father of Johanan.
10 Johanan was the father of Azariah, the high priest at the Temple built by Solomon in Jerusalem.
11 Azariah was the father of Amariah. Amariah was the father of Ahitub.
12 Ahitub was the father of Zadok. Zadok was the father of Shallum.
13 Shallum was the father of Hilkiah. Hilkiah was the father of Azariah.
14 Azariah was the father of Seraiah. Seraiah was the father of Jehozadak, 15who went into exile when the LORD sent the people of Judah and Jerusalem into captivity under Nebuchadnezzar.

The Levite Clans

16The sons of Levi were Gershon,* Kohath, and Merari.
17The descendants of Gershon included Libni and Shimei.
18The descendants of Kohath included Amram, Izhar, Hebron, and Uzziel.
19The descendants of Merari included Mahli and Mushi.

The following were the Levite clans, listed according to their ancestral descent:

20The descendants of Gershon included Libni, Jahath, Zimmah, 21Joah, Iddo, Zerah, and Jeatherai.
22The descendants of Kohath included Amminadab, Korah, Assir, 23Elkanah, Abiasaph,* Assir, 24Tahath, Uriel, Uzziah, and Shaul.
25The descendants of Elkanah included Amasai, Ahimoth, 26Elkanah, Zophai, Nahath, 27Eliab, Jeroham, Elkanah, and Samuel.*

28The sons of Samuel were Joel* (the older) and Abijah (the second).
29The descendants of Merari included Mahli, Libni, Shimei, Uzzah, 30Shimea, Haggiah, and Asaiah.

The Temple Musicians

31David assigned the following men to lead the music at the house of the LORD after he put the Ark there. 32They ministered with music there at the Tabernacle* until Solomon built the Temple of the LORD in Jerusalem. Then they carried on their work there, following all the regulations handed down to them. 33These are the men who served, along with their sons:

Heman the musician was from the clan of Kohath. His genealogy was traced back through Joel, Samuel, 34Elkanah, Jeroham, Eliel, Toah, 35Zuph, Elkanah, Mahath, Amasai, 36Elkanah, Joel, Azariah, Zephaniah, 37Tahath, Assir, Abiasaph, Korah, 38Izhar, Kohath, Levi, and Israel.*
39Heman's first assistant was Asaph from the clan of Gershon.* Asaph's genealogy was traced back through Berekiah, Shimea, 40Michael, Baaseiah, Malkijah, 41Ethni, Zerah, Adaiah, 42Ethan, Zimmah, Shimei, 43Jahath, Gershon, and Levi.
44Heman's second assistant was Ethan from the clan of Merari. Ethan's genealogy was traced back through Kishi, Abdi, Malluch, 45Hashabiah, Amaziah, Hilkiah, 46Amzi, Bani, Shemer, 47Mahli, Mushi, Merari, and Levi.

48Their relatives, also Levites, were appointed to various other tasks in the Tabernacle, the house of God.

Aaron's Descendants

49Only Aaron and his descendants served as priests. They presented the offerings on the altar of burnt offering and the altar of incense, and they performed all the other duties related to the Most Holy Place. They made atonement for Israel by following all the commands that Moses, the servant of God, had given them.

50The descendants of Aaron were Eleazar, Phinehas, Abishua, 51Bukki, Uzzi, Zerahiah, 52Meraioth, Amariah, Ahitub, 53Zadok, and Ahimaaz.

6:16 Hebrew *Gershom*, a variant name for Gershon (see 6:1); also in 6:17, 20, 43, 62, 71.   6:23 Hebrew *Ebiasaph*, a variant name for Abiasaph (also in 6:37); compare parallel text at Exod 6:24.   6:27 As in some Greek manuscripts (see also 6:33-34); Hebrew lacks *and Samuel.*   6:28 As in some Greek manuscripts and the Syriac version (see also 6:33 and 1 Sam 8:2); Hebrew lacks *Joel.*   6:32 Hebrew *the Tabernacle, the Tent of Meeting.*   6:38 *Israel* is the name that God gave to Jacob.   6:39 Hebrew lacks *from the clan of Gershon*; see 6:43.

Territory for the Levites

⁵⁴This is a record of the towns and territory assigned by means of sacred lots to the descendants of Aaron who were from the clan of Kohath. ⁵⁵This included Hebron and its surrounding pasturelands in Judah, ⁵⁶but the fields and outlying areas were given to Caleb son of Jephunneh. ⁵⁷So the descendants of Aaron were given the following towns, each with its surrounding pasturelands: Hebron (a city of refuge), Libnah, Jattir, Eshtemoa, ⁵⁸Holon,* Debir, ⁵⁹Ain,* Juttah,* and Bethshemesh. ⁶⁰And from the territory of Benjamin they were given Gibeon,* Geba, Alemeth, and Anathoth, each with its pasturelands. So a total of thirteen towns was given to the descendants of Aaron. ⁶¹The remaining descendants of Kohath received ten towns from the territory of the half-tribe of Manasseh by means of sacred lots.

⁶²The descendants of Gershon received by sacred lots thirteen towns from the territories of Issachar, Asher, Naphtali, and from the Bashan area of Manasseh, east of the Jordan.

⁶³The descendants of Merari received by sacred lots twelve towns from the territories of Reuben, Gad, and Zebulun.

⁶⁴So the people of Israel assigned all these towns and pasturelands to the Levites. ⁶⁵The towns in the territories of Judah, Simeon, and Benjamin, mentioned above, were also assigned by means of sacred lots.

⁶⁶The descendants of Kohath received from the territory of Ephraim these towns, each with its surrounding pasturelands: ⁶⁷Shechem (a city of refuge in the hill country of Ephraim), Gezer, ⁶⁸Jokmeam, Beth-horon, ⁶⁹Aijalon, and Gathrimmon. ⁷⁰The remaining descendants of Kohath were assigned these towns from the territory of the half-tribe of Manasseh: Aner and Bileam, each with its pasturelands.

⁷¹The descendants of Gershon received from the territory of the half-tribe of Manasseh the town of Golan in Bashan with its pasturelands and Ashtaroth with its pasturelands. ⁷²From the territory of Issachar, they were given Kedesh, Daberath, ⁷³Ramoth, and Anem, with their pasturelands. ⁷⁴From the territory of Asher, they received Mashal, Abdon, ⁷⁵Hukok, and Rehob, each with its pasturelands. ⁷⁶From the territory of Naphtali, they were given Kedesh in Galilee, Hammon, and Kiriathaim, each with its pasturelands.

⁷⁷The remaining descendants of Merari re-

ceived from the territory of Zebulun the towns of Jokneam, Kartah,* Rimmono, and Tabor, each with its pasturelands. ⁷⁸From the territory of Reuben, east of the Jordan River opposite Jericho, they received Bezer (a desert town), Jahaz,* ⁷⁹Kedemoth, and Mephaath, each with its pasturelands. ⁸⁰And from the territory of Gad, they received Ramoth in Gilead, Mahanaim, ⁸¹Heshbon, and Jazer, each with its pasturelands.

CHAPTER 7
Descendants of Issachar

The four sons of Issachar were Tola, Puah, Jashub, and Shimron.

²The sons of Tola were Uzzi, Rephaiah, Jeriel, Jahmai, Ibsam, and Shemuel. Each of them was the leader of an ancestral clan. At the time of King David, the total number of men available for military service from these families was 22,600.

³The son of Uzzi was Izrahiah. The sons of Izrahiah were Michael, Obadiah, Joel, and Isshiah. These five became the leaders of clans. ⁴The total number of men available for military service among their descendants was 36,000, for all five of them had many wives and many sons.

⁵The total number of men available for military service from all the clans of the tribe of Issachar was 87,000. All of them were listed in their tribal genealogy.

Descendants of Benjamin

⁶Three of Benjamin's sons were Bela, Beker, and Jediael.

⁷The sons of Bela were Ezbon, Uzzi, Uzziel, Jerimoth, and Iri. These five warriors were the leaders of clans. The total number of men available for military service among their descendants was 22,034. All of them were listed in their family genealogy.

⁸The sons of Beker were Zemirah, Joash, Eliezer, Elioenai, Omri, Jeremoth, Abijah, Anathoth, and Alemeth. ⁹According to their family genealogy, there were 20,200 men available for military service among their descendants, in addition to their clan leaders.

¹⁰The son of Jediael was Bilhan. The sons of Bilhan were Jeush, Benjamin, Ehud, Kenaanah, Zethan, Tarshish, and Ahishahar.

[11]They were the leaders of the clans of Jediael, and their descendants included 17,200 men available for military service. [12]The sons of Ir were Shuppim and Huppim. Hushim was the son of Aher.

Descendants of Naphtali

[13]The sons of Naphtali were Jahzeel,* Guni, Jezer, and Shillem.* They were all descendants of Jacob's wife Bilhah.

Descendants of Manasseh

[14]The sons of Manasseh, born to his Aramean concubine, were Asriel and Makir. Makir was the father of Gilead.

[15]Makir found wives for Huppim and Shuppim. Makir's sister was named Maacah. One of his descendants was Zelophehad, who had only daughters.

[16]Makir's wife, Maacah, gave birth to a son whom she named Peresh. His brother's name was Sheresh. The sons of Peresh were Ulam and Rakem. [17]The son of Ulam was Bedan. All these were considered Gileadites, descendants of Makir son of Manasseh.

[18]Makir's sister Hammoleketh gave birth to Ishhod, Abiezer, and Mahlah.

[19]The sons of Shemida were Ahian, Shechem, Likhi, and Aniam.

Descendants of Ephraim

[20]The descendants of Ephraim were Shuthelah, Bered, Tahath, Eleadah, Tahath, [21]Zabad, and Shuthelah.

Ephraim's sons Ezer and Elead were killed trying to steal livestock from the local farmers near Gath. [22]Their father, Ephraim, mourned for them a long time, and his relatives came to comfort him. [23]Afterward Ephraim slept with his wife, and she became pregnant and gave birth to a son. Ephraim named him Beriah* because of the tragedy his family had suffered.

[24]Ephraim had a daughter named Sheerah. She built the towns of Lower and Upper Beth-horon and Uzzen-sheerah.

[25]Ephraim's line of descent was Rephah, Resheph, Telah, Tahan, [26]Ladan, Ammihud, Elishama, [27]Nun, and Joshua.

[28]The descendants of Ephraim lived in the ter-ritory that included Bethel and its surrounding towns to the south, Naaran to the east, Gezer and its villages to the west, and Shechem and its surrounding villages to the north as far as Ayyah and its towns. [29]Along the border of Manasseh were the towns of Beth-shan,* Taanach, Megiddo, Dor, and their surrounding villages. The descendants of Joseph son of Israel* lived in these towns.

Descendants of Asher

[30]The sons of Asher were Imnah, Ishvah, Ishvi, and Beriah. They had a sister named Serah. [31]The sons of Beriah were Heber and Malkiel (the father of Birzaith). [32]The sons of Heber were Japhlet, Shomer, and Hotham. They had a sister named Shua. [33]The sons of Japhlet were Pasach, Bimhal, and Ashvath. [34]The sons of Shomer were Ahi, Rohgah, Hubbah, and Aram. [35]The sons of his brother Helem* were Zophah, Imna, Shelesh, and Amal. [36]The sons of Zophah were Suah, Harnepher, Shual, Beri, Imrah, [37]Bezer, Hod, Shamma, Shilshah, Ithran,* and Beera. [38]The sons of Jether were Jephunneh, Pispah, and Ara. [39]The sons of Ulla were Arah, Hanniel, and Rizia.

[40]Each of these descendants of Asher was the head of an ancestral clan. They were all skilled warriors and prominent leaders. There were 26,000 men available for military service among the descendants listed in their tribal genealogy.

CHAPTER **8**

Descendants of Benjamin

The sons of Benjamin, in order of age, included Bela (the oldest), Ashbel, Aharah, [2]Nohah, and Rapha.

[3]The sons of Bela were Addar, Gera, Abihud,* [4]Abishua, Naaman, Ahoah, [5]Gera, Shephuphan, and Huram.

[6]The sons of Ehud, leaders of the clans living at Geba, were driven out and moved to Manahath. [7]Ehud's sons were Naaman, Ahijah, and Gera. Gera, the father of Uzza and Ahihud, led them when they moved.

[8]After Shaharaim divorced his wives Hushim and Baara, he had children in the land of

---

7:13a As in parallel text at Gen 46:24; Hebrew reads *Jahziel*, a variant name for Jahzeel.   7:13b As in some Hebrew and Greek manuscripts (see also Gen 46:24; Num 26:49); most Hebrew manuscripts read *Shallum*.   7:23 *Beriah* sounds like a Hebrew term meaning "tragedy" or "misfortune."   7:29a Hebrew *Beth-shean*, a variant name for Beth-shan.   7:29b *Israel* is the name that God gave to Jacob.   7:35 Possibly another name for *Hotham*; compare 7:32.   7:37 Possibly another name for *Jether*; compare 7:38.   8:3 Possibly *Gera the father of Ehud*; compare 8:6.

Moab. ⁹Hodesh, his new wife, gave birth to Jobab, Zibia, Mesha, Malcam, ¹⁰Jeuz, Sakia, and Mirmah. These sons all became the leaders of clans.

¹¹Shaharaim's wife Hushim had already given birth to Abitub and Elpaal. ¹²The sons of Elpaal were Eber, Misham, Shemed (who built Ono and Lod and their villages), ¹³Beriah, and Shema. They were the leaders of the clans living in Aijalon, and they drove out the inhabitants of Gath.

¹⁴Ahio, Shashak, Jeremoth, ¹⁵Zebadiah, Arad, Eder, ¹⁶Michael, Ishpah, and Joha were the sons of Beriah.

¹⁷Zebadiah, Meshullam, Hizki, Heber, ¹⁸Ishmerai, Izliah, and Jobab were the sons of Elpaal.

¹⁹Jakim, Zicri, Zabdi, ²⁰Elienai, Zillethai, Eliel, ²¹Adaiah, Beraiah, and Shimrath were the sons of Shimei.

²²Ishpan, Eber, Eliel, ²³Abdon, Zicri, Hanan, ²⁴Hananiah, Elam, Anthothijah, ²⁵Iphdeiah, and Penuel were the sons of Shashak.

²⁶Shamsherai, Shehariah, Athaliah, ²⁷Jaareshiah, Elijah, and Zicri were the sons of Jeroham.

²⁸These were the leaders of the ancestral clans, and they were listed in their tribal genealogy. They all lived in Jerusalem.

The Family of Saul

²⁹Jeiel* (the father of* Gibeon) lived in Gibeon. His wife's name was Maacah, ³⁰and his oldest son was named Abdon. Jeiel's other sons were Zur, Kish, Baal, Ner,* Nadab, ³¹Gedor, Ahio, Zechariah,* ³²and Mikloth, who was the father of Shimeam.* All these families lived near each other in Jerusalem.

³³Ner was the father of Kish. Kish was the father of Saul. Saul was the father of Jonathan, Malkishua, Abinadab, and Eshbaal.

³⁴Jonathan was the father of Meribbaal. Meribbaal was the father of Micah. ³⁵Micah was the father of Pithon, Melech, Tahrea,* and Ahaz.

³⁶ Ahaz was the father of Jadah.* Jadah was the father of Alemeth, Azmaveth, and Zimri. Zimri was the father of Moza.

³⁷ Moza was the father of Binea. Binea was the father of Rephaiah.* Rephaiah was the father of Eleasah. Eleasah was the father of Azel.

³⁸Azel had six sons: Azrikam, Bokeru, Ishmael, Sheariah, Obadiah, and Hanan. These were the sons of Azel.

³⁹Azel's brother Eshek had three sons: Ulam (the oldest), Jeush (the second), and Eliphelet (the third). ⁴⁰The sons of Ulam were all skilled warriors and expert archers. They had many sons and grandsons—150 in all.

All these were descendants of Benjamin.

CHAPTER 9

All Israel was listed in the genealogical record in *The Book of the Kings of Israel.*

The Returning Exiles

The people of Judah were exiled to Babylon because they were unfaithful to the Lord. ²The first to return to their property in their former towns were common people. With them came some of the priests, Levites, and Temple assistants. ³People from the tribes of Judah, Benjamin, Ephraim, and Manasseh came and settled in Jerusalem.

⁴One family that returned was that of Uthai son of Ammihud, son of Omri, son of Imri, son of Bani, a descendant of Perez son of Judah.

⁵Others returned from the Shilonite clan, including Asaiah (the oldest) and his sons.

⁶From the Zerahite clan, Jeuel returned with his relatives.

In all, 690 families from the tribe of Judah returned.

⁷From the tribe of Benjamin came Sallu son of Meshullam, son of Hodaviah, son of Hassenuah; ⁸Ibneiah son of Jeroham; Elah son of Uzzi, son of Micri; Meshullam son of Shephatiah, son of Reuel, son of Ibnijah.

⁹These men were all leaders of clans, and they were listed in their tribal genealogy. In all, 956 families from the tribe of Benjamin returned.

The Returning Priests

¹⁰Among the priests who returned were Jedaiah, Jehoiarib, Jakin, ¹¹Azariah son of

---

8:29a As in some Greek manuscripts (see also 9:35); Hebrew lacks *Jeiel.*   8:29b Or *the founder of.*   8:30 As in some Greek manuscripts (see also 9:36); Hebrew lacks *Ner.*   8:31 As in parallel text at 9:37; Hebrew reads *Zeker,* a variant name for Zechariah.   8:32 As in parallel text at 9:38; Hebrew reads *Shimeah,* a variant name for Shimeam.   8:35 As in parallel text at 9:41; Hebrew reads *Tarea,* a variant name for Tahrea.   8:36 As in parallel text at 9:42; Hebrew reads *Jehoaddah,* a variant name for Jadah.   8:37 As in parallel text at 9:43; Hebrew reads *Raphah,* a variant name for Rephaiah.

Hilkiah, son of Meshullam, son of Zadok, son of Meraioth, son of Ahitub. Azariah was the chief officer of the house of God. ¹²Other returning priests were Adaiah son of Jeroham, son of Pashhur, son of Malkijah, and Maasai son of Adiel, son of Jahzerah, son of Meshullam, son of Meshillemith, son of Immer.

¹³In all, 1,760 priests returned. They were heads of clans and very able men. They were responsible for ministering at the house of God.

The Returning Levites

¹⁴The Levites who returned were Shemaiah son of Hasshub, son of Azrikam, son of Hashabiah, a descendant of Merari; ¹⁵Bakbakkar; Heresh; Galal; Mattaniah son of Mica, son of Zicri, son of Asaph; ¹⁶Obadiah son of Shemaiah, son of Galal, son of Jeduthun; and Berekiah son of Asa, son of Elkanah, who lived in the area of Netophah.

¹⁷The gatekeepers who returned were Shallum, Akkub, Talmon, Ahiman, and their relatives. Shallum was the chief gatekeeper. ¹⁸Prior to this time, they were responsible for the King's Gate on the east side. These men served as gatekeepers for the camps of the Levites. ¹⁹Shallum was the son of Kore, a descendant of Abiasaph,* from the clan of Korah. He and his relatives, the Korahites, were responsible for guarding the entrance to the sanctuary, just as their ancestors had guarded the Tabernacle in the camp of the LORD.

²⁰Phinehas son of Eleazar had been in charge of the gatekeepers in earlier times, and the LORD had been with him. ²¹And later Zechariah son of Meshelemiah had been responsible for guarding the entrance to the Tabernacle.*

²²In all, there were 212 gatekeepers in those days, and they were listed by genealogies in their villages. David and Samuel the seer had appointed their ancestors because they were reliable men. ²³These gatekeepers and their descendants, by their divisions, were responsible for guarding the entrance to the house of the LORD, the house that was formerly a tent. ²⁴The gatekeepers were stationed on all four sides—east, west, north, and south. ²⁵From time to time, their relatives in the villages came to share their duties for seven-day periods.

²⁶The four chief gatekeepers, all Levites, were in an office of great trust, for they were responsible for the rooms and treasuries at the house of God. ²⁷They would spend the night around the house of God, since it was their duty to guard it. It was also their job to open the gates every morning.

²⁸Some of the gatekeepers were assigned to care for the various utensils used in worship. They checked them in and out to avoid any loss. ²⁹Others were responsible for the furnishings, the items in the sanctuary, and the supplies such as choice flour, wine, olive oil, incense, and spices. ³⁰But it was the priests who prepared the spices and incense. ³¹Mattithiah, a Levite and the oldest son of Shallum the Korahite, was entrusted with baking the bread used in the offerings. ³²And some members of the clan of Kohath were in charge of preparing the bread to be set on the table each Sabbath day.

³³The musicians, all prominent Levites, lived at the Temple. They were exempt from other responsibilities there since they were on duty at all hours. ³⁴All these men lived in Jerusalem. They were the heads of Levite families and were listed as prominent leaders in their tribal genealogy.

King Saul's Family Tree

³⁵Jeiel (the father of* Gibeon) lived in Gibeon. His wife's name was Maacah, ³⁶and his oldest son was named Abdon. Jeiel's other sons were Zur, Kish, Baal, Ner, Nadab, ³⁷Gedor, Ahio, Zechariah, and Mikloth. ³⁸Mikloth was the father of Shimeam. All these families lived near each other in Jerusalem.

³⁹Ner was the father of Kish. Kish was the father of Saul. Saul was the father of Jonathan, Malkishua, Abinadab, and Eshbaal.

⁴⁰Jonathan was the father of Meribbaal. Meribbaal was the father of Micah. ⁴¹The sons of Micah were Pithon, Melech, Tahrea, and Ahaz.*

⁴² Ahaz was the father of Jadah.* Jadah was the father of Alemeth, Azmaveth, and Zimri.

Zimri was the father of Moza.

⁴³ Moza was the father of Binea. Binea's son was Rephaiah.

9:19 Hebrew *Ebiasaph*, a variant name for Abiasaph; compare Exod 6:24. 9:21 Hebrew *Tent of Meeting*. 9:35 Or *the founder of*. 9:41 As in Syriac version and Latin Vulgate (see also 8:35); Hebrew lacks *and Ahaz*. 9:42 As in some Hebrew manuscripts and Greek version (see also 8:36); Hebrew reads *Jarah*.

Rephaiah's son was Eleasah.
Eleasah's son was Azel.

⁴⁴Azel had six sons, and their names were Azrikam, Bokeru, Ishmael, Sheariah, Obadiah, and Hanan. These were the sons of Azel.

CHAPTER 10
The Death of King Saul

Now the Philistines attacked Israel, forcing the Israelites to flee. Many were slaughtered on the slopes of Mount Gilboa. ²The Philistines closed in on Saul and his sons, and they killed three of his sons—Jonathan, Abinadab, and Malkishua. ³The fighting grew very fierce around Saul, and the Philistine archers caught up with him and wounded him severely. ⁴Saul groaned to his armor bearer, "Take your sword and run me through before these pagan Philistines come and humiliate me." But his armor bearer was afraid and would not do it. So Saul took his own sword and fell on it. ⁵When his armor bearer realized that Saul was dead, he fell on his own sword and died. ⁶So Saul and his three sons died there together, bringing his dynasty to an end.

⁷When the Israelites in the Jezreel Valley saw that their army had been routed and that Saul and his sons were dead, they abandoned their towns and fled. So the Philistines moved in and occupied their towns.

⁸The next day when the Philistines went out to strip the dead, they found the bodies of Saul and his sons on Mount Gilboa. ⁹So they stripped off Saul's armor and cut off his head. Then they proclaimed the news of Saul's death before their idols and to the people throughout the land of Philistia. ¹⁰They placed his armor in the temple of their gods, and they fastened his head to the wall in the temple of Dagon.

¹¹But when the people of Jabesh-gilead heard what the Philistines had done to Saul, ¹²their warriors went out and brought the bodies of Saul and his three sons back to Jabesh. Then they buried their remains beneath the oak tree at Jabesh, and they fasted for seven days.

¹³So Saul died because he was unfaithful to the LORD. He failed to obey the LORD's command, and he even consulted a medium ¹⁴instead of asking the LORD for guidance. So the LORD killed him and turned his kingdom over to David son of Jesse.

CHAPTER 11
David Becomes King of All Israel

Then all Israel went to David at Hebron and told him, "We are all members of your family. ²For a long time, even while Saul was our king, you were the one who really led Israel. And the LORD your God has told you, 'You will be the shepherd of my people Israel. You will be their leader.'" ³So there at Hebron David made a covenant with the leaders of Israel before the LORD. They anointed him king of Israel, just as the LORD had promised through Samuel.

David Captures Jerusalem

⁴Then David and all Israel went to Jerusalem (or Jebus, as it used to be called), where the Jebusites, original inhabitants of the land, lived. ⁵The people of Jebus said to David, "You will never get in here!" But David captured the fortress of Zion, now called the City of David.

⁶David had said to his troops, "Whoever leads the attack against the Jebusites will become the commander of my armies!" And Joab, the son of David's sister Zeruiah, led the attack, so he became the commander of David's armies.

⁷David made the fortress his home, and that is why it is called the City of David. ⁸He extended the city from the Millo* to the surrounding area, while Joab rebuilt the rest of Jerusalem. ⁹And David became more and more powerful, because the LORD Almighty was with him.

David's Mightiest Men

¹⁰These are the leaders of David's mighty men. Together with all Israel, they determined to make David their king, just as the LORD had promised concerning Israel. ¹¹Here is the record of David's mightiest men:

The first was Jashobeam the Hacmonite, who was commander of the Three—the three greatest warriors among David's men.* He once used his spear to kill three hundred enemy warriors in a single battle.

¹²Next in rank among the Three was Eleazar son of Dodai,* a descendant of Ahoah. ¹³He was with David in the battle against the Philistines at Pas-dammim. The battle took place in a field full of barley, and the Israelite army fled. ¹⁴But Eleazar and David held their ground in the middle of the field and beat back the Philistines. So the LORD saved them by giving them a great victory.

¹⁵Once when David was at the rock near the cave of Adullam, the Philistine army was camped

11:8 Or *the supporting terraces.* The meaning of the Hebrew is uncertain.   11:11 As in some Greek manuscripts (see also 2 Sam 23:8); Hebrew *commander of the Thirty,* or *commander of the captains.*   11:12 As in parallel text at 2 Sam 23:9 (see also 1 Chr 27:4); Hebrew reads *Dodo,* a variant name for Dodai.

in the valley of Rephaim. The Three (who were among the Thirty—an elite group among David's fighting men) went down to meet him there. ¹⁶David was staying in the stronghold at the time, and a Philistine detachment had occupied the town of Bethlehem. ¹⁷David remarked longingly to his men, "Oh, how I would love some of that good water from the well in Bethlehem, the one by the gate." ¹⁸So the Three broke through the Philistine lines, drew some water from the well, and brought it back to David. But David refused to drink it. Instead, he poured it out before the LORD. ¹⁹"God forbid that I should drink this!" he exclaimed. "This water is as precious as the blood of these men who risked their lives to bring it to me." So David did not drink it. This is an example of the exploits of the Three.

David's Thirty Mighty Men
²⁰Abishai, the brother of Joab, was the leader of the Thirty.* He once used his spear to kill three hundred enemy warriors in a single battle. It was by such feats that he became as famous as the Three. ²¹Abishai was the most famous of the Thirty and was their commander, though he was not one of the Three.

²²There was also Benaiah son of Jehoiada, a valiant warrior from Kabzeel. He did many heroic deeds, which included killing two of Moab's mightiest warriors. Another time he chased a lion down into a pit. Then, despite the snow and slippery ground, he caught the lion and killed it. ²³Another time, armed with only a club, he killed an Egyptian warrior who was seven and a half feet* tall and whose spear was as thick as a weaver's beam. Benaiah wrenched the spear from the Egyptian's hand and killed him with it. ²⁴These are some of the deeds that made Benaiah as famous as the Three. ²⁵He was more honored than the other members of the Thirty, though he was not one of the Three. And David made him commander of his bodyguard.

²⁶These were also included among David's mighty men:

Asahel, Joab's brother;
Elhanan son of Dodo from Bethlehem;
²⁷ Shammah from Harod;*
Helez from Pelon;
²⁸ Ira son of Ikkesh from Tekoa;
Abiezer from Anathoth;

²⁹ Sibbecai from Hushah;
Zalmon* from Ahoah;
³⁰ Maharai from Netophah;
Heled son of Baanah from Netophah;
³¹ Ithai son of Ribai from Gibeah (from the tribe of Benjamin);
Benaiah from Pirathon;
³² Hurai from near Nahale-gaash*;
Abi-albon* the Arbathite;
³³ Azmaveth from Bahurim*;
Eliahba from Shaalbon;
³⁴ the sons of Jashen* from Gizon;
Jonathan son of Shagee from Harar;
³⁵ Ahiam son of Sharar* from Harar;
Eliphal son of Ur;
³⁶ Hepher from Mekerah;
Ahijah from Pelon;
³⁷ Hezro from Carmel;
Paarai* son of Ezbai;
³⁸ Joel, the brother of Nathan;
Mibhar son of Hagri;
³⁹ Zelek from Ammon;
Naharai from Beeroth (Joab's armor bearer);
⁴⁰ Ira from Jattir;
Gareb from Jattir;
⁴¹ Uriah the Hittite;
Zabad son of Ahlai;
⁴² Adina son of Shiza, the Reubenite leader who had thirty men with him;
⁴³ Hanan son of Maacah;
Joshaphat from Mithna;
⁴⁴ Uzzia from Ashtaroth;
Shama and Jeiel, the sons of Hotham, from Aroer;
⁴⁵ Jediael son of Shimri;
Joha, his brother, from Tiz;
⁴⁶ Eliel from Mahavah;
Jeribai and Joshaviah, the sons of Elnaam;
Ithmah from Moab;
⁴⁷ Eliel and Obed;
Jaasiel from Zobah.

CHAPTER **12**
Warriors Join David's Army
The following men joined David at Ziklag while he was hiding from Saul son of Kish. They were among the warriors who fought beside David in battle. ²All of them were expert archers, and they could shoot arrows or sling stones with their left hand as well as their right. They were all relatives

11:20 As in Syriac version; Hebrew reads *the Three*; also in 11:21.   11:23 Hebrew *5 cubits* [2.3 meters].   11:27 As in parallel text at 2 Sam 23:25; Hebrew reads *Shammoth from Haror.*   11:29 As in parallel text at 2 Sam 23:28; Hebrew reads *Ilai.*   11:32a Or *from the ravines of Gaash.*   11:32b As in parallel text at 2 Sam 23:31; Hebrew reads *Abiel.*   11:33 As in parallel text at 2 Sam 23:31; Hebrew reads *Baharum.*   11:34 As in parallel text at 2 Sam 23:32; Hebrew reads *sons of Hashem.*   11:35 As in parallel text at 2 Sam 23:33; Hebrew reads *son of Sacar.*   11:37 As in parallel text at 2 Sam 23:35; Hebrew reads *Naarai.*

of Saul from the tribe of Benjamin. ³Their leader was Ahiezer son of Shemaah from Gibeah; his brother Joash was second-in-command. These were the other warriors:

Jeziel and Pelet, sons of Azmaveth;
Beracah and Jehu from Anathoth;
⁴ Ishmaiah from Gibeon, a famous warrior and leader among the Thirty;
Jeremiah, Jahaziel, Johanan, and Jozabad from Gederah;
⁵ Eluzai, Jerimoth, Bealiah, Shemariah, and Shephatiah from Haruph;
⁶ Elkanah, Isshiah, Azarel, Joezer, and Jashobeam, who were Korahites;
⁷ Joelah and Zebadiah, sons of Jeroham from Gedor.

⁸Some brave and experienced warriors from the tribe of Gad also defected to David while he was at the stronghold in the wilderness. They were expert with both shield and spear, as fierce as lions and as swift as deer on the mountains.

⁹ Ezer was their leader.
Obadiah was second.
Eliab was third.
¹⁰ Mishmannah was fourth.
Jeremiah was fifth.
¹¹ Attai was sixth.
Eliel was seventh.
¹² Johanan was eighth.
Elzabad was ninth.
¹³ Jeremiah was tenth.
Macbannai was eleventh.

¹⁴These warriors from Gad were army commanders. The weakest among them could take on a hundred regular troops, and the strongest could take on a thousand! ¹⁵They crossed the Jordan River during its seasonal flooding at the beginning of the year and drove out all the people living in the lowlands on both the east and west banks.

¹⁶Others from Benjamin and Judah came to David at the stronghold. ¹⁷David went out to meet them and said, "If you have come in peace to help me, we are friends. But if you have come to betray me to my enemies when I am innocent, then may the God of our ancestors see and judge you."

¹⁸Then the Spirit came upon Amasai, who later became a leader among the Thirty, and he said,

"We are yours, David!
We are on your side, son of Jesse.
Peace and prosperity be with you,
and success to all who help you,
for your God is the one who helps you."

So David let them join him, and he made them officers over his troops.

¹⁹Some men from Manasseh defected from the Israelite army and joined David when he went with the Philistines to fight against Saul. But as it turned out, the Philistine leaders refused to let David and his men go with them. After much discussion, they sent them back, for they said, "It will cost us our lives if David switches loyalties to Saul and turns against us."

²⁰Here is a list of the men from Manasseh who defected to David as he was returning to Ziklag: Adnah, Jozabad, Jediael, Michael, Jozabad, Elihu, and Zillethai. Each commanded a thousand troops from the tribe of Manasseh. ²¹They helped David chase down bands of raiders, for they were all brave and able warriors who became commanders in his army. ²²Day after day more men joined David until he had a great army, like the army of God.

²³These are the numbers of armed warriors who joined David at Hebron. They were all eager to see David become king instead of Saul, just as the LORD had promised.

²⁴From the tribe of Judah, there were 6,800 warriors armed with shields and spears.
²⁵From the tribe of Simeon, there were 7,100 warriors.
²⁶From the tribe of Levi, there were 4,600 troops. ²⁷This included Jehoiada, leader of the family of Aaron, who had 3,700 under his command. ²⁸This also included Zadok, a young warrior, with twenty-two members of his family who were all officers.
²⁹From the tribe of Benjamin, Saul's relatives, there were 3,000 warriors. Most of the men from Benjamin had remained loyal to Saul until this time.
³⁰From the tribe of Ephraim, there were 20,800 warriors, each famous in his own clan.
³¹From the half-tribe of Manasseh west of the Jordan, 18,000 men were sent for the express purpose of helping David become king.
³²From the tribe of Issachar, there were 200 leaders of the tribe with their relatives. All these men understood the temper of the times and knew the best course for Israel to take.
³³From the tribe of Zebulun, there were 50,000 skilled warriors. They were fully armed and prepared for battle and completely loyal to David.

³⁴From the tribe of Naphtali, there were 1,000 officers and 37,000 warriors armed with shields and spears. ³⁵From the tribe of Dan, there were 28,600 warriors, all prepared for battle. ³⁶From the tribe of Asher, there were 40,000 trained warriors, all prepared for battle. ³⁷From the east side of the Jordan River—where the tribes of Reuben and Gad and the half-tribe of Manasseh lived—there were 120,000 troops armed with every kind of weapon.

³⁸All these men came in battle array to Hebron with the single purpose of making David the king of Israel. In fact, all Israel agreed that David should be their king. ³⁹They feasted and drank with David for three days, for preparations had been made by their relatives for their arrival. ⁴⁰And people from as far away as Issachar, Zebulun, and Naphtali brought food on donkeys, camels, mules, and oxen. Vast supplies of flour, fig cakes, raisins, wine, olive oil, cattle, and sheep were brought to the celebration. There was great joy throughout the land of Israel.

CHAPTER **13**
David Attempts to Move the Ark
David consulted with all his officials, including the generals and captains of his army. ²Then he addressed the entire assembly of Israel as follows: "If you approve and if it is the will of the LORD our God, let us send messages to all the Israelites throughout the land, including the priests and Levites in their towns and pasturelands. Let us invite them to come and join us. ³It is time to bring back the Ark of our God, for we neglected it during the reign of Saul."

⁴The whole assembly agreed to this, for the people could see it was the right thing to do. ⁵So David summoned all the people of Israel, from one end of the country to the other,* to join in bringing the Ark of God from Kiriath-jearim. ⁶Then David and all Israel went to Baalah of Judah (also called Kiriath-jearim) to bring back the Ark of God, which bears the name of the LORD who is enthroned between the cherubim. ⁷They transported the Ark of God from the house of Abinadab on a new cart, with Uzzah and Ahio guiding it. ⁸David and all Israel were celebrating before God with all their might, singing and playing all kinds of musical instruments—lyres, harps, tambourines, cymbals, and trumpets.

⁹But when they arrived at the threshing floor of Nacon,* the oxen stumbled, and Uzzah put out his hand to steady the Ark. ¹⁰Then the LORD's anger blazed out against Uzzah, and he struck him dead because he had laid his hand on the Ark. So Uzzah died there in the presence of God. ¹¹David was angry because the LORD's anger blazed out against Uzzah. He named that place Perez-uzzah (which means "outbreak against Uzzah"). It is still called that today.

¹²David was now afraid of God and asked, "How can I ever bring the Ark of God back into my care?" ¹³So David decided not to move the Ark into the City of David. He took it instead to the home of Obed-edom of Gath. ¹⁴The Ark of God remained there with the family of Obed-edom for three months, and the LORD blessed him and his entire household.

CHAPTER **14**
David's Palace and Family
Now King Hiram of Tyre sent messengers to David, along with stonemasons and carpenters to build him a palace. Hiram also sent many cedar logs for lumber. ²And David realized that the LORD had made him king over Israel and had made his kingdom very great for the sake of his people Israel.

³Then David married more wives in Jerusalem, and they had many sons and daughters. ⁴These are the names of David's sons who were born in Jerusalem: Shimea,* Shobab, Nathan, Solomon, ⁵Ibhar, Elishua, Elpelet, ⁶Nogah, Nepheg, Japhia, ⁷Elishama, Eliada,* and Eliphelet.

David Conquers the Philistines
⁸When the Philistines heard that David had been anointed king over all Israel, they mobilized all their forces to capture him. But David was told they were coming, so he and his men marched out to meet them. ⁹The Philistines had arrived in the valley of Rephaim and raided it. ¹⁰So David asked God, "Should I go out to fight the Philistines? Will you hand them over to me?"

The LORD replied, "Yes, go ahead. I will give you the victory."

¹¹So David and his troops went to Baal-perazim and defeated the Philistines there. "God has done it!" David exclaimed. "He used me to burst through my enemies like a raging flood!" So that place was named Baal-perazim (which means "the Lord who bursts through"). ¹²The

---

13:5 Hebrew *from the Shihor of Egypt to Lebo-hamath.*   **13:9** As in parallel text at 2 Sam 6:6; Hebrew reads *Kidon.*   **14:4** Hebrew *Shammua,* a variant name for Shimea; compare 3:5.   **14:7** Hebrew *Beeliada,* a variant name for Eliada; compare 3:8 and parallel text at 2 Sam 5:16.

Philistines had abandoned their idols* there, so David gave orders to burn them up.

13But after a while, the Philistines returned and raided the valley again. 14And once again David asked God what to do. "Do not attack them straight on," God replied. "Instead, circle around behind them and attack them near the balsam trees. 15When you hear a sound like marching feet in the tops of the balsam trees, attack! That will be the signal that God is moving ahead of you to strike down the Philistines." 16So David did what God commanded, and he struck down the Philistine army all the way from Gibeon to Gezer.

17So David's fame spread everywhere, and the LORD caused all the nations to fear David.

CHAPTER **15**

Preparing to Move the Ark

David now built several buildings for himself in the City of David. He also prepared a place for the Ark of God and set up a special tent there to shelter it. 2Then he issued these instructions: "When we transport the Ark of God this time, no one except the Levites may carry it. The LORD has chosen them to carry the Ark of the LORD and to minister before him forever."

3Then David summoned all the Israelites to Jerusalem to bring the Ark of the LORD to the place he had prepared for it. 4These are the priests* and Levites who were called together:

5There were 120 from the clan of Kohath, with Uriel as their leader.

6There were 220 from the clan of Merari, with Asaiah as their leader.

7There were 130 from the clan of Gershon,* with Joel as their leader.

8There were 200 descendants of Elizaphan, with Shemaiah as their leader.

9There were 80 descendants of Hebron, with Eliel as their leader.

10There were 112 descendants of Uzziel, with Amminadab as their leader.

11Then David summoned the priests, Zadok and Abiathar, and these Levite leaders: Uriel, Asaiah, Joel, Shemaiah, Eliel, and Amminadab. 12He said to them, "You are the leaders of the Levite families. You must purify yourselves and all your fellow Levites, so you can bring the Ark of the LORD, the God of Israel, to the place I have prepared for it. 13Because you Levites did not

carry the Ark the first time, the anger of the LORD our God burst out against us. We failed to ask God how to move it in the proper way." 14So the priests and the Levites purified themselves in order to bring the Ark of the LORD, the God of Israel, to Jerusalem. 15Then the Levites carried the Ark of God on their shoulders with its carrying poles, just as the LORD had instructed Moses.

16David also ordered the Levite leaders to appoint a choir of Levites who were singers and musicians to sing joyful songs to the accompaniment of lyres, harps, and cymbals. 17So the Levites appointed Heman son of Joel, Asaph son of Berekiah, and Ethan son of Kushaiah from the clan of Merari to direct the musicians. 18The following men were chosen as their assistants: Zechariah, Jaaziel, Shemiramoth, Jehiel, Unni, Eliab, Benaiah, Maaseiah, Mattithiah, Eliphelehu, Mikneiah, and the gatekeepers, Obed-edom and Jeiel.

19Heman, Asaph, and Ethan were chosen to sound the bronze cymbals. 20Zechariah, Aziel, Shemiramoth, Jehiel, Unni, Eliab, Maaseiah, and Benaiah were chosen to play the lyres.* 21Mattithiah, Eliphelehu, Mikneiah, Obed-edom, Jeiel, and Azaziah were chosen to play the harps.* 22Kenaniah, the head Levite, was chosen as the choir leader because of his skill.

23Berekiah and Elkanah were chosen to guard the Ark. 24Shebaniah, Joshaphat, Nethanel, Amasai, Zechariah, Benaiah, and Eliezer—all of whom were priests—were chosen to blow the trumpets as they marched in front of the Ark of God. Obed-edom and Jehiah were chosen to guard the Ark.

Moving the Ark to Jerusalem

25Then David and the leaders of Israel and the generals of the army went to the home of Obed-edom to bring the Ark of the LORD's covenant up to Jerusalem with a great celebration. 26And because God was clearly helping the Levites as they carried the Ark of the LORD's covenant, they sacrificed seven bulls and seven lambs. 27David was dressed in a robe of fine linen, as were the Levites who carried the Ark, the singers, and Kenaniah the song leader. David was also wearing a priestly tunic.* 28So all Israel brought up the Ark of the LORD's covenant to Jerusalem with shouts of joy, the blowing of horns and trumpets, the crashing of cymbals, and loud playing on harps and lyres.

14:12 Hebrew *their gods*; compare parallel text at 2 Sam 5:21.   15:4 Hebrew *descendants of Aaron*.   15:7 Hebrew *Gershom*, a variant name for Gershon.   15:20 Hebrew adds *according to Alamoth*, which is probably a musical term. The meaning of the Hebrew is uncertain.   15:21 Hebrew adds *according to the Sheminith*, which is probably a musical term. The meaning of the Hebrew is uncertain.   15:27 Hebrew *a linen ephod.*

²⁹But as the Ark of the LORD's covenant entered the City of David, Michal, the daughter of Saul, looked down from her window. When she saw King David dancing and leaping for joy, she was filled with contempt for him.

CHAPTER **16**

So they brought the Ark of God into the special tent David had prepared for it, and they sacrificed burnt offerings and peace offerings before God. ²When he had finished, David blessed the people in the name of the LORD. ³Then he gave a gift of food to every man and woman in Israel: a loaf of bread, a cake of dates,* and a cake of raisins.

⁴David appointed the following Levites to lead the people in worship before the Ark of the LORD by asking for his blessings and giving thanks and praise to the LORD, the God of Israel. ⁵Asaph, the leader of this group, sounded the cymbals. His assistants were Zechariah (the second), then Jeiel, Shemiramoth, Jehiel, Mattithiah, Eliab, Benaiah, Obed-edom, and Jeiel. They played the harps and lyres. ⁶The priests, Benaiah and Jahaziel, played the trumpets regularly before the Ark of God's covenant.

David's Song of Praise

⁷That day David gave to Asaph and his fellow Levites this song of thanksgiving to the LORD:

8 Give thanks to the LORD and proclaim his greatness.
    Let the whole world know what he has done.
9 Sing to him; yes, sing his praises.
    Tell everyone about his miracles.
10 Exult in his holy name;
    O worshipers of the LORD, rejoice!
11 Search for the LORD and for his strength,
    and keep on searching.
12 Think of the wonderful works he has done,
    the miracles, and the judgments he handed down,
13 O children of Israel, God's servant,
    O descendants of Jacob, God's chosen one.

14 He is the LORD our God.
    His rule is seen throughout the land.
15 He always stands by his covenant* —
    the commitment he made to a thousand generations.
16 This is the covenant he made with Abraham

and the oath he swore to Isaac.
17 He confirmed it to Jacob as a decree,
    to the people of Israel as a never-ending treaty:
18 "I will give you the land of Canaan
    as your special possession."

19 He said this when they were few in number,
    a tiny group of strangers in Canaan.
20 They wandered back and forth between nations,
    from one kingdom to another.
21 Yet he did not let anyone oppress them.
    He warned kings on their behalf:
22 "Do not touch these people I have chosen,
    and do not hurt my prophets."

23 Let the whole earth sing to the LORD!
    Each day proclaim the good news that he saves.
24 Publish his glorious deeds among the nations.
    Tell everyone about the amazing things he does.
25 Great is the LORD! He is most worthy of praise!
    He is to be revered above all gods.
26 The gods of other nations are merely idols,
    but the LORD made the heavens!
27 Honor and majesty surround him;
    strength and beauty are in his dwelling.

28 O nations of the world, recognize the LORD,
    recognize that the LORD is glorious and strong.
29 Give to the LORD the glory he deserves!
    Bring your offering and come to worship him.
    Worship the LORD in all his holy splendor.
30 Let all the earth tremble before him.
    The world is firmly established and cannot be shaken.

31 Let the heavens be glad, and let the earth rejoice!
    Tell all the nations that the LORD is king.
32 Let the sea and everything in it shout his praise!
    Let the fields and their crops burst forth with joy!
33 Let the trees of the forest rustle with praise
    before the LORD!
    For he is coming to judge the earth.
34 Give thanks to the LORD, for he is good!
    His faithful love endures forever.

16:3 Or *a portion of meat.* The meaning of the Hebrew is uncertain. **16:15** As in some Greek manuscripts (see also Ps 105:8); Hebrew reads *Remember his covenant forever.*

³⁵ Cry out, "Save us, O God of our salvation!
 Gather and rescue us from among the
  nations,
 so we can thank your holy name
  and rejoice and praise you."

³⁶ Blessed be the LORD, the God of Israel,
  from everlasting to everlasting!

And all the people shouted "Amen!" and
praised the LORD.

Worship at Jerusalem and Gibeon

³⁷David arranged for Asaph and his fellow Levites to minister regularly before the Ark of the LORD's covenant, doing whatever needed to be done each day. ³⁸This group included Obed-edom (son of Jeduthun), Hosah, and sixty-eight other Levites as gatekeepers.

³⁹Meanwhile, David stationed Zadok the priest and his fellow priests at the Tabernacle of the LORD on the hill of Gibeon, where they continued to minister before the LORD. ⁴⁰They sacrificed the regular burnt offerings to the LORD each morning and evening on the altar set aside for that purpose, obeying everything written in the law of the LORD, which he had given to Israel. ⁴¹David also appointed Heman, Jeduthun, and the others chosen by name to give thanks to the LORD, "for his faithful love endures forever." ⁴²They used their trumpets, cymbals, and other instruments to accompany the songs of praise to God. And the sons of Jeduthun were appointed as gatekeepers.

⁴³Then all the people returned to their homes, and David returned home to bless his family.

CHAPTER 17

The LORD's Covenant Promise to David

Now when David was settled in his palace, he said to Nathan the prophet, "Here I am living in this beautiful cedar palace, but the Ark of the LORD's covenant is out in a tent!"

²Nathan replied, "Go ahead with what you have in mind, for God is with you."

³But that same night God said to Nathan,

⁴ "Go and tell my servant David, 'This is what the LORD says: You are not the one to build me a temple to live in. ⁵I have never lived in a temple, from the day I brought the Israelites out of Egypt until now. My home has always been a tent, moving from one place to another. ⁶And I never once complained to Israel's leaders,* the shepherds of my people. I have never asked them, "Why haven't you built me a beautiful cedar temple?" '

⁷"Now go and say to my servant David, 'This is what the LORD Almighty says: I chose you to lead my people Israel when you were just a shepherd boy, tending your sheep out in the pasture. ⁸I have been with you wherever you have gone, and I have destroyed all your enemies. Now I will make your name famous throughout the earth! ⁹And I have provided a permanent homeland for my people Israel, a secure place where they will never be disturbed. It will be their own land where wicked nations won't oppress them as they did in the past, ¹⁰from the time I appointed judges to rule my people. And I will subdue all your enemies.

" 'And now I declare that the LORD will build a house for you—a dynasty of kings! ¹¹For when you die, I will raise up one of your sons, and I will make his kingdom strong. ¹²He is the one who will build a house—a temple—for me. And I will establish his throne forever. ¹³I will be his father, and he will be my son. I will not take my unfailing love from him as I took it from Saul, who ruled before you. ¹⁴I will establish him over my dynasty and my kingdom for all time, and his throne will be secure forever.' "

¹⁵So Nathan went back to David and told him everything the LORD had said.

David's Prayer of Thanks

¹⁶Then King David went in and sat before the LORD and prayed, "Who am I, O LORD God, and what is my family, that you have brought me this far? ¹⁷And now, O God, in addition to everything else, you speak of giving me a lasting dynasty! You speak as though I were someone very great,* O LORD God! ¹⁸What more can I say about the way you have honored me? You know what I am really like. ¹⁹For my sake, O LORD, and according to your will, you have done all these great things and have made them known.

²⁰O LORD, there is no one like you—there is no other God. We have never even heard of another god like you! ²¹What other nation on earth is like Israel? What other nation, O God, have you redeemed from slavery to be your own people? You made a great name for yourself when you rescued your people from Egypt. You

17:6 As in Greek version (see also 2 Sam 7:7); Hebrew reads *judges.*   17:17 The meaning of the Hebrew is uncertain.

performed awesome miracles and drove out the nations that stood in their way. ²²You chose Israel to be your people forever, and you, O LORD, have become their God.

²³"And now, O LORD, do as you have promised concerning me and my family. May it be a promise that will last forever. ²⁴And may your name be established and honored forever so that all the world will say, 'The LORD Almighty is God over Israel!' And may the dynasty of your servant David be established in your presence.

²⁵"O my God, I have been bold enough to pray this prayer because you have revealed that you will build a house for me—an eternal dynasty! ²⁶For you are God, O LORD. And you have promised these good things to me, your servant. ²⁷And now, it has pleased you to bless me and my family so that our dynasty will continue forever before you. For when you grant a blessing, O LORD, it is an eternal blessing!"

CHAPTER **18**
David's Military Victories
After this, David subdued and humbled the Philistines by conquering Gath and its surrounding towns. ²David also conquered the land of Moab, and the Moabites became David's subjects and brought him tribute money.

³Then David destroyed the forces of King Hadadezer of Zobah, as far as Hamath,* when Hadadezer marched out to strengthen his control along the Euphrates River. ⁴David captured one thousand chariots, seven thousand charioteers, and twenty thousand foot soldiers. Then he crippled all but one hundred of the chariot horses.

⁵When Arameans from Damascus arrived to help Hadadezer, David killed twenty-two thousand of them. ⁶Then he placed several army garrisons in Damascus, the Aramean capital, and the Arameans became David's subjects and brought him tribute money. So the LORD gave David victory wherever he went. ⁷David brought the gold shields of Hadadezer's officers to Jerusalem, ⁸along with a large amount of bronze from Hadadezer's cities of Tebah* and Cun. Later Solomon melted the bronze and used it for the Temple. He molded it into the bronze Sea, the pillars, and the various bronze utensils used at the Temple.

⁹When King Toi* of Hamath heard that David had destroyed the army of King Hadadezer of Zobah, ¹⁰he sent his son Joram* to congratulate David on his success. Hadadezer and Toi had long been enemies, and there had been many wars between them. Joram presented David with many gifts of gold, silver, and bronze. ¹¹King David dedicated all these gifts to the LORD, along with the silver and gold he had taken from the other nations he had subdued—Edom, Moab, Ammon, Philistia, and Amalek.

¹²Abishai son of Zeruiah destroyed eighteen thousand Edomites in the Valley of Salt. ¹³He placed army garrisons throughout Edom, and all the Edomites became David's subjects. This was another example of how the LORD made David victorious wherever he went.

¹⁴David reigned over all Israel and was fair to everyone. ¹⁵Joab son of Zeruiah was commander of the army. Jehoshaphat son of Ahilud was the royal historian. ¹⁶Zadok son of Ahitub and Ahimelech* son of Abiathar were the priests. Seraiah* was the court secretary. ¹⁷Benaiah son of Jehoiada was captain of the king's bodyguard.* David's sons served as the king's chief assistants.

CHAPTER **19**
David Defeats the Ammonites
Some time after this, King Nahash of the Ammonites died, and his son Hanun* became king. ²David said, "I am going to show complete loyalty to Hanun because his father, Nahash, was always completely loyal to me." So David sent ambassadors to express sympathy to Hanun about his father's death.

But when David's ambassadors arrived in the land of Ammon, ³Hanun's advisers said to him, "Do you really think these men are coming here to honor your father? No! David has sent them to spy out the land so that they can come in and conquer it!" ⁴So Hanun seized David's ambassadors and shaved their beards, cut off their robes at the buttocks, and sent them back to David in shame. ⁵When David heard what had happened, he sent messengers to tell the men to stay at Jericho until their beards grew out, for they were very embarrassed by their appearance.

⁶Now the people of Ammon realized how seriously they had angered David, so Hanun and the Ammonites sent thirty-eight tons* of silver to hire chariots and troops from Aram-naharaim,

18:3 The meaning of the Hebrew is uncertain.   **18:8** Hebrew reads *Tibhath*, a variant name for Tebah; compare parallel text at 2 Sam 8:8.   **18:9** As in parallel text at 2 Sam 8:9; Hebrew reads *Tou*; also in 18:10.   **18:10** As in parallel text at 2 Sam 8:10; Hebrew reads *Hadoram*, a variant name for Joram.   **18:16a** As in some Hebrew manuscripts, Syriac version, and Latin Vulgate (see also 2 Sam 8:17); most Hebrew manuscripts read *Abimelech*.   **18:16b** As in parallel text at 2 Sam 8:17; Hebrew reads *Shavsha*.   **18:17** Hebrew *of the Kerethites and Pelethites*.   **19:1** Hebrew lacks *Hanun*; compare parallel text at 2 Sam 10:1.   **19:6** Hebrew *1,000 talents* [34 metric tons].

Aram-maacah, and Zobah. 7They also hired thirty-two thousand chariots and secured the support of the king of Maacah and his army. These forces camped at Medeba, where they were joined by the Ammonite troops that Hanun had recruited from his own towns. 8When David heard about this, he sent Joab and all his warriors to fight them. 9The Ammonite troops drew up their battle lines at the gate of the city, while the other kings positioned themselves to fight in the open fields.

10When Joab saw that he would have to fight on two fronts, he chose the best troops in his army. He placed them under his personal command and led them out to fight the Arameans in the fields. 11He left the rest of the army under the command of his brother Abishai, who was to attack the Ammonites. 12"If the Arameans are too strong for me, then come over and help me," Joab told his brother. "And if the Ammonites are too strong for you, I will help you. 13Be courageous! Let us fight bravely to save our people and the cities of our God. May the LORD's will be done."

14When Joab and his troops attacked, the Arameans began to run away. 15And when the Ammonites saw the Arameans running, they ran from Abishai and retreated into the city. Then Joab returned to Jerusalem.

16The Arameans now realized that they were no match for Israel, so they summoned additional Aramean troops from the other side of the Euphrates River.* These troops arrived under the command of Shobach,* the commander of all Hadadezer's forces. 17When David heard what was happening, he mobilized all Israel, crossed the Jordan River, and positioned his troops in battle formation. Then he engaged the enemy troops in battle, and they fought against him. 18But again the Arameans fled from the Israelites. This time David's forces killed seven thousand charioteers and forty thousand foot soldiers, including Shobach, the commander of their army. 19When the servants of Hadadezer realized they had been defeated by Israel, they surrendered to David and became his subjects. After that, the Arameans were no longer willing to help the Ammonites.

CHAPTER **20**
The Capture of Rabbah

The following spring, the time of year when kings go to war, Joab led the Israelite army in successful attacks against the towns and villages of the Ammonites. In the process they laid siege to the city of Rabbah and destroyed it. But David had stayed behind in Jerusalem.

2When David arrived at Rabbah, he removed the crown from the king's head,* and it was placed on David's own head. The crown was made of gold and set with gems, and it weighed about seventy-five pounds.* David took a vast amount of plunder from the city. 3He also made slaves of the people of Rabbah and forced them to labor with saws, picks, and axes.* That is how he dealt with the people of all the Ammonite cities. Then David and his army returned to Jerusalem.

Battles against the Philistines

4After this, war broke out with the Philistines at Gezer. As they fought, Sibbecai from Hushah killed Saph,* a descendant of the giants,* and so the Philistines were subdued. 5During another battle with the Philistines, Elhanan son of Jair killed Lahmi, the brother of Goliath of Gath. The handle of Lahmi's spear was as thick as a weaver's beam! 6In another battle with the Philistines at Gath, a huge man with six fingers on each hand and six toes on each foot—a descendant of the giants—7defied and taunted Israel. But he was killed by Jonathan, the son of David's brother Shimea. 8These Philistines were descendants of the giants of Gath, but they were killed by David and his warriors.

CHAPTER **21**
David Takes a Census

Satan rose up against Israel and caused David to take a census of the Israelites. 2David gave these orders to Joab and his commanders: "Take a census of all the people in the land—from Beersheba in the south to Dan in the north—and bring me the totals so I may know how many there are."

3But Joab replied, "May the LORD increase the number of his people a hundred times over! But why, my lord, do you want to do this? Are they not all your servants? Why must you cause Israel to sin?"

4But the king insisted that Joab take the census, so Joab traveled throughout Israel to count the people. Then he returned to Jerusalem 5and reported the number of people to David. There were 1,100,000 men of military age in Israel, and

19:16a Hebrew *the river.* 19:16b As in parallel text at 2 Sam 10:16; Hebrew reads *Shophach;* also in 19:18. 20:2a Greek version and Latin Vulgate read *removed the crown of Milcom;* compare 1 Kgs 11:5. Milcom, also called Molech, was the god of the Ammonites. 20:2b Hebrew *1 talent* [34 kilograms]. 20:3 As in parallel text at 2 Sam 12:31; Hebrew reads *and saws.* 20:4a As in parallel text at 2 Sam 21:18; Hebrew reads *Sippai.* 20:4b Hebrew *descendant of the Rephaites;* also in 20:6, 8.

470,000 in Judah. ⁶But Joab did not include the tribes of Levi and Benjamin in the census because he was so distressed at what the king had made him do.

Judgment for David's Sin

⁷God was very displeased with the census, and he punished Israel for it. ⁸Then David said to God, "I have sinned greatly and shouldn't have taken the census. Please forgive me for doing this foolish thing."

⁹Then the LORD spoke to Gad, David's seer. This was the message: ¹⁰"Go and say to David, 'This is what the LORD says: I will give you three choices. Choose one of these punishments, and I will do it.'"

¹¹So Gad came to David and said, "These are the choices the LORD has given you. ¹²You may choose three years of famine, three months of destruction by your enemies, or three days of severe plague as the angel of the LORD brings devastation throughout the land of Israel. Think this over and let me know what answer to give the LORD."

¹³"This is a desperate situation!" David replied to Gad. "But let me fall into the hands of the LORD, for his mercy is very great. Do not let me fall into human hands."

¹⁴So the LORD sent a plague upon Israel, and seventy thousand people died as a result. ¹⁵And God sent an angel to destroy Jerusalem. But just as the angel was preparing to destroy it, the LORD relented and said to the death angel, "Stop! That is enough!" At that moment the angel of the LORD was standing by the threshing floor of Araunah* the Jebusite.

¹⁶David looked up and saw the angel of the LORD standing between heaven and earth with his sword drawn, stretched out over Jerusalem. So David and the leaders of Israel put on sackcloth to show their distress and fell down with their faces to the ground. ¹⁷And David said to God, "I am the one who called for the census! I am the one who has sinned and done wrong! But these people are innocent—what have they done? O LORD my God, let your anger fall against me and my family, but do not destroy your people."

David Builds an Altar

¹⁸Then the angel of the LORD told Gad to instruct David to build an altar to the LORD at the threshing floor of Araunah the Jebusite. ¹⁹So David obeyed the instructions the LORD had given him

through Gad. ²⁰Araunah, who was busy threshing wheat at the time, turned and saw the angel there. His four sons, who were with him, ran away and hid. ²¹When Araunah saw the king approaching, he left his threshing floor and bowed to the ground before David.

²²David said to Araunah, "Let me buy this threshing floor from you at its full price. Then I will build an altar to the LORD there, so that he will stop the plague."

²³"Take it, my lord, and use it as you wish," Araunah said to David. "Here are oxen for the burnt offerings, and you can use the threshing tools for wood to build a fire on the altar. And take the wheat for the grain offering. I will give it all to you."

²⁴But the king replied to Araunah, "No, I insist on paying what it is worth. I cannot take what is yours and give it to the LORD. I will not offer a burnt offering that has cost me nothing!" ²⁵So David gave Araunah six hundred pieces of gold* in payment for the threshing floor. ²⁶David built an altar there to the LORD and sacrificed burnt offerings and peace offerings. And when David prayed, the LORD answered him by sending fire from heaven to burn up the offering on the altar. ²⁷Then the LORD spoke to the angel, who put the sword back into its sheath.

²⁸When David saw that the LORD had answered his prayer, he offered sacrifices there at Araunah's threshing floor. ²⁹At that time, the Tabernacle of the LORD and the altar that Moses made in the wilderness were located at the hill of Gibeon. ³⁰But David was not able to go there to inquire of God, because he was terrified by the drawn sword of the angel of the LORD.

CHAPTER 22

Then David said, "This will be the location for the Temple of the LORD God and the place of the altar for Israel's burnt offerings!"

Preparations for the Temple

²So David gave orders to call together the foreigners living in Israel, and he assigned them the task of preparing blocks of stone for building the Temple of God. ³David provided large amounts of iron for the nails that would be needed for the doors in the gates and for the clamps, and more bronze than they could ever weigh. ⁴He also provided innumerable cedar logs, for the men of Tyre and Sidon had brought vast amounts of

---

21:15 As in parallel text at 2 Sam 24:16; Hebrew reads *Ornan,* another name for Araunah; also in 21:18-28. **21:25** Hebrew *600 shekels of gold,* about 15 pounds or 6.8 kilograms in weight.

cedar to David. 5David said, "My son Solomon is still young and inexperienced, and the Temple of the LORD must be a magnificent structure, famous and glorious throughout the world. So I will begin making preparations for it now." So David collected vast amounts of building materials before his death.

6Then David sent for his son Solomon and instructed him to build a Temple for the LORD, the God of Israel. 7"I wanted to build a Temple to honor the name of the LORD my God," David told him. 8"But the LORD said to me, 'You have killed many men in the great battles you have fought. And since you have shed so much blood before me, you will not be the one to build a Temple to honor my name. 9But you will have a son who will experience peace and rest. I will give him peace with his enemies in all the surrounding lands. His name will be Solomon,* and I will give peace and quiet to Israel during his reign. 10He is the one who will build a Temple to honor my name. He will be my son, and I will be his father. And I will establish the throne of his kingdom over Israel forever.'

11"Now, my son, may the LORD be with you and give you success as you follow his instructions in building the Temple of the LORD your God. 12And may the LORD give you wisdom and understanding, that you may obey the law of the LORD your God as you rule over Israel. 13For if you carefully obey the laws and regulations that the LORD gave to Israel through Moses, you will be successful. Be strong and courageous; do not be afraid or lose heart!

14"I have worked hard to provide materials for building the Temple of the LORD—nearly four thousand tons of gold, nearly forty thousand tons of silver,* and so much iron and bronze that it cannot be weighed. I have also gathered lumber and stone for the walls, though you may need to add more. 15You have many skilled stonemasons and carpenters and craftsmen of every kind available to you. 16They are expert goldsmiths and silversmiths and workers of bronze and iron. Now begin the work, and may the LORD be with you!"

17Then David ordered all the leaders of Israel to assist Solomon in this project. 18"The LORD your God is with you," he declared. "He has given you peace with the surrounding nations. He has handed them over to me, and they are now subject to the LORD and his people. 19Now seek the LORD

your God with all your heart. Build the sanctuary of the LORD God so that you can bring the Ark of the LORD's covenant and the holy vessels of God into the Temple built to honor the LORD's name."

CHAPTER **23**

Duties of the Levites

When David was an old man, he appointed his son Solomon to be king over Israel. 2David summoned all the political leaders of Israel, together with the priests and Levites, for the coronation ceremony. 3All the Levites who were thirty years old or older were counted, and the total came to thirty-eight thousand. 4Then David said, "Twenty-four thousand of them will supervise the work at the Temple of the LORD. Six thousand are to serve as officials and judges. 5Four thousand will work as gatekeepers, and another four thousand will praise the LORD with the musical instruments I have made." 6Then David divided the Levites into divisions named after the clans descended from the three sons of Levi—Gershon, Kohath, and Merari.

The Gershonites

7The Gershonite family units were defined by their lines of descent from Libni* and Shimei, the sons of Gershon. 8Three of the descendants of Libni were Jehiel (the family leader), Zetham, and Joel. 9These were the leaders of the family of Libni.

Three of the descendants of Shimei were Shelomoth, Haziel, and Haran. 10Four other descendants of Shimei were Jahath, Ziza,* Jeush, and Beriah. 11Jahath was the family leader, and Ziza was next. Jeush and Beriah were counted as a single family because neither had many sons.

The Kohathites

12The descendants of Kohath included Amram, Izhar, Hebron, and Uzziel.
13The sons of Amram were Aaron and Moses. Aaron and his descendants were set apart to dedicate the most holy things, to offer sacrifices in the LORD's presence, to serve the LORD, and to pronounce blessings in his name forever.

14As for Moses, the man of God, his sons were included with the tribe of Levi. 15The sons of Moses were Gershom and Eliezer. 16 The descendants of Gershom included Shebuel, the family leader.

22:9 *Solomon* sounds like and is probably derived from the Hebrew word for "peace." **22:14** Hebrew *100,000 talents* [3,400 metric tons] *of gold, 1,000,000 talents* [34,000 metric tons] *of silver.* **23:7** Hebrew *Ladan* (also in 23:8-9), another name for Libni; compare 6:17. **23:10** As in Greek version and Latin Vulgate (see also 23:11); Hebrew reads *Zina.*

17 Eliezer had only one son, Rehabiah, the family leader. Rehabiah had numerous descendants.

18 The descendants of Izhar included Shelomith, the family leader.

19 The descendants of Hebron included Jeriah (the family leader), Amariah (the second), Jahaziel (the third), and Jekameam (the fourth).

20 The descendants of Uzziel included Micah (the family leader) and Isshiah (the second).

The Merarites

21 The descendants of Merari included Mahli and Mushi.

The sons of Mahli were Eleazar and Kish. 22 Eleazar died with no sons, only daughters. His daughters married their cousins, the sons of Kish. 23 The three sons of Mushi were Mahli, Eder, and Jerimoth.

24 These were the descendants of Levi by clans, the leaders of their family groups, registered carefully by name. Each had to be twenty years old or older to qualify for service in the house of the LORD. 25 For David said, "The LORD, the God of Israel, has given us peace, and he will always live in Jerusalem. 26 Now the Levites will no longer need to carry the Tabernacle and its utensils from place to place." 27 It was according to David's final instructions that all the Levites twenty years old or older were registered for service.

28 The work of the Levites was to assist the priests, the descendants of Aaron, as they served at the house of the LORD. They also took care of the courtyards and side rooms, helped perform the ceremonies of purification, and served in many other ways in the house of God. 29 They were in charge of the sacred bread that was set out on the table, the choice flour for the grain offerings, the wafers made without yeast, the cakes cooked in olive oil, and the other mixed breads. They were also responsible to check all the weights and measures. 30 And each morning and evening they stood before the LORD to sing songs of thanks and praise to him. 31 They assisted with the burnt offerings that were presented to the LORD on Sabbath days, at new moon celebrations, and at all the appointed festivals. The proper number of Levites served in the LORD's presence at all times, following all the procedures they had been given.

32 And so, under the supervision of the priests, the Levites watched over the Tabernacle and Temple* and faithfully carried out their duties of service at the house of the LORD.

23:32 Hebrew *the Tent of Meeting and the sanctuary.*

CHAPTER 24
Duties of the Priests

This is how Aaron's descendants, the priests, were divided into groups for service. The sons of Aaron were Nadab, Abihu, Eleazar, and Ithamar. 2 But Nadab and Abihu died before their father did, and they had no sons. So only Eleazar and Ithamar were left to carry on as priests.

3 With the help of Zadok, who was a descendant of Eleazar, and of Ahimelech, who was a descendant of Ithamar, David divided Aaron's descendants into groups according to their various duties. 4 Eleazar's descendants were divided into sixteen groups and Ithamar's into eight, for there were more family leaders among the descendants of Eleazar.

5 All tasks were assigned to the various groups by means of sacred lots so that no preference would be shown, for there were many qualified officials serving God in the sanctuary from among the descendants of both Eleazar and Ithamar. 6 Shemaiah son of Nethanel, a Levite, acted as secretary and wrote down the names and assignments in the presence of the king, Zadok the priest, Ahimelech son of Abiathar, and the family leaders of the priests and Levites. The descendants of Eleazar and Ithamar took turns casting lots.

7 The first lot fell to Jehoiarib.
The second lot fell to Jedaiah.
8 The third lot fell to Harim.
The fourth lot fell to Seorim.
9 The fifth lot fell to Malkijah.
The sixth lot fell to Mijamin.
10 The seventh lot fell to Hakkoz.
The eighth lot fell to Abijah.
11 The ninth lot fell to Jeshua.
The tenth lot fell to Shecaniah.
12 The eleventh lot fell to Eliashib.
The twelfth lot fell to Jakim.
13 The thirteenth lot fell to Huppah.
The fourteenth lot fell to Jeshebeab.
14 The fifteenth lot fell to Bilgah.
The sixteenth lot fell to Immer.
15 The seventeenth lot fell to Hezir.
The eighteenth lot fell to Happizzez.
16 The nineteenth lot fell to Pethahiah.
The twentieth lot fell to Jehezkel.
17 The twenty-first lot fell to Jakin.
The twenty-second lot fell to Gamul.
18 The twenty-third lot fell to Delaiah.
The twenty-fourth lot fell to Maaziah.

¹⁹Each group carried out its duties in the house of the LORD according to the procedures established by their ancestor Aaron in obedience to the commands of the LORD, the God of Israel.

Family Leaders among the Levites

²⁰These were the other family leaders descended from Levi:

From the descendants of Amram, the leader was Shebuel.*

From the descendants of Shebuel, the leader was Jehdeiah.

²¹ From the descendants of Rehabiah, the leader was Isshiah.

²² From the descendants of Izhar, the leader was Shelomith.*

From the descendants of Shelomith, the leader was Jahath.

²³ From the descendants of Hebron, Jeriah was the leader,* Amariah was second-in-command, Jahaziel was third, and Jekameam was fourth.

²⁴ From the descendants of Uzziel, the leader was Micah.

From the descendants of Micah, the leader was Shamir, ²⁵along with Isshiah, the brother of Micah.

From the descendants of Isshiah, the leader was Zechariah.

²⁶ From the descendants of Merari, the leaders were Mahli and Mushi.

From the descendants of Jaaziah, the leader was Beno.

²⁷ From the descendants of Merari through Jaaziah, the leaders were Beno, Shoham, Zaccur, and Ibri.

²⁸ From the descendants of Mahli, the leader was Eleazar, though he had no sons.

²⁹ From the descendants of Kish, the leader was Jerahmeel.

³⁰ From the descendants of Mushi, the leaders were Mahli, Eder, and Jerimoth.

These were the descendants of Levi in their various families. ³¹Like the descendants of Aaron, they were assigned to their duties by means of sacred lots, without regard to age or rank. It was done in the presence of King David, Zadok, Ahimelech, and the family leaders of the priests and the Levites.

CHAPTER **25**
Duties of the Musicians

David and the army commanders then appointed men from the families of Asaph, Heman, and Jeduthun to proclaim God's messages to the accompaniment of harps, lyres, and cymbals. Here is a list of their names and their work:

²From the sons of Asaph, there were Zaccur, Joseph, Nethaniah, and Asarelah. They worked under the direction of their father, Asaph, who proclaimed God's messages by the king's orders.

³Jeduthun had six sons: Gedaliah, Zeri, Jeshaiah, Shimei,* Hashabiah, and Mattithiah. They worked under the direction of their father, Jeduthun, who proclaimed God's messages to the accompaniment of the harp, offering thanks and praise to the LORD.

⁴Heman's sons were Bukkiah, Mattaniah, Uzziel, Shubael,* Jerimoth, Hananiah, Hanani, Eliathah, Geddalti, Romamti-ezer, Joshbekashah, Mallothi, Hothir, and Mahazioth. ⁵All these were the sons of Heman, the king's seer, for God had honored him with fourteen sons and three daughters.

⁶All these men were under the direction of their fathers as they made music at the house of the LORD. Their responsibilities included the playing of cymbals, lyres, and harps at the house of God. Asaph, Jeduthun, and Heman reported directly to the king. ⁷They and their families were all trained in making music before the LORD, and each of them—288 in all—was an accomplished musician. ⁸The musicians were appointed to their particular term of service by means of sacred lots, without regard to whether they were young or old, teacher or student.

⁹ The first lot fell to Joseph of the Asaph clan and twelve of his sons and relatives.*

The second lot fell to Gedaliah and twelve of his sons and relatives.

¹⁰ The third lot fell to Zaccur and twelve of his sons and relatives.

¹¹ The fourth lot fell to Zeri* and twelve of his sons and relatives.

¹² The fifth lot fell to Nethaniah and twelve of his sons and relatives.

24:20 Hebrew *Shubael* (also in 24:20b), a variant name for Shebuel; compare 23:16 and 26:24.   24:22 Hebrew *Shelomoth* (also in 24:22b), a variant name for Shelomith; compare 23:18.   24:23 Hebrew *From the descendants of Jeriah*; compare 23:19.   25:3 As in one Hebrew manuscript and some Greek manuscripts (see also 25:17); most Hebrew manuscripts lack *Shimei.*   25:4 Hebrew *Shebuel,* a variant name for Shubael; compare 25:20.   25:9 As in Greek version; Hebrew lacks *and twelve of his sons and relatives.*   25:11 Hebrew *Izri,* a variant name for Zeri; compare 25:3.

13 The sixth lot fell to Bukkiah and twelve of his sons and relatives.

14 The seventh lot fell to Asarelah* and twelve of his sons and relatives.

15 The eighth lot fell to Jeshaiah and twelve of his sons and relatives.

16 The ninth lot fell to Mattaniah and twelve of his sons and relatives.

17 The tenth lot fell to Shimei and twelve of his sons and relatives.

18 The eleventh lot fell to Uzziel* and twelve of his sons and relatives.

19 The twelfth lot fell to Hashabiah and twelve of his sons and relatives.

20 The thirteenth lot fell to Shubael and twelve of his sons and relatives.

21 The fourteenth lot fell to Mattithiah and twelve of his sons and relatives.

22 The fifteenth lot fell to Jerimoth* and twelve of his sons and relatives.

23 The sixteenth lot fell to Hananiah and twelve of his sons and relatives.

24 The seventeenth lot fell to Joshbekashah* and twelve of his sons and relatives.

25 The eighteenth lot fell to Hanani and twelve of his sons and relatives.

26 The nineteenth lot fell to Mallothi and twelve of his sons and relatives.

27 The twentieth lot fell to Eliathah and twelve of his sons and relatives.

28 The twenty-first lot fell to Hothir and twelve of his sons and relatives.

29 The twenty-second lot fell to Geddalti* and twelve of his sons and relatives.

30 The twenty-third lot fell to Mahazioth and twelve of his sons and relatives.

31 The twenty-fourth lot fell to Romamti-ezer and twelve of his sons and relatives.

CHAPTER **26**
Duties of the Gatekeepers
These are the divisions of the gatekeepers:

From the Korahites, there was Meshelemiah son of Kore, of the family of Asaph. 2The sons of Meshelemiah were Zechariah (the oldest), Jediael (the second), Zebadiah (the third), Jathniel (the fourth), 3Elam (the fifth), Jehohanan (the sixth), and Eliehoenai (the seventh).

4The sons of Obed-edom, also gatekeepers, were Shemaiah (the oldest), Jehozabad (the second), Joah (the third), Sacar (the fourth), Nethanel (the fifth), 5Ammiel (the sixth), Issachar (the seventh), and Peullethai (the eighth). God had richly blessed Obed-edom.

6Obed-edom's son Shemaiah had sons with great ability who earned positions of great authority in the clan. 7Their names were Othni, Rephael, Obed, and Elzabad. Their relatives, Elihu and Semakiah, were also very capable men.

8All of these descendants of Obed-edom, including their sons and grandsons—sixty-two of them in all—were very capable men, well qualified for their work.

9Meshelemiah's eighteen sons and relatives were also very capable men.

10Hosah, of the Merari clan, appointed Shimri as the leader among his sons, though he was not the oldest. 11His other sons included Hilkiah (the second), Tebaliah (the third), and Zechariah (the fourth). Hosah's sons and relatives, who served as gatekeepers, numbered thirteen in all.

12These divisions of the gatekeepers were named for their family leaders, and like the other Levites, they served at the house of the LORD. 13They were assigned by families for guard duty at the various gates, without regard to age or training, for it was all decided by means of sacred lots.

14The responsibility for the east gate went to Meshelemiah* and his group. The north gate was assigned to his son Zechariah, a man of unusual wisdom. 15The south gate went to Obed-edom, and his sons were put in charge of the storehouses. 16Shuppim and Hosah were assigned the west gate and the gateway leading up to the Temple.* Guard duties were divided evenly. 17Six Levites were assigned each day to the east gate, four to the north gate, four to the south gate, and two to each of the storehouses. 18Six were assigned each day to the west gate, four to the gateway leading up to the Temple, and two to the courtyard.*

19These were the divisions of the gatekeepers from the clans of Korah and Merari.

25:14 Hebrew *Jesharelah,* a variant name for Asarelah; compare 25:2. 25:18 Hebrew *Azarel,* a variant name for Uzziel; compare 25:4. 25:22 Hebrew *Jeremoth,* a variant name for Jerimoth; compare 25:4. 25:24 Hebrew *Joshbekasha,* a variant name for Joshbekashah; compare 25:4. 25:29 Hebrew *Giddalti,* a variant name for Geddalti; compare 25:4. 26:14 Hebrew *Shelemiah,* a variant name for Meshelemiah; compare 26:2. 26:16 Or *the gate of Shalleketh on the upper road* (also in 26:18). The meaning of the Hebrew is uncertain. 26:18 Or *the colonnade.* The meaning of the Hebrew is uncertain.

Treasurers and Other Officials

20Other Levites, led by Ahijah, were in charge of the treasuries of the house of God and the storerooms. 21From the family of Libni* in the clan of Gershon, Jehiel* was the leader. 22The sons of Jehiel, Zetham and his brother Joel, were in charge of the treasuries of the house of the LORD.

23These are the leaders that descended from Amram, Izhar, Hebron, and Uzziel:

24From the clan of Amram, Shebuel was a descendant of Gershom son of Moses. He was the chief officer of the treasuries. 25His relatives through Eliezer were Rehabiah, Jeshaiah, Joram, Zicri, and Shelomoth.

26Shelomoth and his relatives were in charge of the treasuries that held all the things dedicated to the LORD by King David, the family leaders, and the generals and captains and other officers of the army. 27These men had dedicated some of the plunder they had gained in battle to maintain the house of the LORD. 28Shelomoth and his relatives also cared for the items dedicated to the LORD by Samuel the seer, Saul son of Kish, Abner son of Ner, and Joab son of Zeruiah. All the other dedicated items were in their care, too.

29From the clan of Izhar came Kenaniah. He and his sons were appointed to serve as public administrators and judges throughout Israel.

30From the clan of Hebron came Hashabiah. He and his relatives—seventeen hundred capable men—were put in charge of the Israelite lands west of the Jordan River. They were responsible for all matters related to the things of the LORD and the service of the king in that area.

31Also from the clan of Hebron came Jeriah,* who was the leader of the Hebronites according to the genealogical records. (In the fortieth year of David's reign, a search was made in the records, and capable men from the clan of Hebron were found at Jazer in the land of Gilead.) 32There were twenty-seven hundred capable men among the relatives of Jeriah. King David sent them to the east side of the Jordan River and put them in charge of the tribes of Reuben and Gad and the half-tribe of Manasseh. They were responsible for all matters related to the things of God and the service of the king.

CHAPTER 27

Military Commanders and Divisions

This is the list of Israelite generals and captains, and their officers, who served the king by supervising the army divisions that were on duty each month of the year. Each division served for one month and had twenty-four thousand troops.

2Jashobeam son of Zabdiel was commander of the first division, which was on duty during the first month. There were twenty-four thousand troops in his division. 3He was a descendant of Perez and was in charge of all the army officers for the first month.

4Dodai, a descendant of Ahoah, was commander of the second division, which was on duty during the second month. There were twenty-four thousand troops in his division, and Mikloth was his chief officer.

5Benaiah son of Jehoiada the priest was commander of the third division, which was on duty during the third month. There were twenty-four thousand troops in his division. 6This was the Benaiah who commanded David's elite military group known as the Thirty. His son Ammizabad was his chief officer.

7Asahel, the brother of Joab, was commander of the fourth division, which was on duty during the fourth month. There were twenty-four thousand troops in his division. Asahel was succeeded by his son Zebadiah. 8Shammah* the Izrahite was commander of the fifth division, which was on duty during the fifth month. There were twenty-four thousand troops in his division.

9Ira son of Ikkesh from Tekoa was commander of the sixth division, which was on duty during the sixth month. There were twenty-four thousand troops in his division. 10Helez, a descendant of Ephraim from Pelon, was commander of the seventh division, which was on duty during the seventh month. There were twenty-four thousand troops in his division.

11Sibbecai, a descendant of Zerah from Hushah, was commander of the eighth division, which was on duty during the

---

26:21a Hebrew *Ladan*, another name for Libni; compare 6:17.   26:21b Hebrew *Jehieli* (also in 26:22), a variant name for Jehiel; compare 23:8.   26:31 Hebrew *Jerijah*, a variant name for Jeriah; compare 23:19.   27:8 Hebrew *Shamhuth*, another name for Shammah; compare 11:27 and 2 Sam 23:25.

eighth month. There were twenty-four thousand troops in his division.

12Abiezer from Anathoth in the territory of Benjamin was commander of the ninth division, which was on duty during the ninth month. There were twenty-four thousand troops in his division.

13Maharai, a descendant of Zerah from Netophah, was commander of the tenth division, which was on duty during the tenth month. There were twenty-four thousand troops in his division.

14Benaiah from Pirathon in Ephraim was commander of the eleventh division, which was on duty during the eleventh month. There were twenty-four thousand troops in his division.

15Heled,* a descendant of Othniel from Netophah, was commander of the twelfth division, which was on duty during the twelfth month. There were twenty-four thousand troops in his division.

Leaders of the Tribes

16The following were the tribes of Israel and their leaders:

Tribe	Leader
Reuben	Eliezer son of Zicri
Simeon	Shephatiah son of Maacah
17 Levi	Hashabiah son of Kemuel
Aaron (the priests)	Zadok
18 Judah	Elihu (a brother of David)
Issachar	Omri son of Michael
19 Zebulun	Ishmaiah son of Obadiah
Naphtali	Jeremoth son of Azriel
20 Ephraim	Hoshea son of Azaziah
Manasseh (west)	Joel son of Pedaiah
21 Manasseh (east*)	Iddo son of Zechariah
Benjamin	Jaasiel son of Abner
22 Dan	Azarel son of Jeroham

These were the leaders of the tribes of Israel.

23When David took his census, he did not count those who were younger than twenty years of age, because the LORD had promised to make the Israelites as numerous as the stars in heaven. 24Joab began the census but never finished it because the anger of God broke out against Israel. The final total was never recorded in King David's official records.

Officials of David's Kingdom

25Azmaveth son of Adiel was in charge of the palace treasuries.

Jonathan son of Uzziah was in charge of the regional treasuries throughout the towns, villages, and fortresses of Israel.

26Ezri son of Kelub was in charge of the field workers who farmed the king's lands.

27Shimei from Ramah was in charge of the king's vineyards.

Zabdi from Shepham was responsible for the grapes and the supplies of wine.

28Baal-hanan from Geder was in charge of the king's olive groves and sycamore-fig trees in the foothills of Judah.*

Joash was responsible for the supplies of olive oil.

29Shitrai from Sharon was in charge of the cattle on the Sharon Plain.

Shaphat son of Adlai was responsible for the cattle in the valleys.

30Obil the Ishmaelite was in charge of the camels.

Jehdeiah from Meronoth was in charge of the donkeys.

31Jaziz the Hagrite was in charge of the king's sheep.

All these officials were overseers of King David's property.

32Jonathan, David's uncle, was a wise counselor to the king, a man of great insight, and a scribe. Jehiel the Hacmonite was responsible to teach the king's sons. 33Ahithophel was the royal adviser. Hushai the Arkite was the king's friend. 34Ahithophel was succeeded by Jehoiada son of Benaiah and by Abiathar. Joab was commander of the Israelite army.

CHAPTER 28
David's Instructions to Solomon

David summoned all his officials to Jerusalem—the leaders of the tribes, the commanders of the twelve army divisions, the other generals and captains, the overseers of the royal property and livestock, the palace officials, the mighty men, and all the other warriors in the kingdom. 2David rose and stood before them and addressed them as follows: "My brothers and my people! It was my desire to build a temple where the Ark of the LORD's covenant, God's footstool, could rest permanently. I made the necessary preparations for building it, 3but God said to me, 'You must not build a temple to honor my name, for you are a warrior and have shed much blood.'

4"Yet the LORD, the God of Israel, has chosen me from among all my father's family to be king over Israel forever. For he has chosen the tribe of Judah to rule, and from among the families of

---

27:15 Hebrew *Heldai*, a variant name for Heled; compare 11:30 and 2 Sam 23:29.   27:21 Hebrew *in Gilead*.   27:28 Hebrew *the Shephelah*.

Judah, he chose my father's family. And from among my father's sons, the LORD was pleased to make me king over all Israel. 5And from among my sons—for the LORD has given me many children—he chose Solomon to succeed me on the throne of his kingdom of Israel. 6He said to me, 'Your son Solomon will build my Temple and its courtyards, for I have chosen him as my son, and I will be his father. 7And if he continues to obey my commands and regulations as he does now, I will make his kingdom last forever.' 8So now, with God as our witness, I give you this charge for all Israel, the LORD's assembly: Be careful to obey all the commands of the LORD your God, so that you may possess this good land and leave it to your children as a permanent inheritance.

9"And Solomon, my son, get to know the God of your ancestors. Worship and serve him with your whole heart and with a willing mind. For the LORD sees every heart and understands and knows every plan and thought. If you seek him, you will find him. But if you forsake him, he will reject you forever. 10So take this seriously. The LORD has chosen you to build a Temple as his sanctuary. Be strong, and do the work."

11Then David gave Solomon the plans for the Temple and its surroundings, including the treasuries, the upstairs rooms, the inner rooms, and the inner sanctuary where the Ark's cover—the place of atonement—would be kept. 12David also gave Solomon all the plans he had in mind* for the courtyards of the LORD's Temple, the outside rooms, the treasuries of God's Temple, and the rooms for the dedicated gifts. 13The king also gave Solomon the instructions concerning the work of the various divisions of priests and Levites in the Temple of the LORD. And he gave specifications for the items in the LORD's Temple which were to be used for worship and sacrifice.

14David gave instructions regarding how much gold and silver should be used to make the necessary items. 15He told Solomon the amount of gold needed for the gold lampstands and lamps, and the amount of silver for the silver lampstands and lamps, depending on how each would be used. 16He designated the amount of gold for the table on which the Bread of the Presence would be placed and the amount of silver for other tables.

17David also designated the amount of gold for the solid gold meat hooks used to handle the sacrificial meat and for the basins, pitchers, and dishes, as well as the amount of silver for every dish. 18Finally, he designated the amount of refined gold for the altar of incense and for the gold cherubim, whose wings were stretched out over the Ark of the LORD's covenant. 19"Every part of this plan," David told Solomon, "was given to me in writing from the hand of the LORD.*"

20Then David continued, "Be strong and courageous, and do the work. Don't be afraid or discouraged by the size of the task, for the LORD God, my God, is with you. He will not fail you or forsake you. He will see to it that all the work related to the Temple of the LORD is finished correctly. 21The various divisions of priests and Levites will serve in the Temple of God. Others with skills of every kind will volunteer, and the leaders and the entire nation are at your command."

CHAPTER **29**
Gifts for Building the Temple
Then King David turned to the entire assembly and said, "My son Solomon, whom God has chosen to be the next king of Israel, is still young and inexperienced. The work ahead of him is enormous, for the Temple he will build is not just another building—it is for the LORD God himself! 2Using every resource at my command, I have gathered as much as I could for building the Temple of my God. Now there is enough gold, silver, bronze, iron, and wood, as well as great quantities of onyx, other precious stones, costly jewels, and all kinds of fine stone and marble. 3And now because of my devotion to the Temple of my God, I am giving all of my own private treasures of gold and silver to help in the construction. This is in addition to the building materials I have already collected for his holy Temple. 4I am donating more than 112 tons of gold* from Ophir and over 262 tons of refined silver* to be used for overlaying the walls of the buildings 5and for the other gold and silver work to be done by the craftsmen. Now then, who will follow my example? Who is willing to give offerings to the LORD today?"

6Then the family leaders, the leaders of the tribes of Israel, the generals and captains of the army, and the king's administrative officers all gave willingly. 7For the construction of the Temple of God, they gave almost 188 tons of gold,* 10,000 gold coins,* about 375 tons of silver,* about 675 tons of bronze,* and about 3,750 tons of iron.* 8They also contributed nu-

---

28:12 Or *the plans of the spirit that was with him.* **28:19** Or *was written under the direction of the LORD.* **29:4a** Hebrew *3,000 talents* [102 metric tons] *of gold.* **29:4b** Hebrew *7,000 talents* [238 metric tons] *of silver.* **29:7a** Hebrew *5,000 talents* [170 metric tons] *of gold.* **29:7b** Hebrew *10,000 darics* [a Persian coin] *of gold,* about 185 pounds or 84 kilograms in weight. **29:7c** Hebrew *10,000 talents* [340 metric tons] *of silver.* **29:7d** Hebrew *18,000 talents* [612 metric tons] *of bronze.* **29:7e** Hebrew *100,000 talents* [3,400 metric tons] *of iron.*

merous precious stones, which were deposited in the treasury of the house of the LORD under the care of Jehiel, a descendant of Gershon. 9The people rejoiced over the offerings, for they had given freely and wholeheartedly to the LORD, and King David was filled with joy.

David's Prayer of Praise

10Then David praised the LORD in the presence of the whole assembly: "O LORD, the God of our ancestor Israel,* may you be praised forever and ever! 11Yours, O LORD, is the greatness, the power, the glory, the victory, and the majesty. Everything in the heavens and on earth is yours, O LORD, and this is your kingdom. We adore you as the one who is over all things. 12Riches and honor come from you alone, for you rule over everything. Power and might are in your hand, and it is at your discretion that people are made great and given strength.

13"O our God, we thank you and praise your glorious name! 14But who am I, and who are my people, that we could give anything to you? Everything we have has come from you, and we give you only what you have already given us! 15We are here for only a moment, visitors and strangers in the land as our ancestors were before us. Our days on earth are like a shadow, gone so soon without a trace.

16"O LORD our God, even these materials that we have gathered to build a Temple to honor your holy name come from you! It all belongs to you! 17I know, my God, that you examine our hearts and rejoice when you find integrity there. You know I have done all this with good motives, and I have watched your people offer their gifts willingly and joyously.

18"O LORD, the God of our ancestors Abraham, Isaac, and Israel, make your people always want to obey you. See to it that their love for you never changes. 19Give my son Solomon the wholehearted desire to obey all your com-

29:10 *Israel* is the name that God gave to Jacob.

mands, decrees, and principles, and to build this Temple, for which I have made all these preparations."

20Then David said to the whole assembly, "Give praise to the LORD your God!" And the entire assembly praised the LORD, the God of their ancestors, and they bowed low and knelt before the LORD and the king.

Solomon Named as King

21The next day they brought a thousand bulls, a thousand rams, and a thousand male lambs as burnt offerings to the LORD. They also brought drink offerings and many other sacrifices on behalf of Israel. 22They feasted and drank in the LORD's presence with great joy that day.

And again they crowned David's son Solomon as their new king. They anointed him before the LORD as their leader, and they anointed Zadok as their priest. 23So Solomon took the throne of the LORD in place of his father, David, and he prospered greatly, and all Israel obeyed him. 24All the royal officials, the army commanders, and the sons of King David pledged their loyalty to King Solomon. 25And the LORD exalted Solomon so the entire nation of Israel stood in awe of him, and he gave Solomon even greater wealth and honor than his father.

Summary of David's Reign

26So David son of Jesse reigned over all Israel. 27He ruled Israel for forty years in all, seven years from Hebron and thirty-three years from Jerusalem. 28He died at a ripe old age, having enjoyed long life, wealth, and honor. Then his son Solomon ruled in his place. 29All the events of King David's reign, from beginning to end, are written in *The Record of Samuel the Seer, The Record of Nathan the Prophet,* and *The Record of Gad the Seer.* 30These accounts include the mighty deeds of his reign and everything that happened to him and to Israel and to all the surrounding kingdoms.

2 Chronicles

CHAPTER 1

Solomon Asks for Wisdom

Solomon, the son of King David, now took firm control of the kingdom, for the LORD his God was with him and made him very powerful. 2He called together all Israel—the generals and captains of the army, the judges, and all the political and clan leaders. 3Then Solomon led the entire assembly to the hill at Gibeon where God's Tabernacle* was located. This was the Tabernacle that Moses, the LORD's servant, had constructed in the wilderness. 4David had already moved the Ark of God from Kiriath-jearim to the special tent he had prepared for it in Jerusalem. 5But the bronze altar made by Bezalel son of Uri and grandson of Hur was still at Gibeon in front of the Tabernacle of the LORD. So Solomon and the people gathered in front of it to consult the LORD. 6There in front of the Tabernacle, Solomon went up to the bronze altar in the LORD's presence and sacrificed a thousand burnt offerings on it.

7That night God appeared to Solomon in a dream and said, "What do you want? Ask, and I will give it to you!"

8Solomon replied to God, "You have been so faithful and kind to my father, David, and now you have made me king in his place. 9Now, LORD God, please keep your promise to David my father, for you have made me king over a people as numerous as the dust of the earth! 10Give me wisdom and knowledge to rule them properly, for who is able to govern this great nation of yours?"

11God said to Solomon, "Because your greatest desire is to help your people, and you did not ask for personal wealth and honor or the death of your enemies or even a long life, but rather you asked for wisdom and knowledge to properly govern my people, 12I will certainly give you the wisdom and knowledge you requested. And I will also give you riches, wealth, and honor such as no other king has ever had before you or will ever have again!" 13Then Solomon returned to Jerusalem from the Tabernacle at the hill of Gibeon, and he reigned over Israel.

14Solomon built up a huge military force, which included fourteen hundred chariots and twelve thousand horses.* He stationed many of them in the chariot cities, and some near him in Jerusalem. 15During Solomon's reign, silver and gold were as plentiful in Jerusalem as stones. And valuable cedarwood was as common as the sycamore wood that grows in the foothills of Judah.* 16Solomon's horses were imported from Egypt* and from Cilicia*; the king's traders acquired them from Cilicia at the standard price. 17At that time, Egyptian chariots delivered to Jerusalem could be purchased for 600 pieces of silver,* and horses could be bought for 150 pieces of silver.* Many of these were then resold to the kings of the Hittites and the kings of Aram.

CHAPTER 2

Preparations for Building the Temple

Solomon now decided that the time had come to build a Temple for the LORD and a royal palace for himself. 2He enlisted a force of 70,000 common laborers, 80,000 stonecutters in the hill country, and 3,600 foremen. 3Solomon also sent this message to King Hiram* at Tyre:

"Send me cedar logs like the ones that were supplied to my father, David, when he was building his palace. 4I am about to build a

---

1:3 Hebrew *Tent of Meeting;* also in 1:6, 13.   1:14 Or *12,000 charioteers.*   1:15 Hebrew *the Shephelah.*   1:16a Possibly *Muzur,* a district near Cilicia; also in 1:17.   1:16b Hebrew *Kue,* probably another name for Cilicia.   1:17a Hebrew *600 shekels of silver,* about 15 pounds or 6.8 kilograms in weight.   1:17b Hebrew *150 shekels,* about 3.8 pounds or 1.7 kilograms in weight.   2:3 Hebrew *Huram,* a variant name for Hiram; also in 2:11, 12.

Temple to honor the name of the LORD my God. It will be a place set apart to burn incense and sweet spices before him, to display the special sacrificial bread, and to sacrifice burnt offerings each morning and evening, on the Sabbaths, at new moon celebrations, and at the other appointed festivals of the LORD our God. He has commanded Israel to do these things forever.

5 "This will be a magnificent Temple because our God is an awesome God, greater than any other. 6 But who can really build him a worthy home? Not even the highest heavens can contain him! So who am I to consider building a Temple for him, except as a place to burn sacrifices to him?

7 "So send me a master craftsman who can work with gold, silver, bronze, and iron; someone who is expert at dyeing purple, scarlet, and blue cloth; and a skilled engraver who can work with the craftsmen of Judah and Jerusalem who were selected by my father, David. 8 Also send me cedar, cypress, and almug* logs from Lebanon, for I know that your men are without equal at cutting timber. I will send my men to help them. 9 An immense amount of timber will be needed, for the Temple I am going to build will be very large and magnificent. 10 I will pay your men 100,000 bushels of crushed wheat, 100,000 bushels of barley,* 110,000 gallons of wine, and 110,000 gallons of olive oil.*"

11 King Hiram sent this letter of reply to Solomon:

"It is because the LORD loves his people that he has made you their king! 12 Blessed be the LORD, the God of Israel, who made the heavens and the earth! He has given David a wise son, gifted with skill and understanding, who will build a Temple for the LORD and a royal palace for himself.

13 "I am sending you a master craftsman named Huram-abi. He is a brilliant man, 14 the son of a woman from Dan in Israel; his father is from Tyre. He is skillful at making things from gold, silver, bronze, and iron. He also knows all about stonework, carpentry, and weaving. He is an expert in dyeing purple, blue, and scarlet cloth and in working with linen. He is also an engraver and can follow any design given to him. He will work with your craftsmen and those appointed by my lord David, your father.

15 "Send along the wheat, barley, olive oil, and wine that you mentioned. 16 We will cut whatever timber you need from the Lebanon mountains and will float the logs in rafts down the coast of the Mediterranean Sea to Joppa. From there you can transport the logs up to Jerusalem."

17 Solomon took a census of all foreigners in the land of Israel, like the census his father had taken, and he counted 153,600. 18 He enlisted 70,000 of them as common laborers, 80,000 as stonecutters in the hill country, and 3,600 as foremen.

CHAPTER **3**

Solomon Builds the Temple

So Solomon began to build the Temple of the LORD in Jerusalem on Mount Moriah, where the LORD had appeared to Solomon's father, King David. The Temple was built on the threshing floor of Araunah* the Jebusite, the site that David had selected. 2 The construction began in midspring,* during the fourth year of Solomon's reign.

3 The foundation for the Temple of God was ninety feet long and thirty feet wide.* 4 The foyer at the front of the Temple was thirty feet wide, running across the entire width of the Temple. The inner walls of the foyer and the ceiling were overlaid with pure gold. The roof of the foyer was thirty feet* high.

5 The main room of the Temple was paneled with cypress wood, overlaid with pure gold, and decorated with carvings of palm trees and chains. 6 The walls of the Temple were decorated with beautiful jewels and with pure gold from the land of Parvaim. 7 All the walls, beams, doors, and thresholds throughout the Temple were overlaid with gold, and figures of cherubim were carved on the walls.

8 The Most Holy Place was thirty feet wide, corresponding to the width of the Temple, and it was also thirty feet deep. Its interior was overlaid with about twenty-three tons* of pure gold. 9 They used gold nails that weighed about twenty

---

2:8 Hebrew *algum,* a variant name for almug; compare 9:10-11 and parallel text at 1 Kgs 10:11-12.   2:10a Hebrew *20,000 cors* [3,640 kiloliters] *of crushed wheat, 20,000 cors of barley.*   2:10b Hebrew *20,000 baths* [420 kiloliters] *of wine, and 20,000 baths of olive oil.*   3:1 Hebrew reads *Ornan,* another name for Araunah; compare 2 Sam 24:16.   3:2 Hebrew *on the second day of the second month.* This day of the Hebrew lunar calendar occurs in April or early May.   3:3 Hebrew *60 cubits* [27 meters] *long and 20 cubits* [9 meters] *wide.* In this chapter, the distance measures are calculated from the Hebrew cubit at a ratio of 18 inches or 45 centimeters per cubit.   3:4 As in some Greek and Syriac manuscripts, which read *20 cubits* [9 meters]; Hebrew reads *120 cubits,* which is 180 feet or 54 meters.   3:8 Hebrew *600 talents* [20.4 metric tons].

ounces* each. The walls of the upper rooms were also overlaid with pure gold.

¹⁰Solomon made two figures shaped like cherubim and overlaid them with gold. These were placed in the Most Holy Place. ¹¹The total wingspan of the two cherubim standing side by side was 30 feet. One wing of the first figure was 7½ feet long, and it touched the Temple wall. The other wing, also 7½ feet long, touched one of the wings of the second figure. ¹²In the same way, the second figure had one wing 7½ feet long that touched the opposite wall. The other wing, also 7½ feet long, touched the wing of the first figure. ¹³So the wingspan of both cherubim together was 30 feet. They both stood and faced out toward the main room of the Temple. ¹⁴Across the entrance of the Most Holy Place, Solomon hung a curtain made of fine linen and blue, purple, and scarlet yarn, with figures of cherubim embroidered on it.

¹⁵For the front of the Temple, Solomon made two pillars that were 27 feet* tall, each topped by a capital extending upward another 7½ feet. ¹⁶He made a network of interwoven chains and used them to decorate the tops of the pillars. He also made one hundred decorative pomegranates and attached them to the chains. ¹⁷Then he set up the two pillars at the entrance of the Temple, one to the south of the entrance and the other to the north. He named the one on the south Jakin, and the one on the north Boaz.*

CHAPTER **4**
Furnishings for the Temple
Solomon also made a bronze altar 30 feet long, 30 feet wide, and 15 feet high.* ²Then he cast a large round tank, 15 feet across from rim to rim; it was called the Sea. It was 7½ feet deep and about 45 feet in circumference. ³The Sea was encircled just below its rim by two rows of figures that resembled oxen. There were about six oxen per foot* all the way around, and they had been cast as part of the tank. ⁴The Sea rested on a base of twelve bronze oxen, all facing outward. Three faced north, three faced west, three faced south, and three faced east. ⁵The walls of the Sea were about three inches* thick, and its rim flared out like a cup and resembled a lily blossom. It could hold about 16,500 gallons* of water.

⁶He also made ten basins for water to wash the offerings, five to the south of the Sea and five to the north. The priests used the Sea itself, and not the basins, for their own washing.

⁷Solomon then cast ten gold lampstands according to the specifications that had been given and put them in the Temple. Five were placed against the south wall, and five were placed against the north wall. ⁸He also built ten tables and placed them in the Temple, five along the south wall and five along the north wall. Then he molded one hundred gold basins.

⁹Solomon also built a courtyard for the priests and the large outer courtyard. He made doors for the courtyard entrances and overlaid them with bronze. ¹⁰The Sea was placed near the southeast corner of the Temple.

¹¹Huram-abi also made the necessary pots, shovels, and basins.

So at last Huram-abi completed everything King Solomon had assigned him to make for the Temple of God:

¹² two pillars,
two bowl-shaped capitals on top of the pillars,
two networks of chains that decorated the capitals,
¹³ four hundred pomegranates that hung from the chains on the capitals (two rows of pomegranates for each of the chain networks that were hung around the capitals on top of the pillars),
¹⁴ the water carts holding the basins,
¹⁵ the Sea and the twelve oxen under it,
¹⁶ the pots, the shovels, the meat hooks, and all the related utensils.

Huram-abi made all these things out of burnished bronze for the Temple of the LORD, just as King Solomon had requested. ¹⁷The king had them cast in clay molds in the Jordan Valley between Succoth and Zarethan.* ¹⁸Such great quantities of bronze were used that its weight could not be determined.

¹⁹So Solomon made all the furnishings for the Temple of God:

the gold altar;
the tables for the Bread of the Presence;

3:9 Hebrew *50 shekels* [570 grams]. 3:15 As in Syriac version (see also 1 Kgs 7:15; 2 Kgs 25:17; Jer 52:21), which reads *18 cubits* [8.1 meters]; Hebrew reads *35 cubits*, which is 52.5 feet or 15.8 meters. 3:17 Jakin probably means "he establishes"; Boaz probably means "in him is strength." 4:1 Hebrew *20 cubits* [9 meters] *long, 20 cubits wide, and 10 cubits* [4.5 meters] *high.* In this chapter, the distance measures are calculated from the Hebrew cubit at a ratio of 18 inches or 45 centimeters per cubit. 4:3 Or *20 oxen per meter;* Hebrew reads *10 per cubit.* 4:5a Hebrew *a handbreadth* [8 centimeters]. 4:5b Hebrew *3,000 baths* [63 kiloliters]. 4:17 As in parallel text at 1 Kgs 7:46; Hebrew reads *Zeredah.*

20 the lampstands and their lamps of pure gold to burn in front of the Most Holy Place as prescribed;

21 the flower decorations, lamps, and tongs, all of pure gold;

22 the lamp snuffers, basins, dishes, and firepans, all of pure gold;

the doors for the entrances to the Most Holy Place and the main room of the Temple, overlaid with gold.

CHAPTER 5

The Ark Brought to the Temple

When Solomon had finished all the work related to building the Temple of the LORD, he brought in the gifts dedicated by his father, King David, including all the silver and gold and all the utensils. These were stored in the treasuries of the Temple of God.

2Solomon then summoned the leaders of all the tribes and families of Israel to assemble in Jerusalem. They were to bring the Ark of the LORD's covenant from its location in the City of David, also known as Zion, to its new place in the Temple. 3They all assembled before the king at the annual Festival of Shelters in early autumn.* 4When all the leaders of Israel arrived, the Levites moved the Ark, 5along with the special tent* and all its sacred utensils. The Levitical priests carried them all up to the Temple. 6King Solomon and the entire community of Israel sacrificed sheep and oxen before the Ark in such numbers that no one could keep count!

7Then the priests carried the Ark of the LORD's covenant into the inner sanctuary of the Temple—the Most Holy Place—and placed it beneath the wings of the cherubim. 8The cherubim spread their wings out over the Ark, forming a canopy over the Ark and its carrying poles. 9These poles were so long that their ends could be seen from the front entrance of the Temple's main room—the Holy Place—but not from outside it. They are still there to this day. 10Nothing was in the Ark except the two stone tablets that Moses had placed there at Mount Sinai,* when the LORD made a covenant with the people of Israel after they left Egypt.

11Then the priests left the Holy Place. All the priests who were present had purified themselves, whether or not they were on duty that day. 12And the Levites who were musicians—Asaph, Heman, Jeduthun, and all their sons and brothers—were dressed in fine linen robes and stood at the east side of the altar playing cymbals, harps, and lyres. They were joined by 120 priests who were playing trumpets. 13The trumpeters and singers performed together in unison to praise and give thanks to the LORD. Accompanied by trumpets, cymbals, and other instruments, they raised their voices and praised the LORD with these words:

"He is so good!
His faithful love endures forever!"

At that moment a cloud filled the Temple of the LORD. 14The priests could not continue their work because the glorious presence of the LORD filled the Temple of God.

CHAPTER 6

Solomon Blesses the People

Then Solomon prayed, "O LORD, you have said that you would live in thick darkness. 2But I have built a glorious Temple for you, where you can live forever!"

3Then the king turned around to the entire community of Israel standing before him and gave this blessing: 4"Blessed be the LORD, the God of Israel, who has kept the promise he made to my father, David. For he told my father, 5'From the day I brought my people out of Egypt, I have never chosen a city among the tribes of Israel as the place where a temple should be built to honor my name. Nor have I chosen a king to lead my people Israel. 6But now I have chosen Jerusalem as that city, and David as that king.'"

7Then Solomon said, "My father, David, wanted to build this Temple to honor the name of the LORD, the God of Israel. 8But the LORD told him, 'It is right for you to want to build the Temple to honor my name, 9but you will not be the one to do it. One of your sons will build it instead.'

10"And now the LORD has done what he promised, for I have become king in my father's place. I have built this Temple to honor the name of the LORD, the God of Israel. 11There I have placed the Ark, and in the Ark is the covenant that the LORD made with the people of Israel."

Solomon's Prayer of Dedication

12Then Solomon stood with his hands spread out before the altar of the LORD in front of the entire community of Israel. 13He had made a

5:3 Hebrew *at the festival that is in the seventh month.* The Festival of Shelters began on the fifteenth day of the seventh month of the Hebrew lunar calendar. This occurs on our calendar in late September or early October. 5:5 Hebrew *Tent of Meeting.* 5:10 Hebrew *Horeb,* another name for Sinai.

bronze platform 7½ feet long, 7½ feet wide, and 4½ feet high* and had placed it at the center of the Temple's outer courtyard. He stood on the platform before the entire assembly, and then he knelt down and lifted his hands toward heaven. 14He prayed, "O LORD, God of Israel, there is no God like you in all of heaven and earth. You keep your promises and show unfailing love to all who obey you and are eager to do your will. 15You have kept your promise to your servant David, my father. You made that promise with your own mouth, and today you have fulfilled it with your own hands. 16And now, O LORD, God of Israel, carry out your further promise to your servant David, my father. For you said to him, 'If your descendants guard their behavior and obey my law as you have done, they will always reign over Israel.' 17Now, O LORD, God of Israel, fulfill this promise to your servant David.

18"But will God really live on earth among people? Why, even the highest heavens cannot contain you. How much less this Temple I have built! 19Listen to my prayer and my request, O LORD my God. Hear the cry and the prayer that your servant is making to you. 20May you watch over this Temple both day and night, this place where you have said you would put your name. May you always hear the prayers I make toward this place. 21May you hear the humble and earnest requests from me and your people Israel when we pray toward this place. Yes, hear us from heaven where you live, and when you hear, forgive.

22"If someone wrongs another person and is required to take an oath of innocence in front of the altar at this Temple, 23then hear from heaven and judge between your servants—the accuser and the accused. Punish the guilty party, and acquit the one who is innocent.

24"If your people Israel are defeated by their enemies because they have sinned against you, and if they turn to you and call on your name and pray to you here in this Temple, 25then hear from heaven and forgive their sins and return them to this land you gave their ancestors.

26"If the skies are shut up and there is no rain because your people have sinned against you, and then they pray toward this Temple and confess your name and turn from their sins because you have punished them, 27then hear from heaven and forgive the sins of your servants, your people Israel. Teach them to do what is right, and send rain on your land that you have given to your people as their special possession.

28"If there is a famine in the land, or plagues, or

crop disease, or attacks of locusts or caterpillars, or if your people's enemies are in the land besieging their towns—whatever the trouble is— 29and if your people offer a prayer concerning their troubles or sorrow, raising their hands toward this Temple, 30then hear from heaven where you live, and forgive. Give your people whatever they deserve, for you alone know the human heart. 31Then they will fear you and walk in your ways as long as they live in the land you gave to our ancestors.

32"And when foreigners hear of you and your mighty miracles, and they come from distant lands to worship your great name and to pray toward this Temple, 33then hear from heaven where you live, and grant what they ask of you. Then all the people of the earth will come to know and fear you, just as your own people Israel do. They, too, will know that this Temple I have built bears your name.

34"If your people go out at your command to fight their enemies, and if they pray to you toward this city that you have chosen and toward this Temple that I have built for your name, 35then hear their prayers from heaven and uphold their cause.

36"If they sin against you—and who has never sinned?—you may become angry with them and let their enemies conquer them and take them captive to a foreign land far or near. 37But in that land of exile, they may turn to you again in repentance and pray, 'We have sinned, done evil, and acted wickedly.' 38Then if they turn to you with their whole heart and soul and pray toward the land you gave to their ancestors, toward this city you have chosen, and toward this Temple I have built to honor your name, 39then hear their prayers from heaven where you live. Uphold their cause and forgive your people who have sinned against you.

40"O my God, be attentive to all the prayers made to you in this place. 41And now, O LORD God, arise and enter this resting place of yours, where your magnificent Ark has been placed. May your priests, O LORD God, be clothed with salvation, and may your saints rejoice in your goodness. 42O LORD God, do not reject your anointed one. Remember your unfailing love for your servant David.*"

CHAPTER **7**
The Dedication of the Temple
When Solomon finished praying, fire flashed down from heaven and burned up the burnt

6:13 Hebrew *5 cubits* [2.3 meters] *long, 5 cubits wide, and 3 cubits* [1.4 meters] *high.*   6:42 Or *Remember the faithfulness of your servant David.*

offerings and sacrifices, and the glorious presence of the LORD filled the Temple. [2]The priests could not even enter the Temple of the LORD because the glorious presence of the LORD filled it. [3]When all the people of Israel saw the fire coming down and the glorious presence of the LORD filling the Temple, they fell face down on the ground and worshiped and praised the LORD, saying,

"He is so good!
His faithful love endures forever!"

[4]Then the king and all the people offered sacrifices to the LORD. [5]King Solomon offered a sacrifice of 22,000 oxen and 120,000 sheep. And so the king and all the people dedicated the Temple of God. [6]The priests took their assigned positions, and so did the Levites who were singing, "His faithful love endures forever!" They accompanied the singing with music from the instruments King David had made for praising the LORD. On the other side of the Levites, the priests blew the trumpets, while all Israel stood.

[7]Solomon then dedicated the central area of the courtyard in front of the LORD's Temple so they could present burnt offerings and the fat from peace offerings there. He did this because the bronze altar he had built could not handle all the burnt offerings, grain offerings, and sacrificial fat.

[8]For the next seven days they celebrated the Festival of Shelters* with huge crowds gathered from all the tribes of Israel. They came from as far away as Lebo-hamath in the north, to the brook of Egypt in the south. [9]On the eighth day they had a closing ceremony, for they had celebrated the dedication of the altar for seven days and the Festival of Shelters for seven days. [10]Then at the end of the celebration,* Solomon sent the people home. They were all joyful and happy because the LORD had been so good to David and Solomon and to his people Israel.

The LORD's Response to Solomon

[11]So Solomon finished building the Temple of the LORD, as well as the royal palace. He completed everything he had planned to do. [12]Then one night the LORD appeared to Solomon and said, "I have heard your prayer and have chosen this Temple as the place for making sacrifices. [13]At times I might shut up the heavens so that no rain falls, or I might command locusts to devour your crops, or I might send plagues

among you. [14]Then if my people who are called by my name will humble themselves and pray and seek my face and turn from their wicked ways, I will hear from heaven and will forgive their sins and heal their land. [15]I will listen to every prayer made in this place, [16]for I have chosen this Temple and set it apart to be my home forever. My eyes and my heart will always be here.

[17]"As for you, if you follow me as your father, David, did and obey all my commands, laws, and regulations, [18]then I will not let anyone take away your throne. This is the same promise I gave your father, David, when I said, 'You will never fail to have a successor who rules over Israel.'

[19]"But if you abandon me and disobey the laws and commands I have given you, and if you go and worship other gods, [20]then I will uproot the people of Israel from this land of mine that I have given them. I will reject this Temple that I have set apart to honor my name. I will make it a spectacle of contempt among the nations. [21]And though this Temple is impressive now, it will become an appalling sight to all who pass by. They will ask, 'Why has the LORD done such terrible things to his land and to his Temple?' [22]And the answer will be, 'Because his people abandoned the LORD, the God of their ancestors, who brought them out of Egypt, and they worshiped other gods instead. That is why he brought all these disasters upon them.'"

CHAPTER 8
Solomon's Many Achievements

It was now twenty years since Solomon had become king, and the great building projects of the LORD's Temple and his own royal palace were completed. [2]Solomon now turned his attention to rebuilding the towns that King Hiram* had given him, and he settled Israelites in them. [3]It was at this time, too, that Solomon fought against the city of Hamath-zobah and conquered it. [4]He rebuilt Tadmor in the desert and built towns in the region of Hamath as supply centers. [5]He fortified the cities of Upper Beth-horon and Lower Beth-horon, rebuilding their walls and installing barred gates. [6]He also rebuilt Baalath and other supply centers at this time and constructed cities where his chariots and horses* could be kept. He built to his heart's

7:8 Hebrew *the festival* (also in 7:9); see note on 5:3.   7:10 Hebrew *Then on the twenty-seventh day of the seventh month.* This day of the Hebrew lunar calendar occurs in late September or early October.   8:2 Hebrew *Huram,* a variant name for Hiram; also in 8:18.   8:6 Or *and charioteers.*

What Is Revival? Read 2 CHRONICLES 7:14

As we witness the moral breakdown in society and see the blatant disregard of God and his absolutes, we know that things have to change. Politicians aren't the answer. Laws alone aren't going to solve the problem. More social programs won't help. Remember, the Bible tells us that Satan is the "god" of this world (see Ephesians 2:2, p. 1024). It is Satan who is responsible for the gross perversion, the injustice, the violence, and the rebellion against God and his laws. That is why all attempts to reform this world, this culture, and this society, apart from a change of heart, are futile. The only hope for our country and the rest of the world is a return to God and his Word, in short, a revival!

Unfortunately, many people do not understand what a revival is. It is not a series of organized meetings. In fact, you don't organize for revival—you agonize for it in prayer. No revival in American history has ever been brought about by a bunch of committees getting together and setting up a series of meetings. Revival is something God sovereignly does. It is a supernatural work of the Holy Spirit.

Revival Begins with Believers. As we look at the problems in our country today, we in the church tend to shift the blame to non-Christians. Yet whenever God speaks of revival in the Bible, he doesn't direct his comments to nonbelievers. You see, the world doesn't need reviving. The church does. In the first century, the church turned the world upside down. Today, in many ways, the world has turned the church upside down. Though our numbers have never been larger, we are not influencing our culture as effectively as we could. Our passion for the Lord needs to be revived.

Revival Is Characterized by Prayer. How do we turn things around? As the verse says, we must humble ourselves and *pray.* Every revival in history has been characterized by fervent prayer. The word used for *prayer* in 2 Chronicles is worth noting. Of the twelve words used to express the single verb *to pray* in the Hebrew language, the one used in this verse means "to judge self habitually." James explains why this is so essential: "Let there be tears for the wrong things you have done. Let there be sorrow and deep grief. Let there be sadness instead of laughter, and gloom instead of joy. When you bow down before the Lord and admit your dependence on him, he will lift you up and give you honor" (James 4:9-10).

Revival Comes As We Put God First. God knew that his people, the Israelites, would one day disobey and even forsake him. So he gave Solomon, the Israelite king, a prescription for revival. The prescription contained three parts: The Israelites had to (1) humble themselves before God, (2) pray to God, and (3) turn from their sin. If the Israelites would follow this prescription, *then* God would bless them and bring healing to their land.

Like the Israelites of old, many of us in the church have turned away from God and are living for ourselves. In order for revival to happen, we need to place God first in our lives again. We need to have a consistent time of Bible study and prayer. It is time to become an active part of the church, not just an idle spectator. It is time to care for the old, the sick, and the poor. It is time to share our faith with nonbelievers. And above all else, it is time to honor and obey God by rooting out sin from our lives.

As you do these things, you will see revival come to your own life—and it may even help to spark revival in the lives of those around you.

For the next "Big Question" note, turn to p. 853.

BIG QUESTIONS ?

---

content in Jerusalem and Lebanon and throughout the entire realm.

7There were still some people living in the land who were not Israelites, including Hittites, Amorites, Perizzites, Hivites, and Jebusites. 8These were descendants of the nations that Israel had not completely destroyed. So Solomon conscripted them for his labor force, and they serve in the labor force to this day. 9But Solomon did not conscript any of the Israelites for forced labor. Instead, he assigned them to serve as fighting men, officers in his army, commanders of his chariots, and charioteers. [10]King Solomon also appointed 250 of them to supervise the various projects.

[11]Solomon moved his wife, Pharaoh's daughter, from the City of David to the new palace he had built for her. He said, "My wife must not live in King David's palace, for the Ark of the LORD has been there, and it is holy ground."

[12]Then Solomon sacrificed burnt offerings to the LORD on the altar he had built in front of the foyer of the Temple. [13]The number of sacrifices varied from day to day according to the commands Moses had given. Extra sacrifices were offered on the Sabbaths, on new moon festivals, and at the three annual festivals—the Passover celebration, the Festival of Harvest,* and the Festival of Shelters. [14]In assigning the priests to their duties, Solomon followed the regulations of his father, David. He also assigned the Levites to lead the people in praise and to assist the priests in their daily duties. And he assigned the gatekeepers to their gates by their divisions, following the commands of David, the man of God. [15]Solomon did not deviate in any way from David's commands concerning the priests and Levites and the treasuries.

[16]So Solomon made sure that all the work related to building the Temple of the LORD was carried out, from the day its foundation was laid to the day of its completion.

[17]Later Solomon went to Ezion-geber and Elath,* ports in the land of Edom, along the shore of the Red Sea.* [18]Hiram sent him ships commanded by his own officers and manned by experienced crews of sailors. These ships sailed to the land of Ophir with Solomon's men and brought back to Solomon almost seventeen tons* of gold.

CHAPTER **9**

The Queen of Sheba's Visit

When the queen of Sheba heard of Solomon's reputation, she came to Jerusalem to test him with hard questions. She arrived with a large group of attendants and a great caravan of camels loaded with spices, huge quantities of gold, and precious jewels. [2]When she met with Solomon, they talked about everything she had on her mind. Solomon answered all her questions; nothing was too hard for him to explain to her. [3]When the queen of Sheba realized how wise Solomon was, and when she saw the palace he had built, [4]she was breath-

less. She was also amazed at the food on his tables, the organization of his officials and their splendid clothing, the cup-bearers and their robes, and the burnt offerings Solomon made at the Temple of the LORD.

[5]She exclaimed to the king, "Everything I heard in my country about your achievements and wisdom is true! [6]I didn't believe it until I arrived here and saw it with my own eyes. Truly I had not heard the half of it! Your wisdom is far greater than what I was told. [7]How happy these people must be! What a privilege for your officials to stand here day after day, listening to your wisdom! [8]The LORD your God is great indeed! He delights in you and has placed you on the throne to rule for him. Because God loves Israel so much and desires this kingdom to last forever, he has made you king so you can rule with justice and righteousness."

[9]Then she gave the king a gift of nine thousand pounds* of gold, and great quantities of spices and precious jewels. Never before had there been spices as fine as those the queen of Sheba gave to Solomon.

[10](When the crews of Hiram and Solomon brought gold from Ophir, they also brought rich cargoes of almug wood* and precious jewels. [11]The king used the almug wood to make steps* for the Temple of the LORD and the royal palace, and to construct harps and lyres for the musicians. Never before had there been such beautiful instruments in Judah.)

[12]King Solomon gave the queen of Sheba whatever she asked for—gifts of greater value than the gifts she had given him. Then she and all her attendants left and returned to their own land.

Solomon's Wealth and Splendor

[13]Each year Solomon received about 25 tons* of gold. [14]This did not include the additional revenue he received from merchants and traders. All the kings of Arabia and the governors of the land also brought gold and silver to Solomon.

[15]King Solomon made two hundred large shields of hammered gold, each containing over 15 pounds* of gold. [16]He also made three hundred smaller shields of hammered gold, each containing about 7½ pounds* of gold. The king placed these shields in the Palace of the Forest of Lebanon.

[17]Then the king made a huge ivory throne

8:13 Or *Festival of Weeks.*   **8:17a** As in Greek version (see also 2 Kgs 14:22; 16:6); Hebrew reads *Eloth.*   **8:17b** Hebrew *the sea.*
8:18 Hebrew *450 talents* [15.3 metric tons].   **9:9** Hebrew *120 talents* [4 metric tons].   **9:10** Hebrew *algum wood* (also in 9:11); compare parallel text at 1 Kgs 10:11-12.   **9:11** Or *gateways.* The meaning of the Hebrew is uncertain.   **9:13** Hebrew *666 talents* [23 metric tons].
9:15 Hebrew *600 shekels* [6.8 kilograms].   **9:16** Hebrew *300 shekels* [3.4 kilograms].

and overlaid it with pure gold. [18]The throne had six steps, and there was a footstool of gold attached to it. On both sides of the seat were armrests, with the figure of a lion standing on each side of the throne. [19]Solomon made twelve other lion figures, one standing on each end of each of the six steps. No other throne in all the world could be compared with it! [20]All of King Solomon's drinking cups were solid gold, as were all the utensils in the Palace of the Forest of Lebanon. They were not made of silver because silver was considered of little value in Solomon's day! [21]The king had a fleet of trading ships* manned by the sailors sent by Hiram.* Once every three years the ships returned, loaded down with gold, silver, ivory, apes, and peacocks.*

[22]So King Solomon became richer and wiser than any other king in all the earth. [23]Kings from every nation came to visit him and to hear the wisdom God had given him. [24]Year after year, everyone who came to visit him brought him gifts of silver and gold, clothing, weapons, spices, horses, and mules. [25]Solomon had four thousand stalls for his chariot horses and twelve thousand horses.* He stationed many of them in the chariot cities, and some near him in Jerusalem. [26]He ruled over all the kings from the Euphrates River* to the land of the Philistines and the border of Egypt. [27]The king made silver as plentiful in Jerusalem as stones. And valuable cedarwood was as common as the sycamore wood that grows in the foothills of Judah.* [28]Solomon's horses were imported from Egypt* and many other countries.

Summary of Solomon's Reign

[29]The rest of the events of Solomon's reign, from beginning to end, are recorded in *The Record of Nathan the Prophet* and in *The Prophecy of Ahijah from Shiloh*, and also in *The Visions of Iddo the Seer*, concerning Jeroboam son of Nebat. [30]Solomon ruled in Jerusalem over all Israel for forty years. [31]When he died, he was buried in the city of his father, David. Then his son Rehoboam became the next king.

CHAPTER **10**

The Northern Tribes Revolt

Rehoboam went to Shechem, where all Israel had gathered to make him king. [2]When Jeroboam son of Nebat heard of Solomon's death, he returned from Egypt, for he had fled to Egypt to escape from King Solomon. [3]The leaders of Israel sent for Jeroboam, and he and all Israel went together to speak with Rehoboam. [4]"Your father was a hard master," they said. "Lighten the harsh labor demands and heavy taxes that your father imposed on us. Then we will be your loyal subjects."

[5]Rehoboam replied, "Come back in three days for my answer." So the people went away.

[6]Then King Rehoboam went to discuss the matter with the older men who had counseled his father, Solomon. "What is your advice?" he asked. "How should I answer these people?"

[7]The older counselors replied, "If you are good to the people and show them kindness and do your best to please them, they will always be your loyal subjects."

[8]But Rehoboam rejected the advice of the elders and instead asked the opinion of the young men who had grown up with him and who were now his advisers. [9]"What is your advice?" he asked them. "How should I answer these people who want me to lighten the burdens imposed by my father?"

[10]The young men replied, "This is what you should tell those complainers: 'My little finger is thicker than my father's waist—if you think he was hard on you, just wait and see what I'll be like! [11]Yes, my father was harsh on you, but I'll be even harsher! My father used whips on you, but I'll use scorpions!'"

[12]Three days later, Jeroboam and all the people returned to hear Rehoboam's decision, just as the king had requested. [13]But Rehoboam spoke harshly to them, for he rejected the advice of the older counselors [14]and followed the counsel of his younger advisers. He told the people, "My father was harsh on you, but I'll be even harsher! My father used whips on you, but I'll use scorpions!" [15]So the king paid no attention to the people's demands. This turn of events was the will of God, for it fulfilled the prophecy of the LORD spoken to Jeroboam son of Nebat by the prophet Ahijah from Shiloh.

[16]When all Israel realized that the king had rejected their request, they shouted, "Down with David and his dynasty! We have no share in Jesse's son! Let's go home, Israel! Look out for your own house, O David!" So all Israel returned home. [17]But Rehoboam continued to rule over the Israelites who lived in the towns of Judah.

[18]King Rehoboam sent Adoniram,* who was

in charge of the labor force, to restore order, but the Israelites stoned him to death. When this news reached King Rehoboam, he quickly jumped into his chariot and fled to Jerusalem. ¹⁹The northern tribes of Israel have refused to be ruled by a descendant of David to this day.

CHAPTER 11
Shemaiah's Prophecy
When Rehoboam arrived at Jerusalem, he mobilized the armies of Judah and Benjamin— 180,000 select troops—to fight against the army of Israel and to restore the kingdom to himself. ²But the LORD said to Shemaiah, the man of God, ³"Say to Rehoboam son of Solomon, king of Judah, and to all the Israelites in Judah and Benjamin: ⁴'This is what the LORD says: Do not fight against your relatives. Go back home, for what has happened is my doing!'" So they obeyed the message of the LORD and did not fight against Jeroboam.

Rehoboam Fortifies Judah
⁵Rehoboam remained in Jerusalem and fortified various cities for the defense of Judah. ⁶He built up Bethlehem, Etam, Tekoa, ⁷Beth-zur, Soco, Adullam, ⁸Gath, Mareshah, Ziph, ⁹Adoraim, Lachish, Azekah, ¹⁰Zorah, Aijalon, and Hebron. These became the fortified cities of Judah and Benjamin. ¹¹Rehoboam strengthened their defenses and stationed commanders in them. In each of them, he stored supplies of food, olive oil, and wine. ¹²He also put shields and spears in these towns as a further safety measure. So only Judah and Benjamin remained under his control.

¹³But all the priests and Levites living among the northern tribes of Israel sided with Rehoboam. ¹⁴The Levites even abandoned their homes and property and moved to Judah and Jerusalem, because Jeroboam and his sons would not allow them to serve the LORD as priests. ¹⁵Jeroboam appointed his own priests to serve at the pagan shrines, where they worshiped the goat and calf idols he had made. ¹⁶From all over Israel, those who sincerely wanted to worship the LORD, the God of Israel, followed the Levites to Jerusalem, where they could offer sacrifices to the LORD, the God of their ancestors. ¹⁷This strengthened the kingdom of Judah, and for three years they supported Rehoboam son of Solomon and earnestly sought to obey the LORD as they had done during the reigns of David and Solomon.

Rehoboam's Family
¹⁸Rehoboam married his cousin Mahalath, the daughter of David's son Jerimoth and of Abihail, the daughter of Eliab. (Eliab was one of David's brothers, a son of Jesse.) ¹⁹Mahalath had three sons—Jeush, Shemariah, and Zaham.

²⁰Later Rehoboam married another cousin, Maacah, the daughter of Absalom. Maacah gave birth to Abijah, Attai, Ziza, and Shelomith. ²¹Rehoboam loved Maacah more than any of his other wives and concubines. In all, he had eighteen wives and sixty concubines, and they gave birth to twenty-eight sons and sixty daughters. ²²Rehoboam made Maacah's son Abijah chief among the princes, making it clear that he would be the next king. ²³Rehoboam also wisely gave responsibilities to his other sons and stationed them in the fortified cities throughout the land of Judah and Benjamin. He provided them with generous provisions and arranged for each of them to have several wives.

CHAPTER 12
Egypt Invades Judah
But when Rehoboam was firmly established and strong, he abandoned the law of the LORD, and all Israel followed him in this sin. ²Because they were unfaithful to the LORD, King Shishak of Egypt attacked Jerusalem in the fifth year of King Rehoboam's reign. ³He came with twelve hundred chariots, sixty thousand horsemen, and a countless army of foot soldiers, including Libyans, Sukkites, and Ethiopians.* ⁴Shishak conquered Judah's fortified cities and then advanced to attack Jerusalem.

⁵The prophet Shemaiah then met with Rehoboam and Judah's leaders, who had all fled to Jerusalem because of Shishak. Shemaiah told them, "This is what the LORD says: You have abandoned me, so I am abandoning you to Shishak."

⁶The king and the leaders of Israel humbled themselves and said, "The LORD is right in doing this to us!"

⁷When the LORD saw their change of heart, he gave this message to Shemaiah: "Since the people have humbled themselves, I will not completely destroy them and will soon give them some relief. I will not use Shishak to pour out my anger on Jerusalem. ⁸But they will become his subjects, so that they can learn how much better it is to serve me than to serve earthly rulers."

⁹So King Shishak of Egypt came to Jerusalem and took away all the treasures of the Temple of

12:3 Hebrew *and Cushites.*

the LORD and of the royal palace, including all of Solomon's gold shields. ¹⁰King Rehoboam later replaced them with bronze shields and entrusted them to the care of the captain of his bodyguard. ¹¹Whenever the king went to the Temple of the LORD, the guards would carry them along and then return them to the guardroom. ¹²Because Rehoboam humbled himself, the LORD's anger was turned aside, and he did not destroy him completely. And there was still goodness in the land of Judah.

Summary of Rehoboam's Reign
¹³King Rehoboam firmly established himself in Jerusalem and continued to rule. He was forty-one years old when he became king, and he reigned seventeen years in Jerusalem, the city the LORD had chosen from among all the tribes of Israel as the place to honor his name. Rehoboam's mother was Naamah, a woman from Ammon. ¹⁴But he was an evil king, for he did not seek the LORD with all his heart.

¹⁵The rest of the events of Rehoboam's reign, from beginning to end, are recorded in *The Record of Shemaiah the Prophet* and in *The Record of Iddo the Seer*, which are part of the genealogical record. Rehoboam and Jeroboam were continually at war with each other. ¹⁶When Rehoboam died, he was buried in the City of David. Then his son Abijah became the next king.

CHAPTER **13**
Abijah's War with Jeroboam
Abijah began to rule over Judah in the eighteenth year of Jeroboam's reign in Israel. ²He reigned in Jerusalem three years. His mother was Maacah,* a daughter of Uriel from Gibeah.

Then war broke out between Abijah and Jeroboam. ³Judah, led by King Abijah, fielded 400,000 seasoned warriors, while Jeroboam mustered 800,000 courageous men from Israel. ⁴When the army of Judah arrived in the hill country of Ephraim, Abijah stood on Mount Zemaraim and shouted to Jeroboam and the Israelite army: "Listen to me! ⁵Don't you realize that the LORD, the God of Israel, made an unbreakable covenant* with David, giving him and his descendants the throne of Israel forever? ⁶Yet Jeroboam son of Nebat, who was a mere servant of David's son Solomon, became a traitor to his master. ⁷Then a whole gang of scoundrels joined him, defying Solomon's son Rehoboam when he was young and inexperienced and could not stand

up to them. ⁸Do you really think you can stand against the kingdom of the LORD that is led by the descendants of David? Your army is vast indeed, but with you are those gold calves that Jeroboam made as your gods! ⁹And you have chased away the priests of the LORD and the Levites and have appointed your own priests, just like the pagan nations. You let anyone become a priest these days! Whoever comes to be dedicated with a young bull and seven rams can become a priest of these so-called gods of yours!

¹⁰"But as for us, the LORD is our God, and we have not abandoned him. Only the descendants of Aaron serve the LORD as priests, and the Levites alone may help them in their work. ¹¹They present burnt offerings and fragrant incense to the LORD every morning and evening. They place the Bread of the Presence on the holy table, and they light the gold lampstand every evening. We are following the instructions of the LORD our God, but you have abandoned him. ¹²So you see, God is with us. He is our leader. His priests blow their trumpets and lead us into battle against you. O people of Israel, do not fight against the LORD, the God of your ancestors, for you will not succeed!"

¹³Meanwhile, Jeroboam had secretly sent part of his army around behind the men of Judah to ambush them. ¹⁴When Judah realized that they were being attacked from the front and the rear, they cried out to the LORD for help. Then the priests blew the trumpets, ¹⁵and the men of Judah began to shout. At the sound of their battle cry, God defeated Jeroboam and the Israelite army and routed them before Abijah and the army of Judah. ¹⁶The Israelite army fled from Judah, and God handed them over to Judah in defeat. ¹⁷Abijah and his army inflicted heavy losses on them; there were 500,000 casualties among Israel's finest troops that day. ¹⁸So Judah defeated Israel because they trusted in the LORD, the God of their ancestors. ¹⁹Abijah and his army pursued Jeroboam's troops and captured some of his towns, including Bethel, Jeshanah, and Ephron, along with their surrounding villages.

²⁰So Jeroboam of Israel never regained his power during Abijah's lifetime, and finally the LORD struck him down and he died. ²¹By contrast, Abijah of Judah grew more and more powerful. He married fourteen wives and had twenty-two sons and sixteen daughters. ²²The rest of the events of Abijah's reign, including his words and deeds, are recorded in *The Commentary of Iddo the Prophet.*

13:2 As in most Greek manuscripts and Syriac version (see also 2 Chr 11:20-21; 1 Kgs 15:2); Hebrew reads *Micaiah.* **13:5** Hebrew *a covenant of salt.*

CHAPTER 14
Early Years of Asa's Reign

When Abijah died, he was buried in the City of David. Then his son Asa became the next king. There was peace in the land for ten years, ²for Asa did what was pleasing and good in the sight of the LORD his God. ³He removed the pagan altars and the shrines. He smashed the sacred pillars and cut down the Asherah poles. ⁴He commanded the people of Judah to seek the LORD, the God of their ancestors, and to obey his law and his commands. ⁵Asa also removed the pagan shrines, as well as the incense altars from every one of Judah's towns. So Asa's kingdom enjoyed a period of peace. ⁶During those peaceful years, he was able to build up the fortified cities throughout Judah. No one tried to make war against him at this time, for the LORD was giving him rest from his enemies. ⁷Asa told the people of Judah, "Let us build towns and fortify them with walls, towers, gates, and bars. The land is ours because we sought the LORD our God, and he has given us rest from our enemies." So they went ahead with these projects and brought them to completion.

⁸King Asa had an army of 300,000 warriors from the tribe of Judah, armed with large shields and spears. He also had an army of 280,000 warriors from the tribe of Benjamin, armed with small shields and bows. Both armies were composed of courageous fighting men.

⁹Once an Ethiopian* named Zerah attacked Judah with an army of a million men* and three hundred chariots. They advanced to the city of Mareshah, ¹⁰so Asa deployed his armies for battle in the valley north of Mareshah.* ¹¹Then Asa cried out to the LORD his God, "O LORD, no one but you can help the powerless against the mighty! Help us, O LORD our God, for we trust in you alone. It is in your name that we have come against this vast horde. O LORD, you are our God; do not let mere men prevail against you!"

¹²So the LORD defeated the Ethiopians* in the presence of Asa and the army of Judah, and the enemy fled. ¹³Asa and his army pursued them as far as Gerar, and so many Ethiopians fell that they were unable to rally. They were destroyed by the LORD and his army, and the army of Judah carried off vast quantities of plunder. ¹⁴While they were at Gerar, they attacked all the towns in that area, and terror from the LORD came upon the people there. As a result, vast quantities of plunder were taken from these towns, too.

¹⁵They also attacked the camps of herdsmen and captured many sheep and camels before finally returning to Jerusalem.

CHAPTER 15
Asa's Religious Reforms

Then the Spirit of God came upon Azariah son of Oded, ²and he went out to meet King Asa as he was returning from the battle. "Listen to me, Asa!" he shouted. "Listen, all you people of Judah and Benjamin! The LORD will stay with you as long as you stay with him! Whenever you seek him, you will find him. But if you abandon him, he will abandon you. ³For a long time, Israel was without the true God, without a priest to teach them, and without God's law. ⁴But whenever you were in distress and turned to the LORD, the God of Israel, and sought him out, you found him. ⁵During those dark times, it was not safe to travel. Problems troubled the nation on every hand. ⁶Nation fought against nation, and city against city, for God was troubling you with every kind of problem. ⁷And now, you men of Judah, be strong and courageous, for your work will be rewarded."

⁸When Asa heard this message from Azariah the prophet,* he took courage and removed all the idols in the land of Judah and Benjamin and in the towns he had captured in the hill country of Ephraim. And he repaired the altar of the LORD, which stood in front of the foyer of the LORD's Temple.

⁹Then Asa called together all the people of Judah and Benjamin, along with the people of Ephraim, Manasseh, and Simeon who had settled among them. Many had moved to Judah during Asa's reign when they saw that the LORD his God was with him. ¹⁰The people gathered at Jerusalem in late spring,* during the fifteenth year of Asa's reign. ¹¹On that day they sacrificed to the LORD some of the animals they had taken as plunder in the battle—seven hundred oxen and seven thousand sheep and goats. ¹²Then they entered into a covenant to seek the LORD, the God of their ancestors, with all their heart and soul. ¹³They agreed that anyone who refused to seek the LORD, the God of Israel, would be put to death—whether young or old, man or woman. ¹⁴They shouted out their oath of loyalty to the LORD with trumpets blaring and horns sounding. ¹⁵All were happy about this covenant, for they had entered into it with all their hearts.

14:9a Hebrew *a Cushite.* 14:9b Or *an army of thousands and thousands;* Hebrew reads *an army of a thousand thousands.* 14:10 Or *in the Zephathah Valley near Mareshah.* 14:12 Hebrew *Cushites;* also in 14:13. 15:8 As in Syriac version and Latin Vulgate (see also 15:1); Hebrew reads *from Oded the prophet.* 15:10 Hebrew *in the third month.* This month of the Hebrew lunar calendar usually occurs in May and June.

Eagerly they sought after God, and they found him. And the LORD gave them rest from their enemies on every side.

16King Asa even deposed his grandmother Maacah from her position as queen mother because she had made an obscene Asherah pole. He cut down the pole, broke it up, and burned it in the Kidron Valley. 17Although the pagan shrines were not completely removed from Israel, Asa remained fully committed to the LORD throughout his life. 18He brought into the Temple of God the silver and gold and the utensils that he and his father had dedicated. 19So there was no more war until the thirty-fifth year of Asa's reign.

CHAPTER 16
Final Years of Asa's Reign
In the thirty-sixth year of Asa's reign, King Baasha of Israel invaded Judah and fortified Ramah in order to prevent anyone from entering or leaving King Asa's territory in Judah. 2Asa responded by taking the silver and gold from the treasuries of the LORD's Temple and from the royal palace. He sent it to King Ben-hadad of Aram, who was ruling in Damascus, along with this message:

3"Let us renew the treaty that existed between your father and my father. See, I am sending you a gift of silver and gold. Break your treaty with King Baasha of Israel so that he will leave me alone."

4Ben-hadad agreed to King Asa's request and sent his armies to attack Israel. They conquered the towns of Ijon, Dan, Abel-beth-maacah,* and all the store cities in Naphtali. 5As soon as Baasha of Israel heard what was happening, he abandoned his project of fortifying Ramah. 6Then King Asa called out all the men of Judah to carry away the building stones and timbers that Baasha had been using to fortify Ramah. Asa used these materials to fortify the towns of Geba and Mizpah.

7At that time Hanani the seer came to King Asa and told him, "Because you have put your trust in the king of Aram instead of in the LORD your God, you missed your chance to destroy the army of the king of Aram. 8Don't you remember what happened to the Ethiopians* and Libyans and their vast army, with all of their chariots and horsemen*? At that time you relied on the LORD, and he handed them all over to you. 9The eyes

of the LORD search the whole earth in order to strengthen those whose hearts are fully committed to him. What a fool you have been! From now on, you will be at war." 10Asa became so angry with Hanani for saying this that he threw him into prison. At that time, Asa also began to oppress some of his people.

Summary of Asa's Reign
11The rest of the events of Asa's reign, from beginning to end, are recorded in *The Book of the Kings of Judah and Israel.* 12In the thirty-ninth year of his reign, Asa developed a serious foot disease. Even when the disease became life threatening, he did not seek the LORD's help but sought help only from his physicians. 13So he died in the forty-first year of his reign. 14He was buried in the tomb he had carved out for himself in the City of David. He was laid on a bed perfumed with sweet spices and ointments, and at his funeral the people built a huge fire in his honor.

CHAPTER 17
Jehoshaphat Rules in Judah
Then Jehoshaphat, Asa's son, became the next king. He strengthened Judah to stand against any attack from Israel. 2He stationed troops in all the fortified cities of Judah, and he assigned additional garrisons to the land of Judah and to the towns of Ephraim that his father, Asa, had conquered.

3The LORD was with Jehoshaphat because he followed the example of his father's early years* and did not worship the images of Baal. 4He sought his father's God and obeyed his commands instead of following the practices of the kingdom of Israel. 5So the LORD established Jehoshaphat's control over the kingdom of Judah. All the people of Judah brought gifts to Jehoshaphat, so he became very wealthy and highly esteemed. 6He was committed to the ways of the LORD. He knocked down the pagan shrines and destroyed the Asherah poles.

7In the third year of his reign, Jehoshaphat sent out his officials to teach in all the towns of Judah. These officials included Ben-hail, Obadiah, Zechariah, Nethanel, and Micaiah. 8He sent Levites along with them, including Shemaiah, Nethaniah, Zebadiah, Asahel, Shemiramoth, Jehonathan, Adonijah, Tobijah, and Tob-adonijah. He also sent out the priests, Elishama and Jehoram. 9They took copies of the

16:4 As in parallel text at 1 Kgs 15:20; Hebrew reads *Abel-maim*, another name for Abel-beth-maacah.   16:8a Hebrew *Cushites*.   16:8b Or *and charioteers*.   17:3 Some Hebrew manuscripts read *the example of his father, David*.

Book of the Law of the LORD and traveled around through all the towns of Judah, teaching the people.

10Then the fear of the LORD fell over all the surrounding kingdoms so that none of them declared war on Jehoshaphat. 11Some of the Philistines brought him gifts and silver as tribute, and the Arabs brought seventy-seven hundred rams and seventy-seven hundred male goats.

12So Jehoshaphat became more and more powerful and built fortresses and store cities throughout Judah. 13He stored numerous supplies in Judah's towns and stationed an army of seasoned troops at Jerusalem. 14His army was enrolled according to ancestral clans.

From Judah, there were 300,000 troops organized in units of one thousand, under the command of Adnah. 15Next in command was Jehohanan, who commanded 280,000 troops. 16Next was Amasiah son of Zicri, who volunteered for the LORD's service, with 200,000 troops under his command.

17From Benjamin, there were 200,000 troops equipped with bows and shields. They were under the command of Eliada, a veteran soldier. 18Next in command was Jehozabad, who commanded 180,000 armed men.

19These were the troops stationed in Jerusalem to serve the king, besides those Jehoshaphat stationed in the fortified cities throughout Judah.

CHAPTER **18**
Jehoshaphat and Ahab
Now Jehoshaphat enjoyed great riches and high esteem, and he arranged for his son to marry the daughter of King Ahab of Israel. 2A few years later, he went to Samaria to visit Ahab, who prepared a great banquet for him and his officials. They butchered great numbers of sheep and oxen for the feast. Then Ahab enticed Jehoshaphat to join forces with him to attack Ramoth-gilead. 3"Will you join me in fighting against Ramoth-gilead?" Ahab asked.

And Jehoshaphat replied, "Why, of course! You and I are brothers, and my troops are yours to command. We will certainly join you in battle." 4Then Jehoshaphat added, "But first let's find out what the LORD says."

5So King Ahab summoned his prophets, four hundred of them, and asked them, "Should we go to war against Ramoth-gilead or not?"

They all replied, "Go ahead, for God will give you a great victory!"

6But Jehoshaphat asked, "Isn't there a prophet of the LORD around, too? I would like to ask him the same question."

7King Ahab replied, "There is still one prophet of the LORD, but I hate him. He never prophesies anything but bad news for me! His name is Micaiah son of Imlah."

"You shouldn't talk like that," Jehoshaphat said. "Let's hear what he has to say."

8So the king of Israel called one of his officials and said, "Quick! Go and get Micaiah son of Imlah."

Micaiah Prophesies against Ahab
9King Ahab of Israel and King Jehoshaphat of Judah, dressed in their royal robes, were sitting on thrones at the threshing floor near the gate of Samaria. All of Ahab's prophets were prophesying there in front of them. 10One of them, Zedekiah son of Kenaanah, made some iron horns and proclaimed, "This is what the LORD says: With these horns you will gore the Arameans to death!"

11All the other prophets agreed. "Yes," they said, "go up to Ramoth-gilead and be victorious. The LORD will give you a glorious victory!"

12Meanwhile, the messenger who went to get Micaiah said to him, "Look, all the prophets are

OFF AND RUNNING

Watch the Legacy You Leave   Read 2 CHRONICLES 17:3-6

Never underestimate the influence of your faith upon the lives of your children. As this passage illustrates, the influence of your faith is especially important in your child's early, formative years. Even though Jehoshaphat's father, Asa, had chosen to disobey God later in life, Jehoshaphat remembered his father's faith. And Asa's faith had a positive effect on the way Jehoshaphat lived his life.

promising victory for the king. Be sure that you agree with them and promise success."

¹³But Micaiah replied, "As surely as the LORD lives, I will say only what my God tells me to say."

¹⁴When Micaiah arrived before the king, Ahab asked him, "Micaiah, should we go to war against Ramoth-gilead or not?"

And Micaiah replied, "Go right ahead! It will be a glorious victory!"

¹⁵But the king replied sharply, "How many times must I demand that you speak only the truth when you speak for the LORD?"

¹⁶So Micaiah told him, "In a vision I saw all Israel scattered on the mountains, like sheep without a shepherd. And the LORD said, 'Their master has been killed. Send them home in peace.'"

¹⁷"Didn't I tell you?" the king of Israel said to Jehoshaphat. "He does it every time. He never prophesies anything but bad news for me."

¹⁸Then Micaiah continued, "Listen to what the LORD says! I saw the LORD sitting on his throne with all the armies of heaven on his right and on his left. ¹⁹And the LORD said, 'Who can entice King Ahab of Israel to go into battle against Ramoth-gilead so that he can be killed there?' There were many suggestions, ²⁰until finally a spirit approached the LORD and said, 'I can do it!'

" 'How will you do this?' the LORD asked.

²¹"And the spirit replied, 'I will go out and inspire all Ahab's prophets to speak lies.'

" 'You will succeed,' said the LORD. 'Go ahead and do it.'

²²"So you see, the LORD has put a lying spirit in the mouths of your prophets. For the LORD has determined disaster for you."

²³Then Zedekiah son of Kenaanah walked up to Micaiah and slapped him across the face. "When did the Spirit of the LORD leave me to speak to you?" he demanded.

²⁴And Micaiah replied, "You will find out soon enough, when you find yourself hiding in some secret room!"

²⁵King Ahab of Israel then ordered, "Arrest Micaiah and take him back to Amon, the governor of the city, and to my son Joash. ²⁶Give them this order from the king: 'Put this man in prison, and feed him nothing but bread and water until I return safely from the battle!'"

²⁷But Micaiah replied, "If you return safely, the LORD has not spoken through me!" Then he added to those standing around, "Take note of what I have said."

The Death of Ahab

²⁸So the king of Israel and King Jehoshaphat of Judah led their armies against Ramoth-gilead. ²⁹Now King Ahab said to Jehoshaphat, "As we go into battle, I will disguise myself so no one will recognize me, but you wear your royal robes." So Ahab disguised himself, and they went into battle.

³⁰Now the king of Aram had issued these orders to his charioteers: "Attack only the king of Israel!" ³¹So when the Aramean charioteers saw Jehoshaphat in his royal robes, they went after him. "There is the king of Israel!" they shouted. But Jehoshaphat cried out to the LORD to save him, and God helped him by turning the attack away from him. ³²As soon as the charioteers realized he was not the king of Israel, they stopped chasing him.

³³An Aramean soldier, however, randomly shot an arrow at the Israelite troops, and the arrow hit the king of Israel between the joints of his armor. "Get me out of here!" Ahab groaned to the driver of his chariot. "I have been badly wounded!" ³⁴The battle raged all that day, and Ahab propped himself up in his chariot facing the Arameans until evening. Then, just as the sun was setting, he died.

CHAPTER 19

Jehoshaphat Appoints Judges

When King Jehoshaphat of Judah arrived safely home to Jerusalem, ²Jehu son of Hanani the seer went out to meet him. "Why should you help the

---

Take a moment to reevaluate your Christian witness in the home. What sort of books line your bookshelves? How often do you spend time in Christian activities versus watching television? What sort of music do you listen to? How do you go about making decisions? How do you communicate with your spouse? Remember, little eyes are watching, little ears are listening, and little lives will often imitate what you do. What sort of legacy are you leaving behind?

For the next note on "Children," turn to p. 560.

wicked and love those who hate the LORD?" he asked the king. "What you have done has brought the LORD's anger against you. ³There is some good in you, however, for you have removed the Asherah poles throughout the land, and you have committed yourself to seeking God."

⁴So Jehoshaphat lived in Jerusalem, but he went out among the people, traveling from Beersheba to the hill country of Ephraim, encouraging the people to return to the LORD, the God of their ancestors. ⁵He appointed judges throughout the nation in all the fortified cities, ⁶and he gave them these instructions: "Always think carefully before pronouncing judgment. Remember that you do not judge to please people but to please the LORD. He will be with you when you render the verdict in each case that comes before you. ⁷Fear the LORD and judge with care, for the LORD our God does not tolerate perverted justice, partiality, or the taking of bribes."

⁸Jehoshaphat appointed some of the Levites and priests and clan leaders in Israel to serve as judges in Jerusalem for cases concerning both the law of the LORD and civil disputes. ⁹These were his instructions to them: "You must always act in the fear of the LORD, with integrity and with undivided hearts. ¹⁰Whenever a case comes to you from fellow citizens in an outlying town, whether a murder case or some other violation of God's instructions, commands, laws, or regulations, you must warn them not to sin against the LORD, so that his anger will not come against you and them. Do this and you will not be guilty. ¹¹Amariah the high priest will have final say in all cases concerning the LORD. Zebadiah son of Ishmael, a leader from the tribe of Judah, will have final say in all civil cases. The Levites will assist you in making sure that justice is served. Take courage as you fulfill your duties, and may the LORD be with those who do what is right."

CHAPTER **20**

War with Moab, Ammon, and Edom

After this, the armies of the Moabites, Ammonites, and some of the Meunites* declared war on Jehoshaphat. ²Messengers came and told Jehoshaphat, "A vast army from Edom* is marching against you from beyond the Dead Sea.* They are already at Hazazon-tamar." (This was another name for Engedi.) ³Jehoshaphat was alarmed by this news and sought the LORD for guidance. He also gave orders that everyone throughout Judah should observe a fast. ⁴So people from all the towns of Judah came to Jerusalem to seek the LORD.

⁵Jehoshaphat stood before the people of Judah and Jerusalem in front of the new courtyard at the Temple of the LORD. ⁶He prayed, "O LORD, God of our ancestors, you alone are the God who is in heaven. You are ruler of all the kingdoms of the earth. You are powerful and mighty; no one can stand against you! ⁷O our God, did you not drive out those who lived in this land when your people arrived? And did you not give this land forever to the descendants of your friend Abraham? ⁸Your people settled here and built this Temple for you. ⁹They said, 'Whenever we are faced with any calamity such as war, disease, or famine, we can come to stand in your presence before this Temple where your name is honored. We can cry out to you to save us, and you will hear us and rescue us.'

¹⁰"And now see what the armies of Ammon, Moab, and Mount Seir are doing. You would not let our ancestors invade those nations when Israel left Egypt, so they went around them and did not destroy them. ¹¹Now see how they reward us! For they have come to throw us out of your land, which you gave us as an inheritance. ¹²O our God, won't you stop them? We are powerless against this mighty army that is about to attack us. We do not know what to do, but we are looking to you for help."

¹³As all the men of Judah stood before the LORD with their little ones, wives, and children, ¹⁴the Spirit of the LORD came upon one of the men standing there. His name was Jahaziel son of Zechariah, son of Benaiah, son of Jeiel, son of Mattaniah, a Levite who was a descendant of Asaph. ¹⁵He said, "Listen, King Jehoshaphat! Listen, all you people of Judah and Jerusalem! This is what the LORD says: Do not be afraid! Don't be discouraged by this mighty army, for the battle is not yours, but God's. ¹⁶Tomorrow, march out against them. You will find them coming up through the ascent of Ziz at the end of the valley that opens into the wilderness of Jeruel. ¹⁷But you will not even need to fight. Take your positions; then stand still and watch the LORD's victory. He is with you, O people of Judah and Jerusalem. Do not be afraid or discouraged. Go out there tomorrow, for the LORD is with you!"

¹⁸Then King Jehoshaphat bowed down with his face to the ground. And all the people of Judah and Jerusalem did the same, worshiping the LORD. ¹⁹Then the Levites from the clans of

---

20:1 As in some Greek manuscripts (see also 26:7); Hebrew reads *Ammonites.* 20:2a As in one Hebrew manuscript; most Hebrew manuscripts and ancient versions read *Aram.* 20:2b Hebrew *the sea.*

Kohath and Korah stood to praise the LORD, the God of Israel, with a very loud shout. ²⁰Early the next morning the army of Judah went out into the wilderness of Tekoa. On the way Jehoshaphat stopped and said, "Listen to me, all you people of Judah and Jerusalem! Believe in the LORD your God, and you will be able to stand firm. Believe in his prophets, and you will succeed." ²¹After consulting the leaders of the people, the king appointed singers to walk ahead of the army, singing to the LORD and praising him for his holy splendor. This is what they sang:

"Give thanks to the LORD;
his faithful love endures forever!"

²²At the moment they began to sing and give praise, the LORD caused the armies of Ammon, Moab, and Mount Seir to start fighting among themselves. ²³The armies of Moab and Ammon turned against their allies from Mount Seir and killed every one of them. After they had finished off the army of Seir, they turned on each other.

²⁴So when the army of Judah arrived at the lookout point in the wilderness, there were dead bodies lying on the ground for as far as they could see. Not a single one of the enemy had escaped. ²⁵King Jehoshaphat and his men went out to gather the plunder. They found vast amounts of equipment, clothing,* and other valuables—more than they could carry. There was so much plunder that it took them three days just to collect it all! ²⁶On the fourth day they gathered in the Valley of Blessing,* which got its name that day because the people praised and thanked the LORD there. It is still called the Valley of Blessing today.

²⁷Then they returned to Jerusalem, with Jehoshaphat leading them, full of joy that the LORD had given them victory over their enemies. ²⁸They marched into Jerusalem to the music of harps, lyres, and trumpets and proceeded to the Temple of the LORD. ²⁹When the surrounding kingdoms heard that the LORD himself had fought against the enemies of Israel, the fear of God came over them. ³⁰So Jehoshaphat's kingdom was at peace, for his God had given him rest on every side.

Summary of Jehoshaphat's Reign

³¹So Jehoshaphat ruled over the land of Judah. He was thirty-five years old when he became king, and he reigned in Jerusalem twenty-five

years. His mother was Azubah, the daughter of Shilhi. ³²Jehoshaphat was a good king, following the ways of his father, Asa. He did what was pleasing in the LORD's sight. ³³During his reign, however, he failed to remove all the pagan shrines, and the people never fully committed themselves to following the God of their ancestors. ³⁴The rest of the events of Jehoshaphat's reign, from beginning to end, are recorded in *The Record of Jehu Son of Hanani*, which is included in *The Book of the Kings of Israel.*

³⁵But near the end of his life, King Jehoshaphat of Judah made an alliance with King Ahaziah of Israel, who was a very wicked man.* ³⁶Together they built a fleet of trading ships* at the port of Ezion-geber. ³⁷Then Eliezer son of Dodavahu from Mareshah prophesied against Jehoshaphat. He said, "Because you have allied yourself with King Ahaziah, the LORD will destroy your work." So the ships met with disaster and never put out to sea.*

CHAPTER **21**
Jehoram Rules in Judah

When Jehoshaphat died, he was buried with his ancestors in the City of David. Then his son Jehoram became the next king. ²Jehoram's brothers— the other sons of Jehoshaphat—were Azariah, Jehiel, Zechariah, Azariahu, Michael, and Shephatiah. ³Their father had given each of them valuable gifts of silver, gold, and costly items, and also the ownership of some of Judah's fortified cities. However, Jehoram became king because he was the oldest. ⁴But when Jehoram had become solidly established as king, he killed all his brothers and some of the other leaders of Israel.

⁵Jehoram was thirty-two years old when he became king, and he reigned in Jerusalem eight years. ⁶But Jehoram followed the example of the kings of Israel and was as wicked as King Ahab, for he had married one of Ahab's daughters. So Jehoram did what was evil in the LORD's sight. ⁷But the LORD was not willing to destroy David's dynasty, for he had made a covenant with David and promised that his descendants would continue to rule forever.*

⁸During Jehoram's reign, the Edomites revolted against Judah and crowned their own king. ⁹So Jehoram went to attack Edom with his full army and all his chariots. The Edomites surrounded him and his charioteers, but he escaped

---

20:25 As in some Hebrew manuscripts and Latin Vulgate; most Hebrew manuscripts read *corpses.* **20:26** Hebrew *valley of Beracah.*
20:35 Or *who made him do what was wrong.* **20:36** Hebrew *fleet of ships that could go to Tarshish.* **20:37** Hebrew *never set sail for Tarshish.*
21:7 Hebrew *promised to give a lamp to David and his descendants forever.*

at night under cover of darkness. ¹⁰Edom has been independent from Judah to this day. The town of Libnah revolted about that same time, because Jehoram had abandoned the LORD, the God of his ancestors. ¹¹He had built pagan shrines in the hill country of Judah and had led the people of Jerusalem and Judah to give themselves to pagan gods.

¹²Then Elijah the prophet wrote Jehoram this letter:

"This is what the LORD, the God of your ancestor David, says: You have not followed the good example of your father, Jehoshaphat, or your grandfather King Asa of Judah. ¹³Instead, you have been as evil as the kings of Israel. You have led the people of Jerusalem and Judah to worship idols, just as King Ahab did in Israel. And you have even killed your own brothers, men who were better than you. ¹⁴So now the LORD is about to strike you, your people, your children, your wives, and all that is yours with a heavy blow. ¹⁵You yourself will be stricken with a severe intestinal disease until it causes your bowels to come out."

¹⁶Then the LORD stirred up the Philistines and the Arabs, who lived near the Ethiopians,* to attack Jehoram. ¹⁷They marched against Judah, broke down its defenses, and carried away everything of value in the royal palace, including his sons and his wives. Only his youngest son, Ahaziah,* was spared.

¹⁸It was after this that the LORD struck Jehoram with the severe intestinal disease. ¹⁹In the course of time, at the end of two years, the disease caused his bowels to come out, and he died in agony. His people did not build a great fire to honor him at his funeral as they had done for his ancestors. ²⁰Jehoram was thirty-two years old when he became king, and he reigned in Jerusalem eight years. No one was sorry when he died. He was buried in the City of David, but not in the royal cemetery.

CHAPTER 22

Ahaziah Rules in Judah

Then the people of Jerusalem made Ahaziah, Jehoram's youngest son, their next king. The marauding bands of Arabs had killed all the older sons. So Ahaziah son of Jehoram reigned as king of Judah. ²Ahaziah was twenty-two* years old when he became king, and he reigned in Jerusalem one year. His mother was Athaliah, a granddaughter of King Omri of Israel. ³Ahaziah also followed the evil example of King Ahab's family, for his mother encouraged him in doing wrong. ⁴He did what was evil in the LORD's sight, just as Ahab had done. After the death of his father, members of Ahab's family became his advisers, and they led him to ruin.

⁵Following their evil advice, Ahaziah made an alliance with King Joram,* the son of King Ahab of Israel. They went out to fight King Hazael of Aram at Ramoth-gilead, and the Arameans wounded Joram in the battle. ⁶Joram returned to Jezreel to recover from his wounds, and King Ahaziah* of Judah went to Jezreel to visit him. ⁷But this turned out to be a fatal mistake, for God decided to punish Ahaziah. It was during this visit that Ahaziah went out with Joram to meet Jehu son of Nimshi, whom the LORD had appointed to end the dynasty of Ahab.

⁸While Jehu was executing judgment against the family of Ahab, he happened to meet some of Judah's officials and Ahaziah's relatives* who were attending Ahaziah. So Jehu killed them all. ⁹Then Jehu's men searched for Ahaziah, and they found him hiding in the city of Samaria. They brought him to Jehu, who killed him. Ahaziah was given a decent burial because the people said, "He was the grandson of Jehoshaphat—a man who sought the LORD with all his heart." None of the surviving members of Ahaziah's family was capable of ruling the kingdom.

Athaliah Rules in Judah

¹⁰When Athaliah, the mother of King Ahaziah of Judah, learned that her son was dead, she set out to destroy the rest of Judah's royal family. ¹¹But Ahaziah's sister Jehosheba,* the daughter of King Jehoram, took Ahaziah's infant son, Joash, and stole him away from among the rest of the king's children, who were about to be killed. She put Joash and his nurse in a bedroom. In this way, Jehosheba, the wife of Jehoiada the priest, hid the child so that Athaliah could not murder him. ¹²Joash remained hidden in the Temple of God for six years while Athaliah ruled over the land.

21:16 Hebrew *the Cushites.* 21:17 Hebrew *Jehoahaz,* a variant name for Ahaziah; compare 22:1. 22:2 As in some Greek manuscripts and Syriac version (see also 2 Kgs 8:26); Hebrew reads *forty-two.* 22:5 Hebrew *Jehoram,* a variant name for Joram; also in 22:6, 7. 22:6 Some Hebrew manuscripts, Greek and Syriac versions, and Latin Vulgate (see also 2 Kgs 8:29); most Hebrew manuscripts read *Azariah.* 22:8 As in Greek version (see also 2 Kgs 10:13); Hebrew reads *and sons of the brothers of Ahaziah.* 22:11 As in parallel text at 2 Kgs 11:2; Hebrew reads *Jehoshabeath,* a variant name for Jehosheba.

CHAPTER **23**

Revolt against Athaliah

In the seventh year of Athaliah's reign, Jehoiada the priest decided to act. He got up his courage and made a pact with five army commanders: Azariah son of Jeroham, Ishmael son of Jehohanan, Azariah son of Obed, Maaseiah son of Adaiah, and Elishaphat son of Zicri. ²These men traveled secretly throughout Judah and summoned the Levites and clan leaders in Judah's towns to come to Jerusalem. ³They all gathered at the Temple of God, where they made a covenant with Joash, the young king.

Jehoiada said to them, "The time has come for the king's son to reign! The LORD has promised that a descendant of David will be our king. ⁴This is what you must do. When the priests and Levites come on duty on the Sabbath, a third of them will serve as gatekeepers. ⁵Another third will go over to the royal palace, and the final third will be at the Foundation Gate. Everyone else should stay in the courtyards of the LORD's Temple. ⁶Remember, only the priests and Levites on duty may enter the Temple of the LORD, for they are set apart as holy. The rest of the people must obey the LORD's instructions and stay outside. ⁷You Levites, form a bodyguard for the king and keep your weapons in hand. Any unauthorized person who enters the Temple must be killed. Stay right beside the king at all times."

⁸So the Levites and the people did everything just as Jehoiada the priest ordered. The commanders took charge of the men reporting for duty that Sabbath, as well as those who were going off duty. Jehoiada the priest did not let anyone go home after their shift ended. ⁹Then Jehoiada supplied the commanders with the spears and shields that had once belonged to King David and were stored in the Temple of God. ¹⁰He stationed the guards around the king, with their weapons ready. They formed a line from the south side of the Temple around to the north side and all around the altar.

¹¹Then Jehoiada and his sons brought out Joash, the king's son, and placed the crown on his head. They presented Joash with a copy of God's laws and proclaimed him king. Then they anointed him, and everyone shouted, "Long live the king!"

The Death of Athaliah

¹²When Athaliah heard the noise of the people running and the shouts of praise to the king, she hurried to the LORD's Temple to see what was happening. ¹³And she saw the newly crowned king standing in his place of authority by the pillar at the Temple entrance. The officers and trumpeters were surrounding him, and people from all over the land were rejoicing and blowing trumpets. Singers with musical instruments were leading the people in a great celebration. When Athaliah saw all this, she tore her clothes in despair and shouted, "Treason! Treason!"

¹⁴Then Jehoiada the priest ordered the commanders who were in charge of the troops, "Take her out of the Temple, and kill anyone who tries to rescue her. Do not kill her here in the Temple of the LORD." ¹⁵So they seized her and led her out to the gate where horses enter the palace grounds, and they killed her there.

Jehoiada's Religious Reforms

¹⁶Then Jehoiada made a covenant between himself and the king and the people that they would be the LORD's people. ¹⁷And all the people went over to the temple of Baal and tore it down. They demolished the altars and smashed the idols, and they killed Mattan the priest of Baal in front of the altars.

¹⁸Jehoiada now put the Levitical priests in charge of the Temple of the LORD, following all the instructions given by David. He also commanded them to present burnt offerings to the LORD, as prescribed by the law of Moses, and to sing and rejoice as David had instructed. ¹⁹He stationed gatekeepers at the gates of the LORD's Temple to keep those who were ceremonially unclean from entering.

²⁰Then the commanders, nobles, rulers, and all the people escorted the king from the Temple of the LORD. They went through the Upper Gate and into the palace, and they seated the king on the royal throne. ²¹So all the people of the land rejoiced, and the city was peaceful because Athaliah had been killed.

CHAPTER **24**

Joash Repairs the Temple

Joash was seven years old when he became king, and he reigned in Jerusalem forty years. His mother was Zibiah, from Beersheba. ²Joash did what was pleasing in the LORD's sight throughout the lifetime of Jehoiada the priest. ³Jehoiada chose two wives for Joash, and he had sons and daughters.

⁴Some time later, Joash decided to repair and restore the Temple of the LORD. ⁵He summoned the priests and Levites and gave them these instructions: "Go at once to all the towns of Judah and collect the required annual offerings, so that

we can repair the Temple of your God. Do not delay!" But the Levites did not act right away.

6So the king called for Jehoiada the high priest and asked him, "Why haven't you demanded that the Levites go out and collect the Temple taxes from the towns of Judah and from Jerusalem? Moses, the servant of the LORD, levied this tax on the community of Israel in order to maintain the Tabernacle of the Covenant.*"

7Over the years, the followers of wicked Athaliah had broken into the Temple of God, and they had used all the dedicated things from the Temple of the LORD to worship the images of Baal. 8So now Joash gave instructions for a chest to be made and set outside the gate leading to the Temple of the LORD. 9Then a proclamation was sent throughout Judah and Jerusalem, telling the people to bring to the LORD the tax that Moses, the servant of God, had required of the Israelites in the wilderness. 10This pleased all the leaders and the people, and they gladly brought their money and filled the chest with it.

11Whenever the chest became full, the Levites carried it to the king's officials. Then the court secretary and an officer of the high priest counted the money and took the chest back to the Temple again. This went on day after day, and a large amount of money was collected. 12The king and Jehoiada gave the money to the construction supervisors, who hired masons and carpenters to restore the Temple of the LORD. They also hired metalworkers, who made articles of iron and bronze for the LORD's Temple.

13So the men in charge of the renovation worked hard, and they made steady progress. They restored the Temple of God according to its original design and strengthened it. 14When all the repairs were finished, they brought the remaining money to the king and Jehoiada. It was used to make utensils for the Temple of the LORD—utensils for worship services and for burnt offerings, including ladles and other vessels made of gold and silver. And the burnt offerings were sacrificed continually in the Temple of the LORD during the lifetime of Jehoiada the priest.

15Jehoiada lived to a very old age, finally dying at 130. 16He was buried among the kings in the City of David, because he had done so much good in Israel for God and his Temple.

Jehoiada's Reforms Reversed

17But after Jehoiada's death, the leaders of Judah came and bowed before King Joash and persuaded the king to listen to their advice. 18They decided to abandon the Temple of the LORD, the God of their ancestors, and they worshiped Asherah poles and idols instead! Then the anger of God burned against Judah and Jerusalem because of their sin. 19The LORD sent prophets to bring them back to him, but the people would not listen.

20Then the Spirit of God came upon Zechariah son of Jehoiada the priest. He stood before the people and said, "This is what God says: Why do you disobey the LORD's commands so that you cannot prosper? You have abandoned the LORD, and now he has abandoned you!"

21Then the leaders plotted to kill Zechariah, and by order of King Joash himself, they stoned him to death in the courtyard of the LORD's Temple. 22That was how King Joash repaid Jehoiada for his love and loyalty—by killing his son. Zechariah's last words as he died were, "May the LORD see what they are doing and hold them accountable!"

The End of Joash's Reign

23At the beginning of the year, the Aramean army marched against Joash. They invaded Judah and Jerusalem and killed all the leaders of the nation. Then they sent all the plunder back to their king in Damascus. 24Although the Arameans attacked with only a small army, the LORD helped them conquer the much larger army of Judah. The people of Judah had abandoned the LORD, the God of their ancestors, so judgment was executed against Joash.

25The Arameans withdrew, leaving Joash severely wounded. But his own officials decided to kill him for murdering the son of Jehoiada the priest. They assassinated him as he lay in bed. Then he was buried in the City of David, but not in the royal cemetery. 26The assassins were Jozabad,* the son of an Ammonite woman named Shimeath, and Jehozabad, the son of a Moabite woman named Shomer.* 27The complete story about the sons of Joash, the prophecies about him, and the record of his restoration of the Temple of God are written in *The Commentary on the Book of the Kings.* When Joash died, his son Amaziah became the next king.

CHAPTER 25
Amaziah Rules in Judah

Amaziah was twenty-five years old when he became king, and he reigned in Jerusalem twenty-

24:6 Hebrew *Tent of the Testimony.* 24:26a As in parallel text at 2 Kgs 12:21; Hebrew reads *Zabad.* 24:26b As in parallel text at 2 Kgs 12:21; Hebrew reads *Shimrith.*

nine years. His mother was Jehoaddin,* from Jerusalem. ²Amaziah did what was pleasing in the LORD's sight, but not wholeheartedly.

³When Amaziah was well established as king, he executed the men who had assassinated his father. ⁴However, he did not kill the children of the assassins, for he obeyed the command of the LORD written in the Book of the Law of Moses: "Parents must not be put to death for the sins of their children, nor the children for the sins of their parents. Those worthy of death must be executed for their own crimes."*

⁵Another thing Amaziah did was to organize the army, assigning leaders to each clan from Judah and Benjamin. Then he took a census and found that he had an army of 300,000 men twenty years old and older, all trained in the use of spear and shield. ⁶He also paid about 7,500 pounds* of silver to hire 100,000 experienced fighting men from Israel.

⁷But a man of God came to the king and said, "O king, do not hire troops from Israel, for the LORD is not with Israel. He will not help those people of Ephraim! ⁸If you let them go with your troops into battle, you will be defeated no matter how well you fight. God will overthrow you, for he has the power to help or to frustrate."

⁹Amaziah asked the man of God, "But what should I do about the silver I paid to hire the army of Israel?"

The man of God replied, "The LORD is able to give you much more than this!" ¹⁰So Amaziah discharged the hired troops and sent them back to Ephraim. This made them angry with Judah, and they returned home in a great rage.

¹¹Then Amaziah summoned his courage and led his army to the Valley of Salt, where they killed ten thousand Edomite troops from Seir. ¹²They captured another ten thousand and took them to the top of a cliff and threw them off, dashing them to pieces on the rocks below.

¹³Meanwhile, the hired troops that Amaziah had sent home raided several of the towns of Judah between Samaria and Beth-horon, killing three thousand people and carrying off great quantities of plunder.

¹⁴When King Amaziah returned from defeating the Edomites, he brought with him idols taken from the people of Seir. He set them up as his own gods, bowed down in front of them, and presented sacrifices to them! ¹⁵This made the LORD very angry, and he sent a prophet to ask,

"Why have you worshiped gods who could not even save their own people from you?"

¹⁶But the king interrupted him and said, "Since when have I asked your advice? Be quiet now before I have you killed!"

So the prophet left with this warning: "I know that God has determined to destroy you because you have done this and have not accepted my counsel."

¹⁷After consulting with his advisers, King Amaziah of Judah sent this challenge to Israel's king Jehoash,* the son of Jehoahaz and grandson of Jehu: "Come and meet me in battle!"

¹⁸But King Jehoash of Israel replied to King Amaziah of Judah with this story: "Out in the Lebanon mountains, a thistle sent a message to a mighty cedar tree: 'Give your daughter in marriage to my son.' But just then a wild animal came by and stepped on the thistle, crushing it! ¹⁹You may be very proud of your conquest of Edom, but my advice is to stay home. Why stir up trouble that will bring disaster on you and the people of Judah?"

²⁰But Amaziah would not listen, for God was arranging to destroy him for worshiping the gods of Edom. ²¹So King Jehoash of Israel mobilized his army against King Amaziah of Judah. The two armies drew up their battle lines at Beth-shemesh in Judah. ²²Judah was routed by the army of Israel, and its army scattered and fled for home. ²³King Jehoash of Israel captured King Amaziah of Judah at Beth-shemesh and brought him back to Jerusalem. Then Jehoash ordered his army to demolish six hundred feet* of Jerusalem's wall, from the Ephraim Gate to the Corner Gate. ²⁴He carried off all the gold and silver and all the utensils from the Temple of God that had been in the care of Obed-edom. He also seized the treasures of the royal palace, along with hostages, and then returned to Samaria.

²⁵King Amaziah of Judah lived on for fifteen years after the death of King Jehoash of Israel. ²⁶The rest of the events of Amaziah's reign, from beginning to end, are recorded in *The Book of the Kings of Judah and Israel.* ²⁷After Amaziah turned away from the LORD, there was a conspiracy against his life in Jerusalem, and he fled to Lachish. But his enemies sent assassins after him, and they killed him there. ²⁸They brought him back to Jerusalem on a horse, and he was buried with his ancestors in the City of David.*

25:1 As in parallel text at 2 Kgs 14:2; Hebrew reads *Jehoaddan,* a variant name for Jehoaddin. 25:4 Deut 24:16. 25:6 Hebrew *100 talents* [3.4 metric tons]. 25:17 Hebrew *Joash,* a variant name for Jehoash; also in 25:18, 21, 23, 25. 25:23 Hebrew *400 cubits* [180 meters]. 25:28 As in some Hebrew manuscripts and other ancient versions (see also 2 Kgs 14:20); most Hebrew manuscripts read *the city of Judah.*

CHAPTER 26

Uzziah Rules in Judah

The people of Judah then crowned Amaziah's sixteen-year-old son, Uzziah, as their next king. ²After his father's death, Uzziah rebuilt the town of Elath* and restored it to Judah. ³Uzziah was sixteen when he became king, and he reigned in Jerusalem fifty-two years. His mother was Jecoliah, from Jerusalem. ⁴He did what was pleasing in the LORD's sight, just as his father, Amaziah, had done. ⁵Uzziah sought God during the days of Zechariah, who instructed him in the fear of God. And as long as the king sought the LORD, God gave him success.

⁶He declared war on the Philistines and broke down the walls of Gath, Jabneh, and Ashdod. Then he built new towns in the Ashdod area and in other parts of Philistia. ⁷God helped him not only with his wars against the Philistines, but also in his battles with the Arabs of Gur* and in his wars with the Meunites. ⁸The Meunites* paid annual tribute to him, and his fame spread even to Egypt, for he had become very powerful.

⁹Uzziah built fortified towers in Jerusalem at the Corner Gate, at the Valley Gate, and at the angle in the wall. ¹⁰He also constructed forts in the wilderness and dug many water cisterns, because he kept great herds of livestock in the foothills of Judah* and on the plains. He was also a man who loved the soil. He had many workers who cared for his farms and vineyards, both on the hillsides and in the fertile valleys.

¹¹Uzziah had an army of well-trained warriors, ready to march into battle, unit by unit. This great army of fighting men had been mustered and organized by Jeiel, the secretary of the army, and his assistant, Maaseiah. They were under the direction of Hananiah, one of the king's officials. ¹²Twenty-six hundred clan leaders commanded these regiments of seasoned warriors. ¹³The army consisted of 307,500 men, all elite troops. They were prepared to assist the king against any enemy. ¹⁴Uzziah provided the entire army with shields, spears, helmets, coats of mail, bows, and sling stones. ¹⁵And he produced machines mounted on the walls of Jerusalem, designed by brilliant men to shoot arrows and hurl stones* from the towers and the corners of the wall. His fame spread far and wide, for the LORD helped him wonderfully until he became very powerful.

Uzziah's Sin and Punishment

¹⁶But when he had become powerful, he also became proud, which led to his downfall. He sinned against the LORD his God by entering the sanctuary of the LORD's Temple and personally burning incense on the altar. ¹⁷Azariah the high priest went in after him with eighty other priests of the LORD, all brave men. ¹⁸They confronted King Uzziah and said, "It is not for you, Uzziah, to burn incense to the LORD. That is the work of the priests alone, the sons of Aaron who are set apart for this work. Get out of the sanctuary, for you have sinned. The LORD God will not honor you for this!"

¹⁹Uzziah was furious and refused to set down the incense burner he was holding. But as he was standing there with the priests before the incense altar in the LORD's Temple, leprosy* suddenly broke out on his forehead. ²⁰When Azariah and the other priests saw the leprosy, they rushed him out. And the king himself was eager to get out because the LORD had struck him. ²¹So King Uzziah had leprosy until the day he died. He lived in isolation, excluded from the Temple of the LORD. His son Jotham was put in charge of the royal palace, and he governed the people of the land.

²²The rest of the events of Uzziah's reign, from beginning to end, are recorded by the prophet Isaiah son of Amoz. ²³So Uzziah died, and since he had leprosy, he was buried nearby in a burial field belonging to the kings. Then his son Jotham became the next king.

CHAPTER 27

Jotham Rules in Judah

Jotham was twenty-five years old when he became king, and he reigned in Jerusalem sixteen years. His mother was Jerusha, the daughter of Zadok. ²He did what was pleasing in the LORD's sight, just as his father, Uzziah, had done. But unlike him, Jotham did not enter the Temple of the LORD. Nevertheless, the people continued in their corrupt ways.

³Jotham rebuilt the Upper Gate to the LORD's Temple and also did extensive rebuilding on the wall at the hill of Ophel. ⁴He built towns in the hill country of Judah and constructed fortresses and towers in the wooded areas. ⁵Jotham waged war against the Ammonites and conquered them. For the next three years, he received from them an annual tribute of 7,500 pounds* of

---

26:2 As in Greek version (see also 2 Kgs 14:22; 16:6); Hebrew reads *Eloth.* 26:7 As in Greek version; Hebrew reads *Gur-baal.* 26:8 As in Greek version; Hebrew reads *Ammonites.* Compare 26:7. 26:10 Hebrew *the Shephelah.* 26:15 Or *designed by brilliant men to protect those who shot arrows and stones.* 26:19 Or *a contagious skin disease.* The Hebrew word used here and throughout this passage can describe various skin diseases. 27:5a Hebrew *100 talents* [3.4 metric tons].

silver, 50,000 bushels of wheat, and 50,000 bushels of barley.*

6King Jotham became powerful because he was careful to live in obedience to the LORD his God.

7The rest of the events of Jotham's reign, including his wars and other activities, are recorded in *The Book of the Kings of Israel and Judah.* 8He was twenty-five years old when he became king, and he reigned in Jerusalem sixteen years. 9When he died, he was buried in the City of David, and his son Ahaz became the next king.

CHAPTER **28**

Ahaz Rules in Judah

Ahaz was twenty years old when he became king, and he reigned in Jerusalem sixteen years. He did not do what was pleasing in the sight of the LORD, as his ancestor David had done. 2Instead, he followed the example of the kings of Israel and cast images for the worship of Baal. 3He offered sacrifices in the valley of the son of Hinnom, even sacrificing his own sons in the fire.* He imitated the detestable practices of the pagan nations whom the LORD had driven from the land ahead of the Israelites. 4He offered sacrifices and burned incense at the pagan shrines and on the hills and under every green tree.

5That is why the LORD his God allowed the king of Aram to defeat Ahaz and to exile large numbers of his people to Damascus. The armies of Israel also defeated Ahaz and inflicted many casualties on his army. 6In a single day Pekah son of Remaliah, Israel's king, killed 120,000 of Judah's troops because they had abandoned the LORD, the God of their ancestors. 7Then Zicri, a warrior from Ephraim, killed Maaseiah, the king's son; Azrikam, the king's palace commander; and Elkanah, the king's second-in-command. 8The armies of Israel captured 200,000 women and children from Judah and took tremendous amounts of plunder, which they took back to Samaria.

9But a prophet of the LORD named Oded was there in Samaria when the army of Israel returned home. He went out to meet them and said, "The LORD, the God of your ancestors, was angry with Judah and let you defeat them. But you have gone too far, killing them without mercy, and all heaven is disturbed. 10And now you are planning to make slaves of these people

from Judah and Jerusalem. What about your own sins against the LORD your God? 11Listen to me and return these captives you have taken, for they are your own relatives. Watch out, because now the LORD's fierce anger has been turned against you!"

12Then some of the leaders of Israel*—Azariah son of Jehohanan, Berekiah son of Meshillemoth, Jehizkiah son of Shallum, and Amasa son of Hadlai—agreed with this and confronted the men returning from battle. 13"You must not bring the prisoners here!" they declared. "We cannot afford to add to our sins and guilt. Our guilt is already great, and the LORD's fierce anger is already turned against Israel."

14So the warriors released the prisoners and handed over the plunder in the sight of all the leaders and people. 15Then the four men mentioned by name came forward and distributed clothes from the plunder to the prisoners who were naked. They provided clothing and sandals to wear, gave them enough food and drink, and dressed their wounds with olive oil. They put those who were weak on donkeys and took all the prisoners back to their own land—to Jericho, the city of palms. Then they returned to Samaria.

Ahaz Closes the Temple

16About that time King Ahaz of Judah asked the king of Assyria for help against his enemies. 17The armies of Edom had again invaded Judah and taken captives. 18And the Philistines had raided towns located in the foothills of Judah* and in the Negev. They had already captured Beth-shemesh, Aijalon, Gederoth, Soco with its villages, Timnah with its villages, and Gimzo with its villages, and the Philistines had occupied these towns. 19The LORD was humbling Judah because of King Ahaz of Judah,* for he had encouraged his people to sin and had been utterly unfaithful to the LORD. 20So when King Tiglath-pileser* of Assyria arrived, he oppressed King Ahaz instead of helping him. 21Ahaz took valuable items from the LORD's Temple, the royal palace, and from the homes of his officials and gave them to the king of Assyria as tribute. But even this did not help him.

22And when trouble came to King Ahaz, he became even more unfaithful to the LORD. 23He offered sacrifices to the gods of Damascus who had defeated him, for he said, "These gods helped the kings of Aram, so they will help me,

27:5b Hebrew *10,000 cors* [1,820 kiloliters] *of wheat, and 10,000 cors of barley.*   28:3 Or *even making his sons pass through the fire.*
28:12 Hebrew *Ephraim*, referring to the northern kingdom of Israel.   28:18 Hebrew *the Shephelah.*   28:19 Hebrew *of Israel.*   28:20 Hebrew *Tilgath-pileser*, a variant name for Tiglath-pileser.

too, if I sacrifice to them." But instead, they led to his ruin and the ruin of all Israel. ²⁴The king took the utensils from the Temple of God and broke them into pieces. He shut the doors of the LORD's Temple so that no one could worship there and then set up altars to pagan gods in every corner of Jerusalem. ²⁵He made pagan shrines in all the towns of Judah for offering sacrifices to other gods. In this way, he aroused the anger of the LORD, the God of his ancestors.

²⁶The rest of the events of Ahaz's reign and all his dealings, from beginning to end, are recorded in *The Book of the Kings of Judah and Israel.* ²⁷When King Ahaz died, he was buried in Jerusalem but not in the royal cemetery. Then his son Hezekiah became the next king.

CHAPTER 29
Hezekiah Rules in Judah

Hezekiah was twenty-five years old when he became the king of Judah, and he reigned in Jerusalem twenty-nine years. His mother was Abijah, the daughter of Zechariah. ²He did what was pleasing in the LORD's sight, just as his ancestor David had done.

Hezekiah Reopens the Temple

³In the very first month of the first year of his reign, Hezekiah reopened the doors of the Temple of the LORD and repaired them. ⁴He summoned the priests and Levites to meet him at the courtyard east of the Temple. ⁵He said to them, "Listen to me, you Levites! Purify yourselves, and purify the Temple of the LORD, the God of your ancestors. Remove all the defiled things from the sanctuary. ⁶Our ancestors were unfaithful and did what was evil in the sight of the LORD our God. They abandoned the LORD and his Temple; they turned their backs on him. ⁷They also shut the doors to the Temple's foyer, and they snuffed out the lamps. They stopped burning incense and presenting burnt offerings at the sanctuary of the God of Israel. ⁸That is why the LORD's anger has fallen upon Judah and Jerusalem. He has made us an object of dread, horror, and ridicule, as you can so plainly see. ⁹Our fathers have been killed in battle, and our sons and daughters and wives are in captivity. ¹⁰But now I will make a covenant with the LORD, the God of Israel, so that his fierce anger will turn away from us. ¹¹My dear Levites, do not neglect your duties any longer! The LORD has chosen you to stand in his presence, to minister

to him, and to lead the people in worship and make offerings to him."

¹²Then these Levites got right to work:

From the clan of Kohath: Mahath son of Amasai and Joel son of Azariah.
From the clan of Merari: Kish son of Abdi and Azariah son of Jehallelel.
From the clan of Gershon: Joah son of Zimmah and Eden son of Joah.
¹³ From the family of Elizaphan: Shimri and Jeiel.
From the family of Asaph: Zechariah and Mattaniah.
¹⁴ From the family of Heman: Jehiel and Shimei.
From the family of Jeduthun: Shemaiah and Uzziel.

¹⁵These men called together their fellow Levites, and they purified themselves. Then they began to purify the Temple of the LORD, just as the king had commanded. They were careful to follow all the LORD's instructions in their work. ¹⁶The priests went into the sanctuary of the Temple of the LORD to cleanse it, and they took out to the Temple courtyard all the defiled things they found. From there the Levites carted it all out to the Kidron Valley.

¹⁷The work began on a day in early spring,* and in eight days they had reached the foyer of the LORD's Temple. Then they purified the Temple of the LORD itself, which took another eight days. So the entire task was completed in sixteen days.

The Temple Rededication

¹⁸Then the Levites went to King Hezekiah and gave him this report: "We have purified the Temple of the LORD, the altar of burnt offering with all its utensils, and the table of the Bread of the Presence with all its utensils. ¹⁹We have also recovered all the utensils taken by King Ahaz when he was unfaithful and closed the Temple. They are now in front of the altar of the LORD, purified and ready for use."

²⁰Early the next morning King Hezekiah gathered the city officials and went to the Temple of the LORD. ²¹They brought seven bulls, seven rams, seven lambs, and seven male goats as a sin offering for the kingdom, for the Temple, and for Judah. The king commanded the priests, who were descendants of Aaron, to sacrifice the animals on the altar of the LORD. ²²So they killed the bulls, and the priests took the blood and sprin-

29:17 Hebrew *on the first day of the first month.* This day of the Hebrew lunar calendar occurs in March or early April.

kled it on the altar. Next they killed the rams and sprinkled their blood on the altar. And finally, they did the same with the lambs. 23The male goats for the sin offering were then brought before the king and the assembly of people, who laid their hands on them. 24The priests then killed the goats as a sin offering and sprinkled their blood on the altar to make atonement for the sins of all Israel. The king had specifically commanded that this burnt offering and sin offering should be made for all Israel.

25King Hezekiah then stationed the Levites at the Temple of the LORD with cymbals, harps, and lyres. He obeyed all the commands that the LORD had given to King David through Gad, the king's seer, and the prophet Nathan. 26The Levites then took their positions around the Temple with the instruments of David, and the priests took their positions with the trumpets. 27Then Hezekiah ordered that the burnt offering be placed on the altar. As the burnt offering was presented, songs of praise to the LORD were begun, accompanied by the trumpets and other instruments of David, king of Israel. 28The entire assembly worshiped the LORD as the singers sang and the trumpets blew, until all the burnt offerings were finished. 29Then the king and everyone with him bowed down in worship. 30King Hezekiah and the officials ordered the Levites to praise the LORD with the psalms of David and Asaph the seer. So they offered joyous praise and bowed down in worship.

31Then Hezekiah declared, "The dedication ceremony has come to an end. Now bring your sacrifices and thanksgiving offerings to the Temple of the LORD." So the people brought their sacrifices and thanksgiving offerings, and those whose hearts were willing brought burnt offerings, too. 32The people brought to the LORD seventy bulls, one hundred rams, and two hundred lambs for burnt offerings. 33They also brought six hundred bulls and three thousand sheep as sacrifices. 34But there were too few priests to prepare all the burnt offerings, so their relatives the Levites helped them until the work was finished and until more priests had been purified. For the Levites had been more conscientious about purifying themselves than the priests. 35There was an abundance of burnt offerings, along with the usual drink offerings, and a great deal of fat from the many peace offerings. So the Temple of the LORD was restored to service. 36And Hezekiah and all the people rejoiced greatly because of what God had done for the people, for everything had been accomplished so quickly.

CHAPTER **30**
Preparations for Passover
King Hezekiah now sent word to all Israel and Judah, and he wrote letters of invitation to Ephraim and Manasseh. He asked everyone to come to the Temple of the LORD at Jerusalem to celebrate the Passover of the LORD, the God of Israel. 2The king, his officials, and all the community of Jerusalem decided to celebrate Passover a month later than usual.* 3They were unable to celebrate it at the regular time because not enough priests could be purified by then, and the people had not yet assembled at Jerusalem. 4This plan for keeping the Passover seemed right to the king and all the people. 5So they sent a proclamation throughout all Israel, from Beersheba in the south to Dan in the north, inviting everyone to come to Jerusalem to celebrate the Passover of the LORD, the God of Israel. The people had not been celebrating it in great numbers as prescribed in the law.

6At the king's command, messengers were sent throughout Israel and Judah. They carried letters which said:

"O people of Israel, return to the LORD, the God of Abraham, Isaac, and Israel,* so that he will return to the few of us who have survived the conquest of the Assyrian kings. 7Do not be like your ancestors and relatives who abandoned the LORD, the God of their ancestors, and became an object of derision, as you yourselves can see. 8Do not be stubborn, as they were, but submit yourselves to the LORD. Come to his Temple which he has set apart as holy forever. Worship the LORD your God so that his fierce anger will turn away from you. 9For if you return to the LORD, your relatives and your children will be treated mercifully by their captors, and they will be able to return to this land. For the LORD your God is gracious and merciful. If you return to him, he will not continue to turn his face from you."

Celebration of Passover
10The messengers went from town to town throughout Ephraim and Manasseh and as far as the territory of Zebulun. But most of the people just laughed at the messengers and made fun of them. 11However, some from Asher, Manasseh,

30:2 Hebrew *in the second month*. This month of the Hebrew lunar calendar usually occurs in April and May.   30:6 *Israel* is the name that God gave to Jacob.

and Zebulun humbled themselves and went to Jerusalem. 12At the same time, God's hand was on the people in the land of Judah, giving them a strong desire to unite in obeying the orders of the king and his officials, who were following the word of the LORD. 13And so a huge crowd assembled at Jerusalem in midspring* to celebrate Passover and the Festival of Unleavened Bread. 14They set to work and removed the pagan altars from Jerusalem. They took away all the incense altars and threw them into the Kidron Valley.

15On the appointed day in midspring, one month later than usual,* the people slaughtered their Passover lambs. Then the priests and Levites became ashamed, so they purified themselves and brought burnt offerings to the Temple of the LORD. 16They took their places at the Temple according to the regulations found in the law of Moses, the man of God. The Levites brought the sacrificial blood to the priests, who then sprinkled it on the altar. 17Since many of the people there had not purified themselves, the Levites had to slaughter their Passover lambs for them, to set them apart for the LORD. 18Most of those who came from Ephraim, Manasseh, Issachar, and Zebulun had not purified themselves. But King Hezekiah prayed for them, and they were allowed to eat the Passover meal anyway, even though this was contrary to God's laws. For Hezekiah said, "May the LORD, who is good, pardon those 19who decide to follow the LORD, the God of their ancestors, even though they are not properly cleansed for the ceremony." 20And the LORD listened to Hezekiah's prayer and healed the people.

21So the people of Israel who were present in Jerusalem celebrated the Festival of Unleavened Bread for seven days with great joy. Each day the Levites and priests sang to the LORD, accompanied by loud instruments.* 22Hezekiah encouraged the Levites for the skill they displayed as they served the LORD. So for seven days the celebration continued. Peace offerings were sacrificed, and the people confessed their sins to the LORD, the God of their ancestors.

23The entire assembly then decided to continue the festival another seven days, so they celebrated joyfully for another week. 24King Hezekiah gave the people one thousand bulls and seven thousand sheep for offerings, and the officials donated one thousand bulls and ten

thousand sheep. Meanwhile, many more priests purified themselves.

25The entire assembly of Judah rejoiced, including the priests, the Levites, all who came from the land of Israel, the foreigners who came to the festival, and all those who lived in Judah. 26There was great joy in the city, for Jerusalem had not seen a celebration like this one since the days of Solomon, King David's son. 27Then the Levitical priests stood and blessed the people, and God heard them from his holy dwelling in heaven.

CHAPTER 31
Hezekiah's Religious Reforms

Now when the festival ended, the Israelites who attended went to all the towns of Judah, Benjamin, Ephraim, and Manasseh, and they smashed the sacred pillars, cut down the Asherah poles, and removed the pagan shrines and altars. After this, the Israelites returned to their own towns and homes.

2Hezekiah then organized the priests and Levites into divisions to offer the burnt offerings and peace offerings, and to worship and give thanks and praise to the LORD at the gates of the Temple. 3The king also made a personal contribution of animals for the daily morning and evening burnt offerings, as well as for the weekly Sabbath festivals and monthly new moon festivals, and for the other annual festivals as required in the law of the LORD. 4In addition, he required the people in Jerusalem to bring the prescribed portion of their income to the priests and Levites, so they could devote themselves fully to the law of the LORD.

5The people responded immediately and generously with the first of their crops and grain, new wine, olive oil, honey, and all the produce of their fields. They brought a tithe of all they owned. 6The people who had moved to Judah from Israel, and the people of Judah themselves, brought in the tithes of their cattle and sheep and a tithe of the things that had been dedicated to the LORD their God, and they piled them up in great heaps. 7The first of these tithes was brought in late spring,* and the heaps continued to grow until early autumn.* 8When Hezekiah and his officials came and saw these huge piles, they thanked the LORD and his people Israel!

9"Where did all this come from?" Hezekiah asked the priests and Levites.

10And Azariah the high priest, from the family

30:13 Hebrew *in the second month*. This month of the Hebrew lunar calendar usually occurs in April and May.   30:15 Hebrew *On the fourteenth day of the second month*. This day of the Hebrew lunar calendar occurs in late April or early May.   30:21 Or *sang to the LORD with all their strength*.   31:7a Hebrew *in the third month*. This month of the Hebrew lunar calendar usually occurs in May and June.   31:7b Hebrew *in the seventh month*. This month of the Hebrew lunar calendar usually occurs in September and October.

of Zadok, replied, "Since the people began bringing their gifts to the LORD's Temple, we have had enough to eat and plenty to spare, for the LORD has blessed his people."

11Hezekiah decided to have storerooms prepared in the Temple of the LORD, and this was done. 12Then all the gifts and tithes were faithfully brought to the Temple. Conaniah the Levite was put in charge, assisted by his brother Shimei. 13The supervisors under them were Jehiel, Azaziah, Nahath, Asahel, Jerimoth, Jozabad, Eliel, Ismakiah, Mahath, and Benaiah. These appointments were made by King Hezekiah and Azariah, the chief official in the Temple of God.

14Kore son of Imnah the Levite, who was the gatekeeper at the East Gate, was put in charge of distributing the freewill offerings of God, the gifts, and the things that had been dedicated to the LORD. 15His faithful assistants were Eden, Miniamin, Jeshua, Shemaiah, Amariah, and Shecaniah. They distributed the gifts among the families of priests in their towns, by their divisions, dividing the gifts fairly among young and old alike. 16They also distributed the gifts to all males three years old or older, regardless of their place in the genealogical records, who came daily to the LORD's Temple to perform their official duties, by their divisions. 17And they distributed gifts to the priests who were listed in the genealogical records by families, and to the Levites twenty years old or older who were listed according to their jobs and their divisions. 18Food allotments were also given to all the families listed in the genealogical records, including the little babies, the wives, and the sons and daughters. For they had all been faithful in purifying themselves. 19As for the priests, the descendants of Aaron, who were living in the open villages around the towns, men were appointed to distribute portions to every male among the priests and to all the Levites listed in the genealogical records.

20In this way, King Hezekiah handled the distribution throughout all Judah, doing what was pleasing and good in the sight of the LORD his God. 21In all that he did in the service of the Temple of God and in his efforts to follow the law and the commands, Hezekiah sought his God wholeheartedly. As a result, he was very successful.

CHAPTER **32**

Assyria Invades Judah

After Hezekiah had faithfully carried out this work, King Sennacherib of Assyria invaded

32:5 Or *the supporting terraces.*

Judah. He laid siege to the fortified cities, giving orders for his army to break through their walls. 2When Hezekiah realized that Sennacherib also intended to attack Jerusalem, 3he consulted with his officials and military advisers, and they decided to stop the flow of the springs outside the city. 4They organized a huge work crew to stop the flow of the springs, cutting off the brook that ran through the fields. For they said, "Why should the kings of Assyria come here and find plenty of water?"

5Then Hezekiah further strengthened his defenses by repairing the wall wherever it was broken down and by adding to the fortifications and constructing a second wall outside the first. He also reinforced the Millo* in the City of David and manufactured large numbers of weapons and shields. 6He appointed military officers over the people and asked them to assemble before him in the square at the city gate. Then Hezekiah encouraged them with this address: 7"Be strong and courageous! Don't be afraid of the king of Assyria or his mighty army, for there is a power far greater on our side! 8He may have a great army, but they are just men. We have the LORD our God to help us and to fight our battles for us!" These words greatly encouraged the people.

Sennacherib Threatens Jerusalem

9Then King Sennacherib of Assyria, while still besieging the town of Lachish, sent officials to Jerusalem with this message for Hezekiah and all the people in the city:

10"This is what King Sennacherib of Assyria says: What are you trusting in that makes you think you can survive my siege of Jerusalem? 11Hezekiah has said, 'The LORD our God will rescue us from the king of Assyria.' Surely Hezekiah is misleading you, sentencing you to death by famine and thirst! 12Surely you must realize that Hezekiah is the very person who destroyed all the LORD's shrines and altars. He commanded Judah and Jerusalem to worship at only the one altar at the Temple and to make sacrifices on it alone.

13"Surely you must realize what I and the other kings of Assyria before me have done to all the people of the earth! Were any of the gods of those nations able to rescue their people from my power? 14Name just one time when any god, anywhere, was able to rescue his people from me! What makes you think your God can do any better? 15Don't let Hezekiah fool you! Don't let him deceive you like this! I say it again—no god of any nation has ever yet been able to rescue his people from me or my ancestors. How much less will your God rescue you from my power!"

16And Sennacherib's officials further mocked the LORD God and his servant Hezekiah, heaping insult upon insult. 17The king also sent letters scorning the LORD, the God of Israel. He wrote, "Just as the gods of all the other nations failed to rescue their people from my power, so the God of Hezekiah will also fail." 18The Assyrian officials who brought the letters shouted this in the Hebrew language to the people gathered on the walls of the city, trying to terrify them so it would be easier to capture the city. 19These officials talked about the God of Jerusalem as though he were one of the pagan gods, made by human hands.

20Then King Hezekiah and the prophet Isaiah son of Amoz cried out in prayer to God in heaven. 21And the LORD sent an angel who destroyed the Assyrian army with all its commanders and officers. So Sennacherib returned home in disgrace to his own land. And when he entered the temple of his god, some of his own sons killed him there with a sword. 22That is how the LORD rescued Hezekiah and the people of Jerusalem from King Sennacherib of Assyria and from all the others who threatened them. So there was peace at last throughout the land. 23From then on King Hezekiah became highly respected among the surrounding nations, and many gifts for the LORD arrived at Jerusalem, with valuable presents for King Hezekiah, too.

Hezekiah's Sickness and Recovery

24About that time, Hezekiah became deathly ill. He prayed to the LORD, who healed him and gave him a miraculous sign. 25But Hezekiah did not respond appropriately to the kindness shown him, and he became proud. So the LORD's anger came against him and against Judah and Jerusalem. 26Then Hezekiah repented of his pride, and the people of Jerusalem humbled themselves. So the LORD's anger did not come against them during Hezekiah's lifetime.

27Hezekiah was very wealthy and held in high esteem. He had to build special treasury buildings for his silver, gold, precious stones, and spices, and for his shields and other valuable items. 28He also constructed many storehouses for his grain, new wine, and olive oil; and he made many stalls for his cattle and folds for his flocks of sheep and goats. 29He built many towns and acquired vast flocks and herds, for God had given him great wealth. 30He blocked up the upper spring of Gihon and brought the water down through a tunnel to the west side of the City of David. And so he succeeded in everything he did.

31However, when ambassadors arrived from Babylon to ask about the remarkable events that had taken place in the land, God withdrew from Hezekiah in order to test him and to see what was really in his heart.

Summary of Hezekiah's Reign

32The rest of the events of Hezekiah's reign and his acts of devotion are recorded in *The Vision of the Prophet Isaiah Son of Amoz*, which is included in *The Book of the Kings of Judah and Israel*. 33When Hezekiah died, he was buried in the upper area of the royal cemetery, and all Judah and Jerusalem honored him at his death. Then his son Manasseh became the next king.

CHAPTER **33**

Manasseh Rules in Judah

Manasseh was twelve years old when he became king, and he reigned in Jerusalem fifty-five years. 2He did what was evil in the LORD's sight, imitating the detestable practices of the pagan nations whom the LORD had driven from the land ahead of the Israelites. 3He rebuilt the pagan shrines his father Hezekiah had destroyed. He constructed altars for the images of Baal and set up Asherah poles. He also bowed before all the stars of heaven and worshiped them. 4He even built pagan altars in the Temple of the LORD, the place where the LORD had said his name should be honored forever. 5He put these altars for the stars of heaven in both courtyards of the LORD's Temple. 6Manasseh even sacrificed his own sons in the fire* in the valley of the son of Hinnom. He practiced sorcery, divination, and witchcraft, and he consulted with mediums and psychics. He did much that was evil in the LORD's sight, arousing his anger.

7Manasseh even took a carved idol he had made and set it up in God's Temple, the very place where God had told David and his son Solomon: "My name will be honored here forever in this Temple and in Jerusalem—the city I have chosen from among all the other tribes of Israel. 8If the Israelites will obey my com-

33:6 Or *even made his sons pass through the fire.*

mands—all the instructions, laws, and regulations given through Moses—I will not send them into exile from this land that I gave their ancestors." 9But Manasseh led the people of Judah and Jerusalem to do even more evil than the pagan nations whom the LORD had destroyed when the Israelites entered the land.

10The LORD spoke to Manasseh and his people, but they ignored all his warnings. 11So the LORD sent the Assyrian armies, and they took Manasseh prisoner. They put a ring through his nose, bound him in bronze chains, and led him away to Babylon. 12But while in deep distress, Manasseh sought the LORD his God and cried out humbly to the God of his ancestors. 13And when he prayed, the LORD listened to him and was moved by his request for help. So the LORD let Manasseh return to Jerusalem and to his kingdom. Manasseh had finally realized that the LORD alone is God!

14It was after this that Manasseh rebuilt the outer wall of the City of David, from west of the Gihon Spring in the Kidron Valley to the Fish Gate, and continuing around the hill of Ophel, where it was built very high. And he stationed his military officers in all of the fortified cities of Judah. 15Manasseh also removed the foreign gods from the hills and the idol from the LORD's Temple. He tore down all the altars he had built on the hill where the Temple stood and all the altars that were in Jerusalem, and he dumped them outside the city. 16Then he restored the altar of the LORD and sacrificed peace offerings and thanksgiving offerings on it. He also encouraged the people of Judah to worship the LORD, the God of Israel. 17However, the people still sacrificed at the pagan shrines, but only to the LORD their God.

18The rest of the events of Manasseh's reign, his prayer to God, and the words the seers spoke to him in the name of the LORD, the God of Israel, are recorded in The Book of the Kings of Israel. 19Manasseh's prayer, the account of the way God answered him, and an account of all his sins and unfaithfulness are recorded in The Record of the Seers.* It includes a list of the locations where he built pagan shrines and set up Asherah poles and idols before he repented. 20When Manasseh died, he was buried at his palace. Then his son Amon became the next king.

Amon Rules in Judah

21Amon was twenty-two years old when he became king, and he reigned in Jerusalem two years.

33:19 Or The Record of Hozai.

22He did what was evil in the LORD's sight, just as his father Manasseh had done. He worshiped and sacrificed to all the idols his father had made. 23But unlike his father, he did not humble himself before the LORD. Instead, Amon sinned even more. 24At last Amon's own officials plotted against him and assassinated him in his palace. 25But the people of the land killed all those who had conspired against King Amon, and they made his son Josiah the next king.

CHAPTER **34**
Josiah Rules in Judah

Josiah was eight years old when he became king, and he reigned in Jerusalem thirty-one years. 2He did what was pleasing in the LORD's sight and followed the example of his ancestor David. He did not turn aside from doing what was right.

3During the eighth year of his reign, while he was still young, Josiah began to seek the God of his ancestor David. Then in the twelfth year, he began to purify Judah and Jerusalem, destroying all the pagan shrines, the Asherah poles, and the carved idols and cast images. 4He saw to it that the altars for the images of Baal and their incense altars were torn down. He also made sure that the Asherah poles, the carved idols, and the cast images were smashed and scattered over the graves of those who had sacrificed to them. 5Then he burned the bones of the pagan priests on their own altars, and so he purified Judah and Jerusalem.

6He did the same thing in the towns of Manasseh, Ephraim, and Simeon, even as far as Naphtali. 7He destroyed the pagan altars and the Asherah poles, and he crushed the idols into dust. He cut down the incense altars throughout the land of Israel and then returned to Jerusalem.

8In the eighteenth year of his reign, after he had purified the land and the Temple, Josiah appointed Shaphan son of Azaliah, Maaseiah the governor of Jerusalem, and Joah son of Joahaz, the royal historian, to repair the Temple of the LORD his God. 9They gave Hilkiah the high priest the money that had been collected by the Levites who served as gatekeepers at the Temple of God. The gifts were brought by people from Manasseh, Ephraim, and from all the remnant of Israel, as well as from all Judah, Benjamin, and the people of Jerusalem. 10He entrusted the money to the men assigned to supervise the restoration of the LORD's Temple. Then they paid the workers who did the repairs and renovation.

¹¹Thus, they hired carpenters and masons and purchased cut stone for the walls and timber for the rafters and beams. They restored what earlier kings of Judah had allowed to fall into ruin.

¹²The workers served faithfully under the leadership of Jahath and Obadiah, Levites of the Merarite clan, and Zechariah and Meshullam, Levites of the Kohathite clan. Other Levites, all of whom were skilled musicians, ¹³were put in charge of the laborers of the various trades. Still others assisted as secretaries, officials, and gatekeepers.

Hilkiah Discovers God's Law

¹⁴As Hilkiah the high priest was recording the money collected at the LORD's Temple, he found the Book of the Law of the LORD as it had been given through Moses. ¹⁵Hilkiah said to Shaphan the court secretary, "I have found the Book of the Law in the LORD's Temple!" Then Hilkiah gave the scroll to Shaphan.

¹⁶Shaphan took the scroll to the king and reported, "Your officials are doing everything they were assigned to do. ¹⁷The money that was collected at the Temple of the LORD has been given to the supervisors and workmen." ¹⁸Shaphan also said to the king, "Hilkiah the priest has given me a scroll." So Shaphan read it to the king.

¹⁹When the king heard what was written in the law, he tore his clothes in despair. ²⁰Then he gave these orders to Hilkiah, Ahikam son of Shaphan, Acbor son of Micaiah,* Shaphan the court secretary, and Asaiah the king's personal adviser: ²¹"Go to the Temple and speak to the LORD for me and for all the remnant of Israel and Judah. Ask him about the words written in this scroll that has been found. The LORD's anger has been poured out against us because our ancestors have not obeyed the word of the LORD. We have not been doing what this scroll says we must do."

²²So Hilkiah and the other men went to the newer Mishneh section* of Jerusalem to consult with the prophet Huldah. She was the wife of Shallum son of Tikvah and grandson of Harhas,* the keeper of the Temple wardrobe. ²³She said to them, "The LORD, the God of Israel, has spoken! Go and tell the man who sent you, ²⁴'This is what the LORD says: I will certainly destroy this city and its people. All the curses written in the scroll you have read will come true. ²⁵For the people of Judah have abandoned me and worshiped pagan gods, and I am very

angry with them for everything they have done. My anger will be poured out against this place, and nothing will be able to stop it.'

²⁶"But go to the king of Judah who sent you to seek the LORD and tell him: 'This is what the LORD, the God of Israel, says concerning the message you have just heard: ²⁷You were sorry and humbled yourself before God when you heard what I said against this city and its people. You humbled yourself and tore your clothing in despair and wept before me in repentance. So I have indeed heard you, says the LORD. ²⁸I will not send the promised disaster against this city and its people until after you have died and been buried in peace. You will not see the disaster I am going to bring on this place.'" So they took her message back to the king.

Josiah's Religious Reforms

²⁹Then the king summoned all the leaders of Judah and Jerusalem. ³⁰And the king went up to the Temple of the LORD with all the people of Judah and Jerusalem and the priests and the Levites—all the people from the greatest to the least. There the king read to them the entire Book of the Covenant that had been found in the LORD's Temple. ³¹The king took his place of authority beside the pillar and renewed the covenant in the LORD's presence. He pledged to obey the LORD by keeping all his commands, regulations, and laws with all his heart and soul. He promised to obey all the terms of the covenant that were written in the scroll. ³²And he required everyone in Jerusalem and the people of Benjamin to make a similar pledge. As the people of Jerusalem did this, they renewed their covenant with God, the God of their ancestors.

³³So Josiah removed all detestable idols from the entire land of Israel and required everyone to worship the LORD their God. And throughout the rest of his lifetime, they did not turn away from the LORD, the God of their ancestors.

CHAPTER 35

Josiah Celebrates Passover

Then Josiah announced that the Passover of the LORD would be celebrated in Jerusalem on the appointed day in early spring.* The Passover lambs were slaughtered at twilight of that day. ²Josiah also assigned the priests to their duties and encouraged them in their work at the

---

34:20 As in parallel text at 2 Kgs 22:12; Hebrew reads *Abdon son of Micah.* **34:22a** Or *the Second Quarter,* a newer section of Jerusalem. **34:22b** As in parallel text at 2 Kgs 22:14; Hebrew reads *son of Tokhath, son of Hasrah.* **35:1** Hebrew *on the fourteenth day of the first month.* This day of the Hebrew lunar calendar occurs in late March or early April.

Temple of the LORD. ³He issued this order to the Levites, who had been set apart to serve the LORD and were teachers in Israel: "Since the Ark is now in Solomon's Temple and you do not need to carry it back and forth on your shoulders, spend your time serving the LORD your God and his people Israel. ⁴Report for duty according to the family divisions of your ancestors, following the written instructions of King David of Israel and the instructions of his son Solomon. ⁵Then stand in your appointed holy places and help the families assigned to you as they bring their offerings to the Temple. ⁶Slaughter the Passover lambs, purify yourselves, and prepare to help those who come. Follow all the instructions that the LORD gave through Moses."

⁷Then Josiah contributed from his personal property thirty thousand lambs and young goats for the people's Passover offerings, and three thousand bulls. ⁸The king's officials also made willing contributions to the people, priests, and Levites. Hilkiah, Zechariah, and Jehiel, the administrators of God's Temple, gave the priests twenty-six hundred lambs and young goats and three hundred bulls as Passover offerings. ⁹The Levite leaders—Conaniah and his brothers Shemaiah and Nethanel, and Hashabiah, Jeiel, and Jozabad—gave five thousand lambs and young goats and five hundred bulls to the Levites for their Passover offerings.

¹⁰When everything was ready for the Passover celebration, the priests and the Levites took their places, organized by their divisions, according to the king's orders. ¹¹The Levites then slaughtered the Passover lambs and presented the blood to the priests, who sprinkled the blood on the altar while the Levites prepared the animals. ¹²They divided the burnt offerings among the people by their family groups, so they could offer them to the LORD according to the instructions recorded in the Book of Moses. They did the same with the bulls. ¹³Then they roasted the Passover lambs as prescribed; and they boiled the holy offerings in pots, kettles, and pans, and brought them out quickly so the people could eat them. ¹⁴Afterward the Levites prepared a meal for themselves and for the priests, because the priests had been busy from morning till night offering the burnt offerings and the fat portions. The Levites took responsibility for all these preparations. ¹⁵The musicians, descendants of Asaph, were in their assigned places, following the orders given by David, Asaph, Heman, and Jeduthun, the king's seer. The gatekeepers guarded the gates and did not need to leave their posts of duty, for their meals were brought to them by their fellow Levites.

¹⁶The entire ceremony for the LORD's Passover was completed that day. All the burnt offerings were sacrificed on the altar of the LORD, as King Josiah had ordered. ¹⁷All the Israelites present in Jerusalem celebrated Passover and the Festival of Unleavened Bread for seven days. ¹⁸Never since the time of the prophet Samuel had there been such a Passover. None of the kings of Israel had ever kept a Passover as Josiah did, involving all the priests and Levites, all the people of Jerusalem, and people from all over Judah and Israel. ¹⁹This Passover celebration took place in the eighteenth year of Josiah's reign.

Josiah Dies in Battle

²⁰After Josiah had finished restoring the Temple, King Neco of Egypt led his army up from Egypt to do battle at Carchemish on the Euphrates River, and Josiah and his army marched out to fight him. ²¹But King Neco sent ambassadors to Josiah with this message:

"What do you want with me, king of Judah? I have no quarrel with you today! I only want to fight the nation with which I am at war. And God has told me to hurry! Do not interfere with God, who is with me, or he will destroy you."

²²But Josiah refused to listen to Neco, to whom God had indeed spoken, and he would not turn back. Instead, he led his army into battle on the plain of Megiddo. He laid aside his royal robes so the enemy would not recognize him. ²³But the enemy archers hit King Josiah with their arrows and wounded him. He cried out to his men, "Take me from the battle, for I am badly wounded!"

²⁴So they lifted Josiah out of his chariot and placed him in another chariot. Then they brought him back to Jerusalem, where he died. He was buried there in the royal cemetery. And all Judah and Jerusalem mourned for him. ²⁵The prophet Jeremiah composed funeral songs for Josiah, and to this day choirs still sing these sad songs about his death. These songs of sorrow have become a tradition and are recorded in *The Book of Laments*. ²⁶The rest of the events of Josiah's reign and his acts of devotion done according to the written law of the LORD, ²⁷from beginning to end, are recorded in *The Book of the Kings of Israel and Judah*.

CHAPTER **36**

Jehoahaz Rules in Judah

Then the people of the land took Josiah's son Jehoahaz and made him the next king in Jerusalem. ²Jehoahaz* was twenty-three years old when he became king, but he reigned only three months. ³Then he was deposed by Neco, the king of Egypt, who demanded a tribute from Judah of 7,500 pounds of silver and 75 pounds of gold.* ⁴The king of Egypt appointed Eliakim, the brother of Jehoahaz, as the next king of Judah and Jerusalem, and he changed Eliakim's name to Jehoiakim. Then Neco took Jehoahaz to Egypt as a prisoner.

Jehoiakim Rules in Judah

⁵Jehoiakim was twenty-five years old when he became king, and he reigned in Jerusalem eleven years. But he did what was evil in the sight of the LORD his God. ⁶Then King Nebuchadnezzar of Babylon came to Jerusalem and captured it, and he bound Jehoiakim in chains and led him away to Babylon. ⁷Nebuchadnezzar also took some of the treasures from the Temple of the LORD, and he placed them in his palace* in Babylon. ⁸The rest of the events of Jehoiakim's reign, including all the evil things he did and everything found against him, are recorded in *The Book of the Kings of Israel and Judah.* Then his son Jehoiachin became the next king.

Jehoiachin Rules in Judah

⁹Jehoiachin was eighteen* years old when he became king, but he reigned in Jerusalem only three months and ten days. Jehoiachin did what was evil in the LORD's sight. ¹⁰In the spring of the following year, Jehoiachin was summoned to Babylon by King Nebuchadnezzar. Many treasures from the Temple of the LORD were taken to Babylon at that time. And Nebuchadnezzar appointed Jehoiachin's uncle,* Zedekiah, to be the next king in Judah and Jerusalem.

Zedekiah Rules in Judah

¹¹Zedekiah was twenty-one years old when he became king, and he reigned in Jerusalem eleven years. ¹²He did what was evil in the sight of the LORD his God, and he refused to humble himself in the presence of the prophet Jeremiah, who spoke for the LORD. ¹³He also rebelled against King Nebuchadnezzar, even though he had taken an oath of loyalty in God's name. Zede-

kiah was a hard and stubborn man, refusing to turn to the LORD, the God of Israel.

¹⁴All the leaders of the priests and the people became more and more unfaithful. They followed the pagan practices of the surrounding nations, desecrating the Temple of the LORD in Jerusalem.

¹⁵The LORD, the God of their ancestors, repeatedly sent his prophets to warn them, for he had compassion on his people and his Temple. ¹⁶But the people mocked these messengers of God and despised their words. They scoffed at the prophets until the LORD's anger could no longer be restrained and there was no remedy.

The Fall of Jerusalem

¹⁷So the LORD brought the king of Babylon against them. The Babylonians* killed Judah's young men, even chasing after them into the Temple. They had no pity on the people, killing both young and old, men and women, healthy and sick. God handed them all over to Nebuchadnezzar. ¹⁸The king also took home to Babylon all the utensils, large and small, used in the Temple of God, and the treasures from both the LORD's Temple and the royal palace. He also took with him all the royal princes. ¹⁹Then his army set fire to the Temple of God, broke down the walls of Jerusalem, burned all the palaces, and completely destroyed everything of value.* ²⁰The few who survived were taken away to Babylon, and they became servants to the king and his sons until the kingdom of Persia came to power. ²¹So the message of the LORD spoken through Jeremiah was fulfilled. The land finally enjoyed its Sabbath rest, lying desolate for seventy years, just as the prophet had said.

Cyrus Allows the Exiles to Return

²²In the first year of King Cyrus of Persia,* the LORD fulfilled Jeremiah's prophecy by stirring the heart of Cyrus to put this proclamation into writing and to send it throughout his kingdom:

²³"This is what King Cyrus of Persia says: The LORD, the God of heaven, has given me all the kingdoms of the earth. He has appointed me to build him a Temple at Jerusalem in the land of Judah. All of you who are the LORD's people may return to Israel for this task. May the LORD your God be with you!"

36:2 Hebrew *Joahaz,* a variant name for Jehoahaz; also in 36:4.   **36:3** Hebrew *100 talents* [3.4 metric tons] *of silver and 1 talent* [34 kilograms] *of gold.*   **36:7** Or *temple.*   **36:9** As in one Hebrew manuscript, some Greek manuscripts, and Syriac version (see also 2 Kgs 24:8); most Hebrew manuscripts read *eight.*   **36:10** As in parallel text at 2 Kgs 24:17; Hebrew reads *brother,* or *relative.*   **36:17** Or *Chaldeans.*   **36:19** Or *destroyed all the valuable Temple utensils.*   **36:22** The first year of Cyrus's reign was 538 B.C.

Ezra

CHAPTER 1

Cyrus Allows the Exiles to Return

In the first year of King Cyrus of Persia,* the LORD fulfilled Jeremiah's prophecy by stirring the heart of Cyrus to put this proclamation into writing and to send it throughout his kingdom:

2 "This is what King Cyrus of Persia says: The LORD, the God of heaven, has given me all the kingdoms of the earth. He has appointed me to build him a Temple at Jerusalem in the land of Judah. 3All of you who are his people may return to Jerusalem in Judah to rebuild this Temple of the LORD, the God of Israel, who lives in Jerusalem. And may your God be with you! 4Those who live in any place where Jewish survivors are found should contribute toward their expenses by supplying them with silver and gold, supplies for the journey, and livestock, as well as a freewill offering for the Temple of God in Jerusalem."

5Then God stirred the hearts of the priests and Levites and the leaders of the tribes of Judah and Benjamin to return to Jerusalem to rebuild the Temple of the LORD. 6And all their neighbors assisted by giving them vessels of silver and gold, supplies for the journey, and livestock. They gave them many choice gifts in addition to all the freewill offerings.

7King Cyrus himself brought out the valuable items which King Nebuchadnezzar had taken from the LORD's Temple in Jerusalem and had placed in the temple of his own gods. 8Cyrus directed Mithredath, the treasurer of Persia, to count these items and present them to Sheshbazzar, the leader of the exiles returning to Judah.*

9These were the items Cyrus donated:

gold trays	30
silver trays	1,000
silver censers*	29
10gold bowls	30
silver bowls	410
other items	1,000

11In all, 5,400 gold and silver items were turned over to Sheshbazzar to take back to Jerusalem when the exiles returned there from Babylon.

CHAPTER 2

Exiles Who Returned with Zerubbabel

Here is the list of the Jewish exiles of the provinces who returned from their captivity to Jerusalem and to the other towns of Judah. They had been deported to Babylon by King Nebuchadnezzar. 2Their leaders were Zerubbabel, Jeshua, Nehemiah, Seraiah, Reelaiah, Mordecai, Bilshan, Mispar, Bigvai, Rehum, and Baanah. This is the number of the men of Israel who returned from exile:

3 The family of Parosh	2,172
4 The family of Shephatiah	372
5 The family of Arah	775
6 The family of Pahath-moab (descendants of Jeshua and Joab)	2,812
7 The family of Elam	1,254
8 The family of Zattu	945
9 The family of Zaccai	760
10The family of Bani	642
11The family of Bebai	623
12The family of Azgad	1,222
13The family of Adonikam	666
14The family of Bigvai	2,056
15The family of Adin	454
16The family of Ater (descendants of Hezekiah)	98
17The family of Bezai	323
18The family of Jorah	112

1:1 The first year of Cyrus's reign was 538 B.C. 1:8 Hebrew *Sheshbazzar, the prince of Judah.* 1:9 The meaning of this Hebrew word is uncertain.

19The family of Hashum 223
20The family of Gibbar 95
21The people of Bethlehem 123
22The people of Netophah 56
23The people of Anathoth 128
24The people of Beth-azmaveth* 42
25The peoples of Kiriath-jearim,* Kephirah, and
  Beeroth 743
26The peoples of Ramah and Geba 621
27The people of Micmash 122
28The peoples of Bethel and Ai 223
29The citizens of Nebo 52
30The citizens of Magbish 156
31The citizens of Elam 1,254
32The citizens of Harim 320
33The citizens of Lod, Hadid, and Ono 725
34The citizens of Jericho 345
35The citizens of Senaah 3,630

36These are the priests who returned from exile:

The family of Jedaiah (through the line of
  Jeshua) 973
37The family of Immer 1,052
38The family of Pashhur 1,247
39The family of Harim 1,017

40These are the Levites who returned from exile:

The families of Jeshua and Kadmiel (descendants
  of Hodaviah) 74
41The singers of the family of Asaph 128
42The gatekeepers of the families of Shallum, Ater,
  Talmon, Akkub, Hatita, and Shobai 139

43The descendants of the following Temple
  servants returned from exile:
  Ziha, Hasupha, Tabbaoth,
44 Keros, Siaha, Padon,
45 Lebanah, Hagabah, Akkub,
46 Hagab, Shalmai,* Hanan,
47 Giddel, Gahar, Reaiah,
48 Rezin, Nekoda, Gazzam,
49 Uzza, Paseah, Besai,
50 Asnah, Meunim, Nephusim,
51 Bakbuk, Hakupha, Harhur,
52 Bazluth, Mehida, Harsha,
53 Barkos, Sisera, Temah,
54 Neziah, and Hatipha.

55The descendants of these servants of King
  Solomon returned from exile:
  Sotai, Sophereth,* Peruda,
56 Jaalah, Darkon, Giddel,
57 Shephatiah, Hattil, Pokereth-hazzebaim,
  and Ami.

58In all, the Temple servants and the descendants of Solomon's servants numbered 392.

59Another group returned to Jerusalem at this time from the towns of Tel-melah, Tel-harsha, Kerub, Addan, and Immer. However, they could not prove that they or their families were descendants of Israel. 60This group consisted of the families of Delaiah, Tobiah, and Nekoda—a total of 652 people.

61Three families of priests—Hobaiah, Hakkoz, and Barzillai—also returned to Jerusalem. (This Barzillai had married a woman who was a descendant of Barzillai of Gilead, and he had taken her family name.) 62But they had lost their genealogical records, so they were not allowed to serve as priests. 63The governor would not even let them eat the priests' share of food from the sacrifices until there was a priest who could consult the LORD about the matter by means of sacred lots.*

64So a total of 42,360 people returned to Judah, 65in addition to 7,337 servants and 200 singers, both men and women. 66They took with them 736 horses, 245 mules, 67435 camels, and 6,720 donkeys.

68When they arrived at the Temple of the LORD in Jerusalem, some of the family leaders gave generously toward the rebuilding of God's Temple on its original site, 69and each leader gave as much as he could. The total of their gifts came to 61,000 gold coins,* 6,250 pounds* of silver, and 100 robes for the priests.

70So the priests, the Levites, the singers, the gatekeepers, the Temple servants, and some of the common people settled in villages near Jerusalem. The rest of the people returned to the other towns of Judah from which they had come.

CHAPTER **3**
The Altar Is Rebuilt
Now in early autumn,* when the Israelites had settled in their towns, all the people assembled together as one person in Jerusalem. 2Then Jeshua son of Jehozadak* with his fellow priests and Zerubbabel son of Shealtiel with his family began to rebuild the altar of the God of Israel so they could sacrifice burnt offerings on it, as instructed in the law of Moses, the man of God. 3Even though the people were afraid of the local residents, they rebuilt the altar at its old site.

2:24 As in parallel text at Neh 7:28; Hebrew reads *Azmaveth*.   2:25 As in some Hebrew manuscripts and Greek version (see also Neh 7:29); Hebrew reads *Kiriath-arim*.   2:46 As in the marginal *Qere* reading of the Masoretic Text (see also Neh 7:48); Hebrew text reads *Shamlai*.   2:55 As in parallel text at Neh 7:57; Hebrew reads *Hassophereth*.   2:63 Hebrew *consult the Urim and Thummim about the matter*.   2:69a Hebrew *61,000 darics of gold*, about 1,100 pounds or 500 kilograms in weight.   2:69b Hebrew *5,000 minas* [3 metric tons].   3:1 Hebrew *in the seventh month*. The year is not specific, so it may have been during Cyrus's first year (538 B.C.) or second year (537 B.C.). The seventh month of the Hebrew lunar calendar occurred in September/October 538 B.C. and October/November 537 B.C.   3:2 Hebrew *Jozadak*, a variant name for Jehozadak; also in 3:8.

Then they immediately began to sacrifice burnt offerings on the altar to the LORD. They did this each morning and evening.

⁴They celebrated the Festival of Shelters as prescribed in the law of Moses, sacrificing the burnt offerings specified for each day of the festival. ⁵They also offered the regular burnt offerings and the offerings required for the new moon celebrations and the other annual festivals to the LORD. Freewill offerings were also sacrificed to the LORD by the people. ⁶Fifteen days before the Festival of Shelters began,* the priests had begun to sacrifice burnt offerings to the LORD. This was also before they had started to lay the foundation of the LORD's Temple.

The People Rebuild the Temple

⁷Then they hired masons and carpenters and bought cedar logs from the people of Tyre and Sidon, paying them with food, wine, and olive oil. The logs were brought down from the Lebanon mountains and floated along the coast of the Mediterranean Sea to Joppa, for King Cyrus had given permission for this.

⁸The construction of the Temple of God began in midspring,* during the second year after they arrived in Jerusalem. The work force was made up of everyone who had returned from exile, including Zerubbabel son of Shealtiel, Jeshua son of Jehozadak and his fellow priests, and all the Levites. The Levites who were twenty years old or older were put in charge of rebuilding the LORD's Temple. ⁹The workers at the Temple of God were supervised by Jeshua with his sons and relatives, and Kadmiel and his sons, all descendants of Hodaviah.* They were helped in this task by the Levites of the family of Henadad.

¹⁰When the builders completed the foundation of the LORD's Temple, the priests put on their robes and took their places to blow their trumpets. And the Levites, descendants of Asaph, clashed their cymbals to praise the LORD, just as King David had prescribed. ¹¹With praise and thanks, they sang this song to the LORD:

"He is so good!
    His faithful love for Israel endures
        forever!"

Then all the people gave a great shout, praising the LORD because the foundation of the LORD's Temple had been laid.

¹²Many of the older priests, Levites, and other leaders remembered the first Temple, and they wept aloud when they saw the new Temple's foundation. The others, however, were shouting for joy. ¹³The joyful shouting and weeping mingled together in a loud commotion that could be heard far in the distance.

CHAPTER 4

Enemies Oppose the Rebuilding

The enemies of Judah and Benjamin heard that the exiles were rebuilding a Temple to the LORD, the God of Israel. ²So they approached Zerubbabel and the other leaders and said, "Let us build with you, for we worship your God just as you do. We have sacrificed to him ever since King Esarhaddon of Assyria brought us here."

³But Zerubbabel, Jeshua, and the other leaders of Israel replied, "You may have no part in this work, for we have nothing in common. We alone will build the Temple for the LORD, the God of Israel, just as King Cyrus of Persia commanded us."

⁴Then the local residents tried to discourage and frighten the people of Judah to keep them from their work. ⁵They bribed agents to work against them and to frustrate their aims. This went on during the entire reign of King Cyrus of Persia and lasted until King Darius of Persia took the throne.

Later Opposition under King Artaxerxes

⁶Years later when Xerxes* began his reign, the enemies of Judah wrote him a letter of accusation against the people of Judah and Jerusalem. ⁷And even later, during the reign of King Artaxerxes of Persia,* the enemies of Judah, led by Bishlam, Mithredath, and Tabeel, sent a letter to Artaxerxes in the Aramaic language, and it was translated for the king. ⁸Rehum* the governor and Shimshai the court secretary wrote the letter, telling King Artaxerxes about the situation in Jerusalem. ⁹They greeted the king for all their colleagues—the judges and local leaders, the people of Tarpel, the Persians, the Babylonians, and the people of Erech and Susa (that is, Elam). ¹⁰They also sent greetings from the rest of the people whom the great and noble Ashurbanipal* had deported and relocated in Samaria and throughout the neighboring lands of the province west of the Euphrates River. ¹¹This is a copy of the letter they sent him:

3:6 Hebrew *On the first day of the seventh month.* This day of the Hebrew lunar calendar occurs in September or October. The Festival of Shelters began on the fifteenth day of the seventh month.   3:8 Hebrew *in the second month.* This month of the Hebrew lunar calendar occurred in April and May 536 B.C.   3:9 Hebrew *sons of Judah* (i.e., *bene Yehudah*). *Bene* might also be read here as the proper name Binnui; *Yehudah* is probably another name for Hodaviah. Compare 2:40; Neh 7:43; 1 Esdras 5:58.   4:6 Hebrew *Ahasuerus,* another name for Xerxes. He reigned 486–465 B.C.
4:7 Artxzerxes reigned 465–424 B.C.   4:8 The original text of 4:8–6:18 is in Aramaic.   4:10 Aramaic *Osnappar,* another name for Ashurbanipal.

"To Artaxerxes, from your loyal subjects in the province west of the Euphrates River.

12 "Please be informed that the Jews who came here to Jerusalem from Babylon are rebuilding this rebellious and evil city. They have already laid the foundation for its walls and will soon complete them. 13But we wish you to know that if this city is rebuilt and its walls are completed, it will be much to your disadvantage, for the Jews will then refuse to pay their tribute, customs, and tolls to you.

14 "Since we are loyal to you as your subjects and we do not want to see you dishonored in this way, we have sent you this information. 15We suggest that you search your ancestors' records, where you will discover what a rebellious city this has been in the past. In fact, it was destroyed because of its long history of sedition against the kings and countries who attempted to control it. 16We declare that if this city is rebuilt and its walls are completed, the province west of the Euphrates River will be lost to you."

17Then Artaxerxes made this reply:

"To Rehum the governor, Shimshai the court secretary, and their colleagues living in Samaria and throughout the province west of the Euphrates River.

18 "Greetings. The letter you sent has been translated and read to me. 19I have ordered a search to be made of the records and have indeed found that Jerusalem has in times past been a hotbed of insurrection against many kings. In fact, rebellion and sedition are normal there! 20Powerful kings have ruled over Jerusalem and the entire province west of the Euphrates River and have received vast tribute, customs, and tolls. 21Therefore, issue orders to have these people stop their work. That city must not be rebuilt except at my express command. 22Do not delay, for we must not permit the situation to get out of control."

23When this letter from King Artaxerxes was read to Rehum, Shimshai, and their colleagues, they hurried to Jerusalem and forced the Jews to stop building.

The Rebuilding Resumes

24The work on the Temple of God in Jerusalem had stopped, and it remained at a standstill until the second year of the reign of King Darius of Persia.*

CHAPTER **5**

At that time the prophets Haggai and Zechariah son of Iddo prophesied in the name of the God of Israel to the Jews in Judah and Jerusalem. 2Zerubbabel son of Shealtiel and Jeshua son of Jehozadak* responded by beginning the task of rebuilding the Temple of God in Jerusalem. And the prophets of God were with them and helped them.

3But Tattenai, governor of the province west of the Euphrates, and Shethar-bozenai and their colleagues soon arrived in Jerusalem and asked, "Who gave you permission to rebuild this Temple and restore this structure?" 4They also asked for a list of the names of all the people who were working on the Temple. 5But because their God was watching over them, the leaders of the Jews were not prevented from building until a report was sent to Darius and he returned his decision.

Tattenai's Letter to King Darius

6This is the letter that Tattenai the governor, Shethar-bozenai, and the other officials of the province west of the Euphrates River sent to King Darius:

7 "Greetings to King Darius. 8We wish to inform you that we went to the construction site of the Temple of the great God in the province of Judah. It is being rebuilt with specially prepared stones, and timber is being laid in its walls. The work is going forward with great energy and success. 9We asked the leaders, 'Who gave you permission to rebuild this Temple and restore this structure?' 10And we demanded their names so that we could tell you who the leaders were.

11 "This was their answer: 'We are the servants of the God of heaven and earth, and we are rebuilding the Temple that was built here many years ago by a great king of Israel. 12But because our ancestors angered the God of heaven, he abandoned them to King Nebuchadnezzar of Babylon,* who destroyed this Temple and exiled the people to Babylonia.

4:24 The second year of Darius's reign was 520 B.C.   5:2 Aramaic *Jozadak,* a variant name for Jehozadak.   5:12 Aramaic *Nebuchadnezzar the Chaldean.*

13However, King Cyrus of Babylon,* during the first year of his reign, issued a decree that the Temple of God should be rebuilt. 14King Cyrus returned the gold and silver utensils that Nebuchadnezzar had taken from the Temple of God in Jerusalem and had placed in the temple of Babylon. These items were taken from that temple and delivered into the safekeeping of a man named Sheshbazzar, whom King Cyrus appointed as governor of Judah. 15The king instructed him to return the utensils to their place in Jerusalem and to rebuild the Temple of God there as it had been before. 16So this Sheshbazzar came and laid the foundations of the Temple of God in Jerusalem. The people have been working on it ever since, though it is not yet completed.'

17"So now, if it pleases the king, we request that you search in the royal archives of Babylon to discover whether King Cyrus ever issued a decree to rebuild God's Temple in Jerusalem. And then let the king send us his decision in this matter."

CHAPTER **6**

Darius Approves the Rebuilding

So King Darius issued orders that a search be made in the Babylonian archives, where treasures were stored. 2But it was at the fortress at Ecbatana in the province of Media that a scroll was found. This is what it said:

3"Memorandum:

"In the first year of King Cyrus's reign, a decree was sent out concerning the Temple of God at Jerusalem. It must be rebuilt on the site where Jews used to offer their sacrifices, retaining the original foundations. Its height will be ninety feet, and its width will be ninety feet.* 4Every three layers of specially prepared stones will be topped by a layer of timber. All expenses will be paid by the royal treasury. 5And the gold and silver utensils, which were taken to Babylon by Nebuchadnezzar from the Temple of God in Jerusalem, will be taken back to Jerusalem and put into God's Temple as they were before."

6So King Darius sent this message:

"To Tattenai, governor of the province west of the Euphrates River, to Shethar-bozenai, and to your colleagues and other officials west of the Euphrates:

"Stay away from there! 7Do not disturb the construction of the Temple of God. Let it be rebuilt on its former site, and do not hinder the governor of Judah and the leaders of the Jews in their work. 8Moreover I hereby decree that you are to help these leaders of the Jews as they rebuild this Temple of God. You must pay the full construction costs without delay from my taxes collected in your province so that the work will not be discontinued. 9Give the priests in Jerusalem whatever is needed in the way of young bulls, rams, and lambs for the burnt offerings presented to the God of heaven. And without fail, provide them with the wheat, salt, wine, and olive oil that they need each day. 10Then they will be able to offer acceptable sacrifices to the God of heaven and pray for me and my sons.

11"Those who violate this decree in any way will have a beam pulled from their house. Then they will be tied to it and flogged, and their house will be reduced to a pile of rubble.* 12May the God who has chosen the city of Jerusalem as the place to honor his name destroy any king or nation that violates this command and destroys this Temple. I, Darius, have issued this decree. Let it be obeyed with all diligence."

The Temple's Dedication

13Tattenai, governor of the province west of the Euphrates River, and Shethar-bozenai and their colleagues complied at once with the command of King Darius. 14So the Jewish leaders continued their work, and they were greatly encouraged by the preaching of the prophets Haggai and Zechariah son of Iddo. The Temple was finally finished, as had been commanded by the God of Israel and decreed by Cyrus, Darius, and Artaxerxes, the kings of Persia. 15The Temple was completed on March 12,* during the sixth year of King Darius's reign.

16The Temple of God was then dedicated with great joy by the people of Israel, the priests, the

---

5:13 King Cyrus of Persia is here identified as the king of Babylon because Persia had conquered the Babylonian Empire. **6:3** Aramaic *Its height will be 60 cubits [27 meters], and its width will be 60 cubits.* It is commonly held that this verse should be emended to read: "Its height will be 45 feet, its length will be 90 feet, and its width will be 30 feet"; compare 1 Kgs 6:2. The emendation regarding the width is supported by the Syriac version. **6:11** Aramaic *a dunghill.* **6:15** Aramaic *on the third day of the month Adar*, of the Hebrew calendar. This event occurred on March 12, 515 B.C.; also see note on 3:1.

Levites, and the rest of the people who had returned from exile. 17During the dedication ceremony for the Temple of God, one hundred young bulls, two hundred rams, and four hundred lambs were sacrificed. And twelve male goats were presented as a sin offering for the twelve tribes of Israel. 18Then the priests and Levites were divided into their various divisions to serve at the Temple of God in Jerusalem, following all the instructions recorded in the Book of Moses.

Celebration of Passover

19On April 21* the returned exiles celebrated Passover. 20The priests and Levites had purified themselves and were ceremonially clean. So they slaughtered the Passover lamb for all the returned exiles, for the other priests, and for themselves. 21The Passover meal was eaten by the people of Israel who had returned from exile and by the others in the land who had turned from their immoral customs to worship the LORD, the God of Israel. 22They ate the Passover meal and celebrated the Festival of Unleavened Bread for seven days. There was great joy throughout the land because the LORD had changed the attitude of the king of Assyria* toward them, so that he helped them to rebuild the Temple of God, the God of Israel.

CHAPTER 7

Ezra Arrives in Jerusalem

Many years later, during the reign of King Artaxerxes of Persia,* there was a man named Ezra. He was the son* of Seraiah, son of Azariah, son of Hilkiah, 2son of Shallum, son of Zadok, son of Ahitub, 3son of Amariah, son of Azariah, son* of Meraioth, 4son of Zerahiah, son of Uzzi, son of Bukki, 5son of Abishua, son of Phinehas, son of Eleazar, son of Aaron the high priest. 6This Ezra was a scribe, well versed in the law of Moses, which the LORD, the God of Israel, had given to the people of Israel. He came up to Jerusalem from Babylon, and the king gave him everything he asked for, because the gracious hand of the LORD his God was on him. 7Some of the people of Israel, as well as some of the priests, Levites, singers, gatekeepers, and Temple servants, traveled up to Jerusalem with him in the seventh year of King Artaxerxes' reign.

8Ezra arrived in Jerusalem in August* of that year. 9He had left Babylon on April 8* and came to Jerusalem on August 4,* for the gracious hand of his God was on him. 10This was because Ezra had determined to study and obey the law of the LORD and to teach those laws and regulations to the people of Israel.

Artaxerxes' Letter to Ezra

11King Artaxerxes had given a copy of the following letter to Ezra, the priest and scribe who studied and taught the commands and laws of the LORD to Israel:

12"Greetings* from Artaxerxes, the king of kings, to Ezra the priest, the teacher of the law of the God of heaven.

13"I decree that any of the people of Israel in my kingdom, including the priests and Levites, may volunteer to return to Jerusalem with you. 14I and my Council of Seven hereby instruct you to conduct an inquiry into the situation in Judah and Jerusalem, based on your God's law, which is in your hand. 15We also commission you to take with you some silver and gold, which we are freely presenting as an offering to the God of Israel who lives in Jerusalem.

16"Moreover you are to take any silver and gold which you may obtain from the province of Babylon, as well as the freewill offerings of the people and the priests that are presented for the Temple of their God in Jerusalem. 17These donations are to be used specifically for the purchase of bulls, rams, lambs, and the appropriate grain offerings and drink offerings, all of which will be offered on the altar of the Temple of your God in Jerusalem. 18Any money that is left over may be used in whatever way you and your colleagues feel is the will of your God. 19But as for the utensils we are entrusting to you for the service of the Temple of your God, deliver them in full to the God of Jerusalem. 20If you run short of money for anything necessary for your God's Temple or for any similar needs, you may requisition funds from the royal treasury.

21"I, Artaxerxes the king, hereby send this decree to all the treasurers in the province

---

6:19 Hebrew *On the fourteenth day of the first month,* of the Hebrew calendar. This event occurred on April 21, 515 B.C.; also see note on 3:1.
6:22 King Darius of Persia is here identified as the king of Assyria because Persia had conquered the Babylonian Empire, which included the earlier Assyrian Empire.   7:1a Artaxerxes reigned 465–424 B.C.   7:1b Or *descendant;* see 1 Chr 6:14.   7:3 Or *descendant;* see 1 Chr 6:6-10.
7:8 Hebrew *in the fifth month.* This month of the Hebrew lunar calendar occurred in August and September 458 B.C.   7:9a Hebrew *on the first day of the first month,* of the Hebrew calendar. This event occurred on April 8, 458 B.C.; also see note on 3:1.   7:9b Hebrew *on the first day of the fifth month,* of the Hebrew calendar. This event occurred on August 4, 458 B.C.; also see note on 3:1.   7:12 The original text of 7:12-26 is in Aramaic.

west of the Euphrates River: 'You are to give Ezra whatever he requests of you, for he is a priest and teacher of the law of the God of heaven. 22You are to give him up to 7,500 pounds* of silver, 500 bushels* of wheat, 550 gallons of wine, 550 gallons of olive oil,* and an unlimited supply of salt. 23Be careful to provide whatever the God of heaven demands for his Temple, for why should we risk bringing God's anger against the realm of the king and his sons? 24I also decree that no priest, Levite, singer, gatekeeper, Temple servant, or other worker in this Temple of God will be required to pay taxes of any kind.'

25"And you, Ezra, are to use the wisdom God has given you to appoint magistrates and judges who know your God's laws to govern all the people in the province west of the Euphrates River. If the people are not familiar with those laws, you must teach them. 26Anyone who refuses to obey the law of your God and the law of the king will be punished immediately by death, banishment, confiscation of goods, or imprisonment."

Ezra Praises the LORD

27Praise the LORD, the God of our ancestors, who made the king want to beautify the Temple of the LORD in Jerusalem! 28And praise him for demonstrating such unfailing love to me by honoring me before the king, his council, and all his mighty princes! I felt encouraged because the gracious hand of the LORD my God was on me. And I gathered some of the leaders of Israel to return with me to Jerusalem.

CHAPTER **8**
Exiles Who Returned with Ezra

Here is a list of the family leaders and the genealogies of those who came with me from Babylon during the reign of King Artaxerxes:

2 From the family of Phinehas: Gershom.
  From the family of Ithamar: Daniel.
3 From the family of David: Hattush son of Shecaniah.
  From the family of Parosh: Zechariah and 150 other men.
4 From the family of Pahath-moab: Eliehoenai son of Zerahiah and 200 other men.

5 From the family of Zattu*: Shecaniah son of Jahaziel and 300 other men.
6 From the family of Adin: Ebed son of Jonathan and 50 other men.
7 From the family of Elam: Jeshaiah son of Athaliah and 70 other men.
8 From the family of Shephatiah: Zebadiah son of Michael and 80 other men.
9 From the family of Joab: Obadiah son of Jehiel and 218 other men.
10 From the family of Bani*: Shelomith son of Josiphiah and 160 other men.
11 From the family of Bebai: Zechariah son of Bebai and 28 other men.
12 From the family of Azgad: Johanan son of Hakkatan and 110 other men.
13 From the family of Adonikam, who came later*: Eliphelet, Jeuel, Shemaiah, and 60 other men.
14 From the family of Bigvai: Uthai, Zaccur, and 70 other men.

Ezra's Journey to Jerusalem

15I assembled the exiles at the Ahava Canal, and we camped there for three days while I went over the lists of the people and the priests who had arrived. I found that not one Levite had volunteered to come along. 16So I sent for Eliezer, Ariel, Shemaiah, Elnathan, Jarib, Elnathan, Nathan, Zechariah, and Meshullam, who were leaders of the people. I also sent for Joiarib and Elnathan, who were very wise men. 17I sent them to Iddo, the leader of the Levites at Casiphia, to ask him and his relatives and the Temple servants to send us ministers for the Temple of God at Jerusalem. 18Since the gracious hand of our God was on us, they sent us a man named Sherebiah, along with eighteen of his sons and brothers. He was a very astute man and a descendant of Mahli, who was a descendant of Levi son of Israel.* 19They also sent Hashabiah, together with Jeshaiah from the descendants of Merari, and twenty of his sons and brothers, 20and 220 Temple servants. The Temple servants were assistants to the Levites—a group of Temple workers first instituted by King David. They were all listed by name.

21And there by the Ahava Canal, I gave orders for all of us to fast and humble ourselves before our God. We prayed that he would give us a safe journey and protect us, our children, and our goods as we traveled. 22For I was ashamed to ask

---

7:22a Aramaic *100 talents* [3.4 metric tons].   7:22b Aramaic *100 cors* [18.2 kiloliters].   7:22c Aramaic *100 baths* [2.1 kiloliters] *of wine, 100 baths of olive oil.*   8:5 As in some Greek manuscripts (see also 1 Esdras 8:32); Hebrew lacks *Zattu.*   8:10 As in some Greek manuscripts (see also 1 Esdras 8:36); Hebrew lacks *Bani.*   8:13 The meaning of the Hebrew for this phrase is uncertain.   8:18 *Israel* is the name that God gave to Jacob.

the king for soldiers and horsemen to accompany us and protect us from enemies along the way. After all, we had told the king, "Our God protects all those who worship him, but his fierce anger rages against those who abandon him." ²³So we fasted and earnestly prayed that our God would take care of us, and he heard our prayer.

²⁴I appointed twelve leaders of the priests—Sherebiah, Hashabiah, and ten other priests—²⁵to be in charge of transporting the silver, the gold, the gold bowls, and the other items that the king, his council, his leaders, and the people of Israel had presented for the Temple of God. ²⁶I weighed the treasure as I gave it to them and found the totals to be as follows:

24 tons* of silver,
7,500 pounds* of silver utensils,
7,500 pounds* of gold,
²⁷ 20 gold bowls, equal in value to 1,000 gold coins,*
2 fine articles of polished bronze, as precious as gold.

²⁸And I said to these priests, "You and these treasures have been set apart as holy to the LORD. This silver and gold is a freewill offering to the LORD, the God of our ancestors. ²⁹Guard these treasures well until you present them, without an ounce lost, to the leading priests, the Levites, and the leaders of Israel at the storerooms of the LORD's Temple in Jerusalem." ³⁰So the priests and the Levites accepted the task of transporting these treasures to the Temple of our God in Jerusalem.

³¹We broke camp at the Ahava Canal on April 19* and started off to Jerusalem. And the gracious hand of our God protected us and saved us from enemies and bandits along the way. ³²So at last we arrived safely in Jerusalem, where we rested for three days.

³³On the fourth day after our arrival, the silver, gold, and other valuables were weighed at the Temple of our God and entrusted to Meremoth son of Uriah the priest and to Eleazar son of Phinehas, along with Jozabad son of Jeshua and Noadiah son of Binnui—both of whom were Levites. ³⁴Everything was accounted for by number and weight, and the total weight was officially recorded.

³⁵Then the exiles who had returned from captivity sacrificed burnt offerings to the God of Israel. They presented twelve oxen for the people of Israel, as well as ninety-six rams and seventy-seven lambs. They also offered twelve goats as a sin offering. All this was given as a burnt offering to the LORD. ³⁶The king's decrees were delivered to his lieutenants and the governors of the province west of the Euphrates River, who then cooperated by supporting the people and the Temple of God.

CHAPTER 9

Ezra's Prayer concerning Intermarriage

But then the Jewish leaders came to me and said, "Many of the people of Israel, and even some of the priests and Levites, have not kept themselves separate from the other peoples living in the land. They have taken up the detestable practices of the Canaanites, Hittites, Perizzites, Jebusites, Ammonites, Moabites, Egyptians, and Amorites. ²For the men of Israel have married women from these people and have taken them as wives for their sons. So the holy race has become polluted by these mixed marriages. To make matters worse, the officials and leaders are some of the worst offenders."

³When I heard this, I tore my clothing, pulled hair from my head and beard, and sat down utterly shocked. ⁴Then all who trembled at the words of the God of Israel came and sat with me because of this unfaithfulness of his people. And I sat there utterly appalled until the time of the evening sacrifice.

⁵At the time of the sacrifice, I stood up from where I had sat in mourning with my clothes torn. I fell to my knees, lifted my hands to the LORD my God. ⁶I prayed, "O my God, I am utterly ashamed; I blush to lift up my face to you. For our sins are piled higher than our heads, and our guilt has reached to the heavens. ⁷Our whole history has been one of great sin. That is why we and our kings and our priests have been at the mercy of the pagan kings of the land. We have been killed, captured, robbed, and disgraced, just as we are today.

⁸"But now we have been given a brief moment of grace, for the LORD our God has allowed a few of us to survive as a remnant. He has given us security in this holy place. Our God has brightened our eyes and granted us some relief from our slavery. ⁹For we were slaves, but in his unfailing love our God did not abandon us in our slavery. Instead, he caused the kings of Persia to treat us favorably. He revived us so that we

8:26a Hebrew *650 talents* [22 metric tons]. 8:26b Hebrew *100 talents* [3.4 metric tons]. 8:26c Hebrew *100 talents* [3.4 metric tons]. 8:27 Hebrew *1,000 darics*, about 19 pounds or 8.6 kilograms in weight. 8:31 Hebrew *on the twelfth day of the first month*, of the Hebrew calendar. This event occurred on April 19, 458 B.C.; see note on 7:9a.

were able to rebuild the Temple of our God and repair its ruins. He has given us a protective wall in Judah and Jerusalem.

¹⁰"And now, O our God, what can we say after all of this? For once again we have ignored your commands! ¹¹Your servants the prophets warned us that the land we would possess was totally defiled by the detestable practices of the people living there. From one end to the other, the land is filled with corruption. ¹²You told us not to let our daughters marry their sons, and not to let our sons marry their daughters, and not to help those nations in any way. You promised that if we avoided these things, we would become a prosperous nation. You promised that we would enjoy the good produce of the land and leave this prosperity to our children as an inheritance forever.

¹³"Now we are being punished because of our wickedness and our great guilt. But we have actually been punished far less than we deserve, for you, our God, have allowed some of us to survive as a remnant. ¹⁴But now we are again breaking your commands and intermarrying with people who do these detestable things. Surely your anger will destroy us until even this little remnant no longer survives. ¹⁵O LORD, God of Israel, you are just. We stand before you in our guilt as nothing but an escaped remnant, though in such a condition none of us can stand in your presence."

CHAPTER **10**

The People Confess Their Sin

While Ezra prayed and made this confession, weeping and throwing himself to the ground in front of the Temple of God, a large crowd of people from Israel—men, women, and children—gathered and wept bitterly with him. ²Then Shecaniah son of Jehiel, a descendant of Elam, said to Ezra, "We confess that we have been unfaithful to our God, for we have married these pagan women of the land. But there is hope for Israel in spite of this. ³Let us now make a covenant with our God to divorce our pagan wives and to send them away with their children. We will follow the advice given by you and by the others who respect the commands of our God. We will obey the law of God. ⁴Take courage, for it is your duty to tell us how to proceed in setting things straight, and we will cooperate fully."

⁵So Ezra stood up and demanded that the leaders of the priests and the Levites and all the people of Israel swear that they would do as Shecaniah had said. And they all swore a solemn oath. ⁶Then Ezra left the front of the Temple of God and went to the room of Jehohanan son of Eliashib. He spent the night* there, but he did not eat any food or drink. He was still in mourning because of the unfaithfulness of the returned exiles. ⁷Then a proclamation was made throughout Judah and Jerusalem that all the returned exiles should come to Jerusalem. ⁸Those who failed to come within three days would, if the leaders and elders so decided, forfeit all their property and be expelled from the assembly of the exiles.

⁹Within three days, all the people of Judah and Benjamin had gathered in Jerusalem. This took place on December 19,* and all the people were sitting in the square before the Temple of God. They were trembling both because of the seriousness of the matter and because it was raining. ¹⁰Then Ezra the priest stood and said to them: "You have sinned, for you have married pagan women. Now we are even more deeply under condemnation than we were before. ¹¹Confess your sin to the LORD, the God of your ancestors, and do what he demands. Separate yourselves from the people of the land and from these pagan women."

¹²Then the whole assembly raised their voices and answered, "Yes, you are right; we must do as you say!" ¹³Then they added, "This isn't something that can be done in a day or two, for many of us are involved in this extremely sinful affair. This is the rainy season, so we cannot stay out here much longer. ¹⁴Let our leaders act on behalf of us all. Everyone who has a pagan wife will come at the scheduled time with the leaders and judges of his city, so that the fierce anger of our God may be turned away from us concerning this affair." ¹⁵Only Jonathan son of Asahel and Jahzeiah son of Tikvah opposed this course of action, and Meshullam and Shabbethai the Levite supported them.

¹⁶So this was the plan that they followed. Ezra selected leaders to represent their families, designating each of the representatives by name. On December 29,* the leaders sat down to investigate the matter. ¹⁷By March 27 of the next year* they had finished dealing with all the men who had married pagan wives.

10:6 As in parallel text at 1 Esdras 9:2; Hebrew reads *He went.*   10:9 Hebrew *on the twentieth day of the ninth month,* of the Hebrew calendar. This event occurred on December 19, 458 B.C.; also see note on 7:9a.   10:16 Hebrew *On the first day of the tenth month,* of the Hebrew calendar. This event occurred on December 29, 458 B.C.; also see note on 7:9a.   10:17 Hebrew *By the first day of the first month,* of the Hebrew calendar. This event occurred on March 27, 457 B.C.; also see note on 7:9a.

Those Guilty of Intermarriage

18These are the priests who had married pagan wives:

From the family of Jeshua son of Jehozadak* and his brothers: Maaseiah, Eliezer, Jarib, and Gedaliah. 19They vowed to divorce their wives, and they each acknowledged their guilt by offering a ram as a guilt offering.

20From the family of Immer: Hanani and Zebadiah.

21From the family of Harim: Maaseiah, Elijah, Shemaiah, Jehiel, and Uzziah.

22From the family of Pashhur: Elioenai, Maaseiah, Ishmael, Nethanel, Jozabad, and Elasah.

23These are the Levites who were guilty: Jozabad, Shimei, Kelaiah (also called Kelita), Pethahiah, Judah, and Eliezer.

24This is the singer who was guilty: Eliashib.

These are the gatekeepers who were guilty: Shallum, Telem, and Uri.

25These are the other people of Israel who were guilty:

From the family of Parosh: Ramiah, Izziah, Malkijah, Mijamin, Eleazar, Hashabiah,* and Benaiah.

26From the family of Elam: Mattaniah, Zechariah, Jehiel, Abdi, Jeremoth, and Elijah.

27From the family of Zattu: Elioenai, Eliashib, Mattaniah, Jeremoth, Zabad, and Aziza.

28From the family of Bebai: Jehohanan, Hananiah, Zabbai, and Athlai.

29From the family of Bani: Meshullam, Malluch, Adaiah, Jashub, Sheal, and Jeremoth.

30From the family of Pahath-moab: Adna, Kelal, Benaiah, Maaseiah, Mattaniah, Bezalel, Binnui, and Manasseh.

31From the family of Harim: Eliezer, Ishijah, Malkijah, Shemaiah, Shimeon, 32Benjamin, Malluch, and Shemariah.

33From the family of Hashum: Mattenai, Mattattah, Zabad, Eliphelet, Jeremai, Manasseh, and Shimei.

34From the family of Bani: Maadai, Amram, Uel, 35Benaiah, Bedeiah, Keluhi, 36Vaniah, Meremoth, Eliashib, 37Mattaniah, Mattenai, and Jaasu.

38From the family of Binnui*: Shimei, 39Shelemiah, Nathan, Adaiah, 40Macnadebai, Shashai, Sharai, 41Azarel, Shelemiah, Shemariah, 42Shallum, Amariah, and Joseph.

43From the family of Nebo: Jeiel, Mattithiah, Zabad, Zebina, Jaddai, Joel, and Benaiah.

44Each of these men had a pagan wife, and some even had children by these wives.*

10:18 Hebrew *Jozadak,* a variant name for Jehozadak.   10:25 As in parallel text at 1 Esdras 9:26; Hebrew reads *Malkijah.*   10:37-38 As in Greek version; Hebrew reads *Jaasu,* 38*Bani, Binnui.*   10:44 Or *and they sent them away with their children.* The meaning of the Hebrew is uncertain.

Nehemiah

CHAPTER **1**

These are the memoirs of Nehemiah son of Hacaliah.

Nehemiah's Concern for Jerusalem

In late autumn of the twentieth year of King Artaxerxes' reign,* I was at the fortress of Susa. ²Hanani, one of my brothers, came to visit me with some other men who had just arrived from Judah. I asked them about the Jews who had survived the captivity and about how things were going in Jerusalem. ³They said to me, "Things are not going well for those who returned to the province of Judah. They are in great trouble and disgrace. The wall of Jerusalem has been torn down, and the gates have been burned."

⁴When I heard this, I sat down and wept. In fact, for days I mourned, fasted, and prayed to the God of heaven. ⁵Then I said, "O LORD, God of heaven, the great and awesome God who keeps his covenant of unfailing love with those who love him and obey his commands, ⁶listen to my prayer! Look down and see me praying night and day for your people Israel. I confess that we have sinned against you. Yes, even my own family and I have sinned! ⁷We have sinned terribly by not obeying the commands, laws, and regulations that you gave us through your servant Moses.

⁸"Please remember what you told your servant Moses: 'If you sin, I will scatter you among the nations. ⁹But if you return to me and obey my commands, even if you are exiled to the ends of the earth, I will bring you back to the place I have chosen for my name to be honored.'

¹⁰"We are your servants, the people you rescued by your great power and might. ¹¹O Lord, please hear my prayer! Listen to the prayers of those of us who delight in honoring you. Please grant me success now as I go to ask the king* for a great favor. Put it into his heart to be kind to me."

In those days I was the king's cup-bearer.

CHAPTER **2**

Nehemiah Goes to Jerusalem

Early the following spring,* during the twentieth year of King Artaxerxes' reign, I was serving the king his wine. I had never appeared sad in his presence before this time. ²So the king asked me, "Why are you so sad? You aren't sick, are you? You look like a man with deep troubles."

Then I was badly frightened, ³but I replied, "Long live the king! Why shouldn't I be sad? For the city where my ancestors are buried is in ruins, and the gates have been burned down."

⁴The king asked, "Well, how can I help you?"

With a prayer to the God of heaven, ⁵I replied, "If it please Your Majesty and if you are pleased with me, your servant, send me to Judah to rebuild the city where my ancestors are buried."

⁶The king, with the queen sitting beside him, asked, "How long will you be gone? When will you return?" So the king agreed, and I set a date for my departure.

⁷I also said to the king, "If it please Your Majesty, give me letters to the governors of the province west of the Euphrates River, instructing them to let me travel safely through their territories on my way to Judah. ⁸And please send a letter to Asaph, the manager of the king's forest, instructing him to give me timber. I will need it to make beams for the gates of the Temple fortress, for the city walls, and for a house for

---

1:1 Hebrew *In the month of Kislev of the twentieth year.* A number of dates in the book of Nehemiah can be cross-checked with dates in surviving Persian records and related accurately to our modern calendar. This month of the Hebrew lunar calendar occurred in November and December 446 B.C. The *twentieth year* probably refers to the reign of King Artaxerxes I; compare 2:1; 5:14. 1:11 Hebrew *stand before this man.* 2:1 Hebrew *In the month of Nisan.* This month of the Hebrew lunar calendar occurred in April and May 445 B.C.

myself." And the king granted these requests, because the gracious hand of God was on me.

9When I came to the governors of the province west of the Euphrates River, I delivered the king's letters to them. The king, I should add, had sent along army officers and horsemen to protect me. 10But when Sanballat the Horonite and Tobiah the Ammonite official heard of my arrival, they were very angry that someone had come who was interested in helping Israel.

Nehemiah Inspects Jerusalem's Wall

11Three days after my arrival at Jerusalem, 12I slipped out during the night, taking only a few others with me. I had not told anyone about the plans God had put in my heart for Jerusalem. We took no pack animals with us, except the donkey that I myself was riding. 13I went out through the Valley Gate, past the Jackal's Well,* and over to the Dung Gate to inspect the broken walls and burned gates. 14Then I went to the Fountain Gate and to the King's Pool, but my donkey couldn't get through the rubble. 15So I went up the Kidron Valley* instead, inspecting the wall before I turned back and entered again at the Valley Gate.

16The city officials did not know I had been out there or what I was doing, for I had not yet said anything to anyone about my plans. I had not yet spoken to the religious and political leaders, the officials, or anyone else in the administration. 17But now I said to them, "You know full well the tragedy of our city. It lies in ruins, and its gates are burned. Let us rebuild the wall of Jerusalem and rid ourselves of this disgrace!" 18Then I told them about how the gracious hand of God had been on me, and about my conversation with the king.

They replied at once, "Good! Let's rebuild the wall!" So they began the good work.

19But when Sanballat, Tobiah, and Geshem the Arab heard of our plan, they scoffed contemptuously. "What are you doing, rebelling against the king like this?" they asked.

20But I replied, "The God of heaven will help us succeed. We his servants will start rebuilding this wall. But you have no stake or claim in Jerusalem."

CHAPTER **3**
Rebuilding the Wall of Jerusalem

Then Eliashib the high priest and the other priests started to rebuild at the Sheep Gate. They dedicated it and set up its doors, building the wall as far as the Tower of the Hundred, which they dedicated, and the Tower of Hananel. 2People from the city of Jericho worked next to them, and beyond them was Zaccur son of Imri.

3The Fish Gate was built by the sons of Hassenaah. They did the whole thing—laid the beams, hung the doors, and put the bolts and bars in place. 4Meremoth son of Uriah and grandson of Hakkoz repaired the next section of wall. Beside him were Meshullam son of Berekiah and grandson of Meshezabel, and then Zadok son of Baana. 5Next were the people from Tekoa, though their leaders refused to help.

6The Old City Gate* was repaired by Joiada son of Paseah and Meshullam son of Besodeiah. They laid the beams, set up the doors, and installed the bolts and bars. 7Next to them were Melatiah from Gibeon, Jadon from Meronoth, and people from Gibeon and Mizpah, the headquarters of the governor of the province west of the Euphrates River. 8Next was Uzziel son of Harhaiah, a goldsmith by trade, who also worked on the wall. Beyond him was Hananiah, a manufacturer of perfumes. They left out* a section of Jerusalem as far as the Broad Wall.

9Rephaiah son of Hur, the leader of half the district of Jerusalem, was next to them on the wall. 10Next Jedaiah son of Harumaph repaired the wall beside his own house, and next to him was Hattush son of Hashabneiah. 11Then came Malkijah son of Harim and Hasshub son of Pahath-moab, who repaired the Tower of the Ovens, in addition to another section of the wall. 12Shallum son of Hallohesh and his daughters repaired the next section. He was the leader of the other half of the district of Jerusalem.

13The people from Zanoah, led by Hanun, rebuilt the Valley Gate, hung its doors, and installed the bolts and bars. They also repaired the fifteen hundred feet* of wall to the Dung Gate.

14The Dung Gate was repaired by Malkijah son of Recab, the leader of the Beth-hakkerem district. After rebuilding it, he hung the doors and installed the bolts and bars.

15Shallum son of Col-hozeh, the leader of the Mizpah district, repaired the Fountain Gate. He rebuilt it, roofed it, hung its doors, and installed its bolts and bars. Then he repaired the wall of the pool of Siloam* near the king's garden, and he rebuilt the wall as far as the stairs that descend from the City of David. 16Next to him was Nehemiah son of Azbuk, the leader of half the district of Beth-zur. He rebuilt the wall to a place

2:13 Or *Serpent's Well.* 2:15 Hebrew *the valley.* 3:6 Or *The Mishneh Gate,* or *The Jeshanah Gate.* 3:8 Or *They restored.* 3:13 Hebrew *1,000 cubits* [450 meters]. 3:15 Hebrew *pool of Shelah,* another name for the pool of Siloam.

opposite the royal cemetery as far as the water reservoir and the House of the Warriors.

¹⁷Next was a group of Levites working under the supervision of Rehum under of Bani. Then came Hashabiah, the leader of half the district of Keilah, who supervised the building of the wall on behalf of his own district. ¹⁸Next down the line were his countrymen led by Binnui* son of Henadad, the leader of the other half of the district of Keilah.

¹⁹Next to them, Ezer son of Jeshua, the leader of Mizpah, repaired another section of wall opposite the armory by the buttress. ²⁰Next to him was Baruch son of Zabbai, who repaired an additional section from the buttress to the door of the home of Eliashib the high priest. ²¹Meremoth son of Uriah and grandson of Hakkoz rebuilt another section of the wall extending from a point opposite the door of Eliashib's house to the side of the house.

²²Then came the priests from the surrounding region. ²³After them, Benjamin, Hasshub, and Azariah son of Maaseiah and grandson of Ananiah repaired the sections next to their own houses. ²⁴Next was Binnui son of Henadad, who rebuilt another section of the wall from Azariah's house to the buttress and the corner. ²⁵Palal son of Uzai carried on the work from a point opposite the buttress and the corner to the upper tower that projects from the king's house beside the court of the guard. Next to him were Pedaiah son of Parosh ²⁶and the Temple servants living on the hill of Ophel, who repaired the wall as far as the Water Gate toward the east and the projecting tower. ²⁷Then came the people of Tekoa, who repaired another section opposite the great projecting tower and over to the wall of Ophel.

²⁸The priests repaired the wall up the hill from the Horse Gate, each one doing the section immediately opposite his own house. ²⁹Next Zadok son of Immer also rebuilt the wall next to his own house, and beyond him was Shemaiah son of Shecaniah, the gatekeeper of the East Gate. ³⁰Next Hananiah son of Shelemiah and Hanun, the sixth son of Zalaph, repaired another section, while Meshullam son of Berekiah rebuilt the wall next to his own house. ³¹Malkijah, one of the goldsmiths, repaired the wall as far as the housing for the Temple servants and merchants, opposite the Inspection Gate. Then he continued as far as the upper room at the corner. ³²The other goldsmiths and merchants repaired the wall from that corner to the Sheep Gate.

CHAPTER **4**

Enemies Oppose the Rebuilding

Sanballat was very angry when he learned that we were rebuilding the wall. He flew into a rage and mocked the Jews, ²saying in front of his friends and the Samarian army officers, "What does this bunch of poor, feeble Jews think they are doing? Do they think they can build the wall in a day if they offer enough sacrifices? Look at those charred stones they are pulling out of the rubbish and using again!"

³Tobiah the Ammonite, who was standing beside him, remarked, "That stone wall would collapse if even a fox walked along the top of it!"

⁴Then I prayed, "Hear us, O our God, for we are being mocked. May their scoffing fall back on their own heads, and may they themselves become captives in a foreign land! ⁵Do not ignore their guilt. Do not blot out their sins, for they have provoked you to anger here in the presence of* the builders."

⁶At last the wall was completed to half its original height around the entire city, for the people had worked very hard. ⁷But when Sanballat and Tobiah and the Arabs, Ammonites, and Ashdodites heard that the work was going ahead and that the gaps in the wall were being repaired, they became furious. ⁸They all made plans to come and fight against Jerusalem and to bring about confusion there. ⁹But we prayed to our God and guarded the city day and night to protect ourselves.

¹⁰Then the people of Judah began to complain that the workers were becoming tired. There was so much rubble to be moved that we could never get it done by ourselves. ¹¹Meanwhile, our enemies were saying, "Before they know what's happening, we will swoop down on them and kill them and end their work."

¹²The Jews who lived near the enemy came and told us again and again, "They will come from all directions and attack us!"* ¹³So I placed armed guards behind the lowest parts of the wall in the exposed areas. I stationed the people to stand guard by families, armed with swords, spears, and bows.

¹⁴Then as I looked over the situation, I called together the leaders and the people and said to them, "Don't be afraid of the enemy! Remember the Lord, who is great and glorious, and fight for your friends, your families, and your homes!"

¹⁵When our enemies heard that we knew of their plans and that God had frustrated them,

3:18 As in a few Hebrew manuscripts, some Greek manuscripts, and Syriac version (see also 3:24; 10:9); most Hebrew manuscripts read *Bavvai.* **4:5** Or *for they have thrown insults in the face of.* **4:12** The meaning of the Hebrew is uncertain.

we all returned to our work on the wall. 16But from then on, only half my men worked while the other half stood guard with spears, shields, bows, and coats of mail. The officers stationed themselves behind the people of Judah 17who were building the wall. The common laborers carried on their work with one hand supporting their load and one hand holding a weapon. 18All the builders had a sword belted to their side. The trumpeter stayed with me to sound the alarm.

19Then I explained to the nobles and officials and all the people, "The work is very spread out, and we are widely separated from each other along the wall. 20When you hear the blast of the trumpet, rush to wherever it is sounding. Then our God will fight for us!"

21We worked early and late, from sunrise to sunset. And half the men were always on guard. 22I also told everyone living outside the walls to move into Jerusalem. That way they and their servants could go on guard duty at night as well as work during the day. 23During this time, none of us—not I, nor my relatives, nor my servants, nor the guards who were with me— ever took off our clothes. We carried our weapons with us at all times, even when we went for water.*

CHAPTER 5
Nehemiah Defends the Oppressed

About this time some of the men and their wives raised a cry of protest against their fellow Jews. 2They were saying, "We have such large families. We need more money just so we can buy the food we need to survive." 3Others said, "We have mortgaged our fields, vineyards, and homes to get food during the famine." 4And others said, "We have already borrowed to the limit on our fields and vineyards to pay our taxes. 5We belong to the same family, and our children are just like theirs. Yet we must sell our children into slavery just to get enough money to live. We have already sold some of our daughters, and we are helpless to do anything about it, for our fields and vineyards are already mortgaged to others."

6When I heard their complaints, I was very angry. 7After thinking about the situation, I spoke out against these nobles and officials. I told them, "You are oppressing your own relatives by charging them interest when they bor-

row money!" Then I called a public meeting to deal with the problem.

8At the meeting I said to them, "The rest of us are doing all we can to redeem our Jewish relatives who have had to sell themselves to pagan foreigners, but you are selling them back into slavery again. How often must we redeem them?" And they had nothing to say in their defense.

9Then I pressed further, "What you are doing is not right! Should you not walk in the fear of our God in order to avoid being mocked by enemy nations? 10I myself, as well as my brothers and my workers, have been lending the people money and grain, but now let us stop this business of loans. 11You must restore their fields, vineyards, olive groves, and homes to them this very day. Repay the interest you charged on their money, grain, wine, and olive oil."

12Then they replied, "We will give back everything and demand nothing more from the people. We will do as you say." Then I called the priests and made the nobles and officials formally vow to do what they had promised.

13I shook out the fold of my robe and said, "If you fail to keep your promise, may God shake you from your homes and from your property!"

The whole assembly responded, "Amen," and they praised the LORD. And the people did as they had promised.

14I would like to mention that for the entire twelve years that I was governor of Judah— from the twentieth until the thirty-second year of the reign of King Artaxerxes*—neither I nor my officials drew on our official food allowance. 15This was quite a contrast to the former governors who had laid heavy burdens on the people, demanding a daily ration of food and wine, besides a pound* of silver. Even their assistants took advantage of the people. But because of my fear of God, I did not act that way. 16I devoted myself to working on the wall and refused to acquire any land. And I required all my officials to spend time working on the wall. 17I asked for nothing, even though I regularly fed 150 Jewish officials at my table, besides all the visitors from other lands! 18The provisions required at my expense for each day were one ox, six fat sheep, and a large number of domestic fowl. And every ten days we needed a large supply of all kinds of wine. Yet I refused to claim the governor's food allow-

4:23 Hebrew *Each his weapon the water.* The meaning of the Hebrew is uncertain.   5:14 That is, from 445 to 433 B.C.   5:15 Hebrew *40 shekels* [456 grams].

ance because the people were already having a difficult time.

19Remember, O my God, all that I have done for these people, and bless me for it.

CHAPTER 6
Continued Opposition to Rebuilding

When Sanballat, Tobiah, Geshem the Arab, and the rest of our enemies found out that I had finished rebuilding the wall and that no gaps remained—though we had not yet hung the doors in the gates—2Sanballat and Geshem sent me a message asking me to meet them at one of the villages* in the plain of Ono. But I realized they were plotting to harm me, 3so I replied by sending this message to them: "I am doing a great work! I cannot stop to come and meet with you."

4Four times they sent the same message, and each time I gave the same reply. 5The fifth time, Sanballat's servant came with an open letter in his hand, 6and this is what it said:

"Geshem* tells me that everywhere he goes he hears that you and the Jews are planning to rebel and that is why you are building the wall. According to his reports, you plan to be their king. 7He also reports that you have appointed prophets to prophesy about you in Jerusalem, saying, 'Look! There is a king in Judah!'

"You can be very sure that this report will get back to the king, so I suggest that you come and talk it over with me."

8My reply was, "You know you are lying. There is no truth in any part of your story." 9They were just trying to intimidate us, imagining that they could break our resolve and stop the work. So I prayed for strength to continue the work.

10Later I went to visit Shemaiah son of Delaiah and grandson of Mehetabel, who was confined to his home. He said, "Let us meet together inside the Temple of God and bolt the doors shut. Your enemies are coming to kill you tonight."

11But I replied, "Should someone in my position run away from danger? Should someone in my position enter the Temple to save his life? No, I won't do it!" 12I realized that God had not spoken to him, but that he had uttered this prophecy against me because Tobiah and Sanballat had hired him. 13They were hoping to intimidate me and make me sin by following his

suggestion. Then they would be able to accuse and discredit me.

14Remember, O my God, all the evil things that Tobiah and Sanballat have done. And remember Noadiah the prophet and all the prophets like her who have tried to intimidate me.

The Builders Complete the Wall

15So on October 2* the wall was finally finished—just fifty-two days after we had begun. 16When our enemies and the surrounding nations heard about it, they were frightened and humiliated. They realized that this work had been done with the help of our God.

17During those fifty-two days, many letters went back and forth between Tobiah and the officials of Judah. 18For many in Judah had sworn allegiance to him because his father-in-law was Shecaniah son of Arah and because his son Jehohanan was married to the daughter of Meshullam son of Berekiah. 19They kept telling me what a wonderful man Tobiah was, and then they told him everything I said. And Tobiah sent many threatening letters to intimidate me.

CHAPTER 7

After the wall was finished and I had hung the doors in the gates, the gatekeepers, singers, and Levites were appointed. 2I gave the responsibility of governing Jerusalem to my brother Hanani, along with Hananiah, the commander of the fortress, for he was a faithful man who feared God more than most. 3I said to them, "Do not leave the gates open during the hottest part of the day.* And while the gatekeepers are still on duty, have them shut and bar the doors. Appoint the residents of Jerusalem to act as guards, everyone on a regular watch. Some will serve at their regular posts and some in front of their own homes."

Nehemiah Registers the People

4At that time the city was large and spacious, but the population was small. And only a few houses were scattered throughout the city. 5So my God gave me the idea to call together all the leaders of the city, along with the ordinary citizens, for registration. I had found the genealogical record of those who had first returned to Judah. This is what was written there:

6:2 As in Greek version; Hebrew reads *at Kephirim.* 6:6 Hebrew *Gashmu,* another name for Geshem. 6:15 Hebrew *on the twenty-fifth day of the month Elul,* of the Hebrew calendar. This event occurred on October 2, 445 B.C.; also see note on 1:1. 7:3 Or *Keep the gates of Jerusalem closed until the sun is hot.*

Studying God's Word Helps Us to Experience His Joy
Read NEHEMIAH 8:1-18

In looking at this story, we see that the study of God's Word should lead to joy. Since the Bible has been the number one best-seller in America for years, you would think that we would have a country of joyful people—but that is obviously not the case. As this text shows, simply reading the Bible and studying its contents is not enough. Several things must take place before we can truly experience the joy of the Lord.

- We must make the study of God's Word a priority (verses 1-5).
- Our study of God's Word should lead to worship (verse 6).
- We need to take time to understand what passages mean (verses 7-8).
- We need to rejoice about what we have learned and share with others (verses 9-12).
- We need to apply what we have learned (verses 13-18).

When you study, understand, and obey God's Word, it produces joy in your life. And that joy of the Lord will be your strength, carrying you through the trials and tribulations of life.

For the next note on "Joy," turn to p. 1094.

CORNER STONES

6 "Here is the list of the Jewish exiles of the provinces who returned from their captivity to Jerusalem and to the other towns of Judah. They had been deported to Babylon by King Nebuchadnezzar. 7Their leaders were Zerubbabel, Jeshua, Nehemiah, Seraiah,* Reelaiah,* Nahamani, Mordecai, Bilshan, Mispar,* Bigvai, Rehum,* and Baanah. This is the number of men of Israel who returned from exile:

8 The family of Parosh	2,172
9 The family of Shephatiah	372
10 The family of Arah	652
11 The family of Pahath-moab (descendants of Jeshua and Joab)	2,818
12 The family of Elam	1,254
13 The family of Zattu	845
14 The family of Zaccai	760
15 The family of Bani*	648
16 The family of Bebai	628
17 The family of Azgad	2,322
18 The family of Adonikam	667
19 The family of Bigvai	2,067
20 The family of Adin	655
21 The family of Ater (descendants of Hezekiah)	98
22 The family of Hashum	328
23 The family of Bezai	324
24 The family of Jorah*	112
25 The family of Gibbar*	95
26 The peoples of Bethlehem and Netophah	188
27 The people of Anathoth	128
28 The people of Beth-azmaveth	42
29 The peoples of Kiriath-jearim, Kephirah, and Beeroth	743
30 The peoples of Ramah and Geba	621
31 The people of Micmash	122
32 The peoples of Bethel and Ai	123
33 The people of Nebo	52
34 The citizens of Elam	1,254
35 The citizens of Harim	320
36 The citizens of Jericho	345
37 The citizens of Lod, Hadid, and Ono	721
38 The citizens of Senaah	3,930

39 "These are the priests who returned from exile:

The family of Jedaiah (through the line of Jeshua)	973
40 The family of Immer	1,052
41 The family of Pashhur	1,247
42 The family of Harim	1,017

43 "These are the Levites who returned from exile:

The families of Jeshua and Kadmiel (descendants of Hodaviah*)	74
44 The singers of the family of Asaph	148
45 The gatekeepers of the families of Shallum, Ater, Talmon, Akkub, Hatita, and Shobai	138

46 "The descendants of the following Temple servants returned from exile:
Ziha, Hasupha, Tabbaoth,
47 Keros, Siaha,* Padon,

7:7a As in parallel text at Ezra 2:2; Hebrew reads *Azariah*.   7:7b As in parallel text at Ezra 2:2; Hebrew reads *Raamiah*.   7:7c As in parallel text at Ezra 2:2; Hebrew reads *Mispereth*.   7:7d As in parallel text at Ezra 2:2; Hebrew reads *Nehum*.   7:15 As in parallel text at Ezra 2:10; Hebrew reads *Binnui*.   7:24 As in parallel text at Ezra 2:18; Hebrew reads *Hariph*.   7:25 As in parallel text at Ezra 2:20; Hebrew reads *Gibeon*.   7:43 As in parallel text at Ezra 2:40; Hebrew reads *Hodevah*.   7:47 As in parallel text at Ezra 2:44; Hebrew reads *Sia*.

⁴⁸ Lebanah, Hagabah, Shalmai,
⁴⁹ Hanan, Giddel, Gahar,
⁵⁰ Reaiah, Rezin, Nekoda,
⁵¹ Gazzam, Uzza, Paseah,
⁵² Besai, Meunim, Nephusim,*
⁵³ Bakbuk, Hakupha, Harhur,
⁵⁴ Bazluth,* Mehida, Harsha,
⁵⁵ Barkos, Sisera, Temah,
⁵⁶ Neziah, and Hatipha.

⁵⁷ "The descendants of these servants of King Solomon returned from exile:
Sotai, Sophereth, Peruda,*
⁵⁸ Jaalah,* Darkon, Giddel,
⁵⁹ Shephatiah, Hattil, Pokereth-hazzebaim, and Ami.*

⁶⁰ "In all, the Temple servants and the descendants of Solomon's servants numbered 392.

⁶¹ "Another group returned to Jerusalem at this time from the towns of Tel-melah, Tel-harsha, Kerub, Addan,* and Immer. However, they could not prove that they or their families were descendants of Israel. ⁶²This group included the families of Delaiah, Tobiah, and Nekoda—a total of 642 people.

⁶³ "Three families of priests—Hobaiah, Hakkoz, and Barzillai—also returned to Jerusalem. (This Barzillai had married a woman who was a descendant of Barzillai of Gilead, and he had taken her family name.) ⁶⁴But they had lost their genealogical records, so they were not allowed to serve as priests. ⁶⁵The governor would not even let them eat the priests' share of food from the sacrifices until there was a priest who could consult the LORD about the matter by means of sacred lots.*

⁶⁶ "So a total of 42,360 people returned to Judah, ⁶⁷in addition to 7,337 servants and 245 singers, both men and women. ⁶⁸They took with them 736 horses, 245 mules,* ⁶⁹435 camels, and 6,720 donkeys.

⁷⁰ "Some of the family leaders gave gifts for the work. The governor gave to the treasury 1,000 gold coins,* 50 gold basins, and 530 robes for the priests. ⁷¹The other leaders gave to the treasury a total of 20,000 gold coins* and some 2,750 pounds* of silver for the work. ⁷²The rest of the people gave 20,000 gold coins,

about 2,500 pounds* of silver, and 67 robes for the priests.

⁷³ "So the priests, the Levites, the gatekeepers, the singers, the Temple servants, along with some of the people—that is to say, all Israel—settled in their own towns."

Ezra Reads the Law

Now in midautumn,* when the Israelites had settled in their towns, ¹all the people assembled together as one person at the square just inside the Water Gate. They asked Ezra the scribe to bring out the Book of the Law of Moses, which the LORD had given for Israel to obey.

CHAPTER **8**

²So on October 8* Ezra the priest brought the scroll of the law before the assembly, which included the men and women and all the children old enough to understand. ³He faced the square just inside the Water Gate from early morning until noon and read aloud to everyone who could understand. All the people paid close attention to the Book of the Law. ⁴Ezra the scribe stood on a high wooden platform that had been made for the occasion. To his right stood Mattithiah, Shema, Anaiah, Uriah, Hilkiah, and Maaseiah. To his left stood Pedaiah, Mishael, Malkijah, Hashum, Hashbaddanah, Zechariah, and Meshullam. ⁵Ezra stood on the platform in full view of all the people. When they saw him open the book, they all rose to their feet.

⁶Then Ezra praised the LORD, the great God, and all the people chanted, "Amen! Amen!" as they lifted their hands toward heaven. Then they bowed down and worshiped the LORD with their faces to the ground.

⁷Now the Levites—Jeshua, Bani, Sherebiah, Jamin, Akkub, Shabbethai, Hodiah, Maaseiah, Kelita, Azariah, Jozabad, Hanan, and Pelaiah—instructed the people who were standing there. ⁸They read from the Book of the Law of God and clearly explained the meaning of what was being read, helping the people understand each passage. ⁹Then Nehemiah the governor, Ezra the priest and scribe, and the Levites who were interpreting for the people said to them, "Don't weep on such a day as this! For today is a sacred day

---

7:52 As in parallel text at Ezra 2:50; Hebrew reads *Nephushesim.* 7:54 As in parallel text at Ezra 2:52; Hebrew reads *Bazlith.* 7:57 As in parallel text at Ezra 2:55; Hebrew reads *Perida.* 7:58 As in parallel text at Ezra 2:56; Hebrew reads *Jaala.* 7:59 As in parallel text at Ezra 2:57; Hebrew reads *Amon.* 7:61 As in parallel text at Ezra 2:59; Hebrew reads *Addon.* 7:65 Hebrew *consult the Urim and Thummim about the matter.* 7:68 As in some Hebrew manuscripts (see also Ezra 2:66); most Hebrew manuscripts lack this verse. 7:70 Hebrew *1,000 darics of gold,* about 19 pounds or 8.6 kilograms in weight; also in 7:72. 7:71a Hebrew *20,000 darics of gold,* about 375 pounds or 170 kilograms in weight; also in 7:72. 7:71b Hebrew *2,000 minas* [1.3 metric tons]. 7:72 Hebrew *2,000 minas* [1.2 metric tons]. 7:73 Hebrew *in the seventh month.* This month of the Hebrew lunar calendar occurred in October and November 445 B.C. 8:2 Hebrew *on the first day of the seventh month,* of the Hebrew calendar. This event occurred on October 8, 445 B.C.; also see note on 1:1.

before the LORD your God." All the people had been weeping as they listened to the words of the law.

10And Nehemiah* continued, "Go and celebrate with a feast of choice foods and sweet drinks, and share gifts of food with people who have nothing prepared. This is a sacred day before our Lord. Don't be dejected and sad, for the joy of the LORD is your strength!"

11And the Levites, too, quieted the people, telling them, "Hush! Don't weep! For this is a sacred day." 12So the people went away to eat and drink at a festive meal, to share gifts of food, and to celebrate with great joy because they had heard God's words and understood them.

The Festival of Shelters

13On October 9* the family leaders and the priests and Levites met with Ezra to go over the law in greater detail. 14As they studied the law, they discovered that the LORD had commanded through Moses that the Israelites should live in shelters during the festival to be held that month.* 15He had said that a proclamation should be made throughout their towns and especially in Jerusalem, telling the people to go to the hills to get branches from olive, wild olive, myrtle, palm, and fig trees. They were to use these branches to make shelters in which they would live during the festival, as it was prescribed in the law.

16So the people went out and cut branches and used them to build shelters on the roofs of their houses, in their courtyards, in the courtyards of God's Temple, or in the squares just inside the Water Gate and the Ephraim Gate. 17So everyone who had returned from captivity lived in these shelters for the seven days of the festival, and everyone was filled with great joy! The Israelites had not celebrated this way since the days of Joshua son of Nun. 18Ezra read from the Book of the Law of God on each of the seven days of the festival. Then on October 15* they held a solemn assembly, as the law of Moses required.

CHAPTER 9

The People Confess Their Sins

On October 31* the people returned for another observance. This time they fasted and dressed in sackcloth and sprinkled dust on their heads. 2Those of Israelite descent separated themselves from all foreigners as they confessed their own sins and the sins of their ancestors. 3The Book of the Law of the LORD their God was read aloud to them for about three hours.* Then for three more hours they took turns confessing their sins and worshiping the LORD their God. 4Some of the Levites were standing on the stairs, crying out to the LORD their God. Their names were Jeshua, Bani, Kadmiel, Shebaniah, Bunni, Sherebiah, Bani, and Kenani.

5Then the leaders of the Levites—Jeshua, Kadmiel, Bani, Hashabneiah, Sherebiah, Hodiah, Shebaniah, and Pethahiah—called out to the people: "Stand up and praise the LORD your God, for he lives from everlasting to everlasting!"

Then they continued, "Praise his glorious name! It is far greater than we can think or say. 6You alone are the LORD. You made the skies and the heavens and all the stars. You made the earth and the seas and everything in them. You preserve and give life to everything, and all the angels of heaven worship you.

7"You are the LORD God, who chose Abram and brought him from Ur of the Chaldeans and renamed him Abraham. 8When he had proved himself faithful, you made a covenant with him to give him and his descendants the land of the Canaanites, Hittites, Amorites, Perizzites, Jebusites, and Girgashites. And you have done what you promised, for you are always true to your word.

9"You saw the sufferings and sorrows of our ancestors in Egypt, and you heard their cries from beside the Red Sea.* 10You displayed miraculous signs and wonders against Pharaoh, his servants, and all his people, for you knew how arrogantly the Egyptians were treating them. You have a glorious reputation that has never been forgotten. 11You divided the sea for your people so they could walk through on dry land! And then you hurled their enemies into the depths of the sea. They sank like stones beneath the mighty waters. 12You led our ancestors by a pillar of cloud during the day and a pillar of fire at night so that they could find their way.

13"You came down on Mount Sinai and spoke to them from heaven. You gave them regulations and instructions that were just, and laws and commands that were true. 14You instructed them concerning the laws of your holy Sabbath. And you commanded them, through

8:10 Hebrew *he.*   8:13 Hebrew *On the second day,* of the seventh month of the Hebrew calendar. This event occurred on October 9, 445 B.C.; also see notes on 1:1 and 8:2.   8:14 Hebrew *in the seventh month.* This month of the Hebrew lunar calendar usually occurs in September and October. See Lev 23:39-43.   8:18 Hebrew *on the eighth day,* of the seventh month of the Hebrew calendar. This event occurred on October 15, 445 B.C.; also see notes on 1:1 and 8:2.   9:1 Hebrew *On the twenty-fourth day of that same month,* the seventh month of the Hebrew calendar. This event occurred on October 31, 445 B.C.; also see note on 1:1.   9:3 Hebrew *for a quarter of a day.*   9:9 Hebrew *sea of reeds.*

Moses your servant, to obey all your commands, laws, and instructions.

15"You gave them bread from heaven when they were hungry and water from the rock when they were thirsty. You commanded them to go and take possession of the land you had sworn to give them. 16But our ancestors were a proud and stubborn lot, and they refused to obey your commands.

17"They refused to listen and did not remember the miracles you had done for them. Instead, they rebelled and appointed a leader to take them back to their slavery in Egypt! But you are a God of forgiveness, gracious and merciful, slow to become angry, and full of unfailing love and mercy. You did not abandon them, 18even though they made an idol shaped like a calf and said, 'This is your god who brought you out of Egypt!' They sinned and committed terrible blasphemies. 19But in your great mercy you did not abandon them to die in the wilderness. The pillar of cloud still led them forward by day, and the pillar of fire showed them the way through the night. 20You sent your good Spirit to instruct them, and you did not stop giving them bread from heaven or water for their thirst. 21For forty years you sustained them in the wilderness. They lacked nothing in all that time. Their clothes did not wear out, and their feet did not swell!

22"Then you helped our ancestors conquer great kingdoms and many nations, and you placed your people in every corner of the land. They completely took over the land of King Sihon of Heshbon and the land of King Og of Bashan. 23You made their descendants as numerous as the stars in the sky and brought them into the land you had promised to their ancestors. 24They went in and took possession of the land. You subdued whole nations before them. Even the kings and the Canaanites, who inhabited the land, were powerless! Your people could deal with them as they pleased. 25Our ancestors captured fortified cities and fertile land. They took over houses full of good things, with cisterns already dug and vineyards and olive groves and orchards in abundance. So they ate until they were full and grew fat and enjoyed themselves in all your blessings.

26"But despite all this, they were disobedient and rebelled against you. They threw away your law, they killed the prophets who encouraged them to return to you, and they committed terrible blasphemies. 27So you handed them over

9:38 Or Because of all this.

to their enemies. But in their time of trouble they cried to you, and you heard them from heaven. In great mercy, you sent them deliverers who rescued them from their enemies.

28"But when all was going well, your people turned to sin again, and once more you let their enemies conquer them. Yet whenever your people cried to you again for help, you listened once more from heaven. In your wonderful mercy, you rescued them repeatedly! 29You warned them to return to your law, but they became proud and obstinate and disobeyed your commands. They did not follow your regulations, by which people will find life if only they obey. They stubbornly turned their backs on you and refused to listen. 30In your love, you were patient with them for many years. You sent your Spirit, who, through the prophets, warned them about their sins. But still they wouldn't listen! So once again you allowed the pagan inhabitants of the land to conquer them. 31But in your great mercy, you did not destroy them completely or abandon them forever. What a gracious and merciful God you are!

32"And now, our God, the great and mighty and awesome God, who keeps his covenant of unfailing love, do not let all the hardships we have suffered be as nothing to you. Great trouble has come upon us and upon our kings and princes and priests and prophets and ancestors from the days when the kings of Assyria first triumphed over us until now. 33Every time you punished us you were being just. We have sinned greatly, and you gave us only what we deserved. 34Our kings, princes, priests, and ancestors did not obey your law or listen to your commands and solemn warnings. 35Even while they had their own kingdom, they did not serve you even though you showered your goodness on them. You gave them a large, fertile land, but they refused to turn from their wickedness.

36"So now today we are slaves here in the land of plenty that you gave to our ancestors! We are slaves among all this abundance! 37The lush produce of this land piles up in the hands of the kings whom you have set over us because of our sins. They have power over us and our cattle. We serve them at their pleasure, and we are in great misery.

38"Yet in spite of all this,* we are making a solemn promise and putting it in writing. On this sealed document are the names of our princes and Levites and priests."

CHAPTER 10

The People Agree to Obey

The document was ratified and sealed with the following names:

Nehemiah the governor, the son of Hacaliah. The priests who signed were Zedekiah, ²Seraiah, Azariah, Jeremiah, ³Pashhur, Amariah, Malkijah, ⁴Hattush, Shebaniah, Malluch, ⁵Harim, Meremoth, Obadiah, ⁶Daniel, Ginnethon, Baruch, ⁷Meshullam, Abijah, Mijamin, ⁸Maaziah, Bilgai, and Shemaiah. These were the priests.

⁹The Levites who signed were Jeshua son of Azaniah, Binnui from the family of Henadad, Kadmiel, ¹⁰and their fellow Levites: Shebaniah, Hodiah, Kelita, Pelaiah, Hanan, ¹¹Mica, Rehob, Hashabiah, ¹²Zaccur, Sherebiah, Shebaniah, ¹³Hodiah, Bani, and Beninu.

¹⁴The leaders who signed were Parosh, Pahath-moab, Elam, Zattu, Bani, ¹⁵Bunni, Azgad, Bebai, ¹⁶Adonijah, Bigvai, Adin, ¹⁷Ater, Hezekiah, Azzur, ¹⁸Hodiah, Hashum, Bezai, ¹⁹Hariph, Anathoth, Nebai, ²⁰Magpiash, Meshullam, Hezir, ²¹Meshezabel, Zadok, Jaddua, ²²Pelatiah, Hanan, Anaiah, ²³Hoshea, Hananiah, Hasshub, ²⁴Hallohesh, Pilha, Shobek, ²⁵Rehum, Hashabnah, Maaseiah, ²⁶Ahiah, Hanan, Anan, ²⁷Malluch, Harim, and Baanah.

²⁸The rest of the people—the priests, Levites, gatekeepers, singers, Temple servants, and all who had separated themselves from the pagan people of the land in order to serve God, and who were old enough to understand—²⁹now all heartily bound themselves with an oath. They vowed to accept the curse of God if they failed to obey the law of God as issued by his servant Moses. They solemnly promised to carefully follow all the commands, laws, and regulations of the LORD their Lord.

The Vow of the People

³⁰"We promise not to let our daughters marry the pagan people of the land, nor to let our sons marry their daughters. ³¹We further promise that if the people of the land should bring any merchandise or grain to be sold on the Sabbath or on any other holy day, we will refuse to buy it. And we promise not to do any work every seventh year and to cancel the debts owed to us by other Jews.

³²"In addition, we promise to obey the command to pay the annual Temple tax of an eighth of an ounce of silver,* so that there will be enough money to care for the Temple of our God. ³³This will provide for the Bread of the Presence; for the regular grain offerings and burnt offerings; for the offerings on the Sabbaths, the new moon celebrations, and the annual festivals; for the holy offerings; and for the sin offerings to make atonement for Israel. It will also provide for the other items necessary for the work of the Temple of our God.

³⁴"We have cast sacred lots to determine when—at regular times each year—the families of the priests, Levites, and the common people should bring wood to God's Temple to be burned on the altar of the LORD our God, as required in the law.

³⁵"We promise always to bring the first part of every harvest to the LORD's Temple—whether it be a crop from the soil or from our fruit trees. ³⁶We agree to give to God our oldest sons and the firstborn of all our herds and flocks, just as the law requires. We will present them to the priests who minister in the Temple of our God. ³⁷We will store the produce in the storerooms of the Temple of our God. We will bring the best of our flour and other grain offerings, the best of our fruit, and the best of our new wine and olive oil. And we promise to bring to the Levites a tenth of everything our land produces, for it is the Levites who collect the tithes in all our rural towns. ³⁸A priest—a descendant of Aaron—will be with the Levites as they receive these tithes. And a tenth of all that is collected as tithes will be delivered by the Levites to the Temple of our God and placed in the storerooms. ³⁹The people and the Levites must bring these offerings of grain, new wine, and olive oil to the Temple and place them in the sacred containers near the ministering priests, the gatekeepers, and the singers.

"So we promise together not to neglect the Temple of our God."

CHAPTER 11

The People Occupy Jerusalem

Now the leaders of the people were living in Jerusalem, the holy city, at this time. A tenth of the people from the other towns of Judah and Benjamin were chosen by sacred lots to live there, too, while the rest stayed where they were. ²And the people commended everyone who volunteered to resettle in Jerusalem.

10:32 Hebrew *tax of ¹/₃ of a shekel* [4 grams].

³Here is a list of the names of the provincial officials who came to Jerusalem. Most of the people, priests, Levites, Temple servants, and descendants of Solomon's servants continued to live in their own homes in the various towns of Judah, ⁴but some of the people from Judah and Benjamin resettled in Jerusalem.

From the tribe of Judah: Athaiah son of Uzziah, son of Zechariah, son of Amariah, son of Shephatiah, son of Mahalalel, of the family of Perez; ⁵and Maaseiah son of Baruch, son of Col-hozeh, son of Hazaiah, son of Adaiah, son of Joiarib, son of Zechariah, of the family of Shelah.* ⁶There were also 468 descendants of Perez who lived in Jerusalem—all outstanding men. ⁷From the tribe of Benjamin: Sallu son of Meshullam, son of Joed, son of Pedaiah, son of Kolaiah, son of Maaseiah, son of Ithiel, son of Jeshaiah; ⁸and after him there were Gabbai and Sallai, and a total of 928 relatives. ⁹Their chief officer was Joel son of Zicri, who was assisted by Judah son of Hassenuah, second-in-command over the city. ¹⁰From the priests: Jedaiah son of Joiarib; Jakin; ¹¹and Seraiah son of Hilkiah, son of Meshullam, son of Zadok, son of Meraioth, son of Ahitub, the supervisor of the Temple of God; ¹²together with 822 of their associates, who worked at the Temple. Also, there was Adaiah son of Jeroham, son of Pelaliah, son of Amzi, son of Zechariah, son of Pashhur, son of Malkijah; ¹³and 242 of his associates, who were heads of their families. There were also Amashsai son of Azarel, son of Ahzai, son of Meshillemoth, son of Immer, ¹⁴and 128 of his outstanding associates. Their chief officer was Zabdiel son of Haggedolim.

¹⁵From the Levites: Shemaiah son of Hasshub, son of Azrikam, son of Hashabiah, son of Bunni; ¹⁶Shabbethai and Jozabad, who were in charge of the work outside the Temple of God; ¹⁷Mattaniah son of Mica, son of Zabdi, a descendant of Asaph, who opened the thanksgiving services with prayer; Bakbukiah, who was Mattaniah's assistant; and Abda son of Shammua, son of Galal, son of Jeduthun. ¹⁸In all, there were 284 Levites in the holy city. ¹⁹From the gatekeepers: Akkub, Talmon, and 172 of their associates, who guarded the gates.

²⁰The other priests, Levites, and the rest of the Israelites lived wherever their family inheritance was located in any of the towns of Judah. ²¹However, the Temple servants, whose leaders were Ziha and Gishpa, all lived on the hill of Ophel.

²²The chief officer of the Levites in Jerusalem was Uzzi son of Bani, son of Hashabiah, son of Mattaniah, son of Mica, a descendant of Asaph, whose family served as singers at God's Temple. ²³They were under royal orders, which determined their daily activities.

²⁴Pethahiah son of Meshezabel, a descendant of Zerah son of Judah, was the king's agent in all matters of public administration.

²⁵Some of the people of Judah lived in Kiriath-arba with its villages, Dibon with its villages, and Jekabzeel with its villages. ²⁶They also lived in Jeshua, Moladah, Beth-pelet, ²⁷Hazar-shual, Beersheba with its villages, ²⁸Ziklag, and Meconah with its villages. ²⁹They were also in En-rimmon, Zorah, Jarmuth, ³⁰Zanoah, and Adullam with their villages. They were also in Lachish and its nearby fields and Azekah with its surrounding villages. So the people of Judah were living all the way from Beersheba to the valley of Hinnom.

³¹Some of the people of Benjamin lived at Geba, Micmash, Aija, and Bethel with its surrounding villages. ³²They were also in Anathoth, Nob, Ananiah, ³³Hazor, Ramah, Gittaim, ³⁴Hadid, Zeboim, Neballat, ³⁵Lod, Ono, and the Valley of Craftsmen.* ³⁶Some of the Levites who lived in Judah were sent to live with the tribe of Benjamin.

CHAPTER 12

A History of the Priests and Levites

Here is the list of the priests and Levites who had returned with Zerubbabel son of Shealtiel and Jeshua the high priest:

Seraiah, Jeremiah, Ezra,
² Amariah, Malluch, Hattush,
³ Shecaniah, Harim,* Meremoth,
⁴ Iddo, Ginnethon,* Abijah,
⁵ Miniamin, Moadiah,* Bilgah,
⁶ Shemaiah, Joiarib, Jedaiah,
⁷ Sallu, Amok, Hilkiah, and Jedaiah.

These were the leaders of the priests and their associates in the days of Jeshua.

⁸The Levites who had returned with them were Jeshua, Binnui, Kadmiel, Sherebiah, Judah,

---

11:5 Hebrew *son of the Shilonite.*   11:35 Or *and Ge-harashim.*   12:3 Hebrew *Rehum;* compare 7:42; 12:15; Ezra 2:39.   12:4 As in some Hebrew manuscripts and Latin Vulgate (see also 12:16); most Hebrew manuscripts read *Ginnethoi.*   12:5 Hebrew *Mijamin, Maadiah;* compare 12:17.

and Mattaniah, who with his associates was in charge of the songs of thanksgiving. 9Their associates, Bakbukiah and Unni, stood opposite them during the service.

10 Jeshua the high priest was the father of Joiakim.
Joiakim was the father of Eliashib.
Eliashib was the father of Joiada.
11 Joiada was the father of Johanan.*
Johanan was the father of Jaddua.

12Now when Joiakim was high priest, the family leaders of the priests were as follows:

Meraiah was leader of the family of Seraiah.
Hananiah was leader of the family of Jeremiah.
13 Meshullam was leader of the family of Ezra.
Jehohanan was leader of the family of Amariah.
14 Jonathan was leader of the family of Malluch.*
Joseph was leader of the family of Shecaniah.*
15 Adna was leader of the family of Harim.
Helkai was leader of the family of Meremoth.*
16 Zechariah was leader of the family of Iddo.
Meshullam was leader of the family of Ginnethon.
17 Zicri was leader of the family of Abijah.
There was also a* leader of the family of Miniamin.
Piltai was leader of the family of Moadiah.
18 Shammua was leader of the family of Bilgah.
Jehonathan was leader of the family of Shemaiah.
19 Mattenai was leader of the family of Joiarib.
Uzzi was leader of the family of Jedaiah.
20 Kallai was leader of the family of Sallu.*
Eber was leader of the family of Amok.
21 Hashabiah was leader of the family of Hilkiah.
Nethanel was leader of the family of Jedaiah.

22During the reign of Darius II of Persia,* a list was compiled of the family leaders of the Levites and the priests in the days of the following high priests: Eliashib, Joiada, Johanan, and Jaddua. 23The heads of the Levite families were

recorded in *The Book of History* down to the days of Johanan, the grandson* of Eliashib.

24These were the family leaders of the Levites: Hashabiah, Sherebiah, Jeshua, Binnui,* Kadmiel, and other associates, who stood opposite them during the ceremonies of praise and thanksgiving, one section responding to the other, just as commanded by David, the man of God. 25This included Mattaniah, Bakbukiah, and Obadiah.

Meshullam, Talmon, and Akkub were the gatekeepers in charge of the storerooms at the gates. 26These all served in the days of Joiakim son of Jeshua, son of Jehozadak,* and in the days of Nehemiah the governor and of Ezra the priest and scribe.

Dedication of Jerusalem's Wall

27During the dedication of the new wall of Jerusalem, the Levites throughout the land were asked to come to Jerusalem to assist in the ceremonies. They were to take part in the joyous occasion with their songs of thanksgiving and with the music of cymbals, lyres, and harps. 28The singers were brought together from Jerusalem and its surrounding villages and from the villages of the Netophathites. 29They also came from Beth-gilgal and the area of Geba and Azmaveth, for the singers had built their own villages around Jerusalem. 30The priests and Levites first dedicated themselves, then the people, the gates, and the wall.

31I led the leaders of Judah to the top of the wall and organized two large choirs to give thanks. One of the choirs proceeded southward* along the top of the wall to the Dung Gate. 32Hoshaiah and half the leaders of Judah followed them, 33along with Azariah, Ezra, Meshullam, 34Judah, Benjamin, Shemaiah, Jeremiah, 35and some priests who played trumpets. Then came Zechariah son of Jonathan, son of Shemaiah, son of Mattaniah, son of Micaiah, son of Zaccur, a descendant of Asaph. 36And finally came Zechariah's colleagues Shemaiah, Azarel, Milalai, Gilalai, Maai, Nethanel, Judah, and Hanani. They used the musical instruments prescribed by David, the man of God. Ezra the scribe led this procession. 37At the Fountain Gate they went straight up the steps on the ascent of the city wall toward the City of David.

12:11 Hebrew *Jonathan;* compare 12:22. 12:14a As in Greek version (see also 10:4; 12:2); Hebrew reads *Malluchi.* 12:14b As in many Hebrew manuscripts, some Greek manuscripts, and Syriac version (see also 12:3); most Hebrew manuscripts read *Shebaniah.* 12:15 As in some Greek manuscripts (see also 12:3); Hebrew reads *Meraioth.* 12:17 Hebrew lacks the name of this family leader. 12:20 Hebrew *Sallai;* compare 12:7. 12:22 Hebrew *Darius the Persian.* 12:23 Hebrew *son;* compare 12:10-11. 12:24 Hebrew *son of* (i.e., *ben*), which should probably be read here as the proper name Binnui; compare Ezra 3:9 and the note there. 12:26 Hebrew *Jozadak,* a variant name for Jehozadak. 12:31 Hebrew *to the right.*

They passed the house of David and then proceeded to the Water Gate on the east. 38The second choir went northward* around the other way to meet them. I followed them, with the other half of the people, along the top of the wall past the Tower of the Ovens to the Broad Wall, 39then past the Ephraim Gate to the Old City Gate,* past the Fish Gate and the Tower of Hananel, and went on to the Tower of the Hundred. Then we continued on to the Sheep Gate and stopped at the Guard Gate.

40The two choirs that were giving thanks then proceeded to the Temple of God, where they took their places. So did I, together with the group of leaders who were with me. 41We went together with the trumpet-playing priests—Eliakim, Maaseiah, Miniamin, Micaiah, Elioenai, Zechariah, and Hananiah—42and the singers—Maaseiah, Shemaiah, Eleazar, Uzzi, Jehohanan, Malkijah, Elam, and Ezer. They played and sang loudly and clearly under the direction of Jezrahiah the choir director.

43Many sacrifices were offered on that joyous day, for God had given the people cause for great joy. The women and children also participated in the celebration, and the joy of the people of Jerusalem could be heard far away.

Provisions for Temple Worship
44On that day men were appointed to be in charge of the storerooms for the gifts, the first part of the harvest, and the tithes. They were responsible to collect these from the fields as required by the law for the priests and Levites, for all the people of Judah valued the priests and Levites and their work. 45They performed the service of their God and the service of purification, as required by the laws of David and his son Solomon, and so did the singers and the gatekeepers. 46The custom of having choir directors to lead the choirs in hymns of praise and thanks to God began long ago in the days of David and Asaph. 47So now, in the days of Zerubbabel and of Nehemiah, the people brought a daily supply of food for the singers, the gatekeepers, and the Levites. The Levites, in turn, gave a portion of what they received to the priests, the descendants of Aaron.

CHAPTER **13**
Nehemiah's Various Reforms
On that same day, as the Book of Moses was being read, the people found a statement which said that no Ammonite or Moabite should ever

be permitted to enter the assembly of God. 2For they had not been friendly to the Israelites when they left Egypt. Instead, they hired Balaam to curse them, though our God turned the curse into a blessing. 3When this law was read, all those of mixed ancestry were immediately expelled from the assembly.

4Before this had happened, Eliashib the priest, who had been appointed as supervisor of the storerooms of the Temple of our God and who was also a relative of Tobiah, 5had converted a large storage room and placed it at Tobiah's disposal. The room had previously been used for storing the grain offerings, frankincense, Temple utensils, and tithes of grain, new wine, olive oil, and the special portion set aside for the priests. Moses had decreed that these offerings belonged to the Levites, the singers, and the gatekeepers.

6I was not in Jerusalem at that time, for I had returned to the king in the thirty-second year of the reign of King Artaxerxes of Babylon,* though I later received his permission to return. 7When I arrived back in Jerusalem and learned the extent of this evil deed of Eliashib—that he had provided Tobiah with a room in the courtyards of the Temple of God—8I became very upset and threw all of Tobiah's belongings from the room. 9Then I demanded that the rooms be purified, and I brought back the utensils for God's Temple, the grain offerings, and the frankincense.

10I also discovered that the Levites had not been given what was due them, so they and the singers who were to conduct the worship services had all returned to work their fields. 11I immediately confronted the leaders and demanded, "Why has the Temple of God been neglected?" Then I called all the Levites back again and restored them to their proper duties. 12And once more all the people of Judah began bringing their tithes of grain, new wine, and olive oil to the Temple storerooms.

13I put Shelemiah the priest, Zadok the scribe, and Pedaiah, one of the Levites, in charge of the storerooms. And I appointed Hanan son of Zaccur and grandson of Mattaniah as their assistant. These men had an excellent reputation, and it was their job to make honest distributions to their fellow Levites.

14Remember this good deed, O my God, and do not forget all that I have faithfully done for the Temple of my God.

12:38 Hebrew *to the left.*   12:39 Or *the Mishneh Gate,* or *the Jeshanah Gate.*   13:6 The thirty-second year of Artaxerxes was 433 B.C.

¹⁵One Sabbath day I saw some men of Judah treading their winepresses. They were also bringing in bundles of grain and loading them on their donkeys. And on that day they were bringing in their wine, grapes, figs, and all sorts of produce to Jerusalem to sell. So I rebuked them for selling their produce on the Sabbath. ¹⁶There were also some men from Tyre bringing in fish and all kinds of merchandise. They were selling it on the Sabbath to the people of Judah—and in Jerusalem at that!

¹⁷So I confronted the leaders of Judah, "Why are you profaning the Sabbath in this evil way? ¹⁸Wasn't it enough that your ancestors did this sort of thing, so that our God brought the present troubles upon us and our city? Now you are bringing even more wrath upon the people of Israel by permitting the Sabbath to be desecrated in this way!" ¹⁹So I commanded that from then on the gates of the city should be shut as darkness fell every Friday evening,* not to be opened until the Sabbath ended. I also sent some of my own servants to guard the gates so that no merchandise could be brought in on the Sabbath day. ²⁰The merchants and tradesmen with a variety of wares camped outside Jerusalem once or twice. ²¹But I spoke sharply to them and said, "What are you doing out here, camping around the wall? If you do this again, I will arrest you!" And that was the last time they came on the Sabbath. ²²Then I commanded the Levites to purify themselves and to guard the gates in order to preserve the holiness of the Sabbath.

Remember this good deed also, O my God! Have compassion on me according to your great and unfailing love.

²³About the same time I realized that some of the men of Judah had married women from Ashdod, Ammon, and Moab. ²⁴Even worse, half their children spoke in the language of Ashdod or some other people and could not speak the language of Judah at all. ²⁵So I confronted them and called down curses on them. I beat some of them and pulled out their hair. I made them swear before God that they would not let their children intermarry with the pagan people of the land.

²⁶"Wasn't this exactly what led King Solomon of Israel into sin?" I demanded. "There was no king from any nation who could compare to him, and God loved him and made him king over all Israel. But even he was led into sin by his foreign wives. ²⁷How could you even think of committing this sinful deed and acting unfaithfully toward God by marrying foreign women?"

²⁸One of the sons of Joiada* son of Eliashib the high priest had married a daughter of Sanballat the Horonite, so I banished him from my presence.

²⁹Remember them, O my God, for they have defiled the priesthood and the promises and vows of the priests and Levites.

³⁰So I purged out everything foreign and assigned tasks to the priests and Levites, making certain that each knew his work. ³¹I also made sure that the supply of wood for the altar was brought at the proper times and that the first part of the harvest was collected for the priests.

Remember this in my favor, O my God.

13:19 Hebrew *on the day before the Sabbath.*   **13:28** Hebrew *Jehoiada,* a variant name for Joiada.

Esther

The King's Banquet

This happened in the days of King Xerxes,* who reigned over 127 provinces stretching from India to Ethiopia.* ²At that time he ruled his empire from his throne at the fortress of Susa. ³In the third year of his reign, he gave a banquet for all his princes and officials. He invited all the military officers of Media and Persia, as well as the noblemen and provincial officials. ⁴The celebration lasted six months*—a tremendous display of the opulent wealth and glory of his empire.

⁵When it was all over, the king gave a special banquet for all the palace servants and officials—from the greatest to the least. It lasted for seven days and was held at Susa in the courtyard of the palace garden. ⁶The courtyard was decorated with beautifully woven white and blue linen hangings, fastened by purple ribbons to silver rings embedded in marble pillars. Gold and silver couches stood on a mosaic pavement of porphyry, marble, mother-of-pearl, and other costly stones. ⁷Drinks were served in gold goblets of many designs, and there was an abundance of royal wine, just as the king had commanded. ⁸The only restriction on the drinking was that no one should be compelled to take more than he wanted. But those who wished could have as much as they pleased, for the king had instructed his staff to let everyone decide this matter for himself.

⁹Queen Vashti gave a banquet for the women of the palace at the same time.

Queen Vashti Deposed

¹⁰On the seventh day of the feast, when King Xerxes was half drunk with wine, he told Mehuman, Biztha, Harbona, Bigtha, Abagtha, Zethar, and Carcas, the seven eunuchs who attended him, ¹¹to bring Queen Vashti to him with the royal crown on her head. He wanted all the men to gaze on her beauty, for she was a very beautiful woman. ¹²But when they conveyed the king's order to Queen Vashti, she refused to come. This made the king furious, and he burned with anger.

¹³He immediately consulted with his advisers, who knew all the Persian laws and customs, for he always asked their advice. ¹⁴The names of these men were Carshena, Shethar, Admatha, Tarshish, Meres, Marsena, and Memucan—seven high officials of Persia and Media. They were his closest associates and held the highest positions in the empire. ¹⁵"What must be done to Queen Vashti?" the king demanded. "What penalty does the law provide for a queen who refuses to obey the king's orders, properly sent through his eunuchs?"

¹⁶Memucan answered the king and his princes, "Queen Vashti has wronged not only the king but also every official and citizen throughout your empire. ¹⁷Women everywhere will begin to despise their husbands when they learn that Queen Vashti has refused to appear before the king. ¹⁸Before this day is out, the wife of every one of us, your officials throughout the empire, will hear what the queen did and will start talking to their husbands the same way. There will be no end to the contempt and anger throughout your realm. ¹⁹So if it please the king, we suggest that you issue a written decree, a law of the Persians and Medes that cannot be revoked. It should order that Queen Vashti be forever banished from your presence and that you choose another queen more worthy than she. ²⁰When this decree is published throughout your vast

1:1a Hebrew *Ahasuerus*, another name for Xerxes; also throughout the book of Esther. 1:1b Hebrew *to Cush.* 1:4 Hebrew *180 days.*

empire, husbands everywhere, whatever their rank, will receive proper respect from their wives!"

21The king and his princes thought this made good sense, so he followed Memucan's counsel. 22He sent letters to all parts of the empire, to each province in its own script and language, proclaiming that every man should be the ruler of his home.

CHAPTER 2
Esther Becomes Queen

But after Xerxes' anger had cooled, he began thinking about Vashti and what she had done and the decree he had made. 2So his attendants suggested, "Let us search the empire to find beautiful young virgins for the king. 3Let the king appoint agents in each province to bring these beautiful young women into the royal harem at Susa. Hegai, the eunuch in charge, will see that they are all given beauty treatments. 4After that, the young woman who pleases you most will be made queen instead of Vashti." This advice was very appealing to the king, so he put the plan into effect immediately.

5Now at the fortress of Susa there was a certain Jew named Mordecai son of Jair. He was from the tribe of Benjamin and was a descendant of Kish and Shimei. 6His family* had been exiled from Jerusalem to Babylon by King Nebuchadnezzar, along with King Jehoiachin* of Judah and many others. 7This man had a beautiful and lovely young cousin, Hadassah, who was also called Esther. When her father and mother had died, Mordecai adopted her into his family and raised her as his own daughter. 8As a result of the king's decree, Esther, along with many other young women, was brought to the king's harem at the fortress of Susa and placed in Hegai's care. 9Hegai was very impressed with Esther and treated her kindly. He quickly ordered a special menu for her and provided her with beauty treatments. He also assigned her seven maids specially chosen from the king's palace, and he moved her and her maids into the best place in the harem.

10Esther had not told anyone of her nationality and family background, for Mordecai had told her not to. 11Every day Mordecai would take a walk near the courtyard of the harem to ask about Esther and to find out what was happening to her.

12Before each young woman was taken to the king's bed, she was given the prescribed twelve months of beauty treatments—six months with oil of myrrh, followed by six months with special perfumes and ointments. 13When the time came for her to go in to the king, she was given her choice of whatever clothing or jewelry she wanted to enhance her beauty. 14That evening she was taken to the king's private rooms, and the next morning she was brought to the second harem,* where the king's wives lived. There she would be under the care of Shaashgaz, another of the king's eunuchs. She would live there for the rest of her life, never going to the king again unless he had especially enjoyed her and requested her by name.

15When it was Esther's turn* to go to the king, she accepted the advice of Hegai, the eunuch in charge of the harem. She asked for nothing except what he suggested, and she was admired by everyone who saw her. 16When Esther was taken to King Xerxes at the royal palace in early winter* of the seventh year of his reign, 17the king loved her more than any of the other young women. He was so delighted with her that he set the royal crown on her head and declared her queen instead of Vashti. 18To celebrate the occasion, he gave a banquet in Esther's honor for all his princes and servants, giving generous gifts to everyone and declaring a public festival for the provinces.

19Even after all the young women had been transferred to the second harem* and Mordecai had become a palace official, 20Esther continued to keep her nationality and family background a secret. She was still following Mordecai's orders, just as she did when she was living in his home.

Mordecai's Loyalty to the King

21One day as Mordecai was on duty at the palace, two of the king's eunuchs, Bigthana* and Teresh—who were guards at the door of the king's private quarters—became angry at King Xerxes and plotted to assassinate him. 22But Mordecai heard about the plot and passed the information on to Queen Esther. She then told the king about it and gave Mordecai credit for the report. 23When an investigation was made and Mordecai's story was found to be true, the two men were hanged on a gallows.* This was all duly recorded in *The Book of the History of King Xerxes' Reign.*

2:6a Hebrew *He.* 2:6b Hebrew *Jeconiah,* a variant name for Jehoiachin. 2:14 Or *to another part of the harem.* 2:15 Hebrew *the turn of Esther, the daughter of Abihail, who was Mordecai's uncle, who had adopted her.* 2:16 Hebrew *in the tenth month, the month of Tebeth.* A number of dates in the book of Esther can be cross-checked with dates in surviving Persian records and related accurately to our modern calendar. This month of the Hebrew lunar calendar occurred in December 479 B.C. and January 478 B.C. 2:19 The meaning of the Hebrew is uncertain. 2:21 Hebrew *Bigthan;* compare 6:2. 2:23 Or *on a pole.*

CHAPTER 3
Haman's Plot against the Jews

Some time later, King Xerxes promoted Haman son of Hammedatha the Agagite to prime minister, making him the most powerful official in the empire next to the king himself. 2All the king's officials would bow down before Haman to show him respect whenever he passed by, for so the king had commanded. But Mordecai refused to bow down or show him respect.

3Then the palace officials at the king's gate asked Mordecai, "Why are you disobeying the king's command?" 4They spoke to him day after day, but still he refused to comply with the order. So they spoke to Haman about this to see if he would tolerate Mordecai's conduct, since Mordecai had told them he was a Jew.

5When Haman saw that Mordecai would not bow down or show him respect, he was filled with rage. 6So he decided it was not enough to lay hands on Mordecai alone. Since he had learned that Mordecai was a Jew, he decided to destroy all the Jews throughout the entire empire of Xerxes.

7So in the month of April,* during the twelfth year of King Xerxes' reign, lots were cast (the lots were called *purim*) to determine the best day and month to take action. And the day selected was March 7, nearly a year later.*

8Then Haman approached King Xerxes and said, "There is a certain race of people scattered through all the provinces of your empire. Their laws are different from those of any other nation, and they refuse to obey even the laws of the king. So it is not in the king's interest to let them live. 9If it please Your Majesty, issue a decree that they be destroyed, and I will give 375 tons* of silver to the government administrators so they can put it into the royal treasury."

10The king agreed, confirming his decision by removing his signet ring from his finger and giving it to Haman son of Hammedatha the Agagite—the enemy of the Jews. 11"Keep the money," the king told Haman, "but go ahead and do as you like with these people."

12On April 17* Haman called in the king's secretaries and dictated letters to the princes, the governors of the respective provinces, and the local officials of each province in their own scripts and languages. These letters were signed in the name of King Xerxes, sealed with his ring, 13and sent by messengers into all the provinces of the empire. The letters decreed that all Jews— young and old, including women and children— must be killed, slaughtered, and annihilated on a single day. This was scheduled to happen nearly a year later on March 7.* The property of the Jews would be given to those who killed them. 14A copy of this decree was to be issued in every province and made known to all the people, so that they would be ready to do their duty on the appointed day. 15At the king's command, the decree went out by the swiftest messengers, and it was proclaimed in the fortress of Susa. Then the king and Haman sat down to drink, but the city of Susa fell into confusion.

CHAPTER 4
Mordecai Requests Esther's Help

When Mordecai learned what had been done, he tore his clothes, put on sackcloth and ashes, and went out into the city, crying with a loud and bitter wail. 2He stood outside the gate of the palace, for no one was allowed to enter while wearing clothes of mourning. 3And as news of the king's decree reached all the provinces, there was great mourning among the Jews. They fasted, wept, and wailed, and many people lay in sackcloth and ashes.

4When Queen Esther's maids and eunuchs came and told her about Mordecai, she was deeply distressed. She sent clothing to him to replace the sackcloth, but he refused it. 5Then Esther sent for Hathach, one of the king's eunuchs who had been appointed as her attendant. She ordered him to go to Mordecai and find out what was troubling him and why he was in mourning. 6So Hathach went out to Mordecai in the square in front of the palace gate.

7Mordecai told him the whole story and told him how much money Haman had promised to pay into the royal treasury for the destruction of the Jews. 8Mordecai gave Hathach a copy of the decree issued in Susa that called for the death of all Jews, and he asked Hathach to show it to Esther. He also asked Hathach to explain it to her and to urge her to go to the king to beg for mercy and plead for her people. 9So Hathach returned to Esther with Mordecai's message.

10Then Esther told Hathach to go back and

3:7a Hebrew *in the first month, the month of Nisan.* This month of the Hebrew lunar calendar occurred in April and May 474 B.C.; also see note on 2:16.   **3:7b** As in Greek version, which reads *the thirteenth day of the twelfth month, the month of Adar* (see also 3:13). Hebrew reads *in the twelfth month,* of the Hebrew calendar. The date selected was March 7, 473 B.C.; also see note on 2:16.   **3:9** Hebrew *10,000 talents* [340 metric tons].   **3:12** Hebrew *On the thirteenth day of the first month,* of the Hebrew calendar. This event occurred on April 17, 474 B.C.; also see note on 2:16.   **3:13** Hebrew *on the thirteenth day of the twelfth month, the month of Adar,* of the Hebrew calendar. The date selected was March 7, 473 B.C.; also see note on 2:16.

relay this message to Mordecai: ¹¹"The whole world knows that anyone who appears before the king in his inner court without being invited is doomed to die unless the king holds out his gold scepter. And the king has not called for me to come to him in more than a month." ¹²So Hathach gave Esther's message to Mordecai.

¹³Mordecai sent back this reply to Esther: "Don't think for a moment that you will escape there in the palace when all other Jews are killed. ¹⁴If you keep quiet at a time like this, deliverance for the Jews will arise from some other place, but you and your relatives will die. What's more, who can say but that you have been elevated to the palace for just such a time as this?"

¹⁵Then Esther sent this reply to Mordecai: ¹⁶"Go and gather together all the Jews of Susa and fast for me. Do not eat or drink for three days, night or day. My maids and I will do the same. And then, though it is against the law, I will go in to see the king. If I must die, I am willing to die." ¹⁷So Mordecai went away and did as Esther told him.

CHAPTER 5
Esther's Request to the King

Three days later, Esther put on her royal robes and entered the inner court of the palace, just across from the king's hall. The king was sitting on his royal throne, facing the entrance. ²When he saw Queen Esther standing there in the inner court, he welcomed her, holding out the gold scepter to her. So Esther approached and touched its tip.

³Then the king asked her, "What do you want, Queen Esther? What is your request? I will give it to you, even if it is half the kingdom!"

⁴And Esther replied, "If it please Your Majesty, let the king and Haman come today to a banquet I have prepared for the king."

⁵The king turned to his attendants and said, "Tell Haman to come quickly to a banquet, as Esther has requested." So the king and Haman went to Esther's banquet.

⁶And while they were drinking wine, the king said to Esther, "Now tell me what you really want. What is your request? I will give it to you, even if it is half the kingdom!"

⁷Esther replied, "This is my request and deepest wish. ⁸If Your Majesty is pleased with me and wants to grant my request, please come with Haman tomorrow to the banquet I will prepare for you. Then tomorrow I will explain what this is all about."

Haman's Plan to Kill Mordecai

⁹What a happy man Haman was as he left the banquet! But when he saw Mordecai sitting at the gate, not standing up or trembling nervously before him, he was furious. ¹⁰However, he restrained himself and went on home. Then he gathered together his friends and Zeresh, his wife, ¹¹and boasted to them about his great wealth and his many children. He bragged about the honors the king had given him and how he had been promoted over all the other officials and leaders.

¹²Then Haman added, "And that's not all! Queen Esther invited only me and the king himself to the banquet she prepared for us. And she has invited me to dine with her and the king again tomorrow!" ¹³Then he added, "But all this is meaningless as long as I see Mordecai the Jew just sitting there at the palace gate."

¹⁴So Haman's wife, Zeresh, and all his friends suggested, "Set up a gallows* that stands seventy-five feet* tall, and in the morning ask the king to hang Mordecai on it. When this is done, you can go on your merry way to the banquet with the king." This pleased Haman immensely, and he ordered the gallows set up.

CHAPTER 6
The King Honors Mordecai

That night the king had trouble sleeping, so he ordered an attendant to bring the historical records of his kingdom so they could be read to him. ²In those records he discovered an account of how Mordecai had exposed the plot of Bigthana and Teresh, two of the eunuchs who guarded the door to the king's private quarters. They had plotted to assassinate the king. ³"What reward or recognition did we ever give Mordecai for this?" the king asked.

His attendants replied, "Nothing has been done."

⁴"Who is that in the outer court?" the king inquired. Now, as it happened, Haman had just arrived in the outer court of the palace to ask the king to hang Mordecai from the gallows* he had prepared.

⁵So the attendants replied to the king, "Haman is out there."

"Bring him in," the king ordered. ⁶So Haman came in, and the king said, "What should I do to honor a man who truly pleases me?"

Haman thought to himself, "Whom would the king wish to honor more than me?" ⁷So he replied, "If the king wishes to honor someone,

5:14a Or *a pole*.   5:14b Hebrew *50 cubits* [22.5 meters].   6:4 Or *from the pole*.

8he should bring out one of the king's own royal robes, as well as the king's own horse with a royal emblem on its head. 9Instruct one of the king's most noble princes to dress the man in the king's robe and to lead him through the city square on the king's own horse. Have the prince shout as they go, 'This is what happens to those the king wishes to honor!'"

10"Excellent!" the king said to Haman. "Hurry and get the robe and my horse, and do just as you have said for Mordecai the Jew, who sits at the gate of the palace. Do not fail to carry out everything you have suggested."

11So Haman took the robe and put it on Mordecai, placed him on the king's own horse, and led him through the city square, shouting, "This is what happens to those the king wishes to honor!" 12Afterward Mordecai returned to the palace gate, but Haman hurried home dejected and completely humiliated.

13When Haman told his wife, Zeresh, and all his friends what had happened, they said, "Since Mordecai—this man who has humiliated you— is a Jew, you will never succeed in your plans against him. It will be fatal to continue to oppose him." 14While they were still talking, the king's eunuchs arrived to take Haman to the banquet Esther had prepared.

CHAPTER **7**
The King Executes Haman

So the king and Haman went to Queen Esther's banquet. 2And while they were drinking wine that day, the king again asked her, "Tell me what you want, Queen Esther. What is your request? I will give it to you, even if it is half the kingdom!"

3And so Queen Esther replied, "If Your Majesty is pleased with me and wants to grant my request, my petition is that my life and the lives of my people will be spared. 4For my people and I have been sold to those who would kill, slaughter, and annihilate us. If we had only been sold as slaves, I could remain quiet, for that would have been a matter too trivial to warrant disturbing the king."

5"Who would do such a thing?" King Xerxes demanded. "Who would dare touch you?"

6Esther replied, "This wicked Haman is our enemy." Haman grew pale with fright before the king and queen. 7Then the king jumped to his feet in a rage and went out into the palace garden. But Haman stayed behind to plead for his life with Queen Esther, for he knew that he was

doomed. 8In despair he fell on the couch where Queen Esther was reclining, just as the king returned from the palace garden. "Will he even assault the queen right here in the palace, before my very eyes?" the king roared. And as soon as the king spoke, his attendants covered Haman's face, signaling his doom.

9Then Harbona, one of the king's eunuchs, said, "Haman has set up a gallows* that stands seventy-five feet* tall in his own courtyard. He intended to use it to hang Mordecai, the man who saved the king from assassination."

"Then hang Haman on it!" the king ordered. 10So they hanged Haman on the gallows he had set up for Mordecai, and the king's anger was pacified.

CHAPTER **8**
A Decree to Help the Jews

On that same day King Xerxes gave the estate of Haman, the enemy of the Jews, to Queen Esther. Then Mordecai was brought before the king, for Esther had told the king how they were related. 2The king took off his signet ring—which he had taken back from Haman—and gave it to Mordecai. And Esther appointed Mordecai to be in charge of Haman's property.

3Now once more Esther came before the king, falling down at his feet and begging him with tears to stop Haman's evil plot against the Jews. 4Again the king held out the gold scepter to Esther. So she rose and stood before him 5and said, "If Your Majesty is pleased with me and if he thinks it is right, send out a decree reversing Haman's orders to destroy the Jews throughout all the provinces of the king. 6For how can I endure to see my people and my family slaughtered and destroyed?"

7Then King Xerxes said to Queen Esther and Mordecai the Jew, "I have given Esther the estate of Haman, and he has been hanged on the gallows* because he tried to destroy the Jews. 8Now go ahead and send a message to the Jews in the king's name, telling them whatever you want, and seal it with the king's signet ring. But remember that whatever is written in the king's name and sealed with his ring can never be revoked."

9So on June 25* the king's secretaries were summoned. As Mordecai dictated, they wrote a decree to the Jews and to the princes, governors, and local officials of all the 127 provinces stretching from India to Ethiopia.* The decree was written in the scripts and languages of all the

---

7:9a Or *a pole;* also in 7:10.   7:9b Hebrew *50 cubits* [22.5 meters].   8:7 Or *on the pole.*   8:9a Hebrew *on the twenty-third day of the third month, the month of Sivan,* of the Hebrew calendar. This event occurred on June 25, 474 B.C.; also see note on 2:16.   8:9b Hebrew *to Cush.*

peoples of the empire, including the Jews. [10]Mordecai wrote in the name of King Xerxes and sealed the message with the king's signet ring. He sent the letters by swift messengers, who rode horses especially bred for the king's service.

[11]The king's decree gave the Jews in every city authority to unite to defend their lives. They were allowed to kill, slaughter, and annihilate anyone of any nationality or province who might attack them or their children and wives, and to take the property of their enemies. [12]The day chosen for this event throughout all the provinces of King Xerxes was March 7 of the next year.* [13]A copy of this decree was to be recognized as law in every province and proclaimed to all the people. That way the Jews would be ready on that day to take revenge on their enemies. [14]So urged on by the king's command, the messengers rode out swiftly on horses bred for the king's service. The same decree was also issued at the fortress of Susa.

[15]Then Mordecai put on the royal robe of blue and white and the great crown of gold, and he wore an outer cloak of fine linen and purple. And the people of Susa celebrated the new decree. [16]The Jews were filled with joy and gladness and were honored everywhere. [17]In every city and province, wherever the king's decree arrived, the Jews rejoiced and had a great celebration and declared a public festival and holiday. And many of the people of the land became Jews themselves, for they feared what the Jews might do to them.

CHAPTER 9
The Victory of the Jews

So on March 7* the two decrees of the king were put into effect. On that day, the enemies of the Jews had hoped to destroy them, but quite the opposite happened. [2]The Jews gathered in their cities throughout all the king's provinces to defend themselves against anyone who might try to harm them. But no one could make a stand against them, for everyone was afraid of them. [3]And all the commanders of the provinces, the princes, the governors, and the royal officials helped the Jews for fear of Mordecai. [4]For Mordecai had been promoted in the king's palace,

and his fame spread throughout all the provinces as he became more and more powerful.

[5]But the Jews went ahead on the appointed day and struck down their enemies with the sword. They killed and annihilated their enemies and did as they pleased with those who hated them. [6]They killed five hundred people in the fortress of Susa. [7]They also killed Parshandatha, Dalphon, Aspatha, [8]Poratha, Adalia, Aridatha, [9]Parmashta, Arisai, Aridai, and Vaizatha—[10]the ten sons of Haman son of Hammedatha, the enemy of the Jews. But they did not take any plunder.

[11]That evening, when the king was informed of the number of people killed in the fortress of Susa, [12]he called for Queen Esther and said, "The Jews have killed five hundred people in the fortress of Susa alone and also Haman's ten sons. If they have done that here, what has happened in the rest of the provinces? But now, what more do you want? It will be granted to you; tell me and I will do it."

[13]And Esther said, "If it please Your Majesty, give the Jews in Susa permission to do again tomorrow as they have done today, and have the bodies of Haman's ten sons hung from the gallows.*"

[14]So the king agreed, and the decree was announced in Susa. They also hung the bodies of Haman's ten sons from the gallows. [15]Then the Jews at Susa gathered together on March 8* and killed three hundred more people, though again they took no plunder.

[16]Meanwhile, the other Jews throughout the king's provinces had gathered together to defend their lives. They gained relief from all their enemies, killing seventy-five thousand of those who hated them. But they did not take any plunder. [17]Throughout the provinces this was done on March 7.* Then on the following day* they rested, celebrating their victory with a day of feasting and gladness. [18]But the Jews at Susa continued killing their enemies on the second day also, and then rested on the third day,* making that their day of feasting and gladness. [19]So to this day, rural Jews living in unwalled villages celebrate an annual festival and holiday in late winter,* when they rejoice and send gifts to each other.

8:12 Hebrew *the thirteenth day of the twelfth month, the month of Adar,* of the Hebrew calendar. The date selected was March 7, 473 B.C.; also see note on 2:16. **9:1** Hebrew *on the thirteenth day of the twelfth month, the month of Adar,* of the Hebrew calendar. This event occurred on March 7, 473 B.C.; also see note on 2:16. **9:13** Or *the pole;* also in 9:14, 25. **9:15** Hebrew *the fourteenth day of the month of Adar,* of the Hebrew calendar. This event occurred on March 8, 473 B.C.; also see note on 2:16. **9:17a** Hebrew *on the thirteenth day of the month of Adar,* of the Hebrew calendar. This event occurred on March 7, 473 B.C.; also see note on 2:16. **9:17b** Hebrew *on the fourteenth day,* of the Hebrew month of Adar. **9:18** Hebrew *killing their enemies on the thirteenth day and the fourteenth day, and then rested on the fifteenth day,* of the Hebrew month of Adar. **9:19** Hebrew *on the fourteenth day of the month of Adar.* This day of the Hebrew lunar calendar usually occurs in March.

The Festival of Purim

20Mordecai recorded these events and sent letters to the Jews near and far, throughout all the king's provinces, 21encouraging them to celebrate an annual festival on these two days. 22He told them to celebrate these days with feasting and gladness and by giving gifts to each other and to the poor. This would commemorate a time when the Jews gained relief from their enemies, when their sorrow was turned into gladness and their mourning into joy.

23So the Jews adopted Mordecai's suggestion and began this annual custom. 24Haman son of Hammedatha the Agagite, the enemy of the Jews, had plotted to crush and destroy them on the day and month determined by casting lots (the lots were called *purim*). 25But when Esther came before the king, he issued a decree causing Haman's evil plot to backfire, and Haman and his sons were hanged on the gallows. 26(That is why this celebration is called Purim, because it is the ancient word for casting lots.) So because of Mordecai's letter and because of what they had experienced, 27the Jews throughout the realm agreed to inaugurate this tradition and to pass it on to their descendants and to all who became Jews. They declared they would never fail to celebrate these two prescribed days at the appointed time each year. 28These days would be remembered and kept from generation to generation and celebrated by every family throughout the provinces and cities of the empire. These days would never cease to be celebrated among the Jews, nor would the memory of what happened ever die out among their descendants.

29Then Queen Esther, the daughter of Abihail, along with Mordecai the Jew, wrote another letter putting the queen's full authority behind Mordecai's letter to establish the Festival of Purim. 30In addition, letters wishing peace and security were sent to the Jews throughout the 127 provinces of the empire of Xerxes. 31These letters established the Festival of Purim—an annual celebration of these days at the appointed time, decreed by both Mordecai the Jew and Queen Esther. (The people decided to observe this festival, just as they had decided for themselves and their descendants to establish the times of fasting and mourning.) 32So the command of Esther confirmed the practices of Purim, and it was all written down in the records.

CHAPTER **10**

The Greatness of Xerxes and Mordecai

King Xerxes imposed tribute throughout his empire, even to the distant coastlands. 2His great achievements and the full account of the greatness of Mordecai, whom the king had promoted, are recorded in *The Book of the History of the Kings of Media and Persia.* 3Mordecai the Jew became the prime minister, with authority next to that of King Xerxes himself. He was very great among the Jews, who held him in high esteem, because he worked for the good of his people and was a friend at the royal court for all of them.

Job

Prologue

There was a man named Job who lived in the land of Uz. He was blameless, a man of complete integrity. He feared God and stayed away from evil. ²He had seven sons and three daughters. ³He owned seven thousand sheep, three thousand camels, five hundred teams of oxen, and five hundred female donkeys, and he employed many servants. He was, in fact, the richest person in that entire area.

⁴Every year when Job's sons had birthdays, they invited their brothers and sisters to join them for a celebration. On these occasions they would get together to eat and drink. ⁵When these celebrations ended—and sometimes they lasted several days—Job would purify his children. He would get up early in the morning and offer a burnt offering for each of them. For Job said to himself, "Perhaps my children have sinned and have cursed God in their hearts." This was Job's regular practice.

Job's First Test

⁶One day the angels* came to present themselves before the LORD, and Satan the Accuser came with them. ⁷"Where have you come from?" the LORD asked Satan.

And Satan answered the LORD, "I have been going back and forth across the earth, watching everything that's going on."

⁸Then the LORD asked Satan, "Have you noticed my servant Job? He is the finest man in all the earth—a man of complete integrity. He fears God and will have nothing to do with evil."

⁹Satan replied to the LORD, "Yes, Job fears God, but not without good reason! ¹⁰You have always protected him and his home and his property from harm. You have made him prosperous in everything he does. Look how rich he is! ¹¹But take away everything he has, and he will surely curse you to your face!"

¹²"All right, you may test him," the LORD said to Satan. "Do whatever you want with everything he possesses, but don't harm him physically." So Satan left the LORD's presence.

¹³One day when Job's sons and daughters were dining at the oldest brother's house, ¹⁴a messenger arrived at Job's home with this news: "Your oxen were plowing, with the donkeys feeding beside them, ¹⁵when the Sabeans raided us. They stole all the animals and killed all the farmhands. I am the only one who escaped to tell you."

¹⁶While he was still speaking, another messenger arrived with this news: "The fire of God has fallen from heaven and burned up your sheep and all the shepherds. I am the only one who escaped to tell you."

¹⁷While he was still speaking, a third messenger arrived with this news: "Three bands of Chaldean raiders have stolen your camels and killed your servants. I am the only one who escaped to tell you."

¹⁸While he was still speaking, another messenger arrived with this news: "Your sons and daughters were feasting in their oldest brother's home. ¹⁹Suddenly, a powerful wind swept in from the desert and hit the house on all sides. The house collapsed, and all your children are dead. I am the only one who escaped to tell you."

²⁰Job stood up and tore his robe in grief. Then he shaved his head and fell to the ground before God. ²¹He said,

"I came naked from my mother's womb,
    and I will be stripped of everything when
        I die.

1:6 Hebrew *the sons of God.*

What Are Satan's Limitations? Read JOB 1:1–2:10

For all of his apparent abilities, Satan still does not come anywhere close to equaling the power of God—even on his best day! He would love to have us think he is God's equal, but as this story points out, Satan does have some definite limitations.

Satan Cannot Be Everywhere at Once. While he can freely move throughout the earth to do his work, he cannot be in more than one place at one time. Unlike God, who can be everywhere at one time, Satan is limited to the scope of his travels.

Satan Is Not All-Powerful. Satan does have certain powers and abilities, but his power is far from unlimited. For example, Satan did not have the ability to cause Job to break under his attacks.

Satan Is Limited in What He Can Do in the Life of a Christian. Before Satan could do anything to Job, he had to seek God's permission. While Satan was allowed by God to murder Job's servants, kill Job's children in a storm, steal Job's goods, and strike Job with sickness, God still kept a hedge of protection around Job.

For the next note on "Who Is the Devil?" turn to p. 6.

CORNER STONES

The LORD gave me everything I had,
   and the LORD has taken it away.
Praise the name of the LORD!"

22In all of this, Job did not sin by blaming God.

CHAPTER **2**
Job's Second Test
One day the angels* came again to present themselves before the LORD, and Satan the Accuser came with them. 2"Where have you come from?" the LORD asked Satan.

And Satan answered the LORD, "I have been going back and forth across the earth, watching everything that's going on."

3Then the LORD asked Satan, "Have you noticed my servant Job? He is the finest man in all the earth—a man of complete integrity. He fears God and will have nothing to do with evil. And he has maintained his integrity, even though you persuaded me to harm him without cause."

4Satan replied to the LORD, "Skin for skin—he blesses you only because you bless him. A man will give up everything he has to save his life. 5But take away his health, and he will surely curse you to your face!"

6"All right, do with him as you please," the LORD said to Satan. "But spare his life." 7So Satan left the LORD's presence, and he struck Job with a terrible case of boils from head to foot.

8Then Job scraped his skin with a piece of

2:1 Hebrew *the sons of God.*

broken pottery as he sat among the ashes. 9His wife said to him, "Are you still trying to maintain your integrity? Curse God and die."

10But Job replied, "You talk like a godless woman. Should we accept only good things from the hand of God and never anything bad?" So in all this, Job said nothing wrong.

Job's Three Friends Share His Anguish
11Three of Job's friends were Eliphaz the Temanite, Bildad the Shuhite, and Zophar the Naamathite. When they heard of the tragedy he had suffered, they got together and traveled from their homes to comfort and console him. 12When they saw Job from a distance, they scarcely recognized him. Wailing loudly, they tore their robes and threw dust into the air over their heads to demonstrate their grief. 13Then they sat on the ground with him for seven days and nights. And no one said a word, for they saw that his suffering was too great for words.

CHAPTER **3**
Job's First Speech
At last Job spoke, and he cursed the day of his birth. 2He said:

3"Cursed be the day of my birth, and cursed be the night when I was conceived. 4Let that day be turned to darkness. Let it be lost even to God on high, and let it be shrouded in darkness. 5Yes, let the darkness and utter gloom claim it for its own. Let a black cloud overshadow it, and let the darkness terrify it. 6Let that night be blotted off the calendar, never again to be counted among the days of the year, never again to appear among the months. 7Let that night be barren. Let it have no joy. 8Let those who are experts at cursing—those who are ready to rouse the sea monster*—curse that day. 9Let its morning stars remain dark. Let it hope for light, but in vain; may it never see the morning light. 10Curse it for its failure to shut my mother's womb, for letting me be born to all this trouble.

11 "Why didn't I die at birth as I came from the womb? 12Why did my mother let me live? Why did she nurse me at her breasts? 13For if I had died at birth, I would be at peace now, asleep and at rest. 14I would rest with the world's kings and prime ministers, famous for their great construction projects. 15I would rest with wealthy princes whose palaces were filled with gold and silver. 16Why was I not buried like a stillborn child, like a baby who never lives to see the light? 17For in death the wicked cease from troubling, and the weary are at rest. 18Even prisoners are at ease in death, with no guards to curse them. 19Rich and poor are there alike, and the slave is free from his master.

20"Oh, why should light be given to the weary, and life to those in misery? 21They long for death, and it won't come. They search for death more eagerly than for hidden treasure. 22It is a blessed relief when they finally die, when they find the grave. 23Why is life given to those with no future, those destined by God to live in distress? 24I cannot eat for sighing; my groans pour out like water. 25What I always feared has happened to me. What I dreaded has come to be. 26I have no peace, no quietness. I have no rest; instead, only trouble comes."

CHAPTER **4**
Eliphaz's First Response to Job
Then Eliphaz the Temanite replied to Job:

2 "Will you be patient and let me say a word? For who could keep from speaking out?

3 "In the past you have encouraged many a troubled soul to trust in God; you have supported those who were weak. 4Your words have strengthened the fallen; you steadied those who wavered. 5But now when trouble strikes, you faint and are broken. 6Does your reverence for God give you no confidence? Shouldn't you believe that God will care for those who are upright?

7 "Stop and think! Does the innocent person perish? When has the upright person been destroyed? 8My experience shows that those who plant trouble and cultivate evil will harvest the same. 9They perish by a breath from God. They vanish in a blast of his anger. 10Though they are fierce young lions, they will all be broken and destroyed. 11The fierce lion will starve, and the cubs of the lioness will be scattered.

12 "This truth was given me in secret, as though whispered in my ear. 13It came in a vision at night as others slept. 14Fear gripped me; I trembled and shook with terror. 15A spirit* swept past my face. Its wind sent shivers up my spine. 16It stopped, but I couldn't see its shape. There was a form before my eyes, and a hushed voice said, 17'Can a mortal be just and upright before God? Can a person be pure before the Creator?'

18 "If God cannot trust his own angels and has charged some of them with folly, 19how much less will he trust those made of clay! Their foundation is dust, and they are crushed as easily as moths. 20They are alive in the morning, but by evening they are dead, gone forever without a trace. 21Their tent collapses; they die in ignorance.

CHAPTER **5**
Eliphaz's Response Continues
"You may cry for help, but no one listens. You may turn to the angels,* but they give you no help. 2Surely resentment destroys the fool, and jealousy kills the simple. 3From my experience, I know that fools who turn from God may be successful for the moment, but then comes sudden disaster. 4Their children are abandoned far from help, with no one to defend them. 5Their harvests are stolen, and their wealth satisfies the thirst of many others, not themselves! 6But evil does not spring from the soil, and trouble does not sprout from the earth. 7People are born for trouble as predictably as sparks fly upward from a fire.

8 "My advice to you is this: Go to God and present your case to him. 9For he does great works too marvelous to understand. He performs miracles without number. 10He gives rain for the earth. He sends water for the fields. 11He gives prosperity to the poor and humble, and he takes sufferers to safety. 12He frustrates the plans of the crafty, so their efforts will not succeed. 13He catches those who think they are wise in their own cleverness, so that their cunning schemes are thwarted. 14They grope in the daylight as though they were blind; they see no

3:8 Hebrew *rouse Leviathan.*   **4:15** Or *wind.*   **5:1** Hebrew *the holy ones.*

better in the daytime than at night. 15He rescues the poor from the cutting words of the strong. He saves them from the clutches of the powerful. 16And so at last the poor have hope, and the fangs of the wicked are broken.

17"But consider the joy of those corrected by God! Do not despise the chastening of the Almighty when you sin. 18For though he wounds, he also bandages. He strikes, but his hands also heal. 19He will rescue you again and again so that no evil can touch you. 20He will save you from death in time of famine, from the power of the sword in time of war. 21You will be safe from slander and will have no fear of destruction when it comes. 22You will laugh at destruction and famine; wild animals will not terrify you. 23You will be at peace with the stones of the field, and its wild animals will be at peace with you. 24You will know that your home is kept safe. When you visit your pastures, nothing will be missing. 25Your children will be many; your descendants will be as plentiful as grass! 26You will live to a good old age. You will not be harvested until the proper time!

27"We have found from experience that all this is true. Listen to my counsel, and apply it to yourself."

CHAPTER **6**

Job's Second Speech: A Response to Eliphaz
Then Job spoke again:

2"If my sadness could be weighed and my troubles be put on the scales, 3they would be heavier than all the sands of the sea. That is why I spoke so rashly. 4For the Almighty has struck me down with his arrows. He has sent his poisoned arrows deep within my spirit. All God's terrors are arrayed against me. 5Don't I have a right to complain? Wild donkeys bray when they find no green grass, and oxen low when they have no food. 6People complain when there is no salt in their food. And how tasteless is the uncooked white of an egg! 7My appetite disappears when I look at it; I gag at the thought of eating it!

8"Oh, that I might have my request, that God would grant my hope. 9I wish he would crush me. I wish he would reach out his hand and kill me. 10At least I can take comfort in this: Despite the pain, I have not denied the words of the Holy One. 11But I do not have the strength to endure. I do not have a goal that encourages me to carry on. 12Do I have strength as hard as

6:27 Hebrew *even gamble over an orphan.*

stone? Is my body made of bronze? 13No, I am utterly helpless, without any chance of success.

14"One should be kind to a fainting friend, but you have accused me without the slightest fear of the Almighty. 15My brother, you have proved as unreliable as a seasonal brook that overflows its banks in the spring 16when it is swollen with ice and melting snow. 17But when the hot weather arrives, the water disappears. The brook vanishes in the heat. 18The caravans turn aside to be refreshed, but there is nothing there to drink, and so they perish in the desert. 19With high hopes, the caravans from Tema and from Sheba stop for water, 20but finding none, their hopes are dashed. 21You, too, have proved to be of no help. You have seen my calamity, and you are afraid. 22But why? Have I ever asked you for a gift? Have I begged you to use any of your wealth on my behalf? 23Have I ever asked you to rescue me from my enemies? Have I asked you to save me from ruthless people?

24"All I want is a reasonable answer—then I will keep quiet. Tell me, what have I done wrong? 25Honest words are painful, but what do your criticisms amount to? 26Do you think your words are convincing when you disregard my cry of desperation? 27You would even send an orphan into slavery* or sell a friend. 28Look at me! Would I lie to your face? 29Stop assuming my guilt, for I am righteous. Don't be so unjust. 30Do you think I am lying? Don't I know the difference between right and wrong?

CHAPTER **7**

"Is this not the struggle of all humanity? A person's life is long and hard, like that of a hired hand, 2like a worker who longs for the day to end, like a servant waiting to be paid. 3I, too, have been assigned months of futility, long and weary nights of misery. 4When I go to bed, I think, 'When will it be morning?' But the night drags on, and I toss till dawn. 5My skin is filled with worms and scabs. My flesh breaks open, full of pus.

Job Cries Out to God
6"My days are swifter than a weaver's shuttle flying back and forth. They end without hope. 7O God, remember that my life is but a breath, and I will never again experience pleasure. 8You see me now, but not for long. Your eyes will be on me, but I will be dead. 9Just as a cloud dissipates and vanishes, those who die will not

come back. ¹⁰They are gone forever from their home—never to be seen again.

¹¹"I cannot keep from speaking. I must express my anguish. I must complain in my bitterness. ¹²Am I a sea monster that you place a guard on me? ¹³If I think, 'My bed will comfort me, and I will try to forget my misery with sleep,' ¹⁴you shatter me with dreams. You terrify me with visions. ¹⁵I would rather die of strangulation than go on and on like this. ¹⁶I hate my life. I do not want to go on living. Oh, leave me alone for these few remaining days.

¹⁷"What are mere mortals, that you should make so much of us? ¹⁸For you examine us every morning and test us every moment. ¹⁹Why won't you leave me alone—even for a moment*? ²⁰Have I sinned? What have I done to you, O watcher of all humanity? Why have you made me your target? Am I a burden to you? ²¹Why not just pardon my sin and take away my guilt? For soon I will lie down in the dust and die. When you look for me, I will be gone."

CHAPTER 8
Bildad's First Response to Job

Then Bildad the Shuhite replied to Job:

²"How long will you go on like this? Your words are a blustering wind. ³Does God twist justice? Does the Almighty twist what is right? ⁴Your children obviously sinned against him, so their punishment was well deserved. ⁵But if you pray to God and seek the favor of the Almighty, ⁶if you are pure and live with complete integrity, he will rise up and restore your happy home. ⁷And though you started with little, you will end with much.

⁸"Just ask the former generation. Pay attention to the experience of our ancestors. ⁹For we were born but yesterday and know so little. Our days on earth are as transient as a shadow. ¹⁰But those who came before us will teach you. They will teach you from the wisdom of former generations.

¹¹"Can papyrus reeds grow where there is no marsh? Can bulrushes flourish where there is no water? ¹²While they are still flowering, not ready to be cut, they begin to wither. ¹³Such is the fate of all who forget God. The hope of the godless comes to nothing. ¹⁴Everything they count on will collapse. They are leaning on a spiderweb. ¹⁵They cling to their home for security, but it won't last. They try to hold it fast, but it will not endure. ¹⁶The godless seem so strong, like a lush plant growing in the sunshine, its branches spreading across the garden. ¹⁷Its roots grow down through a pile of rocks to hold it firm. ¹⁸But when it is uprooted, it isn't even missed! ¹⁹That is the end of its life, and others spring up from the earth to replace it.

²⁰"But look! God will not reject a person of integrity, nor will he make evildoers prosper. ²¹He will yet fill your mouth with laughter and your lips with shouts of joy. ²²Those who hate you will be clothed with shame, and the tent of the wicked will be destroyed."

CHAPTER 9
Job's Third Speech: A Response to Bildad

Then Job spoke again:

²"Yes, I know this is all true in principle. But how can a person be declared innocent in the eyes of God? ³If someone wanted to take God to court,* would it be possible to answer him even once in a thousand times? ⁴For God is so wise and so mighty. Who has ever challenged him successfully?

⁵"Without warning, he moves the mountains, overturning them in his anger. ⁶He shakes the earth from its place, and its foundations tremble. ⁷If he commands it, the sun won't rise and the stars won't shine. ⁸He alone has spread out the heavens and marches on the waves of the sea. ⁹He made all the stars—the Bear, Orion, the Pleiades, and the constellations of the southern sky. ¹⁰His great works are too marvelous to understand. He performs miracles without number.

¹¹Yet when he comes near, I cannot see him. When he moves on, I do not see him go. ¹²If he sends death to snatch someone away, who can stop him? Who dares to ask him, 'What are you doing?' ¹³And God does not restrain his anger. The mightiest forces against him* are crushed beneath his feet.

¹⁴"And who am I, that I should try to answer God or even reason with him? ¹⁵Even if I were innocent, I would have no defense. I could only plead for mercy. ¹⁶And even if I summoned him and he responded, he would never listen to me. ¹⁷For he attacks me without reason,* and he multiplies my wounds without cause. ¹⁸He will not let me catch my breath, but fills me instead with bitter sorrows. ¹⁹As for strength, he has it. As for justice, who can challenge him? ²⁰Though I am innocent, my own mouth would pronounce me guilty. Though I am blameless, it* would prove me wicked.

7:19 Hebrew *long enough to swallow my spittle.* 9:3 Or *If God wanted to take a person to court.* 9:13 Hebrew *The helpers of Rahab,* the name of a mythical sea monster that represents chaos in ancient literature. 9:17 As in Syriac version; Hebrew reads *with a storm.* 9:20 Or *he.*

21 "I am innocent, but it makes no difference to me—I despise my life. 22Innocent or wicked, it is all the same to him. That is why I say, 'He destroys both the blameless and the wicked.' 23He laughs when a plague suddenly kills the innocent. 24The whole earth is in the hands of the wicked, and God blinds the eyes of the judges and lets them be unfair. If not he, then who?

25 "My life passes more swiftly than a runner. It flees away, filled with tragedy. 26It disappears like a swift boat, like an eagle that swoops down on its prey. 27If I decided to forget my complaints, if I decided to end my sadness and be cheerful, 28I would dread all the pain he would send. For I know you will not hold me innocent, O God. 29Whatever happens, I will be found guilty. So what's the use of trying? 30Even if I were to wash myself with soap and cleanse my hands with lye to make them absolutely clean, 31you would plunge me into a muddy ditch, and I would be so filthy my own clothing would hate me.

32 "God is not a mortal like me, so I cannot argue with him or take him to trial. 33If only there were a mediator who could bring us together, but there is none. 34The mediator could make God stop beating me, and I would no longer live in terror of his punishment. 35Then I could speak to him without fear, but I cannot do that in my own strength.

CHAPTER 10
Job Frames His Plea to God

"I am disgusted with my life. Let me complain freely. I will speak in the bitterness of my soul. 2I will say to God, 'Don't simply condemn me—tell me the charge you are bringing against me. 3What do you gain by oppressing me? Why do you reject me, the work of your own hands, while sending joy and prosperity to the wicked? 4Are your eyes only those of a human? Do you see things as people see them? 5Is your lifetime merely human? Is your life so short 6that you are in a hurry to probe for my guilt, to search for my sin? 7Although you know I am not guilty, no one can rescue me from your power.

8 " 'You formed me with your hands; you made me, and yet you completely destroy me. 9Remember that I am made of dust—will you turn me back to dust so soon? 10You guided my conception and formed me in the womb.* 11You clothed me with skin and flesh, and you knit my bones and sinews together. 12You gave me life and showed me your unfailing love. My life was preserved by your care.

13 " 'Yet your real motive—I know this was your intent—14was to watch me, and if I sinned, you would not forgive my iniquity. 15If I am guilty, too bad for me. And even if I'm innocent, I am filled with shame and misery so that I can't hold my head high. 16And if I hold my head high, you hunt me like a lion and display your awesome power against me. 17Again and again you witness against me. You pour out an ever-increasing volume of anger upon me and bring fresh armies against me.

18 " 'Why, then, did you bring me out of my mother's womb? Why didn't you let me die at birth? 19Then I would have been spared this miserable existence. I would have gone directly from the womb to the grave. 20I have only a little time left, so leave me alone—that I may have a little moment of comfort 21before I leave for the land of darkness and utter gloom, never to return. 22It is a land as dark as midnight, a land of utter gloom where confusion reigns and the light is as dark as midnight.' "

CHAPTER 11
Zophar's First Response to Job

Then Zophar the Naamathite replied to Job:

2 "Shouldn't someone answer this torrent of words? Is a person proved innocent just by talking a lot? 3Should I remain silent while you babble on? When you mock God, shouldn't someone make you ashamed? 4You claim, 'My teaching is pure,' and 'I am clean in the sight of God.' 5If only God would speak; if only he would tell you what he thinks! 6If only he would tell you the secrets of wisdom, for true wisdom is not a simple matter. Listen! God is doubtless punishing you far less than you deserve!

7 "Can you solve the mysteries of God? Can you discover everything there is to know about the Almighty? 8Such knowledge is higher than the heavens—but who are you? It is deeper than the underworld*—what can you know in comparison to him? 9It is broader than the earth and wider than the sea. 10If God comes along and puts a person in prison, or if he calls the court to order, who is going to stop him? 11For he knows those who are false, and he takes note of all their sins. 12An empty-headed person won't become wise any more than a wild donkey can bear human offspring*!

13 "If only you would prepare your heart and lift up your hands to him in prayer! 14Get rid of your sins and leave all iniquity behind you. 15Then your face will brighten in innocence. You

---

10:10 Hebrew *You poured me out like milk and curdled me like cheese.*   11:8 Hebrew *Sheol.*   11:12 Or *bear a tame colt.*

will be strong and free of fear. 16You will forget your misery. It will all be gone like water under the bridge. 17Your life will be brighter than the noonday. Any darkness will be as bright as morning. 18You will have courage because you will have hope. You will be protected and will rest in safety. 19You will lie down unafraid, and many will look to you for help. 20But the wicked will lose hope. They have no escape. Their hope becomes despair."

CHAPTER 12
Job's Fourth Speech: A Response to Zophar
Then Job spoke again:

2"You really know everything, don't you? And when you die, wisdom will die with you! 3Well, I know a few things myself—and you're no better than I am. Who doesn't know these things you've been saying? 4Yet my friends laugh at me. I am a man who calls on God and receives an answer. I am a just and blameless man, yet they laugh at me. 5People who are at ease mock those in trouble. They give a push to people who are stumbling. 6But even robbers are left in peace, and those who provoke God—and God has them in his power—live in safety!

7"Ask the animals, and they will teach you. Ask the birds of the sky, and they will tell you. 8Speak to the earth, and it will instruct you. Let the fish of the sea speak to you. 9They all know that the LORD has done this. 10For the life of every living thing is in his hand, and the breath of all humanity. 11Just as the mouth tastes good food, so the ear tests the words it hears. 12Wisdom belongs to the aged, and understanding to those who have lived many years.

13"But true wisdom and power are with God; counsel and understanding are his. 14What he destroys cannot be rebuilt. When he closes in on someone, there is no escape. 15If he holds back the rain, the earth becomes a desert. If he releases the waters, they flood the earth.

16"Yes, strength and wisdom are with him; deceivers and deceived are both in his power. 17He leads counselors away stripped of good judgment; he drives judges to madness. 18He removes the royal robe of kings. With ropes around their waist, they are led away. 19He leads priests away stripped of status; he overthrows the mighty. 20He silences the trusted adviser, and he removes the insight of the elders. 21He pours disgrace upon princes and confiscates weapons from the strong.

22"He floods the darkness with light; he brings light to the deepest gloom. 23He raises up nations, and he destroys them. He makes nations expand, and he abandons them. 24He takes away the understanding of kings, and he leaves them wandering in a wasteland without a path. 25They grope in the darkness without a light. He makes them stagger like drunkards.

CHAPTER 13
Job Wants to Argue His Case with God
"Look, I have seen many instances such as you describe. I understand what you are saying. 2I know as much as you do. You are no better than I am. 3Oh, how I long to speak directly to the Almighty. I want to argue my case with God himself. 4For you are smearing me with lies. As doctors, you are worthless quacks. 5Please be quiet! That's the smartest thing you could do. 6Listen to my charge; pay attention to my arguments.

7"Are you defending God by means of lies and dishonest arguments? 8You should be impartial witnesses, but will you slant your testimony in his favor? Will you argue God's case for him? 9Be careful that he doesn't find out what you are doing! Or do you think you can fool him as easily as you fool people? 10No, you will be in serious trouble with him if even in your hearts you slant your testimony in his favor. 11Doesn't his majesty strike terror into your heart? Does not your fear of him seize you? 12Your statements have about as much value as ashes. Your defense is as fragile as a clay pot.

13"Be silent now and leave me alone. Let me speak—and I will face the consequences. 14Yes, I will take my life in my hands and say what I really think. 15God might kill me, but I cannot wait. I am going to argue my case with him. 16But this is what will save me: that I am not godless. If I were, I would be thrown from his presence.

17"Listen closely to what I am about to say. Hear me out. 18I have prepared my case; I will be proved innocent. 19Who can argue with me over this? If you could prove me wrong, I would remain silent until I die.

Job Asks How He Has Sinned
20"O God, there are two things I beg of you, and I will be able to face you. 21Remove your hand from me, and don't terrify me with your awesome presence. 22Now summon me, and I will answer! Or let me speak to you, and you reply. 23Tell me, what have I done wrong? Show me my rebellion and my sin. 24Why do you turn away from me? Why do you consider me your enemy?

25Would you terrify a leaf that is blown by the wind? Would you chase a dry stalk of grass? 26"You write bitter accusations against me and bring up all the sins of my youth. 27You put my feet in stocks. You watch all my paths. You trace all my footprints. 28I waste away like rotting wood, like a moth-eaten coat.

CHAPTER 14

"How frail is humanity! How short is life, and how full of trouble! 2Like a flower, we blossom for a moment and then wither. Like the shadow of a passing cloud, we quickly disappear. 3Must you keep an eye on such a frail creature and demand an accounting from me? 4Who can create purity in one born impure? No one! 5You have decided the length of our lives. You know how many months we will live, and we are not given a minute longer. 6So give us a little rest, won't you? Turn away your angry stare. We are like hired hands, so let us finish the task you have given us.

7"If a tree is cut down, there is hope that it will sprout again and grow new branches. 8Though its roots have grown old in the earth and its stump decays, 9at the scent of water it may bud and sprout again like a new seedling. 10"But when people die, they lose all strength. They breathe their last, and then where are they? 11As water evaporates from a lake and as a river disappears in drought, 12people lie down and do not rise again. Until the heavens are no more, they will not wake up nor be roused from their sleep.

13"I wish you would hide me with the dead and forget me there until your anger has passed. But mark your calendar to think of me again! 14If mortals die, can they live again? This thought would give me hope, and through my struggle I would eagerly wait for release. 15You would call and I would answer, and you would yearn for me, your handiwork. 16For then you would count my steps, instead of watching for my sins. 17My sins would be sealed in a pouch, and you would cover over my iniquity.

18"But as mountains fall and crumble and as rocks fall from a cliff, 19as water wears away the stones and floods wash away the soil, so you destroy people's hope. 20You always overpower them, and then they pass from the scene. You disfigure them in death and send them away. 21They never know if their sons grow up in honor or sink to insignificance. 22They are absorbed in their own pain and grief."

CHAPTER 15

Eliphaz's Second Response to Job

Then Eliphaz the Temanite replied:

2"You are supposed to be a wise man, and yet you give us all this foolish talk. You are nothing but a windbag. 3It isn't right to speak so foolishly. What good do such words do? 4Have you no fear of God, no reverence for him? 5Your sins are telling your mouth what to say. Your words are based on clever deception. 6But why should I condemn you? Your own mouth does!

7"Were you the first person ever born? Were you born before the hills were made? 8Were you listening at God's secret council? Do you have a monopoly on wisdom? 9What do you know that we don't? What do you understand that we don't? 10On our side are aged, gray-haired men much older than your father!

11"Is God's comfort too little for you? Is his gentle word not enough? 12What has captured your reason? What has weakened your vision, 13that you turn against God and say all these evil things? 14Can a mortal be pure? Can a human be just? 15Why, God doesn't even trust the angels*! Even the heavens cannot be absolutely pure in his sight. 16How much less pure is a corrupt and sinful person with a thirst for wickedness!

17"If you will listen, I will answer you from my own experience. 18And it is confirmed by the experience of wise men who have heard the same thing from their fathers, 19those to whom the land was given long before any foreigners arrived.

20"Wicked people are in pain throughout their lives. 21They are surrounded by terrors, and even on good days they fear the attack of the destroyer. 22They dare not go out into the darkness for fear they will be murdered. 23They wander abroad for bread, saying, 'Where is it?'* They know their ruin is certain. 24That dark day terrifies them. They live in distress and anguish, like a king preparing for an attack. 25For they have clenched their fists against God, defying the Almighty. 26Holding their strong shields, they defiantly charge against him.

27"These wicked people are fat and rich, 28but their cities will be ruined. They will live in abandoned houses that are ready to tumble down. 29They will not continue to be rich. Their wealth will not endure, and their possessions will no longer spread across the horizon.

30"They will not escape the darkness. The flame will burn them up, and the breath of God

15:15 Hebrew *the holy ones.*   15:23 Greek version reads *He is appointed to be food for a vulture.*

will destroy everything they have. ³¹Let them no longer trust in empty riches. They are only fooling themselves, for emptiness will be their only reward. ³²They will be cut down in the prime of life, and all they counted on will disappear. ³³They will be like a vine whose grapes are harvested before they are ripe, like an olive tree that sheds its blossoms so the fruit cannot form. ³⁴For the godless are barren. Their homes, enriched through bribery, will be consumed by fire. ³⁵They conceive trouble and evil, and their hearts give birth only to deceit."

CHAPTER 16
Job's Fifth Speech: A Response to Eliphaz

Then Job spoke again:

²"I have heard all this before. What miserable comforters you are! ³Won't you ever stop your flow of foolish words? What have I said that makes you speak so endlessly? ⁴I could say the same things if you were in my place. I could spout off my criticisms against you and shake my head at you. ⁵But that's not what I would do. I would speak in a way that helps you. I would try to take away your grief. ⁶But as it is, my grief remains no matter how I defend myself. And it does not help if I refuse to speak.

⁷"O God, you have ground me down and devastated my family. ⁸You have reduced me to skin and bones—as proof, they say, of my sins. ⁹God hates me and tears angrily at my flesh. He gnashes his teeth at me and pierces me with his eyes. ¹⁰People jeer and laugh at me. They slap my cheek in contempt. A mob gathers against me. ¹¹God has handed me over to sinners. He has tossed me into the hands of the wicked.

¹²"I was living quietly until he broke me apart. He took me by the neck and dashed me to pieces. Then he set me up as his target. ¹³His archers surrounded me, and his arrows pierced me without mercy. The ground is wet with my blood.* ¹⁴Again and again he smashed me, charging at me like a warrior. ¹⁵Here I sit in sackcloth. I have surrendered, and I sit in the dust. ¹⁶My eyes are red with weeping; darkness covers my eyes. ¹⁷Yet I am innocent, and my prayer is pure.

¹⁸"O earth, do not conceal my blood. Let it cry out on my behalf. ¹⁹Even now my witness is in heaven. My advocate is there on high. ²⁰My friends scorn me, but I pour out my tears to God. ²¹Oh, that someone would mediate between God and me, as a person mediates between

16:13 Hebrew *my gall.*

friends. ²²For soon I must go down that road from which I will never return.

CHAPTER 17
Job Continues to Defend His Innocence

"My spirit is crushed, and I am near death. The grave is ready to receive me. ²I am surrounded by mockers. I watch how bitterly they taunt me.

³"You must defend my innocence, O God, since no one else will stand up for me. ⁴You have closed their minds to understanding, but do not let them triumph. ⁵They denounce their companions for their own advantage, so let their children faint with hunger.

⁶"God has made a mockery of me among the people; they spit in my face. ⁷My eyes are dim with weeping, and I am but a shadow of my former self. ⁸The upright are astonished when they see me. The innocent are aroused against the ungodly. ⁹The righteous will move onward and forward, and those with pure hearts will become stronger and stronger.

¹⁰"As for all of you, come back and try again! But I will not find a wise man among you. ¹¹My days are over. My hopes have disappeared. My heart's desires are broken. ¹²They say that night is day and day is night; how they pervert the truth! ¹³I might go to the grave and make my bed in darkness. ¹⁴And I might call the grave my father, and the worm my mother and my sister. ¹⁵But where then is my hope? Can anyone find it? ¹⁶No, my hope will go down with me to the grave. We will rest together in the dust!"

CHAPTER 18
Bildad's Second Response to Job

Then Bildad the Shuhite replied:

²"How long before you stop talking? Speak sense if you want us to answer! ³Do you think we are cattle? Do you think we have no intelligence? ⁴You may tear your hair out in anger, but will that cause the earth to be abandoned? Will it make rocks fall from a cliff?

⁵"The truth remains that the light of the wicked will be snuffed out. The sparks of their fire will not glow. ⁶The light in their tent will grow dark. The lamp hanging above them will be quenched. ⁷The confident stride of the wicked will be shortened. Their own schemes will be their downfall.

⁸"The wicked walk into a net. They fall into a pit that's been dug in the path. ⁹A trap grabs

them by the heel. A noose tightens around them. ¹⁰A snare lies hidden in the ground. A rope lies coiled on their path.

¹¹ "Terrors surround the wicked and trouble them at every step. ¹²Their vigor is depleted by hunger, and calamity waits for them to stumble. ¹³Disease eats their skin; death devours their limbs. ¹⁴They are torn from the security of their tent, and they are brought down to the king of terrors. ¹⁵The home of the wicked will disappear beneath a fiery barrage of burning sulfur. ¹⁶Their roots will dry up, and their branches will wither. ¹⁷All memory of their existence will perish from the earth. No one will remember them. ¹⁸They will be thrust from light into darkness, driven from the world. ¹⁹They will have neither children nor grandchildren, nor any survivor in their home country. ²⁰People in the west are appalled at their fate; people in the east are horrified. ²¹They will say, 'This was the home of a wicked person, the place of one who rejected God.' "

CHAPTER 19
Job's Sixth Speech: A Response to Bildad

Then Job spoke again:

2 "How long will you torture me? How long will you try to break me with your words? ³Ten times now you have meant to insult me. You should be ashamed of dealing with me so harshly. ⁴And even if I have sinned, that is my concern, not yours. ⁵You are trying to overcome me, using my humiliation as evidence of my sin, ⁶but it is God who has wronged me. I cannot defend myself, for I am like a city under siege.

7 "I cry out for help, but no one hears me. I protest, but there is no justice. ⁸God has blocked my way and plunged my path into darkness. ⁹He has stripped me of my honor and removed the crown from my head. ¹⁰He has demolished me on every side, and I am finished. He has destroyed my hope. ¹¹His fury burns against me; he counts me as an enemy. ¹²His troops advance. They build up roads to attack me. They camp all around my tent.

13 "My relatives stay far away, and my friends have turned against me. ¹⁴My neighbors and my close friends are all gone. ¹⁵The members of my household have forgotten me. The servant girls consider me a stranger. I am like a foreigner to them. ¹⁶I call my servant, but he doesn't come; I even plead with him! ¹⁷My breath is repulsive to my wife. I am loathsome to my own family. ¹⁸Even young children despise me. When I stand to speak, they turn their backs on me. ¹⁹My close friends abhor me. Those I loved

19:26 Or *without my body I will see God.*

have turned against me. ²⁰I have been reduced to skin and bones and have escaped death by the skin of my teeth.

21 "Have mercy on me, my friends, have mercy, for the hand of God has struck me. ²²Why must you persecute me as God does? Why aren't you satisfied with my anguish?

23 "Oh, that my words could be written. Oh, that they could be inscribed on a monument, ²⁴carved with an iron chisel and filled with lead, engraved forever in the rock.

25 "But as for me, I know that my Redeemer lives, and that he will stand upon the earth at last. ²⁶And after my body has decayed, yet in my body I will see God*! ²⁷I will see him for myself. Yes, I will see him with my own eyes. I am overwhelmed at the thought!

28 "How dare you go on persecuting me, saying, 'It's his own fault'? ²⁹I warn you, you yourselves are in danger of punishment for your attitude. Then you will know that there is judgment."

CHAPTER 20
Zophar's Second Response to Job

Then Zophar the Naamathite replied:

2 "I must reply because I am greatly disturbed. ³I have had to endure your insults, but now my spirit prompts me to reply.

4 "Don't you realize that ever since people were first placed on the earth, ⁵the triumph of the wicked has been short-lived and the joy of the godless has been only temporary? ⁶Though the godless man's pride reaches to the heavens and though his head touches the clouds, ⁷yet he will perish forever, thrown away like his own dung. Those who knew him will ask, 'Where is he?' ⁸He will fade like a dream and not be found. He will vanish like a vision in the night. ⁹Neither his friends nor his family will ever see him again. ¹⁰His children will beg from the poor, for he must give back his ill-gotten wealth. ¹¹He was just a young man, but his bones will lie in the dust.

12 "He enjoyed the taste of his wickedness, letting it melt under his tongue. ¹³He savored it, holding it long in his mouth. ¹⁴But suddenly, the food he has eaten turns sour within him, a poisonous venom in his stomach. ¹⁵He will vomit the wealth he swallowed. God won't let him keep it down. ¹⁶He will suck the poison of snakes. The viper will kill him. ¹⁷He will never again enjoy abundant streams of olive oil or rivers of milk and honey. ¹⁸His labors will not

be rewarded. His wealth will bring him no joy. ¹⁹For he oppressed the poor and left them destitute. He foreclosed on their homes. ²⁰He was always greedy but never satisfied. Of all the things he dreamed about, nothing remains. ²¹Nothing is left after he finishes gorging himself; therefore, his prosperity will not endure.

²²"In the midst of plenty, he will run into trouble, and disasters will destroy him. ²³May God give him a bellyful of trouble. May God rain down his anger upon him. ²⁴He will try to escape, but God's arrow will pierce him. ²⁵The arrow is pulled from his body, and the arrowhead glistens with blood.* The terrors of death are upon him.

²⁶"His treasures will be lost in deepest darkness. A wildfire will devour his goods, consuming all he has left. ²⁷The heavens will reveal his guilt, and the earth will give testimony against him. ²⁸A flood will sweep away his house. God's anger will descend on him in torrents. ²⁹This is the fate that awaits the wicked. It is the inheritance decreed by God."

CHAPTER **21**
Job's Seventh Speech: A Response to Zophar
Then Job spoke again:

²"Listen closely to what I am saying. You can console me by listening to me. ³Bear with me, and let me speak. After I have spoken, you may mock me.

⁴"My complaint is with God, not with people. No wonder I'm so impatient. ⁵Look at me and be stunned. Put your hand over your mouth in shock. ⁶When I think about what I am saying, I shudder. My body trembles.

⁷"The truth is that the wicked live to a good old age. They grow old and wealthy. ⁸They live to see their children grow to maturity, and they enjoy their grandchildren. ⁹Their homes are safe from every fear, and God does not punish them. ¹⁰Their bulls never fail to breed. Their cows bear calves without miscarriage. ¹¹Their children skip about like lambs in a flock of sheep. ¹²They sing with tambourine and harp. They make merry to the sound of the flute. ¹³They spend their days in prosperity; then they go down to the grave in peace. ¹⁴All this, even though they say to God, 'Go away. We want no part of you and your ways. ¹⁵Who is the Almighty, and why should we obey him? What good will it do us if we pray?' ¹⁶But their prosperity is not of their own doing, so I will have nothing to do with that kind of thinking.

²⁰:²⁵ Hebrew *with gall.*

¹⁷"Yet the wicked get away with it time and time again. They rarely have trouble, and God skips them when he distributes sorrows in his anger. ¹⁸Are they driven before the wind like straw? Are they carried away by the storm? Not at all!

¹⁹" 'Well,' you say, 'at least God will punish their children!' But I say that God should punish the ones who sin, not their children! Let them feel their own penalty. ²⁰Let their own eyes see their destruction. Let them drink deeply of the anger of the Almighty. ²¹For when they are dead, they will not care what happens to their family.

²²"But who can teach a lesson to God, the supreme Judge? ²³One person dies in prosperity and security, ²⁴the very picture of good health. ²⁵Another person dies in bitter poverty, never having tasted the good life. ²⁶Both alike are buried in the same dust, both eaten by the same worms.

²⁷"Look, I know your thoughts. I know the schemes you plot against me. ²⁸You will tell me of rich and wicked people who came to disaster because of their sins. ²⁹But I tell you to ask those who have been around, and they can tell you the truth. ³⁰Evil people are spared in times of calamity and are allowed to escape. ³¹No one rebukes them openly. No one repays them for what they have done. ³²When they are carried to the grave, an honor guard keeps watch at their tomb. ³³A great funeral procession goes to the cemetery. Many pay their respects as the body is laid to rest and the earth gives sweet repose.

³⁴"How can you comfort me? All your explanations are wrong!"

CHAPTER **22**
Eliphaz's Third Response to Job
Then Eliphaz the Temanite replied:

²"Can a person's actions be of benefit to God? Can even a wise person be helpful to him? ³Is it any pleasure to the Almighty if you are righteous? Would it be any gain to him if you were perfect? ⁴Is it because of your reverence for him that he accuses and judges you? ⁵Not at all! It is because of your wickedness! Your guilt has no limit!

⁶"For example, you must have lent money to your friend and then kept the clothing he gave you as a pledge. Yes, you stripped him to the bone. ⁷You must have refused water for the thirsty and food for the hungry. ⁸After all, you think the land belongs to the powerful and that those who are privileged have a right to it! ⁹You

must have sent widows away without helping them and crushed the strength of orphans. ¹⁰That is why you are surrounded by traps and sudden fears. ¹¹That is why you cannot see in the darkness, and waves of water cover you.

¹²"God is so great—higher than the heavens, higher than the farthest stars. ¹³But you reply, 'That's why God can't see what I am doing! How can he judge through the thick darkness? ¹⁴For thick clouds swirl about him, and he cannot see us. He is way up there, walking on the vault of heaven.'

¹⁵"Will you continue on the old paths where evil people have walked? ¹⁶They were snatched away in the prime of life, and the foundations of their lives were washed away forever. ¹⁷For they said to God, 'Leave us alone! What can the Almighty do for us?' ¹⁸But they forgot that he had filled their homes with good things, so I will have nothing to do with that kind of thinking.

¹⁹"Now the righteous will be happy to see the wicked destroyed, and the innocent will laugh them to scorn. ²⁰They will say, 'Surely our enemies have been destroyed. The last of them have been consumed in the fire.'

²¹"Stop quarreling with God! If you agree with him, you will have peace at last, and things will go well for you. ²²Listen to his instructions, and store them in your heart. ²³If you return to the Almighty and clean up your life, you will be restored. ²⁴Give up your lust for money, and throw your precious gold into the river. ²⁵Then the Almighty himself will be your treasure. He will be your precious silver!

²⁶"Then you will delight yourself in the Almighty and look up to God. ²⁷You will pray to him, and he will hear you, and you will fulfill your vows to him. ²⁸Whatever you decide to do will be accomplished, and light will shine on the road ahead of you. ²⁹If someone is brought low and you say, 'Help him up,' God will save the downcast. ³⁰Then even sinners will be rescued by your pure hands."

CHAPTER 23

Job's Eighth Speech: A Response to Eliphaz
Then Job spoke again:

²"My complaint today is still a bitter one, and I try hard not to groan aloud. ³If only I knew where to find God, I would go to his throne and talk with him there. ⁴I would lay out my case and present my arguments. ⁵Then I would listen to his reply and understand what he says to me. ⁶Would he merely argue with me in his greatness? No, he would give me a fair hearing. ⁷Fair

and honest people can reason with him, so I would be acquitted by my Judge.

⁸"I go east, but he is not there. I go west, but I cannot find him. ⁹I do not see him in the north, for he is hidden. I turn to the south, but I cannot find him. ¹⁰But he knows where I am going. And when he has tested me like gold in a fire, he will pronounce me innocent.

¹¹"For I have stayed in God's paths; I have followed his ways and not turned aside. ¹²I have not departed from his commands but have treasured his word in my heart. ¹³Nevertheless, his mind concerning me remains unchanged, and who can turn him from his purposes? Whatever he wants to do, he does. ¹⁴So he will do for me all he has planned. He controls my destiny. ¹⁵No wonder I am so terrified in his presence. When I think of it, terror grips me. ¹⁶God has made my heart faint; the Almighty has terrified me. ¹⁷Darkness is all around me; thick, impenetrable darkness is everywhere.

CHAPTER 24

Job Asks Why the Wicked Are Not Punished
"Why doesn't the Almighty open the court and bring judgment? Why must the godly wait for him in vain? ²Evil people steal land by moving the boundary markers. They steal flocks of sheep, ³and they even take donkeys from the poor and fatherless. A poor widow must surrender her valuable ox as collateral for a loan. ⁴The poor are kicked aside; the needy must hide together for safety. ⁵Like the wild donkeys in the desert, the poor must spend all their time just getting enough to keep body and soul together. They go into the desert to search for food for their children. ⁶They harvest a field they do not own, and they glean in the vineyards of the wicked. ⁷All night they lie naked in the cold, without clothing or covering. ⁸They are soaked by mountain showers, and they huddle against the rocks for want of a home.

⁹"The wicked snatch a widow's child from her breast; they take the baby as a pledge for a loan. ¹⁰The poor must go about naked, without any clothing. They are forced to carry food while they themselves are starving. ¹¹They press out olive oil without being allowed to taste it, and they tread in the winepress as they suffer from thirst. ¹²The groans of the dying rise from the city, and the wounded cry for help, yet God does not respond to their moaning.

¹³"Wicked people rebel against the light. They refuse to acknowledge its ways. They will not stay in its paths. ¹⁴The murderer rises in the

early dawn to kill the poor and needy; at night he is a thief. ¹⁵The adulterer waits for the twilight, for he says, 'No one will see me then.' He masks his face so no one will know him. ¹⁶They break into houses at night and sleep in the daytime. They are not acquainted with the light. ¹⁷The black night is their morning. They ally themselves with the terrors of the darkness.

¹⁸"But they disappear from the earth as quickly as foam is swept down a river. Everything they own is cursed, so that no one enters their vineyard. ¹⁹Death consumes sinners just as drought and heat consume snow. ²⁰Even the sinner's own mother will forget him. Worms will find him sweet to eat. No one will remember him. Wicked people are broken like a tree in the storm. ²¹For they have taken advantage of the childless who have no protecting sons. They refuse to help the needy widows.

²²"God, in his power, drags away the rich. They may rise high, but they have no assurance in life. ²³They may be allowed to live in security, but God is always watching them. ²⁴And though they are great now, in a moment they will be gone like all others, withered like heads of grain. ²⁵"Can anyone claim otherwise? Who can prove me wrong?"

CHAPTER 25
Bildad's Third Response to Job
Then Bildad the Shuhite replied:

²"God is powerful and dreadful. He enforces peace in the heavens. ³Who is able to count his heavenly army? Does his light not shine on all the earth? ⁴How can a mere mortal stand before God and claim to be righteous? Who in all the earth is pure? ⁵God is so glorious that even the moon and stars scarcely shine compared to him. ⁶How much less are mere people, who are but worms in his sight?"

CHAPTER 26
Job's Ninth Speech: A Response to Bildad
Then Job spoke again:

²"How you have helped the powerless! How you have saved a person who has no strength! ³How you have enlightened my stupidity! What wise things you have said! ⁴Where have you gotten all these wise sayings? Whose spirit speaks through you?

⁵"The dead tremble in their place beneath the waters. ⁶The underworld* is naked in God's presence. There is no cover for the place of destruc-

tion. ⁷God stretches the northern sky over empty space and hangs the earth on nothing. ⁸He wraps the rain in his thick clouds, and the clouds do not burst with the weight. ⁹He shrouds his throne with his clouds. ¹⁰He created the horizon when he separated the waters; he set the boundaries for day and night. ¹¹The foundations of heaven tremble at his rebuke. ¹²By his power the sea grew calm. By his skill he crushed the great sea monster.* ¹³His Spirit made the heavens beautiful, and his power pierced the gliding serpent.

¹⁴"These are some of the minor things he does, merely a whisper of his power. Who can understand the thunder of his power?"

CHAPTER 27
Job's Final Speech
Job continued speaking:

²"I make this vow by the living God, who has taken away my rights, by the Almighty who has embittered my soul. ³As long as I live, while I have breath from God, ⁴my lips will speak no evil, and my tongue will speak no lies. ⁵I will never concede that you are right; until I die, I will defend my innocence. ⁶I will maintain my innocence without wavering. My conscience is clear for as long as I live.

⁷"May my enemy be punished like the wicked, my adversary like evil men. ⁸For what hope do the godless have when God cuts them off and takes away their life? ⁹Will God listen to their cry when trouble comes upon them? ¹⁰Can they take delight in the Almighty? Can they call to God at any time?

¹¹"I will teach you about God's power. I will not conceal anything that concerns the Almighty. ¹²But I don't need to, for you yourselves have seen all this; yet you are saying all these useless things to me.

¹³"This is what the wicked will receive from God; this is their inheritance from the Almighty. ¹⁴If they have a multitude of children, their children will die in war or starve to death. ¹⁵Those who survive will be brought down to the grave by a plague, with no one to mourn them, not even their wives.

¹⁶"Evil people may have all the money in the world, and they may store away mounds of clothing. ¹⁷But the righteous will wear that clothing, and the innocent will divide all that money. ¹⁸The houses built by the wicked are as fragile as a spiderweb, as flimsy as a shelter made of branches.

26:6 Hebrew *Sheol.*   26:12 Hebrew *Rahab,* the name of a mythical sea monster that represents chaos in ancient literature.

19"The wicked go to bed rich but wake up to find that all their wealth is gone. 20Terror overwhelms them, and they are blown away in the storms of the night. 21The east wind carries them away, and they are gone. It sweeps them away. 22It whirls down on them without mercy. They struggle to flee from its power. 23But everyone jeers at them and mocks them.

CHAPTER 28

Job Speaks of Wisdom and Understanding

"People know how to mine silver and refine gold. 2They know how to dig iron from the earth and smelt copper from stone. 3They know how to put light into darkness and explore the farthest, darkest regions of the earth as they search for ore. 4They sink a mine shaft into the earth far from where anyone lives. They descend on ropes, swinging back and forth. 5Bread comes from the earth, but below the surface the earth is melted as by fire.

6"People know how to find sapphires and gold dust—7treasures that no bird of prey can see, no falcon's eye observe—8for they are deep within the mines. No wild animal has ever walked upon those treasures; no lion has set his paw there. 9People know how to tear apart flinty rocks and overturn the roots of mountains. 10They cut tunnels in the rocks and uncover precious stones. 11They dam up the trickling streams and bring to light the hidden treasures.

12"But do people know where to find wisdom? Where can they find understanding? 13No one knows where to find it, for it is not found among the living. 14'It is not here,' says the ocean. 'Nor is it here,' says the sea.

15"It cannot be bought for gold or silver. 16Its value is greater than all the gold of Ophir, greater than precious onyx stone or sapphires. 17Wisdom is far more valuable than gold and crystal. It cannot be purchased with jewels mounted in fine gold. 18Coral and valuable rock crystal are worthless in trying to get it. The price of wisdom is far above pearls. 19Topaz from Ethiopia* cannot be exchanged for it. Its value is greater than the purest gold.

20"But do people know where to find wisdom? Where can they find understanding? 21For it is hidden from the eyes of all humanity. Even the sharp-eyed birds in the sky cannot discover it. 22But Destruction and Death say, 'We have heard a rumor of where wisdom can be found.'

23"God surely knows where it can be found,

24for he looks throughout the whole earth, under all the heavens. 25He made the winds blow and determined how much rain should fall. 26He made the laws of the rain and prepared a path for the lightning. 27Then, when he had done all this, he saw wisdom and measured it. He established it and examined it thoroughly. 28And this is what he says to all humanity: 'The fear of the Lord is true wisdom; to forsake evil is real understanding.'"

CHAPTER 29

Job Speaks of His Former Blessings

Job continued speaking:

2"I long for the years gone by when God took care of me, 3when he lighted the way before me and I walked safely through the darkness. 4In my early years, the friendship of God was felt in my home. 5The Almighty was still with me, and my children were around me. 6In those days my cows produced milk in abundance, and my olive groves poured out streams of olive oil.

7"Those were the days when I went to the city gate and took my place among the honored leaders. 8The young stepped aside when they saw me, and even the aged rose in respect at my coming. 9The princes stood in silence and put their hands over their mouths. 10The highest officials of the city stood quietly, holding their tongues in respect.

11"All who heard of me praised me. All who saw me spoke well of me. 12For I helped the poor in their need and the orphans who had no one to help them. 13I helped those who had lost hope, and they blessed me. And I caused the widows' hearts to sing for joy. 14All I did was just and honest. Righteousness covered me like a robe, and I wore justice like a turban. 15I served as eyes for the blind and feet for the lame. 16I was a father to the poor and made sure that even strangers received a fair trial. 17I broke the jaws of godless oppressors and made them release their victims.

18"I thought, 'Surely I will die surrounded by my family after a long, good life. 19For I am like a tree whose roots reach the water, whose branches are refreshed with the dew. 20New honors are constantly bestowed on me, and my strength is continually renewed.'

21"Everyone listened to me and valued my advice. They were silent as they waited for me to speak. 22And after I spoke, they had nothing to add, for my counsel satisfied them. 23They longed for me to speak as they longed for rain.

28:19 Hebrew *from Cush.*

They waited eagerly, for my words were as refreshing as the spring rain. ²⁴When they were discouraged, I smiled at them. My look of approval was precious to them. ²⁵I told them what they should do and presided over them as their chief. I lived as a king among his troops and as one who comforts those who mourn.

CHAPTER 30
Job Speaks of His Anguish

"But now I am mocked by those who are younger than I, by young men whose fathers are not worthy to run with my sheepdogs. ²A lot of good they are to me—those worn-out wretches! ³They are gaunt with hunger and flee to the deserts and the wastelands, desolate and gloomy. ⁴They eat coarse leaves, and they burn the roots of shrubs for heat. ⁵They are driven from civilization, and people shout after them as if they were thieves. ⁶So now they live in frightening ravines and in caves and among the rocks. ⁷They sound like animals as they howl among the bushes; they huddle together for shelter beneath the nettles. ⁸They are nameless fools, outcasts of civilization.

⁹"And now their sons mock me with their vulgar song! They taunt me! ¹⁰They despise me and won't come near me, except to spit in my face. ¹¹For God has cut the cords of my tent. He has humbled me, so they have thrown off all restraint. ¹²These outcasts oppose me to my face. They send me sprawling; they lay traps in my path. ¹³They block my road and do everything they can to hasten my calamity, knowing full well that I have no one to help me. ¹⁴They come at me from all directions. They rush upon me when I am down. ¹⁵I live in terror now. They hold me in contempt, and my prosperity has vanished as a cloud before a strong wind.

¹⁶"And now my heart is broken. Depression haunts my days. ¹⁷My weary nights are filled with pain as though something were relentlessly gnawing at my bones. ¹⁸With a strong hand, God grabs my garment. He grips me by the collar of my tunic. ¹⁹He has thrown me into the mud. I have become as dust and ashes.

²⁰"I cry to you, O God, but you don't answer me. I stand before you, and you don't bother to look. ²¹You have become cruel toward me. You persecute me with your great power. ²²You throw me into the whirlwind and destroy me in the storm. ²³And I know that you are sending me to my death—the destination of all who live.

²⁴"Surely no one would turn against the needy when they cry for help. ²⁵Did I not weep for those in trouble? Was I not deeply grieved for the needy? ²⁶So I looked for good, but evil came instead. I waited for the light, but darkness fell. ²⁷My heart is troubled and restless. Days of affliction have come upon me. ²⁸I walk in gloom, without sunlight. I stand in the public square and cry for help. ²⁹But instead, I am considered a brother to jackals and a companion to ostriches. ³⁰My skin has turned dark, and my bones burn with fever. ³¹My harp plays sad music, and my flute accompanies those who weep.

CHAPTER 31
Job's Final Protest of Innocence

"I made a covenant with my eyes not to look with lust upon a young woman. ²What has God above chosen for us? What is our inheritance from the Almighty on high? ³It is calamity for the wicked, misfortune for those who do evil. ⁴He sees everything I do and every step I take.

⁵"Have I lied to anyone or deceived anyone? ⁶Let God judge me on the scales of justice, for he knows my integrity. ⁷If I have strayed from his pathway, or if my heart has lusted for what my eyes have seen, or if I am guilty of any other sin, ⁸then let someone else harvest the crops I have planted, and let all that I have planted be uprooted.

⁹"If my heart has been seduced by a woman, or if I have lusted for my neighbor's wife, ¹⁰then may my wife belong to another man; may other men sleep with her. ¹¹For lust is a shameful sin, a crime that should be punished. ¹²It is a devastating fire that destroys to hell. It would wipe out everything I own.

¹³"If I have been unfair to my male or female servants, if I have refused to hear their complaints, ¹⁴how could I face God? What could I say when he questioned me about it? ¹⁵For God created both me and my servants. He created us both.

¹⁶"Have I refused to help the poor, or crushed the hopes of widows who looked to me for help? ¹⁷Have I been stingy with my food and refused to share it with hungry orphans? ¹⁸No, from childhood I have cared for orphans, and all my life I have cared for widows. ¹⁹Whenever I saw someone who was homeless and without clothes, ²⁰did they not praise me for providing wool clothing to keep them warm? ²¹If my arm has abused an orphan because I thought I could get away with it, ²²then let my shoulder be wrenched out of place! Let my arm be torn from its socket! ²³That would be better than facing the judgment sent by God. For if the majesty of God opposes me, what hope is there?

24"Have I put my trust in money or felt secure because of my gold? 25Does my happiness depend on my wealth and all that I own? 26Have I looked at the sun shining in the skies, or the moon walking down its silver pathway, 27and been secretly enticed in my heart to worship them? 28If so, I should be punished by the judges, for it would mean I had denied the God of heaven.

29"Have I ever rejoiced when my enemies came to ruin or become excited when harm came their way? 30No, I have never cursed anyone or asked for revenge. 31My servants have never let others go hungry. 32I have never turned away a stranger but have opened my doors to everyone. 33Have I tried to hide my sins as people normally do, hiding my guilt in a closet? 34Have I feared the crowd and its contempt, so that I refused to acknowledge my sin and would not go outside?

35"If only I had someone who would listen to me and try to see my side! Look, I will sign my name to my defense. Let the Almighty show me that I am wrong. Let my accuser write out the charges against me. 36I would face the accusation proudly. I would treasure it like a crown. 37For I would tell him exactly what I have done. I would come before him like a prince.

38"If my land accuses me and all its furrows weep together, 39or if I have stolen its crops or murdered its owners, 40then let thistles grow on that land instead of wheat and weeds instead of barley."

Job's words are ended.

CHAPTER 32
Elihu Responds to Job's Friends

Job's three friends refused to reply further to him because he kept insisting on his innocence.

2Then Elihu son of Barakel the Buzite, of the clan of Ram, became angry. He was angry because Job refused to admit that he had sinned and that God was right in punishing him. 3He was also angry with Job's three friends because they had condemned God* by their inability to answer Job's arguments. 4Elihu had waited for the others to speak because they were older than he. 5But when he saw that they had no further reply, he spoke out angrily.

6Elihu son of Barakel the Buzite said, "I am young and you are old, so I held back and did not dare to tell you what I think. 7I thought, 'Those who are older should speak, for wisdom comes with age.' 8Surely it is God's Spirit within people, the breath of the Almighty within them,

that makes them intelligent. 9But sometimes the elders are not wise. Sometimes the aged do not understand justice. 10So listen to me and let me express my opinion.

11"I have waited all this time, listening very carefully to your arguments, listening to you grope for words. 12I have listened, but not one of you has refuted Job or answered his arguments. 13And don't tell me, 'He is too wise for us. Only God can convince him.' 14If Job had been arguing with me, I would not answer with that kind of logic! 15You sit there baffled, with no further response. 16Should I continue to wait, now that you are silent? Must I also remain silent? 17No, I will say my piece. I will speak my mind. I surely will. 18For I am pent up and full of words, and the spirit within me urges me on. 19I am like a wine cask without a vent. My words are ready to burst out! 20I must speak to find relief, so let me give my answers. 21I won't play favorites or try to flatter anyone. 22And if I tried, my Creator would soon do away with me.

CHAPTER 33
Elihu Presents His Case against Job

"Listen, Job, to what I have to say. 2Now that I have begun to speak, let me continue. 3I speak with all sincerity; I speak the truth. 4For the Spirit of God has made me, and the breath of the Almighty gives me life. 5Answer me, if you can; make your case and take your stand.

6"Look, you and I are the same before God. I, too, was formed from clay. 7So you don't need to be afraid of me. I am not some great person to make you nervous and afraid.

8"You have said it in my hearing. I have heard your very words. 9You said, 'I am pure; I am innocent; I have not sinned. 10God is picking a quarrel with me, and he considers me to be his enemy. 11He puts my feet in the stocks and watches every move I make.'

12"In this you are not right, and I will show you why. As you yourself have said, 'God is greater than any person.' 13So why are you bringing a charge against him? You say, 'He does not respond to people's complaints.' 14But God speaks again and again, though people do not recognize it. 15He speaks in dreams, in visions of the night when deep sleep falls on people as they lie in bed. 16He whispers in their ear and terrifies them with his warning. 17He causes them to change their minds; he keeps them from pride. 18He keeps them from the grave, from

32:3 As in ancient Hebrew scribal tradition; the Masoretic Text makes no reference to God.

crossing over the river of death. ¹⁹Or God disciplines people with sickness and pain, with ceaseless aching in their bones. ²⁰They lose their appetite and do not care for even the most delicious food. ²¹They waste away to skin and bones. ²²They are at death's door; the angels of death wait for them.

²³"But if a special messenger from heaven is there to intercede for a person, to declare that he is upright, ²⁴God will be gracious and say, 'Set him free. Do not make him die, for I have found a ransom for his life.' ²⁵Then his body will become as healthy as a child's, firm and youthful again. ²⁶When he prays to God, he will be accepted. And God will receive him with joy and restore him to good standing. ²⁷He will declare to his friends, 'I sinned, but it was not worth it. ²⁸God rescued me from the grave, and now my life is filled with light.'

²⁹"Yes, God often does these things for people. ³⁰He rescues them from the grave so they may live in the light of the living. ³¹Mark this well, Job. Listen to me, and let me say more. ³²But if you have anything to say, go ahead. I want to hear it, for I am anxious to see you justified. ³³But if not, then listen to me. Keep silent and I will teach you wisdom!"

CHAPTER 34

Elihu Accuses Job of Arrogance

Then Elihu said:

²"Listen to me, you wise men. Pay attention, you who have knowledge. ³'Just as the mouth tastes good food, the ear tests the words it hears.' ⁴So let us discern for ourselves what is right; let us learn together what is good. ⁵For Job has said, 'I am innocent, but God has taken away my rights. ⁶I am innocent, but they call me a liar. My suffering is incurable, even though I have not sinned.'

⁷"Has there ever been a man as arrogant as Job, with his thirst for irreverent talk? ⁸He seeks the companionship of evil people. He spends his time with wicked men. ⁹He has even said, 'Why waste time trying to please God?'

¹⁰"Listen to me, you who have understanding. Everyone knows that God doesn't sin! The Almighty can do no wrong. ¹¹He repays people according to their deeds. He treats people according to their ways. ¹²There is no truer statement than this: God will not do wrong. The Almighty cannot twist justice. ¹³Who put the world in his care? Who has set the whole world in place? ¹⁴If God were to take back his spirit* and withdraw

his breath, ¹⁵all life would cease, and humanity would turn again to dust.

¹⁶"Listen now and try to understand. ¹⁷Could God govern if he hated justice? Are you going to condemn the almighty Judge? ¹⁸For he says to kings and nobles, 'You are wicked and unjust.' ¹⁹He doesn't care how great a person may be, and he doesn't pay any more attention to the rich than to the poor. He made them all. ²⁰In a moment they die. At midnight they all pass away; the mighty are removed without human hand.

²¹"For God carefully watches the way people live; he sees everything they do. ²²No darkness is thick enough to hide the wicked from his eyes. ²³For it is not up to mortals to decide when to come before God in judgment. ²⁴He brings the mighty to ruin without asking anyone, and he sets up others in their places. ²⁵He watches what they do, and in the night he overturns them, destroying them. ²⁶He openly strikes them down for their wickedness. ²⁷For they turned aside from following him. They have no respect for any of his ways. ²⁸So they cause the poor to cry out, catching God's attention. Yes, he hears the cries of the needy. ²⁹When he is quiet, who can make trouble? But when he hides his face, who can find him? ³⁰He prevents the godless from ruling so they cannot be a snare to the people.

³¹"Why don't people say to God, 'I have sinned, but I will sin no more'? ³²Or 'I don't know what evil I have done; tell me, and I will stop at once'?

³³"Must God tailor his justice to your demands? But you have rejected him! The choice is yours, not mine. Go ahead, share your wisdom with us. ³⁴After all, bright people will tell me, and wise people will hear me say, ³⁵'Job speaks without knowledge; his words lack insight.' ³⁶Job, you deserve the maximum penalty for the wicked way you have talked. ³⁷For now you have added rebellion and blasphemy against God to your other sins."

CHAPTER 35

Elihu Reminds Job of God's Justice

Then Elihu said:

²"Do you think it is right for you to claim, 'I am righteous before God'? ³Yet you also ask, 'What's the use of living a righteous life? How will it benefit me?'

⁴"I will answer you and all your friends, too. ⁵Look up into the sky and see the clouds high

34:14 Or *his Spirit.*

above you. 6If you sin, what do you accomplish against him? Even if you sin again and again, what effect will it have on him? 7If you are good, is this some great gift to him? What could you possibly give him? 8No, your sins affect only people like yourself, and your good deeds affect only other people.

9"The oppressed cry out beneath the wrongs that are done to them. They groan beneath the power of the mighty. 10Yet they don't ask, 'Where is God my Creator, the one who gives songs in the night? 11Where is the one who makes us wiser than the animals and birds?'

12"And if they do cry out and God does not answer, it is because of their pride. 13But it is wrong to say God doesn't listen, to say the Almighty isn't concerned. 14And it is even more false to say he doesn't see what is going on. He will bring about justice if you will only wait. 15But do you cry out against him because he does not respond in anger? 16Job, you have protested in vain. You have spoken like a fool."

CHAPTER 36

Elihu continued speaking:

2"Let me go on, and I will show you the truth of what I am saying. For I have not finished defending God! 3I will give you many illustrations of the righteousness of my Creator. 4I am telling you the honest truth, for I am a man of well-rounded knowledge.

5"God is mighty, yet he does not despise anyone! He is mighty in both power and understanding. 6He does not let the wicked live but gives justice to the afflicted. 7His eyes never leave the innocent, but he establishes and exalts them with kings forever. 8If troubles come upon them and they are enslaved and afflicted, 9he takes the trouble to show them the reason. He shows them their sins, for they have behaved proudly. 10He gets their attention and says they must turn away from evil.

11"If they listen and obey God, then they will be blessed with prosperity throughout their lives. All their years will be pleasant. 12But if they refuse to listen to him, they will perish in battle and die from lack of understanding. 13For the godless are full of resentment. Even when he punishes them, they refuse to cry out to him for help. 14They die young after wasting their lives in immoral living. 15But by means of their suffering, he rescues those who suffer. For he gets their attention through adversity.

16"God has led you away from danger, giving

you freedom. You have prospered in a wide and pleasant valley. 17But you are too obsessed with judgment on the godless. Don't worry, justice will be upheld. 18But watch out, or you may be seduced with wealth. Don't let yourself be bribed into sin. 19Could all your wealth and mighty efforts keep you from distress? 20Do not long for the cover of night, for that is when people will be destroyed. 21Be on guard! Turn back from evil, for it was to prevent you from getting into a life of evil that God sent this suffering.

Elihu Reminds Job of God's Power

22"Look, God is all-powerful. Who is a teacher like him? 23No one can tell him what to do. No one can say to him, 'You have done wrong.' 24Instead, glorify his mighty works, singing songs of praise. 25Everyone has seen these things, but only from a distance.

26"Look, God is exalted beyond what we can understand. His years are without number. 27He draws up the water vapor and then distills it into rain. 28The rain pours down from the clouds, and everyone benefits from it. 29Can anyone really understand the spreading of the clouds and the thunder that rolls forth from heaven? 30See how he spreads the lightning around him and how it lights up the depths of the sea. 31By his mighty acts he governs the people, giving them food in abundance. 32He fills his hands with lightning bolts. He hurls each at its target. 33The thunder announces his presence; the storm announces his indignant anger.*

CHAPTER 37

"My heart pounds as I think of this. It leaps within me. 2Listen carefully to the thunder of God's voice as it rolls from his mouth. 3It rolls across the heavens, and his lightning flashes out in every direction. 4Then comes the roaring of the thunder—the tremendous voice of his majesty. He does not restrain the thunder when he speaks. 5God's voice is glorious in the thunder. We cannot comprehend the greatness of his power.

6"He directs the snow to fall on the earth and tells the rain to pour down. 7Everyone stops working at such a time so they can recognize his power. 8The wild animals hide in the rocks or in their dens. 9The stormy wind comes from its chamber, and the driving winds bring the cold. 10God's breath sends the ice, freezing wide expanses of water. 11He loads the clouds with moisture, and they flash with his lightning.

36:33 Or *even the cattle know when a storm is coming.* The meaning of the Hebrew is uncertain.

¹²The clouds turn around and around under his direction. They do whatever he commands throughout the earth. ¹³He causes things to happen on earth, either as a punishment or as a sign of his unfailing love.

¹⁴"Listen, Job; stop and consider the wonderful miracles of God! ¹⁵Do you know how God controls the storm and causes the lightning to flash forth from his clouds? ¹⁶Do you understand how he balances the clouds with wonderful perfection and skill? ¹⁷When you are sweltering in your clothes and the south wind dies down and everything is still, ¹⁸he makes the skies reflect the heat like a giant mirror. Can you do that?

¹⁹"You think you know so much, so teach the rest of us what to say to God. We are too ignorant to make our own arguments. ²⁰Should God be told that I want to speak? Can we speak when we are confused? ²¹We cannot look at the sun, for it shines brightly in the sky when the wind clears away the clouds. ²²Golden splendor comes from the mountain of God. He is clothed in dazzling splendor. ²³We cannot imagine the power of the Almighty, yet he is so just and merciful that he does not oppress us. ²⁴No wonder people everywhere fear him. People who are truly wise show him reverence."

CHAPTER **38**

The LORD Challenges Job

Then the LORD answered Job from the whirlwind:

²"Who is this that questions my wisdom with such ignorant words? ³Brace yourself, because I have some questions for you, and you must answer them.

⁴"Where were you when I laid the foundations of the earth? Tell me, if you know so much. ⁵Do you know how its dimensions were determined and who did the surveying? ⁶What supports its foundations, and who laid its cornerstone ⁷as the morning stars sang together and all the angels* shouted for joy?

⁸"Who defined the boundaries of the sea as it burst from the womb, ⁹and as I clothed it with clouds and thick darkness? ¹⁰For I locked it behind barred gates, limiting its shores. ¹¹I said, 'Thus far and no farther will you come. Here your proud waves must stop!'

¹²"Have you ever commanded the morning to appear and caused the dawn to rise in the east? ¹³Have you ever told the daylight to spread to the ends of the earth, to bring an end to the

night's wickedness? ¹⁴For the features of the earth take shape as the light approaches, and the dawn is robed in red. ¹⁵The light disturbs the haunts of the wicked, and it stops the arm that is raised in violence.

¹⁶"Have you explored the springs from which the seas come? Have you walked about and explored their depths? ¹⁷Do you know where the gates of death are located? Have you seen the gates of utter gloom? ¹⁸Do you realize the extent of the earth? Tell me about it if you know!

¹⁹"Where does the light come from, and where does the darkness go? ²⁰Can you take it to its home? Do you know how to get there? ²¹But of course you know all this! For you were born before it was all created, and you are so very experienced!

²²"Have you visited the treasuries of the snow? Have you seen where the hail is made and stored? ²³I have reserved it for the time of trouble, for the day of battle and war. ²⁴Where is the path to the origin of light? Where is the home of the east wind?

²⁵"Who created a channel for the torrents of rain? Who laid out the path for the lightning? ²⁶Who makes the rain fall on barren land, in a desert where no one lives? ²⁷Who sends the rain that satisfies the parched ground and makes the tender grass spring up?

²⁸"Does the rain have a father? Where does dew come from? ²⁹Who is the mother of the ice? Who gives birth to the frost from the heavens? ³⁰For the water turns to ice as hard as rock, and the surface of the water freezes.

³¹"Can you hold back the movements of the stars? Are you able to restrain the Pleiades or Orion? ³²Can you ensure the proper sequence of the seasons or guide the constellation of the Bear with her cubs across the heavens? ³³Do you know the laws of the universe and how God rules the earth?

³⁴"Can you shout to the clouds and make it rain? ³⁵Can you make lightning appear and cause it to strike as you direct it? ³⁶Who gives intuition and instinct? ³⁷Who is wise enough to count all the clouds? Who can tilt the water jars of heaven, ³⁸turning the dry dust to clumps of mud?

³⁹"Can you stalk prey for a lioness and satisfy the young lions' appetites ⁴⁰as they lie in their dens or crouch in the thicket? ⁴¹Who provides food for the ravens when their young cry out to God as they wander about in hunger?

38:7 Hebrew *sons of God.*

CHAPTER **39**

The LORD's Challenge Continues

" Do you know when the mountain goats give birth? Have you watched as the wild deer are born? ²Do you know how many months they carry their young? Are you aware of the time of their delivery? ³They crouch down to give birth to their young and deliver their offspring. ⁴Their young grow up in the open fields, then leave their parents and never return.

⁵"Who makes the wild donkey wild? ⁶I have placed it in the wilderness; its home is the wasteland. ⁷It hates the noise of the city, and it has no driver to shout at it. ⁸The mountains are its pastureland, where it searches for every blade of grass.

⁹"Will the wild ox consent to being tamed? Will it stay in your stall? ¹⁰Can you hitch a wild ox to a plow? Will it plow a field for you? ¹¹Since it is so strong, can you trust it? Can you go away and trust the ox to do your work? ¹²Can you rely on it to return, bringing your grain to the threshing floor?

¹³"The ostrich flaps her wings grandly, but they are no match for the feathers of the stork. ¹⁴She lays her eggs on top of the earth, letting them be warmed in the dust. ¹⁵She doesn't worry that a foot might crush them or that wild animals might destroy them. ¹⁶She is harsh toward her young, as if they were not her own. She is unconcerned though they die, ¹⁷for God has deprived her of wisdom. He has given her no understanding. ¹⁸But whenever she jumps up to run, she passes the swiftest horse with its rider.

¹⁹"Have you given the horse its strength or clothed its neck with a flowing mane? ²⁰Did you give it the ability to leap forward like a locust? Its majestic snorting is something to hear! ²¹It paws the earth and rejoices in its strength. When it charges to war, ²²it is unafraid. It does not run from the sword. ²³The arrows rattle against it, and the spear and javelin flash. ²⁴Fiercely it paws the ground and rushes forward into battle when the trumpet blows. ²⁵It snorts at the sound of the bugle. It senses the battle even at a distance. It quivers at the noise of battle and the shout of the captain's commands.

²⁶"Are you the one who makes the hawk soar and spread its wings to the south? ²⁷Is it at your command that the eagle rises to the heights to make its nest? ²⁸It lives on the cliffs, making its home on a distant, rocky crag. ²⁹From there it hunts its prey, keeping watch with piercing eyes. ³⁰Its nestlings gulp down blood, for it feeds on the carcass of the slaughtered."

CHAPTER **40**

Then the LORD said to Job, ²"Do you still want to argue with the Almighty? You are God's critic, but do you have the answers?"

Job Responds to the LORD

³Then Job replied to the LORD, ⁴"I am nothing—how could I ever find the answers? I will put my hand over my mouth in silence. ⁵I have said too much already. I have nothing more to say."

The LORD Challenges Job Again

⁶Then the LORD answered Job from the whirlwind:

⁷"Brace yourself, because I have some questions for you, and you must answer them. ⁸Are you going to discredit my justice and condemn me so you can say you are right? ⁹Are you as strong as God, and can you thunder with a voice like his? ¹⁰All right then, put on your robes of state, your majesty and splendor. ¹¹Give vent to your anger. Let it overflow against the proud. ¹²Humiliate the proud with a glance; walk on the wicked where they stand. ¹³Bury them in the dust. Imprison them in the world of the dead. ¹⁴Then even I would praise you, for your own strength would save you.

¹⁵"Take a look at the mighty hippopotamus.* I made it, just as I made you. It eats grass like an ox. ¹⁶See its powerful loins and the muscles of its belly. ¹⁷Its tail is as straight as a cedar. The sinews of its thighs are tightly knit together. ¹⁸Its bones are tubes of bronze. Its limbs are bars of iron. ¹⁹It is a prime example of God's amazing handiwork. Only its Creator can threaten it. ²⁰The mountains offer it their best food, where all the wild animals play. ²¹It lies down under the lotus plants, hidden by the reeds. ²²The lotus plants give it shade among the willows beside the stream. ²³It is not disturbed by raging rivers, not even when the swelling Jordan rushes down upon it. ²⁴No one can catch it off guard or put a ring in its nose and lead it away.

CHAPTER **41**

The LORD's Challenge Continues

"Can you catch a crocodile* with a hook or put a noose around its jaw? ²Can you tie it with a rope through the nose or pierce its jaw with a spike? ³Will it beg you for mercy or implore you

---

40:15 Hebrew *at behemoth.*   41:1 Hebrew *Leviathan;* also throughout the following passage.

for pity? 4Will it agree to work for you? Can you make it be your slave for life? 5Can you make it a pet like a bird, or give it to your little girls to play with? 6Will merchants try to buy it? Will they sell it in their shops? 7Will its hide be hurt by darts, or its head by a harpoon? 8If you lay a hand on it, you will never forget the battle that follows, and you will never try it again!

9"No, it is useless to try to capture it. The hunter who attempts it will be thrown down. 10And since no one dares to disturb the crocodile, who would dare to stand up to me? 11Who will confront me and remain safe*? Everything under heaven is mine.

12"I want to emphasize the tremendous strength in the crocodile's limbs and throughout its enormous frame. 13Who can strip off its hide, and who can penetrate its double layer of armor*? 14Who could pry open its jaws? For its teeth are terrible! 15The overlapping scales on its back make a shield. 16They are close together so no air can get between them. 17They lock together so nothing can penetrate them.

18"When it sneezes, it flashes light! Its eyes are like the red of dawn. 19Fire and sparks leap from its mouth. 20Smoke streams from its nostrils like steam from a boiling pot on a fire of dry rushes. 21Yes, its breath would kindle coals, for flames shoot from its mouth.

22"The tremendous strength in its neck strikes terror wherever it goes. 23Its flesh is hard and firm, not soft and fat. 24Its heart is as hard as rock, as hard as a millstone. 25When it rises, the mighty are afraid, gripped by terror. 26No sword can stop it, nor spear nor dart nor pointed shaft. 27To the crocodile, iron is nothing but straw, and bronze is rotten wood. 28Arrows cannot make it flee. Stones shot from a sling are as ineffective as straw. 29Clubs do no good, and it laughs at the swish of the javelins. 30Its belly is covered with scales as sharp as glass. They tear up the ground as it drags through the mud.

31"The crocodile makes the water boil with its commotion. It churns the depths. 32The water glistens in its wake. One would think the sea had turned white. 33There is nothing else so fearless anywhere on earth. 34Of all the creatures, it is the proudest. It is the king of beasts."

CHAPTER **42**
Job Responds to the LORD
Then Job replied to the LORD:

2"I know that you can do anything, and no

one can stop you. 3You ask, 'Who is this that questions my wisdom with such ignorance?' It is I. And I was talking about things I did not understand, things far too wonderful for me.

4"You said, 'Listen and I will speak! I have some questions for you, and you must answer them.'

5"I had heard about you before, but now I have seen you with my own eyes. 6I take back everything I said, and I sit in dust and ashes to show my repentance."

Conclusion: The LORD Blesses Job
7After the LORD had finished speaking to Job, he said to Eliphaz the Temanite: "I am angry with you and with your two friends, for you have not been right in what you said about me, as my servant Job was. 8Now take seven young bulls and seven rams and go to my servant Job and offer a burnt offering for yourselves. My servant Job will pray for you, and I will accept his prayer on your behalf. I will not treat you as you deserve, for you have not been right in what you said about me, as my servant Job was."

9So Eliphaz the Temanite, Bildad the Shuhite, and Zophar the Naamathite did as the LORD commanded them, and the LORD accepted Job's prayer.

10When Job prayed for his friends, the LORD restored his fortunes. In fact, the LORD gave him twice as much as before! 11Then all his brothers, sisters, and former friends came and feasted with him in his home. And they consoled him and comforted him because of all the trials the LORD had brought against him. And each of them brought him a gift of money* and a gold ring.

12So the LORD blessed Job in the second half of his life even more than in the beginning. For now he had fourteen thousand sheep, six thousand camels, one thousand teams of oxen, and one thousand female donkeys. 13He also gave Job seven more sons and three more daughters. 14He named his first daughter Jemimah, the second Keziah, and the third Keren-happuch. 15In all the land there were no other women as lovely as the daughters of Job. And their father put them into his will along with their brothers.

16Job lived 140 years after that, living to see four generations of his children and grandchildren. 17Then he died, an old man who had lived a long, good life.

41:11 As in Greek version; Hebrew reads *confront me that I must pay.* 41:13 As in Greek version; Hebrew reads *its bridle.* 42:11 Hebrew *a kesitah;* the value or weight of the kesitah is no longer known.

Psalms

BOOK ONE (Psalms 1–41)

PSALM 1

1 Oh, the joys of those
    who do not follow the advice of the wicked,
    or stand around with sinners,
    or join in with scoffers.
2 But they delight in doing everything the
        LORD wants;
    day and night they think about his law.
3 They are like trees planted along the
        riverbank,
    bearing fruit each season without fail.
Their leaves never wither,
    and in all they do, they prosper.

4 But this is not true of the wicked.
    They are like worthless chaff, scattered by
        the wind.
5 They will be condemned at the time of
        judgment.
    Sinners will have no place among the godly.

6 For the LORD watches over the path of the
        godly,
    but the path of the wicked leads to
        destruction.

PSALM 2

1 Why do the nations rage?
    Why do the people waste their time with
        futile plans?
2 The kings of the earth prepare for battle;
    the rulers plot together
against the LORD
    and against his anointed one.
3 "Let us break their chains," they cry,
    "and free ourselves from this slavery."

4 But the one who rules in heaven laughs.
    The Lord scoffs at them.
5 Then in anger he rebukes them,
    terrifying them with his fierce fury.
6 For the LORD declares, "I have placed my
        chosen king on the throne
    in Jerusalem, my holy city.*"

7 The king proclaims the LORD's decree:
    "The LORD said to me, 'You are my son.*
    Today I have become your Father.*
8 Only ask, and I will give you the nations as
        your inheritance,
    the ends of the earth as your possession.
9 You will break them with an iron rod
    and smash them like clay pots.'"

10 Now then, you kings, act wisely!
    Be warned, you rulers of the earth!
11 Serve the LORD with reverent fear,
    and rejoice with trembling.
12 Submit to God's royal son, or he will
        become angry,
    and you will be destroyed in the midst of
        your pursuits—
    for his anger can flare up in an instant.

But what joy for all who find protection in
        him!

PSALM 3

*A psalm of David, regarding the time David fled from his
son Absalom.*

1 O LORD, I have so many enemies;
    so many are against me.
2 So many are saying,
    "God will never rescue him!"   *Interlude**

2:6 Hebrew *on Zion, my holy mountain.*   2:7a Or *Son;* also in 2:12.   2:7b Or *Today I reveal you as my son.*   3:2 Hebrew *Selah.* The meaning
of this word is uncertain, though it is probably a musical or literary term. It is rendered *Interlude* throughout the Psalms.

3 But you, O LORD, are a shield around me,
  my glory, and the one who lifts my head
    high.
4 I cried out to the LORD,
  and he answered me from his holy
    mountain.   *Interlude*

5 I lay down and slept.
  I woke up in safety,
  for the LORD was watching over me.
6 I am not afraid of ten thousand enemies
  who surround me on every side.

7 Arise, O LORD!
  Rescue me, my God!
  Slap all my enemies in the face!
  Shatter the teeth of the wicked!

8 Victory comes from you, O LORD.
  May your blessings rest on your people.
                                Interlude

PSALM 4

*For the choir director: A psalm of David, to be
accompanied by stringed instruments.*

1 Answer me when I call,
  O God who declares me innocent.
  Take away my distress.
    Have mercy on me and hear my prayer.

2 How long will you people ruin my
    reputation?
  How long will you make these
    groundless accusations?
  How long will you pursue lies? *Interlude*

3 You can be sure of this:
  The LORD has set apart the godly for
    himself.
  The LORD will answer when I call to him.

4 Don't sin by letting anger gain control over
    you.
  Think about it overnight and remain
    silent.   *Interlude*
5 Offer proper sacrifices,
  and trust in the LORD.

6 Many people say, "Who will show us better
    times?"
  Let the smile of your face shine on us,
    LORD.
7 You have given me greater joy
  than those who have abundant harvests
    of grain and wine.

8 I will lie down in peace and sleep,
  for you alone, O LORD, will keep me
    safe.

PSALM 5

*For the choir director: A psalm of David, to be
accompanied by the flute.*

1 O LORD, hear me as I pray;
  pay attention to my groaning.
2 Listen to my cry for help, my King and my
    God,
  for I will never pray to anyone but you.
3 Listen to my voice in the morning, LORD.
  Each morning I bring my requests to you
    and wait expectantly.

4 O God, you take no pleasure in
    wickedness;
  you cannot tolerate the slightest sin.
5 Therefore, the proud will not be allowed to
    stand in your presence,
  for you hate all who do evil.
6 You will destroy those who tell lies.
  The LORD detests murderers and deceivers.

OFF AND RUNNING ▰▰▰▰▰

Don't Associate with Those Who Mock God Read PSALM 1:1-6

If you have recently become a Christian, you have probably gone
through a radical lifestyle change. As a result, you no longer
have all of the same interests and priorities that many of your
non-Christian friends do. Yet, it may be hard to influence—or in some cases
end—those friendships. This passage illustrates the need for Christians to avoid
keeping company with those who have a bad influence on them. To understand why this is
necessary, compare the differences between those who follow God and those who don't:

• Those who are close to God delight in following God's Word. . . . Those who are not follow evil men's advice.
• Those who are close to God meditate on his laws day and night. . . . Those who are not hang around with
sinners.

7 Because of your unfailing love, I can enter
    your house;
  with deepest awe I will worship at your
    Temple.
8 Lead me in the right path, O LORD,
    or my enemies will conquer me.
  Tell me clearly what to do,
    and show me which way to turn.

9 My enemies cannot speak one truthful word.
    Their deepest desire is to destroy others.
  Their talk is foul, like the stench from an
    open grave.
    Their speech is filled with flattery.
10 O God, declare them guilty.
    Let them be caught in their own traps.
  Drive them away because of their many sins,
    for they rebel against you.

11 But let all who take refuge in you rejoice;
    let them sing joyful praises forever.
  Protect them,
    so all who love your name may be filled
    with joy.
12 For you bless the godly, O LORD,
    surrounding them with your shield of
    love.

PSALM **6**

*For the choir director: A psalm of David, to be
accompanied by an eight-stringed instrument.* *

1 O LORD, do not rebuke me in your anger
    or discipline me in your rage.
2 Have compassion on me, LORD, for I am
    weak.
  Heal me, LORD, for my body is in agony.
3 I am sick at heart.
  How long, O LORD, until you restore me?

6:TITLE Hebrew *with stringed instruments; according to the sheminith.*

4 Return, O LORD, and rescue me.
  Save me because of your unfailing love.
5 For in death, who remembers you?
  Who can praise you from the grave?

6 I am worn out from sobbing.
  Every night tears drench my bed;
    my pillow is wet from weeping.
7 My vision is blurred by grief;
  my eyes are worn out because of all my
    enemies.

8 Go away, all you who do evil,
    for the LORD has heard my crying.
9 The LORD has heard my plea;
    the LORD will answer my prayer.
10 May all my enemies be disgraced and terrified.
  May they suddenly turn back in shame.

PSALM **7**

*A psalm of David, which he sang to the LORD concerning
Cush of the tribe of Benjamin.*

1 I come to you for protection, O LORD my God.
  Save me from my persecutors—rescue
    me!
2 If you don't, they will maul me like a lion,
  tearing me to pieces with no one to
    rescue me.

3 O LORD my God, if I have done wrong
    or am guilty of injustice,
4 if I have betrayed a friend
    or plundered my enemy without cause,
5 then let my enemies capture me.
  Let them trample me into the ground.
  Let my honor be left in the dust. *Interlude*

6 Arise, O LORD, in anger!
  Stand up against the fury of my enemies!
  Wake up, my God, and bring justice!

- Those who are close to God think about ways to follow God more closely. . . . Those who are not scoff at the things of God.
- Those who are close to God are like a strong, fruit-bearing tree. . . . Those who are not are like the chaff that blows away.
- Those who are close to God have God's protection. . . . Those who are not face certain destruction.

  While it is important to share your faith with those who do not know God, it is important that you do not allow their lifestyle to influence you. Jude, in speaking of how to reach such people, wrote, "Rescue others by snatching them from the flames of judgment. There are still others to whom you need to show mercy, but be careful that you aren't contaminated by their sins" (Jude 1:23).

  Reach out in God's love to your old friends, but also look for new friends who share your love for the Lord and will encourage you in your faith.

For the next note on "Relationships," turn to p. 1010.

7 Gather the nations before you.
  Sit on your throne high above them.
8 The LORD passes judgment on the nations.
  Declare me righteous, O LORD,
  for I am innocent, O Most High!
9 End the wickedness of the ungodly,
  but help all those who obey you.
  For you look deep within the mind and
    heart,
    O righteous God.

10 God is my shield,
  saving those whose hearts are true and
    right.
11 God is a judge who is perfectly fair.
  He is angry with the wicked every day.

12 If a person does not repent,
  God* will sharpen his sword;
  he will bend and string his bow.
13 He will prepare his deadly weapons
  and ignite his flaming arrows.

14 The wicked conceive evil;
  they are pregnant with trouble
  and give birth to lies.
15 They dig a pit to trap others
  and then fall into it themselves.
16 They make trouble,
  but it backfires on them.
  They plan violence for others,
  but it falls on their own heads.

17 I will thank the LORD because he is just;
  I will sing praise to the name of the LORD
    Most High.

PSALM 8

*For the choir director: A psalm of David, to be
accompanied by a stringed instrument.* *

1 O LORD, our Lord, the majesty of your name
    fills the earth!
  Your glory is higher than the heavens.

2 You have taught children and nursing infants
    to give you praise.*
  They silence your enemies
  who were seeking revenge.

3 When I look at the night sky and see the
    work of your fingers—
    the moon and the stars you have set in
    place—
4 what are mortals that you should think of us,

mere humans that you should care for
    us?*
5 For you made us only a little lower than
    God,*
  and you crowned us with glory and
    honor.
6 You put us in charge of everything you
    made,
  giving us authority over all things—
7 the sheep and the cattle
  and all the wild animals,
8 the birds in the sky, the fish in the sea,
  and everything that swims the ocean
    currents.

9 O LORD, our Lord, the majesty of your name
    fills the earth!

PSALM 9

*For the choir director: A psalm of David, to be sung to the
tune "Death of the Son."*

1 I will thank you, LORD, with all my heart;
  I will tell of all the marvelous things you
    have done.
2 I will be filled with joy because of you.
  I will sing praises to your name, O Most
    High.

3 My enemies turn away in retreat;
  they are overthrown and destroyed
    before you.
4 For you have judged in my favor;
  from your throne, you have judged with
    fairness.

5 You have rebuked the nations and
    destroyed the wicked;
  you have wiped out their names forever.
6 My enemies have met their doom;
  their cities are perpetual ruins.
  Even the memory of their uprooted cities
    is lost.

7 But the LORD reigns forever,
  executing judgment from his throne.
8 He will judge the world with justice
  and rule the nations with fairness.

9 The LORD is a shelter for the oppressed,
  a refuge in times of trouble.
10 Those who know your name trust in you,
  for you, O LORD, have never abandoned
    anyone who searches for you.

7:12 Hebrew *he.*   8:TITLE Hebrew *according to the gittith.*   8:2 As in Greek version; Hebrew reads *to show strength.*   8:4 Hebrew *what is man
that you should think of him, the son of man that you should care for him?*   8:5 Or *a little lower than the angels;* Hebrew reads *Elohim.*

¹¹ Sing praises to the LORD who reigns in
    Jerusalem.*
    Tell the world about his unforgettable deeds.
¹² For he who avenges murder cares for the
    helpless.
    He does not ignore those who cry to him
    for help.

¹³ LORD, have mercy on me.
    See how I suffer at the hands of those
    who hate me.
    Snatch me back from the jaws of death.
¹⁴ Save me, so I can praise you publicly at
    Jerusalem's gates,
    so I can rejoice that you have rescued me.

¹⁵ The nations have fallen into the pit they
    dug for others.
    They have been caught in their own trap.
¹⁶ The LORD is known for his justice.
    The wicked have trapped themselves in
    their own snares.   *Quiet Interlude**

¹⁷ The wicked will go down to the grave.*
    This is the fate of all the nations who
    ignore God.
¹⁸ For the needy will not be forgotten forever;
    the hopes of the poor will not always be
    crushed.

¹⁹ Arise, O LORD!
    Do not let mere mortals defy you!
    Let the nations be judged in your presence!
²⁰ Make them tremble in fear, O LORD.
    Let them know they are merely human.
                                    Interlude

PSALM **10**

¹ O LORD, why do you stand so far away?
    Why do you hide when I need you the
    most?
² Proud and wicked people viciously oppress
    the poor.
    Let them be caught in the evil they plan
    for others.
³ For they brag about their evil desires;
    they praise the greedy and curse the LORD.
⁴ These wicked people are too proud to seek
    God.
    They seem to think that God is dead.
⁵ Yet they succeed in everything they do.
    They do not see your punishment
    awaiting them.
    They pour scorn on all their enemies.

⁶ They say to themselves, "Nothing bad will
    ever happen to us!
    We will be free of trouble forever!"
⁷ Their mouths are full of cursing, lies, and
    threats.
    Trouble and evil are on the tips of their
    tongues.
⁸ They lurk in dark alleys,
    murdering the innocent who pass by.

They are always searching
    for some helpless victim.
⁹ Like lions they crouch silently,
    waiting to pounce on the helpless.
    Like hunters they capture their victims
    and drag them away in nets.
¹⁰ The helpless are overwhelmed and collapse;
    they fall beneath the strength of the wicked.

Studying the Bible Helps Us Apply Its Truth to Our Lives
Read PSALM 1:1-3

Have you ever eaten your food so quickly that you could not enjoy or savor its taste? Reading God's Word quickly is much like "inhaling" your food. In order to really understand what we are reading, we need to slow down, read through a passage more than once, and think about it. As you meditate upon God's Word, you will know what is right and true.

While it is excellent to read through the Bible, to study it, and to memorize it, the truth of God's Word must also go through you. You must apply what you have learned from the Bible to your life. It is not how you mark your Bible, but how your Bible marks you. What you meditate upon must affect the way you live.

When you meditate on God's Word and apply its truths to your life, you will experience the promise in verse 3, and everything you do you will prosper. That does not mean you necessarily will be the richest, most successful person in the world. It does mean, however, that your work, life, and attitude will be blessed because you are living by God's principles and experiencing the rewards of obedience to him.

To begin the next topic, turn to p. A26.

9:11 Hebrew *Zion;* also in 9:14. 9:16 Hebrew *Higgaion Selah.* The meaning of this phrase is uncertain. 9:17 Hebrew *to Sheol.*

11 The wicked say to themselves, "God isn't
watching!
He will never notice!"

12 Arise, O LORD!
Punish the wicked, O God!
Do not forget the helpless!
13 Why do the wicked get away with cursing God?
How can they think, "God will never call
us to account"?

14 But you do see the trouble and grief they cause.
You take note of it and punish them.
The helpless put their trust in you.
You are the defender of orphans.

15 Break the arms of these wicked, evil people!
Go after them until the last one is destroyed!
16 The LORD is king forever and ever!
Let those who worship other gods be
swept from the land.

17 LORD, you know the hopes of the helpless.
Surely you will listen to their cries and
comfort them.
18 You will bring justice to the orphans and
the oppressed,
so people can no longer terrify them.

PSALM 11

For the choir director: A psalm of David.

1 I trust in the LORD for protection.
So why do you say to me,
"Fly to the mountains for safety!
2 The wicked are stringing their bows
and setting their arrows in the bowstrings.
They shoot from the shadows at those
who do right.
3 The foundations of law and order have
collapsed.
What can the righteous do?"

4 But the LORD is in his holy Temple;
the LORD still rules from heaven.
He watches everything closely,
examining everyone on earth.
5 The LORD examines both the righteous and
the wicked.
He hates everyone who loves violence.
6 He rains down blazing coals on the wicked,
punishing them with burning sulfur and
scorching winds.
7 For the LORD is righteous, and he loves justice.
Those who do what is right will see his
face.

12:TITLE Hebrew *according to the sheminith.*

PSALM 12

*For the choir director: A psalm of David, to be
accompanied by an eight-stringed instrument.* *

1 Help, O LORD, for the godly are fast
disappearing!
The faithful have vanished from the
earth!
2 Neighbors lie to each other,
speaking with flattering lips and
insincere hearts.
3 May the LORD bring their flattery to an end
and silence their proud tongues.
4 They say, "We will lie to our hearts' content.
Our lips are our own—who can stop
us?"

5 The LORD replies, "I have seen violence
done to the helpless,
and I have heard the groans of the poor.
Now I will rise up to rescue them,
as they have longed for me to do."
6 The LORD's promises are pure,
like silver refined in a furnace,
purified seven times over.

7 Therefore, LORD, we know you will protect
the oppressed,
preserving them forever from this lying
generation,
8 even though the wicked strut about,
and evil is praised throughout the land.

PSALM 13

For the choir director: A psalm of David.

1 O LORD, how long will you forget me?
Forever?
How long will you look the other way?
2 How long must I struggle with anguish in
my soul,
with sorrow in my heart every day?
How long will my enemy have the upper
hand?

3 Turn and answer me, O LORD my God!
Restore the light to my eyes, or I will die.
4 Don't let my enemies gloat, saying, "We
have defeated him!"
Don't let them rejoice at my downfall.

5 But I trust in your unfailing love.
I will rejoice because you have rescued
me.
6 I will sing to the LORD
because he has been so good to me.

PSALM 14

For the choir director: A psalm of David.

1 Only fools say in their hearts,
"There is no God."
They are corrupt, and their actions are evil;
no one does good!

2 The LORD looks down from heaven
on the entire human race;
he looks to see if there is even one with real
understanding,
one who seeks for God.

3 But no, all have turned away from God;
all have become corrupt.
No one does good,
not even one!

4 Will those who do evil never learn?
They eat up my people like bread;
they wouldn't think of praying to the LORD.

5 Terror will grip them,
for God is with those who obey him.

6 The wicked frustrate the plans of the
oppressed,
but the LORD will protect his people.

7 Oh, that salvation would come from Mount
Zion to rescue Israel!
For when the LORD restores his people,
Jacob will shout with joy, and Israel will
rejoice.

PSALM 15

A psalm of David.

1 Who may worship in your sanctuary, LORD?
Who may enter your presence on your
holy hill?

2 Those who lead blameless lives
and do what is right,
speaking the truth from sincere hearts.

3 Those who refuse to slander others
or harm their neighbors
or speak evil of their friends.

4 Those who despise persistent sinners,
and honor the faithful followers of the
LORD
and keep their promises even when it hurts.

5 Those who do not charge interest on the
money they lend,
and who refuse to accept bribes to testify
against the innocent.

Such people will stand firm forever.

PSALM 16

A psalm of David.

1 Keep me safe, O God,
for I have come to you for refuge.

2 I said to the LORD, "You are my Master!
All the good things I have are from you."

3 The godly people in the land
are my true heroes!
I take pleasure in them!

4 Those who chase after other gods will be
filled with sorrow.
I will not take part in their sacrifices
or even speak the names of their gods.

5 LORD, you alone are my inheritance, my cup
of blessing.
You guard all that is mine.

6 The land you have given me is a pleasant land.
What a wonderful inheritance!

7 I will bless the LORD who guides me;
even at night my heart instructs me.

8 I know the LORD is always with me.
I will not be shaken, for he is right beside
me.

9 No wonder my heart is filled with joy,
and my mouth* shouts his praises!
My body rests in safety.

10 For you will not leave my soul among the
dead*
or allow your godly one* to rot in the
grave.

11 You will show me the way of life,
granting me the joy of your presence
and the pleasures of living with you
forever.

PSALM 17

A prayer of David.

1 O LORD, hear my plea for justice.
Listen to my cry for help.
Pay attention to my prayer,
for it comes from an honest heart.

2 Declare me innocent,
for you know those who do right.

3 You have tested my thoughts and examined
my heart in the night.
You have scrutinized me and found
nothing amiss,
for I am determined not to sin in what I
say.

16:9 As in Greek version; Hebrew reads *glory.* 16:10a Hebrew *in Sheol.* 16:10b Or *your Holy One.*

4 I have followed your commands,
  which have kept me from going along
    with cruel and evil people.
5 My steps have stayed on your path;
  I have not wavered from following you.

6 I am praying to you because I know you
    will answer, O God.
  Bend down and listen as I pray.
7 Show me your unfailing love in wonderful
    ways.
  You save with your strength
    those who seek refuge from their enemies.
8 Guard me as the apple of your eye.
  Hide me in the shadow of your wings.
9 Protect me from wicked people who attack
    me,
  from murderous enemies who surround
    me.

10 They are without pity.
  Listen to their boasting.
11 They track me down, surround me,
  and throw me to the ground.
12 They are like hungry lions, eager to tear me
    apart—
  like young lions in hiding, waiting for
    their chance.

13 Arise, O LORD!
  Stand against them and bring them to
    their knees!
  Rescue me from the wicked with your
    sword!
14 Save me by your mighty hand, O LORD,
  from those whose only concern is earthly
    gain.
  May they have their punishment in full.
  May their children inherit more of the same,
  and may the judgment continue to their
    children's children.

15 But because I have done what is right, I will
    see you.
  When I awake, I will be fully satisfied,
  for I will see you face to face.

PSALM 18

For the choir director: A psalm of David, the servant of
the LORD. He sang this song to the LORD on the day the
LORD rescued him from all his enemies and from Saul.

1 I love you, LORD; you are my strength.
2 The LORD is my rock, my fortress, and my
    savior;

my God is my rock, in whom I find
    protection.
  He is my shield, the strength of my
    salvation, and my stronghold.
3 I will call on the LORD, who is worthy of
    praise,
  for he saves me from my enemies.

4 The ropes of death surrounded me;
  the floods of destruction swept over me.
5 The grave* wrapped its ropes around me;
  death itself stared me in the face.
6 But in my distress I cried out to the LORD;
  yes, I prayed to my God for help.
  He heard me from his sanctuary;
  my cry reached his ears.

7 Then the earth quaked and trembled;
  the foundations of the mountains shook;
  they quaked because of his anger.
8 Smoke poured from his nostrils;
  fierce flames leaped from his mouth;
  glowing coals flamed forth from him.
9 He opened the heavens and came down;
  dark storm clouds were beneath his feet.
10 Mounted on a mighty angel,* he flew,
  soaring on the wings of the wind.
11 He shrouded himself in darkness,
  veiling his approach with dense rain
    clouds.
12 The brilliance of his presence broke through
    the clouds,
  raining down hail and burning coals.
13 The LORD thundered from heaven;
  the Most High gave a mighty shout.*
14 He shot his arrows and scattered his enemies;
  his lightning flashed, and they were
    greatly confused.
15 Then at your command, O LORD,
  at the blast of your breath,
  the bottom of the sea could be seen,
  and the foundations of the earth were
    laid bare.

16 He reached down from heaven and rescued
    me;
  he drew me out of deep waters.
17 He delivered me from my powerful enemies,
  from those who hated me and were too
    strong for me.
18 They attacked me at a moment when I was
    weakest,
  but the LORD upheld me.
19 He led me to a place of safety;
  he rescued me because he delights in me.

18:5 Hebrew *Sheol*.   18:10 Hebrew *a cherub*.   18:13 As in Greek version (see also 2 Sam 22:14); Hebrew adds *raining down hail and burning coals*.

20 The LORD rewarded me for doing right;
    he compensated me because of my
    innocence.
21 For I have kept the ways of the LORD;
    I have not turned from my God to follow
    evil.
22 For all his laws are constantly before me;
    I have never abandoned his principles.
23 I am blameless before God;
    I have kept myself from sin.
24 The LORD rewarded me for doing right,
    because of the innocence of my hands in
    his sight.

25 To the faithful you show yourself faithful;
    to those with integrity you show integrity.
26 To the pure you show yourself pure,
    but to the wicked you show yourself
    hostile.
27 You rescue those who are humble,
    but you humiliate the proud.
28 LORD, you have brought light to my life;
    my God, you light up my darkness.
29 In your strength I can crush an army;
    with my God I can scale any wall.

30 As for God, his way is perfect.
    All the LORD's promises prove true.
    He is a shield for all who look to him for
    protection.
31 For who is God except the LORD?
    Who but our God is a solid rock?
32 God arms me with strength;
    he has made my way safe.
33 He makes me as surefooted as a deer,
    leading me safely along the mountain
    heights.
34 He prepares me for battle;
    he strengthens me to draw a bow of
    bronze.
35 You have given me the shield of your
    salvation.
    Your right hand supports me;
    your gentleness has made me great.
36 You have made a wide path for my feet
    to keep them from slipping.

37 I chased my enemies and caught them;
    I did not stop until they were conquered.
38 I struck them down so they could not get up;
    they fell beneath my feet.
39 You have armed me with strength for the
    battle;
    you have subdued my enemies under my
    feet.

40 You made them turn and run;
    I have destroyed all who hated me.
41 They called for help, but no one came to
    rescue them.
    They cried to the LORD, but he refused to
    answer them.
42 I ground them as fine as dust carried by the
    wind.
    I swept them into the gutter like dirt.

43 You gave me victory over my accusers.
    You appointed me as the ruler over nations;
    people I don't even know now serve me.
44 As soon as they hear of me, they submit;
    foreigners cringe before me.
45 They all lose their courage
    and come trembling from their
    strongholds.

46 The LORD lives! Blessed be my rock!
    May the God of my salvation be exalted!
47 He is the God who pays back those who
    harm me;
    he subdues the nations under me
48   and rescues me from my enemies.
    You hold me safe beyond the reach of my
    enemies;
    you save me from violent opponents.
49 For this, O LORD, I will praise you among
    the nations;
    I will sing joyfully to your name.
50 You give great victories to your king;
    you show unfailing love to your anointed,
    to David and all his descendants forever.

PSALM **19**

For the choir director: A psalm of David.

1 The heavens tell of the glory of God.
    The skies display his marvelous
    craftsmanship.
2 Day after day they continue to speak;
    night after night they make him known.
3 They speak without a sound or a word;
    their voice is silent in the skies;*
4 yet their message has gone out to all the earth,
    and their words to all the world.

    The sun lives in the heavens
    where God placed it.
5 It bursts forth like a radiant bridegroom
    after his wedding.
    It rejoices like a great athlete
    eager to run the race.
6 The sun rises at one end of the heavens

19:3 Or *There is no speech or language where their voice is not heard.*

and follows its course to the other end.
Nothing can hide from its heat.

7 The law of the LORD is perfect,
reviving the soul.
The decrees of the LORD are trustworthy,
making wise the simple.
8 The commandments of the LORD are right,
bringing joy to the heart.
The commands of the LORD are clear,
giving insight to life.
9 Reverence for the LORD is pure,
lasting forever.
The laws of the LORD are true;
each one is fair.
10 They are more desirable than gold,
even the finest gold.
They are sweeter than honey,
even honey dripping from the comb.
11 They are a warning to those who hear them;
there is great reward for those who obey
them.
12 How can I know all the sins lurking in my
heart?
Cleanse me from these hidden faults.
13 Keep me from deliberate sins!
Don't let them control me.
Then I will be free of guilt
and innocent of great sin.
14 May the words of my mouth and the
thoughts of my heart
be pleasing to you,
O LORD, my rock and my redeemer.

PSALM 20

For the choir director: A psalm of David.

1 In times of trouble, may the LORD respond
to your cry.
May the God of Israel* keep you safe
from all harm.
2 May he send you help from his sanctuary
and strengthen you from Jerusalem.*
3 May he remember all your gifts
and look favorably on your burnt
offerings. *Interlude*
4 May he grant your heart's desire
and fulfill all your plans.
5 May we shout for joy when we hear of your
victory,
flying banners to honor our God.
May the LORD answer all your prayers.

6 Now I know that the LORD saves his
anointed king.
He will answer him from his holy heaven
and rescue him by his great power.
7 Some nations boast of their armies and
weapons,*
but we boast in the LORD our God.
8 Those nations will fall down and collapse,
but we will rise up and stand firm.
9 Give victory to our king, O LORD!
Respond to our cry for help.

PSALM 21

For the choir director: A psalm of David.

1 How the king rejoices in your strength,
O LORD!
He shouts with joy because of your
victory.
2 For you have given him his heart's desire;
you have held back nothing that he
requested. *Interlude*

3 You welcomed him back with success and
prosperity.
You placed a crown of finest gold on his
head.
4 He asked you to preserve his life,
and you have granted his request.
The days of his life stretch on forever.
5 Your victory brings him great honor,
and you have clothed him with splendor
and majesty.
6 You have endowed him with eternal
blessings.
You have given him the joy of being in
your presence.
7 For the king trusts in the LORD.
The unfailing love of the Most High will
keep him from stumbling.

8 You will capture all your enemies.
Your strong right hand will seize all those
who hate you.
9 You will destroy them as in a flaming
furnace
when you appear.
The LORD will consume them in his anger;
fire will devour them.
10 You will wipe their children from the face of
the earth;
they will never have descendants.
11 Although they plot against you,
their evil schemes will never succeed.

20:1 Hebrew *of Jacob.*   20:2 Hebrew *Zion.*   20:7 Hebrew *chariots and horses.*

12 For they will turn and run
   when they see your arrows aimed at
   them.
13 We praise you, LORD, for all your glorious
   power.
   With music and singing we celebrate
   your mighty acts.

PSALM 22

*For the choir director: A psalm of David, to be sung to the
tune "Doe of the Dawn."*

1 My God, my God! Why have you forsaken
   me?
   Why do you remain so distant?
   Why do you ignore my cries for help?
2 Every day I call to you, my God, but you do
   not answer.
   Every night you hear my voice, but I find
   no relief.

3 Yet you are holy.
   The praises of Israel surround your
   throne.
4 Our ancestors trusted in you,
   and you rescued them.
5 You heard their cries for help and saved them.
   They put their trust in you and were
   never disappointed.

6 But I am a worm and not a man.
   I am scorned and despised by all!
7 Everyone who sees me mocks me.
   They sneer and shake their heads, saying,
8 "Is this the one who relies on the LORD?
   Then let the LORD save him!
   If the LORD loves him so much,
   let the LORD rescue him!"

9 Yet you brought me safely from my
   mother's womb
   and led me to trust you when I was a
   nursing infant.
10 I was thrust upon you at my birth.
   You have been my God from the
   moment I was born.

11 Do not stay so far from me,
   for trouble is near,
   and no one else can help me.
12 My enemies surround me like a herd of bulls;
   fierce bulls of Bashan have hemmed
   me in!
13 Like roaring lions attacking their prey,
   they come at me with open mouths.

14 My life is poured out like water,
   and all my bones are out of joint.
   My heart is like wax,
   melting within me.
15 My strength has dried up like sunbaked
   clay.
   My tongue sticks to the roof of my
   mouth.
   You have laid me in the dust and left me
   for dead.

16 My enemies surround me like a pack of dogs;
   an evil gang closes in on me.
   They have pierced my hands and feet.
17 I can count every bone in my body.
   My enemies stare at me and gloat.
18 They divide my clothes among themselves
   and throw dice* for my garments.

19 O LORD, do not stay away!
   You are my strength; come quickly to my
   aid!
20 Rescue me from a violent death;
   spare my precious life from these dogs.
21 Snatch me from the lions' jaws,
   and from the horns of these wild oxen.

22 Then I will declare the wonder of your
   name to my brothers and sisters.
   I will praise you among all your people.
23 Praise the LORD, all you who fear him!
   Honor him, all you descendants of Jacob!
   Show him reverence, all you descendants
   of Israel!
24 For he has not ignored the suffering of the
   needy.
   He has not turned and walked away.
   He has listened to their cries for help.

25 I will praise you among all the people;
   I will fulfill my vows in the presence of
   those who worship you.
26 The poor will eat and be satisfied.
   All who seek the LORD will praise him.
   Their hearts will rejoice with everlasting
   joy.
27 The whole earth will acknowledge the LORD
   and return to him.
   People from every nation will bow down
   before him.
28 For the LORD is king!
   He rules all the nations.

29 Let the rich of the earth feast and worship.
   Let all mortals—those born to die—bow
   down in his presence.

22:18 Hebrew *cast lots.*

³⁰ Future generations will also serve him.
Our children will hear about the
wonders of the Lord.
³¹ His righteous acts will be told to those yet
unborn.
They will hear about everything he has
done.

PSALM 23
A psalm of David.

¹ The LORD is my shepherd;
I have everything I need.
² He lets me rest in green meadows;
he leads me beside peaceful streams.
³ He renews my strength.
He guides me along right paths,
bringing honor to his name.

⁴ Even when I walk
through the dark valley of death,*
I will not be afraid,
for you are close beside me.
Your rod and your staff
protect and comfort me.

⁵ You prepare a feast for me
in the presence of my enemies.
You welcome me as a guest,
anointing my head with oil.
My cup overflows with blessings.
⁶ Surely your goodness and unfailing love
will pursue me
all the days of my life,
and I will live in the house of the LORD
forever.

PSALM 24
A psalm of David.

¹ The earth is the LORD's, and everything in it.
The world and all its people belong to
him.
² For he laid the earth's foundation on the seas
and built it on the ocean depths.

³ Who may climb the mountain of the LORD?
Who may stand in his holy place?
⁴ Only those whose hands and hearts are
pure,
who do not worship idols
and never tell lies.
⁵ They will receive the LORD's blessing
and have right standing with God their
savior.

⁶ They alone may enter God's presence
and worship the God of Israel.* *Interlude*

⁷ Open up, ancient gates!
Open up, ancient doors,
and let the King of glory enter.
⁸ Who is the King of glory?
The LORD, strong and mighty,
the LORD, invincible in battle.
⁹ Open up, ancient gates!
Open up, ancient doors,
and let the King of glory enter.
¹⁰ Who is the King of glory?
The LORD Almighty—
he is the King of glory. *Interlude*

PSALM 25
A psalm of David.

¹ To you, O LORD, I lift up my soul.
² I trust in you, my God!
Do not let me be disgraced,
or let my enemies rejoice in my defeat.
³ No one who trusts in you will ever be
disgraced,
but disgrace comes to those who try to
deceive others.

⁴ Show me the path where I should walk,
O LORD;
point out the right road for me to follow.
⁵ Lead me by your truth and teach me,
for you are the God who saves me.
All day long I put my hope in you.

⁶ Remember, O LORD, your unfailing love and
compassion,
which you have shown from long ages
past.
⁷ Forgive the rebellious sins of my youth;
look instead through the eyes of your
unfailing love,
for you are merciful, O LORD.

⁸ The LORD is good and does what is right;
he shows the proper path to those who
go astray.
⁹ He leads the humble in what is right,
teaching them his way.
¹⁰ The LORD leads with unfailing love and
faithfulness
all those who keep his covenant and
obey his decrees.

¹¹ For the honor of your name, O LORD,
forgive my many, many sins.

23:4 Or *the darkest valley.* 24:6 Hebrew *of Jacob.*

12 Who are those who fear the LORD?
  He will show them the path they should
    choose.
13 They will live in prosperity,
  and their children will inherit the
    Promised Land.
14 Friendship with the LORD is reserved for
    those who fear him.
  With them he shares the secrets of his
    covenant.
15 My eyes are always looking to the LORD for
    help,
  for he alone can rescue me from the traps
    of my enemies.

16 Turn to me and have mercy on me,
  for I am alone and in deep distress.
17 My problems go from bad to worse.
  Oh, save me from them all!
18 Feel my pain and see my trouble.
  Forgive all my sins.
19 See how many enemies I have,
  and how viciously they hate me!
20 Protect me! Rescue my life from them!
  Do not let me be disgraced, for I trust in
    you.
21 May integrity and honesty protect me,
  for I put my hope in you.

22 O God, ransom Israel
  from all its troubles.

PSALM 26

A psalm of David.

1 Declare me innocent, O LORD,
  for I have acted with integrity;
  I have trusted in the LORD without
    wavering.
2 Put me on trial, LORD, and cross-examine me.
  Test my motives and affections.
3 For I am constantly aware of your unfailing
    love,
  and I have lived according to your truth.

4 I do not spend time with liars
  or go along with hypocrites.
5 I hate the gatherings of those who do evil,
  and I refuse to join in with the wicked.

6 I wash my hands to declare my innocence.
  I come to your altar, O LORD,
7 singing a song of thanksgiving
  and telling of all your miracles.

8 I love your sanctuary, LORD,
  the place where your glory shines.

9 Don't let me suffer the fate of sinners.
  Don't condemn me along with murderers.
10 Their hands are dirty with wicked schemes,
  and they constantly take bribes.

11 But I am not like that; I do what is right.
  So in your mercy, save me.
12 I have taken a stand,
  and I will publicly praise the LORD.

PSALM 27

A psalm of David.

1 The LORD is my light and my salvation—
  so why should I be afraid?
  The LORD protects me from danger—
  so why should I tremble?

2 When evil people come to destroy me,
  when my enemies and foes attack me,
  they will stumble and fall.
3 Though a mighty army surrounds me,
  my heart will know no fear.
  Even if they attack me,
  I remain confident.

4 The one thing I ask of the LORD—
  the thing I seek most—
  is to live in the house of the LORD all the
    days of my life,
  delighting in the LORD's perfections
  and meditating in his Temple.
5 For he will conceal me there when troubles
    come;
  he will hide me in his sanctuary.
  He will place me out of reach on a high
    rock.
6 Then I will hold my head high,
  above my enemies who surround me.
  At his Tabernacle I will offer sacrifices with
    shouts of joy,
  singing and praising the LORD with music.

7 Listen to my pleading, O LORD.
  Be merciful and answer me!
8 My heart has heard you say, "Come and
    talk with me."
  And my heart responds, "LORD, I am
    coming."
9 Do not hide yourself from me.
  Do not reject your servant in anger.
  You have always been my helper.
  Don't leave me now; don't abandon me,
  O God of my salvation!
10 Even if my father and mother abandon me,
  the LORD will hold me close.

11 Teach me how to live, O LORD.
  Lead me along the path of honesty,
  for my enemies are waiting for me to
    fall.
12 Do not let me fall into their hands.
  For they accuse me of things I've never
    done
  and breathe out violence against me.
13 Yet I am confident that I will see the LORD's
    goodness
  while I am here in the land of the living.
14 Wait patiently for the LORD.
  Be brave and courageous.
  Yes, wait patiently for the LORD.

P S A L M **28**

A psalm of David.

1 O LORD, you are my rock of safety.
  Please help me; don't refuse to answer
    me.
  For if you are silent,
  I might as well give up and die.
2 Listen to my prayer for mercy
    as I cry out to you for help,
    as I lift my hands toward your holy
      sanctuary.

3 Don't drag me away with the wicked—
    with those who do evil—
  those who speak friendly words to their
      neighbors
    while planning evil in their hearts.
4 Give them the punishment they so richly
      deserve!
    Measure it out in proportion to their
      wickedness.
  Pay them back for all their evil deeds!
    Give them a taste of what they have done
      to others.
5 They care nothing for what the LORD has
      done
    or for what his hands have made.
  So he will tear them down like old
      buildings,
    and they will never be rebuilt!

6 Praise the LORD!
  For he has heard my cry for mercy.
7 The LORD is my strength, my shield from
      every danger.
  I trust in him with all my heart.
  He helps me, and my heart is filled with joy.
  I burst out in songs of thanksgiving.

8 The LORD protects his people
  and gives victory to his anointed king.
9 Save your people!
  Bless Israel, your special possession!
  Lead them like a shepherd,
  and carry them forever in your arms.

P S A L M **29**

A psalm of David.

1 Give honor to the LORD, you angels;
  give honor to the LORD for his glory and
    strength.
2 Give honor to the LORD for the glory of his
    name.
  Worship the LORD in the splendor of his
    holiness.

3 The voice of the LORD echoes above the sea.
  The God of glory thunders.
  The LORD thunders over the mighty sea.
4 The voice of the LORD is powerful;
  the voice of the LORD is full of majesty.
5 The voice of the LORD splits the mighty cedars;
  the LORD shatters the cedars of Lebanon.
6 He makes Lebanon's mountains skip like a
    calf
  and Mount Hermon* to leap like a
    young bull.
7 The voice of the LORD strikes with lightning
    bolts.
8 The voice of the LORD makes the desert quake;
  the LORD shakes the desert of Kadesh.
9 The voice of the LORD twists mighty oaks*
  and strips the forests bare.
  In his Temple everyone shouts, "Glory!"

10 The LORD rules over the floodwaters.
  The LORD reigns as king forever.
11 The LORD gives his people strength.
  The LORD blesses them with peace.

P S A L M **30**

A psalm of David, sung at the dedication of the Temple.

1 I will praise you, LORD, for you have rescued
    me.
  You refused to let my enemies triumph
    over me.
2 O LORD my God, I cried out to you for help,
  and you restored my health.
3 You brought me up from the grave, O LORD.
  You kept me from falling into the pit of
    death.

29:6 Hebrew *Sirion*, another name for Mount Hermon. 29:9 Or *causes the deer to writhe in labor.*

4 Sing to the L‍ORD, all you godly ones!
    Praise his holy name.
5 His anger lasts for a moment,
    but his favor lasts a lifetime!
Weeping may go on all night,
    but joy comes with the morning.
6 When I was prosperous I said,
    "Nothing can stop me now!"
7 Your favor, O L‍ORD, made me as secure as a
    mountain.
Then you turned away from me, and I
    was shattered.
8 I cried out to you, O L‍ORD.
    I begged the Lord for mercy, saying,
9 "What will you gain if I die,
    if I sink down into the grave?
Can my dust praise you from the grave?
    Can it tell the world of your faithfulness?
10 Hear me, L‍ORD, and have mercy on me.
    Help me, O L‍ORD."
11 You have turned my mourning into joyful
    dancing.
You have taken away my clothes of
    mourning and clothed me with joy,
12 that I might sing praises to you and not be
    silent.
O L‍ORD my God, I will give you thanks
    forever!

P S A L M **31**
For the choir director: A psalm of David.

1 O L‍ORD, I have come to you for protection;
    don't let me be put to shame.
Rescue me, for you always do what is right.
2 Bend down and listen to me;
    rescue me quickly.
Be for me a great rock of safety,
    a fortress where my enemies cannot
    reach me.
3 You are my rock and my fortress.
    For the honor of your name, lead me out
    of this peril.
4 Pull me from the trap my enemies set for me,
    for I find protection in you alone.
5 I entrust my spirit into your hand.
    Rescue me, L‍ORD, for you are a faithful God.
6 I hate those who worship worthless idols.
    I trust in the L‍ORD.
7 I am overcome with joy because of your
    unfailing love,

for you have seen my troubles,
    and you care about the anguish of my
    soul.
8 You have not handed me over to my enemy
    but have set me in a safe place.
9 Have mercy on me, L‍ORD, for I am in
    distress.
My sight is blurred because of my tears.
    My body and soul are withering away.
10 I am dying from grief;
    my years are shortened by sadness.
Misery* has drained my strength;
    I am wasting away from within.
11 I am scorned by all my enemies
    and despised by my neighbors—
    even my friends are afraid to come near
    me.
When they see me on the street,
    they turn the other way.
12 I have been ignored as if I were dead,
    as if I were a broken pot.
13 I have heard the many rumors about me,
    and I am surrounded by terror.
My enemies conspire against me,
    plotting to take my life.
14 But I am trusting you, O L‍ORD,
    saying, "You are my God!"
15 My future is in your hands.
    Rescue me from those who hunt me
    down relentlessly.
16 Let your favor shine on your servant.
    In your unfailing love, save me.
17 Don't let me be disgraced, O L‍ORD,
    for I call out to you for help.
Let the wicked be disgraced;
    let them lie silent in the grave.
18 May their lying lips be silenced—
    those proud and arrogant lips that accuse
    the godly.
19 Your goodness is so great!
    You have stored up great blessings for
    those who honor you.
You have done so much for those who
    come to you for protection,
    blessing them before the watching
    world.
20 You hide them in the shelter of your
    presence,
    safe from those who conspire against
    them.
You shelter them in your presence,
    far from accusing tongues.

31:10 Or *Sin.*

the LORD,
he has shown me his unfailing love.
e kept me safe when my city was under
attack.

22 In sudden fear I had cried out,
"I have been cut off from the LORD!"
But you heard my cry for mercy
and answered my call for help.

23 Love the LORD, all you faithful ones!
For the LORD protects those who are loyal
to him,
but he harshly punishes all who are
arrogant.

24 So be strong and take courage,
all you who put your hope in the LORD!

PSALM 32

A psalm of David.

1 Oh, what joy for those
whose rebellion is forgiven,
whose sin is put out of sight!

2 Yes, what joy for those
whose record the LORD has cleared of sin,
whose lives are lived in complete honesty!

3 When I refused to confess my sin,
I was weak and miserable,
and I groaned all day long.

4 Day and night your hand of discipline was
heavy on me.
My strength evaporated like water in the
summer heat. *Interlude*

5 Finally, I confessed all my sins to you
and stopped trying to hide them.
I said to myself, "I will confess my rebellion
to the LORD."
And you forgave me! All my guilt is gone.
Interlude

6 Therefore, let all the godly confess their
rebellion to you while there is time,
that they may not drown in the
floodwaters of judgment.

7 For you are my hiding place;
you protect me from trouble.
You surround me with songs of victory.
Interlude

8 The LORD says, "I will guide you along the
best pathway for your life.
I will advise you and watch over you.

9 Do not be like a senseless horse or mule
that needs a bit and bridle to keep it
under control."

10 Many sorrows come to the wicked,
but unfailing love surrounds those who
trust the LORD.

11 So rejoice in the LORD and be glad, all you
who obey him!
Shout for joy, all you whose hearts are
pure!

PSALM 33

1 Let the godly sing with joy to the LORD,
for it is fitting to praise him.

2 Praise the LORD with melodies on the lyre;
make music for him on the ten-stringed
harp.

3 Sing new songs of praise to him;
play skillfully on the harp and sing with
joy.

4 For the word of the LORD holds true,
and everything he does is worthy of our
trust.

5 He loves whatever is just and good,
and his unfailing love fills the earth.

6 The LORD merely spoke,
and the heavens were created.
He breathed the word,
and all the stars were born.

7 He gave the sea its boundaries
and locked the oceans in vast reservoirs.

8 Let everyone in the world fear the LORD,
and let everyone stand in awe of him.

9 For when he spoke, the world began!
It appeared at his command.

10 The LORD shatters the plans of the nations
and thwarts all their schemes.

11 But the LORD's plans stand firm forever;
his intentions can never be shaken.

12 What joy for the nation whose God is the
LORD,
whose people he has chosen for his own.

13 The LORD looks down from heaven
and sees the whole human race.

14 From his throne he observes
all who live on the earth.

15 He made their hearts,
so he understands everything they do.

16 The best-equipped army cannot save a king,
nor is great strength enough to save a
warrior.

17 Don't count on your warhorse to give you
victory—
for all its strength, it cannot save you.

18 But the LORD watches over those who fear
    him,
    those who rely on his unfailing love.
19 He rescues them from death
    and keeps them alive in times of famine.
20 We depend on the LORD alone to save us.
    Only he can help us, protecting us like a
    shield.
21 In him our hearts rejoice,
    for we are trusting in his holy name.
22 Let your unfailing love surround us, LORD,
    for our hope is in you alone.

PSALM **34**

*A psalm of David, regarding the time he pretended to be
insane in front of Abimelech, who sent him away.*

1 I will praise the LORD at all times.
    I will constantly speak his praises.
2 I will boast only in the LORD;
    let all who are discouraged take heart.
3 Come, let us tell of the LORD's greatness;
    let us exalt his name together.

4 I prayed to the LORD, and he answered me,
    freeing me from all my fears.
5 Those who look to him for help will be
    radiant with joy;
    no shadow of shame will darken their
    faces.
6 I cried out to the LORD in my suffering, and
    he heard me.
    He set me free from all my fears.
7 For the angel of the LORD guards all who
    fear him,
    and he rescues them.

8 Taste and see that the LORD is good.
    Oh, the joys of those who trust in him!
9 Let the LORD's people show him reverence,
    for those who honor him will have all
    they need.
10 Even strong young lions sometimes go
    hungry,
    but those who trust in the LORD will
    never lack any good thing.

11 Come, my children, and listen to me,
    and I will teach you to fear the LORD.
12 Do any of you want to live
    a life that is long and good?
13 Then watch your tongue!
    Keep your lips from telling lies!
14 Turn away from evil and do good.
    Work hard at living in peace with others.

15 The eyes of the LORD watch over those who
    do right;
    his ears are open to their cries for help.
16 But the LORD turns his face against those
    who do evil;
    he will erase their memory from the earth.

17 The LORD hears his people when they call to
    him for help.
    He rescues them from all their troubles.
18 The LORD is close to the brokenhearted;
    he rescues those who are crushed in spirit.

19 The righteous face many troubles,
    but the LORD rescues them from each and
    every one.
20 For the LORD protects them from harm—
    not one of their bones* will be broken!

21 Calamity will surely overtake the wicked,
    and those who hate the righteous will be
    punished.
22 But the LORD will redeem those who serve
    him.
    Everyone who trusts in him will be freely
    pardoned.

PSALM **35**

A psalm of David.

1 O LORD, oppose those who oppose me.
    Declare war on those who are attacking me.
2 Put on your armor, and take up your shield.
    Prepare for battle, and come to my aid.
3 Lift up your spear and javelin
    and block the way of my enemies.
    Let me hear you say,
    "I am your salvation!"

4 Humiliate and disgrace those trying to kill
    me;
    turn them back in confusion.
5 Blow them away like chaff in the wind—
    a wind sent by the angel of the LORD.
6 Make their path dark and slippery,
    with the angel of the LORD pursuing them.
7 Although I did them no wrong,
    they laid a trap for me.
    Although I did them no wrong,
    they dug a pit for me.
8 So let sudden ruin overtake them!
    Let them be caught in the snare they set
    for me!
    Let them fall to destruction in the pit
    they dug for me.

34:20 Hebrew *protects him from harm—not one of his bones.*

9 Then I will rejoice in the LORD.
I will be glad because he rescues me.
10 I will praise him from the bottom of my
heart:
"LORD, who can compare with you?
Who else rescues the weak and helpless
from the strong?
Who else protects the poor and needy
from those who want to rob them?"

11 Malicious witnesses testify against me.
They accuse me of things I don't even
know about.
12 They repay me with evil for the good I do.
I am sick with despair.
13 Yet when they were ill,
I grieved for them.
I even fasted and prayed for them,
but my prayers returned unanswered.
14 I was sad, as though they were my friends or
family,
as if I were grieving for my own mother.

15 But they are glad now that I am in trouble;
they gleefully join together against me.
I am attacked by people I don't even
know;
they hurl slander at me continually.
16 They mock me with the worst kind of
profanity,
and they snarl at me.

17 How long, O Lord, will you look on and do
nothing?
Rescue me from their fierce attacks.
Protect my life from these lions!
18 Then I will thank you in front of the entire
congregation.
I will praise you before all the people.

19 Don't let my treacherous enemies
rejoice over my defeat.
Don't let those who hate me without cause
gloat over my sorrow.
20 They don't talk of peace;
they plot against innocent people
who are minding their own business.
21 They shout that they have seen me doing
wrong.
"Aha," they say. "Aha!
With our own eyes we saw him do it!"

22 O LORD, you know all about this.
Do not stay silent.
Don't abandon me now, O Lord.
23 Wake up! Rise to my defense!
Take up my case, my God and my Lord.

24 Declare me "not guilty," O LORD my God,
for you give justice.
Don't let my enemies laugh about me in
my troubles.
25 Don't let them say, "Look! We have what
we wanted!
Now we will eat him alive!"

26 May those who rejoice at my troubles
be humiliated and disgraced.
May those who triumph over me
be covered with shame and dishonor.

27 But give great joy to those
who have stood with me in my defense.
Let them continually say, "Great is the LORD,
who enjoys helping his servant."
28 Then I will tell everyone of your justice and
goodness,
and I will praise you all day long.

PSALM **36**

*For the choir director: A psalm of David, the servant of
the* LORD.

1 Sin whispers to the wicked, deep within
their hearts.
They have no fear of God to restrain them.
2 In their blind conceit,
they cannot see how wicked they really are.
3 Everything they say is crooked and deceitful.
They refuse to act wisely or do what is
good.
4 They lie awake at night, hatching sinful plots.
Their course of action is never good.
They make no attempt to turn from evil.

5 Your unfailing love, O LORD, is as vast as the
heavens;
your faithfulness reaches beyond the
clouds.
6 Your righteousness is like the mighty
mountains,
your justice like the ocean depths.
You care for people and animals alike,
O LORD.
7 How precious is your unfailing love,
O God!
All humanity finds shelter
in the shadow of your wings.
8 You feed them from the abundance of your
own house,
letting them drink from your rivers of
delight.
9 For you are the fountain of life,
the light by which we see.

10 Pour out your unfailing love on those who
   love you;
   give justice to those with honest hearts.
11 Don't let the proud trample me;
   don't let the wicked push me around.
12 Look! They have fallen!
   They have been thrown down, never to
   rise again.

PSALM **37**
A psalm of David.

1 Don't worry about the wicked.
   Don't envy those who do wrong.
2 For like grass, they soon fade away.
   Like springtime flowers, they soon wither.
3 Trust in the LORD and do good.
   Then you will live safely in the land and
   prosper.
4 Take delight in the LORD,
   and he will give you your heart's desires.
5 Commit everything you do to the LORD.
   Trust him, and he will help you.
6 He will make your innocence as clear as the
   dawn,
   and the justice of your cause will shine
   like the noonday sun.

7 Be still in the presence of the LORD,
   and wait patiently for him to act.
   Don't worry about evil people who prosper
   or fret about their wicked schemes.

8 Stop your anger!
   Turn from your rage!
   Do not envy others—
   it only leads to harm.
9 For the wicked will be destroyed,
   but those who trust in the LORD will
   possess the land.

10 In a little while, the wicked will disappear.
   Though you look for them, they will be gone.
11 Those who are gentle and lowly will possess
   the land;
   they will live in prosperous security.

12 The wicked plot against the godly;
   they snarl at them in defiance.
13 But the Lord just laughs,
   for he sees their day of judgment coming.

14 The wicked draw their swords
   and string their bows
   to kill the poor and the oppressed,
   to slaughter those who do right.

15 But they will be stabbed through the heart
   with their own swords,
   and their bows will be broken.

16 It is better to be godly and have little
   than to be evil and possess much.
17 For the strength of the wicked will be
   shattered,
   but the LORD takes care of the godly.

18 Day by day the LORD takes care of the
   innocent,
   and they will receive a reward that lasts
   forever.
19 They will survive through hard times;
   even in famine they will have more than
   enough.

20 But the wicked will perish.
   The LORD's enemies are like flowers in a
   field—
   they will disappear like smoke.

21 The wicked borrow and never repay,
   but the godly are generous givers.
22 Those blessed by the LORD will inherit the
   land,
   but those cursed by him will die.

23 The steps of the godly are directed by the
   LORD.
   He delights in every detail of their lives.
24 Though they stumble, they will not fall,
   for the LORD holds them by the hand.

25 Once I was young, and now I am old.
   Yet I have never seen the godly forsaken,
   nor seen their children begging for bread.
26 The godly always give generous loans to
   others,
   and their children are a blessing.

27 Turn from evil and do good,
   and you will live in the land forever.
28 For the LORD loves justice,
   and he will never abandon the godly.

   He will keep them safe forever,
   but the children of the wicked will perish.
29 The godly will inherit the land
   and will live there forever.

30 The godly offer good counsel;
   they know what is right from wrong.
31 They fill their hearts with God's law,
   so they will never slip from his path.

32 Those who are evil spy on the godly,
   waiting for an excuse to kill them.

³³ But the LORD will not let the wicked succeed
or let the godly be condemned when
they are brought before the judge.

³⁴ Don't be impatient for the LORD to act!
Travel steadily along his path.
He will honor you, giving you the land.
You will see the wicked destroyed.

³⁵ I myself have seen it happen—
proud and evil people thriving like
mighty trees.

³⁶ But when I looked again, they were gone!
Though I searched for them, I could not
find them!

³⁷ Look at those who are honest and good,
for a wonderful future lies before those
who love peace.

³⁸ But the wicked will be destroyed;
they have no future.

³⁹ The LORD saves the godly;
he is their fortress in times of trouble.

⁴⁰ The LORD helps them,
rescuing them from the wicked.
He saves them,
and they find shelter in him.

PSALM **38**

*A psalm of David, to bring us to the LORD's
remembrance.*

¹ O LORD, don't rebuke me in your anger!
Don't discipline me in your rage!

² Your arrows have struck deep,
and your blows are crushing me.

³ Because of your anger, my whole body is sick;
my health is broken because of my sins.

⁴ My guilt overwhelms me—
it is a burden too heavy to bear.

⁵ My wounds fester and stink
because of my foolish sins.

⁶ I am bent over and racked with pain.
My days are filled with grief.

⁷ A raging fever burns within me,
and my health is broken.

⁸ I am exhausted and completely crushed.
My groans come from an anguished heart.

⁹ You know what I long for, Lord;
you hear my every sigh.

¹⁰ My heart beats wildly, my strength fails,
and I am going blind.

¹¹ My loved ones and friends stay away,
fearing my disease.
Even my own family stands at a distance.

¹² Meanwhile, my enemies lay traps for me;
they make plans to ruin me.
They think up treacherous deeds all day
long.

¹³ But I am deaf to all their threats.
I am silent before them as one who
cannot speak.

¹⁴ I choose to hear nothing,
and I make no reply.

¹⁵ For I am waiting for you, O LORD.
You must answer for me, O Lord my God.

¹⁶ I prayed, "Don't let my enemies gloat over
me
or rejoice at my downfall."

¹⁷ I am on the verge of collapse,
facing constant pain.

¹⁸ But I confess my sins;
I am deeply sorry for what I have done.

¹⁹ My enemies are many;
they hate me though I have done
nothing against them.

²⁰ They repay me evil for good
and oppose me because I stand for the
right.

²¹ Do not abandon me, LORD.
Do not stand at a distance, my God.

²² Come quickly to help me, O Lord my savior.

OFF AND RUNNING

Don't Waste Time Pursuing Things
That Won't Last   Read PSALM 39:1-7

David made at least three profound realizations in these seven
verses. First, he recognized that everyone's time on earth is short.
Second, he realized that a person's efforts to accumulate wealth
are futile. That is because the person who works for wealth may not get to enjoy it. In
addition, the time he or she spends doing so could be better spent pursuing God. Third,
David understood that his only hope was in God.

All of these points are just as important for us to realize today. When we focus our attention on the
problems, pursuits, and pleasures of this life, we will always get sidetracked from the thing that really

PSALM **39**

For Jeduthun, the choir director: A psalm of David.

1 I said to myself, "I will watch what I do
   and not sin in what I say.
   I will curb my tongue
   when the ungodly are around me."
2 But as I stood there in silence—
   not even speaking of good things—
   the turmoil within me grew to the
   bursting point.
3 My thoughts grew hot within me
   and began to burn,
   igniting a fire of words:
4 "LORD, remind me how brief my time on
   earth will be.
   Remind me that my days are numbered,
   and that my life is fleeing away.
5 My life is no longer than the width of my hand.
   An entire lifetime is just a moment to you;
   human existence is but a breath."

Interlude

6 We are merely moving shadows,
   and all our busy rushing ends in nothing.
   We heap up wealth for someone else to
   spend.

7 And so, Lord, where do I put my hope?
   My only hope is in you.
8 Rescue me from my rebellion,
   for even fools mock me when I rebel.
9 I am silent before you; I won't say a word.
   For my punishment is from you.
10 Please, don't punish me anymore!
   I am exhausted by the blows from your hand.
11 When you discipline people for their sins,
   their lives can be crushed like the life of a
   moth.
   Human existence is as frail as breath.

Interlude

12 Hear my prayer, O LORD!

Listen to my cries for help!
   Don't ignore my tears.
For I am your guest—
   a traveler passing through,
   as my ancestors were before me.
13 Spare me so I can smile again
   before I am gone and exist no more.

PSALM **40**

For the choir director: A psalm of David.

1 I waited patiently for the LORD to help me,
   and he turned to me and heard my cry.
2 He lifted me out of the pit of despair,
   out of the mud and the mire.
   He set my feet on solid ground
   and steadied me as I walked along.
3 He has given me a new song to sing,
   a hymn of praise to our God.
   Many will see what he has done and be
   astounded.
   They will put their trust in the LORD.

4 Oh, the joys of those who trust the LORD,
   who have no confidence in the proud,
   or in those who worship idols.
5 O LORD my God, you have done many
   miracles for us.
   Your plans for us are too numerous to list.
   If I tried to recite all your wonderful deeds,
   I would never come to the end of them.

6 You take no delight in sacrifices or offerings.
   Now that you have made me listen, I
   finally understand—
   you don't require burnt offerings or sin
   offerings.
7 Then I said, "Look, I have come.
   And this has been written about me in
   your scroll:
8 I take joy in doing your will, my God,
   for your law is written on my heart."

matters—knowing Jesus. But if we focus on God, we will realize how frail and short our life is, and we will see that our hope is in God alone. For that reason, we should pursue things of eternal value. That may include financially supporting some missionaries, faithfully praying for an unbelieving relative, sharing Christ with a coworker, or showing Christ's love by providing food and shelter for a family in need.

What is your greatest pursuit? money? power? a meaningful career? a nice house or car? As you evaluate your pursuits, remember the words of Jesus: "Don't store up treasures here on earth, where they can be eaten by moths and get rusty, and where thieves break in and steal. Store your treasures in heaven, where they will never become moth-eaten or rusty and where they will be safe from thieves. Wherever your treasure is, there your heart and thoughts will also be" (Matthew 6:19-21).

For the next note on "Priorities," turn to p. 614.

9 I have told all your people about your
justice.
I have not been afraid to speak out,
as you, O Lord, well know.
10 I have not kept this good news hidden in
my heart;
I have talked about your faithfulness and
saving power.
I have told everyone in the great assembly
of your unfailing love and
faithfulness.

11 Lord, don't hold back your tender mercies
from me.
My only hope is in your unfailing love
and faithfulness.
12 For troubles surround me—
too many to count!
They pile up so high
I can't see my way out.
They are more numerous than the hairs on
my head.
I have lost all my courage.

13 Please, Lord, rescue me!
Come quickly, Lord, and help me.
14 May those who try to destroy me
be humiliated and put to shame.
May those who take delight in my trouble
be turned back in disgrace.
15 Let them be horrified by their shame,
for they said, "Aha! We've got him now!"

16 But may all who search for you
be filled with joy and gladness.
May those who love your salvation
repeatedly shout, "The Lord is great!"

17 As for me, I am poor and needy,
but the Lord is thinking about me right
now.
You are my helper and my savior.
Do not delay, O my God.

PSALM 41

For the choir director: A psalm of David.

1 Oh, the joys of those who are kind to the
poor.
The Lord rescues them in times of
trouble.
2 The Lord protects them
and keeps them alive.
He gives them prosperity
and rescues them from their enemies.
3 The Lord nurses them when they are sick
and eases their pain and discomfort.

4 "O Lord," I prayed, "have mercy on me.
Heal me, for I have sinned against you."
5 But my enemies say nothing but evil about
me.
"How soon will he die and be
forgotten?" they ask.
6 They visit me as if they are my friends,
but all the while they gather gossip,
and when they leave, they spread it
everywhere.
7 All who hate me whisper about me,
imagining the worst for me.
8 "Whatever he has, it is fatal," they say.
"He will never get out of that bed!"
9 Even my best friend, the one I trusted
completely,
the one who shared my food,
has turned against me.

10 Lord, have mercy on me.
Make me well again, so I can pay them
back!
11 I know that you are pleased with me,
for you have not let my enemy triumph
over me.
12 You have preserved my life because I am
innocent;
you have brought me into your presence
forever.

13 Bless the Lord, the God of Israel,
who lives forever from eternal ages past.
Amen and amen!

BOOK TWO (Psalms 42–72)

PSALM 42

*For the choir director: A psalm of the descendants
of Korah.*

1 As the deer pants for streams of water,
so I long for you, O God.
2 I thirst for God, the living God.
When can I come and stand before
him?
3 Day and night, I have only tears for food,
while my enemies continually taunt me,
saying,
"Where is this God of yours?"

4 My heart is breaking
as I remember how it used to be:
I walked among the crowds of worshipers,
leading a great procession to the house
of God,
singing for joy and giving thanks—
it was the sound of a great celebration!

5 Why am I discouraged?
  Why so sad?
  I will put my hope in God!
  I will praise him again—
  my Savior and 6my God!

Now I am deeply discouraged,
  but I will remember your kindness—
  from Mount Hermon, the source of the Jordan,
  from the land of Mount Mizar.
7 I hear the tumult of the raging seas
  as your waves and surging tides sweep over me.

8 Through each day the LORD pours his unfailing love upon me,
  and through each night I sing his songs,
  praying to God who gives me life.

9 "O God my rock," I cry,
  "Why have you forsaken me?
  Why must I wander in darkness,
  oppressed by my enemies?"
10 Their taunts pierce me like a fatal wound.
  They scoff, "Where is this God of yours?"

11 Why am I discouraged?
  Why so sad?
  I will put my hope in God!
  I will praise him again—
  my Savior and my God!

PSALM 43

1 O God, take up my cause!
  Defend me against these ungodly people.
  Rescue me from these unjust liars.
2 For you are God, my only safe haven.
  Why have you tossed me aside?
  Why must I wander around in darkness,
  oppressed by my enemies?

3 Send out your light and your truth;
  let them guide me.
  Let them lead me to your holy mountain,
  to the place where you live.
4 There I will go to the altar of God,
  to God—the source of all my joy.
  I will praise you with my harp,
  O God, my God!

5 Why am I discouraged?
  Why so sad?
  I will put my hope in God!
  I will praise him again—
  my Savior and my God!

44:4 Hebrew *for Jacob.*

PSALM 44

For the choir director: A psalm of the descendants of Korah.

1 O God, we have heard it with our own ears—
  our ancestors have told us
  of all you did in other days,
  in days long ago:
2 You drove out the pagan nations
  and gave all the land to our ancestors;
  you crushed their enemies,
  setting our ancestors free.
3 They did not conquer the land with their swords;
  it was not their own strength that gave them victory.
  It was by your mighty power that they succeeded;
  it was because you favored them and smiled on them.

4 You are my King and my God.
  You command victories for your people.*
5 Only by your power can we push back our enemies;
  only in your name can we trample our foes.
6 I do not trust my bow;
  I do not count on my sword to save me.
7 It is you who gives us victory over our enemies;
  it is you who humbles those who hate us.
8 O God, we give glory to you all day long
  and constantly praise your name. *Interlude*

9 But now you have tossed us aside in dishonor.
  You no longer lead our armies to battle.
10 You make us retreat from our enemies
  and allow them to plunder our land.
11 You have treated us like sheep waiting to be slaughtered;
  you have scattered us among the nations.
12 You sold us—your precious people—for a pittance.
  You valued us at nothing at all.

13 You have caused all our neighbors to mock us.
  We are an object of scorn and derision to the nations around us.
14 You have made us the butt of their jokes;
  we are scorned by the whole world.
15 We can't escape the constant humiliation;
  shame is written across our faces.
16 All we hear are the taunts of our mockers.
  All we see are our vengeful enemies.

17 All this has happened despite our loyalty to
   you.
   We have not violated your covenant.
18 Our hearts have not deserted you.
   We have not strayed from your path.
19 Yet you have crushed us in the desert.
   You have covered us with darkness and
   death.

20 If we had turned away from worshiping our
   God
   or spread our hands in prayer to foreign
   gods,
21 God would surely have known it,
   for he knows the secrets of every heart.
22 For your sake we are killed every day;
   we are being slaughtered like sheep.

23 Wake up, O Lord! Why do you sleep?
   Get up! Do not reject us forever.
24 Why do you look the other way?
   Why do you ignore our suffering and
   oppression?
25 We collapse in the dust,
   lying face down in the dirt.
26 Rise up! Come and help us!
   Save us because of your unfailing love.

PSALM 45

*For the choir director: A psalm of the descendants of
Korah, to be sung to the tune "Lilies." A love song.*

1 My heart overflows with a beautiful thought!
   I will recite a lovely poem to the king,
   for my tongue is like the pen of a skillful
   poet.

2 You are the most handsome of all.
   Gracious words stream from your lips.
   God himself has blessed you forever.
3 Put on your sword, O mighty warrior!
   You are so glorious, so majestic!
4 In your majesty, ride out to victory,
   defending truth, humility, and justice.
   Go forth to perform awe-inspiring deeds!
5 Your arrows are sharp,
   piercing your enemies' hearts.
   The nations fall before you,
   lying down beneath your feet.

6 Your throne, O God,* endures forever and ever.
   Your royal power is expressed in justice.
7 You love what is right and hate what is wrong.
   Therefore God, your God, has anointed
   you,

pouring out the oil of joy on you more
   than on anyone else.
8 Your robes are perfumed with myrrh, aloes,
   and cassia.
   In palaces decorated with ivory,
   you are entertained by the music of harps.
9 Kings' daughters are among your
   concubines.
   At your right side stands the queen,
   wearing jewelry of finest gold from
   Ophir!

10 Listen to me, O royal daughter; take to heart
   what I say.
   Forget your people and your homeland
   far away.
11 For your royal husband delights in your
   beauty;
   honor him, for he is your lord.
12 The princes of Tyre* will shower you with
   gifts.
   People of great wealth will entreat your
   favor.

13 The bride, a princess, waits within her
   chamber,
   dressed in a gown woven with gold.
14 In her beautiful robes, she is led to the king,
   accompanied by her bridesmaids.
15 What a joyful, enthusiastic procession
   as they enter the king's palace!

16 Your sons will become kings like their father.
   You will make them rulers over many
   lands.

17 I will bring honor to your name in every
   generation.
   Therefore, the nations will praise you
   forever and ever.

PSALM 46

*For the choir director: A psalm of the descendants of
Korah, to be sung by soprano voices.* A song.*

1 God is our refuge and strength,
   always ready to help in times of trouble.
2 So we will not fear, even if earthquakes
   come
   and the mountains crumble into the sea.
3 Let the oceans roar and foam.
   Let the mountains tremble as the waters
   surge!   *Interlude*

4 A river brings joy to the city of our God,
   the sacred home of the Most High.

45:6 Or *Your divine throne.*   45:12 Hebrew *The daughter of Tyre.*   46:TITLE Hebrew *according to alamoth.*

5 God himself lives in that city; it cannot be
  destroyed.
  God will protect it at the break of day.
6 The nations are in an uproar,
  and kingdoms crumble!
  God thunders,
  and the earth melts!

7 The Lord Almighty is here among us;
  the God of Israel* is our fortress.
  Interlude

8 Come, see the glorious works of the Lord:
  See how he brings destruction upon the
  world
9 and causes wars to end throughout the
  earth.
  He breaks the bow and snaps the spear
  in two;
  he burns the shields with fire.

10 "Be silent, and know that I am God!
   I will be honored by every nation.
   I will be honored throughout the world."

11 The Lord Almighty is here among us;
   the God of Israel is our fortress. *Interlude*

PSALM 47

*For the choir director: A psalm of the descendants
of Korah.*

1 Come, everyone, and clap your hands for
  joy!
  Shout to God with joyful praise!
2 For the Lord Most High is awesome.
  He is the great King of all the earth.
3 He subdues the nations before us,
  putting our enemies beneath our feet.
4 He chose the Promised Land as our
  inheritance,
  the proud possession of Jacob's
  descendants, whom he loves. *Interlude*

5 God has ascended with a mighty shout.
  The Lord has ascended with trumpets
  blaring.
6 Sing praise to God, sing praises;
  sing praise to our King, sing praises!
7 For God is the King over all the earth.
  Praise him with a psalm!
8 God reigns above the nations,
  sitting on his holy throne.
9 The rulers of the world have gathered
  together.

They join us in praising the God of
  Abraham.
For all the kings of the earth belong to God.
  He is highly honored everywhere.

PSALM 48

A psalm of the descendants of Korah. A song.

1 How great is the Lord,
  and how much we should praise him
  in the city of our God,
  which is on his holy mountain!
2 It is magnificent in elevation—
  the whole earth rejoices to see it!
  Mount Zion, the holy mountain,*
  is the city of the great King!
3 God himself is in Jerusalem's towers.
  He reveals himself as her defender.

4 The kings of the earth joined forces
  and advanced against the city.
5 But when they saw it, they were stunned;
  they were terrified and ran away.
6 They were gripped with terror,
  like a woman writhing in the pain of
  childbirth
7 or like the mighty ships of Tarshish
  being shattered by a powerful east wind.

8 We had heard of the city's glory,
  but now we have seen it ourselves—
  the city of the Lord Almighty.
  It is the city of our God;
  he will make it safe forever. *Interlude*

9 O God, we meditate on your unfailing love
  as we worship in your Temple.
10 As your name deserves, O God,
   you will be praised to the ends of the
   earth.
   Your strong right hand is filled with
   victory.
11 Let the people on Mount Zion rejoice.
   Let the towns of Judah be glad,
   for your judgments are just.

12 Go, inspect the city of Jerusalem.*
   Walk around and count the many towers.
13 Take note of the fortified walls,
   and tour all the citadels,
   that you may describe them
   to future generations.
14 For that is what God is like.
   He is our God forever and ever,
   and he will be our guide until we die.

46:7 Hebrew *of Jacob;* also in 46:11. **48:2** Or *Mount Zion, in the far north;* Hebrew reads *Mount Zion, the heights of Zaphon.* **48:12** Hebrew *Zion.*

PSALM **49**

For the choir director: A psalm of the descendants of Korah.

1 Listen to this, all you people!
    Pay attention, everyone in the world!
2 High and low,
    rich and poor—listen!
3 For my words are wise,
    and my thoughts are filled with insight.
4 I listen carefully to many proverbs
    and solve riddles with inspiration from a
      harp.

5 There is no need to fear when times of
      trouble come,
    when enemies are surrounding me.
6 They trust in their wealth
    and boast of great riches.
7 Yet they cannot redeem themselves from
      death*
    by paying a ransom to God.
8 Redemption does not come so easily,
    for no one can ever pay enough
9 to live forever
    and never see the grave.

10 Those who are wise must finally die,
     just like the foolish and senseless,
     leaving all their wealth behind.
11 The grave is their eternal home,
     where they will stay forever.
    They may name their estates after
       themselves,
     but they leave their wealth to others.
12 They will not last long despite their riches—
     they will die like the animals.
13 This is the fate of fools,
     though they will be remembered as
       being so wise.   *Interlude*

14 Like sheep, they are led to the grave,
     where death will be their shepherd.
    In the morning the godly will rule over them.
     Their bodies will rot in the grave,
     far from their grand estates.
15 But as for me, God will redeem my life.
     He will snatch me from the power of
       death.   *Interlude*

16 So don't be dismayed when the wicked
       grow rich,
     and their homes become ever more
       splendid.
17 For when they die, they carry nothing with
       them.

49:7 Or *no one can redeem the life of another.*

Their wealth will not follow them into
  the grave.
18 In this life they consider themselves fortunate,
     and the world loudly applauds their
       success.
19 But they will die like all others before them
     and never again see the light of day.
20 People who boast of their wealth don't
       understand
     that they will die like the animals.

PSALM **50**

A psalm of Asaph.

1 The mighty God, the LORD, has spoken;
    he has summoned all humanity from
      east to west!
2 From Mount Zion, the perfection of beauty,
    God shines in glorious radiance.
3 Our God approaches with the noise of
      thunder.
    Fire devours everything in his way,
    and a great storm rages around him.
4 Heaven and earth will be his witnesses
    as he judges his people:
5 "Bring my faithful people to me—
    those who made a covenant with me by
      giving sacrifices."
6 Then let the heavens proclaim his justice,
    for God himself will be the judge.
                             Interlude

7 "O my people, listen as I speak.
    Here are my charges against you, O Israel:
    I am God, your God!
8 I have no complaint about your sacrifices
    or the burnt offerings you constantly
      bring to my altar.
9 But I want no more bulls from your barns;
    I want no more goats from your pens.
10 For all the animals of the forest are mine,
     and I own the cattle on a thousand hills.
11 Every bird of the mountains
     and all the animals of the field belong to
       me.
12 If I were hungry, I would not mention it to
       you,
     for all the world is mine and everything
       in it.
13 I don't need the bulls you sacrifice;
     I don't need the blood of goats.
14 What I want instead is your true thanks to God;
     I want you to fulfill your vows to the
       Most High.

¹⁵ Trust me in your times of trouble,
  and I will rescue you,
  and you will give me glory."

¹⁶ But God says to the wicked:
  "Recite my laws no longer,
  and don't pretend that you obey me.
¹⁷ For you refuse my discipline
  and treat my laws like trash.
¹⁸ When you see a thief, you help him,
  and you spend your time with adulterers.
¹⁹ Your mouths are filled with wickedness,
  and your tongues are full of lies.
²⁰ You sit around and slander a brother—
  your own mother's son.
²¹ While you did all this, I remained silent,
  and you thought I didn't care.
  But now I will rebuke you,
  listing all my charges against you.
²² Repent, all of you who ignore me,
  or I will tear you apart,
  and no one will help you.
²³ But giving thanks is a sacrifice that truly
    honors me.
  If you keep to my path,
  I will reveal to you the salvation of God."

PSALM 51

For the choir director: A psalm of David, regarding the time Nathan the prophet came to him after David had committed adultery with Bathsheba.

¹ Have mercy on me, O God,
  because of your unfailing love.
  Because of your great compassion,
  blot out the stain of my sins.
² Wash me clean from my guilt.
  Purify me from my sin.

³ For I recognize my shameful deeds—
  they haunt me day and night.
⁴ Against you, and you alone, have I sinned;
  I have done what is evil in your sight.
  You will be proved right in what you say,
  and your judgment against me is just.

⁵ For I was born a sinner—
  yes, from the moment my mother
    conceived me.
⁶ But you desire honesty from the heart,
  so you can teach me to be wise in my
    inmost being.

⁷ Purify me from my sins,* and I will be clean;
  wash me, and I will be whiter than snow.

51:7 Hebrew *Purify me with the hyssop branch.*

⁸ Oh, give me back my joy again;
  you have broken me—
  now let me rejoice.
⁹ Don't keep looking at my sins.
  Remove the stain of my guilt.
¹⁰ Create in me a clean heart, O God.
  Renew a right spirit within me.
¹¹ Do not banish me from your presence,
  and don't take your Holy Spirit from me.
¹² Restore to me again the joy of your salvation,
  and make me willing to obey you.
¹³ Then I will teach your ways to sinners,
  and they will return to you.
¹⁴ Forgive me for shedding blood, O God who saves;
  then I will joyfully sing of your forgiveness.
¹⁵ Unseal my lips, O Lord,
  that I may praise you.

¹⁶ You would not be pleased with sacrifices,
  or I would bring them.
  If I brought you a burnt offering,
  you would not accept it.
¹⁷ The sacrifice you want is a broken spirit.
  A broken and repentant heart, O God,
  you will not despise.

¹⁸ Look with favor on Zion and help her;
  rebuild the walls of Jerusalem.
¹⁹ Then you will be pleased with worthy sacrifices
  and with our whole burnt offerings;
  and bulls will again be sacrificed on your
    altar.

PSALM 52

For the choir director: A psalm of David, regarding the time Doeg the Edomite told Saul that Ahimelech had given refuge to David.

¹ You call yourself a hero, do you?
  Why boast about this crime of yours,
  you who have disgraced God's people?
² All day long you plot destruction.
  Your tongue cuts like a sharp razor;
  you're an expert at telling lies.
³ You love evil more than good
  and lies more than truth.   *Interlude*

⁴ You love to say things that harm others,
  you liar!
⁵ But God will strike you down once and for all.
  He will pull you from your home
  and drag you from the land of the living.
                                      Interlude

⁶ The righteous will see it and be amazed.
  They will laugh and say,

If You Fall, Ask God to Forgive You and Purify Your Heart and Desires Read PSALM 51:7-15

This psalm was written by David after Nathan had informed him of God's judgment against him for his affair with Bathsheba. David had not confessed his sin to God for a full year—and what a miserable year that had been. He writes, "When I refused to confess my sin, I was weak and miserable, and I groaned all day long. Day and night your hand of discipline was heavy on me. My strength evaporated like water in the summer heat" (Psalm 32:3-4).

Like David, we will be miserable until we confess our sin. But we must also ask God to help purify our heart. In the Bible, the heart is an expression that is used to describe the center of who we are. It indicates our will, thoughts, and emotions.

David recognized the wicked inclinations of his heart, and he realized that he could not change them on his own. Only God could fill his heart with pure desires.

If you have already crossed the line of adultery, turn to God and ask for his forgiveness, and put  a stop to that relationship now. Avoid the situations and relationships that could lead you back down that perilous road. Aggressively seek to fill your mind and life with things that are spiritually uplifting: "Fix your thoughts on what is true and honorable and right. Think about things that are pure and lovely and admirable. Think about things that are excellent and worthy of praise" (Philippians 4:8). Ultimately, only God can help you get through the rough waters of sexual temptation.

For the next note on "Purity," turn to p. 1102.

CORNER STONES

---

7 "Look what happens to mighty warriors
    who do not trust in God.
They trust their wealth instead
    and grow more and more bold in their
        wickedness."

8 But I am like an olive tree,
    thriving in the house of God.
I trust in God's unfailing love
    forever and ever.
9 I will praise you forever, O God,
    for what you have done.
I will wait for your mercies
    in the presence of your people.

PSALM 53

For the choir director: A meditation of David.

1 Only fools say in their hearts,
    "There is no God."
They are corrupt, and their actions are evil;
    no one does good!

2 God looks down from heaven
    on the entire human race;
he looks to see if there is even one with real
    understanding,
    one who seeks for God.

3 But no, all have turned away from God;
    all have become corrupt.
No one does good,
    not even one!

4 Will those who do evil never learn?
    They eat up my people like bread;
    they wouldn't think of praying to God.
5 But then terror will grip them,
    terror like they have never known before.
God will scatter the bones of your enemies.
    You will put them to shame, for God has
        rejected them.

6 Oh, that salvation would come from Mount
        Zion to rescue Israel!
    For when God restores his people,
    Jacob will shout with joy, and Israel will
        rejoice.

PSALM 54

For the choir director: A meditation of David, regarding the time the Ziphites came and said to Saul, "We know where David is hiding." To be accompanied by stringed instruments.

1 Come with great power, O God, and rescue
        me!
    Defend me with your might.

² O God, listen to my prayer.
Pay attention to my plea.

³ For strangers are attacking me;
violent men are trying to kill me.
They care nothing for God.   *Interlude*

⁴ But God is my helper.
The Lord is the one who keeps me alive!

⁵ May my enemies' plans for evil be turned
against them.
Do as you promised and put an end to
them.

⁶ I will sacrifice a voluntary offering to you;
I will praise your name, O LORD,
for it is good.

⁷ For you will rescue me from my troubles
and help me to triumph over my enemies.

PSALM 55

For the choir director: A psalm of David, to be
accompanied by stringed instruments.

¹ Listen to my prayer, O God.
Do not ignore my cry for help!

² Please listen and answer me,
for I am overwhelmed by my troubles.

³ My enemies shout at me,
making loud and wicked threats.
They bring trouble on me,
hunting me down in their anger.

⁴ My heart is in anguish.
The terror of death overpowers me.

⁵ Fear and trembling overwhelm me.
I can't stop shaking.

⁶ Oh, how I wish I had wings like a dove;
then I would fly away and rest!

⁷ I would fly far away
to the quiet of the wilderness.   *Interlude*

⁸ How quickly I would escape—
far away from this wild storm of hatred.

⁹ Destroy them, Lord, and confuse their speech,
for I see violence and strife in the city.

¹⁰ Its walls are patrolled day and night against
invaders,
but the real danger is wickedness within
the city.

¹¹ Murder and robbery are everywhere there;
threats and cheating are rampant in the
streets.

¹² It is not an enemy who taunts me—
I could bear that.

55:15 Hebrew *let Sheol.*

It is not my foes who so arrogantly insult
me—
I could have hidden from them.

¹³ Instead, it is you—my equal,
my companion and close friend.

¹⁴ What good fellowship we enjoyed
as we walked together to the house of God.

¹⁵ Let death seize my enemies by surprise;
let the grave* swallow them alive,
for evil makes its home within them.

¹⁶ But I will call on God,
and the LORD will rescue me.

¹⁷ Morning, noon, and night
I plead aloud in my distress,
and the LORD hears my voice.

¹⁸ He rescues me and keeps me safe
from the battle waged against me,
even though many still oppose me.

¹⁹ God, who is king forever,
will hear me and will humble them.
Interlude
For my enemies refuse to change their
ways;
they do not fear God.

²⁰ As for this friend of mine, he betrayed me;
he broke his promises.

²¹ His words are as smooth as cream,
but in his heart is war.
His words are as soothing as lotion,
but underneath are daggers!

²² Give your burdens to the LORD,
and he will take care of you.
He will not permit the godly to slip and
fall.

²³ But you, O God, will send the wicked
down to the pit of destruction.
Murderers and liars will die young,
but I am trusting you to save me.

PSALM 56

For the choir director: A psalm of David, regarding the
time the Philistines seized him in Gath. To be sung to the
tune "Dove on Distant Oaks."

¹ O God, have mercy on me.
The enemy troops press in on me.
My foes attack me all day long.

² My slanderers hound me constantly,
and many are boldly attacking me.

³ But when I am afraid,
I put my trust in you.

⁴ O God, I praise your word.
  I trust in God, so why should I be afraid?
  What can mere mortals do to me?

⁵ They are always twisting what I say;
  they spend their days plotting ways to
    harm me.
⁶ They come together to spy on me—
  watching my every step, eager to kill me.
⁷ Don't let them get away with their
    wickedness;
  in your anger, O God, throw them to the
    ground.

⁸ You keep track of all my sorrows.
  You have collected all my tears in your
    bottle.
  You have recorded each one in your book.

⁹ On the very day I call to you for help,
  my enemies will retreat.
  This I know: God is on my side.*
¹⁰ O God, I praise your word.
  Yes, LORD, I praise your word.
¹¹ I trust in God, so why should I be afraid?
  What can mere mortals do to me?

¹² I will fulfill my vows to you, O God,
  and offer a sacrifice of thanks for your
    help.
¹³ For you have rescued me from death;
  you have kept my feet from slipping.
  So now I can walk in your presence, O God,
  in your life-giving light.

PSALM 57

For the choir director: A psalm of David, regarding the time he fled from Saul and went into the cave. To be sung to the tune "Do Not Destroy!"

¹ Have mercy on me, O God, have mercy!
  I look to you for protection.
  I will hide beneath the shadow of your
    wings
  until this violent storm is past.

56:9 Or *By this I will know that God is on my side.*

² I cry out to God Most High,
  to God who will fulfill his purpose for me.
³ He will send help from heaven to save me,
  rescuing me from those who are out to
    get me.   *Interlude*
  My God will send forth his unfailing love
  and faithfulness.

⁴ I am surrounded by fierce lions
  who greedily devour human prey—
  whose teeth pierce like spears and arrows,
  and whose tongues cut like swords.

⁵ Be exalted, O God, above the highest
    heavens!
  May your glory shine over all the earth.

⁶ My enemies have set a trap for me.
  I am weary from distress.
  They have dug a deep pit in my path,
  but they themselves have fallen into it.
                                    Interlude

⁷ My heart is confident in you, O God;
  no wonder I can sing your praises!
⁸ Wake up, my soul!
  Wake up, O harp and lyre!
  I will waken the dawn with my song.
⁹ I will thank you, Lord, in front of all the
    people.
  I will sing your praises among the nations.
¹⁰ For your unfailing love is as high as the
    heavens.
  Your faithfulness reaches to the clouds.

¹¹ Be exalted, O God, above the highest
    heavens.
  May your glory shine over all the earth.

PSALM 58

For the choir director: A psalm of David, to be sung to the tune "Do Not Destroy!"

¹ Justice—do you rulers know the meaning
    of the word?
  Do you judge the people fairly?

OFF AND RUNNING

Pray Regularly Read PSALM 55:16-17

Prayer often seems like an obligation. Some only do it when they need something or because it is a specific time of day. Once someone opens his or her heart to Jesus, however, prayer becomes a thing of joy, not a duty. Prayer becomes an opportunity to converse with the Creator, our Lord. And the more often we pray, the closer and deeper our relationship with Jesus becomes. As the psalmist suggests in this

2 No, all your dealings are crooked;
   you hand out violence instead of justice.
3 These wicked people are born sinners;
   even from birth they have lied and gone
     their own way.
4 They spit poison like deadly snakes;
   they are like cobras that refuse to listen,
5 ignoring the tunes of the snake charmers,
   no matter how skillfully they play.

6 Break off their fangs, O God!
   Smash the jaws of these lions, O LORD!
7 May they disappear like water into thirsty
    ground.
   Make their weapons useless in their
    hands.*
8 May they be like snails that dissolve into
    slime,
   like a stillborn child who will never see
    the sun.
9 God will sweep them away, both young and
    old,
   faster than a pot heats on an open flame.

10 The godly will rejoice when they see
    injustice avenged.
   They will wash their feet in the blood of
    the wicked.
11 Then at last everyone will say,
   "There truly is a reward for those who
    live for God;
   surely there is a God who judges justly
    here on earth."

PSALM 59

For the choir director: A psalm of David, regarding the time Saul sent soldiers to watch David's house in order to kill him. To be sung to the tune "Do Not Destroy!"

1 Rescue me from my enemies, O God.
   Protect me from those who have come to
    destroy me.
2 Rescue me from these criminals;
   save me from these murderers.

3 They have set an ambush for me.
   Fierce enemies are out there waiting,
   though I have done them no wrong,
    O LORD.
4 Despite my innocence, they prepare to kill me.
   Rise up and help me! Look on my plight!
5 O LORD God Almighty, the God of Israel,
   rise up to punish hostile nations.
   Show no mercy to wicked traitors. *Interlude*

6 They come at night,
   snarling like vicious dogs
    as they prowl the streets.
7 Listen to the filth that comes from their
    mouths,
   the piercing swords that fly from their lips.
   "Who can hurt us?" they sneer.

8 But LORD, you laugh at them.
   You scoff at all the hostile nations.
9 You are my strength; I wait for you to rescue
    me,
   for you, O God, are my place of safety.
10 In his unfailing love, my God will come and
    help me.
   He will let me look down in triumph on
    all my enemies.

11 Don't kill them, for my people soon forget
    such lessons;
   stagger them with your power, and bring
    them to their knees,
    O Lord our shield.
12 Because of the sinful things they say,
   because of the evil that is on their lips,
   let them be captured by their pride,
    their curses, and their lies.
13 Destroy them in your anger!
   Wipe them out completely!
   Then the whole world will know
    that God reigns in Israel.*   *Interlude*

14 My enemies come out at night,
   snarling like vicious dogs
    as they prowl the streets.

58:7 Or *Let them be trodden down and wither like grass.* The meaning of the Hebrew is uncertain. 59:13 Hebrew *in Jacob.*

---

passage, we should pray morning, noon, and night—ever aware that God is listening and that he *will* answer.

   Not only will prayer transform your life, it will transform your problems. Sometimes it will even eliminate them! For as verse 22 proclaims, "Give your burdens to the LORD, and he will take care of you. He will not permit the godly to slip and fall." As a believer, prayer should be a daily practice of devotion, not an occasional pleading of need.

   For the next note on "Prayer Time," turn to p. 616.

15 They scavenge for food
   but go to sleep unsatisfied.*

16 But as for me, I will sing about your power.
   I will shout with joy each morning
      because of your unfailing love.
   For you have been my refuge,
      a place of safety in the day of distress.

17 O my Strength, to you I sing praises,
   for you, O God, are my refuge,
      the God who shows me unfailing love.

PSALM 60

*For the choir director: A psalm of David useful for teaching,
regarding the time David fought Aram-naharaim and
Aram-zobah, and Joab returned and killed twelve thousand
Edomites in the Valley of Salt. To be sung to the tune "Lily of
the Testimony."*

1 You have rejected us, O God, and broken
      our defenses.
   You have been angry with us; now restore
      us to your favor.
2 You have shaken our land and split it open.
   Seal the cracks before it completely
      collapses.
3 You have been very hard on us,
   making us drink wine that sent us reeling.
4 But you have raised a banner for those who
      honor you—
   a rallying point in the face of attack.
                                   Interlude

5 Use your strong right arm to save us,
   and rescue your beloved people.
6 God has promised this by his holiness*:
   "I will divide up Shechem with joy.
   I will measure out the valley of Succoth.
7 Gilead is mine,
   and Manasseh is mine.
   Ephraim will produce my warriors,
      and Judah will produce my kings.
8 Moab will become my lowly servant,
   and Edom will be my slave.
   I will shout in triumph over the
      Philistines."

9 But who will bring me into the fortified city?
   Who will bring me victory over Edom?
10 Have you rejected us, O God?
   Will you no longer march with our armies?
11 Oh, please help us against our enemies,
   for all human help is useless.
12 With God's help we will do mighty things,
   for he will trample down our foes.

59:15 Or *and growl if they don't get enough.*   60:6 Or *in his sanctuary.*

PSALM 61

*For the choir director: A psalm of David, to be
accompanied by stringed instruments.*

1 O God, listen to my cry!
   Hear my prayer!
2 From the ends of the earth,
   I will cry to you for help,
      for my heart is overwhelmed.
   Lead me to the towering rock of safety,
3   for you are my safe refuge,
      a fortress where my enemies cannot
         reach me.
4 Let me live forever in your sanctuary,
   safe beneath the shelter of your wings!
                                   Interlude
5 For you have heard my vows, O God.
   You have given me an inheritance
      reserved for those who fear your name.

6 Add many years to the life of the king!
   May his years span the generations!
7 May he reign under God's protection forever.
   Appoint your unfailing love and
      faithfulness to watch over him.

8 Then I will always sing praises to your name
   as I fulfill my vows day after day.

PSALM 62

For Jeduthun, the choir director: A psalm of David.

1 I wait quietly before God,
   for my salvation comes from him.
2 He alone is my rock and my salvation,
   my fortress where I will never be shaken.

3 So many enemies against one man—
   all of them trying to kill me.
   To them I'm just a broken-down wall
      or a tottering fence.
4 They plan to topple me from my high
      position.
   They delight in telling lies about me.
   They are friendly to my face,
      but they curse me in their hearts.   *Interlude*

5 I wait quietly before God,
   for my hope is in him.
6 He alone is my rock and my salvation,
   my fortress where I will not be shaken.
7 My salvation and my honor come from
      God alone.
   He is my refuge, a rock where no enemy
      can reach me.

8 O my people, trust in him at all times.
   Pour out your heart to him,
   for God is our refuge. *Interlude*

9 From the greatest to the lowliest—
   all are nothing in his sight.
   If you weigh them on the scales,
   they are lighter than a puff of air.
10 Don't try to get rich
   by extortion or robbery.
   And if your wealth increases,
   don't make it the center of your life.

11 God has spoken plainly,
   and I have heard it many times:
   Power, O God, belongs to you;
12   unfailing love, O Lord, is yours.
   Surely you judge all people
   according to what they have done.

PSALM 63

A psalm of David, regarding a time when David was in the wilderness of Judah.

1 O God, you are my God;
   I earnestly search for you.
   My soul thirsts for you;
   my whole body longs for you
   in this parched and weary land
   where there is no water.

2 I have seen you in your sanctuary
   and gazed upon your power and glory.
3 Your unfailing love is better to me than life
   itself;
   how I praise you!
4 I will honor you as long as I live,
   lifting up my hands to you in prayer.
5 You satisfy me more than the richest of
   foods.
   I will praise you with songs of joy.

6 I lie awake thinking of you,
   meditating on you through the night.
7 I think how much you have helped me;
   I sing for joy in the shadow of your
   protecting wings.
8 I follow close behind you;
   your strong right hand holds me
   securely.

9 But those plotting to destroy me will come
   to ruin.
   They will go down into the depths of the
   earth.
10 They will die by the sword
   and become the food of jackals.

11 But the king will rejoice in God.
   All who trust in him will praise him,
   while liars will be silenced.

PSALM 64

For the choir director: A psalm of David.

1 O God, listen to my complaint.
   Do not let my enemies' threats
   overwhelm me.
2 Protect me from the plots of the wicked,
   from the scheming of those who do evil.
3 Sharp tongues are the swords they wield;
   bitter words are the arrows they aim.
4 They shoot from ambush at the innocent,
   attacking suddenly and fearlessly.
5 They encourage each other to do evil
   and plan how to set their traps.
   "Who will ever notice?" they ask.
6 As they plot their crimes, they say,
   "We have devised the perfect plan!"
   Yes, the human heart and mind are cunning.

7 But God himself will shoot them down.
   Suddenly, his arrows will pierce them.
8 Their own words will be turned against
   them, destroying them.
   All who see it happening will shake their
   heads in scorn.
9 Then everyone will stand in awe,
   proclaiming the mighty acts of God,
   realizing all the amazing things he does.

10 The godly will rejoice in the LORD
   and find shelter in him.
   And those who do what is right
   will praise him.

PSALM 65

For the choir director: A psalm of David. A song.

1 What mighty praise, O God,
   belongs to you in Zion.
   We will fulfill our vows to you,
2   for you answer our prayers,
   and to you all people will come.
3 Though our hearts are filled with sins,
   you forgive them all.
4 What joy for those you choose to bring near,
   those who live in your holy courts.
   What joys await us
   inside your holy Temple.

5 You faithfully answer our prayers with
   awesome deeds,
   O God our savior.

You are the hope of everyone on earth,
even those who sail on distant seas.
6 You formed the mountains by your power
and armed yourself with mighty strength.
7 You quieted the raging oceans
with their pounding waves
and silenced the shouting of the nations.
8 Those who live at the ends of the earth
stand in awe of your wonders.
From where the sun rises to where it sets,
you inspire shouts of joy.

9 You take care of the earth and water it,
making it rich and fertile.
The rivers of God will not run dry;
they provide a bountiful harvest of grain,
for you have ordered it so.
10 You drench the plowed ground with rain,
melting the clods and leveling the ridges.
You soften the earth with showers
and bless its abundant crops.
11 You crown the year with a bountiful harvest;
even the hard pathways overflow with
abundance.
12 The wilderness becomes a lush pasture,
and the hillsides blossom with joy.
13 The meadows are clothed with flocks of sheep,
and the valleys are carpeted with grain.
They all shout and sing for joy!

PSALM 66

For the choir director: A psalm. A song.

1 Shout joyful praises to God, all the earth!
2 Sing about the glory of his name!
Tell the world how glorious he is.
3 Say to God, "How awesome are your deeds!
Your enemies cringe before your mighty
power.
4 Everything on earth will worship you;
they will sing your praises,
shouting your name in glorious songs."
Interlude

5 Come and see what our God has done,
what awesome miracles he does for his
people!
6 He made a dry path through the Red Sea,*
and his people went across on foot.
Come, let us rejoice in who he is.
7 For by his great power he rules forever.
He watches every movement of the
nations;
let no rebel rise in defiance. *Interlude*

8 Let the whole world bless our God
and sing aloud his praises.
9 Our lives are in his hands,
and he keeps our feet from stumbling.
10 You have tested us, O God;
you have purified us like silver melted in
a crucible.
11 You captured us in your net
and laid the burden of slavery on our backs.
12 You sent troops to ride across our broken
bodies.
We went through fire and flood.
But you brought us to a place of great
abundance.

13 Now I come to your Temple with burnt
offerings
to fulfill the vows I made to you—
14 yes, the sacred vows you heard me make
when I was in deep trouble.
15 That is why I am sacrificing burnt offerings
to you—
the best of my rams as a pleasing aroma.
And I will sacrifice bulls and goats.
Interlude

16 Come and listen, all you who fear God,
and I will tell you what he did for me.
17 For I cried out to him for help,
praising him as I spoke.
18 If I had not confessed the sin in my heart,
my Lord would not have listened.
19 But God did listen!
He paid attention to my prayer.

20 Praise God, who did not ignore my prayer
and did not withdraw his unfailing love
from me.

PSALM 67

*For the choir director: A psalm, to be accompanied by
stringed instruments. A song.*

1 May God be merciful and bless us.
May his face shine with favor upon us.
Interlude
2 May your ways be known throughout the earth,
your saving power among people everywhere.
3 May the nations praise you, O God.
Yes, may all the nations praise you.

4 How glad the nations will be, singing for joy,
because you govern them with justice
and direct the actions of the whole world.
Interlude

66:6 Hebrew *the sea.*

5 May the nations praise you, O God.
Yes, may all the nations praise you.

6 Then the earth will yield its harvests,
and God, our God, will richly bless us.

7 Yes, God will bless us,
and people all over the world will fear him.

PSALM 68

For the choir director: A psalm of David. A song.

1 Arise, O God, and scatter your enemies.
Let those who hate God run for their
lives.

2 Drive them off like smoke blown by the wind.
Melt them like wax in fire.
Let the wicked perish in the presence of
God.

3 But let the godly rejoice.
Let them be glad in God's presence.
Let them be filled with joy.

4 Sing praises to God and to his name!
Sing loud praises to him who rides the
clouds.
His name is the LORD—
rejoice in his presence!

5 Father to the fatherless, defender of
widows—
this is God, whose dwelling is holy.

6 God places the lonely in families;
he sets the prisoners free and gives them
joy.
But for rebels, there is only famine and
distress.

7 O God, when you led your people from
Egypt,
when you marched through the
wilderness,   *Interlude*

8 the earth trembled, and the heavens poured
rain
before you, the God of Sinai,
before God, the God of Israel.

9 You sent abundant rain, O God,
to refresh the weary Promised Land.

10 There your people finally settled,
and with a bountiful harvest, O God,
you provided for your needy people.

11 The Lord announces victory,
and throngs of women shout the happy
news.

12 Enemy kings and their armies flee,
while the women of Israel divide the
plunder.

13 Though they lived among the sheepfolds,
now they are covered with silver and
gold,
as a dove is covered by its wings.

14 The Almighty scattered the enemy kings
like a blowing snowstorm on Mount
Zalmon.

15 The majestic mountains of Bashan
stretch high into the sky.

16 Why do you look with envy, O rugged
mountains,
at Mount Zion, where God has chosen to
live,
where the LORD himself will live forever?

17 Surrounded by unnumbered thousands of
chariots,
the Lord came from Mount Sinai into his
sanctuary.

18 When you ascended to the heights,
you led a crowd of captives.
You received gifts from the people,
even from those who rebelled against
you.
Now the LORD God will live among us
here.

19 Praise the Lord; praise God our savior!
For each day he carries us in his arms.
                                Interlude

20 Our God is a God who saves!
The Sovereign LORD rescues us from death.

21 But God will smash the heads of his
enemies,
crushing the skulls of those who love
their guilty ways.

22 The Lord says, "I will bring my enemies
down from Bashan;
I will bring them up from the depths of
the sea.

23 You, my people, will wash your feet in their
blood,
and even your dogs will get their share!"

24 Your procession has come into view,
O God—
the procession of my God and King
as he goes into the sanctuary.

25 Singers are in front, musicians are behind;
with them are young women playing
tambourines.

26 Praise God, all you people of Israel;
praise the LORD, the source of Israel's life.

27 Look, the little tribe of Benjamin leads
the way.

Then comes a great throng of rulers from
   Judah
   and all the rulers of Zebulun and Naphtali.

28 Summon your might, O God.
   Display your power, O God, as you have
      in the past.
29 The kings of the earth are bringing tribute
      to your Temple in Jerusalem.
30 Rebuke these enemy nations—
      these wild animals lurking in the reeds,
      this herd of bulls among the weaker calves.
   Humble those who demand tribute from
      us.*
   Scatter the nations that delight in war.
31 Let Egypt come with gifts of precious metals;
      let Ethiopia* bow in submission to God.
32 Sing to God, you kingdoms of the earth.
   Sing praises to the Lord.   *Interlude*

33 Sing to the one who rides across the ancient
      heavens,
      his mighty voice thundering from the sky.
34 Tell everyone about God's power.
   His majesty shines down on Israel;
      his strength is mighty in the heavens.
35 God is awesome in his sanctuary.
   The God of Israel gives power and
      strength to his people.

   Praise be to God!

PSALM **69**

*For the choir director: A psalm of David, to be sung to the
tune "Lilies."*

1 Save me, O God,
      for the floodwaters are up to my neck.
2 Deeper and deeper I sink into the mire;
      I can't find a foothold to stand on.
   I am in deep water,
      and the floods overwhelm me.
3 I am exhausted from crying for help;
      my throat is parched and dry.
   My eyes are swollen with weeping,
      waiting for my God to help me.

4 Those who hate me without cause
      are more numerous than the hairs on my
      head.
   These enemies who seek to destroy me
      are doing so without cause.
   They attack me with lies,
      demanding that I give back what I didn't
      steal.

5 O God, you know how foolish I am;
      my sins cannot be hidden from you.
6 Don't let those who trust in you stumble
      because of me,
      O Sovereign Lord Almighty.
   Don't let me cause them to be humiliated,
      O God of Israel.
7 For I am mocked and shamed for your sake;
      humiliation is written all over my face.
8 Even my own brothers pretend they don't
      know me;
      they treat me like a stranger.

9 Passion for your house burns within me,
      so those who insult you are also
      insulting me.
10 When I weep and fast before the Lord,
      they scoff at me.
11 When I dress in sackcloth to show sorrow,
      they make fun of me.
12 I am the favorite topic of town gossip,
      and all the drunkards sing about me.

13 But I keep right on praying to you, Lord,
      hoping this is the time you will show me
      favor.
   In your unfailing love, O God,
      answer my prayer with your sure salvation.
14 Pull me out of the mud;
      don't let me sink any deeper!
   Rescue me from those who hate me,
      and pull me from these deep waters.
15 Don't let the floods overwhelm me,
      or the deep waters swallow me,
      or the pit of death devour me.

16 Answer my prayers, O Lord,
      for your unfailing love is wonderful.
   Turn and take care of me,
      for your mercy is so plentiful.
17 Don't hide from your servant;
      answer me quickly, for I am in deep trouble!
18 Come and rescue me;
      free me from all my enemies.

19 You know the insults I endure—
      the humiliation and disgrace.
   You have seen all my enemies
      and know what they have said.
20 Their insults have broken my heart,
      and I am in despair.
   If only one person would show some pity;
      if only one would turn and comfort me.
21 But instead, they give me poison for food;
      they offer me sour wine to satisfy my thirst.

68:30 Or *Humble them until they submit, bringing pieces of silver as tribute.*   **68:31** Hebrew *Cush.*

²² Let the bountiful table set before them
  become a snare,
  and let their security become a trap.
²³ Let their eyes go blind so they cannot see,
  and let their bodies grow weaker and
  weaker.
²⁴ Pour out your fury on them;
  consume them with your burning anger.
²⁵ May their homes become desolate
  and their tents be deserted.
²⁶ To those you have punished, they add insult
  to injury;
  they scoff at the pain of those you have
  hurt.
²⁷ Pile their sins up high,
  and don't let them go free.
²⁸ Erase their names from the Book of Life;
  don't let them be counted among the
  righteous.

²⁹ I am suffering and in pain.
  Rescue me, O God, by your saving power.

³⁰ Then I will praise God's name with singing,
  and I will honor him with thanksgiving.
³¹ For this will please the LORD more than
  sacrificing an ox
  or presenting a bull with its horns and
  hooves.
³² The humble will see their God at work and
  be glad.
  Let all who seek God's help live in joy.
³³ For the LORD hears the cries of his needy ones;
  he does not despise his people who are
  oppressed.

³⁴ Praise him, O heaven and earth,
  the seas and all that move in them.
³⁵ For God will save Jerusalem*
  and rebuild the towns of Judah.
  His people will live there
  and take possession of the land.
³⁶ The descendants of those who obey him
  will inherit the land,
  and those who love him will live there in
  safety.

PSALM **70**

*For the choir director: A psalm of David, to bring us to
the LORD's remembrance.*

¹ Please, God, rescue me!
  Come quickly, LORD, and help me.
² May those who try to destroy me
  be humiliated and put to shame.

May those who take delight in my trouble
  be turned back in disgrace.
³ Let them be horrified by their shame,
  for they said, "Aha! We've got him now!"
⁴ But may all who search for you
  be filled with joy and gladness.
  May those who love your salvation
  repeatedly shout, "God is great!"
⁵ But I am poor and needy;
  please hurry to my aid, O God.
  You are my helper and my savior;
  O LORD, do not delay!

PSALM **71**

¹ O LORD, you are my refuge;
  never let me be disgraced.
² Rescue me! Save me from my enemies, for
  you are just.
  Turn your ear to listen and set me free.
³ Be to me a protecting rock of safety,
  where I am always welcome.
  Give the order to save me,
  for you are my rock and my fortress.

⁴ My God, rescue me from the power of the
  wicked,
  from the clutches of cruel oppressors.
⁵ O Lord, you alone are my hope.
  I've trusted you, O LORD, from childhood.
⁶ Yes, you have been with me from birth;
  from my mother's womb you have cared
  for me.
  No wonder I am always praising you!

⁷ My life is an example to many,
  because you have been my strength and
  protection.
⁸ That is why I can never stop praising you;
  I declare your glory all day long.

⁹ And now, in my old age, don't set me aside.
  Don't abandon me when my strength is
  failing.
¹⁰ For my enemies are whispering against me.
  They are plotting together to kill me.
¹¹ They say, "God has abandoned him.
  Let's go and get him,
  for there is no one to help him now."

¹² O God, don't stay away.
  My God, please hurry to help me.
¹³ Bring disgrace and destruction on those
  who accuse me.
  May humiliation and shame cover
  those who want to harm me.

69:35 Hebrew *Zion.*

¹⁴ But I will keep on hoping for you to help me;
  I will praise you more and more.
¹⁵ I will tell everyone about your righteousness.
  All day long I will proclaim your saving
    power,
  for I am overwhelmed by how much you
    have done for me.
¹⁶ I will praise your mighty deeds, O Sovereign
    LORD.
  I will tell everyone that you alone are just
    and good.

¹⁷ O God, you have taught me from my
    earliest childhood,
  and I have constantly told others about
    the wonderful things you do.
¹⁸ Now that I am old and gray,
  do not abandon me, O God.
  Let me proclaim your power to this new
    generation,
    your mighty miracles to all who come
      after me.

¹⁹ Your righteousness, O God, reaches to the
    highest heavens.
  You have done such wonderful things.
  Who can compare with you, O God?
²⁰ You have allowed me to suffer much
    hardship,
  but you will restore me to life again
  and lift me up from the depths of the
    earth.
²¹ You will restore me to even greater honor
  and comfort me once again.

²² Then I will praise you with music on the
    harp,
  because you are faithful to your
    promises, O God.
  I will sing for you with a lyre,
  O Holy One of Israel.
²³ I will shout for joy and sing your praises,
  for you have redeemed me.
²⁴ I will tell about your righteous deeds
    all day long,
  for everyone who tried to hurt me
    has been shamed and humiliated.

PSALM **72**

A psalm of Solomon.

¹ Give justice to the king, O God,
  and righteousness to the king's son.
² Help him judge your people in the right way;
  let the poor always be treated fairly.

³ May the mountains yield prosperity for all,
  and may the hills be fruitful,
  because the king does what is right.
⁴ Help him to defend the poor,
  to rescue the children of the needy,
  and to crush their oppressors.
⁵ May he live* as long as the sun shines,
  as long as the moon continues in the
    skies.
  Yes, forever!
⁶ May his reign be as refreshing as the
    springtime rains—
  like the showers that water the earth.
⁷ May all the godly flourish during his reign.
  May there be abundant prosperity until
    the end of time.

⁸ May he reign from sea to sea,
  and from the Euphrates River* to the
    ends of the earth.
⁹ Desert nomads will bow before him;
  his enemies will fall before him in the
    dust.
¹⁰ The western kings of Tarshish and the
    islands
  will bring him tribute.
  The eastern kings of Sheba and Seba
  will bring him gifts.
¹¹ All kings will bow before him,
  and all nations will serve him.

¹² He will rescue the poor when they cry to
    him;
  he will help the oppressed, who have no
    one to defend them.
¹³ He feels pity for the weak and the needy,
  and he will rescue them.
¹⁴ He will save them from oppression and
    from violence,
  for their lives are precious to him.

¹⁵ Long live the king!
  May the gold of Sheba be given to him.
  May the people always pray for him
  and bless him all day long.
¹⁶ May there be abundant crops throughout
    the land,
  flourishing even on the mountaintops.
  May the fruit trees flourish as they do in
    Lebanon,
  sprouting up like grass in a field.
¹⁷ May the king's name endure forever;
  may it continue as long as the sun shines.
  May all nations be blessed through him
  and bring him praise.

72:5 As in Greek version; Hebrew reads *May they fear you.* 72:8 Hebrew *the river.*

18 Bless the LORD God, the God of Israel,
   who alone does such wonderful things.
19 Bless his glorious name forever!
   Let the whole earth be filled with his
      glory.
   Amen and amen!

20 (This ends the prayers of David son of Jesse.)

BOOK THREE (Psalms 73–89)

P S A L M **73**

A psalm of Asaph.

1 Truly God is good to Israel,
   to those whose hearts are pure.

2 But as for me, I came so close to the edge of
      the cliff!
   My feet were slipping, and I was almost
      gone.
3 For I envied the proud
   when I saw them prosper despite their
      wickedness.
4 They seem to live such a painless life;
   their bodies are so healthy and strong.
5 They aren't troubled like other people
   or plagued with problems like everyone
      else.
6 They wear pride like a jeweled necklace,
   and their clothing is woven of cruelty.
7 These fat cats have everything
   their hearts could ever wish for!
8 They scoff and speak only evil;
   in their pride they seek to crush others.
9 They boast against the very heavens,
   and their words strut throughout the
      earth.
10 And so the people are dismayed and
      confused,
   drinking in all their words.
11 "Does God realize what is going on?" they
      ask.
   "Is the Most High even aware of what is
      happening?"
12 Look at these arrogant people—
   enjoying a life of ease while their riches
      multiply.

13 Was it for nothing that I kept my heart pure
   and kept myself from doing wrong?
14 All I get is trouble all day long;
   every morning brings me pain.

15 If I had really spoken this way,
   I would have been a traitor to your people.

16 So I tried to understand why the wicked
      prosper.
   But what a difficult task it is!
17 Then one day I went into your sanctuary,
      O God,
   and I thought about the destiny of the
      wicked.
18 Truly, you put them on a slippery path
   and send them sliding over the cliff to
      destruction.
19 In an instant they are destroyed,
   swept away by terrors.
20 Their present life is only a dream
   that is gone when they awake.
   When you arise, O Lord,
   you will make them vanish from this life.

21 Then I realized how bitter I had become,
   how pained I had been by all I had seen.
22 I was so foolish and ignorant—
   I must have seemed like a senseless
      animal to you.
23 Yet I still belong to you;
   you are holding my right hand.
24 You will keep on guiding me with your
      counsel,
   leading me to a glorious destiny.
25 Whom have I in heaven but you?
   I desire you more than anything on earth.
26 My health may fail, and my spirit may grow
      weak,
   but God remains the strength of my heart;
   he is mine forever.

27 But those who desert him will perish,
   for you destroy those who abandon you.
28 But as for me, how good it is to be near God!
   I have made the Sovereign LORD my
      shelter,
   and I will tell everyone about the
      wonderful things you do.

P S A L M **74**

A psalm of Asaph.

1 O God, why have you rejected us forever?
   Why is your anger so intense against the
      sheep of your own pasture?
2 Remember that we are the people you chose
      in ancient times,
   the tribe you redeemed as your own
      special possession!
   And remember Jerusalem,* your home
      here on earth.

74:2 Hebrew *Mount Zion.*

3 Walk through the awful ruins of the city;
see how the enemy has destroyed your
sanctuary.
4 There your enemies shouted their victorious
battle cries;
there they set up their battle standards.
5 They chopped down the entrance
like woodcutters in a forest.
6 With axes and picks,
they smashed the carved paneling.
7 They set the sanctuary on fire, burning it to
the ground.
They utterly defiled the place that bears
your holy name.
8 Then they thought, "Let's destroy
everything!"
So they burned down all the places
where God was worshiped.

9 We see no miraculous signs
as evidence that you will save us.
All the prophets are gone;
no one can tell us when it will end.
10 How long, O God, will you allow our
enemies to mock you?
Will you let them dishonor your name
forever?
11 Why do you hold back your strong right
hand?
Unleash your powerful fist and deliver a
deathblow.

12 You, O God, are my king from ages past,
bringing salvation to the earth.
13 You split the sea by your strength
and smashed the sea monster's heads.
14 You crushed the heads of Leviathan
and let the desert animals eat him.
15 You caused the springs and streams to gush
forth,
and you dried up rivers that never run dry.
16 Both day and night belong to you;
you made the starlight* and the sun.
17 You set the boundaries of the earth,
and you make both summer and winter.

18 See how these enemies scoff at you, LORD.
A foolish nation has dishonored your
name.
19 Don't let these wild beasts destroy your doves.
Don't forget your afflicted people forever.
20 Remember your covenant promises,
for the land is full of darkness and
violence!

21 Don't let the downtrodden be constantly
disgraced!
Instead, let these poor and needy ones
give praise to your name.

22 Arise, O God, and defend your cause.
Remember how these fools insult you all
day long.
23 Don't overlook these things your enemies
have said.
Their uproar of rebellion grows ever
louder.

PSALM **75**

For the choir director: A psalm of Asaph, to be sung to the tune "Do Not Destroy!" A song.

1 We thank you, O God!
We give thanks because you are near.
People everywhere tell of your mighty
miracles.

2 God says, "At the time I have planned,
I will bring justice against the wicked.
3 When the earth quakes and its people live
in turmoil,
I am the one who keeps its foundations
firm.   *Interlude*

4 "I warned the proud, 'Stop your boasting!'
I told the wicked, 'Don't raise your fists!
5 Don't lift your fists in defiance at the
heavens
or speak with rebellious arrogance.'"

6 For no one on earth—from east or west,
or even from the wilderness—
can raise another person up.
7 It is God alone who judges;
he decides who will rise and who will
fall.
8 For the LORD holds a cup in his hand;
it is full of foaming wine mixed with
spices.
He pours the wine out in judgment,
and all the wicked must drink it,
draining it to the dregs.

9 But as for me, I will always proclaim what
God has done;
I will sing praises to the God of Israel.*

10 For God says, "I will cut off the strength of
the wicked,
but I will increase the power of the
godly."

74:16 Or *moon;* Hebrew reads *light.*   75:9 Hebrew *of Jacob.*

PSALM 76

For the choir director: A psalm of Asaph, to be accompanied by stringed instruments. A song.

1 God is well known in Judah;
   his name is great in Israel.
2 Jerusalem* is where he lives;
   Mount Zion is his home.
3 There he breaks the arrows of the enemy,
   the shields and swords and weapons of
   his foes.   *Interlude*

4 You are glorious and more majestic
   than the everlasting mountains.*
5 The mightiest of our enemies have been
   plundered.
   They lie before us in the sleep of death.
   No warrior could lift a hand against us.
6 When you rebuked them, O God of Jacob,
   their horses and chariots stood still.

7 No wonder you are greatly feared!
   Who can stand before you when your
   anger explodes?
8 From heaven you sentenced your enemies;
   the earth trembled and stood silent
   before you.
9 You stand up to judge those who do evil,
   O God,
   and to rescue the oppressed of the earth.
                              Interlude

10 Human opposition only enhances your glory,
    for you use it as a sword of judgment.*

11 Make vows to the LORD your God, and fulfill
    them.
    Let everyone bring tribute to the
    Awesome One.
12 For he breaks the spirit of princes
    and is feared by the kings of the earth.

PSALM 77

For Jeduthun, the choir director: A psalm of Asaph.

1 I cry out to God without holding back.
   Oh, that God would listen to me!
2 When I was in deep trouble,
   I searched for the Lord.
   All night long I pray, with hands lifted
   toward heaven, pleading.
   There can be no joy for me until he acts.
3 I think of God, and I moan,
   overwhelmed with longing for his help.
                              Interlude

4 You don't let me sleep.
   I am too distressed even to pray!
5 I think of the good old days, long since ended,
6 when my nights were filled with joyful songs.
   I search my soul and think about the
   difference now.
7 Has the Lord rejected me forever?
   Will he never again show me favor?
8 Is his unfailing love gone forever?
   Have his promises permanently failed?
9 Has God forgotten to be kind?
   Has he slammed the door on his
   compassion?   *Interlude*

10 And I said, "This is my fate,
    that the blessings of the Most High have
    changed to hatred."
11 I recall all you have done, O LORD;
    I remember your wonderful deeds of
    long ago.
12 They are constantly in my thoughts.
    I cannot stop thinking about them.

13 O God, your ways are holy.
    Is there any god as mighty as you?
14 You are the God of miracles and wonders!
    You demonstrate your awesome power
    among the nations.
15 You have redeemed your people by your
    strength,
    the descendants of Jacob and of Joseph
    by your might.   *Interlude*

16 When the Red Sea* saw you, O God,
    its waters looked and trembled!
    The sea quaked to its very depths.
17 The clouds poured down their rain;
    the thunder rolled and crackled in the sky.
    Your arrows of lightning flashed.
18 Your thunder roared from the whirlwind;
    the lightning lit up the world!
    The earth trembled and shook.
19 Your road led through the sea,
    your pathway through the mighty waters—
    a pathway no one knew was there!
20 You led your people along that road like a
    flock of sheep,
    with Moses and Aaron as their shepherds.

PSALM 78

A psalm of Asaph.

1 O my people, listen to my teaching.
   Open your ears to what I am saying,

76:2 Hebrew *Salem,* another name for Jerusalem.   76:4 As in Greek version; Hebrew reads *than mountains filled with beasts of prey.*
76:10 The meaning of the Hebrew is uncertain.   77:16 Hebrew *the waters.*

2 for I will speak to you in a parable.
I will teach you hidden lessons from our
    past—
3 stories we have heard and know,
    stories our ancestors handed down to us.
4 We will not hide these truths from our
    children
        but will tell the next generation about
        the glorious deeds of the LORD.
    We will tell of his power and the mighty
    miracles he did.
5 For he issued his decree to Jacob;
    he gave his law to Israel.
He commanded our ancestors
    to teach them to their children,
6 so the next generation might know them—
    even the children not yet born—
        that they in turn might teach their
        children.
7 So each generation can set its hope anew on
    God,
        remembering his glorious miracles
        and obeying his commands.
8 Then they will not be like their ancestors—
    stubborn, rebellious, and unfaithful,
    refusing to give their hearts to God.

9 The warriors of Ephraim, though fully
    armed,
        turned their backs and fled when the day
        of battle came.
10 They did not keep God's covenant,
    and they refused to live by his law.
11 They forgot what he had done—
    the wonderful miracles he had shown
    them,
12   the miracles he did for their ancestors in
    Egypt, on the plain of Zoan.
13 For he divided the sea before them and led
    them through!
    The water stood up like walls beside
    them!
14 In the daytime he led them by a cloud,
    and at night by a pillar of fire.
15 He split open the rocks in the wilderness
    to give them plenty of water, as from a
    gushing spring.
16 He made streams pour from the rock,
    making the waters flow down like a river!

17 Yet they kept on with their sin,
    rebelling against the Most High in the
    desert.
18 They willfully tested God in their hearts,
    demanding the foods they craved.

19 They even spoke against God himself, saying,
    "God can't give us food in the desert."
20 Yes, he can strike a rock so water gushes out,
    but he can't give his people bread and
    meat."
21 When the LORD heard them, he was angry.
    The fire of his wrath burned against
    Jacob.
    Yes, his anger rose against Israel,
22   for they did not believe God
    or trust him to care for them.
23 But he commanded the skies to open—
    he opened the doors of heaven—
24   and rained down manna for them to eat.
    He gave them bread from heaven.
25   They ate the food of angels!
    God gave them all they could hold.
26 He released the east wind in the heavens
    and guided the south wind by his mighty
    power.
27 He rained down meat as thick as dust—
    birds as plentiful as the sands along the
    seashore!
28 He caused the birds to fall within their camp
    and all around their tents.
29 The people ate their fill.
    He gave them what they wanted.
30 But before they finished eating this food
    they had craved,
    while the meat was yet in their mouths,
31 the anger of God rose against them,
    and he killed their strongest men;
    he struck down the finest of Israel's
    young men.
32 But in spite of this, the people kept on
    sinning.
    They refused to believe in his miracles.
33 So he ended their lives in failure
    and gave them years of terror.

34 When God killed some of them, the rest
    finally sought him.
    They repented and turned to God.
35 Then they remembered that God was their
    rock,
    that their redeemer was the Most High.
36 But they followed him only with their
    words;
    they lied to him with their tongues.
37 Their hearts were not loyal to him.
    They did not keep his covenant.
38 Yet he was merciful and forgave their sins
    and didn't destroy them all.
    Many a time he held back his anger
    and did not unleash his fury!

39 For he remembered that they were merely
  mortal,
    gone in a moment like a breath of wind,
    never to return.
40 Oh, how often they rebelled against him in
  the desert
    and grieved his heart in the wilderness.
41 Again and again they tested God's patience
    and frustrated the Holy One of Israel.
42 They forgot about his power
    and how he rescued them from their
    enemies.
43 They forgot his miraculous signs in Egypt,
    his wonders on the plain of Zoan.
44 For he turned their rivers into blood,
    so no one could drink from the streams.
45 He sent vast swarms of flies to consume them
    and hordes of frogs to ruin them.
46 He gave their crops to caterpillars;
    their harvest was consumed by locusts.
47 He destroyed their grapevines with hail
    and shattered their sycamores with sleet.
48 He abandoned their cattle to the hail,
    their livestock to bolts of lightning.
49 He loosed on them his fierce anger—
    all his fury, rage, and hostility.
  He dispatched against them
    a band of destroying angels.
50 He turned his anger against them;
    he did not spare the Egyptians' lives
    but handed them over to the plague.
51 He killed the oldest son in each Egyptian
  family,
    the flower of youth throughout the land
    of Egypt.*
52 But he led his own people like a flock of
  sheep,
    guiding them safely through the
    wilderness.
53 He kept them safe so they were not afraid;
    but the sea closed in upon their enemies.
54 He brought them to the border of his holy
  land,
    to this land of hills he had won for them.
55 He drove out the nations before them;
    he gave them their inheritance by lot.
  He settled the tribes of Israel into their
  homes.

56 Yet though he did all this for them,
    they continued to test his patience.
  They rebelled against the Most High
    and refused to follow his decrees.

57 They turned back and were as faithless as
    their parents had been.
  They were as useless as a crooked bow.
58 They made God angry by building altars to
  other gods;
    they made him jealous with their idols.
59 When God heard them, he was very angry,
    and he rejected Israel completely.
60 Then he abandoned his dwelling at Shiloh,
    the Tabernacle where he had lived
    among the people.
61 He allowed the Ark of his might to be
  captured;
    he surrendered his glory into enemy hands.
62 He gave his people over to be butchered by
  the sword,
    because he was so angry with his own
    people—his special possession.
63 Their young men were killed by fire;
    their young women died before singing
    their wedding songs.
64 Their priests were slaughtered,
    and their widows could not mourn their
    deaths.
65 Then the Lord rose up as though waking
  from sleep,
    like a mighty man aroused from a
    drunken stupor.
66 He routed his enemies
    and sent them to eternal shame.
67 But he rejected Joseph's descendants;
    he did not choose the tribe of Ephraim.
68 He chose instead the tribe of Judah,
    Mount Zion, which he loved.
69 There he built his towering sanctuary,
    as solid and enduring as the earth itself.
70 He chose his servant David,
    calling him from the sheep pens.
71 He took David from tending the ewes and
  lambs
    and made him the shepherd of Jacob's
    descendants—
    God's own people, Israel.
72 He cared for them with a true heart
    and led them with skillful hands.

PSALM 79

A psalm of Asaph.

1 O God, pagan nations have conquered your
    land, your special possession.
  They have defiled your holy Temple
    and made Jerusalem a heap of ruins.

78:51 Hebrew *in the tents of Ham.*

2 They have left the bodies of your servants
   as food for the birds of heaven.
   The flesh of your godly ones
   has become food for the wild animals.
3 Blood has flowed like water all around
   Jerusalem;
   no one is left to bury the dead.
4 We are mocked by our neighbors,
   an object of scorn and derision to those
   around us.

5 O LORD, how long will you be angry with
   us? Forever?
   How long will your jealousy burn like fire?
6 Pour out your wrath on the nations that
   refuse to recognize you—
   on kingdoms that do not call upon your
   name.
7 For they have devoured your people Israel,*
   making the land a desolate wilderness.
8 Oh, do not hold us guilty for our former
   sins!
   Let your tenderhearted mercies quickly
   meet our needs,
   for we are brought low to the dust.
9 Help us, O God of our salvation!
   Help us for the honor of your name.
   Oh, save us and forgive our sins
   for the sake of your name.
10 Why should pagan nations be allowed to
   scoff,
   asking, "Where is their God?"
   Show us your vengeance against the nations,
   for they have spilled the blood of your
   servants.
11 Listen to the moaning of the prisoners.
   Demonstrate your great power by saving
   those condemned to die.

12 O Lord, take sevenfold vengeance on our
   neighbors
   for the scorn they have hurled at you.
13 Then we your people, the sheep of your
   pasture,
   will thank you forever and ever,
   praising your greatness from generation
   to generation.

PSALM 80

*For the choir director: A psalm of Asaph, to be sung to the
tune "Lilies of the Covenant."*

1 Please listen, O Shepherd of Israel,
   you who lead Israel* like a flock.

O God, enthroned above the cherubim,
   display your radiant glory
2 to Ephraim, Benjamin, and Manasseh.
   Show us your mighty power.
   Come to rescue us!

3 Turn us again to yourself, O God.
   Make your face shine down upon us.
   Only then will we be saved.

4 O LORD God Almighty,
   how long will you be angry and reject
   our prayers?
5 You have fed us with sorrow
   and made us drink tears by the bucketful.
6 You have made us the scorn of neighboring
   nations.
   Our enemies treat us as a joke.

7 Turn us again to yourself, O God Almighty.
   Make your face shine down upon us.
   Only then will we be saved.
8 You brought us from Egypt as though we
   were a tender vine;
   you drove away the pagan nations and
   transplanted us into your land.
9 You cleared the ground for us,
   and we took root and filled the land.
10 The mountains were covered with our
   shade;
   the mighty cedars were covered with our
   branches.
11 We spread our branches west to the
   Mediterranean Sea,
   our limbs east to the Euphrates River.*
12 But now, why have you broken down our
   walls
   so that all who pass may steal our fruit?
13 The boar from the forest devours us,
   and the wild animals feed on us.

14 Come back, we beg you, O God Almighty.
   Look down from heaven and see our
   plight.
   Watch over and care for this vine
15   that you yourself have planted,
   this son you have raised for yourself.
16 For we are chopped up and burned by our
   enemies.
   May they perish at the sight of your frown.
17 Strengthen the man you love,
   the son of your choice.
18 Then we will never forsake you again.
   Revive us so we can call on your name
   once more.

79:7 Hebrew *Jacob.* **80:1** Hebrew *Joseph.* **80:11** Hebrew *west to the sea, . . . east to the river.*

^19 Turn us again to yourself, O Lord God
Almighty.
Make your face shine down upon us.
Only then will we be saved.

PSALM **81**

*For the choir director: A psalm of Asaph, to be
accompanied by a stringed instrument.* *

^1 Sing praises to God, our strength.
Sing to the God of Israel. *
^2 Sing! Beat the tambourine.
Play the sweet lyre and the harp.
^3 Sound the trumpet for a sacred feast
when the moon is new,
when the moon is full.
^4 For this is required by the laws of Israel;
it is a law of the God of Jacob.
^5 He made it a decree for Israel*
when he attacked Egypt to set us free.

I heard an unknown voice that said,
^6 "Now I will relieve your shoulder of its
burden;
I will free your hands from their heavy
tasks.
^7 You cried to me in trouble, and I saved you;
I answered out of the thundercloud.
I tested your faith at Meribah,
when you complained that there was no
water.   *Interlude*

^8 "Listen to me, O my people, while I give
you stern warnings.
O Israel, if you would only listen!
^9 You must never have a foreign god;
you must not bow down before a false
god.
^10 For it was I, the Lord your God,
who rescued you from the land of Egypt.
Open your mouth wide, and I will fill it
with good things.

^11 "But no, my people wouldn't listen.
Israel did not want me around.
^12 So I let them follow their blind and
stubborn way,
living according to their own desires.
^13 But oh, that my people would listen to me!
Oh, that Israel would follow me, walking
in my paths!
^14 How quickly I would then subdue their
enemies!
How soon my hands would be upon
their foes!

^15 Those who hate the Lord would cringe
before him;
their desolation would last forever.
^16 But I would feed you with the best of foods.
I would satisfy you with wild honey from
the rock."

PSALM **82**

A psalm of Asaph.

^1 God presides over heaven's court;
he pronounces judgment on the judges:
^2 "How long will you judges hand down
unjust decisions?
How long will you shower special favors
on the wicked?   *Interlude*

^3 "Give fair judgment to the poor and the
orphan;
uphold the rights of the oppressed and
the destitute.
^4 Rescue the poor and helpless;
deliver them from the grasp of evil people.
^5 But these oppressors know nothing;
they are so ignorant!
And because they are in darkness,
the whole world is shaken to the core.
^6 I say, 'You are gods
and children of the Most High.
^7 But in death you are mere men.
You will fall as any prince,
for all must die.'"

^8 Rise up, O God, and judge the earth,
for all the nations belong to you.

PSALM **83**

A psalm of Asaph. A song.

^1 O God, don't sit idly by,
silent and inactive!
^2 Don't you hear the tumult of your enemies?
Don't you see what your arrogant
enemies are doing?
^3 They devise crafty schemes against your people,
laying plans against your precious ones.
^4 "Come," they say, "let us wipe out Israel as
a nation.
We will destroy the very memory of its
existence."
^5 This was their unanimous decision.
They signed a treaty as allies against you—
^6 these Edomites and Ishmaelites,
Moabites and Hagrites,

81:title Hebrew *according to the gittith.*   81:1 Hebrew *of Jacob.*   81:5 Hebrew *for Joseph.*

7 Gebalites, Ammonites, and Amalekites,
and people from Philistia and Tyre.
8 Assyria has joined them, too,
and is allied with the descendants of Lot.

Interlude

9 Do to them as you did to the Midianites
or as you did to Sisera and Jabin at the
Kishon River.
10 They were destroyed at Endor,
and their decaying corpses fertilized the
soil.
11 Let their mighty nobles die as Oreb and
Zeeb did.
Let all their princes die like Zebah and
Zalmunna,
12 for they said, "Let us seize for our own use
these pasturelands of God!"

13 O my God, blow them away like whirling
dust,
like chaff before the wind!
14 As a fire roars through a forest
and as a flame sets mountains ablaze,
15 chase them with your fierce storms;
terrify them with your tempests.
16 Utterly disgrace them
until they submit to your name, O LORD.
17 Let them be ashamed and terrified forever.
Make them failures in everything they
do,
18 until they learn that you alone are called
the LORD,
that you alone are the Most High,
supreme over all the earth.

PSALM 84

*For the choir director: A psalm of the descendants of
Korah, to be accompanied by a stringed instrument.**

1 How lovely is your dwelling place,
O LORD Almighty.
2 I long, yes, I faint with longing
to enter the courts of the LORD.
With my whole being, body and soul,
I will shout joyfully to the living God.
3 Even the sparrow finds a home there,
and the swallow builds her nest
and raises her young—
at a place near your altar,
O LORD Almighty, my King and my God!
4 How happy are those who can live in your
house,
always singing your praises.   *Interlude*

5 Happy are those who are strong in the LORD,
who set their minds on a pilgrimage to
Jerusalem.
6 When they walk through the Valley of
Weeping,*
it will become a place of refreshing springs,
where pools of blessing collect after the
rains!
7 They will continue to grow stronger,
and each of them will appear before God
in Jerusalem.*

8 O LORD God Almighty, hear my prayer.
Listen, O God of Israel.*   *Interlude*
9 O God, look with favor upon the king, our
protector!
Have mercy on the one you have anointed.

10 A single day in your courts
is better than a thousand anywhere else!
I would rather be a gatekeeper in the house
of my God
than live the good life in the homes of
the wicked.
11 For the LORD God is our light and protector.
He gives us grace and glory.
No good thing will the LORD withhold
from those who do what is right.
12 O LORD Almighty,
happy are those who trust in you.

PSALM 85

*For the choir director: A psalm of the descendants
of Korah.*

1 LORD, you have poured out amazing
blessings on your land!
You have restored the fortunes of Israel.*
2 You have forgiven the guilt of your people—
yes, you have covered all their sins.

Interlude

3 You have withdrawn your fury.
You have ended your blazing anger.
4 Now turn to us again, O God of our
salvation.
Put aside your anger against us.
5 Will you be angry with us always?
Will you prolong your wrath to distant
generations?
6 Won't you revive us again,
so your people can rejoice in you?
7 Show us your unfailing love, O LORD,
and grant us your salvation.

84:TITLE Hebrew *according to the gittith.*   84:6 Hebrew *valley of Baca.*   84:7 Hebrew *Zion.*   84:8 Hebrew *of Jacob.*   85:1 Hebrew *of Jacob.*

8 I listen carefully to what God the LORD is
saying,
for he speaks peace to his people, his
faithful ones.
But let them not return to their foolish ways.
9 Surely his salvation is near to those who
honor him;
our land will be filled with his glory.

10 Unfailing love and truth have met together.
Righteousness and peace have kissed!
11 Truth springs up from the earth,
and righteousness smiles down from
heaven.
12 Yes, the LORD pours down his blessings.
Our land will yield its bountiful crops.
13 Righteousness goes as a herald before him,
preparing the way for his steps.

PSALM 86
A prayer of David.

1 Bend down, O LORD, and hear my prayer;
answer me, for I need your help.
2 Protect me, for I am devoted to you.
Save me, for I serve you and trust you.
You are my God.
3 Be merciful, O Lord,
for I am calling on you constantly.
4 Give me happiness, O Lord,
for my life depends on you.
5 O Lord, you are so good, so ready to forgive,
so full of unfailing love for all who ask
your aid.
6 Listen closely to my prayer, O LORD;
hear my urgent cry.
7 I will call to you whenever trouble strikes,
and you will answer me.

8 Nowhere among the pagan gods is there a
god like you, O Lord.
There are no other miracles like yours.
9 All the nations—and you made each one—
will come and bow before you, Lord;
they will praise your great and holy name.
10 For you are great and perform great miracles.
You alone are God.

11 Teach me your ways, O LORD,
that I may live according to your truth!
Grant me purity of heart,
that I may honor you.
12 With all my heart I will praise you, O Lord
my God.

I will give glory to your name forever,
13 for your love for me is very great.
You have rescued me from the depths of
death*!

14 O God, insolent people rise up against me;
violent people are trying to kill me.
And you mean nothing to them.
15 But you, O Lord, are a merciful and
gracious God,
slow to get angry,
full of unfailing love and truth.
16 Look down and have mercy on me.
Give strength to your servant;
yes, save me, for I am your servant.
17 Send me a sign of your favor.
Then those who hate me will be put to
shame,
for you, O LORD, help and comfort me.

PSALM 87
A psalm of the descendants of Korah. A song.

1 On the holy mountain stands the city
founded by the LORD.
2 He loves the city of Jerusalem
more than any other city in Israel.*
3 O city of God,
what glorious things are said of you!
Interlude

4 I will record Egypt* and Babylon among
those who know me—
also Philistia and Tyre, and even distant
Ethiopia.*
They have all become citizens of Jerusalem!
5 And it will be said of Jerusalem,*
"Everyone has become a citizen here."
And the Most High will personally bless
this city.
6 When the LORD registers the nations,
he will say, "This one has become a
citizen of Jerusalem." *Interlude*

7 At all the festivals, the people will sing,
"The source of my life is in Jerusalem!"

PSALM 88
*For the choir director: A psalm of the descendants of
Korah, to be sung to the tune "The Suffering of
Affliction." A psalm of Heman the Ezrahite. A song.*

1 O LORD, God of my salvation,
I have cried out to you day and night.

86:13 Hebrew *of Sheol.* 87:2 Hebrew *He loves the gates of Zion more than all the dwellings of Jacob.* 87:4a Hebrew *Rahab,* the name of a mythical sea
monster that represents chaos in ancient literature. The name is used here as a poetic name for Egypt. 87:4b Hebrew *Cush.* 87:5 Hebrew *Zion.*

2 Now hear my prayer;
    listen to my cry.
3 For my life is full of troubles,
    and death draws near.
4 I have been dismissed as one who is dead,
    like a strong man with no strength left.
5 They have abandoned me to death,
    and I am as good as dead.
  I am forgotten,
    cut off from your care.
6 You have thrust me down to the lowest pit,
    into the darkest depths.
7 Your anger lies heavy on me;
    wave after wave engulfs me.   *Interlude*

8 You have caused my friends to loathe me;
    you have sent them all away.
  I am in a trap with no way of escape.
9   My eyes are blinded by my tears.
  Each day I beg for your help, O LORD;
    I lift my pleading hands to you for mercy.
10 Of what use to the dead are your miracles?
    Do the dead get up and praise you? *Interlude*

11 Can those in the grave declare your
      unfailing love?
  In the place of destruction, can they
      proclaim your faithfulness?
12 Can the darkness speak of your miracles?
    Can anyone in the land of forgetfulness
      talk about your righteousness?

13 O LORD, I cry out to you.
    I will keep on pleading day by day.
14 O LORD, why do you reject me?
    Why do you turn your face away from me?
15 I have been sickly and close to death since
      my youth.
  I stand helpless and desperate before
      your terrors.
16 Your fierce anger has overwhelmed me.
    Your terrors have cut me off.
17 They swirl around me like floodwaters all
      day long.
  They have encircled me completely.
18 You have taken away my companions and
      loved ones;
    only darkness remains.

PSALM **89**

A psalm of Ethan the Ezrahite.

1   I will sing of the tender mercies of the LORD
      forever!
  Young and old will hear of your faithfulness.

2 Your unfailing love will last forever.
    Your faithfulness is as enduring as the
      heavens.

3 The LORD said, "I have made a solemn
      agreement with David, my chosen
      servant.
  I have sworn this oath to him:
4 'I will establish your descendants as kings
      forever;
    they will sit on your throne from now
      until eternity.'"   *Interlude*

5 All heaven will praise your miracles, LORD;
    myriads of angels will praise you for your
      faithfulness.
6 For who in all of heaven can compare with
      the LORD?
  What mightiest angel is anything like the
      LORD?
7 The highest angelic powers stand in awe of
      God.
  He is far more awesome than those who
      surround his throne.
8 O LORD God Almighty!
    Where is there anyone as mighty as you,
      LORD?
  Faithfulness is your very character.

9 You are the one who rules the oceans.
    When their waves rise in fearful storms,
      you subdue them.
10 You are the one who crushed the great sea
      monster.*
  You scattered your enemies with your
      mighty arm.
11 The heavens are yours, and the earth is
      yours;
    everything in the world is yours—you
      created it all.
12 You created north and south.
    Mount Tabor and Mount Hermon praise
      your name.
13 Powerful is your arm!
    Strong is your hand!
  Your right hand is lifted high in glorious
      strength.
14 Your throne is founded on two strong
      pillars—righteousness and justice.
  Unfailing love and truth walk before you
      as attendants.
15 Happy are those who hear the joyful call to
      worship,
    for they will walk in the light of your
      presence, LORD.

89:10 Hebrew *Rahab*, the name of a mythical sea monster that represents chaos in ancient literature.

¹⁶ They rejoice all day long in your wonderful
reputation.
They exult in your righteousness.
¹⁷ You are their glorious strength.
Our power is based on your favor.
¹⁸ Yes, our protection comes from the LORD,
and he, the Holy One of Israel, has given
us our king.

¹⁹ You once spoke in a vision to your prophet
and said,
"I have given help to a warrior.
I have selected him from the common
people to be king.
²⁰ I have found my servant David.
I have anointed him with my holy oil.
²¹ I will steady him,
and I will make him strong.
²² His enemies will not get the best of him,
nor will the wicked overpower him.
²³ I will beat down his adversaries before him
and destroy those who hate him.
²⁴ My faithfulness and unfailing love will be
with him,
and he will rise to power because of me.
²⁵ I will extend his rule from the
Mediterranean Sea in the west
to the Tigris and Euphrates rivers in the
east.*
²⁶ And he will say to me, 'You are my Father,
my God, and the Rock of my salvation.'
²⁷ I will make him my firstborn son,
the mightiest king on earth.
²⁸ I will love him and be kind to him forever;
my covenant with him will never end.
²⁹ I will preserve an heir for him;
his throne will be as endless as the days
of heaven.
³⁰ But if his sons forsake my law
and fail to walk in my ways,
³¹ if they do not obey my decrees
and fail to keep my commands,
³² then I will punish their sin with the rod,
and their disobedience with beating.
³³ But I will never stop loving him,
nor let my promise to him fail.
³⁴ No, I will not break my covenant;
I will not take back a single word I said.
³⁵ I have sworn an oath to David,
and in my holiness I cannot lie:
³⁶ His dynasty will go on forever;
his throne is as secure as the sun,
³⁷ as eternal as the moon,
my faithful witness in the sky!" *Interlude*

³⁸ But now you have rejected him.
Why are you so angry with the one you
chose as king?
³⁹ You have renounced your covenant with
him,
for you have thrown his crown in the
dust.
⁴⁰ You have broken down the walls protecting
him
and laid in ruins every fort defending him.
⁴¹ Everyone who comes along has robbed him
while his neighbors mock.
⁴² You have strengthened his enemies against
him
and made them all rejoice.
⁴³ You have made his sword useless
and have refused to help him in battle.
⁴⁴ You have ended his splendor
and overturned his throne.
⁴⁵ You have made him old before his time
and publicly disgraced him. *Interlude*

⁴⁶ O LORD, how long will this go on?
Will you hide yourself forever?
How long will your anger burn like fire?
⁴⁷ Remember how short my life is,
how empty and futile this human
existence!
⁴⁸ No one can live forever; all will die.
No one can escape the power of the grave.
Interlude

⁴⁹ Lord, where is your unfailing love?
You promised it to David with a faithful
pledge.
⁵⁰ Consider, Lord, how your servants are
disgraced!
I carry in my heart the insults of so many
people.
⁵¹ Your enemies have mocked me, O LORD;
they mock the one you anointed as king.

⁵² Blessed be the LORD forever!
Amen and amen!

BOOK FOUR (Psalms 90–106)
P S A L M **90**
A prayer of Moses, the man of God.

¹ Lord, through all the generations
you have been our home!
² Before the mountains were created,
before you made the earth and the world,
you are God, without beginning or end.

89:25 Hebrew *I will set his hand on the sea, his right hand on the rivers.*

What Do Angels Do in the Life of a Christian? Read PSALM 91:1-16

People often wonder if Christians have "guardian angels," meaning that each person has a specific angel assigned to him or her. In this matter, the Bible is not clear. Certainly Scripture teaches that angels are actively involved in the lives of believers. This is illustrated throughout both the Old and New Testament (for examples, see 1 Kings 19:5, p. 311; Daniel 6:22, p. 727; Matthew 18:10, p. 812; Luke 16:22, p. 879; Acts 12:7, p. 938).

This passage contains some wonderful promises concerning angels. Yet these promises are "conditional." In other words, they will only be met once a person has fulfilled the specified condition. In this case, a person has to have a relationship with God to receive his promise of angelic protection. Once this condition is met, God will command his angels to keep his followers from danger and to rescue them from threatening situations, according to his will.

For the next note on "What Are Angels?" turn to p. 730.

CORNER STONES

---

3 You turn people back to dust, saying,
    "Return to dust!"
4 For you, a thousand years are as yesterday!
    They are like a few hours!
5 You sweep people away like dreams that
        disappear
    or like grass that springs up in the
        morning.
6 In the morning it blooms and flourishes,
    but by evening it is dry and withered.
7 We wither beneath your anger;
    we are overwhelmed by your fury.
8 You spread out our sins before you—
    our secret sins—and you see them all.
9 We live our lives beneath your wrath.
    We end our lives with a groan.

10 Seventy years are given to us!
    Some may even reach eighty.
    But even the best of these years are filled
        with pain and trouble;
    soon they disappear, and we are gone.
11 Who can comprehend the power of your
        anger?
    Your wrath is as awesome as the fear you
        deserve.
12 Teach us to make the most of our time,
    so that we may grow in wisdom.

13 O LORD, come back to us!
    How long will you delay?
    Take pity on your servants!
14 Satisfy us in the morning with your
        unfailing love,
    so we may sing for joy to the end of our
        lives.

15 Give us gladness in proportion to our
        former misery!
    Replace the evil years with good.
16 Let us see your miracles again;
    let our children see your glory at work.
17 And may the Lord our God show us his
        approval
    and make our efforts successful.
    Yes, make our efforts successful!

PSALM **91**
1 Those who live in the shelter of the Most
        High
    will find rest in the shadow of the
        Almighty.
2 This I declare of the LORD:
    He alone is my refuge, my place of safety;
    he is my God, and I am trusting him.
3 For he will rescue you from every trap
    and protect you from the fatal plague.
4 He will shield you with his wings.
    He will shelter you with his feathers.
    His faithful promises are your armor and
        protection.
5 Do not be afraid of the terrors of the night,
    nor fear the dangers of the day,
6 nor dread the plague that stalks in darkness,
    nor the disaster that strikes at midday.
7 Though a thousand fall at your side,
    though ten thousand are dying around
        you,
    these evils will not touch you.
8 But you will see it with your eyes;
    you will see how the wicked are
        punished.

9 If you make the LORD your refuge,
  if you make the Most High your shelter,
10 no evil will conquer you;
  no plague will come near your dwelling.
11 For he orders his angels
  to protect you wherever you go.
12 They will hold you with their hands
  to keep you from striking your foot on a
  stone.
13 You will trample down lions and poisonous
  snakes;
  you will crush fierce lions and serpents
  under your feet!

14 The LORD says, "I will rescue those who love
  me.
  I will protect those who trust in my
  name.
15 When they call on me, I will answer;
  I will be with them in trouble.
  I will rescue them and honor them.
16 I will satisfy them with a long life
  and give them my salvation."

PSALM 92

A psalm to be sung on the LORD's Day. A song.

1 It is good to give thanks to the LORD,
  to sing praises to the Most High.
2 It is good to proclaim your unfailing love in
  the morning,
  your faithfulness in the evening,
3 accompanied by the harp and lute
  and the harmony of the lyre.
4 You thrill me, LORD, with all you have done
  for me!
  I sing for joy because of what you have
  done.

5 O LORD, what great miracles you do!
  And how deep are your thoughts.
6 Only an ignorant person would not know
  this!
  Only a fool would not understand it.
7 Although the wicked flourish like weeds,
  and evildoers blossom with success,
  there is only eternal destruction ahead of
  them.
8 But you are exalted in the heavens.
  You, O LORD, continue forever.
9 Your enemies, LORD, will surely perish;
  all evildoers will be scattered.

10 But you have made me as strong as a wild
  bull.
  How refreshed I am by your power!

11 With my own eyes I have seen the downfall
  of my enemies;
  with my own ears I have heard the defeat
  of my wicked opponents.
12 But the godly will flourish like palm trees
  and grow strong like the cedars of
  Lebanon.
13 For they are transplanted into the LORD's
  own house.
  They flourish in the courts of our God.
14 Even in old age they will still produce fruit;
  they will remain vital and green.
15 They will declare, "The LORD is just!
  He is my rock!
  There is nothing but goodness in him!"

PSALM 93

1 The LORD is king! He is robed in majesty.
  Indeed, the LORD is robed in majesty and
  armed with strength.
  The world is firmly established;
  it cannot be shaken.

2 Your throne, O LORD, has been established
  from time immemorial.
  You yourself are from the everlasting past.
3 The mighty oceans have roared, O LORD.
  The mighty oceans roar like thunder;
  the mighty oceans roar as they pound the
  shore.
4 But mightier than the violent raging of the
  seas,
  mightier than the breakers on the shore—
  the LORD above is mightier than these!
5 Your royal decrees cannot be changed.
  The nature of your reign, O LORD, is
  holiness forever.

PSALM 94

1 O LORD, the God to whom vengeance belongs,
  O God of vengeance, let your glorious
  justice be seen!
2 Arise, O judge of the earth.
  Sentence the proud to the penalties they
  deserve.
3 How long, O LORD?
  How long will the wicked be allowed to
  gloat?
4 Hear their arrogance!
  How these evildoers boast!
5 They oppress your people, LORD,
  hurting those you love.
6 They kill widows and foreigners
  and murder orphans.

7 "The LORD isn't looking," they say,
"and besides, the God of Israel* doesn't
care."

8 Think again, you fools!
When will you finally catch on?
9 Is the one who made your ears deaf?
Is the one who formed your eyes blind?
10 He punishes the nations—won't he also
punish you?
He knows everything—doesn't he also
know what you are doing?
11 The LORD knows people's thoughts,
that they are worthless!

12 Happy are those whom you discipline, LORD,
and those whom you teach from your
law.
13 You give them relief from troubled times
until a pit is dug for the wicked.
14 The LORD will not reject his people;
he will not abandon his own special
possession.
15 Judgment will come again for the righteous,
and those who are upright will have a
reward.

16 Who will protect me from the wicked?
Who will stand up for me against
evildoers?
17 Unless the LORD had helped me,
I would soon have died.
18 I cried out, "I'm slipping!"
and your unfailing love, O LORD,
supported me.
19 When doubts filled my mind,
your comfort gave me renewed hope and
cheer.

20 Can unjust leaders claim that God is on
their side—
leaders who permit injustice by their laws?
21 They attack the righteous
and condemn the innocent to death.
22 But the LORD is my fortress;
my God is a mighty rock where I can hide.
23 God will make the sins of evil people fall
back upon them.
He will destroy them for their sins.
The LORD our God will destroy them.

PSALM 95

1 Come, let us sing to the LORD!
Let us give a joyous shout to the rock of
our salvation!

2 Let us come before him with thanksgiving.
Let us sing him psalms of praise.
3 For the LORD is a great God,
the great King above all gods.
4 He owns the depths of the earth,
and even the mightiest mountains are his.
5 The sea belongs to him, for he made it.
His hands formed the dry land, too.

6 Come, let us worship and bow down.
Let us kneel before the LORD our maker,
7 for he is our God.
We are the people he watches over,
the sheep under his care.

Oh, that you would listen to his voice today!
8 The LORD says, "Don't harden your hearts as
Israel did at Meribah,
as they did at Massah in the wilderness.
9 For there your ancestors tried my patience;
they courted my wrath though they had
seen my many miracles.
10 For forty years I was angry with them, and I
said,
'They are a people whose hearts turn
away from me.
They refuse to do what I tell them.'
11 So in my anger I made a vow:
'They will never enter my place of rest.'"

PSALM 96

1 Sing a new song to the LORD!
Let the whole earth sing to the LORD!
2 Sing to the LORD; bless his name.
Each day proclaim the good news that he
saves.
3 Publish his glorious deeds among the
nations.
Tell everyone about the amazing things
he does.
4 Great is the LORD! He is most worthy of
praise!
He is to be revered above all the gods.
5 The gods of other nations are merely idols,
but the LORD made the heavens!
6 Honor and majesty surround him;
strength and beauty are in his sanctuary.

7 O nations of the world, recognize the LORD;
recognize that the LORD is glorious and
strong.
8 Give to the LORD the glory he deserves!
Bring your offering and come to worship
him.

94:7 Hebrew *of Jacob.*

⁹ Worship the LORD in all his holy splendor.
Let all the earth tremble before him.
¹⁰ Tell all the nations that the LORD is king.
The world is firmly established and
cannot be shaken.
He will judge all peoples fairly.

¹¹ Let the heavens be glad, and let the earth
rejoice!
Let the sea and everything in it shout his
praise!
¹² Let the fields and their crops burst forth
with joy!
Let the trees of the forest rustle with praise
¹³ before the LORD!
For the LORD is coming!
He is coming to judge the earth.
He will judge the world with righteousness
and all the nations with his truth.

P S A L M **97**

¹ The LORD is king! Let the earth rejoice!
Let the farthest islands be glad.
² Clouds and darkness surround him.
Righteousness and justice are the
foundation of his throne.
³ Fire goes forth before him
and burns up all his foes.
⁴ His lightning flashes out across the world.
The earth sees and trembles.
⁵ The mountains melt like wax before the
LORD,
before the Lord of all the earth.
⁶ The heavens declare his righteousness;
every nation sees his glory.
⁷ Those who worship idols are disgraced—
all who brag about their worthless gods—
for every god must bow to him.
⁸ Jerusalem* has heard and rejoiced,
and all the cities of Judah are glad
because of your justice, LORD!
⁹ For you, O LORD, are most high over all the
earth;
you are exalted far above all gods.

¹⁰ You who love the LORD, hate evil!
He protects the lives of his godly people
and rescues them from the power of the
wicked.
¹¹ Light shines on the godly,
and joy on those who do right.
¹² May all who are godly be happy in the LORD
and praise his holy name!

P S A L M **98**

A psalm.

¹ Sing a new song to the LORD,
for he has done wonderful deeds.
He has won a mighty victory
by his power and holiness.
² The LORD has announced his victory
and has revealed his righteousness to
every nation!
³ He has remembered his promise to love
and be faithful to Israel.
The whole earth has seen the salvation of
our God.

⁴ Shout to the LORD, all the earth;
break out in praise and sing for joy!
⁵ Sing your praise to the LORD with the harp,
with the harp and melodious song,
⁶ with trumpets and the sound of the
ram's horn.
Make a joyful symphony before the LORD,
the King!

⁷ Let the sea and everything in it shout his
praise!
Let the earth and all living things join in.
⁸ Let the rivers clap their hands in glee!
Let the hills sing out their songs of joy
⁹ before the LORD.
For the LORD is coming to judge the earth.
He will judge the world with justice,
and the nations with fairness.

P S A L M **99**

¹ The LORD is king!
Let the nations tremble!
He sits on his throne between the cherubim.
Let the whole earth quake!
² The LORD sits in majesty in Jerusalem,*
supreme above all the nations.
³ Let them praise your great and awesome
name.
Your name is holy!
⁴ Mighty king, lover of justice,
you have established fairness.
You have acted with justice
and righteousness throughout Israel.*
⁵ Exalt the LORD our God!
Bow low before his feet, for he is holy!

⁶ Moses and Aaron were among his priests;
Samuel also called on his name.
They cried to the LORD for help,
and he answered them.

97:8 Hebrew *Zion.*   99:2 Hebrew *Zion.*   99:4 Hebrew *Jacob.*

7 He spoke to them from the pillar of cloud,
and they followed the decrees and
principles he gave them.
8 O LORD our God, you answered them.
You were a forgiving God,
but you punished them when they went
wrong.

9 Exalt the LORD our God
and worship at his holy mountain in
Jerusalem,
for the LORD our God is holy!

PSALM 100

A psalm of thanksgiving.

1 Shout with joy to the LORD, O earth!
2 Worship the LORD with gladness.
Come before him, singing with joy.
3 Acknowledge that the LORD is God!
He made us, and we are his.
We are his people, the sheep of his
pasture.

4 Enter his gates with thanksgiving;
go into his courts with praise.
Give thanks to him and bless his name.
5 For the LORD is good.
His unfailing love continues forever,
and his faithfulness continues to each
generation.

PSALM 101

A psalm of David.

1 I will sing of your love and justice.
I will praise you, LORD, with songs.
2 I will be careful to live a blameless life—
when will you come to my aid?
I will lead a life of integrity
in my own home.
3 I will refuse to look at
anything vile and vulgar.
I hate all crooked dealings;
I will have nothing to do with them.
4 I will reject perverse ideas
and stay away from every evil.
5 I will not tolerate people who slander their
neighbors.
I will not endure conceit and pride.

6 I will keep a protective eye on the godly,
so they may dwell with me in safety.
Only those who are above reproach
will be allowed to serve me.

7 I will not allow deceivers to serve me,
and liars will not be allowed to enter my
presence.
8 My daily task will be to ferret out criminals
and free the city of the LORD from their
grip.

PSALM 102

*A prayer of one overwhelmed with trouble, pouring out
problems before the LORD.*

1 LORD, hear my prayer!
Listen to my plea!
2 Don't turn away from me
in my time of distress.
Bend down your ear
and answer me quickly when I call to you,
3 for my days disappear like smoke,
and my bones burn like red-hot coals.
4 My heart is sick, withered like grass,
and I have lost my appetite.
5 Because of my groaning,
I am reduced to skin and bones.
6 I am like an owl in the desert,
like a lonely owl in a far-off wilderness.
7 I lie awake,
lonely as a solitary bird on the roof.
8 My enemies taunt me day after day.
They mock and curse me.
9 I eat ashes instead of my food.
My tears run down into my drink
10 because of your anger and wrath.
For you have picked me up and thrown
me out.
11 My life passes as swiftly as the evening
shadows.
I am withering like grass.

12 But you, O LORD, will rule forever.
Your fame will endure to every
generation.
13 You will arise and have mercy on
Jerusalem*—
and now is the time to pity her,
now is the time you promised to help.
14 For your people love every stone in her walls
and show favor even to the dust in her
streets.
15 And the nations will tremble before the
LORD.
The kings of the earth will tremble before
his glory.
16 For the LORD will rebuild Jerusalem.
He will appear in his glory.

102:13 Hebrew *Zion;* also in 102:16.

¹⁷ He will listen to the prayers of the destitute.
    He will not reject their pleas.

¹⁸ Let this be recorded for future generations,
    so that a nation yet to be created will
        praise the LORD.
¹⁹ Tell them the LORD looked down
    from his heavenly sanctuary.
    He looked to the earth from heaven
²⁰   to hear the groans of the prisoners,
    to release those condemned to die.
²¹ And so the LORD's fame will be celebrated in
        Zion,
    his praises in Jerusalem,
²² when multitudes gather together
    and kingdoms come to worship the LORD.

²³ He has cut me down in midlife,
    shortening my days.
²⁴ But I cried to him, "My God, who lives
        forever,
    don't take my life while I am still so
        young!
²⁵ In ages past you laid the foundation of the
        earth,
    and the heavens are the work of your hands.
²⁶ Even they will perish, but you remain forever;
    they will wear out like old clothing.
    You will change them like a garment,
    and they will fade away.
²⁷ But you are always the same;
    your years never end.
²⁸ The children of your people
    will live in security.
    Their children's children
    will thrive in your presence."

P S A L M **103**

A psalm of David.

¹ Praise the LORD, I tell myself;
    with my whole heart, I will praise his
        holy name.
² Praise the LORD, I tell myself,
    and never forget the good things he does
        for me.
³ He forgives all my sins
    and heals all my diseases.
⁴ He ransoms me from death
    and surrounds me with love and tender
        mercies.
⁵ He fills my life with good things.
    My youth is renewed like the eagle's!
⁶ The LORD gives righteousness
    and justice to all who are treated unfairly.

⁷ He revealed his character to Moses
    and his deeds to the people of Israel.
⁸ The LORD is merciful and gracious;
    he is slow to get angry and full of
        unfailing love.
⁹ He will not constantly accuse us,
    nor remain angry forever.
¹⁰ He has not punished us for all our sins,
    nor does he deal with us as we deserve.
¹¹ For his unfailing love toward those who fear
        him
    is as great as the height of the heavens
        above the earth.
¹² He has removed our rebellious acts
    as far away from us as the east is from the
        west.
¹³ The LORD is like a father to his children,
    tender and compassionate to those who
        fear him.
¹⁴ For he understands how weak we are;
    he knows we are only dust.
¹⁵ Our days on earth are like grass;
    like wildflowers, we bloom and die.
¹⁶ The wind blows, and we are gone—
    as though we had never been here.
¹⁷ But the love of the LORD remains forever
    with those who fear him.
    His salvation extends to the children's
        children
¹⁸   of those who are faithful to his covenant,
    of those who obey his commandments!

¹⁹ The LORD has made the heavens his throne;
    from there he rules over everything.
²⁰ Praise the LORD, you angels of his,
    you mighty creatures who carry out his plans,
    listening for each of his commands.
²¹ Yes, praise the LORD, you armies of angels
    who serve him and do his will!
²² Praise the LORD, everything he has created,
    everywhere in his kingdom.
    As for me—I, too, will praise the LORD.

P S A L M **104**

¹ Praise the LORD, I tell myself;
    O LORD my God, how great you are!
    You are robed with honor and with majesty;
²   you are dressed in a robe of light.
    You stretch out the starry curtain of the
        heavens;
³   you lay out the rafters of your home in
        the rain clouds.
    You make the clouds your chariots;
    you ride upon the wings of the wind.

4 The winds are your messengers;
    flames of fire are your servants.

5 You placed the world on its foundation
    so it would never be moved.
6 You clothed the earth with floods of water,
    water that covered even the mountains.
7 At the sound of your rebuke, the water fled;
    at the sound of your thunder, it fled away.
8 Mountains rose and valleys sank
    to the levels you decreed.
9 Then you set a firm boundary for the seas,
    so they would never again cover the earth.

10 You make the springs pour water into ravines,
    so streams gush down from the
        mountains.
11 They provide water for all the animals,
    and the wild donkeys quench their thirst.
12 The birds nest beside the streams
    and sing among the branches of the trees.
13 You send rain on the mountains from your
        heavenly home,
    and you fill the earth with the fruit of
        your labor.
14 You cause grass to grow for the cattle.
    You cause plants to grow for people to
        use.
    You allow them to produce food from the
        earth—
15   wine to make them glad,
    olive oil as lotion for their skin,
    and bread to give them strength.
16 The trees of the LORD are well cared for—
    the cedars of Lebanon that he planted.
17 There the birds make their nests,
    and the storks make their homes in the
        firs.
18 High in the mountains are pastures for the
        wild goats,
    and the rocks form a refuge for rock
        badgers.*
19 You made the moon to mark the seasons
    and the sun that knows when to set.
20 You send the darkness, and it becomes
        night,
    when all the forest animals prowl about.
21 Then the young lions roar for their food,
    but they are dependent on God.
22 At dawn they slink back
    into their dens to rest.
23 Then people go off to their work;
    they labor until the evening shadows fall
        again.

24 O LORD, what a variety of things you have
        made!
    In wisdom you have made them all.
    The earth is full of your creatures.
25 Here is the ocean, vast and wide,
    teeming with life of every kind,
    both great and small.
26 See the ships sailing along,
    and Leviathan, which you made to play
        in the sea.
27 Every one of these depends on you
    to give them their food as they need it.
28 When you supply it, they gather it.
    You open your hand to feed them, and
        they are satisfied.
29 But if you turn away from them, they panic.
    When you take away their breath, they die
    and turn again to dust.
30 When you send your Spirit, new life is born
    to replenish all the living of the earth.

31 May the glory of the LORD last forever!
    The LORD rejoices in all he has made!
32 The earth trembles at his glance;
    the mountains burst into flame at his
        touch.
33 I will sing to the LORD as long as I live.
    I will praise my God to my last breath!
34 May he be pleased by all these thoughts
        about him,
    for I rejoice in the LORD.
35 Let all sinners vanish from the face of the
        earth;
    let the wicked disappear forever.
    As for me—I will praise the LORD!

Praise the LORD!

PSALM **105**
1 Give thanks to the LORD and proclaim his
        greatness.
    Let the whole world know what he has
        done.
2 Sing to him; yes, sing his praises.
    Tell everyone about his miracles.
3 Exult in his holy name;
    O worshipers of the LORD, rejoice!
4 Search for the LORD and for his strength,
    and keep on searching.
5 Think of the wonderful works he has done,
    the miracles and the judgments he
        handed down,
6 O children of Abraham, God's servant,
    O descendants of Jacob, God's chosen one.

104:18 Or *coneys,* or *hyraxes.*

7 He is the LORD our God.
His rule is seen throughout the land.
8 He always stands by his covenant—
the commitment he made to a thousand
generations.
9 This is the covenant he made with Abraham
and the oath he swore to Isaac.
10 He confirmed it to Jacob as a decree,
to the people of Israel as a never-ending
treaty:
11 "I will give you the land of Canaan
as your special possession."

12 He said this when they were few in number,
a tiny group of strangers in Canaan.
13 They wandered back and forth between
nations,
from one kingdom to another.
14 Yet he did not let anyone oppress them.
He warned kings on their behalf:
15 "Do not touch these people I have chosen,
and do not hurt my prophets."
16 He called for a famine on the land of
Canaan,
cutting off its food supply.
17 Then he sent someone to Egypt ahead of
them—
Joseph, who was sold as a slave.
18 There in prison, they bruised his feet with
fetters
and placed his neck in an iron collar.
19 Until the time came to fulfill his word,
the LORD tested Joseph's character.
20 Then Pharaoh sent for him and set him free;
the ruler of the nation opened his prison
door.
21 Joseph was put in charge of all the king's
household;
he became ruler over all the king's
possessions.
22 He could instruct the king's aides as he pleased
and teach the king's advisers.

23 Then Israel arrived in Egypt;
Jacob lived as a foreigner in the land of
Ham.
24 And the LORD multiplied the people of Israel
until they became too mighty for their
enemies.
25 Then he turned the Egyptians against the
Israelites,
and they plotted against the LORD's
servants.

26 But the LORD sent Moses his servant,
along with Aaron, whom he had chosen.

27 They performed miraculous signs among
the Egyptians,
and miracles in the land of Ham.
28 The LORD blanketed Egypt in darkness,
for they had defied his commands to let
his people go.
29 He turned the nation's water into blood,
poisoning all the fish.
30 Then frogs overran the land;
they were found even in the king's
private rooms.
31 When he spoke, flies descended on the
Egyptians,
and gnats swarmed across Egypt.
32 Instead of rain, he sent murderous hail,
and flashes of lightning overwhelmed
the land.
33 He ruined their grapevines and fig trees
and shattered all the trees.
34 He spoke, and hordes of locusts came—
locusts beyond number.
35 They ate up everything green in the land,
destroying all the crops.
36 Then he killed the oldest child in each
Egyptian home,
the pride and joy of each family.

37 But he brought his people safely out of
Egypt, loaded with silver and gold;
there were no sick or feeble people
among them.
38 Egypt was glad when they were gone,
for the dread of them was great.
39 The LORD spread out a cloud above them as
a covering
and gave them a great fire to light the
darkness.
40 They asked for meat, and he sent them quail;
he gave them manna—bread from heaven.
41 He opened up a rock, and water gushed out
to form a river through the dry and
barren land.
42 For he remembered his sacred promise
to Abraham his servant.
43 So he brought his people out of Egypt with
joy,
his chosen ones with rejoicing.
44 He gave his people the lands of pagan nations,
and they harvested crops that others had
planted.
45 All this happened so they would follow his
principles
and obey his laws.

Praise the LORD!

PSALM **106**

1 Praise the LORD!

Give thanks to the LORD, for he is good!
His faithful love endures forever.
2 Who can list the glorious miracles of the
LORD?
Who can ever praise him half enough?
3 Happy are those who deal justly with others
and always do what is right.

4 Remember me, too, LORD, when you show
favor to your people;
come to me with your salvation.
5 Let me share in the prosperity of your
chosen ones.
Let me rejoice in the joy of your people;
let me praise you with those who are
your heritage.

6 Both we and our ancestors have sinned.
We have done wrong! We have acted
wickedly!
7 Our ancestors in Egypt
were not impressed by the LORD's miracles.
They soon forgot his many acts of kindness
to them.
Instead, they rebelled against him at the
Red Sea.*
8 Even so, he saved them—
to defend the honor of his name
and to demonstrate his mighty power.
9 He commanded the Red Sea* to divide, and
a dry path appeared.
He led Israel across the sea bottom that
was as dry as a desert.
10 So he rescued them from their enemies
and redeemed them from their foes.
11 Then the water returned and covered their
enemies;
not one of them survived.
12 Then at last his people believed his promises.
Then they finally sang his praise.

13 Yet how quickly they forgot what he had
done!
They wouldn't wait for his counsel!
14 In the wilderness, their desires ran wild,
testing God's patience in that dry land.
15 So he gave them what they asked for,
but he sent a plague along with it.
16 The people in the camp were jealous of Moses
and envious of Aaron, the LORD's holy
priest.

17 Because of this, the earth opened up;
it swallowed Dathan
and buried Abiram and the other rebels.
18 Fire fell upon their followers;
a flame consumed the wicked.
19 The people made a calf at Mount Sinai*;
they bowed before an image made of
gold.
20 They traded their glorious God
for a statue of a grass-eating ox!
21 They forgot God, their savior,
who had done such great things in
Egypt—
22 such wonderful things in that land,
such awesome deeds at the Red Sea.
23 So he declared he would destroy them.
But Moses, his chosen one, stepped
between the LORD and the people.
He begged him to turn from his anger
and not destroy them.

24 The people refused to enter the pleasant
land,
for they wouldn't believe his promise to
care for them.
25 Instead, they grumbled in their tents
and refused to obey the LORD.
26 Therefore, he swore
that he would kill them in the wilderness,
27 that he would scatter their descendants
among the nations,
exiling them to distant lands.

28 Then our ancestors joined in the worship of
Baal at Peor;
they even ate sacrifices offered to the dead!
29 They angered the LORD with all these things,
so a plague broke out among them.
30 But Phinehas had the courage to step in,
and the plague was stopped.
31 So he has been regarded as a righteous man
ever since that time.

32 At Meribah, too, they angered the LORD,
causing Moses serious trouble.
33 They made Moses angry,*
and he spoke foolishly.

34 Israel failed to destroy the nations in the land,
as the LORD had told them to.
35 Instead, they mingled among the pagans
and adopted their evil customs.
36 They worshiped their idols,
and this led to their downfall.

106:7 Hebrew *at the sea, the sea of reeds.*   **106:9** Hebrew *sea of reeds;* also in 106:22.   **106:19** Hebrew *at Horeb,* another name for Sinai.
106:33 Hebrew *They embittered his spirit.*

37 They even sacrificed their sons
   and their daughters to the demons.
38 They shed innocent blood,
   the blood of their sons and daughters.
   By sacrificing them to the idols of Canaan,
   they polluted the land with murder.
39 They defiled themselves by their evil deeds,
   and their love of idols was adultery in
   the LORD's sight.

40 That is why the LORD's anger burned against
   his people,
   and he abhorred his own special
   possession.
41 He handed them over to pagan nations,
   and those who hated them ruled over
   them.
42 Their enemies crushed them
   and brought them under their cruel
   power.
43 Again and again he delivered them,
   but they continued to rebel against him,
   and they were finally destroyed by their
   sin.
44 Even so, he pitied them in their distress
   and listened to their cries.
45 He remembered his covenant with them
   and relented because of his unfailing love.
46 He even caused their captors
   to treat them with kindness.

47 O LORD our God, save us!
   Gather us back from among the nations,
   so we can thank your holy name
   and rejoice and praise you.

48 Blessed be the LORD, the God of Israel,
   from everlasting to everlasting!
   Let all the people say, "Amen!"

   Praise the LORD!

BOOK FIVE (Psalms 107–150)
P S A L M **107**

1 Give thanks to the LORD, for he is good!
   His faithful love endures forever.
2 Has the LORD redeemed you? Then speak
   out!
   Tell others he has saved you from your
   enemies.
3 For he has gathered the exiles from many
   lands,
   from east and west, from north and south.

4 Some wandered in the desert,
   lost and homeless.

5 Hungry and thirsty,
   they nearly died.
6 "LORD, help!" they cried in their trouble,
   and he rescued them from their distress.
7 He led them straight to safety,
   to a city where they could live.
8 Let them praise the LORD for his great love
   and for all his wonderful deeds to them.
9 For he satisfies the thirsty
   and fills the hungry with good things.

10 Some sat in darkness and deepest gloom,
   miserable prisoners in chains.
11 They rebelled against the words of God,
   scorning the counsel of the Most High.
12 That is why he broke them with hard labor;
   they fell, and no one helped them rise
   again.
13 "LORD, help!" they cried in their trouble,
   and he saved them from their distress.
14 He led them from the darkness and deepest
   gloom;
   he snapped their chains.
15 Let them praise the LORD for his great love
   and for all his wonderful deeds to them.
16 For he broke down their prison gates of bronze;
   he cut apart their bars of iron.

17 Some were fools in their rebellion;
   they suffered for their sins.
18 Their appetites were gone,
   and death was near.
19 "LORD, help!" they cried in their trouble,
   and he saved them from their distress.
20 He spoke, and they were healed—
   snatched from the door of death.
21 Let them praise the LORD for his great love
   and for all his wonderful deeds to them.
22 Let them offer sacrifices of thanksgiving
   and sing joyfully about his glorious acts.

23 Some went off in ships,
   plying the trade routes of the world.
24 They, too, observed the LORD's power in action,
   his impressive works on the deepest seas.
25 He spoke, and the winds rose,
   stirring up the waves.
26 Their ships were tossed to the heavens
   and sank again to the depths;
   the sailors cringed in terror.
27 They reeled and staggered like drunkards
   and were at their wits' end.
28 "LORD, help!" they cried in their trouble,
   and he saved them from their distress.
29 He calmed the storm to a whisper
   and stilled the waves.

30 What a blessing was that stillness
   as he brought them safely into harbor!
31 Let them praise the LORD for his great love
   and for all his wonderful deeds to them.
32 Let them exalt him publicly before the
    congregation
   and before the leaders of the nation.

33 He changes rivers into deserts,
   and springs of water into dry land.
34 He turns the fruitful land into salty
    wastelands,
   because of the wickedness of those who
    live there.
35 But he also turns deserts into pools of water,
   the dry land into flowing springs.
36 He brings the hungry to settle there
   and build their cities.
37 They sow their fields, plant their vineyards,
   and harvest their bumper crops.
38 How he blesses them!
   They raise large families there,
   and their herds of cattle increase.

39 When they decrease in number and become
    impoverished
   through oppression, trouble, and sorrow,
40 the LORD pours contempt on their princes,
   causing them to wander in trackless
    wastelands.
41 But he rescues the poor from their distress
   and increases their families like vast
    flocks of sheep.
42 The godly will see these things and be glad,
   while the wicked are stricken silent.
43 Those who are wise will take all this to
    heart;
   they will see in our history the faithful
    love of the LORD.

PSALM **108**
A psalm of David. A song.

1 My heart is confident in you, O God;
   no wonder I can sing your praises!
   Wake up, my soul!
2 Wake up, O harp and lyre!
   I will waken the dawn with my song.
3 I will thank you, LORD, in front of all the
    people.
   I will sing your praises among the nations.
4 For your unfailing love is higher than the
    heavens.
   Your faithfulness reaches to the clouds.

108:7 Or *in his sanctuary.*

5 Be exalted, O God, above the highest heavens.
   May your glory shine over all the earth.

6 Use your strong right arm to save me,
   and rescue your beloved people.
7 God has promised this by his holiness*:
   "I will divide up Shechem with joy.
   I will measure out the valley of Succoth.
8 Gilead is mine,
   and Manasseh is mine.
 Ephraim will produce my warriors,
   and Judah will produce my kings.
9 Moab will become my lowly servant,
   and Edom will be my slave.
   I will shout in triumph over the
    Philistines."

10 But who will bring me into the fortified city?
   Who will bring me victory over Edom?
11 Have you rejected us, O God?
   Will you no longer march with our armies?
12 Oh, please help us against our enemies,
   for all human help is useless.
13 With God's help we will do mighty things,
   for he will trample down our foes.

PSALM **109**
For the choir director: A psalm of David.

1 O God, whom I praise,
   don't stand silent and aloof
2 while the wicked slander me
   and tell lies about me.
3 They are all around me with their hateful
    words,
   and they fight against me for no reason.
4 I love them, but they try to destroy me—
   even as I am praying for them!
5 They return evil for good,
   and hatred for my love.

6 Arrange for an evil person to turn on him.
   Send an accuser to bring him to trial.
7 When his case is called for judgment,
   let him be pronounced guilty.
   Count his prayers as sins.
8 Let his years be few;
   let his position be given to someone else.
9 May his children become fatherless,
   and may his wife become a widow.
10 May his children wander as beggars;
   may they be evicted from their ruined
    homes.
11 May creditors seize his entire estate,
   and strangers take all he has earned.

12 Let no one be kind to him;
   let no one pity his fatherless children.
13 May all his offspring die.
   May his family name be blotted out in a
   single generation.
14 May the LORD never forget the sins of his
   ancestors;
   may his mother's sins never be erased
   from the record.
15 May these sins always remain before the LORD,
   but may his name be cut off from human
   memory.
16 For he refused all kindness to others;
   he persecuted the poor and needy,
   and he hounded the brokenhearted to
   death.
17 He loved to curse others;
   now you curse him.
   He never blessed others;
   now don't you bless him.
18 Cursing is as much a part of him as his
   clothing,
   or as the water he drinks,
   or the rich food he eats.
19 Now may his curses return and cling to him
   like clothing;
   may they be tied around him like a belt.

20 May those curses become the LORD's
   punishment for my accusers
   who are plotting against my life.
21 But deal well with me, O Sovereign LORD,
   for the sake of your own reputation!
   Rescue me because you are so faithful and
   good.
22 For I am poor and needy,
   and my heart is full of pain.
23 I am fading like a shadow at dusk;
   I am falling like a grasshopper that is
   brushed aside.
24 My knees are weak from fasting,
   and I am skin and bones.
25 I am an object of mockery to people everywhere;
   when they see me, they shake their heads.
26 Help me, O LORD my God!
   Save me because of your unfailing love.
27 Let them see that this is your doing,
   that you yourself have done it, LORD.
28 Then let them curse me if they like,
   but you will bless me!
   When they attack me, they will be disgraced!
   But I, your servant, will go right on
   rejoicing!

110:2 Hebrew *Zion*.

29 Make their humiliation obvious to all;
   clothe my accusers with disgrace.
30 But I will give repeated thanks to the LORD,
   praising him to everyone.
31 For he stands beside the needy,
   ready to save them from those who
   condemn them.

PSALM 110

A psalm of David.

1 The LORD said to my Lord,
   "Sit in honor at my right hand
   until I humble your enemies,
   making them a footstool under your feet."

2 The LORD will extend your powerful
   dominion from Jerusalem*;
   you will rule over your enemies.
3 In that day of battle,
   your people will serve you willingly.
   Arrayed in holy garments,
   your vigor will be renewed each day like
   the morning dew.
4 The LORD has taken an oath and will not
   break his vow:
   "You are a priest forever in the line of
   Melchizedek."
5 The Lord stands at your right hand to
   protect you.
   He will strike down many kings in the
   day of his anger.
6 He will punish the nations
   and fill them with their dead;
   he will shatter heads
   over the whole earth.
7 But he himself will be refreshed from
   brooks along the way.
   He will be victorious.

PSALM 111

1 Praise the LORD!

   I will thank the LORD with all my heart
   as I meet with his godly people.
2 How amazing are the deeds of the LORD!
   All who delight in him should ponder them.
3 Everything he does reveals his glory and
   majesty.
   His righteousness never fails.
4 Who can forget the wonders he performs?
   How gracious and merciful is our LORD!
5 He gives food to those who trust him;
   he always remembers his covenant.

6 He has shown his great power to his people
by giving them the lands of other nations.
7 All he does is just and good,
and all his commandments are trustworthy.
8 They are forever true,
to be obeyed faithfully and with integrity.
9 He has paid a full ransom for his people.
He has guaranteed his covenant with
them forever.
What a holy, awe-inspiring name he has!
10 Reverence for the LORD is the foundation of
true wisdom.
The rewards of wisdom come to all who
obey him.

Praise his name forever!

PSALM 112

1 Praise the LORD!

Happy are those who fear the LORD.
Yes, happy are those who delight in
doing what he commands.
2 Their children will be successful everywhere;
an entire generation of godly people will
be blessed.
3 They themselves will be wealthy,
and their good deeds will never be
forgotten.
4 When darkness overtakes the godly, light
will come bursting in.
They are* generous, compassionate, and
righteous.
5 All goes well for those who are generous,
who lend freely and conduct their
business fairly.
6 Such people will not be overcome by evil
circumstances.
Those who are righteous will be long
remembered.
7 They do not fear bad news;
they confidently trust the LORD to care for
them.
8 They are confident and fearless
and can face their foes triumphantly.
9 They give generously to those in need.
Their good deeds will never be forgotten.
They will have influence and honor.
10 The wicked will be infuriated when they see
this.
They will grind their teeth in anger;
they will slink away, their hopes
thwarted.

PSALM 113

1 Praise the LORD!

Yes, give praise, O servants of the LORD.
Praise the name of the LORD!
2 Blessed be the name of the LORD
forever and ever.
3 Everywhere—from east to west—
praise the name of the LORD.
4 For the LORD is high above the nations;
his glory is far greater than the heavens.

5 Who can be compared with the LORD our
God,
who is enthroned on high?
6 Far below him are the heavens and the earth.
He stoops to look,
7 and he lifts the poor from the dirt
and the needy from the garbage dump.
8 He sets them among princes,
even the princes of his own people!
9 He gives the barren woman a home,
so that she becomes a happy mother.

Praise the LORD!

PSALM 114

1 When the Israelites escaped from Egypt—
when the family of Jacob left that foreign
land—
2 the land of Judah became God's sanctuary,
and Israel became his kingdom.

3 The Red Sea* saw them coming and hurried
out of their way!
The water of the Jordan River turned away.
4 The mountains skipped like rams,
the little hills like lambs!
5 What's wrong, Red Sea, that made you
hurry out of their way?
What happened, Jordan River, that you
turned away?
6 Why, mountains, did you skip like rams?
Why, little hills, like lambs?

7 Tremble, O earth, at the presence of the Lord,
at the presence of the God of Israel.*
8 He turned the rock into pools of water;
yes, springs of water came from solid
rock.

PSALM 115

1 Not to us, O LORD, but to you goes all the
glory
for your unfailing love and faithfulness.

112:4 Greek version reads *The LORD is.*   114:3 Hebrew *the sea;* also in 114:5.   114:7 Hebrew *of Jacob.*

2 Why let the nations say,
   "Where is their God?"
3 For our God is in the heavens,
   and he does as he wishes.
4 Their idols are merely things of silver and
      gold,
   shaped by human hands.
5 They cannot talk, though they have mouths,
   or see, though they have eyes!
6 They cannot hear with their ears,
   or smell with their noses,
7 or feel with their hands,
   or walk with their feet,
   or utter sounds with their throats!
8 And those who make them are just like
      them,
   as are all who trust in them.

9 O Israel, trust the LORD!
   He is your helper; he is your shield.
10 O priests of Aaron, trust the LORD!
   He is your helper; he is your shield.
11 All you who fear the LORD, trust the LORD!
   He is your helper; he is your shield.

12 The LORD remembers us,
   and he will surely bless us.
   He will bless the people of Israel
   and the family of Aaron, the priests.
13 He will bless those who fear the LORD,
   both great and small.

14 May the LORD richly bless
   both you and your children.
15 May you be blessed by the LORD,
   who made heaven and earth.
16 The heavens belong to the LORD,
   but he has given the earth to all humanity.

17 The dead cannot sing praises to the LORD,
   for they have gone into the silence of the
      grave.
18 But we can praise the LORD
   both now and forever!

   Praise the LORD!

PSALM 116

1 I love the LORD because he hears
   and answers my prayers.
2 Because he bends down and listens,
   I will pray as long as I have breath!
3 Death had its hands around my throat;
   the terrors of the grave* overtook me.
   I saw only trouble and sorrow.

116:3 Hebrew *of Sheol.*

4 Then I called on the name of the LORD:
   "Please, LORD, save me!"
5 How kind the LORD is! How good he is!
   So merciful, this God of ours!
6 The LORD protects those of childlike faith;
   I was facing death, and then he saved me.
7 Now I can rest again,
   for the LORD has been so good to me.
8 He has saved me from death,
   my eyes from tears,
   my feet from stumbling.
9 And so I walk in the LORD's presence
   as I live here on earth!
10 I believed in you, so I prayed,
   "I am deeply troubled, LORD."
11 In my anxiety I cried out to you,
   "These people are all liars!"
12 What can I offer the LORD
   for all he has done for me?
13 I will lift up a cup symbolizing his salvation;
   I will praise the LORD's name for saving me.
14 I will keep my promises to the LORD
   in the presence of all his people.

15 The LORD's loved ones are precious to him;
   it grieves him when they die.
16 O LORD, I am your servant;
   yes, I am your servant, the son of your
      handmaid,
   and you have freed me from my bonds!
17 I will offer you a sacrifice of thanksgiving
   and call on the name of the LORD.
18 I will keep my promises to the LORD
   in the presence of all his people,
19 in the house of the LORD,
   in the heart of Jerusalem.

   Praise the LORD!

PSALM 117

1 Praise the LORD, all you nations.
   Praise him, all you people of the earth.
2 For he loves us with unfailing love;
   the faithfulness of the LORD endures
      forever.

   Praise the LORD!

PSALM 118

1 Give thanks to the LORD, for he is good!
   His faithful love endures forever.

2 Let the congregation of Israel repeat:
   "His faithful love endures forever."

3 Let Aaron's descendants, the priests, repeat:
"His faithful love endures forever."
4 Let all who fear the LORD repeat:
"His faithful love endures forever."

5 In my distress I prayed to the LORD,
and the LORD answered me and rescued
me.
6 The LORD is for me, so I will not be afraid.
What can mere mortals do to me?
7 Yes, the LORD is for me; he will help me.
I will look in triumph at those who hate me.
8 It is better to trust the LORD
than to put confidence in people.
9 It is better to trust the LORD
than to put confidence in princes.

10 Though hostile nations surrounded me,
I destroyed them all in the name of the
LORD.
11 Yes, they surrounded and attacked me,
but I destroyed them all in the name of
the LORD.
12 They swarmed around me like bees;
they blazed against me like a roaring
flame.
But I destroyed them all in the name of
the LORD.
13 You did your best to kill me, O my enemy,
but the LORD helped me.
14 The LORD is my strength and my song;
he has become my victory.
15 Songs of joy and victory are sung in the
camp of the godly.
The strong right arm of the LORD has
done glorious things!
16 The strong right arm of the LORD is raised in
triumph.
The strong right arm of the LORD has
done glorious things!
17 I will not die, but I will live
to tell what the LORD has done.
18 The LORD has punished me severely,
but he has not handed me over to death.

19 Open for me the gates where the righteous
enter,
and I will go in and thank the LORD.
20 Those gates lead to the presence of the LORD,
and the godly enter there.
21 I thank you for answering my prayer
and saving me!

22 The stone rejected by the builders
has now become the cornerstone.

23 This is the LORD's doing,
and it is marvelous to see.
24 This is the day the LORD has made.
We will rejoice and be glad in it.
25 Please, LORD, please save us.
Please, LORD, please give us success.
26 Bless the one who comes in the name of the
LORD.
We bless you from the house of the LORD.
27 The LORD is God, shining upon us.
Bring forward the sacrifice and put it on
the altar.
28 You are my God, and I will praise you!
You are my God, and I will exalt you!

29 Give thanks to the LORD, for he is good!
His faithful love endures forever.

PSALM 119

1 Happy are people of integrity,
who follow the law of the LORD.
2 Happy are those who obey his decrees
and search for him with all their hearts.
3 They do not compromise with evil,
and they walk only in his paths.
4 You have charged us
to keep your commandments carefully.
5 Oh, that my actions would consistently
reflect your principles!
6 Then I will not be disgraced
when I compare my life with your
commands.
7 When I learn your righteous laws,
I will thank you by living as I should!
8 I will obey your principles.
Please don't give up on me!

9 How can a young person stay pure?
By obeying your word and following its rules.
10 I have tried my best to find you—
don't let me wander from your commands.
11 I have hidden your word in my heart,
that I might not sin against you.
12 Blessed are you, O LORD;
teach me your principles.
13 I have recited aloud
all the laws you have given us.
14 I have rejoiced in your decrees
as much as in riches.
15 I will study your commandments
and reflect on your ways.
16 I will delight in your principles
and not forget your word.

119 This psalm is a Hebrew acrostic poem; there are 22 stanzas, one for each letter of the Hebrew alphabet. The 8 verses within each stanza
begin with the Hebrew letter of its section.

17 Be good to your servant,
  that I may live and obey your word.
18 Open my eyes to see
  the wonderful truths in your law.
19 I am but a foreigner here on earth;
  I need the guidance of your commands.
  Don't hide them from me!
20 I am overwhelmed continually
  with a desire for your laws.
21 You rebuke those cursed proud ones
  who wander from your commands.
22 Don't let them scorn and insult me,
  for I have obeyed your decrees.
23 Even princes sit and speak against me,
  but I will meditate on your principles.
24 Your decrees please me;
  they give me wise advice.

25 I lie in the dust, completely discouraged;
  revive me by your word.
26 I told you my plans, and you answered.
  Now teach me your principles.
27 Help me understand the meaning of your
  commandments,
  and I will meditate on your wonderful
  miracles.
28 I weep with grief;
  encourage me by your word.
29 Keep me from lying to myself;
  give me the privilege of knowing your
  law.
30 I have chosen to be faithful;
  I have determined to live by your laws.
31 I cling to your decrees.
  LORD, don't let me be put to shame!
32 If you will help me,
  I will run to follow your commands.

33 Teach me, O LORD,
  to follow every one of your principles.
34 Give me understanding and I will obey your
  law;
  I will put it into practice with all my heart.
35 Make me walk along the path of your
  commands,
  for that is where my happiness is found.
36 Give me an eagerness for your decrees;
  do not inflict me with love for money!
37 Turn my eyes from worthless things,
  and give me life through your word.*
38 Reassure me of your promise,
  which is for those who honor you.
39 Help me abandon my shameful ways;
  your laws are all I want in life.

119:37 Some manuscripts read *in your ways.*

Studying the Bible Keeps Us Spiritually Strong
Read PSALM 119:9-18

Although it is good to carry a Bible in your briefcase, your pocket, or your purse, the best place to carry the Bible is in your heart. Psalm 119 gives a wonderful illustration of what can happen in our lives when we fill our minds with God's Word. It is highly beneficial to read this entire psalm. The particular passage chosen here, however, gives us at least three good principles regarding the importance of regular Bible study:

1. The Study and Application of God's Word Will Keep Us Pure. If we really study and apply God's Word to our lives, we will be able to live a pure and holy life—even though we live in a blatantly evil world.

2. The Memorization of God's Word Will Keep Us from Sin. When Jesus squared off with the devil for forty days in the wilderness (see Luke 4:1-14, pp. 857-858), he faced serious temptation. His response to the temptations was simple but effective—he quoted Scripture. Once Scripture is ingrained in our memory, we will be amazed at how often a verse will suddenly come to mind and speak to our situation and strengthen our hearts. The famous early twentieth-century evangelist Billy Sunday used to say of the Bible, "This Book will keep you from sin, and sin will keep you from this Book." He was right. The greatest deterrent for sin and temptation is the Word of God stored in our hearts.

3. The Study of God's Laws Will Give Us a Sense of Joy and Peace. Some people view God's laws as a long list of don'ts. The author of this psalm, however, did not view God's laws as shackles but as shelter. He held this view because he understood that God's principles for living were good for him. When we begin to do the same, we will have a greater awareness of God's concern for us as individuals. Then we will not see God's laws as barriers to happiness but as walls of protection!

For the next note on "Study the Bible," turn to p. 165.

40 I long to obey your commandments!
   Renew my life with your goodness.

41 LORD, give to me your unfailing love,
   the salvation that you promised me.
42 Then I will have an answer for those who
   taunt me,
   for I trust in your word.
43 Do not snatch your word of truth from me,
   for my only hope is in your laws.
44 I will keep on obeying your law
   forever and forever.
45 I will walk in freedom,
   for I have devoted myself to your
   commandments.
46 I will speak to kings about your decrees,
   and I will not be ashamed.
47 How I delight in your commands!
   How I love them!
48 I honor and love your commands.
   I meditate on your principles.

49 Remember your promise to me,
   for it is my only hope.
50 Your promise revives me;
   it comforts me in all my troubles.
51 The proud hold me in utter contempt,
   but I do not turn away from your law.
52 I meditate on your age-old laws;
   O LORD, they comfort me.
53 I am furious with the wicked,
   those who reject your law.
54 Your principles have been the music of my
   life
   throughout the years of my pilgrimage.
55 I reflect at night on who you are, O LORD,
   and I obey your law because of this.
56 This is my happy way of life:
   obeying your commandments.

57 LORD, you are mine!
   I promise to obey your words!
58 With all my heart I want your blessings.
   Be merciful just as you promised.
59 I pondered the direction of my life,
   and I turned to follow your statutes.
60 I will hurry, without lingering,
   to obey your commands.
61 Evil people try to drag me into sin,
   but I am firmly anchored to your law.
62 At midnight I rise to thank you
   for your just laws.
63 Anyone who fears you is my friend—
   anyone who obeys your commandments.
64 O LORD, the earth is full of your unfailing love;
   teach me your principles.

65 You have done many good things for me,
   LORD,
   just as you promised.
66 I believe in your commands;
   now teach me good judgment and
   knowledge.
67 I used to wander off until you disciplined me;
   but now I closely follow your word.
68 You are good and do only good;
   teach me your principles.
69 Arrogant people have made up lies about
   me,
   but in truth I obey your commandments
   with all my heart.
70 Their hearts are dull and stupid,
   but I delight in your law.
71 The suffering you sent was good for me,
   for it taught me to pay attention to your
   principles.
72 Your law is more valuable to me
   than millions in gold and silver!

73 You made me; you created me.
   Now give me the sense to follow your
   commands.
74 May all who fear you find in me a cause for
   joy,
   for I have put my hope in your word.
75 I know, O LORD, that your decisions are fair;
   you disciplined me because I needed it.
76 Now let your unfailing love comfort me,
   just as you promised me, your servant.
77 Surround me with your tender mercies so I
   may live,
   for your law is my delight.
78 Bring disgrace upon the arrogant people
   who lied about me;
   meanwhile, I will concentrate on your
   commandments.
79 Let me be reconciled
   with all who fear you and know your
   decrees.
80 May I be blameless in keeping your
   principles;
   then I will never have to be ashamed.

81 I faint with longing for your salvation;
   but I have put my hope in your word.
82 My eyes are straining to see your promises
   come true.
   When will you comfort me?
83 I am shriveled like a wineskin in the smoke,
   exhausted with waiting.
   But I cling to your principles and obey
   them.

84 How long must I wait?
   When will you punish those who
      persecute me?
85 These arrogant people who hate your law
   have dug deep pits for me to fall into.
86 All your commands are trustworthy.
   Protect me from those who hunt me
      down without cause.
87 They almost finished me off,
   but I refused to abandon your
      commandments.
88 In your unfailing love, spare my life;
   then I can continue to obey your decrees.

89 Forever, O LORD,
   your word stands firm in heaven.
90 Your faithfulness extends to every generation,
   as enduring as the earth you created.
91 Your laws remain true today,
   for everything serves your plans.
92 If your law hadn't sustained me with joy,
   I would have died in my misery.
93 I will never forget your commandments,
   for you have used them to restore my joy
      and health.
94 I am yours; save me!
   For I have applied myself to obey your
      commandments.
95 Though the wicked hide along the way to
      kill me,
   I will quietly keep my mind on your
      decrees.
96 Even perfection has its limits,
   but your commands have no limit.

97 Oh, how I love your law!
   I think about it all day long.
98 Your commands make me wiser than my
      enemies,
   for your commands are my constant guide.
99 Yes, I have more insight than my teachers,
   for I am always thinking of your decrees.
100 I am even wiser than my elders,
   for I have kept your commandments.
101 I have refused to walk on any path of evil,
   that I may remain obedient to your word.
102 I haven't turned away from your laws,
   for you have taught me well.
103 How sweet are your words to my taste;
   they are sweeter than honey.
104 Your commandments give me
      understanding;
   no wonder I hate every false way of life.

105 Your word is a lamp for my feet
   and a light for my path.

106 I've promised it once, and I'll promise again:
   I will obey your wonderful laws.
107 I have suffered much, O LORD;
   restore my life again, just as you promised.
108 LORD, accept my grateful thanks
   and teach me your laws.
109 My life constantly hangs in the balance,
   but I will not stop obeying your law.
110 The wicked have set their traps for me along
      your path,
   but I will not turn from your
      commandments.
111 Your decrees are my treasure;
   they are truly my heart's delight.
112 I am determined to keep your principles,
   even forever, to the very end.

113 I hate those who are undecided about you,
   but my choice is clear—I love your law.
114 You are my refuge and my shield;
   your word is my only source of hope.
115 Get out of my life, you evil-minded people,
   for I intend to obey the commands of my
      God.
116 LORD, sustain me as you promised, that I
      may live!
   Do not let my hope be crushed.
117 Sustain me, and I will be saved;
   then I will meditate on your principles
      continually.
118 But you have rejected all who stray from
      your principles.
   They are only fooling themselves.
119 All the wicked of the earth are the scum you
      skim off;
   no wonder I love to obey your decrees!
120 I tremble in fear of you;
   I fear your judgments.

121 Don't leave me to the mercy of my enemies,
   for I have done what is just and right.
122 Please guarantee a blessing for me.
   Don't let those who are arrogant oppress
      me!
123 My eyes strain to see your deliverance,
   to see the truth of your promise fulfilled.
124 I am your servant;
   deal with me in unfailing love,
   and teach me your principles.
125 Give discernment to me, your servant;
   then I will understand your decrees.
126 LORD, it is time for you to act,
   for these evil people have broken your law.
127 Truly, I love your commands
   more than gold, even the finest gold.

A Love for God's Word Brings Peace of Mind Read PSALM 119:165-168

ome people today claim you can find peace by becoming "at peace" with yourself. Or they insist that, so long as we accept that what is right for one person may not be right for another, we will have a better understanding of the world around us. Thus, things won't seem so out of control or chaotic. But reality paints a different picture. For instance, the moral foundation America once had is quickly crumbling. Our streets are characterized by violence, and our families are characterized by turmoil. What is missing?

This passage gives us the missing piece of the puzzle. In order to find "great peace of heart and mind," you must love God's laws. Not only must the Bible become your standard for living, but you must also cherish what it says. To obey God's laws without a love for the Lawgiver is legalism, and you will never be completely satisfied. But to obey God's commands with a love for the Lord and his gift of salvation is true liberty, and you will find tremendous peace and assurance.

For the next note on "Peace," turn to p. 1042.

CORNER STONES

---

128 Truly, each of your commandments is right.
That is why I hate every false way.

129 Your decrees are wonderful.
No wonder I obey them!

130 As your words are taught, they give light;
even the simple can understand them.

131 I open my mouth, panting expectantly,
longing for your commands.

132 Come and show me your mercy,
as you do for all who love your name.

133 Guide my steps by your word,
so I will not be overcome by any evil.

134 Rescue me from the oppression of evil
people;
then I can obey your commandments.

135 Look down on me with love;
teach me all your principles.

136 Rivers of tears gush from my eyes
because people disobey your law.

137 O LORD, you are righteous,
and your decisions are fair.

138 Your decrees are perfect;
they are entirely worthy of our trust.

139 I am overwhelmed with rage,
for my enemies have disregarded your words.

140 Your promises have been thoroughly tested;
that is why I love them so much.

141 I am insignificant and despised,
but I don't forget your commandments.

142 Your justice is eternal,
and your law is perfectly true.

143 As pressure and stress bear down on me,
I find joy in your commands.

144 Your decrees are always fair;
help me to understand them, that I may
live.

145 I pray with all my heart; answer me, LORD!
I will obey your principles.

146 I cry out to you; save me,
that I may obey your decrees.

147 I rise early, before the sun is up;
I cry out for help and put my hope in
your words.

148 I stay awake through the night,
thinking about your promise.

149 In your faithful love, O LORD, hear my cry;
in your justice, save my life.

150 Those lawless people are coming near to
attack me;
they live far from your law.

151 But you are near, O LORD,
and all your commands are true.

152 I have known from my earliest days
that your decrees never change.

153 Look down upon my sorrows and rescue me,
for I have not forgotten your law.

154 Argue my case; take my side!
Protect my life as you promised.

155 The wicked are far from salvation,
for they do not bother with your
principles.

156 LORD, how great is your mercy;
in your justice, give me back my life.

157 Many persecute and trouble me,
yet I have not swerved from your
decrees.

158 I hate these traitors
  because they care nothing for your word.
159 See how I love your commandments, LORD.
  Give back my life because of your
    unfailing love.
160 All your words are true;
  all your just laws will stand forever.

161 Powerful people harass me without cause,
  but my heart trembles only at your word.
162 I rejoice in your word
  like one who finds a great treasure.
163 I hate and abhor all falsehood,
  but I love your law.
164 I will praise you seven times a day
  because all your laws are just.
165 Those who love your law have great peace
  and do not stumble.
166 I long for your salvation, LORD,
  so I have obeyed your commands.
167 I have obeyed your decrees,
  and I love them very much.
168 Yes, I obey your commandments and
    decrees,
  because you know everything I do.

169 O LORD, listen to my cry;
  give me the discerning mind you
    promised.
170 Listen to my prayer;
  rescue me as you promised.
171 Let my lips burst forth with praise,
  for you have taught me your principles.
172 Let my tongue sing about your word,
  for all your commands are right.
173 Stand ready to help me,
  for I have chosen to follow your
    commandments.
174 O LORD, I have longed for your salvation,
  and your law is my delight.
175 Let me live so I can praise you,
  and may your laws sustain me.
176 I have wandered away like a lost sheep;
  come and find me,
  for I have not forgotten your
    commands.

PSALM 120

A song for the ascent to Jerusalem.

1 I took my troubles to the LORD;
  I cried out to him, and he answered my
    prayer.
2 Rescue me, O LORD, from liars
  and from all deceitful people.

3 O deceptive tongue, what will God do to you?
  How will he increase your punishment?
4 You will be pierced with sharp arrows
  and burned with glowing coals.
5 How I suffer among these scoundrels of
    Meshech!
  It pains me to live with these people
    from Kedar!
6 I am tired of living here
  among people who hate peace.
7 As for me, I am for peace;
  but when I speak, they are for war!

PSALM 121

A song for the ascent to Jerusalem.

1 I look up to the mountains—
  does my help come from there?
2 My help comes from the LORD,
  who made the heavens and the earth!

3 He will not let you stumble and fall;
  the one who watches over you will not
    sleep.
4 Indeed, he who watches over Israel
  never tires and never sleeps.

5 The LORD himself watches over you!
  The LORD stands beside you as your
    protective shade.
6 The sun will not hurt you by day,
  nor the moon at night.
7 The LORD keeps you from all evil
  and preserves your life.
8 The LORD keeps watch over you as you come
    and go,
  both now and forever.

PSALM 122

A song for the ascent to Jerusalem. A psalm of David.

1 I was glad when they said to me,
  "Let us go to the house of the LORD."
2 And now we are standing here
  inside your gates, O Jerusalem.
3 Jerusalem is a well-built city,
  knit together as a single unit.
4 All the people of Israel—the LORD's people—
  make their pilgrimage here.
  They come to give thanks to the name of
    the LORD
  as the law requires.
5 Here stand the thrones where judgment is
    given,
  the thrones of the dynasty of David.

Sharing Your Faith Results in Joy Read PSALM 126:5-6

While these two verses reflect the restoration of joy in one's life, they may also hold particular significance for the person who longs to see others come to faith in Jesus Christ. As Christians, our hearts should break for those who do not know the Lord. The apostle Paul reflected this compassion when he wrote, "My heart is filled with bitter sorrow and unending grief for my people, my Jewish brothers and sisters. I would be willing to be forever cursed—cut off from Christ!—if that would save them" (Romans 9:2-3).

Because of Paul's compelling desire to see people come to Christ, many came to faith as a result of his prayers and preaching. And his joy will be great in heaven when he sees the fruit of his labor.

This joy of seeing others come to Christ is not only ours on this earth, but it is also reflected in heaven itself. The Bible tells us, "In the same way, heaven will be happier over one lost sinner who returns to God than over ninety-nine others who are righteous and haven't strayed away!" (Luke 15:7).

It is not enough to wish for people's salvation. First, your heart must break for their salvation ("plant in tears"). Second, you must actively pray and share your faith ("go to plant their seed"). Third, rejoice when you see that person turn to God ("harvest with shouts of joy"). Sharing your faith with others is not always an easy task, but the joy you will experience afterward is well worth the effort. So keep on praying for that loved one who doesn't yet know the Lord. Remember, the harvest isn't over until the Harvester returns.

For the next note on "Joy," turn to p. 984.

CORNERSTONES

---

6 Pray for the peace of Jerusalem.
  May all who love this city prosper.
7 O Jerusalem, may there be peace within
      your walls
    and prosperity in your palaces.
8 For the sake of my family and friends, I will
      say,
    "Peace be with you."
9 For the sake of the house of the LORD our
      God,
    I will seek what is best for you,
      O Jerusalem.

PSALM 123
A song for the ascent to Jerusalem.

1 I lift my eyes to you,
    O God, enthroned in heaven.
2 We look to the LORD our God for his mercy,
    just as servants keep their eyes on their
      master,
    as a slave girl watches her mistress for the
      slightest signal.
3 Have mercy on us, LORD, have mercy,
    for we have had our fill of contempt.
4 We have had our fill of the scoffing of the
      proud
    and the contempt of the arrogant.

PSALM 124
A song for the ascent to Jerusalem. A psalm of David.

1 If the LORD had not been on our side—
    let Israel now say—
2 if the LORD had not been on our side
    when people rose up against us,
3 they would have swallowed us alive
    because of their burning anger against us.
4 The waters would have engulfed us;
    a torrent would have overwhelmed us.
5 Yes, the raging waters of their fury
    would have overwhelmed our very lives.

6 Blessed be the LORD,
    who did not let their teeth tear us apart!
7 We escaped like a bird from a hunter's trap.
    The trap is broken, and we are free!
8 Our help is from the LORD,
    who made the heavens and the earth.

PSALM 125
A song for the ascent to Jerusalem.

1 Those who trust in the LORD are as secure as
      Mount Zion;
    they will not be defeated but will endure
      forever.
2 Just as the mountains surround and protect
      Jerusalem,

so the LORD surrounds and protects his
people, both now and forever.
3 The wicked will not rule the godly,
for then the godly might be forced to do
wrong.
4 O LORD, do good to those who are good,
whose hearts are in tune with you.
5 But banish those who turn to crooked ways,
O LORD.
Take them away with those who do evil.
And let Israel have quietness and peace.

P S A L M 126
A song for the ascent to Jerusalem.

1 When the LORD restored his exiles to
Jerusalem,*
it was like a dream!
2 We were filled with laughter,
and we sang for joy.
And the other nations said,
"What amazing things the LORD has done
for them."
3 Yes, the LORD has done amazing things for us!
What joy!

4 Restore our fortunes, LORD,
as streams renew the desert.
5 Those who plant in tears
will harvest with shouts of joy.
6 They weep as they go to plant their seed,
but they sing as they return with the
harvest.

P S A L M 127
A song for the ascent to Jerusalem. A psalm of Solomon.

1 Unless the LORD builds a house,
the work of the builders is useless.
Unless the LORD protects a city,
guarding it with sentries will do no good.
2 It is useless for you to work so hard
from early morning until late at night,
anxiously working for food to eat;
for God gives rest to his loved ones.

3 Children are a gift from the LORD;
they are a reward from him.
4 Children born to a young man
are like sharp arrows in a warrior's hands.
5 How happy is the man whose quiver is full
of them!
He will not be put to shame when he
confronts his accusers at the city gates.

126:1 Hebrew *Zion.*   129:5 Hebrew *Zion.*

P S A L M 128
A song for the ascent to Jerusalem.

1 How happy are those who fear the LORD—
all who follow his ways!
2 You will enjoy the fruit of your labor.
How happy you will be! How rich your
life!
3 Your wife will be like a fruitful vine,
flourishing within your home.
And look at all those children!
There they sit around your table
as vigorous and healthy as young olive trees.
4 That is the LORD's reward
for those who fear him.

5 May the LORD continually bless you from Zion.
May you see Jerusalem prosper as long as
you live.
6 May you live to enjoy your grandchildren.
And may Israel have quietness and peace.

P S A L M 129
A song for the ascent to Jerusalem.

1 From my earliest youth my enemies have
persecuted me—
let Israel now say—
2 from my earliest youth my enemies have
persecuted me,
but they have never been able to finish
me off.
3 My back is covered with cuts,
as if a farmer had plowed long furrows.
4 But the LORD is good;
he has cut the cords used by the ungodly
to bind me.

5 May all who hate Jerusalem*
be turned back in shameful defeat.
6 May they be as useless as grass on a rooftop,
turning yellow when only half grown,
7 ignored by the harvester,
despised by the binder.
8 And may those who pass by refuse to give
them this blessing:
"The LORD's blessings be upon you;
we bless you in the LORD's name."

P S A L M 130
A song for the ascent to Jerusalem.

1 From the depths of despair, O LORD,
I call for your help.
2 Hear my cry, O Lord.
Pay attention to my prayer.

³ LORD, if you kept a record of our sins,
  who, O Lord, could ever survive?
⁴ But you offer forgiveness,
  that we might learn to fear you.

⁵ I am counting on the LORD;
  yes, I am counting on him.
  I have put my hope in his word.
⁶ I long for the Lord
  more than sentries long for the dawn,
  yes, more than sentries long for the dawn.

⁷ O Israel, hope in the LORD;
  for with the LORD there is unfailing love
  and an overflowing supply of salvation.
⁸ He himself will free Israel
  from every kind of sin.

PSALM 131

A song for the ascent to Jerusalem. A psalm of David.

¹ LORD, my heart is not proud;
  my eyes are not haughty.
  I don't concern myself with matters too
    great
  or awesome for me.
² But I have stilled and quieted myself,
  just as a small child is quiet with its
    mother.
  Yes, like a small child is my soul within
    me.

³ O Israel, put your hope in the LORD—
  now and always.

PSALM 132

A song for the ascent to Jerusalem.

¹ LORD, remember David
  and all that he suffered.
² He took an oath before the LORD.
  He vowed to the Mighty One of Israel,*
³ "I will not go home;
  I will not let myself rest.
⁴ I will not let my eyes sleep
  nor close my eyelids in slumber
⁵ until I find a place to build a house for
    the LORD,
  a sanctuary for the Mighty One of
    Israel."
⁶ We heard that the Ark was in Ephrathah;
  then we found it in the distant
    countryside of Jaar.
⁷ Let us go to the dwelling place of the LORD;
  let us bow low before him.

⁸ Arise, O LORD, and enter your sanctuary,
  along with the Ark, the symbol of your
    power.
⁹ Your priests will be agents of salvation;
  may your loyal servants sing for joy.

¹⁰ For the sake of your servant David,
  do not reject the king you chose for your
    people.
¹¹ The LORD swore to David
  a promise he will never take back:
  "I will place one of your descendants on your
    throne.
¹² If your descendants obey the terms of my
    covenant
  and follow the decrees that I teach them,
  then your royal line will never end."

¹³ For the LORD has chosen Jerusalem*;
  he has desired it as his home.
¹⁴ "This is my home where I will live forever,"
  he said.
  "I will live here, for this is the place I desired.
¹⁵ I will make this city prosperous
  and satisfy its poor with food.
¹⁶ I will make its priests the agents of salvation;
  its godly people will sing for joy.
¹⁷ Here I will increase the power of David;
  my anointed one will be a light for my
    people.
¹⁸ I will clothe his enemies with shame,
  but he will be a glorious king."

PSALM 133

A song for the ascent to Jerusalem. A psalm of David.

¹ How wonderful it is, how pleasant,
  when brothers live together in harmony!
² For harmony is as precious as the fragrant
    anointing oil
  that was poured over Aaron's head,
  that ran down his beard
  and onto the border of his robe.
³ Harmony is as refreshing as the dew from
    Mount Hermon
  that falls on the mountains of Zion.
  And the LORD has pronounced his blessing,
  even life forevermore.

PSALM 134

A song for the ascent to Jerusalem.

¹ Oh, bless the LORD, all you servants of the
    LORD,

132:2 Hebrew *of Jacob;* also in 132:5.   132:13 Hebrew *Zion.*

you who serve as night watchmen in the
house of the LORD.
2 Lift your hands in holiness,
and bless the LORD.

3 May the LORD, who made heaven and earth,
bless you from Jerusalem.*

PSALM 135

1 Praise the LORD!

Praise the name of the LORD!
Praise him, you who serve the LORD,
2 you who serve in the house of the LORD,
in the courts of the house of our God.
3 Praise the LORD, for the LORD is good;
celebrate his wonderful name with music.
4 For the LORD has chosen Jacob for himself,
Israel for his own special treasure.

5 I know the greatness of the LORD—
that our Lord is greater than any other
god.
6 The LORD does whatever pleases him
throughout all heaven and earth,
and on the seas and in their depths.
7 He causes the clouds to rise over the earth.
He sends the lightning with the rain
and releases the wind from his
storehouses.
8 He destroyed the firstborn in each Egyptian
home,
both people and animals.
9 He performed miraculous signs and
wonders in Egypt;
Pharaoh and all his people watched.
10 He struck down great nations
and slaughtered mighty kings—
11 Sihon king of the Amorites,
Og king of Bashan,
and all the kings of Canaan.
12 He gave their land as an inheritance,
a special possession to his people Israel.
13 Your name, O LORD, endures forever;
your fame, O LORD, is known to every
generation.
14 For the LORD will vindicate his people
and have compassion on his servants.

15 Their idols are merely things of silver and gold,
shaped by human hands.
16 They cannot talk, though they have mouths,
or see, though they have eyes!
17 They cannot hear with their ears
or smell with their noses.

18 And those who make them are just like
them,
as are all who trust in them.

19 O Israel, praise the LORD!
O priests of Aaron, praise the LORD!
20 O Levites, praise the LORD!
All you who fear the LORD, praise the
LORD!
21 The LORD be praised from Zion,
for he lives here in Jerusalem.

Praise the LORD!

PSALM 136

1 Give thanks to the LORD, for he is good!
His faithful love endures forever.
2 Give thanks to the God of gods.
His faithful love endures forever.
3 Give thanks to the Lord of lords.
His faithful love endures forever.

4 Give thanks to him who alone does mighty
miracles.
His faithful love endures forever.
5 Give thanks to him who made the heavens
so skillfully.
His faithful love endures forever.
6 Give thanks to him who placed the earth on
the water.
His faithful love endures forever.
7 Give thanks to him who made the heavenly
lights—
His faithful love endures forever.
8 the sun to rule the day,
His faithful love endures forever.
9 and the moon and stars to rule the night.
His faithful love endures forever.

10 Give thanks to him who killed the firstborn
of Egypt.
His faithful love endures forever.
11 He brought Israel out of Egypt.
His faithful love endures forever.
12 He acted with a strong hand and powerful
arm.
His faithful love endures forever.
13 Give thanks to him who parted the Red Sea.*
His faithful love endures forever.
14 He led Israel safely through,
His faithful love endures forever.
15 but he hurled Pharaoh and his army into
the sea.
His faithful love endures forever.

134:3 Hebrew *Zion.*   136:13 Hebrew *sea of reeds;* also in 136:15.

God Is All-Knowing, Ever-Present, and All-Powerful
Read PSALM 139:1-24

Scripture teaches us about many of God's characteristics. This psalm highlights two of them and alludes to a third.

1. God Is All-Knowing. As verses 1-6 attest, God knows every little detail about what is going on in his creation. Scientists tell us that there are 100 billion stars and more than a billion galaxies. Yet Scripture tells us that God counts the stars and calls them by name (Psalm 147:4, p. 539)! If God pays that much attention to detail, you can be assured that he is always aware of what is happening in your life. God is also able to "chart the path ahead of [you]" because he lives in the eternal realm, where he can see the future as clearly as we see the past.

2. God Is Ever-Present. The psalmist beautifully illustrates a second characteristic of God in verses 7-12—his omnipresence. There is no place the psalmist can go to escape God's presence. This fact brings comfort to the psalmist because anywhere he goes he can depend on God to be there to guide, strengthen, and support him. At the same time, God's omnipresence brings the psalmist discomfort. Because God is present everywhere, he is aware of the psalmist's sin. The darkness cannot hide him (verse 12). God's omnipresence should not only bring us comfort but also motivate us to live lives that are pleasing to him.

3. God Is All-Powerful. In asking God to destroy the wicked (verse 19), the psalmist alludes to another of God's characteristics—his omnipotence. God's omnipotence is further displayed in

other passages of Scripture. Job 42:2 says, "I know that you can do anything, and no one can stop you." As the writer of Ecclesiastes acknowledged, "And I know that whatever God does is final. Nothing can be added to it or taken from it. God's purpose in this is that people should fear him" (Ecclesiastes 3:14). There is no one more powerful than God. He is ultimately in control of the universe—and your life.

For the next note on "Who Is God?" turn to p. 580.

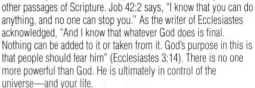

CORNER STONES

---

16 Give thanks to him who led his people
through the wilderness.
His faithful love endures forever.

17 Give thanks to him who struck down
mighty kings.
His faithful love endures forever.

18 He killed powerful kings—
His faithful love endures forever.

19 Sihon king of the Amorites,
His faithful love endures forever.

20 and Og king of Bashan.
His faithful love endures forever.

21 God gave the land of these kings as an
inheritance—
His faithful love endures forever.

22 a special possession to his servant Israel.
His faithful love endures forever.

23 He remembered our utter weakness.
His faithful love endures forever.

24 He saved us from our enemies.
His faithful love endures forever.

25 He gives food to every living thing.
His faithful love endures forever.

26 Give thanks to the God of heaven.
His faithful love endures forever.

PSALM **137**

1 Beside the rivers of Babylon, we sat and wept
as we thought of Jerusalem.*

2 We put away our lyres,
hanging them on the branches of the
willow trees.

3 For there our captors demanded a song of us.
Our tormentors requested a joyful hymn:
"Sing us one of those songs of
Jerusalem!"

4 But how can we sing the songs of the LORD
while in a foreign land?

137:1 Hebrew *Zion;* also in 137:3.

⁵ If I forget you, O Jerusalem,
let my right hand forget its skill upon the
harp.
⁶ May my tongue stick to the roof of my mouth
if I fail to remember you,
if I don't make Jerusalem my highest joy.

⁷ O LORD, remember what the Edomites did
on the day the armies of Babylon
captured Jerusalem.
"Destroy it!" they yelled.
"Level it to the ground!"
⁸ O Babylon, you will be destroyed.
Happy is the one who pays you back
for what you have done to us.
⁹ Happy is the one who takes your babies
and smashes them against the rocks!

PSALM **138**
A psalm of David.

¹ I give you thanks, O LORD, with all my
heart;
I will sing your praises before the gods.
² I bow before your holy Temple as I
worship.
I will give thanks to your name
for your unfailing love and faithfulness,
because your promises are backed
by all the honor of your name.
³ When I pray, you answer me;
you encourage me by giving me the
strength I need.

⁴ Every king in all the earth will give you
thanks, O LORD,
for all of them will hear your words.
⁵ Yes, they will sing about the LORD's ways,
for the glory of the LORD is very great.
⁶ Though the LORD is great, he cares for the
humble,
but he keeps his distance from the proud.

⁷ Though I am surrounded by troubles,
you will preserve me against the anger of
my enemies.
You will clench your fist against my angry
enemies!
Your power will save me.
⁸ The LORD will work out his plans for my
life—
for your faithful love, O LORD, endures
forever.
Don't abandon me, for you made me.

PSALM **139**
For the choir director: A psalm of David.

¹ O LORD, you have examined my heart
and know everything about me.
² You know when I sit down or stand up.
You know my every thought when far away.
³ You chart the path ahead of me
and tell me where to stop and rest.
Every moment you know where I am.
⁴ You know what I am going to say
even before I say it, LORD.
⁵ You both precede and follow me.
You place your hand of blessing on my
head.
⁶ Such knowledge is too wonderful for me,
too great for me to know!

⁷ I can never escape from your spirit!
I can never get away from your presence!
⁸ If I go up to heaven, you are there;
if I go down to the place of the dead,*
you are there.
⁹ If I ride the wings of the morning,
if I dwell by the farthest oceans,
¹⁰ even there your hand will guide me,
and your strength will support me.
¹¹ I could ask the darkness to hide me
and the light around me to become night—
¹² but even in darkness I cannot hide from
you.
To you the night shines as bright as day.
Darkness and light are both alike to you.

¹³ You made all the delicate, inner parts of my
body
and knit me together in my mother's
womb.
¹⁴ Thank you for making me so wonderfully
complex!
Your workmanship is marvelous—and
how well I know it.
¹⁵ You watched me as I was being formed in
utter seclusion,
as I was woven together in the dark of
the womb.
¹⁶ You saw me before I was born.
Every day of my life was recorded in your
book.
Every moment was laid out
before a single day had passed.

¹⁷ How precious are your thoughts about me,*
O God!
They are innumerable!

139:8 Hebrew *to Sheol.*   **139:17** Or *How precious to me are your thoughts.*

18 I can't even count them;
   they outnumber the grains of sand!
   And when I wake up in the morning,
   you are still with me!

19 O God, if only you would destroy the wicked!
   Get out of my life, you murderers!
20 They blaspheme you;
   your enemies take your name in vain.
21 O Lord, shouldn't I hate those who hate you?
   Shouldn't I despise those who resist you?
22 Yes, I hate them with complete hatred,
   for your enemies are my enemies.

23 Search me, O God, and know my heart;
   test me and know my thoughts.
24 Point out anything in me that offends you,
   and lead me along the path of everlasting
   life.

PSALM **140**

For the choir director: A psalm of David.

1 O Lord, rescue me from evil people.
   Preserve me from those who are violent,
2 those who plot evil in their hearts
   and stir up trouble all day long.
3 Their tongues sting like a snake;
   the poison of a viper drips from their lips.
                                    Interlude

4 O Lord, keep me out of the hands of the
   wicked.
   Preserve me from those who are violent,
   for they are plotting against me.
5 The proud have set a trap to catch me;
   they have stretched out a net;
   they have placed traps all along the way.
                                    Interlude

6 I said to the Lord, "You are my God!"
   Listen, O Lord, to my cries for mercy!
7 O Sovereign Lord, my strong savior,
   you protected me on the day of battle.
8 Lord, do not give in to their evil desires.
   Do not let their evil schemes succeed,
   O God.   *Interlude*

9 Let my enemies be destroyed
   by the very evil they have planned for me.
10 Let burning coals fall down on their heads,
   or throw them into the fire,
   or into deep pits from which they can't
   escape.
11 Don't let liars prosper here in our land.
   Cause disaster to fall with great force on
   the violent.

12 But I know the Lord will surely help those
   they persecute;
   he will maintain the rights of the poor.
13 Surely the godly are praising your name,
   for they will live in your presence.

PSALM **141**

A psalm of David.

1 O Lord, I am calling to you. Please hurry!
   Listen when I cry to you for help!
2 Accept my prayer as incense offered to
   you,
   and my upraised hands as an evening
   offering.

3 Take control of what I say, O Lord,
   and keep my lips sealed.
4 Don't let me lust for evil things;
   don't let me participate in acts of
   wickedness.
   Don't let me share in the delicacies
   of those who do evil.

5 Let the godly strike me!
   It will be a kindness!
   If they reprove me, it is soothing medicine.
   Don't let me refuse it.

   But I am in constant prayer
   against the wicked and their deeds.
6 When their leaders are thrown down from a
   cliff,
   they will listen to my words and find
   them pleasing.
7 Even as a farmer breaks up the soil and
   brings up rocks,
   so the bones of the wicked will be
   scattered without a decent burial.

8 I look to you for help, O Sovereign Lord.
   You are my refuge; don't let them kill me.
9 Keep me out of the traps they have set
   for me,
   out of the snares of those who do evil.
10 Let the wicked fall into their own snares,
   but let me escape.

PSALM **142**

A psalm of David, regarding his experience in the cave.
A prayer.

1 I cry out to the Lord;
   I plead for the Lord's mercy.
2 I pour out my complaints before him
   and tell him all my troubles.

³ For I am overwhelmed,
and you alone know the way I should turn.
Wherever I go,
my enemies have set traps for me.
⁴ I look for someone to come and help me,
but no one gives me a passing thought!
No one will help me;
no one cares a bit what happens to me.
⁵ Then I pray to you, O LORD.
I say, "You are my place of refuge.
You are all I really want in life.
⁶ Hear my cry,
for I am very low.
Rescue me from my persecutors,
for they are too strong for me.
⁷ Bring me out of prison
so I can thank you.
The godly will crowd around me,
for you treat me kindly."

PSALM 143

A psalm of David.

¹ Hear my prayer, O LORD;
listen to my plea!
Answer me because you are faithful and
righteous.
² Don't bring your servant to trial!
Compared to you, no one is perfect.
³ My enemy has chased me.
He has knocked me to the ground.
He forces me to live in darkness like
those in the grave.
⁴ I am losing all hope;
I am paralyzed with fear.
⁵ I remember the days of old.
I ponder all your great works.
I think about what you have done.
⁶ I reach out for you.
I thirst for you as parched land thirsts for
rain.   *Interlude*

⁷ Come quickly, LORD, and answer me,
for my depression deepens.
Don't turn away from me,
or I will die.
⁸ Let me hear of your unfailing love to me in
the morning,
for I am trusting you.
Show me where to walk,
for I have come to you in prayer.
⁹ Save me from my enemies, LORD;
I run to you to hide me.
¹⁰ Teach me to do your will,

for you are my God.
May your gracious Spirit lead me forward
on a firm footing.
¹¹ For the glory of your name, O LORD, save me.
In your righteousness, bring me out of
this distress.
¹² In your unfailing love, cut off all my enemies
and destroy all my foes,
for I am your servant.

PSALM 144

A psalm of David.

¹ Bless the LORD, who is my rock.
He gives me strength for war
and skill for battle.
² He is my loving ally and my fortress,
my tower of safety, my deliverer.
He stands before me as a shield, and I take
refuge in him.
He subdues the nations* under me.

³ O LORD, what are mortals that you should
notice us,
mere humans that you should care for us?
⁴ For we are like a breath of air;
our days are like a passing shadow.

⁵ Bend down the heavens, LORD, and come
down.
Touch the mountains so they billow smoke.
⁶ Release your lightning bolts and scatter your
enemies!
Release your arrows and confuse them!
⁷ Reach down from heaven and rescue me;
deliver me from deep waters,
from the power of my enemies.
⁸ Their mouths are full of lies;
they swear to tell the truth, but they lie.

⁹ I will sing a new song to you, O God!
I will sing your praises with a
ten-stringed harp.
¹⁰ For you grant victory to kings!
You are the one who rescued your
servant David.
¹¹ Save me from the fatal sword!
Rescue me from the power of my enemies.
Their mouths are full of lies;
they swear to tell the truth, but they lie.

¹² May our sons flourish in their youth
like well-nurtured plants.
May our daughters be like graceful pillars,
carved to beautify a palace.

144:2 Some manuscripts read *my people.*

13 May our farms be filled
with crops of every kind.
May the flocks in our fields multiply by the
thousands,
even tens of thousands,
14 and may our oxen be loaded down with
produce.
May there be no breached walls, no forced
exile,
no cries of distress in our squares.
15 Yes, happy are those who have it like this!
Happy indeed are those whose God is
the LORD.

PSALM 145

A psalm of praise of David.

1 I will praise you, my God and King,
and bless your name forever and ever.
2 I will bless you every day,
and I will praise you forever.
3 Great is the LORD! He is most worthy of
praise!
His greatness is beyond discovery!

4 Let each generation tell its children
of your mighty acts.
5 I will meditate* on your majestic, glorious
splendor
and your wonderful miracles.
6 Your awe-inspiring deeds will be on every
tongue;
I will proclaim your greatness.
7 Everyone will share the story of your
wonderful goodness;
they will sing with joy of your
righteousness.

8 The LORD is kind and merciful,
slow to get angry, full of unfailing love.
9 The LORD is good to everyone.
He showers compassion on all his creation.
10 All of your works will thank you, LORD,
and your faithful followers will bless you.
11 They will talk together about the glory of
your kingdom;
they will celebrate examples of your
power.
12 They will tell about your mighty deeds
and about the majesty and glory of your
reign.
13 For your kingdom is an everlasting
kingdom.
You rule generation after generation.

The LORD is faithful in all he says;
he is gracious in all he does.*
14 The LORD helps the fallen
and lifts up those bent beneath their
loads.
15 All eyes look to you for help;
you give them their food as they need it.
16 When you open your hand,
you satisfy the hunger and thirst of every
living thing.
17 The LORD is righteous in everything he does;
he is filled with kindness.
18 The LORD is close to all who call on him,
yes, to all who call on him sincerely.
19 He fulfills the desires of those who fear him;
he hears their cries for help and rescues
them.
20 The LORD protects all those who love him,
but he destroys the wicked.

21 I will praise the LORD,
and everyone on earth will bless his holy
name
forever and forever.

PSALM 146

1 Praise the LORD!

Praise the LORD, I tell myself.
2 I will praise the LORD as long as I live.
I will sing praises to my God even with
my dying breath.

3 Don't put your confidence in powerful people;
there is no help for you there.
4 When their breathing stops, they return to
the earth,
and in a moment all their plans come to
an end.
5 But happy are those who have the God of
Israel* as their helper,
whose hope is in the LORD their God.
6 He is the one who made heaven and earth,
the sea, and everything in them.
He is the one who keeps every promise
forever,
7 who gives justice to the oppressed
and food to the hungry.
The LORD frees the prisoners.
8 The LORD opens the eyes of the blind.
The LORD lifts the burdens of those bent
beneath their loads.
The LORD loves the righteous.

145:5 Some manuscripts read *They will speak.* 145:13 The last two lines of 145:13 are not found in many of the ancient manuscripts.
146:5 Hebrew *of Jacob.*

⁹ The LORD protects the foreigners among us.
  He cares for the orphans and widows,
  but he frustrates the plans of the wicked.

¹⁰ The LORD will reign forever.
  O Jerusalem,* your God is King in every
  generation!

Praise the LORD!

P S A L M **147**

¹ Praise the LORD!

How good it is to sing praises to our God!
  How delightful and how right!

² The LORD is rebuilding Jerusalem
  and bringing the exiles back to Israel.

³ He heals the brokenhearted,
  binding up their wounds.

⁴ He counts the stars
  and calls them all by name.

⁵ How great is our Lord! His power is absolute!
  His understanding is beyond
  comprehension!

⁶ The LORD supports the humble,
  but he brings the wicked down into the
  dust.

⁷ Sing out your thanks to the LORD;
  sing praises to our God, accompanied by
  harps.

⁸ He covers the heavens with clouds,
  provides rain for the earth,
  and makes the green grass grow in
  mountain pastures.

⁹ He feeds the wild animals,
  and the young ravens cry to him for food.

¹⁰ The strength of a horse does not impress
  him;
  how puny in his sight is the strength of a
  man.

¹¹ Rather, the LORD's delight is in those who
  honor him,
  those who put their hope in his unfailing
  love.

¹² Praise the LORD, O Jerusalem!
  Praise your God, O Zion!

¹³ For he has fortified the bars of your gates
  and blessed your children within you.

¹⁴ He sends peace across your nation
  and satisfies you with plenty of the finest
  wheat.

¹⁵ He sends his orders to the world—
  how swiftly his word flies!

146:10 Hebrew *Zion.*

¹⁶ He sends the snow like white wool;
  he scatters frost upon the ground like
  ashes.

¹⁷ He hurls the hail like stones.
  Who can stand against his freezing cold?

¹⁸ Then, at his command, it all melts.
  He sends his winds, and the ice thaws.

¹⁹ He has revealed his words to Jacob,
  his principles and laws to Israel.

²⁰ He has not done this with any other nation;
  they do not know his laws.

Praise the LORD!

P S A L M **148**

¹ Praise the LORD!

Praise the LORD from the heavens!
  Praise him from the skies!

² Praise him, all his angels!
  Praise him, all the armies of heaven!

³ Praise him, sun and moon!
  Praise him, all you twinkling stars!

⁴ Praise him, skies above!
  Praise him, vapors high above the
  clouds!

⁵ Let every created thing give praise to the
  LORD,
  for he issued his command, and they
  came into being.

⁶ He established them forever and forever.
  His orders will never be revoked.

⁷ Praise the LORD from the earth,
  you creatures of the ocean depths,

⁸ fire and hail, snow and storm,
  wind and weather that obey him,

⁹ mountains and all hills,
  fruit trees and all cedars,

¹⁰ wild animals and all livestock,
  reptiles and birds,

¹¹ kings of the earth and all people,
  rulers and judges of the earth,

¹² young men and maidens,
  old men and children.

¹³ Let them all praise the name of the LORD.
  For his name is very great;
  his glory towers over the earth and
  heaven!

¹⁴ He has made his people strong,
  honoring his godly ones—
  the people of Israel who are close to him.

Praise the LORD!

PSALM **149**

1 Praise the LORD!

Sing to the LORD a new song.
  Sing his praises in the assembly of the
  faithful.
2 O Israel, rejoice in your Maker.
  O people of Jerusalem,* exult in your
  King.
3 Praise his name with dancing,
  accompanied by tambourine and
  harp.
4 For the LORD delights in his people;
  he crowns the humble with salvation.
5 Let the faithful rejoice in this honor.
  Let them sing for joy as they lie on their
  beds.
6 Let the praises of God be in their
  mouths,
  and a sharp sword in their hands—
7 to execute vengeance on the nations
  and punishment on the peoples,
8 to bind their kings with shackles
  and their leaders with iron chains,

149:2 Hebrew *Zion.*

9 to execute the judgment written against
  them.
  This is the glory of his faithful ones.

Praise the LORD!

PSALM **150**

1 Praise the LORD!

Praise God in his heavenly dwelling;
  praise him in his mighty heaven!
2 Praise him for his mighty works;
  praise his unequaled greatness!
3 Praise him with a blast of the trumpet;
  praise him with the lyre and harp!
4 Praise him with the tambourine and dancing;
  praise him with stringed instruments and
  flutes!
5 Praise him with a clash of cymbals;
  praise him with loud clanging cymbals.
6 Let everything that lives sing praises to the
  LORD!

Praise the LORD!

Proverbs

CHAPTER 1

The Purpose of Proverbs

These are the proverbs of Solomon, David's son, king of Israel.

²The purpose of these proverbs is to teach people wisdom and discipline, and to help them understand wise sayings. ³Through these proverbs, people will receive instruction in discipline, good conduct, and doing what is right, just, and fair. ⁴These proverbs will make the simpleminded clever. They will give knowledge and purpose to young people.

⁵Let those who are wise listen to these proverbs and become even wiser. And let those who understand receive guidance ⁶by exploring the depth of meaning in these proverbs, parables, wise sayings, and riddles.

⁷Fear of the LORD is the beginning of knowledge. Only fools despise wisdom and discipline.

A Father's Exhortation: Acquire Wisdom

⁸Listen, my child,* to what your father teaches you. Don't neglect your mother's teaching. ⁹What you learn from them will crown you with grace and clothe you with honor.

¹⁰My child, if sinners entice you, turn your back on them! ¹¹They may say, "Come and join us. Let's hide and kill someone! Let's ambush the innocent! ¹²Let's swallow them alive as the grave swallows its victims. Though they are in the prime of life, they will go down into the pit of death. ¹³And the loot we'll get! We'll fill our houses with all kinds of things! ¹⁴Come on, throw in your lot with us; we'll split our loot with you."

¹⁵Don't go along with them, my child! Stay far away from their paths. ¹⁶They rush to commit crimes. They hurry to commit murder. ¹⁷When a bird sees a trap being set, it stays away. ¹⁸But not these people! They set an ambush for themselves; they booby-trap their own lives! ¹⁹Such is the fate of all who are greedy for gain. It ends up robbing them of life.

Wisdom Shouts in the Streets

²⁰Wisdom shouts in the streets. She cries out in the public square. ²¹She calls out to the crowds along the main street, and to those in front of city hall. ²²"You simpletons!" she cries. "How long will you go on being simpleminded? How long will you mockers relish your mocking? How long will you fools fight the facts? ²³Come here and listen to me! I'll pour out the spirit of wisdom upon you and make you wise.

²⁴"I called you so often, but you didn't come. I reached out to you, but you paid no attention. ²⁵You ignored my advice and rejected the correction I offered. ²⁶So I will laugh when you are in trouble! I will mock you when disaster overtakes you—²⁷when calamity overcomes you like a storm, when you are engulfed by trouble, and when anguish and distress overwhelm you.

²⁸"I will not answer when they cry for help. Even though they anxiously search for me, they will not find me. ²⁹For they hated knowledge and chose not to fear the LORD. ³⁰They rejected my advice and paid no attention when I corrected them. ³¹That is why they must eat the bitter fruit of living their own way. They must experience the full terror of the path they have chosen. ³²For they are simpletons who turn away from me—to death. They are fools, and their own complacency will destroy them. ³³But all who listen to me will live in peace and safety, unafraid of harm."

CHAPTER 2

The Benefits of Wisdom

My child,* listen to me and treasure my instructions. ²Tune your ears to wisdom, and concen-

1:8 Hebrew *my son;* also in 1:10, 15.   2:1 Hebrew *My son.*

trate on understanding. ³Cry out for insight and understanding. ⁴Search for them as you would for lost money or hidden treasure. ⁵Then you will understand what it means to fear the LORD, and you will gain knowledge of God. ⁶For the LORD grants wisdom! From his mouth come knowledge and understanding. ⁷He grants a treasure of good sense to the godly. He is their shield, protecting those who walk with integrity. ⁸He guards the paths of justice and protects those who are faithful to him.

⁹Then you will understand what is right, just, and fair, and you will know how to find the right course of action every time. ¹⁰For wisdom will enter your heart, and knowledge will fill you with joy. ¹¹Wise planning will watch over you. Understanding will keep you safe.

¹²Wisdom will save you from evil people, from those whose speech is corrupt. ¹³These people turn from right ways to walk down dark and evil paths. ¹⁴They rejoice in doing wrong, and they enjoy evil as it turns things upside down. ¹⁵What they do is crooked, and their ways are wrong.

¹⁶Wisdom will save you from the immoral woman, from the flattery of the adulterous woman. ¹⁷She has abandoned her husband and ignores the covenant she made before God. ¹⁸Entering her house leads to death; it is the road to hell.* ¹⁹The man who visits her is doomed. He will never reach the paths of life.

²⁰Follow the steps of good men instead, and stay on the paths of the righteous. ²¹For only the upright will live in the land, and those who have integrity will remain in it. ²²But the wicked will be removed from the land, and the treacherous will be destroyed.

CHAPTER **3**
Trusting in the LORD
My child,* never forget the things I have taught you. Store my commands in your heart, ²for they will give you a long and satisfying life. ³Never let loyalty and kindness get away from you! Wear them like a necklace; write them deep within your heart. ⁴Then you will find favor with both God and people, and you will gain a good reputation.

⁵Trust in the LORD with all your heart; do not depend on your own understanding. ⁶Seek his will in all you do, and he will direct your paths.

⁷Don't be impressed with your own wisdom. Instead, fear the LORD and turn your back on

evil. ⁸Then you will gain renewed health and vitality.

⁹Honor the LORD with your wealth and with the best part of everything your land produces. ¹⁰Then he will fill your barns with grain, and your vats will overflow with the finest wine.

¹¹My child, don't ignore it when the LORD disciplines you, and don't be discouraged when he corrects you. ¹²For the LORD corrects those he loves, just as a father corrects a child* in whom he delights.

¹³Happy is the person who finds wisdom and gains understanding. ¹⁴For the profit of wisdom is better than silver, and her wages are better than gold. ¹⁵Wisdom is more precious than rubies; nothing you desire can compare with her. ¹⁶She offers you life in her right hand, and riches and honor in her left. ¹⁷She will guide you down delightful paths; all her ways are satisfying. ¹⁸Wisdom is a tree of life to those who embrace her; happy are those who hold her tightly.

¹⁹By wisdom the LORD founded the earth; by understanding he established the heavens. ²⁰By his knowledge the deep fountains of the earth burst forth, and the clouds poured down rain.

²¹My child, don't lose sight of good planning and insight. Hang on to them, ²²for they fill you with life and bring you honor and respect. ²³They keep you safe on your way and keep your feet from stumbling. ²⁴You can lie down without fear and enjoy pleasant dreams. ²⁵You need not be afraid of disaster or the destruction that comes upon the wicked, ²⁶for the LORD is your security. He will keep your foot from being caught in a trap.

²⁷Do not withhold good from those who deserve it when it's in your power to help them. ²⁸If you can help your neighbor now, don't say, "Come back tomorrow, and then I'll help you."

²⁹Do not plot against your neighbors, for they trust you. ³⁰Don't make accusations against someone who hasn't wronged you.

³¹Do not envy violent people; don't copy their ways. ³²Such wicked people are an abomination to the LORD, but he offers his friendship to the godly.

³³The curse of the LORD is on the house of the wicked, but his blessing is on the home of the upright.

³⁴The LORD mocks at mockers, but he shows favor to the humble.

³⁵The wise inherit honor, but fools are put to shame!

2:18 Hebrew *to the spirits of the dead.*   3:1 Hebrew *My son;* also in 3:11, 21.   3:12 Hebrew *a son.*

CHAPTER **4**
A Father's Wise Advice

My children,* listen to me. Listen to your father's instruction. Pay attention and grow wise, ²for I am giving you good guidance. Don't turn away from my teaching. ³For I, too, was once my father's son, tenderly loved by my mother as an only child.

⁴My father told me, "Take my words to heart. Follow my instructions and you will live. ⁵Learn to be wise, and develop good judgment. Don't forget or turn away from my words. ⁶Don't turn your back on wisdom, for she will protect you. Love her, and she will guard you. ⁷Getting wisdom is the most important thing you can do! And whatever else you do, get good judgment. ⁸If you prize wisdom, she will exalt you. Embrace her and she will honor you. ⁹She will place a lovely wreath on your head; she will present you with a beautiful crown."

¹⁰My child,* listen to me and do as I say, and you will have a long, good life. ¹¹I will teach you wisdom's ways and lead you in straight paths. ¹²If you live a life guided by wisdom, you won't limp or stumble as you run. ¹³Carry out my instructions; don't forsake them. Guard them, for they will lead you to a fulfilled life.

¹⁴Do not do as the wicked do or follow the path of evildoers. ¹⁵Avoid their haunts. Turn away and go somewhere else, ¹⁶for evil people cannot sleep until they have done their evil deed for the day. They cannot rest unless they have caused someone to stumble. ¹⁷They eat wickedness and drink violence!

¹⁸The way of the righteous is like the first gleam of dawn, which shines ever brighter until the full light of day. ¹⁹But the way of the wicked is like complete darkness. Those who follow it have no idea what they are stumbling over.

²⁰Pay attention, my child, to what I say. Listen carefully. ²¹Don't lose sight of my words. Let them penetrate deep within your heart, ²²for they bring life and radiant health to anyone who discovers their meaning.

²³Above all else, guard your heart, for it affects everything you do.* ²⁴Avoid all perverse talk; stay far from corrupt speech.

²⁵Look straight ahead, and fix your eyes on what lies before you. ²⁶Mark out a straight path for your feet; then stick to the path and stay safe. ²⁷Don't get sidetracked; keep your feet from following evil.

4:1 Hebrew *My sons.*   4:10 Hebrew *My son;* also in 4:20.
4:23 Hebrew *for from it flow the springs of life.*

CHAPTER **5**
Avoid Immoral Women

My son, pay attention to my wisdom; listen carefully to my wise counsel. ²Then you will learn to be discreet and will store up knowledge.

³The lips of an immoral woman are as sweet as honey, and her mouth is smoother than oil. ⁴But the result is as bitter as poison, sharp as a double-edged sword. ⁵Her feet go down to death; her steps lead straight to the grave.* ⁶For she does not care about the path to life. She staggers down a crooked trail and doesn't even realize where it leads.

⁷So now, my sons, listen to me. Never stray from what I am about to say: ⁸Run from her! Don't go near the door of her house! ⁹If you do,

5:5 Hebrew *to Sheol.*

Trust God Completely
Read PROVERBS 3:5-8

One of the most difficult things for us to do as human beings is to fully entrust something to someone. We have an inherent desire to be in control, to make our own plans and decisions. Yet, this verse flies in the face of this philosophy. To find God's will, you need to completely trust God and his judgment and timing. How do you practically do this in your life?

• Always ask God for his will to supersede your own in your prayers.
• Seek God before you start making decisions, not afterward.
• Spend time looking for what God's Word has to say about a certain decision.
• Honor God by turning your back on evil.

To "put God first" is the same principle Jesus gave us in Matthew 6:33 (p. 796), where he reminded us of the importance of giving him "first place in [our] lives." This simply means that we consider his will as revealed in Scripture as we grapple with the decisions of life. Not only will you find his will in this process, but you also will "gain renewed health and vitality" (verse 8). Remember this passage of Scripture whenever you are faced with a moment of decision or uncertainty. You can rest assured, knowing that God wants to be an integral part of every decision you make and every step you take.

For the next note on "Seek God's Will," turn to p. 311.

you will lose your honor and hand over to merciless people everything you have achieved in life. 10Strangers will obtain your wealth, and someone else will enjoy the fruit of your labor. 11Afterward you will groan in anguish when disease consumes your body, 12and you will say, "How I hated discipline! If only I had not demanded my own way! 13Oh, why didn't I listen to my teachers? Why didn't I pay attention to those who gave me instruction? 14I have come to the brink of utter ruin, and now I must face public disgrace."

15Drink water from your own well—share your love only with your wife.* 16Why spill the water of your springs in public, having sex with just anyone?* 17You should reserve it for yourselves. Don't share it with strangers.

18Let your wife be a fountain of blessing for you. Rejoice in the wife of your youth. 19She is a loving doe, a graceful deer. Let her breasts satisfy you always. May you always be captivated by her love. 20Why be captivated, my son, with an immoral woman, or embrace the breasts of an adulterous woman?

21For the LORD sees clearly what a man does, examining every path he takes. 22An evil man is held captive by his own sins; they are ropes that catch and hold him. 23He will die for lack of self-control; he will be lost because of his incredible folly.

CHAPTER 6

Lessons for Daily Life

My child,* if you co-sign a loan for a friend or guarantee the debt of someone you hardly know—2if you have trapped yourself by your agreement and are caught by what you said—3quick, get out of it if you possibly can! You have placed yourself at your friend's mercy. Now swallow your pride; go and beg to have your name erased. 4Don't put it off. Do it now! Don't rest

until you do. 5Save yourself like a deer escaping from a hunter, like a bird fleeing from a net.

6Take a lesson from the ants, you lazybones. Learn from their ways and be wise! 7Even though they have no prince, governor, or ruler to make them work, 8they labor hard all summer, gathering food for the winter. 9But you, lazybones, how long will you sleep? When will you wake up? I want you to learn this lesson: 10A little extra sleep, a little more slumber, a little folding of the hands to rest—11and poverty will pounce on you like a bandit; scarcity will attack you like an armed robber.

12Here is a description of worthless and wicked people: They are constant liars, 13signaling their true intentions to their friends by making signs with their eyes and feet and fingers. 14Their perverted hearts plot evil. They stir up trouble constantly. 15But they will be destroyed suddenly, broken beyond all hope of healing.

16There are six things the LORD hates—no, seven things he detests:
17 haughty eyes,
   a lying tongue,
   hands that kill the innocent,
18 a heart that plots evil,
   feet that race to do wrong,
19 a false witness who pours out lies,
   a person who sows discord among brothers.

20My son, obey your father's commands, and don't neglect your mother's teaching. 21Keep their words always in your heart. Tie them around your neck. 22Wherever you walk, their counsel can lead you. When you sleep, they will protect you. When you wake up in the morning, they will advise you. 23For these commands and this teaching are a lamp to light the way ahead of you. The correction of discipline is the way to life.

24These commands and this teaching will keep you from the immoral woman, from the smooth tongue of an adulterous woman. 25Don't lust for

5:15 Hebrew Drink water from your own cistern, flowing water from your own well.   5:16 Hebrew Why spill your springs in public, your streams in the streets?   6:1 Hebrew My son.

OFF AND RUNNING

The Boundaries of Marriage Are to Be Honored and Enjoyed Read PROVERBS 5:15-20

Marriage is a unique, fragile bond between a man and a woman. It is unique in the sense that no other relationship between a man and a woman allows them to become one. It is fragile in the sense that the intimacy and trust built up over years can be destroyed in one careless moment.

To preserve and protect this bond, God established boundaries for conduct. One important boundary contained

her beauty. Don't let her coyness seduce you. 26For a prostitute will bring you to poverty, and sleeping with another man's wife may cost you your very life. 27Can a man scoop fire into his lap and not be burned? 28Can he walk on hot coals and not blister his feet? 29So it is with the man who sleeps with another man's wife. He who embraces her will not go unpunished.

30Excuses might be found for a thief who steals because he is starving. 31But if he is caught, he will be fined seven times as much as he stole, even if it means selling everything in his house to pay it back.

32But the man who commits adultery is an utter fool, for he destroys his own soul. 33Wounds and constant disgrace are his lot. His shame will never be erased. 34For the woman's husband will be furious in his jealousy, and he will have no mercy in his day of vengeance. 35There is no compensation or bribe that will satisfy him.

CHAPTER **7**

Another Warning about Immoral Women

Follow my advice, my son; always treasure my commands. 2Obey them and live! Guard my teachings as your most precious possession.* 3Tie them on your fingers as a reminder. Write them deep within your heart.

4Love wisdom like a sister; make insight a beloved member of your family. 5Let them hold you back from an affair with an immoral woman, from listening to the flattery of an adulterous woman.

6I was looking out the window of my house one day 7and saw a simpleminded young man who lacked common sense. 8He was crossing the street near the house of an immoral woman. He was strolling down the path by her house 9at twilight, as the day was fading, as the dark of night set in. 10The woman approached him, dressed seductively and sly of heart. 11She was

7:2 Hebrew *as the apple of your eye.*   7:27 Hebrew *to Sheol.*

the brash, rebellious type who never stays at home. 12She is often seen in the streets and markets, soliciting at every corner.

13She threw her arms around him and kissed him, and with a brazen look she said, 14"I've offered my sacrifices and just finished my vows. 15It's you I was looking for! I came out to find you, and here you are! 16My bed is spread with colored sheets of finest linen imported from Egypt. 17I've perfumed my bed with myrrh, aloes, and cinnamon. 18Come, let's drink our fill of love until morning. Let's enjoy each other's caresses, 19for my husband is not home. He's away on a long trip. 20He has taken a wallet full of money with him, and he won't return until later in the month."

21So she seduced him with her pretty speech. With her flattery she enticed him. 22He followed her at once, like an ox going to the slaughter or like a trapped stag, 23awaiting the arrow that would pierce its heart. He was like a bird flying into a snare, little knowing it would cost him his life.

24Listen to me, my sons, and pay attention to my words. 25Don't let your hearts stray away toward her. Don't wander down her wayward path. 26For she has been the ruin of many; numerous men have been her victims. 27Her house is the road to the grave.* Her bedroom is the den of death.

CHAPTER **8**

Wisdom Calls for a Hearing

Listen as wisdom calls out! Hear as understanding raises her voice! 2She stands on the hilltop and at the crossroads. 3At the entrance to the city, at the city gates, she cries aloud, 4"I call to you, to all of you! I am raising my voice to all people. 5How naive you are! Let me give you common sense. O foolish ones, let me give you understanding. 6Listen to me! For I have excellent things to tell you. Everything I say is right,

---

in this passage is sexual fidelity. When this boundary is crossed, the sacred bond of marriage is jeopardized. Not only does sexual infidelity hurt a couple's relationship, but it can cause pain and problems for an entire family.

Although God has established boundaries within which people can seek sexual satisfaction, he is not a killjoy. In fact, he created sex to be enjoyed between a husband and wife. He never intended for marriages to become lifeless and dull. If a couple keeps the romance alive in their own marriage, the temptation to look for someone else to meet their needs will be much less appealing. As this passage explains, a husband and wife can find true sexual fulfillment if they stay within the boundaries God has given them.

For the next note on "Marriage," turn to p. 1082.

7for I speak the truth and hate every kind of deception. 8My advice is wholesome and good. There is nothing crooked or twisted in it. 9My words are plain to anyone with understanding, clear to those who want to learn.

10"Choose my instruction rather than silver, and knowledge over pure gold. 11For wisdom is far more valuable than rubies. Nothing you desire can be compared with it.

12"I, Wisdom, live together with good judgment. I know where to discover knowledge and discernment. 13All who fear the LORD will hate evil. That is why I hate pride, arrogance, corruption, and perverted speech. 14Good advice and success belong to me. Insight and strength are mine. 15Because of me, kings reign, and rulers make just laws. 16Rulers lead with my help, and nobles make righteous judgments.

17"I love all who love me. Those who search for me will surely find me. 18Unending riches, honor, wealth, and justice are mine to distribute. 19My gifts are better than the purest gold, my wages better than sterling silver! 20I walk in righteousness, in paths of justice. 21Those who love me inherit wealth, for I fill their treasuries.

22"The LORD formed me from the beginning, before he created anything else. 23I was appointed in ages past, at the very first, before the earth began. 24I was born before the oceans were created, before the springs bubbled forth their waters. 25Before the mountains and the hills were formed, I was born—26before he had made the earth and fields and the first handfuls of soil. 27"I was there when he established the heavens, when he drew the horizon on the oceans. 28I was there when he set the clouds above, when he established the deep fountains of the earth. 29I was there when he set the limits of the seas, so they would not spread beyond their boundaries. And when he marked off the earth's foundations, 30I was the architect at his side. I was his constant delight, rejoicing always in his presence. 31And how happy I was with what he created—his wide world and all the human family!

32"And so, my children,* listen to me, for happy are all who follow my ways. 33Listen to my counsel and be wise. Don't ignore it.

34"Happy are those who listen to me, watching for me daily at my gates, waiting for me outside my home! 35For whoever finds me finds life and wins approval from the LORD. 36But those who miss me have injured themselves. All who hate me love death."

CHAPTER **9**

Wisdom has built her spacious house with seven pillars. 2She has prepared a great banquet, mixed the wines, and set the table. 3She has sent her servants to invite everyone to come. She calls out from the heights overlooking the city. 4"Come home with me," she urges the simple. To those without good judgment, she says, 5"Come, eat my food, and drink the wine I have mixed. 6Leave your foolish ways behind, and begin to live; learn how to be wise."

7Anyone who rebukes a mocker will get a smart retort. Anyone who rebukes the wicked will get hurt. 8So don't bother rebuking mockers; they will only hate you. But the wise, when rebuked, will love you all the more. 9Teach the wise, and they will be wiser. Teach the righteous, and they will learn more.

10Fear of the LORD is the beginning of wisdom. Knowledge of the Holy One results in understanding.

11Wisdom will multiply your days and add years to your life. 12If you become wise, you will be the one to benefit. If you scorn wisdom, you will be the one to suffer.

Folly Calls for a Hearing

13The woman named Folly is loud and brash. She is ignorant and doesn't even know it. 14She sits in her doorway on the heights overlooking the city. 15She calls out to men going by who are minding their own business. 16"Come home with me," she urges the simple. To those without good judgment, she says, 17"Stolen water is refreshing; food eaten in secret tastes the best!" 18But the men don't realize that her former guests are now in the grave.*

CHAPTER **10**

The Proverbs of Solomon

The proverbs of Solomon:

A wise child* brings joy to a father; a foolish child brings grief to a mother.

2Ill-gotten gain has no lasting value, but right living can save your life.

3The LORD will not let the godly starve to death, but he refuses to satisfy the craving of the wicked.

4Lazy people are soon poor; hard workers get rich.

5A wise youth works hard all summer; a youth who sleeps away the hour of opportunity brings shame.

8:32 Hebrew *my sons*. **9:18** Hebrew *in Sheol*. **10:1** Hebrew *son*; also in 10:1b.

6The godly are showered with blessings; evil people cover up their harmful intentions.

7We all have happy memories of the godly, but the name of a wicked person rots away.

8The wise are glad to be instructed, but babbling fools fall flat on their faces.

9People with integrity have firm footing, but those who follow crooked paths will slip and fall.

10People who wink at wrong cause trouble, but a bold reproof promotes peace.*

11The words of the godly lead to life; evil people cover up their harmful intentions.

12Hatred stirs up quarrels, but love covers all offenses.

13Wise words come from the lips of people with understanding, but fools will be punished with a rod.

14Wise people treasure knowledge, but the babbling of a fool invites trouble.

15The wealth of the rich is their fortress; the poverty of the poor is their calamity.

16The earnings of the godly enhance their lives, but evil people squander their money on sin.

17People who accept correction are on the pathway to life, but those who ignore it will lead others astray.

18To hide hatred is to be a liar; to slander is to be a fool.

19Don't talk too much, for it fosters sin. Be sensible and turn off the flow!

20The words of the godly are like sterling silver; the heart of a fool is worthless.

21The godly give good advice, but fools are destroyed by their lack of common sense.

22The blessing of the LORD makes a person rich, and he adds no sorrow with it.

23Doing wrong is fun for a fool, while wise conduct is a pleasure to the wise.

24The fears of the wicked will all come true; so will the hopes of the godly.

25Disaster strikes like a cyclone, whirling the wicked away, but the godly have a lasting foundation.

26Lazy people are a pain to their employer. They are like smoke in the eyes or vinegar that sets the teeth on edge.

27Fear of the LORD lengthens one's life, but the years of the wicked are cut short.

28The hopes of the godly result in happiness, but the expectations of the wicked are all in vain.

29The LORD protects the upright but destroys the wicked.

30The godly will never be disturbed, but the wicked will be removed from the land.

31The godly person gives wise advice, but the tongue that deceives will be cut off.

32The godly speak words that are helpful, but the wicked speak only what is corrupt.

CHAPTER **11**

The LORD hates cheating, but he delights in honesty.

2Pride leads to disgrace, but with humility comes wisdom.

3Good people are guided by their honesty; treacherous people are destroyed by their dishonesty.

4Riches won't help on the day of judgment, but right living is a safeguard against death.

5The godly are directed by their honesty; the wicked fall beneath their load of sin.

6The godliness of good people rescues them; the ambition of treacherous people traps them.

7When the wicked die, their hopes all perish, for they rely on their own feeble strength.

8God rescues the godly from danger, but he lets the wicked fall into trouble.

9Evil words destroy one's friends; wise discernment rescues the godly.

10The whole city celebrates when the godly succeed; they shout for joy when the godless die.

11Upright citizens bless a city and make it prosper, but the talk of the wicked tears it apart.

12It is foolish to belittle a neighbor; a person with good sense remains silent.

13A gossip goes around revealing secrets, but those who are trustworthy can keep a confidence.

14Without wise leadership, a nation falls; with many counselors, there is safety.

15Guaranteeing a loan for a stranger is dangerous; it is better to refuse than to suffer later.

16Beautiful women obtain wealth, and violent men get rich.

17Your own soul is nourished when you are kind, but you destroy yourself when you are cruel.

18Evil people get rich for the moment, but the reward of the godly will last.

19Godly people find life; evil people find death.

20The LORD hates people with twisted hearts, but he delights in those who have integrity.

21You can be sure that evil people will be punished, but the children of the godly will go free.

22A woman who is beautiful but lacks discretion is like a gold ring in a pig's snout.

10:10 As in Greek version; Hebrew reads *but babbling fools fall flat on their faces.*

23The godly can look forward to happiness, while the wicked can expect only wrath.

24It is possible to give freely and become more wealthy, but those who are stingy will lose everything.

25The generous prosper and are satisfied; those who refresh others will themselves be refreshed.

26People curse those who hold their grain for higher prices, but they bless the one who sells to them in their time of need.

27If you search for good, you will find favor; but if you search for evil, it will find you!

28Trust in your money and down you go! But the godly flourish like leaves in spring.

29Those who bring trouble on their families inherit only the wind. The fool will be a servant to the wise.

30The godly are like trees that bear life-giving fruit, and those who save lives are wise.

31If the righteous are rewarded here on earth, how much more true that the wicked and the sinner will get what they deserve!

CHAPTER **12**

To learn, you must love discipline; it is stupid to hate correction.

2The LORD approves of those who are good, but he condemns those who plan wickedness.

3Wickedness never brings stability; only the godly have deep roots.

4A worthy wife is her husband's joy and crown; a shameful wife saps his strength.

5The plans of the godly are just; the advice of the wicked is treacherous.

6The words of the wicked are like a murderous ambush, but the words of the godly save lives.

7The wicked perish and are gone, but the children of the godly stand firm.

8Everyone admires a person with good sense, but a warped mind is despised.

9It is better to be a nobody with a servant than to be self-important but have no food.

10The godly are concerned for the welfare of their animals, but even the kindness of the wicked is cruel.

11Hard work means prosperity; only fools idle away their time.

12Thieves are jealous of each other's loot, while the godly bear their own fruit.

13The wicked are trapped by their own words, but the godly escape such trouble.

14People can get many good things by the words they say; the work of their hands also gives them many benefits.

15Fools think they need no advice, but the wise listen to others.

16A fool is quick-tempered, but a wise person stays calm when insulted.

17An honest witness tells the truth; a false witness tells lies.

18Some people make cutting remarks, but the words of the wise bring healing.

19Truth stands the test of time; lies are soon exposed.

20Deceit fills hearts that are plotting evil; joy fills hearts that are planning peace!

21No real harm befalls the godly, but the wicked have their fill of trouble.

22The LORD hates those who don't keep their word, but he delights in those who do.

23Wise people don't make a show of their knowledge, but fools broadcast their folly.

24Work hard and become a leader; be lazy and become a slave.

25Worry weighs a person down; an encouraging word cheers a person up.

26The godly give good advice to their friends;* the wicked lead them astray.

27Lazy people don't even cook the game they catch, but the diligent make use of everything they find.

28The way of the godly leads to life; their path does not lead to death.

CHAPTER **13**

A wise child* accepts a parent's discipline; a young mocker refuses to listen.

2Good people enjoy the positive results of their words, but those who are treacherous crave violence.

3Those who control their tongue will have a long life; a quick retort can ruin everything.

4Lazy people want much but get little, but those who work hard will prosper and be satisfied.

5Those who are godly hate lies; the wicked come to shame and disgrace.

6Godliness helps people all through life, while the evil are destroyed by their wickedness.

7Some who are poor pretend to be rich; others who are rich pretend to be poor.

8The rich can pay a ransom, but the poor won't even get threatened.

9The life of the godly is full of light and joy, but the sinner's light is snuffed out.

10Pride leads to arguments; those who take advice are wise.

12:26 Or *The godly are cautious in friendship,* or *the godly are freed from evil.* The meaning of the Hebrew is uncertain. **13:1** Hebrew *son.*

11Wealth from get-rich-quick schemes quickly disappears; wealth from hard work grows.

12Hope deferred makes the heart sick, but when dreams come true, there is life and joy.

13People who despise advice will find themselves in trouble; those who respect it will succeed.

14The advice of the wise is like a life-giving fountain; those who accept it avoid the snares of death.

15A person with good sense is respected; a treacherous person walks a rocky road.

16Wise people think before they act; fools don't and even brag about it!

17An unreliable messenger stumbles into trouble, but a reliable messenger brings healing.

18If you ignore criticism, you will end in poverty and disgrace; if you accept criticism, you will be honored.

19It is pleasant to see dreams come true, but fools will not turn from evil to attain them.

20Whoever walks with the wise will become wise; whoever walks with fools will suffer harm.

21Trouble chases sinners, while blessings chase the righteous!

22Good people leave an inheritance to their grandchildren, but the sinner's wealth passes to the godly.

23A poor person's farm may produce much food, but injustice sweeps it all away.

24If you refuse to discipline your children, it proves you don't love them; if you love your children, you will be prompt to discipline them.

25The godly eat to their hearts' content, but the belly of the wicked goes hungry.

CHAPTER 14

A wise woman builds her house; a foolish woman tears hers down with her own hands.

2Those who follow the right path fear the LORD; those who take the wrong path despise him.

3The talk of fools is a rod for their backs,* but the words of the wise keep them out of trouble.

4An empty stable stays clean, but no income comes from an empty stable.

5A truthful witness does not lie; a false witness breathes lies.

6A mocker seeks wisdom and never finds it, but knowledge comes easily to those with understanding.

7Stay away from fools, for you won't find knowledge there.

8The wise look ahead to see what is coming, but fools deceive themselves.

9Fools make fun of guilt, but the godly acknowledge it and seek reconciliation.

10Each heart knows its own bitterness, and no one else can fully share its joy.

11The house of the wicked will perish, but the tent of the godly will flourish.

12There is a path before each person that seems right, but it ends in death.

13Laughter can conceal a heavy heart; when the laughter ends, the grief remains.

14Backsliders get what they deserve; good people receive their reward.

15Only simpletons believe everything they are told! The prudent carefully consider their steps.

16The wise are cautious* and avoid danger; fools plunge ahead with great confidence.

17Those who are short-tempered do foolish things, and schemers are hated.

18The simpleton is clothed with folly, but the wise person is crowned with knowledge.

19Evil people will bow before good people; the wicked will bow at the gates of the godly.

20The poor are despised even by their neighbors, while the rich have many "friends."

21It is sin to despise one's neighbors; blessed are those who help the poor.

22If you plot evil, you will be lost; but if you plan good, you will be granted unfailing love and faithfulness.

23Work brings profit, but mere talk leads to poverty!

24Wealth is a crown for the wise; the effort of fools yields only folly.

25A truthful witness saves lives, but a false witness is a traitor.

26Those who fear the LORD are secure; he will be a place of refuge for their children.

27Fear of the LORD is a life-giving fountain; it offers escape from the snares of death.

28A growing population is a king's glory; a dwindling nation is his doom.

29Those who control their anger have great understanding; those with a hasty temper will make mistakes.

30A relaxed attitude lengthens life; jealousy rots it away.

31Those who oppress the poor insult their Maker, but those who help the poor honor him.

32The wicked are crushed by their sins, but the godly have a refuge when they die.

33Wisdom is enshrined in an understanding heart; wisdom is not* found among fools.

14:3 Hebrew *a rod of pride.* 14:16 Hebrew *The wise fear.* 14:33 As in Greek version; Hebrew lacks *not.*

³⁴Godliness exalts a nation, but sin is a disgrace to any people.

³⁵A king rejoices in servants who know what they are doing; he is angry with those who cause trouble.

CHAPTER 15

A gentle answer turns away wrath, but harsh words stir up anger.

²The wise person makes learning a joy; fools spout only foolishness.

³The LORD is watching everywhere, keeping his eye on both the evil and the good.

⁴Gentle words bring life and health; a deceitful tongue crushes the spirit.

⁵Only a fool despises a parent's discipline; whoever learns from correction is wise.

⁶There is treasure in the house of the godly, but the earnings of the wicked bring trouble.

⁷Only the wise can give good advice; fools cannot do so.

⁸The LORD hates the sacrifice of the wicked, but he delights in the prayers of the upright.

⁹The LORD despises the way of the wicked, but he loves those who pursue godliness.

¹⁰Whoever abandons the right path will be severely punished; whoever hates correction will die.

¹¹Even the depths of Death and Destruction* are known by the LORD. How much more does he know the human heart!

¹²Mockers don't love those who rebuke them, so they stay away from the wise.

¹³A glad heart makes a happy face; a broken heart crushes the spirit.

¹⁴A wise person is hungry for truth, while the fool feeds on trash.

¹⁵For the poor, every day brings trouble; for the happy heart, life is a continual feast.

¹⁶It is better to have little with fear for the LORD than to have great treasure with turmoil.

¹⁷A bowl of soup with someone you love is better than steak with someone you hate.

15:11 Hebrew *Sheol and Abaddon.*   15:24 Hebrew *Sheol.*

¹⁸A hothead starts fights; a cool-tempered person tries to stop them.

¹⁹A lazy person has trouble all through life; the path of the upright is easy!

²⁰Sensible children bring joy to their father; foolish children despise their mother.

²¹Foolishness brings joy to those who have no sense; a sensible person stays on the right path.

²²Plans go wrong for lack of advice; many counselors bring success.

²³Everyone enjoys a fitting reply; it is wonderful to say the right thing at the right time!

²⁴The path of the wise leads to life above; they leave the grave* behind.

²⁵The LORD destroys the house of the proud, but he protects the property of widows.

²⁶The LORD despises the thoughts of the wicked, but he delights in pure words.

²⁷Dishonest money brings grief to the whole family, but those who hate bribes will live.

²⁸The godly think before speaking; the wicked spout evil words.

²⁹The LORD is far from the wicked, but he hears the prayers of the righteous.

³⁰A cheerful look brings joy to the heart; good news makes for good health.

³¹If you listen to constructive criticism, you will be at home among the wise.

³²If you reject criticism, you only harm yourself; but if you listen to correction, you grow in understanding.

³³Fear of the LORD teaches a person to be wise; humility precedes honor.

CHAPTER 16

We can gather our thoughts, but the LORD gives the right answer.

²People may be pure in their own eyes, but the LORD examines their motives.

³Commit your work to the LORD, and then your plans will succeed.

⁴The LORD has made everything for his own purposes, even the wicked for punishment.

OFF AND RUNNING

Think before You Speak Read PROVERBS 16:23-24

You might say these verses are directed to those of us who suffer from the foot-in-mouth syndrome. It is so easy to say things without really thinking about the implications of our words. Yet, as Christ's ambassadors, we especially need to weigh our words. The only way we can do this is to develop a wise mind.

5The LORD despises pride; be assured that the proud will be punished.

6Unfailing love and faithfulness cover sin; evil is avoided by fear of the LORD.

7When the ways of people please the LORD, he makes even their enemies live at peace with them.

8It is better to be poor and godly than rich and dishonest.

9We can make our plans, but the LORD determines our steps.

10The king speaks with divine wisdom; he must never judge unfairly.

11The LORD demands fairness in every business deal; he sets the standard.

12A king despises wrongdoing, for his rule depends on his justice.

13The king is pleased with righteous lips; he loves those who speak honestly.

14The anger of the king is a deadly threat; the wise do what they can to appease it.

15When the king smiles, there is life; his favor refreshes like a gentle rain.

16How much better to get wisdom than gold, and understanding than silver!

17The path of the upright leads away from evil; whoever follows that path is safe.

18Pride goes before destruction, and haughtiness before a fall.

19It is better to live humbly with the poor than to share plunder with the proud.

20Those who listen to instruction will prosper; those who trust the LORD will be happy.

21The wise are known for their understanding, and instruction is appreciated if it's well presented.

22Discretion is a life-giving fountain to those who possess it, but discipline is wasted on fools.

23From a wise mind comes wise speech; the words of the wise are persuasive.

24Kind words are like honey—sweet to the soul and healthy for the body.

25There is a path before each person that seems right, but it ends in death.

26It is good for workers to have an appetite; an empty stomach drives them on.

27Scoundrels hunt for scandal; their words are a destructive blaze.

28A troublemaker plants seeds of strife; gossip separates the best of friends.

29Violent people deceive their companions, leading them down a harmful path.

30With narrowed eyes, they plot evil; without a word, they plan their mischief.

31Gray hair is a crown of glory; it is gained by living a godly life.

32It is better to be patient than powerful; it is better to have self-control than to conquer a city.

33We may throw the dice, but the LORD determines how they fall.

CHAPTER **17**

A dry crust eaten in peace is better than a great feast with strife.

2A wise slave will rule over the master's shameful sons and will share their inheritance.

3Fire tests the purity of silver and gold, but the LORD tests the heart.

4Wrongdoers listen to wicked talk; liars pay attention to destructive words.

5Those who mock the poor insult their Maker; those who rejoice at the misfortune of others will be punished.

6Grandchildren are the crowning glory of the aged; parents are the pride of their children.

7Eloquent speech is not fitting for a fool; even less are lies fitting for a ruler.

8A bribe seems to work like magic for those who give it; they succeed in all they do.

9Disregarding another person's faults preserves love; telling about them separates close friends.

10A single rebuke does more for a person of understanding than a hundred lashes on the back of a fool.

11Evil people seek rebellion, but they will be severely punished.

12It is safer to meet a bear robbed of her cubs than to confront a fool caught in folly.

13If you repay evil for good, evil will never leave your house.

How do we develop a wise mind? The Bible teaches that trust and reverence for the Lord is the first step to obtaining wisdom (see Proverbs 1:7, p. 541). Carrying that thought over to this verse, if we are truly wise, then our conversation should reflect a holy respect for our heavenly Father. When we allow this pattern to guide our speech, our words will have greater value. They will build up rather than tear down. And ultimately, they will draw attention to the Lord rather than ourselves.

For the next note on "Conversation," turn to p. 1088.

¹⁴Beginning a quarrel is like opening a floodgate, so drop the matter before a dispute breaks out.

¹⁵The LORD despises those who acquit the guilty and condemn the innocent.

¹⁶It is senseless to pay tuition to educate a fool who has no heart for wisdom.

¹⁷A friend is always loyal, and a brother is born to help in time of need.

¹⁸It is poor judgment to co-sign a friend's note, to become responsible for a neighbor's debts.

¹⁹Anyone who loves to quarrel loves sin; anyone who speaks boastfully* invites disaster.

²⁰The crooked heart will not prosper; the twisted tongue tumbles into trouble.

²¹It is painful to be the parent of a fool; there is no joy for the father of a rebel.

²²A cheerful heart is good medicine, but a broken spirit saps a person's strength.

²³The wicked accept secret bribes to pervert justice.

²⁴Sensible people keep their eyes glued on wisdom, but a fool's eyes wander to the ends of the earth.

²⁵A foolish child* brings grief to a father and bitterness to a mother.

²⁶It is wrong to fine the godly for being good or to punish nobles for being honest!

²⁷A truly wise person uses few words; a person with understanding is even-tempered.

²⁸Even fools are thought to be wise when they keep silent; when they keep their mouths shut, they seem intelligent.

CHAPTER **18**

A recluse is self-indulgent, snarling at every sound principle of conduct.

²Fools have no interest in understanding; they only want to air their own opinions.

³When the wicked arrive, contempt, shame, and disgrace are sure to follow.

⁴A person's words can be life-giving water; words of true wisdom are as refreshing as a bubbling brook.

⁵It is wrong for a judge to favor the guilty or condemn the innocent.

⁶Fools get into constant quarrels; they are asking for a beating.

⁷The mouths of fools are their ruin; their lips get them into trouble.

⁸What dainty morsels rumors are—but they sink deep into one's heart.

⁹A lazy person is as bad as someone who destroys things.

¹⁰The name of the LORD is a strong fortress; the godly run to him and are safe.

¹¹The rich think of their wealth as an impregnable defense; they imagine it is a high wall of safety.

¹²Haughtiness goes before destruction; humility precedes honor.

¹³What a shame, what folly, to give advice before listening to the facts!

¹⁴The human spirit can endure a sick body, but who can bear it if the spirit is crushed?

¹⁵Intelligent people are always open to new ideas. In fact, they look for them.

¹⁶Giving a gift works wonders; it may bring you before important people!

¹⁷Any story sounds true until someone sets the record straight.

¹⁸Casting lots can end arguments and settle disputes between powerful opponents.

¹⁹It's harder to make amends with an offended friend than to capture a fortified city. Arguments separate friends like a gate locked with iron bars.

²⁰Words satisfy the soul as food satisfies the

17:19 Or *who builds up defenses;* Hebrew reads *who makes a high gate.*   17:25 Hebrew *son.*

OFF AND RUNNING

Marriage Is for Companionship Read PROVERBS 18:22

When two people get married, they become many things. They become husband and wife. They become lovers. Eventually they may become mother and father, and even grandmother and grandfather. They essentially become partners in life, and even in business. All of these things are a part of the marriage relationship. Yet, as the years go by, it is easy for that couple to lose sight of the one thing that brought them together in the first place: friendship.

This verse reminds us that marriage is not just some simple agreement two people make. It is a unique blessing from God himself. While God has given some people the ability to be happily single (see "Marriage Is Not for Everyone," p. 990), he has given others the gift of a companion for life. For that reason, we should never take the friendship of our husband or our wife for granted.

stomach; the right words on a person's lips bring satisfaction.

21 Those who love to talk will experience the consequences, for the tongue can kill or nourish life.

22The man who finds a wife finds a treasure and receives favor from the LORD.

23The poor plead for mercy; the rich answer with insults.

24There are "friends" who destroy each other, but a real friend sticks closer than a brother.

CHAPTER **19**

It is better to be poor and honest than to be a fool and dishonest.

2Zeal without knowledge is not good; a person who moves too quickly may go the wrong way.

3People ruin their lives by their own foolishness and then are angry at the LORD.

4Wealth makes many "friends"; poverty drives them away.

5A false witness will not go unpunished, nor will a liar escape.

6Many beg favors from a prince; everyone is the friend of a person who gives gifts!

7If the relatives of the poor despise them, how much more will their friends avoid them. The poor call after them, but they are gone.

8To acquire wisdom is to love oneself; people who cherish understanding will prosper.

9A false witness will not go unpunished, and a liar will be destroyed.

10It isn't right for a fool to live in luxury or for a slave to rule over princes!

11People with good sense restrain their anger; they earn esteem by overlooking wrongs.

12The king's anger is like a lion's roar, but his favor is like dew on the grass.

13A foolish child* is a calamity to a father; a nagging wife annoys like a constant dripping.

19:13 Hebrew *son;* also in 19:27.

14Parents can provide their sons with an inheritance of houses and wealth, but only the LORD can give an understanding wife.

15A lazy person sleeps soundly—and goes hungry.

16Keep the commandments and keep your life; despising them leads to death.

17If you help the poor, you are lending to the LORD—and he will repay you!

18Discipline your children while there is hope. If you don't, you will ruin their lives.

19Short-tempered people must pay their own penalty. If you rescue them once, you will have to do it again.

20Get all the advice and instruction you can, and be wise the rest of your life.

21You can make many plans, but the LORD's purpose will prevail.

22Loyalty makes a person attractive. And it is better to be poor than dishonest.

23Fear of the LORD gives life, security, and protection from harm.

24Some people are so lazy that they won't even lift a finger to feed themselves.

25If you punish a mocker, the simpleminded will learn a lesson; if you reprove the wise, they will be all the wiser.

26Children who mistreat their father or chase away their mother are a public disgrace and an embarrassment.

27If you stop listening to instruction, my child, you have turned your back on knowledge.

28A corrupt witness makes a mockery of justice; the mouth of the wicked gulps down evil.

29Mockers will be punished, and the backs of fools will be beaten.

CHAPTER **20**

Wine produces mockers; liquor leads to brawls. Whoever is led astray by drink cannot be wise.

When you trace marriage back to its roots, you see that God brought the very first couple—Adam and Eve—together because of Adam's need for companionship (see Genesis 2:18, p. 4). That is pretty amazing when you think about it. Adam—made in the image of God, placed in a flawless creation which God had told him to enjoy, with free and constant access to his Creator—still felt that something was missing in his life. That is when God decided to bring Eve into the picture. He did not want man to be alone.

If you are married, make a point to constantly cultivate the friendship in your marriage. Look as great for one another as you did when you were dating. Listen to each other as much as you did at the beginning of your relationship. Tell your spouse often how much you appreciate him or her. Make time to pray and study the Bible together to deepen your spiritual bond. Above all, remember that your husband or wife is a precious gift—a lifelong companion—from the Lord.

For the next note on "Marriage," turn to p. 572.

²The king's fury is like a lion's roar; to rouse his anger is to risk your life.

³Avoiding a fight is a mark of honor; only fools insist on quarreling.

⁴If you are too lazy to plow in the right season, you will have no food at the harvest.

⁵Though good advice lies deep within a person's heart, the wise will draw it out.

⁶Many will say they are loyal friends, but who can find one who is really faithful?

⁷The godly walk with integrity; blessed are their children after them.

⁸When a king judges, he carefully weighs all the evidence, distinguishing the bad from the good.

⁹Who can say, "I have cleansed my heart; I am pure and free from sin"?

¹⁰The LORD despises double standards of every kind.

¹¹Even children are known by the way they act, whether their conduct is pure and right.

¹²Ears to hear and eyes to see—both are gifts from the LORD.

¹³If you love sleep, you will end in poverty. Keep your eyes open, and there will be plenty to eat!

¹⁴The buyer haggles over the price, saying, "It's worthless," then brags about getting a bargain!

¹⁵Wise speech is rarer and more valuable than gold and rubies.

¹⁶Be sure to get collateral from anyone who guarantees the debt of a stranger. Get a deposit if someone guarantees the debt of a foreigner.*

¹⁷Stolen bread tastes sweet, but it turns to gravel in the mouth.

¹⁸Plans succeed through good counsel; don't go to war without the advice of others.

¹⁹A gossip tells secrets, so don't hang around with someone who talks too much.

²⁰If you curse your father or mother, the lamp of your life will be snuffed out.

²¹An inheritance obtained early in life is not a blessing in the end.

²²Don't say, "I will get even for this wrong." Wait for the LORD to handle the matter.

²³The LORD despises double standards; he is not pleased by dishonest scales.

²⁴How can we understand the road we travel? It is the LORD who directs our steps.

²⁵It is dangerous to make a rash promise to God before counting the cost.

²⁶A wise king finds the wicked, lays them out like wheat, then runs the crushing wheel over them.

²⁷The LORD's searchlight penetrates the human spirit,* exposing every hidden motive.

²⁸Unfailing love and faithfulness protect the king; his throne is made secure through love.

²⁹The glory of the young is their strength; the gray hair of experience is the splendor of the old.

³⁰Physical punishment cleanses away evil;* such discipline purifies the heart.

CHAPTER **21**

The king's heart is like a stream of water directed by the LORD; he turns it wherever he pleases.

²People may think they are doing what is right, but the LORD examines the heart.

³The LORD is more pleased when we do what is just and right than when we give him sacrifices.

⁴Haughty eyes, a proud heart, and evil actions are all sin.

⁵Good planning and hard work lead to prosperity, but hasty shortcuts lead to poverty.

⁶Wealth created by lying is a vanishing mist and a deadly trap.*

⁷Because the wicked refuse to do what is just, their violence boomerangs and destroys them.

⁸The guilty walk a crooked path; the innocent travel a straight road.

⁹It is better to live alone in the corner of an attic than with a contentious wife in a lovely home.

20:16 An alternate reading in the Hebrew text is *the debt of an adulterous woman;* compare 27:13.   20:27 Or *The human spirit is the LORD's searchlight.*   20:30 The meaning of the Hebrew is uncertain.   21:6 As in Greek version; Hebrew reads *mist for those who seek death.*

OFF AND RUNNING

Children Are Never Too Young to Learn about God
Read PROVERBS 22:6

The original Hebrew meaning of the word *teach* in this verse connotes the actions of a midwife. During biblical times, a midwife, after helping to deliver a baby, would dip her finger in crushed dates and then put her sweetened finger in the infant's mouth. This would help create a thirst for milk in the infant. That is the main idea behind this verse—to create a thirst in your child for the things of God from infancy to adulthood.

¹⁰Evil people love to harm others; their neighbors get no mercy from them.

¹¹A simpleton can learn only by seeing mockers punished; a wise person learns from instruction.

¹²The Righteous One* knows what is going on in the homes of the wicked; he will bring the wicked to disaster.

¹³Those who shut their ears to the cries of the poor will be ignored in their own time of need.

¹⁴A secret gift calms anger; a secret bribe pacifies fury.

¹⁵Justice is a joy to the godly, but it causes dismay among evildoers.

¹⁶The person who strays from common sense will end up in the company of the dead.

¹⁷Those who love pleasure become poor; wine and luxury are not the way to riches.

¹⁸Sometimes the wicked are punished to save the godly, and the treacherous for the upright.

¹⁹It is better to live alone in the desert than with a crabby, complaining wife.

²⁰The wise have wealth and luxury, but fools spend whatever they get.

²¹Whoever pursues godliness and unfailing love will find life, godliness, and honor.

²²The wise conquer the city of the strong and level the fortress in which they trust.

²³If you keep your mouth shut, you will stay out of trouble.

²⁴Mockers are proud and haughty; they act with boundless arrogance.

²⁵The desires of lazy people will be their ruin, for their hands refuse to work. ²⁶They are always greedy for more, while the godly love to give!

²⁷God loathes the sacrifice of an evil person, especially when it is brought with ulterior motives.

²⁸A false witness will be cut off, but an attentive witness will be allowed to speak.

²⁹The wicked put up a bold front, but the upright proceed with care.

³⁰Human plans, no matter how wise or well advised, cannot stand against the LORD.

21:12 Or *The righteous man.*

³¹The horses are prepared for battle, but the victory belongs to the LORD.

CHAPTER **22**

Choose a good reputation over great riches, for being held in high esteem is better than having silver or gold.

²The rich and the poor have this in common: The LORD made them both.

³A prudent person foresees the danger ahead and takes precautions; the simpleton goes blindly on and suffers the consequences.

⁴True humility and fear of the LORD lead to riches, honor, and long life.

⁵The deceitful walk a thorny, treacherous road; whoever values life will stay away.

⁶Teach your children to choose the right path, and when they are older, they will remain upon it.

⁷Just as the rich rule the poor, so the borrower is servant to the lender.

⁸Those who plant seeds of injustice will harvest disaster, and their reign of terror will end.

⁹Blessed are those who are generous, because they feed the poor.

¹⁰Throw out the mocker, and fighting, quarrels, and insults will disappear.

¹¹Anyone who loves a pure heart and gracious speech is the king's friend.

¹²The LORD preserves knowledge, but he ruins the plans of the deceitful.

¹³The lazy person is full of excuses, saying, "If I go outside, I might meet a lion in the street and be killed!"

¹⁴The mouth of an immoral woman is a deep pit; those living under the LORD's displeasure will fall into it.

¹⁵A youngster's heart is filled with foolishness, but discipline will drive it away.

¹⁶A person who gets ahead by oppressing the poor or by showering gifts on the rich will end in poverty.

To teach or train also speaks of breaking and bringing into submission, much like breaking in a wild horse by putting a bit in its mouth. How do we apply this principle to our children? We establish outward boundaries for them while we seek to create an inward thirst for God. That does not mean that we "mold" them into something we think they should be. It means that we tailor our teaching and discipline to their God-given bent so that their unique personality can come into full bloom and bring glory to God.

For the next note on "Children," turn to p. 944.

Thirty Sayings of the Wise

17Listen to the words of the wise; apply your heart to my instruction. 18For it is good to keep these sayings deep within yourself, always ready on your lips. 19I am teaching you today—yes, you—so you will trust in the LORD. 20I have written thirty sayings for you, filled with advice and knowledge. 21In this way, you may know the truth and bring an accurate report to those who sent you.

22Do not rob the poor because they are poor or exploit the needy in court. 23For the LORD is their defender. He will injure anyone who injures them.

24Keep away from angry, short-tempered people, 25or you will learn to be like them and endanger your soul.

26Do not co-sign another person's note or put up a guarantee for someone else's loan. 27If you can't pay it, even your bed will be snatched from under you.

28Do not steal your neighbor's property by moving the ancient boundary markers set up by your ancestors.

29Do you see any truly competent workers? They will serve kings rather than ordinary people.

CHAPTER **23**

When dining with a ruler, pay attention to what is put before you. 2If you are a big eater, put a knife to your throat, 3and don't desire all the delicacies—deception may be involved.

4Don't weary yourself trying to get rich. Why waste your time? 5For riches can disappear as though they had the wings of a bird!

6Don't eat with people who are stingy; don't desire their delicacies. 7"Eat and drink," they say, but they don't mean it. They are always thinking about how much it costs. 8You will vomit up the delicious food they serve, and you will have to take back your words of appreciation for their "kindness."

9Don't waste your breath on fools, for they will despise the wisest advice.

10Don't steal the land of defenseless orphans by moving the ancient boundary markers, 11for their Redeemer is strong. He himself will bring their charges against you.

12Commit yourself to instruction; attune your ears to hear words of knowledge.

13Don't fail to correct your children. They won't die if you spank them. 14Physical discipline may well save them from death.*

15My child,* how I will rejoice if you become wise. 16Yes, my heart will thrill when you speak what is right and just.

17Don't envy sinners, but always continue to fear the LORD. 18For surely you have a future ahead of you; your hope will not be disappointed.

19My child, listen and be wise. Keep your heart on the right course. 20Do not carouse with drunkards and gluttons, 21for they are on their way to poverty. Too much sleep clothes a person with rags.

22Listen to your father, who gave you life, and don't despise your mother's experience when she is old. 23Get the truth and don't ever sell it; also get wisdom, discipline, and discernment. 24The father of godly children has cause for joy. What a pleasure it is to have wise children.* 25So give your parents joy! May she who gave you birth be happy.

26O my son, give me your heart. May your eyes delight in my ways of wisdom. 27A prostitute is a deep pit; an adulterous woman is treacherous.* 28She hides and waits like a robber, looking for another victim who will be unfaithful to his wife.

29Who has anguish? Who has sorrow? Who is always fighting? Who is always complaining? Who has unnecessary bruises? Who has bloodshot eyes? 30It is the one who spends long hours in the taverns, trying out new drinks. 31Don't let the sparkle and smooth taste of wine deceive you. 32For in the end it bites like a poisonous serpent; it stings like a viper. 33You will see hallucinations, and you will say crazy things. 34You will stagger like a sailor tossed at sea, clinging to a swaying mast. 35And you will say, "They hit me, but I didn't feel it. I didn't even know it when they beat me up. When will I wake up so I can have another drink?"

CHAPTER **24**

Don't envy evil people; don't desire their company. 2For they spend their days plotting violence, and their words are always stirring up trouble.

3A house is built by wisdom and becomes strong through good sense. 4Through knowledge its rooms are filled with all sorts of precious riches and valuables.

5A wise man is mightier than a strong man,* and a man of knowledge is more powerful than a strong man. 6So don't go to war without wise guidance; victory depends on having many counselors.

7Wisdom is too much for a fool. When the leaders gather, the fool has nothing to say.

8A person who plans evil will get a reputation

23:14 Hebrew *from Sheol.* **23:15** Hebrew *My son;* also in 23:19. **23:24** Hebrew *a wise son.* **23:27** Hebrew *is a narrow well.* **24:5** As in Greek version; Hebrew reads *A wise man is strength.*

as a troublemaker. ⁹The schemes of a fool are sinful; everyone despises a mocker.

¹⁰If you fail under pressure, your strength is not very great.

¹¹Rescue those who are unjustly sentenced to death; don't stand back and let them die. ¹²Don't try to avoid responsibility by saying you didn't know about it. For God knows all hearts, and he sees you. He keeps watch over your soul, and he knows you knew! And he will judge all people according to what they have done.

¹³My child,* eat honey, for it is good, and the honeycomb is sweet to the taste. ¹⁴In the same way, wisdom is sweet to your soul. If you find it, you will have a bright future, and your hopes will not be cut short.

¹⁵Do not lie in wait like an outlaw at the home of the godly. And don't raid the house where the godly live. ¹⁶They may trip seven times, but each time they will rise again. But one calamity is enough to lay the wicked low.

¹⁷Do not rejoice when your enemies fall into trouble. Don't be happy when they stumble. ¹⁸For the LORD will be displeased with you and will turn his anger away from them.

¹⁹Do not fret because of evildoers; don't envy the wicked. ²⁰For the evil have no future; their light will be snuffed out.

²¹My child, fear the LORD and the king, and don't associate with rebels. ²²For you will go down with them to sudden disaster. Who knows where the punishment from the LORD and the king will end?

More Sayings of the Wise

²³Here are some further sayings of the wise:

It is wrong to show favoritism when passing judgment. ²⁴A judge who says to the wicked, "You are innocent," will be cursed by many people and denounced by the nations. ²⁵But blessings are showered on those who convict the guilty.

²⁶It is an honor to receive an honest reply.

²⁷Develop your business first before building your house.

²⁸Do not testify spitefully against innocent neighbors; don't lie about them. ²⁹And don't say, "Now I can pay them back for all their meanness to me! I'll get even!"

³⁰I walked by the field of a lazy person, the vineyard of one lacking sense. ³¹I saw that it was overgrown with thorns. It was covered with weeds, and its walls were broken down. ³²Then, as I looked and thought about it, I learned this

24:13 Hebrew *My son;* also in 24:21.

lesson: ³³A little extra sleep, a little more slumber, a little folding of the hands to rest—³⁴and poverty will pounce on you like a bandit; scarcity will attack you like an armed robber.

CHAPTER **25**
More Proverbs of Solomon

These are more proverbs of Solomon, collected by the advisers of King Hezekiah of Judah.

²It is God's privilege to conceal things and the king's privilege to discover them.

³No one can discover the height of heaven, the depth of the earth, or all that goes on in the king's mind!

⁴Remove the dross from silver, and the sterling will be ready for the silversmith. ⁵Remove the wicked from the king's court, and his reign will be made secure by justice.

⁶Don't demand an audience with the king or push for a place among the great. ⁷It is better to wait for an invitation than to be sent to the end of the line, publicly disgraced!

Just because you see something, ⁸don't be in a hurry to go to court. You might go down before your neighbors in shameful defeat. ⁹So discuss the matter with them privately. Don't tell anyone else, ¹⁰or others may accuse you of gossip. Then you will never regain your good reputation.

¹¹Timely advice is as lovely as golden apples in a silver basket.

¹²Valid criticism is as treasured by the one who heeds it as jewelry made from finest gold.

¹³Faithful messengers are as refreshing as snow in the heat of summer. They revive the spirit of their employer.

¹⁴A person who doesn't give a promised gift is like clouds and wind that don't bring rain.

¹⁵Patience can persuade a prince, and soft speech can crush strong opposition.

¹⁶Do you like honey? Don't eat too much of it, or it will make you sick!

¹⁷Don't visit your neighbors too often, or you will wear out your welcome.

¹⁸Telling lies about others is as harmful as hitting them with an ax, wounding them with a sword, or shooting them with a sharp arrow.

¹⁹Putting confidence in an unreliable person is like chewing with a toothache or walking on a broken foot.

²⁰Singing cheerful songs to a person whose heart is heavy is as bad as stealing someone's jacket in cold weather or rubbing salt in a wound.

²¹If your enemies are hungry, give them food

to eat. If they are thirsty, give them water to drink. 22You will heap burning coals on their heads, and the LORD will reward you.

23As surely as a wind from the north brings rain, so a gossiping tongue causes anger!

24It is better to live alone in the corner of an attic than with a contentious wife in a lovely home.

25Good news from far away is like cold water to the thirsty.

26If the godly compromise with the wicked, it is like polluting a fountain or muddying a spring.

27Just as it is not good to eat too much honey, it is not good for people to think about all the honors they deserve.

28A person without self-control is as defenseless as a city with broken-down walls.

CHAPTER 26

Honor doesn't go with fools any more than snow with summer or rain with harvest.

2Like a fluttering sparrow or a darting swallow, an unfair curse will not land on its intended victim.

3Guide a horse with a whip, a donkey with a bridle, and a fool with a rod to his back!

4When arguing with fools, don't answer their foolish arguments, or you will become as foolish as they are.

5When arguing with fools, be sure to answer their foolish arguments, or they will become wise in their own estimation.

6Trusting a fool to convey a message is as foolish as cutting off one's feet or drinking poison!

7In the mouth of a fool, a proverb becomes as limp as a paralyzed leg.

8Honoring a fool is as foolish as tying a stone to a slingshot.

9A proverb in a fool's mouth is as dangerous as a thornbush brandished by a drunkard.

10An employer who hires a fool or a bystander is like an archer who shoots recklessly.

11As a dog returns to its vomit, so a fool repeats his folly.

12There is more hope for fools than for people who think they are wise.

13The lazy person is full of excuses, saying, "I can't go outside because there might be a lion on the road! Yes, I'm sure there's a lion out there!"

14As a door turns back and forth on its hinges, so the lazy person turns over in bed.

15Some people are so lazy that they won't lift a finger to feed themselves.

16Lazy people consider themselves smarter than seven wise counselors.

17Yanking a dog's ears is as foolish as interfering in someone else's argument.

18Just as damaging as a mad man shooting a lethal weapon 19is someone who lies to a friend and then says, "I was only joking."

20Fire goes out for lack of fuel, and quarrels disappear when gossip stops.

21A quarrelsome person starts fights as easily as hot embers light charcoal or fire lights wood.

22What dainty morsels rumors are—but they sink deep into one's heart.

23Smooth* words may hide a wicked heart, just as a pretty glaze covers a common clay pot.

24People with hate in their hearts may sound pleasant enough, but don't believe them. 25Though they pretend to be kind, their hearts are full of all kinds of evil. 26While their hatred may be concealed by trickery, it will finally come to light for all to see.

27If you set a trap for others, you will get caught in it yourself. If you roll a boulder down on others, it will roll back and crush you.

28A lying tongue hates its victims, and flattery causes ruin.

CHAPTER 27

Don't brag about tomorrow, since you don't know what the day will bring.

2Don't praise yourself; let others do it!

3A stone is heavy and sand is weighty, but the resentment caused by a fool is heavier than both.

4Anger is cruel, and wrath is like a flood, but who can survive the destructiveness of jealousy?

5An open rebuke is better than hidden love!

6Wounds from a friend are better than many kisses from an enemy.

7Honey seems tasteless to a person who is full, but even bitter food tastes sweet to the hungry.

8A person who strays from home is like a bird that strays from its nest.

9The heartfelt counsel of a friend is as sweet as perfume and incense.

10Never abandon a friend—either yours or your father's. Then in your time of need, you won't have to ask your relatives for assistance. It is better to go to a neighbor than to a relative who lives far away.

11My child,* how happy I will be if you turn out to be wise! Then I will be able to answer my critics.

12A prudent person foresees the danger ahead

26:23 As in Greek version; Hebrew reads *Burning.*　27:11 Hebrew *My son.*

and takes precautions. The simpleton goes blindly on and suffers the consequences.

¹³Be sure to get collateral from anyone who guarantees the debt of a stranger. Get a deposit if someone guarantees the debt of an adulterous woman.

¹⁴If you shout a pleasant greeting to your neighbor too early in the morning, it will be counted as a curse!

¹⁵A nagging wife is as annoying as the constant dripping on a rainy day. ¹⁶Trying to stop her complaints is like trying to stop the wind or hold something with greased hands.

¹⁷As iron sharpens iron, a friend sharpens a friend.

¹⁸Workers who tend a fig tree are allowed to eat its fruit. In the same way, workers who protect their employer's interests will be rewarded.

¹⁹As a face is reflected in water, so the heart reflects the person.

²⁰Just as Death and Destruction* are never satisfied, so human desire is never satisfied.

²¹Fire tests the purity of silver and gold, but a person is tested by being praised.

²²You cannot separate fools from their foolishness, even though you grind them like grain with mortar and pestle.

²³Know the state of your flocks, and put your heart into caring for your herds, ²⁴for riches don't last forever, and the crown might not be secure for the next generation. ²⁵After the hay is harvested, the new crop appears, and the mountain grasses are gathered in, ²⁶your sheep will provide wool for clothing, and your goats will be sold for the price of a field. ²⁷And you will have enough goats' milk for you, your family, and your servants.

CHAPTER **28**

The wicked run away when no one is chasing them, but the godly are as bold as lions.

²When there is moral rot within a nation, its government topples easily. But with wise and knowledgeable leaders, there is stability.

³A poor person who oppresses the poor is like a pounding rain that destroys the crops.

⁴To reject the law is to praise the wicked; to obey the law is to fight them.

⁵Evil people don't understand justice, but those who follow the LORD understand completely.

⁶It is better to be poor and honest than rich and crooked.

⁷Young people who obey the law are wise; those who seek out worthless companions bring shame to their parents.

⁸A person who makes money by charging interest will lose it. It will end up in the hands of someone who is kind to the poor.

⁹The prayers of a person who ignores the law are despised.

¹⁰Those who lead the upright into sin will fall into their own trap, but the honest will inherit good things.

¹¹Rich people picture themselves as wise, but their real poverty is evident to the poor.

¹²When the godly succeed, everyone is glad. When the wicked take charge, people go into hiding.

¹³People who cover over their sins will not prosper. But if they confess and forsake them, they will receive mercy.

¹⁴Blessed are those who have a tender conscience,* but the stubborn are headed for serious trouble.

¹⁵A wicked ruler is as dangerous to the poor as a lion or bear attacking them.

¹⁶Only a stupid prince will oppress his people, but a king will have a long reign if he hates dishonesty and bribes.

¹⁷A murderer's tormented conscience will drive him into the grave. Don't protect him!

¹⁸The honest will be rescued from harm, but those who are crooked will be destroyed.

¹⁹Hard workers have plenty of food; playing around brings poverty.

²⁰The trustworthy will get a rich reward. But the person who wants to get rich quick will only get into trouble.

²¹Showing partiality is never good, yet some will do wrong for something as small as a piece of bread.

²²A greedy person tries to get rich quick, but it only leads to poverty.

²³In the end, people appreciate frankness more than flattery.

²⁴Robbing your parents and then saying, "What's wrong with that?" is as serious as committing murder.

²⁵Greed causes fighting; trusting the LORD leads to prosperity.

²⁶Trusting oneself is foolish, but those who walk in wisdom are safe.

²⁷Whoever gives to the poor will lack nothing. But a curse will come upon those who close their eyes to poverty.

²⁸When the wicked take charge, people hide. When the wicked meet disaster, the godly multiply.

27:20 Hebrew *Sheol and Abaddon.* 28:14 Hebrew *those who fear.*

CHAPTER **29**

Whoever stubbornly refuses to accept criticism will suddenly be broken beyond repair.

²When the godly are in authority, the people rejoice. But when the wicked are in power, they groan.

³The man who loves wisdom brings joy to his father, but if he hangs around with prostitutes, his wealth is wasted.

⁴A just king gives stability to his nation, but one who demands bribes destroys it.

⁵To flatter people is to lay a trap for their feet.

⁶Evil people are trapped by sin, but the righteous escape, shouting for joy.

⁷The godly know the rights of the poor; the wicked don't care to know.

⁸Mockers can get a whole town agitated, but those who are wise will calm anger.

⁹If a wise person takes a fool to court, there will be ranting and ridicule but no satisfaction.

¹⁰The bloodthirsty hate the honest, but the upright seek out the honest.

¹¹A fool gives full vent to anger, but a wise person quietly holds it back.

¹²If a ruler honors liars, all his advisers will be wicked.

¹³The poor and the oppressor have this in common—the LORD gives light to the eyes of both.

¹⁴A king who is fair to the poor will have a long reign.

¹⁵To discipline and reprimand a child produces wisdom, but a mother is disgraced by an undisciplined child.

¹⁶When the wicked are in authority, sin increases. But the godly will live to see the tyrant's downfall.

¹⁷Discipline your children, and they will give you happiness and peace of mind.

¹⁸When people do not accept divine guidance, they run wild. But whoever obeys the law is happy.

¹⁹For a servant, mere words are not enough—discipline is needed. For the words may be understood, but they are not heeded.

²⁰There is more hope for a fool than for someone who speaks without thinking.

²¹A servant who is pampered from childhood will later become a rebel.

²²A hot-tempered person starts fights and gets into all kinds of sin.

²³Pride ends in humiliation, while humility brings honor.

²⁴If you assist a thief, you are only hurting yourself. You will be punished if you report the crime, but you will be cursed if you don't.

²⁵Fearing people is a dangerous trap, but to trust the LORD means safety.

²⁶Many seek the ruler's favor, but justice comes from the LORD.

²⁷The godly despise the wicked; the wicked despise the godly.

CHAPTER **30**
The Sayings of Agur

The message of Agur son of Jakeh. An oracle.*

I am weary, O God; I am weary and worn out, O God.* ²I am too ignorant to be human, and I lack common sense. ³I have not mastered human wisdom, nor do I know the Holy One.

⁴Who but God goes up to heaven and comes back down? Who holds the wind in his fists? Who wraps up the oceans in his cloak? Who has created the whole wide world? What is his name—and his son's name? Tell me if you know!

⁵Every word of God proves true. He defends all who come to him for protection. ⁶Do not add to his words, or he may rebuke you, and you will be found a liar. ⁷O God, I beg two favors from you before I die. ⁸First, help me never to tell a lie. Second, give me neither poverty nor riches! Give me just enough to satisfy my needs. ⁹For if I grow rich, I may deny you and say, "Who is the LORD?" And if I am too poor, I may steal and thus insult God's holy name.

¹⁰Never slander a person to his employer. If

30:1a Or *son of Jakeh from Massa.* 30:1b The Hebrew can also be translated *The man declares this to Ithiel, to Ithiel and to Ucal.*

OFF AND RUNNING
Discipline Your Children Read PROVERBS 29:15

The concept of discipline seems to have disappeared from our culture of late. But look at the results: More and more children are committing violent crimes; far too many teens no longer know the difference between right and wrong; and young people show little or no respect for those in authority. That is why this verse states that a child who receives no discipline is a disgrace to his or her mother.

you do, the person will curse you, and you will pay for it.

¹¹Some people curse their father and do not thank their mother. ¹²They feel pure, but they are filthy and unwashed. ¹³They are proud beyond description and disdainful. ¹⁴They devour the poor with teeth as sharp as swords or knives. They destroy the needy from the face of the earth.

¹⁵The leech has two suckers that cry out, "More, more!"* There are three other things— no, four!—that are never satisfied:
¹⁶ the grave,
the barren womb,
the thirsty desert,
the blazing fire.

¹⁷The eye that mocks a father and despises a mother will be plucked out by ravens of the valley and eaten by vultures.

¹⁸There are three things that amaze me—no, four things I do not understand:
¹⁹ how an eagle glides through the sky,
how a snake slithers on a rock,
how a ship navigates the ocean,
how a man loves a woman.

²⁰Equally amazing is how an adulterous woman can satisfy her sexual appetite, shrug her shoulders, and then say, "What's wrong with that?"

²¹There are three things that make the earth tremble—no, four it cannot endure:
²² a slave who becomes a king,
an overbearing fool who prospers,
²³ a bitter woman who finally gets a husband,
a servant girl who supplants her mistress.

²⁴There are four things on earth that are small but unusually wise:
²⁵ Ants—they aren't strong,
but they store up food for the winter.
²⁶ Rock badgers*—they aren't powerful,
but they make their homes among the rocky cliffs.

²⁷ Locusts—they have no king,
but they march like an army in ranks.
²⁸ Lizards—they are easy to catch,
but they are found even in kings' palaces.

²⁹There are three stately monarchs on the earth—no, four:
³⁰ the lion, king of animals, who won't turn aside for anything,
³¹ the strutting rooster,
the male goat,
a king as he leads his army.

³²If you have been a fool by being proud or plotting evil, don't brag about it—cover your mouth with your hand in shame.

³³As the beating of cream yields butter, and a blow to the nose causes bleeding, so anger causes quarrels.

CHAPTER 31

The Sayings of King Lemuel

These are the sayings of King Lemuel, an oracle* that his mother taught him.

²O my son, O son of my womb, O son of my promises, ³do not spend your strength on women, on those who ruin kings.

⁴And it is not for kings, O Lemuel, to guzzle wine. Rulers should not crave liquor. ⁵For if they drink, they may forget their duties and be unable to give justice to those who are oppressed. ⁶Liquor is for the dying, and wine for those in deep depression. ⁷Let them drink to forget their poverty and remember their troubles no more.

⁸Speak up for those who cannot speak for themselves; ensure justice for those who are perishing. ⁹Yes, speak up for the poor and helpless, and see that they get justice.

A Wife of Noble Character

¹⁰Who can find a virtuous and capable wife? She is worth more than precious rubies. ¹¹Her husband can trust her, and she will greatly enrich his

---

30:15 Hebrew *two daughters who cry out, "Give, give!"*   30:26 Or *coneys,* or *hyraxes.*   31:1 Or *of Lemuel, king of Massa.*

Children need to learn right from wrong. They cannot do this without parental leadership and guidance, which at times may require "the board of education applied to the seat of understanding."

Scripture gives us yet another reason for the importance of discipline: "For the Lord disciplines those he loves, and he punishes those he accepts as his children" (Hebrews 12:6). Just as God's punishment of us demonstrates his love for us as part of his family, so the discipline of our children shows our love for them as our sons or daughters. Discipline, when given for the right reasons and administered in love, gives a child a sense of security and belonging.

For the next note on "Children," turn to p. 1042.

life. 12She will not hinder him but help him all her life.

13She finds wool and flax and busily spins it. 14She is like a merchant's ship; she brings her food from afar. 15She gets up before dawn to prepare breakfast for her household and plan the day's work for her servant girls. 16She goes out to inspect a field and buys it; with her earnings she plants a vineyard.

17She is energetic and strong, a hard worker. 18She watches for bargains; her lights burn late into the night. 19Her hands are busy spinning thread, her fingers twisting fiber.

20She extends a helping hand to the poor and opens her arms to the needy.

21She has no fear of winter for her household because all of them have warm* clothes. 22She quilts her own bedspreads. She dresses like royalty in gowns of finest cloth.

31:21 As in Greek version; Hebrew *scarlet.*

23Her husband is well known, for he sits in the council meeting with the other civic leaders. 24She makes belted linen garments and sashes to sell to the merchants. 25She is clothed with strength and dignity, and she laughs with no fear of the future. 26When she speaks, her words are wise, and kindness is the rule when she gives instructions. 27She carefully watches all that goes on in her household and does not have to bear the consequences of laziness.

28Her children stand and bless her. Her husband praises her: 29"There are many virtuous and capable women in the world, but you surpass them all!"

30Charm is deceptive, and beauty does not last; but a woman who fears the LORD will be greatly praised. 31Reward her for all she has done. Let her deeds publicly declare her praise.

Ecclesiastes

CHAPTER **1**

These are the words of the Teacher,* King David's son, who ruled in Jerusalem.

Everything Is Meaningless

2"Everything is meaningless," says the Teacher, "utterly meaningless!"

3What do people get for all their hard work? 4Generations come and go, but nothing really changes. 5The sun rises and sets and hurries around to rise again. 6The wind blows south and north, here and there, twisting back and forth, getting nowhere. 7The rivers run into the sea, but the sea is never full. Then the water returns again to the rivers and flows again to the sea. 8Everything is so weary and tiresome! No matter how much we see, we are never satisfied. No matter how much we hear, we are not content.

9History merely repeats itself. It has all been done before. Nothing under the sun is truly new. 10What can you point to that is new? How do you know it didn't already exist long ago? 11We don't remember what happened in those former times. And in future generations, no one will remember what we are doing now.

The Futility of Wisdom

12I, the Teacher, was king of Israel, and I lived in Jerusalem. 13I devoted myself to search for understanding and to explore by wisdom everything being done in the world. I soon discovered that God has dealt a tragic existence to the human race. 14Everything under the sun is meaningless, like chasing the wind. 15What is wrong cannot be righted. What is missing cannot be recovered.

16I said to myself, "Look, I am wiser than any of the kings who ruled in Jerusalem before me. I have greater wisdom and knowledge than any of them." 17So I worked hard to distinguish wisdom from foolishness. But now I realize that even this was like chasing the wind. 18For the greater my wisdom, the greater my grief. To increase knowledge only increases sorrow.

CHAPTER **2**

The Futility of Pleasure

I said to myself, "Come now, let's give pleasure a try. Let's look for the 'good things' in life." But I found that this, too, was meaningless. 2"It is silly to be laughing all the time," I said. "What good does it do to seek only pleasure?" 3After much thought, I decided to cheer myself with wine. While still seeking wisdom, I clutched at foolishness. In this way, I hoped to experience the only happiness most people find during their brief life in this world.

4I also tried to find meaning by building huge homes for myself and by planting beautiful vineyards. 5I made gardens and parks, filling them with all kinds of fruit trees. 6I built reservoirs to collect the water to irrigate my many flourishing groves. 7I bought slaves, both men and women, and others were born into my household. I also owned great herds and flocks, more than any of the kings who lived in Jerusalem before me. 8I collected great sums of silver and gold, the treasure of many kings and provinces. I hired wonderful singers, both men and women, and had many beautiful concubines. I had everything a man could desire!

9So I became greater than any of the kings who ruled in Jerusalem before me. And with it all, I remained clear-eyed so that I could evaluate all these things. 10Anything I wanted, I took. I did not restrain myself from any joy. I even found great pleasure in hard work, an additional reward for all

1:1 Hebrew *Koheleth*; this term is rendered "the Teacher" throughout this book.

my labors. [11]But as I looked at everything I had worked so hard to accomplish, it was all so meaningless. It was like chasing the wind. There was nothing really worthwhile anywhere.

The Wise and the Foolish

[12]So I decided to compare wisdom and folly, and anyone else would come to the same conclusions I did. [13]Wisdom is of more value than foolishness, just as light is better than darkness. [14]For the wise person sees, while the fool is blind. Yet I saw that wise and foolish people share the same fate. [15]Both of them die. Just as the fool will die, so will I. So of what value is all my wisdom? Then I said to myself, "This is all so meaningless!" [16]For the wise person and the fool both die, and in the days to come, both will be forgotten.

The Futility of Work

[17]So now I hate life because everything done here under the sun is so irrational. Everything is meaningless, like chasing the wind. [18]I am disgusted that I must leave the fruits of my hard work to others. [19]And who can tell whether my successors will be wise or foolish? And yet they will control everything I have gained by my skill and hard work. How meaningless!

[20]So I turned in despair from hard work. It was not the answer to my search for satisfaction in this life. [21]For though I do my work with wisdom, knowledge, and skill, I must leave everything I gain to people who haven't worked to earn it. This is not only foolish but highly unfair. [22]So what do people get for all their hard work? [23]Their days of labor are filled with pain and grief; even at night they cannot rest. It is all utterly meaningless.

[24]So I decided there is nothing better than to enjoy food and drink and to find satisfaction in work. Then I realized that this pleasure is from the hand of God. [25]For who can eat or enjoy anything apart from him? [26]God gives wisdom, knowledge, and joy to those who please him. But if a sinner becomes wealthy, God takes the wealth away and gives it to those who please him. Even this, however, is meaningless, like chasing the wind.

CHAPTER **3**

A Time for Everything

1 There is a time for everything,
   a season for every activity under heaven.
2 A time to be born and a time to die.
   A time to plant and a time to harvest.
3 A time to kill and a time to heal.
   A time to tear down and a time to rebuild.
4 A time to cry and a time to laugh.
   A time to grieve and a time to dance.
5 A time to scatter stones and a time to gather
      stones.
   A time to embrace and a time to turn away.
6 A time to search and a time to lose.
   A time to keep and a time to throw away.
7 A time to tear and a time to mend.
   A time to be quiet and a time to speak up.
8 A time to love and a time to hate.
   A time for war and a time for peace.

[9]What do people really get for all their hard work? [10]I have thought about this in connection with the various kinds of work God has given people to do. [11]God has made everything beautiful for its own time. He has planted eternity in the human heart, but even so, people cannot see the whole scope of God's work from beginning to end. [12]So I concluded that there is nothing better for people than to be happy and to enjoy themselves as long as they can. [13]And people should eat and drink and enjoy the fruits of their labor, for these are gifts from God.

[14]And I know that whatever God does is final. Nothing can be added to it or taken from it. God's purpose in this is that people should fear him. [15]Whatever exists today and whatever will exist in the future has already existed in the past. For God calls each event back in its turn.*

The Injustices of Life

[16]I also noticed that throughout the world there is evil in the courtroom. Yes, even the courts of law are corrupt! [17]I said to myself, "In due season God will judge everyone, both good and bad, for all their deeds."

[18]Then I realized that God allows people to continue in their sinful ways so he can test them. That way, they can see for themselves that they are no better than animals. [19]For humans and animals both breathe the same air,* and both die. So people have no real advantage over the animals. How meaningless! [20]Both go to the same place—the dust from which they came and to which they must return. [21]For who can prove that the human spirit goes upward and the spirit of animals goes downward into the earth? [22]So I saw that there is nothing better for people than to be happy in their work. That is why they are here! No one will bring them back from death to enjoy life in the future.

3:15 Hebrew *For God calls the past to account.*   3:19 Or *both have the same spirit.*

CHAPTER 4

Again I observed all the oppression that takes place in our world. I saw the tears of the oppressed, with no one to comfort them. The oppressors have great power, and the victims are helpless. ²So I concluded that the dead are better off than the living. ³And most fortunate of all are those who were never born. For they have never seen all the evil that is done in our world.

⁴Then I observed that most people are motivated to success by their envy of their neighbors. But this, too, is meaningless, like chasing the wind.

⁵Foolish people refuse to work and almost starve. ⁶They feel it is better to be lazy and barely survive than to work hard, especially when in the long run everything is so futile.

The Advantages of Companionship

⁷I observed yet another example of meaninglessness in our world. ⁸This is the case of a man who is all alone, without a child or a brother, yet who works hard to gain as much wealth as he can. But then he asks himself, "Who am I working for? Why am I giving up so much pleasure now?" It is all so meaningless and depressing.

⁹Two people can accomplish more than twice as much as one; they get a better return for their labor. ¹⁰If one person falls, the other can reach out and help. But people who are alone when they fall are in real trouble. ¹¹And on a cold night, two under the same blanket can gain warmth from each other. But how can one be warm alone? ¹²A person standing alone can be attacked and defeated, but two can stand back-to-back and conquer. Three are even better, for a triple-braided cord is not easily broken.

The Futility of Political Power

¹³It is better to be a poor but wise youth than to be an old and foolish king who refuses all advice. ¹⁴Such a youth could come from prison and succeed. He might even become king, though he was born in poverty. ¹⁵Everyone is eager to help such a youth, even to help him take the throne. ¹⁶He might become the leader of millions and be very popular. But then the next generation grows up and rejects him! So again, it is all meaningless, like chasing the wind.

CHAPTER 5

The Importance of Fearing God

As you enter the house of God, keep your ears open and your mouth shut! Don't be a fool who

doesn't realize that mindless offerings to God are evil. ²And don't make rash promises to God, for he is in heaven, and you are only here on earth. So let your words be few.

³Just as being too busy gives you nightmares, being a fool makes you a blabbermouth.

⁴So when you make a promise to God, don't delay in following through, for God takes no pleasure in fools. Keep all the promises you make to him. ⁵It is better to say nothing than to promise something that you don't follow through on. ⁶In such cases, your mouth is making you sin. And don't defend yourself by telling the Temple messenger that the promise you made was a mistake. That would make God angry, and he might wipe out everything you have achieved.

⁷Dreaming all the time instead of working is foolishness. And there is ruin in a flood of empty words. Fear God instead.

The Futility of Wealth

⁸If you see a poor person being oppressed by the powerful and justice being miscarried throughout the land, don't be surprised! For every official is under orders from higher up, and matters of justice only get lost in red tape and bureaucracy. ⁹Even the king milks the land for his own profit! *

¹⁰Those who love money will never have enough. How absurd to think that wealth brings true happiness! ¹¹The more you have, the more people come to help you spend it. So what is the advantage of wealth—except perhaps to watch it run through your fingers!

¹²People who work hard sleep well, whether they eat little or much. But the rich are always worrying and seldom get a good night's sleep.

¹³There is another serious problem I have seen in the world. Riches are sometimes hoarded to the harm of the saver, ¹⁴or they are put into risky investments that turn sour, and everything is lost. In the end, there is nothing left to pass on to one's children. ¹⁵People who live only for wealth come to the end of their lives as naked and empty-handed as on the day they were born.

¹⁶And this, too, is a very serious problem. As people come into this world, so they depart. All their hard work is for nothing. They have been working for the wind, and everything will be swept away. ¹⁷Throughout their lives, they live under a cloud—frustrated, discouraged, and angry.

¹⁸Even so, I have noticed one thing, at least, that is good. It is good for people to eat well, drink a good glass of wine, and enjoy their

5:9 The meaning of the Hebrew is uncertain.

work—whatever they do under the sun—for however long God lets them live. ¹⁹And it is a good thing to receive wealth from God and the good health to enjoy it. To enjoy your work and accept your lot in life—that is indeed a gift from God. ²⁰People who do this rarely look with sorrow on the past, for God has given them reasons for joy.

CHAPTER **6**

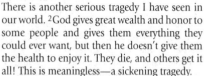

There is another serious tragedy I have seen in our world. ²God gives great wealth and honor to some people and gives them everything they could ever want, but then he doesn't give them the health to enjoy it. They die, and others get it all! This is meaningless—a sickening tragedy.

³A man might have a hundred children and live to be very old. But if he finds no satisfaction in life and in the end does not even get a decent burial, I say he would have been better off born dead. ⁴I realize that his birth would have been meaningless and ended in darkness. He wouldn't even have had a name, ⁵and he would never have seen the sun or known of its existence. Yet he would have had more peace than he has in growing up to be an unhappy man. ⁶He might live a thousand years twice over but not find contentment. And since he must die like everyone else—well, what's the use?

⁷All people spend their lives scratching for food, but they never seem to have enough. ⁸Considering this, do wise people really have any advantage over fools? Do poor people gain anything by being wise and knowing how to act in front of others?

⁹Enjoy what you have rather than desiring what you don't have. Just dreaming about nice things is meaningless; it is like chasing the wind.

The Future—Determined and Unknown

¹⁰Everything has already been decided. It was known long ago what each person would be. So there's no use arguing with God about your destiny.

¹¹The more words you speak, the less they mean. So why overdo it?

¹²In the few days of our empty lives, who knows how our days can best be spent? And who can tell what will happen in the future after we are gone?

CHAPTER **7**

Wisdom for Life

A good reputation is more valuable than the most expensive perfume. In the same way, the day you die is better than the day you are born.

²It is better to spend your time at funerals than at festivals. For you are going to die, and you should think about it while there is still time.

³Sorrow is better than laughter, for sadness has a refining influence on us.

⁴A wise person thinks much about death, while the fool thinks only about having a good time now.

⁵It is better to be criticized by a wise person than to be praised by a fool! ⁶Indeed, a fool's laughter is quickly gone, like thorns crackling in a fire. This also is meaningless.

⁷Extortion turns wise people into fools, and bribes corrupt the heart.

⁸Finishing is better than starting. Patience is better than pride.

⁹Don't be quick-tempered, for anger is the friend of fools.

¹⁰Don't long for "the good old days," for you don't know whether they were any better than today.

¹¹Being wise is as good as being rich; in fact, it is better. ¹²Wisdom or money can get you almost anything, but it's important to know that only wisdom can save your life.

¹³Notice the way God does things; then fall into line. Don't fight the ways of God, for who can straighten out what he has made crooked?

¹⁴Enjoy prosperity while you can. But when hard times strike, realize that both come from God. That way you will realize that nothing is certain in this life.

The Limits of Human Wisdom

¹⁵In this meaningless life, I have seen everything, including the fact that some good people die young and some wicked people live on and on. ¹⁶So don't be too good or too wise! Why destroy yourself? ¹⁷On the other hand, don't be too wicked either—don't be a fool! Why should you die before your time? ¹⁸So try to walk a middle course—but those who fear God will succeed either way.

¹⁹A wise person is stronger than the ten leading citizens of a town!

²⁰There is not a single person in all the earth who is always good and never sins.

²¹Don't eavesdrop on others—you may hear your servant laughing at you. ²²For you know how often you yourself have laughed at others.

²³All along I have tried my best to let wisdom guide my thoughts and actions. I said to myself, "I am determined to be wise." But it didn't really work. ²⁴Wisdom is always distant and very diffi-

cult to find. ²⁵I searched everywhere, determined to find wisdom and to understand the reason for things. I was determined to prove to myself that wickedness is stupid and that foolishness is madness.

²⁶I discovered that a seductive woman is more bitter than death. Her passion is a trap, and her soft hands will bind you. Those who please God will escape from her, but sinners will be caught in her snare.

²⁷"This is my conclusion," says the Teacher. "I came to this result after looking into the matter from every possible angle. ²⁸Just one out of every thousand men I interviewed can be said to be upright, but not one woman! ²⁹I discovered that God created people to be upright, but they have each turned to follow their own downward path."

CHAPTER 8

How wonderful to be wise, to be able to analyze and interpret things. Wisdom lights up a person's face, softening its hardness.

Obedience to the King

²Obey the king because you have vowed before God to do this. ³Don't try to avoid doing your duty, and don't take a stand with those who plot evil. For the king will punish those who disobey him. ⁴The king's command is backed by great power. No one can resist or question it. ⁵Those who obey him will not be punished. Those who are wise will find a time and a way to do what is right. ⁶Yes, there is a time and a way for everything, even as people's troubles lie heavily upon them.

⁷Indeed, how can people avoid what they don't know is going to happen? ⁸None of us can hold back our spirit from departing. None of us has the power to prevent the day of our death. There is no escaping that obligation, that dark battle. And in the face of death, wickedness will certainly not rescue those who practice it.

The Wicked and the Righteous

⁹I have thought deeply about all that goes on here in the world, where people have the power to hurt each other. ¹⁰I have seen wicked people buried with honor. How strange that they were the very ones who frequented the Temple and are praised* in the very city where they committed their crimes! ¹¹When a crime is not punished, people feel it is safe to do wrong. ¹²But even though a person sins a hundred times and still lives a long

time, I know that those who fear God will be better off. ¹³The wicked will never live long, good lives, for they do not fear God. Their days will never grow long like the evening shadows.

¹⁴And this is not all that is meaningless in our world. In this life, good people are often treated as though they were wicked, and wicked people are often treated as though they were good. This is so meaningless!

¹⁵So I recommend having fun, because there is nothing better for people to do in this world than to eat, drink, and enjoy life. That way they will experience some happiness along with all the hard work God gives them.

¹⁶In my search for wisdom, I tried to observe everything that goes on all across the earth. I discovered that there is ceaseless activity, day and night. ¹⁷This reminded me that no one can discover everything God has created in our world, no matter how hard they work at it. Not even the wisest people know everything, even if they say they do.

CHAPTER 9
Death Comes to All

This, too, I carefully explored: Even though the actions of godly and wise people are in God's hands, no one knows whether or not God will show them favor in this life. ²The same destiny ultimately awaits everyone, whether they are righteous or wicked, good or bad,* ceremonially clean or unclean, religious or irreligious. Good people receive the same treatment as sinners, and people who take oaths are treated like people who don't.

³It seems so tragic that one fate comes to all. That is why people are not more careful to be good. Instead, they choose their own mad course, for they have no hope. There is nothing ahead but death anyway. ⁴There is hope only for the living. For as they say, "It is better to be a live dog than a dead lion!"

⁵The living at least know they will die, but the dead know nothing. They have no further reward, nor are they remembered. ⁶Whatever they did in their lifetime—loving, hating, envying—is all long gone. They no longer have a part in anything here on earth. ⁷So go ahead. Eat your food and drink your wine with a happy heart, for God approves of this! ⁸Wear fine clothes, with a dash of cologne!

⁹Live happily with the woman you love

through all the meaningless days of life that God has given you in this world. The wife God gives you is your reward for all your earthly toil. 10Whatever you do, do well. For when you go to the grave, there will be no work or planning or knowledge or wisdom.

11I have observed something else in this world of ours. The fastest runner doesn't always win the race, and the strongest warrior doesn't always win the battle. The wise are often poor, and the skillful are not necessarily wealthy. And those who are educated don't always lead successful lives. It is all decided by chance, by being at the right place at the right time.

12People can never predict when hard times might come. Like fish in a net or birds in a snare, people are often caught by sudden tragedy.

Thoughts on Wisdom and Folly

13Here is another bit of wisdom that has impressed me as I have watched the way our world works. 14There was a small town with only a few people living in it, and a great king came with his army and besieged it. 15There was a poor, wise man living there who knew how to save the town, and so it was rescued. But afterward no one thought any more about him. 16Then I realized that though wisdom is better than strength, those who are wise will be despised if they are poor. What they say will not be appreciated for long. 17But even so, the quiet words of a wise person are better than the shouts of a foolish king. 18A wise person can overcome weapons of war, but one sinner can destroy much that is good.

CHAPTER 10

Dead flies will cause even a bottle of perfume to stink! Yes, an ounce of foolishness can outweigh a pound of wisdom and honor.

2The hearts of the wise lead them to do right, and the hearts of the foolish lead them to do evil. 3You can identify fools just by the way they walk down the street!

4If your boss is angry with you, don't quit! A quiet spirit can overcome even great mistakes.

5There is another evil I have seen as I have watched the world go by. Kings and rulers make a grave mistake 6if they give foolish people great authority, and if they fail to give people of proven worth their rightful place of dignity. 7I have even seen servants riding like princes—and princes walking like servants.

8When you dig a well, you may fall in. When you demolish an old wall, you could be bitten by a snake. 9When you work in a quarry, stones might fall and crush you! When you chop wood, there is danger with each stroke of your ax! Such are the risks of life.

10Since a dull ax requires great strength, sharpen the blade. That's the value of wisdom; it helps you succeed.

11It does no good to charm a snake after it has bitten you.

12It is pleasant to listen to wise words, but the speech of fools brings them to ruin. 13Since fools base their thoughts on foolish premises, their conclusions will be wicked madness. 14Foolish people claim to know all about the future and tell everyone the details! But who can really know what is going to happen?

15Fools are so exhausted by a little work that they have no strength for even the simplest tasks.

16Destruction is certain for the land whose king is a child* and whose leaders feast in the morning. 17Happy is the land whose king is a nobleman and whose leaders feast only to gain strength for their work, not to get drunk.

18Laziness lets the roof leak, and soon the rafters begin to rot.

19A party gives laughter, and wine gives happiness, and money gives everything!

20Never make light of the king, even in your thoughts. And don't make fun of a rich man, either. A little bird may tell them what you have said.

CHAPTER 11

Generosity and Diligence

Give generously, for your gifts will return to you later.* 2Divide your gifts among many, for you do not know what risks might lie ahead.

3When the clouds are heavy, the rains come down.

When a tree falls, whether south or north, there it lies.

4If you wait for perfect conditions, you will never get anything done.

5God's ways are as hard to discern as the pathways of the wind, and as mysterious as a tiny baby being formed in a mother's womb.

6Be sure to stay busy and plant a variety of crops, for you never know which will grow—perhaps they all will.

10:16 Or *whose king is a servant.*   11:1 Hebrew *Throw your bread on the waters, for after many days you will find it again.*

Advice for Old and Young

7Light is sweet; it's wonderful to see the sun! 8When people live to be very old, let them rejoice in every day of life. But let them also remember that the dark days will be many. Everything still to come is meaningless.

9Young man, it's wonderful to be young! Enjoy every minute of it. Do everything you want to do; take it all in. But remember that you must give an account to God for everything you do. 10So banish grief and pain, but remember that youth, with a whole life before it, still faces the threat of meaninglessness.

CHAPTER **12**

Don't let the excitement of youth cause you to forget your Creator. Honor him in your youth before you grow old and no longer enjoy living. 2It will be too late then to remember him, when the light of the sun and moon and stars is dim to your old eyes, and there is no silver lining left among the clouds. 3Your limbs will tremble with age, and your strong legs will grow weak. Your teeth will be too few to do their work, and you will be blind, too. 4And when your teeth are gone, keep your lips tightly closed when you eat! Even the chirping of birds will wake you up. But you yourself will be deaf and tuneless, with a quavering voice. 5You will be afraid of heights and of falling, white-haired and withered, dragging along without any sexual desire.

12:12 Hebrew *my son.*

You will be standing at death's door. And as you near your everlasting home, the mourners will walk along the streets.

6Yes, remember your Creator now while you are young, before the silver cord of life snaps and the golden bowl is broken. Don't wait until the water jar is smashed at the spring and the pulley is broken at the well. 7For then the dust will return to the earth, and the spirit will return to God who gave it.

8"All is meaningless," says the Teacher, "utterly meaningless."

Concluding Thoughts

9Because the Teacher was wise, he taught the people everything he knew. He collected proverbs and classified them. 10Indeed, the Teacher taught the plain truth, and he did so in an interesting way.

11A wise teacher's words spur students to action and emphasize important truths. The collected sayings of the wise are like guidance from a shepherd.

12But, my child,* be warned: There is no end of opinions ready to be expressed. Studying them can go on forever and become very exhausting!

13Here is my final conclusion: Fear God and obey his commands, for this is the duty of every person. 14God will judge us for everything we do, including every secret thing, whether good or bad.

Song of Songs

CHAPTER **1**

This is Solomon's song of songs, more wonderful than any other.

*Young Woman:** 2"Kiss me again and again, for your love is sweeter than wine. 3How fragrant your cologne, and how pleasing your name! No wonder all the young women love you! 4Take me with you. Come, let's run! Bring me into your bedroom, O my king.*"

Young Women of Jerusalem: "How happy we are for him! We praise his love even more than wine."

Young Woman: "How right that the young women love you!

5"I am dark and beautiful, O women of Jerusalem, tanned as the dark tents of Kedar. Yes, even as the tents of Solomon!

6"Don't look down on me, you fair city girls, just because my complexion is so dark. The sun has burned my skin. My brothers were angry with me and sent me out to tend the vineyards in the hot sun. Now see what it has done to me!*

7"Tell me, O my love, where are you leading your flock today? Where will you rest your sheep at noon? For why should I wander like a prostitute* among the flocks of your companions?"

Young Man: 8"If you don't know, O most beautiful woman, follow the trail of my flock to the shepherds' tents, and there feed your young goats. 9What a lovely filly you are, my beloved one!* 10How lovely are your cheeks, with your earrings setting them afire! How stately is your neck, accented with a long string of jewels. 11We will make earrings of gold for you and beads of silver."

Young Woman: 12"The king is lying on his couch, enchanted by the fragrance of my perfume. 13My lover is like a sachet of myrrh lying between my breasts. 14He is like a bouquet of flowers in the gardens of En-gedi."

Young Man: 15"How beautiful you are, my beloved, how beautiful! Your eyes are soft like doves."

Young Woman: 16"What a lovely, pleasant sight you are, my love, as we lie here on the grass, 17shaded by cedar trees and spreading firs."

CHAPTER **2**

Young Woman: "I am the rose of Sharon, the lily of the valley."

Young Man: 2"Yes, compared to other women, my beloved is like a lily among thorns."

Young Woman: 3"And compared to other youths, my lover is like the finest apple tree in the orchard. I am seated in his delightful shade, and his fruit is delicious to eat. 4He brings me to the banquet hall, so everyone can see how much he loves me. 5Oh, feed me with your love—your 'raisins' and your 'apples'—for I am utterly lovesick! 6His left hand is under my head, and his right hand embraces me.

7"Promise me, O women of Jerusalem, by the swift gazelles and the deer of the wild, not to awaken love until the time is right.*

8"Ah, I hear him—my lover! Here he comes, leaping on the mountains and bounding over the hills. 9My lover is like a swift gazelle or a young deer. Look, there he

---

1:1 The headings identifying the speakers are not in the original text, though the Hebrew usually gives clues by means of the gender of the person speaking.   1:4 Or *The king has brought me into his bedroom.*   1:6 Hebrew *My own vineyard I have neglected.*   1:7 Hebrew *like a veiled woman.*   1:9 Hebrew *I compare you, my beloved, to a mare among Pharaoh's chariots.*   2:7 Or *not to awaken love until it is ready.*

is behind the wall! Now he is looking in through the window, gazing into the room. ¹⁰"My lover said to me, 'Rise up, my beloved, my fair one, and come away. ¹¹For the winter is past, and the rain is over and gone. ¹²The flowers are springing up, and the time of singing birds has come, even the cooing of turtledoves. ¹³The fig trees are budding, and the grapevines are in blossom. How delicious they smell! Yes, spring is here! Arise, my beloved, my fair one, and come away.'"

Young Man: ¹⁴"My dove is hiding behind some rocks, behind an outcrop on the cliff. Let me see you; let me hear your voice. For your voice is pleasant, and you are lovely."

Young Women of Jerusalem: ¹⁵"Quick! Catch all the little foxes before they ruin the vineyard of your love, for the grapevines are all in blossom."

Young Woman: ¹⁶"My lover is mine, and I am his. He feeds among the lilies! ¹⁷Before the dawn comes and the shadows flee away, come back to me, my love. Run like a gazelle or a young stag on the rugged mountains.*"

CHAPTER **3**

Young Woman: "One night as I lay in bed, I yearned deeply for my lover, but he did not come. ²So I said to myself, 'I will get up now and roam the city, searching for him in all its streets and squares.' But my search was in vain. ³The watchmen stopped me as they made their rounds, and I said to them, 'Have you seen him anywhere, this one I love so much?' ⁴A little while later I found him and held him. I didn't let him go until

I had brought him to my childhood home, into my mother's bedroom, where I had been conceived.

⁵"Promise me, O women of Jerusalem, by the swift gazelles and the deer of the wild, not to awaken love until the time is right.*"

Young Women of Jerusalem: ⁶"Who is this sweeping in from the deserts like a cloud of smoke along the ground? Who is it that smells of myrrh and frankincense and every other spice? ⁷Look, it is Solomon's carriage, with sixty of Israel's mightiest men surrounding it. ⁸They are all skilled swordsmen and experienced warriors. Each one wears a sword on his thigh, ready to defend the king against an attack during the night.

⁹"King Solomon has built a carriage for himself from wood imported from Lebanon's forests. ¹⁰Its posts are of silver, its canopy is gold, and its seat is upholstered in purple cloth. Its interior was a gift of love from the young women of Jerusalem."

Young Woman: ¹¹"Go out to look upon King Solomon, O young women of Jerusalem.* See the crown with which his mother crowned him on his wedding day, the day of his gladness."

CHAPTER **4**

Young Man: "How beautiful you are, my beloved, how beautiful! Your eyes behind your veil are like doves. Your hair falls in waves, like a flock of goats frisking down the slopes of Gilead. ²Your teeth are as white as sheep, newly shorn and washed. They are perfectly matched; not one is missing. ³Your lips are like a ribbon of scarlet. Oh, how

2:17 Or *on the hills of Bether.*   3:5 Or *not to awaken love until it is ready.*   3:11 Hebrew *Zion.*

OFF AND RUNNING
There Is an Intimacy in Marriage That Can Be Found Nowhere Else Read SONG OF SONGS 4:1–5:1

Intimacy, or sex, has been perhaps one of the most misunderstood subjects throughout the ages. Various aberrant views on the subject of "sex" have been taught. In earlier times, some considered sex simply as the means of having children. To use it as a means of enjoyment was considered "sinful" or "vulgar." Current opinion has now gone to the opposite extreme. Now, if you put any restrictions on sex, you are considered "narrow" and "inhibited." Both views fall far short of God's biblical design.

It may surprise you to know that God wants all married couples to have a fulfilling, enjoyable sex life. But the only way they will find it is within the parameters of marriage. Many forget that God is the definitive authority on the subject. After all, it was he who brought the first woman and man together and created the sexual drive to begin with. He wanted

beautiful your mouth! Your cheeks behind your veil are like pomegranate halves—lovely and delicious. 4Your neck is as stately as the tower of David, jeweled with the shields of a thousand heroes. 5Your breasts are like twin fawns of a gazelle, feeding among the lilies. 6Before the dawn comes and the shadows flee away, I will go to the mountain of myrrh and to the hill of frankincense. 7You are so beautiful, my beloved, so perfect in every part.

8"Come with me from Lebanon, my bride. Come down* from the top of Mount Amana, from Mount Senir and Mount Hermon, where lions have their dens and panthers prowl. 9You have ravished my heart, my treasure, my bride. I am overcome by one glance of your eyes, by a single bead of your necklace. 10How sweet is your love, my treasure, my bride! How much better it is than wine! Your perfume is more fragrant than the richest of spices. 11Your lips, my bride, are as sweet as honey. Yes, honey and cream are under your tongue. The scent of your clothing is like that of the mountains and the cedars of Lebanon.

12"You are like a private garden, my treasure, my bride! You are like a spring that no one else can drink from, a fountain of my own. 13You are like a lovely orchard bearing precious fruit, with the rarest of perfumes: 14nard and saffron, calamus and cinnamon, myrrh and aloes, perfume from every incense tree, and every other lovely spice. 15You are a garden fountain, a well of living water, as refreshing as the streams from the Lebanon mountains."

Young Woman: 16"Awake, north wind! Come, south wind! Blow on my garden and waft its

4:8 Or *Look down.*

lovely perfume to my lover. Let him come into his garden and eat its choicest fruits."

CHAPTER 5

Young Man: "I am here in my garden, my treasure, my bride! I gather my myrrh with my spices and eat my honeycomb with my honey. I drink my wine with my milk."

Young Women of Jerusalem: "Oh, lover and beloved, eat and drink! Yes, drink deeply of this love!"

Young Woman: 2"One night as I was sleeping, my heart awakened in a dream. I heard the voice of my lover. He was knocking at my bedroom door. 'Open to me, my darling, my treasure, my lovely dove,' he said, 'for I have been out in the night. My head is soaked with dew, my hair with the wetness of the night.'

3"But I said, 'I have taken off my robe. Should I get dressed again? I have washed my feet. Should I get them soiled?'

4"My lover tried to unlatch the door, and my heart thrilled within me. 5I jumped up to open it. My hands dripped with perfume, my fingers with lovely myrrh, as I pulled back the bolt. 6I opened to my lover, but he was gone. I yearned for even his voice! I searched for him, but I couldn't find him anywhere. I called to him, but there was no reply. 7The watchmen found me as they were making their rounds; they struck and wounded me. The watchman on the wall tore off my veil.

8"Make this promise to me, O women of Jerusalem! If you find my beloved one, tell him that I am sick with love."

---

them to become as "one person" (see Genesis 2:24, p. 4). And before they gave in to the temptation to disobey God, Scripture says that they were naked, yet not ashamed or embarrassed (see Genesis 2:25, p. 4).

This passage of Scripture vividly portrays the intimacy God desires a husband and wife to have. It describes the wedding night of Solomon and his bride in poetic detail. The two newlyweds not only express their love to one another by their actions, but also through their words. Verse 12 emphasizes the sacredness of their union. In describing his bride as a private garden, a spring that no one else can have, Solomon focuses upon his wife's virginity. She has saved herself for her husband, and now she is his alone. Theirs is a bond no one else can breach.

Intimacy within marriage is unlike anything else. Disregarding God's original marriage design will only produce short-lived thrills (at best) and long-lasting regret. Following God's plan for marriage will bring a couple closer than they could ever have imagined. Don't allow a moment of pleasure (and a guilty one, at that) to lead to a lifetime of regret. If you are single and desire to be married, save yourself for that right man or woman God has for you.

For the next note on "Marriage," turn to p. 784.

Young Women of Jerusalem: 9 "O woman of rare beauty, what is it about your loved one that brings you to tell us this?"

Young Woman: 10 "My lover is dark and dazzling, better than ten thousand others! 11His head is the finest gold, and his hair is wavy and black. 12His eyes are like doves beside brooks of water; they are set like jewels. 13His cheeks are like sweetly scented beds of spices. His lips are like perfumed lilies. His breath is like myrrh. 14His arms are like round bars of gold, set with chrysolite. His body is like bright ivory, aglow with sapphires. 15His legs are like pillars of marble set in sockets of the finest gold, strong as the cedars of Lebanon. None can rival him. 16His mouth is altogether sweet; he is lovely in every way. Such, O women of Jerusalem, is my lover, my friend."

CHAPTER 6

Young Women of Jerusalem: "O rarest of beautiful women, where has your lover gone? We will help you find him."

Young Woman: 2 "He has gone down to his garden, to his spice beds, to graze and to gather the lilies. 3I am my lover's, and my lover is mine. He grazes among the lilies!"

Young Man: 4 "O my beloved, you are as beautiful as the lovely town of Tirzah. Yes, as beautiful as Jerusalem! You are as majestic as an army with banners! 5Look away, for your eyes overcome me! Your hair falls in waves, like a flock of goats frisking down the slopes of Gilead. 6Your teeth are as white as newly washed sheep. They are perfectly matched; not one is missing. 7Your cheeks behind your veil are like pomegranate halves—lovely and delicious. 8There may be sixty wives, all queens, and eighty concubines and unnumbered virgins available to me. 9But I would still choose my dove, my perfect one, the only beloved daughter of her mother! The young women are delighted when they see her; even queens and concubines sing her praises! 10'Who is this,' they ask, 'arising like the dawn, as fair as the moon, as bright as the sun, as majestic as an army with banners?'

11 "I went down into the grove of nut trees and out to the valley to see the new growth brought on by spring. I wanted to see whether the grapevines were budding yet, or whether the pomegranates were blossoming. 12Before I realized it, I found myself in my princely bed with my beloved one.*"

Young Women of Jerusalem: 13 "Return, return to us, O maid of Shulam. Come back, come back, that we may see you once again."

Young Man: "Why do you gaze so intently at this young woman of Shulam, as she moves so gracefully between two lines of dancers?*"

CHAPTER 7

Young Man: "How beautiful are your sandaled feet, O queenly maiden. Your rounded thighs are like jewels, the work of a skilled craftsman. 2Your navel is as delicious as a goblet filled with wine. Your belly is lovely, like a heap of wheat set about with lilies. 3Your breasts are like twin fawns of a gazelle. 4Your neck is as stately as an ivory tower. Your eyes are like the sparkling pools in Heshbon by the gate of Bath-rabbim. Your nose is as fine as the tower of Lebanon overlooking Damascus. 5Your head is as majestic as Mount Carmel, and the sheen of your hair radiates royalty. A king is held captive in your queenly tresses.

6 "Oh, how delightful you are, my beloved; how pleasant for utter delight! 7You are tall and slim like a palm tree, and your breasts are like its clusters of dates. 8I said, 'I will climb up into the palm tree and take hold of its branches.' Now may your breasts be like grape clusters, and the scent of your breath like apples. 9May your kisses be as exciting as the best wine, smooth and sweet, flowing gently over lips and teeth.*"

Young Woman: 10 "I am my lover's, the one he desires. 11Come, my love, let us go out into the fields and spend the night among the wildflowers.* 12Let us get up early and go out to the vineyards. Let us see whether the vines have budded, whether the blossoms have opened, and whether the pomegranates are in flower. And there I will give you my love. 13There the mandrakes give forth their fragrance, and the rarest fruits are at our doors, the new as well as old, for I have stored them up for you, my lover."

6:12 Or *among the royal chariots of my people,* or *among the chariots of Amminadab.* The meaning of the Hebrew is uncertain. 6:13 Or *as you would at the movements of two armies?* or *as you would at the dance of Mahanaim?* The meaning of the Hebrew is uncertain. 7:9 As in Greek and Syriac versions and Latin Vulgate; Hebrew reads *over lips of sleepers.* 7:11 Or *in the villages.*

CHAPTER **8**

Young Woman: "Oh, if only you were my brother, who nursed at my mother's breast. Then I could kiss you no matter who was watching, and no one would criticize me. ²I would bring you to my childhood home, and there you would teach me. I would give you spiced wine to drink, my sweet pomegranate wine. ³Your left hand would be under my head and your right hand would embrace me.

⁴"I want you to promise, O women of Jerusalem, not to awaken love until the time is right.*"

Young Women of Jerusalem: ⁵"Who is this coming up from the desert, leaning on her lover?"

Young Woman: "I aroused you under the apple tree, where your mother gave you birth, where in great pain she delivered you. ⁶Place me like a seal over your heart, or like a seal on your arm. For love is as strong as death, and its jealousy is as enduring as the grave. Love flashes like fire, the brightest kind of flame. ⁷Many waters cannot quench love; neither can rivers drown it. If a man tried to buy love with everything he owned, his offer would be utterly despised."

The Young Woman's Brothers: ⁸"We have a little sister too young for breasts. What will we do if someone asks to marry her? ⁹If she is chaste, we will strengthen and encourage her. But if she is promiscuous, we will shut her off from men.*"

Young Woman: ¹⁰"I am chaste, and I am now full breasted. And my lover is content with me.

¹¹"Solomon has a vineyard at Baal-hamon, which he rents to some farmers there. Each of them pays one thousand pieces of silver* for its use. ¹²But as for my own vineyard, O Solomon, you can take my thousand pieces of silver. And I will give two hundred pieces of silver* to those who care for its vines."

Young Man: ¹³"O my beloved, lingering in the gardens, how wonderful that your companions can listen to your voice. Let me hear it, too!"

Young Woman: ¹⁴"Come quickly, my love! Move like a swift gazelle or a young deer on the mountains of spices."

8:4 Or *not to awaken love until it is ready.*   8:9 Hebrew *If she is a wall, we will build battlements of silver on her; but if she is a door, we will surround her with panels of cedar.*   8:11 Hebrew *1,000 shekels of silver,* about 25 pounds or 11.4 kilograms in weight; also in 8:12. 8:12 Hebrew *200 [shekels],* about 5 pounds or 2.3 kilograms in weight.

Isaiah

These visions concerning Judah and Jerusalem came to Isaiah son of Amoz during the reigns of Uzziah, Jotham, Ahaz, and Hezekiah—all kings of Judah.

A Message for Rebellious Judah

2Hear, O heavens! Listen, O earth! This is what the LORD says: "The children I raised and cared for have turned against me. 3Even the animals—the donkey and the ox—know their owner and appreciate his care, but not my people Israel. No matter what I do for them, they still do not understand."

4Oh, what a sinful nation they are! They are loaded down with a burden of guilt. They are evil and corrupt children who have turned away from the LORD. They have despised the Holy One of Israel, cutting themselves off from his help.

5Why do you continue to invite punishment? Must you rebel forever? Your head is injured, and your heart is sick. 6You are sick from head to foot—covered with bruises, welts, and infected wounds—without any ointments or bandages. 7Your country lies in ruins, and your cities are burned. As you watch, foreigners plunder your fields and destroy everything they see. 8Jerusalem* stands abandoned like a watchman's shelter in a vineyard or field after the harvest is over. It is as helpless as a city under siege. 9If the LORD Almighty had not spared a few of us, we would have been wiped out as completely as Sodom and Gomorrah.

10Listen to the LORD, you leaders of Israel! Listen to the law of our God, people of Israel. You act just like the rulers and people of Sodom and Gomorrah. 11"I am sick of your sacrifices," says the LORD. "Don't bring me any more burnt offerings! I don't want the fat from your rams or other animals. I don't want to see the blood from your offerings of bulls and rams and goats. 12Why do you keep parading through my courts with your worthless sacrifices? 13The incense you bring me is a stench in my nostrils! Your celebrations of the new moon and the Sabbath day, and your special days for fasting—even your most pious meetings—are all sinful and false. I want nothing more to do with them. 14I hate all your festivals and sacrifices. I cannot stand the sight of them! 15From now on, when you lift up your hands in prayer, I will refuse to look. Even though you offer many prayers, I will not listen. For your hands are covered with the blood of your innocent victims. 16Wash yourselves and be clean! Let me no longer see your evil deeds. Give up your wicked ways. 17Learn to do good. Seek justice. Help the oppressed. Defend the orphan. Fight for the rights of widows.

18"Come now, let us argue this out," says the LORD. "No matter how deep the stain of your sins, I can remove it. I can make you as clean as freshly fallen snow. Even if you are stained as red as crimson, I can make you as white as wool. 19If you will only obey me and let me help you, then you will have plenty to eat. 20But if you keep turning away and refusing to listen, you will be destroyed by your enemies. I, the LORD, have spoken!"

Unfaithful Jerusalem

21See how Jerusalem, once so faithful, has become a prostitute. Once the home of justice and righteousness, she is now filled with murderers. 22Once like pure silver, you have become like worthless slag. Once so pure, you are now like watered-down wine. 23Your leaders are rebels, the companions of thieves. All of them take bribes and refuse to defend the orphans and the widows.

1:8 Hebrew *The daughter of Zion.*

24Therefore, the Lord, the LORD Almighty, the Mighty One of Israel, says, "I will pour out my fury on you, my enemies! 25I will turn against you. I will melt you down and skim off your slag. I will remove all your impurities. 26Afterward I will give you good judges and wise counselors like the ones you used to have. Then Jerusalem will again be called the Home of Justice and the Faithful City."

27Because the LORD is just and righteous, the repentant people of Jerusalem* will be redeemed. 28But all sinners will be completely destroyed, for they refuse to come to the LORD.

29Shame will cover you when you think of the times you offered sacrifices to idols in your groves of sacred oaks. You will blush when you think of all the sins you committed in your sacred gardens. 30You will wither away like an oak or garden without water. 31The strongest among you will disappear like burning straw. Your evil deeds are the spark that will set the straw on fire, and no one will be able to put it out.

CHAPTER 2
The LORD's Future Reign

This is another vision that Isaiah son of Amoz saw concerning Judah and Jerusalem:

2In the last days, the Temple of the LORD in Jerusalem will become the most important place on earth. People from all over the world will go there to worship. 3Many nations will come and say, "Come, let us go up to the mountain of the LORD, to the Temple of the God of Israel.* There he will teach us his ways, so that we may obey him." For in those days the LORD's teaching and his word will go out from Jerusalem.

4The LORD will settle international disputes. All the nations will beat their swords into plowshares and their spears into pruning hooks. All wars will stop, and military training will come to an end. 5Come, people of Israel, let us walk in the light of the LORD!

A Warning of Judgment

6The LORD has rejected the people of Israel because they have made alliances with foreigners from the East who practice magic and divination, just like the Philistines. 7Israel has vast treasures of silver and gold and many horses and chariots. 8The land is filled with idols. The people bow down and worship these things they have made. 9So now everyone will be humbled and brought low. The LORD cannot simply ignore their sins!

10Crawl into caves in the rocks. Hide from the terror of the LORD and the glory of his majesty. 11The day is coming when your pride will be brought low and the LORD alone will be exalted. 12In that day the LORD Almighty will punish the proud, bringing them down to the dust. 13He will cut down the tall cedars of Lebanon and the mighty oaks of Bashan. 14He will level the high mountains and hills. 15He will break down every high tower and wall. 16He will destroy the great trading ships* and all the small boats in the harbor. 17The arrogance of all people will be brought low. Their pride will lie in the dust. The LORD alone will be exalted! 18Idols will be utterly abolished and destroyed.

19When the LORD rises to shake the earth, his enemies will crawl with fear into holes in the ground. They will hide in caves in the rocks from the terror of the LORD and the glory of his majesty. 20They will abandon their gold and silver idols to the moles and bats. 21They will crawl into caverns and hide among the jagged rocks at the tops of cliffs. In this way, they will try to escape the terror of the LORD and the glory of his majesty as he rises to shake the earth.

22Stop putting your trust in mere humans. They are as frail as breath. How can they be of help to anyone?

CHAPTER 3
Judgment against Judah

The Lord, the LORD Almighty, will cut off the supplies of food and water from Jerusalem and Judah. 2He will destroy all the nation's leaders—the heroes, soldiers, judges, prophets, diviners, elders, 3army officers, honorable citizens, advisers, skilled magicians, and expert enchanters. 4Then he will appoint children to rule over them, and anarchy will prevail. 5People will take advantage of each other—man against man, neighbor fighting neighbor. Young people will revolt against authority, and nobodies will sneer at honorable people.

6In those days a man will say to his brother, "Since you have a cloak, you be our leader! Take charge of this heap of ruins!"

7"No!" he will reply. "I can't help. I don't have any extra food or clothes. Don't ask me to get involved!"

8Judah and Jerusalem will lie in ruins because they speak out against the LORD and refuse to obey him. They have offended his glorious presence among them. 9The very look on their faces gives them away and displays their guilt. They sin openly like the people of Sodom. They are not one bit ashamed. How terrible it will be for them! They have brought about their own destruction.

[10]But all will be well for those who are godly. Tell them, "You will receive a wonderful reward!" [11]But say to the wicked, "Your destruction is sure. You, too, will get what you deserve. Your well-earned punishment is on the way."

[12]Children oppress my people, and women rule over them. O my people, can't you see what fools your rulers are? They are leading you down a pretty garden path to destruction.

[13]The LORD takes his place in court. He is the great prosecuting attorney, presenting his case against his people! [14]The leaders and the princes will be the first to feel the LORD's judgment. "You have ruined Israel, which is my vineyard. You have taken advantage of the poor, filling their barns with grain extorted from helpless people. [15]How dare you grind my people into the dust like that!" demands the Lord, the LORD Almighty.

A Warning for Jerusalem's Women
[16]Next the LORD will judge the women of Jerusalem,* who walk around with their noses in the air, with tinkling ornaments on their ankles. Their eyes rove among the crowds, flirting with the men. [17]The Lord will send a plague of scabs to ornament their heads. Yes, the LORD will make them bald for all to see!

[18]The Lord will strip away their artful beauty—their ornaments, headbands, and crescent necklaces; [19]their earrings, bracelets, and veils of shimmering gauze. [20]Gone will be their scarves, ankle chains, sashes, perfumes, and charms; [21]their rings, jewels, [22]party clothes, gowns, capes, and purses; [23]their mirrors, linen garments, head ornaments, and shawls. [24]Instead of smelling of sweet perfume, they will stink. They will wear ropes for sashes, and their well-set hair will fall out. They will wear rough sackcloth instead of rich robes. Their beauty will be gone. Only shame will be left to them.

[25]The men of the city will die in battle. [26]The gates of Jerusalem* will weep and mourn. The city will be like a ravaged woman, huddled on the ground.

In that day few men will be left alive. Seven women will fight over each of them and say, "Let us all marry you! We will provide our own food

and clothing. Only let us be called by your name so we won't be mocked as old maids."

A Promise of Restoration
[2]But in the future, Israel—the branch of the LORD—will be lush and beautiful, and the fruit of the land will be the pride of its people. [3]All those whose names are written down, who have survived the destruction of Jerusalem, will be a holy people. [4]The Lord will wash the moral filth from the women of Jerusalem.* He will cleanse Jerusalem of its bloodstains by a spirit of judgment that burns like fire. [5]Then the LORD will provide shade for Jerusalem* and all who assemble there. There will be a canopy of smoke and cloud throughout the day and clouds of fire at night, covering the glorious land. [6]It will be a shelter from daytime heat and a hiding place from storms and rain.

A Song about the LORD's Vineyard
Now I will sing a song for the one I love about his vineyard:

> My beloved has a vineyard
>   on a rich and fertile hill.
> [2] He plowed the land, cleared its stones,
>   and planted it with choice vines.
> In the middle he built a watchtower
>   and carved a winepress in the nearby rocks.
> Then he waited for a harvest of sweet grapes,
>   but the grapes that grew were wild and
>   sour.
> [3] "Now, you people of Jerusalem and Judah,
>   you have heard the case; you be the
>   judges.
> [4] What more could I have done
>   to cultivate a rich harvest?
> Why did my vineyard give me wild grapes
>   when I expected sweet ones?
> [5] Now this is what I am going to do to my
>   vineyard:
> I will tear down its fences
>   and let it be destroyed.
> I will break down its walls
>   and let the animals trample it.
> [6] I will make it a wild place.
>   I will not prune the vines or hoe the
>   ground.
> I will let it be overgrown with briers and
>   thorns.
> I will command the clouds
>   to drop no more rain on it."

3:16 Hebrew *the daughters of Zion.*   3:26 Hebrew *Zion.*   4:4 Hebrew *from the daughters of Zion.*   4:5 Hebrew *Mount Zion.*

God Is Holy Read ISAIAH 6:1-8

The Bible states that God's eyes are too pure to look on evil (Habakkuk 1:13, p. 765). Unlike God, we all are flawed by sin. We are not perfect as he is. We are full of impure and selfish motives, while no impure or selfish motive exists in him. He is absolutely pure and flawless. Scripture says, "God is light and in him is no darkness at all" (1 John 1:5).

This passage gives us a glimpse into God's purity and perfection—otherwise known as his holiness. Here we see God's holiness in Isaiah's description *of* God, the angels' behavior *before* God, and Isaiah's response *to* God.

Isaiah's Description of God. Isaiah described God as "sitting on a lofty throne." *Lofty* means "elevated in status, superior." Only God occupies this throne, not the seraphim, not Isaiah. This means that only God is worthy of the elevated, superior status of sitting there.

The Angels' Behavior before God. The seraphim are one type of angel. Although they are without sin and are constantly in the very presence of God, they showed their reverence and awe for him by covering their faces and their feet with their wings. Also, they sang a chorus of praise to God, in which they described him as "holy" three times. In the Hebrew language, repetition is used to indicate the superlative. In essence, the word *superlative* means "surpassing all others." Therefore, the repetition of *holy* indicates that God is the most holy. There is no one holier than he.

Isaiah's Response to God. Isaiah realized what an unholy man he was when he saw the holy God. He feared for his life because he knew he was sinful and was standing before the perfect God. But after the angel purified Isaiah from his guilt, Isaiah quickly volunteered to be God's messenger to Israel. His realization of his sinfulness and his willingness to be God's messenger were motivated by God's holy character.

Like Isaiah, we should realize our sinfulness before the only pure and perfect God. When we do, we will realize our true need for forgiveness and salvation from our sin. In addition, we will not only understand why God alone deserves our praise and worship, but we will desire to serve him.

For the next note on "Who Is God?" turn to p. 1100.

CORNER STONES

---

7 This is the story of the LORD's people.
They are the vineyard of the LORD
Almighty.
Israel and Judah are his pleasant garden.
He expected them to yield a crop of justice,
but instead he found bloodshed.
He expected to find righteousness,
but instead he heard cries of oppression.

Judah's Guilt and Judgment

8Destruction is certain for you who buy up property so others have no place to live. Your homes are built on great estates so you can be alone in the land. 9But the LORD Almighty has sealed your awful fate. With my own ears I heard him say, "Many beautiful homes will stand deserted, the owners dead or gone. 10Ten acres* of vineyard will not produce even six gallons* of wine. Ten measures of seed will yield only one measure* of grain."

11Destruction is certain for you who get up early to begin long drinking bouts that last late into the night. 12You furnish lovely music and wine at your grand parties; the harps, lyres, tambourines, and flutes are superb! But you never think about the LORD or notice what he is doing. 13So I will send my people into exile far away because they do not know me. The great and honored among them will starve, and the common people will die of thirst.

14The grave* is licking its chops in anticipation of Jerusalem, this delicious morsel. Her great and lowly will be swallowed up, with all her drunken crowds. 15In that day the arrogant will be brought down to the dust; the proud will be humbled. 16But the LORD Almighty is exalted

5:10a Hebrew *A ten yoke,* that is, the area of land plowed by ten teams of oxen in one day.   5:10b Hebrew *a bath* [21 liters].   5:10c Hebrew *A homer* [5 bushels or 182 liters] *of seed will yield only an ephah* [0.5 bushels or 18.2 liters].   5:14 Hebrew *Sheol.*

by his justice. The holiness of God is displayed by his righteousness. 17In those days flocks will feed among the ruins; lambs and kids* will pasture there.

18Destruction is certain for those who drag their sins behind them, tied with cords of falsehood. 19They even mock the Holy One of Israel and say, "Hurry up and do something! Quick, show us what you can do. We want to see what you have planned."

20Destruction is certain for those who say that evil is good and good is evil; that dark is light and light is dark; that bitter is sweet and sweet is bitter.

21Destruction is certain for those who think they are wise and consider themselves to be clever.

22Destruction is certain for those who are heroes when it comes to drinking, who boast about all the liquor they can hold. 23They take bribes to pervert justice. They let the wicked go free while punishing the innocent.

24Therefore, they will all disappear like burning straw. Their roots will rot and their flowers wither, for they have rejected the law of the LORD Almighty. They have despised the word of the Holy One of Israel. 25That is why the anger of the LORD burns against his people. That is why he has raised his fist to crush them. The hills tremble, and the rotting bodies of his people are thrown as garbage into the streets. But even then the LORD's anger will not be satisfied. His fist is still poised to strike!

26He will send a signal to the nations far away. He will whistle to those at the ends of the earth, and they will come racing toward Jerusalem. 27They will not get tired or stumble. They will run without stopping for rest or sleep. Not a belt will be loose, not a sandal thong broken. 28Their arrows will be sharp and their bows ready for battle. Sparks will fly from their horses' hooves as the wheels of their chariots spin like the wind. 29Roaring like lions, they will pounce on their prey. They will seize my people and carry them off into captivity, and no one will be there to rescue them. 30The enemy nations will growl over their victims like the roaring of the sea. A cloud of darkness and sorrow will hover over Israel. The clouds will blot out the light.

CHAPTER 6
Isaiah's Cleansing and Call
In the year King Uzziah died, I saw the Lord. He was sitting on a lofty throne, and the train of his robe filled the Temple. 2Hovering around him were mighty seraphim, each with six wings. With two wings they covered their faces, with two they covered their feet, and with the remaining two they flew. 3In a great chorus they sang, "Holy, holy, holy is the LORD Almighty! The whole earth is filled with his glory!" 4The glorious singing shook the Temple to its foundations, and the entire sanctuary was filled with smoke.

5Then I said, "My destruction is sealed, for I am a sinful man and a member of a sinful race. Yet I have seen the King, the LORD Almighty!"

6Then one of the seraphim flew over to the altar, and he picked up a burning coal with a pair of tongs. 7He touched my lips with it and said, "See, this coal has touched your lips. Now your guilt is removed, and your sins are forgiven."

8Then I heard the Lord asking, "Whom should I send as a messenger to my people? Who will go for us?"

And I said, "Lord, I'll go! Send me."

9And he said, "Yes, go. But tell my people this: 'You will hear my words, but you will not understand. You will see what I do, but you will not perceive its meaning.' 10Harden the hearts of these people. Close their ears, and shut their eyes. That way, they will not see with their eyes, hear with their ears, understand with their hearts, and turn to me for healing."

11Then I said, "Lord, how long must I do this?"

And he replied, "Until their cities are destroyed, with no one left in them. Until their houses are deserted and the whole country is an utter wasteland. 12Do not stop until the LORD has sent everyone away to distant lands and the entire land of Israel lies deserted. 13Even if only a tenth—a remnant—survive, it will be invaded again and burned. Israel will remain a stump, like a tree that is cut down, but the stump will be a holy seed that will grow again."

CHAPTER 7
A Message for Ahaz
During the reign of Ahaz son of Jotham and grandson of Uzziah, Jerusalem was attacked by King Rezin of Aram and King Pekah of Israel, the son of Remaliah. The city withstood the attack, however, and was not taken.

2The news had come to the royal court: "Aram is allied with Israel* against us!" So the hearts of the king and his people trembled with fear, just as trees shake in a storm.

5:17 As in Greek version; Hebrew reads strangers. 7:2 Hebrew Ephraim, referring to the northern kingdom of Israel; also in 7:5, 8, 9, 17.

3Then the LORD said to Isaiah, "Go out to meet King Ahaz, you and your son Shear-jashub.* You will find the king at the end of the aqueduct that feeds water into the upper pool, near the road leading to the field where cloth is bleached. 4Tell him to stop worrying. Tell him he doesn't need to fear the fierce anger of those two burned-out embers, King Rezin of Aram and Pekah son of Remaliah.

5"Yes, the kings of Aram and Israel are coming against you. They are saying, 6'We will invade Judah and throw its people into panic. Then we will fight our way into Jerusalem and install the son of Tabeel as Judah's king.'

7"But this is what the Sovereign LORD says: This invasion will never happen, 8because Aram is no stronger than its capital, Damascus. And Damascus is no stronger than its king, Rezin. As for Israel, within sixty-five years it will be crushed and completely destroyed. 9Israel is no stronger than its capital, Samaria. And Samaria is no stronger than its king, Pekah son of Remaliah. You do not believe me? If you want me to protect you, learn to believe what I say."

The Sign of Immanuel

10Not long after this, the LORD sent this message to King Ahaz: 11"Ask me for a sign, Ahaz, to prove that I will crush your enemies as I have promised. Ask for anything you like, and make it as difficult as you want."

12But the king refused. "No," he said, "I wouldn't test the LORD like that."

13Then Isaiah said, "Listen well, you royal family of David! You aren't satisfied to exhaust my patience. You exhaust the patience of God as well! 14All right then, the Lord himself will choose the sign. Look! The virgin* will conceive a child! She will give birth to a son and will call him Immanuel—'God is with us.' 15By the time this child is old enough to eat curds and honey, he will know enough to choose what is right and reject what is wrong. 16But before he knows right from wrong, the two kings you fear so much—the kings of Israel and Aram—will both be dead.

17"The LORD will bring a terrible curse on you, your nation, and your family. You will soon experience greater terror than has been known in all the years since Solomon's empire was divided into Israel and Judah. The mighty king of Assyria will come with his great army!"

18In that day the LORD will whistle for the army of Upper Egypt and for the army of Assyria. They will swarm around you like flies. Like bees, they will sting and kill. 19They will come in vast hordes, spreading across the whole land. They will settle in the fertile areas and also in the desolate valleys, caves, and thorny places. 20In that day the Lord will take this "razor"—these Assyrians you have hired to protect you—and use it to shave off everything: your land, your crops, and your people.*

21When they finally stop plundering, a farmer will be fortunate to have a cow and two sheep left. 22The few people still left in the land will live on curds and wild honey because that is all the land will produce. 23In that day the lush vineyards, now worth as much as a thousand pieces of silver,* will become patches of briers and thorns. 24The entire land will be one vast brier patch, a hunting ground overrun by wildlife. 25No one will go to the fertile hillsides where the gardens once grew, for briers and thorns will cover them. Cattle, sheep, and goats will graze there.

CHAPTER 8

The Coming Assyrian Invasion

Again the LORD said to me, "Make a large signboard and clearly write this name on it: Maher-shalal-hash-baz.* " 2I asked Uriah the priest and Zechariah son of Jeberekiah, both known as honest men, to testify that I had written it before the child was conceived.

3Then I slept with my wife, and she became pregnant and had a son. And the LORD said, "Call him Maher-shalal-hash-baz. 4This name prophesies that within a couple of years, before this child is old enough to say 'Papa' or 'Mama,' the king of Assyria will invade both Damascus and Samaria and carry away their riches."

5Then the LORD spoke to me again and said, 6"The people of Judah have rejected my gentle care* and are rejoicing over what will happen to King Rezin and King Pekah. 7Therefore, the Lord will overwhelm them with a mighty flood from the Euphrates River*—the king of Assyria and all his mighty armies. 8This flood will overflow all its channels and sweep into Judah. It will submerge Immanuel's land from one end to the other.

9"The Assyrians will cry, 'Do your best to defend yourselves, but you will be shattered! Listen all you nations. Prepare for battle—and

---

7:3 *Shear-jashub* means "A remnant will return." 7:14 Or *young woman.* 7:20 Hebrew *shave off the head, the hair of the legs, and the beard.* 7:23 Hebrew *1,000 shekels of silver*, about 25 pounds or 11.4 kilograms in weight. 8:1 *Maher-shalal-hash-baz* means "Swift to plunder and quick to spoil." 8:6 Hebrew *rejected the gently flowing waters of Shiloah.* 8:7 Hebrew *the river.*

die! Yes, die! ¹⁰Call your councils of war, develop your strategies, prepare your plans of attack—and then die! For God is with us!*'"

A Call to Trust the LORD

¹¹The LORD has said to me in the strongest terms: "Do not think like everyone else does. ¹²Do not be afraid that some plan conceived behind closed doors will be the end of you. ¹³Do not fear anything except the LORD Almighty. He alone is the Holy One. If you fear him, you need fear nothing else. ¹⁴He will keep you safe. But to Israel and Judah he will be a stone that causes people to stumble and a rock that makes them fall. And for the people of Jerusalem he will be a trap that entangles them. ¹⁵Many of them will stumble and fall, never to rise again. Many will be captured."

¹⁶I will write down all these things as a testimony of what the LORD will do. I will entrust it to my disciples, who will pass it down to future generations. ¹⁷I will wait for the LORD to help us, though he has turned away from the people of Israel.* My only hope is in him. ¹⁸I and the children the LORD has given me have names* that reveal the plans the LORD Almighty has for his people. ¹⁹So why are you trying to find out the future by consulting mediums and psychics? Do not listen to their whisperings and mutterings. Can the living find out the future from the dead? Why not ask your God?

²⁰"Check their predictions against my testimony," says the LORD. "If their predictions are different from mine, it is because there is no light or truth in them. ²¹My people will be led away as captives, weary and hungry. And because they are hungry, they will rage and shake their fists at heaven and curse their king and their God. ²²Wherever they look, there will be trouble and anguish and dark despair. They will be thrown out into the darkness."

CHAPTER **9**

Hope in the Messiah

Nevertheless, that time of darkness and despair will not go on forever. The land of Zebulun and Naphtali will soon be humbled, but there will be a time in the future when Galilee of the Gentiles, which lies along the road that runs between the Jordan and the sea, will be filled with glory. ²The people who walk in darkness will see a great light—a light that will shine on all who live in the land where death casts its shadow. ³Israel will again be great, and its people will rejoice as people rejoice at harvesttime. They will shout with joy like warriors dividing the plunder. ⁴For God will break the chains that bind his people and the whip that scourges them, just as he did when he destroyed the army of Midian with Gideon's little band. ⁵In that day of peace, battle gear will no longer be issued. Never again will uniforms be bloodstained by war. All such equipment will be burned.

⁶For a child is born to us, a son is given to us. And the government will rest on his shoulders. These will be his royal titles: Wonderful Counselor,* Mighty God, Everlasting Father, Prince of Peace. ⁷His ever expanding, peaceful government will never end. He will rule forever with fairness and justice from the throne of his ancestor David. The passionate commitment of the LORD Almighty will guarantee this!

The LORD's Anger against Israel

⁸The Lord has spoken out against that braggart Israel, ⁹and the people of Israel* and Samaria will soon discover it. In their pride and arrogance they say, ¹⁰"Our land lies in ruins now, but we will rebuild it better than before. We will replace the broken bricks with cut stone, the fallen sycamore trees with cedars." ¹¹The LORD will reply to their bragging by bringing Rezin's enemies, the Assyrians, against them—¹²along with Arameans from the east and Philistines from the west. With bared fangs, they will devour Israel. But even then the LORD's anger will not be satisfied. His fist is still poised to strike. ¹³For after all this punishment, the people will still not repent and turn to the LORD Almighty.

¹⁴Therefore, in a single day, the LORD will destroy both the head and the tail, the palm branch and the reed. ¹⁵The leaders of Israel are the head, and the lying prophets are the tail. ¹⁶For the leaders of the people have led them down the path of destruction. ¹⁷That is why the Lord has no joy in the young men and no mercy on even the widows and orphans. For they are all hypocrites, speaking wickedness with lies. But even then the LORD's anger will not be satisfied. His fist is still poised to strike.

¹⁸This wickedness is like a brushfire. It burns not only briers and thorns but the forests, too. Its burning sends up vast clouds of smoke. ¹⁹The land is blackened by the fury of the LORD

8:10 Hebrew *Immanuel!* 8:17 Hebrew *the house of Jacob.* 8:18 *Isaiah* means "The LORD will save"; *Shear-jashub* means "A remnant will return"; and *Maher-shalal-hash-baz* means "Swift to plunder and quick to spoil." 9:6 Or *Wonderful, Counselor.* 9:9 Hebrew *of Ephraim,* referring to the northern kingdom of Israel.

Almighty. The people are fuel for the fire, and no one spares anyone else. 20They fight against their own neighbors to steal food, but they will still be hungry. In the end they will even eat their own children.* 21Manasseh will feed on Ephraim, Ephraim will feed on Manasseh, and both will devour Judah. But even then the LORD's anger will not be satisfied. His fist is still poised to strike.

CHAPTER **10**

Destruction is certain for the unjust judges, for those who issue unfair laws. 2They deprive the poor, the widows, and the orphans of justice. Yes, they rob widows and fatherless children! 3What will you do when I send desolation upon you from a distant land? To whom will you turn for help? Where will your treasures be safe? 4I will not help you. You will stumble along as prisoners or lie among the dead. But even then the LORD's anger will not be satisfied. His fist is still poised to strike.

Judgment against Assyria

5 "Destruction is certain for Assyria, the whip of my anger. Its military power is a club in my hand. 6Assyria will enslave my people, who are a godless nation. It will plunder them, trampling them like dirt beneath its feet. 7But the king of Assyria will not know that it is I who sent him. He will merely think he is attacking my people as part of his plan to conquer the world. 8He will say, 'Each of my princes will soon be a king, ruling a conquered land. 9We will destroy Calno just as we did Carchemish. Hamath will fall before us as Arpad did. And we will destroy Samaria just as we did Damascus. 10Yes, we have finished off many a kingdom whose gods were far greater than those in Jerusalem and Samaria. 11So when we have defeated Samaria and her gods, we will destroy Jerusalem with hers.'"

12After the Lord has used the king of Assyria to accomplish his purposes in Jerusalem, he will turn against the king of Assyria and punish him—for he is proud and arrogant. 13He boasts, "By my own power and wisdom I have won these wars. By my own strength I have captured many lands, destroyed their kings, and carried off their treasures. 14By my greatness I have robbed their nests of riches and gathered up kingdoms as a farmer gathers eggs. No one can even flap a wing against me or utter a peep of protest."

15Can the ax boast greater power than the person who uses it? Is the saw greater than the person who saws? Can a whip strike unless a hand is moving it? Can a cane walk by itself?

16Listen now, king of Assyria! Because of all your evil boasting, the Lord, the LORD Almighty, will send a plague among your proud troops, and a flaming fire will ignite your glory. 17The LORD, the Light of Israel and the Holy One, will be a flaming fire that will destroy them. In a single night he will burn those thorns and briers, the Assyrians. 18Assyria's vast army is like a glorious forest, yet it will be destroyed. The LORD will completely destroy Assyria's warriors, and they will waste away like sick people in a plague. 19Only a few from all that mighty army will survive—so few that a child could count them!

Hope for the LORD's People

20Then at last those left in Israel and Judah* will trust the LORD, the Holy One of Israel. They will no longer depend on the Assyrians, who would destroy them. 21A remnant of them will return* to the Mighty God. 22But though the people of Israel are as numerous as the sand on the seashore, only a few of them will return at that time. The LORD has rightly decided to destroy his people. 23Yes, the Lord, the LORD Almighty, has already decided to consume them.

24So this is what the Lord, the LORD Almighty, says: "My people in Jerusalem,* do not be afraid of the Assyrians when they oppress you just as the Egyptians did long ago. 25It will not last very long. In a little while my anger against you will end, and then my anger will rise up to destroy them." 26The LORD Almighty will beat them with his whip, as he did when Gideon triumphed over the Midianites at the rock of Oreb, or when the LORD's staff was raised to drown the Egyptian army in the sea. 27In that day the LORD will end the bondage of his people. He will break the yoke of slavery and lift it from their shoulders.*

28Look, the mighty armies of Assyria are coming! They are now at Aiath, now at Migron. They are storing some of their equipment at Micmash. 29They are crossing the pass and are staying overnight at Geba. Fear strikes the city of Ramah. All the people of Gibeah—the city of Saul—are running for their lives. 30Well may you scream in terror, you people of Gallim! Shout out a warning to Laishah, for the mighty army comes. Poor Anathoth, what a fate is yours! 31There go the people of Madmenah, all fleeing. And the citizens of Gebim are preparing to run. 32But the

9:20 Or *eat their own arms.*   **10:20** Hebrew *and the house of Jacob.*   **10:21** Hebrew *Shear-jashub;* see 7:3; 8:18.   **10:24** Hebrew *Zion.*   **10:27** As in Greek version; Hebrew reads *The yoke will be broken, for you have grown so fat.*

enemy stops at Nob for the rest of that day. He shakes his fist at Mount Zion in Jerusalem.

33But look! The Lord, the LORD Almighty, will chop down the mighty tree! He will destroy all that vast army of Assyria—officers and high officials alike. 34The Mighty One will cut down the enemy as an ax cuts down the forest trees in Lebanon.

CHAPTER 11
A Branch from David's Line

Out of the stump of David's family* will grow a shoot—yes, a new Branch bearing fruit from the old root. 2And the Spirit of the LORD will rest on him—the Spirit of wisdom and understanding, the Spirit of counsel and might, the Spirit of knowledge and the fear of the LORD. 3He will delight in obeying the LORD. He will never judge by appearance, false evidence, or hearsay. 4He will defend the poor and the exploited. He will rule against the wicked and destroy them with the breath of his mouth. 5He will be clothed with fairness and truth.

6In that day the wolf and the lamb will live together; the leopard and the goat will be at peace. Calves and yearlings will be safe among lions, and a little child will lead them all. 7The cattle will graze among bears. Cubs and calves will lie down together. And lions will eat grass as the livestock do. 8Babies will crawl safely among poisonous snakes. Yes, a little child will put its hand in a nest of deadly snakes and pull it out unharmed. 9Nothing will hurt or destroy in all my holy mountain. And as the waters fill the sea, so the earth will be filled with people who know the LORD.

10In that day the heir to David's throne* will be a banner of salvation to all the world. The nations will rally to him, for the land where he lives will be a glorious place. 11In that day the Lord will bring back a remnant of his people for the second time, returning them to the land of Israel from Assyria, Lower Egypt, Upper Egypt, Ethiopia,* Elam, Babylonia,* Hamath, and all the distant coastlands.

12He will raise a flag among the nations for Israel to rally around. He will gather the scattered people of Judah from the ends of the earth. 13Then at last the jealousy between Israel* and Judah will end. They will not fight against each other anymore. 14They will join forces to swoop down on Philistia to the west. Together they will attack and plunder the na-

tions to the east. They will occupy all the lands of Edom, Moab, and Ammon.

15The LORD will make a dry path through the Red Sea.* He will wave his hand over the Euphrates River,* sending a mighty wind to divide it into seven streams that can easily be crossed. 16He will make a highway from Assyria for the remnant there, just as he did for Israel long ago when they returned from Egypt.

CHAPTER 12
Songs of Praise for Salvation

In that day you will sing:

"Praise the LORD!
He was angry with me,
 but now he comforts me.
2 See, God has come to save me.
 I will trust in him and not be afraid.
The LORD GOD is my strength and my song;
 he has become my salvation."

3With joy you will drink deeply from the fountain of salvation! 4In that wonderful day you will sing:

"Thank the LORD!
 Praise his name!
Tell the world what he has done.
 Oh, how mighty he is!
5 Sing to the LORD,
 for he has done wonderful things.
 Make known his praise around the world.
6 Let all the people of Jerusalem* shout his
 praise with joy!
 For great is the Holy One of Israel who
 lives among you."

CHAPTER 13
A Message about Babylon

Isaiah son of Amoz received this message concerning the destruction of Babylon:

2"See the flags waving as the enemy attacks. Cheer them on, O Israel! Wave to them as they march against Babylon to destroy the palaces of the high and mighty. 3I, the LORD, have assigned this task to these armies, and they will rejoice when I am exalted. I have called them to satisfy my anger."

4Hear the noise on the mountains! Listen, as the armies march! It is the noise and the shout of many nations. The LORD Almighty has brought them here to form an army. 5They came

11:1 Hebrew *the line of Jesse.* Jesse was King David's father.   11:10 Hebrew *the root of Jesse.*   11:11a Hebrew *Pathros, Cush.*   11:11b Hebrew *Shinar.*   11:13 Hebrew *Ephraim,* referring to the northern kingdom of Israel.   11:15a Hebrew *sea of Egypt.*   11:15b Hebrew *the river.* 12:6 Hebrew *Zion.*

from countries far away. They are the LORD's weapons; they carry his anger with them and will destroy the whole land. ⁶Scream in terror, for the LORD's time has arrived—the time for the Almighty to destroy. ⁷Every arm is paralyzed with fear. Even the strongest hearts melt ⁸and are afraid. Fear grips them with terrible pangs, like those of a woman about to give birth. They look helplessly at one another as the flames of the burning city reflect on their faces. ⁹For see, the day of the LORD is coming—the terrible day of his fury and fierce anger. The land will be destroyed and all the sinners with it. ¹⁰The heavens will be black above them. No light will shine from stars or sun or moon.

¹¹ "I, the LORD, will punish the world for its evil and the wicked for their sin. I will crush the arrogance of the proud and the haughtiness of the mighty. ¹²Few will be left alive when I have finished my work. People will be as scarce as gold—more rare than the gold of Ophir. ¹³For I will shake the heavens, and the earth will move from its place. I, the LORD Almighty, will show my fury and fierce anger."

¹⁴Everyone will run until exhausted, rushing back to their own lands like hunted deer, wandering like sheep without a shepherd. ¹⁵Anyone who is captured will be run through with a sword. ¹⁶Their little children will be dashed to death right before their eyes. Their homes will be sacked and their wives raped by the attacking hordes. ¹⁷For I will stir up the Medes against Babylon, and no amount of silver or gold will buy them off. ¹⁸The attacking armies will shoot down the young people with arrows. They will have no mercy on helpless babies and will show no compassion for the children.

¹⁹Babylon, the most glorious of kingdoms, the flower of Chaldean culture, will be devastated like Sodom and Gomorrah when God destroyed them. ²⁰Babylon will never rise again. Generation after generation will come and go, but the land will never again be lived in. Nomads will refuse to camp there, and shepherds will not allow their sheep to stay overnight. ²¹Wild animals of the desert will move into the ruined city. The houses will be haunted by howling creatures. Ostriches will live among the ruins, and wild goats will come there to dance. ²²Hyenas will howl in its fortresses, and jackals will make their dens in its palaces. Babylon's days are numbered; its time of destruction will soon arrive.

CHAPTER **14**
A Taunt for Babylon's King

But the LORD will have mercy on the descendants of Jacob. Israel will be his special people once again. He will bring them back to settle once again in their own land. And people from many different nations will come and join them there and become a part of the people of Israel.* ²The nations of the world will help the LORD's people to return, and those who come to live in their land will serve them. Those who captured Israel will be captured, and Israel will rule over its enemies.

³In that wonderful day when the LORD gives his people rest from sorrow and fear, from slavery and chains, ⁴you will taunt the king of Babylon. You will say, "The mighty man has been destroyed. Yes, your insolence is ended. ⁵For the LORD has crushed your wicked power and broken your evil rule. ⁶You persecuted the people with unceasing blows of rage and held the nations in your angry grip. Your tyranny was unrestrained. ⁷But at last the land is at rest and is quiet. Finally it can sing again! ⁸Even the trees of the forest— the cypress trees and the cedars of Lebanon— sing out this joyous song: 'Your power is broken! No one will come to cut us down now!'

⁹"In the place of the dead* there is excitement over your arrival. World leaders and mighty kings long dead are there to see you. ¹⁰With one voice they all cry out, 'Now you are as weak as we are! ¹¹Your might and power are gone; they were buried with you. All the pleasant music in your palace has ceased. Now maggots are your sheet and worms your blanket.'

¹²"How you are fallen from heaven, O shining star, son of the morning! You have been thrown down to the earth, you who destroyed the nations of the world. ¹³For you said to yourself, 'I will ascend to heaven and set my throne above God's stars. I will preside on the mountain of the gods far away in the north. ¹⁴I will climb to the highest heavens and be like the Most High.' ¹⁵But instead, you will be brought down to the place of the dead, down to its lowest depths. ¹⁶Everyone there will stare at you and ask, 'Can this be the one who shook the earth and the kingdoms of the world? ¹⁷Is this the one who destroyed the world and made it into a wilderness? Is this the king who demolished the world's greatest cities and had no mercy on his prisoners?'

¹⁸"The kings of the nations lie in stately glory in their tombs, ¹⁹but you will be thrown out of your grave like a worthless branch. Like a corpse

14:1 Hebrew *the house of Jacob.*   14:9 Hebrew *Sheol*; also in 14:15.

trampled underfoot, you will be dumped into a mass grave with those killed in battle. You will descend to the pit. 20You will not be given a proper burial, for you have destroyed your nation and slaughtered your people. Your son will not succeed you as king. 21Kill the children of this sinner! Do not let them rise and conquer the land or rebuild the cities of the world."

22This is what the LORD Almighty says: "I, myself, have risen against him! I will destroy his children and his children's children, so they will never sit on his throne. 23I will make Babylon into a desolate land, a place of porcupines, filled with swamps and marshes. I will sweep the land with the broom of destruction. I, the LORD Almighty, have spoken!"

A Message about Assyria

24The LORD Almighty has sworn this oath: "It will all happen as I have planned. It will come about according to my purposes. 25I will break the Assyrians when they are in Israel; I will trample them on my mountains. My people will no longer be their slaves. 26I have a plan for the whole earth, for my mighty power reaches throughout the world. 27The LORD Almighty has spoken—who can change his plans? When his hand moves, who can stop him?"

A Message about Philistia

28This message came to me the year King Ahaz died:

29Do not rejoice, you Philistines, that the king who attacked you is dead. For even though that whip is broken, his son will be worse than his father ever was. From that snake a poisonous snake will be born, a fiery serpent to destroy you! 30I will feed the poor in my pasture; the needy will lie down in peace. But as for you, I will wipe you out with famine. I will destroy the few who remain.

31Weep, you Philistine cities, for you are doomed! Melt in fear, for everyone will be destroyed. A powerful army is coming out of the north. Each soldier rushes forward ready to fight. 32What should we tell the enemy messengers? Tell them that the LORD has built Jerusalem,* and that the poor of his people will find refuge in its walls.

CHAPTER 15
A Message about Moab

This message came to me concerning Moab:

In one night your cities of Ar and Kir will be destroyed. 2Your people in Dibon will mourn at their temples and shrines, weeping for the fate of Nebo and Medeba. They will shave their heads in sorrow and cut off their beards. 3They will wear sackcloth as they wander the streets. From every home will come the sound of weeping. 4The cries from the cities of Heshbon and Elealeh will be heard far away, even in Jahaz! The bravest warriors of Moab will cry out in utter terror.

5My heart weeps for Moab. Its people flee to Zoar and Eglath-shelishiyah. Weeping, they climb the road to Luhith. Their crying can be heard all along the road to Horonaim. 6Even the waters of Nimrim are dried up! The grassy banks are scorched, and the tender plants are gone. 7The desperate refugees take only the possessions they can carry and flee across the Ravine of Willows. 8The whole land of Moab is a land of weeping from one end to the other—from Eglaim to Beerelim. 9The stream near Dibon* runs red with blood, but I am still not finished with Dibon! Lions will hunt down the survivors, both those who try to run and those who remain behind.

CHAPTER 16

Moab's refugees at Sela send lambs to Jerusalem* as a token of alliance with the king of Judah. 2The women of Moab are left like homeless birds at the shallow crossings of the Arnon River. 3"Help us," they cry. "Defend us against our enemies. Protect us from their relentless attack. Do not betray us. 4Let our outcasts stay among you. Hide them from our enemies until the terror is past."

When oppression and destruction have ceased and enemy raiders have disappeared, 5then David's throne will be established by love. From that throne a faithful king will reign, one who always does what is just and right.

6Is this Moab, the proud land we have heard so much about? Its pride and insolence are all gone now! 7The entire land of Moab weeps. Yes, you people of Moab, mourn for the delicacies of Kir-hareseth. 8Weep for the abandoned farms of Heshbon and the vineyards at Sibmah. The wine from those vineyards used to make the rulers of the nations drunk. Moab was once like a spreading grapevine. Her tendrils spread out as far as Jazer and trailed out into the desert. Her shoots once reached as far as the Dead Sea.* 9But now the enemy has completely destroyed that vine. So I wail and lament for Jazer and the vineyards

14:32 Hebrew *Zion.*   15:9 As in Dead Sea Scrolls, some Greek manuscripts, and Latin Vulgate; Masoretic Text reads *Dimon;* also in 15:9b.   16:1 Hebrew *to the daughter of Zion.*   16:8 Hebrew *the sea.*

of Sibmah. My tears will flow for Heshbon and Elealeh, for their summer fruits and harvests have all been destroyed.

10Gone now is the gladness; gone is the joy of harvest. The happy singing in the vineyards will be heard no more. The treading out of grapes in the winepresses has ceased forever. I have ended all their harvest joys. 11I will weep for Moab. My sorrow for Kir-hareseth* will be very great. 12On the hilltops the people of Moab will pray in anguish to their idols, but it will do them no good. They will cry to the gods in their temples, but no one will come to save them.

13The LORD has already said this about Moab in the past. 14But now the LORD says, "Within three years, without fail, the glory of Moab will be ended, and few of its people will be left alive."

CHAPTER 17
A Message about Damascus and Israel

This message came to me concerning Damascus:

"Look, Damascus will disappear! It will become a heap of ruins. 2The cities of Aroer will be deserted. Sheep will graze in the streets and lie down unafraid. There will be no one to chase them away. 3The fortified cities of Israel* will also be destroyed, and the power of Damascus will end. The few left in Aram will share the fate of Israel's departed glory," says the LORD Almighty.

4"In that day the glory of Israel* will be very dim, for poverty will stalk the land. 5Israel will be abandoned like the grainfields in the valley of Rephaim after the harvest. 6Only a few of its people will be left, like the stray olives left on the tree after the harvest. Only two or three remain in the highest branches, four or five out on the tips of the limbs. Yes, Israel will be stripped bare of people," says the LORD, the God of Israel.

7Then at last the people will think of their Creator and have respect for the Holy One of Israel. 8They will no longer ask their idols for help or worship what their own hands have made. They will never again bow down to their Asherah poles or burn incense on the altars they built.

9Their largest cities will be as deserted as overgrown thickets. They will become like the cities the Amorites abandoned when the Israelites came here so long ago. 10Why? Because you have turned from the God who can save you— the Rock who can hide you. You may plant the finest imported grapevines, 11and they may grow so well that they blossom on the very morning

you plant them, but you will never pick any grapes from them. Your only harvest will be a load of grief and incurable pain.

12Look! The armies rush forward like waves thundering toward the shore. 13But though they roar like breakers on a beach, God will silence them. They will flee like chaff scattered by the wind or like dust whirling before a storm. 14In the evening Israel waits in terror, but by dawn its enemies are dead. This is the just reward of those who plunder and destroy the people of God.

CHAPTER 18
A Message about Ethiopia

Destruction is certain for the land of Ethiopia,* which lies at the headwaters of the Nile. Its winged sailboats glide along the river, 2and ambassadors are sent in fast boats down the Nile. Go home, swift messengers! Take a message to your land divided by rivers, to your tall, smooth-skinned people, who are feared far and wide for their conquests and destruction.

3When I raise my battle flag on the mountain, let all the world take notice. When I blow the trumpet, listen! 4For the LORD has told me this: "I will watch quietly from my dwelling place— as quietly as the heat rises on a summer day, or as the dew forms on an autumn morning during the harvest."

5Even before you begin your attack, while your plans are ripening like grapes, the LORD will cut you off as though with pruning shears. He will snip your spreading branches. 6Your mighty army will be left dead in the fields for the mountain birds and wild animals to eat. The vultures will tear at corpses all summer. The wild animals will gnaw at bones all winter.

7But the time will come when the LORD Almighty will receive gifts from this land divided by rivers, from this tall, smooth-skinned people, who are feared far and wide for their conquests and destruction. They will bring the gifts to the LORD Almighty in Jerusalem,* the place where his name dwells.

CHAPTER 19
A Message about Egypt

This message came to me concerning Egypt:

Look! The LORD is advancing against Egypt, riding on a swift cloud. The idols of Egypt tremble. The hearts of the Egyptians melt with fear.

2"I will make the Egyptians fight against each

16:11 Hebrew *Kir-heres,* a variant name for Kir-hareseth.   17:3 Hebrew *of Ephraim,* referring to the northern kingdom of Israel.
17:4 Hebrew *of Jacob.*   18:1 Hebrew *Cush.*   18:7 Hebrew *on Mount Zion.*

other—brother against brother, neighbor against neighbor, city against city, province against province. ³The Egyptians will lose heart, and I will confuse their plans. They will plead with their idols for wisdom. They will call on spirits, mediums, and psychics to show them which way to turn. ⁴I will hand Egypt over to a hard, cruel master, to a fierce king," says the Lord, the LORD Almighty.

⁵The waters of the Nile will fail to rise and flood the fields. The riverbed will be parched and dry. ⁶The canals of the Nile will dry up, and the streams of Egypt will become foul with rotting reeds and rushes. ⁷All the greenery along the riverbank will wither and blow away. All the crops will dry up, and everything will die. ⁸The fishermen will weep for lack of work. Those who fish with hooks and those who use nets will all be unemployed. ⁹The weavers will have no flax or cotton, for the crops will fail. ¹⁰The weavers and all the workers will be sick at heart.

¹¹What fools are the counselors of Zoan! Their best counsel to the king of Egypt is stupid and wrong. Will they still boast of their wisdom? Will they dare tell Pharaoh about their long line of wise ancestors? ¹²What has happened to your wise counselors, Pharaoh? If they are so wise, let them tell you what the LORD Almighty is going to do to Egypt. ¹³The wise men from Zoan are fools, and those from Memphis* are deluded. The leaders of Egypt have ruined the land with their foolish counsel. ¹⁴The LORD has sent a spirit of foolishness on them, so all their suggestions are wrong. They cause the land of Egypt to stagger like a sick drunkard. ¹⁵Nobody in Egypt, whether rich or poor, important or unknown, can offer any help.

¹⁶In that day the Egyptians will be as weak as women. They will cower in fear beneath the upraised fist of the LORD Almighty. ¹⁷Just to speak the name of Israel will strike deep terror in their hearts, for the LORD Almighty has laid out his plans against them.

¹⁸In that day five of Egypt's cities will follow the LORD Almighty. They will even begin to speak the Hebrew language.* One of these will be Heliopolis, the City of the Sun. ¹⁹In that day there will be an altar to the LORD in the heart of Egypt, and there will be a monument to the LORD at its border. ²⁰It will be a sign and a witness to the LORD Almighty in the land of Egypt. When the people cry to the LORD for help against those who oppress them, he will send them a savior who will rescue them.

²¹In that day the LORD will make himself known to the Egyptians. Yes, they will know the LORD and will give their sacrifices and offerings to him. They will make promises to the LORD and keep them. ²²The LORD will strike Egypt in a way that will bring healing. For the Egyptians will turn to the LORD, and he will listen to their pleas and heal them.

²³In that day Egypt and Assyria will be connected by a highway. The Egyptians and Assyrians will move freely between their lands, and they will worship the same God. ²⁴And Israel will be their ally. The three will be together, and Israel will be a blessing to them. ²⁵For the LORD Almighty will say, "Blessed be Egypt, my people. Blessed be Assyria, the land I have made. Blessed be Israel, my special possession!"

CHAPTER **20**

A Message about Egypt and Ethiopia

In the year when King Sargon of Assyria captured the Philistine city of Ashdod, ²the LORD told Isaiah son of Amoz, "Take off all your clothes, including your sandals." Isaiah did as he was told and walked around naked and barefoot.

³Then the LORD said, "My servant Isaiah has been walking around naked and barefoot for the last three years. This is a sign—a symbol of the terrible troubles I will bring upon Egypt and Ethiopia.* ⁴For the king of Assyria will take away the Egyptians and Ethiopians* as prisoners. He will make them walk naked and barefoot, both young and old, their buttocks uncovered, to the shame of Egypt. ⁵How dismayed will be the Philistines, who counted on the power of Ethiopia and boasted of their allies in Egypt! ⁶They will say, 'If this can happen to Egypt, what chance do we have? For we counted on Egypt to protect us from the king of Assyria.'"

CHAPTER **21**

A Message about Babylon

This message came to me concerning the land of Babylonia*:

Disaster is roaring down on you from the desert, like a whirlwind sweeping in from the Negev. ²I see an awesome vision: I see you plundered and destroyed. Go ahead, you Elamites and Medes, take part in the siege. Babylon will fall, and the groaning of all the nations she enslaved will end. ³My stomach aches and burns with pain. Sharp pangs of horror are upon me,

19:13 Hebrew *Noph.* **19:18** Hebrew *the language of Canaan.* **20:3** Hebrew *Cush;* also in 20:5. **20:4** Hebrew *Cushites.* **21:1** Hebrew *the desert of the sea.*

like the pangs of a woman giving birth. I grow faint when I hear what God is planning; I am blinded with dismay. 4My mind reels; my heart races. The sleep I once enjoyed at night is now a faint memory. I lie awake, trembling.

5Look! They are preparing a great feast. They are spreading rugs for people to sit on. Everyone is eating and drinking. Quick! Grab your shields and prepare for battle! You are being attacked!

6Meanwhile, the Lord said to me, "Put a watchman on the city wall to shout out what he sees. 7Tell him to sound the alert when he sees chariots drawn by horses and warriors mounted on donkeys and camels."

8Then the watchman* called out, "Day after day I have stood on the watchtower, my lord. Night after night I have remained at my post. 9Now at last—look! Here come the chariots and warriors!" Then the watchman said, "Babylon is fallen! All the idols of Babylon lie broken on the ground!"

10O my people, threshed and winnowed, I have told you everything the LORD Almighty, the God of Israel, has said.

A Message about Edom

11This message came to me concerning Edom*:

Someone from Edom* keeps calling to me, "Watchman, how much longer until morning? When will the night be over?"

12The watchman replies, "Morning is coming, but night will soon follow. If you wish to ask again, then come back and ask."

A Message about Arabia

13This message came to me concerning Arabia:

O caravans from Dedan, hide in the deserts of Arabia. 14O people of Tema, bring food and water to these weary refugees. 15They have fled from drawn swords and sharp arrows and the terrors of war. 16"But within a year,"* says the Lord, "all the glory of Kedar will come to an end. 17Only a few of its courageous archers will survive. I, the LORD, the God of Israel, have spoken!"

CHAPTER **22**

A Message about Jerusalem

This message came to me concerning Jerusalem*:

What is happening? Why is everyone running to the rooftops? 2The whole city is in a terrible uproar. What do I see in this reveling city? Bodies are lying everywhere, killed by famine and disease.* 3All your leaders flee. They surrender without resistance. The people try to slip away, but they are captured, too. 4Leave me alone to weep; do not try to comfort me. Let me cry for my people as I watch them being destroyed.

5Oh, what a day of crushing trouble! What a day of confusion and terror the Lord, the LORD Almighty, has brought upon the Valley of Vision! The walls of Jerusalem have been broken, and cries of death echo from the mountainsides. 6Elamites are the archers; Arameans drive the chariots. The men of Kir hold up the shields. 7They fill your beautiful valleys and crowd against your gates. 8Judah's defenses have been stripped away. You run to the armory for your weapons. 9You inspect the walls of Jerusalem* to see what needs to be repaired. You store up water in the lower pool. 10You check the houses and tear some down to get stone to fix the walls. 11Between the city walls, you build a reservoir for water from the old pool. But all your feverish plans are to no avail because you never ask God for help. He is the one who planned this long ago.

12The Lord, the LORD Almighty, called you to weep and mourn. He told you to shave your heads in sorrow for your sins and to wear clothes of sackcloth to show your remorse. 13But instead, you dance and play; you slaughter sacrificial animals, feast on meat, and drink wine. "Let's eat, drink, and be merry," you say. "What's the difference, for tomorrow we die." 14The LORD Almighty has revealed to me that this sin will never be forgiven you until the day you die. That is the judgment of the Lord, the LORD Almighty.

A Message for Shebna

15Furthermore, the Lord, the LORD Almighty, told me to confront Shebna, the palace administrator, and to give him this message: 16"Who do you think you are, building a beautiful tomb for yourself in the rock? 17For the LORD is about to seize you and hurl you away. He is going to send you into captivity, you strong man! 18He will crumple you up into a ball and toss you away into a distant, barren land. There you will die, and there your glorious chariots will remain, broken and useless. You are a disgrace to your master.

19"Yes, I will drive you out of office," says the LORD. "I will pull you down from your high position. 20And then I will call my servant Elia-

21:8 As in Dead Sea Scrolls and Syriac version; Masoretic Text reads *a lion.*   21:11a Hebrew *Dumah,* which means "silence" or "stillness." It is a wordplay on the word *Edom.*   21:11b Hebrew *Seir,* another name for Edom.   21:16 Hebrew *Within a year, like the years of a hired hand.* Some ancient manuscripts read *Within three years,* as in 16:14.   22:1 Hebrew *concerning the Valley of Vision.*   22:2 Hebrew *killed, but not by sword and not in battle.*   22:9 Hebrew *the city of David.*

kim son of Hilkiah to replace you. 21He will have your royal robes, your title, and your authority. And he will be a father to the people of Jerusalem and Judah. 22I will give him the key to the house of David—the highest position in the royal court. He will open doors, and no one will be able to shut them; he will close doors, and no one will be able to open them. 23He will bring honor to his family name, for I will drive him firmly in place like a tent stake. 24He will be loaded down with responsibility, and he will bring honor to even the lowliest members of his family."

25The LORD Almighty says: "When that time comes, I will pull out the stake that seemed so firm. It will come out and fall to the ground. Everything it supports will fall with it. I, the LORD, have spoken!"

CHAPTER 23
A Message about Tyre

This message came to me concerning Tyre:

Weep, O ships of Tarshish, returning home from distant lands! Weep for your harbor at Tyre because it is gone! The rumors you heard in Cyprus* are all true. 2Mourn in silence, you people of the coast and you merchants of Sidon. Your traders crossed the sea, 3sailing over deep waters. They brought you grain from Egypt* and harvests from along the Nile. You were the merchandise mart of the world.

4But now you are put to shame, city of Sidon, fortress on the sea. For the sea says, "Now I am childless; I have no sons or daughters." 5When Egypt hears the news about Tyre, there will be great sorrow. 6Flee now to Tarshish! Wail, you people who live by the sea! 7How can this silent ruin be all that is left of your once joyous city? What a history was yours! Think of all the colonists you sent to distant lands.

8Who has brought this disaster on Tyre, empire builder and chief trader of the world? 9The LORD Almighty has done it to destroy your pride and show his contempt for all human greatness. 10Come, Tarshish, sweep over your mother Tyre like the flooding Nile, for the city is defenseless. 11The LORD holds out his hand over the seas. He shakes the kingdoms of the earth. He has spoken out against Phoenicia* and depleted its strength. 12He says, "Never again will you rejoice, O daughter of Sidon. Once you were a lovely city, but you will never again be strong. Even if you flee to Cyprus, you will find no rest."

13Look at the land of Babylonia*—the people of that land are gone! The Assyrians have handed Babylon over to the wild beasts. They have built siege ramps against its walls, torn down its palaces, and turned it into a heap of rubble.

14Wail, O ships of Tarshish, for your home port is destroyed! 15For seventy years, the length of a king's life, Tyre will be forgotten. But then the city will come back to life and sing sweet songs like a prostitute. 16Long absent from her lovers, she will take a harp, walk the streets, and sing her songs, so that she will again be remembered. 17Yes, after seventy years the LORD will revive Tyre. But she will be no different than she was before. She will return again to all her evil ways around the world. 18But in the end her businesses will give their profits to the LORD. Her wealth will not be hoarded but will be used to provide good food and fine clothing for the LORD's priests.

CHAPTER 24
Destruction of the Earth

Look! The LORD is about to destroy the earth and make it a vast wasteland. See how he is scattering the people over the face of the earth. 2Priests and laypeople, servants and masters, maids and mistresses, buyers and sellers, lenders and borrowers, bankers and debtors—none will be spared. 3The earth will be completely emptied and looted. The LORD has spoken!

4The earth dries up, the crops wither, the skies refuse to rain. 5The earth suffers for the sins of its people, for they have twisted the instructions of God, violated his laws, and broken his everlasting covenant. 6Therefore, a curse consumes the earth and its people. They are left desolate, destroyed by fire. Few will be left alive.

7All the joys of life will be gone. The grape harvest will fail, and there will be no wine. The merrymakers will sigh and mourn. 8The clash of tambourines will be stilled; the happy cries of celebration will be heard no more. The melodious chords of the harp will be silent. 9Gone are the joys of wine and song; strong drink now turns bitter in the mouth.

10The city writhes in chaos; every home is locked to keep out looters. 11Mobs gather in the streets, crying out for wine. Joy has reached its lowest ebb. Gladness has been banished from the land. 12The city is left in ruins, with its gates battered down. 13Throughout the earth the story is the same—like the stray olives left on the tree or the few grapes left on the vine after harvest, only a remnant is left.

23:1 Hebrew *Kittim;* also in 23:12. 23:3 Hebrew *from Shihor,* a branch of the Nile River. 23:11 Hebrew *Canaan.* 23:13 Or *Chaldea.*

Perfect Peace Builds upon Total Trust Read ISAIAH 26:3

One test of a true Christian is whether his or her thoughts are occupied with God or those things that hamper spiritual growth. If most of the Christian's thoughts are focused on his or her problems, then God is probably not the center of his or her life. On the other hand, if the believer's thoughts frequently turn to God, then it is likely that he or she has a close walk with the Lord.

The Bible tells us, "Let heaven fill your thoughts. Do not think only about things down here on earth" (Colossians 3:2). You may have heard the cynical expression, "They are so heavenly minded that they are of no earthly good." In reality, the opposite is true. If you truly are "heavenly" or spiritually minded, you will be of the greatest earthly good.

Those "whose thoughts turn often to the Lord" have also been described as having a "steadfast" mind. Their trust in God is unwavering. So how does one put this verse into practice? Here are four suggestions that will help you place your total trust in God and experience his promised "perfect peace" in your daily life:

1. Meditate upon God's Attributes. For instance, verse 4 calls God our "everlasting strength." Think about what that really means.

2. Turn to God First When a Problem Arises. It is easy to pick up the phone and call a friend or relative, but make sure that you have told the Lord your concerns first.

3. Thank God for the Good Things in Your Life. Sometimes we forget about God when things seem to be going smoothly. Make a point of thanking him throughout the day.

4. Spend Time in God's Word. Don't just read your Bible. Think about what you have read, and memorize it as you go through your day.

For the next note on "Peace," turn to p. 974.

CORNER STONES

---

¹⁴But all who are left will shout and sing for joy. Those in the west will praise the LORD's majesty. ¹⁵In eastern lands, give glory to the LORD. In the coastlands of the sea, praise the name of the LORD, the God of Israel. ¹⁶Listen to them as they sing to the LORD from the ends of the earth. Hear them singing praises to the Righteous One!

But my heart is heavy with grief. I am discouraged, for evil still prevails, and treachery is everywhere. ¹⁷Terror and traps and snares will be your lot, you people of the earth. ¹⁸Those who flee in terror will fall into a trap, and those who escape the trap will step into a snare.

Destruction falls on you from the heavens. The world is shaken beneath you. ¹⁹The earth has broken down and has utterly collapsed. Everything is lost, abandoned, and confused. ²⁰The earth staggers like a drunkard. It trembles like a tent in a storm. It falls and will not rise again, for its sins are very great.

²¹In that day the LORD will punish the fallen angels in the heavens and the proud rulers of the nations on earth. ²²They will be rounded up and put in prison until they are tried and condemned. ²³Then the LORD Almighty will mount his throne on Mount Zion. He will rule gloriously in Jerusalem, in the sight of all the leaders of his people. There will be such glory that the brightness of the sun and moon will seem to fade away.

CHAPTER 25
Praise for Judgment and Salvation

O LORD, I will honor and praise your name, for you are my God. You do such wonderful things! You planned them long ago, and now you have accomplished them. ²You turn mighty cities into heaps of ruins. Cities with strong walls are turned to rubble. Beautiful palaces in distant lands disappear and will never be rebuilt. ³Therefore, strong nations will declare your glory; ruthless nations will revere you.

⁴But to the poor, O LORD, you are a refuge from the storm. To the needy in distress, you are a shelter from the rain and the heat. For the oppressive acts of ruthless people are like a storm beating

against a wall, ⁵or like the relentless heat of the desert. But you silence the roar of foreign nations. You cool the land with the shade of a cloud. So the boastful songs of ruthless people are stilled.

⁶In Jerusalem,* the LORD Almighty will spread a wonderful feast for everyone around the world. It will be a delicious feast of good food, with clear, well-aged wine and choice beef. ⁷In that day he will remove the cloud of gloom, the shadow of death that hangs over the earth. ⁸He will swallow up death forever! The Sovereign LORD will wipe away all tears. He will remove forever all insults and mockery against his land and people. The LORD has spoken!

⁹In that day the people will proclaim, "This is our God. We trusted in him, and he saved us. This is the LORD, in whom we trusted. Let us rejoice in the salvation he brings!" ¹⁰For the LORD's good hand will rest on Jerusalem.

Moab will be crushed like trampled straw and left to rot. ¹¹God will push down Moab's people as a swimmer pushes down water with his hands. He will end their pride and all their evil works. ¹²The high walls of Moab will be demolished and ground to dust.

CHAPTER **26**

A Song of Praise to the LORD

In that day, everyone in the land of Judah will sing this song:

Our city is now strong!
    We are surrounded by the walls of God's
        salvation.
2 Open the gates to all who are righteous;
    allow the faithful to enter.
3 You will keep in perfect peace all who trust
        in you,
    whose thoughts are fixed on you!
4 Trust in the LORD always,
    for the LORD GOD is the eternal Rock.
5 He humbles the proud
    and brings the arrogant city to the dust.
    Its walls come crashing down!
6   The poor and oppressed trample it underfoot.

7 But for those who are righteous,
    the path is not steep and rough.
    You are a God of justice,
    and you smooth out the road ahead of them.
8 LORD, we love to obey your laws;
    our heart's desire is to glorify your name.
9 All night long I search for you;
    earnestly I seek for God.

25:6 Hebrew *On this mountain;* also in 25:10.

For only when you come to judge the earth
    will people turn from wickedness and do
        what is right.
¹⁰ Your kindness to the wicked does not make
        them do good.
    They keep doing wrong and take no
        notice of the LORD's majesty.
¹¹ O LORD, they do not listen when you threaten.
    They do not see your upraised fist.
    Show them your eagerness to defend your
        people.
    Perhaps then they will be ashamed.
    Let your fire consume your enemies.

¹² LORD, you will grant us peace,
    for all we have accomplished is really
        from you.
¹³ O LORD our God, others have ruled us,
    but we worship you alone.
¹⁴ Those we served before are dead and gone.
    Never again will they return!
    You attacked them and destroyed them,
    and they are long forgotten.
¹⁵ We praise you, LORD!
    You have made our nation great;
    you have extended our borders!

¹⁶ LORD, in distress we searched for you.
    We were bowed beneath the burden of
        your discipline.
¹⁷ We were like a woman about to give birth,
    writhing and crying out in pain.
    When we are in your presence, LORD,
¹⁸   we, too, writhe in agony,
    but nothing comes of our suffering.
    We have done nothing to rescue the world;
    no one has been born to populate the
        earth.
¹⁹ Yet we have this assurance:
    Those who belong to God will live;
    their bodies will rise again!
    Those who sleep in the earth
    will rise up and sing for joy!
    For God's light of life will fall like dew
    on his people in the place of the dead!

Restoration for Israel

²⁰Go home, my people, and lock your doors! Hide until the LORD's anger against your enemies has passed. ²¹Look! The LORD is coming from heaven to punish the people of the earth for their sins. The earth will no longer hide those who have been murdered. They will be brought out for all to see.

CHAPTER **27**

In that day the LORD will take his terrible, swift sword and punish Leviathan, the swiftly moving serpent, the coiling, writhing serpent, the dragon of the sea.

2 "In that day we will sing of the pleasant vineyard. 3 I, the LORD, will watch over it and tend its fruitful vines. Each day I will water them; day and night I will watch to keep enemies away. 4 My anger against Israel will be gone. If I find briers and thorns bothering her, I will burn them up. 5 These enemies will be spared only if they surrender and beg for peace and protection."

6 The time is coming when my people will take root. Israel will bud and blossom and fill the whole earth with her fruit! 7 Has the LORD punished Israel in the same way he has punished her enemies? No, for he devastated her enemies, 8 but he has punished Israel only a little. He has exiled her from her land as though blown away in a storm from the east. 9 The LORD did this to purge away Israel's* sin. When he has finished, all the pagan altars will be crushed to dust. There won't be an Asherah pole or incense altar left standing. 10 Israel's fortified cities will be silent and empty, the houses abandoned, the streets covered with grass. Cattle will graze there, chewing on twigs and branches.

11 The people are like the dead branches of a tree, broken off and used for kindling beneath the cooking pots. Israel is a foolish and stupid nation, for its people have turned away from God. Therefore, the one who made them will show them no pity or mercy. 12 Yet the time will come when the LORD will gather them together one by one like handpicked grain. He will bring them to his great threshing floor—from the Euphrates River* in the east to the brook of Egypt in the west. 13 In that day the great trumpet will sound. Many who were dying in exile in Assyria and Egypt will return to Jerusalem to worship the LORD on his holy mountain.

CHAPTER **28**

A Message about Samaria

Destruction is certain for the city of Samaria—the pride and joy of the drunkards of Israel*! It sits in a rich valley, but its glorious beauty will suddenly disappear. Destruction is certain for that city—the pride of a people brought low by wine. 2 For the Lord will send the mighty Assyrian army against it. Like a mighty hailstorm and

a torrential rain, they will burst upon it and dash it to the ground. 3 The proud city of Samaria—the pride and joy of the drunkards of Israel—will be trampled beneath its enemies' feet. 4 It sits in a fertile valley, but its glorious beauty will suddenly disappear. It will be greedily snatched up, as an early fig is hungrily picked and eaten.

5 Then at last the LORD Almighty will himself be Israel's crowning glory. He will be the pride and joy of the remnant of his people. 6 He will give a longing for justice to their judges. He will give great courage to their warriors who stand at the gates.

7 Now, however, Israel is being led by drunks! The priests and prophets reel and stagger from beer and wine. They make stupid mistakes as they carry out their responsibilities. 8 Their tables are covered with vomit; filth is everywhere. 9 They say, "Who does the LORD think we are? Why does he speak to us like this? Are we little children, barely old enough to talk? 10 He tells us everything over and over again, a line at a time, in very simple words!*"

11 Since they refuse to listen, God will speak to them through foreign oppressors who speak an unknown language! 12 God's people could have rest in their own land if they would only obey him, but they will not listen. 13 So the LORD will spell out his message for them again, repeating it over and over, a line at a time, in very simple words. Yet they will stumble over this simple, straightforward message. They will be injured, trapped, and captured.

14 Therefore, listen to this message from the LORD, you scoffing rulers in Jerusalem. 15 You boast that you have struck a bargain to avoid death and have made a deal to dodge the grave.* You say, "The Assyrians can never touch us, for we have built a strong refuge made of lies and deception." 16 Therefore, this is what the Sovereign LORD says: "Look! I am placing a foundation stone in Jerusalem.* It is firm, a tested and precious cornerstone that is safe to build on. Whoever believes need never run away again.*

17 "I will take the measuring line of justice and the plumb line of righteousness to check the foundation wall you have built. Your refuge looks strong, but since it is made of lies, a hailstorm will knock it down. Since it is made of deception, the enemy will come like a flood to sweep it away. 18 I will cancel the bargain you made to avoid death, and I will overturn your

---

27:9 Hebrew *Jacob's*. **27:12** Hebrew *the river*. **28:1** Hebrew *of Ephraim*, referring to the northern kingdom of Israel; also in 28:3.
28:10 The Hebrew text for this verse may simply be childish sounds that have no meaning, or perhaps a childish mimicking of the prophet's words. Also in 28:13. **28:15** Hebrew *Sheol*; also in 28:18. **28:16a** Hebrew *in Zion*. **28:16b** Greek version reads *Anyone who believes in him will not be disappointed*.

deal to dodge the grave. When the terrible enemy floods in, you will be trampled into the ground. ¹⁹Again and again that flood will come, morning after morning, day and night, until you are carried away."

This message will bring terror to your people. ²⁰For you have no place of refuge—the bed you have made is too short to lie on. The blankets are too narrow to cover you. ²¹The LORD will come suddenly and in anger, as he did against the Philistines at Mount Perazim and against the Amorites at Gibeon. He will come to do a strange, unusual thing: He will destroy his own people! ²²So scoff no more, or your punishment will be even greater. For the Lord, the LORD Almighty, has plainly told me that he is determined to crush you.

²³Listen to me; listen as I plead! ²⁴Does a farmer always plow and never sow? Is he forever cultivating the soil and never planting it? ²⁵Does he not finally plant his seeds for dill, cumin, wheat, barley, and spelt, each in its own section of his land? ²⁶The farmer knows just what to do, for God has given him understanding. ²⁷He doesn't thresh all his crops the same way. A heavy sledge is never used on dill; rather, it is beaten with a light stick. A threshing wheel is never rolled on cumin; instead, it is beaten softly with a flail. ²⁸Bread grain is easily crushed, so he doesn't keep on pounding it. He threshes it under the wheels of a cart, but he doesn't pulverize it. ²⁹The LORD Almighty is a wonderful teacher, and he gives the farmer great wisdom.

CHAPTER 29
A Message about Jerusalem

"Destruction is certain for Ariel,* the City of David. Year after year you offer your many sacrifices. ²Yet I will bring disaster upon you, and there will be much weeping and sorrow. For Jerusalem will become as her name Ariel means—an altar covered with blood. ³I will be your enemy, surrounding Jerusalem and attacking its walls. I will build siege towers around it and will destroy it. ⁴Your voice will whisper like a ghost from the earth where you will lie buried.

⁵"But suddenly, your ruthless enemies will be driven away like chaff before the wind. ⁶In an instant, I, the LORD Almighty, will come against them with thunder and earthquake and great noise, with whirlwind and storm and consuming fire. ⁷All the nations fighting against Jerusalem* will vanish like a dream! Those who are attacking her walls will vanish like a vision in the night. ⁸A hungry person dreams of eating but is still hungry. A thirsty person dreams of drinking but is still faint from thirst when morning comes. In the same way, your enemies will dream of a victorious conquest over Jerusalem,* but all to no avail."

⁹Are you amazed and incredulous? Do you not believe it? Then go ahead and be blind if you must. You are stupid, but not from wine! You stagger, but not from beer! ¹⁰For the LORD has poured out on you a spirit of deep sleep. He has closed the eyes of your prophets and visionaries. ¹¹All these future events are a sealed book to them. When you give it to those who can read, they will say, "We can't read it because it is sealed." ¹²When you give it to those who cannot read, they will say, "Sorry, we don't know how to read."

¹³And so the Lord says, "These people say they are mine. They honor me with their lips, but their hearts are far away. And their worship of me amounts to nothing more than human laws learned by rote.* ¹⁴Because of this, I will do wonders among these hypocrites. I will show that human wisdom is foolish and even the most brilliant people lack understanding."

¹⁵Destruction is certain for those who try to hide their plans from the LORD, who try to keep him in the dark concerning what they do! "The LORD can't see us," you say to yourselves. "He doesn't know what is going on!" ¹⁶How stupid can you be? He is the Potter, and he is certainly greater than you. You are only the jars he makes! Should the thing that was created say to the one who made it, "He didn't make us"? Does a jar ever say, "The potter who made me is stupid"?

¹⁷Soon—and it will not be very long—the wilderness of Lebanon will be a fertile field once again. And the fertile fields will become a lush and fertile forest. ¹⁸In that day deaf people will hear words read from a book, and blind people will see through the gloom and darkness. ¹⁹The humble will be filled with fresh joy from the LORD. Those who are poor will rejoice in the Holy One of Israel. ²⁰Those who intimidate and harass will be gone, and all those who plot evil will be killed. ²¹Those who make the innocent guilty by their false testimony will disappear. And those who use trickery to pervert justice and tell lies to tear down the innocent will be no more.

²²That is why the LORD, who redeemed Abraham, says to the people of Israel,* "My people will no longer pale with fear or be ashamed. ²³For when they see their many children and

---

29:1 *Ariel* sounds like a Hebrew term that means "hearth" or "altar." 29:7 Hebrew *Ariel.* 29:8 Hebrew *Mount Zion.* 29:13 Greek version reads *Their worship is a farce, for they merely teach human commands and teachings.* 29:22 Hebrew *of Jacob*; also in 29:23.

material blessings, they will recognize the holiness of the Holy One of Israel. They will stand in awe of the God of Israel. ²⁴Those in error will then believe the truth, and those who constantly complain will accept instruction.

CHAPTER **30**

Judah's Worthless Treaty with Egypt
"Destruction is certain for my rebellious children," says the LORD. "You make plans that are contrary to my will. You weave a web of plans that are not from my Spirit, thus piling up your sins. ²For without consulting me, you have gone down to Egypt to find help. You have put your trust in Pharaoh for his protection. ³But in trusting Pharaoh, you will be humiliated and disgraced. ⁴For though his power extends to Zoan and Hanes, ⁵it will all turn out to your shame. He will not help you even one little bit."

⁶Look at the animals moving slowly across the terrible desert to Egypt—donkeys and camels loaded with treasure to pay for Egypt's aid. On through the wilderness they go, where lions and poisonous snakes live. All this, and Egypt will give you nothing in return. ⁷Egypt's promises are worthless! I call her the Harmless Dragon.*

A Warning for Rebellious Judah
⁸Now go and write down these words concerning Egypt. They will then stand until the end of time as a witness to Israel's unbelief. ⁹For these people are stubborn rebels who refuse to pay any attention to the LORD's instructions. ¹⁰They tell the prophets, "Shut up! We don't want any more of your reports." They say, "Don't tell us the truth. Tell us nice things. Tell us lies. ¹¹Forget all this gloom. We have heard more than enough about your 'Holy One of Israel.' We are tired of listening to what he has to say."

¹²This is the reply of the Holy One of Israel: "Because you despise what I tell you and trust instead in oppression and lies, ¹³calamity will come upon you suddenly. It will be like a bulging wall that bursts and falls. In an instant it will collapse and come crashing down. ¹⁴You will be smashed like a piece of pottery—shattered so completely that there won't be a piece left that is big enough to carry coals from a fireplace or a little water from the well."

¹⁵The Sovereign LORD, the Holy One of Israel, says, "Only in returning to me and waiting for me will you be saved. In quietness and confidence is

your strength. But you would have none of it. ¹⁶You said, 'No, we will get our help from Egypt. They will give us swift horses for riding into battle.' But the only swiftness you are going to see is the swiftness of your enemies chasing you! ¹⁷One of them will chase a thousand of you. Five of them will make all of you flee. You will be left like a lonely flagpole on a distant mountaintop."

Blessings for the LORD's People
¹⁸But the LORD still waits for you to come to him so he can show you his love and compassion. For the LORD is a faithful God. Blessed are those who wait for him to help them.

¹⁹O people of Zion, who live in Jerusalem, you will weep no more. He will be gracious if you ask for help. He will respond instantly to the sound of your cries. ²⁰Though the Lord gave you adversity for food and affliction for drink, he will still be with you to teach you. You will see your teacher with your own eyes, ²¹and you will hear a voice say, "This is the way; turn around and walk here." ²²Then you will destroy all your silver idols and gold images. You will throw them out like filthy rags. "Ugh!" you will say to them. "Begone!"

²³Then the LORD will bless you with rain at planting time. There will be wonderful harvests and plenty of pastureland for your cattle. ²⁴The oxen and donkeys that till the ground will eat good grain, its chaff having been blown away by the wind. ²⁵In that day, when your enemies are slaughtered, there will be streams of water flowing down every mountain and hill. ²⁶The moon will be as bright as the sun, and the sun will be seven times brighter—like the light of seven days! So it will be when the LORD begins to heal his people and cure the wounds he gave them.

²⁷Look! The LORD is coming from far away, burning with anger, surrounded by a thick, rising smoke. His lips are filled with fury; his words consume like fire. ²⁸His anger pours out like a flood on his enemies, sweeping them all away. He will sift out the proud nations. He will bridle them and lead them off to their destruction.

²⁹But the people of God will sing a song of joy, like the songs at the holy festivals. You will be filled with joy, as when a flutist leads a group of pilgrims to Jerusalem—the mountain of the LORD—to the Rock of Israel. ³⁰And the LORD will make his majestic voice heard. With angry indignation he will bring down his mighty arm on his enemies. It will descend with devouring flames, with cloudbursts, thunderstorms, and huge hail-

30:7 Hebrew *Rahab who sits still*. Rahab is the name of a mythical sea monster that represents chaos in ancient literature. The name is used here as a poetic name for Egypt.

stones, bringing their destruction. ³¹At the LORD's command, the Assyrians will be shattered. He will strike them down with his rod. ³²And as the LORD strikes them, his people will keep time with the music of tambourines and harps. ³³Topheth—the place of burning—has long been ready for the Assyrian king; it has been piled high with wood. The breath of the LORD, like fire from a volcano, will set it ablaze.

CHAPTER **31**

The Futility of Relying on Egypt

Destruction is certain for those who look to Egypt for help, trusting their cavalry and chariots instead of looking to the LORD, the Holy One of Israel. ²In his wisdom, the LORD will send great disaster; he will not change his mind. He will rise against those who are wicked, and he will crush their allies, too. ³For these Egyptians are mere humans, not God! Their horses are puny flesh, not mighty spirits! When the LORD clenches his fist against them, they will stumble and fall among those they are trying to help. They will all fall down and die together.

⁴But the LORD has told me this: "When a lion, even a young one, kills a sheep, it pays no attention to the shepherd's shouts and noise. It just goes right on eating. In the same way, the LORD Almighty will come and fight on Mount Zion. He will not be frightened away! ⁵The LORD Almighty will hover over Jerusalem as a bird hovers around its nest. He will defend and save the city; he will pass over it and rescue it."

⁶Therefore, my people, though you are such wicked rebels, come and return to the LORD. 7I know the glorious day will come when every one of you will throw away the gold idols and silver images that your sinful hands have made.

⁸"The Assyrians will be destroyed, but not by the swords of men. The sword of God will strike them, and they will panic and flee. The strong young Assyrians will be taken away as captives. ⁹Even their generals will quake with terror and flee when they see the battle flags," says the LORD, whose flame burns brightly in Jerusalem.

CHAPTER **32**

Israel's Ultimate Deliverance

Look, a righteous king is coming! And honest princes will rule under him. ²He will shelter Israel from the storm and the wind. He will refresh her as a river in the desert and as the cool

shadow of a large rock in a hot and weary land. ³Then everyone who can see will be looking for God, and those who can hear will listen to his voice. ⁴Even the hotheads among them will be full of sense and understanding. Those who stammer in uncertainty will speak out plainly.

⁵In that day ungodly fools will not be heroes. Wealthy cheaters will not be respected as outstanding citizens. ⁶Everyone will recognize ungodly fools for what they are. They spread lies about the LORD; they deprive the hungry of food and give no water to the thirsty. ⁷The smooth tricks of evil people will be exposed, including all the lies they use to oppress the poor in the courts. ⁸But good people will be generous to others and will be blessed for all they do.

⁹Listen, you women who lie around in lazy ease. Listen to me, and I will tell you of your reward. ¹⁰In a short time—in just a little more than a year—you careless ones will suddenly begin to care. For your fruit crop will fail, and the harvest will never take place. ¹¹Tremble, you women of ease; throw off your unconcern. Strip off your pretty clothes, and wear sackcloth in your grief. ¹²Beat your breasts in sorrow for your bountiful farms that will soon be gone, and for those fruitful vines of other years. ¹³For your land will be overgrown with thorns and briers. Your joyful homes and happy cities will be gone. ¹⁴The palace and the city will be deserted, and busy towns will be empty. Herds of donkeys and goats will graze on the hills where the watchtowers are, ¹⁵until at last the Spirit is poured down upon us from heaven. Then the wilderness will become a fertile field, and the fertile field will become a lush and fertile forest. ¹⁶Justice will rule in the wilderness and righteousness in the fertile field. ¹⁷And this righteousness will bring peace. Quietness and confidence will fill the land forever.

¹⁸My people will live in safety, quietly at home. They will be at rest. ¹⁹Even though the forest will be destroyed and the city torn down, ²⁰God will greatly bless his people. Wherever they plant seed, bountiful crops will spring up. Their flocks and herds will graze in green pastures.

CHAPTER **33**

A Message about Assyria

Destruction is certain for you Assyrians,* who have destroyed everything around you but have never felt destruction yourselves. You expect others to respect their promises to you, while

33:1 Hebrew *for you, O destroyer . . . O betrayer.* The Hebrew text does not specifically name Assyria as the object of this prophecy.

you betray your promises to them. Now you, too, will be betrayed and destroyed!

²But LORD, be merciful to us, for we have waited for you. Be our strength each day and our salvation in times of trouble. ³The enemy runs at the sound of your voice. When you stand up, the nations flee! ⁴Just as locusts strip the fields and vines, so Jerusalem will strip the fallen army of Assyria!

⁵Though the LORD is very great and lives in heaven, he will make Jerusalem* his home of justice and righteousness. ⁶In that day he will be your sure foundation, providing a rich store of salvation, wisdom, and knowledge. The fear of the LORD is the key to this treasure.

⁷But now your ambassadors weep in bitter disappointment, for Assyria has refused their petition for peace. ⁸Your roads are deserted; no one travels them anymore. The Assyrians have broken their peace pact and care nothing for the promises they made before witnesses.* They have no respect for anyone. ⁹All the land of Israel is in trouble. Lebanon has been destroyed. The plain of Sharon is now a wilderness. Bashan and Carmel have been plundered.

¹⁰But the LORD says: "I will stand up and show my power and might. ¹¹You Assyrians will gain nothing by all your efforts. Your own breath will turn to fire and kill you. ¹²Your people will be burned up completely, like thorns cut down and tossed in a fire. ¹³Listen to what I have done, you nations far away! And you that are near, acknowledge my might!"

¹⁴The sinners in Jerusalem* shake with fear. "Which one of us," they cry, "can live here in the presence of this all-consuming fire?" ¹⁵The ones who can live here are those who are honest and fair, who reject making a profit by fraud, who stay far away from bribes, who refuse to listen to those who plot murder, who shut their eyes to all enticement to do wrong. ¹⁶These are the ones who will dwell on high. The rocks of the mountains will be their fortress of safety. Food will be supplied to them, and they will have water in abundance.

¹⁷Your eyes will see the king in all his splendor, and you will see a land that stretches into the distance. ¹⁸You will think back to this time of terror when the Assyrian officers outside your walls counted your towers and estimated how much plunder they would get from your fallen city. ¹⁹But soon they will be all be gone. These fierce, violent people with a strange, unknown language will disappear.

²⁰Instead, you will see Zion as a place of worship and celebration. You will see Jerusalem, a city quiet and secure. ²¹The LORD will be our Mighty One. He will be like a wide river of protection that no enemy can cross. ²²For the LORD is our judge, our lawgiver, and our king. He will care for us and save us. ²³The enemies' sails hang loose on broken masts with useless tackle. Their treasure will be divided by the people of God. Even the lame will win their share! ²⁴The people of Israel will no longer say, "We are sick and helpless," for the LORD will forgive their sins.

CHAPTER **34**

A Message for the Nations

Come here and listen, O nations of the earth. Let the world and everything in it hear my words. ²For the LORD is enraged against the nations. His fury is against all their armies. He will completely destroy* them, bringing about their slaughter. ³Their dead will be left unburied, and the stench of rotting bodies will fill the land. The mountains will flow with their blood. ⁴The heavens above will melt away and disappear like a rolled-up scroll. The stars will fall from the sky, just as withered leaves and fruit fall from a tree.

⁵And when my sword has finished its work in the heavens, then watch. It will fall upon Edom, the nation I have completely destroyed. ⁶The sword of the LORD is drenched with blood. It is covered with fat as though it had been used for killing lambs and goats and rams for a sacrifice. Yes, the LORD will offer a great sacrifice in the rich city of Bozrah. He will make a mighty slaughter in Edom. ⁷The strongest will die—veterans and young men, too. The land will be soaked with blood and the soil enriched with fat. ⁸For it is the day of the LORD's vengeance, the year when Edom will be paid back for all it did to Israel.* ⁹The streams of Edom will be filled with burning pitch, and the ground will be covered with fire.

¹⁰This judgment on Edom will never end; the smoke of its burning will rise forever. The land will lie deserted from generation to generation. No one will live there anymore. ¹¹It will be haunted by the horned owl, the hawk, the screech owl, and the raven.* For God will bring chaos and destruction to that land. ¹²It will be called the Land of Nothing, and its princes soon will all be gone. ¹³Thorns will overrun its palaces; nettles will grow in its forts. The ruins will

---

33:5 Hebrew *Zion.* **33:8** As in Dead Sea Scrolls; Masoretic Text reads *care nothing for the cities.* **33:14** Hebrew *in Zion.* **34:2** The Hebrew term used here refers to the complete consecration of things or people to the LORD, either by destroying them or by giving them as an offering; also in 34:5. **34:8** Hebrew *to Zion.* **34:11** The identification of some of these birds is uncertain.

become a haunt for jackals and a home for ostriches. ¹⁴Wild animals of the desert will mingle there with hyenas, their howls filling the night. Wild goats will bleat at one another among the ruins, and night creatures will come there to rest. ¹⁵There the owl will make her nest and lay her eggs. She will hatch her young and cover them with her wings. And the vultures will come, each one with its mate.

¹⁶Search the book of the LORD, and see what he will do. He will not miss a single detail. Not one of these birds and animals will be missing, and none will lack a mate, for the LORD has promised this. His Spirit will make it all come true. ¹⁷He has surveyed and divided the land and deeded it over to those creatures. They will possess it forever, from generation to generation.

CHAPTER 35
Hope for Restoration

Even the wilderness will rejoice in those days. The desert will blossom with flowers. ²Yes, there will be an abundance of flowers and singing and joy! The deserts will become as green as the mountains of Lebanon, as lovely as Mount Carmel's pastures and the plain of Sharon. There the LORD will display his glory, the splendor of our God.

³With this news, strengthen those who have tired hands, and encourage those who have weak knees. ⁴Say to those who are afraid, "Be strong, and do not fear, for your God is coming to destroy your enemies. He is coming to save you." ⁵And when he comes, he will open the eyes of the blind and unstop the ears of the deaf. ⁶The lame will leap like a deer, and those who cannot speak will shout and sing! Springs will gush forth in the wilderness, and streams will water the desert. ⁷The parched ground will become a pool, and springs of water will satisfy the thirsty land. Marsh grass and reeds and rushes will flourish where desert jackals once lived.

⁸And a main road will go through that once deserted land. It will be named the Highway of Holiness. Evil-hearted people will never travel on it. It will be only for those who walk in God's ways; fools will never walk there. ⁹Lions will not lurk along its course, and there will be no other dangers. Only the redeemed will follow it. ¹⁰Those who have been ransomed by the LORD will return to Jerusalem,* singing songs of everlasting joy. Sorrow and mourning will disappear, and they will be overcome with joy and gladness.

35:10 Hebrew *Zion.* 36:9 Or *and charioteers.*

CHAPTER 36
Assyria Invades Judah

In the fourteenth year of King Hezekiah's reign, King Sennacherib of Assyria came to attack the fortified cities of Judah and conquered them. ²Then the king of Assyria sent his personal representative with a huge army from Lachish to confront King Hezekiah in Jerusalem. The Assyrians stopped beside the aqueduct that feeds water into the upper pool, near the road leading to the field where cloth is bleached.

³These are the officials who went out to meet with them: Eliakim son of Hilkiah, the palace administrator, Shebna the court secretary, and Joah son of Asaph, the royal historian. ⁴Then the Assyrian king's personal representative sent this message to King Hezekiah:

"This is what the great king of Assyria says: What are you trusting in that makes you so confident? ⁵Do you think that mere words can substitute for military skill and strength? Which of your allies will give you any military backing against Assyria? ⁶Will Egypt? If you lean on Egypt, you will find it to be a stick that breaks beneath your weight and pierces your hand. The Pharaoh of Egypt is completely unreliable!

⁷"But perhaps you will say, 'We are trusting in the LORD our God!' But isn't he the one who was insulted by King Hezekiah? Didn't Hezekiah tear down his shrines and altars and make everyone in Judah worship only at the altar here in Jerusalem?

⁸"I'll tell you what! My master, the king of Assyria, will strike a bargain with you. If you can find two thousand horsemen in your entire army, he will give you two thousand horses for them to ride on! ⁹With your tiny army, how can you think of challenging even the weakest contingent of my master's troops, even with the help of Egypt's chariots and horsemen*? ¹⁰What's more, do you think we have invaded your land without the LORD's direction? The LORD himself told us, 'Go and destroy it!'"

¹¹Then Eliakim, Shebna, and Joah said to the king's representative, "Please speak to us in Aramaic, for we understand it well. Don't speak in Hebrew, for the people on the wall will hear."

¹²But Sennacherib's representative replied, "My master wants everyone in Jerusalem to hear this, not just you. He wants them to know that

if you do not surrender, this city will be put under siege. The people will become so hungry and thirsty that they will eat their own dung and drink their own urine."

13Then he stood and shouted in Hebrew to the people on the wall, "Listen to this message from the great king of Assyria! 14This is what the king says: Don't let King Hezekiah deceive you. He will never be able to rescue you. 15Don't let him fool you into trusting in the LORD by saying, 'The LORD will rescue us! This city will never be handed over to the Assyrian king.'

16"Don't listen to Hezekiah! These are the terms the king of Assyria is offering: Make peace with me—open the gates and come out. Then I will allow each of you to continue eating from your own garden and drinking from your own well. 17Then I will arrange to take you to another land like this one—a country with bountiful harvests of grain and wine, bread and vineyards—a land of plenty.

18"Don't let Hezekiah mislead you by saying, 'The LORD will rescue us!' Have the gods of any other nations ever saved their people from the king of Assyria? 19What happened to the gods of Hamath and Arpad? And what about the gods of Sepharvaim? Did they rescue Samaria from my power? 20What god of any nation has ever been able to save its people from my power? Name just one! So what makes you think that the LORD can rescue Jerusalem?"

21But the people were silent and did not answer because Hezekiah had told them not to speak. 22Then Eliakim son of Hilkiah, the palace administrator, Shebna the court secretary, and Joah son of Asaph, the royal historian, went back to Hezekiah. They tore their clothes in despair, and they went in to see the king and told him what the Assyrian representative had said.

CHAPTER 37
Hezekiah Seeks the LORD's Help

When King Hezekiah heard their report, he tore his clothes and put on sackcloth and went into the Temple of the LORD to pray. 2And he sent Eliakim the palace administrator, Shebna the court secretary, and the leading priests, all dressed in sackcloth, to the prophet Isaiah son of Amoz. 3They told him, "This is what King Hezekiah says: This is a day of trouble, insult, and disgrace. It is like when a child is ready to be born, but the mother has no strength to deliver it. 4But perhaps the LORD your God has heard the Assyrian representative defying the living God

37:9 Hebrew *of Cush.*

and will punish him for his words. Oh, pray for those of us who are left!"

5After King Hezekiah's officials delivered the king's message to Isaiah, 6the prophet replied, "Say to your master, 'This is what the LORD says: Do not be disturbed by this blasphemous speech against me from the Assyrian king's messengers. 7Listen! I myself will make sure that the king will receive a report from Assyria telling him that he is needed at home. Then I will make him want to return to his land, where I will have him killed with a sword.'"

8Meanwhile, the Assyrian representative left Jerusalem and went to consult his king, who had left Lachish and was attacking Libnah. 9Soon afterward King Sennacherib received word that King Tirhakah of Ethiopia* was leading an army to fight against him. Before leaving to meet the attack, he sent this message back to Hezekiah in Jerusalem:

10"This message is for King Hezekiah of Judah. Don't let this God you trust deceive you with promises that Jerusalem will not be captured by the king of Assyria. 11You know perfectly well what the kings of Assyria have done wherever they have gone. They have crushed everyone who stood in their way! Why should you be any different? 12Have the gods of other nations rescued them—such nations as Gozan, Haran, Rezeph, and the people of Eden who were in Tel-assar? The former kings of Assyria destroyed them all! 13What happened to the king of Hamath and the king of Arpad? What happened to the kings of Sepharvaim, Hena, and Ivvah?"

14After Hezekiah received the letter and read it, he went up to the LORD's Temple and spread it out before the LORD. 15And Hezekiah prayed this prayer before the LORD: 16"O LORD Almighty, God of Israel, you are enthroned between the mighty cherubim! You alone are God of all the kingdoms of the earth. You alone created the heavens and the earth. 17Listen to me, O LORD, and hear! Open your eyes, O LORD, and see! Listen to Sennacherib's words of defiance against the living God.

18"It is true, LORD, that the kings of Assyria have destroyed all these nations, just as the message says. 19And they have thrown the gods of these nations into the fire and burned them. But of course the Assyrians could destroy them! They were not gods at all—only idols of wood and stone shaped by human hands. ²⁰Now, O Lord our God, rescue us from his power; then all the kingdoms of the earth will know that you alone, O Lord, are God."

Isaiah Predicts Judah's Deliverance
²¹Then Isaiah son of Amoz sent this message to Hezekiah: "This is what the Lord, the God of Israel, says: This is my answer to your prayer concerning King Sennacherib of Assyria. ²²This is the message that the Lord has spoken against him:

'The virgin daughter of Zion
    despises you and laughs at you.
The daughter of Jerusalem
    scoffs and shakes her head as you flee.

²³ 'Whom do you think you have been
        insulting and ridiculing?
Against whom did you raise your voice?
At whom did you look in such proud
        condescension?
    It was the Holy One of Israel!

²⁴ By your messengers you have mocked the
        Lord.
You have said, "With my many chariots
I have conquered the highest mountains—
    yes, the remotest peaks of Lebanon.
I have cut down its tallest cedars
    and its choicest cypress trees.
I have reached its farthest corners
    and explored its deepest forests.

²⁵ I have dug wells in many a foreign land
    and refreshed myself with their water.
I even stopped up the rivers of Egypt
    so that my armies could go across!"

²⁶ 'But have you not heard?
    It was I, the Lord, who decided this long
        ago.
Long ago I planned what I am now causing
        to happen,
    that you should crush fortified cities into
        heaps of rubble.

²⁷ That is why their people have so little power
    and are such easy prey for you.
They are as helpless as the grass,
    as easily trampled as tender green shoots.
They are like grass sprouting on a housetop,
    easily scorched by the sun.

²⁸ 'But I know you well—
    your comings and goings and all you do.
    I know the way you have raged against me.

²⁹ And because of your arrogance against me,
    which I have heard for myself,
I will put my hook in your nose
    and my bridle in your mouth.
I will make you return
    by the road on which you came.' "

³⁰Then Isaiah said to Hezekiah, "Here is the proof that the Lord will protect this city from Assyria's king. This year you will eat only what grows up by itself, and next year you will eat what springs up from that. But in the third year you will plant crops and harvest them; you will tend vineyards and eat their fruit. ³¹And you who are left in Judah, who have escaped the ravages of the siege, will take root again in your own soil, and you will flourish and multiply. ³²For a remnant of my people will spread out from Jerusalem, a group of survivors from Mount Zion. The passion of the Lord Almighty will make this happen!

³³"And this is what the Lord says about the king of Assyria: His armies will not enter Jerusalem to shoot their arrows. They will not march outside its gates with their shields and build banks of earth against its walls. ³⁴The king will return to his own country by the road on which he came. He will not enter this city, says the Lord. ³⁵For my own honor and for the sake of my servant David, I will defend it."

³⁶That night the angel of the Lord went out to the Assyrian camp and killed 185,000 Assyrian troops. When the surviving Assyrians* woke up the next morning, they found corpses everywhere. ³⁷Then King Sennacherib of Assyria broke camp and returned to his own land. He went home to his capital of Nineveh and stayed there. ³⁸One day while he was worshiping in the temple of his god Nisroch, his sons Adrammelech and Sharezer killed him with their swords. They then escaped to the land of Ararat, and another son, Esarhaddon, became the next king of Assyria.

CHAPTER **38**
Hezekiah's Sickness and Recovery
About that time Hezekiah became deathly ill, and the prophet Isaiah son of Amoz went to visit him. He gave the king this message: "This is what the Lord says: Set your affairs in order, for you are going to die. You will not recover from this illness."

²When Hezekiah heard this, he turned his face to the wall and prayed to the Lord, ³"Remember,

37:36 Hebrew *When they.*

O LORD, how I have always tried to be faithful to you and do what is pleasing in your sight." Then he broke down and wept bitterly.

4Then this message came to Isaiah from the LORD: 5"Go back to Hezekiah and tell him, 'This is what the LORD, the God of your ancestor David, says: I have heard your prayer and seen your tears. I will add fifteen years to your life, 6and I will rescue you and this city from the king of Assyria. Yes, I will defend this city.

7" 'And this is the sign that the LORD will give you to prove he will do as he promised: 8I will cause the sun's shadow to move ten steps backward on the sundial of Ahaz!'" So the shadow on the sundial moved backward ten steps.

Hezekiah's Poem of Praise

9When King Hezekiah was well again, he wrote this poem about his experience:

10 I said, "In the prime of my life,
    must I now enter the place of the dead?
    Am I to be robbed of my normal years?"
11 I said, "Never again will I see the LORD GOD
    while still in the land of the living.
  Never again will I see my friends
    or laugh with those who live in this world.
12 My life has been blown away
    like a shepherd's tent in a storm.
  It has been cut short,
    as when a weaver cuts cloth from a loom.
  Suddenly, my life was over.
13 I waited patiently all night,
    but I was torn apart as though by lions.
  Suddenly, my life was over.
14 Delirious, I chattered like a swallow or a
    crane,
    and then I moaned like a mourning dove.
  My eyes grew tired of looking to heaven for
    help.
  I am in trouble, Lord. Help me!"

15 But what could I say?
    For he himself had sent this sickness.
  Now I will walk humbly throughout my
    years
    because of this anguish I have felt.
16 Lord, your discipline is good,
    for it leads to life and health.
  You have restored my health
    and have allowed me to live!
17 Yes, it was good for me to suffer this
    anguish,
    for you have rescued me from death
    and have forgiven all my sins.

18 For the dead cannot praise you;
    they cannot raise their voices in praise.
  Those who go down to destruction
    can no longer hope in your faithfulness.
19 Only the living can praise you as I do today.
  Each generation can make known your
    faithfulness to the next.
20 Think of it—the LORD has healed me!
  I will sing his praises with instruments
  every day of my life
    in the Temple of the LORD.

21Isaiah had said to Hezekiah's servants, "Make an ointment from figs and spread it over the boil, and Hezekiah will recover."

22And Hezekiah had asked, "What sign will prove that I will go to the Temple of the LORD three days from now?"

CHAPTER 39

Envoys from Babylon

Soon after this, Merodach-baladan son of Baladan, king of Babylon, sent Hezekiah his best wishes and a gift. He had heard that Hezekiah had been very sick and that he had recovered. 2Hezekiah welcomed the Babylonian envoys and showed them everything in his treasure-houses— the silver, the gold, the spices, and the aromatic oils. He also took them to see his armory and showed them all his other treasures—everything! There was nothing in his palace or kingdom that Hezekiah did not show them.

3Then Isaiah the prophet went to King Hezekiah and asked him, "What did those men want? Where were they from?"

Hezekiah replied, "They came from the distant land of Babylon."

4"What did they see in your palace?" asked Isaiah.

"They saw everything," Hezekiah replied. "I showed them everything I own—all my treasures."

5Then Isaiah said to Hezekiah, "Listen to this message from the LORD Almighty: 6The time is coming when everything you have—all the treasures stored up by your ancestors—will be carried off to Babylon. Nothing will be left, says the LORD. 7Some of your own descendants will be taken away into exile. They will become eunuchs who will serve in the palace of Babylon's king."

8Then Hezekiah said to Isaiah, "This message you have given me from the LORD is good." But the king was thinking, "At least there will be peace and security during my lifetime."

CHAPTER **40**

Comfort for God's People

"Comfort, comfort my people," says your God. ²"Speak tenderly to Jerusalem. Tell her that her sad days are gone and that her sins are pardoned. Yes, the LORD has punished her in full for all her sins."

³Listen! I hear the voice of someone shouting, "Make a highway for the LORD through the wilderness. Make a straight, smooth road through the desert for our God. ⁴Fill the valleys and level the hills. Straighten out the curves and smooth off the rough spots. ⁵Then the glory of the LORD will be revealed, and all people will see it together. The LORD has spoken!"

⁶A voice said, "Shout!"

I asked, "What should I shout?"

"Shout that people are like the grass that dies away. Their beauty fades as quickly as the beauty of flowers in a field. ⁷The grass withers, and the flowers fade beneath the breath of the LORD. And so it is with people. ⁸The grass withers, and the flowers fade, but the word of our God stands forever."

⁹Messenger of good news, shout to Zion from the mountaintops! Shout louder to Jerusalem— do not be afraid. Tell the towns of Judah, "Your God is coming!" ¹⁰Yes, the Sovereign LORD is coming in all his glorious power. He will rule with awesome strength. See, he brings his reward with him as he comes. ¹¹He will feed his flock like a shepherd. He will carry the lambs in his arms, holding them close to his heart. He will gently lead the mother sheep with their young.

¹²Who else has held the oceans in his hand? Who has measured off the heavens with his fingers? Who else knows the weight of the earth or has weighed out the mountains and the hills? ¹³Who is able to advise the Spirit of the LORD? Who knows enough to be his teacher or counselor? ¹⁴Has the LORD ever needed anyone's advice? Does he need instruction about what is good or what is best? ¹⁵No, for all the nations of the world are nothing in comparison with him. They are but a drop in the bucket, dust on the scales. He picks up the islands as though they had no weight at all. ¹⁶All Lebanon's forests do not contain sufficient fuel to consume a sacrifice large enough to honor him. All Lebanon's sacrificial animals would not make an offering worthy of our God. ¹⁷The nations of the world are as nothing to him. In his eyes they are less than nothing—mere emptiness and froth.

¹⁸To whom, then, can we compare God? What image might we find to resemble him? ¹⁹Can he be compared to an idol formed in a mold, overlaid with gold, and decorated with silver chains? ²⁰Or is a poor person's wooden idol better? Can God be compared to an idol that must be placed on a stand so it won't fall down?

²¹Have you never heard or understood? Are you deaf to the words of God—the words he gave before the world began? Are you so ignorant? ²²It is God who sits above the circle of the earth. The people below must seem to him like grasshoppers! He is the one who spreads out the heavens like a curtain and makes his tent from them. ²³He judges the great people of the world and brings them all to nothing. ²⁴They hardly get started, barely taking root, when he blows on them and their work withers. The wind carries them off like straw.

²⁵"To whom will you compare me? Who is my equal?" asks the Holy One. ²⁶Look up into the heavens. Who created all the stars? He brings them out one after another, calling each by its name. And he counts them to see that none are lost or have strayed away.

²⁷O Israel, how can you say the LORD does not see your troubles? How can you say God refuses to hear your case? ²⁸Have you never heard or understood? Don't you know that the LORD is the everlasting God, the Creator of all the earth? He never grows faint or weary. No one can measure the depths of his understanding. ²⁹He gives power to those who are tired and worn out; he offers strength to the weak. ³⁰Even youths will become exhausted, and young men will give up. ³¹But those who wait on the LORD will find new strength. They will fly high on wings like eagles. They will run and not grow weary. They will walk and not faint.

CHAPTER **41**

God's Help for Israel

"Listen in silence before me, you lands beyond the sea. Bring your strongest arguments. Come now and speak. The court is ready for your case.

²"Who has stirred up this king from the east, who meets victory at every step? Who, indeed, but the LORD? He gives him victory over many nations and permits him to trample their kings underfoot. He puts entire armies to the sword. He scatters them in the wind with his bow. ³He chases them away and goes on safely, though he is walking over unfamiliar ground. ⁴Who has done such mighty deeds, directing the affairs of the human race as each new generation marches by? It is I, the LORD, the First and the Last. I alone am he."

5The lands beyond the sea watch in fear. Remote lands tremble and mobilize for war. 6They encourage one another with the words, "Be strong!" 7The craftsmen rush to make new idols. The carver hurries the goldsmith, and the molder helps at the anvil. "Good," they say. "It's coming along fine." Carefully they join the parts together, then fasten the thing in place so it won't fall over.

8"But as for you, Israel my servant, Jacob my chosen one, descended from my friend Abraham, 9I have called you back from the ends of the earth so you can serve me. For I have chosen you and will not throw you away. 10Don't be afraid, for I am with you. Do not be dismayed, for I am your God. I will strengthen you. I will help you. I will uphold you with my victorious right hand.

11"See, all your angry enemies lie there, confused and ashamed. Anyone who opposes you will die. 12You will look for them in vain. They will be all gone! 13I am holding you by your right hand—I, the LORD your God. And I say to you, 'Do not be afraid. I am here to help you. 14Despised though you are, O Israel, don't be afraid, for I will help you. I am the LORD, your Redeemer. I am the Holy One of Israel.' 15You will be a new threshing instrument with many sharp teeth. You will tear all your enemies apart, making chaff of mountains. 16You will toss them in the air, and the wind will blow them all away; a whirlwind will scatter them. And the joy of the LORD will fill you to overflowing. You will glory in the Holy One of Israel.

17"When the poor and needy search for water and there is none, and their tongues are parched from thirst, then I, the LORD, will answer them. I, the God of Israel, will never forsake them. 18I will open up rivers for them on high plateaus. I will give them fountains of water in the valleys. In the deserts they will find pools of water. Rivers fed by springs will flow across the dry, parched ground. 19I will plant trees—cedar, acacia, myrtle, olive, cypress, fir, and pine—on barren land. 20Everyone will see this miracle and understand that it is the LORD, the Holy One of Israel, who did it.

21"Can your idols make such claims as these? Let them come and show what they can do!" says the LORD, the King of Israel.* 22"Let them try to tell us what happened long ago or what the future holds. 23Yes, that's it! If you are gods, tell what will occur in the days ahead. Or perform a mighty miracle that will fill us with amazement

41:21 Hebrew *the King of Jacob.*

and fear. Do something, whether good or bad! 24But no! You are less than nothing and can do nothing at all. Anyone who chooses you becomes filthy, just like you!

25"But I have stirred up a leader from the north and east. He will come against the nations and call on my name, and I will give him victory over kings and princes. He will trample them as a potter treads on clay.

26"Who but I have told you this would happen? Who else predicted this, making you admit that he was right? No one else said a word! 27I was the first to tell Jerusalem, 'Look! Help is on the way!' 28Not one of your idols told you this. Not one gave any answer when I asked. 29See, they are all foolish, worthless things. Your idols are all as empty as the wind.

CHAPTER **42**

The LORD's Chosen Servant

"Look at my servant, whom I strengthen. He is my chosen one, and I am pleased with him. I have put my Spirit upon him. He will reveal justice to the nations. 2He will be gentle—he will not shout or raise his voice in public. 3He will not crush those who are weak or quench the smallest hope. He will bring full justice to all who have been wronged. 4He will not stop until truth and righteousness prevail throughout the earth. Even distant lands beyond the sea will wait for his instruction."

5God, the LORD, created the heavens and stretched them out. He created the earth and everything in it. He gives breath and life to everyone in all the world. And it is he who says, 6"I, the LORD, have called you to demonstrate my righteousness. I will guard and support you, for I have given you to my people as the personal confirmation of my covenant with them. And you will be a light to guide all nations to me. 7You will open the eyes of the blind and free the captives from prison. You will release those who sit in dark dungeons.

8"I am the LORD; that is my name! I will not give my glory to anyone else. I will not share my praise with carved idols. 9Everything I prophesied has come true, and now I will prophesy again. I will tell you the future before it happens."

A Song of Praise to the LORD

10 Sing a new song to the LORD!

Sing his praises from the ends of the earth!

Sing, all you who sail the seas,
all you who live in distant coastlands.
11 Join in the chorus, you desert towns;
let the villages of Kedar rejoice!
Let the people of Sela sing for joy;
shout praises from the mountaintops!
12 Let the coastlands glorify the LORD;
let them sing his praise.
13 The LORD will march forth like a mighty man;
he will come out like a warrior, full of
fury.
He will shout his thundering battle cry,
and he will crush all his enemies.
14 He will say, "I have long been silent;
yes, I have restrained myself.
But now I will give full vent to my fury;
I will gasp and pant like a woman giving
birth.
15 I will level the mountains and hills
and bring a blight on all their greenery.
I will turn the rivers into dry land
and will dry up all the pools.
16 I will lead blind Israel down a new path,
guiding them along an unfamiliar way.
I will make the darkness bright before them
and smooth out the road ahead of them.
Yes, I will indeed do these things;
I will not forsake them.
17 But those who trust in idols,
calling them their gods—
they will be turned away in shame.

Israel's Failure to See and Listen
18 "Oh, how deaf and blind you are toward me!
Why won't you listen? Why do you refuse to see?
19 Who in all the world is as blind as my own
people, my servant? Who is as deaf as my messengers? Who is as blind as my chosen people,
the servant of the LORD? 20 You see and understand what is right but refuse to act on it. You
hear, but you don't really listen."

21 The LORD has magnified his law and made
it truly glorious. Through it he had planned to
show the world that he is righteous. 22 But what
a sight his people are, for they have been robbed,
enslaved, imprisoned, and trapped. They are fair
game for all and have no one to protect them.
23 Will not even one of you apply these lessons
from the past and see the ruin that awaits you?
24 Who allowed Israel to be robbed and hurt?
Was it not the LORD? It was the LORD whom we
sinned against, for the people would not go
where he sent them, nor would they obey his

law. 25 That is why he poured out such fury on
them and destroyed them in battle. They were
set on fire and burned, but they still refused to
understand.

CHAPTER **43**
The Savior of Israel
But now, O Israel, the LORD who created you
says: "Do not be afraid, for I have ransomed you.
I have called you by name; you are mine. 2 When
you go through deep waters and great trouble, I
will be with you. When you go through rivers of
difficulty, you will not drown! When you walk
through the fire of oppression, you will not be
burned up; the flames will not consume you.
3 For I am the LORD, your God, the Holy One of
Israel, your Savior. I gave Egypt, Ethiopia,* and
Seba as a ransom for your freedom. 4 Others died
that you might live. I traded their lives for yours
because you are precious to me. You are honored, and I love you.

5 "Do not be afraid, for I am with you. I will
gather you and your children from east and west
6 and from north and south. I will bring my sons
and daughters back to Israel from the distant
corners of the earth. 7 All who claim me as their
God will come, for I have made them for my
glory. It was I who created them."

8 Bring out the people who have eyes but are
blind, who have ears but are deaf. 9 Gather the
nations together! Which of their idols has ever
foretold such things? Can any of them predict
something even a single day in advance? Where
are the witnesses of such predictions? Who can
verify that they spoke the truth?

10 "But you are my witnesses, O Israel!" says the
LORD. "And you are my servant. You have been
chosen to know me, believe in me, and understand that I alone am God. There is no other God;
there never has been and never will be. 11 I am the
LORD, and there is no other Savior. 12 First I predicted your deliverance; I declared what I would
do, and then I did it—I saved you. No foreign god
has ever done this before. You are witnesses that I
am the only God," says the LORD. 13 "From eternity
to eternity I am God. No one can oppose what I
do. No one can reverse my actions."

The LORD's Promise of Victory
14 The LORD your Redeemer, the Holy One of
Israel, says: "For your sakes I will send an invading army against Babylon. And the Babylonians* will be forced to flee in those ships they are

43:3 Hebrew *Cush.* 43:14 Or *Chaldeans.*

so proud of. 15I am the LORD, your Holy One, Israel's Creator and King. 16I am the LORD, who opened a way through the waters, making a dry path through the sea. 17I called forth the mighty army of Egypt with all its chariots and horses. I drew them beneath the waves, and they drowned, their lives snuffed out like a smoldering candlewick.

18"But forget all that—it is nothing compared to what I am going to do. 19For I am about to do a brand-new thing. See, I have already begun! Do you not see it? I will make a pathway through the wilderness for my people to come home. I will create rivers for them in the desert! 20The wild animals in the fields will thank me, the jackals and ostriches, too, for giving them water in the wilderness. Yes, I will make springs in the desert, so that my chosen people can be refreshed. 21I have made Israel for myself, and they will someday honor me before the whole world.

22"But, my dear people, you refuse to ask for my help. You have grown tired of me! 23You have not brought me lambs for burnt offerings. You have not honored me with sacrifices, though I have not burdened and wearied you with my requests for grain offerings and incense. 24You have not brought me fragrant incense or pleased me with the fat from sacrifices. Instead, you have burdened me with your sins and wearied me with your faults.

25"I—yes, I alone—am the one who blots out your sins for my own sake and will never think of them again. 26Let us review the situation together, and you can present your case if you have one. 27From the very beginning, your ancestors sinned against me—all your leaders broke my laws. 28That is why I have disgraced your priests and assigned Israel a future of complete destruction* and shame.

CHAPTER 44

"But now, listen to me, Jacob my servant, Israel my chosen one. 2The LORD who made you and helps you says: O Jacob, my servant, do not be afraid. O Israel,* my chosen one, do not fear. 3For I will give you abundant water to quench your thirst and to moisten your parched fields. And I will pour out my Spirit and my blessings on your children. 4They will thrive like watered grass, like willows on a riverbank. 5Some will proudly claim, 'I belong to the LORD.' Others will say, 'I am a descendant of Jacob.'

Some will write the LORD's name on their hands and will take the honored name of Israel as their own.

The Foolishness of Idols

6"This is what the LORD, Israel's King and Redeemer, the LORD Almighty, says: I am the First and the Last; there is no other God. 7Who else can tell you what is going to happen in the days ahead? Let them tell you if they can and thus prove their power. Let them do as I have done since ancient times. 8Do not tremble; do not be afraid. Have I not proclaimed from ages past what my purposes are for you? You are my witnesses—is there any other God? No! There is no other Rock—not one!"

9How foolish are those who manufacture idols to be their gods. These highly valued objects are really worthless. They themselves are witnesses that this is so, for their idols neither see nor know. No wonder those who worship them are put to shame. 10Who but a fool would make his own god—an idol that cannot help him one bit! 11All who worship idols will stand before the LORD in shame, along with all these craftsmen—mere humans—who claim they can make a god. Together they will stand in terror and shame.

12The blacksmith stands at his forge to make a sharp tool, pounding and shaping it with all his might. His work makes him hungry and thirsty, weak and faint. 13Then the wood-carver measures and marks out a block of wood, takes the tool, and carves the figure of a man. Now he has a wonderful idol that cannot even move from where it is placed! 14He cuts down cedars; he selects the cypress and the oak; he plants the cedar in the forest to be nourished by the rain. 15And after his care, he uses part of the wood to make a fire to warm himself and bake his bread. Then—yes, it's true—he takes the rest of it and makes himself a god for people to worship! He makes an idol and bows down and praises it! 16He burns part of the tree to roast his meat and to keep himself warm. 17Then he takes what's left and makes his god: a carved idol! He falls down in front of it, worshiping and praying to it. "Rescue me!" he says. "You are my god!"

18Such stupidity and ignorance! Their eyes are closed, and they cannot see. Their minds are shut, and they cannot think. 19The person who made the idol never stops to reflect, "Why, it's just a block of wood! I burned half of it for heat and used it to bake my bread and roast my meat.

43:28 The Hebrew term used here refers to the complete consecration of things or people to the LORD, either by destroying them or by giving them as an offering.   44:2 Hebrew *Jeshurun*, a term of endearment for Israel.

How can the rest of it be a god? Should I bow down to worship a chunk of wood?" 20The poor, deluded fool feeds on ashes. He is trusting something that can give him no help at all. Yet he cannot bring himself to ask, "Is this thing, this idol that I'm holding in my hand, a lie?"

Restoration for Jerusalem

21 "Pay attention, O Israel, for you are my servant. I, the LORD, made you, and I will not forget to help you. 22I have swept away your sins like the morning mists. I have scattered your offenses like the clouds. Oh, return to me, for I have paid the price to set you free."

23Sing, O heavens, for the LORD has done this wondrous thing. Shout, O earth! Break forth into song, O mountains and forests and every tree! For the LORD has redeemed Jacob and is glorified in Israel.

24The LORD, your Redeemer and Creator, says: "I am the LORD, who made all things. I alone stretched out the heavens. By myself I made the earth and everything in it. 25I am the one who exposes the false prophets as liars by causing events to happen that are contrary to their predictions. I cause wise people to give bad advice, thus proving them to be fools. 26But I carry out the predictions of my prophets! When they say Jerusalem will be saved and the towns of Judah will be lived in once again, it will be done! 27When I speak to the rivers and say, 'Be dry!' they will be dry. 28When I say of Cyrus, 'He is my shepherd,' he will certainly do as I say. He will command that Jerusalem be rebuilt and that the Temple be restored."

CHAPTER 45
Cyrus, the LORD's Chosen One

This is what the LORD says to Cyrus, his anointed one, whose right hand he will empower. Before him, mighty kings will be paralyzed with fear. Their fortress gates will be opened, never again to shut against him. 2This is what the LORD says: "I will go before you, Cyrus, and level the mountains.* I will smash down gates of bronze and cut through bars of iron. 3And I will give you treasures hidden in the darkness—secret riches. I will do this so you may know that I am the LORD, the God of Israel, the one who calls you by name.

4 "And why have I called you for this work? It is for the sake of Jacob my servant, Israel my chosen one. I called you by name when you did not know me. 5I am the LORD; there is no other

God. I have prepared you, even though you do not know me, 6so all the world from east to west will know there is no other God. I am the LORD, and there is no other. 7I am the one who creates the light and makes the darkness. I am the one who sends good times and bad times. I, the LORD, am the one who does these things. 8Open up, O heavens, and pour out your righteousness. Let the earth open wide so salvation and righteousness can sprout up together. I, the LORD, created them.

9 "Destruction is certain for those who argue with their Creator. Does a clay pot ever argue with its maker? Does the clay dispute with the one who shapes it, saying, 'Stop, you are doing it wrong!' Does the pot exclaim, 'How clumsy can you be!' 10How terrible it would be if a newborn baby said to its father and mother, 'Why was I born? Why did you make me this way?'"

11This is what the LORD, the Creator and Holy One of Israel, says: "Do you question what I do? Do you give me orders about the work of my hands? 12I am the one who made the earth and created people to live on it. With my hands I stretched out the heavens. All the millions of stars are at my command. 13I will raise up Cyrus to fulfill my righteous purpose, and I will guide all his actions. He will restore my city and free my captive people—and not for a reward! I, the LORD Almighty, have spoken!"

Future Conversion of Gentiles

14This is what the LORD says: "The Egyptians, Ethiopians,* and Sabeans will be subject to you. They will come to you with all their merchandise, and it will all be yours. They will follow you as prisoners in chains. They will fall to their knees in front of you and say, 'God is with you, and he is the only God.'"

15Truly, O God of Israel, our Savior, you work in strange and mysterious ways. 16All who make idols will be humiliated and disgraced. 17But the LORD will save the people of Israel with eternal salvation. They will never again be humiliated and disgraced throughout everlasting ages. 18For the LORD is God, and he created the heavens and earth and put everything in place. He made the world to be lived in, not to be a place of empty chaos. "I am the LORD," he says, "and there is no other. 19I publicly proclaim bold promises. I do not whisper obscurities in some dark corner so no one can understand what I mean. And I did not tell the people of Israel* to ask me for

45:2 As in Dead Sea Scrolls and Greek version; Masoretic Text reads *the swellings.* 45:14 Hebrew *Cushites.* 45:19 Hebrew *of Jacob.*

The God of the Bible Is the One True God Read ISAIAH 45:9-23

Many people have asked the question, Don't all religions lead to God? The answer, as laid out in this passage, is an emphatic no. The God of the Bible is the one, true God, and at some time in the future, the entire world will acknowledge this fact (verse 23). This passage shows three reasons why God is the one, true God to be worshiped:

1. God Created the World with a Purpose in Mind. The uniqueness of creation testifies to the uniqueness of its Creator. God did not randomly put the world together. He created every living thing with a purpose in mind: to glorify God (verses 9–18).

2. God's Word Is Tested and True. All that God says will come to pass (verses 20–21). He sees all and knows all because he is eternal. While we are limited by space and time and can see things only from the beginning to the end, God sees things from the end to the beginning. For instance, the words God spoke concerning the coming of the Messiah, Jesus Christ, in the Old Testament were fulfilled to the letter and recorded in the New Testament. For that reason, when God speaks of the future—such as Christ's return to earth for all believers—you can bank on it. What other god can make this same claim?

3. God Offers Salvation to All. God does not just limit himself to a select group of people who must follow certain rituals in order to be acceptable to him. He has made his offer of salvation to all who will turn to him. In the end, whether everyone believes or not, all the world will indeed bow before him as the one, true God (verses 22–23).

To begin the next topic, turn to p. A12.

CORNER STONES

---

something I did not plan to give. I, the LORD, speak only what is true and right.

20 "Gather together and come, you fugitives from surrounding nations. What fools they are who carry around their wooden idols and pray to gods that cannot save! 21Consult together, argue your case, and state your proofs that idol worship pays. Who made these things known long ago? What idol ever told you they would happen? Was it not I, the LORD? For there is no other God but me—a just God and a Savior—no, not one! 22Let all the world look to me for salvation! For I am God; there is no other. 23I have sworn by my own name, and I will never go back on my word: Every knee will bow to me, and every tongue will confess allegiance to my name."

24The people will declare, "The LORD is the source of all my righteousness and strength." And all who were angry with him will come to him and be ashamed. 25In the LORD all the generations of Israel will be justified, and in him they will boast.

CHAPTER **46**
Babylon's False Gods
The idols of Babylon, Bel and Nebo, are being hauled away on ox carts. But look! The beasts are staggering under the weight! 2Both the idols and the ones carrying them are bowed down. The gods cannot protect the people, and the people cannot protect the gods. They go off into captivity together.

3 "Listen to me, all you who are left in Israel. I created you and have cared for you since before you were born. 4I will be your God throughout your lifetime—until your hair is white with age. I made you, and I will care for you. I will carry you along and save you.

5 "To whom will you compare me? Who is my equal? 6Some people pour out their silver and gold and hire a craftsman to make a god from it. Then they bow down and worship it! 7They carry it around on their shoulders, and when they set it down, it stays there. It cannot even move! And when someone prays to it, there is no answer. It has no power to get anyone out of trouble.

8 "Do not forget this, you guilty ones. 9And do not forget the things I have done throughout history. For I am God—I alone! I am God, and there is no one else like me. 10Only I can tell you what is going to happen even before it happens. Everything I plan will come to pass, for I do whatever I wish. 11I will call a swift bird of prey from the east—a leader from a distant land who

will come and do my bidding. I have said I would do it, and I will. 12Listen to me, you stubborn, evil people! 13For I am ready to set things right, not in the distant future, but right now! I am ready to save Jerusalem* and give my glory to Israel.

CHAPTER 47
Prediction of Babylon's Fall
"Come, Babylon, unconquered one, sit in the dust. For your days of glory, pomp, and honor have ended. O daughter of Babylonia,* never again will you be the lovely princess, tender and delicate. 2Take heavy millstones and grind the corn. Remove your veil and strip off your robe. Expose yourself to public view. 3You will be naked and burdened with shame. I will take vengeance against you and will not negotiate."

4Our Redeemer, whose name is the LORD Almighty, is the Holy One of Israel.

5"O daughter of Babylonia, sit now in darkness and silence. Never again will you be known as the queen of kingdoms. 6For I was angry with my chosen people and began their punishment by letting them fall into your hands. But you, Babylon, showed them no mercy. You have forced even the elderly to carry heavy burdens. 7You thought, 'I will reign forever as queen of the world!' You did not care at all about my people or think about the consequences of your actions.

8"You are a pleasure-crazy kingdom, living at ease and feeling secure, bragging as if you were the greatest in the world! You say, 'I'm self-sufficient and not accountable to anyone! I will never be a widow or lose my children.' 9Well, those two things will come upon you in a moment: widowhood and the loss of your children. Yes, these calamities will come upon you, despite all your witchcraft and magic.

10"You felt secure in all your wickedness. 'No one sees me,' you said. Your 'wisdom' and 'knowledge' have caused you to turn away from me and claim, 'I am self-sufficient and not accountable to anyone!' 11So disaster will overtake you suddenly, and you won't be able to charm it away. Calamity will fall upon you, and you won't be able to buy your way out. A catastrophe will arise so fast that you won't know what hit you.

12"Call out the demon hordes you have worshiped all these years. Ask them to help you strike terror into the hearts of people once again. 13You have more than enough advisers, astrologers, and stargazers. Let them stand up and save you from

what the future holds. 14But they are as useless as dried grass burning in a fire. They cannot even save themselves! You will get no help from them at all. Their hearth is not a place to sit for warmth. 15And all your friends, those with whom you have done business since childhood, will slip away and disappear, unable to help.

CHAPTER 48
God's Stubborn People
"Listen to me, O family of Jacob, who are called by the name of Israel and born into the family of Judah. Listen, you who take oaths in the name of the LORD and call on the God of Israel. You don't follow through on any of your promises, 2even though you call yourself the holy city and talk about depending on the God of Israel, whose name is the LORD Almighty. 3Time and again I warned you about what was going to happen in the future. Then suddenly I took action, and all my predictions came true.

4"I know how stubborn and obstinate you are. Your necks are as unbending as iron. You are as hardheaded as bronze. 5That is why I told you ahead of time what I was going to do. That way, you could never say, 'My idols did it. My wooden image and metal god commanded it to happen!' 6You have heard my predictions and seen them fulfilled, but you refuse to admit it. Now I will tell you new things I have not mentioned before, secrets you have not yet heard. 7They are brand new, not things from the past. So you cannot say, 'We knew that all the time!'

8"Yes, I will tell you of things that are entirely new, for I know so well what traitors you are. You have been rebels from your earliest childhood, rotten through and through. 9Yet for my own sake and for the honor of my name, I will hold back my anger and not wipe you out. 10I have refined you but not in the way silver is refined. Rather, I have refined you in the furnace of suffering. 11I will rescue you for my sake—yes, for my own sake! That way, the pagan nations will not be able to claim that their gods have conquered me. I will not let them have my glory!

Freedom from Babylon
12"Listen to me, O family of Jacob, Israel my chosen one! I alone am God, the First and the Last. 13It was my hand that laid the foundations of the earth. The palm of my right hand spread out the heavens above. I spoke, and they came into being.

14"Have any of your idols ever told you this?

46:13 Hebrew *Zion.*   47:1 Or *Chaldea;* also in 47:5.

Come, all of you, and listen: 'The LORD has chosen Cyrus as his ally. He will use him to put an end to the empire of Babylon, destroying the Babylonian* armies.' 15I have said it: I am calling Cyrus! I will send him on this errand and will help him succeed. 16Come closer and listen. I have always told you plainly what would happen so you would have no trouble understanding."

And now the Sovereign LORD and his Spirit have sent me with this message: 17"The LORD, your Redeemer, the Holy One of Israel, says: I am the LORD your God, who teaches you what is good and leads you along the paths you should follow. 18Oh, that you had listened to my commands! Then you would have had peace flowing like a gentle river and righteousness rolling like waves. 19Then you would have become as numerous as the sands along the seashore—too many to count! There would have been no need for your destruction."

20Yet even now, be free from your captivity! Leave Babylon and the Babylonians,* singing as you go! Shout to the ends of the earth that the LORD has redeemed his servants, the people of Israel.* 21They were not thirsty when he led them through the desert. He divided the rock, and water gushed out for them to drink.

22"But there is no peace for the wicked," says the LORD.

CHAPTER 49
The LORD's Servant Commissioned

Listen to me, all of you in far-off lands! The LORD called me before my birth; from within the womb he called me by name. 2He made my words of judgment as sharp as a sword. He has hidden me in the shadow of his hand. I am like a sharp arrow in his quiver.

3He said to me, "You are my servant, Israel, and you will bring me glory."

4I replied, "But my work all seems so useless! I have spent my strength for nothing and to no purpose at all. Yet I leave it all in the LORD's hand; I will trust God for my reward."

5And now the LORD speaks—he who formed me in my mother's womb to be his servant, who commissioned me to bring his people of Israel back to him. The LORD has honored me, and my God has given me strength. 6He says, "You will do more than restore the people of Israel to me. I will make you a light to the Gentiles, and you will bring my salvation to the ends of the earth."

7The LORD, the Redeemer and Holy One of Israel, says to the one who is despised and rejected by a nation, to the one who is the servant of rulers: "Kings will stand at attention when you pass by. Princes will bow low because the LORD has chosen you. He, the faithful LORD, the Holy One of Israel, chooses you."

Promises of Israel's Restoration

8This is what the LORD says: "At just the right time, I will respond to you. On the day of salvation, I will help you. I will give you as a token and pledge to Israel. This will prove that I will reestablish the land of Israel and reassign it to its own people again. 9Through you I am saying to the prisoners of darkness, 'Come out! I am giving you your freedom!' They will be my sheep, grazing in green pastures and on hills that were previously bare. 10They will neither hunger nor thirst. The searing sun and scorching desert winds will not reach them anymore. For the LORD in his mercy will lead them beside cool waters. 11And I will make my mountains into level paths for them. The highways will be raised above the valleys. 12See, my people will return from far away, from lands to the north and west, and from as far south as Egypt.*"

13Sing for joy, O heavens! Rejoice, O earth! Burst into song, O mountains! For the LORD has comforted his people and will have compassion on them in their sorrow.

14Yet Jerusalem* says, "The LORD has deserted us; the Lord has forgotten us."

15"Never! Can a mother forget her nursing child? Can she feel no love for a child she has borne? But even if that were possible, I would not forget you! 16See, I have written your name on my hand. Ever before me is a picture of Jerusalem's walls in ruins. 17Soon your descendants will come back, and all who are trying to destroy you will go away. 18Look and see, for all your children will come back to you. As surely as I live," says the LORD, "they will be like jewels or bridal ornaments for you to display.

19"Even the most desolate parts of your abandoned land will soon be crowded with your people. Your enemies who enslaved you will be far away. 20The generations born in exile will return and say, 'We need more room! It's crowded here!' 21Then you will think to yourself, 'Who has given me all these descendants? For most of my children were killed, and the rest were carried away into exile. I was left here all

48:14 Or *Chaldean*. 48:20a Or *the Chaldeans*. 48:20b Hebrew *his servant, Jacob*. 49:12 As in Dead Sea Scrolls, which read *from the region of Aswan*, which is in southern Egypt. Masoretic Text reads *from the region of Sinim*. 49:14 Hebrew *Zion*.

alone. Who bore these children? Who raised them for me?'"

22This is what the Sovereign LORD says: "See, I will give a signal to the godless nations. They will carry your little sons back to you in their arms; they will bring your daughters on their shoulders. 23Kings and queens will serve you. They will care for all your needs. They will bow to the earth before you and lick the dust from your feet. Then you will know that I am the LORD. Those who wait for me will never be put to shame."

24Who can snatch the plunder of war from the hands of a warrior? Who can demand that a tyrant* let his captives go? 25But the LORD says, "The captives of warriors will be released, and the plunder of tyrants will be retrieved. For I will fight those who fight you, and I will save your children. 26I will feed your enemies with their own flesh. They will be drunk with rivers of their own blood. All the world will know that I, the LORD, am your Savior and Redeemer, the Mighty One of Israel.*"

CHAPTER **50**

The LORD asks, "Did I sell you as slaves to my creditors? Is that why you are not here? Is your mother gone because I divorced her and sent her away? No, you went away as captives because of your sins. And your mother, too, was taken because of your sins. 2Was I too weak to save you? Is that why the house is silent and empty when I come home? Is it because I have no power to rescue? No, that is not the reason! For I can speak to the sea and make it dry! I can turn rivers into deserts covered with dying fish. 3I am the one who sends darkness out across the skies, bringing it to a state of mourning."

The LORD's Obedient Servant
4The Sovereign LORD has given me his words of wisdom, so that I know what to say to all these weary ones. Morning by morning he wakens me and opens my understanding to his will. 5The Sovereign LORD has spoken to me, and I have listened. I do not rebel or turn away. 6I give my back to those who beat me and my cheeks to those who pull out my beard. I do not hide from shame, for they mock me and spit in my face. 7Because the Sovereign LORD helps me, I will not be dismayed. Therefore, I have set my face like a stone, determined to do his will. And I

know that I will triumph. 8He who gives me justice is near. Who will dare to oppose me now? Where are my enemies? Let them appear! 9See, the Sovereign LORD is on my side! Who will declare me guilty? All my enemies will be destroyed like old clothes that have been eaten by moths!

10Who among you fears the LORD and obeys his servant? If you are walking in darkness, without a ray of light, trust in the LORD and rely on your God. 11But watch out, you who live in your own light and warm yourselves by your own fires. This is the reward you will receive from me: You will soon lie down in great torment.

CHAPTER **51**
A Call to Trust the LORD
"Listen to me, all who hope for deliverance—all who seek the LORD! Consider the quarry from which you were mined, the rock from which you were cut! 2Yes, think about your ancestors Abraham and Sarah, from whom you came. Abraham was alone when I called him. But when I blessed him, he became a great nation."

3The LORD will comfort Israel* again and make her deserts blossom. Her barren wilderness will become as beautiful as Eden—the garden of the LORD. Joy and gladness will be found there. Lovely songs of thanksgiving will fill the air.

4"Listen to me, my people. Hear me, Israel, for my law will be proclaimed, and my justice will become a light to the nations. 5My mercy and justice are coming soon. Your salvation is on the way. I will rule the nations. They will wait for me and long for my power. 6Look up to the skies above, and gaze down on the earth beneath. For the skies will disappear like smoke, and the earth will wear out like a piece of clothing. The people of the earth will die like flies, but my salvation lasts forever. My righteous rule will never end!

7"Listen to me, you who know right from wrong and cherish my law in your hearts. Do not be afraid of people's scorn or their slanderous talk. 8For the moth will destroy them as it destroys clothing. The worm will eat away at them as it eats wool. But my righteousness will last forever. My salvation will continue from generation to generation."

9Wake up, LORD! Robe yourself with strength! Rouse yourself as in the days of old when you slew Egypt, the dragon of the Nile.* 10Are you

49:24 As in Dead Sea Scrolls, Syriac version, and Latin Vulgate (also see 49:25); Masoretic Text reads *a righteous person.* 49:26 Hebrew *of Jacob.* 51:3 Hebrew *Zion;* also in 51:16. 51:9 Hebrew *slew Rahab the dragon.* Rahab is the name of a mythical sea monster that represents chaos in ancient literature. The name is used here as a poetic name for Egypt.

Jesus Made the Ultimate Sacrifice Read ISAIAH 53:1-12

The cross was not a rude interruption of an otherwise wonderful ministry of a great humanitarian and moral teacher. Jesus chose to take the punishment for our sins because he knew that there was no other way for you to approach a holy God. The fact that Jesus knew what was waiting for him at the cross makes his journey to earth even more amazing. Here are three things his death on the cross shows us:

1. The Cross Shows the Depth of Human Sin. When we look at the cross of Jesus Christ, we should see a representation of human sin and recognize how lost we really are. Ultimately, each one of us drove those spikes into his flesh because of our sins. Jesus took our punishment upon himself as he hung upon that cross. That thought alone should make us realize the depth of our sinful nature.

2. The Cross Demonstrates the Overwhelming Love of God. Although our sins drove the nails through his hands, it was his love for us that held him to the cross. As the apostle Paul so eloquently writes, "He [Jesus] loved me and gave himself for me" (Galatians 2:20).

3. The Cross Represents the Only Way of Salvation. Jesus himself said, "I am the way, the truth, and the life. No one can come to the Father except through me" (John 14:6). If there had been any other way for us to be forgiven, Jesus surely would have found it. To say there are other ways to know and have a relationship with God is to make a mockery of what happened at Calvary.

For the next note on "Who Is Jesus?" turn to p. 926.

CORNER STONES

not the same today, the one who dried up the sea, making a path of escape when you saved your people? ¹¹Those who have been ransomed by the LORD will return to Jerusalem,* singing songs of everlasting joy. Sorrow and mourning will disappear, and they will be overcome with joy and gladness.

¹²"I, even I, am the one who comforts you. So why are you afraid of mere humans, who wither like the grass and disappear? ¹³Yet you have forgotten the LORD, your Creator, the one who put the stars in the sky and established the earth. Will you remain in constant dread of human oppression? Will you continue to fear the anger of your enemies from morning till night? ¹⁴Soon all you captives will be released! Imprisonment, starvation, and death will not be your fate! ¹⁵For I am the LORD your God, who stirs up the sea, causing its waves to roar. My name is the LORD Almighty. ¹⁶And I have put my words in your mouth and hidden you safely within my hand. I set all the stars in space and established the earth. I am the one who says to Israel, 'You are mine!'"

¹⁷Wake up, wake up, O Jerusalem! You have drunk enough from the cup of the LORD's fury.

51:11 Hebrew *Zion*.

You have drunk the cup of terror, tipping out its last drops. ¹⁸Not one of your children is left alive to help you or tell you what to do. ¹⁹These two things have been your lot: desolation and destruction, famine and war. And who is left to sympathize? Who is left to comfort you? ²⁰For your children have fainted and lie in the streets, helpless as antelopes caught in a net. The LORD has poured out his fury; God has rebuked them.

²¹But now listen to this, you afflicted ones, who sit in a drunken stupor, though not from drinking wine. ²²This is what the Sovereign LORD, your God and Defender, says: "See, I am taking the terrible cup from your hands. You will drink no more of my fury. It is gone at last! ²³But I will put that cup into the hands of those who tormented you. I will give it to those who trampled you into the dust and walked on your backs."

CHAPTER 52
Deliverance for Jerusalem

Wake up, wake up, O Zion! Clothe yourselves with strength. Put on your beautiful clothes, O holy city of Jerusalem, for unclean and godless people will no longer enter your gates. ²Rise from the dust, O Jerusalem. Remove the slave bands from your neck, O captive daughter of Zion. ³For this is what the LORD says: "When I sold you into exile, I received no payment. Now I can redeem you without paying for you."

⁴This is what the Sovereign LORD says: "Long ago my people went to live as resident foreigners in Egypt. Now they have been oppressed without cause by Assyria. ⁵And now, what is this?" asks the LORD. "Why are my people enslaved again? Those who rule them shout in exultation. My name is being blasphemed all day long. ⁶But I will reveal my name to my people, and they will come to know its power. Then at last they will recognize that it is I who speaks to them."

⁷How beautiful on the mountains are the feet of those who bring good news of peace and salvation, the news that the God of Israel* reigns! ⁸The watchmen shout and sing with joy, for before their very eyes they see the LORD bringing his people home to Jerusalem.* ⁹Let the ruins of Jerusalem break into joyful song, for the LORD has comforted his people. He has redeemed Jerusalem. ¹⁰The LORD will demonstrate his holy power before the eyes of all the nations. The ends of the earth will see the salvation of our God.

¹¹Go now, leave your bonds and slavery. Put Babylon behind you, with everything it represents, for it is unclean to you. You are the LORD's holy people. Purify yourselves, you who carry home the vessels of the LORD. ¹²You will not leave in a hurry, running for your lives. For the LORD will go ahead of you, and the God of Israel will protect you from behind.

The LORD's Suffering Servant

¹³See, my servant will prosper; he will be highly exalted. ¹⁴Many were amazed when they saw him*—beaten and bloodied, so disfigured one would scarcely know he was a person. ¹⁵And he will again startle* many nations. Kings will stand speechless in his presence. For they will see what they had not previously been told about; they will understand what they had not heard about.

CHAPTER **53**

Who has believed our message? To whom will the LORD reveal his saving power? ²My servant grew up in the LORD's presence like a tender green shoot, sprouting from a root in dry and sterile ground. There was nothing beautiful or majestic about his appearance, nothing to at-

tract us to him. ³He was despised and rejected—a man of sorrows, acquainted with bitterest grief. We turned our backs on him and looked the other way when he went by. He was despised, and we did not care.

⁴Yet it was our weaknesses he carried; it was our sorrows* that weighed him down. And we thought his troubles were a punishment from God for his own sins! ⁵But he was wounded and crushed for our sins. He was beaten that we might have peace. He was whipped, and we were healed! ⁶All of us have strayed away like sheep. We have left God's paths to follow our own. Yet the LORD laid on him the guilt and sins of us all.

⁷He was oppressed and treated harshly, yet he never said a word. He was led as a lamb to the slaughter. And as a sheep is silent before the shearers, he did not open his mouth. ⁸From prison and trial they led him away to his death. But who among the people realized that he was dying for their sins—that he was suffering their punishment? ⁹He had done no wrong, and he never deceived anyone. But he was buried like a criminal; he was put in a rich man's grave.

¹⁰But it was the LORD's good plan to crush him and fill him with grief. Yet when his life is made an offering for sin, he will have a multitude of children, many heirs. He will enjoy a long life, and the LORD's plan will prosper in his hands. ¹¹When he sees all that is accomplished by his anguish, he will be satisfied. And because of what he has experienced, my righteous servant will make it possible for many to be counted righteous, for he will bear all their sins. ¹²I will give him the honors of one who is mighty and great, because he exposed himself to death. He was counted among those who were sinners. He bore the sins of many and interceded for sinners.

CHAPTER **54**

Future Glory for Jerusalem

"Sing, O childless woman! Break forth into loud and joyful song, O Jerusalem, even though you never gave birth to a child. For the woman who could bear no children now has more than all the other women," says the LORD. ²"Enlarge your house; build an addition; spread out your home! ³For you will soon be bursting at the seams. Your descendants will take over other nations and live in their cities.

⁴"Fear not; you will no longer live in shame. The shame of your youth and the sorrows of

52:7 Hebrew *of Zion.* 52:8 Hebrew *to Zion.* 52:14 As in Syriac version; Hebrew reads *you.* 52:15 Or *cleanse.* 53:4 Or *Yet it was our sicknesses he carried; it was our diseases.*

widowhood will be remembered no more, 5for your Creator will be your husband. The LORD Almighty is his name! He is your Redeemer, the Holy One of Israel, the God of all the earth. 6For the LORD has called you back from your grief—as though you were a young wife abandoned by her husband," says your God. 7"For a brief moment I abandoned you, but with great compassion I will take you back. 8In a moment of anger I turned my face away for a little while. But with everlasting love I will have compassion on you," says the LORD, your Redeemer.

9"Just as I swore in the time of Noah that I would never again let a flood cover the earth and destroy its life, so now I swear that I will never again pour out my anger on you. 10For the mountains may depart and the hills disappear, but even then I will remain loyal to you. My covenant of blessing will never be broken," says the LORD, who has mercy on you.

11"O storm-battered city, troubled and desolate! I will rebuild you on a foundation of sapphires and make the walls of your houses from precious jewels. 12I will make your towers of sparkling rubies and your gates and walls of shining gems. 13I will teach all your citizens, and their prosperity will be great. 14You will live under a government that is just and fair. Your enemies will stay far away; you will live in peace. Terror will not come near. 15If any nation comes to fight you, it will not be because I sent them to punish you. Your enemies will always be defeated because I am on your side. 16I have created the blacksmith who fans the coals beneath the forge and makes the weapons of destruction. And I have created the armies that destroy. 17But in that coming day, no weapon turned against you will succeed. And everyone who tells lies in court will be brought to justice. These benefits are enjoyed by the servants of the LORD; their vindication will come from me. I, the LORD, have spoken!

CHAPTER 55
Invitation to the LORD's Salvation

"Is anyone thirsty? Come and drink—even if you have no money! Come, take your choice of wine or milk—it's all free! 2Why spend your money on food that does not give you strength? Why pay for food that does you no good? Listen, and I will tell you where to get food that is good for the soul!

3"Come to me with your ears wide open. Listen, for the life of your soul is at stake. I am ready to make an everlasting covenant with you. I will give you all the mercies and unfailing love that I promised to David. 4He displayed my power by being my witness and a leader among the nations. 5You also will command the nations, and they will come running to obey, because I, the LORD your God, the Holy One of Israel, have made you glorious."

6Seek the LORD while you can find him. Call on him now while he is near. 7Let the people turn from their wicked deeds. Let them banish from their minds the very thought of doing wrong! Let them turn to the LORD that he may have mercy on them. Yes, turn to our God, for he will abundantly pardon.

8"My thoughts are completely different from yours," says the LORD. "And my ways are far beyond anything you could imagine. 9For just as the heavens are higher than the earth, so are my ways higher than your ways and my thoughts higher than your thoughts.

10"The rain and snow come down from the heavens and stay on the ground to water the earth. They cause the grain to grow, producing seed for the farmer and bread for the hungry. 11It is the same with my word. I send it out, and it always produces fruit. It will accomplish all I want it to, and it will prosper everywhere I send it. 12You will live in joy and peace. The mountains and hills will burst into song, and the trees of the field will clap their hands! 13Where once there were thorns, cypress trees will grow. Where briers grew, myrtles will sprout up. This miracle will bring great honor to the LORD's name; it will be an everlasting sign of his power and love.

CHAPTER 56
Blessings for All Nations

"Be just and fair to all," says the LORD. "Do what

OFF AND RUNNING ◢◢◢ ◢◢ ◢

Spend Time Feeding Your Soul Read ISAIAH 55:1-13

It has been said that seven days without God's Word makes one weak. When we neglect to feed our soul with God's Word, we become spiritually malnourished. Instead, we fill our lives and time with things that do not really satisfy our spiritual hunger. We look forward to the next weekend off more than our next quiet time with God. We spend more time watching TV than reading our Bibles. We choose a day at the beach over a day at

is right and good, for I am coming soon to rescue you. ²Blessed are those who are careful to do this. Blessed are those who honor my Sabbath days of rest by refusing to work. And blessed are those who keep themselves from doing wrong.

³"And my blessings are for Gentiles, too, when they commit themselves to the LORD. Do not let them think that I consider them second-class citizens. And my blessings are also for the eunuchs. They are as much mine as anyone else. ⁴For I say this to the eunuchs who keep my Sabbath days holy, who choose to do what pleases me and commit their lives to me: ⁵I will give them—in my house, within my walls—a memorial and a name far greater than the honor they would have received by having sons and daughters. For the name I give them is an everlasting one. It will never disappear!

⁶"I will also bless the Gentiles who commit themselves to the LORD and serve him and love his name, who worship him and do not desecrate the Sabbath day of rest, and who have accepted his covenant. ⁷I will bring them also to my holy mountain of Jerusalem and will fill them with joy in my house of prayer. I will accept their burnt offerings and sacrifices, because my Temple will be called a house of prayer for all nations. ⁸For the Sovereign LORD, who brings back the outcasts of Israel, says: I will bring others, too, besides my people Israel."

Sinful Leaders Condemned

⁹Come, wild animals of the field! Come, wild animals of the forest! Come and devour my people! ¹⁰For the leaders of my people—the LORD's watchmen, his shepherds—are blind to every danger. They are like silent watchdogs that give no warning when danger comes. They love to lie around, sleeping and dreaming. ¹¹And they are as greedy as dogs, never satisfied. They are stupid shepherds, all following

57:9a Or *to the king.* 57:9b Hebrew *into Sheol.*

their own path, all of them intent on personal gain.

¹²"Come," they say. "We will get some wine and have a party. Let's all get drunk. Let this go on and on, and tomorrow will be even better."

CHAPTER **57**

The righteous pass away; the godly often die before their time. And no one seems to care or wonder why. No one seems to understand that God is protecting them from the evil to come. ²For the godly who die will rest in peace.

Idolatrous Worship Condemned

³"But you—come here, you witches' children, you offspring of adulterers and prostitutes! ⁴Whom do you mock, making faces and sticking out your tongues? You children of sinners and liars! ⁵You worship your idols with great passion beneath every green tree. You slaughter your children as human sacrifices down in the valleys, under overhanging rocks. ⁶Your gods are the smooth stones in the valleys. You worship them with drink offerings and grain offerings. They, not I, are your inheritance. Does all this make me happy? ⁷You have committed adultery on the mountaintops by worshiping idols there, and so you have been unfaithful to me. ⁸Behind closed doors, you have set up your idols and worship them instead of me. This is adultery, for you are loving these idols instead of loving me. You have climbed right into bed with these detestable gods. ⁹You have given olive oil and perfume to Molech* as your gift. You have traveled far, even into the world of the dead,* to find new gods to love. ¹⁰You grew weary in your search, but you never gave up. You strengthened yourself and went on. ¹¹Why were you more afraid of them than of me? How is it that you don't even remember me or think about me? Is it because I have not corrected you that you have no fear of me?

¹²"Now I will expose your so-called good deeds that you consider so righteous. None of

church. When this happens, we need to heed God's advice to the spiritually hungry Israelites: We need to seek and call upon the Lord, come to him with open ears, and listen attentively to what he says.

God promises that if you do these things, you will feed your soul. Why settle for the crumbs that fall on the floor when you can have the finest gourmet food at the Master's table? Make a commitment to stay spiritually fit by making your time with God and his Word a priority.

For the next note on "Priorities," turn to p. 972.

them will benefit or save you. 13Let's see if your idols can do anything for you when you cry to them for help. They are so helpless that a breath of wind can knock them down! But whoever trusts in me will possess the land and inherit my holy mountain. 14I will say, 'Rebuild the road! Clear away the rocks and stones so my people can return from captivity.'"

God Forgives the Repentant

15The high and lofty one who inhabits eternity, the Holy One, says this: "I live in that high and holy place with those whose spirits are contrite and humble. I refresh the humble and give new courage to those with repentant hearts. 16For I will not fight against you forever; I will not always show my anger. If I did, all people would pass away—all the souls I have made. 17I was angry and punished these greedy people. I withdrew myself from them, but they went right on sinning. 18I have seen what they do, but I will heal them anyway! I will lead them and comfort those who mourn. 19Then words of praise will be on their lips. May they have peace, both near and far, for I will heal them all," says the LORD. 20"But those who still reject me are like the restless sea. It is never still but continually churns up mire and dirt. 21There is no peace for the wicked," says my God.

CHAPTER **58**
True and False Worship

"Shout with the voice of a trumpet blast. Tell my people Israel* of their sins! 2Yet they act so pious! They come to the Temple every day and seem delighted to hear my laws. You would almost think this was a righteous nation that

58:1 Hebrew *Jacob.*

would never abandon its God. They love to make a show of coming to me and asking me to take action on their behalf. 3'We have fasted before you!' they say. 'Why aren't you impressed? We have done much penance, and you don't even notice it!'

"I will tell you why! It's because you are living for yourselves even while you are fasting. You keep right on oppressing your workers. 4What good is fasting when you keep on fighting and quarreling? This kind of fasting will never get you anywhere with me. 5You humble yourselves by going through the motions of penance, bowing your heads like a blade of grass in the wind. You dress in sackcloth and cover yourselves with ashes. Is this what you call fasting? Do you really think this will please the LORD?

6"No, the kind of fasting I want calls you to free those who are wrongly imprisoned and to stop oppressing those who work for you. Treat them fairly and give them what they earn. 7I want you to share your food with the hungry and to welcome poor wanderers into your homes. Give clothes to those who need them, and do not hide from relatives who need your help.

8"If you do these things, your salvation will come like the dawn. Yes, your healing will come quickly. Your godliness will lead you forward, and the glory of the LORD will protect you from behind. 9Then when you call, the LORD will answer. 'Yes, I am here,' he will quickly reply.

"Stop oppressing the helpless and stop making false accusations and spreading vicious rumors! 10Feed the hungry and help those in trouble. Then your light will shine out from the darkness, and the darkness around you will be

OFF AND RUNNING ▰▰ ▰▰ ▰▰

Pray without Hinderance Read ISAIAH 59:1-2

Just as there are things you can do to make your prayers more effective, there are also things you can do (or not do) to make your prayers ineffective. Here are four specific obstacles to effective prayer.

1. Selfishness or Pride. When it comes to having effective prayers, motives are of the greatest importance. If a person comes to God praying for something with a selfish motive, that prayer will not get any higher than the ceiling. God will not answer prayers that come from a selfish motive.

2. Idolatry. Idolatry is not limited to bowing down to images of gold, wood, or bronze. An idol could also be defined as anything or anyone that takes the place of God in your life. It could be a person, a relationship, a career, or even a leisure activity. When you place something other than God on the throne of your heart, your prayers will go unanswered. As Ezekiel 14:3 says, "Son of man, these leaders have set up idols in their hearts. . . . Why should I let them ask me anything?"

as bright as day. ¹¹The LORD will guide you continually, watering your life when you are dry and keeping you healthy, too. You will be like a well-watered garden, like an ever-flowing spring. ¹²Your children will rebuild the deserted ruins of your cities. Then you will be known as the people who rebuild their walls and cities.

¹³"Keep the Sabbath day holy. Don't pursue your own interests on that day, but enjoy the Sabbath and speak of it with delight as the LORD's holy day. Honor the LORD in everything you do, and don't follow your own desires or talk idly. If you do this, ¹⁴the LORD will be your delight. I will give you great honor and give you your full share of the inheritance I promised to Jacob, your ancestor. I, the LORD, have spoken!"

CHAPTER **59**
Warnings against Sin

Listen! The LORD is not too weak to save you, and he is not becoming deaf. He can hear you when you call. ²But there is a problem—your sins have cut you off from God. Because of your sin, he has turned away and will not listen anymore. ³Your hands are the hands of murderers, and your fingers are filthy with sin. Your mouth is full of lies, and your lips are tainted with corruption.

⁴No one cares about being fair and honest. Their lawsuits are based on lies. They spend their time plotting evil deeds and then doing them. ⁵They spend their time and energy spinning evil plans that end up in deadly actions. ⁶They cheat and shortchange everyone. Nothing they do is productive; all their activity is filled with sin. Violence is their trademark. ⁷Their feet run to do evil, and they rush to commit murder. They think only about sinning. Wherever they go, misery and destruction follow them. ⁸They do not know what true peace is or what it means to be just and good. They continually do wrong, and those who follow them cannot experience a moment's peace.

⁹It is because of all this evil that deliverance is far from us. That is why God doesn't punish those who injure us. No wonder we are in darkness when we expected light. No wonder we are walking in the gloom. ¹⁰No wonder we grope like blind people and stumble along. Even at brightest noontime, we fall down as though it were dark. No wonder we are like corpses when compared to vigorous young men! ¹¹We growl like hungry bears; we moan like mournful doves. We look for justice, but it is nowhere to be found. We look to be rescued, but it is far away from us. ¹²For our sins are piled up before God and testify against us. Yes, we know what sinners we are. ¹³We know that we have rebelled against the LORD. We have turned our backs on God. We know how unfair and oppressive we have been, carefully planning our deceitful lies. ¹⁴Our courts oppose people who are righteous, and justice is nowhere to be found. Truth falls dead in the streets, and fairness has been outlawed. ¹⁵Yes, truth is gone, and anyone who tries to live a godly life is soon attacked.

The LORD looked and was displeased to find that there was no justice. ¹⁶He was amazed to see that no one intervened to help the oppressed. So he himself stepped in to save them with his mighty power and justice. ¹⁷He put on righteousness as his body armor and placed the helmet of salvation on his head. He clothed himself with the robes of vengeance and godly fury. ¹⁸He will repay his enemies for their evil deeds. His fury will fall on his foes in distant

3. Unforgiveness. In Mark 11:25, Jesus says, "But when you are praying, first forgive anyone you are holding a grudge against, so that your Father in heaven will forgive your sins, too." If you are harboring a grudge against someone right now, your prayer life will suffer. Get rid of that root of bitterness before it destroys you and those around you. If you don't release it, you will be sinning, and that sin will hinder your prayers.

4. Unconfessed Sin. Psalm 66:18 says, "If I had not confessed the sin in my heart, my Lord would not have listened." If you feel like your prayers are going unanswered, you may want to consider whether you are harboring some unconfessed sin in your life. Maybe you are committing a sin right now that you do not even categorize as a sin because "everybody is doing it." Yet, if the Bible characterizes that activity as sin, then it is.

If you can identify with any of the problems listed above, confess your sins to God and turn away from that attitude or activity. Once that obstacle is removed, you will again see God working through your prayers.

For the next note on "Prayer Time," turn to p. 1108.

lands. 19Then at last they will respect and glorify the name of the LORD throughout the world. For he will come like a flood tide driven by the breath of the LORD.

20"The Redeemer will come to Jerusalem,*" says the LORD, "to buy back those in Israel* who have turned from their sins. 21And this is my covenant with them," says the LORD. "My Spirit will not leave them, and neither will these words I have given you. They will be on your lips and on the lips of your children and your children's children forever. I, the LORD, have spoken!

CHAPTER 60
Future Glory for Jerusalem

"Arise, Jerusalem! Let your light shine for all the nations to see! For the glory of the LORD is shining upon you. 2Darkness as black as night will cover all the nations of the earth, but the glory of the LORD will shine over you. 3All nations will come to your light. Mighty kings will come to see your radiance.

4"Look and see, for everyone is coming home! Your sons are coming from distant lands; your little daughters will be carried home. 5Your eyes will shine, and your hearts will thrill with joy, for merchants from around the world will come to you. They will bring you the wealth of many lands. 6Vast caravans of camels will converge on you, the camels of Midian and Ephah. From Sheba they will bring gold and incense for the worship of the LORD. 7The flocks of Kedar will be given to you, and the rams of Nebaioth will be brought for my altars. In that day I will make my Temple glorious.

8"And what do I see flying like clouds to Israel, like doves to their nests? 9They are the ships of Tarshish, reserved to bring the people of Israel home. They will bring their wealth with them, and it will bring great honor to the LORD your God, the Holy One of Israel, for he will fill you with splendor.

10"Foreigners will come to rebuild your cities. Kings and rulers will send you aid. For though I have destroyed you in my anger, I will have mercy on you through my grace. 11Your gates will stay open around the clock to receive the wealth of many lands. The kings of the world will be led as captives in a victory procession. 12For the nations that refuse to be your allies will be destroyed. 13The glory of Lebanon will be yours—the forests of cypress, fir, and pine—to beautify my sanctuary. My Temple will be glorious!

14"The children of your tormentors will come and bow before you. Those who despised you will kiss your feet. They will call you the City of the LORD, and Zion of the Holy One of Israel.

15"Though you were once despised and hated and rebuffed by all, you will be beautiful forever. You will be a joy to all generations, for I will make you so. 16Powerful kings and mighty nations will bring the best of their goods to satisfy your every need. You will know at last that I, the LORD, am your Savior and Redeemer, the Mighty One of Israel.* 17I will exchange your bronze for gold, your iron for silver, your wood for bronze, and your stones for iron. Peace and righteousness will be your leaders! 18Violence will disappear from your land; the desolation and destruction of war will end. Salvation will surround you like city walls, and praise will be on the lips of all who enter there.

19"No longer will you need the sun or moon to give you light, for the LORD your God will be your everlasting light, and he will be your glory. 20The sun will never set; the moon will not go down. For the LORD will be your everlasting light. Your days of mourning will come to an end. 21All your people will be righteous. They will possess their land forever, for I will plant them there with my own hands in order to bring myself glory. 22The smallest family will multiply into a large clan. The tiniest group will become a mighty nation. I, the LORD, will bring it all to pass at the right time."

CHAPTER 61
Good News for the Oppressed

The Spirit of the Sovereign LORD is upon me, because the LORD has appointed me to bring good news to the poor. He has sent me to comfort the brokenhearted and to announce that captives will be released and prisoners will be freed.* 2He has sent me to tell those who mourn that the time of the LORD's favor has come,* and with it, the day of God's anger against their enemies. 3To all who mourn in Israel,* he will give beauty for ashes, joy instead of mourning, praise instead of despair. For the LORD has planted them like strong and graceful oaks for his own glory.

4They will rebuild the ancient ruins, repairing cities long ago destroyed. They will revive them, though they have been empty for many generations. 5Foreigners will be your servants. They will feed your flocks and plow your fields and tend your vineyards. 6You will be called priests of the LORD, ministers of our God. You will be fed with the treasures of the nations and will boast in their riches. 7Instead of shame and dishonor, you will inherit a double portion of prosperity and everlasting joy.

8 "For I, the LORD, love justice. I hate robbery and wrongdoing. I will faithfully reward my people for their suffering and make an everlasting covenant with them. 9Their descendants will be known and honored among the nations. Everyone will realize that they are a people the LORD has blessed."

10I am overwhelmed with joy in the LORD my God! For he has dressed me with the clothing of salvation and draped me in a robe of righteousness. I am like a bridegroom in his wedding suit or a bride with her jewels. 11The Sovereign LORD will show his justice to the nations of the world. Everyone will praise him! His righteousness will be like a garden in early spring, filled with young plants springing up everywhere.

CHAPTER 62
Isaiah's Prayer for Jerusalem

Because I love Zion, because my heart yearns for Jerusalem, I cannot remain silent. I will not stop praying for her until her righteousness shines like the dawn, and her salvation blazes like a burning torch.

2The nations will see your righteousness. Kings will be blinded by your glory. And the LORD will give you a new name. 3The LORD will hold you in his hands for all to see—a splendid crown in the hands of God. 4Never again will you be called the Godforsaken City* or the Desolate Land.* Your new name will be the City of God's Delight* and the Bride of God,* for the LORD delights in you and will claim you as his own. 5Your children will care for you with joy, O Jerusalem, just as a young man cares for his bride. Then God will rejoice over you as a bridegroom rejoices over his bride.

6O Jerusalem, I have posted watchmen on your walls; they will pray to the LORD day and night for the fulfillment of his promises. Take no rest, all you who pray. 7Give the LORD no rest until he makes Jerusalem the object of praise throughout the earth. 8The LORD has sworn to Jerusalem by his own strength: "I will never again hand you over to your enemies. Never again will foreign warriors come and take away

your grain and wine. 9You raised it, and you will keep it, praising the LORD. Within the courtyards of the Temple, you yourselves will drink the wine that you have pressed."

10Go out! Prepare the highway for my people to return! Smooth out the road; pull out the boulders; raise a flag for all the nations to see. 11The LORD has sent this message to every land: "Tell the people of Israel,* 'Look, your Savior is coming. See, he brings his reward with him as he comes.'" 12They will be called the Holy People and the People Redeemed by the LORD. And Jerusalem will be known as the Desirable Place and the City No Longer Forsaken.

CHAPTER 63
Judgment against the LORD's Enemies

Who is this who comes from Edom, from the city of Bozrah, with his clothing stained red? Who is this in royal robes, marching in the greatness of his strength?

"It is I, the LORD, announcing your salvation! It is I, the LORD, who is mighty to save!"

2Why are your clothes so red, as if you have been treading out grapes?

3 "I have trodden the winepress alone; no one was there to help me. In my anger I have trampled my enemies as if they were grapes. In my fury I have trampled my foes. It is their blood that has stained my clothes. 4For the time has come for me to avenge my people, to ransom them from their oppressors. 5I looked, but no one came to help my people. I was amazed and appalled at what I saw. So I executed vengeance alone; unaided, I passed down judgment. 6I crushed the nations in my anger and made them stagger and fall to the ground."

Praise for Deliverance

7I will tell of the LORD's unfailing love. I will praise the LORD for all he has done. I will rejoice in his great goodness to Israel, which he has granted according to his mercy and love. 8He said, "They are very own people. Surely they will not be false again." And he became their Savior. 9In all their suffering he also suffered, and he personally rescued them. In his love and mercy he redeemed them. He lifted them up and carried them through all the years.

10But they rebelled against him and grieved his Holy Spirit. That is why he became their enemy and fought against them. 11Then they remem-

---

62:4a Hebrew *Azubah*, which means "forsaken." 62:4b Hebrew *Shemamah*, which means "desolate." 62:4c Hebrew *Hephzibah*, which means "my delight is in her." 62:4d Hebrew *Beulah*, which means "married." 62:11 Hebrew *Tell the daughter of Zion.*

bered those days of old when Moses led his people out of Egypt. They cried out, "Where is the one who brought Israel through the sea, with Moses as their shepherd? Where is the one who sent his Holy Spirit to be among his people? 12Where is the one whose power divided the sea before them, when Moses lifted up his hand, establishing his reputation forever? 13Where is the one who led them through the bottom of the sea? They were like fine stallions racing through the desert, never stumbling. 14As with cattle going down into a peaceful valley, the Spirit of the LORD gave them rest. You led your people, LORD, and gained a magnificent reputation."

Prayer for Mercy and Pardon

15LORD, look down from heaven and see us from your holy, glorious home. Where is the passion and the might you used to show on our behalf? Where are your mercy and compassion now? 16Surely you are still our Father! Even if Abraham and Jacob* would disown us, LORD, you would still be our Father. You are our Redeemer from ages past. 17LORD, why have you allowed us to turn from your path? Why have you given us stubborn hearts so we no longer fear you? Return and help us, for we are your servants and your special possession. 18How briefly your holy people possessed the holy place, and now our enemies have destroyed it. 19LORD, why do you treat us as though we never belonged to you? Why do you act as though we had never been known as your people?

CHAPTER 64

Oh, that you would burst from the heavens and come down! How the mountains would quake in your presence! 2As fire causes wood to burn and water to boil, your coming would make the nations tremble. Then your enemies would learn the reason for your fame! 3When you came down long ago, you did awesome things beyond our highest expectations. And oh, how the mountains quaked! 4For since the world began, no ear has heard, and no eye has seen a God like you, who works for those who wait for him! 5You welcome those who cheerfully do good, who follow godly ways.

But we are not godly. We are constant sinners, so your anger is heavy on us. How can people like us be saved? 6We are all infected and impure with sin. When we proudly display our righteous deeds, we find they are but filthy rags. Like autumn leaves, we wither and fall. And our sins,

like the wind, sweep us away. 7Yet no one calls on your name or pleads with you for mercy. Therefore, you have turned away from us and turned us over to our sins.

8And yet, LORD, you are our Father. We are the clay, and you are the potter. We are all formed by your hand. 9Oh, don't be so angry with us, LORD. Please don't remember our sins forever. Look at us, we pray, and see that we are all your people.

10Your holy cities are destroyed; even Jerusalem is a desolate wilderness. 11The holy, beautiful Temple where our ancestors praised you has been burned down, and all the things of beauty are destroyed. 12After all this, LORD, must you still refuse to help us? Will you continue to be silent and punish us?

CHAPTER 65

Judgment and Final Salvation

The LORD says, "People who never before inquired about me are now asking about me. I am being found by people who were not looking for me. To them I have said, 'I am here!'

2"I opened my arms to my own people all day long, but they have rebelled. They follow their own evil paths and thoughts. 3All day long they insult me to my face by worshiping idols in their sacred gardens. They burn incense on the rooftops of their homes. 4At night they go out among the graves and secret places to worship evil spirits. They also eat pork and other forbidden foods. 5Yet they say to each other, 'Don't come too close or you will defile me! I am holier than you!' They are a stench in my nostrils, an acrid smell that never goes away.

6"Look, my decree is written out in front of me: I will not stand silent; I will repay them in full! Yes, I will repay them—7both for their own sins and for those of their ancestors," says the LORD. "For they also burned incense on the mountains and insulted me on the hills. I will pay them back in full!

8"But I will not destroy them all," says the LORD. "For just as good grapes are found among a cluster of bad ones (and someone will say, 'Don't throw them all away—there are some good grapes there!'), so I will not destroy all Israel. For I still have true servants there. 9I will preserve a remnant of the people of Israel* and of Judah to possess my land. Those I choose will inherit it and serve me there. 10For my people who have searched for me, the plain of Sharon will again be filled with flocks, and the valley of Achor will be a place to pasture herds.

63:16 Hebrew *Israel.*   65:9 Hebrew *remnant of Jacob.*

11 "But because the rest of you have forsaken the LORD and his Temple and worship the gods of Fate and Destiny, 12I will 'destine' you to the sword. All of you will bow before the executioner, for when I called, you did not answer. When I spoke, you did not listen. You deliberately sinned—before my very eyes—and chose to do what you know I despise."

13Therefore, this is what the Sovereign LORD says: "You will starve, but my servants will eat. You will be thirsty, but they will drink. You will be sad and ashamed, but they will rejoice. 14You will cry in sorrow and despair, while my servants sing for joy. 15Your name will be a curse word among my people, for the Sovereign LORD will destroy you and call his true servants by another name. 16All who invoke a blessing or take an oath will do so by the God of truth. For I will put aside my anger and forget the evil of earlier days.

17"Look! I am creating new heavens and a new earth—so wonderful that no one will even think about the old ones anymore. 18Be glad; rejoice forever in my creation! And look! I will create Jerusalem as a place of happiness. Her people will be a source of joy. 19I will rejoice in Jerusalem and delight in my people. And the sound of weeping and crying will be heard no more.

20"No longer will babies die when only a few days old. No longer will adults die before they have lived a full life. No longer will people be considered old at one hundred! Only sinners will die that young! 21In those days, people will live in the houses they build and eat the fruit of their own vineyards. 22It will not be like the past, when invaders took the houses and confiscated the vineyards. For my people will live as long as trees and will have time to enjoy their hard-won gains. 23They will not work in vain, and their children will not be doomed to misfortune. For they are people blessed by the LORD, and their children, too, will be blessed. 24I will answer them before they even call to me. While they are still talking to me about their needs, I will go ahead and answer their prayers! 25The wolf and lamb will feed together. The lion will eat straw like the ox. Poisonous snakes will strike no more. In those days, no one will be hurt or destroyed on my holy mountain. I, the LORD, have spoken!"

CHAPTER **66**

This is what the LORD says: "Heaven is my throne, and the earth is my footstool. Could you

66:8 Hebrew *Zion's.*

ever build me a temple as good as that? Could you build a dwelling place for me? 2My hands have made both heaven and earth, and they are mine. I, the LORD, have spoken!

"I will bless those who have humble and contrite hearts, who tremble at my word. 3But those who choose their own ways, delighting in their sins, are cursed. Their offerings will not be accepted. When such people sacrifice an ox, it is no more acceptable than a human sacrifice. When they sacrifice a lamb or bring an offering of grain, it is as bad as putting a dog or the blood of a pig on the altar! When they burn incense, it is as if they had blessed an idol. 4I will send great troubles against them—all the things they feared. For when I called, they did not answer. When I spoke, they did not listen. They deliberately sinned—before my very eyes—and chose to do what they know I despise."

5Hear this message from the LORD, and tremble at his words: "Your close relatives hate you and throw you out for being loyal to my name. 'Let the LORD be honored!' they scoff. 'Be joyful in him!' But they will be put to shame. 6What is all the commotion in the city? What is that terrible noise from the Temple? It is the voice of the LORD taking vengeance against his enemies.

7"Before the birth pains even begin, Jerusalem gives birth to a son. 8Who has ever seen or heard of anything as strange as this? Has a nation ever been born in a single day? Has a country ever come forth in a mere moment? But by the time Jerusalem's* birth pains begin, the baby will be born; the nation will come forth. 9Would I ever bring this nation to the point of birth and then not deliver it?" asks the LORD. "No! I would never keep this nation from being born," says your God.

10"Rejoice with Jerusalem! Be glad with her, all you who love her and mourn for her. 11Delight in Jerusalem! Drink deeply of her glory even as an infant drinks at its mother's generous breasts. 12Peace and prosperity will overflow Jerusalem like a river," says the LORD. "The wealth of the nations will flow to her. Her children will be nursed at her breasts, carried in her arms, and treated with love. 13I will comfort you there as a child is comforted by its mother."

14When you see these things, your heart will rejoice. Vigorous health will be yours! Everyone will see the good hand of the LORD on his people—and his anger against his enemies. 15See, the LORD is coming with fire, and his swift chariots of destruction roar like a whirlwind. He will bring punishment with the fury of his anger and the flaming fire of his hot rebuke. [16]The LORD will punish the world by fire and by his sword, and many will be killed by the LORD.

[17]"Those who 'purify' themselves in a sacred garden, feasting on pork and rats and other forbidden meats, will come to a terrible end," says the LORD. [18]"I can see what they are doing, and I know what they are thinking. So I will gather all nations and peoples together, and they will see my glory. [19]I will perform a sign among them. And I will send those who survive to be messengers to the nations—to Tarshish, to the Libyans* and Lydians* (who are famous as archers), to Tubal and Greece,* and to all the lands beyond the sea that have not heard of my fame or seen my glory. There they will declare my glory to the nations. [20]They will bring the remnant of your people back from every nation. They will bring them to my holy mountain in Jerusalem as an offering to the LORD. They will ride on horses, in chariots and wagons, and on mules and camels," says the LORD. [21]"And I will appoint some of those who return to be my priests and Levites. I, the LORD, have spoken!

[22]"As surely as my new heavens and earth will remain, so will you always be my people, with a name that will never disappear," says the LORD. [23]"All humanity will come to worship me from week to week and from month to month. [24]And as they go out, they will see the dead bodies of those who have rebelled against me. For the worms that devour them will never die, and the fire that burns them will never go out. All who pass by will view them with utter horror."

66:19a As in some Greek manuscripts, which read *Put* [Libya]; Hebrew reads *Pul.* **66:19b** Hebrew *Lud.* **66:19c** Hebrew *Javan.*

Jeremiah

CHAPTER 1

These are the words of Jeremiah son of Hilkiah, one of the priests from Anathoth, a town in the land of Benjamin. ²The LORD first gave messages to Jeremiah during the thirteenth year of King Josiah's reign in Judah.* ³He continued to give messages throughout the reign of Josiah's son, King Jehoiakim, until the eleventh year of King Zedekiah's reign in Judah. In August of that year,* the people of Jerusalem were taken away as captives.

Jeremiah's Call and First Visions

⁴The LORD gave me a message. He said, ⁵"I knew you before I formed you in your mother's womb. Before you were born I set you apart and appointed you as my spokesman to the world."

⁶"O Sovereign LORD," I said, "I can't speak for you! I'm too young!"

⁷"Don't say that," the LORD replied, "for you must go wherever I send you and say whatever I tell you. ⁸And don't be afraid of the people, for I will be with you and take care of you. I, the LORD, have spoken!"

⁹Then the LORD touched my mouth and said, "See, I have put my words in your mouth! ¹⁰Today I appoint you to stand up against nations and kingdoms. You are to uproot some and tear them down, to destroy and overthrow them. You are to build others up and plant them."

¹¹Then the LORD said to me, "Look, Jeremiah! What do you see?"

And I replied, "I see a branch from an almond tree."

¹²And the LORD said, "That's right, and it means that I am watching,* and I will surely carry out my threats of punishment."

¹³Then the LORD spoke to me again and asked, "What do you see now?"

And I replied, "I see a pot of boiling water, tipping from the north."

¹⁴"Yes," the LORD said, "for terror from the north will boil out on the people of this land. ¹⁵Listen! I am calling the armies of the kingdoms of the north to come to Jerusalem. They will set their thrones at the gates of the city. They will attack its walls and all the other towns of Judah. ¹⁶I will pronounce judgment on my people for all their evil—for deserting me and worshiping other gods. Yes, they worship idols that they themselves have made!

¹⁷"Get up and get dressed. Go out, and tell them whatever I tell you to say. Do not be afraid of them, or I will make you look foolish in front of them. ¹⁸For see, today I have made you immune to their attacks. You are strong like a fortified city that cannot be captured, like an iron pillar or a bronze wall. None of the kings, officials, priests, or people of Judah will be able to stand against you. ¹⁹They will try, but they will fail. For I am with you, and I will take care of you. I, the LORD, have spoken!"

CHAPTER 2

The LORD's Case against His People

The LORD gave me another message. He said, ²"Go and shout in Jerusalem's streets: 'This is what the LORD says: I remember how eager you were to please me as a young bride long ago, how you loved me and followed me even through the barren wilderness. ³In those days Israel was holy to the LORD, the first of my children.* All who harmed my people were

---

1:2 The thirteenth year of Josiah's reign was 627 B.C.   1:3 Hebrew In the fifth month, of the Hebrew calendar. A number of events in Jeremiah can be cross-checked with dates in surviving Babylonian records and related accurately to our modern calendar. This month in the eleventh year of Zedekiah's reign occurred in August and September 586 B.C. Also see 52:12 and the note there.   1:12 The Hebrew word for "watching" sounds like the word for "almond tree."   2:3 Hebrew the firstfruits of his harvest.

considered guilty, and disaster fell upon them. I, the LORD, have spoken!' "

4Listen to the word of the LORD, people of Jacob—all you families of Israel! 5This is what the LORD says: "What sin did your ancestors find in me that led them to stray so far? They worshiped foolish idols, only to become foolish themselves. 6They did not ask, 'Where is the LORD who brought us safely out of Egypt and led us through the barren wilderness—a land of deserts and pits, of drought and death, where no one lives or even travels?'

7"And when I brought you into a fruitful land to enjoy its bounty and goodness, you defiled my land and corrupted the inheritance I had promised you. 8The priests did not ask, 'Where is the LORD?' The judges ignored me, the rulers turned against me, and the prophets spoke in the name of Baal, wasting their time on nonsense. 9Therefore, I will bring my case against you and will keep on accusing you, even against your children's children in the years to come. I, the LORD, have spoken!

10"Go west to the land of Cyprus*; go east to the land of Kedar. Think about what you see there. See if anyone has ever heard of anything as strange as this. 11Has any nation ever exchanged its gods for another god, even though its gods are nothing? Yet my people have exchanged their glorious God* for worthless idols! 12The heavens are shocked at such a thing and shrink back in horror and dismay, says the LORD. 13For my people have done two evil things: They have forsaken me—the fountain of living water. And they have dug for themselves cracked cisterns that can hold no water at all!

The Results of Israel's Sin

14"Why has Israel become a nation of slaves? Why has she been carried away as plunder? 15Lions have roared against her. The land has been destroyed, and the cities are now in ruins. No one lives in them anymore. 16Egyptians, marching from their cities of Memphis* and Tahpanhes, have utterly destroyed Israel's glory and power. 17And you have brought this on yourselves by rebelling against the LORD your God when he wanted to lead you and show you the way! 18"What have you gained by your alliances with Egypt and Assyria? What good to you are the waters of the Nile* and the Euphrates*? 19Your own wickedness will punish you. You will see what an evil, bitter thing it is to forsake the LORD

your God, having no fear of him. I, the Lord, the LORD Almighty, have spoken! 20Long ago I broke your yoke and tore away the chains of your slavery, but still you would not obey me. On every hill and under every green tree, you have prostituted yourselves by bowing down to idols.

21"How could this happen? When I planted you, I chose a vine of the purest stock—the very best. How did you grow into this corrupt wild vine? 22No amount of soap or lye can make you clean. You are stained with guilt that cannot be washed away. I, the Sovereign LORD, have spoken!

Israel, an Unfaithful Wife

23"You say, 'That's not true! We haven't worshiped the images of Baal!' But how can you say that? Go and look in any valley in the land! Face the awful sins you have done. You are like a restless female camel, desperate for a male! 24You are like a wild donkey, sniffing the wind at mating time. Who can restrain your lust? Those who desire you do not even need to search, for you come running to them! 25Why do you refuse to turn from all this running after other gods? But you say, 'Don't waste your breath. I have fallen in love with these foreign gods, and I can't stop loving them now!'

26"Like a thief, Israel feels shame only when she gets caught. Kings, officials, priests, and prophets—all are alike in this. 27To an image carved from a piece of wood they say, 'You are my father.' To an idol chiseled out of stone they say, 'You are my mother.' They turn their backs on me, but in times of trouble they cry out for me to save them! 28Why don't you call on these gods you have made? When danger comes, let them save you if they can! For you have as many gods as there are cities and towns in Judah. 29Why do you accuse me of doing wrong? You are the ones who have rebelled, says the LORD. 30I have punished your children, but it did them no good. They still refuse to obey. You yourselves have killed your prophets as a lion kills its prey.

31"O my people, listen to the words of the LORD! Have I been like a desert to Israel? Have I been to them a land of darkness? Why then do my people say, 'At last we are free from God! We won't have anything to do with him anymore!' 32Does a young woman forget her jewelry? Does a bride hide her wedding dress? No! Yet for years on end my people have forgotten me.

33"How you plot and scheme to win your lovers. The most experienced prostitute could

2:10 Hebrew *Kittim.* 2:11 Hebrew *their Glory.* 2:16 Hebrew *Noph.* 2:18a Hebrew *of Shihor,* a branch of the Nile River. 2:18b Hebrew *the river.*

learn from you! 34Your clothing is stained with the blood of the innocent and the poor. You killed them even though they didn't break into your houses! 35And yet you say, 'I haven't done anything wrong. Surely he isn't angry with me!' Now I will punish you severely because you claim you have not sinned.

36"First here, then there—you flit from one ally to another asking for help. But your new friends in Egypt will let you down, just as Assyria did before. 37In despair, you will be led into exile with your hands on your heads, for the LORD has rejected the nations you trust. You will not succeed despite their help.

CHAPTER 3

"If a man divorces a woman and she marries someone else, he is not to take her back again, for that would surely corrupt the land. But you have prostituted yourself with many lovers, says the LORD. Yet I am still calling you to come back to me. 2"Look all around you. Is there anywhere in the entire land where you have not been defiled by your adulteries? You sit like a prostitute beside the road waiting for a client. You sit alone like a nomad in the desert. You have polluted the land with your prostitution and wickedness. 3That is why even the spring rains have failed. For you are a prostitute and are completely unashamed. 4Yet you say to me, 'Father, you have been my guide since the days of my youth. 5Surely you won't be angry about such a little thing! Surely you can forget it!' So you talk, and keep right on doing all the evil you can."

Judah Follows Israel's Example

6During the reign of King Josiah, the LORD said to me, "Have you seen what fickle Israel does? Like a wife who commits adultery, Israel has worshiped other gods on every hill and under every green tree. 7I thought that after she had done all this she would return to me. But she did not come back. And though her faithless sister Judah saw this, 8she paid no attention. She saw that I had divorced faithless Israel and sent her away. But now Judah, too, has left me and given herself to prostitution. 9Israel treated it all so lightly—she thought nothing of committing adultery by worshiping idols made of wood and stone. So now the land has been greatly defiled. 10But in spite of all this, her faithless sister Judah has never sincerely returned to me. She has only pretended to be sorry," says the LORD.

Hope for Wayward Israel

11Then the LORD said to me, "Even faithless Israel is less guilty than treacherous Judah! 12Therefore, go and say these words to Israel,* 'This is what the LORD says: O Israel, my faithless people, come home to me again, for I am merciful. I will not be angry with you forever. 13Only acknowledge your guilt. Admit that you rebelled against the LORD your God and committed adultery against him by worshiping idols under every green tree. Confess that you refused to follow me. I, the LORD, have spoken!'"

14"Return home, you wayward children," says the LORD, "for I am your husband. I will bring you again to the land of Israel*—one from here and two from there, from wherever you are scattered. 15And I will give you leaders after my own heart, who will guide you with knowledge and understanding.

16"And when your land is once more filled with people," says the LORD, "you will no longer wish for 'the good old days' when you possessed the Ark of the LORD's covenant. Those days will not be missed or even thought about, and there will be no need to rebuild the Ark. 17In that day Jerusalem will be known as The Throne of the LORD. All nations will come there to honor the LORD. They will no longer stubbornly follow their own evil desires. 18In those days the people of Judah and Israel will return together from exile in the north. They will return to the land I gave their ancestors as an inheritance forever.

19"I thought to myself, 'I would love to treat you as my own children!' I wanted nothing more than to give you this beautiful land—the finest inheritance in the world. I looked forward to your calling me 'Father,' and I thought you would never turn away from me again. 20But you have betrayed me, you people of Israel! You have been like a faithless wife who leaves her husband," says the LORD.

21Voices are heard high on the windswept mountains, the weeping and pleading of Israel's people. For they have forgotten the LORD their God and wandered far from his ways.

22"My wayward children," says the LORD, "come back to me, and I will heal your wayward hearts."

"Yes, we will come," the people reply, "for you are the LORD our God. 23Our worship of idols and our religious orgies on the hills and mountains are completely false. Only in the LORD our God will Israel ever find salvation.

3:12 Hebrew *toward the north*. 3:14 Hebrew *to Zion*.

24From childhood we have watched as everything our ancestors worked for—their flocks and herds, their sons and daughters—was squandered on a delusion. 25Let us now lie down in shame and dishonor, for we and our ancestors have always sinned against the LORD our God. We have never obeyed him."

CHAPTER 4

"O Israel, come back to me," says the LORD. "If you will throw away your detestable idols and go astray no more, 2and if you will swear by my name alone, and begin to live good, honest lives and uphold justice, then you will be a blessing to the nations of the world, and all people will come and praise my name."

Coming Judgment against Judah

3This is what the LORD says to the people of Judah and Jerusalem: "Plow up the hard ground of your hearts! Do not waste your good seed among thorns. 4Cleanse your minds and hearts before the LORD, or my anger will burn like an unquenchable fire because of all your sins.

5"Shout to Jerusalem and to all Judah! Tell them to sound the alarm throughout the land: 'Run for your lives! Flee to the fortified cities!' 6Send a signal toward Jerusalem*: 'Flee now! Do not delay!' For I am bringing terrible destruction upon you from the north."

7A lion stalks from its den, a destroyer of nations. And it is headed for your land! Your towns will lie in ruins, empty of people. 8So put on clothes of mourning and weep with broken hearts, for the fierce anger of the LORD is still upon us.

9"In that day," says the LORD, "the king and the officials will tremble in fear. The priests and the prophets will be struck with horror."

10Then I said, "O Sovereign LORD, the people have been deceived by what you said, for you promised peace for Jerusalem. Yet the sword is even now poised to strike them dead!"

11The time is coming when the LORD will say to the people of Jerusalem, "A burning wind is blowing in from the desert. It is not a gentle breeze useful for winnowing grain. 12It is a roaring blast sent by me! Now I will pronounce your destruction!"

13Our enemy rushes down on us like a storm wind! His chariots are like whirlwinds; his horses are swifter than eagles. How terrible it will be! Our destruction is sure! 14O Jerusalem, cleanse your hearts that you may be saved. How

4:6 Hebrew *Zion*.

long will you harbor your evil thoughts? 15From Dan and the hill country of Ephraim, your destruction has been announced.

16"Warn the surrounding nations and announce to Jerusalem: 'The enemy is coming from a distant land, raising a battle cry against the towns of Judah. 17They surround Jerusalem like watchmen surrounding a field, for my people have rebelled against me,'" says the LORD. 18"Your own actions have brought this upon you. This punishment is a bitter dose of your own medicine. It has pierced you to the heart!"

Jeremiah Weeps for His People

19My heart, my heart—I writhe in pain! My heart pounds within me! I cannot be still. For I have heard the blast of enemy trumpets and the roar of their battle cries. 20Waves of destruction roll over the land, until it lies in complete desolation. Suddenly, every tent is destroyed; in a moment, every shelter is crushed. 21How long must this go on? How long must I be surrounded by war and death?

22"My people are foolish and do not know me," says the LORD. "They are senseless children who have no understanding. They are clever enough at doing wrong, but they have no talent at all for doing right!"

Jeremiah's Vision of Coming Disaster

23I looked at the earth, and it was empty and formless. I looked at the heavens, and there was no light. 24I looked at the mountains and hills, and they trembled and shook. 25I looked, and all the people were gone. All the birds of the sky had flown away. 26I looked, and the fertile fields had become a wilderness. The cities lay in ruins, crushed by the LORD's fierce anger.

27This is what the LORD says: "The whole land will be ruined, but I will not destroy it completely. 28The earth will mourn, the heavens will be draped in black, because of my decree against my people. I have made up my mind and will not change it."

29At the noise of marching armies, the people flee in terror from the cities. They hide in the bushes and run for the mountains. All the cities have been abandoned—not a person remains! 30What are you doing, you who have been plundered? Why do you dress up in your most beautiful clothing and jewelry? Why do you brighten your eyes with mascara? It will do you no good! Your allies despise you and will kill you.

³¹I hear a great cry, like that of a woman giving birth to her first child. It is the cry of Jerusalem's people* gasping for breath, pleading for help, prostrate before their murderers.

CHAPTER **5**

The Sins of Judah

"Run up and down every street in Jerusalem," says the LORD. "Look high and low; search throughout the city! If you can find even one person who is just and honest, I will not destroy the city. ²Even when they are under oath, saying, 'As surely as the LORD lives,' they all tell lies!"

³LORD, you are searching for honesty. You struck your people, but they paid no attention. You crushed them, but they refused to turn from sin. They are determined, with faces set like stone; they have refused to repent.

⁴Then I said, "But what can we expect from the poor and ignorant? They don't know the ways of the LORD. They don't understand what God expects of them. ⁵I will go and speak to their leaders. Surely they will know the LORD's ways and what God requires of them." But the leaders, too, had utterly rejected their God. ⁶So now a lion from the forest will attack them; a wolf from the desert will pounce on them. A leopard will lurk near their towns, tearing apart any who dare to venture out. For their rebellion is great, and their sins are many.

⁷"How can I pardon you? For even your children have turned from me. They have sworn by gods that are not gods at all! I fed my people until they were fully satisfied. But they thanked me by committing adultery and lining up at the city's brothels. ⁸They are well-fed, lusty stallions, each neighing for his neighbor's wife. ⁹Should I not punish them for this?" asks the LORD. "Should I not avenge myself against a nation such as this?

¹⁰"Go down the rows of the vineyards and destroy them, but leave a scattered few alive. Strip the branches from the vine, for they do not belong to the LORD. ¹¹The people of Israel and Judah are full of treachery against me," says the LORD. ¹²"They have lied about the LORD and have said, 'He won't bother us! No disasters will come upon us! There will be no war or famine! ¹³God's prophets are windbags full of words with no divine authority. Their predictions of disaster will fall on themselves!'"

¹⁴Therefore, this is what the LORD God Almighty says: "Because the people are talking like this, I will give you messages that will burn them up as if they were kindling wood. ¹⁵O Israel, I will bring a distant nation against you," says the LORD. "It is a mighty nation, an ancient nation, a people whose language you do not know, whose speech you cannot understand. ¹⁶Their weapons are deadly; their warriors are mighty. ¹⁷They will eat your harvests and your children's bread, your flocks of sheep and your herds of cattle. Yes, they will eat your grapes and figs. And they will destroy your fortified cities, which you think are so safe.

¹⁸"Yet even in those days I will not blot you out completely," says the LORD. ¹⁹"And when your people ask, 'Why is the LORD our God doing this to us?' you must reply, 'You rejected him and gave yourselves to foreign gods in your own land. Now you will serve foreigners in a land that is not your own.'

A Warning for God's People

²⁰"Make this announcement to Israel* and to Judah: ²¹Listen, you foolish and senseless people—who have eyes but do not see, who have ears but do not hear. ²²Do you have no respect for me? Why do you not tremble in my presence? I, the LORD, am the one who defines the ocean's sandy shoreline, an everlasting boundary that the waters cannot cross. The waves may toss and roar, but they can never pass the bounds I set.

²³"But my people have stubborn and rebellious hearts. They have turned against me and have chosen to practice idolatry. ²⁴They do not say from the heart, 'Let us live in awe of the LORD our God, for he gives us rain each spring and fall, assuring us of plentiful harvests.' ²⁵Your wickedness has deprived you of these wonderful blessings. Your sin has robbed you of all these good things.

²⁶"Among my people are wicked men who lie in wait for victims like a hunter hiding in a blind. They are continually setting traps for other people. ²⁷Like a cage filled with birds, their homes are filled with evil plots. And the result? Now they are great and rich. ²⁸They are well fed and well groomed, and there is no limit to their wicked deeds. They refuse justice to orphans and deny the rights of the poor. ²⁹Should I not punish them for this?" asks the LORD. "Should I not avenge myself against a nation such as this?

³⁰"A horrible and shocking thing has happened in this land—³¹the prophets give false prophecies, and the priests rule with an iron

4:31 Hebrew *the daughter of Zion.*   5:20 Hebrew *to the house of Jacob.*

hand. And worse yet, my people like it that way! But what will you do when the end comes?

CHAPTER 6
Jerusalem's Last Warning

"Run for your lives, you people of Benjamin! Flee from Jerusalem! Sound the alarm in Tekoa! Send up a signal at Beth-hakkerem! Warn everyone that a powerful army is coming from the north to destroy this nation. ²O Jerusalem,* you are my beautiful and delicate daughter—but I will destroy you! ³Enemy shepherds will surround you. They will set up camp around the city and divide your pastures for their flocks. ⁴They shout, 'Prepare for battle and attack at noon! But now the day is fading, and the evening shadows are falling. ⁵So let us attack by night and destroy her palaces!'"

⁶This is what the LORD Almighty says: "Cut down the trees for battering rams. Build ramps against the walls of Jerusalem. This is the city to be punished, for she is wicked through and through. ⁷She spouts evil like a fountain! Her streets echo with the sounds of violence and destruction. Her sickness and sores are ever before me. ⁸This is your last warning, Jerusalem! If you do not listen, I will empty the land."

⁹This is what the LORD Almighty says: "Disaster will fall upon you. Even the few who remain in Israel will be gleaned again, as when a harvester checks each vine a second time to pick the grapes that were missed."

Israel's Constant Rebellion

¹⁰To whom can I give warning? Who will listen when I speak? Their ears are closed, and they cannot hear. They scorn the word of the LORD. They don't want to listen at all. ¹¹So now I am filled with the LORD's fury. Yes, I am weary of holding it in!

"I will pour out my fury over Jerusalem, even on children playing in the streets, on gatherings of young men, and on husbands and wives and grandparents. ¹²Their homes will be turned over to their enemies, and so will their fields and their wives. For I will punish the people of this land," says the LORD.

¹³"From the least to the greatest, they trick others to get what does not belong to them. Yes, even my prophets and priests are like that! ¹⁴They offer superficial treatments for my people's mortal wound. They give assurances of peace when all is war. ¹⁵Are they ashamed when they do these disgusting things? No, not at all— they don't even blush! Therefore, they will lie among the slaughtered. They will be humbled beneath my punishing anger," says the LORD.

Israel Rejects the LORD's Way

¹⁶So now the LORD says, "Stop right where you are! Look for the old, godly way, and walk in it. Travel its path, and you will find rest for your souls. But you reply, 'No, that's not the road we want!' ¹⁷I set watchmen over you who said, 'Listen for the sound of the trumpet!' But you replied, 'No! We won't pay attention!'

¹⁸"Therefore, listen to this, all you nations. Take note of my people's condition. ¹⁹Listen, all the earth! I will bring disaster upon my people. It is the fruit of their own sin because they refuse to listen to me. They have rejected all my instructions. ²⁰There is no use now in offering me sweet incense from Sheba. Keep your expensive perfumes! I cannot accept your burnt offerings. Your sacrifices have no sweet fragrance for me."

²¹Therefore, this is what the LORD says: "I will put obstacles in my people's path. Fathers and sons will both fall over them. Neighbors and friends will collapse together."

An Invasion from the North

²²This is what the LORD says: "See a great army marching from the north! A great nation is rising against you from far-off lands. ²³They are fully armed for slaughter. They are cruel and show no mercy. As they ride forward, the noise of their army is like a roaring sea. They are marching in battle formation to destroy you, Jerusalem.*"

²⁴We have heard reports about the enemy, and we are weak with fright. Fear and pain have gripped us, like that of a woman about to give birth. ²⁵Don't go out to the fields! Don't travel the roads! The enemy is everywhere, and they are ready to kill. We are terrorized at every turn! ²⁶Now my people, dress yourselves in sackcloth, and sit among the ashes. Mourn and weep bitterly, as for the loss of an only son. For suddenly, the destroying armies will be upon you!

²⁷"Jeremiah, I have made you a tester of metals, that you may determine the quality of my people. ²⁸Are they not the worst of rebels, full of slander? They are as insolent as bronze, as hard and cruel as iron. All of them lead others into corruption. ²⁹The bellows blow fiercely. The refining fire grows hotter. But it will

6:2 Hebrew *Zion*.   6:23 Hebrew *daughter of Zion*.

never purify and cleanse them because there is no purity in them to refine. ³⁰I will label them 'Rejected Silver' because I, the LORD, am discarding them."

CHAPTER **7**
Jeremiah Speaks at the Temple
The LORD gave another message to Jeremiah. He said, ²"Go to the entrance of the LORD's Temple, and give this message to the people: 'O Judah, listen to this message from the LORD! Listen to it, all of you who worship here! ³The LORD Almighty, the God of Israel, says: Even now, if you quit your evil ways, I will let you stay in your own land. ⁴But do not be fooled by those who repeatedly promise your safety because the Temple of the LORD is here. ⁵I will be merciful only if you stop your wicked thoughts and deeds and are fair to others; ⁶and if you stop exploiting foreigners, orphans, and widows; and if you stop your murdering; and if you stop worshiping idols as you now do to your own harm. ⁷Then I will let you stay in this land that I gave to your ancestors to keep forever.

⁸" 'Do you think that because the Temple is here you will never suffer? Don't fool yourselves! ⁹Do you really think you can steal, murder, commit adultery, lie, and worship Baal and all those other new gods of yours, ¹⁰and then come here and stand before me in my Temple and chant, "We are safe!"—only to go right back to all those evils again? ¹¹Do you think this Temple, which honors my name, is a den of thieves? I see all the evil going on there, says the LORD.

¹²" 'Go to the place at Shiloh where I once put the Tabernacle to honor my name. See what I did there because of all the wickedness of my people, the Israelites. ¹³While you were doing these wicked things, says the LORD, I spoke to you about it repeatedly, but you would not listen. I called out to you, but you refused to answer. ¹⁴So just as I destroyed Shiloh, I will now destroy this Temple that was built to honor my name, this Temple that you trust for help, this place that I gave to you and your ancestors. ¹⁵And I will send you into exile, just as I did your relatives, the people of Israel.*'

Judah's Persistent Idolatry
¹⁶"Pray no more for these people, Jeremiah. Do not weep or pray for them, and don't beg me to help them, for I will not listen to you. ¹⁷Do you not see what they are doing throughout the

7:15 Hebrew *of Ephraim,* referring to the northern kingdom of Israel.

towns of Judah and in the streets of Jerusalem? ¹⁸No wonder I am so angry! Watch how the children gather wood and the fathers build sacrificial fires. See how the women knead dough and make cakes to offer to the Queen of Heaven. And they give drink offerings to their other idol gods! ¹⁹Am I the one they are hurting?" asks the LORD. "Most of all, they hurt themselves, to their own shame."

²⁰So the Sovereign LORD says: "I will pour out my terrible fury on this place. Its people, animals, trees, and crops will be consumed by the unquenchable fire of my anger."

²¹This is what the LORD Almighty, the God of Israel, says: "Away with your burnt offerings and sacrifices! Eat them yourselves! ²²When I led your ancestors out of Egypt, it was not burnt offerings and sacrifices I wanted from them. ²³This is what I told them: 'Obey me, and I will be your God, and you will be my people. Only do as I say, and all will be well!'

²⁴"But my people would not listen to me. They kept on doing whatever they wanted, following the stubborn desires of their evil hearts. They went backward instead of forward. ²⁵From the day your ancestors left Egypt until now, I have continued to send my prophets—day in and day out. ²⁶But my people have not listened to me or even tried to hear. They have been stubborn and sinful—even worse than their ancestors.

²⁷"Tell them all this, but do not expect them to listen. Shout out your warnings, but do not expect them to respond. ²⁸Say to them, 'This is the nation whose people will not obey the LORD their God and who refuse to be taught. Truth has vanished from among them; it is no longer heard on their lips. ²⁹O Jerusalem, shave your head in mourning, and weep alone on the mountains. For the LORD has rejected and forsaken this generation that has provoked his fury.'

The Valley of Slaughter
³⁰"The people of Judah have sinned before my very eyes," says the LORD. "They have set up their abominable idols right in my own Temple, defiling it. ³¹They have built the pagan shrines of Topheth in the valley of the son of Hinnom, where they sacrifice their little sons and daughters in the fire. I have never commanded such a horrible deed; it never even crossed my mind to command such a thing! ³²So beware, for the time is coming," says the LORD, "when that place

will no longer be called Topheth or the valley of the son of Hinnom, but the Valley of Slaughter. They will bury so many bodies in Topheth that there won't be room for all the graves. ³³The corpses of my people will be food for the vultures and wild animals, and no one will be left to scare them away. ³⁴I will put an end to the happy singing and laughter in the streets of Jerusalem. The joyful voices of bridegrooms and brides will no longer be heard in the towns of Judah. The land will lie in complete desolation.

CHAPTER 8

"In that day," says the LORD, "the enemy will break open the graves of the kings and officials of Judah, and the graves of the priests, prophets, and common people. ²They will dig out their bones and spread them out on the ground before the sun, moon, and stars—the gods my people have loved, served, and worshiped. Their bones will not be gathered up again or buried but will be scattered on the ground like dung. ³And the people of this evil nation who survive will wish to die rather than live where I will send them. I, the LORD Almighty, have spoken!

Deception by False Prophets

⁴"Jeremiah, say to the people, 'This is what the LORD says: When people fall down, don't they get up again? When they start down the wrong road and discover their mistake, don't they turn back? ⁵Then why do these people keep going along their self-destructive path, refusing to turn back, even though I have warned them? ⁶I listen to their conversations, and what do I hear? Is anyone sorry for sin? Does anyone say, "What a terrible thing I have done"? No! All are running down the path of sin as swiftly as a horse rushing into battle! ⁷The stork knows the time of her migration, as do the turtledove, the swallow, and the crane.* They all return at the proper time each year. But not my people! They do not know what the LORD requires of them.

⁸"'How can you say, "We are wise because we have the law of the LORD," when your teachers have twisted it so badly? ⁹These wise teachers will be shamed by exile for their sin, for they have rejected the word of the LORD. Are they so wise after all? ¹⁰I will give their wives and their farms to others. From the least to the greatest, they trick others to get what does not belong to them. Yes, even my prophets and priests are like that. ¹¹They offer superficial treatments for my people's mortal wound. They give assurances of peace when all is war. ¹²Are they ashamed when they do these disgusting things? No, not at all—they don't even blush! Therefore, they will lie among the slaughtered. They will be humbled when they are punished, says the LORD. ¹³I will take away their rich harvests of figs and grapes. Their fruit trees will all die. All the good things I prepared for them will soon be gone. I, the LORD, have spoken!'

¹⁴"Then the people will say, 'Why should we wait here to die? Come, let's go to the fortified cities to die there. For the LORD our God has decreed our destruction and has given us a cup of poison to drink because we sinned against the LORD. ¹⁵We hoped for peace, but no peace came. We hoped for a time of healing, but found only terror. ¹⁶The snorting of the enemies' warhorses can be heard all the way from the land of Dan in the north! The whole land trembles at the approach of the terrible army, for it is coming to devour the land and everything in it—cities and people alike.'

¹⁷"I will send these enemy troops among you like poisonous snakes you cannot charm," says the LORD. "No matter what you do, they will bite you, and you will die."

Jeremiah Weeps for Sinful Judah

¹⁸My grief is beyond healing; my heart is broken. ¹⁹Listen to the weeping of my people; it can be heard all across the land.

"Has the LORD abandoned Jerusalem*?" the people ask. "Is her King no longer there?"

"Oh, why have they angered me with their carved idols and worthless gods?" asks the LORD.

²⁰"The harvest is finished, and the summer is gone," the people cry, "yet we are not saved!"

²¹I weep for the hurt of my people. I am stunned and silent, mute with grief. ²²Is there no medicine in Gilead? Is there no physician there? Why is there no healing for the wounds of my people?

CHAPTER 9

Oh, that my eyes were a fountain of tears; I would weep forever! I would sob day and night for all my people who have been slaughtered. ²Oh, that I could go away and forget them and live in a shack in the desert, for they are all adulterous and treacherous.

Judgment for Disobedience

³"My people bend their tongues like bows to shoot lies. They refuse to stand up for the truth.

8:7 The identification of some of these birds is uncertain. 8:19 Hebrew *Zion.*

And they only go from bad to worse! They care nothing for me," says the LORD.

4 "Beware of your neighbor! Beware of your brother! They all take advantage of one another and spread their slanderous lies. 5They all fool and defraud each other; no one tells the truth. With practiced tongues they tell lies; they wear themselves out with all their sinning. 6They pile lie upon lie and utterly refuse to come to me," says the LORD.

7Therefore, the LORD Almighty says, "See, I will melt them in a crucible and test them like metal. What else can I do with them? 8For their tongues aim lies like poisoned arrows. They promise peace to their neighbors while planning to kill them. 9Should I not punish them for this?" asks the LORD. "Should I not avenge myself against a nation such as this?"

10I will weep for the mountains and wail for the desert pastures. For they are desolate and empty of life; the lowing of cattle is heard no more; the birds and wild animals all have fled.

11 "I will make Jerusalem into a heap of ruins," says the LORD. "It will be a place haunted by jackals. The towns of Judah will be ghost towns, with no one living in them."

12Who is wise enough to understand all this? Who has been instructed by the LORD and can explain it to others? Why has the land been ruined so completely that no one even dares to travel through it?

13The LORD replies, "This has happened because my people have abandoned the instructions I gave them; they have refused to obey my law. 14Instead, they have stubbornly followed their own desires and worshiped the images of Baal, as their ancestors taught them. 15So now, listen to what the LORD Almighty, the God of Israel, says: Look! I will feed them with bitterness and give them poison to drink. 16I will scatter them around the world, and they will be strangers in distant lands. Their enemies will chase them with the sword until I have destroyed them completely."

Weeping in Jerusalem

17This is what the LORD Almighty says: "Think about what is going on! Call for the mourners to come. 18Quick! Begin your weeping! Let the tears flow from your eyes. 19Hear the people of Jerusalem* crying in despair, 'We are ruined! Disaster has come upon us! We must leave our land, because our homes have been torn down.'"

20Listen, you women, to the words of the

LORD; open your ears to what he has to say. Teach your daughters to wail; teach one another how to lament. 21For death has crept in through our windows and has entered our mansions. It has killed off the flower of our youth: Children no longer play in the streets, and young men no longer gather in the squares. 22And the LORD says, "Bodies will be scattered across the fields like dung, or like bundles of grain after the harvest. No one will be left to bury them."

23This is what the LORD says: "Let not the wise man gloat in his wisdom, or the mighty man in his might, or the rich man in his riches. 24Let them boast in this alone: that they truly know me and understand that I am the LORD who is just and righteous, whose love is unfailing, and that I delight in these things. I, the LORD, have spoken!

25"A time is coming," says the LORD, "when I will punish all those who are circumcised in body but not in spirit—26the Egyptians, Edomites, Ammonites, Moabites, the people who live in distant places,* and yes, even the people of Judah. Like all these pagan nations, the people of Israel also have uncircumcised hearts."

CHAPTER 10

Idolatry Brings Destruction

Hear the word of the LORD, O Israel! 2This is what the LORD says: "Do not act like other nations who try to read their future in the stars. Do not be afraid of their predictions, even though other nations are terrified by them. 3Their ways are futile and foolish. They cut down a tree and carve an idol. 4They decorate it with gold and silver and then fasten it securely with hammer and nails so it won't fall over. 5There stands their god like a helpless scarecrow in a garden! It cannot speak, and it needs to be carried because it cannot walk. Do not be afraid of such gods, for they can neither harm you nor do you any good."

6LORD, there is no one like you! For you are great, and your name is full of power. 7Who would not fear you, O King of nations? That title belongs to you alone! Among all the wise people of the earth and in all the kingdoms of the world, there is no one like you.

8The wisest of people who worship idols are stupid and foolish. The things they worship are made of wood! 9They bring beaten sheets of silver from Tarshish and gold from Uphaz, and they give these materials to skillful craftsmen who make their idols. Then they dress these

9:19 Hebrew *Zion.*   9:26 Or *the people who clip the corners of their hair.*

gods in royal purple robes made by expert tailors. 10But the LORD is the only true God, the living God. He is the everlasting King! The whole earth trembles at his anger. The nations hide before his wrath.

11Say this to those who worship other gods: "Your so-called gods, who did not make the heavens and earth, will vanish from the earth."*

12 But God made the earth by his power,
and he preserves it by his wisdom.
He has stretched out the heavens
by his understanding.
13 When he speaks, there is thunder in the
heavens.
He causes the clouds to rise over the earth.
He sends the lightning with the rain
and releases the wind from his storehouses.
14 Compared to him, all people are foolish
and have no knowledge at all!
They make idols, but the idols will disgrace
their makers,
for they are frauds.
They have no life or power in them.
15 Idols are worthless; they are lies!
The time is coming when they will all be
destroyed.
16 But the God of Israel* is no idol!
He is the Creator of everything that exists,
including Israel, his own special
possession.
The LORD Almighty is his name!

The Coming Destruction

17"Pack your bag and prepare to leave; the siege is about to begin," 18says the LORD. "For suddenly, I will fling you from this land and pour great troubles upon you. At last you will feel my anger."

19My wound is desperate, and my grief is great. My sickness is incurable, but I must bear it. 20My home is gone, and no one is left to help me rebuild it. My children have been taken away, and I will never see them again. 21The shepherds of my people have lost their senses. They no longer follow the LORD or ask what he wants of them. Therefore, they fail completely, and their flocks are scattered. 22Listen! Hear the terrifying roar of great armies as they roll down from the north. The towns of Judah will be destroyed and will become a haunt for jackals.

Jeremiah's Prayer

23I know, LORD, that a person's life is not his own. No one is able to plan his own course. 24So correct me, LORD, but please be gentle. Do not correct me in anger, for I would die. 25Pour out your wrath on the nations that refuse to recognize you—on nations that do not call upon your name. For they have utterly devoured your people Israel,* making the land a desolate wilderness.

CHAPTER 11
Judah's Broken Covenant

The LORD gave another message to Jeremiah. He said, 2"Remind the people of Judah and Jerusalem about the terms of their covenant with me. 3Say to them, 'This is what the LORD, the God of Israel, says: Cursed is anyone who does not obey the terms of my covenant! 4For I said to your ancestors when I brought them out of slavery in Egypt, "If you obey me and do whatever I command you, then you will be my people, and I will be your God." 5I said this so I could keep my promise to your ancestors to give you a land flowing with milk and honey—the land you live in today.'"

Then I replied, "So be it,* LORD!"

6Then the LORD said, "Broadcast this message in the streets of Jerusalem. Go from town to town throughout the land and say, 'Remember the covenant your ancestors made, and do everything they promised. 7For I solemnly warned your ancestors when I brought them out of Egypt, repeating over and over again to this day: "Obey me!" 8But your ancestors did not pay any attention; they would not even listen. Instead, they stubbornly followed their own evil desires. And because they refused to obey, I brought upon them all the curses described in our covenant.'"

9Again the LORD spoke to me and said, "I have discovered a conspiracy against me among the people of Judah and Jerusalem. 10They have returned to the sins of their forefathers. They have refused to listen to me and are worshiping idols. Israel and Judah have both broken the covenant I made with their ancestors. 11Therefore, says the LORD, I am going to bring calamity upon them, and they will not escape. Though they beg for mercy, I will not listen to their cries. 12Then the people of Judah and Jerusalem will pray to their idols and offer incense before them. But the idols will not save them when disaster strikes! 13Look now, people of Judah, you have as many gods as there are cities and towns. Your altars of shame—altars for burning incense to your god Baal—are along every street in Jerusalem.

10:11 The original text of this verse is in Aramaic. 10:16 Hebrew *the Portion of Jacob.* 10:25 Hebrew *Jacob.* 11:5 Hebrew *Amen.*

14 "Pray no more for these people, Jeremiah. Do not weep or pray for them, for I will not listen to them when they cry out to me in distress. 15What right do my beloved people have to come to my Temple, where they have done so many immoral things? Can their sacrifices avert their destruction? They actually rejoice in doing evil! 16 "I, the LORD, once called them a thriving olive tree, beautiful to see and full of good fruit. But now I have sent the fury of their enemies to burn them with fire, leaving them charred and broken. 17I, the LORD Almighty, who planted this olive tree, have ordered it destroyed. For the people of Israel and Judah have done evil, provoking my anger by offering incense to Baal."

A Plot against Jeremiah
18Then the LORD told me about the plots my enemies were making against me. 19I had been as unaware as a lamb on the way to its slaughter. I had no idea that they were planning to kill me! "Let's destroy this man and all his words," they said. "Let's kill him, so his name will be forgotten forever."

20O LORD Almighty, you are just, and you examine the deepest thoughts of hearts and minds. Let me see your vengeance against them, for I have committed my cause to you.

21The men of Anathoth wanted me dead. They said they would kill me if I did not stop speaking in the LORD's name. 22So this is what the LORD Almighty says about them: "I will punish them! Their young men will die in battle, and their little boys and girls will starve. 23Not one of these plotters from Anathoth will survive, for I will bring disaster upon them when their time of punishment comes."

CHAPTER 12
Jeremiah Questions the LORD's Justice
LORD, you always give me justice when I bring a case before you. Now let me bring you this complaint: Why are the wicked so prosperous? Why are evil people so happy? 2You have planted them, and they have taken root and prospered. Your name is on their lips, but in their hearts they give you no credit at all. 3But as for me, LORD, you know my heart. You see me and test my thoughts. Drag these people away like helpless sheep to be butchered! Set them aside to be slaughtered!

4How long must this land weep? Even the grass in the fields has withered. The wild animals and birds have disappeared because of the evil in the land. Yet the people say, "The LORD won't do anything!"

The LORD's Reply to Jeremiah
5Then the LORD replied to me, "If racing against mere men makes you tired, how will you race against horses? If you stumble and fall on open ground, what will you do in the thickets near the Jordan? 6Even your own brothers, members of your own family, have turned on you. They have plotted, raising a cry against you. Do not trust them, no matter how pleasantly they speak.

7"I have abandoned my people, my special possession. I have surrendered my dearest ones to their enemies. 8My chosen people have roared at me like a lion of the forest, so I have treated them as though I hated them. 9My chosen people have become as disgusting to me as a vulture. And indeed, they are surrounded by vultures. Bring on the wild beasts to pick their corpses clean!

10 "Many rulers have ravaged my vineyard, trampling down the vines and turning all its beauty into a barren wilderness. 11They have made it an empty wasteland; I hear its mournful cry. The whole land is desolate, and no one even cares. 12Destroying armies plunder the land. The sword of the LORD kills people from one end of the nation to the other. No one will escape! 13My people have planted wheat but are harvesting thorns. They have worked hard, but it has done them no good. They will harvest a crop of shame, for the fierce anger of the LORD is upon them."

A Message for Israel's Neighbors
14Now this is what the LORD says: "As for all the evil nations reaching out for the inheritance I gave my people Israel, I will uproot them from their lands just as Judah will be uprooted from hers. 15But afterward I will return and have compassion on all of them. I will bring them home to their own lands again, each nation to its own inheritance. 16And if these nations quickly learn the ways of my people, and if they learn to swear by my name, saying, 'As surely as the LORD lives' (just as they taught my people to swear by the name of Baal), then they will be given a place among my people. 17But any nation who refuses to obey me will be uprooted and destroyed. I, the LORD, have spoken!"

CHAPTER 13
Jeremiah's Linen Belt
This is what the LORD said to me: "Go and buy a linen belt and put it around your waist, but do not wash it." 2So I bought the belt as the LORD directed me and put it around my waist. 3Then the LORD

gave me another message: 4"Take the linen belt you are wearing, and go to the Euphrates River.* Hide it there in a hole in the rocks." 5So I went and hid it at the Euphrates as the LORD had instructed me.

6A long time afterward, the LORD said to me, "Go back to the Euphrates and get the linen belt that I told you to hide there." 7So I went to the Euphrates and dug it out of the hole where I had hidden it. But now it was mildewed and falling apart. The belt was useless.

8Then I received this message from the LORD: 9"The LORD says: This illustrates how I will rot away the pride of Judah and Jerusalem. 10These wicked people refuse to listen to me. They stubbornly follow their own desires and worship idols. Therefore, they will become like this linen belt—good for nothing! 11As a belt clings to a person's waist, so I created Judah and Israel to cling to me," says the LORD. "They were to be my people, my pride, my glory—an honor to my name. But they would not listen to me.

12"So tell them, 'The LORD, the God of Israel, says: All your wineskins will be full of wine.' And they will reply, 'Of course, you don't need to tell us how prosperous we will be!' 13Then tell them, 'No, this is what the LORD means: I will make everyone in this land so confused that they will seem drunk—from the king sitting on David's throne and from the priests and the prophets, right on down to the common people. 14I will smash them one against the other, even parents against children, says the LORD. I will not let my pity or mercy or compassion keep me from destroying them.'"

A Warning against Pride

15Listen! Do not be proud, for the LORD has spoken. 16Give glory to the LORD your God before it is too late. Acknowledge him before he brings darkness upon you, causing you to stumble and fall on the dark mountains. For then, when you look for light, you will find only terrible darkness. 17And if you still refuse to listen, I will weep alone because of your pride. My eyes will overflow with tears because the LORD's flock will be led away into exile.

18Say to the king and his mother, "Come down from your thrones and sit in the dust, for your glorious crowns will soon be snatched from your heads." 19The towns of the Negev will close their gates, and no one will be able to open them. The people of Judah will be taken away as captives. They will all be carried into exile.

13:4 Hebrew *Perath;* also in 13:5, 6, 7. 13:23 Hebrew *a Cushite.*

20See the armies marching down from the north! Where is your flock—your beautiful flock—that he gave you to care for? 21How will you feel when the LORD sets your foreign allies over you as rulers? You will writhe in pain like a woman giving birth! 22You may ask yourself, "Why is all this happening to me?" It is because of your many sins! That is why you have been raped and destroyed by invading armies. 23Can an Ethiopian* change the color of his skin? Can a leopard take away its spots? Neither can you start doing good, for you always do evil.

24"I will scatter you, just as chaff is scattered by the winds blowing in from the desert. 25This is your allotment, that which is due you," says the LORD. "I have measured it out especially for you, because you have forgotten me and put your trust in false gods. 26I myself will expose you to shame. 27I am keenly aware of your adultery and lust, and your abominable idol worship out in the fields and on the hills. Your destruction is sure, Jerusalem! How long will it be before you are pure?"

CHAPTER 14

Judah's Terrible Drought

This message came to Jeremiah from the LORD, explaining why he was holding back the rain: 2"Judah wilts; her businesses have ground to a halt. All the people sit on the ground in mourning, and a great cry rises from Jerusalem. 3The nobles send servants to get water, but all the wells are dry. The servants return with empty pitchers, confused and desperate, covering their heads in grief. 4The ground is parched and cracked for lack of rain. The farmers are afraid; they, too, cover their heads. 5The deer abandons her newborn fawn because there is no grass. 6The wild donkeys stand on the bare hills panting like thirsty jackals. They strain their eyes looking for grass to eat, but there is none to be found."

7The people say, "LORD, our wickedness has caught up with us. We have sinned against you. So please, help us for the sake of your own reputation. 8O Hope of Israel, our Savior in times of trouble! Why are you like a stranger to us? Why are you like someone passing through the land, stopping only for the night? 9Are you also confused? Are you helpless to save us? You are right here among us, LORD. We are known as your people. Please don't abandon us now!"

10So the LORD replies to his people, "You love to wander far from me and do not follow in my paths. Now I will no longer accept you as my people. I will remember all your wickedness and will punish you for your sins."

The LORD Forbids Jeremiah to Intercede
¹¹Then the LORD said to me, "Do not pray for these people anymore. ¹²When they fast in my presence, I will pay no attention. When they present their burnt offerings and grain offerings to me, I will not accept them. In return, I will give them only war, famine, and disease."

¹³Then I said, "O Sovereign LORD, their prophets are telling them, 'All is well—no war or famine will come. The LORD will surely send you peace.'"

¹⁴Then the LORD said, "These prophets are telling lies in my name. I did not send them or tell them to speak. I did not give them any messages. They prophesy of visions and revelations they have never seen or heard. They speak foolishness made up in their own lying hearts. ¹⁵Therefore, says the LORD, I will punish these lying prophets, for they have spoken in my name even though I never sent them. They say that no war or famine will come, but they themselves will die by war and famine! ¹⁶As for the people to whom they prophesy—their bodies will be thrown out into the streets of Jerusalem, victims of famine and war. There will be no one left to bury them. Husbands, wives, sons, and daughters—all will be gone. For I will pour out their own wickedness on them.

¹⁷"Now, Jeremiah, say this to them: 'Night and day my eyes overflow with tears. I cannot stop weeping, for my virgin daughter—my precious people—has been run through with a sword and lies mortally wounded on the ground. ¹⁸If I go out into the fields, I see the bodies of people slaughtered by the enemy. If I walk the city streets, there I see people who have died of starvation. The prophets and priests continue with their work, but they do not know what they are doing.'"

A Prayer for Healing
¹⁹LORD, have you completely rejected Judah? Do you really hate Jerusalem*? Why have you wounded us past all hope of healing? We hoped for peace, but no peace came. We hoped for a time of healing but found only terror.

²⁰LORD, we confess our wickedness and that of our ancestors, too. We all have sinned against you. ²¹For the sake of your own name, LORD, do not abandon us. Do not disgrace yourself and

14:19 Hebrew *Zion.*

the throne of your glory. Do not break your covenant with us. Please don't forget us!

²²Can any of the foreign gods send us rain? Does it fall from the sky by itself? No, it comes from you, the LORD our God! Only you can do such things. So we will wait for you to help us.

CHAPTER 15

Judah's Inevitable Doom
Then the LORD said to me, "Even if Moses and Samuel stood before me pleading for these people, I wouldn't help them. Away with them! Get them out of my sight! ²And if they say to you, 'But where can we go?' tell them, 'This is what the LORD says: Those who are destined for death, to death; those who are destined for war, to war; those who are destined for famine, to famine; those who are destined for captivity, to captivity.'

³"I will send four kinds of destroyers against them," says the LORD. "I will send the sword to kill, the dogs to drag away, the vultures to devour, and the wild animals to finish up what is left. ⁴Because of the wicked things Manasseh son of Hezekiah, king of Judah, did in Jerusalem, I will make my people an object of horror to all the kingdoms of the earth.

⁵"Who will feel sorry for you, Jerusalem? Who will weep for you? Who will even bother to ask how you are? ⁶You have forsaken me and turned your back on me," says the LORD. "Therefore, I will raise my clenched fists to destroy you. I am tired of always giving you another chance. ⁷I will winnow you like grain at the gates of your cities and take away everything you hold dear. I will destroy my own people, because they refuse to turn back to me from all their evil ways.

⁸"There will be more widows than the grains of sand along the seashore. At noontime I will bring a destroyer against the mothers of young men. I will cause anguish and terror to come upon them suddenly. ⁹The mother of seven grows faint and gasps for breath; her sun has gone down while it is yet day. She sits childless now, disgraced and humiliated. And those who are left, I will hand over to the enemy to be killed," says the LORD.

Jeremiah's Complaint
¹⁰Then I said, "What sadness is mine, my mother. Oh, that I had died at birth! I am hated everywhere I go. I am neither a lender who has threatened to foreclose nor a borrower who refuses to pay—yet they all curse me."

11The Lord replied, "All will be well with you, Jeremiah. Your enemies will ask you to plead on their behalf in times of trouble and distress. 12Can a man break a bar of iron from the north, or a bar of bronze? 13Because of all my people's sins against me, I will hand over their wealth and treasures as plunder to the enemy. 14I will tell their enemies to take them as captives to a foreign land. For my anger blazes forth like fire, and it will consume them."

15Then I said, "Lord, you know I am suffering for your sake. Punish my persecutors! Don't let them kill me! Be merciful to me and give them what they deserve! 16Your words are what sustain me. They bring me great joy and are my heart's delight, for I bear your name, O Lord God Almighty. 17I never joined the people in their merry feasts. I sat alone because your hand was on me. I burst with indignation at their sins. 18Why then does my suffering continue? Why is my wound so incurable? Your help seems as uncertain as a seasonal brook. It is like a spring that has gone dry."

19The Lord replied, "If you return to me, I will restore you so you can continue to serve me. If you speak words that are worthy, you will be my spokesman. You are to influence them; do not let them influence you! 20They will fight against you like an attacking army, but I will make you as secure as a fortified wall. They will not conquer you, for I will protect and deliver you. I, the Lord, have spoken! 21Yes, I will certainly keep you safe from these wicked men. I will rescue you from their cruel hands."

CHAPTER **16**
Jeremiah Forbidden to Marry
The Lord gave me another message. He said, 2"Do not marry or have children in this place. 3For this is what the Lord says about the children born here in this city and about their mothers and fathers: 4They will die from terrible diseases. No one will mourn for them or bury them, and they will lie scattered on the ground like dung. They will die from war and famine, and their bodies will be food for the vultures and wild animals.

Judah's Coming Punishment
5"Do not go to their funerals to mourn and show sympathy for them," says the Lord, "for I have removed my protection and peace from them. I have taken away my unfailing love and my mercy. 6Both the great and the lowly will die in this land. No one will bury them or mourn for them. Their friends will not cut themselves or shave their heads in sadness. 7No one will offer a meal to comfort those who mourn for the dead—not even for the death of a mother or a father. No one will send a cup of wine to console them.

8"And do not go to their feasts and parties. Do not eat and drink with them at all. 9For the Lord Almighty, the God of Israel, says: In your own lifetime, before your very eyes, I will put an end to the happy singing and laughter in this land. The joyful voices of bridegrooms and brides will no longer be heard.

10"When you tell the people all these things, they will ask, 'Why has the Lord decreed such terrible things against us? What have we done to deserve such treatment? What is our sin against the Lord our God?' 11Tell them that this is the Lord's reply: It is because your ancestors were unfaithful to me. They worshiped other gods and served them. They abandoned me. They did not keep my law. 12And you are even worse than your ancestors! You stubbornly follow your own evil desires and refuse to listen to me. 13So I will throw you out of this land and send you into a foreign land where you and your ancestors have never been. There you can worship idols all you like—and I will grant you no favors!

Hope despite the Disaster
14"But the time is coming," says the Lord, "when people who are taking an oath will no longer say, 'As surely as the Lord lives, who rescued the people of Israel from the land of Egypt.' 15Instead, they will say, 'As surely as the Lord lives, who brought the people of Israel back to their own land from the land of the north and from all the countries to which he had exiled them.' For I will bring them back to this land that I gave their ancestors.

16"But now I am sending for many fishermen who will catch them," says the Lord. "I am sending for hunters who will search for them in the forests and caves. 17I am watching them closely, and I see every sin. They cannot hope to hide from me. 18I will punish them doubly for all their sins, because they have defiled my land with lifeless images of their detestable gods and filled my inheritance with their evil deeds."

Jeremiah's Prayer of Confidence
19Lord, you are my strength and fortress, my refuge in the day of trouble! Nations from around the world will come to you and say,

"Our ancestors were foolish, for they worshiped worthless idols. 20Can people make their own god? The gods they make are not real gods at all!"

21"So now I will show them my power and might," says the LORD. "At last they will know that I am the LORD."

CHAPTER 17
Judah's Sin and Punishment

The LORD says, "My people act as though their evil ways are laws to be obeyed, inscribed with a diamond point on their stony hearts, or with an iron chisel on the corners of their altars. 2Even their children go to worship at their sacred altars and Asherah poles, beneath every green tree and on every high hill. 3So I will give all your wealth and treasures—together with your pagan shrines—as plunder to your enemies, for sin runs rampant in your land. 4The wonderful inheritance I have reserved for you will slip out of your hands, and I will send you away as captives to a foreign land. For you have kindled my anger into a roaring fire that will burn forever."

Wisdom from the LORD

5This is what the LORD says: "Cursed are those who put their trust in mere humans and turn their hearts away from the LORD. 6They are like stunted shrubs in the desert, with no hope for the future. They will live in the barren wilderness, on the salty flats where no one lives.

7"But blessed are those who trust in the LORD and have made the LORD their hope and confidence. 8They are like trees planted along a riverbank, with roots that reach deep into the water. Such trees are not bothered by the heat or worried by long months of drought. Their leaves stay green, and they go right on producing delicious fruit.

9"The human heart is most deceitful and desperately wicked. Who really knows how bad it is? 10But I know! I, the LORD, search all hearts and examine secret motives. I give all people their due rewards, according to what their actions deserve."

Jeremiah's Trust in the LORD

11Like a bird that hatches eggs she has not laid, so are those who get their wealth by unjust means. Sooner or later they will lose their riches and, at the end of their lives, will become poor old fools.

17:26 Hebrew *the Shephelah.*

12But we worship at your throne—eternal, high, and glorious! 13O LORD, the hope of Israel, all who turn away from you will be disgraced and shamed. They will be buried in a dry and dusty grave, for they have forsaken the LORD, the fountain of living water.

14O LORD, you alone can heal me; you alone can save. My praises are for you alone! 15People scoff at me and say, "What is this 'message from the LORD' you keep talking about? Why don't your predictions come true?"

16LORD, I have not abandoned my job as a shepherd for your people. I have not urged you to send disaster. It is your message I have given them, not my own. 17LORD, do not desert me now! You alone are my hope in the day of disaster. 18Bring shame and terror on all who persecute me, but give me peace. Yes, bring double destruction upon them!

Observing the Sabbath

19Then the LORD said to me, "Go and stand in the gates of Jerusalem, first at the gate where the king goes out, and then at each of the other gates. 20Say to all the people, 'Listen to this message from the LORD, you kings of Judah and all you people of Judah and everyone living in Jerusalem. 21This is what the LORD says: Listen to my warning and live! Stop carrying on your trade at Jerusalem's gates on the Sabbath day. 22Do not do your work on the Sabbath, but make it a holy day. I gave this command to your ancestors, 23but they did not listen or obey. They stubbornly refused to pay attention and would not respond to discipline.

24"But if you obey me, says the LORD, and do not carry on your trade or work on the Sabbath day, and if you keep it holy, 25then this nation will continue forever. There will always be a descendant of David sitting on the throne here in Jerusalem. Kings and their officials will always ride among the people of Judah in chariots and on horses, and this city will remain forever. 26And from all around Jerusalem, from the towns of Judah and Benjamin, from the western foothills* and the hill country and the Negev, the people will come with their burnt offerings and sacrifices. They will bring their grain offerings, incense, and thanksgiving offerings to the LORD's Temple.

27"But if you do not listen to me and refuse to keep the Sabbath holy, and if on the Sabbath day you bring loads of merchandise through the gates of Jerusalem just as on other days, then I will set fire to these gates. The fire will spread to the palaces, and no one will be able to put out the roaring flames.'"

CHAPTER 18
The Potter and the Clay

The LORD gave another message to Jeremiah. He said, 2"Go down to the shop where clay pots and jars are made. I will speak to you while you are there." 3So I did as he told me and found the potter working at his wheel. 4But the jar he was making did not turn out as he had hoped, so the potter squashed the jar into a lump of clay and started again.

5Then the LORD gave me this message: 6"O Israel, can I not do to you as this potter has done to his clay? As the clay is in the potter's hand, so are you in my hand. 7If I announce that a certain nation or kingdom is to be uprooted, torn down, and destroyed, 8but then that nation renounces its evil ways, I will not destroy it as I had planned. 9And if I announce that I will build up and plant a certain nation or kingdom, making it strong and great, 10but then that nation turns to evil and refuses to obey me, I will not bless that nation as I had said I would.

11"Therefore, Jeremiah, go and warn all Judah and Jerusalem. Say to them, 'This is what the LORD says: I am planning disaster against you instead of good. So turn from your evil ways, each of you, and do what is right.'"

12But they replied, "Don't waste your breath. We will continue to live as we want to, following our own evil desires."

13Then the LORD said, "Has anyone ever heard of such a thing, even among the pagan nations? My virgin Israel has done something too terrible to understand! 14Does the snow ever melt high up in the mountains of Lebanon? Do the cold, flowing streams from the crags of Mount Hermon ever run dry? 15These can be counted on, but not my people! For they have deserted me and turned to worthless idols. They have stumbled off the ancient highways of good, and they walk the muddy paths of sin. 16Therefore, their land will become desolate, a monument to their stupidity. All who pass by will be astonished and shake their heads in amazement at its utter desolation. 17I will scatter my people before their enemies as the east wind scatters dust. And in all their trouble I will turn my back on them and refuse to notice their distress."

A Plot against Jeremiah

18Then the people said, "Come on, let's find a way to stop Jeremiah. We have our own priests and wise men and prophets. We don't need him to teach the law and give us advice and prophecies. Let's spread rumors about him and ignore what he says."

19LORD, help me! Listen to what they are planning to do to me! 20Should they repay evil for good? They have set a trap to kill me, though I pleaded for them and tried to protect them from your anger. 21So let their children starve! Let the sword pour out their blood! Let their wives become widows without any children! Let their old men die in a plague, and let their young men be killed in battle! 22Let screaming be heard from their homes as warriors come suddenly upon them. For they have dug a pit for me, and they have hidden traps along my path.

23LORD, you know all about their murderous plots against me. Don't forgive their crimes and blot out their sins. Let them die before you. Deal with them in your anger.

CHAPTER 19
Jeremiah's Shattered Jar

The LORD said to me, "Go and buy a clay jar. Then ask some of the leaders of the people and of the priests to follow you. 2Go out into the valley of the son of Hinnom by the entrance to the Potsherd Gate, and repeat to them the words that I give you. 3Say to them, 'Listen to this message from the LORD, you kings of Judah and citizens of Jerusalem! This is what the LORD Almighty, the God of Israel, says: I will bring such a terrible disaster on this place that the ears of those who hear about it will ring!

4"'For Israel has forsaken me and turned this valley into a place of wickedness. The people burn incense to foreign gods—idols never before worshiped by this generation, by their ancestors, or by the kings of Judah. And they have filled this place with the blood of innocent children. 5They have built pagan shrines to Baal, and there they burn their sons as sacrifices to Baal. I have never commanded such a horrible deed; it never even crossed my mind to command such a thing! 6So beware, for the time is coming, says the LORD, when this place will no longer be called Topheth or the valley of the son of Hinnom, but the Valley of Slaughter. 7For I will upset the battle plans of Judah and Jerusalem and let invading armies slaughter them. The enemy will leave the dead bodies as food for the vultures and wild animals. 8I will wipe Jerusalem from the face of the earth, making it a monument to their stupidity. All who pass by will be appalled and will gasp at the destruction they see there. [9]I will see to it that your enemies lay siege to the city until all the food is gone. Then those trapped inside will have to eat their own sons and daughters and friends. They will be driven to utter despair.'

[10]"As these men watch, Jeremiah, smash the jar you brought with you. [11]Then say to them, 'This is what the LORD Almighty says: As this jar lies shattered, so I will shatter the people of Judah and Jerusalem beyond all hope of repair. They will bury the bodies in Topheth until there is no more room. [12]This is what I will do to this place and its people, says the LORD. I will cause this city to become defiled like Topheth. [13]Yes, all the houses in Jerusalem, including the palace of Judah's kings, will become like Topheth—all the houses where you burned incense on the rooftops to your star gods, and where drink offerings were poured out to your idols.'"

[14]Then Jeremiah returned from Topheth where he had delivered this message, and he stopped in front of the Temple of the LORD. He said to the people there, [15]"This is what the LORD Almighty, the God of Israel, says: I will bring disaster upon this city and its surrounding towns just as I promised, because you have stubbornly refused to listen to me."

CHAPTER 20
Jeremiah and Pashhur

Now Pashhur son of Immer, the priest in charge of the Temple of the LORD, heard what Jeremiah was saying. [2]So he arrested Jeremiah the prophet and had him whipped and put in stocks at the Benjamin Gate of the LORD's Temple.

[3]The next day, when Pashhur finally released him, Jeremiah said, "Pashhur, the LORD has changed your name. From now on you are to be called 'The Man Who Lives in Terror.'* [4]For this is what the LORD says: I will send terror upon you and all your friends, and you will watch as they are slaughtered by the swords of the enemy. I will hand the people of Judah over to the king of Babylon. He will take them captive to Babylon or run them through with the sword. [5]And I will let your enemies plunder Jerusalem. All the famed treasures of the city—the precious jewels and gold and silver of your kings—will be carried off to Babylon. [6]As for you, Pashhur, you

and all your household will go as captives to Babylon. There you will die and be buried, you and all your friends to whom you promised that everything would be all right."

Jeremiah's Complaint

[7]O LORD, you persuaded me, and I allowed myself to be persuaded. You are stronger than I am, and you overpowered me. Now I am mocked by everyone in the city. [8]Whenever I speak, the words come out in a violent outburst. "Violence and destruction!" I shout. So these messages from the LORD have made me a household joke. [9]And I can't stop! If I say I'll never mention the LORD or speak in his name, his word burns in my heart like a fire. It's like a fire in my bones! I am weary of holding it in!

[10]I have heard the many rumors about me. They call me "The Man Who Lives in Terror." And they say, "If you say anything, we will report it." Even my old friends are watching me, waiting for a fatal slip. "He will trap himself," they say, "and then we will get our revenge on him."

[11]But the LORD stands beside me like a great warrior. Before him they will stumble. They cannot defeat me. They will be shamed and thoroughly humiliated. Their dishonor will never be forgotten. [12]O LORD Almighty! You know those who are righteous, and you examine the deepest thoughts of hearts and minds. Let me see your vengeance against them, for I have committed my cause to you. [13]Now I will sing out my thanks to the LORD! Praise the LORD! For though I was poor and needy, he delivered me from my oppressors.

[14]Yet I curse the day I was born! May the day of my birth not be blessed. [15]I curse the messenger who told my father, "Good news—you have a son!" [16]Let him be destroyed like the cities of old that the LORD overthrew without mercy. Terrify him all day long with battle shouts, [17]for he did not kill me at birth. Oh, that I had died in my mother's womb, that her body had been my grave! [18]Why was I ever born? My entire life has been filled with trouble, sorrow, and shame.

CHAPTER 21
No Deliverance from Babylon

The LORD spoke through Jeremiah when King Zedekiah sent Pashhur son of Malkijah and Zephaniah son of Maaseiah, the priest, to speak with him. They begged Jeremiah, [2]"Please ask the LORD to help us. King Nebuchadnezzar* of Babylon has begun his attack on Judah. Perhaps the LORD will be gracious and do a mighty miracle as he has done in the past. Perhaps he will force Nebuchadnezzar to withdraw his armies."

³Jeremiah replied, "Go back to King Zedekiah and tell him, ⁴'This is what the LORD, the God of Israel, says: I will make your weapons useless against the king of Babylon and the Babylonians* who are attacking you. Yes, I will bring your enemies right into the heart of this city. ⁵I myself will fight against you with great power, for I am very angry. You have made me furious! ⁶I will send a terrible plague upon this city, and both people and animals will die. ⁷And then, says the LORD, even after King Zedekiah, his officials, and everyone else in the city have survived war, famine, and disease, I will hand them over to King Nebuchadnezzar of Babylon. He will slaughter them all without mercy, pity, or compassion.'

⁸"Tell all the people, 'This is what the LORD says: Take your choice of life or death! ⁹Everyone who stays in Jerusalem will die from war, famine, or disease, but those who go out and surrender to the Babylonians will live. ¹⁰For I have decided to bring disaster and not good upon this city, says the LORD. It will be captured by the king of Babylon, and he will reduce it to ashes.'

Judgment on Judah's Kings

¹¹"Say to the royal family of Judah, 'Listen to this message from the LORD! ¹²This is what the LORD says to the dynasty of David: Give justice to the people you judge! Help those who have been robbed; rescue them from their oppressors. Do what is right, or my anger will burn like an unquenchable fire because of all your sins. ¹³I will fight against this city of Jerusalem that boasts, "We are safe on our mountain! No one can touch us here." ¹⁴And I myself will punish you for your sinfulness, says the LORD. I will light a fire in your forests that will burn up everything around you.'"

CHAPTER 22

A Message for Judah's Kings

Then the LORD said to me, "Go over and speak directly to the king of Judah. Say to him, ²'Listen to this message from the LORD, you king of Judah, sitting on David's throne. Let your officials and your people listen, too. ³This is what the LORD says: Be fair-minded and just. Do what is right! Help those who have been robbed; rescue them from their oppressors. Quit your

evil deeds! Do not mistreat foreigners, orphans, and widows. Stop murdering the innocent! ⁴If you obey me, there will always be a descendant of David sitting on the throne here in Jerusalem. The king will ride through the palace gates in chariots and on horses, with his parade of officials and subjects. ⁵But if you refuse to pay attention to this warning, I swear by my own name, says the LORD, that this palace will become a pile of rubble.'"

A Message about the Palace

⁶Now this is what the LORD says concerning the royal palace: "You are as beloved to me as fruitful Gilead and the green forests of Lebanon. But I will destroy you and leave you deserted, with no one living within your walls. ⁷I will call for wreckers, who will bring out their tools to dismantle you. They will tear out all your fine cedar beams and throw them on the fire. ⁸People from many nations will pass by the ruins of this city and say to one another, 'Why did the LORD destroy such a great city?' ⁹And the answer will be, 'Because they violated their covenant with the LORD their God by worshiping other gods.'"

A Message about Jehoahaz

¹⁰Do not weep for the dead king or mourn his loss. Instead, weep for the captive king being led away! For he will never return to see his native land again. ¹¹For this is what the LORD says about Jehoahaz,* who succeeded his father, King Josiah, and was taken away as a captive: "He will never return. ¹²He will die in a distant land and never again see his own country."

A Message about Jehoiakim

¹³And the LORD says, "Destruction is certain for Jehoiakim, who builds his palace with forced labor.* By not paying wages, he builds injustice into its walls and oppression into its doorframes and ceilings. ¹⁴He says, 'I will build a magnificent palace with huge rooms and many windows, paneled throughout with fragrant cedar and painted a lovely red.'

¹⁵"But a beautiful palace does not make a great king! Why did your father, Josiah, reign so long? Because he was just and right in all his dealings. That is why God blessed him. ¹⁶He made sure that justice and help were given to the poor and needy, and everything went well for him. Isn't that what it means to know me?" asks the LORD. ¹⁷"But you! You are full of selfish

21:4 Or *Chaldeans*; also in 21:9.   22:11 Hebrew *Shallum*, another name for Jehoahaz.   22:13a The brother and successor of the exiled Jehoahaz.   22:13b Hebrew *by unrighteousness*.

greed and dishonesty! You murder the innocent, oppress the poor, and reign ruthlessly."

18Therefore, this is the LORD's decree of punishment against King Jehoiakim, who succeeded his father, Josiah, on the throne: "His family will not weep for him when he dies. His subjects will not even care that he is dead. 19He will be buried like a dead donkey—dragged out of Jerusalem and dumped outside the gate! 20Weep, for your allies are all gone. Search for them in Lebanon. Shout for them at Bashan. Search for them in the regions east of the river.* See, they are all destroyed. Not one is left to help you.

21"When you were prosperous, I warned you, but you replied, 'Don't bother me.' Since childhood you have been that way—you simply will not listen! 22And now your allies have all disappeared with a puff of wind. All your friends have been taken away as captives. Surely at last you will see your wickedness and be ashamed. 23It may be nice to live in a beautiful palace lined with lumber from the cedars of Lebanon, but soon you will cry and groan in anguish—anguish like that of a woman about to give birth.

A Message for Jehoiachin

24"And as surely as I live," says the LORD, "I will abandon you, Jehoiachin* son of Jehoiakim, king of Judah. Even if you were the signet ring on my right hand, I would pull you off. 25I will hand you over to those who seek to kill you, of whom you are so desperately afraid—to King Nebuchadnezzar* of Babylon and the mighty Babylonian* army. 26I will expel you and your mother from this land, and you will die in a foreign country. 27You will never again return to the land of your desire.

28"Why is this man Jehoiachin like a discarded, broken dish? Why are he and his children to be exiled to distant lands? 29O earth, earth, earth! Listen to this message from the LORD! 30This is what the LORD says: Let the record show that this man Jehoiachin was childless, for none of his children will ever sit on the throne of David to rule in Judah. His life will amount to nothing."

CHAPTER **23**
The Righteous Branch
"I will send disaster upon the leaders of my people—the shepherds of my sheep—for they have destroyed and scattered the very ones they were expected to care for," says the LORD.

2This is what the LORD, the God of Israel, says to these shepherds: "Instead of leading my flock to safety, you have deserted them and driven them to destruction. Now I will pour out judgment on you for the evil you have done to them. 3But I will gather together the remnant of my flock from wherever I have driven them. I will bring them back into their own fold, and they will be fruitful and increase in number. 4Then I will appoint responsible shepherds to care for them, and they will never be afraid again. Not a single one of them will be lost or missing," says the LORD.

5"For the time is coming," says the LORD, "when I will place a righteous Branch on King David's throne. He will be a King who rules with wisdom. He will do what is just and right throughout the land. 6And this is his name: 'The LORD Is Our Righteousness.'* In that day Judah will be saved, and Israel will live in safety.

7"In that day," says the LORD, "when people are taking an oath, they will no longer say, 'As surely as the LORD lives, who rescued the people of Israel from the land of Egypt.' 8Instead, they will say, 'As surely as the LORD lives, who brought the people of Israel back to their own land from the land of the north and from all the countries to which he had exiled them.' Then they will live in their own land."

Judgment on False Prophets

9My heart is broken because of the false prophets, and I tremble uncontrollably. I stagger like a drunkard, like someone overcome by wine, because of the holy words the LORD has spoken against them. 10For the land is full of adultery, and it lies under a curse. The land itself is in mourning—its pastures are dried up. For the prophets do evil and abuse their power.

11"The priests are like the prophets, all ungodly, wicked men. I have seen their despicable acts right here in my own Temple," says the LORD. 12"Therefore, their paths will be dark and slippery. They will be chased down dark and treacherous trails, where they will fall. For I will bring disaster upon them when their time of punishment comes. I, the LORD, have spoken!

13"I saw that the prophets of Samaria were terribly evil, for they prophesied by Baal and led my people of Israel into sin. 14But now I see that the prophets of Jerusalem are even worse! They commit adultery, and they love dishonesty. They encourage those who are doing evil instead of turning them away from their sins. These prophets

---

22:20 Hebrew in *Abarim.*   22:24 Hebrew *Coniah,* a variant name for Jehoiachin; also in 22:28, 30.   22:25a Hebrew *Nebuchadrezzar,* a variant name for Nebuchadnezzar.   22:25b Or *Chaldean.*   23:6 Hebrew *Yahweh Tsidqenu.*

are as wicked as the people of Sodom and Gomorrah once were."

15Therefore, this is what the LORD Almighty says concerning the prophets: "I will feed them with bitterness and give them poison to drink. For it is because of Jerusalem's prophets that wickedness fills this land. 16This is my warning to my people," says the LORD Almighty. "Do not listen to these prophets when they prophesy to you, filling you with futile hopes. They are making up everything they say. They do not speak for the LORD! 17They keep saying to these rebels who despise my word, 'Don't worry! The LORD says you will have peace!' And to those who stubbornly follow their own evil desires, they say, 'No harm will come your way!'

18"But can you name even one of these prophets who knows the LORD well enough to hear what he is saying? Has even one of them cared enough to listen? 19Look! The LORD's anger bursts out like a storm, a whirlwind that swirls down on the heads of the wicked. 20The anger of the LORD will not diminish until it has finished all his plans. In the days to come, you will understand all this very clearly.

21"I have not sent these prophets, yet they claim to speak for me. I have given them no message, yet they prophesy. 22If they had listened to me, they would have spoken my words and turned my people from their evil ways. 23Am I a God who is only in one place?" asks the LORD. "Do they think I cannot see what they are doing? 24Can anyone hide from me? Am I not everywhere in all the heavens and earth?" asks the LORD.

25"I have heard these prophets say, 'Listen to the dream I had from God last night.' And then they proceed to tell lies in my name. 26How long will this go on? If they are prophets, they are prophets of deceit, inventing everything they say. 27By telling these false dreams, they are trying to get my people to forget me, just as their ancestors did by worshiping the idols of Baal. 28Let these false prophets tell their dreams, but let my true messengers faithfully proclaim my every word. There is a difference between chaff and wheat! 29Does not my word burn like fire?" asks the LORD. "Is it not like a mighty hammer that smashes rock to pieces?

30"Therefore," says the LORD, "I stand against these prophets who get their messages from each other—31these smooth-tongued prophets who say, 'This prophecy is from the LORD!' 32Their imaginary dreams are flagrant lies that lead my people into sin. I did not send or appoint them, and they have no message at all for my people," says the LORD.

False Prophecies and False Prophets

33"Suppose one of the people or one of the prophets or priests asks you, 'What prophecy has the LORD burdened you with now?' You must reply, 'You are the burden!* The LORD says he will abandon you!' 34If any prophet, priest, or anyone else says, 'I have a prophecy from the LORD,' I will punish that person along with his entire family. 35You should keep asking each other, 'What is the LORD's answer?' or 'What is the LORD saying?' 36But stop using this phrase, 'prophecy from the LORD.' For people are using it to give authority to their own ideas, turning upside down the words of our God, the living God, the LORD Almighty.

37"This is what you should say to the prophets: 'What is the LORD's answer?' or 'What is the LORD saying?' 38But suppose they respond, 'This is a prophecy from the LORD!' Then you should say, 'This is what the LORD says: Because you have used this phrase, "prophecy from the LORD," even though I warned you not to use it, 39I will forget you completely. I will expel you from my presence, along with this city that I gave to you and your ancestors. 40And I will make you an object of ridicule, and your name will be infamous throughout the ages.'"

CHAPTER 24

Good and Bad Figs

After King Nebuchadnezzar* of Babylon exiled Jehoiachin* son of Jehoiakim, king of Judah, to Babylon along with the princes of Judah and all the skilled craftsmen, the LORD gave me this vision. I saw two baskets of figs placed in front of the LORD's Temple in Jerusalem. 2One basket was filled with fresh, ripe figs, while the other was filled with figs that were spoiled and could not be eaten.

3Then the LORD said to me, "What do you see, Jeremiah?"

I replied, "Figs, some very good and some very bad."

4Then the LORD gave me this message: 5"This is what the LORD, the God of Israel, says: The good figs represent the exiles I sent from Judah to the land of the Babylonians.* 6I have sent them into captivity for their own good. I will see that they are well treated, and I will bring them

---

23:33 As in Greek version and Latin Vulgate; Hebrew reads *What burden?*   24:1a Hebrew *Nebuchadrezzar,* a variant name for Nebuchadnezzar.   24:1b Hebrew *Jeconiah,* a variant name for Jehoiachin.   24:5 Or *Chaldeans.*

back here again. I will build them up and not tear them down. I will plant them and not uproot them. 7I will give them hearts that will recognize me as the LORD. They will be my people, and I will be their God, for they will return to me wholeheartedly.

8"But the rotten figs," the LORD said, "represent King Zedekiah of Judah, his officials, all the people left in Jerusalem, and those who live in Egypt. I will treat them like spoiled figs, too rotten to eat. 9I will make them an object of horror and evil to every nation on earth. They will be disgraced and mocked, taunted and cursed, wherever I send them. 10I will send war, famine, and disease until they have vanished from the land of Israel, which I gave to them and their ancestors."

CHAPTER **25**

Seventy Years of Captivity

This message for all the people of Judah came to Jeremiah from the LORD during the fourth year of Jehoiakim's reign* over Judah. This was the year when King Nebuchadnezzar* of Babylon began his reign.

2Jeremiah the prophet said to the people in Judah and Jerusalem, 3"For the past twenty-three years—from the thirteenth year of Josiah son of Amon,* king of Judah, until now—the LORD has been giving me his messages. I have faithfully passed them on to you, but you have not listened.

4"Again and again, the LORD has sent you his prophets, but you have not listened or even tried to hear. 5Each time the message was this: 'Turn from the evil road you are traveling and from the evil things you are doing. Only then will I let you live in this land that the LORD gave to you and your ancestors forever. 6Do not make me angry by worshiping the idols you have made. Then I will not harm you.'

7"But you would not listen to me," says the LORD. "You made me furious by worshiping your idols, bringing on yourselves all the disasters you now suffer. 8And now the LORD Almighty says: Because you have not listened to me, 9I will gather together all the armies of the north under King Nebuchadnezzar of Babylon, whom I have appointed as my deputy. I will bring them all against this land and its people and against the other nations near you. I will completely destroy* you and make you an object of horror and contempt and a ruin forever. 10I will take

away your happy singing and laughter. The joyful voices of bridegrooms and brides will no longer be heard. Your businesses will fail, and all your homes will stand silent and dark. 11This entire land will become a desolate wasteland. Israel and her neighboring lands will serve the king of Babylon for seventy years.

12"Then, after the seventy years of captivity are over, I will punish the king of Babylon and his people for their sins, says the LORD. I will make the country of the Babylonians* an everlasting wasteland. 13I will bring upon them all the terrors I have promised in this book—all the penalties announced by Jeremiah against the nations. 14Many nations and great kings will enslave the Babylonians, just as they enslaved my people. I will punish them in proportion to the suffering they cause my people."

The Cup of the LORD's Anger

15Then the LORD, the God of Israel, said to me, "Take from my hand this cup filled to the brim with my anger, and make all the nations to whom I send you drink from it. 16When they drink from it, they will stagger, crazed by the warfare I will send against them."

17So I took the cup of anger from the LORD and made all the nations drink from it—every nation the LORD sent me to. 18I went to Jerusalem and the other towns of Judah, and their kings and officials drank from the cup. From that day until this, they have been a desolate ruin, an object of horror, contempt, and cursing. 19I went to Egypt and spoke to Pharaoh, his officials, his princes, and his people. They, too, drank from that terrible cup, 20along with all the foreigners living in that land. So did all the kings of the land of Uz and the kings of the Philistine cities of Ashkelon, Gaza, Ekron, and what remains of Ashdod. 21Then I went to the nations of Edom, Moab, and Ammon, 22and the kings of Tyre and Sidon, and the kings of the regions across the sea. 23I went to Dedan, Tema, and Buz, and to the people who live in distant places.* 24I went to the kings of Arabia, the kings of the nomadic tribes of the desert, 25and to the kings of Zimri, Elam, and Media. 26And I went to the kings of the northern countries, far and near, one after the other—all the kingdoms of the world. And finally, the king of Babylon* himself drank from the cup of the LORD's anger.

25:1a The fourth year of Jehoiakim's reign and the accession year of Nebuchadnezzar's reign was 605 B.C. 25:1b Hebrew *Nebuchadrezzar*, a variant name for Nebuchadnezzar; also in 25:9. 25:3 The thirteenth year of Josiah's reign was 627 B.C. 25:9 The Hebrew term used here refers to the complete consecration of things or people to the LORD, either by destroying them or by giving them as an offering. 25:12 Or *Chaldeans.* 25:23 Or *who clip the corners of their hair.* 25:26 Hebrew *of Sheshach*, a code name for Babylon.

27Then the LORD said to me, "Now tell them, 'The LORD Almighty, the God of Israel, says: Drink from this cup of my anger. Get drunk and vomit, and you will fall to rise no more, for I am sending terrible wars against you.' 28And if they refuse to accept the cup, tell them, 'The LORD Almighty says: You must drink from it. You cannot escape! 29I have begun to punish Jerusalem, the city where my own name is honored. Now should I let you go unpunished? No, you will not escape disaster. I will call for war against all the nations of the earth. I, the LORD Almighty, have spoken!'

30"Now prophesy all these things, and say to them, 'The LORD will roar loudly against his own land from his holy dwelling in heaven. He will shout against everyone on the earth, like the harvesters do as they crush juice from the grapes. 31His cry of judgment will reach the ends of the earth, for the LORD will bring his case against all the nations. He will judge all the people of the earth, slaughtering the wicked with his sword. The LORD has spoken!'"

32This is what the LORD Almighty says: "Look! Disaster will fall upon nation after nation! A great whirlwind of fury is rising from the most distant corners of the earth!"

33In that day those the LORD has slaughtered will fill the earth from one end to the other. No one will mourn for them or gather up their bodies to bury them. They will be scattered like dung on the ground.

34Weep and moan, you evil shepherds! Roll in the dust, you leaders of the flock! The time of your slaughter has arrived; you will fall and shatter like fragile pottery. 35You will find no place to hide; there will be no way to escape.

36Listen to the frantic cries of the shepherds, to the leaders of the flock shouting in despair, for the LORD is spoiling their pastures. 37Peaceful meadows will be turned into a wasteland by the LORD's fierce anger. 38He has left his den like a lion seeking its prey, and their land will be made desolate by the sword of the enemy and the LORD's fierce anger.

CHAPTER **26**

Jeremiah's Escape from Death

This message came to Jeremiah from the LORD early in the reign of Jehoiakim son of Josiah,* king of Judah. 2The LORD said, "Stand out in front of the Temple of the LORD, and make an announcement to the people who have come there to worship from all over Judah. Give

26:1 The first year of Jehoiakim's reign was 608 B.C.

them my entire message; include every word. 3Perhaps they will listen and turn from their evil ways. Then I will be able to withhold the disaster I am ready to pour out on them because of their sins.

4"Say to them, 'This is what the LORD says: If you will not listen to me and obey the law I have given you, 5and if you will not listen to my servants, the prophets—for I sent them again and again to warn you, but you would not listen to them—6then I will destroy this Temple as I destroyed Shiloh, the place where the Tabernacle was located. And I will make Jerusalem an object of cursing in every nation on earth.'"

7The priests, the prophets, and all the people listened to Jeremiah as he spoke in front of the LORD's Temple. 8But when Jeremiah had finished his message, saying everything the LORD had told him to say, the priests and prophets and all the people at the Temple mobbed him. "Kill him!" they shouted. 9"What right do you have to prophesy in the LORD's name that this Temple will be destroyed like Shiloh? What do you mean, saying that Jerusalem will be destroyed?" And all the people threatened him as he stood in front of the Temple.

10When the officials of Judah heard what was happening, they rushed over from the palace and sat down at the New Gate of the Temple to hold court. 11The priests and prophets presented their accusations to the officials and the people. "This man should die!" they said. "You have heard with your own ears what a traitor he is, for he has prophesied against this city."

12Then Jeremiah spoke in his own defense. "The LORD sent me to prophesy against this Temple and this city," he said. "The LORD gave me every word that I have spoken. 13But if you stop your sinning and begin to obey the LORD your God, he will cancel this disaster that he has announced against you. 14As for me, I am helpless and in your power—do with me as you think best. 15But if you kill me, rest assured that you will be killing an innocent man! The responsibility for such a deed will lie on you, on this city, and on every person living in it. For it is absolutely true that the LORD sent me to speak every word you have heard."

16Then the officials and the people said to the priests and prophets, "This man does not deserve the death sentence, for he has spoken to us in the name of the LORD our God."

17Then some of the wise old men stood and

spoke to the people there. 18They said, "Think back to the days when Micah of Moresheth prophesied during the reign of King Hezekiah of Judah. He told the people of Judah, 'This is what the LORD Almighty says: Mount Zion will be plowed like an open field; Jerusalem will be reduced to rubble! A great forest will grow on the hilltop, where the Temple now stands.'* 19But did King Hezekiah and the people kill him for saying this? No, they turned from their sins and worshiped the LORD. They begged him to have mercy on them. Then the LORD held back the terrible disaster he had pronounced against them. If we kill Jeremiah, who knows what will happen to us?"

20(At this time, Uriah son of Shemaiah from Kiriath-jearim was also prophesying for the LORD. And he predicted the same terrible disaster against the city and nation as Jeremiah did. 21When King Jehoiakim and the army officers and officials heard what he was saying, the king sent someone to kill him. But Uriah heard about the plot and escaped to Egypt. 22Then King Jehoiakim sent Elnathan son of Acbor to Egypt along with several other men to capture Uriah. 23They took him prisoner and brought him back to King Jehoiakim. The king then killed Uriah with a sword and had him buried in an unmarked grave.)

24Ahikam son of Shaphan also stood with Jeremiah and persuaded the court not to turn him over to the mob to be killed.

CHAPTER **27**
Jeremiah Wears an Ox Yoke
This message came to Jeremiah from the LORD early in the reign of Zedekiah* son of Josiah, king of Judah.

2The LORD said to me, "Make a yoke, and fasten it on your neck with leather thongs. 3Then send messages to the kings of Edom, Moab, Ammon, Tyre, and Sidon through their ambassadors to King Zedekiah in Jerusalem. 4Give them this message for their masters: 'This is what the LORD Almighty, the God of Israel, says: 5By my great power I have made the earth and all its people and every animal. I can give these things of mine to anyone I choose. 6Now I will give your countries to King Nebuchadnezzar of Babylon, who is my servant. I have put everything, even the wild animals, under his control. 7All the nations will serve him and his son and his grandson until his time is up. But then many

nations and great kings will conquer and rule over Babylon. 8So you must submit to Babylon's king and serve him; put your neck under Babylon's yoke! I will punish any nation that refuses to be his slave, says the LORD. I will send war, famine, and disease upon that nation until Babylon has conquered it.

9"'Do not listen to your false prophets, fortune-tellers, interpreters of dreams, mediums, and sorcerers who say, "The king of Babylon will not conquer you." 10They are all liars, and I will drive you from your land and send you far away to die. 11But the people of any nation that submits to the king of Babylon will be allowed to stay in their own country to farm the land as usual. I, the LORD, have spoken!'"

12Then I repeated this same message to King Zedekiah of Judah. "If you want to live, submit to the king of Babylon and his people," I said. 13"Why do you insist on dying—you and your people? Why should you choose war, famine, and disease, which the LORD will bring against every nation that refuses to submit to Babylon's king? 14Do not listen to the false prophets who keep telling you, 'The king of Babylon will not conquer you.' They are liars. 15This is what the LORD says: I have not sent these prophets! They are telling you lies in my name, so I will drive you from this land. You will all die—you and all these prophets, too."

16Then I spoke to the priests and the people and said, "This is what the LORD says: Do not listen to your prophets who claim that soon the gold utensils taken from my Temple will be returned from Babylon. It is all a lie! 17Do not listen to them. Surrender to the king of Babylon, and you will live. Why should this whole city be destroyed? 18If they really are the LORD's prophets, let them pray to the LORD Almighty about the gold utensils that are still left in the LORD's Temple and in the king's palace and in the palaces of Jerusalem. Let them pray that these remaining articles will not be carried away with you to Babylon!

19"For this is what the LORD Almighty says about the bronze pillars in front of the Temple, the bronze Sea in the Temple courtyard, the bronze water carts, and all the other ceremonial articles. 20King Nebuchadnezzar of Babylon left them here when he exiled Jehoiachin* son of Jehoiakim, king of Judah, to Babylon, along with all the other important people of Judah and Jerusalem. 21Yes, this is what the LORD Almighty, the God of Israel, says about the precious things kept

---

26:18 Mic 3:12. 27:1 As in some Hebrew manuscripts and Syriac version (see also 27:3, 12); most Hebrew manuscripts read *Jehoiakim*. 27:20 Hebrew *Jeconiah*, a variant name for Jehoiachin.

in the Temple and in the palace of Judah's king: 22They will all be carried away to Babylon and will stay there until I send for them, says the LORD. But someday I will bring them back to Jerusalem again."

CHAPTER 28
Jeremiah Condemns Hananiah

One day in late summer* of that same year—the fourth year of the reign of Zedekiah, king of Judah—Hananiah son of Azzur, a prophet from Gibeon, addressed me publicly in the Temple while all the priests and people listened. He said, 2"The LORD Almighty, the God of Israel, says: I will remove the yoke of the king of Babylon from your necks. 3Within two years, I will bring back all the Temple treasures that King Nebuchadnezzar carried off to Babylon. 4And I will bring back Jehoiachin* son of Jehoiakim, king of Judah, and all the other captives that were taken to Babylon. I will surely break the yoke that the king of Babylon has put on your necks. I, the LORD, have spoken!"

5Jeremiah responded to Hananiah as they stood in front of all the priests and people at the Temple. 6He said, "Amen! May your prophecies come true! I hope the LORD does everything you say. I hope he does bring back from Babylon the treasures of this Temple and all our loved ones. 7But listen now to the solemn words I speak to you in the presence of all these people. 8The ancient prophets who preceded you and me spoke against many nations, always warning of war, famine, and disease. 9So a prophet who predicts peace must carry the burden of proof. Only when his predictions come true can it be known that he is really from the LORD."

10Then Hananiah the prophet took the yoke off Jeremiah's neck and broke it. 11And Hananiah said again to the crowd that had gathered, "The LORD has promised that within two years he will break the yoke of oppression from all the nations now subject to King Nebuchadnezzar of Babylon." At that, Jeremiah left the Temple area.

12Soon afterward the LORD gave this message to Jeremiah: 13"Go and tell Hananiah, 'This is what the LORD says: You have broken a wooden yoke, but you have replaced it with a yoke of iron. 14The LORD Almighty, the God of Israel, says: I have put a yoke of iron on the necks of all these nations, forcing them into slavery under King Nebuchadnezzar of Babylon. I have put

everything, even the wild animals, under his control.'"

15Then Jeremiah the prophet said to Hananiah, "Listen, Hananiah! The LORD has not sent you, but the people believe your lies. 16Therefore, the LORD says you must die. Your life will end this very year because you have rebelled against the LORD."

17Two months later,* Hananiah died.

CHAPTER 29
A Letter to the Exiles

Jeremiah wrote a letter from Jerusalem to the elders, priests, prophets, and all the people who had been exiled to Babylon by King Nebuchadnezzar. 2This was after King Jehoiachin,* the queen mother, the court officials, the leaders of Judah, and all the craftsmen had been deported from Jerusalem. 3He sent the letter with Elasah son of Shaphan and Gemariah son of Hilkiah, when they went to Babylon as King Zedekiah's ambassadors to Nebuchadnezzar. This is what Jeremiah's letter said:

4The LORD Almighty, the God of Israel, sends this message to all the captives he has exiled to Babylon from Jerusalem: 5"Build homes, and plan to stay. Plant gardens, and eat the food you produce. 6Marry, and have children. Then find spouses for them, and have many grandchildren. Multiply! Do not dwindle away! 7And work for the peace and prosperity of Babylon. Pray to the LORD for that city where you are held captive, for if Babylon has peace, so will you."

8The LORD Almighty, the God of Israel, says, "Do not let the prophets and mediums who are there in Babylon trick you. Do not listen to their dreams 9because they prophesy lies in my name. I have not sent them," says the LORD. 10"The truth is that you will be in Babylon for seventy years. But then I will come and do for you all the good things I have promised, and I will bring you home again. 11For I know the plans I have for you," says the LORD. "They are plans for good and not for disaster, to give you a future and a hope. 12In those days when you pray, I will listen. 13If you look for me in earnest, you will find me when you seek me. 14I will be found by you," says the LORD. "I will end your captivity and

---

28:1 Hebrew *In the fifth month,* of the Hebrew calendar. This month in the fourth year of Zedekiah's reign occurred in August and September 593 B.C. Also see note on 1:3. 28:4 Hebrew *Jeconiah,* a variant name for Jehoiachin. 28:17 Hebrew *In the seventh month of that same year.* See 28:1 and the note there. 29:2 Hebrew *Jeconiah,* a variant name for Jehoiachin.

restore your fortunes. I will gather you out of the nations where I sent you and bring you home again to your own land."

¹⁵You may claim that the LORD has raised up prophets for you in Babylon. ¹⁶But this is what the LORD says about the king who sits on David's throne and all those still living here in Jerusalem—your relatives who were not exiled to Babylon. ¹⁷This is what the LORD Almighty says: "I will send war, famine, and disease upon them and make them like rotting figs—too bad to eat. ¹⁸Yes, I will pursue them with war, famine, and disease, and I will scatter them around the world. In every nation where I send them, I will make them an object of damnation, horror, contempt, and mockery. ¹⁹For they refuse to listen to me, though I have spoken to them repeatedly through my prophets. And you who are in exile have not listened either," says the LORD.

²⁰Therefore, listen to this message from the LORD, all you captives there in Babylon. ²¹This is what the LORD Almighty, the God of Israel, says about your prophets—Ahab son of Kolaiah and Zedekiah son of Maaseiah—who are telling you lies in my name: "I will turn them over to Nebuchadnezzar* for a public execution. ²²Their terrible fate will become proverbial, so that whenever the Judean exiles want to curse someone they will say, 'May the LORD make you like Zedekiah and Ahab, whom the king of Babylon burned alive!' ²³For these men have done terrible things among my people. They have committed adultery with their neighbors' wives and have lied in my name. I am a witness to this," says the LORD.

A Message for Shemaiah

²⁴The LORD sent this message to Shemaiah the Nehelamite in Babylon: ²⁵"This is what the LORD Almighty, the God of Israel, says: You wrote a letter on your own authority to Zephaniah son of Maaseiah, the priest, and you sent copies to the other priests and people in Jerusalem. You said to Zephaniah, ²⁶'The LORD has appointed you to replace Jehoiada as the priest in charge of the house of the LORD. You are responsible to put anyone who claims to be a prophet in the stocks and neck irons. ²⁷So why have you done nothing to stop Jeremiah from Anathoth, who pretends to be a prophet

29:21 Hebrew *Nebuchadrezzar*, a variant name for Nebuchadnezzar.

Realize That God Has a Plan for Your Life Read JEREMIAH 29:11

If you happen to be in the process of making an important decision, remember that God has a plan and purpose for your life and that he wants to reveal his will to you. Here are three basic principles that may help you in discovering God's will for your life:

1. God Speaks to Us through His Word. The Bible has been described as a lamp that shines a light on our path (see Psalm 119:105, p. 527). Without exception, God will never—under any circumstances—lead us contrary to what is plainly written in Scripture. This is one compelling reason we should become thoroughly familiar with its contents. If it is not in the Word, then it is not of the Lord.

2. God Can Speak to Us through Circumstances. In the Old Testament we have the story of Gideon, who was called by God to lead the Israelites into battle. Gideon, afraid and unsure about this seemingly daunting task, asked the Lord to confirm it to him through a sign. He prayed, "If you are truly going to use me to rescue Israel as you promised, prove it to me in this way. I will put some wool on the threshing floor tonight. If the fleece is wet with dew in the morning but the ground is dry, then I will know that you are going to help me rescue Israel as you promised" (Judges 6:36-37). God condescended to Gideon's weak faith and answered Gideon's request. Although we shouldn't necessarily ask God to confirm his will to us in such a tangible way, this story shows that at times God can and does circumstantially reinforce what he has called us to do.

3. God Will Place a Peace in Your Heart. If you are in the will of God, you will find yourself encompassed by his peace. His peace reassures you that you are following his will.

The great British Bible teacher F. B. Meyer once said, "When we want to know God's will, there are three things which always concur: the inward impulse, the Word of God, and the trend of the circumstances—God in the heart, impelling you forward; God in His Book, corroborating whatever He says in the heart; and God in circumstances, indicating His will. Never start until these three things agree."

For the next note on "Seek God's Will," turn to p. 1047.

We Are Responsible for Our Own Sins and Mistakes
Read JEREMIAH 31:30

We live in an age when it is popular to shift the blame for our actions. Some blame society for their problems with drugs and alcohol, or they blame their family for the problems they now have as an adult. Yet this verse makes it abundantly clear that God views each person as responsible for his or her own actions.

While the sins and failings of the people around us can affect us, we are still held accountable for our own mistakes. That is why each person must come to grips with his or her own sinful nature, turn to God for forgiveness and salvation through Jesus Christ, and move forward. The apostle Paul would never have had such an effective ministry had he been so absorbed in his past. After all, he had led a murderous assault against the early church. Instead of dwelling on the past or blaming the religious establishment that had endorsed these killings, he said, "Forgetting the past and looking forward to what lies ahead, I strain to reach the end of the race and receive the prize for which God, through Christ Jesus, is calling us up to heaven" (Philippians 3:13-14).

When Paul speaks of forgetting the past, he is not implying that he has no memory of what he has done, but that he is no longer brought under the power of his past. May we have the same attitude as we face the sins of our past and confront the failings of our present in the light of God's forgiveness and grace.

For the next note on "Accountability," turn to p. 882.

CORNER STONES

---

among you? 28Jeremiah sent a letter here to Babylon, predicting that our captivity will be a long one. He said we should build homes and plan to stay for many years. He said we should plant fruit trees, because we will be here to eat the fruit for many years to come.'"

29But when Zephaniah the priest received Shemaiah's letter, he took it to Jeremiah and read it to him. 30Then the LORD gave this message to Jeremiah: 31"Send an open letter to all the exiles in Babylon. Tell them, 'This is what the LORD says concerning Shemaiah the Nehelamite: Since he has prophesied to you when I did not send him and has tricked you into believing his lies, 32I will punish him and his family. None of his descendants will see the good things I will do for my people, for he has taught you to rebel against me. I, the LORD, have spoken!'"

CHAPTER 30
Promises of Deliverance

The LORD gave another message to Jeremiah. He said, 2"This is what the LORD, the God of Israel, says: Write down for the record everything I have said to you, Jeremiah. 3For the time is coming when I will restore the fortunes of my people of Israel and Judah. I will bring them home to this land that I gave to their ancestors, and they will possess it and live here again. I, the LORD, have spoken!"

4This is the message the LORD gave concerning Israel and Judah: 5"This is what the LORD says: I have heard the people crying; there is only fear and trembling. 6Now let me ask you a question: Do men give birth to babies? Then why do they stand there, ashen-faced, hands pressed against their sides like women about to give birth? 7In all history there has never been such a time of terror. It will be a time of trouble for my people Israel.* Yet in the end, they will be saved!

8"For in that day, says the LORD Almighty, I will break the yoke from their necks and snap their chains. Foreigners will no longer be their masters. 9For my people will serve the LORD their God and David their king, whom I will raise up for them.

10"So do not be afraid, Jacob, my servant; do not be dismayed, Israel, says the LORD. For I will bring you home again from distant lands, and your children will return from their exile. Israel will return and will have peace and quiet in their own land, and no one will make them afraid. 11For I am with you and will save you, says the LORD. I will completely destroy the nations

30:7 Hebrew *Jacob;* also in 30:10b.

where I have scattered you, but I will not destroy you. But I must discipline you; I cannot let you go unpunished.

12 "This is what the LORD says: Yours is an incurable bruise, a terrible wound. 13 There is no one to help you or bind up your injury. You are beyond the help of any medicine. 14 All your allies have left you and do not care about you anymore. I have wounded you cruelly, as though I were your enemy. For your sins are many, and your guilt is great. 15 Why do you protest your punishment—this wound that has no cure? I have had to punish you because your sins are many and your guilt is great.

16 "But in that coming day, all who destroy you will be destroyed, and all your enemies will be sent into exile. Those who plunder you will be plundered, and those who attack you will be attacked. 17 I will give you back your health and heal your wounds, says the LORD.

"Now you are called an outcast—'Jerusalem* for whom nobody cares.' 18 But the LORD says this: When I bring you home again from your captivity and restore your fortunes, Jerusalem will be rebuilt on her ruins. The palace will be reconstructed as it was before. 19 There will be joy and songs of thanksgiving, and I will multiply my people and make of them a great and honored nation. 20 Their children will prosper as they did long ago. I will establish them as a nation before me, and I will punish anyone who hurts them. 21 They will have their own ruler again, and he will not be a foreigner. I will invite him to approach me, says the LORD, for who would dare to come unless invited? 22 You will be my people, and I will be your God."

23 Look! The LORD's anger bursts out like a storm, a driving wind that swirls down on the heads of the wicked. 24 The fierce anger of the LORD will not diminish until it has finished all his plans. In the days to come, you will understand all this.

CHAPTER **31**
Hope for Restoration
"In that day," says the LORD, "I will be the God of all the families of Israel, and they will be my people. 2 I will care for the survivors as they travel through the wilderness. I will again come to give rest to the people of Israel."

3 Long ago the LORD said to Israel: "I have loved you, my people, with an everlasting love. With unfailing love I have drawn you to myself.

4 I will rebuild you, my virgin Israel. You will again be happy and dance merrily with tambourines. 5 Again you will plant your vineyards on the mountains of Samaria and eat from your own gardens there. 6 The day will come when watchmen will shout from the hill country of Ephraim, 'Come, let us go up to Jerusalem* to worship the LORD our God.'"

7 Now this is what the LORD says: "Sing with joy for Israel*! Shout for the greatest of nations! Shout out with praise and joy: 'Save your people, O LORD, the remnant of Israel!' 8 For I will bring them from the north and from the distant corners of the earth. I will not forget the blind and lame, the expectant mothers and women about to give birth. A great company will return! 9 Tears of joy will stream down their faces, and I will lead them home with great care. They will walk beside quiet streams and not stumble. For I am Israel's father, and Ephraim is my oldest child.

10 "Listen to this message from the LORD, you nations of the world; proclaim it in distant coastlands: The LORD, who scattered his people, will gather them together and watch over them as a shepherd does his flock. 11 For the LORD has redeemed Israel from those too strong for them. 12 They will come home and sing songs of joy on the heights of Jerusalem. They will be radiant because of the many gifts the LORD has given them—the good crops of wheat, wine, and oil, and the healthy flocks and herds. Their life will be like a watered garden, and all their sorrows will be gone. 13 The young women will dance for joy, and the men—old and young—will join in the celebration. I will turn their mourning into joy. I will comfort them and exchange their sorrow for rejoicing. 14 I will supply the priests with an abundance of offerings. I will satisfy my people with my bounty. I, the LORD, have spoken!"

Rachel's Sadness Turns to Joy
15 This is what the LORD says: "A cry of anguish is heard in Ramah—mourning and weeping unrestrained. Rachel weeps for her children, refusing to be comforted—for her children are dead."

16 But now the LORD says, "Do not weep any longer, for I will reward you. Your children will come back to you from the distant land of the enemy. 17 There is hope for your future," says the LORD. "Your children will come again to their own land. 18 I have heard Israel* saying, 'You disciplined me severely, but I deserved it. I was like a calf that needed to be trained for the yoke

30:17 Hebrew *Zion.* **31:6** Hebrew *Zion;* also in 31:12. **31:7** Hebrew *Jacob;* also in 31:11. **31:18** Hebrew *Ephraim,* referring to the northern kingdom of Israel; also in 31:20.

and plow. Turn me again to you and restore me, for you alone are the LORD my God. ¹⁹I turned away from God, but then I was sorry. I kicked myself for my stupidity! I was thoroughly ashamed of all I did in my younger days.'

²⁰"Is not Israel still my son, my darling child?" asks the LORD. "I had to punish him, but I still love him. I long for him and surely will have mercy on him.

²¹"Set up road signs; put up guideposts. Mark well the path by which you came. Come back again, my virgin Israel; return to your cities here. ²²How long will you wander, my wayward daughter? For the LORD will cause something new and different to happen—Israel will embrace her God.*"

²³This is what the LORD Almighty, the God of Israel, says: "When I bring them back again, the people of Judah and its cities will again say, 'The LORD bless you—O righteous home, O holy mountain!' ²⁴And city dwellers and farmers and shepherds alike will live together in peace and happiness. ²⁵For I have given rest to the weary and joy to the sorrowing."

²⁶At this, I woke up and looked around. My sleep had been very sweet.

²⁷"The time will come," says the LORD, "when I will greatly increase the population and multiply the number of cattle here in Israel and Judah. ²⁸In the past I uprooted and tore down this nation. I overthrew it, destroyed it, and brought disaster upon it. But in the future I will plant it and build it up," says the LORD.

²⁹"The people will no longer quote this proverb: 'The parents eat sour grapes, but their children's mouths pucker at the taste.' ³⁰All people will die for their own sins—those who eat the sour grapes will be the ones whose mouths will pucker.

³¹"The day will come," says the LORD, "when I will make a new covenant with the people of Israel and Judah. ³²This covenant will not be like the one I made with their ancestors when I took them by the hand and brought them out of the land of Egypt. They broke that covenant, though I loved them as a husband loves his wife," says the LORD.

³³"But this is the new covenant I will make with the people of Israel on that day," says the LORD. "I will put my laws in their minds, and I will write them on their hearts. I will be their God, and they will be my people. ³⁴And they will not need to teach their neighbors, nor will they need to teach their family, saying, 'You should know the LORD.' For everyone, from the least to the greatest, will already know me," says the LORD. "And I will forgive their wickedness and will never again remember their sins."

³⁵It is the LORD who provides the sun to light the day and the moon and stars to light the night. It is he who stirs the sea into roaring waves. His name is the LORD Almighty, and this is what he says: ³⁶"I am as likely to reject my people Israel as I am to do away with the laws of nature! ³⁷Just as the heavens cannot be measured and the foundation of the earth cannot be explored, so I will not consider casting them away forever for their sins. I, the LORD, have spoken!

³⁸"The time is coming," says the LORD, "when all Jerusalem will be rebuilt for me, from the Tower of Hananel to the Corner Gate. ³⁹A measuring line will be stretched out over the hill of Gareb and across to Goah. ⁴⁰And the entire area—including the graveyard and ash dump in the valley, and all the fields out to the Kidron Valley on the east as far as the Horse Gate—will be holy to the LORD. The city will never again be captured or destroyed."

CHAPTER **32**

Jeremiah's Land Purchase

The following message came to Jeremiah from the LORD in the tenth year of the reign of Zedekiah,* king of Judah. This was also the eighteenth year of the reign of King Nebuchadnezzar.* ²Jerusalem was under siege from the Babylonian army, and Jeremiah was imprisoned in the courtyard of the guard in the royal palace. ³King Zedekiah had put him there because he continued to give this prophecy: "This is what the LORD says: I am about to hand this city over to the king of Babylon. ⁴King Zedekiah will be captured by the Babylonians* and taken to the king of Babylon to be judged and sentenced. ⁵I will take Zedekiah to Babylon and will deal with him there. If you fight against the Babylonians, you will never succeed."

⁶At that time the LORD sent me a message. He said, ⁷"Your cousin Hanamel son of Shallum will come and say to you, 'Buy my field at Anathoth. By law you have the right to buy it before it is offered to anyone else.'"

⁸Then, just as the LORD had said he would, Hanamel came and visited me in the prison. He said, "Buy my field at Anathoth in the land of Benjamin. By law you have the right to buy it before it is offered to anyone else, so buy it for

---

31:22 Hebrew *a woman will court a suitor.*   **32:1a** The tenth year of Zedekiah's reign and the eighteenth year of Nebuchadnezzar's reign was 587 B.C.   **32:1b** Hebrew *Nebuchadrezzar,* a variant name for Nebuchadnezzar; also in 32:28.   **32:4** Or *Chaldeans;* also in 32:5, 24, 25, 28, 29, 43.

yourself." Then I knew for sure that the message I had heard was from the LORD.

⁹So I bought the field at Anathoth, paying Hanamel seventeen pieces* of silver for it. ¹⁰I signed and sealed the deed of purchase before witnesses, weighed out the silver, and paid him. ¹¹Then I took the sealed deed and an unsealed copy of the deed, which contained the terms and conditions of the purchase, ¹²and I handed them to Baruch son of Neriah and grandson of Mahseiah. I did all this in the presence of my cousin Hanamel, the witnesses who had signed the deed, and all the men of Judah who were there.

¹³Then I said to Baruch as they all listened, ¹⁴"The LORD Almighty, the God of Israel, says: Take both this sealed deed and the unsealed copy, and put them into a pottery jar to preserve them for a long time. ¹⁵For the LORD Almighty, the God of Israel, says: Someday people will again own property here in this land and will buy and sell houses and vineyards and fields."

Jeremiah's Prayer

¹⁶Then after I had given the papers to Baruch, I prayed to the LORD: ¹⁷"O Sovereign LORD! You have made the heavens and earth by your great power. Nothing is too hard for you! ¹⁸You are loving and kind to thousands, though children suffer for their parents' sins. You are the great and powerful God, the LORD Almighty. ¹⁹You have all wisdom and do great and mighty miracles. You are very aware of the conduct of all people, and you reward them according to their deeds. ²⁰You performed miraculous signs and wonders in the land of Egypt—things still remembered to this day! And you have continued to do great miracles in Israel and all around the world. You have made your name very great, as it is today.

²¹"You brought Israel out of Egypt with mighty signs and wonders, with great power and overwhelming terror. ²²You gave the people of Israel this land that you had promised their ancestors long before—a land flowing with milk and honey. ²³Our ancestors came and conquered it and lived in it, but they refused to obey you or follow your law. They have hardly done one thing you told them to! That is why you have sent this terrible disaster upon them.

²⁴"See how the siege ramps have been built against the city walls! Because of war, famine, and disease, the city has been handed over to the Babylonians, who will conquer it. Everything has happened just as you said it would. ²⁵And

32:9 Hebrew *17 shekels*, about 7 ounces or 194 grams in weight.

yet, O Sovereign LORD, you have told me to buy the field—paying good money for it before these witnesses—even though the city will soon belong to the Babylonians."

A Prediction of Jerusalem's Fall

²⁶Then this message came to Jeremiah from the LORD: ²⁷"I am the LORD, the God of all the peoples of the world. Is anything too hard for me? ²⁸I will hand this city over to the Babylonians and to Nebuchadnezzar, king of Babylon, and he will capture it. ²⁹The Babylonians outside the walls will come in and set fire to the city. They will burn down all these houses, where the people caused my fury to rise by offering incense to Baal on the rooftops and by pouring out drink offerings to other gods. ³⁰Israel and Judah have done nothing but wrong since their earliest days. They have infuriated me with all their evil deeds," says the LORD. ³¹"From the time this city was built until now, it has done nothing but anger me, so I am determined to get rid of it.

³²"The sins of Israel and Judah—the sins of the people of Jerusalem, the kings, the officials, the priests, and the prophets—stir up my anger. ³³My people have turned their backs on me and have refused to return. Day after day, year after year, I taught them right from wrong, but they would not listen or obey. ³⁴They have set up their abominable idols right in my own Temple, defiling it. ³⁵They have built pagan shrines to Baal in the valley of the son of Hinnom, and there they sacrifice their sons and daughters to Molech. I have never commanded such a horrible deed; it never even crossed my mind to command such a thing. What an incredible evil, causing Judah to sin so greatly!

A Promise of Restoration

³⁶Now I want to say something more about this city. You have been saying, 'It will fall to the king of Babylon through war, famine, and disease.' But this is what the LORD, the God of Israel, says: ³⁷I will surely bring my people back again from all the countries where I will scatter them in my fury. I will bring them back to this very city and let them live in peace and safety. ³⁸They will be my people, and I will be their God. ³⁹And I will give them one heart and mind to worship me forever, for their own good and for the good of all their descendants.

⁴⁰"And I will make an everlasting covenant with them, promising not to stop doing good for them. I will put a desire in their hearts to

worship me, and they will never leave me. ⁴¹I will rejoice in doing good to them and will faithfully and wholeheartedly replant them in this land. ⁴²Just as I have sent all these calamities upon them, so I will do all the good I have promised them. I, the LORD, have spoken!

⁴³"Fields will again be bought and sold in this land about which you now say, 'It has been ravaged by the Babylonians, a land where people and animals have all disappeared.' ⁴⁴Yes, fields will once again be bought and sold—deeds signed and sealed and witnessed—in the land of Benjamin and here in Jerusalem, in the towns of Judah and in the hill country, in the foothills of Judah* and in the Negev, too. For someday I will restore prosperity to them. I, the LORD, have spoken!"

CHAPTER **33**
Promises of Peace and Prosperity
While Jeremiah was still confined in the courtyard of the guard, the LORD gave him this second message: ²"The LORD, the Maker of the heavens and earth—the LORD is his name—says this: ³Ask me and I will tell you some remarkable secrets about what is going to happen here. ⁴For this is what the LORD, the God of Israel, says: Though you have torn down the houses of this city and even the king's palace to get materials to strengthen the walls against the siege weapons of the enemy, ⁵the Babylonians* will still enter. The men of this city are already as good as dead, for I have determined to destroy them in my terrible anger. I have abandoned them because of all their wickedness.

⁶"Nevertheless, the time will come when I will heal Jerusalem's damage and give her prosperity and peace. ⁷I will restore the fortunes of Judah and Israel and rebuild their cities. ⁸I will cleanse away their sins against me, and I will forgive all their sins of rebellion. ⁹Then this city will bring me joy, glory, and honor before all the nations of the earth! The people of the world will see the good I do for my people and will tremble with awe!

¹⁰"This is what the LORD says: You say, 'This land has been ravaged, and the people and animals have all disappeared.' Yet in the empty streets of Jerusalem and Judah's other towns, there will be heard once more ¹¹the sounds of joy and laughter. The joyful voices of bridegrooms and brides will be heard again, along with the joyous songs of people bringing thanksgiving offerings to the LORD. They will sing,

'Give thanks to the LORD Almighty, for the
　LORD is good.
His faithful love endures forever!'

For I will restore the prosperity of this land to what it was in the past, says the LORD.

¹²"This is what the LORD Almighty says: This land—though it is now desolate and the people and animals have all disappeared—will once more see shepherds leading sheep and lambs. ¹³Once again their flocks will prosper in the towns of the hill country, the foothills of Judah,* the Negev, the land of Benjamin, the vicinity of Jerusalem, and all the towns of Judah. I, the LORD, have spoken!

¹⁴"The day will come, says the LORD, when I will do for Israel and Judah all the good I have promised them. ¹⁵At that time I will bring to the throne of David a righteous descendant,* and he will do what is just and right throughout the land. ¹⁶In that day Judah will be saved, and Jerusalem will live in safety. And their motto will be 'The LORD is our righteousness!' ¹⁷For this is what the LORD says: David will forever have a descendant sitting on the throne of Israel. ¹⁸And there will always be Levitical priests to offer burnt offerings and grain offerings and sacrifices to me."

¹⁹Then this message came to Jeremiah from the LORD: ²⁰"If you can break my covenant with the day and the night so that they do not come on their usual schedule, ²¹only then will my covenant with David, my servant, be broken. Only then will he no longer have a descendant to reign on his throne. The same is true for my covenant with the Levitical priests who minister before me. ²²And as the stars cannot be counted and the sand on the seashores cannot be measured, so I will multiply the descendants of David, my servant, and the Levites who minister before me."

²³The LORD gave another message to Jeremiah. He said, ²⁴"Have you heard what people are saying?—'The LORD chose Judah and Israel and then abandoned them!' They are sneering and saying that Israel is not worthy to be counted as a nation. ²⁵But this is the LORD's reply: I would no more reject my people than I would change my laws of night and day, of earth and sky. ²⁶I will never abandon the descendants of Jacob or David, my servant, or change the plan that David's descendants will rule the descendants of Abraham, Isaac, and Jacob. Instead, I will restore them to their land and have mercy on them."

32:44 Hebrew *the Shephelah*.　**33:5** Or *Chaldeans*.　**33:13** Hebrew *the Shephelah*.　**33:15** Hebrew *a righteous Branch*.

CHAPTER **34**

A Warning for Zedekiah

King Nebuchadnezzar of Babylon came with all the armies from the kingdoms he ruled, and he fought against Jerusalem and the towns of Judah. At that time this message came to Jeremiah from the LORD. 2"Go to King Zedekiah of Judah, and tell him, 'This is what the LORD, the God of Israel, says: I am about to hand this city over to the king of Babylon, and he will burn it. 3You will not escape his grasp but will be taken into captivity. You will stand before the king of Babylon to be judged and sentenced. Then you will be exiled to Babylon.'

4"But listen to this promise from the LORD, O Zedekiah, king of Judah. This is what the LORD says: 'You will not be killed in war 5but will die peacefully among your people. They will burn incense in your memory, just as they did for your ancestors. They will weep for you and say, "Alas, our king is dead!" This I have decreed, says the LORD.'"

6So Jeremiah the prophet delivered the message to King Zedekiah of Judah. 7At this time the Babylonian army was besieging Jerusalem, Lachish, and Azekah—the only cities of Judah with their walls still standing.

Freedom for Hebrew Slaves

8This message came to Jeremiah from the LORD after King Zedekiah made a covenant with the people, proclaiming freedom for the slaves. 9He had ordered all the people to free their Hebrew slaves—both men and women. No one was to keep a fellow Judean in bondage. 10The officials and all the people had obeyed the king's command, 11but later they changed their minds. They took back the people they had freed, making them slaves again.

12So the LORD gave them this message through Jeremiah: 13"This is what the LORD, the God of Israel, says: I made a covenant with your ancestors long ago when I rescued them from their slavery in Egypt. 14I told them that every Hebrew slave must be freed after serving six years. But this was never done. 15Recently you repented and did what was right, following my command. You freed your slaves and made a solemn covenant with me in my Temple. 16But now you have shrugged off your oath and defiled my name by taking back the men and women you had freed, making them slaves once again.

17"Therefore, this is what the LORD says: Since you have not obeyed me by setting your country-

Prayer Increases Our Spiritual Knowledge and Maturity Read JEREMIAH 33:3

One way to increase our knowledge of God and grow in our faith is to study his Word. But study alone will only help us to grow so much spiritually. To deepen our faith even more, we need to follow the three points God gave to the prophet Jeremiah in this verse:

1. Call Upon God. Often we don't seek God's guidance until after we make a critical decision. Here we find that to receive greater spiritual wisdom and understanding, we must simply ask God in prayer.

2. Listen for His Answer. God says that when we call upon him, he will answer us. Many times we may think that God has not answered our prayers. But in reality, he may have already answered, and we may not have been listening. So how can we become more attentive to his answer? One way is to study the Bible. God has given us a wealth of spiritual knowledge and wisdom in his Word. Studying the Bible gives the Holy Spirit an opportunity to help us understand God's Word and how it applies not only to our life but also to specific situations in our life. In addition, we can pay attention to the circumstances that surround our prayer requests. How are they changing—or not changing—in light of our prayers? God's answer may sometimes be found in the outcome of these events and situations.

3. Deepen Your Spiritual Understanding. Only God, through the Holy Spirit, can reveal deep spiritual things to us. He does this because he loves us and longs for us to know him intimately. But don't expect God to reveal deep things to you in a casual prayer. If you want the deep spiritual answers that God longs to share with you, spend quantity and quality time with him in prayer and Bible study.

A growing and mature Christian is someone who seeks God and his guidance daily. The more you commune with God, the more the Holy Spirit will open your eyes to who he is and how he works in your life and in the world. Ask God to open your eyes to fresh insights from his Word. The more you understand God's Word, the easier it will be to follow his will for your life.

To begin the next topic, turn to p. A26.

To begin the next topic, turn to p. A26.

men free, I will set you free to be destroyed by war, famine, and disease. You will be considered a disgrace by all the nations of the earth. 18Because you have refused the terms of our covenant, I will cut you apart just as you cut apart the calf when you walked between its halves to solemnize your vows. 19Yes, I will cut you apart, whether you are officials of Judah or Jerusalem, court officials, priests, or common people—for you have broken your oath. 20I will give you to your enemies, and they will kill you. Your bodies will be food for the vultures and wild animals. 21I will hand over King Zedekiah of Judah and his officials to the army of the king of Babylon. And though Babylon's king has left this city for a while, 22I will call the Babylonian armies back again. They will fight against this city and will capture and burn it. I will see to it that all the towns of Judah are destroyed and left completely empty."

CHAPTER 35
The Faithful Recabites

This is the message the LORD gave Jeremiah when Jehoiakim son of Josiah was king of Judah: 2 "Go to the settlement where the families of the Recabites live, and invite them to the LORD's Temple. Take them into one of the inner rooms, and offer them some wine."

3So I went to see Jaazaniah son of Jeremiah and grandson of Habazziniah and all his brothers and sons—representing all the Recabite families. 4I took them to the Temple, and we went into the room assigned to the sons of Hanan son of Igdaliah, a man of God. This room was located next to the one used by the palace officials, directly above the room of Maaseiah son of Shallum, the Temple gatekeeper.

5I set cups and jugs of wine before them and invited them to have a drink, 6but they refused. "No," they said. "We don't drink wine, because Jehonadab* son of Recab, our ancestor, gave us this command: 'You and your descendants must never drink wine. 7And do not build houses or plant crops or vineyards, but always live in tents. If you follow these commands, you will live long, good lives in the land.' 8So we have obeyed him in all these things. We have never had a drink of wine since then, nor have our wives, our sons, or our daughters. 9We haven't built houses or owned vineyards or farms or planted crops. 10We have lived in tents and have fully obeyed all the

commands of Jehonadab, our ancestor. 11But when King Nebuchadnezzar* of Babylon arrived in this country, we were afraid of the Babylonian* and Aramean armies. So we decided to move to Jerusalem. That is why we are here."

12Then the LORD gave this message to Jeremiah: 13 "The LORD Almighty, the God of Israel, says: Go and say to the people in Judah and Jerusalem, 'Come and learn a lesson about how to obey me. 14The Recabites do not drink wine because their ancestor Jehonadab told them not to. But I have spoken to you again and again, and you refuse to listen or obey. 15I have sent you prophet after prophet to tell you to turn from your wicked ways and to stop worshiping other gods, so that you might live in peace here in the land I gave to you and your ancestors. But you would not listen to me or obey. 16The families of Recab have obeyed their ancestor completely, but you have refused to listen to me.'

17 "Therefore, the LORD God Almighty, the God of Israel, says: Because you refuse to listen or answer when I call, I will send upon Judah and Jerusalem all the disasters I have threatened."

18Then Jeremiah turned to the Recabites and said, "This is what the LORD Almighty, the God of Israel, says: You have obeyed your ancestor Jehonadab in every respect, following all his instructions. 19Because of this, Jehonadab son of Recab will always have descendants who serve me. I, the LORD Almighty, the God of Israel, have spoken!"

CHAPTER 36
Baruch Reads the LORD's Messages

During the fourth year that Jehoiakim son of Josiah was king in Judah,* the LORD gave this message to Jeremiah: 2 "Get a scroll, and write down all my messages against Israel, Judah, and the other nations. Begin with the first message back in the days of Josiah, and write down every message you have given, right up to the present time. 3Perhaps the people of Judah will repent if they see in writing all the terrible things I have planned for them. Then I will be able to forgive their sins and wrongdoings."

4So Jeremiah sent for Baruch son of Neriah, and as Jeremiah dictated, Baruch wrote down all the prophecies that the LORD had given him. 5Then Jeremiah said to Baruch, "I am a prisoner here and unable to go to the Temple. 6So you go to the Temple on the next day of fasting, and read

---

35:6 Hebrew *Jonadab*, a variant name for Jehonadab; also in 35:10, 14, 18, 19. See 2 Kgs 10:15.   35:11a Hebrew *Nebuchadrezzar*, a variant name for Nebuchadnezzar.   35:11b Or *Chaldean*.   36:1 The fourth year of Jehoiakim's reign was 605 B.C.

the messages from the LORD that are on this scroll. On that day people will be there from all over Judah. 7Perhaps even yet they will turn from their evil ways and ask the LORD's forgiveness before it is too late. For the LORD's terrible anger has been pronounced against them."

8Baruch did as Jeremiah told him and read these messages from the LORD to the people at the Temple. 9This happened on the day of sacred fasting held in late autumn,* during the fifth year of the reign of Jehoiakim son of Josiah. People from all over Judah came to attend the services at the Temple on that day. 10Baruch read Jeremiah's words to all the people from the Temple room of Gemariah son of Shaphan. This room was just off the upper courtyard of the Temple, near the New Gate entrance.

11When Micaiah son of Gemariah and grandson of Shaphan heard the messages from the LORD, 12he went down to the secretary's room in the palace where the administrative officials were meeting. Elishama the secretary was there, along with Delaiah son of Shemaiah, Elnathan son of Acbor, Gemariah son of Shaphan, Zedekiah son of Hananiah, and all the others with official responsibilities. 13When Micaiah told them about the messages Baruch was reading to the people, 14the officials sent Jehudi son of Nethaniah, grandson of Shelemiah, and greatgrandson of Cushi, to ask Baruch to come and read the messages to them, too. So Baruch took the scroll and went to them. 15"Sit down and read the scroll to us," the officials said, and Baruch did as they requested.

16By the time Baruch had finished reading, they were badly frightened. "We must tell the king what we have heard," they said. 17"But first, tell us how you got these messages. Did they come directly from Jeremiah?"

18So Baruch explained, "Jeremiah dictated them to me word by word, and I wrote down his words with ink on this scroll."

19"You and Jeremiah should both hide," the officials told Baruch. "Don't tell anyone where you are!" 20Then the officials left the scroll for safekeeping in the room of Elishama the secretary and went to tell the king.

King Jehoiakim Burns the Scroll

21The king sent Jehudi to get the scroll. Jehudi brought it from Elishama's room and read it to the king as all his officials stood by. 22It was late autumn, and the king was in a winterized part of the palace, sitting in front of a fire to keep warm. 23Whenever Jehudi finished reading three or four columns, the king took his knife and cut off that section of the scroll. He then threw it into the fire, section by section, until the whole scroll was burned up. 24Neither the king nor his officials showed any signs of fear or repentance at what they heard. 25Even when Elnathan, Delaiah, and Gemariah begged the king not to burn the scroll, he wouldn't listen.

26Then the king commanded his son Jerahmeel, Seraiah son of Azriel, and Shelemiah son of Abdeel to arrest Baruch and Jeremiah. But the LORD had hidden them.

Jeremiah Rewrites the Scroll

27After the king had burned Jeremiah's scroll, the LORD gave Jeremiah another message. He said, 28"Get another scroll, and write everything again just as you did on the scroll King Jehoiakim burned. 29Then say to the king, 'This is what the LORD says: You burned the scroll because it said the king of Babylon would destroy this land and everything in it. 30Now this is what the LORD says about King Jehoiakim of Judah: He will have no heirs to sit on the throne of David. His dead body will be thrown out to lie unburied—exposed to hot days and frosty nights. 31I will punish him and his family and his officials because of their sins. I will pour out on them and on all the people of Judah and Jerusalem all the disasters I have promised, for they would not listen to my warnings.'"

32Then Jeremiah took another scroll and dictated again to his secretary Baruch. He wrote everything that had been on the scroll King Jehoiakim had burned in the fire. Only this time, he added much more!

CHAPTER **37**
Zedekiah Calls for Jeremiah

Zedekiah son of Josiah succeeded Jehoiachin* son of Jehoiakim as the king of Judah. He was appointed by King Nebuchadnezzar* of Babylon. 2But neither King Zedekiah nor his officials nor the people who were left in the land listened to what the LORD said through Jeremiah. 3Nevertheless, King Zedekiah sent Jehucal son of Shelemiah and Zephaniah the priest, son of Maaseiah, to ask Jeremiah, "Please pray

36:9 Hebrew *in the ninth month,* of the Hebrew calendar (also in 36:22). This month in the fifth year of Jehoiakim's reign occurred in November and December 604 B.C. Also see note on 1:3.   37:1a Hebrew *Coniah,* a variant name for Jehoiachin.   37:1b Hebrew *Nebuchadrezzar,* a variant name for Nebuchadnezzar.

to the LORD our God for us." ⁴Jeremiah had not yet been imprisoned, so he could come and go as he pleased.

⁵At this time the army of Pharaoh Hophra* of Egypt appeared at the southern border of Judah. When the Babylonian* army heard about it, they withdrew from their siege of Jerusalem. ⁶Then the LORD gave this message to Jeremiah: ⁷"This is what the LORD, the God of Israel, says: Tell the king of Judah, who sent you to ask me what is going to happen, that Pharaoh's army is about to return to Egypt, though he came here to help you. ⁸Then the Babylonians* will come back and capture this city and burn it to the ground. ⁹The LORD says: Do not fool yourselves that the Babylonians are gone for good. They aren't! ¹⁰Even if you were to destroy the entire Babylonian army, leaving only a handful of wounded survivors, they would still stagger from their tents and burn this city to the ground!"

Jeremiah Is Imprisoned

¹¹When the Babylonian army left Jerusalem because of Pharaoh's approaching army, ¹²Jeremiah started to leave the city on his way to the land of Benjamin, to see the property he had bought. ¹³But as he was walking through the Benjamin Gate, a sentry arrested him and said, "You are defecting to the Babylonians!" The sentry making the arrest was Irijah son of Shelemiah and grandson of Hananiah.

¹⁴"That's not true!" Jeremiah protested. "I had no intention of doing any such thing." But Irijah wouldn't listen, and he took Jeremiah before the officials. ¹⁵They were furious with Jeremiah and had him flogged and imprisoned in the house of Jonathan the secretary. Jonathan's house had been converted into a prison. ¹⁶Jeremiah was put into a dungeon cell, where he remained for many days.

¹⁷Later King Zedekiah secretly requested that Jeremiah come to the palace, where the king asked him, "Do you have any messages from the LORD?"

"Yes, I do!" said Jeremiah. "You will be defeated by the king of Babylon."

¹⁸Then Jeremiah asked the king, "What crime have I committed? What have I done against you, your officials, or the people that I should be imprisoned like this? ¹⁹Where are your prophets now who told you the king of Babylon would not attack you? ²⁰Listen, my lord the king, I beg you.

Don't send me back to the dungeon in the house of Jonathan the secretary, for I will die there."

²¹So King Zedekiah commanded that Jeremiah not be returned to the dungeon. Instead, he was imprisoned in the courtyard of the guard in the royal palace. The king also commanded that Jeremiah be given a loaf of fresh bread every day as long as there was any left in the city. So Jeremiah was put in the palace prison.

CHAPTER **38**

Jeremiah in a Cistern

Now Shephatiah son of Mattan, Gedaliah son of Pashhur, Jehucal* son of Shelemiah, and Pashhur son of Malkijah heard what Jeremiah had been telling the people. He was saying, ²"This is what the LORD says: Everyone who stays in Jerusalem will die from war, famine, or disease, but those who surrender to the Babylonians* will live. ³The LORD also says: The city of Jerusalem will surely be handed over to the army of the king of Babylon, who will capture it."

⁴So these officials went to the king and said, "Sir, this man must die! That kind of talk will undermine the morale of the few fighting men we have left, as well as that of all the people, too. This man is a traitor!"

⁵So King Zedekiah agreed. "All right," he said. "Do as you like. I will do nothing to stop you."

⁶So the officials took Jeremiah from his cell and lowered him by ropes into an empty cistern in the prison yard. It belonged to Malkijah, a member of the royal family. There was no water in the cistern, but there was a thick layer of mud at the bottom, and Jeremiah sank down into it.

⁷But Ebed-melech the Ethiopian,* an important palace official, heard that Jeremiah was in the cistern. At that time the king was holding court at the Benjamin Gate, ⁸so Ebed-melech rushed from the palace to speak with him. ⁹"My lord the king," he said, "these men have done a very evil thing in putting Jeremiah the prophet into the cistern. He will soon die of hunger, for almost all the bread in the city is gone."

¹⁰So the king told Ebed-melech, "Take along thirty of my men, and pull Jeremiah out of the cistern before he dies."

¹¹So Ebed-melech took the men with him and went to a room in the palace beneath the treasury, where he found some old rags and discarded clothing. He carried these to the cistern and lowered them to Jeremiah on a rope.

37:5a Hebrew *army of Pharaoh;* see 44:30. **37:5b** Or *Chaldean;* also in 37:10, 11. **37:8** Or *Chaldeans;* also in 37:9, 13. **38:1** Hebrew *Jucal,* a variant name for Jehucal; see 37:3. **38:2** Or *Chaldeans;* also in 38:18, 19, 23. **38:7** Hebrew *the Cushite.*

¹²Ebed-melech called down to Jeremiah, "Put these rags under your armpits to protect you from the ropes." Then when Jeremiah was ready, ¹³they pulled him out. So Jeremiah was returned to the courtyard of the guard—the palace prison—where he remained.

Zedekiah Questions Jeremiah

¹⁴One day King Zedekiah sent for Jeremiah to meet him at the third entrance of the LORD's Temple. "I want to ask you something," the king said. "And don't try to hide the truth."

¹⁵Jeremiah said, "If I tell you the truth, you will kill me. And if I give you advice, you won't listen to me anyway."

¹⁶So King Zedekiah secretly promised him, "As surely as the LORD our Creator lives, I will not kill you or hand you over to the men who want you dead."

¹⁷Then Jeremiah said to Zedekiah, "The LORD God Almighty, the God of Israel, says: If you surrender to Babylon, you and your family will live, and the city will not be burned. ¹⁸But if you refuse to surrender, you will not escape! This city will be handed over to the Babylonians, and they will burn it to the ground."

¹⁹"But I am afraid to surrender," the king said, "for the Babylonians will hand me over to the Judeans who have defected to them. And who knows what they will do to me?"

²⁰Jeremiah replied, "You won't be handed over to them if you choose to obey the LORD. Your life will be spared, and all will go well for you. ²¹But if you refuse to surrender, this is what the LORD has revealed to me: ²²All the women left in your palace will be brought out and given to the officers of the Babylonian army. Then the women will taunt you, saying, 'What fine friends you have! They have betrayed and misled you. When your feet sank in the mud, they left you to your fate!' ²³All your wives and children will be led out to the Babylonians, and you will not escape. You will be seized by the king of Babylon, and this city will be burned."

²⁴Then Zedekiah said to Jeremiah, "Don't tell anyone you told me this, or you will die! ²⁵My officials may hear that I spoke to you. Then they may say to you, 'Tell us what you and the king were talking about. If you don't tell us, we will kill you.' ²⁶If this happens, just tell them you

begged me not to send you back to Jonathan's dungeon, for fear you would die there."

²⁷Sure enough, it wasn't long before the king's officials came to Jeremiah and asked him why the king had called for him. But Jeremiah followed the king's instructions, and they left without finding out the truth. No one had overheard the conversation between Jeremiah and the king. ²⁸And Jeremiah remained a prisoner in the courtyard of the guard until the day Jerusalem was captured.

CHAPTER **39**
The Fall of Jerusalem

It was in January* during the ninth year of King Zedekiah's reign that King Nebuchadnezzar* and his army returned to besiege Jerusalem. ²Two and a half years later, on July 18,* the Babylonians broke through the wall, and the city fell. ³All the officers of the Babylonian army came in and sat in triumph at the Middle Gate: Nergal-sharezer of Samgar, and Nebo-sarsekim,* a chief officer, and Nergal-sharezer, the king's adviser, and many others.

⁴King Zedekiah and his royal guard saw the Babylonians in the city gate, so they fled when the darkness of night arrived. They went out through a gate between the two walls behind the king's garden and headed toward the Jordan Valley.* ⁵But the Babylonians* chased the king and caught him on the plains of Jericho. They took him to King Nebuchadnezzar of Babylon, who was at Riblah in the land of Hamath. There the king of Babylon pronounced judgment upon Zedekiah. ⁶He made Zedekiah watch as they killed his sons and all the nobles of Judah. ⁷Then he gouged out Zedekiah's eyes, bound him in chains, and sent him away to exile in Babylon.

⁸Meanwhile, the Babylonians burned Jerusalem, including the palace, and tore down the walls of the city. ⁹Then Nebuzaradan, the captain of the guard, sent to Babylon the remnant of the population as well as those who had defected to him. ¹⁰But Nebuzaradan left a few of the poorest people in Judah, and he assigned them fields and vineyards to care for.

Jeremiah Remains in Judah

¹¹King Nebuchadnezzar had told Nebuzaradan to find Jeremiah. ¹²"See that he isn't hurt," he

---

39:1a Hebrew *in the tenth month*, of the Hebrew calendar. A number of events in Jeremiah can be cross-checked with dates in surviving Babylonian records and related accurately to our modern calendar. This event occurred on January 15, 588 B.C.; see 52:4 and the note there. 39:1b Hebrew *Nebuchadrezzar*, a variant name for Nebuchadnezzar; also in 39:11. 39:2 Hebrew *On the ninth day of the fourth month of the eleventh year of Zedekiah*. This event occurred on July 18, 586 B.C.; also see note on 39:1. 39:3 Or *Nergal-sharezer, Samgar-nebo, Sarsekim*. 39:4 Hebrew *the Arabah*. 39:5 Or *Chaldeans*; also in 39:8.

had said. "Look after him well, and give him anything he wants." 13So Nebuzaradan, the captain of the guard, and Nebushazban, a chief officer, and Nergal-sharezer, the king's adviser, and the other officers of Babylon's king 14sent messengers to bring Jeremiah out of the prison. They put him under the care of Gedaliah son of Ahikam and grandson of Shaphan, who was to take him back to his home. So Jeremiah stayed in Judah among his own people.

15The LORD had given the following message to Jeremiah while he was still in prison: 16"Say to Ebed-melech the Ethiopian,* 'The LORD Almighty, the God of Israel, says: I will do to this city everything I have threatened. I will send disaster, not prosperity. You will see its destruction, 17but I will rescue you from those you fear so much. 18Because you trusted me, I will preserve your life and keep you safe. I, the LORD, have spoken!'"

CHAPTER **40**

The LORD gave a message to Jeremiah after Nebuzaradan, captain of the guard, had released him at Ramah. He had found Jeremiah bound in chains among the captives of Jerusalem and Judah who were being sent to exile in Babylon.

2The captain of the guard called for Jeremiah and said, "The LORD your God has brought this disaster on this land, 3just as he said he would. For these people have sinned against the LORD and disobeyed him. That is why it happened. 4Now I am going to take off your chains and let you go. If you want to come with me to Babylon, you are welcome. I will see that you are well cared for. But if you don't want to come, you may stay here. The whole land is before you—go wherever you like. 5If you decide to stay, then return to Gedaliah son of Ahikam and grandson of Shaphan. He has been appointed governor of Judah by the king of Babylon. Stay there with the people he rules. But it's up to you; go wherever you like."

Then Nebuzaradan gave Jeremiah some food and money and let him go. 6So Jeremiah returned to Gedaliah son of Ahikam at Mizpah and lived in Judah with the few who were still left in the land.

Gedaliah Governs in Judah

7The leaders of the Judean guerrilla bands in the countryside heard that the king of Babylon had appointed Gedaliah son of Ahikam as governor over the poor people who were left behind in Judah, and that he hadn't exiled everyone to Babylon. 8So they came to see Gedaliah at Mizpah. These are the names of the leaders who came: Ishmael son of Nethaniah, Johanan and Jonathan, sons of Kareah, Seraiah son of Tanhumeth, the sons of Ephai the Netophathite, Jaazaniah* son of the Maacathite, and all their men.

9Gedaliah assured them that it would be safe for them to surrender to the Babylonians.* "Stay here, and serve the king of Babylon," he said, "and all will go well for you. 10As for me, I will stay at Mizpah to represent you before the Babylonians who come to meet with us. Settle in any town you wish, and live off the land. Harvest the grapes and summer fruits and olives, and store them away."

11When the Judeans in Moab, Ammon, Edom, and the other nearby countries heard that the king of Babylon had left a few people in Judah and that Gedaliah was the governor, 12they began to return to Judah from the places to which they had fled. They stopped at Mizpah to discuss their plans with Gedaliah and then went out into the Judean countryside to gather a great harvest of grapes and other crops.

A Plot against Gedaliah

13Soon after this, Johanan son of Kareah and the other guerrilla leaders came to Gedaliah at Mizpah. 14They said to him, "Did you know that Baalis, king of Ammon, has sent Ishmael son of Nethaniah to assassinate you?" But Gedaliah refused to believe them.

15Later Johanan had a private conference with Gedaliah and volunteered to kill Ishmael secretly. "Why should we let him come and murder you?" Johanan asked. "What will happen then to the Judeans who have returned? Why should the few of us who are still left be scattered and lost?"

16But Gedaliah said to Johanan, "I forbid you to do any such thing, for you are lying about Ishmael."

CHAPTER **41**
The Murder of Gedaliah

But in midautumn,* Ishmael son of Nethaniah and grandson of Elishama, who was a member of the royal family, arrived in Mizpah accompanied by ten men. Gedaliah invited them to dinner.

39:16 Hebrew *the Cushite.*   40:8 As in parallel text at 2 Kgs 25:23; Hebrew reads *Jezaniah,* a variant name for Jaazaniah.   40:9 Or *Chaldeans;* also in 40:10.   41:1 Hebrew *in the seventh month,* of the Hebrew calendar. This month occurred in October and November 586 B.C. Also see note on 39:1.

While they were eating, ²Ishmael and his ten men suddenly drew their swords and killed Gedaliah, whom the king of Babylon had appointed governor. ³Then they went out and slaughtered all the Judean officials and Babylonian* soldiers who were with Gedaliah at Mizpah.

⁴The next day, before anyone had heard about Gedaliah's murder, ⁵eighty men arrived from Shechem, Shiloh, and Samaria. They had come to worship at the Temple of the LORD. They had shaved off their beards, torn their clothes, and cut themselves, and had brought along grain offerings and incense. ⁶Ishmael left Mizpah to meet them, weeping as he went. When he reached them, he said, "Oh, come and see what has happened to Gedaliah!"

⁷But as soon as they were all inside the town, Ishmael and his men killed all but ten of them and threw their bodies into a cistern. ⁸The other ten had talked Ishmael into letting them go by promising to bring him their stores of wheat, barley, oil, and honey that they had hidden away. ⁹The cistern where Ishmael dumped the bodies of the men he murdered was the large one made by King Asa when he fortified Mizpah to protect himself against King Baasha of Israel. Ishmael son of Nethaniah filled it with corpses.

¹⁰Ishmael made captives of the king's daughters and the other people who had been left under Gedaliah's care in Mizpah by Nebuzaradan, captain of the guard. Taking them with him, he started back toward the land of Ammon.

¹¹But when Johanan son of Kareah and the rest of the guerrilla leaders heard what Ishmael had done, ¹²they took all their men and set out to stop him. They caught up with him at the pool near Gibeon. ¹³The people Ishmael had captured shouted for joy when they saw Johanan and his men. ¹⁴And all the captives from Mizpah escaped and began to help Johanan. ¹⁵Meanwhile, Ishmael and eight of his men escaped from Johanan into the land of Ammon.

¹⁶Then Johanan son of Kareah and his officers led away all the people they had rescued—warriors, women, children, and palace officials.* ¹⁷They took them all to the village of Geruth-kimham near Bethlehem, where they prepared to leave for Egypt. ¹⁸They were afraid of what the Babylonians* would do when they heard that Ishmael had killed Gedaliah, the governor appointed by the Babylonian king.

CHAPTER 42

Warning to Stay in Judah

Then all the army officers, including Johanan son of Kareah and Jezaniah* son of Hoshaiah, and all the people, from the least to the greatest, approached ²Jeremiah the prophet. They said, "Please pray to the LORD your God for us. As you know, we are only a tiny remnant compared to what we were before. ³Beg the LORD your God to show us what to do and where to go."

⁴"All right," Jeremiah replied. "I will pray to the LORD your God, and I will tell you everything he says. I will hide nothing from you."

⁵Then they said to Jeremiah, "May the LORD your God be a faithful witness against us if we refuse to obey whatever he tells us to do! ⁶Whether we like it or not, we will obey the LORD our God to whom we send you with our plea. For if we obey him, everything will turn out well for us."

⁷Ten days later, the LORD gave his reply to Jeremiah. ⁸So he called for Johanan son of Kareah and the army officers, and for all the people, from the least to the greatest. ⁹He said to them, "You sent me to the LORD, the God of Israel, with your request, and this is his reply: ¹⁰'Stay here in this land. If you do, I will build you up and not tear you down; I will plant you and not uproot you. For I am sorry for all the punishment I have had to bring upon you. ¹¹Do not fear the king of Babylon anymore, says the LORD. For I am with you and will save you and rescue you from his power. ¹²I will be merciful to you by making him kind, so he will let you stay here in your land.'

¹³"But if you refuse to obey the LORD your God and say, 'We will not stay here,' ¹⁴and if you insist on going to live in Egypt where you think you will be free from war, famine, and alarms, ¹⁵then this is what the LORD says to the remnant of Judah. The LORD Almighty, the God of Israel, says: 'If you insist on going to Egypt, ¹⁶the war and famine you fear will follow close behind you, and you will die there. ¹⁷That is the fate awaiting every one of you who insists on going to live in Egypt. Yes, you will die from war, famine, and disease. None of you will escape from the disaster I will bring upon you there.'

¹⁸"For the LORD Almighty, the God of Israel, says: 'Just as my anger and fury were poured out on the people of Jerusalem, so they will be poured out on you when you enter Egypt. You will become an object of damnation, horror,

41:3 Or *Chaldean.*   41:16 Or *eunuchs.*   41:18 Or *Chaldeans.*   42:1 Greek version reads *Azariah;* compare 43:2.

cursing, and mockery. And you will never see your homeland again.'

19"Listen, you remnant of Judah. The LORD has told you: 'Do not go to Egypt!' Don't forget this warning I have given you today. 20For you were deceitful when you sent me to pray to the LORD your God for you, saying, 'Just tell us what the LORD our God says, and we will do it!' 21And today I have told you exactly what he said, but you will not obey the LORD your God any better now than you have in the past. 22So you can be sure that you will die from war, famine, and disease in Egypt, where you insist on going."

CHAPTER 43
Jeremiah Taken to Egypt

When Jeremiah had finished giving this message from the LORD their God to all the people, 2Azariah son of Hoshaiah and Johanan son of Kareah and all the other proud men said to Jeremiah, "You lie! The LORD our God hasn't forbidden us to go to Egypt! 3Baruch son of Neriah has convinced you to say this, so we will stay here and be killed by the Babylonians* or be carried off into exile."

4So Johanan and all the army officers and all the people refused to obey the LORD's command to stay in Judah. 5Johanan and his officers took with them all the people who had returned from the nearby countries to which they had fled. 6In the crowd were men, women, and children, the king's daughters, and all those whom Nebuzaradan, the captain of the guard, had left with Gedaliah. Also included were the prophet Jeremiah and Baruch. 7The people refused to obey the LORD and went to Egypt, going as far as the city of Tahpanhes.

8Then at Tahpanhes, the LORD gave another message to Jeremiah. He said, 9"While the people of Judah are watching, bury large rocks between the pavement stones at the entrance of Pharaoh's palace here in Tahpanhes. 10Then say to the people of Judah, 'The LORD Almighty, the God of Israel, says: I will surely bring my servant Nebuchadnezzar,* king of Babylon, here to Egypt. I will set his throne on these stones that I have hidden. He will spread his royal canopy over them. 11And when he comes, he will destroy the land of Egypt. He will bring death to those destined for death; he will bring captivity to those destined for captivity; he will bring the sword against those destined for the sword. 12He will set fire to the temples of Egypt's gods, burning all their idols and carrying away the people as captives. He will pick clean the

land of Egypt as a shepherd picks fleas from his cloak. And he himself will leave unharmed. 13He will break down the sacred pillars standing in the temple of the sun* in Egypt, and he will burn down the temples of Egypt's gods.'"

CHAPTER 44
Judgment for Idolatry

This is the message Jeremiah received concerning the Judeans living in northern Egypt in the cities of Migdol, Tahpanhes, and Memphis,* and throughout southern Egypt as well: 2"This is what the LORD Almighty, the God of Israel, says: You saw what I did to Jerusalem and to all the towns of Judah. They now lie in ruins, and no one lives in them. 3Because of all their wickedness, my anger rose high against them. They burned incense and worshiped other gods— gods that neither they nor you nor any of your ancestors have ever known.

4"Again and again I sent my servants, the prophets, to plead with them, 'Don't do these horrible things that I hate so much.' 5But my people would not listen or turn back from their wicked ways. They kept right on burning incense to these gods. 6And so my fury boiled over and fell like fire on the towns of Judah and into the streets of Jerusalem, and now they are a desolate ruin.

7"And now the LORD God Almighty, the God of Israel, asks you: Why are you destroying yourselves? For not one of you will survive—not a man, woman, or child among you who has come here from Judah, not even the babies in your arms. 8Why arouse my anger by burning incense to the idols you have made here in Egypt? You will only destroy yourselves and make yourselves an object of cursing and mockery for all the nations of the earth. 9Have you forgotten the sins of your ancestors, the sins of the kings and queens of Judah, and the sins you and your wives committed in Judah and Jerusalem? 10To this very hour you have shown no remorse or reverence. No one has chosen to follow my law and the decrees I gave to you and your ancestors before you.

11"Therefore, the LORD Almighty, the God of Israel, says: I have made up my mind to destroy every one of you! 12I will take this remnant of Judah that insisted on coming here to Egypt, and I will consume them. They will fall here in Egypt, killed by war and famine. All will die, from the least to the greatest. They will be an object of damnation, horror, cursing, and mockery. 13I will

---

43:3 Or *Chaldeans.*   43:10 Hebrew *Nebuchadrezzar,* a variant name for Nebuchadnezzar.   43:13 Or *in Heliopolis.*   44:1 Hebrew *Noph.*

punish them in Egypt just as I punished them in Jerusalem, by war, famine, and disease. 14Of those who fled to Egypt with dreams of returning home to Judah, only a handful will escape."

15Then all the women present and all the men who knew that their wives had burned incense to idols—a great crowd of all the Judeans living in Pathros, the southern region of Egypt—answered Jeremiah, 16"We will not listen to your messages from the LORD! 17We will do whatever we want. We will burn incense to the Queen of Heaven and sacrifice to her just as much as we like—just as we and our ancestors did before us, and as our kings and princes have always done in the towns of Judah and in the streets of Jerusalem. For in those days we had plenty to eat, and we were well off and had no troubles! 18But ever since we quit burning incense to the Queen of Heaven and stopped worshiping her, we have been in great trouble and have suffered the effects of war and famine."

19"And," the women added, "do you suppose that we were worshiping the Queen of Heaven, pouring out drink offerings to her, and making cakes marked with her image, without our husbands knowing it and helping us? Of course not!"

20Then Jeremiah said to all of them, men and women alike, who had given him that answer, 21"Do you think the LORD did not know that you and your ancestors, your kings and officials, and all the people were burning incense to idols in the towns of Judah and in the streets of Jerusalem? 22It was because the LORD could no longer bear all the evil things you were doing that he made your land an object of cursing—a desolate ruin without a single inhabitant—as it is today. 23The very reason all these terrible things have happened to you is because you have burned incense to idols and sinned against the LORD, refusing to obey him and follow his instructions, laws, and stipulations."

24Then Jeremiah said to them all, including the women, "Listen to this message from the LORD, all you citizens of Judah who live in Egypt. 25The LORD Almighty, the God of Israel, says: You and your wives have said that you will never give up your devotion and sacrifices to the Queen of Heaven, and you have proved it by your actions. Then go ahead and carry out your promises and vows to her!

26"But listen to this message from the LORD, all you Judeans now living in Egypt: I have sworn by my great name, says the LORD, that my name will no longer be spoken by any of the Judeans in the land of Egypt. None of you may invoke my name or use this oath: 'As surely as the Sovereign LORD lives!' 27For I will watch over you to bring you disaster and not good. You will suffer war and famine until all of you are dead.

28"Only a small number will escape death and return to Judah from Egypt. Then all those who came to Egypt will find out whose words are true, mine or theirs! 29And this is the proof I give you, says the LORD, that all I have threatened will happen to you and that I will punish you here: 30I will turn Pharaoh Hophra, king of Egypt, over to his enemies who want to kill him, just as I turned King Zedekiah of Judah over to King Nebuchadnezzar* of Babylon. I, the LORD, have spoken!"

CHAPTER **45**
A Message for Baruch

The prophet Jeremiah gave a message to Baruch son of Neriah in the fourth year of the reign of Jehoiakim son of Josiah,* after Baruch had written down everything Jeremiah had dictated to him. He said, 2"This is what the LORD, the God of Israel, says to you, Baruch: 3You have said, 'I am overwhelmed with trouble! Haven't I had enough pain already? And now the LORD has added more! I am weary of my own sighing and can find no rest.'

4"Baruch, this is what the LORD says: I will destroy this nation that I built. I will uproot what I planted. 5Are you seeking great things for yourself? Don't do it! But don't be discouraged. I will bring great disaster upon all these people, but I will protect you wherever you go. I, the LORD, have spoken!"

CHAPTER **46**
Messages for the Nations

The following messages were given to Jeremiah the prophet from the LORD concerning foreign nations.

Messages about Egypt

2This message concerning Egypt was given in the fourth year of the reign of Jehoiakim son of Josiah,* the king of Judah, on the occasion of the battle of Carchemish when Pharaoh Neco, king of Egypt, and his army were defeated beside the Euphrates River by King Nebuchadnezzar* of Babylon.

3"Buckle on your armor and advance into

44:30 Hebrew *Nebuchadrezzar*, a variant name for Nebuchadnezzar. 45:1 The fourth year of Jehoiakim's reign was 605 B.C. 46:2a The fourth year of Jehoiakim's reign was 605 B.C. 46:2b Hebrew *Nebuchadrezzar*, a variant name for Nebuchadnezzar; also in 46:13, 26.

battle! ⁴Harness the horses, and prepare to mount them. Put on your helmets, sharpen your spears, and prepare your armor. ⁵But look! The Egyptian army flees in terror. The bravest of its fighting men run without a backward glance. They are terrorized at every turn, says the LORD. ⁶The swiftest cannot flee; the mightiest warriors cannot escape. By the Euphrates River to the north they stumble and fall.

⁷"Who is this, rising like the Nile River at floodtime, overflowing all the land? ⁸It is the Egyptian army, boasting that it will cover the earth like a flood, destroying every foe. ⁹Then come, you horses and chariots and mighty warriors of Egypt! Come, all you allies from Ethiopia, Libya, and Lydia* who are skilled with the shield and bow! ¹⁰For this is the day of the Lord, the LORD Almighty, a day of vengeance on his enemies. The sword will devour until it is satisfied, yes, drunk with your blood! The Lord, the LORD Almighty, will receive a sacrifice today in the north country beside the Euphrates River. ¹¹Go up to Gilead to get ointment, O virgin daughter of Egypt! But your many medicines will bring you no healing. ¹²The nations have heard of your shame. The earth is filled with your cries of despair. Your mightiest warriors will stumble across each other and fall together."

¹³Then the LORD gave the prophet Jeremiah this message about King Nebuchadnezzar's plans to attack Egypt.

¹⁴"Shout it out in Egypt! Publish it in the cities of Migdol, Memphis,* and Tahpanhes! Mobilize for battle, for the sword of destruction will devour everyone around you. ¹⁵Why have your warriors fled in terror? They cannot stand because the LORD has driven them away. ¹⁶They stumble and fall over each other and say among themselves, 'Come, let's go back to our homeland where we were born. Let's get away from the sword of the enemy!' ¹⁷There they will say, 'Pharaoh, the king of Egypt, is a loudmouth who missed his opportunity!'

¹⁸"As surely as I live," says the King, whose name is the LORD Almighty, "one is coming against Egypt who is as tall as Mount Tabor or Mount Carmel by the sea! ¹⁹Pack up! Get ready to leave for exile, you citizens of Egypt! The city of Memphis will be destroyed, without a single person living there. ²⁰Egypt is as sleek as a young cow, but a gadfly from the north is on its way! ²¹Egypt's famed mercenaries have become like fattened calves. They turn and run, for it is a day of great disaster for Egypt, a time of great pun-

ishment. ²²Silent as a serpent gliding away, Egypt flees. The invading army marches in; they come against her with axes like woodsmen. ²³They will cut down her people like trees," says the LORD, "for they are more numerous than grasshoppers. ²⁴Egypt will be humiliated; she will be handed over to men from the north."

²⁵The LORD Almighty, the God of Israel, says: "I will punish Amon, the god of Thebes,* and all the other gods of Egypt. I will punish its rulers and Pharaoh, too, and all who trust in him. ²⁶I will hand them over to those who want them killed—to King Nebuchadnezzar of Babylon and his army. But afterward the land will recover from the ravages of war. I, the LORD, have spoken!

²⁷"But do not be afraid, Jacob, my servant; do not be dismayed, Israel. For I will bring you home again from distant lands, and your children will return from their exile. Israel* will return and will have peace and quiet, and nothing will make them afraid. ²⁸Fear not, Jacob, my servant," says the LORD, "for I am with you. I will destroy the nations to which I have exiled you, but I will not destroy you. But I must discipline you; I cannot let you go unpunished."

CHAPTER **47**

A Message about Philistia

This is the LORD's message to the prophet Jeremiah concerning the Philistines of Gaza, before it was captured by the Egyptian army.

²This is what the LORD says: "A flood is coming from the north to overflow the land. It will destroy the land and everything in it—cities and people alike. People will scream in terror, and everyone in the land will weep. ³Hear the clatter of hooves and the rumble of wheels as the chariots rush by. Terrified fathers run madly, without a backward glance at their helpless children.

⁴"The time has come for the Philistines to be destroyed, along with their allies from Tyre and Sidon. Yes, the LORD is destroying the Philistines, those colonists from Crete.* ⁵The city of Gaza will be demolished; Ashkelon will lie in ruins. You remnant of the Mediterranean plain,* how long will you lament and mourn?

⁶"Now, O sword of the LORD, when will you be at rest again? Go back into your sheath; rest and be still! ⁷But how can it be still when the LORD has sent it on an errand? For the city of Ashkelon and the people living along the sea must be destroyed."

46:9 Hebrew *Cush, Put, and Lud.*   46:14 Hebrew *Noph;* also in 46:19.   46:25 Hebrew *No.*   46:27 Hebrew *Jacob.*   47:4 Hebrew *from Caphtor.*   47:5 Hebrew *the plain.*

CHAPTER **48**

A Message about Moab

This message was given concerning Moab.

This is what the LORD Almighty, the God of Israel, says: "Destruction is certain for the city of Nebo; it will soon lie in ruins. The city of Kiriathaim will be humiliated and captured; the fortress will be humiliated and broken down. ²No one will ever brag about Moab again, for there is a plot against her life. In Heshbon plans have been completed to destroy her. 'Come,' they say, 'we will cut her off from being a nation.' The city of Madmen,* too, will be silenced; the sword will follow you there. ³And then the roar of battle will surge against Horonaim, ⁴for all Moab is being destroyed. Her little ones will cry out.* ⁵Her refugees will climb the hills of Luhith, weeping bitterly, while cries of terror rise from Horonaim below. ⁶Flee for your lives! Hide in the wilderness!* ⁷Because you have trusted in your wealth and skill, you will be taken captive. Your god Chemosh, with his priests and princes, will be exiled to distant lands!

⁸"All the towns will be destroyed, both on the plateaus and in the valleys, for the LORD has spoken. ⁹Oh, that Moab had wings so she could fly away, for her cities will be left empty, with no one living in them. ¹⁰Cursed be those who refuse to do the work the LORD has given them, who hold back their swords from shedding blood!

¹¹"From her earliest history, Moab has lived in peace. She is like wine that has been allowed to settle. She has not been poured from flask to flask, and she is now fragrant and smooth. ¹²But the time is coming soon," says the LORD, "when I will send troublemakers to pour her from her jar. They will pour her out, then shatter the jar! ¹³At last Moab will be ashamed of her idol Chemosh, as Israel was ashamed of her gold calf at Bethel.*

¹⁴"You used to boast, 'We are heroes, mighty men of war.' ¹⁵But now Moab and her towns will be destroyed. Her most promising youth are doomed to slaughter," says the King, whose name is the LORD Almighty. ¹⁶"Calamity is coming fast to Moab; it threatens ominously.

¹⁷"You friends of Moab, weep for her and cry! See how the strong scepter is broken, how the beautiful staff is shattered! ¹⁸Come down from your glory and sit in the dust, you people of Dibon, for those who destroy Moab will shatter Dibon, too. They will tear down all your towers. ¹⁹The people of Aroer stand anxiously beside the road to watch. They shout to those who flee from Moab, 'What has happened there?'

²⁰"And the reply comes back, 'Moab lies in ruins; weep and wail! Tell it by the banks of the Arnon River: Moab has been destroyed!' ²¹All the cities of the plateau lie in ruins, too. Judgment has been poured out on them all—on Holon and Jahaz* and Mephaath, ²²and on Dibon and Nebo and Beth-diblathaim, ²³and on Kiriathaim and Beth-gamul and Beth-meon, ²⁴and on Kerioth and Bozrah—all the cities of Moab, far and near.

²⁵"The strength of Moab has ended. Her horns have been cut off, and her arms have been broken," says the LORD. ²⁶"Let her stagger and fall like a drunkard, for she has rebelled against the LORD. Moab will wallow in her own vomit, ridiculed by all. ²⁷Did you not make Israel the object of your ridicule? Was she caught in the company of thieves that you should despise her as you do?

²⁸"You people of Moab, flee from your cities and towns! Live in the caves like doves that nest in the clefts of the rocks. ²⁹We have heard of the pride of Moab, for it is very great. We know of her loftiness, her arrogance, and her haughty heart. ³⁰I know about her insolence," says the LORD, "but her boasts are false; they accomplish nothing. ³¹Yes, I wail for Moab; my heart is broken for the men of Kir-hareseth.*

³²"You people of Sibmah, rich in vineyards, I will weep for you even more than I did for Jazer. Your spreading vines once reached as far as the Dead Sea,* but the destroyer has stripped you bare! He has harvested your grapes and summer fruits. ³³Joy and gladness are gone from fruitful Moab. The presses yield no wine. No one treads the grapes with shouts of joy. There is shouting, yes, but not of joy. ³⁴Instead, their awful cries of terror can be heard from Heshbon clear across to Elealeh and Jahaz; from Zoar all the way to Horonaim and Eglath-shelishiyah. Even the waters of Nimrim are dried up now.

³⁵"I will put an end to Moab," says the LORD, "for they offer sacrifices at the pagan shrines and burn incense to their false gods. ³⁶My heart moans like a flute for Moab and Kir-hareseth, for all their wealth has disappeared. ³⁷They shave their heads and beards in mourning. They slash

---

48:2 *Madmen* sounds like the Hebrew word for "silence"; it should not be confused with the English word *madmen*. **48:4** Greek version reads *Her cries are heard as far away as Zoar.* **48:6** Or *Be like* [the town of] *Aroer in the wilderness.* **48:13** Hebrew *ashamed when they trusted in Bethel.* **48:21** Hebrew *Jahzah,* a variant name for Jahaz. **48:31** Hebrew *Kir-heres,* a variant name for Kir-hareseth; also in 48:36. **48:32** Hebrew *the sea of Jazer.*

their hands and put on clothes made of sackcloth. 38Crying and sorrow will be in every Moabite home and on every street. For I have smashed Moab like an old, unwanted bottle. 39How it is broken! Hear the wailing! See the shame of Moab! She has become an object of ridicule, an example of ruin to all her neighbors.

40"An eagle swoops down on the land of Moab," says the LORD. 41"Her cities will fall; her strongholds will be seized. Even the mightiest warriors will be as frightened as a woman about to give birth. 42Moab will no longer be a nation, for she has boasted against the LORD.

43"Terror and traps and snares will be your lot, O Moab," says the LORD. 44"Those who flee in terror will fall into a trap, and those who escape the trap will step into a snare. I will see to it that you do not get away, for the time of your judgment has come," says the LORD. 45"The people flee as far as Heshbon but are unable to go on. For a fire comes from Heshbon, King Sihon's ancestral home, to devour the entire land with all its rebellious people.

46"O Moab, your destruction is sure! The people of the god Chemosh are destroyed! Your sons and daughters have been taken away as captives. 47But in the latter days I will restore the fortunes of Moab," says the LORD.

This is the end of Jeremiah's prophecy concerning Moab.

CHAPTER **49**

A Message about Ammon

This message was given concerning the Ammonites.

This is what the LORD says: "What are you doing? Are there no descendants of Israel to inherit the land of Gad? Why are you, who worship Molech,* living in its towns? 2I will punish you for this," says the LORD, "by destroying your city of Rabbah. It will become a desolate heap, and the neighboring towns will be burned. Then Israel will come and take back the land you took from her," says the LORD.

3"Cry out, O Heshbon, for the town of Ai is destroyed. Weep, O people of Rabbah! Put on your clothes of mourning. Weep and wail, hiding in the hedges, for your god Molech will be exiled along with his princes and priests. 4You are proud of your fertile valleys, but they will soon be ruined. You rebellious daughter, you trusted in your wealth and thought no one could ever harm you. 5But look! I will bring terror upon you," says the Lord, the LORD Almighty. "Your neighbors will chase you from your land, and no one will help your exiles as they flee. 6But afterward I will restore the fortunes of the Ammonites," says the LORD.

Messages about Edom

7This message was given concerning Edom.

This is what the LORD Almighty says: "Where are all the wise men of Teman? Is there no one left to give wise counsel? 8Turn and flee! Hide in deep caves, you people of Dedan! For when I bring disaster on Edom,* I will punish you, too! 9Those who harvest grapes always leave a few for the poor. If thieves came at night, even they would not take everything. 10But I will strip bare the land of Edom, and there will be no place left to hide. Its children, its brothers, and its neighbors—all will be destroyed—and Edom itself will be no more. 11But I will preserve the orphans who remain among you. Your widows, too, will be able to depend on me for help."

12And this is what the LORD says: "If the innocent must suffer, how much more must you! You will not go unpunished! You must drink this cup of judgment! 13For I have sworn by my own name," says the LORD, "that Bozrah will become an object of horror and a heap of rubble; it will be mocked and cursed. All its towns and villages will be desolate forever."

14I have heard a message from the LORD that an ambassador was sent to the nations to say, "Form a coalition against Edom, and prepare for battle!"

15This is what the LORD says: "I will cut you down to size among the nations, Edom. You will be despised by all. 16You are proud that you inspire fear in others. And you are proud because you live in a rock fortress and hide high in the mountains. But don't fool yourselves! Though you live among the peaks with the eagles, I will bring you crashing down," says the LORD.

17"Edom will be an object of horror. All who pass by will be appalled and will gasp at the destruction they see there. 18It will be like the destruction of Sodom and Gomorrah and their neighboring towns," says the LORD. "No one will live there anymore. 19I will come like a lion from the thickets of the Jordan, leaping on the sheep in the pasture. I will chase Edom from its land, and I will appoint the leader of my choice. For who is like me, and who can challenge me? What ruler can oppose my will?"

20Listen to the LORD's plans for Edom and the

49:1 Hebrew *Milcom,* a variant name for Molech; also in 49:3. 49:8 Hebrew *Esau;* also in 49:10.

people of Teman. Even the little children will be dragged off, and their homes will be empty. ²¹The earth will shake with the noise of Edom's fall, and its cry of despair will be heard all the way to the Red Sea.* ²²The enemy will come as swiftly as an eagle, and he will spread his wings against Bozrah. Even the mightiest warriors will be as frightened as a woman about to give birth.

A Message about Damascus

²³This message was given concerning Damascus.

This is what the LORD says: "The towns of Hamath and Arpad are struck with fear, for they have heard the news of their destruction. Their hearts are troubled like a wild sea in a raging storm. ²⁴Damascus has become feeble, and all her people turn to flee. Fear, anguish, and pain have gripped her as they do a woman giving birth. ²⁵That famous city, a city of joy, will be forsaken! ²⁶Her young men will fall in the streets and die. Her warriors will all be killed," says the LORD Almighty. ²⁷"And I will start a fire at the edge of Damascus that will burn up the palaces of Ben-hadad."

A Message about Kedar and Hazor

²⁸This message was given concerning Kedar and the kingdoms of Hazor, which were attacked by King Nebuchadnezzar* of Babylon.

This is what the LORD says: "Advance against Kedar! Blot out the warriors from the East! ²⁹Their flocks and tents will be captured, and their household goods and camels will be taken away. Everywhere shouts of panic will be heard: 'We are terrorized at every turn!' ³⁰Flee for your lives," says the LORD. "Hide yourselves in deep caves, you people of Hazor, for King Nebuchadnezzar of Babylon has plotted against you and is preparing to destroy you.

³¹"Go up and attack those self-sufficient nomadic tribes," says the LORD. "They live alone in the desert without walls or gates. ³²Their camels and cattle will all be yours. I will scatter to the winds these people who live in distant places.* I will bring calamity upon them from every direction," says the LORD. ³³"Hazor will be inhabited by jackals, and it will be desolate forever. No one will live there anymore."

A Message about Elam

³⁴This message concerning Elam came to the prophet Jeremiah from the LORD at the beginning of the reign of King Zedekiah of Judah.

³⁵This is what the LORD Almighty says: "I will destroy the archers of Elam—the best of their marksmen. ³⁶I will bring enemies from all directions, and I will scatter the people of Elam to the four winds. They will be exiled to countries around the world. ³⁷I myself will go with Elam's enemies to shatter it. My fierce anger will bring great disaster upon the people of Elam," says the LORD. "Their enemies will chase them with the sword until I have destroyed them completely. ³⁸I will set my throne in Elam," says the LORD, "and I will destroy its king and princes. ³⁹But in the latter days I will restore the fortunes of Elam," says the LORD.

CHAPTER 50

A Message about Babylon

The LORD gave Jeremiah the prophet this message concerning Babylon and the land of the Babylonians.*

²This is what the LORD says: "Tell the whole world, and keep nothing back! Raise a signal flag so everyone will know that Babylon will fall! Her images and idols will be shattered. Her gods Bel and Marduk will be utterly disgraced. ³For a nation will attack her from the north and bring such destruction that no one will live in her again. Everything will be gone; both people and animals will flee.

Hope for Israel and Judah

⁴"Then the people of Israel and Judah will join together," says the LORD, "weeping and seeking the LORD their God. ⁵They will ask the way to Jerusalem* and will start back home again. They will bind themselves to the LORD with an eternal covenant that will never again be broken.

⁶"My people have been lost sheep. Their shepherds have led them astray and turned them loose in the mountains. They have lost their way and cannot remember how to get back to the fold. ⁷All who found them devoured them. Their enemies said, 'We are allowed to attack them freely, for they have sinned against the LORD, their place of rest, the hope of their ancestors.'

⁸"But now, flee from Babylon! Leave the land of the Babylonians. Lead my people home again. ⁹For look, I am raising up an army of great nations from the north. I will bring them against Babylon to attack her, and she will be captured. The enemies' arrows will go straight to the mark; they will not miss! ¹⁰Babylonia* will be plundered until the attackers are glutted with plunder," says the LORD.

49:21 Hebrew *sea of reeds.* 49:28 Hebrew *Nebuchadrezzar,* a variant name for Nebuchadnezzar; also in 49:30. 49:32 Or *who clip the corners of their hair.* 50:1 Or *Chaldeans;* also in 50:8, 25, 35, 45. 50:5 Hebrew *Zion;* also in 50:28. 50:10 Or *Chaldea.*

Babylon's Sure Fall

11 "You rejoice and are glad, you plunderers of my chosen people. You frisk about like a calf in a meadow and neigh like a stallion. 12But your homeland* will be overwhelmed with shame and disgrace. You will become the least of nations—a wilderness, a dry and desolate land. 13Because of the LORD's anger, Babylon will become a deserted wasteland. All who pass by will be horrified and will gasp at the destruction they see there.

14"Yes, prepare to attack Babylon, all you nations round about. Let your archers shoot at her. Spare no arrows, for she has sinned against the LORD. 15Shout against her from every side. Look! She surrenders! Her walls have fallen. The LORD has taken vengeance, so do not spare her. Do to her as she has done to others! 16Lead from Babylon all those who plant crops; send all the harvesters away. Let the captives escape the sword of the enemy and rush back to their own lands.

Hope for God's People

17"The Israelites are like sheep that have been scattered by lions. First the king of Assyria ate them up. Then King Nebuchadnezzar* of Babylon cracked their bones." 18Therefore, the LORD Almighty, the God of Israel, says: "Now I will punish the king of Babylon and his land, just as I punished the king of Assyria. 19And I will bring Israel home again to her own land, to feed in the fields of Carmel and Bashan, and to be satisfied once more on the hill country of Ephraim and Gilead. 20In those days," says the LORD, "no sin will be found in Israel or in Judah, for I will forgive the remnant I preserve.

The LORD's Judgment on Babylon

21 "Go up, my warriors, against the land of Merathaim and against the people of Pekod. Yes, march against Babylon, the land of rebels, a land that I will judge! Pursue, kill, and completely destroy* them, as I have commanded you," says the LORD. 22"Let the battle cry be heard in the land, a shout of great destruction. 23Babylon, the mightiest hammer in all the earth, lies broken and shattered. Babylon is desolate among the nations! 24Listen, Babylon, for I have set a trap for you. You are caught, for you have fought against the LORD. 25"The LORD has opened his armory and brought out weapons to vent his fury against his enemies. The terror that falls upon the Babylonians will be the work of the Sovereign LORD Almighty. 26Yes, come against her from distant lands. Break open her granaries. Crush her walls and houses into heaps of rubble. Destroy her completely, and leave nothing! 27Even destroy her cattle—it will be terrible for them, too! Slaughter them all! For the time has come for Babylon to be devastated. 28Listen to the people who have escaped from Babylon, as they declare in Jerusalem how the LORD our God has taken vengeance against those who destroyed his Temple.

29"Send out a call for archers to come to Babylon. Surround the city so none can escape. Do to her as she has done to others, for she has defied the LORD, the Holy One of Israel. 30Her young men will fall in the streets and die. Her warriors will all be killed," says the LORD.

31 "See, I am your enemy, O proud people," says the Lord, the LORD Almighty. "Your day of reckoning has arrived. 32O land of pride, you will stumble and fall, and no one will raise you up. For I will light a fire in the cities of Babylon that will burn everything around them."

33And now the LORD Almighty says this: "The people of Israel and Judah have been wronged. Their captors hold them and refuse to let them go. 34But the one who redeems them is strong. His name is the LORD Almighty. He will defend them and give them rest again in Israel. But the people of Babylon—there will be no rest for them!

35"The sword of destruction will strike the Babylonians," says the LORD. "It will strike the people of Babylon—her princes and wise men, too. 36And when it strikes her wise counselors, they will become fools! When it strikes her mightiest warriors, panic will seize them! 37When it strikes her horses and chariots, her allies from other lands will become as weak as women. When it strikes her treasures, they all will be plundered. 38It will even strike her water supply, causing it to dry up. And why? Because the whole land is filled with idols, and the people are madly in love with them.

39"Soon this city of Babylon will be inhabited by ostriches and jackals. It will be a home for the wild animals of the desert. Never again will people live there; it will lie desolate forever. 40I will destroy it just as I* destroyed Sodom and Gomorrah and their neighboring towns," says the LORD. "No one will live there anymore.

50:12 Hebrew *your mother.*   50:17 Hebrew *Nebuchadrezzar,* a variant name for Nebuchadnezzar.   50:21 The Hebrew term used here refers to the complete consecration of things or people to the LORD, either by destroying them or by giving them as an offering.   50:40 Hebrew *just as God.*

⁴¹"Look! A great army is marching from the north! A great nation and many kings are rising against you from far-off lands. ⁴²They are fully armed for slaughter. They are cruel and show no mercy. As they ride forward, the noise of their army is like a roaring sea. They are marching in battle formation to destroy you, Babylon. ⁴³The king of Babylon has received reports about the enemy, and he is weak with fright. Fear and pain have gripped him, like that of a woman about to give birth.

⁴⁴"I will come like a lion from the thickets of the Jordan, leaping on the sheep in the pasture. I will chase Babylon from its land, and I will appoint the leader of my choice. For who is like me, and who can challenge me? What ruler can oppose my will?"

⁴⁵Listen to the Lᴏʀᴅ's plans against Babylon and the land of the Babylonians. Even little children will be dragged off, and their homes will be empty. ⁴⁶The earth will shake with the noise of Babylon's fall, and her cry of despair will be heard around the world.

CHAPTER **51**

This is what the Lᴏʀᴅ says: "I will stir up a destroyer against Babylon and the people of Babylonia.* ²Foreigners will come and winnow her, blowing her away as chaff. They will come from every side to rise against her in her day of trouble. ³Don't let the archers put on their armor or draw their bows. No one will be spared! Young and old alike will be completely destroyed.* ⁴They will fall dead in the land of the Babylonians,* slashed to death in her streets. ⁵For the Lᴏʀᴅ Almighty has not forsaken Israel and Judah. He is still their God, even though their land was filled with sin against the Holy One of Israel."

⁶Flee from Babylon! Save yourselves! Don't get trapped in her punishment! It is the Lᴏʀᴅ's time for vengeance; he will fully repay her. ⁷Babylon has been like a golden cup in the Lᴏʀᴅ's hands, a cup from which he made the whole earth drink and go mad. ⁸But now suddenly, Babylon, too, has fallen. Weep for her, and give her medicine. Perhaps she can yet be healed. ⁹We would have helped her if we could, but nothing can save her now. Let her go; abandon her. Return now to your own land, for her judgment will be so great it cannot be measured.

¹⁰The Lᴏʀᴅ has vindicated us. Come, let us announce in Jerusalem* everything the Lᴏʀᴅ our God has done.

¹¹Sharpen the arrows! Lift up the shields! For the Lᴏʀᴅ has stirred up the spirit of the kings of the Medes to march against Babylon and destroy her. This is his vengeance against those who desecrated his Temple. ¹²Raise the battle flag against Babylon! Reinforce the guard and station the watchmen. Prepare an ambush, for the Lᴏʀᴅ will fulfill all his plans against Babylon.

¹³You are a city rich with water, a great center of commerce, but your end has come. The thread of your life is cut. ¹⁴The Lᴏʀᴅ Almighty has taken this vow and has sworn to it by his own name: "Your cities will be filled with enemies, like fields filled with locusts, and they will lift their shouts of triumph over you."

A Hymn of Praise to the Lᴏʀᴅ
¹⁵ He made the earth by his power,
and he preserves it by his wisdom.
He has stretched out the heavens
by his understanding.
¹⁶ When he speaks, there is thunder in the heavens.
He causes the clouds to rise over the earth.
He sends the lightning with the rain
and releases the wind from his storehouses.
¹⁷ Compared to him, all people are foolish
and have no knowledge at all!
They make idols, but the idols will disgrace their makers,
for they are frauds.
They have no life or power in them.
¹⁸ Idols are worthless; they are lies!
The time is coming when they will all be destroyed.
¹⁹ But the God of Israel* is no idol!
He is the Creator of everything that exists,
including his people, his own special possession.
The Lᴏʀᴅ Almighty is his name!

Babylon's Great Punishment
²⁰"You* are my battle-ax and sword," says the Lᴏʀᴅ. "With you I will shatter nations and destroy many kingdoms. ²¹With you I will shatter armies, destroying the horse and rider, the chariot and charioteer. ²²With you I will shatter men and women, old people and children, young

---

51:1 Hebrew *of Leb-kamai*, a code name for Babylonia.   51:3 The Hebrew term used here refers to the complete consecration of things or people to the Lᴏʀᴅ, either by destroying them or by giving them as an offering.   51:4 Or *Chaldeans*; also in 51:54.   51:10 Hebrew *Zion*; also in 51:24, 35a.   51:19 Hebrew *the Portion of Jacob.*   51:20 Possibly Cyrus, who was used of God to conquer Babylon. Compare Isa 44:28; 45:1.

men and maidens. 23With you I will shatter shepherds and flocks, farmers and oxen, captains and rulers.

24"As you watch, I will repay Babylon and the people of Babylonia* for all the wrong they have done to my people in Jerusalem," says the LORD. 25"Look, O mighty mountain, destroyer of the earth! I am your enemy," says the LORD. "I will raise my fist against you, to roll you down from the heights. When I am finished, you will be nothing but a heap of rubble. 26You will be desolate forever. Even your stones will never again be used for building. You will be completely wiped out," says the LORD.

27Signal many nations to mobilize for war against Babylon. Sound the battle cry! Bring out the armies of Ararat, Minni, and Ashkenaz. Appoint a leader, and bring a multitude of horses! 28Bring against her the armies of the kings of the Medes and their generals, and the armies of all the countries they rule.

29Babylon trembles and writhes in pain, for everything the LORD has planned against her stands unchanged. Babylon will be left desolate without a single inhabitant. 30Her mightiest warriors no longer fight. They stay in their barracks. Their courage is gone. They have become as fearful as women. The invaders have burned the houses and broken down the city gates. 31Messengers from every side come running to the king to tell him all is lost! 32All the escape routes are blocked. The fortifications are burning, and the army is in panic.

33For the LORD Almighty, the God of Israel, says: "Babylon is like wheat on a threshing floor, about to be trampled. In just a little while her harvest will begin."

34"King Nebuchadnezzar* of Babylon has eaten and crushed us and emptied out our strength. He has swallowed us like a great monster and filled his belly with our riches. He has thrown us out of our own country. 35May Babylon be repaid for all the violence she did to us," say the people of Jerusalem. "May the people of Babylonia be paid in full for all the blood they spilled," says Jerusalem.

The LORD's Vengeance on Babylon

36The LORD says to Jerusalem, "I will be your lawyer to plead your case, and I will avenge you. I will dry up her river, her water supply, 37and Babylon will become a heap of rubble, haunted by jackals. It will be an object of horror and contempt, without a single person living there.

38"In their drunken feasts, the people of Babylon roar like lions. 39And while they lie inflamed with all their wine, I will prepare a different kind of feast for them. I will make them drink until they fall asleep, never again to waken," says the LORD. 40"I will bring them like lambs to the slaughter, like rams and goats to be sacrificed.

41"How Babylon* is fallen—great Babylon, praised throughout the earth! The world can scarcely believe its eyes at her fall! 42The sea has risen over Babylon; she is covered by its waves. 43Her cities now lie in ruins; she is a dry wilderness where no one lives or even passes by. 44And I will punish Bel, the god of Babylon, and pull from his mouth what he has taken. The nations will no longer come and worship him. The wall of Babylon has fallen.

A Message for the Exiles

45"Listen, my people, flee from Babylon. Save yourselves! Run from the LORD's fierce anger. 46But do not panic when you hear the first rumor of approaching forces. For rumors will keep coming year by year. Then there will be a time of violence as the leaders fight against each other. 47For the time is surely coming when I will punish this great city and all her idols. Her whole land will be disgraced, and her dead will lie in the streets. 48The heavens and earth will rejoice, for out of the north will come destroying armies against Babylon," says the LORD. 49"Just as Babylon killed the people of Israel and others throughout the world, so must her people be killed. 50Go, you who escaped the sword! Do not stand and watch—flee while you can! Remember the LORD, even though you are in a far-off land, and think about your home in Jerusalem."

51"We are ashamed," the people say. "We are insulted and disgraced because the LORD's Temple has been defiled by foreigners."

52"Yes," says the LORD, "but the time is coming when Babylon's idols will be destroyed. The groans of her wounded people will be heard throughout the land. 53Though Babylon reaches as high as the heavens, and though she increases her strength immeasurably, I will send enemies to plunder her," says the LORD.

Babylon's Complete Destruction

54Listen! Hear the cry of Babylon, the sound of great destruction from the land of the Babyloni-

51:24 Or *Chaldea;* also in 51:35. 51:34 Hebrew *Nebuchadrezzar,* a variant name for Nebuchadnezzar. 51:41 Hebrew *Sheshach,* a code name for Babylon.

ans. ⁵⁵For the LORD is destroying Babylon. He will silence her. Waves of enemies pound against her; the noise of battle rings through the city. ⁵⁶Destroying armies come against Babylon. Her mighty men are captured, and their weapons break in their hands. For the LORD is a God who gives just punishment, and he is giving Babylon all she deserves.

⁵⁷"I will make drunk her officials, wise men, rulers, captains, and warriors," says the King, whose name is the LORD Almighty. "They will fall asleep and never wake up again!"

⁵⁸This is what the LORD Almighty says: "The wide walls of Babylon will be leveled to the ground, and her high gates will be burned. The builders from many lands have worked in vain, for their work will be destroyed by fire!"

Jeremiah's Message Sent to Babylon

⁵⁹The prophet Jeremiah gave this message to Zedekiah's staff officer, Seraiah son of Neriah and grandson of Mahseiah, when he went to Babylon with King Zedekiah of Judah. This was during the fourth year of Zedekiah's reign.* ⁶⁰Jeremiah had recorded on a scroll all the terrible disasters that would soon come upon Babylon. ⁶¹He said to Seraiah, "When you get to Babylon, read aloud everything on this scroll. ⁶²Then say, 'LORD, you have said that you will destroy Babylon so that neither people nor animals will remain here. She will lie empty and abandoned forever.' ⁶³Then, when you have finished reading the scroll, tie it to a stone, and throw it into the Euphrates River. ⁶⁴Then say, 'In this same way Babylon and her people will sink, never again to rise, because of the disasters I will bring upon her.'"

This is the end of Jeremiah's messages.

CHAPTER 52
The Fall of Jerusalem

Zedekiah was twenty-one years old when he became king, and he reigned in Jerusalem eleven years. His mother's name was Hamutal, the daughter of Jeremiah from Libnah. ²But Zedekiah did what was evil in the LORD's sight, just as Jehoiakim had done. ³So the LORD, in his anger, finally banished the people of Jerusalem and Judah from his presence and sent them into exile.

Then Zedekiah rebelled against the king of Babylon. ⁴So on January 15,* during the ninth year of Zedekiah's reign, King Nebuchadnezzar* of Babylon led his entire army against Jerusalem. They surrounded the city and built siege ramps against its walls. ⁵Jerusalem was kept under siege until the eleventh year of King Zedekiah's reign.

⁶By July 18 of Zedekiah's eleventh year,* the famine in the city had become very severe, with the last of the food entirely gone. ⁷Then a section of the city wall was broken down, and all the soldiers made plans to escape from the city. But since the city was surrounded by the Babylonians,* they waited for nightfall and fled through the gate between the two walls behind the king's gardens. They made a dash across the fields, in the direction of the Jordan Valley.*

⁸But the Babylonians chased after them and caught King Zedekiah on the plains of Jericho, for by then his men had all abandoned him. ⁹They brought him to the king of Babylon at Riblah, in the land of Hamath, where sentence was passed against him. ¹⁰There at Riblah, the king of Babylon made Zedekiah watch as all his sons were killed; they also killed all the other leaders of Judah. ¹¹Then they gouged out Zedekiah's eyes, bound him in bronze chains, and led him away to Babylon. Zedekiah remained there in prison for the rest of his life.

The Temple Destroyed

¹²On August 17 of that year,* which was the nineteenth year of Nebuchadnezzar's reign, Nebuzaradan, captain of the guard, an official of the Babylonian king, arrived in Jerusalem. ¹³He burned down the Temple of the LORD, the royal palace, and all the houses of Jerusalem. He destroyed all the important buildings in the city. ¹⁴Then the captain of the guard supervised the entire Babylonian* army as they tore down the walls of Jerusalem. ¹⁵Nebuzaradan, captain of the guard, then took some of the poorest of the people and those who remained in the city, along with the rest of the craftsmen and the troops who had declared their allegiance to the king of Babylon. ¹⁶But Nebuzaradan allowed some of the poorest people to stay behind in Judah to care for the vineyards and fields.

¹⁷The Babylonians broke up the bronze pillars, the bronze water carts, and the bronze Sea

---

51:59 The fourth year of Zedekiah's reign was 593 B.C. 52:4a Hebrew *on the tenth day of the tenth month,* of the Hebrew calendar. A number of events in Jeremiah can be cross-checked with dates in surviving Babylonian records and related accurately to our modern calendar. This event occurred on January 15, 588 B.C. 52:4b Hebrew *Nebuchadrezzar,* a variant name for Nebuchadnezzar; also in 52:12, 28, 29, 30. 52:6 Hebrew *By the ninth day of the fourth month* [of Zedekiah's eleventh year]. This event of the Hebrew lunar calendar occurred on July 18, 586 B.C.; also see note on 52:4a. 52:7a Or *Chaldeans;* also in 52:8, 17. 52:7b Hebrew *the Arabah.* 52:12 Hebrew *On the tenth day of the fifth month,* of the Hebrew calendar. This day was August 17, 586 B.C.; also see note on 52:4a. 52:14 Or *Chaldean.*

that were at the LORD's Temple, and they carried all the bronze away to Babylon. 18They also took all the pots, shovels, lamp snuffers, basins, dishes, and all the other bronze utensils used for making sacrifices at the Temple. 19Nebuzaradan, captain of the guard, also took the small bowls, firepans, basins, pots, lampstands, dishes, bowls used for drink offerings, and all the other utensils made of pure gold or silver.

20The bronze from the two pillars, the water carts, and the Sea with the twelve bulls beneath it was too great to be measured. These things had been made for the LORD's Temple in the days of King Solomon. 21Each of the pillars was 27 feet tall and 18 feet in circumference.* They were hollow, with walls 3 inches thick.* 22The bronze capital on top of each pillar was 7½ feet* high and was decorated with a network of bronze pomegranates all the way around. 23There were ninety-six pomegranates on the sides, and a total of one hundred on the network around the top.

24The captain of the guard took with him as prisoners Seraiah the chief priest, his assistant Zephaniah, and the three chief gatekeepers. 25And of the people still hiding in the city, he took an officer of the Judean army, seven of the king's personal advisers, the army commander's chief secretary, who was in charge of recruit-

ment, and sixty other citizens. 26Nebuzaradan the commander took them all to the king of Babylon at Riblah. 27And there at Riblah in the land of Hamath, the king of Babylon had them all put to death. So the people of Judah were sent into exile from their land.

28The number of captives taken to Babylon in the seventh year of Nebuchadnezzar's reign* was 3,023. 29Then in Nebuchadnezzar's eighteenth year* he took 832 more. 30In his twenty-third year* he sent Nebuzaradan, his captain of the guard, who took 745 more—a total of 4,600 captives in all.

Hope for Israel's Royal Line

31In the thirty-seventh year of King Jehoiachin's exile in Babylon, Evil-merodach ascended to the Babylonian throne. He was kind to Jehoiachin and released him from prison on March 31 of that year.* 32He spoke pleasantly to Jehoiachin and gave him preferential treatment over all the other exiled kings in Babylon. 33He supplied Jehoiachin with new clothes to replace his prison garb and allowed him to dine at the king's table for the rest of his life. 34The Babylonian king also gave him a regular allowance to cover his living expenses until the day of his death.

52:21a Hebrew *18 cubits* [8.1 meters] *tall and 12 cubits* [5.4 meters] *in circumference.*   52:21b Hebrew *4 fingers thick* [8 centimeters].   52:22 Hebrew *5 cubits* [2.3 meters].   52:28 This exile in the seventh year of Nebuchadnezzar's reign occurred in 597 B.C.   52:29 This exile in the eighteenth year of Nebuchadnezzar's reign occurred in 586 B.C.   52:30 This exile in the twenty-third year of Nebuchadnezzar's reign occurred in 581 B.C.   52:31 Hebrew *on the twenty-fifth day of the twelfth month,* of the Hebrew calendar. This day was March 31, 561 B.C.; also see note on 52:4a.

Lamentations

CHAPTER 1

Sorrow in Jerusalem

Jerusalem's streets, once bustling with people, are now silent. Like a widow broken with grief, she sits alone in her mourning. Once the queen of nations, she is now a slave.

²She sobs through the night; tears stream down her cheeks. Among all her lovers, there is no one left to help her. All her friends have betrayed her; they are now her enemies.

³Judah has been led away into captivity, afflicted and enslaved. She lives among foreign nations and has no place of rest. Her enemies have chased her down, and she has nowhere to turn.

⁴The roads to Jerusalem* are in mourning, no longer filled with crowds on their way to celebrate the Temple festivals. The city gates are silent, her priests groan, her young women are crying—how bitterly Jerusalem weeps!

⁵Her oppressors have become her masters, and her enemies prosper, for the LORD has punished Jerusalem for her many sins. Her children have been captured and taken away to distant lands.

⁶All the beauty and majesty of Jerusalem* are gone. Her princes are like starving deer searching for pasture, too weak to run from the pursuing enemy.

⁷And now in the midst of her sadness and wandering, Jerusalem remembers her ancient splendor. But then she fell to her enemy, and there was no one to help her. Her enemy struck her down and laughed as she fell.

⁸Jerusalem has sinned greatly, so she has been tossed away like a filthy rag. All who once honored her now despise her, for they have seen her stripped naked and humiliated. All she can do is groan and hide her face.

⁹She defiled herself with immorality with no thought of the punishment that would follow. Now she lies in the gutter with no one to lift her out. "LORD, see my deep misery," she cries. "The enemy has triumphed."

¹⁰The enemy has plundered her completely, taking everything precious that she owns. She has seen foreigners violate her sacred Temple, the place the LORD had forbidden them to enter.

¹¹Her people groan as they search for bread. They have sold their treasures for food to stay alive. "O LORD, look," she mourns, "and see how I am despised.

¹²"Is it nothing to you, all you who pass by? Look around and see if there is any suffering like mine, which the LORD brought on me in the day of his fierce anger.

¹³"He has sent fire from heaven that burns in my bones. He has placed a trap in my path and turned me back. He has made me desolate, racked with sickness all day long.

¹⁴"He wove my sins into ropes to hitch me to a yoke of captivity. The Lord sapped my strength and gave me to my enemies; I am helpless in their hands.

¹⁵"The Lord has treated my mighty men with contempt. At his command a great army has come to crush my young warriors. The Lord has trampled his beloved city* as grapes are trampled in a winepress.

¹⁶"For all these things I weep; tears flow down my cheeks. No one is here to comfort me; any who might encourage me are far away. My children have no future, for the enemy has conquered us."

¹⁷Jerusalem pleads for help, but no one comforts her. Regarding his people,* the LORD has

---

1:1 Each of the first four chapters of this book is an acrostic, laid out in the order of the Hebrew alphabet. The first word of each verse begins with a successive Hebrew letter. Chapters 1, 2, and 4 have one verse for each of the 22 Hebrew letters. Chapter 3 contains 22 stanzas of three verses each. Though chapter 5 is not an acrostic, it also has 22 verses.   1:4 Hebrew *Zion*; also in 1:17.   1:6 Hebrew *the daughter of Zion.*
1:15 Hebrew *the virgin daughter of Judah.*   1:17 Hebrew *Jacob.*

said, "Let their neighbors be their enemies! Let them be thrown away like a filthy rag!"

18 "And the LORD is right," she groans, "for I rebelled against him. Listen, people everywhere; look upon my anguish and despair, for my sons and daughters have been taken captive to distant lands.

19 "I begged my allies for help, but they betrayed me. My priests and leaders starved to death in the city, even as they searched for food to save their lives.

20 "LORD, see my anguish! My heart is broken and my soul despairs, for I have rebelled against you. In the streets the sword kills, and at home there is only death.

21 "Others heard my groans, but no one turned to comfort me. When my enemies heard of my troubles, they were happy to see what you had done. Oh, bring the day you promised, when you will destroy them as you have destroyed me.

22 "Look at all their evil deeds, LORD. Punish them, as you have punished me for all my sins. My groans are many, and my heart is faint."

CHAPTER 2
God's Anger at Sin

The Lord in his anger has cast a dark shadow over Jerusalem.* The fairest of Israel's cities lies in the dust, thrown down from the heights of heaven. In his day of awesome fury, the Lord has shown no mercy even to his Temple.*

2 Without mercy the Lord has destroyed every home in Israel.* In his anger he has broken down the fortress walls of Jerusalem.* He has brought to dust the kingdom and all its rulers.

3 All the strength of Israel vanishes beneath his fury. The Lord has withdrawn his protection as the enemy attacks. He consumes the whole land of Israel like a raging fire.

4 He bends his bow against his people as though he were their enemy. His strength is used against them to kill their finest youth. His fury is poured out like fire on beautiful Jerusalem.*

5 Yes, the Lord has vanquished Israel like an enemy. He has destroyed her forts and palaces. He has brought unending sorrow and tears to Jerusalem.

6 He has broken down his Temple as though it were merely a garden shelter. The LORD has blotted out all memory of the holy festivals and Sabbath days. Kings and priests fall together before his anger.

7 The Lord has rejected his own altar; he despises his own sanctuary. He has given Jerusalem's palaces to her enemies. They shout in the LORD's Temple as though it were a day of celebration.

8 The LORD was determined to destroy the walls of Jerusalem. He made careful plans for their destruction, then he went ahead and did it. Therefore, the ramparts and walls have fallen down before him.

9 Jerusalem's gates have sunk into the ground. All their locks and bars are destroyed, for he has smashed them. Her kings and princes have been exiled to distant lands; the law is no more. Her prophets receive no more visions from the LORD.

10 The leaders of Jerusalem sit on the ground in silence, clothed in sackcloth. They throw dust on their heads in sorrow and despair. The young women of Jerusalem hang their heads in shame.

11 I have cried until the tears no longer come. My heart is broken, my spirit poured out, as I see what has happened to my people. Little children and tiny babies are fainting and dying in the streets.

12 "Mama, we want food," they cry, and then collapse in their mothers' arms. Their lives ebb away like the life of a warrior wounded in battle.

13 In all the world has there ever been such sorrow? O daughter of Jerusalem, to what can I compare your anguish? O virgin daughter of Zion, how can I comfort you? For your wound is as deep as the sea. Who can heal you?

14 Your "prophets" have said so many foolish things, false to the core. They did not try to hold you back from exile by pointing out your sins. Instead, they painted false pictures, filling you with false hope.

15 All who pass by jeer at you. They scoff and insult Jerusalem,* saying, "Is this the city called 'Most Beautiful in All the World' and 'Joy of All the Earth'?"

16 All your enemies deride you. They scoff and grind their teeth and say, "We have destroyed her at last! Long have we awaited this day, and it is finally here!"

17 But it is the LORD who did it just as he warned. He has fulfilled the promises of disaster he made long ago. He has destroyed Jerusalem without mercy and caused her enemies to rejoice over her and boast of their power.

18 Cry aloud* before the Lord, O walls of Jerusalem! Let your tears flow like a river. Give yourselves no rest from weeping day or night.

19 Rise during the night and cry out. Pour out your hearts like water to the Lord. Lift up your

---

2:1a Hebrew *the daughter of Zion;* also in 2:8, 10, 18.   2:1b Hebrew *footstool.*   2:2a Hebrew *Jacob;* also in 2:3.   2:2b Hebrew *the daughter of Judah;* also in 2:5.   2:4 Hebrew *on the tent of the daughter of Zion.*   2:15 Hebrew *the daughter of Jerusalem.*   2:18 Hebrew *Their heart cried.*

hands to him in prayer. Plead for your children as they faint with hunger in the streets.

20"O Lord, think about this!" Jerusalem cries. "You are doing this to your own people! Should mothers eat their little children, those they once bounced on their knees? Should priests and prophets die within the Lord's Temple?

21"See them lying in the streets—young and old, boys and girls, killed by the swords of the enemy. You have killed them in your anger, slaughtering them without mercy.

22"You have invited terrors from all around as though you were calling them to a day of feasting. In the day of the Lord's anger, no one has escaped or survived. The enemy has killed all the children I bore and raised."

CHAPTER 3

Hope in the Lord's Faithfulness

I am the one who has seen the afflictions that come from the rod of the Lord's anger. 2He has brought me into deep darkness, shutting out all light. 3He has turned against me. Day and night his hand is heavy upon me.

4He has made my skin and flesh grow old. He has broken my bones. 5He has attacked me and surrounded me with anguish and distress. 6He has buried me in a dark place, like a person long dead.

7He has walled me in, and I cannot escape. He has bound me in heavy chains. 8And though I cry and shout, he shuts out my prayers. 9He has blocked my path with a high stone wall. He has twisted the road before me with many detours.

10He hid like a bear or a lion, waiting to attack me. 11He dragged me off the path and tore me with his claws, leaving me helpless and desolate. 12He bent his bow and aimed it squarely at me.

13He shot his arrows deep into my heart. 14My own people laugh at me. All day long they sing their mocking songs. 15He has filled me with bitterness. He has given me a cup of deep sorrow to drink.

16He has made me grind my teeth on gravel. He has rolled me in the dust. 17Peace has been stripped away, and I have forgotten what prosperity is. 18I cry out, "My splendor is gone! Everything I had hoped for from the Lord is lost!"

19The thought of my suffering and homelessness is bitter beyond words.* 20I will never forget this awful time, as I grieve over my loss. 21Yet I still dare to hope when I remember this:

22The unfailing love of the Lord never ends! By his mercies we have been kept from complete destruction. 23Great is his faithfulness; his mercies begin afresh each day. 24I say to myself, "The Lord is my inheritance; therefore, I will hope in him!"

25The Lord is wonderfully good to those who wait for him and seek him. 26So it is good to wait quietly for salvation from the Lord. 27And it is good for the young to submit to the yoke of his discipline.

28Let them sit alone in silence beneath the Lord's demands. 29Let them lie face down in the dust; then at last there is hope for them. 30Let them turn the other cheek to those who strike them. Let them accept the insults of their enemies.

31For the Lord does not abandon anyone forever. 32Though he brings grief, he also shows compassion according to the greatness of his unfailing love. 33For he does not enjoy hurting people or causing them sorrow.

34But the leaders of his people trampled prisoners underfoot. 35They deprived people of their God-given rights in defiance of the Most High. 36They perverted justice in the courts. Do they think the Lord didn't see it?

37Can anything happen without the Lord's permission? 38Is it not the Most High who helps one and harms another? 39Then why should we, mere humans, complain when we are punished for our sins?

40Instead, let us test and examine our ways. Let us turn again in repentance to the Lord. 41Let us lift our hearts and hands to God in heaven and say, 42"We have sinned and rebelled, and you have not forgiven us.

43"You have engulfed us with your anger, chased us down, and slaughtered us without mercy. 44You have hidden yourself in a cloud so our prayers cannot reach you. 45You have discarded us as refuse and garbage among the nations.

46"All our enemies have spoken out against us. 47We are filled with fear, for we are trapped, desolate, and ruined." 48Streams of tears flow from my eyes because of the destruction of my people!

49My tears flow down endlessly. They will not stop 50until the Lord looks down from heaven and sees. 51My heart is breaking over the fate of all the women of Jerusalem.

52My enemies, whom I have never harmed, chased me like a bird. 53They threw me into a pit

---

3:19 Hebrew *is wormwood and gall.*

and dropped stones on me. ⁵⁴The water flowed above my head, and I cried out, "This is the end!"

⁵⁵But I called on your name, LORD, from deep within the well, ⁵⁶and you heard me! You listened to my pleading; you heard my weeping! ⁵⁷Yes, you came at my despairing cry and told me, "Do not fear."

⁵⁸Lord, you are my lawyer! Plead my case! For you have redeemed my life. ⁵⁹You have seen the wrong they have done to me, LORD. Be my judge, and prove me right. ⁶⁰You have seen the plots my enemies have laid against me.

⁶¹LORD, you have heard the vile names they call me. You know all about the plans they have made—⁶²the plots my enemies whisper and mutter against me all day long. ⁶³Look at them! In all their activities, they constantly mock me with their songs.

⁶⁴Pay them back, LORD, for all the evil they have done. ⁶⁵Give them hard and stubborn hearts, and then let your curse fall upon them! ⁶⁶Chase them down in your anger, destroying them from beneath the LORD's heavens.

CHAPTER 4
God's Anger Satisfied

How the gold has lost its luster! Even the finest gold has become dull. The sacred gemstones lie scattered in the streets!

²See how the precious children of Jerusalem,* worth their weight in gold, are now treated like pots of clay.

³Even the jackals feed their young, but not my people Israel. They ignore their children's cries, like the ostriches of the desert.

⁴The parched tongues of their little ones stick with thirst to the roofs of their mouths. The children cry for bread, but no one has any to give them.

⁵The people who once ate only the richest foods now beg in the streets for anything they can get. Those who once lived in palaces now search the garbage pits for food.

⁶The guilt* of my people is greater than that of Sodom, where utter disaster struck in a moment with no one to help them.

⁷Our princes were once glowing with health; they were as clean as snow and as elegant as jewels.

⁸But now their faces are blacker than soot. No one even recognizes them. Their skin sticks to their bones; it is as dry and hard as wood.

⁹Those killed by the sword are far better off than those who die of hunger, wasting away for want of food.

¹⁰Tenderhearted women have cooked their own children and eaten them in order to survive the siege.

¹¹But now the anger of the LORD is satisfied. His fiercest anger has now been poured out. He started a fire in Jerusalem* that burned the city to its foundations.

¹²Not a king in all the earth—no one in all the world—would have believed an enemy could march through the gates of Jerusalem.

¹³Yet it happened because of the sins of her prophets and priests, who defiled the city by shedding innocent blood.

¹⁴They wandered blindly through the streets, so defiled by blood that no one dared to touch them.

¹⁵"Get away!" the people shouted at them. "You are defiled! Don't touch us!" So they fled to distant lands and wandered there among foreign nations, but none would let them stay.

¹⁶The LORD himself has scattered them, and he no longer helps them. The priests and leaders are no longer honored and respected.

¹⁷We looked in vain for our allies to come and save us, but we were looking to nations that could offer no help at all.

¹⁸We couldn't go into the streets without danger to our lives. Our end was near; our days were numbered. We were doomed!

¹⁹Our enemies were swifter than the eagles. If we fled to the mountains, they found us. If we hid in the wilderness, they were waiting for us there.

²⁰Our king, the LORD's anointed, the very life of our nation, was caught in their snares. We had foolishly boasted that under his protection we could hold our own against any nation on earth!

²¹Are you rejoicing in the land of Uz, O people of Edom? But you, too, must drink from the cup of the LORD's anger. You, too, will be stripped naked in your drunkenness.

²²O Jerusalem,* your punishment will end; you will soon return from exile. But Edom, your punishment is just beginning; soon your many sins will be revealed.

CHAPTER 5
Prayer for Restoration

LORD, remember everything that has happened to us. See all the sorrows we bear! ²Our inheritance has been turned over to strangers, our homes to foreigners. ³We are orphaned and fa-

4:2 Hebrew *sons of Zion.*   4:6 Or *punishment.*   4:11 Hebrew *in Zion.*   4:22 Hebrew *daughter of Zion.*

therless. Our mothers are widowed. 4We have to pay for water to drink, and even firewood is expensive. 5Those who pursue us are at our heels; we are exhausted but are given no rest. 6We submitted to Egypt and Assyria to get enough food to survive. 7It was our ancestors who sinned, but they died before the hand of judgment fell. We have suffered the punishment they deserved!

8Slaves have now become our masters; there is no one left to rescue us. 9We must hunt for food in the wilderness at the risk of our lives. 10Because of the famine, our skin has been blackened as though baked in an oven. 11Our enemies rape the women and young girls in Jerusalem* and throughout the towns of Judah. 12Our princes are being hanged by their thumbs, and the old men are treated with contempt. 13The young men are led away to work at mill-

stones, and the children stagger under heavy loads of wood. 14The old men no longer sit in the city gates; the young men no longer dance and sing.

15The joy of our hearts has ended; our dancing has turned to mourning. 16The garlands have* fallen from our heads. Disaster has fallen upon us because we have sinned. 17Our hearts are sick and weary, and our eyes grow dim with tears. 18For Jerusalem* is empty and desolate, a place haunted by jackals.

19But LORD, you remain the same forever! Your throne continues from generation to generation. 20Why do you continue to forget us? Why have you forsaken us for so long? 21Restore us, O LORD, and bring us back to you again! Give us back the joys we once had! 22Or have you utterly rejected us? Are you angry with us still?

5:11 Hebrew *Zion.*   5:16 Or *The crown has.*   5:18 Hebrew *Mount Zion.*

Ezekiel

CHAPTER 1

A Vision of Living Beings

On July 31* of my thirtieth year,* while I was with the Judean exiles beside the Kebar River in Babylon, the heavens were opened to me, and I saw visions of God. ²This happened during the fifth year of King Jehoiachin's captivity. ³The LORD gave a message to me, Ezekiel son of Buzi, a priest, there beside the Kebar River in the land of the Babylonians,* and I felt the hand of the LORD take hold of me.

⁴As I looked, I saw a great storm coming toward me from the north, driving before it a huge cloud that flashed with lightning and shone with brilliant light. The fire inside the cloud glowed like gleaming amber. ⁵From the center of the cloud came four living beings that looked human, ⁶except that each had four faces and two pairs of wings. ⁷Their legs were straight like human legs, but their feet were split like calves' feet and shone like burnished bronze. ⁸Beneath each of their wings I could see human hands. ⁹The wings of each living being touched the wings of the two beings beside it. The living beings were able to fly in any direction without turning around. ¹⁰Each had a human face in the front, the face of a lion on the right side, the face of an ox on the left side, and the face of an eagle at the back. ¹¹Each had two pairs of outstretched wings—one pair stretched out to touch the wings of the living beings on either side of it, and the other pair covered its body. ¹²They went in whatever direction the spirit chose, and they moved straight forward in all directions without having to turn around.

¹³The living beings looked like bright coals of fire or brilliant torches, and it looked as though lightning was flashing back and forth among them. ¹⁴And the living beings darted to and fro like flashes of lightning.

¹⁵As I looked at these beings, I saw four wheels on the ground beneath them, one wheel belonging to each. ¹⁶The wheels sparkled as if made of chrysolite. All four wheels looked the same; each wheel had a second wheel turning crosswise within it. ¹⁷The beings could move forward in any of the four directions they faced, without turning as they moved. ¹⁸The rims of the four wheels were awesomely tall, and they were covered with eyes all around the edges. ¹⁹When the four living beings moved, the wheels moved with them. When they flew upward, the wheels went up, too. ²⁰The spirit of the four living beings was in the wheels. So wherever the spirit went, the wheels and the living beings went, too. ²¹When the living beings moved, the wheels moved. When the living beings stopped, the wheels stopped. When the living beings flew into the air, the wheels rose up. For the spirit of the living beings was in the wheels.

²²There was a surface spread out above them like the sky. It sparkled like crystal. ²³Beneath this surface the wings of each living being stretched out to touch the others' wings, and each had two wings covering its body. ²⁴As they flew their wings roared like waves crashing against the shore, or like the voice of the Almighty,* or like the shouting of a mighty army. When they stopped, they let down their wings. ²⁵As they stood with their wings lowered, a voice spoke from beyond the crystal surface above them.

²⁶Above the surface over their heads was what looked like a throne made of blue sapphire. And high above this throne was a figure

---

1:1a Hebrew *On the fifth day of the fourth month,* of the Hebrew calendar. A number of dates in Ezekiel can be cross-checked with dates in surviving Babylonian records and related accurately to our modern calendar. This event occurred on July 31, 593 B.C. **1:1b** Or *in the thirtieth year.* **1:3** Or *Chaldeans.* **1:24** Hebrew *Shaddai.*

whose appearance was like that of a man. 27From his waist up, he looked like gleaming amber, flickering like a fire. And from his waist down, he looked like a burning flame, shining with splendor. 28All around him was a glowing halo, like a rainbow shining through the clouds. This was the way the glory of the LORD appeared to me. When I saw it, I fell face down in the dust, and I heard someone's voice speaking to me.

CHAPTER 2

Ezekiel's Call and Commission

"Stand up, son of man," said the voice. "I want to speak with you." 2The Spirit came into me as he spoke and set me on my feet. I listened carefully to his words. 3"Son of man," he said, "I am sending you to the nation of Israel, a nation that is rebelling against me. Their ancestors have rebelled against me from the beginning, and they are still in revolt to this very day. 4They are a hard-hearted and stubborn people. But I am sending you to say to them, 'This is what the Sovereign LORD says!' 5And whether they listen or not—for remember, they are rebels—at least they will know they have had a prophet among them.

6"Son of man, do not fear them. Don't be afraid even though their threats are sharp as thorns and barbed like briers, and they sting like scorpions. Do not be dismayed by their dark scowls. For remember, they are rebels! 7You must give them my messages whether they listen or not. But they won't listen, for they are completely rebellious! 8Son of man, listen to what I say to you. Do not join them in being a rebel. Open your mouth, and eat what I give you."

9Then I looked and saw a hand reaching out to me, and it held a scroll. 10He unrolled it, and I saw that both sides were covered with funeral songs, other words of sorrow, and pronouncements of doom.

CHAPTER 3

The voice said to me, "Son of man, eat what I am giving you—eat this scroll! Then go and give its message to the people of Israel." 2So I opened my mouth, and he fed me the scroll. 3"Eat it all," he said. And when I ate it, it tasted as sweet as honey.

4Then he said, "Son of man, go to the people of Israel with my messages. 5I am not sending you to some foreign people whose language you cannot understand. 6No, I am not sending you

to people with strange and difficult speech. If I did, they would listen! 7I am sending you to the people of Israel, but they won't listen to you any more than they listen to me! For the whole lot of them are hard-hearted and stubborn. 8But look, I have made you as hard and stubborn as they are. 9I have made you as hard as rock! So don't be afraid of them or fear their angry looks, even though they are such rebels."

10Then he added, "Son of man, let all my words sink deep into your own heart first. Listen to them carefully for yourself. 11Then go to your people in exile and say to them, 'This is what the Sovereign LORD says!' Do this whether they listen to you or not."

12Then the Spirit lifted me up, and I heard a loud rumbling sound behind me. (May the glory of the LORD be praised in his place!)* 13It was the sound of the wings of the living beings as they brushed against each other and the rumbling of their wheels beneath them.

14The Spirit lifted me up and took me away. I went in bitterness and turmoil, but the LORD's hold on me was strong. 15Then I came to the colony of Judean exiles in Tel-abib, beside the Kebar River. I sat there among them for seven days, overwhelmed.

A Watchman for Israel

16At the end of the seven days, the LORD gave me a message. He said, 17"Son of man, I have appointed you as a watchman for Israel. Whenever you receive a message from me, pass it on to the people immediately. 18If I warn the wicked, saying, 'You are under the penalty of death,' but you fail to deliver the warning, they will die in their sins. And I will hold you responsible, demanding your blood for theirs. 19If you warn them and they keep on sinning and refuse to repent, they will die in their sins. But you will have saved your life because you did what you were told to do. 20If good people turn bad and don't listen to my warning, they will die. If you did not warn them of the consequences, then they will die in their sins. Their previous good deeds won't help them, and I will hold you responsible, demanding your blood for theirs. 21But if you warn them and they repent, they will live, and you will have saved your own life, too."

22Then the LORD took hold of me, and he said to me, "Go out into the valley, and I will talk to you there." 23So I got up and went, and there I saw the glory of the LORD, just as I had seen it

---

3:12 A likely reading for this verse is *Then the Spirit lifted me up, and as the glory of the LORD rose from its place, I heard behind me a loud rumbling sound.*

in my first vision by the Kebar River. And I fell face down in the dust.

24Then the Spirit came into me and set me on my feet. He talked to me and said, "Go, shut yourself up in your house. 25There you will be bound with ropes so you cannot go out among the people. 26And I will make your tongue stick to the roof of your mouth so you won't be able to pray for them, for they are rebellious. 27But whenever I give you a message, I will loosen your tongue and let you speak. Then you will say to them, 'This is what the Sovereign LORD says!' Some of them will listen, but some will ignore you, for they are rebels.

A Sign of the Coming Siege

"And now, son of man, take a large brick and set it down in front of you. Then draw a map of the city of Jerusalem on it. 2Build siege ramps against the city walls. Surround it with enemy camps and battering rams. 3Then take an iron griddle and place it between you and the city. Turn toward it and demonstrate how the enemy will attack Jerusalem. This will be a warning to the people of Israel.

4"Now lie on your left side and place the sins of Israel on yourself. You are to bear their sins for the number of days you lie there on your side. 5You will bear Israel's sins for 390 days—one day for each year of their sin. 6After that, turn over and lie on your right side for 40 days—one day for each year of Judah's sin.

7"Meanwhile, continue your demonstration of the siege of Jerusalem. Lie there with your arm bared and prophesy her destruction. 8I will tie you up with ropes so you won't be able to turn from side to side until the days of your siege have been completed.

9"Now go and get some wheat, barley, beans, lentils, millet, and spelt, and mix them together in a storage jar. Use this food to make bread for yourself during the 390 days you will be lying on your side. 10Ration this out to yourself, eight ounces* of food for each day, and eat it at set times. 11Then measure out a jar* of water for each day, and drink it at set times. 12Each day prepare your bread as you would barley cakes. While all the people are watching, bake it over a fire using dried human dung as fuel and then eat the bread. 13For this is what the LORD says: Israel will eat defiled bread in the Gentile lands, where I will banish them!"

14Then I said, "O Sovereign LORD, must I be defiled by using human dung? For I have never been defiled before. From the time I was a child until now I have never eaten any animal that died of sickness or that I found dead. And I have never eaten any of the animals that our laws forbid."

15"All right," the LORD said. "You may bake your bread with cow dung instead of human dung." 16Then he told me, "Son of man, I will cause food to be very scarce in Jerusalem. It will be weighed out with great care and eaten fearfully. The water will be portioned out drop by drop, and the people will drink it with dismay. 17Food and water will be so scarce that the people will look at one another in terror, and they will waste away under their punishment.

A Sign of the Coming Judgment

"Son of man, take a sharp sword and use it as a razor to shave your head and beard. Use a scale to weigh the hair into three equal parts. 2Place a third of it at the center of your map of Jerusalem. After acting out the siege, burn it there. Scatter another third across your map and slash at it with a sword. Scatter the last third to the wind, for I will scatter my people with the sword. 3Keep just a bit of the hair and tie it up in your robe. 4Then take a few of these hairs out and throw them into the fire, burning them up. A fire will then spread from this remnant and destroy all of Israel.

5"This is what the Sovereign LORD says: This is an illustration of what will happen to Jerusalem. I placed her at the center of the nations, 6but she has rebelled against my regulations and has been even more wicked than the surrounding nations. She has refused to obey the laws I gave her to follow. 7So this is what the Sovereign LORD says: Since you have refused to obey my laws and regulations and have behaved even worse than your neighbors, 8I myself, the Sovereign LORD, am now your enemy. I will punish you publicly while all the nations watch. 9Because of your detestable idols, I will punish you more severely than I have punished anyone before or ever will again. 10Parents will eat their own children, and children will eat their parents. And I will punish you by scattering the few who survive to the far reaches of the earth.

11"As surely as I live, says the Sovereign LORD, I will cut you off completely. I will show you no pity at all because you have defiled my Temple with idols and vile practices. 12A third of your

---

4:10 Hebrew *20 shekels* [228 grams].   4:11 Hebrew *⅙ of a hin*, about 1.3 pints or 0.6 liters.

people will die in the city from famine and disease. A third of them will be slaughtered by the enemy outside the city walls. And I will scatter a third to the winds and chase them with my sword. 13Then at last my anger will be spent, and I will be satisfied. And when my fury against them has subsided, all Israel will know that I, the LORD, have spoken to them in my jealous anger.

14"So I will turn you into a ruin, a mockery in the eyes of the surrounding nations and to everyone who travels by. 15You will become an object of mockery and taunting and horror. You will be a warning to all the nations around you. They will see what happens when the LORD turns against a nation in furious rebuke. I, the LORD, have spoken!

16"I will shower you with the deadly arrows of famine to destroy you. The famine will become more and more severe until every crumb of food is gone. 17And along with the famine, wild animals will attack you, robbing you of your children. Disease and war will stalk your land, and I will bring the sword of the enemy against you. I, the LORD, have spoken!"

CHAPTER 6
Judgment against Israel's Mountains

Again a message came to me from the LORD: 2"Son of man, look over toward the mountains of Israel and prophesy against them. 3Give the mountains of Israel this message from the Sovereign LORD. This is what the Sovereign LORD says to the mountains and hills and to the ravines and valleys: I am about to bring war upon you, and I will destroy your pagan shrines. 4All your altars will be demolished, and your incense altars will be smashed. I will kill your people in front of your idols. 5I will lay your corpses in front of your idols and scatter your bones around your altars. 6Wherever you live there will be desolation. I will destroy your pagan shrines, your altars, your idols, your incense altars, and all the other religious objects you have made. 7Then when the place is littered with corpses, you will know that I am the LORD.

8"But I will let a few of my people escape destruction, and they will be scattered among the nations of the world. 9Then when they are exiled among the nations, they will remember me. They will recognize how grieved I am by their unfaithful hearts and lustful eyes that long for other gods. Then at last they will hate themselves for all their wickedness. 10They will know that I alone

am the LORD and that I was serious when I predicted that all this would happen to them.

11"This is what the Sovereign LORD says: Clap your hands in horror, and stamp your feet. Cry out, 'Alas!' because of all the evil that the people of Israel have done. Now they are going to die from war and famine and disease. 12Disease will strike down those who are far away in exile. War will destroy those who are nearby. And anyone who survives will be killed by famine. So at last I will spend my fury on them. 13When their dead lie scattered among their idols and altars, on every hill and mountain and under every green tree and great oak where they offered incense to their gods, then they will know that I alone am the LORD. 14I will crush them and make their cities desolate from the wilderness in the south to Riblah* in the north. Then they will know that I am the LORD."

CHAPTER 7
The Coming of the End

Then this message came to me from the LORD: 2"Son of man, this is what the Sovereign LORD says to Israel: The end is here! Wherever you look—east, west, north, or south—your land is finished. 3No hope remains, for I will unleash my anger against you. I will call you to account for all your disgusting behavior. 4I will turn my eyes away and show no pity, repaying you in full for all your evil. Then you will know that I am the LORD!

5"This is what the Sovereign LORD says: With one blow after another I will bring total disaster! 6The end has come! It has finally arrived! Your final doom is waiting! 7O people of Israel, the day of your destruction is dawning. The time has come; the day of trouble is near. It will ring with shouts of anguish, not shouts of joy. 8Soon I will pour out my fury to complete your punishment for all your disgusting behavior. 9I will neither spare nor pity you. I will repay you for all your detestable practices. Then you will know that it is I, the LORD, who is striking the blow.

10"The day of judgment is here; your destruction awaits! The people's wickedness and pride have reached a climax. 11Their violence will fall back on them as punishment for their wickedness. None of these proud and wicked people will survive. All their wealth will be swept away. 12Yes, the time has come; the day is here! There is no reason for buyers to rejoice over the bargains they find or for sellers to grieve over their losses, for all of them will fall under my terrible

6:14 As in some Hebrew manuscripts; most Hebrew manuscripts read *Diblah*.

anger. ¹³And if any merchants should survive, they will never return to their business. For what God has said applies to everyone—it will not be changed! Not one person whose life is twisted by sin will recover.

The Desolation of Israel

¹⁴"The trumpets call Israel's army to mobilize, but no one listens, for my fury is against them all. ¹⁵Any who leave the city walls will be killed by enemy swords. Those who stay inside will die of famine and disease. ¹⁶The few who survive and escape to the mountains will moan like doves, weeping for their sins. ¹⁷Everyone's hands will be feeble; their knees will be as weak as water. ¹⁸They will dress themselves in sackcloth; horror and shame will cover them. They will shave their heads in sorrow and remorse.

¹⁹"They will throw away their money, tossing it out like worthless trash. It won't buy their deliverance in that day of the LORD's anger. It will neither satisfy nor feed them, for their love of money made them stumble into sin. ²⁰They were proud of their gold jewelry and used it to make vile and detestable idols. That is why I will make all their wealth disgusting to them. ²¹I will give it as plunder to foreigners from the most wicked of nations, and they will defile it. ²²I will hide my eyes as these robbers invade my treasured land and corrupt it.

²³"Prepare chains for my people, for the land is bloodied by terrible crimes. Jerusalem is filled with violence. ²⁴I will bring the most ruthless of nations to occupy their homes. I will break down their proud fortresses and defile their sanctuaries. ²⁵Terror and trembling will overcome my people. They will look for peace but will not find it. ²⁶Calamity will follow calamity; rumor will follow rumor. They will look in vain for a vision from the prophets. They will receive no teaching from the priests and no counsel from the leaders. ²⁷The king and the prince will stand helpless, weeping in despair, and the people's hands will tremble with fear. I will bring against them the evil they have done to others, and they will receive the punishment they so richly deserve. Then they will know that I am the LORD!"

CHAPTER 8
Idolatry in the Temple

Then on September 17,* during the sixth year of King Jehoiachin's captivity, while the leaders of Judah were in my home, the Sovereign LORD took hold of me. ²I saw a figure that appeared to be a man. From the waist down he looked like a burning flame. From the waist up he looked like gleaming amber. ³He put out what seemed to be a hand and took me by the hair. Then the Spirit lifted me up into the sky and transported me in a vision of God to Jerusalem. I was taken to the north gate of the inner courtyard of the Temple, where there is a large idol that has made the LORD very angry. ⁴Suddenly, the glory of the God of Israel was there, just as I had seen it before in the valley.

⁵Then the LORD said to me, "Son of man, look toward the north." So I looked, and there to the north, beside the entrance to the gate of the altar, stood the idol that had made the LORD so angry.

⁶"Son of man," he said, "do you see what they are doing? Do you see the great sins the people of Israel are doing to drive me from my Temple? But come, and you will see even greater sins than these!" ⁷Then he brought me to the door of the Temple courtyard, where I could see an opening in the wall. ⁸He said to me, "Now, son of man, dig into the wall." So I dug into the wall and uncovered a door to a hidden room.

⁹"Go in," he said, "and see the unspeakable wickedness going on in there!" ¹⁰So I went in and saw the walls engraved with all kinds of snakes, lizards, and hideous creatures. I also saw the various idols worshiped by the people of Israel. ¹¹Seventy leaders of Israel were standing there with Jaazaniah son of Shaphan in the middle. Each of them held an incense burner, so there was a thick cloud of incense above their heads.

¹²Then the LORD said to me, "Son of man, have you seen what the leaders of Israel are doing with their idols in dark rooms? They are saying, 'The LORD doesn't see us; he has deserted our land!'" ¹³Then he added, "Come, and I will show you greater sins than these!"

¹⁴He brought me to the north gate of the LORD's Temple, and some women were sitting there, weeping for the god Tammuz. ¹⁵"Have you seen this?" he asked. "But I will show you even greater sins than these!"

¹⁶Then he brought me into the inner courtyard of the LORD's Temple. At the entrance, between the foyer and the bronze altar, about twenty-five men were standing with their backs to the LORD's Temple. They were facing eastward, worshiping the sun!

¹⁷"Have you seen this, son of man?" he

8:1 Hebrew *on the fifth day of the sixth month,* of the Hebrew calendar. This event occurred on September 17, 592 B.C.; also see note on 1:1.

asked. "Is it nothing to the people of Judah that they commit these terrible sins, leading the whole nation into violence, thumbing their noses at me, and rousing my fury against them? 18Therefore, I will deal with them in fury. I will neither pity nor spare them. And though they scream for mercy, I will not listen."

CHAPTER 9
The Slaughter of Idolaters

Then the LORD thundered, "Bring on the men appointed to punish the city! Tell them to bring their weapons with them!" 2Six men soon appeared from the upper gate that faces north, each carrying a battle club in his hand. One of them was dressed in linen and carried a writer's case strapped to his side. They all went into the Temple courtyard and stood beside the bronze altar.

3Then the glory of the God of Israel rose up from between the cherubim, where it had rested, and moved to the entrance of the Temple. And the LORD called to the man dressed in linen who was carrying the writer's case. 4He said to him, "Walk through the streets of Jerusalem and put a mark on the foreheads of all those who weep and sigh because of the sins they see around them."

5Then I heard the LORD say to the other men, "Follow him through the city and kill everyone whose forehead is not marked. Show no mercy; have no pity! 6Kill them all—old and young, girls and women and little children. But do not touch anyone with the mark. Begin your task right here at the Temple." So they began by killing the seventy leaders. 7"Defile the Temple!" the LORD commanded. "Fill its courtyards with the bodies of those you kill! Go!" So they went throughout the city and did as they were told.

8While they were carrying out their orders, I was all alone. I fell face down in the dust and cried out, "O Sovereign LORD! Will your fury against Jerusalem wipe out everyone left in Israel?"

9Then he said to me, "The sins of the people of Israel and Judah are very great. The entire land is full of murder; the city is filled with injustice. They are saying, 'The LORD doesn't see it! The LORD has forsaken the land!' 10So I will not spare them or have any pity on them. I will fully repay them for all they have done."

11Then the man in linen clothing, who carried the writer's case, reported back and said, "I have finished the work you gave me to do."

10:14 Hebrew *the face of a cherub*; compare 1:10.

CHAPTER 10
The LORD's Glory Leaves the Temple

As I looked, I saw what appeared to be a throne of blue sapphire above the crystal surface over the heads of the cherubim. 2Then the LORD spoke to the man in linen clothing and said, "Go in between the whirling wheels beneath the cherubim, and take a handful of glowing coals and scatter them over the city." He did this as I watched. 3The cherubim were standing at the south end of the Temple when the man went in, and the cloud of glory filled the inner courtyard. 4Then the glory of the LORD rose up from above the cherubim and went over to the door of the Temple. The Temple was filled with this cloud of glory, and the Temple courtyard glowed brightly with the glory of the LORD. 5The moving wings of the cherubim sounded like the voice of God Almighty and could be heard clearly in the outer courtyard.

6The LORD said to the man in linen clothing, "Go between the cherubim and take some burning coals from between the wheels." So the man went in and stood beside one of the wheels. 7Then one of the cherubim reached out his hand and took some live coals from the fire burning among them. He put the coals into the hands of the man in linen clothing, and the man took them and went out. 8(All the cherubim had what looked like human hands hidden beneath their wings.)

9Each of the four cherubim had a wheel beside him, and the wheels sparkled like chrysolite. 10All four wheels looked the same; each wheel had a second wheel turning crosswise within it. 11The cherubim could move forward in any of the four directions they faced, without turning as they moved. They went straight in the direction in which their heads were turned, never turning aside. 12Both the cherubim and the wheels were covered with eyes. The cherubim had eyes all over their bodies, including their hands, their backs, and their wings. 13I heard someone refer to the wheels as "the whirling wheels." 14Each of the four cherubim had four faces—the first was the face of an ox,* the second was a human face, the third was the face of a lion, and the fourth was the face of an eagle.

15Then the cherubim rose upward. These were the same living beings I had seen beside the Kebar River. 16When the cherubim moved, the wheels moved with them. When they rose into the air, the wheels stayed beside them, going with them as they flew. 17When the cherubim stood still, the wheels also stopped, for the spirit of the living beings was in the wheels.

18Then the glory of the LORD moved from the door of the Temple and hovered above the cherubim. 19And as I watched, the cherubim flew with their wheels to the east gate of the LORD's Temple. And the glory of the God of Israel hovered above them.

20These were the same living beings I had seen beneath the God of Israel when I was by the Kebar River. I knew they were cherubim, 21for each had four faces and four wings and what looked like human hands under their wings. 22Their faces, too, were just like the faces of the beings I had seen at the Kebar, and they traveled straight ahead, just as the others had.

CHAPTER **11**

Judgment on Israel's Leaders

Then the Spirit lifted me and brought me over to the east gateway of the LORD's Temple, where I saw twenty-five prominent men of the city. Among them were Jaazaniah son of Azzur and Pelatiah son of Benaiah, who were leaders among the people.

2Then the Spirit said to me, "Son of man, these are the men who are responsible for the wicked counsel being given in this city. 3They say to the people, 'Is it not a good time to build houses? Our city is like an iron pot. Inside it we will be like meat—safe from all harm.*' 4Therefore, son of man, prophesy against them loudly and clearly."

5Then the Spirit of the LORD came upon me, and he told me to say, "This is what the LORD says to the people of Israel: Is that what you are saying? Yes, I know it is, for I know every thought that comes into your minds. 6You have murdered endlessly and filled your streets with the dead.

7"Therefore, this is what the Sovereign LORD says: This city is an iron pot, but the victims of your injustice are the pieces of meat. And you are not safe, for I will soon drag you from the city. 8I will expose you to the war you so greatly fear, says the Sovereign LORD. 9I will drive you out of Jerusalem and hand you over to foreigners who will carry out my judgments against you. 10You will be slaughtered all the way to the borders of Israel, and then you will know that I am the LORD. 11No, this city will not be an iron pot for you, and you will not be the meat, safe inside. I will judge you even to the borders of Israel, 12and you will know that I am the LORD. For you

have refused to obey me; instead, you have copied the sins of the nations around you."

13While I was still speaking, Pelatiah son of Benaiah suddenly died. Then I fell face down in the dust and cried out, "O Sovereign LORD, are you going to kill everyone in Israel?"

Hope for Exiled Israel

14Then this message came to me from the LORD: 15"Son of man, the people still left in Jerusalem are talking about their relatives in exile, saying, 'They are far away from the LORD, so now he has given their land to us!' 16Therefore, give the exiles this message from the Sovereign LORD: Although I have scattered you in the countries of the world, I will be a sanctuary to you during your time in exile. 17I, the Sovereign LORD, will gather you back from the nations where you are scattered, and I will give you the land of Israel once again.

18"When the people return to their homeland, they will remove every trace of their detestable idol worship. 19And I will give them singleness of heart and put a new spirit within them. I will take away their hearts of stone and give them tender hearts* instead, 20so they will obey my laws and regulations. Then they will truly be my people, and I will be their God. 21But as for those who long for idols, I will repay them fully for their sins, says the Sovereign LORD."

The LORD's Glory Leaves Jerusalem

22Then the cherubim lifted their wings and rose into the air with their wheels beside them, and the glory of the God of Israel hovered above them. 23Then the glory of the LORD went up from the city and stopped above the mountain to the east. 24Afterward the Spirit of God carried me back again to Babylonia,* to the Judeans in exile there. And so ended the vision of my visit to Jerusalem. 25And I told the exiles everything the LORD had shown me.

CHAPTER **12**

Signs of the Coming Exile

Again a message came to me from the LORD: 2"Son of man, you live among rebels who could see the truth if they wanted to, but they don't want to. They could hear me if they would listen, but they won't listen because they are rebellious. 3So now put on a demonstration to show them what it will be like to go off into exile. Pack whatever you can carry on your back and leave your home to go on a journey.

11:3 Hebrew *This city is the pot, and we are the meat.* 11:19 Hebrew *hearts of flesh.* 11:24 Or *Chaldea.*

Make your preparations in broad daylight so the people can see you, for perhaps they will even yet consider what this means, even though they are such rebels. ⁴Bring your baggage outside during the day so they can watch you. Then as they are watching, leave your house in the evening, just as captives do when they begin a long march to distant lands. ⁵Dig a hole through the wall while they are watching and carry your possessions out through it. ⁶As they watch, lift your pack to your shoulders and walk away into the night. Cover your face and don't look around. All of these actions will be a sign for the people of Israel."

⁷So I did as I was told. In broad daylight I brought my pack outside, filled with the things I might carry into exile. Then in the evening while the people looked on, I dug through the wall with my hands and went out into the darkness with my pack on my shoulder.

⁸The next morning this message came to me from the LORD: ⁹"Son of man, these rebels, the people of Israel, have asked you what all this means. ¹⁰Say to them, 'This is what the Sovereign LORD says: These actions contain a message for Zedekiah in Jerusalem* and for all the people of Israel.' ¹¹Then explain that your actions are a demonstration of what will soon happen to them, for they will be driven from their homes and sent away into exile.

¹²"Even Zedekiah will leave Jerusalem at night through a hole in the wall, taking only what he can carry with him. He will cover his face, and his eyes will never see his homeland again. ¹³Then I will spread out my net and capture him in my snare. I will bring him to Babylon, the land of the Babylonians,* though he will never see it, and he will die there. ¹⁴I will scatter his servants and guards to the four winds and send the sword after them. ¹⁵And when I scatter them among the nations, they will know that I am the LORD. ¹⁶But I will spare a few of them from death by war, famine, or disease, so they can confess to their captors about how wicked they have been. Then they will know that I am the LORD!"

¹⁷Then this message came to me from the LORD: ¹⁸"Son of man, tremble as you eat your food. Drink your water with fear, as if it were your last. ¹⁹Give the people this message from the Sovereign LORD concerning those living in Israel and Jerusalem: They will eat their food with trembling and sip their tiny portions of water in utter despair, because their land will be stripped bare on account of their violence. ²⁰The cities will be destroyed and the farmland deserted. Then you will know that I am the LORD."

A New Proverb for Israel

²¹Again a message came to me from the LORD: ²²"Son of man, what is that proverb they quote in Israel: 'Time passes, making a liar of every prophet'? ²³Give the people this message from the Sovereign LORD: I will put an end to this proverb, and you will soon stop quoting it. Now give them this new proverb to replace the old one: 'The time has come for every prophecy to be fulfilled!'

²⁴"Then you will see what becomes of all the false visions and misleading predictions about peace in Israel. ²⁵For I am the LORD! What I threaten always happens. There will be no more delays, you rebels of Israel! I will fulfill my threat of destruction in your own lifetime, says the Sovereign LORD."

²⁶Then this message came to me from the LORD: ²⁷"Son of man, the people of Israel are saying, 'His visions won't come true for a long, long time.' ²⁸Therefore, give them this message from the Sovereign LORD: No more delay! I will now do everything I have threatened! I, the Sovereign LORD, have spoken!"

CHAPTER **13**
Judgment against False Prophets

Then this message came to me from the LORD: ²"Son of man, speak against the false prophets of Israel who are inventing their own prophecies. Tell them to listen to the word of the LORD. ³This is what the Sovereign LORD says: Destruction is certain for the false prophets who are following their own imaginations and have seen nothing at all!

⁴"O people of Israel, these prophets of yours are like jackals digging around in the ruins. ⁵They have done nothing to strengthen the breaks in the walls around the nation. They have not helped it to stand firm in battle on the day of the LORD. ⁶Instead, they have lied and said, 'My message is from the LORD,' even though the LORD never sent them. And yet they expect him to fulfill their prophecies! ⁷Can your visions be anything but false if you claim, 'This message is from the LORD,' when I have not even spoken to you?

⁸"Therefore, this is what the Sovereign LORD says: Because what you say is false and your visions are a lie, I will stand against you, says the Sovereign LORD. ⁹I will raise my fist against all

12:10 Hebrew *the prince in Jerusalem;* also in 12:12. 12:13 Or *Chaldeans.*

the lying prophets, and they will be banished from the community of Israel. I will blot their names from Israel's record books, and they will never again see their own land. Then you will know that I am the Sovereign LORD!

10"These evil prophets deceive my people by saying, 'All is peaceful!' when there is no peace at all! It's as if the people have built a flimsy wall, and these prophets are trying to hold it together by covering it with whitewash! 11Tell these whitewashers that their wall will soon fall down. A heavy rainstorm will undermine it; great hailstones and mighty winds will knock it down. 12And when the wall falls, the people will cry out, 'Where is the whitewash you applied?'

13"Therefore, this is what the Sovereign LORD says: I will sweep away your whitewashed wall with a storm of indignation, with a great flood of anger, and with hailstones of fury. 14I will break down your wall right to the foundation, and when it falls, it will crush you. Then you will know that I am the LORD! 15At last my anger against the wall and those who covered it with whitewash will be satisfied. Then I will say to you: 'The wall and those who whitewashed it are both gone. 16They were lying prophets who claimed peace would come to Jerusalem when there was no peace. I, the Sovereign LORD, have spoken!'

Judgment against False Women Prophets

17"Now, son of man, also speak out against the women who prophesy from their own imaginations. 18This is what the Sovereign LORD says: Destruction is certain for you women who are ensnaring the souls of my people, both young and old alike. You tie magic charms on their wrists and furnish them with magic veils. Do you think you can trap others without bringing destruction on yourselves? 19You turn my people away from me for a few handfuls of barley or a piece of bread. By lying to my people who love to listen to lies, you kill those who should not die, and you promise life to those who should not live.

20"And so the Sovereign LORD says: I am against all your magic charms, which you use to ensnare my people like birds. I will tear them from your arms, setting my people free like birds set free from a cage. 21I will tear off the magic veils and save my people from your grasp. They will no longer be your victims. Then you will know that I am the LORD. 22You have discouraged the righteous with your lies, when I didn't want them to suffer grief. And you have encouraged the wicked by promising them life, even

though they continue in their sins. 23But you will no longer talk of seeing visions that you never saw, nor will you practice your magic. For I will rescue my people from your grasp. Then you will know that I am the LORD."

CHAPTER **14**

The Idolatry of Israel's Leaders

Then some of the leaders of Israel visited me, and while they were there, 2this message came to me from the LORD: 3"Son of man, these leaders have set up idols in their hearts. They have embraced things that lead them into sin. Why should I let them ask me anything? 4Give them this message from the Sovereign LORD: I, the LORD, will punish the people of Israel who set up idols in their hearts so they fall into sin and then come to a prophet asking for help. 5I will do this to capture the minds and hearts of all my people who have turned from me to worship their detestable idols.

6"Therefore, give the people of Israel this message from the Sovereign LORD: Repent and turn away from your idols, and stop all your loathsome practices. 7I, the LORD, will punish all those, both Israelites and foreigners, who reject me and set up idols in their hearts so they fall into sin, and who then come to a prophet asking for my advice. 8I will turn against such people and make a terrible example of them, destroying them. Then you will know that I am the LORD. 9And if a prophet is deceived and gives a message anyway, it is because I, the LORD, have deceived that prophet. I will stand against such prophets and cut them off from the community of Israel. 10False prophets and hypocrites—evil people who claim to want my advice—will all be punished for their sins. 11In this way, the people of Israel will learn not to stray from me, polluting themselves with sin. They will be my people, and I will be their God, says the Sovereign LORD."

The Certainty of the LORD's Judgment

12Then this message came to me from the LORD: 13"Son of man, suppose the people of a country were to sin against me, and I lifted my fist to crush them, cutting off their food supply and sending a famine to destroy both people and animals alike. 14Even if Noah, Daniel, and Job were there, their righteousness would save no one but themselves, declares the Sovereign LORD.

15"Or suppose I were to send an invasion of dangerous wild animals to devastate the land and kill the people. 16Even if these three men were there, the Sovereign LORD swears that it would do no good—it wouldn't save the people from destruction. Those three alone would be saved, but the land would be devastated.

17 "Or suppose I were to bring war against the land, and I told enemy armies to come and destroy everything. 18Even if these three men were in the land, the Sovereign LORD swears that they could not save the people. They alone would be saved.

19 "Or suppose I were to pour out my fury by sending an epidemic of disease into the land, and the plague killed people and animals alike. 20Even if Noah, Daniel, and Job were living there, the Sovereign LORD swears that they could not save the people. They alone would be saved by their righteousness.

21 "Now this is what the Sovereign LORD says: How terrible it will be when all four of these fearsome punishments fall upon Jerusalem— war, famine, beasts, and plague—destroying all her people and animals. 22Yet there will be survivors, and they will come here to join you as exiles in Babylon. You will see with your own eyes how wicked they are, and then you will feel better about what I have done to Jerusalem. 23When you meet them and see their behavior, you will agree that these things are not being done to Israel without cause, says the Sovereign LORD."

CHAPTER **15**
Jerusalem—a Useless Vine
Then this message came to me from the LORD: 2 "Son of man, how does a grapevine compare to a tree? Is a vine's wood as useful as the wood of a tree? 3Can its wood be used for making things, like pegs to hang up pots and pans? 4No, it can only be used for fuel, and even as fuel, it burns too quickly. 5Vine branches are useless both before and after being put into the fire!

6 "And this is what the Sovereign LORD says: The people of Jerusalem are like grapevines growing among the trees of the forest. Since they are useless, I have set them aside to be burned! 7And I will see to it that if they escape from one fire, they will fall into another. When this happens, you will know that I am the LORD. 8And I will make the land desolate because my people have been unfaithful to me, says the Sovereign LORD."

CHAPTER **16**
Jerusalem—an Unfaithful Wife
Then another message came to me from the LORD. 2 "Son of man, confront Jerusalem with her loath-

some sins. 3Give her this message from the Sovereign LORD: You are nothing but a Canaanite! Your father was an Amorite and your mother a Hittite! 4When you were born, no one cared about you. Your umbilical cord was left uncut, and you were never washed, rubbed with salt, and dressed in warm clothing. 5No one had the slightest interest in you; no one pitied you or cared for you. On the day you were born, you were dumped in a field and left to die, unwanted.

6 "But I came by and saw you there, helplessly kicking about in your own blood. As you lay there, I said, 'Live!' 7And I helped you to thrive like a plant in the field. You grew up and became a beautiful jewel. Your breasts became full, and your hair grew, though you were still naked. 8And when I passed by and saw you again, you were old enough to be married. So I wrapped my cloak around you to cover your nakedness and declared my marriage vows. I made a covenant with you, says the Sovereign LORD, and you became mine.

9 "Then I bathed you and washed off your blood, and I rubbed fragrant oils into your skin. 10I gave you expensive clothing of linen and silk, beautifully embroidered, and sandals made of fine leather. 11I gave you lovely jewelry, bracelets, and beautiful necklaces, 12a ring for your nose and earrings for your ears, and a lovely crown for your head. 13And so you were made beautiful with gold and silver. Your clothes were made of fine linen and were beautifully embroidered. You ate the finest foods—fine flour, honey, and olive oil—and became more beautiful than ever. You looked like a queen, and so you were! 14Your fame soon spread throughout the world on account of your beauty, because the splendor I bestowed on you perfected your beauty, says the Sovereign LORD.

15 "But you thought you could get along without me, so you trusted instead in your fame and beauty. You gave yourself as a prostitute to every man who came along. Your beauty was theirs for the asking! 16You used the lovely things I gave you to make shrines for idols, where you carried out your acts of prostitution. Unbelievable! How could such a thing ever happen? 17You took the very jewels and gold and silver ornaments I had given you and made statues of men and worshiped them, which is adultery against me. 18You used the beautifully embroidered clothes I gave you to cover your idols. Then you used my oil and incense to worship them. 19Imagine it! You set before them as a lovely

sacrifice the fine flour and oil and honey I had given you, says the Sovereign LORD.

20"Then you took your sons and daughters—the children you had borne to me—and sacrificed them to your gods. Was it not enough that you should be a prostitute? 21Must you also slaughter my children by sacrificing them to idols? 22In all your years of adultery and loathsome sin, you have not once thought of the days long ago when you lay naked in a field, kicking about in your own blood.

23"Your destruction is certain, says the Sovereign LORD. In addition to all your other wickedness, 24you built a pagan shrine and put altars to idols in every town square. 25On every street corner you defiled your beauty, offering your body to every passerby in an endless stream of prostitution. 26Then you added lustful Egypt to your lovers, fanning the flames of my anger with your increasing promiscuity. 27That is why I struck you with my fist and reduced your boundaries. I handed you over to your enemies, the Philistines, and even they were shocked by your lewd conduct! 28You have prostituted yourselves with the Assyrians, too. It seems you can never find enough new lovers! And after your prostitution there, you still were not satisfied. 29You added to your lovers by embracing that great merchant land of Babylonia*—but you still weren't satisfied!

30"What a sick heart you have, says the Sovereign LORD, to do such things as these, acting like a shameless prostitute. 31You build your pagan shrines on every street corner and your altars to idols in every square. You have been worse than a prostitute, so eager for sin that you have not even demanded payment for your love! 32Yes, you are an adulterous wife who takes in strangers instead of her own husband. 33Prostitutes charge for their services—but not you! You give gifts to your lovers, bribing them to come to you. 34So you are the opposite of other prostitutes. No one pays you; instead, you pay them!

Judgment on Jerusalem's Prostitution

35"Therefore, you prostitute, listen to this message from the LORD! 36This is what the Sovereign LORD says: Because you have exposed yourself in prostitution to all your lovers, and because you have worshiped detestable idols, and because you have slaughtered your children as sacrifices to your gods, 37this is what I am going to do. I will gather together all your allies—these lovers of yours with whom you have sinned, both

16:29 Or *Chaldea.*

those you loved and those you hated—and I will strip you naked in front of them so they can stare at you. 38I will punish you for your murder and adultery. I will cover you with blood in my jealous fury. 39Then I will give you to your lovers—these many nations—and they will destroy you. They will knock down your pagan shrines and the altars to your idols. They will strip you and take your beautiful jewels, leaving you completely naked and ashamed. 40They will band together in a mob to stone you and run you through with swords. 41They will burn your homes and punish you in front of many women. I will see to it that you stop your prostitution and end your payments to your many lovers.

42"Then at last my fury against you will be spent, and my jealous anger will subside. I will be calm and will not be angry with you anymore. 43But first, because you have not remembered your youth but have angered me by doing all these evil things, I will fully repay you for all of your sins, says the Sovereign LORD. For to all your disgusting sins, you have added these lewd acts. 44Everyone who makes up proverbs will say of you, 'Like mother, like daughter.' 45For your mother loathed her husband and her children, and so do you. And you are exactly like your sisters, for they despised their husbands and their children. Truly your mother must have been a Hittite and your father an Amorite.

46"Your older sister was Samaria, who lived with her daughters in the north. Your younger sister was Sodom, who lived with her daughters in the south. 47But you have not merely sinned as they did—no, that was nothing to you. In a very short time you far surpassed them! 48As surely as I live, says the Sovereign LORD, Sodom and her daughters were never as wicked as you and your daughters. 49Sodom's sins were pride, laziness, and gluttony, while the poor and needy suffered outside her door. 50She was proud and did loathsome things, so I wiped her out, as you have seen.

51"Even Samaria did not commit half your sins. You have done far more loathsome things than your sisters ever did. They seem righteous compared to you! 52You should be deeply ashamed because your sins are so terrible. In comparison, you make your sisters seem innocent!

53"But someday I will restore the fortunes of Sodom and Samaria, and I will restore you, too. 54Then you will be truly ashamed of everything you have done, for your sins make them feel good in comparison. 55Yes, your sisters, Sodom and

Samaria, and all their people will be restored, and at that time you also will be restored. ⁵⁶In your proud days you held Sodom in contempt. ⁵⁷But now your greater wickedness has been exposed to all the world, and you are the one who is scorned—by Edom* and all her neighbors and by Philistia. ⁵⁸This is your punishment for all your disgusting sins, says the LORD.

⁵⁹"Now this is what the Sovereign LORD says: I will give you what you deserve, for you have taken your solemn vows lightly by breaking your covenant. ⁶⁰Yet I will keep the covenant I made with you when you were young, and I will establish an everlasting covenant with you. ⁶¹Then you will remember with shame all the evil you have done. I will make your sisters, Samaria and Sodom, to be your daughters, even though they are not part of our covenant. ⁶²And I will reaffirm my covenant with you, and you will know that I am the LORD. ⁶³You will remember your sins and cover your mouth in silence and shame when I forgive you of all that you have done, says the Sovereign LORD."

CHAPTER 17
A Story of Two Eagles

Then this message came to me from the LORD: ²"Son of man, tell this story to the people of Israel. ³Give them this message from the Sovereign LORD: A great eagle with broad wings full of many-colored feathers came to Lebanon. He took hold of the highest branch of a cedar tree ⁴and plucked off its topmost shoot. Then he carried it away to a city filled with merchants, where he planted it.

⁵"Then he planted one of its seedlings in fertile ground beside a broad river, where it would grow as quickly as a willow tree. ⁶It took root there and grew into a low, spreading vine. Its branches turned up toward the eagle, and its roots grew down beneath it. It soon produced strong branches and luxuriant leaves. ⁷But then another great eagle with broad wings and full plumage came along. So the vine sent its roots and branches out toward him for water. ⁸The vine did this even though it was already planted in good soil and had plenty of water so it could grow into a splendid vine and produce rich leaves and luscious fruit.

⁹"So now the Sovereign LORD asks: Should I let this vine grow and prosper? No! I will pull it out, roots and all! I will cut off its fruit and let its leaves wither and die. I will pull it out easily enough—it won't take a strong arm or a large army to do it.

¹⁰Then when the vine is transplanted, will it thrive? No, it will wither away completely when the east wind blows against it. It will die in the same good soil where it had grown so well."

The Riddle Explained

¹¹Then this message came to me from the LORD: ¹²"Say to these rebels of Israel: Don't you understand the meaning of this riddle of the eagles? I will tell you, says the Sovereign LORD. The king of Babylon came to Jerusalem, took away her king and princes, and brought them to Babylon. ¹³He made a treaty with a member of the royal family and made him take an oath of loyalty. He also exiled Israel's most influential leaders, ¹⁴so Israel would not become strong again and revolt. Only by keeping her treaty with Babylon could Israel maintain her national identity.

¹⁵"Nevertheless, this man of Israel's royal family rebelled against Babylon, sending ambassadors to Egypt to request a great army and many horses. Can Israel break her sworn treaties like that and get away with it? ¹⁶No! For as surely as I live, says the Sovereign LORD, the king of Israel will die in Babylon, the land of the king who put him in power and whose treaty he despised and broke. ¹⁷Pharaoh and all his mighty army will fail to help Israel when the king of Babylon lays siege to Jerusalem again and destroys the lives of many. ¹⁸For the king of Israel broke his treaty after swearing to obey; therefore, he will not escape.

¹⁹"So this is what the Sovereign LORD says: As surely as I live, I will punish him for breaking my covenant and despising the solemn oath he made in my name. ²⁰I will throw my net over him and capture him in my snare. I will bring him to Babylon and deal with him there for this treason against me. ²¹And all the best warriors of Israel will be killed in battle, and those remaining in the city will be scattered to the four winds. Then you will know that I, the LORD, have spoken these words.

²²"And the Sovereign LORD says: I will take a tender shoot from the top of a tall cedar, and I will plant it on the top of Israel's highest mountain. ²³It will become a noble cedar, sending forth its branches and producing seed. Birds of every sort will nest in it, finding shelter beneath its branches. ²⁴And all the trees will know that it is I, the LORD, who cuts down the tall tree and helps the short tree to grow tall. It is I who makes the green tree wither and gives new life to the dead tree. I, the LORD, have spoken! I will do what I have said."

16:57 Many ancient manuscripts read *Aram.*

CHAPTER **18**

The Justice of a Righteous God

Then another message came to me from the LORD: 2 "Why do you quote this proverb in the land of Israel: 'The parents have eaten sour grapes, but their children's mouths pucker at the taste'? 3 As surely as I live, says the Sovereign LORD, you will not say this proverb anymore in Israel. 4 For all people are mine to judge—both parents and children alike. And this is my rule: The person who sins will be the one who dies.

5 "Suppose a certain man is just and does what is lawful and right, 6 and he has not feasted in the mountains before Israel's idols or worshiped them. And suppose he does not commit adultery or have intercourse with a woman during her menstrual period. 7 Suppose he is a merciful creditor, not keeping the items given in pledge by poor debtors, and does not rob the poor but instead gives food to the hungry and provides clothes for people in need. 8 And suppose he grants loans without interest, stays away from injustice, is honest and fair when judging others, 9 and faithfully obeys my laws and regulations. Anyone who does these things is just and will surely live, says the Sovereign LORD.

10 "But suppose that man has a son who grows up to be a robber or murderer and refuses to do what is right. 11 And suppose that son does all the evil things his father would never do—worships idols on the mountains, commits adultery, 12 oppresses the poor and helpless, steals from debtors by refusing to let them redeem what they have given in pledge, worships idols and takes part in loathsome practices, 13 and lends money at interest. Should such a sinful person live? No! He must die and must take full blame.

14 "But suppose that sinful son, in turn, has a son who sees his father's wickedness but decides against that kind of life. 15 Suppose this son refuses to worship idols on the mountains, does not commit adultery, 16 and does not exploit the poor, but instead is fair to debtors and does not rob them. And suppose this son feeds the hungry, provides clothes for the needy, 17 helps the poor, does not lend money at interest, and obeys all my regulations and laws. Such a person will not die because of his father's sins; he will surely live. 18 But the father will die for the many sins he committed—for being cruel and robbing close relatives, doing what was clearly wrong among his people.

19 " 'What?' you ask. 'Doesn't the child pay for the parent's sins?' No! For if the child does what is right and keeps my laws, that child will surely live. 20 The one who sins is the one who dies. The child will not be punished for the parent's sins, and the parent will not be punished for the child's sins. Righteous people will be rewarded for their own goodness, and wicked people will be punished for their own wickedness. 21 But if wicked people turn away from all their sins and begin to obey my laws and do what is just and right, they will surely live and not die. 22 All their past sins will be forgotten, and they will live because of the righteous things they have done.

23 "Do you think, asks the Sovereign LORD, that I like to see wicked people die? Of course not! I only want them to turn from their wicked ways and live. 24 However, if righteous people turn to sinful ways and start acting like other sinners, should they be allowed to live? No, of course not! All their previous goodness will be forgotten, and they will die for their sins.

25 "Yet you say, 'The Lord isn't being just!' Listen to me, O people of Israel. Am I the one who is unjust, or is it you? 26 When righteous people turn from being good and start doing sinful things, they will die for it. Yes, they will die because of their sinful deeds. 27 And if wicked people turn away from their wickedness, obey the law, and do what is just and right, they will save their lives. 28 They will live, because after thinking it over, they decided to turn from their sins. Such people will not die. 29 And yet the people of Israel keep saying, 'The Lord is unjust!' O people of Israel, it is you who are unjust, not I.

30 "Therefore, I will judge each of you, O people of Israel, according to your actions, says the Sovereign LORD. Turn from your sins! Don't let them destroy you! 31 Put all your rebellion behind you, and get for yourselves a new heart and a new spirit. For why should you die, O people of Israel? 32 I don't want you to die, says the Sovereign LORD. Turn back and live!

CHAPTER **19**

A Funeral Song for Israel's Kings

"Sing this funeral song for the princes of Israel:

2 'What is your mother?
    A lioness among lions!
She lay down among the young lions
    and reared her cubs.
3 She raised one of her cubs
    to become a strong young lion.
He learned to catch and devour prey,
    and he became a man-eater.

4 Then the nations heard about him,
    and he was trapped in their pit.
They led him away in chains
    to the land of Egypt.

5 'When the mother lion saw
    that all her hopes for him were gone,
she took another of her cubs
    and taught him to be a strong lion.
6 He prowled among the other lions
    and became a leader among them.
He learned to catch and devour prey,
    and he, too, became a man-eater.
7 He demolished fortresses in nearby nations*
    and destroyed their towns and cities.
Their farms were desolated,
    and their crops were destroyed.
Everyone in the land trembled in fear
    when they heard him roar.
8 Then the armies of the nations attacked him,
    surrounding him from every direction.
They spread out their nets for him
    and captured him in their pit.
9 With hooks, they dragged him into a cage
    and brought him before the king of
    Babylon.
They held him in captivity,
    so his voice could never again be heard
    on the mountains of Israel.

10 'Your mother was like a vine
    planted by the water's edge.
It had lush, green foliage
    because of the abundant water.
11 Its branches became very strong,
    strong enough to be a ruler's scepter.
It soon became very tall,
    towering above all the others.
It stood out because of its height
    and because of its many lush branches.
12 But the vine was uprooted in fury
    and thrown down to the ground.
The desert wind dried up its fruit
    and tore off its branches.
Its stem was destroyed by fire.
13 Now the vine is growing in the wilderness,
    where the ground is hard and dry.
14 A fire has come from its branches
    and devoured its fruit.
None of the remaining limbs
    is strong enough to be a ruler's scepter.'

This is a funeral song, and it is now time for the funeral."

CHAPTER 20
The Rebellion of Israel

On August 14,* during the seventh year of King Jehoiachin's captivity, some of the leaders of Israel came to request a message from the LORD. They sat down in front of me to wait for his reply. 2Then this message came to me from the LORD: 3"Son of man, give the leaders of Israel this message from the Sovereign LORD: How dare you come to ask for my help? As surely as I live, I will tell you nothing. This is the word of the Sovereign LORD!

4"Son of man, bring judgment against them and condemn them. Make them realize how loathsome the actions of their ancestors really were. 5Give them this message from the Sovereign LORD: When I chose Israel and revealed myself to her in Egypt, I swore that I, the LORD, would be her God. 6I promised that I would bring her and her descendants out of Egypt to a land I had discovered and explored for them—a good land, a land flowing with milk and honey, the best of all lands anywhere. 7Then I said to them, 'Each of you, get rid of your idols. Do not defile yourselves with the Egyptian gods, for I am the LORD your God.'

8"But they rebelled against me and would not listen. They did not get rid of their idols or forsake the gods of Egypt. Then I threatened to pour out my fury on them to satisfy my anger while they were still in Egypt. 9But I didn't do it, for I acted to protect the honor of my name. That way the surrounding nations wouldn't be able to laugh at Israel's God, who had promised to deliver his people. 10So I brought my people out of Egypt and led them into the wilderness. 11There I gave them my laws so they could live by keeping them. Yes, all those who keep them will live! 12And I gave them my Sabbath days of rest as a sign between them and me. It was to remind them that I, the LORD, had set them apart to be holy, making them my special people.

13"But the people of Israel rebelled against me, and they refused to obey my laws there in the wilderness. They wouldn't obey my instructions even though obedience would have given them life. And they also violated my Sabbath days. So I threatened to pour out my fury on them, and I made plans to utterly consume them in the desert. 14But again I held back in order to protect the honor of my name. That way the nations who saw me lead my people out of Egypt wouldn't be able to claim I destroyed them because I couldn't take care of them. 15But I swore to them in the wilder-

---

19:7 As in Greek version; Hebrew reads *He consorted with widows.* **20:1** Hebrew *In the fifth month, on the tenth day,* of the Hebrew calendar. This event occurred on August 14, 591 B.C.; also see note on 1:1.

ness that I would not bring them into the land I had given them, a land flowing with milk and honey, the most beautiful place on earth. 16I told them this because they had rejected my laws, ignored my will for them, and violated my Sabbath days. Their hearts were given to their idols. 17Nevertheless, I pitied them and held back from destroying them in the wilderness.

18"Then I warned their children and told them not to follow in their parents' footsteps, defiling themselves with their idols. 19'I am the LORD your God,' I told them. 'Follow my laws, pay attention to my instructions, 20and keep my Sabbath days holy, for they are a sign to remind you that I am the LORD your God.'

21"But their children, too, rebelled against me. They refused to keep my laws and follow my instructions, even though obeying them would have given them life. And they also violated my Sabbath days. So again I threatened to pour out my fury on them in the wilderness. 22Nevertheless, I withdrew my judgment against them to protect the honor of my name among the nations who had seen my power in bringing them out of Egypt. 23But I took a solemn oath against them while they were in the wilderness. I vowed I would scatter them among all the nations 24because they did not obey my laws. They scorned my instructions by violating my Sabbath days and longing for the idols of their ancestors. 25I gave them over to worthless customs and laws that would not lead to life. 26I let them pollute themselves with the very gifts I had given them, and I allowed them to give their firstborn children as offerings to their gods—so I might devastate them and show them that I alone am the LORD.

Judgment and Restoration

27"Therefore, son of man, give the people of Israel this message from the Sovereign LORD: Your ancestors continued to blaspheme and betray me, 28for when I brought them into the land I had promised them, they offered sacrifices and incense on every high hill and under every green tree they saw! They roused my fury as they offered up sacrifices to their gods. They brought their perfumes and incense and poured out their drink offerings to them! 29I said to them, 'What is this high place where you are going?' (This idol shrine has been called Bamah—'high place'—ever since.)

30"Therefore, give the people of Israel this message from the Sovereign LORD: Do you plan to pollute yourselves just as your ancestors did? Do you intend to keep prostituting yourselves by worshiping detestable idols? 31For when you offer gifts to them and give your little children to be burned as sacrifices,* you continue to pollute yourselves to this day. Should I listen to you or help you, O people of Israel? As surely as I live, says the Sovereign LORD, I will not give you a message even though you have come to me requesting one.

32"You say, 'We want to be like the nations all around us, who serve idols of wood and stone.' But what you have in mind will never happen. 33As surely as I live, says the Sovereign LORD, I will rule you with an iron fist in great anger and with awesome power. 34With might and fury I will bring you out from the lands where you are scattered. 35I will bring you into the wilderness of the nations, and there I will judge you face to face. 36I will judge you there just as I did your ancestors in the wilderness after bringing them out of Egypt, says the Sovereign LORD. 37I will count you carefully and hold you to the terms of the covenant. 38I will purge you of all those who rebel and sin against me. I will bring them out of the countries where they are in exile, but they will never enter the land of Israel. And when that happens, you will know that I am the LORD.

39"As for you, O people of Israel, this is what the Sovereign LORD says: If you insist, go right ahead and worship your idols, but then don't turn around and bring gifts to me. Such desecration of my holy name must stop! 40For on my holy mountain, says the Sovereign LORD, the people of Israel will someday worship me, and I will accept them. There I will require that you bring me all your offerings and choice gifts and sacrifices. 41When I bring you home from exile, you will be as pleasing to me as an offering of perfumed incense. And I will display my holiness in you as all the nations watch. 42Then when I have brought you home to the land I promised your ancestors, you will know that I am the LORD. 43You will look back at all your sins and hate yourselves because of the evil you have done. 44You will know that I am the LORD, O people of Israel, when I have honored my name by treating you mercifully in spite of your wickedness, says the Sovereign LORD."

Judgment against the Negev

45Then this message came to me from the LORD: 46"Son of man, look toward the south* and speak out against it; prophesy against the fields of the Negev. 47Give the southern wilderness this mes-

20:31 Or *and make your little children pass through the fire.*   20:46 Hebrew *Teman.*

sage from the Sovereign LORD: Hear the word of the LORD! I will set you on fire, O forest, and every tree will be burned—green and dry trees alike. The terrible flames will not be quenched; they will scorch everything from south to north. 48And all the world will see that I, the LORD, have set this fire. It will not be put out."

49Then I said, "O Sovereign LORD, they are saying of me, 'He only talks in riddles!'"

CHAPTER 21
The LORD's Sword of Judgment

Then this message came to me from the LORD: 2"Son of man, look toward Jerusalem and prophesy against Israel and her sanctuaries. 3Give her this message from the LORD: I am your enemy, O Israel, and I am about to unsheath my sword to destroy your people—the righteous and the wicked alike. 4Yes, I will not spare even the righteous! I will make a clean sweep throughout the land from south to north. 5All the world will know that I am the LORD. My sword is in my hand, and it will not return to its sheath until its work is finished.

6"Son of man, groan before the people! Groan before them with bitter anguish and a broken heart. 7When they ask you why, tell them, 'I groan because of the terrifying news I have heard. When it comes true, the boldest heart will melt with fear; all strength will disappear. Every spirit will faint; strong knees will tremble and become as weak as water. And the Sovereign LORD says: It is coming! It's on its way!'"

8Then the LORD said to me, 9"Son of man, give the people this message from the LORD: A sword is being sharpened and polished. 10It is being prepared for terrible slaughter; it will flash like lightning! Now will you laugh? Those far stronger than you have fallen beneath its power!* 11Yes, the sword is now being sharpened and polished; it is being prepared for the executioner!

12"Son of man, cry out and wail; pound your thighs in anguish, for that sword will slaughter my people and their leaders—everyone will die! 13It will put them all to the test! So now the Sovereign LORD asks: What chance do they have?*

14"Son of man, prophesy to them and clap your hands vigorously. Then take the sword and brandish it twice, even three times, to symbolize the great massacre they will face! 15Let their hearts melt with terror, for the sword glitters at every gate. It flashes like lightning; it is polished for slaughter! 16O sword, slash to the right, and

slash to the left, wherever you will, wherever you want. 17I, too, will clap my hands, and I will satisfy my fury. I, the LORD, have spoken!"

A Signpost for Babylon's King

18Then this message came to me from the LORD: 19"Son of man, make a map and trace two routes on it for the sword of Babylon's king to follow. Put a signpost on the road that comes out of Babylon where the road forks into two—20one road going to Ammon and its capital, Rabbah, and the other to Judah and fortified Jerusalem. 21The king of Babylon now stands at the fork, uncertain whether to attack Jerusalem or Rabbah. He will call his magicians to use divination. They will cast lots by shaking arrows from the quiver. They will inspect the livers of their animal sacrifices. 22Then they will decide to turn toward Jerusalem! With battering rams they will go against the gates, shouting for the kill. They will put up siege towers and build ramps against the walls to reach the top. 23The people of Jerusalem will think it is a mistake, because of their treaty with the Babylonians. But the king of Babylon will remind the people of their rebellion. Then he will attack and capture them.

24"Therefore, this is what the Sovereign LORD says: Again and again your guilt cries out against you, for you are not ashamed of your sin. You don't even try to hide it! Wherever you go, whatever you do, all your actions are filled with sin. So now the time of your punishment has come!

25"O you corrupt and wicked prince of Israel, your final day of reckoning is here! 26Take off your jeweled crown, says the Sovereign LORD. The old order changes—now the lowly are exalted, and the mighty are brought low. 27Destruction! Destruction! I will surely destroy the kingdom. And it will not be restored until the one appears who has the right to judge it. Then I will hand it over to him.

A Message for the Ammonites

28"And now, son of man, prophesy concerning the Ammonites and their mockery. Give them this message from the Sovereign LORD: My sword is drawn for your slaughter; it is sharpened to destroy, flashing like lightning! 29Your magicians and false prophets have given false visions and told lies about the sword. And now it will fall with even greater force on the wicked for whom the day of final reckoning has come. 30Should I return my sword to its sheath before I deal with you? No, I

21:10 The meaning of the Hebrew is uncertain.   21:13 The meaning of the Hebrew is uncertain.

will destroy you in your own country, the land of your birth. ³¹I will pour out my fury on you and blow on you with the fire of my anger. I will hand you over to cruel men who are skilled in destruction. ³²You are fuel for the fire, and your blood will be spilled in your own land. You will be utterly wiped out, your memory lost to history. I, the LORD, have spoken!"

CHAPTER 22

The Sins of Jerusalem

Now this message came to me from the LORD: ²"Son of man, are you ready to judge Jerusalem? Are you ready to judge this city of murderers? Denounce her terrible deeds in public, ³and give her this message from the Sovereign LORD: O city of murderers, doomed and damned—city of idols, filthy and foul—⁴you are guilty of both murder and idolatry. Your day of destruction has come! You have reached the end of your years. I will make you an object of mockery throughout the world. ⁵O infamous city, filled with confusion, you will be mocked by people both far and near.

⁶"Every leader in Israel who lives within your walls is bent on murder. ⁷Fathers and mothers are contemptuously ignored. Resident foreigners are forced to pay for protection. Orphans and widows are wronged and oppressed. ⁸Inside your walls you despise my holy things and violate my Sabbath days of rest. ⁹People accuse others falsely and send them to their death. You are filled with idol worshipers and people who take part in lewd activities. ¹⁰Men sleep with their fathers' wives and have intercourse with women who are menstruating. ¹¹Within your walls live men who commit adultery with their neighbors' wives, who defile their daughters-in-law or who rape their own sisters. ¹²There are hired murderers, loan racketeers, and extortioners everywhere! They never even think of me and my commands, says the Sovereign LORD.

¹³"But now I clap my hands in indignation over your dishonest gain and bloodshed. ¹⁴How strong and courageous will you be in my day of reckoning? I, the LORD, have spoken! I will do what I have said. ¹⁵I will scatter you among the nations and purge you of your wickedness. ¹⁶And when you have been dishonored among the nations, you will know that I am the LORD."

The LORD's Refining Furnace

¹⁷Then this message came to me from the LORD: ¹⁸"Son of man, the people of Israel are the worth-

less slag that remains after silver is smelted. They are the dross that is left over—a useless mixture of copper, tin, iron, and lead. ¹⁹So give them this message from the Sovereign LORD: Because you are all worthless slag, I will bring you to my crucible in Jerusalem. ²⁰I will melt you down in the heat of my fury, just as copper, tin, iron, and lead are melted down in a furnace. ²¹I will gather you together and blow the fire of my anger upon you, ²²and you will melt like silver in fierce heat. Then you will know that I, the LORD, have poured out my fury on you."

The Sins of Israel's Leaders

²³Again a message came to me from the LORD: ²⁴"Son of man, give the people of Israel this message: In the day of my indignation, you will become like an uncleared wilderness or a desert without rain. ²⁵Your princes* plot conspiracies just as lions stalk their prey. They devour innocent people, seizing treasures and extorting wealth. They increase the number of widows in the land. ²⁶Your priests have violated my laws and defiled my holy things. To them there is no difference between what is holy and what is not. And they do not teach my people the difference between what is ceremonially clean and unclean. They disregard my Sabbath days so that my holy name is greatly dishonored among them. ²⁷Your leaders are like wolves, who tear apart their victims. They actually destroy people's lives for profit! ²⁸And your prophets announce false visions and speak false messages. They say, 'My message is from the Sovereign LORD,' when the LORD hasn't spoken a single word to them. They repair cracked walls with whitewash! ²⁹Even common people oppress the poor, rob the needy, and deprive foreigners of justice.

³⁰"I looked for someone who might rebuild the wall of righteousness that guards the land. I searched for someone to stand in the gap in the wall so I wouldn't have to destroy the land, but I found no one. ³¹So now I will pour out my fury on them, consuming them in the fire of my anger. I will heap on them the full penalty for all their sins, says the Sovereign LORD."

CHAPTER 23

The Adultery of Two Sisters

This message came to me from the LORD: ²"Son of man, once there were two sisters who were daughters of the same mother. ³They became

22:25 As in Greek version; Hebrew reads *prophets.*

prostitutes in Egypt. Even as young girls, they allowed themselves to be fondled and caressed. ⁴The older girl was named Oholah, and her sister was Oholibah. I married them, and they bore me sons and daughters. I am speaking of Samaria and Jerusalem, for Oholah is Samaria and Oholibah is Jerusalem.

⁵"Then Oholah lusted after other lovers instead of me, and she gave her love to the Assyrians, her neighbors. ⁶They were all attractive young men, captains and commanders dressed in handsome blue, dashing about on their horses. ⁷And so she prostituted herself with the most desirable men of Assyria, worshiping their idols and defiling herself. ⁸For when she left Egypt, she did not leave her spirit of prostitution behind. She was still as lewd as in her youth, when the Egyptians satisfied their lusts with her and robbed her of her virginity. ⁹And so I handed her over to her Assyrian lovers, whom she desired so much. ¹⁰They stripped her and killed her and took away her children as their slaves. Her name was known to every woman in the land as a sinner who had received what she deserved.

¹¹"Yet even though Oholibah saw what had happened to Oholah, her sister, she followed right in her footsteps. And she was even more depraved, abandoning herself to her lust and prostitution. ¹²She fawned over her Assyrian neighbors, those handsome young men on fine horses, those captains and commanders in handsome uniforms—all of them desirable. ¹³I saw the way she was going, defiling herself just like her older sister.

¹⁴"Then she carried her prostitution even further. She fell in love with pictures that were painted on a wall—pictures of Babylonian* military officers, outfitted in striking red uniforms. ¹⁵Handsome belts encircled their waists, and flowing turbans crowned their heads. They were dressed like chariot officers from the land of Babylonia.* ¹⁶When she saw these paintings, she longed to give herself to them, so she sent messengers to Babylonia to invite them to come to her. ¹⁷So they came and committed adultery with her, defiling her in the bed of love. But later, she became disgusted with them and broke off their relationship.

¹⁸"So I became disgusted with Oholibah, just as I was with her sister, because she flaunted herself before them and gave herself to satisfy their lusts. ¹⁹But that didn't bother her. She turned to even greater prostitution, remembering her youth

23:14 Or *Chaldean.*   23:15 Or *Chaldea;* also in 23:16.

when she was a prostitute in Egypt. ²⁰She lusted after lovers whose attentions were gross and bestial. ²¹And so, Oholibah, you celebrated your former days as a young girl in Egypt, when you first allowed yourself to be fondled and caressed.

The LORD's Judgment of Oholibah

²²"Therefore, Oholibah, this is what the Sovereign LORD says: I will send your lovers against you— those very nations from which you turned away in disgust. ²³For the Babylonians will come with all the Chaldeans from Pekod and Shoa and Koa. And all the Assyrians will come with them— handsome young captains, commanders, chariot officers, and other high-ranking officers, riding their horses. ²⁴They will all come against you from the north with chariots, wagons, and a great army fully prepared for attack. They will take up positions on every side, surrounding you with men armed for battle. And I will hand you over to them so they can do with you as they please. ²⁵I will turn my jealous anger against you, and they will deal furiously with you. They will cut off your nose and ears, and any survivors will then be slaughtered by the sword. Your children will be taken away as captives, and everything that is left will be burned. ²⁶They will strip you of your beautiful clothes and jewels. ²⁷In this way, I will put a stop to the lewdness and prostitution you brought from Egypt. You will never again cast longing eyes on those things or fondly remember your time in Egypt.

²⁸"For this is what the Sovereign LORD says: I will surely hand you over to your enemies, to those you loathe. ²⁹They will deal with you in hatred and rob you of all you own, leaving you naked and bare. The shame of your prostitution will be exposed to all the world. ³⁰You brought all this on yourself by prostituting yourself to other nations, defiling yourself with all their idols. ³¹Because you have followed in your sister's footsteps, I will punish you with the same terrors that destroyed her.

³²"Yes, this is what the Sovereign LORD says: You will drink from the same cup of terror as your sister—a cup that is large and deep. And all the world will mock and scorn you in your desolation. ³³You will reel like a drunkard beneath the awful blows of sorrow and distress, just as your sister Samaria did. ³⁴In deep anguish you will drain that cup of terror to the very bottom. Then you will smash it to pieces and beat your breast in anguish. For I, the Sovereign LORD, have spoken! ³⁵And because you have

forgotten me and turned your back on me, says the Sovereign LORD, you must bear the consequences of all your lewdness and prostitution."

The LORD's Judgment on Both Sisters

36The LORD said to me, "Son of man, you must accuse Oholah and Oholibah of all their awful deeds. 37They have committed both adultery and murder—adultery by worshiping idols and murder by burning their children as sacrifices on their altars. 38Then after doing these terrible things, they defiled my Temple and violated my Sabbath day! 39On the very day that they murdered their children in front of their idols, they boldly came into my Temple to worship! They came in and defiled my house!

40"You sisters sent messengers to distant lands to get men. Then when they arrived, you bathed yourselves, painted your eyelids, and put on your finest jewels for them. 41You sat with them on a beautifully embroidered couch and put my incense and my oil on a table that was spread before you. 42From your room came the sound of many men carousing. They were lustful men and drunkards from the wilderness, who put bracelets on your wrists and beautiful crowns on your heads. 43Then I said, 'If they really want to sleep with worn-out, old prostitutes like these, let them!' 44And that is what they did. They slept with Oholah and Oholibah, these shameless prostitutes, with all the zest of lustful young men. 45But righteous people will judge these sister cities for what they really are—adulteresses and murderers. They will sentence them to all the punishment they deserve.

46"Now this is what the Sovereign LORD says: Bring an army against them and hand them over to be terrorized and plundered. 47For their enemies will stone them and kill them with swords. They will butcher their sons and daughters and burn their homes. 48In this way, I will put an end to lewdness and idolatry in the land, and my judgment will be a warning to others not to follow their wicked example. 49You will be fully repaid for all your prostitution—your worship of idols. Yes, you will suffer the full penalty! Then you will know that I am the Sovereign LORD."

CHAPTER 24
The Sign of the Cooking Pot

On January 15,* during the ninth year of King Jehoiachin's captivity, this message came to me from the LORD: 2"Son of man, write down to-day's date, because on this very day the king of Babylon is beginning his attack against Jerusalem. 3Then show these rebels an illustration; give them a message from the Sovereign LORD. Put a pot of water on the fire to boil. 4Fill it with choice meat—the rump and the shoulder and all the most tender cuts. 5Use only the best sheep from the flock and heap fuel on the fire beneath the pot. Bring the pot to a boil, and cook the bones along with the meat.

6"Now this is what the Sovereign LORD says: Destruction is certain for Jerusalem, the city of murderers! She is a pot filled with corruption. So take the meat out chunk by chunk in whatever order it comes, 7for her wickedness is evident to all. She murders boldly, leaving blood on the rocks for all to see. She doesn't even try to cover it! 8So I will splash her blood on a rock as an open expression of my anger and vengeance against her.

9"This is what the Sovereign LORD says: Destruction is certain for Jerusalem, the city of murderers! I myself will pile up the fuel beneath her. 10Yes, heap on the wood! Let the fire roar to make the pot boil. Cook the meat well with many spices. Then empty the pot and burn the bones. 11Now set the empty pot on the coals to scorch away the filth and corruption. 12But it's hopeless; the corruption remains. So throw it into the fire! 13It is the filth and corruption of your lewdness and idolatry. And now, because I tried to cleanse you but you refused, you will remain filthy until my fury against you has been satisfied. 14I, the LORD, have spoken! The time has come and I won't hold back; I will not change my mind. You will be judged on the basis of all your wicked actions, says the Sovereign LORD."

The Death of Ezekiel's Wife

15Then this message came to me from the LORD: 16"Son of man, I am going to take away your dearest treasure. Suddenly she will die. Yet you must not show any sorrow. Do not weep; let there be no tears. 17You may sigh but only quietly. Let there be no wailing at her grave. Do not uncover your head or take off your sandals. Do not perform the rituals of mourning or accept any food brought to you by consoling friends."

18So I proclaimed this to the people the next morning, and in the evening my wife died. The next morning I did everything I had been told to do. 19Then the people asked, "What does all this mean? What are you trying to tell us?"

24:1 Hebrew *On the tenth day of the tenth month,* of the Hebrew calendar. This event occurred on January 15, 588 B.C.; also see note on 1:1.

20So I said to them, "A message came to me from the LORD, 21and I was told to give this message to the people of Israel. This is what the Sovereign LORD says: I will desecrate my Temple, the source of your security and pride. Your sons and daughters in Judea will be slaughtered by the sword. 22Then you will do as Ezekiel has done. You will not mourn in public or console yourselves by eating the food brought to you by sympathetic friends. 23Your heads must remain covered, and your sandals must not be taken off. You will not mourn or weep, but you will waste away because of your sins. You will mourn privately for all the evil you have done. 24Ezekiel is an example for you to follow; you will do as he has done. And when that time comes, you will know that I am the LORD."

25Then the LORD said to me, "Son of man, on the day I take away their stronghold—their joy and glory, their heart's desire, their dearest treasure—I will also take away their sons and daughters. 26And on that day a refugee from Jerusalem will come to you in Babylon and tell you what has happened. 27And when he arrives, your voice will suddenly return so you can talk to him, and you will be a symbol for these people. Then they will know that I am the LORD."

CHAPTER 25
A Message for Ammon

Then this message came to me from the LORD: 2"Son of man, look toward the land of Ammon and prophesy against its people. 3Give the Ammonites this message from the Sovereign LORD: Hear the word of the Sovereign LORD! Because you scoffed when my Temple was desecrated, mocked Israel in her desolation, and laughed at Judah as she went away into exile, 4I will allow nomads from the eastern deserts to overrun your country. They will set up their camps among you and pitch their tents on your land. They will harvest all your fruit and steal your livestock. 5And I will turn the city of Rabbah into a pasture for camels, and all the land of the Ammonites into an enclosure for sheep. Then you will know that I am the LORD.

6"And the Sovereign LORD says: Because you clapped and stamped and cheered with glee at the destruction of my people, 7I will lift up my fist against you. I will give you as plunder to many nations. I will cut you off from being a

nation and destroy you completely. Then you will know that I am the LORD.

A Message for Moab

8"And the Sovereign LORD says: Because the people of Moab have said that Judah is just like all the other nations, 9I will open up their eastern flank and wipe out their glorious frontier cities— Beth-jeshimoth, Baal-meon, and Kiriathaim. 10And I will hand Moab over to nomads from the eastern deserts, just as I handed over Ammon. Yes, the Ammonites will no longer be counted among the nations. 11And in the same way, I will bring my judgment down on the Moabites. Then they will know that I am the LORD.

A Message for Edom

12"And the Sovereign LORD says: The people of Edom have sinned greatly by avenging themselves against the people of Judah. 13Therefore, says the Sovereign LORD, I will raise my fist of judgment against Edom. I will wipe out their people, cattle, and flocks with the sword. I will make a wasteland of everything from Teman to Dedan. 14By the hand of my people of Israel, I will accomplish this. They will carry out my furious vengeance, and Edom will know it is from me. I, the Sovereign LORD, have spoken!

A Message for Philistia

15"And the Sovereign LORD says: The people of Philistia have acted against Judah out of revenge and long-standing contempt. 16Therefore, says the Sovereign LORD, I will raise my fist of judgment against the land of the Philistines. I will wipe out the Kerethites and utterly destroy the people who live by the sea. 17I will execute terrible vengeance against them to rebuke them for what they have done. And when I have inflicted my revenge, then they will know that I am the LORD."

CHAPTER 26
A Message for Tyre

On February 3, during the twelfth year of King Jehoiachin's captivity,* this message came to me from the LORD: 2"Son of man, Tyre has rejoiced over the fall of Jerusalem, saying, 'Ha! She who controlled the rich trade routes to the east has been broken, and I am the heir! Because she has been destroyed, I will become wealthy!'

3"Therefore, this is what the Sovereign LORD says: I am your enemy, O Tyre, and I will bring

26:1 Hebrew In the eleventh year, on the first day of the month, of the Hebrew calendar year. Since an element is missing in the date formula here, scholars have reconstructed this probable reading: In the eleventh [month of the twelfth] year, on the first day of the month. This reading would put this message on February 3, 585 B.C.; also see note on 1:1.

many nations against you, like the waves of the sea crashing against your shoreline. ⁴They will destroy the walls of Tyre and tear down its towers. I will scrape away its soil and make it a bare rock! ⁵The island of Tyre will become uninhabited. It will be a place for fishermen to spread their nets, for I have spoken, says the Sovereign LORD. Tyre will become the prey of many nations, ⁶and its mainland villages will be destroyed by the sword. Then they will know that I am the LORD.

⁷"For the Sovereign LORD says: I will bring King Nebuchadnezzar* of Babylon—the king of kings from the north—against Tyre with his cavalry, chariots, and great army. ⁸First he will destroy your mainland villages. Then he will attack you by building a siege wall, constructing a ramp, and raising a roof of shields against you. ⁹He will pound your walls with battering rams and demolish your towers with sledgehammers. ¹⁰The hooves of his cavalry will choke the city with dust, and your walls will shake as the horses gallop through your broken gates, pulling chariots behind them. ¹¹His horsemen will trample every street in the city. They will butcher your people, and your famous pillars will topple.

¹²"They will plunder all your riches and merchandise and break down your walls. They will destroy your lovely homes and dump your stones and timbers and even your dust into the sea. ¹³I will stop the music of your songs. No more will the sound of harps be heard among your people. ¹⁴I will make your island a bare rock, a place for fishermen to spread their nets. You will never be rebuilt, for I, the LORD, have spoken! This is the word of the Sovereign LORD.

The Effect of Tyre's Destruction

¹⁵"This is what the Sovereign LORD says to Tyre: The whole coastline will tremble at the sound of your fall, as the screams of the wounded echo in the continuing slaughter. ¹⁶All the seaport rulers will step down from their thrones and take off their royal robes and beautiful clothing. They will sit on the ground trembling with horror at what they have seen. ¹⁷Then they will wail for you, singing this funeral song:

'O famous island city,
　once ruler of the sea,
　how you have been destroyed!
Your people, with their naval power,
　once spread fear around the world.

¹⁸ Now the coastlands tremble at your fall.
　The islands are dismayed as you pass away.'

¹⁹"For the Sovereign LORD says: I will make Tyre an uninhabited ruin. You will sink beneath the terrible waves of enemy attack. Great seas will swallow you. ²⁰I will send you to the pit to lie there with those who descended there long ago. Your city will lie in ruins, buried beneath the earth, like those in the pit who have entered the world of the dead. Never again will you be given a position of respect here in the land of the living. ²¹I will bring you to a terrible end, and you will be no more. You will be looked for, but you will never be found. I, the Sovereign LORD, have spoken!"

CHAPTER **27**
The End of Tyre's Glory

Then this message came to me from the LORD: ²"Son of man, sing a funeral song for Tyre, ³that mighty gateway to the sea, the trading center of the world. Give Tyre this message from the Sovereign LORD: You claimed, O Tyre, to be perfect in beauty. ⁴You extended your boundaries into the sea. Your builders made you glorious! ⁵You were like a great ship built of the finest cypress from Senir.* They took a cedar from Lebanon to make a mast for you. ⁶They carved oars for you from the oaks of Bashan. They made your deck of pine wood, brought from the southern coasts of Cyprus.* Then they inlaid it with ivory. ⁷Your sails were made of Egypt's finest linen, and they flew as a banner above you. You stood beneath blue and purple awnings made bright with dyes from the coasts of Elishah.

⁸"Your oarsmen came from Sidon and Arvad; your helmsmen were skilled men from Tyre itself. ⁹Wise old craftsmen from Gebal did all the caulking. Ships came with goods from every land to barter for your trade. ¹⁰Men from distant Persia, Lydia, and Libya* served in your great army. They hung their shields and helmets on your walls, giving you great honor. ¹¹Men from Arvad and from Helech stood on your walls as sentinels. Your towers were manned by men from Gammad. Their shields hung on your walls, perfecting your splendor.

¹²"Tarshish was your agent, trading your wares in exchange for silver, iron, tin, and lead. ¹³Merchants from Greece,* Tubal, and Meshech brought slaves and bronze dishes. ¹⁴From Togarmah came riding horses, chariot horses, and

---

26:7 Hebrew *Nebuchadrezzar*, a variant name for Nebuchadnezzar.　27:5 Or *Hermon*.　27:6 Hebrew *Kittim*.　27:10 Hebrew *Paras, Lud, and Put*.　27:13 Hebrew *Javan*.

Where Did Satan Come From? Read EZEKIEL 28:12-19

The Bible teaches that God did not create Satan as we know him today. Satan, formerly known as Lucifer, was once a high-ranking angelic being. According to this passage, he held a position of great power and influence. So what went wrong? This text, although it was directed to the king of Tyre, includes at least four revealing facts regarding the devil and his irreversible fall from glory:

1. Lucifer Had Been Created Perfect. Verse 12 says that he was "the perfection of wisdom and beauty." Another way of interpreting this verse is, "You had the seal of perfection. You were full of wisdom, perfect in beauty." Clearly Lucifer was a magnificent angelic being.

2. Lucifer Had Been Given a Position of Privilege. Not only was Lucifer a picture of perfection, but he had been given a position of great responsibility and honor. He was appointed to be the anointed "guardian angel." Moreover, he had access to God, and he had special abilities.

3. Lucifer's Fall Was Rooted in Pride. Lucifer was not satisfied to worship God. He wanted to be worshiped. Scripture says that he desired to "climb to the highest heavens and be like the Most High" (Isaiah 14:14). Instead of being grateful for the many blessings God had given him, he sought to use those blessings to his own advantage. As a result, he lost his position in heaven and will one day be brought down to the lowest depths of the pit of hell (see Isaiah 14:15, p. 586).

4. Lucifer Now Wants to Create As Much Havoc As Possible. Because he knows his time is limited and his sentence sure, Satan is dramatically stepping up his efforts in these last days. In fact, the Bible tells us that he is trying to lead people away from the faith by causing them to follow teachers with "teachings that come from demons" (1 Timothy 4:1). He wants to pull down as many people with him as he can.

For the next note on "Who Is the Devil?" turn to p. 1006.

CORNER STONES

---

mules. All these things were exchanged for your manufactured goods. [15]Merchants came to you from Dedan.* Numerous coastlands were your captive markets; they brought payment in ivory tusks and ebony wood.

[16]"Aram* sent merchants to buy your wares. They traded turquoise, purple dyes, embroidery, fine linen, and jewelry of coral and rubies. [17]Judah and Israel traded for your wares, offering wheat from Minnith, early figs,* honey, oil, and balm. [18]Damascus traded for your rich variety of goods, bringing wine from Helbon and white wool from Zahar. [19]Greeks from Uzal* came to trade for your merchandise. Wrought iron, cassia, and calamus were bartered for your wares. [20]Dedan traded their expensive saddle blankets with you.

[21]"The Arabians and the princes of Kedar brought lambs and rams and goats in trade for your goods. [22]The merchants of Sheba and Raamah came with all kinds of spices, jewels, and gold in exchange for your wares. [23]Haran, Canneh, Eden, Sheba, Asshur, and Kilmad came with their merchandise, too. [24]They brought choice fabrics to trade—blue cloth, embroidery, and many-colored carpets bound with cords and made secure. [25]The ships of Tarshish were your ocean caravans. Your island warehouse was filled to the brim!

The Destruction of Tyre

[26]"But look! Your oarsmen are rowing your ship of state into a hurricane! Your mighty vessel flounders in the heavy eastern gale. You are shipwrecked in the heart of the sea! [27]Everything is lost—your riches and wares, your sailors and helmsmen, your ship builders, merchants, and warriors. On that day of vast ruin, everyone on board sinks into the depths of the sea.

[28]"Your cities by the sea tremble as your helmsmen cry out in terror. [29]All the oarsmen abandon their ships; the sailors and helmsmen come to stand on the shore. [30]They weep bitterly as they throw dust on their heads and roll in

27:15 Greek version reads *Rhodes.*   27:16 Some manuscripts read *Edom.*   27:17 The meaning of the Hebrew is uncertain.   27:19 Hebrew *Vedan and Javan from Uzal.* The meaning of the Hebrew is uncertain.

ashes. [31]They shave their heads in grief because of you and dress themselves in sackcloth. They weep for you with bitter anguish and deep mourning. [32]As they wail and mourn, they sing this sad funeral song:

'Was there ever such a city as Tyre,
now silent at the bottom of the sea?
[33] The merchandise you traded
satisfied the needs of many nations.
Kings at the ends of the earth
were enriched by your trade.
[34] Now you are a wrecked ship,
broken at the bottom of the sea.
All your merchandise and your crew
have passed away with you.
[35] All who live along the coastlands
are appalled at your terrible fate.
Their kings are filled with horror
and look on with twisted faces.
[36] The merchants of the nations
shake their heads at the sight of you,*
for you have come to a horrible end
and will be no more.'"

CHAPTER 28

A Message for Tyre's King

Then this message came to me from the LORD: [2]"Son of man, give the prince of Tyre this message from the Sovereign LORD: In your great pride you claim, 'I am a god! I sit on a divine throne in the heart of the sea.' But you are only a man and not a god, though you boast that you are like a god. [3]You regard yourself as wiser than Daniel and think no secret is hidden from you. [4]With your wisdom and understanding you have amassed great wealth—gold and silver for your treasuries. [5]Yes, your wisdom has made you very rich, and your riches have made you very proud.

[6]"Therefore, this is what the Sovereign LORD says: Because you think you are as wise as a god, [7]I will bring against you an enemy army, the terror of the nations. They will suddenly draw their swords against your marvelous wisdom and defile your splendor! [8]They will bring you down to the pit, and you will die there on your island home in the heart of the sea, pierced with many wounds. [9]Will you then boast, 'I am a god!' to those who kill you? To them you will be no god but merely a man! [10]You will die like an outcast at the hands of foreigners. I, the Sovereign LORD, have spoken!"

[11]Then this further message came to me from the LORD: [12]"Son of man, weep for the king of Tyre. Give him this message from the Sovereign LORD: You were the perfection of wisdom and beauty. [13]You were in Eden, the garden of God. Your clothing was adorned with every precious stone*—red carnelian, chrysolite, white moonstone, beryl, onyx, jasper, sapphire, turquoise, and emerald—all beautifully crafted for you and set in the finest gold. They were given to you on the day you were created. [14]I ordained and anointed you as the mighty angelic guardian.* You had access to the holy mountain of God and walked among the stones of fire.

[15]"You were blameless in all you did from the day you were created until the day evil was found in you. [16]Your great wealth filled you with violence, and you sinned. So I banished you from the mountain of God. I expelled you, O mighty guardian, from your place among the stones of fire. [17]Your heart was filled with pride because of all your beauty. You corrupted your wisdom for the sake of your splendor. So I threw you to the earth and exposed you to the curious gaze of kings. [18]You defiled your sanctuaries with your many sins and your dishonest trade. So I brought fire from within you, and it consumed you. I let it burn you to ashes on the ground in the sight of all who were watching. [19]All who knew you are appalled at your fate. You have come to a terrible end, and you are no more."

A Message for Sidon

[20]Then another message came to me from the LORD: [21]"Son of man, look toward the city of Sidon and prophesy against it. [22]Give the people of Sidon this message from the Sovereign LORD: I am your enemy, O Sidon, and I will reveal my glory by what happens to you. When I bring judgment against you and reveal my holiness among you, everyone watching will know that I am the LORD. [23]I will send a plague against you, and blood will be spilled in your streets. The attack will come from every direction, and your people will lie slaughtered within your walls. Then everyone will know that I am the LORD. [24]No longer will Israel's scornful neighbors prick and tear at her like thorns and briers. For then they will know that I am the Sovereign LORD.

Restoration for Israel

[25]"This is what the Sovereign LORD says: The people of Israel will again live in their own land, the land I gave my servant Jacob. For I will gather them from the distant lands where I have scattered them. I will reveal to the nations of the

27:36 Hebrew *hiss at you.*   28:13 The identification of some of these gemstones is uncertain.   28:14 Hebrew *guardian cherub;* also in 28:16.

world my holiness among my people. 26They will live safely in Israel and build their homes and plant their vineyards. And when I punish the neighboring nations that treated them with contempt, they will know that I am the LORD their God."

CHAPTER 29
A Message for Egypt

On January 7,* during the tenth year of King Jehoiachin's captivity, this message came to me from the LORD: 2"Son of man, turn toward Egypt and prophesy against Pharaoh the king and all the people of Egypt. 3Give them this message from the Sovereign LORD: I am your enemy, O Pharaoh, king of Egypt—you great monster, lurking in the streams of the Nile. For you have said, 'The Nile River is mine; I made it for myself!' 4I will put hooks in your jaws and drag you out on the land with fish sticking to your scales. 5I will leave you and all your fish stranded in the desert to die. You will lie unburied on the open ground, for I have given you as food to the wild animals and birds.

6"All the people of Egypt will discover that I am the LORD, for you collapsed like a reed when Israel looked to you for help. 7Israel leaned on you, but like a cracked staff, you splintered and stabbed her in the armpit. When she put her weight on you, you gave way, and her back was thrown out of joint. 8So now the Sovereign LORD says: I will bring an army against you, O Egypt, and destroy both people and animals. 9The land of Egypt will become a desolate wasteland, and the Egyptians will know that I am the LORD.

"Because you said, 'The Nile River is mine; I made it,' 10I am now the enemy of both you and your river. I will utterly destroy the land of Egypt, from Migdol to Aswan, as far south as the border of Ethiopia.* 11For forty years not a soul will pass that way, neither people nor animals. It will be completely uninhabited. 12I will make Egypt desolate, and it will be surrounded by other desolate nations. Its cities will be empty and desolate for forty years, surrounded by other desolate cities. I will scatter the Egyptians to distant lands.

13"But the Sovereign LORD also says: At the end of the forty years I will bring the Egyptians home again from the nations to which they have been scattered. 14I will restore the prosperity of Egypt and bring its people back to the land of Pathros in southern Egypt from which they came. But Egypt will remain an unimportant, minor kingdom. 15It will be the lowliest of all the nations, never again great enough to rise above its neighbors.

16"Then Israel will no longer be tempted to trust in Egypt for help. Egypt's shattered condition will remind Israel of how sinful she was to trust Egypt in earlier days. Then Israel will know that I alone am the Sovereign LORD."

Nebuchadnezzar to Conquer Egypt

17On April 26,* during the twenty-seventh year of King Jehoiachin's captivity, this message came to me from the LORD: 18"Son of man, the army of King Nebuchadnezzar* of Babylon fought so hard against Tyre that the warriors' heads were rubbed bare and their shoulders were raw and blistered. Yet Nebuchadnezzar and his army won no plunder to compensate them for all their work. 19Therefore, this is what the Sovereign LORD says: I will give the land of Egypt to Nebuchadnezzar, king of Babylon. He will carry off their wealth, plundering everything they have to pay his army. 20Yes, I have given him the land of Egypt as a reward for his work, says the Sovereign LORD, because he was working for me when he destroyed Tyre.

21"And the day will come when I will cause the ancient glory of Israel to revive, and then at last your words will be respected. Then they will know that I am the LORD."

CHAPTER 30
A Sad Day for Egypt

This is another message that came to me from the LORD: 2"Son of man, prophesy and give this message from the Sovereign LORD: Weep, 3for the terrible day is almost here—the day of the LORD! It is a day of clouds and gloom, a day of despair for the nations! 4A sword will come against Egypt, and those who are slaughtered will cover the ground. Their wealth will be carried away and their foundations destroyed. The land of Ethiopia* will be ravished. 5Ethiopia, Libya,* Lydia,* and Arabia, with all their other allies, will be destroyed in that war.

6"For this is what the LORD says: All of Egypt's allies will fall, and the pride of their power will end. From Migdol to Aswan they will be slaugh-

29:1 Hebrew *On the twelfth day of the tenth month,* of the Hebrew calendar. A number of dates in Ezekiel can be cross-checked with dates in surviving Babylonian records and related accurately to our modern calendar. This event occurred on January 7, 587 B.C. 29:10 Hebrew *Cush.* 29:17 Hebrew *On the first day of the first month,* of the Hebrew calendar. This event occurred on April 26, 571 B.C.; also see note on 29:1. 29:18 Hebrew *Nebuchadrezzar,* a variant name for Nebuchadnezzar; also in 29:19. 30:4 Hebrew *Cush;* also in 30:5, 9. 30:5a Hebrew *Put . . . Kub.* Both *Put* and *Kub* are associated with Libya. 30:5b Hebrew *Lud.*

tered by the sword, says the Sovereign LORD. 7Egypt will be desolate, surrounded by desolate nations, and its cities will be in ruins, surrounded by other ruined cities. 8And the people of Egypt will know that I am the LORD when I have set Egypt on fire and destroyed all their allies. 9At that time I will send swift messengers in ships to terrify the complacent Ethiopians. Great panic will come upon them on that day of Egypt's certain destruction.

10"For this is what the Sovereign LORD says: Through King Nebuchadnezzar* of Babylon, I will destroy the hordes of Egypt. 11He and his armies—ruthless among the nations—have been sent to demolish the land. They will make war against Egypt until slaughtered Egyptians cover the ground. 12I will dry up the Nile River and hand the land over to wicked men. I will destroy the land of Egypt and everything in it, using foreigners to do it. I, the LORD, have spoken! 13"This is what the Sovereign LORD says: I will smash the idols of Egypt and the images at Memphis.* There will be no rulers left in Egypt; anarchy will prevail throughout the land! 14I will destroy Pathros, Zoan, and Thebes,* and they will lie in ruins, burned up by my anger. 15I will pour out my fury on Pelusium,* the strongest fortress of Egypt, and I will stamp out the people of Thebes. 16Yes, I will set fire to all Egypt! Pelusium will be racked with pain; Thebes will be torn apart; Memphis will be in constant terror. 17The young men of Heliopolis and Bubastis* will die in battle, and the women* will be taken away as slaves. 18When I come to break the proud strength of Egypt, it will be a dark day for Tahpanhes, too. A dark cloud will cover Tahpanhes, and its daughters will be led away as captives. 19And so I will greatly punish Egypt, and they will know that I am the LORD."

The Broken Arms of Pharaoh

20On April 29,* during the eleventh year of King Jehoiachin's captivity, this message came to me from the LORD: 21 "Son of man, I have broken the arm of Pharaoh, the king of Egypt. His arm has not been put in a cast so that it may heal. Neither has it been bound up with a splint to make it strong enough to hold a sword. 22Therefore, this is what the Sovereign LORD says: I am the enemy of Pharaoh, the king of Egypt! I will break both of his arms—the good arm along with the bro-

ken one—and I will make his sword clatter to the ground. 23I will scatter the Egyptians to many lands throughout the world. 24I will strengthen the arms of Babylon's king and put my sword in his hand. But I will break the arms of Pharaoh, king of Egypt, and he will lie there mortally wounded, groaning in pain. 25I will strengthen the arms of the king of Babylon, while the arms of Pharaoh fall useless to his sides. And when I put my sword in the hand of Babylon's king and he brings it against the land of Egypt, Egypt will know that I am the LORD. 26I will scatter the Egyptians among the nations. Then they will know that I am the LORD."

CHAPTER **31**
Egypt Compared to Fallen Assyria

On June 21,* during the eleventh year of King Jehoiachin's captivity, this message came to me from the LORD: 2"Son of man, give this message to Pharaoh, king of Egypt, and all his people: To whom would you compare your greatness? 3You are as Assyria was—a great and mighty nation. Assyria, too, was once like a cedar of Lebanon, full of thick branches that cast deep forest shade with its top high among the clouds. 4Deep springs watered it and helped it to grow tall and luxuriant. The water was so abundant that there was enough for all the trees nearby. 5This great tree towered above all the other trees around it. It prospered and grew long thick branches because of all the water at its roots. 6The birds nested in its branches, and in its shade all the wild animals gave birth to their young. All the great nations of the world lived in its shadow. 7It was strong and beautiful, for its roots went deep into abundant water. 8This tree became taller than any of the other cedars in the garden of God. No cypress had branches equal to it; no plane tree had boughs to compare. No tree in the garden of God came close to it in beauty. 9Because of the magnificence I gave this tree, it was the envy of all the other trees of Eden, the garden of God.

10"Therefore, this is what the Sovereign LORD says: Because it became proud and arrogant, and because it set itself so high above the others, reaching to the clouds, 11I handed it over to a mighty nation that destroyed it as its wickedness deserved. I myself discarded it. 12A foreign army—the terror of the nations—cut it down and left it fallen on the ground. Its branches

---

30:10 Hebrew *Nebuchadrezzar*, a variant name for Nebuchadnezzar. **30:13** Hebrew *Noph*; also in 30:16. **30:14** Hebrew *No*; also in 30:15, 16. **30:15** Hebrew *Sin*; also in 30:16. **30:17a** Hebrew of *Awen and Pi-beseth*. **30:17b** Or *her cities*. **30:20** Hebrew *On the seventh day of the first month*, of the Hebrew calendar. This event occurred on April 29, 587 B.C.; also see note on 29:1. **31:1** Hebrew *On the first day of the third month*, of the Hebrew calendar. This event occurred on June 21, 587 B.C.; also see note on 29:1.

were scattered across the mountains and valleys and ravines of the land. All those who lived beneath its shadow went away and left it lying there. 13The birds roosted on its fallen trunk, and the wild animals lay among its branches. 14Let no other nation proudly exult in its own prosperity, though it be higher than the clouds, for all are doomed. They will land in the pit along with all the proud people of the world.

15"This is what the Sovereign LORD says: When Assyria went down into the grave,* I made the deep places mourn, and I restrained the mighty waters. I clothed Lebanon in black and caused the trees of the field to wilt. 16I made the nations shake with fear at the sound of its fall, for I sent it down to the grave with all the others like it. And all the other proud trees of Eden, the most beautiful and the best of Lebanon, the ones whose roots went deep into the water, were relieved to find it there with them in the pit. 17Its allies, too, were all destroyed and had passed away. They had gone down to the grave—all those nations that had lived in its shade.

18"O Egypt, to which of the trees of Eden will you compare your strength and glory? You, too, will be brought down to the pit with all these other nations. You will lie there among the outcasts who have died by the sword. This will be the fate of Pharaoh and all his teeming hordes. I, the Sovereign LORD, have spoken!"

CHAPTER 32

A Warning for Pharaoh

On March 3,* during the twelfth year of King Jehoiachin's captivity, this message came to me from the LORD: 2"Son of man, mourn for Pharaoh, king of Egypt, and give him this message: You think of yourself as a strong young lion among the nations, but you are really just a sea monster, heaving around in your own rivers, stirring up mud with your feet.

3"Therefore, this is what the Sovereign LORD says: I will send many people to catch you in my net and haul you out of the water. 4I will leave you stranded on the land to die. All the birds of the heavens will land on you, and the wild animals of the whole earth will gorge themselves on you. 5I will cover the hills with your flesh and fill the valleys with your bones. 6I will drench the earth with your gushing blood all the way to the

mountains, filling the ravines to the brim. 7When I blot you out, I will veil the heavens and darken the stars. I will cover the sun with a cloud, and the moon will not give you its light. 8Yes, I will bring darkness everywhere across your land. Even the brightest stars will become dark above you. I, the Sovereign LORD, have spoken!

9"And when I bring your shattered remains to distant nations that you have never seen, I will disturb many hearts. 10Yes, I will bring terror to many lands, and their kings will be terrified because of all I do to you. They will shudder in fear for their lives as I brandish my sword before them on the day of your fall.

11"For this is what the Sovereign LORD says: The sword of the king of Babylon will come against you. 12I will destroy you with the swords of mighty warriors—the terror of the nations. They will shatter the pride of Egypt, and all its hordes will be destroyed. 13I will destroy all your flocks and herds that graze beside the streams. Never again will people or animals disturb those waters with their feet. 14Then I will let the waters of Egypt become calm again, and they will flow as smoothly as olive oil, says the Sovereign LORD. 15And when I destroy Egypt and wipe out everything you have and strike down all your people, then you will know that I am the LORD. 16Yes, this is the funeral song they will sing for Egypt. Let all the nations mourn for Egypt and its hordes. I, the Sovereign LORD, have spoken!"

Egypt Falls into the Pit

17On March 17,* during the twelfth year, another message came to me from the LORD: 18"Son of man, weep for the hordes of Egypt and for the other mighty nations. For I will send them down to the world below in company with those who descend to the pit. 19Say to them, 'O Egypt, are you lovelier than the other nations? No! So go down to the pit and lie there among the outcasts.' 20The Egyptians will fall with the many who have died by the sword, for the sword is drawn against them. Egypt will be dragged away to its judgment. 21Down in the grave* mighty leaders will mockingly welcome Egypt and its allies, saying, 'They have come down; they lie among the outcasts, all victims of the sword.'

22"Assyria lies there surrounded by the graves of all its people, those who were slaughtered by

31:15 Hebrew *to Sheol*; also in 31:16, 17. 32:1 Hebrew *On the first day of the twelfth month*, of the Hebrew calendar. This event occurred on March 3, 585 B.C.; also see note on 29:1. 32:17 Hebrew *On the fifteenth day of the month*, presumably in the twelfth month of the Hebrew calendar (see 32:1). This would put this message at the end of King Jehoiachin's twelfth year of captivity, on March 17, 585 B.C.; also see note on 29:1. Greek version reads *On the fifteenth day of the first month*, which would put this message on April 27, 586 B.C., at the beginning of Jehoiachin's twelfth year. 32:21 Hebrew *in Sheol*.

the sword. 23Their graves are in the depths of the pit, and they are surrounded by their allies. These mighty men who once struck terror in the hearts of people everywhere are now dead at the hands of their enemies.

24 "Elam lies there buried with its hordes who descended as outcasts to the world below. They terrorized the nations while they lived, but now they lie in the pit and share the humiliation of those who have gone to the world of the dead. 25They have a resting place among the slaughtered, surrounded by the graves of all their people. Yes, they terrorized the nations while they lived, but now they lie in shame in the pit, all of them outcasts, slaughtered by the sword.

26 "Meshech and Tubal are there, surrounded by the graves of all their hordes. They once struck terror into the hearts of all people. But now they are outcasts, all victims of the sword. 27They are not buried in honor like the fallen heroes of the outcasts, who went down to the grave* with their weapons—their shields covering their bodies,* and their swords beneath their heads. They brought terror to everyone while they were still alive.

28 "You too, Egypt, will lie crushed and broken among the outcasts, all victims of the sword.

29 "Edom is there with its kings and princes. Mighty as they were, they also lie among those killed by the sword, with the outcasts who have gone down to the pit. 30All the princes of the north and the Sidonians are there, all victims of the sword. Once a terror, they now lie there in shame. They lie there as outcasts with all the other dead who have descended to the pit.

31 "When Pharaoh arrives, he will be relieved to find that he is not alone in having his entire army killed, says the Sovereign LORD. 32For I have caused my terror to fall upon all the living. And Pharaoh and his hordes will lie there among the outcasts who have died by the sword. I, the Sovereign LORD, have spoken!"

CHAPTER 33
Ezekiel as Israel's Watchman

Once again a message came to me from the LORD: 2 "Son of man, give your people this message: When I bring an army against a country, the people of that land choose a watchman. 3When the watchman sees the enemy coming, he blows the alarm to warn the people. 4Then if those who hear the alarm refuse to take action—well, it is their own fault if they die. 5They heard the

warning but wouldn't listen, so the responsibility is theirs. If they had listened to the warning, they could have saved their lives. 6But if the watchman sees the enemy coming and doesn't sound the alarm to warn the people, he is responsible for their deaths. They will die in their sins, but I will hold the watchman accountable.

7 "Now, son of man, I am making you a watchman for the people of Israel. Therefore, listen to what I say and warn them for me. 8If I announce that some wicked people are sure to die and you fail to warn them about changing their ways, then they will die in their sins, but I will hold you responsible for their deaths. 9But if you warn them to repent and they don't repent, they will die in their sins, but you will not be held responsible.

The Watchman's Message

10 "Son of man, give the people of Israel this message: You are saying, 'Our sins are heavy upon us; we are wasting away! How can we survive?' 11As surely as I live, says the Sovereign LORD, I take no pleasure in the death of wicked people. I only want them to turn from their wicked ways so they can live. Turn! Turn from your wickedness, O people of Israel! Why should you die?

12 "Son of man, give your people this message: The good works of righteous people will not save them if they turn to sin, nor will the sins of evil people destroy them if they repent and turn from their sins. 13When I tell righteous people that they will live, but then they sin, expecting their past righteousness to save them, then none of their good deeds will be remembered. I will destroy them for their sins. 14And suppose I tell some wicked people that they will surely die, but then they turn from their sins and do what is just and right. 15For instance, they might give back a borrower's pledge, return what they have stolen, and obey my life-giving laws, no longer doing what is evil. If they do this, then they will surely live and not die. 16None of their past sins will be brought up again, for they have done what is just and right, and they will surely live.

17 "Your people are saying, 'The Lord is not just,' but it is they who are not just. 18For again I say, when righteous people turn to evil, they will die. 19But if wicked people turn from their wickedness and do what is just and right, they will live. 20O people of Israel, you are saying, 'The Lord is not just.' But I will judge each of you according to your deeds."

32:27a Hebrew *to Sheol.*   32:27b The meaning of the Hebrew phrase here is uncertain.

Explanation of Jerusalem's Fall

21On January 8,* during the twelfth year of our captivity, a man who had escaped from Jerusalem came to me and said, "The city has fallen!" 22The previous evening the LORD had taken hold of me and opened my mouth, so I would be able to speak when this man arrived the next morning.

23Then this message came to me from the LORD: 24"Son of man, the scattered remnants of Judah living among the ruined cities keep saying, 'Abraham was only one man, and yet he gained possession of the entire land! We are many; surely the land should be given to us as a possession.' 25Now give these people this message from the Sovereign LORD: You eat meat with blood in it, you worship idols, and you murder the innocent. Do you really think the land should be yours? 26Murderers! Idolaters! Adulterers! Should the land belong to you?

27"Give them this message from the Sovereign LORD: As surely as I live, those living in the ruins will die by the sword. Those living in the open fields will be eaten by wild animals. Those hiding in the forts and caves will die of disease. 28I will destroy the land and demolish her pride. Her arrogant power will come to an end. The mountains of Israel will be so ruined that no one will even travel through them. 29When I have ruined the land because of their disgusting sins, then they will know that I am the LORD.

30"Son of man, your people are whispering behind your back. They talk about you in their houses and whisper about you at the doors, saying, 'Come on, let's have some fun! Let's go hear the prophet tell us what the LORD is saying!' 31So they come pretending to be sincere and sit before you listening. But they have no intention of doing what I tell them. They express love with their mouths, but their hearts seek only after money. 32You are very entertaining to them, like someone who sings love songs with a beautiful voice or plays fine music on an instrument. They hear what you say, but they don't do it! 33But when all these terrible things happen to them— as they certainly will—then they will know a prophet has been among them."

CHAPTER **34**

The Shepherds of Israel

Then this message came to me from the LORD: 2"Son of man, prophesy against the shepherds, the leaders of Israel. Give them this message from the Sovereign LORD: Destruction is certain for you shepherds who feed yourselves instead of your flocks. Shouldn't shepherds feed their sheep? 3You drink the milk, wear the wool, and butcher the best animals, but you let your flocks starve. 4You have not taken care of the weak. You have not tended the sick or bound up the broken bones. You have not gone looking for those who have wandered away and are lost. Instead, you have ruled them with force and cruelty. 5So my sheep have been scattered without a shepherd. They are easy prey for any wild animal. 6They have wandered through the mountains and hills, across the face of the earth, yet no one has gone to search for them.

7"Therefore, you shepherds, hear the word of the LORD: 8As surely as I live, says the Sovereign LORD, you abandoned my flock and left them to be attacked by every wild animal. Though you were my shepherds, you didn't search for my sheep when they were lost. You took care of yourselves and left the sheep to starve. 9Therefore, you shepherds, hear the word of the LORD. 10This is what the Sovereign LORD says: I now consider these shepherds my enemies, and I will hold them responsible for what has happened to my flock. I will take away their right to feed the flock, along with their right to feed themselves. I will rescue my flock from their mouths; the sheep will no longer be their prey.

The Good Shepherd

11"For this is what the Sovereign LORD says: I myself will search and find my sheep. 12I will be like a shepherd looking for his scattered flock. I will find my sheep and rescue them from all the places to which they were scattered on that dark and cloudy day. 13I will bring them back home to their own land of Israel from among the peoples and nations. I will feed them on the mountains of Israel and by the rivers in all the places where people live. 14Yes, I will give them good pastureland on the high hills of Israel. There they will lie down in pleasant places and feed in lush mountain pastures. 15I myself will tend my sheep and cause them to lie down in peace, says the Sovereign LORD. 16I will search for my lost ones who strayed away, and I will bring them safely home again. I will bind up the injured and strengthen the weak. But I will destroy those who are fat and powerful. I will feed them, yes—feed them justice!

17"And as for you, my flock, my people, this is what the Sovereign LORD says: I will judge between one sheep and another, separating the sheep from the goats. 18Is it not enough for you

33:21 Hebrew *On the fifth day of the tenth month,* of the Hebrew calendar. This event occurred on January 8, 585 B.C.; also see note on 29:1.

to keep the best of the pastures for yourselves? Must you also trample down the rest? Is it not enough for you to take the best water for yourselves? Must you also muddy the rest with your feet? 19All that is left for my flock to eat is what you have trampled down. All they have to drink is water that you have fouled.

20"Therefore, this is what the Sovereign LORD says: I will surely judge between the fat sheep and the scrawny sheep. 21For you fat sheep push and butt and crowd my sick and hungry flock until they are scattered to distant lands. 22So I will rescue my flock, and they will no longer be abused and destroyed. And I will judge between one sheep and another. 23And I will set one shepherd over them, even my servant David. He will feed them and be a shepherd to them. 24And I, the LORD, will be their God, and my servant David will be a prince among my people. I, the LORD, have spoken!

The LORD's Covenant of Peace

25"I will make a covenant of peace with them and drive away the dangerous animals from the land. Then my people will be able to camp safely in the wildest places and sleep in the woods without fear. 26I will cause my people and their homes around my holy hill to be a blessing. And I will send showers, showers of blessings, which will come just when they are needed. 27The orchards and fields of my people will yield bumper crops, and everyone will live in safety. When I have broken their chains of slavery and rescued them from those who enslaved them, then they will know that I am the LORD. 28They will no longer be prey for other nations, and wild animals will no longer attack them. They will live in safety, and no one will make them afraid.

29"And I will give them a land famous for its crops, so my people will never again go hungry or be shamed by the scorn of foreign nations. 30In this way, they will know that I, the LORD their God, am with them. And they will know that they, the people of Israel, are my people, says the Sovereign LORD. 31You are my flock, the sheep of my pasture. You are my people, and I am your God, says the Sovereign LORD."

CHAPTER 35
A Message for Edom

Again a message came to me from the LORD: 2"Son of man, turn toward Mount Seir, and prophesy against its people. 3Give them this message from the Sovereign LORD: I am your enemy, O Mount Seir, and I will raise my fist

against you to destroy you completely. 4I will demolish your cities and make you desolate, and then you will know that I am the LORD. 5Your continual hatred for the people of Israel led you to butcher them when they were helpless, when I had already punished them for all their sins. 6As surely as I live, says the Sovereign LORD, since you show no distaste for blood, I will give you a bloodbath of your own. Your turn has come! 7I will make Mount Seir utterly desolate, killing off all who try to escape and any who return. 8I will fill your mountains with the dead. Your hills, your valleys, and your streams will be filled with people slaughtered by the sword. 9I will make you desolate forever. Your cities will never be rebuilt. Then you will know that I am the LORD.

10"For you said, 'The lands of Israel and Judah will be ours. We will take possession of them. What do we care that the LORD is there!' 11Therefore, as surely as I live, says the Sovereign LORD, I will pay back your angry deeds with mine. I will punish you for all your acts of anger, envy, and hatred. And I will bring honor to my name by what I do to you. 12Then you will know that I, the LORD, have heard every contemptuous word you spoke against the mountains of Israel. For you said, 'They have been destroyed; they have been given to us as food to eat!' 13In saying that, you boasted proudly against me, and I have heard it all!

14"This is what the Sovereign LORD says: The whole world will rejoice when I make you desolate. 15You rejoiced at the desolation of Israel's inheritance. Now I will rejoice at yours! You will be wiped out, you people of Mount Seir and all who live in Edom! Then you will know that I am the LORD!

CHAPTER 36
Restoration for Israel

"Son of man, prophesy to Israel's mountains. Give them this message: O mountains of Israel, hear the word of the LORD! 2This is what the Sovereign LORD says: Your enemies have taunted you, saying, 'Aha! Now the ancient heights belong to us!' 3Therefore, son of man, give the mountains of Israel this message from the Sovereign LORD: Your enemies have attacked you from all directions, and now you are possessed by many nations. You are the object of much mocking and slander. 4Therefore, O mountains of Israel, hear the word of the Sovereign LORD. He speaks to the hills and mountains, ravines and valleys, and to ruined wastes and long-deserted cities that have been destroyed and mocked by foreign nations everywhere. 5This is what the Sovereign LORD says: My jealous anger is on fire against these nations, especially Edom, because they have shown utter contempt for me by gleefully taking my land for themselves as plunder.

6"Therefore, prophesy to the hills and mountains, the ravines and valleys of Israel. Give them this message from the Sovereign LORD: I am full of fury because you have suffered shame before the surrounding nations. 7Therefore, says the Sovereign LORD, I have raised my hand and sworn an oath that those nations will soon have their turn at suffering shame. 8But the mountains of Israel will produce heavy crops of fruit to prepare for my people's return—and they will be coming home again soon! 9See, I am concerned for you, and I will come to help you. Your ground will be tilled and your crops planted. 10I will greatly increase the population of Israel, and the ruined cities will be rebuilt and filled with people. 11Not only the people, but your flocks and herds will also greatly multiply. O mountains of Israel, I will bring people to live on you once again. I will make you even more prosperous than you were before. Then you will know that I am the LORD. 12I will cause my people to walk on you once again, and you will be their inheritance. You will never again devour their children.

13"This is what the Sovereign LORD says: Now the other nations taunt you, saying, 'Israel is a land that devours her own people!' 14But you will never again devour your people or bereave your nation, says the Sovereign LORD. 15I will not allow those foreign nations to sneer at you, and you will no longer be shamed by them or cause your nation to fall, says the Sovereign LORD."

16Then this further message came to me from the LORD: 17"Son of man, when the people of Israel were living in their own land, they defiled it by their evil deeds. To me their conduct was as filthy as a bloody rag. 18They polluted the land with murder and by worshiping idols, so I poured out my fury on them. 19I scattered them to many lands to punish them for the evil way they had lived. 20But when they were scattered among the nations, they brought dishonor to my holy name. For the nations said, 'These are the people of the LORD, and he couldn't keep them safe in his own land!' 21Then I was concerned for my holy name, which had been dishonored by my people throughout the world.

22"Therefore, give the people of Israel this

message from the Sovereign LORD: I am bringing you back again but not because you deserve it. I am doing it to protect my holy name, which you dishonored while you were scattered among the nations. 23I will show how holy my great name is—the name you dishonored among the nations. And when I reveal my holiness through you before their very eyes, says the Sovereign LORD, then the nations will know that I am the LORD. 24For I will gather you up from all the nations and bring you home again to your land.

25"Then I will sprinkle clean water on you, and you will be clean. Your filth will be washed away, and you will no longer worship idols. 26And I will give you a new heart with new and right desires, and I will put a new spirit in you. I will take out your stony heart of sin and give you a new, obedient heart.* 27And I will put my Spirit in you so you will obey my laws and do whatever I command.

28"And you will live in Israel, the land I gave your ancestors long ago. You will be my people, and I will be your God. 29I will cleanse you of your filthy behavior. I will give you good crops, and I will abolish famine in the land. 30I will give you great harvests from your fruit trees and fields, and never again will the surrounding nations be able to scoff at your land for its famines. 31Then you will remember your past sins and hate yourselves for all the evil things you did. 32But remember, says the Sovereign LORD, I am not doing this because you deserve it. O my people of Israel, you should be utterly ashamed of all you have done!

33"This is what the Sovereign LORD says: When I cleanse you from your sins, I will bring people to live in your cities, and the ruins will be rebuilt. 34The fields that used to lie empty and desolate—a shock to all who passed by—will again be farmed. 35And when I bring you back, people will say, 'This godforsaken land is now like Eden's garden! The ruined cities now have strong walls, and they are filled with people!' 36Then the nations all around—all those still left—will know that I, the LORD, rebuilt the ruins and planted lush crops in the wilderness. For I, the LORD, have promised this, and I will do it.

37"This is what the Sovereign LORD says: I am ready to hear Israel's prayers for these blessings, and I am ready to grant them their requests. 38I will multiply them like the sacred flocks that fill Jerusalem's streets at the time of her festivals. The ruined cities will be crowded with people once more, and everyone will know that I am the LORD."

36:26 Hebrew *a heart of flesh.*

CHAPTER **37**
A Valley of Dry Bones

The LORD took hold of me, and I was carried away by the Spirit of the LORD to a valley filled with bones. ²He led me around among the old, dry bones that covered the valley floor. They were scattered everywhere across the ground. ³Then he asked me, "Son of man, can these bones become living people again?"

"O Sovereign LORD," I replied, "you alone know the answer to that."

⁴Then he said to me, "Speak to these bones and say, 'Dry bones, listen to the word of the LORD! ⁵This is what the Sovereign LORD says: Look! I am going to breathe into you and make you live again! ⁶I will put flesh and muscles on you and cover you with skin. I will put breath into you, and you will come to life. Then you will know that I am the LORD.'"

⁷So I spoke these words, just as he told me. Suddenly as I spoke, there was a rattling noise all across the valley. The bones of each body came together and attached themselves as they had been before. ⁸Then as I watched, muscles and flesh formed over the bones. Then skin formed to cover their bodies, but they still had no breath in them.

⁹Then he said to me, "Speak to the winds and say: 'This is what the Sovereign LORD says: Come, O breath, from the four winds! Breathe into these dead bodies so that they may live again.'"

¹⁰So I spoke as he commanded me, and the wind entered the bodies, and they began to breathe. They all came to life and stood up on their feet—a great army of them.

¹¹Then he said to me, "Son of man, these bones represent the people of Israel. They are saying, 'We have become old, dry bones—all hope is gone.' ¹²Now give them this message from the Sovereign LORD: O my people, I will open your graves of exile and cause you to rise again. Then I will bring you back to the land of Israel. ¹³When this happens, O my people, you will know that I am the LORD. ¹⁴I will put my Spirit in you, and you will live and return home to your own land. Then you will know that I am the LORD. You will see that I have done everything just as I promised. I, the LORD, have spoken!"

Reunion of Israel and Judah

¹⁵Again a message came to me from the LORD: ¹⁶"Son of man, take a stick and carve on it these words: 'This stick represents Judah and its allied tribes.' Then take another stick and carve these

words on it: 'This stick represents the northern tribes of Israel.'* ¹⁷Now hold them together in your hand as one stick. ¹⁸When your people ask you what your actions mean, ¹⁹say to them, 'This is what the Sovereign LORD says: I will take the northern tribes and join them to Judah. I will make them one stick in my hand.' ²⁰Then hold out the sticks you have inscribed, so the people can see them. ²¹And give them this message from the Sovereign LORD: I will gather the people of Israel from among the nations. I will bring them home to their own land from the places where they have been scattered. ²²I will unify them into one nation in the land. One king will rule them all; no longer will they be divided into two nations. ²³They will stop polluting themselves with their detestable idols and other sins, for I will save them from their sinful backsliding. I will cleanse them. Then they will truly be my people, and I will be their God.

²⁴"My servant David will be their king, and they will have only one shepherd. They will obey my regulations and keep my laws. ²⁵They will live in the land of Israel where their ancestors

37:16 Hebrew *Ephraim's stick, representing Joseph and all the house of Israel.*

God's Spirit Will Encourage You to Be Obedient
Read EZEKIEL 36:26-27

As a new believer, you may be wondering if your old lifestyle will lure you away from the Lord you love. Make no mistake about it: You will be tempted to do some of the things you have now tried to put out of your life. But you don't have to give in to those temptations. In fact, this passage should encourage you.

You see, God has already performed "heart surgery" on you, so to speak. To keep that new heart healthy and strong, he has given you an in-house physician: the Holy Spirit.

The Holy Spirit will not only fill your heart with a love for God, but he will also help you to obey God's commands and follow the principles found in the Bible. So when those temptations come your way—and they will—ask the Holy Spirit to give your heart a checkup and any necessary maintenance. And he will.

For the next note on "Live in God's Power," turn to p. 967.

lived, the land I gave my servant Jacob. They and their children and their grandchildren after them will live there forever, generation after generation. And my servant David will be their prince forever. 26And I will make a covenant of peace with them, an everlasting covenant. I will give them their land and multiply them, and I will put my Temple among them forever. 27I will make my home among them. I will be their God, and they will be my people. 28And since my Temple will remain among them forever, the nations will know that I, the LORD, have set Israel apart for myself to be holy."

CHAPTER **38**

A Message for Gog

This is another message that came to me from the LORD: 2"Son of man, prophesy against Gog of the land of Magog, the prince who rules over the nations of Meshech and Tubal. 3Give him this message from the Sovereign LORD: Gog, I am your enemy! 4I will turn you around and put hooks into your jaws to lead you out to your destruction. I will mobilize your troops and cavalry and make you a vast and mighty horde, all fully armed. 5Persia, Ethiopia, and Libya* will join you, too, with all their weapons. 6Gomer and all its hordes will also join you, along with the armies of Beth-togarmah from the distant north and many others.

7"Get ready; be prepared! Keep all the armies around you mobilized, and take command of them. 8A long time from now you will be called into action. In the distant future you will swoop down on the land of Israel, which will be lying in peace after her recovery from war and after the return of her people from many lands. 9You and all your allies—a vast and awesome horde—will roll down on them like a storm and cover the land like a cloud.

10"This is what the Sovereign LORD says: At that time evil thoughts will come to your mind, and you will devise a wicked scheme. 11You will say, 'Israel is an unprotected land filled with unwalled villages! I will march against her and destroy these people who live in such confidence! 12I will go to those once-desolate cities that are again filled with people who have returned from exile in many nations. I will capture vast amounts of plunder and take many slaves, for the people are rich with cattle now, and they think the whole world revolves around them!' 13But Sheba and Dedan and the merchants of Tarshish will ask,

'Who are you to rob them of silver and gold? Who are you to drive away their cattle and seize their goods and make them poor?'

14"Therefore, son of man, prophesy against Gog. Give him this message from the Sovereign LORD: When my people are living in peace in their land, then you will rouse yourself.* 15You will come from your homeland in the distant north with your vast cavalry and your mighty army, 16and you will cover the land like a cloud. This will happen in the distant future. I will bring you against my land as everyone watches, and my holiness will be displayed by what happens to you. Then all the nations will know that I am the LORD.

17"This is what the Sovereign LORD says: You are the one I was talking about long ago, when I announced through Israel's prophets that in future days I would bring you against my people. 18But when Gog invades the land of Israel, says the Sovereign LORD, my fury will rise! 19For in my jealousy and blazing anger, I promise a mighty shaking in the land of Israel on that day. 20All living things—all the fish, birds, animals, and people—will quake in terror at my presence. Mountains will be thrown down; cliffs will crumble; walls will fall to the earth. 21I will summon the sword against you throughout Israel, says the Sovereign LORD. Your men will turn against each other in mortal combat. 22I will punish you and your hordes with disease and bloodshed; I will send torrential rain, hailstones, fire, and burning sulfur! 23Thus will I show my greatness and holiness, and I will make myself known to all the nations of the world. Then they will know that I am the LORD!

CHAPTER **39**

The Slaughter of Gog's Armies

"Son of man, prophesy against Gog. Give him this message from the Sovereign LORD: I am your enemy, O Gog, ruler of the nations of Meshech and Tubal. 2I will turn you and drive you toward the mountains of Israel, bringing you from the distant north. 3I will knock your weapons from your hands and leave you helpless. 4You and all your vast hordes will die on the mountains. I will give you as food to the vultures and wild animals. 5You will fall in the open fields, for I have spoken, says the Sovereign LORD. 6And I will rain down fire on Magog and on all your allies who live safely on the coasts. Then they will know that I am the LORD.

7"Thus, I will make known my holy name among my people of Israel. I will not let it be

38:5 Hebrew *Paras, Cush, and Put.* 38:14 As in Greek version; Hebrew reads *then you will know.*

desecrated anymore. And the nations, too, will know that I am the LORD, the Holy One of Israel. ⁸That day of judgment will come, says the Sovereign LORD. Everything will happen just as I have declared it.

⁹"Then the people in the towns of Israel will go out and pick up your small and large shields, bows and arrows, javelins and spears, and they will use them for fuel. There will be enough to last them seven years! ¹⁰They will need nothing else for their fires. They won't need to cut wood from the fields or forests, for these weapons will give them all they need. They will take plunder from those who planned to plunder them, says the Sovereign LORD.

¹¹"And I will make a vast graveyard for Gog and his hordes in the Valley of the Travelers, east of the Dead Sea.* The path of those who travel there will be blocked by this burial ground, and they will change the name of the place to the Valley of Gog's Hordes. ¹²It will take seven months for the people of Israel to cleanse the land by burying the bodies. ¹³Everyone in Israel will help, for it will be a glorious victory for Israel when I demonstrate my glory on that day, says the Sovereign LORD. ¹⁴At the end of the seven months, special crews will be appointed to search the land for any skeletons and to bury them, so the land will be made clean again. ¹⁵Whenever some bones are found, a marker will be set up beside them so the burial crews will see them and take them to be buried in the Valley of Gog's Hordes. ¹⁶(There will be a town there named Hamonah—which means 'horde.') And so the land will finally be cleansed.

¹⁷"And now, son of man, call all the birds and wild animals, says the Sovereign LORD. Say to them: Gather together for my great sacrificial feast. Come from far and near to the mountains of Israel, and there eat the flesh and drink the blood! ¹⁸Eat the flesh of mighty men and drink the blood of princes as though they were rams, lambs, goats, and fat young bulls of Bashan! ¹⁹Gorge yourselves with flesh until you are glutted; drink blood until you are drunk. This is the sacrificial feast I have prepared for you. ²⁰Feast at my banquet table—feast on horses, riders, and valiant warriors, says the Sovereign LORD.

²¹"Thus, I will demonstrate my glory among the nations. Everyone will see the punishment I have inflicted on them and the power I have demonstrated. ²²And from that time on the people of Israel will know that I am the LORD their God. ²³The nations will then know why Israel was sent away to exile—it was punishment for sin, for they acted in treachery against their God. Therefore, I turned my back on them and let their enemies destroy them. ²⁴I turned my face away and punished them in proportion to the vileness of their sins.

Restoration for God's People

²⁵"So now the Sovereign LORD says: I will end the captivity of my people*; I will have mercy on Israel, for I am jealous for my holy reputation! ²⁶They will accept responsibility for their past shame and treachery against me after they come home to live in peace and safety in their own land. And then no one will bother them or make them afraid. ²⁷When I bring them home from the lands of their enemies, my holiness will be displayed to the nations. ²⁸Then my people will know that I am the LORD their God—responsible for sending them away to exile and responsible for bringing them home. I will leave none of my people behind. ²⁹And I will never again turn my back on them, for I will pour out my Spirit upon them, says the Sovereign LORD."

CHAPTER 40

The New Temple Area

On April 28,* during the twenty-fifth year of our captivity—fourteen years after the fall of Jerusalem—the LORD took hold of me. ²In a vision of God he took me to the land of Israel and set me down on a very high mountain. From there I could see what appeared to be a city across from me toward the south. ³As he brought me nearer, I saw a man whose face shone like bronze standing beside a gateway entrance. He was holding in his hand a measuring tape and a measuring rod.

⁴He said to me, "Son of man, watch and listen. Pay close attention to everything I show you. You have been brought here so I can show you many things. Then you will return to the people of Israel and tell them everything you have seen."

The East Gateway

⁵I could see a wall completely surrounding the Temple area. The man took a measuring rod that was 10½ feet* long and measured the wall, and the wall was 10½ feet thick and 10½ feet high.

39:11 Hebrew *the sea.* **39:25** Hebrew *of Jacob.* **40:1** Hebrew *At the beginning of the year, on the tenth day of the month,* of the Hebrew calendar. A number of dates in Ezekiel can be cross-checked with dates in surviving Babylonian records and related accurately to our modern calendar. This event occurred on April 28, 573 B.C. **40:5** Hebrew *6 long cubits* [3.2 meters], *each being a cubit* [18 inches or 45 centimeters] *and a handbreadth* [3 inches or 8 centimeters] *in length.* In this chapter, the distance measures are calculated using the Hebrew long cubit, which equals 21 inches or 53 centimeters.

⁶Then he went over to the gateway that goes through the eastern wall. He climbed the steps and measured the threshold of the gateway; it was 10½ feet deep.* ⁷There were guard alcoves on each side built into the gateway passage. Each of these alcoves was 10½ feet square, with a distance between them of 8¾ feet along the passage wall. The gateway's inner threshold, which led to the foyer at the inner end of the gateway passage, was 10½ feet deep. ⁸He also measured the foyer of the gateway* ⁹and found it to be 14 feet deep, with supporting columns 3½ feet thick. This foyer was at the inner end of the gateway structure, facing toward the Temple.

¹⁰There were three guard alcoves on each side of the gateway passage. Each had the same measurements, and the dividing walls separating them were also identical. ¹¹The man measured the gateway entrance, which was 17½ feet wide at the opening and 22¾ feet wide in the gateway passage. ¹²In front of each of the guard alcoves was a 21-inch curb. The alcoves themselves were 10½ feet square. ¹³Then he measured the entire width of the gateway, measuring the distance between the back walls of facing guard alcoves; this distance was 43¾ feet. ¹⁴He measured the dividing walls all along the inside of the gateway up to the gateway's foyer; this distance was 105 feet.* ¹⁵The full length of the gateway passage was 87½ feet from one end to the other. ¹⁶There were recessed windows that narrowed inward through the walls of the guard alcoves and their dividing walls. There were also windows in the foyer structure. The surfaces of the dividing walls were decorated with carved palm trees.

The Outer Courtyard

¹⁷Then the man brought me through the gateway into the outer courtyard of the Temple. A stone pavement ran along the walls of the courtyard, and thirty rooms were built against the walls, opening onto the pavement. ¹⁸This pavement flanked the gates and extended out from the walls into the courtyard the same distance as the gateway entrance. This was the lower pavement. ¹⁹Then the man measured across the Temple's outer courtyard between the outer and inner gateways; the distance was 175 feet.

The North Gateway

²⁰There was a gateway on the north just like the one on the east, and the man measured it. ²¹Here,

too, there were three guard alcoves on each side, with dividing walls and a foyer. All the measurements matched those of the east gateway. The gateway passage was 87½ feet long and 43¾ feet wide between the back walls of facing guard alcoves. ²²The windows, the foyer, and the palm tree decorations were identical to those in the east gateway. There were seven steps leading up to the gateway entrance, and the foyer was at the inner end of the gateway passage. ²³Here on the north side, just as on the east, there was another gateway leading to the Temple's inner courtyard directly opposite this outer gateway. The distance between the two gateways was 175 feet.

The South Gateway

²⁴Then the man took me around to the south gateway and measured its various parts, and he found they were exactly the same as in the others. ²⁵It had windows along the walls as the others did, and there was a foyer where the gateway passage opened into the outer courtyard. And like the others, the gateway passage was 87½ feet long and 43¾ feet wide between the back walls of facing guard alcoves. ²⁶This gateway also had a stairway of seven steps leading up to it, and there were palm tree decorations along the dividing walls. ²⁷And here again, directly opposite the outer gateway, was another gateway that led into the inner courtyard. The distance between the two gateways was 175 feet.

Gateways to the Inner Courtyard

²⁸Then the man took me to the south gateway leading into the inner courtyard. He measured it and found that it had the same measurements as the other gateways. ²⁹Its guard alcoves, dividing walls, and foyer were the same size as those in the others. It also had windows along its walls and in the foyer structure. And like the others, the gateway passage was 87½ feet long and 43¾ feet wide. ³⁰(The foyers of the gateways leading into the inner courtyard were 8¾ feet deep and 43¾ feet wide.) ³¹The foyer of the south gateway faced into the outer courtyard. It had palm tree decorations on its columns, and there were eight steps leading to its entrance.

³²Then he took me to the east gateway leading to the inner courtyard. He measured it and found that it had the same measurements as the other gateways. ³³Its guard alcoves, dividing walls, and foyer were the same size as those of

the others, and there were windows along the walls and in the foyer structure. The gateway passage measured 87½ feet long and 43¾ feet wide. ³⁴Its foyer faced into the outer courtyard. It had palm tree decorations on its columns, and there were eight steps leading to its entrance.

³⁵Then he took me around to the north gateway leading to the inner courtyard. He measured it and found that it had the same measurements as the other gateways. ³⁶The guard alcoves, dividing walls, and foyer of this gateway had the same measurements as in the others and the same window arrangements. The gateway passage measured 87½ feet long and 43¾ feet wide. ³⁷Its foyer faced into the outer courtyard, and it had palm tree decorations on the columns. There were eight steps leading to its entrance.

Rooms for Preparing Sacrifices

³⁸A door led from the foyer of the inner gateway on the north side into a side room where the meat for sacrifices was washed before being taken to the altar. ³⁹On each side of this foyer were two tables, where the sacrificial animals were slaughtered for the burnt offerings, sin offerings, and guilt offerings. ⁴⁰Outside the foyer, on each side of the stairs going up to the north entrance, there were two more tables. ⁴¹So there were eight tables in all, four inside and four outside, where the sacrifices were cut up and prepared. ⁴²There were also four tables of hewn stone for preparation of the burnt offerings, each 31½ inches square and 21 inches high. On these tables were placed the butchering knives and other implements and the sacrificial animals. ⁴³There were hooks, each three inches* long, fastened to the foyer walls and set on the tables where the sacrificial meat was to be laid.

Rooms for the Priests

⁴⁴Inside the inner courtyard there were two one-room buildings for the singers, one beside the north gateway, facing south, and the other beside the south* gateway, facing north. ⁴⁵And the man said to me, "The building beside the north inner gate is for the priests who supervise the Temple maintenance. ⁴⁶The building beside the south inner gate is for the priests in charge of the altar—the descendants of Zadok—for they alone of all the Levites may approach the LORD to minister to him."

The Inner Courtyard and Temple

⁴⁷Then the man measured the inner courtyard and found it to be 175 feet square. The altar stood there in the courtyard in front of the Temple. ⁴⁸Then he brought me to the foyer of the Temple. He measured its supporting columns and found them to be 8¾ feet square. The entrance was 24½ feet wide with walls 5¼ feet thick. ⁴⁹The depth of the foyer was 35 feet and the width was 19¼ feet. There were ten steps leading up to it, with a column on each side.

CHAPTER 41

After that, the man brought me into the Holy Place, the large main room of the Temple, and he measured the columns that framed its doorway. They were 10½ feet* square. ²The entrance was 17½ feet wide, and the walls on each side were 8¾ feet wide. The Holy Place itself was 70 feet long and 35 feet wide.

³Then he went into the inner room at the end of the Holy Place. He measured the columns at the entrance and found them to be 3½ feet thick. The entrance was 10½ feet wide, and the walls on each side of the entrance extended 12¼ feet to the corners of the inner room. ⁴The inner room was 35 feet square. "This," he told me, "is the Most Holy Place."

⁵Then he measured the wall of the Temple and found that it was 10½ feet thick. There was a row of rooms along the outside wall; each room was 7 feet wide. ⁶These rooms were built in three levels, one above the other, with thirty rooms on each level. The supports for these rooms rested on ledges in the Temple wall, but the supports did not extend into the wall. ⁷Each level was wider than the one below it, corresponding to the narrowing of the Temple wall as it rose higher. A stairway led up from the bottom level through the middle level to the top level.

⁸I noticed that the Temple was built on a terrace, which provided a foundation for the side rooms. This terrace was 10½ feet high. ⁹The outer wall of the Temple's side rooms was 8¾ feet thick. This left an open area between these side rooms ¹⁰and the row of rooms along the outer wall of the inner courtyard. This open area measured 35 feet in width, and it went all the way around the Temple. ¹¹Two doors opened from the side rooms into the terrace yard, which was 8¾ feet wide. One door faced north and the other south.

¹²A large building stood on the west, facing

the Temple courtyard. It was 122½ feet wide and 157½ feet long, and its walls were 8¾ feet thick. ¹³Then the man measured the Temple, and he found it to be 175 feet long. The courtyard around the building, including its walls, was an additional 175 feet in length. ¹⁴The inner courtyard to the east of the Temple was also 175 feet wide. ¹⁵The building to the west, including its two walls, was also 175 feet wide.

The Holy Place, the Most Holy Place, and the foyer of the Temple were all paneled with wood, ¹⁶as were the frames of the recessed windows. The inner walls of the Temple were paneled with wood above and below the windows. ¹⁷The space above the door leading into the Most Holy Place was also paneled. ¹⁸All the walls were decorated with carvings of cherubim, each with two faces, and there was a palm tree carving between each of the cherubim. ¹⁹One face—that of a man—looked toward the palm tree on one side. The other face—that of a young lion—looked toward the palm tree on the other side. The figures were carved all along the inside of the Temple, ²⁰from the floor to the top of the walls, including the outer wall of the Holy Place.

²¹There were square columns at the entrance to the Holy Place, and the ones at the entrance of the Most Holy Place were similar. ²²There was an altar made of wood, 3½ feet square and 5¼ feet high. Its corners, base, and sides were all made of wood. "This," the man told me, "is the table that stands in the LORD's presence."

²³Both the Holy Place and the Most Holy Place had double doorways, ²⁴each with two swinging doors. ²⁵The doors leading into the Holy Place were decorated with carved cherubim and palm trees just as on the walls. And there was a wooden canopy over the front of the Temple's foyer. ²⁶On both sides of the foyer there were recessed windows decorated with carved palm trees.

CHAPTER **42**
Rooms for the Priests
Then the man led me out of the Temple courtyard by way of the north gateway. We entered the outer courtyard and came to a group of rooms against the north wall of the inner courtyard. ²This group of structures, whose entrance opened toward the north, was 175 feet long and 87½ feet wide.* ³One block of rooms overlooked the 35-foot width of the inner courtyard. Another block of rooms looked out onto the pavement of the outer courtyard. The

two blocks were built three levels high and stood across from each other. ⁴Between the two blocks of rooms ran a walkway 17½ feet wide. It extended the entire 175 feet of the complex, and all the doors faced toward the north. ⁵Each of the two upper levels of rooms was narrower than the one beneath it because the upper levels had to allow space for walkways in front of them. ⁶Since there were three levels and they did not have supporting columns as in the courtyards, each of the upper levels was set back from the level beneath it. ⁷There was an outer wall that separated the rooms from the outer courtyard; it was 87½ feet long. ⁸This wall added length to the outer block of rooms, which extended for only 87½ feet, while the inner block—the rooms toward the Temple—extended for 175 feet. ⁹There was an entrance from the outer courtyard to these rooms from the east.

¹⁰On the south* side of the Temple there were two blocks of rooms just south of the inner courtyard between the Temple and the outer courtyard. These rooms were arranged just like the rooms on the north. ¹¹There was a walkway between the two blocks of rooms just like the complex on the north side of the Temple. This complex of rooms was the same length and width as the other one, and it had the same entrances and doors. The dimensions of each were identical. ¹²So there was an entrance in the wall facing the doors of the inner block of rooms, and another on the east at the end of the interior walkway.

¹³Then the man told me, "These rooms that overlook the Temple from the north and south are holy. It is there that the priests who offer sacrifices to the LORD will eat the most holy offerings. And they will use these rooms to store the grain offerings, sin offerings, and guilt offerings because these rooms are holy. ¹⁴When the priests leave the Holy Place, they must not go directly to the outer courtyard. They must first take off the clothes they wore while ministering because these clothes are holy. They must put on other clothes before entering the parts of the building complex open to the public."

¹⁵When the man had finished taking these measurements, he led me out through the east gateway to measure the entire Temple area. ¹⁶He measured the east side; it was 875 feet long. ¹⁷He also measured the north side and got the same measurement. ¹⁸The south side was the same length, ¹⁹and so was the west side. ²⁰So the area was 875 feet on each side with a wall all around it to separate the holy places from the common.

42:2 Hebrew *100 cubits* [53 meters] *long and 50 cubits* [26.5 meters] *wide*. In this chapter, the distance measures are calculated using the Hebrew long cubit, which equals 21 inches or 53 centimeters. 42:10 As in Greek version; Hebrew reads *east*.

CHAPTER **43**

The LORD's Glory Returns

After this, the man brought me back around to the east gateway. ²Suddenly, the glory of the God of Israel appeared from the east. The sound of his coming was like the roar of rushing waters, and the whole landscape shone with his glory. ³This vision was just like the others I had seen, first by the Kebar River and then when he came to destroy Jerusalem. And I fell down before him with my face in the dust. ⁴And the glory of the LORD came into the Temple through the east gateway.

⁵Then the Spirit took me up and brought me into the inner courtyard, and the glory of the LORD filled the Temple. ⁶And I heard someone speaking to me from within the Temple. (The man who had been measuring was still standing beside me.) ⁷And the LORD said to me, "Son of man, this is the place of my throne and the place where I will rest my feet. I will remain here forever, living among the people of Israel. They and their kings will not defile my holy name any longer by their adulterous worship of other gods or by raising monuments in honor of their dead kings.* ⁸They put their idol altars right next to mine with only a wall between them and me. They defiled my holy name by such wickedness, so I consumed them in my anger. ⁹Now let them put away their idols and the sacred pillars erected to honor their kings, and I will live among them forever.

¹⁰"Son of man, describe to the people of Israel the Temple I have shown you. Tell them its appearance and its plan so they will be ashamed of all their sins. ¹¹And if they are ashamed of what they have done, describe to them all the specifications of its construction—including its entrances and doors—and everything else about it. Write down all these specifications and directions as they watch so they will be sure to remember them. ¹²And this is the basic law of the Temple: absolute holiness! The entire top of the hill where the Temple is built is holy. Yes, this is the primary law of the Temple.

The Altar

¹³"These are the measurements of the altar*: There is a gutter all around the altar 21 inches wide and 21 inches deep, with a curb 9 inches* wide around its edge. And this is the height of the altar: ¹⁴From the gutter the altar rises 3½ feet to a ledge that surrounds the altar; this lower ledge is 21 inches wide. From the lower ledge the

altar rises 7 feet to the upper ledge; this upper ledge is also 21 inches wide. ¹⁵The top of the altar, the hearth, rises still 7 feet higher, with a horn rising up from each of the four corners. ¹⁶The top of the altar is square, measuring 21 feet by 21 feet. ¹⁷The upper ledge also forms a square, measuring 24½ feet on each side, with a 21-inch gutter and a 10½-inch curb all around the edge. There are steps going up the east side of the altar."

¹⁸Then he said to me, "Son of man, this is what the Sovereign LORD says: These will be the regulations for the burning of offerings and the sprinkling of blood when the altar is built. ¹⁹At that time, the Levitical priests of the family of Zadok, who minister before me, are to be given a young bull for a sin offering, says the Sovereign LORD. ²⁰You will take some of its blood and smear it on the four horns of the altar, the four corners of the upper ledge, and the curb that runs around that ledge. This will cleanse and make atonement for the altar. ²¹Then take the young bull for the sin offering and burn it at the appointed place outside the Temple area.

²²"On the second day, sacrifice as a sin offering a young male goat that has no physical defects. Then cleanse and make atonement for the altar again, just as you did with the young bull. ²³When you have finished the cleansing ceremony, offer another young bull that has no defects and a perfect ram from the flock. ²⁴You are to present them to the LORD, and the priests are to sprinkle salt on them and offer them as a burnt offering to the LORD.

²⁵"Every day for seven days a male goat, a young bull, and a ram from the flock will be sacrificed as a sin offering. None of these animals may have physical defects of any kind. ²⁶Do this each day for seven days to cleanse and make atonement for the altar, thus setting it apart for holy use. ²⁷On the eighth day, and on each day afterward, the priests will sacrifice on the altar the burnt offerings and peace offerings of the people. Then I will accept you, says the Sovereign LORD."

CHAPTER **44**

The Prince, Levites, and Priests

Then the man brought me back to the east gateway in the outer wall, but it was closed. ²And the LORD said to me, "This gate must remain closed; it

---

43:7 Or *by raising pillars on their high places.* 43:13a Hebrew *measurements of the altar in long cubits, each being a cubit* [18 inches or 45 centimeters] *and a handbreadth* [3 inches or 8 centimeters] *in length. In this chapter, the distance measures are calculated using the Hebrew long cubit, which equals 21 inches or 53 centimeters. 43:13b Hebrew 1 span* [23 centimeters].

will never again be opened. No man will ever pass through it, for the LORD, the God of Israel, entered here. Thus, it must always remain shut. ³Only the prince himself may sit inside this gateway to feast in the LORD's presence. But he may come and go only through the gateway's foyer."

⁴Then the man brought me through the north gateway to the front of the Temple. I looked and saw that the glory of the LORD filled the Temple of the LORD, and I fell to the ground with my face in the dust.

⁵And the LORD said to me, "Son of man, take careful notice; use your eyes and ears. Listen to everything I tell you about the regulations concerning the LORD's Temple. Take careful note of who may be admitted to the Temple and who is to be excluded from it. ⁶And give these rebels, the people of Israel, this message from the Sovereign LORD: O people of Israel, enough of your disgusting sins! ⁷You have brought uncircumcised foreigners into my sanctuary—people who have no heart for God. In this way, you profaned my Temple even as you offered me my food, the fat and blood of sacrifices. Thus, in addition to all your other disgusting sins, you have broken my covenant. ⁸You have not kept the laws I gave you concerning these sacred rituals, for you have hired foreigners to take charge of my sanctuary.

⁹"So this is what the Sovereign LORD says: No foreigners, including those who live among the people of Israel, will enter my sanctuary if they have not been circumcised and do not love the LORD. ¹⁰And the men of the tribe of Levi who abandoned me when Israel strayed away from me to worship idols must bear the consequences of their unfaithfulness. ¹¹They may still be Temple guards and gatemen, and they may still slaughter the animals brought for burnt offerings and be present to help the people. ¹²But they encouraged my people to worship other gods, causing Israel to fall into deep sin. So I have raised my hand and taken an oath that they must bear the consequences for their sins, says the Sovereign LORD. ¹³They may not approach me to minister as priests. They may not touch any of my holy things or the holy offerings, for they must bear the shame of all the sins they have committed. ¹⁴They are to serve as the Temple caretakers and are relegated to doing maintenance work and helping the people in a general way.

¹⁵"However, the Levitical priests of the family of Zadok continued to minister faithfully in the Temple when Israel abandoned me for idols.

These men will serve as my ministers. They will stand in my presence and offer the fat and blood of the sacrifices, says the Sovereign LORD. ¹⁶They are the ones who will enter my sanctuary and approach my table to serve me. They are the ones who will fulfill all my requirements. ¹⁷When they enter the gateway to the inner courtyard, they must wear only linen clothing. They must wear no wool while on duty in the inner courtyard or in the Temple itself. ¹⁸They must wear linen turbans and linen undergarments. They must not wear anything that would cause them to perspire. ¹⁹When they return to the outer courtyard where the people are, they must take off the clothes they wear while ministering to me. They must leave them in the sacred rooms and put on other clothes so they do not harm the people by transmitting holiness to them through this clothing.

²⁰"They must neither let their hair grow too long nor shave it off completely. Instead, they must trim it regularly. ²¹The priests must never drink wine before entering the inner courtyard. ²²They may choose their wives only from among the virgins of Israel or the widows of the priests. They may not marry other widows or divorced women. ²³They will teach my people the difference between what is holy and what is common, what is ceremonially clean and unclean.

²⁴"They will serve as judges to resolve any disagreements among my people. Their decisions must be based on my regulations. And the priests themselves must obey my instructions and laws at all the sacred festivals, and they will see to it that the Sabbath is set apart as a holy day. ²⁵A priest must never defile himself by being in the presence of a dead person unless it is his father, mother, child, brother, or unmarried sister. In such cases it is permitted. ²⁶But such a priest can only return to his Temple duties after being ritually cleansed and then waiting for seven days. ²⁷The first day he returns to work and enters the inner courtyard and the sanctuary, he must offer a sin offering for himself, says the Sovereign LORD.

²⁸"As to property, the priests will not have any, for I alone am their inheritance. ²⁹Their food will come from the gifts and sacrifices brought to the Temple by the people—the grain offerings, the sin offerings, and the guilt offerings. Whatever anyone sets apart* for the LORD will belong to the priests. ³⁰The first of the ripe fruits and all the gifts brought to the LORD will

44:29 The Hebrew term used here refers to the complete consecration of things or people to the LORD, either by destroying them or by giving them as an offering.

go to the priests. The first samples of each grain harvest and the first of your flour must also be given to the priests so the LORD will bless your homes. ³¹The priests may never eat meat from any bird or animal that dies a natural death or that dies after being attacked by another animal.

CHAPTER 45
Division of the Land

"When you divide the land among the tribes of Israel, you must set aside a section of it for the LORD as his holy portion. This piece of land will be 8⅓ miles long and 6⅔ miles wide.* The entire area will be holy ground. ²A section of this land, measuring 875 feet by 875 feet, will be set aside for the Temple. An additional strip of land 87½ feet wide is to be left empty all around it. ³Within the larger sacred area, measure out a portion of land 8⅓ miles long and 3⅓ miles wide. Within it the sanctuary of the Most Holy Place will be located. ⁴This area will be a holy land, set aside for the priests who minister to the LORD in the sanctuary. They will use it for their homes, and my Temple will be located within it. ⁵The strip of sacred land next to it, also 8⅓ miles long and 3⅓ miles wide, will be a living area for the Levites who work at the Temple. It will be their possession and a place for their towns.*

⁶"Adjacent to the larger sacred area will be a section of land 8⅓ miles long and 1⅔ miles wide. This will be set aside to be a city where anyone in Israel can come and live.

⁷"Two special sections of land will be set apart for the prince. One section will share a border with the east side of the sacred lands and city, and the second section will share a border on the west side. Then the far eastern and western borders of the prince's lands will line up with the eastern and western boundaries of the tribal areas. ⁸These sections of land will be the prince's allotment.

Rules for the Prince

"My princes will no longer oppress and rob my people; they will assign the rest of the land to the people, giving an allotment to each tribe. ⁹For this is what the Sovereign LORD says: Enough, you princes of Israel! Stop all your violence and

oppression and do what is just and right. Quit robbing and cheating my people out of their land! Stop expelling them from their homes! ¹⁰You must use only honest weights and scales, honest dry volume measures, and honest liquid volume measures.* ¹¹The homer* will be your standard unit for measuring volume. The ephah and the bath* will each measure one-tenth of a homer. ¹²The standard unit for weight will be the silver shekel.* One shekel consists of twenty gerahs, and sixty shekels are equal to one mina.*

Special Offerings and Celebrations

¹³"This is the tax you must give to the prince: one bushel of wheat or barley for every sixty* you harvest, ¹⁴one percent of your olive oil,* ¹⁵and one sheep for every two hundred in your flocks in Israel. These will be the grain offerings, burnt offerings, and peace offerings that will make atonement for the people who bring them, says the Sovereign LORD. ¹⁶All the people of Israel must join the prince in bringing their offerings. ¹⁷The prince will be required to provide offerings that are given at the religious festivals, the new moon celebrations, the Sabbath days, and all other similar occasions. He will provide the sin offerings, burnt offerings, grain offerings, drink offerings, and peace offerings to make reconciliation for the people of Israel.

¹⁸"This is what the Sovereign LORD says: In early spring, on the first day of each new year,* sacrifice a young bull with no physical defects to purify the Temple. ¹⁹The priest will take some of the blood of this sin offering and put it on the doorposts of the Temple, the four corners of the upper ledge on the altar, and the gateposts at the entrance to the inner courtyard. ²⁰Do this also on the seventh day of the new year for anyone who has sinned through error or ignorance. In that way, you will make atonement for the Temple.

²¹"On the fourteenth day of the new year, you must celebrate the Passover. This festival will last for seven days. Only bread without yeast may be eaten during that time. ²²On the day of Passover the prince will provide a young bull as a sin offering for himself and the people of Israel. ²³On each of the seven days of the feast he will

45:1 Reflecting the Greek reading *25,000 cubits* [13.3 kilometers] *long and 20,000 cubits* [10.6 kilometers] *wide;* Hebrew reads *25,000 cubits long and 10,000 cubits wide.* Compare 45:3, 5; 48:9. In this chapter, the distance measures are calculated using the Hebrew long cubit, which equals 21 inches or 53 centimeters. **45:5** As in Greek version; Hebrew reads *They will have as their possession 20 rooms.* **45:10** Hebrew *use honest scales, an honest ephah, and an honest bath.* **45:11a** The *homer* measures about 40 gallons or 182 liters. **45:11b** The *ephah* is a dry measure; the *bath* is a liquid measure. **45:12a** The shekel weighs about 0.4 ounces or 11 grams. **45:12b** Elsewhere the mina is equated to 50 shekels. **45:13** Hebrew *⅙ of an ephah from each homer of wheat . . . and of barley.* **45:14** Hebrew *the portion of oil, measured by the bath, is ¹/₁₀ of a bath from each cor, which consists of 10 baths or 1 homer, for 10 baths are equivalent to a homer.* **45:18** Hebrew *On the first day of the first month,* of the Hebrew calendar. This day of the Hebrew lunar calendar occurs in late March or early April.

prepare a burnt offering to the LORD. This daily offering will consist of seven young bulls and seven rams without any defects. A male goat will also be given each day for a sin offering. 24The prince will provide a half bushel of flour as a grain offering and a gallon of olive oil* with each young bull and ram.

25"During the seven days of the Festival of Shelters, which occurs every year in early autumn,* the prince will provide these same sacrifices for the sin offering, the burnt offering, and the grain offering, along with the required olive oil.

CHAPTER 46

"This is what the Sovereign LORD says: The east gateway of the inner wall will be closed during the six workdays each week, but it will be open on Sabbath days and the days of new moon celebrations. 2The prince will enter the foyer of the gateway from the outside. Then he will stand by the gatepost while the priest offers his burnt offering and peace offering. He will worship inside the gateway passage and then go back out the way he came. The gateway will not be closed until evening. 3The common people will worship the LORD in front of this gateway on Sabbath days and the days of new moon celebrations.

4"Each Sabbath day the prince will present to the LORD a burnt offering of six lambs and one ram, all with no physical defects. 5He will present a grain offering of a half bushel of flour to go with the ram and whatever amount of flour he chooses to go with each lamb. He is to offer one gallon of olive oil* for each half bushel of flour. 6At the new moon celebrations, he will bring one young bull, six lambs, and one ram, all with no physical defects. 7With the young bull he must bring a half bushel of flour for a grain offering. With the ram he must bring another half bushel of flour. And with each lamb he is to bring whatever amount of flour that he decides to give. With each half bushel of flour he must offer one gallon of olive oil.

8"The prince must enter the gateway through the foyer, and he must leave the same way he came. 9But when the people come in through the north gateway to worship the LORD during the religious festivals, they must leave by the south gateway. And those who entered through the south gateway must leave by the north gateway. They must never leave by the same gateway they came in; they must always use the opposite

gateway. 10The prince will enter and leave with the people on these occasions.

11"So at the special feasts and sacred festivals, the grain offering will be a half bushel of flour with each young bull, another half bushel of flour with each ram, and as much flour as the prince chooses to give with each lamb. One gallon of oil is to be given with each half bushel of flour. 12Whenever the prince offers a voluntary burnt offering or peace offering to the LORD, the east gateway to the inner courtyard will be opened for him to enter, and he will offer his sacrifices just as he does on Sabbath days. Then he will turn and leave the way he entered, and the gateway will be shut behind him.

13"Each morning a year-old lamb with no physical defects must be sacrificed as a burnt offering to the LORD. 14With the lamb, a grain offering must also be given to the LORD—about two and a half quarts of flour with a third of a gallon of olive oil* to moisten the flour. This will be a permanent law for you. 15The lamb, the grain offering, and the olive oil must be given as a daily sacrifice every morning without fail.

16"This is what the Sovereign LORD says: If the prince gives a gift of land to one of his sons, it will belong to him and his descendants forever. 17But if he gives a gift of land to one of his servants, the servant may keep it only until the Year of Jubilee, which comes every fiftieth year.* At that time the servant will be set free, and the land will return to the prince. Only the gifts given to the prince's sons will be permanent. 18And the prince may never take anyone's property by force. If he gives property to his sons, it must be from his own land, for I do not want any of my people unjustly evicted from their property."

The Temple Kitchens

19Then the man brought me through the entrance beside the gateway and led me to the sacred rooms assigned to the priests, which faced toward the north. He showed me a place at the extreme west end of these rooms. 20He explained, "This is where the priests will cook the meat from the guilt offerings and sin offerings and bake the flour from the grain offerings into bread. They will do it here to avoid carrying the sacrifices through the outer courtyard and harming the people by transmitting holiness to them."

45:24 Hebrew *an ephah* [18 liters] *of flour . . . a hin* [3.8 liters] *of olive oil.* 45:25 Hebrew *the festival which begins on the fifteenth day of the seventh month* (see Lev 23:33). This day of the Hebrew lunar calendar occurs in late September or October. 46:5 Hebrew *an ephah* [18 liters] *of flour . . . a hin* [3.8 liters] *of olive oil*; also in 46:7, 11. 46:14 Hebrew 1/6 *of an ephah* [2.9 liters] *of flour with* 1/3 *of a hin* [1.3 liters] *of olive oil.* 46:17 Hebrew *until the Year of Release*; see Lev 25:8-17.

²¹Then he brought me back to the outer courtyard and led me to each of its four corners. In each corner I saw an enclosure. ²²Each of these enclosures was 70 feet long and 52½ feet wide,* surrounded by walls. ²³Along the inside of these walls was a ledge of stone with fireplaces under the ledge all the way around. ²⁴The man said to me, "These are the kitchens to be used by the Temple assistants to boil the sacrifices offered by the people."

CHAPTER **47**
The River of Healing
Then the man brought me back to the entrance of the Temple. There I saw a stream flowing eastward from beneath the Temple threshold. This stream then passed to the right of the altar on its south side. ²The man brought me outside the wall through the north gateway and led me around to the eastern entrance. There I could see the stream flowing out through the south side of the east gateway. ³Measuring as he went, he led me along the stream for 1,750 feet* and told me to go across. At that point the water was up to my ankles. ⁴He measured off another 1,750 feet and told me to go across again. This time the water was up to my knees. After another 1,750 feet, it was up to my waist. ⁵Then he measured another 1,750 feet, and the river was too deep to cross without swimming.

⁶He told me to keep in mind what I had seen; then he led me back along the riverbank. ⁷Suddenly, to my surprise, many trees were now growing on both sides of the river! ⁸Then he said to me, "This river flows east through the desert into the Jordan Valley,* where it enters the Dead Sea.* The waters of this stream will heal the salty waters of the Dead Sea and make them fresh and pure. ⁹Everything that touches the water of this river will live. Fish will abound in the Dead Sea, for its waters will be healed. Wherever this water flows, everything will live. ¹⁰Fishermen will stand along the shores of the Dead Sea, fishing all the way from En-gedi to En-eglaim. The shores will be covered with nets drying in the sun. Fish of every kind will fill the Dead Sea, just as they fill the Mediterranean*! ¹¹But the marshes and swamps will not be purified; they will be sources of salt. ¹²All kinds of fruit trees will grow along both sides of the river. The leaves of these trees will never turn brown and fall, and

there will always be fruit on their branches. There will be a new crop every month, without fail! For they are watered by the river flowing from the Temple. The fruit will be for food and the leaves for healing."

Boundaries for the Land
¹³This is what the Sovereign LORD says: "Follow these instructions for dividing the land for the twelve tribes of Israel: The tribe of Joseph will be given two shares of land.* ¹⁴Otherwise each tribe will receive an equal share. I swore that I would give this land to your ancestors, and it will now come to you as your inheritance.

¹⁵"The northern border will run from the Mediterranean toward Hethlon, then on through Lebo-hamath to Zedad; ¹⁶then it will run to Berothah and Sibraim, which are on the border between Damascus and Hamath, and finally to Hazer-hatticon, on the border of Hauran. ¹⁷So the northern border will run from the Mediterranean to Hazar-enan, on the border between Hamath to the north and Damascus to the south.

¹⁸"The eastern border starts at a point between Hauran and Damascus and runs southward along the Jordan River between Israel and Gilead, past the Dead Sea* and as far south as Tamar.* This will be the eastern border.

¹⁹"The southern border will go west from Tamar to the waters of Meribah at Kadesh* and then follow the course of the brook of Egypt to the Mediterranean. This will be the southern border.

²⁰"On the west side the Mediterranean itself will be your border from the southern border to the point where the northern border begins, opposite Lebo-hamath.

²¹"Divide the land within these boundaries among the tribes of Israel. ²²Distribute the land as an inheritance for yourselves and for the foreigners who have joined you and are raising their families among you. They will be just like native-born Israelites to you, and they will receive an inheritance among the tribes. ²³All these immigrants are to be given land within the territory of the tribe with whom they now live. I, the Sovereign LORD, have spoken!

46:22 Hebrew *40 cubits* [21.2 meters] *long and 30 cubits* [15.9 meters] *wide.* The distances are calculated using the Hebrew long cubit, which equals 21 inches or 53 centimeters.   **47:3** Hebrew *1,000 cubits* [530 meters]; also in 47:4, 5. The distances are calculated using the Hebrew long cubit, which equals 21 inches or 53 centimeters.   **47:8a** Hebrew *the Arabah.*   **47:8b** Hebrew *the sea;* also in 47:10.   **47:10** Hebrew *the great sea;* also in 47:15, 17, 19, 20.   **47:13** A share of land for each of Joseph's two oldest sons, Ephraim and Manasseh.   **47:18a** Hebrew *the eastern sea.*   **47:18b** As in Greek version; Hebrew reads *you will measure.*   **47:19** Hebrew *waters of Meribath-kadesh.*

CHAPTER **48**
Division of the Land
"Here is the list of the tribes of Israel and the territory each is to receive. The territory of Dan is in the extreme north. Its boundary line follows the Hethlon road to Lebo-hamath and then runs on to Hazar-enan on the border of Damascus, with Hamath to the north. Dan's territory extends all the way across the land of Israel from east to west. ²Asher's territory lies south of Dan's and also extends from east to west. ³Naphtali's land lies south of Asher's, also extending from east to west. ⁴Then comes Manasseh south of Naphtali, and its territory also extends from east to west. ⁵South of Manasseh is Ephraim, ⁶and then Reuben, ⁷and then Judah, all of whose boundaries extend from east to west.

⁸"South of Judah is the land set aside for a special purpose. It will be 8⅓ miles wide and will extend as far east and west as the tribal territories, with the Temple at the center. ⁹"The area set aside for the LORD's Temple will be 8⅓ miles long and 6⅔ miles wide.* ¹⁰For the priests there will be a strip of land measuring 8⅓ miles long by 3⅓ miles wide, with the LORD's Temple at the center. ¹¹This area is set aside for the ordained priests, the descendants of Zadok who obeyed me and did not go astray when the people of Israel and the rest of the Levites did. ¹²It will be their special portion when the land is distributed, the most sacred land of all. Next to the priests' territory will lie the land where the other Levites will live. ¹³The land allotted to the Levites will be the same size and shape as that belonging to the priests—8⅓ miles long and 3⅓ miles wide. Together these portions of land will measure 8⅓ miles long by 6⅔ miles wide.* ¹⁴None of this special land will ever be sold or traded or used by others, for it belongs to the LORD; it is set apart as holy.

¹⁵"An additional strip of land 8⅓ miles long by 1⅔ miles wide, south of the sacred Temple area, will be allotted for public use—homes, pasturelands, and common lands, with a city at the center. ¹⁶The city will measure 1½ miles* on each side. ¹⁷Open lands will surround the city for 150 yards* in every direction. ¹⁸Outside the city there will be a farming area that stretches 3⅓ miles to the east and 3⅓ miles to the west

along the border of the sacred area. This farmland will produce food for the people working in the city. ¹⁹Those who come from the various tribes to work in the city may farm it. ²⁰This entire area—including the sacred lands and the city—is a square that measures 8⅓ miles on each side.

²¹"The areas that remain, to the east and to the west of the sacred lands and the city, will belong to the prince. Each of these areas will be 8⅓ miles wide, extending in opposite directions to the eastern and western borders of Israel. ²²So the prince's land will include everything between the territories allotted to Judah and Benjamin, except for the areas set aside for the sacred lands and the city.

²³"These are the territories allotted to the rest of the tribes. Benjamin's territory lies just south of the prince's lands, and it extends across the entire land of Israel from east to west. ²⁴South of Benjamin's territory lies that of Simeon, also extending across the land from east to west. ²⁵Next is the territory of Issachar with the same eastern and western boundaries. ²⁶Then comes the territory of Zebulun, which also extends across the land from east to west. ²⁷The territory of Gad is just south of Zebulun with the same borders to the east and west. ²⁸The southern border of Gad runs from Tamar to the waters of Meribah at Kadesh* and then follows the brook of Egypt to the Mediterranean.* ²⁹These are the allotments that will be set aside for each tribe's inheritance, says the Sovereign LORD.

The Gates of the City
³⁰"These will be the exits to the city: On the north wall, which is 1½ miles long, ³¹there will be three gates, each one named after a tribe of Israel. The first will be named for Reuben, the second for Judah, and the third for Levi. ³²On the east wall, also 1½ miles long, the gates will be named for Joseph, Benjamin, and Dan. ³³The south wall, also 1½ miles long, will have gates named for Simeon, Issachar, and Zebulun. ³⁴And on the west wall, also 1½ miles long, the gates will be named for Gad, Asher, and Naphtali.

³⁵"The distance around the entire city will be six miles.* And from that day the name of the city will be 'The LORD Is There.'* "

48:9 Reflecting the Greek reading in 45:1: *25,000 cubits* [13.3 kilometers] *long and 20,000 cubits* [10.6 kilometers] *wide;* Hebrew reads *25,000 cubits long and 10,000 cubits wide.* Compare 45:1-5; 48:10-13. In this chapter, the distance measures are calculated using the Hebrew long cubit, which equals 21 inches or 53 centimeters.   48:13 See note on 48:9.   48:16 Hebrew *4,500 cubits* [2.4 kilometers]; also in 48:30, 32, 33, 34.   48:17 Hebrew *250 cubits* [133 meters].   48:28a Hebrew *waters of Meribath-kadesh.*   48:28b Hebrew *the great sea.*   48:35a Hebrew *18,000 cubits* [9.6 kilometers].   48:35b Hebrew *Yahweh Shammah.*

Daniel

CHAPTER 1

Daniel in Nebuchadnezzar's Court

During the third year of King Jehoiakim's reign in Judah,* King Nebuchadnezzar of Babylon came to Jerusalem and besieged it with his armies. ²The Lord gave him victory over King Jehoiakim of Judah. When Nebuchadnezzar returned to Babylon, he took with him some of the sacred objects from the Temple of God and placed them in the treasure-house of his god in the land of Babylonia.*

³Then the king ordered Ashpenaz, who was in charge of the palace officials, to bring to the palace some of the young men of Judah's royal family and other noble families, who had been brought to Babylon as captives. ⁴"Select only strong, healthy, and good-looking young men," he said. "Make sure they are well versed in every branch of learning, are gifted with knowledge and good sense, and have the poise needed to serve in the royal palace. Teach these young men the language and literature of the Babylonians.*" ⁵The king assigned them a daily ration of the best food and wine from his own kitchens. They were to be trained for a three-year period, and then some of them would be made his advisers in the royal court.

⁶Daniel, Hananiah, Mishael, and Azariah were four of the young men chosen, all from the tribe of Judah. ⁷The chief official renamed them with these Babylonian names:

Daniel was called Belteshazzar.
Hananiah was called Shadrach.
Mishael was called Meshach.
Azariah was called Abednego.

⁸But Daniel made up his mind not to defile himself by eating the food and wine given to them by the king. He asked the chief official for permission to eat other things instead. ⁹Now God had given the chief official great respect for Daniel. ¹⁰But he was alarmed by Daniel's suggestion. "My lord the king has ordered that you eat this food and wine," he said. "If you become pale and thin compared to the other youths your age, I am afraid the king will have me beheaded for neglecting my duties."

¹¹Daniel talked it over with the attendant who had been appointed by the chief official to look after Daniel, Hananiah, Mishael, and Azariah. ¹²"Test us for ten days on a diet of vegetables and water," Daniel said. ¹³"At the end of the ten days, see how we look compared to the other young men who are eating the king's rich food. Then you can decide whether or not to let us continue eating our diet." ¹⁴So the attendant agreed to Daniel's suggestion and tested them for ten days.

¹⁵At the end of the ten days, Daniel and his three friends looked healthier and better nourished than the young men who had been eating the food assigned by the king. ¹⁶So after that, the attendant fed them only vegetables instead of the rich foods and wines. ¹⁷God gave these four young men an unusual aptitude for learning the literature and science of the time. And God gave Daniel special ability in understanding the meanings of visions and dreams.

¹⁸When the three-year training period ordered by the king was completed, the chief official brought all the young men to King Nebuchadnezzar. ¹⁹The king talked with each of them, and none of them impressed him as much as Daniel, Hananiah, Mishael, and Azariah. So they were appointed to his regular staff of advisers. ²⁰In all matters requiring wisdom and balanced judgment, the king found the advice of these young men to be ten times better than that

1:1 The third year of Jehoiakim's reign, according to the Hebrew system of reckoning, was 605 B.C.   1:2 Hebrew *the land of Shinar.*   1:4 Or *of the Chaldeans.*

of all the magicians and enchanters in his entire kingdom. 21Daniel remained there until the first year of King Cyrus's reign.*

CHAPTER 2
Nebuchadnezzar's Dream

One night during the second year of his reign,* Nebuchadnezzar had a dream that disturbed him so much that he couldn't sleep. 2He called in his magicians, enchanters, sorcerers, and astrologers,* and he demanded that they tell him what he had dreamed. As they stood before the king, 3he said, "I have had a dream that troubles me. Tell me what I dreamed, for I must know what it means."

4Then the astrologers answered the king in Aramaic,* "Long live the king! Tell us the dream, and we will tell you what it means."

5But the king said to the astrologers, "I am serious about this. If you don't tell me what my dream was and what it means, you will be torn limb from limb, and your houses will be demolished into heaps of rubble! 6But if you tell me what I dreamed and what the dream means, I will give you many wonderful gifts and honors. Just tell me the dream and what it means!"

7They said again, "Please, Your Majesty. Tell us the dream, and we will tell you what it means."

8The king replied, "I can see through your trick! You are trying to stall for time because you know I am serious about what I said. 9If you don't tell me the dream, you will be condemned. You have conspired to tell me lies in hopes that something will change. But tell me the dream, and then I will know that you can tell me what it means."

10The astrologers replied to the king, "There isn't a man alive who can tell Your Majesty his dream! And no king, however great and powerful, has ever asked such a thing of any magician, enchanter, or astrologer! 11This is an impossible thing the king requires. No one except the gods can tell you your dream, and they do not live among people."

12The king was furious when he heard this, and he sent out orders to execute all the wise men of Babylon. 13And because of the king's decree, men were sent to find and kill Daniel and his friends. 14When Arioch, the commander of the king's guard, came to kill them, Daniel handled the situation with wisdom and discretion. 15He asked Arioch, "Why has the king issued such a harsh decree?" So Arioch told him all that had happened. 16Daniel went at once to see the king and requested more time so he could tell the king what the dream meant.

17Then Daniel went home and told his friends Hananiah, Mishael, and Azariah what had happened. 18He urged them to ask the God of heaven to show them his mercy by telling them the secret, so they would not be executed along with the other wise men of Babylon. 19That night the secret was revealed to Daniel in a vision. Then Daniel praised the God of heaven, 20saying,

"Praise the name of God forever and ever,
  for he alone has all wisdom and power.
21 He determines the course of world events;
  he removes kings and sets others on the
    throne.
He gives wisdom to the wise
  and knowledge to the scholars.
22 He reveals deep and mysterious things
  and knows what lies hidden in darkness,
    though he himself is surrounded by light.
23 I thank and praise you, God of my ancestors,
  for you have given me wisdom and
    strength.
You have told me what we asked of you
  and revealed to us what the king
    demanded."

Daniel Interprets the Dream

24Then Daniel went in to see Arioch, who had been ordered to execute the wise men of Babylon. Daniel said to him, "Don't kill the wise men. Take me to the king, and I will tell him the meaning of his dream."

25Then Arioch quickly took Daniel to the king and said, "I have found one of the captives from Judah who will tell Your Majesty the meaning of your dream!"

26The king said to Daniel (also known as Belteshazzar), "Is this true? Can you tell me what my dream was and what it means?"

27Daniel replied, "There are no wise men, enchanters, magicians, or fortune-tellers who can tell the king such things. 28But there is a God in heaven who reveals secrets, and he has shown King Nebuchadnezzar what will happen in the future. Now I will tell you your dream and the visions you saw as you lay on your bed.

29"While Your Majesty was sleeping, you dreamed about coming events. The revealer of mysteries has shown you what is going to hap-

1:21 The first year of Cyrus's reign was 538 B.C.   2:1 The second year of Nebuchadnezzar's reign was 603 B.C.   2:2 Or *Chaldeans;* also in 2:4, 5, 10.   2:4 The original text from this point through chapter 7 is in Aramaic.

pen. 30And it is not because I am wiser than any living person that I know the secret of your dream, but because God wanted you to understand what you were thinking about.

31"Your Majesty, in your vision you saw in front of you a huge and powerful statue of a man, shining brilliantly, frightening and awesome. 32The head of the statue was made of fine gold, its chest and arms were of silver, its belly and thighs were of bronze, 33its legs were of iron, and its feet were a combination of iron and clay. 34But as you watched, a rock was cut from a mountain by supernatural means.* It struck the feet of iron and clay, smashing them to bits. 35The whole statue collapsed into a heap of iron, clay, bronze, silver, and gold. The pieces were crushed as small as chaff on a threshing floor, and the wind blew them all away without a trace. But the rock that knocked the statue down became a great mountain that covered the whole earth.

36"That was the dream; now I will tell Your Majesty what it means. 37Your Majesty, you are a king over many kings. The God of heaven has given you sovereignty, power, strength, and honor. 38He has made you the ruler over all the inhabited world and has put even the animals and birds under your control. You are the head of gold.

39"But after your kingdom comes to an end, another great kingdom, inferior to yours, will rise to take your place. After that kingdom has fallen, yet a third great kingdom, represented by the bronze belly and thighs, will rise to rule the world. 40Following that kingdom, there will be a fourth great kingdom, as strong as iron. That kingdom will smash and crush all previous empires, just as iron smashes and crushes everything it strikes. 41The feet and toes you saw that were a combination of iron and clay show that this kingdom will be divided. 42Some parts of it will be as strong as iron, and others as weak as clay. 43This mixture of iron and clay also shows that these kingdoms will try to strengthen themselves by forming alliances with each other through intermarriage. But this will not succeed, just as iron and clay do not mix.

44"During the reigns of those kings, the God of heaven will set up a kingdom that will never be destroyed; no one will ever conquer it. It will shatter all these kingdoms into nothingness, but it will stand forever. 45That is the meaning of the rock cut from the mountain by supernatural

means, crushing to dust the statue of iron, bronze, clay, silver, and gold.

"The great God has shown Your Majesty what will happen in the future. The dream is true, and its meaning is certain."

Nebuchadnezzar Rewards Daniel

46Then King Nebuchadnezzar bowed to the ground before Daniel and worshiped him, and he commanded his people to offer sacrifices and burn sweet incense before him. 47The king said to Daniel, "Truly, your God is the God of gods, the Lord over kings, a revealer of mysteries, for you have been able to reveal this secret."

48Then the king appointed Daniel to a high position and gave him many valuable gifts. He made Daniel ruler over the whole province of Babylon, as well as chief over all his wise men. 49At Daniel's request, the king appointed Shadrach, Meshach, and Abednego to be in charge of all the affairs of the province of Babylon, while Daniel remained in the king's court.

CHAPTER 3
Nebuchadnezzar's Gold Statue

King Nebuchadnezzar made a gold statue ninety feet tall and nine feet wide* and set it up on the plain of Dura in the province of Babylon. 2Then he sent messages to the princes, prefects, governors, advisers, counselors, judges, magistrates, and all the provincial officials to come to the dedication of the statue he had set up. 3When all these officials* had arrived and were standing before the image King Nebuchadnezzar had set up, 4a herald shouted out, "People of all races and nations and languages, listen to the king's command! 5When you hear the sound of the horn, flute, zither, lyre, harp, pipes, and other instruments,* bow to the ground to worship King Nebuchadnezzar's gold statue. 6Anyone who refuses to obey will immediately be thrown into a blazing furnace."

7So at the sound of the musical instruments,* all the people, whatever their race or nation or language, bowed to the ground and worshiped the statue that King Nebuchadnezzar had set up.

8But some of the astrologers* went to the king and informed on the Jews. 9They said to King Nebuchadnezzar, "Long live the king! 10You issued a decree requiring all the people to bow down and worship the gold statue when they hear the sound of the musical instruments.*

2:34 Aramaic *not by human hands;* also in 2:45.   3:1 Aramaic *60 cubits* [27 meters] *tall and 6 cubits* [2.7 meters] *wide.*   3:3 Aramaic *the princes, prefects, governors, advisers, counselors, judges, magistrates, and all the provincial officials.*   3:5 The identification of some of these musical instruments is uncertain.   3:7 Aramaic *the horn, flute, zither, lyre, harp, and other instruments of the musical ensemble.*   3:8 Aramaic *Chaldeans.*   3:10 Aramaic *the horn, flute, zither, lyre, harp, pipes, and other instruments of the musical ensemble;* also in 3:15.

11That decree also states that those who refuse to obey must be thrown into a blazing furnace. 12But there are some Jews—Shadrach, Meshach, and Abednego—whom you have put in charge of the province of Babylon. They have defied Your Majesty by refusing to serve your gods or to worship the gold statue you have set up."

13Then Nebuchadnezzar flew into a rage and ordered Shadrach, Meshach, and Abednego to be brought before him. When they were brought in, 14Nebuchadnezzar said to them, "Is it true, Shadrach, Meshach, and Abednego, that you refuse to serve my gods or to worship the gold statue I have set up? 15I will give you one more chance. If you bow down and worship the statue I have made when you hear the sound of the musical instruments, all will be well. But if you refuse, you will be thrown immediately into the blazing furnace. What god will be able to rescue you from my power then?"

16Shadrach, Meshach, and Abednego replied, "O Nebuchadnezzar, we do not need to defend ourselves before you. 17If we are thrown into the blazing furnace, the God whom we serve is able to save us. He will rescue us from your power, Your Majesty. 18But even if he doesn't, Your Majesty can be sure that we will never serve your gods or worship the gold statue you have set up."

The Blazing Furnace
19Nebuchadnezzar was so furious with Shadrach, Meshach, and Abednego that his face became distorted with rage. He commanded that the furnace be heated seven times hotter than usual. 20Then he ordered some of the strongest men of his army to bind Shadrach, Meshach, and Abednego and throw them into the blazing furnace. 21So they tied them up and threw them into the furnace, fully clothed. 22And because the king, in his anger, had demanded such a hot fire in the furnace, the flames leaped out and killed the soldiers as they threw the three men in! 23So Shadrach, Meshach, and Abednego, securely tied, fell down into the roaring flames.

24But suddenly, as he was watching, Nebuchadnezzar jumped up in amazement and exclaimed to his advisers, "Didn't we tie up three men and throw them into the furnace?"

"Yes," they said, "we did indeed, Your Majesty."

25"Look!" Nebuchadnezzar shouted. "I see four men, unbound, walking around in the fire. They aren't even hurt by the flames! And the fourth looks like a divine being*!"

26Then Nebuchadnezzar came as close as he could to the door of the flaming furnace and shouted: "Shadrach, Meshach, and Abednego, servants of the Most High God, come out! Come here!" So Shadrach, Meshach, and Abednego stepped out of the fire. 27Then the princes, prefects, governors, and advisers crowded around them and saw that the fire had not touched them. Not a hair on their heads was singed, and their clothing was not scorched. They didn't even smell of smoke!

28Then Nebuchadnezzar said, "Praise to the God of Shadrach, Meshach, and Abednego! He sent his angel to rescue his servants who trusted in him. They defied the king's command and were willing to die rather than serve or worship any god except their own God. 29Therefore, I make this decree: If any people, whatever their race or nation or language, speak a word against the God of Shadrach, Meshach, and Abednego, they will be torn limb from limb, and their houses will be crushed into heaps of rubble. There is no other god who can rescue like this!" 30Then the king promoted Shadrach, Meshach, and Abednego to even higher positions in the province of Babylon.

CHAPTER **4**
Nebuchadnezzar's Dream about a Tree
King Nebuchadnezzar sent this message to the people of every race and nation and language throughout the world:

"Peace and prosperity to you!

2 "I want you all to know about the miraculous signs and wonders the Most High God has performed for me.

3 How great are his signs,
    how powerful his wonders!
His kingdom will last forever,
    his rule through all generations.

4 "I, Nebuchadnezzar, was living in my palace in comfort and prosperity. 5But one night I had a dream that greatly frightened me; I saw visions that terrified me as I lay in my bed. 6So I issued an order calling in all the wise men of Babylon, so they could tell me what my dream meant. 7When all the magicians, enchanters, astrologers,* and fortune-tellers came in, I told them the dream, but they could not tell me what it meant. 8At last Daniel came in before me, and I told him the dream. (He was named

3:25 Aramaic *like a son of the gods.* 4:7 Or *Chaldeans.*

Belteshazzar after my god, and the spirit of the holy gods is in him.)

9 "I said to him, 'O Belteshazzar, master magician, I know that the spirit of the holy gods is in you and that no mystery is too great for you to solve. Now tell me what my dream means.
10 " 'While I was lying in my bed, this is what I dreamed. I saw a large tree in the middle of the earth. 11 The tree grew very tall and strong, reaching high into the heavens for all the world to see. 12 It had fresh green leaves, and it was loaded with fruit for all to eat. Wild animals lived in its shade, and birds nested in its branches. All the world was fed from this tree.
13 " 'Then as I lay there dreaming, I saw a messenger,* a holy one, coming down from heaven. 14 The messenger shouted, "Cut down the tree; lop off its branches! Shake off its leaves, and scatter its fruit! Chase the animals from its shade and the birds from its branches. 15 But leave the stump and the roots in the ground, bound with a band of iron and bronze and surrounded by tender grass. Now let him be drenched with the dew of heaven, and let him live like an animal among the plants of the fields. 16 For seven periods of time, let him have the mind of an animal instead of a human. 17 For this has been decreed by the messengers*; it is commanded by the holy ones. The purpose of this decree is that the whole world may understand that the Most High rules over the kingdoms of the world and gives them to anyone he chooses—even to the lowliest of humans."
18 " 'O Belteshazzar, that was the dream that I, King Nebuchadnezzar, had. Now tell me what it means, for no one else can help me. All the wisest men of my kingdom have failed me. But you can tell me because the spirit of the holy gods is in you.'

Daniel Explains the Dream

19 "Upon hearing this, Daniel (also known as Belteshazzar) was overcome for a time, aghast at the meaning of the dream. Finally, the king said to him, 'Belteshazzar, don't be alarmed by the dream and what it means.'

"Belteshazzar replied, 'Oh, how I wish the events foreshadowed in this dream would happen to your enemies, my lord, and not to you! 20 You saw a tree growing very tall and strong, reaching high into the heavens for all the world to see. 21 It had fresh green leaves,

and it was loaded with fruit for all to eat. Wild animals lived in its shade, and birds nested in its branches. 22 That tree, Your Majesty, is you. For you have grown strong and great; your greatness reaches up to heaven, and your rule to the ends of the earth.
23 " 'Then you saw a messenger, a holy one, coming down from heaven and saying, "Cut down the tree and destroy it. But leave the stump and the roots in the ground, bound with a band of iron and bronze and surrounded by tender grass. Let him be drenched with the dew of heaven. Let him eat grass with the animals of the field for seven periods of time."
24 " 'This is what the dream means, Your Majesty, and what the Most High has declared will happen to you. 25 You will be driven from human society, and you will live in the fields with the wild animals. You will eat grass like a cow, and you will be drenched with the dew of heaven. Seven periods of time will pass while you live this way, until you learn that the Most High rules over the kingdoms of the world and gives them to anyone he chooses. 26 But the stump and the roots were left in the ground. This means that you will receive your kingdom back again when you have learned that heaven rules.
27 " 'O King Nebuchadnezzar, please listen to me. Stop sinning and do what is right. Break from your wicked past by being merciful to the poor. Perhaps then you will continue to prosper.'

The Dream's Fulfillment

28 "But all these things did happen to King Nebuchadnezzar. 29 Twelve months later, he was taking a walk on the flat roof of the royal palace in Babylon. 30 As he looked out across the city, he said, 'Just look at this great city of Babylon! I, by my own mighty power, have built this beautiful city as my royal residence and as an expression of my royal splendor.'

31 "While he was still speaking these words, a voice called down from heaven, 'O King Nebuchadnezzar, this message is for you! You are no longer ruler of this kingdom. 32 You will be driven from human society. You will live in the fields with the wild animals, and you will eat grass like a cow. Seven periods of time will pass while you live this way, until you learn that the Most High rules over the

4:13 Aramaic *a watcher;* also in 4:23.   4:17 Aramaic *the watchers.*

kingdoms of the world and gives them to anyone he chooses.'

33"That very same hour the prophecy was fulfilled, and Nebuchadnezzar was driven from human society. He ate grass like a cow, and he was drenched with the dew of heaven. He lived this way until his hair was as long as eagles' feathers and his nails were like birds' claws.

Nebuchadnezzar Praises God

34"After this time had passed, I, Nebuchadnezzar, looked up to heaven. My sanity returned, and I praised and worshiped the Most High and honored the one who lives forever.

> His rule is everlasting,
> and his kingdom is eternal.
> 35 All the people of the earth
> are nothing compared to him.
> He has the power to do as he pleases
> among the angels of heaven
> and with those who live on earth.
> No one can stop him or challenge him,
> saying, 'What do you mean by doing
> these things?'

36"When my sanity returned to me, so did my honor and glory and kingdom. My advisers and officers sought me out, and I was reestablished as head of my kingdom, with even greater honor than before.

37"Now I, Nebuchadnezzar, praise and glorify and honor the King of heaven. All his acts are just and true, and he is able to humble those who are proud."

CHAPTER 5
The Writing on the Wall

A number of years later, King Belshazzar gave a great feast for a thousand of his nobles and drank wine with them. 2While Belshazzar was drinking,

5:2 Aramaic *father;* also in 5:11, 13, 18.   5:7 Or *Chaldeans;* also in 5:11.

he gave orders to bring in the gold and silver cups that his predecessor,* Nebuchadnezzar, had taken from the Temple in Jerusalem, so that he and his nobles, his wives, and his concubines might drink from them. 3So they brought these gold cups taken from the Temple of God in Jerusalem, and the king and his nobles, his wives, and his concubines drank from them. 4They drank toasts from them to honor their idols made of gold, silver, bronze, iron, wood, and stone.

5At that very moment they saw the fingers of a human hand writing on the plaster wall of the king's palace, near the lampstand. The king himself saw the hand as it wrote, 6and his face turned pale with fear. Such terror gripped him that his knees knocked together and his legs gave way beneath him.

7The king shouted for the enchanters, astrologers,* and fortune-tellers to be brought before him. He said to these wise men of Babylon, "Whoever can read this writing and tell me what it means will be dressed in purple robes of royal honor and will wear a gold chain around his neck. He will become the third highest ruler in the kingdom!" 8But when all the king's wise men came in, none of them could read the writing or tell him what it meant. 9So the king grew even more alarmed, and his face turned ashen white. His nobles, too, were shaken.

10But when the queen mother heard what was happening, she hurried to the banquet hall. She said to Belshazzar, "Long live the king! Don't be so pale and afraid about this. 11There is a man in your kingdom who has within him the spirit of the holy gods. During Nebuchadnezzar's reign, this man was found to have insight, understanding, and wisdom as though he himself were a god. Your predecessor, King Nebuchadnezzar, made him chief over all the magicians, enchanters, astrologers, and fortune-tellers of Babylon. 12This man Daniel, whom the king named Belteshazzar,

OFF AND RUNNING ▟▟▟
Honor Christ with Your Hard Work Read DANIEL 6:1-28

Your work ethic and attitude can make a great deal of difference to those around you. Take Daniel, for instance. He was a man of purpose. He would not compromise his faith, nor would he perform sloppy work. Even when he was unjustly accused of disobeying one of the king's decrees, he held his ground. As the well-known story goes, he spent the night in the lions' den and survived without a scratch. When all was said and done, his uncompromising faith had made such an impact on the king that the king declared "that everyone throughout my kingdom should tremble with fear before the God of Daniel. For he is the living God, and he has a sharp mind and is filled with divine knowledge and understanding. He can interpret dreams, explain riddles, and solve difficult problems. Call for Daniel, and he will tell you what the writing means."

Daniel Explains the Writing

13So Daniel was brought in before the king. The king asked him, "Are you Daniel, who was exiled from Judah by my predecessor, King Nebuchadnezzar? 14I have heard that you have the spirit of the gods within you and that you are filled with insight, understanding, and wisdom. 15My wise men and enchanters have tried to read this writing on the wall, but they cannot. 16I am told that you can give interpretations and solve difficult problems. If you can read these words and tell me their meaning, you will be clothed in purple robes of royal honor, and you will wear a gold chain around your neck. You will become the third highest ruler in the kingdom."

17Daniel answered the king, "Keep your gifts or give them to someone else, but I will tell you what the writing means. 18Your Majesty, the Most High God gave sovereignty, majesty, glory, and honor to your predecessor, Nebuchadnezzar. 19He made him so great that people of all races and nations and languages trembled before him in fear. He killed those he wanted to kill and spared those he wanted to spare. He honored those he wanted to honor and disgraced those he wanted to disgrace. 20But when his heart and mind were hardened with pride, he was brought down from his royal throne and stripped of his glory. 21He was driven from human society. He was given the mind of an animal, and he lived among the wild donkeys. He ate grass like a cow, and he was drenched with the dew of heaven, until he learned that the Most High God rules the kingdoms of the world and appoints anyone he desires to rule over them.

22"You are his successor,* O Belshazzar, and you knew all this, yet you have not humbled yourself. 23For you have defied the Lord of heaven and have had these cups from his Temple brought before you. You and your nobles and your wives and concubines have been drinking wine from them while praising gods of silver, gold, bronze, iron, wood, and stone—gods that neither see nor hear nor know anything at all. But you have not honored the God who gives you the breath of life and controls your destiny! 24So God has sent this hand to write a message.

25"This is the message that was written: MENE, MENE, TEKEL, PARSIN. 26This is what these words mean:

Mene means 'numbered'—God has numbered the days of your reign and has brought it to an end.
27 Tekel means 'weighed'—you have been weighed on the balances and have failed the test.
28 Parsin* means 'divided'—your kingdom has been divided and given to the Medes and Persians."

29Then at Belshazzar's command, Daniel was dressed in purple robes, a gold chain was hung around his neck, and he was proclaimed the third highest ruler in the kingdom.

30That very night Belshazzar, the Babylonian* king, was killed.* 31And Darius the Mede took over the kingdom at the age of sixty-two.

CHAPTER **6**
Daniel in the Lions' Den

Darius the Mede decided to divide the kingdom into 120 provinces, and he appointed a prince to rule over each province. 2The king also chose Daniel and two others as administrators to supervise the princes and to watch out for the king's interests. 3Daniel soon proved himself more capable than all the other administrators and princes. Because of his great

5:22 Aramaic son.   5:28 Aramaic Peres, the singular of Parsin.   5:30a Or Chaldean.   5:30b The Persians and Medes conquered Babylon in October 539 B.C.

will endure forever. His kingdom will never be destroyed, and his rule will never end" (Daniel 6:26).
Sometimes others may discourage you from living a life completely dedicated to God. That is because your changed life will convict them of their sinful living. But you need to stand for your convictions. If others see you using deception or treachery to obtain a certain position, or if they can tell you are giving less than your all, or if they detect that you have a bad attitude toward your superiors, then you have given God and his followers a bad name.
Your faith, your attitude, and your work all speak loudly to those around you. Will you bring honor or dishonor to God's name?

For the next note on "Job Performance," turn to p. 872.

We Should Be above Criticism Read DANIEL 6:3-4

What set Daniel apart from the other administrators? Why was he promoted to such great responsibility? Verse 3 tells us that he had great ability, which has also been translated as "an excellent spirit." In other words, Daniel's spiritual life was not merely an afterthought or something he pursued when he found the time in his busy schedule. His life revolved around his commitment to God. It affected and permeated everything he did.

His faith produced such a high level of integrity and excellence in his work that his peers could find nothing in him to criticize. They couldn't label him as a hypocrite, and he left them nothing to hang their doubts on. So these jealous administrators devised a plan to make Daniel fall. They had the king pass a law that made it illegal for any person—including Daniel—to pray to anyone other than the king. Daniel's uncompromising faith got him thrown into the lions' den for violating this law. But God protected Daniel, and his testimony became even greater.

Living a life above reproach is one of the greatest testimonies we can have for the Lord. Like Daniel, we need to strive to live honestly and with integrity. That means we work hard and do a good job when we are at our place of employment. It also means that we don't cheat or steal and that we live by high standards of moral conduct at home as well.

Show that you really are dependable, trustworthy, and honest. As you do, you will bring glory to God.

For the next note on "Honesty and Integrity," turn to p. 1096.

CORNER STONES

---

ability, the king made plans to place him over the entire empire. ⁴Then the other administrators and princes began searching for some fault in the way Daniel was handling his affairs, but they couldn't find anything to criticize. He was faithful and honest and always responsible. ⁵So they concluded, "Our only chance of finding grounds for accusing Daniel will be in connection with the requirements of his religion."

⁶So the administrators and princes went to the king and said, "Long live King Darius! ⁷We administrators, prefects, princes, advisers, and other officials have unanimously agreed that Your Majesty should make a law that will be strictly enforced. Give orders that for the next thirty days anyone who prays to anyone, divine or human—except to Your Majesty—will be thrown to the lions. ⁸And let Your Majesty issue and sign this law so it cannot be changed, a law of the Medes and Persians, which cannot be revoked." ⁹So King Darius signed the law.

¹⁰But when Daniel learned that the law had been signed, he went home and knelt down as usual in his upstairs room, with its windows open toward Jerusalem. He prayed three times a day, just as he had always done, giving thanks to his God. ¹¹The officials went together to Daniel's house and found him praying and asking for God's help. ¹²So they went back to the king and reminded him about his law. "Did you not sign a law that for the next thirty days anyone who prays to anyone, divine or human—except to Your Majesty—will be thrown to the lions?"

"Yes," the king replied, "that decision stands; it is a law of the Medes and Persians, which cannot be revoked."

¹³Then they told the king, "That man Daniel, one of the captives from Judah, is paying no attention to you or your law. He still prays to his God three times a day."

¹⁴Hearing this, the king was very angry with himself for signing the law, and he tried to find a way to save Daniel. He spent the rest of the day looking for a way to get Daniel out of this predicament. ¹⁵In the evening the men went together to the king and said, "Your Majesty knows that according to the law of the Medes and the Persians, no law that the king signs can be changed."

¹⁶So at last the king gave orders for Daniel to be arrested and thrown into the den of lions. The king said to him, "May your God, whom you worship continually, rescue you." ¹⁷A stone was brought and placed over the mouth of the den. The king sealed the stone with his own royal seal and the seals of his nobles, so that no one could rescue Daniel from the lions. ¹⁸Then the king returned to his palace and spent the night fasting. He refused his usual entertainment and couldn't sleep at all that night.

¹⁹Very early the next morning, the king hurried out to the lions' den. ²⁰When he got there, he called out in anguish, "Daniel, servant of the living God! Was your God, whom you worship continually, able to rescue you from the lions?"

²¹Daniel answered, "Long live the king! ²²My God sent his angel to shut the lions' mouths so that they would not hurt me, for I have been found innocent in his sight. And I have not wronged you, Your Majesty."

²³The king was overjoyed and ordered that Daniel be lifted from the den. Not a scratch was found on him because he had trusted in his God. ²⁴Then the king gave orders to arrest the men who had maliciously accused Daniel. He had them thrown into the lions' den, along with their wives and children. The lions leaped on them and tore them apart before they even hit the floor of the den.

²⁵Then King Darius sent this message to the people of every race and nation and language throughout the world:

"Peace and prosperity to you!

²⁶"I decree that everyone throughout my kingdom should tremble with fear before the God of Daniel.

For he is the living God,
    and he will endure forever.
His kingdom will never be destroyed,
    and his rule will never end.
²⁷ He rescues and saves his people;
    he performs miraculous signs and wonders
    in the heavens and on earth.
He has rescued Daniel
    from the power of the lions."

²⁸So Daniel prospered during the reign of Darius and the reign of Cyrus the Persian.*

CHAPTER 7

Daniel's Vision of Four Beasts

Earlier, during the first year of King Belshazzar's reign in Babylon, Daniel had a dream and saw visions as he lay in his bed. He wrote the dream down, and this is what he saw.

²In my vision that night, I, Daniel, saw a great storm churning the surface of a great sea, with strong winds blowing from every direction. ³Then four huge beasts came up out of the water, each different from the others.

⁴The first beast was like a lion with eagles' wings. As I watched, its wings were pulled off, and it was left standing with its two hind feet on the ground, like a human being. And a human mind was given to it.

⁵Then I saw a second beast, and it looked like a bear. It was rearing up on one side, and it had three ribs in its mouth between its teeth. And I heard a voice saying to it, "Get up! Devour many people!"

⁶Then the third of these strange beasts appeared, and it looked like a leopard. It had four wings like birds' wings on its back, and it had four heads. Great authority was given to this beast.

⁷Then in my vision that night, I saw a fourth beast, terrifying, dreadful, and very strong. It devoured and crushed its victims with huge iron teeth and trampled what was left beneath its feet. It was different from any of the other beasts, and it had ten horns. ⁸As I was looking at the horns, suddenly another small horn appeared among them. Three of the first horns were wrenched out, roots and all, to make room for it. This little horn had eyes like human eyes and a mouth that was boasting arrogantly.

⁹I watched as thrones were put in place and the Ancient One* sat down to judge. His clothing was as white as snow, his hair like whitest wool. He sat on a fiery throne with wheels of blazing fire, ¹⁰and a river of fire flowed from his presence. Millions of angels ministered to him, and a hundred million stood to attend him. Then the court began its session, and the books were opened.

¹¹I continued to watch because I could hear the little horn's boastful speech. I kept watching until the fourth beast was killed and its body was destroyed by fire. ¹²As for the other three beasts, their authority was taken from them, but they were allowed to live for a while longer.*

¹³As my vision continued that night, I saw someone who looked like a man* coming with the clouds of heaven. He approached the Ancient One and was led into his presence. ¹⁴He was given authority, honor, and royal power over all the nations of the world, so that people of every race and nation and language would obey him. His rule is eternal—it will never end. His kingdom will never be destroyed.

The Vision Is Explained

¹⁵I, Daniel, was troubled by all I had seen, and my visions terrified me. ¹⁶So I approached one of those standing beside the throne and asked him what it all meant. He explained it to me like this: ¹⁷"These four huge beasts represent four kingdoms that will arise from the earth.

6:28 Or *of Darius, that is, the reign of Cyrus the Persian.*   7:9 Aramaic *an Ancient of Days;* also in 7:13, 22.   7:12 Aramaic *for a season and a time.*   7:13 Or *like a Son of Man;* Aramaic reads *like a son of man.*

18But in the end, the holy people of the Most High will be given the kingdom, and they will rule forever and ever."

19Then I wanted to know the true meaning of the fourth beast, the one so different from the others and so terrifying. It devoured and crushed its victims with iron teeth and bronze claws, and it trampled what was left beneath its feet. 20I also asked about the ten horns on the fourth beast's head and the little horn that came up afterward and destroyed three of the other horns. This was the horn that seemed greater than the others and had human eyes and a mouth that was boasting arrogantly. 21As I watched, this horn was waging war against the holy people and was defeating them, 22until the Ancient One came and judged in favor of the holy people of the Most High. Then the time arrived for the holy people to take over the kingdom.

23Then he said to me, "This fourth beast is the fourth world power that will rule the earth. It will be different from all the others. It will devour the whole world, trampling everything in its path. 24Its ten horns are ten kings that will rule that empire. Then another king will arise, different from the other ten, who will subdue three of them. 25He will defy the Most High and wear down the holy people of the Most High. He will try to change their sacred festivals and laws, and they will be placed under his control for a time, times, and half a time.

26"But then the court will pass judgment, and all his power will be taken away and completely destroyed. 27Then the sovereignty, power, and greatness of all the kingdoms under heaven will be given to the holy people of the Most High. They will rule forever, and all rulers will serve and obey them."

28That was the end of the vision. I, Daniel, was terrified by my thoughts and my face was pale with fear, but I kept these things to myself.

CHAPTER **8**
Daniel's Vision of a Ram and Goat

During the third year of King Belshazzar's reign, I, Daniel, saw another vision, following the one that had already appeared to me. 2This time I was at the fortress of Susa, in the province of Elam, standing beside the Ulai River.* 3As I looked up, I saw in front of me a ram with two long horns standing beside the river.* One of the horns was longer than the other, even though it had begun to grow later than the shorter one.

4The ram butted everything out of its way to the west, to the north, and to the south, and no one could stand against it or help its victims. It did as it pleased and became very great.

5While I was watching, suddenly a male goat appeared from the west, crossing the land so swiftly that it didn't even touch the ground. This goat, which had one very large horn between its eyes, 6headed toward the two-horned ram that I had seen standing beside the river. 7The goat charged furiously at the ram and struck it, breaking off both its horns. Now the ram was helpless, and the goat knocked it down and trampled it. There was no one who could rescue the ram from the goat's power.

8The goat became very powerful. But at the height of its power, its large horn was broken off. In the large horn's place grew four prominent horns pointing in the four directions of the earth. 9From one of the prominent horns came a small horn whose power grew very great. It extended toward the south and the east and toward the glorious land of Israel. 10His power reached to the heavens where it attacked the heavenly armies, throwing some of the heavenly beings and stars to the ground and trampling them. 11He even challenged the Commander of heaven's armies by canceling the daily sacrifices offered to him and by destroying his Temple. 12But the army of heaven was restrained from destroying him for this sin. As a result, sacrilege was committed against the Temple ceremonies, and truth was overthrown. The horn succeeded in everything it did.*

13Then I heard two of the holy ones talking to each other. One of them said, "How long will the events of this vision last? How long will the rebellion that causes desecration stop the daily sacrifices? How long will the Temple and heaven's armies be trampled on?"

14The other replied, "It will take twenty-three hundred evenings and mornings; then the Temple will be restored."

Gabriel Explains the Vision

15As I, Daniel, was trying to understand the meaning of this vision, someone who looked like a man suddenly stood in front of me. 16And I heard a human voice calling out from the Ulai River, "Gabriel, tell this man the meaning of his vision."

17As Gabriel approached the place where I was standing, I became so terrified that I fell to the ground. "Son of man," he said, "you must understand that the events you have seen in your vision relate to the time of the end."

8:2 Or *the Ulai Gate;* also in 8:16.   8:3 Or *the gate;* also in 8:6.   8:11-12 The meaning of the Hebrew for these verses is uncertain.

18While he was speaking, I fainted and lay there with my face to the ground. But Gabriel roused me with a touch and helped me to my feet. 19Then he said, "I am here to tell you what will happen later in the time of wrath. What you have seen pertains to the very end of time. 20The two-horned ram represents the kings of Media and Persia. 21The shaggy male goat represents the king of Greece,* and the large horn between its eyes represents the first king of the Greek Empire. 22The four prominent horns that replaced the one large horn show that the Greek Empire will break into four sections with four kings, none of them as great as the first.

23 " At the end of their rule, when their sin is at its height, a fierce king, a master of intrigue, will rise to power. 24He will become very strong, but not by his own power. He will cause a shocking amount of destruction and succeed in everything he does. He will destroy powerful leaders and devastate the holy people. 25He will be a master of deception, defeating many by catching them off guard. Without warning he will destroy them. He will even take on the Prince of princes in battle, but he will be broken, though not by human power.

26"This vision about the twenty-three hundred evenings and mornings* is true. But none of these things will happen for a long time, so do not tell anyone about them yet."

27Then I, Daniel, was overcome and lay sick for several days. Afterward I got up and performed my duties for the king, but I was greatly troubled by the vision and could not understand it.

CHAPTER 9
Daniel's Prayer for His People

It was the first year of the reign of Darius the Mede, the son of Ahasuerus, who became king of the Babylonians.* 2During the first year of his reign, I, Daniel, was studying the writings of the prophets. I learned from the word of the LORD, as recorded by Jeremiah the prophet, that Jerusalem must lie desolate for seventy years.* 3So I turned to the Lord God and pleaded with him in prayer and fasting. I wore rough sackcloth and sprinkled myself with ashes.

4I prayed to the LORD my God and confessed: "O Lord, you are a great and awesome God! You always fulfill your promises of unfailing love to those who love you and keep your commands. 5But we have sinned and done wrong. We have rebelled against you and scorned your commands and regulations. 6We have refused to listen to your servants the prophets, who spoke your messages to our kings and princes and ancestors and to all the people of the land.

7"Lord, you are in the right; but our faces are covered with shame, just as you see us now. This is true of us all, including the people of Judah and Jerusalem and all Israel, scattered near and far, wherever you have driven us because of our disloyalty to you. 8O LORD, we and our kings, princes, and ancestors are covered with shame because we have sinned against you. 9But the Lord our God is merciful and forgiving, even though we have rebelled against him. 10We have not obeyed the LORD our God, for we have not followed the laws he gave us through his servants the prophets. 11All Israel has disobeyed your law and turned away, refusing to listen to your voice.

"So now the solemn curses and judgments written in the law of Moses, the servant of God, have been poured out against us because of our sin. 12You have done exactly what you warned you would do against us and our rulers. Never in all history has there been a disaster like the one that happened in Jerusalem. 13Every curse written against us in the law of Moses has come true. All the troubles he predicted have taken place. But we have refused to seek mercy from the LORD our God by turning from our sins and recognizing his truth. 14The LORD has brought against us the disaster he prepared, for we did not obey him, and the LORD our God is just in everything he does.

15"O Lord our God, you brought lasting honor to your name by rescuing your people from Egypt in a great display of power. But we have sinned and are full of wickedness. 16In view of all your faithful mercies, Lord, please turn your furious anger away from your city of Jerusalem, your holy mountain. All the neighboring nations mock Jerusalem and your people because of our sins and the sins of our ancestors.

17"O our God, hear your servant's prayer! Listen as I plead. For your own sake, Lord, smile again on your desolate sanctuary.

18"O my God, listen to me and hear my request. Open your eyes and see our wretchedness. See how your city lies in ruins—for everyone knows that it is yours. We do not ask because we deserve help, but because you are so merciful.

19"O Lord, hear. O Lord, forgive. O Lord, listen and act! For your own sake, O my God, do not delay, for your people and your city bear your name."

8:21 Hebrew *of Javan.* 8:26 Hebrew *about the evenings and mornings;* compare 8:14. 9:1 Or *the Chaldeans.* 9:2 See Jer 25:11-12; 29:10.

How Are Angels Involved in Our Prayers? Read DANIEL 10:1–11:1

This is an amazing behind-the-scenes look at what takes place when people pray. Here we see the battle that rages between the angelic activity on God's side and the demonic activity on the devil's side. According to the story, Daniel was praying on earth. God heard him in heaven and dispatched an angel with a special message in answer to his prayer. Yet, somewhere between heaven and earth, between the visible and the invisible, this angel was accosted by an evil angel, and a battle ensued. After a number of days of warfare (twenty-one, to be exact), God dispatched a higher ranking angel, Michael the archangel. And finally Daniel received his message.

Many times we don't realize how important and significant our prayers really are—especially when we are praying for the salvation of a loved one. But this passage should show you what a high priority God places upon answering your prayers. God answers our prayers in one of three ways: yes, no, or wait. Yet, as in Daniel's case, the "wait" may be more complex than we realize. While an angel may not directly deliver our message, an affirmative answer to your prayer could spark a powerful supernatural battle. Perhaps you have been praying for someone to come to Christ, or for a "spiritual awakening" in your city, or for a specific opportunity to share your faith, but your prayer seems to be going unanswered. Take heart, and remember that God does hear your prayers. In the meantime, however, keep praying. If Daniel had given up, he could have missed out on this great spiritual blessing. Bear in mind that delays are not necessarily denials.

For the next note on "What Are Angels?" turn to p. 1128.

CORNER STONES

Gabriel's Message about the Exile

20I went on praying and confessing my sin and the sins of my people, pleading with the LORD my God for Jerusalem, his holy mountain. 21As I was praying, Gabriel, whom I had seen in the earlier vision, came swiftly to me at the time of the evening sacrifice. 22He explained to me, "Daniel, I have come here to give you insight and understanding. 23The moment you began praying, a command was given. I am here to tell you what it was, for God loves you very much. Now listen, so you can understand the meaning of your vision.

24 "A period of seventy sets of seven* has been decreed for your people and your holy city to put down rebellion, to bring an end to sin, to atone for guilt, to bring in everlasting righteousness, to confirm the prophetic vision, and to anoint the Most Holy Place.* 25Now listen and understand! Seven sets of seven plus sixty-two sets of seven* will pass from the time the command is given to rebuild Jerusalem until the Anointed One* comes. Jerusalem will be rebuilt with streets and strong defenses,* despite the perilous times.

26"After this period of sixty-two sets of seven,* the Anointed One will be killed, appearing to have accomplished nothing, and a ruler will arise whose armies will destroy the city and the Temple. The end will come with a flood, and war and its miseries are decreed from that time to the very end. 27He will make a treaty with the people for a period of one set of seven,* but after half this time, he will put an end to the sacrifices and offerings. Then as a climax to all his terrible deeds,* he will set up a sacrilegious object that causes desecration,* until the end that has been decreed is poured out on this defiler."

CHAPTER 10

Daniel's Vision of a Messenger

In the third year of the reign of King Cyrus of Persia, Daniel (also known as Belteshazzar) had another vision. It concerned events certain to happen in the future—times of war and great hardship—and Daniel understood what the vision meant.

2When this vision came to me, I, Daniel, had been in mourning for three weeks. 3All that time I had eaten no rich food or meat, had drunk no wine, and had used no fragrant oils. 4On

9:24a Hebrew *70 sevens.* 9:24b Or *the Most Holy One.* 9:25a Hebrew *Seven sevens plus 62 sevens.* 9:25b Or *an anointed one.* 9:25c Or *and a moat,* or *and trenches.* 9:26 Hebrew *After 62 sevens.* 9:27a Hebrew *for one seven.* 9:27b Hebrew *on the wing of abominations;* the meaning of the Hebrew is uncertain. 9:27c Hebrew *an abomination of desolation.*

April 23,* as I was standing beside the great Tigris River, 5I looked up and saw a man dressed in linen clothing, with a belt of pure gold around his waist. 6His body looked like a dazzling gem. From his face came flashes like lightning, and his eyes were like flaming torches. His arms and feet shone like polished bronze, and his voice was like the roaring of a vast multitude of people.

7I, Daniel, am the only one who saw this vision. The men with me saw nothing, but they were suddenly terrified and ran away to hide. 8So I was left there all alone to watch this amazing vision. My strength left me, my face grew deathly pale, and I felt very weak. 9When I heard him speak, I fainted and lay there with my face to the ground.

10Just then a hand touched me and lifted me, still trembling, to my hands and knees. 11And the man said to me, "O Daniel, greatly loved of God, listen carefully to what I have to say to you. Stand up, for I have been sent to you." When he said this to me, I stood up, still trembling with fear.

12Then he said, "Don't be afraid, Daniel. Since the first day you began to pray for understanding and to humble yourself before your God, your request has been heard in heaven. I have come in answer to your prayer. 13But for twenty-one days the spirit prince* of the kingdom of Persia blocked my way. Then Michael, one of the archangels,* came to help me, and I left him there with the spirit prince of the kingdom of Persia.* 14Now I am here to explain what will happen to your people in the future, for this vision concerns a time yet to come."

15While he was speaking to me, I looked down at the ground, unable to say a word. 16Then the one who looked like a man* touched my lips, and I opened my mouth and began to speak. I said to the one standing in front of me, "I am terrified by the vision I have seen, my lord, and I am very weak. 17How can someone like me, your servant, talk to you, my lord? My strength is gone, and I can hardly breathe."

18Then the one who looked like a man touched me again, and I felt my strength returning. 19"Don't be afraid," he said, "for you are deeply loved by God. Be at peace; take heart and be strong!"

As he spoke these words, I suddenly felt stronger and said to him, "Now you may speak, my lord, for you have strengthened me."

20He replied, "Do you know why I have come?

Soon I must return to fight against the spirit prince of the kingdom of Persia, and then against the spirit prince of the kingdom of Greece.* 21But before I do that, I will tell you what is written in the Book of Truth. (There is no one to help me against these spirit princes except Michael, your spirit prince.* 1I have been standing beside Michael* as his support and defense since the first year of the reign of Darius the Mede.)

CHAPTER 11

Kings of the South and North

2 "Now then, I will reveal the truth to you. Three more Persian kings will reign, to be succeeded by a fourth, far richer than the others. Using his wealth for political advantage, he will stir up everyone to war against the kingdom of Greece.*

3 "Then a mighty king will rise to power who will rule a vast kingdom and accomplish everything he sets out to do. 4But at the height of his power, his kingdom will be broken apart and divided into four parts. It will not be ruled by the king's descendants, nor will the kingdom hold the authority it once had. For his empire will be uprooted and given to others.

5 "The king of the south will increase in power, but one of this king's own officials will become more powerful than he and will rule his kingdom with great strength.

6 "Some years later, an alliance will be formed between the king of the north and the king of the south. The daughter of the king of the south will be given in marriage to the king of the north to secure the alliance, but she will lose her influence over him, and so will her father. She will be given up along with her supporters. 7But when one of her relatives* becomes king of the south, he will raise an army and enter the fortress of the king of the north and defeat him. 8When he returns again to Egypt, he will carry back their idols with him, along with priceless gold and silver dishes. For some years afterward he will leave the king of the north alone.

9 "Later the king of the north will invade the realm of the king of the south but will soon return to his own land. 10However, the sons of the king of the north will assemble a mighty army that will advance like a flood and carry the battle as far as the enemy's fortress. 11Then the king of the south, in great anger, will rally

10:4 Hebrew *On the twenty-fourth day of the first month.* This date in the book of Daniel can be cross-checked with dates in surviving Persian records and can be related accurately to our modern calendar. This day of the Hebrew lunar calendar occurred on April 23, 536 B.C. 10:13a Hebrew *the prince;* also in 10:13c, 20. 10:13b Hebrew *the chief princes.* 10:13c As in one Greek version; Hebrew reads *and I was left there with the kings of Persia.* The meaning of the Hebrew is uncertain. 10:16 As in most manuscripts of the Masoretic Text; one manuscript of the Masoretic Text and one Greek version read *Then something that looked like a human hand.* 10:20 Hebrew *of Javan.* 10:21 Hebrew *against these except Michael, your prince.* 11:1 Hebrew *him.* 11:2 Hebrew *of Javan.* 11:7 Hebrew *a branch from her roots.*

against the vast forces assembled by the king of the north and will defeat them. ¹²After the enemy army is swept away, the king of the south will be filled with pride and will have many thousands of his enemies killed. But his success will be short lived.

¹³ "A few years later, the king of the north will return with a fully equipped army far greater than the one he lost. ¹⁴At that time there will be a general uprising against the king of the south. Lawless ones among your own people will join them in order to fulfill the vision, but they will not succeed. ¹⁵Then the king of the north will come and lay siege to a fortified city and capture it. The best troops of the south will not be able to stand in the face of the onslaught.

¹⁶ "The king of the north will march onward unopposed; none will be able to stop him. He will pause in the glorious land of Israel, intent on destroying it. ¹⁷He will make plans to come with the might of his entire kingdom and will form an alliance with the king of the south. He will give him a daughter in marriage in order to overthrow the kingdom from within, but his plan will fail.

¹⁸ "After this, he will turn his attention to the coastal cities and conquer many. But a commander from another land will put an end to his insolence and will cause him to retreat in shame. ¹⁹He will take refuge in his own fortresses but will stumble and fall, and he will be seen no more.

²⁰ "His successor will be remembered as the king who sent a tax collector to maintain the royal splendor, but after a very brief reign, he will die, though neither in battle nor open conflict.

²¹ "The next to come to power will be a despicable man who is not directly in line for royal succession. But he will slip in when least expected and take over the kingdom by flattery and intrigue. ²²Before him great armies will be swept away, including a covenant prince. ²³By making deceitful promises, he will make various alliances. With a mere handful of followers, he will become strong. ²⁴Without warning he will enter the richest areas of the land and do something that none of his predecessors ever did—distribute among his followers the plunder and wealth of the rich. He will plot the overthrow of strongholds, but this will last for only a short while.

²⁵ "Then he will stir up his courage and raise a great army against the king of the south. The king of the south will go to battle with a mighty army, but to no avail, for plots against him will succeed.

²⁶Those of his own household will bring his downfall. His army will be swept away, and many will be killed. ²⁷Seeking nothing but each other's harm, these kings will plot against each other at the conference table, attempting to deceive each other. But it will make no difference, for an end will still come at the appointed time.

²⁸ "The king of the north will then return home with great riches. On the way he will set himself against the people of the holy covenant, doing much damage before continuing his journey.

²⁹ "Then at the appointed time he will once again invade the south, but this time the result will be different. ³⁰For warships from western coastlands* will scare him off, and he will withdraw and return home. But he will vent his anger against the people of the holy covenant and reward those who forsake the covenant. ³¹His army will take over the Temple fortress, polluting the sanctuary, putting a stop to the daily sacrifices, and setting up the sacrilegious object that causes desecration.* ³²He will flatter those who have violated the covenant and win them over to his side. But the people who know their God will be strong and will resist him.

³³ "Those who are wise will give instruction to many. But for a time many of these teachers will die by fire and sword, or they will be jailed and robbed. ³⁴While all these persecutions are going on, a little help will arrive, though many who join them will not be sincere. ³⁵And some who are wise will fall victim to persecution. In this way, they will be refined and cleansed and made pure until the time of the end, for the appointed time is still to come.

³⁶ "The king will do as he pleases, exalting himself and claiming to be greater than every god there is, even blaspheming the God of gods. He will succeed—until the time of wrath is completed. For what has been determined will surely take place. ³⁷He will have no regard for the gods of his ancestors, or for the god beloved of women, or for any other god, for he will boast that he is greater than them all. ³⁸Instead of these, he will worship the god of fortresses—a god his ancestors never knew—and lavish on him gold, silver, precious stones, and costly gifts. ³⁹Claiming this foreign god's help, he will attack the strongest fortresses. He will honor those who submit to him, appointing them to positions of authority and dividing the land among them as their reward.*

11:30 Hebrew *from Kittim.*   11:31 Hebrew *the abomination of desolation.*   11:39 Or *at a price.*

40"Then at the time of the end, the king of the south will attack him, and the king of the north will storm out against him with chariots, cavalry, and a vast navy. He will invade various lands and sweep through them like a flood. 41He will enter the glorious land of Israel, and many nations will fall, but Moab, Edom, and the best part of Ammon will escape. 42He will conquer many countries, and Egypt will not escape. 43He will gain control over the gold, silver, and treasures of Egypt, and the Libyans and Ethiopians* will be his servants.

44"But then news from the east and the north will alarm him, and he will set out in great anger to destroy many as he goes. 45He will halt between the glorious holy mountain and the sea and will pitch his royal tents there, but while he is there, his time will suddenly run out, and there will be no one to help him.

CHAPTER **12**
The Time of the End
"At that time Michael, the archangel* who stands guard over your nation, will arise. Then there will be a time of anguish greater than any since nations first came into existence. But at that time every one of your people whose name is written in the book will be rescued. 2Many of those whose bodies lie dead and buried will rise up, some to everlasting life and some to shame and everlasting contempt. 3Those who are wise will shine as bright as the sky, and those who turn many to righteousness will shine like stars forever. 4But you, Daniel, keep this prophecy a secret; seal up the book until the time of the end. Many will rush here and there, and knowledge will increase."

5Then I, Daniel, looked and saw two others standing on opposite banks of the river. 6One of them asked the man dressed in linen, who was now standing above the river, "How long will it be until these shocking events happen?"

7The man dressed in linen, who was standing above the river, raised both his hands toward heaven and took this solemn oath by the one who lives forever: "It will go on for a time, times, and half a time. When the shattering of the holy people has finally come to an end, all these things will have happened."

8I heard what he said, but I did not understand what he meant. So I asked, "How will all this finally end, my lord?"

9But he said, "Go now, Daniel, for what I have said is for the time of the end. 10Many will be purified, cleansed, and refined by these trials. But the wicked will continue in their wickedness, and none of them will understand. Only those who are wise will know what it means.

11"From the time the daily sacrifice is taken away and the sacrilegious object that causes desecration* is set up to be worshiped, there will be 1,290 days. 12And blessed are those who wait and remain until the end of the 1,335 days!

13"As for you, go your way until the end. You will rest, and then at the end of the days, you will rise again to receive the inheritance set aside for you."

11:43 Hebrew *Cushites.*   12:1 Hebrew *the great prince.*   12:11 Hebrew *the abomination of desolation.*

Hosea

CHAPTER 1

The LORD gave these messages to Hosea son of Beeri during the years when Uzziah, Jotham, Ahaz, and Hezekiah were kings of Judah, and Jeroboam son of Jehoash* was king of Israel.

Hosea's Wife and Children

2When the LORD first began speaking to Israel through Hosea, he said to him, "Go and marry a prostitute,* so some of her children will be born to you from other men. This will illustrate the way my people have been untrue to me, openly committing adultery against the LORD by worshiping other gods."

3So Hosea married Gomer, the daughter of Diblaim, and she became pregnant and gave Hosea a son. 4And the LORD said, "Name the child Jezreel, for I am about to punish King Jehu's dynasty to avenge the murders he committed at Jezreel. 5In fact, I will put an end to Israel's independence by breaking its military power in the Jezreel Valley."

6Soon Gomer became pregnant again and gave birth to a daughter. And the LORD said to Hosea, "Name your daughter Lo-ruhamah—'Not loved'—for I will no longer show love to the people of Israel or forgive them. 7But I, the LORD their God, will show love to the people of Judah. I will personally free them from their enemies without any help from weapons or armies."

8After Gomer had weaned Lo-ruhamah, she again became pregnant and gave birth to a second son. 9And the LORD said, "Name him Lo-ammi—'Not my people'—for Israel is not my people, and I am not their God. 10Yet the time will come when Israel will prosper and become a great nation. In that day its people will be like the sands of the seashore—too many to count! Then,

at the place where they were told, 'You are not my people,' it will be said, 'You are children of the living God.' 11Then the people of Judah and Israel will unite under one leader, and they will return from exile together. What a day that will be—the day of Jezreel*—when God will again plant his people in his land. 1In that day you will call your brothers Ammi—'My people.' And you will call your sisters Ruhamah—'The ones I love.'

CHAPTER 2

Charges against an Unfaithful Wife

2"But now, call Israel* to account, for she is no longer my wife, and I am no longer her husband. Tell her to take off her garish makeup and suggestive clothing and to stop playing the prostitute. 3If she doesn't, I will strip her as naked as she was on the day she was born. I will leave her to die of thirst, as in a desert or a dry and barren wilderness. 4And I will not love her children as I would my own because they are not my children! They were conceived in adultery. 5For their mother is a shameless prostitute and became pregnant in a shameful way. She said, 'I'll run after other lovers and sell myself to them for food and drink, for clothing of wool and linen, and for olive oil.'

6"But I will fence her in with thornbushes. I will block the road to make her lose her way. 7When she runs after her lovers, she won't be able to catch up with them. She will search for them but not find them. Then she will think, 'I might as well return to my husband because I was better off with him than I am now.' 8She doesn't realize that it was I who gave her everything she has—the grain, the wine, the olive oil. Even the gold and silver she used in worshiping the god Baal were gifts from me!

1:1 Hebrew *Joash*, a variant name for Jehoash.   1:2 Or *a promiscuous woman*.   1:11 *Jezreel* means "God plants."   2:2 Hebrew *call your mother*.

9 "But now I will take back the wine and ripened grain I generously provided each harvest season. I will take away the linen and wool clothing I gave her to cover her nakedness. 10 I will strip her naked in public, while all her lovers look on. No one will be able to rescue her from my hands. 11 I will put an end to her annual festivals, her new moon celebrations, and her Sabbath days—all her appointed festivals. 12 I will destroy her vineyards and orchards, things she claims her lovers gave her. I will let them grow into tangled thickets, where only wild animals will eat the fruit. 13 I will punish her for all the times she deserted me, when she burned incense to her images of Baal, put on her earrings and jewels, and went out looking for her lovers," says the LORD.

The LORD's Love for Unfaithful Israel

14 "But then I will win her back once again. I will lead her out into the desert and speak tenderly to her there. 15 I will return her vineyards to her and transform the Valley of Trouble* into a gateway of hope. She will give herself to me there, as she did long ago when she was young, when I freed her from her captivity in Egypt.

16 "In that coming day," says the LORD, "you will call me 'my husband' instead of 'my master.'* 17 O Israel, I will cause you to forget your images of Baal; even their names will no longer be spoken. 18 At that time I will make a covenant with all the wild animals and the birds and the animals that scurry along the ground so that they will not harm you. I will remove all weapons of war from the land, all swords and bows, so you can live unafraid in peace and safety. 19 I will make you my wife forever, showing you righteousness and justice, unfailing love and compassion. 20 I will be faithful to you and make you mine, and you will finally know me as LORD.

21 "In that day," says the LORD, "I will answer the pleading of the sky for clouds, which will pour down water on the earth in answer to its cries for rain. 22 Then the earth will answer the thirsty cries of the grain, the grapes, and the olive trees for moisture. And the whole grand chorus will sing together, 'Jezreel'—'God plants!'

23 "At that time I will plant a crop of Israelites and raise them for myself! I will show love to those I called 'Not loved.'* And to those I called 'Not my people,'* I will say, 'Now you are my people.' Then they will reply, 'You are our God!'"

CHAPTER 3

Hosea's Wife Is Redeemed

Then the LORD said to me, "Go and get your wife again. Bring her back to you and love her, even though she loves adultery. For the LORD still loves Israel even though the people have turned to other gods, offering them choice gifts.*"

2 So I bought her back for fifteen pieces of silver* and about five bushels of barley and a measure of wine.* 3 Then I said to her, "You must live in my house for many days and stop your prostitution. During this time, you will not have sexual intercourse with anyone, not even with me.*"

4 This illustrates that Israel will be a long time without a king or prince, and without sacrifices, temple, priests, or even idols! 5 But afterward the people will return to the LORD their God and to David's descendant, their king.* They will come trembling in awe to the LORD, and they will receive his good gifts in the last days.

CHAPTER 4

The LORD's Case against Israel

Hear the word of the LORD, O people of Israel! The LORD has filed a lawsuit against you, saying: "There is no faithfulness, no kindness, no knowledge of God in your land. 2 You curse and lie and kill and steal and commit adultery. There is violence everywhere, with one murder after another. 3 That is why your land is not producing. It is filled with sadness, and all living things are becoming sick and dying. Even the animals, birds, and fish have begun to disappear.

4 "Don't point your finger at someone else and try to pass the blame! Look, you priests, my complaint is with you!* 5 As a sentence for your crimes, you will stumble in broad daylight, just as you might at night, and so will your false prophets. And I will destroy your mother, Israel. 6 My people are being destroyed because they don't know me. It is all your fault, you priests, for you yourselves refuse to know me. Now I refuse to recognize you as my priests. Since you have forgotten the laws of your God, I will forget to bless your children. 7 The more priests there are, the more they sin against me. They have exchanged* the glory of God for the disgrace of idols.

8 "The priests get fed when the people sin and bring their sin offerings to them. So the priests are glad when the people sin! 9 Like priests, like

2:15 Hebrew *valley of Achor.* 2:16 Hebrew *'my baal.'* 2:23a Hebrew *Lo-ruhamah;* see 1:6. 2:23b Hebrew *Lo-ammi;* see 1:9. 3:1 Hebrew *raisin cakes.* 3:2a Hebrew *15 shekels of silver,* about 6 ounces or 171 grams in weight. 3:2b As in Greek version, which reads *a homer* [182 liters] *of barley and a measure of wine;* Hebrew reads *a homer of barley and a lethech* [2.5 bushels or 91 liters] *of barley.* 3:3 Or *and I will live with you.* 3:5 Hebrew *to David their king.* 4:4 Hebrew *Your people are like those with a complaint against the priests.* 4:7 As in Syriac version and an ancient Hebrew tradition; Masoretic Text reads *I will exchange.*

people'—since the priests are wicked, the people are wicked, too. So now I will punish both priests and people for all their wicked deeds. 10They will eat and still be hungry. Though they do a big business as prostitutes, they will have no children, for they have deserted the LORD to worship other gods.

11"Alcohol and prostitution have robbed my people of their brains. 12They are asking a piece of wood to tell them what to do! They think a stick can tell them the future! Longing after idols has made them foolish. They have played the prostitute, serving other gods and deserting their God. 13They offer sacrifices to idols on the tops of mountains. They go up into the hills to burn incense in the pleasant shade of oaks, poplars, and other trees.

"That is why your daughters turn to prostitution, and your daughters-in-law commit adultery. 14Why should I punish them? For you men are doing the same thing, sinning with whores and shrine prostitutes. O foolish people! You will be destroyed, for you refuse to understand.

15"Though Israel is a prostitute, may Judah avoid such guilt. O Judah, do not join with those who worship me insincerely at Gilgal and at Beth-aven.* Their worship is mere pretense as they take oaths in the LORD's name. 16Israel is as stubborn as a heifer, so the LORD will put her out to pasture. She will stand alone and unprotected, like a helpless lamb in an open field. 17Leave her alone because she is married to idolatry. 18The men of Israel finish up their drinking bouts and off they go to find some prostitutes. Their love for shame is greater than their love for honor.* 19So a mighty wind will sweep them away. They will die in shame because they offer sacrifices to idols.

CHAPTER 5
The Failure of Israel's Leaders

"Hear this, you priests and all of Israel's leaders! Listen, all you men of the royal family! These words of judgment are for you: You are doomed! For you have led the people into a snare by worshiping the idols at Mizpah and Tabor. 2You have dug a deep pit to trap them at Acacia.* But never forget—I will settle with all of you for what you have done. 3I know what you are like, O Israel! You have left me as a prostitute leaves her husband; you are utterly defiled. 4Your deeds won't let you return to your God. You are a prostitute through and through, and you cannot know the LORD.

5"The arrogance of Israel* testifies against her; she will stumble under her load of guilt. Judah, too, will fall with her. 6Then at last, they will come with their flocks and herds to offer sacrifices to the LORD. But it will be too late! They will not find him, because he has withdrawn from them, and they are now alone. 7For they have betrayed the honor of the LORD, bearing children that aren't his. Now their false religion will devour them, along with their wealth.

8"Blow the ram's horn in Gibeah! Sound the alarm in Ramah! Raise the battle cry in Beth-aven*! Lead on into battle, O warriors of Benjamin! 9One thing is certain, Israel*: When your day of punishment comes, you will become a heap of rubble.

10"The leaders of Judah have become as bad as thieves.* So I will pour my anger down on them like a waterfall. 11The people of Israel will be crushed and broken by my judgment because they are determined to worship idols. 12I will destroy Israel as a moth consumes wool. I will sap Judah's strength as dry rot weakens wood.

13"When Israel and Judah saw how sick they were, Israel turned to Assyria, to the great king there, but he could neither help nor cure them. 14I will tear at Israel and Judah as a lion rips apart its prey. I will carry them off, and there will be no one left to rescue them. 15Then I will return to my place until they admit their guilt and look to me for help. For as soon as trouble comes, they will search for me."

CHAPTER 6
A Call to Repentance

"Come, let us return to the LORD! He has torn us in pieces; now he will heal us. He has injured us; now he will bandage our wounds. 2In just a short time, he will restore us so we can live in his presence. 3Oh, that we might know the LORD! Let us press on to know him! Then he will respond to us as surely as the arrival of dawn or the coming of rains in early spring."

4"O Israel* and Judah, what should I do with you?" asks the LORD. "For your love vanishes like the morning mist and disappears like dew in the sunlight. 5I sent my prophets to cut you to pieces. I have slaughtered you with my words,

---

4:15 Beth-aven means "house of wickedness"; it is being used as another name for Bethel, which means "house of God."   4:18 As in Greek version; the meaning of the Hebrew is uncertain.   5:2 Hebrew at Shittim. The meaning of the Hebrew for this sentence is uncertain.
5:5 Hebrew Israel and Ephraim.   5:8 Beth-aven means "house of wickedness"; it is being used as another name for Bethel, which means "house of God."   5:9 Hebrew Ephraim, referring to the northern kingdom of Israel; also in 5:11, 12, 13, 14.   5:10 Hebrew have become as those who move a boundary marker.   6:4 Hebrew Ephraim, referring to the northern kingdom of Israel.

threatening you with death. My judgment will strike you as surely as day follows night. ⁶I want you to be merciful; I don't want your sacrifices. I want you to know God; that's more important than burnt offerings.

⁷"But like Adam, you broke my covenant and rebelled against me. ⁸Gilead is a city of sinners, tracked with footprints of blood. ⁹Its citizens are bands of robbers, lying in ambush for their victims. Gangs of priests murder travelers along the road to Shechem and practice every kind of sin. ¹⁰Yes, I have seen a horrible thing in Israel: My people have defiled themselves by chasing after other gods!

¹¹"O Judah, a harvest of punishment is also waiting for you, though I wanted so much to restore the fortunes of my people!

CHAPTER 7
Israel's Love for Wickedness

"I wanted to heal Israel, but its sins were far too great. Samaria is filled with liars, thieves, and bandits! ²Its people don't realize I am watching them. Their sinful deeds are all around them; I see them all! ³The people make the king glad with their wickedness. The princes laugh about the people's many lies. ⁴They are all adulterers, always aflame with lust. They are like an oven that is kept hot even while the baker is still kneading the dough.

⁵"On royal holidays, the princes get drunk. The king makes a fool of himself and drinks with those who are making fun of him. ⁶Their hearts blaze like a furnace with intrigue. Their plot smolders through the night, and in the morning it flames forth like a raging fire. ⁷They kill their kings one after another, and no one cries out to me for help.

⁸"My people of Israel* mingle with godless foreigners, picking up their evil ways. Now they have become as worthless as a half-baked cake! ⁹Worshiping foreign gods has sapped their strength, but they don't even know it. Israel is like an old man with graying hair, unaware of how weak and old he has become. ¹⁰His arrogance testifies against him, yet he doesn't return to the LORD his God or even try to find him.

¹¹"The people of Israel have become like silly, witless doves, first calling to Egypt, then flying to Assyria. ¹²But as they fly about, I will throw my net over them and bring them down like a bird from the sky. I will punish them for all their evil ways.*

¹³"How terrible it will be for my people who have deserted me! Let them die, for they have rebelled against me. I wanted to redeem them, but they have only spoken lies about me. ¹⁴They do not cry out to me with sincere hearts. Instead, they sit on their couches and wail. They cut themselves, begging foreign gods for crops and prosperity.

¹⁵"I trained them and made them strong, yet now they plot evil against me. ¹⁶They look everywhere except to heaven, to the Most High. They are like a crooked bow that always misses its target. Their leaders will be killed by their enemies because of their insolence toward me. Then the people of Egypt will laugh at them.

CHAPTER 8
Israel Harvests the Whirlwind

"Sound the alarm! The enemy descends like an eagle on the people of the LORD, for they have broken my covenant and revolted against my law. ²Now Israel pleads with me, 'Help us, for you are our God!' ³But it is too late! The people of Israel have rejected what is good, and now their enemies will chase after them. ⁴The people have appointed kings and princes, but not with my consent. By making idols for themselves from their silver and gold, they have brought about their own destruction.

⁵"O Samaria, I reject this calf—this idol you have made. My fury burns against you. How long will you be incapable of innocence? ⁶This calf you worship was crafted by your own hands! It is not God! Therefore, it must be smashed to bits.

⁷"They have planted the wind and will harvest the whirlwind. The stalks of wheat wither, producing no grain. And if there is any grain, foreigners will eat it. ⁸The people of Israel have been swallowed up; they lie among the nations like an old pot that no one wants. ⁹Like a wild donkey looking for a mate, they have gone up to Assyria. The people of Israel* have sold themselves to many lovers. ¹⁰But though they have sold themselves to many lands, I will now gather them together. Then they will writhe under the burden of the great king!

¹¹"Israel has built many altars to take away sin, but these very altars became places for sinning! ¹²Even though I gave them all my laws, they act as if those laws don't apply to them. ¹³The people of Israel love their rituals of sacrifice, but to me their sacrifices are all meaningless! I will call my people to account for their sins, and I will punish them. They will go back down to Egypt.

¹⁴"Israel has built great palaces, and Judah has fortified its cities. But they have both forgotten their Maker. Therefore, I will send down fire on their palaces and burn their fortresses."

7:8 Hebrew *Ephraim,* referring to the northern kingdom of Israel; also in 7:11.   7:12 Hebrew *I will punish them because of what was reported against them in the assembly.*   8:9 Hebrew *Ephraim,* referring to the northern kingdom of Israel; also in 8:11.

CHAPTER 9
Hosea Announces Israel's Punishment

O people of Israel, do not rejoice as others do. For you have been unfaithful to your God, hiring yourselves out like prostitutes, offering sacrifices to other gods on every threshing floor. ²So now your harvests will be too small to feed you. The grapes you gather will not quench your thirst. ³You may no longer stay here in this land of the LORD. You will be carried off to Egypt and Assyria, where you will live on food that is ceremonially unclean.

⁴There, far from home, you will not be allowed to pour out wine as a sacrifice to the LORD. None of the sacrifices you offer there will please him. Such sacrifices will be unclean, just as food touched by a person in mourning is unclean. All who present such sacrifices will be defiled. They may eat this food to feed themselves, but they may not offer it to the LORD.

⁵What then will you do on festival days? What will you do on days of feasting in the LORD's presence? ⁶Even if you escape destruction from Assyria, you will be conquered by Egypt. Memphis* will bury you. Briers will take over your treasures of silver; brambles will fill your homes.

⁷The time of Israel's punishment has come; the day of payment is almost here. Soon Israel will know this all too well. "The prophets are crazy!" the people shout. "The inspired men are mad!" So they taunt, for the nation is burdened with sin and shows only hatred for those who love God.

⁸The prophet is a watchman for my God over Israel,* yet traps are laid in front of him wherever he goes. He faces hostility even in the house of God. ⁹The things my people do are as depraved as what they did in Gibeah long ago. God will not forget. He will surely punish them for their sins.

¹⁰The LORD says, "O Israel, when I first found you, it was like finding fresh grapes in the desert! When I saw your ancestors, it was like seeing the first ripe figs of the season! But then they deserted me for Baal-peor, giving themselves to that shameful idol. Soon they became as vile as the god they worshiped. ¹¹The glory of Israel will fly away like a bird, for your children will die at birth or perish in the womb or never even be conceived. ¹²Even if your children do survive to grow up, I will take them from you. It will be a terrible day when I turn away and leave you alone. ¹³I have watched Israel become as beautiful and pleasant as Tyre. But now Israel will bring out her children to be slaughtered."

¹⁴O LORD, what should I request for your people? I will ask for wombs that don't give birth and breasts that give no milk.

¹⁵The LORD says, "All their wickedness began at Gilgal; there I began to hate them. I will drive them from my land because of their evil actions. I will love them no more because all their leaders are rebels. ¹⁶The people of Israel are stricken. Their roots are dried up; they will bear no more fruit. And if they give birth, I will slaughter their beloved children."

¹⁷My God will reject the people of Israel because they will not listen or obey. They will be wanderers, homeless among the nations.

CHAPTER 10
The LORD's Judgment against Israel

How prosperous Israel is—a luxuriant vine loaded with fruit! But the more wealth the people got, the more they poured it on the altars of their foreign gods. The richer the harvests they brought in, the more beautiful the statues and idols they built. ²The hearts of the people are fickle; they are guilty and must be punished. The LORD will break down their foreign altars and smash their many idols.

³Then they will say, "We have no king because we didn't fear the LORD. But what's the difference? What could a king do for us anyway?" ⁴They spout empty words and make promises they don't intend to keep. So perverted justice springs up among them like poisonous weeds in a farmer's field.

⁵The people of Samaria tremble for their calf idol at Beth-aven.* The people mourn over it, and the priests wail for it, because its glory will be stripped away. ⁶This idol they love so much will be carted away with them when they go as captives to Assyria, a gift to the great king there. Israel will be laughed at and shamed because its people have trusted in this idol. ⁷Samaria will be cut off, and its king will disappear like a chip of wood on an ocean wave. ⁸And the pagan shrines of Aven,* the place of Israel's sin, will crumble. Thorns and thistles will grow up around them. They will beg the mountains to bury them and the hills to fall on them.

⁹The LORD says, "O Israel, ever since that awful night in Gibeah, there has been only sin and more sin! You have made no progress whatsoever. Was it not right that the wicked men of Gibeah were attacked? ¹⁰Now I will attack you,

9:6 Memphis was the capital of northern Egypt.   9:8 Hebrew *Ephraim*, referring to the northern kingdom of Israel; also in 9:11, 13, 16.
10:5 *Beth-aven* means "house of wickedness"; it is being used as another name for Bethel, which means "house of God."   10:8 *Aven* is a reference to Beth-aven; see 10:5 and the note there.

too, for your rebellion and disobedience. I will call out the armies of the nations to punish you for your multiplied sins.

11 "Israel* is like a trained heifer accustomed to treading out the grain—an easy job that she loves. Now I will put a heavy yoke on her tender neck. I will drive her in front of the plow. Israel* and Judah must now break up the hard ground; their days of ease are gone. 12I said, 'Plant the good seeds of righteousness, and you will harvest a crop of my love. Plow up the hard ground of your hearts, for now is the time to seek the LORD, that he may come and shower righteousness upon you.'

13 "But you have cultivated wickedness and raised a thriving crop of sins. You have eaten the fruit of lies—trusting in your military might, believing that great armies could make your nation safe! 14Now the terrors of war will rise among your people. All your fortifications will fall, just as they did when Shalman destroyed Beth-arbel. Even mothers and children were dashed to death there. 15You will share that fate, Bethel, because of your great wickedness. When the day of judgment dawns, the king of Israel will be completely destroyed.

CHAPTER 11
The LORD's Love for Israel

"When Israel was a child, I loved him as a son, and I called my son out of Egypt. 2But the more I* called to him, the more he rebelled, offering sacrifices to the images of Baal and burning incense to idols. 3It was I who taught Israel* how to walk, leading him along by the hand. But he doesn't know or even care that it was I who took care of him. 4I led Israel along with my ropes of kindness and love. I lifted the yoke from his neck, and I myself stooped to feed him.

5 "But since my people refuse to return to me, they will go back to Egypt and will be forced to serve Assyria. 6War will swirl through their cities; their enemies will crash through their gates and destroy them, trapping them in their own evil plans. 7For my people are determined to desert me. They call me the Most High, but they don't truly honor me.

8 "Oh, how can I give you up, Israel? How can I let you go? How can I destroy you like Admah and Zeboiim? My heart is torn within me, and my compassion overflows. 9No, I will not pun-

ish you as much as my burning anger tells me to. I will not completely destroy Israel, for I am God and not a mere mortal. I am the Holy One living among you, and I will not come to destroy.

10 "For someday the people will follow the LORD. I will roar like a lion, and my people will return trembling from the west. 11Like a flock of birds, they will come from Egypt. Flying like doves, they will return from Assyria. And I will bring them home again," says the LORD.

Charges against Israel and Judah

12Israel surrounds me with lies and deceit, but Judah still walks with God and is faithful to the Holy One.*

CHAPTER 12

The people of Israel* feed on the wind; they chase after the east wind all day long. They multiply lies and violence; they make alliances with Assyria and cut deals with the Egyptians.

2Now the LORD is bringing a lawsuit against Judah. He is about to punish Jacob* for all his deceitful ways. 3Before Jacob was born, he struggled with his brother; when he became a man, he even fought with God. 4Yes, he wrestled with the angel and won. He wept and pleaded for a blessing from him. There at Bethel he met God face to face, and God spoke to him*—5the LORD God Almighty, the LORD is his name! 6So now, come back to your God! Act on the principles of love and justice, and always live in confident dependence on your God.

7But no, the people are like crafty merchants selling from dishonest scales—they love to cheat. 8Israel boasts, "I am rich, and I've gotten it all by myself! No one can say I got it by cheating! My record is spotless!"

9 "I am the LORD your God, who rescued you from your slavery in Egypt. And I will make you live in tents again, as you do each year when you celebrate the Festival of Shelters.* 10I sent my prophets to warn you with many visions and parables."

11But Gilead is filled with sinners who worship idols. And in Gilgal, too, they sacrifice bulls; their altars are lined up like the heaps of stone along the edges of a plowed field. 12Jacob fled to the land of Aram and earned a wife by tending sheep. 13Then the LORD led Jacob's descendants, the Israelites, out of Egypt by a

---

11:10a Hebrew *Ephraim*, referring to the northern kingdom of Israel.   11:10b Hebrew *Jacob*.   11:2 As in Greek version; Hebrew reads *they*.
11:3 Hebrew *Ephraim*, referring to the northern kingdom of Israel; also in 11:8, 9, 12.   11:12 Or *and Judah is unruly against God, the faithful Holy One.*   12:1 Hebrew *Ephraim*, referring to the northern kingdom of Israel; also in 12:8, 14.   12:2 *Jacob* means "he grasps at the heel"; this can also figuratively mean "he deceives."   12:4 As in Greek and Syriac versions; Hebrew reads *to us.*   12:9 Hebrew *as in the days of your appointed feast.*

prophet, who guided and protected them. 14But the people of Israel have bitterly provoked the LORD, so their Lord will now sentence them to death in payment for their sins.

CHAPTER 13
The LORD's Anger against Israel

In the past when the tribe of Ephraim spoke, the people shook with fear because the other Israelite tribes looked up to them. But the people of Ephraim sinned by worshiping Baal and thus sealed their destruction. 2Now they keep on sinning by making silver idols to worship—images shaped skillfully with human hands. "Sacrifice to these," they cry, "and kiss the calf idols!" 3Therefore, they will disappear like the morning mist, like dew in the morning sun, like chaff blown by the wind, like smoke from a chimney.

4"I am the LORD your God, who rescued you from your slavery in Egypt. You have no God but me, for there is no other savior. 5I took care of you in the wilderness, in that dry and thirsty land. 6But when you had eaten and were satisfied, then you became proud and forgot me. 7So now I will attack you like a lion, or like a leopard that lurks along the road. 8I will rip you to pieces like a bear whose cubs have been taken away. I will tear you apart and devour you like a hungry lion.

9"You are about to be destroyed, O Israel, though I am your helper. 10Where now is* your king? Why don't you call on him for help? Where are all the leaders of the land? You asked for them, now let them save you! 11In my anger I gave you kings, and in my fury I took them away.

12"The sins of Ephraim have been collected and stored away for punishment. 13The people have been offered new birth, but they are like a child who resists being born. How stubborn they are! How foolish! 14Should I ransom them from the grave? Should I redeem them from death? O death, bring forth your terrors! O grave, bring forth your plagues! For I will not relent! 15Ephraim was the most fruitful of all his brothers, but the east wind—a blast from the LORD—will arise in the desert. It will blow hard against the people of Ephraim, drying up their land. All their flowing springs and wells will disappear. Every precious thing they have will be plundered and carried away. 16The people of Samaria must bear the consequences of their

13:10 As in Greek and Syriac versions and Latin Vulgate; Hebrew reads *I will be.*

Prayer Enables Us to Seek Forgiveness Read HOSEA 14:1-7

Have you been weighted down by guilt over something you have said or done recently that displeases the Lord? Do you feel "crushed" by your sins like the people of Israel? If so, then your spiritual warning system is intact. Just as your body has a warning system called pain that alerts you to danger, your soul has a warning system called a conscience. Pain alerts us to a physical problem that needs attention in order to keep our bodies from suffering. A guilty conscience signals that something in our heart needs to be confronted and cleansed to keep our relationship with God from suffering.

The only real and effective way to remove our guilt is to confess our sin before God and ask his forgiveness. This is exactly what the Lord was asking of the Israelites in this passage, and he expects no less of us when we have fallen into sin. Notice the key elements of the type of prayer God desires when we ask for his forgiveness:

- Acknowledge that he is the Lord of your life.
- Confess your sin and ask for God's forgiveness.
- Make a commitment to praise him.
- Recognize that you cannot live the Christian life in your own strength.
- Commit yourself to turn to him in your times of trouble and temptation.

Once we have sincerely prayed a prayer for forgiveness, God makes a wonderful promise that relates to us today as well. He says that he will heal us from our idolatry or backsliding. His love for us will "know no bounds," and he will refresh us. Just as he promised to restore the Israelites, he wants to restore us and help us live productive and fruitful Christian lives.

Don't let your guilty conscience continue to weigh you down. Remember, God will convict you of your sins in a loving way to draw you to the Cross for forgiveness. Satan, on the other hand, will condemn you for your sins in a hateful way to drive you from it. If you are living in sin, pray for God's forgiveness today, so that you can begin to experience the full measure of his mercy.

For the next note on "Pray," turn to p. 1037.

guilt because they rebelled against their God. They will be killed by an invading army, their little ones dashed to death against the ground, their pregnant women ripped open by swords."

CHAPTER **14**
Healing for the Repentant

Return, O Israel, to the LORD your God, for your sins have brought you down. ²Bring your petitions, and return to the LORD. Say to him, "Forgive all our sins and graciously receive us, so that we may offer you the sacrifice of praise. ³Assyria cannot save us, nor can our strength in battle. Never again will we call the idols we have made 'our gods.' No, in you alone do the orphans find mercy."

⁴The LORD says, "Then I will heal you of your idolatry and faithlessness, and my love will know no bounds, for my anger will be gone

14:8 Hebrew *Ephraim*, referring to the northern kingdom of Israel.

forever! ⁵I will be to Israel like a refreshing dew from heaven. It will blossom like the lily; it will send roots deep into the soil like the cedars in Lebanon. ⁶Its branches will spread out like those of beautiful olive trees, as fragrant as the cedar forests of Lebanon. ⁷My people will return again to the safety of their land. They will flourish like grain and blossom like grapevines. They will be as fragrant as the wines of Lebanon.

⁸"O Israel,* stay away from idols! I am the one who looks after you and cares for you. I am like a tree that is always green, giving my fruit to you all through the year."

⁹Let those who are wise understand these things. Let those who are discerning listen carefully. The paths of the LORD are true and right, and righteous people live by walking in them. But sinners stumble and fall along the way.

Joel

CHAPTER 1

The LORD gave this message to Joel son of Pethuel.

Mourning over the Locust Plague

²Hear this, you leaders of the people! Everyone listen! In all your history, has anything like this ever happened before? ³Tell your children about it in the years to come. Pass the awful story down from generation to generation. ⁴After the cutting locusts finished eating the crops, the swarming locusts took what was left! After them came the hopping locusts, and then the stripping locusts,* too!

⁵Wake up, you drunkards, and weep! All the grapes are ruined, and all your new wine is gone! ⁶A vast army of locusts* has invaded my land. It is a terrible army, too numerous to count! Its teeth are as sharp as the teeth of lions! ⁷They have destroyed my grapevines and fig trees, stripping their bark and leaving the branches white and bare.

⁸Weep with sorrow, as a virgin weeps when her fiancé has died. ⁹There is no grain or wine to offer at the Temple of the LORD. The priests are mourning because there are no offerings. Listen to the weeping of these ministers of the LORD! ¹⁰The fields are ruined and empty of crops. The grain, the wine, and the olive oil are gone.

¹¹Despair, all you farmers! Wail, all you vine growers! Weep, because the wheat and barley—yes, all the field crops—are ruined. ¹²The grapevines and the fig trees have all withered. The pomegranate trees, palm trees, and apple trees—yes, all the fruit trees—have dried up. All joy has dried up with them.

¹³Dress yourselves in sackcloth, you priests! Wail, you who serve before the altar! Come, spend the night in sackcloth, you ministers of my God! There is no grain or wine to offer at the Temple of your God. ¹⁴Announce a time of fasting; call the people together for a solemn meeting. Bring the leaders and all the people into the Temple of the LORD your God, and cry out to him there. ¹⁵The day of the LORD is on the way, the day when destruction comes from the Almighty. How terrible that day will be!

¹⁶We watch as our food disappears before our very eyes. There are no joyful celebrations in the house of our God. ¹⁷The seeds die in the parched ground, and the grain crops fail. The barns and granaries stand empty and abandoned. ¹⁸How the animals moan with hunger! The cattle wander about confused because there is no pasture for them. The sheep bleat in misery.

¹⁹LORD, help us! The fire has consumed the pastures and burned up all the trees. ²⁰Even the wild animals cry out to you because they have no water to drink. The streams have dried up, and fire has consumed the pastures.

CHAPTER 2

Locusts Invade like an Army

Blow the trumpet in Jerusalem*! Sound the alarm on my holy mountain! Let everyone tremble in fear because the day of the LORD is upon us. ²It is a day of darkness and gloom, a day of thick clouds and deep blackness. Suddenly, like dawn spreading across the mountains, a mighty army appears! How great and powerful they are! The likes of them have not been seen before and never will be seen again.

³Fire burns in front of them and follows them in every direction! Ahead of them the land lies as fair as the Garden of Eden in all its beauty. Behind them is nothing but desolation; not one thing escapes. ⁴They look like tiny horses, and they run as fast. ⁵Look at them as they leap along

---

1:4 The precise identification of the four kinds of locusts mentioned here is uncertain.   1:6 Hebrew *A nation.*   2:1 Hebrew *Zion;* also in 2:15, 23.

the mountaintops! Listen to the noise they make—like the rumbling of chariots, like the roar of a fire sweeping across a field, or like a mighty army moving into battle.

6Fear grips all the people; every face grows pale with fright. 7The attackers march like warriors and scale city walls like trained soldiers. Straight forward they march, never breaking rank. 8They never jostle each other; each moves in exactly the right place. They lunge through the gaps, and no weapon can stop them. 9They swarm over the city and run along its walls. They enter all the houses, climbing like thieves through the windows.

10The earth quakes as they advance, and the heavens tremble. The sun and moon grow dark, and the stars no longer shine. 11The LORD leads them with a shout! This is his mighty army, and they follow his orders. The day of the LORD is an awesome, terrible thing. Who can endure it?

A Call to Repentance

12That is why the LORD says, "Turn to me now, while there is time! Give me your hearts. Come with fasting, weeping, and mourning. 13Don't tear your clothing in your grief; instead, tear your hearts." Return to the LORD your God, for he is gracious and merciful. He is not easily angered. He is filled with kindness and is eager not to punish you. 14Who knows? Perhaps even yet he will give you a reprieve, sending you a blessing instead of this terrible curse. Perhaps he will give you so much that you will be able to offer grain and wine to the LORD your God as before!

15Blow the trumpet in Jerusalem! Announce a time of fasting; call the people together for a solemn meeting. 16Bring everyone—the elders, the children, and even the babies. Call the bridegroom from his quarters and the bride from her private room. 17The priests, who minister in the LORD's presence, will stand between the people and the altar, weeping. Let them pray, "Spare your people, LORD! They belong to you, so don't let them become an object of mockery. Don't let their name become a proverb of unbelieving foreigners who say, 'Where is the God of Israel? He must be helpless!'"

The LORD's Promise of Restoration

18Then the LORD will pity his people and be indignant for the honor of his land! 19He will reply, "Look! I am sending you grain and wine and olive oil, enough to satisfy your needs. You will no longer be an object of mockery among the surrounding nations. 20I will remove these armies from the north and send them far away. I will drive them back into the parched wastelands, where they will die. Those in the rear will go into the Dead Sea; those at the front will go into the Mediterranean.* The stench of their rotting bodies will rise over the land."

Surely the LORD has done great things! 21Don't be afraid, my people! Be glad now and rejoice because the LORD has done great things. 22Don't be afraid, you animals of the field! The pastures will soon be green. The trees will again be filled with luscious fruit; fig trees and grapevines will flourish once more. 23Rejoice, you people of Jerusalem! Rejoice in the LORD your God! For the rains he sends are an expression of his grace. Once more the autumn rains will come, as well as the rains of spring. 24The threshing floors will again be piled high with grain, and the presses will overflow with wine and olive oil.

25The LORD says, "I will give you back what you lost to the stripping locusts, the cutting locusts, the swarming locusts, and the hopping locusts.* It was I who sent this great destroying army against you. 26Once again you will have all the food you want, and you will praise the LORD your God, who does these miracles for you. Never again will my people be disgraced like this. 27Then you will know that I am here among my people of Israel and that I alone am the LORD your God. My people will never again be disgraced like this.

The LORD's Promise of His Spirit

28"Then after I have poured out my rains again, I will pour out my Spirit upon all people. Your sons and daughters will prophesy. Your old men will dream dreams. Your young men will see visions. 29In those days, I will pour out my Spirit even on servants, men and women alike.

30"I will cause wonders in the heavens and on the earth—blood and fire and pillars of smoke. 31The sun will be turned into darkness, and the moon will turn bloodred before that great and terrible day of the LORD arrives. 32And anyone who calls on the name of the LORD will be saved. There will be people on Mount Zion in Jerusalem who escape, just as the LORD has said. These will be among the survivors whom the LORD has called.

CHAPTER **3**

Judgment against Enemy Nations

"At that time, when I restore the prosperity of Judah and Jerusalem," says the LORD, 2"I will

---

2:20 Hebrew *the eastern sea; . . . the western sea.*   2:25 The precise identification of the four kinds of locusts mentioned here is uncertain.

gather the armies of the world into the valley of Jehoshaphat.* There I will judge them for harming my people, for scattering my inheritance among the nations, and for dividing up my land. 3They cast lots to decide which of my people would be their slaves. They traded young boys for prostitutes and little girls for enough wine to get drunk.

4"What do you have against me, Tyre and Sidon and you cities of Philistia? Are you trying to take revenge on me? If you are, then watch out! I will strike swiftly and pay you back for everything you have done. 5You have taken my silver and gold and all my precious treasures, and you have carried them off to your pagan temples. 6You have sold the people of Judah and Jerusalem to the Greeks,* who took them far from their homeland. 7But I will bring them back again from all these places to which you sold them, and I will pay you back for all you have done. 8I will sell your sons and daughters to the people of Judah, and they will sell them to the peoples of Arabia,* a nation far away. I, the LORD, have spoken!"

9Say to the nations far and wide: "Get ready for war! Call out your best warriors! Let all your fighting men advance for the attack! 10Beat your plowshares into swords and your pruning hooks into spears. Train even your weaklings to be warriors. 11Come quickly, all you nations everywhere! Gather together in the valley."

And now, O LORD, call out your warriors!

12"Let the nations be called to arms. Let them march to the valley of Jehoshaphat. There I, the LORD, will sit to pronounce judgment on them all. 13Now let the sickle do its work, for the harvest is ripe. Come, tread the winepress because it is full. The storage vats are overflowing with the wickedness of these people."

14Thousands upon thousands are waiting in the valley of decision. It is there that the day of the LORD will soon arrive. 15The sun and moon will grow dark, and the stars will no longer shine. 16The LORD's voice will roar from Zion and thunder from Jerusalem, and the earth and heavens will begin to shake. But to his people of Israel, the LORD will be a welcoming refuge and a strong fortress.

Blessings for God's People

17"Then you will know that I, the LORD your God, live in Zion, my holy mountain. Jerusalem will be holy forever, and foreign armies will never conquer her again. 18In that day the mountains will drip with sweet wine, and the hills will flow with milk. Water will fill the dry streambeds of Judah, and a fountain will burst forth from the LORD's Temple, watering the arid valley of acacias.* 19Egypt will become a wasteland and Edom a wilderness, because they attacked Judah and killed her innocent people.

20"But Judah will remain forever, and Jerusalem will endure through all future generations. 21I will pardon my people's crimes, which I have not yet pardoned; and I, the LORD, will make my home in Jerusalem* with my people."

3:2 *Jehoshaphat* means "the LORD judges." 3:6 Hebrew *to the peoples of Javan.* 3:8 Hebrew *to the Sabeans.* 3:18 Hebrew *valley of Shittim.* 3:21 Hebrew *Zion.*

Amos

This message was given to Amos, a shepherd from the town of Tekoa in Judah. He received this message in visions two years before the earthquake, when Uzziah was king of Judah and Jeroboam II, the son of Jehoash,* was king of Israel.

²This is his report of what he saw and heard: "The LORD's voice roars from his Temple on Mount Zion; he thunders from Jerusalem! Suddenly, the lush pastures of the shepherds dry up. All the grass on Mount Carmel withers and dies."

God's Judgment on Israel's Neighbors

³This is what the LORD says: "The people of Damascus have sinned again and again, and I will not forget it. I will not let them go unpunished any longer! They beat down my people in Gilead as grain is threshed with threshing sledges of iron. ⁴So I will send down fire on King Hazael's palace, and the fortresses of King Benhadad will be destroyed. ⁵I will break down the gates of Damascus and slaughter its people all the way to the valley of Aven.* I will destroy the ruler in Beth-eden, and the people of Aram will return to Kir as slaves. I, the LORD, have spoken!"

⁶This is what the LORD says: "The people of Gaza have sinned again and again, and I will not forget it. I will not let them go unpunished any longer! They sent my people into exile, selling them as slaves in Edom. ⁷So I will send down fire on the walls of Gaza, and all its fortresses will be destroyed. ⁸I will slaughter the people of Ashdod and destroy the king of Ashkelon. Then I will turn to attack Ekron, and the few Philistines still left will be killed. I, the Sovereign LORD, have spoken!"

⁹This is what the LORD says: "The people of Tyre have sinned again and again, and I will not forget it. I will not let them go unpunished any longer! They broke their treaty of brotherhood with Israel, selling whole villages as slaves to Edom. ¹⁰So I will send down fire on the walls of Tyre, and all its fortresses will be destroyed."

¹¹This is what the LORD says: "The people of Edom have sinned again and again, and I will not forget it. I will not let them go unpunished any longer! They chased down their relatives, the Israelites, with swords. They showed them no mercy and were unrelenting in their anger. ¹²So I will send down fire on Teman, and the fortresses of Bozrah will be destroyed."

¹³This is what the LORD says: "The people of Ammon have sinned again and again, and I will not forget it. I will not let them go unpunished any longer! When they attacked Gilead to extend their borders, they committed cruel crimes, ripping open pregnant women with their swords. ¹⁴So I will send down fire on the walls of Rabbah, and all its fortresses will be destroyed. There will be wild shouts during the battle, swirling like a whirlwind in a mighty storm. ¹⁵And their king* and his princes will go into exile together. I, the LORD, have spoken!"

This is what the LORD says: "The people of Moab have sinned again and again, and I will not forget it. I will not let them go unpunished any longer! They desecrated the tomb of Edom's king and burned his bones to ashes. ²So I will send down fire on the land of Moab, and all the fortresses in Kerioth will be destroyed. The people will fall in the noise of battle, as the warriors shout and the trumpets blare. ³And I will destroy their king and slaughter all their princes. I, the LORD, have spoken!"

1:1 Hebrew *Joash,* a variant name for Jehoash. 1:5 *Aven* means "wickedness." 1:15 Hebrew *malcam,* possibly referring to their god Molech.

God's Judgment on Judah and Israel

⁴This is what the LORD says: "The people of Judah have sinned again and again, and I will not forget it. I will not let them go unpunished any longer! They have rejected the laws of the LORD, refusing to obey him. They have been led astray by the same lies that deceived their ancestors. ⁵So I will send down fire on Judah, and all the fortresses of Jerusalem will be destroyed."

⁶This is what the LORD says: "The people of Israel have sinned again and again, and I will not forget it. I will not let them go unpunished any longer! They have perverted justice by selling honest people for silver and poor people for a pair of sandals. ⁷They trample helpless people in the dust and deny justice to those who are oppressed. Both father and son sleep with the same woman, corrupting my holy name. ⁸At their religious festivals, they lounge around in clothing stolen from their debtors. In the house of their god, they present offerings of wine purchased with stolen money.

⁹"Yet think of all I did for my people! I destroyed the Amorites before my people arrived in the land. The Amorites were as tall as cedar trees and strong as oaks, but I destroyed their fruit and dug out their roots. ¹⁰It was I who rescued you from Egypt and led you through the desert for forty years so you could possess the land of the Amorites. ¹¹I chose some of your sons to be prophets and others to be Nazirites. Can you deny this, my people of Israel?" asks the LORD. ¹²"But you caused the Nazirites to sin by making them drink your wine, and you said to my prophets, 'Shut up!'

¹³"So I will make you groan as a wagon groans when it is loaded down with grain. ¹⁴Your fastest runners will not get away. The strongest among you will become weak. Even the mightiest warriors will be unable to save themselves. ¹⁵The archers will fail to stand their ground. The swiftest soldiers won't be fast enough to escape. Even warriors on horses won't be able to outrun the danger. ¹⁶On that day, the most courageous of your fighting men will drop their weapons and run for their lives. I, the LORD, have spoken!"

CHAPTER 3

Listen to this message that the LORD has spoken against you, O people of Israel and Judah—the entire family I rescued from Egypt: ²"From among all the families on the earth, I chose you alone. That is why I must punish you for all your sins."

Witnesses against Guilty Israel

³Can two people walk together without agreeing on the direction? ⁴Does a lion ever roar in a thicket without first finding a victim? Does a young lion growl in its den without first catching its prey? ⁵Does a bird ever get caught in a trap that has no bait? Does a trap ever spring shut when there's nothing there to catch? ⁶When the war trumpet blares, shouldn't the people be alarmed? When disaster comes to a city, isn't it because the LORD planned it?

⁷"But always, first of all, I warn you through my servants the prophets. I, the Sovereign LORD, have now done this."

⁸The lion has roared—tremble in fear! The Sovereign LORD has spoken—I dare not refuse to proclaim his message!

⁹Announce this to the leaders of Philistia* and Egypt: "Take your seats now on the hills around Samaria, and witness the scandalous spectacle of all Israel's crimes."

¹⁰"My people have forgotten what it means to do right," says the LORD. "Their fortresses are filled with wealth taken by theft and violence. ¹¹Therefore," says the Sovereign LORD, "an enemy is coming! He will surround them and shatter their defenses. Then he will plunder all their fortresses."

¹²This is what the LORD says: "A shepherd who tries to rescue a sheep from a lion's mouth will recover only two legs and a piece of ear. So it will be when the Israelites in Samaria are rescued with only a broken chair and a tattered pillow. ¹³Now listen to this, and announce it throughout all Israel,* " says the Lord, the LORD God Almighty. ¹⁴"On the very day I punish Israel for its sins, I will destroy the pagan altars at Bethel. The horns of the altar will be cut off and fall to the ground. ¹⁵And I will destroy the beautiful homes of the wealthy—their winter mansions and their summer houses, too—all their palaces filled with ivory. I, the LORD, have spoken!"

CHAPTER 4

Israel's Failure to Learn

Listen to me, you "fat cows" of Samaria, you women who oppress the poor and crush the needy and who are always asking your husbands for another drink! ²The Sovereign LORD has sworn this by his holiness: "The time will come when you will be led away with hooks in your noses. Every last one of you will be dragged away like a fish on a hook! ³You will leave by going straight through the breaks in the wall; you will be thrown from your fortresses.* I, the LORD, have spoken!

3:9 Hebrew *Ashdod.* 3:13 Hebrew *the house of Jacob.* 4:3 Hebrew *thrown out toward Harmon,* possibly a reference to Mount Hermon.

4 "Go ahead and offer your sacrifices to the idols at Bethel and Gilgal. Keep on disobeying— your sins are mounting up! Offer sacrifices each morning and bring your tithes every three days! 5Present your bread made with yeast as an offering of thanksgiving. Then give your extra voluntary offerings so you can brag about it everywhere! This is the kind of thing you Israelites love to do," says the Sovereign LORD.

6 "I brought hunger to every city and famine to every town. But still you wouldn't return to me," says the LORD.

7 "I kept the rain from falling when you needed it the most, ruining all your crops. I sent rain on one town but withheld it from another. Rain fell on one field, while another field withered away. 8People staggered from one town to another for a drink of water, but there was never enough. But still you wouldn't return to me," says the LORD.

9 "I struck your farms and vineyards with blight and mildew. Locusts devoured all your fig and olive trees. But still you wouldn't return to me," says the LORD.

10 "I sent plagues against you like the plagues I sent against Egypt long ago. I killed your young men in war and slaughtered all your horses. The stench of death filled the air! But still you wouldn't return to me," says the LORD.

11 "I destroyed some of your cities, as I destroyed* Sodom and Gomorrah. Those of you who survived were like half-burned sticks snatched from a fire. But still you wouldn't return to me," says the LORD.

12 "Therefore, I will bring upon you all these further disasters I have announced. Prepare to meet your God as he comes in judgment, you people of Israel!"

13For the LORD is the one who shaped the mountains, stirs up the winds, and reveals his every thought. He turns the light of dawn into darkness and treads the mountains under his feet. The LORD God Almighty is his name!

CHAPTER 5
A Call to Repentance

Listen, you people of Israel! Listen to this funeral song I am singing:

2   "The virgin Israel has fallen,
        never to rise again!
    She lies forsaken on the ground,
        with none to raise her up."

3The Sovereign LORD says: "When one of your cities sends a thousand men to battle, only a hundred will return. When a town sends a hundred, only ten will come back alive."

4Now this is what the LORD says to the family of Israel: "Come back to me and live! 5Don't go to worship the idols of Bethel, Gilgal, or Beersheba. For the people of Gilgal will be dragged off into exile, and the people of Bethel will come to nothing."

6Come back to the LORD and live! If you don't, he will roar through Israel* like a fire, devouring you completely. Your gods in Bethel certainly won't be able to quench the flames! 7You wicked people! You twist justice, making it a bitter pill for the poor and oppressed. Righteousness and fair play are meaningless fictions to you.

8It is the LORD who created the stars, the Pleiades and Orion. It is he who turns darkness into morning and day into night. It is he who draws up water from the oceans and pours it down as rain on the land. The LORD is his name! 9With blinding speed and power he destroys the strong, crushing all their defenses.

10How you hate honest judges! How you despise people who tell the truth! 11You trample the poor and steal what little they have through taxes and unfair rent. Therefore, you will never live in the beautiful stone houses you are building. You will never drink wine from the lush vineyards you are planting. 12For I know the vast number of your sins and rebellions. You oppress good people by taking bribes and deprive the poor of justice in the courts. 13So those who are wise will keep quiet, for it is an evil time.

14Do what is good and run from evil—that you may live! Then the LORD God Almighty will truly be your helper, just as you have claimed he is. 15Hate evil and love what is good; remodel your courts into true halls of justice. Perhaps even yet the LORD God Almighty will have mercy on his people who remain.*

16Therefore, this is what the Lord, the LORD God Almighty, says: "There will be crying in all the public squares and in every street. Call for the farmers to weep with you, and summon professional mourners to wail and lament. 17There will be wailing in every vineyard, for I will pass through and destroy them all. I, the LORD, have spoken!"

Warning of Coming Judgment

18How terrible it will be for you who say, "If only the day of the LORD were here! For then the LORD would rescue us from all our enemies." But you have no idea what you are wishing for. That day

4:11 Hebrew *as when God destroyed.*   5:6 Hebrew *the house of Joseph.*   5:15 Hebrew *on the remnant of Joseph.*

will not bring light and prosperity, but darkness and disaster. 19In that day you will be like a man who runs from a lion—only to meet a bear. After escaping the bear, he leans his hand against a wall in his house—and is bitten by a snake. 20Yes, the day of the LORD will be a dark and hopeless day, without a ray of joy or hope.

21"I hate all your show and pretense—the hypocrisy of your religious festivals and solemn assemblies. 22I will not accept your burnt offerings and grain offerings. I won't even notice all your choice peace offerings. 23Away with your hymns of praise! They are only noise to my ears. I will not listen to your music, no matter how lovely it is. 24Instead, I want to see a mighty flood of justice, a river of righteous living that will never run dry.

25"Was it to me you were bringing sacrifices and offerings during the forty years in the wilderness, Israel? 26No, your real interest was in your pagan gods—Sakkuth your king god and Kaiwan your star god—the images you yourselves made.* 27So I will send you into exile, to a land east of Damascus," says the LORD, whose name is God Almighty.

CHAPTER 6

How terrible it will be for you who lounge in luxury and think you are secure in Jerusalem* and Samaria! You are famous and popular in Israel, you to whom the people go for help. 2Go over to Calneh and see what happened there. Then go to the great city of Hamath and on down to the Philistine city of Gath. You are no better than they were, and look at how they were destroyed. 3You push away every thought of coming disaster, but your actions only bring the day of judgment closer.

4How terrible it will be for you who sprawl on ivory beds surrounded with luxury, eating the meat of tender lambs and choice calves. 5You sing idle songs to the sound of the harp, and you fancy yourselves to be great musicians, as King David was. 6You drink wine by the bowlful, and you perfume yourselves with exotic fragrances, caring nothing at all that your nation* is going to ruin. 7Therefore, you will be the first to be led away as captives. Suddenly, all your revelry will end.

8The Sovereign LORD has sworn by his own name, and this is what he, the LORD God Almighty, says: "I despise the pride and false glory of Israel,* and I hate their beautiful homes. I will give this city and everything in it to their enemies."

9If there are ten men left in one house, they will all die. 10And when a close relative—one who is responsible for burning the dead—goes into the house to carry away a dead body, he will ask the last survivor, "Is there anyone else with you?" And the person will answer, "No!" Then he will say, "Hush! Don't even whisper the name of the LORD. He might hear you!"

11When the LORD gives the command, homes both great and small will be smashed to pieces. 12Can horses gallop over rocks? Can oxen be used to plow rocks? Stupid even to ask—but that's how stupid you are when you turn justice into poison and make bitter the sweet fruit of righteousness. 13And just as stupid is this bragging about your conquest of Lo-debar.* You boast, "Didn't we take Karnaim* by our own strength and power?"

14"O people of Israel, I am about to bring an enemy nation against you," says the LORD God Almighty. "It will oppress you bitterly throughout your land—from Lebo-hamath in the north to the Arabah Valley in the south."

CHAPTER 7

A Vision of Locusts

The Sovereign LORD showed me a vision. I saw him preparing to send a vast swarm of locusts over the land. This was after the king's share had been harvested from the fields and as the main crop was coming up. 2In my vision the locusts ate everything in sight that was green. Then I said, "O Sovereign LORD, please forgive your people! Unless you relent, Israel* will not survive, for we are only a small nation."

3So the LORD relented and did not fulfill the vision. "I won't do it," he said.

A Vision of Fire

4Then the Sovereign LORD showed me another vision. I saw him preparing to punish his people with a great fire. The fire had burned up the depths of the sea and was devouring the entire land. 5Then I said, "O Sovereign LORD, please don't do it. Unless you relent, Israel will not survive, for we are only a small nation."

6Then the LORD turned from this plan, too. "I won't do that either," said the Sovereign LORD.

A Vision of a Plumb Line

7Then he showed me another vision. I saw the Lord standing beside a wall that had been built using a plumb line. He was checking it with a

---

5:26 Greek version reads *You took up the shrine of Molech, and the star of your god Rephan, and the images you made for yourselves.*   6:1 Hebrew *Zion.*   6:6 Hebrew *Joseph.*   6:8 Hebrew *Jacob.*   6:13a *Lo-debar* means "nothing."   6:13b *Karnaim* means "horns," a term that symbolizes strength.   7:2 Hebrew *Jacob;* also in 7:5.

plumb line to see if it was straight. ⁸And the LORD said to me, "Amos, what do you see?"

I answered, "A plumb line."

And the Lord replied, "I will test my people with this plumb line. I will no longer ignore all their sins. ⁹The pagan shrines of your ancestors* and the temples of Israel will be destroyed, and I will bring the dynasty of King Jeroboam to a sudden end."

Amos and Amaziah

¹⁰But when Amaziah, the priest of Bethel, heard what Amos was saying, he rushed a message to King Jeroboam: "Amos is hatching a plot against you right here on your very doorstep! What he is saying is intolerable. It will lead to rebellion all across the land. ¹¹He is saying, 'Jeroboam will soon be killed and the people of Israel will be sent away into exile.'"

¹²Then Amaziah sent orders to Amos: "Get out of here, you seer! Go on back to the land of Judah and do your preaching there! ¹³Don't bother us here in Bethel with your prophecies, especially not here where the royal sanctuary is!"

¹⁴But Amos replied, "I'm not one of your professional prophets. I certainly never trained to be one. I'm just a shepherd, and I take care of fig trees. ¹⁵But the LORD called me away from my flock and told me, 'Go and prophesy to my people in Israel.'

¹⁶"Now then, listen to this message from the LORD! You say, 'Don't prophesy against Israel. Stop preaching against my people.*' ¹⁷But this is what the LORD says: Because you have refused to listen, your wife will become a prostitute in this city, and your sons and daughters will be killed. Your land will be divided up, and you yourself will die in a foreign land. And the people of Israel will certainly become captives in exile, far from their homeland."

CHAPTER 8

A Vision of Ripe Fruit

Then the Sovereign LORD showed me another vision. In it I saw a basket filled with ripe fruit. ²"What do you see, Amos?" he asked.

I replied, "A basket full of ripe fruit."

Then the LORD said, "This fruit represents my people of Israel—ripe for punishment! I will not delay their punishment again. ³In that day the riotous sounds of singing in the Temple will turn to wailing. Dead bodies will be scattered everywhere. They will be carried out of the city in silence. I, the Sovereign LORD, have spoken!"

⁴Listen to this, you who rob the poor and trample the needy! ⁵You can't wait for the Sabbath day to be over and the religious festivals to end so you can get back to cheating the helpless. You measure out your grain in false measures and weigh it out on dishonest scales. ⁶And you mix the wheat you sell with chaff swept from the floor! Then you enslave poor people for a debt of one piece of silver or a pair of sandals.

⁷Now the LORD has sworn this oath by his own name, the Pride of Israel*: "I will never forget the wicked things you have done! ⁸The earth will tremble for your deeds, and everyone will mourn. The land will rise up like the Nile River at floodtime, toss about, and sink again. ⁹At that time," says the Sovereign LORD, "I will make the sun go down at noon and darken the earth while it is still day. ¹⁰I will turn your celebrations into times of mourning, and your songs of joy will be turned to weeping. You will wear funeral clothes and shave your heads as signs of sorrow, as if your only son had died. How very bitter that day will be!

¹¹"The time is surely coming," says the Sovereign LORD, "when I will send a famine on the land—not a famine of bread or water but of hearing the words of the LORD. ¹²People will stagger everywhere from sea to sea, searching for the word of the LORD, running here and going there, but they will not find it. ¹³Beautiful girls and fine young men will grow faint and weary, thirsting for the LORD's word. ¹⁴And those who worship and swear by the idols of Samaria, Dan, and Beersheba will fall down, never to rise again."

CHAPTER 9

A Vision of God at the Altar

Then I saw a vision of the Lord standing beside the altar. He said, "Strike the tops of the Temple columns so hard that the foundation will shake. Smash the columns so the roof will crash down on the people below. Then those who survive will be slaughtered in battle. No one will escape!

²"Even if they dig down to the place of the dead,* I will reach down and pull them up. Even if they climb up into the heavens, I will bring them down. ³Even if they hide at the very top of Mount Carmel, I will search them out and capture them. Even if they hide at the bottom of the ocean, I will send the great sea serpent after them to bite and destroy them. ⁴Even if they are driven into exile, I will command the sword to kill them there. I am determined to bring disaster upon them and not to help them."

7:9 Hebrew of Isaac. 7:16 Hebrew against the house of Isaac. 8:7 Hebrew the pride of Jacob. 9:2 Hebrew to Sheol.

⁵The Lord, the LORD Almighty, touches the land and it melts, and all its people mourn. The ground rises like the Nile River at floodtime, and then it sinks again. ⁶The upper stories of the LORD's home are in the heavens, while its foundation is on the earth. He draws up water from the oceans and pours it down as rain on the land. The LORD is his name!

⁷"Do you Israelites think you are more important to me than the Ethiopians*?" asks the LORD. "I brought you out of Egypt, but have I not done as much for other nations, too? I brought the Philistines from Crete* and led the Arameans out of Kir.

⁸"I, the Sovereign LORD, am watching this sinful nation of Israel, and I will uproot it and scatter its people across the earth. Yet I have promised that I will never completely destroy the family of Israel,*" says the LORD. ⁹"For I have commanded that Israel be persecuted by the other nations as grain is sifted in a sieve, yet not one true kernel will be lost. ¹⁰But all the sinners will die by the sword—all those who say, 'Nothing bad will happen to us.'

A Promise of Restoration

¹¹"In that day I will restore the fallen kingdom of David. It is now like a house in ruins, but I will rebuild its walls and restore its former glory. ¹²And Israel will possess what is left of Edom and all the nations I have called to be mine. I, the LORD, have spoken, and I will do these things.

¹³"The time will come," says the LORD, "when the grain and grapes will grow faster than they can be harvested. Then the terraced vineyards on the hills of Israel will drip with sweet wine! ¹⁴I will bring my exiled people of Israel back from distant lands, and they will rebuild their ruined cities and live in them again. They will plant vineyards and gardens; they will eat their crops and drink their wine. ¹⁵I will firmly plant them there in the land I have given them," says the LORD your God. "Then they will never be uprooted again."

9:7a Hebrew *the Cushites.*   9:7b Hebrew *Caphtor.*   9:8 Hebrew *the house of Jacob.*

Obadiah

This is the vision that the Sovereign LORD revealed to Obadiah concerning the land of Edom.

Edom's Judgment Announced

We have heard a message from the LORD that an ambassador was sent to the nations to say, "Get ready, everyone! Let's assemble our armies and attack Edom!"

2The LORD says, "I will cut you down to size among the nations, Edom; you will be small and despised. 3You are proud because you live in a rock fortress and make your home high in the mountains. 'Who can ever reach us way up here?' you ask boastfully. Don't fool yourselves! 4Though you soar as high as eagles and build your nest among the stars, I will bring you crashing down. I, the LORD, have spoken!

5"If thieves came at night and robbed you, they would not take everything. Those who harvest grapes always leave a few for the poor. But your enemies will wipe you out completely! 6Every nook and cranny of Edom* will be searched and looted. Every treasure will be found and taken.

7"All your allies will turn against you. They will help to chase you from your land. They will promise you peace, while plotting your destruction. Your trusted friends will set traps for you, and you won't even know about it. 8At that time not a single wise person will be left in the whole land of Edom!" says the LORD. "For on the mountains of Edom I will destroy everyone who has wisdom and understanding. 9The mightiest warriors of Teman will be terrified, and everyone on the mountains of Edom will be cut down in the slaughter.

Reasons for Edom's Punishment

10"And why? Because of the violence you did to your close relatives in Israel.* Now you will be destroyed completely and filled with shame forever. 11For you deserted your relatives in Israel during their time of greatest need. You stood aloof, refusing to lift a finger to help when foreign invaders carried off their wealth and cast lots to divide up Jerusalem. You acted as though you were one of Israel's enemies.

12"You shouldn't have done this! You shouldn't have gloated when they exiled your relatives to distant lands. You shouldn't have rejoiced because they were suffering such misfortune. You shouldn't have crowed over them as they suffered these disasters. 13You shouldn't have plundered the land of Israel when they were suffering such calamity. You shouldn't have gloated over the destruction of your relatives, looting their homes and making yourselves rich at their expense. 14You shouldn't have stood at the crossroads, killing those who tried to escape. You shouldn't have captured the survivors, handing them over to their enemies in that terrible time of trouble.

Edom Destroyed, Israel Restored

15"The day is near when I, the LORD, will judge the godless nations! As you have done to Israel, so it will be done to you. All your evil deeds will fall back on your own heads. 16Just as you swallowed up my people on my holy mountain, so you and the surrounding nations will swallow the punishment I pour out on you. Yes, you nations will drink and stagger and disappear from history, as though you had never even existed.

17"But Jerusalem* will become a refuge for those who escape; it will be a holy place. And the people of Israel* will come back to reclaim their inheritance. 18At that time Israel will be a raging fire, and Edom, a field of dry stubble. The fire will roar across the field, devouring everything

6 Hebrew *Esau;* also in 8b, 9, 18, 19, 21.   10 Hebrew *your brother Jacob.*   17a Hebrew *Mount Zion.*   17b Hebrew *house of Jacob;* also in 18.

and leaving no survivors in Edom. I, the LORD, have spoken!

19 "Then my people living in the Negev will occupy the mountains of Edom. Those living in the foothills of Judah* will possess the Philistine plains and take over the fields of Ephraim and Samaria. And the people of Benjamin will occupy the land of Gilead. 20 The exiles of Israel will return to their land and occupy the Phoenician coast as far north as Zarephath. The captives from Jerusalem exiled in the north* will return to their homeland and resettle the villages of the Negev. 21 Deliverers will go up to* Mount Zion in Jerusalem to rule over the mountains of Edom. And the LORD himself will be king!"

19 Hebrew *the Shephelah.*   20 Hebrew *in Sepharad.*   21 Or *from.*

Jonah

CHAPTER 1
Jonah Runs from the LORD

The LORD gave this message to Jonah son of Amittai: 2"Get up and go to the great city of Nineveh! Announce my judgment against it because I have seen how wicked its people are."

3But Jonah got up and went in the opposite direction in order to get away from the LORD. He went down to the seacoast, to the port of Joppa, where he found a ship leaving for Tarshish. He bought a ticket and went on board, hoping that by going away to the west he could escape from the LORD.

4But as the ship was sailing along, suddenly the LORD flung a powerful wind over the sea, causing a violent storm that threatened to send them to the bottom. 5Fearing for their lives, the desperate sailors shouted to their gods for help and threw the cargo overboard to lighten the ship. And all this time Jonah was sound asleep down in the hold. 6So the captain went down after him. "How can you sleep at a time like this?" he shouted. "Get up and pray to your god! Maybe he will have mercy on us and spare our lives."

7Then the crew cast lots to see which of them had offended the gods and caused the terrible storm. When they did this, Jonah lost the toss. 8"What have you done to bring this awful storm down on us?" they demanded. "Who are you? What is your line of work? What country are you from? What is your nationality?"

9And Jonah answered, "I am a Hebrew, and I worship the LORD, the God of heaven, who made the sea and the land." 10Then he told them that he was running away from the LORD.

The sailors were terrified when they heard this. "Oh, why did you do it?" they groaned. 11And since the storm was getting worse all the time, they asked him, "What should we do to you to stop this storm?"

12"Throw me into the sea," Jonah said, "and it will become calm again. For I know that this terrible storm is all my fault."

13Instead, the sailors tried even harder to row the boat ashore. But the stormy sea was too violent for them, and they couldn't make it. 14Then they cried out to the LORD, Jonah's God. "O LORD," they pleaded, "don't make us die for this man's sin. And don't hold us responsible for his death, because it isn't our fault. O LORD, you have sent this storm upon him for your own good reasons."

15Then the sailors picked Jonah up and threw him into the raging sea, and the storm stopped at once! 16The sailors were awestruck by the LORD's great power, and they offered him a sacrifice and vowed to serve him.

17Now the LORD had arranged for a great fish to swallow Jonah. And Jonah was inside the fish for three days and three nights.

CHAPTER 2
Jonah's Prayer

Then Jonah prayed to the LORD his God from inside the fish. 2He said, "I cried out to the LORD in my great trouble, and he answered me. I called to you from the world of the dead,* and LORD, you heard me! 3You threw me into the ocean depths, and I sank down to the heart of the sea. I was buried beneath your wild and stormy waves. 4Then I said, 'O LORD, you have driven me from your presence. How will I ever again see your holy Temple?'

5"I sank beneath the waves, and death was very near. The waters closed in around me, and seaweed wrapped itself around my head. 6I sank down to the very roots of the mountains. I was locked out of life and imprisoned in the land of

2:2 Hebrew from Sheol.

the dead. But you, O LORD my God, have snatched me from the yawning jaws of death!

7 "When I had lost all hope, I turned my thoughts once more to the LORD. And my earnest prayer went out to you in your holy Temple. 8 Those who worship false gods turn their backs on all God's mercies. 9 But I will offer sacrifices to you with songs of praise, and I will fulfill all my vows. For my salvation comes from the LORD alone."

10 Then the LORD ordered the fish to spit up Jonah on the beach, and it did.

CHAPTER 3
Jonah Goes to Nineveh

Then the LORD spoke to Jonah a second time: 2 "Get up and go to the great city of Nineveh, and deliver the message of judgment I have given you."

3 This time Jonah obeyed the LORD's command and went to Nineveh, a city so large that it took three days to see it all. 4 On the day Jonah entered the city, he shouted to the crowds: "Forty days from now Nineveh will be destroyed!" 5 The people of Nineveh believed God's message, and from the greatest to the least, they decided to go without food and wear sackcloth to show their sorrow.

6 When the king of Nineveh heard what Jonah was saying, he stepped down from his throne and took off his royal robes. He dressed himself in sackcloth and sat on a heap of ashes. 7 Then the king and his nobles sent this decree throughout the city: "No one, not even the animals, may eat or drink anything at all. 8 Everyone is required to wear sackcloth and pray earnestly to God. Everyone must turn from their evil ways and stop all their violence. 9 Who can tell? Perhaps even yet God will have pity on us and hold back his fierce anger from destroying us."

10 When God saw that they had put a stop to their evil ways, he had mercy on them and didn't carry out the destruction he had threatened.

4:11 Hebrew *people who don't know their right hands from their left.*

CHAPTER 4
Jonah's Anger at the LORD's Mercy

This change of plans upset Jonah, and he became very angry. 2 So he complained to the LORD about it: "Didn't I say before I left home that you would do this, LORD? That is why I ran away to Tarshish! I knew that you were a gracious and compassionate God, slow to get angry and filled with unfailing love. I knew how easily you could cancel your plans for destroying these people. 3 Just kill me now, LORD! I'd rather be dead than alive because nothing I predicted is going to happen."

4 The LORD replied, "Is it right for you to be angry about this?"

5 Then Jonah went out to the east side of the city and made a shelter to sit under as he waited to see if anything would happen to the city. 6 And the LORD God arranged for a leafy plant to grow there, and soon it spread its broad leaves over Jonah's head, shading him from the sun. This eased some of his discomfort, and Jonah was very grateful for the plant.

7 But God also prepared a worm! The next morning at dawn the worm ate through the stem of the plant, so that it soon died and withered away. 8 And as the sun grew hot, God sent a scorching east wind to blow on Jonah. The sun beat down on his head until he grew faint and wished to die. "Death is certainly better than this!" he exclaimed.

9 Then God said to Jonah, "Is it right for you to be angry because the plant died?"

"Yes," Jonah retorted, "even angry enough to die!"

10 Then the LORD said, "You feel sorry about the plant, though you did nothing to put it there. And a plant is only, at best, short lived. 11 But Nineveh has more than 120,000 people living in spiritual darkness,* not to mention all the animals. Shouldn't I feel sorry for such a great city?"

Micah

The LORD gave these messages to Micah of Moresheth during the years when Jotham, Ahaz, and Hezekiah were kings of Judah. The messages concerned both Samaria and Jerusalem, and they came to Micah in the form of visions.

Grief over Samaria and Jerusalem

²Attention! Let all the people of the world listen! The Sovereign LORD has made accusations against you; the Lord speaks from his holy Temple.

³Look! The LORD is coming! He leaves his throne in heaven and comes to earth, walking on the high places. ⁴They melt beneath his feet and flow into the valleys like wax in a fire, like water pouring down a hill.

⁵And why is this happening? Because of the sins and rebellion of Israel and Judah.* Who is to blame for Israel's rebellion? Samaria, its capital city! Where is the center of idolatry in Judah? In Jerusalem, its capital!

⁶"So I, the LORD, will make the city of Samaria a heap of rubble. Her streets will be plowed up for planting vineyards. I will roll the stones of her walls down into the valley below, exposing all her foundations. ⁷All her carved images will be smashed to pieces. All her sacred treasures will be burned up. These things were bought with the money earned by her prostitution, and they will now be carried away to pay prostitutes elsewhere."

⁸Because of all this, I will mourn and lament. I will walk around naked and barefoot in sorrow and shame. I will howl like a jackal and wail like an ostrich. ⁹For my people's wound is far too deep to heal. It has reached into Judah, even to the gates of Jerusalem.

¹⁰Don't tell our enemies in the city of Gath*; don't weep at all.* You people in Beth-leaphrah,* roll in the dust to show your anguish and despair. ¹¹You people of Shaphir,* go as captives into exile—naked and ashamed. The people of Zaanan* dare not come outside their walls. The people of Beth-ezel* mourn because the very foundations of their city have been swept away. ¹²The people of Maroth* anxiously wait for relief, but only bitterness awaits them as the LORD's judgment reaches even to the gates of Jerusalem.

¹³Quick! Use your swiftest chariots and flee, you people of Lachish.* You were the first city in Judah to follow Israel in the sin of idol worship, and so you led Jerusalem* into sin. ¹⁴Send a farewell gift to Moresheth-gath; there is no hope of saving it. The town of Aczib* has deceived the kings of Israel, for it promised help it could not give. ¹⁵You people of Mareshah,* I will bring a conqueror to capture your town. And the leaders* of Israel will go to Adullam.

¹⁶Weep, you people of Judah! Shave your heads in sorrow, for the children you love will be snatched away, and you will never see them again. Make yourselves as bald as an eagle, for your little ones will be exiled to distant lands.

Judgment against Wealthy Oppressors

How terrible it will be for you who lie awake at night, thinking up evil plans. You rise at dawn and hurry to carry out any of the wicked schemes you have power to accomplish. ²When you want a certain piece of land, you find a way to seize it. When you want someone's house, you take it by

---

1:5 Hebrew *and Jacob.* 1:10a *Gath* sounds like the Hebrew term for "tell." 1:10b Greek version reads *weep not in Acco.* 1:10c *Beth-leaphrah* means "house of dust." 1:11a *Shaphir* means "pleasant." 1:11b *Zaanan* sounds like the Hebrew term for "come out." 1:11c *Beth-ezel* means "adjoining house." 1:12 *Maroth* sounds like the Hebrew term for "bitter." 1:13a *Lachish* sounds like the Hebrew term for "team of horses." 1:13b Hebrew *the daughter of Zion.* 1:14 *Aczib* means "deception." 1:15a *Mareshah* sounds like the Hebrew term for "conqueror." 1:15b Hebrew *the glory.*

fraud and violence. No one's family or inheritance is safe with you around!

³But this is what the LORD says: "I will reward your evil with evil; you won't be able to escape! After I am through with you, none of you will ever again walk proudly in the streets."

⁴In that day your enemies will make fun of you by singing this song of despair about your experience:

"We are finished,
    completely ruined!
God has confiscated our land,
    taking it from us.
He has given our fields
    to those who betrayed us.*"

⁵Others will set your boundaries then, and the LORD's people will have no say in how the land is divided.

True and False Prophets

⁶"Don't say such things," the people say. "Don't prophesy like that. Such disasters will never come our way!"

⁷Should you talk that way, O family of Israel*? Will the LORD have patience with such behavior? If you would do what is right, you would find my words to be good. ⁸Yet to this very hour my people rise against me! You steal the shirts right off the backs of those who trusted you, making them as ragged as men who have just come home from battle. ⁹You have evicted women from their homes and stripped their children of all their God-given rights. ¹⁰Up! Begone! This is no longer your land and home, for you have filled it with sin and ruined it completely.

¹¹Suppose a prophet full of lies were to say to you, "I'll preach to you the joys of wine and drink!" That's just the kind of prophet you would like!

Hope for Restoration

¹²"Someday, O Israel, I will gather the few of you who are left. I will bring you together again like sheep in a fold, like a flock in its pasture. Yes, your land will again be filled with noisy crowds! ¹³Your leader will break out and lead you out of exile. He will bring you through the gates of your cities of captivity, back to your own land. Your king will lead you; the LORD himself will guide you."

CHAPTER 3
Judgment against Israel's Leaders

Listen, you leaders of Israel! You are supposed to know right from wrong, ²but you are the very ones who hate good and love evil. You skin my people alive and tear the flesh off their bones. ³You eat my people's flesh, cut away their skin, and break their bones. You chop them up like meat for the cooking pot. ⁴Then you beg the LORD for help in times of trouble! Do you really expect him to listen? After all the evil you have done, he won't even look at you!

⁵This is what the LORD says to you false prophets: "You are leading my people astray! You promise peace for those who give you food, but you declare war on anyone who refuses to pay you. ⁶Now the night will close around you, cutting off all your visions. Darkness will cover you, making it impossible for you to predict the future. The sun will set for you prophets, and your day will come to an end. ⁷Then you seers will cover your faces in shame, and you diviners will be disgraced. And you will admit that your messages were not from God."

⁸But as for me, I am filled with power and the Spirit of the LORD. I am filled with justice and might, fearlessly pointing out Israel's sin and rebellion. ⁹Listen to me, you leaders of Israel! You hate justice and twist all that is right. ¹⁰You are building Jerusalem on a foundation of murder and corruption. ¹¹You rulers govern for the bribes you can get; you priests teach God's laws only for a price; you prophets won't prophesy unless you are paid. Yet all of you claim you are depending on the LORD. "No harm can come to us," you say, "for the LORD is here among us."

¹²So because of you, Mount Zion will be plowed like an open field; Jerusalem will be reduced to rubble! A great forest will grow on the hilltop, where the Temple now stands.

CHAPTER 4
The LORD's Future Reign

In the last days, the Temple of the LORD in Jerusalem will become the most important place on earth. People from all over the world will go there to worship. ²Many nations will come and say, "Come, let us go up to the mountain of the LORD, to the Temple of the God of Israel.* There he will teach us his ways, so that we may obey him." For in those days the LORD's teaching and his word will go out from Jerusalem.

³The LORD will settle international disputes. All the nations will beat their swords into plowshares and their spears into pruning hooks. All wars will stop, and military training will come to an end. ⁴Everyone will live quietly in their own

---

2:4 Or *to those who took us captive.*   2:7 Hebrew *house of Jacob.*   4:2 Hebrew *of Jacob.*

homes in peace and prosperity, for there will be nothing to fear. The LORD Almighty has promised this! ⁵Even though the nations around us worship idols, we will follow the LORD our God forever and ever.

Israel's Return from Exile
⁶"In that coming day," says the LORD, "I will gather together my people who are lame, who have been exiles, filled with grief. ⁷They are weak and far from home, but I will make them strong again, a mighty nation. Then I, the LORD, will rule from Jerusalem* as their king forever."

⁸As for you, O Jerusalem, the citadel of God's people, your royal might and power will come back to you again. The kingship will be restored to my precious Jerusalem. ⁹But why are you now screaming in terror? Have you no king to lead you? He is dead! Have you no wise people to counsel you? All are gone! Pain has gripped you like it does a woman in labor. ¹⁰Writhe and groan in terrible pain, you people of Jerusalem,* for you must leave this city to live in the open fields. You will soon be sent into exile in distant Babylon. But the LORD will rescue you there; he will redeem you from the grip of your enemies.

¹¹True, many nations have gathered together against you, calling for your blood, eager to gloat over your destruction. ¹²But they do not know the LORD's thoughts or understand his plan. These nations don't know that he is gathering them together to be beaten and trampled like bundles of grain on a threshing floor.

¹³"Rise up and destroy the nations, O Jerusalem!"* says the LORD. "For I will give you iron horns and bronze hooves, so you can trample many nations to pieces. Then you will give all the wealth they acquired as offerings to me, the Lord of all the earth."

CHAPTER **5**
A Ruler from Bethlehem
Mobilize! Marshal your troops! The enemy is laying siege to Jerusalem. With a rod they will strike the leader of Israel in the face.

²But you, O Bethlehem Ephrathah, are only a small village in Judah. Yet a ruler of Israel will come from you, one whose origins are from the distant past. ³The people of Israel will be abandoned to their enemies until the time when the woman in labor gives birth to her son. Then at last his fellow countrymen will return from exile to their own land. ⁴And he will stand to lead his flock with the LORD's strength, in the majesty of the name of the LORD his God. Then his people will live there undisturbed, for he will be highly honored all around the world. ⁵And he will be the source of our peace.

When the Assyrians invade our land and break through our defenses, we will appoint seven rulers to watch over us, eight princes to lead us. ⁶They will rule Assyria with drawn swords and enter the gates of the land of Nimrod. They* will rescue us from the Assyrians when they pour over the borders to invade our land.

The Remnant Purified
⁷Then the few left in Israel* will go out among the nations. They will be like dew sent by the LORD or like rain falling on the grass, which no one can hold back. ⁸The remnant of Israel will go out among the nations and be as strong as a lion. And the other nations will be like helpless sheep, with no one to rescue them. ⁹The people of Israel will stand up to their foes, and all their enemies will be wiped out.

¹⁰"At that same time," says the LORD, "I will destroy all your weapons—your horses and chariots. ¹¹I will tear down your walls and demolish the defenses of your cities. ¹²I will put an end to all witchcraft; there will be no more fortune-tellers to consult. ¹³I will destroy all your idols and sacred pillars, so you will never again worship the work of your own hands. ¹⁴I will abolish your pagan shrines with their Asherah poles and destroy the cities where your idol temples stand. ¹⁵I will pour out my vengeance on all the nations that refuse to obey me."

CHAPTER **6**
The LORD's Case against Israel
Listen to what the LORD is saying: "Stand up and state your case against me. Let the mountains and hills be called to witness your complaints.

²"And now, O mountains, listen to the LORD's complaint! He has a case against his people Israel! He will prosecute them to the full extent of the law. ³O my people, what have I done to make you turn from me? Tell me why your patience is exhausted! Answer me! ⁴For I brought you out of Egypt and redeemed you from your slavery. I sent Moses, Aaron, and Miriam to help you.

⁵"Don't you remember, my people, how King Balak of Moab tried to have you cursed and how

4:7 Hebrew *Mount Zion.*   4:10 Hebrew *O daughter of Zion.*   4:13 Hebrew *"Rise up and thresh, O daughter of Zion."*   5:6 Hebrew *He.*
5:7 Hebrew *Jacob;* also in 5:8.

Balaam son of Beor blessed you instead? And remember your journey from Acacia* to Gilgal, when I, the LORD, did everything I could to teach you about my faithfulness."

6What can we bring to the LORD to make up for what we've done? Should we bow before God with offerings of yearling calves? 7Should we offer him thousands of rams and tens of thousands of rivers of olive oil? Would that please the LORD? Should we sacrifice our first-born children to pay for the sins of our souls? Would that make him glad?

8No, O people, the LORD has already told you what is good, and this is what he requires: to do what is right, to love mercy, and to walk humbly with your God.

Israel's Guilt and Punishment
9Listen! Fear the LORD if you are wise! His voice is calling out to everyone in Jerusalem: "The armies of destruction are coming; the LORD is sending them.* 10Will there be no end of your getting rich by cheating? The homes of the wicked are filled with treasures gained by dishonestly measuring out grain in short measures.* 11And how can I tolerate all your merchants who use dishonest scales and weights? 12The rich among you have become wealthy through extortion and violence. Your citizens are so used to lying that their tongues can no longer tell the truth.

13"Therefore, I will wound you! I will bring you to ruin for all your sins. 14You will eat but never have enough. Your hunger pangs and emptiness will still remain. And though you try to save your money, it will come to nothing in the end. You will save a little, but I will give it to those who conquer you. 15You will plant crops but not harvest them. You will press your olives but not get enough oil to anoint yourselves. You will trample the grapes but get no juice to make your wine.

16"The only laws you keep are those of evil King Omri; the only example you follow is that of wicked King Ahab! Therefore, I will make an example of you, bringing you to complete ruin. You will be treated with contempt, mocked by all who see you."

CHAPTER **7**
Misery Turned to Hope
What misery is mine! I feel like the fruit picker after the harvest who can find nothing to eat. Not a cluster of grapes or a single fig can be found to satisfy my hunger. 2The godly people have all disappeared; not one fair-minded person is left on the earth. They are all murderers, even setting traps for their own brothers. 3They go about their evil deeds with both hands. How skilled they are at using them! Officials and judges alike demand bribes. The people with money and influence pay them off, and together they scheme to twist justice. 4Even the best of them is like a brier; the straightest is more crooked than a hedge of thorns. But your judgment day is coming swiftly now. Your time of punishment is here.

5Don't trust anyone—not your best friend or even your wife! 6For the son despises his father. The daughter defies her mother. The daughter-in-law defies her mother-in-law. Your enemies will be right in your own household.

7As for me, I look to the LORD for his help. I wait confidently for God to save me, and my God will certainly hear me. 8Do not gloat over me, my enemies! For though I fall, I will rise again. Though I sit in darkness, the LORD himself will be my light. 9I will be patient as the LORD punishes me, for I have sinned against him. But after that, he will take up my case and punish my enemies for all the evil they have done to me. The LORD will bring me out of my darkness into the light, and I will see his righteousness. 10Then my enemies will see that the LORD is on my side. They will be ashamed that they taunted me, saying, "Where is the LORD—that God of yours?" With my own eyes I will see them trampled down like mud in the streets.

11In that day, Israel, your cities will be rebuilt, and your borders will be extended. 12People from many lands will come and honor you—from Assyria all the way to the towns of Egypt, and from Egypt all the way to the Euphrates River,* and from many distant seas and mountains. 13But the land* will become empty and desolate because of the wickedness of those who live there.

The LORD's Compassion on Israel
14O LORD, come and rule your people; lead your flock in green pastures. Help them to live in peace and prosperity. Let them enjoy the fertile pastures of Bashan and Gilead as they did long ago.

15"Yes," says the LORD, "I will do mighty miracles for you, like those I did when I rescued you from slavery in Egypt."

16All the nations of the world will stand amazed at what the LORD will do for you. They will be embarrassed that their power is so insig-

6:5 Hebrew *Shittim.* 6:9 Hebrew *"Listen to the rod. Who appointed it?"* 6:10 Hebrew *by using the short ephah;* the ephah was a unit for measuring grain. 7:12 Hebrew *the river.* 7:13 Or *earth.*

nificant. They will stand in silent awe, deaf to everything around them. 17They will come to realize what lowly creatures they really are. Like snakes crawling from their holes, they will come out to meet the LORD our God. They will fear him greatly, trembling in terror at his presence.

18Where is another God like you, who pardons the sins of the survivors among his people? You cannot stay angry with your people forever, because you delight in showing mercy. 19Once again you will have compassion on us. You will trample our sins under your feet and throw them into the depths of the ocean! 20You will show us your faithfulness and unfailing love as you promised with an oath to our ancestors Abraham and Jacob long ago.

Nahum

This message concerning Nineveh came as a vision to Nahum, who lived in Elkosh.

The LORD's Anger against Nineveh

2The LORD is a jealous God, filled with vengeance and wrath. He takes revenge on all who oppose him and furiously destroys his enemies! 3The LORD is slow to get angry, but his power is great, and he never lets the guilty go unpunished. He displays his power in the whirlwind and the storm. The billowing clouds are the dust beneath his feet. 4At his command the oceans and rivers dry up, the lush pastures of Bashan and Carmel fade, and the green forests of Lebanon wilt. 5In his presence the mountains quake, and the hills melt away; the earth trembles, and its people are destroyed. 6Who can stand before his fierce anger? Who can survive his burning fury? His rage blazes forth like fire, and the mountains crumble to dust in his presence.

7The LORD is good. When trouble comes, he is a strong refuge. And he knows everyone who trusts in him. 8But he sweeps away his enemies in an overwhelming flood. He pursues his foes into the darkness of night.

9Why are you scheming against the LORD? He will destroy you with one blow; he won't need to strike twice! 10His enemies, tangled up like thorns, staggering like drunks, will be burned like dry straw in a field. 11Who is this king of yours who dares to plot evil against the LORD?

12This is what the LORD says: "Even though the Assyrians have many allies, they will be destroyed and disappear. O my people, I have already punished you once, and I will not do it again. 13Now I will break your chains and release you from Assyrian oppression."

14And this is what the LORD says concerning the Assyrians in Nineveh: "You will have no more children to carry on your name. I will destroy all the idols in the temples of your gods. I am preparing a grave for you because you are despicable and don't deserve to live!"

15Look! A messenger is coming over the mountains with good news! He is bringing a message of peace. Celebrate your festivals, O people of Judah, and fulfill all your vows, for your enemies from Nineveh will never invade your land again. They have been completely destroyed!

The Fall of Nineveh

Nineveh, you are already surrounded by enemy armies! Sound the alarm! Man the ramparts! Muster your defenses, and keep a sharp watch for the enemy attack to begin! 2For the land of Israel lies empty and broken after your attacks, but the LORD will restore its honor and power again.

3Shields flash red in the sunlight! The attack begins! See their scarlet uniforms! Watch as their glittering chariots move into position, with a forest of spears waving above them. 4The chariots race recklessly along the streets and through the squares, swift as lightning, flickering like torches. 5The king shouts to his officers; they stumble in their haste, rushing to the walls to set up their defenses. 6But too late! The river gates are open! The enemy has entered! The palace is about to collapse!

7Nineveh's exile has been decreed, and all the servant girls mourn its capture. Listen to them moan like doves; watch them beat their breasts in sorrow. 8Nineveh is like a leaking water reservoir! The people are slipping away. "Stop, stop!"

someone shouts, but the people just keep on running. 9Loot the silver! Plunder the gold! There seems no end to Nineveh's many treasures—its vast, uncounted wealth. 10Soon the city is an empty shambles, stripped of its wealth. Hearts melt in horror, and knees shake. The people stand aghast, their faces pale and trembling.

11Where now is that great Nineveh, lion of the nations, full of fight and boldness, where the old and feeble and the young and tender lived with nothing to fear? 12O Nineveh, you were once a mighty lion! You crushed your enemies to feed your cubs and your mate. You filled your city and your homes with captives and plunder.

13"I am your enemy!" says the LORD Almighty. "Your chariots will soon go up in smoke. The finest of your youth will be killed in battle. Never again will you bring back plunder from conquered nations. Never again will the voices of your proud messengers be heard."

CHAPTER **3**
The LORD's Judgment against Nineveh
How terrible it will be for Nineveh, the city of murder and lies! She is crammed with wealth to be plundered. 2Listen! Hear the crack of the whips as the chariots rush forward against her. Wheels rumble, horses' hooves pound, and chariots clatter as they bump wildly through the streets. 3See the flashing swords and glittering spears in the upraised arms of the cavalry! The dead are lying in the streets—dead bodies, heaps of bodies, everywhere. People stumble over them, scramble to their feet, and fall again. 4All this because Nineveh, the beautiful and faithless city, mistress of deadly charms, enticed the nations with her beauty. She taught them all to worship her false gods, enchanting people everywhere.

5"No wonder I am your enemy!" declares the LORD Almighty. "And now I will lift your skirts so all the earth will see your nakedness and shame. 6I will cover you with filth and show the world how vile you really are. 7All who see you

3:8 Hebrew *No-amon;* also in 3:10. 3:9 Hebrew *Cush.*

will shrink back in horror and say, 'Nineveh lies in utter ruin.' Yet no one anywhere will regret your destruction."

8Are you any better than Thebes,* surrounded by rivers, protected by water on all sides? 9Ethiopia* and the land of Egypt were the source of her strength, which seemed without limit. The nations of Put and Libya also helped and supported her. 10Yet Thebes fell, and her people were led away as captives. Her babies were dashed to death against the stones of the streets. Soldiers cast lots to see who would get the Egyptian officers as servants. All their leaders were bound in chains.

11And you, Nineveh, will also stagger like a drunkard. You will hide for fear of the attacking enemy. 12All your fortresses will fall. They will be devoured like the ripe figs that fall into the mouths of those who shake the trees. 13Your troops will be as weak and helpless as women. The gates of your land will be opened wide to the enemy and set on fire and burned.

14Get ready for the siege! Store up water! Strengthen the defenses! Make bricks to repair the walls! Go into the pits to trample clay, and pack it into molds! 15But in the middle of your preparations, the fire will devour you; the sword will cut you down. The enemy will consume you like locusts, devouring everything they see. There will be no escape, even if you multiply like grasshoppers. 16Merchants, as numerous as the stars, have filled your city with vast wealth. But like a swarm of locusts, they strip the land and then fly away. 17Your princes and officials are also like locusts, crowding together in the hedges to survive the cold. But like locusts that fly away when the sun comes up to warm the earth, all of them will fly away and disappear.

18O Assyrian king, your princes lie dead in the dust. Your people are scattered across the mountains. There is no longer a shepherd to gather them together. 19There is no healing for your wound; your injury is fatal. All who hear of your destruction will clap their hands for joy. Where can anyone be found who has not suffered from your cruelty?

Habakkuk

CHAPTER 1

This is the message that the prophet Habakkuk received from the LORD in a vision.

Habakkuk's Complaint

2 How long, O LORD, must I call for help? But you do not listen! "Violence!" I cry, but you do not come to save. 3 Must I forever see this sin and misery all around me? Wherever I look, I see destruction and violence. I am surrounded by people who love to argue and fight. 4 The law has become paralyzed and useless, and there is no justice given in the courts. The wicked far outnumber the righteous, and justice is perverted with bribes and trickery.

The LORD's Reply

5 The LORD replied, "Look at the nations and be amazed! Watch and be astounded at what I will do! For I am doing something in your own day, something you wouldn't believe even if someone told you about it. 6 I am raising up the Babylonians* to be a new power on the world scene. They are a cruel and violent nation who will march across the world and conquer it. 7 They are notorious for their cruelty. They do as they like, and no one can stop them. 8 Their horses are swifter than leopards. They are a fierce people, more fierce than wolves at dusk. Their horsemen race forward from distant places. Like eagles they swoop down to pounce on their prey.

9 "On they come, all of them bent on violence. Their hordes advance like a wind from the desert, sweeping captives ahead of them like sand. 10 They scoff at kings and princes and scorn all their defenses. They simply pile ramps of earth against their walls and capture them! 11 They sweep past like the wind and are gone.

1:6 Or Chaldeans.

But they are deeply guilty, for their own strength is their god."

Habakkuk's Second Complaint

12 O LORD my God, my Holy One, you who are eternal—is your plan in all of this to wipe us out? Surely not! O LORD our Rock, you have decreed the rise of these Babylonians to punish and correct us for our terrible sins. 13 You are perfectly just in this. But will you, who cannot allow sin in any form, stand idly by while they swallow us up? Should you be silent while the wicked destroy people who are more righteous than they?

14 Are we but fish to be caught and killed? Are we but creeping things that have no leader to defend them from their enemies? 15 Must we be strung up on their hooks and dragged out in their nets while they rejoice? 16 Then they will worship their nets and burn incense in front of them. "These nets are the gods who have made us rich!" they will claim.

17 Will you let them get away with this forever? Will they succeed forever in their heartless conquests?

CHAPTER 2

I will climb up into my watchtower now and wait to see what the LORD will say to me and how he will answer my complaint.

The LORD's Second Reply

2 Then the LORD said to me, "Write my answer in large, clear letters on a tablet, so that a runner can read it and tell everyone else. 3 But these things I plan won't happen right away. Slowly, steadily, surely, the time approaches when the vision will be fulfilled. If it seems slow, wait

God Is in Control Read HABAKKUK 3:2-19

The prophet Habakkuk penned these words during a time of great trial. His heart was broken by the apparent success of the wicked around him. He brought his concerns before the Lord in the first two chapters of this book. Here he reflects upon the fact that God is sovereign and is ultimately in control of all events. In the end, God will sustain his people.

Many people today question how a good God could allow wars, natural disasters, sickness, crime, and suffering. Yet, as Habakkuk realized, the character of God remains unchanged. He still is "the keeper of the keys," so to speak. When faced with doubts and questions in your life, try doing what Habakkuk did to bolster his faith.

- Recognize God's incredible power and give him honor and glory (verses 2-7).
- Realize that God's ultimate purpose will prevail, even if it is unclear at the present time (verses 8-15).
- Patiently wait for the Lord to act in your life and circumstances (verse 16).
- Choose to praise God in spite of how bleak your situation may appear, remembering how he saved you (verses 17-18).
- Rest assured that God will give you the strength to get through the most difficult of trials (verse 19).

For the next note on "Who Is God?" turn to p. 608.

CORNER STONES

---

patiently, for it will surely take place. It will not be delayed.

⁴"Look at the proud! They trust in themselves, and their lives are crooked;* but the righteous will live by their faith.* ⁵Wealth* is treacherous, and the arrogant are never at rest. They range far and wide, with their mouths opened as wide as death,* but they are never satisfied. In their greed they have gathered up many nations and peoples. ⁶But the time is coming when all their captives will taunt them, saying, 'You thieves! At last justice has caught up with you! Now you will get what you deserve for your oppression and extortion!' ⁷Suddenly, your debtors will rise up in anger. They will turn on you and take all you have, while you stand trembling and helpless. ⁸You have plundered many nations; now they will plunder you. You murderers! You have filled the countryside with violence and all the cities, too.

⁹"How terrible it will be for you who get rich by unjust means! You believe your wealth will buy security, putting your families beyond the reach of danger. ¹⁰But by the murders you committed, you have shamed your name and forfeited your lives. ¹¹The very stones in the walls of your houses cry out against you, and the beams in the ceilings echo the complaint.

¹²"How terrible it will be for you who build cities with money gained by murder and corruption! ¹³Has not the LORD Almighty promised that the wealth of nations will turn to ashes? They work so hard, but all in vain! ¹⁴For the time will come when all the earth will be filled, as the waters fill the sea, with an awareness of the glory of the LORD.

¹⁵"How terrible it will be for you who make your neighbors drunk! You force your cup on them so that you can gloat over their nakedness and shame. ¹⁶But soon it will be your turn! Come, drink and be exposed! Drink from the cup of the LORD's judgment, and all your glory will be turned to shame. ¹⁷You cut down the forests of Lebanon. Now you will be cut down! You terrified the wild animals you caught in your traps. Now terror will strike you because of your murder and violence in cities everywhere!

¹⁸"What have you gained by worshiping all your man-made idols? How foolish to trust in something made by your own hands! What fools you are to believe such lies! ¹⁹How terrible it will be for you who beg lifeless wooden idols to save you. You ask speechless stone images to tell you what to do. Can an idol speak for God? They may be overlaid with gold and

2:4a Greek version reads *I will have no pleasure in anyone who turns away.* **2:4b** Or *the just will live by their faithfulness.* **2:5a** As in Dead Sea Scroll 1QpHab; other Hebrew manuscripts read *Wine.* **2:5b** Hebrew *as Sheol.*

silver, but they are lifeless inside. 20But the LORD is in his holy Temple. Let all the earth be silent before him."

CHAPTER 3
Habakkuk's Prayer

This prayer was sung by the prophet Habakkuk:*

2I have heard all about you, LORD, and I am filled with awe by the amazing things you have done. In this time of our deep need, begin again to help us, as you did in years gone by. Show us your power to save us. And in your anger, remember your mercy.

3I see God, the Holy One, moving across the deserts from Edom* and Mount Paran.* His brilliant splendor fills the heavens, and the earth is filled with his praise! What a wonderful God he is! 4Rays of brilliant light flash from his hands. He rejoices in his awesome power.* 5Pestilence marches before him; plague follows close behind. 6When he stops, the earth shakes. When he looks, the nations tremble. He shatters the everlasting mountains and levels the eternal hills. But his power is not diminished in the least! 7I see the peoples of Cushan and Midian trembling in terror.

8Was it in anger, LORD, that you struck the rivers and parted the sea? Were you displeased with them? No, you were sending your chariots of salvation! 9You were commanding your weapons of power! You split open the earth with flowing rivers! 10The mountains watched and trembled. Onward swept the raging waters. The mighty deep cried out, lifting its hands to the LORD. 11The lofty sun and moon began to fade, obscured by brilliance from your arrows and the flashing of your glittering spear.

12You marched across the land in awesome anger and trampled the nations in your fury. 13You went out to rescue your chosen people, to save your anointed ones. You crushed the heads of the wicked and laid bare their bones from head to toe. 14With their own weapons, you destroyed those who rushed out like a whirlwind, thinking Israel would be easy prey. 15You trampled the sea with your horses, and the mighty waters piled high.

16I trembled inside when I heard all this; my lips quivered with fear. My legs gave way beneath me,* and I shook in terror. I will wait quietly for the coming day when disaster will strike the people who invade us. 17Even though the fig trees have no blossoms, and there are no grapes on the vine; even though the olive crop fails, and the fields lie empty and barren; even though the flocks die in the fields, and the cattle barns are empty, 18yet I will rejoice in the LORD! I will be joyful in the God of my salvation! 19The Sovereign LORD is my strength! He will make me as surefooted as a deer* and bring me safely over the mountains.

(For the choir director: This prayer is to be accompanied by stringed instruments.)

3:1 Hebrew adds *according to shigionoth,* probably indicating the musical setting for the prayer.   3:3a Hebrew *Teman.*   3:3b Hebrew adds *selah;* also in 3:9, 13. The meaning of this Hebrew term is uncertain; it is probably a musical or literary term.   3:4 Or *He veils his awesome power.*   3:16 Hebrew *Decay entered my bones.*   3:19 Or *will give me the speed of a deer.*

Zephaniah

CHAPTER **1**

The LORD gave these messages to Zephaniah when Josiah son of Amon was king of Judah. Zephaniah was the son of Cushi, son of Gedaliah, son of Amariah, son of Hezekiah.

Coming Judgment against Judah

2 "I will sweep away everything in all your land," says the LORD. 3 "I will sweep away both people and animals alike. Even the birds of the air and the fish in the sea will die. I will reduce the wicked to heaps of rubble,* along with the rest of humanity," says the LORD. 4 "I will crush Judah and Jerusalem with my fist and destroy every last trace of their Baal worship. I will put an end to all the idolatrous priests, so that even the memory of them will disappear. 5For they go up to their roofs and bow to the sun, moon, and stars. They claim to follow the LORD, but then they worship Molech,* too. So now I will destroy them! 6And I will destroy those who used to worship me but now no longer do. They no longer ask for the LORD's guidance or seek my blessings."

7Stand in silence in the presence of the Sovereign LORD, for the awesome day of the LORD's judgment has come. The LORD has prepared his people for a great slaughter and has chosen their executioners.* 8 "On that day of judgment," says the LORD, "I will punish the leaders and princes of Judah and all those following pagan customs. 9Yes, I will punish those who participate in pagan worship ceremonies, and those who steal and kill to fill their masters' homes with loot.

10 "On that day," says the LORD, "a cry of alarm will come from the Fish Gate and echo throughout the newer Mishneh section* of the city. And a great crashing sound will come from the surrounding hills. 11Wail in sorrow, all you who live in the market area, for all who buy and sell there will die.

12 "I will search with lanterns in Jerusalem's darkest corners to find and punish those who sit contented in their sins, indifferent to the LORD, thinking he will do nothing at all to them. 13They are the very ones whose property will be plundered by the enemy, whose homes will be ransacked. They will never have a chance to live in the new homes they have built. They will never drink wine from the vineyards they have planted.

14 "That terrible day of the LORD is near. Swiftly it comes—a day when strong men will cry bitterly. 15It is a day when the LORD's anger will be poured out. It is a day of terrible distress and anguish, a day of ruin and desolation, a day of darkness and gloom, of clouds, blackness, 16trumpet calls, and battle cries. Down go the walled cities and strongest battlements!

17 "Because you have sinned against the LORD, I will make you as helpless as a blind man searching for a path. Your blood will be poured out into the dust, and your bodies will lie there rotting on the ground."

18Your silver and gold will be of no use to you on that day of the LORD's anger. For the whole land will be devoured by the fire of his jealousy. He will make a terrifying end of all the people on earth.*

CHAPTER **2**

A Call to Repentance

Gather together and pray, you shameless nation. 2Gather while there is still time, before judgment begins and your opportunity is blown away like chaff. Act now, before the fierce fury of

---

1:3 The meaning of the Hebrew is uncertain.   1:5 Hebrew *Malcam*, another name for Molech; or it could possibly mean *their king.*
1:7 Hebrew *has prepared a sacrifice and sanctified his guests.*   1:10 Or *the Second Quarter,* a newer section of Jerusalem.   1:18 Or *the people living in the land.*

the LORD falls and the terrible day of the LORD's anger begins. ³Beg the LORD to save you—all you who are humble, all you who uphold justice. Walk humbly and do what is right. Perhaps even yet the LORD will protect you from his anger on that day of destruction.

Judgment against Philistia

⁴Gaza, Ashkelon, Ashdod, Ekron—these Philistine cities, too, will be rooted out and left in desolation. ⁵And how terrible it will be for you Philistines* who live along the coast and in the land of Canaan, for this judgment is against you, too! The LORD will destroy you until not one of you is left. ⁶The coastal area will become a pasture, a place of shepherd camps and enclosures for sheep.

⁷The few survivors of the tribe of Judah will pasture there. They will lie down to rest in the abandoned houses in Ashkelon. For the LORD their God will visit his people in kindness and restore their prosperity again.

Judgment against Moab and Ammon

⁸"I have heard the taunts of the people of Moab and Ammon, mocking my people and invading their borders. ⁹Now, as surely as I live," says the LORD Almighty, the God of Israel, "Moab and Ammon will be destroyed as completely as Sodom and Gomorrah. Their land will become a place of stinging nettles, salt pits, and eternal desolation. Those of my people who are left will plunder them and take their land."

¹⁰They will receive the wages of their pride, for they have scoffed at the people of the LORD Almighty. ¹¹The LORD will terrify them as he destroys all the gods in the land. Then people from nations around the world will worship the LORD, each in their own land.

Judgment against Ethiopia and Assyria

¹²"You Ethiopians* will also be slaughtered by my sword," says the LORD.

¹³And the LORD will strike the lands of the north with his fist. He will destroy Assyria and make its great capital, Nineveh, a desolate wasteland, parched like a desert. ¹⁴The city that once was so proud will become a pasture for sheep and cattle. All sorts of wild animals will settle there. Owls of many kinds will live among the ruins of its palaces, hooting from the gaping windows. Rubble will block all the doorways, and the cedar paneling will lie open to the wind and weather.

¹⁵This is the fate of that boisterous city, once so secure. "In all the world there is no city as great as I," it boasted. But now, look how it has become an utter ruin, a place where animals live! Everyone passing that way will laugh in derision or shake a defiant fist.

CHAPTER 3

Jerusalem's Rebellion and Redemption

How terrible it will be for rebellious, polluted Jerusalem, the city of violence and crime. ²It proudly refuses to listen even to the voice of the LORD. No one can tell it anything; it refuses all correction. It does not trust in the LORD or draw near to its God.

³Its leaders are like roaring lions hunting for their victims—out for everything they can get. Its judges are like ravenous wolves at evening time, who by dawn have left no trace of their prey. ⁴Its prophets are arrogant liars seeking their own gain. Its priests defile the Temple by disobeying God's laws. ⁵But the LORD is still there in the city, and he does no wrong. Day by day his justice is more evident, but no one takes notice—the wicked know no shame.

⁶"I have wiped out many nations, devastating their fortress walls and towers. Their cities are now deserted; their streets are in silent ruin. There are no survivors to even tell what happened. ⁷I thought, 'Surely they will have reverence for me now! Surely they will listen to my warnings, so I won't need to strike again.' But no; however much I punish them, they continue their evil practices from dawn till dusk and dusk till dawn." ⁸So now the LORD says: "Be patient; the time is coming soon when I will stand up and accuse these evil nations. For it is my decision to gather together the kingdoms of the earth and pour out my fiercest anger and fury on them. All the earth will be devoured by the fire of my jealousy.

⁹"On that day I will purify the lips of all people, so that everyone will be able to worship the LORD together. ¹⁰My scattered people who live beyond the rivers of Ethiopia* will come to present their offerings. ¹¹And then you will no longer need to be ashamed of yourselves, for you will no longer be rebels against me. I will remove all the proud and arrogant people from among you. There will be no pride on my holy mountain. ¹²Those who are left will be the lowly and the humble, for it is they who trust in the name of the LORD. ¹³The people of Israel who survive

2:5 Hebrew *Kerethites.* 2:12 Hebrew *Cushites.* 3:10 Hebrew *Cush.*

will do no wrong to each other, never telling lies or deceiving one another. They will live peaceful lives, lying down to sleep in safety; there will be no one to make them afraid."

14Sing, O daughter of Zion; shout aloud, O Israel! Be glad and rejoice with all your heart, O daughter of Jerusalem! 15For the LORD will remove his hand of judgment and will disperse the armies of your enemy. And the LORD himself, the King of Israel, will live among you! At last your troubles will be over, and you will fear disaster no more.

16On that day the announcement to Jerusalem will be, "Cheer up, Zion! Don't be afraid! 17For the LORD your God has arrived to live among you. He is a mighty savior. He will rejoice

3:18 The meaning of the Hebrew for this verse is uncertain.

over you with great gladness. With his love, he will calm all your fears. He will exult over you by singing a happy song."

18"I will gather you who mourn for the appointed festivals; you will be disgraced no more.* 19And I will deal severely with all who have oppressed you. I will save the weak and helpless ones; I will bring together those who were chased away. I will give glory and renown to my former exiles, who have been mocked and shamed. 20On that day I will gather you together and bring you home again. I will give you a good name, a name of distinction among all the nations of the earth. They will praise you as I restore your fortunes before their very eyes. I, the LORD, have spoken!"

Haggai

A Call to Rebuild the Temple

On August 29* of the second year of King Darius's reign, the LORD gave a message through the prophet Haggai to Zerubbabel son of Shealtiel, governor of Judah, and to Jeshua* son of Jehozadak, the high priest. 2 "This is what the LORD Almighty says: The people are saying, 'The time has not yet come to rebuild the LORD's house—the Temple.'"

3 So the LORD sent this message through the prophet Haggai: 4 "Why are you living in luxurious houses while my house lies in ruins? 5 This is what the LORD Almighty says: Consider how things are going for you! 6 You have planted much but harvested little. You have food to eat, but not enough to fill you up. You have wine to drink, but not enough to satisfy your thirst. You have clothing to wear, but not enough to keep you warm. Your wages disappear as though you were putting them in pockets filled with holes!

7 "This is what the LORD Almighty says: Consider how things are going for you! 8 Now go up into the hills, bring down timber, and rebuild my house. Then I will take pleasure in it and be honored, says the LORD. 9 You hoped for rich harvests, but they were poor. And when you brought your harvest home, I blew it away. Why? Because my house lies in ruins, says the LORD Almighty, while you are all busy building your own fine houses. 10 That is why the heavens have withheld the dew and the earth has withheld its crops. 11 I have called for a drought on your fields and hills—a drought to wither the grain and grapes and olives and all your other crops, a drought to starve both you and your cattle and to ruin everything you have worked so hard to get."

Obedience to God's Call

12 Then Zerubbabel son of Shealtiel, Jeshua son of Jehozadak, the high priest, and the whole remnant of God's people obeyed the message from the LORD their God. It had been delivered by the prophet Haggai, whom the LORD their God had sent, and the people worshiped the LORD in earnest. 13 Then Haggai, the LORD's messenger, gave the people this message from the LORD: "I am with you, says the LORD!" 14 So the LORD sparked the enthusiasm of Zerubbabel son of Shealtiel, governor of Judah, Jeshua son of Jehozadak, the high priest, and the whole remnant of God's people. They came and began their work on the house of the LORD Almighty, their God. 15 This was on September 21* of the second year of King Darius's reign.

The New Temple's Splendor

Then on October 17* of that same year, the LORD sent another message through the prophet Haggai. 2 "Say this to Zerubbabel son of Shealtiel, governor of Judah, and to Jeshua* son of Jehozadak, the high priest, and to the remnant of God's people there in the land: 3 Is there anyone who can remember this house—the Temple—as it was before? In comparison, how does it look to you now? It must seem like nothing at all! 4 But now take courage, Zerubbabel, says the LORD. Take courage, Jeshua son of Jehozadak, the

---

1:1a Hebrew *On the first day of the sixth month,* of the Hebrew calendar. A number of dates in Haggai can be cross-checked with dates in surviving Persian records and related accurately to our modern calendar. This event occurred on August 29, 520 B.C. 1:1b Hebrew *Joshua,* a variant name for Jeshua; also in 1:12, 14. 1:15 Hebrew *on the twenty-fourth day of the sixth month,* of the Hebrew calendar. This event occurred on September 21, 520 B.C.; also see note on 1:1a. 2:1 Hebrew *on the twenty-first day of the seventh month,* of the Hebrew calendar. This event occurred on October 17, 520 B.C.; also see note on 1:1a. 2:2 Hebrew *Joshua,* a variant name for Jeshua; also in 2:4.

high priest. Take courage, all you people still left in the land, says the LORD. Take courage and work, for I am with you, says the LORD Almighty. 5My Spirit remains among you, just as I promised when you came out of Egypt. So do not be afraid.

6"For this is what the LORD Almighty says: In just a little while I will again shake the heavens and the earth. I will shake the oceans and the dry land, too. 7I will shake all the nations, and the treasures of all the nations will come to this Temple. I will fill this place with glory, says the LORD Almighty. 8The silver is mine, and the gold is mine, says the LORD Almighty. 9The future glory of this Temple will be greater than its past glory, says the LORD Almighty. And in this place I will bring peace. I, the LORD Almighty, have spoken!"

Blessings Promised for Obedience

10On December 18* of the second year of King Darius's reign, the LORD sent this message to the prophet Haggai: 11"This is what the LORD Almighty says! Ask the priests this question about the law: 12If one of you is carrying a holy sacrifice in his robes and happens to brush against some bread or stew, wine or oil, or any other kind of food, will it also become holy?"

The priests replied, "No."

13Then Haggai asked, "But if someone becomes ceremonially unclean by touching a dead person and then brushes against any of the things mentioned, will it be defiled?"

And the priests answered, "Yes."

14Then Haggai said, "That is how it is with this people and this nation, says the LORD. Everything they do and everything they offer is defiled. 15So think about this from now on—consider how things were going for you before you began to lay the foundation of the LORD's Temple. 16When you hoped for a twenty-bushel crop, you harvested only ten. When you expected to draw fifty gallons from the winepress, you found only twenty. 17I sent blight and mildew and hail to destroy all the produce of your labor. Yet, even so, you refused to return to me, says the LORD.

18"On this eighteenth day of December—the day when the foundation of the LORD's Temple was laid—carefully consider this: 19I am giving you a promise now while the seed is still in the barn, before you have harvested your grain and before the grapevine, the fig tree, the pomegranate, and the olive tree have produced their crops. From this day onward I will bless you."

Promises for Zerubbabel

20The LORD sent this second message to Haggai on December 18*: 21"Tell Zerubbabel, the governor of Judah, that I am about to shake the heavens and the earth. 22I will overthrow royal thrones, destroying the power of foreign kingdoms. I will overturn their chariots and charioteers. The horses will fall, and their riders will kill each other. 23But when this happens, says the LORD Almighty, I will honor you, Zerubbabel son of Shealtiel, my servant. I will treat you like a signet ring on my finger, says the LORD, for I have specially chosen you. I, the LORD Almighty, have spoken!"

2:10 Hebrew *On the twenty-fourth day of the ninth month*, of the Hebrew calendar (also in 2:18). This event occurred on December 18, 520 B.C.; also see note on 1:1a. 2:20 Hebrew *on the twenty-fourth day of the month*; see note on 2:10.

Zechariah

CHAPTER 1

A Call to Return to the LORD

In midautumn* of the second year of King Darius's reign, the LORD gave this message to the prophet Zechariah son of Berekiah and grandson of Iddo.

2 "I, the LORD, was very angry with your ancestors. 3 Therefore, say to the people, 'This is what the LORD Almighty says: Return to me, and I will return to you, says the LORD Almighty.' 4 Do not be like your ancestors who would not listen when the earlier prophets said to them, 'This is what the LORD Almighty says: Turn from your evil ways and stop all your evil practices.'

5 "Your ancestors and their prophets are now long dead. 6 But all the things I said through my servants the prophets happened to your ancestors, just as I said they would. As a result, they repented and said, 'We have received what we deserved from the LORD Almighty. He has done what he said he would do.' "

A Man among the Myrtle Trees

7 Then on February 15* of the second year of King Darius's reign, the LORD sent another message to the prophet Zechariah son of Berekiah and grandson of Iddo. Zechariah said:

8 In a vision during the night, I saw a man sitting on a red horse that was standing among some myrtle trees in a small valley. Behind him were red, brown, and white horses, each with its own rider. 9 I asked the angel who was talking with me, "My lord, what are all those horses for?"

"I will show you," the angel replied.

10 So the man standing among the myrtle trees explained, "They are the ones the LORD has sent out to patrol the earth."

11 Then the other riders reported to the angel of the LORD, who was standing among the myrtle trees, "We have patrolled the earth, and the whole earth is at peace."

12 Upon hearing this, the angel of the LORD prayed this prayer: "O LORD Almighty, for seventy years now you have been angry with Jerusalem and the towns of Judah. How long will it be until you again show mercy to them?" 13 And the LORD spoke kind and comforting words to the angel who talked with me.

14 Then the angel said to me, "Shout this message for all to hear: 'This is what the LORD Almighty says: My love for Jerusalem and Mount Zion is passionate and strong. 15 But I am very angry with the other nations that enjoy peace and security. I was only a little angry with my people, but the nations punished them far beyond my intentions.

16 " 'Therefore, this is what the LORD says: I have returned to show mercy to Jerusalem. My Temple will be rebuilt, says the LORD Almighty, and plans will be made for the reconstruction of Jerusalem.*' 17 Say this also: 'This is what the LORD Almighty says: The towns of Israel will again overflow with prosperity, and the LORD will again comfort Zion and choose Jerusalem as his own.' "

Four Horns and Four Blacksmiths

18 Then I looked up and saw four animal horns. 19 "What are these?" I asked the angel who was talking with me.

He replied, "These horns represent the world powers that scattered Judah, Israel, and Jerusalem."

1:1 Hebrew *In the eighth month.* A number of dates in Zechariah can be cross-checked with dates in surviving Persian records and related accurately to our modern calendar. This month of the Hebrew lunar calendar occurred in October and November 520 B.C. 1:7 Hebrew *on the twenty-fourth day of the eleventh month, the month of Shebat,* of the Hebrew calendar. This event occurred on February 15, 519 B.C.; also see note on 1:1. 1:16 Hebrew *and the measuring line will be stretched out over Jerusalem.*

20Then the LORD showed me four blacksmiths. 21"What are these men coming to do?" I asked.

The angel replied, "The blacksmiths have come to terrify the four horns that scattered and humbled Judah. They will throw them down and destroy them."

CHAPTER 2
Future Prosperity of Jerusalem

When I looked around me again, I saw a man with a measuring line in his hand. 2"Where are you going?" I asked.

He replied, "I am going to measure Jerusalem, to see how wide and how long it is."

3Then the angel who was with me went to meet a second angel who was coming toward him. 4The other angel said, "Hurry, and say to that young man, 'Jerusalem will someday be so full of people that it won't have room enough for everyone! Many will live outside the city walls, with all their livestock—and yet they will be safe. 5For I, myself, will be a wall of fire around Jerusalem, says the LORD. And I will be the glory inside the city!'"

The Exiles Are Called Home

6The LORD says, "Come away! Flee from the north, for I have scattered you to the four winds. 7Come away! Escape to Jerusalem,* you who are exiled in Babylon!"

8"After a period of glory, the LORD Almighty sent me against the nations who oppressed you. For he said, 'Anyone who harms you harms my most precious possession.* 9I will raise my fist to crush them, and their own slaves will plunder them.' Then you will know that the LORD Almighty has sent me."

10The LORD says, "Shout and rejoice, O Jerusalem,* for I am coming to live among you. 11Many nations will join themselves to the LORD on that day, and they, too, will be my people. I will live among you, and you will know that the LORD Almighty sent me to you. 12The land of Judah will be the LORD's inheritance in the holy land, and he will once again choose Jerusalem to be his own city. 13Be silent before the LORD, all humanity, for he is springing into action from his holy dwelling."

CHAPTER 3
Cleansing for the High Priest

Then the angel showed me Jeshua* the high priest standing before the angel of the LORD. Satan* was there at the angel's right hand, accusing Jeshua of many things. 2And the LORD said to Satan, "I, the LORD, reject your accusations, Satan. Yes, the LORD, who has chosen Jerusalem, rebukes you. This man is like a burning stick that has been snatched from a fire."

3Jeshua's clothing was filthy as he stood there before the angel. 4So the angel said to the others standing there, "Take off his filthy clothes." And turning to Jeshua he said, "See, I have taken away your sins, and now I am giving you these fine new clothes."

5Then I said, "Please, could he also have a clean turban on his head?" So they put a clean priestly turban on his head and dressed him in new clothes while the angel of the LORD stood by.

6Then the angel of the LORD spoke very solemnly to Jeshua and said, 7"This is what the LORD Almighty says: If you follow my ways and obey my requirements, then you will be given authority over my Temple and its courtyards. I will let you walk in and out of my presence along with these others standing here. 8Listen to me, O Jeshua the high priest, and all you other priests. You are symbols of the good things to come. Soon I am going to bring my servant, the Branch. 9Now look at the jewel I have set before Jeshua, a single stone with seven facets.* I will engrave an inscription on it, says the LORD Almighty, and I will remove the sins of this land in a single day. 10And on that day, says the LORD Almighty, each of you will invite your neighbor into your home to share your peace and prosperity."

CHAPTER 4
A Lampstand and Two Olive Trees

Then the angel who had been talking with me returned and woke me, as though I had been asleep. 2"What do you see now?" he asked.

I answered, "I see a solid gold lampstand with a bowl of oil on top of it. Around the bowl are seven lamps, each one having seven spouts with wicks. 3And I see two olive trees, one on each side of the bowl."

4Then I asked the angel, "What are these, my lord? What do they mean?"

5"Don't you know?" the angel asked.

"No, my lord," I replied.

6Then he said to me, "This is what the LORD says to Zerubbabel: It is not by force nor by strength, but by my Spirit, says the LORD Almighty. 7Nothing, not even a mighty mountain, will stand in Zerubbabel's way; it will flatten out before him! Then Zerubbabel will set the final stone of the

2:7 Hebrew *to Zion.* 2:8 Hebrew *harms the apple of my eye.* 2:10 Hebrew *O daughter of Zion.* 3:1a Hebrew *Joshua,* a variant name for Jeshua; also in 3:3, 4, 6, 8, 9. 3:1b Or *The Accuser;* Hebrew reads *The Adversary;* also in 3:2. 3:9 Hebrew *7 eyes.*

Temple in place, and the people will shout: 'May God bless it! May God bless it!'"

8Then another message came to me from the LORD. 9"Zerubbabel is the one who laid the foundation of this Temple, and he will complete it. Then you will know that the LORD Almighty has sent me. 10Do not despise these small beginnings, for the LORD rejoices to see the work begin, to see the plumb line in Zerubbabel's hand. For these seven lamps represent the eyes of the LORD that search all around the world."

11Then I asked the angel, "What are these two olive trees on each side of the lampstand, 12and what are the two olive branches that pour out golden oil through two gold tubes?"

13"Don't you know?" he asked.

"No, my lord," I replied.

14Then he said to me, "They represent the two anointed ones who assist the Lord of all the earth."

CHAPTER 5
A Flying Scroll

I looked up again and saw a scroll flying through the air.

2"What do you see?" the angel asked.

"I see a flying scroll," I replied. "It appears to be about thirty feet long and fifteen feet wide.*"

3Then he said to me, "This scroll contains the curse that is going out over the entire land. One side says that those who steal will be banished from the land; the other side says that those who swear falsely will be banished from the land. 4And this is what the LORD Almighty says: I am sending this curse into the house of every thief and into the house of everyone who swears falsely by my name. And my curse will remain in that house until it is completely destroyed—even its timbers and stones."

A Woman in a Basket

5Then the angel who was talking with me came forward and said, "Look up! Something is appearing in the sky."

6"What is it?" I asked.

He replied, "It is a basket for measuring grain,* and it is filled with the sins* of everyone throughout the land."

7When the heavy lead cover was lifted off the basket, there was a woman sitting inside it. 8The angel said, "The woman's name is Wickedness," and he pushed her back into the basket and closed the heavy lid again.

9Then I looked up and saw two women flying toward us, with wings gliding on the wind. Their wings were like those of a stork, and they picked up the basket and flew with it into the sky.

10"Where are they taking the basket?" I asked the angel.

11He replied, "To the land of Babylonia,* where they will build a temple for the basket. And when the temple is ready, they will set the basket there on its pedestal."

CHAPTER 6
Four Chariots

Then I looked up again and saw four chariots coming from between two bronze mountains. 2The first chariot was pulled by red horses, the second by black horses, 3the third by white horses, and the fourth by dappled-gray horses. 4"And what are these, my lord?" I asked the angel who was talking with me.

5He replied, "These are the four spirits* of heaven who stand before the Lord of all the earth. They are going out to do his work. 6The chariot with black horses is going north, the chariot with white horses is going west,* and the chariot with dappled-gray horses is going south."

7The powerful horses were eager to be off, to patrol back and forth across the earth. And the LORD said, "Go and patrol the earth!" So they left at once on their patrol.

8Then the LORD summoned me and said, "Those who went north have vented the anger of my Spirit* there."

The Crowning of Jeshua

9Then I received another message from the LORD. 10"Heldai, Tobijah, and Jedaiah will bring gifts of silver and gold from the Jews exiled in Babylon. As soon as they arrive, meet them at the home of Josiah son of Zephaniah. 11Accept their gifts and make a crown* from the silver and gold. Then put the crown on the head of Jeshua* son of Jehozadak, the high priest. 12Tell him that the LORD Almighty says: Here is the man called the Branch. He will branch out where he is and build the Temple of the LORD. 13He will build the LORD's Temple, and he will receive royal honor and will rule as king from his throne. He will also serve as priest from his throne,* and there will be perfect harmony between the two.

5:2 Hebrew 20 cubits [9 meters] long and 10 cubits [4.5 meters] wide. 5:6a Hebrew an ephah, about half a bushel or 18 liters; also in 5:7, 8, 9, 10, 11. 5:6b As in Greek version; Hebrew reads the appearance. 5:11 Hebrew the land of Shinar. 6:5 Or the four winds. 6:6 Hebrew is going after them. 6:8 Hebrew have given my Spirit rest. 6:11a As in Greek and Syriac versions; Hebrew reads crowns. 6:11b Hebrew Joshua, a variant name for Jeshua. 6:13 Or There will be a priest by his throne.

14 "The crown will be a memorial in the Temple of the LORD to honor those who gave it—Heldai,* Tobijah, Jedaiah, and Josiah* son of Zephaniah."

15 Many will come from distant lands to rebuild the Temple of the LORD. And when this happens, you will know my messages have been from the LORD Almighty. All this will happen if you carefully obey the commands of the LORD your God.

CHAPTER 7
A Call to Justice and Mercy

On December 7* of the fourth year of King Darius's reign, another message came to Zechariah from the LORD. 2 The people of Bethel had sent Sharezer and Regemmelech,* along with their men, to seek the LORD's favor. 3 They were to ask this question of the prophets and of the priests at the Temple of the LORD Almighty: "Should we continue to mourn and fast each summer on the anniversary of the Temple's destruction,* as we have done for so many years?"

4 The LORD Almighty sent me this message: 5 "Say to all your people and your priests, 'During those seventy years of exile, when you fasted and mourned in the summer and at the festival in early autumn,* was it really for me that you were fasting? 6 And even now in your holy festivals, you don't think about me but only of pleasing yourselves. 7 Isn't this the same message the LORD proclaimed through the prophets years ago when Jerusalem and the towns of Judah were bustling with people, and the Negev and the foothills of Judah* were populated areas?'"

8 Then this message came to Zechariah from the LORD: 9 "This is what the LORD Almighty says: Judge fairly and honestly, and show mercy and kindness to one another. 10 Do not oppress widows, orphans, foreigners, and poor people. And do not make evil plans to harm each other.

11 "Your ancestors would not listen to this message. They turned stubbornly away and put their fingers in their ears to keep from hearing. 12 They made their hearts as hard as stone, so they could not hear the law or the messages that the LORD Almighty had sent them by his Spirit through the earlier prophets. That is why the LORD Almighty was so angry with them.

13 "Since they refused to listen when I called to them, I would not listen when they called to me, says the LORD Almighty. 14 I scattered them as with a whirlwind among the distant nations, where they lived as strangers. Their land became so desolate that no one even traveled through it. The land that had been so pleasant became a desert."

CHAPTER 8
Promised Blessings for Jerusalem

Then another message came to me from the LORD Almighty: 2 "This is what the LORD Almighty says: My love for Mount Zion is passionate and strong; I am consumed with passion for Jerusalem! 3 And now the LORD says: I am returning to Mount Zion, and I will live in Jerusalem. Then Jerusalem will be called the Faithful City; the mountain of the LORD Almighty will be called the Holy Mountain. 4 This is what the LORD Almighty says: Once again old men and women will walk Jerusalem's streets with a cane and sit together in the city squares. 5 And the streets of the city will be filled with boys and girls at play.

6 "This is what the LORD Almighty says: All this may seem impossible to you now, a small and discouraged remnant of God's people. But do you think this is impossible for me, the LORD Almighty? 7 This is what the LORD Almighty says: You can be sure that I will rescue my people from the east and from the west. 8 I will bring them home again to live safely in Jerusalem. They will be my people, and I will be faithful and just toward them as their God.

9 "This is what the LORD Almighty says: Take heart and finish the task! You have heard what the prophets have been saying about building the Temple of the LORD Almighty ever since the foundation was laid. 10 Before the work on the Temple began, there were no jobs and no wages for either people or animals. No traveler was safe from the enemy, for there were enemies on all sides. I had turned everyone against each other. 11 But now I will not treat the remnant of my people as I treated them before, says the LORD Almighty. 12 For I am planting seeds of peace and prosperity among you. The grapevines will be heavy with fruit. The earth will produce its crops, and the sky will release the dew. Once more I will make the remnant in Judah and Israel the heirs of these blessings.

6:14a As in Syriac version (compare 6:10); Hebrew reads *Helem.*   6:14b As in Syriac version (compare 6:10); Hebrew reads *Hen.*
7:1 Hebrew *On the fourth day of the ninth month, the month of Kislev,* of the Hebrew calendar. This event occurred on December 7, 518 B.C.; also see note on 1:1.   7:2 Or *Bethel-sharezer had sent Regemmelech.*   7:3 Hebrew *mourn and fast in the fifth month.* This month of the Hebrew lunar calendar usually occurs in July and August.   7:5 Hebrew *fasted and mourned in the fifth and seventh months.* The fifth month of the Hebrew lunar calendar usually occurs in July and August. The seventh month usually occurs in September and October; both the Day of Atonement and the Festival of Shelters were celebrated in the seventh month.   7:7 Hebrew *the Shephelah.*

13Among the nations, Judah and Israel had become symbols of what it means to be cursed. But no longer! Now I will rescue you and make you both a symbol and a source of blessing! So don't be afraid or discouraged, but instead get on with rebuilding the Temple!

14"For this is what the LORD Almighty says: I did not change my mind when your ancestors angered me and I promised to punish them, says the LORD Almighty. 15Neither will I change my decision to bless Jerusalem and the people of Judah. So don't be afraid. 16But this is what you must do: Tell the truth to each other. Render verdicts in your courts that are just and that lead to peace. 17Do not make evil plots to harm each other. And stop this habit of swearing to things that are false. I hate all these things, says the LORD."

18Here is another message that came to me from the LORD Almighty. 19"This is what the LORD Almighty says: The traditional fasts and times of mourning you have kept in early summer, midsummer, autumn, and winter* are now ended. They will become festivals of joy and celebration for the people of Judah. So love truth and peace.

20"This is what the LORD Almighty says: People from nations and cities around the world will travel to Jerusalem. 21The people of one city will say to the people in another, 'Let us go to Jerusalem to ask the LORD to bless us and to seek the LORD Almighty. We are planning to go ourselves.' 22People from many nations, even powerful nations, will come to Jerusalem to seek the LORD Almighty and to ask the LORD to bless them.

23"This is what the LORD Almighty says: In those days ten people from nations and languages around the world will clutch at the hem of one Jew's robe. And they will say, 'Please let us walk with you, for we have heard that God is with you.'"

CHAPTER 9

Judgment against Israel's Enemies

This is the message* from the LORD against the land of Aram* and the city of Damascus, for the eyes of all humanity, including the people of Israel, are on the LORD. 2Doom is certain for Hamath, near Damascus, and for the cities of Tyre and Sidon, too, though they are so clever. 3Tyre has built a strong fortress and has piled up so much silver and gold that it is as common as dust in the streets! 4But now the Lord will strip away Tyre's possessions and hurl its fortifications into the Mediterranean Sea.* Tyre will be set on fire and burned to the ground.

5The city of Ashkelon will see Tyre fall and will be filled with fear. Gaza will shake with terror, and so will Ekron, for their hopes will be dashed. Gaza will be conquered and its king killed, and Ashkelon will be completely deserted. 6Foreigners will occupy the city of Ashdod. Thus, I will destroy the pride of the Philistines. 7They will no longer eat meat with blood in it or feed on other forbidden foods. All the surviving Philistines will worship our God and be adopted as a new clan in Judah.* And the Philistines of Ekron will join my people, just as the Jebusites once did. 8I will guard my Temple and protect it from invading armies. I am closely watching their movements. No foreign oppressor will ever again overrun my people's land.

Zion's Coming King

9Rejoice greatly, O people* of Zion! Shout in triumph, O people of Jerusalem! Look, your king is coming to you. He is righteous and victorious, yet he is humble, riding on a donkey—even on a donkey's colt. 10I will remove the battle chariots from Israel* and the warhorses from Jerusalem, and I will destroy all the weapons used in battle. Your king will bring peace to the nations. His realm will stretch from sea to sea and from the Euphrates River* to the ends of the earth.*

11Because of the covenant I made with you, sealed with blood, I will free your prisoners from death in a waterless dungeon. 12Come back to the place of safety, all you prisoners, for there is yet hope! I promise this very day that I will repay you two mercies for each of your woes! 13Judah is my bow, and Israel is my arrow! Jerusalem* is my sword, and like a warrior, I will brandish it against the Greeks.*

14The LORD will appear above his people; his arrows will fly like lightning! The Sovereign LORD will sound the trumpet; he will go out against his enemies like a whirlwind from the southern desert. 15The LORD Almighty will protect his people, and they will subdue their enemies with sling stones. They will shout in battle as though drunk with wine, shedding the blood of their enemies.

8:19 Hebrew *in the fourth, fifth, seventh, and tenth months.* The fourth month of the Hebrew lunar calendar usually occurs in June and July. The fifth month usually occurs in July and August. The seventh month usually occurs in September and October. The tenth month usually occurs in December and January. 9:1a Hebrew *An Oracle: The message.* 9:1b Hebrew *land of Hadrach.* 9:4 Hebrew *the sea.* 9:7 Hebrew *and will become a leader in Judah.* 9:9 Hebrew *daughter.* 9:10a Hebrew *from Ephraim;* also in 9:13. 9:10b Hebrew *the river.* 9:10c Or *the end of the land.* 9:13a Hebrew *Zion.* 9:13b Hebrew *the sons of Javan.*

They will be filled with blood like a bowl, drenched with blood like the corners of the altar.

16When that day arrives, the LORD their God will rescue his people, just as a shepherd rescues his sheep. They will sparkle in his land like jewels in a crown. 17How wonderful and beautiful they will be! The young men and women will thrive on the abundance of grain and new wine.

CHAPTER **10**

The LORD Will Restore His People

Ask the LORD for rain in the spring, and he will give it. It is the LORD who makes storm clouds that drop showers of rain so that every field becomes a lush pasture.

2Household gods give false advice, fortunetellers predict only lies, and interpreters of dreams pronounce comfortless falsehoods. So my people are wandering like lost sheep, without a shepherd to protect and guide them.

3"My anger burns against your shepherds, and I will punish these leaders.* For the LORD Almighty has arrived to look after his flock of Judah; he will make them strong and glorious, like a proud warhorse in battle. 4From Judah will come the cornerstone, the tent peg, the battle bow, and all the rulers. 5They will be like mighty warriors in battle, trampling their enemies in the mud under their feet. Since the LORD is with them as they fight, they will overthrow even the horsemen of the enemy.

6"I will strengthen Judah and save Israel*; I will reestablish them because I love them. It will be as though I had never rejected them, for I am the LORD their God, who will hear their cries. 7The people of Israel* will become like mighty warriors, and their hearts will be happy as if by wine. Their children, too, will see it all and be glad; their hearts will rejoice in the LORD. 8When I whistle to them, they will come running, for I have redeemed them. From the few that are left, their population will grow again to its former size. 9Though I have scattered them like seeds among the nations, still they will remember me in distant lands. With their children, they will survive and come home again to Israel. 10I will bring them back from Egypt and Assyria and resettle them in Gilead and Lebanon. There won't be enough room for them all! 11They will pass safely through the sea of distress,* for the waves of the sea will be held back. And the waters of the

Nile will become dry. The pride of Assyria will be crushed, and the rule of Egypt will end. 12I will make my people strong in my power, and they will go wherever they wish by my authority. I, the LORD, have spoken!"

CHAPTER **11**

Open your doors, Lebanon, so that fire may sweep through your cedar forests. 2Weep, you cypress trees, for all the ruined cedars; the tallest and most beautiful of them are fallen. Weep, you oaks of Bashan, as you watch the thickest forests being felled. 3Listen to the wailing of the shepherds, for their wealth is gone. Hear the young lions roaring, for their thickets in the Jordan Valley have been destroyed.

The Good and Evil Shepherds

4This is what the LORD my God says: "Go and care for a flock that is intended for slaughter. 5The buyers will slaughter their sheep without remorse. The sellers will say, 'Praise the LORD, I am now rich!' Even the shepherds have no compassion for them. 6And likewise, I will no longer have pity on the inhabitants of the land," says the LORD. "I will let them fall into each other's clutches, as well as into the clutches of their king. They will turn the land into a wilderness, and I will not protect them."

7So I cared for the flock intended for slaughter—the flock that was oppressed. Then I took two shepherd's staffs and named one Favor and the other Union. 8I got rid of their three evil shepherds in a single month. But I became impatient with these sheep—this nation—and they hated me, too. 9So I told them, "I won't be your shepherd any longer. If you die, you die. If you are killed, you are killed. And those who remain will devour each other!"

10Then I took my staff called Favor and snapped it in two, showing that I had revoked the covenant I had made with all the nations. 11That was the end of my covenant with them. Those who bought and sold sheep were watching me, and they knew that the LORD was speaking to them through my actions. 12And I said to them, "If you like, give me my wages, whatever I am worth; but only if you want to." So they counted out for my wages thirty pieces* of silver.

13And the LORD said to me, "Throw it to the potters*"—this magnificent sum at which they valued me! So I took the thirty coins and threw

---

10:3 Or *these male goats.*   10:6 Hebrew *save the house of Joseph.*   10:7 Hebrew *of Ephraim.*   10:11 Or *the sea of Egypt,* referring to the Red Sea.   11:12 Hebrew *30 shekels,* about 12 ounces or 342 grams in weight.   11:13 Syriac version reads *into the treasury;* also in 11:13b.

them to the potters in the Temple of the LORD. [14]Then I broke my other staff, Union, to show that the bond of unity between Judah and Israel was broken.

[15]Then the LORD said to me, "Go again and play the part of a worthless shepherd. [16]This will illustrate how I will give this nation a shepherd who will not care for the sheep that are threatened by death, nor look after the young, nor heal the injured, nor feed the healthy. Instead, this shepherd will eat the meat of the fattest sheep and tear off their hooves. [17]Doom is certain for this worthless shepherd who abandons the flock! The sword will cut his arm and pierce his right eye! His arm will become useless, and his right eye completely blind!"

CHAPTER **12**

Future Deliverance for Jerusalem

This* message concerning the fate of Israel came from the LORD: "This message is from the LORD, who stretched out the heavens, laid the foundations of the earth, and formed the spirit within humans. [2]I will make Jerusalem and Judah like an intoxicating drink to all the nearby nations that send their armies to besiege Jerusalem. [3]On that day I will make Jerusalem a heavy stone, a burden for the world. None of the nations who try to lift it will escape unscathed.

[4]"On that day, says the LORD, I will cause every horse to panic and every rider to lose his nerve. I will watch over the people of Judah, but I will blind the horses of her enemies. [5]And the clans of Judah will say to themselves, 'The people of Jerusalem have found strength in the LORD Almighty, their God.'

[6]"On that day I will make the clans of Judah like a brazier that sets a woodpile ablaze or like a burning torch among sheaves of grain. They will burn up all the neighboring nations right and left, while the people living in Jerusalem remain secure. [7]The LORD will give victory to the rest of Judah first, before Jerusalem, so that the people of Jerusalem and the royal line of David will not have greater honor than the rest of Judah. [8]On that day the LORD will defend the people of Jerusalem; the weakest among them will be as mighty as King David! And the royal descendants will be like God, like the angel of the LORD who goes before them! [9]For my plan is to destroy all the nations that come against Jerusalem.

[10]"Then I will pour out a spirit of grace and prayer on the family of David and on all the people of Jerusalem. They will look on me whom they have pierced and mourn for him as for an only son. They will grieve bitterly for him as for a firstborn son who has died. [11]The sorrow and mourning in Jerusalem on that day will be like the grievous mourning of Hadad-rimmon in the valley of Megiddo.

[12]"All Israel will weep in profound sorrow, each family by itself, with the husbands and wives in separate groups. The family of David will mourn, along with the family of Nathan, [13]the family of Levi, and the family of Shimei. [14]Each of the surviving families from Judah will mourn separately, husbands and wives apart.

CHAPTER **13**

A Fountain of Cleansing

"On that day a fountain will be opened for the dynasty of David and for the people of Jerusalem, a fountain to cleanse them from all their sins and defilement.

[2]"And on that day, says the LORD Almighty, I will get rid of every trace of idol worship throughout the land, so that even the names of the idols will be forgotten. I will remove from the land all false prophets and the unclean spirits that inspire them. [3]If anyone begins prophesying again, his own father and mother will tell him, 'You must die, for you have prophesied lies in the name of the LORD.' Then his own father and mother will stab him.

[4]"No one will be boasting then of a prophetic gift! No one will wear prophet's clothes to try to fool the people. [5]'No,' he will say. 'I'm not a prophet; I'm a farmer. The soil has been my means of livelihood from my earliest youth.' [6]And if someone asks, 'Then what are those scars on your chest*?' he will say, 'I was wounded at the home of friends!'

The Scattering of the Sheep

[7]"Awake, O sword, against my shepherd, the man who is my partner, says the LORD Almighty. Strike down the shepherd, and the sheep will be scattered, and I will turn against the lambs. [8]Two-thirds of the people in the land will be cut off and die, says the LORD. But a third will be left in the land. [9]I will bring that group through the fire and make them pure, just as gold and silver are refined and purified by fire. They will call on my name, and I will answer them. I will say, 'These are my people,' and they will say, 'The LORD is our God.'"

12:1 Hebrew *An Oracle: This.*   13:6 Or *scars between your hands.*

CHAPTER **14**

The LORD Will Rule the Earth

Watch, for the day of the LORD is coming when your possessions will be plundered right in front of you! ²On that day I will gather all the nations to fight against Jerusalem. The city will be taken, the houses plundered, and the women raped. Half the population will be taken away into captivity, and half will be left among the ruins of the city.

³Then the LORD will go out to fight against those nations, as he has fought in times past. ⁴On that day his feet will stand on the Mount of Olives, which faces Jerusalem on the east. And the Mount of Olives will split apart, making a wide valley running from east to west, for half the mountain will move toward the north and half toward the south. ⁵You will flee through this valley, for it will reach across to Azal.* Yes, you will flee as you did from the earthquake in the days of King Uzziah of Judah. Then the LORD my God will come, and all his holy ones with him.*

⁶On that day the sources of light will no longer shine,* ⁷yet there will be continuous day! Only the LORD knows how this could happen! There will be no normal day and night, for at evening time it will still be light. ⁸On that day life-giving waters will flow out from Jerusalem, half toward the Dead Sea and half toward the Mediterranean,* flowing continuously both in summer and in winter.

⁹And the LORD will be king over all the earth. On that day there will be one LORD—his name alone will be worshiped. ¹⁰All the land from Geba, north of Judah, to Rimmon, south of Jerusalem, will become one vast plain. But Jerusalem will be raised up in its original place and will be inhabited all the way from the Benjamin Gate over to the site of the old gate, then to the Corner Gate, and from the Tower of Hananel to the king's winepresses. ¹¹And Jerusalem will be filled, safe at last, never again to be cursed and destroyed.

¹²And the LORD will send a plague on all the nations that fought against Jerusalem. Their people will become like walking corpses, their flesh rotting away. Their eyes will shrivel in their sockets, and their tongues will decay in their mouths. ¹³On that day they will be terrified, stricken by the LORD with great panic. They will fight against each other in hand-to-hand combat; ¹⁴Judah, too, will be fighting at Jerusalem. The wealth of all the neighboring nations will be captured— great quantities of gold and silver and fine clothing. ¹⁵This same plague will strike the horses, mules, camels, donkeys, and all the other animals in the enemy camps.

¹⁶In the end, the enemies of Jerusalem who survive the plague will go up to Jerusalem each year to worship the King, the LORD Almighty, and to celebrate the Festival of Shelters. ¹⁷And any nation anywhere in the world that refuses to come to Jerusalem to worship the King, the LORD Almighty, will have no rain. ¹⁸And if the people of Egypt refuse to attend the festival, the LORD will punish them with the same plague that he sends on the other nations who refuse to go. ¹⁹Egypt and the other nations will all be punished if they don't go to celebrate the festival.

²⁰On that day even the harness bells of the horses will be inscribed with these words: SET APART AS HOLY TO THE LORD. And the cooking pots in the Temple of the LORD will be as sacred as the basins used beside the altar. ²¹In fact, every cooking pot in Jerusalem and Judah will be set apart as holy to the LORD Almighty. All who come to worship will be free to use any of these pots to boil their sacrifices. And on that day there will no longer be traders* in the Temple of the LORD Almighty.

14:5a The meaning of the Hebrew is uncertain.   14:5b As in Greek version; Hebrew reads *with you.*   14:6 Hebrew *there will be no light, no cold or frost.* The meaning of the Hebrew is uncertain.   14:8 Hebrew *half toward the eastern sea and half toward the western sea.*   14:21 Hebrew *Canaanites.*

Malachi

CHAPTER 1

This is the message* that the LORD gave to Israel through the prophet Malachi.*

The LORD's Love for Israel

2 "I have loved you deeply," says the LORD.

But you retort, " Really? How have you loved us?"

And the LORD replies, "I showed my love for you by loving your ancestor Jacob. Yet Esau was Jacob's brother, 3and I rejected Esau and devastated his hill country. I turned Esau's inheritance into a desert for jackals."

4And Esau's descendants in Edom may say, "We have been shattered, but we will rebuild the ruins."

But this is what the LORD Almighty says: "They may try to rebuild, but I will demolish them again! Their country will be known as 'The Land of Wickedness,' and their people will be called 'The People with Whom the LORD Is Forever Angry.' 5When you see the destruction for yourselves, you will say, 'Truly, the LORD's great power reaches far beyond our borders!'"

Unworthy Sacrifices

6The LORD Almighty says to the priests: "A son honors his father, and a servant respects his master. I am your father and master, but where are the honor and respect I deserve? You have despised my name!

"But you ask, 'How have we ever despised your name?'

7"You have despised my name by offering defiled sacrifices on my altar.

"Then you ask, 'How have we defiled the sacrifices*?'

"You defile them by saying the altar of the LORD deserves no respect. 8When you give blind animals as sacrifices, isn't that wrong? And isn't it wrong to offer animals that are crippled and diseased? Try giving gifts like that to your governor, and see how pleased he is!" says the LORD Almighty.

9"Go ahead, beg God to be merciful to you! But when you bring that kind of offering, why should he show you any favor at all?" asks the LORD Almighty.

10"I wish that someone among you would shut the Temple doors so that these worthless sacrifices could not be offered! I am not at all pleased with you," says the LORD Almighty, "and I will not accept your offerings. 11But my name is honored by people of other nations from morning till night. All around the world they offer sweet incense and pure offerings in honor of my name. For my name is great among the nations," says the LORD Almighty. 12"But you dishonor my name with your actions. By bringing contemptible food, you are saying it's all right to defile the Lord's table. 13You say, 'It's too hard to serve the LORD,' and you turn up your noses at his commands," says the LORD Almighty. "Think of it! Animals that are stolen and mutilated, crippled and sick—presented as offerings! Should I accept from you such offerings as these?" asks the LORD. 14"Cursed is the cheat who promises to give a fine ram from his flock but then sacrifices a defective one to the Lord. For I am a great king," says the LORD Almighty, "and my name is feared among the nations!

CHAPTER 2

A Warning for the Priests

"Listen, you priests; this command is for you! 2Listen to me and take it to heart. Honor my

1:1a Hebrew *An Oracle: The message.*   1:1b *Malachi* means "my messenger."   1:7 As in Greek version; Hebrew reads *defiled you.*

name," says the LORD Almighty, "or I will bring a terrible curse against you. I will curse even the blessings you receive. Indeed, I have already cursed them, because you have not taken my warning seriously. ³I will rebuke your descendants and splatter your faces with the dung of your festival sacrifices, and I will add you to the dung heap. ⁴Then at last you will know it was I who sent you this warning so that my covenant with the Levites may continue," says the LORD Almighty.

⁵"The purpose of my covenant with the Levites was to bring life and peace, and this is what I gave them. This called for reverence from them, and they greatly revered me and stood in awe of my name. ⁶They passed on to the people all the truth they received from me. They did not lie or cheat; they walked with me, living good and righteous lives, and they turned many from lives of sin. ⁷The priests' lips should guard knowledge, and people should go to them for instruction, for the priests are the messengers of the LORD Almighty. ⁸But not you! You have left God's paths. Your 'guidance' has caused many to stumble into sin. You have corrupted the covenant I made with the Levites," says the LORD

2:12 Hebrew *from the tents of Jacob.*

Almighty. ⁹"So I have made you despised and humiliated in the eyes of all the people. For you have not obeyed me but have shown partiality in your interpretation of the law."

A Call to Faithfulness

¹⁰Are we not all children of the same Father? Are we not all created by the same God? Then why are we faithless to each other, violating the covenant of our ancestors? ¹¹In Judah, in Israel, and in Jerusalem there is treachery, for the men of Judah have defiled the LORD's beloved sanctuary by marrying women who worship idols. ¹²May the LORD cut off from the nation of Israel* every last man who has done this and yet brings an offering to the LORD Almighty.

¹³Here is another thing you do. You cover the LORD's altar with tears, weeping and groaning because he pays no attention to your offerings, and he doesn't accept them with pleasure. ¹⁴You cry out, "Why has the LORD abandoned us?" I'll tell you why! Because the LORD witnessed the vows you and your wife made to each other on your wedding day when you were young. But you have been disloyal to her, though she remained your faithful companion, the wife of

OFF AND RUNNING ▰▰▰ ▰▰▰ ▰▰▰

A Strong Marriage Is an Ideal Environment for Raising Godly Children Read MALACHI 2:15

God does not just want you to cultivate the oneness and intimacy in your marriage for your own benefit. He also wants you and your spouse to remain united so that godly children can come from your union. Since God has given us this great privilege and responsibility, we should want to do everything we can to make—and keep—our marriages strong.

Scripture tells us that "a triple-braided cord is not easily broken" (Ecclesiastes 4:12). A strong marriage is not simply built upon emotions or dreams, but upon a solid relationship with Jesus Christ. Such a couple recognizes that God is the one who has placed them together and that he is the one who will keep them together for the long haul.

Those children who see their parents united by their love for God and one another have a distinct advantage over those who do not—they have a chance to see the love of God in action. They witness the power of prayer when they watch their parents pray and see God answer. They observe the value of unconditional love when their parents forgive each other instead of harboring a grudge. They understand the concept of trust when they see Mom and Dad stay true to their wedding vows. They learn to respect God's Word when they witness the way their parents obey the principles found in its pages. In essence, they see firsthand what it means to be a Christian.

Our home should be a place where our children are encouraged to follow God and his Word because of how we live, not just what we say. They need our example—as a couple committed to God and to each other—to give them hope and stability in this uncertain world. As the Bible says, "Reverence for God gives a man deep strength; his children have a place of refuge and security" (Proverbs 14:26).

To begin the next topic, turn to p. A34.

your marriage vows. ¹⁵Didn't the LORD make you one with your wife? In body and spirit you are his.* And what does he want? Godly children from your union. So guard yourself; remain loyal to the wife of your youth. ¹⁶"For I hate divorce!" says the LORD, the God of Israel. "It is as cruel as putting on a victim's bloodstained coat," says the LORD Almighty. "So guard yourself; always remain loyal to your wife."

¹⁷You have wearied the LORD with your words. "Wearied him?" you ask. "How have we wearied him?"

You have wearied him by suggesting that the LORD favors evildoers since he does not punish them. You have wearied him by asking, "Where is the God of justice?"

CHAPTER **3**

The Coming Day of Judgment

"Look! I am sending my messenger, and he will prepare the way before me. Then the Lord you are seeking will suddenly come to his Temple. The messenger of the covenant, whom you look for so eagerly, is surely coming," says the LORD Almighty. ²"But who will be able to endure it when he comes? Who will be able to stand and face him when he appears? For he will be like a blazing fire that refines metal or like a strong soap that whitens clothes. ³He will sit and judge like a refiner of silver, watching closely as the dross is burned away. He will purify the Levites, refining them like gold or silver, so that they may once again offer acceptable sacrifices to the LORD. ⁴Then once more the LORD will accept the offerings brought to him by the people of Judah and Jerusalem, as he did in former times. ⁵At that time I will put you on trial. I will be a ready witness against all sorcerers and adulterers and liars. I will speak against those who cheat employees of their wages, who oppress widows and orphans, or who deprive the foreigners living among you of justice, for these people do not fear me," says the LORD Almighty.

A Call to Repentance

⁶"I am the LORD, and I do not change. That is why you descendants of Jacob are not already completely destroyed. ⁷Ever since the days of your ancestors, you have scorned my laws and failed to obey them. Now return to me, and I will return to you," says the LORD Almighty.

2:15 Or *Did not one God make us and preserve our life and breath?* or *Did not one God make her, both flesh and spirit?* The meaning of the Hebrew is uncertain.

Why Should You Give a Portion of Your Financial Resources to God?

Read MALACHI 3:8-11

Here we find the only instance in the Bible where God actually challenges us to test him. And the challenge involves the giving of our financial resources.

Tithing Has a Long History. The word *tithe* actually means "one-tenth." In the Old Testament, Abraham presented a tithe to the priest-king of Jerusalem, Melchizedek (see Genesis 14:18-20, p. 13). Jacob also pledged to offer God a tithe of all his possessions upon his safe return home (see Genesis 28:22, p. 25).

In the New Testament, Jesus mentioned it as well, though he warned that strict tithing must accompany concern for the more important demands of the law—namely those which dealt with just and merciful living (see Matthew 23:23, p. 819; and Luke 11:42, p. 872).

Tithing Strengthens the Church. The "tithe" was for the "House of the Lord." For Old Testament believers, this meant the financial support of the Temple and the priests. In the New Testament, this meant support of the church. As Christians, it is vitally important that we become an active part of a local body of believers. As part of that body, we should support the ministry of our church on a regular basis with our tithes and offerings.

Tithing Brings God's Blessings. This brings us to God's personal challenge. If we are faithful to keep our priorities in order, God promises to "open the windows of heaven" for us and provide for our needs. This does not mean that God will provide everything we want. God only promises to provide for our *needs*, not our *greeds*.

God is not asking us to give because he needs our resources. The whole world is at his disposal. In essence, he is challenging us to make *him* the focus of our lives, rather than our money or possessions. He does not want us to "give to get" but to give because we have received. When we express our love to God by giving our resources, he promises to tangibly display his faithfulness to us in return.

For the next note on "Give to God," turn to p. 845.

FIRST STEPS

"But you ask, 'How can we return when we have never gone away?'

8 "Should people cheat God? Yet you have cheated me!

"But you ask, 'What do you mean? When did we ever cheat you?'

"You have cheated me of the tithes and offerings due to me. 9 You are under a curse, for your whole nation has been cheating me. 10 Bring all the tithes into the storehouse so there will be enough food in my Temple. If you do," says the LORD Almighty, "I will open the windows of heaven for you. I will pour out a blessing so great you won't have enough room to take it in! Try it! Let me prove it to you! 11 Your crops will be abundant, for I will guard them from insects and disease.* Your grapes will not shrivel before they are ripe," says the LORD Almighty. 12 "Then all nations will call you blessed, for your land will be such a delight," says the LORD Almighty.

13 "You have said terrible things about me," says the LORD.

"But you say, 'What do you mean? How have we spoken against you?'

14 "You have said, 'What's the use of serving God? What have we gained by obeying his commands or by trying to show the LORD Almighty that we are sorry for our sins? 15 From now on we will say, "Blessed are the arrogant." For those who do evil get rich, and those who dare God to punish them go free of harm.'"

The LORD's Promise of Mercy

16 Then those who feared the LORD spoke with each other, and the LORD listened to what they said. In his presence, a scroll of remembrance was written to record the names of those who feared him and loved to think about him. 17 "They will be my people," says the LORD Almighty. "On the day when I act, they will be my own special treasure. I will spare them as a father spares an obedient and dutiful child. 18 Then you will again see the difference between the righteous and the wicked, between those who serve God and those who do not."

CHAPTER **4**
The Coming Day of Judgment

The LORD Almighty says, "The day of judgment is coming, burning like a furnace. The arrogant and the wicked will be burned up like straw on that day. They will be consumed like a tree—roots and all.

2 "But for you who fear my name, the Sun of Righteousness will rise with healing in his wings.* And you will go free, leaping with joy like calves let out to pasture. 3 On the day when I act, you will tread upon the wicked as if they were dust under your feet," says the LORD Almighty.

4 "Remember to obey the instructions of my servant Moses, all the laws and regulations that I gave him on Mount Sinai* for all Israel.

5 "Look, I am sending you the prophet Elijah before the great and dreadful day of the LORD arrives. 6 His preaching will turn the hearts of parents* to their children, and the hearts of children to their parents. Otherwise I will come and strike the land with a curse."

3:11 Hebrew *from the devourer.*   4:2 Or *the sun of righteousness will rise with healing in its wings.*   4:4 Hebrew *Horeb,* another name for Sinai.
4:6 Hebrew *fathers;* also in 4:6b.

OFF AND RUNNING ▰▰ ▰▰ ▰▰
Make a Habit of Talking about the Lord Read Malachi 3:16

Some people mistakenly assume that the only place holy and sacred things take place is within the walls of the church. Yet this verse explains that every time you talk about the Lord with another believer, God is paying close attention. In fact, the phrase Malachi uses here means "to bend down so as not to miss a word."

What an incredible thought! God deeply desires that we spend time with other believers discussing him, his attributes, and what he is doing in our lives. That should give us all more reasons to make friends with other believers and take part in Bible studies and church gatherings.

The next time you get together with your Christian friends, don't just discuss the weather or the latest news headlines. Make the Lord a central part of your conversation. He is listening.

For the next note on "Conversation," turn to p. 1044.

The
NEW
Testament

Matthew

CHAPTER **1**

The Record of Jesus' Ancestors

This is a record of the ancestors of Jesus the Messiah, a descendant of King David and of Abraham:

2 Abraham was the father of Isaac.
Isaac was the father of Jacob.
Jacob was the father of Judah and his brothers.

3 Judah was the father of Perez and Zerah (their mother was Tamar).
Perez was the father of Hezron.
Hezron was the father of Ram.*

4 Ram was the father of Amminadab.
Amminadab was the father of Nahshon.
Nahshon was the father of Salmon.

5 Salmon was the father of Boaz (his mother was Rahab).
Boaz was the father of Obed (his mother was Ruth).
Obed was the father of Jesse.

6 Jesse was the father of King David.
David was the father of Solomon (his mother was Bathsheba, the widow of Uriah).

7 Solomon was the father of Rehoboam.
Rehoboam was the father of Abijah.
Abijah was the father of Asaph.*

8 Asaph was the father of Jehoshaphat.
Jehoshaphat was the father of Jehoram.*
Jehoram was the father* of Uzziah.

9 Uzziah was the father of Jotham.
Jotham was the father of Ahaz.
Ahaz was the father of Hezekiah.

10 Hezekiah was the father of Manasseh.
Manasseh was the father of Amos.*

Amos was the father of Josiah.

11 Josiah was the father of Jehoiachin* and his brothers (born at the time of the exile to Babylon).

12 After the Babylonian exile:
Jehoiachin was the father of Shealtiel.
Shealtiel was the father of Zerubbabel.

13 Zerubbabel was the father of Abiud.
Abiud was the father of Eliakim.
Eliakim was the father of Azor.

14 Azor was the father of Zadok.
Zadok was the father of Akim.
Akim was the father of Eliud.

15 Eliud was the father of Eleazar.
Eleazar was the father of Matthan.
Matthan was the father of Jacob.

16 Jacob was the father of Joseph, the husband of Mary.
Mary was the mother of Jesus, who is called the Messiah.

17All those listed above include fourteen generations from Abraham to King David, and fourteen from David's time to the Babylonian exile, and fourteen from the Babylonian exile to the Messiah.

The Birth of Jesus the Messiah

18Now this is how Jesus the Messiah was born. His mother, Mary, was engaged to be married to Joseph. But while she was still a virgin, she became pregnant by the Holy Spirit. 19Joseph, her fiancé, being a just man, decided to break the engagement quietly, so as not to disgrace her publicly.

20As he considered this, he fell asleep, and an angel of the Lord appeared to him in a dream.

1:3 Greek *Aram;* also in 1:4. See 1 Chr 2:9-10.   1:7 *Asaph* is the same person as Asa; also in 1:8. See 1 Chr 3:10.   1:8a Greek *Joram.* See 1 Kgs 22:50 and note at 1 Chr 3:11.   1:8b Or *ancestor;* also in 1:11.   1:10 *Amos* is the same person as Amon. See 1 Chr 3:14.   1:11 Greek *Jeconiah;* also in 1:12. See 2 Kgs 24:6 and note at 1 Chr 3:16.

"Joseph, son of David," the angel said, "do not be afraid to go ahead with your marriage to Mary. For the child within her has been conceived by the Holy Spirit. 21And she will have a son, and you are to name him Jesus,* for he will save his people from their sins." 22All of this happened to fulfill the Lord's message through his prophet:

23 "Look! The virgin will conceive a child!
    She will give birth to a son,
    and he will be called Immanuel*
    (meaning, God is with us)."

24When Joseph woke up, he did what the angel of the Lord commanded. He brought Mary home to be his wife, 25but she remained a virgin until her son was born. And Joseph named him Jesus.

CHAPTER **2**

The Visit of the Wise Men

Jesus was born in the town of Bethlehem in Judea, during the reign of King Herod. About that time some wise men* from eastern lands arrived in Jerusalem, asking, 2"Where is the newborn king of the Jews? We have seen his star as it arose,* and we have come to worship him."

3Herod was deeply disturbed by their question, as was all of Jerusalem. 4He called a meeting of the leading priests and teachers of religious law. "Where did the prophets say the Messiah would be born?" he asked them.

5"In Bethlehem," they said, "for this is what the prophet wrote:

6 'O Bethlehem of Judah,
    you are not just a lowly village in Judah,
    for a ruler will come from you
        who will be the shepherd for my people
        Israel.'* "

7Then Herod sent a private message to the wise men, asking them to come see him. At this meeting he learned the exact time when they first saw the star. 8Then he told them, "Go to Bethlehem and search carefully for the child. And when you find him, come back and tell me so that I can go and worship him, too!"

9After this interview the wise men went their way. Once again the star appeared to them, guiding them to Bethlehem. It went ahead of them and stopped over the place where the child was. 10When they saw the star, they were filled with

joy! 11They entered the house where the child and his mother, Mary, were, and they fell down before him and worshiped him. Then they opened their treasure chests and gave him gifts of gold, frankincense, and myrrh. 12But when it was time to leave, they went home another way, because God had warned them in a dream not to return to Herod.

The Escape to Egypt

13After the wise men were gone, an angel of the Lord appeared to Joseph in a dream. "Get up and flee to Egypt with the child and his mother," the angel said. "Stay there until I tell you to return, because Herod is going to try to kill the child." 14That night Joseph left for Egypt with the child and Mary, his mother, 15and they stayed there until Herod's death. This fulfilled what the Lord had spoken through the prophet: "I called my Son out of Egypt."*

16Herod was furious when he learned that the wise men had outwitted him. He sent soldiers to kill all the boys in and around Bethlehem who were two years old and under, because the wise men had told him the star first appeared to them about two years earlier.* 17Herod's brutal action fulfilled the prophecy of Jeremiah:

18 "A cry of anguish is heard in Ramah—
    weeping and mourning unrestrained.
    Rachel weeps for her children,
        refusing to be comforted—for they are
        dead."*

The Return to Nazareth

19When Herod died, an angel of the Lord appeared in a dream to Joseph in Egypt and told him, 20"Get up and take the child and his mother back to the land of Israel, because those who were trying to kill the child are dead." 21So Joseph returned immediately to Israel with Jesus and his mother. 22But when he learned that the new ruler was Herod's son Archelaus, he was afraid. Then, in another dream, he was warned to go to Galilee. 23So they went and lived in a town called Nazareth. This fulfilled what was spoken by the prophets concerning the Messiah: "He will be called a Nazarene." .

CHAPTER **3**

John the Baptist Prepares the Way

In those days John the Baptist began preaching in the Judean wilderness. His message was,

---

1:21 *Jesus* means "The Lord saves." **1:23** Isa 7:14; 8:8, 10. **2:1** Or *royal astrologers;* Greek reads *Magi;* also in 2:7, 16. **2:2** Or *in the east.* **2:6** Mic 5:2; 2 Sam 5:2. **2:15** Hos 11:1. **2:16** Or *according to the time he calculated from the wise men.* **2:18** Jer 31:15.

2"Turn from your sins and turn to God, because the Kingdom of Heaven is near.*" 3Isaiah had spoken of John when he said,

"He is a voice shouting in the wilderness:
'Prepare a pathway for the Lord's coming!
Make a straight road for him!'"*

4John's clothes were woven from camel hair, and he wore a leather belt; his food was locusts and wild honey. 5People from Jerusalem and from every section of Judea and from all over the Jordan Valley went out to the wilderness to hear him preach. 6And when they confessed their sins, he baptized them in the Jordan River.

7But when he saw many Pharisees and Sadducees coming to be baptized, he denounced them. "You brood of snakes!" he exclaimed. "Who warned you to flee God's coming judgment? 8Prove by the way you live that you have really turned from your sins and turned to God. 9Don't just say, 'We're safe—we're the descendants of Abraham.' That proves nothing. God can change these stones here into children of Abraham. 10Even now the ax of God's judgment is poised, ready to sever your roots. Yes, every tree that does not produce good fruit will be chopped down and thrown into the fire.

11"I baptize with* water those who turn from their sins and turn to God. But someone is coming soon who is far greater than I am—so much greater that I am not even worthy to be his slave.* He will baptize you with the Holy Spirit and with fire.* 12He is ready to separate the chaff from the grain with his winnowing fork. Then he will clean up the threshing area, storing the grain in his barn but burning the chaff with never-ending fire."

The Baptism of Jesus

13Then Jesus went from Galilee to the Jordan River to be baptized by John. 14But John didn't want to baptize him. "I am the one who needs to be baptized by you," he said, "so why are you coming to me?"

15But Jesus said, "It must be done, because we must do everything that is right.*" So then John baptized him.

16After his baptism, as Jesus came up out of the water, the heavens were opened and he saw the Spirit of God descending like a dove and settling on him. 17And a voice from heaven said, "This is my beloved Son, and I am fully pleased with him."

CHAPTER 4
The Temptation of Jesus

Then Jesus was led out into the wilderness by the Holy Spirit to be tempted there by the Devil. 2For forty days and forty nights he ate nothing and became very hungry. 3Then the Devil* came and said to him, "If you are the Son of God, change these stones into loaves of bread."

4But Jesus told him, "No! The Scriptures say,

'People need more than bread for their life;
they must feed on every word of God.'*"

5Then the Devil took him to Jerusalem, to the highest point of the Temple, 6and said, "If you are the Son of God, jump off! For the Scriptures say,

'He orders his angels to protect you.
And they will hold you with their hands
to keep you from striking your foot on a
stone.'*"

7Jesus responded, "The Scriptures also say, 'Do not test the Lord your God.'*"

8Next the Devil took him to the peak of a very high mountain and showed him the nations of the world and all their glory. 9"I will give it all to you," he said, "if you will only kneel down and worship me."

10"Get out of here, Satan," Jesus told him. "For the Scriptures say,

'You must worship the Lord your God;
serve only him.'*"

11Then the Devil went away, and angels came and cared for Jesus.

The Ministry of Jesus Begins

12When Jesus heard that John had been arrested, he left Judea and returned to Galilee. 13But instead of going to Nazareth, he went to Capernaum, beside the Sea of Galilee, in the region of Zebulun and Naphtali. 14This fulfilled Isaiah's prophecy:

15 "In the land of Zebulun and of Naphtali,
beside the sea, beyond the Jordan River—
in Galilee where so many Gentiles live—
16 the people who sat in darkness
have seen a great light.
And for those who lived in the land where
death casts its shadow,
a light has shined."*

17From then on, Jesus began to preach, "Turn

3:2 Or *has come* or *is coming soon.* 3:3 Isa 40:3. 3:11a Or *in.* 3:11b Greek *to carry his sandals.* 3:11c Or *in the Holy Spirit and in fire.* 3:15 Or *we must fulfill all righteousness.* 4:3 Greek *the tempter.* 4:4 Deut 8:3. 4:6 Ps 91:11-12. 4:7 Deut 6:16. 4:10 Deut 6:13. 4:15-16 Isa 9:1-2.

from your sins and turn to God, because the Kingdom of Heaven is near.*"

The First Disciples

18One day as Jesus was walking along the shore beside the Sea of Galilee, he saw two brothers—Simon, also called Peter, and Andrew—fishing with a net, for they were commercial fishermen. 19Jesus called out to them, "Come, be my disciples, and I will show you how to fish for people!" 20And they left their nets at once and went with him.

21A little farther up the shore he saw two other brothers, James and John, sitting in a boat with their father, Zebedee, mending their nets. And he called them to come, too. 22They immediately followed him, leaving the boat and their father behind.

The Ministry of Jesus in Galilee

23Jesus traveled throughout Galilee teaching in the synagogues, preaching everywhere the Good News about the Kingdom. And he healed people who had every kind of sickness and disease. 24News about him spread far beyond the borders of Galilee so that the sick were soon coming to be healed from as far away as Syria. And whatever their illness and pain, or if they were possessed by demons, or were epileptics, or were paralyzed—he healed them all. 25Large crowds followed him wherever he went—people from Galilee, the Ten Towns,* Jerusalem, from all over Judea, and from east of the Jordan River.

CHAPTER 5
The Sermon on the Mount

One day as the crowds were gathering, Jesus went up the mountainside with his disciples and sat down to teach them.

The Beatitudes

2This is what he taught them:

3 "God blesses those who realize their need
    for him,*
        for the Kingdom of Heaven is given to
        them.
4 God blesses those who mourn,
        for they will be comforted.
5 God blesses those who are gentle and lowly,
        for the whole earth will belong to them.
6 God blesses those who are hungry and
        thirsty for justice,
        for they will receive it in full.
7 God blesses those who are merciful,
        for they will be shown mercy.
8 God blesses those whose hearts are pure,
        for they will see God.
9 God blesses those who work for peace,
        for they will be called the children of
        God.
10 God blesses those who are persecuted
        because they live for God,
        for the Kingdom of Heaven is theirs.

11"God blesses you when you are mocked and persecuted and lied about because you are my followers. 12Be happy about it! Be very glad! For a great reward awaits you in heaven. And remember, the ancient prophets were persecuted, too.

Teaching about Salt and Light

13"You are the salt of the earth. But what good is salt if it has lost its flavor? Can you make it useful again? It will be thrown out and trampled underfoot as worthless. 14You are the light of the world—like a city on a mountain, glowing in

4:17 Or *has come* or *is coming soon.*   **4:25** Greek *Decapolis.*   **5:3** Greek *the poor in spirit.*

OFF AND RUNNING ▰▰▰▰▰
We Need to Recognize Our True Condition
Read MATTHEW 5:3-5

Jesus shows us the way to true happiness in this text. Interestingly, not a word is said about seeking "personal fulfillment." Here Jesus gives us a three-step prescription to spiritual health and happiness:

1. See Yourself as You Really Are. When you realize your need for God (verse 3), you see yourself as you really are: a sinner, in desperate need of God's forgiveness. This is the first "rung on the ladder." The phrase "need for God" in this verse comes from a verb meaning "to shrink, cower, or cringe," as beggars often did in that day. It speaks of someone who is destitute and completely dependent on others for help. Therefore, to "realize your need for God" is to admit that you are spiritually destitute apart from God.

2. Take Action. Another way to translate verse 4 is "happy are the unhappy." Because we see ourselves as we really are, we mourn over, or are sorry for, our condition. This leads us to begin making changes in our

the night for all to see. 15Don't hide your light under a basket! Instead, put it on a stand and let it shine for all. 16In the same way, let your good deeds shine out for all to see, so that everyone will praise your heavenly Father.

Teaching about the Law

17"Don't misunderstand why I have come. I did not come to abolish the law of Moses or the writings of the prophets. No, I came to fulfill them. 18I assure you, until heaven and earth disappear, even the smallest detail of God's law will remain until its purpose is achieved. 19So if you break the smallest commandment and teach others to do the same, you will be the least in the Kingdom of Heaven. But anyone who obeys God's laws and teaches them will be great in the Kingdom of Heaven.

20"But I warn you—unless you obey God better than the teachers of religious law and the Pharisees do, you can't enter the Kingdom of Heaven at all!

Teaching about Anger

21"You have heard that the law of Moses says, 'Do not murder. If you commit murder, you are subject to judgment.'* 22But I say, if you are angry with someone,* you are subject to judgment! If you call someone an idiot,* you are in danger of being brought before the high council. And if you curse someone,* you are in danger of the fires of hell.

23"So if you are standing before the altar in the Temple, offering a sacrifice to God, and you suddenly remember that someone has some-thing against you, 24leave your sacrifice there beside the altar. Go and be reconciled to that person. Then come and offer your sacrifice to God. 25Come to terms quickly with your enemy before it is too late and you are dragged into court, handed over to an officer, and thrown in jail. 26I assure you that you won't be free again until you have paid the last penny.

Teaching about Adultery

27"You have heard that the law of Moses says, 'Do not commit adultery.'* 28But I say, anyone who even looks at a woman with lust in his eye has already committed adultery with her in his heart. 29So if your eye—even if it is your good eye*—causes you to lust, gouge it out and throw it away. It is better for you to lose one part of your body than for your whole body to be thrown into hell. 30And if your hand—even if it is your stronger hand*—causes you to sin, cut it off and throw it away. It is better for you to lose one part of your body than for your whole body to be thrown into hell.

Teaching about Divorce

31"You have heard that the law of Moses says, 'A man can divorce his wife by merely giving her a letter of divorce.'* 32But I say that a man who divorces his wife, unless she has been unfaithful, causes her to commit adultery. And anyone who marries a divorced woman commits adultery.

Teaching about Vows

33"Again, you have heard that the law of Moses says, 'Do not break your vows; you must carry out the vows you have made to the Lord.'* 34But I say,

5:21 Exod 20:13; Deut 5:17.   5:22a Greek your brother; also in 5:23. Some manuscripts add without cause.   5:22b Greek uses an Aramaic term of contempt: If you say to your brother, 'Raca.'   5:22c Greek if you say, 'You fool.'   5:27 Exod 20:14; Deut 5:18.   5:29 Greek your right eye.   5:30 Greek your right hand.   5:31 Deut 24:1.   5:33 Num 30:2.

lives. Scripture tells us, "For God can use sorrow in our lives to help us turn away from sin and seek salvation. We will never regret that kind of sorrow. But sorrow without repentance is the kind that results in death" (2 Corinthians 7:10). Our true sorrow will lead to joy—salvation in Jesus Christ. But without that sorrow, there will be no joy.

3. Pursue Meekness. Seeing ourselves as we really are produces two vital spiritual qualities: gentleness and lowliness (verse 5). We are no longer inflated with pride. We have an accurate and honest assessment of ourselves that, in turn, affects how we approach others. This contradicts the world's way of thinking, which advocates standing up for your rights and asserting yourself in order to get "your piece of the pie." The meekness Jesus describes here is not some sort of weakness or cowardice, but rather "power under constraint," much like a powerful stallion submitting to the control of the bit.

The more we humble ourselves and admit our weaknesses, the more we will rely on God's grace—and the happier we will be with ourselves and others.

For the next note on "Attitude toward Self," turn to p. 1084.

Beware of the Sins of the Heart Read MATTHEW 5:27-30

Some people have the mistaken notion that unless you commit the act of adultery, you have not really sinned. They think it is OK to fantasize about or look at someone, so long as you don't become involved in a sinful relationship with that person. But Jesus "cuts to the chase" in this passage. He lets us know that even a lustful glance is as sinful as committing the act of adultery.

In the original Greek, one of the meanings for the word Jesus uses for "look" is intentional and repeated gazing. Jesus' remedy for someone who has a problem in this area seems rather harsh, but you really have to look at the context and the culture of the day to understand this radical but important statement.

In the Jewish culture, the right eye and the right hand were thought of as the best one had. The right eye represented one's best vision and the right hand represented one's best skills. In essence, Jesus is saying that you should be willing to give up whatever is necessary to keep you from falling into this sin. That may mean terminating a relationship, canceling a cable channel or magazine subscription, or changing how or where you spend your spare time. In other words, remove yourself from those things that can have a spiritually destructive effect on your life. Then take practical steps to fill your mind with the things of God: "Fix your thoughts on what is true and honorable and right. Think about things that are pure and lovely and admirable. Think about things that are excellent and worthy of praise" (Philippians 4:8).

For the next note on "Purity," turn to p. 1048.

CORNER STONES

---

don't make any vows! If you say, 'By heaven!' it is a sacred vow because heaven is God's throne. ³⁵And if you say, 'By the earth!' it is a sacred vow because the earth is his footstool. And don't swear, 'By Jerusalem!' for Jerusalem is the city of the great King. ³⁶Don't even swear, 'By my head!' for you can't turn one hair white or black. ³⁷Just say a simple, 'Yes, I will,' or 'No, I won't.' Your word is enough. To strengthen your promise with a vow shows that something is wrong.*

Teaching about Revenge

³⁸"You have heard that the law of Moses says, 'If an eye is injured, injure the eye of the person who did it. If a tooth gets knocked out, knock out the tooth of the person who did it.'* ³⁹But I say, don't resist an evil person! If you are slapped on the right cheek, turn the other, too. ⁴⁰If you are ordered to court and your shirt is taken from you, give your coat, too. ⁴¹If a soldier demands that you carry his gear for a mile,* carry it two miles. ⁴²Give to those who ask, and don't turn away from those who want to borrow.

Teaching about Love for Enemies

⁴³"You have heard that the law of Moses says, 'Love your neighbor'* and hate your enemy.

⁴⁴But I say, love your enemies!* Pray for those who persecute you! ⁴⁵In that way, you will be acting as true children of your Father in heaven. For he gives his sunlight to both the evil and the good, and he sends rain on the just and on the unjust, too. ⁴⁶If you love only those who love you, what good is that? Even corrupt tax collectors do that much. ⁴⁷If you are kind only to your friends,* how are you different from anyone else? Even pagans do that. ⁴⁸But you are to be perfect, even as your Father in heaven is perfect.

CHAPTER 6

Teaching about Giving to the Needy

"Take care! Don't do your good deeds publicly, to be admired, because then you will lose the reward from your Father in heaven. ²When you give a gift to someone in need, don't shout about it as the hypocrites do—blowing trumpets in the synagogues and streets to call attention to their acts of charity! I assure you, they have received all the reward they will ever get. ³But when you give to someone, don't tell your left hand what your right hand is doing. ⁴Give

5:37 Or *Anything beyond this is from the evil one.*　**5:38** Greek *'An eye for an eye and a tooth for a tooth.'* Exod 21:24; Lev 24:20; Deut 19:21.
5:41 Greek *milion* [4,854 feet or 1,478 meters].　**5:43** Lev 19:18.　**5:44** Some manuscripts add *Bless those who curse you, do good to those who hate you.*　**5:47** Greek *your brothers.*

your gifts in secret, and your Father, who knows all secrets, will reward you.

Teaching about Prayer and Fasting

5"And now about prayer. When you pray, don't be like the hypocrites who love to pray publicly on street corners and in the synagogues where everyone can see them. I assure you, that is all the reward they will ever get. 6But when you pray, go away by yourself, shut the door behind you, and pray to your Father secretly. Then your Father, who knows all secrets, will reward you.

7"When you pray, don't babble on and on as people of other religions do. They think their prayers are answered only by repeating their words again and again. 8Don't be like them, because your Father knows exactly what you need even before you ask him! 9Pray like this:

Our Father in heaven,
　　may your name be honored.
10 May your Kingdom come soon.
　　May your will be done here on earth,
　　　　just as it is in heaven.
11 Give us our food for today,*
12 and forgive us our sins,
　　just as we have forgiven those who have
　　　　sinned against us.
13 And don't let us yield to temptation,
　　but deliver us from the evil one.*

14"If you forgive those who sin against you, your heavenly Father will forgive you. 15But if you refuse to forgive others, your Father will not forgive your sins.

16"And when you fast, don't make it obvious, as the hypocrites do, who try to look pale and disheveled so people will admire them for their fasting. I assure you, that is the only reward they will ever get. 17But when you fast, comb your hair and wash your face. 18Then no one will suspect you are fasting, except your Father, who knows what you do in secret. And your Father, who knows all secrets, will reward you.

Teaching about Money and Possessions

19"Don't store up treasures here on earth, where they can be eaten by moths and get rusty, and where thieves break in and steal. 20Store your treasures in heaven, where they will never become moth-eaten or rusty and where they will

6:11 Or *for tomorrow.*　6:13 Or *from evil.* Some manuscripts add *For yours is the kingdom and the power and the glory forever. Amen.*

Prayer Was Modeled for Us by Christ Read MATTHEW 6:5-15

You have probably heard what has been called "the Lord's Prayer." Jesus gave us this particular prayer to show us *how* to pray. Incidentally, just because we call this prayer "the Lord's Prayer" does not mean that Jesus prayed it for himself. He had no reason to ask for forgiveness because he never sinned. Instead, it is more accurate to call this prayer "the Disciples' Prayer," for it was given by Jesus as a response to the disciples' request, "Lord, teach us how to pray."

To better understand this prayer, we can break it down into two sets of petitions:

The first three petitions focus on the glory of God.

- "Our Father in heaven": Recognize that you are addressing a holy God who sees you as his child.
- "May your name be honored": Begin your prayers with reverence and praise to God for who he is. This will enable you to put your needs or problems in their proper perspective.
- "May your Kingdom come soon. May your will be done here on earth, just as it is in heaven": Ask God for his will to reign supreme in your life. You cannot pray "your Kingdom come" until you pray "my kingdom go."

The second three petitions focus on our personal needs.

- "Give us our food for today": Make your physical and personal needs known to God. Remember, Scripture tells us that God will provide for all of our needs (see Philippians 4:19, p. 1037).
- "And forgive us our sins, just as we have forgiven those who have sinned against us": Confess your sins to God. Psalm 66:18 says, "If I had not confessed the sin in my heart, my Lord would not have listened." If you are clinging to some sin, your prayer life will come to a screeching halt.
- "And don't let us yield to temptation, but deliver us from the evil one": Recognize your inclination to fall into sin, and pray that the opportunity to sin and the desire to do so will never coincide.

Make it a point to include these important aspects in your personal prayers. By doing so, you will begin to understand how immense your God is and how small your problems are in comparison to him.

For the next note on "Pray," turn to p. 969.

Forgiveness Is Not Selective Read MATTHEW 5:43-48

As one Bible commentator has put it, "To return evil for good is devilish; to return good for good is human. To return good for evil is divine." Although we are not divine, we, as believers, do not have the liberty to choose whom we will forgive and not forgive. This means that we must do as Jesus has commanded and not only forgive our enemies, but love them as well.

Loving our enemies is certainly something that does not come easily—or naturally. In fact, if we wait for some feeling of love to suddenly overtake us, it simply won't happen. We must begin to pray for our enemies even before we are conscious of loving them. This is absolutely impossible to do apart from the help of the Holy Spirit. If you feel you fall short in the area of forgiveness, take heart. The Bible is full of examples of that "divine" ability to forgive, which can only come from the working of the Holy Spirit in our lives:

- God's Spirit enabled Abraham to give the best land to his traveling partner and nephew, Lot (see Genesis 13:1-12, p. 12).
- God's Spirit gave Joseph the ability to embrace and kiss the very brothers who had sold him into slavery (see Genesis 45:1-15, pp. 42-43).
- God's Spirit kept David from taking advantage of an opportunity to kill King Saul, who was then seeking David's life (see 1 Samuel 24, pp. 256-257).
- God's Spirit caused Stephen (the first Christian martyr) to pray for those who were stoning him to death (see Acts 7:59-60, p. 933).

The ultimate example of forgiving one's enemies, however, comes from Jesus. He clearly modeled this principle for us when, while hanging on the cross, he prayed, "Father, forgive these people, because they don't know what they are doing" (see Luke 23:34, p. 890). If the cruel torture of crucifixion would not silence Jesus' prayer for his enemies, what pain, prejudice, or unfair treatment could justify the silencing of our prayers for our enemies? Just as God's Spirit worked in the lives of the individuals above, he will enable you to love, pray, and do good to those who hate and hurt you.

For the next note on "Forgiveness," turn to p. 42.

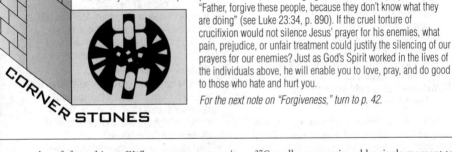

CORNER STONES

---

be safe from thieves. 21Wherever your treasure is, there your heart and thoughts will also be.

22"Your eye is a lamp for your body. A pure eye lets sunshine into your soul. 23But an evil eye shuts out the light and plunges you into darkness. If the light you think you have is really darkness, how deep that darkness will be!

24"No one can serve two masters. For you will hate one and love the other, or be devoted to one and despise the other. You cannot serve both God and money.

25"So I tell you, don't worry about everyday life—whether you have enough food, drink, and clothes. Doesn't life consist of more than food and clothing? 26Look at the birds. They don't need to plant or harvest or put food in barns because your heavenly Father feeds them. And you are far more valuable to him than they are.

27Can all your worries add a single moment to your life? Of course not.

28"And why worry about your clothes? Look at the lilies and how they grow. They don't work or make their clothing, 29yet Solomon in all his glory was not dressed as beautifully as they are. 30And if God cares so wonderfully for flowers that are here today and gone tomorrow, won't he more surely care for you? You have so little faith!

31"So don't worry about having enough food or drink or clothing. 32Why be like the pagans who are so deeply concerned about these things? Your heavenly Father already knows all your needs, 33and he will give you all you need from day to day if you live for him and make the Kingdom of God your primary concern.

34"So don't worry about tomorrow, for tomorrow will bring its own worries. Today's trouble is enough for today.

CHAPTER **7**

Don't Condemn Others

"Stop judging others, and you will not be judged. ²For others will treat you as you treat them.* Whatever measure you use in judging others, it will be used to measure how you are judged. ³And why worry about a speck in your friend's eye* when you have a log in your own? ⁴How can you think of saying, 'Let me help you get rid of that speck in your eye,' when you can't see past the log in your own eye? ⁵Hypocrite! First get rid of the log from your own eye; then perhaps you will see well enough to deal with the speck in your friend's eye.

⁶"Don't give what is holy to unholy people.* Don't give pearls to swine! They will trample the pearls, then turn and attack you.

Effective Prayer

⁷"Keep on asking, and you will be given what you ask for. Keep on looking, and you will find. Keep on knocking, and the door will be opened. ⁸For everyone who asks, receives. Everyone who seeks, finds. And the door is opened to everyone who knocks. ⁹You parents—if your children ask for a loaf of bread, do you give them a stone instead? ¹⁰Or if they ask for a fish, do you give them a snake? Of course not! ¹¹If you sinful people know how to give good gifts to your children, how much more will your heavenly Father give good gifts to those who ask him.

The Golden Rule

¹²"Do for others what you would like them to do for you. This is a summary of all that is taught in the law and the prophets.

The Narrow Gate

¹³"You can enter God's Kingdom only through the narrow gate. The highway to hell* is broad, and its gate is wide for the many who choose the easy way. ¹⁴But the gateway to life is small, and the road is narrow, and only a few ever find it.

The Tree and Its Fruit

¹⁵"Beware of false prophets who come disguised as harmless sheep, but are really wolves that will tear you apart. ¹⁶You can detect them by the way they act, just as you can identify a tree by its fruit. You don't pick grapes from thornbushes, or figs from thistles. ¹⁷A healthy tree produces good fruit, and an unhealthy tree produces bad fruit. ¹⁸A good tree can't

---

7:2 Or *For God will treat you as you treat others;* Greek reads *For with the judgment you judge you will be judged.* 7:3 Greek *your brother's eye;* also in 7:5. 7:6 Greek *Don't give the sacred to dogs.* 7:13 Greek *The way that leads to destruction.*

How Should You View Material Wealth? Read MATTHEW 6:19-34

This passage is part of Jesus' famous Sermon on the Mount. Here Jesus deals with possibly the greatest distraction to following him wholeheartedly: wealth. This series of verses gives us at least three warnings about wealth and one prescription to overcome its enslaving effects:

1. We Must Watch How and What We Store. Verse 19 says that we should not "store up treasures." The idea here is not simply saving, but stockpiling. Jesus is not condemning saving your resources or providing for your family (see Proverbs 6:6, p. 544; and 1 Timothy 5:8, p. 1058). He is condemning the accumulation of possessions to flaunt or to impress others. We need to be able to enjoy what God has given us without making those possessions our primary ambition.

2. We Must Keep Our Vision Clear. While we can enjoy what God gives us, we need to understand that the material things of this world are only temporary. Our personal possessions and investments can be devalued by inflation or deflation, destroyed by natural disasters, or stolen by thieves. That is the problem with making the accumulation of "things" your life's passion. It is so fleeting, temporary, unfulfilling, and even enslaving. When we don't have this perspective, we can become easily enslaved to consumption and accumulation. Then we are no longer serving God but money, and our vision is dark, shutting out the light of God's Word (verses 22-24).

3. We Should Not Worry about Material Things. Worry is a powerful force that can divide or distract us. You can worry about your future, your job, your health, or even about what others think about you. But Jesus tells you to stop worrying, because God will *always* meet your needs (verses 25-30). Quite simply, worry is a waste of your valuable time as his servant on earth.

4. We Must Put God First in Our Lives Our main concern should not be the acquiring of material possessions or prestige. Our primary pursuit should be seeking the reign of Jesus Christ in our lives above all else (verses 31-34). It makes a lot of sense to place your temporary needs and worries in the hands of an eternal God.

For the next note on "Give to God," turn to p. 1057.

Our Walk Should Match Our Talk Read MATTHEW 7:21

I n this verse, Jesus gets down to the heart of every person's belief. He states that calling him "Lord" is not enough to get into heaven. That is because anyone can say the word but not mean it. What counts is a person's changed life—a life of obedience to God's will.

Regarding the Christian life, it has been said, "It is not how high you can jump that matters, but how straight you can walk when you hit the ground again." You may be able to say all of the "right things," but if your faith does not impact the way you live, it is meaningless—even offensive. In truth, you do not have a real relationship with God.

An engraving on a cathedral wall in Germany bears these soul-searching words:

Thus speaketh Christ our Lord to us,
"You call me Master and obey me not;
You call me light and see me not;
You call me the Way and walk me not;
You call me life and live me not;
You call me wise and follow me not;
You call me fair and love me not;
You call me rich and ask me not;
You call me eternal and seek me not;
If I condemn you, blame me not."

The more we learn about what God has done for us, the more we will want to know what we can do for him. In addition, our motives will come from a pure heart, not from selfish ambition. God is looking for genuine believers whose walk matches their talk. Can you be counted as one?

To begin the next topic, turn to p. A21.

CORNER STONES

---

produce bad fruit, and a bad tree can't produce good fruit. [19]So every tree that does not produce good fruit is chopped down and thrown into the fire. [20]Yes, the way to identify a tree or a person is by the kind of fruit that is produced.

True Disciples

[21]"Not all people who sound religious are really godly. They may refer to me as 'Lord,' but they still won't enter the Kingdom of Heaven. The decisive issue is whether they obey my Father in heaven. [22]On judgment day many will tell me, 'Lord, Lord, we prophesied in your name and cast out demons in your name and performed many miracles in your name.' [23]But I will reply, 'I never knew you. Go away; the things you did were unauthorized.*'

Building on a Solid Foundation

[24]"Anyone who listens to my teaching and obeys me is wise, like a person who builds a house on solid rock. [25]Though the rain comes in torrents

7:23 Or *unlawful.*

and the floodwaters rise and the winds beat against that house, it won't collapse, because it is built on rock. [26]But anyone who hears my teaching and ignores it is foolish, like a person who builds a house on sand. [27]When the rains and floods come and the winds beat against that house, it will fall with a mighty crash."

[28]After Jesus finished speaking, the crowds were amazed at his teaching, [29]for he taught as one who had real authority—quite unlike the teachers of religious law.

CHAPTER **8**
Jesus Heals a Man with Leprosy
Large crowds followed Jesus as he came down the mountainside. [2]Suddenly, a man with leprosy approached Jesus. He knelt before him, worshiping. "Lord," the man said, "if you want to, you can make me well again."

[3]Jesus touched him. "I want to," he said. "Be

healed!" And instantly the leprosy disappeared. ⁴Then Jesus said to him, "Go right over to the priest and let him examine you. Don't talk to anyone along the way. Take along the offering required in the law of Moses for those who have been healed of leprosy, so everyone will have proof of your healing."

Faith of the Roman Officer

⁵When Jesus arrived in Capernaum, a Roman officer came and pleaded with him, ⁶"Lord, my young servant lies in bed, paralyzed and racked with pain."

⁷Jesus said, "I will come and heal him."

⁸Then the officer said, "Lord, I am not worthy to have you come into my home. Just say the word from where you are, and my servant will be healed! ⁹I know, because I am under the authority of my superior officers and I have authority over my soldiers. I only need to say, 'Go,' and they go, or 'Come,' and they come. And if I say to my slaves, 'Do this or that,' they do it."

¹⁰When Jesus heard this, he was amazed. Turning to the crowd, he said, "I tell you the truth, I haven't seen faith like this in all the land of Israel! ¹¹And I tell you this, that many Gentiles will come from all over the world and sit down with Abraham, Isaac, and Jacob at the feast in the Kingdom of Heaven. ¹²But many Israelites— those for whom the Kingdom was prepared— will be cast into outer darkness, where there will be weeping and gnashing of teeth."

¹³Then Jesus said to the Roman officer, "Go on home. What you have believed has happened." And the young servant was healed that same hour.

Jesus Heals Many People

¹⁴When Jesus arrived at Peter's house, Peter's mother-in-law was in bed with a high fever. ¹⁵But when Jesus touched her hand, the fever left her. Then she got up and prepared a meal for him.

¹⁶That evening many demon-possessed people were brought to Jesus. All the spirits fled when he commanded them to leave; and he healed all the sick. ¹⁷This fulfilled the word of the Lord through Isaiah, who said, "He took our sicknesses and removed our diseases."*

The Cost of Following Jesus

¹⁸When Jesus noticed how large the crowd was growing, he instructed his disciples to cross to the other side of the lake.

¹⁹Then one of the teachers of religious law said to him, "Teacher, I will follow you no matter where you go!"

²⁰But Jesus said, "Foxes have dens to live in, and birds have nests, but I, the Son of Man, have no home of my own, not even a place to lay my head."

²¹Another of his disciples said, "Lord, first let me return home and bury my father."

²²But Jesus told him, "Follow me now! Let those who are spiritually dead care for their own dead."*

Jesus Calms the Storm

²³Then Jesus got into the boat and started across the lake with his disciples. ²⁴Suddenly, a terrible storm came up, with waves breaking into the boat. But Jesus was sleeping. ²⁵The disciples went to him and woke him up, shouting, "Lord, save us! We're going to drown!"

²⁶And Jesus answered, "Why are you afraid? You have so little faith!" Then he stood up and rebuked the wind and waves, and suddenly all was calm. ²⁷The disciples just sat there in awe. "Who is this?" they asked themselves. "Even the wind and waves obey him!"

Jesus Heals Two Demon-Possessed Men

²⁸When Jesus arrived on the other side of the lake in the land of the Gadarenes,* two men who were possessed by demons met him. They lived in a cemetery and were so dangerous that no one could go through that area. ²⁹They began screaming at him, "Why are you bothering us, Son of God? You have no right to torture us before God's appointed time!" ³⁰A large herd of pigs was feeding in the distance, ³¹so the demons begged, "If you cast us out, send us into that herd of pigs."

³²"All right, go!" Jesus commanded them. So the demons came out of the men and entered the pigs, and the whole herd plunged down the steep hillside into the lake and drowned in the water. ³³The herdsmen fled to the nearby city, telling everyone what happened to the demon-possessed men. ³⁴The entire town came out to meet Jesus, but they begged him to go away and leave them alone.

Jesus Heals a Paralyzed Man

Jesus climbed into a boat and went back across the lake to his own town. ²Some people brought

8:17 Isa 53:4. 8:22 Greek *Let the dead bury their own dead.* 8:28 Some manuscripts read *Gerasenes;* other manuscripts read *Gergesenes.* See Mark 5:1; Luke 8:26.

to him a paralyzed man on a mat. Seeing their faith, Jesus said to the paralyzed man, "Take heart, son! Your sins are forgiven."

3 "Blasphemy! This man talks like he is God!" some of the teachers of religious law said among themselves.

4Jesus knew what they were thinking, so he asked them, "Why are you thinking such evil thoughts? 5Is it easier to say, 'Your sins are forgiven' or 'Get up and walk'? 6I will prove that I, the Son of Man, have the authority on earth to forgive sins." Then Jesus turned to the paralyzed man and said, "Stand up, take your mat, and go on home, because you are healed!"

7And the man jumped up and went home! 8Fear swept through the crowd as they saw this happen right before their eyes. They praised God for sending a man with such great authority.

Jesus Calls Matthew

9As Jesus was going down the road, he saw Matthew sitting at his tax-collection booth. "Come, be my disciple," Jesus said to him. So Matthew got up and followed him.

10That night Matthew invited Jesus and his disciples to be his dinner guests, along with his fellow tax collectors and many other notorious sinners. 11The Pharisees were indignant. "Why does your teacher eat with such scum*?" they asked his disciples.

12When he heard this, Jesus replied, "Healthy people don't need a doctor—sick people do." 13Then he added, "Now go and learn the meaning of this Scripture: 'I want you to be merciful; I don't want your sacrifices.'* For I have come to call sinners, not those who think they are already good enough."

A Discussion about Fasting

14One day the disciples of John the Baptist came to Jesus and asked him, "Why do we and the Pharisees fast, but your disciples don't fast?"

15Jesus responded, "Should the wedding guests mourn while celebrating with the groom? Someday he will be taken from them, and then they will fast. 16And who would patch an old garment with unshrunk cloth? For the patch shrinks and pulls away from the old cloth, leaving an even bigger hole than before. 17And no one puts new wine into old wineskins. The old skins would burst from the pressure, spilling the wine and ruining the skins. New wine must be

9:11 Greek *with tax collectors and sinners.* 9:13 Hos 6:6.

stored in new wineskins. That way both the wine and the wineskins are preserved."

Jesus Heals in Response to Faith

18As Jesus was saying this, the leader of a synagogue came and knelt down before him. "My daughter has just died," he said, "but you can bring her back to life again if you just come and lay your hand upon her."

19As Jesus and the disciples were going to the official's home, 20a woman who had had a hemorrhage for twelve years came up behind him. She touched the fringe of his robe, 21for she thought, "If I can just touch his robe, I will be healed."

22Jesus turned around and said to her, "Daughter, be encouraged! Your faith has made you well." And the woman was healed at that moment.

23When Jesus arrived at the official's home, he noticed the noisy crowds and heard the funeral music. 24He said, "Go away, for the girl isn't dead; she's only asleep." But the crowd laughed at him. 25When the crowd was finally outside, Jesus went in and took the girl by the hand, and she stood up! 26The report of this miracle swept through the entire countryside.

Jesus Heals the Blind and Mute

27After Jesus left the girl's home, two blind men followed along behind him, shouting, "Son of David, have mercy on us!"

28They went right into the house where he was staying, and Jesus asked them, "Do you believe I can make you see?"

"Yes, Lord," they told him, "we do."

29Then he touched their eyes and said, "Because of your faith, it will happen." 30And suddenly they could see! Jesus sternly warned them, "Don't tell anyone about this." 31But instead, they spread his fame all over the region.

32When they left, some people brought to him a man who couldn't speak because he was possessed by a demon. 33So Jesus cast out the demon, and instantly the man could talk. The crowds marveled. "Nothing like this has ever happened in Israel!" they exclaimed.

34But the Pharisees said, "He can cast out demons because he is empowered by the prince of demons."

The Need for Workers

35Jesus traveled through all the cities and villages of that area, teaching in the synagogues and announcing the Good News about the Kingdom. And wherever he went, he healed people of every sort of disease and illness. 36He felt great pity for the crowds that came, because their problems were so great and they didn't know where to go for help. They were like sheep without a shepherd. 37He said to his disciples, "The harvest is so great, but the workers are so few. 38So pray to the Lord who is in charge of the harvest; ask him to send out more workers for his fields."

CHAPTER **10**

Jesus Sends Out the Twelve Apostles
Jesus called his twelve disciples to him and gave them authority to cast out evil spirits and to heal every kind of disease and illness. 2Here are the names of the twelve apostles:

first Simon (also called Peter),
then Andrew (Peter's brother),
James (son of Zebedee),
John (James's brother),
3 Philip,
Bartholomew,
Thomas,
Matthew (the tax collector),
James (son of Alphaeus),
Thaddaeus,
4 Simon (the Zealot*),
Judas Iscariot (who later betrayed him).

5Jesus sent the twelve disciples out with these instructions: "Don't go to the Gentiles or the Samaritans, 6but only to the people of Israel—God's lost sheep. 7Go and announce to them that the Kingdom of Heaven is near.* 8Heal the sick, raise the dead, cure those with leprosy, and cast out demons. Give as freely as you have received!

9"Don't take any money with you. 10Don't carry a traveler's bag with an extra coat and sandals or even a walking stick. Don't hesitate to accept hospitality, because those who work deserve to be fed.* 11Whenever you enter a city or village, search for a worthy man and stay in his home until you leave for the next town. 12When you are invited into someone's home, give it your blessing. 13If it turns out to be a worthy home, let your blessing stand; if it is not, take back the blessing. 14If a village doesn't welcome you or listen to you, shake off the dust of that place from your feet as you leave. 15I assure you, the wicked cities of Sodom and Gomorrah will

be better off on the judgment day than that place will be.

16"Look, I am sending you out as sheep among wolves. Be as wary as snakes and harmless as doves. 17But beware! For you will be handed over to the courts and beaten in the synagogues. 18And you must stand trial before governors and kings because you are my followers. This will be your opportunity to tell them about me—yes, to witness to the world. 19When you are arrested, don't worry about what to say in your defense, because you will be given the right words at the right time. 20For it won't be you doing the talking—it will be the Spirit of your Father speaking through you.

21"Brother will betray brother to death, fathers will betray their own children, and children will rise against their parents and cause them to be killed. 22And everyone will hate you because of your allegiance to me. But those who endure to the end will be saved. 23When you are persecuted in one town, flee to the next. I assure you that I, the Son of Man, will return before you have reached all the towns of Israel.

24"A student is not greater than the teacher. A servant is not greater than the master. 25The student shares the teacher's fate. The servant shares the master's fate. And since I, the master of the household, have been called the prince of demons,* how much more will it happen to you, the members of the household! 26But don't be afraid of those who threaten you. For the time is coming when everything will be revealed; all that is secret will be made public. 27What I tell you now in the darkness, shout abroad when daybreak comes. What I whisper in your ears, shout from the housetops for all to hear!

28"Don't be afraid of those who want to kill you. They can only kill your body; they cannot touch your soul. Fear only God, who can destroy both soul and body in hell. 29Not even a sparrow, worth only half a penny, can fall to the ground without your Father knowing it. 30And the very hairs on your head are all numbered. 31So don't be afraid; you are more valuable to him than a whole flock of sparrows.

32"If anyone acknowledges me publicly here on earth, I will openly acknowledge that person before my Father in heaven. 33But if anyone denies me here on earth, I will deny that person before my Father in heaven.

34"Don't imagine that I came to bring peace to the earth! No, I came to bring a sword. 35I

Peace Begins When We Relinquish Control of Our Lives to God Read MATTHEW 11:28-30

In this passage, Jesus teaches us three things we must do in order to find true peace, or "rest." Yet, for some odd reason, we sometimes find these things difficult to do:

1. Come to Christ. If you have already accepted Jesus Christ as Lord and Savior in your life, you have already completed this step. If you are still searching, you might be right at the door. But know this: You will not find peace from anyone or anything else. Sure, you may have temporary peace of mind when you feel financially secure or if you think you have discovered that "perfect" relationship. But when the bottom falls out, what happens then? Only Christ can guarantee you unending peace.

2. Exchange Your Yoke for His Yoke. A yoke is a heavy wooden harness that is placed over the neck of one or more oxen in order to help pull a wagon or other piece of equipment. It enables a farmer to direct the oxen. Shifting the analogy to humans, our "heavy yoke" could be the weight of guilt, or the burden of keeping God's commands and trying to please him through our own good works. Jesus wants you to exchange that load for his lighter load—God's grace. You can rest in knowing that you do not have to work for God's favor; you need only to accept his Son.

3. Let Jesus Lead. This is undoubtedly one of the hardest parts of this promise. That is because we want to be in control. But God says that we need to give him the reins so that he can "teach" us. Are you ready and willing to leave your abilities, your future, and your problems in God's hands? Then—and only then—will you experience God's promised "rest" for your soul.

For the next note on "Peace," turn to p. 592.

CORNER STONES

---

have come to set a man against his father, and a daughter against her mother, and a daughter-in-law against her mother-in-law. ³⁶Your enemies will be right in your own household! ³⁷If you love your father or mother more than you love me, you are not worthy of being mine; or if you love your son or daughter more than me, you are not worthy of being mine. ³⁸If you refuse to take up your cross and follow me, you are not worthy of being mine. ³⁹If you cling to your life, you will lose it; but if you give it up for me, you will find it.

⁴⁰"Anyone who welcomes you is welcoming me, and anyone who welcomes me is welcoming the Father who sent me. ⁴¹If you welcome a prophet as one who speaks for God,* you will receive the same reward a prophet gets. And if you welcome good and godly people because of their godliness, you will be given a reward like theirs. ⁴²And if you give even a cup of cold water to one of the least of my followers, you will surely be rewarded."

CHAPTER **11**
Jesus and John the Baptist
When Jesus had finished giving these instructions to his twelve disciples, he went off teaching and preaching in towns throughout the country.

²John the Baptist, who was now in prison, heard about all the things the Messiah was doing. So he sent his disciples to ask Jesus, ³"Are you really the Messiah we've been waiting for, or should we keep looking for someone else?"

⁴Jesus told them, "Go back to John and tell him about what you have heard and seen—⁵the blind see, the lame walk, the lepers are cured, the deaf hear, the dead are raised to life, and the Good News is being preached to the poor. ⁶And tell him: 'God blesses those who are not offended by me.*'"

⁷When John's disciples had gone, Jesus began talking about him to the crowds. "Who is this man in the wilderness that you went out to see? Did you find him weak as a reed, moved by every breath of wind? ⁸Or were you expecting to see a

10:41 Greek *welcome a prophet in the name of a prophet.* **11:6** Or *who don't fall away because of me.*

man dressed in expensive clothes? Those who dress like that live in palaces, not out in the wilderness. 9Were you looking for a prophet? Yes, and he is more than a prophet. 10John is the man to whom the Scriptures refer when they say,

'Look, I am sending my messenger before
  you,
and he will prepare your way before you.'*

11"I assure you, of all who have ever lived, none is greater than John the Baptist. Yet even the most insignificant person in the Kingdom of Heaven is greater than he is! 12And from the time John the Baptist began preaching and baptizing until now, the Kingdom of Heaven has been forcefully advancing, and violent people attack it.* 13For before John came, all the teachings of the Scriptures looked forward to this present time. 14And if you are willing to accept what I say, he is Elijah, the one the prophets said would come.* 15Anyone who is willing to hear should listen and understand!

16"How shall I describe this generation? These people are like a group of children playing a game in the public square. They complain to their friends, 17'We played wedding songs, and you weren't happy, so we played funeral songs, but you weren't sad.' 18For John the Baptist didn't drink wine and he often fasted, and you say, 'He's demon possessed.' 19And I, the Son of Man, feast and drink, and you say, 'He's a glutton and a drunkard, and a friend of the worst sort of sinners!' But wisdom is shown to be right by what results from it."

Judgment for the Unbelievers

20Then Jesus began to denounce the cities where he had done most of his miracles, because they hadn't turned from their sins and turned to God. 21"What horrors await you, Korazin and Bethsaida! For if the miracles I did in you had been done in wicked Tyre and Sidon, their people would have sat in deep repentance long ago, clothed in sackcloth and throwing ashes on their heads to show their remorse. 22I assure you, Tyre and Sidon will be better off on the judgment day than you! 23And you people of Capernaum, will you be exalted to heaven? No, you will be brought down to the place of the dead.* For if the miracles I did for you had been done in Sodom, it would still be here today. 24I assure you, Sodom will be better off on the judgment day than you."

Jesus' Prayer of Thanksgiving

25Then Jesus prayed this prayer: "O Father, Lord of heaven and earth, thank you for hiding the truth from those who think themselves so wise and clever, and for revealing it to the childlike. 26Yes, Father, it pleased you to do it this way!

27"My Father has given me authority over everything. No one really knows the Son except the Father, and no one really knows the Father except the Son and those to whom the Son chooses to reveal him."

28Then Jesus said, "Come to me, all of you who are weary and carry heavy burdens, and I will give you rest. 29Take my yoke upon you. Let me teach you, because I am humble and gentle, and you will find rest for your souls. 30For my yoke fits perfectly, and the burden I give you is light."

CHAPTER 12

Controversy about the Sabbath

At about that time Jesus was walking through some grainfields on the Sabbath. His disciples were hungry, so they began breaking off heads of wheat and eating the grain. 2Some Pharisees saw them do it and protested, "Your disciples shouldn't be doing that! It's against the law to work by harvesting grain on the Sabbath."

3But Jesus said to them, "Haven't you ever read in the Scriptures what King David did when he and his companions were hungry? 4He went into the house of God, and they ate the special bread reserved for the priests alone. That was breaking the law, too. 5And haven't you ever read in the law of Moses that the priests on duty in the Temple may work on the Sabbath? 6I tell you, there is one here who is even greater than the Temple! 7But you would not have condemned those who aren't guilty if you knew the meaning of this Scripture: 'I want you to be merciful; I don't want your sacrifices.'* 8For I, the Son of Man, am master even of the Sabbath."

9Then he went over to the synagogue, 10where he noticed a man with a deformed hand. The Pharisees asked Jesus, "Is it legal to work by healing on the Sabbath day?" (They were, of course, hoping he would say yes, so they could bring charges against him.)

11And he answered, "If you had one sheep, and it fell into a well on the Sabbath, wouldn't you get to work and pull it out? Of course you

---

11:10 Mal 3:1.   11:12 Or *until now, eager multitudes have been pressing into the Kingdom of Heaven.*   11:14 See Mal 4:5.   11:23 Greek *to Hades.*   12:7 Hos 6:6.

would. 12And how much more valuable is a person than a sheep! Yes, it is right to do good on the Sabbath." 13Then he said to the man, "Reach out your hand." The man reached out his hand, and it became normal, just like the other one. 14Then the Pharisees called a meeting and discussed plans for killing Jesus.

Jesus, God's Chosen Servant

15But Jesus knew what they were planning. He left that area, and many people followed him. He healed all the sick among them, 16but he warned them not to say who he was. 17This fulfilled the prophecy of Isaiah concerning him:

18 "Look at my Servant,
  whom I have chosen.
He is my Beloved,
  and I am very pleased with him.
I will put my Spirit upon him,
  and he will proclaim justice to the
    nations.
19 He will not fight or shout;
  he will not raise his voice in public.
20 He will not crush those who are weak,
  or quench the smallest hope,
    until he brings full justice with his final
      victory.
21 And his name will be the hope
  of all the world."*

Jesus and the Prince of Demons

22Then a demon-possessed man, who was both blind and unable to talk, was brought to Jesus. He healed the man so that he could both speak and see. 23The crowd was amazed. "Could it be that Jesus is the Son of David, the Messiah?" they wondered out loud.

24But when the Pharisees heard about the miracle, they said, "No wonder he can cast out demons. He gets his power from Satan,* the prince of demons."

25Jesus knew their thoughts and replied, "Any kingdom at war with itself is doomed. A city or home divided against itself is doomed. 26And if Satan is casting out Satan, he is fighting against himself. His own kingdom will not survive. 27And if I am empowered by the prince of demons,* what about your own followers? They cast out demons, too, so they will judge you for what you have said. 28But if I am casting out demons by the Spirit of God, then the Kingdom of God has arrived among you. 29Let me illustrate this. You can't enter a strong man's house and rob him without first tying him up. Only then can his house be robbed!* 30Anyone who isn't helping me opposes me, and anyone who isn't working with me is actually working against me.

31"Every sin or blasphemy can be forgiven—except blasphemy against the Holy Spirit, which can never be forgiven. 32Anyone who blasphemes against me, the Son of Man, can be forgiven, but blasphemy against the Holy Spirit will never be forgiven, either in this world or in the world to come.

33"A tree is identified by its fruit. Make a tree good, and its fruit will be good. Make a tree bad, and its fruit will be bad. 34You brood of snakes! How could evil men like you speak what is good and right? For whatever is in your heart determines what you say. 35A good person produces good words from a good heart, and an evil person produces evil words from an evil heart. 36And I tell you this, that you must give an account on judgment day of every idle word you speak. 37The words you say now reflect your fate then; either you will be justified by them or you will be condemned."

12:18-21 Isa 42:1-4.   12:24 Greek *Beelzeboul.*   12:27 Greek *by Beelzeboul.*   12:29 Or *One cannot rob Satan's kingdom without first tying him up. Only then can his demons be cast out.*

OFF AND RUNNING

Refrain from Idle Talk Read MATTHEW 12:35-37

The verse preceding this text says, "For whatever is in your heart determines what you say." Your speech mirrors the condition of your heart. Your heart represents your innermost thoughts, desires, and emotions. If your heart is filled with bitterness, your speech will be tainted by it. If it is filled with the love of God, your words will also express that love. If we take seriously Jesus' warning about being held accountable for our idle words, then we should not only weigh our words, but we should also examine our hearts—the source of our speech. Here is a good rule to apply before you speak: THINK.

The Sign of Jonah

38One day some teachers of religious law and Pharisees came to Jesus and said, "Teacher, we want you to show us a miraculous sign to prove that you are from God."

39But Jesus replied, "Only an evil, faithless generation would ask for a miraculous sign; but the only sign I will give them is the sign of the prophet Jonah. 40For as Jonah was in the belly of the great fish for three days and three nights, so I, the Son of Man, will be in the heart of the earth for three days and three nights. 41The people of Nineveh will rise up against this generation on judgment day and condemn it, because they repented at the preaching of Jonah. And now someone greater than Jonah is here—and you refuse to repent. 42The queen of Sheba* will also rise up against this generation on judgment day and condemn it, because she came from a distant land to hear the wisdom of Solomon. And now someone greater than Solomon is here—and you refuse to listen to him.

43"When an evil spirit leaves a person, it goes into the desert, seeking rest but finding none. 44Then it says, 'I will return to the person I came from.' So it returns and finds its former home empty, swept, and clean. 45Then the spirit finds seven other spirits more evil than itself, and they all enter the person and live there. And so that person is worse off than before. That will be the experience of this evil generation."

The True Family of Jesus

46As Jesus was speaking to the crowd, his mother and brothers were outside, wanting to talk with him. 47Someone told Jesus, "Your mother and your brothers are outside, and they want to speak to you."

48Jesus asked, "Who is my mother? Who are my brothers?" 49Then he pointed to his disciples

12:42 Greek *The queen of the south.*

and said, "These are my mother and brothers. 50Anyone who does the will of my Father in heaven is my brother and sister and mother!"

CHAPTER **13**

Story of the Farmer Scattering Seed

Later that same day, Jesus left the house and went down to the shore, 2where an immense crowd soon gathered. He got into a boat, where he sat and taught as the people listened on the shore. 3He told many stories such as this one:

"A farmer went out to plant some seed. 4As he scattered it across his field, some seeds fell on a footpath, and the birds came and ate them. 5Other seeds fell on shallow soil with underlying rock. The plants sprang up quickly, 6but they soon wilted beneath the hot sun and died because the roots had no nourishment in the shallow soil. 7Other seeds fell among thorns that shot up and choked out the tender blades. 8But some seeds fell on fertile soil and produced a crop that was thirty, sixty, and even a hundred times as much as had been planted. 9Anyone who is willing to hear should listen and understand!"

10His disciples came and asked him, "Why do you always tell stories when you talk to the people?"

11Then he explained to them, "You have been permitted to understand the secrets of the Kingdom of Heaven, but others have not. 12To those who are open to my teaching, more understanding will be given, and they will have an abundance of knowledge. But to those who are not listening, even what they have will be taken away from them. 13That is why I tell these stories, because people see what I do, but they don't really see. They hear what I say, but they don't really hear, and they don't understand. 14This fulfills the prophecy of Isaiah, which says:

T— Is it true?
H—Is it helpful?
I— Is it inspiring?
N—Is it necessary?
K—Is it kind?

If the content of what you want to say doesn't pass this test, you really do not need to say it. Otherwise, you will have to give an explanation when you stand before the Lord.

For the next note on "Conversation," turn to p. 786.

Beware of Satan's Clever Imitations Read MATTHEW 13:24-30

This is known as the parable of the wheat and the tares. Jesus gave this illustration to expose the Satanic tactic of imitation and infiltration.

The thistles, or tares, were actually a plant that came from the darnel seed. In the initial stages of growth, this plant looked exactly like wheat. But in time the wild weed would show itself for what it really was—a plant that actually uprooted the wheat.

In essence, Satan has followed the pattern of the darnel seed in his attacks against the church. He has "flooded the market" with his imitations of the real thing. There are numerous examples of this throughout the Bible. In Exodus (the second book of the Old Testament), the Egyptian magicians imitated some of the miracles performed by God through Moses—like turning a rod into a snake, turning the waters of the Nile into blood, and bringing forth a plague of frogs. In Acts (the fifth book of the New Testament), the sorcerer Simon imitated Philip (see Acts 8:9-24, pp. 933-934).

In fact, whenever the church has experienced a great revival, a false movement has grown up by its side proclaiming half-truths and deceptions.

Satan knows that half of a truth is more dangerous than a lie. For those who have modified the truth have always injured the truth more than those who have denied it openly. Therefore we must guard against falling for half-truths and gospel imitations at all costs.

CORNER STONES

For the next note on "Discernment," turn to p. 1056.

'You will hear my words,
　but you will not understand;
you will see what I do,
　but you will not perceive its meaning.
15 For the hearts of these people are hardened,
　and their ears cannot hear,
　and they have closed their eyes—
so their eyes cannot see,
　and their ears cannot hear,
　and their hearts cannot understand,
and they cannot turn to me
　and let me heal them.'*

16 "But blessed are your eyes, because they see; and your ears, because they hear. 17 I assure you, many prophets and godly people have longed to see and hear what you have seen and heard, but they could not.

18 "Now here is the explanation of the story I told about the farmer sowing grain: 19 The seed that fell on the hard path represents those who hear the Good News about the Kingdom and don't understand it. Then the evil one comes and snatches the seed away from their hearts. 20 The rocky soil represents those who hear the message and receive it with joy. 21 But like young plants in such soil, their roots don't go very deep. At first they get along fine, but they wilt as soon as they have problems or are persecuted

13:14-15 Isa 6:9-10.

because they believe the word. 22 The thorny ground represents those who hear and accept the Good News, but all too quickly the message is crowded out by the cares of this life and the lure of wealth, so no crop is produced. 23 The good soil represents the hearts of those who truly accept God's message and produce a huge harvest—thirty, sixty, or even a hundred times as much as had been planted."

Story of the Wheat and Weeds
24 Here is another story Jesus told: "The Kingdom of Heaven is like a farmer who planted good seed in his field. 25 But that night as everyone slept, his enemy came and planted weeds among the wheat. 26 When the crop began to grow and produce grain, the weeds also grew. 27 The farmer's servants came and told him, 'Sir, the field where you planted that good seed is full of weeds!'

28 " 'An enemy has done it!' the farmer exclaimed.

" 'Shall we pull out the weeds?' they asked.

29 "He replied, 'No, you'll hurt the wheat if you do. 30 Let both grow together until the harvest. Then I will tell the harvesters to sort out the weeds and burn them and to put the wheat in the barn.' "

Illustration of the Mustard Seed

31Here is another illustration Jesus used: "The Kingdom of Heaven is like a mustard seed planted in a field. 32It is the smallest of all seeds, but it becomes the largest of garden plants and grows into a tree where birds can come and find shelter in its branches."

Illustration of the Yeast

33Jesus also used this illustration: "The Kingdom of Heaven is like yeast used by a woman making bread. Even though she used a large amount* of flour, the yeast permeated every part of the dough."

34Jesus always used stories and illustrations like these when speaking to the crowds. In fact, he never spoke to them without using such parables. 35This fulfilled the prophecy that said,

"I will speak to you in parables.
I will explain mysteries hidden since the creation of the world."*

The Wheat and Weeds Explained

36Then, leaving the crowds outside, Jesus went into the house. His disciples said, "Please explain the story of the weeds in the field."

37"All right," he said. "I, the Son of Man, am the farmer who plants the good seed. 38The field is the world, and the good seed represents the people of the Kingdom. The weeds are the people who belong to the evil one. 39The enemy who planted the weeds among the wheat is the Devil. The harvest is the end of the world, and the harvesters are the angels.

40"Just as the weeds are separated out and burned, so it will be at the end of the world. 41I, the Son of Man, will send my angels, and they will remove from my Kingdom everything that causes sin and all who do evil, 42and they will throw them into the furnace and burn them. There will be weeping and gnashing of teeth. 43Then the godly will shine like the sun in their Father's Kingdom. Anyone who is willing to hear should listen and understand!

Illustration of the Hidden Treasure

44"The Kingdom of Heaven is like a treasure that a man discovered hidden in a field. In his excitement, he hid it again and sold everything he owned to get enough money to buy the field—and to get the treasure, too!

Illustration of the Pearl Merchant

45"Again, the Kingdom of Heaven is like a pearl merchant on the lookout for choice pearls.

46When he discovered a pearl of great value, he sold everything he owned and bought it!

Illustration of the Fishing Net

47"Again, the Kingdom of Heaven is like a fishing net that is thrown into the water and gathers fish of every kind. 48When the net is full, they drag it up onto the shore, sit down, sort the good fish into crates, and throw the bad ones away. 49That is the way it will be at the end of the world. The angels will come and separate the wicked people from the godly, 50throwing the wicked into the fire. There will be weeping and gnashing of teeth. 51Do you understand?"

"Yes," they said, "we do."

52Then he added, "Every teacher of religious law who has become a disciple in the Kingdom of Heaven is like a person who brings out of the storehouse the new teachings as well as the old."

Jesus Rejected at Nazareth

53When Jesus had finished telling these stories, he left that part of the country. 54He returned to Nazareth, his hometown. When he taught there in the synagogue, everyone was astonished and said, "Where does he get his wisdom and his miracles? 55He's just a carpenter's son, and we know Mary, his mother, and his brothers—James, Joseph, Simon, and Judas. 56All his sisters live right here among us. What makes him so great?" 57And they were deeply offended and refused to believe in him.

Then Jesus told them, "A prophet is honored everywhere except in his own hometown and among his own family." 58And so he did only a few miracles there because of their unbelief.

C H A P T E R **14**

The Death of John the Baptist

When Herod Antipas* heard about Jesus, 2he said to his advisers, "This must be John the Baptist come back to life again! That is why he can do such miracles." 3For Herod had arrested and imprisoned John as a favor to his wife Herodias (the former wife of Herod's brother Philip). 4John kept telling Herod, "It is illegal for you to marry her." 5Herod would have executed John, but he was afraid of a riot, because all the people believed John was a prophet.

6But at a birthday party for Herod, Herodias's daughter performed a dance that greatly pleased him, 7so he promised with an oath to

---

13:33 Greek *3 measures.* **13:35** Ps 78:2. **14:1** Greek *Herod the tetrarch.* He was a son of King Herod and was ruler over one of the four districts in Palestine.

give her anything she wanted. 8At her mother's urging, the girl asked, "I want the head of John the Baptist on a tray!" 9The king was sorry, but because of his oath and because he didn't want to back down in front of his guests, he issued the necessary orders. 10So John was beheaded in the prison, 11and his head was brought on a tray and given to the girl, who took it to her mother. 12John's disciples came for his body and buried it. Then they told Jesus what had happened.

Jesus Feeds Five Thousand

13As soon as Jesus heard the news, he went off by himself in a boat to a remote area to be alone. But the crowds heard where he was headed and followed by land from many villages. 14A vast crowd was there as he stepped from the boat, and he had compassion on them and healed their sick.

15That evening the disciples came to him and said, "This is a desolate place, and it is getting late. Send the crowds away so they can go to the villages and buy food for themselves."

16But Jesus replied, "That isn't necessary— you feed them."

17"Impossible!" they exclaimed. "We have only five loaves of bread and two fish!"

18"Bring them here," he said. 19Then he told the people to sit down on the grass. And he took the five loaves and two fish, looked up toward heaven, and asked God's blessing on the food. Breaking the loaves into pieces, he gave some of the bread and fish to each disciple, and the disciples gave them to the people. 20They all ate as much as they wanted, and they picked up twelve baskets of leftovers. 21About five thousand men had eaten from those five loaves, in addition to all the women and children!

Jesus Walks on Water

22Immediately after this, Jesus made his disciples get back into the boat and cross to the other side of the lake while he sent the people home. 23Afterward he went up into the hills by himself to pray. Night fell while he was there alone. 24Meanwhile, the disciples were in trouble far away from land, for a strong wind had risen, and they were fighting heavy waves.

25About three o'clock in the morning* Jesus came to them, walking on the water. 26When the disciples saw him, they screamed in terror, thinking he was a ghost. 27But Jesus spoke to them at once. "It's all right," he said. "I am here! Don't be afraid."

28Then Peter called to him, "Lord, if it's really you, tell me to come to you by walking on water."

29"All right, come," Jesus said.

So Peter went over the side of the boat and walked on the water toward Jesus. 30But when he looked around at the high waves, he was terrified and began to sink. "Save me, Lord!" he shouted.

31Instantly Jesus reached out his hand and grabbed him. "You don't have much faith," Jesus said. "Why did you doubt me?" 32And when they climbed back into the boat, the wind stopped.

33Then the disciples worshiped him. "You really are the Son of God!" they exclaimed.

34After they had crossed the lake, they landed at Gennesaret. 35The news of their arrival spread quickly throughout the whole surrounding area, and soon people were bringing all their sick to be healed. 36The sick begged him to let them touch even the fringe of his robe, and all who touched it were healed.

CHAPTER **15**

Jesus Teaches about Inner Purity

Some Pharisees and teachers of religious law now arrived from Jerusalem to interview Jesus. 2"Why do your disciples disobey our age-old traditions?" they demanded. "They ignore our tradition of ceremonial hand washing before they eat."

3Jesus replied, "And why do you, by your traditions, violate the direct commandments of God? 4For instance, God says, 'Honor your father and mother,' and 'Anyone who speaks evil of father or mother must be put to death.'* 5But you say, 'You don't need to honor your parents by caring for their needs if you give the money to God instead.' 6And so, by your own tradition, you nullify the direct commandment of God. 7You hypocrites! Isaiah was prophesying about you when he said,

8 'These people honor me with their lips,
but their hearts are far away.
9 Their worship is a farce,
for they replace God's commands with
their own man-made teachings.'* "

10Then Jesus called to the crowds and said, "Listen to what I say and try to understand.

14:25 Greek *In the fourth watch of the night.* 15:4 Exod 20:12; 21:17; Lev 20:9; Deut 5:16. 15:8-9 Isa 29:13.

¹¹You are not defiled by what you eat; you are defiled by what you say and do.*"

¹²Then the disciples came to him and asked, "Do you realize you offended the Pharisees by what you just said?"

¹³Jesus replied, "Every plant not planted by my heavenly Father will be rooted up, ¹⁴so ignore them. They are blind guides leading the blind, and if one blind person guides another, they will both fall into a ditch."

¹⁵Then Peter asked Jesus, "Explain what you meant when you said people aren't defiled by what they eat."

¹⁶"Don't you understand?" Jesus asked him. ¹⁷"Anything you eat passes through the stomach and then goes out of the body. ¹⁸But evil words come from an evil heart and defile the person who says them. ¹⁹For from the heart come evil thoughts, murder, adultery, all other sexual immorality, theft, lying, and slander. ²⁰These are what defile you. Eating with unwashed hands could never defile you and make you unacceptable to God!"

The Faith of a Gentile Woman

²¹Jesus then left Galilee and went north to the region of Tyre and Sidon. ²²A Gentile* woman who lived there came to him, pleading, "Have mercy on me, O Lord, Son of David! For my daughter has a demon in her, and it is severely tormenting her."

²³But Jesus gave her no reply—not even a word. Then his disciples urged him to send her away. "Tell her to leave," they said. "She is bothering us with all her begging."

²⁴Then he said to the woman, "I was sent only to help the people of Israel—God's lost sheep—not the Gentiles."

²⁵But she came and worshiped him and pleaded again, "Lord, help me!"

²⁶"It isn't right to take food from the children and throw it to the dogs," he said.

²⁷"Yes, Lord," she replied, "but even dogs are permitted to eat crumbs that fall beneath their master's table."

²⁸"Woman," Jesus said to her, "your faith is great. Your request is granted." And her daughter was instantly healed.

Jesus Heals Many People

²⁹Jesus returned to the Sea of Galilee and climbed a hill and sat down. ³⁰A vast crowd brought him the lame, blind, crippled, mute, and many others with physical difficulties, and they laid them before Jesus. And he healed them all. ³¹The crowd was amazed! Those who hadn't been able to speak were talking, the crippled were made well, the lame were walking around, and those who had been blind could see again! And they praised the God of Israel.

Jesus Feeds Four Thousand

³²Then Jesus called his disciples to him and said, "I feel sorry for these people. They have been here with me for three days, and they have nothing left to eat. I don't want to send them away hungry, or they will faint along the road."

³³The disciples replied, "And where would we get enough food out here in the wilderness for all of them to eat?"

³⁴Jesus asked, "How many loaves of bread do you have?"

They replied, "Seven, and a few small fish."

³⁵So Jesus told all the people to sit down on the ground. ³⁶Then he took the seven loaves and the fish, thanked God for them, broke them into pieces, and gave them to the disciples, who distributed the food to the crowd.

³⁷They all ate until they were full, and when the scraps were picked up, there were seven large baskets of food left over! ³⁸There were four thousand men who were fed that day, in addition to all the women and children. ³⁹Then Jesus sent the people home, and he got into a boat and crossed over to the region of Magadan.

CHAPTER 16

Leaders Demand a Miraculous Sign

One day the Pharisees and Sadducees came to test Jesus' claims by asking him to show them a miraculous sign from heaven.

²He replied, "You know the saying, 'Red sky at night means fair weather tomorrow, ³red sky in the morning means foul weather all day.' You are good at reading the weather signs in the sky, but you can't read the obvious signs of the times!* ⁴Only an evil, faithless generation would ask for a miraculous sign, but the only sign I will give them is the sign of the prophet Jonah." Then Jesus left them and went away.

Yeast of the Pharisees and Sadducees

⁵Later, after they crossed to the other side of the lake, the disciples discovered they had forgotten to bring any food. ⁶"Watch out!" Jesus warned

15:11 Or *what comes out of the mouth defiles a person.*   **15:22** Greek *Canaanite.*   **16:2-3** Several manuscripts do not include any of the words in 16:2-3 after *He replied.*

them. "Beware of the yeast of the Pharisees and Sadducees."

7They decided he was saying this because they hadn't brought any bread. 8Jesus knew what they were thinking, so he said, "You have so little faith! Why are you worried about having no food? 9Won't you ever understand? Don't you remember the five thousand I fed with five loaves, and the baskets of food that were left over? 10Don't you remember the four thousand I fed with seven loaves, with baskets of food left over? 11How could you even think I was talking about food? So again I say, 'Beware of the yeast of the Pharisees and Sadducees.'"

12Then at last they understood that he wasn't speaking about yeast or bread but about the false teaching of the Pharisees and Sadducees.

Peter's Declaration about Jesus

13When Jesus came to the region of Caesarea Philippi, he asked his disciples, "Who do people say that the Son of Man is?"

14"Well," they replied, "some say John the Baptist, some say Elijah, and others say Jeremiah or one of the other prophets."

15Then he asked them, "Who do you say I am?"

16Simon Peter answered, "You are the Messiah, the Son of the living God."

17Jesus replied, "You are blessed, Simon son of John,* because my Father in heaven has revealed this to you. You did not learn this from any human being. 18Now I say to you that you are Peter,* and upon this rock I will build my church, and all the powers of hell* will not conquer it. 19And I will give you the keys of the Kingdom of Heaven. Whatever you lock on earth will be locked in heaven, and whatever you open on earth will be opened in heaven." 20Then he sternly warned them not to tell anyone that he was the Messiah.

Jesus Predicts His Death

21From then on Jesus began to tell his disciples plainly that he had to go to Jerusalem, and he told them what would happen to him there. He would suffer at the hands of the leaders and the leading priests and the teachers of religious law. He would be killed, and he would be raised on the third day.

22But Peter took him aside and corrected him. "Heaven forbid, Lord," he said. "This will never happen to you!"

23Jesus turned to Peter and said, "Get away from me, Satan! You are a dangerous trap to me. You are seeing things merely from a human point of view, and not from God's."

24Then Jesus said to the disciples, "If any of you wants to be my follower, you must put aside your selfish ambition, shoulder your cross, and follow me. 25If you try to keep your life for yourself, you will lose it. But if you give up your life for me, you will find true life. 26And how do you benefit if you gain the whole world but lose your own soul* in the process? Is anything worth more than your soul? 27For I, the Son of Man, will come in the glory of my Father with his angels and will judge all people according to their deeds. 28And I assure you that some of you standing here right now will not die before you see me, the Son of Man, coming in my Kingdom."

16:17 Greek *Simon son of Jonah;* see John 1:42; 21:15-17.   16:18a *Peter* means "stone" or "rock."   16:18b Greek *and the gates of Hades.*
16:26 Or *your life.*

OFF AND RUNNING ▰▰▰ ▰ ▰

We Must Surrender Our Dreams and Seek God's Will Read MATTHEW 16:24-26

Jesus' words in this passage may seem extremely harsh. Yet in reality they are compassionate, because they point the way to real life. Anyone who wants this real life must become a disciple of Jesus. That means obeying Jesus' commands and adopting an attitude of self-denial. This text makes three points on what it means to adopt that attitude and follow Jesus:

1. We Must "Lose Our Life." We "find life" not in seeking it but in coming into a proper alignment with God and his plan for us. As you "lose your life," you find it again. This "life" Jesus speaks of not only includes life after death, but also "life during life." Jesus tells us that he came to "give life in all its fullness" (John 10:10). You should never be afraid to trust an unknown future to a known God. God's plan for you is good. In fact, it is better than any plan you may have for yourself. God tells us in his Word, "For I know the plans I have for you. . . . They are plans for good and not for disaster, to give you a future and a hope" (Jeremiah 29:11).

CHAPTER **17**
The Transfiguration

Six days later Jesus took Peter and the two brothers, James and John, and led them up a high mountain. ²As the men watched, Jesus' appearance changed so that his face shone like the sun, and his clothing became dazzling white. ³Suddenly, Moses and Elijah appeared and began talking with Jesus. ⁴Peter blurted out, "Lord, this is wonderful! If you want me to, I'll make three shrines,* one for you, one for Moses, and one for Elijah."

⁵But even as he said it, a bright cloud came over them, and a voice from the cloud said, "This is my beloved Son, and I am fully pleased with him. Listen to him." ⁶The disciples were terrified and fell face down on the ground.

⁷Jesus came over and touched them. "Get up," he said, "don't be afraid." ⁸And when they looked, they saw only Jesus with them. ⁹As they descended the mountain, Jesus commanded them, "Don't tell anyone what you have seen until I, the Son of Man, have been raised from the dead."

¹⁰His disciples asked, "Why do the teachers of religious law insist that Elijah must return before the Messiah comes*?"

¹¹Jesus replied, "Elijah is indeed coming first to set everything in order. ¹²But I tell you, he has already come, but he wasn't recognized, and he was badly mistreated. And soon the Son of Man will also suffer at their hands." ¹³Then the disciples realized he had been speaking of John the Baptist.

Jesus Heals a Demon-Possessed Boy

¹⁴When they arrived at the foot of the mountain, a huge crowd was waiting for them. A man came and knelt before Jesus and said, ¹⁵"Lord, have mercy on my son, because he has seizures and suffers terribly. He often falls into the fire or into the water. ¹⁶So I brought him to your disciples, but they couldn't heal him."

¹⁷Jesus replied, "You stubborn, faithless people! How long must I be with you until you believe? How long must I put up with you? Bring the boy to me." ¹⁸Then Jesus rebuked the demon in the boy, and it left him. From that moment the boy was well.

¹⁹Afterward the disciples asked Jesus privately, "Why couldn't we cast out that demon?"

²⁰"You didn't have enough faith," Jesus told them. "I assure you, even if you had faith as small as a mustard seed you could say to this mountain, 'Move from here to there,' and it would move. Nothing would be impossible."*

Jesus Again Predicts His Death

²²One day after they had returned to Galilee, Jesus told them, "The Son of Man is going to be betrayed. ²³He will be killed, but three days later he will be raised from the dead." And the disciples' hearts were filled with grief.

Payment of the Temple Tax

²⁴On their arrival in Capernaum, the tax collectors for the Temple tax came to Peter and asked him, "Doesn't your teacher pay the Temple tax?"

²⁵"Of course he does," Peter replied. Then he went into the house to talk to Jesus about it. But before he had a chance to speak, Jesus asked him, "What do you think, Peter*? Do kings tax their own people or the foreigners they have conquered?"

17:4 Or shelters; Greek reads tabernacles. 17:10 Greek that Elijah must come first. 17:20 Some manuscripts add verse 21, But this kind of demon won't leave unless you have prayed and fasted. 17:25 Greek Simon.

2. We Must Deny Ourselves. To "deny ourselves" means that we put the will and purposes of God above our own. We discover God's will for our lives as we search, study, and obey God's Word.

3. We Must Take Up Our Cross. This speaks of "dying" to our own will and selfish ambition. Don't let this passage frighten you. It is through this dying to ourselves that we find God's plan and purpose for our lives.

The Christian life is not one of morbid misery and hyper self-examination. It is a life of peace and joy as we walk in harmony with the God who made us. Paul sums it up perfectly when he writes, "I have been crucified with Christ. I myself no longer live, but Christ lives in me. So I live my life in this earthly body by trusting in the Son of God, who loved me and gave himself for me" (Galatians 2:19-20). It is only when the bulb of a tulip goes into the ground and dies that a beautiful flower can grow in its place. Be willing to entrust yourself to God's plan for your life. You won't regret it.

To begin the next reading track, turn to p. A41.

Forgiveness Knows No Limits Read MATTHEW 18:21-35

The religious leaders of that day taught that one who had been wronged was to forgive the person who wronged him two to three times—at the most! In this text, Peter, mustering up as much forgiveness as he could, wondered if forgiving someone seven times would be enough in Jesus' eyes. Imagine Peter's shock when Jesus told him that he should forgive up to "seventy times seven," or *490* times.

Does this mean that if someone needed forgiveness after the four-hundred-ninety-first time that we should say no? Of course not. Rather, Jesus was teaching that we should extend unlimited forgiveness to others. He then went on to tell this dramatic story of a man who was forgiven for so much (possibly $10 million), yet was unwilling to even work out terms with a person who owed him far less (around two thousand dollars). The point of Jesus' message is that we, as sinners, have been forgiven much. Therefore, we ought to forgive those who have hurt us, no matter how badly. For they owe us little, compared to what we had owed to God.

For the next note on "Forgiveness," turn to p. 796.

CORNER STONES

26"They tax the foreigners," Peter replied.

"Well, then," Jesus said, "the citizens are free! 27However, we don't want to offend them, so go down to the lake and throw in a line. Open the mouth of the first fish you catch, and you will find a coin. Take the coin and pay the tax for both of us."

CHAPTER 18
The Greatest in the Kingdom

About that time the disciples came to Jesus and asked, "Which of us is greatest in the Kingdom of Heaven?"

2Jesus called a small child over to him and put the child among them. 3Then he said, "I assure you, unless you turn from your sins and become as little children, you will never get into the Kingdom of Heaven. 4Therefore, anyone who becomes as humble as this little child is the greatest in the Kingdom of Heaven. 5And anyone who welcomes a little child like this on my behalf is welcoming me. 6But if anyone causes one of these little ones who trusts in me to lose faith, it would be better for that person to be thrown into the sea with a large millstone tied around the neck.

7"How terrible it will be for anyone who causes others to sin. Temptation to do wrong is inevitable, but how terrible it will be for the person who does the tempting. 8So if your hand or foot causes you to sin, cut it off and throw it away. It is better to enter heaven* crippled or lame than to be thrown into the unquenchable fire with both of your hands and feet. 9And if your eye causes you to sin, gouge it out and throw it away. It is better to enter heaven half blind than to have two eyes and be thrown into hell.

10"Beware that you don't despise a single one of these little ones. For I tell you that in heaven their angels are always in the presence of my heavenly Father.*

Story of the Lost Sheep

12"If a shepherd has one hundred sheep, and one wanders away and is lost, what will he do? Won't he leave the ninety-nine others and go out into the hills to search for the lost one? 13And if he finds it, he will surely rejoice over it more than over the ninety-nine that didn't wander away! 14In the same way, it is not my heavenly Father's will that even one of these little ones should perish.

Correcting a Fellow Believer

15"If another believer* sins against you, go privately and point out the fault. If the other person listens and confesses it, you have won that person back. 16But if you are unsuccessful, take one or two others with you and go back again, so that everything you say may be confirmed by two or three witnesses. 17If that person still refuses to listen, take your case to the church. If the church decides you are right, but the other person won't accept it, treat that person as a pagan or a corrupt tax collector. 18I tell you this: Whatever you prohibit on earth is prohibited in

18:8 Greek *enter life;* also in 18:9. **18:10** Some manuscripts add verse 11, *And I, the Son of Man, have come to save the lost.* **18:15** Greek *your brother*

heaven, and whatever you allow on earth is allowed in heaven.

19 "I also tell you this: If two of you agree down here on earth concerning anything you ask, my Father in heaven will do it for you. 20For where two or three gather together because they are mine,* I am there among them."

Story of the Unforgiving Debtor
21Then Peter came to him and asked, "Lord, how often should I forgive someone* who sins against me? Seven times?"

22 "No!" Jesus replied, "seventy times seven!*

23 "For this reason, the Kingdom of Heaven can be compared to a king who decided to bring his accounts up to date with servants who had borrowed money from him. 24In the process, one of his debtors was brought in who owed him millions of dollars.* 25He couldn't pay, so the king ordered that he, his wife, his children, and everything he had be sold to pay the debt. 26But the man fell down before the king and begged him, 'Oh, sir, be patient with me, and I will pay it all.' 27Then the king was filled with pity for him, and he released him and forgave his debt.

28 "But when the man left the king, he went to a fellow servant who owed him a few thousand dollars.* He grabbed him by the throat and demanded instant payment. 29His fellow servant fell down before him and begged for a little more time. 'Be patient and I will pay it,' he pleaded. 30But his creditor wouldn't wait. He had the man arrested and jailed until the debt could be paid in full.

31 "When some of the other servants saw this, they were very upset. They went to the king and told him what had happened. 32Then the king called in the man he had forgiven and said, 'You evil servant! I forgave you that tremendous debt because you pleaded with me. 33Shouldn't you have mercy on your fellow servant, just as I had mercy on you?' 34Then the angry king sent the man to prison until he had paid every penny.

35 "That's what my heavenly Father will do to you if you refuse to forgive your brothers and sisters* in your heart."

CHAPTER **19**
Discussion about Divorce and Marriage
After Jesus had finished saying these things, he left Galilee and went southward to the region of Judea and into the area east of the Jordan River. 2Vast crowds followed him there, and he healed their sick.

3Some Pharisees came and tried to trap him with this question: "Should a man be allowed to divorce his wife for any reason?"

4 "Haven't you read the Scriptures?" Jesus replied. "They record that from the beginning 'God made them male and female.'* 5And he said, 'This explains why a man leaves his father and mother and is joined to his wife, and the two are united into one.'* 6Since they are no longer two but one, let no one separate them, for God has joined them together."

7 "Then why did Moses say a man could merely write an official letter of divorce and send her away?"* they asked.

8Jesus replied, "Moses permitted divorce as a concession to your hard-hearted wickedness, but it was not what God had originally intended. 9And I tell you this, a man who divorces his wife and marries another commits adultery—unless his wife has been unfaithful.*"

10Jesus' disciples then said to him, "Then it is better not to marry!"

11 "Not everyone can accept this statement," Jesus said. "Only those whom God helps. 12Some are born as eunuchs, some have been made that way by others, and some choose not to marry for the sake of the Kingdom of Heaven. Let anyone who can, accept this statement."

Jesus Blesses the Children
13Some children were brought to Jesus so he could lay his hands on them and pray for them. The disciples told them not to bother him. 14But Jesus said, "Let the children come to me. Don't stop them! For the Kingdom of Heaven belongs to such as these." 15And he put his hands on their heads and blessed them before he left.

The Rich Young Man
16Someone came to Jesus with this question: "Teacher,* what good things must I do to have eternal life?"

17 "Why ask me about what is good?" Jesus replied. "Only God is good. But to answer your question, you can receive eternal life if you keep the commandments."

18 "Which ones?" the man asked.

And Jesus replied: " 'Do not murder. Do not commit adultery. Do not steal. Do not testify

18:20 Greek *gather together in my name.* 18:21 Greek *my brother.* 18:22 Or *77 times.* 18:24 Greek *10,000 talents.* 18:28 Greek *100 denarii.* A denarius was the equivalent of a full day's wage. 18:35 Greek *your brother.* 19:4 Gen 1:27; 5:2. 19:5 Gen 2:24. 19:7 Deut 24:1. 19:9 Some manuscripts add *And the man who marries a divorced woman commits adultery.* 19:16 Some manuscripts read *Good Teacher.*

falsely. ¹⁹Honor your father and mother. Love your neighbor as yourself.'* "

²⁰"I've obeyed all these commandments," the young man replied. "What else must I do?"

²¹Jesus told him, "If you want to be perfect, go and sell all you have and give the money to the poor, and you will have treasure in heaven. Then come, follow me." ²²But when the young man heard this, he went sadly away because he had many possessions.

²³Then Jesus said to his disciples, "I tell you the truth, it is very hard for a rich person to get into the Kingdom of Heaven. ²⁴I say it again—it is easier for a camel to go through the eye of a needle than for a rich person to enter the Kingdom of God!"

²⁵The disciples were astounded. "Then who in the world can be saved?" they asked.

²⁶Jesus looked at them intently and said, "Humanly speaking, it is impossible. But with God everything is possible."

²⁷Then Peter said to him, "We've given up everything to follow you. What will we get out of it?"

²⁸And Jesus replied, "I assure you that when I, the Son of Man, sit upon my glorious throne in the Kingdom,* you who have been my followers will also sit on twelve thrones, judging the twelve tribes of Israel. ²⁹And everyone who has given up houses or brothers or sisters or father or mother or children or property, for my sake, will receive a hundred times as much in return and will have eternal life. ³⁰But many who seem to be important now will be the least important then, and those who are considered least here will be the greatest then.*

CHAPTER 20

Story of the Vineyard Workers

"For the Kingdom of Heaven is like the owner of an estate who went out early one morning to hire workers for his vineyard. ²He agreed to pay the normal daily wage* and sent them out to work.

³"At nine o'clock in the morning he was passing through the marketplace and saw some people standing around doing nothing. ⁴So he hired them, telling them he would pay them whatever was right at the end of the day. ⁵At noon and again around three o'clock he did the same thing. ⁶At five o'clock that evening he was in town again and saw some more people standing around. He asked them, 'Why haven't you been working today?'

⁷"They replied, 'Because no one hired us.'

"The owner of the estate told them, 'Then go on out and join the others in my vineyard.'

⁸"That evening he told the foreman to call the workers in and pay them, beginning with the last workers first. ⁹When those hired at five o'clock were paid, each received a full day's wage. ¹⁰When those hired earlier came to get their pay, they assumed they would receive more. But they, too, were paid a day's wage. ¹¹When they received their pay, they protested, ¹²'Those people worked only one hour, and yet you've paid them just as much as you paid us who worked all day in the scorching heat.'

¹³"He answered one of them, 'Friend, I haven't been unfair! Didn't you agree to work all day for the usual wage? ¹⁴Take it and go. I wanted to pay this last worker the same as you. ¹⁵Is it against the law for me to do what I want with my money? Should you be angry because I am kind?'

¹⁶"And so it is, that many who are first now will be last then; and those who are last now will be first then."

Jesus Again Predicts His Death

¹⁷As Jesus was on the way to Jerusalem, he took the twelve disciples aside privately and told them what was going to happen to him. ¹⁸"When we get to Jerusalem," he said, "the Son of Man will be betrayed to the leading priests and the teachers of religious law. They will sentence him to die. ¹⁹Then they will hand him over to the Romans to be mocked, whipped, and crucified. But on the third day he will be raised from the dead."

Jesus Teaches about Serving Others

²⁰Then the mother of James and John, the sons of Zebedee, came to Jesus with her sons. She knelt respectfully to ask a favor. ²¹"What is your request?" he asked.

She replied, "In your Kingdom, will you let my two sons sit in places of honor next to you, one at your right and the other at your left?"

²²But Jesus told them, "You don't know what you are asking! Are you able to drink from the bitter cup of sorrow I am about to drink?"

"Oh yes," they replied, "we are able!"

²³"You will indeed drink from it," he told them. "But I have no right to say who will sit on

19:18-19 Exod 20:12-16; Lev 19:18; Deut 5:16-20. **19:28** Greek *in the regeneration.* **19:30** Greek *But many who are first will be last; and the last, first.* **20:2** Greek *a denarius,* the payment for a full day's labor; also in 20:9, 10, 13.

the thrones next to mine. My Father has prepared those places for the ones he has chosen."

24When the ten other disciples heard what James and John had asked, they were indignant. 25But Jesus called them together and said, "You know that in this world kings are tyrants, and officials lord it over the people beneath them. 26But among you it should be quite different. Whoever wants to be a leader among you must be your servant, 27and whoever wants to be first must become your slave. 28For even I, the Son of Man, came here not to be served but to serve others, and to give my life as a ransom for many."

Jesus Heals Two Blind Men

29As Jesus and the disciples left the city of Jericho, a huge crowd followed behind. 30Two blind men were sitting beside the road. When they heard that Jesus was coming that way, they began shouting, "Lord, Son of David, have mercy on us!" 31The crowd told them to be quiet, but they only shouted louder, "Lord, Son of David, have mercy on us!"

32Jesus stopped in the road and called, "What do you want me to do for you?"

33"Lord," they said, "we want to see!" 34Jesus felt sorry for them and touched their eyes. Instantly they could see! Then they followed him.

CHAPTER **21**
The Triumphal Entry

As Jesus and the disciples approached Jerusalem, they came to the town of Bethphage on the Mount of Olives. Jesus sent two of them on ahead. 2"Go into the village over there," he said, "and you will see a donkey tied there, with its colt beside it. Untie them and bring them here. 3If anyone asks what you are doing, just say, 'The Lord needs them,' and he will immediately send them." 4This was done to fulfill the prophecy,

5 "Tell the people of Israel,*
'Look, your King is coming to you.
He is humble, riding on a donkey—
even on a donkey's colt.'"*

6The two disciples did as Jesus said. 7They brought the animals to him and threw their garments over the colt, and he sat on it.*

8Most of the crowd spread their coats on the road ahead of Jesus, and others cut branches from the trees and spread them on the road. 9He

was in the center of the procession, and the crowds all around him were shouting,

"Praise God* for the Son of David!
Bless the one who comes in the name of the Lord!
Praise God in highest heaven!"*

10The entire city of Jerusalem was stirred as he entered. "Who is this?" they asked.

11And the crowds replied, "It's Jesus, the prophet from Nazareth in Galilee."

Jesus Clears the Temple

12Jesus entered the Temple and began to drive out the merchants and their customers. He knocked over the tables of the money changers and the stalls of those selling doves. 13He said, "The Scriptures declare, 'My Temple will be called a place of prayer,' but you have turned it into a den of thieves!"*

14The blind and the lame came to him, and he healed them there in the Temple. 15The leading priests and the teachers of religious law saw these wonderful miracles and heard even the little children in the Temple shouting, "Praise God for the Son of David." But they were indignant 16and asked Jesus, "Do you hear what these children are saying?"

"Yes," Jesus replied. "Haven't you ever read the Scriptures? For they say, 'You have taught children and infants to give you praise.'* " 17Then he returned to Bethany, where he stayed overnight.

Jesus Curses the Fig Tree

18In the morning, as Jesus was returning to Jerusalem, he was hungry, 19and he noticed a fig tree beside the road. He went over to see if there were any figs on it, but there were only leaves. Then he said to it, "May you never bear fruit again!" And immediately the fig tree withered up.

20The disciples were amazed when they saw this and asked, "How did the fig tree wither so quickly?"

21Then Jesus told them, "I assure you, if you have faith and don't doubt, you can do things like this and much more. You can even say to this mountain, 'May God lift you up and throw you into the sea,' and it will happen. 22If you believe, you will receive whatever you ask for in prayer."

The Authority of Jesus Challenged

23When Jesus returned to the Temple and began teaching, the leading priests and other leaders

---

21:5a Greek *Tell the daughter of Zion.* Isa 62:11. **21:5b** Zech 9:9. **21:7** Greek *over them, and he sat on them.* **21:9a** Greek *Hosanna,* an exclamation of praise that literally means "save now"; also in 21:9b, 15. **21:9b** Pss 118:25-26; 148:1. **21:13** Isa 56:7; Jer 7:11. **21:16** Ps 8:2.

Will We Recognize People in Heaven? Read MATTHEW 22:23-33

A number of the people in Jesus' day had some aberrant views of life after death. The particular group of religious leaders mentioned here, the Sadducees, did not believe in life beyond the grave. So when Jesus answered their question (which they had asked to test him), he immediately addressed the error of their teaching: "Your problem is that you don't know the Scriptures, and you don't know the power of God" (verse 29). In refuting the error and arrogance of the Sadducees, Jesus revealed these three insights about life in heaven:

1. We Will Not Be Married. We will not participate in the same activities we do now, such as marriage and family life. In fact, it would appear that the majority of our time will be spent worshiping God (see Revelation 19:5, p. 1131).

2. We Will Recognize One Another. Jesus said that we will be as the angels. We won't become angels, but we will probably have some of the same capabilities or characteristics. We will not simply be a spirit, but we will actually have a resurrected body. While no specific passage of Scripture guarantees that we will recognize one another in heaven, many verses suggest that we will. Jesus' disciples were able to recognize his resurrected body, so he must have retained certain physical characteristics. In the parable of Lazarus and the rich man (see Luke 16:19-31, p. 879), both men retained their identity. The Bible also says that we will have increased knowledge in heaven: "Now we see things imperfectly as in a poor mirror, but then we will see everything with perfect clarity. All that I know now is partial and incomplete, but then I will know everything completely, just as God knows me now" (1 Corinthians 13:12). With that kind of knowledge, we will probably recognize more people in heaven than we do here on earth!

3. We Will Have a Distinct Personality. Notice that at the end of the text Jesus refers to the Old Testament passage that says, "I *am* the God of Abraham, the God of Isaac, and the God of Jacob." Not only does this verse give great proof for a bodily resurrection, but it also refers to these men by name. When we read that God writes our names in the Book of Life, it indicates that we are distinct personalities in heaven. God didn't write a number—he wrote your *name*.

Some day, "in the blinking of an eye," Christ will call us home to heaven, and our bodies will be transformed into "heavenly bodies that will never die" (see 1 Corinthians 15:50-53, p. 1001).

To live forever in these present bodies of ours would be a curse. But to live forever in new bodies—free of sickness and pain—in the presence of God will be a blessing.

For the next note on "What Is Heaven?" turn to p. 1122.

CORNER STONES

---

came up to him. They demanded, "By whose authority did you drive out the merchants from the Temple?* Who gave you such authority?"

24"I'll tell you who gave me the authority to do these things if you answer one question," Jesus replied. 25"Did John's baptism come from heaven or was it merely human?"

They talked it over among themselves. "If we say it was from heaven, he will ask why we didn't believe him. 26But if we say it was merely human, we'll be mobbed, because the people think he was a prophet." 27So they finally replied, "We don't know."

And Jesus responded, "Then I won't answer your question either.

Story of the Two Sons

28"But what do you think about this? A man with two sons told the older boy, 'Son, go out and work in the vineyard today.' 29The son answered, 'No, I won't go,' but later he changed his mind and went anyway. 30Then the father told the other son, 'You go,' and he said, 'Yes, sir, I will.' But he didn't go. 31Which of the two was obeying his father?"

They replied, "The first, of course."

21:23 Or *By whose authority do you do these things?*

Then Jesus explained his meaning: "I assure you, corrupt tax collectors and prostitutes will get into the Kingdom of God before you do. 32For John the Baptist came and showed you the way to life, and you didn't believe him, while tax collectors and prostitutes did. And even when you saw this happening, you refused to turn from your sins and believe him.

Story of the Evil Farmers

33"Now listen to this story. A certain landowner planted a vineyard, built a wall around it, dug a pit for pressing out the grape juice, and built a lookout tower. Then he leased the vineyard to tenant farmers and moved to another country. 34At the time of the grape harvest he sent his servants to collect his share of the crop. 35But the farmers grabbed his servants, beat one, killed one, and stoned another. 36So the landowner sent a larger group of his servants to collect for him, but the results were the same.

37"Finally, the owner sent his son, thinking, 'Surely they will respect my son.'

38"But when the farmers saw his son coming, they said to one another, 'Here comes the heir to this estate. Come on, let's kill him and get the estate for ourselves!' 39So they grabbed him, took him out of the vineyard, and murdered him.

40"When the owner of the vineyard returns," Jesus asked, "what do you think he will do to those farmers?"

41The religious leaders replied, "He will put the wicked men to a horrible death and lease the vineyard to others who will give him his share of the crop after each harvest."

42Then Jesus asked them, "Didn't you ever read this in the Scriptures?

'The stone rejected by the builders
   has now become the cornerstone.
This is the Lord's doing,
   and it is marvelous to see.'*

43What I mean is that the Kingdom of God will be taken away from you and given to a nation that will produce the proper fruit. 44Anyone who stumbles over that stone will be broken to pieces, and it will crush anyone on whom it falls.*"

45When the leading priests and Pharisees heard Jesus, they realized he was pointing at them—that they were the farmers in his story. 46They wanted to arrest him, but they were afraid to try because the crowds considered Jesus to be a prophet.

CHAPTER 22

Story of the Great Feast

Jesus told them several other stories to illustrate the Kingdom. He said, 2"The Kingdom of Heaven can be illustrated by the story of a king who prepared a great wedding feast for his son. 3Many guests were invited, and when the banquet was ready, he sent his servants to notify everyone that it was time to come. But they all refused! 4So he sent other servants to tell them, 'The feast has been prepared, and choice meats have been cooked. Everything is ready. Hurry!' 5But the guests he had invited ignored them and went about their business, one to his farm, another to his store. 6Others seized his messengers and treated them shamefully, even killing some of them.

7"Then the king became furious. He sent out his army to destroy the murderers and burn their city. 8And he said to his servants, 'The wedding feast is ready, and the guests I invited aren't worthy of the honor. 9Now go out to the street corners and invite everyone you see.'

10"So the servants brought in everyone they could find, good and bad alike, and the banquet hall was filled with guests. 11But when the king came in to meet the guests, he noticed a man who wasn't wearing the proper clothes for a wedding. 12'Friend,' he asked, 'how is it that you are here without wedding clothes?' And the man had no reply. 13Then the king said to his aides, 'Bind him hand and foot and throw him out into the outer darkness, where there is weeping and gnashing of teeth.' 14For many are called, but few are chosen."

Taxes for Caesar

15Then the Pharisees met together to think of a way to trap Jesus into saying something for which they could accuse him. 16They decided to send some of their disciples, along with the supporters of Herod, to ask him this question: "Teacher, we know how honest you are. You teach about the way of God regardless of the consequences. You are impartial and don't play favorites. 17Now tell us what you think about this: Is it right to pay taxes to the Roman government or not?"

18But Jesus knew their evil motives. "You hypocrites!" he said. "Whom are you trying to fool with your trick questions? 19Here, show me the Roman coin used for the tax." When they handed him the coin,* 20he asked, "Whose picture and title are stamped on it?"

21:42 Ps 118:22-23.   21:44 This verse is omitted in some early manuscripts.   22:19 Greek a denarius.

21 "Caesar's," they replied.

"Well, then," he said, "give to Caesar what belongs to him. But everything that belongs to God must be given to God." 22His reply amazed them, and they went away.

Discussion about Resurrection

23That same day some Sadducees stepped forward—a group of Jews who say there is no resurrection after death. They posed this question: 24"Teacher, Moses said, 'If a man dies without children, his brother should marry the widow and have a child who will be the brother's heir.'* 25Well, there were seven brothers. The oldest married and then died without children, so the second brother married the widow. 26This brother also died without children, and the wife was married to the next brother, and so on until she had been the wife of each of them. 27And then she also died. 28So tell us, whose wife will she be in the resurrection? For she was the wife of all seven of them!"

29Jesus replied, "Your problem is that you don't know the Scriptures, and you don't know the power of God. 30For when the dead rise, they won't be married. They will be like the angels in heaven. 31But now, as to whether there will be a resurrection of the dead—haven't you ever read about this in the Scriptures? Long after Abraham, Isaac, and Jacob had died, God said,* 32'I am the God of Abraham, the God of Isaac, and the God of Jacob.'* So he is the God of the living, not the dead."

33When the crowds heard him, they were impressed with his teaching.

The Most Important Commandment

34But when the Pharisees heard that he had silenced the Sadducees with his reply, they thought up a fresh question of their own to ask him. 35One of them, an expert in religious law,

tried to trap him with this question: 36"Teacher, which is the most important commandment in the law of Moses?"

37Jesus replied, "'You must love the Lord your God with all your heart, all your soul, and all your mind.'* 38This is the first and greatest commandment. 39A second is equally important: 'Love your neighbor as yourself.'* 40All the other commandments and all the demands of the prophets are based on these two commandments."

Whose Son Is the Messiah?

41Then, surrounded by the Pharisees, Jesus asked them a question: 42"What do you think about the Messiah? Whose son is he?"

They replied, "He is the son of David."

43Jesus responded, "Then why does David, speaking under the inspiration of the Holy Spirit, call him Lord? For David said,

44 'The LORD said to my Lord,
   Sit in honor at my right hand
      until I humble your enemies beneath
      your feet.'*

45Since David called him Lord, how can he be his son at the same time?"

46No one could answer him. And after that, no one dared to ask him any more questions.

CHAPTER **23**
Jesus Warns the Religious Leaders
Then Jesus said to the crowds and to his disciples, 2 "The teachers of religious law and the Pharisees are the official interpreters of the Scriptures. 3So practice and obey whatever they say to you, but don't follow their example. For they don't practice what they teach. 4They crush you with impossible religious demands and never lift a finger to help ease the burden.

22:24 Deut 25:5-6.   22:31 Greek *in the Scriptures? God said.*   22:32 Exod 3:6.   22:37 Deut 6:5.   22:39 Lev 19:18.   22:44 Ps 110:1.

OFF AND RUNNING
We Will Find Happiness in Loving God and Others
Read MATTHEW 22:37-39

In two commands Jesus summarized the entire Old Testament law. His summarization shows us what is important for us as his followers to do: to love God wholeheartedly and to love our neighbors as ourselves. When we do these two things, we will not only please God by our obedience, but we will also experience real happiness.

Ironically, real happiness is not found in fulfilling our own appetites and desires. Rather, it is found in loving God and others. This is not by chance, either. God designed it that way. He knew the value of loving

5 "Everything they do is for show. On their arms they wear extra wide prayer boxes with Scripture verses inside,* and they wear extra long tassels on their robes. 6And how they love to sit at the head table at banquets and in the most prominent seats in the synagogue! 7They enjoy the attention they get on the streets, and they enjoy being called 'Rabbi.'* 8Don't ever let anyone call you 'Rabbi,' for you have only one teacher, and all of you are on the same level as brothers and sisters.* 9And don't address anyone here on earth as 'Father,' for only God in heaven is your spiritual Father. 10And don't let anyone call you 'Master,' for there is only one master, the Messiah. 11The greatest among you must be a servant. 12But those who exalt themselves will be humbled, and those who humble themselves will be exalted.

13 "How terrible it will be for you teachers of religious law and you Pharisees. Hypocrites! For you won't let others enter the Kingdom of Heaven, and you won't go in yourselves.* 15Yes, how terrible it will be for you teachers of religious law and you Pharisees. For you cross land and sea to make one convert, and then you turn him into twice the son of hell as you yourselves are.

16 "Blind guides! How terrible it will be for you! For you say that it means nothing to swear 'by God's Temple'—you can break that oath. But then you say that it is binding to swear 'by the gold in the Temple.' 17Blind fools! Which is greater, the gold, or the Temple that makes the gold sacred? 18And you say that to take an oath 'by the altar' can be broken, but to swear 'by the gifts on the altar' is binding! 19How blind! For which is greater, the gift on the altar, or the altar that makes the gift sacred? 20When you swear 'by the altar,' you are swearing by it and by everything on it. 21And when you swear 'by the

Temple,' you are swearing by it and by God, who lives in it. 22And when you swear 'by heaven,' you are swearing by the throne of God and by God, who sits on the throne.

23 "How terrible it will be for you teachers of religious law and you Pharisees. Hypocrites! For you are careful to tithe even the tiniest part of your income,* but you ignore the important things of the law—justice, mercy, and faith. You should tithe, yes, but you should not leave undone the more important things. 24Blind guides! You strain your water so you won't accidentally swallow a gnat; then you swallow a camel!

25 "How terrible it will be for you teachers of religious law and you Pharisees. Hypocrites! You are so careful to clean the outside of the cup and the dish, but inside you are filthy—full of greed and self-indulgence! 26Blind Pharisees! First wash the inside of the cup, and then the outside will become clean, too.

27 "How terrible it will be for you teachers of religious law and you Pharisees. Hypocrites! You are like whitewashed tombs—beautiful on the outside but filled on the inside with dead people's bones and all sorts of impurity. 28You try to look like upright people outwardly, but inside your hearts are filled with hypocrisy and lawlessness.

29 "How terrible it will be for you teachers of religious law and you Pharisees. Hypocrites! For you build tombs for the prophets your ancestors killed and decorate the graves of the godly people your ancestors destroyed. 30Then you say, 'We never would have joined them in killing the prophets.'

31 "In saying that, you are accusing yourselves of being the descendants of those who murdered the prophets. 32Go ahead. Finish what they

23:5 Greek *They enlarge their phylacteries.* 23:7 *Rabbi,* from Aramaic, means "master" or "teacher." 23:8 Greek *brothers.* 23:13 Some manuscripts add verse 14, *How terrible it will be for you teachers of religious law and you Pharisees. Hypocrites! You shamelessly cheat widows out of their property, and then, to cover up the kind of people you really are, you make long prayers in public. Because of this, your punishment will be the greater.* 23:23 Greek *to tithe the mint, the dill, and the cumin.*

others even before he proved his love for us on the cross. He also knew how self-absorbed we are as humans and that we would fill our lives with empty pursuits in search of happiness if he didn't command us to love him and to love others.

As Paul tells us, all of our works will be tested by fire on Judgment Day (see 1 Corinthians 3:13, p. 986). Those works that were done out of selfishness will not last. But those works done out of love for God and others will. Because this love—and the works motivated by it—are everlasting, we will find real meaning in doing them. In addition, we will experience real joy in giving of ourselves to God and others out of love. It is in giving that we find purpose in life. From purpose we gain true happiness.

For the next note on "Attitude toward Self," turn to p. 810.

started. 33Snakes! Sons of vipers! How will you escape the judgment of hell? 34I will send you prophets and wise men and teachers of religious law. You will kill some by crucifixion and whip others in your synagogues, chasing them from city to city. 35As a result, you will become guilty of murdering all the godly people from righteous Abel to Zechariah son of Barachiah, whom you murdered in the Temple between the altar and the sanctuary. 36I assure you, all the accumulated judgment of the centuries will break upon the heads of this very generation.

Jesus Grieves over Jerusalem

37"O Jerusalem, Jerusalem, the city that kills the prophets and stones God's messengers! How often I have wanted to gather your children together as a hen protects her chicks beneath her wings, but you wouldn't let me. 38And now look, your house is left to you, empty and desolate. 39For I tell you this, you will never see me again until you say, 'Bless the one who comes in the name of the Lord!'* "

CHAPTER **24**

Jesus Foretells the Future

As Jesus was leaving the Temple grounds, his disciples pointed out to him the various Temple buildings. 2But he told them, "Do you see all these buildings? I assure you, they will be so completely demolished that not one stone will be left on top of another!"

3Later, Jesus sat on the slopes of the Mount of Olives. His disciples came to him privately and asked, "When will all this take place? And will there be any sign ahead of time to signal your return and the end of the world*?"

4Jesus told them, "Don't let anyone mislead you. 5For many will come in my name, saying, 'I am the Messiah.' They will lead many astray. 6And wars will break out near and far, but don't panic. Yes, these things must come, but the end won't follow immediately. 7The nations and kingdoms will proclaim war against each other, and there will be famines and earthquakes in many parts of the world. 8But all this will be only the beginning of the horrors to come.

9"Then you will be arrested, persecuted, and killed. You will be hated all over the world because of your allegiance to me. 10And many will turn away from me and betray and hate each other. 11And many false prophets will appear

and will lead many people astray. 12Sin will be rampant everywhere, and the love of many will grow cold. 13But those who endure to the end will be saved. 14And the Good News about the Kingdom will be preached throughout the whole world, so that all nations will hear it; and then, finally, the end will come.

15"The time will come when you will see what Daniel the prophet spoke about: the sacrilegious object that causes desecration* standing in the Holy Place"—reader, pay attention! 16"Then those in Judea must flee to the hills. 17A person outside the house* must not go inside to pack. 18A person in the field must not return even to get a coat. 19How terrible it will be for pregnant women and for mothers nursing their babies in those days. 20And pray that your flight will not be in winter or on the Sabbath. 21For that will be a time of greater horror than anything the world has ever seen or will ever see again. 22In fact, unless that time of calamity is shortened, the entire human race will be destroyed. But it will be shortened for the sake of God's chosen ones.

23"Then if anyone tells you, 'Look, here is the Messiah,' or 'There he is,' don't pay any attention. 24For false messiahs and false prophets will rise up and perform great miraculous signs and wonders so as to deceive, if possible, even God's chosen ones. 25See, I have warned you.

26"So if someone tells you, 'Look, the Messiah is out in the desert,' don't bother to go and look. Or, 'Look, he is hiding here,' don't believe it! 27For as the lightning lights up the entire sky, so it will be when the Son of Man comes. 28Just as the gathering of vultures shows there is a carcass nearby, so these signs indicate that the end is near.*

29"Immediately after those horrible days end,

the sun will be darkened,
the moon will not give light,
the stars will fall from the sky,
and the powers of heaven will be
shaken.*

30And then at last, the sign of the coming of the Son of Man will appear in the heavens, and there will be deep mourning among all the nations of the earth. And they will see the Son of Man arrive on the clouds of heaven with power and great glory.* 31And he will send forth his angels with the sound of a mighty trumpet blast, and they will gather together his chosen ones from the farthest ends of the earth and heaven.

23:39 Ps 118:26. **24:3** Or *the age.* **24:15** Greek *the abomination of desolation.* See Dan 9:27; 11:31; 12:11. **24:17** Greek *on the roof.*
24:28 Greek *Wherever the carcass is, the vultures gather.* **24:29** See Isa 13:10; 34:4; Joel 2:10. **24:30** See Dan 7:13.

32 "Now learn a lesson from the fig tree. When its buds become tender and its leaves begin to sprout, you know without being told that summer is near. 33 Just so, when you see the events I've described beginning to happen, you can know his return is very near, right at the door. 34 I assure you, this generation* will not pass from the scene before all these things take place. 35 Heaven and earth will disappear, but my words will remain forever.

36 "However, no one knows the day or the hour when these things will happen, not even the angels in heaven or the Son himself.* Only the Father knows.

37 "When the Son of Man returns, it will be like it was in Noah's day. 38 In those days before the Flood, the people were enjoying banquets and parties and weddings right up to the time Noah entered his boat. 39 People didn't realize what was going to happen until the Flood came and swept them all away. That is the way it will be when the Son of Man comes.

40 "Two men will be working together in the field; one will be taken, the other left. 41 Two women will be grinding flour at the mill; one will be taken, the other left. 42 So be prepared, because you don't know what day your Lord is coming.

43 "Know this: A homeowner who knew exactly when a burglar was coming would stay alert and not permit the house to be broken into. 44 You also must be ready all the time. For the Son of Man will come when least expected.

45 "Who is a faithful, sensible servant, to whom the master can give the responsibility of managing his household and feeding his family? 46 If the master returns and finds that the servant has done a good job, there will be a reward. 47 I assure you, the master will put that servant in charge of all he owns. 48 But if the servant is evil and thinks, 'My master won't be back for a while,' 49 and begins oppressing the other servants, partying, and getting drunk— 50 well, the master will return unannounced and unexpected. 51 He will tear the servant apart and banish him with the hypocrites. In that place there will be weeping and gnashing of teeth.

CHAPTER **25**
Story of the Ten Bridesmaids
"The Kingdom of Heaven can be illustrated by the story of ten bridesmaids* who took their lamps and went to meet the bridegroom. 2 Five of them were foolish, and five were wise. 3 The five who were foolish took no oil for their lamps, 4 but the other five were wise enough to take along extra oil. 5 When the bridegroom was delayed, they all lay down and slept. 6 At midnight they were roused by the shout, 'Look, the bridegroom is coming! Come out and welcome him!'

7 "All the bridesmaids got up and prepared their lamps. 8 Then the five foolish ones asked the others, 'Please give us some of your oil because our lamps are going out.' 9 But the others replied, 'We don't have enough for all of us. Go to a shop and buy some for yourselves.'

10 "But while they were gone to buy oil, the bridegroom came, and those who were ready went in with him to the marriage feast, and the door was locked. 11 Later, when the other five bridesmaids returned, they stood outside, calling, 'Sir, open the door for us!' 12 But he called back, 'I don't know you!'

13 "So stay awake and be prepared, because you do not know the day or hour of my return.

Story of the Three Servants
14 "Again, the Kingdom of Heaven can be illustrated by the story of a man going on a trip. He called together his servants and gave them money to invest for him while he was gone. 15 He gave five bags of gold* to one, two bags of gold to another, and one bag of gold to the last—dividing it in proportion to their abilities—and then left on his trip. 16 The servant who received the five bags of gold began immediately to invest the money and soon doubled it. 17 The servant with two bags of gold also went right to work and doubled the money. 18 But the servant who received the one bag of gold dug a hole in the ground and hid the master's money for safekeeping.

19 "After a long time their master returned from his trip and called them to give an account of how they had used his money. 20 The servant to whom he had entrusted the five bags of gold said, 'Sir, you gave me five bags of gold to invest, and I have doubled the amount.' 21 The master was full of praise. 'Well done, my good and faithful servant. You have been faithful in handling this small amount, so now I will give you many more responsibilities. Let's celebrate together!'

22 "Next came the servant who had received the two bags of gold, with the report, 'Sir, you

24:34 Or *this age,* or *this nation.*   24:36 Some manuscripts omit the phrase *or the Son himself.*   25:1 Or *virgins;* also in 25:7, 11.
25:15 Greek *talents;* also throughout the story. A talent is equal to 75 pounds or 34 kilograms.

gave me two bags of gold to invest, and I have doubled the amount.' 23The master said, 'Well done, my good and faithful servant. You have been faithful in handling this small amount, so now I will give you many more responsibilities. Let's celebrate together!'

24"Then the servant with the one bag of gold came and said, 'Sir, I know you are a hard man, harvesting crops you didn't plant and gathering crops you didn't cultivate. 25I was afraid I would lose your money, so I hid it in the earth and here it is.'

26"But the master replied, 'You wicked and lazy servant! You think I'm a hard man, do you, harvesting crops I didn't plant and gathering crops I didn't cultivate? 27Well, you should at least have put my money into the bank so I could have some interest. 28Take the money from this servant and give it to the one with the ten bags of gold. 29To those who use well what they are given, even more will be given, and they will have an abundance. But from those who are unfaithful,* even what little they have will be taken away. 30Now throw this useless servant into outer darkness, where there will be weeping and gnashing of teeth.'

The Final Judgment

31"But when the Son of Man comes in his glory, and all the angels with him, then he will sit upon his glorious throne. 32All the nations will be gathered in his presence, and he will separate them as a shepherd separates the sheep from the goats. 33He will place the sheep at his right hand and the goats at his left. 34Then the King will say to those on the right, 'Come, you who are blessed by my Father, inherit the Kingdom prepared for you from the foundation of the world. 35For I was hungry, and you fed me. I was thirsty, and you gave me a drink. I was a stranger, and you invited me into your home. 36I was naked, and you gave me clothing. I was sick, and you cared for me. I was in prison, and you visited me.'

37"Then these righteous ones will reply, 'Lord, when did we ever see you hungry and feed you? Or thirsty and give you something to drink? 38Or a stranger and show you hospitality? Or naked and give you clothing? 39When did we ever see you sick or in prison, and visit you?' 40And the King will tell them, 'I assure you, when you did it to one of the least of these my brothers and sisters,* you were doing it to me!'

41"Then the King will turn to those on the left and say, 'Away with you, you cursed ones, into the eternal fire prepared for the Devil and his demons! 42For I was hungry, and you didn't feed me. I was thirsty, and you didn't give me anything to drink. 43I was a stranger, and you didn't invite me into your home. I was naked, and you gave me no clothing. I was sick and in prison, and you didn't visit me.'

44"Then they will reply, 'Lord, when did we ever see you hungry or thirsty or a stranger or naked or sick or in prison, and not help you?' 45And he will answer, 'I assure you, when you refused to help the least of these my brothers and sisters, you were refusing to help me.' 46And they will go away into eternal punishment, but the righteous will go into eternal life."

CHAPTER **26**

The Plot to Kill Jesus

When Jesus had finished saying these things, he said to his disciples, 2"As you know, the Passover celebration begins in two days, and I, the Son of Man, will be betrayed and crucified."

3At that same time the leading priests and other leaders were meeting at the residence of Caiaphas, the high priest, 4to discuss how to capture Jesus secretly and put him to death. 5"But not during the Passover," they agreed, "or there will be a riot."

Jesus Anointed at Bethany

6Meanwhile, Jesus was in Bethany at the home of Simon, a man who had leprosy. 7During supper, a woman came in with a beautiful jar* of expensive perfume and poured it over his head. 8The disciples were indignant when they saw this. "What a waste of money," they said. 9"She could have sold it for a fortune and given the money to the poor."

10But Jesus replied, "Why berate her for doing such a good thing to me? 11You will always have the poor among you, but I will not be here with you much longer. 12She has poured this perfume on me to prepare my body for burial. 13I assure you, wherever the Good News is preached throughout the world, this woman's deed will be talked about in her memory."

Judas Agrees to Betray Jesus

14Then Judas Iscariot, one of the twelve disciples, went to the leading priests 15and asked, "How much will you pay me to betray Jesus to you?" And they gave him thirty pieces of silver.

25:29 Or *who have nothing.*   25:40 Greek *my brothers.*   26:7 Greek *an alabaster jar.*

16From that time on, Judas began looking for the right time and place to betray Jesus.

The Last Supper

17On the first day of the Festival of Unleavened Bread, the disciples came to Jesus and asked, "Where do you want us to prepare the Passover supper?"

18"As you go into the city," he told them, "you will see a certain man. Tell him, 'The Teacher says, My time has come, and I will eat the Passover meal with my disciples at your house.'" 19So the disciples did as Jesus told them and prepared the Passover supper there.

20When it was evening, Jesus sat down at the table with the twelve disciples. 21While they were eating, he said, "The truth is, one of you will betray me."

22Greatly distressed, one by one they began to ask him, "I'm not the one, am I, Lord?"

23He replied, "One of you who is eating with me now* will betray me. 24For I, the Son of Man, must die, as the Scriptures declared long ago. But how terrible it will be for my betrayer. Far better for him if he had never been born!"

25Judas, the one who would betray him, also asked, "Teacher, I'm not the one, am I?"

And Jesus told him, "You have said it yourself."

26As they were eating, Jesus took a loaf of bread and asked God's blessing on it. Then he broke it in pieces and gave it to the disciples, saying, "Take it and eat it, for this is my body."

27And he took a cup of wine and gave thanks to God for it. He gave it to them and said, "Each of you drink from it, 28for this is my blood, which seals the covenant* between God and his people. It is poured out to forgive the sins of many. 29Mark my words—I will not drink wine again until the day I drink it new with you in my Father's Kingdom." 30Then they sang a hymn and went out to the Mount of Olives.

Jesus Predicts Peter's Denial

31"Tonight all of you will desert me," Jesus told them. "For the Scriptures say,

'God* will strike the Shepherd,
    and the sheep of the flock will be
        scattered.'*

32But after I have been raised from the dead, I will go ahead of you to Galilee and meet you there."

33Peter declared, "Even if everyone else deserts you, I never will."

34"Peter," Jesus replied, "the truth is, this very night, before the rooster crows, you will deny me three times."

35"No!" Peter insisted. "Not even if I have to die with you! I will never deny you!" And all the other disciples vowed the same.

Jesus Prays in Gethsemane

36Then Jesus brought them to an olive grove called Gethsemane, and he said, "Sit here while I go on ahead to pray." 37He took Peter and Zebedee's two sons, James and John, and he began to be filled with anguish and deep distress. 38He told them, "My soul is crushed with grief to the point of death. Stay here and watch with me."

39He went on a little farther and fell face down on the ground, praying, "My Father! If it is possible, let this cup of suffering be taken away from me. Yet I want your will, not mine." 40Then he returned to the disciples and found them asleep. He said to Peter, "Couldn't you stay awake and watch with me even one hour? 41Keep alert and pray. Otherwise temptation will overpower you. For though the spirit is willing enough, the body is weak!"

42Again he left them and prayed, "My Father! If this cup cannot be taken away until I drink it, your will be done." 43He returned to them again and found them sleeping, for they just couldn't keep their eyes open.

44So he went back to pray a third time, saying the same things again. 45Then he came to the disciples and said, "Still sleeping? Still resting?* Look, the time has come. I, the Son of Man, am betrayed into the hands of sinners. 46Up, let's be going. See, my betrayer is here!"

Jesus Is Arrested

47And even as he said this, Judas, one of the twelve disciples, arrived with a mob that was armed with swords and clubs. They had been sent out by the leading priests and other leaders of the people. 48Judas had given them a prearranged signal: "You will know which one to arrest when I go over and give him the kiss of greeting." 49So Judas came straight to Jesus. "Greetings, Teacher!" he exclaimed and gave him the kiss.

50Jesus said, "My friend, go ahead and do what you have come for." Then the others

---

26:23 Or *The one who has dipped his hand in the bowl with me.*   26:28 Some manuscripts read *the new covenant.*   26:31a Greek *I.*
26:31b Zech 13:7.   26:45 Or *Sleep on, take your rest.*

grabbed Jesus and arrested him. ⁵¹One of the men with Jesus pulled out a sword and slashed off an ear of the high priest's servant.

⁵²"Put away your sword," Jesus told him. "Those who use the sword will be killed by the sword. ⁵³Don't you realize that I could ask my Father for thousands* of angels to protect us, and he would send them instantly? ⁵⁴But if I did, how would the Scriptures be fulfilled that describe what must happen now?"

⁵⁵Then Jesus said to the crowd, "Am I some dangerous criminal, that you have come armed with swords and clubs to arrest me? Why didn't you arrest me in the Temple? I was there teaching every day. ⁵⁶But this is all happening to fulfill the words of the prophets as recorded in the Scriptures." At that point, all the disciples deserted him and fled.

Jesus before the Council

⁵⁷Then the people who had arrested Jesus led him to the home of Caiaphas, the high priest, where the teachers of religious law and other leaders had gathered. ⁵⁸Meanwhile, Peter was following far behind and eventually came to the courtyard of the high priest's house. He went in, sat with the guards, and waited to see what was going to happen to Jesus.

⁵⁹Inside, the leading priests and the entire high council* were trying to find witnesses who would lie about Jesus, so they could put him to death. ⁶⁰But even though they found many who agreed to give false witness, there was no testimony they could use. Finally, two men were found ⁶¹who declared, "This man said, 'I am able to destroy the Temple of God and rebuild it in three days.'"

⁶²Then the high priest stood up and said to Jesus, "Well, aren't you going to answer these charges? What do you have to say for yourself?" ⁶³But Jesus remained silent. Then the high priest said to him, "I demand in the name of the living God that you tell us whether you are the Messiah, the Son of God."

⁶⁴Jesus replied, "Yes, it is as you say. And in the future you will see me, the Son of Man, sitting at God's right hand in the place of power and coming back on the clouds of heaven."*

⁶⁵Then the high priest tore his clothing to show his horror, shouting, "Blasphemy! Why do we need other witnesses? You have all heard his blasphemy. ⁶⁶What is your verdict?"

"Guilty!" they shouted. "He must die!"

⁶⁷Then they spit in Jesus' face and hit him with their fists. And some slapped him, ⁶⁸saying, "Prophesy to us, you Messiah! Who hit you that time?"

Peter Denies Jesus

⁶⁹Meanwhile, as Peter was sitting outside in the courtyard, a servant girl came over and said to him, "You were one of those with Jesus the Galilean."

⁷⁰But Peter denied it in front of everyone. "I don't know what you are talking about," he said.

⁷¹Later, out by the gate, another servant girl noticed him and said to those standing around, "This man was with Jesus of Nazareth."

⁷²Again Peter denied it, this time with an oath. "I don't even know the man," he said.

⁷³A little later some other bystanders came over to him and said, "You must be one of them; we can tell by your Galilean accent."

⁷⁴Peter said, "I swear by God, I don't know the man." And immediately the rooster crowed. ⁷⁵Suddenly, Jesus' words flashed through Peter's mind: "Before the rooster crows, you will deny me three times." And he went away, crying bitterly.

CHAPTER 27

Judas Hangs Himself

Very early in the morning, the leading priests and other leaders met again to discuss how to persuade the Roman government to sentence Jesus to death. ²Then they bound him and took him to Pilate, the Roman governor.

³When Judas, who had betrayed him, realized that Jesus had been condemned to die, he was filled with remorse. So he took the thirty pieces of silver back to the leading priests and other leaders. ⁴"I have sinned," he declared, "for I have betrayed an innocent man."

"What do we care?" they retorted. "That's your problem." ⁵Then Judas threw the money onto the floor of the Temple and went out and hanged himself. ⁶The leading priests picked up the money. "We can't put it in the Temple treasury," they said, "since it's against the law to accept money paid for murder." ⁷After some discussion they finally decided to buy the potter's field, and they made it into a cemetery for foreigners. ⁸That is why the field is still called the Field of Blood. ⁹This fulfilled the prophecy of Jeremiah that says,

26:53 Greek *12 legions*. 26:59 Greek *the Sanhedrin*. 26:64 See Ps 110:1; Dan 7:13.

"They took* the thirty pieces of silver—
the price at which he was valued by the
people of Israel—
10 and purchased the potter's field,
as the Lord directed.*"

Jesus' Trial before Pilate
11Now Jesus was standing before Pilate, the Roman governor. "Are you the King of the Jews?"
the governor asked him.

Jesus replied, "Yes, it is as you say."

12But when the leading priests and other
leaders made their accusations against him,
Jesus remained silent. 13"Don't you hear their
many charges against you?" Pilate demanded.
14But Jesus said nothing, much to the governor's
great surprise.

15Now it was the governor's custom to release
one prisoner to the crowd each year during the
Passover celebration—anyone they wanted.
16This year there was a notorious criminal in
prison, a man named Barabbas.* 17As the
crowds gathered before Pilate's house that
morning, he asked them, "Which one do you
want me to release to you—Barabbas, or Jesus
who is called the Messiah?" 18(He knew very
well that the Jewish leaders had arrested Jesus
out of envy.)

19Just then, as Pilate was sitting on the judgment seat, his wife sent him this message:
"Leave that innocent man alone, because I had
a terrible nightmare about him last night."

20Meanwhile, the leading priests and other
leaders persuaded the crowds to ask for Barabbas to be released and for Jesus to be put to
death. 21So when the governor asked again,
"Which of these two do you want me to release
to you?" the crowd shouted back their reply:
"Barabbas!"

22"But if I release Barabbas," Pilate asked
them, "what should I do with Jesus who is called
the Messiah?"

And they all shouted, "Crucify him!"

23"Why?" Pilate demanded. "What crime has
he committed?"

But the crowd only roared the louder, "Crucify him!"

24Pilate saw that he wasn't getting anywhere
and that a riot was developing. So he sent for a
bowl of water and washed his hands before the
crowd, saying, "I am innocent of the blood of
this man. The responsibility is yours!"

25And all the people yelled back, "We will
take responsibility for his death—we and our
children!"*

26So Pilate released Barabbas to them. He
ordered Jesus flogged with a lead-tipped whip,
then turned him over to the Roman soldiers to
crucify him.

The Soldiers Mock Jesus
27Some of the governor's soldiers took Jesus into
their headquarters and called out the entire battalion. 28They stripped him and put a scarlet
robe on him. 29They made a crown of long,
sharp thorns and put it on his head, and they
placed a stick in his right hand as a scepter. Then
they knelt before him in mockery, yelling, "Hail!
King of the Jews!" 30And they spit on him and
grabbed the stick and beat him on the head with
it. 31When they were finally tired of mocking
him, they took off the robe and put his own
clothes on him again. Then they led him away to
be crucified.

The Crucifixion
32As they were on the way, they came across a
man named Simon, who was from Cyrene,* and
they forced him to carry Jesus' cross. 33Then they
went out to a place called Golgotha (which
means Skull Hill). 34The soldiers gave him wine
mixed with bitter gall, but when he had tasted it,
he refused to drink it.

35After they had nailed him to the cross, the
soldiers gambled for his clothes by throwing
dice.* 36Then they sat around and kept guard as
he hung there. 37A signboard was fastened to the
cross above Jesus' head, announcing the charge
against him. It read: "This is Jesus, the King of
the Jews."

38Two criminals were crucified with him,
their crosses on either side of his. 39And the
people passing by shouted abuse, shaking their
heads in mockery. 40"So! You can destroy the
Temple and build it again in three days, can you?
Well then, if you are the Son of God, save yourself and come down from the cross!"

41The leading priests, the teachers of religious
law, and the other leaders also mocked Jesus.
42"He saved others," they scoffed, "but he can't
save himself! So he is the king of Israel, is he? Let
him come down from the cross, and we will
believe in him! 43He trusted God—let God
show his approval by delivering him! For he

27:9 Or *I took.* 27:9-10 Greek *as the Lord directed me.* Zech 11:12-13; Jer 32:6-9. 27:16 Some manuscripts read *Jesus Barabbas;* also in
27:17. 27:25 Greek *"His blood be on us and on our children."* 27:32 *Cyrene* was a city in northern Africa. 27:35 Greek *by casting lots.* A few
late manuscripts add *This fulfilled the word of the prophet: "They divided my clothes among themselves and cast lots for my robe."* See Ps 22:18.

said, 'I am the Son of God.' " ⁴⁴And the criminals who were crucified with him also shouted the same insults at him.

The Death of Jesus

⁴⁵At noon, darkness fell across the whole land until three o'clock. ⁴⁶At about three o'clock, Jesus called out with a loud voice, "*Eli, Eli, lema sabachthani?*" which means, "My God, my God, why have you forsaken me?"*

⁴⁷Some of the bystanders misunderstood and thought he was calling for the prophet Elijah. ⁴⁸One of them ran and filled a sponge with sour wine, holding it up to him on a stick so he could drink. ⁴⁹But the rest said, "Leave him alone. Let's see whether Elijah will come and save him."*

⁵⁰Then Jesus shouted out again, and he gave up his spirit. ⁵¹At that moment the curtain in the Temple was torn in two, from top to bottom. The earth shook, rocks split apart, ⁵²and tombs opened. The bodies of many godly men and women who had died were raised from the dead ⁵³after Jesus' resurrection. They left the cemetery, went into the holy city of Jerusalem, and appeared to many people.*

⁵⁴The Roman officer and the other soldiers at the crucifixion were terrified by the earthquake and all that had happened. They said, "Truly, this was the Son of God!"

⁵⁵And many women who had come from Galilee with Jesus to care for him were watching from a distance. ⁵⁶Among them were Mary Magdalene, Mary (the mother of James and Joseph), and Zebedee's wife, the mother of James and John.

The Burial of Jesus

⁵⁷As evening approached, Joseph, a rich man from Arimathea who was one of Jesus' followers, ⁵⁸went to Pilate and asked for Jesus' body. And Pilate issued an order to release it to him. ⁵⁹Joseph took the body and wrapped it in a long linen cloth. ⁶⁰He placed it in his own new tomb, which had been carved out of the rock. Then he rolled a great stone across the entrance as he left. ⁶¹Both Mary Magdalene and the other Mary were sitting nearby watching.

The Guard at the Tomb

⁶²The next day—on the first day of the Passover ceremonies*—the leading priests and Pharisees went to see Pilate. ⁶³They told him, "Sir, we remember what that deceiver once said while he was still alive: 'After three days I will be raised from the dead.' ⁶⁴So we request that you seal the tomb until the third day. This will prevent his disciples from coming and stealing his body and then telling everyone he came back to life! If that happens, we'll be worse off than we were at first."

⁶⁵Pilate replied, "Take guards and secure it the best you can." ⁶⁶So they sealed the tomb and posted guards to protect it.

CHAPTER 28

The Resurrection

Early on Sunday morning,* as the new day was dawning, Mary Magdalene and the other Mary went out to see the tomb. ²Suddenly there was a great earthquake, because an angel of the Lord came down from heaven and rolled aside the stone and sat on it. ³His face shone like lightning, and his clothing was as white as snow. ⁴The guards shook with fear when they saw him, and they fell into a dead faint.

⁵Then the angel spoke to the women. "Don't be afraid!" he said. "I know you are looking for Jesus, who was crucified. ⁶He isn't here! He has been raised from the dead, just as he said would happen. Come, see where his body was lying. ⁷And now, go quickly and tell his disciples he has been raised from the dead, and he is going ahead of you to Galilee. You will see him there. Remember, I have told you."

⁸The women ran quickly from the tomb. They were very frightened but also filled with great joy, and they rushed to find the disciples to give them the angel's message. ⁹And as they went, Jesus met them. "Greetings!" he said. And they ran to him, held his feet, and worshiped him. ¹⁰Then Jesus said to them, "Don't be afraid! Go tell my brothers to leave for Galilee, and they will see me there."

The Report of the Guard

¹¹As the women were on their way into the city, some of the men who had been guarding the tomb went to the leading priests and told them what had happened. ¹²A meeting of all the religious leaders was called, and they decided to bribe the soldiers. ¹³They told the soldiers, "You must say, 'Jesus' disciples came during the night

27:46 Ps 22:1. 27:49 Some manuscripts add *And another took a spear and pierced his side, and out came water and blood.* 27:51-53 Or *The earth shook, rocks split apart, tombs opened, and the bodies of many godly men and women who had died were raised from the dead. After Jesus' resurrection, they left the cemetery, went into the holy city of Jerusalem, and appeared to many people.* 27:62 Or *On the next day, which is after the Preparation.* 28:1 Greek *After the Sabbath, on the first day of the week.*

while we were sleeping, and they stole his body.' ¹⁴If the governor hears about it, we'll stand up for you and everything will be all right." ¹⁵So the guards accepted the bribe and said what they were told to say. Their story spread widely among the Jews, and they still tell it today.

The Great Commission
¹⁶Then the eleven disciples left for Galilee, going to the mountain where Jesus had told them to go. ¹⁷When they saw him, they worshiped him—but some of them still doubted!

¹⁸Jesus came and told his disciples, "I have been given complete authority in heaven and on earth. ¹⁹Therefore, go and make disciples of all the nations, baptizing them in the name of the Father and the Son and the Holy Spirit. ²⁰Teach these new disciples to obey all the commands I have given you. And be sure of this: I am with you always, even to the end of the age."

Mark

CHAPTER 1

John the Baptist Prepares the Way

Here begins the Good News about Jesus the Messiah, the Son of God.*

2In the book of the prophet Isaiah, God said,

"Look, I am sending my messenger before you,
and he will prepare your way.*
3 He is a voice shouting in the wilderness:
'Prepare a pathway for the Lord's coming!
Make a straight road for him!'* "

4This messenger was John the Baptist. He lived in the wilderness and was preaching that people should be baptized to show that they had turned from their sins and turned to God to be forgiven.* 5People from Jerusalem and from all over Judea traveled out into the wilderness to see and hear John. And when they confessed their sins, he baptized them in the Jordan River. 6His clothes were woven from camel hair, and he wore a leather belt; his food was locusts and wild honey. 7He announced: "Someone is coming soon who is far greater than I am—so much greater that I am not even worthy to be his slave.* 8I baptize you with* water, but he will baptize you with the Holy Spirit!"

The Baptism of Jesus

9One day Jesus came from Nazareth in Galilee, and he was baptized by John in the Jordan River. 10And when Jesus came up out of the water, he saw the heavens split open and the Holy Spirit descending like a dove on him. 11And a voice came from heaven saying, "You are my beloved Son, and I am fully pleased with you."

The Temptation of Jesus

12Immediately the Holy Spirit compelled Jesus to go into the wilderness. 13He was there for forty days, being tempted by Satan. He was out among the wild animals, and angels took care of him.

The First Disciples

14Later on, after John was arrested by Herod Antipas, Jesus went to Galilee to preach God's Good News. 15"At last the time has come!" he announced. "The Kingdom of God is near! Turn from your sins and believe this Good News!"

16One day as Jesus was walking along the shores of the Sea of Galilee, he saw Simon* and his brother, Andrew, fishing with a net, for they were commercial fishermen. 17Jesus called out to them, "Come, be my disciples, and I will show you how to fish for people!" 18And they left their nets at once and went with him.

19A little farther up the shore Jesus saw Zebedee's sons, James and John, in a boat mending their nets. 20He called them, too, and immediately they left their father, Zebedee, in the boat with the hired men and went with him.

Jesus Casts Out an Evil Spirit

21Jesus and his companions went to the town of Capernaum, and every Sabbath day he went into the synagogue and taught the people. 22They were amazed at his teaching, for he taught as one who had real authority—quite unlike the teachers of religious law.

23A man possessed by an evil spirit was in the synagogue, 24and he began shouting, "Why are you bothering us, Jesus of Nazareth? Have you come to destroy us? I know who you are—the Holy One sent from God!"

25Jesus cut him short. "Be silent! Come out of the man." 26At that, the evil spirit screamed

1:1 Some manuscripts do not include *the Son of God.* 1:2 Mal 3:1. 1:3 Isa 40:3. 1:4 Greek *preaching a baptism of repentance for the forgiveness of sins.* 1:7 Greek *to stoop down and untie his sandals.* 1:8 Or *in.* 1:16 *Simon* is called *Peter* in 3:16 and thereafter.

and threw the man into a convulsion, but then he left him.

27Amazement gripped the audience, and they began to discuss what had happened. "What sort of new teaching is this?" they asked excitedly. "It has such authority! Even evil spirits obey his orders!" 28The news of what he had done spread quickly through that entire area of Galilee.

Jesus Heals Many People

29After Jesus and his disciples left the synagogue, they went over to Simon and Andrew's home, and James and John were with them. 30Simon's mother-in-law was sick in bed with a high fever. They told Jesus about her right away. 31He went to her bedside, and as he took her by the hand and helped her to sit up, the fever suddenly left, and she got up and prepared a meal for them.

32That evening at sunset, many sick and demon-possessed people were brought to Jesus. 33And a huge crowd of people from all over Capernaum gathered outside the door to watch. 34So Jesus healed great numbers of sick people who had many different kinds of diseases, and he ordered many demons to come out of their victims. But because they knew who he was, he refused to allow the demons to speak.

Jesus Preaches in Galilee

35The next morning Jesus awoke long before daybreak and went out alone into the wilderness to pray. 36Later Simon and the others went out to find him. 37They said, "Everyone is asking for you."

38But he replied, "We must go on to other towns as well, and I will preach to them, too, because that is why I came." 39So he traveled throughout the region of Galilee, preaching in the synagogues and expelling demons from many people.

Jesus Heals a Man with Leprosy

40A man with leprosy came and knelt in front of Jesus, begging to be healed. "If you want to, you can make me well again," he said.

41Moved with pity,* Jesus touched him. "I want to," he said. "Be healed!" 42Instantly the leprosy disappeared—the man was healed. 43Then Jesus sent him on his way and told him sternly, 44"Go right over to the priest and let him examine you. Don't talk to anyone along the way. Take along the offering required in the law of Moses for those who have been healed of

1:41 Some manuscripts read *Moved with anger.*

leprosy, so everyone will have proof of your healing."

45But as the man went on his way, he spread the news, telling everyone what had happened to him. As a result, such crowds soon surrounded Jesus that he couldn't enter a town anywhere publicly. He had to stay out in the secluded places, and people from everywhere came to him there.

CHAPTER **2**

Jesus Heals a Paralyzed Man

Several days later Jesus returned to Capernaum, and the news of his arrival spread quickly through the town. 2Soon the house where he was staying was so packed with visitors that there wasn't room for one more person, not even outside the door. And he preached the word to them. 3Four men arrived carrying a paralyzed man on a mat. 4They couldn't get to Jesus through the crowd, so they dug through the clay roof above his head. Then they lowered the sick man on his mat, right down in front of Jesus. 5Seeing their faith, Jesus said to the paralyzed man, "My son, your sins are forgiven."

6But some of the teachers of religious law who were sitting there said to themselves, 7"What? This is blasphemy! Who but God can forgive sins!"

8Jesus knew what they were discussing among themselves, so he said to them, "Why do you think this is blasphemy? 9Is it easier to say to the paralyzed man, 'Your sins are forgiven' or 'Get up, pick up your mat, and walk'? 10I will prove that I, the Son of Man, have the authority on earth to forgive sins." Then Jesus turned to the paralyzed man and said, 11"Stand up, take your mat, and go on home, because you are healed!"

12The man jumped up, took the mat, and pushed his way through the stunned onlookers. Then they all praised God. "We've never seen anything like this before!" they exclaimed.

Jesus Calls Levi (Matthew)

13Then Jesus went out to the lakeshore again and taught the crowds that gathered around him. 14As he walked along, he saw Levi son of Alphaeus sitting at his tax-collection booth. "Come, be my disciple," Jesus said to him. So Levi got up and followed him.

15That night Levi invited Jesus and his disciples to be his dinner guests, along with his fellow tax collectors and many other notorious sinners. (There were many people of this kind among the crowds that followed Jesus.) 16But when some of the teachers of religious law who were Pharisees* saw him eating with people like that, they said to his disciples, "Why does he eat with such scum*?"

17When Jesus heard this, he told them, "Healthy people don't need a doctor—sick people do. I have come to call sinners, not those who think they are already good enough."

A Discussion about Fasting

18John's disciples and the Pharisees sometimes fasted. One day some people came to Jesus and asked, "Why do John's disciples and the Pharisees fast, but your disciples don't fast?"

19Jesus replied, "Do wedding guests fast while celebrating with the groom? Of course not. They can't fast while they are with the groom. 20But someday he will be taken away from them, and then they will fast. 21And who would patch an old garment with unshrunk cloth? For the new patch shrinks and pulls away from the old cloth, leaving an even bigger hole than before. 22And no one puts new wine into old wineskins. The wine would burst the wineskins, spilling the wine and ruining the skins. New wine needs new wineskins."

A Discussion about the Sabbath

23One Sabbath day as Jesus was walking through some grainfields, his disciples began breaking off heads of wheat. 24But the Pharisees said to Jesus, "They shouldn't be doing that! It's against the law to work by harvesting grain on the Sabbath."

25But Jesus replied, "Haven't you ever read in the Scriptures what King David did when he and his companions were hungry? 26He went into the house of God (during the days when Abiathar was high priest), ate the special bread reserved for the priests alone, and then gave some to his companions. That was breaking the law, too." 27Then he said to them, "The Sabbath was made to benefit people, and not people to benefit the Sabbath. 28And I, the Son of Man, am master even of the Sabbath!"

CHAPTER 3

Jesus Heals on the Sabbath

Jesus went into the synagogue again and noticed a man with a deformed hand. 2Since it was the Sabbath, Jesus' enemies watched him closely. Would he heal the man's hand on the Sabbath? If he did, they planned to condemn him. 3Jesus said to the man, "Come and stand in front of everyone." 4Then he turned to his critics and asked, "Is it legal to do good deeds on the Sabbath, or is it a day for doing harm? Is this a day to save life or to destroy it?" But they wouldn't answer him. 5He looked around at them angrily, because he was deeply disturbed by their hard hearts. Then he said to the man, "Reach out your hand." The man reached out his hand, and it became normal again! 6At once the Pharisees went away and met with the supporters of Herod to discuss plans for killing Jesus.

Crowds Follow Jesus

7Jesus and his disciples went out to the lake, followed by a huge crowd from all over Galilee, Judea, 8Jerusalem, Idumea, from east of the Jordan River, and even from as far away as Tyre and Sidon. The news about his miracles had spread far and wide, and vast numbers of people came to see him for themselves.

9Jesus instructed his disciples to bring around a boat and to have it ready in case he was crowded off the beach. 10There had been many healings that day. As a result, many sick people were crowding around him, trying to touch him. 11And whenever those possessed by evil spirits caught sight of him, they would fall down in front of him shrieking, "You are the Son of God!" 12But Jesus strictly warned them not to say who he was.

Jesus Chooses the Twelve Apostles

13Afterward Jesus went up on a mountain and called the ones he wanted to go with him. And they came to him. 14Then he selected twelve of them to be his regular companions, calling them apostles.* He sent them out to preach, 15and he gave them authority to cast out demons. 16These are the names of the twelve he chose:

Simon (he renamed him Peter),
17 James and John (the sons of Zebedee, but Jesus nicknamed them "Sons of Thunder"*),
18 Andrew,
Philip,
Bartholomew,
Matthew,

2:16a Greek *the scribes of the Pharisees.* 2:16b Greek *with tax collectors and sinners.* 3:14 Some manuscripts do not include *calling them apostles.* 3:17 Greek *whom he named Boanerges, which means Sons of Thunder.*

Thomas,
James (son of Alphaeus),
Thaddaeus,
Simon (the Zealot*),
19 Judas Iscariot (who later betrayed him).

Jesus and the Prince of Demons

20When Jesus returned to the house where he was staying, the crowds began to gather again, and soon he and his disciples couldn't even find time to eat. 21When his family heard what was happening, they tried to take him home with them. "He's out of his mind," they said.

22But the teachers of religious law who had arrived from Jerusalem said, "He's possessed by Satan,* the prince of demons. That's where he gets the power to cast out demons."

23Jesus called them over and said to them by way of illustration, "How can Satan cast out Satan? 24A kingdom at war with itself will collapse. 25A home divided against itself is doomed. 26And if Satan is fighting against himself, how can he stand? He would never survive. 27Let me illustrate this. You can't enter a strong man's house and rob him without first tying him up. Only then can his house be robbed!*

28"I assure you that any sin can be forgiven, including blasphemy; 29but anyone who blasphemes against the Holy Spirit will never be forgiven. It is an eternal sin." 30He told them this because they were saying he had an evil spirit.

The True Family of Jesus

31Jesus' mother and brothers arrived at the house where he was teaching. They stood outside and sent word for him to come out and talk with them. 32There was a crowd around Jesus, and someone said, "Your mother and your brothers and sisters* are outside, asking for you."

33Jesus replied, "Who is my mother? Who are my brothers?" 34Then he looked at those around him and said, "These are my mother and brothers. 35Anyone who does God's will is my brother and sister and mother."

CHAPTER **4**
Story of the Farmer Scattering Seed

Once again Jesus began teaching by the lakeshore. There was such a large crowd along the shore that he got into a boat and sat down

and spoke from there. 2He began to teach the people by telling many stories such as this one:

3"Listen! A farmer went out to plant some seed. 4As he scattered it across his field, some seed fell on a footpath, and the birds came and ate it. 5Other seed fell on shallow soil with underlying rock. The plant sprang up quickly, 6but it soon wilted beneath the hot sun and died because the roots had no nourishment in the shallow soil. 7Other seed fell among thorns that shot up and choked out the tender blades so that it produced no grain. 8Still other seed fell on fertile soil and produced a crop that was thirty, sixty, and even a hundred times as much as had been planted." Then he said, 9"Anyone who is willing to hear should listen and understand!"

10Later, when Jesus was alone with the twelve disciples and with the others who were gathered around, they asked him, "What do your stories mean?"

11He replied, "You are permitted to understand the secret about the Kingdom of God. But I am using these stories to conceal everything about it from outsiders, 12so that the Scriptures might be fulfilled:

'They see what I do,
    but they don't perceive its meaning.
They hear my words,
    but they don't understand.
So they will not turn from their sins
    and be forgiven.'*

13"But if you can't understand this story, how will you understand all the others I am going to tell? 14The farmer I talked about is the one who brings God's message to others. 15The seed that fell on the hard path represents those who hear the message, but then Satan comes at once and takes it away from them. 16The rocky soil represents those who hear the message and receive it with joy. 17But like young plants in such soil, their roots don't go very deep. At first they get along fine, but they wilt as soon as they have problems or are persecuted because they believe the word. 18The thorny ground represents those who hear and accept the Good News, 19but all too quickly the message is crowded out by the cares of this life, the lure of wealth, and the desire for nice things, so no crop is produced. 20But the good soil represents those who hear and accept God's message and produce a huge harvest—thirty, sixty, or even a hundred times as much as had been planted."

3:18 Greek *the Cananean.*   3:22 Greek *Beelzeboul.*   3:27 Or *One cannot rob Satan's kingdom without first tying him up. Only then can his demons be cast out.*   3:32 Some manuscripts do not include *and sisters.*   4:12 Isa 6:9-10.

Illustration of the Lamp

21Then Jesus asked them, "Would anyone light a lamp and then put it under a basket or under a bed to shut out the light? Of course not! A lamp is placed on a stand, where its light will shine.

22"Everything that is now hidden or secret will eventually be brought to light. 23Anyone who is willing to hear should listen and understand! 24And be sure to pay attention to what you hear. The more you do this, the more you will understand—and even more, besides. 25To those who are open to my teaching, more understanding will be given. But to those who are not listening, even what they have will be taken away from them."

Illustration of the Growing Seed

26Jesus also said, "Here is another illustration of what the Kingdom of God is like: A farmer planted seeds in a field, 27and then he went on with his other activities. As the days went by, the seeds sprouted and grew without the farmer's help, 28because the earth produces crops on its own. First a leaf blade pushes through, then the heads of wheat are formed, and finally the grain ripens. 29And as soon as the grain is ready, the farmer comes and harvests it with a sickle."

Illustration of the Mustard Seed

30Jesus asked, "How can I describe the Kingdom of God? What story should I use to illustrate it? 31It is like a tiny mustard seed. Though this is one of the smallest of seeds, 32it grows to become one of the largest of plants, with long branches where birds can come and find shelter."

33He used many such stories and illustrations to teach the people as much as they were able to understand. 34In fact, in his public teaching he taught only with parables, but afterward when he was alone with his disciples, he explained the meaning to them.

Jesus Calms the Storm

35As evening came, Jesus said to his disciples, "Let's cross to the other side of the lake." 36He was already in the boat, so they started out, leaving the crowds behind (although other boats followed). 37But soon a fierce storm arose. High waves began to break into the boat until it was nearly full of water.

38Jesus was sleeping at the back of the boat with his head on a cushion. Frantically they woke him up, shouting, "Teacher, don't you even care that we are going to drown?"

39When he woke up, he rebuked the wind and said to the water, "Quiet down!" Suddenly the wind stopped, and there was a great calm. 40And he asked them, "Why are you so afraid? Do you still not have faith in me?"

Jesus Is with Us in Life's Storms Read MARK 4:35-41

This story illustrates how God is with us and in control of even the most desperate of circumstances. Here we find the disciples, several of whom were seasoned fishermen and sailors, frantically worried that they would perish in this storm. Although Jesus was with them in the middle of it, they thought he was oblivious to the severity of their situation. Yet Jesus wanted them to discover three important lessons.

1. Jesus Is Aware of Your Situation. Although Jesus, being human, needed physical sleep for his weary body, he was still fully aware of the disciples' predicament. The moment one of them cried to him, he responded immediately and powerfully. Though the shrieking of the storm did not wake him, the cry of one of his disciples did. Psalm 121:3 says, "He will not let you stumble and fall; the one who watches over you will not sleep."

2. Jesus Will Answer Your Call for Help. The Lord will do the same for you in the midst of your trials. Sometimes he just lets us reach the point of desperation so we will recognize that he is our only hope. He wants us to remember that he is "on board" with us, so to speak.

3. You Can Make It Through. Every one of us is going to face hardship. But only the child of God has the promise that God's presence is with him or her in the midst of the storm. As surely as Jesus said to the disciples, "Let's cross to the other side of the lake" (verse 35), God has promised to finish the work he has begun in your life. He will not leave you stranded in the middle of your problem. Although he didn't promise smooth sailing, he did promise safe passage. Paul reminds us that "I am sure that God, who began the good work within you, will continue his work until it is finally finished on that day when Christ Jesus comes back again" (Philippians 1:6).

For the next note on "Have Courage in Trials," turn to p. 909.

⁴¹And they were filled with awe and said among themselves, "Who is this man, that even the wind and waves obey him?"

CHAPTER 5

Jesus Heals a Demon-Possessed Man

So they arrived at the other side of the lake, in the land of the Gerasenes.* ²Just as Jesus was climbing from the boat, a man possessed by an evil spirit ran out from a cemetery to meet him. ³This man lived among the tombs and could not be restrained, even with a chain. ⁴Whenever he was put into chains and shackles—as he often was—he snapped the chains from his wrists and smashed the shackles. No one was strong enough to control him. ⁵All day long and throughout the night, he would wander among the tombs and in the hills, screaming and hitting himself with stones.

⁶When Jesus was still some distance away, the man saw him. He ran to meet Jesus and fell down before him. ⁷He gave a terrible scream, shrieking, "Why are you bothering me, Jesus, Son of the Most High God? For God's sake, don't torture me!" ⁸For Jesus had already said to the spirit, "Come out of the man, you evil spirit."

⁹Then Jesus asked, "What is your name?"

And the spirit replied, "Legion, because there are many of us here inside this man." ¹⁰Then the spirits begged him again and again not to send them to some distant place. ¹¹There happened to be a large herd of pigs feeding on the hillside nearby. ¹²"Send us into those pigs," the evil spirits begged. ¹³Jesus gave them permission. So the evil spirits came out of the man and entered the pigs, and the entire herd of two thousand pigs plunged down the steep hillside into the lake, where they drowned.

¹⁴The herdsmen fled to the nearby city and the surrounding countryside, spreading the news as they ran. Everyone rushed out to see for themselves. ¹⁵A crowd soon gathered around Jesus, but they were frightened when they saw the man who had been demon possessed, for he was sitting there fully clothed and perfectly sane. ¹⁶Those who had seen what happened to the man and to the pigs told everyone about it, ¹⁷and the crowd began pleading with Jesus to go away and leave them alone.

¹⁸When Jesus got back into the boat, the man who had been demon possessed begged to go, too. ¹⁹But Jesus said, "No, go home to your friends, and tell them what wonderful things the Lord has done for you and how merciful he has been." ²⁰So the man started off to visit the Ten Towns* of that region and began to tell everyone about the great things Jesus had done for him; and everyone was amazed at what he told them.

Jesus Heals in Response to Faith

²¹When Jesus went back across to the other side of the lake, a large crowd gathered around him on the shore. ²²A leader of the local synagogue, whose name was Jairus, came and fell down before him, ²³pleading with him to heal his little daughter. "She is about to die," he said in desperation. "Please come and place your hands on her; heal her so she can live."

²⁴Jesus went with him, and the crowd thronged behind. ²⁵And there was a woman in the crowd who had had a hemorrhage for twelve years. ²⁶She had suffered a great deal from many doctors through the years and had spent everything she had to pay them, but she had gotten no better. In fact, she was worse. ²⁷She had heard about Jesus, so she came up behind him through the crowd and touched the fringe of his robe. ²⁸For she thought to herself, "If I can just touch his clothing, I will be healed." ²⁹Immediately the bleeding stopped, and she could feel that she had been healed!

³⁰Jesus realized at once that healing power had gone out from him, so he turned around in the crowd and asked, "Who touched my clothes?"

³¹His disciples said to him, "All this crowd is pressing around you. How can you ask, 'Who touched me?'"

³²But he kept on looking around to see who had done it. ³³Then the frightened woman, trembling at the realization of what had happened to her, came and fell at his feet and told him what she had done. ³⁴And he said to her, "Daughter, your faith has made you well. Go in peace. You have been healed."

³⁵While he was still speaking to her, messengers arrived from Jairus's home with the message, "Your daughter is dead. There's no use troubling the Teacher now."

³⁶But Jesus ignored their comments and said to Jairus, "Don't be afraid. Just trust me." ³⁷Then Jesus stopped the crowd and wouldn't let anyone go with him except Peter and James and John. ³⁸When they came to the home of the synagogue leader, Jesus saw the commotion and the weeping and wailing. ³⁹He went inside and

5:1 Some manuscripts read *Gadarenes;* others read *Gergesenes.* See Matt 8:28; Luke 8:26.   5:20 Greek *Decapolis.*

spoke to the people. "Why all this weeping and commotion?" he asked. "The child isn't dead; she is only asleep."

⁴⁰The crowd laughed at him, but he told them all to go outside. Then he took the girl's father and mother and his three disciples into the room where the girl was lying. ⁴¹Holding her hand, he said to her, "Get up, little girl!"* ⁴²And the girl, who was twelve years old, immediately stood up and walked around! Her parents were absolutely overwhelmed. ⁴³Jesus commanded them not to tell anyone what had happened, and he told them to give her something to eat.

CHAPTER 6
Jesus Rejected at Nazareth

Jesus left that part of the country and returned with his disciples to Nazareth, his hometown. ²The next Sabbath he began teaching in the synagogue, and many who heard him were astonished. They asked, "Where did he get all his wisdom and the power to perform such miracles? ³He's just the carpenter, the son of Mary and brother of James, Joseph,* Judas, and Simon. And his sisters live right here among us." They were deeply offended and refused to believe in him.

⁴Then Jesus told them, "A prophet is honored everywhere except in his own hometown and among his relatives and his own family." ⁵And because of their unbelief, he couldn't do any mighty miracles among them except to place his hands on a few sick people and heal them. ⁶And he was amazed at their unbelief.

Jesus Sends Out the Twelve Apostles

Then Jesus went out from village to village, teaching. ⁷And he called his twelve disciples together and sent them out two by two, with authority to cast out evil spirits. ⁸He told them to take nothing with them except a walking stick—no food, no traveler's bag, no money. ⁹He told them to wear sandals but not to take even an extra coat. ¹⁰"When you enter each village, be a guest in only one home," he said. ¹¹"And if a village won't welcome you or listen to you, shake off its dust from your feet as you leave. It is a sign that you have abandoned that village to its fate."

¹²So the disciples went out, telling all they met to turn from their sins. ¹³And they cast out many demons and healed many sick people, anointing them with olive oil.

The Death of John the Baptist

¹⁴Herod Antipas, the king, soon heard about Jesus, because people everywhere were talking about him. Some were saying,* "This must be John the Baptist come back to life again. That is why he can do such miracles." ¹⁵Others thought Jesus was the ancient prophet Elijah. Still others thought he was a prophet like the other great prophets of the past. ¹⁶When Herod heard about Jesus, he said, "John, the man I beheaded, has come back from the dead." ¹⁷For Herod had sent soldiers to arrest and imprison John as a favor to Herodias. She had been his brother Philip's wife, but Herod had married her. ¹⁸John kept telling Herod, "It is illegal for you to marry your brother's wife." ¹⁹Herodias was enraged and wanted John killed in revenge, but without Herod's approval she was powerless. ²⁰And Herod respected John, knowing that he was a good and holy man, so he kept him under his protection. Herod was disturbed whenever he talked with John, but even so, he liked to listen to him.

²¹Herodias's chance finally came. It was Herod's birthday, and he gave a party for his palace aides, army officers, and the leading citizens of Galilee. ²²Then his daughter, also named Herodias,* came in and performed a dance that greatly pleased them all. "Ask me for anything you like," the king said to the girl, "and I will give it to you." ²³Then he promised, "I will give you whatever you ask, up to half of my kingdom!"

²⁴She went out and asked her mother, "What should I ask for?"

Her mother told her, "Ask for John the Baptist's head!"

²⁵So the girl hurried back to the king and told him, "I want the head of John the Baptist, right now, on a tray!"

²⁶Then the king was very sorry, but he was embarrassed to break his oath in front of his guests. ²⁷So he sent an executioner to the prison to cut off John's head and bring it to him. The soldier beheaded John in the prison, ²⁸brought his head on a tray, and gave it to the girl, who took it to her mother. ²⁹When John's disciples heard what had happened, they came for his body and buried it in a tomb.

5:41 Greek text uses Aramaic "Talitha cumi" and then translates it as "Get up, little girl." 6:3 Greek *Joses*; see Matt 13:55. 6:14 Some manuscripts read *He was saying.* 6:22 Some manuscripts read *the daughter of Herodias herself.*

Jesus Feeds Five Thousand

30The apostles returned to Jesus from their ministry tour and told him all they had done and what they had taught. 31Then Jesus said, "Let's get away from the crowds for a while and rest." There were so many people coming and going that Jesus and his apostles didn't even have time to eat. 32They left by boat for a quieter spot. 33But many people saw them leaving, and people from many towns ran ahead along the shore and met them as they landed. 34A vast crowd was there as he stepped from the boat, and he had compassion on them because they were like sheep without a shepherd. So he taught them many things.

35Late in the afternoon his disciples came to him and said, "This is a desolate place, and it is getting late. 36Send the crowds away so they can go to the nearby farms and villages and buy themselves some food."

37But Jesus said, "You feed them."

"With what?" they asked. "It would take a small fortune* to buy food for all this crowd!"

38"How much food do you have?" he asked. "Go and find out."

They came back and reported, "We have five loaves of bread and two fish." 39Then Jesus told the crowd to sit down in groups on the green grass. 40So they sat in groups of fifty or a hundred.

41Jesus took the five loaves and two fish, looked up toward heaven, and asked God's blessing on the food. Breaking the loaves into pieces, he kept giving the bread and fish to the disciples to give to the people. 42They all ate as much as they wanted, 43and they picked up twelve baskets of leftover bread and fish. 44Five thousand men had eaten from those five loaves!

Jesus Walks on Water

45Immediately after this, Jesus made his disciples get back into the boat and head out across the lake to Bethsaida, while he sent the people home. 46Afterward he went up into the hills by himself to pray.

47During the night, the disciples were in their boat out in the middle of the lake, and Jesus was alone on land. 48He saw that they were in serious trouble, rowing hard and struggling against the wind and waves. About three o'clock in the morning* he came to them, walking on the water. He started to go past them, 49but when

they saw him walking on the water, they screamed in terror, thinking he was a ghost. 50They were all terrified when they saw him. But Jesus spoke to them at once. "It's all right," he said. "I am here! Don't be afraid." 51Then he climbed into the boat, and the wind stopped. They were astonished at what they saw. 52They still didn't understand the significance of the miracle of the multiplied loaves, for their hearts were hard and they did not believe.

53When they arrived at Gennesaret on the other side of the lake, they anchored the boat 54and climbed out. The people standing there recognized him at once, 55and they ran throughout the whole area and began carrying sick people to him on mats. 56Wherever he went—in villages and cities and out on the farms—they laid the sick in the market plazas and streets. The sick begged him to let them at least touch the fringe of his robe, and all who touched it were healed.

CHAPTER 7
Jesus Teaches about Inner Purity

One day some Pharisees and teachers of religious law arrived from Jerusalem to confront Jesus. 2They noticed that some of Jesus' disciples failed to follow the usual Jewish ritual of hand washing before eating. 3(The Jews, especially the Pharisees, do not eat until they have poured water over their cupped hands,* as required by their ancient traditions. 4Similarly, they eat nothing bought from the market unless they have immersed their hands in water. This is but one of many traditions they have clung to—such as their ceremony of washing cups, pitchers, and kettles.*) 5So the Pharisees and teachers of religious law asked him, "Why don't your disciples follow our age-old customs? For they eat without first performing the hand-washing ceremony."

6Jesus replied, "You hypocrites! Isaiah was prophesying about you when he said,

7 'These people honor me with their lips,
    but their hearts are far away.
  Their worship is a farce,
    for they replace God's commands with
      their own man-made teachings.'*

8For you ignore God's specific laws and substitute your own traditions."

9Then he said, "You reject God's laws in order

6:37 Greek *200 denarii.* A denarius was the equivalent of a full day's wage.   6:48 Greek *About the fourth watch of the night.*   7:3 Greek *washed with the fist.*   7:4 Some Greek manuscripts add *and dining couches.*   7:7 Isa 29:13.

to hold on to your own traditions. [10]For instance, Moses gave you this law from God: 'Honor your father and mother,' and 'Anyone who speaks evil of father or mother must be put to death.'* [11]But you say it is all right for people to say to their parents, 'Sorry, I can't help you. For I have vowed to give to God what I could have given to you.'* [12]You let them disregard their needy parents. [13]As such, you break the law of God in order to protect your own tradition. And this is only one example. There are many, many others."

[14]Then Jesus called to the crowd to come and hear. "All of you listen," he said, "and try to understand. [15]You are not defiled by what you eat; you are defiled by what you say and do!*"

[17]Then Jesus went into a house to get away from the crowds, and his disciples asked him what he meant by the statement he had made. [18]"Don't you understand either?" he asked. "Can't you see that what you eat won't defile you? [19]Food doesn't come in contact with your heart, but only passes through the stomach and then comes out again." (By saying this, he showed that every kind of food is acceptable.)

[20]And then he added, "It is the thought-life that defiles you. [21]For from within, out of a person's heart, come evil thoughts, sexual immorality, theft, murder, [22]adultery, greed, wickedness, deceit, eagerness for lustful pleasure, envy, slander, pride, and foolishness. [23]All these vile things come from within; they are what defile you and make you unacceptable to God."

The Faith of a Gentile Woman

[24]Then Jesus left Galilee and went north to the region of Tyre.* He tried to keep it secret that he was there, but he couldn't. As usual, the news of his arrival spread fast. [25]Right away a woman came to him whose little girl was possessed by an evil spirit. She had heard about Jesus, and now she came and fell at his feet. [26]She begged him to release her child from the demon's control.

Since she was a Gentile, born in Syrian Phoenicia, [27]Jesus told her, "First I should help my own family, the Jews.* It isn't right to take food from the children and throw it to the dogs."

[28]She replied, "That's true, Lord, but even the dogs under the table are given some crumbs from the children's plates."

[29]"Good answer!" he said. "And because you have answered so well, I have healed your daughter." [30]And when she arrived home, her little girl was lying quietly in bed, and the demon was gone.

Jesus Heals a Deaf and Mute Man

[31]Jesus left Tyre and went to Sidon, then back to the Sea of Galilee and the region of the Ten Towns.* [32]A deaf man with a speech impediment was brought to him, and the people begged Jesus to lay his hands on the man to heal him. [33]Jesus led him to a private place away from the crowd. He put his fingers into the man's ears. Then, spitting onto his own fingers, he touched the man's tongue with the spittle. [34]And looking up to heaven, he sighed and commanded, "Be opened!"* [35]Instantly the man could hear perfectly and speak plainly!

[36]Jesus told the crowd not to tell anyone, but the more he told them not to, the more they spread the news, [37]for they were completely amazed. Again and again they said, "Everything he does is wonderful. He even heals those who are deaf and mute."

CHAPTER **8**

Jesus Feeds Four Thousand

About this time another great crowd had gathered, and the people ran out of food again. Jesus called his disciples and told them, [2]"I feel sorry for these people. They have been here with me for three days, and they have nothing left to eat. [3]And if I send them home without feeding them, they will faint along the road. For some of them have come a long distance."

[4]"How are we supposed to find enough food for them here in the wilderness?" his disciples asked.

[5]"How many loaves of bread do you have?" he asked.

"Seven," they replied. [6]So Jesus told all the people to sit down on the ground. Then he took the seven loaves, thanked God for them, broke them into pieces, and gave them to his disciples, who distributed the bread to the crowd. [7]A few small fish were found, too, so Jesus also blessed these and told the disciples to pass them out.

[8]They ate until they were full, and when the scraps were picked up, there were seven large baskets of food left over! [9]There were about four thousand people in the crowd that day, and he

---

7:10 Exod 20:12; 21:17; Lev 20:9; Deut 5:16.   **7:11** Greek *'What I could have given to you is Corban' (that is, a gift).*   **7:15** Some manuscripts add verse 16, *Anyone who is willing to hear should listen and understand.*   **7:24** Some Greek manuscripts add *and Sidon.*   **7:27** Greek *Let the children eat first.*   **7:31** Greek *Decapolis.*   **7:34** Greek text uses Aramaic *"Ephphatha"* and then translates it as *"Be opened."*

sent them home after they had eaten. ¹⁰Immediately after this, he got into a boat with his disciples and crossed over to the region of Dalmanutha.

Pharisees Demand a Miraculous Sign

¹¹When the Pharisees heard that Jesus had arrived, they came to argue with him. Testing him to see if he was from God, they demanded, "Give us a miraculous sign from heaven to prove yourself."

¹²When he heard this, he sighed deeply and said, "Why do you people keep demanding a miraculous sign? I assure you, I will not give this generation any such sign." ¹³So he got back into the boat and left them, and he crossed to the other side of the lake.

Yeast of the Pharisees and Herod

¹⁴But the disciples discovered they had forgotten to bring any food, so there was only one loaf of bread with them in the boat. ¹⁵As they were crossing the lake, Jesus warned them, "Beware of the yeast of the Pharisees and of Herod."

¹⁶They decided he was saying this because they hadn't brought any bread. ¹⁷Jesus knew what they were thinking, so he said, "Why are you so worried about having no food? Won't you ever learn or understand? Are your hearts too hard to take it in? ¹⁸You have eyes—can't you see? You have ears—can't you hear?'* Don't you remember anything at all? ¹⁹What about the five thousand men I fed with five loaves of bread? How many baskets of leftovers did you pick up afterward?"

"Twelve," they said.

²⁰"And when I fed the four thousand with seven loaves, how many large baskets of leftovers did you pick up?"

"Seven," they said.

²¹"Don't you understand even yet?" he asked them.

Jesus Heals a Blind Man

²²When they arrived at Bethsaida, some people brought a blind man to Jesus, and they begged him to touch and heal the man. ²³Jesus took the blind man by the hand and led him out of the village. Then, spitting on the man's eyes, he laid his hands on him and asked, "Can you see anything now?"

²⁴The man looked around. "Yes," he said, "I see people, but I can't see them very clearly. They look like trees walking around."

²⁵Then Jesus placed his hands over the man's eyes again. As the man stared intently, his sight was completely restored, and he could see everything clearly. ²⁶Jesus sent him home, saying, "Don't go back into the village on your way home."

Peter's Declaration about Jesus

²⁷Jesus and his disciples left Galilee and went up to the villages of Caesarea Philippi. As they were walking along, he asked them, "Who do people say I am?"

²⁸"Well," they replied, "some say John the Baptist, some say Elijah, and others say you are one of the other prophets."

²⁹Then Jesus asked, "Who do you say I am?"

Peter replied, "You are the Messiah." ³⁰But Jesus warned them not to tell anyone about him.

Jesus Predicts His Death

³¹Then Jesus began to tell them that he, the Son of Man, would suffer many terrible things and be rejected by the leaders, the leading priests, and the teachers of religious law. He would be killed, and three days later he would rise again. ³²As he talked about this openly with his disciples, Peter took him aside and told him he shouldn't say things like that.*

³³Jesus turned and looked at his disciples and then said to Peter very sternly, "Get away from me, Satan! You are seeing things merely from a human point of view, not from God's."

³⁴Then he called his disciples and the crowds to come over and listen. "If any of you wants to be my follower," he told them, "you must put aside your selfish ambition, shoulder your cross, and follow me. ³⁵If you try to keep your life for yourself, you will lose it. But if you give up your life for my sake and for the sake of the Good News, you will find true life. ³⁶And how do you benefit if you gain the whole world but lose your own soul* in the process? ³⁷Is anything worth more than your soul? ³⁸If a person is ashamed of me and my message in these adulterous and sinful days, I, the Son of Man, will be ashamed of that person when I return in the glory of my Father with the holy angels."

CHAPTER 9

Jesus went on to say, "I assure you that some of you standing here right now will not die before you see the Kingdom of God arrive in great power!"

8:18 Jer 5:21.   8:32 Or *and began to correct him.*   8:36 Or *your life;* also in 8:37.

The Transfiguration

2Six days later Jesus took Peter, James, and John to the top of a mountain. No one else was there. As the men watched, Jesus' appearance changed, 3and his clothing became dazzling white, far whiter than any earthly process could ever make it. 4Then Elijah and Moses appeared and began talking with Jesus.

5"Teacher, this is wonderful!" Peter exclaimed. "We will make three shrines*—one for you, one for Moses, and one for Elijah." 6He didn't really know what to say, for they were all terribly afraid.

7Then a cloud came over them, and a voice from the cloud said, "This is my beloved Son. Listen to him." 8Suddenly they looked around, and Moses and Elijah were gone, and only Jesus was with them. 9As they descended the mountainside, he told them not to tell anyone what they had seen until he, the Son of Man, had risen from the dead. 10So they kept it to themselves, but they often asked each other what he meant by "rising from the dead."

11Now they began asking him, "Why do the teachers of religious law insist that Elijah must return before the Messiah comes?"

12Jesus responded, "Elijah is indeed coming first to set everything in order. Why then is it written in the Scriptures that the Son of Man must suffer and be treated with utter contempt? 13But I tell you, Elijah has already come, and he was badly mistreated, just as the Scriptures predicted."

Jesus Heals a Boy Possessed by an Evil Spirit

14At the foot of the mountain they found a great crowd surrounding the other disciples, as some teachers of religious law were arguing with them. 15The crowd watched Jesus in awe as he came toward them, and then they ran to greet him. 16"What is all this arguing about?" he asked.

17One of the men in the crowd spoke up and said, "Teacher, I brought my son for you to heal him. He can't speak because he is possessed by an evil spirit that won't let him talk. 18And whenever this evil spirit seizes him, it throws him violently to the ground and makes him foam at the mouth and grind his teeth and become rigid.* So I asked your disciples to cast out the evil spirit, but they couldn't do it."

19Jesus said to them, "You faithless people! How long must I be with you until you believe? How long must I put up with you? Bring the boy

to me." 20So they brought the boy. But when the evil spirit saw Jesus, it threw the child into a violent convulsion, and he fell to the ground, writhing and foaming at the mouth. 21"How long has this been happening?" Jesus asked the boy's father.

He replied, "Since he was very small. 22The evil spirit often makes him fall into the fire or into water, trying to kill him. Have mercy on us and help us. Do something if you can."

23"What do you mean, 'If I can'?" Jesus asked. "Anything is possible if a person believes."

24The father instantly replied, "I do believe, but help me not to doubt!"

25When Jesus saw that the crowd of onlookers was growing, he rebuked the evil spirit. "Spirit of deafness and muteness," he said, "I command you to come out of this child and never enter him again!" 26Then the spirit screamed and threw the boy into another violent convulsion and left him. The boy lay there motionless, and he appeared to be dead. A murmur ran through the crowd, "He's dead." 27But Jesus took him by the hand and helped him to his feet, and he stood up.

28Afterward, when Jesus was alone in the house with his disciples, they asked him, "Why couldn't we cast out that evil spirit?"

29Jesus replied, "This kind can be cast out only by prayer.*"

Jesus Again Predicts His Death

30Leaving that region, they traveled through Galilee. Jesus tried to avoid all publicity 31in order to spend more time with his disciples and teach them. He said to them, "The Son of Man is going to be betrayed. He will be killed, but three days later he will rise from the dead." 32But they didn't understand what he was saying, and they were afraid to ask him what he meant.

The Greatest in the Kingdom

33After they arrived at Capernaum, Jesus and his disciples settled in the house where they would be staying. Jesus asked them, "What were you discussing out on the road?" 34But they didn't answer, because they had been arguing about which of them was the greatest. 35He sat down and called the twelve disciples over to him. Then he said, "Anyone who wants to be the first must take last place and be the servant of everyone else."

36Then he put a little child among them. Taking the child in his arms, he said to them,

9:5 Or *shelters;* Greek reads *tabernacles.*   9:18 Or *become weak.*   9:29 Some manuscripts add *and fasting.*

37"Anyone who welcomes a little child like this on my behalf welcomes me, and anyone who welcomes me welcomes my Father who sent me."

Using the Name of Jesus
38John said to Jesus, "Teacher, we saw a man using your name to cast out demons, but we told him to stop because he isn't one of our group."

39"Don't stop him!" Jesus said. "No one who performs miracles in my name will soon be able to speak evil of me. 40Anyone who is not against us is for us. 41If anyone gives you even a cup of water because you belong to the Messiah, I assure you, that person will be rewarded.

42"But if anyone causes one of these little ones who trusts in me to lose faith, it would be better for that person to be thrown into the sea with a large millstone tied around the neck. 43If your hand causes you to sin, cut it off. It is better to enter heaven* with only one hand than to go into the unquenchable fires of hell with two hands.* 45If your foot causes you to sin, cut it off. It is better to enter heaven with only one foot than to be thrown into hell with two feet.* 47And if your eye causes you to sin, gouge it out. It is better to enter the Kingdom of God half blind than to have two eyes and be thrown into hell, 48'where the worm never dies and the fire never goes out.'*

49"For everyone will be purified with fire.* 50Salt is good for seasoning. But if it loses its flavor, how do you make it salty again? You must have the qualities of salt among yourselves and live in peace with each other."

CHAPTER **10**
Discussion about Divorce and Marriage
Then Jesus left Capernaum and went southward to the region of Judea and into the area east of the Jordan River. As always there were the crowds, and as usual he taught them.

2Some Pharisees came and tried to trap him with this question: "Should a man be allowed to divorce his wife?"

3"What did Moses say about divorce?" Jesus asked them.

4"Well, he permitted it," they replied. "He said a man merely has to write his wife an official letter of divorce and send her away."*

5But Jesus responded, "He wrote those instructions only as a concession to your hard-hearted wickedness. 6But God's plan was seen from the beginning of creation, for 'He made them male and female.'* 7This explains why a man leaves his father and mother and is joined to his wife,* 8and the two are united into one.'* Since they are no longer two but one, 9let no one separate them, for God has joined them together."

10Later, when he was alone with his disciples in the house, they brought up the subject again. 11He told them, "Whoever divorces his wife and marries someone else commits adultery against her. 12And if a woman divorces her husband and remarries, she commits adultery."

Jesus Blesses the Children
13One day some parents brought their children to Jesus so he could touch them and bless them, but the disciples told them not to bother him.

9:43a Greek *enter life*; also in 9:45.   9:43b Some manuscripts add verse 44 (which is identical with 9:48).   9:45 Some manuscripts add verse 46 (which is identical with 9:48).   9:48 Isa 66:24.   9:49 Greek *salted with fire*. Some manuscripts add *and every sacrifice will be salted with salt*.   10:4 Deut 24:1.   10:6 Gen 1:27; 5:2.   10:7 Some manuscripts do not include *and is joined to his wife*.   10:7-8 Gen 2:24.

OFF AND RUNNING ▰▰▰▰
Divorce Is Not Part of God's Plan Read MARK 10:2-12

At the time Jesus was asked this question about divorce, some people had a liberal attitude toward it. Much like today, one could dissolve a marriage for practically any reason. But Jesus reminded the people of God's original plan for marriage (verses 6-9). God desires that a man and woman make a lifelong commitment to each other. Divorce should not even be a consideration.

Perhaps one of the greatest deterrents for divorce is to see how much God really hates it:

"You cry out, 'Why has the LORD abandoned us?' I'll tell you why! Because the LORD witnessed the vows you and your wife made to each other on your wedding day when you were young. But you have been disloyal to her, though she remained your faithful companion, the wife of your marriage vows. Didn't the LORD make you one with your wife? In body and spirit you are his. And what does he want? Godly children from your union. So guard yourself; remain loyal to the wife of your youth. 'For I hate divorce!'" (Malachi 2:14-16).

14But when Jesus saw what was happening, he was very displeased with his disciples. He said to them, "Let the children come to me. Don't stop them! For the Kingdom of God belongs to such as these. 15I assure you, anyone who doesn't have their kind of faith will never get into the Kingdom of God." 16Then he took the children into his arms and placed his hands on their heads and blessed them.

The Rich Man

17As he was starting out on a trip, a man came running up to Jesus, knelt down, and asked, "Good Teacher, what should I do to get eternal life?"

18"Why do you call me good?" Jesus asked. "Only God is truly good. 19But as for your question, you know the commandments: 'Do not murder. Do not commit adultery. Do not steal. Do not testify falsely. Do not cheat. Honor your father and mother.'* "

20"Teacher," the man replied, "I've obeyed all these commandments since I was a child."

21Jesus felt genuine love for this man as he looked at him. "You lack only one thing," he told him. "Go and sell all you have and give the money to the poor, and you will have treasure in heaven. Then come, follow me." 22At this, the man's face fell, and he went sadly away because he had many possessions.

23Jesus looked around and said to his disciples, "How hard it is for rich people to get into the Kingdom of God!" 24This amazed them. But Jesus said again, "Dear children, it is very hard* to get into the Kingdom of God. 25It is easier for a camel to go through the eye of a needle than for a rich person to enter the Kingdom of God!"

26The disciples were astounded. "Then who in the world can be saved?" they asked.

27Jesus looked at them intently and said, "Humanly speaking, it is impossible. But not with God. Everything is possible with God."

28Then Peter began to mention all that he and the other disciples had left behind. "We've given up everything to follow you," he said.

29And Jesus replied, "I assure you that everyone who has given up house or brothers or sisters or mother or father or children or property, for my sake and for the Good News, 30will receive now in return, a hundred times over, houses, brothers, sisters, mothers, children, and property—with persecutions. And in the world to come they will have eternal life. 31But many who seem to be important now will be the least important then, and those who are considered least here will be the greatest then.* "

Jesus Again Predicts His Death

32They were now on the way to Jerusalem, and Jesus was walking ahead of them. The disciples were filled with dread and the people following behind were overwhelmed with fear. Taking the twelve disciples aside, Jesus once more began to describe everything that was about to happen to him in Jerusalem. 33"When we get to Jerusalem," he told them, "the Son of Man will be betrayed to the leading priests and the teachers of religious law. They will sentence him to die and hand him over to the Romans. 34They will mock him, spit on him, beat him with their

10:19 Exod 20:12-16; Deut 5:16-20. 10:24 Some manuscripts add *for those who trust in riches.* 10:31 Greek *But many who are first will be last; and the last, first.*

Just as one should count the cost of getting married, one should also count the cost of getting divorced. Not only does it devastate the "companionship" God desires between a husband and wife, but it will also greatly affect any children they may have. As God says here, he wants his people to bring up godly children from the union between husband and wife. When a home is broken by divorce, it can become more difficult to raise children in obedience to the Lord.

Does God ever permit divorce? While the Bible cites two instances (adultery, and if a nonbelieving spouse chooses to leave a believing spouse), God's will is that a married couple stay together. Any confusion about the subject arises when we try to accommodate the divine standard to the lack of standards in our contemporary morality.

Winston Churchill astutely observed, "Victory is not obtained through evacuation." If you are married, ask God to strengthen your marriage today. Remember that God has joined you and your spouse together. Stand by your commitment. Don't retreat from your problems, but ask God to help you face and overcome them. Cultivate "oneness" and friendship in your marriage, and get back to God's original design.

For the next note on "Marriage," turn to p. 992.

Forgiveness First Comes from God Read MARK 11:25

As verse 25 of this passage implies, an attitude of unforgiveness can actually hinder our prayer life. The psalmist wrote, "He would not have listened if I had not confessed my sins" (Psalm 66:18).

In verse 25, Jesus is not saying that God's forgiveness is dependent upon your forgiveness of others. God's acceptance and forgiveness is entirely dependent upon what he did for you at the cross. He is simply stressing that if you are truly a forgiven person, you—of all people—should be willing to forgive others. At the same time, if you are not willing to forgive others, one would wonder if you personally know anything of God's forgiveness.

Don't let unforgiveness rob you of your joy. Forgive as Christ forgave you.

For the next note on "Forgiveness," turn to p. 812.

CORNER STONES

---

whips, and kill him, but after three days he will rise again."

Jesus Teaches about Serving Others

35Then James and John, the sons of Zebedee, came over and spoke to him. "Teacher," they said, "we want you to do us a favor."

36"What is it?" he asked.

37"In your glorious Kingdom, we want to sit in places of honor next to you," they said, "one at your right and the other at your left."

38But Jesus answered, "You don't know what you are asking! Are you able to drink from the bitter cup of sorrow I am about to drink? Are you able to be baptized with the baptism of suffering I must be baptized with?"

39"Oh yes," they said, "we are able!"

And Jesus said, "You will indeed drink from my cup and be baptized with my baptism, 40but I have no right to say who will sit on the thrones next to mine. God has prepared those places for the ones he has chosen."

41When the ten other disciples discovered what James and John had asked, they were indignant. 42So Jesus called them together and said, "You know that in this world kings are tyrants, and officials lord it over the people beneath them. 43But among you it should be quite different. Whoever wants to be a leader among you must be your servant, 44and whoever wants to be first must be the slave of all. 45For even I, the Son of Man, came here not to be served but to serve others, and to give my life as a ransom for many."

10:52 Or *on the way.*

Jesus Heals Blind Bartimaeus

46And so they reached Jericho. Later, as Jesus and his disciples left town, a great crowd was following. A blind beggar named Bartimaeus (son of Timaeus) was sitting beside the road as Jesus was going by. 47When Bartimaeus heard that Jesus from Nazareth was nearby, he began to shout out, "Jesus, Son of David, have mercy on me!"

48"Be quiet!" some of the people yelled at him.

But he only shouted louder, "Son of David, have mercy on me!"

49When Jesus heard him, he stopped and said, "Tell him to come here."

So they called the blind man. "Cheer up," they said. "Come on, he's calling you!" 50Bartimaeus threw aside his coat, jumped up, and came to Jesus.

51"What do you want me to do for you?" Jesus asked.

"Teacher," the blind man said, "I want to see!"

52And Jesus said to him, "Go your way. Your faith has healed you." And instantly the blind man could see! Then he followed Jesus down the road.*

CHAPTER 11

The Triumphal Entry

As Jesus and his disciples approached Jerusalem, they came to the towns of Bethphage and Bethany, on the Mount of Olives. Jesus sent two of them on ahead. 2"Go into that village over there," he told them, "and as soon as you enter it, you will see a colt tied there that has never been ridden. Untie it and bring it here. ³If anyone asks what you are doing, just say, 'The Lord needs it and will return it soon.'"

⁴The two disciples left and found the colt standing in the street, tied outside a house. ⁵As they were untying it, some bystanders demanded, "What are you doing, untying that colt?" ⁶They said what Jesus had told them to say, and they were permitted to take it. ⁷Then they brought the colt to Jesus and threw their garments over it, and he sat on it.

⁸Many in the crowd spread their coats on the road ahead of Jesus, and others cut leafy branches in the fields and spread them along the way. ⁹He was in the center of the procession, and the crowds all around him were shouting,

"Praise God!*
Bless the one who comes in the name of
the Lord!
¹⁰ Bless the coming kingdom of our ancestor
David!
Praise God in highest heaven!"*

¹¹So Jesus came to Jerusalem and went into the Temple. He looked around carefully at everything, and then he left because it was late in the afternoon. Then he went out to Bethany with the twelve disciples.

Jesus Curses the Fig Tree

¹²The next morning as they were leaving Bethany, Jesus felt hungry. ¹³He noticed a fig tree a little way off that was in full leaf, so he went over to see if he could find any figs on it. But there were only leaves because it was too early in the season for fruit. ¹⁴Then Jesus said to the tree, "May no one ever eat your fruit again!" And the disciples heard him say it.

Jesus Clears the Temple

¹⁵When they arrived back in Jerusalem, Jesus entered the Temple and began to drive out the merchants and their customers. He knocked over the tables of the money changers and the stalls of those selling doves, ¹⁶and he stopped everyone from bringing in merchandise. ¹⁷He taught them, "The Scriptures declare, 'My Temple will be called a place of prayer for all nations,' but you have turned it into a den of thieves."*

¹⁸When the leading priests and teachers of religious law heard what Jesus had done, they began planning how to kill him. But they were afraid of him because the people were so enthusiastic about Jesus' teaching. ¹⁹That evening Jesus and the disciples* left the city.

²⁰The next morning as they passed by the fig tree he had cursed, the disciples noticed it was withered from the roots. ²¹Peter remembered what Jesus had said to the tree on the previous day and exclaimed, "Look, Teacher! The fig tree you cursed has withered!"

²²Then Jesus said to the disciples, "Have faith in God. ²³I assure you that you can say to this mountain, 'May God lift you up and throw you into the sea,' and your command will be obeyed. All that's required is that you really believe and do not doubt in your heart. ²⁴Listen to me! You can pray for anything, and if you believe, you will have it. ²⁵But when you are praying, first forgive anyone you are holding a grudge against, so that your Father in heaven will forgive your sins, too.*"

The Authority of Jesus Challenged

²⁷By this time they had arrived in Jerusalem again. As Jesus was walking through the Temple area, the leading priests, the teachers of religious law, and the other leaders came up to him. They demanded, ²⁸"By whose authority did you drive out the merchants from the Temple?* Who gave you such authority?"

²⁹"I'll tell who gave me authority to do these things if you answer one question," Jesus replied. ³⁰"Did John's baptism come from heaven or was it merely human? Answer me!"

³¹They talked it over among themselves. "If we say it was from heaven, he will ask why we didn't believe him. ³²But do we dare say it was merely human?" For they were afraid that the people would start a riot, since everyone thought that John was a prophet. ³³So they finally replied, "We don't know."

And Jesus responded, "Then I won't answer your question either."

CHAPTER **12**
Story of the Evil Farmers

Then Jesus began telling them stories: "A man planted a vineyard, built a wall around it, dug a pit for pressing out the grape juice, and built a lookout tower. Then he leased the vineyard to tenant farmers and moved to another country.

11:9 Greek *Hosanna*, an exclamation of praise that literally means "save now"; also in 11:10.   11:9-10 Pss 118:25-26; 148:1.   11:17 Isa 56:7; Jer 7:11.   11:19 Greek *they*; some manuscripts read *he*.   11:25 Some manuscripts add verse 26, *But if you do not forgive, neither will your Father who is in heaven forgive your sins.*   11:28 Or *By whose authority do you do these things?*

²At grape-picking time he sent one of his servants to collect his share of the crop. ³But the farmers grabbed the servant, beat him up, and sent him back empty-handed.

⁴"The owner then sent another servant, but they beat him over the head and treated him shamefully. ⁵The next servant he sent was killed. Others who were sent were either beaten or killed, ⁶until there was only one left—his son whom he loved dearly. The owner finally sent him, thinking, 'Surely they will respect my son.'

⁷"But the farmers said to one another, 'Here comes the heir to this estate. Let's kill him and get the estate for ourselves!' ⁸So they grabbed him and murdered him and threw his body out of the vineyard.

⁹"What do you suppose the owner of the vineyard will do?" Jesus asked. "I'll tell you—he will come and kill them all and lease the vineyard to others. ¹⁰Didn't you ever read this in the Scriptures?

'The stone rejected by the builders
    has now become the cornerstone.
¹¹ This is the Lord's doing,
    and it is marvelous to see.'* "

¹²The Jewish leaders wanted to arrest him for using this illustration because they realized he was pointing at them—they were the wicked farmers in his story. But they were afraid to touch him because of the crowds. So they left him and went away.

Taxes for Caesar

¹³The leaders sent some Pharisees and supporters of Herod to try to trap Jesus into saying something for which he could be arrested. ¹⁴"Teacher," these men said, "we know how honest you are. You are impartial and don't play favorites. You sincerely teach the ways of God. Now tell us—is it right to pay taxes to the Roman government or not? ¹⁵Should we pay them, or should we not?"

Jesus saw through their hypocrisy and said, "Whom are you trying to fool with your trick questions? Show me a Roman coin,* and I'll tell you." ¹⁶When they handed it to him, he asked, "Whose picture and title are stamped on it?"

"Caesar's," they replied.

¹⁷"Well, then," Jesus said, "give to Caesar what belongs to him. But everything that belongs to God must be given to God." This reply completely amazed them.

Discussion about Resurrection

¹⁸Then the Sadducees stepped forward—a group of Jews who say there is no resurrection after death. They posed this question: ¹⁹"Teacher, Moses gave us a law that if a man dies, leaving a wife without children, his brother should marry the widow and have a child who will be the brother's heir.* ²⁰Well, there were seven brothers. The oldest of them married and then died without children. ²¹So the second brother married the widow, but soon he too died and left no children. Then the next brother married her and died without children. ²²This continued until all the brothers had married her and died, and still there were no children. Last of all, the woman died, too. ²³So tell us, whose wife will she be in the resurrection? For all seven were married to her."

²⁴Jesus replied, "Your problem is that you don't know the Scriptures, and you don't know the power of God. ²⁵For when the dead rise, they won't be married. They will be like the angels in heaven. ²⁶But now, as to whether the dead will be raised—haven't you ever read about this in the writings of Moses, in the story of the burning bush? Long after Abraham, Isaac, and Jacob had died, God said to Moses,* 'I am the God of Abraham, the God of Isaac, and the God of Jacob.'* ²⁷So he is the God of the living, not the dead. You have made a serious error."

The Most Important Commandment

²⁸One of the teachers of religious law was standing there listening to the discussion. He realized that Jesus had answered well, so he asked, "Of all the commandments, which is the most important?"

²⁹Jesus replied, "The most important commandment is this: 'Hear, O Israel! The Lord our God is the one and only Lord. ³⁰And you must love the Lord your God with all your heart, all your soul, all your mind, and all your strength.'* ³¹The second is equally important: 'Love your neighbor as yourself.'* No other commandment is greater than these."

³²The teacher of religious law replied, "Well said, Teacher. You have spoken the truth by saying that there is only one God and no other. ³³And I know it is important to love him with all my heart and all my understanding and all my strength, and to love my neighbors as myself. This is more important than to offer all of

12:10-11 Ps 118:22-23.   12:15 Greek *a denarius*.   12:19 Deut 25:5-6.   12:26a Greek *in the story of the bush? God said to him*.
12:26b Exod 3:6.   12:29-30 Deut 6:4-5.   12:31 Lev 19:18.

the burnt offerings and sacrifices required in the law."

³⁴Realizing this man's understanding, Jesus said to him, "You are not far from the Kingdom of God." And after that, no one dared to ask him any more questions.

Whose Son Is the Messiah?

³⁵Later, as Jesus was teaching the people in the Temple, he asked, "Why do the teachers of religious law claim that the Messiah will be the son of David? ³⁶For David himself, speaking under the inspiration of the Holy Spirit, said,

'The LORD said to my Lord,
Sit in honor at my right hand
until I humble your enemies beneath
your feet.'*

³⁷Since David himself called him Lord, how can he be his son at the same time?" And the crowd listened to him with great interest.

³⁸Here are some of the other things he taught them at this time: "Beware of these teachers of religious law! For they love to parade in flowing robes and to have everyone bow to them as they walk in the marketplaces. ³⁹And how they love the seats of honor in the synagogues and at banquets. ⁴⁰But they shamelessly cheat widows out of their property, and then, to cover up the kind of people they really are, they make long prayers in public. Because of this, their punishment will be the greater."

The Widow's Offering

⁴¹Jesus went over to the collection box in the Temple and sat and watched as the crowds dropped in their money. Many rich people put in large amounts. ⁴²Then a poor widow came and dropped in two pennies.* ⁴³He called his disciples to him and said, "I assure you, this poor widow has given more than all the others have given. ⁴⁴For they gave a tiny part of their surplus, but she, poor as she is, has given everything she has."

CHAPTER **13**

Jesus Foretells the Future

As Jesus was leaving the Temple that day, one of his disciples said, "Teacher, look at these tremendous buildings! Look at the massive stones in the walls!"

²Jesus replied, "These magnificent buildings

12:36 Ps 110:1.   12:42 Greek 2 lepta, which is a kodrantes.

will be so completely demolished that not one stone will be left on top of another."

³Later, Jesus sat on the slopes of the Mount of Olives across the valley from the Temple. Peter, James, John, and Andrew came to him privately and asked him, ⁴"When will all this take place? And will there be any sign ahead of time to show us when all this will be fulfilled?"

⁵Jesus replied, "Don't let anyone mislead you, ⁶because many will come in my name, claiming to be the Messiah.* They will lead many astray. ⁷And wars will break out near and far, but don't panic. Yes, these things must come, but the end won't follow immediately. ⁸Nations and kingdoms will proclaim war against each other, and there will be earth-

13:6 Greek name, saying, 'I am.'

How Much Should You Give?
Read MARK 12:41-44

Generosity is not measured by the size of the gift itself, but by the motivation. In this story, we see how Jesus valued the small offering of this poor widow over the large sums of money from the wealthy people. Jesus knew that she had given all she had. He could see that her heart was in the right place.

The great psalmist, David, king of Israel, said he would not give to the Lord that which cost him nothing. In other words, we are not to give our "leftovers" to God, but our best. When you think about it, is that really too much to ask? After all, he gave his best to us when he sent us his own dear Son to die in our place.

Our attitude toward giving should be like that of the generous believers in Macedonia, who eagerly came to the aid of the church in Jerusalem during its time of need: "For I can testify that they gave not only what they could afford but far more. And they did it of their own free will. They begged us again and again for the gracious privilege of sharing in the gift for the Christians in Jerusalem" (2 Corinthians 8:3-4).

When you question how much of your income should be spent on God's work, remember this promise from the book of Proverbs: "The generous prosper and are satisfied; those who refresh others will themselves be refreshed" (Proverbs 11:25).

For the next note on "Give to God," turn to p. 1013.

quakes in many parts of the world, and famines. But all this will be only the beginning of the horrors to come. 9But when these things begin to happen, watch out! You will be handed over to the courts and beaten in the synagogues. You will be accused before governors and kings of being my followers. This will be your opportunity to tell them about me.* 10And the Good News must first be preached to every nation. 11But when you are arrested and stand trial, don't worry about what to say in your defense. Just say what God tells you to. Then it is not you who will be speaking, but the Holy Spirit.

12"Brother will betray brother to death, fathers will betray their own children, and children will rise against their parents and cause them to be killed. 13And everyone will hate you because of your allegiance to me. But those who endure to the end will be saved.

14"The time will come when you will see the sacrilegious object that causes desecration* standing where it should not be"—reader, pay attention! "Then those in Judea must flee to the hills. 15A person outside the house* must not go back into the house to pack. 16A person in the field must not return even to get a coat. 17How terrible it will be for pregnant women and for mothers nursing their babies in those days. 18And pray that your flight will not be in winter. 19For those will be days of greater horror than at any time since God created the world. And it will never happen again. 20In fact, unless the Lord shortens that time of calamity, the entire human race will be destroyed. But for the sake of his chosen ones he has shortened those days.

21"And then if anyone tells you, 'Look, here is the Messiah,' or, 'There he is,' don't pay any attention. 22For false messiahs and false prophets will rise up and perform miraculous signs and wonders so as to deceive, if possible, even God's chosen ones. 23Watch out! I have warned you!

24"At that time, after those horrible days end,

the sun will be darkened,
the moon will not give light,
25 the stars will fall from the sky,
and the powers of heaven will be shaken.*

26Then everyone will see the Son of Man arrive on the clouds with great power and glory.*

27And he will send forth his angels to gather together his chosen ones from all over the world—from the farthest ends of the earth and heaven.

28"Now, learn a lesson from the fig tree. When its buds become tender and its leaves begin to sprout, you know without being told that summer is near. 29Just so, when you see the events I've described beginning to happen, you can be sure that his return is very near, right at the door. 30I assure you, this generation* will not pass from the scene until all these events have taken place. 31Heaven and earth will disappear, but my words will remain forever.

32"However, no one knows the day or hour when these things will happen, not even the angels in heaven or the Son himself. Only the Father knows. 33And since you don't know when they will happen, stay alert and keep watch.*

34"The coming of the Son of Man can be compared with that of a man who left home to go on a trip. He gave each of his employees instructions about the work they were to do, and he told the gatekeeper to watch for his return. 35So keep a sharp lookout! For you do not know when the homeowner will return—at evening, midnight, early dawn, or late daybreak. 36Don't let him find you sleeping when he arrives without warning. 37What I say to you I say to everyone: Watch for his return!"

CHAPTER **14**
Jesus Anointed at Bethany
It was now two days before the Passover celebration and the Festival of Unleavened Bread. The leading priests and the teachers of religious law were still looking for an opportunity to capture Jesus secretly and put him to death. 2"But not during the Passover," they agreed, "or there will be a riot."

3Meanwhile, Jesus was in Bethany at the home of Simon, a man who had leprosy. During supper, a woman came in with a beautiful jar of expensive perfume.* She broke the seal and poured the perfume over his head. 4Some of those at the table were indignant. "Why was this expensive perfume wasted?" they asked. 5"She could have sold it for a small fortune* and given the money to the poor!" And they scolded her harshly.

13:9 Or *This will be your testimony against them.* 13:14 Greek *the abomination of desolation.* See Dan 9:27; 11:31; 12:11. 13:15 Greek *on the roof.* 13:24-25 See Isa 13:10; 34:4; Joel 2:10. 13:26 See Dan 7:13. 13:30 Or *this age,* or *this nation.* 13:33 Some manuscripts add *and pray.* 14:3 Greek *an alabaster jar of expensive ointment, pure nard.* 14:5 Greek *300 denarii.* A denarius was the equivalent of a full day's wage.

6But Jesus replied, "Leave her alone. Why berate her for doing such a good thing to me? 7You will always have the poor among you, and you can help them whenever you want to. But I will not be here with you much longer. 8She has done what she could and has anointed my body for burial ahead of time. 9I assure you, wherever the Good News is preached throughout the world, this woman's deed will be talked about in her memory."

Judas Agrees to Betray Jesus

10Then Judas Iscariot, one of the twelve disciples, went to the leading priests to arrange to betray Jesus to them. 11The leading priests were delighted when they heard why he had come, and they promised him a reward. So he began looking for the right time and place to betray Jesus.

The Last Supper

12On the first day of the Festival of Unleavened Bread (the day the Passover lambs were sacrificed), Jesus' disciples asked him, "Where do you want us to go to prepare the Passover supper?"

13So Jesus sent two of them into Jerusalem to make the arrangements. "As you go into the city," he told them, "a man carrying a pitcher of water will meet you. Follow him. 14At the house he enters, say to the owner, 'The Teacher asks, Where is the guest room where I can eat the Passover meal with my disciples?' 15He will take you upstairs to a large room that is already set up. That is the place; go ahead and prepare our supper there." 16So the two disciples went on ahead into the city and found everything just as Jesus had said, and they prepared the Passover supper there.

17In the evening Jesus arrived with the twelve disciples. 18As they were sitting around the table eating, Jesus said, "The truth is, one of you will betray me, one of you who is here eating with me."

19Greatly distressed, one by one they began to ask him, "I'm not the one, am I?"

20He replied, "It is one of you twelve, one who is eating with me now.* 21For I, the Son of Man, must die, as the Scriptures declared long ago. But how terrible it will be for my betrayer. Far better for him if he had never been born!"

22As they were eating, Jesus took a loaf of bread and asked God's blessing on it. Then he broke it in pieces and gave it to the disciples, saying, "Take it, for this is my body."

23And he took a cup of wine and gave thanks to God for it. He gave it to them, and they all drank from it. 24And he said to them, "This is my blood, poured out for many, sealing the covenant* between God and his people. 25I solemnly declare that I will not drink wine again until that day when I drink it new in the Kingdom of God." 26Then they sang a hymn and went out to the Mount of Olives.

Jesus Predicts Peter's Denial

27"All of you will desert me," Jesus told them. "For the Scriptures say,

'God* will strike the Shepherd,
    and the sheep will be scattered.'*

28But after I am raised from the dead, I will go ahead of you to Galilee and meet you there."

29Peter said to him, "Even if everyone else deserts you, I never will."

30"Peter," Jesus replied, "the truth is, this very night, before the rooster crows twice, you will deny me three times."

31"No!" Peter insisted. "Not even if I have to die with you! I will never deny you!" And all the others vowed the same.

Jesus Prays in Gethsemane

32And they came to an olive grove called Gethsemane, and Jesus said, "Sit here while I go and pray." 33He took Peter, James, and John with him, and he began to be filled with horror and deep distress. 34He told them, "My soul is crushed with grief to the point of death. Stay here and watch with me."

35He went on a little farther and fell face down on the ground. He prayed that, if it were possible, the awful hour awaiting him might pass him by. 36"Abba,* Father," he said, "everything is possible for you. Please take this cup of suffering away from me. Yet I want your will, not mine."

37Then he returned and found the disciples asleep. "Simon!" he said to Peter. "Are you asleep? Couldn't you stay awake and watch with me even one hour? 38Keep alert and pray. Otherwise temptation will overpower you. For though the spirit is willing enough, the body is weak."

39Then Jesus left them again and prayed, repeating his pleadings. 40Again he returned to

14:20 Or *one who is dipping bread into the bowl with me.*   **14:24** Some manuscripts read *the new covenant.*   **14:27a** Greek *I.*   **14:27b** Zech 13:7.   **14:36** *Abba* is an Aramaic term for "father."

them and found them sleeping, for they just couldn't keep their eyes open. And they didn't know what to say.

⁴¹When he returned to them the third time, he said, "Still sleeping? Still resting?* Enough! The time has come. I, the Son of Man, am betrayed into the hands of sinners. ⁴²Up, let's be going. See, my betrayer is here!"

Jesus Is Betrayed and Arrested

⁴³And immediately, as he said this, Judas, one of the twelve disciples, arrived with a mob that was armed with swords and clubs. They had been sent out by the leading priests, the teachers of religious law, and the other leaders. ⁴⁴Judas had given them a prearranged signal: "You will know which one to arrest when I go over and give him the kiss of greeting. Then you can take him away under guard."

⁴⁵As soon as they arrived, Judas walked up to Jesus. "Teacher!" he exclaimed, and gave him the kiss. ⁴⁶Then the others grabbed Jesus and arrested him. ⁴⁷But someone pulled out a sword and slashed off an ear of the high priest's servant.

⁴⁸Jesus asked them, "Am I some dangerous criminal, that you come armed with swords and clubs to arrest me? ⁴⁹Why didn't you arrest me in the Temple? I was there teaching every day. But these things are happening to fulfill what the Scriptures say about me."

⁵⁰Meanwhile, all his disciples deserted him and ran away. ⁵¹There was a young man following along behind, clothed only in a linen nightshirt. When the mob tried to grab him, ⁵²they tore off his clothes, but he escaped and ran away naked.

Jesus before the Council

⁵³Jesus was led to the high priest's home where the leading priests, other leaders, and teachers of religious law had gathered. ⁵⁴Meanwhile, Peter followed far behind and then slipped inside the gates of the high priest's courtyard. For a while he sat with the guards, warming himself by the fire.

⁵⁵Inside, the leading priests and the entire high council* were trying to find witnesses who would testify against Jesus, so they could put him to death. But their efforts were in vain. ⁵⁶Many false witnesses spoke against him, but they contradicted each other. ⁵⁷Finally, some men stood up to testify against him with this lie: ⁵⁸"We heard him say, 'I will destroy this Temple made with human hands, and in three days I will build another, made without human

hands.'" ⁵⁹But even then they didn't get their stories straight!

⁶⁰Then the high priest stood up before the others and asked Jesus, "Well, aren't you going to answer these charges? What do you have to say for yourself?" ⁶¹Jesus made no reply. Then the high priest asked him, "Are you the Messiah, the Son of the blessed God?"

⁶²Jesus said, "I am, and you will see me, the Son of Man, sitting at God's right hand in the place of power and coming back on the clouds of heaven."*

⁶³Then the high priest tore his clothing to show his horror and said, "Why do we need other witnesses? ⁶⁴You have all heard his blasphemy. What is your verdict?" And they all condemned him to death.

⁶⁵Then some of them began to spit at him, and they blindfolded him and hit his face with their fists. "Who hit you that time, you prophet?" they jeered. And even the guards were hitting him as they led him away.

Peter Denies Jesus

⁶⁶Meanwhile, Peter was below in the courtyard. One of the servant girls who worked for the high priest ⁶⁷noticed Peter warming himself at the fire. She looked at him closely and then said, "You were one of those with Jesus, the Nazarene."

⁶⁸Peter denied it. "I don't know what you're talking about," he said, and he went out into the entryway. Just then, a rooster crowed.*

⁶⁹The servant girl saw him standing there and began telling the others, "That man is definitely one of them!" ⁷⁰Peter denied it again.

A little later some other bystanders began saying to Peter, "You must be one of them because you are from Galilee."

⁷¹Peter said, "I swear by God, I don't know this man you're talking about." ⁷²And immediately the rooster crowed the second time. Suddenly, Jesus' words flashed through Peter's mind: "Before the rooster crows twice, you will deny me three times." And he broke down and cried.

CHAPTER 15

Jesus' Trial before Pilate

Very early in the morning the leading priests, other leaders, and teachers of religious law—the entire high council*—met to discuss their next step. They bound Jesus and took him to Pilate, the Roman governor.

14:41 Or *Sleep on, take your rest.*   14:55 Greek *the Sanhedrin.*   14:62 See Ps 110:1; Dan 7:13.   14:68 Some manuscripts do not include *Just then, a rooster crowed.*   15:1 Greek *the Sanhedrin;* also in 15:43.

[2]Pilate asked Jesus, "Are you the King of the Jews?"

Jesus replied, "Yes, it is as you say."

[3]Then the leading priests accused him of many crimes, [4]and Pilate asked him, "Aren't you going to say something? What about all these charges against you?" [5]But Jesus said nothing, much to Pilate's surprise.

[6]Now it was the governor's custom to release one prisoner each year at Passover time—anyone the people requested. [7]One of the prisoners at that time was Barabbas, convicted along with others for murder during an insurrection. [8]The mob began to crowd in toward Pilate, asking him to release a prisoner as usual. [9]"Should I give you the King of the Jews?" Pilate asked. [10](For he realized by now that the leading priests had arrested Jesus out of envy.) [11]But at this point the leading priests stirred up the mob to demand the release of Barabbas instead of Jesus. [12]"But if I release Barabbas," Pilate asked them, "what should I do with this man you call the King of the Jews?"

[13]They shouted back, "Crucify him!"

[14]"Why?" Pilate demanded. "What crime has he committed?"

But the crowd only roared the louder, "Crucify him!"

[15]So Pilate, anxious to please the crowd, released Barabbas to them. He ordered Jesus flogged with a lead-tipped whip, then turned him over to the Roman soldiers to crucify him.

The Soldiers Mock Jesus

[16]The soldiers took him into their headquarters* and called out the entire battalion. [17]They dressed him in a purple robe and made a crown of long, sharp thorns and put it on his head. [18]Then they saluted, yelling, "Hail! King of the Jews!" [19]And they beat him on the head with a stick, spit on him, and dropped to their knees in mock worship. [20]When they were finally tired of mocking him, they took off the purple robe and put his own clothes on him again. Then they led him away to be crucified.

The Crucifixion

[21]A man named Simon, who was from Cyrene,* was coming in from the country just then, and they forced him to carry Jesus' cross. (Simon is the father of Alexander and Rufus.) [22]And they brought Jesus to a place called Golgotha (which means Skull Hill).

[23]They offered him wine drugged with myrrh, but he refused it. [24]Then they nailed him to the cross. They gambled for his clothes, throwing dice* to decide who would get them.

[25]It was nine o'clock in the morning when the crucifixion took place. [26]A signboard was fastened to the cross above Jesus' head, announcing the charge against him. It read: "The King of the Jews." [27]Two criminals were crucified with him, their crosses on either side of his.* [29]And the people passing by shouted abuse, shaking their heads in mockery. "Ha! Look at you now!" they yelled at him. "You can destroy the Temple and rebuild it in three days, can you? [30]Well then, save yourself and come down from the cross!"

[31]The leading priests and teachers of religious law also mocked Jesus. "He saved others," they scoffed, "but he can't save himself! [32]Let this Messiah, this king of Israel, come down from the cross so we can see it and believe him!" Even the two criminals who were being crucified with Jesus ridiculed him.

The Death of Jesus

[33]At noon, darkness fell across the whole land until three o'clock. [34]Then, at that time Jesus called out with a loud voice, "*Eloi, Eloi, lema sabachthani?*" which means, "My God, my God, why have you forsaken me?"*

[35]Some of the bystanders misunderstood and thought he was calling for the prophet Elijah. [36]One of them ran and filled a sponge with sour wine, holding it up to him on a stick so he could drink. "Leave him alone. Let's see whether Elijah will come and take him down!" he said.

[37]Then Jesus uttered another loud cry and breathed his last. [38]And the curtain in the Temple was torn in two, from top to bottom. [39]When the Roman officer who stood facing him saw how he had died, he exclaimed, "Truly, this was the Son of God!"

[40]Some women were there, watching from a distance, including Mary Magdalene, Mary (the mother of James the younger and of Joseph*), and Salome. [41]They had been followers of Jesus and had cared for him while he was in Galilee. Then they and many other women had come with him to Jerusalem.

The Burial of Jesus

[42]This all happened on Friday, the day of preparation,* the day before the Sabbath. As evening

---

15:16 Greek *the courtyard, which is the praetorium.*   **15:21** *Cyrene* was a city in northern Africa.   **15:24** Greek *casting lots.* See Ps 22:18.
15:27 Some manuscripts add verse 28, *And the Scripture was fulfilled that said, "He was counted among those who were rebels."* See Isa 53:12.
15:34 Ps 22:1.   **15:40** Greek *Joses;* also in 15:47. See Matt 27:56.   **15:42** Greek *on the day of preparation.*

approached, ⁴³an honored member of the high council, Joseph from Arimathea (who was waiting for the Kingdom of God to come), gathered his courage and went to Pilate to ask for Jesus' body. ⁴⁴Pilate couldn't believe that Jesus was already dead, so he called for the Roman military officer in charge and asked him. ⁴⁵The officer confirmed the fact, and Pilate told Joseph he could have the body. ⁴⁶Joseph bought a long sheet of linen cloth, and taking Jesus' body down from the cross, he wrapped it in the cloth and laid it in a tomb that had been carved out of the rock. Then he rolled a stone in front of the entrance. ⁴⁷Mary Magdalene and Mary the mother of Joseph saw where Jesus' body was laid.

CHAPTER **16**
The Resurrection
The next evening, when the Sabbath ended, Mary Magdalene and Salome and Mary the mother of James went out and purchased burial spices to put on Jesus' body. ²Very early on Sunday morning,* just at sunrise, they came to the tomb. ³On the way they were discussing who would roll the stone away from the entrance to the tomb. ⁴But when they arrived, they looked up and saw that the stone—a very large one—had already been rolled aside. ⁵So they entered the tomb, and there on the right sat a young man clothed in a white robe. The women were startled, ⁶but the angel said, "Do not be so surprised. You are looking for Jesus, the Nazarene, who was crucified. He isn't here! He has been raised from the dead! Look, this is where they laid his body. ⁷Now go and give this message to his disciples, including Peter: Jesus is going ahead of you to Galilee. You will see him there, just as he told you before he died!" ⁸The women fled from the tomb, trembling and bewildered, saying nothing to anyone because they were too frightened to talk.*

[Shorter Ending of Mark]

Then they reported all these instructions briefly to Peter and his companions. Afterward Jesus himself sent them out from east to west with the sacred and unfailing message of salvation that gives eternal life. Amen.

[Longer Ending of Mark]

⁹It was early on Sunday morning when Jesus rose from the dead, and the first person who saw him was Mary Magdalene, the woman from whom he had cast out seven demons. ¹⁰She went and found the disciples, who were grieving and weeping. ¹¹But when she told them that Jesus was alive and she had seen him, they didn't believe her.

¹²Afterward he appeared to two who were walking from Jerusalem into the country, but they didn't recognize him at first because he had changed his appearance. ¹³When they realized who he was, they rushed back to tell the others, but no one believed them.

¹⁴Still later he appeared to the eleven disciples as they were eating together. He rebuked them for their unbelief—their stubborn refusal to believe those who had seen him after he had risen.

¹⁵And then he told them, "Go into all the world and preach the Good News to everyone, everywhere. ¹⁶Anyone who believes and is baptized will be saved. But anyone who refuses to believe will be condemned. ¹⁷These signs will accompany those who believe: They will cast out demons in my name, and they will speak new languages.* ¹⁸They will be able to handle snakes with safety, and if they drink anything poisonous, it won't hurt them. They will be able to place their hands on the sick and heal them."

¹⁹When the Lord Jesus had finished talking with them, he was taken up into heaven and sat down in the place of honor at God's right hand. ²⁰And the disciples went everywhere and preached, and the Lord worked with them, confirming what they said by many miraculous signs.

16:2 Greek *on the first day of the week;* also in 16:9. **16:8** The most reliable early manuscripts conclude the Gospel of Mark at verse 8. Other manuscripts include various endings to the Gospel. Two of the more noteworthy endings are printed here. **16:17** Or *new tongues.* Some manuscripts omit *new.*

Luke

CHAPTER 1

Introduction

Most honorable Theophilus:

Many people have written accounts about the events that took place* among us. ²They used as their source material the reports circulating among us from the early disciples and other eyewitnesses of what God has done in fulfillment of his promises. ³Having carefully investigated all of these accounts from the beginning, I have decided to write a careful summary for you, ⁴to reassure you of the truth of all you were taught.

The Birth of John the Baptist Foretold

⁵It all begins with a Jewish priest, Zechariah, who lived when Herod was king of Judea. Zechariah was a member of the priestly order of Abijah. His wife, Elizabeth, was also from the priestly line of Aaron. ⁶Zechariah and Elizabeth were righteous in God's eyes, careful to obey all of the Lord's commandments and regulations. ⁷They had no children because Elizabeth was barren, and now they were both very old.

⁸One day Zechariah was serving God in the Temple, for his order was on duty that week. ⁹As was the custom of the priests, he was chosen by lot to enter the sanctuary and burn incense in the Lord's presence. ¹⁰While the incense was being burned, a great crowd stood outside, praying.

¹¹Zechariah was in the sanctuary when an angel of the Lord appeared, standing to the right of the incense altar. ¹²Zechariah was overwhelmed with fear. ¹³But the angel said, "Don't be afraid, Zechariah! For God has heard your prayer, and your wife, Elizabeth, will bear you a son! And you are to name him John. ¹⁴You will have great joy and gladness, and many will rejoice with you at his birth, ¹⁵for he will be great

in the eyes of the Lord. He must never touch wine or hard liquor, and he will be filled with the Holy Spirit, even before his birth.* ¹⁶And he will persuade many Israelites to turn to the Lord their God. ¹⁷He will be a man with the spirit and power of Elijah, the prophet of old. He will precede the coming of the Lord, preparing the people for his arrival. He will turn the hearts of the fathers to their children, and he will change disobedient minds to accept godly wisdom."*

¹⁸Zechariah said to the angel, "How can I know this will happen? I'm an old man now, and my wife is also well along in years."

¹⁹Then the angel said, "I am Gabriel! I stand in the very presence of God. It was he who sent me to bring you this good news! ²⁰And now, since you didn't believe what I said, you won't be able to speak until the child is born. For my words will certainly come true at the proper time."

²¹Meanwhile, the people were waiting for Zechariah to come out, wondering why he was taking so long. ²²When he finally did come out, he couldn't speak to them. Then they realized from his gestures that he must have seen a vision in the Temple sanctuary.

²³He stayed at the Temple until his term of service was over, and then he returned home. ²⁴Soon afterward his wife, Elizabeth, became pregnant and went into seclusion for five months. ²⁵"How kind the Lord is!" she exclaimed. "He has taken away my disgrace of having no children!"

The Birth of Jesus Foretold

²⁶In the sixth month of Elizabeth's pregnancy, God sent the angel Gabriel to Nazareth, a village in Galilee, ²⁷to a virgin named Mary. She was engaged to be married to a man named Joseph,

1:1 Or *have been fulfilled.* 1:15 Or *even from birth.* 1:17 See Mal 4:5-6.

a descendant of King David. 28Gabriel appeared to her and said, "Greetings, favored woman! The Lord is with you!*"

29Confused and disturbed, Mary tried to think what the angel could mean. 30"Don't be frightened, Mary," the angel told her, "for God has decided to bless you! 31You will become pregnant and have a son, and you are to name him Jesus. 32He will be very great and will be called the Son of the Most High. And the Lord God will give him the throne of his ancestor David. 33And he will reign over Israel* forever; his Kingdom will never end!"

34Mary asked the angel, "But how can I have a baby? I am a virgin."

35The angel replied, "The Holy Spirit will come upon you, and the power of the Most High will overshadow you. So the baby born to you will be holy, and he will be called the Son of God. 36What's more, your relative Elizabeth has become pregnant in her old age! People used to say she was barren, but she's already in her sixth month. 37For nothing is impossible with God."

38Mary responded, "I am the Lord's servant, and I am willing to accept whatever he wants. May everything you have said come true." And then the angel left.

Mary Visits Elizabeth

39A few days later Mary hurried to the hill country of Judea, to the town 40where Zechariah lived. She entered the house and greeted Elizabeth. 41At the sound of Mary's greeting, Elizabeth's child leaped within her, and Elizabeth was filled with the Holy Spirit.

42Elizabeth gave a glad cry and exclaimed to Mary, "You are blessed by God above all other women, and your child is blessed. 43What an honor this is, that the mother of my Lord should visit me! 44When you came in and greeted me, my baby jumped for joy the instant I heard your voice! 45You are blessed, because you believed that the Lord would do what he said."

The Magnificat: Mary's Song of Praise

46Mary responded,

"Oh, how I praise the Lord.
47 How I rejoice in God my Savior!
48 For he took notice of his lowly servant girl,
    and now generation after generation
       will call me blessed.
49 For he, the Mighty One, is holy,

and he has done great things for me.
50 His mercy goes on from generation to
       generation,
    to all who fear him.
51 His mighty arm does tremendous things!
    How he scatters the proud and haughty
       ones!
52 He has taken princes from their thrones
    and exalted the lowly.
53 He has satisfied the hungry with good things
    and sent the rich away with empty hands.
54 And how he has helped his servant Israel!
    He has not forgotten his promise to be
       merciful.
55 For he promised our ancestors—Abraham
       and his children—
    to be merciful to them forever."

56Mary stayed with Elizabeth about three months and then went back to her own home.

The Birth of John the Baptist

57Now it was time for Elizabeth's baby to be born, and it was a boy. 58The word spread quickly to her neighbors and relatives that the Lord had been very kind to her, and everyone rejoiced with her.

59When the baby was eight days old, all the relatives and friends came for the circumcision ceremony. They wanted to name him Zechariah, after his father. 60But Elizabeth said, "No! His name is John!"

61"What?" they exclaimed. "There is no one in all your family by that name." 62So they asked the baby's father, communicating to him by making gestures. 63He motioned for a writing tablet, and to everyone's surprise he wrote, "His name is John!" 64Instantly Zechariah could speak again, and he began praising God.

65Wonder fell upon the whole neighborhood, and the news of what had happened spread throughout the Judean hills. 66Everyone who heard about it reflected on these events and asked, "I wonder what this child will turn out to be? For the hand of the Lord is surely upon him in a special way."

Zechariah's Prophecy

67Then his father, Zechariah, was filled with the Holy Spirit and gave this prophecy:

68 "Praise the Lord, the God of Israel,
    because he has visited his people and
       redeemed them.

1:28 Some manuscripts add *Blessed are you among women.* 1:33 Greek *over the house of Jacob.*

Is the Bible Believable? Read LUKE 1:1-4

In writing this Gospel, Luke took painstaking efforts to confirm the accuracy of his work. He made it clear that he meticulously put this book together, going so far as to "recheck" the disciples' accounts "from the beginning."

Although Luke and other writers of the books of the Bible have taken great pains to accurately record the events within, some people have tried to point out alleged contradictions or inconsistencies in the Bible. These same people argue that the Bible is not credible based on what they believe to be contradictions. But here are three reasons why the Bible is believable:

1. God Is the Author. Despite the fact that the Bible was written by more than forty authors, we must recognize one important fact: The people who put the pen to the paper were but instruments in the hand of God. The real author of the Bible is God. As the apostle Paul wrote, "All Scripture is inspired by God" (2 Timothy 3:16). God chose to speak through these different people much like an artist uses different brushes to paint on a canvas. Each one had his own unique style, but the truth was the same.

2. The Main Story of the Bible Is Too Complex to Be a Hoax. The renowned historian Will Durant, who devoted his life to the study of records of antiquity, made this observation concerning the accounts of Jesus and the early church in Scripture: "That a few simple men should in one generation have invented so powerful and appealing a personality, so lofty an ethic, and so inspiring a vision of human brotherhood, would be a miracle far more incredible than any recorded in the Gospels. After two centuries of Higher Criticism the outlines of life, character, and teaching of Christ remain reasonably clear, and constitute the most fascinating feature in the history of Western man" [*Caesar and Christ,* in The Story of Civilization, vol. 3 (New York: Simon & Schuster, 1944), p. 557].

3. Scientific Evidence Supports the Bible's Accuracy. Archaeological findings have supported many of the complex historical passages found in the Bible. In addition, the Bible has greater documented accuracy than any other ancient literary work [see Norman L. Geisler & William E. Nix, *A General Introduction to the Bible* (Chicago: Moody Press, Moody Bible Institute, 1986)].

In spite of the evidence, God's Word must be accepted by faith. You, as an individual, must come to recognize that the words of the Lord are perfect, trustworthy, and right (see Psalm 19:7-11). Your belief in and practice of the truths found in this book—God's message to us—will make the most profound impact on your life for time and eternity.

For the next "Big Question" note, turn to p. 889.

For the next "Big Question" note, turn to p. 889.

---

⁶⁹ He has sent us a mighty Savior
  from the royal line of his servant David,
⁷⁰ just as he promised
  through his holy prophets long ago.
⁷¹ Now we will be saved from our enemies
  and from all who hate us.
⁷² He has been merciful to our ancestors
  by remembering his sacred covenant
   with them,
⁷³ the covenant he gave to our ancestor
   Abraham.
⁷⁴ We have been rescued from our enemies,
  so we can serve God without fear,
⁷⁵ in holiness and righteousness forever.

⁷⁶ "And you, my little son,
  will be called the prophet of the Most
   High,
  because you will prepare the way for the
   Lord.
⁷⁷ You will tell his people how to find
   salvation
  through forgiveness of their sins.
⁷⁸ Because of God's tender mercy,
  the light from heaven is about to break
   upon us,
⁷⁹ to give light to those who sit in darkness
  and in the shadow of death,
  and to guide us to the path of peace."

80John grew up and became strong in spirit. Then he lived out in the wilderness until he began his public ministry to Israel.

CHAPTER 2

The Birth of Jesus

At that time the Roman emperor, Augustus, decreed that a census should be taken throughout the Roman Empire. 2(This was the first census taken when Quirinius was governor of Syria.) 3All returned to their own towns to register for this census. 4And because Joseph was a descendant of King David, he had to go to Bethlehem in Judea, David's ancient home. He traveled there from the village of Nazareth in Galilee. 5He took with him Mary, his fiancée, who was obviously pregnant by this time.

6And while they were there, the time came for her baby to be born. 7She gave birth to her first child, a son. She wrapped him snugly in strips of cloth and laid him in a manger, because there was no room for them in the village inn.

The Shepherds and Angels

8That night some shepherds were in the fields outside the village, guarding their flocks of sheep. 9Suddenly, an angel of the Lord appeared among them, and the radiance of the Lord's glory surrounded them. They were terribly frightened, 10but the angel reassured them. "Don't be afraid!" he said. "I bring you good news of great joy for everyone! 11The Savior—yes, the Messiah, the Lord—has been born tonight in Bethlehem, the city of David! 12And this is how you will recognize him: You will find a baby lying in a manger, wrapped snugly in strips of cloth!"

13Suddenly, the angel was joined by a vast host of others—the armies of heaven—praising God:

14 "Glory to God in the highest heaven,
     and peace on earth to all whom God
          favors.*"

15When the angels had returned to heaven, the shepherds said to each other, " Come on, let's go to Bethlehem! Let's see this wonderful thing that has happened, which the Lord has told us about."

16They ran to the village and found Mary and Joseph. And there was the baby, lying in the manger. 17Then the shepherds told everyone what had happened and what the angel had said to them about this child. 18All who heard the shepherds'

story were astonished, 19but Mary quietly treasured these things in her heart and thought about them often. 20The shepherds went back to their fields and flocks, glorifying and praising God for what the angels had told them, and because they had seen the child, just as the angel had said.

Jesus Is Presented in the Temple

21Eight days later, when the baby was circumcised, he was named Jesus, the name given him by the angel even before he was conceived.

22Then it was time for the purification offering, as required by the law of Moses after the birth of a child; so his parents took him to Jerusalem to present him to the Lord. 23The law of the Lord says, "If a woman's first child is a boy, he must be dedicated to the Lord."* 24So they offered a sacrifice according to what was required in the law of the Lord—"either a pair of turtledoves or two young pigeons."*

The Prophecy of Simeon

25Now there was a man named Simeon who lived in Jerusalem. He was a righteous man and very devout. He was filled with the Holy Spirit, and he eagerly expected the Messiah to come and rescue Israel. 26The Holy Spirit had revealed to him that he would not die until he had seen the Lord's Messiah. 27That day the Spirit led him to the Temple. So when Mary and Joseph came to present the baby Jesus to the Lord as the law required, 28Simeon was there. He took the child in his arms and praised God, saying,

29 "Lord, now I can die in peace!
     As you promised me,
30 I have seen the Savior
31   you have given to all people.
32 He is a light to reveal God to the nations,
          and he is the glory of your people Israel!"

33Joseph and Mary were amazed at what was being said about Jesus. 34Then Simeon blessed them, and he said to Mary, "This child will be rejected by many in Israel, and it will be their undoing. But he will be the greatest joy to many others. 35Thus, the deepest thoughts of many hearts will be revealed. And a sword will pierce your very soul."

The Prophecy of Anna

36Anna, a prophet, was also there in the Temple. She was the daughter of Phanuel, of the tribe of Asher, and was very old. She was a widow, for her

2:14 Or *and peace on earth for all those pleasing God.* Some manuscripts read *and peace on earth, goodwill among people.* 2:23 Exod 13:2.
2:24 Lev 12:8.

husband had died when they had been married only seven years. ³⁷She was now eighty-four years old. She never left the Temple but stayed there day and night, worshiping God with fasting and prayer. ³⁸She came along just as Simeon was talking with Mary and Joseph, and she began praising God. She talked about Jesus to everyone who had been waiting for the promised King to come and deliver Jerusalem.

³⁹When Jesus' parents had fulfilled all the requirements of the law of the Lord, they returned home to Nazareth in Galilee. ⁴⁰There the child grew up healthy and strong. He was filled with wisdom beyond his years, and God placed his special favor upon him.

Jesus Speaks with the Teachers
⁴¹Every year Jesus' parents went to Jerusalem for the Passover festival. ⁴²When Jesus was twelve years old, they attended the festival as usual. ⁴³After the celebration was over, they started home to Nazareth, but Jesus stayed behind in Jerusalem. His parents didn't miss him at first, ⁴⁴because they assumed he was with friends among the other travelers. But when he didn't show up that evening, they started to look for him among their relatives and friends. ⁴⁵When they couldn't find him, they went back to Jerusalem to search for him there. ⁴⁶Three days later they finally discovered him. He was in the Temple, sitting among the religious teachers, discussing deep questions with them. ⁴⁷And all who heard him were amazed at his understanding and his answers.

⁴⁸His parents didn't know what to think. "Son!" his mother said to him. "Why have you done this to us? Your father and I have been frantic, searching for you everywhere."

⁴⁹"But why did you need to search?" he asked. "You should have known that I would be in my Father's house."* ⁵⁰But they didn't understand what he meant.

⁵¹Then he returned to Nazareth with them and was obedient to them; and his mother stored all these things in her heart. ⁵²So Jesus grew both in height and in wisdom, and he was loved by God and by all who knew him.

CHAPTER 3
John the Baptist Prepares the Way
It was now the fifteenth year of the reign of Tiberius, the Roman emperor. Pilate was governor over Judea; Herod Antipas was ruler* over Galilee; his brother Philip was ruler* over Iturea and Traconitis; Lysanias was ruler over Abilene. ²Annas and Caiaphas were the high priests. At this time a message from God came to John son of Zechariah, who was living out in the wilderness. ³Then John went from place to place on both sides of the Jordan River, preaching that people should be baptized to show that they had turned from their sins and turned to God to be forgiven.* ⁴Isaiah had spoken of John when he said,

"He is a voice shouting in the wilderness:
'Prepare a pathway for the Lord's coming!
    Make a straight road for him!
⁵ Fill in the valleys,
    and level the mountains and hills!
Straighten the curves,
    and smooth out the rough places!
⁶ And then all people will see
    the salvation sent from God.'"*

⁷Here is a sample of John's preaching to the crowds that came for baptism: "You brood of snakes! Who warned you to flee God's coming judgment? ⁸Prove by the way you live that you have really turned from your sins and turned to God. Don't just say, 'We're safe—we're the descendants of Abraham.' That proves nothing. God can change these stones here into children of Abraham. ⁹Even now the ax of God's judgment is poised, ready to sever your roots. Yes, every tree that does not produce good fruit will be chopped down and thrown into the fire."

¹⁰The crowd asked, "What should we do?"

¹¹John replied, "If you have two coats, give one to the poor. If you have food, share it with those who are hungry."

¹²Even corrupt tax collectors came to be baptized and asked, "Teacher, what should we do?"

¹³"Show your honesty," he replied. "Make sure you collect no more taxes than the Roman government requires you to."

¹⁴"What should we do?" asked some soldiers.

John replied, "Don't extort money, and don't accuse people of things you know they didn't do. And be content with your pay."

¹⁵Everyone was expecting the Messiah to come soon, and they were eager to know whether John might be the Messiah. ¹⁶John answered their questions by saying, "I baptize with* water; but someone is coming soon who is greater than I am—so much greater that I am

Jesus Had a Specific Mission to Accomplish Read LUKE 4:16-21

Jesus quoted from Isaiah 61:1-2 to describe the purpose of his ministry. This portion of Scripture describes five goals of Jesus' personal ministry on earth:

1. Preach the Good News to the Poor. Jesus ministered to people from all walks of life—from the wealthy tax collectors, to the "blue collar" fishermen, to the beggars on the street. It was not people's financial status that he was concerned with. Rather, he looked beyond people's outward need to their inward need. He saw the poverty of their soul. And to those who will listen, Jesus offers the good news of the gospel.

2. Heal the Brokenhearted. When your heart is broken, you may feel as though no one understands or cares. Yet Jesus understands. He knows what it is like to be abandoned by friends. He has experienced what it is like to be let down. He understands the sting of death. For that reason, he wants to heal your broken heart.

3. Bring Deliverance to the Captives. The Bible teaches that before we give our lives to God, we are held captive by sin. If you find yourself a slave to some vice or sin that you just can't overcome, Jesus wants to release you from that spiritual bondage. Just admit your sinful condition and turn from it, and ask God to give you a new heart. Then begin to yield yourself to the help and power of the Holy Spirit, and you will know true freedom.

4. Give Sight to the Blind. The Bible also teaches that before we give our lives to Jesus Christ, we are spiritually blind: "Satan, the god of this evil world, has blinded the minds of those who don't believe, so they are unable to see the glorious light of the Good News that is shining upon them. They don't understand the message we preach about the glory of Christ, who is the exact likeness of God" (2 Corinthians 4:4). Jesus wants to open our eyes so that we can understand and respond to the gospel message.

5. Bring Liberty to the Oppressed. The word *downtrodden* can also be translated "those who are crushed with life." Jesus understands your worries and hurts, and he wants to lift those burdens from your shoulders.

For the next note on "Who Is Jesus?" turn to p. 612.

CORNERSTONES

---

not even worthy to be his slave.* He will baptize you with the Holy Spirit and with fire.* [17]He is ready to separate the chaff from the grain with his winnowing fork. Then he will clean up the threshing area, storing the grain in his barn but burning the chaff with never-ending fire." [18]John used many such warnings as he announced the Good News to the people.

[19]John also publicly criticized Herod Antipas, ruler of Galilee, for marrying Herodias, his brother's wife, and for many other wrongs he had done. [20]So Herod put John in prison, adding this sin to his many others.

The Baptism of Jesus

[21]One day when the crowds were being baptized, Jesus himself was baptized. As he was praying, the heavens opened, [22]and the Holy Spirit descended on him in the form of a dove. And a voice from heaven said, "You are my beloved Son, and I am fully pleased with you.*"

The Record of Jesus' Ancestors

[23]Jesus was about thirty years old when he began his public ministry.

Jesus was known as the son of Joseph.
Joseph was the son of Heli.
[24] Heli was the son of Matthat.
Matthat was the son of Levi.
Levi was the son of Melki.
Melki was the son of Jannai.
Jannai was the son of Joseph.
[25] Joseph was the son of Mattathias.

3:16b Greek *to untie his sandals.* 3:16c Or *in the Holy Spirit and in fire.* 3:22 Some manuscripts read *and today I have become your Father.*

Mattathias was the son of Amos.
Amos was the son of Nahum.
Nahum was the son of Esli.
Esli was the son of Naggai.
²⁶ Naggai was the son of Maath.
Maath was the son of Mattathias.
Mattathias was the son of Semein.
Semein was the son of Josech.
Josech was the son of Joda.
²⁷ Joda was the son of Joanan.
Joanan was the son of Rhesa.
Rhesa was the son of Zerubbabel.
Zerubbabel was the son of Shealtiel.
Shealtiel was the son of Neri.
²⁸ Neri was the son of Melki.
Melki was the son of Addi.
Addi was the son of Cosam.
Cosam was the son of Elmadam.
Elmadam was the son of Er.
²⁹ Er was the son of Joshua.
Joshua was the son of Eliezer.
Eliezer was the son of Jorim.
Jorim was the son of Matthat.
Matthat was the son of Levi.
³⁰ Levi was the son of Simeon.
Simeon was the son of Judah.
Judah was the son of Joseph.
Joseph was the son of Jonam.
Jonam was the son of Eliakim.
³¹ Eliakim was the son of Melea.
Melea was the son of Menna.
Menna was the son of Mattatha.
Mattatha was the son of Nathan.
Nathan was the son of David.
³² David was the son of Jesse.
Jesse was the son of Obed.
Obed was the son of Boaz.
Boaz was the son of Salmon.*
Salmon was the son of Nahshon.
³³ Nahshon was the son of Amminadab.
Amminadab was the son of Admin.
Admin was the son of Arni.*
Arni was the son of Hezron.
Hezron was the son of Perez.
Perez was the son of Judah.
³⁴ Judah was the son of Jacob.
Jacob was the son of Isaac.
Isaac was the son of Abraham.
Abraham was the son of Terah.
Terah was the son of Nahor.
³⁵ Nahor was the son of Serug.
Serug was the son of Reu.
Reu was the son of Peleg.

Peleg was the son of Eber.
Eber was the son of Shelah.
³⁶ Shelah was the son of Cainan.
Cainan was the son of Arphaxad.
Arphaxad was the son of Shem.
Shem was the son of Noah.
Noah was the son of Lamech.
³⁷ Lamech was the son of Methuselah.
Methuselah was the son of Enoch.
Enoch was the son of Jared.
Jared was the son of Mahalalel.
Mahalalel was the son of Kenan.
³⁸ Kenan was the son of Enosh.*
Enosh was the son of Seth.
Seth was the son of Adam.
Adam was the son of God.

CHAPTER **4**

The Temptation of Jesus

Then Jesus, full of the Holy Spirit, left the Jordan River. He was led by the Spirit to go out into the wilderness, ²where the Devil tempted him for forty days. He ate nothing all that time and was very hungry.

³Then the Devil said to him, "If you are the Son of God, change this stone into a loaf of bread."

⁴But Jesus told him, "No! The Scriptures say, 'People need more than bread for their life.'* "

⁵Then the Devil took him up and revealed to him all the kingdoms of the world in a moment of time. ⁶The Devil told him, "I will give you the glory of these kingdoms and authority over them—because they are mine to give to anyone I please. ⁷I will give it all to you if you will bow down and worship me."

⁸Jesus replied, "The Scriptures say,

'You must worship the Lord your God;
    serve only him.'* "

⁹Then the Devil took him to Jerusalem, to the highest point of the Temple, and said, "If you are the Son of God, jump off! ¹⁰For the Scriptures say,

'He orders his angels to protect and guard you.
¹¹ And they will hold you with their hands
    to keep you from striking your foot on a
    stone.'* "

¹²Jesus responded, "The Scriptures also say, 'Do not test the Lord your God.'* "

¹³When the Devil had finished tempting Jesus, he left him until the next opportunity came.

3:32 Greek *Sala;* see Ruth 4:22.   **3:33** *Arni* is the same person as Ram; see 1 Chr 2:9-10.   **3:38** Greek *Enos;* see Gen 5:6.   **4:4** Deut 8:3.
4:8 Deut 6:13.   **4:10-11** Ps 91:11-12.   **4:12** Deut 6:16.

Jesus Rejected at Nazareth

[14]Then Jesus returned to Galilee, filled with the Holy Spirit's power. Soon he became well known throughout the surrounding country. [15]He taught in their synagogues and was praised by everyone.

[16]When he came to the village of Nazareth, his boyhood home, he went as usual to the synagogue on the Sabbath and stood up to read the Scriptures. [17]The scroll containing the messages of Isaiah the prophet was handed to him, and he unrolled the scroll to the place where it says:

[18] "The Spirit of the Lord is upon me,
> for he has appointed me to preach Good News to the poor.
He has sent me to proclaim
> that captives will be released,
> that the blind will see,
> that the downtrodden will be freed from their oppressors,
[19]   and that the time of the Lord's favor has come.*"

[20]He rolled up the scroll, handed it back to the attendant, and sat down. Everyone in the synagogue stared at him intently. [21]Then he said, "This Scripture has come true today before your very eyes!"

[22]All who were there spoke well of him and were amazed by the gracious words that fell from his lips. "How can this be?" they asked. "Isn't this Joseph's son?"

[23]Then he said, "Probably you will quote me that proverb, 'Physician, heal yourself'—meaning, 'Why don't you do miracles here in your hometown like those you did in Capernaum?' [24]But the truth is, no prophet is accepted in his own hometown.

[25]"Certainly there were many widows in Israel who needed help in Elijah's time, when there was no rain for three and a half years and hunger stalked the land. [26]Yet Elijah was not sent to any of them. He was sent instead to a widow of Zarephath—a foreigner in the land of Sidon. [27]Or think of the prophet Elisha, who healed Naaman, a Syrian, rather than the many lepers in Israel who needed help."

[28]When they heard this, the people in the synagogue were furious. [29]Jumping up, they mobbed him and took him to the edge of the hill on which the city was built. They intended to push him over the cliff, [30]but he slipped away through the crowd and left them.

Jesus Casts Out a Demon

[31]Then Jesus went to Capernaum, a town in Galilee, and taught there in the synagogue every Sabbath day. [32]There, too, the people were amazed at the things he said, because he spoke with authority.

[33]Once when he was in the synagogue, a man possessed by a demon began shouting at Jesus, [34]"Go away! Why are you bothering us, Jesus of Nazareth? Have you come to destroy us? I know who you are—the Holy One sent from God."

[35]Jesus cut him short. "Be silent!" he told the demon. "Come out of the man!" The demon threw the man to the floor as the crowd watched; then it left him without hurting him further.

[36]Amazed, the people exclaimed, "What authority and power this man's words possess! Even evil spirits obey him and flee at his command!" [37]The story of what he had done spread like wildfire throughout the whole region.

Jesus Heals Many People

[38]After leaving the synagogue that day, Jesus went to Simon's home, where he found Simon's mother-in-law very sick with a high fever. "Please heal her," everyone begged. [39]Standing at her bedside, he spoke to the fever, rebuking it, and immediately her temperature returned to normal. She got up at once and prepared a meal for them.

[40]As the sun went down that evening, people throughout the village brought sick family members to Jesus. No matter what their diseases were, the touch of his hand healed every one. [41]Some were possessed by demons; and the demons came out at his command, shouting, "You are the Son of God." But because they knew he was the Messiah, he stopped them and told them to be silent.

Jesus Continues to Preach

[42]Early the next morning Jesus went out into the wilderness. The crowds searched everywhere for him, and when they finally found him, they begged him not to leave them. [43]But he replied, "I must preach the Good News of the Kingdom of God in other places, too, because that is why I was sent." [44]So he continued to travel around, preaching in synagogues throughout Judea.*

CHAPTER **5**
The First Disciples

One day as Jesus was preaching on the shore of the Sea of Galilee,* great crowds pressed in on him to listen to the word of God. [2]He noticed two empty

---

4:18-19 Or *and to proclaim the acceptable year of the Lord.* Isa 61:1-2. **4:44** Some manuscripts read *Galilee.* **5:1** Greek *Lake Gennesaret,* another name for the Sea of Galilee.

boats at the water's edge, for the fishermen had left them and were washing their nets. ³Stepping into one of the boats, Jesus asked Simon, * its owner, to push it out into the water. So he sat in the boat and taught the crowds from there.

⁴When he had finished speaking, he said to Simon, "Now go out where it is deeper and let down your nets, and you will catch many fish."

⁵"Master," Simon replied, "we worked hard all last night and didn't catch a thing. But if you say so, we'll try again." ⁶And this time their nets were so full they began to tear! ⁷A shout for help brought their partners in the other boat, and soon both boats were filled with fish and on the verge of sinking.

⁸When Simon Peter realized what had happened, he fell to his knees before Jesus and said, "Oh, Lord, please leave me—I'm too much of a sinner to be around you." ⁹For he was awestruck by the size of their catch, as were the others with him. ¹⁰His partners, James and John, the sons of Zebedee, were also amazed.

Jesus replied to Simon, "Don't be afraid! From now on you'll be fishing for people!" ¹¹And as soon as they landed, they left everything and followed Jesus.

Jesus Heals a Man with Leprosy

¹²In one of the villages, Jesus met a man with an advanced case of leprosy. When the man saw Jesus, he fell to the ground, face down in the dust, begging to be healed. "Lord," he said, "if you want to, you can make me well again."

¹³Jesus reached out and touched the man. "I want to," he said. "Be healed!" And instantly the leprosy disappeared. ¹⁴Then Jesus instructed him not to tell anyone what had happened. He said, "Go right to the priest and let him examine you. Take along the offering required in the law of Moses for those who have been healed of leprosy, so everyone will have proof of your healing." ¹⁵Yet despite Jesus' instructions, the report of his power spread even faster, and vast crowds came to hear him preach and to be healed of their diseases. ¹⁶But Jesus often withdrew to the wilderness for prayer.

Jesus Heals a Paralyzed Man

¹⁷One day while Jesus was teaching, some Pharisees and teachers of religious law were sitting nearby. (It seemed that these men showed up from every village in all Galilee and Judea, as well as from Jerusalem.) And the Lord's healing power was strongly with Jesus. ¹⁸Some men came carrying a paralyzed man on a sleeping mat. They tried to push through the crowd to Jesus, ¹⁹but they couldn't reach him. So they went up to the roof, took off some tiles, and lowered the sick man down into the crowd, still on his mat, right in front of Jesus. ²⁰Seeing their faith, Jesus said to the man, "Son, your sins are forgiven."

²¹"Who does this man think he is?" the Pharisees and teachers of religious law said to each other. "This is blasphemy! Who but God can forgive sins?"

²²Jesus knew what they were thinking, so he asked them, "Why do you think this is blasphemy? ²³Is it easier to say, 'Your sins are forgiven' or 'Get up and walk'? ²⁴I will prove that I, the Son of Man, have the authority on earth to forgive sins." Then Jesus turned to the paralyzed man and said, "Stand up, take your mat, and go on home, because you are healed!"

²⁵And immediately, as everyone watched, the man jumped to his feet, picked up his mat, and went home praising God. ²⁶Everyone was gripped with great wonder and awe. And they praised God, saying over and over again, "We have seen amazing things today."

Jesus Calls Levi (Matthew)

²⁷Later, as Jesus left the town, he saw a tax-collector named Levi sitting at his tax-collection booth. "Come, be my disciple!" Jesus said to him. ²⁸So Levi got up, left everything, and followed him.

²⁹Soon Levi held a banquet in his home with Jesus as the guest of honor. Many of Levi's fellow tax collectors and other guests were there. ³⁰But the Pharisees and their teachers of religious law complained bitterly to Jesus' disciples, "Why do you eat and drink with such scum*?"

³¹Jesus answered them, "Healthy people don't need a doctor—sick people do. ³²I have come to call sinners to turn from their sins, not to spend my time with those who think they are already good enough."

A Discussion about Fasting

³³The religious leaders complained that Jesus' disciples were feasting instead of fasting. "John the Baptist's disciples always fast and pray," they declared, "and so do the disciples of the Pharisees. Why are yours always feasting?"

³⁴Jesus asked, "Do wedding guests fast while celebrating with the groom? ³⁵Someday he will be taken away from them, and then they will fast."

5:3 *Simon* is called *Peter* in 6:14 and thereafter.   5:30 Greek *with tax collectors and sinners.*

36Then Jesus gave them this illustration: "No one tears a piece of cloth from a new garment and uses it to patch an old garment. For then the new garment would be torn, and the patch wouldn't even match the old garment. 37And no one puts new wine into old wineskins. The new wine would burst the old skins, spilling the wine and ruining the skins. 38New wine must be put into new wineskins. 39But no one who drinks the old wine seems to want the fresh and the new. 'The old is better,' they say."

CHAPTER 6

A Discussion about the Sabbath

One Sabbath day as Jesus was walking through some grainfields, his disciples broke off heads of wheat, rubbed off the husks in their hands, and ate the grains. 2But some Pharisees said, "You shouldn't be doing that! It's against the law to work by harvesting grain on the Sabbath."

3Jesus replied, "Haven't you ever read in the Scriptures what King David did when he and his companions were hungry? 4He went into the house of God, ate the special bread reserved for the priests alone, and then gave some to his friends. That was breaking the law, too." 5And Jesus added, "I, the Son of Man, am master even of the Sabbath."

Jesus Heals on the Sabbath

6On another Sabbath day, a man with a deformed right hand was in the synagogue while Jesus was teaching. 7The teachers of religious law and the Pharisees watched closely to see whether Jesus would heal the man on the Sabbath, because they were eager to find some legal charge to bring against him. 8But Jesus knew their thoughts. He said to the man with the deformed hand, "Come and stand here where everyone can see." So the man came forward. 9Then Jesus said to his critics, "I have a question for you. Is it legal to do good deeds on the Sabbath, or is it a day for doing harm? Is this a day to save life or to destroy it?" 10He looked around at them one by one and then said to the man, "Reach out your hand." The man reached out his hand, and it became normal again! 11At this, the enemies of Jesus were wild with rage and began to discuss what to do with him.

Jesus Chooses the Twelve Apostles

12One day soon afterward Jesus went to a mountain to pray, and he prayed to God all night. 13At daybreak he called together all of his disciples and chose twelve of them to be apostles. Here are their names:

14 Simon (he also called him Peter),
  Andrew (Peter's brother),
  James,
  John,
  Philip,
  Bartholomew,
15 Matthew,
  Thomas,
  James (son of Alphaeus),
  Simon (the Zealot),
16 Judas (son of James),
  Judas Iscariot (who later betrayed him).

Crowds Follow Jesus

17When they came down the slopes of the mountain, the disciples stood with Jesus on a large, level area, surrounded by many of his followers and by the crowds. There were people from all over Judea and from Jerusalem and from as far north as the seacoasts of Tyre and Sidon. 18They had come to hear him and to be healed, and Jesus cast out many evil spirits. 19Everyone was trying to touch him, because healing power went out from him, and they were all cured.

The Beatitudes

20Then Jesus turned to his disciples and said,

"God blesses you who are poor,
  for the Kingdom of God is given to you.
21 God blesses you who are hungry now,
  for you will be satisfied.
God blesses you who weep now,
  for the time will come when you will
  laugh with joy.
22 God blesses you who are hated and
  excluded and mocked and cursed
  because you are identified with me, the
  Son of Man.

23"When that happens, rejoice! Yes, leap for joy! For a great reward awaits you in heaven. And remember, the ancient prophets were also treated that way by your ancestors.

Sorrows Foretold

24 "What sorrows await you who are rich,
  for you have your only happiness now.
25 What sorrows await you who are satisfied
  and prosperous now,
  for a time of awful hunger is before you.

What sorrows await you who laugh carelessly,
for your laughing will turn to mourning and sorrow.
²⁶ What sorrows await you who are praised by the crowds,
for their ancestors also praised false prophets.

Love for Enemies

²⁷ "But if you are willing to listen, I say, love your enemies. Do good to those who hate you. ²⁸Pray for the happiness of those who curse you. Pray for those who hurt you. ²⁹If someone slaps you on one cheek, turn the other cheek. If someone demands your coat, offer your shirt also. ³⁰Give what you have to anyone who asks you for it; and when things are taken away from you, don't try to get them back. ³¹Do for others as you would like them to do for you.

³²"Do you think you deserve credit merely for loving those who love you? Even the sinners do that! ³³And if you do good only to those who do good to you, is that so wonderful? Even sinners do that much! ³⁴And if you lend money only to those who can repay you, what good is that? Even sinners will lend to their own kind for a full return.

³⁵"Love your enemies! Do good to them! Lend to them! And don't be concerned that they might not repay. Then your reward from heaven will be very great, and you will truly be acting as children of the Most High, for he is kind to the unthankful and to those who are wicked. ³⁶You must be compassionate, just as your Father is compassionate.

Don't Condemn Others

³⁷"Stop judging others, and you will not be judged. Stop criticizing others, or it will all come back on you. If you forgive others, you will be forgiven. ³⁸If you give, you will receive. Your gift will return to you in full measure, pressed down, shaken together to make room for more, and running over. Whatever measure you use in giving—large or small—it will be used to measure what is given back to you."

³⁹Then Jesus gave the following illustration: "What good is it for one blind person to lead another? The first one will fall into a ditch and pull the other down also. ⁴⁰A student is not greater than the teacher. But the student who works hard will become like the teacher.

⁴¹"And why worry about a speck in your friend's eye* when you have a log in your own?

⁴²How can you think of saying, 'Friend,* let me help you get rid of that speck in your eye,' when you can't see past the log in your own eye? Hypocrite! First get rid of the log from your own eye; then perhaps you will see well enough to deal with the speck in your friend's eye.

The Tree and Its Fruit

⁴³"A good tree can't produce bad fruit, and a bad tree can't produce good fruit. ⁴⁴A tree is identified by the kind of fruit it produces. Figs never grow on thornbushes or grapes on bramble

6:41 Greek *your brother's eye;* also in 6:42. 6:42 Greek *Brother.*

Trials Test Our Foundation
Read LUKE 6:48-49

From all outward appearances, these homes probably looked alike. They may have even had similar floor plans. The only thing that set them apart was their foundation. This became apparent when the storm hit. In the same way, when the storms of life hit us, the true foundation of our lives will be revealed. Upon which foundation have you built your life?

The Faulty (or Nonexistent) Foundation. The person who builds upon this foundation is known as a "hearer." This individual may be quick to read, listen, or talk about what Jesus has to say in his Word but will fail to apply those teachings to his or her own life. When the storms of life come—and they will—this person will be spiritually weakened and will likely "throw in the towel" on his or her faith because he or she does not have a good foothold.

The Rock Solid Foundation. The person who builds upon this foundation is known as a "doer." This individual not only listens to Jesus' teachings, but follows them in his or her day-to-day life. Such a person will be able to withstand even the most devastating tempest, because he or she is grounded in the teachings of the Lord.

If you find yourself on the faulty foundation, you still have time to remodel. But you are the only architect who can make that change.

For the next note on "Have Courage in Trials," turn to p. 833.

bushes. 45A good person produces good deeds from a good heart, and an evil person produces evil deeds from an evil heart. Whatever is in your heart determines what you say.

Building on a Solid Foundation

46"So why do you call me 'Lord,' when you won't obey me? 47I will show you what it's like when someone comes to me, listens to my teaching, and then obeys me. 48It is like a person who builds a house on a strong foundation laid upon the underlying rock. When the floodwaters rise and break against the house, it stands firm because it is well built. 49But anyone who listens and doesn't obey is like a person who builds a house without a foundation. When the floods sweep down against that house, it will crumble into a heap of ruins."

CHAPTER **7**

Faith of the Roman Officer

When Jesus had finished saying all this, he went back to Capernaum. 2Now the highly valued slave of a Roman officer was sick and near death. 3When the officer heard about Jesus, he sent some respected Jewish leaders to ask him to come and heal his slave. 4So they earnestly begged Jesus to come with them and help the man. "If anyone deserves your help, it is he," they said, 5"for he loves the Jews and even built a synagogue for us."

6So Jesus went with them. But just before they arrived at the house, the officer sent some friends to say, "Lord, don't trouble yourself by coming to my home, for I am not worthy of such an honor. 7I am not even worthy to come and meet you. Just say the word from where you are, and my servant will be healed. 8I know because I am under the authority of my superior officers, and I have authority over my soldiers. I only need to say, 'Go,' and they go, or 'Come,' and they come. And if I say to my slaves, 'Do this or that,' they do it."

9When Jesus heard this, he was amazed. Turning to the crowd, he said, "I tell you, I haven't seen faith like this in all the land of Israel!" 10And when the officer's friends returned to his house, they found the slave completely healed.

Jesus Raises a Widow's Son

11Soon afterward Jesus went with his disciples to the village of Nain, with a great crowd following

him. 12A funeral procession was coming out as he approached the village gate. The boy who had died was the only son of a widow, and many mourners from the village were with her. 13When the Lord saw her, his heart overflowed with compassion. "Don't cry!" he said. 14Then he walked over to the coffin and touched it, and the bearers stopped. "Young man," he said, "get up." 15Then the dead boy sat up and began to talk to those around him! And Jesus gave him back to his mother.

16Great fear swept the crowd, and they praised God, saying, "A mighty prophet has risen among us," and "We have seen the hand of God at work today." 17The report of what Jesus had done that day spread all over Judea and even out across its borders.

Jesus and John the Baptist

18The disciples of John the Baptist told John about everything Jesus was doing. So John called for two of his disciples, 19and he sent them to the Lord to ask him, "Are you the Messiah we've been expecting, or should we keep looking for someone else?"

20John's two disciples found Jesus and said to him, "John the Baptist sent us to ask, 'Are you the Messiah we've been expecting, or should we keep looking for someone else?'"

21At that very time, he cured many people of their various diseases, and he cast out evil spirits and restored sight to the blind. 22Then he told John's disciples, "Go back to John and tell him what you have seen and heard—the blind see, the lame walk, the lepers are cured, the deaf hear, the dead are raised to life, and the Good News is being preached to the poor. 23And tell him, 'God blesses those who are not offended by me.*'"

24After they left, Jesus talked to the crowd about John. "Who is this man in the wilderness that you went out to see? Did you find him weak as a reed, moved by every breath of wind? 25Or were you expecting to see a man dressed in expensive clothes? No, people who wear beautiful clothes and live in luxury are found in palaces, not in the wilderness. 26Were you looking for a prophet? Yes, and he is more than a prophet. 27John is the man to whom the Scriptures refer when they say,

'Look, I am sending my messenger before
   you,
   and he will prepare your way before
      you.'*

7:23 Or *who don't fall away because of me.*   7:27 Mal 3:1.

28I tell you, of all who have ever lived, none is greater than John. Yet even the most insignificant person in the Kingdom of God is greater than he is!"

29When they heard this, all the people, including the unjust tax collectors, agreed that God's plan was right,* for they had been baptized by John. 30But the Pharisees and experts in religious law had rejected God's plan for them, for they had refused John's baptism.

31"How shall I describe this generation?" Jesus asked. "With what will I compare them? 32They are like a group of children playing a game in the public square. They complain to their friends, 'We played wedding songs, and you weren't happy, so we played funeral songs, but you weren't sad.' 33For John the Baptist didn't drink wine and he often fasted, and you say, 'He's demon possessed.' 34And I, the Son of Man, feast and drink, and you say, 'He's a glutton and a drunkard, and a friend of the worst sort of sinners!' 35But wisdom is shown to be right by the lives of those who follow it.*"

Jesus Anointed by a Sinful Woman

36One of the Pharisees asked Jesus to come to his home for a meal, so Jesus accepted the invitation and sat down to eat. 37A certain immoral woman heard he was there and brought a beautiful jar* filled with expensive perfume. 38Then she knelt behind him at his feet, weeping. Her tears fell on his feet, and she wiped them off with her hair. Then she kept kissing his feet and putting perfume on them.

39When the Pharisee who was the host saw what was happening and who the woman was, he said to himself, "This proves that Jesus is no prophet. If God had really sent him, he would know what kind of woman is touching him. She's a sinner!"

40Then Jesus spoke up and answered his thoughts. "Simon," he said to the Pharisee, "I have something to say to you."

"All right, Teacher," Simon replied, "go ahead."

41Then Jesus told him this story: "A man loaned money to two people—five hundred pieces of silver* to one and fifty pieces to the other. 42But neither of them could repay him, so he kindly forgave them both, canceling their debts. Who do you suppose loved him more after that?"

43Simon answered, "I suppose the one for whom he canceled the larger debt."

"That's right," Jesus said. 44Then he turned to the woman and said to Simon, "Look at this woman kneeling here. When I entered your home, you didn't offer me water to wash the dust from my feet, but she has washed them with her tears and wiped them with her hair. 45You didn't give me a kiss of greeting, but she has kissed my feet again and again from the time I first came in. 46You neglected the courtesy of olive oil to anoint my head, but she has anointed my feet with rare perfume. 47I tell you, her sins—and they are many—have been forgiven, so she has shown me much love. But a person who is forgiven little shows only little love." 48Then Jesus said to the woman, "Your sins are forgiven."

49The men at the table said among themselves, "Who does this man think he is, going around forgiving sins?"

50And Jesus said to the woman, "Your faith has saved you; go in peace."

CHAPTER 8

Women Who Followed Jesus

Not long afterward Jesus began a tour of the nearby cities and villages to announce the Good News concerning the Kingdom of God. He took his twelve disciples with him, 2along with some women he had healed and from whom he had cast out evil spirits. Among them were Mary Magdalene, from whom he had cast out seven demons; 3Joanna, the wife of Chuza, Herod's business manager; Susanna; and many others who were contributing from their own resources to support Jesus and his disciples.

Story of the Farmer Scattering Seed

4One day Jesus told this story to a large crowd that had gathered from many towns to hear him: 5"A farmer went out to plant some seed. As he scattered it across his field, some seed fell on a footpath, where it was stepped on, and the birds came and ate it. 6Other seed fell on shallow soil with underlying rock. This seed began to grow, but soon it withered and died for lack of moisture. 7Other seed fell among thorns that shot up and choked out the tender blades. 8Still other seed fell on fertile soil. This seed grew and produced a crop one hundred times as much as had been planted." When he had said this, he called out, "Anyone who is willing to hear should listen and understand!"

9His disciples asked him what the story

7:29 Or praised God.   7:35 Or But wisdom is justified by all her children.   7:37 Greek an alabaster jar.   7:41 Greek 500 denarii. A denarius was the equivalent of a full day's wage.

Perseverance Produces Results Read LUKE 8:15

In verses 4 through 8 of this chapter, Jesus tells the well-known parable of the sower to illustrate four different reactions to his message. The verses following that parable explain what those responses are.

The seed that falls on the roadside represents those who hear the gospel, but who do not allow it to penetrate their hearts and minds (verse 12). The seed that lands on the rocky soil depicts those who hear God's Word and initially receive it with joy, but their "commitment" is shown to be shallow and superficial through time (verse 13). The seed that lands among the thorns portrays those who appear to believe, but who let the cares of this life slowly choke out any growth (verse 14). The seed that falls on the fertile soil is the seed that actually takes root to produce spiritual fruit.

What is the difference between this group of individuals and the rest? The key to their success can be broken down into three steps: (1) They *listen* to God's Word; (2) they *obey* God's Word; and (3) they *persevere* to "produce a huge harvest."

Describing their perseverance in the faith, Jesus uses the Greek word *hupomone,* which speaks of "a patient enduring." It is this type of perseverance that produces spiritual fruit in the form of new believers.

By letting God's Word take root in your heart and life, you will not only grow stronger and be able to withstand the storms of life, but your life will help to draw many others to the Lord Jesus Christ.

For the next note on "Perseverance," turn to p. 1086.

CORNER STONES

---

meant. ¹⁰He replied, "You have been permitted to understand the secrets of the Kingdom of God. But I am using these stories to conceal everything about it from outsiders, so that the Scriptures might be fulfilled:

'They see what I do,
but they don't really see;
they hear what I say,
but they don't understand.'*

¹¹"This is the meaning of the story: The seed is God's message. ¹²The seed that fell on the hard path represents those who hear the message, but then the Devil comes and steals it away and prevents them from believing and being saved. ¹³The rocky soil represents those who hear the message with joy. But like young plants in such soil, their roots don't go very deep. They believe for a while, but they wilt when the hot winds of testing blow. ¹⁴The thorny ground represents those who hear and accept the message, but all too quickly the message is crowded out by the cares and riches and pleasures of this life. And so they never grow into maturity. ¹⁵But the good soil represents honest, good-hearted people who hear God's message, cling to it, and steadily produce a huge harvest.

8:10 Isa 6:9.

Illustration of the Lamp

¹⁶"No one would light a lamp and then cover it up or put it under a bed. No, lamps are mounted in the open, where they can be seen by those entering the house. ¹⁷For everything that is hidden or secret will eventually be brought to light and made plain to all. ¹⁸So be sure to pay attention to what you hear. To those who are open to my teaching, more understanding will be given. But to those who are not listening, even what they think they have will be taken away from them."

The True Family of Jesus

¹⁹Once when Jesus' mother and brothers came to see him, they couldn't get to him because of the crowds. ²⁰Someone told Jesus, "Your mother and your brothers are outside, and they want to see you."

²¹Jesus replied, "My mother and my brothers are all those who hear the message of God and obey it."

Jesus Calms the Storm

²²One day Jesus said to his disciples, "Let's cross over to the other side of the lake." So they got into a boat and started out. ²³On the way across, Jesus lay down for a nap, and while he was

sleeping the wind began to rise. A fierce storm developed that threatened to swamp them, and they were in real danger.

24The disciples woke him up, shouting, "Master, Master, we're going to drown!"

So Jesus rebuked the wind and the raging waves. The storm stopped and all was calm! 25Then he asked them, "Where is your faith?"

And they were filled with awe and amazement. They said to one another, "Who is this man, that even the winds and waves obey him?"

Jesus Heals a Demon-Possessed Man

26So they arrived in the land of the Gerasenes,* across the lake from Galilee. 27As Jesus was climbing out of the boat, a man who was possessed by demons came out to meet him. Homeless and naked, he had lived in a cemetery for a long time. 28As soon as he saw Jesus, he shrieked and fell to the ground before him, screaming, "Why are you bothering me, Jesus, Son of the Most High God? Please, I beg you, don't torture me!" 29For Jesus had already commanded the evil spirit to come out of him. This spirit had often taken control of the man. Even when he was shackled with chains, he simply broke them and rushed out into the wilderness, completely under the demon's power.

30"What is your name?" Jesus asked.

"Legion," he replied—for the man was filled with many demons. 31The demons kept begging Jesus not to send them into the Bottomless Pit. 32A large herd of pigs was feeding on the hillside nearby, and the demons pleaded with him to let them enter into the pigs. Jesus gave them permission. 33So the demons came out of the man and entered the pigs, and the whole herd plunged down the steep hillside into the lake, where they drowned.

34When the herdsmen saw it, they fled to the nearby city and the surrounding countryside, spreading the news as they ran. 35A crowd soon gathered around Jesus, for they wanted to see for themselves what had happened. And they saw the man who had been possessed by demons sitting quietly at Jesus' feet, clothed and sane. And the whole crowd was afraid. 36Then those who had seen what happened told the others how the demon-possessed man had been healed. 37And all the people in that region begged Jesus to go away and leave them alone, for a great wave of fear swept over them.

So Jesus returned to the boat and left, crossing back to the other side of the lake. 38The man who had been demon possessed begged to go, too, but Jesus said, 39"No, go back to your family and tell them all the wonderful things God has done for you." So he went all through the city telling about the great thing Jesus had done for him.

Jesus Heals in Response to Faith

40On the other side of the lake the crowds received Jesus with open arms because they had been waiting for him. 41And now a man named Jairus, a leader of the local synagogue, came and fell down at Jesus' feet, begging him to come home with him. 42His only child was dying, a little girl twelve years old.

As Jesus went with him, he was surrounded by the crowds. 43And there was a woman in the crowd who had had a hemorrhage for twelve years. She had spent everything she had on doctors* and still could find no cure. 44She came up behind Jesus and touched the fringe of his robe. Immediately, the bleeding stopped.

45"Who touched me?" Jesus asked.

Everyone denied it, and Peter said, "Master, this whole crowd is pressing up against you."

46But Jesus told him, "No, someone deliberately touched me, for I felt healing power go out from me." 47When the woman realized that Jesus knew, she began to tremble and fell to her knees before him. The whole crowd heard her explain why she had touched him and that she had been immediately healed. 48"Daughter," he said to her, "your faith has made you well. Go in peace."

49While he was still speaking to her, a messenger arrived from Jairus's home with the message, "Your little girl is dead. There's no use troubling the Teacher now."

50But when Jesus heard what had happened, he said to Jairus, "Don't be afraid. Just trust me, and she will be all right."

51When they arrived at the house, Jesus wouldn't let anyone go in with him except Peter, James, John, and the little girl's father and mother. 52The house was filled with people weeping and wailing, but he said, "Stop the weeping! She isn't dead; she is only asleep."

53But the crowd laughed at him because they all knew she had died. 54Then Jesus took her by the hand and said in a loud voice, "Get up, my child!" 55And at that moment her life returned, and she immediately stood up! Then Jesus told

---

8:26 Some manuscripts read *Gadarenes;* other manuscripts read *Gergesenes.* See Matt 8:28; Mark 5:1.   **8:43** Some manuscripts omit *She had spent everything she had on doctors.*

them to give her something to eat. 56Her parents were overwhelmed, but Jesus insisted that they not tell anyone what had happened.

CHAPTER **9**

Jesus Sends Out the Twelve Apostles

One day Jesus called together his twelve apostles and gave them power and authority to cast out demons and to heal all diseases. 2Then he sent them out to tell everyone about the coming of the Kingdom of God and to heal the sick. 3"Don't even take along a walking stick," he instructed them, "nor a traveler's bag, nor food, nor money. Not even an extra coat. 4When you enter each village, be a guest in only one home. 5If the people of the village won't receive your message when you enter it, shake off its dust from your feet as you leave. It is a sign that you have abandoned that village to its fate."

6So they began their circuit of the villages, preaching the Good News and healing the sick.

Herod's Confusion

7When reports of Jesus' miracles reached Herod Antipas,* he was worried and puzzled because some were saying, "This is John the Baptist come back to life again." 8Others were saying, "It is Elijah or some other ancient prophet risen from the dead."

9"I beheaded John," Herod said, "so who is this man about whom I hear such strange stories?" And he tried to see him.

Jesus Feeds Five Thousand

10When the apostles returned, they told Jesus everything they had done. Then he slipped quietly away with them toward the town of Bethsaida. 11But the crowds found out where he was going, and they followed him. And he welcomed them, teaching them about the Kingdom of God and curing those who were ill. 12Late in the afternoon the twelve disciples came to him and said, "Send the crowds away to the nearby villages and farms, so they can find food and lodging for the night. There is nothing to eat here in this deserted place."

13But Jesus said, "You feed them."

"Impossible!" they protested. "We have only five loaves of bread and two fish. Or are you expecting us to go and buy enough food for this whole crowd?" 14For there were about five thousand men there.

"Just tell them to sit down on the ground in groups of about fifty each," Jesus replied. 15So the people all sat down. 16Jesus took the five loaves and two fish, looked up toward heaven, and asked God's blessing on the food. Breaking the loaves into pieces, he kept giving the bread and fish to the disciples to give to the people. 17They all ate as much as they wanted, and they picked up twelve baskets of leftovers!

Peter's Declaration about Jesus

18One day as Jesus was alone, praying, he came over to his disciples and asked them, "Who do people say I am?"

19"Well," they replied, "some say John the Baptist, some say Elijah, and others say you are one of the other ancient prophets risen from the dead."

20Then he asked them, "Who do you say I am?"

Peter replied, "You are the Messiah sent from God!"

Jesus Predicts His Death

21Jesus warned them not to tell anyone about this. 22"For I, the Son of Man, must suffer many terrible things," he said. "I will be rejected by the leaders, the leading priests, and the teachers of religious law. I will be killed, but three days later I will be raised from the dead."

23Then he said to the crowd, "If any of you wants to be my follower, you must put aside your selfish ambition, shoulder your cross daily, and follow me. 24If you try to keep your life for yourself, you will lose it. But if you give up your life for me, you will find true life. 25And how do you benefit if you gain the whole world but lose or forfeit your own soul in the process? 26If a person is ashamed of me and my message, I, the Son of Man, will be ashamed of that person when I return in my glory and in the glory of the Father and the holy angels. 27And I assure you that some of you standing here right now will not die before you see the Kingdom of God."

The Transfiguration

28About eight days later Jesus took Peter, James, and John to a mountain to pray. 29And as he was praying, the appearance of his face changed, and his clothing became dazzling white. 30Then two men, Moses and Elijah, appeared and began talking with Jesus. 31They were glorious to see. And they were speaking of how he was about to fulfill God's plan by dying in Jerusalem.

32Peter and the others were very drowsy and

9:7 Greek *Herod the tetrarch.* He was a son of King Herod and was ruler over one of the four districts in Palestine.

had fallen asleep. Now they woke up and saw Jesus' glory and the two men standing with him. 33As Moses and Elijah were starting to leave, Peter, not even knowing what he was saying, blurted out, "Master, this is wonderful! We will make three shrines*—one for you, one for Moses, and one for Elijah." 34But even as he was saying this, a cloud came over them; and terror gripped them as it covered them.

35Then a voice from the cloud said, "This is my Son, my Chosen One.* Listen to him." 36When the voice died away, Jesus was there alone. They didn't tell anyone what they had seen until long after this happened.

Jesus Heals a Demon-Possessed Boy

37The next day, after they had come down the mountain, a huge crowd met Jesus. 38A man in the crowd called out to him, "Teacher, look at my boy, who is my only son. 39An evil spirit keeps seizing him, making him scream. It throws him into convulsions so that he foams at the mouth. It is always hitting and injuring him. It hardly ever leaves him alone. 40I begged your disciples to cast the spirit out, but they couldn't do it."

41"You stubborn, faithless people," Jesus said, "how long must I be with you and put up with you? Bring him here." 42As the boy came forward, the demon knocked him to the ground and threw him into a violent convulsion. But Jesus rebuked the evil spirit and healed the boy. Then he gave him back to his father. 43Awe gripped the people as they saw this display of God's power.

Jesus Again Predicts His Death

While everyone was marveling over all the wonderful things he was doing, Jesus said to his disciples, 44"Listen to me and remember what I say. The Son of Man is going to be betrayed." 45But they didn't know what he meant. Its significance was hidden from them, so they could not understand it, and they were afraid to ask him about it.

The Greatest in the Kingdom

46Then there was an argument among them as to which of them would be the greatest. 47But Jesus knew their thoughts, so he brought a little child to his side. 48Then he said to them, "Anyone who welcomes a little child like this on my behalf welcomes me, and anyone who

9:33 Or *shelters*; Greek reads *tabernacles*. 9:35 Some manuscripts read *This is my beloved Son.*

A Disciple Takes Up His or Her Cross and Follows Christ

Read LUKE 9:23-25

Choosing to be a disciple of Jesus Christ takes more than just some verbal affirmation. It takes daily sacrifice and commitment. But when you follow Christ's guidelines for discipleship, you will find that the end result is far better than you could ever have imagined. Here are three things a true disciple of Christ should do:

1. Your Desires Must Take a Backseat to His Desires for Your Life. Being a disciple means recognizing that God's plans for your life are ultimately better than your own. That may mean making some sacrifices in your life, such as spending more of your time in God's Word than in the newspaper, volunteering your services for teaching children's Sunday school, or putting off that vacation to work on a ministry project. Yet, in relinquishing your own plans, you will find yourself drawn closer to the Lord.

2. You Must Take Up Your Cross Daily. Jesus is not simply referring to a religious symbol. At this time in history, a cross symbolized the cruelest of deaths. Anyone seen carrying a cross was headed for a horrible death. Some have misunderstood this statement by Jesus to mean that your cross is your personal inconvenience or problem. In this passage, however, Jesus is talking about the act of dying to yourself. In essence, he wants you to lay yourself at his feet and say, "I want your will more than my own." Once you have taken up that cross, you will experience the abundant life that Jesus promises to those who follow him.

3. You Must Lose Yourself to Save Yourself. Verse 24 may sound like a contradiction when you first read it. Yet, if you truly want to find happiness and fulfillment, you must relinquish full control of your life to Jesus Christ. Paul wrote, "I myself no longer live, but Christ lives in me" (Galatians 2:20). Taking up the cross is no more a burden to the disciple than wings are to a bird, or sails are to a ship. A surrendered life holds the key to a fulfilling walk.

Though it is true that it costs to be a disciple, it is also true that it costs a lot more not to be!

For the next note on "Live as a Disciple," *turn to p. 877.*

What Makes Demons Powerless? Read LUKE 10:1-20

Some Christians cower in fear of Satan and his army of demons. Yet every person who has put his or her faith and trust in Jesus Christ comes under God's protection. In fact, Scripture says that God has placed a wall of protection around us (see Job 1:10, p. 439). So even though demons have real powers, we do not have to be paralyzed at their presence in this world. In fact, we need to recognize the power Christ has given us in the face of our enemy.

As Jesus' disciples found out, demons are drastically limited in their power before the true follower of Christ (verse 17). The power they had was not of themselves but from God. And Jesus was quick to warn them not to rejoice in the power they had been given over demons. Rather, Jesus told them to rejoice that their names were "registered as citizens of heaven" (verse 20).

Today you may find people who allege to have "conversations" with demons and reminding them how powerless they are. Yet even Michael the archangel, when arguing with Satan about Moses' body, did not taunt the devil, but simply said, "The Lord rebuke you" (see Jude 1:9, p. 1115). Our focus should not be upon the power we have been given but on the Giver of that power.

To begin the next topic, turn to p. A15.

CORNER STONES

---

welcomes me welcomes my Father who sent me. Whoever is the least among you is the greatest."

Using the Name of Jesus

⁴⁹John said to Jesus, "Master, we saw someone using your name to cast out demons. We tried to stop him because he isn't in our group."

⁵⁰But Jesus said, "Don't stop him! Anyone who is not against you is for you."

Opposition from Samaritans

⁵¹As the time drew near for his return to heaven, Jesus resolutely set out for Jerusalem. ⁵²He sent messengers ahead to a Samaritan village to prepare for his arrival. ⁵³But they were turned away. The people of the village refused to have anything to do with Jesus because he had resolved to go to Jerusalem. ⁵⁴When James and John heard about it, they said to Jesus, "Lord, should we order down fire from heaven to burn them up*?" ⁵⁵But Jesus turned and rebuked them.* ⁵⁶So they went on to another village.

The Cost of Following Jesus

⁵⁷As they were walking along someone said to Jesus, "I will follow you no matter where you go."

⁵⁸But Jesus replied, "Foxes have dens to live in, and birds have nests, but I, the Son of Man, have no home of my own, not even a place to lay my head."

⁵⁹He said to another person, "Come, be my disciple."

The man agreed, but he said, "Lord, first let me return home and bury my father."

⁶⁰Jesus replied, "Let those who are spiritually dead care for their own dead.* Your duty is to go and preach the coming of the Kingdom of God."

⁶¹Another said, "Yes, Lord, I will follow you, but first let me say good-bye to my family."

⁶²But Jesus told him, "Anyone who puts a hand to the plow and then looks back is not fit for the Kingdom of God."

CHAPTER 10

Jesus Sends Out His Disciples

The Lord now chose seventy-two* other disciples and sent them on ahead in pairs to all the towns and villages he planned to visit. ²These were his instructions to them: "The harvest is so great, but the workers are so few. Pray to the Lord who is in charge of the harvest, and ask him to send out more workers for his fields. ³Go now, and remember that I am sending you out as lambs among wolves. ⁴Don't take along any money, or a traveler's bag, or even an extra pair of sandals. And don't stop to greet anyone on the road.

⁵ "Whenever you enter a home, give it your blessing. ⁶If those who live there are worthy, the blessing will stand; if they are not, the blessing

9:54 Some manuscripts add *as Elijah did.*   9:55 Some manuscripts add *And he said, "You don't realize what your hearts are like. ⁵⁶For the Son of Man has not come to destroy men's lives, but to save them."*   9:60 Greek *Let the dead bury their own dead.*   10:1 Some manuscripts read *70;* also in 10:17.

will return to you. [7]When you enter a town, don't move around from home to home. Stay in one place, eating and drinking what they provide you. Don't hesitate to accept hospitality, because those who work deserve their pay.

[8]"If a town welcomes you, eat whatever is set before you [9]and heal the sick. As you heal them, say, 'The Kingdom of God is near you now.' [10]But if a town refuses to welcome you, go out into its streets and say, [11]'We wipe the dust of your town from our feet as a public announcement of your doom. And don't forget the Kingdom of God is near!' [12]The truth is, even wicked Sodom will be better off than such a town on the judgment day.

[13]"What horrors await you, Korazin and Bethsaida! For if the miracles I did in you had been done in wicked Tyre and Sidon, their people would have sat in deep repentance long ago, clothed in sackcloth and throwing ashes on their heads to show their remorse. [14]Yes, Tyre and Sidon will be better off on the judgment day than you. [15]And you people of Capernaum, will you be exalted to heaven? No, you will be brought down to the place of the dead.*"

[16]Then he said to the disciples, "Anyone who accepts your message is also accepting me. And anyone who rejects you is rejecting me. And anyone who rejects me is rejecting God who sent me."

[17]When the seventy-two disciples returned, they joyfully reported to him, "Lord, even the demons obey us when we use your name!"

[18]"Yes," he told them, "I saw Satan falling from heaven as a flash of lightning! [19]And I have given you authority over all the power of the enemy, and you can walk among snakes and scorpions and crush them. Nothing will injure you. [20]But don't rejoice just because evil spirits obey you; rejoice because your names are registered as citizens of heaven."

Jesus' Prayer of Thanksgiving

[21]Then Jesus was filled with the joy of the Holy Spirit and said, "O Father, Lord of heaven and earth, thank you for hiding the truth from those who think themselves so wise and clever, and for revealing it to the childlike. Yes, Father, it pleased you to do it this way.

[22]"My Father has given me authority over everything. No one really knows the Son except the Father, and no one really knows the Father

except the Son and those to whom the Son chooses to reveal him."

[23]Then when they were alone, he turned to the disciples and said, "How privileged you are to see what you have seen. [24]I tell you, many prophets and kings have longed to see and hear what you have seen and heard, but they could not."

The Most Important Commandment

[25]One day an expert in religious law stood up to test Jesus by asking him this question: "Teacher, what must I do to receive eternal life?"

[26]Jesus replied, "What does the law of Moses say? How do you read it?"

[27]The man answered, " 'You must love the Lord your God with all your heart, all your soul, all your strength, and all your mind.' And, 'Love your neighbor as yourself.' "*

[28]"Right!" Jesus told him. "Do this and you will live!"

[29]The man wanted to justify his actions, so he asked Jesus, "And who is my neighbor?"

Story of the Good Samaritan

[30]Jesus replied with an illustration: "A Jewish man was traveling on a trip from Jerusalem to Jericho, and he was attacked by bandits. They stripped him of his clothes and money, beat him up, and left him half dead beside the road.

[31]"By chance a Jewish priest came along; but when he saw the man lying there, he crossed to the other side of the road and passed him by. [32]A Temple assistant* walked over and looked at him lying there, but he also passed by on the other side.

[33]"Then a despised Samaritan came along, and when he saw the man, he felt deep pity. [34]Kneeling beside him, the Samaritan soothed his wounds with medicine and bandaged them. Then he put the man on his own donkey and took him to an inn, where he took care of him. [35]The next day he handed the innkeeper two pieces of silver* and told him to take care of the man. 'If his bill runs higher than that,' he said, 'I'll pay the difference the next time I am here.'

[36]"Now which of these three would you say was a neighbor to the man who was attacked by bandits?" Jesus asked.

[37]The man replied, "The one who showed him mercy."

Then Jesus said, "Yes, now go and do the same."

10:15 Greek *to Hades.*   10:27 Deut 6:5; Lev 19:18.   10:32 Greek *A Levite.*   10:35 Greek *2 denarii.* A denarius was the equivalent of a full day's wage.

Jesus Visits Martha and Mary

38As Jesus and the disciples continued on their way to Jerusalem, they came to a village where a woman named Martha welcomed them into her home. 39Her sister, Mary, sat at the Lord's feet, listening to what he taught. 40But Martha was worrying over the big dinner she was preparing. She came to Jesus and said, "Lord, doesn't it seem unfair to you that my sister just sits here while I do all the work? Tell her to come and help me."

41But the Lord said to her, "My dear Martha, you are so upset over all these details! 42There is really only one thing worth being concerned about. Mary has discovered it—and I won't take it away from her."

CHAPTER 11
Teaching about Prayer

Once when Jesus had been out praying, one of his disciples came to him as he finished and said, "Lord, teach us to pray, just as John taught his disciples."

2He said, "This is how you should pray:

"Father, may your name be honored.
    May your Kingdom come soon.
3 Give us our food day by day.
4 And forgive us our sins—
    just as we forgive those who have sinned
        against us.
And don't let us yield to temptation.*"

5Then, teaching them more about prayer, he used this illustration: "Suppose you went to a friend's house at midnight, wanting to borrow three loaves of bread. You would say to him, 6'A friend of mine has just arrived for a visit, and I have nothing

for him to eat.' 7He would call out from his bedroom, 'Don't bother me. The door is locked for the night, and we are all in bed. I can't help you this time.' 8But I tell you this—though he won't do it as a friend, if you keep knocking long enough, he will get up and give you what you want so his reputation won't be damaged.*

9"And so I tell you, keep on asking, and you will be given what you ask for. Keep on looking, and you will find. Keep on knocking, and the door will be opened. 10For everyone who asks, receives. Everyone who seeks, finds. And the door is opened to everyone who knocks.

11"You fathers—if your children ask* for a fish, do you give them a snake instead? 12Or if they ask for an egg, do you give them a scorpion? Of course not! 13If you sinful people know how to give good gifts to your children, how much more will your heavenly Father give the Holy Spirit to those who ask him."

Jesus and the Prince of Demons

14One day Jesus cast a demon out of a man who couldn't speak, and the man's voice returned to him. The crowd was amazed, 15but some said, "No wonder he can cast out demons. He gets his power from Satan,* the prince of demons!" 16Trying to test Jesus, others asked for a miraculous sign from heaven to see if he was from God.

17He knew their thoughts, so he said, "Any kingdom at war with itself is doomed. A divided home is also doomed. 18You say I am empowered by the prince of demons.* But if Satan is fighting against himself by empowering me to cast out his demons, how can his kingdom survive? 19And if I am empowered by

11:2-4 Some manuscripts add additional portions of the Lord's Prayer as it reads in Matt 6:9-13.   11:8 Greek *in order to avoid shame,* or *because of [your] persistence.*   11:11 Some manuscripts add *for bread, do you give them a stone? Or if they ask.*   11:15 Greek *Beelzeboul.*
11:18 Greek *by Beelzeboul;* also in 11:19.

OFF AND RUNNING
Balance Christian Service with Worship Read LUKE 10:38-42

It is easy to lose sight of Jesus in the midst of all our activity for him. This story shows the necessity of balancing our work with our worship. Here we see two personalities, represented by Martha and Mary.

Martha: the Doer. Martha was a practical type of person who wanted to get things done. Deep down, she probably wanted to please the Lord, but she made the common mistake of offering work for worship. She received Jesus into her house, then neglected Jesus in the process. Jesus wanted her attention, and she offered him a flurry of activity. As a result, she felt tired and overworked. Like Martha, we can become weary in our work for the Lord when we fail to take time to sit at his feet and draw from the spiritual resources available to us.

Mary: the Worshiper. Mary had a balanced life. She recognized that there was a time to work and a time to

the prince of demons, what about your own followers? They cast out demons, too, so they will judge you for what you have said. 20But if I am casting out demons by the power of God, then the Kingdom of God has arrived among you. 21For when Satan,* who is completely armed, guards his palace, it is safe—22until someone who is stronger attacks and overpowers him, strips him of his weapons, and carries off his belongings.

23"Anyone who isn't helping me opposes me, and anyone who isn't working with me is actually working against me.

24"When an evil spirit leaves a person, it goes into the desert, searching for rest. But when it finds none, it says, 'I will return to the person I came from.' 25So it returns and finds that its former home is all swept and clean. 26Then the spirit finds seven other spirits more evil than itself, and they all enter the person and live there. And so that person is worse off than before."

27As he was speaking, a woman in the crowd called out, "God bless your mother—the womb from which you came, and the breasts that nursed you!"

28He replied, "But even more blessed are all who hear the word of God and put it into practice."

The Sign of Jonah

29As the crowd pressed in on Jesus, he said, "These are evil times, and this evil generation keeps asking me to show them a miraculous sign. But the only sign I will give them is the sign of the prophet Jonah. 30What happened to him was a sign to the people of Nineveh that God had sent him. What happens to me will be a sign

that God has sent me, the Son of Man, to these people.

31"The queen of Sheba* will rise up against this generation on judgment day and condemn it, because she came from a distant land to hear the wisdom of Solomon. And now someone greater than Solomon is here—and you refuse to listen to him. 32The people of Nineveh, too, will rise up against this generation on judgment day and condemn it, because they repented at the preaching of Jonah. And now someone greater than Jonah is here—and you refuse to repent.

Receiving the Light

33"No one lights a lamp and then hides it or puts it under a basket. Instead, it is put on a lampstand to give light to all who enter the room. 34Your eye is a lamp for your body. A pure eye lets sunshine into your soul. But an evil eye shuts out the light and plunges you into darkness. 35Make sure that the light you think you have is not really darkness. 36If you are filled with light, with no dark corners, then your whole life will be radiant, as though a floodlight is shining on you."

Jesus Criticizes the Religious Leaders

37As Jesus was speaking, one of the Pharisees invited him home for a meal. So he went in and took his place at the table. 38His host was amazed to see that he sat down to eat without first performing the ceremonial washing required by Jewish custom. 39Then the Lord said to him, "You Pharisees are so careful to clean the outside of the cup and the dish, but inside you are still filthy—full of greed and wickedness! 40Fools! Didn't God make the inside as well as the outside? 41So give to the needy

11:21 Greek *the strong one*.   11:31 Greek *the queen of the south*.

---

worship, a time to do and a time to pray. She knew when it was time to take off the apron and converse with this most honored guest. While Martha essentially wanted to "get the dishes done," Mary wanted to seize this wonderful moment to sit at the feet of the Creator of the universe.

Few things are as damaging to the Christian life as trying to work for Christ without taking time to commune with him. In his letter to young Timothy, the apostle Paul writes, "Hardworking farmers are the first to enjoy the fruit of their labor" (2 Timothy 2:6). In other words, you can't effectively feed others until you yourself have been fed.

What we do *with* Christ is far more important than what we do *for* Christ. Those who strike a balance between work and worship will keep themselves from spiritual burnout and will become more effective in their service to the Lord.

For the next note on "Priorities," turn to p. 480.

what you greedily possess, and you will be clean all over.

42"But how terrible it will be for you Pharisees! For you are careful to tithe even the tiniest part of your income,* but you completely forget about justice and the love of God. You should tithe, yes, but you should not leave undone the more important things.

43"How terrible it will be for you Pharisees! For how you love the seats of honor in the synagogues and the respectful greetings from everyone as you walk through the markets! 44Yes, how terrible it will be for you. For you are like hidden graves in a field. People walk over them without knowing the corruption they are stepping on."

45"Teacher," said an expert in religious law, "you have insulted us, too, in what you just said."

46"Yes," said Jesus, "how terrible it will be for you experts in religious law! For you crush people beneath impossible religious demands, and you never lift a finger to help ease the burden. 47How terrible it will be for you! For you build tombs for the very prophets your ancestors killed long ago. 48Murderers! You agree with your ancestors that what they did was right. You would have done the same yourselves. 49This is what God in his wisdom said about you:* 'I will send prophets and apostles to them, and they will kill some and persecute the others.'

50"And you of this generation will be held responsible for the murder of all God's prophets from the creation of the world—51from the murder of Abel to the murder of Zechariah, who was killed between the altar and the sanctuary. Yes, it will surely be charged against you.

52"How terrible it will be for you experts in religious law! For you hide the key to knowledge from the people. You don't enter the Kingdom yourselves, and you prevent others from entering."

53As Jesus finished speaking, the Pharisees

11:42 Greek *to tithe the mint and the rue and every herb.*   11:49 Greek *Therefore, the wisdom of God said.*

and teachers of religious law were furious. From that time on they grilled him with many hostile questions, 54trying to trap him into saying something they could use against him.

CHAPTER 12
A Warning against Hypocrisy
Meanwhile, the crowds grew until thousands were milling about and crushing each other. Jesus turned first to his disciples and warned them, "Beware of the yeast of the Pharisees—beware of their hypocrisy. 2The time is coming when everything will be revealed; all that is secret will be made public. 3Whatever you have said in the dark will be heard in the light, and what you have whispered behind closed doors will be shouted from the housetops for all to hear!

4"Dear friends, don't be afraid of those who want to kill you. They can only kill the body; they cannot do any more to you. 5But I'll tell you whom to fear. Fear God, who has the power to kill people and then throw them into hell.

6"What is the price of five sparrows? A couple of pennies? Yet God does not forget a single one of them. 7And the very hairs on your head are all numbered. So don't be afraid; you are more valuable to him than a whole flock of sparrows.

8"And I assure you of this: If anyone acknowledges me publicly here on earth, I, the Son of Man, will openly acknowledge that person in the presence of God's angels. 9But if anyone denies me here on earth, I will deny that person before God's angels. 10Yet those who speak against the Son of Man may be forgiven, but anyone who speaks blasphemies against the Holy Spirit will never be forgiven.

11"And when you are brought to trial in the synagogues and before rulers and authorities, don't worry about what to say in your defense, 12for the Holy Spirit will teach you what needs to be said even as you are standing there."

OFF AND RUNNING
Don't Neglect Your Spiritual Health Read LUKE 12:16-21

As this parable illustrates, it is easy to allow other pursuits to cloud our spiritual vision. We have to make enough money to get that new car, buy that house, or take that dream vacation. Sometimes we can get so caught up in chasing after money and success that we leave God out of the equation altogether.

Story of the Rich Fool

13Then someone called from the crowd, "Teacher, please tell my brother to divide our father's estate with me."

14Jesus replied, "Friend, who made me a judge over you to decide such things as that?" 15Then he said, "Beware! Don't be greedy for what you don't have. Real life is not measured by how much we own."

16And he gave an illustration: "A rich man had a fertile farm that produced fine crops. 17In fact, his barns were full to overflowing. 18So he said, 'I know! I'll tear down my barns and build bigger ones. Then I'll have room enough to store everything. 19And I'll sit back and say to myself, My friend, you have enough stored away for years to come. Now take it easy! Eat, drink, and be merry!'

20"But God said to him, 'You fool! You will die this very night. Then who will get it all?'

21"Yes, a person is a fool to store up earthly wealth but not have a rich relationship with God."

Teaching about Money and Possessions

22Then turning to his disciples, Jesus said, "So I tell you, don't worry about everyday life— whether you have enough food to eat or clothes to wear. 23For life consists of far more than food and clothing. 24Look at the ravens. They don't need to plant or harvest or put food in barns because God feeds them. And you are far more valuable to him than any birds! 25Can all your worries add a single moment to your life? Of course not! 26And if worry can't do little things like that, what's the use of worrying over bigger things?

27"Look at the lilies and how they grow. They don't work or make their clothing, yet Solomon in all his glory was not dressed as beautifully as they are. 28And if God cares so wonderfully for flowers that are here today and gone tomorrow, won't he more surely care for you? You have so little faith! 29And don't worry about food—

12:38 Greek *in the second or third watch.*

what to eat and drink. Don't worry whether God will provide it for you. 30These things dominate the thoughts of most people, but your Father already knows your needs. 31He will give you all you need from day to day if you make the Kingdom of God your primary concern.

32"So don't be afraid, little flock. For it gives your Father great happiness to give you the Kingdom.

33"Sell what you have and give to those in need. This will store up treasure for you in heaven! And the purses of heaven have no holes in them. Your treasure will be safe—no thief can steal it and no moth can destroy it. 34Wherever your treasure is, there your heart and thoughts will also be.

Be Ready for the Lord's Coming

35"Be dressed for service and well prepared, 36as though you were waiting for your master to return from the wedding feast. Then you will be ready to open the door and let him in the moment he arrives and knocks. 37There will be special favor for those who are ready and waiting for his return. I tell you, he himself will seat them, put on an apron, and serve them as they sit and eat! 38He may come in the middle of the night or just before dawn.* But whenever he comes, there will be special favor for his servants who are ready!

39"Know this: A homeowner who knew exactly when a burglar was coming would not permit the house to be broken into. 40You must be ready all the time, for the Son of Man will come when least expected."

41Peter asked, "Lord, is this illustration just for us or for everyone?"

42And the Lord replied, "I'm talking to any faithful, sensible servant to whom the master gives the responsibility of managing his household and feeding his family. 43If the master returns and finds that the servant has done a good job, there will be a reward. 44I assure you, the master will put that servant in charge of all he

---

God's answer to this dilemma is for us to seek first his reign and will in our lives. Then everything else will come into balance. It is simple. The more you channel your energy, your ambition, and your life into this one, holy pursuit, the less obsessed you will be with the cares and concerns of this world. For the sake of your spiritual health, seek God's kingdom in all that you do. Failure to do so will only guarantee confusion, failure, emptiness, and dissatisfaction.

To begin the next topic, turn to p. A39.

The More We Know, the Greater Our Responsibility Will Be
Read LUKE 12:48

According to this verse, you will be held accountable for what you know. This can refer to your personal behavior, as well as the work you do for God's Kingdom. For instance, you now know that you should not lie, cheat, steal, or live an immoral lifestyle. If you disregard God's commands, you know that you will reap the consequences. On the other hand, you must also share your spiritual knowledge with others—especially those who are on their way to spending eternity in hell. Our attitude should be as Paul's, who wrote, "For we speak as messengers who have been approved by God to be entrusted with the Good News. Our purpose is to please God, not people. He is the one who examines the motives of our hearts" (1 Thessalonians 2:4).

What are you doing with the spiritual knowledge and insight God has given you? Are you using it to his glory?

For the next note on "Accountability," turn to p. 648.

CORNER STONES

---

owns. ⁴⁵But if the servant thinks, 'My master won't be back for a while,' and begins oppressing the other servants, partying, and getting drunk—⁴⁶well, the master will return unannounced and unexpected. He will tear the servant apart and banish him with the unfaithful. ⁴⁷The servant will be severely punished, for though he knew his duty, he refused to do it.

⁴⁸"But people who are not aware that they are doing wrong will be punished only lightly. Much is required from those to whom much is given, and much more is required from those to whom much more is given.

Jesus Causes Division

⁴⁹"I have come to bring fire to the earth, and I wish that my task were already completed! ⁵⁰There is a terrible baptism ahead of me, and I am under a heavy burden until it is accomplished. ⁵¹Do you think I have come to bring peace to the earth? No, I have come to bring strife and division! ⁵²From now on families will be split apart, three in favor of me, and two against—or the other way around. ⁵³There will be a division between father and son, mother and daughter, mother-in-law and daughter-in-law."

⁵⁴Then Jesus turned to the crowd and said, "When you see clouds beginning to form in the west, you say, 'Here comes a shower.' And you are right. ⁵⁵When the south wind blows, you say, 'Today will be a scorcher.' And it is. ⁵⁶You hypocrites! You know how to interpret the appearance of the earth and the sky, but you can't interpret these present times.

⁵⁷"Why can't you decide for yourselves what is right? ⁵⁸If you are on the way to court and you meet your accuser, try to settle the matter before it reaches the judge, or you may be sentenced and handed over to an officer and thrown in jail. ⁵⁹And if that happens, you won't be free again until you have paid the last penny."

CHAPTER 13
A Call to Repentance

About this time Jesus was informed that Pilate had murdered some people from Galilee as they were sacrificing at the Temple in Jerusalem. ²"Do you think those Galileans were worse sinners than other people from Galilee?" he asked. "Is that why they suffered? ³Not at all! And you will also perish unless you turn from your evil ways and turn to God. ⁴And what about the eighteen men who died when the Tower of Siloam fell on them? Were they the worst sinners in Jerusalem? ⁵No, and I tell you again that unless you repent, you will also perish."

Illustration of the Barren Fig Tree

⁶Then Jesus used this illustration: "A man planted a fig tree in his garden and came again and again to see if there was any fruit on it, but he was always disappointed. ⁷Finally, he said to his gardener, 'I've waited three years, and there hasn't been a single fig! Cut it down. It's taking up space we can use for something else.'

⁸"The gardener answered, 'Give it one more

chance. Leave it another year, and I'll give it special attention and plenty of fertilizer. ⁹If we get figs next year, fine. If not, you can cut it down.'"

Jesus Heals on the Sabbath

¹⁰One Sabbath day as Jesus was teaching in a synagogue, ¹¹he saw a woman who had been crippled by an evil spirit. She had been bent double for eighteen years and was unable to stand up straight. ¹²When Jesus saw her, he called her over and said, "Woman, you are healed of your sickness!" ¹³Then he touched her, and instantly she could stand straight. How she praised and thanked God!

¹⁴But the leader in charge of the synagogue was indignant that Jesus had healed her on the Sabbath day. "There are six days of the week for working," he said to the crowd. "Come on those days to be healed, not on the Sabbath."

¹⁵But the Lord replied, "You hypocrite! You work on the Sabbath day! Don't you untie your ox or your donkey from their stalls on the Sabbath and lead them out for water? ¹⁶Wasn't it necessary for me, even on the Sabbath day, to free this dear woman* from the bondage in which Satan has held her for eighteen years?" ¹⁷This shamed his enemies. And all the people rejoiced at the wonderful things he did.

Illustration of the Mustard Seed

¹⁸Then Jesus said, "What is the Kingdom of God like? How can I illustrate it? ¹⁹It is like a tiny mustard seed planted in a garden; it grows and becomes a tree, and the birds come and find shelter among its branches."

Illustration of the Yeast

²⁰He also asked, "What else is the Kingdom of God like? ²¹It is like yeast used by a woman making bread. Even though she used a large amount* of flour, the yeast permeated every part of the dough."

The Narrow Door

²²Jesus went through the towns and villages, teaching as he went, always pressing on toward Jerusalem. ²³Someone asked him, "Lord, will only a few be saved?"

He replied, ²⁴"The door to heaven is narrow. Work hard to get in, because many will try to enter, ²⁵but when the head of the house has locked the door, it will be too late. Then you will

stand outside knocking and pleading, 'Lord, open the door for us!' But he will reply, 'I do not know you.' ²⁶You will say, 'But we ate and drank with you, and you taught in our streets.' ²⁷And he will reply, 'I tell you, I don't know you. Go away, all you who do evil.'

²⁸"And there will be great weeping and gnashing of teeth, for you will see Abraham, Isaac, Jacob, and all the prophets within the Kingdom of God, but you will be thrown out. ²⁹Then people will come from all over the world to take their places in the Kingdom of God. ³⁰And note this: Some who are despised now will be greatly honored then; and some who are greatly honored now will be despised then.*"

Jesus Grieves over Jerusalem

³¹A few minutes later some Pharisees said to him, "Get out of here if you want to live, because Herod Antipas wants to kill you!"

³²Jesus replied, "Go tell that fox that I will keep on casting out demons and doing miracles of healing today and tomorrow; and the third day I will accomplish my purpose. ³³Yes, today, tomorrow, and the next day I must proceed on my way. For it wouldn't do for a prophet of God to be killed except in Jerusalem!

³⁴"O Jerusalem, Jerusalem, the city that kills the prophets and stones God's messengers! How often I have wanted to gather your children together as a hen protects her chicks beneath her wings, but you wouldn't let me. ³⁵And now look, your house is left to you empty. And you will never see me again until you say, 'Bless the one who comes in the name of the Lord!'*"

CHAPTER **14**
Jesus Heals on the Sabbath

One Sabbath day Jesus was in the home of a leader of the Pharisees. The people were watching him closely, ²because there was a man there whose arms and legs were swollen.* ³Jesus asked the Pharisees and experts in religious law, "Well, is it permitted in the law to heal people on the Sabbath day, or not?" ⁴When they refused to answer, Jesus touched the sick man and healed him and sent him away. ⁵Then he turned to them and asked, "Which of you doesn't work on the Sabbath? If your son* or your cow falls into a pit, don't you proceed at once to get him out?" ⁶Again they had no answer.

13:16 Greek *this woman, a daughter of Abraham.*   13:21 Greek *3 measures.*   13:30 Greek *Some are last who will be first, and some are first who will be last.*   13:35 Ps 118:26.   14:2 Traditionally translated *who had dropsy.*   14:5 Some manuscripts read *donkey.*

Jesus Teaches about Humility

7When Jesus noticed that all who had come to the dinner were trying to sit near the head of the table, he gave them this advice: 8"If you are invited to a wedding feast, don't always head for the best seat. What if someone more respected than you has also been invited? 9The host will say, 'Let this person sit here instead.' Then you will be embarrassed and will have to take whatever seat is left at the foot of the table!

10"Do this instead—sit at the foot of the table. Then when your host sees you, he will come and say, 'Friend, we have a better place than this for you!' Then you will be honored in front of all the other guests. 11For the proud will be humbled, but the humble will be honored."

12Then he turned to his host. "When you put on a luncheon or a dinner," he said, "don't invite your friends, brothers, relatives, and rich neighbors. For they will repay you by inviting you back. 13Instead, invite the poor, the crippled, the lame, and the blind. 14Then at the resurrection of the godly, God will reward you for inviting those who could not repay you."

Story of the Great Feast

15Hearing this, a man sitting at the table with Jesus exclaimed, "What a privilege it would be to have a share in the Kingdom of God!"

16Jesus replied with this illustration: "A man prepared a great feast and sent out many invitations. 17When all was ready, he sent his servant around to notify the guests that it was time for them to come. 18But they all began making excuses. One said he had just bought a field and wanted to inspect it, so he asked to be excused. 19Another said he had just bought five pair of oxen and wanted to try them out. 20Another had just been married, so he said he couldn't come.

21"The servant returned and told his master what they had said. His master was angry and said, 'Go quickly into the streets and alleys of the city and invite the poor, the crippled, the lame, and the blind.' 22After the servant had done this, he reported, 'There is still room for more.' 23So his master said, 'Go out into the country lanes and behind the hedges and urge anyone you find to come, so that the house will be full. 24For none of those I invited first will get even the smallest taste of what I had prepared for them.'"

The Cost of Being a Disciple

25Great crowds were following Jesus. He turned around and said to them, 26"If you want to be

14:26 Greek *you must hate.*

my follower you must love me more than* your own father and mother, wife and children, brothers and sisters—yes, more than your own life. Otherwise, you cannot be my disciple. 27And you cannot be my disciple if you do not carry your own cross and follow me.

28"But don't begin until you count the cost. For who would begin construction of a building without first getting estimates and then checking to see if there is enough money to pay the bills? 29Otherwise, you might complete only the foundation before running out of funds. And then how everyone would laugh at you! 30They would say, 'There's the person who started that building and ran out of money before it was finished!'

31"Or what king would ever dream of going to war without first sitting down with his counselors and discussing whether his army of ten thousand is strong enough to defeat the twenty thousand soldiers who are marching against him? 32If he is not able, then while the enemy is still far away, he will send a delegation to discuss terms of peace. 33So no one can become my disciple without giving up everything for me.

34"Salt is good for seasoning. But if it loses its flavor, how do you make it salty again? 35Flavorless salt is good neither for the soil nor for fertilizer. It is thrown away. Anyone who is willing to hear should listen and understand!"

CHAPTER 15

Story of the Lost Sheep

Tax collectors and other notorious sinners often came to listen to Jesus teach. 2This made the Pharisees and teachers of religious law complain that he was associating with such despicable people—even eating with them!

3So Jesus used this illustration: 4"If you had one hundred sheep, and one of them strayed away and was lost in the wilderness, wouldn't you leave the ninety-nine others to go and search for the lost one until you found it? 5And then you would joyfully carry it home on your shoulders. 6When you arrived, you would call together your friends and neighbors to rejoice with you because your lost sheep was found. 7In the same way, heaven will be happier over one lost sinner who returns to God than over ninety-nine others who are righteous and haven't strayed away!

Story of the Lost Coin

8 "Or suppose a woman has ten valuable silver coins* and loses one. Won't she light a lamp and look in every corner of the house and sweep every nook and cranny until she finds it? 9And when she finds it, she will call in her friends and neighbors to rejoice with her because she has found her lost coin. 10In the same way, there is joy in the presence of God's angels when even one sinner repents."

Story of the Lost Son

11To illustrate the point further, Jesus told them this story: "A man had two sons. 12The younger son told his father, 'I want my share of your estate now, instead of waiting until you die.' So his father agreed to divide his wealth between his sons.

13 "A few days later this younger son packed all his belongings and took a trip to a distant land, and there he wasted all his money on wild living. 14About the time his money ran out, a great famine swept over the land, and he began to starve. 15He persuaded a local farmer to hire him to feed his pigs. 16The boy became so hungry that even the pods he was feeding the pigs looked good to him. But no one gave him anything.

17 "When he finally came to his senses, he said to himself, 'At home even the hired men have food enough to spare, and here I am, dying of hunger! 18I will go home to my father and say, "Father, I have sinned against both heaven and you, 19and I am no longer worthy of being called your son. Please take me on as a hired man." '

20 "So he returned home to his father. And while he was still a long distance away, his father saw him coming. Filled with love and compassion, he ran to his son, embraced him, and kissed him. 21His son said to him, 'Father, I have sinned against both heaven and you, and I am no longer worthy of being called your son.*'

22 "But his father said to the servants, 'Quick! Bring the finest robe in the house and put it on him. Get a ring for his finger, and sandals for his feet. 23And kill the calf we have been fattening in the pen. We must celebrate with a feast, 24for this son of mine was dead and has now returned to life. He was lost, but now he is found.' So the party began.

25 "Meanwhile, the older son was in the fields working. When he returned home, he heard

15:8 Greek *10 drachmas.* A drachma was the equivalent of a full day's wage. 15:21 Some manuscripts add *Please take me on as a hired man.*

music and dancing in the house, 26and he asked one of the servants what was going on. 27'Your brother is back,' he was told, 'and your father has killed the calf we were fattening and has prepared a great feast. We are celebrating because of his safe return.'

28 "The older brother was angry and wouldn't go in. His father came out and begged him, 29but he replied, 'All these years I've worked hard for you and never once refused to do a single thing you told me to. And in all that time you never gave me even one young goat for a feast with my friends. 30Yet when this son of yours comes back

A Disciple Counts the Cost
Read LUKE 14:25-33

At the time Jesus said these words, he had become quite a popular figure. Crowds flocked around him wherever he went. But they did not always do so for the right reasons. Consequently, Jesus directed his solemn and searching words to those people who followed him for selfish purposes or because it was the thing to do.

Likewise, Jesus doesn't want you to follow him only when it is convenient or socially acceptable. He wants you to be his disciple for the long haul—regardless of how easy or difficult it might be. That is why you must count the cost of being a true disciple of Jesus Christ. What does it mean to count the cost? The following four questions will give you a concrete idea:

• Do you love Jesus more than anyone or anything else in your life?
• Do you love Jesus and desire his will for your life over your own?
• Are you willing to accept ridicule and sacrifice for the cause of Christ?
• Will you commit to following Jesus, whether or not it is popular or expedient?

If you have carefully examined your heart, counted the cost, and can truthfully answer yes to these questions, then you are on the road to discipleship and are now ready to spend the rest of your life as his disciple and friend.

Jesus is not looking for half-hearted followers. He wants wholehearted commitment.

For the next note on "Live as a Disciple," turn to p. 911.

What Is Hell Like? Read LUKE 16:19-31

Jesus gave us a rare glimpse of life in hell in this parable. Here is what he revealed about this dark place of punishment.

People's Lifestyles on Earth Will Not Be the Same in Eternity. Things dramatically changed for the rich man when he passed into eternity. Because he did not have a personal relationship with God, he immediately entered into the dark torment of hell, penniless and in agony. Those whose hearts are not right with God face the same future as the rich man in this story. After death they will be held in hell until they are brought before God at what is called the Great White Throne Judgment (see "Why Would a Good God Send Anyone to Hell?" p. 1073).

Hell Is a Place of Flames and Torment. The rich man in this parable experienced unrelenting heat and an unquenchable thirst. He was in so much agony that he called out to Abraham to have Lazarus come and dip his finger in water to cool his (the rich man's) tongue. If you have ever been badly burned, then you have an idea of the torment that awaits those who will spend eternity in hell. Add to that darkness and isolation, and you have an incredibly bleak scenario.

People Do Not "Have a Good Time" in Hell. Some people say, "I want to go to hell. All of my friends will be there." That may be true. But hell holds no parties. As this parable states, the rich man is so alarmed by his situation that he wants Lazarus to go and warn his brothers, so that they will not join him in torment.

If you want to know about the reality of hell, you don't need some tabloid account of someone who has supposedly had an out-of-body experience. You can study the words of the living God, who died and rose again, and who can tell you exactly what to expect in eternity. Our acceptance or rejection of his words determines on which side of the divide we will spend the rest of our lives.

For the next note on "What Is Hell?" turn to p. 1132.

CORNER STONES

---

after squandering your money on prostitutes, you celebrate by killing the finest calf we have.'

31 "His father said to him, 'Look, dear son, you and I are very close, and everything I have is yours. 32We had to celebrate this happy day. For your brother was dead and has come back to life! He was lost, but now he is found!'"

CHAPTER 16
Story of the Shrewd Manager

Jesus told this story to his disciples: "A rich man hired a manager to handle his affairs, but soon a rumor went around that the manager was thoroughly dishonest. 2So his employer called him in and said, 'What's this I hear about your stealing from me? Get your report in order, because you are going to be dismissed.'

3 "The manager thought to himself, 'Now what? I'm through here, and I don't have the strength to go out and dig ditches, and I'm too proud to beg. 4I know just the thing! And then I'll have plenty of friends to take care of me when I leave!'

5 "So he invited each person who owed money to his employer to come and discuss the situation. He asked the first one, 'How much do you owe him?' 6The man replied, 'I owe him eight hundred gallons of olive oil.' So the manager told him, 'Tear up that bill and write another one for four hundred gallons.*'

7 " 'And how much do you owe my employer?' he asked the next man. 'A thousand bushels of wheat,' was the reply. 'Here,' the manager said, 'take your bill and replace it with one for only eight hundred bushels.*'

8 "The rich man had to admire the dishonest rascal for being so shrewd. And it is true that the citizens of this world are more shrewd than the godly are. 9I tell you, use your worldly resources to

16:6 Greek *100 baths . . . 50 [baths].*   16:7 Greek *100 korous . . . 80 [korous].*

benefit others and make friends. In this way, your generosity stores up a reward for you in heaven.*

10"Unless you are faithful in small matters, you won't be faithful in large ones. If you cheat even a little, you won't be honest with greater responsibilities. 11And if you are untrustworthy about worldly wealth, who will trust you with the true riches of heaven? 12And if you are not faithful with other people's money, why should you be trusted with money of your own?

13"No one can serve two masters. For you will hate one and love the other, or be devoted to one and despise the other. You cannot serve both God and money."

14The Pharisees, who dearly loved their money, naturally scoffed at all this. 15Then he said to them, "You like to look good in public, but God knows your evil hearts. What this world honors is an abomination in the sight of God.

16"Until John the Baptist began to preach, the laws of Moses and the messages of the prophets were your guides. But now the Good News of the Kingdom of God is preached, and eager multitudes are forcing their way in. 17But that doesn't mean that the law has lost its force in even the smallest point. It is stronger and more permanent than heaven and earth.

18"Anyone who divorces his wife and marries someone else commits adultery, and anyone who marries a divorced woman commits adultery."

The Rich Man and Lazarus

19Jesus said, "There was a certain rich man who was splendidly clothed and who lived each day in luxury. 20At his door lay a diseased beggar named Lazarus. 21As Lazarus lay there longing for scraps from the rich man's table, the dogs would come and lick his open sores. 22Finally, the beggar died and was carried by the angels to be with Abraham.* The rich man also died and was buried, 23and his soul went to the place of the dead.* There, in torment, he saw Lazarus in the far distance with Abraham.

24"The rich man shouted, 'Father Abraham, have some pity! Send Lazarus over here to dip the tip of his finger in water and cool my tongue, because I am in anguish in these flames.'

25"But Abraham said to him, 'Son, remember that during your lifetime you had everything you wanted, and Lazarus had nothing. So now he is here being comforted, and you are in anguish. 26And besides, there is a great chasm separating us. Anyone who wanted to cross over to you

from here is stopped at its edge, and no one there can cross over to us.'

27"Then the rich man said, 'Please, Father Abraham, send him to my father's home. 28For I have five brothers, and I want him to warn them about this place of torment so they won't have to come here when they die.'

29"But Abraham said, 'Moses and the prophets have warned them. Your brothers can read their writings anytime they want to.'

30"The rich man replied, 'No, Father Abraham! But if someone is sent to them from the dead, then they will turn from their sins.'

31"But Abraham said, 'If they won't listen to Moses and the prophets, they won't listen even if someone rises from the dead.'"

CHAPTER 17

Teachings about Forgiveness and Faith

One day Jesus said to his disciples, "There will always be temptations to sin, but how terrible it will be for the person who does the tempting. 2It would be better to be thrown into the sea with a large millstone tied around the neck than to face the punishment in store for harming one of these little ones. 3I am warning you! If another believer* sins, rebuke him; then if he repents, forgive him. 4Even if he wrongs you seven times a day and each time turns again and asks forgiveness, forgive him."

5One day the apostles said to the Lord, "We need more faith; tell us how to get it."

6"Even if you had faith as small as a mustard seed," the Lord answered, "you could say to this mulberry tree, 'May God uproot you and throw you into the sea,' and it would obey you!

7"When a servant comes in from plowing or taking care of sheep, he doesn't just sit down and eat. 8He must first prepare his master's meal and serve him his supper before eating his own. 9And the servant is not even thanked, because he is merely doing what he is supposed to do. 10In the same way, when you obey me you should say, 'We are not worthy of praise. We are servants who have simply done our duty.'"

Ten Healed of Leprosy

11As Jesus continued on toward Jerusalem, he reached the border between Galilee and Samaria. 12As he entered a village there, ten lepers stood at a distance, 13crying out, "Jesus, Master, have mercy on us!"

16:9 Or Then when you run out at the end of this life, your friends will welcome you into eternal homes.   16:22 Greek into Abraham's bosom.   16:23 Greek to Hades.   17:3 Greek your brother.

¹⁴He looked at them and said, "Go show yourselves to the priests." And as they went, their leprosy disappeared.

¹⁵One of them, when he saw that he was healed, came back to Jesus, shouting, "Praise God, I'm healed!" ¹⁶He fell face down on the ground at Jesus' feet, thanking him for what he had done. This man was a Samaritan.

¹⁷Jesus asked, "Didn't I heal ten men? Where are the other nine? ¹⁸Does only this foreigner return to give glory to God?" ¹⁹And Jesus said to the man, "Stand up and go. Your faith has made you well."

The Coming of the Kingdom

²⁰One day the Pharisees asked Jesus, "When will the Kingdom of God come?"

Jesus replied, "The Kingdom of God isn't ushered in with visible signs.* ²¹You won't be able to say, 'Here it is!' or 'It's over there!' For the Kingdom of God is among you.*"

²²Later he talked again about this with his disciples. "The time is coming when you will long to share in the days of the Son of Man, but you won't be able to," he said. ²³"Reports will reach you that the Son of Man has returned and that he is in this place or that. Don't believe such reports or go out to look for him. ²⁴For when the Son of Man returns, you will know it beyond all doubt. It will be as evident as the lightning that flashes across the sky. ²⁵But first the Son of Man must suffer terribly* and be rejected by this generation.

²⁶"When the Son of Man returns, the world will be like the people were in Noah's day. ²⁷In those days before the flood, the people enjoyed banquets and parties and weddings right up to the time Noah entered his boat and the flood came to destroy them all.

²⁸"And the world will be as it was in the days of Lot. People went about their daily business— eating and drinking, buying and selling, farming and building—²⁹until the morning Lot left Sodom. Then fire and burning sulfur rained down from heaven and destroyed them all. ³⁰Yes, it will be 'business as usual' right up to the hour when the Son of Man returns.* ³¹On that day a person outside the house* must not go into the house to pack. A person in the field must not return to town. ³²Remember what happened to Lot's wife! ³³Whoever clings to this life will lose it, and whoever loses this life will save it. ³⁴That night two people will be asleep in one bed; one will be taken away, and the other will be left. ³⁵Two women will be grinding flour together at the mill; one will be taken, the other left.*"

³⁷"Lord, where will this happen?" the disciples asked.

Jesus replied, "Just as the gathering of vultures shows there is a carcass nearby, so these signs indicate that the end is near."*

CHAPTER 18

Story of the Persistent Widow

One day Jesus told his disciples a story to illustrate their need for constant prayer and to show them that they must never give up. ²"There was a judge in a certain city," he said, "who was a godless man with great contempt for everyone. ³A widow of that city came to him repeatedly, appealing for justice against someone who had harmed her. ⁴The judge ignored her for a while, but eventually she wore him out. 'I fear neither God nor man,' he said to himself, ⁵'but this woman is driving me crazy. I'm going to see that she gets justice, because she is wearing me out with her constant requests!'"

⁶Then the Lord said, "Learn a lesson from this evil judge. ⁷Even he rendered a just decision

---

17:20 Or *by your speculations.* 17:21 Or *within you.* 17:25 Or *suffer many things.* 17:30 Or *on the day the Son of Man is revealed.*
17:31 Greek *on the roof.* 17:35 Some manuscripts add verse 36, *Two men will be working in the field; one will be taken, the other left.*
17:37 Greek *Wherever the carcass is, the vultures gather.*

OFF AND RUNNING ▰▰▰ ▰ ▰ ▰

Pray Persistently Read LUKE 18:1-8

This parable illustrates the need for persistence in prayer. Interestingly enough, Jesus chose two unlikely characters for this parable: a poor, widowed woman, and a corrupt judge. These characters hardly seem like the proper comparison for describing our relationship with God, but Jesus wants to us to focus upon several important contrasts in this story:

• The widow had to go to a corrupt judge. . . . We can go to our heavenly Father (see Ephesians 3:14, p. 1025).
• The widow was a stranger. . . . We are God's children (see John 1:12, p. 893).

in the end, so don't you think God will surely give justice to his chosen people who plead with him day and night? Will he keep putting them off? 8I tell you, he will grant justice to them quickly! But when I, the Son of Man, return, how many will I find who have faith?"

Story of the Pharisee and Tax Collector
9Then Jesus told this story to some who had great self-confidence and scorned everyone else: 10"Two men went to the Temple to pray. One was a Pharisee, and the other was a dishonest tax collector. 11The proud Pharisee stood by himself and prayed this prayer: 'I thank you, God, that I am not a sinner like everyone else, especially like that tax collector over there! For I never cheat, I don't sin, I don't commit adultery, 12I fast twice a week, and I give you a tenth of my income.'

13"But the tax collector stood at a distance and dared not even lift his eyes to heaven as he prayed. Instead, he beat his chest in sorrow, saying, 'O God, be merciful to me, for I am a sinner.' 14I tell you, this sinner, not the Pharisee, returned home justified before God. For the proud will be humbled, but the humble will be honored."

Jesus Blesses the Children
15One day some parents brought their little children to Jesus so he could touch them and bless them, but the disciples told them not to bother him. 16Then Jesus called for the children and said to the disciples, "Let the children come to me. Don't stop them! For the Kingdom of God belongs to such as these. 17I assure you, anyone who doesn't have their kind of faith will never get into the Kingdom of God."

The Rich Man
18Once a religious leader asked Jesus this question: "Good teacher, what should I do to get eternal life?"

18:20 Exod 20:12-16; Deut 5:16-20.

19"Why do you call me good?" Jesus asked him. "Only God is truly good. 20But as for your question, you know the commandments: 'Do not commit adultery. Do not murder. Do not steal. Do not testify falsely. Honor your father and mother.'* "

21The man replied, "I've obeyed all these commandments since I was a child."

22"There is still one thing you lack," Jesus said. "Sell all you have and give the money to the poor, and you will have treasure in heaven. Then come, follow me." 23But when the man heard this, he became sad because he was very rich.

24Jesus watched him go and then said to his disciples, "How hard it is for rich people to get into the Kingdom of God! 25It is easier for a camel to go through the eye of a needle than for a rich person to enter the Kingdom of God!"

26Those who heard this said, "Then who in the world can be saved?"

27He replied, "What is impossible from a human perspective is possible with God."

28Peter said, "We have left our homes and followed you."

29"Yes," Jesus replied, "and I assure you, everyone who has given up house or wife or brothers or parents or children, for the sake of the Kingdom of God, 30will be repaid many times over in this life, as well as receiving eternal life in the world to come."

Jesus Again Predicts His Death
31Gathering the twelve disciples around him, Jesus told them, "As you know, we are going to Jerusalem. And when we get there, all the predictions of the ancient prophets concerning the Son of Man will come true. 32He will be handed over to the Romans to be mocked, treated shamefully, and spit upon. 33They will whip him and kill him, but on the third day he will rise again." 34But they didn't understand a thing he said.

- The widow had no access to the judge. . . . We have constant access to God (see Hebrews 10:19, p. 1079).
- The widow came to the court of law. . . . We come to the throne of grace (see Hebrews 4:16, p. 1074).
- The widow had no lawyer. . . . We have Jesus as our advocate (see 1 John 2:1, p. 1103).
- The widow had to wear down the judge before he really listened. . . . We already know that God hears our requests (see Psalm 4:3, p. 462).

If this poor woman received what she deserved from a corrupt judge, how much more will we receive from our loving heavenly Father. As Jesus illustrated, persistence pays off. Keep on praying!

To begin the next topic, turn to p. A36.

We Need to Invest Our Abilities and Resources in God's Kingdom Read LUKE 19:11-26

This parable explains what Jesus expects of us as we await his return to earth. The nobleman in this story represents Christ. The servants refer to us, his followers. In essence, the crux of the parable is that we are to work diligently on his behalf until he returns.

In this parable, each man was given ten pounds of silver. Likewise, every believer has been given equal opportunity to invest his or her life in God's Kingdom, a common responsibility. It is the simple commission to proclaim the gospel to the world and make disciples. We then see three levels of investment.

1. The Servant with Tremendous Gain. This ambitious servant gave the king back ten times the amount he originally had been given. This type of person is truly a disciple. He or she actively shares his or her faith with one person after another, then takes these individuals under his or her wing to help them mature in their faith.

2. The Servant with Splendid Gain. The second servant was a little less ambitious than the first, but he did make some gain. This type of person seems somewhat satisfied with the status quo. He or she gets the gospel out slowly but surely, but he or she doesn't see the same results as the first type of person. This person fails to use all of the resources God has given him or her, so he or she always falls a little short of his or her full potential.

3. The Servant with No Gain. The third servant wanted to "play it safe," so he buried his money. He did so because he had a false perception of his master. He claimed that his master was hard and unfair. In the same way, this person is often motivated out of fear of God rather than a love for God. He or she sees witnessing as a duty rather than a privilege. That is why Paul tells us that Christ's love needs to be the motivating force in all that we do (see 2 Corinthians 5:14, pp. 1006-1007). We can only give out what we ourselves have taken in. And this person knows little of the Savior he or she serves.

In the Kingdom of God, God expects investment as well as results. Don't take this sacred trust he has given to you and bury it in the ground. Use it. Multiply it. Remember, God isn't asking you to work *for* him. He is asking to work *through* you. Yield to the power of the Holy Spirit and ask God for directions as to how you can be used by him. Then you will see results.

For the next note on "Accountability," turn to p. 986.

CORNER STONES

Its significance was hidden from them, and they failed to grasp what he was talking about.

Jesus Heals a Blind Beggar

35As they approached Jericho, a blind beggar was sitting beside the road. 36When he heard the noise of a crowd going past, he asked what was happening. 37They told him that Jesus of Nazareth was going by. 38So he began shouting, "Jesus, Son of David, have mercy on me!" 39The crowds ahead of Jesus tried to hush the man, but he only shouted louder, "Son of David, have mercy on me!"

40When Jesus heard him, he stopped and ordered that the man be brought to him. 41Then Jesus asked the man, "What do you want me to do for you?"

"Lord," he pleaded, "I want to see!"

42And Jesus said, "All right, you can see! Your faith has healed you." 43Instantly the man could see, and he followed Jesus, praising God. And all who saw it praised God, too.

CHAPTER **19**

Jesus and Zacchaeus

Jesus entered Jericho and made his way through the town. 2There was a man there named Zacchaeus. He was one of the most influential Jews in the Roman tax-collecting business, and he had become very rich. 3He tried to get a look at Jesus, but he was too short to see over the crowds. 4So he ran ahead and climbed a sycamore tree beside the road, so he could watch from there.

⁵When Jesus came by, he looked up at Zacchaeus and called him by name. "Zacchaeus!" he said. "Quick, come down! For I must be a guest in your home today."

⁶Zacchaeus quickly climbed down and took Jesus to his house in great excitement and joy. ⁷But the crowds were displeased. "He has gone to be the guest of a notorious sinner," they grumbled.

⁸Meanwhile, Zacchaeus stood there and said to the Lord, "I will give half my wealth to the poor, Lord, and if I have overcharged people on their taxes, I will give them back four times as much!"

⁹Jesus responded, "Salvation has come to this home today, for this man has shown himself to be a son of Abraham. ¹⁰And I, the Son of Man, have come to seek and save those like him who are lost."

Story of the Ten Servants

¹¹The crowd was listening to everything Jesus said. And because he was nearing Jerusalem, he told a story to correct the impression that the Kingdom of God would begin right away. ¹²He said, "A nobleman was called away to a distant empire to be crowned king and then return. ¹³Before he left, he called together ten servants and gave them ten pounds of silver* to invest for him while he was gone. ¹⁴But his people hated him and sent a delegation after him to say they did not want him to be their king.

¹⁵"When he returned, the king called in the servants to whom he had given the money. He wanted to find out what they had done with the money and what their profits were. ¹⁶The first servant reported a tremendous gain—ten times as much as the original amount! ¹⁷'Well done!' the king exclaimed. 'You are a trustworthy servant. You have been faithful with the little I entrusted to you, so you will be governor of ten cities as your reward.'

¹⁸"The next servant also reported a good gain—five times the original amount. ¹⁹'Well done!' the king said. 'You can be governor over five cities.'

²⁰"But the third servant brought back only the original amount of money and said, 'I hid it and kept it safe. ²¹I was afraid because you are a

hard man to deal with, taking what isn't yours and harvesting crops you didn't plant.'

²²"'You wicked servant!' the king roared. 'Hard, am I? If you knew so much about me and how tough I am, ²³why didn't you deposit the money in the bank so I could at least get some interest on it?' ²⁴Then turning to the others standing nearby, the king ordered, 'Take the money from this servant, and give it to the one who earned the most.'

²⁵"'But, master,' they said, 'that servant has enough already!'

²⁶"'Yes,' the king replied, 'but to those who use well what they are given, even more will be given. But from those who are unfaithful,* even what little they have will be taken away. ²⁷And now about these enemies of mine who didn't want me to be their king—bring them in and execute them right here in my presence.'"

The Triumphal Entry

²⁸After telling this story, Jesus went on toward Jerusalem, walking ahead of his disciples. ²⁹As they came to the towns of Bethphage and Bethany, on the Mount of Olives, he sent two disciples ahead. ³⁰"Go into that village over there," he told them, "and as you enter it, you will see a colt tied there that has never been ridden. Untie it and bring it here. ³¹If anyone asks what you are doing, just say, 'The Lord needs it.'"

³²So they went and found the colt, just as Jesus had said. ³³And sure enough, as they were untying it, the owners asked them, "Why are you untying our colt?"

³⁴And the disciples simply replied, "The Lord needs it." ³⁵So they brought the colt to Jesus and threw their garments over it for him to ride on.

³⁶Then the crowds spread out their coats on the road ahead of Jesus. ³⁷As they reached the place where the road started down from the Mount of Olives, all of his followers began to shout and sing as they walked along, praising God for all the wonderful miracles they had seen.

³⁸ "Bless the King who comes in the name of
　　　the Lord!
　Peace in heaven
　　　and glory in highest heaven!"*

³⁹But some of the Pharisees among the crowd said, "Teacher, rebuke your followers for saying things like that!"

⁴⁰He replied, "If they kept quiet, the stones along the road would burst into cheers!"

19:13 Greek *10 minas; 1 mina was worth about 3 months' wages.*　**19:26** Or *who have nothing.*　**19:38** Pss 118:26; 148:1.

Jesus Weeps over Jerusalem

41But as they came closer to Jerusalem and Jesus saw the city ahead, he began to cry. 42"I wish that even today you would find the way of peace. But now it is too late, and peace is hidden from you. 43Before long your enemies will build ramparts against your walls and encircle you and close in on you. 44They will crush you to the ground, and your children with you. Your enemies will not leave a single stone in place, because you have rejected the opportunity God offered you."

Jesus Clears the Temple

45Then Jesus entered the Temple and began to drive out the merchants from their stalls. 46He told them, "The Scriptures declare, 'My Temple will be a place of prayer,' but you have turned it into a den of thieves."*

47After that, he taught daily in the Temple, but the leading priests, the teachers of religious law, and the other leaders of the people began planning how to kill him. 48But they could think of nothing, because all the people hung on every word he said.

CHAPTER **20**

The Authority of Jesus Challenged

One day as Jesus was teaching and preaching the Good News in the Temple, the leading priests and teachers of religious law and other leaders came up to him. 2They demanded, "By whose authority did you drive out the merchants from the Temple?* Who gave you such authority?"

3"Let me ask you a question first," he replied. 4"Did John's baptism come from heaven, or was it merely human?"

5They talked it over among themselves. "If we say it was from heaven, he will ask why we didn't believe him. 6But if we say it was merely human, the people will stone us, because they are convinced he was a prophet." 7Finally they replied, "We don't know."

8And Jesus responded, "Then I won't answer your question either."

Story of the Evil Farmers

9Now Jesus turned to the people again and told them this story: "A man planted a vineyard, leased it out to tenant farmers, and moved to another country to live for several years. 10At grape-picking time, he sent one of his servants to collect his share of the crop. But the farmers attacked the servant, beat him up, and sent him back empty-handed. 11So the owner sent another servant, but the same thing happened; he was beaten up and treated shamefully, and he went away empty-handed. 12A third man was sent and the same thing happened. He, too, was wounded and chased away.

13" 'What will I do?' the owner asked himself. 'I know! I'll send my cherished son. Surely they will respect him.'

14"But when the farmers saw his son, they said to each other, 'Here comes the heir to this estate. Let's kill him and get the estate for ourselves!' 15So they dragged him out of the vineyard and murdered him.

"What do you suppose the owner of the vineyard will do to those farmers?" Jesus asked. 16"I'll tell you—he will come and kill them all and lease the vineyard to others."

"But God forbid that such a thing should ever happen," his listeners protested.

17Jesus looked at them and said, "Then what do the Scriptures mean?

'The stone rejected by the builders
  has now become the cornerstone.'*

18All who stumble over that stone will be broken to pieces, and it will crush anyone on whom it falls."

19When the teachers of religious law and the leading priests heard this story, they wanted to arrest Jesus immediately because they realized he was pointing at them—that they were the farmers in the story. But they were afraid there would be a riot if they arrested him.

Taxes for Caesar

20Watching for their opportunity, the leaders sent secret agents pretending to be honest men. They tried to get Jesus to say something that could be reported to the Roman governor so he would arrest Jesus. 21They said, "Teacher, we know that you speak and teach what is right and are not influenced by what others think. You sincerely teach the ways of God. 22Now tell us—is it right to pay taxes to the Roman government or not?"

23He saw through their trickery and said, 24"Show me a Roman coin.* Whose picture and title are stamped on it?"

"Caesar's," they replied.

25"Well then," he said, "give to Caesar what belongs to him. But everything that belongs to

19:46 Isa 56:7; Jer 7:11.   20:2 Or *By whose authority do you do these things?*   20:17 Ps 118:22.   20:24 Greek *a denarius.*

God must be given to God." 26So they failed to trap him in the presence of the people. Instead, they were amazed by his answer, and were silenced.

Discussion about Resurrection
27Then some Sadducees stepped forward—a group of Jews who say there is no resurrection after death. 28They posed this question: "Teacher, Moses gave us a law that if a man dies, leaving a wife but no children, his brother should marry the widow and have a child who will be the brother's heir.* 29Well, there were seven brothers. The oldest married and then died without children. 30His brother married the widow, but he also died. Still no children. 31And so it went, one after the other, until each of the seven had married her and died, leaving no children. 32Finally, the woman died, too. 33So tell us, whose wife will she be in the resurrection? For all seven were married to her!"

34Jesus replied, "Marriage is for people here on earth. 35But that is not the way it will be in the age to come. For those worthy of being raised from the dead won't be married then. 36And they will never die again. In these respects they are like angels. They are children of God raised up to new life. 37But now, as to whether the dead will be raised—even Moses proved this when he wrote about the burning bush. Long after Abraham, Isaac, and Jacob had died, he referred to the Lord* as 'the God of Abraham, the God of Isaac, and the God of Jacob.'* 38So he is the God of the living, not the dead. They are all alive to him."

39"Well said, Teacher!" remarked some of the teachers of religious law who were standing there. 40And that ended their questions; no one dared to ask any more.

Whose Son Is the Messiah?
41Then Jesus presented them with a question. "Why is it," he asked, "that the Messiah is said to be the son of David? 42For David himself wrote in the book of Psalms:

'The LORD said to my Lord,
Sit in honor at my right hand
43   until I humble your enemies,
    making them a footstool under your
    feet.'*

44Since David called him Lord, how can he be his son at the same time?"

45Then, with the crowds listening, he turned to his disciples and said, 46"Beware of these teachers of religious law! For they love to parade in flowing robes and to have everyone bow to them as they walk in the marketplaces. And how they love the seats of honor in the synagogues and at banquets. 47But they shamelessly cheat widows out of their property, and then, to cover up the kind of people they really are, they make long prayers in public. Because of this, their punishment will be the greater."

CHAPTER **21**
The Widow's Offering
While Jesus was in the Temple, he watched the rich people putting their gifts into the collection box. 2Then a poor widow came by and dropped in two pennies.* 3"I assure you," he said, "this poor widow has given more than all the rest of them. 4For they have given a tiny part of their surplus, but she, poor as she is, has given everything she has."

Jesus Foretells the Future
5Some of his disciples began talking about the beautiful stonework of the Temple and the memorial decorations on the walls. But Jesus said, 6"The time is coming when all these things will be so completely demolished that not one stone will be left on top of another."

7"Teacher," they asked, "when will all this take place? And will there be any sign ahead of time?"

8He replied, "Don't let anyone mislead you. For many will come in my name, claiming to be the Messiah* and saying, 'The time has come!' But don't believe them. 9And when you hear of wars and insurrections, don't panic. Yes, these things must come, but the end won't follow immediately." 10Then he added, "Nations and kingdoms will proclaim war against each other. 11There will be great earthquakes, and there will be famines and epidemics in many lands, and there will be terrifying things and great miraculous signs in the heavens.

12"But before all this occurs, there will be a time of great persecution. You will be dragged into synagogues and prisons, and you will be accused before kings and governors of being my followers. 13This will be your opportunity to tell them about me. 14So don't worry about how to answer the charges against you, 15for I will give you the right words and such wisdom that none

20:28 Deut 25:5-6. 20:37a Greek *when he wrote about the bush. He referred to the Lord.* 20:37b Exod 3:6. 20:42-43 Ps 110:1. 21:2 Greek *2 lepta.* 21:8 Greek *name, saying, 'I am.'*

of your opponents will be able to reply! ¹⁶Even those closest to you—your parents, brothers, relatives, and friends—will betray you. And some of you will be killed. ¹⁷And everyone will hate you because of your allegiance to me. ¹⁸But not a hair of your head will perish! ¹⁹By standing firm, you will win your souls.

²⁰"And when you see Jerusalem surrounded by armies, then you will know that the time of its destruction has arrived. ²¹Then those in Judea must flee to the hills. Let those in Jerusalem escape, and those outside the city should not enter it for shelter. ²²For those will be days of God's vengeance, and the prophetic words of the Scriptures will be fulfilled. ²³How terrible it will be for pregnant women and for mothers nursing their babies. For there will be great distress in the land and wrath upon this people. ²⁴They will be brutally killed by the sword or sent away as captives to all the nations of the world. And Jerusalem will be conquered and trampled down by the Gentiles until the age of the Gentiles comes to an end.

²⁵"And there will be strange events in the skies—signs in the sun, moon, and stars. And down here on earth the nations will be in turmoil, perplexed by the roaring seas and strange tides. ²⁶The courage of many people will falter because of the fearful fate they see coming upon the earth, because the stability of the very heavens will be broken up. ²⁷Then everyone will see the Son of Man arrive on the clouds with power and great glory.* ²⁸So when all these things begin to happen, stand straight and look up, for your salvation is near!"

²⁹Then he gave them this illustration: "Notice the fig tree, or any other tree. ³⁰When the leaves come out, you know without being told that summer is near. ³¹Just so, when you see the events I've described taking place, you can be sure that the Kingdom of God is near. ³²I assure you, this generation* will not pass from the scene until all these events have taken place. ³³Heaven and earth will disappear, but my words will remain forever.

³⁴"Watch out! Don't let me find you living in careless ease and drunkenness, and filled with the worries of this life. Don't let that day catch you unaware, ³⁵as in a trap. For that day will come upon everyone living on the earth. ³⁶Keep a constant watch. And pray that, if possible, you may escape these horrors and stand before the Son of Man."

²¹:²⁷ See Dan 7:13. ²¹:³² Or *this age,* or *this nation.*

³⁷Every day Jesus went to the Temple to teach, and each evening he returned to spend the night on the Mount of Olives. ³⁸The crowds gathered early each morning to hear him.

CHAPTER **22**

Judas Agrees to Betray Jesus

The Festival of Unleavened Bread, which begins with the Passover celebration, was drawing near. ²The leading priests and teachers of religious law were actively plotting Jesus' murder. But they wanted to kill him without starting a riot, a possibility they greatly feared.

³Then Satan entered into Judas Iscariot, who was one of the twelve disciples, ⁴and he went over to the leading priests and captains of the Temple guard to discuss the best way to betray Jesus to them. ⁵They were delighted that he was ready to help them, and they promised him a reward. ⁶So he began looking for an opportunity to betray Jesus so they could arrest him quietly when the crowds weren't around.

The Last Supper

⁷Now the Festival of Unleavened Bread arrived, when the Passover lambs were sacrificed. ⁸Jesus sent Peter and John ahead and said, "Go and prepare the Passover meal, so we can eat it together."

⁹"Where do you want us to go?" they asked him.

¹⁰He replied, "As soon as you enter Jerusalem, a man carrying a pitcher of water will meet you. Follow him. At the house he enters, ¹¹say to the owner, 'The Teacher asks, Where is the guest room where I can eat the Passover meal with my disciples?' ¹²He will take you upstairs to a large room that is already set up. That is the place. Go ahead and prepare our supper there." ¹³They went off to the city and found everything just as Jesus had said, and they prepared the Passover supper there.

¹⁴Then at the proper time Jesus and the twelve apostles sat down together at the table. ¹⁵Jesus said, "I have looked forward to this hour with deep longing, anxious to eat this Passover meal with you before my suffering begins. ¹⁶For I tell you now that I won't eat it again until it comes to fulfillment in the Kingdom of God."

¹⁷Then he took a cup of wine, and when he had given thanks for it, he said, "Take this and share it among yourselves. ¹⁸For I will not drink wine again until the Kingdom of God has come."

19Then he took a loaf of bread; and when he had thanked God for it, he broke it in pieces and gave it to the disciples, saying, "This is my body, given for you. Do this in remembrance of me." 20After supper he took another cup of wine and said, "This wine is the token of God's new covenant to save you—an agreement sealed with the blood I will pour out for you.*

21 "But here at this table, sitting among us as a friend, is the man who will betray me. 22For I, the Son of Man, must die since it is part of God's plan. But how terrible it will be for my betrayer!" 23Then the disciples began to ask each other which of them would ever do such a thing.

24And they began to argue among themselves as to who would be the greatest in the coming Kingdom. 25Jesus told them, "In this world the kings and great men order their people around, and yet they are called 'friends of the people.' 26But among you, those who are the greatest should take the lowest rank, and the leader should be like a servant. 27Normally the master sits at the table and is served by his servants. But not here! For I am your servant. 28You have remained true to me in my time of trial. 29And just as my Father has granted me a Kingdom, I now grant you the right 30to eat and drink at my table in that Kingdom. And you will sit on thrones, judging the twelve tribes of Israel.

Jesus Predicts Peter's Denial

31 "Simon, Simon, Satan has asked to have all of you, to sift you like wheat. 32But I have pleaded in prayer for you, Simon, that your faith should not fail. So when you have repented and turned to me again, strengthen and build up your brothers."

33Peter said, "Lord, I am ready to go to prison with you, and even to die with you."

34But Jesus said, "Peter, let me tell you something. The rooster will not crow tomorrow morning until you have denied three times that you even know me."

35Then Jesus asked them, "When I sent you out to preach the Good News and you did not have money, a traveler's bag, or extra clothing, did you lack anything?"

"No," they replied.

36"But now," he said, "take your money and a traveler's bag. And if you don't have a sword, sell your clothes and buy one! 37For the time has come for this prophecy about me to be fulfilled: 'He was counted among those who were reb-els.'* Yes, everything written about me by the prophets will come true."

38"Lord," they replied, "we have two swords among us."

"That's enough," he said.

Jesus Prays on the Mount of Olives

39Then, accompanied by the disciples, Jesus left the upstairs room and went as usual to the Mount of Olives. 40There he told them, "Pray that you will not be overcome by temptation."

41He walked away, about a stone's throw, and knelt down and prayed, 42"Father, if you are willing, please take this cup of suffering away from me. Yet I want your will, not mine." 43Then an angel from heaven appeared and strengthened him. 44He prayed more fervently, and he was in such agony of spirit that his sweat fell to the ground like great drops of blood.* 45At last he stood up again and returned to the disciples, only to find them asleep, exhausted from grief. 46"Why are you sleeping?" he asked. "Get up and pray. Otherwise temptation will overpower you."

Jesus Is Betrayed and Arrested

47But even as he said this, a mob approached, led by Judas, one of his twelve disciples. Judas walked over to Jesus and greeted him with a kiss. 48But Jesus said, "Judas, how can you betray me, the Son of Man, with a kiss?"

49When the other disciples saw what was about to happen, they exclaimed, "Lord, should we fight? We brought the swords!" 50And one of them slashed at the high priest's servant and cut off his right ear.

51But Jesus said, "Don't resist anymore." And he touched the place where the man's ear had been and healed him. 52Then Jesus spoke to the leading priests and captains of the Temple guard and the other leaders who headed the mob. "Am I some dangerous criminal," he asked, "that you have come armed with swords and clubs to arrest me? 53Why didn't you arrest me in the Temple? I was there every day. But this is your moment, the time when the power of darkness reigns."

Peter Denies Jesus

54So they arrested him and led him to the high priest's residence, and Peter was following far behind. 55The guards lit a fire in the courtyard and sat around it, and Peter joined them there.

22:19-20 Some manuscripts omit 22:19b-20, *given for you . . . I will pour out for you.*   22:37 Isa 53:12.   22:43-44 These verses are not included in many ancient manuscripts.

56A servant girl noticed him in the firelight and began staring at him. Finally she said, "This man was one of Jesus' followers!"

57Peter denied it. "Woman," he said, "I don't even know the man!"

58After a while someone else looked at him and said, "You must be one of them!"

"No, man, I'm not!" Peter replied.

59About an hour later someone else insisted, "This must be one of Jesus' disciples because he is a Galilean, too."

60But Peter said, "Man, I don't know what you are talking about." And as soon as he said these words, the rooster crowed. 61At that moment the Lord turned and looked at Peter. Then Peter remembered that the Lord had said, "Before the rooster crows tomorrow morning, you will deny me three times." 62And Peter left the courtyard, crying bitterly.

63Now the guards in charge of Jesus began mocking and beating him. 64They blindfolded him; then they hit him and asked, "Who hit you that time, you prophet?" 65And they threw all sorts of terrible insults at him.

Jesus before the Council

66At daybreak all the leaders of the people assembled, including the leading priests and the teachers of religious law. Jesus was led before this high council,* 67and they said, "Tell us if you are the Messiah."

But he replied, "If I tell you, you won't believe me. 68And if I ask you a question, you won't answer. 69But the time is soon coming when I, the Son of Man, will be sitting at God's right hand in the place of power."*

70They all shouted, "Then you claim you are the Son of God?"

And he replied, "You are right in saying that I am."

71"What need do we have for other witnesses?" they shouted. "We ourselves heard him say it."

CHAPTER 23
Jesus' Trial before Pilate

Then the entire council took Jesus over to Pilate, the Roman governor. 2They began at once to state their case: "This man has been leading our people to ruin by telling them not to pay their taxes to the Roman government and by claiming he is the Messiah, a king."

3So Pilate asked him, "Are you the King of the Jews?"

Jesus replied, "Yes, it is as you say."

4Pilate turned to the leading priests and to the crowd and said, "I find nothing wrong with this man!"

5Then they became desperate. "But he is causing riots everywhere he goes, all over Judea, from Galilee to Jerusalem!"

6"Oh, is he a Galilean?" Pilate asked. 7When they answered that he was, Pilate sent him to Herod Antipas, because Galilee was under Herod's jurisdiction, and Herod happened to be in Jerusalem at the time.

8Herod was delighted at the opportunity to see Jesus, because he had heard about him and had been hoping for a long time to see him perform a miracle. 9He asked Jesus question after question, but Jesus refused to answer. 10Meanwhile, the leading priests and the teachers of religious law stood there shouting their accusations. 11Now Herod and his soldiers began mocking and ridiculing Jesus. Then they put a royal robe on him and sent him back to Pilate. 12Herod and Pilate, who had been enemies before, became friends that day.

13Then Pilate called together the leading priests and other religious leaders, along with the people, 14and he announced his verdict. "You brought this man to me, accusing him of leading a revolt. I have examined him thoroughly on this point in your presence and find him innocent. 15Herod came to the same conclusion and sent him back to us. Nothing this man has done calls for the death penalty. 16So I will have him flogged, but then I will release him."*

18Then a mighty roar rose from the crowd, and with one voice they shouted, "Kill him, and release Barabbas to us!" 19(Barabbas was in prison for murder and for taking part in an insurrection in Jerusalem against the government.) 20Pilate argued with them, because he wanted to release Jesus. 21But they shouted, "Crucify him! Crucify him!"

22For the third time he demanded, "Why? What crime has he committed? I have found no reason to sentence him to death. I will therefore flog him and let him go."

23But the crowd shouted louder and louder for Jesus' death, and their voices prevailed. 24So Pilate sentenced Jesus to die as they demanded. 25As they had requested, he released Barabbas,

22:66 Greek *before their Sanhedrin.*   22:69 See Ps 110:1.   23:16 Some manuscripts add verse 17, *For it was necessary for him to release one [prisoner] for them during the feast.*

What Is Backsliding? Read LUKE 22:31-62

As believers we have been given a "new nature"—a part of us that spiritually hungers after God, a supernatural inclination to do what is right. Unfortunately, being human, we also have an "old nature"—a natural inclination to do wrong. Sometimes Christians begin to fall back spiritually or "backslide." God speaks of this in Jeremiah 3:22, where he says, "Come back to me, and I will heal your wayward hearts."

Perhaps the best way to understand the dangers of backsliding is to examine the biblical account of how one believer fell into this trap. He was none other than Simon Peter, one of Jesus' closest disciples. In Luke 22 we are given the account of his spiritual regression. His story serves as a warning that even the most mature believers have the potential to fall if they let their guard down.

Self-Confidence and False Security. Not only did Peter reveal his unfounded confidence in himself (his claim that he would "die" with Jesus), but he also directly contradicted the Lord's prediction that he would fall (verse 34). He denied his own weakness to sin. The Bible warns, "If you think you are standing strong, be careful, for you, too, may fall into the same sin" (1 Corinthians 10:12).

Prayerlessness. Even after Jesus specifically instructed Peter to pray, he decided to sleep instead. In Matthew's account of this incident, Jesus had even warned them, "For though the spirit is willing enough, the body is weak!" (Matthew 26:41). Yet he felt no weakness and saw no need to be prayerful and watchful. Prayerlessness is as much a sin as directly breaking a commandment, for throughout Scripture God has specifically instructed us to pray.

Following God at a Distance. A lack of closeness and fellowship with the Lord will always be at the foundation of all spiritual regression. Although Peter was still following Jesus, he wasn't following as closely as he could have been. There are some Christians who want to try to live in both worlds. They want to be believers, but they don't want to be too committed. You endanger yourself when you live this way.

Warming Up at the Enemies' Fire. Following in the distance, Peter became cold and was attracted to the fire. Peter hoped to go unnoticed in the larger crowd, so he settled in with the very people who were responsible for arresting his Lord. The Bible tells us, "Oh, the joys of those who do not follow the advice of the wicked, or stand around with sinners, or join in with scoffers" (Psalm 1:1). Tragically, Peter was doing exactly the opposite. When that spiritual passion in our heart begins to die, that fire for Jesus Christ will grow cold, and we will look elsewhere for warmth.

Denial and Disassociations. Peter reached this final step of spiritual regression when he denied knowing or ever being with Jesus. Matthew's Gospel tells us that he began to curse and swear, which means that he took an oath, saying, "May God kill and damn me if I am not speaking the truth (26:74)." Peter had lost all sense of reality and seemingly all awareness of God.

Despite Peter's fall, he was restored. In verse 61, his eyes met those of Jesus, and Peter cried bitterly. As he grieved over his sin, Jesus saw his heart. The Bible says, "God can use sorrow in our lives to help us turn away from sin and seek salvation" (2 Corinthians 7:10). Interestingly enough, three days later, after Jesus' resurrection, the angel at the tomb specifically told Mary, "Now go and give this message to his disciples, *including Peter:* 'Jesus is going ahead of you to Galilee. You will see him there" (Mark 16:7, emphasis added). Jesus wanted Peter to know that he still loved him.

As Christians we will sin. Scripture says, "If we say that we have no sin, we are only fooling ourselves and refusing to accept the truth" (1 John 1:8). But the Holy Spirit will lovingly convict us of that sin and lead us back to the cross, where we can confess it and turn from it. Remember, when we sin we should run to—not away from—the Lord.

For the next "Big Question" note, turn to p. 927.

the man in prison for insurrection and murder. But he delivered Jesus over to them to do as they wished.

The Crucifixion

²⁶As they led Jesus away, Simon of Cyrene,* who was coming in from the country just then, was forced to follow Jesus and carry his cross. ²⁷Great crowds trailed along behind, including many grief-stricken women. ²⁸But Jesus turned and said to them, "Daughters of Jerusalem, don't weep for me, but weep for yourselves and for your children. ²⁹For the days are coming when they will say, 'Fortunate indeed are the women who are childless, the wombs that have not borne a child and the breasts that have never nursed.' ³⁰People will beg the mountains to fall on them and the hills to bury them. ³¹For if these things are done when the tree is green, what will happen when it is dry?*"

³²Two others, both criminals, were led out to be executed with him. ³³Finally, they came to a place called The Skull.* All three were crucified there—Jesus on the center cross, and the two criminals on either side.

³⁴Jesus said, "Father, forgive these people, because they don't know what they are doing."* And the soldiers gambled for his clothes by throwing dice.*

³⁵The crowd watched, and the leaders laughed and scoffed. "He saved others," they said, "let him save himself if he is really God's Chosen One, the Messiah." ³⁶The soldiers mocked him, too, by offering him a drink of sour wine. ³⁷They called out to him, "If you are the King of the Jews, save yourself!" ³⁸A signboard was nailed to the cross above him with these words: "This is the King of the Jews."

³⁹One of the criminals hanging beside him scoffed, "So you're the Messiah, are you? Prove it by saving yourself—and us, too, while you're at it!"

⁴⁰But the other criminal protested, "Don't you fear God even when you are dying? ⁴¹We deserve to die for our evil deeds, but this man hasn't done anything wrong." ⁴²Then he said, "Jesus, remember me when you come into your Kingdom."

⁴³And Jesus replied, "I assure you, today you will be with me in paradise."

The Death of Jesus

⁴⁴By this time it was noon, and darkness fell across the whole land until three o'clock. ⁴⁵The light from the sun was gone. And suddenly, the thick veil hanging in the Temple was torn apart. ⁴⁶Then Jesus shouted, "Father, I entrust my spirit into your hands!"* And with those words he breathed his last.

⁴⁷When the captain of the Roman soldiers handling the executions saw what had happened, he praised God and said, "Surely this man was innocent.*" ⁴⁸And when the crowd that came to see the crucifixion saw all that had happened, they went home in deep sorrow.* ⁴⁹But Jesus' friends, including the women who had followed him from Galilee, stood at a distance watching.

The Burial of Jesus

⁵⁰Now there was a good and righteous man named Joseph. He was a member of the Jewish high council, ⁵¹but he had not agreed with the decision and actions of the other religious leaders. He was from the town of Arimathea in Judea, and he had been waiting for the Kingdom of God to come. ⁵²He went to Pilate and asked for Jesus' body. ⁵³Then he took the body down from the cross and wrapped it in a long linen cloth and laid it in a new tomb that had been carved out of rock. ⁵⁴This was done late on Friday afternoon, the day of preparation* for the Sabbath.

⁵⁵As his body was taken away, the women from Galilee followed and saw the tomb where they placed his body. ⁵⁶Then they went home and prepared spices and ointments to embalm him. But by the time they were finished it was the Sabbath, so they rested all that day as required by the law.

CHAPTER 24

The Resurrection

But very early on Sunday morning* the women came to the tomb, taking the spices they had prepared. ²They found that the stone covering the entrance had been rolled aside. ³So they went in, but they couldn't find the body of the Lord Jesus. ⁴They were puzzled, trying to think what could have happened to it. Suddenly, two men appeared to them, clothed in dazzling robes. ⁵The women were terrified and bowed

23:26 *Cyrene* was a city in northern Africa. **23:31** Or *If these things are done to me, the living tree, what will happen to you, the dry tree?* **23:33** Sometimes rendered *Calvary*, which comes from the Latin word for "skull." **23:34a** This sentence is not included in many ancient manuscripts. **23:34b** Greek *by casting lots.* See Ps 22:18. **23:46** Ps 31:5. **23:47** Or *righteous.* **23:48** Greek *beating their breasts.* **23:54** Greek *on the day of preparation.* **24:1** Greek *But on the first day of the week, very early in the morning.*

low before them. Then the men asked, "Why are you looking in a tomb for someone who is alive? ⁶He isn't here! He has risen from the dead! Don't you remember what he told you back in Galilee, ⁷that the Son of Man must be betrayed into the hands of sinful men and be crucified, and that he would rise again the third day?"

⁸Then they remembered that he had said this. ⁹So they rushed back to tell his eleven disciples—and everyone else—what had happened. ¹⁰The women who went to the tomb were Mary Magdalene, Joanna, Mary the mother of James, and several others. They told the apostles what had happened, ¹¹but the story sounded like nonsense, so they didn't believe it. ¹²However, Peter ran to the tomb to look. Stooping, he peered in and saw the empty linen wrappings; then he went home again, wondering what had happened.*

The Walk to Emmaus

¹³That same day two of Jesus' followers were walking to the village of Emmaus, seven miles* out of Jerusalem. ¹⁴As they walked along they were talking about everything that had happened. ¹⁵Suddenly, Jesus himself came along and joined them and began walking beside them. ¹⁶But they didn't know who he was, because God kept them from recognizing him.

¹⁷"You seem to be in a deep discussion about something," he said. "What are you so concerned about?"

They stopped short, sadness written across their faces. ¹⁸Then one of them, Cleopas, replied, "You must be the only person in Jerusalem who hasn't heard about all the things that have happened there the last few days."

¹⁹"What things?" Jesus asked.

"The things that happened to Jesus, the man from Nazareth," they said. "He was a prophet who did wonderful miracles. He was a mighty teacher, highly regarded by both God and all the people. ²⁰But our leading priests and other religious leaders arrested him and handed him over to be condemned to death, and they crucified him. ²¹We had thought he was the Messiah who had come to rescue Israel. That all happened three days ago. ²²Then some women from our group of his followers were at his tomb early this morning, and they came back with an amazing report. ²³They said his body was missing, and they had seen angels who told them Jesus is alive! ²⁴Some of our men ran out to see, and

sure enough, Jesus' body was gone, just as the women had said."

²⁵Then Jesus said to them, "You are such foolish people! You find it so hard to believe all that the prophets wrote in the Scriptures. ²⁶Wasn't it clearly predicted by the prophets that the Messiah would have to suffer all these things before entering his time of glory?" ²⁷Then Jesus quoted passages from the writings of Moses and all the prophets, explaining what all the Scriptures said about himself.

²⁸By this time they were nearing Emmaus and the end of their journey. Jesus would have gone on, ²⁹but they begged him to stay the night with them, since it was getting late. So he went home with them. ³⁰As they sat down to eat, he took a small loaf of bread, asked God's blessing on it, broke it, then gave it to them. ³¹Suddenly, their eyes were opened, and they recognized him. And at that moment he disappeared!

³²They said to each other, "Didn't our hearts feel strangely warm as he talked with us on the road and explained the Scriptures to us?" ³³And within the hour they were on their way back to Jerusalem, where the eleven disciples and the other followers of Jesus were gathered. When they arrived, they were greeted with the report, ³⁴"The Lord has really risen! He appeared to Peter*!"

Jesus Appears to the Disciples

³⁵Then the two from Emmaus told their story of how Jesus had appeared to them as they were walking along the road and how they had recognized him as he was breaking the bread. ³⁶And just as they were telling about it, Jesus himself was suddenly standing there among them. He said, "Peace be with you."* ³⁷But the whole group was terribly frightened, thinking they were seeing a ghost! ³⁸"Why are you frightened?" he asked. "Why do you doubt who I am? ³⁹Look at my hands. Look at my feet. You can see that it's really me. Touch me and make sure that I am not a ghost, because ghosts don't have bodies, as you see that I do!" ⁴⁰As he spoke, he held out his hands for them to see, and he showed them his feet.*

⁴¹Still they stood there doubting, filled with joy and wonder. Then he asked them, "Do you have anything here to eat?" ⁴²They gave him a piece of broiled fish, ⁴³and he ate it as they watched.

⁴⁴Then he said, "When I was with you before,

24:12 Some manuscripts do not include this verse. 24:13 Greek *60 stadia* [11.1 kilometers]. 24:34 Greek *Simon.* 24:36 Some manuscripts do not include *He said, "Peace be with you."* 24:40 Some manuscripts do not include this verse.

I told you that everything written about me by Moses and the prophets and in the Psalms must all come true." ⁴⁵Then he opened their minds to understand these many Scriptures. ⁴⁶And he said, "Yes, it was written long ago that the Messiah must suffer and die and rise again from the dead on the third day. ⁴⁷With my authority, take this message of repentance to all the nations, beginning in Jerusalem: 'There is forgiveness of sins for all who turn to me.' ⁴⁸You are witnesses of all these things.

⁴⁹"And now I will send the Holy Spirit, just as my Father promised. But stay here in the city until the Holy Spirit comes and fills you with power from heaven."

The Ascension

⁵⁰Then Jesus led them to Bethany, and lifting his hands to heaven, he blessed them. ⁵¹While he was blessing them, he left them and was taken up to heaven.* ⁵²They worshiped him and* then returned to Jerusalem filled with great joy. ⁵³And they spent all of their time in the Temple, praising God.

24:51 Some manuscripts do not include *and was taken up to heaven.*   24:52 Some manuscripts do not include *worshiped him and.*

John

Christ, the Eternal Word

In the beginning the Word already existed. He was with God, and he was God. ²He was in the beginning with God. ³He created everything there is. Nothing exists that he didn't make. ⁴Life itself was in him, and this life gives light to everyone. ⁵The light shines through the darkness, and the darkness can never extinguish it.

⁶God sent John the Baptist ⁷to tell everyone about the light so that everyone might believe because of his testimony. ⁸John himself was not the light; he was only a witness to the light. ⁹The one who is the true light, who gives light to everyone, was going to come into the world.

¹⁰But although the world was made through him, the world didn't recognize him when he came. ¹¹Even in his own land and among his own people, he was not accepted. ¹²But to all who believed him and accepted him, he gave the right to become children of God. ¹³They are reborn! This is not a physical birth resulting from human passion or plan—this rebirth comes from God.

¹⁴So the Word became human and lived here on earth among us. He was full of unfailing love and faithfulness.* And we have seen his glory, the glory of the only Son of the Father.

¹⁵John pointed him out to the people. He shouted to the crowds, "This is the one I was talking about when I said, 'Someone is coming who is far greater than I am, for he existed long before I did.'"

¹⁶We have all benefited from the rich blessings he brought to us—one gracious blessing after another.* ¹⁷For the law was given through Moses; God's unfailing love and faithfulness came through Jesus Christ. ¹⁸No one has ever seen God. But his only Son, who is himself God,* is near to the Father's heart; he has told us about him.

The Testimony of John the Baptist

¹⁹This was the testimony of John when the Jewish leaders sent priests and Temple assistants* from Jerusalem to ask John whether he claimed to be the Messiah. ²⁰He flatly denied it. "I am not the Messiah," he said.

²¹"Well then, who are you?" they asked. "Are you Elijah?"

"No," he replied.

"Are you the Prophet?"*

"No."

²²"Then who are you? Tell us, so we can give an answer to those who sent us. What do you have to say about yourself?"

²³John replied in the words of Isaiah:

"I am a voice shouting in the wilderness,
  'Prepare a straight pathway for the Lord's
    coming!'"*

²⁴Then those who were sent by the Pharisees ²⁵asked him, "If you aren't the Messiah or Elijah or the Prophet, what right do you have to baptize?"

²⁶John told them, "I baptize with* water, but right here in the crowd is someone you do not know, ²⁷who will soon begin his ministry. I am not even worthy to be his slave.*" ²⁸This incident took place at Bethany, a village east of the Jordan River, where John was baptizing.

Jesus, the Lamb of God

²⁹The next day John saw Jesus coming toward him and said, "Look! There is the Lamb of God who takes away the sin of the world! ³⁰He is the one I was talking about when I said, 'Soon a

1:14 Greek *grace and truth;* also in 1:17.   1:16 Greek *grace upon grace.*   1:18 Some manuscripts read *his one and only Son.*   1:19 Greek *and Levites.*   1:21 See Deut 18:15, 18; Mal 4:5-6.   1:23 Isa 40:3.   1:26 Or *in;* also in 1:31, 33.   1:27 Greek *to untie his sandals.*

man is coming who is far greater than I am, for he existed long before I did.' ³¹I didn't know he was the one, but I have been baptizing with water in order to point him out to Israel."

³²Then John said, "I saw the Holy Spirit descending like a dove from heaven and resting upon him. ³³I didn't know he was the one, but when God sent me to baptize with water, he told me, 'When you see the Holy Spirit descending and resting upon someone, he is the one you are looking for. He is the one who baptizes with the Holy Spirit.' ³⁴I saw this happen to Jesus, so I testify that he is the Son of God.*"

The First Disciples

³⁵The following day, John was again standing with two of his disciples. ³⁶As Jesus walked by, John looked at him and then declared, "Look! There is the Lamb of God!" ³⁷Then John's two disciples turned and followed Jesus.

³⁸Jesus looked around and saw them following. "What do you want?" he asked them.

They replied, "Rabbi" (which means Teacher), "where are you staying?"

³⁹"Come and see," he said. It was about four o'clock in the afternoon when they went with him to the place, and they stayed there the rest of the day.

⁴⁰Andrew, Simon Peter's brother, was one of these men who had heard what John said and then followed Jesus. ⁴¹The first thing Andrew did was to find his brother, Simon, and tell him, "We have found the Messiah" (which means the Christ).

⁴²Then Andrew brought Simon to meet Jesus. Looking intently at Simon, Jesus said, "You are Simon, the son of John—but you will be called Cephas" (which means Peter*).

⁴³The next day Jesus decided to go to Galilee. He found Philip and said to him, "Come, be my disciple." ⁴⁴Philip was from Bethsaida, Andrew and Peter's hometown.

⁴⁵Philip went off to look for Nathanael and told him, "We have found the very person Moses and the prophets wrote about! His name is Jesus, the son of Joseph from Nazareth."

⁴⁶"Nazareth!" exclaimed Nathanael. "Can anything good come from there?"

"Just come and see for yourself," Philip said.

⁴⁷As they approached, Jesus said, "Here comes an honest man—a true son of Israel."

⁴⁸"How do you know about me?" Nathanael asked.

And Jesus replied, "I could see you under the fig tree before Philip found you."

⁴⁹Nathanael replied, "Teacher, you are the Son of God—the King of Israel!"

⁵⁰Jesus asked him, "Do you believe all this just because I told you I had seen you under the fig tree? You will see greater things than this." ⁵¹Then he said, "The truth is, you will all see heaven open and the angels of God going up and down upon the Son of Man."*

CHAPTER **2**

The Wedding at Cana

The next day* Jesus' mother was a guest at a wedding celebration in the village of Cana in Galilee. ²Jesus and his disciples were also invited to the celebration. ³The wine supply ran out during the festivities, so Jesus' mother spoke to him about the problem. "They have no more wine," she told him.

⁴"How does that concern you and me?" Jesus asked. "My time has not yet come."

⁵But his mother told the servants, "Do whatever he tells you."

⁶Six stone waterpots were standing there; they were used for Jewish ceremonial purposes and held twenty to thirty gallons* each. ⁷Jesus told the servants, "Fill the jars with water." When the jars had been filled to the brim, ⁸he said, "Dip some out and take it to the master of ceremonies." So they followed his instructions.

⁹When the master of ceremonies tasted the water that was now wine, not knowing where it had come from (though, of course, the servants knew), he called the bridegroom over. ¹⁰"Usually a host serves the best wine first," he said. "Then, when everyone is full and doesn't care, he brings out the less expensive wines. But you have kept the best until now!"

¹¹This miraculous sign at Cana in Galilee was Jesus' first display of his glory. And his disciples believed in him.

¹²After the wedding he went to Capernaum for a few days with his mother, his brothers, and his disciples.

Jesus Clears the Temple

¹³It was time for the annual Passover celebration, and Jesus went to Jerusalem. ¹⁴In the Temple area he saw merchants selling cattle, sheep, and doves for sacrifices; and he saw money changers behind their counters. ¹⁵Jesus made a whip from some

---

1:34 Some manuscripts read *the chosen One of God.*   1:42 The names *Cephas* and *Peter* both mean "rock."   1:51 See Gen 28:10-17, the account of Jacob's ladder.   2:1 Greek *On the third day;* see 1:35, 43.   2:6 Greek *2 or 3 measures* [75 to 113 liters].

ropes and chased them all out of the Temple. He drove out the sheep and oxen, scattered the money changers' coins over the floor, and turned over their tables. 16Then, going over to the people who sold doves, he told them, "Get these things out of here. Don't turn my Father's house into a marketplace!"

17Then his disciples remembered this prophecy from the Scriptures: "Passion for God's house burns within me."*

18"What right do you have to do these things?" the Jewish leaders demanded. "If you have this authority from God, show us a miraculous sign to prove it."

19"All right," Jesus replied. "Destroy this temple, and in three days I will raise it up."

20"What!" they exclaimed. "It took forty-six years to build this Temple, and you can do it in three days?" 21But by "this temple," Jesus meant his body. 22After he was raised from the dead, the disciples remembered that he had said this. And they believed both Jesus and the Scriptures.

23Because of the miraculous signs he did in Jerusalem at the Passover celebration, many people were convinced that he was indeed the Messiah. 24But Jesus didn't trust them, because he knew what people were really like. 25No one needed to tell him about human nature.

CHAPTER 3

Jesus and Nicodemus

After dark one evening, a Jewish religious leader named Nicodemus, a Pharisee, 2came to speak with Jesus. "Teacher," he said, "we all know that God has sent you to teach us. Your miraculous signs are proof enough that God is with you."

3Jesus replied, "I assure you, unless you are born again,* you can never see the Kingdom of God."

4"What do you mean?" exclaimed Nicodemus. "How can an old man go back into his mother's womb and be born again?"

5Jesus replied, "The truth is, no one can enter the Kingdom of God without being born of water and the Spirit.* 6Humans can reproduce only human life, but the Holy Spirit gives new life from heaven. 7So don't be surprised at my statement that you* must be born again. 8Just as you can hear the wind but can't tell where it comes from or where it is going, so you can't explain how people are born of the Spirit."

9"What do you mean?" Nicodemus asked.

10Jesus replied, "You are a respected Jewish teacher, and yet you don't understand these things? 11I assure you, I am telling you what we know and have seen, and yet you won't believe us. 12But if you don't even believe me when I tell you about things that happen here on earth, how can you possibly believe if I tell you what is going on in heaven? 13For only I, the Son of Man,* have come to earth and will return to heaven again. 14And as Moses lifted up the bronze snake on a pole in the wilderness, so I, the Son of Man, must be lifted up on a pole,* 15so that everyone who believes in me will have eternal life.

16"For God so loved the world that he gave his only Son, so that everyone who believes in him will not perish but have eternal life. 17God did not send his Son into the world to condemn it, but to save it.

18"There is no judgment awaiting those who trust him. But those who do not trust him have already been judged for not believing in the only Son of God. 19Their judgment is based on this fact: The light from heaven came into the world, but they loved the darkness more than the light, for their actions were evil. 20They hate the light because they want to sin in the darkness. They stay away from the light for fear their sins will be exposed and they will be punished. 21But those who do what is right come to the light gladly, so everyone can see that they are doing what God wants."

John the Baptist Exalts Jesus

22Afterward Jesus and his disciples left Jerusalem, but they stayed in Judea for a while and baptized there.

23At this time John the Baptist was baptizing at Aenon, near Salim, because there was plenty of water there and people kept coming to him for baptism. 24This was before John was put into prison. 25At that time a certain Jew began an argument with John's disciples over ceremonial cleansing. 26John's disciples came to him and said, "Teacher, the man you met on the other side of the Jordan River, the one you said was the Messiah, is also baptizing people. And everybody is going over there instead of coming here to us."

27John replied, "God in heaven appoints each person's work. 28You yourselves know how plainly I told you that I am not the Messiah. I am here to prepare the way for him—that is all. 29The bride will go where the bridegroom is. A

2:17 Or "Concern for God's house will be my undoing." Ps 69:9. 3:3 Or born from above; also in 3:7. 3:5 Or spirit. The Greek word for Spirit can also be translated wind; see 3:8. 3:7 The Greek word for you is plural; also in 3:12. 3:13 Some manuscripts add who lives in heaven. 3:14 Greek must be lifted up.

Do not hide in darkness and sin! Go to the light and follow the Lord for eternal life!

bridegroom's friend rejoices with him. I am the bridegroom's friend, and I am filled with joy at his success. 30He must become greater and greater, and I must become less and less.

31"He has come from above and is greater than anyone else. I am of the earth, and my understanding is limited to the things of earth, but he has come from heaven.* 32He tells what he has seen and heard, but how few believe what he tells them! 33Those who believe him discover that God is true. 34For he is sent by God. He speaks God's words, for God's Spirit is upon him without measure or limit. 35The Father loves his Son, and he has given him authority over everything. 36And all who believe in God's Son have eternal life. Those who don't obey the Son will never experience eternal life, but the wrath of God remains upon them."

CHAPTER **4**

Jesus and the Samaritan Woman

Jesus* learned that the Pharisees had heard, "Jesus is baptizing and making more disciples than John" 2(though Jesus himself didn't baptize them—his disciples did). 3So he left Judea to return to Galilee.

4He had to go through Samaria on the way. 5Eventually he came to the Samaritan village of Sychar, near the parcel of ground that Jacob gave to his son Joseph. 6Jacob's well was there; and Jesus, tired from the long walk, sat wearily beside the well about noontime. 7Soon a Samaritan woman came to draw water, and Jesus said to her, "Please give me a drink." 8He was alone at the time because his disciples had gone into the village to buy some food.

9The woman was surprised, for Jews refuse to have anything to do with Samaritans. She said to Jesus, "You are a Jew, and I am a Samaritan woman. Why are you asking me for a drink?"

10Jesus replied, "If you only knew the gift God has for you and who I am, you would ask me, and I would give you living water."

11"But sir, you don't have a rope or a bucket," she said, "and this is a very deep well. Where would you get this living water? 12And besides, are you greater than our ancestor Jacob who gave us this well? How can you offer better water than he and his sons and his cattle enjoyed?"

13Jesus replied, "People soon become thirsty again after drinking this water. 14But the water I give them takes away thirst altogether. It be-

comes a perpetual spring within them, giving them eternal life."

15"Please, sir," the woman said, "give me some of that water! Then I'll never be thirsty again, and I won't have to come here to haul water."

16"Go and get your husband," Jesus told her.

17"I don't have a husband," the woman replied.

Jesus said, "You're right! You don't have a husband—18for you have had five husbands, and you aren't even married to the man you're living with now."

19"Sir," the woman said, "you must be a prophet. 20So tell me, why is it that you Jews insist that Jerusalem is the only place of worship, while we Samaritans claim it is here at Mount Gerizim,* where our ancestors worshiped?"

21Jesus replied, "Believe me, the time is coming when it will no longer matter whether you worship the Father here or in Jerusalem. 22You Samaritans know so little about the one you worship, while we Jews know all about him, for salvation comes through the Jews. 23But the time is coming and is already here when true worshipers will worship the Father in spirit and in truth. The Father is looking for anyone who will worship him that way. 24For God is Spirit, so those who worship him must worship in spirit and in truth."

25The woman said, "I know the Messiah will come—the one who is called Christ. When he comes, he will explain everything to us."

26Then Jesus told her, "I am the Messiah!"*

27Just then his disciples arrived. They were astonished to find him talking to a woman, but none of them asked him why he was doing it or what they had been discussing. 28The woman left her water jar beside the well and went back to the village and told everyone, 29"Come and meet a man who told me everything I ever did! Can this be the Messiah?" 30So the people came streaming from the village to see him.

31Meanwhile, the disciples were urging Jesus to eat. 32"No," he said, "I have food you don't know about."

33"Who brought it to him?" the disciples asked each other.

34Then Jesus explained: "My nourishment comes from doing the will of God, who sent me, and from finishing his work. 35Do you think the work of harvesting will not begin until the summer ends four months from now? Look around

3:31 Some manuscripts omit *but he has come from heaven.*   **4:1** Some manuscripts read *The Lord.*   **4:20** Greek *on this mountain.*   **4:26** Greek *"I am, the one speaking to you."*

you! Vast fields are ripening all around us and are ready now for the harvest. 36The harvesters are paid good wages, and the fruit they harvest is people brought to eternal life. What joy awaits both the planter and the harvester alike! 37You know the saying, 'One person plants and someone else harvests.' And it's true. 38I sent you to harvest where you didn't plant; others had already done the work, and you will gather the harvest."

Many Samaritans Believe
39Many Samaritans from the village believed in Jesus because the woman had said, "He told me everything I ever did!" 40When they came out to see him, they begged him to stay at their village. So he stayed for two days, 41long enough for many of them to hear his message and believe. 42Then they said to the woman, "Now we believe because we have heard him ourselves, not just because of what you told us. He is indeed the Savior of the world."

Jesus Heals an Official's Son
43At the end of the two days' stay, Jesus went on into Galilee. 44He had previously said, "A prophet is honored everywhere except in his own country." 45The Galileans welcomed him, for they had been in Jerusalem at the Passover celebration and had seen all his miraculous signs.

46In the course of his journey through Galilee, he arrived at the town of Cana, where he had turned the water into wine. There was a government official in the city of Capernaum whose son was very sick. 47When he heard that Jesus had come from Judea and was traveling in Galilee, he went over to Cana. He found Jesus and begged him to come to Capernaum with him to heal his son, who was about to die.

48Jesus asked, "Must I do miraculous signs and wonders before you people will believe in me?"

49The official pleaded, "Lord, please come now before my little boy dies."

50Then Jesus told him, "Go back home. Your son will live!" And the man believed Jesus' word and started home.

51While he was on his way, some of his servants met him with the news that his son was alive and well. 52He asked them when the boy had begun to feel better, and they replied, "Yesterday afternoon at one o'clock his fever suddenly disappeared!" 53Then the father realized it was the same time that Jesus had told him,

"Your son will live." And the officer and his entire household believed in Jesus. 54This was Jesus' second miraculous sign in Galilee after coming from Judea.

CHAPTER 5
Jesus Heals a Lame Man
Afterward Jesus returned to Jerusalem for one of the Jewish holy days. 2Inside the city, near the Sheep Gate, was the pool of Bethesda,* with five covered porches. 3Crowds of sick people— blind, lame, or paralyzed—lay on the porches.* 5One of the men lying there had been sick for thirty-eight years. 6When Jesus saw him and knew how long he had been ill, he asked him, "Would you like to get well?"

7"I can't, sir," the sick man said, "for I have no one to help me into the pool when the water is stirred up. While I am trying to get there, someone else always gets in ahead of me."

8Jesus told him, "Stand up, pick up your sleeping mat, and walk!"

9Instantly, the man was healed! He rolled up the mat and began walking! But this miracle happened on the Sabbath day. 10So the Jewish leaders objected. They said to the man who was cured, "You can't work on the Sabbath! It's illegal to carry that sleeping mat!"

11He replied, "The man who healed me said to me, 'Pick up your sleeping mat and walk.' "

12"Who said such a thing as that?" they demanded.

13The man didn't know, for Jesus had disappeared into the crowd. 14But afterward Jesus found him in the Temple and told him, "Now you are well; so stop sinning, or something even worse may happen to you." 15Then the man went to find the Jewish leaders and told them it was Jesus who had healed him.

Jesus Claims to Be the Son of God
16So the Jewish leaders began harassing Jesus for breaking the Sabbath rules. 17But Jesus replied, "My Father never stops working, so why should I?" 18So the Jewish leaders tried all the more to kill him. In addition to disobeying the Sabbath rules, he had spoken of God as his Father, thereby making himself equal with God.

19Jesus replied, "I assure you, the Son can do nothing by himself. He does only what he sees the Father doing. Whatever the Father does, the Son also does. 20For the Father loves the Son and

5:2 Some manuscripts read *Beth-zatha;* other manuscripts read *Bethsaida.*   5:3 Some manuscripts add *waiting for a certain movement of the water,* 4*for an angel of the Lord came from time to time and stirred up the water. And the first person to step down into it afterward was healed.*

tells him everything he is doing, and the Son will do far greater things than healing this man. You will be astonished at what he does. 21He will even raise from the dead anyone he wants to, just as the Father does. 22And the Father leaves all judgment to his Son, 23so that everyone will honor the Son, just as they honor the Father. But if you refuse to honor the Son, then you are certainly not honoring the Father who sent him.

24"I assure you, those who listen to my message and believe in God who sent me have eternal life. They will never be condemned for their sins, but they have already passed from death into life.

25"And I assure you that the time is coming, in fact it is here, when the dead will hear my voice—the voice of the Son of God. And those who listen will live. 26The Father has life in himself, and he has granted his Son to have life in himself. 27And he has given him authority to judge all mankind because he is the Son of Man. 28Don't be so surprised! Indeed, the time is coming when all the dead in their graves will hear the voice of God's Son, 29and they will rise again. Those who have done good will rise to eternal life, and those who have continued in evil will rise to judgment. 30But I do nothing without consulting the Father. I judge as I am told. And my judgment is absolutely just, because it is according to the will of God who sent me; it is not merely my own.

Witnesses to Jesus

31"If I were to testify on my own behalf, my testimony would not be valid. 32But someone else is also testifying about me, and I can assure you that everything he says about me is true. 33In fact, you sent messengers to listen to John the Baptist, and he preached the truth. 34But the best testimony about me is not from a man, though I have reminded you about John's testimony so you might be saved. 35John shone brightly for a while, and you benefited and rejoiced. 36But I have a greater witness than John—my teachings and my miracles. They have been assigned to me by the Father, and they testify that the Father has sent me. 37And the Father himself has also testified about me. You have never heard his voice or seen him face to face, 38and you do not have his message in your hearts, because you do not believe me—the one he sent to you.

39"You search the Scriptures because you believe they give you eternal life. But the Scriptures point to me! 40Yet you refuse to come to me so that I can give you this eternal life.

41"Your approval or disapproval means nothing to me, 42because I know you don't have God's love within you. 43For I have come to you representing my Father, and you refuse to welcome me, even though you readily accept others who represent only themselves. 44No wonder you can't believe! For you gladly honor each other, but you don't care about the honor that comes from God alone.

45"Yet it is not I who will accuse you of this before the Father. Moses will accuse you! Yes, Moses, on whom you set your hopes. 46But if you had believed Moses, you would have believed me because he wrote about me. 47And since you don't believe what he wrote, how will you believe what I say?"

CHAPTER **6**

Jesus Feeds Five Thousand

After this, Jesus crossed over the Sea of Galilee, also known as the Sea of Tiberias. 2And a huge crowd kept following him wherever he went, because they saw his miracles as he healed the sick. 3Then Jesus went up into the hills and sat down with his disciples around him. 4(It was nearly time for the annual Passover celebration.) 5Jesus soon saw a great crowd of people climbing the hill, looking for him. Turning to Philip, he asked, "Philip, where can we buy bread to feed all these people?" 6He was testing Philip, for he already knew what he was going to do.

7Philip replied, "It would take a small fortune* to feed them!"

8Then Andrew, Simon Peter's brother, spoke up. 9"There's a young boy here with five barley loaves and two fish. But what good is that with this huge crowd?"

10"Tell everyone to sit down," Jesus ordered. So all of them—the men alone numbered five thousand—sat down on the grassy slopes. 11Then Jesus took the loaves, gave thanks to God, and passed them out to the people. Afterward he did the same with the fish. And they all ate until they were full. 12"Now gather the leftovers," Jesus told his disciples, "so that nothing is wasted." 13There were only five barley loaves to start with, but twelve baskets were filled with the pieces of bread the people did not eat!

14When the people saw this miraculous sign, they exclaimed, "Surely, he is the Prophet* we have been expecting!" 15Jesus saw that they were ready to take him by force and make him king, so he went higher into the hills alone.

6:7 Greek *200 denarii. A denarius was the equivalent of a full day's wage.* 6:14 See Deut 18:15, 18.

Jesus Walks on Water

16That evening his disciples went down to the shore to wait for him. 17But as darkness fell and Jesus still hadn't come back, they got into the boat and headed out across the lake toward Capernaum. 18Soon a gale swept down upon them as they rowed, and the sea grew very rough. 19They were three or four miles* out when suddenly they saw Jesus walking on the water toward the boat. They were terrified, 20but he called out to them, "I am here! Don't be afraid." 21Then they were eager to let him in, and immediately the boat arrived at their destination!

Jesus, the Bread of Life

22The next morning, back across the lake, crowds began gathering on the shore, waiting to see Jesus. For they knew that he and his disciples had come over together and that the disciples had gone off in their boat, leaving him behind. 23Several boats from Tiberias landed near the place where the Lord had blessed the bread and the people had eaten. 24When the crowd saw that Jesus wasn't there, nor his disciples, they got into the boats and went across to Capernaum to look for him. 25When they arrived and found him, they asked, "Teacher, how did you get here?"

26Jesus replied, "The truth is, you want to be with me because I fed you, not because you saw the miraculous sign. 27But you shouldn't be so concerned about perishable things like food. Spend your energy seeking the eternal life that I, the Son of Man, can give you. For God the Father has sent me for that very purpose."

28They replied, "What does God want us to do?"

29Jesus told them, "This is what God wants you to do: Believe in the one he has sent."

30They replied, "You must show us a miraculous sign if you want us to believe in you. What will you do for us? 31After all, our ancestors ate manna while they journeyed through the wilderness! As the Scriptures say, 'Moses gave them bread from heaven to eat.'* "

32Jesus said, "I assure you, Moses didn't give them bread from heaven. My Father did. And now he offers you the true bread from heaven. 33The true bread of God is the one who comes down from heaven and gives life to the world."

34"Sir," they said, "give us that bread every day of our lives."

35Jesus replied, "I am the bread of life. No one who comes to me will ever be hungry again.

Those who believe in me will never thirst. 36But you haven't believed in me even though you have seen me. 37However, those the Father has given me will come to me, and I will never reject them. 38For I have come down from heaven to do the will of God who sent me, not to do what I want. 39And this is the will of God, that I should not lose even one of all those he has given me, but that I should raise them to eternal life at the last day. 40For it is my Father's will that all who see his Son and believe in him should have eternal life— that I should raise them at the last day."

41Then the people* began to murmur in disagreement because he had said, "I am the bread from heaven." 42They said, "This is Jesus, the son of Joseph. We know his father and mother. How can he say, 'I came down from heaven'?"

43But Jesus replied, "Don't complain about what I said. 44For people can't come to me unless the Father who sent me draws them to me, and at the last day I will raise them from the dead. 45As it is written in the Scriptures, 'They will all be taught by God.'* Everyone who hears and learns from the Father comes to me. 46(Not that anyone has ever seen the Father; only I, who was sent from God, have seen him.)

47"I assure you, anyone who believes in me already has eternal life. 48Yes, I am the bread of life! 49Your ancestors ate manna in the wilderness, but they all died. 50However, the bread from heaven gives eternal life to everyone who eats it. 51I am the living bread that came down out of heaven. Anyone who eats this bread will live forever; this bread is my flesh, offered so the world may live."

52Then the people began arguing with each other about what he meant. "How can this man give us his flesh to eat?" they asked.

53So Jesus said again, "I assure you, unless you eat the flesh of the Son of Man and drink his blood, you cannot have eternal life within you. 54But those who eat my flesh and drink my blood have eternal life, and I will raise them at the last day. 55For my flesh is the true food, and my blood is the true drink. 56All who eat my flesh and drink my blood remain in me, and I in them. 57I live by the power of the living Father who sent me; in the same way, those who partake of me will live because of me. 58I am the true bread from heaven. Anyone who eats this bread will live forever and not die as your ancestors did, even though they ate the manna."

6:19 Greek 25 or 30 stadia [4.6 or 5.5 kilometers]. 6:31 Exod 16:4; Ps 78:24. 6:41 Greek Jewish people; also in 6:52. 6:45 Isa 54:13.

59He said these things while he was teaching in the synagogue in Capernaum.

Many Disciples Desert Jesus

60Even his disciples said, "This is very hard to understand. How can anyone accept it?"

61Jesus knew within himself that his disciples were complaining, so he said to them, "Does this offend you? 62Then what will you think if you see me, the Son of Man, return to heaven again? 63It is the Spirit who gives eternal life. Human effort accomplishes nothing. And the very words I have spoken to you are spirit and life. 64But some of you don't believe me." (For Jesus knew from the beginning who didn't believe, and he knew who would betray him.) 65Then he said, "That is what I meant when I said that people can't come to me unless the Father brings them to me."

66At this point many of his disciples turned away and deserted him. 67Then Jesus turned to the Twelve and asked, "Are you going to leave, too?"

68Simon Peter replied, "Lord, to whom would we go? You alone have the words that give eternal life. 69We believe them, and we know you are the Holy One of God."

70Then Jesus said, "I chose the twelve of you, but one is a devil." 71He was speaking of Judas, son of Simon Iscariot, one of the Twelve, who would betray him.

CHAPTER 7

Jesus and His Brothers

After this, Jesus stayed in Galilee, going from village to village. He wanted to stay out of Judea where the Jewish leaders were plotting his death. 2But soon it was time for the Festival of Shelters, 3and Jesus' brothers urged him to go to Judea for the celebration. "Go where your followers can see your miracles!" they scoffed. 4"You can't become a public figure if you hide like this! If you can do such wonderful things, prove it to the world!" 5For even his brothers didn't believe in him.

6Jesus replied, "Now is not the right time for me to go. But you can go anytime, and it will make no difference. 7The world can't hate you, but it does hate me because I accuse it of sin and evil. 8You go on. I am not yet* ready to go to this festival, because my time has not yet come." 9So Jesus remained in Galilee.

Jesus Teaches Openly at the Temple

10But after his brothers had left for the festival, Jesus also went, though secretly, staying out of

public view. 11The Jewish leaders tried to find him at the festival and kept asking if anyone had seen him. 12There was a lot of discussion about him among the crowds. Some said, "He's a wonderful man," while others said, "He's nothing but a fraud, deceiving the people." 13But no one had the courage to speak favorably about him in public, for they were afraid of getting in trouble with the Jewish leaders.

14Then, midway through the festival, Jesus went up to the Temple and began to teach. 15The Jewish leaders were surprised when they heard him. "How does he know so much when he hasn't studied everything we've studied?" they asked.

16So Jesus told them, "I'm not teaching my own ideas, but those of God who sent me. 17Anyone who wants to do the will of God will know whether my teaching is from God or is merely my own. 18Those who present their own ideas are looking for praise for themselves, but those who seek to honor the one who sent them are good and genuine. 19None of you obeys the law of Moses! In fact, you are trying to kill me."

20The crowd replied, "You're demon possessed! Who's trying to kill you?"

21Jesus replied, "I worked on the Sabbath by healing a man, and you were offended. 22But you work on the Sabbath, too, when you obey Moses' law of circumcision. (Actually, this tradition of circumcision is older than the law of Moses; it goes back to Abraham.) 23For if the correct time for circumcising your son falls on the Sabbath, you go ahead and do it, so as not to break the law of Moses. So why should I be condemned for making a man completely well on the Sabbath? 24Think this through and you will see that I am right."

Is Jesus the Messiah?

25Some of the people who lived there in Jerusalem said among themselves, "Isn't this the man they are trying to kill? 26But here he is, speaking in public, and they say nothing to him. Can it be that our leaders know that he really is the Messiah? 27But how could he be? For we know where this man comes from. When the Messiah comes, he will simply appear; no one will know where he comes from."

28While Jesus was teaching in the Temple, he called out, "Yes, you know me, and you know where I come from. But I represent one you don't know, and he is true. 29I know him be-

7:8 Some manuscripts omit *yet*.

cause I have come from him, and he sent me to you." 30Then the leaders tried to arrest him; but no one laid a hand on him, because his time had not yet come.

31Many among the crowds at the Temple believed in him. "After all," they said, "would you expect the Messiah to do more miraculous signs than this man has done?"

32When the Pharisees heard that the crowds were murmuring such things, they and the leading priests sent Temple guards to arrest Jesus. 33But Jesus told them, "I will be here a little longer. Then I will return to the one who sent me. 34You will search for me but not find me. And you won't be able to come where I am."

35The Jewish leaders were puzzled by this statement. "Where is he planning to go?" they asked. "Maybe he is thinking of leaving the country and going to the Jews in other lands, or maybe even to the Gentiles! 36What does he mean when he says, 'You will search for me but not find me,' and 'You won't be able to come where I am'?"

Jesus Promises Living Water

37On the last day, the climax of the festival, Jesus stood and shouted to the crowds, "If you are thirsty, come to me! 38If you believe in me, come and drink! For the Scriptures declare that rivers of living water will flow out from within."* 39(When he said "living water," he was speaking of the Spirit, who would be given to everyone believing in him. But the Spirit had not yet been given, because Jesus had not yet entered into his glory.)

Division and Unbelief

40When the crowds heard him say this, some of them declared, "This man surely is the Prophet."* 41Others said, "He is the Messiah." Still others said, "But he can't be! Will the Messiah come from Galilee? 42For the Scriptures clearly state that the Messiah will be born of the royal line of David, in Bethlehem, the village where King David was born."* 43So the crowd was divided in their opinion about him. 44And some wanted him arrested, but no one touched him.

45The Temple guards who had been sent to arrest him returned to the leading priests and Pharisees. "Why didn't you bring him in?" they demanded.

46"We have never heard anyone talk like this!" the guards responded.

47"Have you been led astray, too?" the Phari-

sees mocked. 48"Is there a single one of us rulers or Pharisees who believes in him? 49These ignorant crowds do, but what do they know about it? A curse on them anyway!"

50Nicodemus, the leader who had met with Jesus earlier, then spoke up. 51"Is it legal to convict a man before he is given a hearing?" he asked.

52They replied, "Are you from Galilee, too? Search the Scriptures and see for yourself—no prophet ever comes from Galilee!"

[The most ancient Greek manuscripts do not include John 7:53–8:11.]

53Then the meeting broke up and everybody went home.

CHAPTER 8

A Woman Caught in Adultery

Jesus returned to the Mount of Olives, 2but early the next morning he was back again at the Temple. A crowd soon gathered, and he sat down and taught them. 3As he was speaking, the teachers of religious law and Pharisees brought a woman they had caught in the act of adultery. They put her in front of the crowd.

4"Teacher," they said to Jesus, "this woman was caught in the very act of adultery. 5The law of Moses says to stone her. What do you say?"

6They were trying to trap him into saying something they could use against him, but Jesus stooped down and wrote in the dust with his finger. 7They kept demanding an answer, so he stood up again and said, "All right, stone her. But let those who have never sinned throw the first stones!" 8Then he stooped down again and wrote in the dust.

9When the accusers heard this, they slipped away one by one, beginning with the oldest, until only Jesus was left in the middle of the crowd with the woman. 10Then Jesus stood up again and said to her, "Where are your accusers? Didn't even one of them condemn you?"

11"No, Lord," she said.

And Jesus said, "Neither do I. Go and sin no more."

Jesus, the Light of the World

12Jesus said to the people, "I am the light of the world. If you follow me, you won't be stumbling through the darkness, because you will have the light that leads to life."

7:37-38 Or *"Let anyone who is thirsty come to me and drink.* 38*For the Scriptures declare that rivers of living water will flow from the heart of those who believe in me."* 7:40 See Deut 18:15, 18. 7:42 See Mic 5:2.

13The Pharisees replied, "You are making false claims about yourself!"

14Jesus told them, "These claims are valid even though I make them about myself. For I know where I came from and where I am going, but you don't know this about me. 15You judge me with all your human limitations,* but I am not judging anyone. 16And if I did, my judgment would be correct in every respect because I am not alone—I have with me the Father who sent me. 17Your own law says that if two people agree about something, their witness is accepted as fact.* 18I am one witness, and my Father who sent me is the other."

19"Where is your father?" they asked.

Jesus answered, "Since you don't know who I am, you don't know who my Father is. If you knew me, then you would know my Father, too." 20Jesus made these statements while he was teaching in the section of the Temple known as the Treasury. But he was not arrested, because his time had not yet come.

The Unbelieving People Warned

21Later Jesus said to them again, "I am going away. You will search for me and die in your sin. You cannot come where I am going."

22The Jewish leaders asked, "Is he planning to commit suicide? What does he mean, 'You cannot come where I am going'?"

23Then he said to them, "You are from below; I am from above. You are of this world; I am not. 24That is why I said that you will die in your sins; for unless you believe that I am who I say I am, you will die in your sins."

25"Tell us who you are," they demanded.

Jesus replied, "I am the one I have always claimed to be.* 26I have much to say about you and much to condemn, but I won't. For I say only what I have heard from the one who sent me, and he is true." 27But they still didn't understand that he was talking to them about his Father.

28So Jesus said, "When you have lifted up the Son of Man on the cross, then you will realize that I am he and that I do nothing on my own, but I speak what the Father taught me. 29And the one who sent me is with me—he has not deserted me. For I always do those things that are pleasing to him." 30Then many who heard him say these things believed in him.

Jesus and Abraham

31Jesus said to the people* who believed in him, "You are truly my disciples if you keep obeying my teachings. 32And you will know the truth, and the truth will set you free."

33"But we are descendants of Abraham," they said. "We have never been slaves to anyone on earth. What do you mean, 'set free'?"

34Jesus replied, "I assure you that everyone who sins is a slave of sin. 35A slave is not a permanent member of the family, but a son is part of the family forever. 36So if the Son sets you free, you will indeed be free. 37Yes, I realize that you are descendants of Abraham. And yet some of you are trying to kill me because my message does not find a place in your hearts. 38I am telling you what I saw when I was with my Father. But you are following the advice of your father."

39"Our father is Abraham," they declared.

"No," Jesus replied, "for if you were children of Abraham, you would follow his good example.* 40I told you the truth I heard from God, but you are trying to kill me. Abraham wouldn't do a thing like that. 41No, you are obeying your real father when you act that way."

They replied, "We were not born out of wedlock! Our true Father is God himself."

42Jesus told them, "If God were your Father, you would love me, because I have come to you from God. I am not here on my own, but he sent me. 43Why can't you understand what I am saying? It is because you are unable to do so! 44For you are the children of your father the Devil, and you love to do the evil things he does. He was a murderer from the beginning and has always hated the truth. There is no truth in him. When he lies, it is consistent with his character; for he is a liar and the father of lies. 45So when I tell the truth, you just naturally don't believe me! 46Which of you can truthfully accuse me of sin? And since I am telling you the truth, why don't you believe me? 47Anyone whose Father is God listens gladly to the words of God. Since you don't, it proves you aren't God's children."

48The people retorted, "You Samaritan devil! Didn't we say all along that you were possessed by a demon?"

49"No," Jesus said, "I have no demon in me. For I honor my Father—and you dishonor me. 50And though I have no wish to glorify myself, God wants to glorify me. Let him be the judge. 51I assure you, anyone who obeys my teaching will never die!"

52The people said, "Now we know you are possessed by a demon. Even Abraham and the prophets died, but you say that those who obey

8:15 Or *judge me by human standards.* 8:17 See Deut 19:15. 8:25 Or *"Why do I speak to you at all?"* 8:31 Greek *Jewish people;* also in 8:48, 52, 57. 8:39 Some manuscripts read *if you are children of Abraham, follow his example.*

your teaching will never die! ⁵³Are you greater than our father Abraham, who died? Are you greater than the prophets, who died? Who do you think you are?"

⁵⁴Jesus answered, "If I am merely boasting about myself, it doesn't count. But it is my Father who says these glorious things about me. You say, 'He is our God,' ⁵⁵but you do not even know him. I know him. If I said otherwise, I would be as great a liar as you! But it is true—I know him and obey him. ⁵⁶Your ancestor Abraham rejoiced as he looked forward to my coming. He saw it and was glad."

⁵⁷The people said, "You aren't even fifty years old. How can you say you have seen Abraham?*"

⁵⁸Jesus answered, "The truth is, I existed before Abraham was even born!"* ⁵⁹At that point they picked up stones to kill him. But Jesus hid himself from them and left the Temple.

CHAPTER **9**

Jesus Heals a Man Born Blind

As Jesus was walking along, he saw a man who had been blind from birth. ²"Teacher," his disciples asked him, "why was this man born blind? Was it a result of his own sins or those of his parents?"

³"It was not because of his sins or his parents' sins," Jesus answered. "He was born blind so the power of God could be seen in him. ⁴All of us must quickly carry out the tasks assigned us by the one who sent me, because there is little time left before the night falls and all work comes to an end. ⁵But while I am still here in the world, I am the light of the world."

⁶Then he spit on the ground, made mud with the saliva, and smoothed the mud over the blind man's eyes. ⁷He told him, "Go and wash in the pool of Siloam" (Siloam means Sent). So the man went and washed, and came back seeing!

⁸His neighbors and others who knew him as a blind beggar asked each other, "Is this the same man—that beggar?" ⁹Some said he was, and others said, "No, but he surely looks like him!"

And the beggar kept saying, "I am the same man!"

¹⁰They asked, "Who healed you? What happened?"

¹¹He told them, "The man they call Jesus made mud and smoothed it over my eyes and told me, 'Go to the pool of Siloam and wash off the mud.' I went and washed, and now I can see!"

8:57 Some manuscripts read *How can you say Abraham has seen you?* 8:58 Or *"Truly, truly, before Abraham was, I am."*

¹²"Where is he now?" they asked.

"I don't know," he replied.

¹³Then they took the man to the Pharisees. ¹⁴Now as it happened, Jesus had healed the man on a Sabbath. ¹⁵The Pharisees asked the man all about it. So he told them, "He smoothed the mud over my eyes, and when it was washed away, I could see!"

¹⁶Some of the Pharisees said, "This man Jesus is not from God, for he is working on the Sabbath." Others said, "But how could an ordinary sinner do such miraculous signs?" So there was a deep division of opinion among them.

You Don't Need Any Training to Share Read JOHN 9:1-41

Perhaps one of the biggest reasons many Christians haven't shared their faith is that they feel God could never use them to draw people to himself. You might say, "I am not qualified to speak for God!" In reality, once you invite Jesus Christ into your life as Savior and Lord, you can begin to tell others about your newfound faith.

This passage tells the story of a blind man whose sight was restored when Jesus touched his eyes. After Jesus healed this man, certain religious rulers known as Pharisees challenged him, asking him some rather complex questions about Jesus. The man's response was classic. He said, "I know this: I was blind, and now I can see!"

In many ways, we as believers are like this formerly blind man. We, too, were once blinded by the power and deception of sin. Scripture tells us that "Satan, the god of this evil world" made us "blind" and "unable to see the glorious light of the Good News" (2 Corinthians 4:4). But one day God lovingly "opened our eyes" to see our real spiritual need, and we responded to the message of the Gospel.

Although we may not yet be great scholars of Scripture, we still know more about the gospel than many, and we can start with that. Like that blind man, we can, in a spiritual sense, say to others, "Once I was blind, but now I can see. . . ." As we study the Bible on a regular basis, we will be able to answer many of the questions people have about our faith.

For the next note on "Share Your Faith," turn to p. 933.

17Then the Pharisees once again questioned the man who had been blind and demanded, "This man who opened your eyes—who do you say he is?"

The man replied, "I think he must be a prophet."

18The Jewish leaders wouldn't believe he had been blind, so they called in his parents. 19They asked them, "Is this your son? Was he born blind? If so, how can he see?"

20His parents replied, "We know this is our son and that he was born blind, 21but we don't know how he can see or who healed him. He is old enough to speak for himself. Ask him." 22They said this because they were afraid of the Jewish leaders, who had announced that anyone saying Jesus was the Messiah would be expelled from the synagogue. 23That's why they said, "He is old enough to speak for himself. Ask him."

24So for the second time they called in the man who had been blind and told him, "Give glory to God by telling the truth,* because we know Jesus is a sinner."

25"I don't know whether he is a sinner," the man replied. "But I know this: I was blind, and now I can see!"

26"But what did he do?" they asked. "How did he heal you?"

27"Look!" the man exclaimed. "I told you once. Didn't you listen? Why do you want to hear it again? Do you want to become his disciples, too?"

28Then they cursed him and said, "You are his disciple, but we are disciples of Moses. 29We know God spoke to Moses, but as for this man, we don't know anything about him."

30"Why, that's very strange!" the man replied. "He healed my eyes, and yet you don't know anything about him! 31Well, God doesn't listen to sinners, but he is ready to hear those who worship him and do his will. 32Never since the world began has anyone been able to open the eyes of someone born blind. 33If this man were not from God, he couldn't do it."

34"You were born in sin!" they answered. "Are you trying to teach us?" And they threw him out of the synagogue.

Spiritual Blindness

35When Jesus heard what had happened, he found the man and said, "Do you believe in the Son of Man*?"

36The man answered, "Who is he, sir, because I would like to."

37"You have seen him," Jesus said, "and he is speaking to you!"

38"Yes, Lord," the man said, "I believe!" And he worshiped Jesus.

39Then Jesus told him, "I have come to judge the world. I have come to give sight to the blind and to show those who think they see that they are blind."

40The Pharisees who were standing there heard him and asked, "Are you saying we are blind?"

41"If you were blind, you wouldn't be guilty," Jesus replied. "But you remain guilty because you claim you can see.

CHAPTER **10**

The Good Shepherd and His Sheep

"I assure you, anyone who sneaks over the wall of a sheepfold, rather than going through the gate, must surely be a thief and a robber! 2For a shepherd enters through the gate. 3The gatekeeper opens the gate for him, and the sheep hear his voice and come to him. He calls his own sheep by name and leads them out. 4After he has gathered his own flock, he walks ahead of them, and they follow him because they recognize his voice. 5They won't follow a stranger; they will run from him because they don't recognize his voice."

6Those who heard Jesus use this illustration didn't understand what he meant, 7so he explained it to them. "I assure you, I am the gate for the sheep," he said. 8"All others who came before me were thieves and robbers. But the true sheep did not listen to them. 9Yes, I am the gate. Those who come in through me will be saved. Wherever they go, they will find green pastures. 10The thief's purpose is to steal and kill and destroy. My purpose is to give life in all its fullness.

11"I am the good shepherd. The good shepherd lays down his life for the sheep. 12A hired hand will run when he sees a wolf coming. He will leave the sheep because they aren't his and he isn't their shepherd. And so the wolf attacks them and scatters the flock. 13The hired hand runs away because he is merely hired and has no real concern for the sheep.

14"I am the good shepherd; I know my own sheep, and they know me, 15just as my Father knows me and I know the Father. And I lay down my life for the sheep. ¹⁶I have other sheep, too, that are not in this sheepfold. I must bring them also, and they will listen to my voice; and there will be one flock with one shepherd.

¹⁷"The Father loves me because I lay down my life that I may have it back again. ¹⁸No one can take my life from me. I lay down my life voluntarily. For I have the right to lay it down when I want to and also the power to take it again. For my Father has given me this command."

¹⁹When he said these things, the people* were again divided in their opinions about him. ²⁰Some of them said, "He has a demon, or he's crazy. Why listen to a man like that?" ²¹Others said, "This doesn't sound like a man possessed by a demon! Can a demon open the eyes of the blind?"

Jesus Claims to Be the Son of God

²²It was now winter, and Jesus was in Jerusalem at the time of Hanukkah.* ²³He was at the Temple, walking through the section known as Solomon's Colonnade. ²⁴The Jewish leaders surrounded him and asked, "How long are you going to keep us in suspense? If you are the Messiah, tell us plainly."

²⁵Jesus replied, "I have already told you, and you don't believe me. The proof is what I do in the name of my Father. ²⁶But you don't believe me because you are not part of my flock. ²⁷My sheep recognize my voice; I know them, and they follow me. ²⁸I give them eternal life, and they will never perish. No one will snatch them away from me, ²⁹for my Father has given them to me, and he is more powerful than anyone else. So no one can take them from me. ³⁰The Father and I are one."

³¹Once again the Jewish leaders picked up stones to kill him. ³²Jesus said, "At my Father's direction I have done many things to help the people. For which one of these good deeds are you killing me?"

³³They replied, "Not for any good work, but for blasphemy, because you, a mere man, have made yourself God."

³⁴Jesus replied, "It is written in your own law that God said to certain leaders of the people, 'I say, you are gods!'* ³⁵And you know that the Scriptures cannot be altered. So if those people, who received God's message, were called 'gods,' ³⁶why do you call it blasphemy when the Holy One who was sent into the world by the Father

says, 'I am the Son of God'? ³⁷Don't believe me unless I carry out my Father's work. ³⁸But if I do his work, believe in what I have done, even if you don't believe me. Then you will realize that the Father is in me, and I am in the Father."

³⁹Once again they tried to arrest him, but he got away and left them. ⁴⁰He went beyond the Jordan River to stay near the place where John was first baptizing. ⁴¹And many followed him. "John didn't do miracles," they remarked to one another, "but all his predictions about this man have come true." ⁴²And many believed in him there.

CHAPTER **11**
The Death of Lazarus

A man named Lazarus was sick. He lived in Bethany with his sisters, Mary and Martha. ²This is the Mary who poured the expensive perfume on the Lord's feet and wiped them with her hair.* Her brother, Lazarus, was sick. ³So the two sisters sent a message to Jesus telling him, "Lord, the one you love is very sick."

⁴But when Jesus heard about it he said, "Lazarus's sickness will not end in death. No, it is for the glory of God. I, the Son of God, will receive glory from this." ⁵Although Jesus loved Martha, Mary, and Lazarus, ⁶he stayed where he was for the next two days and did not go to them. ⁷Finally after two days, he said to his disciples, "Let's go to Judea again."

⁸But his disciples objected. "Teacher," they said, "only a few days ago the Jewish leaders in Judea were trying to kill you. Are you going there again?"

⁹Jesus replied, "There are twelve hours of daylight every day. As long as it is light, people can walk safely. They can see because they have the light of this world. ¹⁰Only at night is there danger of stumbling because there is no light."

¹¹Then he said, "Our friend Lazarus has fallen asleep, but now I will go and wake him up."

¹²The disciples said, "Lord, if he is sleeping, that means he is getting better!" ¹³They thought Jesus meant Lazarus was having a good night's rest, but Jesus meant Lazarus had died.

¹⁴Then he told them plainly, "Lazarus is dead. ¹⁵And for your sake, I am glad I wasn't there, because this will give you another opportunity to believe in me. Come, let's go see him."

¹⁶Thomas, nicknamed the Twin,* said to his fellow disciples, "Let's go, too—and die with Jesus."

10:19 Greek *Jewish people.* **10:22** Or *the Festival of Dedication.* **10:34** Ps 82:6. **11:2** This incident is recorded in chapter 12. **11:16** Greek *the one who was called Didymus.*

17When Jesus arrived at Bethany, he was told that Lazarus had already been in his grave for four days. 18Bethany was only a few miles* down the road from Jerusalem, 19and many of the people* had come to pay their respects and console Martha and Mary on their loss. 20When Martha got word that Jesus was coming, she went to meet him. But Mary stayed at home. 21Martha said to Jesus, "Lord, if you had been here, my brother would not have died. 22But even now I know that God will give you whatever you ask."

23Jesus told her, "Your brother will rise again."

24"Yes," Martha said, "when everyone else rises, on resurrection day."

25Jesus told her, "I am the resurrection and the life.* Those who believe in me, even though they die like everyone else, will live again. 26They are given eternal life for believing in me and will never perish. Do you believe this, Martha?"

27"Yes, Lord," she told him. "I have always believed you are the Messiah, the Son of God, the one who has come into the world from God." 28Then she left him and returned to Mary. She called Mary aside from the mourners and told her, "The Teacher is here and wants to see you." 29So Mary immediately went to him.

30Now Jesus had stayed outside the village, at the place where Martha met him. 31When the people who were at the house trying to console Mary saw her leave so hastily, they assumed she was going to Lazarus's grave to weep. So they followed her there. 32When Mary arrived and saw Jesus, she fell down at his feet and said, "Lord, if you had been here, my brother would not have died."

33When Jesus saw her weeping and saw the other people wailing with her, he was moved with indignation and was deeply troubled. 34"Where have you put him?" he asked them.

They told him, "Lord, come and see." 35Then Jesus wept. 36The people who were standing nearby said, "See how much he loved him." 37But some said, "This man healed a blind man. Why couldn't he keep Lazarus from dying?"

Jesus Raises Lazarus from the Dead

38And again Jesus was deeply troubled. Then they came to the grave. It was a cave with a stone rolled across its entrance. 39"Roll the stone aside," Jesus told them.

But Martha, the dead man's sister, said, "Lord, by now the smell will be terrible because he has been dead for four days."

40Jesus responded, "Didn't I tell you that you will see God's glory if you believe?" 41So they rolled the stone aside. Then Jesus looked up to heaven and said, "Father, thank you for hearing me. 42You always hear me, but I said it out loud for the sake of all these people standing here, so they will believe you sent me." 43Then Jesus shouted, "Lazarus, come out!" 44And Lazarus came out, bound in graveclothes, his face wrapped in a headcloth. Jesus told them, "Unwrap him and let him go!"

The Plot to Kill Jesus

45Many of the people who were with Mary believed in Jesus when they saw this happen. 46But some went to the Pharisees and told them what Jesus had done. 47Then the leading priests and Pharisees called the high council* together to discuss the situation. "What are we going to do?" they asked each other. "This man certainly performs many miraculous signs. 48If we leave him alone, the whole nation will follow him, and then the Roman army will come and destroy both our Temple and our nation."

49And one of them, Caiaphas, who was high priest that year, said, "How can you be so stupid? 50Why should the whole nation be destroyed? Let this one man die for the people."

51This prophecy that Jesus should die for the entire nation came from Caiaphas in his position as high priest. He didn't think of it himself; he was inspired to say it. 52It was a prediction that Jesus' death would be not for Israel only, but for the gathering together of all the children of God scattered around the world.

53So from that time on the Jewish leaders began to plot Jesus' death. 54As a result, Jesus stopped his public ministry among the people and left Jerusalem. He went to a place near the wilderness, to the village of Ephraim, and stayed there with his disciples.

55It was now almost time for the celebration of Passover, and many people from the country arrived in Jerusalem several days early so they could go through the cleansing ceremony before the Passover began. 56They wanted to see Jesus, and as they talked in the Temple, they asked each other, "What do you think? Will he come for the Passover?" 57Meanwhile, the leading priests and Pharisees had publicly announced that anyone seeing Jesus must report him immediately so they could arrest him.

11:18 Greek *was about 15 stadia* [about 2.8 kilometers]. 11:19 Greek *Jewish people;* also 11:31, 33, 36, 45, 54. 11:25 Some manuscripts do not include *and the life.* 11:47 Greek *the Sanhedrin.*

CHAPTER **12**

Jesus Anointed at Bethany

Six days before the Passover ceremonies began, Jesus arrived in Bethany, the home of Lazarus—the man he had raised from the dead. 2A dinner was prepared in Jesus' honor. Martha served, and Lazarus sat at the table with him. 3Then Mary took a twelve-ounce jar* of expensive perfume made from essence of nard, and she anointed Jesus' feet with it and wiped his feet with her hair. And the house was filled with fragrance.

4But Judas Iscariot, one of his disciples—the one who would betray him—said, 5"That perfume was worth a small fortune.* It should have been sold and the money given to the poor." 6Not that he cared for the poor—he was a thief who was in charge of the disciples' funds, and he often took some for his own use.

7Jesus replied, "Leave her alone. She did it in preparation for my burial. 8You will always have the poor among you, but I will not be here with you much longer."

9When all the people* heard of Jesus' arrival, they flocked to see him and also to see Lazarus, the man Jesus had raised from the dead. 10Then the leading priests decided to kill Lazarus, too, 11for it was because of him that many of the people had deserted them and believed in Jesus.

The Triumphal Entry

12The next day, the news that Jesus was on the way to Jerusalem swept through the city. A huge crowd of Passover visitors 13took palm branches and went down the road to meet him. They shouted,

"Praise God!*
Bless the one who comes in the name of the Lord!
Hail to the King of Israel!"*

14Jesus found a young donkey and sat on it, fulfilling the prophecy that said:

15 "Don't be afraid, people of Israel.*
Look, your King is coming,
sitting on a donkey's colt."*

16His disciples didn't realize at the time that this was a fulfillment of prophecy. But after Jesus entered into his glory, they remembered that these Scriptures had come true before their eyes.

17Those in the crowd who had seen Jesus call Lazarus back to life were telling others all about it. 18That was the main reason so many went out to meet him—because they had heard about this mighty miracle. 19Then the Pharisees said to each other, "We've lost. Look, the whole world has gone after him!"

Jesus Predicts His Death

20Some Greeks who had come to Jerusalem to attend the Passover 21paid a visit to Philip, who was from Bethsaida in Galilee. They said, "Sir, we want to meet Jesus." 22Philip told Andrew about it, and they went together to ask Jesus.

23Jesus replied, "The time has come for the Son of Man to enter into his glory. 24The truth is, a kernel of wheat must be planted in the soil. Unless it dies it will be alone—a single seed. But its death will produce many new kernels—a plentiful harvest of new lives. 25Those who love their life in this world will lose it. Those who despise their life in this world will keep it for eternal life. 26All those who want to be my disciples must come and follow me, because my servants must be where I am. And if they follow me, the Father will honor them. 27Now my soul is deeply troubled. Should I pray, 'Father, save me from what lies ahead'? But that is the very reason why I came! 28Father, bring glory to your name."

Then a voice spoke from heaven, saying, "I have already brought it glory, and I will do it again." 29When the crowd heard the voice, some thought it was thunder, while others declared an angel had spoken to him.

30Then Jesus told them, "The voice was for your benefit, not mine. 31The time of judgment for the world has come, when the prince of this world* will be cast out. 32And when I am lifted up on the cross,* I will draw everyone to myself." 33He said this to indicate how he was going to die.

34"Die?" asked the crowd. "We understood from Scripture that the Messiah would live forever. Why are you saying the Son of Man will die? Who is this Son of Man you are talking about?"

35Jesus replied, "My light will shine out for you just a little while longer. Walk in it while you can, so you will not stumble when the darkness falls. If you walk in the darkness, you cannot see where you are going. 36Believe in the light while there is still time; then you will become children of the light." After saying these things, Jesus went away and was hidden from them.

The Unbelief of the People

37But despite all the miraculous signs he had done, most of the people did not believe in him.

12:3 Greek *took 1 litra* [327 grams]. 12:5 Greek *300 denarii.* A denarius was equivalent to a full day's wage. 12:9 Greek *Jewish people;* also in 12:11. 12:13a Greek *Hosanna,* an exclamation of praise that literally means "save now." 12:13b Ps 118:25-26; Zeph 3:15. 12:15a Greek *daughter of Zion.* 12:15b Zech 9:9. 12:31 *The prince of this world* is a name for Satan. 12:32 Greek *lifted up from the earth.*

38This is exactly what Isaiah the prophet had predicted:

"Lord, who has believed our message?
To whom will the Lord reveal his saving
power?"*

39But the people couldn't believe, for as Isaiah also said,

40 "The Lord has blinded their eyes
and hardened their hearts—
so their eyes cannot see,
and their hearts cannot understand,
and they cannot turn to me
and let me heal them."*

41Isaiah was referring to Jesus when he made this prediction, because he was given a vision of the Messiah's glory. 42Many people, including some of the Jewish leaders, believed in him. But they wouldn't admit it to anyone because of their fear that the Pharisees would expel them from the synagogue. 43For they loved human praise more than the praise of God.

44Jesus shouted to the crowds, "If you trust me, you are really trusting God who sent me. 45For when you see me, you are seeing the one who sent me. 46I have come as a light to shine in this dark world, so that all who put their trust in me will no longer remain in the darkness. 47If anyone hears me and doesn't obey me, I am not his judge—for I have come to save the world and not to judge it. 48But all who reject me and my message will be judged at the day of judgment by the truth I have spoken. 49I don't speak on my own authority. The Father who sent me gave me his own instructions as to what I should say. 50And I know his instructions lead to eternal life; so I say whatever the Father tells me to say!"

CHAPTER **13**

Jesus Washes His Disciples' Feet

Before the Passover celebration, Jesus knew that his hour had come to leave this world and return to his Father. He now showed the disciples the full extent of his love.* 2It was time for supper, and the Devil had already enticed Judas, son of Simon Iscariot, to carry out his plan to betray Jesus. 3Jesus knew that the Father had given him authority over everything and that he had come from God and would return to God. 4So he got up from the table, took off his robe, wrapped a towel around his waist, 5and poured water into a basin. Then he began to wash the disciples' feet and to wipe them with the towel he had around him.

6When he came to Simon Peter, Peter said to him, "Lord, why are you going to wash my feet?"

7Jesus replied, "You don't understand now why I am doing it; someday you will."

8"No," Peter protested, "you will never wash my feet!"

Jesus replied, "But if I don't wash you, you won't belong to me."

9Simon Peter exclaimed, "Then wash my hands and head as well, Lord, not just my feet!"

10Jesus replied, "A person who has bathed all over does not need to wash, except for the feet,* to be entirely clean. And you are clean, but that isn't true of everyone here." 11For Jesus knew who would betray him. That is what he meant when he said, "Not all of you are clean."

12After washing their feet, he put on his robe again and sat down and asked, "Do you understand what I was doing? 13You call me 'Teacher' and 'Lord,' and you are right, because it is true. 14And since I, the Lord and Teacher, have washed your feet, you ought to wash each other's feet. 15I have given you an example to follow. Do as I have done to you. 16How true it is that a servant is not greater than the master. Nor are messengers more important than the one who sends them. 17You know these things—now do them! That is the path of blessing.

Jesus Predicts His Betrayal

18"I am not saying these things to all of you; I know so well each one of you I chose. The Scriptures declare, 'The one who shares my food has turned against me,'* and this will soon come true. 19I tell you this now, so that when it happens you will believe I am the Messiah. 20Truly, anyone who welcomes my messenger is welcoming me, and anyone who welcomes me is welcoming the Father who sent me."

21Now Jesus was in great anguish of spirit, and he exclaimed, "The truth is, one of you will betray me!"

22The disciples looked at each other, wondering whom he could mean. 23One of Jesus' disciples, the one Jesus loved, was sitting next to Jesus at the table.* 24Simon Peter motioned to him to ask who would do this terrible thing. 25Leaning toward Jesus, he asked, "Lord, who is it?"

26Jesus said, "It is the one to whom I give the bread dipped in the sauce." And when he had

---

12:38 Isa 53:1.   12:40 Isa 6:10.   13:1 Or *He loved his disciples to the very end.*   13:10 Some manuscripts do not include *except for the feet.*
13:18 Ps 41:9.   13:23 Greek *was reclining on Jesus' bosom.* The "disciple whom Jesus loved" was probably John.

dipped it, he gave it to Judas, son of Simon Iscariot. ²⁷As soon as Judas had eaten the bread, Satan entered into him. Then Jesus told him, "Hurry. Do it now." ²⁸None of the others at the table knew what Jesus meant. ²⁹Since Judas was their treasurer, some thought Jesus was telling him to go and pay for the food or to give some money to the poor. ³⁰So Judas left at once, going out into the night.

Jesus Predicts Peter's Denial

³¹As soon as Judas left the room, Jesus said, "The time has come for me, the Son of Man, to enter into my glory, and God will receive glory because of all that happens to me. ³²And God will bring* me into my glory very soon. ³³Dear children, how brief are these moments before I must go away and leave you! Then, though you search for me, you cannot come to me—just as I told the Jewish leaders. ³⁴So now I am giving you a new commandment: Love each other. Just as I have loved you, you should love each other. ³⁵Your love for one another will prove to the world that you are my disciples."

³⁶Simon Peter said, "Lord, where are you going?"

And Jesus replied, "You can't go with me now, but you will follow me later."

³⁷"But why can't I come now, Lord?" he asked. "I am ready to die for you."

³⁸Jesus answered, "Die for me? No, before the rooster crows tomorrow morning, you will deny three times that you even know me.

CHAPTER **14**

Jesus, the Way to the Father

"Don't be troubled. You trust God, now trust in me. ²There are many rooms in my Father's home, and I am going to prepare a place for you. If this were not so, I would tell you plainly. ³When everything is ready, I will come and get you, so that you will always be with me where I am. ⁴And you know where I am going and how to get there."

⁵"No, we don't know, Lord," Thomas said. "We haven't any idea where you are going, so how can we know the way?"

⁶Jesus told him, "I am the way, the truth, and the life. No one can come to the Father except through me. ⁷If you had known who I am, then you would have known who my Father is.* From now on you know him and have seen him!"

13:32 Some manuscripts read *And if God is glorified in him [the Son of Man], God will bring.*   14:7 Some manuscripts read *If you really have known me, you will know who my Father is.*

⁸Philip said, "Lord, show us the Father and we will be satisfied."

⁹Jesus replied, "Philip, don't you even yet know who I am, even after all the time I have

---

God Gives Hope to Our Troubled Hearts Read JOHN 14:1-4

Have you ever felt troubled and uncertain about your future? Have you ever questioned whether God realizes that your world has turned upside down? The disciples may have been experiencing these feelings when Jesus gave them this message. He had just told them that he was going to leave them, and they were extremely concerned. Yet he tells them to not be troubled, then gives them three reasons why they should have peace in their hearts:

1. We Can Take God at His Word. When Jesus said, "You trust God, now trust in me," he was reminding his disciples to trust in God's Word (verse 1). Scripture had spoken not only of Jesus' impending crucifixion but also of his resurrection. Somehow they had missed that. Sometimes we forget to look at the whole picture when our circumstances seem overwhelming. But we must remember that the words found in these pages will "remain forever" (Matthew 24:35). We can always take God's promises at face value.

2. We Are Going to Heaven. The next time you face some kind of difficulty—be it an illness, a family problem, or an unexpected change in your life—remember that you are going to heaven (verse 2). That will help to keep everything in perspective. Your trials are only temporary. One day you will be in the presence of the Lord, and there will be no more fear, no more death, no more pain, and no more sorrow.

3. Jesus Is Coming Back for Us. Notice that Jesus says, "I will come and get you" (verse 3). The Lord is not merely going to send for us. He is going to personally escort us to the Father's house. The Bible tells us to *"comfort* and encourage each other with these words" (1 Thessalonians 4:18). In the midst of your trials, remember that God cares for you so much that he is coming back so that you can be with him forever.

To begin the next reading track, turn to p. A33.

Who Will Enter Heaven? Read JOHN 14:2-6

Hollywood has often depicted the gates of heaven as the place where you "plead your case" for the merits of your entrance. In this passage, Jesus clearly explains that the only ones who will enter heaven will be those who have accepted him as the way, the truth, and the life—not those who have the best "arguments" or who have performed the greatest number of good deeds.

Heaven is not a court but a prepared place for prepared people. If you are a Christian, you can rest assured that your reservation for heaven was made the moment you received Christ. And when it comes to accommodations, you don't need to worry, for Jesus himself has promised to prepare a place for you.

The Bible tells us to prepare to meet our God. Is your reservation in place?

For the next note on "What Is Heaven?" turn to p. 1008.

CORNER STONES

been with you? Anyone who has seen me has seen the Father! So why are you asking to see him? 10Don't you believe that I am in the Father and the Father is in me? The words I say are not my own, but my Father who lives in me does his work through me. 11Just believe that I am in the Father and the Father is in me. Or at least believe because of what you have seen me do.

12"The truth is, anyone who believes in me will do the same works I have done, and even greater works, because I am going to be with the Father. 13You can ask for anything in my name, and I will do it, because the work of the Son brings glory to the Father. 14Yes, ask anything in my name, and I will do it!

Jesus Promises the Holy Spirit

15"If you love me, obey my commandments. 16And I will ask the Father, and he will give you another Counselor,* who will never leave you. 17He is the Holy Spirit, who leads into all truth. The world at large cannot receive him, because it isn't looking for him and doesn't recognize him. But you do, because he lives with you now and later will be in you. 18No, I will not abandon you as orphans—I will come to you. 19In just a little while the world will not see me again, but you will. For I will live again, and you will, too. 20When I am raised to life again, you will know that I am in my Father, and you are in me, and I am in you. 21Those who obey my commandments are the ones who love me. And because they love me, my Father will love them, and I will love them. And I will reveal myself to each one of them."

22Judas (not Judas Iscariot, but the other dis-

ciple with that name) said to him, "Lord, why are you going to reveal yourself only to us and not to the world at large?"

23Jesus replied, "All those who love me will do what I say. My Father will love them, and we will come to them and live with them. 24Anyone who doesn't love me will not do what I say. And remember, my words are not my own. This message is from the Father who sent me. 25I am telling you these things now while I am still with you. 26But when the Father sends the Counselor as my representative—and by the Counselor I mean the Holy Spirit—he will teach you everything and will remind you of everything I myself have told you.

27"I am leaving you with a gift—peace of mind and heart. And the peace I give isn't like the peace the world gives. So don't be troubled or afraid. 28Remember what I told you: I am going away, but I will come back to you again. If you really love me, you will be very happy for me, because now I can go to the Father, who is greater than I am. 29I have told you these things before they happen so that you will believe when they do happen.

30"I don't have much more time to talk to you, because the prince of this world approaches. He has no power over me, 31but I will do what the Father requires of me, so that the world will know that I love the Father. Come, let's be going.

CHAPTER 15
Jesus, the True Vine

"I am the true vine, and my Father is the gardener. 2He cuts off every branch that doesn't

14:16 Or *Comforter,* or *Encourager,* or *Advocate.* Greek *Paraclete;* also in 14:26.

produce fruit, and he prunes the branches that do bear fruit so they will produce even more. ³You have already been pruned for greater fruitfulness by the message I have given you. ⁴Remain in me, and I will remain in you. For a branch cannot produce fruit if it is severed from the vine, and you cannot be fruitful apart from me.

⁵"Yes, I am the vine; you are the branches. Those who remain in me, and I in them, will produce much fruit. For apart from me you can do nothing. ⁶Anyone who parts from me is thrown away like a useless branch and withers. Such branches are gathered into a pile to be burned. ⁷But if you stay joined to me and my words remain in you, you may ask any request you like, and it will be granted! ⁸My true disciples produce much fruit. This brings great glory to my Father.

⁹"I have loved you even as the Father has loved me. Remain in my love. ¹⁰When you obey me, you remain in my love, just as I obey my Father and remain in his love. ¹¹I have told you this so that you will be filled with my joy. Yes, your joy will overflow! ¹²I command you to love each other in the same way that I love you. ¹³And here is how to measure it—the greatest love is shown when people lay down their lives for their friends. ¹⁴You are my friends if you obey me. ¹⁵I no longer call you servants, because a master doesn't confide in his servants. Now you are my friends, since I have told you everything the Father told me. ¹⁶You didn't choose me. I chose you. I appointed you to go and produce fruit that will last, so that the Father will give you whatever you ask for, using my name. ¹⁷I command you to love each other.

The World's Hatred

¹⁸"When the world hates you, remember it hated me before it hated you. ¹⁹The world would love you if you belonged to it, but you don't. I chose you to come out of the world, and so it hates you. ²⁰Do you remember what I told you? 'A servant is not greater than the master.' Since they persecuted me, naturally they will persecute you. And if they had listened to me, they would listen to you! ²¹The people of the world will hate you because you belong to me, for they don't know God who sent me. ²²They would not be guilty if I had not come and spoken to them. But now they have no excuse for their sin. ²³Anyone who

hates me hates my Father, too. ²⁴If I hadn't done such miraculous signs among them that no one else could do, they would not be counted guilty. But as it is, they saw all that I

A Disciple Abides in Christ
Read JOHN 15:1-17

Jesus knows that his true followers desire to live productive, fulfilling, joy-filled lives. In this passage, he lays out four predominant characteristics of a growing disciple:

1. A Disciple Stays Close to the Master. Jesus encourages us to remain in him (verses 4-5). Another way to translate that is "to abide in him." The word *abide* signifies a permanence of position. It means that you sink your roots deep into your relationship with Jesus, allowing him to fill every part of your life and daily activities. If you maintain this unbroken fellowship with God, a changed lifestyle will result.

2. A Disciple Is Fruitful. Just as a branch can only be fruitful when attached to the vine, we can only be productive when we draw our strength from Jesus (verses 6, 16). The Bible describes the fruit Jesus is talking about as love, joy, peace, patience, kindness, goodness, faithfulness, gentleness, and self-control (see Galatians 5:22, p. 1020).

3. A Disciple Obeys the Master. Another clear sign that you are Christ's disciple is your obedience to the principles and guidelines found in his Word, the Bible (verse 10). Then, and only then, will you discover what it means to live in God's love.

4. A Disciple Loves Others. Jesus gave us the ultimate example of love by laying down his life for us. He, in essence, is asking us to do nothing less. Although that may not mean actually dying for someone, it may mean placing someone else's needs before our own.

In verse 11 we find Jesus' reason for sharing these principles: He wants us to be filled with joy. If you try to find happiness by pursuing it in and of itself, it will elude you. The only way to find happiness is through the pursuit of God. If you prioritize your life as Jesus has laid out in these verses, then "your joy will overflow."

For the next note on "Live as a Disciple," turn to p. 1105.

How the Holy Spirit Works in Our Lives Read JOHN 14:15-17

The Bible uses three different Greek prepositions in the New Testament to describe the different ways in which the Holy Spirit works in our lives. This verse shows two of these ways, and a third can be found elsewhere in Scripture:

1. He Works *with* Us as Nonbelievers (*para*). Prior to our conversion to faith in Jesus Christ, the Holy Spirit convicts us of our sin and reveals Christ as the answer (see John 16:8, p. 912). Some might dismiss his working as the prodding of one's personal conscience. Yet it is the Holy Spirit who opens our eyes to our terminally sinful condition, exposing our lack of righteousness so that we will see the need to turn our lives over to Jesus Christ.

2. He Comes *into* Our Lives When We Turn to Christ (*en*). Once we accept Jesus Christ as our Savior and invite him into our lives, the Holy Spirit moves into our lives and sets up residence, so to speak. First, he produces the process of salvation in our heart. As Jesus said, "No one can enter the Kingdom of God without being born of . . . the Spirit" (John 3:5). Second, he assures us that we have done the right thing. For Scripture tells us, "For his Holy Spirit speaks to us deep in our hearts and tells us that we are God's children" (Romans 8:16). He gives us the inner knowledge that Christ is living in us. Now he can begin changing us from the inside out and develop the new nature within us.

3. He Will Come *upon* Us to Empower Us as Believers (*epi*). This aspect of the Holy Spirit's work is described in Luke 24:49, where Jesus says, "And now I will send the Holy Spirit, just as my

Father promised." Here Jesus describes the dynamic empowering of the Holy Spirit upon our lives. This is what the early Christians experienced in Acts chapter 2, and it dramatically emboldened their witness for Jesus Christ. This power is available to believers today, for Scripture says of the giving of his Spirit, "This promise is to you and your children, and even to the Gentiles—all who have been called by the Lord our God!" (Acts 2:39).

For the next note on "Who Is the Holy Spirit?" turn to p. 928.

CORNER STONES

---

did and yet hated both of us—me and my Father. 25This has fulfilled what the Scriptures said: 'They hated me without cause.'*

26"But I will send you the Counselor*—the Spirit of truth. He will come to you from the Father and will tell you all about me. 27And you must also tell others about me because you have been with me from the beginning.

CHAPTER **16**

"I have told you these things so that you won't fall away. 2For you will be expelled from the synagogues, and the time is coming when those who kill you will think they are doing God a service. 3This is because they have never known the Father or me. 4Yes, I'm telling you these things now, so that when they happen, you will remember I warned you. I didn't tell you earlier because I was going to be with you for a while longer.

The Work of the Holy Spirit

5"But now I am going away to the one who sent me, and none of you has asked me where I am going. 6Instead, you are very sad. 7But it is actually best for you that I go away, because if I don't, the Counselor* won't come. If I do go away, he will come because I will send him to you. 8And when he comes, he will convince the world of its sin, and of God's righteousness, and of the coming judgment. 9The world's sin is unbelief in me. 10Righteousness is available because I go to the Father, and you will see me no more. 11Judgment will come because the prince of this world has already been judged.

12"Oh, there is so much more I want to tell you, but you can't bear it now. 13When the Spirit of truth comes, he will guide you into all truth. He will not be presenting his own ideas; he will be telling you what he has heard. He will tell you

15:25 Pss 35:19; 69:4. **15:26** Or *Comforter*, or *Encourager*, or *Advocate*. Greek *Paraclete*. **16:7** Or *Comforter*, or *Encourager*, or *Advocate*. Greek *Paraclete*.

about the future. ¹⁴He will bring me glory by revealing to you whatever he receives from me. ¹⁵All that the Father has is mine; this is what I mean when I say that the Spirit will reveal to you whatever he receives from me.

Sadness Will Be Turned to Joy

¹⁶"In just a little while I will be gone, and you won't see me anymore. Then, just a little while after that, you will see me again."

¹⁷The disciples asked each other, "What does he mean when he says, 'You won't see me, and then you will see me'? And what does he mean when he says, 'I am going to the Father'? ¹⁸And what does he mean by 'a little while'? We don't understand."

¹⁹Jesus realized they wanted to ask him, so he said, "Are you asking yourselves what I meant? I said in just a little while I will be gone, and you won't see me anymore. Then, just a little while after that, you will see me again. ²⁰Truly, you will weep and mourn over what is going to happen to me, but the world will rejoice. You will grieve, but your grief will suddenly turn to wonderful joy when you see me again. ²¹It will be like a woman experiencing the pains of labor. When her child is born, her anguish gives place to joy because she has brought a new person into the world. ²²You have sorrow now, but I will see you again; then you will rejoice, and no one can rob you of that joy. ²³At that time you won't need to ask me for anything. The truth is, you can go directly to the Father and ask him, and he will grant your request because you use my name. ²⁴You haven't done this before. Ask, using my name, and you will receive, and you will have abundant joy.

²⁵"I have spoken of these matters in parables, but the time will come when this will not be necessary, and I will tell you plainly all about the Father. ²⁶Then you will ask in my name. I'm not saying I will ask the Father on your behalf, ²⁷for the Father himself loves you dearly because you love me and believe that I came from God. ²⁸Yes, I came from the Father into the world, and I will leave the world and return to the Father."

²⁹Then his disciples said, "At last you are speaking plainly and not in parables. ³⁰Now we understand that you know everything and don't need anyone to tell you anything.* From this we believe that you came from God."

³¹Jesus asked, "Do you finally believe? ³²But the time is coming—in fact, it is already here—when you will be scattered, each one going his

16:30 Or *don't need that anyone should ask you anything.*

Live in God's Love Read JOHN 15:9-11

This passage is a portion of Jesus' last message to his disciples before his death. In preparing them for his departure, he wanted to emphasize his love for them and how that love should affect their lives. He wanted them to realize that they could experience true and lasting joy in their walk with God—even if he could not personally be with them. For that reason this intimate message and command from Christ applies to us today as well. In this text Jesus gives four simple points that will enable us to live in his love:

1. Realize That You Have the Love of Jesus and Your Heavenly Father. Jesus is not simply some authoritative figure who demands our respect. He is a personal being who loved us so much that he died in our place. In return, he requires our obedience. Knowing that you are loved by Jesus frees you to love him in return. The best way to show your love for him is to obey his commands. Trying to obey his commands out of obligation rather than love can produce resentment toward him. That is because there is no joy in mere obligation. But obeying Jesus out of love produces joy.

2. Live within God's Love by Obeying His Commands. This is one of the earmarks of a true follower of Christ. It is easy to boast of our great love for God or the wonderful affection and devotion we feel toward him. But as the saying goes, The proof is in the pudding. If we really love God, we will obey him. If we do not obey him, it is questionable as to just how deep our love for him really is.

3. Follow Jesus' Example. Jesus is our perfect model of obedience. Pay careful attention to how Jesus obeyed his heavenly Father throughout the Gospels of Matthew, Mark, Luke, and John.

4. Experience the Reward of Obedience: Overflowing Joy. The obedient Christian is the happy Christian. If you want more joy in your life, make sure that you are following the guidelines God has given you in his Word.

Do you find it hard to obey God and his principles? If so, it is probably time to reexamine your priorities and make sure that getting to know your Creator is right at the top of the list. Then you will discover the joy that comes from living in God's love every day.

For the next note on "Obey God," turn to p. 977.

own way, leaving me alone. Yet I am not alone because the Father is with me. ³³I have told you all this so that you may have peace in me. Here on earth you will have many trials and sorrows. But take heart, because I have overcome the world."

CHAPTER 17
The Prayer of Jesus

When Jesus had finished saying all these things, he looked up to heaven and said, "Father, the time has come. Glorify your Son so he can give glory back to you. ²For you have given him authority over everyone in all the earth. He gives eternal life to each one you have given him. ³And this is the way to have eternal life—to know you, the only true God, and Jesus Christ, the one you sent to earth. ⁴I brought glory to you here on earth by doing everything you told me to do. ⁵And now, Father, bring me into the glory we shared before the world began.

⁶"I have told these men about you. They were in the world, but then you gave them to me. Actually, they were always yours, and you gave them to me; and they have kept your word. ⁷Now they know that everything I have is a gift from you, ⁸for I have passed on to them the words you gave me; and they accepted them and know that I came from you, and they believe you sent me.

⁹"My prayer is not for the world, but for those you have given me, because they belong to you. ¹⁰And all of them, since they are mine, belong to you; and you have given them back to me, so they are my glory! ¹¹Now I am departing the world; I am leaving them behind and coming to you. Holy Father, keep them and care for them—all those you have given me—so that they will be united just as we are. ¹²During my time here, I have kept them safe.* I guarded them so that not one was lost, except the one headed for destruction, as the Scriptures foretold.

¹³"And now I am coming to you. I have told them many things while I was with them so they would be filled with my joy. ¹⁴I have given them your word. And the world hates them because they do not belong to the world, just as I do not. ¹⁵I'm not asking you to take them out of the world, but to keep them safe from the evil one. ¹⁶They are not part of this world any more than I am. ¹⁷Make them pure and holy by teaching them your words of truth. ¹⁸As you sent me into

the world, I am sending them into the world. ¹⁹And I give myself entirely to you so they also might be entirely yours.

²⁰"I am praying not only for these disciples but also for all who will ever believe in me because of their testimony. ²¹My prayer for all of them is that they will be one, just as you and I are one, Father—that just as you are in me and I am in you, so they will be in us, and the world will believe you sent me.

²²"I have given them the glory you gave me, so that they may be one, as we are—²³I in them and you in me, all being perfected into one. Then the world will know that you sent me and will understand that you love them as much as you love me. ²⁴Father, I want these whom you've given me to be with me, so they can see my glory. You gave me the glory because you loved me even before the world began!

²⁵"O righteous Father, the world doesn't know you, but I do; and these disciples know you sent me. ²⁶And I have revealed you to them and will keep on revealing you. I will do this so that your love for me may be in them and I in them."

CHAPTER 18
Jesus Is Betrayed and Arrested

After saying these things, Jesus crossed the Kidron Valley with his disciples and entered a grove of olive trees. ²Judas, the betrayer, knew this place, because Jesus had gone there many times with his disciples. ³The leading priests and Pharisees had given Judas a battalion of Roman soldiers and Temple guards to accompany him. Now with blazing torches, lanterns, and weapons, they arrived at the olive grove.

⁴Jesus fully realized all that was going to happen to him. Stepping forward to meet them, he asked, "Whom are you looking for?"

⁵"Jesus of Nazareth," they replied.

"I am he,"* Jesus said. Judas was standing there with them when Jesus identified himself. ⁶And as he said, "I am he," they all fell backward to the ground! ⁷Once more he asked them, "Whom are you searching for?"

And again they replied, "Jesus of Nazareth."

⁸"I told you that I am he," Jesus said. "And since I am the one you want, let these others go." ⁹He did this to fulfill his own statement: "I have not lost a single one of those you gave me."*

¹⁰Then Simon Peter drew a sword and slashed off the right ear of Malchus, the high

17:12 Greek *I have kept in your name those whom you have given me.*   18:5 Greek *I am;* also in 18:6, 8.   18:9 See John 6:39 and 17:12.

priest's servant. [11]But Jesus said to Peter, "Put your sword back into its sheath. Shall I not drink from the cup the Father has given me?"

Annas Questions Jesus

[12]So the soldiers, their commanding officer, and the Temple guards arrested Jesus and tied him up. [13]First they took him to Annas, the father-in-law of Caiaphas, the high priest that year. [14]Caiaphas was the one who had told the other Jewish leaders, "Better that one should die for all."

Peter's First Denial

[15]Simon Peter followed along behind, as did another of the disciples. That other disciple was acquainted with the high priest, so he was allowed to enter the courtyard with Jesus. [16]Peter stood outside the gate. Then the other disciple spoke to the woman watching at the gate, and she let Peter in. [17]The woman asked Peter, "Aren't you one of Jesus' disciples?"

"No," he said, "I am not."

[18]The guards and the household servants were standing around a charcoal fire they had made because it was cold. And Peter stood there with them, warming himself.

The High Priest Questions Jesus

[19]Inside, the high priest began asking Jesus about his followers and what he had been teaching them. [20]Jesus replied, "What I teach is widely known, because I have preached regularly in the synagogues and the Temple. I have been heard by people* everywhere, and I teach nothing in private that I have not said in public. [21]Why are you asking me this question? Ask those who heard me. They know what I said."

[22]One of the Temple guards standing there struck Jesus on the face. "Is that the way to answer the high priest?" he demanded.

[23]Jesus replied, "If I said anything wrong, you must give evidence for it. Should you hit a man for telling the truth?"

[24]Then Annas bound Jesus and sent him to Caiaphas, the high priest.

Peter's Second and Third Denials

[25]Meanwhile, as Simon Peter was standing by the fire, they asked him again, "Aren't you one of his disciples?"

"I am not," he said.

[26]But one of the household servants of the high priest, a relative of the man whose ear Peter had cut off, asked, "Didn't I see you out there in

18:20 Greek *Jewish people;* also in 18:38.

the olive grove with Jesus?" [27]Again Peter denied it. And immediately a rooster crowed.

Jesus' Trial before Pilate

[28]Jesus' trial before Caiaphas ended in the early hours of the morning. Then he was taken to the headquarters of the Roman governor. His accusers didn't go in themselves because it would

---

God's Spirit Will Guide You
Read JOHN 16:13-15

The work of the Holy Spirit in the life of a Christian is multidimensional. We are told that, among other things, the Holy Spirit "speaks to us deep in our hearts and tells us that we are God's children" (Romans 8:16). In this passage, we see that the Holy Spirit serves as a teacher and a guide.

The Holy Spirit Will Help Us Understand the Bible. Before you became a Christian, understanding the Bible may have been like walking around with blinders on. But those "blinders" you once had were taken off, so to speak, when the Holy Spirit took up residence in your heart. The Holy Spirit teaches you the truth of the Scripture, helping you grasp hard-to-understand passages.

The Holy Spirit Will Reveal More and More about God and Jesus. The Bible makes it abundantly clear that one of the primary roles of the Holy Spirit is to glorify Christ. The moment you invited Jesus into your heart, God's Spirit began to help you grasp the awesome, praiseworthy attributes of Jesus. Those who do not have a personal relationship with Christ cannot see or understand the full glory of God, because they do not have the Holy Spirit's assistance.

The Holy Spirit wants to be actively involved in your life, helping you grow in the knowledge of God and his Word so that you can better understand God's will for your life. Every time you open the Bible, pray for the Holy Spirit to show you how the passages you read can apply to your life.

For the next note on "Live in God's Power," turn to p. 923.

defile them, and they wouldn't be allowed to celebrate the Passover feast. 29So Pilate, the governor, went out to them and asked, "What is your charge against this man?"

30"We wouldn't have handed him over to you if he weren't a criminal!" they retorted.

31"Then take him away and judge him by your own laws," Pilate told them.

"Only the Romans are permitted to execute someone," the Jewish leaders replied. 32This fulfilled Jesus' prediction about the way he would die.*

33Then Pilate went back inside and called for Jesus to be brought to him. "Are you the King of the Jews?" he asked him.

34Jesus replied, "Is this your own question, or did others tell you about me?"

35"Am I a Jew?" Pilate asked. "Your own people and their leading priests brought you here. Why? What have you done?"

36Then Jesus answered, "I am not an earthly king. If I were, my followers would have fought when I was arrested by the Jewish leaders. But my Kingdom is not of this world."

37Pilate replied, "You are a king then?"

"You say that I am a king, and you are right," Jesus said. "I was born for that purpose. And I came to bring truth to the world. All who love the truth recognize that what I say is true."

38"What is truth?" Pilate asked. Then he went out again to the people and told them, "He is not guilty of any crime. 39But you have a custom of asking me to release someone from prison each year at Passover. So if you want me to, I'll release the King of the Jews."

40But they shouted back, "No! Not this man, but Barabbas!" (Barabbas was a criminal.)

CHAPTER 19
Jesus Sentenced to Death

Then Pilate had Jesus flogged with a lead-tipped whip. 2The soldiers made a crown of long, sharp thorns and put it on his head, and they put a royal purple robe on him. 3"Hail! King of the Jews!" they mocked, and they hit him with their fists.

4Pilate went outside again and said to the people, "I am going to bring him out to you now, but understand clearly that I find him not guilty." 5Then Jesus came out wearing the crown of thorns and the purple robe. And Pilate said, "Here is the man!"

6When they saw him, the leading priests and Temple guards began shouting, "Crucify! Crucify!"

"You crucify him," Pilate said. "I find him not guilty."

7The Jewish leaders replied, "By our laws he ought to die because he called himself the Son of God."

8When Pilate heard this, he was more frightened than ever. 9He took Jesus back into the headquarters again and asked him, "Where are you from?" But Jesus gave no answer. 10"You won't talk to me?" Pilate demanded. "Don't you realize that I have the power to release you or to crucify you?"

11Then Jesus said, "You would have no power over me at all unless it were given to you from above. So the one who brought me to you has the greater sin."

12Then Pilate tried to release him, but the Jewish leaders told him, "If you release this man, you are not a friend of Caesar. Anyone who declares himself a king is a rebel against Caesar."

13When they said this, Pilate brought Jesus out to them again. Then Pilate sat down on the judgment seat on the platform that is called the Stone Pavement (in Hebrew, *Gabbatha*). 14It was now about noon of the day of preparation for the Passover. And Pilate said to the people,* "Here is your king!"

15"Away with him," they yelled. "Away with him—crucify him!"

"What? Crucify your king?" Pilate asked.

"We have no king but Caesar," the leading priests shouted back.

16Then Pilate gave Jesus to them to be crucified.

The Crucifixion

So they took Jesus and led him away. 17Carrying the cross by himself, Jesus went to the place called Skull Hill (in Hebrew, *Golgotha*). 18There they crucified him. There were two others crucified with him, one on either side, with Jesus between them. 19And Pilate posted a sign over him that read, "Jesus of Nazareth, the King of the Jews." 20The place where Jesus was crucified was near the city; and the sign was written in Hebrew, Latin, and Greek, so that many people could read it.

21Then the leading priests said to Pilate, "Change it from 'The King of the Jews' to 'He said, I am King of the Jews.'"

22Pilate replied, "What I have written, I have written. It stays exactly as it is."

18:32 See John 12:32-33. 19:14 Greek *Jewish people*; also in 19:20.

23When the soldiers had crucified Jesus, they divided his clothes among the four of them. They also took his robe, but it was seamless, woven in one piece from the top. 24So they said, "Let's not tear it but throw dice* to see who gets it." This fulfilled the Scripture that says, "They divided my clothes among themselves and threw dice for my robe."* 25So that is what they did.

Standing near the cross were Jesus' mother, and his mother's sister, Mary (the wife of Clopas), and Mary Magdalene. 26When Jesus saw his mother standing there beside the disciple he loved, he said to her, "Woman, he is your son." 27And he said to this disciple, "She is your mother." And from then on this disciple took her into his home.

The Death of Jesus

28Jesus knew that everything was now finished, and to fulfill the Scriptures he said, "I am thirsty."* 29A jar of sour wine was sitting there, so they soaked a sponge in it, put it on a hyssop branch, and held it up to his lips. 30When Jesus had tasted it, he said, "It is finished!" Then he bowed his head and gave up his spirit.

31The Jewish leaders didn't want the victims hanging there the next day, which was the Sabbath (and a very special Sabbath at that, because it was the Passover), so they asked Pilate to hasten their deaths by ordering that their legs be broken. Then their bodies could be taken down. 32So the soldiers came and broke the legs of the two men crucified with Jesus. 33But when they came to Jesus, they saw that he was dead already, so they didn't break his legs. 34One of the soldiers, however, pierced his side with a spear, and blood and water flowed out. 35This report is from an eyewitness giving an accurate account; it is presented so that you also can believe. 36These things happened in fulfillment of the Scriptures that say, "Not one of his bones will be broken,"* 37and "They will look on him whom they pierced."*

The Burial of Jesus

38Afterward Joseph of Arimathea, who had been a secret disciple of Jesus (because he feared the Jewish leaders), asked Pilate for permission to take Jesus' body down. When Pilate gave him permission, he came and took the body away. 39Nicodemus, the man who had come to Jesus at night, also came, bringing about seventy-five pounds* of embalming ointment made from myrrh and aloes. 40Together they wrapped Jesus' body in a long linen cloth with the spices, as is the Jewish custom of burial. 41The place of crucifixion was near a garden, where there was a new tomb, never used before. 42And so, because it was the day of preparation before the Passover and since the tomb was close at hand, they laid Jesus there.

CHAPTER 20
The Resurrection

Early Sunday morning,* while it was still dark, Mary Magdalene came to the tomb and found that the stone had been rolled away from the entrance. 2She ran and found Simon Peter and the other disciple, the one whom Jesus loved. She said, "They have taken the Lord's body out of the tomb, and I don't know where they have put him!"

3Peter and the other disciple ran to the tomb to see. 4The other disciple outran Peter and got there first. 5He stooped and looked in and saw the linen cloth lying there, but he didn't go in. 6Then Simon Peter arrived and went inside. He also noticed the linen wrappings lying there, 7while the cloth that had covered Jesus' head was folded up and lying to the side. 8Then the other disciple also went in, and he saw and believed—9for until then they hadn't realized that the Scriptures said he would rise from the dead. 10Then they went home.

Jesus Appears to Mary Magdalene

11Mary was standing outside the tomb crying, and as she wept, she stooped and looked in. 12She saw two white-robed angels sitting at the head and foot of the place where the body of Jesus had been lying. 13"Why are you crying?" the angels asked her.

"Because they have taken away my Lord," she replied, "and I don't know where they have put him."

14She glanced over her shoulder and saw someone standing behind her. It was Jesus, but she didn't recognize him. 15"Why are you crying?" Jesus asked her. "Who are you looking for?"

She thought he was the gardener. "Sir," she said, "if you have taken him away, tell me where you have put him, and I will go and get him."

16"Mary!" Jesus said.

She turned toward him and exclaimed, "Teacher!"*

17"Don't cling to me," Jesus said, "for I haven't

19:24a Greek *cast lots.* 19:24b Ps 22:18. 19:28 See Pss 22:15; 69:21. 19:36 Exod 12:46; Num 9:12; Ps 34:20. 19:37 Zech 12:10. 19:39 Greek *100 litras* [32.7 kilograms]. 20:1 Greek *On the first day of the week.* 20:16 Greek *and said in Hebrew, "Rabboni," which means "Teacher."*

Our Love for God Prepares Us for Service Read JOHN 21:15-17

Peter knew that he had let Jesus down by denying him three times prior to the Crucifixion. But Peter also knew that Jesus had forgiven him. So Jesus tested Peter by asking him the searching question, "Do you love me?" three times.

Peter's response to Jesus' questions has great significance in the original language of the text. When Jesus posed the questions, he had basically asked, "Peter, do you love me with a sacrificial, committed love?" Peter, however, responded with a different word for "love" than Jesus had suggested. Peter essentially said, "Lord, I like you. I love you as a friend."

At least Peter was being honest. He told Jesus the truth about his commitment. Interestingly enough, Jesus still enlisted Peter in his service, to feed and care for his sheep. Jesus just wanted Peter to affirm his devotion to the Lord before giving him his directions for ministry.

As this story implies, we must love God before we can serve him faithfully. Do you love God? Here are five ways to tell if you really love God and are growing in that love for him:

1. If You Love the Lord, You Will Long for Personal Communion with Him. Can you relate to the words of the psalmist, "As the deer pants for streams of water, so I long for you, O God" (Psalm 42:1)? When you really love God, you will delight in praising and worshiping him. That is because your praise and worship will overflow from a heart filled with love for God. And this love will cause you to look forward to spending time with him and his people.

2. If You Love God, You Will Love the Things He Loves. We know what God loves by what he has declared in his Word, the Bible. So if you love God, you will love his Word. Bible study will not be a drudgery, but a delight.

3. If You Love the Lord, You Will Hate What He Hates. As the Lord's nature becomes your nature, his likes and dislikes become your likes and dislikes. His outlook becomes your outlook. We know from his Word that he hates sin. If we love him, then we should also hate sin.

4. If You Love the Lord, You Will Long for His Return. Jesus described himself as a bridegroom (Mark 2:19). His bride is the church—the body of believers (Ephesians 5:23-29). When Jesus returns, he will be united with his bride. Therefore, if you love the Lord, you will long for his return as a bride and bridegroom long to be together.

5. If You Love the Lord, You Will Keep His Commandments. Jesus says, "If you love me, obey my commandments" (John 14:15). That does not mean that you will never sin. Though it is impossible for any of us who love God to go on an endless course of sin, it is quite possible to fall into individual sins. But if we love God, we will repent of those sins and seek his forgiveness, and our lifestyle will conform to the truths we find in his Word.

Do you love the Lord? Like Peter, you may be tempted to believe that you have no love for Jesus when you sin. Maybe you feel that God could never use you in his service again. Be honest with God; then start rebuilding that relationship by following the steps above. As you reaffirm your love for him, God will open up opportunities for you to serve him and share that love with others. A committed heart leads to committed service.

For the next note on "Love," turn to p. 1104.

CORNER STONES

---

yet ascended to the Father. But go find my brothers and tell them that I am ascending to my Father and your Father, my God and your God."

18Mary Magdalene found the disciples and told them, "I have seen the Lord!" Then she gave them his message.

Jesus Appears to His Disciples

19That evening, on the first day of the week, the disciples were meeting behind locked doors because they were afraid of the Jewish leaders. Suddenly, Jesus was standing there among them! "Peace be with you," he said. 20As he spoke, he held out his hands for them to see, and he showed them his side. They were filled with joy when they saw their Lord! 21He spoke to them again and said, "Peace be with you. As the Father has sent me, so I send you." 22Then he breathed on them and said to them, "Receive the Holy Spirit. 23If you forgive anyone's sins, they are forgiven. If you refuse to forgive them, they are unforgiven."

Jesus Appears to Thomas

24One of the disciples, Thomas (nicknamed the Twin*), was not with the others when Jesus came. 25They told him, "We have seen the Lord!" But he replied, "I won't believe it unless I see the nail wounds in his hands, put my fingers into them, and place my hand into the wound in his side."

26Eight days later the disciples were together again, and this time Thomas was with them. The doors were locked; but suddenly, as before, Jesus was standing among them. He said, "Peace be with you." 27Then he said to Thomas, "Put your finger here and see my hands. Put your hand into the wound in my side. Don't be faithless any longer. Believe!"

28"My Lord and my God!" Thomas exclaimed.

29Then Jesus told him, "You believe because you have seen me. Blessed are those who haven't seen me and believe anyway."

Purpose of the Book

30Jesus' disciples saw him do many other miraculous signs besides the ones recorded in this book. 31But these are written so that you may believe* that Jesus is the Messiah, the Son of God, and that by believing in him you will have life.

CHAPTER 21

Jesus Appears to Seven Disciples

Later Jesus appeared again to the disciples beside the Sea of Galilee.* This is how it happened. 2Several of the disciples were there—Simon Peter, Thomas (nicknamed the Twin*), Nathanael from Cana in Galilee, the sons of Zebedee, and two other disciples.

3Simon Peter said, "I'm going fishing."

"We'll come, too," they all said. So they went out in the boat, but they caught nothing all night.

4At dawn the disciples saw Jesus standing on the beach, but they couldn't see who he was. 5He called out, "Friends, have you caught any fish?"

"No," they replied.

6Then he said, "Throw out your net on the right-hand side of the boat, and you'll get plenty of fish!" So they did, and they couldn't draw in the net because there were so many fish in it.

7Then the disciple whom Jesus loved said to Peter, "It is the Lord!" When Simon Peter heard that it was the Lord, he put on his tunic (for he had stripped for work), jumped into the water, and swam ashore. 8The others stayed with the boat and pulled the loaded net to the shore, for they were only out about three hundred feet.* 9When they got there, they saw that a charcoal fire was burning and fish were frying over it, and there was bread.

10"Bring some of the fish you've just caught," Jesus said. 11So Simon Peter went aboard and dragged the net to the shore. There were 153 large fish, and yet the net hadn't torn.

12"Now come and have some breakfast!" Jesus said. And no one dared ask him if he really was the Lord because they were sure of it. 13Then Jesus served them the bread and the fish. 14This was the third time Jesus had appeared to his disciples since he had been raised from the dead.

Jesus Challenges Peter

15After breakfast Jesus said to Simon Peter, "Simon son of John, do you love me more than these?"

"Yes, Lord," Peter replied, "you know I love you."

"Then feed my lambs," Jesus told him.

16Jesus repeated the question: "Simon son of John, do you love me?"

"Yes, Lord," Peter said, "you know I love you."

"Then take care of my sheep," Jesus said.

17Once more he asked him, "Simon son of John, do you love me?"

Peter was grieved that Jesus asked the question a third time. He said, "Lord, you know everything. You know I love you."

Jesus said, "Then feed my sheep. 18The truth is, when you were young, you were able to do as you liked and go wherever you wanted to. But when you are old, you will stretch out your hands, and others will direct you and take you where you don't want to go." 19Jesus said this to let him know what kind of death he would die

---

20:24 Greek *the one who was called Didymus.* 20:31 Some manuscripts read *may continue to believe.* 21:1 Greek *Sea of Tiberias,* another name for the Sea of Galilee. 21:2 Greek *the one who was called Didymus.* 21:8 Greek *200 cubits* [90 meters].

to glorify God. Then Jesus told him, "Follow me."

20Peter turned around and saw the disciple Jesus loved following them—the one who had leaned over to Jesus during supper and asked, "Lord, who among us will betray you?" 21Peter asked Jesus, "What about him, Lord?"

22Jesus replied, "If I want him to remain alive until I return, what is that to you? You follow me." 23So the rumor spread among the community of believers* that that disciple wouldn't die.

21:23 Greek *the brothers.*

But that isn't what Jesus said at all. He only said, "If I want him to remain alive until I return, what is that to you?"

Conclusion
24This is that disciple who saw these events and recorded them here. And we all know that his account of these things is accurate.

25And I suppose that if all the other things Jesus did were written down, the whole world could not contain the books.

Acts

CHAPTER 1

The Promise of the Holy Spirit

Dear Theophilus:

In my first book* I told you about everything Jesus began to do and teach ²until the day he ascended to heaven after giving his chosen apostles further instructions from the Holy Spirit. ³During the forty days after his crucifixion, he appeared to the apostles from time to time and proved to them in many ways that he was actually alive. On these occasions he talked to them about the Kingdom of God.

⁴In one of these meetings as he was eating a meal with them, he told them, "Do not leave Jerusalem until the Father sends you what he promised. Remember, I have told you about this before. ⁵John baptized with* water, but in just a few days you will be baptized with the Holy Spirit."

The Ascension of Jesus

⁶When the apostles were with Jesus, they kept asking him, "Lord, are you going to free Israel now and restore our kingdom?"

⁷"The Father sets those dates," he replied, "and they are not for you to know. ⁸But when the Holy Spirit has come upon you, you will receive power and will tell people about me everywhere—in Jerusalem, throughout Judea, in Samaria, and to the ends of the earth."

⁹It was not long after he said this that he was taken up into the sky while they were watching, and he disappeared into a cloud. ¹⁰As they were straining their eyes to see him, two white-robed men suddenly stood there among them. ¹¹They said, "Men of Galilee, why are you standing here staring at the sky? Jesus has been taken away from you into heaven. And someday, just as you saw him go, he will return!"

Matthias Replaces Judas

¹²The apostles were at the Mount of Olives when this happened, so they walked the half mile* back to Jerusalem. ¹³Then they went to the upstairs room of the house where they were staying. Here is the list of those who were present:

Peter,
John,
James,
Andrew,
Philip,
Thomas,
Bartholomew,
Matthew,
James (son of Alphaeus),
Simon (the Zealot),
and Judas (son of James).

¹⁴They all met together continually for prayer, along with Mary the mother of Jesus, several other women, and the brothers of Jesus.

¹⁵During this time, on a day when about 120 believers* were present, Peter stood up and addressed them as follows:

¹⁶"Brothers, it was necessary for the Scriptures to be fulfilled concerning Judas, who guided the Temple police to arrest Jesus. This was predicted long ago by the Holy Spirit, speaking through King David. ¹⁷Judas was one of us, chosen to share in the ministry with us.

¹⁸(Judas bought a field with the money he received for his treachery, and falling there, he burst open, spilling out his intestines. ¹⁹The news of his death spread rapidly among all the people of Jerusalem, and they gave the place the Aramaic name *Akeldama*, which means "Field of Blood.")

1:1 The reference is to the book of Luke.   1:5 Or *in;* also in 1:5b.   1:12 Greek *a Sabbath day's journey.*   1:15 Greek *brothers.*

Who the Holy Spirit Helps Read ACTS 2:1-41

Who is the Holy Spirit here to help? The Holy Spirit has been given to all believers to deepen their spiritual walk and to enable them to make an impact upon their world for Jesus Christ. This passage illustrates three aspects of the Holy Spirit's unique work in the lives of believers:

1. The Holy Spirit Fills All Believers. In the Old Testament, the Holy Spirit was given only to a select few to perform specific tasks. This chapter indicates a change in that pattern. The Holy Spirit was poured out on all the believers in the house that day (verse 4), and he continued to be present in each of their lives from that day forward. This outpouring of the Holy Spirit was used by God to establish the church—and to spread the message of the gospel around the world (see verse 39).

2. The Holy Spirit Draws Attention to the Savior. Notice that Peter did not focus on the unique happening that had just taken place but turned the crowd's attention to the message of Jesus Christ and their need for repentance. Likewise, the Holy Spirit does not draw attention to himself but to the Savior. And when he fills your life, he radically increases your ability to share the gospel with others.

3. The Holy Spirit Inspired Peter's Message. Peter's sermon, inspired by the Holy Spirit, led many in the crowd to a point of decision: "What should we do?" (verse 37). The people were not attracted to Peter but to his message. As stated in point 2 above, one of the primary roles of the Holy Spirit is to draw people to God. As stated above, the Holy Spirit worked powerfully this day, and three thousand people responded to the message.

The Holy Spirit is promised to all who repent and receive Jesus Christ into their lives. Many people fail to understand who the Holy Spirit is and what dimension of power is available to them through him. It may help to examine what took place after the disciples received the filling of the Holy Spirit that Jesus had promised (see Acts 1:8, p. 921).

For the next note on "Who Is the Holy Spirit?" turn to p. 1092.

CORNER STONES

20Peter continued, "This was predicted in the book of Psalms, where it says, 'Let his home become desolate, with no one living in it.' And again, 'Let his position be given to someone else.'*

21"So now we must choose another man to take Judas's place. It must be someone who has been with us all the time that we were with the Lord Jesus—22from the time he was baptized by John until the day he was taken from us into heaven. Whoever is chosen will join us as a witness of Jesus' resurrection."

23So they nominated two men: Joseph called Barsabbas (also known as Justus) and Matthias. 24Then they all prayed for the right man to be chosen. "O Lord," they said, "you know every heart. Show us which of these men you have chosen 25as an apostle to replace Judas the traitor in this ministry, for he has deserted us and gone where he belongs." 26Then they cast lots,

and in this way Matthias was chosen and became an apostle with the other eleven.

CHAPTER **2**
The Holy Spirit Comes
On the day of Pentecost, seven weeks after Jesus' resurrection,* the believers were meeting together in one place. 2Suddenly, there was a sound from heaven like the roaring of a mighty windstorm in the skies above them, and it filled the house where they were meeting. 3Then, what looked like flames or tongues of fire appeared and settled on each of them. 4And everyone present was filled with the Holy Spirit and began speaking in other languages,* as the Holy Spirit gave them this ability.

5Godly Jews from many nations were living in Jerusalem at that time. 6When they heard this sound, they came running to see what it was all

1:20 Pss 69:25; 109:8.   2:1 Greek *When the day of Pentecost arrived.* This annual celebration came 50 days after the Passover ceremonies. See Lev 23:16.   2:4 Or *in other tongues.*

about, and they were bewildered to hear their own languages being spoken by the believers.

[7]They were beside themselves with wonder. "How can this be?" they exclaimed. "These people are all from Galilee, [8]and yet we hear them speaking the languages of the lands where we were born! [9]Here we are—Parthians, Medes, Elamites, people from Mesopotamia, Judea, Cappadocia, Pontus, the province of Asia, [10]Phrygia, Pamphylia, Egypt, and the areas of Libya toward Cyrene, visitors from Rome (both Jews and converts to Judaism), [11]Cretans, and Arabians. And we all hear these people speaking in our own languages about the wonderful things God has done!" [12]They stood there amazed and perplexed. "What can this mean?" they asked each other. [13]But others in the crowd were mocking. "They're drunk, that's all!" they said.

Peter Preaches to a Crowd

[14]Then Peter stepped forward with the eleven other apostles and shouted to the crowd, "Listen carefully, all of you, fellow Jews and residents of Jerusalem! Make no mistake about this. [15]Some of you are saying these people are drunk. It isn't true! It's much too early for that. People don't get drunk by nine o'clock in the morning. [16]No, what you see this morning was predicted centuries ago by the prophet Joel:

[17] 'In the last days, God said,
    I will pour out my Spirit upon all people.
  Your sons and daughters will prophesy,
    your young men will see visions,
    and your old men will dream dreams.
[18] In those days I will pour out my Spirit
    upon all my servants, men and women alike,
    and they will prophesy.
[19] And I will cause wonders in the heavens above
    and signs on the earth below—
    blood and fire and clouds of smoke.
[20] The sun will be turned into darkness,
    and the moon will turn bloodred,
    before that great and glorious day of the Lord arrives.
[21] And anyone who calls on the name of the Lord
    will be saved.'*

[22]"People of Israel, listen! God publicly endorsed Jesus of Nazareth by doing wonderful miracles, wonders, and signs through him, as

2:17-21 Joel 2:28-32.

you well know. [23]But you followed God's prearranged plan. With the help of lawless Gentiles, you nailed him to the cross and murdered him. [24]However, God released him from the horrors of death and raised him back to life again, for death could not keep him in its grip. [25]King David said this about him:

'I know the Lord is always with me.
  I will not be shaken, for he is right beside me.
[26] No wonder my heart is filled with joy,
    and my mouth shouts his praises!
  My body rests in hope.
[27] For you will not leave my soul among the dead*

2:27 Greek *in Hades*; also in 2:31.

God's Spirit Will Empower Your Witness Read ACTS 1:8

One of the greatest things the Holy Spirit wants to do in the life of the believer is empower his or her witness. The word for *power* in this verse comes from the Greek word *dunamis*, from which we get the words *dynamite, dynamic,* and *dynamo*. God didn't give us the power of the Holy Spirit to *feel* something, but to *accomplish* something.

Sometimes the Holy Spirit's power acts like dynamite in our lives, blasting us with zeal, jolting us out of complacency, and motivating us to greater spiritual growth. At other times God's Spirit is like a dynamic, generating power that will help us live from day to day at a level we could not achieve on our own. We need to remember the encouraging words the apostle Paul gave to young Timothy: "For God has not given us a spirit of fear and timidity, but of power, love, and self-discipline" (2 Timothy 1:7).

Are you timid in your witness for Christ? Is it hard for you to speak up for what you believe? Then you need to tap in to that power he has made available to you through his Spirit. God's Holy Spirit will give you an added dimension of boldness, power, and persuasiveness in your witness that you have never experienced before.

For the next note on "Live in God's Power," turn to p. 707.

or allow your Holy One to rot in the grave.

28 You have shown me the way of life,
and you will give me wonderful joy in
your presence.'*

29 "Dear brothers, think about this! David wasn't referring to himself when he spoke these words I have quoted, for he died and was buried, and his tomb is still here among us. 30 But he was a prophet, and he knew God had promised with an oath that one of David's own descendants would sit on David's throne as the Messiah. 31 David was looking into the future and predicting the Messiah's resurrection. He was saying that the Messiah would not be left among the dead and that his body would not rot in the grave.

32 "This prophecy was speaking of Jesus, whom God raised from the dead, and we all are witnesses of this. 33 Now he sits on the throne of highest honor in heaven, at God's right hand. And the Father, as he had promised, gave him the Holy Spirit to pour out upon us, just as you see and hear today. 34 For David himself never ascended into heaven, yet he said,

'The LORD said to my Lord,
Sit in honor at my right hand
35   until I humble your enemies,
making them a footstool under your
feet.'*

36 So let it be clearly known by everyone in Israel that God has made this Jesus whom you crucified to be both Lord and Messiah!"

37 Peter's words convicted them deeply, and they said to him and to the other apostles, "Brothers, what should we do?"

38 Peter replied, "Each of you must turn from your sins and turn to God, and be baptized in the name of Jesus Christ for the forgiveness of your sins. Then you will receive the gift of the Holy Spirit. 39 This promise is to you and to your children, and even to the Gentiles*—all who have been called by the Lord our God." 40 Then Peter continued preaching for a long time, strongly urging all his listeners, "Save yourselves from this generation that has gone astray!"

41 Those who believed what Peter said were baptized and added to the church—about three thousand in all. 42 They joined with the other believers and devoted themselves to the apostles' teaching and fellowship, sharing in the Lord's Supper and in prayer.

The Believers Meet Together

43 A deep sense of awe came over them all, and the apostles performed many miraculous signs and wonders. 44 And all the believers met together constantly and shared everything they had. 45 They sold their possessions and shared the proceeds with those in need. 46 They worshiped together at the Temple each day, met in homes for the Lord's Supper, and shared their meals with great joy and generosity—47 all the while praising God and enjoying the goodwill of all the people. And each day the Lord added to their group those who were being saved.

CHAPTER **3**

Peter Heals a Crippled Beggar

Peter and John went to the Temple one afternoon to take part in the three o'clock prayer service. 2 As they approached the Temple, a man lame from birth was being carried in. Each day he was put beside the Temple gate, the one called the Beautiful Gate, so he could beg from the people going into the Temple. 3 When he saw Peter and John about to enter, he asked them for some money.

4 Peter and John looked at him intently, and Peter said, "Look at us!" 5 The lame man looked at them eagerly, expecting a gift. 6 But Peter said, "I don't have any money for you. But I'll give you what I have. In the name of Jesus Christ of Nazareth, get up and walk!"

7 Then Peter took the lame man by the right hand and helped him up. And as he did, the man's feet and anklebones were healed and strengthened. 8 He jumped up, stood on his feet, and began to walk! Then, walking, leaping, and praising God, he went into the Temple with them.

9 All the people saw him walking and heard him praising God. 10 When they realized he was the lame beggar they had seen so often at the Beautiful Gate, they were absolutely astounded! 11 They all rushed out to Solomon's Colonnade, where he was holding tightly to Peter and John. Everyone stood there in awe of the wonderful thing that had happened.

Peter Preaches in the Temple

12 Peter saw his opportunity and addressed the crowd. "People of Israel," he said, "what is so astounding about this? And why look at us as though we had made this man walk by our own power and godliness? 13 For it is the God of

2:25-28 Ps 16:8-11. 2:34-35 Ps 110:1. 2:39 Greek *to those far away.*

Abraham, the God of Isaac, the God of Jacob, the God of all our ancestors who has brought glory to his servant Jesus by doing this. This is the same Jesus whom you handed over and rejected before Pilate, despite Pilate's decision to release him. [14]You rejected this holy, righteous one and instead demanded the release of a murderer. [15]You killed the author of life, but God raised him to life. And we are witnesses of this fact!

[16]"The name of Jesus has healed this man— and you know how lame he was before. Faith in Jesus' name has caused this healing before your very eyes. *

[17]"Friends,* I realize that what you did to Jesus was done in ignorance; and the same can be said of your leaders. [18]But God was fulfilling what all the prophets had declared about the Messiah beforehand—that he must suffer all these things. [19]Now turn from your sins and turn to God, so you can be cleansed of your sins. [20]Then wonderful times of refreshment will come from the presence of the Lord, and he will send Jesus your Messiah to you again. [21]For he must remain in heaven until the time for the final restoration of all things, as God promised long ago through his prophets. [22]Moses said, 'The Lord your God will raise up a Prophet like me from among your own people. Listen carefully to everything he tells you.'* [23]Then Moses said, 'Anyone who will not listen to that Prophet will be cut off from God's people and utterly destroyed.'*

[24]"Starting with Samuel, every prophet spoke about what is happening today. [25]You are the children of those prophets, and you are included in the covenant God promised to your ancestors. For God said to Abraham, 'Through your descendants all the families on earth will be blessed.'* [26]When God raised up his servant, he sent him first to you people of Israel, to bless you by turning each of you back from your sinful ways."

CHAPTER **4**

Peter and John before the Council

While Peter and John were speaking to the people, the leading priests, the captain of the Temple guard, and some of the Sadducees came over to them. [2]They were very disturbed that Peter and John were claiming, on the authority of Jesus, that there is a resurrection of the dead. [3]They arrested them and, since it was already

3:17 Greek *Brothers.*   **3:22** Deut 18:15.   **3:23** Deut 18:19; Lev 23:29.   **3:25** Gen 22:18.

What to Look for in a Church
Read ACTS 2:42, 44-47

The first-century church turned the world upside down with its message (see Acts 17:6, p. 945). What made the early church so dynamic was the commitment of its members to follow Christ wholeheartedly. When you look for a church to attend, make sure it has these five characteristics of a healthy church:

1. Look for a Church That Meets Together Regularly. The early believers did not view church as a social club, but as a place for devoted fellowship and valuable instruction. We miss out on a tremendous blessing when we neglect meeting together with God's people. When we are spiritually weak, we should not run *from* church but *to* church!

2. Look for a Church That Places a High Priority on Bible Study. The first-century Christians "devoted themselves to the apostles' teaching." The apostles' teachings on the life and ministry of Jesus eventually became the Gospel portion of the New Testament. Studying the Bible is important to every Christian's spiritual growth. Without Bible study, Christians cannot know and understand God's commands and truth.

3. Look for a Church That Is a Place of Corporate Worship and Prayer. The early church recognized the importance of corporate worship and prayer. Corporate worship focused their attention on the praiseworthy character of God and gave them an opportunity to express their thanks to God. Corporate prayer allowed them to express their thanks to God as well, but it was also an opportunity to seek God together and present their requests before him as a body.

4. Look for a Church That Looks after Its Members. The early believers shared food, clothing, and housing with each other. The Bible reminds us to care for fellow believers who are in need (see 2 Corinthians 9:1-15).

5. Look for a Church That Is Growing. Church growth is not our responsibility but God's. If we do our part as a church, God will do his. We see proof of this in verse 47.

For the next note on "Look For and Attend the Right Church," turn to p. 1079.

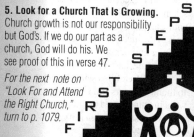

S
P
E
T
S

T
S
R
I
F

Jesus Has Great Power to Transform People Read ACTS 4:1-13

The entire book of Acts is a testimony to the transformation that takes place in the life of a true follower of Jesus Christ. Consider the case of Peter and John. Immediately after Christ's crucifixion, Peter and John went into hiding. In fact, Peter denied knowing Jesus three times before Jesus even died! These men were far from bold. Yet when Jesus came back to life, met with them, and told them to wait for the promised Holy Spirit once he returned to heaven, everything changed.

Why were Peter and John so bold? What made their witness so effective, and how can our lives be so dramatically transformed?

Peter and John Spent Time with Jesus. For three years Peter and John followed Jesus throughout Israel. During this time they saw Jesus perform many miracles. They also listened to his teaching and observed his lifestyle. But they weren't just casual observers. They talked with Jesus and shared their lives with him. In doing so, they made Jesus a significant part of their lives. Even though we did not walk alongside Jesus during his time on earth, we can invite him into our hearts. In addition, we have his teachings to study and the ability to spend time with him in prayer. In other words, we don't have to live in Bible times to have a relationship with Jesus.

Peter and John Modeled Their Lives after Jesus' Life and Teachings. Christ's life and resurrection had such an impact on Peter and John that they began to imitate Jesus in their behavior. We can see the impact Jesus made on these two disciples in the first few chapters of Acts. Here Peter and John speak boldly for Jesus in public, heal a crippled beggar, and endure persecution for Jesus. Their actions prove an important point: We need to put into practice what we have learned from spending time with Jesus.

Peter and John Put Their Confidence in Christ, Not in Their Own Abilities. Remember, Peter and John were common fishermen. They had no impressive credentials to flash in front of these

CORNER STONES

people. They simply relied upon Jesus to guide them and help them through any obstacles, and that gave them all the confidence they needed. We should do no less.

If you want to see the power of Jesus Christ in action today, take a look at some of the lives he has turned around. Some of the greatest evidence for Jesus Christ today consists of the countless lives that have been dramatically changed by his touch.

For the next note on "Who Is Jesus?" turn to p. 1118.

For the next note on "Who Is Jesus?" turn to p. 1118.

---

evening, jailed them until morning. ⁴But many of the people who heard their message believed it, so that the number of believers totaled about five thousand men, not counting women and children.*

⁵The next day the council of all the rulers and elders and teachers of religious law met in Jerusalem. ⁶Annas the high priest was there, along with Caiaphas, John, Alexander, and other relatives of the high priest. ⁷They brought in the two disciples and demanded, "By what power, or in whose name, have you done this?"

⁸Then Peter, filled with the Holy Spirit, said to them, "Leaders and elders of our nation, ⁹are we being questioned because we've done a good

deed for a crippled man? Do you want to know how he was healed? ¹⁰Let me clearly state to you and to all the people of Israel that he was healed in the name and power of Jesus Christ from Nazareth, the man you crucified, but whom God raised from the dead. ¹¹For Jesus is the one referred to in the Scriptures, where it says,

'The stone that you builders rejected
has now become the cornerstone.'*

¹²There is salvation in no one else! There is no other name in all of heaven for people to call on to save them."

¹³The members of the council were amazed when they saw the boldness of Peter and John,

4:4 Greek *5,000 adult males.*   4:11 Ps 118:22.

Why Is Jesus Christ the Only Way to God? Read ACTS 4:12

One of the most common criticisms of Christianity is that it is too narrow. Many people just cannot believe that there is only one way to heaven. Because Christians have championed this truth, they have been criticized for implying that they are better than those who do not believe in Jesus Christ. But it is important to note that the reason Christians believe Jesus Christ is the only way to heaven is because he himself said it. Jesus said, "I am the way, the truth, and the life. No one can come to the Father except through me" (John 14:6).

If humankind could have reached God any other way, Jesus would not have had to die. His voluntary death on the cross clearly illustrates the fact that there is no other way. Those who reject his loving offer of forgiveness—which is extended to all of humankind—do so at their own peril.

For the next "Big Question" note, turn to p. 929.

---

for they could see that they were ordinary men who had had no special training. They also recognized them as men who had been with Jesus. [14]But since the man who had been healed was standing right there among them, the council had nothing to say. [15]So they sent Peter and John out of the council chamber* and conferred among themselves.

[16]"What should we do with these men?" they asked each other. "We can't deny they have done a miraculous sign, and everybody in Jerusalem knows about it. [17]But perhaps we can stop them from spreading their propaganda. We'll warn them not to speak to anyone in Jesus' name again." [18]So they called the apostles back in and told them never again to speak or teach about Jesus.

[19]But Peter and John replied, "Do you think God wants us to obey you rather than him? [20]We cannot stop telling about the wonderful things we have seen and heard."

[21]The council then threatened them further, but they finally let them go because they didn't know how to punish them without starting a riot. For everyone was praising God [22]for this miraculous sign—the healing of a man who had been lame for more than forty years.

The Believers Pray for Courage

[23]As soon as they were freed, Peter and John found the other believers and told them what the leading priests and elders had said. [24]Then all the believers were united as they lifted their voices in prayer: "O Sovereign Lord, Creator of heaven and earth, the sea, and everything in them—[25]you spoke long ago by the Holy Spirit through our ancestor King David, your servant, saying,

'Why did the nations rage?
  Why did the people waste their time with futile plans?
[26] The kings of the earth prepared for battle;
  the rulers gathered together
against the Lord
  and against his Messiah.'*

[27]"That is what has happened here in this city! For Herod Antipas, Pontius Pilate the governor, the Gentiles, and the people of Israel were all united against Jesus, your holy servant, whom you anointed. [28]In fact, everything they did occurred according to your eternal will and plan. [29]And now, O Lord, hear their threats, and give your servants great boldness in their preaching. [30]Send your healing power; may miraculous signs and wonders be done through the name of your holy servant Jesus."

[31]After this prayer, the building where they were meeting shook, and they were all filled with the Holy Spirit. And they preached God's message with boldness.

4:15 Greek *the Sanhedrin.*   4:25-26 Ps 2:1-2.

When the Holy Spirit Can Be Sinned Against Read ACTS 5:1-10

One way Scripture supports the concept that the Holy Spirit is a person rather than a force is by showing how one can sin against him. It is important to understand that the Holy Spirit is indeed *God* at work and that to commit a sin against him is to commit a sin against God. In this passage we see one way in which we can sin against the Holy Spirit. But other passages inform us of at least five additional ways in which a person can sin against the Spirit.

1. Lying to the Holy Spirit. Ananias and Sapphira lied to the Holy Spirit by pretending to be thoroughly devoted to God when they really were not. One way people continue to do this today is by "going through the [spiritual] motions" without really meaning it in their hearts.

2. Grieving the Holy Spirit. Only believers can grieve the Holy Spirit (see Ephesians 4:30, p. 1028). We grieve the Holy Spirit when we carry anger in our heart, slander others, or do things that we know go against the new nature that is inside of us.

3. Quenching the Holy Spirit. When the Holy Spirit convicts us of something we need to change in our life and we ignore his promptings, we are extinguishing his power in our life (1 Thessalonians 5:19). He is still in our life, but we are holding back from giving him complete control.

4. Resisting the Holy Spirit. When Stephen, the first recorded Christian martyr, spoke to his persecutors, he shared the message of Jesus Christ but closed with the words: "You stubborn people! . . . Must you forever resist the Holy Spirit?" (Acts 7:51). People who commit this sin may know that the Holy Spirit is trying to bring them to Jesus, but their pride keeps them from acknowledging Christ as Savior and Lord. The danger with this sin is that every time a person resists God's Spirit, he or she makes it more difficult for him or herself to come to Christ.

5. Insulting the Holy Spirit. To insult the Holy Spirit means to treat "the blood of the covenant as if it were common and unholy" (Hebrews 10:29). The person who commits this sin essentially dismisses the great price that Jesus paid for him or her at the cross of Calvary. This person has refused to accept the tremendous gift of salvation that God has offered to him or her.

6. Blaspheming the Holy Spirit. The two sins listed above, resisting and insulting the Holy Spirit, can lead to what is termed the "unforgivable sin": blasphemy against the Holy Spirit (see Matthew 12:31-32, p. 804). Since the Bible tells us that Christ is the only way of salvation, and the Holy Spirit's initial work in our life as a nonbeliever is to draw us to Christ, to blaspheme the Holy Spirit is to reject Jesus Christ as our Lord and Savior. That is the point of no return. Every time a person resists the Spirit and insults him, he or she gets a step closer to this ultimate sin.

For the next note on "Who Is the Holy Spirit?" turn to p. 1016.

CORNER STONES

The Believers Share Their Possessions

³²All the believers were of one heart and mind, and they felt that what they owned was not their own; they shared everything they had. ³³And the apostles gave powerful witness to the resurrection of the Lord Jesus, and God's great favor was upon them all. ³⁴There was no poverty among them, because people who owned land or houses sold them ³⁵and brought the money to the apostles to give to others in need.

³⁶For instance, there was Joseph, the one the apostles nicknamed Barnabas (which means "Son of Encouragement"). He was from the tribe of Levi and came from the island of Cyprus. ³⁷He sold a field he owned and brought the money to the apostles for those in need.

CHAPTER 5
Ananias and Sapphira

There was also a man named Ananias who, with his wife, Sapphira, sold some property. ²He brought part of the money to the apostles, but he claimed it was the full amount. His wife had agreed to this deception.

³Then Peter said, "Ananias, why has Satan filled your heart? You lied to the Holy Spirit, and

Aren't Other Religions Just As Good As Christianity? Read ACTS 4:12

{ome people say that all religions basically say and teach the same thing, so they must all be "true." To quote another well-used phrase, "If a person is really sincere in what he or she believes, he or she will get to heaven."

In reality, all belief systems cannot be true, because they contradict one another. Many would like to think that all religions blend together beautifully, but they do not. Look at the differences between what the followers of three major world religions believe compared with what Christians believe.

The Existence of a Personal God.
- Buddhists deny the existence of a personal God.
- Hindus believe in two major gods, Vishnu and Siva, as well as in millions of lesser gods.
- Muslims believe in one God named Allah.
- Christians believe that God is a being who created humans in his own image and who loves them and wants to have a personal relationship with them.

The Subject of Salvation.
- Buddhists believe salvation is by self-effort only.
- Hindus believe you achieve salvation by devotion, works, and self-control.
- Muslims believe that people earn their own salvation and pay for their own sins.
- Christians believe that Jesus Christ died for their sins. If people turn from their sins and follow Jesus, they can be forgiven and have the hope of being with Jesus in heaven.

The Person of Jesus Christ.
- Buddhists believe that Jesus Christ was a good teacher, though less important then Buddha.
- Hindus believe that Jesus was just one of many incarnations—or sons —of God. Yet they also assert that Christ was not the unique Son of God. He was no more divine then any other man, and he did not die for people's sins.
- Muslims believe that Jesus Christ was the greatest of the prophets below Muhammad. In addition, they do not believe that Christ died for people's sin.
- Christians believe that Jesus is God as well as man, that he was sinless, and that he died to redeem humankind.

As you can see, you cannot believe in all of the major religious beliefs. That is because each religion eventually contradicts the claims of Christianity [Fritz Ridenour, *So What's the Difference?* (Glendale: Gospel Light Publications, 1967)].

For the next "Big Question" note, turn to p. 963.

---

you kept some of the money for yourself. 4The property was yours to sell or not sell, as you wished. And after selling it, the money was yours to give away. How could you do a thing like this? You weren't lying to us but to God."

5As soon as Ananias heard these words, he fell to the floor and died. Everyone who heard about it was terrified. 6Then some young men wrapped him in a sheet and took him out and buried him.

7About three hours later his wife came in, not knowing what had happened. 8Peter asked her, "Was this the price you and your husband received for your land?"

"Yes," she replied, "that was the price."

9And Peter said, "How could the two of you even think of doing a thing like this—conspiring together to test the Spirit of the Lord? Just outside that door are the young men who buried your husband, and they will carry you out, too."

10Instantly, she fell to the floor and died. When the young men came in and saw that she was dead, they carried her out and buried her beside her husband. 11Great fear gripped the entire church and all others who heard what had happened.

The Apostles Heal Many
12Meanwhile, the apostles were performing many miraculous signs and wonders among the

people. And the believers were meeting regularly at the Temple in the area known as Solomon's Colonnade. 13No one else dared to join them, though everyone had high regard for them. 14And more and more people believed and were brought to the Lord—crowds of both men and women. 15As a result of the apostles' work, sick people were brought out into the streets on beds and mats so that Peter's shadow might fall across some of them as he went by. 16Crowds came in from the villages around Jerusalem, bringing their sick and those possessed by evil spirits, and they were all healed.

The Apostles Meet Opposition

17The high priest and his friends, who were Sadducees, reacted with violent jealousy. 18They arrested the apostles and put them in the jail. 19But an angel of the Lord came at night, opened the gates of the jail, and brought them out. Then he told them, 20"Go to the Temple and give the people this message of life!" 21So the apostles entered the Temple about daybreak and immediately began teaching.

When the high priest and his officials arrived, they convened the high council,* along with all the elders of Israel. Then they sent for the apostles to be brought for trial. 22But when the Temple guards went to the jail, the men were gone. So they returned to the council and reported, 23"The jail was locked, with the guards standing outside, but when we opened the gates, no one was there!"

24When the captain of the Temple guard and the leading priests heard this, they were perplexed, wondering where it would all end. 25Then someone arrived with the news that the men they had jailed were out in the Temple, teaching the people.

26The captain went with his Temple guards and arrested them, but without violence, for they were afraid the people would kill them if they treated the apostles roughly. 27Then they brought the apostles in before the council. 28"Didn't we tell you never again to teach in this man's name?" the high priest demanded. "Instead, you have filled all Jerusalem with your teaching about Jesus, and you intend to blame us for his death!"

29But Peter and the apostles replied, "We must obey God rather than human authority. 30The God of our ancestors raised Jesus from the dead after you killed him by crucifying him. 31Then God put him in the place of honor at his right hand as Prince and Savior. He did this to give the people of Israel an opportunity to turn from their sins and turn to God so their sins would be forgiven. 32We are witnesses of these things and so is the Holy Spirit, who is given by God to those who obey him."

33At this, the high council was furious and decided to kill them. 34But one member had a different perspective. He was a Pharisee named Gamaliel, who was an expert on religious law and was very popular with the people. He stood up and ordered that the apostles be sent outside the council chamber for a while. 35Then he addressed his colleagues as follows: "Men of Israel, take care what you are planning to do to these men! 36Some time ago there was that fellow Theudas, who pretended to be someone great. About four hundred others joined him, but he was killed, and his followers went their various ways. The whole movement came to nothing. 37After him, at the time of the census, there was Judas of Galilee. He got some people to follow him, but he was killed, too, and all his followers were scattered.

38"So my advice is, leave these men alone. If they are teaching and doing these things merely on their own, it will soon be overthrown. 39But if it is of God, you will not be able to stop them. You may even find yourselves fighting against God."

40The council accepted his advice. They called in the apostles and had them flogged. Then they ordered them never again to speak in the name of Jesus, and they let them go. 41The apostles left the high council rejoicing that God had counted them worthy to suffer dishonor for the name of Jesus. 42And every day, in the Temple and in their homes,* they continued to teach and preach this message: "The Messiah you are looking for is Jesus."

CHAPTER 6

Seven Men Chosen to Serve

But as the believers* rapidly multiplied, there were rumblings of discontent. Those who spoke Greek complained against those who spoke Hebrew, saying that their widows were being discriminated against in the daily distribution of food. 2So the Twelve called a meeting of all the believers.

"We apostles should spend our time preaching and teaching the word of God, not adminis-

---

5:21 Greek *Sanhedrin;* also in 5:27, 41.   5:42 Greek *from house to house.*   6:1 Greek *disciples;* also in 6:2, 7.

tering a food program," they said. 3"Now look around among yourselves, brothers, and select seven men who are well respected and are full of the Holy Spirit and wisdom. We will put them in charge of this business. 4Then we can spend our time in prayer and preaching and teaching the word."

5This idea pleased the whole group, and they chose the following: Stephen (a man full of faith and the Holy Spirit), Philip, Procorus, Nicanor, Timon, Parmenas, and Nicolas of Antioch (a Gentile convert to the Jewish faith, who had now become a Christian). 6These seven were presented to the apostles, who prayed for them as they laid their hands on them.

7God's message was preached in ever-widening circles. The number of believers greatly increased in Jerusalem, and many of the Jewish priests were converted, too.

Stephen Is Arrested

8Stephen, a man full of God's grace and power, performed amazing miracles and signs among the people. 9But one day some men from the Synagogue of Freed Slaves, as it was called, started to debate with him. They were Jews from Cyrene, Alexandria, Cilicia, and the province of Asia. 10None of them was able to stand against the wisdom and Spirit by which Stephen spoke.

11So they persuaded some men to lie about Stephen, saying, "We heard him blaspheme Moses, and even God." 12Naturally, this roused the crowds, the elders, and the teachers of religious law. So they arrested Stephen and brought him before the high council.* 13The lying witnesses said, "This man is always speaking against the Temple and against the law of Moses. 14We have heard him say that this Jesus of Nazareth will destroy the Temple and change the customs Moses handed down to us." 15At this point everyone in the council stared at Stephen because his face became as bright as an angel's.

CHAPTER 7
Stephen Addresses the Council

Then the high priest asked Stephen, "Are these accusations true?"

2This was Stephen's reply: "Brothers and honorable fathers, listen to me. Our glorious God appeared to our ancestor Abraham in Mesopotamia before he moved to Haran.* 3God told him, 'Leave your native land and your rela-

tives, and come to the land that I will show you.'* 4So Abraham left the land of the Chaldeans and lived in Haran until his father died. Then God brought him here to the land where you now live. 5But God gave him no inheritance here, not even one square foot of land. God did promise, however, that eventually the whole country would belong to Abraham and his descendants—though he had no children yet. 6But God also told him that his descendants would live in a foreign country where they would be mistreated as slaves for four hundred years. 7'But I will punish the nation that enslaves them,' God told him, 'and in the end they will come out and worship me in this place.'* 8God also gave Abraham the covenant of circumcision at that time. And so Isaac, Abraham's son, was circumcised when he was eight days old. Isaac became the father of Jacob, and Jacob was the father of the twelve patriarchs of the Jewish nation.

9"These sons of Jacob were very jealous of their brother Joseph, and they sold him to be a slave in Egypt. But God was with him 10and delivered him from his anguish. And God gave him favor before Pharaoh, king of Egypt. God also gave Joseph unusual wisdom, so that Pharaoh appointed him governor over all of Egypt and put him in charge of all the affairs of the palace.

11"But a famine came upon Egypt and Canaan. There was great misery for our ancestors, as they ran out of food. 12Jacob heard that there was still grain in Egypt, so he sent his sons* to buy some. 13The second time they went, Joseph revealed his identity to his brothers, and they were introduced to Pharaoh. 14Then Joseph sent for his father, Jacob, and all his relatives to come to Egypt, seventy-five persons in all. 15So Jacob went to Egypt. He died there, as did all his sons. 16All of them were taken to Shechem and buried in the tomb Abraham had bought from the sons of Hamor in Shechem.

17"As the time drew near when God would fulfill his promise to Abraham, the number of our people in Egypt greatly increased. 18But then a new king came to the throne of Egypt who knew nothing about Joseph. 19This king plotted against our people and forced parents to abandon their newborn babies so they would die.

20"At that time Moses was born—a beautiful child in God's eyes. His parents cared for him at home for three months. 21When at last they had to abandon him, Pharaoh's daughter found him

6:12 Greek *Sanhedrin*; also in 6:15. 7:2 *Mesopotamia* was the region now called Iraq. *Haran* was a city in what is now called Syria. 7:3 Gen 12:1. 7:5-7 Gen 12:7; 15:13-14; Exod 3:12. 7:12 Greek *our fathers*; also in 7:15.

and raised him as her own son. 22Moses was taught all the wisdom of the Egyptians, and he became mighty in both speech and action.

23"One day when he was forty years old, he decided to visit his relatives, the people of Israel. 24During this visit, he saw an Egyptian mistreating a man of Israel. So Moses came to his defense and avenged him, killing the Egyptian. 25Moses assumed his brothers would realize that God had sent him to rescue them, but they didn't.

26"The next day he visited them again and saw two men of Israel fighting. He tried to be a peacemaker. 'Men,' he said, 'you are brothers. Why are you hurting each other?'

27"But the man in the wrong pushed Moses aside and told him to mind his own business. 'Who made you a ruler and judge over us?' he asked. 28'Are you going to kill me as you killed that Egyptian yesterday?' 29When Moses heard that, he fled the country and lived as a foreigner in the land of Midian, where his two sons were born.

30"Forty years later, in the desert near Mount Sinai, an angel appeared to Moses in the flame of a burning bush. 31Moses saw it and wondered what it was. As he went to see, the voice of the Lord called out to him, 32'I am the God of your ancestors—the God of Abraham, Isaac, and Jacob.' Moses shook with terror and dared not look.

33"And the Lord said to him, 'Take off your sandals, for you are standing on holy ground. 34You can be sure that I have seen the misery of my people in Egypt. I have heard their cries. So I have come to rescue them. Now go, for I will send you to Egypt.'* 35And so God sent back the same man his people had previously rejected by demanding, 'Who made you a ruler and judge over us?' Through the angel who appeared to him in the burning bush, Moses was sent to be their ruler and savior. 36And by means of many miraculous signs and wonders, he led them out of Egypt, through the Red Sea, and back and forth through the wilderness for forty years.

37"Moses himself told the people of Israel, 'God will raise up a Prophet like me from among your own people.'* 38Moses was with the assembly of God's people in the wilderness. He was the mediator between the people of Israel and the angel who gave him life-giving words on Mount Sinai to pass on to us.

39"But our ancestors rejected Moses and wanted to return to Egypt. 40They told Aaron, 'Make us some gods who can lead us, for we don't know what has become of this Moses, who brought us out of Egypt.' 41So they made an idol shaped like a calf, and they sacrificed to it and rejoiced in this thing they had made. 42Then God turned away from them and gave them up to serve the sun, moon, and stars as their gods! In the book of the prophets it is written,

'Was it to me you were bringing sacrifices
    during those forty years in the
        wilderness, Israel?
43 No, your real interest was in your pagan
        gods—
    the shrine of Molech,
    the star god Rephan,
    and the images you made to worship
        them.
So I will send you into captivity
    far away in Babylon.'*

44"Our ancestors carried the Tabernacle* with them through the wilderness. It was constructed in exact accordance with the plan shown to Moses by God. 45Years later, when Joshua led the battles against the Gentile nations that God drove out of this land, the Tabernacle was taken with them into their new territory. And it was used there until the time of King David. 46David found favor with God and asked for the privilege of building a permanent Temple for the God of Jacob.* 47But it was Solomon who actually built it. 48However, the Most High doesn't live in temples made by human hands. As the prophet says,

49 'Heaven is my throne,
    and the earth is my footstool.
Could you ever build me a temple as good
        as that?'
    asks the Lord.
'Could you build a dwelling place for me?
50   Didn't I make everything in heaven and
        earth?'*

51"You stubborn people! You are heathen at heart and deaf to the truth. Must you forever resist the Holy Spirit? But your ancestors did, and so do you! 52Name one prophet your ancestors didn't persecute! They even killed the ones who predicted the coming of the Righteous One—the Messiah whom you betrayed and

7:31-34 Exod 3:5-10. 7:37 Deut 18:15. 7:42-43 Amos 5:25-27. 7:44 Greek *the tent of witness.* 7:46 Some manuscripts read *the house of Jacob.* 7:49-50 Isa 66:1-2.

murdered. 53You deliberately disobeyed God's law, though you received it from the hands of angels.*"

54The Jewish leaders were infuriated by Stephen's accusation, and they shook their fists in rage.* 55But Stephen, full of the Holy Spirit, gazed steadily upward into heaven and saw the glory of God, and he saw Jesus standing in the place of honor at God's right hand. 56And he told them, "Look, I see the heavens opened and the Son of Man standing in the place of honor at God's right hand!"

57Then they put their hands over their ears, and drowning out his voice with their shouts, they rushed at him. 58They dragged him out of the city and began to stone him. The official witnesses took off their coats and laid them at the feet of a young man named Saul.*

59And as they stoned him, Stephen prayed, "Lord Jesus, receive my spirit." 60And he fell to his knees, shouting, "Lord, don't charge them with this sin!" And with that, he died.

CHAPTER 8

Saul was one of the official witnesses at the killing of Stephen.

Persecution Scatters the Believers

A great wave of persecution began that day, sweeping over the church in Jerusalem, and all the believers except the apostles fled into Judea and Samaria. 2(Some godly men came and buried Stephen with loud weeping.) 3Saul was going everywhere to devastate the church. He went from house to house, dragging out both men and women to throw them into jail.

Philip Preaches in Samaria

4But the believers who had fled Jerusalem went everywhere preaching the Good News about Jesus. 5Philip, for example, went to the city of Samaria and told the people there about the Messiah. 6Crowds listened intently to what he had to say because of the miracles he did. 7Many evil spirits were cast out, screaming as they left their victims. And many who had been paralyzed or lame were healed. 8So there was great joy in that city.

9A man named Simon had been a sorcerer there for many years, claiming to be someone great. 10The Samaritan people, from the least to

7:53 Greek *received the Law as it was ordained by angels.* 7:54 Greek *they were grinding their teeth against him.* 7:58 *Saul* is later called Paul; see 13:9.

Be Open to God's Leading
Read ACTS 8:4-8, 26-38

This text shows two forms of evangelism. In the beginning of this passage, we see Philip engaged in "mass evangelism" (verses 4-8). Toward the end of the chapter, we see Philip taking part in personal, "one-on-one evangelism" with the Ethiopian (verses 26-38). The text also gives us three principles to follow for effective evangelism:

1. Philip Was Led by God's Spirit. This principle (verse 29) can make all the difference in sharing one's faith. This leading will often come in the form of an "impression" or a burden—such as a compelling desire to talk to someone about your faith (see Acts 17:16-31, pp. 945-946). Like Philip, we should simply be open and available to what God would have us to do.

2. Philip Obeyed God's Leading. Philip did exactly what the Lord told him to do without delay (verse 27). Jesus said, "My sheep recognize my voice; I know them, and they follow me" (John 10:27). So when God said, "Go," Philip went! Likewise, we need to be on duty at all times, ready to "preach the word of God" (2 Timothy 4:2).

3. Philip Knew Scripture. Philip used the Scripture this man was reading as a starting point. Then he used a number of other passages to tell the Ethiopian about Jesus (verse 35). Knowing God's Word is essential for any person who wants to lead others to Jesus Christ. Arguments will not have nearly the impact that God's Word will when we share our faith with others.

The same God who led Philip in his evangelistic work also wants to direct your steps. You might start each day with a prayer like the prophet Isaiah: "Lord, I'll go! Send me" (Isaiah 6:8). Remember, God is not looking so much for a person's ability as his or her availability. God is not looking for "strong" people to be his witnesses so much as he is looking for people through whom he can show his strength.

For the next note on "Share Your Faith," *turn to p. 985.*

the greatest, often spoke of him as "the Great One—the Power of God." 11He was very influential because of the magic he performed. 12But now the people believed Philip's message of Good News concerning the Kingdom of God and the name of Jesus Christ. As a result, many men and women were baptized. 13Then Simon himself believed and was baptized. He began following Philip wherever he went, and he was amazed by the great miracles and signs Philip performed.

14When the apostles back in Jerusalem heard that the people of Samaria had accepted God's message, they sent Peter and John there. 15As soon as they arrived, they prayed for these new Christians to receive the Holy Spirit. 16The Holy Spirit had not yet come upon any of them, for they had only been baptized in the name of the Lord Jesus. 17Then Peter and John laid their hands upon these believers, and they received the Holy Spirit.

18When Simon saw that the Holy Spirit was given when the apostles placed their hands upon people's heads, he offered money to buy this power. 19"Let me have this power, too," he exclaimed, "so that when I lay my hands on people, they will receive the Holy Spirit!"

20But Peter replied, "May your money perish with you for thinking God's gift can be bought! 21You can have no part in this, for your heart is not right before God. 22Turn from your wickedness and pray to the Lord. Perhaps he will forgive your evil thoughts, 23for I can see that you are full of bitterness and held captive by sin."

24"Pray to the Lord for me," Simon exclaimed, "that these terrible things won't happen to me!"

25After testifying and preaching the word of the Lord in Samaria, Peter and John returned to Jerusalem. And they stopped in many Samaritan villages along the way to preach the Good News to them, too.

Philip and the Ethiopian Eunuch

26As for Philip, an angel of the Lord said to him, "Go south* down the desert road that runs from Jerusalem to Gaza." 27So he did, and he met the treasurer of Ethiopia, a eunuch of great authority under the queen of Ethiopia.* The eunuch had gone to Jerusalem to worship, 28and he was now returning. Seated in his carriage, he was reading aloud from the book of the prophet Isaiah.

29The Holy Spirit said to Philip, "Go over and walk along beside the carriage."

30Philip ran over and heard the man reading from the prophet Isaiah; so he asked, "Do you understand what you are reading?"

31The man replied, "How can I, when there is no one to instruct me?" And he begged Philip to come up into the carriage and sit with him. 32The passage of Scripture he had been reading was this:

"He was led as a sheep to the slaughter.
And as a lamb is silent before the
    shearers,
he did not open his mouth.
33 He was humiliated and received no justice.
Who can speak of his descendants?
For his life was taken from the earth."*

34The eunuch asked Philip, "Was Isaiah talking about himself or someone else?" 35So Philip began with this same Scripture and then used many others to tell him the Good News about Jesus.

36As they rode along, they came to some water, and the eunuch said, "Look! There's some water! Why can't I be baptized?"* 38He ordered the carriage to stop, and they went down into the water, and Philip baptized him.

39When they came up out of the water, the Spirit of the Lord caught Philip away. The eunuch never saw him again but went on his way rejoicing. 40Meanwhile, Philip found himself farther north at the city of Azotus! He preached the Good News there and in every city along the way until he came to Caesarea.

CHAPTER 9
Saul's Conversion

Meanwhile, Saul was uttering threats with every breath. He was eager to destroy the Lord's followers,* so he went to the high priest. 2He requested letters addressed to the synagogues in Damascus, asking their cooperation in the arrest of any followers of the Way he found there. He wanted to bring them—both men and women—back to Jerusalem in chains.

3As he was nearing Damascus on this mission, a brilliant light from heaven suddenly beamed down upon him! 4He fell to the ground and heard a voice saying to him, "Saul! Saul! Why are you persecuting me?"

8:26 Or *Go at noon.*   8:27 Greek *under the Candace, the queen of Ethiopia.*   8:32-33 Isa 53:7-8.   8:36 Some manuscripts add verse 37, *"You can," Philip answered, "if you believe with all your heart." And the eunuch replied, "I believe that Jesus Christ is the Son of God."*   9:1 Greek *disciples.*

5"Who are you, sir?" Saul asked.

And the voice replied, "I am Jesus, the one you are persecuting! 6Now get up and go into the city, and you will be told what you are to do."

7The men with Saul stood speechless with surprise, for they heard the sound of someone's voice, but they saw no one! 8As Saul picked himself up off the ground, he found that he was blind. 9So his companions led him by the hand to Damascus. He remained there blind for three days. And all that time he went without food and water.

10Now there was a believer* in Damascus named Ananias. The Lord spoke to him in a vision, calling, "Ananias!"

"Yes, Lord!" he replied.

11The Lord said, "Go over to Straight Street, to the house of Judas. When you arrive, ask for Saul of Tarsus. He is praying to me right now. 12I have shown him a vision of a man named Ananias coming in and laying his hands on him so that he can see again."

13"But Lord," exclaimed Ananias, "I've heard about the terrible things this man has done to the believers in Jerusalem! 14And we hear that he is authorized by the leading priests to arrest every believer in Damascus."

15But the Lord said, "Go and do what I say. For Saul is my chosen instrument to take my message to the Gentiles and to kings, as well as to the people of Israel. 16And I will show him how much he must suffer for me."

17So Ananias went and found Saul. He laid his hands on him and said, "Brother Saul, the Lord Jesus, who appeared to you on the road, has sent me so that you may get your sight back and be filled with the Holy Spirit." 18Instantly something like scales fell from Saul's eyes, and he regained his sight. Then he got up and was baptized. 19Afterward he ate some food and was strengthened.

Saul in Damascus and Jerusalem

Saul stayed with the believers* in Damascus for a few days. 20And immediately he began preaching about Jesus in the synagogues, saying, "He is indeed the Son of God!"

21All who heard him were amazed. "Isn't this the same man who persecuted Jesus' followers with such devastation in Jerusalem?" they asked. "And we understand that he came here to arrest them and take them in chains to the leading priests."

22Saul's preaching became more and more powerful, and the Jews in Damascus couldn't refute his proofs that Jesus was indeed the Messiah. 23After a while the Jewish leaders decided to kill him. 24But Saul was told about their plot, and that they were watching for him day and night at the city gate so they could murder him. 25So during the night, some of the other believers* let him down in a large basket through an opening in the city wall.

26When Saul arrived in Jerusalem, he tried to meet with the believers, but they were all afraid of him. They thought he was only pretending to be a believer! 27Then Barnabas brought him to the apostles and told them how Saul had seen the Lord on the way to Damascus. Barnabas also told them what the Lord had said to Saul and how he boldly preached in the name of Jesus in Damascus. 28Then the apostles accepted Saul, and after that he was constantly with them in Jerusalem, preaching boldly in the name of the Lord. 29He debated with some Greek-speaking Jews, but they plotted to murder him. 30When the believers* heard about it, however, they took him to Caesarea and sent him on to his hometown of Tarsus.

31The church then had peace throughout Judea, Galilee, and Samaria, and it grew in strength and numbers. The believers were walking in the fear of the Lord and in the comfort of the Holy Spirit.

Peter Heals Aeneas and Raises Dorcas

32Peter traveled from place to place to visit the believers, and in his travels he came to the Lord's people in the town of Lydda. 33There he met a man named Aeneas, who had been paralyzed and bedridden for eight years. 34Peter said to him, "Aeneas, Jesus Christ heals you! Get up and make your bed!" And he was healed instantly. 35Then the whole population of Lydda and Sharon turned to the Lord when they saw Aeneas walking around.

36There was a believer in Joppa named Tabitha (which in Greek is Dorcas*). She was always doing kind things for others and helping the poor. 37About this time she became ill and died. Her friends prepared her for burial and laid her in an upstairs room. 38But they had heard that Peter was nearby at Lydda, so they sent two men to beg him, "Please come as soon as possible!"

9:10 Greek *disciple;* also in 9:36.   9:19 Greek *disciples;* also in 9:26.   9:25 Greek *his disciples.*   9:30 Greek *brothers.*   9:36 The names *Tabitha* in Aramaic and *Dorcas* in Greek both mean "gazelle."

39So Peter returned with them; and as soon as he arrived, they took him to the upstairs room. The room was filled with widows who were weeping and showing him the coats and other garments Dorcas had made for them. 40But Peter asked them all to leave the room; then he knelt and prayed. Turning to the body he said, "Get up, Tabitha." And she opened her eyes! When she saw Peter, she sat up! 41He gave her his hand and helped her up. Then he called in the widows and all the believers, and he showed them that she was alive.

42The news raced through the whole town, and many believed in the Lord. 43And Peter stayed a long time in Joppa, living with Simon, a leatherworker.

CHAPTER 10

Cornelius Calls for Peter

In Caesarea there lived a Roman army officer named Cornelius, who was a captain of the Italian Regiment. 2He was a devout man who feared the God of Israel, as did his entire household. He gave generously to charity and was a man who regularly prayed to God. 3One afternoon about three o'clock, he had a vision in which he saw an angel of God coming toward him. "Cornelius!" the angel said.

4Cornelius stared at him in terror. "What is it, sir?" he asked the angel.

And the angel replied, "Your prayers and gifts to the poor have not gone unnoticed by God! 5Now send some men down to Joppa to find a man named Simon Peter. 6He is staying with Simon, a leatherworker who lives near the shore. Ask him to come and visit you."

7As soon as the angel was gone, Cornelius called two of his household servants and a devout soldier, one of his personal attendants. 8He told them what had happened and sent them off to Joppa.

Peter Visits Cornelius

9The next day as Cornelius's messengers were nearing the city, Peter went up to the flat roof to pray. It was about noon, 10and he was hungry. But while lunch was being prepared, he fell into a trance. 11He saw the sky open, and something like a large sheet was let down by its four corners. 12In the sheet were all sorts of animals, reptiles, and birds. 13Then a voice said to him, "Get up, Peter; kill and eat them."

14"Never, Lord," Peter declared. "I have never in all my life eaten anything forbidden by our Jewish laws.*"

15The voice spoke again, "If God says something is acceptable, don't say it isn't."* 16The same vision was repeated three times. Then the sheet was pulled up again to heaven.

17Peter was very perplexed. What could the vision mean? Just then the men sent by Cornelius found the house and stood outside at the gate. 18They asked if this was the place where Simon Peter was staying. 19Meanwhile, as Peter was puzzling over the vision, the Holy Spirit said to him, "Three men have come looking for you. 20Go down and go with them without hesitation. All is well, for I have sent them."

21So Peter went down and said, "I'm the man you are looking for. Why have you come?"

22They said, "We were sent by Cornelius, a Roman officer. He is a devout man who fears the God of Israel and is well respected by all the Jews. A holy angel instructed him to send for you so you can go to his house and give him a message." 23So Peter invited the men to be his guests for the night. The next day he went with them, accompanied by some other believers* from Joppa.

24They arrived in Caesarea the following day. Cornelius was waiting for him and had called together his relatives and close friends to meet Peter. 25As Peter entered his home, Cornelius fell to the floor before him in worship. 26But Peter pulled him up and said, "Stand up! I'm a human being like you!" 27So Cornelius got up, and they talked together and went inside where the others were assembled.

28Peter told them, "You know it is against the Jewish laws for me to come into a Gentile home like this. But God has shown me that I should never think of anyone as impure. 29So I came as soon as I was sent for. Now tell me why you sent for me."

30Cornelius replied, "Four days ago I was praying in my house at three o'clock in the afternoon. Suddenly, a man in dazzling clothes was standing in front of me. 31He told me, 'Cornelius, your prayers have been heard, and your gifts to the poor have been noticed by God! 32Now send some men to Joppa and summon Simon Peter. He is staying in the home of Simon, a leatherworker who lives near the shore.' 33So I sent for you at once, and it was good of you to come. Now here we are, waiting before God to hear the message the Lord has given you."

10:14 Greek *anything common and unclean.*   **10:15** Greek *"What God calls clean you must not call unclean."*   **10:23** Greek *brothers.*

The Gentiles Hear the Good News

³⁴Then Peter replied, "I see very clearly that God doesn't show partiality. ³⁵In every nation he accepts those who fear him and do what is right. ³⁶I'm sure you have heard about the Good News for the people of Israel—that there is peace with God through Jesus Christ, who is Lord of all. ³⁷You know what happened all through Judea, beginning in Galilee after John the Baptist began preaching. ³⁸And no doubt you know that God anointed Jesus of Nazareth with the Holy Spirit and with power. Then Jesus went around doing good and healing all who were oppressed by the Devil, for God was with him.

³⁹"And we apostles are witnesses of all he did throughout Israel and in Jerusalem. They put him to death by crucifying him, ⁴⁰but God raised him to life three days later. Then God allowed him to appear, ⁴¹not to the general public,* but to us whom God had chosen beforehand to be his witnesses. We were those who ate and drank with him after he rose from the dead. ⁴²And he ordered us to preach everywhere and to testify that Jesus is ordained of God to be the judge of all—the living and the dead. ⁴³He is the one all the prophets testified about, saying that everyone who believes in him will have their sins forgiven through his name."

The Gentiles Receive the Holy Spirit

⁴⁴Even as Peter was saying these things, the Holy Spirit fell upon all who had heard the message. ⁴⁵The Jewish believers who came with Peter were amazed that the gift of the Holy Spirit had been poured out upon the Gentiles, too. ⁴⁶And there could be no doubt about it, for they heard them speaking in tongues and praising God.

Then Peter asked, ⁴⁷"Can anyone object to their being baptized, now that they have received the Holy Spirit just as we did?" ⁴⁸So he gave orders for them to be baptized in the name of Jesus Christ. Afterward Cornelius asked him to stay with them for several days.

CHAPTER 11

Peter Explains His Actions

Soon the news reached the apostles and other believers* in Judea that the Gentiles had received the word of God. ²But when Peter arrived back in Jerusalem, some of the Jewish believers* criticized him. ³"You entered the home of Gentiles* and even ate with them!" they said.

⁴Then Peter told them exactly what had happened. ⁵"One day in Joppa," he said, "while I was praying, I went into a trance and saw a vision. Something like a large sheet was let down by its four corners from the sky. And it came right down to me. ⁶When I looked inside the sheet, I saw all sorts of small animals, wild animals, reptiles, and birds that we are not allowed to eat. ⁷And I heard a voice say, 'Get up, Peter; kill and eat them.'

⁸" 'Never, Lord,' I replied. 'I have never eaten anything forbidden by our Jewish laws.*'

⁹"But the voice from heaven came again, 'If God says something is acceptable, don't say it isn't.'*

¹⁰"This happened three times before the sheet and all it contained was pulled back up to heaven. ¹¹Just then three men who had been sent from Caesarea arrived at the house where I was staying. ¹²The Holy Spirit told me to go with them and not to worry about their being Gentiles. These six brothers here accompanied me, and we soon arrived at the home of the man who had sent for us. ¹³He told us how an angel had appeared to him in his home and had told him, 'Send messengers to Joppa to find Simon Peter. ¹⁴He will tell you how you and all your household will be saved!'

¹⁵"Well, I began telling them the Good News, but just as I was getting started, the Holy Spirit fell on them, just as he fell on us at the beginning. ¹⁶Then I thought of the Lord's words when he said, 'John baptized with* water, but you will be baptized with the Holy Spirit.' ¹⁷And since God gave these Gentiles the same gift he gave us when we believed in the Lord Jesus Christ, who was I to argue?"

¹⁸When the others heard this, all their objections were answered and they began praising God. They said, "God has also given the Gentiles the privilege of turning from sin and receiving eternal life."

The Church in Antioch of Syria

¹⁹Meanwhile, the believers who had fled from Jerusalem during the persecution after Stephen's death traveled as far as Phoenicia, Cyprus, and Antioch of Syria. They preached the Good News, but only to Jews. ²⁰However, some of the believers who went to Antioch from Cyprus and Cyrene began preaching to Gentiles* about the

---

10:41 Greek *the people.* 11:1 Greek *brothers.* 11:2 Greek *those of the circumcision.* 11:3 Greek *of uncircumcised men.* 11:8 Greek *anything common or unclean.* 11:9 Greek *'What God calls clean you must not call unclean.'* 11:16 Or *in;* also in 11:16b. 11:20 Greek *the Greeks;* other manuscripts read *the Hellenists.*

Lord Jesus. 21The power of the Lord was upon them, and large numbers of these Gentiles believed and turned to the Lord.

22When the church at Jerusalem heard what had happened, they sent Barnabas to Antioch. 23When he arrived and saw this proof of God's favor, he was filled with joy, and he encouraged the believers to stay true to the Lord. 24Barnabas was a good man, full of the Holy Spirit and strong in faith. And large numbers of people were brought to the Lord.

25Then Barnabas went on to Tarsus to find Saul. 26When he found him, he brought him back to Antioch. Both of them stayed there with the church for a full year, teaching great numbers of people. (It was there at Antioch that the believers* were first called Christians.)

27During this time, some prophets traveled from Jerusalem to Antioch. 28One of them named Agabus stood up in one of the meetings to predict by the Spirit that a great famine was coming upon the entire Roman world. (This was fulfilled during the reign of Claudius.) 29So the believers in Antioch decided to send relief to the brothers and sisters* in Judea, everyone giving as much as they could. 30This they did, entrusting their gifts to Barnabas and Saul to take to the elders of the church in Jerusalem.

CHAPTER **12**
James Is Killed and Peter Is Imprisoned
About that time King Herod Agrippa* began to persecute some believers in the church. 2He had the apostle James (John's brother) killed with a sword. 3When Herod saw how much this pleased the Jewish leaders, he arrested Peter during the Passover celebration* 4and imprisoned him, placing him under the guard of four squads of four soldiers each. Herod's intention was to bring Peter out for public trial after the Passover. 5But while Peter was in prison, the church prayed very earnestly for him.

Peter's Miraculous Escape from Prison
6The night before Peter was to be placed on trial, he was asleep, chained between two soldiers, with others standing guard at the prison gate. 7Suddenly, there was a bright light in the cell, and an angel of the Lord stood before Peter. The angel tapped him on the side to awaken him and said, "Quick! Get up!" And the chains fell off his wrists. 8Then the angel told him, "Get dressed and put on your sandals." And he did. "Now put on your coat and follow me," the angel ordered.

9So Peter left the cell, following the angel. But all the time he thought it was a vision. He didn't realize it was really happening. 10They passed the first and second guard posts and came to the iron gate to the street, and this opened to them all by itself. So they passed through and started walking down the street, and then the angel suddenly left him.

11Peter finally realized what had happened. "It's really true!" he said to himself. "The Lord has sent his angel and saved me from Herod and from what the Jews were hoping to do to me!"

12After a little thought, he went to the home of Mary, the mother of John Mark, where many were gathered for prayer. 13He knocked at the door in the gate, and a servant girl named Rhoda

11:26 Greek *disciples;* also in 11:29.   11:29 Greek *the brothers.*   12:1 Greek *Herod the king.* He was the nephew of Herod Antipas and a grandson of Herod the Great.   12:3 Greek *the days of unleavened bread.*

OFF AND RUNNING ▰▰▰▰
Pray Effectively Read ACTS 12:1-17

This Bible story vividly illustrates how God works in response to the prayers of his people. Though all appeared hopeless for Peter, the body of believers did all that they could for him—they called on God. What made the prayers of these believers so effective? Their secret is found in verse 5. There we see the three basic steps these Christians took in response to what appeared to be a hopeless situation:

1. They Directed Their Prayer to God. Ironically, many times our prayers often contain little thought of God himself. We fill our mind with thoughts about our own needs instead of our heavenly Father. But Jesus himself encouraged us to respectfully consider whom we are praying to when he gave us the Lord's Prayer (see Matthew 6:9-13, p. 795). This will allow you to take your eyes off of your dilemma and to place them on Jesus, and it will also help to align your will or desire with his.

2. They Prayed Earnestly. These believers offered constant, fervent prayer on Peter's behalf. Another way

came to open it. [14]When she recognized Peter's voice, she was so overjoyed that, instead of opening the door, she ran back inside and told everyone, "Peter is standing at the door!"

[15]"You're out of your mind," they said. When she insisted, they decided, "It must be his angel."

[16]Meanwhile, Peter continued knocking. When they finally went out and opened the door, they were amazed. [17]He motioned for them to quiet down and told them what had happened and how the Lord had led him out of jail. "Tell James and the other brothers what happened," he said. And then he went to another place.

[18]At dawn, there was a great commotion among the soldiers about what had happened to Peter. [19]Herod Agrippa ordered a thorough search for him. When he couldn't be found, Herod interrogated the guards and sentenced them to death. Afterward Herod left Judea to stay in Caesarea for a while.

The Death of Herod Agrippa

[20]Now Herod was very angry with the people of Tyre and Sidon. So they sent a delegation to make peace with him because their cities were dependent upon Herod's country for their food. They made friends with Blastus, Herod's personal assistant, [21]and an appointment with Herod was granted. When the day arrived, Herod put on his royal robes, sat on his throne, and made a speech to them. [22]The people gave him a great ovation, shouting, "It is the voice of a god, not of a man!"

[23]Instantly, an angel of the Lord struck Herod with a sickness, because he accepted the people's

worship instead of giving the glory to God. So he was consumed with worms and died.

[24]But God's Good News was spreading rapidly, and there were many new believers.

[25]When Barnabas and Saul had finished their mission in Jerusalem, they returned to Antioch, taking John Mark with them.

CHAPTER 13

Barnabas and Saul Are Sent Out

Among the prophets and teachers of the church at Antioch of Syria were Barnabas, Simeon (called "the black man"*), Lucius (from Cyrene), Manaen (the childhood companion of King Herod Antipas*), and Saul. [2]One day as these men were worshiping the Lord and fasting, the Holy Spirit said, "Dedicate Barnabas and Saul for the special work I have for them." [3]So after more fasting and prayer, the men laid their hands on them and sent them on their way.

Paul's First Missionary Journey

[4]Sent out by the Holy Spirit, Saul and Barnabas went down to the seaport of Seleucia and then sailed for the island of Cyprus. [5]There, in the town of Salamis, they went to the Jewish synagogues and preached the word of God. (John Mark went with them as their assistant.)

[6]Afterward they preached from town to town across the entire island until finally they reached Paphos, where they met a Jewish sorcerer, a false prophet named Bar-Jesus. [7]He had attached himself to the governor, Sergius Paulus, a man of considerable insight and understanding. The governor invited Barnabas and Saul to visit him, for he wanted to hear the word of God. [8]But

13:1a Greek *who was called Niger.*   13:1b Greek *Herod the tetrarch.*

---

to translate this verse is, "They prayed with agony." It is the same phrase used to describe the way Jesus prayed in the garden of Gethsemane. Their prayers had intensity. Many of our prayers have no power because they have little or no heart in them. If we put so little heart into our prayers, we cannot expect God to put much heart into answering them.

3. They Prayed as a Body. There is power in united prayer. Jesus said in Matthew 18:19, "I also tell you this: If two of you agree down here on earth concerning anything you ask, my Father in heaven will do it for you." What Jesus meant is that if two or more people who share the same God-given burden are sure of God's will and are in agreement with the Spirit of God and one another as they pray—they will see dynamic results.

Someone once said, "Satan trembles when he sees the weakest saint upon his knees." If you are in a bleak situation today, consider how God worked through the prayers of these early Christians. Don't give up. If you follow these principles, you will see results done God's way and in God's timing.

For the next note on "Prayer Time," turn to p. 880.

Elymas, the sorcerer (as his name means in Greek), interfered and urged the governor to pay no attention to what Saul and Barnabas said. He was trying to turn the governor away from the Christian faith.

9Then Saul, also known as Paul, filled with the Holy Spirit, looked the sorcerer in the eye and said, 10"You son of the Devil, full of every sort of trickery and villainy, enemy of all that is good, will you never stop perverting the true ways of the Lord? 11And now the Lord has laid his hand of punishment upon you, and you will be stricken awhile with blindness." Instantly mist and darkness fell upon him, and he began wandering around begging for someone to take his hand and lead him. 12When the governor saw what had happened, he believed and was astonished at what he learned about the Lord.

Paul Preaches in Antioch of Pisidia

13Now Paul and those with him left Paphos by ship for Pamphylia,* landing at the port town of Perga. There John Mark left them and returned to Jerusalem. 14But Barnabas and Paul traveled inland to Antioch of Pisidia.*

On the Sabbath they went to the synagogue for the services. 15After the usual readings from the books of Moses and from the Prophets, those in charge of the service sent them this message: "Brothers, if you have any word of encouragement for us, come and give it!"

16So Paul stood, lifted his hand to quiet them, and started speaking. "People of Israel," he said, "and you devout Gentiles who fear the God of Israel, listen to me.

17"The God of this nation of Israel chose our ancestors and made them prosper in Egypt. Then he powerfully led them out of their slavery. 18He put up with them* through forty years of wandering around in the wilderness. 19Then he destroyed seven nations in Canaan and gave their land to Israel as an inheritance. 20All this took about 450 years. After that, judges ruled until the time of Samuel the prophet. 21Then the people begged for a king, and God gave them Saul son of Kish, a man of the tribe of Benjamin, who reigned for forty years. 22But God removed him from the kingship and replaced him with David, a man about whom God said, 'David son of Jesse is a man after my own heart, for he will do everything I want him to.'*

23"And it is one of King David's descendants,

Jesus, who is God's promised Savior of Israel! 24But before he came, John the Baptist preached the need for everyone in Israel to turn from sin and turn to God and be baptized. 25As John was finishing his ministry he asked, 'Do you think I am the Messiah? No! But he is coming soon—and I am not even worthy to be his slave.*'

26"Brothers—you sons of Abraham, and also all of you devout Gentiles who fear the God of Israel—this salvation is for us! 27The people in Jerusalem and their leaders fulfilled prophecy by condemning Jesus to death. They didn't recognize him or realize that he is the one the prophets had written about, though they hear the prophets' words read every Sabbath. 28They found no just cause to execute him, but they asked Pilate to have him killed anyway.

29"When they had fulfilled all the prophecies concerning his death, they took him down from the cross and placed him in a tomb. 30But God raised him from the dead! 31And he appeared over a period of many days to those who had gone with him from Galilee to Jerusalem—these are his witnesses to the people of Israel.

32"And now Barnabas and I are here to bring you this Good News. God's promise to our ancestors has come true in our own time, 33in that God raised Jesus. This is what the second psalm is talking about when it says concerning Jesus,

'You are my Son.
Today I have become your Father.*'

34For God had promised to raise him from the dead, never again to die. This is stated in the Scripture that says, 'I will give you the sacred blessings I promised to David.'* 35Another psalm explains more fully, saying, 'You will not allow your Holy One to rot in the grave.'* 36Now this is not a reference to David, for after David had served his generation according to the will of God, he died and was buried, and his body decayed. 37No, it was a reference to someone else—someone whom God raised and whose body did not decay.

38"Brothers, listen! In this man Jesus there is forgiveness for your sins. 39Everyone who believes in him is freed from all guilt and declared right with God—something the Jewish law could never do. 40Be careful! Don't let the prophets' words apply to you. For they said,

41 'Look you mockers,

13:13-14 *Pamphylia* and *Pisidia* were districts in the land now called Turkey. 13:18 Other manuscripts read *He cared for them;* compare Deut 1:31. 13:22 1 Sam 13:14. 13:25 Greek *to untie his sandals.* 13:33 Or *Today I reveal you as my Son.* Ps 2:7. 13:34 Isa 55:3. 13:35 Ps 16:10.

be amazed and die!
For I am doing something in your own day,
something you wouldn't believe
even if someone told you about it.'* "

42As Paul and Barnabas left the synagogue that day, the people asked them to return again and speak about these things the next week. 43Many Jews and godly converts to Judaism who worshiped at the synagogue followed Paul and Barnabas, and the two men urged them, "By God's grace, remain faithful."

Paul Turns to the Gentiles
44The following week almost the entire city turned out to hear them preach the word of the Lord. 45But when the Jewish leaders saw the crowds, they were jealous; so they slandered Paul and argued against whatever he said.

46Then Paul and Barnabas spoke out boldly and declared, "It was necessary that this Good News from God be given first to you Jews. But since you have rejected it and judged yourselves unworthy of eternal life—well, we will offer it to Gentiles. 47For this is as the Lord commanded us when he said,

'I have made you a light to the Gentiles,
to bring salvation to the farthest corners
of the earth.'* "

48When the Gentiles heard this, they were very glad and thanked the Lord for his message; and all who were appointed to eternal life became believers. 49So the Lord's message spread throughout that region.

50Then the Jewish leaders stirred up both the influential religious women and the leaders of the city, and they incited a mob against Paul and Barnabas and ran them out of town. 51But they shook off the dust of their feet against them and went to the city of Iconium. 52And the believers* were filled with joy and with the Holy Spirit.

CHAPTER **14**
Paul and Barnabas in Iconium
In Iconium,* Paul and Barnabas went together to the synagogue and preached with such power that a great number of both Jews and Gentiles believed. 2But the Jews who spurned God's message stirred up distrust among the Gentiles against Paul and Barnabas, saying all sorts of evil things about them. 3The apostles stayed there a long time, preaching boldly

about the grace of the Lord. The Lord proved their message was true by giving them power to do miraculous signs and wonders. 4But the people of the city were divided in their opinion about them. Some sided with the Jews, and some with the apostles.

5A mob of Gentiles and Jews, along with their leaders, decided to attack and stone them. 6When the apostles learned of it, they fled for their lives. They went to the region of Lycaonia, to the cities of Lystra and Derbe and the surrounding area, 7and they preached the Good News there.

Paul and Barnabas in Lystra and Derbe
8While they were at Lystra, Paul and Barnabas came upon a man with crippled feet. He had been that way from birth, so he had never walked. 9He was listening as Paul preached, and Paul noticed him and realized he had faith to be healed. 10So Paul called to him in a loud voice, "Stand up!" And the man jumped to his feet and started walking.

11When the listening crowd saw what Paul had done, they shouted in their local dialect, "These men are gods in human bodies!" 12They decided that Barnabas was the Greek god Zeus and that Paul, because he was the chief speaker, was Hermes. 13The temple of Zeus was located on the outskirts of the city. The priest of the temple and the crowd brought oxen and wreaths of flowers, and they prepared to sacrifice to the apostles at the city gates.

14But when Barnabas and Paul heard what was happening, they tore their clothing in dismay and ran out among the people, shouting, 15"Friends,* why are you doing this? We are merely human beings like yourselves! We have come to bring you the Good News that you should turn from these worthless things to the living God, who made heaven and earth, the sea, and everything in them. 16In earlier days he permitted all the nations to go their own ways, 17but he never left himself without a witness. There were always his reminders, such as sending you rain and good crops and giving you food and joyful hearts." 18But even so, Paul and Barnabas could scarcely restrain the people from sacrificing to them.

19Now some Jews arrived from Antioch and Iconium and turned the crowds into a murderous mob. They stoned Paul and dragged him out of the city, apparently dead. 20But as the believ-

13:41 Hab 1:5.   13:47 Isa 49:6.   13:52 Greek *the disciples.*   14:1 *Iconium,* as well as *Lystra* and *Derbe* (14:6), were cities in the land now called Turkey.   14:15 Greek *Men.*

ers* stood around him, he got up and went back into the city. The next day he left with Barnabas for Derbe.

Paul and Barnabas Return to Antioch of Syria

21After preaching the Good News in Derbe and making many disciples, Paul and Barnabas returned again to Lystra, Iconium, and Antioch of Pisidia, 22where they strengthened the believers. They encouraged them to continue in the faith, reminding them that they must enter into the Kingdom of God through many tribulations. 23Paul and Barnabas also appointed elders in every church and prayed for them with fasting, turning them over to the care of the Lord, in whom they had come to trust. 24Then they traveled back through Pisidia to Pamphylia. 25They preached again in Perga, then went on to Attalia.

26Finally, they returned by ship to Antioch of Syria, where their journey had begun and where they had been committed to the grace of God for the work they had now completed. 27Upon arriving in Antioch, they called the church together and reported about their trip, telling all that God had done and how he had opened the door of faith to the Gentiles, too. 28And they stayed there with the believers in Antioch for a long time.

CHAPTER **15**
The Council at Jerusalem

While Paul and Barnabas were at Antioch of Syria, some men from Judea arrived and began to teach the Christians*: "Unless you keep the ancient Jewish custom of circumcision taught by Moses, you cannot be saved." 2Paul and Barnabas, disagreeing with them, argued forcefully and at length. Finally, Paul and Barnabas were sent to Jerusalem, accompanied by some local believers, to talk to the apostles and elders about this question. 3The church sent the delegates to Jerusalem, and they stopped along the way in Phoenicia and Samaria to visit the believers.* They told them—much to everyone's joy—that the Gentiles, too, were being converted.

4When they arrived in Jerusalem, Paul and Barnabas were welcomed by the whole church, including the apostles and elders. They reported on what God had been doing through their ministry. 5But then some of the men who had been Pharisees before their conversion stood up and declared that all Gentile converts must be circumcised and be required to follow the law of Moses.

6So the apostles and church elders got together to decide this question. 7At the meeting, after a long discussion, Peter stood and addressed them as follows: "Brothers, you all know that God chose me from among you some time ago to preach to the Gentiles so that they could hear the Good News and believe. 8God, who knows people's hearts, confirmed that he accepts Gentiles by giving them the Holy Spirit, just as he gave him to us. 9He made no distinction between us and them, for he also cleansed their hearts through faith. 10Why are you now questioning God's way by burdening the Gentile believers* with a yoke that neither we nor our ancestors were able to bear? 11We believe that we are all saved the same way, by the special favor of the Lord Jesus."

12There was no further discussion, and everyone listened as Barnabas and Paul told about the miraculous signs and wonders God had done through them among the Gentiles.

13When they had finished, James stood and said, "Brothers, listen to me. 14Peter* has told you about the time God first visited the Gentiles to take from them a people for himself. 15And this conversion of Gentiles agrees with what the prophets predicted. For instance, it is written:

16 'Afterward I will return,
    and I will restore the fallen kingdom of
      David.
  From the ruins I will rebuild it,
    and I will restore it,
17 so that the rest of humanity might find the
      Lord,
    including the Gentiles—
    all those I have called to be mine.
  This is what the Lord says,
18   he who made these things known long
      ago.'*

19And so my judgment is that we should stop troubling the Gentiles who turn to God, 20except that we should write to them and tell them to abstain from eating meat sacrificed to idols, from sexual immorality, and from consuming blood or eating the meat of strangled animals. 21For these laws of Moses have been preached in Jewish synagogues in every city on every Sabbath for many generations."

The Letter for Gentile Believers

22Then the apostles and elders and the whole church in Jerusalem chose delegates, and they

---

14:20 Greek *disciples*; also in 14:22, 28.   15:1 Greek *brothers*; also in 15:32, 33.   15:3 Greek *brothers*; also in 15:23, 36, 40.   15:10 Greek *disciples*.   15:14 Greek *Simon*.   15:16-18 Amos 9:11-12; Isa 45:21.

sent them to Antioch of Syria with Paul and Barnabas to report on this decision. The men chosen were two of the church leaders*—Judas (also called Barsabbas) and Silas. 23This is the letter they took along with them:

"This letter is from the apostles and elders, your brothers in Jerusalem. It is written to the Gentile believers in Antioch, Syria, and Cilicia. Greetings!

24"We understand that some men from here have troubled you and upset you with their teaching, but they had no such instructions from us. 25So it seemed good to us, having unanimously agreed on our decision, to send you these official representatives, along with our beloved Barnabas and Paul, 26who have risked their lives for the sake of our Lord Jesus Christ. 27So we are sending Judas and Silas to tell you what we have decided concerning your question.

28"For it seemed good to the Holy Spirit and to us to lay no greater burden on you than these requirements: 29You must abstain from eating food offered to idols, from consuming blood or eating the meat of strangled animals, and from sexual immorality. If you do this, you will do well. Farewell."

30The four messengers went at once to Antioch, where they called a general meeting of the Christians and delivered the letter. 31And there was great joy throughout the church that day as they read this encouraging message.

32Then Judas and Silas, both being prophets, spoke extensively to the Christians, encouraging and strengthening their faith. 33They stayed for a while, and then Judas and Silas were sent back to Jerusalem, with the blessings of the Christians, to those who had sent them.* 35Paul and Barnabas stayed in Antioch to assist many others who were teaching and preaching the word of the Lord there.

Paul and Barnabas Separate
36After some time Paul said to Barnabas, "Let's return to each city where we previously preached the word of the Lord, to see how the new believers are getting along." 37Barnabas agreed and wanted to take along John Mark. 38But Paul disagreed strongly, since John Mark had deserted

them in Pamphylia and had not shared in their work. 39Their disagreement over this was so sharp that they separated. Barnabas took John Mark with him and sailed for Cyprus. 40Paul chose Silas, and the believers sent them off, entrusting them to the Lord's grace. 41So they traveled throughout Syria and Cilicia to strengthen the churches there.

CHAPTER 16
Paul's Second Missionary Journey
Paul and Silas went first to Derbe and then on to Lystra. There they met Timothy, a young disciple whose mother was a Jewish believer, but whose father was a Greek. 2Timothy was well thought of by the believers* in Lystra and Iconium, 3so Paul wanted him to join them on their journey. In deference to the Jews of the area, he arranged for Timothy to be circumcised before they left, for everyone knew that his father was a Greek. 4Then they went from town to town, explaining the decision regarding the commandments that were to be obeyed, as decided by the apostles and elders in Jerusalem. 5So the churches were strengthened in their faith and grew daily in numbers.

A Call from Macedonia
6Next Paul and Silas traveled through the area of Phrygia and Galatia, because the Holy Spirit had told them not to go into the province of Asia at that time. 7Then coming to the borders of Mysia, they headed for the province of Bithynia,* but again the Spirit of Jesus did not let them go. 8So instead, they went on through Mysia to the city of Troas.

9That night Paul had a vision. He saw a man from Macedonia in northern Greece, pleading with him, "Come over here and help us." 10So we* decided to leave for Macedonia at once, for we could only conclude that God was calling us to preach the Good News there.

Lydia of Philippi Believes in Jesus
11We boarded a boat at Troas and sailed straight across to the island of Samothrace, and the next day we landed at Neapolis. 12From there we reached Philippi, a major city of the district of Macedonia and a Roman colony; we stayed there several days.

13On the Sabbath we went a little way outside the city to a riverbank, where we supposed that some people met for prayer, and we sat down to

15:22 Greek *were leaders among the brothers.* 15:33 Some manuscripts add verse 34, *But Silas decided to stay there.* 16:2 Greek *brothers;* also in 16:40. 16:6-7 *Phrygia, Galatia, Asia, Mysia,* and *Bithynia* were all districts in the land now called Turkey. 16:10 Luke, the writer of this book, here joined Paul and accompanied him on his journey.

speak with some women who had come to-gether. 14One of them was Lydia from Thyatira, a merchant of expensive purple cloth. She was a worshiper of God. As she listened to us, the Lord opened her heart, and she accepted what Paul was saying. 15She was baptized along with other members of her household, and she asked us to be her guests. "If you agree that I am faithful to the Lord," she said, "come and stay at my home." And she urged us until we did.

Paul and Silas in Prison

16One day as we were going down to the place of prayer, we met a demon-possessed slave girl. She was a fortune-teller who earned a lot of money for her masters. 17She followed along behind us shouting, "These men are servants of the Most High God, and they have come to tell you how to be saved."

18This went on day after day until Paul got so exasperated that he turned and spoke to the demon within her. "I command you in the name of Jesus Christ to come out of her," he said. And instantly it left her.

19Her masters' hopes of wealth were now shattered, so they grabbed Paul and Silas and dragged them before the authorities at the marketplace. 20"The whole city is in an uproar because of these Jews!" they shouted. 21"They are teaching the people to do things that are against Roman customs."

22A mob quickly formed against Paul and Silas, and the city officials ordered them stripped and beaten with wooden rods. 23They were severely beaten, and then they were thrown into prison. The jailer was ordered to make sure they didn't escape. 24So he took no chances but put them into the inner dungeon and clamped their feet in the stocks.

25Around midnight, Paul and Silas were pray-ing and singing hymns to God, and the other prisoners were listening. 26Suddenly, there was a great earthquake, and the prison was shaken to its foundations. All the doors flew open, and the chains of every prisoner fell off! 27The jailer woke up to see the prison doors wide open. He assumed the prisoners had escaped, so he drew his sword to kill himself. 28But Paul shouted to him, "Don't do it! We are all here!"

29Trembling with fear, the jailer called for lights and ran to the dungeon and fell down before Paul and Silas. 30He brought them out and asked, "Sirs, what must I do to be saved?"

31They replied, "Believe on the Lord Jesus and you will be saved, along with your entire household." 32Then they shared the word of the Lord with him and all who lived in his household. 33That same hour the jailer washed their wounds, and he and everyone in his household were immediately baptized. 34Then he brought them into his house and set a meal before them. He and his entire household rejoiced because they all believed in God.

35The next morning the city officials sent the police to tell the jailer, "Let those men go!" 36So the jailer told Paul, "You and Silas are free to leave. Go in peace."

37But Paul replied, "They have publicly beaten us without trial and jailed us—and we are Roman citizens. So now they want us to leave secretly? Certainly not! Let them come themselves to release us!"

38When the police made their report, the city officials were alarmed to learn that Paul and Silas were Roman citizens. 39They came to the jail and apologized to them. Then they brought them out and begged them to leave the city. 40Paul and Silas then returned to the home of Lydia, where they met with the believers and encouraged them once more before leaving town.

OFF AND RUNNING ▰▰ ▰ ▰ ▰

Make Sure Your Children Hear the Gospel Message
Read ACTS 16:29-34

In this wonderful story, we see how one man looked out for the spiritual welfare of his family. He took the opportunity at hand to expose his family to the message of Christ through the testimony of Paul and Silas.

We, too, need to take advantage of every opportunity to share Christ with our family—and particularly our children. They are never too young (or too old) to be taught about the things of God. Here are four suggestions to help you share the gospel with your family:

1. Set Aside Time for Family Devotions. Study the Bible, pray together, and share how God has been working in your life.

CHAPTER **17**

Paul Preaches in Thessalonica

Now Paul and Silas traveled through the towns of Amphipolis and Apollonia and came to Thessalonica, where there was a Jewish synagogue. ²As was Paul's custom, he went to the synagogue service, and for three Sabbaths in a row he interpreted the Scriptures in the people. ³He was explaining and proving the prophecies about the sufferings of the Messiah and his rising from the dead. He said, "This Jesus I'm telling you about is the Messiah." ⁴Some who listened were persuaded and became converts, including a large number of godly Greek men and also many important women of the city.*

⁵But the Jewish leaders were jealous, so they gathered some worthless fellows from the streets to form a mob and start a riot. They attacked the home of Jason, searching for Paul and Silas so they could drag them out to the crowd.* ⁶Not finding them there, they dragged out Jason and some of the other believers* instead and took them before the city council. "Paul and Silas have turned the rest of the world upside down, and now they are here disturbing our city," they shouted. ⁷"And Jason has let them into his home. They are all guilty of treason against Caesar, for they profess allegiance to another king, Jesus."

⁸The people of the city, as well as the city officials, were thrown into turmoil by these reports. ⁹But the officials released Jason and the other believers after they had posted bail.

Paul and Silas in Berea

¹⁰That very night the believers sent Paul and Silas to Berea. When they arrived there, they went to the synagogue. ¹¹And the people of Berea were more open-minded than those in Thessalonica, and they listened eagerly to Paul's message. They searched the Scriptures day after day to check up on Paul and Silas, to see if they were really teaching the truth. ¹²As a result, many Jews believed, as did some of the prominent Greek women and many men.

¹³But when some Jews in Thessalonica learned that Paul was preaching the word of God in Berea, they went there and stirred up trouble. ¹⁴The believers acted at once, sending Paul on to the coast, while Silas and Timothy remained behind. ¹⁵Those escorting Paul went with him to Athens; then they returned to Berea with a message for Silas and Timothy to hurry and join him.

Paul Preaches in Athens

¹⁶While Paul was waiting for them in Athens, he was deeply troubled by all the idols he saw everywhere in the city. ¹⁷He went to the synagogue to debate with the Jews and the God-fearing Gentiles, and he spoke daily in the public square to all who happened to be there.

¹⁸He also had a debate with some of the Epicurean and Stoic philosophers. When he told them about Jesus and his resurrection, they said, "This babbler has picked up some strange ideas." Others said, "He's pushing some foreign religion."

¹⁹Then they took him to the Council of Philosophers.* "Come and tell us more about this new religion," they said. ²⁰"You are saying some rather startling things, and we want to know what it's all about." ²¹(It should be explained that all the Athenians as well as the foreigners in Athens seemed to spend all their time discussing the latest ideas.)

17:4 Some manuscripts read *many of the wives of the leading men.*   17:5 Or *the city council.*   17:6 Greek *brothers;* also in 17:10, 14.
17:19 Greek *the Areopagus.*

2. Invite Other Believers to Your Home. This jailer invited Paul and Silas over for dinner, and we read how the whole household rejoiced because all were now believers. This type of fellowship can be an enriching time for your family.

3. Bring Your Children to Church with You. Your children will probably learn lessons here that they will carry with them the rest of their lives. If they are young enough, bring them. If they are older, strongly encourage them to join you.

4. Pray for Your Children Daily. As a parent, you cannot "make" your children Christians, but you can pray that their hearts will be sensitive and open to the gospel message.

For the next note on "Children," turn to p. 1046.

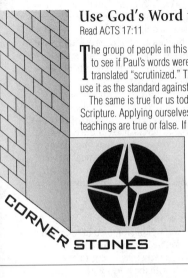

Use God's Word to Evaluate Someone's Teachings
Read ACTS 17:11

The group of people in this passage—the Bereans—actually searched the written Word of God to see if Paul's words were true. In the original Greek, the word for "searched" could also be translated "scrutinized." They did this because they knew that they could trust God's Word and use it as the standard against which to evaluate others' teachings.

The same is true for us today. Everything we need to know about God is found in the pages of Scripture. Applying ourselves in the study of his Word helps us determine whether someone's teachings are true or false. If we fail to study the Bible, we may be lured into believing false teachings. But if we consistently study God's Word, it—along with the illumination of the Holy Spirit—will enable us to distinguish truth from error.

Here is a trustworthy saying to keep in mind: If someone says they "have a new 'word' or 'revelation' from the Lord," rest assured that it is not true. If it is true, it is not new. If it is new, it is not true! If it is not in the Word, it is not of the Lord.

To begin the next topic, turn to p. A21.

CORNER STONES

22So Paul, standing before the Council,* addressed them as follows: "Men of Athens, I notice that you are very religious, 23for as I was walking along I saw your many altars. And one of them had this inscription on it—'To an Unknown God.' You have been worshiping him without knowing who he is, and now I wish to tell you about him.

24"He is the God who made the world and everything in it. Since he is Lord of heaven and earth, he doesn't live in man-made temples, 25and human hands can't serve his needs—for he has no needs. He himself gives life and breath to everything, and he satisfies every need there is. 26From one man he created all the nations throughout the whole earth. He decided beforehand which should rise and fall, and he determined their boundaries.

27"His purpose in all of this was that the nations should seek after God and perhaps feel their way toward him and find him—though he is not far from any one of us. 28For in him we live and move and exist. As one of your own poets says, 'We are his offspring.' 29And since this is true, we shouldn't think of God as an idol designed by craftsmen from gold or silver or stone. 30God overlooked people's former ignorance about these things, but now he commands everyone everywhere to turn away from idols and turn to him.* 31For he has set a day for

judging the world with justice by the man he has appointed, and he proved to everyone who this is by raising him from the dead."

32When they heard Paul speak of the resurrection of a person who had been dead, some laughed, but others said, "We want to hear more about this later." 33That ended Paul's discussion with them, 34but some joined him and became believers. Among them were Dionysius, a member of the Council,* a woman named Damaris, and others.

CHAPTER 18
Paul Meets Priscilla and Aquila in Corinth
Then Paul left Athens and went to Corinth.* 2There he became acquainted with a Jew named Aquila, born in Pontus, who had recently arrived from Italy with his wife, Priscilla. They had been expelled from Italy as a result of Claudius Caesar's order to deport all Jews from Rome. 3Paul lived and worked with them, for they were tentmakers* just as he was.

4Each Sabbath found Paul at the synagogue, trying to convince the Jews and Greeks alike. 5And after Silas and Timothy came down from Macedonia, Paul spent his full time preaching and testifying to the Jews, telling them, "The Messiah you are looking for is Jesus." 6But when the Jews opposed him and insulted him, Paul

17:22 Or *in the middle of Mars Hill;* Greek reads *in the middle of the Areopagus.* **17:30** Greek *everywhere to repent.* **17:34** Greek *an Areopagite.* **18:1** *Athens* and *Corinth* were major cities in Achaia, the region on the southern end of the Greek peninsula. **18:3** Or *leatherworkers.*

shook the dust from his robe and said, "Your blood be upon your own heads—I am innocent. From now on I will go to the Gentiles."

7After that he stayed with Titius Justus, a Gentile who worshiped God and lived next door to the synagogue. 8Crispus, the leader of the synagogue, and all his household believed in the Lord. Many others in Corinth also became believers and were baptized.

9One night the Lord spoke to Paul in a vision and told him, "Don't be afraid! Speak out! Don't be silent! 10For I am with you, and no one will harm you because many people here in this city belong to me." 11So Paul stayed there for the next year and a half, teaching the word of God.

12But when Gallio became governor of Achaia, some Jews rose in concerted action against Paul and brought him before the governor for judgment. 13They accused Paul of "persuading people to worship God in ways that are contrary to the law." 14But just as Paul started to make his defense, Gallio turned to Paul's accusers and said, "Listen, you Jews, if this were a case involving some wrongdoing or a serious crime, I would be obliged to listen to you. 15But since it is merely a question of words and names and your Jewish laws, you take care of it. I refuse to judge such matters." 16And he drove them out of the courtroom. 17The mob had grabbed Sosthenes, the leader of the synagogue, and had beaten him right there in the courtroom. But Gallio paid no attention.

Paul Returns to Antioch of Syria

18Paul stayed in Corinth for some time after that and then said good-bye to the brothers and sisters* and sailed for the coast of Syria, taking Priscilla and Aquila with him. (Earlier, at Cenchrea, Paul had shaved his head according to Jewish custom, for he had taken a vow.) 19When they arrived at the port of Ephesus, Paul left the others behind. But while he was there, he went to the synagogue to debate with the Jews. 20They asked him to stay longer, but he declined. 21So he left, saying, "I will come back later,* God willing." Then he set sail from Ephesus. 22The next stop was at the port of Caesarea. From there he went up and visited the church at Jerusalem* and then went back to Antioch.

23After spending some time in Antioch, Paul went back to Galatia and Phrygia, visiting all the believers,* encouraging them and helping them to grow in the Lord.

Apollos Instructed at Ephesus

24Meanwhile, a Jew named Apollos, an eloquent speaker who knew the Scriptures well, had just arrived in Ephesus from Alexandria in Egypt. 25He had been taught the way of the Lord and talked to others with great enthusiasm and accuracy about Jesus. However, he knew only about John's baptism. 26When Priscilla and Aquila heard him preaching boldly in the synagogue, they took him aside and explained the way of God more accurately.

27Apollos had been thinking about going to Achaia, and the brothers and sisters in Ephesus encouraged him in this. They wrote to the believers in Achaia, asking them to welcome him. When he arrived there, he proved to be of great benefit to those who, by God's grace, had believed. 28He refuted all the Jews with powerful arguments in public debate. Using the Scriptures, he explained to them, "The Messiah you are looking for is Jesus."

CHAPTER 19
Paul's Third Missionary Journey

While Apollos was in Corinth, Paul traveled through the interior provinces. Finally, he came to Ephesus, where he found several believers.* 2"Did you receive the Holy Spirit when you believed?" he asked them.

"No," they replied, "we don't know what you mean. We haven't even heard that there is a Holy Spirit."

3"Then what baptism did you experience?" he asked.

And they replied, "The baptism of John."

4Paul said, "John's baptism was to demonstrate a desire to turn from sin and turn to God. John himself told the people to believe in Jesus, the one John said would come later."

5As soon as they heard this, they were baptized in the name of the Lord Jesus. 6Then when Paul laid his hands on them, the Holy Spirit came on them, and they spoke in other tongues and prophesied. 7There were about twelve men in all.

Paul Ministers in Ephesus

8Then Paul went to the synagogue and preached boldly for the next three months, arguing persuasively about the Kingdom of God. 9But some rejected his message and publicly spoke against the Way, so Paul left the synagogue and took the believers with him. Then he began preaching

---

18:18 Greek *brothers;* also in 18:27.   **18:21** Some manuscripts read *"I must by all means be at Jerusalem for the upcoming festival, but I will come back later."*   **18:22** Greek *the church.*   **18:23** Greek *disciples;* also in 18:27.   **19:1** Greek *disciples;* also in 19:9, 30.

God Is Personal Read ACTS 17:22-33

Paul's audience in this passage included people of two different beliefs. There were those who did not believe in life after death and lived only for pleasure. They were known as the Epicureans. There were also those who believed that God existed in every material object and strived to be at peace with the world. These people were known as the Stoics. In speaking to these two groups, Paul showed them how their philosophies fell short of grasping the true nature of God. He did this by bringing out the following truths about who God is.

God Is the All-Powerful Creator
- God made heaven and earth, and every living creature.
- God is too great to be housed in man-made temples or shrines.
- God created all the people of the world from one man.
- God is the architect behind the world stage.

God Is the Personal Supreme Being
- His purpose behind creation was to draw people to himself.
- He is concerned about people's needs.
- He is not far from any of us.
- He makes it easy for us to know him personally (salvation through Jesus Christ).
- He can and will judge every thought and motive on Judgment Day.

CORNER STONES

The people who listened to Paul speak responded in one of three ways: (1) Some mocked him; (2) some procrastinated and said they would make a decision after listening to him again later; and (3) some believed him and accepted Jesus as their Savior. People today react to the gospel message in much the same way. However, if someone really wants to know the powerful God who created him or her and who is personally interested in his or her life, only the last response will do.

For the next note on "Who Is God?" turn to p. 766.

---

daily at the lecture hall of Tyrannus. ¹⁰This went on for the next two years, so that people throughout the province of Asia—both Jews and Greeks—heard the Lord's message.

¹¹God gave Paul the power to do unusual miracles, ¹²so that even when handkerchiefs or cloths that had touched his skin were placed on sick people, they were healed of their diseases, and any evil spirits within them came out.

¹³A team of Jews who were traveling from town to town casting out evil spirits tried to use the name of the Lord Jesus. The incantation they used was this: "I command you by Jesus, whom Paul preaches, to come out!" ¹⁴Seven sons of Sceva, a leading priest, were doing this. ¹⁵But when they tried it on a man possessed by an evil spirit, the spirit replied, "I know Jesus, and I know Paul. But who are you?" ¹⁶And he leaped on them and attacked them with such violence that they fled from the house, naked and badly injured.

¹⁷The story of what happened spread quickly all through Ephesus, to Jews and Greeks alike. A solemn fear descended on the city, and the name of the Lord Jesus was greatly honored. ¹⁸Many who became believers confessed their sinful practices. ¹⁹A number of them who had been practicing magic brought their incantation books and burned them at a public bonfire. The value of the books was several million dollars.* ²⁰So the message about the Lord spread widely and had a powerful effect.

The Riot in Ephesus
²¹Afterward Paul felt impelled by the Holy Spirit* to go over to Macedonia and Achaia before returning to Jerusalem. "And after that," he said, "I must go on to Rome!" ²²He sent his two assistants, Timothy and Erastus, on ahead to Macedonia while he stayed awhile longer in the province of Asia.

²³But about that time, serious trouble developed in Ephesus concerning the Way. ²⁴It began

19:19 Greek *50,000 pieces of silver*, each of which was the equivalent of a day's wage.　19:21 Or *purposed in his spirit.*

with Demetrius, a silversmith who had a large business manufacturing silver shrines of the Greek goddess Artemis.* He kept many craftsmen busy. 25He called the craftsmen together, along with others employed in related trades, and addressed them as follows:

"Gentlemen, you know that our wealth comes from this business. 26As you have seen and heard, this man Paul has persuaded many people that handmade gods aren't gods at all. And this is happening not only here in Ephesus but throughout the entire province! 27Of course, I'm not just talking about the loss of public respect for our business. I'm also concerned that the temple of the great goddess Artemis will lose its influence and that Artemis—this magnificent goddess worshiped throughout the province of Asia and all around the world—will be robbed of her prestige!"

28At this their anger boiled, and they began shouting, "Great is Artemis of the Ephesians!" 29A crowd began to gather, and soon the city was filled with confusion. Everyone rushed to the amphitheater, dragging along Gaius and Aristarchus, who were Paul's traveling companions from Macedonia. 30Paul wanted to go in, but the believers wouldn't let him. 31Some of the officials of the province, friends of Paul, also sent a message to him, begging him not to risk his life by entering the amphitheater.

32Inside, the people were all shouting, some one thing and some another. Everything was in confusion. In fact, most of them didn't even know why they were there. 33Alexander was thrust forward by some of the Jews, who encouraged him to explain the situation. He motioned for silence and tried to speak in defense. 34But when the crowd realized he was a Jew, they started shouting again and kept it up for two hours: "Great is Artemis of the Ephesians! Great is Artemis of the Ephesians!"

35At last the mayor was able to quiet them down enough to speak. "Citizens of Ephesus," he said. "Everyone knows that Ephesus is the official guardian of the temple of the great Artemis, whose image fell down to us from heaven. 36Since this is an indisputable fact, you shouldn't be disturbed, no matter what is said. Don't do anything rash. 37You have brought these men here, but they have stolen nothing from the temple and have not spoken against our goddess. 38If Demetrius and the craftsmen have a case against them, the courts are in ses-

sion and the judges can take the case at once. Let them go through legal channels. 39And if there are complaints about other matters, they can be settled in a legal assembly. 40I am afraid we are in danger of being charged with rioting by the Roman government, since there is no cause for all this commotion. And if Rome demands an explanation, we won't know what to say." 41Then he dismissed them, and they dispersed.

CHAPTER 20

Paul Goes to Macedonia and Greece

When it was all over, Paul sent for the believers* and encouraged them. Then he said good-bye and left for Macedonia. 2Along the way, he encouraged the believers in all the towns he passed through. Then he traveled down to Greece, 3where he stayed for three months. He was preparing to sail back to Syria when he discovered a plot by some Jews against his life, so he decided to return through Macedonia.

4Several men were traveling with him. They were Sopater of Berea, the son of Pyrrhus; Aristarchus and Secundus, from Thessalonica; Gaius, from Derbe; Timothy; and Tychicus and Trophimus, who were from the province of Asia. 5They went ahead and waited for us at Troas. 6As soon as the Passover season* ended, we boarded a ship at Philippi in Macedonia and five days later arrived in Troas, where we stayed a week.

Paul's Final Visit to Troas

7On the first day of the week, we gathered to observe the Lord's Supper.* Paul was preaching; and since he was leaving the next day, he talked until midnight. 8The upstairs room where we met was lighted with many flickering lamps. 9As Paul spoke on and on, a young man named Eutychus, sitting on the windowsill, became very drowsy. Finally, he sank into a deep sleep and fell three stories to his death below. 10Paul went down, bent over him, and took him into his arms. "Don't worry," he said, "he's alive!" 11Then they all went back upstairs and ate the Lord's Supper together.* And Paul continued talking to them until dawn; then he left. 12Meanwhile, the young man was taken home unhurt, and everyone was greatly relieved.

Paul Meets the Ephesian Elders

13Paul went by land to Assos, where he had arranged for us to join him, and we went on

19:24 Artemis is otherwise known as Diana.   20:1 Greek disciples.   20:6 Greek the days of unleavened bread.   20:7 Greek to break bread.
20:11 Greek broke the bread.

Can Demons Personally Harm You? Read ACTS 19:13-20

While Christians have the promise of angelic protection over their lives, non-Christians are open targets for the Devil and his demon forces. As this passage relates, demons will only respond to or avoid the "genuine" believer. They will not answer to someone who simply uses the name of Jesus without really knowing who Jesus is. Religion will not keep them away, nor will symbols like a crucifix. Certainly the Devil hates what Jesus did on the literal cross, but wearing a cross will not drive these evil spirits away.

The only thing that will secure you from the Devil's domination—and even possession—of your soul is the presence of Jesus Christ in your life. Once you trust in him, you come under divine protection and become his property. He said that you are his sheep and that no one can take you out of his hand (see John 10:27-29, p. 905). But if you are not a Christian, you are open game that the Devil can take at his will.

For the next note on "What Are Demons?" turn to p. 868.

CORNER STONES

---

ahead by ship. ¹⁴He joined us there and we sailed together to Mitylene. ¹⁵The next day we passed the island of Kios. The following day, we crossed to the island of Samos. And a day later we arrived at Miletus.

¹⁶Paul had decided against stopping at Ephesus this time because he didn't want to spend further time in the province of Asia. He was hurrying to get to Jerusalem, if possible, for the Festival of Pentecost. ¹⁷But when we landed at Miletus, he sent a message to the elders of the church at Ephesus, asking them to come down to meet him.

¹⁸When they arrived he declared, "You know that from the day I set foot in the province of Asia until now ¹⁹I have done the Lord's work humbly—yes, and with tears. I have endured the trials that came to me from the plots of the Jews. ²⁰Yet I never shrank from telling you the truth, either publicly or in your homes. ²¹I have had one message for Jews and Gentiles alike—the necessity of turning from sin and turning to God, and of faith in our Lord Jesus.

²²"And now I am going to Jerusalem, drawn there irresistibly by the Holy Spirit,* not knowing what awaits me, ²³except that the Holy Spirit has told me in city after city that jail and suffering lie ahead. ²⁴But my life is worth nothing unless I use it for doing the work assigned me by the Lord Jesus—the work of telling others the Good News about God's wonderful kindness and love.

²⁵"And now I know that none of you to whom I have preached the Kingdom will ever see me again. ²⁶Let me say plainly that I have been faithful. No one's damnation can be blamed on me,* ²⁷for I didn't shrink from declaring all that God wants for you.

²⁸"And now beware! Be sure that you feed and shepherd God's flock—his church, purchased with his blood—over whom the Holy Spirit has appointed you as elders.* ²⁹I know full well that false teachers, like vicious wolves, will come in among you after I leave, not sparing the flock. ³⁰Even some of you will distort the truth in order to draw a following. ³¹Watch out! Remember the three years I was with you—my constant watch and care over you night and day, and my many tears for you.

³²"And now I entrust you to God and the word of his grace—his message that is able to build you up and give you an inheritance with all those he has set apart for himself.

³³"I have never coveted anyone's money or fine clothing. ³⁴You know that these hands of mine have worked to pay my own way, and I have even supplied the needs of those who were with me. ³⁵And I have been a constant example of how you can help the poor by working hard. You should remember the words of the Lord Jesus: 'It is more blessed to give than to receive.' "

³⁶When he had finished speaking, he knelt and prayed with them. ³⁷They wept aloud as they embraced him in farewell, ³⁸sad most of all because he had said that they would never see him again. Then they accompanied him down to the ship.

20:22 Or *by my spirit,* or *by an inner compulsion;* Greek reads *by the spirit.*   **20:26** Greek *I am innocent of the blood of all.*   **20:28** Greek *overseers.*

CHAPTER 21

Paul's Journey to Jerusalem

After saying farewell to the Ephesian elders, we sailed straight to the island of Cos. The next day we reached Rhodes and then went to Patara. ²There we boarded a ship sailing for the Syrian province of Phoenicia. ³We sighted the island of Cyprus, passed it on our left, and landed at the harbor of Tyre, in Syria, where the ship was to unload. ⁴We went ashore, found the local believers,* and stayed with them a week. These disciples prophesied through the Holy Spirit that Paul should not go on to Jerusalem. ⁵When we returned to the ship at the end of the week, the entire congregation, including wives and children, came down to the shore with us. There we knelt, prayed, ⁶and said our farewells. Then we went aboard, and they returned home.

⁷The next stop after leaving Tyre was Ptolemais, where we greeted the brothers and sisters* but stayed only one day. ⁸Then we went on to Caesarea and stayed at the home of Philip the Evangelist, one of the seven men who had been chosen to distribute food. ⁹He had four unmarried daughters who had the gift of prophecy.

¹⁰During our stay of several days, a man named Agabus, who also had the gift of prophecy, arrived from Judea. ¹¹When he visited us, he took Paul's belt and bound his own feet and hands with it. Then he said, "The Holy Spirit declares, 'So shall the owner of this belt be bound by the Jewish leaders in Jerusalem and turned over to the Romans.'" ¹²When we heard this, we who were traveling with him, as well as the local believers, begged Paul not to go on to Jerusalem.

¹³But he said, "Why all this weeping? You are breaking my heart! For I am ready not only to be jailed at Jerusalem but also to die for the sake of the Lord Jesus." ¹⁴When it was clear that we couldn't persuade him, we gave up and said, "The will of the Lord be done."

Paul Arrives at Jerusalem

¹⁵Shortly afterward we packed our things and left for Jerusalem. ¹⁶Some believers from Caesarea accompanied us, and they took us to the home of Mnason, a man originally from Cyprus and one of the early disciples. ¹⁷All the brothers and sisters in Jerusalem welcomed us cordially.

¹⁸The next day Paul went in with us to meet with James, and all the elders of the Jerusalem church were present. ¹⁹After greetings were exchanged, Paul gave a detailed account of the things God had accomplished among the Gentiles through his ministry.

²⁰After hearing this, they praised God. But then they said, "You know, dear brother, how many thousands of Jews have also believed, and they all take the law of Moses very seriously. ²¹Our Jewish Christians here at Jerusalem have been told that you are teaching all the Jews living in the Gentile world to turn their backs on the laws of Moses. They say that you teach people not to circumcise their children or follow other Jewish customs. ²²Now what can be done? For they will certainly hear that you have come.

²³"Here's our suggestion. We have four men here who have taken a vow and are preparing to shave their heads. ²⁴Go with them to the Temple and join them in the purification ceremony, and pay for them to have their heads shaved. Then everyone will know that the rumors are all false and that you yourself observe the Jewish laws.

²⁵"As for the Gentile Christians, all we ask of them is what we already told them in a letter: They should not eat food offered to idols, nor consume blood, nor eat meat from strangled animals, and they should stay away from all sexual immorality."

Paul Is Arrested

²⁶So Paul agreed to their request, and the next day he went through the purification ritual with the men and went to the Temple. Then he publicly announced the date when their vows would end and sacrifices would be offered for each of them.

²⁷The seven days were almost ended when some Jews from the province of Asia saw Paul in the Temple and roused a mob against him. They grabbed him, ²⁸yelling, "Men of Israel! Help! This is the man who teaches against our people and tells everybody to disobey the Jewish laws. He speaks against the Temple—and he even defiles it by bringing Gentiles in!" ²⁹(For earlier that day they had seen him in the city with Trophimus, a Gentile from Ephesus,* and they assumed Paul had taken him into the Temple.)

³⁰The whole population of the city was rocked by these accusations, and a great riot followed. Paul was dragged out of the Temple, and immediately the gates were closed behind him. ³¹As they were trying to kill him, word reached the commander of the Roman regiment that all Jerusalem was in an uproar. ³²He

21:4 Greek *disciples;* also in 21:16.   21:7 Greek *brothers;* also in 21:17.   21:29 Greek *Trophimus, the Ephesian.*

immediately called out his soldiers and officers and ran down among the crowd. When the mob saw the commander and the troops coming, they stopped beating Paul. 33The commander arrested him and ordered him bound with two chains. Then he asked the crowd who he was and what he had done. 34Some shouted one thing and some another. He couldn't find out the truth in all the uproar and confusion, so he ordered Paul to be taken to the fortress. 35As they reached the stairs, the mob grew so violent the soldiers had to lift Paul to their shoulders to protect him. 36And the crowd followed behind shouting, "Kill him, kill him!"

Paul Speaks to the Crowd

37As Paul was about to be taken inside, he said to the commander, "May I have a word with you?"

"Do you know Greek?" the commander asked, surprised. 38"Aren't you the Egyptian who led a rebellion some time ago and took four thousand members of the Assassins out into the desert?"

39"No," Paul replied, "I am a Jew from Tarsus in Cilicia, which is an important city. Please, let me talk to these people." 40The commander agreed, so Paul stood on the stairs and motioned to the people to be quiet. Soon a deep silence enveloped the crowd, and he addressed them in their own language, Aramaic.*

CHAPTER 22

"Brothers and esteemed fathers," Paul said, "listen to me as I offer my defense." 2When they heard him speaking in their own language,* the silence was even greater. 3"I am a Jew, born in Tarsus, a city in Cilicia, and I was brought up and educated here in Jerusalem under Gamaliel. At his feet I learned to follow our Jewish laws and customs very carefully. I became very zealous to honor God in everything I did, just as all of you are today. 4And I persecuted the followers of the Way, hounding some to death, binding and delivering both men and women to prison. 5The high priest and the whole council of leaders can testify that this is so. For I received letters from them to our Jewish brothers in Damascus, authorizing me to bring the Christians from there to Jerusalem, in chains, to be punished.

6"As I was on the road, nearing Damascus, about noon a very bright light from heaven suddenly shone around me. 7I fell to the ground

and heard a voice saying to me, 'Saul, Saul, why are you persecuting me?'

8" 'Who are you, sir?' I asked. And he replied, 'I am Jesus of Nazareth, the one you are persecuting.' 9The people with me saw the light but didn't hear the voice.

10"I said, 'What shall I do, Lord?' And the Lord told me, 'Get up and go into Damascus, and there you will be told all that you are to do.'

11"I was blinded by the intense light and had to be led into Damascus by my companions. 12A man named Ananias lived there. He was a godly man in his devotion to the law, and he was well thought of by all the Jews of Damascus. 13He came to me and stood beside me and said, 'Brother Saul, receive your sight.' And that very hour I could see him!

14"Then he told me, 'The God of our ancestors has chosen you to know his will and to see the Righteous One and hear him speak. 15You are to take his message everywhere, telling the whole world what you have seen and heard. 16And now, why delay? Get up and be baptized, and have your sins washed away, calling on the name of the Lord.'

17"One day after I returned to Jerusalem, I was praying in the Temple, and I fell into a trance. 18I saw a vision of Jesus saying to me, 'Hurry! Leave Jerusalem, for the people here won't believe you when you give them your testimony about me.'

19" 'But Lord,' I argued, 'they certainly know that I imprisoned and beat those in every synagogue who believed on you. 20And when your witness Stephen was killed, I was standing there agreeing. I kept the coats they laid aside as they stoned him.'

21"But the Lord said to me, 'Leave Jerusalem, for I will send you far away to the Gentiles!' "

22The crowd listened until Paul came to that word; then with one voice they shouted, "Away with such a fellow! Kill him! He isn't fit to live!" 23They yelled, threw off their coats, and tossed handfuls of dust into the air.

Paul Reveals His Roman Citizenship

24The commander brought Paul inside and ordered him lashed with whips to make him confess his crime. He wanted to find out why the crowd had become so furious. 25As they tied Paul down to lash him, Paul said to the officer standing there, "Is it legal for you to whip a Roman citizen who hasn't even been tried?"

21:40 Or *Hebrew.* 22:2 Greek *in Aramaic.*

26The officer went to the commander and asked, "What are you doing? This man is a Roman citizen!"

27So the commander went over and asked Paul, "Tell me, are you a Roman citizen?"

"Yes, I certainly am," Paul replied.

28"I am, too," the commander muttered, "and it cost me plenty!"

"But I am a citizen by birth!"

29The soldiers who were about to interrogate Paul quickly withdrew when they heard he was a Roman citizen, and the commander was frightened because he had ordered him bound and whipped.

Paul before the High Council

30The next day the commander freed Paul from his chains and ordered the leading priests into session with the Jewish high council.* He had Paul brought in before them to try to find out what the trouble was all about.

CHAPTER **23**

Gazing intently at the high council,* Paul began: "Brothers, I have always lived before God in all good conscience!"

2Instantly Ananias the high priest commanded those close to Paul to slap him on the mouth. 3But Paul said to him, "God will slap you, you whitewashed wall! What kind of judge are you to break the law yourself by ordering me struck like that?"

4Those standing near Paul said to him, "Is that the way to talk to God's high priest?"

5"I'm sorry, brothers. I didn't realize he was the high priest," Paul replied, "for the Scriptures say, 'Do not speak evil of anyone who rules over you.'*"

6Paul realized that some members of the high council were Sadducees and some were Pharisees, so he shouted, "Brothers, I am a Pharisee, as were all my ancestors! And I am on trial because my hope is in the resurrection of the dead!"

7This divided the council—the Pharisees against the Sadducees—8for the Sadducees say there is no resurrection or angels or spirits, but the Pharisees believe in all of these. 9So a great clamor arose. Some of the teachers of religious law who were Pharisees jumped up to argue that Paul was all right. "We see nothing wrong with him," they shouted. "Perhaps a spirit or an angel spoke to him." 10The shouting grew louder and louder, and the men were tugging at Paul from both sides, pulling him this way and that. Finally, the commander, fearing they would tear him apart, ordered his soldiers to take him away from them and bring him back to the fortress.

11That night the Lord appeared to Paul and said, "Be encouraged, Paul. Just as you have told the people about me here in Jerusalem, you must preach the Good News in Rome."

The Plan to Kill Paul

12The next morning a group of Jews got together and bound themselves with an oath to neither eat nor drink until they had killed Paul. 13There were more than forty of them. 14They went to the leading priests and other leaders and told them what they had done. "We have bound ourselves under oath to neither eat nor drink until we have killed Paul. 15You and the high council should tell the commander to bring Paul back to the council again," they requested. "Pretend you want to examine his case more fully. We will kill him on the way."

16But Paul's nephew heard of their plan and went to the fortress and told Paul. 17Paul called one of the officers and said, "Take this young man to the commander. He has something important to tell him."

18So the officer did, explaining, "Paul, the prisoner, called me over and asked me to bring this young man to you because he has something to tell you."

19The commander took him by the arm, led him aside, and asked, "What is it you want to tell me?"

20Paul's nephew told him, "Some Jews are going to ask you to bring Paul before the Jewish high council tomorrow, pretending they want to get some more information. 21But don't do it! There are more than forty men hiding along the way ready to jump him and kill him. They have vowed not to eat or drink until they kill him. They are ready, expecting you to agree to their request."

22"Don't let a soul know you told me this," the commander warned the young man as he sent him away.

Paul Is Sent to Caesarea

23Then the commander called two of his officers and ordered, "Get two hundred soldiers ready to leave for Caesarea at nine o'clock tonight. Also take two hundred spearmen and

22:30 Greek *Sanhedrin*. 23:1 Greek *Sanhedrin*; also in 23:6, 15, 20, 28. 23:5 Exod 22:28.

seventy horsemen. 24Provide horses for Paul to ride, and get him safely to Governor Felix." 25Then he wrote this letter to the governor:

26"From Claudius Lysias, to his Excellency, Governor Felix. Greetings! 27This man was seized by some Jews, and they were about to kill him when I arrived with the troops. When I learned that he was a Roman citizen, I removed him to safety. 28Then I took him to their high council to try to find out what he had done. 29I soon discovered it was something regarding their religious law—certainly nothing worthy of imprisonment or death. 30But when I was informed of a plot to kill him, I immediately sent him on to you. I have told his accusers to bring their charges before you."

31So that night, as ordered, the soldiers took Paul as far as Antipatris. 32They returned to the fortress the next morning, while the horsemen took him on to Caesarea. 33When they arrived in Caesarea, they presented Paul and the letter to Governor Felix. 34He read it and then asked Paul what province he was from. "Cilicia," Paul answered.

35"I will hear your case myself when your accusers arrive," the governor told him. Then the governor ordered him kept in the prison at Herod's headquarters.

CHAPTER **24**

Paul Appears before Felix

Five days later Ananias, the high priest, arrived with some of the Jewish leaders and the lawyer* Tertullus, to press charges against Paul. 2When Paul was called in, Tertullus laid charges against Paul in the following address to the governor:

"Your Excellency, you have given peace to us Jews and have enacted reforms for us. 3And for all of this we are very grateful to you. 4But lest I bore you, kindly give me your attention for only a moment as I briefly outline our case against this man. 5For we have found him to be a troublemaker, a man who is constantly inciting the Jews throughout the world to riots and rebellions against the Roman government. He is a ringleader of the sect known as the Nazarenes. 6Moreover he was trying to defile the Temple when we arrested him.* 8You can find out the truth of our accusations by examining him your-

self." 9Then the other Jews chimed in, declaring that everything Tertullus said was true.

10Now it was Paul's turn. The governor motioned for him to rise and speak. Paul said, "I know, sir, that you have been a judge of Jewish affairs for many years, and this gives me confidence as I make my defense. 11You can quickly discover that it was no more than twelve days ago that I arrived in Jerusalem to worship at the Temple. 12I didn't argue with anyone in the Temple, nor did I incite a riot in any synagogue or on the streets of the city. 13These men certainly cannot prove the things they accuse me of doing.

14"But I admit that I follow the Way, which they call a sect. I worship the God of our ancestors, and I firmly believe the Jewish law and everything written in the books of prophecy. 15I have hope in God, just as these men do, that he will raise both the righteous and the ungodly. 16Because of this, I always try to maintain a clear conscience before God and everyone else.

17"After several years away, I returned to Jerusalem with money to aid my people and to offer sacrifices to God. 18My accusers saw me in the Temple as I was completing a purification ritual. There was no crowd around me and no rioting. 19But some Jews from the province of Asia were there—and they ought to be here to bring charges if they have anything against me! 20Ask these men here what wrongdoing the Jewish high council* found in me, 21except for one thing I said when I shouted out, 'I am on trial before you today because I believe in the resurrection of the dead!'"

22Felix, who was quite familiar with the Way, adjourned the hearing and said, "Wait until Lysias, the garrison commander, arrives. Then I will decide the case." 23He ordered an officer to keep Paul in custody but to give him some freedom and allow his friends to visit him and take care of his needs.

24A few days later Felix came with his wife, Drusilla, who was Jewish. Sending for Paul, they listened as he told them about faith in Christ Jesus. 25As he reasoned with them about righteousness and self-control and the judgment to come, Felix was terrified. "Go away for now," he replied. "When it is more convenient, I'll call for you again." 26He also hoped that Paul would bribe him, so he sent for him quite often and talked with him.

24:1 Greek *some elders and an orator.* 24:6 Some manuscripts add *We would have judged him by our law,* 7but *Lysias, the commander of the garrison, came and took him violently away from us,* 8commanding *his accusers to come before you.* 24:20 Greek *Sanhedrin.*

27Two years went by in this way; then Felix was succeeded by Porcius Festus. And because Felix wanted to gain favor with the Jewish leaders, he left Paul in prison.

CHAPTER 25

Paul Appears before Festus

Three days after Festus arrived in Caesarea to take over his new responsibilities, he left for Jerusalem, 2where the leading priests and other Jewish leaders met with him and made their accusations against Paul. 3They asked Festus as a favor to transfer Paul to Jerusalem. (Their plan was to waylay and kill him.) 4But Festus replied that Paul was at Caesarea and he himself would be returning there soon. 5So he said, "Those of you in authority can return with me. If Paul has done anything wrong, you can make your accusations."

6Eight or ten days later he returned to Caesarea, and on the following day Paul's trial began. 7On Paul's arrival in court, the Jewish leaders from Jerusalem gathered around and made many serious accusations they couldn't prove. 8Paul denied the charges. "I am not guilty," he said. "I have committed no crime against the Jewish laws or the Temple or the Roman government."

9Then Festus, wanting to please the Jews, asked him, "Are you willing to go to Jerusalem and stand trial before me there?"

10But Paul replied, "No! This is the official Roman court, so I ought to be tried right here. You know very well I am not guilty. 11If I have done something worthy of death, I don't refuse to die. But if I am innocent, neither you nor anyone else has a right to turn me over to these men to kill me. I appeal to Caesar!"

12Festus conferred with his advisers and then replied, "Very well! You have appealed to Caesar, and to Caesar you shall go!"

13A few days later King Agrippa arrived with his sister, Bernice,* to pay their respects to Festus. 14During their stay of several days, Festus discussed Paul's case with the king. "There is a prisoner here," he told him, "whose case was left for me by Felix. 15When I was in Jerusalem, the leading priests and other Jewish leaders pressed charges against him and asked me to sentence him. 16Of course, I quickly pointed out to them that Roman law does not convict people without a trial. They are given an opportunity to defend themselves face to face with their accusers.

17"When they came here for the trial, I called the case the very next day and ordered Paul brought in. 18But the accusations made against him weren't at all what I expected. 19It was something about their religion and about someone called Jesus who died, but whom Paul insists is alive. 20I was perplexed as to how to conduct an investigation of this kind, and I asked him whether he would be willing to stand trial on these charges in Jerusalem. 21But Paul appealed to the emperor. So I ordered him back to jail until I could arrange to send him to Caesar."

22"I'd like to hear the man myself," Agrippa said.

And Festus replied, "You shall—tomorrow!"

Paul Speaks to Agrippa

23So the next day Agrippa and Bernice arrived at the auditorium with great pomp, accompanied by military officers and prominent men of the city. Festus ordered that Paul be brought in. 24Then Festus said, "King Agrippa and all present, this is the man whose death is demanded both by the local Jews and by those in Jerusalem. 25But in my opinion he has done nothing worthy of death. However, he appealed his case to the emperor, and I decided to send him. 26But what shall I write the emperor? For there is no real charge against him. So I have brought him before all of you, and especially you, King Agrippa, so that after we examine him, I might have something to write. 27For it doesn't seem reasonable to send a prisoner to the emperor without specifying the charges against him!"

CHAPTER 26

Then Agrippa said to Paul, "You may speak in your defense."

So Paul, with a gesture of his hand, started his defense: 2"I am fortunate, King Agrippa, that you are the one hearing my defense against all these accusations made by the Jewish leaders, 3for I know you are an expert on Jewish customs and controversies. Now please listen to me patiently!

4"As the Jewish leaders are well aware, I was given a thorough Jewish training from my earliest childhood among my own people and in Jerusalem. 5If they would admit it, they know that I have been a member of the Pharisees, the strictest sect of our religion. 6Now I am on trial because I am looking forward to the fulfillment

25:13 Greek *Agrippa the king and Bernice arrived.*

of God's promise made to our ancestors. ⁷In fact, that is why the twelve tribes of Israel worship God night and day, and they share the same hope I have. Yet, O king, they say it is wrong for me to have this hope! ⁸Why does it seem incredible to any of you that God can raise the dead?

⁹"I used to believe that I ought to do everything I could to oppose the followers of Jesus of Nazareth.* ¹⁰Authorized by the leading priests, I caused many of the believers in Jerusalem to be sent to prison. And I cast my vote against them when they were condemned to death. ¹¹Many times I had them whipped in the synagogues to try to get them to curse Christ. I was so violently opposed to them that I even hounded them in distant cities of foreign lands.

¹²"One day I was on such a mission to Damascus, armed with the authority and commission of the leading priests. ¹³About noon, Your Majesty, a light from heaven brighter than the sun shone down on me and my companions. ¹⁴We all fell down, and I heard a voice saying to me in Aramaic,* 'Saul, Saul, why are you persecuting me? It is hard for you to fight against my will.*'

¹⁵"'Who are you, sir?' I asked.

"And the Lord replied, 'I am Jesus, the one you are persecuting. ¹⁶Now stand up! For I have appeared to you to appoint you as my servant and my witness. You are to tell the world about this experience and about other times I will appear to you. ¹⁷And I will protect you from both your own people and the Gentiles. Yes, I am going to send you to the Gentiles, ¹⁸to open their eyes so they may turn from darkness to light, and from the power of Satan to God. Then they will receive forgiveness for their sins and be given a place among God's people, who are set apart by faith in me.'

¹⁹"And so, O King Agrippa, I was not disobedient to that vision from heaven. ²⁰I preached first to those in Damascus, then in Jerusalem and throughout all Judea, and also to the Gentiles, that all must turn from their sins and turn to God—and prove they have changed by the good things they do. ²¹Some Jews arrested me in the Temple for preaching this, and they tried to kill me. ²²But God protected me so that I am still alive today to tell these facts to everyone, from the least to the greatest. I teach nothing except what the prophets and Moses said would happen—²³that the Messiah would suffer and be

the first to rise from the dead as a light to Jews and Gentiles alike."

²⁴Suddenly, Festus shouted, "Paul, you are insane. Too much study has made you crazy!"

²⁵But Paul replied, "I am not insane, Most Excellent Festus. I am speaking the sober truth. ²⁶And King Agrippa knows about these things. I speak frankly, for I am sure these events are all familiar to him, for they were not done in a corner! ²⁷King Agrippa, do you believe the prophets? I know you do—"

²⁸Agrippa interrupted him. "Do you think you can make me a Christian so quickly?"*

²⁹Paul replied, "Whether quickly or not, I pray to God that both you and everyone here in this audience might become the same as I am, except for these chains."

³⁰Then the king, the governor, Bernice, and all the others stood and left. ³¹As they talked it over they agreed, "This man hasn't done anything worthy of death or imprisonment." ³²And Agrippa said to Festus, "He could be set free if he hadn't appealed to Caesar!"

CHAPTER **27**
Paul Sails for Rome

When the time came, we set sail for Italy. Paul and several other prisoners were placed in the custody of an army officer named Julius, a captain of the Imperial Regiment. ²And Aristarchus, a Macedonian from Thessalonica, was also with us. We left on a boat whose home port was Adramyttium; it was scheduled to make several stops at ports along the coast of the province of Asia.

³The next day when we docked at Sidon, Julius was very kind to Paul and let him go ashore to visit with friends so they could provide for his needs. ⁴Putting out to sea from there, we encountered headwinds that made it difficult to keep the ship on course, so we sailed north of Cyprus between the island and the mainland. ⁵We passed along the coast of the provinces of Cilicia and Pamphylia, landing at Myra, in the province of Lycia. ⁶There the officer found an Egyptian ship from Alexandria that was bound for Italy, and he put us on board.

⁷We had several days of rough sailing, and after great difficulty we finally neared Cnidus. But the wind was against us, so we sailed down to the leeward side of Crete, past the cape of Salmone. ⁸We struggled along the coast with great difficulty

and finally arrived at Fair Havens, near the city of Lasea. 9We had lost a lot of time. The weather was becoming dangerous for long voyages by then because it was so late in the fall,* and Paul spoke to the ship's officers about it.

10"Sirs," he said, "I believe there is trouble ahead if we go on—shipwreck, loss of cargo, injuries, and danger to our lives." 11But the officer in charge of the prisoners listened more to the ship's captain and the owner than to Paul. 12And since Fair Havens was an exposed harbor—a poor place to spend the winter—most of the crew wanted to go to Phoenix, farther up the coast of Crete, and spend the winter there. Phoenix was a good harbor with only a southwest and northwest exposure.

The Storm at Sea

13When a light wind began blowing from the south, the sailors thought they could make it. So they pulled up anchor and sailed along close to shore. 14But the weather changed abruptly, and a wind of typhoon strength (a "northeaster," they called it) caught the ship and blew it out to sea. 15They couldn't turn the ship into the wind, so they gave up and let it run before the gale.

16We sailed behind a small island named Cauda,* where with great difficulty we hoisted aboard the lifeboat that was being towed behind us. 17Then we banded the ship with ropes to strengthen the hull. The sailors were afraid of being driven across to the sandbars of Syrtis off the African coast, so they lowered the sea anchor and were thus driven before the wind. 18The next day, as gale-force winds continued to batter the ship, the crew began throwing the cargo overboard. 19The following day they even threw out the ship's equipment and anything else they could lay their hands on. 20The terrible storm raged unabated for many days, blotting out the sun and the stars, until at last all hope was gone.

21No one had eaten for a long time. Finally, Paul called the crew together and said, "Men, you should have listened to me in the first place and not left Fair Havens. You would have avoided all this injury and loss. 22But take courage! None of you will lose your lives, even though the ship will go down. 23For last night an angel of the God to whom I belong and whom I serve stood beside me, 24and he said, 'Don't be afraid, Paul, for you

27:9 Greek *because the fast was now already gone by.* This fast happened on the Day of Atonement (*Yom Kippur*), which occurred in late September or early October. 27:16 Some manuscripts read *Clauda.*

will surely stand trial before Caesar! What's more, God in his goodness has granted safety to everyone sailing with you.' 25So take courage! For I believe God. It will be just as he said. 26But we will be shipwrecked on an island."

The Shipwreck

27About midnight on the fourteenth night of the storm, as we were being driven across the Sea of Adria,* the sailors sensed land was near. 28They took soundings and found the water was only 120 feet deep. A little later they sounded again and found only 90 feet.* 29At this rate they were

27:27 The *Sea of Adria* is in the central Mediterranean; it is not to be confused with the Adriatic Sea. 27:28 Greek *20 fathoms . . . 15 fathoms* [37 meters . . . 27 meters].

Share Your Own Story
Read ACTS 26:1-23

Another useful tool in our "evangelistic toolbox" is the story, or testimony, of how we came to personally know Jesus Christ. Paul used this method effectively when he appeared before King Agrippa. As was often his style, he began his presentation of the gospel by explaining how he had personally come into a relationship with Christ. Then he segued into the proclamation of the gospel message (verses 19-23).

Every believer has a testimony. Some may be more dramatic than others. Such was the case with Paul, formerly the notorious Saul of Tarsus, an aggressive persecutor of the church. Regardless of how incredible your testimony may seem, your personal salvation story will help you find common ground with a nonbeliever. You can tell him or her of your former life and attitude before coming to Christ, then explain the changes that came afterward. When a nonbeliever sees that you can relate to his or her own life, he or she may be more open to what you have to say.

Why don't you take a moment to think about the changes that have taken place in your life now that you are a Christian? You may even want to write down your testimony so that you will be ready to share it at the next opportunity.

To begin the next topic, turn to p. A30.

afraid we would soon be driven against the rocks along the shore, so they threw out four anchors from the stern and prayed for daylight. 30Then the sailors tried to abandon the ship; they lowered the lifeboat as though they were going to put out anchors from the prow. 31But Paul said to the commanding officer and the soldiers, "You will all die unless the sailors stay aboard." 32So the soldiers cut the ropes and let the boat fall off.

33As the darkness gave way to the early morning light, Paul begged everyone to eat. "You haven't touched food for two weeks," he said. 34"Please eat something now for your own good. For not a hair of your heads will perish." 35Then he took some bread, gave thanks to God before them all, and broke off a piece and ate it. 36Then everyone was encouraged, 37and all 276 of us began eating—for that is the number we had aboard. 38After eating, the crew lightened the ship further by throwing the cargo of wheat overboard.

39When morning dawned, they didn't recognize the coastline, but they saw a bay with a beach and wondered if they could get between the rocks and get the ship safely to shore. 40So they cut off the anchors and left them in the sea. Then they lowered the rudders, raised the foresail, and headed toward shore. 41But the ship hit a shoal and ran aground. The bow of the ship stuck fast, while the stern was repeatedly smashed by the force of the waves and began to break apart.

42The soldiers wanted to kill the prisoners to make sure they didn't swim ashore and escape. 43But the commanding officer wanted to spare Paul, so he didn't let them carry out their plan. Then he ordered all who could swim to jump overboard first and make for land, 44and he told the others to try for it on planks and debris from the broken ship. So everyone escaped safely ashore!

CHAPTER **28**

Paul on the Island of Malta

Once we were safe on shore, we learned that we were on the island of Malta. 2The people of the island were very kind to us. It was cold and rainy, so they built a fire on the shore to welcome us and warm us.

3As Paul gathered an armful of sticks and was laying them on the fire, a poisonous snake, driven out by the heat, fastened itself onto his hand. 4The people of the island saw it hanging there and said to each other, "A murderer, no doubt! Though he escaped the sea, justice will not permit him to live." 5But Paul shook off the snake into the fire and was unharmed. 6The people waited for him to swell up or suddenly drop dead. But when they had waited a long time and saw no harm come to him, they changed their minds and decided he was a god.

7Near the shore where we landed was an estate belonging to Publius, the chief official of the island. He welcomed us courteously and fed us for three days. 8As it happened, Publius's father was ill with fever and dysentery. Paul went in and prayed for him, and laying his hands on him, he healed him. 9Then all the other sick people on the island came and were cured. 10As a result we were showered with honors, and when the time came to sail, people put on board all sorts of things we would need for the trip.

Paul Arrives at Rome

11It was three months after the shipwreck that we set sail on another ship that had wintered at the island—an Alexandrian ship with the twin gods* as its figurehead. 12Our first stop was Syracuse,* where we stayed three days. 13From there we sailed across to Rhegium.* A day later a south wind began blowing, so the following day we sailed up the coast to Puteoli. 14There we found some believers,* who invited us to stay with them seven days. And so we came to Rome.

15The brothers and sisters* in Rome had heard we were coming, and they came to meet us at the Forum* on the Appian Way. Others joined us at The Three Taverns.* When Paul saw them, he thanked God and took courage.

16When we arrived in Rome, Paul was permitted to have his own private lodging, though he was guarded by a soldier.

Paul Preaches at Rome under Guard

17Three days after Paul's arrival, he called together the local Jewish leaders. He said to them, "Brothers, I was arrested in Jerusalem and handed over to the Roman government, even though I had done nothing against our people or the customs of our ancestors. 18The Romans tried me and wanted to release me, for they found no cause for the death sentence. 19But

28:11 The *twin gods* were the Roman gods Castor and Pollux.   **28:12** *Syracuse* was on the island of Sicily.   **28:13** *Rhegium* was on the southern tip of Italy.   **28:14** Greek *brothers*.   **28:15a** Greek *brothers*.   **28:15b** *The Forum* was about 43 miles (70 kilometers) from Rome. **28:15c** *The Three Taverns* was about 35 miles (57 kilometers) from Rome.

when the Jewish leaders protested the decision, I felt it necessary to appeal to Caesar, even though I had no desire to press charges against my own people. 20I asked you to come here today so we could get acquainted and so I could tell you that I am bound with this chain because I believe that the hope of Israel—the Messiah—has already come."

21They replied, "We have heard nothing against you. We have had no letters from Judea or reports from anyone who has arrived here. 22But we want to hear what you believe, for the only thing we know about these Christians* is that they are denounced everywhere."

23So a time was set, and on that day a large number of people came to Paul's house. He told them about the Kingdom of God and taught them about Jesus from the Scriptures—from the five books of Moses and the books of the prophets. He began lecturing in the morning and went on into the evening. 24Some believed and some didn't. 25But after they had argued back and forth among themselves, they left with this final word from Paul: "The Holy Spirit was right when he said to our ancestors through Isaiah the prophet,

26 'Go and say to my people,
   You will hear my words,
      but you will not understand;
   you will see what I do,
      but you will not perceive its meaning.
27 For the hearts of these people are hardened,
      and their ears cannot hear,
      and they have closed their eyes—
   so their eyes cannot see,
      and their ears cannot hear,
      and their hearts cannot understand,
   and they cannot turn to me
      and let me heal them.'*

28So I want you to realize that this salvation from God is also available to the Gentiles, and they will accept it."*

30For the next two years, Paul lived in his own rented house.* He welcomed all who visited him, 31proclaiming the Kingdom of God with all boldness and teaching about the Lord Jesus Christ. And no one tried to stop him.

28:22 Greek *this sect.*   28:26-27 Isa 6:9-10.   28:28 Some manuscripts add verse 29, *And when he had said these words, the Jews departed, greatly disagreeing with each other.*   28:30 Or *at his own expense.*

Romans

CHAPTER 1

Greetings from Paul

This letter is from Paul, Jesus Christ's slave, chosen by God to be an apostle and sent out to preach his Good News. 2This Good News was promised long ago by God through his prophets in the holy Scriptures. 3It is the Good News about his Son, Jesus, who came as a man, born into King David's royal family line. 4And Jesus Christ our Lord was shown to be the Son of God when God powerfully raised him from the dead by means of the Holy Spirit.* 5Through Christ, God has given us the privilege and authority to tell Gentiles everywhere what God has done for them, so that they will believe and obey him, bringing glory to his name.

6You are among those who have been called to belong to Jesus Christ, 7dear friends in Rome. God loves you dearly, and he has called you to be his very own people.

May grace and peace be yours from God our Father and the Lord Jesus Christ.

God's Good News

8Let me say first of all that your faith in God is becoming known throughout the world. How I thank God through Jesus Christ for each one of you. 9God knows how often I pray for you. Day and night I bring you and your needs in prayer to God, whom I serve with all my heart* by telling others the Good News about his Son.

10One of the things I always pray for is the opportunity, God willing, to come at last to see you. 11For I long to visit you so I can share a spiritual blessing with you that will help you grow strong in the Lord. 12I'm eager to encourage you in your faith, but I also want to be encouraged by yours. In this way, each of us will be a blessing to the other.

13I want you to know, dear brothers and sisters,* that I planned many times to visit you, but I was prevented until now. I want to work among you and see good results, just as I have done among other Gentiles. 14For I have a great sense of obligation to people in our culture and to people in other cultures,* to the educated and uneducated alike. 15So I am eager to come to you in Rome, too, to preach God's Good News.

16For I am not ashamed of this Good News about Christ. It is the power of God at work, saving everyone who believes—Jews first and also Gentiles. 17This Good News tells us how God makes us right in his sight. This is accomplished from start to finish by faith. As the Scriptures say, "It is through faith that a righteous person has life."*

God's Anger at Sin

18But God shows his anger from heaven against all sinful, wicked people who push the truth away from themselves.* 19For the truth about God is known to them instinctively.* God has put this knowledge in their hearts. 20From the time the world was created, people have seen the earth and sky and all that God made. They can clearly see his invisible qualities—his eternal power and divine nature. So they have no excuse whatsoever for not knowing God.

21Yes, they knew God, but they wouldn't worship him as God or even give him thanks. And they began to think up foolish ideas of what God was like. The result was that their minds became dark and confused. 22Claiming to be wise, they became utter fools instead. 23And instead of worshiping the glorious, ever-living

1:4 Or the Spirit of holiness.   1:9 Or in my spirit.   1:13 Greek brothers.   1:14 Greek to Greeks and to barbarians.   1:17 Hab 2:4.   1:18 Or who prevent the truth from being known.   1:19 Greek is manifest in them.

God, they worshiped idols made to look like mere people, or birds and animals and snakes.

24So God let them go ahead and do whatever shameful things their hearts desired. As a result, they did vile and degrading things with each other's bodies. 25Instead of believing what they knew was the truth about God, they deliberately chose to believe lies. So they worshiped the things God made but not the Creator himself, who is to be praised forever. Amen.

26That is why God abandoned them to their shameful desires. Even the women turned against the natural way to have sex and instead indulged in sex with each other. 27And the men, instead of having normal sexual relationships with women, burned with lust for each other. Men did shameful things with other men and, as a result, suffered within themselves the penalty they so richly deserved.

28When they refused to acknowledge God, he abandoned them to their evil minds and let them do things that should never be done. 29Their lives became full of every kind of wickedness, sin, greed, hate, envy, murder, fighting, deception, malicious behavior, and gossip. 30They are backstabbers, haters of God, insolent, proud, and boastful. They are forever inventing new ways of sinning and are disobedient to their parents. 31They refuse to understand, break their promises, and are heartless and unforgiving. 32They are fully aware of God's death penalty for those who do these things, yet they go right ahead and do them anyway. And, worse yet, they encourage others to do them, too.

CHAPTER **2**

God's Judgment of Sin

You may be saying, "What terrible people you have been talking about!" But you are just as bad, and you have no excuse! When you say they are wicked and should be punished, you are condemning yourself, for you do these very same things. 2And we know that God, in his justice, will punish anyone who does such things. 3Do you think that God will judge and condemn others for doing them and not judge you when you do them, too? 4Don't you realize how kind, tolerant, and patient God is with you? Or don't you care? Can't you see how kind he has been in giving you time to turn from your sin?

5But no, you won't listen. So you are storing up terrible punishment for yourself because of

2:24 Isa 52:5.

your stubbornness in refusing to turn from your sin. For there is going to come a day of judgment when God, the just judge of all the world, 6will judge all people according to what they have done. 7He will give eternal life to those who persist in doing what is good, seeking after the glory and honor and immortality that God offers. 8But he will pour out his anger and wrath on those who live for themselves, who refuse to obey the truth and practice evil deeds. 9There will be trouble and calamity for everyone who keeps on sinning—for the Jew first and also for the Gentile. 10But there will be glory and honor and peace from God for all who do good—for the Jew first and also for the Gentile. 11For God does not show favoritism.

12God will punish the Gentiles when they sin, even though they never had God's written law. And he will punish the Jews when they sin, for they do have the law. 13For it is not merely knowing the law that brings God's approval. Those who obey the law will be declared right in God's sight. 14Even when Gentiles, who do not have God's written law, instinctively follow what the law says, they show that in their hearts they know right from wrong. 15They demonstrate that God's law is written within them, for their own consciences either accuse them or tell them they are doing what is right. 16The day will surely come when God, by Jesus Christ, will judge everyone's secret life. This is my message.

The Jews and the Law

17If you are a Jew, you are relying on God's law for your special relationship with him. You boast that all is well between yourself and God. 18Yes, you know what he wants; you know right from wrong because you have been taught his law. 19You are convinced that you are a guide for the blind and a beacon light for people who are lost in darkness without God. 20You think you can instruct the ignorant and teach children the ways of God. For you are certain that in God's law you have complete knowledge and truth.

21Well then, if you teach others, why don't you teach yourself? You tell others not to steal, but do you steal? 22You say it is wrong to commit adultery, but do you do it? You condemn idolatry, but do you steal from pagan temples? 23You are so proud of knowing the law, but you dishonor God by breaking it. 24No wonder the Scriptures say, "The world blasphemes the name of God because of you."*

[handwritten margin note: Sinner's Being gay is a sin and looked to be shameful!]

What Happens to Those Who Have Never Heard the Gospel?
Read ROMANS 1:18-20

Sometimes the person who asks this question is not so much concerned about those who have never heard the gospel. Rather, this person may be more concerned about trying to put up a "smoke screen" to keep you—the Christian—from showing his or her need for God. We might remind that person that God is loving and compassionate, and that he will deal fairly and justly with those who have never heard the gospel. But the person who asks you this question needs to recognize that knowledge brings responsibility. Those who know the truth of the gospel will be held accountable.

As we know from the Bible, God will judge us according to what we know of him (see Luke 12:48, p. 874). We will not be held accountable for what we do not know. Still, that does not excuse us from all responsibility. Otherwise we might say, "Ignorance is bliss." But this is not to say that the person who has not heard of Jesus will never know of him.

We, as humans, no matter where we live on God's earth, were born with a soul, an emptiness, a sense that life should have meaning and purpose. In spite of that spiritual longing, we have disregarded God and his Word. But if we are truly seeking God, he will reveal himself to us. We find proof of this in Acts 10:1-48 (pp. 936-937). There, a man named Cornelius—a religious man who constantly prayed to God—asked the Lord to reveal himself to him. Although Cornelius may have heard of Jesus Christ, he did not know God's plan for salvation. But that did not stop God from answering his prayer by sending the apostle Peter to preach the gospel to him. When Cornelius heard that wonderful message, he believed!

The Bible tells us that God is unchanging (see Malachi 3:6, p. 785, and James 1:17, p. 1085). He is the same yesterday, today, and tomorrow. If he heard Cornelius's prayer, he will also hear the prayers of those who do not know him but desire to.

For the next "Big Question" note, turn to p. 965.

BIG QUESTIONS?

25The Jewish ceremony of circumcision is worth something only if you obey God's law. But if you don't obey God's law, you are no better off than an uncircumcised Gentile. 26And if the Gentiles obey God's law, won't God give them all the rights and honors of being his own people? 27In fact, uncircumcised Gentiles who keep God's law will be much better off than you Jews who are circumcised and know so much about God's law but don't obey it.

28For you are not a true Jew just because you were born of Jewish parents or because you have gone through the Jewish ceremony of circumcision. 29No, a true Jew is one whose heart is right with God. And true circumcision is not a cutting of the body but a change of heart produced by God's Spirit. Whoever has that kind of change seeks praise from God, not from people.

CHAPTER **3**
God Remains Faithful
Then what's the advantage of being a Jew? Is

there any value in the Jewish ceremony of circumcision? 2Yes, being a Jew has many advantages. First of all, the Jews were entrusted with the whole revelation of God.*

3True, some of them were unfaithful; but just because they broke their promises, does that mean God will break his promises? 4Of course not! Though everyone else in the world is a liar, God is true. As the Scriptures say, "He will be proved right in what he says, and he will win his case in court."*

5"But," some say, "our sins serve a good purpose, for people will see God's goodness when he declares us sinners to be innocent. Isn't it unfair, then, for God to punish us?" (That is actually the way some people talk.) 6Of course not! If God is not just, how is he qualified to judge the world? 7"But," some might still argue, "how can God judge and condemn me as a sinner if my dishonesty highlights his truthfulness and brings him more glory?" 8If you follow that kind of thinking, however, you might as

3:2 Greek *the oracles of God.* 3:4 Ps 51:4.

well say that the more we sin the better it is! Those who say such things deserve to be condemned, yet some slander me by saying this is what I preach!

All People Are Sinners

9Well then, are we Jews better than others?* No, not at all, for we have already shown that all people, whether Jews or Gentiles, are under the power of sin. 10As the Scriptures say,

"No one is good—
  not even one.
11 No one has real understanding;
  no one is seeking God.
12 All have turned away from God;
  all have gone wrong.
No one does good,
  not even one."*
13 "Their talk is foul, like the stench from an
    open grave.
  Their speech is filled with lies."
"The poison of a deadly snake drips from
    their lips."*
14   "Their mouths are full of cursing and
    bitterness."*
15 "They are quick to commit murder.
16   Wherever they go, destruction and
    misery follow them.
17 They do not know what true peace is."*
18   "They have no fear of God to restrain
    them."*

19Obviously, the law applies to those to whom it was given, for its purpose is to keep people from having excuses and to bring the entire world into judgment before God. 20For no one can ever be made right in God's sight by doing what his law commands. For the more we know God's law, the clearer it becomes that we aren't obeying it.

Christ Took Our Punishment

21But now God has shown us a different way of being right in his sight—not by obeying the law but by the way promised in the Scriptures long ago. 22We are made right in God's sight when we trust in Jesus Christ to take away our sins. And we all can be saved in this same way, no matter who we are or what we have done.

23For all have sinned; all fall short of God's glorious standard. 24Yet now God in his gracious kindness declares us not guilty. He has done this through Christ Jesus, who has freed us by taking

away our sins. 25For God sent Jesus to take the punishment for our sins and to satisfy God's anger against us. We are made right with God when we believe that Jesus shed his blood, sacrificing his life for us. God was being entirely fair and just when he did not punish those who sinned in former times. 26And he is entirely fair and just in this present time when he declares sinners to be right in his sight because they believe in Jesus.

27Can we boast, then, that we have done anything to be accepted by God? No, because our acquittal is not based on our good deeds. It is based on our faith. 28So we are made right with God through faith and not by obeying the law.

29After all, God is not the God of the Jews only, is he? Isn't he also the God of the Gentiles? Of course he is. 30There is only one God, and there is only one way of being accepted by him. He makes people right with himself only by faith, whether they are Jews or Gentiles. 31Well then, if we emphasize faith, does this mean that we can forget about the law? Of course not! In fact, only when we have faith do we truly fulfill the law.

CHAPTER 4
The Faith of Abraham

Abraham was, humanly speaking, the founder of our Jewish nation. What were his experiences concerning this question of being saved by faith? 2Was it because of his good deeds that God accepted him? If so, he would have had something to boast about. But from God's point of view Abraham had no basis at all for pride. 3For the Scriptures tell us, "Abraham believed God, so God declared him to be righteous."*

4When people work, their wages are not a gift. Workers earn what they receive. 5But people are declared righteous because of their faith, not because of their work.

6King David spoke of this, describing the happiness of an undeserving sinner who is declared to be righteous:

7 "Oh, what joy for those whose
      disobedience is forgiven,
    whose sins are put out of sight.
8 Yes, what joy for those
    whose sin is no longer counted against
      them by the Lord."*

3:9 Greek *Are we better?* 3:10-12 Pss 14:1-3; 53:1-3. 3:13 Pss 5:9; 140:3. 3:14 Ps 10:7. 3:15-17 Isa 59:7-8. 3:18 Ps 36:1. 4:3 Gen 15:6. 4:7-8 Ps 32:1-2.

If God Is So Good, Why Do Bad Things Happen to His People? Read ROMANS 5:1-5

Sickness, war, accidents, natural disasters, tragedies—they come to the just and the unjust, the Christian and the non-Christian, the moral and the immoral. Yet, if God is so good and all-powerful, why doesn't he just wipe out evil things in this world? This question often arises after any tragedy, but especially when it affects people who you would think should be "immune" to such things.

In addressing this question, it is important to remember that God originally created the world perfect. But he also gave man the freedom to obey or disobey. When Adam sinned, death and suffering became an inevitable part of life (verse 12). Yet, as the Christian thinker C. S. Lewis observed, it is idle for us to speculate about the *origin* of evil. The problem we all face is the *fact* of evil. The only *solution* to the fact of evil is God's solution, Jesus Christ [Paul Little, *How to Give Away Your Faith* (Downers Grove, Ill.: InterVarsity Press, 1966), p. 72].

How is Jesus Christ the solution to the fact of evil? The moment you surrendered your life to Jesus Christ, you entered into the master plan that God has for you. Though it is true that you may not know what the future holds, you know who holds the future. And he has promised that all things work together for good to those that love God (see Romans 8:28, p. 971). Not just the good things, but all things. As Scripture says, "Everything serves [God's] plans" (Psalm 119:91).

That is easy to say when things are going smoothly. But when something unexpected comes into the picture, we may wonder if God is paying attention. That is when we need to realize that God is painting on a large canvas. He is looking at the big picture. We only see what is in front of us at the given moment.

God will allow many events to come into our life—good things, bad things, things that make sense, things that make no sense at all. But every one of these incidents in our lives serves as a part of his plan for us. Tragedy in itself is not good. But God can take tragedy and hardship and use them for his glory. As God's children, we know that everything that happens to us first goes through his screen of protection. And he will never give us more than we can handle (see 1 Corinthians 10:13, p. 994). For that reason we can follow the advice in verse 3 and rejoice. We have the assurance that God is working in our lives to strengthen and develop our character. More important, he will never leave our side (see Hebrews 13:5, p. 1084).

For the next "Big Question" note, turn to p. 975.

For the next "Big Question" note, turn to p. 975.

9Now then, is this blessing only for the Jews, or is it for Gentiles, too? Well, what about Abraham? We have been saying he was declared righteous by God because of his faith. 10But how did his faith help him? Was he declared righteous only after he had been circumcised, or was it before he was circumcised? The answer is that God accepted him first, and then he was circumcised later!

11The circumcision ceremony was a sign that Abraham already had faith and that God had already accepted him and declared him to be righteous—even before he was circumcised. So Abraham is the spiritual father of those who have faith but have not been circumcised. They are made right with God by faith. 12And Abraham is also the spiritual father of those who have been circumcised, but only if they have the same kind of faith Abraham had before he was circumcised.

13It is clear, then, that God's promise to give the whole earth to Abraham and his descendants was not based on obedience to God's law, but on the new relationship with God that comes by faith. 14So if you claim that God's promise is for those who obey God's law and think they are "good enough" in God's sight, then you are saying that faith is useless. And in that case, the promise is also meaningless. 15But the law brings punishment on those who try to obey it. (The only way to avoid breaking the law is to have no law to break!)

16So that's why faith is the key! God's promise is given to us as a free gift. And we are certain to receive it, whether or not we follow Jewish customs, if we have faith like Abraham's. For Abraham is the father of all who believe. 17That is what the Scriptures mean when God told him, "I have made you the father of many nations."* This happened because Abraham believed in the God who brings the dead back to life and who brings into existence what didn't exist before.

18When God promised Abraham that he would become the father of many nations, Abraham believed him. God had also said, "Your descendants will be as numerous as the stars,"* even though such a promise seemed utterly impossible! 19And Abraham's faith did not weaken, even though he knew that he was too old to be a father at the age of one hundred and that Sarah, his wife, had never been able to have children.

20Abraham never wavered in believing God's promise. In fact, his faith grew stronger, and in this he brought glory to God. 21He was absolutely convinced that God was able to do anything he promised. 22And because of Abraham's faith, God declared him to be righteous.

23Now this wonderful truth—that God declared him to be righteous—wasn't just for Abraham's benefit. 24It was for us, too, assuring us that God will also declare us to be righteous if we believe in God, who brought Jesus our Lord back from the dead. 25He was handed over to die because of our sins, and he was raised from the dead to make us right with God.

CHAPTER **5**
Faith Brings Joy

Therefore, since we have been made right in God's sight by faith, we have peace with God because of what Jesus Christ our Lord has done for us. 2Because of our faith, Christ has brought us into this place of highest privilege where we now stand, and we confidently and joyfully look forward to sharing God's glory.

3We can rejoice, too, when we run into problems and trials, for we know that they are good for us—they help us learn to endure. 4And endurance develops strength of character in us, and character strengthens our confident expectation of salvation. 5And this expectation will not disappoint us. For we know how dearly God loves us, because he has given us the Holy Spirit to fill our hearts with his love.

6When we were utterly helpless, Christ came at just the right time and died for us sinners. 7Now, no one is likely to die for a good person,

4:17 Gen 17:5. 4:18 Gen 15:5.

though someone might be willing to die for a person who is especially good. 8But God showed his great love for us by sending Christ to die for us while we were still sinners. 9And since we have been made right in God's sight by the blood of Christ, he will certainly save us from God's judgment. 10For since we were restored to friendship with God by the death of his Son while we were still his enemies, we will certainly be delivered from eternal punishment by his life. 11So now we can rejoice in our wonderful new relationship with God—all because of what our Lord Jesus Christ has done for us in making us friends of God.

Adam and Christ Contrasted

12When Adam sinned, sin entered the entire human race. Adam's sin brought death, so death spread to everyone, for everyone sinned. 13Yes, people sinned even before the law was given. And though there was no law to break, since it had not yet been given, 14they all died anyway—even though they did not disobey an explicit commandment of God, as Adam did. What a contrast between Adam and Christ, who was yet to come! 15And what a difference between our sin and God's generous gift of forgiveness. For this one man, Adam, brought death to many through his sin. But this other man, Jesus Christ, brought forgiveness to many through God's bountiful gift. 16And the result of God's gracious gift is very different from the result of that one man's sin. For Adam's sin led to condemnation, but we have the free gift of being accepted by God, even though we are guilty of many sins. 17The sin of this one man, Adam, caused death to rule over us, but all who receive God's wonderful, gracious gift of righteousness will live in triumph over sin and death through this one man, Jesus Christ.

18Yes, Adam's one sin brought condemnation upon everyone, but Christ's one act of righteousness makes all people right in God's sight and gives them life. 19Because one person disobeyed God, many people became sinners. But because one other person obeyed God, many people will be made right in God's sight.

20God's law was given so that all people could see how sinful they were. But as people sinned more and more, God's wonderful kindness became more abundant. 21So just as sin ruled over all people and brought them to death, now

God's wonderful kindness rules instead, giving us right standing with God and resulting in eternal life through Jesus Christ our Lord.

CHAPTER 6
Sin's Power Is Broken

Well then, should we keep on sinning so that God can show us more and more kindness and forgiveness? 2Of course not! Since we have died to sin, how can we continue to live in it? 3Or have you forgotten that when we became Christians and were baptized to become one with Christ Jesus, we died with him? 4For we died and were buried with Christ by baptism. And just as Christ was raised from the dead by the glorious power of the Father, now we also may live new lives.

5Since we have been united with him in his death, we will also be raised as he was. 6Our old sinful selves were crucified with Christ so that sin might lose its power in our lives. We are no longer slaves to sin. 7For when we died with Christ, we were set free from the power of sin. 8And since we died with Christ, we know we will also share his new life. 9We are sure of this because Christ rose from the dead, and he will never die again. Death no longer has any power over him. 10He died once to defeat sin, and now he lives for the glory of God. 11So you should consider yourselves dead to sin and able to live for the glory of God through Christ Jesus.

12Do not let sin control the way you live;* do not give in to its lustful desires. 13Do not let any part of your body become a tool of wickedness, to be used for sinning. Instead, give yourselves completely to God since you have been given new life. And use your whole body as a tool to do what is right for the glory of God. 14Sin is no longer your master, for you are no longer subject to the law, which enslaves you to sin. Instead, you are free by God's grace.

Freedom to Obey God

15So since God's grace has set us free from the law, does this mean we can go on sinning? Of course not! 16Don't you realize that whatever you choose to obey becomes your master? You can choose sin, which leads to death, or you can choose to obey God and receive his approval. 17Thank God! Once you were slaves of sin, but now you have obeyed with all your heart the new teaching God has given you. 18Now you are free from sin, your old master,

6:12 Or Do not let sin reign in your body, which is subject to death.

and you have become slaves to your new master, righteousness.

19I speak this way, using the illustration of slaves and masters, because it is easy to understand. Before, you let yourselves be slaves of impurity

---

God's Spirit Will Help You Overcome Sin Read ROMANS 8:9-14

This powerful passage of Scripture contains some critical truths we need to know about letting the Holy Spirit lead our lives. Remember, once you became a Christian, God gave you his Holy Spirit to help you live out your faith, guide your steps, empower your witness, and, as this passage attests, overcome sin. Look at four key points the apostle Paul makes here:

1. You Are Controlled by a New Nature. Your old, sinful nature will still try to get a hand on the steering wheel. But now your new nature is in the driver's seat, and your old nature has become like an annoying backseat driver. You can either give in to your old nature's nagging and bad directions, or you can ignore it and let the Holy Spirit direct your path.

2. Even Though You Will Face Physical Death, You Will Not Face Spiritual Death. As a believer, physical death is simply a transition to eternal life in heaven. You have been spared from spiritual death, which leads to everlasting torment and hell (see Revelation 21:8, p. 1133). This important fact should reassure you when the devil tries to throw doubts your way.

3. The Same Spirit of God That Raised Jesus from the Dead Resides in You. Did you catch that? The Holy Spirit, who had the power to raise Jesus from the dead, now lives in you! If that is indeed true—and God's Word says it is—just think of the supernatural power you now have in your life to resist sin!

4. We Do Not Have to Give In to Our Sinful Nature and Urges. Paul wasn't talking about New Year's resolutions here. If we try to live a morally upright, godly life in our own strength, we will fail—and fail miserably. But, if we rely on the power of the Holy Spirit to help us, we will be overcomers.

To begin the next topic, turn to p. A29.

Our Lives Should Show That God Is at Work in Our Hearts
Read ROMANS 7:4

While we still live on this side of heaven, we will always struggle between the desire to obey God and the desire to follow our sinful instincts. Even the apostle Paul knew what it was like to struggle with sin. In the verses surrounding this text, he describes the six keys to winning this battle and living a life that not only pleases God, but shows that God is working in our heart:

1. Admit the Power of Sin in Your Life (see Romans 7:14, p. 969). Recognize that you have that "combustible nature" within you, a vulnerability to the enticements of sin. If we fail to see our potential weaknesses, we are even more vulnerable to fall to them. The Bible warns against such an attitude, saying, "If you think you are standing strong, be careful, for you too may fall into the same sin" (1 Corinthians 10:12).

2. Realize That You Are Powerless to Change on Your Own (see Romans 7:18, p. 969). Your sinful nature is the source of the problem. You will never "master" sin and live a life pleasing to God on your own. Apart from God, you can do nothing.

3. Become "Fed Up" with Your Condition and Cry for Help (see Romans 7:24, p. 969). You cannot control evil in your life by simply determining to do so. You have to come to the end of yourself and ask for God's help in this struggle.

4. Accept Your Freedom (see Romans 7:25, p. 969). Take the hand of help that is offered to you by Jesus.

5. Accept God's Forgiveness and Lack of Condemnation (see Romans 8:1-2, pp. 969-970). Because of your unique union with Christ, God will forgive you—not condemn you—when you acknowledge your failures, struggles, and broken commitments.

6. Cut the Instinctive Actions of Your Sinful Nature (see Romans 8:3-8, p. 970). The only way to stop committing instinctive sinful actions is to stop living by your sinful nature and start

living by the power of the Holy Spirit. How do you do this? As verse 6 implies, you must relinquish control of your mind to the Spirit. When you do this, you will be "controlled by the Holy Spirit [and] think about things that please the Spirit" (Romans 8:5).

You will always have the potential to sin. But God has given you the power to overcome sin through his Holy Spirit. The key to drawing on his power is to be obedient to the Holy Spirit.

For the next note on "Faith and Works," turn to p. 1088.

CORNER STONES

and lawlessness. Now you must choose to be slaves of righteousness so that you will become holy.

20In those days, when you were slaves of sin, you weren't concerned with doing what was right. 21And what was the result? It was not good, since now you are ashamed of the things you used to do, things that end in eternal doom. 22But now you are free from the power of sin and have become slaves of God. Now you do those things that lead to holiness and result in eternal life. 23For the wages of sin is death, but the free gift of God is eternal life through Christ Jesus our Lord.

7:1 Greek *brothers.*

CHAPTER **7**
No Longer Bound to the Law
Now, dear brothers and sisters*—you who are familiar with the law—don't you know that the law applies only to a person who is still living? 2Let me illustrate. When a woman marries, the law binds her to her husband as long as he is alive. But if he dies, the laws of marriage no longer apply to her. 3So while her husband is alive, she would be committing adultery if she married another man. But if her husband dies, she is free from that law and does not commit adultery when she remarries.

4So this is the point: The law no longer holds

you in its power, because you died to its power when you died with Christ on the cross. And now you are united with the one who was raised from the dead. As a result, you can produce good fruit, that is, good deeds for God. 5When we were controlled by our old nature, sinful desires were at work within us, and the law aroused these evil desires that produced sinful deeds, resulting in death. 6But now we have been released from the law, for we died with Christ, and we are no longer captive to its power. Now we can really serve God, not in the old way by obeying the letter of the law, but in the new way, by the Spirit.

God's Law Reveals Our Sin

7Well then, am I suggesting that the law of God is evil? Of course not! The law is not sinful, but it was the law that showed me my sin. I would never have known that coveting is wrong if the law had not said, "Do not covet."* 8But sin took advantage of this law and aroused all kinds of forbidden desires within me! If there were no law, sin would not have that power.

9I felt fine when I did not understand what the law demanded. But when I learned the truth, I realized I had broken the law and was a sinner, doomed to die. 10So the good law, which was supposed to show me the way of life, instead gave me the death penalty. 11Sin took advantage of the law and fooled me; it took the good law and used it to make me guilty of death. 12But still, the law itself is holy and right and good.

13But how can that be? Did the law, which is good, cause my doom? Of course not! Sin used what was good to bring about my condemnation. So we can see how terrible sin really is. It uses God's good commandment for its own evil purposes.

Struggling with Sin

14The law is good, then. The trouble is not with the law but with me, because I am sold into slavery, with sin as my master. 15I don't understand myself at all, for I really want to do what is right, but I don't do it. Instead, I do the very thing I hate. 16I know perfectly well that what I am doing is wrong, and my bad conscience shows that I agree that the law is good. 17But I can't help myself, because it is sin inside me that makes me do these evil things.

18I know I am rotten through and through so far as my old sinful nature is concerned. No matter which way I turn, I can't make myself do

7:7 Exod 20:17; Deut 5:21.

right. I want to, but I can't. 19When I want to do good, I don't. And when I try not to do wrong, I do it anyway. 20But if I am doing what I don't want to do, I am not really the one doing it; the sin within me is doing it.

21It seems to be a fact of life that when I want to do what is right, I inevitably do what is wrong. 22I love God's law with all my heart. 23But there is another law at work within me that is at war with my mind. This law wins the fight and makes me a slave to the sin that is still within me. 24Oh, what a miserable person I am! Who will free me from this life that is dominated by sin?* 25Thank God! The answer is in Jesus Christ our Lord. So you see how it is: In my mind I really want to obey God's law, but because of my sinful nature I am a slave to sin.

CHAPTER **8**
Life in the Spirit

So now there is no condemnation for those who belong to Christ Jesus. 2For the power* of the life-giving Spirit has freed you* through Christ Jesus

7:24 Greek *from this body of death?*   8:2a Greek *the law;* also in 8:2b.

Prayer Is Not a Solitary Experience Read ROMANS 8:26-27

Have you ever wondered what to say to God? Perhaps you have a sick friend that you don't know how to pray for. Or maybe you are unsure of how to pray for your spiritual needs. This portion of Scripture will encourage you. From the moment you asked Jesus to be your personal Lord and Savior, you received a resident guest in your heart: the Holy Spirit.

One of the many things he does is to help you in prayer—especially at those times when you don't know what to pray. As you realize how intimately God is involved in your prayers, you will begin to feel a unique closeness to your Father in heaven. You may even discover a freshness in your prayer life that you never had before.

The next time you don't know what to pray for, ask the Holy Spirit to help you voice your concerns and needs to God.

For the next note on "Pray," turn to p. 1087.

Live to Please God Read ROMANS 8:5-8

Living to please God may seem like a daunting task. And for some, it is. They struggle to live up to a list of do's and don'ts. They try to obtain God's favor through acts of kindness and compassion. They attempt to "appease" God for their sinful behavior by going to church or making a "confession." But this passage—in fact, this entire chapter in Romans—lets you know that it *is* possible to live a life that is pure and pleasing to God.

The beginning verses of this chapter explain that once we enter into a relationship with Jesus Christ, God frees us from the "vicious circle" of sin and death through the power of his Holy Spirit. This terminology illustrates the basis of our freedom: In essence, the Holy Spirit you received by accepting Jesus Christ into your life has made you a "slave" of Jesus Christ—not a "slave" of your sinful nature.

The apostle Paul often identified himself as a slave of Jesus Christ in his writings. He used the word *doulos,* which means "servant by choice." This word was readily understood by those in the Roman culture. A "doulos," or "bondslave," was a slave who had been granted freedom by his master, but who loved his master so deeply that he voluntarily chose to continue on as that master's servant. Likewise, Paul was not a slave to Christ because he had to be; he was a slave to Christ because he *wanted* to be. He had totally surrendered himself to his Master.

The only way to be free from sin is to be "bound" to Jesus. Unless you completely surrender your life to the Lord, all of your efforts to lead a pure life will be futile. That old sinful nature will continue to rear its ugly head and influence your thoughts and actions. But if you are a bondslave of Jesus, following the leading of the Holy Spirit (verse 5), you will not serve God out of fear and duty but out of love and gratitude. Your service will not be motivated by a desire to earn God's approval but will be motivated by a desire to be close to Jesus, recognizing that you already have that approval because of what Jesus did for you. This "blessed" bondage gives you the will, the power, and the motivation to live a life that is pleasing to God.

To begin the next topic, turn to p. A19.

CORNER STONES

---

from the power of sin that leads to death. ³The law of Moses could not save us, because of our sinful nature. But God put into effect a different plan to save us. He sent his own Son in a human body like ours, except that ours are sinful. God destroyed sin's control over us by giving his Son as a sacrifice for our sins. ⁴He did this so that the requirement of the law would be fully accomplished for us* who no longer follow our sinful nature but instead follow the Spirit.

⁵Those who are dominated by the sinful nature think about sinful things, but those who are controlled by the Holy Spirit think about things that please the Spirit. ⁶If your sinful nature controls your mind, there is death. But if the Holy Spirit controls your mind, there is life and peace. ⁷For the sinful nature is always hostile to God. It never did obey God's laws, and it never will. ⁸That's why those who are still under the control of their sinful nature can never please God.

⁹But you are not controlled by your sinful nature. You are controlled by the Spirit if you have the Spirit of God living in you. (And remember that those who do not have the Spirit of Christ living in them are not Christians at all.) ¹⁰Since Christ lives within you, even though your body will die because of sin, your spirit is alive* because you have been made right with God. ¹¹The Spirit of God, who raised Jesus from the dead, lives in you. And just as he raised Christ from the dead, he will give life to your mortal body by this same Spirit living within you.

¹²So, dear brothers and sisters,* you have no obligation whatsoever to do what your sinful nature urges you to do. ¹³For if you keep on following it, you will perish. But if through the power of the Holy Spirit you turn from it* and

8:2b Some manuscripts read *me.*   8:4 Or *accomplished by us.*   8:10 Or *the Spirit will bring you eternal life.*   8:12 Greek *brothers;* also in 8:29.
8:13 Greek *put it to death.*

its evil deeds, you will live. 14For all who are led by the Spirit of God are children* of God.

15So you should not be like cowering, fearful slaves. You should behave instead like God's very own children, adopted into his family*— calling him "Father, dear Father."* 16For his Holy Spirit speaks to us deep in our hearts and tells us that we are God's children. 17And since we are his children, we will share his treasures— for everything God gives to his Son, Christ, is ours, too. But if we are to share his glory, we must also share his suffering.

The Future Glory

18Yet what we suffer now is nothing compared to the glory he will give us later. 19For all creation is waiting eagerly for that future day when God will reveal who his children really are. 20Against its will, everything on earth was subjected to God's curse. 21All creation anticipates the day when it will join God's children in glorious freedom from death and decay. 22For we know that all creation has been groaning as in the pains of childbirth right up to the present time. 23And even we Christians, although we have the Holy Spirit within us as a foretaste of future glory, also groan to be released from pain and suffering. We, too, wait anxiously for that day when God will give us our full rights as his children,* including the new bodies he has promised us. 24Now that we are saved, we eagerly look forward to this freedom. For if you already have something, you don't need to hope for it. 25But if we look forward to something we don't have yet, we must wait patiently and confidently.

26And the Holy Spirit helps us in our distress. For we don't even know what we should pray for, nor how we should pray. But the Holy Spirit prays for us with groanings that cannot be expressed in words. 27And the Father who knows all hearts knows what the Spirit is saying, for the Spirit pleads for us believers in harmony with God's own will. 28And we know that God causes everything to work together* for the good of those who love God and are called according to his purpose for them. 29For God knew his people in advance, and he chose them to become like his Son, so that his Son would be the firstborn, with many brothers and sisters. 30And having chosen them, he called them to come to

8:14 Greek *sons;* also in 8:19.   8:15a Greek *You received a spirit of sonship.*   8:15b Greek *"Abba, Father." Abba* is an Aramaic term for "father."   8:23 Greek *wait anxiously for sonship.*   8:28 Some manuscripts read *And we know that everything works together.*

Unconditionally Surrender Your Life Read ROMANS 12:1-2

This passage of Scripture is what we call a conditional promise. The last part of verse 2 contains the promise. Yet if we want to discover God's perfect will for our lives, we must meet the three conditions mentioned at the beginning of these verses.

1. We Must Present Ourselves to God as Living Sacrifices. We need to recognize that we, as Christians, belong to God. The Bible tells us that we no longer own our bodies because Christ paid for them when he died on the cross (see 1 Corinthians 6:19b-20, p. 990). Because our bodies belong to him, we must refrain from sinning. This is what is meant by living sacrifice—putting aside our own will and replacing it with God's.

2. We Must Not Be Conformed to This World. The next step to prepare our hearts to know the will of God is to keep from copying "the behavior and customs of this world." When the Bible speaks of the "world," it is not referring to the earth. Rather it is speaking of the mentality and thinking of the times—the spiritually bankrupt mind-set that is hostile toward the things of God and primarily focuses on mankind's own selfish desires.

3. We Must Be Transformed by the Renewing of Our Minds. One of the best ways to become "a new and different person" is to literally saturate your mind and heart with those things that spiritually build you up. You can do this by studying God's Word, singing hymns and praises, spending time in prayer, and fellowshiping with other believers. As the apostle Paul tells us, "Fix your thoughts on what is true and honorable and right. Think about things that are pure and lovely and admirable. Think about things that are excellent and worthy of praise" (Philippians 4:8).

As we take these preliminary steps, we will be able to more accurately discern the will of God for our lives.

For the next note on "Seek God's Will," turn to p. 647.

For the next note on "Seek God's Will," turn to p. 647.

him. And he gave them right standing with himself, and he promised them his glory.

Nothing Can Separate Us from God's Love

³¹What can we say about such wonderful things as these? If God is for us, who can ever be against us? ³²Since God did not spare even his own Son but gave him up for us all, won't God, who gave us Christ, also give us everything else?

³³Who dares accuse us whom God has chosen for his own? Will God? No! He is the one who has given us right standing with himself. ³⁴Who then will condemn us? Will Christ Jesus? No, for he is the one who died for us and was raised to life for us and is sitting at the place of highest honor next to God, pleading for us.

³⁵Can anything ever separate us from Christ's love? Does it mean he no longer loves us if we have trouble or calamity, or are persecuted, or are hungry or cold or in danger or threatened with death? ³⁶(Even the Scriptures say, "For your sake we are killed every day; we are being slaughtered like sheep."*) ³⁷No, despite all these things, overwhelming victory is ours through Christ, who loved us.

³⁸And I am convinced that nothing can ever separate us from his love. Death can't, and life can't. The angels can't, and the demons can't. Our fears for today, our worries about tomorrow, and even the powers of hell can't keep God's love away. ³⁹Whether we are high above the sky or in the deepest ocean, nothing in all creation will ever be able to separate us from the love of God that is revealed in Christ Jesus our Lord.

CHAPTER **9**
God's Selection of Israel

In the presence of Christ, I speak with utter truthfulness—I do not lie—and my conscience and the Holy Spirit confirm that what I am saying is true. ²My heart is filled with bitter sorrow and unending grief ³for my people, my Jewish brothers and sisters.* I would be willing to be forever cursed—cut off from Christ!—if that would save them. ⁴They are the people of Israel, chosen to be God's special children.* God revealed his glory to them. He made covenants with them and gave his law to them. They have the privilege of worshiping him and receiving his wonderful promises. ⁵Their ancestors were great people of God, and Christ himself was a Jew as far as his human nature is concerned. And he is God, who rules over everything and is worthy of eternal praise! Amen.*

⁶Well then, has God failed to fulfill his promise to the Jews? No, for not everyone born into a Jewish family is truly a Jew! ⁷Just the fact that they are descendants of Abraham doesn't make them truly Abraham's children. For the Scriptures say, "Isaac is the son through whom your descendants will be counted,"* though Abraham had other children, too. ⁸This means that Abraham's physical descendants are not necessarily children of God. It is the children of the promise who are considered to be Abraham's children. ⁹For God had promised, "Next year I will return, and Sarah will have a son."*

¹⁰This son was our ancestor Isaac. When he grew up, he married Rebekah, who gave birth to twins. ¹¹But before they were born, before they had done anything good or bad, she received a message from God. (This message proves that God chooses according to his own plan, ¹²not according to our good or bad works.) She was told, "The descendants of your older son will serve the descendants of your younger son."* ¹³In the words of the Scriptures, "I loved Jacob, but I rejected Esau."*

8:36 Ps 44:22.   9:3 Greek *my brothers.*   9:4 Greek *chosen for sonship.*   9:5 Or *May God, who rules over everything, be praised forever. Amen.*
9:7 Gen 21:12.   9:9 Gen 18:10, 14.   9:12 Gen 25:23.   9:13 Mal 1:2-3.

OFF AND RUNNING ◢◢◢◢
Keep Your Spiritual Zeal Alive Read ROMANS 12:11

This verse not only encourages us to keep our zeal for God alive, but it commands us to do so. Another meaning of the phrase "serve the Lord enthusiastically" is to have a burning heart for God. The importance of this is seen in the book of Revelation. There Jesus warned the church in Laodicea that they were in danger of being "spit . . . out of [his] mouth" because they were lukewarm (Revelation 3:15-16). In essence, they had lost the fire of their spiritual zeal and were an offense to Christ. Therefore, Jesus told them to repent or he would reject them.

So what can be done to keep our spiritual zeal alive? We can keep our spiritual fire fueled by spending time

14What can we say? Was God being unfair? Of course not! 15For God said to Moses,

"I will show mercy to anyone I choose,
and I will show compassion to anyone I choose."*

16So receiving God's promise is not up to us. We can't get it by choosing it or working hard for it. God will show mercy to anyone he chooses.

17For the Scriptures say that God told Pharaoh, "I have appointed you for the very purpose of displaying my power in you, and so that my fame might spread throughout the earth."* 18So you see, God shows mercy to some just because he wants to, and he chooses to make some people refuse to listen.

19Well then, you might say, "Why does God blame people for not listening? Haven't they simply done what he made them do?"

20No, don't say that. Who are you, a mere human being, to criticize God? Should the thing that was created say to the one who made it, "Why have you made me like this?" 21When a potter makes jars out of clay, doesn't he have a right to use the same lump of clay to make one jar for decoration and another to throw garbage into? 22God has every right to exercise his judgment and his power, but he also has the right to be very patient with those who are the objects of his judgment and are fit only for destruction. 23He also has the right to pour out the riches of his glory upon those he prepared to be the objects of his mercy—24even upon us, whom he selected, both from the Jews and from the Gentiles.

25Concerning the Gentiles, God says in the prophecy of Hosea,

"Those who were not my people,
I will now call my people.
And I will love those
whom I did not love before."*

26And,

"Once they were told,
'You are not my people.'
But now he will say,
'You are children of the living God.'*"

27Concerning Israel, Isaiah the prophet cried out,

"Though the people of Israel are as
numerous as the sand on the
seashore,
only a small number will be saved.
28 For the Lord will carry out his sentence
upon the earth
quickly and with finality."*

29And Isaiah said in another place,

"If the Lord Almighty
had not spared a few of us,
we would have been wiped out
as completely as Sodom and
Gomorrah."*

Israel's Unbelief

30Well then, what shall we say about these things? Just this: The Gentiles have been made right with God by faith, even though they were not seeking him. 31But the Jews, who tried so hard to get right with God by keeping the law, never succeeded. 32Why not? Because they were trying to get right with God by keeping the law and being good instead of by depending on faith. They stumbled over the great rock in their path. 33God warned them of this in the Scriptures when he said,

9:15 Exod 33:19.   9:17 Exod 9:16.   9:25 Hos 2:23.   9:26 Greek *You are sons of the living God.* Hos 1:10.   9:27-28 Isa 10:22-23.   9:29 Isa 1:9.

with God's people in fellowship and prayer. We can also feed the fire with constant input from God's Word. As two discouraged disciples realized, listening to the words of Jesus can rekindle a person's zeal for God: "They said to each other, 'Didn't our hearts feel strangely warm as he talked with us on the road and explained the Scriptures to us?'" (Luke 24:32).

What is your spiritual temperature? Are you passionate about the Lord you serve? Do you make the most of every opportunity to tell others about Jesus? The English evangelist John Wesley once said, "Give me a hundred men who love God with all of their hearts and fear nothing but sin, and I will move the world." If you are aglow with the Spirit, serving the Lord with zeal and enthusiasm, your life *will* make a difference.

To begin the next topic, turn to p. A35.

Our Peace Continues As We Follow the Holy Spirit Read ROMANS 8:5-8

Even if you are a Christian, you still must struggle with your sinful nature. However, if you allow God's Holy Spirit to control your life, that struggle will be much less intense. For, as this passage says, you will want to live to please God.

If you follow your old evil desires, you "can never please God" (verse 8). Your life—whether you realize it or not—will be empty. But if you live the Spirit-controlled life, you will experience "life and peace" (verse 6). To enter into the Spirit-controlled life, follow the advice of the apostle Paul, "Let heaven fill your thoughts. Do not think only about things down here on earth. For you died when Christ died, and your real life is hidden with Christ in God" (Colossians 3:2-3).

For the next note on "Peace," turn to p. 528.

CORNER STONES

"I am placing a stone in Jerusalem* that
  causes people to stumble,
and a rock that makes them fall.*
But anyone who believes in him
  will not be disappointed.*"

CHAPTER **10**

Dear brothers and sisters,* the longing of my heart and my prayer to God is that the Jewish people might be saved. 2I know what enthusiasm they have for God, but it is misdirected zeal. 3For they don't understand God's way of making people right with himself. Instead, they are clinging to their own way of getting right with God by trying to keep the law. They won't go along with God's way. 4For Christ has accomplished the whole purpose* of the law. All who believe in him are made right with God.

Salvation Is for Everyone

5For Moses wrote that the law's way of making a person right with God requires obedience to all of its commands.* 6But the way of getting right with God through faith says, "You don't need to go to heaven" (to find Christ and bring him down to help you). 7And it says, "You don't need to go to the place of the dead" (to bring Christ back to life again). 8Salvation that comes from trusting Christ—which is the message we preach—is already within easy reach. In fact, the Scriptures say, "The message is close at hand; it is on your lips and in your heart."* 9For if you confess with your mouth that Jesus is Lord and believe in your heart that God raised him from the dead, you will be saved.

10For it is by believing in your heart that you are made right with God, and it is by confessing with your mouth that you are saved. 11As the Scriptures tell us, "Anyone who believes in him will not be disappointed."* 12Jew and Gentile are the same in this respect. They all have the same Lord, who generously gives his riches to all who ask for them. 13For "Anyone who calls on the name of the Lord will be saved."*

14But how can they call on him to save them unless they believe in him? And how can they believe in him if they have never heard about him? And how can they hear about him unless someone tells them? 15And how will anyone go and tell them without being sent? That is what the Scriptures mean when they say, "How beautiful are the feet of those who bring good news!"*

16But not everyone welcomes the Good News, for Isaiah the prophet said, "Lord, who has believed our message?"* 17Yet faith comes from listening to this message of good news—the Good News about Christ.

18But what about the Jews? Have they actually heard the message? Yes, they have:

"The message of God's creation has gone
    out to everyone,
  and its words to all the world."*

19But did the people of Israel really understand? Yes, they did, for even in the time of Moses, God had said,

"I will rouse your jealousy by blessing other
    nations.
  I will make you angry by blessing the
    foolish Gentiles."*

9:33a Greek *in Zion.* 9:33b Isa 8:14. 9:33c Or *will not be put to shame.* Isa 28:16. 10:1 Greek *Brothers.* 10:4 Or *the end.* 10:5 Lev 18:5. 10:6-8 Deut 30:12-14. 10:11 Or *will not be put to shame.* Isa 28:16. 10:13 Joel 2:32. 10:15 Isa 52:7. 10:16 Isa 53:1. 10:18 Ps 19:4. 10:19 Deut 32:21.

How Should I View Authority? Read ROMANS 13:1-2

When dealing with the subject of authority—particularly how one should act toward those in the government—the Bible gives us some important things to consider.

God Raises Up Rulers. It is true that not every government official has been obedient to God. In fact, far too many have directly violated his Word. Yet God has allowed certain people to rule for his purposes. In the Old Testament God often allowed certain "evil" countries to come to power in order to punish Israel for their wrongdoing and to remind them of their need to return to God. Therefore, we need to respect those in authority, since God has divinely appointed them.

God Uses Those in Government Who Fear Him. While God is ultimately in control of every event that takes place in the world, he still uses his people in strategic positions of power. When Queen Esther, a Jew, faced the prospect of seeing her people put to death, her Uncle Mordecai challenged her with these words: "If you keep quiet at a time like this, deliverance for the Jews will arise from some other place, but you and your relatives will die. What's more, who can say but that you have been elevated to the palace for just such a time as this" (Esther 4:14)? Certainly, God does not forbid us to be part of the political process. Sometimes he will even use Christians in government to accomplish his purposes.

We Are to Be a Witness to Those in Authority. Your obedience to the laws of the land serves as a witness to the God you serve. Peter, addressing the early Christians who were suffering persecution under the cruel tyranny of Nero, still challenged believers to be law-abiding citizens (see 1 Peter 2:13-15, p. 1093).

Our Allegiance to God Should Always Come First. What about those times when a law or government does something that directly contradicts God's law? We are accountable to a higher authority. In the Old Testament we read how Daniel defied the king's decree that forbade people to pray to anyone but him (see Daniel 6:1-28, pp. 725-727). Daniel knew that God had said to worship him alone, so he obeyed God's law instead of man's. As you may recall, he was sent to the lions' den, but God spared his life by shutting the lions' mouths. In the New Testament, Peter told the high priest, when he had been warned not to talk about Jesus, "We must obey God rather than human authority" (Acts 5:29). In more recent times, Christians in Communist and Muslim countries continue to share Christ and distribute Bibles, despite laws that make such actions illegal.

Perhaps the best approach to those in authority over us is to follow the advice found in 1 Peter 2:17: "Fear God. Show respect for the king." Here we see a perfect balance, for as we fear God in our daily lives, we will live above reproach and be examples to those in authority. At the same time, we will be able to discern when human laws contradict the divine laws established by God.

For the next "Big Question" note, turn to p. 987.

BIG QUESTIONS?

20And later Isaiah spoke boldly for God:

"I was found by people
  who were not looking for me.
I showed myself to those
  who were not asking for me."*

21But regarding Israel, God said,

"All day long I opened my arms to them,
  but they kept disobeying me and arguing
  with me."*

10:20 Isa 65:1. 10:21 Isa 65:2.

CHAPTER 11
God's Mercy on Israel

I ask, then, has God rejected his people, the Jews? Of course not! Remember that I myself am a Jew, a descendant of Abraham and a member of the tribe of Benjamin.

2No, God has not rejected his own people, whom he chose from the very beginning. Do you remember what the Scriptures say about this? Elijah the prophet complained to God about the people of Israel and said, 3 "Lord, they have killed your prophets and torn down your altars. I alone am left, and now they are trying to kill me, too."*

4And do you remember God's reply? He said, "You are not the only one left. I have seven thousand others who have never bowed down to Baal!"*

5It is the same today, for not all the Jews have turned away from God. A few* are being saved as a result of God's kindness in choosing them. 6And if they are saved by God's kindness, then it is not by their good works. For in that case, God's wonderful kindness would not be what it really is—free and undeserved.

7So this is the situation: Most of the Jews have not found the favor of God they are looking for so earnestly. A few have—the ones God has chosen—but the rest were made unresponsive. 8As the Scriptures say,

"God has put them into a deep sleep.
To this very day he has shut their eyes so
 they do not see,
 and closed their ears so they do not hear."*

9David spoke of this same thing when he said,

"Let their bountiful table become a snare,
 a trap that makes them think all is well.
 Let their blessings cause them to stumble.
10 Let their eyes go blind so they cannot see,
 and let their backs grow weaker and
 weaker."*

11Did God's people stumble and fall beyond recovery? Of course not! His purpose was to make his salvation available to the Gentiles, and then the Jews would be jealous and want it for themselves. 12Now if the Gentiles were enriched because the Jews turned down God's offer of salvation, think how much greater a blessing the world will share when the Jews finally accept it.

13I am saying all of this especially for you Gentiles. God has appointed me as the apostle to the Gentiles. I lay great stress on this, 14for I want to find a way to make the Jews want what you Gentiles have, and in that way I might save some of them. 15For since the Jews' rejection meant that God offered salvation to the rest of the world, how much more wonderful their acceptance will be. It will be life for those who were dead! 16And since Abraham and the other patriarchs were holy, their children will also be holy.* For if the roots of the tree are holy, the branches will be, too.

17But some of these branches from Abraham's tree, some of the Jews, have been broken off. And you Gentiles, who were branches from a wild olive tree, were grafted in. So now you also receive the blessing God has promised Abraham and his children, sharing in God's rich nourishment of his special olive tree. 18But you must be careful not to brag about being grafted in to replace the branches that were broken off. Remember, you are just a branch, not the root.

19"Well," you may say, "those branches were broken off to make room for me." 20Yes, but remember—those branches, the Jews, were broken off because they didn't believe God, and you are there because you do believe. Don't think highly of yourself, but fear what could happen. 21For if God did not spare the branches he put there in the first place, he won't spare you either.

22Notice how God is both kind and severe. He is severe to those who disobeyed, but kind to you as you continue to trust in his kindness. But if you stop trusting, you also will be cut off. 23And if the Jews turn from their unbelief, God will graft them back into the tree again. He has the power to do it.

24For if God was willing to take you who were, by nature, branches from a wild olive tree and graft you into his own good tree—a very unusual thing to do—he will be far more eager to graft the Jews back into the tree where they belong.

God's Mercy Is for Everyone

25I want you to understand this mystery, dear brothers and sisters,* so that you will not feel proud and start bragging. Some of the Jews have hard hearts, but this will last only until the complete number of Gentiles comes to Christ. 26And so all Israel will be saved. Do you remember what the prophets said about this?

"A Deliverer will come from Jerusalem,*
 and he will turn Israel* from all ungodliness.
27 And then I will keep my covenant with them
 and take away their sins."*

28Many of the Jews are now enemies of the Good News. But this has been to your benefit, for God has given his gifts to you Gentiles. Yet the Jews are still his chosen people because of his promises to Abraham, Isaac, and Jacob. 29For God's gifts and his call can never be withdrawn. 30Once, you Gentiles were rebels against God, but when the Jews refused his mercy, God was merciful to you instead.

11:3 1 Kgs 19:10, 14.   11:4 1 Kgs 19:18.   11:5 Greek *A remnant.*   11:8 Deut 29:4; Isa 29:10.   11:9-10 Ps 69:22-23.   11:16 Greek *If the dough offered as firstfruits is holy, so is the whole lump.*   11:25 Greek *brothers.*   11:26a Greek *from Zion.*   11:26b Greek *Jacob.*   11:26-27 Isa 59:20-21.

31And now, in the same way, the Jews are the rebels, and God's mercy has come to you. But someday they,* too, will share in God's mercy. 32For God has imprisoned all people in their own disobedience so he could have mercy on everyone.

33Oh, what a wonderful God we have! How great are his riches and wisdom and knowledge! How impossible it is for us to understand his decisions and his methods! 34For who can know what the Lord is thinking? Who knows enough to be his counselor?* 35And who could ever give him so much that he would have to pay it back? 36For everything comes from him; everything exists by his power and is intended for his glory. To him be glory evermore. Amen.

CHAPTER **12**
A Living Sacrifice to God
And so, dear brothers and sisters,* I plead with you to give your bodies to God. Let them be a living and holy sacrifice—the kind he will accept. When you think of what he has done for you, is this too much to ask? 2Don't copy the behavior and customs of this world, but let God transform you into a new person by changing the way you think. Then you will know what God wants you to do, and you will know how good and pleasing and perfect his will really is.

3As God's messenger, I give each of you this warning: Be honest in your estimate of yourselves, measuring your value by how much faith God has given you. 4Just as our bodies have many parts and each part has a special function, 5so it is with Christ's body. We are all parts of his one body, and each of us has different work to do. And since we are all one body in Christ, we belong to each other, and each of us needs all the others.

6God has given each of us the ability to do certain things well. So if God has given you the ability to prophesy, speak out when you have faith that God is speaking through you. 7If your gift is that of serving others, serve them well. If you are a teacher, do a good job of teaching. 8If your gift is to encourage others, do it! If you have money, share it generously. If God has given you leadership ability, take the responsibility seriously. And if you have a gift for showing kindness to others, do it gladly.

9Don't just pretend that you love others. Really love them. Hate what is wrong. Stand on the side of the good. 10Love each other with

genuine affection,* and take delight in honoring each other. 11Never be lazy in your work, but serve the Lord enthusiastically.

12Be glad for all God is planning for you. Be patient in trouble, and always be prayerful. 13When God's children are in need, be the one to help them out. And get into the habit of inviting guests home for dinner or, if they need lodging, for the night.

14If people persecute you because you are a Christian, don't curse them; pray that God will

Put on God's Armor
Read ROMANS 13:11-14

Another way the last verse of this text has been translated is "Be Christ's men from head to foot, and give no chances to the flesh to have its fling." In other words, we need to "clothe ourselves" with Christ. To do this, you need to let him be a part of everything that you do. Let him go with you everywhere you go. Let him act through you in every decision you make. Remember these three simple truths as you strive to obey Christ:

1. Time Is Short. Jesus Christ will return soon, and we need to be the best possible witness for him that we can be.

2. Live in the Light. As Ephesians 5:8 says, "For though your hearts were once full of darkness, now you are full of light from the Lord, and your behavior should show it!" The more you live in God's light, the less you will want to be influenced by the darkness of the world around you.

3. Rely upon Christ for Your Strength. You will never be able to stand against the temptations of life on your own. As you follow Christ and his example, you will find it much easier to avoid spiritual pitfalls. As it has been said, "The best defense is a good offense."

Some people want to put God in a little compartment. They will worship God from nine to eleven on Sunday morning, but the rest of the week is theirs. That is not the Christian life. As true followers of Jesus Christ, we need to be identified with our Master twenty-four hours a day, seven days a week, for the rest of our lives.

For the next note on "Obey God," *turn to p. 1041.*

11:31 Some manuscripts read *But now they;* other manuscripts read *But they.*   **11:34** See Isa 40:13.   **12:1** Greek *brothers.*
12:10 Greek *with brotherly love.*

bless them. 15When others are happy, be happy with them. If they are sad, share their sorrow. 16Live in harmony with each other. Don't try to act important, but enjoy the company of ordinary people. And don't think you know it all!

17Never pay back evil for evil to anyone. Do things in such a way that everyone can see you are honorable. 18Do your part to live in peace with everyone, as much as possible.

19Dear friends, never avenge yourselves. Leave that to God. For it is written,

"I will take vengeance;
   I will repay those who deserve it,"*
says the Lord.

20Instead, do what the Scriptures say:

"If your enemies are hungry, feed them.
If they are thirsty, give them something to
   drink,
   and they will be ashamed of what they
      have done to you."*

21Don't let evil get the best of you, but conquer evil by doing good.

CHAPTER 13
Respect for Authority

Obey the government, for God is the one who put it there. All governments have been placed in power by God. 2So those who refuse to obey the laws of the land are refusing to obey God, and punishment will follow. 3For the authorities do not frighten people who are doing right, but they frighten those who do wrong. So do what they say, and you will get along well. 4The authorities are sent by God to help you. But if you are doing something wrong, of course you should be afraid, for you will be punished. The authorities are established by God for that very purpose, to punish those who do wrong. 5So you must obey the government for two reasons: to keep from being punished and to keep a clear conscience.

6Pay your taxes, too, for these same reasons. For government workers need to be paid so they can keep on doing the work God intended them to do. 7Give to everyone what you owe them: Pay your taxes and import duties, and give respect and honor to all to whom it is due.

Love Fulfills God's Requirements

8Pay all your debts, except the debt of love for others. You can never finish paying that! If you love your neighbor, you will fulfill all the requirements of God's law. 9For the commandments against adultery and murder and stealing and coveting—and any other commandment— are all summed up in this one commandment: "Love your neighbor as yourself."* 10Love does no wrong to anyone, so love satisfies all of God's requirements.

11Another reason for right living is that you know how late it is; time is running out. Wake up, for the coming of our salvation is nearer now than when we first believed. 12The night is almost gone; the day of salvation will soon be here. So don't live in darkness. Get rid of your evil deeds. Shed them like dirty clothes. Clothe yourselves with the armor of right living, as those who live in the light. 13We should be decent and true in everything we do, so that everyone can approve of our behavior. Don't participate in wild parties and getting drunk, or in adultery and immoral living, or in fighting and jealousy. 14But let the Lord Jesus Christ take control of you, and don't think of ways to indulge your evil desires.

CHAPTER 14
The Danger of Criticism

Accept Christians who are weak in faith, and don't argue with them about what they think is right or wrong. 2For instance, one person believes it is all right to eat anything. But another believer who has a sensitive conscience will eat only vegetables. 3Those who think it is all right to eat anything must not look down on those who won't. And those who won't eat certain foods must not condemn those who do, for God

12:19 Deut 32:35.   12:20 Greek *and you will heap burning coals on their heads.* Prov 25:21-22.   13:9 Lev 19:18.

OFF AND RUNNING ▰▰▰▰▰

Could This Activity Cause Other Christians to Stumble in Their Faith? Read ROMANS 14:15

Don't do anything that will bring criticism against yourself, even if you know that a certain activity is all right. What we do and become has a direct effect on others—not only for our

has accepted them. 4Who are you to condemn God's servants? They are responsible to the Lord, so let him tell them whether they are right or wrong. The Lord's power will help them do as they should.

5In the same way, some think one day is more holy than another day, while others think every day is alike. Each person should have a personal conviction about this matter. 6Those who have a special day for worshiping the Lord are trying to honor him. Those who eat all kinds of food do so to honor the Lord, since they give thanks to God before eating. And those who won't eat everything also want to please the Lord and give thanks to God. 7For we are not our own masters when we live or when we die. 8While we live, we live to please the Lord. And when we die, we go to be with the Lord. So in life and in death, we belong to the Lord. 9Christ died and rose again for this very purpose, so that he might be Lord of those who are alive and of those who have died.

10So why do you condemn another Christian*? Why do you look down on another Christian? Remember, each of us will stand personally before the judgment seat of God. 11For the Scriptures say,

" 'As surely as I live,' says the Lord,
'every knee will bow to me
    and every tongue will confess allegiance
        to God.' "*

12Yes, each of us will have to give a personal account to God. 13So don't condemn each other anymore. Decide instead to live in such a way that you will not put an obstacle in another Christian's path.

14I know and am perfectly sure on the authority of the Lord Jesus that no food, in and of itself, is wrong to eat. But if someone believes it is wrong, then for that person it is wrong. 15And if another Christian is distressed by what you eat, you are not acting in love if you eat it. Don't let your eating ruin someone for whom Christ died.

16Then you will not be condemned for doing something you know is all right.

17For the Kingdom of God is not a matter of what we eat or drink, but of living a life of goodness and peace and joy in the Holy Spirit. 18If you serve Christ with this attitude, you will please God. And other people will approve of you, too. 19So then, let us aim for harmony in the church and try to build each other up.

20Don't tear apart the work of God over what you eat. Remember, there is nothing wrong with these things in themselves. But it is wrong to eat anything if it makes another person stumble. 21Don't eat meat or drink wine or do anything else if it might cause another Christian to stumble. 22You may have the faith to believe that there is nothing wrong with what you are doing, but keep it between yourself and God. Blessed are those who do not condemn themselves by doing something they know is all right. 23But if people have doubts about whether they should eat something, they shouldn't eat it. They would be condemned for not acting in faith before God. If you do anything you believe is not right, you are sinning.

CHAPTER **15**

Living to Please Others

We may know that these things make no difference, but we cannot just go ahead and do them to please ourselves. We must be considerate of the doubts and fears of those who think these things are wrong. 2We should please others. If we do what helps them, we will build them up in the Lord. 3For even Christ didn't please himself. As the Scriptures say, "Those who insult you are also insulting me."* 4Such things were written in the Scriptures long ago to teach us. They give us hope and encouragement as we wait patiently for God's promises.

5May God, who gives this patience and encouragement, help you live in complete harmony with each other—each with the attitude of Christ Jesus toward the other. 6Then all of you can join

14:10 Greek *your brother*; also in 14:10b, 13, 15, 21.   **14:11** Isa 45:23.   **15:3** Ps 69:9.

---

life here on this earth, but also for eternity. We not only need to live our lives conscious of God's opinion, but we also need to live our lives with consideration for others. We do not want to do anything that has the potential of causing another Christian brother or sister to stumble or fall.

To begin the next topic, turn to p. A38.

together with one voice, giving praise and glory to God, the Father of our Lord Jesus Christ.

7So accept each other just as Christ has accepted you; then God will be glorified. 8Remember that Christ came as a servant to the Jews to show that God is true to the promises he made to their ancestors. 9And he came so the Gentiles might also give glory to God for his mercies to them. That is what the psalmist meant when he wrote:

"I will praise you among the Gentiles;
I will sing praises to your name."*

10And in another place it is written,

"Rejoice, O you Gentiles,
along with his people, the Jews."*

11And yet again,

"Praise the Lord, all you Gentiles;
praise him, all you people of the earth."*

12And the prophet Isaiah said,

"The heir to David's throne* will come,
and he will rule over the Gentiles.
They will place their hopes on him."*

13So I pray that God, who gives you hope, will keep you happy and full of peace as you believe in him. May you overflow with hope through the power of the Holy Spirit.

Paul's Reason for Writing

14I am fully convinced, dear brothers and sisters,* that you are full of goodness. You know these things so well that you are able to teach others all about them. 15Even so, I have been bold enough to emphasize some of these points, knowing that all you need is this reminder from me. For I am, by God's grace, 16a special messenger from Christ Jesus to you Gentiles. I bring you the Good News and offer you up as a fragrant sacrifice to God so that you might be pure and pleasing to him by the

Holy Spirit. 17So it is right for me to be enthusiastic about all Christ Jesus has done through me in my service to God. 18I dare not boast of anything else. I have brought the Gentiles to God by my message and by the way I lived before them. 19I have won them over by the miracles done through me as signs from God—all by the power of God's Spirit. In this way, I have fully presented the Good News of Christ all the way from Jerusalem clear over into Illyricum.*

20My ambition has always been to preach the Good News where the name of Christ has never been heard, rather than where a church has already been started by someone else. 21I have been following the plan spoken of in the Scriptures, where it says,

"Those who have never been told about
him will see,
and those who have never heard of him
will understand."*

22In fact, my visit to you has been delayed so long because I have been preaching in these places.

Paul's Travel Plans

23But now I have finished my work in these regions, and after all these long years of waiting, I am eager to visit you. 24I am planning to go to Spain, and when I do, I will stop off in Rome. And after I have enjoyed your fellowship for a little while, you can send me on my way again.

25But before I come, I must go down to Jerusalem to take a gift to the Christians there. 26For you see, the believers in Greece* have eagerly taken up an offering for the Christians in Jerusalem, who are going through such hard times. 27They were very glad to do this because they feel they owe a real debt to them. Since the Gentiles received the wonderful spiritual blessings of the Good News from the Jewish Christians, they feel the least they can do in return is help them financially. 28As soon as I have deliv-

15:9 Ps 18:49.   15:10 Deut 32:43.   15:11 Ps 117:1.   15:12a Greek *The root of Jesse.*   15:12b Isa 11:10.   15:14 Greek *brothers;* also in 15:30.   15:19 *Illyricum* was a region northeast of Italy.   15:21 Isa 52:15.   15:26 Greek *Macedonia and Achaia,* the northern and southern regions of Greece.

OFF AND RUNNING

Do I Have an Uneasy Conscience about This Activity?

Read ROMANS 14:23

When it comes to participating in questionable activities, it is easy to rationalize joining in because others are doing it. Yet this verse places the responsibility of your choice squarely on your shoulders. You may protest and say, "Well, so-and-so is doing it!" But you are not that person. You must be obedient to what God tells *you* to do.

ered this money and completed this good deed of theirs, I will come to see you on my way to Spain. 29And I am sure that when I come, Christ will give me a great blessing for you.

30Dear brothers and sisters, I urge you in the name of our Lord Jesus Christ to join me in my struggle by praying to God for me. Do this because of your love for me, given to you by the Holy Spirit. 31Pray that I will be rescued from those in Judea who refuse to obey God. Pray also that the Christians there will be willing to accept the donation I am bringing them. 32Then, by the will of God, I will be able to come to you with a happy heart, and we will be an encouragement to each other.

33And now may God, who gives us his peace, be with you all. Amen.

CHAPTER **16**
Paul Greets His Friends
Our sister Phoebe, a deacon in the church in Cenchrea, will be coming to see you soon. 2Receive her in the Lord, as one who is worthy of high honor. Help her in every way you can, for she has helped many in their needs, including me.

3Greet Priscilla and Aquila. They have been co-workers in my ministry for Christ Jesus. 4In fact, they risked their lives for me. I am not the only one who is thankful to them; so are all the Gentile churches. 5Please give my greetings to the church that meets in their home.

Greet my dear friend Epenetus. He was the very first person to become a Christian in the province of Asia. 6Give my greetings to Mary, who has worked so hard for your benefit. 7Then there are Andronicus and Junia,* my relatives,* who were in prison with me. They are respected among the apostles and became Christians before I did. Please give them my greetings. 8Say hello to Ampliatus, whom I love as one of the

Lord's own children, 9and Urbanus, our co-worker in Christ, and beloved Stachys.

10Give my greetings to Apelles, a good man whom Christ approves. And give my best regards to the members of the household of Aristobulus. 11Greet Herodion, my relative.* Greet the Christians in the household of Narcissus. 12Say hello to Tryphena and Tryphosa, the Lord's workers, and to dear Persis, who has worked so hard for the Lord. 13Greet Rufus, whom the Lord picked out to be his very own; and also his dear mother, who has been a mother to me.

14And please give my greetings to Asyncritus, Phlegon, Hermes, Patrobas, Hermas, and the brothers and sisters* who are with them. 15Give my greetings to Philologus, Julia, Nereus and his sister, and to Olympas and all the other believers who are with them. 16Greet each other in Christian love.* All the churches of Christ send you their greetings.

Paul's Final Instructions
17And now I make one more appeal, my dear brothers and sisters. Watch out for people who cause divisions and upset people's faith by teaching things that are contrary to what you have been taught. Stay away from them. 18Such people are not serving Christ our Lord; they are serving their own personal interests. By smooth talk and glowing words they deceive innocent people. 19But everyone knows that you are obedient to the Lord. This makes me very happy. I want you to see clearly what is right and to stay innocent of any wrong. 20The God of peace will soon crush Satan under your feet. May the grace of our Lord Jesus Christ be with you.

21Timothy, my fellow worker, and Lucius, Jason, and Sosipater, my relatives, send you their good wishes.

22I, Tertius, the one who is writing this letter for Paul, send my greetings, too, as a Christian brother.

16:7a Or *Junias;* some manuscripts read *Julia.* **16:7b** Or *compatriots;* also in 16:21. **16:11** Or *compatriot.* **16:14** Greek *brothers;* also in 16:17. **16:16** Greek *with a sacred kiss.*

How do you know when you should not participate in a certain activity? God's Holy Spirit will often give you an uneasy conscience about something you should not be doing. For example, you may have a sense that you are in the wrong place, with the wrong people, about to do the wrong thing. Or, you may have a lack of peace in your heart about an activity in which you are participating. When this happens, it is up to you to pay attention to your conscience and follow through by being obedient to God.

For the next note on "Responsibility," turn to p. 978.

Knowing Whom You Belong to and What the Future Holds
Brings True Joy Read ROMANS 15:13

This verse touches upon three important facets of the Christian life that should give you great joy:

1. You Have a New Identity. When you accept Jesus Christ into your life, God gives you a new identity. You discover that you are not merely some product of random chance. You are not a speck in the universe. You are a child of God. And as God's child you can rest assured that you will be loved and cared for by your heavenly Father.

2. You Have Power to Face Life. With that new identity and hope in Christ, you also have the promise of the Holy Spirit's presence and power in your life. The Holy Spirit works constantly in your heart, helping you to understand God's Word and to transform your attitudes and behavior (see "Who Is the Holy Spirit?" p. A2). An expanded translation of this verse says that by the power of the Holy Spirit, your whole life and outlook will be "radiant with hope." God has not left you to face life on your own. He has promised to guide and strengthen you with his Spirit.

3. You Have Hope for the Future. As a Christian, you have the hope and knowledge that there is life beyond the grave. Your last breath on earth will be followed by your first breath in heaven. We know this is true, because God has promised it in his Word (see "What Is Heaven?" p. A5). This verse asserts that your belief in Jesus and his promises to us as his followers will fill you with joy and peace.

The world offers many roads to happiness: sex, money, power, personal success. But they are all cheap and worthless substitutes in comparison to knowing that you are God's child and that you have the hope of heaven. This is the only road to lasting—indeed, eternal—joy.

To begin the next topic, turn to p. A22.

CORNER STONES

---

²³Gaius says hello to you. I am his guest, and the church meets here in his home. Erastus, the city treasurer, sends you his greetings, and so does Quartus, a Christian brother.*

²⁵God is able to make you strong, just as the Good News says. It is the message about Jesus Christ and his plan for you Gentiles, a plan kept secret from the beginning of time. ²⁶But now as the prophets* foretold and as the eternal God has commanded, this message is made known to all Gentiles everywhere, so that they might believe and obey Christ. ²⁷To God, who alone is wise, be the glory forever through Jesus Christ. Amen.

16:23 Some manuscripts add verse 24, *May the grace of our Lord Jesus Christ be with you all. Amen.*   16:26 Greek *the prophetic writings.*

1 Corinthians

Greetings from Paul

This letter is from Paul, chosen by the will of God to be an apostle of Christ Jesus, and from our brother Sosthenes.

²We are writing to the church of God in Corinth, you who have been called by God to be his own holy people. He made you holy by means of Christ Jesus, just as he did all Christians everywhere—whoever calls upon the name of Jesus Christ, our Lord and theirs.

³May God our Father and the Lord Jesus Christ give you his grace and peace.

Paul Gives Thanks to God

⁴I can never stop thanking God for all the generous gifts he has given you, now that you belong to Christ Jesus. ⁵He has enriched your church with the gifts of eloquence and every kind of knowledge. ⁶This shows that what I told you about Christ is true. ⁷Now you have every spiritual gift you need as you eagerly wait for the return of our Lord Jesus Christ. ⁸He will keep you strong right up to the end, and he will keep you free from all blame on the great day when our Lord Jesus Christ returns. ⁹God will surely do this for you, for he always does just what he says, and he is the one who invited you into this wonderful friendship with his Son, Jesus Christ our Lord.

Divisions in the Church

¹⁰Now, dear brothers and sisters,* I appeal to you by the authority of the Lord Jesus Christ to stop arguing among yourselves. Let there be real harmony so there won't be divisions in the church. I plead with you to be of one mind, united in thought and purpose. ¹¹For some members of Chloe's household have told me about your arguments, dear brothers and sisters. ¹²Some of you are saying, "I am a follower of Paul." Others are saying, "I follow Apollos," or "I follow Peter,*" or "I follow only Christ." ¹³Can Christ be divided into pieces?

Was I, Paul, crucified for you? Were any of you baptized in the name of Paul? ¹⁴I thank God that I did not baptize any of you except Crispus and Gaius, ¹⁵for now no one can say they were baptized in my name. ¹⁶(Oh yes, I also baptized the household of Stephanas. I don't remember baptizing anyone else.) ¹⁷For Christ didn't send me to baptize, but to preach the Good News—and not with clever speeches and high-sounding ideas, for fear that the cross of Christ would lose its power.

The Wisdom of God

¹⁸I know very well how foolish the message of the cross sounds to those who are on the road to destruction. But we who are being saved recognize this message as the very power of God. ¹⁹As the Scriptures say,

"I will destroy human wisdom
    and discard their most brilliant ideas."*

²⁰So where does this leave the philosophers, the scholars, and the world's brilliant debaters? God has made them all look foolish and has shown their wisdom to be useless nonsense. ²¹Since God in his wisdom saw to it that the world would never find him through human wisdom, he has used our foolish preaching to save all who believe. ²²God's way seems foolish to the Jews because they want a sign from heaven to prove it is true. And it is foolish to the Greeks because they believe only what agrees with their own wisdom. ²³So when we preach that Christ

1:10 Greek *brothers*; also in 1:11, 26.   1:12 Greek *Cephas*.   1:19 Isa 29:14.

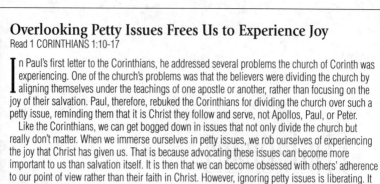

Overlooking Petty Issues Frees Us to Experience Joy
Read 1 CORINTHIANS 1:10-17

In Paul's first letter to the Corinthians, he addressed several problems the church of Corinth was experiencing. One of the church's problems was that the believers were dividing the church by aligning themselves under the teachings of one apostle or another, rather than focusing on the joy of their salvation. Paul, therefore, rebuked the Corinthians for dividing the church over such a petty issue, reminding them that it is Christ they follow and serve, not Apollos, Paul, or Peter.

Like the Corinthians, we can get bogged down in issues that not only divide the church but really don't matter. When we immerse ourselves in petty issues, we rob ourselves of experiencing the joy that Christ has given us. That is because advocating these issues can become more important to us than salvation itself. It is then that we can become obsessed with others' adherence to our point of view rather than their faith in Christ. However, ignoring petty issues is liberating. It frees us to focus on our own salvation and experience the joy of Christ's forgiveness.

How do we do this? Here are four ways to overlook petty issues and experience joy in Christ:

1. Be Single-Minded in Purpose. The purpose of our life is to serve Christ (see Philippians 1:21, p. 1033).

2. Adopt God's Priorities As Your Own. Put God first, others second, and yourself third (see Philippians 2:5-6, p. 1034).

3. Keep Moving Forward Spiritually. Acknowledge that you haven't "arrived" spiritually, and keep pressing on to know God more (see Philippians 3:13-14, p. 1036).

4. Have a Rejoicing Mind. Don't rejoice in circumstances, but rejoice in God and his faithfulness (see Philippians 4:4-5, p. 1036).

Failure to maintain the joy of the Lord in our personal lives leads to spiritual breakdown. Failure to keep the joy of the Lord in our churches cripples the cause of Christ. Let his joy overflow from your life.

For the next note on "Joy," turn to p. 982.

CORNER STONES

---

was crucified, the Jews are offended, and the Gentiles say it's all nonsense. 24But to those called by God to salvation, both Jews and Gentiles,* Christ is the mighty power of God and the wonderful wisdom of God. 25This "foolish" plan of God is far wiser than the wisest of human plans, and God's weakness is far stronger than the greatest of human strength.

26Remember, dear brothers and sisters, that few of you were wise in the world's eyes, or powerful, or wealthy when God called you. 27Instead, God deliberately chose things the world considers foolish in order to shame those who think they are wise. And he chose those who are powerless to shame those who are powerful. 28God chose things despised by the world, things counted as nothing at all, and used them to bring to nothing what the world considers important, 29so that no one can ever boast in the presence of God.

30God alone made it possible for you to be in Christ Jesus. For our benefit God made Christ to be wisdom itself. He is the one who made us acceptable to God. He made us pure and holy, and he gave himself to purchase our freedom. 31As the Scriptures say,

"The person who wishes to boast
   should boast only of what the Lord has
      done."*

CHAPTER 2
Paul Preaches Wisdom

Dear brothers and sisters,* when I first came to you I didn't use lofty words and brilliant ideas to tell you God's message.* 2For I decided to concentrate only on Jesus Christ and his death on the cross. 3I came to you in weakness—timid and trembling. 4And my message and my preaching were very plain. I did not use wise and

1:24 Greek *Greeks.* 1:31 Jer 9:24. 2:1a Greek *Brothers.* 2:1b Greek *mystery;* other manuscripts read *testimony.*

persuasive speeches, but the Holy Spirit was powerful among you. ⁵I did this so that you might trust the power of God rather than human wisdom.

⁶Yet when I am among mature Christians, I do speak with words of wisdom, but not the kind of wisdom that belongs to this world, and not the kind that appeals to the rulers of this world, who are being brought to nothing. ⁷No, the wisdom we speak of is the secret wisdom of God,* which was hidden in former times, though he made it for our benefit before the world began. ⁸But the rulers of this world have not understood it; if they had, they would never have crucified our glorious Lord. ⁹That is what the Scriptures mean when they say,

"No eye has seen, no ear has heard,
    and no mind has imagined
what God has prepared
    for those who love him."*

¹⁰But we know these things because God has revealed them to us by his Spirit, and his Spirit searches out everything and shows us even God's deep secrets. ¹¹No one can know what anyone else is really thinking except that person alone, and no one can know God's thoughts except God's own Spirit. ¹²And God has actually given us his Spirit (not the world's spirit) so we can know the wonderful things God has freely given us. ¹³When we tell you this, we do not use words of human wisdom. We speak words given to us by the Spirit, using the Spirit's words to explain spiritual truths.* ¹⁴But people who aren't Christians can't understand these truths from God's Spirit. It all sounds foolish to them because only those who have the Spirit can understand what the Spirit means. ¹⁵We who have the Spirit understand these things, but others can't understand us at all. ¹⁶How could they? For,

"Who can know what the Lord is thinking?
    Who can give him counsel?"*

But we can understand these things, for we have the mind of Christ.

CHAPTER **3**
Paul and Apollos, Servants of Christ
Dear brothers and sisters,* when I was with you I couldn't talk to you as I would to mature

2:7 Greek *we speak God's wisdom in a mystery.* 2:9 Isa 64:4. 2:13 Or *explaining spiritual truths in spiritual language,* or *explaining spiritual truths to spiritual people.* 2:16 Isa 40:13. 3:1a Greek *Brothers.*

Christians. I had to talk as though you belonged to this world or as though you were infants in the Christian life.* ²I had to feed you with milk and not with solid food, because you couldn't handle anything stronger. And you still aren't ready, ³for you are still controlled by your own sinful desires. You are jealous of one another and quarrel with each other. Doesn't that prove you are controlled by your own desires? You are acting like people who don't belong to the Lord.

3:1b Greek *in Christ.*

Understand the Simplicity of the Gospel Read 1 CORINTHIANS 2:1-5

Paul reminds us in this text that the heartbeat of the gospel message is the story of the life, death, and resurrection of Jesus Christ. The apostles emphasized this message in their preaching throughout the New Testament—especially in the book of Acts, which chronicles the start of the early church. As you share your faith with others, keep in mind these two points demonstrated in the apostles' own efforts to spread the gospel:

1. Remember the Simplicity of the Gospel. People need to know that they are sinners and that their sin separates them from God. But Jesus came to bring God and humankind together. When he died on the cross, the sins of humankind were placed upon him, and the penalty for those sins was paid in full. Three days after his crucifixion, he rose from the dead, proving that he was the true Son of God, the only one who could pay for our sins.

2. Recognize the Power of the Gospel. Although our message is simple, it is incredibly powerful. Paul wrote, "For I am not ashamed of this Good News about Christ. It is the power of God at work, saving everyone who believes" (Romans 1:16). The word Paul uses to describe the power of the gospel is the root for our English words *dynamite* and *dynamic*.

Remember there is power in the simple message of the life, death, and resurrecton of Jesus Christ. We should not be ashamed of it but boldly proclaim it.

For the next note on "Share Your Faith,"
turn to p. 957.

The Value of Our Work on Earth Will Be Tested
Read 1 CORINTHIANS 3:10-15

The British preacher Alan Redpath once said, "It is possible to have a saved soul and a lost life." In other words, it is possible to be saved and forgiven of one's sin but to waste one's life by not serving the Lord.

That is what Paul warned the Corinthians about in this passage. Here Paul describes another judgment—besides the Great White Throne Judgment—specifically for believers. You might call it the Christian's award ceremony. Yet it won't be like any awards ceremony on earth. There the quality of our work for the Lord will be tested, as well as our motives for doing it. Our reward will reflect what we have or haven't done with the talents and abilities God has given us.

One day you are going to stand before Jesus. When you do, you want to be welcomed into the arms of Jesus and hear him say, "Well done, my good and faithful servant" (Matthew 25:21).

Be an "expert builder." Take the gifts and abilities God has given you—however insignificant they may seem to you—and use them for his glory. Then you will have a saved soul *and* an abundant life.

To begin the next reading track, turn to p. A25.

CORNER STONES

4When one of you says, "I am a follower of Paul," and another says, "I prefer Apollos," aren't you acting like those who are not Christians?*

5Who is Apollos, and who is Paul, that we should be the cause of such quarrels? Why, we're only servants. Through us God caused you to believe. Each of us did the work the Lord gave us. 6My job was to plant the seed in your hearts, and Apollos watered it, but it was God, not we, who made it grow. 7The ones who do the planting or watering aren't important, but God is important because he is the one who makes the seed grow. 8The one who plants and the one who waters work as a team with the same purpose. Yet they will be rewarded individually, according to their own hard work. 9We work together as partners who belong to God. You are God's field, God's building—not ours.

10Because of God's special favor to me, I have laid the foundation like an expert builder. Now others are building on it. But whoever is building on this foundation must be very careful. 11For no one can lay any other foundation than the one we already have—Jesus Christ. 12Now anyone who builds on that foundation may use gold, silver, jewels, wood, hay, or straw. 13But there is going to come a time of testing at the judgment day to see what kind of work each builder has done. Everyone's work will be put

through the fire to see whether or not it keeps its value. 14If the work survives the fire, that builder will receive a reward. 15But if the work is burned up, the builder will suffer great loss. The builders themselves will be saved, but like someone escaping through a wall of flames.

16Don't you realize that all of you together are the temple of God and that the Spirit of God lives in* you? 17God will bring ruin upon anyone who ruins this temple. For God's temple is holy, and you Christians are that temple.

18Stop fooling yourselves. If you think you are wise by this world's standards, you will have to become a fool so you can become wise by God's standards. 19For the wisdom of this world is foolishness to God. As the Scriptures say,

"God catches those who think they are wise
    in their own cleverness."*

20And again,

"The Lord knows the thoughts of the wise,
    that they are worthless."*

21So don't take pride in following a particular leader. Everything belongs to you: 22Paul and Apollos and Peter*; the whole world and life and death; the present and the future. Everything belongs to you, 23and you belong to Christ, and Christ belongs to God.

3:4 Greek *aren't you merely human?* 3:16 Or *among.* 3:19 Job 5:13. 3:20 Ps 94:11. 3:22 Greek *Cephas.*

Does God Approve of Alternative Lifestyles? Read 1 CORINTHIANS 6:9-10, 15-20

In this day and age we hear a lot of talk about "alternative lifestyles." But what does God have to say about homosexuality, living together as an unmarried couple, or being promiscuous? While some say that God is accepting of any relationship, the Bible paints a very different picture. Just because these relationships exist does not make them right. In fact, God clearly labels them as sin.

About Homosexuality. Saying that homosexuality is wrong is not a popular thing to do in our culture today. Yet God is not concerned with what is and what is not popular. He is concerned with people's salvation and their obedience to his Word. Just because homosexuality is viewed as an acceptable lifestyle does not mean that it is not a sin. God declared it to be just that when he gave his law to the Israelites (see Leviticus 18:22, p. 103). Paul reiterated God's command on abstaining from homosexual sex in his letter to the Romans (see Romans 1:26-27, p. 962), as well as in some of his other letters to the early church.

About Living Together before Marriage and Premarital Sex. Have you ever thought that something was OK to do because "everybody is doing it"? Today, couples living together outside of marriage has become acceptable. In addition, it seems that premarital sex is the norm, rather than the exception. But God has not given his approval of these relationships (see Hebrews 13:4, p. 1083). Although God created sex, he did not intend us to have it before marriage. That is because he created sex to be a means by which a husband and wife would grow closer in their relationship. He did not create sex to be something cheaply enjoyed outside the bonds of marital commitment, which is what living together and premarital sex are.

About Promiscuity. *Promiscuity* is a word that we do not hear as often today as we used to. The problem with promiscuity is that it involves having many sexual partners. We know from God's Word that he intended us to have one sexual partner—our spouse. When a person has more than one partner (with the exception of remarriage after a spouse's death or a divorce on solid biblical grounds), he or she is involved in sexual immorality, if not married, or adultery, if married (see Ephesians 5:3, p. 1029, and Matthew 5:27-28, p. 793).

Some have questions about whether God's Word on these subjects still applies to us today, or if it was simply meant for the people of that particular time and culture. Yet God has instructed us to obey all of his commands and not to add or subtract from any of them (see Deuteronomy 12:32, p. 166). In addition, we are told that the Word of the Lord stands forever (see 1 Peter 1:25, p. 1092). Consequently, these instructions apply just as much to us today as they did to their original audience centuries ago.

God gave us our sexual desires to enjoy within the bounds of marriage (see 1 Corinthians 7:1-5, p. 990). If you go against God's divinely instituted plan and do not repent, you will reap the consequences—not only in this life, but in eternity. For you cannot be close to God if you are engaged in any immoral behavior. At the same time, you won't be engaged in this type of behavior if you are truly close to God.

For the next "Big Question" note, turn to p. 1027.

CHAPTER **4**
Paul and the Corinthians
So look at Apollos and me as mere servants of Christ who have been put in charge of explaining God's secrets. 2Now, a person who is put in charge as a manager must be faithful. 3What about me? Have I been faithful? Well, it matters very little what you or anyone else thinks. I don't even trust my own judgment on this point. 4My conscience is clear, but that isn't what matters. It is the Lord himself who will examine me and decide.

5So be careful not to jump to conclusions before the Lord returns as to whether or not someone is faithful. When the Lord comes, he will bring our deepest secrets to light and will reveal our private motives. And then God will give to everyone whatever praise is due.

6Dear brothers and sisters,* I have used Apollos and myself to illustrate what I've been saying. If you pay attention to the Scriptures,* you won't brag about one of your leaders at the expense of another. 7What makes you better than anyone else? What do you have that God hasn't given you? And if all you have is from God, why boast as though you have accomplished something on your own?

8You think you already have everything you need! You are already rich! Without us you have become kings! I wish you really were on your thrones already, for then we would be reigning with you! 9But sometimes I think God has put us apostles on display, like prisoners of war at the end of a victor's parade, condemned to die. We have become a spectacle to the entire world—to people and angels alike.

10Our dedication to Christ makes us look like fools, but you are so wise! We are weak, but you are so powerful! You are well thought of, but we are laughed at. 11To this very hour we go hungry and thirsty, without enough clothes to keep us warm. We have endured many beatings, and we have no homes of our own. 12We have worked wearily with our own hands to earn our living. We bless those who curse us. We are patient with those who abuse us. 13We respond gently when evil things are said about us. Yet we are treated like the world's garbage, like everybody's trash—right up to the present moment.

14I am not writing these things to shame you, but to warn you as my beloved children. 15For even if you had ten thousand others to teach you about Christ, you have only one spiritual father. For I became your father in Christ Jesus when I

preached the Good News to you. 16So I ask you to follow my example and do as I do.

17That is the very reason I am sending Timothy—to help you do this. For he is my beloved and trustworthy child in the Lord. He will remind you of what I teach about Christ Jesus in all the churches wherever I go.

18I know that some of you have become arrogant, thinking I will never visit you again. 19But I will come—and soon—if the Lord will let me, and then I'll find out whether these arrogant people are just big talkers or whether they really have God's power. 20For the Kingdom of God is not just fancy talk; it is living by God's power. 21Which do you choose? Should I come with punishment and scolding, or should I come with quiet love and gentleness?

CHAPTER 5
Paul Condemns Spiritual Pride

I can hardly believe the report about the sexual immorality going on among you, something so evil that even the pagans don't do it. I am told that you have a man in your church who is living in sin with his father's wife. 2And you are so proud of yourselves! Why aren't you mourning in sorrow and shame? And why haven't you removed this man from your fellowship?

3Even though I am not there with you in person, I am with you in the Spirit.* Concerning the one who has done this, I have already passed judgment 4in the name of the Lord Jesus. You are to call a meeting of the church,* and I will be there in spirit, and the power of the Lord Jesus will be with you as you meet. 5Then you must cast this man out of the church and into Satan's hands, so that his sinful nature will be destroyed* and he himself* will be saved when the Lord returns.

6How terrible that you should boast about your spirituality, and yet you let this sort of thing

4:6a Greek *Brothers.*   4:6b Or *You must learn not to go beyond "what is written," so that.*   5:3 Or *in spirit.*   5:4 Or *In the name of the Lord Jesus, you are to call a meeting of the church.*   5:5a Or *So that he will die;* Greek reads *for the destruction of the flesh.*   5:5b Greek *and the spirit.*

OFF AND RUNNING ////////
Does This Activity Bring Me under Its Power?
Read 1 CORINTHIANS 6:12

Some have mistakenly assumed that following Christ means drudgingly obeying a list of "do's and don'ts." In reality, the Christian life, if lived according to Scripture, is one of joy and satisfaction. This verse serves as a case in point. To follow the principle laid out here is not overly restricting but truly liberating!

Some people are controlled by pleasure. For example, they may live for a certain sport and become so

go on. Don't you realize that if even one person is allowed to go on sinning, soon all will be affected? 7Remove this wicked person from among you so that you can stay pure.* Christ, our Passover Lamb, has been sacrificed for us. 8So let us celebrate the festival, not by eating the old bread* of wickedness and evil, but by eating the new bread* of purity and truth.

9When I wrote to you before, I told you not to associate with people who indulge in sexual sin. 10But I wasn't talking about unbelievers who indulge in sexual sin, or who are greedy or are swindlers or idol worshipers. You would have to leave this world to avoid people like that. 11What I meant was that you are not to associate with anyone who claims to be a Christian* yet indulges in sexual sin, or is greedy, or worships idols, or is abusive, or a drunkard, or a swindler. Don't even eat with such people.

12It isn't my responsibility to judge outsiders, but it certainly is your job to judge those inside the church who are sinning in these ways. 13God will judge those on the outside; but as the Scriptures say, "You must remove the evil person from among you."*

CHAPTER **6**
Avoiding Lawsuits with Christians
When you have something against another Christian, why do you file a lawsuit and ask a secular court to decide the matter, instead of taking it to other Christians to decide who is right? 2Don't you know that someday we Christians are going to judge the world? And since you are going to judge the world, can't you decide these little things among yourselves? 3Don't you realize that we Christians will judge angels? So you should surely be able to resolve ordinary disagreements here on earth. 4If you have legal disputes about such matters, why do you go to outside judges who are not

respected by the church? 5I am saying this to shame you. Isn't there anyone in all the church who is wise enough to decide these arguments? 6But instead, one Christian* sues another—right in front of unbelievers!

7To have such lawsuits at all is a real defeat for you. Why not just accept the injustice and leave it at that? Why not let yourselves be cheated? 8But instead, you yourselves are the ones who do wrong and cheat even your own Christian brothers and sisters.*

Avoiding Sexual Sin
9Don't you know that those who do wrong will have no share in the Kingdom of God? Don't fool yourselves. Those who indulge in sexual sin, who are idol worshipers, adulterers, male prostitutes, homosexuals, 10thieves, greedy people, drunkards, abusers, and swindlers—none of these will have a share in the Kingdom of God. 11There was a time when some of you were just like that, but now your sins have been washed away,* and you have been set apart for God. You have been made right with God because of what the Lord Jesus Christ and the Spirit of our God have done for you.

12You may say, "I am allowed to do anything." But I reply, "Not everything is good for you." And even though "I am allowed to do anything," I must not become a slave to anything. 13You say, "Food is for the stomach, and the stomach is for food." This is true, though someday God will do away with both of them. But our bodies were not made for sexual immorality. They were made for the Lord, and the Lord cares about our bodies. 14And God will raise our bodies from the dead by his marvelous power, just as he raised our Lord from the dead. 15Don't you realize that your bodies are actually parts of Christ? Should a man take his body, which belongs to Christ, and join

5:6-7 Greek *Don't you realize that even a little leaven spreads quickly through the whole batch of dough? 7Purge out the old leaven so that you can be a new batch of dough, just as you are already unleavened.* 5:8a Greek *not with old leaven.* 5:8b Greek *but with unleavened [bread].* 5:11 Greek *a brother.* 5:13 Deut 17:7. 6:6 Greek *one brother.* 6:8 Greek *brothers.* 6:11 Or *you have been cleansed.*

fanatical about it that it turns into an obsession. Others may be hooked on soap operas, food, or some particular habit that has them under its power. Yet, as a Christian, you should only want to be controlled by and under the power of Jesus Christ.

We need to so treasure our relationship with God—and the ensuing freedom from sin it has brought—that we jealously guard that relationship, wanting no thing or person to get in its way. As the Psalmist prayed, we, too, should pray, "Search me, O God, and know my heart; test me and know my thoughts. Point out anything in me that offends you, and lead me along the path of everlasting life" (Psalm 139:23-24).

For the next note on "Responsibility," turn to p. 980.

it to a prostitute? Never! 16And don't you know that if a man joins himself to a prostitute, he becomes one body with her? For the Scriptures say, "The two are united into one."* 17But the person who is joined to the Lord becomes one spirit with him.

18Run away from sexual sin! No other sin so clearly affects the body as this one does. For sexual immorality is a sin against your own body. 19Or don't you know that your body is the temple of the Holy Spirit, who lives in you and was given to you by God? You do not belong to yourself, 20for God bought you with a high price. So you must honor God with your body.

CHAPTER **7**

Instruction on Marriage

Now about the questions you asked in your letter. Yes, it is good to live a celibate life. 2But because there is so much sexual immorality, each man should have his own wife, and each woman should have her own husband.

3The husband should not deprive his wife of sexual intimacy, which is her right as a married woman, nor should the wife deprive her husband. 4The wife gives authority over her body to her husband, and the husband also gives authority over his body to his wife. 5So do not deprive each other of sexual relations. The only exception to this rule would be the agreement of both husband and wife to refrain from sexual intimacy for a limited time, so they can give themselves more completely to prayer. Afterward they should come together again so that Satan won't be able to tempt them because of their lack of self-control. 6This is only my sug-

gestion. It's not meant to be an absolute rule. 7I wish everyone could get along without marrying, just as I do. But we are not all the same. God gives some the gift of marriage, and to others he gives the gift of singleness.

8Now I say to those who aren't married and to widows—it's better to stay unmarried, just as I am. 9But if they can't control themselves, they should go ahead and marry. It's better to marry than to burn with lust.

10Now, for those who are married I have a command that comes not from me, but from the Lord.* A wife must not leave her husband. 11But if she does leave him, let her remain single or else go back to him. And the husband must not leave his wife.

12Now, I will speak to the rest of you, though I do not have a direct command from the Lord. If a Christian man* has a wife who is an unbeliever and she is willing to continue living with him, he must not leave her. 13And if a Christian woman has a husband who is an unbeliever, and he is willing to continue living with her, she must not leave him. 14For the Christian wife brings holiness to her marriage, and the Christian husband brings holiness to his marriage. Otherwise, your children would not have a godly influence, but now they are set apart for him. 15(But if the husband or wife who isn't a Christian insists on leaving, let them go. In such cases the Christian husband or wife is not required to stay with them, for God wants his children to live in peace.) 16You wives must remember that your husbands might be converted because of you. And you husbands must remember that your wives might be converted because of you.

6:16 Gen 2:24. 7:10 See Matt 5:32; 19:9; Mark 10:11-12; Luke 16:18. 7:12 Greek *a brother.*

OFF AND RUNNING ▰▰▰▰▰

Marriage Is Not for Everyone Read 1 CORINTHIANS 7:1-40

Contrary to what popular opinion suggests, God has given some the ability to remain "happily unmarried." Verse 35 of this passage reminds us that, when it comes to marrying, it is vitally important to make sure that your decision "will help you serve the Lord best." If you are contemplating marriage, here are four important things to consider:

1. Take Time Getting to Know One Another. Don't rush into marriage. If you are really in love with someone, you will want to build your friendship with that person as well. That is the foundation of your marriage. As Benjamin Franklin humorously said, "Keep your eyes wide open before marriage and half shut afterwards"—not the other way around!

2. Test the Depth of Your Love. Love is more than some gooey emotion. It is a commitment. In the Greek language, love was described in three different ways: *eros* (physical attraction), *philos* (love between friends), and *agape* (unconditional love). Marriages that are simply based upon *eros* or *phileo* love are destined for

17You must accept whatever situation the Lord has put you in, and continue on as you were when God first called you. This is my rule for all the churches. 18For instance, a man who was circumcised before he became a believer should not try to reverse it. And the man who was uncircumcised when he became a believer should not be circumcised now. 19For it makes no difference whether or not a man has been circumcised. The important thing is to keep God's commandments.

20You should continue on as you were when God called you. 21Are you a slave? Don't let that worry you—but if you get a chance to be free, take it. 22And remember, if you were a slave when the Lord called you, the Lord has now set you free from the awful power of sin. And if you were free when the Lord called you, you are now a slave of Christ. 23God purchased you at a high price. Don't be enslaved by the world.* 24So, dear brothers and sisters,* whatever situation you were in when you became a believer, stay there in your new relationship with God.

25Now, about the young women who are not yet married. I do not have a command from the Lord for them. But the Lord in his kindness has given me wisdom that can be trusted, and I will share it with you. 26Because of the present crisis,* I think it is best to remain just as you are. 27If you have a wife, do not end the marriage. If you do not have a wife, do not get married. 28But if you do get married, it is not a sin. And if a young woman gets married, it is not a sin. However, I am trying to spare you the extra problems that come with marriage.

29Now let me say this, dear brothers and sis-ters: The time that remains is very short, so husbands should not let marriage be their major concern. 30Happiness or sadness or wealth should not keep anyone from doing God's work. 31Those in frequent contact with the things of the world should make good use of them without becoming attached to them, for this world and all it contains will pass away. 32In everything you do, I want you to be free from the concerns of this life. An unmarried man can spend his time doing the Lord's work and thinking how to please him. 33But a married man can't do that so well. He has to think about his earthly responsibilities and how to please his wife. 34His interests are divided. In the same way, a woman who is no longer married or has never been married can be more devoted to the Lord in body and in spirit, while the married woman must be concerned about her earthly responsibilities and how to please her husband.

35I am saying this for your benefit, not to place restrictions on you. I want you to do whatever will help you serve the Lord best, with as few distractions as possible. 36But if a man thinks he ought to marry his fiancée because he has trouble controlling his passions and time is passing, it is all right; it is not a sin. Let them marry. 37But if he has decided firmly not to marry and there is no urgency and he can control his passion, he does well not to marry. 38So the person who marries does well, and the person who doesn't marry does even better.

39A wife is married to her husband as long as he lives. If her husband dies, she is free to marry whomever she wishes, but this must be a marriage acceptable to the Lord.* 40But in my opinion it

7:23 Greek *don't become slaves of people.* 7:24 Greek *brothers;* also in 7:29. 7:26 Or *pressures of life.* 7:39 Or *but only to a Christian;* Greek reads *but only in the Lord.*

trouble, but marriages built around the *agape* love that Christ displayed will last. Emotions will come and go, but true love is far more than that. The Bible says, "Many waters cannot quench love; neither can rivers drown it" (Song of Songs 8:7).

3. Make Sure of Your Commitment. Ask yourself the following questions: Are you ready to spend the rest of your life with this person? Can you see yourselves going through parenthood together? Are you willing to make sacrifices in relationships, hobbies, and even your career for the sake of your marriage?

4. Consider Your Witness for Christ. If this other person is not a believer, don't even consider marriage. Scripture gives stern warnings against being teamed with those who are unbelievers (2 Corinthians 6:14, p. 1008). You need to also consider the spiritual implications of this relationship. Will the two of you together be a more effective and powerful witness for Christ than the two of you apart?

Whether you marry or remain single, learn to be content in whatever situation the Lord places you. Then you will possess one of the keys to true happiness.

For the next note on "Marriage," turn to p. 552.

will be better for her if she doesn't marry again, and I think I am giving you counsel from God's Spirit when I say this.

CHAPTER 8
Food Sacrificed to Idols

Now let's talk about food that has been sacrificed to idols. You think that everyone should agree with your perfect knowledge. While knowledge may make us feel important, it is love that really builds up the church. 2Anyone who claims to know all the answers doesn't really know very much. 3But the person who loves God is the one God knows and cares for.

4So now, what about it? Should we eat meat that has been sacrificed to idols? Well, we all know that an idol is not really a god and that there is only one God and no other. 5According to some people, there are many so-called gods and many lords, both in heaven and on earth. 6But we know that there is only one God, the Father, who created everything, and we exist for him. And there is only one Lord, Jesus Christ, through whom God made everything and through whom we have been given life.

7However, not all Christians realize this. Some are accustomed to thinking of idols as being real, so when they eat food that has been offered to idols, they think of it as the worship of real gods, and their weak consciences are violated. 8It's true that we can't win God's approval by what we eat. We don't miss out on anything if we don't eat it, and we don't gain anything if we do. 9But you must be careful with this freedom of yours. Do not cause a brother or sister with a weaker conscience to stumble.

10You see, this is what can happen: Weak Christians who think it is wrong to eat this food will see you eating in the temple of an idol. You know there's nothing wrong with it, but they will be encouraged to violate their conscience by eating food that has been dedicated to the idol. 11So because of your superior knowledge, a weak Christian,* for whom Christ died, will be destroyed. 12And you are sinning against Christ when you sin against other Christians* by encouraging them to do something they believe is wrong. 13If what I eat is going to make another Christian sin, I will never eat meat again as long as I live—for I don't want to make another Christian stumble.

CHAPTER 9
Paul Gives Up His Rights

Do I not have as much freedom as anyone else?* Am I not an apostle? Haven't I seen Jesus our Lord with my own eyes? Isn't it because of my hard work that you are in the Lord? 2Even if others think I am not an apostle, I certainly am to you, for you are living proof that I am the Lord's apostle.

3This is my answer to those who question my authority as an apostle.* 4Don't we have the right to live in your homes and share your meals? 5Don't we have the right to bring a Christian wife* along with us as the other disciples and the Lord's brothers and Peter* do? 6Or is it only Barnabas and I who have to work to support ourselves? 7What soldier has to pay his own expenses? And have you ever heard of a farmer who harvests his crop and doesn't have the right to eat some of it? What shepherd takes care of a flock of sheep and isn't allowed to drink some of the milk? 8And this isn't merely human opinion. Doesn't God's law say the same thing? 9For the law of Moses says, "Do not keep an ox from eating as it treads out the grain."* Do you suppose God was thinking only about oxen when

8:11 Greek *brother;* also in 8:13.   8:12 Greek *brothers.*   9:1 Greek *Am I not free?*   9:3 Greek *those who examine me.*   9:5a Greek *a sister, a wife.*   9:5b Greek *Cephas.*   9:9 Deut 25:4.

OFF AND RUNNING ▱▱▱
A Christian Should Not Leave a Non-Christian Spouse
Read 1 CORINTHIANS 7:12-16

While it is easy to rationalize leaving an unbelieving spouse who does not support or encourage your faith, it is not biblical. As Paul reiterates here, divorce is not God's intent for married couples. In the case of a Christian and non-Christian spouse, there are two additional reasons to remain married:

1. A Christian Spouse Serves as a Witness to an Unbelieving Spouse. A Christian may play an important role in winning his or her spouse to the Lord. Scripture says that the Christian wife of a nonbelieving husband can have a powerful influence on her spouse through her godly actions and

he said this? 10Wasn't he also speaking to us? Of course he was. Just as farm workers who plow fields and thresh the grain expect a share of the harvest, Christian workers should be paid by those they serve.

11We have planted good spiritual seed among you. Is it too much to ask, in return, for mere food and clothing? 12If you support others who preach to you, shouldn't we have an even greater right to be supported? Yet we have never used this right. We would rather put up with anything than put an obstacle in the way of the Good News about Christ.

13Don't you know that those who work in the Temple get their meals from the food brought to the Temple as offerings? And those who serve at the altar get a share of the sacrificial offerings. 14In the same way, the Lord gave orders that those who preach the Good News should be supported by those who benefit from it. 15Yet I have never used any of these rights. And I am not writing this to suggest that I would like to start now. In fact, I would rather die than lose my distinction of preaching without charge. 16For preaching the Good News is not something I can boast about. I am compelled by God to do it. How terrible for me if I didn't do it!

17If I were doing this of my own free will, then I would deserve payment. But God has chosen me and given me this sacred trust, and I have no choice. 18What then is my pay? It is the satisfaction I get from preaching the Good News without expense to anyone, never demanding my rights as a preacher.

19This means I am not bound to obey people just because they pay me, yet I have become a servant of everyone so that I can bring them to Christ. 20When I am with the Jews, I become one of them so that I can bring them to Christ. When I am with those who follow the Jewish laws, I do the same, even though I am not subject to the law, so that I can bring them to Christ. 21When I am with the Gentiles who do not have the Jewish law,* I fit in with them as much as I can. In this way, I gain their confidence and bring them to Christ. But I do not discard the law of God; I obey the law of Christ.

22When I am with those who are oppressed, I share their oppression so that I might bring them to Christ. Yes, I try to find common ground with everyone so that I might bring them to Christ. 23I do all this to spread the Good News, and in doing so I enjoy its blessings.

24Remember that in a race everyone runs, but only one person gets the prize. You also must run in such a way that you will win. 25All athletes practice strict self-control. They do it to win a prize that will fade away, but we do it for an eternal prize. 26So I run straight to the goal with purpose in every step. I am not like a boxer who misses his punches.* 27I discipline my body like an athlete, training it to do what it should. Otherwise, I fear that after preaching to others I myself might be disqualified.

CHAPTER 10
Warnings against Idolatry

I don't want you to forget, dear brothers and sisters,* what happened to our ancestors in the wilderness long ago. God guided all of them by sending a cloud that moved along ahead of them, and he brought them all safely through the waters of the sea on dry ground. 2As followers of Moses, they were all baptized in the cloud and the sea. 3And all of them ate the same miraculous* food, 4and all of them drank the same miraculous water. For they all drank from the miraculous rock that traveled with them, and that rock was Christ. 5Yet after all this, God

9:21 Greek *those without the law.*   9:26 Or *I am not just shadowboxing.*   10:1 Greek *brothers.*   10:3 Greek *spiritual;* also in 10:4.

example, which may encourage him to come to faith in Christ (see 1 Peter 3:1-2, p. 1094). The same is true for Christian husbands.

2. A Christian Spouse Can Influence the Couple's Children for Christ. If you separate, as Paul states, there is a good chance your children may not come to faith. It will help them to see your faith in the context of a united family.

If, however, your unbelieving spouse abandons you, and you have done everything you could to keep the marriage together, God will not hold you to that relationship. This is one of the few marriage "release clauses" found in Scripture. God will not force you to stay married to an unbelieving partner who doesn't want to stay married to you.

For the next note on "Marriage," turn to p. 990.

was not pleased with most of them, and he destroyed them in the wilderness.

6These events happened as a warning to us, so that we would not crave evil things as they did 7or worship idols as some of them did. For the Scriptures say, "The people celebrated with feasting and drinking, and they indulged themselves in pagan revelry."* 8And we must not engage in sexual immorality as some of them did, causing 23,000 of them to die in one day. 9Nor should we put Christ* to the test, as some of them did and then died from snakebites. 10And don't grumble as some of them did, for that is why God sent his angel of death to destroy them. 11All these events happened to them as examples for us. They were written down to warn us, who live at the time when this age is drawing to a close.

12If you think you are standing strong, be careful, for you, too, may fall into the same sin. 13But remember that the temptations that come into your life are no different from what others experience. And God is faithful. He will keep the temptation from becoming so strong that you can't stand up against it. When you are tempted, he will show you a way out so that you will not give in to it.

14So, my dear friends, flee from the worship of idols. 15You are reasonable people. Decide for yourselves if what I am about to say is true. 16When we bless the cup at the Lord's Table, aren't we sharing in the benefits of the blood of Christ? And when we break the loaf of bread, aren't we sharing in the benefits of the body of Christ? 17And we all eat from one loaf, showing that we are one body. 18And think about the nation of Israel; all who eat the sacrifices are united by that act.

19What am I trying to say? Am I saying that the idols to whom the pagans bring sacrifices are real gods and that these sacrifices are of some value? 20No, not at all. What I am saying is that these sacrifices are offered to demons, not to God. And I don't want any of you to be partners with demons. 21You cannot drink from the cup of the Lord and from the cup of demons, too. You cannot eat at the Lord's Table and at the table of demons, too. 22What? Do you dare to rouse the Lord's jealousy as Israel did? Do you think we are stronger than he is?

23You say, "I am allowed to do anything"— but not everything is helpful. You say, "I am allowed to do anything"—but not everything is beneficial. 24Don't think only of your own good. Think of other Christians and what is best for them.

25Here's what you should do. You may eat any meat that is sold in the marketplace. Don't ask whether or not it was offered to idols, and then your conscience won't be bothered. 26For "the earth is the Lord's, and everything in it."*

27If someone who isn't a Christian asks you home for dinner, go ahead; accept the invitation if you want to. Eat whatever is offered to you and don't ask any questions about it. Your conscience should not be bothered by this. 28But suppose someone warns you that this meat has been offered to an idol. Don't eat it, out of consideration for the conscience of the one who told you. 29It might not be a matter of conscience for you, but it is for the other person. Now, why should my freedom be limited by what someone else thinks? 30If I can thank God for the food and enjoy it, why should I be condemned for eating it? 31Whatever you eat or drink or whatever you do, you must do all for the glory of God. 32Don't give offense to Jews or Gentiles or the church of God. 33That is the plan I follow, too. I try to please everyone in everything I do. I don't just do what I like or what is best for me, but what is best for them so they may be saved.

CHAPTER **11**

And you should follow my example, just as I follow Christ's.

Instructions for Public Worship

2I am so glad, dear friends, that you always keep me in your thoughts and you are following the Christian teaching I passed on to you. 3But there is one thing I want you to know: A man is responsible to Christ, a woman is responsible to her husband, and Christ is responsible to God. 4A man dishonors Christ* if he covers his head while praying or prophesying. 5But a woman dishonors her husband* if she prays or prophesies without a covering on her head, for this is the same as shaving her head. 6Yes, if she refuses to wear a head covering, she should cut off all her hair. And since it is shameful for a woman to have her hair cut or her head shaved, then she should wear a covering.* 7A man should not wear anything on his head when worshiping, for man is God's glory, made in God's own image,

10:7 Exod 32:6.   10:9 Some manuscripts read *the Lord*.   10:26 Ps 24:1.   11:4 Greek *his head*.   11:5 Greek *her head*.   11:6 Or *then she should have long hair.*

but woman is the glory of man. ⁸For the first man didn't come from woman, but the first woman came from man. ⁹And man was not made for woman's benefit, but woman was made for man. ¹⁰So a woman should wear a covering on her head as a sign of authority because the angels are watching.

¹¹But in relationships among the Lord's people, women are not independent of men, and men are not independent of women. ¹²For although the first woman came from man, all men have been born from women ever since, and everything comes from God.

¹³What do you think about this? Is it right for a woman to pray to God in public without covering her head? ¹⁴Isn't it obvious that it's disgraceful for a man to have long hair? ¹⁵And isn't it obvious that long hair is a woman's pride and joy? For it has been given to her as a covering. ¹⁶But if anyone wants to argue about this, all I can say is that we have no other custom than this, and all the churches of God feel the same way about it.

Order at the Lord's Supper

¹⁷But now when I mention this next issue, I cannot praise you. For it sounds as if more harm than good is done when you meet together. ¹⁸First of all, I hear that there are divisions among you when you meet as a church, and to some extent I believe it. ¹⁹But, of course, there must be divisions among you so that those of you who are right will be recognized!

²⁰It's not the Lord's Supper you are concerned about when you come together. ²¹For I am told that some of you hurry to eat your own meal without sharing with others. As a result, some go hungry while others get drunk. ²²What? Is this really true? Don't you have your own homes for eating and drinking? Or do you really want to disgrace the church of God and shame the poor? What am I supposed to say about these things? Do you want me to praise you? Well, I certainly do not!

²³For this is what the Lord himself said, and I pass it on to you just as I received it. On the night when he was betrayed, the Lord Jesus took a loaf of bread, ²⁴and when he had given thanks, he broke it and said, "This is my body, which is given* for you. Do this in remembrance of me." ²⁵In the same way, he took the cup of wine after supper, saying, "This cup is the new covenant between God and you, sealed by the shedding of

11:24 Some manuscripts read *broken.*

my blood. Do this in remembrance of me as often as you drink it." ²⁶For every time you eat this bread and drink this cup, you are announcing the Lord's death until he comes again.

²⁷So if anyone eats this bread or drinks this cup of the Lord unworthily, that person is guilty of sinning against the body and the blood of the Lord. ²⁸That is why you should examine yourself before eating the bread and drinking from the cup. ²⁹For if you eat the bread or drink the cup unworthily, not honoring the body of Christ,* you are eating and drinking God's judgment upon yourself. ³⁰That is why many of you are weak and sick and some have even died.

11:29 Greek *the body;* some manuscripts read *the Lord's body.*

Rejoice Because Victory Is Yours in Christ Jesus
Read 1 CORINTHIANS 10:13

God realizes that we as humans will be tempted by one thing or another in this world. Fortunately for us, God cares so deeply about us that he has taken action to help us through times of temptation. This verse provides two rays of hope for you when you are tempted:

1. Jesus Understands Your Situation. Any temptation you are facing or will face has been faced before. Better yet, Jesus understands what it is like to be tempted, for the Bible teaches that he can sympathize with us, for he "faced all of the same temptations we do, yet he did not sin" (Hebrews 4:15).

2. God Will Always Give You the Strength to Get Through the Temptation. When you face temptation, God will always give you the power to resist it or give you a way to escape it. Sometimes the way out of temptation is literal. For instance, if you are at the movie theater and an explicit sexual scene appears on the screen, the way of escape means walking out of the theater. At other times, it may mean relying on God's Holy Spirit to give you the power to resist.

The next time you are tempted or tested, remember this: God will allow hardship in the life of the Christian, but it will always be filtered through the screen of his love. He will never give you more than you can handle.

For the next note on "Resist Temptation," turn to p. 37.

31But if we examine ourselves, we will not be examined by God and judged in this way. 32But when we are judged and disciplined by the Lord, we will not be condemned with the world. 33So, dear brothers and sisters,* when you gather for the Lord's Supper, wait for each other. 34If you are really hungry, eat at home so you won't bring judgment upon yourselves when you meet together.

I'll give you instructions about the other matters after I arrive.

CHAPTER 12
Spiritual Gifts

And now, dear brothers and sisters,* I will write about the special abilities the Holy Spirit gives to each of us, for I must correct your misunderstandings about them. 2You know that when you were still pagans you were led astray and swept along in worshiping speechless idols. 3So I want you to know how to discern what is truly from God: No one speaking by the Spirit of God can curse Jesus, and no one is able to say, "Jesus is Lord," except by the Holy Spirit.

4Now there are different kinds of spiritual gifts, but it is the same Holy Spirit who is the source of them all. 5There are different kinds of service in the church, but it is the same Lord we are serving. 6There are different ways God works in our lives, but it is the same God who does the work through all of us. 7A spiritual gift is given to each of us as a means of helping the entire church.

8To one person the Spirit gives the ability to give wise advice; to another he gives the gift of special knowledge. 9The Spirit gives special faith to another, and to someone else he gives the power to heal the sick. 10He gives one person the power to perform miracles, and to another the ability to prophesy. He gives someone else the ability to know whether it is really the Spirit of God or another spirit that is speaking. Still another person is given the ability to speak in unknown languages,* and another is given the ability to interpret what is being said. 11It is the one and only Holy Spirit who distributes these gifts. He alone decides which gift each person should have.

One Body with Many Parts

12The human body has many parts, but the many parts make up only one body. So it is with the body of Christ. 13Some of us are Jews, some are Gentiles, some are slaves, and some are free. But we have all been baptized into Christ's body by one Spirit, and we have all received the same Spirit.*

14Yes, the body has many different parts, not just one part. 15If the foot says, "I am not a part of the body because I am not a hand," that does not make it any less a part of the body. 16And if the ear says, "I am not part of the body because I am only an ear and not an eye," would that make it any less a part of the body? 17Suppose the whole body were an eye—then how would you hear? Or if your whole body were just one big ear, how could you smell anything?

18But God made our bodies with many parts, and he has put each part just where he wants it. 19What a strange thing a body would be if it had only one part! 20Yes, there are many parts, but only one body. 21The eye can never say to the hand, "I don't need you." The head can't say to the feet, "I don't need you."

22In fact, some of the parts that seem weakest and least important are really the most necessary. 23And the parts we regard as less honorable are those we clothe with the greatest care. So we carefully protect from the eyes of others those parts that should not be seen, 24while other parts do not require this special care. So God has put the body together in such a way that extra honor and care are given to those parts that have less dignity. 25This makes for harmony among

11:33 Greek *brothers.* 12:1 Greek *brothers.* 12:10 Or *in tongues;* also in 12:28, 30. 12:13 Greek *we were all given one Spirit to drink.*

OFF AND RUNNING ////
Does This Activity Build Me Up Spiritually?
Read 1 CORINTHIANS 10:23

This verse tackles the issue of whether certain activities will be spiritually constructive in your life—even if it falls into a so-called "gray" area. A more literal translation of that verse is "All things are permissible, but not all things promote growth in Christian character." The next time you question whether you should be seeing a certain movie, participating in a specific activity, or engaging in a certain habit, ask yourself the following questions:

the members, so that all the members care for each other equally. 26If one part suffers, all the parts suffer with it, and if one part is honored, all the parts are glad.

27Now all of you together are Christ's body, and each one of you is a separate and necessary part of it. 28Here is a list of some of the members that God has placed in the body of Christ:

first are apostles,
second are prophets,
third are teachers,
then those who do miracles,
those who have the gift of healing,
those who can help others,
those who can get others to work together,
those who speak in unknown languages.

29Is everyone an apostle? Of course not. Is everyone a prophet? No. Are all teachers? Does everyone have the power to do miracles? 30Does everyone have the gift of healing? Of course not. Does God give all of us the ability to speak in unknown languages? Can everyone interpret unknown languages? No! 31And in any event, you should desire the most helpful gifts.

Love Is the Greatest
First, however, let me tell you about something else that is better than any of them!

CHAPTER **13**
If I could speak in any language in heaven or on earth* but didn't love others, I would only be making meaningless noise like a loud gong or a clanging cymbal. 2If I had the gift of prophecy, and if I knew all the mysteries of the future and knew everything about everything, but didn't love others, what good would I be? And if I had the gift of faith so that I could speak to a mountain and make it move, without love I would be no good to anybody. 3If I gave everything I have

to the poor and even sacrificed my body, I could boast about it;* but if I didn't love others, I would be of no value whatsoever.

4Love is patient and kind. Love is not jealous or boastful or proud 5or rude. Love does not demand its own way. Love is not irritable, and it keeps no record of when it has been wronged. 6It is never glad about injustice but rejoices whenever the truth wins out. 7Love never gives up, never loses faith, is always hopeful, and endures through every circumstance.

8Love will last forever, but prophecy and speaking in unknown languages* and special knowledge will all disappear. 9Now we know only a little, and even the gift of prophecy reveals little! 10But when the end comes, these special gifts will all disappear.

11It's like this: When I was a child, I spoke and thought and reasoned as a child does. But when I grew up, I put away childish things. 12Now we see things imperfectly as in a poor mirror, but then we will see everything with perfect clarity.* All that I know now is partial and incomplete, but then I will know everything completely, just as God knows me now.

13There are three things that will endure— faith, hope, and love—and the greatest of these is love.

CHAPTER **14**
The Gifts of Tongues and Prophecy
Let love be your highest goal, but also desire the special abilities the Spirit gives, especially the gift of prophecy. 2For if your gift is the ability to speak in tongues,* you will be talking to God but not to people, since they won't be able to understand you. You will be speaking by the power of the Spirit, but it will all be mysterious. 3But one who prophesies is helping others grow in the Lord, encouraging and comforting them. 4A person who speaks in tongues is strength-

13:1 Greek *in tongues of people and angels.* 13:3 Some manuscripts read *and even gave my body to be burned.* 13:8 Or *in tongues.* 13:12 Greek *see face to face.* 14:2 Or *in unknown languages;* also in 14:4, 5, 13, 14, 18, 22, 28, 39.

• Will this activity make the things of this world more appealing than the things of God?
• Will it keep me from prayer?
• Will it diminish my hunger for God's Word?
• Will it spiritually tear me down by pulling me away from other Christian believers?

You do not have time for anything that would make this world more attractive, dull your desire for prayer, take away your appetite for Bible study, or keep you from Christian fellowship. Instead, look for things that will benefit and build your Christian character.

For the next note on "Responsibility," turn to p. 988.

ened personally in the Lord, but one who speaks a word of prophecy strengthens the entire church.

5I wish you all had the gift of speaking in tongues, but even more I wish you were all able to prophesy. For prophecy is a greater and more useful gift than speaking in tongues, unless someone interprets what you are saying so that the whole church can get some good out of it.

6Dear brothers and sisters,* if I should come to you talking in an unknown language,* how would that help you? But if I bring you some revelation or some special knowledge or some prophecy or some teaching—that is what will help you. 7Even musical instruments like the flute or the harp, though they are lifeless, are examples of the need for speaking in plain language. For no one will recognize the melody unless the notes are played clearly. 8And if the bugler doesn't sound a clear call, how will the soldiers know they are being called to battle? 9And it's the same for you. If you talk to people in a language they don't understand, how will they know what you mean? You might as well be talking to an empty room.

10There are so many different languages in the world, and all are excellent for those who understand them, 11but to me they mean nothing. I will not understand people who speak those languages, and they will not understand me. 12Since you are so eager to have spiritual gifts, ask God for those that will be of real help to the whole church.

13So anyone who has the gift of speaking in tongues should pray also for the gift of interpretation in order to tell people plainly what has been said. 14For if I pray in tongues, my spirit is praying, but I don't understand what I am saying.

15Well then, what shall I do? I will do both. I will pray in the spirit,* and I will pray in words I understand. I will sing in the spirit, and I will sing in words I understand. 16For if you praise God only in the spirit, how can those who don't understand you praise God along with you? How can they join you in giving thanks when they don't understand what you are saying? 17You will be giving thanks very nicely, no doubt, but it doesn't help the other people present.

18I thank God that I speak in tongues more than all of you. 19But in a church meeting I would much rather speak five understandable

words that will help others than ten thousand words in an unknown language.

20Dear brothers and sisters, don't be childish in your understanding of these things. Be innocent as babies when it comes to evil, but be mature and wise in understanding matters of this kind. 21It is written in the Scriptures,*

"I will speak to my own people
    through unknown languages
    and through the lips of foreigners.
But even then, they will not listen to me,"*
    says the Lord.

22So you see that speaking in tongues is a sign, not for believers, but for unbelievers; prophecy, however, is for the benefit of believers, not unbelievers. 23Even so, if unbelievers or people who don't understand these things come into your meeting and hear everyone talking in an unknown language, they will think you are crazy. 24But if all of you are prophesying, and unbelievers or people who don't understand these things come into your meeting, they will be convicted of sin, and they will be condemned by what you say. 25As they listen, their secret thoughts will be laid bare, and they will fall down on their knees and worship God, declaring, "God is really here among you."

A Call to Orderly Worship

26Well, my brothers and sisters, let's summarize what I am saying. When you meet, one will sing, another will teach, another will tell some special revelation God has given, one will speak in an unknown language, while another will interpret what is said. But everything that is done must be useful to all and build them up in the Lord. 27No more than two or three should speak in an unknown language. They must speak one at a time, and someone must be ready to interpret what they are saying. 28But if no one is present who can interpret, they must be silent in your church meeting and speak in tongues to God privately.

29Let two or three prophesy, and let the others evaluate what is said. 30But if someone is prophesying and another person receives a revelation from the Lord, the one who is speaking must stop. 31In this way, all who prophesy will have a turn to speak, one after the other, so that everyone will learn and be encouraged. 32Remember that people who prophesy are in control of their spirit and can wait their turn.

14:6a Greek *brothers;* also in 14:20, 26, 39.   **14:6b** Or *in tongues;* also in 14:19, 23, 26, 27.   **14:15** Or *in the Spirit;* also in 14:15b, 16.
14:21a Greek *in the law.*   **14:21b** Isa 28:11-12.

³³For God is not a God of disorder but of peace, as in all the other churches.*

³⁴Women should be silent during the church meetings. It is not proper for them to speak. They should be submissive, just as the law says. ³⁵If they have any questions to ask, let them ask their husbands at home, for it is improper for women to speak in church meetings.*

³⁶Do you think that the knowledge of God's word begins and ends with you Corinthians? Well, you are mistaken! ³⁷If you claim to be a prophet or think you are very spiritual, you should recognize that what I am saying is a command from the Lord himself. ³⁸But if you do not recognize this, you will not be recognized.*

³⁹So, dear brothers and sisters, be eager to prophesy, and don't forbid speaking in tongues. ⁴⁰But be sure that everything is done properly and in order.

CHAPTER **15**

The Resurrection of Christ

Now let me remind you, dear brothers and sisters,* of the Good News I preached to you before. You welcomed it then and still do now, for your faith is built on this wonderful message. ²And it is this Good News that saves you if you firmly believe it—unless, of course, you believed something that was never true in the first place.

³I passed on to you what was most important and what had also been passed on to me—that Christ died for our sins, just as the Scriptures said. ⁴He was buried, and he was raised from the dead on the third day, as the Scriptures said. ⁵He was seen by Peter* and then by the twelve apostles. ⁶After that, he was seen by more than five hundred of his followers* at one time, most of whom are still alive, though some have died by now. ⁷Then he was seen by James and later by all the apostles. ⁸Last of all, I saw him, too, long after the others, as though I had been born at the wrong time. ⁹For I am the least of all the apostles, and I am not worthy to be called an apostle after the way I persecuted the church of God.

¹⁰But whatever I am now, it is all because God poured out his special favor on me—and not without results. For I have worked harder than all the other apostles, yet it was not I but God who was working through me by his grace. ¹¹So

14:33 The phrase *as in all the other churches* could be joined to the beginning of 14:34.   14:35 Some manuscripts place verses 34-35 after 14:40.   14:38 Some manuscripts read *If you are ignorant of this, stay in your ignorance.*   15:1 Greek *brothers;* also in 15:31, 50, 58.   15:5 Greek *Cephas.*   15:6 Greek *the brothers.*

You Have a Place in the Church Read 1 CORINTHIANS 12:12-27

The apostle Paul used this illustration of the physical body to drive home an important point: Every single person has a vital role to play in the body of Christ. That means God has a specific purpose for *you* to carry out in your local church, and it is up to you to fill that purpose, with God's help. This passage explains why this is so important.

The Church Consists of Different People with Different Roles. When God designed the church, he did not intend for its members to be "Christian clones." Instead, he chose to use the various groups and spiritual gifts found throughout the church to bring attention to the person who unifies us: Jesus Christ (see Ephesians 3:10-11, p. 1025). When the church operates as God intended, it serves as a powerful witness to a watching world.

No One Person Is More Valuable than Another. No gift of the Holy Spirit is "better" than another. Therefore, each individual has a special place of significance within the body of Christ. Even though your role may not seem as visible as others—for instance, God may be using you to visit convalescent homes while someone else leads a Bible study—your role is just as vital.

We Need One Another to Function as God Intended. If you fail to use the special gifts and abilities God has given you, you do a disservice to the church. God wants you to realize the importance of working together and building friendships with other committed Christians. One could liken the church to a group of coals burning brightly together. Each coal not only emanates its own heat, but also helps to keep the others hot, all the while benefiting from their warmth, as well. If you were to isolate one of those coals from the others, it would only be a matter of time until its heat dissipated. The same holds true for us as believers. We need one another to function as individuals and as the body of Christ.

To begin the next topic, turn to p. A27.

Love Surpasses All Spiritual Gifts Read 1 CORINTHIANS 13:1-13

This passage gives one of the most complete descriptions of love in the Bible. More importantly, it shows that love needs to be the one thing in life we seek more than anything else. For without it, whatever we do or say really has no lasting value. Compare the love described here with the superficial love found in this world:

- God says love should be directed toward others (verses 1-3).
  The world says love should be directed toward ourselves.
- God says love is patient and kind (verse 4).
  The world says love satisfies your immediate needs.
- God says love is never jealous or envious (verse 4).
  The world says love means that you deserve the "best."
- God says love is never boastful or proud (verse 4).
  The world says love isn't necessary to make people respect you.
- God says love is never rude (verse 5).
  The world says love lets you act as you please.
- God says love does not demand its own way (verse 5).
  The world says love gets in the way of what is in it for me.
- God says love is not irritable or touchy, and it holds no grudges (verse 5).
  The world says love takes a backseat when it comes to seeking revenge.
- God says love rejoices in justice and truth (verse 6).
  The world says love understands—even ignores—evil.
- God says love is loyal (verse 7).
  The world says love should be self-serving.

CORNER STONES

The kind of love God wants you to give others is impossible to "manufacture" on our own. You might say that it is a "supernatural" love. It is a natural outflow of God's presence in our lives. That is why the Bible says, "[God] has given us the Holy Spirit to fill our hearts with his love" (Romans 5:5).

If you feel your love for others is falling short of God's ideal, ask the Holy Spirit to strengthen you in this area. Your relationships with others will never be the same.

For the next note on "Love," turn to p. 918.

---

it makes no difference whether I preach or they preach. The important thing is that you believed what we preached to you.

The Resurrection of the Dead

12But tell me this—since we preach that Christ rose from the dead, why are some of you saying there will be no resurrection of the dead? 13For if there is no resurrection of the dead, then Christ has not been raised either. 14And if Christ was not raised, then all our preaching is useless, and your trust in God is useless. 15And we apostles would all be lying about God, for we have said that God raised Christ from the grave, but that can't be true if there is no resurrection of the dead. 16If there is no resurrection of the dead, then Christ has not been raised. 17And if Christ has not been raised, then your faith is useless, and you are still under condemnation for your sins. 18In that case, all who have died believing in Christ have perished! 19And if we have hope in Christ only for this life, we are the most miserable people in the world.

20But the fact is that Christ has been raised from the dead. He has become the first of a great harvest of those who will be raised to life again.

21So you see, just as death came into the world through a man, Adam, now the resurrection from the dead has begun through another man, Christ. 22Everyone dies because all of us are related to Adam, the first man. But all who are related to Christ, the other man, will be given new life. 23But there is an order to this resurrection: Christ was raised first; then when Christ comes back, all his people will be raised.

24After that the end will come, when he will turn the Kingdom over to God the Father, having put down all enemies of every kind.* 25For Christ must reign until he humbles all his enemies beneath his feet. 26And the last enemy to be destroyed is death. 27For the Scriptures say, "God has given him authority over all things."* (Of course, when it says "authority over all things," it does not include God himself, who gave Christ his authority.) 28Then, when he has conquered all things, the Son will present himself to God, so that God, who gave his Son authority over all things, will be utterly supreme over everything everywhere.

29If the dead will not be raised, then what point is there in people being baptized for those who are dead? Why do it unless the dead will someday rise again?

30And why should we ourselves be continually risking our lives, facing death hour by hour? 31For I swear, dear brothers and sisters, I face death daily. This is as certain as my pride in what the Lord Jesus Christ has done in you. 32And what value was there in fighting wild beasts—those men of Ephesus*—if there will be no resurrection from the dead? If there is no resurrection,

"Let's feast and get drunk,
for tomorrow we die!"*

33Don't be fooled by those who say such things, for "bad company corrupts good character." 34Come to your senses and stop sinning. For to your shame I say that some of you don't even know God.

The Resurrection Body

35But someone may ask, "How will the dead be raised? What kind of bodies will they have?" 36What a foolish question! When you put a seed into the ground, it doesn't grow into a plant unless it dies first. 37And what you put in the ground is not the plant that will grow, but only a dry little seed of wheat or whatever it is you are planting. 38Then God gives it a new body—just the kind he wants it to have. A different kind of plant grows from each kind of seed. 39And just as there are different kinds of seeds and plants, so also there are different kinds of flesh—whether of humans, animals, birds, or fish. 40There are bodies in the heavens, and there are bodies on earth. The glory of the heavenly

bodies is different from the beauty of the earthly bodies. 41The sun has one kind of glory, while the moon and stars each have another kind. And even the stars differ from each other in their beauty and brightness.

42It is the same way for the resurrection of the dead. Our earthly bodies, which die and decay, will be different when they are resurrected, for they will never die. 43Our bodies now disappoint us, but when they are raised, they will be full of glory. They are weak now, but when they are raised, they will be full of power. 44They are natural human bodies now, but when they are raised, they will be spiritual bodies. For just as there are natural bodies, so also there are spiritual bodies.

45The Scriptures tell us, "The first man, Adam, became a living person."* But the last Adam—that is, Christ—is a life-giving Spirit. 46What came first was the natural body, then the spiritual body comes later. 47Adam, the first man, was made from the dust of the earth, while Christ, the second man, came from heaven. 48Every human being has an earthly body just like Adam's, but our heavenly bodies will be just like Christ's. 49Just as we are now like Adam, the man of the earth, so we will someday be like Christ, the man from heaven.

50What I am saying, dear brothers and sisters, is that flesh and blood cannot inherit the Kingdom of God. These perishable bodies of ours are not able to live forever.

51But let me tell you a wonderful secret God has revealed to us. Not all of us will die, but we will all be transformed! 52It will happen in a moment, in the blinking of an eye, when the last trumpet is blown. For when the trumpet sounds, the Christians who have died* will be raised with transformed bodies. And then we who are living will be transformed so that we will never die. 53For our perishable earthly bodies must be transformed into heavenly bodies that will never die.

54When this happens—when our perishable earthly bodies have been transformed into heavenly bodies that will never die—then at last the Scriptures will come true:

"Death is swallowed up in victory.*
55 O death, where is your victory?
O death, where is your sting?"*

56For sin is the sting that results in death, and the law gives sin its power. 57How we thank God,

15:24 Greek *every ruler and every authority and power.* 15:27 Ps 8:6. 15:32a Greek *fighting wild beasts in Ephesus.* 15:32b Isa 22:13.
15:45 Gen 2:7. 15:52 Greek *the dead.* 15:54 Isa 25:8. 15:55 Hos 13:14.

who gives us victory over sin and death through Jesus Christ our Lord!

58So, my dear brothers and sisters, be strong and steady, always enthusiastic about the Lord's work, for you know that nothing you do for the Lord is ever useless.

CHAPTER **16**
The Collection for Jerusalem
Now about the money being collected for the Christians in Jerusalem: You should follow the same procedures I gave to the churches in Galatia. 2On every Lord's Day,* each of you should put aside some amount of money in relation to what you have earned and save it for this offering. Don't wait until I get there and then try to collect it all at once. 3When I come I will write letters of recommendation for the messengers you choose to deliver your gift to Jerusalem. 4And if it seems appropriate for me also to go along, then we can travel together.

Paul's Final Instructions
5I am coming to visit you after I have been to Macedonia, for I am planning to travel through Macedonia. 6It could be that I will stay awhile with you, perhaps all winter, and then you can send me on my way to the next destination. 7This time I don't want to make just a short visit and then go right on. I want to come and stay awhile, if the Lord will let me. 8In the meantime, I will be staying here at Ephesus until the Festival of Pentecost, 9for there is a wide-open door for a great work here, and many people are responding. But there are many who oppose me.

10When Timothy comes, treat him with respect. He is doing the Lord's work, just as I am.

11Don't let anyone despise him. Send him on his way with your blessings when he returns to me. I am looking forward to seeing him soon, along with the other brothers.

12Now about our brother Apollos—I urged him to join the other brothers when they visit you, but he was not willing to come right now. He will be seeing you later, when the time is right.

13Be on guard. Stand true to what you believe. Be courageous. Be strong. 14And everything you do must be done with love.

15You know that Stephanas and his household were the first to become Christians in Greece,* and they are spending their lives in service to other Christians. I urge you, dear brothers and sisters,* 16to respect them fully and others like them who serve with such real devotion. 17I am so glad that Stephanas, Fortunatus, and Achaicus have come here. They have been making up for the help you weren't here to give me. 18They have been a wonderful encouragement to me, as they have been to you, too. You must give proper honor to all who serve so well.

Paul's Final Greetings
19The churches here in the province of Asia* greet you heartily in the Lord, along with Aquila and Priscilla and all the others who gather in their home for church meetings. 20All the brothers and sisters here have asked me to greet you for them. Greet each other in Christian love.*

21Here is my greeting, which I write with my own hand—PAUL.

22If anyone does not love the Lord, that person is cursed. Our Lord, come!*

23May the grace of the Lord Jesus be with you. 24My love to all of you in Christ Jesus.*

16:2 Greek *every first day of the week.* **16:15a** Greek *were the firstfruits in Achaia,* the southern region of the Greek peninsula. **16:15b** Greek *brothers;* also in 16:20. **16:19** *Asia* was a Roman province in what is now western Turkey. **16:20** Greek *with a sacred kiss.* **16:22** From Aramaic, *Marana tha.* **16:24** Some manuscripts add *Amen.*

2 Corinthians

CHAPTER **1**

Greetings from Paul

This letter is from Paul, appointed by God to be an apostle of Christ Jesus, and from our dear brother Timothy.

We are writing to God's church in Corinth and to all the Christians throughout Greece.*

2May God our Father and the Lord Jesus Christ give you his grace and peace.

God Offers Comfort to All

3All praise to the God and Father of our Lord Jesus Christ. He is the source* of every mercy and the God who comforts us. 4He comforts us in all our troubles so that we can comfort others. When others are troubled, we will be able to give them the same comfort God has given us. 5You can be sure that the more we suffer for Christ, the more God will shower us with his comfort through Christ. 6So when we are weighed down with troubles, it is for your benefit and salvation! For when God comforts us, it is so that we, in turn, can be an encouragement to you. Then you can patiently endure the same things we suffer. 7We are confident that as you share in suffering, you will also share God's comfort.

8I think you ought to know, dear brothers and sisters,* about the trouble we went through in the province of Asia. We were crushed and completely overwhelmed, and we thought we would never live through it. 9In fact, we expected to die. But as a result, we learned not to rely on ourselves, but on God who can raise the dead. 10And he did deliver us from mortal danger. And we are confident that he will continue to deliver us. 11He will rescue us because you are helping by praying for us. As a result, many will give thanks to God because so many people's prayers for our safety have been answered.

Paul's Change of Plans

12We can say with confidence and a clear conscience that we have been honest* and sincere in all our dealings. We have depended on God's grace, not on our own earthly wisdom. That is how we have acted toward everyone, and especially toward you. 13My letters have been straightforward, and there is nothing written between the lines and nothing you can't understand. I hope someday you will fully understand us, 14even if you don't fully understand us now. Then on the day when our Lord Jesus comes back again, you will be proud of us in the same way we are proud of you.

15Since I was so sure of your understanding and trust, I wanted to give you a double blessing. 16I wanted to stop and see you on my way to Macedonia and again on my return trip. Then you could send me on my way to Judea.

17You may be asking why I changed my plan. Hadn't I made up my mind yet? Or am I like people of the world who say yes when they really mean no? 18As surely as God is true, I am not that sort of person. My yes means yes 19because Jesus Christ, the Son of God, never wavers between yes and no. He is the one whom Timothy, Silas,* and I preached to you, and he is the divine Yes—God's affirmation. 20For all of God's promises have been fulfilled in him. That is why we say "Amen" when we give glory to God through Christ. 21It is God who gives us, along with you, the ability to stand firm for Christ.* He has commissioned us, 22and he has identified us as his own by placing the Holy Spirit in our hearts as the first installment of everything he will give us.

1:1 Greek *Achaia*, the southern region of the Greek peninsula. 1:3 Greek *the Father.* 1:8 Greek *brothers.* 1:12 Some manuscripts read *holy.* 1:19 Greek *Silvanus.* 1:21 Or *who has identified us and you as genuine Christians.*

23Now I call upon God as my witness that I am telling the truth. The reason I didn't return to Corinth was to spare you from a severe rebuke. 24But that does not mean we want to tell you exactly how to put your faith into practice.* We want to work together with you so you will be full of joy as you stand firm in your faith.

CHAPTER **2**

So I said to myself, "No, I won't do it. I won't make them unhappy with another painful visit." 2For if I cause you pain and make you sad, who is going to make me glad? 3That is why I wrote as I did in my last letter, so that when I do come, I will not be made sad by the very ones who ought to give me the greatest joy. Surely you know that my happiness depends on your happiness. 4How painful it was to write that letter! Heartbroken, I cried over it. I didn't want to hurt you, but I wanted you to know how very much I love you.

Forgiveness for the Sinner

5I am not overstating it when I say that the man who caused all the trouble hurt your entire church more than he hurt me. 6He was punished enough when most of you were united in your judgment against him. 7Now it is time to forgive him and comfort him. Otherwise he may become so discouraged that he won't be able to recover. 8Now show him that you still love him.

9I wrote to you as I did to find out how far you would go in obeying me. 10When you forgive this man, I forgive him, too. And when I forgive him (for whatever is to be forgiven), I do so with Christ's authority for your benefit, 11so that Satan will not outsmart us. For we are very familiar with his evil schemes.

Ministers of the New Covenant

12Well, when I came to the city of Troas to preach the Good News of Christ, the Lord gave me tremendous opportunities. 13But I couldn't rest because my dear brother Titus hadn't yet arrived with a report from you. So I said goodbye and went on to Macedonia to find him.

14But thanks be to God, who made us his captives and leads us along in Christ's triumphal procession. Now wherever we go he uses us to tell others about the Lord and to spread the Good News like a sweet perfume. 15Our lives are a fragrance presented by Christ to God. But this fragrance is perceived differently by those being

saved and by those perishing. 16To those who are perishing we are a fearful smell of death and doom. But to those who are being saved we are a life-giving perfume. And who is adequate for such a task as this? 17You see, we are not like those hucksters—and there are many of them—who preach just to make money. We preach God's message with sincerity and with Christ's authority. And we know that the God who sent us is watching us.

CHAPTER **3**

Are we beginning again to tell you how good we are? Some people need to bring letters of recommendation with them or ask you to write letters of recommendation for them. 2But the only letter of recommendation we need is you yourselves! Your lives are a letter written in our* hearts, and everyone can read it and recognize our good work among you. 3Clearly, you are a letter from Christ prepared by us. It is written not with pen and ink, but with the Spirit of the living God. It is carved not on stone, but on human hearts.

4We are confident of all this because of our great trust in God through Christ. 5It is not that we think we can do anything of lasting value by ourselves. Our only power and success come from God. 6He is the one who has enabled us to represent his new covenant. This is a covenant, not of written laws, but of the Spirit. The old way ends in death; in the new way, the Holy Spirit gives life.

The Glory of the New Covenant

7That old system of law etched in stone led to death, yet it began with such glory that the people of Israel could not bear to look at Moses' face. For his face shone with the glory of God, even though the brightness was already fading away. 8Shouldn't we expect far greater glory when the Holy Spirit is giving life? 9If the old covenant, which brings condemnation, was glorious, how much more glorious is the new covenant, which makes us right with God! 10In fact, that first glory was not glorious at all compared with the overwhelming glory of the new covenant. 11So if the old covenant, which has been set aside, was full of glory, then the new covenant, which remains forever, has far greater glory.

12Since this new covenant gives us such confidence, we can be very bold. 13We are not like

1:24 Greek *want to lord it over your faith.*   3:2 Some manuscripts read *your.*

Moses, who put a veil over his face so the people of Israel would not see the glory fading away. [14]But the people's minds were hardened, and even to this day whenever the old covenant is being read, a veil covers their minds so they cannot understand the truth. And this veil can be removed only by believing in Christ. [15]Yes, even today when they read Moses' writings, their hearts are covered with that veil, and they do not understand.

[16]But whenever anyone turns to the Lord, then the veil is taken away. [17]Now, the Lord is the Spirit, and wherever the Spirit of the Lord is, he gives freedom. [18]And all of us have had that veil removed so that we can be mirrors that brightly reflect* the glory of the Lord. And as the Spirit of the Lord works within us, we become more and more like him and reflect his glory even more.

CHAPTER **4**

Treasure in Perishable Containers

And so, since God in his mercy has given us this wonderful ministry, we never give up. [2]We reject all shameful and underhanded methods. We do not try to trick anyone, and we do not distort the word of God. We tell the truth before God, and all who are honest know that.

[3]If the Good News we preach is veiled from anyone, it is a sign that they are perishing. [4]Satan, the god of this evil world, has blinded the minds of those who don't believe, so they are unable to see the glorious light of the Good News that is shining upon them. They don't understand the message we preach about the glory of Christ, who is the exact likeness of God.

[5]We don't go around preaching about ourselves; we preach Christ Jesus, the Lord. All we say about ourselves is that we are your servants because of what Jesus has done for us. [6]For God, who said, "Let there be light in the darkness," has made us understand that this light is the brightness of the glory of God that is seen in the face of Jesus Christ.

[7]But this precious treasure—this light and power that now shine within us—is held in perishable containers, that is, in our weak bodies.* So everyone can see that our glorious power is from God and is not our own.

[8]We are pressed on every side by troubles, but we are not crushed and broken. We are perplexed, but we don't give up and quit. [9]We are

hunted down, but God never abandons us. We get knocked down, but we get up again and keep going. [10]Through suffering, these bodies of ours constantly share in the death of Jesus so that the life of Jesus may also be seen in our bodies.

[11]Yes, we live under constant danger of death because we serve Jesus, so that the life of Jesus will be obvious in our dying bodies. [12]So we live in the face of death, but it has resulted in eternal life for you.

[13]But we continue to preach because we have the same kind of faith the psalmist had when he said, "I believed in God, and so I speak."* [14]We know that the same God who raised our Lord Jesus will also raise us with Jesus and present us to himself along with you. [15]All of these things are for your benefit. And as God's grace brings more and more people to Christ, there will be great thanksgiving, and God will receive more and more glory.

[16]That is why we never give up. Though our bodies are dying, our spirits are* being renewed

4:13 Ps 116:10.   4:16 Greek *our inner being is.*

Trials Help Us Comfort Others   Read 2 CORINTHIANS 1:3-7

The apostle Paul penned these words from personal experience. He had seen his share of suffering over the years—particularly for the sake of the gospel of Jesus Christ. He was thrown into prison on more than one occasion, but he continued to praise God and share his faith in Christ. He was shipwrecked, abandoned by former friends, pelted by stones, and left for dead. His faith, however, remained firm. Why? Because he learned to draw his comfort from the Lord. This then enabled him to be a greater source of comfort to those around him.

The next time someone ridicules or rejects you because of your commitment to Christ, remember Paul's words. You do not need to fear trials in your life. No matter how great a hardship you face, realize that Jesus *will* comfort and strengthen you. In turn, you will be better equipped to comfort those around you who suffer the same hardships.

For the next note on "Have Courage in Trials," turn to p. 1007.

For the next note on "Have Courage in Trials," turn to p. 1007.

3:18 Or *so that we can see in a mirror.*   4:7 Greek *But we have this treasure in earthen vessels.*

What Are Satan's Abilities? Read 2 CORINTHIANS 4:3-4

Ever since Satan lost his privileges and was cast to this earth, he has been using his abilities to oppose the work that God has been seeking to accomplish. Paul's second letter to the Corinthians reveals at least three of Satan's abilities:

1. He Is the God of This World. This becomes more and more evident as you survey the increasing wickedness around you. While Christ conquered sin and death at the cross, this world is still flawed and evil. But Satan will lose his reign in this world when Christ returns to establish his Kingdom on earth.

2. He Blinds the Minds of Unbelievers. According to this text, Satan wants to keep those who do not have a relationship with God from coming to God. The unbelieving mind has a difficult time understanding the message of the gospel because Satan has darkened or blinded that person's mind. Yet Christ can break through that barrier (see 2 Timothy 2:24-26, p. 1063).

3. He Is a Master Counterfeiter. One of Satan's greatest abilities is deception. He is good at deception because he makes lies look like truth. Paul describes Satan as someone who disguises himself as an angel of light (see 2 Corinthians 11:14, p. 1012). That is, he fools people by making them think the lies he offers are truth. His lies take on various forms, such as cults and false doctrines. But we can discern the difference between truth and error when we test them against what is found in God's Word.

For the next note on "Who Is the Devil?" turn to p. 440.

CORNER STONES

---

every day. [17]For our present troubles are quite small and won't last very long. Yet they produce for us an immeasurably great glory that will last forever! [18]So we don't look at the troubles we can see right now; rather, we look forward to what we have not yet seen. For the troubles we see will soon be over, but the joys to come will last forever.

CHAPTER 5
New Bodies

For we know that when this earthly tent we live in is taken down—when we die and leave these bodies—we will have a home in heaven, an eternal body made for us by God himself and not by human hands. [2]We grow weary in our present bodies, and we long for the day when we will put on our heavenly bodies like new clothing. [3]For we will not be spirits without bodies, but we will put on new heavenly bodies. [4]Our dying bodies make us groan and sigh, but it's not that we want to die and have no bodies at all. We want to slip into our new bodies so that these dying bodies will be swallowed up by everlasting life. [5]God himself has prepared us for this, and as a guarantee he has given us his Holy Spirit.

5:14a Or *urges us on.*

[6]So we are always confident, even though we know that as long as we live in these bodies we are not at home with the Lord. [7]That is why we live by believing and not by seeing. [8]Yes, we are fully confident, and we would rather be away from these bodies, for then we will be at home with the Lord. [9]So our aim is to please him always, whether we are here in this body or away from this body. [10]For we must all stand before Christ to be judged. We will each receive whatever we deserve for the good or evil we have done in our bodies.

We Are God's Ambassadors

[11]It is because we know this solemn fear of the Lord that we work so hard to persuade others. God knows we are sincere, and I hope you know this, too. [12]Are we trying to pat ourselves on the back again? No, we are giving you a reason to be proud of us, so you can answer those who brag about having a spectacular ministry rather than having a sincere heart before God. [13]If it seems that we are crazy, it is to bring glory to God. And if we are in our right minds, it is for your benefit. [14]Whatever we do, it is because Christ's love controls us.* Since we believe that Christ died

for everyone, we also believe that we have all died to the old life we used to live.* ¹⁵He died for everyone so that those who receive his new life will no longer live to please themselves. Instead, they will live to please Christ, who died and was raised for them.

¹⁶So we have stopped evaluating others by what the world thinks about them. Once I mistakenly thought of Christ that way, as though he were merely a human being. How differently I think about him now! ¹⁷What this means is that those who become Christians become new persons. They are not the same anymore, for the old life is gone. A new life has begun!

¹⁸All this newness of life is from God, who brought us back to himself through what Christ did. And God has given us the task of reconciling people to him. ¹⁹For God was in Christ, reconciling the world to himself, no longer counting people's sins against them. This is the wonderful message he has given us to tell others. ²⁰We are Christ's ambassadors, and God is using us to speak to you. We urge you, as though Christ himself were here pleading with you, "Be reconciled to God!" ²¹For God made Christ, who never sinned, to be the offering for our sin, so that we could be made right with God through Christ.

CHAPTER **6**

As God's partners,* we beg you not to reject this marvelous message of God's great kindness. ²For God says,

"At just the right time, I heard you.
On the day of salvation, I helped you."*

Indeed, God is ready to help you right now. Today is the day of salvation.

Paul's Hardships

³We try to live in such a way that no one will be hindered from finding the Lord by the way we act, and so no one can find fault with our ministry. ⁴In everything we do we try to show that we are true ministers of God. We patiently endure troubles and hardships and calamities of every kind. ⁵We have been beaten, been put in jail, faced angry mobs, worked to exhaustion, endured sleepless nights, and gone without food. ⁶We have proved ourselves by our purity, our understanding, our patience, our kindness, our sincere love, and the power of the Holy Spirit.*

5:14b Greek *Since one died on behalf of all, then all died.* 6:1 Or *As we work together.* 6:2 Isa 49:8. 6:6 Or *the holiness of spirit.*

Trials Are Survivable
Read 2 CORINTHIANS 4:7-18

When we face trials in our lives, we can do one of two things. We can either become self-absorbed with our problems and say, "Look at how tough things are!" Or we can keep our eyes on Jesus and say, "This is only temporary." The apostle Paul was able to focus on the temporary nature of his problems because he accepted five important facts:

1. Our Bodies Are Weak and Mortal. Paul wasn't the type to be caught up in his bodily aches and pains. He didn't strive for the perfect body or the perfect image because he knew his body was a "perishable container." The Bible does not teach that we should neglect our bodies, but it does say that spiritual exercise is more important and beneficial (see 1 Timothy 4:8, p. 1058).

2. God's Power Is Displayed in Our Weakness. If we become overly obsessed with ourselves, we will never give God the chance to work through our lives. Paul recognized that God's glory shines through our weaknesses.

3. God Does Not Abandon Us. Even though we may be "crushed" and "perplexed," we have the hope that God will protect and strengthen us through these trials.

4. Trials Can Be Witnessing Opportunities. When people see the inner strength we have in Christ, they will take notice. This is well illustrated in the story of Paul and Silas, who were put in prison for preaching the gospel (see Acts 16:16-36, p. 944). Though they had been whipped and had their legs clamped in stocks in a damp, dark dungeon, they began to pray and worship the Lord in song. In an unusual string of events, these men were able to lead their jailer, as well as his entire family, to the Lord. Paul and Silas's godly attitude, which enabled them to rejoice in such a time of trouble, prepared the soil of this man's heart, opening him up to the gospel they preached.

5. We Have the Hope of Heaven. These trials are only a momentary blink in time compared to the eternal joys and blessings of heaven.

For the next note on "Have Courage in Trials," turn to p. 861.

When Does a Christian Enter Heaven? Read 2 CORINTHIANS 5:6-9

S ome people teach that when we die we go into a state of suspended animation. Then later on we are called into the presence of God. But this passage clearly explains that when a believer dies, he or she will go directly to heaven to "be at home with the Lord." This is illustrated in at least two other instances in Scripture:

1. The Thief on the Cross. As Jesus was being crucified, a thief hanging on a cross next to him asked Jesus to remember him when Jesus entered his Kingdom. To this request, Jesus replied, *"Today* you will be with me in paradise" (Luke 23:40-43).

2. The Apostle Paul. The apostle Paul wrote, "I long to go and be with Christ" (Philippians 1:23). He didn't say, "I long to depart and be suspended in a soul sleep for a few thousand years." Paul understood better than most this truth about entering heaven, because he had already had a glimpse of heaven. It is probable that when Paul had been stoned, he died and entered the presence of the Lord. But God still had work for Paul to do on earth. So he sent Paul back to earth to carry out God's work (see 2 Corinthians 12:2-4, p. 1013).

The moment you take your last breath on earth, you will take your first breath in heaven. So don't be afraid of death. Instead, enjoy your life in Christ on earth, and spend the rest of your time here introducing others to the one with whom you will spend eternity.

For the next note on "What Is Heaven?" turn to p. 816.

CORNER STONES

7We have faithfully preached the truth. God's power has been working in us. We have righteousness as our weapon, both to attack and to defend ourselves. 8We serve God whether people honor us or despise us, whether they slander us or praise us. We are honest, but they call us impostors. 9We are well known, but we are treated as unknown. We live close to death, but here we are, still alive. We have been beaten within an inch of our lives. 10Our hearts ache, but we always have joy. We are poor, but we give spiritual riches to others. We own nothing, and yet we have everything.

11Oh, dear Corinthian friends! We have spoken honestly with you. Our hearts are open to you. 12If there is a problem between us, it is not because of a lack of love on our part, but because you have withheld your love from us. 13I am talking now as I would to my own children. Open your hearts to us!

The Temple of the Living God

14Don't team up with those who are unbelievers. How can goodness be a partner with wickedness? How can light live with darkness? 15What harmony can there be between Christ and the Devil*? How can a believer be a part-

ner with an unbeliever? 16And what union can there be between God's temple and idols? For we are the temple of the living God. As God said:

"I will live in them
and walk among them.
I will be their God,
and they will be my people.*
17 Therefore, come out from them
and separate yourselves from them, says
the Lord.
Don't touch their filthy things,
and I will welcome you.*
18 And I will be your Father,
and you will be my sons and daughters,
says the Lord Almighty.*"

CHAPTER 7

Because we have these promises, dear friends, let us cleanse ourselves from everything that can defile our body or spirit. And let us work toward complete purity because we fear God.

Paul's Joy at the Church's Repentance

2Please open your hearts to us. We have not done wrong to anyone. We have not led anyone

6:15 Greek *and Beliar.*   6:16 Lev 26:12; Ezek 37:27.   6:17 Isa 52:11; Ezek 20:34.   6:18 2 Sam 7:14.

astray. We have not taken advantage of anyone. [3]I'm not saying this to condemn you, for I said before that you are in our hearts forever. We live or die together with you. [4]I have the highest confidence in you, and my pride in you is great. You have greatly encouraged me; you have made me happy despite all our troubles.

[5]When we arrived in Macedonia there was no rest for us. Outside there was conflict from every direction, and inside there was fear. [6]But God, who encourages those who are discouraged, encouraged us by the arrival of Titus. [7]His presence was a joy, but so was the news he brought of the encouragement he received from you. When he told me how much you were looking forward to my visit, and how sorry you were about what had happened, and how loyal your love is for me, I was filled with joy!

[8]I am no longer sorry that I sent that letter to you, though I was sorry for a time, for I know that it was painful to you for a little while. [9]Now I am glad I sent it, not because it hurt you, but because the pain caused you to have remorse and change your ways. It was the kind of sorrow God wants his people to have, so you were not harmed by us in any way. [10]For God can use sorrow in our lives to help us turn away from sin and seek salvation. We will never regret that kind of sorrow. But sorrow without repentance is the kind that results in death.

[11]Just see what this godly sorrow produced in you! Such earnestness, such concern to clear yourselves, such indignation, such alarm, such longing to see me, such zeal, and such a readiness to punish the wrongdoer. You showed that you have done everything you could to make things right. [12]My purpose was not to write about who did the wrong or who was wronged. I wrote to you so that in the sight of God you could show how much you really do care for us. [13]We have been encouraged by this.

In addition to our own encouragement, we were especially delighted to see how happy Titus was at the way you welcomed him and set his mind at ease. [14]I had told him how proud I was of you—and you didn't disappoint me. I have always told you the truth, and now my boasting to Titus has also proved true! [15]Now he cares for you more than ever when he remembers the way you listened to him and welcomed him with such respect and deep concern. [16]I am very happy now because I have complete confidence in you.

CHAPTER **8**
A Call to Generous Giving
Now I want to tell you, dear brothers and sisters,* what God in his kindness has done for the churches in Macedonia. [2]Though they have been going through much trouble and hard times, their wonderful joy and deep poverty have overflowed in rich generosity. [3]For I can testify that they gave not only what they could

8:1 Greek *brothers.*

Recognize That You Are a New Creation Read 2 CORINTHIANS 5:14-17

Although outwardly you may appear to be the same person, when you received Christ you underwent a radical heart transplant. You literally became a "new person" (or "creation") inside. This short passage of Scripture highlights some encouraging points as you endeavor to be obedient to God.

- As "new creations," Christ's love compels us to please God rather than ourselves.
- As "new creations," we can look beyond the "packaging" of a person to what is inside.
- As "new creations," we have become altogether different people.
- As "new creations," we have been given a clean slate, a fresh start, and a new nature.

The new nature you have received is like a tender little flower. It takes time and effort to cultivate. You may find it hard at times to obey God and leave certain old habits behind at first. But as you cultivate that new nature by spending more time with God through activities like prayer and Bible study, you will notice changes as the weeks, months, and years go by.

A man from India was heard to compare our new spiritual nature and our old selfish one to two dogs constantly fighting with each other. He went on to say that he could determine which dog would win. When asked how he determined which dog won, his response was, "The one I feed the most, of course." When you take time to "feed" your new spiritual nature (as you are doing right now), you give it the edge in this ongoing conflict between good and evil.

For the next note on "Obey God," turn to p. 197.

afford but far more. And they did it of their own free will. 4They begged us again and again for the gracious privilege of sharing in the gift for the Christians in Jerusalem. 5Best of all, they went beyond our highest hopes, for their first action was to dedicate themselves to the Lord and to us for whatever directions God might give them.

6So we have urged Titus, who encouraged your giving in the first place, to return to you and encourage you to complete your share in this ministry of giving. 7Since you excel in so many ways—you have so much faith, such gifted speakers, such knowledge, such enthusiasm, and such love for us*—now I want you to excel also in this gracious ministry of giving. 8I am not saying you must do it, even though the other churches are eager to do it. This is one way to prove your love is real.

9You know how full of love and kindness our Lord Jesus Christ was. Though he was very rich, yet for your sakes he became poor, so that by his poverty he could make you rich.

10I suggest that you finish what you started a year ago, for you were the first to propose this idea, and you were the first to begin doing something about it. 11Now you should carry this project through to completion just as enthusiastically as you began it. Give whatever you can according to what you have. 12If you are really eager to give, it isn't important how much you are able to give. God wants you to give what you have, not what you don't have. 13Of course, I don't mean you should give so much that you suffer from having too little. I only mean that there should be some equality. 14Right now you have plenty and can help them. Then at some other time they can share with you when you need it. In this way, everyone's needs will be met. 15Do you remember what the Scriptures say about this? "Those who gathered a lot had nothing left over, and those who gathered only a little had enough."*

Titus and His Companions
16I am thankful to God that he has given Titus the same enthusiasm for you that I have. 17He welcomed our request that he visit you again. In fact, he himself was eager to go and see you. 18We are also sending another brother with Titus. He is highly praised in all the churches as a preacher of the Good News. 19He was appointed by the churches to accompany us as we take the offering to Jerusalem*—a service that glorifies the Lord and shows our eagerness to help. 20By traveling together we will guard against any suspicion, for we are anxious that no one should find fault with the way we are handling this generous gift. 21We are careful to be honorable before the Lord, but we also want everyone else to know we are honorable.

22And we are also sending with them another brother who has been thoroughly tested and has shown how earnest he is on many occasions. He is now even more enthusiastic because of his increased confidence in you. 23If anyone asks about Titus, say that he is my partner who works with me to help you. And these brothers are representatives* of the churches. They are splendid examples of those who bring glory to Christ. 24So show them your love, and prove to all the churches that our boasting about you is justified.

CHAPTER **9**
The Collection for Christians in Jerusalem
I really don't need to write to you about this gift for the Christians in Jerusalem.* 2For I know how eager you are to help, and I have been boasting to our friends in Macedonia that you Christians in Greece* were ready to send an offering a year ago. In fact, it was your enthusiasm that stirred up many of them to begin helping. 3But I am sending these brothers just to be sure that you really are ready, as I told them you would be, with your money all collected. I don't want it to turn out that I was wrong in my boasting about you. 4I would be humiliated—

8:7 Some manuscripts read *love from us to you.*   8:15 Exod 16:18.   8:19 See 1 Cor 16:3-4.   8:23 Greek *apostles.*   9:1 Greek *about the offering for the saints.*   9:2 Greek *Achaia,* the southern region of the Greek peninsula.

OFF AND RUNNING ▰▰▰▰

Avoid Relationships That Could Cause You to Sin
Read 2 CORINTHIANS 6:14–7:1

As a Christian, you should avoid anything that would compromise your relationship with Jesus. That includes entering into a relationship, business deal, or any other association that would tempt you to lower your standards or discredit your integrity. When you team up with someone who does not love and fear the Lord, that relationship can dramatically weaken you spiritually.

and so would you—if some Macedonian Christians came with me, only to find that you still weren't ready after all I had told them! ⁵So I thought I should send these brothers ahead of me to make sure the gift you promised is ready. But I want it to be a willing gift, not one given under pressure.

⁶Remember this—a farmer who plants only a few seeds will get a small crop. But the one who plants generously will get a generous crop. ⁷You must each make up your own mind as to how much you should give. Don't give reluctantly or in response to pressure. For God loves the person who gives cheerfully. ⁸And God will generously provide all you need. Then you will always have everything you need and plenty left over to share with others. ⁹As the Scriptures say,

"Godly people give generously to the poor.
Their good deeds will never be forgotten."*

¹⁰For God is the one who gives seed to the farmer and then bread to eat. In the same way, he will give you many opportunities to do good, and he will produce a great harvest of generosity* in you. ¹¹Yes, you will be enriched so that you can give even more generously. And when we take your gifts to those who need them, they will break out in thanksgiving to God. ¹²So two good things will happen—the needs of the Christians in Jerusalem will be met, and they will joyfully express their thanksgiving to God. ¹³You will be glorifying God through your generous gifts. For your generosity to them will prove that you are obedient to the Good News of Christ. ¹⁴And they will pray for you with deep affection because of the wonderful grace of God shown through you.

¹⁵Thank God for his Son—a gift too wonderful for words!*

CHAPTER 10
Paul Defends His Authority

Now I, Paul, plead with you. I plead with the gentleness and kindness that Christ himself would use, even though some of you say I am bold in my letters but timid in person. ²I hope it won't be necessary, but when I come I may have to be very bold with those who think we act from purely human motives. ³We are human, but we don't wage war with human plans and methods. ⁴We use God's mighty weapons, not mere worldly weapons, to knock down the Devil's strongholds. ⁵With these weapons we break down every proud argument that keeps people from knowing God. With these weapons we conquer their rebellious ideas, and we teach them to obey Christ. ⁶And we will punish those who remained disobedient after the rest of you became loyal and obedient.

⁷The trouble with you is that you make your decisions on the basis of appearance.* You must recognize that we belong to Christ just as much as those who proudly declare that they belong to Christ. ⁸I may seem to be boasting too much about the authority given to us by the Lord. But this authority is to build you up, not to tear you down. And I will not be put to shame by having my work among you destroyed.

⁹Now this is not just an attempt to frighten you by my letters. ¹⁰For some say, "Don't worry about Paul. His letters are demanding and forceful, but in person he is weak, and his speeches are really bad!" ¹¹The ones who say this must realize that we will be just as demanding and forceful in person as we are in our letters.

¹²Oh, don't worry; I wouldn't dare say that I am as wonderful as these other men who tell you how important they are! But they are only comparing themselves with each other, and measuring themselves by themselves. What foolishness!

¹³But we will not boast of authority we do not have. Our goal is to stay within the boundaries of God's plan for us, and this plan includes our working there with you. ¹⁴We are not going too far when we claim authority over you, for we were the first to travel all the way to you with the

9:9 Ps 112:9.   9:10 Greek *righteousness.*   9:15 Greek *Thank God for his indescribable gift.*   10:7 Or *Look at the obvious facts.*

God does not want us to avoid all interaction with nonbelievers. Jesus himself spent time with the "sinners" and social outcasts of his day in order to share the message of salvation. God just wants us to keep from being so closely connected to unbelievers that it ultimately affects our faith and behavior, tempting us to compromise our witness for and obedience to God.

For the next note on "Relationships," turn to p. 1104.

Good News of Christ. 15Nor do we claim credit for the work someone else has done. Instead, we hope that your faith will grow and that our work among you will be greatly enlarged. 16Then we will be able to go and preach the Good News in other places that are far beyond you, where no one else is working. Then there will be no question about being in someone else's territory. 17As the Scriptures say,

"The person who wishes to boast
　　should boast only of what the Lord has
　　done."*

18When people boast about themselves, it doesn't count for much. But when the Lord commends someone, that's different!

CHAPTER 11
Paul and the False Apostles
I hope you will be patient with me as I keep on talking like a fool. Please bear with me. 2I am jealous for you with the jealousy of God himself. For I promised you as a pure bride* to one husband, Christ. 3But I fear that somehow you will be led away from your pure and simple devotion to Christ, just as Eve was deceived by the serpent. 4You seem to believe whatever anyone tells you, even if they preach about a different Jesus than the one we preach, or a different Spirit than the one you received, or a different kind of gospel than the one you believed. 5But I don't think I am inferior to these "super apostles." 6I may not be a trained speaker, but I know what I am talking about. I think you realize this by now, for we have proved it again and again.

7Did I do wrong when I humbled myself and honored you by preaching God's Good News to you without expecting anything in return? 8I "robbed" other churches by accepting their contributions so I could serve you at no cost. 9And when I was with you and didn't have enough to live on, I did not ask you to help me. For the brothers who came from Macedonia brought me another gift. I have never yet asked you for any support, and I never will. 10As surely as the truth of Christ is in me, I will never stop boasting about this all over Greece.* 11Why? Because I don't love you? God knows I do.

12But I will continue doing this to cut the ground out from under the feet of those who boast that their work is just like ours. 13These people are false apostles. They have fooled you by disguising themselves as apostles of Christ.

14But I am not surprised! Even Satan can disguise himself as an angel of light. 15So it is no wonder his servants can also do it by pretending to be godly ministers. In the end they will get every bit of punishment their wicked deeds deserve.

Paul's Many Trials
16Once again, don't think that I have lost my wits to talk like this. But even if you do, listen to me, as you would to a foolish person, while I also boast a little. 17Such bragging is not something the Lord wants, but I am acting like a fool. 18And since others boast about their human achievements, I will, too. 19After all, you, who think you are so wise, enjoy listening to fools! 20You put up with it when they make you their slaves, take everything you have, take advantage of you, put on airs, and slap you in the face. 21I'm ashamed to say that we were not strong enough to do that!

But whatever they dare to boast about—I'm talking like a fool again—I can boast about it, too. 22They say they are Hebrews, do they? So am I. And they say they are Israelites? So am I. And they are descendants of Abraham? So am I. 23They say they serve Christ? I know I sound like a madman, but I have served him far more! I have worked harder, been put in jail more often, been whipped times without number, and faced death again and again. 24Five different times the Jews gave me thirty-nine lashes. 25Three times I was beaten with rods. Once I was stoned. Three times I was shipwrecked. Once I spent a whole night and a day adrift at sea. 26I have traveled many weary miles. I have faced danger from flooded rivers and from robbers. I have faced danger from my own people, the Jews, as well as from the Gentiles. I have faced danger in the cities, in the deserts, and on the stormy seas. And I have faced danger from men who claim to be Christians but are not.* 27I have lived with weariness and pain and sleepless nights. Often I have been hungry and thirsty and have gone without food. Often I have shivered with cold, without enough clothing to keep me warm.

28Then, besides all this, I have the daily burden of how the churches are getting along. 29Who is weak without my feeling that weakness? Who is led astray, and I do not burn with anger?

30If I must boast, I would rather boast about the things that show how weak I am. 31God, the

Father of our Lord Jesus, who is to be praised forever, knows I tell the truth. 32When I was in Damascus, the governor under King Aretas kept guards at the city gates to catch me. 33But I was lowered in a basket through a window in the city wall, and that's how I got away!

CHAPTER **12**

Paul's Vision and His Thorn in the Flesh
This boasting is all so foolish, but let me go on. Let me tell about the visions and revelations I received from the Lord. 2I* was caught up into the third heaven fourteen years ago. 3Whether my body was there or just my spirit, I don't know; only God knows. 4But I do know that I* was caught up into paradise and heard things so astounding that they cannot be told. 5That experience is something worth boasting about, but I am not going to do it. I am going to boast only about my weaknesses. 6I have plenty to boast about and would be no fool in doing it, because I would be telling the truth. But I won't do it. I don't want anyone to think more highly of me than what they can actually see in my life and my message, 7even though I have received wonderful revelations from God. But to keep me from getting puffed up, I was given a thorn in my flesh, a messenger from Satan to torment me and keep me from getting proud.

8Three different times I begged the Lord to take it away. 9Each time he said, "My gracious favor is all you need. My power works best in your weakness." So now I am glad to boast about my weaknesses, so that the power of Christ may work through me. 10Since I know it is all for Christ's good, I am quite content with my weaknesses and with insults, hardships, persecutions, and calamities. For when I am weak, then I am strong.

Paul's Concern for the Corinthians
11You have made me act like a fool—boasting like this. You ought to be writing commendations for me, for I am not at all inferior to these "super apostles," even though I am nothing at all. 12When I was with you, I certainly gave you every proof that I am truly an apostle, sent to you by God himself. For I patiently did many signs and wonders and miracles among you. 13The only thing I didn't do, which I do in the other churches, was to become a burden to you. Please forgive me for this wrong!

14Now I am coming to you for the third time,

12:2 Greek *I know a man in Christ who.*   12:4 Greek *he.*

What Happens When You Give? Read 2 CORINTHIANS 9:6-14

One of Paul's goals in his ministry was to mend the division that existed between Jewish and Gentile believers. To do this, he took up a gift offering from the Gentile believers to be given to the needy Jewish believers in Jerusalem. Apparently the believers in Corinth were lagging behind in their giving. So Paul, in this portion of 2 Corinthians, wrote of the benefits of giving to God and the work of his church. Here are three important truths from this passage about our giving as believers:

1. Our Motives Are Important. The passage says that God prizes cheerful givers (verse 7). The word *cheerfully* could also be translated as "hilariously." We should give hilariously, joyfully—not out of mere duty or guilt. As Jesus said, it is truly "more blessed to give than to receive" (Acts 20:35).

2. As We Give, God Will Give to Us. You can't outgive God (verses 8, 10). As Jesus said, "If you give, you will receive. Your gift will return to you in full measure, pressed down, shaken together to make room for more, and running over. Whatever measure you use in giving—large or small—it will be used to measure what is given back to you" (Luke 6:38). Coming back to our motive for giving, we should not fall into the trap of "giving to get." We should give because God has so graciously and generously given to us.

3. Others Are Helped because of Our Financial Help. We should always be on the lookout to help Christian brothers and sisters who are in need. Paul was not speaking of the tithe you give, but an offering above and beyond your tithe (verses 11-14). Our tithe goes to the church. Our offerings go to other situations, like helping those in need. When these people receive our gifts, they see that our faith is deeper than mere words.

When you give to the Lord's work, that money, which really had no effect in any spiritual sense before, will be used to touch the lives of others for the glory of God. God is looking for openhanded people— people upon whom he can pour out his blessings, and who, in turn, will give it to others.

For the next note on *"Give to God,"* turn to p. 797.

and I will not be a burden to you. I don't want what you have; I want you. And anyway, little children don't pay for their parents' food. It's the other way around; parents supply food for their children. [15]I will gladly spend myself and all I have for your spiritual good, even though it seems that the more I love you, the less you love me.

[16]Some of you admit I was not a burden to you. But they still think I was sneaky and took advantage of you by trickery. [17]But how? Did any of the men I sent to you take advantage of you? [18]When I urged Titus to visit you and sent our other brother with him, did Titus take advantage of you? No, of course not! For we both have the same Spirit and walk in each other's steps, doing things the same way.

[19]Perhaps you think we are saying all this just to defend ourselves. That isn't it at all. We tell you this as Christ's servants, and we know that God is listening. Everything we do, dear friends, is for your benefit. [20]For I am afraid that when I come to visit you I won't like what I find, and then you won't like my response. I am afraid that I will find quarreling, jealousy, outbursts of anger, selfishness, backstabbing, gossip, conceit, and disorderly behavior. [21]Yes, I am afraid that when I come, God will humble me again because of you. And I will have to grieve because many of you who sinned earlier have not repented of your impurity, sexual immorality, and eagerness for lustful pleasure.

CHAPTER **13**
Paul's Final Advice

This is the third time I am coming to visit you. As the Scriptures say, "The facts of every case must be established by the testimony of two or three witnesses."* [2]I have already warned those who had been sinning when I was there on my second visit. Now I again warn them and all

others, just as I did before, that this next time I will not spare them.

[3]I will give you all the proof you want that Christ speaks through me. Christ is not weak in his dealings with you; he is a mighty power among you. [4]Although he died on the cross in weakness, he now lives by the mighty power of God. We, too, are weak, but we live in him and have God's power—the power we use in dealing with you.

[5]Examine yourselves to see if your faith is really genuine. Test yourselves. If you cannot tell that Jesus Christ is among you,* it means you have failed the test. [6]I hope you recognize that we have passed the test and are approved by God.

[7]We pray to God that you will not do anything wrong. We pray this, not to show that our ministry to you has been successful, but because we want you to do right even if we ourselves seem to have failed. [8]Our responsibility is never to oppose the truth, but to stand for the truth at all times. [9]We are glad to be weak, if you are really strong. What we pray for is your restoration to maturity.

[10]I am writing this to you before I come, hoping that I won't need to deal harshly with you when I do come. For I want to use the authority the Lord has given me to build you up, not to tear you down.

Paul's Final Greetings

[11]Dear brothers and sisters,* I close my letter with these last words: Rejoice. Change your ways. Encourage each other. Live in harmony and peace. Then the God of love and peace will be with you.

[12]Greet each other in Christian love.* All the Christians here send you their greetings.

[13]May the grace of our Lord Jesus Christ, the love of God, and the fellowship of the Holy Spirit be with you all.*

13:1 Deut 19:15.   13:5 Or *in you.*   13:11 Greek *brothers.*   13:12 Greek *with a sacred kiss.*   13:12-13 Some English versions divide verse 12 into verses 12 and 13, and then verse 13 becomes verse 14.

Galatians

CHAPTER 1
Greetings from Paul

This letter is from Paul, an apostle. I was not appointed by any group or by human authority. My call is from Jesus Christ himself and from God the Father, who raised Jesus from the dead.

2All the brothers and sisters* here join me in sending greetings to the churches of Galatia.

3May grace and peace be yours from God our Father and from the Lord Jesus Christ. 4He died for our sins, just as God our Father planned, in order to rescue us from this evil world in which we live. 5That is why all glory belongs to God through all the ages of eternity. Amen.

There Is Only One Good News

6I am shocked that you are turning away so soon from God, who in his love and mercy called you to share the eternal life he gives through Christ. You are already following a different way 7that pretends to be the Good News but is not the Good News at all. You are being fooled by those who twist and change the truth concerning Christ.

8Let God's curse fall on anyone, including myself, who preaches any other message than the one we told you about. Even if an angel comes from heaven and preaches any other message, let him be forever cursed. 9I will say it again: If anyone preaches any other gospel than the one you welcomed, let God's curse fall upon that person.

10Obviously, I'm not trying to be a people pleaser! No, I am trying to please God. If I were still trying to please people, I would not be Christ's servant.

Paul's Message Comes from Christ

11Dear brothers and sisters, I solemnly assure you that the Good News of salvation which I preach is not based on mere human reasoning or logic. 12For my message came by a direct revelation from Jesus Christ himself. No one else taught me.

13You know what I was like when I followed the Jewish religion—how I violently persecuted the Christians.* I did my best to get rid of them. 14I was one of the most religious Jews of my own age, and I tried as hard as possible to follow all the old traditions of my religion.

15But then something happened! For it pleased God in his kindness to choose me and call me, even before I was born! What undeserved mercy! 16Then he revealed his Son to me* so that I could proclaim the Good News about Jesus to the Gentiles. When all this happened to me, I did not rush out to consult with anyone else; 17nor did I go up to Jerusalem to consult with those who were apostles before I was. No, I went away into Arabia and later returned to the city of Damascus. 18It was not until three years later that I finally went to Jerusalem for a visit with Peter* and stayed there with him for fifteen days. 19And the only other apostle I met at that time was James, our Lord's brother. 20You must believe what I am saying, for I declare before God that I am not lying. 21Then after this visit, I went north into the provinces of Syria and Cilicia. 22And still the Christians in the churches in Judea didn't know me personally. 23All they knew was that people were saying, "The one who used to persecute us now preaches the very faith he tried to destroy!" 24And they gave glory to God because of me.

CHAPTER 2
The Apostles Accept Paul

Then fourteen years later I went back to Jerusalem again, this time with Barnabas; and Titus

1:2 Greek brothers; also in 1:11.   1:13 Greek the church of God.   1:16 Or in me.   1:18 Greek Cephas.

Why Christians Need the Holy Spirit Read GALATIANS 5:16-26

This text lays out four important reasons we need to let the Holy Spirit have full control of our lives as believers:

1. The Holy Spirit Helps to Conquer Our Sin Nature. The Holy Spirit will help us make the right decisions if we listen to his advice.

2. The Holy Spirit Makes It Easier to Follow God's Guidelines. The Holy Spirit gives us the power to live by God's guidelines. If we listen to and follow the Holy Spirit's promptings, then we won't have to force ourselves to obey the Lord. That is because we will want to obey him.

3. The Holy Spirit Will Produce Godly Qualities in Our Lives. When we live by the Holy Spirit, he develops godly qualities (known as the fruit of the Spirit) in our lives.

4. The Holy Spirit Encourages Us to Seek God's Approval above Man's. We will seek God's glory above our own when we follow the Holy Spirit's leading.

In essence, the Holy Spirit enables Christians to live lives that are pleasing to God—something that is impossible to do on our own. He makes following Christ a joy rather than a duty.

To begin the next topic, turn to p. A13.

CORNER STONES

---

came along, too. ²I went there because God revealed to me that I should go. While I was there I talked privately with the leaders of the church. I wanted them to understand what I had been preaching to the Gentiles. I wanted to make sure they did not disagree, or my ministry would have been useless. ³And they did agree. They did not even demand that my companion Titus be circumcised, though he was a Gentile.*

⁴Even that question wouldn't have come up except for some so-called Christians there— false ones, really*—who came to spy on us and see our freedom in Christ Jesus. They wanted to force us, like slaves, to follow their Jewish regulations. ⁵But we refused to listen to them for a single moment. We wanted to preserve the truth of the Good News for you.

⁶And the leaders of the church who were there had nothing to add to what I was preaching. (By the way, their reputation as great leaders made no difference to me, for God has no favorites.) ⁷They saw that God had given me the responsibility of preaching the Good News to the Gentiles, just as he had given Peter the responsibility of preaching to the Jews. ⁸For the same God who worked through Peter for the benefit of the Jews worked through me for the

benefit of the Gentiles. ⁹In fact, James, Peter,* and John, who were known as pillars of the church, recognized the gift God had given me, and they accepted Barnabas and me as their co-workers. They encouraged us to keep preaching to the Gentiles, while they continued their work with the Jews. ¹⁰The only thing they suggested was that we remember to help the poor, and I have certainly been eager to do that.

Paul Confronts Peter

¹¹But when Peter came to Antioch, I had to oppose him publicly, speaking strongly against what he was doing, for it was very wrong. ¹²When he first arrived, he ate with the Gentile Christians, who don't bother with circumcision. But afterward, when some Jewish friends of James came, Peter wouldn't eat with the Gentiles anymore because he was afraid of what these legalists would say. ¹³Then the other Jewish Christians followed Peter's hypocrisy, and even Barnabas was influenced to join them in their hypocrisy.

¹⁴When I saw that they were not following the truth of the Good News, I said to Peter in front of all the others, "Since you, a Jew by birth, have discarded the Jewish laws and are living like a Gentile, why are you trying to make these

2:3 Greek *a Greek.*   2:4 Greek *some false brothers.*   2:9 Greek *Cephas;* also in 2:11, 14.

Gentiles obey the Jewish laws you abandoned? 15You and I are Jews by birth, not 'sinners' like the Gentiles. 16And yet we Jewish Christians know that we become right with God, not by doing what the law commands, but by faith in Jesus Christ. So we have believed in Christ Jesus, that we might be accepted by God because of our faith in Christ—and not because we have obeyed the law. For no one will ever be saved by obeying the law."*

17But what if we seek to be made right with God through faith in Christ and then find out that we are still sinners? Has Christ led us into sin? Of course not! 18Rather, I make myself guilty if I rebuild the old system I already tore down. 19For when I tried to keep the law, I realized I could never earn God's approval. So I died to the law so that I might live for God. I have been crucified with Christ. 20I myself no longer live, but Christ lives in me. So I live my life in this earthly body by trusting in the Son of God, who loved me and gave himself for me. 21I am not one of those who treats the grace of God as meaningless. For if we could be saved by keeping the law, then there was no need for Christ to die.

CHAPTER 3

The Law and Faith in Christ

Oh, foolish Galatians! What magician has cast an evil spell on you? For you used to see the meaning of Jesus Christ's death as clearly as though I had shown you a signboard with a picture of Christ dying on the cross. 2Let me ask you this one question: Did you receive the Holy Spirit by keeping the law? Of course not, for the Holy Spirit came upon you only after you believed the message you heard about Christ. 3Have you lost your senses? After starting your Christian lives in the Spirit, why are you now trying to become perfect by your own human effort? 4You have suffered so much for the Good News. Surely it was not in vain, was it? Are you now going to just throw it all away?

5I ask you again, does God give you the Holy Spirit and work miracles among you because you obey the law of Moses? Of course not! It is because you believe the message you heard about Christ.

6In the same way, "Abraham believed God, so God declared him righteous because of his faith."* 7The real children of Abraham, then, are all those who put their faith in God.

8What's more, the Scriptures looked forward to this time when God would accept the Gentiles, too, on the basis of their faith. God promised this good news to Abraham long ago when he said, "All nations will be blessed through you."* 9And so it is: All who put their faith in Christ share the same blessing Abraham received because of his faith.

10But those who depend on the law to make them right with God are under his curse, for the Scriptures say, "Cursed is everyone who does not observe and obey all these commands that are written in God's Book of the Law."* 11Consequently, it is clear that no one can ever be right with God by trying to keep the law. For the Scriptures say, "It is through faith that a righteous person has life."* 12How different from this way of faith is the way of law, which says, "If you wish to find life by obeying the law, you must obey all of its commands."* 13But Christ has rescued us from the curse pronounced by the law. When he was hung on the cross, he took upon himself the curse for our wrongdoing. For it is written in the Scriptures, "Cursed is everyone who is hung on a tree."* 14Through the work of Christ Jesus, God has blessed the Gentiles with the same blessing he promised to Abraham, and we Christians receive the promised Holy Spirit through faith.

The Law and God's Promises

15Dear brothers and sisters,* here's an example from everyday life. Just as no one can set aside or amend an irrevocable agreement, so it is in this case. 16God gave the promise to Abraham and his child.* And notice that it doesn't say the promise was to his children,* as if it meant many descendants. But the promise was to his child—and that, of course, means Christ. 17This is what I am trying to say: The agreement God made with Abraham could not be canceled 430 years later when God gave the law to Moses. God would be breaking his promise. 18For if the inheritance could be received only by keeping the law, then it would not be the result of accepting God's promise. But God gave it to Abraham as a promise.

19Well then, why was the law given? It was given to show people how guilty they are. But this system of law was to last only until the coming of the child to whom God's promise was made. And there is this further difference. God

2:16 Some translators hold that the quotation extends through verse 14; others through verse 16; and still others through verse 21. 3:6 Gen 15:6. 3:8 Gen 12:3; 18:18; 22:18. 3:10 Deut 27:26. 3:11 Hab 2:4. 3:12 Lev 18:5. 3:13 Deut 21:23. 3:15 Greek *Brothers*. 3:16a Greek *seed*; also in 3:16c, 19. See Gen 12:7. 3:16b Greek *seeds*.

gave his laws to angels to give to Moses, who was the mediator between God and the people. 20Now a mediator is needed if two people enter into an agreement, but God acted on his own when he made his promise to Abraham.

21Well then, is there a conflict between God's law and God's promises? Absolutely not! If the law could have given us new life, we could have been made right with God by obeying it. 22But the Scriptures have declared that we are all prisoners of sin, so the only way to receive God's promise is to believe in Jesus Christ.

23Until faith in Christ was shown to us as the way of becoming right with God, we were guarded by the law. We were kept in protective custody, so to speak, until we could put our faith in the coming Savior.

God's Children through Faith

24Let me put it another way. The law was our guardian and teacher to lead us until Christ came. So now, through faith in Christ, we are made right with God. 25But now that faith in Christ has come, we no longer need the law as our guardian. 26So you are all children* of God through faith in Christ Jesus. 27And all who have been united with Christ in baptism have been made like him. 28There is no longer Jew or Gentile,* slave or free, male or female. For you are all Christians—you are one in Christ Jesus. 29And now that you belong to Christ, you are the true children of Abraham. You are his heirs, and now all the promises God gave to him belong to you.

CHAPTER **4**

Think of it this way. If a father dies and leaves great wealth for his young children, those children are not much better off than slaves until they grow up, even though they actually own everything their father had. 2They have to obey their guardians until they reach whatever age their father set.

3And that's the way it was with us before Christ came. We were slaves to the spiritual powers of this world. 4But when the right time came, God sent his Son, born of a woman, subject to the law. 5God sent him to buy freedom for us who were slaves to the law, so that he could adopt us as his very own children.* 6And because you Gentiles have become his children, God has sent the Spirit of his Son into your hearts, and now you can call God your dear Father.* 7Now you are no longer a slave but God's own child.* And since you are his child, everything he has belongs to you.

Paul's Concern for the Galatians

8Before you Gentiles knew God, you were slaves to so-called gods that do not even exist. 9And now that you have found God (or should I say, now that God has found you), why do you want to go back again and become slaves once more to the weak and useless spiritual powers of this world? 10You are trying to find favor with God by what you do or don't do on certain days or months or seasons or years. 11I fear for you. I am afraid that all my hard work for you was worth nothing. 12Dear brothers and sisters,* I plead with you to live as I do in freedom from these things, for I have become like you Gentiles were—free from the law.

You did not mistreat me when I first preached to you. 13Surely you remember that I was sick when I first brought you the Good News of Christ. 14But even though my sickness was revolting to you, you did not reject me and turn me away. No, you took me in and cared for me as though I were an angel from God or even Christ Jesus himself. 15Where is that joyful spirit

3:26 Greek *sons.*   3:28 Greek *Jew or Greek.*   4:5 Greek *sons;* also in 4:6.   4:6 Greek *into your hearts, crying, "Abba, Father." Abba* is an Aramaic term for "father."   4:7 Greek *son;* also in 4:7b.   4:12 Greek *brothers;* also in 4:28, 31.

OFF AND RUNNING ▰▰▰▰▰

Find a Close Christian Friend Read GALATIANS 6:1-3

God never intended us to be "solo" Christians. That is why one of the first things you should do after becoming a Christian is find some good, solid Christian friends. Although God wants us to turn to him first in times of trouble, he also knows that we need Christian brothers and sisters here on earth to help us through our difficulties—and they need us, too. Here are three things to look for in a Christian friend:

1. A True Christian Friend Will Let You Know When You Sin. A true friend will care enough about your spiritual condition to tell you the truth. The Bible says, "Wounds from a friend are better than many kisses from an enemy" (Proverbs 27:6).

we felt together then? In those days, I know you would gladly have taken out your own eyes and given them to me if it had been possible. 16Have I now become your enemy because I am telling you the truth?

17Those false teachers who are so anxious to win your favor are not doing it for your good. They are trying to shut you off from me so that you will pay more attention to them. 18Now it's wonderful if you are eager to do good, and especially when I am not with you. 19But oh, my dear children! I feel as if I am going through labor pains for you again, and they will continue until Christ is fully developed in your lives. 20How I wish I were there with you right now, so that I could be more gentle with you. But at this distance I frankly don't know what else to do.

Abraham's Two Children

21Listen to me, you who want to live under the law. Do you know what the law really says? 22The Scriptures say that Abraham had two sons, one from his slave-wife and one from his freeborn wife.* 23The son of the slave-wife was born in a human attempt to bring about the fulfillment of God's promise. But the son of the freeborn wife was born as God's own fulfillment of his promise.

24Now these two women serve as an illustration of God's two covenants. Hagar, the slave-wife, represents Mount Sinai where people first became enslaved to the law. 25And now Jerusalem is just like Mount Sinai in Arabia, because she and her children live in slavery. 26But Sarah, the free woman, represents the heavenly Jerusalem. And she is our mother. 27That is what Isaiah meant when he prophesied,

"Rejoice, O childless woman!
Break forth into loud and joyful song,
even though you never gave birth to a child.

4:22 See Gen 16:15; 21:2-3.   4:27 Isa 54:1.   4:30 Gen 21:10.

For the woman who could bear no children now has more than all the other women!"*

28And you, dear brothers and sisters, are children of the promise, just like Isaac. 29And we who are born of the Holy Spirit are persecuted by those who want us to keep the law, just as Isaac, the child of promise, was persecuted by Ishmael, the son of the slave-wife.

30But what do the Scriptures say about that? "Get rid of the slave and her son, for the son of the slave woman will not share the family inheritance with the free woman's son."* 31So, dear brothers and sisters, we are not children of the slave woman, obligated to the law. We are children of the free woman, acceptable to God because of our faith.

CHAPTER 5
Freedom in Christ

So Christ has really set us free. Now make sure that you stay free, and don't get tied up again in slavery to the law.

2Listen! I, Paul, tell you this: If you are counting on circumcision to make you right with God, then Christ cannot help you. 3I'll say it again. If you are trying to find favor with God by being circumcised, you must obey all of the regulations in the whole law of Moses. 4For if you are trying to make yourselves right with God by keeping the law, you have been cut off from Christ! You have fallen away from God's grace.

5But we who live by the Spirit eagerly wait to receive everything promised to us who are right with God through faith. 6For when we place our faith in Christ Jesus, it makes no difference to God whether we are circumcised or not circumcised. What is important is faith expressing itself in love.

---

2. A True Christian Friend Is Humble. If you fall spiritually, a friend who is a strong Christian can be counted upon to help restore you without spreading rumors. That is because this friend realizes that he or she is just as susceptible to sin as you are.

3. A True Christian Friend Will Help Carry Your Burdens. He will weep with you when you weep and rejoice with you when you rejoice (see Romans 12:15, p. 978).

Having a friend who is a strong Christian is not just a benefit—it is a necessity! And that is how Jesus wants it to be. Therefore, build your Christian friendships, and in so doing, you will help strengthen yourself and the body of Christ.

For the next note on "Relationships," turn to p. 462.

7You were getting along so well. Who has interfered with you to hold you back from following the truth? 8It certainly isn't God, for he is the one who called you to freedom. 9But it takes only one wrong person among you to infect all the others—a little yeast spreads quickly through the whole batch of dough! 10I am trusting the Lord to bring you back to believing as I do about these things. God will judge that person, whoever it is, who has been troubling and confusing you.

11Dear brothers and sisters,* if I were still preaching that you must be circumcised—as some say I do—why would the Jews persecute me? The fact that I am still being persecuted proves that I am still preaching salvation through the cross of Christ alone. 12I only wish that those troublemakers who want to mutilate you by circumcision would mutilate themselves.*

13For you have been called to live in freedom—not freedom to satisfy your sinful nature, but freedom to serve one another in love. 14For the whole law can be summed up in this one command: "Love your neighbor as yourself."* 15But if instead of showing love among yourselves you are always biting and devouring one another, watch out! Beware of destroying one another.

Living by the Spirit's Power
16So I advise you to live according to your new life in the Holy Spirit. Then you won't be doing what your sinful nature craves. 17The old sinful nature loves to do evil, which is just opposite from what the Holy Spirit wants. And the Spirit gives us desires that are opposite from what the sinful nature desires. These two forces are constantly fighting each other, and your choices are never free from this conflict. 18But when you are directed by the Holy Spirit, you are no longer subject to the law.

19When you follow the desires of your sinful nature, your lives will produce these evil results: sexual immorality, impure thoughts, eagerness for lustful pleasure, 20idolatry, participation in demonic activities, hostility, quarreling, jealousy, outbursts of anger, selfish ambition, divisions, the feeling that everyone is wrong except those in your own little group, 21envy, drunkenness, wild parties, and other kinds of sin. Let me tell you again, as I have before, that anyone living that sort of life will not inherit the Kingdom of God.

22But when the Holy Spirit controls our lives, he will produce this kind of fruit in us: love, joy, peace, patience, kindness, goodness, faithfulness, 23gentleness, and self-control. Here there is no conflict with the law.

24Those who belong to Christ Jesus have nailed the passions and desires of their sinful nature to his cross and crucified them there. 25If we are living now by the Holy Spirit, let us follow the Holy Spirit's leading in every part of our lives. 26Let us not become conceited, or irritate one another, or be jealous of one another.

CHAPTER 6
We Reap What We Sow

Dear brothers and sisters, if another Christian* is overcome by some sin, you who are godly should gently and humbly help that person back onto the right path. And be careful not to fall into the same temptation yourself. 2Share each other's troubles and problems, and in this way obey the law of Christ. 3If you think you are too important to help someone in need, you are only fooling yourself. You are really a nobody.

4Be sure to do what you should, for then you will enjoy the personal satisfaction of having done your work well, and you won't need to compare yourself to anyone else. 5For we are each responsible for our own conduct.

6Those who are taught the word of God should help their teachers by paying them.

7Don't be misled. Remember that you can't ignore God and get away with it. You will always reap what you sow! 8Those who live only to satisfy their own sinful desires will harvest the consequences of decay and death. But those who live to please the Spirit will harvest everlasting life from the Spirit. 9So don't get tired of doing what is good. Don't get discouraged and give up, for we will reap a harvest of blessing at the appropriate time. 10Whenever we have the opportunity, we should do good to everyone, especially to our Christian brothers and sisters.

Paul's Final Advice
11Notice what large letters I use as I write these closing words in my own handwriting. 12Those who are trying to force you to be circumcised are doing it for just one reason. They don't want to be persecuted for teaching that the cross of Christ alone can save. 13And even those who

5:11 Greek *Brothers.* 5:12 Or *castrate themselves;* Greek reads *cut themselves off.* 5:14 Lev 19:18. 6:1 Greek *Brothers, if a man.*

advocate circumcision don't really keep the whole law. They only want you to be circumcised so they can brag about it and claim you as their disciples.

¹⁴As for me, God forbid that I should boast about anything except the cross of our Lord Jesus Christ. Because of that cross,* my interest in this world died long ago, and the world's interest in me is also long dead. ¹⁵It doesn't make any difference now whether we have been circum-

cised or not. What counts is whether we really have been changed into new and different people. ¹⁶May God's mercy and peace be upon all those who live by this principle. They are the new people of God.*

¹⁷From now on, don't let anyone trouble me with these things. For I bear on my body the scars that show I belong to Jesus.

¹⁸My dear brothers and sisters,* may the grace of our Lord Jesus Christ be with you all. Amen.

6:14 Or *Because of him.*   6:16 Greek *the Israel of God.*   6:18 Greek *Brothers.*

Ephesians

CHAPTER 1

Greetings from Paul

This letter is from Paul, chosen by God to be an apostle of Christ Jesus.

It is written to God's holy people in Ephesus,* who are faithful followers of Christ Jesus.

2May grace and peace be yours, sent to you from God our Father and Jesus Christ our Lord.

Spiritual Blessings

3How we praise God, the Father of our Lord Jesus Christ, who has blessed us with every spiritual blessing in the heavenly realms because we belong to Christ. 4Long ago, even before he made the world, God loved us and chose us in Christ to be holy and without fault in his eyes. 5His unchanging plan has always been to adopt us into his own family by bringing us to himself through Jesus Christ. And this gave him great pleasure.

6So we praise God for the wonderful kindness he has poured out on us because we belong to his dearly loved Son. 7He is so rich in kindness that he purchased our freedom through the blood of his Son, and our sins are forgiven. 8He has showered his kindness on us, along with all wisdom and understanding.

9God's secret plan has now been revealed to us; it is a plan centered on Christ, designed long ago according to his good pleasure. 10And this is his plan: At the right time he will bring everything together under the authority of Christ—everything in heaven and on earth. 11Furthermore, because of Christ, we have received an inheritance from God,* for he chose us from the beginning, and all things happen just as he decided long ago. 12God's purpose was that we who were the first to trust in Christ should praise our glorious God. 13And now you also have heard the truth, the Good News that God saves you. And when you believed in Christ, he identified you as his own by giving you the Holy Spirit, whom he promised long ago. 14The Spirit is God's guarantee that he will give us everything he promised and that he has purchased us to be his own people. This is just one more reason for us to praise our glorious God.

Paul's Prayer for Spiritual Wisdom

15Ever since I first heard of your strong faith in the Lord Jesus and your love for Christians everywhere, 16I have never stopped thanking God for you. I pray for you constantly, 17asking God, the glorious Father of our Lord Jesus Christ, to give you spiritual wisdom and understanding, so that you might grow in your knowledge of God. 18I pray that your hearts will be flooded with light so that you can understand the wonderful future he has promised to those he called. I want you to realize what a rich and glorious inheritance he has given to his people.*

19I pray that you will begin to understand the incredible greatness of his power for us who believe him. This is the same mighty power 20that raised Christ from the dead and seated him in the place of honor at God's right hand in the heavenly realms. 21Now he is far above any ruler or authority or power or leader or anything else in this world or in the world to come. 22And God has put all things under the authority of Christ, and he gave him this authority for the benefit of the church. 23And the church is his body; it is filled by Christ, who fills everything everywhere with his presence.

1:1 Some manuscripts do not include *in Ephesus.*   1:11 Or *we have become God's inheritance.*   1:18 Or *realize how much God has been honored by acquiring his people.*

Why God Gives Us the Holy Spirit Read EPHESIANS 1:13-14

You might say that the Holy Spirit is our "identifying mark" as a Christian. In this text we see three specific reasons God gives us his Holy Spirit:

1. The Holy Spirit Is a Promise. Once again, Scripture reminds us that God has promised to send the Holy Spirit to all those who have heard the good news of the gospel and trusted Christ as Savior.

2. The Holy Spirit Is a Seal. The Holy Spirit serves as a mark of ownership, showing that we belong to God.

3. The Holy Spirit Is a Guarantee. The Holy Spirit also represents God's pledge to bring us to our final spiritual inheritance. This word could also be translated as a "first installment" or "deposit," signifying that his sealing in our lives is a foretaste of much more to come!

God gives us the Holy Spirit not only to enable us to live out the Christian life but to prove that we are precious in his sight.

For the next note on "Who Is the Holy Spirit?" turn to p. 912.

CORNER STONES

CHAPTER **2**
Made Alive with Christ

Once you were dead, doomed forever because of your many sins. ²You used to live just like the rest of the world, full of sin, obeying Satan, the mighty prince of the power of the air. He is the spirit at work in the hearts of those who refuse to obey God. ³All of us used to live that way, following the passions and desires of our evil nature. We were born with an evil nature, and we were under God's anger just like everyone else.

⁴But God is so rich in mercy, and he loved us so very much, ⁵that even while we were dead because of our sins, he gave us life when he raised Christ from the dead. (It is only by God's special favor that you have been saved!) ⁶For he raised us from the dead along with Christ, and we are seated with him in the heavenly realms— all because we are one with Christ Jesus. ⁷And so God can always point to us as examples of the incredible wealth of his favor and kindness toward us, as shown in all he has done for us through Christ Jesus.

⁸God saved you by his special favor when you believed. And you can't take credit for this; it is a gift from God. ⁹Salvation is not a reward for the good things we have done, so none of us can boast about it. ¹⁰For we are God's masterpiece. He has created us anew in Christ Jesus, so that we can do the good things he planned for us long ago.

Oneness and Peace in Christ

¹¹Don't forget that you Gentiles used to be outsiders by birth. You were called "the uncircumcised ones" by the Jews, who were proud of their circumcision, even though it affected only their bodies and not their hearts. ¹²In those days you were living apart from Christ. You were excluded from God's people, Israel, and you did not know the promises God had made to them. You lived in this world without God and without hope. ¹³But now you belong to Christ Jesus. Though you once were far away from God, now you have been brought near to him because of the blood of Christ.

¹⁴For Christ himself has made peace between us Jews and you Gentiles by making us all one people. He has broken down the wall of hostility that used to separate us. ¹⁵By his death he ended the whole system of Jewish law that excluded the Gentiles. His purpose was to make peace between Jews and Gentiles by creating in himself one new person from the two groups. ¹⁶Together as one body, Christ reconciled both groups to God by means of his death, and our hostility toward each other was put to death. ¹⁷He has brought this Good News of peace to you Gentiles who were far away from him, and to us Jews who were near. ¹⁸Now all of us, both Jews and Gentiles, may come to the Father through the same Holy Spirit because of what Christ has done for us.

A Temple for the Lord

¹⁹So now you Gentiles are no longer strangers and foreigners. You are citizens along with all of God's holy people. You are members of God's family. ²⁰We are his house, built on the foundation of the apostles and the prophets. And the cornerstone is Christ Jesus himself. ²¹We who believe are carefully joined together, becoming a holy temple for the Lord. ²²Through him you Gentiles are also joined together as part of this dwelling where God lives by his Spirit.

CHAPTER 3
God's Secret Plan Revealed

I, Paul, am a prisoner of Christ Jesus because of my preaching to you Gentiles. ²As you already know, God has given me this special ministry of announcing his favor to you Gentiles. ³As I briefly mentioned earlier in this letter, God himself revealed his secret plan to me. ⁴As you read what I have written, you will understand what I know about this plan regarding Christ. ⁵God did not reveal it to previous generations, but now he has revealed it by the Holy Spirit to his holy apostles and prophets.

⁶And this is the secret plan: The Gentiles have an equal share with the Jews in all the riches inherited by God's children. Both groups have believed the Good News, and both are part of the same body and enjoy together the promise of blessings through Christ Jesus. ⁷By God's special favor and mighty power, I have been given the wonderful privilege of serving him by spreading this Good News.

⁸Just think! Though I did nothing to deserve it, and though I am the least deserving Christian there is, I was chosen for this special joy of telling the Gentiles about the endless treasures available to them in Christ. ⁹I was chosen to explain to everyone this plan that God, the Creator of all things, had kept secret from the beginning.

¹⁰God's purpose was to show his wisdom in all its rich variety to all the rulers and authorities in the heavenly realms. They will see this when Jews and Gentiles are joined together in his church. ¹¹This was his plan from all eternity, and it has now been carried out through Christ Jesus our Lord.

¹²Because of Christ and our faith in him, we can now come fearlessly into God's presence, assured of his glad welcome. ¹³So please don't despair because of what they are doing to me

here. It is for you that I am suffering, so you should feel honored and encouraged.

Paul's Prayer for Spiritual Empowering

¹⁴When I think of the wisdom and scope of God's plan, I fall to my knees and pray to the Father,* ¹⁵the Creator of everything in heaven and on earth. ¹⁶I pray that from his glorious, unlimited resources he will give you mighty inner strength through his Holy Spirit. ¹⁷And I pray that Christ will be more and more at home in your hearts as you trust in him. May your roots go down deep into the soil of God's marvelous love. ¹⁸And may you have the power to under-

3:14 Some manuscripts read *the Father of our Lord Jesus Christ.*

Why the Church Needs You
Read EPHESIANS 4:11-16

Not only do you need the church, but the church needs you! As God's child, you are blessed with unique spiritual gifts and talents that can be used to benefit the body of Christ. You can use these gifts in at least two ways to benefit fellow believers:

1. The Gifts God Gives You Promote Spiritual Maturity. God wants you to grow spiritually. In order for this to happen, he has placed gifted people in the church to fulfill different aspects of ministry. If the pastor, teacher, evangelist, and others properly carry out their duties, this not only helps to promote your spiritual growth, but also equips you to do better work for him. For this to take place, however, you must be "fitted together perfectly," with "each part [doing] its own special work, [helping] the other parts grow."

2. The Gifts God Gives You Bless Others. Although you may not hold a prominent position in your church, you may be able to encourage others, care for the sick or those in need, financially support a ministry outreach, or even clean restrooms. If you fail to regularly fellowship in a church with other believers, you are neglecting a tremendous opportunity to use what God has given you.

For the next note on "Look for and Attend the Right Church," turn to p. 999.

God Saved Us for a Purpose Read EPHESIANS 2:10

As a nonbeliever, you had nothing to motivate you to live righteously. You may have searched for purpose and meaning in life but found nothing satisfying. As a believer, however, you are "God's workmanship," which means that his Spirit is working in your life to make you more like Christ and to give you a purpose for living.

This verse describes part of the purpose God has for your life as his child—to do good works by helping others. The amazing and wonderful truth about God's purpose for your life is that he had plans for you to do good works long before you even existed. He has already scheduled the days and events of your life with opportunities to tangibly share his love with others (see Psalm 139:16, p. 535, and Jeremiah 29:11, p. 646).

The next time you see a neighbor in trouble, hear about a friend struggling with a problem, notice a coworker in distress, or see a stranger who genuinely needs a helping hand—take hold of this opportunity God has placed in your path. Let your "light shine" (see Matthew 5:16, p. 793) because you are his child.

For the next note on "Faith and Works," turn to p. 798.

CORNER STONES

---

stand, as all God's people should, how wide, how long, how high, and how deep his love really is. 19May you experience the love of Christ, though it is so great you will never fully understand it. Then you will be filled with the fullness of life and power that comes from God.

20Now glory be to God! By his mighty power at work within us, he is able to accomplish infinitely more than we would ever dare to ask or hope. 21May he be given glory in the church and in Christ Jesus forever and ever through endless ages. Amen.

CHAPTER **4**
Unity in the Body
Therefore I, a prisoner for serving the Lord, beg you to lead a life worthy of your calling, for you have been called by God. 2Be humble and gentle. Be patient with each other, making allowance for each other's faults because of your love. 3Always keep yourselves united in the Holy Spirit, and bind yourselves together with peace.

4We are all one body, we have the same Spirit, and we have all been called to the same glorious future. 5There is only one Lord, one faith, one baptism, 6and there is only one God and Father, who is over us all and in us all and living through us all. 7However, he has given each one of us a special gift according to the generosity of Christ. 8That is why the Scriptures say,

"When he ascended to the heights,
he led a crowd of captives
and gave gifts to his people."*

9Notice that it says "he ascended." This means that Christ first came down to the lowly world in which we live.* 10The same one who came down is the one who ascended higher than all the heavens, so that his rule might fill the entire universe.

11He is the one who gave these gifts to the church: the apostles, the prophets, the evangelists, and the pastors and teachers. 12Their responsibility is to equip God's people to do his work and build up the church, the body of Christ, 13until we come to such unity in our faith and knowledge of God's Son that we will be mature and full grown in the Lord, measuring up to the full stature of Christ.

14Then we will no longer be like children, forever changing our minds about what we believe because someone has told us something different or because someone has cleverly lied to us and made the lie sound like the truth. 15Instead, we will hold to the truth in love, becoming more and more in every way like Christ, who is the head of his body, the church. 16Under his direction, the whole body is fitted together perfectly. As each part does its own special work, it helps the other parts grow, so that the whole body is healthy and growing and full of love.

4:8 Ps 68:18. 4:9 Or *to the lowest parts of the earth.*

What Are Spiritual Gifts? Read EPHESIANS 4:11-16

God has chosen people to do his work. He chose this course of action for reasons only he knows and understands. From a human perspective, we may wonder if this was the best decision. After all, "the sky was the limit" concerning what God could have done. He could have chosen to use angels to speak to lost humanity. He certainly used them on many significant occasions throughout Scripture. Or God could have created a special category of messengers that would never fail him—a "sin-proof" instrument that would faithfully proclaim his Word. For that matter, God himself could have simply poked his face through the heavens and said, "Hello, world! I'm God, and you're not!" But God has chosen men and women to do his work among humankind.

As we seek to follow and be used by Jesus Christ, we need to utilize all that he has made available to us. One of the great blessings Jesus has given to his church and to us as individuals is the gifts of the Spirit. Why has he given these gifts? The Bible has this to say about the vital role they play in the lives of believers:

Spiritual Gifts Enable Us to Grow in the Knowledge of Christ.   Some people get sidetracked with spiritual gifts and become more obsessed with the gifts than with Jesus. Believers begin to follow signs and wonders, instead of signs and wonders following believers. This is a sign of spiritual immaturity. The Christian writer/preacher A. B. Simpson wrote these insightful words:

Once it was the blessing, now it is the Lord.
Once it was the feeling, now it is his Word.
Once his gifts I wanted, now the Giver own.
Once I sought for healing, now himself alone.

Attaining spiritual gifts is not the goal—they are the gateway. They are not a hobby to play with—they are tools to build with, weapons to fight with. We will be more effective as we put them to use for God's glory and not our own.

Spiritual Gifts Are to Be Used.   It is possible to let a gift go unused. In doing this, however, you disobey God and cheat the church of a blessing. For this reason, we must use those unique gifts he has given us. In fact, it must be insulting to God for us to demean some gift his Holy Spirit has instilled in our life by saying that it just isn't important enough to use.

Each Spiritual Gift Has a Special Place in the Body of Christ.   Every gift that God has placed in the body of Christ, the church, is important. Some gifts such as preaching, teaching, and prophesying may seem more important than others such as hospitality or service. But God has given all of these gifts to build up his church. None of these gifts should be looked down upon or treated lightly.

For the next "Big Question" note, turn to p. 1073.

For the next "Big Question" note, turn to p. 1073.

Living as Children of Light

17With the Lord's authority let me say this: Live no longer as the ungodly.* do, for they are hopelessly confused. 18Their closed minds are full of darkness; they are far away from the life of God because they have shut their minds and hardened their hearts against him. 19They don't care anymore about right and wrong, and they have given themselves over to immoral ways. Their lives are filled with all kinds of impurity and greed.

20But that isn't what you were taught when you learned about Christ. 21Since you have heard all about him and have learned the truth that is in Jesus, 22throw off your old evil nature and your former way of life, which is rotten through and through, full of lust and deception. 23Instead, there must be a spiritual renewal of your thoughts and attitudes. 24You must display a new nature because you are a new person, created in God's likeness—righteous, holy, and true.

25So put away all falsehood and "tell your neighbor the truth"* because we belong to each

4:17 Greek *Gentiles.*   4:25 Zech 8:16.

other. 26And "don't sin by letting anger gain control over you."* Don't let the sun go down while you are still angry, 27for anger gives a mighty foothold to the Devil.

28If you are a thief, stop stealing. Begin using your hands for honest work, and then give generously to others in need. 29Don't use foul or abusive language. Let everything you say be good and helpful, so that your words will be an encouragement to those who hear them.

30And do not bring sorrow to God's Holy Spirit by the way you live. Remember, he is the one who has identified you as his own, guaran-

4:26 Ps 4:4.

teeing that you will be saved on the day of redemption.

31Get rid of all bitterness, rage, anger, harsh words, and slander, as well as all types of malicious behavior. 32Instead, be kind to each other, tenderhearted, forgiving one another, just as God through Christ has forgiven you.

CHAPTER **5**
Living in the Light
Follow God's example in everything you do, because you are his dear children. 2Live a life

OFF AND RUNNING

Husbands and Wives Have Distinct Roles in

Marriage Read EPHESIANS 5:21-33

The reason so many marriages fail is that husbands, wives, or both do not obey the standards God has laid out in Scripture. In this text, we find the specific roles God has given the husband and the wife.

God's Plan for the Husband.
• He is to be the head of his wife as Christ is the head of the church
True authority in the marriage relationship has been given by God to the husband. From the beginning, God designated the man as the leader in the marriage relationship (verse 23). Like Christ, a husband should be firm and decisive but also humble and unselfish. Before a husband can expect his wife to submit to him, though, he has to submit to Christ.

• He must love his wife as Christ loved the church
Jesus said, "I . . . came here not to be served but to serve others, and to give my life as a ransom for many" (Matthew 20:28). To love as Jesus loved means that a husband focuses primarily on his wife's needs, not his own (verse 25). The wife's submission hinges upon the husband's fulfillment of this role. Just as the church loves Jesus because of his incredible display of love for it, so the wife will love and submit to her husband as she sees his demonstration of love toward her. One heart burning with love sets another on fire.

• He must encourage his wife's spiritual growth
One of the husband's first priorities is to make sure his wife has a good relationship with God (verse 26). He is to encourage his wife's spiritual growth, recognizing that it affects her personal happiness as a woman, wife, and mother.

• He must love his wife as he loves himself
A husband must recognize that he and his wife are actually "one." Therefore, he must do for his wife what he would do for himself. He should give her needs as much attention as he would his own (verses 28-29).

God's Plan for the Wife.
• She must submit to her husband's leadership
Just as a wife submits to God, seeking his will above her own, so she must submit to her husband and his decisions (verses 21, 24).

These guidelines for the husband and the wife become much easier to follow if they respect the first code of conduct listed: "Submit to one another out of reverence for Christ" (verse 21). The word used for *submit* is a term that means "to arrange or rank under." In other words, we need to put the needs of our spouse before our own—in the fear of God. As we do that, our marriages will flourish as God intended—and you will be a living illustration of Christ's love for the church to an unbelieving world. For marriage is not so much *finding* the right person as it is *being* the right person.

For the next note on "Marriage," turn to p. 544.

filled with love for others, following the example of Christ, who loved you and gave himself as a sacrifice to take away your sins. And God was pleased, because that sacrifice was like sweet perfume to him.

3 Let there be no sexual immorality, impurity, or greed among you. Such sins have no place among God's people. 4 Obscene stories, foolish talk, and coarse jokes—these are not for you. Instead, let there be thankfulness to God. 5 You can be sure that no immoral, impure, or greedy person will inherit the Kingdom of Christ and of God. For a greedy person is really an idolater who worships the things of this world. 6 Don't be fooled by those who try to excuse these sins, for the terrible anger of God comes upon all those who disobey him. 7 Don't participate in the things these people do. 8 For though your hearts were once full of darkness, now you are full of light from the Lord, and your behavior should show it! 9 For this light within you produces only what is good and right and true.

10 Try to find out what is pleasing to the Lord. 11 Take no part in the worthless deeds of evil and darkness; instead, rebuke and expose them. 12 It is shameful even to talk about the things that ungodly people do in secret. 13 But when the light shines on them, it becomes clear how evil these things are. 14 And where your light shines, it will expose their evil deeds. This is why it is said,

"Awake, O sleeper,
 rise up from the dead,
 and Christ will give you light."

Living by the Spirit's Power
15 So be careful how you live, not as fools but as those who are wise. 16 Make the most of every opportunity for doing good in these evil days. 17 Don't act thoughtlessly, but try to understand what the Lord wants you to do. 18 Don't be drunk with wine, because that will ruin your life. Instead, let the Holy Spirit fill and control you. 19 Then you will sing psalms and hymns and spiritual songs among yourselves, making music to the Lord in your hearts. 20 And you will always give thanks for everything to God the Father in the name of our Lord Jesus Christ.

Spirit-Guided Relationships: Wives and Husbands
21 And further, you will submit to one another out of reverence for Christ. 22 You wives will submit to your husbands as you do to the Lord. 23 For a husband is the head of his wife as Christ is the head of his body, the church; he gave his life to be her Savior. 24 As the church submits to Christ, so you wives must submit to your husbands in everything.

25 And you husbands must love your wives

Realize Who Is Tempting You
Read EPHESIANS 6:10-12

In the Bible, the Christian life is not simply compared to a war—it is actually called a war! As in any battle, it helps to know your enemy. In this case, our enemy is the same one who faced off against Christ in the wilderness: the devil. He is incensed that you have surrendered your life to Christ, and he also sees you as a potential threat to his kingdom. But the encouraging news is that the devil is not as powerful as he would like you to think. Here are two things the devil doesn't want you to know:

1. The Devil Was Conquered by Jesus. When Jesus Christ died on the cross, he disarmed the devil and his demon powers. They could no longer control and condemn people for their sin. In addition, they could no longer keep the penalty of death hanging above people's heads (see Colossians 2:13-15, p. 1041; Hebrews 2:14, p. 1073; 1 John 3:8-9, pp. 1105-1106). The fact that Jesus defeated the devil does not mean that the devil has no power today. But it does mean that he does not have the upper hand.

2. The Devil Has Definite Limitations. Satan would love to have us think that he is God's equal, but he has clear and definite limitations as to what he can do (see Job 1:1-12, p. 439). Most important, before he can bring one temptation or hardship our way, he has to go through the protective hedge of Jesus Christ.

Temptation will come your way in the Christian life. But if you are wise, you will cling to the Lord that much tighter when the devil comes with his enticements. Then, once you have stood through the temptation, you will be stronger. As Martin Luther once said, "One Christian who has been tempted is worth a thousand who haven't."

For the next note on "Resist Temptation," turn to p. 1089.

Christ's Love Sets the Standard Read EPHESIANS 5:2

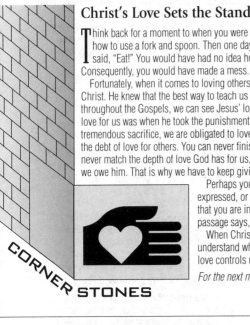

Think back for a moment to when you were a child. What if your parents had never demonstrated how to use a fork and spoon. Then one day they placed you at a table with these utensils and said, "Eat!" You would have had no idea how to use them to get food into your mouth. Consequently, you would have made a mess.

Fortunately, when it comes to loving others, God has given us the greatest example: Jesus Christ. He knew that the best way to teach us how to love was to show us how it is done, and throughout the Gospels, we can see Jesus' love in action. Of course the greatest display of Christ's love for us was when he took the punishment we deserved by dying on the cross. Because of that tremendous sacrifice, we are obligated to love others. Scripture says, "Pay all your debts, except the debt of love for others. You can never finish paying that!" (Romans 13:8). Because we will never match the depth of love God has for us, we will never be able to fully repay the debt of love we owe him. That is why we have to keep giving out that same kind of love to others.

Perhaps you have grown up in a home where love was seldom expressed, or you have had a distorted view of love, and you feel that you are incapable of truly loving others. Take heart, for as this passage says, you can look to Jesus as your example.

When Christ becomes the standard of your love, you will understand what the apostle Paul meant when he said that Christ's love controls us (see 2 Corinthians 5:14, pp. 1006-1007).

For the next note on "Love," turn to p. 1000.

CORNER STONES

---

with the same love Christ showed the church. He gave up his life for her [26]to make her holy and clean, washed by baptism and God's word.* [27]He did this to present her to himself as a glorious church without a spot or wrinkle or any other blemish. Instead, she will be holy and without fault. [28]In the same way, husbands ought to love their wives as they love their own bodies. For a man is actually loving himself when he loves his wife. [29]No one hates his own body but lovingly cares for it, just as Christ cares for his body, which is the church. [30]And we are his body.

[31]As the Scriptures say, "A man leaves his father and mother and is joined to his wife, and the two are united into one."* [32]This is a great mystery, but it is an illustration of the way Christ and the church are one. [33]So again I say, each man must love his wife as he loves himself, and the wife must respect her husband.

CHAPTER 6
Children and Parents

Children, obey your parents because you belong to the Lord, for this is the right thing to do. [2]"Honor your father and mother." This is the first of the Ten Commandments that ends with a promise. [3]And this is the promise: If you honor your father and mother, "you will live a long life, full of blessing."*

[4]And now a word to you fathers. Don't make your children angry by the way you treat them. Rather, bring them up with the discipline and instruction approved by the Lord.

Slaves and Masters

[5]Slaves, obey your earthly masters with deep respect and fear. Serve them sincerely as you would serve Christ. [6]Work hard, but not just to please your masters when they are watching. As slaves of Christ, do the will of God with all your heart. [7]Work with enthusiasm, as though you were working for the Lord rather than for people. [8]Remember that the Lord will reward each one of us for the good we do, whether we are slaves or free.

[9]And in the same way, you masters must treat your slaves right. Don't threaten them; remember, you both have the same Master in heaven, and he has no favorites.

The Whole Armor of God

[10]A final word: Be strong with the Lord's mighty

5:26 Greek *having cleansed her by the washing of water with the word.* 5:31 Gen 2:24. 6:2-3 Exod 20:12; Deut 5:16.

power. [11]Put on all of God's armor so that you will be able to stand firm against all strategies and tricks of the Devil. [12]For we are not fighting against people made of flesh and blood, but against the evil rulers and authorities of the unseen world, against those mighty powers of darkness who rule this world, and against wicked spirits in the heavenly realms.

[13]Use every piece of God's armor to resist the enemy in the time of evil, so that after the battle you will still be standing firm. [14]Stand your ground, putting on the sturdy belt of truth and the body armor of God's righteousness. [15]For shoes, put on the peace that comes from the Good News, so that you will be fully prepared.* [16]In every battle you will need faith as your shield to stop the fiery arrows aimed at you by Satan.* [17]Put on salvation as your helmet, and take the sword of the Spirit, which is the word of God. [18]Pray at all times and on every occasion in the power of the Holy Spirit. Stay alert and be persistent in your prayers for all Christians everywhere.

[19]And pray for me, too. Ask God to give me the right words as I boldly explain God's secret plan that the Good News is for the Gentiles, too.* [20]I am in chains now for preaching this message as God's ambassador. But pray that I will keep on speaking boldly for him, as I should.

Final Greetings

[21]Tychicus, a much loved brother and faithful helper in the Lord's work, will tell you all about how I am getting along. [22]I am sending him to you for just this purpose. He will let you know how we are, and he will encourage you.

[23]May God give you peace, dear brothers and sisters,* and love with faith, from God the Father and the Lord Jesus Christ. [24]May God's grace be upon all who love our Lord Jesus Christ with an undying love.

6:15 Or *For shoes, put on the readiness to preach the Good News of peace with God.*   6:16 Greek *by the evil one.*   6:19 Greek *explain the mystery of the gospel.*   6:23 Greek *brothers.*

Philippians

CHAPTER 1

Greetings from Paul

This letter is from Paul and Timothy, slaves of Christ Jesus.

It is written to all of God's people in Philippi, who believe in Christ Jesus, and to the elders* and deacons.

2May God our Father and the Lord Jesus Christ give you grace and peace.

Paul's Thanksgiving and Prayer

3Every time I think of you, I give thanks to my God. 4I always pray for you, and I make my requests with a heart full of joy 5because you have been my partners in spreading the Good News about Christ from the time you first heard it until now. 6And I am sure that God, who began the good work within you, will continue his work until it is finally finished on that day when Christ Jesus comes back again.

7It is right that I should feel as I do about all of you, for you have a very special place in my heart. We have shared together the blessings of God, both when I was in prison and when I was out, defending the truth and telling others the Good News. 8God knows how much I love you and long for you with the tender compassion of Christ Jesus. 9I pray that your love for each other will overflow more and more, and that you will keep on growing in your knowledge and understanding. 10For I want you to understand what really matters, so that you may live pure and blameless lives until Christ returns. 11May you always be filled with the fruit of your salvation*—those good things that are produced in your life by Jesus Christ—for this will bring much glory and praise to God.

Paul's Joy That Christ Is Preached

12And I want you to know, dear brothers and sisters,* that everything that has happened to me here has helped to spread the Good News. 13For everyone here, including all the soldiers in the palace guard, knows that I am in chains because of Christ. 14And because of my imprisonment, many of the Christians* here have gained confidence and become more bold in telling others about Christ.

15Some are preaching out of jealousy and rivalry. But others preach about Christ with pure motives. 16They preach because they love me, for they know the Lord brought me here to defend the Good News. 17Those others do not have pure motives as they preach about Christ. They preach with selfish ambition, not sincerely, intending to make my chains more painful to me. 18But whether or not their motives are pure, the fact remains that the message about Christ is being preached, so I rejoice. And I will continue to rejoice. 19For I know that as you pray for me and as the Spirit of Jesus Christ helps me, this will all turn out for my deliverance.

Paul's Life for Christ

20For I live in eager expectation and hope that I will never do anything that causes me shame, but that I will always be bold for Christ, as I have been in the past, and that my life will always honor Christ, whether I live or I die. 21For to me, living is for Christ, and dying is even better. 22Yet if I live, that means fruitful service for Christ. I really don't know which is better. 23I'm torn between two desires: Sometimes I want to live, and sometimes I long to go and be with Christ. That would be far better for me, 24but it is better for you that I live.

1:1 Greek overseers.   1:11 Greek the fruit of righteousness.   1:12 Greek brothers.   1:14 Greek brothers in the Lord.

Jesus Is Human Read PHILIPPIANS 2:5-11

This passage of Scripture paints a touching portrait of the Savior while letting us in on some key truths concerning Christ's divinity and humanity. In essence, it shows why we should worship and emulate Jesus in our lives.

Jesus Veiled His Deity without Voiding It. There was never a moment in the life of Jesus when he suddenly "became" God. He was God before he entered this world as a little baby. And he remained God after he became man. When the Scripture says that "made himself nothing," it does not mean that he ceased being God. He simply veiled his deity. But he never voided it. He always was and always will be God.

Jesus Experienced Our Experiences. Another way of saying that Jesus took the disguise of a slave is to say that "he emptied himself." Again, this does not mean that he emptied himself of his deity, but that he emptied himself of the privileges of deity. For instance, he never performed a miracle for his own benefit. He walked this earth as a man, not a spirit. He experienced human limitations. Jesus—God in human form—experienced hunger. He endured sorrow. He grew tired. He felt the sting of loneliness. He felt the pressure of temptation. For these reasons, we can be assured that our God understands what we are going through (see Hebrews 2:17-18, p. 1073).

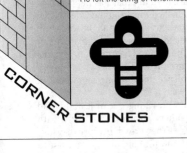

Jesus' Lordship Will Be Acknowledged by All. Regardless of what anyone thinks of Jesus now, in the end every knee will bow and every tongue will confess that Jesus Christ is Lord. The authority of the Bible backs this claim. Christ's divine nature, which he veiled at times during his time on earth, will then be clearly visible for all to see.

For the next note on "Who Is Jesus?" turn to p. 1040.

CORNER STONES

25I am convinced of this, so I will continue with you so that you will grow and experience the joy of your faith. 26Then when I return to you, you will have even more reason to boast about what Christ Jesus has done for me.

Live as Citizens of Heaven

27But whatever happens to me, you must live in a manner worthy of the Good News about Christ, as citizens of heaven. Then, whether I come and see you again or only hear about you, I will know that you are standing side by side, fighting together for the Good News. 28Don't be intimidated by your enemies. This will be a sign to them that they are going to be destroyed, but that you are going to be saved, even by God himself. 29For you have been given not only the privilege of trusting in Christ but also the privilege of suffering for him. 30We are in this fight together. You have seen me suffer for him in the past, and you know that I am still in the midst of this great struggle.

CHAPTER **2**

Unity through Humility

Is there any encouragement from belonging to Christ? Any comfort from his love? Any fellowship together in the Spirit? Are your hearts tender and sympathetic? 2Then make me truly happy by agreeing wholeheartedly with each other, loving one another, and working together with one heart and purpose.

3Don't be selfish; don't live to make a good impression on others. Be humble, thinking of others as better than yourself. 4Don't think only about your own affairs, but be interested in others, too, and what they are doing.

Christ's Humility and Exaltation

5Your attitude should be the same that Christ Jesus had. 6Though he was God, he did not demand and cling to his rights as God. 7He made himself nothing;* he took the humble position of a slave and appeared in human form.* 8And in human form he obediently humbled himself even further by dying a criminal's death on a cross. 9Because of this, God

2:7a Or *He laid aside his mighty power and glory.* 2:7b Greek *and was born in the likeness of men and was found in appearance as a man.*

raised him up to the heights of heaven and gave him a name that is above every other name, ¹⁰so that at the name of Jesus every knee will bow, in heaven and on earth and under the earth, ¹¹and every tongue will confess that Jesus Christ is Lord, to the glory of God the Father.

Shine Brightly for Christ

¹²Dearest friends, you were always so careful to follow my instructions when I was with you. And now that I am away you must be even more careful to put into action God's saving work in your lives, obeying God with deep reverence and fear. ¹³For God is working in you, giving you the desire to obey him and the power to do what pleases him.

¹⁴In everything you do, stay away from complaining and arguing, ¹⁵so that no one can speak a word of blame against you. You are to live clean, innocent lives as children of God in a dark world full of crooked and perverse people. Let your lives shine brightly before them. ¹⁶Hold tightly to the word of life, so that when Christ returns, I will be proud that I did not lose the race and that my work was not useless. ¹⁷But even if my life is to be poured out like a drink offering to complete the sacrifice of your faithful service (that is, if I am to die for you), I will rejoice, and I want to share my joy with all of you. ¹⁸And you should be happy about this and rejoice with me.

Paul Commends Timothy

¹⁹If the Lord Jesus is willing, I hope to send Timothy to you soon. Then when he comes back, he can cheer me up by telling me how you are getting along. ²⁰I have no one else like Timothy, who genuinely cares about your welfare. ²¹All the others care only for themselves and not for what matters to Jesus Christ. ²²But you know how Timothy has proved himself. Like a son with his father, he has helped me in preaching the Good News. ²³I hope to send him to you just as soon as I find out what is going to happen to me here. ²⁴And I have confidence from the Lord that I myself will come to see you soon.

Paul Commends Epaphroditus

²⁵Meanwhile, I thought I should send Epaphroditus back to you. He is a true brother, a faithful worker, and a courageous soldier. And he was your messenger to help me in my need. ²⁶Now I am sending him home again, for he has been longing to see you, and he was very distressed

that you heard he was ill. ²⁷And he surely was ill; in fact, he almost died. But God had mercy on him—and also on me, so that I would not have such unbearable sorrow.

²⁸So I am all the more anxious to send him back to you, for I know you will be glad to see him, and that will lighten all my cares. ²⁹Welcome him with Christian love* and with great joy, and be sure to honor people like him. ³⁰For he risked his life for the work of Christ, and he was at the point of death while trying to do for me the things you couldn't do because you were far away.

CHAPTER 3

The Priceless Gain of Knowing Christ

Whatever happens, dear brothers and sisters,* may the Lord give you joy. I never get tired of telling you this. I am doing this for your own good.

²Watch out for those dogs, those wicked men and their evil deeds, those mutilators who say you must be circumcised to be saved. ³For we who worship God in the Spirit* are the only ones who are truly circumcised. We put no confidence in human effort. Instead, we boast about what Christ Jesus has done for us.

⁴Yet I could have confidence in myself if anyone could. If others have reason for confidence in their own efforts, I have even more! ⁵For I was circumcised when I was eight days old, having been born into a pure-blooded Jewish family that is a branch of the tribe of Benjamin. So I am a real Jew if there ever was one! What's more, I was a member of the Pharisees, who demand the strictest obedience to the Jewish law. ⁶And zealous? Yes, in fact, I harshly persecuted the church. And I obeyed the Jewish law so carefully that I was never accused of any fault.

⁷I once thought all these things were so very important, but now I consider them worthless because of what Christ has done. ⁸Yes, everything else is worthless when compared with the priceless gain of knowing Christ Jesus my Lord. I have discarded everything else, counting it all as garbage, so that I may have Christ ⁹and become one with him. I no longer count on my own goodness or my ability to obey God's law, but I trust Christ to save me. For God's way of making us right with himself depends on faith. ¹⁰As a result, I can really know Christ and experience the mighty power that raised him from the dead. I can learn what it means to suffer with him, sharing in his death, ¹¹so that, somehow, I can experience the resurrection from the dead!

2:29 Greek *in the Lord.*   3:1 Greek *brothers;* also in 3:13, 17.   3:3 Or *in spirit;* some manuscripts read *worship by the Spirit of God.*

Pressing toward the Goal

12I don't mean to say that I have already achieved these things or that I have already reached perfection! But I keep working toward that day when I will finally be all that Christ Jesus saved me for and wants me to be. 13No, dear brothers and sisters, I am still not all I should be,* but I am focusing all my energies on this one thing: Forgetting the past and looking forward to what lies ahead, 14I strain to reach the end of the race and receive the prize for which God, through Christ Jesus, is calling us up to heaven.*

15I hope all of you who are mature Christians will agree on these things. If you disagree on some point, I believe God will make it plain to you. 16But we must be sure to obey the truth we have learned already.

17Dear brothers and sisters, pattern your lives after mine, and learn from those who follow our example. 18For I have told you often before, and I say it again with tears in my eyes, that there are many whose conduct shows they are really enemies of the cross of Christ. 19Their future is eternal destruction. Their god is their appetite, they brag about shameful things, and all they think about is this life here on earth. 20But we are citizens of heaven, where the Lord Jesus Christ lives. And we are eagerly waiting for him to return as our Savior. 21He will take these weak mortal bodies of ours and change them into glorious bodies like his own, using the same mighty power that he will use to conquer everything, everywhere.

CHAPTER 4

Dear brothers and sisters,* I love you and long to see you, for you are my joy and the reward for my work. So please stay true to the Lord, my dear friends.

Paul's Final Thoughts

2And now I want to plead with those two women, Euodia and Syntyche. Please, because you belong to the Lord, settle your disagreement. 3And I ask you, my true teammate,* to help these women, for they worked hard with me in telling others the Good News. And they worked with Clement and the rest of my co-workers, whose names are written in the Book of Life.

4Always be full of joy in the Lord. I say it again—rejoice! 5Let everyone see that you are considerate in all you do. Remember, the Lord is coming soon.

6Don't worry about anything; instead, pray about everything. Tell God what you need, and thank him for all he has done. 7If you do this, you will experience God's peace, which is far more wonderful than the human mind can understand. His peace will guard your hearts and minds as you live in Christ Jesus.

8And now, dear brothers and sisters, let me say one more thing as I close this letter. Fix your thoughts on what is true and honorable and right. Think about things that are pure and lovely and admirable. Think about things that are excellent and worthy of praise. 9Keep putting into practice all you learned from me and

3:13 Some manuscripts read *I am not all I should be.*   3:14 Or *from heaven.*   4:1 Greek *brothers;* also in 4:8.   4:3 Greek *true yokefellow,* or *loyal Syzygus.*

OFF AND RUNNING ▰▰▰

Place Christ before All Else Read PHILIPPIANS 3:4-8

As verses 4-6 attest, the apostle Paul was the epitome of a good Jew. He had been born a member of God's chosen people and had flawlessly kept God's laws. But when Paul met Jesus on the road to Damascus (see Acts 9:1-19, pp. 934-935), Paul realized that everything he was living for was taking him in the wrong direction. For that reason he counted everything else in life—his reputation, his achievements, his pursuits, his possessions—worthless, so that his sole pursuit would be in knowing and serving Jesus.

Do you, like Paul, place Christ above everything else in your life? If you are not sure, ask yourself the following questions: How do you spend your time? What dominates your thoughts? Where are your priorities? What motivates you? If the most important thing in your life is Jesus, then your life will revolve around getting to know him more and more. You will want to spend time learning about his nature, his will, and his purposes for you in his Word. And you will truly be able to say that you have discovered "the priceless gain of knowing Christ Jesus."

For the next note on "Priorities," turn to p. 870.

heard from me and saw me doing, and the God of peace will be with you.

Paul's Thanks for Their Gifts

10How grateful I am, and how I praise the Lord that you are concerned about me again. I know you have always been concerned for me, but for a while you didn't have the chance to help me. 11Not that I was ever in need, for I have learned how to get along happily whether I have much or little. 12I know how to live on almost nothing or with everything. I have learned the secret of living in every situation, whether it is with a full stomach or empty, with plenty or little. 13For I can do everything with the help of Christ who gives me the strength I need. 14But even so, you have done well to share with me in my present difficulty.

15As you know, you Philippians were the only ones who gave me financial help when I brought you the Good News and then traveled on from Macedonia. No other church did this. 16Even when I was in Thessalonica you sent help more than once. 17I don't say this because I want a gift from you. What I want is for you to receive a well-earned reward because of your kindness. 18At the moment I have all I need—more than I need! I am generously supplied with the gifts you sent me with Epaphroditus. They are a sweet-smelling sacrifice that is acceptable to God and pleases him. 19And this same God who takes care of me will supply all your needs from his glorious riches, which have been given to us in Christ Jesus. 20Now glory be to God our Father forever and ever. Amen.

Paul's Final Greetings

21Give my greetings to all the Christians there. The brothers who are with me here send you their greetings. 22And all the other Christians send their greetings, too, especially those who work in Caesar's palace. 23May the grace of the Lord Jesus Christ be with your spirit.

Prayer Helps Us Overcome Worry Read PHILIPPIANS 4:6-7

Have you ever been gripped by worry or fear? Worry is a completely unproductive emotion. It is the advance interest we pay on troubles that seldom come. But these verses give us the best antidote for worry—prayer. God wants to be the first one we turn to in times of worry or crisis. When we do, he promises a special blessing if we do the following four things:

1. Stop Worrying and Start Praying. Don't ever think that your need is too insignificant for God's attention. He wants us to pray about *everything*.

2. Tell God Your Needs. Even though God is all-knowing and is well aware of your situation, he desires that you verbalize your needs to him and place them in his hands.

3. Present Your Requests with Thanks. Instead of praying with feelings of doubt, we can thank God for his answers in advance because of the promises he has made to us in his Word.

4. Receive God's Peace. Once you do these things, verse 7 says that you will experience God's peace. In the original Greek text, this verse literally means that God's peace will "mount a guard or garrison" around your heart and mind to keep and protect you during those difficult times in your life.

The next time you are tempted to worry about something, channel into prayer all of the energy you would have put into worry. Say something like, "Lord, here is my problem. It looms ever larger in my path, so I am putting it into your hands. I am not going to worry, Lord. Instead, I am going to trust you. I am even going to thank you in advance for what you will do, because you know what you are doing." This may not always be an easy thing to do, but if you want to overcome worry and experience God's peace, it is something you must consciously do.

For the next note on "Pray," turn to p. 653.

Colossians

CHAPTER 1

Greetings from Paul

This letter is from Paul, chosen by God to be an apostle of Christ Jesus, and from our brother Timothy.

²It is written to God's holy people in the city of Colosse, who are faithful brothers and sisters* in Christ.

May God our Father give you grace and peace.

Paul's Thanksgiving and Prayer

³We always pray for you, and we give thanks to God the Father of our Lord Jesus Christ, ⁴for we have heard that you trust in Christ Jesus and that you love all of God's people. ⁵You do this because you are looking forward to the joys of heaven—as you have been ever since you first heard the truth of the Good News. ⁶This same Good News that came to you is going out all over the world. It is changing lives everywhere, just as it changed yours that very first day you heard and understood the truth about God's great kindness to sinners.

⁷Epaphras, our much loved co-worker, was the one who brought you the Good News. He is Christ's faithful servant, and he is helping us in your place.* ⁸He is the one who told us about the great love for others that the Holy Spirit has given you.

⁹So we have continued praying for you ever since we first heard about you. We ask God to give you a complete understanding of what he wants to do in your lives, and we ask him to make you wise with spiritual wisdom. ¹⁰Then the way you live will always honor and please the Lord, and you will continually do good, kind things for others. All the while, you will learn to know God better and better.

¹¹We also pray that you will be strengthened with his glorious power so that you will have all the patience and endurance you need. May you be filled with joy, ¹²always thanking the Father, who has enabled you to share the inheritance that belongs to God's holy people, who live in the light. ¹³For he has rescued us from the one who rules in the kingdom of darkness, and he has brought us into the Kingdom of his dear Son. ¹⁴God has purchased our freedom with his blood* and has forgiven all our sins.

Christ Is Supreme

¹⁵Christ is the visible image of the invisible God. He existed before God made anything at all and is supreme over all creation.* ¹⁶Christ is the one through whom God created everything in heaven and earth. He made the things we can see and the things we can't see—kings, kingdoms, rulers, and authorities. Everything has been created through him and for him. ¹⁷He existed before everything else began, and he holds all creation together.

¹⁸Christ is the head of the church, which is his body. He is the first of all who will rise from the dead,* so he is first in everything. ¹⁹For God in all his fullness was pleased to live in Christ, ²⁰and by him God reconciled everything to himself. He made peace with everything in heaven and on earth by means of his blood on the cross. ²¹This includes you who were once so far away from God. You were his enemies, separated from him by your evil thoughts and actions, ²²yet now he has brought you back as his friends. He has done this through his death on the cross in his own human body. As a result, he has brought you into the very presence of God, and you are holy and blameless as you stand before him

1:2 Greek *faithful brothers.* 1:7 Greek *he is ministering on your behalf;* other manuscripts read *he is ministering on our behalf.* 1:14 Some manuscripts do not include *with his blood.* 1:15 Greek *He is the firstborn of all creation.* 1:18 Greek *He is the beginning, the firstborn from the dead.*

Jesus Is Divine Read COLOSSIANS 1:15-20

The most crucial truth of the Christian faith is that Jesus Christ, though he came to earth as a man, was in fact God. This passage lays out six important details about Jesus' divinity and his work in heaven and on earth:

1. Jesus Is Eternal. Being God, Jesus never had a beginning, nor does he have an end (verse 15). The prophet Micah, speaking of the place in which Jesus would be born, said, "But you, O Bethlehem Ephrathah, are only a small village in Judah. Yet a ruler of Israel will come from you, one whose origins are from the distant past" (Micah 5:2). The phrase "distant past" has also been translated "from everlasting," meaning eternal.

2. Jesus Is the Creator of All Things. This concept makes the whole idea of Jesus' coming as a Savior to this earth so amazing. He understood the way people acted and the hardness of humans' hearts because he created them (verse 16). Yet he loved people so much he was willing to come down to earth and die in order to redeem all humankind.

3. Jesus Holds Everything Together. Jesus has and always will be in control (verses 16-17). Our world is not in some chaotic state but has been created with a purpose in mind—to ultimately bring glory to Christ.

4. Jesus Is the Head of the Church. The church was not established by a group of people but by God himself. Although some leaders in the church may let us down at times, we must remember that Christ, the true head of this body of believers (verse 18), will never fail us.

5. Jesus Is the Leader of All Who Will Rise from the Dead. Christ was the first to actually defeat death and return to life in a resurrected body (verse 18). For that reason, we who follow him have the hope—and the evidence—that we, too, will one day rise again after death to spend eternity with him.

6. Jesus Is the Only Way to Peace with God. God was never surprised that man sinned in the Garden of Eden. The Bible even records that Jesus' sacrifice on the cross was known before "the world was made" (Revelation 13:8). That means that God had already made a provision for our sins long before Adam ate the forbidden fruit (verse 20).

Jesus was much more than a mere prophet, teacher, or messenger. In reality, Jesus was nothing less than God himself come to the earth. To deny this central truth is to deny the basis of the Christian faith. Remember, it was this truth that motivated the Christians of the first century to turn their world "upside down" for the sake of the gospel (see Acts 17:6, p. 945).

For the next note on "Who Is Jesus?" turn to p. 856.

CORNER STONES

---

without a single fault. ²³But you must continue to believe this truth and stand in it firmly. Don't drift away from the assurance you received when you heard the Good News. The Good News has been preached all over the world, and I, Paul, have been appointed by God to proclaim it.

Paul's Work for the Church

²⁴I am glad when I suffer for you in my body, for I am completing what remains of Christ's sufferings for his body, the church. ²⁵God has given me the responsibility of serving his church by proclaiming his message in all its fullness to you Gentiles. ²⁶This message was kept secret for centuries and generations past, but now it has been revealed to his own holy people. ²⁷For it has pleased God to tell his people that the riches and glory of Christ are for you Gentiles, too. For this is the secret: Christ lives in you, and this is your assurance that you will share in his glory.

²⁸So everywhere we go, we tell everyone about Christ. We warn them and teach them with all the wisdom God has given us, for we

want to present them to God, perfect* in their relationship to Christ. ²⁹I work very hard at this, as I depend on Christ's mighty power that works within me.

CHAPTER 2

I want you to know how much I have agonized for you and for the church at Laodicea, and for many other friends who have never known me personally. ²My goal is that they will be encouraged and knit together by strong ties of love. I want them to have full confidence because they have complete understanding of God's secret plan, which is Christ himself. ³In him lie hidden all the treasures of wisdom and knowledge.

⁴I am telling you this so that no one will be able to deceive you with persuasive arguments. ⁵For though I am far away from you, my heart is with you. And I am very happy because you are living as you should and because of your strong faith in Christ.

Freedom from Rules and New Life in Christ

⁶And now, just as you accepted Christ Jesus as your Lord, you must continue to live in obedience to him. ⁷Let your roots grow down into him and draw up nourishment from him, so you will grow in faith, strong and vigorous in the truth you were taught. Let your lives overflow with thanksgiving for all he has done.

⁸Don't let anyone lead you astray with empty philosophy and high-sounding nonsense that come from human thinking and from the evil powers of this world,* and not from Christ. ⁹For in Christ the fullness of God lives in a human body,* ¹⁰and you are complete through your union with Christ. He is the Lord over every ruler and authority in the universe.

¹¹When you came to Christ, you were "circumcised," but not by a physical procedure. It was a spiritual procedure—the cutting away of your sinful nature. ¹²For you were buried with Christ when you were baptized. And with him you were raised to a new life because you trusted the mighty power of God, who raised Christ from the dead.

¹³You were dead because of your sins and because your sinful nature was not yet cut away. Then God made you alive with Christ. He forgave all our sins. ¹⁴He canceled the record that contained the charges against us. He

took it and destroyed it by nailing it to Christ's cross. ¹⁵In this way, God disarmed the evil rulers and authorities. He shamed them publicly by his victory over them on the cross of Christ.

¹⁶So don't let anyone condemn you for what you eat or drink, or for not celebrating certain holy days or new-moon ceremonies or Sabbaths. ¹⁷For these rules were only shadows of the real thing, Christ himself. ¹⁸Don't let anyone condemn you by insisting on self-denial. And don't let anyone say you must worship angels, even though they say they have had visions about this. These people claim to be so humble, but their sinful minds have

1:28 Or *mature.*   2:8 Or *from the basic principles of this world;* also in 2:20.   2:9 Greek *in him dwells all the fullness of the Godhead bodily.*

Let God Occupy Your Thoughts Read COLOSSIANS 3:2-4

A song in the church says, "Turn your eyes upon Jesus. Look full in his wonderful face. And the things of earth will grow strangely dim in the light of his glory and grace." These are good words to live by, for one of the strongest deterrents against returning to your old way of life is to focus upon your Savior and future. As a believer, you have been promised eternal life, the hope of heaven, and the assurance of spending eternity in the presence of God. When you think about that, the trappings of this world begin to lose their appeal.

The next time you feel inclined to dabble with your old life, or feel weighed down by the worries of this world, or fear that you won't make it as a Christian, remember to do these things:

- Keep your eyes on your final destination.
- Realize that worry should not be a part of your life.
- Picture yourself as dead to this world and alive in Christ.
- Remember that your Redeemer is returning.

If you allow these truths to occupy your thoughts, you will find it much easier to obey God and say no to the alluring, but damaging, enticements of this sinful world.

To begin the next topic, turn to p. A28.

God's Peace Needs to Rule in Our Hearts Read COLOSSIANS 3:15

One of the most obvious identifying marks of a Christian is peace. As Paul points out in this verse, the peace a Christian has comes from Christ and "rules" in a Christian's heart. The Greek verb Paul uses for *rule* suggests that Christ's peace is to act as an "umpire" or a judge in our lives, deciding our outlook and mood in the midst of all circumstances.

What characterizes Christ's peace? Here are a few more biblical descriptions:

- It is not anxious about anything but trusts God (see Philippians 4:6-7, p. 1036).
- It doesn't doubt that God is in control (see Mark 4:35-41, pp. 833-834).
- It doesn't forget God's blessings and answers to prayer (see Philippians 4:6, p. 1036).
- It should be present in our relationships (see Psalm 34:14, p. 477, and Romans 12:18, p. 978).
- It comes from Christ alone (see John 16:33, p. 914).

- It is produced by the Holy Spirit (see Galatians 5:22, p. 1020).
- It promotes peace with others (see James 3:18, p. 1088).

Does the peace of Christ rule in your life? If not, you are not living as Jesus really intends you to live. Give God your worries and concerns, and ask him to replace them with his peace. This peace will not only calm your heart, but it will also help encourage harmony between you and your Christian brothers and sisters.

To begin the next topic, turn to p. A22.

CORNER STONES

---

made them proud. ¹⁹But they are not connected to Christ, the head of the body. For we are joined together in his body by his strong sinews, and we grow only as we get our nourishment and strength from God.

²⁰You have died with Christ, and he has set you free from the evil powers of this world. So why do you keep on following rules of the world, such as, ²¹"Don't handle, don't eat, don't touch." ²²Such rules are mere human teaching about things that are gone as soon as we use them. ²³These rules may seem wise because they require strong devotion, humility, and severe bodily discipline. But they have no effect when it comes to conquering a person's evil thoughts and desires.

CHAPTER **3**
Living the New Life

Since you have been raised to new life with Christ, set your sights on the realities of heaven, where Christ sits at God's right hand in the place of honor and power. ²Let heaven fill your thoughts. Do not think only about things down

---

OFF AND RUNNING

Avoid Aggravating Your Children Read COLOSSIANS 3:20-21

While discipline is necessary in the lives of children, it is equally necessary that discipline be tempered with love. This means that parents should not scold or nag their children, especially when disciplining them. Other words that have been used for scold and nag are *exasperate* and *aggravate*. The word *aggravate* means to irritate, enrage, harass, tease, and add fuel to the flame.

When discipline is administered in an aggravating manner, the consequences can be devastating. Children may not only be angry with their parents and resent them, but children may also disrespect and dishonor their parents. Even worse, they may one day end their relationship with their parents or act out violently against them.

If you really want your children to honor you as a parent, then you must discipline them with love, praise them when they obey, and train them in the instruction of the Lord.

To begin the next topic, turn to p. A35.

here on earth. 3For you died when Christ died, and your real life is hidden with Christ in God. 4And when Christ, who is your* real life, is revealed to the whole world, you will share in all his glory.

5So put to death the sinful, earthly things lurking within you. Have nothing to do with sexual sin, impurity, lust, and shameful desires. Don't be greedy for the good things of this life, for that is idolatry. 6God's terrible anger will come upon those who do such things. 7You used to do them when your life was still part of this world. 8But now is the time to get rid of anger, rage, malicious behavior, slander, and dirty language. 9Don't lie to each other, for you have stripped off your old evil nature and all its wicked deeds. 10In its place you have clothed yourselves with a brand-new nature that is continually being renewed as you learn more and more about Christ, who created this new nature within you. 11In this new life, it doesn't matter if you are a Jew or a Gentile,* circumcised or uncircumcised, barbaric, uncivilized,* slave, or free. Christ is all that matters, and he lives in all of us.

12Since God chose you to be the holy people whom he loves, you must clothe yourselves with tenderhearted mercy, kindness, humility, gentleness, and patience. 13You must make allowance for each other's faults and forgive the person who offends you. Remember, the Lord forgave you, so you must forgive others. 14And the most important piece of clothing you must wear is love. Love is what binds us all together in perfect harmony. 15And let the peace that comes from Christ rule in your hearts. For as members of one body you are all called to live in peace. And always be thankful.

16Let the words of Christ, in all their richness, live in your hearts and make you wise. Use his words to teach and counsel each other. Sing psalms and hymns and spiritual songs to God with thankful hearts. 17And whatever you do or say, let it be as a representative of the Lord Jesus, all the while giving thanks through him to God the Father.

Instructions for Christian Households

18You wives must submit to your husbands, as is fitting for those who belong to the Lord. 19And you husbands must love your wives and never treat them harshly.

20You children must always obey your parents, for this is what pleases the Lord. 21Fathers, don't aggravate your children. If you do, they will become discouraged and quit trying.

22You slaves must obey your earthly masters in everything you do. Try to please them all the time, not just when they are watching you. Obey them willingly because of your reverent fear of the Lord. 23Work hard and cheerfully at whatever you do, as though you were working for the Lord rather than for people. 24Remember that the Lord will give you an inheritance as your reward, and the Master you are serving is Christ. 25But if you do what is wrong, you will be paid back for the wrong you have done. For God has no favorites who can get away with evil.

CHAPTER 4

You slave owners must be just and fair to your slaves. Remember that you also have a Master— in heaven.

An Encouragement for Prayer

2Devote yourselves to prayer with an alert mind and a thankful heart. 3Don't forget to pray for us, too, that God will give us many opportunities to preach about his secret plan—that Christ is also for you Gentiles. That is why I am here in chains. 4Pray that I will proclaim this message as clearly as I should.

5Live wisely among those who are not Christians, and make the most of every opportunity. 6Let your conversation be gracious and effective so that you will have the right answer for everyone.

Paul's Final Instructions and Greetings

7Tychicus, a much loved brother, will tell you how I am getting along. He is a faithful helper who serves the Lord with me. 8I have sent him on this special trip to let you know how we are doing and to encourage you. 9I am also sending Onesimus, a faithful and much loved brother, one of your own people. He and Tychicus will give you all the latest news.

10Aristarchus, who is in prison with me, sends you his greetings, and so does Mark, Barnabas's cousin. And as you were instructed before, make Mark welcome if he comes your way. 11Jesus (the one we call Justus) also sends his greetings. These are the only Jewish Christians among my co-workers; they are working with me here for the Kingdom of God. And what a comfort they have been!

12Epaphras, from your city, a servant of Christ Jesus, sends you his greetings. He always prays

3:4 Some manuscripts read our.   3:11a Greek Greek.   3:11b Greek Barbarian, Scythian.

OFF AND RUNNING ▰▰▰▰

Work As If You Are Working for the Lord
Read COLOSSIANS 3:22-24

While the world says to work for the sake of your own welfare, Jesus says to work out of your desire to please him. While the world says to work hard to get ahead, Jesus says to work hard to show the world who you are really working for. When you work as though you are working for the Lord, your whole outlook changes.

Do you want to revolutionize your attitude toward your job? Then take this verse to heart. If you are a mother at home, tackle the dishes, laundry, and cooking as if you are serving the Lord, not just your family. If you work in an office, take care of your tasks and treat your co-workers as you would the Lord himself. Your work may be unappreciated and underpaid in this life, but God promises to give you your full reward in heaven (verse 24).

For the next note on "Job Performance," turn to p. 1066.

---

earnestly for you, asking God to make you strong and perfect, fully confident of the whole will of God. 13I can assure you that he has agonized for you and also for the Christians in Laodicea and Hierapolis.

14Dear Doctor Luke sends his greetings, and so does Demas. 15Please give my greetings to our Christian brothers and sisters* at Laodicea, and to Nympha and those who meet in her house.

4:15 Greek *brothers.*

16After you have read this letter, pass it on to the church at Laodicea so they can read it, too. And you should read the letter I wrote to them. 17And say to Archippus, "Be sure to carry out the work the Lord gave you."

18Here is my greeting in my own handwriting—PAUL.

Remember my chains.

May the grace of God be with you.

OFF AND RUNNING ▰▰▰▰

Keep Your Conversation Gracious Read COLOSSIANS 4:6

Witnessing to others about the Lord can be a bit intimidating at first. We never know what kind of response we will receive. But if you follow the three steps found in these verses, you will become much more effective at sharing your faith:

1. Tell the Good News. Center your conversation on the simple gospel message: (1) Man is separated from God by sin; (2) God sent his Son, Jesus Christ, to die on the cross and pay the price for our sin; and (3) if we will turn from that sin, embrace Christ as Savior and Lord, and follow him, we can be forgiven and have a relationship with God.

2. Be Wise When Sharing Your Faith. Use discernment. Don't push the subject of your faith if you sense the person is not interested. On the other hand, don't end the conversation if you feel the person is sincerely interested. Remember, God softens a person's heart. You simply present the message.

3. Let Your Conversation Be Gracious and Sensible. Don't rely upon sophisticated arguments to prove your point. Let Christ's love shine through you as you speak. Another translation adds that your conversation should also be "seasoned with salt." In other words, give the person a thirst to learn more about Christ.

Jesus communicated his message in a unique way to each individual. We must do the same. The more we share our faith, the easier that will become.

For the next note on "Conversation," turn to p. 1094.

1 Thessalonians

CHAPTER 1

Greetings from Paul

This letter is from Paul, Silas,* and Timothy.

It is written to the church in Thessalonica, you who belong to God the Father and the Lord Jesus Christ.

May his grace and peace be yours.

The Faith of the Thessalonian Believers

2We always thank God for all of you and pray for you constantly. 3As we talk to our God and Father about you, we think of your faithful work, your loving deeds, and your continual anticipation of the return of our Lord Jesus Christ.

4We know that God loves you, dear brothers and sisters,* and that he chose you to be his own people. 5For when we brought you the Good News, it was not only with words but also with power, for the Holy Spirit gave you full assurance that what we said was true. And you know that the way we lived among you was further proof of the truth of our message. 6So you received the message with joy from the Holy Spirit in spite of the severe suffering it brought you. In this way, you imitated both us and the Lord. 7As a result, you yourselves became an example to all the Christians in Greece.* 8And now the word of the Lord is ringing out from you to people everywhere, even beyond Greece, for wherever we go we find people telling us about your faith in God. We don't need to tell them about it, 9for they themselves keep talking about the wonderful welcome you gave us and how you turned away from idols to serve the true and living God. 10And they speak of how you are looking forward to the coming of God's Son from heaven—

Jesus, whom God raised from the dead. He is the one who has rescued us from the terrors of the coming judgment.

CHAPTER 2

Paul Remembers His Visit

You yourselves know, dear brothers and sisters,* that our visit to you was not a failure. 2You know how badly we had been treated at Philippi just before we came to you and how much we suffered there. Yet our God gave us the courage to declare his Good News to you boldly, even though we were surrounded by many who opposed us. 3So you can see that we were not preaching with any deceit or impure purposes or trickery.

4For we speak as messengers who have been approved by God to be entrusted with the Good News. Our purpose is to please God, not people. He is the one who examines the motives of our hearts. 5Never once did we try to win you with flattery, as you very well know. And God is our witness that we were not just pretending to be your friends so you would give us money! 6As for praise, we have never asked for it from you or anyone else. 7As apostles of Christ we certainly had a right to make some demands of you, but we were as gentle among you as a mother* feeding and caring for her own children. 8We loved you so much that we gave you not only God's Good News but our own lives, too.

9Don't you remember, dear brothers and sisters, how hard we worked among you? Night and day we toiled to earn a living so that our expenses would not be a burden to anyone there as we preached God's Good News among

---

1:1 Greek *Silvanus.*   1:4 Greek *brothers.*   1:7 Greek *Macedonia and Achaia,* the northern and southern regions of Greece; also in 1:8.
2:1 Greek *brothers;* also in 2:9, 14, 17.   2:7 Some manuscripts read *we were as infants among you; we were as a mother.*

Our Love Should Grow Read 1 THESSALONIANS 3:12-13

Too many of us think that love is some emotional thing that comes and goes. Yet this passage suggests that our love should not only remain steady but that it should also *grow*. This may seem like an impossible task on our own—and it is. That is why the apostle Paul says, "May the *Lord* make your love grow." You cannot manufacture sincere love. Christ's love must motivate and compel you (see 2 Corinthians 5:14, pp. 1006-1007). This love, in turn, will help to strengthen your heart, keep you from sin, and make you holy so that you can be guiltless when Christ returns.

If your love toward God and others seems stagnant, it is likely you have distanced yourself from the Source of that love. Return to the Lord and ask him to refill and refresh your love for him, then look for ways to share that love with others.

To begin the next topic, turn to p. A17.

CORNER STONES

---

you. ¹⁰You yourselves are our witnesses—and so is God—that we were pure and honest and faultless toward all of you believers. ¹¹And you know that we treated each of you as a father treats his own children. ¹²We pleaded with you, encouraged you, and urged you to live your lives in a way that God would consider worthy. For he called you into his Kingdom to share his glory.

¹³And we will never stop thanking God that when we preached his message to you, you didn't think of the words we spoke as being just our own. You accepted what we said as the very word of God—which, of course, it was. And this word continues to work in you who believe.

¹⁴And then, dear brothers and sisters, you suffered persecution from your own countrymen. In this way, you imitated the believers in God's churches in Judea who, because of their belief in Christ Jesus, suffered from their own people, the Jews.

¹⁵For some of the Jews had killed their own prophets, and some even killed the Lord Jesus. Now they have persecuted us and driven us out. They displease God and oppose everyone ¹⁶by trying to keep us from preaching the Good News

---

OFF AND RUNNING

Encourage Your Children's Spiritual Growth
Read 1 THESSALONIANS 2:11-12

The apostle Paul compared his relationship with the Thessalonians to that of a father with his children. Although this passage doesn't necessarily deal with the father-child relationship, it does show three ways in which fathers play an important role in developing their children's faith:

1. Fathers Encourage Children in Their Faith. One way in which fathers can do this is to live out their faith before their children. Doing this will show children how one's faith affects the way a person lives.

2. Fathers Comfort Children in Their Faith. Be available for your children when they face challenges to their faith.

3. Fathers Urge Children to Grow in Their Faith. Set rules and boundaries that will help establish the moral foundation children need to live a life pleasing to God.

Fathers may not be able to be with their children twenty-four hours a day, but they can help build conviction in their children's lives so that their children will make the right choices. This is one of the most important investments fathers will ever make.

For the next note on "Children," turn to p. 388.

to the Gentiles, for fear some might be saved. By doing this, they continue to pile up their sins. But the anger of God has caught up with them at last.

Timothy's Good Report about the Church

¹⁷Dear brothers and sisters, after we were separated from you for a little while (though our hearts never left you), we tried very hard to come back because of our intense longing to see you again. ¹⁸We wanted very much to come, and I, Paul, tried again and again, but Satan prevented us. ¹⁹After all, what gives us hope and joy, and what is our proud reward and crown? It is you! Yes, you will bring us much joy as we stand together before our Lord Jesus when he comes back again. ²⁰For you are our pride and joy.

CHAPTER **3**

Finally, when we could stand it no longer, we decided that I should stay alone in Athens, ²and we sent Timothy to visit you. He is our co-worker for God and our brother in proclaiming the Good News of Christ. We sent him to strengthen you, to encourage you in your faith, ³and to keep you from becoming disturbed by the troubles you were going through. But, of course, you know that such troubles are going to happen to us Christians. ⁴Even while we were with you, we warned you that troubles would soon come—and they did, as you well know.

⁵That is why, when I could bear it no longer, I sent Timothy to find out whether your faith was still strong. I was afraid that the Tempter had gotten the best of you and that all our work had been useless. ⁶Now Timothy has just returned, bringing the good news that your faith and love are as strong as ever. He reports that you remember our visit with joy and that you want to see us just as much as we want to see you. ⁷So we have been greatly comforted, dear brothers and sisters,* in all of our own crushing troubles and suffering, because you have remained strong in your faith. ⁸It gives us new life, knowing you remain strong in the Lord.

⁹How we thank God for you! Because of you we have great joy in the presence of God. ¹⁰Night and day we pray earnestly for you, asking God to let us see you again to fill up anything that may still be missing in your faith.

¹¹May God himself, our Father, and our Lord Jesus make it possible for us to come to you very soon. ¹²And may the Lord make your love grow and overflow to each other and to everyone else,

3:7 Greek *brothers.*

Act upon What God Has Already Revealed in Scripture
Read 1 THESSALONIANS 4:1-5

We often wonder what God's will may be for us concerning a particular situation. Yet Scripture reveals certain things that are clearly the will of God for every believer—without exception. Here are four things Scripture reveals as God's will:

1. God Wants Us to Live under the Control of the Holy Spirit. God doesn't want us to fill our life with cheap substitutes, like alcohol, possessions, or worldly pursuits. Instead, he wants us to seek to live under the control of the Holy Spirit (see Ephesians 5:18, p. 1029), who produces such attributes as love, joy, peace, patience, kindness, goodness, faithfulness, gentleness, and self-control in our lives. To be controlled by anything or anyone else is outside the will of God.

2. God Wants Us to Live a Pure and Holy Life. It is the clear will of God that we as Christians live sexually pure lives (verses 4-5). The only sexual relationship God will bless is that of a man and woman committed to each other in marriage. Premarital and extramarital sexual relationships are never the will of God for the believer, under any circumstances.

3. God Wants Us to Have an Attitude of Gratitude. No matter what happens, God wants us to be thankful, recognizing that he is in control of all the circumstances that surround our life (see 1 Thessalonians 5:18, p. 1050). He has promised to work all things together for good in the life of the Christian. We can rejoice that he has a purpose in mind for whatever we are going through.

4. God Wants Everyone to Come to Repentance. God makes it clear that he desires to see more people come into a relationship with him (see 2 Peter 3:9, p. 1101). For that reason, you should take advantage of every opportunity you have to pray for or witness to someone who needs Christ.

For the next note on "Seek God's Will," turn to p. 543.

Avoid Adulterous Relationships Read 1 THESSALONIANS 4:1-8

This passage gives some strong reasons as to why we should avoid sexual immorality at all costs. Beyond that, there are at least six more damaging consequences the sin of adultery causes:

1. Adultery Inflicts Incredible Pain on the Adulterer's Spouse. A married adulterer violates the oneness with his or her mate by entering into this bond with another person. This sin is so serious that Jesus said it could be grounds for divorce (see Matthew 19:9, p. 813). While a marriage can survive the pain of adultery with God's help, the level of trust will never be the same.

2. Adultery Does Irreparable Damage to the Adulterer. Though God will forgive the person who commits this sin, others will not forgive this person so quickly. This person's reputation will be tarnished, and Satan will undoubtedly riddle him or her with guilt.

3. Adultery Tremendously Hurts the Adulterer's Children. A person who commits this sin may never fully regain his or her children's trust. Worse yet, the adulterer's children may even follow in his or her footsteps and fall to that same sin later in life, as happened in the life of King David.

4. Believers Who Commit Adultery Give the Church a Bad Reputation. Scripture teaches that when one part of the body of Christ suffers, we all suffer (see 1 Corinthians 12:26, p. 997). All Christians are representatives of the church. And when a Christian's sin is exposed, that person has hurt the reputation of the church—especially if that person is in a position of leadership.

5. Adultery Hurts the Cause of Christ. Such behavior hurts a Christian's witness and damages his or her credibility. As the prophet Nathan told David after his adulterous affair, "You have given the enemies of the LORD great opportunity to despise and blaspheme him" (2 Samuel 12:14).

6. Adultery Is a Sin against the Lord. This should be the primary motive for living a pure life.

Remember Joseph's response to Potiphar's wife when faced with this temptation: "How could I ever do such a wicked thing? It would be a great sin against God" (Genesis 39:9).

As Paul reminds us in this text, God has given us his *Holy* Spirit to live in us. The more his Spirit fills and controls our life, the less likely we will be to give in to the temptation of adultery.

For the next note on "Purity," turn to p. 488.

CORNER STONES

---

just as our love overflows toward you. ¹³As a result, Christ will make your hearts strong, blameless, and holy when you stand before God our Father on that day when our Lord Jesus comes with all those who belong to him.

4:1 Greek *brothers;* also in 4:10, 13.

CHAPTER **4**
Live to Please God
Finally, dear brothers and sisters,* we urge you in the name of the Lord Jesus to live in a way that pleases God, as we have taught you. You are

---

OFF AND RUNNING

Strive to Be Responsible Read 1 THESSALONIANS 4:11-12

As a Christian, you should strive to be the best worker you can be. If you don't, then you disgrace the Lord you serve by doing less than quality work. However, if you work hard and lead a responsible life, you will have many more opportunities to share your faith, because people will respect you.

Consider Joseph of the Old Testament. Although he had been sold into slavery by his own brothers, he worked diligently in every position he held. And his hard work made a difference. The Bible

doing this already, and we encourage you to do so more and more. 2For you remember what we taught you in the name of the Lord Jesus. 3God wants you to be holy, so you should keep clear of all sexual sin. 4Then each of you will control your body* and live in holiness and honor— 5not in lustful passion as the pagans do, in their ignorance of God and his ways.

6Never cheat a Christian brother in this matter by taking his wife, for the Lord avenges all such sins, as we have solemnly warned you before. 7God has called us to be holy, not to live impure lives. 8Anyone who refuses to live by these rules is not disobeying human rules but is rejecting God, who gives his Holy Spirit to you.

9But I don't need to write to you about the Christian love* that should be shown among God's people. For God himself has taught you to love one another. 10Indeed, your love is already strong toward all the Christians* in all of Macedonia. Even so, dear brothers and sisters, we beg you to love them more and more. 11This should be your ambition: to live a quiet life, minding your own business and working with your hands, just as we commanded you before. 12As a result, people who are not Christians will respect the way you live, and you will not need to depend on others to meet your financial needs.

The Hope of the Resurrection

13And now, brothers and sisters, I want you to know what will happen to the Christians who have died so you will not be full of sorrow like people who have no hope. 14For since we believe that Jesus died and was raised to life again, we also believe that when Jesus comes, God will bring back with Jesus all the Christians who have died. 15I can tell you this directly from the Lord: We who are still living when the Lord returns will not rise to meet him ahead of those who are in their graves. 16For the Lord himself will come down from heaven with a commanding shout, with the call of the archangel, and with the trumpet call of God. First, all the Christians who have died will rise from their graves. 17Then, together with them, we who are still alive and remain on the earth will be caught up in the clouds to meet the Lord in the air and remain with him forever. 18So comfort and encourage each other with these words.

CHAPTER 5

I really don't need to write to you about how and when all this will happen, dear brothers and sisters.* 2For you know quite well that the day of the Lord will come unexpectedly, like a thief in the night. 3When people are saying, "All is well; everything is peaceful and secure," then disaster will fall upon them as suddenly as a woman's birth pains begin when her child is about to be born. And there will be no escape.

4But you aren't in the dark about these things, dear brothers and sisters, and you won't be surprised when the day of the Lord comes like a thief. 5For you are all children of the light and of the day; we don't belong to darkness and night. 6So be on your guard, not asleep like the others. Stay alert and be sober. 7Night is the time for sleep and the time when people get drunk. 8But let us who live in the light think clearly, protected by the body armor of faith and love, and wearing as our helmet the confidence of our salvation. 9For God decided to save us through our Lord Jesus Christ, not to pour out his anger on us. 10He died for us so that we can live with him forever, whether we are dead or alive at the time of his return. 11So encourage each other and build each other up, just as you are already doing.

Paul's Final Advice

12Dear brothers and sisters, honor those who are your leaders in the Lord's work. They work hard

4:4 Or *will know how to take a wife for himself;* Greek reads *will know how to possess his own vessel.* 4:9 Greek *brotherly love.* 4:10 Greek *the brothers.* 5:1 Greek *brothers;* also in 5:4, 12, 14, 25, 26, 27.

---

records, "The LORD was with Joseph and blessed him greatly as he served in the home of his Egyptian master. Potiphar noticed this and realized that the LORD was with Joseph, giving him success in everything he did" (Genesis 39:2-3).

You can't expect others to take your message seriously if they don't see that you are serious in what you do. Don't draw attention to yourself by your laziness. Instead, draw attention to the Lord by your diligence. Your faithful, responsible lifestyle will be your greatest sermon.

For the next note on "Job Performance," turn to p. 724.

among you and warn you against all that is wrong. 13Think highly of them and give them your wholehearted love because of their work. And remember to live peaceably with each other.

14Brothers and sisters, we urge you to warn those who are lazy. Encourage those who are timid. Take tender care of those who are weak. Be patient with everyone.

15See that no one pays back evil for evil, but always try to do good to each other and to everyone else.

16Always be joyful. 17Keep on praying. 18No matter what happens, always be thankful, for this is God's will for you who belong to Christ Jesus.

19Do not stifle the Holy Spirit. 20Do not scoff

at prophecies, 21but test everything that is said. Hold on to what is good. 22Keep away from every kind of evil.

Paul's Final Greetings

23Now may the God of peace make you holy in every way, and may your whole spirit and soul and body be kept blameless until that day when our Lord Jesus Christ comes again. 24God, who calls you, is faithful; he will do this.

25Dear brothers and sisters, pray for us.

26Greet all the brothers and sisters in Christian love.*

27I command you in the name of the Lord to read this letter to all the brothers and sisters.

28And may the grace of our Lord Jesus Christ be with all of you.

5:26 Greek *with a holy kiss.*

OFF AND RUNNING ▟▟▟ ▟▟▟

Think of Ways to Encourage, Praise, and Build Up Others Read 1 THESSALONIANS 5:11

Do the words you use truly benefit and leave a positive impression upon those to whom you speak? In this passage Paul stresses the importance of speaking wholesomely. Below are three insights from this passage that will help you make your conversations more meaningful:

1. Do Not Use Bad Language. As Christians, our speech should be positive and uplifting, not vulgar and crude. Such speech draws attention away from Christ and does nothing to encourage others.

2. Listen before You Speak. Don't just pretend to be interested—*really* listen. You won't know what would be helpful to say to an individual unless you understand his or her needs, questions, and hurts. James instructs us to be quick to listen and slow to speak (see James 1:19, p. 1085).

3. Strive to Honor Christ in What You Say. The greatest way we can bless or encourage others with our conversation is to point them to our Savior. This verse has also been translated to say that we should use "words suitable for the occasion, which God can use to help other people." For instance, when someone begins talking about a hurt in his or her life, take that opportunity to somehow bring the hope that Jesus Christ gives you into that discussion.

Unfortunately, with our busy, hectic lives, the quality of our conversations with others often suffers. Our discussions seem to revolve around "surface" issues like the weather, sports events, the latest headline, or our workday. Yet, as Christians, we should go the "extra mile" to make our conversations more meaningful so that those who listen to us will be encouraged and refreshed by what we say. Those who follow Paul's advice will not only develop deeper friendships, but will also be effective witnesses for the Lord.

To begin the next topic, turn to p. A37.

2 Thessalonians

CHAPTER 1

Greetings from Paul

This letter is from Paul, Silas,* and Timothy.

It is written to the church in Thessalonica, you who belong to God our Father and the Lord Jesus Christ.

²May God our Father and the Lord Jesus Christ give you grace and peace.

Encouragement during Persecution

³Dear brothers and sisters,* we always thank God for you, as is right, for we are thankful that your faith is flourishing and you are all growing in love for each other. ⁴We proudly tell God's other churches about your endurance and faithfulness in all the persecutions and hardships you are suffering. ⁵But God will use this persecution to show his justice. For he will make you worthy of his Kingdom, for which you are suffering, ⁶and in his justice he will punish those who persecute you. ⁷And God will provide rest for you who are being persecuted and also for us when the Lord Jesus appears from heaven. He will come with his mighty angels, ⁸in flaming fire, bringing judgment on those who don't know God and on those who refuse to obey the Good News of our Lord Jesus. ⁹They will be punished with everlasting destruction, forever separated from the Lord and from his glorious power ¹⁰when he comes to receive glory and praise from his holy people. And you will be among those praising him on that day, for you believed what we testified about him.

¹¹And so we keep on praying for you, that our God will make you worthy of the life to which he called you. And we pray that God, by his power, will fulfill all your good intentions and faithful deeds. ¹²Then everyone will give honor to the name of our Lord Jesus because of you, and you will be honored along with him. This is all made possible because of the undeserved favor of our God and Lord, Jesus Christ.*

CHAPTER 2

Events prior to the Lord's Second Coming

And now, brothers and sisters,* let us tell you about the coming again of our Lord Jesus Christ and how we will be gathered together to meet him. ²Please don't be so easily shaken and troubled by those who say that the day of the Lord has already begun. Even if they claim to have had a vision, a revelation, or a letter supposedly from us, don't believe them. ³Don't be fooled by what they say.

For that day will not come until there is a great rebellion against God and the man of lawlessness is revealed—the one who brings destruction.* ⁴He will exalt himself and defy every god there is and tear down every object of adoration and worship. He will position himself in the temple of God, claiming that he himself is God. ⁵Don't you remember that I told you this when I was with you? ⁶And you know what is holding him back, for he can be revealed only when his time comes.

⁷For this lawlessness is already at work secretly, and it will remain secret until the one who is holding it back steps out of the way. ⁸Then the man of lawlessness will be revealed, whom the Lord Jesus will consume with the breath of his mouth and destroy by the splendor of his coming. ⁹This evil man will come to do the work of Satan with counterfeit power and signs and miracles. ¹⁰He will use every kind of wicked

1:1 Greek *Silvanus.*   1:3 Greek *brothers.*   1:12 Or *of our God and the Lord Jesus Christ.*   2:1 Greek *brothers;* also in 2:13, 15.   2:3 Greek *the son of destruction.*

What Is the Worst Punishment of Hell? Read 2 THESSALONIANS 1:7-10

As this passage states, the real agony of those who go to hell is that they will be eternally separated from the Lord. To understand how terrible a punishment this is, examine the consequences of being separated from God's presence:

Judgment. When Christ comes back, nonbelievers will face a judgment that believers will not. At this judgment nonbelievers will have their deeds revealed before everyone and then will be sentenced to spend eternity in the lake of fire (see Revelation 20:11-15, p. 1133).

Everlasting Destruction. In hell, nonbelievers will be doomed to exist in unending torment with the Devil and his demons. The torment that they will endure is described by Jesus as an unquenchable, eternal fire (see Matthew 18:8, p. 812, and Matthew 25:41, p. 822). Nonbelievers will spend eternity in agony.

Regret. Jesus used many parables to describe the Kingdom of Heaven—who would get into it, and who would not. Those who don't get into the Kingdom are pictured as "weeping and gnashing [their] teeth" (Matthew 13:42). Their response—weeping and gnashing of teeth—is one of regret when they realize what they will be missing out on for eternity.

Hopelessness. Because their punishment is everlasting, nonbelievers have no hope of their condition ever improving. Their existence is not only one of agony, but of despair.

Those who know Christ have much to gain. Those who do not, have everything to lose.

To begin the next topic, turn to p. A17.

CORNER STONES

---

deception to fool those who are on their way to destruction because they refuse to believe the truth that would save them. ¹¹So God will send great deception upon them, and they will believe all these lies. ¹²Then they will be condemned for not believing the truth and for enjoying the evil they do.

Believers Should Stand Firm

¹³As for us, we always thank God for you, dear brothers and sisters loved by the Lord. We are thankful that God chose you to be among the first* to experience salvation, a salvation that came through the Spirit who makes you holy and by your belief in the truth. ¹⁴He called you to salvation when we told you the Good News; now you can share in the glory of our Lord Jesus Christ.

¹⁵With all these things in mind, dear brothers and sisters, stand firm and keep a strong grip on everything we taught you both in person and by letter.

¹⁶May our Lord Jesus Christ and God our Father, who loved us and in his special favor gave us everlasting comfort and good hope, ¹⁷comfort your hearts and give you strength in every good thing you do and say.

CHAPTER 3
Paul's Request for Prayer

Finally, dear brothers and sisters,* I ask you to pray for us. Pray first that the Lord's message will spread rapidly and be honored wherever it goes, just as when it came to you. ²Pray, too, that we will be saved from wicked and evil people, for not everyone believes in the Lord. ³But the Lord is faithful; he will make you strong and guard you from the evil one.* ⁴And we are confident in the Lord that you are practicing the things we commanded you, and that you always will. ⁵May the Lord bring you into an ever deeper understanding of the love of God and the endurance that comes from Christ.

An Exhortation to Proper Living

⁶And now, dear brothers and sisters, we give you this command with the authority of our Lord Jesus Christ: Stay away from any Christian* who lives in idleness and doesn't follow

2:13 Some manuscripts read *God chose you from the very beginning.* 3:1 Greek *brothers*; also in 3:6, 13. 3:3 Or *from evil.* 3:6 Greek *brother*; also in 3:15.

the tradition of hard work we gave you. [7]For you know that you ought to follow our example. We were never lazy when we were with you. [8]We never accepted food from anyone without paying for it. We worked hard day and night so that we would not be a burden to any of you. [9]It wasn't that we didn't have the right to ask you to feed us, but we wanted to give you an example to follow. [10]Even while we were with you, we gave you this rule: "Whoever does not work should not eat."

[11]Yet we hear that some of you are living idle lives, refusing to work and wasting time meddling in other people's business. [12]In the name of the Lord Jesus Christ, we appeal to such people—no, we command them: Settle down and get to work. Earn your own living. [13]And I say to the rest of you, dear brothers and sisters, never get tired of doing good.

[14]Take note of those who refuse to obey what we say in this letter. Stay away from them so they will be ashamed. [15]Don't think of them as enemies, but speak to them as you would to a Christian who needs to be warned.

Paul's Final Greetings

[16]May the Lord of peace himself always give you his peace no matter what happens. The Lord be with you all.

[17]Now here is my greeting, which I write with my own hand—PAUL. I do this at the end of all my letters to prove that they really are from me.

[18]May the grace of our Lord Jesus Christ be with you all.

1 Timothy

CHAPTER 1

Greetings from Paul

This letter is from Paul, an apostle of Christ Jesus, appointed by the command of God our Savior and by Christ Jesus our hope.

2It is written to Timothy, my true child in the faith.

May God our Father and Christ Jesus our Lord give you grace, mercy, and peace.

Warnings against False Teachings

3When I left for Macedonia, I urged you to stay there in Ephesus and stop those who are teaching wrong doctrine. 4Don't let people waste time in endless speculation over myths and spiritual pedigrees.* For these things only cause arguments; they don't help people live a life of faith in God.* 5The purpose of my instruction is that all the Christians there would be filled with love that comes from a pure heart, a clear conscience, and sincere faith.

6But some teachers have missed this whole point. They have turned away from these things and spend their time arguing and talking foolishness. 7They want to be known as teachers of the law of Moses, but they don't know what they are talking about, even though they seem so confident. 8We know these laws are good when they are used as God intended. 9But they were not made for people who do what is right. They are for people who are disobedient and rebellious, who are ungodly and sinful, who consider nothing sacred and defile what is holy, who murder their father or mother or other people. 10These laws are for people who are sexually immoral, for homosexuals and slave traders, for liars and oath breakers, and for those who do anything else that contradicts the right teaching 11that comes from the glorious Good News entrusted to me by our blessed God.

Paul's Gratitude for God's Mercy

12How thankful I am to Christ Jesus our Lord for considering me trustworthy and appointing me to serve him, 13even though I used to scoff at the name of Christ. I hunted down his people, harming them in every way I could. But God had mercy on me because I did it in ignorance and unbelief. 14Oh, how kind and gracious the Lord was! He filled me completely with faith and the love of Christ Jesus.

15This is a true saying, and everyone should believe it: Christ Jesus came into the world to save sinners—and I was the worst of them all. 16But that is why God had mercy on me, so that Christ Jesus could use me as a prime example of his great patience with even the worst sinners. Then others will realize that they, too, can believe in him and receive eternal life. 17Glory and honor to God forever and ever. He is the eternal King, the unseen one who never dies; he alone is God. Amen.

Timothy's Responsibility

18Timothy, my son, here are my instructions for you, based on the prophetic words spoken about you earlier. May they give you the confidence to fight well in the Lord's battles. 19Cling tightly to your faith in Christ, and always keep your conscience clear. For some people have deliberately violated their consciences; as a result, their faith has been shipwrecked. 20Hymenaeus and Alexander are two examples of this. I turned them over to Satan so they would learn not to blaspheme God.

1:4a Greek in myths and endless genealogies, which cause speculation.   1:4b Greek a stewardship of God in faith.

Recognize Satan's Strategies Read 1 TIMOTHY 4:1-2

We must be on our guard against Satan's clever counterfeits, because, as this passage tells us, he will be at work in the last days (which we are in). In fact, we are warned that some in the church will fall prey to these aberrant ideas and teachings. Therefore, as you listen to various teachers and pastors today, remember this:

- Any so-called gospel that distorts the message of Jesus as found in the Bible by adding to it or taking away from it . . .
- Any so-called gospel that offers Christianity without Christ or the Cross . . .
- Any so-called gospel that promises forgiveness without repentance . . .
- Any so-called gospel that presents the hope of heaven without the reality of hell . . .

. . . is not the gospel, but a "watered-down" version that will give you a false assurance. Such teachings are extremely hazardous to your spiritual health. Stay away from them at all costs.

For the next note on "Discernment," turn to p. 1106.

CORNER STONES

CHAPTER **2**

Instructions about Worship

I urge you, first of all, to pray for all people. As you make your requests, plead for God's mercy upon them, and give thanks. ²Pray this way for kings and all others who are in authority, so that we can live in peace and quietness, in godliness and dignity. ³This is good and pleases God our Savior, ⁴for he wants everyone to be saved and to understand the truth. ⁵For there is only one God and one Mediator who can reconcile God and people. He is the man Christ Jesus. ⁶He gave his life to purchase freedom for everyone. This is the message that God gave to the world at the proper time. ⁷And I have been chosen—this is the absolute truth—as a preacher and apostle to teach the Gentiles about faith and truth.

⁸So wherever you assemble, I want men to pray with holy hands lifted up to God, free from anger and controversy. ⁹And I want women to be modest in their appearance. They should wear decent and appropriate clothing and not draw attention to themselves by the way they fix their hair or by wearing gold or pearls or expensive clothes. ¹⁰For women who claim to be devoted to God should make themselves attractive by the good things they do.

¹¹Women should listen and learn quietly and submissively. ¹²I do not let women teach men or have authority over them. Let them listen quietly. ¹³For God made Adam first, and afterward he made Eve. ¹⁴And it was the woman, not Adam, who was deceived by Satan, and sin was the result. ¹⁵But women will be saved through childbearing* and by continuing to live in faith, love, holiness, and modesty.

CHAPTER **3**

Leaders in the Church

It is a true saying that if someone wants to be an elder,* he desires an honorable responsibility. ²For an elder must be a man whose life cannot be spoken against. He must be faithful to his wife.* He must exhibit self-control, live wisely, and have a good reputation. He must enjoy having guests in his home and must be able to teach. ³He must not be a heavy drinker or be violent. He must be gentle, peace loving, and not one who loves money. ⁴He must manage his own family well, with children who respect and obey him. ⁵For if a man cannot manage his own household, how can he take care of God's church?

⁶An elder must not be a new Christian, because he might be proud of being chosen so soon, and the Devil will use that pride to make him fall.* ⁷Also, people outside the church must speak well of him so that he will not fall into the Devil's trap and be disgraced.

⁸In the same way, deacons must be people who are respected and have integrity. They must

---

2:15 Or *will be saved by accepting their role as mothers,* or *will be saved by the birth of the Child.* 3:1 Greek *overseer;* also in 3:2. 3:2 Greek *be the husband of one wife;* also in 3:12. 3:6 Or *he might fall into the same judgment as the Devil.*

not be heavy drinkers and must not be greedy for money. ⁹They must be committed to the revealed truths of the Christian faith and must live with a clear conscience. ¹⁰Before they are appointed as deacons, they should be given other responsibilities in the church as a test of their character and ability. If they do well, then they may serve as deacons.

¹¹In the same way, their wives* must be respected and must not speak evil of others. They must exercise self-control and be faithful in everything they do.

¹²A deacon must be faithful to his wife, and he must manage his children and household well. ¹³Those who do well as deacons will be rewarded with respect from others and will have increased confidence in their faith in Christ Jesus.

The Truths of Our Faith
¹⁴I am writing these things to you now, even though I hope to be with you soon, ¹⁵so that if I can't come for a while, you will know how people must conduct themselves in the household of God. This is the church of the living God, which is the pillar and support of the truth.

¹⁶Without question, this is the great mystery of our faith:

Christ* appeared in the flesh
    and was shown to be righteous by the
    Spirit.*
He was seen by angels
    and was announced to the nations.
He was believed on in the world
    and was taken up into heaven.*

CHAPTER **4**
Warnings against False Teachers
Now the Holy Spirit tells us clearly that in the last times some will turn away from what we believe; they will follow lying spirits and teachings that come from demons. ²These teachers are hypocrites and liars. They pretend to be religious, but their consciences are dead.*

³They will say it is wrong to be married and wrong to eat certain foods. But God created those foods to be eaten with thanksgiving by people who know and believe the truth. ⁴Since everything God created is good, we should not reject any of it. We may receive it gladly, with

3:11 Or *the women deacons.* The Greek word can be translated *women or wives.*   3:16a Greek *Who;* some manuscripts read *God.*
3:16b Or *in his spirit.*   3:16c Greek *in glory.*   4:2 Greek *are seared.*
4:6 Greek *brothers.*

thankful hearts. ⁵For we know it is made holy by the word of God and prayer.

A Good Servant of Christ Jesus
⁶If you explain this to the brothers and sisters,* you will be doing your duty as a worthy servant of Christ Jesus, one who is fed by the message of faith and the true teaching you have followed. ⁷Do not waste time arguing over godless ideas and old

---

Can You Enjoy Wealth?
Read 1 TIMOTHY 6:17-19

The Lord can and may bless you with riches. They may not necessarily be the material kind. As verse 6 of this chapter says, "true religion with contentment is great wealth." Still, if God does bless you with material riches, he requires three things of you:

1. Do Not Be Arrogant or Put Your Ultimate Hope in Your Wealth. As verse 10 of this chapter says, "For the love of money is at the root of all kinds of evil. And some people, craving money, have wandered from the faith and pierced themselves with many sorrows." Wealth is not sinful. Wealth is not godly. It all depends on the heart of the wealthy person. There are godly people who are wealthy, and there are ungodly people who are poor—as well as vice versa. The question you must always ask yourself is, "Do I possess my possessions, or do my possessions possess me?"

2. Enjoy What God Has Given You. If God blesses you materially, don't feel guilty about it. Be thankful, realizing that he wants you to enjoy what you have.

3. Be Generous, Do Good, and Share Your Wealth with Others. With wealth comes responsibility. Recognize that you are a steward of what God has given you, and invest what you have in his work.

If you follow these three principles, they will help you be content with whatever you have. When you give God total control of this area of your life, you will never be controlled by your wealth—or by the wealth you wish you had.

To begin the next topic, turn to p. A32.

wives' tales. Spend your time and energy in training yourself for spiritual fitness. 8Physical exercise has some value, but spiritual exercise is much more important, for it promises a reward in both this life and the next. 9This is true, and everyone should accept it. 10We work hard and suffer much* in order that people will believe the truth, for our hope is in the living God, who is the Savior of all people, and particularly of those who believe.

11Teach these things and insist that everyone learn them. 12Don't let anyone think less of you because you are young. Be an example to all believers in what you teach, in the way you live, in your love, your faith, and your purity. 13Until I get there, focus on reading the Scriptures to the church, encouraging the believers, and teaching them.

14Do not neglect the spiritual gift you received through the prophecies spoken to you when the elders of the church laid their hands on you. 15Give your complete attention to these matters. Throw yourself into your tasks so that everyone will see your progress. 16Keep a close watch on yourself and on your teaching. Stay true to what is right, and God will save you and those who hear you.

CHAPTER **5**

Never speak harshly to an older man,* but appeal to him respectfully as though he were your own father. Talk to the younger men as you would to your own brothers. 2Treat the older women as you would your mother, and treat the younger women with all purity as your own sisters.

Advice about Widows, Elders, and Slaves

3The church should care for any widow who has no one else to care for her. 4But if she has children or grandchildren, their first responsibility is to show godliness at home and repay their parents by taking care of them. This is something that pleases God very much.

5But a woman who is a true widow, one who is truly alone in this world, has placed her hope in God. Night and day she asks God for help and spends much time in prayer. 6But the widow who lives only for pleasure is spiritually dead. 7Give these instructions to the church so that the widows you support* will not be criticized.

8But those who won't care for their own relatives, especially those living in the same household, have denied what we believe. Such people are worse than unbelievers.

9A widow who is put on the list for support must be a woman who is at least sixty years old and was faithful to her husband.* 10She must be well respected by everyone because of the good she has done. Has she brought up her children well? Has she been kind to strangers? Has she served other Christians humbly?* Has she helped those who are in trouble? Has she always been ready to do good?

11The younger widows should not be on the list, because their physical desires will overpower their devotion to Christ and they will want to remarry. 12Then they would be guilty of breaking their previous pledge. 13Besides, they are likely to become lazy and spend their time gossiping from house to house, getting into other people's business and saying things they shouldn't. 14So I advise these younger widows to marry again, have children, and take care of their own homes. Then the enemy will not be able to say anything against them. 15For I am afraid that some of them have already gone astray and now follow Satan.

16If a Christian woman has relatives who are widows, she must take care of them and not put the responsibility on the church. Then the church can care for widows who are truly alone.

17Elders who do their work well should be paid well,* especially those who work hard at both preaching and teaching. 18For the Scripture says, "Do not keep an ox from eating as it treads out the grain." And in another place, "Those who work deserve their pay!"*

19Do not listen to complaints against an elder unless there are two or three witnesses to accuse him. 20Anyone who sins should be rebuked in front of the whole church so that others will have a proper fear of God.

21I solemnly command you in the presence of God and Christ Jesus and the holy angels to obey these instructions without taking sides or showing special favor to anyone. 22Never be in a hurry about appointing an elder. Do not participate in the sins of others. Keep yourself pure.

23Don't drink only water. You ought to drink a little wine for the sake of your stomach because you are sick so often.

24Remember that some people lead sinful lives, and everyone knows they will be judged. But there are others whose sin will not be re-

---

4:10 Some manuscripts read *and strive.*   5:1 Or *an elder.*   5:7 Or *so the church*; Greek reads *so they.*   5:9 Greek *was the wife of one man.*
5:10 Greek *Has she washed the feet of saints?*   5:17 Greek *should be worthy of double honor.*   5:18 Deut 25:4; Luke 10:7.

vealed until later. 25In the same way, everyone knows how much good some people do, but there are others whose good deeds won't be known until later.

CHAPTER 6

Christians who are slaves should give their masters full respect so that the name of God and his teaching will not be shamed. 2If your master is a Christian, that is no excuse for being disrespectful. You should work all the harder because you are helping another believer* by your efforts.

False Teaching and True Riches

Teach these truths, Timothy, and encourage everyone to obey them. 3Some false teachers may deny these things, but these are the sound, wholesome teachings of the Lord Jesus Christ, and they are the foundation for a godly life. 4Anyone who teaches anything different is both conceited and ignorant. Such a person has an unhealthy desire to quibble over the meaning of words. This stirs up arguments ending in jealousy, fighting, slander, and evil suspicions. 5These people always cause trouble. Their minds are corrupt, and they don't tell the truth. To them religion is just a way to get rich.

6Yet true religion with contentment is great wealth. 7After all, we didn't bring anything with us when we came into the world, and we certainly cannot carry anything with us when we die. 8So if we have enough food and clothing, let us be content. 9But people who long to be rich fall into temptation and are trapped by many foolish and harmful desires that plunge them into ruin and destruction. 10For the love of money is at the root of all kinds of evil. And some people, craving money, have wandered from the faith and pierced themselves with many sorrows.

6:2 Greek *a brother.*

Paul's Final Instructions

11But you, Timothy, belong to God; so run from all these evil things, and follow what is right and good. Pursue a godly life, along with faith, love, perseverance, and gentleness. 12Fight the good fight for what we believe. Hold tightly to the eternal life that God has given you, which you have confessed so well before many witnesses. 13And I command you before God, who gives life to all, and before Christ Jesus, who gave a good testimony before Pontius Pilate, 14that you obey his commands with all purity. Then no one can find fault with you from now until our Lord Jesus Christ returns. 15For at the right time Christ will be revealed from heaven by the blessed and only almighty God, the King of kings and Lord of lords. 16He alone can never die, and he lives in light so brilliant that no human can approach him. No one has ever seen him, nor ever will. To him be honor and power forever. Amen.

17Tell those who are rich in this world not to be proud and not to trust in their money, which will soon be gone. But their trust should be in the living God, who richly gives us all we need for our enjoyment. 18Tell them to use their money to do good. They should be rich in good works and should give generously to those in need, always being ready to share with others whatever God has given them. 19By doing this they will be storing up their treasure as a good foundation for the future so that they may take hold of real life.

20Timothy, guard what God has entrusted to you. Avoid godless, foolish discussions with those who oppose you with their so-called knowledge. 21Some people have wandered from the faith by following such foolishness.

May God's grace be with you all.

2 Timothy

CHAPTER 1

Greetings from Paul

This letter is from Paul, an apostle of Christ Jesus by God's will, sent out to tell others about the life he has promised through faith in Christ Jesus.

2It is written to Timothy, my dear son.

May God our Father and Christ Jesus our Lord give you grace, mercy, and peace.

Encouragement to Be Faithful

3Timothy, I thank God for you. He is the God I serve with a clear conscience, just as my ancestors did. Night and day I constantly remember you in my prayers. 4I long to see you again, for I remember your tears as we parted. And I will be filled with joy when we are together again.

5I know that you sincerely trust the Lord, for you have the faith of your mother, Eunice, and your grandmother, Lois. 6This is why I remind you to fan into flames the spiritual gift God gave you when I laid my hands on you. 7For God has not given us a spirit of fear and timidity, but of power, love, and self-discipline. 8So you must never be ashamed to tell others about our Lord. And don't be ashamed of me, either, even though I'm in prison for Christ. With the strength God gives you, be ready to suffer with me for the proclamation of the Good News.

9It is God who saved us and chose us to live a holy life. He did this not because we deserved it, but because that was his plan long before the world began—to show his love and kindness to us through Christ Jesus. 10And now he has made all of this plain to us by the coming of Christ Jesus, our Savior, who broke the power of death and showed us the way to everlasting life

1:12 Or *what has been entrusted to me.*

through the Good News. 11And God chose me to be a preacher, an apostle, and a teacher of this Good News.

12And that is why I am suffering here in prison. But I am not ashamed of it, for I know the one in whom I trust, and I am sure that he is able to guard what I have entrusted to him* until the day of his return. 13Hold on to the pattern of right teaching you learned from me. And remember to live in the faith and love that you have in Christ Jesus. 14With the help of the Holy Spirit who lives within us, carefully guard what has been entrusted to you.

15As you know, all the Christians who came here from the province of Asia have deserted me; even Phygelus and Hermogenes are gone. 16May the Lord show special kindness to Onesiphorus and all his family because he often visited and encouraged me. He was never ashamed of me because I was in prison. 17When he came to Rome, he searched everywhere until he found me. 18May the Lord show him special kindness on the day of Christ's return. And you know how much he helped me at Ephesus.

CHAPTER 2

A Good Soldier of Christ Jesus

Timothy, my dear son, be strong with the special favor God gives you in Christ Jesus. 2You have heard me teach many things that have been confirmed by many reliable witnesses. Teach these great truths to trustworthy people who are able to pass them on to others.

3Endure suffering along with me, as a good soldier of Christ Jesus. 4And as Christ's soldier, do not let yourself become tied up in the affairs of this life, for then you cannot satisfy the one

Guard the Content of Your Thoughts Read 2 TIMOTHY 2:22

In Paul's second letter to Timothy, he gave Timothy helpful advice on how to live a pure life. This advice included (1) recognizing his potential to sin; (2) avoiding influences that could inspire youthful lust; (3) pursuing faith, love, and peace; and (4) spending time with other believers whose hearts are pure.

One of the more difficult challenges of living a pure life is guarding the content of our thoughts. It has been said, "You can't stop a bird from flying over your head, but you can stop it from building a nest in your hair." In the same way, we cannot stop an impure or wicked thought from "knocking" on the door of our imagination, but we certainly can keep that door closed and locked. If we don't, and we allow tempting thoughts to infiltrate our mind, we may fall, allowing our old nature to prevail.

The good news is that even though each one of us is still capable of falling, we don't have to. If we stay close to the Lord and follow Paul's advice in this verse, we will be building a strong "fortress" around our life—including our thoughts—and it will be harder for Satan's arrows of temptation to get through.

For the next note on "Purity," turn to p. 794.

CORNERSTONES

---

who has enlisted you in his army. 5Follow the Lord's rules for doing his work, just as an athlete either follows the rules or is disqualified and wins no prize. 6Hardworking farmers are the first to enjoy the fruit of their labor. 7Think about what I am saying. The Lord will give you understanding in all these things.

8Never forget that Jesus Christ was a man born into King David's family and that he was raised from the dead. This is the Good News I preach. 9And because I preach this Good News, I am suffering and have been chained like a criminal. But the word of God cannot be chained. 10I am willing to endure anything if it will bring salvation and eternal glory in Christ Jesus to those God has chosen.

11This is a true saying:

If we die with him,
  we will also live with him.
12 If we endure hardship,
  we will reign with him.
If we deny him,
  he will deny us.
13 If we are unfaithful,
  he remains faithful,
  for he cannot deny himself.

An Approved Worker

14Remind everyone of these things, and command them in God's name to stop fighting over

words. Such arguments are useless, and they can ruin those who hear them. 15Work hard so God can approve you. Be a good worker, one who does not need to be ashamed and who correctly explains the word of truth. 16Avoid godless, foolish discussions that lead to more and more ungodliness. 17This kind of talk spreads like cancer. Hymenaeus and Philetus are examples of this. 18They have left the path of truth, preaching the lie that the resurrection of the dead has already occurred; and they have undermined the faith of some.

19But God's truth stands firm like a foundation stone with this inscription: "The Lord knows those who are his,"* and "Those who claim they belong to the Lord must turn away from all wickedness."*

20In a wealthy home some utensils are made of gold and silver, and some are made of wood and clay. The expensive utensils are used for special occasions, and the cheap ones are for everyday use. 21If you keep yourself pure, you will be a utensil God can use for his purpose. Your life will be clean, and you will be ready for the Master to use you for every good work.

22Run from anything that stimulates youthful lust. Follow anything that makes you want to do right. Pursue faith and love and peace, and enjoy the companionship of those who call on the Lord with pure hearts.

23Again I say, don't get involved in foolish,

2:19a Num 16:5. 2:19b See Isa 52:11.

ignorant arguments that only start fights. ²⁴The Lord's servants must not quarrel but must be kind to everyone. They must be able to teach effectively and be patient with difficult people. ²⁵They should gently teach those who oppose the truth. Perhaps God will change those people's hearts, and they will believe the truth. ²⁶Then they will come to their senses and escape from the Devil's trap. For they have been held captive by him to do whatever he wants.

CHAPTER 3

The Dangers of the Last Days

You should also know this, Timothy, that in the last days there will be very difficult times. ²For people will love only themselves and their money. They will be boastful and proud, scoffing at God, disobedient to their parents, and ungrateful. They will consider nothing sacred. ³They will be unloving and unforgiving; they will slander others and have no self-control; they will be cruel and have no interest in what is good. ⁴They will betray their friends, be reckless, be puffed up with pride, and love pleasure rather than God. ⁵They will act as if they are religious, but they will reject the power that could make them godly. You must stay away from people like that.

⁶They are the kind who work their way into people's homes and win the confidence of* vulnerable women who are burdened with the guilt of sin and controlled by many desires. ⁷Such women are forever following new teachings, but they never understand the truth. ⁸And these teachers fight the truth just as Jannes and Jambres fought against Moses. Their minds are depraved, and their faith is counterfeit. ⁹But they won't get away with this for long. Someday everyone will recognize what fools they are, just as happened with Jannes and Jambres.

Paul's Charge to Timothy

¹⁰But you know what I teach, Timothy, and how I live, and what my purpose in life is. You know my faith and how long I have suffered. You know my love and my patient endurance. ¹¹You know how much persecution and suffering I have endured. You know all about how I was persecuted in Antioch, Iconium, and Lystra—but the Lord delivered me from all of it. ¹²Yes, and everyone who wants to live a godly life in Christ Jesus will suffer persecution. ¹³But evil people and impostors will flour-

3:6 Greek *and take captive.*

ish. They will go on deceiving others, and they themselves will be deceived.

¹⁴But you must remain faithful to the things you have been taught. You know they are true, for you know you can trust those who taught you. ¹⁵You have been taught the holy Scriptures from childhood, and they have given you the wisdom to receive the salvation that comes by trusting in Christ Jesus. ¹⁶All Scripture is inspired by God and is useful to teach us what is true and to make us realize what is wrong in our lives. It straightens us out and teaches us to do

---

Studying the Bible Is Necessary for Our Spiritual Growth Read 2 TIMOTHY 3:16-17

The primary reason we should study the Bible is because it was inspired by the Creator of the universe to guide us through this adventure called life. This passage of Scripture gives us three more reasons why we should make the Bible part of our day-to-day life:

1. The Bible Teaches Us What Is True. The Bible is the only book we need to discover the foundational truths of how to know and walk with God. Some aberrant religious groups or cults insist we need another book to help us interpret what the Bible says. But the Bible needs no outside interpretation. It speaks for itself. In fact, the best commentary on the Bible is the Bible.

2. The Bible Shows Us What Is Wrong in Our Lives. God's Word serves to reprove us or to make us aware when we are headed in the wrong direction.

3. The Bible Helps Us Do What Is Right. If we read and meditate on God's Word, we will be molded into the man or woman God wants us to be.

When we allow the Bible to teach us in these three areas, we are told that we will be prepared and equipped to do good to everyone (see 2 Timothy 3:14-16). Our foundation will be solid, our motives pure, and our character more refined. What better reasons are there to make a commitment to stick with Bible study!

For the next note on "Study the Bible," turn to p. 525.

what is right. [17]It is God's way of preparing us in every way, fully equipped for every good thing God wants us to do.

CHAPTER 4

And so I solemnly urge you before God and before Christ Jesus—who will someday judge the living and the dead when he appears to set up his Kingdom: [2]Preach the word of God. Be persistent, whether the time is favorable or not. Patiently correct, rebuke, and encourage your people with good teaching.

[3]For a time is coming when people will no longer listen to right teaching. They will follow their own desires and will look for teachers who will tell them whatever they want to hear. [4]They will reject the truth and follow strange myths.

[5]But you should keep a clear mind in every situation. Don't be afraid of suffering for the Lord. Work at bringing others to Christ. Complete the ministry God has given you.

Paul's Final Words

[6]As for me, my life has already been poured out as an offering to God. The time of my death is near. [7]I have fought a good fight, I have finished the race, and I have remained faithful. [8]And now the prize awaits me—the crown of righteousness that the Lord, the righteous Judge, will give me on that great day of his return. And the prize is not just for me but for all who eagerly look forward to his glorious return.

[9]Please come as soon as you can. [10]Demas has deserted me because he loves the things of this life and has gone to Thessalonica. Crescens has gone to Galatia, and Titus has gone to Dalmatia. [11]Only Luke is with me. Bring Mark with you when you come, for he will be helpful to me. [12]I sent Tychicus to Ephesus. [13]When you come, be sure to bring the coat I left with Carpus at Troas. Also bring my books, and especially my papers.*

[14]Alexander the coppersmith has done me much harm, but the Lord will judge him for what he has done. [15]Be careful of him, for he fought against everything we said.

[16]The first time I was brought before the judge, no one was with me. Everyone had abandoned me. I hope it will not be counted against them. [17]But the Lord stood with me and gave me strength, that I might preach the Good News in all its fullness for all the Gentiles to hear. And he saved me from certain death.* [18]Yes, and the Lord will deliver me from every evil attack and will bring me safely to his heavenly Kingdom. To God be the glory forever and ever. Amen.

Paul's Final Greetings

[19]Give my greetings to Priscilla and Aquila and those living at the household of Onesiphorus. [20]Erastus stayed at Corinth, and I left Trophimus sick at Miletus.

[21]Hurry so you can get here before winter. Eubulus sends you greetings, and so do Pudens, Linus, Claudia, and all the brothers and sisters.*

[22]May the Lord be with your spirit. Grace be with you all.

4:13 Greek *especially the parchments.*   4:17 Greek *from the mouth of a lion.*   4:21 Greek *brothers.*

Titus

Greetings from Paul

This letter is from Paul, a slave of God and an apostle of Jesus Christ. I have been sent to bring faith to those God has chosen and to teach them to know the truth that shows them how to live godly lives. 2This truth gives them the confidence of eternal life, which God promised them before the world began—and he cannot lie. 3And now at the right time he has revealed this Good News, and we announce it to everyone. It is by the command of God our Savior that I have been trusted to do this work for him.

4This letter is written to Titus, my true child in the faith that we share.

May God the Father and Christ Jesus our Savior give you grace and peace.

Titus's Work in Crete

5I left you on the island of Crete so you could complete our work there and appoint elders in each town as I instructed you. 6An elder must be well thought of for his good life. He must be faithful to his wife,* and his children must be believers who are not wild or rebellious. 7An elder* must live a blameless life because he is God's minister. He must not be arrogant or quick-tempered; he must not be a heavy drinker, violent, or greedy for money. 8He must enjoy having guests in his home and must love all that is good. He must live wisely and be fair. He must live a devout and disciplined life. 9He must have a strong and steadfast belief in the trustworthy message he was taught; then he will be able to encourage others with right teaching and show those who oppose it where they are wrong.

10For there are many who rebel against right teaching; they engage in useless talk and deceive people. This is especially true of those who insist on circumcision for salvation. 11They must be silenced. By their wrong teaching, they have already turned whole families away from the truth. Such teachers only want your money. 12One of their own men, a prophet from Crete, has said about them, "The people of Crete are all liars; they are cruel animals and lazy gluttons." 13This is true. So rebuke them as sternly as necessary to make them strong in the faith. 14They must stop listening to Jewish myths and the commands of people who have turned their backs on the truth.

15Everything is pure to those whose hearts are pure. But nothing is pure to those who are corrupt and unbelieving, because their minds and consciences are defiled. 16Such people claim they know God, but they deny him by the way they live. They are despicable and disobedient, worthless for doing anything good.

Promote Right Teaching

But as for you, promote the kind of living that reflects right teaching. 2Teach the older men to exercise self-control, to be worthy of respect, and to live wisely. They must have strong faith and be filled with love and patience.

3Similarly, teach the older women to live in a way that is appropriate for someone serving the Lord. They must not go around speaking evil of others and must not be heavy drinkers. Instead, they should teach others what is good. 4These older women must train the younger women to love their husbands and their children, 5to live wisely and be pure, to take care of their homes, to do good, and to be submissive to their husbands. Then they will not bring shame on the word of God.

1:6 Or *have only one wife,* or *be married only once;* Greek reads *be the husband of one wife.*   1:7 Greek *overseer.*

We Need to Set an Example for Others Read TITUS 2:6-8

This passage gives some practical reasons and ways to live out your faith. Though these words were written to Titus, a leader in the early church, they apply to anyone whose life influences the lives of others. That is, the passage speaks to all of us! Take a moment to ponder these simple, yet useful, thoughts:

How Should We Behave?

- We need to be self-controlled and serious about life.
- We should do good deeds often as an example to others.
- We should love the truth.
- We should be earnest and serious in our pursuit of truth.
- We should think before we speak, making sure that our conversation is sound and sensible.

Why Should We Live Godly Lives?

- We represent God, who is holy.
- We are an example to others, particularly young people and new believers.
- Our behavior will silence our critics.

To begin the next topic, turn to p. A20.

CORNER STONES

---

⁶In the same way, encourage the young men to live wisely in all they do. ⁷And you yourself must be an example to them by doing good deeds of every kind. Let everything you do reflect the integrity and seriousness of your teaching. ⁸Let your teaching be so correct that it can't be criticized. Then those who want to argue will be ashamed because they won't have anything bad to say about us.

⁹Slaves must obey their masters and do their best to please them. They must not talk back ¹⁰or steal, but they must show themselves to be entirely trustworthy and good. Then they will make the teaching about God our Savior attractive in every way.

¹¹For the grace of God has been revealed, bringing salvation to all people. ¹²And we are instructed to turn from godless living and sinful pleasures. We should live in this evil world with self-control, right conduct, and devotion to

---

OFF AND RUNNING

Create a Spiritual Hunger in Those around You
Read TITUS 2:9-10

While we are not slaves, this verse could easily apply to workers and employees today—or to anyone who is asked to do something for someone else. Jesus gave a unique example of how this works when he told his disciples, "If a soldier demands that you carry his gear for a mile, carry it two miles" (Matthew 5:41). At that time, Roman law gave soldiers the right to retain private citizens to carry their pack for a mile. Yet Jesus told his disciples to go above and beyond that request. In so doing, they would have a "captive audience" for presenting the gospel.

Today, when everyone seems to be demanding his or her rights, this verse is a direct contradiction to the current wave of thinking. But it all comes back to our frame of reference as Christians: Our goal on earth is not to win our own rights, but to win people to our Lord.

Your work may be difficult. You may even think it is mundane and insignificant. But it is not. God has placed you in your place of employment for a reason—to let your light shine. Your dedicated work may be just the thing that wins your employer or supervisor to Christ. So look for opportunities to "go the extra mile."

For the next note on "Job Performance," turn to p. 1048.

God, 13while we look forward to that wonderful event when the glory of our great God and Savior, Jesus Christ, will be revealed. 14He gave his life to free us from every kind of sin, to cleanse us, and to make us his very own people, totally committed to doing what is right. 15You must teach these things and encourage your people to do them, correcting them when necessary. You have the authority to do this, so don't let anyone ignore you or disregard what you say.

CHAPTER **3**
Do What Is Good
Remind your people to submit to the government and its officers. They should be obedient, always ready to do what is good. 2They must not speak evil of anyone, and they must avoid quarreling. Instead, they should be gentle and show true humility to everyone.

3Once we, too, were foolish and disobedient. We were misled by others and became slaves to many wicked desires and evil pleasures. Our lives were full of evil and envy. We hated others, and they hated us.

4But then God our Savior showed us his kindness and love. 5He saved us, not because of the good things we did, but because of his mercy. He washed away our sins and gave us a new life through the Holy Spirit.* 6He generously poured out the Spirit upon us because of what Jesus Christ our Savior did. 7He declared us not guilty because of his great kindness. And now we know that we will inherit eternal life. 8These things I have told you are all true. I want you to insist on them so that everyone who trusts in God will be careful to do good deeds all the time. These things are good and beneficial for everyone.

Paul's Final Remarks and Greetings
9Do not get involved in foolish discussions about spiritual pedigrees* or in quarrels and fights about obedience to Jewish laws. These kinds of things are useless and a waste of time. 10If anyone is causing divisions among you, give a first and second warning. After that, have nothing more to do with that person. 11For people like that have turned away from the truth. They are sinning, and they condemn themselves.

12I am planning to send either Artemas or Tychicus to you. As soon as one of them arrives, do your best to meet me at Nicopolis as quickly as you can, for I have decided to stay there for the winter. 13Do everything you can to help Zenas the lawyer and Apollos with their trip. See that they are given everything they need. 14For our people should not have unproductive lives. They must learn to do good by helping others who have urgent needs.

15Everybody here sends greetings. Please give my greetings to all of the believers who love us.

May God's grace be with you all.

3:5 Greek *He saved us through the washing of regeneration and renewing of the Holy Spirit.*   3:9 Greek *discussions and genealogies.*

Philemon

Greetings from Paul

This letter is from Paul, in prison for preaching the Good News about Christ Jesus, and from our brother Timothy.

It is written to Philemon, our much loved co-worker, 2and to our sister Apphia and to Archippus, a fellow soldier of the cross. I am also writing to the church that meets in your house. 3May God our Father and the Lord Jesus Christ give you grace and peace.

Paul's Thanksgiving and Prayer

4I always thank God when I pray for you, Philemon, 5because I keep hearing of your trust in the Lord Jesus and your love for all of God's people. 6You are generous because of your faith. And I am praying that you will really put your generosity to work, for in so doing you will come to an understanding of all the good things we can do for Christ. 7I myself have gained much joy and comfort from your love, my brother, because your kindness has so often refreshed the hearts of God's people.

Paul's Appeal for Onesimus

8That is why I am boldly asking a favor of you. I could demand it in the name of Christ because it is the right thing for you to do, 9but because of our love, I prefer just to ask you. So take this as a request from your friend Paul, an old man, now in prison for the sake of Christ Jesus. 10My plea is that you show kindness to Onesimus. I think of him as my own son because he became a believer as a result of my ministry here in prison. 11Onesimus* hasn't been of much use to you in the past, but now he is very useful to both of us. 12I am sending him back to you, and with him comes my own heart.

13I really wanted to keep him here with me while I am in these chains for preaching the Good News, and he would have helped me on your behalf. 14But I didn't want to do anything without your consent. And I didn't want you to help because you were forced to do it but because you wanted to. 15Perhaps you could think of it this way: Onesimus ran away for a little while so you could have him back forever. 16He is no longer just a slave; he is a beloved brother, especially to me. Now he will mean much more to you, both as a slave and as a brother in the Lord.

17So if you consider me your partner, give him the same welcome you would give me if I were coming. 18If he has harmed you in any way or stolen anything from you, charge me for it. 19I, Paul, write this in my own handwriting: "I will repay it." And I won't mention that you owe me your very soul!

20Yes, dear brother, please do me this favor for the Lord's sake. Give me this encouragement in Christ. 21I am confident as I write this letter that you will do what I ask and even more!

22Please keep a guest room ready for me, for I am hoping that God will answer your prayers and let me return to you soon.

Paul's Final Greetings

23Epaphras, my fellow prisoner in Christ Jesus, sends you his greetings. 24So do Mark, Aristarchus, Demas, and Luke, my co-workers.

25The grace of the Lord Jesus Christ be with your spirit.

11 *Onesimus* means "useful."

Hebrews

Jesus Christ Is God's Son

Long ago God spoke many times and in many ways to our ancestors through the prophets. 2But now in these final days, he has spoken to us through his Son. God promised everything to the Son as an inheritance, and through the Son he made the universe and everything in it. 3The Son reflects God's own glory, and everything about him represents God exactly. He sustains the universe by the mighty power of his command. After he died to cleanse us from the stain of sin, he sat down in the place of honor at the right hand of the majestic God of heaven.

Christ Is Greater Than the Angels

4This shows that God's Son is far greater than the angels, just as the name God gave him is far greater than their names. 5For God never said to any angel what he said to Jesus:

"You are my Son.
 Today I have become your Father.*"

And again God said,

"I will be his Father,
 and he will be my Son."*

6And then, when he presented his honored* Son to the world, God said, "Let all the angels of God worship him."* 7God calls his angels

"messengers swift as the wind,
 and servants made of flaming fire."*

8But to his Son he says,

"Your throne, O God, endures forever and
 ever.

Your royal power is expressed in
 righteousness.
9 You love what is right and hate what is
 wrong.
 Therefore God, your God, has anointed
 you,
 pouring out the oil of joy on you more
 than on anyone else."*

10And,

"Lord, in the beginning you laid the
 foundation of the earth,
 and the heavens are the work of your
 hands.
11 Even they will perish, but you remain
 forever.
 They will wear out like old clothing.
12 You will roll them up like an old coat.
 They will fade away like old clothing.
 But you are always the same;
 you will never grow old."*

13And God never said to an angel, as he did to his Son,

"Sit in honor at my right hand
 until I humble your enemies,
 making them a footstool under your
 feet."*

14But angels are only servants. They are spirits sent from God to care for those who will receive salvation.

A Warning against Drifting Away

So we must listen very carefully to the truth we have heard, or we may drift away from it. 2The

1:5a Or *Today I reveal you as my Son.* Ps 2:7. 1:5b 2 Sam 7:14. 1:6a Greek *firstborn.* 1:6b Deut 32:43. 1:7 Ps 104:4. 1:8-9 Ps 45:6-7.
1:10-12 Ps 102:25-27. 1:13 Ps 110:1.

Why Did God Create Angels? Read HEBREWS 1:4-14

Throughout the ages, people have been fascinated with and awed by angels. Some have even tried to worship them. But it is important to understand that angels are distinctly different from God's Son, Jesus Christ. One significant area of distinction is creation. Angels are created beings, while Jesus is not. Because angels are created, it is wrong to worship them.

If they are not to be worshiped, then what did God create angels for? God created angels for several reasons, three of which are the following:

1. Angels Worship God. As verse 6 attests, one of the reasons God created angels was to worship him. Some people may think this is egotistical, but consider how many people worship professional athletes and other celebrities. These people by comparison have done nothing to earn or be worthy of the worship they receive. God, on the other hand, has created angels and humans and given them life. In addition, God is majestic beyond our understanding, so worshiping him is simply the natural response of being in his presence. For it is an incredible privilege to be in the presence of God. Only God is worthy of worship, and his creation, which includes angels, should worship him.

2. Angels Serve as God's Messengers. God uses angels to deliver messages to his followers on earth (verse 7). The Bible records a few instances of this. In Daniel 10 God sent an angel to give Daniel an answer to his prayer. An angel was also sent to Jesus' tomb to tell his followers that he had risen from the dead (Matthew 28).

3. Angels Minister to God's Followers. God also created angels to minister to his followers (verse 14). In Genesis 19, two angels rescued Lot and his family from God's wrath on Sodom and Gomorrah. In Acts 12, an angel freed Peter from prison before he was to be tried in public for being a follower of Christ.

While angels play a significant role in the lives of believers, we must be careful that we do not give them the honor and praise that should be reserved for Jesus Christ alone.

For the next note on "What Are Angels?" turn to p. 510.

CORNER STONES

---

message God delivered through angels has always proved true, and the people were punished for every violation of the law and every act of disobedience. ³What makes us think that we can escape if we are indifferent to this great salvation that was announced by the Lord Jesus himself? It was passed on* to us by those who heard him speak, ⁴and God verified the message by signs and wonders and various miracles and by giving gifts of the Holy Spirit whenever he chose to do so.

Jesus, the Man

⁵And furthermore, the future world we are talking about will not be controlled by angels. ⁶For somewhere in the Scriptures it says,

"What is man that you should think of him,
    and the son of man* that you should
        care for him?

⁷ For a little while you made him lower than
        the angels,
    and you crowned him with glory and
        honor.*
⁸ You gave him authority over all things."*

Now when it says "all things," it means nothing is left out. But we have not yet seen all of this happen. ⁹What we do see is Jesus, who "for a little while was made lower than the angels" and now is "crowned with glory and honor" because he suffered death for us. Yes, by God's grace, Jesus tasted death for everyone in all the world. ¹⁰And it was only right that God—who made everything and for whom everything was made—should bring his many children into glory. Through the suffering of Jesus, God made him a perfect leader, one fit to bring them into their salvation.

2:3 Or *and confirmed.* **2:6** Or *Son of Man.* **2:7** Some manuscripts add *You put him in charge of everything you made.* **2:6-8** Ps 8:4-6.

Why Would a Good God Send Anyone to Hell? Read HEBREWS 2:2-3

I f God loves people, why doesn't he just save everyone? Perhaps you have asked this question or know someone who has. While the question is good, it places the blame for people's damnation on the wrong person: God.

God does not want anyone to spend eternity in hell. In fact, he earnestly desires that everyone spend all eternity with him in heaven. Scripture tells us, "[God] does not want anyone to perish, so he is giving more time for everyone to repent" (2 Peter 3:9). Throughout the Bible we see God's loving and patient invitation for us to come to him:

- "Come to me, all of you who are weary and carry heavy burdens, and I will give you rest." (Matthew 11:28)
- "'Come.' Let the thirsty ones come—anyone who wants to. Let them come and drink the water of life without charge." (Revelation 22:17)

The truth is that there are some things only God can do—such as cleanse us of our sin, forgive us, and justify us. At the same time, there are some things only we can do—such as come to him, believe in him, and repent of our sins. While God does indeed love everyone (see John 3:16, p. 895; and Romans 5:8, p. 966), he has given us a wonderful but dangerous gift. That gift is called "free will." It is the ability to choose between right and wrong, good and evil, God and Satan, and heaven and hell. God will not force his salvation and forgiveness upon our lives. It is our choice to say yes or no.

Anyone who ends up in hell is there because of his or her willful and deliberate decision to reject God's offer of forgiveness. As the famous British author C. S. Lewis put it, "The gates of hell are locked from the inside."

For the next "Big Question" note, turn to p. 1107.

11So now Jesus and the ones he makes holy have the same Father. That is why Jesus is not ashamed to call them his brothers and sisters.* 12For he said to God,

"I will declare the wonder of your name to my brothers and sisters.*
I will praise you among all your people."

13He also said, "I will put my trust in him." And in the same context he said, "Here I am—together with the children God has given me."*

14Because God's children are human beings—made of flesh and blood—Jesus also became flesh and blood by being born in human form. For only as a human being could he die, and only by dying could he break the power of the Devil, who had the power of death. 15Only in this way could he deliver those who have lived all their lives as slaves to the fear of dying.

16We all know that Jesus came to help the descendants of Abraham, not to help the angels. 17Therefore, it was necessary for Jesus to be in every respect like us, his brothers and sisters, so that he could be our merciful and faithful High

Priest before God. He then could offer a sacrifice that would take away the sins of the people. 18Since he himself has gone through suffering and temptation, he is able to help us when we are being tempted.

CHAPTER 3
Jesus Is Greater Than Moses

And so, dear brothers and sisters who belong to God* and are bound for heaven, think about this Jesus whom we declare to be God's Messenger and High Priest. 2For he was faithful to God, who appointed him, just as Moses served faithfully and was entrusted with God's entire house. 3But Jesus deserves far more glory than Moses, just as a person who builds a fine house deserves more praise than the house itself. 4For every house has a builder, but God is the one who made everything.

5Moses was certainly faithful in God's house, but only as a servant. His work was an illustration of the truths God would reveal later. 6But Christ, the faithful Son, was in charge of the entire household. And we are God's household, if we keep up our courage and remain confident

2:11 Greek *his brothers;* also in 2:17.   2:12 Greek *my brothers.* Ps 22:22.   2:13 Isa 8:17-18.   3:1 Greek *And so, holy brothers.*

in our hope in Christ. 7That is why the Holy Spirit says,

"Today you must listen to his voice.
8 Don't harden your hearts against him
as Israel did when they rebelled,
when they tested God's patience in the
wilderness.
9 There your ancestors tried my patience,
even though they saw my miracles for
forty years.
10 So I was angry with them, and I said,
'Their hearts always turn away from me.
They refuse to do what I tell them.'
11 So in my anger I made a vow:
'They will never enter my place of rest.'"*

12Be careful then, dear brothers and sisters.* Make sure that your own hearts are not evil and unbelieving, turning you away from the living God. 13You must warn each other every day, as long as it is called "today," so that none of you will be deceived by sin and hardened against God. 14For if we are faithful to the end, trusting God just as firmly as when we first believed, we will share in all that belongs to Christ. 15But never forget the warning:

"Today you must listen to his voice.
Don't harden your hearts against him
as Israel did when they rebelled."*

16And who were those people who rebelled against God, even though they heard his voice? Weren't they the ones Moses led out of Egypt? 17And who made God angry for forty years? Wasn't it the people who sinned, whose bodies fell in the wilderness? 18And to whom was God speaking when he vowed that they would never enter his place of rest? He was speaking to those who disobeyed him. 19So we see that they were not allowed to enter his rest because of their unbelief.

CHAPTER **4**
Promised Rest for God's People
God's promise of entering his place of rest still stands, so we ought to tremble with fear that some of you might fail to get there. 2For this Good News—that God has prepared a place of rest—has been announced to us just as it was to them. But it did them no good because they didn't believe what God told them.* 3For only we who believe can enter his place of rest. As for those who didn't believe, God said,

"In my anger I made a vow:
'They will never enter my place of rest,'"*

even though his place of rest has been ready since he made the world. 4We know it is ready because the Scriptures mention the seventh day, saying, "On the seventh day God rested from all his work."* 5But in the other passage God said, "They will never enter my place of rest."* 6So God's rest is there for people to enter. But those who formerly heard the Good News failed to enter because they disobeyed God. 7So God set another time for entering his place of rest, and that time is today. God announced this through David a long time later in the words already quoted:

"Today you must listen to his voice.
Don't harden your hearts against him."*

8This new place of rest was not the land of Canaan, where Joshua led them. If it had been, God would not have spoken later about another day of rest. 9So there is a special rest* still waiting for the people of God. 10For all who enter into God's rest will find rest from their labors, just as God rested after creating the world. 11Let us do our best to enter that place of rest. For anyone who disobeys God, as the people of Israel did, will fall.

12For the word of God is full of living power. It is sharper than the sharpest knife, cutting deep into our innermost thoughts and desires. It exposes us for what we really are. 13Nothing in all creation can hide from him. Everything is naked and exposed before his eyes. This is the God to whom we must explain all that we have done.

Christ Is Our High Priest
14That is why we have a great High Priest who has gone to heaven, Jesus the Son of God. Let us cling to him and never stop trusting him. 15This High Priest of ours understands our weaknesses, for he faced all of the same temptations we do, yet he did not sin. 16So let us come boldly to the throne of our gracious God. There we will receive his mercy, and we will find grace to help us when we need it.

CHAPTER **5**
Now a high priest is a man chosen to represent other human beings in their dealings with God. He presents their gifts to God and offers their sacrifices for sins. 2And because he is human, he

3:7-11 Ps 95:7-11. 3:12 Greek *brothers*. 3:15 Ps 95:7-8. 4:2 Some manuscripts read *they didn't share the faith of those who listened [to God]*. 4:3 Ps 95:11. 4:4 Gen 2:2. 4:5 Ps 95:11. 4:7 Ps 95:7-8. 4:9 Or *Sabbath rest*.

is able to deal gently with the people, though they are ignorant and wayward. For he is subject to the same weaknesses they have. ³That is why he has to offer sacrifices, both for their sins and for his own sins. ⁴And no one can become a high priest simply because he wants such an honor. He has to be called by God for this work, just as Aaron was.

⁵That is why Christ did not exalt himself to become High Priest. No, he was chosen by God, who said to him,

"You are my Son.
Today I have become your Father.*"

⁶And in another passage God said to him,

"You are a priest forever
in the line of Melchizedek."*

⁷While Jesus was here on earth, he offered prayers and pleadings, with a loud cry and tears, to the one who could deliver him out of death. And God heard his prayers because of his reverence for God. ⁸So even though Jesus was God's Son, he learned obedience from the things he suffered. ⁹In this way, God qualified him as a perfect High Priest, and he became the source of eternal salvation for all those who obey him. ¹⁰And God designated him to be a High Priest in the line of Melchizedek.

A Call to Spiritual Growth

¹¹There is so much more we would like to say about this. But you don't seem to listen, so it's hard to make you understand. ¹²You have been Christians a long time now, and you ought to be teaching others. Instead, you need someone to teach you again the basic things a beginner must learn about the Scriptures.* You are like babies who drink only milk and cannot eat solid food. ¹³And a person who is living on milk isn't very far along in the Christian life and doesn't know much about doing what is right. ¹⁴Solid food is for those who are mature, who have trained themselves to recognize the difference between right and wrong and then do what is right.

CHAPTER 6

So let us stop going over the basics of Christianity* again and again. Let us go on instead and become mature in our understanding. Surely we don't need to start all over again with the importance of turning away from evil deeds and placing our faith in God. ²You don't need further

instruction about baptisms, the laying on of hands, the resurrection of the dead, and eternal judgment. ³And so, God willing, we will move forward to further understanding.

⁴For it is impossible to restore to repentance those who were once enlightened—those who have experienced the good things of heaven and shared in the Holy Spirit, ⁵who have tasted the goodness of the word of God and the power of the age to come—⁶and who then turn away from God. It is impossible to bring such people to repentance again because they are nailing the Son of God to the cross again by rejecting him, holding him up to public shame.

⁷When the ground soaks up the rain that falls on it and bears a good crop for the farmer, it has the blessing of God. ⁸But if a field bears thistles and thorns, it is useless. The farmer will condemn that field and burn it.

⁹Dear friends, even though we are talking like this, we really don't believe that it applies to you. We are confident that you are meant for better things, things that come with salvation. ¹⁰For God is not unfair. He will not forget how hard you have worked for him and how you have shown your love to him by caring for other Christians, as you still do. ¹¹Our great desire is that you will keep right on loving others as long as life lasts, in order to make certain that what you hope for will come true. ¹²Then you will not become spiritually dull and indifferent. Instead, you will follow the example of those who are going to inherit God's promises because of their faith and patience.

God's Promises Bring Hope

¹³For example, there was God's promise to Abraham. Since there was no one greater to swear by, God took an oath in his own name, saying:

¹⁴ "I will certainly bless you richly,
and I will multiply your descendants into
countless millions."*

¹⁵Then Abraham waited patiently, and he received what God had promised.

¹⁶When people take an oath, they call on someone greater than themselves to hold them to it. And without any question that oath is binding. ¹⁷God also bound himself with an oath, so that those who received the promise could be perfectly sure that he would never change his mind. ¹⁸So God has given us both his promise and his oath. These two things are un-

---

5:5 Or *Today I reveal you as my Son.* Ps 2:7.   5:6 Ps 110:4.   5:12 Or *about the oracles of God.*   6:1 Or *the basics about Christ.*   6:14 Gen 22:17.

changeable because it is impossible for God to lie. Therefore, we who have fled to him for refuge can take new courage, for we can hold on to his promise with confidence.

¹⁹This confidence is like a strong and trustworthy anchor for our souls. It leads us through the curtain of heaven into God's inner sanctuary. ²⁰Jesus has already gone in there for us. He has become our eternal High Priest in the line of Melchizedek.

CHAPTER 7

Melchizedek Is Compared to Abraham

This Melchizedek was king of the city of Salem and also a priest of God Most High. When Abraham was returning home after winning a great battle against many kings, Melchizedek met him and blessed him. ²Then Abraham took a tenth of all he had won in the battle and gave it to Melchizedek. His name means "king of justice." He is also "king of peace" because *Salem* means "peace." ³There is no record of his father or mother or any of his ancestors—no beginning or end to his life. He remains a priest forever, resembling the Son of God.

⁴Consider then how great this Melchizedek was. Even Abraham, the great patriarch of Israel, recognized how great Melchizedek was by giving him a tenth of what he had taken in battle. ⁵Now the priests, who are descendants of Levi, are commanded in the law of Moses to collect a tithe from all the people, even though they are their own relatives.* ⁶But Melchizedek, who was not even related to Levi, collected a tenth from Abraham. And Melchizedek placed a blessing upon Abraham, the one who had already received the promises of God. ⁷And without question, the person who has the power to bless is always greater than the person who is blessed.

⁸In the case of Jewish priests, tithes are paid to men who will die. But Melchizedek is greater than they are, because we are told that he lives on. ⁹In addition, we might even say that Levi's descendants, the ones who collect the tithe, paid a tithe to Melchizedek through their ancestor Abraham. ¹⁰For although Levi wasn't born yet, the seed from which he came was in Abraham's loins when Melchizedek collected the tithe from him.

¹¹And finally, if the priesthood of Levi could have achieved God's purposes—and it was that priesthood on which the law was based—why did God need to send a different priest from the line of Melchizedek, instead of from the line of Levi and Aaron?*

¹²And when the priesthood is changed, the law must also be changed to permit it. ¹³For the one we are talking about belongs to a different tribe, whose members do not serve at the altar. ¹⁴What I mean is, our Lord came from the tribe of Judah, and Moses never mentioned Judah in connection with the priesthood.

Christ Is like Melchizedek

¹⁵The change in God's law is even more evident from the fact that a different priest, who is like Melchizedek, has now come. ¹⁶He became a priest, not by meeting the old requirement of belonging to the tribe of Levi, but by the power of a life that cannot be destroyed. ¹⁷And the psalmist pointed this out when he said of Christ,

"You are a priest forever
    in the line of Melchizedek."*

¹⁸Yes, the old requirement about the priesthood was set aside because it was weak and useless. ¹⁹For the law made nothing perfect, and now a better hope has taken its place. And that is how we draw near to God.

²⁰God took an oath that Christ would always be a priest, but he never did this for any other priest. ²¹Only to Jesus did he say,

"The Lord has taken an oath
    and will not break his vow:
    'You are a priest forever.'"*

²²Because of God's oath, it is Jesus who guarantees the effectiveness of this better covenant.

²³Another difference is that there were many priests under the old system. When one priest died, another had to take his place. ²⁴But Jesus remains a priest forever; his priesthood will never end. ²⁵Therefore he is able, once and forever, to save* everyone who comes to God through him. He lives forever to plead with God on their behalf.

²⁶He is the kind of high priest we need because he is holy and blameless, unstained by sin. He has now been set apart from sinners, and he has been given the highest place of honor in heaven. ²⁷He does not need to offer sacrifices every day like the other high priests. They did this for their own sins first and then for the sins of the people. But Jesus did this once for all when he sacrificed himself on the cross. ²⁸Those

---

7:5 Greek *their brothers, who are descendants of Abraham.*   7:11 Greek *according to the order of Aaron.*   7:17 Ps 110:4.   7:21 Ps 110:4.   7:25 Or *able to save completely.*

who were high priests under the law of Moses were limited by human weakness. But after the law was given, God appointed his Son with an oath, and his Son has been made perfect forever.

CHAPTER 8
Christ Is Our High Priest

Here is the main point: Our High Priest sat down in the place of highest honor in heaven, at God's right hand. ²There he ministers in the sacred tent, the true place of worship that was built by the Lord and not by human hands.

³And since every high priest is required to offer gifts and sacrifices, our High Priest must make an offering, too. ⁴If he were here on earth, he would not even be a priest, since there already are priests who offer the gifts required by the law of Moses. ⁵They serve in a place of worship that is only a copy, a shadow of the real one in heaven. For when Moses was getting ready to build the Tabernacle, God gave him this warning: "Be sure that you make everything according to the design I have shown you here on the mountain."* ⁶But our High Priest has been given a ministry that is far superior to the ministry of those who serve under the old laws, for he is the one who guarantees for us a better covenant with God, based on better promises.

⁷If the first covenant had been faultless, there would have been no need for a second covenant to replace it. ⁸But God himself found fault with the old one when he said:

"The day will come, says the Lord,
    when I will make a new covenant
    with the people of Israel and Judah.
⁹ This covenant will not be like the one
    I made with their ancestors
when I took them by the hand
    and led them out of the land of Egypt.
They did not remain faithful to my
    covenant,
    so I turned my back on them, says the
    Lord.
¹⁰ But this is the new covenant I will make
    with the people of Israel on that day, says
    the Lord:
I will put my laws in their minds
    so they will understand them,
and I will write them on their hearts
    so they will obey them.
I will be their God,
    and they will be my people.

¹¹ And they will not need to teach their
    neighbors,
    nor will they need to teach their family,
    saying, 'You should know the Lord.'
For everyone, from the least to the greatest,
    will already know me.
¹² And I will forgive their wrongdoings,
    and I will never again remember their
    sins."*

¹³When God speaks of a new covenant, it means he has made the first one obsolete. It is now out of date and ready to be put aside.

CHAPTER 9
Old Rules about Worship

Now in that first covenant between God and Israel, there were regulations for worship and a sacred tent here on earth. ²There were two rooms in this tent. In the first room were a lampstand, a table, and loaves of holy bread on the table. This was called the Holy Place. ³Then there was a curtain, and behind the curtain was the second room called the Most Holy Place. ⁴In that room were a gold incense altar and a wooden chest called the Ark of the Covenant, which was covered with gold on all sides. Inside the Ark were a gold jar containing some manna, Aaron's staff that sprouted leaves, and the stone tablets of the covenant with the Ten Commandments written on them. ⁵The glorious cherubim were above the Ark. Their wings were stretched out over the Ark's cover, the place of atonement. But we cannot explain all of these things now.

⁶When these things were all in place, the priests went in and out of the first room* regularly as they performed their religious duties. ⁷But only the high priest goes into the Most Holy Place, and only once a year, and always with blood, which he offers to God to cover his own sins and the sins the people have committed in ignorance. ⁸By these regulations the Holy Spirit revealed that the Most Holy Place was not open to the people as long as the first room and the entire system it represents were still in use.

⁹This is an illustration pointing to the present time. For the gifts and sacrifices that the priests offer are not able to cleanse the consciences of the people who bring them. ¹⁰For that old system deals only with food and drink and ritual washing—external regulations that are in effect only until their limitations can be corrected.

8:5 Exod 25:40; 26:30.   8:8-12 Jer 31:31-34.   9:6 Greek *first tent;* also in 9:8.

Christ Is the Perfect Sacrifice

[11] So Christ has now become the High Priest over all the good things that have come. He has entered that great, perfect sanctuary in heaven, not made by human hands and not part of this created world. [12] Once for all time he took blood into that Most Holy Place, but not the blood of goats and calves. He took his own blood, and with it he secured our salvation forever.

[13] Under the old system, the blood of goats and bulls and the ashes of a young cow could cleanse people's bodies from ritual defilement. [14] Just think how much more the blood of Christ will purify our hearts from deeds that lead to death so that we can worship the living God. For by the power of the eternal Spirit, Christ offered himself to God as a perfect sacrifice for our sins. [15] That is why he is the one who mediates the new covenant between God and people, so that all who are invited can receive the eternal inheritance God has promised them. For Christ died to set them free from the penalty of the sins they had committed under that first covenant.

[16] Now when someone dies and leaves a will, no one gets anything until it is proved that the person who wrote the will* is dead.* [17] The will goes into effect only after the death of the person who wrote it. While the person is still alive, no one can use the will to get any of the things promised to them.

[18] That is why blood was required under the first covenant as a proof of death. [19] For after Moses had given the people all of God's laws, he took the blood of calves and goats, along with water, and sprinkled both the book of God's laws and all the people, using branches of hyssop bushes and scarlet wool. [20] Then he said, "This blood confirms the covenant God has made with you."* [21] And in the same way, he sprinkled blood on the sacred tent and on everything used for worship. [22] In fact, we can say that according to the law of Moses, nearly everything was purified by sprinkling with blood. Without the shedding of blood, there is no forgiveness of sins.

[23] That is why the earthly tent and everything in it—which were copies of things in heaven—had to be purified by the blood of animals. But the real things in heaven had to be purified with far better sacrifices than the blood of animals.

[24] For Christ has entered into heaven itself to appear now before God as our Advocate.* He did not go into the earthly place of worship, for

that was merely a copy of the real Temple in heaven. [25] Nor did he enter heaven to offer himself again and again, like the earthly high priest who enters the Most Holy Place year after year to offer the blood of an animal. [26] If that had been necessary, he would have had to die again and again, ever since the world began. But no! He came once for all time, at the end of the age, to remove the power of sin forever by his sacrificial death for us.

[27] And just as it is destined that each person dies only once and after that comes judgment, [28] so also Christ died only once as a sacrifice to take away the sins of many people. He will come again but not to deal with our sins again. This time he will bring salvation to all those who are eagerly waiting for him.

CHAPTER **10**

Christ's Sacrifice Once for All

The old system in the law of Moses was only a shadow of the things to come, not the reality of the good things Christ has done for us. The sacrifices under the old system were repeated again and again, year after year, but they were never able to provide perfect cleansing for those who came to worship. [2] If they could have provided perfect cleansing, the sacrifices would have stopped, for the worshipers would have been purified once for all time, and their feelings of guilt would have disappeared.

[3] But just the opposite happened. Those yearly sacrifices reminded them of their sins year after year. [4] For it is not possible for the blood of bulls and goats to take away sins. [5] That is why Christ, when he came into the world, said,

"You did not want animal sacrifices and
    grain offerings.
But you have given me a body so that I
    may obey you.
[6] No, you were not pleased with animals
        burned on the altar
    or with other offerings for sin.
[7] Then I said, 'Look, I have come to do your
        will, O God—
    just as it is written about me in the
        Scriptures.'"*

[8] Christ said, "You did not want animal sacrifices or grain offerings or animals burned on the altar or other offerings for sin, nor were you pleased with them" (though they are required by the law

9:16a Or *covenant.*   9:16b Or *Now when someone makes a covenant, it is necessary to ratify it with the death of a sacrifice.*   9:20 Exod 24:8.
9:24 Greek *on our behalf.*   10:5-7 Ps 40:6-8.

of Moses). ⁹Then he added, "Look, I have come to do your will." He cancels the first covenant in order to establish the second. ¹⁰And what God wants is for us to be made holy by the sacrifice of the body of Jesus Christ once for all time.

¹¹Under the old covenant, the priest stands before the altar day after day, offering sacrifices that can never take away sins. ¹²But our High Priest offered himself to God as one sacrifice for sins, good for all time. Then he sat down at the place of highest honor at God's right hand. ¹³There he waits until his enemies are humbled as a footstool under his feet. ¹⁴For by that one offering he perfected forever all those whom he is making holy.

¹⁵And the Holy Spirit also testifies that this is so. First he says,

¹⁶ "This is the new covenant I will make
  with my people on that day, says the
    Lord:
  I will put my laws in their hearts
    so they will understand them,
  and I will write them on their minds
    so they will obey them."

¹⁷Then he adds,

  "I will never again remember
    their sins and lawless deeds."*

¹⁸Now when sins have been forgiven, there is no need to offer any more sacrifices.

A Call to Persevere

¹⁹And so, dear brothers and sisters,* we can boldly enter heaven's Most Holy Place because of the blood of Jesus. ²⁰This is the new, life-giving way that Christ has opened up for us through the sacred curtain, by means of his death for us.*

²¹And since we have a great High Priest who rules over God's people, ²²let us go right into the presence of God, with true hearts fully trusting him. For our evil consciences have been sprinkled with Christ's blood to make us clean, and our bodies have been washed with pure water. ²³Without wavering, let us hold tightly to the hope we say we have, for God can be trusted to keep his promise. ²⁴Think of ways to encourage one another to outbursts of love and good deeds. ²⁵And let us not neglect our meeting together, as some people do, but encourage and warn each other, especially now that the day of his coming back again is drawing near.

²⁶Dear friends, if we deliberately continue

10:16-17 Jer 31:33-34.   **10:19** Greek *brothers*.   **10:20** Greek *his flesh*.

Why We Need Fellowship with Other Believers
Read HEBREWS 10:25

Involvement in a local church is necessary for the spiritual growth of all Christians, and it is something we never outgrow. For the new believer, moreover, such interaction is critical for four reasons:

1. Fellowship Provides Us with Encouragement and Love. As Christians, we need a place where we can be encouraged in our faith and be reminded that we are a member of God's family. When we go to church, we are surrounded by others who share our love for Christ. Being in the presence of other believers can encourage us to live for Christ, as well as give us a sense of belonging and acceptance that we don't receive from the world.

2. Fellowship Allows Us to Learn from Spiritually Mature Christians. In the biblical account of the early church, we are told how the apostle Paul's friends, Priscilla and Aquila, took time to help another believer learn more about Jesus (see Acts 18:26, p. 947). Likewise, younger Christians in the church today will have the opportunity to gain spiritual wisdom and insight from more mature Christians.

3. Fellowship Helps Us Discern False Teachings. The Bible warns of false teachers and teachings, to which the young believer is especially susceptible because he or she lacks basic Bible understanding. A healthy, Bible-teaching church will encourage young believers in their growth and help them discern truth from error.

4. Fellowship Prepares Us for Christ's Return. As the day for Christ's return comes closer, we need to help each other through difficult times and keep our problems in perspective. We also need to encourage each other to live holy lives and to share God's Good News with others in the time that remains. God wants the body of Christ to stand out and be a light in these ever darkening days.

For the next note on "Look for and Attend the Right Church," turn to p. 1025.

Christ Endured Great Pain for Us Read HEBREWS 12:1-3

Throughout the New Testament, the Christian life is compared to a race. With that in mind, we need to realize that it is not a short sprint, but a long-distance run. Sometimes, as we are participating in this race, we can grow discouraged by circumstances or by what others say to us. But just as a successful runner must "keep his eyes on the prize," we, too, must remember what this race is all about. We must bear in mind for whom and to whom we are running: Jesus Christ. In essence, we need to "keep our eyes on Jesus."

Corrie ten Boom, a Dutch Christian who survived the horrors of Hitler's concentration camps during World War II, often said, "Look within and be depressed. Look without and be distressed. Look at Jesus and be at rest."

God will see us through to the end. He has given us his word: "And I am sure that God, who began the good work within you, will continue his work until it is finally finished on that day when Christ Jesus comes back again" (Philippians 1:6).

For the next note on "Perseverance," turn to p. 196.

CORNER STONES

---

sinning after we have received a full knowledge of the truth, there is no other sacrifice that will cover these sins. 27There will be nothing to look forward to but the terrible expectation of God's judgment and the raging fire that will consume his enemies. 28Anyone who refused to obey the law of Moses was put to death without mercy on the testimony of two or three witnesses. 29Think how much more terrible the punishment will be for those who have trampled on the Son of God and have treated the blood of the covenant as if it were common and unholy. Such people have insulted and enraged the Holy Spirit who brings God's mercy to his people.

30For we know the one who said,

"I will take vengeance.
I will repay those who deserve it."

He also said,

"The Lord will judge his own people."*

31It is a terrible thing to fall into the hands of the living God.

32Don't ever forget those early days when you first learned about Christ. Remember how you remained faithful even though it meant terrible suffering. 33Sometimes you were exposed to public ridicule and were beaten, and sometimes you helped others who were suffering the same things. 34You suffered along with those who were thrown into jail. When all you owned was taken from you, you accepted it with joy. You knew you had better things waiting for you in eternity.

35Do not throw away this confident trust in the Lord, no matter what happens. Remember the great reward it brings you! 36Patient endurance is what you need now, so you will continue to do God's will. Then you will receive all that he has promised.

37 "For in just a little while,
    the Coming One will come and not
        delay.
38 And a righteous person will live by faith.
    But I will have no pleasure in anyone
        who turns away."*

39But we are not like those who turn their backs on God and seal their fate. We have faith that assures our salvation.

CHAPTER **11**
Great Examples of Faith
What is faith? It is the confident assurance that what we hope for is going to happen. It is the evidence of things we cannot yet see. 2God gave his approval to people in days of old because of their faith.

3By faith we understand that the entire universe was formed at God's command, that what we now see did not come from anything that can be seen.

10:30 Deut 32:35-36.   **10:37-38** Hab 2:3-4.

⁴It was by faith that Abel brought a more acceptable offering to God than Cain did. God accepted Abel's offering to show that he was a righteous man. And although Abel is long dead, he still speaks to us because of his faith.

⁵It was by faith that Enoch was taken up to heaven without dying—"suddenly he disappeared because God took him."* But before he was taken up, he was approved as pleasing to God. ⁶So, you see, it is impossible to please God without faith. Anyone who wants to come to him must believe that there is a God and that he rewards those who sincerely seek him.

⁷It was by faith that Noah built an ark to save his family from the flood. He obeyed God, who warned him about something that had never happened before. By his faith he condemned the rest of the world and was made right in God's sight.

⁸It was by faith that Abraham obeyed when God called him to leave home and go to another land that God would give him as his inheritance. He went without knowing where he was going. ⁹And even when he reached the land God promised him, he lived there by faith—for he was like a foreigner, living in a tent. And so did Isaac and Jacob, to whom God gave the same promise. ¹⁰Abraham did this because he was confidently looking forward to a city with eternal foundations, a city designed and built by God.

¹¹It was by faith that Sarah together with Abraham was able to have a child, even though they were too old and Sarah was barren. Abraham believed that God would keep his promise.* ¹²And so a whole nation came from this one man, Abraham, who was too old to have any children—a nation with so many people that, like the stars of the sky and the sand on the seashore, there is no way to count them.

¹³All these faithful ones died without receiving what God had promised them, but they saw it all from a distance and welcomed the promises of God. They agreed that they were no more than foreigners and nomads here on earth. ¹⁴And obviously people who talk like that are looking forward to a country they can call their own. ¹⁵If they had meant the country they came from, they would have found a way to go back. ¹⁶But they were looking for a better place, a heavenly homeland. That is why God is not ashamed to be called their God, for he has prepared a heavenly city for them.

¹⁷It was by faith that Abraham offered Isaac as a sacrifice when God was testing him. Abraham, who had received God's promises, was ready to sacrifice his only son, Isaac, ¹⁸though God had promised him, "Isaac is the son through whom your descendants will be counted."* ¹⁹Abraham assumed that if Isaac died, God was able to bring him back to life again. And in a sense, Abraham did receive his son back from the dead.

²⁰It was by faith that Isaac blessed his two sons, Jacob and Esau. He had confidence in what God was going to do in the future.

²¹It was by faith that Jacob, when he was old and dying, blessed each of Joseph's sons and bowed in worship as he leaned on his staff.

²²And it was by faith that Joseph, when he was about to die, confidently spoke of God's bringing the people of Israel out of Egypt. He was so sure of it that he commanded them to carry his bones with them when they left!

²³It was by faith that Moses' parents hid him for three months. They saw that God had given them an unusual child, and they were not afraid of what the king might do.

²⁴It was by faith that Moses, when he grew up, refused to be treated as the son of Pharaoh's daughter. ²⁵He chose to share the oppression of God's people instead of enjoying the fleeting pleasures of sin. ²⁶He thought it was better to suffer for the sake of the Messiah than to own the treasures of Egypt, for he was looking ahead to the great reward that God would give him. ²⁷It was by faith that Moses left the land of Egypt. He was not afraid of the king. Moses kept right on going because he kept his eyes on the one who is invisible. ²⁸It was by faith that Moses commanded the people of Israel to keep the Passover and to sprinkle blood on the doorposts so that the angel of death would not kill their firstborn sons.

²⁹It was by faith that the people of Israel went right through the Red Sea as though they were on dry ground. But when the Egyptians followed, they were all drowned.

³⁰It was by faith that the people of Israel marched around Jericho seven days, and the walls came crashing down.

³¹It was by faith that Rahab the prostitute did not die with all the others in her city who refused to obey God. For she had given a friendly welcome to the spies.

³²Well, how much more do I need to say? It would take too long to recount the stories of

---

11:5 Gen 5:24.   11:11 Some manuscripts read *It was by faith that Sarah was able to have a child, even though she was too old and barren. Sarah believed that God would keep his promise.*   11:18 Gen 21:12.

the faith of Gideon, Barak, Samson, Jephthah, David, Samuel, and all the prophets. 33By faith these people overthrew kingdoms, ruled with justice, and received what God had promised them. They shut the mouths of lions, 34quenched the flames of fire, and escaped death by the edge of the sword. Their weakness was turned to strength. They became strong in battle and put whole armies to flight. 35Women received their loved ones back again from death.

But others trusted God and were tortured, preferring to die rather than turn from God and be free. They placed their hope in the resurrection to a better life. 36Some were mocked, and their backs were cut open with whips. Others were chained in dungeons. 37Some died by stoning, and some were sawed in half; others were killed with the sword. Some went about in skins of sheep and goats, hungry and oppressed and mistreated. 38They were too good for this world. They wandered over deserts and mountains, hiding in caves and holes in the ground.

39All of these people we have mentioned received God's approval because of their faith, yet none of them received all that God had promised. 40For God had far better things in mind for us that would also benefit them, for they can't receive the prize at the end of the race until we finish the race.*

CHAPTER **12**

God's Discipline Proves His Love

Therefore, since we are surrounded by such a huge crowd of witnesses to the life of faith, let us strip off every weight that slows us down, especially the sin that so easily hinders our progress. And let us run with endurance the race that God has set before us. 2We do this by keeping our eyes on Jesus, on whom our faith depends from start to finish.* He was willing to die a shameful death on the cross because of the joy he knew would be his afterward. Now he is seated in the place of highest honor beside God's throne in heaven. 3Think about all he endured when sinful people did such terrible things to him, so that you don't become weary and give up. 4After all, you have not yet given your lives in your struggle against sin.

11:40 Greek *for us, for they apart from us can't finish.* 12:2 Or *Jesus, the Originator and Perfecter of our faith.*

OFF AND RUNNING

Keeping Your Marriage Strong Read HEBREWS 13:4

Tragically, many people do not take marriage seriously today. They forget that their vows are made before God and include the words "till death do us part." So what steps can you take to keep from becoming another marriage "casualty"? Here are four principles that will help you to maintain a strong and flourishing marriage:

1. Walk with God. As you cultivate and deepen your fellowship with God, you will have the power, the will, and the resources to stand when temptation comes knocking.

2. Walk with Your Spouse. Keep the friendship and romance alive in your marriage. Remember what you did when you first started courting your spouse. Compliment one another. Spend time together. Be genuinely interested in one another's lives. Try your best to look attractive for each other. Treat your partner with respect. Take practical steps to keep that fire of love burning.

3. Don't Walk on Thin Ice. Psalm 1 warns of the dangers of close relationships with those who do not love God as you do. You must avoid potentially dangerous and flirtatious relationships at all costs. Find Christian friends (of the same sex) who can be honest with you if they think you are heading into dangerous territory.

4. Count the Cost. Remember the price that comes with adultery and immorality. Are you ready to face the shame? Are you prepared for the disgrace and distrust you will bring upon your spouse and children—as well as the cause of Christ? A few moments of pleasure will result in a lifetime of regret.

An intense love for God and for your husband or wife will see you through the rough waters of sexual temptation. Don't be an easy target for Satan's arrows. Keep moving forward in your relationship with Christ and with your spouse.

For the next note on "Marriage," turn to p. 840.

5And have you entirely forgotten the encouraging words God spoke to you, his children? He said,

"My child, don't ignore it when the Lord disciplines you,
and don't be discouraged when he corrects you.
6 For the Lord disciplines those he loves,
and he punishes those he accepts as his children."*

7As you endure this divine discipline, remember that God is treating you as his own children. Whoever heard of a child who was never disciplined? 8If God doesn't discipline you as he does all of his children, it means that you are illegitimate and are not really his children after all. 9Since we respect our earthly fathers who disciplined us, should we not all the more cheerfully submit to the discipline of our heavenly Father and live forever*?

10For our earthly fathers disciplined us for a few years, doing the best they knew how. But God's discipline is always right and good for us because it means we will share in his holiness. 11No discipline is enjoyable while it is happening—it is painful! But afterward there will be a quiet harvest of right living for those who are trained in this way.

12So take a new grip with your tired hands and stand firm on your shaky legs. 13Mark out a straight path for your feet. Then those who follow you, though they are weak and lame, will not stumble and fall but will become strong.

A Call to Listen to God

14Try to live in peace with everyone, and seek to live a clean and holy life, for those who are not holy will not see the Lord. 15Look after each other so that none of you will miss out on the special favor of God. Watch out that no bitter root of unbelief rises up among you, for whenever it springs up, many are corrupted by its poison. 16Make sure that no one is immoral or godless like Esau. He traded his birthright as the oldest son for a single meal. 17And afterward, when he wanted his father's blessing, he was rejected. It was too late for repentance, even though he wept bitter tears.

18You have not come to a physical mountain, to a place of flaming fire, darkness, gloom, and whirlwind, as the Israelites did at Mount Sinai when God gave them his laws. 19For

they heard an awesome trumpet blast and a voice with a message so terrible that they begged God to stop speaking. 20They staggered back under God's command: "If even an animal touches the mountain, it must be stoned to death."* 21Moses himself was so frightened at the sight that he said, "I am terrified and trembling."*

22No, you have come to Mount Zion, to the city of the living God, the heavenly Jerusalem, and to thousands of angels in joyful assembly. 23You have come to the assembly of God's firstborn children, whose names are written in heaven. You have come to God himself, who is the judge of all people. And you have come to the spirits of the redeemed in heaven who have now been made perfect. 24You have come to Jesus, the one who mediates the new covenant between God and people, and to the sprinkled blood, which graciously forgives instead of crying out for vengeance as the blood of Abel did.

25See to it that you obey God, the one who is speaking to you. For if the people of Israel did not escape when they refused to listen to Moses, the earthly messenger, how terrible our danger if we reject the One who speaks to us from heaven! 26When God spoke from Mount Sinai his voice shook the earth, but now he makes another promise: "Once again I will shake not only the earth but the heavens also."* 27This means that the things on earth will be shaken, so that only eternal things will be left.

28Since we are receiving a kingdom that cannot be destroyed, let us be thankful and please God by worshiping him with holy fear and awe. 29For our God is a consuming fire.

CHAPTER **13**
Concluding Words

Continue to love each other with true Christian love.* 2Don't forget to show hospitality to strangers, for some who have done this have entertained angels without realizing it! 3Don't forget about those in prison. Suffer with them as though you were there yourself. Share the sorrow of those being mistreated, as though you feel their pain in your own bodies.

4Give honor to marriage, and remain faithful to one another in marriage. God will surely judge people who are immoral and those who commit adultery.

12:5-6 Prov 3:11-12. 12:9 Or *really live.* 12:20 Exod 19:13. 12:21 Deut 9:19. 12:26 Hag 2:6. 13:1 Greek *with brotherly love.*

⁵Stay away from the love of money; be satisfied with what you have. For God has said,

"I will never fail you.
I will never forsake you."*

⁶That is why we can say with confidence,

"The Lord is my helper,
so I will not be afraid.
What can mere mortals do to me?"*

⁷Remember your leaders who first taught you the word of God. Think of all the good that has come from their lives, and trust the Lord as they do.

⁸Jesus Christ is the same yesterday, today, and forever. ⁹So do not be attracted by strange, new ideas. Your spiritual strength comes from God's special favor, not from ceremonial rules about food, which don't help those who follow them.

¹⁰We have an altar from which the priests in the Temple on earth have no right to eat. ¹¹Under the system of Jewish laws, the high priest brought the blood of animals into the Holy Place as a sacrifice for sin, but the bodies of the animals were burned outside the camp. ¹²So also Jesus suffered and died outside the city gates in order to make his people holy by shedding his own blood. ¹³So let us go out to him outside the camp and bear the disgrace he bore. ¹⁴For this world is not our home; we are looking forward to our city in heaven, which is yet to come.

¹⁵With Jesus' help, let us continually offer our sacrifice of praise to God by proclaiming the glory of his name. ¹⁶Don't forget to do good and to share what you have with those in need, for such sacrifices are very pleasing to God.

¹⁷Obey your spiritual leaders and do what they say. Their work is to watch over your souls, and they know they are accountable to God. Give them reason to do this joyfully and not with sorrow. That would certainly not be for your benefit.

¹⁸Pray for us, for our conscience is clear and we want to live honorably in everything we do. ¹⁹I especially need your prayers right now so that I can come back to you soon.

²⁰⁻²¹And now, may the God of peace, who brought again from the dead our Lord Jesus, equip you with all you need for doing his will. May he produce in you, through the power of Jesus Christ, all that is pleasing to him. Jesus is the great Shepherd of the sheep by an everlasting covenant, signed with his blood. To him be glory forever and ever. Amen.

²²I urge you, dear brothers and sisters,* please listen carefully to what I have said in this brief letter.

²³I want you to know that our brother Timothy is now out of jail. If he comes here soon, I will bring him with me to see you.

²⁴Give my greetings to all your leaders and to the other believers there. The Christians from Italy send you their greetings.

²⁵May God's grace be with you all.

13:5 Deut 31:6, 8.   13:6 Ps 118:6.   13:22 Greek *brothers.*

OFF AND RUNNING ▰▰▰▰▰
Our Needs Must Come Last Read HEBREWS 13:11-13

Jesus gave us the ultimate example to follow in meekness. Jesus, who is God, came to this earth and humbled himself in an incredible way by becoming a man. It is important to note that he never at any time ceased being God. But he did lay aside the privileges of deity to experience genuine human conditions, such as sorrow, anger, weariness, and pain (see Philippians 2:3-11, pp. 1034-1035). Yet the most dramatic act of his meekness came when he went to a cross to be crucified. Although he was led away to die, no one took his life. That is because Jesus could have called down legions of angels to rescue him. But instead he "suffered and died" for us.

How should Christ's attitude affect the way we treat others? In short, we must put the needs of others before our own. During Jesus' earthly ministry, he always had time for others. We should follow his example. Here is a simple acrostic that will help you keep your priorities in order:

J is for Jesus.
O is for others.
Y is for yourself.

If you put the will of God first and the needs of others above your own, you will find joy.

For the next note on "Attitude toward Self," turn to p. 818.

James

Greetings from James

This letter is from James, a slave of God and of the Lord Jesus Christ.

It is written to Jewish Christians scattered among the nations.* Greetings!

Faith and Endurance

2Dear brothers and sisters,* whenever trouble comes your way, let it be an opportunity for joy. 3For when your faith is tested, your endurance has a chance to grow. 4So let it grow, for when your endurance is fully developed, you will be strong in character and ready for anything.

5If you need wisdom—if you want to know what God wants you to do—ask him, and he will gladly tell you. He will not resent your asking. 6But when you ask him, be sure that you really expect him to answer, for a doubtful mind is as unsettled as a wave of the sea that is driven and tossed by the wind. 7People like that should not expect to receive anything from the Lord. 8They can't make up their minds. They waver back and forth in everything they do.

9Christians who are* poor should be glad, for God has honored them. 10And those who are rich should be glad, for God has humbled them. They will fade away like a flower in the field. 11The hot sun rises and dries up the grass; the flower withers, and its beauty fades away. So also, wealthy people will fade away with all of their achievements.

12God blesses the people who patiently endure testing. Afterward they will receive the crown of life that God has promised to those who love him. 13And remember, no one who wants to do wrong should ever say, "God is tempting me." God is never tempted to do wrong, and he never tempts anyone else either. 14Temptation comes from the lure of our own evil desires. 15These evil desires lead to evil actions, and evil actions lead to death. 16So don't be misled, my dear brothers and sisters.

17Whatever is good and perfect comes to us from God above, who created all heaven's lights.* Unlike them, he never changes or casts shifting shadows. 18In his goodness he chose to make us his own children by giving us his true word. And we, out of all creation, became his choice possession.

Listening and Doing

19My dear brothers and sisters, be quick to listen, slow to speak, and slow to get angry. 20Your anger can never make things right in God's sight.

21So get rid of all the filth and evil in your lives, and humbly accept the message God has planted in your hearts, for it is strong enough to save your souls.

22And remember, it is a message to obey, not just to listen to. If you don't obey, you are only fooling yourself. 23For if you just listen and don't obey, it is like looking at your face in a mirror but doing nothing to improve your appearance. 24You see yourself, walk away, and forget what you look like. 25But if you keep looking steadily into God's perfect law—the law that sets you free—and if you do what it says and don't forget what you heard, then God will bless you for doing it.

26If you claim to be religious but don't control your tongue, you are just fooling yourself, and your religion is worthless. 27Pure and last-

1:1 Greek To the twelve tribes in the dispersion. 1:2 Greek brothers; also in 1:16, 19. 1:9 Greek The brother who is. 1:17 Greek from above, from the Father of lights.

Life's Trials Will Make You Stronger Read JAMES 1:2-4

One of the keys to growing and being able to effectively continue in the Christian life is enduring. A key aspect of endurance is patience. The word used for "endurance" in verse 3 is the Greek word *hupomone*, which means "a patient enduring."

This cheerful, enduring patience, which helps us to continue in our Christian walk, actually comes—and develops—in times of testing and hardship. During these trials or "storms of life," our spiritual roots grow deeper, thus strengthening our faith. If we had our way, most of us would probably try to avoid these difficult times in our lives. Yet God promises that he will never give us more than we can handle (see 1 Corinthians 10:13, p. 994).

These times of trial and testing will make us either better or bitter. It really is up to us and the outlook we choose to take. If we can learn to walk in our relationship with God on the basis of faith as opposed to mere feeling, we will grow stronger and, as this passage says, "be strong in character and ready for anything."

For the next note on "Perseverance," turn to p. 1080.

CORNER STONES

---

ing religion in the sight of God our Father means that we must care for orphans and widows in their troubles, and refuse to let the world corrupt us.

CHAPTER 2
A Warning against Prejudice

My dear brothers and sisters,* how can you claim that you have faith in our glorious Lord Jesus Christ if you favor some people more than others?

2For instance, suppose someone comes into your meeting* dressed in fancy clothes and expensive jewelry, and another comes in who is poor and dressed in shabby clothes. 3If you give special attention and a good seat to the rich person, but you say to the poor one, "You can stand over there, or else sit on the floor"—well, 4doesn't this discrimination show that you are guided by wrong motives?

5Listen to me, dear brothers and sisters. Hasn't God chosen the poor in this world to be rich in faith? Aren't they the ones who will inherit the kingdom God promised to those who love him? 6And yet, you insult the poor man! Isn't it the rich who oppress you and drag you into court? 7Aren't they the ones who slander Jesus Christ, whose noble name you bear?

8Yes indeed, it is good when you truly obey our Lord's royal command found in the Scriptures: "Love your neighbor as yourself."* 9But if you pay special attention to the rich, you are committing a sin, for you are guilty of breaking that law.

10And the person who keeps all of the laws except one is as guilty as the person who has broken all of God's laws. 11For the same God who said, "Do not commit adultery," also said, "Do not murder."* So if you murder someone, you have broken the entire law, even if you do not commit adultery.

12So whenever you speak, or whatever you do, remember that you will be judged by the law of love, the law that set you free. 13For there will be no mercy for you if you have not been merciful to others. But if you have been merciful, then God's mercy toward you will win out over his judgment against you.

Faith without Good Deeds Is Dead

14Dear brothers and sisters, what's the use of saying you have faith if you don't prove it by your actions? That kind of faith can't save anyone. 15Suppose you see a brother or sister who needs food or clothing, 16and you say, "Well, good-bye and God bless you; stay warm and eat well"—but then you don't give that person any food or clothing. What good does that do?

17So you see, it isn't enough just to have faith. Faith that doesn't show itself by good deeds is no faith at all—it is dead and useless.

2:1 Greek *brothers;* also in 2:5, 14.   2:2 Greek *synagogue.*   2:8 Lev 19:18.   2:11 Exod 20:13-14; Deut 5:17-18.

18Now someone may argue, "Some people have faith; others have good deeds." I say, "I can't see your faith if you don't have good deeds, but I will show you my faith through my good deeds."

19Do you still think it's enough just to believe that there is one God? Well, even the demons believe this, and they tremble in terror! 20Fool! When will you ever learn that faith that does not result in good deeds is useless?

21Don't you remember that our ancestor Abraham was declared right with God because of what he did when he offered his son Isaac on the altar? 22You see, he was trusting God so much that he was willing to do whatever God told him to do. His faith was made complete by what he did—by his actions. 23And so it happened just as the Scriptures say: "Abraham believed God, so God declared him to be righteous."* He was even called "the friend of God."* 24So you see, we are made right with God by what we do, not by faith alone.

25Rahab the prostitute is another example of this. She was made right with God by her actions—when she hid those messengers and sent them safely away by a different road. 26Just as the body is dead without a spirit, so also faith is dead without good deeds.

CHAPTER 3
Controlling the Tongue
Dear brothers and sisters,* not many of you should become teachers in the church, for we who teach will be judged by God with greater strictness.

2We all make many mistakes, but those who control their tongues can also control themselves in every other way. 3We can make a large horse turn around and go wherever we want by means of a small bit in its mouth. 4And a tiny rudder makes a huge ship turn wherever the pilot wants it to go, even though the winds are strong. 5So also, the tongue is a small thing, but what enormous damage it can do. A tiny spark can set a great forest on fire. 6And the tongue is a flame of fire. It is full of wickedness that can ruin your whole life. It can turn the entire course of your life into a blazing flame of destruction, for it is set on fire by hell itself.

7People can tame all kinds of animals and birds and reptiles and fish, 8but no one can tame the tongue. It is an uncontrollable evil, full of deadly poison. 9Sometimes it praises our Lord and Father, and sometimes it breaks out into curses against those who have been made in the image of God. 10And so blessing and cursing come pouring out of the same mouth. Surely, my brothers and sisters, this is not right! 11Does a spring of water bubble out with both fresh water and bitter water? 12Can you pick olives from a fig tree or figs from a grapevine? No, and you can't draw fresh water from a salty pool.

True Wisdom Comes from God
13If you are wise and understand God's ways, live a life of steady goodness so that only good deeds will pour forth. And if you don't brag about the good you do, then you will be truly

2:23a Gen 15:6.   2:23b See Isa 41:8.   3:1 Greek *brothers;* also in 3:10.

Prayer Allows Us to Voice Our Requests to God
Read JAMES 4:2-3

There may come a time in your life when you wonder why you are not growing in your faith. Or you might wonder why you don't ever have the opportunity to lead others to Christ. When you ask yourself these kinds of questions, you may be able to answer them with another question: "Have I asked God to help me in this area?"

Understand that this passage does not advocate that you "demand" things from God as though he were some "cosmic butler," prepared to answer your every beck and call. Yet it is equally wrong to fail to ask him to help meet your needs or to bless your life and spiritually strengthen you. God wants to bless you because you are his child. Unfortunately, many of us fail to receive what God has for us because we don't pray.

Take a moment to look at your own spiritual progress. Do you want to have a better understanding of the Bible? Are you looking for some Christian friends? Do you want the Lord to show you what your gifts and talents are? God wants to bless you, but he may be just waiting for your invitation to do so.

For the next note on "Pray," turn to p. 741.

We Must Live Out Our Faith Read JAMES 2:14-17

While you do not need to change your lifestyle before you come to Christ, once you do come to Christ, your lifestyle should show tangible changes. If it does not, then one could doubt whether Christ has really come into your life. The way you live should reflect what you believe. As John the Baptist said, "Prove by the way you live that you have really turned from your sins and turned to God" (Luke 3:8).

James brings out another important reason for backing up our faith with our actions in verses 15 and 16: It makes it easier to share our faith with others. When people see that we genuinely care about them as individuals, then they will be much more open to hearing about what motivates us.

Can people see Jesus in the way you live? If not, it is time to move Jesus into the "pilot seat" of your life.

For the next note on "Faith and Works," turn to p. 1026.

CORNER STONES

---

wise! 14But if you are bitterly jealous and there is selfish ambition in your hearts, don't brag about being wise. That is the worst kind of lie. 15For jealousy and selfishness are not God's kind of wisdom. Such things are earthly, unspiritual, and motivated by the Devil. 16For wherever there is jealousy and selfish ambition, there you will find disorder and every kind of evil.

17But the wisdom that comes from heaven is first of all pure. It is also peace loving, gentle at all times, and willing to yield to others. It is full of mercy and good deeds. It shows no partiality and is always sincere. 18And those who are peacemakers will plant seeds of peace and reap a harvest of goodness.

CHAPTER **4**
Drawing Close to God

What is causing the quarrels and fights among you? Isn't it the whole army of evil desires at war within you? 2You want what you don't have, so you scheme and kill to get it. You are jealous for what others have, and you can't possess it, so you fight and quarrel to take it away from them. And yet the reason you don't have what you want is that you don't ask God for it. 3And even when you do ask, you don't get it because your whole motive is wrong—you want only what will give you pleasure.

4You adulterers! Don't you realize that friendship with this world makes you an enemy of God? I say it again, that if your aim is to enjoy

---

OFF AND RUNNING

Control Your Tongue Read JAMES 3:1-12

It has been said that "A lie is halfway around the world while truth is still putting its shoes on." This illustrates the power of malicious speech. One unfounded rumor, one careless remark, one morsel of gossip can cause the greatest devastation. How correct James was when he wrote that the tongue is a flame of fire and full of wickedness.

Unfortunately, it is the sins of the tongue—backbiting, gossip, and tearing down another person—that we often excuse. We think that because we do not murder, commit adultery, or steal we are basically good people. But James makes it clear that certain kinds of speech are wrong. The content of a Christian's conversation should reflect what has happened in his or her heart. After all, part of the fruit, or evidence, of the Holy Spirit's presence in our lives is self-control (see Galatians 5:22-23, p. 1020). The person who has no control over his or her tongue is usually "out of control" in other areas of life. But the person who has discipline over this area of life has yielded to the control of the Holy Spirit and will undoubtedly be able to keep other areas of his or her life in check as well.

For the next note on "Conversation," turn to p. 804.

this world, you can't be a friend of God. 5What do you think the Scriptures mean when they say that the Holy Spirit, whom God has placed within us, jealously longs for us to be faithful*? 6He gives us more and more strength to stand against such evil desires. As the Scriptures say,

"God sets himself against the proud,
but he shows favor to the humble."*

7So humble yourselves before God. Resist the Devil, and he will flee from you. 8Draw close to God, and God will draw close to you. Wash your hands, you sinners; purify your hearts, you hypocrites. 9Let there be tears for the wrong things you have done. Let there be sorrow and deep grief. Let there be sadness instead of laughter, and gloom instead of joy. 10When you bow down before the Lord and admit your dependence on him, he will lift you up and give you honor.

Warning against Judging Others

11Don't speak evil against each other, my dear brothers and sisters.* If you criticize each other and condemn each other, then you are criticizing and condemning God's law. But you are not a judge who can decide whether the law is right or wrong. Your job is to obey it. 12God alone, who made the law, can rightly judge among us. He alone has the power to save or to destroy. So what right do you have to condemn your neighbor?

Warning about Self-Confidence

13Look here, you people who say, "Today or tomorrow we are going to a certain town and will stay there a year. We will do business there and make a profit." 14How do you know what will happen tomorrow? For your life is like the morning fog—it's here a little while, then it's gone. 15What you ought to say is, "If the Lord wants us to, we will live and do this or that." 16Otherwise you will be boasting about your own plans, and all such boasting is evil.

17Remember, it is sin to know what you ought to do and then not do it.

CHAPTER **5**
Warning to the Rich
Look here, you rich people, weep and groan with anguish because of all the terrible troubles ahead of you. 2Your wealth is rotting away, and

4:5 Or *the spirit that God placed within us tends to envy, or the Holy Spirit, whom God has placed within us, opposes our envy.* 4:6 Prov 3:34.
4:11 Greek *brothers.* 5:3 Or *will eat your flesh like fire.*

your fine clothes are moth-eaten rags. 3Your gold and silver have become worthless. The very wealth you were counting on will eat away your flesh in hell.* This treasure you have accumulated will stand as evidence against you on the day of judgment. 4For listen! Hear the cries of the field workers whom you have cheated of

---

Resist the Devil Read JAMES 4:7-8

Satan recognizes the value of getting a foothold in the realm of our thoughts. He knows that sin is not merely a matter of actions and deeds, but something within the heart and the mind that eventually leads to the sinful action. Here are four practical and effective ways to "resist" the Devil and his temptations:

1. Submit Yourself to God. When you submit yourself to God, you are acknowledging his authority in your life. Because God is holy, which means pure and without sin, he will help you live a life that is pleasing to him. But in order to do this, you must submit to his authority.

2. Resist the Devil. To resist the Devil means to not give in to temptation when it presents itself. Giving in to temptation is an open invitation for the Devil and his demons to continually tempt you. But if you resist giving in to sin, the Devil will flee from you, meaning that he will give up tempting you for the time being.

3. Draw Close to God. The closer you get to God, the more you distance yourself from your old partner, the Devil. And the more time you spend with the Lord, through Bible study and prayer, the less likely you will be to fall. As Psalm 16:8 says, "I am always thinking of the LORD; and because he is so near, I never need to stumble or fall."

4. Wash Your Hands and Purify Your Hearts. This set of instructions is a call to repentance for all those who are harboring sin in their life. To harbor sin in your life is to give the Devil an opportunity to work in you and through you. But God is the one who should work in your life, not the Devil. If you are harboring sin in any area of your life, stop doing it, confess it to God, and ask him to forgive you and then work through you.

For the next note on "Resist Temptation," turn to p. 995.

What Do Demons Believe? Read JAMES 2:19

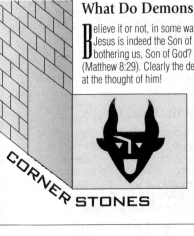

Believe it or not, in some ways demons are quite orthodox in their beliefs. They recognize that Jesus is indeed the Son of God. In Matthew's Gospel, the demons say to Jesus, "Why are you bothering us, Son of God? You have no right to torture us before God's appointed time!" (Matthew 8:29). Clearly the demons understand Jesus' awesome power—and they shudder in fear at the thought of him!

Interestingly enough, many people today do not even accept that Jesus is God's Son. Yet, even if you do believe in God, these verses show that it is not enough to keep you from going to hell. Belief without obedience is worthless. Those who settle for less than a total commitment to Christ may find themselves in the company of the demons at the time of judgment.

For the next note on "What Are Demons?" turn to p. 950.

CORNER STONES

---

their pay. The wages you held back cry out against you. The cries of the reapers have reached the ears of the Lord Almighty.

⁵You have spent your years on earth in luxury, satisfying your every whim. Now your hearts are nice and fat, ready for the slaughter. ⁶You have condemned and killed good people who had no power to defend themselves against you.

Patience in Suffering

⁷Dear brothers and sisters,* you must be patient as you wait for the Lord's return. Consider the farmers who eagerly look for the rains in the fall and in the spring. They patiently wait for the precious harvest to ripen. ⁸You, too, must be patient. And take courage, for the coming of the Lord is near.

⁹Don't grumble about each other, my brothers and sisters, or God will judge you. For look! The great Judge is coming. He is standing at the door!

¹⁰For examples of patience in suffering, dear brothers and sisters, look at the prophets who spoke in the name of the Lord. ¹¹We give great honor to those who endure under suffering. Job is an example of a man who endured patiently. From his experience we see how the Lord's plan finally ended in good, for he is full of tenderness and mercy.

¹²But most of all, my brothers and sisters, never take an oath, by heaven or earth or any-

5:7 Greek *brothers;* also in 5:9, 10, 12, 19.

thing else. Just say a simple yes or no, so that you will not sin and be condemned for it.

The Power of Prayer

¹³Are any among you suffering? They should keep on praying about it. And those who have reason to be thankful should continually sing praises to the Lord.

¹⁴Are any among you sick? They should call for the elders of the church and have them pray over them, anointing them with oil in the name of the Lord. ¹⁵And their prayer offered in faith will heal the sick, and the Lord will make them well. And anyone who has committed sins will be forgiven.

¹⁶Confess your sins to each other and pray for each other so that you may be healed. The earnest prayer of a righteous person has great power and wonderful results. ¹⁷Elijah was as human as we are, and yet when he prayed earnestly that no rain would fall, none fell for the next three and a half years! ¹⁸Then he prayed for rain, and down it poured. The grass turned green, and the crops began to grow again.

Restore Wandering Believers

¹⁹My dear brothers and sisters, if anyone among you wanders away from the truth and is brought back again, ²⁰you can be sure that the one who brings that person back will save that sinner from death and bring about the forgiveness of many sins.

1 Peter

CHAPTER 1

Greetings from Peter

This letter is from Peter, an apostle of Jesus Christ.

I am writing to God's chosen people who are living as foreigners in the lands of Pontus, Galatia, Cappadocia, the province of Asia, and Bithynia. 2God the Father chose you long ago, and the Spirit has made you holy. As a result, you have obeyed Jesus Christ and are cleansed by his blood.

May you have more and more of God's special favor and wonderful peace.

The Hope of Eternal Life

3All honor to the God and Father of our Lord Jesus Christ, for it is by his boundless mercy that God has given us the privilege of being born again. Now we live with a wonderful expectation because Jesus Christ rose again from the dead. 4For God has reserved a priceless inheritance for his children. It is kept in heaven for you, pure and undefiled, beyond the reach of change and decay. 5And God, in his mighty power, will protect you until you receive this salvation, because you are trusting him. It will be revealed on the last day for all to see. 6So be truly glad!* There is wonderful joy ahead, even though it is necessary for you to endure many trials for a while.

7These trials are only to test your faith, to show that it is strong and pure. It is being tested as fire tests and purifies gold—and your faith is far more precious to God than mere gold. So if your faith remains strong after being tried by fiery trials, it will bring you much praise and glory and honor on the day when Jesus Christ is revealed to the whole world.

8You love him even though you have never seen him. Though you do not see him, you trust him; and even now you are happy with a glorious, inexpressible joy. 9Your reward for trusting him will be the salvation of your souls.

10This salvation was something the prophets wanted to know more about. They prophesied about this gracious salvation prepared for you, even though they had many questions as to what it all could mean. 11They wondered what the Spirit of Christ within them was talking about when he told them in advance about Christ's suffering and his great glory afterward. They wondered when and to whom all this would happen.

12They were told that these things would not happen during their lifetime, but many years later, during yours. And now this Good News has been announced by those who preached to you in the power of the Holy Spirit sent from heaven. It is all so wonderful that even the angels are eagerly watching these things happen.

A Call to Holy Living

13So think clearly and exercise self-control. Look forward to the special blessings that will come to you at the return of Jesus Christ. 14Obey God because you are his children. Don't slip back into your old ways of doing evil; you didn't know any better then. 15But now you must be holy in everything you do, just as God—who chose you to be his children—is holy. 16For he himself has said, "You must be holy because I am holy."*

17And remember that the heavenly Father to whom you pray has no favorites when he judges. He will judge or reward you according to what you do. So you must live in reverent fear of him during your time as foreigners here on earth. 18For you know that God paid a ransom to save

1:6 Or *So you are truly glad.*   1:16 Lev 11:44-45; 19:2; 20:7.

How the Holy Spirit Works with the Father and the Son
Read 1 PETER 1:2

The Holy Spirit has the distinct honor of being one of the three members of the Trinity—the other two members being God the Father and Jesus Christ, his Son. This particular verse shows how the Holy Spirit works with the Father and the Son in the life of a believer:

- The Father chooses us and makes us his children.
- Jesus redeems us, having died for us while we were still sinners.
- The Holy Spirit draws us to the Lord and continues to work in our lives to make us pleasing to God.

As you can see, all three members of the Trinity work in concert to bring us into a relationship with God. For that reason, we see that the Holy Spirit is indeed an integral part of what has been called "the Godhead."

For the next note on "Who Is the Holy Spirit?" turn to p. 1024.

CORNER STONES

---

you from the empty life you inherited from your ancestors. And the ransom he paid was not mere gold or silver. ¹⁹He paid for you with the precious lifeblood of Christ, the sinless, spotless Lamb of God. ²⁰God chose him for this purpose long before the world began, but now in these final days, he was sent to the earth for all to see. And he did this for you.

²¹Through Christ you have come to trust in God. And because God raised Christ from the dead and gave him great glory, your faith and hope can be placed confidently in God. ²²Now you can have sincere love for each other as brothers and sisters* because you were cleansed from your sins when you accepted the truth of the Good News. So see to it that you really do love each other intensely with all your hearts.*

²³For you have been born again. Your new life did not come from your earthly parents because the life they gave you will end in death. But this new life will last forever because it comes from the eternal, living word of God. ²⁴As the prophet says,

"People are like grass that dies away;
    their beauty fades as quickly as the
        beauty of wildflowers.
The grass withers,
    and the flowers fall away.
²⁵ But the word of the Lord will last forever."*

And that word is the Good News that was preached to you.

CHAPTER 2

So get rid of all malicious behavior and deceit. Don't just pretend to be good! Be done with hypocrisy and jealousy and backstabbing. ²You must crave pure spiritual milk so that you can grow into the fullness of your salvation. Cry out for this nourishment as a baby cries for milk, ³now that you have had a taste of the Lord's kindness.

Living Stones for God's House

⁴Come to Christ, who is the living cornerstone of God's temple. He was rejected by the people, but he is precious to God who chose him.

⁵And now God is building you, as living stones, into his spiritual temple. What's more, you are God's holy priests, who offer the spiritual sacrifices that please him because of Jesus Christ. ⁶As the Scriptures express it,

"I am placing a stone in Jerusalem,*
    a chosen cornerstone,
and anyone who believes in him
    will never be disappointed.*"

⁷Yes, he is very precious to you who believe. But for those who reject him,

"The stone that was rejected by the builders
    has now become the cornerstone."*

⁸And the Scriptures also say,

"He is the stone that makes people stumble,
    the rock that will make them fall."*

1:22a Greek *can have brotherly love.* **1:22b** Some manuscripts read *with a pure heart.* **1:24-25** Isa 40:6-8. **2:6a** Greek *in Zion.* **2:6b** Or *will never be put to shame.* Isa 28:16. **2:7** Ps 118:22. **2:8** Isa 8:14.

They stumble because they do not listen to God's word or obey it, and so they meet the fate that has been planned for them.

⁹But you are not like that, for you are a chosen people. You are a kingdom of priests, God's holy nation, his very own possession. This is so you can show others the goodness of God, for he called you out of the darkness into his wonderful light.

¹⁰ "Once you were not a people;
  now you are the people of God.
Once you received none of God's mercy;
  now you have received his mercy."*

¹¹Dear brothers and sisters, you are foreigners and aliens here. So I warn you to keep away from evil desires because they fight against your very souls. ¹²Be careful how you live among your unbelieving neighbors. Even if they accuse you of doing wrong, they will see your honorable behavior, and they will believe and give honor to God when he comes to judge the world.*

Respecting People in Authority

¹³For the Lord's sake, accept all authority—the king as head of state, ¹⁴and the officials he has appointed. For the king has sent them to punish all who do wrong and to honor those who do right.

¹⁵It is God's will that your good lives should silence those who make foolish accusations against you. ¹⁶You are not slaves; you are free. But your freedom is not an excuse to do evil. You are free to live as God's slaves. ¹⁷Show respect for everyone. Love your Christian brothers and sisters.* Fear God. Show respect for the king.

Slaves

¹⁸You who are slaves must accept the authority of your masters. Do whatever they tell you—not only if they are kind and reasonable, but even if they are harsh. ¹⁹For God is pleased with you when, for the sake of your conscience, you patiently endure unfair treatment. ²⁰Of course, you get no credit for being patient if you are beaten for doing wrong. But if you suffer for doing right and are patient beneath the blows, God is pleased with you.

²¹This suffering is all part of what God has called you to. Christ, who suffered for you, is your example. Follow in his steps. ²²He never sinned, and he never deceived anyone. ²³He

2:10 Hos 1:6, 9; 2:23. 2:12 Or *on the day of visitation.* 2:17 Greek *Love the brotherhood.*

did not retaliate when he was insulted. When he suffered, he did not threaten to get even. He left his case in the hands of God, who always judges fairly. ²⁴He personally carried away our sins in his own body on the cross so we can be dead to sin and live for what is right. You have been healed by his wounds! ²⁵Once you were wandering like lost sheep. But now you have turned to your Shepherd, the Guardian of your souls.

Trials Sharpen Our Faith
Read 1 PETER 1:3-7

God has selected you for a choice work. But before he can use you, he must toughen the grain of your life. He does this by allowing you to go through difficulties so that your faith can be tested and purified. While this process may not be enjoyable, this passage of Scripture gives us four insights into what we should remember during the testing of our faith, so that our faith will be stronger in the end:

1. Remember *Whose* You Are. You are God's child (verse 3).

2. Remember *What* God Has Promised You. God has promised you the priceless gift of eternal life (verse 4).

3. Remember *Who* Will See You Through. God will protect you until you reach your final destination: heaven (verses 5-6).

4. Remember *Why* God Lets You Go through Trials. God wants to test the genuineness of your faith so that your life will result in praise and glory when Jesus returns (verse 7).

Although it is great to spend time on a "spiritual mountaintop," so to speak, we cannot stay there forever. More often than not, at the bottom of that mountain lies cold, hard reality. Yet fruit grows best in the "valleys" (the hard times of life), not on the mountaintops (when everything is going well). Our greatest character development takes place when we take what we have learned on the mountaintop and put it into practice in the valley.

For the next note on "Have Courage in Trials," turn to p. 1005.

Knowing and Trusting God Is the Source of Inexpressible Joy
Read 1 PETER 1:8

Many people today are seeking joy and happiness but are not finding it. Perhaps they don't understand what happiness really is. At best, they will only find fleeting happiness from possessions, pleasures, or accomplishments. But the joy God gives is not merely some emotional feeling. It is not affected by our circumstances. In fact, it is an unchanging, natural by-product of our faith in Jesus Christ.

As you trust in Jesus and look forward to his return, you will be filled with an "inexpressible joy." It won't be just some sort of emotional high, but it will be a deep, supernatural experience of contentedness based upon the fact that your life is right with God. And this lasting joy and happiness will sustain you for the rest of your life.

For the next note on "Joy," turn to p. 530.

CORNER STONES

CHAPTER **3**

Wives

In the same way, you wives must accept the authority of your husbands, even those who refuse to accept the Good News. Your godly lives will speak to them better than any words. They will be won over ²by watching your pure, godly behavior.

³Don't be concerned about the outward beauty that depends on fancy hairstyles, expensive jewelry, or beautiful clothes. ⁴You should be known for the beauty that comes from within, the unfading beauty of a gentle and quiet spirit, which is so precious to God. ⁵That is the way the holy women of old made themselves beautiful. They trusted God and accepted the authority of their husbands. ⁶For instance, Sarah obeyed her husband, Abraham, when she called him her master. You are her daughters when you do what is right without fear of what your husbands might do.

Husbands

⁷In the same way, you husbands must give honor to your wives. Treat her with understanding as you live together. She may be weaker than you are, but she is your equal partner in God's gift of new life. If you don't treat her as you should, your prayers will not be heard.

All Christians

⁸Finally, all of you should be of one mind, full of sympathy toward each other, loving one another with tender hearts and humble minds. ⁹Don't repay evil for evil. Don't retaliate when people say unkind things about you. Instead, pay them back with a blessing. That is what God wants you to do, and he will bless you for it. ¹⁰For the Scriptures say,

> "If you want a happy life and good days,
>> keep your tongue from speaking evil,
>> and keep your lips from telling lies.
> ¹¹ Turn away from evil and do good.
>> Work hard at living in peace with others.
> ¹² The eyes of the Lord watch over those who
>> do right,
>> and his ears are open to their prayers.

OFF AND RUNNING
Never Use Vulgar Speech Read 1 PETER 3:10

One thing that should certainly change when we come to Christ is the way we talk. If we continue using God's name in vain or keep telling dirty jokes, something is not right. Proverbs 8:13 says, "All who fear the LORD will hate evil." That includes vulgar speech. But when we become indifferent to the way we speak (or the way others speak around us), we are downplaying the destructiveness of sin and doing a disservice to the Lord.

But the Lord turns his face
against those who do evil."*

Suffering for Doing Good

13Now, who will want to harm you if you are eager to do good? 14But even if you suffer for doing what is right, God will reward you for it. So don't be afraid and don't worry. 15Instead, you must worship Christ as Lord of your life. And if you are asked about your Christian hope, always be ready to explain it. 16But you must do this in a gentle and respectful way. Keep your conscience clear. Then if people speak evil against you, they will be ashamed when they see what a good life you live because you belong to Christ. 17Remember, it is better to suffer for doing good, if that is what God wants, than to suffer for doing wrong!

18Christ also suffered when he died for our sins once for all time. He never sinned, but he died for sinners that he might bring us safely home to God. He suffered physical death, but he was raised to life in the Spirit.*

19So he went and preached to the spirits in prison—20those who disobeyed God long ago when God waited patiently while Noah was building his boat. Only eight people were saved from drowning in that terrible flood.* 21And this is a picture of baptism, which now saves you by the power of Jesus Christ's resurrection. Baptism is not a removal of dirt from your body; it is an appeal to God from* a clean conscience.

22Now Christ has gone to heaven. He is seated in the place of honor next to God, and all the angels and authorities and powers are bowing before him.

CHAPTER **4**
Living for God

So then, since Christ suffered physical pain, you must arm yourselves with the same attitude he had, and be ready to suffer, too. For if you are willing to suffer for Christ, you have decided to stop sinning. 2And you won't spend the rest of your life chasing after evil desires, but you will be anxious to do the will of God. 3You have had enough in the past of the evil things that godless people enjoy—their immorality and lust, their feasting and drunkenness and wild parties, and their terrible worship of idols.

4Of course, your former friends are very surprised when you no longer join them in the wicked things they do, and they say evil things about you. 5But just remember that they will have to face God, who will judge everyone, both the living and the dead. 6That is why the Good News was preached even to those who have died—so that although their bodies were punished with death, they could still live in the spirit as God does.

7The end of the world is coming soon. Therefore, be earnest and disciplined in your prayers. 8Most important of all, continue to show deep love for each other, for love covers a multitude of sins. 9Cheerfully share your home with those who need a meal or a place to stay.

10God has given gifts to each of you from his great variety of spiritual gifts. Manage them well so that God's generosity can flow through you. 11Are you called to be a speaker? Then speak as though God himself were speaking through you. Are you called to help others? Do it with all the strength and energy that God supplies. Then God will be given glory in everything through Jesus Christ. All glory and power belong to him forever and ever. Amen.

Suffering for Being a Christian

12Dear friends, don't be surprised at the fiery trials you are going through, as if something strange were happening to you. 13Instead, be very glad—because these trials will make you partners with Christ in his suffering, and afterward you will have the wonderful joy of sharing his glory when it is displayed to all the world.

3:10-12 Ps 34:12-16. 3:18 Or *spirit.* 3:20 Greek *saved through water.* 3:21 Or *for.*

If you find that this area is a trouble spot for you, commit it to God, and he will begin by cleaning up your thoughts. Then consciously replace that coarse language with praise and thankfulness to God for his goodness. As you focus upon God's goodness, your mind will be less filled with the perverse and wicked thoughts of this world.

For the next note on "Conversation," turn to p. 1050.

Our Conduct Should Cause Others to Glorify Christ
Read 1 PETER 2:9-12

Have you ever felt like your life wasn't really important in the grand scheme of things? Have you ever wondered if it was possible to make a difference in the world around you? These verses show that you can—and should—play a significant role in this world.

Remember Who You Are. First, think about who you are. Christians need to be different than those who do not know the Lord. Your godly lifestyle, priorities, and outlook should set you apart from nonbelievers.

Make a Difference. We are not to isolate ourselves from the world. God has placed us in this world so that our lives can have an impact on the people with whom we come into contact. Our Christian character and lifestyle will expose those who are living an ungodly life and confront them with the life-changing message of the gospel.

In many ways, the holiest moment of a church service is when God's people go out the doors of the church and into the world. That is when your godly living will cause people to ask, "What makes you different?"

Some people may criticize, ridicule, or persecute you for living a godly life. Others, however, may come to know Jesus as a result of your faithful obedience to God's Word. If they do, they will glorify God for your testimony and their newfound salvation.

For the next note on "Honesty and Integrity," turn to p. 1066.

CORNER STONES

---

¹⁴Be happy if you are insulted for being a Christian, for then the glorious Spirit of God will come upon you. ¹⁵If you suffer, however, it must not be for murder, stealing, making trouble, or prying into other people's affairs. ¹⁶But it is no shame to suffer for being a Christian. Praise God for the privilege of being called by his wonderful name! ¹⁷For the time has come for judgment, and it must begin first among God's own children. And if even we Christians must be judged, what terrible fate awaits those who have never believed God's Good News? ¹⁸And

"If the righteous are barely saved,
    what chance will the godless and sinners
        have?"*

¹⁹So if you are suffering according to God's will, keep on doing what is right, and trust yourself to the God who made you, for he will never fail you.

CHAPTER **5**
Advice for Elders and Young Men
And now, a word to you who are elders in the churches. I, too, am an elder and a witness to the sufferings of Christ. And I, too, will share his glory and his honor when he returns. As a fellow elder,

this is my appeal to you: ²Care for the flock of God entrusted to you. Watch over it willingly, not grudgingly—not for what you will get out of it, but because you are eager to serve God. ³Don't lord it over the people assigned to your care, but lead them by your good example. ⁴And when the head Shepherd comes, your reward will be a never-ending share in his glory and honor.

⁵You younger men, accept the authority of the elders. And all of you, serve each other in humility, for

"God sets himself against the proud,
    but he shows favor to the humble."*

⁶So humble yourselves under the mighty power of God, and in his good time he will honor you. ⁷Give all your worries and cares to God, for he cares about what happens to you.

⁸Be careful! Watch out for attacks from the Devil, your great enemy. He prowls around like a roaring lion, looking for some victim to devour. ⁹Take a firm stand against him, and be strong in your faith. Remember that your Christian brothers and sisters* all over the world are going through the same kind of suffering you are.

¹⁰In his kindness God called you to his eter-

4:18 Prov 11:31.   5:5 Prov 3:34.   5:9 Greek *your brothers.*

nal glory by means of Jesus Christ. After you have suffered a little while, he will restore, support, and strengthen you, and he will place you on a firm foundation. ¹¹All power is his forever and ever. Amen.

Peter's Final Greetings

¹²I have written this short letter to you with the help of Silas,* whom I consider a faithful brother. My purpose in writing is to encourage you and assure you that the grace of God is with you no matter what happens.

¹³Your sister church here in Rome* sends you greetings, and so does my son Mark. ¹⁴Greet each other in Christian love.*

Peace be to all of you who are in Christ.

5:12 Greek *Silvanus.*   5:13 Greek *The elect one in Babylon.* Babylon was probably a code name for Rome.   5:14 Greek *with a kiss of love.*

2 Peter

Greetings from Peter

This letter is from Simon* Peter, a slave and apostle of Jesus Christ.

I am writing to all of you who share the same precious faith we have, faith given to us by Jesus Christ, our God and Savior, who makes us right with God. ²May God bless you with his special favor and wonderful peace as you come to know Jesus, our God and Lord,* better and better.

Growing in the Knowledge of God

³As we know Jesus better, his divine power gives us everything we need for living a godly life. He has called us to receive his own glory and goodness! ⁴And by that same mighty power, he has given us all of his rich and wonderful promises. He has promised that you will escape the decadence all around you caused by evil desires and that you will share in his divine nature.

⁵So make every effort to apply the benefits of these promises to your life. Then your faith will produce a life of moral excellence. A life of moral excellence leads to knowing God better. ⁶Knowing God leads to self-control. Self-control leads to patient endurance, and patient endurance leads to godliness. ⁷Godliness leads to love for other Christians,* and finally you will grow to have genuine love for everyone. ⁸The more you grow like this, the more you will become productive and useful in your knowledge of our Lord Jesus Christ. ⁹But those who fail to develop these virtues are blind or, at least, very shortsighted. They have already forgotten that God has cleansed them from their old life of sin.

¹⁰So, dear brothers and sisters,* work hard to prove that you really are among those God has called and chosen. Doing this, you will never stumble or fall away. ¹¹And God will open wide the gates of heaven for you to enter into the eternal Kingdom of our Lord and Savior Jesus Christ.

Paying Attention to Scripture

¹²I plan to keep on reminding you of these things—even though you already know them and are standing firm in the truth. ¹³Yes, I believe I should keep on reminding you of these things as long as I live. ¹⁴But the Lord Jesus Christ has shown me that my days here on earth are numbered and I am soon to die.* ¹⁵So I will work hard to make these things clear to you. I want you to remember them long after I am gone.

¹⁶For we were not making up clever stories when we told you about the power of our Lord Jesus Christ and his coming again. We have seen his majestic splendor with our own eyes. ¹⁷And he received honor and glory from God the Father when God's glorious, majestic voice called down from heaven, "This is my beloved Son; I am fully pleased with him." ¹⁸We ourselves heard the voice when we were there with him on the holy mountain.

¹⁹Because of that, we have even greater confidence in the message proclaimed by the prophets. Pay close attention to what they wrote, for their words are like a light shining in a dark place—until the day Christ appears and his brilliant light shines in your hearts.* ²⁰Above all, you must understand that no prophecy in Scripture ever came from the prophets themselves* ²¹or because they wanted to prophesy. It was the Holy Spirit who moved the prophets to speak from God.

1:1 Greek *Simeon.*   1:2 Or *come to know God and Jesus our Lord.*   1:7 Greek *brotherly love.*   1:10 Greek *brothers.*   1:14 Greek *I must soon put off this earthly tent.*   1:19 Or *until the day dawns and the morning star rises in your hearts.*   1:20 Or *is a matter of one's own interpretation.*

God Is Loving and Just Read 2 PETER 3:3-9

The scoffers described in this passage mistook Christ's delayed return to earth to mean that there would be no final judgment at all. Because everything "remained exactly the same since the world was first created," they not only doubted Christ's return but forgot about God's judgment in the past. More importantly, these scoffers overlooked God's love and mercy. It is for their sake that God is restraining his judgment because "he does not want anyone to perish."

This passage shows two important and seemingly contradictory aspects of God's character: love and justice. The Bible tells us that God is love. In spite of his extensive knowledge of our sinfulness and unworthiness, he has declared, "I have loved you, my people, with an everlasting love. With unfailing love I have drawn you to myself" (Jeremiah 31:3). One of the clearest demonstrations of his love is found at the cross on which Jesus died for us: "But God showed his great love for us by sending Christ to die for us while we were still sinners" (Romans 5:8).

God's love, however, is often misunderstood. Many think that because he loves us, he won't judge us. But his love for us does not negate the fact that he is also just. Scripture clearly and repeatedly makes the point that only the godly will see his face (see Psalm 11:7, p. 466). Therefore, we can be certain that our sins must be dealt with. For those who have accepted God's gift of salvation—Jesus' death on the cross—their sins have been forgiven. For those who haven't accepted this gift, God's judgment is certain.

Every day is another opportunity for nonbelievers to come to faith in Jesus Christ. It is also evidence of the tremendous love God has for his creation. In his holiness God is unapproachable, but in his love he approaches us. The next time you are tempted to doubt God's tender love for you, just take a long, hard look at the cross, and remember that it was not the nails that held Jesus there, but his love for you and others!

For the next note on "Who Is God?" turn to p. 948.

CORNER STONES

CHAPTER **2**

The Danger of False Teachers

But there were also false prophets in Israel, just as there will be false teachers among you. They will cleverly teach their destructive heresies about God and even turn against their Master who bought them. Theirs will be a swift and terrible end. ²Many will follow their evil teaching and shameful immorality. And because of them, Christ and his true way will be slandered. ³In their greed they will make up clever lies to get hold of your money. But God condemned them long ago, and their destruction is on the way.

⁴For God did not spare even the angels when they sinned; he threw them into hell,* in gloomy caves* and darkness until the judgment day. ⁵And God did not spare the ancient world—except for Noah and his family of seven. Noah warned the world of God's righteous judgment. Then God destroyed the whole world of ungodly people with a vast flood. ⁶Later, he turned the cities of Sodom and Gomorrah into heaps of ashes and swept them off the face of the earth. He made them an example of what will happen to ungodly people. ⁷But at the same time, God rescued Lot out of Sodom because he was a good man who was sick of all the immorality and wickedness around him. ⁸Yes, he was a righteous man who was distressed by the wickedness he saw and heard day after day.

⁹So you see, the Lord knows how to rescue godly people from their trials, even while punishing the wicked right up until the day of judgment. ¹⁰He is especially hard on those who follow their own evil, lustful desires and who despise authority. These people are proud and arrogant, daring even to scoff at the glorious ones* without so much as trembling. ¹¹But the angels, even though they are far greater in power and strength than these false

2:4a Greek *Tartaros.*   2:4b Some manuscripts read *chains of gloom.*   2:10 *The glorious ones* are probably evil angels; also in 2:11.

teachers, never speak out disrespectfully against* the glorious ones.

¹²These false teachers are like unthinking animals, creatures of instinct, who are born to be caught and killed. They laugh at the terrifying powers they know so little about, and they will be destroyed along with them. ¹³Their destruction is their reward for the harm they have done. They love to indulge in evil pleasures in broad daylight. They are a disgrace and a stain among you. They revel in deceitfulness while they feast with you. ¹⁴They commit adultery with their eyes, and their lust is never satisfied. They make a game of luring unstable people into sin. They train themselves to be greedy; they are doomed and cursed. ¹⁵They have wandered off the right road and followed the way of Balaam son of Beor,* who loved to earn money by doing wrong. ¹⁶But Balaam was stopped from his mad course when his donkey rebuked him with a human voice.

¹⁷These people are as useless as dried-up springs of water or as clouds blown away by the wind—promising much and delivering nothing. They are doomed to blackest darkness. ¹⁸They brag about themselves with empty, foolish boasting. With lustful desire as their bait, they lure back into sin those who have just escaped from such wicked living. ¹⁹They promise freedom, but they themselves are slaves to sin and corruption. For you are a slave to whatever controls you. ²⁰And when people escape from the wicked ways of the world by learning about our Lord and Savior Jesus Christ and then get tangled up with sin and become its slave again, they are worse off than before. ²¹It would be better if they had never known the right way to live than to know it and then reject the holy commandments that were given to them. ²²They make these proverbs come true: "A dog returns to its vomit,"* and "A washed pig returns to the mud."

CHAPTER 3
The Day of the Lord Is Coming

This is my second letter to you, dear friends, and in both of them I have tried to stimulate your wholesome thinking and refresh your memory. ²I want you to remember and understand what the holy prophets said long ago and what our Lord and Savior commanded through your apostles.

³First, I want to remind you that in the last days there will be scoffers who will laugh at the truth and do every evil thing they desire. ⁴This will be their argument: "Jesus promised to come back, did he? Then where is he? Why, as far back as anyone can remember, everything has remained exactly the same since the world was first created."

⁵They deliberately forget that God made the heavens by the word of his command, and he brought the earth up from the water and surrounded it with water. ⁶Then he used the water to destroy the world with a mighty flood. ⁷And God has also commanded that the heavens and the earth will be consumed by fire on the day of judgment, when ungodly people will perish.

⁸But you must not forget, dear friends, that a day is like a thousand years to the Lord, and a thousand years is like a day. ⁹The Lord isn't really being slow about his promise to return, as some people think. No, he is being patient for your sake. He does not want anyone to perish, so he is giving more time for everyone to repent. ¹⁰But the day of the Lord will come as unexpectedly as a thief. Then the heavens will pass away with a terrible noise, and everything in them will disappear in fire, and the earth and everything on it will be exposed to judgment.*

¹¹Since everything around us is going to melt away, what holy, godly lives you should be living! ¹²You should look forward to that day and hurry it along—the day when God will set the heavens on fire and the elements will melt away in the flames. ¹³But we are looking forward to the new heavens and new earth he has promised, a world where everyone is right with God.

¹⁴And so, dear friends, while you are waiting for these things to happen, make every effort to live a pure and blameless life. And be at peace with God.

¹⁵And remember, the Lord is waiting so that people have time to be saved. This is just as our beloved brother Paul wrote to you with the wisdom God gave him—¹⁶speaking of these things in all of his letters. Some of his comments are hard to understand, and those who are ignorant and unstable have twisted his letters around to mean something quite different from what he meant, just as they do the other parts of Scripture—and the result is disaster for them.

2:11 Greek *never bring blasphemous judgment from the Lord against.* 2:15 Other manuscripts read *Bosor.* 2:22 Prov 26:11. 3:10 Some manuscripts read *will be burned up.*

Keep an Eternal Perspective Read 2 PETER 3:10-11

If Jesus were to come today, would you be embarrassed by what you are doing? That is a good question to ask yourself each morning—and especially those times when immoral thoughts pop into your head. Jesus emphasized the importance of keeping a pure heart when he said, "God blesses those whose hearts are pure, for they shall see God" (Matthew 5:8).

A literal definition of the word *pure* is "without hypocrisy," or "single." In other words, Jesus says that we must have a singular, sincere devotion to him in order to see God.

The Bible reminds us that the hope of the coming return of Jesus Christ can have a spiritually purifying effect on our lives: "And all who believe this will keep themselves pure, just as Christ is pure" (1 John 3:3). As we recognize the holiness of God and his imminent return, we should pray along with the psalmist, "Teach me your ways, O LORD, that I may live according to your truth! Grant me purity of heart, that I may honor you" (Psalm 86:11).

For the next note on "Purity," turn to p. 970.

CORNER STONES

Peter's Final Words

17I am warning you ahead of time, dear friends, so that you can watch out and not be carried away by the errors of these wicked people. I don't want you to lose your own secure footing. 18But grow in the special favor and knowledge of our Lord and Savior Jesus Christ.

To him be all glory and honor, both now and forevermore. Amen.

1 John

CHAPTER 1

Introduction

The one who existed from the beginning* is the one we have heard and seen. We saw him with our own eyes and touched him with our own hands. He is Jesus Christ, the Word of life. ²This one who is life from God was shown to us, and we have seen him. And now we testify and announce to you that he is the one who is eternal life. He was with the Father, and then he was shown to us. ³We are telling you about what we ourselves have actually seen and heard, so that you may have fellowship with us. And our fellowship is with the Father and with his Son, Jesus Christ.

⁴We are writing these things so that our* joy will be complete.

Living in the Light

⁵This is the message he has given us to announce to you: God is light and there is no darkness in him at all. ⁶So we are lying if we say we have fellowship with God but go on living in spiritual darkness. We are not living in the truth. ⁷But if we are living in the light of God's presence, just as Christ is, then we have fellowship with each other, and the blood of Jesus, his Son, cleanses us from every sin.

⁸If we say we have no sin, we are only fooling ourselves and refusing to accept the truth. ⁹But if we confess our sins to him, he is faithful and just to forgive us and to cleanse us from every wrong. ¹⁰If we claim we have not sinned, we are calling God a liar and showing that his word has no place in our hearts.

CHAPTER 2

My dear children, I am writing this to you so that you will not sin. But if you do sin, there is someone to plead for you before the Father. He is Jesus Christ, the one who pleases God completely.* ²He is the sacrifice for our sins. He takes away not only our sins but the sins of all the world.

³And how can we be sure that we belong to him? By obeying his commandments. ⁴If someone says, "I belong to God," but doesn't obey God's commandments, that person is a liar and does not live in the truth. ⁵But those who obey God's word really do love him. That is the way to know whether or not we live in him. ⁶Those who say they live in God should live their lives as Christ did.

A New Commandment

⁷Dear friends, I am not writing a new commandment, for it is an old one you have always had, right from the beginning. This commandment—to love one another—is the same message you heard before. ⁸Yet it is also new. This commandment is true in Christ and is true among you, because the darkness is disappearing and the true light is already shining.

⁹If anyone says, "I am living in the light," but hates a Christian brother or sister,* that person is still living in darkness. ¹⁰Anyone who loves other Christians* is living in the light and does not cause anyone to stumble. ¹¹Anyone who hates a Christian brother or sister is living and walking in darkness. Such a person is lost, having been blinded by the darkness.

¹²I am writing to you, my dear children, because your sins have been forgiven because of Jesus.

¹³I am writing to you who are mature

1:1 Greek *What was from the beginning.*   1:4 Some manuscripts read *your.*   2:1 Greek *Jesus Christ, the righteous.*   2:9 Greek *his brother;* also in 2:11.   2:10 Greek *his brother.*

Our Love for Others Mirrors the Condition of Our Heart
Read 1 JOHN 2:9-11

Being a Christian involves more than just vocalizing our love to God. It also means demonstrating God's love to others. Humanly speaking, it is much easier to dislike someone than it is to love him or her. Grudges and resentment come easily. Yet bitterness toward others is a poison. Not only does it affect our relationships with other people, but it spiritually blinds us as well. Worse yet, harboring bitterness toward other people is a sin that can lead to other sins.

If you are having trouble loving others, then you need to learn how to walk "in the light." How do you do that? Verse 6 of this chapter says, "Those who say they live in God should live their lives as Christ did." Take a look at the way you treat the people in your life; then compare your relationships with Jesus' relationships in the Gospels (Matthew, Mark, Luke, and John). Here is a sampling of what you will find:

- Jesus reached out to the unlovable (see Luke 19:1-10, pp. 882-883).
- Jesus gave a second chance to a friend who had let him down (see John 18:25-27, p. 915, and John 21:15-19, pp. 919-920).
- Jesus showed patience toward those who questioned him (see John 20:24-28, p. 919).

- Jesus cared for the sick (see Luke 5:12-16, p. 859).
- Jesus initiated conversations with those whom others despised (see John 4:4-42, pp. 896-897).
- Jesus wept with those who grieved (see John 11:1-44, pp. 905-906).

Ask God to help you love as Jesus loved, and you will see some radical changes in your heart and your life.

For the next note on "Love," turn to p. 1046.

CORNER STONES

---

because you know Christ, the one who is from the beginning.

I am writing to you who are young because you have won your battle with Satan.

¹⁴I have written to you, children, because you have known the Father.

I have written to you who are mature

because you know Christ, the one who is from the beginning.

I have written to you who are young because you are strong with God's word living in your hearts, and you have won your battle with Satan.

¹⁵Stop loving this evil world and all that it offers you, for when you love the world, you show that

---

OFF AND RUNNING
Make Sure Your Friendships Honor God Read 1 JOHN 1:7

What is the key to having a friendship that honors God? First, make sure that you are walking in obedience to God, "living in the light of God's presence." If you are not committed to obeying God, then you will probably make friends with those who also lack this commitment. Any relationship that does not encourage you to live obediently to God and entices you to sin dishonors God.

On the other hand, if you are committed to obeying God, you will seek out friends who are also committed to him. As you walk with those who share the same love for the Lord as you have, you will be filled with joy and have greater impetus to keep from sinning. And your friendships will honor God.

To begin the next topic, turn to p. A37.

you do not have the love of the Father in you. 16For the world offers only the lust for physical pleasure, the lust for everything we see, and pride in our possessions. These are not from the Father. They are from this evil world. 17And this world is fading away, along with everything it craves. But if you do the will of God, you will live forever.

18Dear children, the last hour is here. You have heard that the Antichrist is coming, and already many such antichrists have appeared. From this we know that the end of the world has come. 19These people left our churches because they never really belonged with us; otherwise they would have stayed with us. When they left us, it proved that they do not belong with us. 20But you are not like that, for the Holy Spirit has come upon you,* and all of you know the truth. 21So I am writing to you not because you don't know the truth but because you know the difference between truth and falsehood. 22And who is the great liar? The one who says that Jesus is not the Christ. Such people are antichrists, for they have denied the Father and the Son. 23Anyone who denies the Son doesn't have the Father either. But anyone who confesses the Son has the Father also.

24So you must remain faithful to what you have been taught from the beginning. If you do, you will continue to live in fellowship with the Son and with the Father. 25And in this fellowship we enjoy the eternal life he promised us.

26I have written these things to you because you need to be aware of those who want to lead you astray. 27But you have received the Holy Spirit,* and he lives within you, so you don't need anyone to teach you what is true. For the Spirit teaches you all things, and what he teaches is true—it is not a lie. So continue in what he has taught you, and continue to live in Christ.

28And now, dear children, continue to live in fellowship with Christ so that when he returns, you will be full of courage and not shrink back from him in shame. 29Since we know that God is always right, we also know that all who do what is right are his children.

CHAPTER **3**
Living as Children of God
See how very much our heavenly Father loves us, for he allows us to be called his children, and we really are! But the people who belong to this world don't know God, so they don't under-

2:20 Greek *But you have an anointing from the Holy One.*
2:27 Greek *the anointing.*

stand that we are his children. 2Yes, dear friends, we are already God's children, and we can't even imagine what we will be like when Christ returns. But we do know that when he comes we will be like him, for we will see him as he really is. 3And all who believe this will keep themselves pure, just as Christ is pure.

4Those who sin are opposed to the law of God, for all sin opposes the law of God. 5And you know that Jesus came to take away our sins, for there is no sin in him. 6So if we continue to live in him, we won't sin either. But those who keep on sinning have never known him or understood who he is.

7Dear children, don't let anyone deceive you about this: When people do what is right, it is because they are righteous, even as Christ is righteous. 8But when people keep on sinning, it shows they belong to the Devil, who has been sinning since the beginning. But the Son of God came to destroy these works of the Devil. 9Those who have

A Disciple Walks as Jesus Walked Read 1 JOHN 2:3-6

If you call yourself a disciple, you need to follow in Jesus' footsteps. As verse 6 says, you need to "live [your life] as Christ did." Another translation says that you should "walk as he walked."

Walking implies a steady motion—you put one foot in front of the other, and you keep moving. That is the way we should follow Christ. We need to stick with it and be consistent. How do you practically live as Christ did?

- Make time for God and his Word every single day.
- Spend time in prayer with the Lord throughout the day.
- Take time to be with God's people.

There is a tremendous benefit to the disciple who stays close to Christ. By walking as he walked, the Bible tells us we will have help to keep us from sinning (see 1 John 3:6, p. 1105). For that reason, one of the greatest identifying marks of a disciple is that his or her walk resembles the Master's.

To begin the next topic, turn to p. A31.

Understand the Difference between the True Gospel and a False Gospel Read 1 JOHN 4:1-3

False teachings are not unique to our times. They cropped up in the days of the early church as well. When John wrote this passage, a teaching called Gnosticism (which means "to know") had become popular. It taught that Jesus was a mere human being, born by natural procreation. It also claimed that "the Christ" came upon Jesus at his baptism and left him before his crucifixion. This, of course, was false and unscriptural. Yet it is important to note that this heresy is still taught by some today.

As this text says, we need to "test" these teachings to see if they really come from God. Since false teachers don't carry ID cards, here are three simple questions to ask of anyone you may suspect of being a false teacher:

1. What Is Their Ultimate Hope? Some hope to make a better world. Mormons expect to be equal with God. They also hope that each Mormon couple will be given their own planet to populate. Jehovah's Witnesses believe God will come back to earth at the end of time and establish a paradise here. They hope to live in this paradise on earth. But the hope for the Christian is to spend eternity with Jesus Christ in heaven.

2. What Is the Basis for This Hope? Do they teach that you can only get to heaven by living a good life? Do they say that you obtain salvation by faith in Jesus Christ and by performing certain things or rituals, like baptism, keeping the Sabbath, or other works? You must beware of the "and's." The Bible says, "God saved you by his special favor when you believed. And you can't take credit for this; it is a gift from God. Salvation is not a reward for the good things we have done, so none of us can boast about it" (Ephesians 2:8-9).

3. How Do They View Jesus Christ? Another earmark of a false teacher preaching a false gospel is what he or she claims about the person of Jesus Christ. This is really the central and primary issue. Many cults seek to make their teachings more "palatable" to those in the church by including Jesus Christ in their teachings. They may even use terms like "saved" and "born again," and speak of Jesus dying on the cross. Interestingly enough, some teachings may pass the first two tests but fail this ultimate test, which is believing that Jesus was resurrected from the dead.

Any attempts to cast doubt upon the Bible's sufficiency should be rejected. Any "broadness" that would admit any other way to God outside of Christ is false. To say that Jesus is not the only way to God is to call Jesus a liar! Anytime Jesus, "the unique Son of God," is reduced to merely *"a* son of God" or one of many prophets from God, it is erroneous. The best way to know the false is to be familiar with the true: God's Word, the Bible.

For the next note on "Discernment," turn to p. 946.

CORNER STONES

---

been born into God's family do not sin, because God's life is in them. So they can't keep on sinning, because they have been born of God. ¹⁰So now we can tell who are children of God and who are children of the Devil. Anyone who does not obey God's commands and does not love other Christians* does not belong to God.

Love One Another

¹¹This is the message we have heard from the beginning: We should love one another. ¹²We

must not be like Cain, who belonged to the evil one and killed his brother. And why did he kill him? Because Cain had been doing what was evil, and his brother had been doing what was right. ¹³So don't be surprised, dear brothers and sisters,* if the world hates you.

¹⁴If we love our Christian brothers and sisters, it proves that we have passed from death to eternal life. But a person who has no love is still dead. ¹⁵Anyone who hates another Christian* is really a murderer at heart. And you know that

3:10 Greek *his brother.* **3:13** Greek *brothers;* also in 3:14, 16. **3:15** Greek *his brother.*

How Can I Tell the Difference between True and False Teachings about God? Read 1 JOHN 4:1-2

The Bible tells us that we must be especially careful in these "last days," for the coming Antichrist and false prophet will perform signs and miracles and deceive many (see 2 Thessalonians 2:9-10, pp. 1051-1052).

So how does one tell the true gospel from a counterfeit or false gospel? Here are four tests you can apply to make sure the teachings you hear really come from God:

1. Does the Teaching Recognize Jesus Christ as the Son of God and the Only Way of Salvation? Proper teaching must agree that Jesus Christ is God's unique Son, and that he "became a human being" (verse 2). Most cults deny Christ's deity, recognizing him only as a great teacher or, as Jehovah's Witnesses claim, simply God's first created creature. So find out what this teaching has to say about Jesus.

2. Does the Teaching Agree with Scripture? The apostle Paul commended the Bereans because "they searched the Scriptures day after day to check up on [their statements] to see if they were really teaching the truth" (Acts 17:11). Don't simply take some pastor or teacher's word as gospel without examining it in the light of God's Word first.

3. If Miracles Are Involved, Do They Bring Glory to God or to Someone Else? Remember, God is not the only one who can do miracles. As mentioned above, the Antichrist will deceive many with his miraculous wonders. In the Old Testament, when God enabled Moses to perform miracles in front of Pharaoh to persuade him to release the Hebrews, Pharaoh's own sorcerers—working through the power of the occult—were able to duplicate a number of those miracles (see Exodus 7:10-12, 22, p. 54). While some miracles come from God, others may actually be performed by the Devil himself. Satan is a great imitator. In the last days, "false messiahs and false prophets will rise up and perform great miraculous signs and wonders so as to deceive, if possible, even God's chosen ones" (Matthew 24:24). Do not accept any miracle at face value. Make sure that the person through whom the miracle comes has a strong personal relationship with Jesus Christ (see Matthew 7:21-23, p. 798). More important, be certain the miracle glorifies Jesus Christ and does not contradict what Scripture teaches.

4. Is the Teaching Widely Accepted by the World at Large? Contrary to conventional wisdom, the more popular a teaching is does not make it a more "correct" teaching. For instance, relativism, or the idea that each person can live the way he or she wants to as long as he or she is true to himself or herself, is a popular belief. However, we know that God's Word teaches differently. As shown in this passage, if the message is really from God, the world won't listen to it (1 John 4:6).

The more you study the "real thing"—God's Word—the more you will be able to quickly identify the counterfeits. And remember, "the Spirit who lives in you is greater than the spirit who lives in the world" (1 John 4:4).

BIG QUESTIONS

---

murderers don't have eternal life within them. ¹⁶We know what real love is because Christ gave up his life for us. And so we also ought to give up our lives for our Christian brothers and sisters. ¹⁷But if anyone has enough money to live well and sees a brother or sister in need and refuses to help—how can God's love be in that person?

¹⁸Dear children, let us stop just saying we love each other; let us really show it by our actions. ¹⁹It is by our actions that we know we are living in the truth, so we will be confident when we stand before the Lord, ²⁰even if our hearts condemn us. For God is greater than our hearts, and he knows everything.

²¹Dear friends, if our conscience is clear, we

can come to God with bold confidence. 22And we will receive whatever we request because we obey him and do the things that please him. 23And this is his commandment: We must believe in the name of his Son, Jesus Christ, and love one another, just as he commanded us. 24Those who obey God's commandments live in fellowship with him, and he with them. And we know he lives in us because the Holy Spirit lives in us.

CHAPTER 4
Discerning False Prophets

Dear friends, do not believe everyone who claims to speak by the Spirit. You must test them to see if the spirit they have comes from God. For there are many false prophets in the world. 2This is the way to find out if they have the Spirit of God: If a prophet acknowledges that Jesus Christ became a human being, that person has the Spirit of God. 3If a prophet does not acknowledge Jesus, that person is not from God. Such a person has the spirit of the Antichrist. You have heard that he is going to come into the world, and he is already here.

4But you belong to God, my dear children. You have already won your fight with these false prophets, because the Spirit who lives in you is greater than the spirit who lives in the world. 5These people belong to this world, so they speak from the world's viewpoint, and the world listens to them. 6But we belong to God; that is why those who know God listen to us. If they do not belong to God, they do not listen to us. That is how we know if someone has the Spirit of truth or the spirit of deception.

Loving One Another

7Dear friends, let us continue to love one another, for love comes from God. Anyone who loves is born of God and knows God. 8But anyone who does not love does not know God—for God is love.

9God showed how much he loved us by sending his only Son into the world so that we might have eternal life through him. 10This is real love. It is not that we loved God, but that he loved us and sent his Son as a sacrifice to take away our sins.

11Dear friends, since God loved us that much, we surely ought to love each other. 12No one has ever seen God. But if we love each other, God lives in us, and his love has been brought to full expression through us.

13And God has given us his Spirit as proof that we live in him and he in us. 14Furthermore, we have seen with our own eyes and now testify that the Father sent his Son to be the Savior of the world. 15All who proclaim that Jesus is the Son of God have God living in them, and they live in God. 16We know how much God loves us, and we have put our trust in him.

God is love, and all who live in love live in God, and God lives in them. 17And as we live in God, our love grows more perfect. So we will not be afraid on the day of judgment, but we can face him with confidence because we are like Christ here in this world.

18Such love has no fear because perfect love expels all fear. If we are afraid, it is for fear of judgment, and this shows that his love has not been perfected in us. 19We love each other* as a result of his loving us first.

20If someone says, "I love God," but hates a Christian brother or sister,* that person is a liar; for if we don't love people we can see, how can

4:19 Or We love him; Greek reads We love.   4:20 Greek brother; also in 4:21.

OFF AND RUNNING ▰▰▰

Pray Expecting to Get Answers Read 1 JOHN 5:14-15

Prayer is not getting your will in heaven. It is getting God's will on earth. Prayer is not an argument with God in which you try to persuade him to move things your way. Prayer is an exercise in which his Spirit enables you to move yourself his way. Prayer is not overcoming God's reluctance. It is laying hold of his willingness.

We like to gravitate toward the latter part of these verses. But don't forget the first part. You have to first "stay in Christ" by maintaining a healthy, ongoing relationship with him. When that happens, you will see your will coming in line with his, and your requests will begin to mirror what Christ wants to do in your life and the lives of those around you. At that point, you can be assured that God is listening to you and will answer your prayers.

For the next note on "Prayer Time," turn to p. 938.

we love God, whom we have not seen? ²¹And God himself has commanded that we must love not only him but our Christian brothers and sisters, too.

CHAPTER **5**

Faith in the Son of God

Everyone who believes that Jesus is the Christ is a child of God. And everyone who loves the Father loves his children, too. ²We know we love God's children if we love God and obey his commandments. ³Loving God means keeping his commandments, and really, that isn't difficult. ⁴For every child of God defeats this evil world by trusting Christ to give the victory. ⁵And the ones who win this battle against the world are the ones who believe that Jesus is the Son of God.

⁶And Jesus Christ was revealed as God's Son by his baptism in water and by shedding his blood on the cross*—not by water only, but by water and blood. And the Spirit also gives us the testimony that this is true. ⁷So we have these three witnesses*—⁸the Spirit, the water, and the blood—and all three agree. ⁹Since we believe human testimony, surely we can believe the testimony that comes from God. And God has testified about his Son. ¹⁰All who believe in the Son of God know that this is true. Those who don't believe this are actually calling God a liar because they don't believe what God has testified about his Son.

¹¹And this is what God has testified: He has given us eternal life, and this life is in his Son. ¹²So whoever has God's Son has life; whoever does not have his Son does not have life.

Conclusion

¹³I write this to you who believe in the Son of God, so that you may know you have eternal life. ¹⁴And we can be confident that he will listen to us whenever we ask him for anything in line with his will. ¹⁵And if we know he is listening when we make our requests, we can be sure that he will give us what we ask for.

¹⁶If you see a Christian brother or sister* sinning in a way that does not lead to death, you should pray, and God will give that person life. But there is a sin that leads to death, and I am not saying you should pray for those who commit it. ¹⁷Every wrong is sin, but not all sin leads to death.

¹⁸We know that those who have become part of God's family do not make a practice of sinning, for God's Son holds them securely, and the evil one cannot get his hands on them. ¹⁹We know that we are children of God and that the world around us is under the power and control of the evil one. ²⁰And we know that the Son of God has come, and he has given us understanding so that we can know the true God. And now we are in God because we are in his Son, Jesus Christ. He is the only true God, and he is eternal life.

²¹Dear children, keep away from anything that might take God's place in your hearts.*

5:6 Greek *This is he who came by water and blood.* 5:7 Some very late manuscripts add *in heaven—the Father, the Word, and the Holy Spirit, and these three are one. And we have three witnesses on earth.* 5:16 Greek *your brother.* 5:21 Greek *keep yourselves from idols.*

2 John

Greetings

This letter is from John the Elder.*

It is written to the chosen lady and to her children,* whom I love in the truth, as does everyone else who knows God's truth—²the truth that lives in us and will be in our hearts forever.

³May grace, mercy, and peace, which come from God our Father and from Jesus Christ his Son, be with us who live in truth and love.

Live in the Truth

⁴How happy I was to meet some of your children and find them living in the truth, just as we have been commanded by the Father.

⁵And now I want to urge you, dear lady, that we should love one another. This is not a new commandment, but one we had from the beginning. ⁶Love means doing what God has commanded us, and he has commanded us to love one another, just as you heard from the beginning.

⁷Many deceivers have gone out into the world. They do not believe that Jesus Christ came to earth in a real body. Such a person is a deceiver and an antichrist. ⁸Watch out, so that you do not lose the prize for which we* have been working so hard. Be diligent so that you will receive your full reward. ⁹For if you wander beyond the teaching of Christ, you will not have fellowship with God. But if you continue in the teaching of Christ, you will have fellowship with both the Father and the Son.

¹⁰If someone comes to your meeting and does not teach the truth about Christ, don't invite him into your house or encourage him in any way. ¹¹Anyone who encourages him becomes a partner in his evil work.

Conclusion

¹²Well, I have much more to say to you, but I don't want to say it in a letter. For I hope to visit you soon and to talk with you face to face. Then our joy will be complete.

¹³Greetings from the children of your sister,* chosen by God.

1a Greek *From the elder.* 1b Or *the church God has chosen and her members,* or *the chosen Kyria and her children.* 8 Some manuscripts read *you.* 13 Or *from the members of your sister church.*

3 John

Greetings

This letter is from John the Elder.*

It is written to Gaius, my dear friend, whom I love in the truth.

2 Dear friend, I am praying that all is well with you and that your body is as healthy as I know your soul is. 3 Some of the brothers recently returned and made me very happy by telling me about your faithfulness and that you are living in the truth. 4 I could have no greater joy than to hear that my children live in the truth.

Caring for the Lord's Workers

5 Dear friend, you are doing a good work for God when you take care of the traveling teachers* who are passing through, even though they are strangers to you. 6 They have told the church here of your friendship and your loving deeds. You do well to send them on their way in a manner that pleases God. 7 For they are traveling for the Lord* and accept nothing from those who are not Christians.* 8 So we ourselves should support them so that we may become partners with them for the truth.

9 I sent a brief letter to the church about this, but Diotrephes, who loves to be the leader, does not acknowledge our authority. 10 When I come, I will report some of the things he is doing and the wicked things he is saying about us. He not only refuses to welcome the traveling teachers, he also tells others not to help them. And when they do help, he puts them out of the church.

11 Dear friend, don't let this bad example influence you. Follow only what is good. Remember that those who do good prove that they are God's children, and those who do evil prove that they do not know God. 12 But everyone speaks highly of Demetrius, even truth itself. We ourselves can say the same for him, and you know we speak the truth.

Conclusion

13 I have much to tell you, but I don't want to do it in a letter. 14 For I hope to see you soon, and then we will talk face to face.

15 May God's peace be with you.

Your friends here send you their greetings. Please give my personal greetings to each of our friends there.

1 Greek *From the elder.*   5 Greek *the brothers;* also in verse 10.   7a Greek *the Name.*   7b Greek *from Gentiles.*

Jude

Greetings from Jude

This letter is from Jude, a slave of Jesus Christ and a brother of James.

I am writing to all who are called to live in the love of God the Father and the care of Jesus Christ.

2May you receive more and more of God's mercy, peace, and love.

The Danger of False Teachers

3Dearly loved friends, I had been eagerly planning to write to you about the salvation we all share. But now I find that I must write about something else, urging you to defend the truth of the Good News.* God gave this unchanging truth once for all time to his holy people. 4I say this because some godless people have wormed their way in among you, saying that God's forgiveness allows us to live immoral lives. The fate of such people was determined long ago, for they have turned against our only Master and Lord, Jesus Christ.

5I must remind you—and you know it well—that even though the Lord* rescued the whole nation of Israel from Egypt, he later destroyed every one of those who did not remain faithful. 6And I remind you of the angels who did not stay within the limits of authority God gave them but left the place where they belonged. God has kept them chained in prisons of darkness, waiting for the day of judgment. 7And don't forget the cities of Sodom and Gomorrah and their neighboring towns, which were filled with sexual immorality and every kind of sexual perversion. Those cities were destroyed by fire and are a warning of the eternal fire that will punish all who are evil.

8Yet these false teachers, who claim authority from their dreams, live immoral lives, defy authority, and scoff at the power of the glorious ones.* 9But even Michael, one of the mightiest of the angels, did not dare accuse Satan of blasphemy, but simply said, "The Lord rebuke you." (This took place when Michael was arguing with Satan about Moses' body.) 10But these people mock and curse the things they do not understand. Like animals, they do whatever their instincts tell them, and they bring about their own destruction. 11How terrible it will be for them! For they follow the evil example of Cain, who killed his brother. Like Balaam, they will do anything for money. And like Korah, they will perish because of their rebellion.

12When these people join you in fellowship meals celebrating the love of the Lord, they are like dangerous reefs that can shipwreck you.* They are shameless in the way they care only about themselves. They are like clouds blowing over dry land without giving rain, promising much but producing nothing. They are like trees without fruit at harvesttime. They are not only dead but doubly dead, for they have been pulled out by the roots. 13They are like wild waves of the sea, churning up the dirty foam of their shameful deeds. They are wandering stars, heading for everlasting gloom and darkness.

14Now Enoch, who lived seven generations after Adam, prophesied about these people. He said,

"Look, the Lord is coming
    with thousands of his holy ones.
15 He will bring the people of the world
    to judgment.

3 Greek *to contend for the faith.* 5 Some manuscripts read *Jesus.* 8 *The glorious ones* are probably evil angels. 12 Or *they are contaminants among you,* or *they are stains.*

He will convict the ungodly of all the evil
things
they have done in rebellion
and of all the insults that godless sinners
have spoken against him."*

16These people are grumblers and complainers,
doing whatever evil they feel like. They are loud-
mouthed braggarts, and they flatter others to get
favors in return.

A Call to Remain Faithful

17But you, my dear friends, must remember
what the apostles of our Lord Jesus Christ told
you, 18that in the last times there would be
scoffers whose purpose in life is to enjoy themselves in every evil way imaginable. 19Now they
are here, and they are the ones who are creating
divisions among you. They live by natural instinct because they do not have God's Spirit
living in them.

20But you, dear friends, must continue to
build your lives on the foundation of your holy
faith. And continue to pray as you are directed
by the Holy Spirit.* 21Live in such a way that
God's love can bless you as you wait for the
eternal life that our Lord Jesus Christ in his
mercy is going to give you. 22Show mercy to
those whose faith is wavering. 23Rescue others
by snatching them from the flames of judgment.
There are still others to whom you need to show
mercy, but be careful that you aren't contaminated by their sins.*

A Prayer of Praise

24And now, all glory to God, who is able to keep
you from stumbling, and who will bring you
into his glorious presence innocent of sin and
with great joy. 25All glory to him, who alone is
God our Savior, through Jesus Christ our Lord.
Yes, glory, majesty, power, and authority belong
to him, in the beginning, now, and forevermore.
Amen.

14-15 The quotation comes from the Apocrypha: Enoch 1:9.   **20** Greek *Pray in the Holy Spirit.*   **23** Greek *mercy, hating even the clothing stained by the flesh.*

Revelation

CHAPTER 1

Prologue

This is a revelation from* Jesus Christ, which God gave him concerning the events that will happen soon. An angel was sent to God's servant John so that John could share the revelation with God's other servants. ²John faithfully reported the word of God and the testimony of Jesus Christ—everything he saw.

³God blesses the one who reads this prophecy to the church, and he blesses all who listen to it and obey what it says. For the time is near when these things will happen.

John's Greeting to the Seven Churches

⁴This letter is from John to the seven churches in the province of Asia. Grace and peace from the one who is, who always was, and who is still to come; from the sevenfold Spirit* before his throne; ⁵and from Jesus Christ, who is the faithful witness to these things, the first to rise from the dead, and the commander of all the rulers of the world.

All praise to him who loves us and has freed us from our sins by shedding his blood for us. ⁶He has made us his kingdom and his priests who serve before God his Father. Give to him everlasting glory! He rules forever and ever! Amen!

⁷Look! He comes with the clouds of heaven. And everyone will see him—even those who pierced him. And all the nations of the earth will weep because of him. Yes! Amen!

⁸"I am the Alpha and the Omega—the beginning and the end," says the Lord God. "I am the one who is, who always was, and who is still to come, the Almighty One."

Vision of the Son of Man

⁹I am John, your brother. In Jesus we are partners in suffering and in the Kingdom and in patient endurance. I was exiled to the island of Patmos for preaching the word of God and speaking about Jesus. ¹⁰It was the Lord's Day, and I was worshiping in the Spirit.* Suddenly, I heard a loud voice behind me, a voice that sounded like a trumpet blast. ¹¹It said, "Write down what you see, and send it to the seven churches: Ephesus, Smyrna, Pergamum, Thyatira, Sardis, Philadelphia, and Laodicea."

¹²When I turned to see who was speaking to me, I saw seven gold lampstands. ¹³And standing in the middle of the lampstands was the Son of Man.* He was wearing a long robe with a gold sash across his chest. ¹⁴His head and his hair were white like wool, as white as snow. And his eyes were bright like flames of fire. ¹⁵His feet were as bright as bronze refined in a furnace, and his voice thundered like mighty ocean waves. ¹⁶He held seven stars in his right hand, and a sharp two-edged sword came from his mouth. And his face was as bright as the sun in all its brilliance.

¹⁷When I saw him, I fell at his feet as dead. But he laid his right hand on me and said, "Don't be afraid! I am the First and the Last. ¹⁸I am the living one who died. Look, I am alive forever and ever! And I hold the keys of death and the grave.* ¹⁹Write down what you have seen—both the things that are now happening and the things that will happen later. ²⁰This is the meaning of the seven stars you saw in my right hand and the seven gold lampstands: The seven stars are the angels of* the seven churches, and the seven lampstands are the seven churches.

1:1 Or of. 1:4 Greek the seven spirits. 1:10 Or in spirit. 1:13 Or one who looked like a man; Greek reads one like a son of man.
See Dan 7:13. 1:18 Greek and Hades. 1:20 Or the messengers for.

Jesus Has an Eternal Dominion Read REVELATION 1:4-8

This passage of Scripture confirms two important aspects about Jesus Christ: his majesty and dominion. Yet Jesus is distinctly different than any type of royalty or government we are familiar with. The following six points show that difference:

1. He Is the First to Rise from Death and Die No More. Christ gives us a glimpse of what will happen after we die.

2. He Is Greater than Any King in All the Earth. He is Lord over all creation—no earthly leader can make that claim.

3. He Loves Us and Demonstrated His Love by His Death. Rarely has someone in authority over others offered to die in their place.

4. He Has Set Us Free from Our Sins and Given Us a Place of Honor in His Kingdom. For those of us who have received Jesus into our lives, he has given us a place of tremendous privilege and access to the throne of God.

5. He Will Return Again in Triumph. This king will draw the attention of the entire universe with his return.

6. He Is Eternal. He always has been and always will be. No one else but God could make that claim.

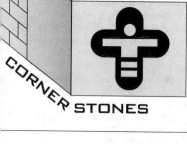

Some people have a rather stereotypical view of Jesus. They picture him as most artists have, with long, flowing hair—perhaps a staff in his hand and a lamb wrapped around his neck. Yet the Bible never does give us a description of Jesus' physical appearance. If it did, we would undoubtedly worship the image instead of the Lord. This description of Christ in Revelation—though it does not give us a physical picture—allows us to see the glorified Christ. And this Christ is full of power and majesty.

CORNER STONES

To begin the next topic, turn to p. A12.

CHAPTER **2**

The Message to the Church in Ephesus

"Write this letter to the angel of* the church in Ephesus. This is the message from the one who holds the seven stars in his right hand, the one who walks among the seven gold lampstands:

² "I know all the things you do. I have seen your hard work and your patient endurance. I know you don't tolerate evil people. You have examined the claims of those who say they are apostles but are not. You have discovered they are liars. ³You have patiently suffered for me without quitting. ⁴But I have this complaint against you. You don't love me or each other as you did at first! ⁵Look how far you have fallen from your first love! Turn back to me again and work as you did at first. If you don't, I will come and remove your lampstand from its place among the churches. ⁶But there is

this about you that is good: You hate the deeds of the immoral Nicolaitans, just as I do.

⁷ "Anyone who is willing to hear should listen to the Spirit and understand what the Spirit is saying to the churches. Everyone who is victorious will eat from the tree of life in the paradise of God.

The Message to the Church in Smyrna

⁸ "Write this letter to the angel of the church in Smyrna. This is the message from the one who is the First and the Last, who died and is alive:

⁹ "I know about your suffering and your poverty—but you are rich! I know the slander of those opposing you. They say they are Jews, but they really aren't because theirs is a synagogue of Satan. ¹⁰Don't be afraid of what you are about to suffer. The Devil will throw some of you into prison

2:1 Or *the messenger for*; also in 2:8, 12, 18.

and put you to the test. You will be persecuted for 'ten days.' Remain faithful even when facing death, and I will give you the crown of life.

11 "Anyone who is willing to hear should listen to the Spirit and understand what the Spirit is saying to the churches. Whoever is victorious will not be hurt by the second death.

The Message to the Church in Pergamum

12 "Write this letter to the angel of the church in Pergamum. This is the message from the one who has a sharp two-edged sword:

13 "I know that you live in the city where that great throne of Satan is located, and yet you have remained loyal to me. And you refused to deny me even when Antipas, my faithful witness, was martyred among you by Satan's followers. 14And yet I have a few complaints against you. You tolerate some among you who are like Balaam, who showed Balak how to trip up the people of Israel. He taught them to worship idols by eating food offered to idols and by committing sexual sin. 15In the same way, you have some Nicolaitans among you—people who follow the same teaching and commit the same sins. 16Repent, or I will come to you suddenly and fight against them with the sword of my mouth.

17 "Anyone who is willing to hear should listen to the Spirit and understand what the Spirit is saying to the churches. Everyone who is victorious will eat of the manna that has been hidden away in heaven. And I will give to each one a white stone, and on the stone will be engraved a new name that no one knows except the one who receives it.

The Message to the Church in Thyatira

18 "Write this letter to the angel of the church in Thyatira. This is the message from the Son of God, whose eyes are bright like flames of fire, whose feet are like polished bronze:

19 "I know all the things you do—your love, your faith, your service, and your patient endurance. And I can see your constant improvement in all these things. 20But I have this complaint against you. You are permitting that woman—that Jezebel who calls herself a prophet—to lead my servants

astray. She is encouraging them to worship idols, eat food offered to idols, and commit sexual sin. 21I gave her time to repent, but she would not turn away from her immorality. 22Therefore, I will throw her upon a sickbed, and she will suffer greatly with all who commit adultery with her, unless they turn away from all their evil deeds. 23I will strike her children dead. And all the churches will know that I am the one who searches out the thoughts and intentions of every person. And I will give to each of you whatever you deserve. 24But I also have a message for the rest of you in Thyatira who have not followed this false teaching ('deeper truths,' as they call them—depths of Satan, really). I will ask nothing more of you 25except that you hold tightly to what you have until I come.

26 "To all who are victorious, who obey me to the very end, I will give authority over all the nations. 27They will rule the nations with an iron rod and smash them like clay pots. 28They will have the same authority I received from my Father, and I will also give them the morning star! 29Anyone who is willing to hear should listen to the Spirit and understand what the Spirit is saying to the churches.

CHAPTER 3

The Message to the Church in Sardis

"Write this letter to the angel of* the church in Sardis. This is the message from the one who has the sevenfold Spirit* of God and the seven stars:

"I know all the things you do, and that you have a reputation for being alive—but you are dead. 2Now wake up! Strengthen what little remains, for even what is left is at the point of death. Your deeds are far from right in the sight of God. 3Go back to what you heard and believed at first; hold to it firmly and turn to me again. Unless you do, I will come upon you suddenly, as unexpected as a thief.

4 "Yet even in Sardis there are some who have not soiled their garments with evil deeds. They will walk with me in white, for they are worthy. 5All who are victorious will be clothed in white. I will never erase their names from the Book of Life, but I will announce before my Father and his angels

3:1a Or *the messenger for;* also in 3:7, 14.   **3:1b** Greek *the seven spirits.*

that they are mine. [6]Anyone who is willing to hear should listen to the Spirit and understand what the Spirit is saying to the churches.

The Message to the Church in Philadelphia

[7]"Write this letter to the angel of the church in Philadelphia. This is the message from the one who is holy and true. He is the one who has the key of David. He opens doors, and no one can shut them; he shuts doors, and no one can open them.

[8]"I know all the things you do, and I have opened a door for you that no one can shut. You have little strength, yet you obeyed my word and did not deny me. [9]Look! I will force those who belong to Satan—those liars who say they are Jews but are not—to come and bow down at your feet. They will acknowledge that you are the ones I love.

[10]"Because you have obeyed my command to persevere, I will protect you from the great time of testing that will come upon the whole world to test those who belong to this world. [11]Look, I am coming quickly. Hold on to what you have, so that no one will take away your crown. [12]All who are victorious will become pillars in the Temple of my God, and they will never have to leave it. And I will write my God's name on them, and they will be citizens in the city of my God—the new Jerusalem that comes down from heaven from my God. And they will have my new name inscribed upon them. [13]Anyone who is willing to hear should listen to the Spirit and understand what the Spirit is saying to the churches.

The Message to the Church in Laodicea

[14]"Write this letter to the angel of the church in Laodicea. This is the message from the one who is the Amen—the faithful and true witness, the ruler* of God's creation:

[15]"I know all the things you do, that you are neither hot nor cold. I wish you were one or the other! [16]But since you are like lukewarm water, I will spit you out of my mouth! [17]You say, 'I am rich. I have everything I want. I don't need a thing!' And you don't realize that you are wretched

and miserable and poor and blind and naked. [18]I advise you to buy gold from me—gold that has been purified by fire. Then you will be rich. And also buy white garments so you will not be shamed by your nakedness. And buy ointment for your eyes so you will be able to see. [19]I am the one who corrects and disciplines everyone I love. Be diligent and turn from your indifference.

[20]"Look! Here I stand at the door and knock. If you hear me calling and open the door, I will come in, and we will share a meal as friends. [21]I will invite everyone who is victorious to sit with me on my throne, just as I was victorious and sat with my Father on his throne. [22]Anyone who is willing to hear should listen to the Spirit and understand what the Spirit is saying to the churches."

CHAPTER **4**
Worship in Heaven

Then as I looked, I saw a door standing open in heaven, and the same voice I had heard before spoke to me with the sound of a mighty trumpet blast. The voice said, "Come up here, and I will show you what must happen after these things." [2]And instantly I was in the Spirit,* and I saw a throne in heaven and someone sitting on it! [3]The one sitting on the throne was as brilliant as gemstones—jasper and carnelian. And the glow of an emerald circled his throne like a rainbow. [4]Twenty-four thrones surrounded him, and twenty-four elders sat on them. They were all clothed in white and had gold crowns on their heads. [5]And from the throne came flashes of lightning and the rumble of thunder. And in front of the throne were seven lampstands with burning flames. They are the seven spirits* of God. [6]In front of the throne was a shiny sea of glass, sparkling like crystal.

In the center and around the throne were four living beings, each covered with eyes, front and back. [7]The first of these living beings had the form of a lion; the second looked like an ox; the third had a human face; and the fourth had the form of an eagle with wings spread out as though in flight. [8]Each of these living beings had six wings, and their wings were covered with eyes, inside and out. Day after day and night after night they keep on saying,

---

3:14 Or *the source.*   4:2 Or *in spirit.*   4:5 See 1:4 and 3:1, where the same expression is translated *the sevenfold Spirit.*

"Holy, holy, holy is the Lord God
Almighty—
the one who always was, who is, and
who is still to come."

⁹Whenever the living beings give glory and honor and thanks to the one sitting on the throne, the one who lives forever and ever, ¹⁰the twenty-four elders fall down and worship the one who lives forever and ever. And they lay their crowns before the throne and say,

¹¹ "You are worthy, O Lord our God,
to receive glory and honor and power.
For you created everything,
and it is for your pleasure that they exist
and were created."

CHAPTER 5
The Lamb Opens the Scroll

And I saw a scroll in the right hand of the one who was sitting on the throne. There was writing on the inside and the outside of the scroll, and it was sealed with seven seals. ²And I saw a strong angel, who shouted with a loud voice: "Who is worthy to break the seals on this scroll and unroll it?" ³But no one in heaven or on earth or under the earth was able to open the scroll and read it.

⁴Then I wept because no one could be found who was worthy to open the scroll and read it. ⁵But one of the twenty-four elders said to me, "Stop weeping! Look, the Lion of the tribe of Judah, the heir to David's throne,* has conquered. He is worthy to open the scroll and break its seven seals."

⁶I looked and I saw a Lamb that had been killed but was now standing between the throne and the four living beings and among the twenty-four elders. He had seven horns and seven eyes, which are the seven spirits* of God that are sent out into every part of the earth. ⁷He stepped forward and took the scroll from the right hand of the one sitting on the throne. ⁸And as he took the scroll, the four living beings and the twenty-four elders fell down before the Lamb. Each one had a harp, and they held gold bowls filled with incense—the prayers of God's people!

⁹And they sang a new song with these words:

"You are worthy to take the scroll
and break its seals and open it.

For you were killed, and your blood has
ransomed people for God
from every tribe and language and
people and nation.
¹⁰ And you have caused them to become
God's kingdom and his priests.
And they will reign* on the earth."

¹¹Then I looked again, and I heard the singing of thousands and millions of angels around the throne and the living beings and the elders. ¹²And they sang in a mighty chorus:

"The Lamb is worthy—the Lamb who was
killed.
He is worthy to receive power and riches
and wisdom and strength
and honor and glory and blessing."

¹³And then I heard every creature in heaven and on earth and under the earth and in the sea. They also sang:

"Blessing and honor and glory and power
belong to the one sitting on the throne
and to the Lamb forever and ever."

¹⁴And the four living beings said, "Amen!" And the twenty-four elders fell down and worshiped God and the Lamb.

CHAPTER 6
The Lamb Breaks the First Six Seals

As I watched, the Lamb broke the first of the seven seals on the scroll. Then one of the four living beings called out with a voice that sounded like thunder, "Come!" ²I looked up and saw a white horse. Its rider carried a bow, and a crown was placed on his head. He rode out to win many battles and gain the victory.

³When the Lamb broke the second seal, I heard the second living being say, "Come!" ⁴And another horse appeared, a red one. Its rider was given a mighty sword and the authority to remove peace from the earth. And there was war and slaughter everywhere.

⁵When the Lamb broke the third seal, I heard the third living being say, "Come!" And I looked up and saw a black horse, and its rider was holding a pair of scales in his hand. ⁶And a voice from among the four living beings said, "A loaf of wheat bread or three loaves of barley for a day's pay.* And don't waste* the olive oil and wine."

⁷And when the Lamb broke the fourth seal, I

5:5 Greek *the root of David.*   5:6 See note on 4:5.   5:10 Some manuscripts read *they are reigning.*   6:6a Greek *A choinix of wheat for a denarius, and 3 choinix of barley for a denarius.*   6:6b Or *hurt.*

What Will Life in Heaven Be Like? Read REVELATION 7:13-17

The apostle Paul had a taste of heaven, either through a vision or by actually dying. He wrote about his experience in 2 Corinthians 12:2-4. Upon entering God's presence, he said, "I was caught up into paradise." The word *paradise* literally means "the royal garden of a king with all kinds of fruit and flowers." This passage of Scripture shows us four aspects of the life we will live in the wonderful place called paradise:

1. We Will Live a Life without Fear and Worry. Heaven is a place of protection (verse 15). We will have no reason to fear anything there. We won't find bars on windows, crime on the streets, or any other type of violence. God will be our shelter.

2. We Will Live a Life without Need. Heaven is a place of complete sufficiency (verse 16). Hunger and thirst will not be a part of our vocabulary there. That is because the Lord will feed us and quench our thirst.

3. We Will Live a Life without Pain. Heaven is a place of comfort (verse 16). Elsewhere, the Bible says that in heaven "there will be no more death or sorrow or crying or pain" (Revelation 21:4). Our heavenly bodies will not be subjected to the illnesses, aches, and pains that we know so well here on earth.

4. We Will Live a Life without Sorrow. Heaven is a place of joy (verse 17). Being in God's presence is a joyful and wonderful experience. Sorrow will not be found in heaven, and God will wipe away all of our tears.

CORNER STONES

While we can look forward to the glories of heaven, one thing far outweighs them all: the fact that we will be able to spend eternity with Jesus. Dwight L. Moody once wrote, "It is not the jeweled walls and pearly gates that are going to make heaven attractive. It is being with God." May that truth inspire you as you live out your life on this earth.

To begin the next topic, turn to p. A16.

---

heard the fourth living being say, "Come!" ⁸And I looked up and saw a horse whose color was pale green like a corpse. And Death was the name of its rider, who was followed around by the Grave.* They were given authority over one-fourth of the earth, to kill with the sword and famine and disease* and wild animals.

⁹And when the Lamb broke the fifth seal, I saw under the altar the souls of all who had been martyred for the word of God and for being faithful in their witness. ¹⁰They called loudly to the Lord and said, "O Sovereign Lord, holy and true, how long will it be before you judge the people who belong to this world for what they have done to us? When will you avenge our blood against these people?" ¹¹Then a white robe was given to each of them. And they were told to rest a little longer until the full number of their brothers and sisters*—their fellow servants of Jesus—had been martyred.

¹²I watched as the Lamb broke the sixth seal, and there was a great earthquake. The sun became as dark as black cloth, and the moon became as red as blood. ¹³Then the stars of the sky fell to the earth like green figs falling from trees shaken by mighty winds. ¹⁴And the sky was rolled up like a scroll and taken away. And all of the mountains and all of the islands disappeared. ¹⁵Then the kings of the earth, the rulers, the generals, the wealthy people, the people with great power, and every slave and every free person—all hid themselves in the caves and among the rocks of the mountains. ¹⁶And they cried to the mountains and the rocks, "Fall on us and hide us from the face of the one who sits on the throne and from the wrath of the Lamb. ¹⁷For the great day of their wrath has come, and who will be able to survive?"

6:8a Greek *by Hades.* 6:8b Greek *death.* 6:11 Greek *their brothers.*

CHAPTER **7**
God's People Will Be Preserved

Then I saw four angels standing at the four corners of the earth, holding back the four winds from blowing upon the earth. Not a leaf rustled in the trees, and the sea became as smooth as glass. 2And I saw another angel coming from the east, carrying the seal of the living God. And he shouted out to those four angels who had been given power to injure land and sea, 3"Wait! Don't hurt the land or the sea or the trees until we have placed the seal of God on the foreheads of his servants."

4And I heard how many were marked with the seal of God. There were 144,000 who were sealed from all the tribes of Israel:

5	from Judah	12,000
	from Reuben	12,000
	from Gad	12,000
6	from Asher	12,000
	from Naphtali	12,000
	from Manasseh	12,000
7	from Simeon	12,000
	from Levi	12,000
	from Issachar	12,000
8	from Zebulun	12,000
	from Joseph	12,000
	from Benjamin	12,000

Praise from the Great Multitude

9After this I saw a vast crowd, too great to count, from every nation and tribe and people and language, standing in front of the throne and before the Lamb. They were clothed in white and held palm branches in their hands. 10And they were shouting with a mighty shout, "Salvation comes from our God on the throne and from the Lamb!"

11And all the angels were standing around the throne and around the elders and the four living beings. And they fell face down before the throne and worshiped God. 12They said,

"Amen! Blessing and glory and wisdom
   and thanksgiving and honor and power
      and strength
   belong to our God forever and forever.
      Amen!"

13Then one of the twenty-four elders asked me, "Who are these who are clothed in white? Where do they come from?"

14And I said to him, "Sir, you are the one who knows."

8:11 Greek *Wormwood.*

Then he said to me, "These are the ones coming out of the great tribulation. They washed their robes in the blood of the Lamb and made them white. 15That is why they are standing in front of the throne of God, serving him day and night in his Temple. And he who sits on the throne will live among them and shelter them. 16They will never again be hungry or thirsty, and they will be fully protected from the scorching noontime heat. 17For the Lamb who stands in front of the throne will be their Shepherd. He will lead them to the springs of life-giving water. And God will wipe away all their tears."

CHAPTER **8**
The Lamb Breaks the Seventh Seal

When the Lamb broke the seventh seal, there was silence throughout heaven for about half an hour. 2And I saw the seven angels who stand before God, and they were given seven trumpets.

3Then another angel with a gold incense burner came and stood at the altar. And a great quantity of incense was given to him to mix with the prayers of God's people, to be offered on the gold altar before the throne. 4The smoke of the incense, mixed with the prayers of the saints, ascended up to God from the altar where the angel had poured them out. 5Then the angel filled the incense burner with fire from the altar and threw it down upon the earth; and thunder crashed, lightning flashed, and there was a terrible earthquake.

The First Four Trumpets

6Then the seven angels with the seven trumpets prepared to blow their mighty blasts.

7The first angel blew his trumpet, and hail and fire mixed with blood were thrown down upon the earth, and one-third of the earth was set on fire. One-third of the trees were burned, and all the grass was burned.

8Then the second angel blew his trumpet, and a great mountain of fire was thrown into the sea. And one-third of the water in the sea became blood. 9And one-third of all things living in the sea died. And one-third of all the ships on the sea were destroyed.

10Then the third angel blew his trumpet, and a great flaming star fell out of the sky, burning like a torch. It fell upon one-third of the rivers and on the springs of water. 11The name of the star was Bitterness.* It made one-third of the water bitter, and many people died because the water was so bitter.

12Then the fourth angel blew his trumpet, and one-third of the sun was struck, and one-third of the moon, and one-third of the stars, and they became dark. And one-third of the day was dark and one-third of the night also.

13Then I looked up. And I heard a single eagle crying loudly as it flew through the air, "Terror, terror, terror to all who belong to this world because of what will happen when the last three angels blow their trumpets."

CHAPTER 9

The Fifth Trumpet Brings the First Terror

Then the fifth angel blew his trumpet, and I saw a star that had fallen to earth from the sky, and he was given the key to the shaft of the bottomless pit. 2When he opened it, smoke poured out as though from a huge furnace, and the sunlight and air were darkened by the smoke.

3Then locusts came from the smoke and descended on the earth, and they were given power to sting like scorpions. 4They were told not to hurt the grass or plants or trees but to attack all the people who did not have the seal of God on their foreheads. 5They were told not to kill them but to torture them for five months with agony like the pain of scorpion stings. 6In those days people will seek death but will not find it. They will long to die, but death will flee away!

7The locusts looked like horses armed for battle. They had gold crowns on their heads, and they had human faces. 8Their hair was long like the hair of a woman, and their teeth were like the teeth of a lion. 9They wore armor made of iron, and their wings roared like an army of chariots rushing into battle. 10They had tails that stung like scorpions, with power to torture people. This power was given to them for five months. 11Their king is the angel from the bottomless pit; his name in Hebrew is *Abaddon*, and in Greek, *Apollyon*—the Destroyer.

12The first terror is past, but look, two more terrors are coming!

The Sixth Trumpet Brings the Second Terror

13Then the sixth angel blew his trumpet, and I heard a voice speaking from the four horns of the gold altar that stands in the presence of God. 14And the voice spoke to the sixth angel who held the trumpet: "Release the four angels who are bound at the great Euphrates River." 15And the four angels who had been prepared for this

hour and day and month and year were turned loose to kill one-third of all the people on earth. 16They led an army of 200 million mounted troops—I heard an announcement of how many there were.

17And in my vision, I saw the horses and the riders sitting on them. The riders wore armor that was fiery red and sky blue and yellow. The horses' heads were like the heads of lions, and fire and smoke and burning sulfur billowed from their mouths. 18One-third of all the people on earth were killed by these three plagues—by the fire and the smoke and burning sulfur that came from the mouths of the horses. 19Their power was in their mouths, but also in their tails. For their tails had heads like snakes, with the power to injure people.

20But the people who did not die in these plagues still refused to turn from their evil deeds. They continued to worship demons and idols made of gold, silver, bronze, stone, and wood—idols that neither see nor hear nor walk! 21And they did not repent of their murders or their witchcraft or their immorality or their thefts.

CHAPTER 10

The Angel and the Small Scroll

Then I saw another mighty angel coming down from heaven, surrounded by a cloud, with a rainbow over his head. His face shone like the sun, and his feet were like pillars of fire. 2And in his hand was a small scroll, which he had unrolled. He stood with his right foot on the sea and his left foot on the land. 3And he gave a great shout, like the roar of a lion. And when he shouted, the seven thunders answered.

4When the seven thunders spoke, I was about to write. But a voice from heaven called to me: "Keep secret what the seven thunders said. Do not write it down."

5Then the mighty angel standing on the sea and on the land lifted his right hand to heaven. 6And he swore an oath in the name of the one who lives forever and ever, who created heaven and everything in it, the earth and everything in it, and the sea and everything in it. He said, "God will wait no longer. 7But when the seventh angel blows his trumpet, God's mysterious plan will be fulfilled. It will happen just as he announced it to his servants the prophets."

8Then the voice from heaven called to me again: "Go and take the unrolled scroll from the angel who is standing on the sea and on the land."

⁹So I approached him and asked him to give me the little scroll. "Yes, take it and eat it," he said. "At first it will taste like honey, but when you swallow it, it will make your stomach sour!" ¹⁰So I took the little scroll from the hands of the angel, and I ate it! It was sweet in my mouth, but it made my stomach sour. ¹¹Then he said to me, "You must prophesy again about many peoples, nations, languages, and kings."

CHAPTER 11
The Two Witnesses

Then I was given a measuring stick, and I was told, "Go and measure the Temple of God and the altar, and count the number of worshipers. ²But do not measure the outer courtyard, for it has been turned over to the nations. They will trample the holy city for 42 months. ³And I will give power to my two witnesses, and they will be clothed in sackcloth and will prophesy during those 1,260 days."

⁴These two prophets are the two olive trees and the two lampstands that stand before the Lord of all the earth. ⁵If anyone tries to harm them, fire flashes from the mouths of the prophets and consumes their enemies. This is how anyone who tries to harm them must die. ⁶They have power to shut the skies so that no rain will fall for as long as they prophesy. And they have the power to turn the rivers and oceans into blood, and to send every kind of plague upon the earth as often as they wish.

⁷When they complete their testimony, the beast that comes up out of the bottomless pit will declare war against them. He will conquer them and kill them. ⁸And their bodies will lie in the main street of Jerusalem,* the city which is called "Sodom" and "Egypt," the city where their Lord was crucified. ⁹And for three and a half days, all peoples, tribes, languages, and nations will come to stare at their bodies. No one will be allowed to bury them. ¹⁰All the people who belong to this world will give presents to each other to celebrate the death of the two prophets who had tormented them.

¹¹But after three and a half days, the spirit of life from God entered them, and they stood up! And terror struck all who were staring at them. ¹²Then a loud voice shouted from heaven, "Come up here!" And they rose to heaven in a cloud as their enemies watched.

11:8 Greek *the great city.*

¹³And in the same hour there was a terrible earthquake that destroyed a tenth of the city. Seven thousand people died in that earthquake. And everyone who did not die was terrified and gave glory to the God of heaven.

¹⁴The second terror is past, but look, now the third terror is coming quickly.

The Seventh Trumpet Brings the Third Terror

¹⁵Then the seventh angel blew his trumpet, and there were loud voices shouting in heaven: "The whole world has now become the kingdom of our Lord and of his Christ, and he will reign forever and ever."

¹⁶And the twenty-four elders sitting on their thrones before God fell on their faces and worshiped him. ¹⁷And they said,

"We give thanks to you, Lord God Almighty,
    the one who is and who always was,
for now you have assumed your great power
    and have begun to reign.
¹⁸ The nations were angry with you,
    but now the time of your wrath has come.
It is time to judge the dead and reward your
    servants.
You will reward your prophets and your
    holy people,
    all who fear your name, from the least to
    the greatest.
And you will destroy all who have caused
    destruction on the earth."

¹⁹Then, in heaven, the Temple of God was opened and the Ark of his covenant could be seen inside the Temple. Lightning flashed, thunder crashed and roared; there was a great hailstorm, and the world was shaken by a mighty earthquake.

CHAPTER 12
The Woman and the Dragon

Then I witnessed in heaven an event of great significance. I saw a woman clothed with the sun, with the moon beneath her feet, and a crown of twelve stars on her head. ²She was pregnant, and she cried out in the pain of labor as she awaited her delivery.

³Suddenly, I witnessed in heaven another significant event. I saw a large red dragon with seven heads and ten horns, with seven crowns on his heads. ⁴His tail dragged down one-third of the stars, which he threw to the earth. He stood before the woman as she was about to give

Who Can Thwart Satan's Agenda? Read REVELATION 12:10-12

God uses his faithful followers to ruin Satan's plans. Here we see three significant ways these martyrs for the gospel overcame the Devil's attacks:

1. They Overcame Him by the Blood of the Lamb. The Bible says, "Without the shedding of blood, there is no forgiveness of sins" (Hebrews 9:22). It is only through what Jesus did for us on the cross that we can approach God. These people knew that they could never go to heaven or overcome Satan's accusations on their own merit or ability. They realized that they had fallen short of God's ideal, but they also knew that the blood of Jesus "cleanses us from every sin" (1 John 1:7).

2. They Overcame Him by Their Testimony. The believers described in these verses had come to understand what God had done for them and were proclaiming it to others. They not only realized that they had unconditional access to God, but they also sought to "invade enemy territory" by reaching out to others with the message of the gospel.

3. They Overcame Him by Their Attitude toward Life. These believers did not love their lives more than Christ. They endured execution for their faith because they realized that a better life was awaiting them in heaven with Christ. As the apostle Paul said, "For to me, living is for Christ, and dying is even better" (Philippians 1:21).

History relates the story of a Christian who was persecuted by Rome for his faith. As he stood before the emperor, he was told, "Give up Christ. If you don't, I'll banish you."

The Christian replied, "You cannot banish me from Christ, for God says, 'I will never leave you or forsake you.'_"

The ruler said, "I'll confiscate your property."

The Christian patiently responded, "My treasures are laid up in heaven. You can't touch them."

The emperor shot back, "I'll kill you!"

The Christian answered, "I've been dead to the world in Christ for forty years. My life is hid with Christ in God. You can't touch it."

The emperor turned to some of the members of his court and said in disgust, "What can you do with such a fanatic?"

May God give his church more men like this man.

To begin the next topic, turn to p. A14.

CORNER STONES

birth to her child, ready to devour the baby as soon as it was born.

5 She gave birth to a boy who was to rule all nations with an iron rod. And the child was snatched away from the dragon and was caught up to God and to his throne. 6 And the woman fled into the wilderness, where God had prepared a place to give her care for 1,260 days.

7 Then there was war in heaven. Michael and the angels under his command fought the dragon and his angels. 8 And the dragon lost the battle and was forced out of heaven. 9 This great dragon—the ancient serpent called the Devil, or Satan, the one deceiving the whole world—was thrown down to the earth with all his angels.

12:10 Greek *brothers*.

10 Then I heard a loud voice shouting across the heavens,

"It has happened at last—the salvation and power and kingdom of our God, and the authority of his Christ! For the Accuser has been thrown down to earth—the one who accused our brothers and sisters* before our God day and night. 11 And they have defeated him because of the blood of the Lamb and because of their testimony. And they were not afraid to die. 12 Rejoice, O heavens! And you who live in the heavens, rejoice! But terror will come on the earth and the sea. For the Devil has come down to you in great anger, and he knows that he has little time."

13And when the dragon realized that he had been thrown down to the earth, he pursued the woman who had given birth to the child. 14But she was given two wings like those of a great eagle. This allowed her to fly to a place prepared for her in the wilderness, where she would be cared for and protected from the dragon* for a time, times, and half a time. 15Then the dragon tried to drown the woman with a flood of water that flowed from its mouth. 16But the earth helped her by opening its mouth and swallowing the river that gushed out from the mouth of the dragon. 17Then the dragon became angry at the woman, and he declared war against the rest of her children—all who keep God's commandments and confess that they belong to Jesus.

The Beast out of the Sea

18Then he stood* waiting on the shore of the sea.

CHAPTER 13

And now in my vision I saw a beast rising up out of the sea. It had seven heads and ten horns, with ten crowns on its horns. And written on each head were names that blasphemed God. 2This beast looked like a leopard, but it had bear's feet and a lion's mouth! And the dragon gave him his own power and throne and great authority.

3I saw that one of the heads of the beast seemed wounded beyond recovery—but the fatal wound was healed! All the world marveled at this miracle and followed the beast in awe. 4They worshiped the dragon for giving the beast such power, and they worshiped the beast. "Is there anyone as great as the beast?" they exclaimed. "Who is able to fight against him?"

5Then the beast was allowed to speak great blasphemies against God. And he was given authority to do what he wanted for forty-two months. 6And he spoke terrible words of blasphemy against God, slandering his name and all who live in heaven, who are his temple. 7And the beast was allowed to wage war against God's holy people and to overcome them. And he was given authority to rule over every tribe and people and language and nation. 8And all the people who belong to this world worshiped the beast. They are the ones whose names were not written in the Book of Life, which belongs to the Lamb who was killed before the world was made.

9Anyone who is willing to hear should listen and understand. 10The people who are destined for prison will be arrested and taken away. Those who are destined for death will be killed. But do not be dismayed, for here is your opportunity to have endurance and faith.

The Beast out of the Earth

11Then I saw another beast come up out of the earth. He had two horns like those of a lamb, and he spoke with the voice of a dragon. 12He exercised all the authority of the first beast. And he required all the earth and those who belong to this world to worship the first beast, whose death-wound had been healed. 13He did astounding miracles, such as making fire flash down to earth from heaven while everyone was watching. 14And with all the miracles he was allowed to perform on behalf of the first beast, he deceived all the people who belong to this world. He ordered the people of the world to make a great statue of the first beast, who was fatally wounded and then came back to life. 15He was permitted to give life to this statue so that it could speak. Then the statue commanded that anyone refusing to worship it must die.

16He required everyone—great and small, rich and poor, slave and free—to be given a mark on the right hand or on the forehead. 17And no one could buy or sell anything without that mark, which was either the name of the beast or the number representing his name. 18Wisdom is needed to understand this. Let the one who has understanding solve the number of the beast, for it is the number of a man.* His number is 666.*

CHAPTER 14

The Lamb and the 144,000

Then I saw the Lamb standing on Mount Zion, and with him were 144,000 who had his name and his Father's name written on their foreheads. 2And I heard a sound from heaven like the roaring of a great waterfall or the rolling of mighty thunder. It was like the sound of many harpists playing together.

3This great choir sang a wonderful new song in front of the throne of God and before the four living beings and the twenty-four elders. And no one could learn this song except those 144,000 who had been redeemed from the earth. 4For they are spiritually undefiled, pure as virgins,*

12:14 Greek *the serpent*; also in 12:15. See 12:9. **12:18** Some manuscripts read *Then I stood,* and some translations put this entire sentence into 13:1. **13:18a** Or *of humanity.* **13:18b** Some manuscripts read *616.* **14:4a** Greek *they are virgins who have not defiled themselves with women.*

What Role Will Angels Play in the End Times? Read REVELATION 14:6-7

The Bible tells us that the last days are going to be spiritually dark. Many people will be deceived into believing "teachings that come from demons" (see 1 Timothy 4:1, p. 1057), and people will become increasingly immoral, proud, and disobedient (see 2 Timothy 3:1-5, p. 1063). We already see this beginning to happen. There is a fresh demand for psychics, an increasing amount of violent crime on the streets, and a blatant lack of values in much of entertainment today.

This text shows that during the Tribulation, which is generally recognized as the last seven years on earth before Christ's return, the demons will not be the only ones at work. The angels of God will fly through the heavens preaching the everlasting gospel to make sure that everyone throughout the world is aware of the upcoming judgment of God. In essence, it will be the final "wake-up call" for people to turn to Jesus Christ.

To begin the next topic, turn to p. A15.

CORNER STONES

---

following the Lamb wherever he goes. They have been purchased from among the people on the earth as a special offering* to God and to the Lamb. ⁵No falsehood can be charged against them; they are blameless.

The Three Angels

⁶And I saw another angel flying through the heavens, carrying the everlasting Good News to preach to the people who belong to this world—to every nation, tribe, language, and people. ⁷"Fear God," he shouted. "Give glory to him. For the time has come when he will sit as judge. Worship him who made heaven and earth, the sea, and all the springs of water."

⁸Then another angel followed him through the skies, shouting, "Babylon is fallen—that great city is fallen—because she seduced the nations of the world and made them drink the wine of her passionate immorality."

⁹Then a third angel followed them, shouting, "Anyone who worships the beast and his statue or who accepts his mark on the forehead or the hand ¹⁰must drink the wine of God's wrath. It is poured out undiluted into God's cup of wrath. And they will be tormented with fire and burning sulfur in the presence of the holy angels and the Lamb. ¹¹The smoke of their torment rises forever and ever, and they will have no relief day or night, for they have worshiped the beast and his statue and have accepted the mark of his name. ¹²Let this encourage God's holy people to endure persecution patiently and remain firm to

the end, obeying his commands and trusting in Jesus."

¹³And I heard a voice from heaven saying, "Write this down: Blessed are those who die in the Lord from now on. Yes, says the Spirit, they are blessed indeed, for they will rest from all their toils and trials; for their good deeds follow them!"

The Harvest of the Earth

¹⁴Then I saw the Son of Man* sitting on a white cloud. He had a gold crown on his head and a sharp sickle in his hand.

¹⁵Then an angel came from the Temple and called out in a loud voice to the one sitting on the cloud, "Use the sickle, for the time has come for you to harvest; the crop is ripe on the earth." ¹⁶So the one sitting on the cloud swung his sickle over the earth, and the whole earth was harvested.

¹⁷After that, another angel came from the Temple in heaven, and he also had a sharp sickle. ¹⁸Then another angel, who has power to destroy the world with fire, shouted to the angel with the sickle, "Use your sickle now to gather the clusters of grapes from the vines of the earth, for they are fully ripe for judgment." ¹⁹So the angel swung his sickle on the earth and loaded the grapes into the great winepress of God's wrath. ²⁰And the grapes were trodden in the winepress outside the city, and blood flowed from the winepress in a stream about 180 miles* long and as high as a horse's bridle.

14:4b Greek *as firstfruits.*   14:14 Or *one who looked like a man;* Greek reads *one like a son of man.*   14:20 Greek *1,600 stadia* [296 kilometers].

CHAPTER 15
The Song of Moses and of the Lamb

Then I saw in heaven another significant event, and it was great and marvelous. Seven angels were holding the seven last plagues, which would bring God's wrath to completion. ²I saw before me what seemed to be a crystal sea mixed with fire. And on it stood all the people who had been victorious over the beast and his statue and the number representing his name. They were all holding harps that God had given them. ³And they were singing the song of Moses, the servant of God, and the song of the Lamb:

"Great and marvelous are your actions,
 Lord God Almighty.
Just and true are your ways,
 O King of the nations.*
⁴ Who will not fear, O Lord, and glorify your
 name?
 For you alone are holy.
All nations will come and worship before
 you,
 for your righteous deeds have been
 revealed."

The Seven Bowls of the Seven Plagues

⁵Then I looked and saw that the Temple in heaven, God's Tabernacle, was thrown wide open! ⁶The seven angels who were holding the bowls of the seven plagues came from the Temple, clothed in spotless white linen* with gold belts across their chests. ⁷And one of the four living beings handed each of the seven angels a gold bowl filled with the terrible wrath of God, who lives forever and forever. ⁸The Temple was filled with smoke from God's glory and power. No one could enter the Temple until the seven angels had completed pouring out the seven plagues.

CHAPTER 16

Then I heard a mighty voice shouting from the Temple to the seven angels, "Now go your ways and empty out the seven bowls of God's wrath on the earth."

²So the first angel left the Temple and poured out his bowl over the earth, and horrible, malignant sores broke out on everyone who had the mark of the beast and who worshiped his statue.

³Then the second angel poured out his bowl on the sea, and it became like the blood of a corpse. And everything in the sea died.

⁴Then the third angel poured out his bowl on the rivers and springs, and they became blood. ⁵And I heard the angel who had authority over all water saying, "You are just in sending this judgment, O Holy One, who is and who always was. ⁶For your holy people and your prophets have been killed, and their blood was poured out on the earth. So you have given their murderers blood to drink. It is their just reward." ⁷And I heard a voice from the altar saying, "Yes, Lord God Almighty, your punishments are true and just."

⁸Then the fourth angel poured out his bowl on the sun, causing it to scorch everyone with its fire. ⁹Everyone was burned by this blast of heat, and they cursed the name of God, who sent all of these plagues. They did not repent and give him glory.

¹⁰Then the fifth angel poured out his bowl on the throne of the beast, and his kingdom was plunged into darkness. And his subjects ground their teeth in anguish, ¹¹and they cursed the God of heaven for their pains and sores. But they refused to repent of all their evil deeds.

¹²Then the sixth angel poured out his bowl on the great Euphrates River, and it dried up so that the kings from the east could march their armies westward without hindrance. ¹³And I saw three evil spirits that looked like frogs leap from the mouth of the dragon, the beast, and the false prophet. ¹⁴These miracle-working demons caused all the rulers of the world to gather for battle against the Lord on that great judgment day of God Almighty.

¹⁵"Take note: I will come as unexpectedly as a thief! Blessed are all who are watching for me, who keep their robes ready so they will not need to walk naked and ashamed."

¹⁶And they gathered all the rulers and their armies to a place called *Armageddon* in Hebrew. ¹⁷Then the seventh angel poured out his bowl into the air. And a mighty shout came from the throne of the Temple in heaven, saying, "It is finished!" ¹⁸Then the thunder crashed and rolled, and lightning flashed. And there was an earthquake greater than ever before in human history. ¹⁹The great city of Babylon split into three pieces, and cities around the world fell into heaps of rubble. And so God remembered all of Babylon's sins, and he made her drink the cup that was filled with the wine of his fierce wrath. ²⁰And every island disappeared, and all the

15:3 Some manuscripts read *King of the ages;* other manuscripts read *King of the saints.* 15:6 Some manuscripts read *in bright and sparkling stone.*

mountains were leveled. ²¹There was a terrible hailstorm, and hailstones weighing seventy-five pounds* fell from the sky onto the people below. They cursed God because of the hailstorm, which was a very terrible plague.

CHAPTER 17
The Great Prostitute

One of the seven angels who had poured out the seven bowls came over and spoke to me. "Come with me," he said, "and I will show you the judgment that is going to come on the great prostitute, who sits on many waters. ²The rulers of the world have had immoral relations with her, and the people who belong to this world have been made drunk by the wine of her immorality."

³So the angel took me in spirit* into the wilderness. There I saw a woman sitting on a scarlet beast that had seven heads and ten horns, written all over with blasphemies against God. ⁴The woman wore purple and scarlet clothing and beautiful jewelry made of gold and precious gems and pearls. She held in her hand a gold goblet full of obscenities and the impurities of her immorality. ⁵A mysterious name was written on her forehead: "Babylon the Great, Mother of All Prostitutes and Obscenities in the World." ⁶I could see that she was drunk—drunk with the blood of God's holy people who were witnesses for Jesus. I stared at her completely amazed.

⁷"Why are you so amazed?" the angel asked. "I will tell you the mystery of this woman and of the beast with seven heads and ten horns. ⁸The beast you saw was alive but isn't now. And yet he will soon come up out of the bottomless pit and go to eternal destruction. And the people who belong to this world, whose names were not written in the Book of Life from before the world began, will be amazed at the reappearance of this beast who had died.

⁹"And now understand this: The seven heads of the beast represent the seven hills of the city where this woman rules. They also represent seven kings. ¹⁰Five kings have already fallen, the sixth now reigns, and the seventh is yet to come, but his reign will be brief. ¹¹The scarlet beast that was alive and then died is the eighth king. He is like the other seven, and he, too, will go to his doom. ¹²His ten horns are ten kings who have not yet risen to power; they will be appointed to their kingdoms for one brief moment to reign with the beast. ¹³They will all agree to give their

power and authority to him. ¹⁴Together they will wage war against the Lamb, but the Lamb will defeat them because he is Lord over all lords and King over all kings, and his people are the called and chosen and faithful ones."

¹⁵And the angel said to me, "The waters where the prostitute is sitting represent masses of people of every nation and language. ¹⁶The scarlet beast and his ten horns—which represent ten kings who will reign with him—all hate the prostitute. They will strip her naked, eat her flesh, and burn her remains with fire. ¹⁷For God has put a plan into their minds, a plan that will carry out his purposes. They will mutually agree to give their authority to the scarlet beast, and so the words of God will be fulfilled. ¹⁸And this woman you saw in your vision represents the great city that rules over the kings of the earth."

CHAPTER 18
The Fall of Babylon

After all this I saw another angel come down from heaven with great authority, and the earth grew bright with his splendor. ²He gave a mighty shout, "Babylon is fallen—that great city is fallen! She has become the hideout of demons and evil spirits, a nest for filthy buzzards, and a den for dreadful beasts. ³For all the nations have drunk the wine of her passionate immorality. The rulers of the world have committed adultery with her, and merchants throughout the world have grown rich as a result of her luxurious living."

⁴Then I heard another voice calling from heaven, "Come away from her, my people. Do not take part in her sins, or you will be punished with her. ⁵For her sins are piled as high as heaven, and God is ready to judge her for her evil deeds. ⁶Do to her as she has done to your people. Give her a double penalty for all her evil deeds. She brewed a cup of terror for others, so give her twice as much as she gave out. ⁷She has lived in luxury and pleasure, so match it now with torments and sorrows. She boasts, 'I am queen on my throne. I am no helpless widow. I will not experience sorrow.' ⁸Therefore, the sorrows of death and mourning and famine will overtake her in a single day. She will be utterly consumed by fire, for the Lord God who judges her is mighty."

⁹And the rulers of the world who took part in her immoral acts and enjoyed her great luxury will mourn for her as they see the smoke rising

16:21 Greek *1 talent* [34 kilograms].   17:3 Or *in the Spirit.*

from her charred remains. [10]They will stand at a distance, terrified by her great torment. They will cry out, "How terrible, how terrible for Babylon, that great city! In one single moment God's judgment came on her."

[11]The merchants of the world will weep and mourn for her, for there is no one left to buy their goods. [12]She bought great quantities of gold, silver, jewels, pearls, fine linen, purple dye, silk, scarlet cloth, every kind of perfumed wood, ivory goods, objects made of expensive wood, bronze, iron, and marble. [13]She also bought cinnamon, spice, incense, myrrh, frankincense, wine, olive oil, fine flour, wheat, cattle, sheep, horses, chariots, and slaves—yes, she even traded in human lives.

[14]"All the fancy things you loved so much are gone," they cry. "The luxuries and splendor that you prized so much will never be yours again. They are gone forever."

[15]The merchants who became wealthy by selling her these things will stand at a distance, terrified by her great torment. They will weep and cry. [16]"How terrible, how terrible for that great city! She was so beautiful—like a woman clothed in finest purple and scarlet linens, decked out with gold and precious stones and pearls! [17]And in one single moment all the wealth of the city is gone!"

And all the shipowners and captains of the merchant ships and their crews will stand at a distance. [18]They will weep as they watch the smoke ascend, and they will say, "Where in all the world is there another city like this?" [19]And they will throw dust on their heads to show their great sorrow. And they will say, "How terrible, how terrible for the great city! She made us all rich from her great wealth. And now in a single hour it is all gone."

[20]But you, O heaven, rejoice over her fate. And you also rejoice, O holy people of God and apostles and prophets! For at last God has judged her on your behalf.

[21]Then a mighty angel picked up a boulder as large as a great millstone. He threw it into the ocean and shouted, "Babylon, the great city, will be thrown down as violently as I have thrown away this stone, and she will disappear forever. [22]Never again will the sound of music be heard there—no more harps, songs, flutes, or trumpets. There will be no industry of any kind, and no more milling of grain. [23]Her nights will be dark, without a single lamp. There will be no

happy voices of brides and grooms. This will happen because her merchants, who were the greatest in the world, deceived the nations with her sorceries. [24]In her streets the blood of the prophets was spilled. She was the one who slaughtered God's people all over the world."

CHAPTER 19
Songs of Victory in Heaven

After this, I heard the sound of a vast crowd in heaven shouting, "Hallelujah! Salvation is from our God. Glory and power belong to him alone. [2]His judgments are just and true. He has punished the great prostitute who corrupted the earth with her immorality, and he has avenged the murder of his servants." [3]Again and again their voices rang, "Hallelujah! The smoke from that city ascends forever and ever!"

[4]Then the twenty-four elders and the four living beings fell down and worshiped God, who was sitting on the throne. They cried out, "Amen! Hallelujah!"

[5]And from the throne came a voice that said, "Praise our God, all his servants, from the least to the greatest, all who fear him."

[6]Then I heard again what sounded like the shout of a huge crowd, or the roar of mighty ocean waves, or the crash of loud thunder: "Hallelujah! For the Lord our God, the Almighty, reigns. [7]Let us be glad and rejoice and honor him. For the time has come for the wedding feast of the Lamb, and his bride has prepared herself. [8]She is permitted to wear the finest white linen." (Fine linen represents the good deeds done by the people of God.)

[9]And the angel said, "Write this: Blessed are those who are invited to the wedding feast of the Lamb." And he added, "These are true words that come from God."

[10]Then I fell down at his feet to worship him, but he said, "No, don't worship me. For I am a servant of God, just like you and other brothers and sisters* who testify of their faith in Jesus. Worship God. For the essence of prophecy is to give a clear witness for Jesus.*"

The Rider on the White Horse

[11]Then I saw heaven opened, and a white horse was standing there. And the one sitting on the horse was named Faithful and True. For he judges fairly and then goes to war. [12]His eyes were bright like flames of fire, and on his head were many crowns. A name was written on him,

19:10a Greek *brothers.* 19:10b Or *is the message confirmed by Jesus.*

Who Will Go to Hell? Read REVELATION 20:11-15

The event described in this passage is the final judgment of humankind, also known as the Great White Throne Judgment. The standard by which you will be judged is simple. If you have accepted God's wonderful gift of salvation through his Son, Jesus Christ, your name will be found in the Book of Life, and you will spend eternity in heaven with God. If you have chosen to reject Christ, then your final destination will be the lake of fire. No arguments. Case closed.

Sadly, many people will unwittingly choose the latter option. They do so, not because they want to spend their eternity in agony, but because they just "go with the flow." They do what everybody else does and don't think for themselves. Jesus called this choice the "easy way." In describing the way to heaven and the way to hell, Jesus said, "You can enter God's Kingdom only through the narrow gate. The highway to hell is broad, and its gate is wide for the many who choose the easy way. But the gateway to life is small, and the road is narrow, and only a few ever find it" (Matthew 7:13-14). The only way to get off this broad road and "cancel" your reservation for hell is to make sure your name is entered into God's reservation book for heaven—the Book of Life.

For the next note on "What Is Hell?" turn to p. 1052.

CORNER STONES

---

and only he knew what it meant. ¹³He was clothed with a robe dipped in blood, and his title was the Word of God. ¹⁴The armies of heaven, dressed in pure white linen, followed him on white horses. ¹⁵From his mouth came a sharp sword, and with it he struck down the nations. He ruled them with an iron rod, and he trod the winepress of the fierce wrath of almighty God. ¹⁶On his robe and thigh was written this title: King of kings and Lord of lords.

¹⁷Then I saw an angel standing in the sun, shouting to the vultures flying high in the sky: "Come! Gather together for the great banquet God has prepared. ¹⁸Come and eat the flesh of kings, captains, and strong warriors; of horses and their riders; and of all humanity, both free and slave, small and great."

¹⁹Then I saw the beast gathering the kings of the earth and their armies in order to fight against the one sitting on the horse and his army. ²⁰And the beast was captured, and with him the false prophet who did mighty miracles on behalf of the beast—miracles that deceived all who had accepted the mark of the beast and who worshiped his statue. Both the beast and his false prophet were thrown alive into the lake of fire that burns with sulfur. ²¹Their entire army was killed by the sharp sword that came out of the mouth of the one riding the white horse. And all the vultures of the sky gorged themselves on the dead bodies.

CHAPTER **20**
The Thousand Years

Then I saw an angel come down from heaven with the key to the bottomless pit and a heavy chain in his hand. ²He seized the dragon—that old serpent, the Devil, Satan—and bound him in chains for a thousand years. ³The angel threw him into the bottomless pit, which he then shut and locked so Satan could not deceive the nations anymore until the thousand years were finished. Afterward he would be released again for a little while.

⁴Then I saw thrones, and the people sitting on them had been given the authority to judge. And I saw the souls of those who had been beheaded for their testimony about Jesus, for proclaiming the word of God. And I saw the souls of those who had not worshiped the beast or his statue, nor accepted his mark on their forehead or their hands. They came to life again, and they reigned with Christ for a thousand years. ⁵This is the first resurrection. (The rest of the dead did not come back to life until the thousand years had ended.) ⁶Blessed and holy are those who share in the first resurrection. For them the second death holds no power, but they will be priests of God and of Christ and will reign with him a thousand years.

The Defeat of Satan

⁷When the thousand years end, Satan will be let out of his prison. ⁸He will go out to deceive the

nations from every corner of the earth, which are called Gog and Magog. He will gather them together for battle—a mighty host, as number-less as sand along the shore. 9And I saw them as they went up on the broad plain of the earth and surrounded God's people and the beloved city. But fire from heaven came down on the attack-ing armies and consumed them.

10Then the Devil, who betrayed them, was thrown into the lake of fire that burns with sulfur, joining the beast and the false prophet. There they will be tormented day and night forever and ever.

The Final Judgment

11And I saw a great white throne, and I saw the one who was sitting on it. The earth and sky fled from his presence, but they found no place to hide. 12I saw the dead, both great and small, standing before God's throne. And the books were opened, including the Book of Life. And the dead were judged according to the things written in the books, according to what they had done. 13The sea gave up the dead in it, and death and the grave* gave up the dead in them. They were all judged according to their deeds. 14And death and the grave were thrown into the lake of fire. This is the second death—the lake of fire. 15And anyone whose name was not found re-corded in the Book of Life was thrown into the lake of fire.

CHAPTER 21

The New Jerusalem

Then I saw a new heaven and a new earth, for the old heaven and the old earth had disappeared. And the sea was also gone. 2And I saw the holy city, the new Jerusalem, coming down from God out of heaven like a beautiful bride prepared for her husband.

3I heard a loud shout from the throne, saying, "Look, the home of God is now among his people! He will live with them, and they will be his people. God himself will be with them.* 4He will remove all of their sorrows, and there will be no more death or sorrow or crying or pain. For the old world and its evils are gone forever."

5And the one sitting on the throne said, "Look, I am making all things new!" And then he said to me, "Write this down, for what I tell you is trustworthy and true." 6And he also said, "It is finished! I am the Alpha and the Omega—

the Beginning and the End. To all who are thirsty I will give the springs of the water of life without charge! 7All who are victorious will inherit all these blessings, and I will be their God, and they will be my children. 8But cowards who turn away from me, and unbelievers, and the corrupt, and murderers, and the immoral, and those who practice witchcraft, and idol worshipers, and all liars—their doom is in the lake that burns with fire and sulfur. This is the second death."

9Then one of the seven angels who held the seven bowls containing the seven last plagues came and said to me, "Come with me! I will show you the bride, the wife of the Lamb."

10So he took me in spirit* to a great, high mountain, and he showed me the holy city, Jerusalem, descending out of heaven from God. 11It was filled with the glory of God and sparkled like a precious gem, crystal clear like jasper. 12Its walls were broad and high, with twelve gates guarded by twelve angels. And the names of the twelve tribes of Israel were written on the gates. 13There were three gates on each side—east, north, south, and west. 14The wall of the city had twelve foundation stones, and on them were written the names of the twelve apostles of the Lamb.

15The angel who talked to me held in his hand a gold measuring stick to measure the city, its gates, and its wall. 16When he measured it, he found it was a square, as wide as it was long. In fact, it was in the form of a cube, for its length and width and height were each 1,400 miles.* 17Then he measured the walls and found them to be 216 feet thick* (the angel used a standard human measure).

18The wall was made of jasper, and the city was pure gold, as clear as glass. 19The wall of the city was built on foundation stones inlaid with twelve gems: the first was jasper, the second sapphire, the third agate, the fourth emerald, 20the fifth onyx, the sixth carnelian, the seventh chrysolite, the eighth beryl, the ninth topaz, the tenth chrysoprase, the eleventh jacinth, the twelfth amethyst.

21The twelve gates were made of pearls—each gate from a single pearl! And the main street was pure gold, as clear as glass.

22No temple could be seen in the city, for the Lord God Almighty and the Lamb are its temple. 23And the city has no need of sun or moon, for the glory of God illuminates the city, and the Lamb is its light. 24The nations of the earth will

20:13 Greek and Hades; also in 20:14.   21:3 Some manuscripts read God himself will be with them, their God.   21:10 Or in the Spirit.
21:16 Greek 12,000 stadia [2,220 kilometers].   21:17 Greek 144 cubits [65 meters].

walk in its light, and the rulers of the world will come and bring their glory to it. 25Its gates never close at the end of day because there is no night. 26And all the nations will bring their glory and honor into the city. 27Nothing evil will be allowed to enter—no one who practices shameful idolatry and dishonesty—but only those whose names are written in the Lamb's Book of Life.

CHAPTER **22**

And the angel showed me a pure river with the water of life, clear as crystal, flowing from the throne of God and of the Lamb, 2coursing down the center of the main street. On each side of the river grew a tree of life, bearing twelve crops of fruit,* with a fresh crop each month. The leaves were used for medicine to heal the nations.

3No longer will anything be cursed. For the throne of God and of the Lamb will be there, and his servants will worship him. 4And they will see his face, and his name will be written on their foreheads. 5And there will be no night there—no need for lamps or sun—for the Lord God will shine on them. And they will reign forever and ever.

6Then the angel said to me, "These words are trustworthy and true: 'The Lord God, who tells his prophets what the future holds, has sent his angel to tell you what will happen soon.'"

Jesus Is Coming

7"Look, I am coming soon! Blessed are those who obey the prophecy written in this scroll."

8I, John, am the one who saw and heard all these things. And when I saw and heard these things, I fell down to worship the angel who showed them to me. 9But again he said, "No, don't worship me. I am a servant of God, just like you and your brothers the prophets, as well as all who obey what is written in this scroll. Worship God!"

10Then he instructed me, "Do not seal up the prophetic words you have written, for the time is near. 11Let the one who is doing wrong continue to do wrong; the one who is vile, continue to be vile; the one who is good, continue to do good; and the one who is holy, continue in holiness."

12"See, I am coming soon, and my reward is with me, to repay all according to their deeds. 13I am the Alpha and the Omega, the First and the Last, the Beginning and the End."

14Blessed are those who wash their robes so they can enter through the gates of the city and eat the fruit from the tree of life. 15Outside the city are the dogs—the sorcerers, the sexually immoral, the murderers, the idol worshipers, and all who love to live a lie.

16"I, Jesus, have sent my angel to give you this message for the churches. I am both the source of David and the heir to his throne.* I am the bright morning star."

17The Spirit and the bride say, "Come." Let each one who hears them say, "Come." Let the thirsty ones come—anyone who wants to. Let them come and drink the water of life without charge. 18And I solemnly declare to everyone who hears the prophetic words of this book: If anyone adds anything to what is written here, God will add to that person the plagues described in this book. 19And if anyone removes any of the words of this prophetic book, God will remove that person's share in the tree of life and in the holy city that are described in this book.

20He who is the faithful witness to all these things says, "Yes, I am coming soon!" Amen! Come, Lord Jesus! 21The grace of the Lord Jesus be with you all.

22:2 Or *12 kinds of fruit.* 22:16 Greek *I am the root and offspring of David.*

TABLE OF WEIGHTS AND MEASURES

WEIGHT

talent (60 minas)	75 pounds	34 kilograms
mina (50 shekels)	1.25 pounds	600 grams
shekel	0.4 ounces	11.4 grams
pim (⅔ shekel)	0.25 ounces	8 grams
beka (½ shekel)	0.2 ounces	5.7 grams
gerah (1/20 shekel)	0.02 ounces	0.6 grams

LENGTH

long cubit	21 inches	53 centimeters
cubit	18 inches	45 centimeters
span	9 inches	23 centimeters
handbreadth	3 inches	8 centimeters

CAPACITY

DRY MEASURE

cor/homer (10 ephahs)	5 bushels	182 liters
lethek (5 ephahs)	2.5 bushels	91 liters
ephah	0.5 bushels	18 liters
seah (⅓ ephah)	5 quarts	6 liters
omer (1/10 ephah)	2 quarts	2 liters
cab (½ omer)	1 quart	1.3 liters

LIQUID MEASURE

bath	5.5 gallons	21 liters
hin (⅙ bath)	1 gallon	3.8 liters
log (1/72 bath)	0.3 quarts	0.3 liters

How to Study the Bible

Now that you are a Christian, one thing you will want to do on a daily basis is study the Bible. You may, however, have some questions about this. For example, you may ask yourself, *How do I study the Bible?* Or, *Where do I begin reading?* This feature will answer those questions and give you the information you need to develop the basic techniques necessary for effective Bible study.

Pray for Wisdom and Understanding. The most often overlooked and under-valued aspect of Bible study is prayer. Yet prayer is essential to gaining wisdom and understanding when you read God's Word. Through prayer, you can approach God and acknowledge your incomplete knowledge of his Word, as well as your need for him to open your heart to his instruction. Therefore, determine to begin each study with prayer. Only God can give you the wisdom to understand his Word.

Read in an Orderly Manner. If you received a letter and read only a few sentences here and there, the letter would not make much sense to you. But if you read the letter in order, you would understand it. The same holds true when you read the Bible.

Sadly, many Christians do not realize the shallowness of this approach. They read a portion of Matthew, a story from Daniel, a verse or two from Exodus, and then a chapter or so from Revelation and wonder why they do not have a good understanding of God's Word. Furthermore, they end up misinterpreting the meaning of these passages because they have failed to grasp the context from which they came.

To avoid developing this poor habit, you need to discipline yourself to read the Bible in an orderly manner. One way to do this is to use an established reading plan. A reading plan lists Scripture passages to be read in a certain order. Many of the existing plans were created with a goal in mind. Some plans break the whole Bible down into 365 daily readings. Others help you read through the Bible in the order that the events actually happened. For now, you may want to use the following plan as your reading guide. Start with the Gospel of John. This Gospel was written so that we might believe that Jesus is the Son of God. Then, after you have finished reading John, read the rest of the New Testament. Once you have finished the New Testament, you should read the books of the Old Testament. There you will see the coming of Jesus foreshadowed.

If you prefer a more structured approach, a one-year New Testament reading plan has been included on p. 1141 to help you get started.

Finish What You Start.   In life, the benefits of doing anything are often not realized until the task is completed. The same is true when reading a book from the Bible. Once you choose a book to read, read it from beginning to end. Although you may benefit spiritually by reading a verse from one book or a story from another, you will benefit more by reading the entire book from which the verse or story came. Reading the entire book puts each verse and story in its proper context. Thus, you will have a better understanding of what each verse and story means. In addition, by reading books from beginning to end you will become more familiar with the Bible as a whole. You may even discover passages that will one day become your favorites.

Meditate on God's Word and Ask Questions.   Thinking about what you have read cannot be overemphasized. Meditating on what you have read helps you to discover the importance of the passage. It also helps you to examine your life in light of what God reveals in his Word.

One of the best ways to begin meditating on God's Word is to ask questions. Here are a few questions to help you get started:

■ What is the main subject of the passage?
■ To whom is this passage addressed?
■ Who is speaking?
■ About what or whom is the person speaking?
■ What is the key verse?
■ What does this passage teach me about God?

To see how the text might apply to you personally, ask yourself these questions:

■ Is there any sin mentioned in the passage that I need to confess or forsake?
■ Is there a command given that I should obey?
■ Is there a promise made that I can apply to my current circumstances?
■ Is there a prayer given that I could pray?

Invest in a Few Good Resource Books.   The Bible alludes to many ancient customs that are completely unfamiliar to us today. Much of the subtle meaning behind these allusions that would give us greater insight into and appreciation for God's Word is therefore lost. To understand the culture in which the Bible was written, you may want to purchase a few good biblical resource books.

There are two types of resource books you should look into purchasing: (1) a one- or two-volume commentary on the whole Bible and (2) a Bible dictionary. Most one- or two-volume commentaries are concise. They give you the necessary information on important words, phrases, and verses from the Bible. They will not give you commentary on each verse, and they will not go into detailed explanations on any one verse. But they are good resources to help you begin to understand God's Word. The price for such a commentary can range from twenty-five to forty dollars per volume.

Bible dictionaries contain short articles (in alphabetical order) on people, places, and objects found in the Bible. Some Bible dictionaries also contain maps, diagrams, and pictures of biblical cities, regions, and artifacts. Bible dictionaries cost between twenty-five and thirty-five dollars. You can find these resources wherever Christian books are sold.

If you apply these practices to your daily personal Bible study, you are bound to develop habits that will help you grow in your faith.

The One Year New Testament Reading Plan

January 1
Matthew 1:1-17
Romans 1:1-7

January 2
Matthew 1:18-25
Romans 1:8-15

January 3
Matthew 2:1-12
Romans 1:16-17

January 4
Matthew 2:13-23
Romans 1:18-32

January 5
Matthew 3:1-12
Romans 2:1-16

January 6
Matthew 3:13-17
Romans 2:17-29

January 7
Matthew 4:1-11
Romans 3:1-8

January 8
Matthew 4:12-25
Romans 3:9-20

January 9
Matthew 5:1-16
Romans 3:21-31

January 10
Matthew 5:17-48
Romans 4:1-12

January 11
Matthew 6:1-18
Romans 4:13-17

January 12
Matthew 6:19-34
Romans 4:18-25

January 13
Matthew 7:1-6
Romans 5:1-5

January 14
Matthew 7:7-12
Romans 5:6-11

January 15
Matthew 7:13-29
Romans 5:12-21

January 16
Matthew 8:1-17
Romans 6:1-14

January 17
Matthew 8:18-22
Romans 6:15-23

January 18
Matthew 8:23-34
Romans 7:1-6

January 19
Matthew 9:1-8
Romans 7:7-13

January 20
Matthew 9:9-13
Romans 7:14-25

January 21
Matthew 9:14-17
Romans 8:1-8

January 22
Matthew 9:18-26
Romans 8:9-17

January 23
Matthew 9:27-38
Romans 8:18-27

January 24
Matthew 10:1-18
Romans 8:28-39

January 25
Matthew 10:19–11:1
Romans 9:1-5

January 26
Matthew 11:2-19
Romans 9:6-18

January 27
Matthew 11:20-30
Romans 9:19-26

January 28
Matthew 12:1-21
Romans 9:27-33

January 29
Matthew 12:22-37
Romans 10:1-13

January 30
Matthew 12:38-50
Romans 10:14-21

January 31
Matthew 13:1-23
Romans 11:1-6

February 1
Matthew 13:24-35
Romans 11:7-12

February 2
Matthew 13:36-43
Romans 11:13-21

February 3
Matthew 13:44-58
Romans 11:22-27

February 4
Matthew 14:1-12
Romans 11:28-36

February 5
Matthew 14:13-21
Romans 12:1-5

February 6
Matthew 14:22-36
Romans 12:6-13

February 7
Matthew 15:1-20
Romans 12:14-21

February 8
Matthew 15:21-28
Romans 13:1-7

February 9
Matthew 15:29-39
Romans 13:8-14

February 10
Matthew 16:1-12
Romans 14:1-4

February 11
Matthew 16:13-28
Romans 14:5-9

February 12
Matthew 17:1-13
Romans 14:10-16

February 13
Matthew 17:14-21
Romans 14:17-23

February 14
Matthew 17:22-27
Romans 15:1-6

February 15
Matthew 18:1-20
Romans 15:7-17

February 16
Matthew 18:21-35
Romans 15:18-22

February 17
Matthew 19:1-12
Romans 15:23-33

February 18
Matthew 19:13-15
Romans 16:1-16

February 19
Matthew 19:16-30
Romans 16:17-27

February 20
Matthew 20:1-19
1 Corinthians 1:1-9

February 21
Matthew 20:20-28
1 Corinthians 1:10-17

February 22
Matthew 20:29-34
1 Corinthians 1:18-25

February 23
Matthew 21:1-17
1 Corinthians 1:26-31

February 24
Matthew 21:18-22
1 Corinthians 2:1-10

February 25
Matthew 21:23-46
1 Corinthians 2:11-16

February 26
Matthew 22:1-14
1 Corinthians 3:1-9

February 27
Matthew 22:15-46
1 Corinthians 3:10-17

February 28
Matthew 23:1-12
1 Corinthians 3:18-23

March 1
Matthew 23:13-39
1 Corinthians 4:1-7

March 2
Matthew 24:1-31
1 Corinthians 4:8-13

March 3
Matthew 24:32-51
1 Corinthians 4:14-21

March 4
Matthew 25:1-13
1 Corinthians 5:1-8

March 5
Matthew 25:14-30
1 Corinthians 5:9-13

March 6
Matthew 25:31-46
1 Corinthians 6:1-9a

March 7
Matthew 26:1-16
1 Corinthians 6:9b-13a

March 8
Matthew 26:17-35
1 Corinthians 6:13b-20

March 9
Matthew 26:36-56
1 Corinthians 7:1-9

March 10
Matthew 26:57-75
1 Corinthians 7:10-17

March 11
Matthew 27:1-10
1 Corinthians 7:18-24

March 12
Matthew 27:11-30
1 Corinthians 7:25-31

March 13
Matthew 27:31-56
1 Corinthians 7:32-40

March 14
Matthew 27:57-66
1 Corinthians 8:1-13

March 15
Matthew 28:1-15
1 Corinthians 9:1-10

March 16
Matthew 28:16-20
1 Corinthians 9:11-18

March 17
Mark 1:1-8
1 Corinthians 9:19-27

March 18
Mark 1:9-13
1 Corinthians 10:1-14

March 19
Mark 1:14-20
1 Corinthians 10:15-22

March 20
Mark 1:21-28
1 Corinthians 10:23–11:1

March 21
Mark 1:29-39
1 Corinthians 11:2-16

March 22
Mark 1:40-45
1 Corinthians 11:17-22

March 23
Mark 2:1-12
1 Corinthians 11:23-34

March 24
Mark 2:13-17
1 Corinthians 12:1-3

March 25
Mark 2:18-22
1 Corinthians 12:4-11

March 26
Mark 2:23–3:6
1 Corinthians 12:12-18

March 27
Mark 3:7-19
1 Corinthians 12:19-27

March 28
Mark 3:20-35
1 Corinthians 12:28-31

March 29
Mark 4:1-20
1 Corinthians 13:1-7

March 30
Mark 4:21-34
1 Corinthians 13:8-13

March 31
Mark 4:35-41
1 Corinthians 14:1-5

April 1
Mark 5:1-20
1 Corinthians 14:6-12

April 2
Mark 5:21-43
1 Corinthians 14:13-17

April 3
Mark 6:1-6
1 Corinthians 14:18-25

April 4
Mark 6:7-13
1 Corinthians 14:26-32

April 5
Mark 6:14-29
1 Corinthians 14:33-40

April 6
Mark 6:30-44
1 Corinthians 15:1-11

April 7
Mark 6:45-56
1 Corinthians 15:12-20

April 8
Mark 7:1-23
1 Corinthians 15:21-28

April 9
Mark 7:24-37
1 Corinthians 15:29-34

April 10
Mark 8:1-10
1 Corinthians 15:35-44

April 11
Mark 8:11-21
1 Corinthians 15:45-49

April 12
Mark 8:22-26
1 Corinthians 15:50-58

April 13
Mark 8:27-38
1 Corinthians 16:1-9

April 14
Mark 9:1-13
1 Corinthians 16:10-18

April 15
Mark 9:14-29
1 Corinthians 16:19-24

April 16
Mark 9:30-37
2 Corinthians 1:1-7

April 17
Mark 9:38-50
2 Corinthians 1:8-14

April 18
Mark 10:1-12
2 Corinthians 1:15-24

April 19
Mark 10:13-16
2 Corinthians 2:1-4

April 20
Mark 10:17-31
2 Corinthians 2:5-11

April 21
Mark 10:32-45
2 Corinthians 2:12-17

April 22
Mark 10:46-52
2 Corinthians 3:1-6

April 23
Mark 11:1-11
2 Corinthians 3:7-18

April 24
Mark 11:12-27
2 Corinthians 4:1-7

April 25
Mark 11:28–12:12
2 Corinthians 4:8-17

April 26
Mark 12:13-34
2 Corinthians 4:18–5:10

April 27
Mark 12:35-44
2 Corinthians 5:11-21

April 28
Mark 13:1-13
2 Corinthians 6:1-7

April 29
Mark 13:14-37
2 Corinthians 6:8-13

April 30
Mark 14:1-11
2 Corinthians 6:14–7:4

May 1
Mark 14:12-31
2 Corinthians 7:5-10

May 2
Mark 14:32-52
2 Corinthians 7:11-16

May 3
Mark 14:53-72
2 Corinthians 8:1-8

May 4
Mark 15:1-20
2 Corinthians 8:9-15

May 5
Mark 15:21-32
2 Corinthians 8:16-24

May 6
Mark 15:33-47
2 Corinthians 9:1-5

May 7
Mark 16:1-20
2 Corinthians 9:6-15

May 8
Luke 1:1-25
2 Corinthians 10:1-6

May 9
Luke 1:26-56
2 Corinthians 10:7-12

May 10
Luke 1:57-80
2 Corinthians 10:13-18

May 11
Luke 2:1-20
2 Corinthians 11:1-6

May 12
Luke 2:21-40
2 Corinthians 11:7-15

May 13
Luke 2:41-52
2 Corinthians 11:16-33

May 14
Luke 3:1-18
2 Corinthians 12:1-10

May 15
Luke 3:19-23a
2 Corinthians 12:11-15

May 16
Luke 3:23b-38
2 Corinthians 12:16-21

May 17
Luke 4:1-13
2 Corinthians 13:1-6

May 18
Luke 4:14-30
2 Corinthians 13:7-14

May 19
Luke 4:31-44
Galatians 1:1-5

May 20
Luke 5:1-11
Galatians 1:6-12

May 21
Luke 5:12-16
Galatians 1:13-24

May 22
Luke 5:17-26
Galatians 2:1-5

May 23
Luke 5:27-39
Galatians 2:6-10

May 24
Luke 6:1-11
Galatians 2:11-16

May 25
Luke 6:12-16
Galatians 2:17-21

May 26
Luke 6:17-38
Galatians 3:1-9

May 27
Luke 6:39-49
Galatians 3:10-14

May 28
Luke 7:1-10
Galatians 3:15-20

May 29
Luke 7:11-17
Galatians 3:21-29

May 30
Luke 7:18-35
Galatians 4:1-7

May 31
Luke 7:36-50
Galatians 4:8-11

June 1
Luke 8:1-3
Galatians 4:12-20

June 2
Luke 8:4-15
Galatians 4:21-31

June 3
Luke 8:16-18
Galatians 5:1-6

June 4
Luke 8:19-21
Galatians 5:7-15

June 5
Luke 8:22-25
Galatians 5:16-21

June 6
Luke 8:26-40
Galatians 5:22-26

June 7
Luke 8:41-56
Galatians 6:1-10

June 8
Luke 9:1-9
Galatians 6:11-18

June 9
Luke 9:10-17
Ephesians 1:1-8

June 10
Luke 9:18-22
Ephesians 1:9-14

June 11
Luke 9:23-27
Ephesians 1:15-23

June 12
Luke 9:28-36
Ephesians 2:1-7

June 13
Luke 9:37-43a
Ephesians 2:8-13

June 14
Luke 9:43b-50
Ephesians 2:14-22

June 15
Luke 9:51-62
Ephesians 3:1-7

June 16
Luke 10:1-24
Ephesians 3:8-13

June 17
Luke 10:25-37
Ephesians 3:14-21

June 18
Luke 10:38-42
Ephesians 4:1-10

June 19
Luke 11:1-13
Ephesians 4:11-16

June 20
Luke 11:14-28
Ephesians 4:17-24

June 21
Luke 11:29-36
Ephesians 4:25-32

June 22
Luke 11:37-54
Ephesians 5:1-9

June 23
Luke 12:1-12
Ephesians 5:10-20

June 24
Luke 12:13-34
Ephesians 5:21-33

June 25
Luke 12:35-48
Ephesians 6:1-4

June 26
Luke 12:49-59
Ephesians 6:5-9

June 27
Luke 13:1-9
Ephesians 6:10-17

June 28
Luke 13:10-17
Ephesians 6:18-24

June 29
Luke 13:18-21
Philippians 1:1-6

June 30
Luke 13:22-30
Philippians 1:7-11

July 1
Luke 13:31-35
Philippians 1:12-18a

July 2
Luke 14:1-6
Philippians 1:18b-30

July 3
Luke 14:7-24
Philippians 2:1-11

July 4
Luke 14:25-35
Philippians 2:12-18

July 5
Luke 15:1-10
Philippians 2:19-30

July 6
Luke 15:11-32
Philippians 3:1-7

July 7
Luke 16:1-14
Philippians 3:8-12

July 8
Luke 16:15-31
Philippians 3:13-16

July 9
Luke 17:1-4
Philippians 3:17-21

July 10
Luke 17:5-10
Philippians 4:1-7

July 11
Luke 17:11-19
Philippians 4:8-14

July 12
Luke 17:20-37
Philippians 4:15-23

July 13
Luke 18:1-8
Colossians 1:1-6

July 14
Luke 18:9-17
Colossians 1:7-9

July 15
Luke 18:18-30
Colossians 1:10-14

July 16
Luke 18:31-34
Colossians 1:15-18

July 17
Luke 18:35-43
Colossians 1:19-23

July 18
Luke 19:1-10
Colossians 1:24-29

July 19
Luke 19:11-27
Colossians 2:1-10

July 20
Luke 19:28-40
Colossians 2:11-15

July 21
Luke 19:41-48
Colossians 2:16-23

July 22
Luke 20:1-19
Colossians 3:1-8

July 23
Luke 20:20-26
Colossians 3:9-14

July 24
Luke 20:27-47
Colossians 3:15-17

July 25
Luke 21:1-4
Colossians 3:18–4:1

July 26
Luke 21:5-19
Colossians 4:2-6

July 27
Luke 21:20-38
Colossians 4:7-18

July 28
Luke 22:1-23
1 Thessalonians 1:1-10

July 29
Luke 22:24-30
1 Thessalonians 2:1-8

July 30
Luke 22:31-34
1 Thessalonians 2:9-13

July 31
Luke 22:35-38
1 Thessalonians 2:14–3:4

August 1
Luke 22:39-53
1 Thessalonians 3:5-8

August 2
Luke 22:54-62
1 Thessalonians 3:9-13

August 3
Luke 22:63-71
1 Thessalonians 4:1-8

August 4
Luke 23:1-25
1 Thessalonians 4:9-12

August 5
Luke 23:26-43
1 Thessalonians 4:13–5:3

August 6
Luke 23:44-56
1 Thessalonians 5:4-11

August 7
Luke 24:1-12
1 Thessalonians 5:12-22

August 8
Luke 24:13-34
1 Thessalonians 5:23-28

August 9
Luke 24:35-53
2 Thessalonians 1:1-12

August 10
John 1:1-14
2 Thessalonians 2:1-6

August 11
John 1:15-34
2 Thessalonians 2:7-17

August 12
John 1:35-51
2 Thessalonians 3:1-5

August 13
John 2:1-12
2 Thessalonians 3:6-18

August 14
John 2:13-25
1 Timothy 1:1-6

August 15
John 3:1-21
1 Timothy 1:7-11

August 16
John 3:22-36
1 Timothy 1:12-17

August 17
John 4:1-30
1 Timothy 1:18-20

August 18
John 4:31-42
1 Timothy 2:1-8

August 19
John 4:43-54
1 Timothy 2:9-15

August 20
John 5:1-24
1 Timothy 3:1-7

August 21
John 5:25-47
1 Timothy 3:8-15

August 22
John 6:1-15
1 Timothy 3:16–4:6

August 23
John 6:16-21
1 Timothy 4:7-11

August 24
John 6:22-46
1 Timothy 4:12–5:2

August 25
John 6:47-71
1 Timothy 5:3-10

August 26
John 7:1-13
1 Timothy 5:11-16

August 27
John 7:14-36
1 Timothy 5:17-25

August 28
John 7:37-53
1 Timothy 6:1-5

August 29
John 8:1-11
1 Timothy 6:6-12

August 30
John 8:12-30
1 Timothy 6:13-16

August 31
John 8:31-59
1 Timothy 6:17-21

September 1
John 9:1-12
2 Timothy 1:1-7

September 2
John 9:13-41
2 Timothy 1:8-14

September 3
John 10:1-21
2 Timothy 1:15-18

September 4
John 10:22-42
2 Timothy 2:1-7

September 5
John 11:1-29
2 Timothy 2:8-14

September 6
John 11:30-46
2 Timothy 2:15-21

September 7
John 11:47-57
2 Timothy 2:22-26

September 8
John 12:1-11
2 Timothy 3:1-9

September 9
John 12:12-19
2 Timothy 3:10-17

September 10
John 12:20-36
2 Timothy 4:1-4

September 11
John 12:37-50
2 Timothy 4:5-8

September 12
John 13:1-20
2 Timothy 4:9-22

September 13
John 13:21-38
Titus 1:1-5

September 14
John 14:1-14
Titus 1:6-16

September 15
John 14:15-31
Titus 2:1-10

September 16
John 15:1-15
Titus 2:11-15

September 17
John 15:16-27
Titus 3:1-8

September 18
John 16:1-15
Titus 3:9-15

September 19
John 16:16-33
Philemon 1:1-7

September 20
John 17:1-26
Philemon 1:8-25

September 21
John 18:1-14
Hebrews 1:1-14

September 22
John 18:15-27
Hebrews 2:1-4

September 23
John 18:28-40
Hebrews 2:5-10

September 24
John 19:1-15
Hebrews 2:11-15

September 25
John 19:16-30
Hebrews 2:16–3:6

September 26
John 19:31-42
Hebrews 3:7-14

September 27
John 20:1-18
Hebrews 3:15-19

September 28
John 20:19-31
Hebrews 4:1-6

September 29
John 21:1-14
Hebrews 4:7-13

September 30
John 21:15-25
Hebrews 4:14–5:6

October 1
Acts 1:1-13
Hebrews 5:7-10

October 2
Acts 1:14-26
Hebrews 5:11-14

October 3
Acts 2:1-13
Hebrews 6:1-6

October 4
Acts 2:14-39
Hebrews 6:7-15

October 5
Acts 2:40-47
Hebrews 6:16-20

October 6
Acts 3:1-26
Hebrews 7:1-11

October 7
Acts 4:1-22
Hebrews 7:12-22

October 8
Acts 4:23-37
Hebrews 7:23-28

October 9
Acts 5:1-11
Hebrews 8:1-6

October 10
Acts 5:12-25
Hebrews 8:7-13

October 11
Acts 5:26-42
Hebrews 9:1-10

October 12
Acts 6:1-7
Hebrews 9:11-15

October 13
Acts 6:8–7:16
Hebrews 9:16-23

October 14
Acts 7:17-43
Hebrews 9:24-28

October 15
Acts 7:44-60
Hebrews 10:1-10

October 16
Acts 8:1-25
Hebrews 10:11-22

October 17
Acts 8:26-40
Hebrews 10:23-25

October 18
Acts 9:1-19a
Hebrews 10:26-31

October 19
Acts 9:19b-31
Hebrews 10:32-39

October 20
Acts 9:32-35
Hebrews 11:1-6

October 21
Acts 9:36-43
Hebrews 11:7-12

October 22
Acts 10:1-23a
Hebrews 11:13-16

October 23
Acts 10:23b-48
Hebrews 11:17-20

October 24
Acts 11:1-18
Hebrews 11:21-23

October 25
Acts 11:19-30
Hebrews 11:24-29

October 26
Acts 12:1-25
Hebrews 11:30-40

October 27
Acts 13:1-12
Hebrews 12:1-4

October 28
Acts 13:13-23
Hebrews 12:5-11

October 29
Acts 13:24-44
Hebrews 12:12-17

October 30
Acts 13:45-52
Hebrews 12:18-24

October 31
Acts 14:1-7
Hebrews 12:25-29

November 1
Acts 14:8-20a
Hebrews 13:1-9

November 2
Acts 14:20b-28
Hebrews 13:10-16

November 3
Acts 15:1-21
Hebrews 13:17-25

November 4
Acts 15:22-41
James 1:1-4

November 5
Acts 16:1-10
James 1:5-8

November 6
Acts 16:11-15
James 1:9-18

November 7
Acts 16:16-40
James 1:19-27

November 8
Acts 17:1-15
James 2:1-9

November 9
Acts 17:16-34
James 2:10-13

November 10
Acts 18:1-8
James 2:14-26

November 11
Acts 18:9-23
James 3:1-12

November 12
Acts 18:24-28
James 3:13-18

November 13
Acts 19:1-10
James 4:1-6

November 14
Acts 19:11-20
James 4:7-10

November 15
Acts 19:21-41
James 4:11-12

November 16
Acts 20:1-12
James 4:13-17

November 17
Acts 20:13-38
James 5:1-6

November 18
Acts 21:1-17
James 5:7-12

November 19
Acts 21:18-36
James 5:13-20

November 20
Acts 21:37–22:16
1 Peter 1:1-7

November 21
Acts 22:17-29
1 Peter 1:8-13

November 22
Acts 22:30–23:11
1 Peter 1:14-25

November 23
Acts 23:12-35
1 Peter 2:1-10

November 24
Acts 24:1-9
1 Peter 2:11-16

November 25
Acts 24:10-27
1 Peter 2:17-25

November 26
Acts 25:1-12
1 Peter 3:1-6

November 27
Acts 25:13-27
1 Peter 3:7-9

November 28
Acts 26:1-32
1 Peter 3:10-16

November 29
Acts 27:1-15
1 Peter 3:17-22

November 30
Acts 27:16-44
1 Peter 4:1-6

December 1
Acts 28:1-10
1 Peter 4:7-11

December 2
Acts 28:11-31
1 Peter 4:12-19

December 3
Revelation 1:1-8
1 Peter 5:1-7

December 4
Revelation 1:9-20
1 Peter 5:8-14

December 5
Revelation 2:1-7
2 Peter 1:1-11

December 6
Revelation 2:8-11
2 Peter 1:12-18

December 7
Revelation 2:12-17
2 Peter 1:19–2:11

December 8
Revelation 2:18-29
2 Peter 2:12-22

December 9
Revelation 3:1-6
2 Peter 3:1-7

December 10
Revelation 3:7-13
2 Peter 3:8-13

December 11
Revelation 3:14-22
2 Peter 3:14-18

December 12
Revelation 4:1-11
1 John 1:1-4

December 13
Revelation 5:1-14
1 John 1:5-10

December 14
Revelation 6:1-17
1 John 2:1-6

December 15
Revelation 7:1-17
1 John 2:7-11

December 16
Revelation 8:1-13
1 John 2:12-17

December 17
Revelation 9:1-21
1 John 2:18-27

December 18
Revelation 10:1-11
1 John 2:28–3:6

December 19
Revelation 11:1-19
1 John 3:7-11

December 20
Revelation 12:1–13:1a
1 John 3:12-24

December 21
Revelation 13:1b-18
1 John 4:1-6

December 22
Revelation 14:1-7
1 John 4:7-15

December 23
Revelation 14:8-20
1 John 4:16-21

December 24
Revelation 15:1-8
1 John 5:1-15

December 25
Revelation 16:1-21
1 John 5:16-21

December 26
Revelation 17:1-18
2 John 1:1-6

December 27
Revelation 18:1-24
2 John 1:7-13

December 28
Revelation 19:1-21
3 John 1:1-15

December 29
Revelation 20:1-15
Jude 1:1-7

December 30
Revelation 21:1–22:6
Jude 1:8-16

December 31
Revelation 22:7-21
Jude 1:17-25

Overview of the Bible

Book
Author
Date Written
Genre
Summary

OLD TESTAMENT

Genesis
Moses
1450–1410 B.C.
Narrative
Genesis is the first book of the Bible. The word *genesis* means "the origin or coming into being of something." Recorded here are such important beginnings as the Creation, the fall of man, and the early years of the nation of Israel.

Exodus
Moses
1450–1410 B.C.
Narrative
Exodus is about deliverance. The Israelites had moved to Egypt during a famine. While there, they had been made slaves. Because the Israelites were God's people, he appointed Moses to lead the Israelites out of Egypt and to the Promised Land, Canaan. On the way there, the Israelites stopped at Mount Sinai, where God gave his people the Ten Commandments.

Leviticus
Moses
1445–1444 B.C.
Law
Leviticus deals with the worship of a holy God. Here God gave the priests and people rules to live by to present themselves holy before him.

Numbers
Moses
1450–1410 B.C.
Narrative
Numbers takes its name from the two censuses (or "numberings") of the people recorded in this book. Yet Numbers is actually a sequel to Exodus. It follows the wanderings of the Israelites through the wilderness of Sinai for the next forty years, until they camped just east of the Promised Land.

Deuteronomy
Moses
1407–1406 B.C.
Narrative
Deuteronomy is a farewell speech given to the people of Israel by Moses just before his death. Moses knew that the people would face many new temptations as they moved into the Promised Land. It was critical that they be reminded of God's promises to them and their responsibility to God and his laws.

Joshua
Joshua and possibly Phinehas
Unknown
Narrative
Joshua is the book of conquest. Here, the Israelites finally took possession of the Promised Land. The conquest was not immediate, though. It was a process of faith and action, through which God displayed his miraclous power.

Judges
Probably Samuel
Unknown
Narrative
This is a book about backsliding, defeat, and God's gracious deliverance. When the Israelites forgot God, he allowed them to be oppressed by a neighboring country. Then they cried out to God, who raised up judges to deliver his people.

Ruth
Unknown
1375–1050 B.C.
Narrative
The events of Ruth take place during some of the darkest days in the history of Israel. It was a time when the nation lapsed again and again into the worship of false gods. In sharp contrast to this is the shining testimony of one Gentile woman from Moab who remained faithful to God.

1 Samuel
Samuel, Nathan, and Gad
Unknown
Narrative
This book records a crucial time in Israel's history. Here the people of Israel rejected God's chosen leader Samuel—a judge—and demanded a king. Despite Samuel's warnings that a king would oppress them, the people insisted that he anoint someone as king. So the leadership of Israel passed from Samuel to Saul, their first king.

2 Samuel
Unknown
930 B.C.
Narrative
Second Samuel focuses on the life and career of Israel's greatest king—David. Under David, the kingdom of Israel doubled in size and its enemies were subdued. Though he was a good leader and

popular with the people, David was not perfect. This book also records David's sin with Bathsheba and his tragic failure as a father.

1 Kings
Unknown
Unknown
Narrative
In 1 Kings, David's reign came to an end and his son Solomon became king. God gave Solomon the gift of wisdom and the blessing of building the temple. By the end of his reign, the kingdom was in an agitated state of unrest due to the excessive taxes for all of his building projects. The book ends as Solomon's son Rehoboam took the throne, which led to the division of the kingdom.

2 Kings
Unknown
Unknown
Narrative
Second Kings shows man's inability to rule himself and the world. The kings of Israel and Judah had turned their backs on God and led their citizens astray. God sent many prophets to warn his people, but they refused to listen. In the end, the kingdoms of Israel and Judah collapsed, and their citizens were taken away into captivity.

1 Chronicles
Ezra
430 B.C.
Narrative
This book emphasizes the spiritual significance of David's righteous reign. Through David's offspring would come the Messiah, Jesus Christ, whose throne and kingdom would be established forever.

2 Chronicles
Ezra
430 B.C.
Narrative
The emphasis in 2 Chronicles is on the southern kingdom, Judah, and on David's descendants. Here God used five outstanding kings to bring periods of revival, renewal, and reformation to the land.

Ezra
Ezra
450 B.C.
Narrative
Ezra relates the account of the two returns from Babylon. It picks up where 2 Chronicles left off by showing how God fulfilled his promise to bring back his people after seventy years of exile and captivity.

Nehemiah
Nehemiah
445–432 B.C.
Narrative
The book of Nehemiah is a wonderful story of how to handle opposition and discouragement when you are seeking to serve the Lord. Nehemiah was a cupbearer for the king of Persia. After hearing about the danger the city of Jerusalem was in, he returned there and, despite local opposition, completed reconstruction of the walls and gates of the city in fifty-two days.

Esther
Unknown
483–471 B.C.
Narrative
The book of Esther shows God's providence at work in a profound way. As one Persian noble close to the king plotted to kill the Jews, Esther, the Jewish queen, interceded on behalf of her people at great personal risk.

Job
Possibly Job
Unknown
Poetry
The book of Job addresses one of life's most-asked questions: Why does God allow suffering? Despite the fact that Job lost everything, suffered greatly, and had doubts about God, he remained faithful to God. In the end, God blessed him greatly.

Psalms
David, Asaph, the sons of Korah, Solomon, Heman, Ethan, and Moses
1440–586 B.C.

Poetry
Psalms contains a variety of themes that touch on every area of life. The central theme, however, is the praise and worship of a sovereign and loving God. Besides being a source of comfort and worship, the Psalms are filled with prophecies about Jesus Christ.

Proverbs
Solomon, Agur, and Lemuel
Early in Solomon's reign
Wisdom Literature
Proverbs is a book of wisdom written by the wisest man who ever lived, Solomon. This book contains God's divine wisdom for every area of life—such as choosing friends, handling temptation, raising children, and knowing God.

Ecclesiastes
Solomon
935 B.C.
Wisdom Literature
Ecclesiastes is Solomon's analysis of life. Solomon had everything—incredible wealth, power, and intellect. He had tried every enterprise and every pleasure known to man. Yet his final conclusion about life was that it is empty and purposeless without God.

Song of Songs
Solomon
Unknown
Poetry
The Song of Songs is one of the most unusual books in the Bible. On one level, it is an expression of pure love—as God intended it—in marriage. On another level, it symbolically speaks of God's love for his people and their love for him.

Isaiah
Isaiah
700–681 B.C.
Prophecy
Isaiah begins the prophetic portion of the Bible. This book includes warnings of God's coming judgment upon the nations of Isaiah's day, as well as prophecies about the future redeemer of humankind—Jesus Christ.

Jeremiah

Jeremiah
627–586 B.C.
Prophecy
Jeremiah is known as the weeping prophet. He delivered God's messages to the people of Judah. Although he passionately pleaded with them to repent of their sins and return to God, the people ignored him and were taken into captivity in Babylon.

Lamentations

Jeremiah
586 B.C.
Poetry and Prophecy
Lamentations is a book of sadness. It opens with Jeremiah weeping over the destruction of Jerusalem and the carting off of captives to Babylon. But near the end, Jeremiah sees hope in the love and compassion of God.

Ezekiel

Ezekiel
571 B.C.
Prophecy
Ezekiel was taken captive to Babylon twelve years before the fall of Jerusalem in 586 B.C. While there, he was called by God to preach to the captives a message of judgment and salvation, to call them to repentance and obedience.

Daniel

Daniel
535 B.C.
Narrative and Prophecy
Like Ezekiel, Daniel had been taken to Babylon in captivity, where he was trained to serve in the courts of the king. Through Daniel's writings, we learn of God's sovereignty and control of man's history. In addition, Daniel contains some of the most well-known stories in the Bible, including Daniel in the lions' den and the three men in the "fiery furnace."

Hosea

Hosea
715 B.C.
Prophecy
Hosea is a tragic love story about God, who loved his people despite their unfaithfulness to him. Hosea warned that one cannot disobey God without disastrous consequences. Yet, this book dramatically portrays God's unending love and mercy as he offers forgiveness to those who repent.

Joel

Joel
835–796 B.C.
Prophecy
This book describes God's inescapable and overwhelming judgment upon sinful man. The prophet Joel was sent to warn the people of the coming judgment of God. He called for the people to turn back to God before judgment fell upon them.

Amos

Amos
760–750 B.C.
Prophecy
Amos prophesied to the northern kingdom during a time of great prosperity. As a result of their prosperity, the people had become self-sufficient and indifferent toward God and others. Amos came to warn them of the dangers of their indifference and spiritual complacency.

Obadiah

Obadiah
Possibly 627–586 B.C.
Prophecy
The book of Obadiah demonstrates God's ongoing protection of his people from their enemies. As the Babylonians carried the Israelites off in captivity, the Edomites watched in indifference. Therefore, Obadiah let them know that they would stand condemned and be destroyed, while Israel would be restored.

Jonah

Jonah
785–760 B.C.
Narrative
This is the story of a man who tried to run from God and quickly learned the futility of it. After repenting of his sin, Jonah was restored and recommissioned. His preaching resulted in a large revival, as the entire city of Nineveh turned to God.

Micah

Micah
Possibly 742–687 B.C.
Prophecy
Micah gives us a glimpse of God's hatred of sin and, at the same time, his love for the sinner. This book also gives us some of the clearest predictions of the coming Messiah. Micah challenges you to live for God and join the faithful remnant of his people who live according to his will.

Nahum

Nahum
663–654 B.C.
Prophecy
Nahum teaches that God is the righteous judge and the supreme ruler over all. Those who continually do evil and oppress God's people, ignoring his repeated warnings, will pay a price.

Habakkuk

Habakkuk
612–589 B.C.
Prophecy
Habakkuk could not understand how God could allow evil and injustice to go on in his country. Yet, 'as Habakkuk sought God, he found his answer in trusting God's character.

Zephaniah

Zephaniah
640–621 B.C.
Prophecy
Zephaniah preached during a time of religious revival in Judah. But the religious zeal was shallow and inconsistent. The people had rid their homes of idols but had not done the same in their hearts. Zephaniah warned them that God did not take sin lightly and that God will punish those who sin.

Haggai

Haggai
520 B.C.
Prophecy
After some of the Jews returned from captivity, they had begun to rebuild the destroyed Temple. But due to opposition and spiritual apathy, they had stopped construction. Haggai

called the Jews to finish the Temple. He encouraged the people to wake up from their apathy and reorder their priorities, putting God first in their lives.

Zechariah

Zechariah
520–480 B.C.
Prophecy
Zechariah ministered with Haggai during the rebuilding of the Temple. He came to bring God's message of encouragement and hope to a discouraged people.

Malachi

Malachi
430 B.C.
Prophecy
Malachi is a beautiful expression of God's mercy and grace to a nation so unworthy of either. Israel, God's chosen people, had willfully disobeyed God. Yet, like a father pleading with his children, God extended a hand of forgiveness to those who would turn and faithfully follow after him.

NEW TESTAMENT

Matthew

Matthew (Levi)
A.D. 60–65
Gospel
This Gospel was written with the Jew in mind and therefore has many references to Old Testament prophecies that were fulfilled by Jesus. It contains at least 129 quotations or allusions to the Old Testament. Matthew's objective was to show the Jewish people that Jesus was indeed their long-awaited Messiah.

Mark

John Mark
A.D. 55–65
Gospel
The Gospel of Mark is the account of the life, ministry, miracles, and words of Jesus Christ. In contrast to Matthew, who primarily presents Jesus as the Messiah, Mark emphasizes the servanthood of the Lord.

Luke

Luke
A.D. 60
Gospel
Luke was a Gentile who put his faith in Jesus Christ. His purpose for writing an account of Jesus Christ's life, death, and resurrection was to make the message of salvation understandable to those outside the Jewish faith and culture.

John

John
A.D. 85–90
Gospel
While the emphasis in the other three Gospels centers around the events in the life of Jesus, John often focuses upon the meaning of those events. For instance, while all four Gospels record the miracle of the feeding of the five thousand, only John gives us Jesus' message on the "Bread of Life" that followed that miracle.

Acts

Luke
A.D. 63–70
History
This book shows the church's early development and rapid growth. It reveals how the dynamic power of the Holy Spirit transformed a diverse group of fishermen, tax collectors, and other ordinary folks into people who turned their world upside-down with the gospel of Jesus Christ.

Romans

Paul
A.D. 70
Epistle
This epistle contains some of the prime secrets of the Christian life. It is a hard-hitting diagnosis of the primary source of man's problems—sin. It also shows the futility of thinking that the answers to our problems lie within ourselves.

1 Corinthians

Paul
A.D. 55
Epistle
Paul wrote this epistle in response to certain situations that had arisen

in the Corinthian church. He straightforwardly dealt with many of the errors that the people of this church believed and practiced. Among these pitfalls were sins of immorality, false teachings, and problems regarding marriage and lawsuits.

2 Corinthians

Paul
A.D. 55–57
Epistle
Some of the Corinthians who were still living in sin after Paul's first letter began denying Paul's authority. Paul wrote this second letter to deal with the problems that persisted within the Corinthian church.

Galatians

Paul
A.D. 49
Epistle
Galatians is a foundational study that shows how complete the work of Jesus' death on the cross was for our salvation. Nothing needs to be added to that work—nor does it need to be improved upon—for you can't improve upon perfection.

Ephesians

Paul
A.D. 60
Epistle
The book of Ephesians shows us our rightful position as children of God "in the heavenlies" with Jesus Christ. It tells us of all that God has done for us, as well as how to fully appreciate and implement it practically in our lives.

Philippians

Paul
A.D. 61
Epistle
This book explains the mind-set, attitude, and outlook the believer must have if he or she is going to experience the joy of the Lord in a troubled world.

Colossians

Paul
A.D. 60
Epistle
Paul wrote this epistle to refute certain false teachings that had found

their way into the church at Colosse. A common theme of this book is the superiority of Jesus Christ.

1 Thessalonians
Paul
A.D. 51
Epistle
The theme of this book focuses upon living a godly and holy life as we await the return of Jesus Christ. Paul also offered words of comfort concerning Christian loved ones who have died.

2 Thessalonians
Paul
A.D. 51
Epistle
This letter offered encouragement to the believers who were facing persecution. It also offered correct teaching on the subject of "the day of the Lord," a confusing matter for some of the Thessalonian believers. In addition, some were not living as they should in light of the return of the Lord, so Paul addressed that issue as well.

1 Timothy
Paul
A.D. 64
Epistle
Paul, under the inspiration of the Holy Spirit, lays out what the conduct of the church and its leaders should be. Though Timothy himself was a pastor, these words apply to all who want to be used by God and have their lives make a difference.

2 Timothy
Paul
A.D. 67
Epistle
Paul wrote this second letter to Timothy to encourage him to be faithful to Christ. Paul also included a glimpse of what the last days would look like.

Titus
Paul
A.D. 65
Epistle
Paul wrote this letter to address the challenges facing Titus as an overseer of the churches on the island of Crete. He included criteria for qualifications of leadership, sound teaching, and good works.

Philemon
Paul
A.D. 60
Epistle
This short but profound epistle contains a wonderful story of the importance of forgiveness among Christians.

Hebrews
Unknown
A.D. 68
Epistle
The book of Hebrews was written for the Jews who had accepted Jesus as their Messiah. They were in danger of slipping back into the traditions of Judaism because they had not put their roots down in the soil of Christianity.

James
James, Jesus' half-brother
A.D. 49
Epistle
James spoke a lot about faith in his book, with an emphasis on results! He stressed the need to live a practical, seven-day-a-week working faith.

1 Peter
Peter
A.D. 65
Epistle
The theme of Peter's first epistle is suffering. He brought inspired words of comfort to those who suffered under persecution.

2 Peter
Peter
A.D. 66
Epistle
In this epistle Peter reminded the believers of certain important spiritual truths. Peter also warned of false teachers and spoke of the hope of the coming of the Lord.

1 John
John
A.D. 90–95
Epistle
In this letter John pointed out that a person either is or is not a child of God. There is no middle ground. John clearly emphasized that if one is really a child of God, it will become evident in one's outward behavior.

2 John
John
A.D. 90–95
Epistle
In this letter John pointed out that true Christian love involves more than just an emotional feeling. It is grounded in what is true. John also warned of false teachers, urging the believers not to receive them.

3 John
John
A.D. 90–95
Epistle
John wrote this letter to commend a believer named Gaius for the hospitality he showed to traveling teachers of the gospel.

Jude
Jude, Jesus' half-brother
A.D. 65
Epistle
The book of Jude is one of the shortest books in the New Testament. Its theme centers around the great apostasy, or falling away from the faith, that will happen on earth before the return of Jesus Christ.

Revelation
John
A.D. 95
Apocalyptic
In this great book, we learn of the return of Jesus Christ to the earth, as well as the events preceding that climactic moment.

Fifty-Two Great Bible Stories

This list not only gives you the fifty-two Bible stories you should be familiar with as a Christian but also provides an interesting reading plan as well. Using the list below, you can read through one great Bible story a week for a whole year.

1. In the Beginning
Genesis 1:1–2:3, p. 1
In an incredible display of majesty and power, God creates the heavens and the earth and everything in them.

2. The First Sin
Genesis 2:4–3:24, p. 4
God's original plan for humankind is spoiled in one small but deliberate act of disobedience that enables sin to enter the human race.

3. Noah and the Ark
Genesis 6:1–9:17, p. 7
One man's faith in and obedience to God spares his family from certain death in the greatest flood ever experienced by humankind.

4. Sodom and Gomorrah
Genesis 18:16–19:29, p. 15
Lot, a God-fearing man, allows outside influences and selfish pursuits to cloud his thinking. Though he escapes the destruction of his evil hometown, his compromising decisions leave a devastating mark on his life and family.

5. Abraham and Isaac
Genesis 22:1-18, p. 19
Abraham learns that complete obedience can mean great sacrifice—but also great blessing.

6. The Story of Joseph
Genesis 37:1-36, p. 33; 39:1–45:28, p. 35
Despite his virtuous lifestyle and his love for God, nothing seems to go right for Joseph. Yet Joseph's personal faith empowers him to rise above his trials and temptations, and he ultimately finds strength and blessing in spite of his hardships.

7. The Burning Bush
Exodus 3:1-22, p. 50
While tending sheep in the desert, Moses sees an unusual sight that leads him into a personal encounter with the living God.

8. The Ten Plagues
Exodus 7:14–12:30, p. 54
Pharaoh refuses to let the Israelites leave Egypt. To convince Pharaoh to change his mind, God sends a series of plagues. Unfortunately, Pharaoh's pride ends up costing him something precious—the life of his firstborn son.

9. The Great Escape
Exodus 12:31–14:31, p. 59
Moses and the Israelites overcome tremendous obstacles and learn the importance of completely trusting in God as they make their way to the Promised Land.

10. The Twelve Scouts and Their Report
Numbers 13:1–14:45, p. 127
When Caleb and Joshua choose to follow God's orders over popular opinion, they appear to be in trouble. God, however, turns the tables in their favor.

11. Balaam and the Talking Donkey
Numbers 22:21-35, p. 136
Balaam tests God by going against his will for profit. Fortunately, Balaam's donkey saves him from God's wrath.

12. Jericho
Joshua 5:13–6:27, p. 188
Marching and music play a strategic role in this unusual battle plan. Nevertheless, when the Israelites follow God's orders, they win a mighty victory.

13. The Story of Gideon and His Army
Judges 6:1–7:25, p. 214
Gideon feels completely unfit for God's service, yet God shows Gideon just how much he can do with so little.

14. The Rise and Fall of Samson
Judges 13:1–16:31, p. 221
God wants to use Samson for his purposes, but Samson allows pride, lust, and self-confidence to ruin his potential.

15. The Story of Ruth
Ruth 1:1–4:22, p. 231
Ruth, young and widowed, chooses to leave her home for an unknown land and an uncertain future in order to care for her mother-in-law and worship the one true God. God blesses Ruth's tender faith in a profound and special way.

16. The Calling of Samuel
1 Samuel 1:1–3:21, p. 235
God uses the most unlikely person, a small child, to deliver a devastating message to Eli the priest.

17. David and Goliath
1 Samuel 17:1-58, p. 249
David overcomes seemingly insurmountable odds and silences his skeptics when he kills Goliath, the mighty Philistine warrior, with a few small stones and an unshakable faith in God.

18. True Friends
1 Samuel 20:1-42, p. 253
David and Jonathan overcome tremendous odds to become the best of friends.

19. David Sins with Bathsheba
2 Samuel 11:1–12:25, p. 271
David underestimates his potential to fall when he allows lust to control his thoughts. He soon discovers that one act of passion can lead to a lifetime of regret.

20. Elijah and the Prophets of Baal
1 Kings 18:16-40, p. 309
The prophet Elijah puts his faith on the line when he challenges the religious leaders of a pagan deity to match the mighty work of his God.

21. Naaman the Leper
2 Kings 5:1-27, p. 321
A servant girl tells Naaman's wife about a prophet in Israel who can heal Naaman of his leprosy. With hope, Naaman looks for the prophet—Elisha—to heal him. But what Elisha tells Naaman to do requires faith.

22. Lepers Discover an Abandoned Camp
2 Kings 7:3-16, p. 323
In desperation, four starving lepers leave the safety of Samaria's gates to surrender to the enemy army that has besieged the city. Hoping to be fed, the lepers discover something even better.

23. Hezekiah's Illness
2 Kings 20:1-11, p. 338
On his deathbed Hezekiah, the king of Judah, prays to the Lord, asking the Lord to remember his faithfulness and devotion. In an incredible act of mercy, God spares Hezekiah's life and even adds fifteen years to his life.

24. Jehoshaphat Defeats Moab and Ammon
2 Chronicles 20:1-30, p. 390
Jehoshaphat leans upon the Lord and his wisdom when faced with a great battle—and Jehoshaphat wins overwhelmingly.

25. Nehemiah Rebuilds the Wall
Nehemiah 1:1–7:3, p. 417
One man's faith helps him persevere through adversity and accomplish a great task.

26. The Story of Queen Esther
Esther 1:1–10:3, p. 431
Queen Esther has it all, yet she is willing to give everything up in order to obey God and save her people, the Jews.

27. The Story of Shadrach, Meshach, and Abednego
Daniel 3:1-30, p. 721
These three men refuse to follow orders that contradict God's Word. In the end, their uncompromising stance changes the heart of a selfish tyrant.

28. Daniel in the Lions' Den
Daniel 6:1-28, p. 725
Daniel takes his faith so seriously that he does not fear when it leads to persecution. He realizes that God is ultimately in control—even in a lions' den.

29. Jonah and the Great Fish
Jonah 1:1–4:11, p. 755
Jonah finds that it does not pay to run away from God and his plan for your life.

30. Jesus' Birth
Luke 1:26-38, p. 851; Luke 2:1-7, p. 854
In the most humble and amazing circumstances, the Savior of the world is born.

31. Jesus Visits the Temple as a Boy
Luke 2:41-52, p. 855
As Jesus' parents return home from the Passover feast in Jerusalem, they notice that Jesus is not with them. Where they find him and what they find him doing astonish them.

32. Jesus' Baptism
Matthew 3:13-17, p. 791; Mark 1:9-11, p. 829; Luke 3:21-22, p. 856
At Jesus' baptism, God expresses his pleasure in his Son and calls him to public ministry.

33. Satan Tempts Jesus
Matthew 4:1-11, p. 791; Mark 1:12-13, p. 829; Luke 4:1-13, p. 857
Jesus withstands temptation from the devil himself, giving his followers a model to follow when they encounter temptation.

34. Jesus Clears the Temple
Matthew 21:12-17, p. 815; Mark 11:15-19, p. 843; Luke 19:45-48, p. 884
In one bold act, Jesus shows his zeal for God's house, making bitter enemies in the process.

35. Jesus and the Miraculous Catch of Fish
Luke 5:1-11, p. 858
Jesus' disciples reap great dividends when they follow Jesus' unusual advice.

36. Jesus and the Samaritan Woman
John 4:1-26, p. 896
A woman who has spent her life looking for love finds true fulfillment and joy in Jesus Christ.

37. Jesus Calms the Storm at Sea
Matthew 8:23-27, p. 799; Mark 4:35-41, p. 833; Luke 8:22-25, p. 864
The disciples discover that although life can be unpredictable, Jesus can calm the storms.

38. Jesus Heals a Lame Man
John 5:1-15, p. 897
A lame man who had been waiting for healing for more than thirty years receives immediate healing when he follows Jesus' instructions.

39. Jesus Feeds Five Thousand
Matthew 14:13-21, p. 808; Mark 6:30-44, p. 855; Luke 9:10-17, p. 836; John 6:1-15, p. 898
A little boy's lunch becomes the focal point of one of Jesus' greatest recorded miracles.

40. The Parable of the Good Samaritan
Luke 10:25-37, p. 869
Our "neighbor," or friend, may not be the person we expect, as this parable explains.

41. Jesus Heals a Blind Man
John 9:1-41, p. 903
This man not only receives his physical sight but also his spiritual sight, as he sees Jesus for who he is.

42. Jesus Raises Lazarus from the Dead
John 11:1-44, p. 905
While Lazarus' sisters expected Jesus to perform a healing, Jesus chooses to do something far greater.

43. The Prodigal Son
Luke 15:11-32, p. 877
Jesus illustrates God's mercy and forgiveness in this parable of a wayward son and shows us how to get right with God.

44. Zacchaeus Climbs a Sycamore Tree
Luke 19:1-10, p. 882

A lonely and despised man finds love and forgiveness in Jesus.

45. The Last Supper
Matthew 26:20-30, p. 823; Mark 14:17-26, p. 847; Luke 22:14-30, p. 886; John 13:1-30, p. 908
Jesus uses some of his last moments with his disciples to teach them important lessons about servanthood and the meaning of his impending sacrifice.

46. Jesus' Crucifixion
Matthew 27:15 66, p. 825; Mark 15:2-47, p. 849; Luke 23:1-56, p. 888; John 18:28–19:42, p. 915
The Son of God shows his tremendous love for people by enduring the most humiliating torture and execution befitting the worst criminal.

47. Jesus' Resurrection
Matthew 28:1-7, p. 826; Mark 16:1-8, p. 850; Luke 24:1-12, p. 890; John 20:1-9, p. 917
Christ's death seems to be a hopeless situation. But what his followers do not know is that he will rise from the dead and break sin's hold on humankind.

48. Peter's First Sermon
Acts 2:14-41, p. 923
A once dejected and disloyal follower, Peter shows his love for Jesus by preaching a powerful sermon through which many come to faith in Christ.

49. Saul's Conversion
Acts 9:1-19, p. 935
One of the earliest persecutors of Christians becomes a believer while he is on his way to arrest Christians in Damascus.

50. An Angel Rescues Peter from Prison
Acts 12:1-19, p. 938
A prayer meeting receives a dramatic answer in the middle of the night.

51. Paul and Silas in Prison
Acts 16:16-40, p. 944
Paul and Silas rise above their circumstances by praising God for his goodness through their trials.

52. Paul's Journey to Rome
Acts 27:1–28:16, p. 956
A seemingly hopeless situation turns into a tremendous witnessing opportunity for the apostle Paul.

Memory Verses

Memorizing Scripture is not really a difficult thing to do. You already have quite a bit in your memory bank: a few key phone numbers, your address, a relative's birthday, and many more essential pieces of information. So you *do* have the ability to memorize. The good news is that Scripture memorization is a refreshing exercise that the Lord will use to bless your life. As his Word says, "But if you keep looking steadily into God's perfect law—the law that sets you free—and if you do what it says and don't forget what you heard, then God will *bless you for doing it*" (James 1:25, italics added).

Below are a few suggestions that may make memorizing God's Word easier for you:

1. When you pick a text to memorize, take time to read the verses surrounding the text so you can better understand the context of the verse. This will help you determine what the verse means.
2. Read the verse(s) several times aloud, and be sure to include the verse reference.
3. Think about the main idea of the verse and how it applies to you personally.
4. You may want to write down the verse several times. You may even choose to write the verse on little cards you can place on your bathroom mirror, in your car, on your refrigerator door, or any other place you frequently find yourself.
5. Review the verse frequently. As someone has said, you memorize a telephone number by dialing, Dialing, DIALING. You can memorize Scripture by reviewing, Reviewing, REVIEWING!
6. Finally, pray over the selected text throughout the day, asking God to help you comprehend its meaning as well as its significance in your own life.

As the verse in James attests, the more you memorize God's Word, the more you will find yourself doing what it says. In effect, filling your mind with Scripture is one of the strongest deterrents for temptation. That is because the more God's Word fills your heart and mind, the less likely you are to want to disregard his commands and displease him. In addition, making the Bible such a central focus of your day will "make you wise" (Colossians 3:16).

Considering the benefits of Scripture memorization, here are some key verses to help you get started in this practice. The following verses have been selected to help you understand the message of salvation, to encourage your spiritual growth, and to remind you of God's promises as you journey through life.

GOD'S PLAN OF SALVATION

▶ *We must acknowledge that we are sinners.*
Romans 3:23. Every person is guilty of sin and has fallen short of God's standard. p. 964
Isaiah 53:6. We all have a basic instinct to follow our own way instead of God's. p. 613
James 2:10. Breaking one of God's laws makes us as guilty as someone who has broken all of God's laws. p. 1086
Romans 3:10. No one can claim innocence before God. p. 964

▶ *We must understand the penalty for our sins.*
Romans 6:23. The wages of sin is death. p. 968

▶ *We must confess and repent of our sins.*
1 John 1:9. God promises to forgive our sins when we confess them. p. 1103
Acts 20:21. We must turn from our sin and turn to God. p. 950

▶ *We must believe that Christ is the only way of salvation.*
John 14:6. Jesus Christ alone leads you to God. p. 909

Acts 4:12. Salvation can be found through no one other than Christ. p. 926
Romans 5:8. Christ's death demonstrates God's unconditional love. p. 966
1 Peter 3:18. Christ, who never sinned, took the punishment for our sins on the cross of Calvary to bring us to God. p. 1095
Romans 10:9-10. Belief in Jesus' death and resurrection is essential to salvation. p. 974

▶ *We must receive Christ into our lives to obtain forgiveness and eternal life.*
John 3:3. We must be spiritually "reborn." p. 895
John 3:16. We are promised salvation by believing in Jesus Christ, God's Son. p. 895
John 10:9. Christ is the gate to salvation. p. 904
Revelation 3:20. Jesus waits for an invitation into our lives. p. 1120
Ephesians 2:8-9. We can only receive salvation through faith in Christ, not through our good works. p. 1024
Titus 3:5. The salvation God extends washes away our sins and brings true joy. p. 1067

▶ *We have the assurance of our salvation.*
John 1:12. We become a child of God by receiving his free gift of salvation. p. 893
Galatians 2:20. We have been given a "new" life in Jesus Christ. p. 1017
Romans 8:1. We no longer have to fear condemnation. p. 969
1 Peter 1:3-4. God has reserved for us the priceless gift of eternal life. p. 1091
1 Peter 1:23. Our new life comes from the living God, not from mortal man. p. 1092
John 10:27-28. The Lord personally guards our salvation. p. 905
1 John 5:13. Our assurance is based upon faith, not feeling. p. 1109
2 Corinthians 1:22. God has placed the Holy Spirit in our hearts as proof that we belong to him. p. 1003
Galatians 4:6-7. We have all the privileges and rights that come from being God's children. p. 1018

GOD'S WORK IN OUR LIVES

▶ *God has a plan and purpose for us.*
Jeremiah 29:11. He wants to give us a future and a hope. p. 646
Romans 8:28. Everything he allows in our lives is for our ultimate good. p. 971
2 Timothy 1:9. He has chosen us to lead holy lives. p. 1061
Psalm 139:16. He has charted every day of our lives. p. 535
1 Corinthians 2:9. He has prepared wonderful things for those who love him. p. 985

▶ *God will change us from the inside out.*
2 Corinthians 5:17. The moment we accept Christ into our lives, we become an altogether "new" person. p. 1007
Colossians 1:27. Jesus Christ has taken residence inside our hearts. p. 1040
Colossians 3:10. We are being conformed to Christ's likeness. p. 1043
Ezekiel 36:26. God will change the nature of our hearts. p. 706
Philippians 1:6. God will complete the work he has started in our lives. p. 1033
Philippians 2:13. God will instill in you the desire to obey him. p. 1035
2 Corinthians 4:16. God will spiritually renew us every day. p. 1005

▶ *He will direct our lives.*
1 Thessalonians 5:23-24. God will help to keep us devoted to him. p. 1050
Psalm 37:23-24. The Lord will direct our steps. p. 479
Jeremiah 10:23. It is God who plans the course of our lives. p. 632
Proverbs 19:21. Man's plans will never supersede God's purposes. p. 553
John 16:13. The Holy Spirit will guide us into all truth. p. 912
Jude 1:24-25. God is able to keep us from slipping and falling. p. 1116

OUR RESPONSE TO GOD'S GOODNESS

▶ *We should honor God with our lives.*
1 Corinthians 6:19-20. We must remember that our body is the home of the Holy Spirit. p. 990
Romans 12:1-2. We must not let this world squeeze us into its mold. p. 977
Psalm 119:9, 11. We need to live according to God's Word. p. 524
Ephesians 2:10. We should spend our lives helping others. p. 1024
2 Timothy 2:22. We should pursue righteousness, faith, love, and peace. p. 1062

Romans 6:13-14. We need to give ourselves completely to God. p. 967
Ephesians 5:18. Our lives need to be controlled by the Holy Spirit. p. 1029
Galatians 5:22-23. Our lives should display the fruit of the Holy Spirit. p. 1020

▶ *We should grow in our knowledge and love of God.*
Joshua 1:8. We need to diligently study and apply God's Word. p. 185
Proverbs 9:10. We need to develop a reverence for God. p. 546
Colossians 3:16. We need to allow Christ's words to enrich our lives. p. 1043
2 Peter 1:2-4. We need to get better acquainted with the Lord in order to lead a godly life. p. 1099
Mark 12:30. We need to love God with all of our heart, soul, mind, and strength. p. 844
Psalm 40:8. We need to allow God's Word to penetrate our hearts so we will want to be obedient. p. 481
John 14:21. We need to follow God's commands. p. 910
Ephesians 3:17-19. We need to make God more at home in our hearts to better comprehend his love for us. p. 1025
James 4:8. As we draw close to God, he will draw close to us. p. 1089

▶ *We should talk to God regularly.*
1 Thessalonians 5:17-18. We should pray continually, throughout the day. p. 1050
Matthew 18:20. We should make a point to pray with other believers. p. 813
Matthew 26:41. We should pray so that we can resist temptation. p. 823
Mark 11:24. We should pray, believing God will answer. p. 843
Luke 11:9. We should pray persistently. p. 870

▶ *We should become an active part of God's family.*
Hebrews 10:24-25. We need to attend church regularly and spend time with other Christians. p. 1079
Romans 12:4-5. God has given each of us a distinct role to play in the church. p. 977
Ephesians 5:19. We spiritually encourage one another by praising God in our conversations. p. 1029
1 John 1:7. The closer we walk with God, the more joyful our relationship with other Christians will be. p. 1103
Philippians 1:2. Love and unity should characterize our Christian fellowship. p. 1033

▶ *We should serve God wholeheartedly.*
Colossians 3:23-24. We must work for the Lord, not just for men. p. 1043
Hebrews 12:2-3. We need to keep our eyes on Jesus to keep from getting discouraged. p. 1082
1 Corinthians 15:58. Nothing we do for the Lord is a wasted effort. p. 1002
Galatians 6:9. We will see positive results if we do not give up. p. 1020

▶ *We should share our faith in Christ with others.*
Matthew 4:19. Jesus wants us to be "fishers" of men and women. p. 792
1 Corinthians 9:22. We should lovingly and tactfully share our faith. p. 993
1 Peter 3:15. We should always be prepared to witness to others. p. 1095
Romans 1:16. We must never be ashamed of the message of the gospel. p. 961
Daniel 12:3. Those who help bring many to the Lord will be blessed. p. 733

▶ *We should persevere in our faith.*
Philippians 3:13-14. We need to focus our sights on the final "prize" of this spiritual race. p. 1036
Ephesians 6:10. We must rely upon God as the source of our strength. p. 1030
Hebrews 12:1. We must rid ourselves of anything that would slow us down. p. 1082
2 Timothy 4:7-8. We must make it our ambition to finish well. p. 1064

GOD'S PROMISES TO US

▶ *We are precious in God's sight.*
John 15:15. We are friends of Christ. p. 911
Jeremiah 31:3. God loves us with an everlasting love. p. 649
Isaiah 43:2. He will never leave us in times of difficulty. p. 605
Romans 8:38-39. Nothing can separate us from his love. p. 972
1 John 5:14-15. He hears our prayers. p. 1109

▶ *God is faithful to us.*
Lamentations 3:23. We can count on his daily faithfulness. p. 673
Hebrews 13:5-6. He will never abandon us. p. 1084

Psalm 46:1. He is a tested help in times of trouble. p. 485
Isaiah 41:10. He is always there to strengthen and help us. p. 604
2 Thessalonians 3:3. He will make us spiritually strong and keep us from evil. p. 1052
1 Peter 3:12. He watches us and hears our prayers. p. 1094

▶ *God watches over us.*
Deuteronomy 33:27. The eternal God is our refuge and protector. p. 184
Psalm 27:1. As God's children, we do not need to fear anyone or anything. p. 473
Proverbs 29:25. We should not fear man but trust God. p. 560
1 Peter 5:7. We can trust him with all of our worries and cares. p. 1096

▶ *God will give us peace.*
Isaiah 26:3. God promises peace to all who trust in him. p. 593
John 14:27. God gives us a lasting peace, not a fragile peace. p. 910
Philippians 4:6-7. Praying to the Lord brings tremendous peace. p. 1036
Psalm 4:8. Trusting God leads to rest and peace. p. 462
Colossians 3:15. It is up to us to allow God's peace to control our lives. p. 1043

▶ *God will give us strength to face life's challenges.*
Isaiah 40:31. The Lord wants to renew our strength. p. 603
John 15:5. We draw our strength from Christ. p. 911
2 Corinthians 3:5. Our competence comes from God. p. 1004
2 Corinthians 12:9. God displays his strength in our weaknesses. p. 1013
1 Corinthians 10:13. God will never allow you to go through more than you can handle. p. 994
Psalm 73:25-26. Regardless of our outward circumstances, God will always be the strength of our life. p. 499
Deuteronomy 31:6. Our strength comes from knowing that God is with us at all times. p. 180
Philippians 4:13. We can do everything through Christ. p. 1037
Hebrews 13:6. We do not have to fear what people may do to us. p. 1084

▶ *God promises forgiveness.*
Psalm 34:18. He rescues those who are humbly sorry for their sins. p. 477
Psalm 86:5. He is always ready to forgive. p. 507
Hebrews 8:12. He will not only forgive our sins but will also forget them. p. 1077
Psalm 103:12. He will remove our sins as far as the east is from the west. p. 515
1 John 2:1. Jesus will stand as our defense before the Father when we ask for forgiveness. p. 1103
Isaiah 55:7. He promises mercy and forgiveness to those who stop their sinful behavior and turn to him. p. 614
Isaiah 1:18. His forgiveness is life changing. p. 577

▶ *God will empower us for his service.*
2 Chronicles 16:9a. He wants to work through those who are truly committed to him. p. 387
Philippians 4:13. We can do everything God asks with the help of Christ. p. 1037
2 Timothy 1:7. The Holy Spirit will give us boldness as we share our faith. p. 1061
Psalm 37:4-5. We need to commit everything we do to the Lord. p. 479
Proverbs 2:6. He provides wisdom and guidance through his Word. p. 542

▶ *God's Word is our infallible guide.*
Mark 13:31. God's Word lasts forever. p. 846
2 Timothy 3:16. All Scripture is inspired by God and will equip us with all we need to know in this life. p. 1063
Psalm 119:105. God's Word sheds light on the path of life. p. 527
Isaiah 55:10-11. God's Word is always effective. p. 614
Hebrews 4:12. God's Word reveals who we really are. p. 1074

Prophecies about Jesus

For the Gospel writers, one of the main reasons for believing in Jesus was the way his life fulfilled the Old Testament prophecies about the Messiah. Following is a list of some of the main prophecies and their fulfillments.

Prophecy	Old Testament Reference	New Testament Fulfillment
Messiah was to be born in Bethlehem	Micah 5:2	Matthew 2:1-6; Luke 2:1-20
Messiah was to be born of a virgin	Isaiah 7:14	Matthew 1:18-25; Luke 1:26-38
Messiah was to be a prophet like Moses	Deuteronomy 18:15, 18-19	John 7:40
Messiah was to enter Jerusalem in triumph	Zechariah 9:9	Matthew 21:1-9; John 12:12-16
Messiah was to be rejected by his own people	Isaiah 53:1-3 Psalm 118:22	Matthew 26:3-4; John 12:37-43; Acts 4:1-12
Messiah was to be betrayed by one of his followers	Psalm 41:9	Matthew 26:14-16, 47-50; Luke 22:16, 47-48
Messiah was to be tried and condemned	Isaiah 53:8	Luke 23:1-25; Matthew 27:1-2
Messiah was to be silent before his accusers	Isaiah 53:7	Matthew 26:62-63; 27:12-14; Mark 15:3-5; Luke 23:8-10
Messiah was to be struck and spit upon by his enemies	Isaiah 50:6	Matthew 26:67; 27:30; Mark 14:65
Messiah was to be mocked and taunted	Psalm 22:7-8	Matthew 27:39-44; Luke 23:11, 35-36
Messiah was to die by crucifixion	Psalm 22:14, 16-17	Matthew 27:31; Mark 15:20, 25
Messiah was to suffer with criminals and pray for his enemies	Isaiah 53:12	Matthew 27:38; Mark 15:27-28; Luke 23:32-34
Messiah was to be given vinegar and gall	Psalm 69:21	Matthew 27:34; John 19:28-30
Others were to cast lots for Messiah's garments	Psalm 22:18	Matthew 27:35; John 19:23-24

Messiah's bones were not to be broken	Exodus 12:46	John 19:31-36
Messiah was to die as a sacrifice for sin	Isaiah 53:5-6, 8, 10-12	John 1:29; 11:49-52; Acts 10:43; 13:38-39
Messiah was to be raised from the dead	Psalm 16:10	Matthew 28:1-10; Mark 16:1-8; Luke 24:1-12; John 20:1-9; Acts 2:22-32
Messiah is now at God's right hand	Psalm 110:1	Mark 16:19; Luke 24:50-51

Glossary of Christian Terms

What does it mean when someone refers to "the flesh"? What is the significance of the phrase "the blood"? And why is it important to "disciple" others? Whether you have just become a Christian or are just interested in learning more about Christianity, you will soon discover that Christians sometimes seem to speak their own language. This basic glossary of commonly used Christian terms and phrases will help you uncover some of the mystery behind the Christian vocabulary. In addition, some entries will point you to areas of further study so that you can see how these expressions apply to your life. If for some reason you still have trouble comprehending what a Christian term means (or if it is not listed here), do not hesitate to ask a more mature Christian, a Bible study leader, or your pastor. As the saying goes, There is only one bad question: the question you never ask. The more you learn about your Christian faith and the God you now serve, the deeper and more meaningful your spiritual walk will be.

Abide: To remain consistently in fellowship with God by maintaining a close relationship with Jesus Christ. Most commonly used in the phrase "abide in Christ." (For further study, turn to "Live as a Disciple," p. A20.)

Accepting Christ: To receive God's gift of salvation by believing in Jesus Christ, asking God to forgive you of your sin that you have repented of, and inviting Christ to take up residence in your heart and allowing the Holy Spirit to change your life. (For further study, turn to "How You Can Know God," p. A33.) See also *Repent*.

Accountability: To be held responsible for your actions. For example, we are accountable to God for what we do with the talents and abilities he gives us. (For further study, turn to "Accountability," p. A12.)

Altar Call: See *Invitation*.

Angels: Spirit messengers who worship God and care for believers. (For further study, turn to "What Are Angels?" p. A4.)

Antichrist: Literally means "false Christ" or "instead of" Christ. The

Bible says that one great Antichrist, or "false Christ," will appear in the final days before Christ's return to earth and will deceive many (see Revelation 13:1-7, p. 1127). This term is also used to describe anyone who opposes Jesus Christ and his teachings (see 1 John 2:18, p. 1105; 1 John 4:3, p. 1108; 2 John 7, p. 1111).

Atonement: The removal of God's punishment for sin through the perfect sacrifice of Jesus Christ (see Romans 3:25, p. 964). (For further study, turn to "The Solution: Jesus Christ," p. A35.)

Backslide: To stop moving forward in the Christian walk; to spiritually regress. (For further study, turn to "What Is Backsliding?" p. 889.)

Baptism: 1. Water baptism is an outward display of what has happened in the life of the believer: the death of the old nature (when one is placed under the water), and the birth of a new nature (when one is raised up) (see Colossians 2:12, p. 1041). While it is not necessary for salvation, it demonstrates a person's submission to Christ. Baptism is also a demonstration of that person's willingness to live God's way.

Jesus himself stressed its importance (see Matthew 28:19, p. 827). 2. Spirit baptism occurs when the Holy Spirit enters a person's life. This baptism only occurs after he or she has received Jesus Christ as Lord and Savior. See also *Filling of the Holy Spirit*.

Burdens: Refers to helping other believers by sharing in their trials, sorrows, and concerns so that they will not feel alone (see Galatians 6:1-3, p. 1020).

Believer: Someone who has accepted Jesus Christ as Savior and Lord.

Blood (the): Refers to the blood Christ shed on the cross of Calvary, where he essentially became the sacrifice for our sins.

Body of Christ (the): Another term for the church—all those who call Jesus Christ their Lord. Throughout the New Testament Jesus Christ is often referred to as the "head" of this body (see Ephesians 1:22-23, p. 1023). See also *Church*.

Book of Life (the): A record found in heaven that lists the names of every individual who has committed his or her life to Jesus Christ and can be called a follower of God (see Daniel

12:1, p. 733; Luke 10:20, p. 869; Revelation 3:5, p. 1119; Revelation 21:27, p. 1134).

Born Again: Describes what takes place when a person accepts Jesus Christ as his or her personal Savior. Essentially, one becomes spiritually "reborn" at that point, escaping spiritual death and receiving eternal life (see John 3:3-7, p. 895).

Bride of Christ (the): Another term for the church or Christian believers as a whole (see 2 Corinthians 11:2, p. 1012). See also *Church.*

Calling: 1. (Noun) God's invitation to men and women to receive the gift and benefits of salvation (see Ephesians 1:18, p. 1023; 1 Thessalonians 2:12, p. 1046; 2 Thessalonians 2:14, p. 1046). 2. (Noun) God's divinely appointed plan or purpose for a believer, as in "He believes that God's calling is for him to . . ." (see Ephesians 4:1, p. 1026; 2 Timothy 1:9, p. 1061). 3. (Verb) When God directs an individual toward a particular vocation or area of service (e.g., "He believes that God is calling him to be a pastor").

Carnal: To be controlled and motivated by one's sinful, human nature rather than the Holy Spirit; a failure to live the Christian life as Jesus meant it to be lived.

Christ: Shortened form of the name "Jesus Christ," the Son of God and Savior of the world; not a name as much as a title. The word *Christ* (or *Christos*) is Greek for "anointed one," which was often used in the description of Jewish kings and high priests. (For further study, turn to "The Solution: Jesus Christ," p. A35)

Church (the): 1. (Proper Noun) The collective body of Christian believers around the world and throughout the ages. 2. (Noun) A place where people come together to fellowship with other believers, learn more about the Christian faith through the leadership of a pastor,

and use their God-given talents and abilities to glorify God. (For further study, turn to "Look for and Attend the Right Church," p. A16.)

Commitment: 1. The decision to accept Jesus Christ as one's Savior and Lord (e.g., "The young woman made a commitment to Christ after the pastor's message"). 2. A person's willingness to stay true to Christ regardless of the cost.

Communion: 1. A time when fellow believers come together to remember the effects of Jesus' sacrifice on the cross for them by receiving and eating the elements Jesus used in the Lord's Supper (also known as the "Last Supper"). The bread symbolizes Jesus' body, broken for us on the cross, while the wine (or juice) represents Jesus' blood, shed on the cross for our sins (see 1 Corinthians 10:16-17, p. 994). See also *Lord's Supper.* 2. The deep closeness and fellowship a person can experience with God as a result of entering into a personal relationship with him (see 1 Corinthians 1:9, p. 983).

Confess: 1. To agree with, as in agreeing with God about our sins and sinful condition. To admit your sins to God and ask for his forgiveness (see 1 John 1:9, p. 1103). 2. To publicly acknowledge your relationship with and commitment to Jesus Christ (see Romans 10:9-10, p. 974).

Consecration: A dedication to serve God wholeheartedly and to be used for his glory (see 1 Chronicles 29:5, p. 372; Romans 12:1, p. 977; 2 Corinthians 8:5, p. 1010).

Conversion: When a person makes a decision to receive Jesus Christ as Savior and Lord, turning from the darkness and futility of this world to the light and hope found in Christ (see Acts 26:18, p. 956).

Conviction: 1. To feel guilt and remorse after committing some wrongdoing. 2. To feel genuine sorrow and concern over one's sinful condition and unworthiness

before God. The Holy Spirit is responsible for this conviction in the life of the unbeliever (see John 16:8, p. 912).

Cross: 1. Reference to Jesus' death on the cross of Calvary and to what his death represents. (For further study, turn to "The Solution: Jesus Christ," p. A35.) 2. Reference to our identification with Jesus Christ; setting aside our personal ambition to follow and serve God (see Matthew 16:24, p. 810). See also *Denying Self.*

Demons: Spirit beings who serve Satan. They are essentially fallen angels (approximately one-third of the original angel population) who lost their former position in heaven along with Satan for their rebellion against God (see Revelation 12:4, p. 1125). (For further study, turn to "What Are Demons?" p. A5.)

Denying Self: To place God's will and desires above your own (see Matthew 16:24).

Devil: See *Satan.*

Devotions: A personal time of fellowship and communion with God that includes Bible study, prayer, and worship. (For further study, turn to "Study the Bible," p. A15 and "Pray," p. A16.)

Disciple: 1. One of the twelve original close followers of Jesus Christ during his earthly ministry. 2. One who learns, follows, and lives by the teachings of Jesus Christ; one who imitates Christ. (For further study, turn to "Live as a Disciple," p. A20.)

Discipleship: The process of making other disciples; the practice of introducing people to Jesus Christ and then encouraging them to grow in their faith by teaching them about the Lord and showing them how to live as a follower of Christ (see Matthew 28:19-20, p. 827).

Divinity: Connotes the self-contained power and holy nature of God.

Doctrine: The fundamental tenets, or cornerstones, of a belief system (in this case, Christianity).

Election: God's choice of an individual or group for a specific purpose or destiny (see Ephesians 1:4-5, p. 1023).

End Times: The final days on this earth before the return of Jesus Christ.

Evangelism: Literally means the sharing of the "good news," or the gospel of Jesus Christ, with others. (For further study, turn to "Share Your Faith," p. A19.)

Faith: 1. A firm conviction that produces a full acknowledgment of God's truth; a belief and hope in God and his Word in response to the message of salvation (see John 1:12, p. 893). 2. Having a certainty in what you hope for even though you may not be able to see it (see Hebrews 11:1-40, p. 1080).

Fall (the): Refers to the first act of disobedience against God, when Adam and Eve ate fruit from the tree that God had forbidden them to touch in the Garden of Eden (see Genesis 3:1-24, p. 4; Romans 5:12, p. 966). (For further study, turn to "The Problem: Sin," p. A33.)

Family of God: Those individuals throughout history who have accepted God's free gift of salvation, which has entitled them to be God's children (see John 1:12, p. 893). (For further study, turn to "Adopted and Assured," p. A41.)

Fasting: When a person voluntarily abstains from food for a given time to devote himself or herself to prayer for a specific need, responsibility, or request (see Matthew 6:17-18, p. 795; Acts 14:23, p. 942).

Father (the): 1. Reference to God, the Father—the source and giver of life, wisdom, and salvation (see Hebrews 12:9, p. 1083; Ephesians 1:17, p. 1023; James 1:17, p. 1085) 2. Used when speaking of God as the Father of Jesus Christ (see 2 Corinthians 1:3, p. 1003). 3. Used to describe God's relationship to a believer after conversion (see John 1:12-13, p. 893). See also *Trinity.*

Fellowship: 1. (Noun) A communion or partnership with other believers. 2. (Verb) To communicate and meet with fellow believers to encourage one another in the Christian faith and to assist those who have special needs (see Acts 2:42, p. 924; Romans 1:12, p. 961; Hebrews 10:25, p. 1079). (For further study, turn to "Look for and Attend the Right Church," p. A16.)

Filling of the Holy Spirit: 1. The entrance of the Holy Spirit into a person's life after he or she has accepted Jesus Christ as personal Savior (see Acts 2:38, p. 924; Galatians 4:6, p. 1018). 2. The empowerment of the Holy Spirit in one's life to perform a certain task (see Acts 1:8, p. 921; Acts 4:31, p. 927). (For further study, turn to "Live in God's Power," p. A18.) See also *Baptism.*

Flesh (the): Speaks of our human, or sinful, nature and tendencies; the weaker element in human nature (see Matthew 26:41, p. 823; Romans 6:19, p. 967; Romans 7:5-6, p. 968).

Foundation: The basis upon which we build our lives. According to the Bible, a strong foundation for living is based upon God and his Word (see Isaiah 28:6, p. 594; Matthew 7:24, p. 798; 2 Timothy 2:19, p. 1062).

Freedom in Christ: Describes the spiritual liberty, or freedom, we have as followers of Jesus Christ. We are freed from the controlling power of sin and released from the obligation of meeting God's righteous require- ments on our own through the death and resurrection of Jesus Christ. This freedom does not give us the "right" to disregard God's laws. It simply allows us to obey God out of love rather than obligation (see Romans 6:7, p. 967; Romans 8:2, p. 969; Galatians 5:13, p. 1020; Galatians 6:1, p. 1020; 1 Peter 2:16, p. 1093). (For further study, turn to "Faith and Works," p. A10.)

Fruit (of the Spirit): 1. Evidence of the presence of the Holy Spirit at work in our lives. This is often displayed through our attitudes and our actions (see Matthew 7:16, p. 797). 2. The character traits the Holy Spirit produces in our lives—love, joy, peace, patience, kindness, goodness, faithfulness, gentleness, and self-control (see Galatians 5:22, p. 1020).

Gifts: See *Spiritual Gifts.*

Gifts of the Spirit: See *Spiritual Gifts.*

Glorification: The ultimate state of the believer after death, when he or she becomes like Christ (see Romans 8:17, p. 971; Philippians 3:21, p. 1036).

Godhead: All that God is (i.e., his person, character, abilities, etc.).

Gospel: 1. The "good news" of salvation; the explanation of how one can be saved from the eternal punishment of hell and receive forgiveness and eternal life through Jesus Christ. 2. This term in the plural also refers to the first four books of the New Testament (see 1 Corinthians 15:1-5, p. 999).

Grace: The undeserved favor, forgiveness, and acceptance we receive from God through our acceptance of Jesus Christ as our Lord and Savior (see Ephesians 2:8-9, p. 1024).

Great Commission: Signifies Christ's command to us to go out into all the world—whether that is across the street or across the ocean—and win people to the Lord so they, too, can become dedicated followers of Jesus Christ (see Matthew 28:19-20, p. 827). (For further study, turn to "Share Your Faith," p. A19.)

Hardness of Heart: The dulling of one's spiritual perception; a built-up stubbornness or animosity toward the will and ways of God (see 2 Corinthians 4:4, p. 1005; Ephesians 4:18, p. 1027).

Harvest (the): Describes the "reaping" of souls through the process of sharing the message of the gospel with others and leading them to Jesus Christ (see John 4:35-36, p. 896; Galatians 6:9, p. 1020).

Holiness: 1. A description of the flawless, sinless character of God. 2. To reflect a devotion to God and his ways in your life; a single-hearted pursuit to become more Christlike in character.

Holy Ghost: See *Holy Spirit.*

Holy Spirit: One of the distinctive, powerful personalities of the three-fold Godhead. His respon-sibilities include convicting us of our sin, leading us to Christ, and helping us grow in character, faith, and knowledge after conversion. (For further study, turn to "Who Is the Holy Spirit?" p. A2.)

Intercession or Interceding: To pray for someone; to make a petition to God on behalf of another (see Psalm 106:23, p. 518; Romans 8:26, p. 971; Ephesians 1:16-17, p. 1023). (For further study, turn to "Pray," p. A16.)

Invitation: The moment (usually at the end of a gospel presentation) when a pastor or evangelist invites people to accept Jesus Christ into their lives. This is also referred to as an "altar call," since people are sometimes asked to come forward to a specified location to make a public stand of their newfound faith.

Jesus: Refers to Jesus Christ, the Son of God and Savior of the World. See also *Christ.*

Judgment: A reference to God's divine judgment, reserved for the end of the age. At that time, each person will stand before God and will be found "guilty" or "innocent" based upon his or her rejection or acceptance of Jesus Christ (see Matthew 25:32, p. 822; Hebrews 9:27, p. 1078; Revelation 20:12, p. 1133).

Justification: Being cleansed of our sins. (For a more in-depth description of justification, see

"What God Has Done for You," p. A39.)

Laborers: Those who are actively serving the Lord and sharing their faith with others (see Matthew 9:37-38, p. 801; 1 Corinthians 3:8-9, p. 986). (For further study, turn to "Share Your Faith," p. A19.)

Lamb (the): A reference to Jesus Christ, who became the "sacrificial lamb" by his death for our sins on the cross of Calvary (see Isaiah 53:7-8, p. 613; John 1:29, p. 893; 1 Peter 1:19, p. 1092).

Last Days: A reference to the last days on earth prior to the return of Jesus Christ. See also *End Times.*

Lord's Supper: Jesus' last supper with his disciples. This is also when fellow believers come together to remember Jesus' sacrifice on the cross for them by receiving and eating the elements Jesus used in the Lord's Supper (also known as the "Last Supper"). The bread symbolizes Jesus' body, broken for us on the cross, while the wine (or juice) represents Jesus' blood, shed on the cross for our sins (see 1 Corinthians 10:16-17, p. 994). See also *Communion.*

Lordship: Signifies the supremacy and authority of the Lord Jesus Christ in the life of the believer and over all the earth (see 1 Corinthians 8:6, p. 992).

Lucifer: Another name for Satan. See *Satan.*

Meditate: To contemplate and reflect upon something. As believers, we are told to ponder such things as the meaning of a passage of Scripture or truths we learn about the Lord through our pastors and teachers (see Joshua 1:8, p. 185; Psalm 63:6, p. 493; Psalm 143:5, p. 537). (For further study, turn to "Study the Bible," p. A15.)

Messiah: The Hebrew word for God's "anointed one" (Jesus Christ) who came to save the world by

taking the punishment for our sins. See also *Christ.*

Millennium: Refers to the thousand-year reign of Jesus Christ on the earth in which there will be no more war (Isaiah 2:4, p. 578; Revelation 20:1-6, p. 1132).

New Creation: A description of what we become once we allow Jesus Christ to take residence in our lives (see 2 Corinthians 5:17, p. 1007). (For further study, turn to "Adopted and Assured," p. A41.)

New Nature: That which enables us to live godly lives through the power of the Holy Spirit. It replaces our "old nature" when we accept Jesus Christ into our lives (see Romans 6:8, p. 967). See also *New Creation.*

Old Nature: That which follows our basic, sinful instincts. Before we came to Christ, we were under this nature's control (see Ephesians 4:22, p. 1027; 2 Peter 1:9, p. 1099).

Original Sin: Refers to the first transgression humankind ever committed, when Adam and Eve took fruit from the tree that God had forbidden them to touch. See also *the Fall.*

Prayer: Conversation with God in which we express praise, needs, thanks, and concerns. (For further study, turn to "Pray," p. A16.)

Predestination: The idea that God knew before the beginning of time those who would follow him (see Romans 8:29, p. 971; Ephesians 1:4, p. 1023). See also *Election.*

Propitiation: See *Atonement.*

Purify: To cleanse or rid oneself of those things that are not pleasing to God (see 2 Corinthians 7:1, p. 1008; James 4:8, p. 1089; 1 John 3:3, p. 1105). (For further study, turn to "Purity," p. A8.)

Quiet Time: Time spent alone in prayer and in the study of God's Word. (For further study, turn to "Study the Bible," p. A15, and "Pray," p. A16.)

Rapture: When Christ takes his followers from earth to be with him (1 Thessalonians 4:17, p. 1049).

Rebirth: See *Born Again.*

Receiving Christ: See *Accepting Christ.*

Recommitment: When a person returns to the Lord after having abandoned his relationship with Christ and gone back to his or her former life. (For further study, turn to "What Is Backsliding?" p. 889.)

Redemption: The price Jesus paid for the sins of the world. (For a more in-depth description of redemption, see "The Problem: Sin," p. A33, and "The Solution: Jesus Christ," p. A35.)

Regeneration: See *New Creation.*

Repent: Literally means "to change your direction." To turn away from those things or activities that displease God and start doing the things that please him. (For further study, turn to "The Response: Accept God's Offer," p. A37.)

Renewal: A time of soul-searching, confession of sin, and spiritual reawakening that leads one to a deeper walk with God (see Psalm 51:10, p. 487; 2 Corinthians 4:16, p. 1005; James 4:8-10, p.1089). See also *Revival.*

Resurrection: 1. When Christ rose from the dead the third day after his crucifixion, breaking the power of death and completing the work of salvation (see Acts 2:23-24, p. 923; Romans 1:4, p. 961; Romans 4:25, p. 966). 2. When all will rise again at the appearance of Jesus Christ (see Daniel 12:2, p. 733; John 5:29, p. 898; John 6:40, p. 899; Acts 24:15, p. 954; 1 Thessalonians 4;16, p. 1049).

Revival: Literally "to flourish anew." A time of spiritual renewal when many come to a committed relationship with Jesus Christ; a time of returning to God (see Psalm 51:12-13, p. 487). (For further study, turn to "What Is Revival?" p. 381.) See also *Renewal.*

Righteousness: Right standing before God; being right before God.

Salvation: The means by which a person can receive eternal life through accepting Jesus Christ as his or her Lord and Savior (see John 3:16, p. 895). See also *Gospel.*

Sanctification: Becoming more and more like Jesus Christ through the work of the Holy Spirit (see Philippians 1:6, p. 1033; 2 Thessalonians 2:13, p. 1052). (For further study, turn to "Live as a Disciple," p. A20.)

Satan: A fallen angel who lost his former position as a high-ranking angel in heaven because of his pride; his chief aim is to foster rebellion against God in the hearts of men and women. (For further study, turn to "Who Is the Devil?" p. A3.)

Savior: A reference to Jesus that signifies his role in bringing us the gift of salvation and freedom from the punishment we deserve.

Second Coming: A reference to Jesus Christ's return to earth to establish his kingdom (see Matthew 26:64, p. 823; Acts 1:11, p. 921; Hebrews 9:28, p. 1078).

Servanthood: 1. A level of commitment that involves a willingness to serve and honor God with your life (see Deuteronomy 10:12, p. 163). 2. The act of following Jesus' humble example toward others by treating them better than yourself and helping to care for their needs (see Philippians 2:3-8, p. 1034).

Sinful Nature: See *Old Nature.*

Sin: 1. (verb) To "miss the mark," or fall short of God's level of perfection; to break God's commands. 2. (noun) The one thing that separates us from a relationship with God. (For further study, turn to "The Problem: Sin," p. A33).

Sinner: Word used to describe what we are by nature. We are not sinners because we sin; rather we sin because we are sinners.

Son (the): See *Son of God.*

Son of God: Another reference for Jesus Christ, signifying Jesus' relationship to God the Father (see Matthew 3:17, p. 791; Hebrews 10:29, p. 1080; 1 John 4:15, p. 1108).

Soul: The vital existence of a human being; the immaterial essence of an individual through which he or she perceives, reflects, feels, and desires.

Soul Winner: A person who actively shares his or her faith with others in order to lead them to Christ. See also *Laborers.*

Sovereignty: A description of God's supreme power and authority.

Spirit (the): See *Holy Spirit.*

Spiritual Gifts: Certain supernatural gifts and abilities given to you by the Holy Spirit in order to build up, edify, and encourage the church (see Romans 12:6, p. 977; Ephesians 4:11, p. 1026). (For further study, turn to "What Are Spiritual Gifts?" p. 1027.)

Stumble: To spiritually regress, or to commit some sin against God, thus hindering your Christian growth. See also *Backslide.*

Surrender: To yield your personal rights and will to the Lord; to fully give your life to the Lord for his service (see Romans 12:1, p. 977).

Testimony: 1. The story of how you came into a relationship with Jesus Christ. 2. An account of what God has been doing in your life.

Tithe: A portion of your earnings (often considered to be 10 percent of gross income) that you set aside to give to the Lord (see Genesis 28:22, p. 25; Malachi 3:10, p. 786). (For further study, turn to "Give to God," p. A21.)

Trials: Difficult times and circumstances that test your faith. (For further study, turn to "Have Courage in Trials," p. A22.)

Tribulation: 1. A time of intense difficulty. 2. A description of the time just prior to the Second Coming of Jesus Christ when the world will go through unprecendented turmoil (see Matthew 24:6-13, p. 820).

Trinity: The three persons that make up the Godhead: God the Father, God the Son (Jesus), and God the Holy Spirit (see Matthew 28:19, p. 827; John 14:26, p. 912; 1 Peter 1:2, p. 1091).

Walk: 1. A description of your spiritual growth or progress. 2. Your daily relationship with God.

Witness: 1. (Verb) To tell others about the message of salvation through Jesus Christ. (For further study, turn to "Share Your Faith," p. A19.) 2. (Noun) The demonstration of God's presence in your life.

Works: Your deeds and actions. (For further study, turn to "Faith and Works," p. A10.)

World (the): 1. Signifies the present condition of human affairs on this earth that are in opposition to God and his ways (see Ephesians 2:2, p. 1024; James 4:4, p. 1088). 2. The temporal possessions of this earth (see Matthew 16:26, p. 810; Colossians 3:2, p. 1042).

Worldly: See *Carnal.*

Worship: A sincere expression of reverence and devotion toward God. Worship can take place through singing songs of praise, praying, and meditating upon God's Word.

Yield: See *Surrender.*